August 17–22, 2014
Chicago, IL, USA



Association for Computing Machinery

*Advancing Computing as a Science & Profession*

# SIGCOMM'14

## Proceedings of the 2014 ACM Conference on Special Interest Group on Data Communication

*Sponsored by:*

***ACM SIGCOMM***

*Supported by:*

***CISCO, VERISIGN, NSF, ERICSSON, CISCO Meraki, AT&T, Google, Microsoft, Northwestern University, Akamai, Conviva, Facebook, HP, Seventh Framework Programme, UIC, and VMware***

Association for Computing Machinery

*Advancing Computing as a Science & Profession*

**The Association for Computing Machinery**
**2 Penn Plaza, Suite 701**
**New York, New York 10121-0701**



**ISBN:** 978-1-4503-2836-4 (Digital)

**ISBN:** 978-1-4503-3260-6 (Print)

Additional copies may be ordered prepaid from:

**ACM Order Department**
PO Box 30777
New York, NY 10087-0777, USA

Phone: 1-800-342-6626 (USA and Canada)
+1-212-626-0500 (Global)
Fax: +1-212-944-1318
E-mail: acmhelp@acm.org
Hours of Operation: 8:30 am – 4:30 pm ET

Printed in the USA

# A Message from the General Chairs

Welcome to Chicago and welcome to the ACM SIGCOMM 2014! It is a great pleasure to host one of ACM's flagship conferences and the leading conference in data communication and networking at the one-of-a-kind city of Chicago.

As it is every year, this SIGCOMM is organized as a weeklong event around the main conference, with workshops and tutorials, posters and demos and several social events for greeting and meeting colleagues and friends. The main program, strong as always, is the result of the great work done by **Sylvia Ratnasamy** and **Arvind Krishnamurthy** and the fantastic program committee they put together. The week's events also include an exciting set of demos and posters organized by **Dave Choffnes** and **Kun Tan**, as well as a new Industrial demo session. Between Monday and Friday, there are 5 workshops on topical subjects and a handful of exciting tutorials. We thank the workshop chairs, **Matt Caesar** and **Ming Zhang**, the tutorial chairs, **Sonia Fahmy** and **Jia Wang**, and the different workshop chairs and tutorial organizers. This year, we have the pleasure to host one additional workshop on Sunday – N2Women. This is a great venue fostering connections among the underrepresented women in computer networking – thanks to **Sami Rollins, Katia Jaffres-Runser** and the N2Women Steering Committee for deciding to collocate their workshop with SIGCOMM 2014.

Organizing a conference such as SIGCOMM is an impressive challenge. That we have been able to pull this off is entirely due to the work of a dedicated organization committee. We are eternally grateful to **Jakob Eriksson** and **Yan Chen**, local chairs, **Randy Berry**, registration chair, **Sujata Banergee**, treasurer, and **Brighten Godfrey**, web chair – all of whom made themselves available, at unscheduled times and for random tasks, to make certain everything runs as smoothly as possible. **Xenofontas Dimitropulos, Phillipa Gil, Bin Liu** and **Claudio Righetti** ensured wide publicity for the conference. **Minlan Yu** and **Robin Kravets**, working with **Lisa M. Tolles** and the folks at Sheridan, have dexterously handled all publication details. The executive committee, and particularly the conference coordinators **Yashar Ganjali** and **Jaudelice de Oliveira**, shared with us their institutional knowledge and invaluable years of experience during these past months.

SIGCOMM has a long tradition of encouraging and financially supporting student participation and we are happy to continue this tradition. We have been able to keep students' registration costs at levels similar to those of the past two years. We have organized a student banquet in a beautiful venue where students can meet and mingle with leaders of the research community (and enjoy the fireworks afterwards). With the help of our corporate sponsors and government agencies, and thanks to the work of our travel grant chairs, **Tilman Wolf, Ignacio Alvarez-Hamelin, Wenjun Hu, Dimitrios Koutsonikolas** and **Marco Melia**, we have been able to offer and distribute tens of travel grants to students and postdocs from around the world.

We are very excited to offer, for the first time, SIGCOMM Kiddie! In cooperation with an experienced childcare provider and with the generous support of Northwestern University, SIGCOMM 2014 will offer day care to our youngest attendees at subsidized prices. This would not have been possible without the constant help of **Renata Cruz Teixeira** and the support of the rest of the SIGCOMM Executive Committee.

We are very grateful to our many supporters from industry, academia and government, for their generosity. Special thanks go out to Cisco and Verisign (Platinum), Ericsson and Meraki (Gold), AT&T, Google, Microsoft and Northwestern University (Silver) and Akamai, Conviva, Facebook, Hewlett Packard, the Flamingo European Project, the University of Illinois at Chicago and VMWare (Bronze). The U.S. National Science Foundation (NSF) is one of SIGCOMM's constant sources of support. We also thank the many people outside the organization who have helped us with the conference, in particular **Svetlana (Lana) Kiperman**, Northwestern University, and our graphic designer **Andrés E. Bustamante** (BDG Design).

A beautiful city in a gorgeous time of the year, Chicago will make it difficult for you to attend the conference. We hope you have made plan to come early and stay longer to explore the many faces of this wonderful and cosmopolitan city, its people, its music, and its food.

**Fabián E. Bustamante**
*SIGCOMM 2014 General Co-Chair*
*Northwestern University, USA*

**Y. Charlie Hu**
*SIGCOMM 2014 General Co-Chair*
*Purdue University, USA*

# Message from the Program Chairs

Welcome to *ACM SIGCOMM 2014!*

This year's conference continues the *SIGCOMM* tradition of being the premier forum for the presentation of research on networking and communications. The technical program this year features a set of outstanding papers that cover a wide variety of areas including network architecture, software defined networks, data center networks, wireless networks, network services, congestion management, security, privacy, measurement and analysis.

This year's call for papers attracted 242 submissions from all over the world. The 54 member Technical Program Committee along with a selected group of external experts carefully considered all of the submissions over two rounds of reviewing – including an author feedback period - with a total of 968 detailed reviews completed. The TPC meeting to select the final program was held at ICSI, Berkeley, in late April 2014. At the conclusion of the meeting, the committee had assembled a wonderful program composed of 45 papers, to be presented over three days at the conference. The quality of submissions was extremely high as reflected in the final technical program.

There are many people who deserve thanks and recognition for the important roles they played in making the 2014 conference possible. We would like to begin by thanking and recognizing the authors who submitted their papers to the conference. The General Chairs Fabián Bustamante and Y. Charlie Hu have put in a great deal of time and effort in arranging and supporting the conference – special thanks to Fabián and Charlie. It has been our honor to work with such a strong and dedicated TPC, and we are very grateful for the many hours spent by everyone on this TPC. Special thanks go to Colin Scott, who set up and maintained all aspects of the HotCRP conference management system, and assisted with other activities. Thanks also to Kattt Atchley for her assistance with organizing the TPC meeting. We thank all other members of the organizing committee, and the members of the *ACM SIGCOMM* executive and technical steering committees for their help and support. Thanks also to Sheridan Communications for their work on preparing these proceedings. Finally, we would like to thank all the attendees and participants in this year's conference.

We hope you will enjoy the *ACM SIGCOMM 2014* program. Now on with the show…

**Arvind Krishnamurthy**
*SIGCOMM 2014 Program Co-Chair*
*University of Washington*

**Sylvia Ratnasamy**
*SIGCOMM 2014 Program Co-Chair*
*University of California at Berkeley*

# Message from the Program Chairs

# Table of Contents

## Middleboxes and Network Services

Session Chair: Vyas Sekar *(Carnegie Mellon University)*



## Wireless 1

Session Chair: Shyamnath Gollakota *(University of Washington, Seattle)*



## Monitoring and Diagnostics

Session Chair: Aditya Akella *(University of Wisconsin)*



## Novel Datacenter Network Designs

Session Chair: Ratul Mahajan *(Microsoft Research)*

## Poster Session II

## Network Architecture 2

Session Chair: John Wroclawski *(ISI)*



## Scheduling in Datacenter Networks

Session Chair: Rodrigo Fonseca *(Brown University)*

## Wireless 2

Session Chair: Kyle Jamieson *(University College London)*



## Network Operations

Session Chair: Andrew Moore *(University of Cambridge, UK)*



## Poster Session 3

# SIGCOMM 2014 Conference Organization

**General Chairs:** Fabián E. Bustamante *(Northwestern University, USA)*
Y. Charlie Hu *(Purdue University, USA)*

**Program Chairs:** Arvind Krishnamurthy *(University of Washington, USA)*
Sylvia Ratnasamy (*University of California, Berkeley, USA)*

**Local Arrangements Chairs:** Yan Chen *(Northwestern University, USA)*
Jakob Eriksson *(University of Illinois, Chicago, USA)*

**Registration Chair:** Randall Berry *(Northwestern University, USA)*

**Workshop Chairs:** Matthew Caesar *(University of Illinois, Urbana-Champaign, USA)*
Ming Zhang *(Microsoft Research, USA)*

**Tutorial Chairs:** Sonia Fahmy *(Purdue University, USA)*
Jia Wang *(AT&T Labs, USA)*

**Poster and Demo Chairs:** David R. Choffnes *(Northeastern University, USA)*
Kun Tan *(Microsoft Research, China)*

**Publicity Chairs:** Xenofontas Dimitropulos *(ETH Zurich, Switzerland)*
Phillipa Gill *(Stony Brook University, USA)*
Bin Liu *(Tsinghua University, China)*
Claudio Righetti *(Universidad de Buenos Aires, Argentina)*

**Publication Chairs:** Robin Kravets *(University of Illinois, Urbana-Champaign, USA)*
Minlan Yu *(University of Southern California, USA)*

**Travel Grant Chairs:** Tilman Wolf *(University of Massachusetts Amherst, USA)*
Ignacio Alvarez-Hamelin *(Universidad de Buenos Aires, Argentina)*
Wenjun Hu *(Yale University, USA)*
Dimitrios Koutsonikolas *(University of Buffalo, SUNY, USA)*
Marco Mellia *(Politecnico di Torino, Italy)*

**Treasurer:** Sujata Banerjee *(HP Labs, USA)*

**Web Chair:** P. Brighten Godfrey *(University of Illinois, Urbana-Champaign, USA)*

**Conference Coordinator:** Yashar Ganjali *(University of Toronto, Canada)*

**Conference Coordinator Emeritus:** Jaudelice de Oliveira *(Drexel University, USA)*

**SIGCOMM Chair:** Srinivasan Keshav *(University of Waterloo, Canada)*

**SIGCOMM Conference Technical Steering Committee:**

Srinivasan Seshan *(Carnegie Mellon University, USA),* Chair
Venkat Padmanabhan *(Microsoft Research, India)*
Anja Feldmann *(Technische Universität Berlin, Germany)*
Scott Shenker *(ICSI/University of California, Berkeley, USA)*
Dina Katabi *(Massachusetts Institute of Technology, USA)*
Srinivasan Keshav *(University of Waterloo, Canada)*
Jeff Mogul *(Google, USA)*

**Program Committee:**

Aditya Akella *(University of Wisconsin, USA)*
Guido Appenzeller *(Big Swtich Networks, USA)*
Katerina Argyraki *(EPFL, Switzerland)*
Hitesh Ballani *(Microsoft Research, UK)*
Paul Barford *(University of Wisconsin, Madison, USA)*
Matt Caesar *(University of Illinois, USA)*
Augustin Chainterau *(Columbia University, USA)*
Bruce Davie *(VMware, USA)*
Christophe Diot *(Technicolor, France)*
Nandita Dukkipati *(Google, USA)*
Rodrigo Fonseca *(Brown University, USA)*
Nate Foster *(Cornell University, USA)*
Ali Ghodsi *(UC Berkeley, USA)*
Paul Francis *(Max Planck Institute, Germany)*
Sharon Goldberg *(Boston University, USA)*
Brighten Godfrey *(University of Illinois, Urbana-Champaign USA)*
Shyam Gollakota *(University of Washington, USA)*
Saikat Guha *(Microsoft Research, India)*
Krishna Gummadi *(Max Planck Institute, Germany)*
Chuanxiong Guo *(Microsoft Research, Asia)*
Polly Huang *(National Taiwan University, Taiwan)*
Kyle Jamieson *(University College London, UK)*
Brad Karp *(University College London, UK)*
Ethan Katz-Bassett *(University of Southern California, USA)*
Teemu Koponen *(VMware, USA)*
Harsha Madhyastha *(University of California, Riverside, USA)*
Ratul Mahajan *(Microsoft Research, USA)*
Nick McKeown *(Stanford University, USA)*
Michael Mitzenmacher *(Harvard University, USA)*
Andrew Moore *(University of Cambridge, UK)*
Robert Morris *(Massachusetts Institute of Technology, USA)*
Jitendra Padhye *(Microsoft Research, USA)*
Vivek Pai *(Princeton University, USA)*
Dina Papagiannaki *(Telefonica, Spain)*
KyoungSoo Park *(KAIST, Korea)*
Adrian Perrig *(ETH Zurich, Switzerland)*

**Program Committee (continued):**

Larry Peterson *(Princeton University and ON.LAB)*
Srinivasan Seshan *(Carnegie Mellon University, USA)*
Vyas Sekar *(Carnegie Mellon University, USA)*
Scott Shenker *(University of California, Berkeley and ICSI, USA)*
Alex Snoeren *(University of California, San Diego, USA)*
Neil Spring *(University of Maryland, USA)*
Kun Tan *(Microsoft Research, Asia)*
Renata Teixeira *(University Pierre et Marie Curie, France)*
Amin Vahdat *(Google and University of California, San Diego, USA)*
Walter Willinger *(Niksun, USA)*
John Wroclawski *(ISI, USA)*
Richard Yang *(Yale University, USA)*
Xiaowei Yang *(Duke University, USA)*
Minlan Yu *(University of Southern California, USA)*
Ellen Zegura *(Georgia Tech, USA)*
Yin Zhang *(University of Texas, Austin, USA)*

**Additional Reviewers:**

Marco Canini *(University College London, UK)*
Ranveer Chandra *(Microsoft Research)*
Krishna Kant Chintalapudi *(Microsoft Research)*
John Chuang *(University of California Berkeley, USA)*
Saurav Das *(Open Networking Foundation, USA)*
Jeff Dean *(Google, USA)*
Yashar Ganjali *(University of Toronto, Canada)*
Hugh Griffiths *(University College London, UK)*
Keon Jang *(KAIST, Korea)*
Ethan Katz-Bassett *(University of Southern California, USA)*
Charles Killian *(Purdue University, USA)*
Yongdae Kim *(KAIST, Korea)*
Ben Liblit *(University of Wisconsin, USA)*
Vishal Misra *(Columbia University, USA)*
Alex Orso *(Georgia Tech, USA)*
Aurojit Panda *(University of California, Berkeley, USA)*
George Porter *(University of California, San Diego, USA)*
Hariharan Rahul *(Massachusetts Institute of Technology, USA)*
Aaron Schulman *(Stanford University, USA)*
Haya Shulman *(Technische Universität Darmstadt, Germany)*
Patrick Traynor *(Georgia Tech, USA)*
Robbert Van Renesse *(Cornell University, USA)*
George Varghese *(Microsoft Research, USA)*
Michael Walfish *(University of Texas and New York University, USA)*
Junfeng Yang *(Columbia University, USA)*
Sergey Yekhanin *(Microsoft Research, USA)*
Ben Yoo *(University of California Davis, USA)*

# ACM SIGCMM 2014 Sponsors & Supporters

**Sponsors:**

**Supporters:**

# Keynote: Life in the Fast Lane

George Varghese
Microsoft Research

## ABSTRACT

The most compelling ideas in systems are *abstractions* such as virtual memory, sockets, or packet scheduling. Algorithmics is the servant of abstraction, allowing system performance to approach that of the underlying hardware, sometimes by using efficient algorithms but often by simply leveraging other aspects of the system. I will survey the trajectory of network algorithmics starting with a focus on speed and scale in the 1990s to measurement and security in the 2000s. While doing so, I will reflect on my experiences in choosing problems and conducting research. I will conclude by describing my passion for the emerging field of network verification and its confluence with programming language research.

## ACM Classification

C.2.0 Computer Systems Organization, COMPUTER-COMMUNICATION NETWORKS, General: Data communications

## BIO

George Varghese worked at DEC designing DECNET protocols before obtaining his Ph.D. in 1992 from MIT. He worked from 1993-1999 at Washington University and from 1999 to 2012 at UCSD, both as professor of computer science. He joined Microsoft Research as a Principal Researcher in 2012. He won the ONR Young Investigator Award in 1996, and was elected to be a Fellow of the Association for Computing Machinery (ACM) in 2002. He helped design the 40 Gbps forwarding engine for Procket Networks, subsequently acquired by Cisco Systems. His book "Network Algorithmics" was published in December 2004 by Morgan-Kaufman. He co-founded NetSift Inc. in May 2004. NetSift was acquired by Cisco in 2005. He was the 2014 winner of the IEEE Koji Kobayashi Computers and Communications Award.


*SIGCOMM'14*, August 17–22, 2014, Chicago, Illinois, USA.
ACM 978-1-4503-2836-4/14/08.
http://dx.doi.org/10.1145/2619239.2626337

# Millions of Little Minions: Using Packets for Low Latency Network Programming and Visibility

Vimalkumar Jeyakumar[1], Mohammad Alizadeh[2], Yilong Geng[1], Changhoon Kim[3], David Mazières[1]
[1]Stanford University, [2]Cisco Systems, [3]Barefoot Networks
{jvimal@cs.,alizade@,gengyl08@}stanford.edu, chkim@barefootnetworks.com

## ABSTRACT

This paper presents a practical approach to rapidly introducing new dataplane functionality into networks: End-hosts embed tiny programs into packets to actively query and manipulate a network's internal state. We show how this "tiny packet program" (TPP) interface gives end-hosts unprecedented visibility into network behavior, enabling them to work with the network to achieve a desired functionality. Our design leverages what each component does best: (a) switches forward and execute tiny packet programs (at most 5 instructions) in-band at line rate, and (b) end-hosts perform arbitrary (and easily updated) computation on network state. By implementing three different research proposals, we show that TPPs are *useful*. Using a hardware prototype on a NetFPGA, we show our design is *feasible* at a reasonable cost.

## Categories and Subject Descriptors

C.2.1 [**Computer-Communication Networks**]: Network Architecture and Design; C.2.3 [**Computer-Communication Networks**]: Network Operations; C.4 [**Performance of Systems**]: Design Studies, Performance Attributes

## Keywords

Active Networks, SDN, Software-Defined Networks, Network Architecture, Switch ASIC Design

## 1 Introduction

Consider a large datacenter network with thousands of switches. Applications complain about poor performance due to high flow completion times for a small subset of their flows. As an operator, you realize this symptom could be due to congestion, either from competing cross traffic or poor routing decisions, or alternatively could be due to packet drops at failed links. In any case, your goal is to diagnose this issue quickly. Unfortunately, the extensive use of multipath routing in today's networks means one often cannot determine the exact path taken by every packet; hence it is quite difficult to triangulate problems to a single switch. Making matters worse, if congestion is intermittent, counters within the network will look "normal" at timescales of minutes or even seconds.


*SIGCOMM'14*, August 17–22, 2014, Chicago, Illinois, USA.

ACM 978-1-4503-2836-4/14/08...$15.00.
http://dx.doi.org/10.1145/2619239.2626292

Such issues would be straightforward to debug if one could examine relevant network state such as switch ID, queue occupancy, input/output ports, port utilization, and matched forwarding rules *at the exact time each packet was forwarded*, so as to reconstruct what exactly transpired in the dataplane. In the above example, end-hosts could use state obtained from millions of successfully delivered packets to explicitly pinpoint network links that have high queue occupancy (for congestion), or use switch and port IDs to verify that packets were correctly routed, or use path information to triangulate network links that cause packet drops due to link failures. In short, the ability to correlate network state to specific packets would be invaluable.

Can packets be instrumented to access and report on switch state? To date such state has been locked inside switches. This paper describes a *simple, programmable* interface that enables end-hosts to query switch memory (counters, forwarding table entries, etc.) from packets, directly in the dataplane. Specifically, a subset of packets carry in their header a tiny packet program (TPP), which consists of a few instructions that read, write, or perform simple, protocol-agnostic computation using switch memory.

A key observation in this paper is that having such programmable and *fast* access to network state benefits a broad class of network tasks—congestion control, measurement, troubleshooting, and verification—which we call *dataplane* tasks. We show how the TPP interface enables end-hosts to rapidly deploy new functionality by refactoring many network tasks into: (a) simple TPPs that execute on switches, and (b) expressive programs at end-hosts.

TPPs contrast to three approaches to introduce new dataplane functionality: (1) build custom hardware for each task, (2) build switches that can execute arbitrary code [33, 36], or (3) use FPGAs and network processors [26]. Each approach has its own drawbacks: Introducing new switch functionality can take many years; switch hardware has stringent performance requirements and cannot incur the penalty of executing arbitrary code; and FPGAs and network processors are simply too expensive at large scale [7]. Instead, we argue that if we could build new hardware to support just *one* simple interface such as the TPP, we can leverage end-hosts to implement *many* complex tasks at software-development timescales.

TPPs can be viewed as a particular, reasoned point within the spectrum of ideas in Active Networking [33, 36]. In many Active Networks formulations, routers execute arbitrary programs that actively control network behavior such as routing, packet compression, and (de-)duplication. By contrast, TPP instructions are so simple they execute within the time to forward packets at line-rate. Just a handful of TPP instructions, shown in Table 1, providing access to the statistics in Table 2, proved sufficient to implement several previous research proposals.

| Instruction | Meaning |
|---|---|
| LOAD, PUSH | Copy values from switch to packet |
| STORE, POP | Copy values from packet to switch |
| CSTORE | Conditionally store and execute subsequent operations |
| CEXEC | Conditionally execute the subsequent instructions |

Table 1: The tasks we present in the paper require support only for the above instructions, whose operands will be clear when we discuss examples. Write instructions may be selectively disabled by the administrator.

## 1.1 Goals

Our main goal is to expose network state to end-hosts through the dataplane. To benefit dataplane tasks, any interface should satisfy the following requirements:

- **Speed**: A recent study shows evidence that switch CPUs are not powerful and are unable to handle more than a few hundred OpenFlow control messages/second [14]. Our experience is that such limitations stand in the way of a whole class of dataplane tasks as they operate at packet and round-trip timescales.
- **Packet-level consistency**: Switch state such as link queue occupancy and forwarding tables varies over time. Today, we lack any means of obtaining a consistent view of such state as it pertains to each packet traveling through the network.
- **Minimality and power**: To be worth the effort, any hardware design should be simple, be sufficiently expressive to enable a diverse class of useful tasks, and incur low-enough overhead to work at line rates.

This paper presents a specific TPP interface whose design is largely guided by the above requirements.

**Non-Goals**: It is worth noting that our goal is not to be flexible enough to implement any, and all dataplane network tasks. For instance, TPPs are not expressive enough to implement per-packet scheduling. Moreover, our design is for networks owned and operated by a single administrative entity (e.g., privately owned WANs and datacenters). We do not advocate exposing network state to untrusted end-hosts connected to the network, but we describe mechanisms to avoid executing untrusted TPPs (§4.3). Finally, a detailed design for inter-operability across devices from multiple vendors is beyond the scope of this paper, though we discuss one plausible approach (§8).

## 1.2 Summary of Results

Through both a software implementation and a NetFPGA prototype, this paper demonstrates that TPPs are both useful and feasible at line rate. Moreover, an analysis using recent data [7] suggests that TPP support within switch hardware can be realized at an acceptable cost.

**Applications**: We show the benefits of TPP by refactoring many recent research proposals using the TPP interface. These tasks broadly fall under the following three categories:

- **Congestion Control**: We show how end-hosts, by periodically querying network link utilization and queue sizes with TPP, can implement a rate-based congestion control algorithm (RCP) providing max-min fairness across flows. We furthermore show how the TPP interface enables fairness metrics beyond the max-min fairness for which RCP was originally designed (§2.2).
- **Network Troubleshooting**: TPPs give end-hosts detailed per-packet visibility into network state that can be used to implement a recently proposed troubleshooting platform called NetSight [13]. In particular, we walk through implementing and deploying `ndb`, a generalization of traceroute introduced by NetSight (§2.3).
- **Network Control**: We also demonstrate how low-latency visibility offered by TPPs enables end-hosts to control how traffic is load balanced across network paths. We refactor CONGA [1], an in-network load-balancing mechanism implemented in Cisco's new ASICs, between end-hosts and a network that supports only the TPP interface.

| Statistics | Examples |
|---|---|
| Per-Switch | Switch ID, counters associated with the global L2 or L3 flow tables, flow table version number, timestamp. |
| Per-Port | Link utilization, bytes received, bytes dropped, bytes enqueued, application-specific registers. |
| Per-Queue | Bytes enqueued, bytes dropped. |
| Per-Packet | Packet's input/output port, queue, matched flow entry, alternate routes for a packet. |

Table 2: A non-exhaustive list of statistics stored in switches memory that TPPs can access when mapped to known memory locations. Many statistics are already tracked today but others, such as flow table version will have to be implemented. Some statistics are read-only (e.g. matched flow entry, bytes received), but others can be modified (e.g. packet's output port). See OpenFlow 1.4 specification [29, Table 5] for a detailed list of available statistics.

**Hardware**: To evaluate the feasibility of building a TPP-capable switch, we synthesized and built a four-port NetFPGA router (at 160MHz) with full TPP support, capable of switching minimum sized packets on each interface at 10Gb/s. We show the hardware and latency costs of adding TPP support are minimal on NetFPGA, and argue the same would hold of a real switch (§6). We find that the key to achieving high performance is restricting TPPs to a handful of instructions per packet (say five), as it ensures that any TPP executes within a fraction of the its transmission time.

**Software**: We also implemented the TPP interface in Open vSwitch [31], which we use to demonstrate research proposals and examples. Additionally, we present a software stack (§4) that enforces security and access control, handles TPP composition, and has a library of useful primitives to ease the path to deploying TPP applications.

The software and hardware implementations of TPP, scripts to run experiments and plots in this paper, and an extended version of this paper describing more TPP applications are all available online at `http://jvimal.github.io/tpp`.

# 2 Example Programs

We start our discussion using examples of dataplane tasks that can be implemented using TPPs, showcasing the utility of exposing network state to end-hosts directly in the dataplane. Each of these tasks typically requires new task-specific hardware changes; however, we show how each task can be refactored such that the network only implements TPPs, while delegating complex task-specific functionality to end-hosts. We will discuss the following tasks: (i) micro-burst detection, (ii) a rate-based congestion control algorithm, (iii) a network troubleshooting platform, (iv) a congestion aware, distributed, network load balancer.

**What is a TPP?** A TPP is any Ethernet packet with a uniquely identifiable header that contains instructions, some additional space (packet memory), and an optional encapsulated Ethernet payload (e.g. IP packet). The TPP exclusively owns its packet memory, but also has access to shared memory on the switch (its SRAM and internal registers) through addresses. TPPs execute directly in the dataplane at every hop, and are forwarded just like other packets. TPPs use a very minimal instruction set listed in Table 1, and we

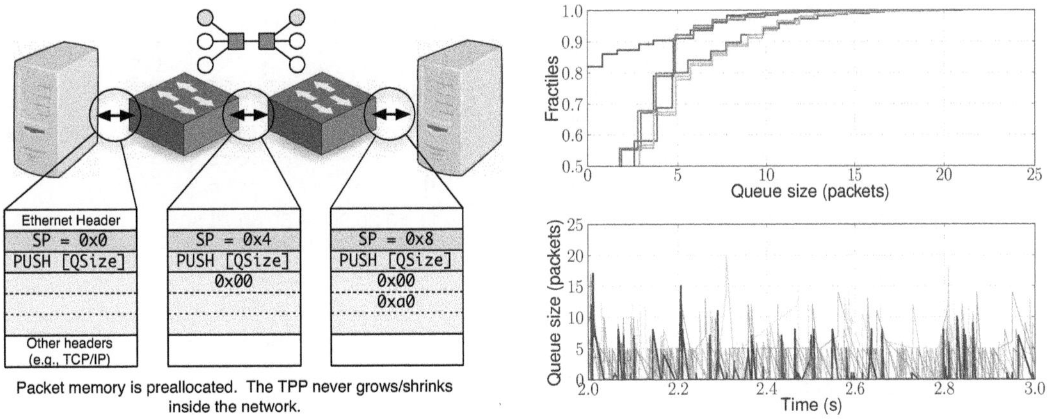


(a) Visualizing the execution of a TPP as it is routed through the network.

(b) CDF and time series of queue occupancy on 6 queues in the network, obtained from *every* packet arriving at one host.

Figure 1: TPPs enable end-hosts to measure queue occupancy evolution at a packet granularity allowing them to detect micro-bursts, which are the spikes in the time series of queue occupancy (bottom of Figure 1b). Notice from the CDF (top) that one of the queues is empty for 80% of the time instants when packet arrives to the queue; a sampling method is likely to miss the bursts.

refer the reader to Section 3 to understand the space overheads. We abuse terminology, and use TPPs to refer both to the programs and the packets that carry them.

We write TPPs in a pseudo-assembly-language with a segmented address space naming various registers, switch RAM, and packet memory. We write addresses using human-readable labels, such as `[Namespace:Statistic]` or `[Queue:QueueOccupancy]`. We posit that these addresses be known upfront at compile time. For example, the mnemonic `[Queue:QueueOccupancy]` could be refer to an address `0xb000` that stores the occupancy of a packet's output queue at each switch.

## 2.1 Micro-burst Detection

Consider the problem of monitoring link queue occupancy within the network to diagnose short-lived congestion events (or "micro-bursts"), which directly quantifies the impact of incast. In low-latency networks such as datacenters, queue occupancy changes rapidly at timescales of a few RTTs. Thus, observing and controlling such bursty traffic requires visibility at timescales orders of magnitude faster than the mechanisms such as SNMP or embedded web servers that we have today, which operate at tens of seconds at best. Moreover, even if the monitoring mechanism is fast, it is not clear which queues to monitor, as (i) the underlying routing could change, and (ii) switch hash functions that affect multipath routing are often proprietary and unknown.

TPPs can provide fine-grained per-RTT, or even per-packet visibility into queue evolution inside the network. Today, switches already track per-port, per-queue occupancy for memory management. The instruction `PUSH [Queue:QueueOccupancy]` could be used to copy the queue register onto the packet. As the packet traverses each hop, the packet memory has snapshots of queue sizes at each hop. The queue sizes are useful in diagnosing micro-bursts, as they are not an average value. They are recorded when the packet traverses the switch. Figure 1a shows the state of a sample packet as it traverses a network. In the figure, `SP` is the stack pointer which points to the next offset inside the packet memory where new values may be pushed. Since the maximum number of hops is small within a datacenter (typically 5–7), the end-host preallocates enough packet memory to store queue sizes. Moreover, the end-host knows exactly how to interpret values in the packet to obtain a detailed breakdown of queueing latencies on all network hops.

This example illustrates how a low-latency, programmatic interface to access dataplane state can be used by software at end-hosts to measure dataplane behavior that is hard to observe in the control plane. Figure 1a shows a six-node dumbell topology on Mininet [12], in which each node sends a small 10kB message to every other node in the topology. The total application-level offered load is 30% of the hosts' network capacity (100Mb/s). We instrumented every packet with a TPP, and collected fully executed TPPs carrying network state at one host. Figure 1b shows the queue evolution of 6 queues inside the network obtained from every packet received at that host.

**Overheads**: The actual TPP consists of three instructions, one each to read the switch ID, the port number, and the queue size, each a 16 bit integer. If the diameter of the network is 5 hops, then each TPP adds only a 54 byte overhead to each packet: 12 bytes for the TPP header (see §3.4), 12 bytes for instructions, and $6 \times 5$ bytes to collect statistics at each hop.

## 2.2 Rate-based Congestion Control

While the previous example shows how TPPs can help observe latency spikes, we now show how such visibility can be used to *control* network congestion. Congestion control is arguably a dataplane task, and the literature has a number of ideas on designing better algorithms, many of which require switch support. However, TCP and its variants still remain the dominant congestion control algorithms. Many congestion control algorithms, such as XCP [20], FCP [11], RCP [9], etc. work by monitoring state that indicates congestion and adjusting flow rates every few RTTs.

We now show how end-hosts can use TPPs to deploy a new congestion control algorithm that enjoys many benefits of in-network algorithms, such as Rate Control Protocol (RCP) [9]. RCP is a congestion control algorithm that rapidly allocates link capacity to help flows finish quickly. An RCP router maintains one fair-share rate $R(t)$ per link (of capacity $C$, regardless of the number of flows), computed periodically (every $T$ seconds) as follows:

$$R(t+T) = R(t)\left(1 - \frac{T}{d} \times \frac{a\,(y(t) - C) + b\,\frac{q(t)}{d}}{C}\right) \qquad (1)$$

Here, $y(t)$ is the average ingress link utilization, $q(t)$ is the average queue size, $d$ is the average round-trip time of flows traversing the link, and $a$ and $b$ are configurable parameters. Each router checks if its estimate of $R(t)$ is smaller than the flow's fair-share (indicated on each packet's header); if so, it replaces the flow's fair share header value with $R(t)$.

We now describe RCP*, an end-host implementation of RCP. The implementation consists of a rate limiter and a rate controller at end-hosts for every flow (since RCP operates at a per-flow granularity). The network control plane allocates two memory addresses per link (`Link:AppSpecific_0` and `Link:AppSpecific_1`) to store fair rates. Each flow's rate controller periodically (using the flow's packets, or using additional probe packets) queries and modifies network state in three phases.

**Phase 1: Collect.** Using the following TPP, the rate controller queries the network for the switch ID on each hop, queue sizes, link utilization, and the link's fair share rate (and its version number), for all links along the path. The receiver simply echos a fully executed TPP back to the sender. The network updates link utilization counters every millisecond. If needed, end-hosts can measure them faster by querying for `[Link:RX-Bytes]`.

```
PUSH [Switch:SwitchID]
PUSH [Link:QueueSize]
PUSH [Link:RX-Utilization]
PUSH [Link:AppSpecific_0] # Version number
PUSH [Link:AppSpecific_1] # Rfair
```

**Phase 2: Compute.** In the second phase, each sender computes a fair share rate $R_{\text{link}}$ for each link: Using the samples collected in phase 1, the rate controller computes the average queue sizes on each link along the path. Then, it computes a per-link rate $R_{\text{link}}$ using the RCP control equation.

**Phase 3: Update.** In the last phase, the rate-controller of each flow asynchronously sends the following TPP to update the fair rates on all links. To ensure correctness due to concurrent updates, we use the `CSTORE` instruction:

```
  CSTORE [Link:AppSpecific_0], \
            [Packet:Hop[0]], [Packet:Hop[1]]
  STORE [Link:AppSpecific_1], [Packet:Hop[2]]
PacketMemory:
  Hop1: V_1, V_1+1, R_new_1, (* 16 bits each*)
  Hop2: V_2, V_2+1, R_new_2, ...
```

where $V_i$ is the version number in the `AppSpecific_0` that the end-host used to derive an updated $R_{\text{new},i}$ for hop $i$, thus ensuring consistency. (`CSTORE dst,old,new` updates `dst` with `new` only if `dst` was `old`, ignoring the rest of the TPP otherwise.) Note that in the TPP, the version numbers and fair rates are read from packet memory at every hop.

**Other allocations**: Although RCP was originally designed to allocate bandwidth in a max-min fair manner among competing flows, Kelly et al. [22] showed how to tweak RCP to allocate bandwidth for a spectrum of fairness criteria—$\alpha$-fairness parameterized by a real number $\alpha \geq 0$. $\alpha$-fairness is achieved as follows: if $R_i$ is the fair rate computed at the $i$-th link traversed by the flow (as per the RCP control equation 1), the flow sets its rate as

$$R = \left(\sum_i R_i^{-\alpha}\right)^{-1/\alpha} \qquad (2)$$

The value $\alpha = 1$ corresponds to proportional fairness, and we can see that in the limit as $\alpha \to \infty$, $R = \min_i R_i$, which is consistent with the notion of max-min fairness. Observe that if the ASIC hardware had been designed for max-min version of RCP, it would have been difficult for end-hosts to achieve other useful notions of fairness. However, TPPs help defer the choice of fairness to deployment time, as the end-hosts can aggregate the per-link $R_i$ according to equation 2 based on *one* chosen $\alpha$. (We do not recommend flows with different $\alpha$ sharing the same links due to reasons in [35].)

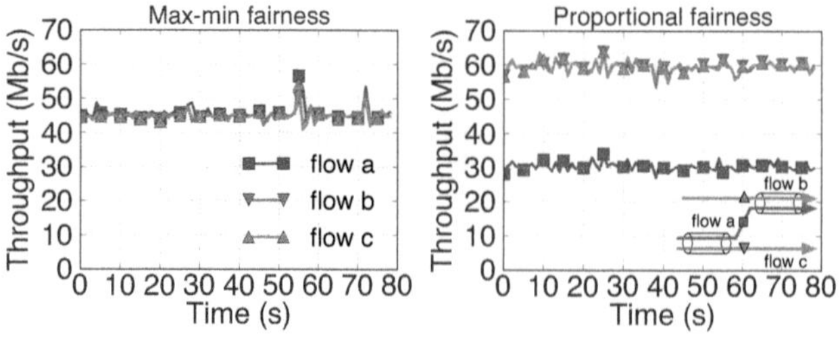


Figure 2: Allocations by max-min and proportional fairness variant of RCP on the traffic pattern shown inset on the right plot; each link has 100Mb/s capacity and all flows start at 1Mb/s at time 0.

Figure 2 shows the throughput of three flows for both max-min RCP* and proportional-fair RCP* in Mininet: Flow 'a' shares one link each with flows 'b' and 'c' (shown inset in the right plot). Flows are basically rate-limited UDP streams, where rates are determined using the control algorithm: Max-min fairness should allocate rates equally across flows, whereas proportional fairness should allocate ⅓ of the link to the flow that traverses two links, and ⅔ to the flows that traverse only one link.

**Overheads**: For the experiment in Figure 2, the bandwidth overhead imposed by TPP control packets was about 1.0–6.0% of the flows' rate as we varied the number of long lived flows from 3 to 30 to 99 (averaged over 3 runs). In the same experiment, TCP had slightly lower overheads: 0.8–2.4%. The RCP* overhead is in the same range as TCP because each flow sends control packets roughly once every RTT. As the number of flows $n$ increases, the average per-flow rate decreases as $1/n$, which causes the RTT of each flow to increase (as the RTT is inversely proportional to flow rate). Therefore, the total overhead does not blow up.

**Are writes absolutely necessary?** RCP* is one of the few TPP applications that *writes* to network state. It is worth asking if this is absolutely necessary. We believe it is necessary for fast convergence since RCP relies on flows traversing a single bottleneck link agreeing on *one* shared rate, which is explicitly enforced in RCP. Alternatively, if rapid convergence isn't critical, flows can converge to their fair rates in an AIMD fashion *without* writing to network state. In fact, XCP implements this AIMD approach, but experiments in [9] show that XCP converges more slowly than RCP.

## 2.3 Network Troubleshooting Framework

There has been recent interest in designing programmatic tools for troubleshooting networks; without doubt, dataplane visibility is central to a troubleshooter. For example, consider the task of verifying that network forwarding rules match the intent specified by the administrator [21, 23]. This task is hard as forwarding rules change constantly, and a network-wide 'consistent' update is not a trivial task [32]. Verification is further complicated by the fact that there can be a mismatch between the control plane's view of routing state and the actual forwarding state in hardware (and such problems have shown up in a cloud provider's production network [24]). Thus, verifying whether packets have been correctly forwarded requires help from the dataplane.

Recently, researchers have proposed a platform called NetSight [13]. NetSight introduced the notion of a 'packet history,'

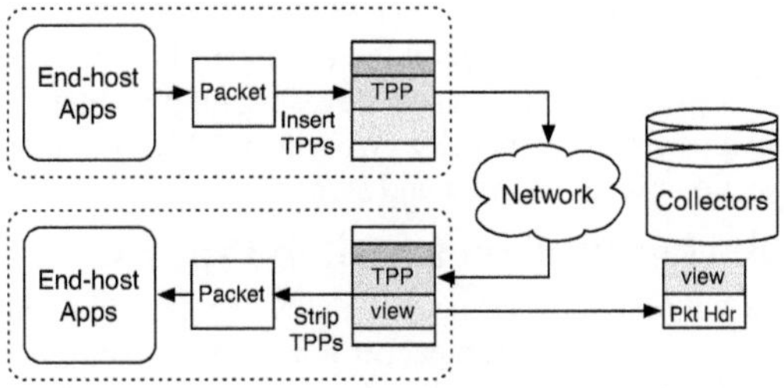


Figure 3: TPPs enable end-hosts to efficiently collect packet histories, which can then be used to implement four different troubleshooting applications described in [13].

which is a record of the packet's path through the network and the switch forwarding state applied to the packet. Using this construct, the authors show how to build four different network troubleshooting applications.

We first show how to efficiently capture packet histories that are central to the NetSight platform. NetSight works by interposing on the control channel between the controller and the network, stamping each flow entry with a unique version number, and modifying flow entries to create truncated copies of packet headers tagged with the version number (without affecting a packet's normal forwarding) and additional metadata (e.g., the packet's input/output ports). These truncated packet copies are reassembled by servers to reconstruct the packet history.

We can refactor the task of collecting packet histories by having a trusted agent at every end-host (§4) insert the TPP shown below on all (or a subset of) its packets. On receiving a TPP that has finished executing on all hops, the end-host gets an accurate view of the network forwarding state that affected the packet's forwarding, without requiring the network to create additional packet copies.

```
PUSH [Switch:ID]
PUSH [PacketMetadata:MatchedEntryID]
PUSH [PacketMetadata:InputPort]
```

Once the end-host constructs a packet history, it is forwarded to collectors where they can be used in many ways. For instance, if the end-host stores the histories, we get the same functionality as `netshark`—a network-wide `tcpdump` distributed across servers. From the stored traces, an administrator can use any query language (e.g., SQL) to extract relevant packet histories, which gives the same functionality as the interactive network debugger `ndb`. Another application, `netwatch` simply uses the packet histories to verify whether network forwarding trace conforms to a policy specified by the control plane (e.g., isolation between tenants).

**Overheads**: The instruction overhead is 12 bytes/packet and 6 bytes of per-hop data. With a TPP header and space for 10 hops, this is 84 bytes/packet. If the average packet size is 1000 bytes, this is a 8.4% bandwidth overhead if we insert the TPP on every packet. If we enable it only for a subset of packets, the overhead will be correspondingly lower.

**Caveats**: Despite its benefits, there are drawbacks to using only TPPs, especially if the network transforms packets in erroneous or non-invertible ways. We can overcome dropped packets by sending packets that will be dropped to a collector (we describe how in §2.5). Some of these assumptions (trusting the dataplane to function correctly) are also made by NetSight, and we believe the advantages of TPPs outweigh its drawbacks. For instance, TPPs can collect more statistics, such as link utilization and queue occupancy, along with a packet's forwarding history.

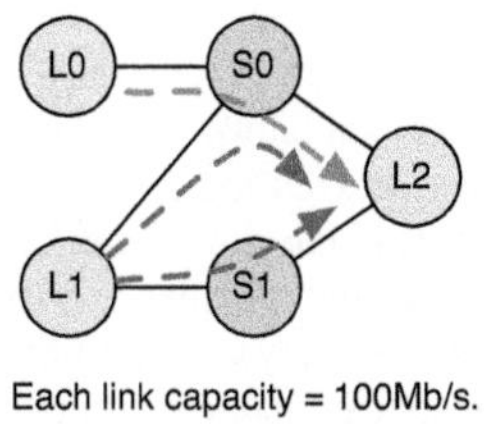


| | | Achieved Thput. | |
|---|---|---|---|
| Flow | Dem. | ECMP | CONGA* |
| L0:L2 | 50 | 45 | 50 |
| L1:L2 | 120 | 115 | 120 |
| Max Util = | | 100 | 85 |

All demand and throughput numbers are in Mb/s.

Figure 4: An example showing the benefits of congestion-aware load balancing: ECMP splits flow from L1 to L2 equally across the two paths resulting in suboptimal network utilization. CONGA*, an end-host refactoring of CONGA [1] is able to detect and reroute flows, achieving optimum in this example.

## 2.4 Distributed Load Balancing

We now show how end-hosts can use TPPs to probe for network congestion, and use this detailed visibility to load balance traffic in a distributed fashion. We demonstrate a simplified version of CONGA [1], which is an in-network scheme for traffic load balancing. CONGA strives to maximize network throughput and minimize the maximum network link utilization in a distributed fashion by having network switches maintain a table of path-level congestion metrics (e.g., quantized link utilization). Using this information, switches route small bursts of flows ("flowlets") selfishly on the least loaded path. CONGA is optimized for datacenter network topologies; we refer the curious reader to [1] for more details.

CONGA's design highlights two benefits relevant to our discussion. First, it uses explicit visibility by having switches stamp quantized congestion information on packet headers. Second, load balancing decisions are made at round-trip timescales to rapidly detect and react to network congestion. Since TPPs also offer similar benefits, we show how we can refactor the load balancing task between end-hosts and the network, without requiring custom hardware (except, of course, to support TPPs).

First, we require the network to install multipath routes that end-hosts can select based on packet header values. This can be done in the slow-path by the control plane by programming a 'group table' available in many switches today for multipath routing [29, §5.6.1], which selects an output port by hashing on header fields (e.g., the VLAN tag). This allows end-hosts to select network paths simply by changing the VLAN ID.

Second, we need end-hosts to query for link utilization across various paths, by inserting the following TPP on a subset of packets destined to hosts within the datacenter:

```
PUSH [Link:ID]
PUSH [Link:TX-Utilization]
PUSH [Link:TX-Bytes]
```

We query for `Link:TX-Bytes` to measure small congestion events if the link utilization isn't updated. The receiver echoes fully executed TPPs back to the sender to communicate the congestion. Note that the header of the echoed TPP also contains the path ID along with the link utilization on each link in the path.

Third, using information in the fully executed TPPs, end-hosts can build a table mapping 'Path $i \rightarrow$ Congestion Metric $(m_i)$,' where $m_i$ is either the maximum or sum of link utilization on each switch–switch network hop on path $i$. The authors of CONGA note that 'sum' is closer to optimal than 'max' in the worst-case scenario (adversarial); however CONGA used 'max' as it does not cause overflows when switches aggregate path-congestion. With TPPs, this is not an issue, and the choice can be deferred to deploy time.

And finally, end-hosts have full context about flows and flowlets, and therefore each end-host can select a flowlet's path by setting the path tag appropriately on the flowlet's packets.

**Overheads**: We implemented a proof-of-concept prototype (CONGA*) in software using UDP flows; Figure 4 reproduces an example from CONGA [1, Figure 4]. We configured switches S0 and S1 to select paths based on destination UDP port. The flow from L0 to L2 uses only one path, whereas the flow from L1 to L2 has two paths. The UDP agents at L0 and L1 query for link utilization and aggregate congestion metrics every millisecond for the two paths. With CONGA*, end-hosts can maximize network throughput meeting the demands for both flows, while simultaneously minimizing the maximum link utilization. In this example, the overhead introduced by TPP packets was minimal (< 1% of the total traffic).

**Remark**: Note that the functionality is *refactored* between the network and end-hosts; not all functionality resides completely at the end-hosts. The network implements TPP and multipath routing. The end-hosts merely select paths based on congestion completely in software.

## 2.5 Other possibilities

The above examples illustrate how a single TPP interface enables end-hosts to achieve many tasks. There are more tasks that we couldn't cover in detail. In the interest of space, we refer the reader to the extended version of this paper for more details on some of the tasks below [28].

**Measurement**: Since TPPs can read network state, they can be used in a straightforward fashion for measuring any network statistic at rapid timescales. As TPPs operate in the dataplane, they are in a unique position to expose path characteristics experienced by a specific packet that an end-host cares about.

**Network verification**: TPPs also help in verifying whether network devices meet certain requirements. For example, the path visibility offered by TPPs help accurately verify that route convergence times are within an acceptable value. This task can be challenging today, if we rely on end-to-end reachability as a way to measure convergence, because backup paths can still maintain end-to-end connectivity when routes change. Also, the explicit visibility eases fault localization.

**Fast network updates**: By allowing secure applications to write to a switch's forwarding tables, network updates can be made very fast. This can reduce the time window of a transient state when network forwarding state hasn't converged. For example, it is possible to add a new route to all switches along a path in half a round-trip time, as updating an IP forwarding table requires only 64 bits of information per-hop: 32 bit address and a 32 bit netmask per hop, tiny enough to fit inside a packet.

**Wireless Networks**: TPPs can also be used in wireless networks where access points can annotate end-host packets with rapidly changing state such as channel SNR. Low-latency access to such rapidly changing state is useful for network diagnosis, allows end-hosts to distinguish between congestive losses and losses due to poor channel quality, and query the bitrate that an AP selected for a particular packet.

# 3 Design of TPP-Capable Switches

In this section, we discuss the TPP instructions, addressing schemes, and the semantics of the TPP interface to a switch and what it means for a switch to be TPP-capable. Network switches have a variety of form factors and implementations; they could be implemented in software (e.g., Click, Open vSwitch), or in network processors (e.g., NetFPGA), or as hardware ASICs. A switch might also be built hierarchically from multiple ASICs, as in 'chassis' based switches [18, Figure 3]. A TPP can be executed on each of these platforms. Thus, it is useful for a TPP-capable switch and the end-host to have a contract that preserves useful properties without imposing a performance penalty. We achieve this by constraining the instruction execution order and atomicity.

## 3.1 Background on a Switch Pipeline

We begin with an abstract model of a switch execution environment shown in Figure 5. The packet flows from input to output(s) through many pipelined modules. Once a packet arrives at an input port, the dataplane tags the packet with metadata (such as its ingress port number). Then, the packet passes through a parser that extracts fields from the packet and passes it further down the pipeline which consists of several match-action stages. This is also known as multiple match table model [7]. For example, one stage might use the parsed fields to route the packet (using a combination of layer 2 MAC table, layer 3 longest-prefix match table, and a flexible TCAM table). Finally, any modifications to the packet are committed and the packet is queued in switch memory. Using metadata (such as the packet's priority), the scheduler decides when it is time for the packet to be transmitted out of the egress port determined earlier in the pipeline. The egress stage also consists of a number of match-action stages.

## 3.2 TPP Semantics

The read/write instructions within a TPP access two distinct memory spaces: memory within the switch (switch memory), and a per-hop scratch space within the packet (packet memory). By all switch memory, we only mean memory at the stages traversed by a TPP, except the memory that stores packet contents. By all packet memory, we mean the TPP related fields in the packet. Now, we state our requirements for read/write instructions accessing the two memory spaces.

**Switch memory**: To expose statistics pertaining to a specific packet as it traverses the network, it is important for the instructions in the TPP to have access to the same values that are used to forward the packet. For read-only values, this requirement means that reads by a TPP to a single memory location must necessarily be atomic and after all writes by the forwarding logic to the *same* memory location. For example, if a TPP accesses the memory that holds the output port of a packet, it must return the same port that the forwarding logic determines, and no other value. This is what we mean by a "packet-consistent" view of network state.

For read-write memory addresses, it is useful if instructions within the TPP were executed in the order specified by the TPP to a given location *after* any modifications by the switch forwarding logic. Thus, writes by a TPP supersede those performed by forwarding logic.

**Packet memory**: Since instructions can read from and write to packet memory using `PUSH` and `POP`, writes to packet memory must take effect sequentially in the order specified by the TPP. This guarantees that if a TPP pushes values at memory locations X, Y, and Z onto packet memory, the end-host sees the values in the packet in the same order. This does not require that reads to X, Y, and Z be issued in the same order.

## 3.3 TPP Execution Model

TPPs are executed in the dataplane pipeline. TPPs are required to fit exactly within an MTU to avoid having the ASIC deal with fragmentation issues. This is not a big limitation, as end-hosts can split a complex task into multiple smaller TPPs if a single packet has insufficient memory to query all the required statistics. By default, a TPP executes at every hop, and instructions are not executed if

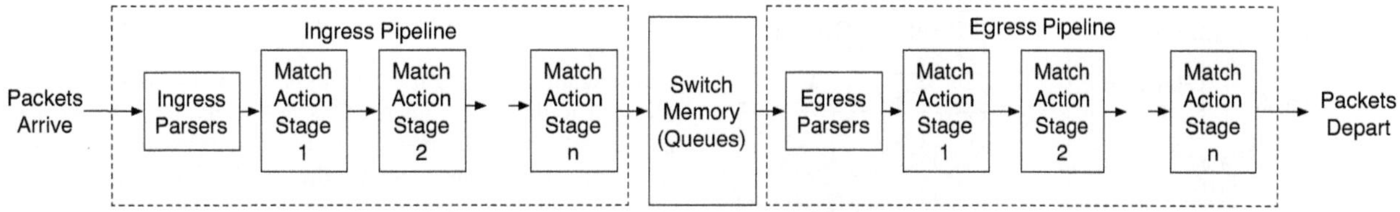


Figure 5: A simplified block diagram of the dataplane pipeline in a switch ASIC. Packets arrive at the ingress, and pass through multiple modules. The scheduler then forwards packets (that are not dropped) to the output ports computed at earlier stages in the pipeline.

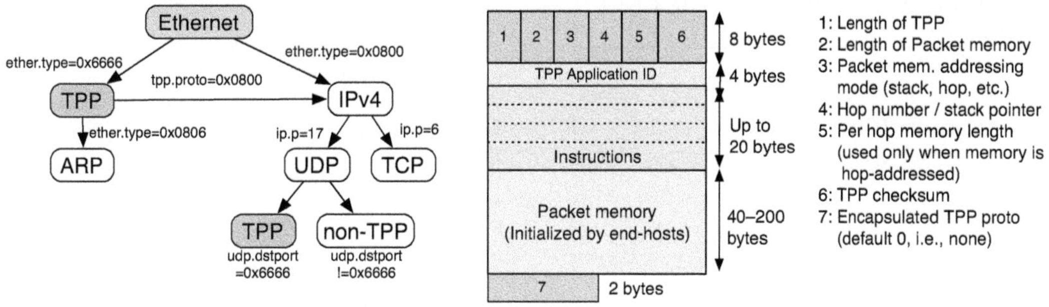


(a) Parse graph for the two ways to parse TPPs: transparent mode, or standalone mode.

(b) TPP's packet structure.

Figure 6: The parse graph and structure of a TPP. We chose `0x6666` as the ethertype and source UDP port that uniquely identifies a TPP. With a programmable switch parser, this choice can be reprogrammed at any time.

they access memory that doesn't exist. This ensures the TPP fails gracefully.

Furthermore, the platform is free to reorder reads and writes so they execute in any order. However, if the programmer needs guarantees on ordering instructions due to data hazards (e.g., for `CEXEC, CSTORE`), they must ensure the TPP accesses memory in the pipeline order. For a vast majority of use cases, we argue this restriction is not severe. From a practical standpoint, this requirement ensures that the switch pipeline remains feed-forward as it is today in a majority of switches.

### *3.3.1 Unified Memory-Mapped IO*

A TPP has access to any statistic computed by the switch that is addressable. The statistics can be broadly namespaced into per-switch (i.e., global), per-port, per-queue and per-packet. Table 2 shows example statistics in each of these namespaces. These statistics may be scattered across different stages in the pipeline, but TPPs access them via a unified address space. For instance, a switch keeps metadata such as input port, the selected route, etc. for every packet that can be made addressable. These address mappings are known upfront to the TPP compiler that converts mnemonics such as `[PacketMetadata:InputPort]` into virtual addresses.

### *3.3.2 Addressing Packet Memory*

Memory is managed using a stack pointer and a `PUSH` instruction that appends values to preallocated packet memory. TPPs also support a hop addressing scheme, similar to the the `base:offset` x86-addressing mode. Here, `base:offset` refers to the word at location `base * hop_size + offset`. Thus, if hop-size is 16 bytes, the instruction "`LOAD [Switch:SwitchID], [Packet:hop[1]]`" will copy the switch ID into `PacketMemory[1]` on the first hop, `PacketMemory[17]` on the second hop, etc. The `offset` is part of the instruction; the `base` value (hop number) and per-hop memory size values are in the TPP header. To simplify memory management in the dataplane, the end-host must preallocate enough space in the TPP to hold per-hop data structures.

### *3.3.3 Synchronization Instructions*

Besides read and write, a useful instruction in a concurrent programming environment is an atomic update instruction, such as a conditional store `CSTORE`, conditioned on a memory location matching a specified value, halting subsequent instructions in the TPP if the update fails. That is, `CSTORE [X],[Packet:hop[Pre]],[Packet:hop[Post]]` works as follows:

```
succeeded = False
if (value at X == value at Packet:hop[Pre]) {
  value at X = value at Packet:hop[Post]
  succeeded = True
}
value at Packet:hop[Pre] = value at X;
if (succeeded) {
  allow subsequent instructions to execute
}
```

By having `CSTORE` return the value of `X`, an end-host can infer if the instruction succeeded. Notice that the second and third operands are read from a unique location at every hop. This is needed to ensure correct semantics when the switch overwrites the value at the second operand.

In a similar vein, we found a conditional execute (`CEXEC`) instruction useful; for example, it may be desirable to execute a network task only on one switch, or on a subset of switches (say all the top of rack switches in a datacenter). The conditional execute instruction specifies a memory address, a 32-bit mask, and a 32-bit value (specified in the packet hop), which instructs the switch to execute all subsequent instructions only when `(switch_value & mask) == value`. All instructions that follow a failed `CEXEC` check will not be executed.

## 3.4 Parsing: TPP Packet Format

As noted in §2, a TPP is any Ethernet frame from which we can uniquely identify a TPP header, the instructions, packet memory, and an optional payload. This allows end-hosts to use TPPs in two ways: (i) piggy-back TPPs on any existing packet by encapsulating

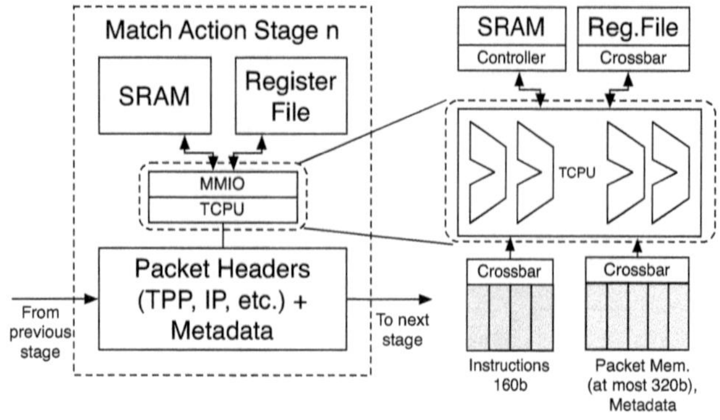


Figure 7: At every stage, the TCPU has execution units that can access only local memory and registers, as well as packet metadata.

the packet within a TPP of ethertype 0x6666, or (ii) embed a TPP into an otherwise normal UDP packet destined for port 0x6666, which is a special port number usurped by TPP-enabled routers.

Figure 6a shows the two parse graphs depicting the two ways in which our prototype uses TPPs. A parse graph depicts a state machine for a packet parser, in which the nodes denote protocols and edges denote state transitions when field values match. We use the same convention as in [7] to show the two ways in which we can parse TPPs.

### 3.5 Putting it together: the TCPU

TPPs execute on a tiny processor, which we call the TCPU. A simple way to implement the TCPU is by having a RISC-like processor at the end of the ingress match-action stages as we described in our earlier position paper [19, Figure 5]. This simple approach could be practical for software, or low-speed hardware switches, but might be impractical in high-speed hardware switches as memory in an ASIC is often distributed across modules. The wiring complexity to provide read and write paths from each module to the TCPU becomes prohibitively expensive within an ASIC, and is simply infeasible across line-cards in a chassis switch.

We overcome this limitation in two ways. First, our execution model permits reordering reads and writes across different ASIC memory locations. Second, end-hosts can statically analyze a desired TPP and split it into smaller TPPs if one TPP is insufficient. For instance, if an end-host requires link utilization on all links at all switches a packet traverses, it can stage the following sequence of TPPs: (i) send one TPP to collect switch ID and link utilizations on links traversed by the packet, and (ii) send a new TPP to each switch link on the switches traversed by TPP 1 to collect the remaining statistics. To summarize:

- Loads and stores in a single packet can be executed in any order, by having end-hosts ensure there are no write-after-write, or read-after-write conflicts.
- The operands for conditional instructions, such as CSTORE and CEXEC, are available before, or at the stages where the subsequent instructions execute; CEXEC can execute when all its operands are available.

By allowing instructions to be executed out of order, we can distribute the single logical TCPU on an ASIC by replicating its functionality at every stage. Each stage has one execution unit for every instruction in the packet, a crossbar to connect the execution units to all registers local to the stage and packet memory, and access to the stage's local memory read/write port. From the decoded instructions, the stage can execute all instructions local to the stage, and once all memory accesses have completed, the packet leaves the stage.

Replicating execution units might seem expensive, but the majority of logic area in an ASIC is due to the large memories (for packet buffers, counters, etc.), so the cost of execution units is not prohibitive [7]. Figure 7 shows the TCPU if we zoom into one of the match-action stages.

**Serializing PUSH/POP instructions**: Finally, there are many techniques to ensure the effect of PUSH and POP instructions appear if they executed inorder. Since the packet memory addresses accessed by PUSH/POP instructions are known immediately when they are parsed, they can be converted to equivalent LOAD/STOREs that can then be executed out of order. For example, consider the following TPP:

```
PUSH [PacketMetadata:OutputPort]
PUSH [PacketMetadata:InputPort]
PUSH [Stage1:Reg1]
POP  [Stage3:Reg3]
```

After parsing the instructions, they can be converted to the following TPP which is equivalent to the above TPP:

```
LOAD  [PacketMetadata:OutputPort], [Packet:Hop[0]]
LOAD  [PacketMetadata:InputPort], [Packet:Hop[1]]
LOAD  [Stage1:Reg1], [Packet:Hop[2]]
STORE [Stage3:Reg3], [Packet:Hop[2]]
```

Now, the TPP loads the values stored in two registers to the packet memory addressed in the hop addressing format. Note that the packet's output port is not known until the packet is routed, i.e., at the end of the ingress stage. The execution proceeds as follows:

- By ingress stage 1, the metadata consists of four instructions, the memory addresses they access (the four registers and the three packet memory offsets), the packet's hop number, the packet's headers, its input port, its CRC, etc.
- At stage 1, the packet's input port is known. Stage 1 executes the second instruction, and stores the input port value at the 2nd word of the packet memory. Stage 1 also executes the third instruction, copying Reg1 to the 3rd word of packet memory.
- At stage 3, the fourth instruction executes, copying the 3rd word from packet memory into Reg3.
- At the end of the ingress stage, the packet's output port is already computed, and the last stage copies the output port number to the 1st word of the packet memory before the packet is stored in the ASIC packet buffers.

## 4 End-host Stack

Now that we have seen how to design a TPP-enabled ASIC, we look at the support needed from end-hosts that use TPPs to achieve a complex network functionality. Since TPP enables a wide range of applications that can be deployed in the network stack (e.g., RCP congestion control), or individual servers (e.g., network monitoring), or a combination of both, we focus our efforts on the common usage patterns.

**End-host architecture**: The purpose of the end-host stack (Figure 8) is to abstract out the common usage patterns of TPPs and implement TPP access control policies. At every end-host, we have a TPP control- and dataplane agent. The control plane is a software agent that does not sit in the critical forwarding path, and interacts with the network control plane if needed. The dataplane shim sits on the critical path between the OS network stack and the network interface and has access to every packet transmitted and received by the end-host. This shim is responsible for transparently adding and removing TPPs from application-generated packets, and enforcing access control.

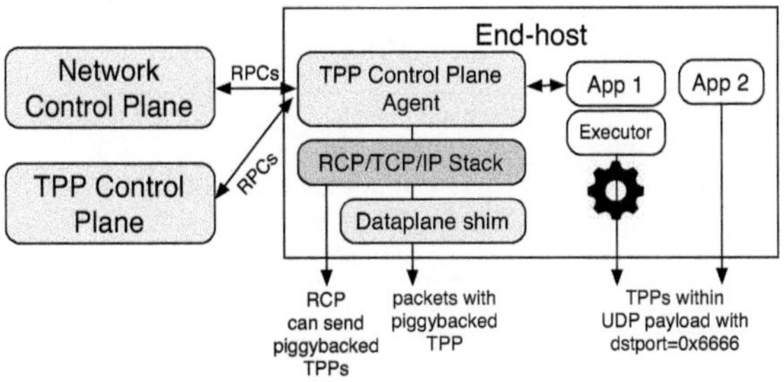


Figure 8: End-host stack for creating and managing TPP-enabled applications. Arrows denote packet flow paths through the stack, and communication paths between the end-host and the network control plane.

## 4.1 Control plane

The TPP control plane (TPP-CP) is a central entity to keep track of running TPP applications and manage switch memory, and has an agent at every end-host that keeps track of the active TPP-enabled applications running locally. Each application is allocated a contiguous set of memory addresses that it can read/write. For example, the RCP application requires access to a switch memory word to store the $R_{\text{fair}}$ at each link, and it owns this memory exclusively. This memory access control information is similar to the x86's global descriptor table, where each entry corresponds to a segment start and end address, and permissions to read/write to memory is granted accordingly.

TPP-CP exports an API which authorized applications can use to insert TPPs on a subset of packets matching certain criteria, with a certain sampling frequency. Note that TPP-CP will know the caller application (e.g. `ndb`) so it can deny the API call if the TPP accesses memory locations other than those permitted. The API definition is as follows:

```
add_tpp(filter, tpp_bytes, sample_frequency, priority)
```

where `filter` is a packet filter (as in `iptables`), and `tpp_bytes` is the compiled TPP, and `sample_frequency` is a non-negative integer that indicates the sampling frequency: if it is $N$, then a packet is stamped with the TPP with probability $1/N$. If $N = 1$, all packets have the TPP. The dataplane stores the list of all TPPs with each filter: This ensures that multiple applications, which want to install TPPs on (say) 1% of all IP packets, can coexist.

TPP-CP also configures the dataplane to enforce access control policies. Each memory access policy is a tuple: `(appid,op,address_range)`. The value `appid` is a 64-bit number, `op` is either `read` or `write`, and `address_range` is an interval denoting the start and end address. The TPPs are statically analyzed, to see if it accesses memories outside the permitted address range; if so, the API call returns a failure and the TPP is never installed.

## 4.2 Dataplane

The end-host dataplane is a software packet processing pipeline that allows applications to inject TPPs into ongoing packets, process executed TPPs from the network, and enforce access control policies.

**Interposition**: The dataplane realizes the TPP-CP API `add_tpp`. It matches outgoing packets against the table of filters and adds a TPP to the first match, or sends the packet as such if there is no match. Only one TPP is added to any packet. The interposition modules in the dataplane also strips incoming packets that have completed TPPs before passing the packet to the network stack, so the applications are oblivious to TPPs.

**Processing executed TPPs**: The dataplane also processes incoming packets from the network, which have fully executed. It echoes any standalone TPPs that have finished executing back to the packet's source IP address. For piggy-backed TPPs, the dataplane checks the table mapping the application ID to its aggregator, and sends the finished TPP to the application-specific aggregator.

## 4.3 Security considerations

There is a great deal of software generating network traffic in any datacenter, and most of it should not be trusted to generate arbitrary TPPs. After all, TPPs can read and write a variety of switch state and affect packet routing. This raises the questions of how to restrict software from generating TPPs, but also how to provide some of the benefits of TPPs to software that is not completely trusted. We now discuss possible mechanisms to enforce such restrictions, under the assumption that switches are trusted, and there is a trusted software layer at end hosts such as a hypervisor.

Fortunately, restricting TPPs is relatively simple, because it boils down to packet filtering, which is already widely deployed. Just as untrusted software should not be able to spoof IP addresses or VLAN IDs, it should not able to originate TPPs. Enforcing this restriction is as easy as filtering based on protocol and port numbers, which can be done either at all ingress switch ports or hypervisors.

In many settings, read-only access to most switch state is harmless. (A big exception is the contents of other buffered packets, to which TPPs do not provide access anyway.) Fortunately, TPPs are relatively amenable to static analysis, particularly since a TPP contains at most five instructions. Hence the hypervisor could be configured to drop any TPPs with write instructions (or write instructions to some subset of switch state). Alternatively, one could imagine the hypervisor implementing higher-level services (such as network visibility) using TPPs and expose them to untrusted software through a restricted API.

At a high level, a compromised hypervisor sending malicious TPPs is as bad as a compromised SDN controller. The difference is that hypervisors are typically spread throughout the datacenter on every machine and may present a larger attack surface than SDN controllers. Hence, for defense in depth, the control plane needs the ability to disable write instructions (`STORE`, `CSTORE`) entirely. A majority of the tasks we presented required only read access to network state.

## 4.4 TPP Executor

Although the default way of executing TPP is to execute at all hops from source to destination, we have built a 'TPP Executor' library that abstracts away common ways in which TPPs can be (i) executed reliably, despite TPPs being dropped in the network, (ii) targeted at one switch, without incurring a full round-trip from one end-host to another, (iii) executed in a scatter-gather fashion across a subset of switches, and many more. In the interest of space, we defer a detailed discussion to the extended version of this paper [28].

# 5 Implementation

We have implemented both hardware and software support needed for TCPU: the distributed TCPU on the 10Gb/s NetFPGA platform, and a software TCPU for the Open vSwitch Linux kernel module. The NetFPGA hardware prototype has a four-stage pipeline at each port, with 64 kbit block RAM and 8 registers at each stage (i.e. a total of 1Mbit RAM and 128 registers). We were able to synthesize the hardware modules at 160 MHz, capable of switching minimum sized (64Byte) packets at a 40Gb/s total data rate.

The end-host stack is a relatively straightforward implementation: We have implemented the TPP-CP, and the TPP executor

| Task | NetFPGA | ASICs |
|---|---|---|
| Parsing | < 1 cycle | 1 cycle |
| Memory access | 1 cycle | 2–5 cycles |
| Instr. Exec.: CSTORE | 1 cycle | 10 cycles |
| Instr. Exec.: (the rest) | < 1 cycle | 1 cycle |
| Packet rewrite | < 1 cycle | 1 cycle |
| Total per-stage | 2–3 cycles | 50–100 cycles† |

Table 3: Summary of hardware latency costs. †The ASIC's per-stage cost is estimated from the total end-to-end latency (200–500ns) and dividing it by the number of stages (typically 4–5). This does not include packetization latency, which is another ~50ns for a 64Byte packet at 10Gb/s.

(with support only for the reliable and scatter-gather execution pattern) as Python programs running in userspace. The software dataplane is a kernel module that acts as a shim between the network stack and the underlying network device, where it can gain access to all network packets on the transmit and receive path. For filtering packets to attach TPPs, we use `iptables` to classify packets and tag them with a TPP number, and the dataplane inserts the appropriate TPP by modifying the packet in place.

# 6 Evaluation

In §2 we have already seen how TPPs enable many dataplane applications. We now delve into targeted benchmarks of the performance of each component in the hardware and software stack.

## 6.1 Hardware

The cost of each instruction is dominated by the memory access latency. Instructions that only access registers complete in less than 1 cycle. On the NetFPGA, we use a single-port 128-bit wide block RAM that has a read (or write) latency of 1 cycle. We measured the total per-stage latency by sending a hundreds of 4 instruction TPP reading the clock from every stage, and found that the total per-stage latency was exactly 2 cycles: thus, parsing, execution, and packet rewrite all complete within a cycle, except for CSTORE, which takes 1 cycle to execute (excluding the time for accessing operands from memory).

The latency cost is different in a real switch: From personal communication with multiple ASIC designers [6, 8], we learned that 1GHz ASIC chips in the market typically use single-port SRAMs 32–128bits wide, and have a 2–5 cycle latency for every operation (read/write). This means that in the worst case, each load/store instruction adds a 5 cycle latency, and a CSTORE adds 10 cycles. Thus, in the worst case, if every instruction is a CSTORE, a TPP can add a maximum of 50ns latency to the pipeline; to avoid losing throughput due to pipeline stalls, we can add 50ns worth of buffering (at 1Tb/s, this is 6.25kB for the entire switch). However, the real cost is likely to be smaller because the ASIC already accesses memory locations that are likely to be accessed by the TPP that is being executed: For instance, the ASIC always looks up the flow entry, and updates queue sizes for memory accounting, so those values needn't be read twice.

Though switch latency costs are different from that of the NetFPGA, they do not significantly impact packet processing latency, as in a typical workload, queueing and propagation delays dominate end-to-end latency and are orders of magnitude larger. Even within a switch, the unloaded ingress-egress latency for a commercial ASIC is about 500ns per packet [3]. The lowest-latency ASICs are in the range of about 200ns per packet [16]. Thus, the extra 50ns worst-case cost per packet adds at most 10–25% extra latency to the packet. Table 3 summarizes the latency costs.

| Resource | Router | +TCPU | %-extra |
|---|---|---|---|
| Slices | 26.8K | 5.8K | 21.6% |
| Slice registers | 64.7K | 14.0K | 21.6% |
| LUTs | 69.1K | 20.8K | 30.1% |
| LUT-flip flop pairs | 88.8K | 21.8K | 24.5% |

Table 4: Hardware cost of TPP modules at 4 pipelines in the NetFPGA (4 outputs, excluding the DMA pipeline).

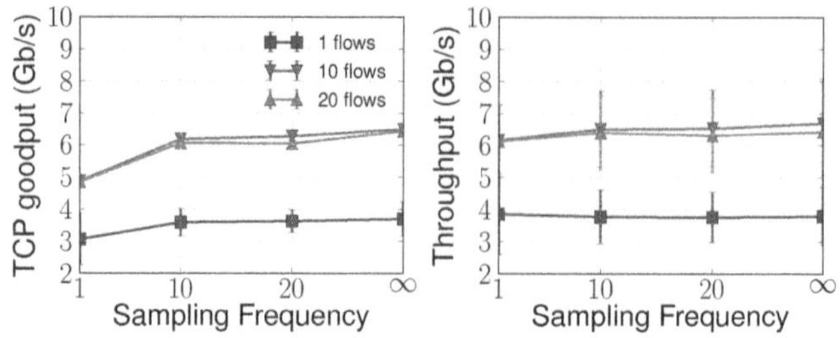


Figure 9: Maximum attainable application-level and network throughput with a 260 byte TPPs inserted on a fraction of packets (1500Byte MTU and 1240Byte MSS). A sampling frequency of ∞ depicts the baseline performance as no TPPs are installed. Error bars denote the standard deviation.

**Die Area**: The NetFPGA costs are summarized in Table 4. Compared to the single-stage reference router, the costs are within 30.1% in terms of the number of gates. However, gate counts by themselves do not account for the total area cost, as logic only accounts for a small fraction of the total area that is dominated by memory. To assess the area cost for a real switch, we use data from Bosshart et al. [7]. In their paper, the authors note that the extra area for a total of 7000 processing units—which support instructions that are similar to the TCPU—distributed across all match-action stages, accounts for less than 7% of the ASIC area [7, §5.4]. We only need $5 \times 64 = 320$ TCPUs, one per instruction per stage in the ingress/egress pipelines; therefore, the area costs are not substantial (0.32%).

## 6.2 End-host Stack

The critical component in the end-host stack is the dataplane. In the transmit side, the dataplane processes every packet, matches against a list of filters, and attaches TPPs. We use a 4-core Intel core i7 machine running Linux 3.12.6.

Figure 9 shows the baseline throughput of a single TCP flow, without segmentation offloads, across a virtual ethernet link, which was able to push about 4Gb/s traffic with one TCP flow, and about 6.5Gb/s of traffic with 20 flows. After adding TPPs, the throughput of the TCP flow reduces, depending on the (uniform random) sampling frequency. If the sampling frequency is infinite, none of the packets have TPPs, which denotes the best possible performance in our setup. As we can see, the network throughput doesn't suffer much, which shows that the CPU overhead to add/remove TPPs is minimal. However, application throughput reduces proportionally, due to header overheads. Table 5 shows the impact on the number of filters in the dataplane, and its effect on network throughput, under three different scenarios: (i) 'first' means we create flows that always match the first rule, (ii) 'last' means flows always match the

| Match | # Rules | | | | |
|---|---|---|---|---|---|
| | 0 | 1 | 10 | 100 | 1000 |
| First | 8.8 | 8.7 | 8.6 | 7.8 | 3.6 |
| Last | 8.8 | 8.7 | 8.6 | 7.7 | 3.6 |
| All | 8.8 | 8.7 | 8.3 | 6.7 | 1.4 |

Table 5: Maximum attainable network throughput in Gb/s with varying number of filters (1500Byte MTU). The numbers are the average of 5 runs.

last rule, and (iii) 'all' means there is at least one flow that matches each rule. In 'first' and 'last,' there are 10 TCP flows. In 'all,' there are as many flows as there are number of rules (with at least 10 flows). Each rule matches on a TCP destination port. As we can see, there is little loss in throughput up to 10 rules. With more rules, throughput does drop, but there is no difference between matching on the first (best case) and last rule (worst case) in the filter chain. With 1000 flows, other overheads (context switches) result in much lower throughput.

# 7 Limitations

Though TPPs help in a wide variety of tasks that were discussed in §2, they are not a panacea to implement any arbitrary functionality due to two reasons: (i) the restricted instruction set, and (ii) restricted programming model in which end-hosts initiate tasks. As we have not presented a formal theory of "network tasks," the classification below is neither complete nor mutually exclusive; it is only meant to be an illustration.

**Tasks that require per-packet computation**: The read and write instructions in TPPs limit end-hosts to high throughput network *updates*, but not arbitrary network computation. As an example, consider the task of implementing an active queue management scheme such as Stochastic Fair Queueing, static priority, dynamic priority queueing (e.g. pFabric [2]), and fair queueing. These tasks require fine-grained control over per-packet transmit and drop schedules, which is better realized using dedicated hardware or FPGAs [34]. In a similar vein, TPPs are not expressive enough to scan packets for specific signatures (e.g., payload analysis using deep packet inspection). Such tasks are better served by other approaches (e.g., middlebox software, or custom packet processors).

**Tasks that are event-driven**: In the examples we discussed, all TPPs originate at end-hosts. This limits end-hosts from implementing tasks that require precisely timed notifications whenever there is some state change within the network. For instance, TPPs by themselves cannot be used to implement flow control mechanisms (e.g., priority flow control, or PFC [15]), or reactive congestion notifications such as Quantized Congestion Notification [30] and FastLane [38]. Such tasks require the network to send special packets when the queue occupancy reaches a certain threshold. However, this isn't a show-stopper for TPPs, as end-hosts can proactively inject TPPs on a subset of packets and be notified quickly of network congestion.

# 8 Discussion

In §2, we showed how TPPs enable end-hosts to access network state with low-latency, which can then act on this state to achieve a certain functionality. This is attractive as it enables interesting functionality to be deployed at software-development timescales. We now discuss a number of important concerns that we haven't covered.

**Handling Device Heterogeneity**: There are two issues here: instruction encoding, and statistics addressing. First, instructions are unlikely to be implemented in an ASIC as hardwired logic, but using microcodes, adding a layer of indirection for platform specific designs. Second, we recommend having two address spaces: (i) a standardized address space where a majority of the important statistics are preloaded at known locations, such as those identified by the OpenFlow standard [29], and (ii) a platform-specific address space through which additional statistics, specific to vendors and switch generations can be accessed. For dealing with multiple vendors, TPPs can support an indirect addressing scheme, so that the the compiler can preload packet memory with platform specific addresses. For example, to load queue sizes from a Broadcom ASIC at hop 1, and an Intel ASIC at hop 2, the compiler generates the TPP below, loading the word from `0xff00` for Broadcom, and `0xfe00` for Intel, obtained out-of-band. For safety, the entire TPP is wrapped around a `CEXEC` as follows:

```
  CEXEC [Switch:VendorID], [Packet:Hop[0]]
  LOAD [[Packet:Hop[1]], [Packet:Hop[1]]
PacketMemory:
  Hop1: $BroadcomVersionID, 0xff00 (* overwritten *)
  Hop2: $IntelVersionID, 0xfe00
```

The TPP compiler can query the ASIC vendor IDs from time to time and change the addresses if the devices at a particular hop suddenly change. However, indirect addressing limits the extent to which a TPP can be statically analyzed.

**MTU issues**: Piggy-backed TPPs are attached to packets at the edge of a network (end-host or a border router). Thus, if the incoming packet is already at the MTU size, there would be no room to add a TPP. This is fortunately not a big issue, as many switches support MTUs up to 9000 bytes. This is already being done today in overlay networks to add headers for network virtualization [1].

# 9 Related Work

TPPs represent a point in the broad design space of programmable networks, ranging from essentially arbitrary in-band programs as formulated by Active Network proposals [33, 36], to switch-centric programmable dataplane pipelines [4, 7, 17, 25], to controller-centric out-of-band proposals such as OpenFlow [27] and Simple Network Management Protocol (SNMP). We do not claim that the TPP approach is a fundamentally novel idea, as it is a specific realization of Active Networks. However, we have been ruthless in simplifying the interface between the end-hosts and switches to a bare minimum. We believe TPPs strike a delicate balance between what is possible in switch hardware at line rate, and what is sufficiently expressive for end-hosts to perform a variety of useful tasks.

TPPs superficially resemble Sprocket, the assembly language in Smart Packets [33]. However, Sprocket represents a far more expressive point in the design space. It allows loops and larger programs that would be hard to realize in hardware at line rate. By contrast, a TPP is a straight-line program whose execution latency is deterministic, small, and known at compile time. TPPs fully execute on the fast-path (i.e., router ASIC), whereas Sprocket exercises the slow-path (router CPU), which has orders of magnitude lower bandwidth. TPPs also resemble the read/write in-band control mechanism for ATM networks as described in a patent [5]; however, we also focus extensively on how to refactor useful dataplane tasks, and a security policy to safeguard the network against malicious TPPs. Wolf et al. [37] focus on designing a high performance Active Network router that supports general purpose instructions. It is unclear whether their model allows end-hosts to obtain a consistent view of network state. Moreover, it is unlikely that ASICs can take on general purpose computations at today's switching capacities at a reasonable cost. Furthermore, out-of-band control mechanisms such as OpenFlow and Simple Network Management Protocol (SNMP) neither meet the performance requirements for dataplane tasks, nor provide a packet-consistent view of network state.

There have been numerous efforts to expose switch statistics through the dataplane, particularly to improve congestion management and network monitoring. One example is Explicit Congestion

Notification in which a router stamps a bit in the IP header whenever the egress queue occupancy exceeds a configurable threshold. Another example is IP Record Route, an IP option that enables routers to insert the interface IP address on the packet. Yet another example is Cisco's Embedded Logic Analyzer Module (ELAM) [10] that traces the packet's path inside the ASIC at layer 2 and layer 3 stages, and generates a summary to the network control plane. Instead of anticipating future requirements and designing specific solutions, we adopt a more generic, protocol-independent approach to accessing switch state.

## 10 Conclusion

We set out with a goal to rapidly introduce new dataplane functionality into the network. We showed how, by presenting a programmatic interface, using which end-hosts can query and manipulate network state directly using tiny packet programs. TPPs support both a distributed programming model in which every end-host participates in a task (e.g., RCP* congestion control), and a logically centralized model in which a central controller can monitor and program the network. We demonstrated that TPPs enable a whole new breed of useful applications at end-hosts: ones that can work *with* the network, have unprecedented visibility nearly instantly, with the ability to tie dataplane events to *actual* packets, umambiguously isolate performance issues, and act on network view without being limited by the control plane's ability to provide such state in a timely manner.

## Acknowledgments

Vimalkumar thanks Brandon Heller, Kok-Kiong Yap, Sarang Dharmapurikar, Srinivas Narayana, Vivek Seshadri, Yiannis Yiakoumis, Patrick Bosshart, Glen Gibb, Swarun Kumar, Lavanya Jose, Michael Chan, Nick McKeown, Balaji Prabhakar, and Navindra Yadav for helpful feedback and discussions that shaped this work. The authors also thank our shepherd John Wroclawski and the anonymous SIGCOMM reviewers for their thoughtful reviews.

The work at Stanford was funded by NSF FIA award CNS–1040190. Opinions, findings, and conclusions do not necessarily reflect the views of NSF or other sponsors.

## References

[1] Mohammad Alizadeh, Tom Essall, Sarang Dharmapurikar, Ramanan Vaidyanathan, Kevin Chu, Andy Fingerhut, Terry Lam, Francis Matus, Rong Pan, Navindra Yadav, and George Varghese. "CONGA: Distributed Congestion-Aware Load Balancing for Datacenters". In: *SIGCOMM* (2014).

[2] Mohammad Alizadeh, Shuang Yang, Milad Sharif, Sachin Katti, Nick McKeown, Balaji Prabhakar, and Scott Shenker. "pFabric: Minimal Near-Optimal Datacenter Transport". In: *SIGCOMM* (2013).

[3] *Arista Networks – 7100 Series Performance Results.* `http://www.aristanetworks.com/media/system/pdf/7148sx-rfc2889-broadcast-with-latency.pdf`, Retrieved January 23, 2014.

[4] Eric A Baden, Mohan Kalkunte, John J Dull, and Venkateshwar Buduma. *Field processor for a network device.* US Patent 7,787,471. 2010.

[5] A.D. Berenbaum, Alexander Gibson Fraser, and Hubert Rae McLellan Jr. *In-band device configuration protocol for ATM transmission convergence devices.* US Patent 08/939,746. 2001.

[6] Pat Bosshart and Glen Gibb. Personal communication, 2014-01-27.

[7] Pat Bosshart, Glen Gibb, Hun-Seok Kim, George Varghese, Nick McKeown, Martin Izzard, Fernando Mujica, and Mark Horowitz. "Forwarding Metamorphosis: Fast Programmable Match-Action Processing in Hardware for SDN". In: *SIGCOMM* (2013).

[8] Sarang Dharmapurikar. Insieme Networks, Personal communication, 2013-07-18.

[9] Nandita Dukkipati and Nick McKeown. "Why Flow-Completion Time is the Right metric for Congestion Control". In: *SIGCOMM CCR* (2006).

[10] *ELAM Overview.* `http://www.cisco.com/c/en/us/support/docs/switches/nexus-7000-series-switches/116648-technote-product-00.html`, Retrieved March 13, 2014.

[11] Dongsu Han, Robert Grandl, Aditya Akella, and Srinivasan Seshan. "FCP: a flexible transport framework for accommodating diversity". In: *SIGCOMM* (2013).

[12] Nikhil Handigol, Brandon Heller, Vimalkumar Jeyakumar, Bob Lantz, and Nick McKeown. "Reproducible network experiments using container-based emulation". In: *CoNEXT* (2012).

[13] Nikhil Handigol, Brandon Heller, Vimalkumar Jeyakumar, David Mazières, and Nick McKeown. "I Know What Your Packet Did Last Hop: Using Packet Histories to Troubleshoot Networks". In: *NSDI* (2014).

[14] Danny Yuxing Huang, Kenneth Yocum, and Alex C Snoeren. "High-Fidelity Switch Models for Software-Defined Network Emulation". In: *HotSDN* (2013).

[15] *IEEE 802.1Qbb – Priority-based Flow Control.* `http://www.ieee802.org/1/pages/802.1bb.html`, Retrieved April 1 2014.

[16] *Intel Fulcrum FM4000 ASIC.* `http://www.intel.com/content/dam/www/public/us/en/documents/datasheets/ethernet-switch-fm4000-datasheet.pdf`, Retrieved July 1, 2013.

[17] *Intel Fulcrum FM6000 ASIC.* `http://www.ethernetsummit.com/English/Collaterals/Proceedings/2013/20130404_S23_Ozdag.pdf`, Retrieved July 1, 2013.

[18] Sushant Jain, Alok Kumar, Subhasree Mandal, Joon Ong, Leon Poutievski, Arjun Singh, Subbaiah Venkata, Jim Wanderer, Junlan Zhou, Min Zhu, et al. "B4: Experience with a globally-deployed software defined WAN". In: *SIGCOMM* (2013).

[19] Vimalkumar Jeyakumar, Mohammad Alizadeh, Changhoon Kim, and David Mazières. "Tiny Packet Programs for low-latency network control and monitoring". In: *HotNets* (2013).

[20] Dina Katabi, Mark Handley, and Charlie Rohrs. "Congestion control for high bandwidth-delay product networks". In: *SIGCOMM* (2002).

[21] Peyman Kazemian, Michael Chang, Hongyi Zeng, George Varghese, Nick McKeown, and Scott Whyte. "Real Time Network Policy Checking using Header Space Analysis". In: *NSDI* (2013).

[22] Frank Kelly, Gaurav Raina, and Thomas Voice. "Stability and fairness of explicit congestion control with small buffers". In: *SIGCOMM CCR* (2008).

[23] Ahmed Khurshid, Xuan Zou, Wenxuan Zhou, Matthew Caesar, and P Brighten Godfrey. "VeriFlow: Verifying Network-Wide Invariants in Real Time". In: *NSDI* (2013).

[24] Changhoon Kim. Windows Azure, Personal communication, 2014-01-26.

[25] Eddie Kohler, Robert Morris, Benjie Chen, John Jannotti, and M Frans Kaashoek. "The Click modular router". In: *TOCS* (2000).

[26] Guohan Lu, Chuanxiong Guo, Yulong Li, Zhiqiang Zhou, Tong Yuan, Haitao Wu, Yongqiang Xiong, Rui Gao, and Yongguang Zhang. "ServerSwitch: a programmable and high performance platform for data center networks". In: *NSDI* (2011).

[27] Nick McKeown, Tom Anderson, Hari Balakrishnan, Guru Parulkar, Larry Peterson, Jennifer Rexford, Scott Shenker, and Jonathan Turner. "OpenFlow: Enabling Innovation in Campus Networks". In: *SIGCOMM CCR* (2008).

[28] *Millions of Little Minions: Using Packets for Low Latency Network Programming and Visibility (extended version).* `http://arxiv.org/abs/1405.7143`. 2014.

[29] *OpenFlow Switch Specification, version 1.4.* `https://www.opennetworking.org/images/stories/downloads/sdn-resources/onf-specifications/openflow/openflow-spec-v1.4.0.pdf`, Retrieved April 1, 2014.

[30] Rong Pan, Balaji Prabhakar, and Ashvin Laxmikantha. "QCN: Quantized congestion notification". In: *IEEE802* 1 (2007).

[31] Ben Pfaff, Justin Pettit, Keith Amidon, Martin Casado, Teemu Koponen, and Scott Shenker. "Extending Networking into the Virtualization Layer." In: *HotNets* (2009).

[32] Mark Reitblatt, Nate Foster, Jennifer Rexford, Cole Schlesinger, and David Walker. "Abstractions for Network Update". In: *SIGCOMM* (2012).

[33] Beverly Schwartz, Alden W Jackson, W Timothy Strayer, Wenyi Zhou, R Dennis Rockwell, and Craig Partridge. "Smart packets for active networks". In: *Open Architectures and Network Programming Proceedings* (1999).

[34] Anirudh Sivaraman, Keith Winstein, Suvinay Subramanian, and Hari Balakrishnan. "No silver bullet: extending SDN to the data plane". In: *HotNets* (2013).

[35] Ao Tang, Jiantao Wang, Steven H Low, and Mung Chiang. "Equilibrium of heterogeneous congestion control: Existence and uniqueness". In: *IEEE TON* (2007).

[36] David L Tennenhouse and David J Wetherall. "Towards an Active Network Architecture". In: *DARPA Active Nets. Conf. and Exposition* (2002).

[37] Tilman Wolf and Jonathan S Turner. "Design Issues for High Performance Active Routers". In: *IEEE Journal on Sel. Areas in Comm.* (2001).

[38] David Zats, Anand Padmanabha Iyer, Randy H Katz, Ion Stoica, and Amin Vahdat. "FastLane: An Agile Congestion Signaling Mechanism for Improving Datacenter Performance". In: *Technical Report UCB/EECS-2013-113* (2013).

# SAX-PAC (Scalable And eXpressive PAcket Classification)

Kirill Kogan
Purdue University and
NetSysAlgo
kirill.kogan@gmail.com

Sergey Nikolenko
Steklov Mathematical Institute
at St. Petersburg,
National Research University
Higher School of Economics
sergey@logic.pdmi.ras.ru

Ori Rottenstreich
Mellanox, Israel
orir@mellanox.com

William Culhane
Purdue University
wculhane@purdue.edu

Patrick Eugster
Purdue University and
Technical University of
Darmstadt
peugster@cs.purdue.edu

## ABSTRACT

Efficient packet classification is a core concern for network services. Traditional multi-field classification approaches, in both software and ternary content-addressable memory (TCAMs), entail tradeoffs between (memory) space and (lookup) time. TCAMs cannot efficiently represent range rules, a common class of classification rules confining values of packet fields to given ranges. The exponential space growth of TCAM entries relative to the number of fields is exacerbated when multiple fields contain ranges. In this work, we present a novel approach which identifies properties of many classifiers which can be implemented in linear space and with worst-case guaranteed logarithmic time *and* allows the addition of more fields including range constraints without impacting space and time complexities. On real-life classifiers from Cisco Systems and additional classifiers from ClassBench [7] (with real parameters), 90-95% of rules are thus handled, and the other 5-10% of rules can be stored in TCAM to be processed in parallel.

## Categories and Subject Descriptors

C.2.6 [**Computer-Communication Networks**]: Internetworking-Routers

## Keywords

packet classification; TCAM

## 1. INTRODUCTION

Packet classification is a core functionality for implementing popular commodity services including Quality of Service (QoS) and access control. Recently packet classification has become even more prominent with the adoption of OpenFlow [25], which expresses features through hierarchical tuple matching with set actions. Multi-field classification, i.e. classification based on more than one field, has become very common. If a classification rule sets exact values for all fields, the rule can be represented by concatenating all its fields. Such classifiers can be implemented in content-addressable memory (CAM) or by a simple hash function in space linear in the number of fields. The problem becomes harder if a field is represented by a prefix (constraint on most significant bits) or a range (confining values inside an interval) since simple concatenation stops working.

Many sophisticated software-based approaches have been proposed (cf. comprehensive survey [40]). Complexity bounds derived from computational geometry imply that a software-based packet classifier with $N$ rules and $k \geq 2$ fields uses either $O(N^k)$ space and $O(\log N)$ time or $O(N)$ space and $O(\log^{k-1} N)$ time [26]. Thus, software-based approaches are either too slow or too memory-intensive even with few prefix- or range-based fields.

Ternary content-addressable memory (TCAM) was introduced to overcome performance problems for prefix matching [24]. TCAM is a fast class of memory for matching packet headers against a set of stored entries represented by tuples of VALUE and MASK words (the latter hides "don't care" bits). Currently, TCAM is the *de facto* standard for classifier implementation. Unlike software-based solutions, TCAM can efficiently represent multi-field classification with prefixes, but suffers an exponential memory blowup from range expansion; each range-based field in a classification rule introduces an additional multiplicative factor. Thus in practice the number of range fields is severely limited.

Defining more sophisticated services requires additional expressiveness on existing classification fields or new ones, and many classifications are naturally represented by ranges. More efficient implementations for classifiers on ranges of IP or MAC addresses, dates, packet lengths, etc. are already highly desired [8]. The state-of-the-art packet classification mechanisms are limited and mostly consider five-tuples with at most two fields which include ranges. This greatly restricts emerging classification possibilities.

In this paper we consider a hybrid software- and TCAM-based approach, which hinges on the *order-independence* of classifiers with respect to the rules they encompass. We identify this property as essential for simple and efficient implementation of classifiers. We show that if a classifier is order-independent then the addition of new classification fields — even those represented by ranges — does not increase the complexity of lookup time or memory space required. We use this to build efficient classification schemes. We also consider the general case with order-dependence, leading to a hybrid approach implementing order-independent rules in software


*SIGCOMM'14*, August 17–22, 2014, Chicago, IL, USA.
Copyright 2014 ACM 978-1-4503-2836-4/14/08 ...$15.00.
http://dx.doi.org/10.1145/2619239.2626294 .

using linear memory and with logarithmic worst-case guaranteed lookup time, and the rest of the rules in TCAM. More precisely, our contributions are the following: (1) we identify classifier properties that guarantee zero cost for additional fields represented by ranges or prefixes transparently to the implementation scheme; (2) we propose a technique to reduce the number of classification fields represented by prefixes or ranges, yielding semantically equivalent classification results; (3) we present a technique to reduce a multi-field classification problem to a classification problem on at most two fields with guaranteed worst-case performance and linear memory which is more sophisticated than previous reducation attempts which do not provide acceptable worst-case guarantees when classifiers start with more than two fields [35, 36]; (4) we demonstrate the viability of our approach through simulations on 12 classifiers from Classbench generated with real parameters [7], each with $\approx$ 50K rules on 6 fields and on 5 real-life classifiers from Cisco Systems; we show that up to 90-95% of the rules can be implemented in software in linear space and with worst-case guaranteed logarithmic time, leaving only $5-10\%$ to be implemented in TCAM.

The rest of this paper is organized as follows. Section 2 details the model underlying our work. Section 3 explains the relevance of order-independence, and Section 4 introduces the main computational problems underlying our approach. Section 5 deals with the Boolean representation of classifiers, comparing it with our approach, whereas Section 6 presents heuristics to efficiently find suboptimal solutions for the computational problems and Section 7 proposes new standard representations of classifiers. Section 8 presents simulation results. Section 9 discusses related prior art and Section 10 concludes the paper.

## 2. MODEL DESCRIPTION

Packets are matched by their headers according to classification rules stored in a classification database. A packet header contains $k$ fields; a field $i$, $1 \leq i \leq k$, is a string of $W_i$ bits. A *classifier* $\mathcal{K}$ is an ordered set of $N$ rules, denoted $R_1 \ldots R_N$. A rule $R_j$ is an ordered set of $k$ fields and an associated action $A_j$; the $i$-th field $F_i$ is represented by a range of values on $W_i$ bits, i.e., each rule contains $k$ ranges $R = (I_1, \ldots, I_k)$, $I_i = [l_i, u_i]$. We assume the last rule of each $\mathcal{K}$ is a "catch-all" rule $R_N = (*, \ldots, *)$ with $A_N =$ TRANSMIT to transmit matched packets without changes. We denote by $\mathcal{K}^{-F}$ the classifier that results from $\mathcal{K}$ by removing the set of fields $F$ from each of its rules; we also usually denote by $\mathcal{K}^{+F}$ a classifier that results from $\mathcal{K}$ by extending its rules with the set of fields $F$ (with values defined separately for every rule), and simplify the notation to $\mathcal{K}^{-|F|}$ and $\mathcal{K}^{+|F|}$ where the fields themselves are clear from context.

Rules are applied sequentially, i.e., the set of rules has non-cyclic ordering $\prec$, and if a header matches both $R_x$ and $R_y$ for $x \prec y$, rule $R_x$ takes precedence. Classifiers are semantically equivalent if they match the same rule for every packet.

A classifier $\mathcal{K}$ is called *order-independent* if for any classifier $\mathcal{K}'$ with the same rules in a different order (except the last "catch-all" rule) and for any packet header $p$, $p$ is matched by the same rule in both $\mathcal{K}$ and $\mathcal{K}'$. This condition for order-independence of a classifier is satisfied exactly when each pair of its rules do not intersect, i.e. for each pair of rules there is at least one field in which the two corresponding ranges (or prefixes) are disjoint. Otherwise, a classifier is called *order-dependent*. For instance, the classifier $\mathcal{K}$ that contains two rules that are based on two fields $R_1 = ([1,3],[4,5])$ and $R_2 = ([5,6],[4,5])$ is order-independent but $\mathcal{K}'$ that contains two rules $R_3 = ([1,3],[4,5])$ and $R_4 = ([2,4],[4,5])$ is order-dependent. This is because $R_1$, $R_2$ do not intersect since the ranges in their first field are disjoint while $R_3$, $R_4$ do intersect. For instance, the input $(3,4)$ matches both rules of $\mathcal{K}'$. $\mathcal{K}(S)$ denotes a classifier that uses only a subset $S$ of fields in classification.

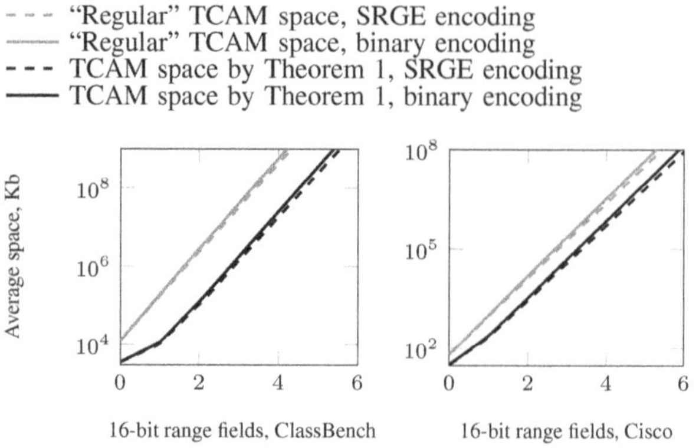


Figure 1: TCAM space required for ClassBench and CISCO classifiers as a function of the number of additional synthetic 16-bit range fields.

## 3. IMPACT OF ORDER-INDEPENDENCE

Order-independence of classifiers, or parts thereof, is a prevalent and powerful property for efficient classifier representation and evaluation. Classifiers using longest-prefix matches on a single field are at least order-independent among all prefixes of the same length; forwarding entries in OpenFlow [25] likely preserve order-independence for simplicity of management; many classifiers representing services and implement "best-match" priority schemes are order-independent. Order-dependent classifiers representing service-level-agreements (SLAs) are often unintended byproducts of uniting several services in a single classifier. In our experience of over a decade of deployments, many classifiers representing services such as QoS or ACLs are order-independent in practice. Increasing the number of rules of a classifier decreases the chance that classifier *as a whole* will stay order-independent, but the size of its *maximal order-independent part* increases. Adding fields to each rule increases the chances of order-independence.

To study the impact of order-independence, we analyze classifiers from ClassBench generated with real parameters [7] and real-life classifiers provided by Cisco Systems. The data in Table 1 indicate new methods for efficient representation of order-independent parts of classifiers can greatly reduce requirements for classification engines. If a classifier is not wholly order-dependent, we can lookup its order-independent and order-dependent parts separately and return the highest-priority match. An order-independent match preempts the need to match the order-dependent part. Alternatively, we can choose rules for the order-independent part which have higher priorities than any rule in the other part.

EXAMPLE 1. Consider an order-independent classifier $\mathcal{K} = (R_1, R_2, R_3)$ with two fields of 5 bits each and rules

$$\begin{aligned} R_1 &= ([1,3],[4,31]), \\ R_2 &= ([4,4],[2,30]), \\ R_3 &= ([7,9],[5,21]). \end{aligned}$$

Let $\mathcal{K}^{+1}$ be a classifier that results from $\mathcal{K}$ by adding one new field of 5 bits, leading to the rules

$$\begin{aligned} R_1^{+1} &= ([1,3],[4,31],[1,28]), \\ R_2^{+1} &= ([4,4],[2,30],[4,27]), \\ R_3^{+1} &= ([7,9],[5,21],[3,18]). \end{aligned}$$

| | Rules | | Original classifier | | | | | | Classifier expanded by two 16-bit ranges | | | | | |
|---|---|---|---|---|---|---|---|---|---|---|---|---|---|---|
| | | | Original $\mathcal{K}$ | | | By Theorem 2 | | | Original $\mathcal{K}^{+2}$ | | | By Theorem 1 | | |
| | Total | order-ind., all fields | Width, bits | Space, Kb Binary | Space, Kb SRGE | Order-ind. width, bits | Space, Kb Binary | Space, Kb SRGE | Width, bits | Space, Kb Binary | Space, Kb SRGE | Order-ind. width, bits | Space, Kb Binary | Space, Kb SRGE |
| acl1 | 49870 | 49779 | 120 | 7922 | 7655 | 31 | 1517 | 1517 | 152 | 1752769 | 1462501 | 31 | 3857 | 3509 |
| acl2 | 47276 | 44178 | 120 | 11289 | 11289 | 82 | 4189 | 4189 | 152 | 2499525 | 2159699 | 82 | 145925 | 126505 |
| acl3 | 49859 | 47674 | 120 | 10771 | 10571 | 91 | 5018 | 5008 | 152 | 2391264 | 2027239 | 91 | 177771 | 152514 |
| acl4 | 49556 | 46670 | 120 | 10079 | 9904 | 97 | 5379 | 5370 | 152 | 2234839 | 1895078 | 97 | 216994 | 186701 |
| acl5 | 40362 | 38962 | 120 | 6121 | 6121 | 63 | 2950 | 2950 | 152 | 1359256 | 1172403 | 63 | 127818 | 110663 |
| fw1 | 47778 | 43675 | 120 | 19454 | 19438 | 72 | 3926 | 3911 | 152 | 4303234 | 3720573 | 72 | 194313 | 164893 |
| fw2 | 48885 | 48826 | 120 | 10866 | 10866 | 52 | 2498 | 2498 | 152 | 2399603 | 2071400 | 52 | 7382 | 6695 |
| fw3 | 46038 | 41615 | 120 | 15090 | 15073 | 84 | 4161 | 4145 | 152 | 3337763 | 2873120 | 84 | 170688 | 144596 |
| fw4 | 45340 | 42857 | 120 | 33500 | 33368 | 76 | 4025 | 4008 | 152 | 7438741 | 6390798 | 76 | 195130 | 165332 |
| fw5 | 45723 | 39962 | 120 | 12478 | 12445 | 76 | 3759 | 3745 | 152 | 2745105 | 2366939 | 76 | 180420 | 152652 |
| ipc1 | 49840 | 48294 | 120 | 8041 | 7924 | 50 | 2580 | 2579 | 152 | 1789100 | 1521153 | 50 | 52378 | 45391 |
| ipc2 | 50000 | 50000 | 120 | 5859 | 5859 | 36 | 1757 | 1757 | 152 | 1301839 | 1123612 | 36 | 1757 | 1757 |
| cisco1 | 584 | 538 | 120 | 78 | 78 | 52 | 34 | 34 | 152 | 17523 | 15088 | 52 | 1650 | 1441 |
| cisco2 | 269 | 249 | 120 | 68 | 68 | 21 | 7 | 7 | 152 | 15662 | 13510 | 21 | 477 | 415 |
| cisco3 | 95 | 92 | 120 | 11 | 11 | 30 | 3 | 3 | 152 | 2505 | 2137 | 30 | 76 | 71 |
| cisco4 | 364 | 329 | 120 | 79 | 79 | 38 | 18 | 18 | 152 | 17827 | 15385 | 38 | 1484 | 1237 |
| cisco5 | 148 | 120 | 120 | 19 | 19 | 17 | 5 | 5 | 152 | 4303 | 3717 | 17 | 695 | 590 |

Table 1: Space comparison. Left to right: number of rules (total and in a maximal order-independent set); a comparison of TCAM space requirements under two encodings (binary [36] and SRGE [3]) for ClassBench classifiers with standard representation and with a representation reduced by Theorem 2; a similar TCAM space comparison for the same classifiers extended with two additional random synthetic 16-bit range fields, with standard representation and with a representation reduced by Theorem 1.

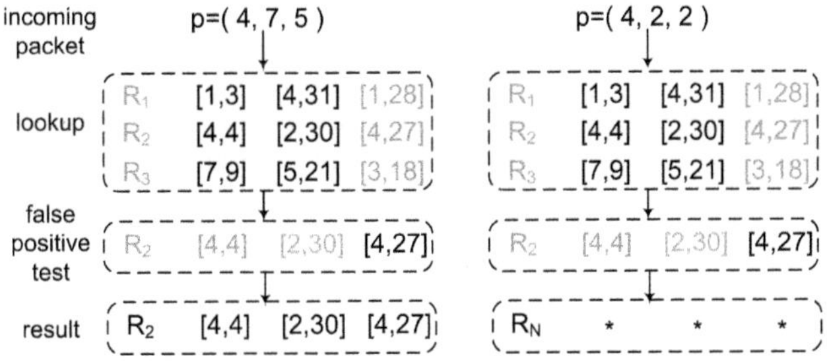


Figure 2: Visualizing the lookup procedure on rules with a subset of fields in Example 1. Fields checked in a certain step are in black; those irrelevant for the step, in grey. Packet $(4, 2, 2)$ matches $R_2$ but fails the false positive check on the added field of $R_2^{+1}$, so the classifier returns the catch-all rule.

Since $\mathcal{K}$ is order-independent, the new fields can be skipped during (the main TCAM-based) classification and a single matched rule verified to avoid false positive matches (see Figure 2). The binary encoding [36] of $\mathcal{K}^{+1}$ requires $42 + 28 + 50 = 120$ TCAM entries and the SRGE encoding [3] requires $24 + 8 + 32 = 64$ entries. On the other hand, the binary and SRGE encodings of $\mathcal{K}$ require only $6 + 7 + 10 = 23$ and $6 + 4 + 8 = 18$ TCAM entries respectively.

THEOREM 1 (FIELDS EXPANSION). *Let $\mathcal{K}^{+m}$ be a classifier that results from an order-independent classifier $\mathcal{K}$ by adding $m$ new fields of any width, i.e., a rule $R = (I_1, \dots, I_k)$ in $\mathcal{K}$ is replaced with $R^{+m} = (I_1, \dots, I_k, \dots, I_{k+m})$ in $\mathcal{K}^{+m}$. Then $\mathcal{K}$ with a false-positive check of a single matched rule is a semantically equivalent representation of $\mathcal{K}^{+m}$.*

PROOF. Adding new fields to an order-independent classifier preserves its order-independence, so $\mathcal{K}^{+m}$ is order-independent. If a header $H$ does not match any rule of $\mathcal{K}$, $H$ cannot match $\mathcal{K}^{+m}$ (we only add constraints). If a header $H$ matches $R_j \in \mathcal{K}$, either $H$ matches $R_j^{+m} \in \mathcal{K}^{+m}$ or $H$ does not match any rule of $\mathcal{K}^{+m}$. If $R_j \in \mathcal{K}$ is matched we check $m$ additional fields to avoid a false-positive match. □

By Theorem 1, introducing additional fields based on prefixes or ranges to an order-dependent classifier affects only the encoding size of its order-dependent part. The space and lookup time complexity of classification in the order-independent do not increase since new fields in the order-independent part can be ignored without affecting the classification outcome; an additional check of at most one matched rule is required to avoid a false positive match. Previously new fields based on prefixes or ranges significantly increased the complexity of software-based solutions (recall $O(\log^{k-1} N)$ lookup time in linear memory). Likewise, in TCAM-based solutions each range is converted to prefixes before configuration, and any new field based on ranges adds an additional multiplicative factor for the required TCAM space. This contributes to the fact that 5-tuple classifiers with only source and destination port fields represented by ranges are the current industry standard. Support for additional fields amenable to range rules would greatly improve classification expressiveness (e.g., ranges on dates, packet length, etc.).

The effect of Theorem 1 is shown in Table 1. We add two new ranges on 16 bits each to benchmark classifiers, garnering significant space savings. We compare memory requirements which result from Theorem 1 with those of two well-known range encoding schemes: binary [36] and SRGE [3]. In addition, Figure 1 demonstrates how average required space depends on the number of range-based fields; for our approach, the exponential growth is significantly deterred. Whereas Theorem 1 shows an equivalent representation of $\mathcal{K}^{+m}$ when new fields are added, Theorem 2 states we can ignore a subset of fields if the remaining fields maintain the order-independence of the classifier. Table 1 shows the effect of Theorem 2: for most benchmarks, significant space savings (by a factor of 2 to 5) caused by order-independence result immediately, on the classifiers themselves rather than their extended versions. The effect is independent of range encoding schemes.

EXAMPLE 2. Consider a classifier $\mathcal{K} = (R_1, R_2, R_3)$ with three fields of 5 bits each and rules

$$\begin{aligned} R_1 &= ([1,3],[4,31],[1,28]), \\ R_2 &= ([4,4],[2,30],[4,27]), \\ R_3 &= ([7,9],[5,21],[3,18]). \end{aligned}$$

In this case the first field is necessary but also sufficient to guarantee order independence, so we have that $\mathcal{K}^{-\{2,3\}} =$

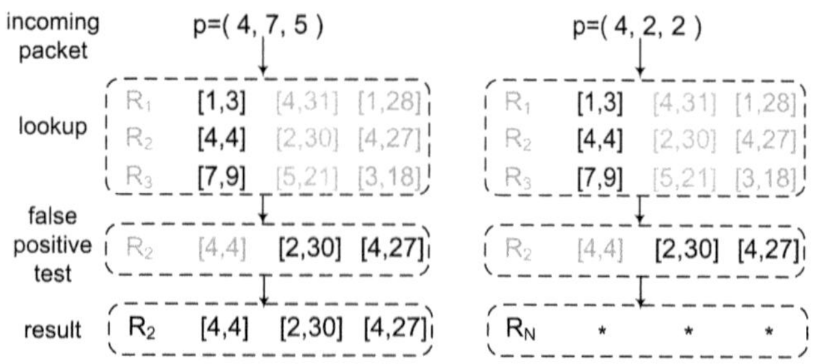


Figure 3: Visualizing the lookup procedure on rules with a subset of fields in Example 2. Fields to be checked in a step are shown in black; irrelevant for the step, in grey. Note that packet $(4, 2, 2)$ matches $R_2^{-\{2,3\}}$ but fails the false positive check, so the classifier returns the catch-all rule.

$\{R_1^{-\{2,3\}}, R_2^{-\{2,3\}}, R_3^{-\{2,3\}}\} = \{([1,3]), ([4,4]), ([7,9])\}$ is order-independent (see Figure 3). That the binary encoding of $\mathcal{K}$ requires $42 + 28 + 50 = 120$ TCAM entries and the SRGE encoding of $\mathcal{K}$ requires $24 + 8 + 32 = 64$ TCAM entries. On the other hand, the binary encoding for $\mathcal{K}^{-\{2,3\}}$ requires $2+1+1 = 4$ TCAM entries and the SRGE encoding requires only $2+1+2 = 5$ TCAM entries.

Note that removing additional classification fields of $\mathcal{K}^{-\{2,3\}}$ based on ranges can significantly reduce space complexity since the same $\mathcal{K}^{-\{2,3\}}$ is sufficient to represent $\mathcal{K}$ in Example 2. Only one false-positive check of a matched rule $R_i^{-\{2,3\}}$ is required. To further improve performance, the removed fields of $R_i$ can be checked in parallel.

THEOREM 2 (FIELDS REDUCTION). *Let $\mathcal{K}^{-m}$ be a classifier that results from an order-independent classifier $\mathcal{K}$ by removing $m$ fields, i.e., each $R = (I_1, \dots, I_k)$ is replaced with $R^{-m} = (I_1, \dots, I_{k-m})$. If $\mathcal{K}^{-m}$ is order-independent then $\mathcal{K}^{-m}$ with a false-positive check of a single matched rule is a semantically equivalent representation of $\mathcal{K}$.*

PROOF. If a header $H$ does not match $\mathcal{K}^{-m}$, $H$ cannot match $\mathcal{K}$ (we only remove new constraints). If a header $H$ matches $R_j^{-m}$, $H$ can match only $R_j$ or $H$ does not match $\mathcal{K}$ (if a header matched both $R_i^{-m}$ and some $R_j$, $i \neq j$, it would contradict the order-independence of $\mathcal{K}^{-m}$). □

By Theorem 2, detecting a false-positive match of a rule $R_i^{-m} \in \mathcal{K}^{-m}$ requires only to check $m$ additional fields of $R_i$. If a false positive is found the catch-all rule is used. At most one rule can match in $\mathcal{K}^{-m}$ classifiers, which hugely impacts the complexity and feasibility of implementation.

There are significantly different complexities involved in adding and removing fields with the suggested approach. In the first case it suffices to maximize the size of the order-independent part on the same set of fields. In the second case, there is an additional tradeoff between the size of the order-independent part and the subset of fields necessary to retain order-independence. In the following section we suggest efficient representations of order-independent parts. The effect of Theorem 2 will be demonstrated in Section 8.

# 4. EFFICIENT REPRESENTATIONS OF CLASSIFIERS

Since the tradeoff between lookup time and memory space for multi-field classification heavily depends on the number of fields $k$ participating in classification, it is reasonable to explore ways to reduce $k$. For software-based solutions, any additional field that is represented by a prefix or range incurs additional complexity on the lookup time or memory space [26]. If the reduced classifier $\mathcal{K}^{-m}$ contains at most two fields, we can efficiently implement lookup in time logarithmic in $N$ with linear memory [36]. For TCAM-based solutions, if a classifier field is represented by a range, removing it reduces the required TCAM space proportionally to the number of prefixes used to express the range. In this section we present optimization problems as a step to achieve this goal. Moreover, removing fields can create a shorter classification format. Common TCAM formats include 72, 144, or 288 bits, so reducing the representation size across one of those barriers halves the required TCAM space.

## 4.1 Semantically Equivalent Representations of All Rules

We begin by optimizing order-independent classifiers based on Theorem 2 (see Example 2).

PROBLEM 1 (FIELDS SUBSET MINIMIZATION (FSM)). *Find a maximal subset of fields $M$ of an order-independent classifier $\mathcal{K}$ such that $\mathcal{K}^{-M}$ is order-independent; if there are several such subsets, choose $M$ with maximal total width (to minimize lookup word width).*

FSM can only be applied to order-independent classifiers, and it does not always reduce the number of classification fields for order-independent classifiers. It is enough that every field of a single rule is required to keep order-independence of a classifier. One way to address these shortcomings is a *multi-group* representation. A subset of classification fields may suffice for order-independence of a subset of rules of a classifier. Assume that the rules of a classifier $\mathcal{K}$ can be assigned to $\beta$ groups such that: (1) each rule belongs to a single group; (2) the rules of each group are order-independent on a subset of $k$ fields of $\mathcal{K}$ (except the "catch-all" rule); (3) different groups can reuse the same fields to keep order-independence. By Theorem 2, a lookup to a group returns a single matched rule to be checked for false-positives on all remaining fields; the matched non-false-positive rule with the highest priority (from exactly $\beta$ matched rules) is returned. We call this the *multi-group* representation of $\mathcal{K}$. Multi-group representations exist for any order-dependent classifier, but each group should be order-independent. The following theorem immediately follows by construction.

THEOREM 3. *The multi-group representation of a classifier is semantically equivalent to the original classifier.*

Lookups to groups can be issued in parallel. If each group in a multi-group representation can be order-independent on at most two fields, we have a semantically equivalent representation of a classifier in linear memory and with worst-case guaranteed logarithmic lookup time. Example 3 shows how the rules of a classifier $\mathcal{K}$ can be split into groups.

EXAMPLE 3. Consider $\mathcal{K} = \{R_1, R_2, R_3, R_4, R_5\}$ with three fields of four bits each and rules

$$\begin{aligned} R_1 &= ([5,10], [4,7], [4,5]),\\ R_2 &= ([1,4], [4,7], [4,5]),\\ R_3 &= ([1,9], [1,3], [4,6]),\\ R_4 &= ([1,9], [4,7], [1,3]),\\ R_5 &= ([1,9], [4,7], [5,6]). \end{aligned}$$

While the set of all rules $\{R_1, R_2, R_3, R_4, R_5\}$ is not order independent (for instance, $R_1 \cap R_5 \neq \emptyset$), the rules can be divided into two independent subsets, $\{R_1, R_2, R_3\}$ and $\{R_4, R_5\}$.

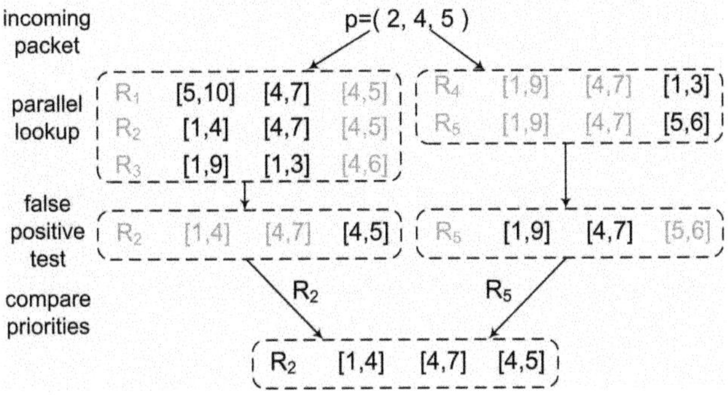


Figure 4: A visualization of the lookup procedure with a multi-group representation of the rules in Example 3. Fields to be checked on a certain step are in black; those that are irrelevant for this step, in grey.

The first two fields are necessary to keep the first group order-independent and the last field is enough to keep the second group order-independent.

Figure 4 shows a visualization of the lookup procedure after the grouping has been accomplished: for an incoming packet $p = (2, 4, 5)$, we issue parallel lookups for the two groups; these lookups return $R_2$ and $R_5$ and look only at fields $\{1, 2\}$ and $\{3\}$ respectively. Then we check if it was a false positive, matching $p$ against the rest of the fields for the returned rules, and then select the match by rule priority. At most one rule will make it to the false positive test for each group. In case when no rule matches or the final test finds that the result was a false positive, the catch-all rule is sent to the priority comparison, so each group sends exactly one rule to the priority comparison for any packet.

In some order-independent classifiers removing any of the fields make it be order-dependent and accordingly the FSM cannot reduce the number of fields. This leads us to the following optimization problem that can be applied also to order-dependent classifiers.

PROBLEM 2 ($l$-GROUPS OF RULES ($l$-MGR)). *Given a classifier $\mathcal{K}$, find an assignment of $\mathcal{K}$'s rules to a minimal number of disjoint groups such that different groups of rules can be based on the same or different subset of at most $l \leq k$ fields, and each group is order-independent on these fields.*

## 4.2 Representation of a Subset of Rules

Problem 2 shows how to deal with order-dependent classifiers. However, the number of lookups that can be issued in parallel is a system parameter, and the minimal number of groups found by solving Problem 2 may be unacceptable. In this situation, we can decompose an order-dependent classifier $\mathcal{K}$ into order-independent part $\mathcal{I}$ and order-dependent part $\mathcal{D}$. We can perform parallel lookups on both parts and return the best matched rule. TCAM or another general implementation can be used to store $\mathcal{D}$. Since in practice a subset of order-dependent rules on $k$ fields should be significantly smaller than $N$, significant TCAM space can be saved. The problem is finding which rules to put in $I$. One possibility is to find a maximal order-independent subset of rules on all $k$ fields and run Problems 1 or 2 on $\mathcal{I}$. Finding maximal order-independent set on $k$ fields is interesting when we extend already existing classifiers with new fields (Theorem 1). Another direction is finding an order-independent part that already has the desired properties.

PROBLEM 3 (MAXIMUM RULES COVERAGE ($l$-MRC)). *Given a classifier $\mathcal{K}$ and a positive number $l \leq k$, find a maximal subset $\mathcal{I} \subseteq \mathcal{K}$ which is order-independent on at most $l$ fields.*

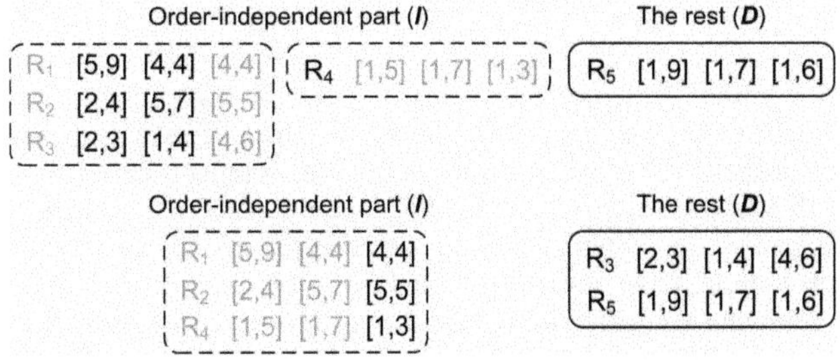


Figure 5: Example 5. Top: a multi-group representation of $\mathcal{I} = \{R_1, R_2, R_3, R_4\}$ and $\mathcal{D} = \{R_5\}$. Bottom: a more compact representation of $\mathcal{I} = \{R_1, R_2, R_4\}$ and $\mathcal{D} = \{R_3, R_5\}$. Fields to be checked in a group lookup are in black; those that are irrelevant for this step, in grey.

EXAMPLE 4. Consider a classifier $\mathcal{K} = \{R_1, R_2, R_3\}$ with three fields and the first three rules from Example 3 $R_1 = ([5, 10], [4, 7], [4, 5])$, $R_2 = ([1, 4], [4, 7], [4, 5])$, $R_3 = ([1, 9], [1, 3], [4, 6])$. If $l = 2$, we can have a maximal subset $\mathcal{K}' = \mathcal{K}$ of three rules, as the first two fields guarantee that the set $\mathcal{K}$ of these three rules is order-independent. Likewise, if $l = 1$ and only one field can be selected to distinguish between the rules, we can have order-independent sets of two rules. By considering the first field, we can have the subset $\mathcal{K}' = (R_1, R_2)$. Using only the second field we can have other possible order-independent subsets such as $\mathcal{K}' = (R_1, R_3)$ or $\mathcal{K}' = (R_2, R_3)$. We can also see that the three rules together are not order-independent based on any single field and accordingly the three mentioned possible subsets are all maximal subsets.

The generalized version of $l$-MRC problem reuses the advantages of the decomposition into $I$ and $D$ and multi-groups representation.

PROBLEM 4 (($(\beta, l)$-MRC). *Given a classifier $\mathcal{K}$ and two positive numbers $l \leq k$ and $\beta$, find a maximal subset of rules $\mathcal{I} \subseteq \mathcal{K}$ that can be assigned to at most $\beta$ groups, where each group is order-independent on at most $l$ fields.*

In some cases, it may be feasible to send a few more rules to $\mathcal{D}$ and thus significantly reduce the number of groups; this usually happens in practice with more general rules at the bottom of a classifier.

EXAMPLE 5. Consider a classifier $\mathcal{K}$ with three fields of five bits each and five rules

$$\begin{aligned} R_1 &= ([5, 9], [4, 4], [4, 4]), \\ R_2 &= ([2, 4], [5, 7], [5, 5]), \\ R_3 &= ([2, 3], [1, 4], [4, 6]), \\ R_4 &= ([1, 5], [1, 7], [1, 3]), \\ R_5 &= ([1, 9], [1, 7], [1, 6]). \end{aligned}$$

The maximal order-independent subset on all three fields is $\mathcal{I} = \{R_1, R_2, R_3, R_4\}$, and one possible multi-group representation of $\mathcal{I}$ consists of two groups: $\{R_1, R_2, R_3\}$ (based on the first two fields) and $\{R_4\}$. But if we set $\mathcal{D} = \{R_3, R_5\}$, the rest will form a single group which is order-independent on a single field, the third one. This example is illustrated on Figure 5.

## 4.3 Efficient Cache Implementation

The $(\beta, l)$-MRC problem maximizes the number of rules in $\mathcal{I}$ that can be assigned to at most $\beta$ groups that are order-independent on at most $l$ fields. Previously, we discussed a decomposition of $\mathcal{K}$ into $\mathcal{I}$ and $\mathcal{D}$, returning the best match between them. We wish to construct $\mathcal{I}$ in such a way that if a non-catch-all rule of $\mathcal{I}$ is matched, the lookup to $\mathcal{D}$ is no longer required. If such $\mathcal{I}$ exists, its content can be configured in cache. If $\mathcal{K}$ is order-independent, $\mathcal{I}$ that is returned by the $(\beta, l)$-MRC problem satisfies the "cache" property. In the order-dependent case we just need to guarantee that there exist no two rules $R_1 \in \mathcal{I}$ and $R_2 \in \mathcal{D}$ such that $R_1$ "intersects" with $R_2$ with priority $R_2 \prec R_1$. As a result, we formulate the following variant of the $(\beta, l)$-MRC problem.

PROBLEM 5 ($(\beta, l)$-MRCC). *Given a classifier $\mathcal{K}$ and two positive numbers $l \leq k$ and $\beta$, find a maximal subset of rules $\mathcal{I} \subseteq \mathcal{K}$ that can be assigned to at most $\beta$ groups, where each group is order-independent on at most $l$ fields and no two rules $R_1 \in \mathcal{I}$ and $R_2 \in \mathcal{D}$ such that $R_1$ "intersects" with $R_2$ and $R_2 \prec R_1$.*

The built $\mathcal{I}$ by $(\beta, l)$-MRCC has not only a space-efficient representation but also implements a power-efficient solution that does not require a lookup to $\mathcal{D}$ (if $\mathcal{I}$ is matched) that is usually will be implemented in TCAMs that suffer from power-inefficiency.

## 4.4 Resolution of Optimization

In case when only a part of the fields are represented by ranges or ranges are remapped to ternary bit-strings the boundaries of real classification fields as SrcIP, DstIP, ToS, etc., are removed. A rule becomes a ternary bitstring where any number of bits can be grouped to *virtual* fields.

EXAMPLE 6. Consider a classifier $\mathcal{K}$ with two fields of four bits each and four rules:

$$\begin{aligned} R_1 &= ( \ \texttt{100}\star, & \texttt{001}\star \ ), \\ R_2 &= ( \ \texttt{1010}, & \texttt{0001} \ ), \\ R_3 &= ( \ \texttt{000}\star, & \star\star\star\star \ ), \\ R_4 &= ( \ \texttt{001}\star, & \star\star\star\star \ ). \end{aligned}$$

In this case, the first field of four bits is enough to ensure order-independence, so if we run FSM on two four-bit fields, we get a classifier

$$\begin{aligned} R_1^{-1} &= (\texttt{100}\star), & R_2^{-1} &= (\texttt{1010}), \\ R_3^{-1} &= (\texttt{000}\star), & R_4^{-1} &= (\texttt{001}\star). \end{aligned}$$

However, note that only the first and third bits suffice to provide order-independence in this case. Hence, if we treat the same $\mathcal{K}$ as 8 one-bit fields, FSM yields a classifier of width two:

$$R_1^{-6} = (10), R_2^{-6} = (11), R_3^{-6} = (00), R_4^{-6} = (01).$$

We have performed experiments on how the resulting reduced classifier width depends on the width of virtual fields. The results are summarized in Figure 6 that shows average widths of ClassBench and CISCO classifiers for different resolutions.

In light of Example 6, solutions to problems in this section are very promising even for the case of a single field represented by a range. This is actually the case of minimization of representation in forwarding tables. Since every prefix corresponds to a single range, finding a maximal order-independent set of ranges is equivalent to maximum independent sets in interval graphs, i.e. a graph in which the nodes are 1-dimensional intervals (e.g., time intervals) and there is an edge between two intervals iff they intersect. This problem can be solved exactly in $O(N \log N)$ time using the earliest-deadline-first (EDF) algorithm [17].

Using the order-independent property of a classifier can in some sense reduce its representation memory size beyond the theoretical entropy lower bounds presented in [27]. Of course, this relates to

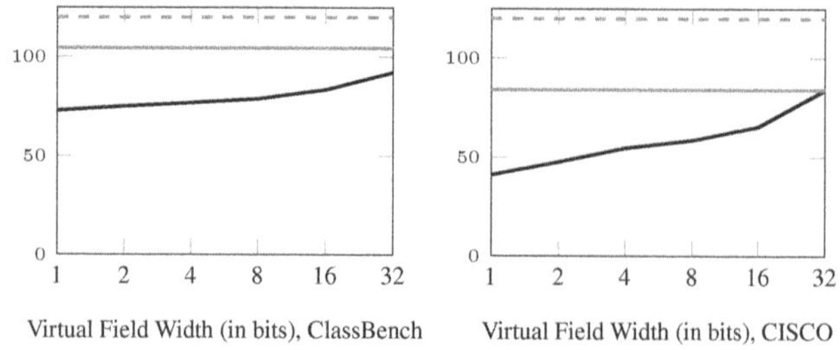


Figure 6: Classifier width (in bits) as a function of virtual field width for ClassBench and CISCO classifiers. Dashed grey line presents average original classifier width; grey solid line shows average classifier width after MinDNF reduction (see Section 5); black line illustrates classifier width after FSM optimization.

the space required in the first step of the classification and does not include the additional memory required to examine the case of a false-positive match.

Consider for instance, a classifier with four rules $R_1, R_2, R_3, R_4$ defined on a single field of $W = 8$ bits such that $R_1 = [148, 148] = (10010100), R_2 = [83, 83] = (01010011), R_3 = [165, 165] = (10100101), R_4 = [102, 102] = (01100110)$. The rules are associated with four distinct actions $A_1, A_2, A_3$ and $A_4$. We can see that two bits are enough in order to distinguish between the rules. These can be for instance the third and the seventh bits which have the values of $00, 01, 10$ and $11$ in the four rules $R_1, R_2, R_3, R_4$, respectively. Accordingly, the representation of this subset of the bits of the rules together with the encoding of the action of each rule (in two additional bits) has a total space of $4 \cdot (2 + 2) = 16$ bits.

For this classifier, the binary tree representation $T$ includes 4 leaves and a total of $27 < (32 = 4 \cdot W)$ nodes since some nodes for the first bits in the rules are shared among more than one rule. The suggested *XBW-l* transform [27] for the tree, denoted xbwl($T$), consists of three strings ($S_{last}$, $S_I$, $S_\alpha$), where the bit length of the binary strings $S_{last}$, $S_I$ that encodes tree structure equals the number of nodes. Likewise, the length of string $S_\alpha$ that encodes the actions equals the number of leaves times the size of each action in bits. This results in a space requirement of $27 + 27 + 4 \cdot 2 = 62$ bits, almost four times the space required in the suggested scheme. Furthermore, the DAG representation [27], a more complicated encoding scheme for the tree $T$, cannot reduce the space required since in this example actions of the rules are disjoint and the tree does not have any isomorphic subtrees. In future work, we plan to compare the size of forwarding table representations computed by heuristics proposed in [27] with the results of semantically equivalent representations considered in this section. We believe that results for representations of IPv6 forwarding tables should be even better since in wider classifiers there is a better chance to find more order-independent rules on fewer bits.

# 5. REPRESENTING CLASSIFIERS AS BOOLEAN EXPRESSIONS

In this section, we discuss a special case when each field is represented by a prefix, and thus fields can be represented by a string of individual bits. This special case lets us represent classifiers as Boolean expressions and apply well known Boolean optimization techniques to reduce the width and number of rules.

We can represent rules and sets of rules as discrete-valued functions. For the purposes of this exposition, we concatenate all fields and treat rules as a ternary bit-string in the Value–Mask–Action format (since fields have a fixed width, we do not lose information with this transformation). In this part we consider the case of order-independent classifiers; we decide whether an action should be applied to an incoming packet, i.e., compute a Boolean function.

A rule $s = s_1 s_2 \dots s_k$, $s_j \in \{0, 1, *\}$, can be expressed as a conjunction $f_s(x_1, \dots, x_k) = \bigwedge_{s_i=1} x_i \wedge \bigwedge_{s_i=0} \bar{x}_i$. Further, an order-independent set of rules $\mathcal{R} = \{R_1, \dots, R_N\}$ with rules $s_1, \dots, s_k$ can be written as an unordered disjunction of individual rules, i.e., as a formula of depth 2 in disjunctive normal form (DNF, disjunction of conjunctions).

EXAMPLE 7. The following set of rules with width 5

$$\begin{array}{l} (0 \;\; 1 \;\; * \;\; * \;\; *) \;\; \to 1 \\ (* \;\; 1 \;\; 0 \;\; * \;\; *) \;\; \to 1 \\ (* \;\; 1 \;\; 1 \;\; * \;\; 0) \;\; \to 1 \\ (* \;\; 1 \;\; 1 \;\; * \;\; 1) \;\; \to 1 \end{array}$$

is order-independent and equivalent to $f(x_1, x_2, x_3, x_4, x_5) = (\bar{x}_1 \wedge x_2) \vee (x_2 \wedge \bar{x}_3) \vee (x_2 \wedge x_3 \wedge \bar{x}_5) \vee (x_2 \wedge x_3 \wedge x_5)$.

Thus, minimizing order-independent TCAMs is equivalent to the following problem.

PROBLEM 6 (MINDNF). *For a given Boolean function $f$, find a minimal size DNF representation for $f$.*

DNF minimization may result in both reducing the number of rules (merging clauses in the DNF) and reducing the width of lookup necessary for classification (removing extra variables in the clauses).

EXAMPLE 8. Let us minimize the set of rules from Example 7. We apply the well-known resolution heuristic to clauses in the DNF representation of $f$:

$$\begin{aligned} (x_1 \wedge \bar{x}_2 \wedge \bar{x}_5) \vee (x_1 \wedge \bar{x}_2 \wedge x_5) &= (x_1 \wedge \bar{x}_2), \\ (x_1 \wedge \bar{x}_2) \vee (x_1 \wedge \bar{x}_2) &= x_2. \end{aligned}$$

At this point, we have $f(x_1, x_2, x_3, x_4, x_5) = (\bar{x}_1 \wedge x_2) \vee x_2$, and we can subsume the first clause into the second: $f(x_1, x_2, x_3, x_4, x_5) = x_2$. After minimizing the corresponding DNF expression, we can express the result as a set of rules, a single rule in this case:

$$(* \;\; 1 \;\; * \;\; * \;\; *) \;\; \to 1$$

Thus, in this example we have reduced the number of rules from four to one and have reduced the number of bits participating in the lookup from four (to apply the rules in Example 7 as stated, we would have to query all bits except bit 4) to one (bit 2).

The *MinDNF* problem has been extensively studied in complexity theory. Its decision version (given a formula $\varphi$ in DNF and a number $k$, find whether there exists an equivalent DNF with size less than $k$) is unlikely to be in NP. It is obviously in $\mathrm{NP}^{\mathrm{NP}}$: to solve this problem, one needs to guess a small DNF and verify with the NP oracle that solves the satisfiability problem that these two formulas are indeed equivalent. In fact, *MinDNF* has been shown to be $\mathrm{NP}^{\mathrm{NP}}$-complete ($\Sigma_2^P$-complete), and some inapproximability results have also been proven [16,37]. In practice, classical heuristics for *MinDNF* were based on Karnaugh maps and the Quine–McCluskey algorithm.

A different view of the problem appeared for the case of functions given by truth tables [1]; this means that the input size is exponential in the number of variables, and an algorithm is thus also allowed to use exponential memory. In this case, one can represent *MinDNF* as a special case of the SetCover problem which leads to using the Greedy SetCover algorithm to find minimal DNFs (see Algorithm 3). This algorithm has been shown to be $O(n)$-approximate, where $n$ is the number of variables in the formula (for functions given by truth tables, $O(\log T)$-approximate, where $T$ is the truth table size), and a matching lower bound has also been provided [1]. However, this approach is impractical for classifier optimization since practical classifiers look up several hundred bits, and it would be infeasible to construct the truth table explicitly.

At the first glance *MinDNF* is a more general problem than *FSM* since it can reduce both classification width and the number of rules. However, due to an additional check for a false-positive match *FSM* can significantly reduce classification width beyond optimal results of *MinDNF*.

EXAMPLE 9. Consider the classifier from Example 6:

$$\begin{array}{lcl} R_1 & = & (\;\texttt{100*}, \quad \texttt{001*}\;), \\ R_2 & = & (\;\texttt{1010}, \quad \texttt{0001}\;), \\ R_3 & = & (\;\texttt{000*}, \quad \texttt{****}\;), \\ R_4 & = & (\;\texttt{001*}, \quad \texttt{****}\;). \end{array}$$

As we have discussed in Example 6, FSM can reduce the width of $\mathcal{K}$ from eight bits to four (if we treat fields as indivisible) or even two (if we are able to get down to the bit level). On the other hand, the only MinDNF heuristic applicable here is the resolution rule that can be applied to $R_3$ and $R_4$, getting

$$\begin{array}{lcl} R_1 & = & (\;\texttt{100*}, \quad \texttt{001*}\;), \\ R_2 & = & (\;\texttt{1010}, \quad \texttt{0001}\;), \\ R_3' & = & (\;\texttt{00**}, \quad \texttt{****}\;). \end{array}$$

This classifier has width 8; if we discard bits with identical values (second bit in the first field), we get width 7, but the width savings are still small compared to FSM.

Table 2 shows how MinDNF heuristics apply to our experimental set of classifiers; we have applied MinDNF to the order-independent set from Table 1. The number of binary rules is sometimes significantly larger than the number of original rules, and MinDNF does not have a significant effect on width, i.e., few bits become purely "don't care" bits even after MinDNF-style reductions. In Table 2, we show both "pure" width (cutting out bits that are purely "don't care") and further reduced width where we have cut out bits that have the same value, not necessarily "don't care". This is a Boolean counterpart of our reduction shown in Section 3 since we can use a single look up to check bits that always have the same value, and they do not change which rule matches an incoming packet. MinDNF does not significantly decrease width even with this reduction.

The example of FSM shows us that algorithms with usage of an additional constant number of checks for false-positive match can significantly reduce a required space of an optimal representation of Boolean expressions. We believe that developing new Boolean expression minimization techniques that are based on the results of Theorem 2 is a very promising direction.

# 6. PROPRIETARY HEURISTICS

The reduction in classifier size with a false-positive check opens new horizons that are not addressed by general Boolean expression minimization. In this section we study the complexity of the algorithms for the problems defined in Section 4.

| | Original classifier | | | | | MinDNF reduced | | | | | | Order-indep. |
|---|---|---|---|---|---|---|---|---|---|---|---|---|
| | Rules, orig. | Rules, order-ind. | Rules, binary | Rules, SRGE | Width, bits | Rules, binary | Width, bits | Red. wid., bits | Rules, SRGE | Width, bits | Red. wid., bits | width, bits |
| acl1 | 49870 | 49779 | 67511 | 65240 | 120 | 67505 | 90 | 90 | 65234 | 90 | 90 | 31 |
| acl2 | 47276 | 44178 | 90772 | 90772 | 120 | 90233 | 104 | 104 | 90230 | 104 | 104 | 82 |
| acl3 | 49859 | 47674 | 85252 | 83630 | 120 | 85226 | 106 | 106 | 83605 | 106 | 106 | 91 |
| acl4 | 49556 | 46670 | 77837 | 76424 | 120 | 77755 | 106 | 106 | 76338 | 106 | 106 | 97 |
| acl5 | 40362 | 38962 | 47514 | 47514 | 120 | 46261 | 96 | 94 | 46249 | 96 | 94 | 63 |
| fw1 | 47778 | 43675 | 159525 | 159519 | 120 | 159461 | 112 | 112 | 159458 | 112 | 112 | 72 |
| fw2 | 48885 | 48826 | 92646 | 92646 | 120 | 92316 | 88 | 88 | 92316 | 88 | 88 | 52 |
| fw3 | 46038 | 41615 | 122495 | 122477 | 120 | 122259 | 112 | 112 | 122244 | 112 | 112 | 84 |
| fw4 | 45340 | 42857 | 278887 | 277921 | 120 | 277799 | 104 | 104 | 276807 | 104 | 104 | 76 |
| fw5 | 45723 | 39962 | 99574 | 99412 | 120 | 99421 | 112 | 112 | 99273 | 112 | 112 | 76 |
| ipc1 | 49840 | 48294 | 66718 | 65734 | 120 | 66715 | 112 | 112 | 65731 | 112 | 112 | 50 |
| ipc2 | 50000 | 50000 | 50000 | 50000 | 120 | 50000 | 112 | 112 | 50000 | 112 | 112 | 36 |
| cisco1 | 584 | 538 | 603 | 603 | 120 | 475 | 104 | 86 | 474 | 104 | 86 | 52 |
| cisco2 | 269 | 249 | 565 | 565 | 120 | 564 | 104 | 84 | 564 | 104 | 84 | 21 |
| cisco3 | 95 | 92 | 92 | 92 | 120 | 92 | 88 | 68 | 92 | 88 | 68 | 30 |
| cisco4 | 364 | 329 | 629 | 629 | 120 | 629 | 104 | 84 | 629 | 104 | 84 | 38 |
| cisco5 | 148 | 120 | 139 | 139 | 120 | 139 | 104 | 84 | 139 | 104 | 84 | 17 |

Table 2: Experimental results of MinDNF reduction in the order-independent subsets of classifiers.

## 6.1 Exact Algorithms

We first consider the existence of algorithms to build exactly the proposed semantically equivalent representations of classifiers.

FSM is NP-complete by reduction from the SetCover problem. Since FSM is exponential on $k$, an exact algorithm is feasible only for a sufficiently small number of fields (e.g., the 5-tuple case).

**Algorithm 1** IsOrderIndependent($M$)

```
for i = 1 → N − 1 do
    for j = i + 1 to N do
        if R_i^{-M} ∩ R_j^{-M} ≠ ∅ then return False
return True
```

**Algorithm 2** FSMBinSearch($k, min, max$)

```
m = ⌊(min+max)/2⌋
if min = max then return m
for M ⊆ {1, ..., k}, |M| = m do
    if IsOrderIndependent(M) then
        min = m
        return FSMBinSearch(k, min, max)
max = m − 1
return FSMBinSearch(k, min, max)
```

Algorithm 1 checks order-independence of a classifier with $N$ rules and a set $M$ of $m$ removed fields with complexity $O(N^2(k-m))$. To solve FSM, we can use a binary search. If the classifier is order-independent for some removed subset with $\frac{k}{2}$ fields, try to find a subset of size $\frac{3k}{4}$, otherwise check order-independence for subsets of size $\frac{k}{4}$, and so on. We call this algorithm FSMBinSearch. At worst we need to run IsOrderIndependent once for each subset of size $\frac{k}{2}$, once for each subset of size $\frac{3k}{4}$ and so on, $\binom{k}{k/2} + \binom{k}{k/4} + \ldots + \binom{k}{1} < 2^{k-1}$ times in total. Thus, we get the following theorem.

Theorem 4. *FSMBinSearch($k, 0, k-1$) finds a minimal subset of $k$ fields for which an original classifier is order-independent in time $O(k2^{k-1}N^2)$.*

When the number of fields grows (e.g, by a resolution increase as in Section 4.4 or adding new fields), FSM requires approximation heuristics.

The 2-MRC problem is NP-complete already for the case when $k = 2$ [4]. Since the $(\beta, l)$-MRC problem simply generalizes the 2-MRC problem when $\beta = 1$, $k = 2$, we can directly deduce based on the hardness of the 2-MRC problem that the $(\beta, l)$-MRC is NP-complete as well. As considered in Section 4.4 for $k = 1$, only the 1-MRC problem has an exact solution by EDF algorithm in $O(N log N)$ time [17]. Unfortunately, even the 2-MRC problem is exponential on $N$, so we do not consider exact algorithms similar to FSM when a number of fields is small.

## 6.2 Approximate Solutions

Algorithms for the FSM problem are exponential in the number of fields $k$; exact algorithms for the other considered problems are exponential even in the number of rules $N$. Therefore, as $k$ and $N$ grow, approximations are needed. In this section, we discuss efficient approximate algorithms that are crucial to achieve TCAM space savings.

### 6.2.1 *Representation of All Rules*

**Algorithm 3** Algorithm GreedySetCover

```
X ← ∅; T ← S
while T not empty do
    Choose S_i in T that contains maximal number of uncovered elements in U
    X ← X ∪ {S_i}
    T ← T \ S_i
return X
```

Theorem 5. *FSM is reducible to SetCover in $O(k \cdot N^2)$ time and has an approximation factor of $2 \cdot \ln(N) + 1$.*

Proof. Given an instance of the FSM problem, i.e., a set of $N$ rules $R_1, ..., R_N$, each with $k$ fields, we would like to find a subset of the fields that can distinguish between any pair of rules. A field distinguishes between two rules if they do not intersect in the field. We look at the (unordered) possible pairs of rules as the universe $U$ that we would like to cover, i.e., to make sure that each of these pairs of rules can be distinguished by one of the fields. We define $U = \{(i,j) | i < j, i,j \in [1,N]\}$. The size of $U$ is $|U| = \binom{N}{2} \leq 1/2 \cdot N^2$. We also define $k$ sets $S_1, ..., S_k$ that are used to cover $U$ such that the set $S_\ell$ represents the $\ell^{\text{th}}$ field out of $k$. For $\ell \in [1,k]$, we define $S_\ell = \{(i,j) | i < j, i,j \in$

$[1, N], R_i(\ell) \cap R_j(\ell) = \emptyset\}$. $S_\ell$ contains all pairs of rules that do not intersect in this field. To construct $S_1, ..., S_k$, one has to check all pairs out of $N$ rules. Therefore, this construction requires a time complexity of $O(k \cdot N^2)$ – polynomial in size of the input to the FSM problem. Given a solution to the set cover instance, i.e., a subset of $S_1, ..., S_k$, the corresponding set of fields are guaranteed to distinguish between any pair of rules and therefore comprise an admissible solution to the FSM problem.

Using Algorithm 3, in which each step selects an additional set with maximal number of uncovered elements, we can achieve an approximate solution to the FSM problem. In such a solution, the number of selected fields is within a constant factor of the optimal number of fields. The approximation ratio is $H(|U|) = H(\binom{N}{2})$, where $H$ is the harmonic number, such that the approximation ratio satisfies $H(|U|) \leq \ln(|U|) + 1 \leq 2 \cdot \ln(N) + 1$. □

Next we consider an estimate for a lower bound on $\beta$ (number of groups) in multi-group representations and how that bound relies on $N$ and $k$ for order-independent classifiers.

THEOREM 6. *1. For each $N$ and $k \geq 2$, there exists an order-independent classifier $\mathcal{K}$ of $N$ rules on $k$ fields such that it cannot be divided into less than $\sqrt{N} - O(1/\sqrt{N})$ groups where each group is order-independent by a single field.*

*2. Moreover, if $k \geq 4$, there exists $\mathcal{K}$ such that it cannot be divided into less than $\sqrt{N} - O(1/\sqrt{N})$ groups where each group is order-independent by two fields.*

*3. Moreover, if $N \geq 2^k$, there exists $\mathcal{K}$ such that it cannot be divided into less than $2^{k-l}$ groups where each group is order-independent by some $l$ fields.*

PROOF. 1. For some natural $n$, consider a classifier on two fields with $n(n-1)$ rules; the rules span all pairs of intervals $([i, i], [j, j])$ for $1 \leq i \neq j \leq n$. Any group of rules that are independent with respect to any single field cannot contain more than $n$ rules (since there are only $n$ distinct intervals in each field), so there are at least $n - 1$ groups.

2. To extend this counterexample to pairs of fields, consider a classifier on 4 fields that contains $n(n-1)(n-2)(n-3)$ rules that implement all quadruples of intervals $([i, i], [j, j], [k, k], [l, l])$, $1 \leq i \neq j \neq k \neq l \leq n$. Now any group of rules that are independent with respect to any pair of rules can contain at most $n(n-1)$ rules, so there are at least $(n-2)(n-3)$ groups in total.

3. Now the example is a classifier consisting of $2^k$ rules that implement all possible combinations of two disjoint intervals (say, $[1, 1]$ and $[2, 2]$) in $k$ rules. Now any group independent with respect to $l$ fields can contain at most $2^l$ rules (exhausting all possible combinations of $[1, 1]$ and $[2, 2]$ of length $l$), so there must be at least $2^{k-l}$ such groups. □

In Section 6.2.2 we propose a simple heuristic to resolve Problem 2 and evaluate its performance in Section 8.

### 6.2.2 Representation of a Maximal Number of Rules

For the case of $k = 2$, the 2-MRC problem can be approximated with factor $O(\log \log N)$ [4]. Consider the $l$-MRC problem in the case of $l = k$, i.e., finding a maximal subset of rules order-independent on all $k$ fields. In this special case, the problem reduces to the maximum independent set problem where each rule represents a node and an edge between two rules exists iff they intersect by some field.

In Theorem 5, we showed how the FSM problem reduces to Set-Cover; in order to find an independent set of rules based on a subset of the fields, we must make sure that each pair of rules does not intersect on at least one of the fields and defined the corresponding coverage problem. We considered the coverage of a field as the set of pairs of rules it can separate. Unfortunately, it is not straightforward to make use of the same idea in order to reduce the $l$-MRC problem to the MSC because a field that separates the maximal number of pairs of rules does not necessarily yield the maximal size of an independent set of rules.

For example, consider the following classifier $\mathcal{K} = (R_1, R_2, R_3, R_4)$ with four rules of two fields: $R_1 = ([0, 1], [0, 0])$, $R_2 = ([2, 3], [1, 1])$, $R_3 = ([0, 1], [2, 2])$ , $R_4 = ([2, 3], [0, 3])$. There are four pairs of rules that do not intersect in the first field. These are pairs $(R_1, R_2)$, $(R_1, R_4)$, $(R_2, R_3)$, $(R_3, R_4)$. Likewise, there are three pairs of rules with disjoint second field: $(R_1, R_2)$, $(R_1, R_3)$ and $(R_2, R_3)$. For this classifier, in the 1-MRC problem we should select the second field to obtain a maximal independent subset of rules although it distinguishes between fewer pairs of rules than the first field. Based only on the first field, the maximal set of independent rules includes two rules ($\{R_1, R_2\}$, $\{R_1, R_4\}$, $\{R_2, R_3\}$, or $\{R_3, R_4\}$). Adding the second field, we get an independent set of three rules $\{R_1, R_2, R_3\}$ because we can separate all pairs of rules in it, so the size of the maximal independent set is not determined by the number of disjoint pairs of rules.

Nevertheless, we can use an algorithm for the $l$-MSC problem as a heuristic to solve the $l$-MRC problem. We give the pairs of rules each field can separate as input to an algorithm that solves $l$-MSC.

PROBLEM 7 (MAXIMUM SET COVERAGE ($l$-MSC)). *Given a set of elements $\mathcal{U} = \{1, 2, \ldots N\}$ (the universe), a set $S$ of $k$ sets whose union equals $\mathcal{U}$, and a positive number $l \leq k$, select at most $l$ sets of $S$ such that as many elements of $\mathcal{U}$ as possible are covered (the union of selected sets has maximal size).*

A variant of Algorithm 3 that stops after $l$ subsets are added solves the $l$-MSC problem and has an approximation factor of $1 - \frac{1}{e} + o(1)$ [10].

To solve $(\beta, l)$-MRC, we can run $l$-MRC; once any unassigned rule "intersects" with any rule assigned to the current group a new group is opened if the total number of groups does not exceed $\beta$. The algorithm for $l$-MGR is the same as for $(\beta, l)$-MRC but now we stop to create new groups once we covered all rules of the original classifier.

The proposed heuristic for the $l$-MRC problem and its variant for $(\beta, l)$-MRC have worst-case guaranteed lookup time $O(\log N)$ and a linear space requirement when $l = 2$. In practice there is an excess of information that preserves order-independence on a relatively small subset of bits (see Section 8)

## 7. CLASSIFIER CONFIGURATION

This section proposes new standard representations of classifiers and discusses updates.

### 7.1 Standardization of Policy Classifiers

We group classifiers into two categories: those required for switching and those implementing service-level-agreement (SLA) policies. The former type can be changed frequently, while the latter is typically static. Dynamic updates for the latter type are significantly less important and we can consider offline computation for more efficient representations.

We suggest explicitly specifying certain classifier characteristics (that can be computed offline) as part of a classifier configuration. The following traits (or variations thereof) are important: (1) maximal size of the order-independent part; (2) minimal subset of fields that preserve order-independence; (3) minimal number of order-independent groups based on at most two fields; (4) assignments of rules to a predefined number of groups based on at most two fields. With these the optimal implementation can be chosen based on the constraints of a configured network element.

## 7.2 Dynamic Updates

Suppose that classifier represents packet flows that can change frequently. It is straightforward to remove a rule from the order-independent part $\mathcal{I}$; for the order-dependent part $\mathcal{D}$, it depends on the representation. Insertion is more complicated. If an inserted rule $R$ is order-dependent with the current $\mathcal{I}$, insert $R$ to $\mathcal{D}$. If $\mathcal{D}$ is full, recompute $\mathcal{I}$ and $\mathcal{D}$ for the new set. If $\mathcal{D}$ is still full, reject $R$. If $R$ is order-independent with $\mathcal{I}$ on $k$ fields and does not increase the subset of fields in FSM, or there is an assignment to one of the groups in MGR without increasing the number of order-independent groups, add $R$ to $\mathcal{I}$. To avoid long delays, recomputation of $\mathcal{I}$ and $\mathcal{D}$ can start in the background. In this case there is a tradeoff between the current optimality of $\mathcal{I}$ representation and the delay before inserting the next rule.

We can increase the chance of successfully inserting a new rule in $\mathcal{I}$. Recall that for order-independent classifiers we must check all $k$ fields for a matched rule to check for false-positive matches on a subset of the fields. We can define an additional parameter $C$: the maximal number of rules that can be checked for false-positives in a line rate. Suppose an inserted rule is order-independent with each rule of the current $\mathcal{I}$ on $k$ fields and increases the number of fields for FSM or requires more groups to keep the order-independence of all groups for MGR. We can still assign $R$ to $\mathcal{I}$ if the number of rules to be checked for false-positives is at most $C$. By doing so, we increase $|\mathcal{I}|$ by up to a factor of $C$.

It is also desirable to support modifications in existing rules. If a rule in $\mathcal{I}$ is only modified in fields not required for order-independence, we can simply change it in additional memory. If the change is in one of the fields required for order-independence, we have to make sure this rule does not intersect other rules in $\mathcal{I}$ after the change. If so, we can simply update this rule in the representation of $\mathcal{I}$, and if it now intersects with some other rule, we can move this modified rule to $\mathcal{D}$. In an offline process, we can recalculate the selection of fields to distinguish among rules to match the recent new rules. As in the rule insertion case, modification of a rule in $\mathcal{D}$ depends on the representation of $\mathcal{D}$.

EXAMPLE 10. Consider a classifier $\mathcal{K} = (R_1, R_2, R_3)$ with three fields of four bits each and rules

$$\begin{aligned} R_1 &= ([1,3],[4,8],[1,5]), \\ R_2 &= ([7,7],[1,8],[4,5]), \\ R_3 &= ([4,5],[6,9],[4,6]). \end{aligned}$$

The first field suffices for order-independence, so we have $\mathcal{K}^{-\{2,3\}} = (([1,3]),([7,7]),([4,5]))$ and $\mathcal{I} = \{R_1, R_2, R_3\}$. Let us try to insert $R_4 = ([2,4],[2,2],[3,3])$; it is order-independent with $\mathcal{I}$ but requires the second field for order-independence with $R_1$ and $R_3$. In this (somewhat unlucky) case we can still use only the first field for $\mathcal{I}$ and test $R_4$ additionally if either $R_1$ or $R_3$ is matched (this requires $C \geq 2$). Note that it is not necessary to match $R_4$ if $R_2$ is matched since it is order-independent with $R_2$ on the first field. This example is illustrated on Figure 7.

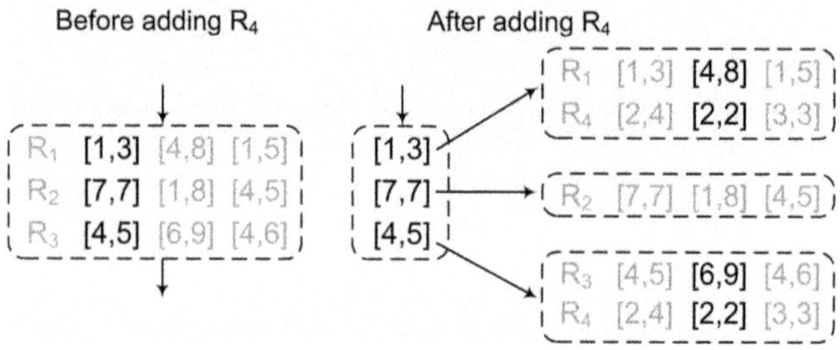


Figure 7: Example 10. Left: a multi-group representation of $\mathcal{I} = \{R_1, R_2, R_3\}$. Right: a representation of the two-step lookup procedure for $C \geq 2$ and recently inserted $R_4$. Fields to be checked in a group lookup are in black; those irrelevant in this step, in grey.

# 8. SIMULATIONS

To validate our scheme, we run simulations on 12 classifiers from Classbench [7] (generated with real parameters), each with $\approx$ 50K rules on 6 fields, and on 5 real life classifiers provided by Cisco Systems. In Figure 1 and Table 1, we have already presented the TCAM space savings resulting from the FSM approach when adding new fields to these classifiers; we have shown that order-independence greatly simplifies adding new fields to classifiers. In Table 2, we compared the proposed FSM approach with MinDNF heuristics, showing that FSM algorithms can have a much greater effect.

The next set of simulations deals with maximal order-independent sets. We use the greedy algorithm for the $l$-MRC problem (see Section 6.2.2) to find a maximal order-independent set on all $k$ fields. Then we apply the FSM problem on the computed maximal order-independent set. To simulate Problem 2 ($l$-MGR) with one- and two-field order-independent groups, we use the algorithm proposed in Section 6.2.2.

The results are summarized in Table 3. In most cases, the vast majority of rules are covered by very few groups of order-independent rules. In some cases the maximal order-independent set constructed with a subset of fields $\mathcal{F} = \{0, 1\}$ is larger than such a set constructed with all fields; this is due to a few rules with large intervals in the first two fields that have been taken up to the set because they are independent on some other field and prevented more rules to join the set later. For example, a rule of the form

0.0.0.0/0 0.0.0.0/0 1234 : 1234 0 : 65535 0x00/0x00 0x0000/0x0000

would block all further rules with source port 1234 if this port has not appeared earlier but would not be taken if only the IP addresses had been taken into account. Thus, interestingly, a greedy approach is not necessarily monotonic as the number of fields taken into account increases.

The effect explained in Example 5 is also seen in simulations. In many cases we see many very small groups (of size $\leq 2$ or $\leq 5$) created by general rules at the bottom of the lists; in practice it makes sense to send these rules to $\mathcal{D}$. Table 3 also shows that a maximal order-independent subset mostly takes care of the small groups, as very few such groups are left when running $l$-MGR on the resulting maximal order-independent set.

The majority of the proposed approximate algorithms are greedy without backtracking (the variants of GreedySetCover algorithm) with $|\mathcal{U}| = O(N^2)$, the running time of these algorithms is $O(kN^2)$, where $N$ is a number of rules and $k$ is a number of fields in a classifier. As a result we do not evaluate a computational time of the proposed algorithms.

# 9. RELATED WORK

Research towards efficient implementations of packet classifiers falls into two main categories: algorithmic solutions (usually software based) and TCAM-based solutions. Algorithmic solutions mainly rely on one of three techniques: decision trees, hashing, or coding-based compression. The works [11,32,39] suggest how

| | Total | $k$-MRC | | | MGR on the entire set | | | | | | | | | | MGR on the $k$-MRC result | | | | | | | | | |
|---|---|---|---|---|---|---|---|---|---|---|---|---|---|---|---|---|---|---|---|---|---|---|---|---|
| | | | | | 1-MGR | | | | | 2-MGR | | | | | 1-MGR | | | | | 2-MGR | | | | |
| | rules | size | FSM | $\{0,1\}$ | all | 95% | 99% | $\leq 2$ | $\leq 5$ | all | 95% | 99% | $\leq 2$ | $\leq 5$ | all | 95% | 99% | $\leq 2$ | $\leq 5$ | all | 95% | 99% | $\leq 2$ | $\leq 5$ |
| acl1 | 49870 | 49779 | 0, 1, 4 | 49768 | 16 | 1 | 1 | 6 | 9 | 12 | 1 | 1 | 5 | 7 | 5 | 1 | 1 | 1 | 2 | 2 | 1 | 1 | 0 | 0 |
| acl2 | 47276 | 44178 | 0, 1, 3, 4 | 43819 | 67 | 5 | 13 | 19 | 32 | 39 | 2 | 5 | 10 | 20 | 17 | 4 | 7 | 1 | 2 | 6 | 1 | 2 | 1 | 1 |
| acl3 | 49859 | 47674 | 0, 1, 2, 3, 4 | 46114 | 31 | 3 | 5 | 11 | 20 | 18 | 2 | 3 | 7 | 10 | 11 | 3 | 4 | 1 | 2 | 6 | 1 | 3 | 1 | 1 |
| acl4 | 49556 | 46670 | 0, 1, 2, 3, 4 | 40518 | 42 | 8 | 14 | 6 | 15 | 16 | 3 | 5 | 3 | 5 | 21 | 7 | 10 | 0 | 3 | 6 | 2 | 3 | 0 | 0 |
| acl5 | 40362 | 38962 | 0, 1, 3, 4 | 22725 | 43 | 18 | 27 | 2 | 6 | 11 | 4 | 6 | 1 | 1 | 37 | 17 | 25 | 0 | 2 | 10 | 4 | 6 | 1 | 1 |
| fw1 | 47778 | 43675 | 0, 1, 2, 3, 4 | 44713 | 71 | 2 | 5 | 18 | 42 | 41 | 2 | 3 | 10 | 19 | 7 | 2 | 2 | 2 | 2 | 4 | 1 | 2 | 0 | 1 |
| fw2 | 48885 | 48826 | 0, 1, 2, 4 | 48755 | 20 | 3 | 3 | 15 | 15 | 12 | 1 | 1 | 5 | 9 | 7 | 3 | 3 | 2 | 3 | 2 | 1 | 1 | 0 | 0 |
| fw3 | 46038 | 41615 | 0, 1, 2, 3, 4 | 40581 | 101 | 2 | 17 | 42 | 57 | 56 | 2 | 7 | 11 | 28 | 17 | 2 | 2 | 2 | 4 | 7 | 1 | 2 | 0 | 0 |
| fw4 | 45340 | 42857 | 0, 1, 2, 3, 4 | 43912 | 109 | 2 | 40 | 9 | 28 | 57 | 1 | 17 | 10 | 16 | 20 | 2 | 2 | 2 | 3 | 8 | 1 | 1 | 0 | 1 |
| fw5 | 45723 | 39794 | 0, 1, 2, 3, 4 | 39007 | 94 | 2 | 13 | 38 | 58 | 49 | 2 | 8 | 6 | 21 | 8 | 2 | 2 | 2 | 3 | 5 | 1 | 2 | 1 | 2 |
| ipc1 | 49840 | 48294 | 0, 1, 3, 4 | 48385 | 22 | 2 | 2 | 9 | 16 | 16 | 1 | 3 | 6 | 11 | 6 | 1 | 2 | 1 | 2 | 4 | 1 | 1 | 0 | 0 |
| ipc2 | 50000 | 50000 | 0, 1 | 50000 | 2 | 2 | 2 | 0 | 0 | 1 | 1 | 1 | 0 | 0 | 2 | 2 | 2 | 0 | 0 | 1 | 1 | 1 | 0 | 0 |
| cisco1 | 584 | 538 | 0, 1, 3, 4 | 406 | 15 | 8 | 13 | 2 | 8 | 10 | 4 | 7 | 3 | 4 | 9 | 5 | 7 | 2 | 3 | 5 | 2 | 4 | 1 | 2 |
| cisco2 | 269 | 249 | 0, 1, 4 | 246 | 4 | 2 | 3 | 1 | 1 | 2 | 2 | 2 | 0 | 0 | 4 | 2 | 3 | 1 | 2 | 2 | 1 | 2 | 0 | 1 |
| cisco3 | 95 | 92 | 0, 1, 3, 4 | 89 | 5 | 3 | 5 | 2 | 3 | 3 | 2 | 3 | 1 | 2 | 4 | 2 | 4 | 2 | 2 | 2 | 1 | 2 | 0 | 1 |
| cisco4 | 364 | 329 | 0, 1, 3, 4 | 324 | 7 | 3 | 5 | 2 | 4 | 4 | 2 | 3 | 1 | 1 | 5 | 2 | 3 | 2 | 3 | 3 | 1 | 2 | 1 | 2 |
| cisco5 | 148 | 120 | 0, 1 | 120 | 3 | 2 | 3 | 0 | 1 | 2 | 2 | 2 | 0 | 0 | 2 | 2 | 2 | 0 | 0 | 1 | 1 | 1 | 0 | 0 |

Table 3: Simulation results. Columns, left to right: total no. of rules $|\mathcal{K}|$; $|\mathcal{I}|$, where $\mathcal{I} = \mathrm{MRC}(\mathcal{K}, \{0, \ldots, 5\})$; minimal size subset of fields w.r.t. which $\mathcal{I}$ is order-independent; $|\mathcal{I}'|$, where $\mathcal{I}' = \mathrm{MRC}(\mathcal{K}, \{0, 1\})$ (i.e., order-independent w.r.t source IP and destination IP); for the one-field result $\{\mathcal{G}\} = MGR(\mathcal{K})$: total number of order-independent groups $|\{\mathcal{G}\}|$, no. of groups covering 95% and 99% of the rules, no. of groups of size $\leq 2$ and of size $\leq 5$; similar statistics for the two-field MGR; similar statistics for one-field and two-field MGR run on $\mathcal{I}$.

to partition the multi-dimensional rule space. Possible matching rules are found by tracing a path in a decision tree. Techniques to balance the partition in each node exist, but rule replication often cannot be avoided. A related approach is described in [43]. There is an inherent tradeoff between space and time complexities in these approaches. Song and Turner's ABC algorithm for filter distribution offers higher throughput with lower memory overhead and the ability to tune the implementation for better time complexity or better space complexity [34]. The works [9, 13] discuss hash-based solutions to match a packet to its possible matching rules. Efficient coding-based representations are shown in [27, 28, 31]. Other works discuss efficient TCAM implementations. TCAMs do not natively support ranges, so one has to translate range fields into prefix representations. Bounds for the maximal number of TCAM entries required to encode a range have been proposed. A range of $W$ bits can be encoded in at most $2W - 2$ entries using only entries with a positive action ("accept") [36]. This bound improves to $2W - 4$ using gray coding [3]. Both schemes encode a multi-field range with a number of entries that is exponential in the number of fields $k$ with upper bounds of $(2W - 2)^k$ and $(2W - 4)^k$, respectively. When including negative action entries ("deny"), the upper bound is improved to $W$ entries [29]. The works [29, 30] suggested schemes to encode a $k$-field range with complexity linear in $k$. Unfortunately, these schemes apply only to the encoding of a single rule; the encoding of a classifier with more rules requires changing the conventional TCAM architecture.

Several works have considered reducing the number of TCAM entries in the encoding of a given classifier by relying on heuristics [5, 23]. These techniques include encoding the most common ranges with additional bits [6, 21], applying block permutations [42], designing tree-based architectures [38], and redundancy removal [20]. While many of these heuristics could be improved with randomization [19], they usually limit the number of fields in a rule or perform badly as the number of fields increases. Rule disjointness is not a new topic; efficient schemes for classification and update supporting that rely on this property have been proposed in [2, 35, 41].

Multi-group representations to reduce power consumption have appeared at [22, 33], while the space-time tradeoff for representation of hierarchical classifiers has been considered in [15]. The relation between packet classifiers and optimization of Boolean expressions was recently studied in [18]. We also note that reusing order-independence can significantly simplify splitting of a classifier over several network elements [12, 14].

# 10. CONCLUSION

Packet classification depends on the number of entries $N$ in a classifier and the classification width $W$ of its rules. In fact, for a given number of entries width is the determining factor for lookup complexity. Once we pass to *multi*-field classification, width, and thus matching complexity, tend to grow significantly. This is especially the case for expressive classification with ranges. In practice, the rules contain excessive information to distinguish between $N$ entries. Various techniques have been proposed to determine similar patterns across table entries and represent and evaluate them efficiently (see, e.g., [27]).

In this work, we take a different route, identifying new properties of classifiers that let us ignore superfluous information in classification lookup. Our proposed concept of order-independence simplifies classifier matching by splitting the problem into two subproblems: (a) the rule selection problem which is based only on parts of rules (not their entire width) and (b) the matching of the selected rule which is based only on the remainder of the fields not considered in (a). As we have demonstrated, the proposed classifier representations can significantly outperform dedicated space minimization approaches. While the proposed techniques are motivated by packet classification problems and demonstrated thereon, we believe that our simple yet effective concepts can be reused for significant improvements also in neighboring areas (e.g., matching in databases or data mining) and can also open new lines of research in other areas (e.g., Boolean minimization).

# 11. ACKNOWLEDGMENTS

We thank the anonymous reviewers and our shepherd Ali Ghodsi for their insightful comments. The work of Patrick Eugster and Kirill Kogan was partially supported by Cisco Systems under grant "A Fog Computing Architecture". The work of Sergey Nikolenko was partially supported by the President Grant for Leading Scientific Schools NSh-3856.2014.1.

## 12. REFERENCES


[1] E. Allender, L. Hellerstein, P. McCabe, T. Pitassi, and M. E. Saks. Minimizing DNF formulas and $AC_d^0$ circuits given a truth table. In *IEEE Conference on Computational Complexity*, 2006.

[2] A. Bremler-Barr, D. Hay, and D. Hendler. Layered interval codes for TCAM-based classification. In *IEEE Infocom*, 2009.

[3] A. Bremler-Barr and D. Hendler. Space-efficient TCAM-based classification using Gray coding. *IEEE Trans. Computers*, 61(1):18–30, 2012.

[4] P. Chalermsook and J. Chuzhoy. Maximum independent set of rectangles. In *ACM-SIAM SODA*, 2009.

[5] Y.K. Chang, C.I. Lee, and C.C. Su. Multi-field range encoding for packet classification in TCAM. In *IEEE Infocom Mini-Conference*, 2011.

[6] H. Che, Z. Wang, K. Zheng, and B. Liu. DRES: Dynamic range encoding scheme for TCAM coprocessors. *IEEE Trans. Computers*, 57(7):902–915, 2008.

[7] ClassBench: A packet classification benchmark. http://www.arl.wustl.edu/classbench/.

[8] Configuring IP ACLs. http://www.cisco.com/en/US/docs/switches/datacenter/sw/4_1/nx-os/security/configuration/guide/sec_ipacls.pdf.

[9] S. Dharmapurikar, H. Song, J. S. Turner, and J. W. Lockwood. Fast packet classification using bloom filters. In *ACM/IEEE ANCS*, 2006.

[10] U. Feige. A threshold of ln $n$ for approximating set cover. *J. ACM*, 45(4):634–652, 1998.

[11] P. Gupta and N. McKeown. Classifying packets with hierarchical intelligent cuttings. *IEEE Micro*, 20(1):34–41, 2000.

[12] N. Kang, Z. Liu, J. Rexford, and D. Walker. Optimizing the "one big switch" abstraction in software-defined networks. In *ACM CoNEXT*, 2013.

[13] Y. Kanizo, D. Hay, and I. Keslassy. Optimal fast hashing. In *IEEE Infocom*, 2009.

[14] Y. Kanizo, D. Hay, and I. Keslassy. Palette: Distributing tables in software-defined networks. In *IEEE INFOCOM*, 2013.

[15] A. Kesselman, K. Kogan, S. Nemzer, and M. Segal. Space and speed tradeoffs in TCAM hierarchical packet classification. *J. Comput. Syst. Sci.*, 79(1):111–121, 2013.

[16] S. Khot and R. Saket. Hardness of minimizing and learning DNF expressions. In *IEEE FOCS*, 2008.

[17] J. M. Kleinberg and É. Tardos. *Algorithm design*. Addison-Wesley, 2006.

[18] K. Kogan, S. I. Nikolenko, W. Culhane, P. Eugster, and E. Ruan. Towards efficient implementation of packet classifiers in sdn/openflow. In *ACM HotSDN*, 2013.

[19] N. Lesh and M. Mitzenmacher. Bubblesearch: A simple heuristic for improving priority-based greedy algorithms. *Inf. Process. Lett.*, 97(4):161–169, 2006.

[20] A. X. Liu, C. R. Meiners, and Y. Zhou. All-match based complete redundancy removal for packet classifiers in TCAMs. In *IEEE Infocom*, 2008.

[21] H. Liu. Efficient mapping of range classifier into Ternary-CAM. In *IEEE Hot Interconnects*, 2002.

[22] Y. Ma and S. Banerjee. A smart pre-classifier to reduce power consumption of tcams for multi-dimensional packet classification. In *ACM SIGCOMM*, 2012.

[23] C. R. Meiners, A. X. Liu, and E. Torng. Bit weaving: A non-prefix approach to compressing packet classifiers in TCAMs. *IEEE/ACM Trans. Netw.*, 20(2):488–500, 2012.

[24] Netlogic Microsystems. Content addressable memory. http://www.netlogicmicro.com.

[25] OpenFlow 1.3 specification, 2012. http://www.openflow.org/wk/index.php/OpenFlow_1_3_proposal.

[26] M. H. Overmars and A. Frank van der Stappen. Range searching and point location among fat objects. *J. Algorithms*, 21(3):629–656, 1996.

[27] G. Rétvári, J. Tapolcai, A. Korösi, A. Majdán, and Z. Heszberger. Compressing ip forwarding tables: towards entropy bounds and beyond. In *ACM SIGCOMM*, 2013.

[28] O. Rottenstreich, A. Berman, Y. Cassuto, and I. Keslassy. Compression for fixed-width memories. In *IEEE ISIT*, 2013.

[29] O. Rottenstreich, R. Cohen, D. Raz, and I. Keslassy. Exact worst-case TCAM rule expansion. *IEEE Trans. Computers*, 62(6):1127–1140, 2013.

[30] O. Rottenstreich, I. Keslassy, A. Hassidim, H. Kaplan, and E. Porat. On finding an optimal TCAM encoding scheme for packet classification. In *IEEE Infocom*, 2013.

[31] O. Rottenstreich, M. Radan, Y. Cassuto, I. Keslassy, C. Arad, T. Mizrahi, Y. Revah, and A. Hassidim. Compressing forwarding tables for datacenter scalability. *IEEE Journal on Selected Areas in Communications*, 32(1):138–151, 2014.

[32] S. Singh, F. Baboescu, G. Varghese, and J. Wang. Packet classification using multidimensional cutting. In *ACM SIGCOMM*, 2003.

[33] M. Somasundaram. Memory and power efficient mechanism for fast table lookup.

[34] H. Song and J. S. Turner. ABC: Adaptive binary cuttings for multidimensional packet classification. *IEEE/ACM Trans. Netw.*, 21(1):98–109, 2013.

[35] V. Srinivasan, S. Suri, and G. Varghese. Packet classification using tuple space search. In *ACM SIGCOMM*, 1999.

[36] V. Srinivasan, G. Varghese, S. Suri, and M. Waldvogel. Fast and scalable layer four switching. In *ACM SIGCOMM*, 1998.

[37] C. Umans. The minimum equivalent DNF problem and shortest implicants. *J. Comput. Syst. Sci.*, 63(4):597–611, 2001.

[38] B. Vamanan and T. N. Vijaykumar. TreeCAM: decoupling updates and lookups in packet classification. In *ACM CoNEXT*, 2011.

[39] B. Vamanan, G. Voskuilen, and T. N. Vijaykumar. EffiCuts: optimizing packet classification for memory and throughput. In *ACM SIGCOMM*, 2010.

[40] G. Varghese. *Network Algorithmics: An Interdisciplinary Approach to Designing Fast Networked Devices*. Morgan Kaufmann, 2005.

[41] Z. Wang, H. Che, M. Kumar, and S. K. Das. CoPTUA: Consistent policy table update algorithm for TCAM without locking. *IEEE Trans. Computers*, 53(12):1602–1614, 2004.

[42] R. Wei, Y. Xu, and H. J. Chao. Block permutations in Boolean space to minimize TCAM for packet classification. In *IEEE Infocom Mini-Conference*, 2012.

[43] X. Zhao, Y. Liu, L. Wang, and B. Zhang. On the aggregatability of router forwarding tables. In *IEEE INFOCOM*, 2010.

# Duet: Cloud Scale Load Balancing with Hardware and Software

Rohan Gandhi† Hongqiang Harry Liu^ Y. Charlie Hu† Guohan Lu*
Jitendra Padhye* Lihua Yuan* Ming Zhang*
Microsoft*, Purdue University†, Yale University^

## ABSTRACT

Load balancing is a foundational function of datacenter infrastructures and is critical to the performance of online services hosted in datacenters. As the demand for cloud services grows, expensive and hard-to-scale dedicated hardware load balancers are being replaced with software load balancers that scale using a distributed data plane that runs on commodity servers. Software load balancers offer low cost, high availability and high flexibility, but suffer high latency and low capacity per load balancer, making them less than ideal for applications that demand either high throughput, or low latency or both. In this paper, we present DUET, which offers all the benefits of software load balancer, along with low latency and high availability – at next to no cost. We do this by exploiting a hitherto overlooked resource in the data center networks – the switches themselves. We show how to embed the load balancing functionality into existing hardware switches, thereby achieving organic scalability at no extra cost. For flexibility and high availability, DUET seamlessly integrates the switch-based load balancer with a small deployment of software load balancer. We enumerate and solve several architectural and algorithmic challenges involved in building such a hybrid load balancer. We evaluate DUET using a prototype implementation, as well as extensive simulations driven by traces from our production data centers. Our evaluation shows that DUET provides 10x more capacity than a software load balancer, at a fraction of a cost, while reducing latency by a factor of 10 or more, and is able to quickly adapt to network dynamics including failures.

**Categories and Subject Descriptors:** C.2.4 [Computer-Communication Networks]: Distributed Systems—Network Operating Systems

**General Terms:** Design, Performance

**Keywords:** Load Balancing, Datacenter, SDN

## 1. INTRODUCTION

A high performance load balancer is one of the most important components of a cloud service infrastructure. Services in the data center scale by running on multiple servers, each with an individual direct IP (DIP). The service exposes one or more virtual IP addresses (VIP) outside the service boundary. The load balancer receives the traffic destined for the VIP, splits it among the DIPs, and routes it to the individual DIPs using IP-in-IP encapsulation.

The load balancer thus touches every packet coming into the data center from the Internet, as well as a significant fraction of all intra-DC traffic. This traffic volume induces heavy load on both data plane and control plane of the load balancer [17]. The performance and reliability of the load balancer directly impact the latency, throughput and the availability of the cloud services hosted in the DC.

Traditional load balancers are dedicated hardware middleboxes [1, 4] that are very expensive. In contrast, Ananta [17] is a software load balancer that runs on commodity servers. Ananta consists of a central controller, and several software Muxes (SMux) that provide a distributed data plane. Each SMux maintains all VIP-to-DIP mappings, and implements traffic splitting and encapsulation functionality in software. The Ananta architecture is flexible, highly scalable and ensures high availability.

However, software load balancers have two fundamental limitations, both of which stem from the fact that they process the packets in software. First, processing packets in software limits *capacity*. Experiments show that the CPU on individual Ananta SMux becomes a bottleneck once the incoming traffic exceeds 300K packets per second. While the aggregate capacity of software load balancer can be scaled out by adding more servers, doing so raises cost. For example, handing 15Tbps traffic (typical for a mid-sized DC) requires over 4000 SMuxes, costing over USD 10 million.

Second, processing packets in software incurs high, and highly variable *latency*. An Ananta SMux, handling as little as 100K packets per second can add anywhere from 200$\mu$sec to 1ms of latency. Applications such as algorithmic stock trading and high performance distributed memory caches demand ultra-low (a few microseconds) latency within the data center. For such applications, the latency inflation by the software load balancer is not acceptable.

In this paper, we propose DUET, which addresses these two drawbacks of software load balancers. DUET uses *existing* switch hardware in data centers to build a high performance, in-situ, organically scalable hardware load balancer and *seamlessly* combines it with a small deployment of software load balancer for enhanced availability and flexibility.

DUET is based on two key ideas. The first idea is to build a load balancer from existing switches in the data center network. The key insight is that the two core functions needed to implement a load balancer – traffic splitting and packet encapsulation – have long been available in commodity switches deployed in data center networks. Traffic splitting is supported using ECMP, while


*SIGCOMM'14*, August 17–22, 2014, Chicago, Illinois, USA.
Copyright 2014 ACM 978-1-4503-2836-4/14/08 ...$15.00.
http://dx.doi.org/10.1145/2619239.2626317

packet encapsulation is supported using tunneling. However, it is only recently that the switch manufacturers have made available APIs that provide detailed, fine-grained control over the data structures (ECMP table and tunneling table) that control these two functions. We re-purpose unused entries in these tables to maintain a database of VIP-to-DIP mappings, thereby enabling the switch to act as a Mux in addition to its normal forwarding function. This gives us an in-situ, hardware Mux (HMux) – without new hardware. Since splitting and encapsulation are handled in the data plane, the switch-based load balancer incurs low latency (microseconds) and high capacity (500 Gbps).

While HMuxes offer high capacity, low latency and low cost, the architecture is less flexible than software load balancers. Specifically, handling certain cases of switch failures is challenging (§5.1). Thus, our second idea is to integrate the HMuxes with a small deployment of SMuxes, to get the best of both worlds. We make the integration seamless using simple routing mechanisms. In the combined design, most of the traffic is handled by the switch-based hardware load balancer, while software load balancer acts as a backstop, to ensure high availability and provide flexibility.

Compared to dedicated hardware load balancers, or pure software load balancers (Ananta), DUET is highly cost effective. It load-balances most of the traffic using *existing* switches (HMuxes), and needs only a small deployment of software load balancer as a backstop. Because most of the traffic is handled by the HMuxes, DUET has significantly lower latency than software load balancers. At the same time, use of software load balancer enables DUET to inherit high availability and flexibility of the software load balancer.

To design DUET, we addressed two main challenges. First, individual switches in the data center do not have enough memory to hold the entire VIP-to-DIP mapping database. Thus, we need to partition the mappings among the switches. We devise a simple greedy algorithm to do this, that attempts to minimize the "leftover" traffic (which is perforce handled by the software load balancer), while taking into account constraints on switch memory and demands of various traffic flows.

The second challenge is that this mapping must be regularly updated as conditions change. For example, VIPs or DIPs are added or removed by customers, switches and links fail and recover etc. We devise a migration scheme that avoids memory deadlocks and minimizes unnecessary VIP movement.

We evaluate DUET using a testbed implementation as well as extensive, large-scale simulations. Our results show that DUET provides 10x more capacity than the pure software load balancer, at a fraction of the SMux cost, while also reducing the latency inflation by 10x or more. Additionally, we show that DUET quickly adapts to the network dynamics in the data center including failures.

In summary, the paper makes the following three contributions. First, We characterize the conditions, design challenges, and design principles for moving load balancing functionality directly into hardware switches which offer significantly lower latency and higher capacity than software servers. Second, we present the design and implementation of a switch-based load balancer. To the best of our knowledge, this is the first such design. Third, we show how to seamlessly combine the switch-based load balancer with software load balancer to achieve high availability and flexibility. Again, to the best of our knowledge, this is the first "hybrid" load balancer design.

## 2. BACKGROUND AND MOTIVATION

We provide background on load balancing functionality in DCs, briefly describe a software-only load balancer architecture (Ananta), and point out its shortcomings.

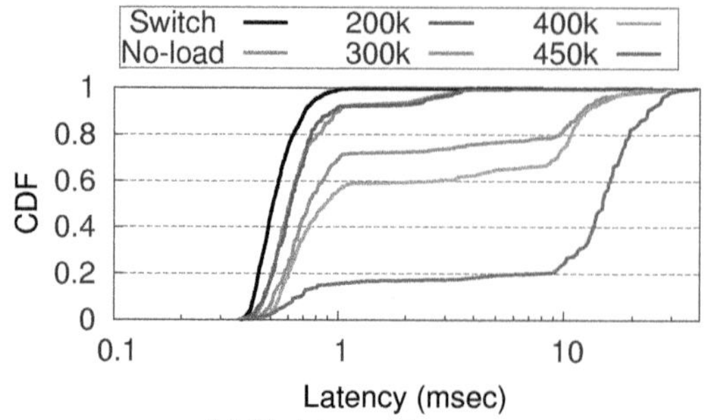

(a) End-to-end latency

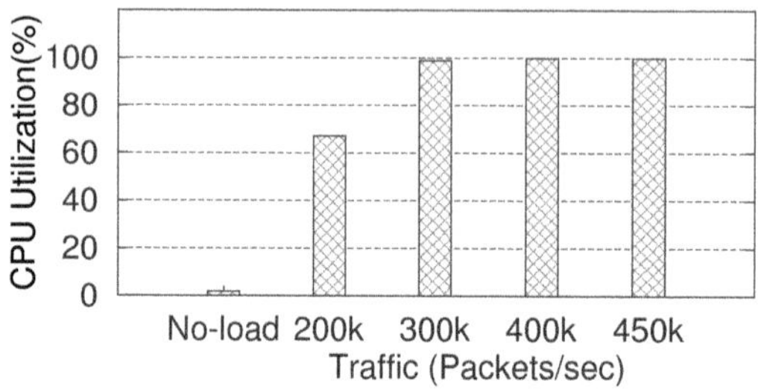

(b) CPU Utilization

**Figure 1: Performance of software Mux.**

A DC typically hosts multiple services. Each service is a set of servers that work together as a single entity. Each server in the set has a unique direct IP (DIP) address. Each service exposes one or more virtual IP (VIP) outside the service boundary. The load balancer forwards the traffic destined to a VIP to one of DIPs for that VIP. Even services within the same DC use VIPs to communicate with each other, since the indirection provided by VIPs offers several benefits. For example, individual servers can be maintained or upgraded without affecting dependent services. Management of firewall rules and ACLs is simplified by expressing them only in terms of VIPs, instead of DIPs, which are far more numerous and are subject to churn.

The key to the efficient functioning of the indirection architecture is the load balancer. A typical DC supports thousands of services [17, 9], each of which has at least one VIP and many DIPs associated with it. All incoming Internet traffic to these services and most inter-service traffic go through the load balancer. As in [17], we observe that almost 70% of the total VIP traffic is generated within DC, and the rest is from the Internet. The load balancer design must not only scale to handle this workload but also minimize the processing latency. This is because to fulfill a single user request, multiple back-end services often need to communicate with each other — traversing the load balancer multiple times. Any extra delay imposed by the load balancer could have a negative impact on end-to-end user experience. Besides that, the load balancer design must also ensure high service availability in face of failures of VIPs, DIPs or network devices.

### 2.1 Ananta Software Load Balancer

We first briefly describe the Ananta [17] software load balancer. Ananta uses a three-tier architecture, consisting of ECMP on the routers, several software Muxes (SMuxes) that run on commodity servers, and are deployed throughout the DC, and a host agent (HA) that runs on each server.

Each SMux stores the VIP to DIP mappings for all the VIPs configured in the DC. Using BGP, every SMux announces itself to be the next hop for every VIP. Incoming packets for a VIP are directed to one of the SMuxes using ECMP. The SMux selects a DIP for the VIP, and encapsulates the packet, setting the destination address of the outer IP header to the chosen DIP. At the DIP, the HA decapsulates the incoming packet, rewrites the destination address and port, and sends it to server. The HA also intercepts outgoing packets, and rewrites their IP source addresses from the DIP to the VIP, and forwards the direct server return (DSR).

Ananta can support essentially an unlimited number of VIPs and DIPs, because it stores this mapping in the large main memory on commodity servers. While a single SMux in Ananta has limited capacity (due to software processing), Ananta can still scale to handle large volumes of traffic. First, Ananta deploys numerous SMuxs, and relies on ECMP to split the incoming traffic among them. Second, DSR ensures that only the incoming or the VIP traffic goes through the load balancer. Ananta also includes a mechanism called fast path to enhance scalability. Fast path allows all inter-service traffic to directly use DIPs, instead of using VIPs. However, this negates the benefits of the VIP indirection. For example, if fast path is enabled, service ACLs have to be expressed in terms of DIPs.

In summary, implementing parts of load balancing functionality in software allows Ananta to be highly scalable and flexible. However, processing packets in software is also the Achilles heel for Ananta, because it adds latency, and limits the throughput, as we discuss next.

## 2.2 Limitations of Software Load Balancer

Figure 1(a) shows the CDF of the RTTs for the VIP traffic load-balanced by a production Ananta SMux as traffic to the VIP varies between 0 and 450K packets/sec. Even at zero load the SMux adds a median latency of 196$\mu$sec. The latency variance is also significant, with the $90^{th}$ percentile being 1ms. The median RTT (without load balancer) in our production DCs is 381$\mu$sec, so the inflation in latency is significant for the intra-DC traffic, which accounts for 70% of the total VIP traffic. (For the remaining traffic from the Internet, it is a lesser problem due to larger WAN latencies). The high latency inflation and high latency variability result from processing the packets in software. We also see that the added latency and the variance get much worse at higher load.

The results also illustrate that an individual SMux instance has low capacity. Beyond 300K packets/sec, the CPU utilization reaches 100% (Figure 1(b)). Thus, for the hardware SKU used in our DCs, each SMux can handle only up to 300K packets/sec, which translates to 3.6 Gbps for 1,500-byte packets. At this rate, supporting 15 Tbps VIP traffic for a mid-sized (40K servers) DC would require over 4K SMuxes, or 10% of the DC size; which is unacceptable[1].

# 3. DUET: CORE IDEAS

In the previous section, we saw that while software load balancers are flexible and scalable, they suffer from low throughput and high latency. In this paper, we propose a new design called DUET that offers scalability, high throughput and low latency, at a small fraction of the software load balancer's cost.

DUET is based on two novel ideas. First, we leverage idle resources of modern, commodity data center switches to construct a hardware load balancer. We call this design Hardware Mux (HMux). HMux offers microsecond latency, and high capacity, without the need for *any* additional hardware. However, the HMux design suffers from certain shortcomings. Thus, our second idea is to combine the HMux with Ananta-like software Mux (SMux). The combined system is called DUET in which the SMux acts as a backstop for the HMux.

We now describe the design of HMux. To simplify the description, we will assume that the DC is not virtualized, *i.e.,* one DIP corresponds to one server. The changes required to support VMs are described in §5.2.

## 3.1 HMux

Ananta's SMux implements two key functions to load balance traffic: (1) for each VIP, split traffic equally among its DIPs, and (2) use IP-in-IP encapsulation to route the VIP traffic to the corresponding DIPs. Both of these functions have long been available on commodity switches, *i.e.,* traffic splitting is supported using ECMP and IP-in-IP encapsulation is supported using tunneling. However, major switch vendors have only recently started to provide the APIs for fine-grained control over ECMP and tunneling functionality.

Our key insight is that by carefully programming the ECMP and tunneling tables using these new APIs, we can make a commodity switch act as a hardware Mux (HMux), in addition to its normal functionality. In fact, this can be easily done on most of the switches used in our DCs today.

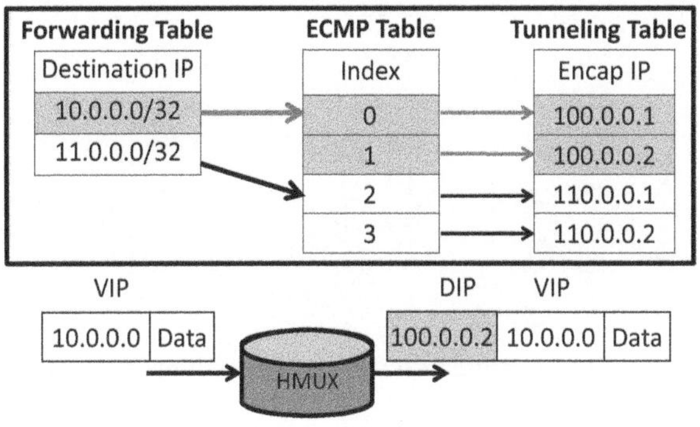


**Figure 2: Storing VIP-DIP mapping on a switch.**

Figure 2 shows the HMux design. A packet arriving at a switch goes through a processing pipeline. We focus on three tables used in the pipeline. The packet matches one entry in the host forwarding table which then points to multiple ECMP table entries. These ECMP table entries correspond to multiple next hops for the packet[2]. The actual next hop for the packet is selected by using the hash of the IP 5-tuple to index into the ECMP table. The tunneling table enables IP-in-IP encapsulation by storing the information needed to prepare the outer IP header for a given packet.

To construct HMux, we link the ECMP and tunneling functionalities. Consider a packet destined for VIP 10.0.0.0 that arrives at the HMux. There are two DIPs (100.0.0.1 and 100.0.0.2) for this VIP. The host forwarding table indicates that the first two entries in the ECMP table pertain to this VIP. The ECMP entries indicate that packets should be encapsulated, and point to appropriate entries in the tunneling table. The switch encapsulates the packet using IP-in-IP encapsulation, and the destination address in the outer IP header is set to the DIP address specified in the tunneling table entry. The packet is then forwarded to the appropriate interface.

Thus, at the expense of some entries in the host forwarding, ECMP and tunneling tables, we can build a load balancer using

[1]Newer technologies such as direct-packet IO and RDMA may help match packet processing capacity of the SMux to that of the NIC (10 Gbps), but they may not match packet processing capacity of the switch (600 Gbps+) as we explain in § 3.1.

[2]The information is split between ECMP group table and ECMP table; we omit such details due to lack of space.

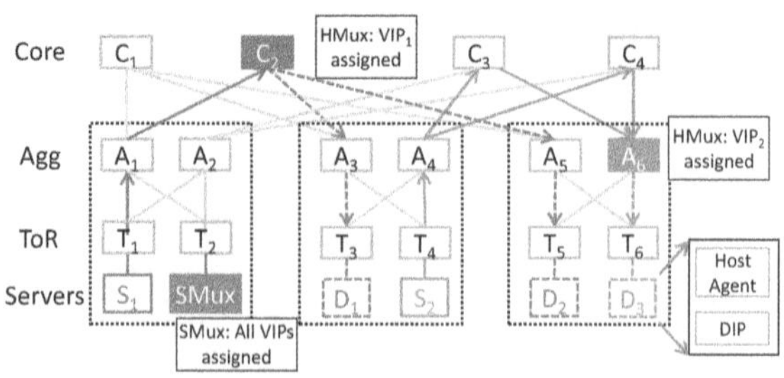


**Figure 3: DUET architecture: VIPs are partitioned across different HMuxes — $VIP_1$ and $VIP_2$ are assigned to HMux $C_2$ and $A_6$. Additionally, SMuxes act as backstop for all the VIPs. Every server (apart from SMuxes) runs host-agent that decapsulates the packets and forwards to the DIP. Links marked with solid lines carry VIP traffic, and links with dotted lines carry DIP traffic.**

commodity switches. In fact, if all the VIP-to-DIP mappings are stored on every top-of-rack (ToR) switch as well as every access switch, this HMux design can provide load balancing functionality to all intra-DC and inter-DC traffic. However, the amount of space available in the three tables is limited, raising two distinct issues.

**Number of VIPs:** The first problem is the size of the host forwarding table. The switches in our DC have 16K entries in the host table. The host table is mostly empty, because it is used only for routing within a rack. But even the 16K entries may not be enough to hold all VIPs in a large DC. One way to address this problem is by using longest prefix match (LPM) forwarding table. However, LPM table is heavily used for routing within and across DCs, and is not available to be used for load balancing. We support higher number of VIPs using SMuxes as explained in §3.3.

**Number of DIPs:** The second problem concerns the sizes of the ECMP and tunneling tables. ECMP table typically holds 4K entries, and is mostly empty (see § 9). The tunneling table typically holds 512 entries. In our DC, few applications use tunneling, so these entries are mostly free as well. The number of DIPs an individual HMux can support is the minimum of the number of free entries in the ECMP and the tunneling tables (see Figure 2). Thus, an individual HMux can support at most 512 DIPs. This is orders of magnitude smaller than the total number of DIPs. We address this challenge next.

## 3.2 Partitioning

We address the problem of limited size of ECMP and tunneling tables using two mechanisms: (1) We divide the VIP-to-DIP mapping across multiple switches. Every switch stores only a small subset of all the VIPs, but stores all the DIPs for those VIPs. This way of partitioning ensures all the traffic for a particular VIP arrives at a single switch and the traffic is then equally split among the DIPs for that VIP. (2) Using BGP, we announce the VIPs that are assigned to the switches, so that other switches can route the VIP packets to the switch where the VIP is assigned.

Figure 3 illustrates this approach. $VIP_1$ has two DIPs ($D_1$ and $D_2$), whereas $VIP_2$ has one ($D_3$). We assign $VIP_1$ and $VIP_2$ to switches $C_2$ and $A_6$ respectively, and flood the routing information in the network. Thus, when a source $S_1$ sends a packet to $VIP_1$, it is routed to switch $C_2$, which then encapsulates the packet with either $D_1$ or $D_2$, and forwards the packet.

Another key benefit of partitioning is that it achieves *organic scalability* of HMuxes — when more servers are added in the DC and hence traffic demand increases, more switches will also be added and hence the aggregate capacity of HMuxes will also increase proportionally.

## 3.3 DUET: HMux + SMux

While partitioning helps increase the number of DIPs HMux can support, that number still remains limited. The HMux design also lacks the flexibility of SMux, because VIPs are partitioned and "pinned" to specific HMuxes. This makes it challenging to achieve high VIP availability during network failures. Although replicating VIP across a few switches may help improve failure resilience, it is still hard to achieve the high availability of Ananta because Ananta stores the complete VIP-DIP mappings on a large number of SMuxes.

This motivates us to architect DUET— a new load balancer design to fuse the flexibility of SMux and the high capacity and low latency of HMux.

### *3.3.1 Design*

DUET's goal is to maximize VIP traffic handled using HMux, while using SMux as a backstop. Thus, besides an HMux on each switch, DUET also deploys a small number of SMuxes on commodity servers (figure 3). The VIPs are partitioned among HMuxes as described earlier. In addition, each SMux announces all the VIPs. The routing protocol preferentially routes VIP traffic to HMux, ensuring that VIP traffic is primarily handled by HMux – thereby providing high capacity and low latency. In case of HMux failure, traffic is automatically diverted to SMux, thereby achieving high availability. To ensure that existing connections do not break as a VIP migrates from HMux to SMux or between HMuxes, all HMuxes and SMuxes use the same hash function to select DIPs for a given VIP.

The preferential routing to HMux can be achieved in several ways. In our current implementation, SMux announces the VIPs in aggregate prefixes, while HMux announces /32 routes to individual VIPs. Longest prefix matching (LPM) prefers /32 routes over aggregate prefix routes, and thus directs incoming VIP traffic to appropriate HMux, unless that HMux is unavailable.

The number of SMuxes needed depends on several factors including the VIP traffic that cannot be assigned to HMux due to switch memory or link bandwidth limits (§4), the VIP traffic that failovers to SMux due to HMux failure (§5.1), and the VIP traffic that is temporarily assigned to SMux during VIP migration (§4.2). We estimate it based on historical traffic and failure data in DC.

### *3.3.2 Benefits*

The key benefits of DUET are summarized below.

**Low cost:** DUET does not require any additional hardware – it uses idle resources on existing switches to provide load balancing functionality. DUET also requires far fewer SMuxes than Ananta, since SMuxes are used only as a backstop for HMuxes, and hence carry far less traffic.

**High capacity and low latency:** this is because VIP traffic is primarily handled by HMux on switch.

**High availability:** by using SMux as a backstop during failures, DUET enjoys the same high availability as Ananta.

**High limit on number of VIPs:** If the number of VIPs exceeds the capacity of the host forwarding table (16K), the additional VIPs can be hosted on SMux. Traffic data (Figure 15) in our production DCs shows that VIP traffic distribution is highly skewed – most of the traffic is destined for a small number of "elephant" VIPs which can be handled by HMux. The remaining traffic to "mice" VIPs can be handled by SMux.

| Notation | Explanation |
|---|---|
| $V$ | Set of VIPs |
| $d_v$ | Set of DIPs for the v-th VIP |
| $S, E$ | Set of switches and links respectively |
| $R$ | Set of resources (switches and links) |
| $C_i$ | Capacity of i-th resource |
| $t_{i,s,v}$ | v-th VIP's traffic on i-th link, when it is assigned to s-th switch |
| $L_{i,s,v}$ | load (additional utilization) on i-th resource if v-th VIP is assigned to s-th switch |
| $U_{i,s,v}$ | Cumulative utilization of i-th resource if v-th VIP is assigned to s-th switch |
| $U_{i,v}$ | Cumulative utilization of i-th resource after v VIPs have been assigned |
| $MRU_{s,v}$ | Max. Resource Utilization (MRU) after v-th VIP is assigned to s-th switch |

**Table 1: Notations used in VIP assignment algorithm.**

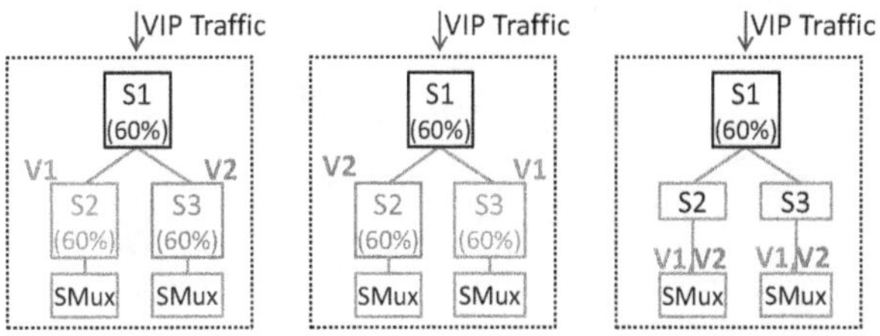


(a) Initial (b) Final (c) Through SMux

**Figure 4: Memory deadlock problem during VIP migration. VIPs V1 and V2 both occupy 60% of switch memory each. The goal of migration is to migrate the VIPs from assignment in (a) to (b);** DUET **eliminates this problem by migrating VIPs through SMuxes, as shown in (c).**

These benefits can only be realized through careful VIP-switch assignment. The assignment must take into account both memory and bandwidth constraints on individual switches, as well as different traffic load of different VIPs. The assignment must dynamically adapt to changes in traffic patterns and network failures. In the next two sections, we describe how DUET solves these problems, as well as provides other load balancing functions.

# 4. VIP ASSIGNMENT ALGORITHM

We formalize the VIP-switch assignment problem using the notations listed in Table 1.

**Input:** The input to the algorithm includes the list of VIPs ($V$), the DIPs for each individual VIP v ($d_v$), and the traffic volume for each VIP. The latter is obtained from network monitoring. The input also includes the network topology, consisting of a set of switches ($S$) and a set of links ($E$). The switches and links constitute the two types of resources ($R$) in the assignment. Each resource instance has a fixed capacity $C_i$, *i.e.,* the link bandwidth for a link, and memory capacity that includes residual ECMP and tunneling table capacity available for DUET on a switch. To absorb the potential transient congestion during VIP migration and network failures, we set the capacity of a link to be 80% of its bandwidth.

**Objective:** Find the VIP-switch assignment that maximizes the VIP traffic handled by HMux. As explained earlier, this will improve latency and reduce cost by cutting the number of SMux needed. We do not attempt to minimize the extra network propagation delay due to indirection because the propagation delay contributes only less than 30$\mu$sec of the 381$\mu$sec RTT in our DC.

**Constraints:** Any VIP-switch assignment should not exceed the capacity of any of the resources.

The VIP assignment problem is a variant of multi-dimensional bin-packing problem [10], where the resources are the bins, and the VIPs are the objects. Multi-dimensional bin-packing problems are NP-hard [10]. DUET approximates it with a greedy algorithm, which works quite well in our simulations based on real topology and traffic load of a large production network.

## 4.1 VIP Assignment

We define the notion of maximum resource utilization (MRU). We have two types of resource – switches and links. MRU represents the maximum utilization across all switches and links.

**Algorithm sketch:** We sort a given set of VIPs in decreasing traffic volume, and attempt to assign them one by one (*i.e.,* VIPs with most traffic are assigned first). To assign a given VIP, we consider all switches as possible candidates to host the VIP. Typically, assigning a VIP to different switches will result in different MRU. We pick the assignment that results in the smallest MRU, breaking ties at random. If the smallest MRU exceeds 100%, *i.e.,* no assignment can accommodate the load of the VIP, the algorithm terminates. The remaining VIPs are not assigned to any switch – their traffic will be handled by the SMuxes. We now describe the process of calculating MRU.

**Calculating MRU:** We calculate the additional utilization (load) on every resource for each potential assignment. If the v-th VIP is assigned to the s-th switch, the extra utilization on the i-th link is $L_{i,s,v} = \frac{t_{i,s,v}}{C_i}$ where traffic $t_{i,s,v}$ is calculated based on the topology and routing information as the source/DIP locations and traffic load are known for every VIP. Similarly, the extra switch memory utilization is calculated as $L_{s,s,v} = \frac{|d_v|}{C_s}$, *i.e.,* the number of DIPs for that VIP over the switch memory capacity.

The cumulative resource utilization when the v-th VIP is assigned to the s-th switch is simply the sum of the resource utilization from previously assigned (v-1) VIPs and the additional utilization due to the v-th VIP:

$$U_{i,s,v} = U_{i,v-1} + L_{i,s,v} \quad (1)$$

The MRU is calculated as:

$$MRU_{s,v} = max(U_{i,s,v}), \forall i \in R \quad (2)$$

## 4.2 VIP Migration

Due to traffic dynamics, network failures, as well as VIP addition and removal, a VIP assignment calculated before may become out-of-date. From time to time, DUET needs to re-calculate the VIP assignment to see if it can handle more VIP traffic through HMux and/or reduce the MRU. If so, it will migrate VIPs from the old assignment to the new one.

There are two challenges here: (1) how to calculate the new assignment that can quickly adapt to network and traffic dynamics without causing too much VIP reshuffling, which may lead to transient congestion and latency inflation. (2) how to migrate from the current assignment to new one.

A simple approach would be to calculate the new assignment from scratch using new inputs (*i.e.,* new traffic, new VIPs etc.), and then migrate the VIPs whose assignment has changed between the current assignment and the new one. To prevent routing black holes during VIP migration, we would use make-before-break — *i.e.,* a VIP would be announced from the new switch before it is withdrawn from the old switch. This simple approach is called *Non-sticky*.

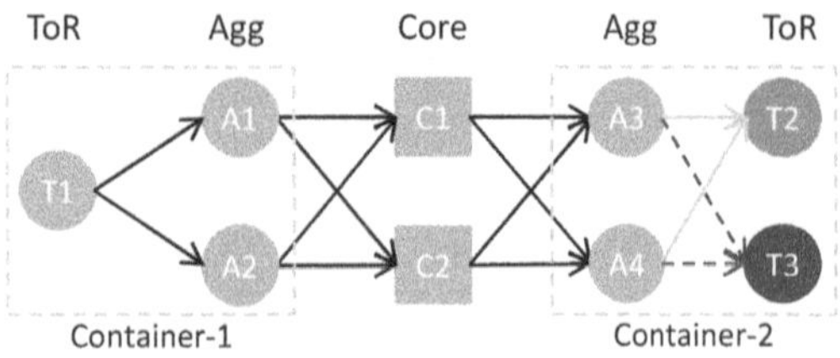


**Figure 5: When the VIP assignment changes from ToR $T_2$ to $T_3$, only the links inside container-2 are affected. As a result, we can first select best ToR in a container based on the links within container, and then scan over all containers and remaining Core and Agg switches.**

The *Non-sticky* approach suffers from two problems. First, it may lead to transitional memory deadlock. Figure 4 shows a simple example where initially VIP V1 and VIP V2 are assigned to switches $S_2$ and $S_3$, respectively, but swap positions in the new assignment. Further, either VIP takes 60% of the switch memory. Because of limited free memory, there is no way to swap the VIPs under the make-before-break approach. When there are a large number of VIPs to migrate, finding a feasible migration plan becomes very challenging. Second, even if there was no such deadlock, calculating a new assignment from scratch may result in a lot of VIP reshuffling, for potentially small gains.

DUET circumvents transitional memory deadlocks by using SMux as a stepping stone. We first withdraw the VIPs that need to be moved from their currently assigned switches and let their traffic hit the SMux[3]. We then announce the VIPs from their newly assigned switches, and let the traffic move to the new switches. This is illustrated in Figure 4(c) where both VIP's (V1 and V2) traffic is handled by SMux during migration.

Because SMux is used as a stepping stone, we want to avoid unnecessary VIP reshuffling to limit the amount of VIP traffic that is handled by SMux during migration. Hence, we devise a *Sticky* version of the greedy VIP assignment algorithm that takes the current assignment into account. A VIP is moved only if doing so results in significant reduction in MRU. Let us say that VIP $v$ was assigned to switch $s_c$ in the current assignment, and the MRU would be the lowest if it is assigned to switch $s_n$ in the new assignment. We assign $v$ to $s_n$ only if $(MRU_{s_c,v} - MRU_{s_n,v})$ is greater than a threshold. Else we leave $v$ at $s_c$.

**Complexity:** It is important for DUET to calculate the new assignment quickly in order to promptly adapt to network dynamics. Since all $L_{i,s,v}$ can be pre-computed, the complexity to find the minimum MRU (Equation 2) for VIP-switch assignment is $O(|V| \cdot |S| \cdot |E|)$.

This complexity can be further reduced by leveraging the hierarchy and symmetry in the data center network topology. The key observation is that assigning a VIP to different ToR switches inside a container will only affect the resource utilization inside the same container (shown in Figure 5). Therefore, when assigning a VIP, we only need to consider one ToR switch with the lowest MRU inside each container. Because ToR switches constitute a majority of the switches in the data center, this will significantly reduce the computation complexity to $O(|V| \cdot ((|S_{core}| + |S_{agg}| + |C|) \cdot |E| + |S_{tor}| \cdot |E_c|))$. Here $C$ and $E_c$ denote the containers and links inside a container. $S_{core}$, $S_{agg}$ and $S_{tor}$ are the Core, Aggregation and ToR switches respectively.

[3]Recall that SMux announces all VIPs to serve as a backstop (§3.3.1)

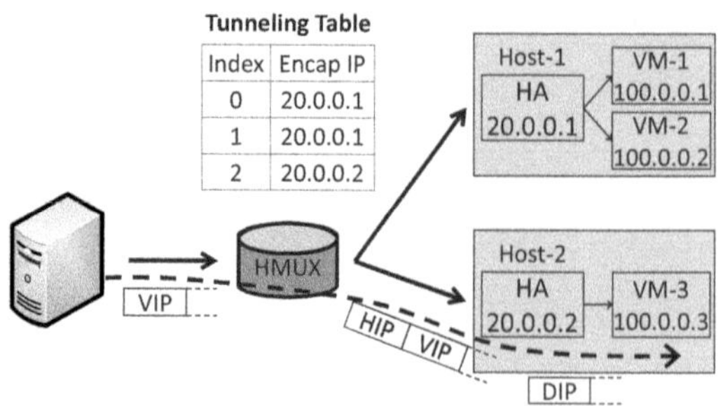


**Figure 6: Load balancing in virtualized clusters.**

# 5. PRACTICAL ISSUES

We now describe how DUET handles important practical issues such as failures and configuration changes.

## 5.1 Failure Recovery

A critical requirement for load balancer is to maintain high availability even during failures. DUET achieves this primarily by using SMuxes as a backstop.

**HMux (switch) failure:** The failure of an HMux is detected by neighboring switches. The routing entries for the VIPs assigned to the failed HMux are removed from all other switches via BGP withdraw messages. After routing convergence, packets for these VIPs are forwarded to SMuxes, since SMuxes announce all VIPs. All HMux and SMux use the same hash function to select DIPs for a given VIP, so existing connections are not broken, although they may suffer some packet drops and/or reorderings during convergence time (<40ms, see §7.2). Because in our production DCs we rarely encounter failures that are more severe than three switch failures or single container failures at a time, we provision sufficient number of SMuxes to handle the failover VIP traffic from HMuxes due to those failures.

**SMux failure:** SMux failure has no impact on VIPs assigned to HMux, and has only a small impact on VIPs that are assigned only to SMuxes. Switches detect SMux failure through BGP, and use ECMP to direct traffic to other SMuxes. Existing connections are not broken, although they may suffer packet drops and/or reorderings during convergence.

**Link failure:** If a link failure isolates a switch, it is handled as a switch failure. Otherwise, it has no impact on availability, although it may cause VIP traffic to re-route.

**DIP failure:** The DUET controller monitors DIP health and removes failed DIP from the set of DIPs for the corresponding VIP. Existing connections to the failed DIP are necessarily terminated. Existing connections to other DIPs for the corresponding VIP are still maintained using resilient hashing [2].

## 5.2 Other Functionalities

**VIP addition:** A new VIP is first added to SMuxes, and then the migration algorithm decides the right destination.

**VIP removal:** When a VIP assigned to an HMux is to be withdrawn, the controller removes it both from that HMux and from all SMuxes. VIPs assigned to *only* SMuxes need to be removed only from SMuxes. BGP withdraw messages remove the corresponding routing entries from all switches.

**DIP addition:** The key issue is to ensure that existing connections are not remapped if DIPs are added to a VIP. For VIPs assigned to SMuxes, this is easily achieved, since SMuxes maintain detailed connection state to ensure that existing connections continue to go to the right DIPs. However, HMuxes can only use a

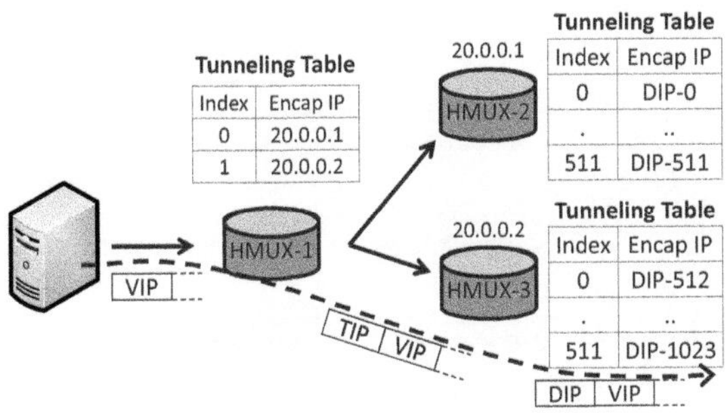


**Figure 7: Large fanout support.**

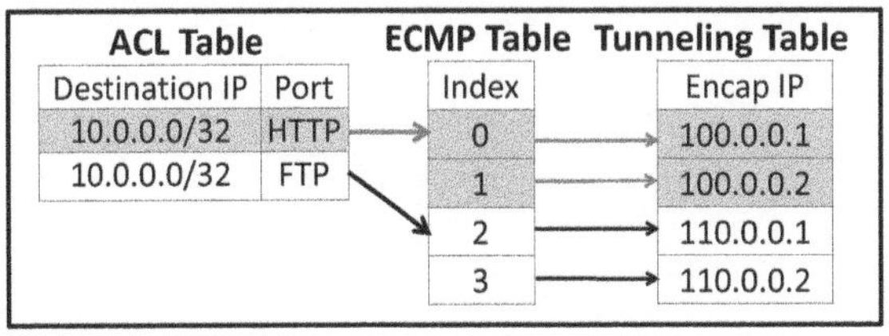


**Figure 8: Port-based load balancing.**

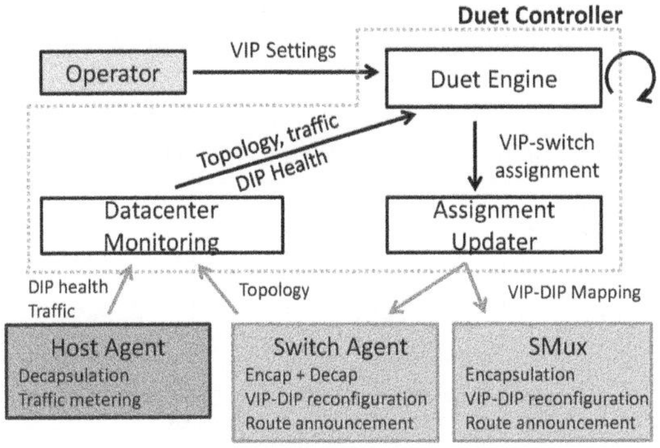


**Figure 9: Components in DUET implementation.**

hash function to map VIPs to DIPs (Figure 2). Resilient hashing only ensures correct mapping in case of DIP *removal* – not DIP *addition*. Thus, to add a DIP to a VIP that is assigned to an HMux, we first remove the VIP from the HMux, causing SMuxes to take it over, as described earlier. We then add the new DIP, and eventually move the VIP back to an appropriate HMux.

**DIP removal:** DIP removal is handled in a manner similar to DIP failure.

**Virtualized clusters:** In virtualized clusters, the HMux would have to encapsulate the packet twice – outer header carries the IP of the host (native) machine, while inner header carries IP of the VM hosting the DIP. However, today's switches cannot encapsulate a single packet twice. So, we use HA in tandem with HMux, as shown in Figure 6. The HMux encapsulates the packet with the IP of the host machine (HIP) that is hosting the DIP. The HA on the DIP decapsulates the packet and forwards it to the right DIP based on the VIP. If a host has multiple DIPs, the ECMP and tunneling table on the HMux holds multiple entries for that HIP (HIP 20.0.0.1 in Figure 6) to ensure equal splitting. At the host, the HA selects the DIP by hashing the 5-tuple.

**Heterogeneity among servers:** When the DIPs for a given VIP have different processing power, we can proportionally split the traffic using WCMP (Weighted Cost Multi-Path) where faster DIPs are assigned larger weights. WCMP can be easily implemented on commodity switches.

**VIPs with large fanout:** Typically the capacity of the tunneling table on a single-chip switch is 512. To support a VIP that has more than 512 DIPs, we use indirection, as shown in Figure 7. We divide the DIPs into multiple partitions, each with at most 512 entries. We assign a single transient IP (TIP) for each partition. As a VIP, a TIP is a routable IP, and is assigned to a switch. When assigning a VIP to an HMux, we store the TIPs (as opposed to DIPs) in the tunneling table (Figure 7). When a packet for such a VIP is received at the HMux, the HMux encapsulates the packet with one of the TIPs and forwards it to the switch to which the TIP is assigned. That switch decapsulates the TIP header and re-encapsulates the packet with one of the DIPs, and forwards it. The latency inflation is negligible, as commodity switches are capable of decapsulating and re-encapsulating a packet at line rate. This allows us to support up to $512 * 512 = 262,144$ DIPs for a single VIP, albeit with small extra propagation delay[4].

**Port-based load balancing:** A VIP can have one set of DIPs for the HTTP port and another for the FTP port. DUET supports this using the tunneling table and ACL rules. ACL (Access Control) Rules are similar to OpenFlow rules, but currently support a wider range of fields. We store the DIPs for different destination ports at different indices in the tunneling table (Figure 8). The ACL rules, match on the IP destination and destination port fields, and the action is forwarding the packet to the corresponding tunneling table entry. Typically the number of ACL rules supported is larger than the tunneling table size, so it is not a bottleneck.

**SNAT:** Source NAT (SNAT) support is needed for DIPs to establish outgoing connections[5]. Ananta supports SNAT by maintaining state on SMuxes [17]. However, as discussed earlier, switches cannot maintain such connection state. Instead, DUET supports SNAT by sharing the hash function used by HMux with the host agent (HA). Like Ananta, DUET assigns disjoint port ranges to the DIPs, but unlike Ananta, the HA on the DIP does not randomly choose an unused port number. Instead, it selects a port such that the hash of the 5-tuple would correctly match the ECMP table entry on HMux. The HA can do this easily since it knows the hash function used by HMux. Note that the HA needs to do this *only* during establishment (*i.e.,* first packet) of outgoing connections. If an HA runs out of available ports, it receives another set from the DUET controller.

# 6. IMPLEMENTATION

In this section, we briefly discuss the implementation of the key components in DUET: (1) DUET Controller, (2) Host Agent, and (3) Switch Agent, and (4) SMux, as shown in Figure 9.

DUET **Controller:** The controller is the heart of DUET. It performs three key functions: (1) Datacenter monitoring: It gathers the topology and traffic information from the underlying network. Additionally, it receives the VIP health status periodically from the host agents. (2) DUET Engine: It receives the VIP-to-DIP mapping from the network operator and the topology and traffic information from the DC-monitoring module, and performs the VIP-switch assignment as described in § 4. (3) Assignment Updater: It takes the VIP-switch assignment from the DUET engine and translates it into rules based on the switch agent interface. All these modules communicate with each other using RESTful APIs.

[4]The VIP assignment algorithm also needs some changes to handle TIPs. We omit details due to lack of space.

[5]Outgoing packets on established connections use DSR.

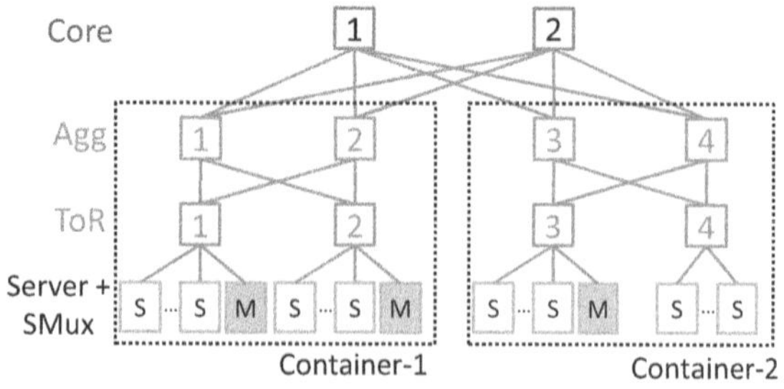

Figure 10: Our testbed. FatTree with two containers of two Agg and two ToR Switches each, connected by two Core switches.

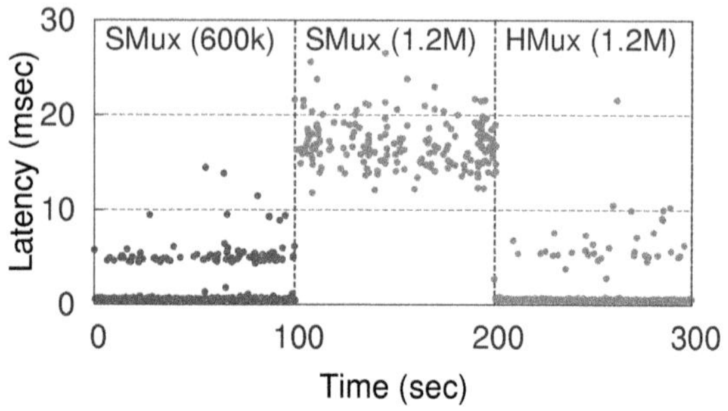

Figure 11: HMux has higher capacity.

**Switch Agent**: The switch agent runs on every switch. It uses vendor-specific APIs to program the ECMP and tunneling tables, and provides RESTful APIs which are used by the assignment updater to add/remove VIP-DIP mapping. On every VIP change, the switch agent fires touting updates over BGP.

**Host Agent and SMux:** The host agent and SMux implementation are the same as in Ananta. The host agent primarily performs packet decapsulation, SNAT and DIP health monitoring. Additionally, the host agents perform traffic metering and report the statistics to the DUET controller.

Same as in Ananta, we run a BGP speaker along side of each SMux to advertise all the VIPs assigned to the SMux.

In total, the controller code consists of 4200 LOC written in C#, and the switch agent code has about 300 LOC in Python.

# 7. TESTBED EXPERIMENTS

Our testbed (Figure 10) consists of 10 Broadcom-based switches and 60 servers. Of the 60 servers, 34 act as DIPs and the others are used to generate traffic. Each of ToRs 1, 2 and 3 is also connected to a server acting as SMux.

Our testbed experiments show: (1) HMuxes provide higher capacity, (2) DUET achieves high availability during HMux failure as the VIP traffic seamlessly falls back to SMuxes, and (3) VIP migration is fast, and DUET maintains high availability during VIP migration.

## 7.1 HMux Capacity

If the load balancer instances have low capacity, packet queues will start building up, and traffic will experience high latency. This experiment illustrates that individual HMuxes instances (*i.e.*, a switch) have significantly higher capacity than individual SMux instances.

The experiment uses 11 VIPs, each with 2 DIPs. We send UDP traffic to 10 of the VIPs, leaving the 11th VIP unloaded.

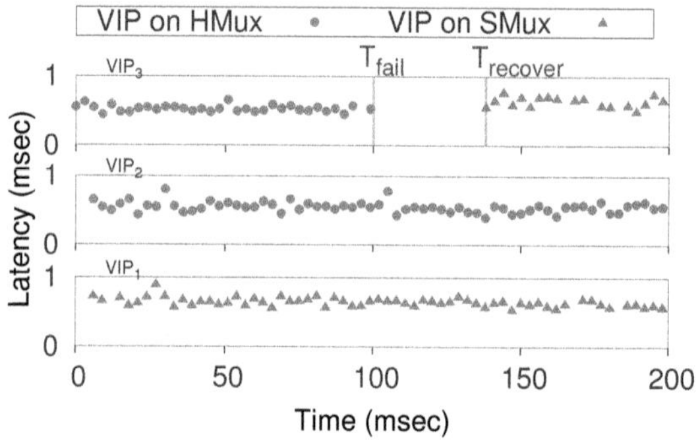

Figure 12: VIP availability during failure.

The experiment has three steps. (1) All 11 VIPs are assigned to the SMuxes, and we generate a total traffic of 600K packets per second to the 10 VIPs (60K per VIP). Since each VIP is announced from every SMux, the traffic is split evenly between all SMuxes, and each SMux is handling 200K packets per second. (2) At time 100 sec, we increase the traffic to 1.2M packets per second, so each SMux is handling 400K packets per second. (3) Finally, at time 200 sec, we switch all VIPs to a *single* HMux hosted on ToR 1.

The metric of interest is the latency to the *unloaded* VIP, measured using pings sent every 3ms. We measure the latency to the unloaded VIP so that the latency *only* reflects the delay suffered at the SMux or HMux – the VIP or the DIP itself is not the bottleneck. The results shown in Figure 11.

We see that until time 100 sec, the latency is mostly below 1ms, with a few outliers. This is because each SMux is handling only 200K packets per second, which is well within its capacity (300K packets per second – see §2), and thus there is no significant queue buildup. At time 100, the latency jumps up – now each SMux is handling 400K packets per second, which is well beyond its ability. Finally, at time 200 sec, when all VIPs are on a single HMux, the latency goes down to 1ms again. This shows that *a single* HMux instance has higher capacity than at least 3 SMux instances.

In fact, since HMux processes all packets in the *data plane* of the switch, it can handle packets at line rate, and no queue buildup will occur till we exceed the link capacity (10Gbps in this experiment).

## 7.2 HMux Failure Mitigation

One of the most important benefits of using the SMux as a backstop is automatic failure mitigation, as described in §5. In this experiment, we investigate the delay involved in failing over from an HMux to an SMux. This delay is important because *during* failover, traffic to the VIP gets disrupted.

We assign 7 VIPs across HMuxes and the remaining 3 to the SMuxes. We fail one switch at 100 msec. We measure the impact of HMux failure on VIP availability by monitoring the ping latency to all 10 VIPs every 3ms.

Figure 12 shows the ping latency for three VIPs: (1) One on the failed HMux ($VIP_3$), (2) One on a healthy HMux ($VIP_2$), and (3) One on an SMux ($VIP_1$), respectively.

We make three observations: (1) The traffic to $VIP_3$ falls over to SMux within 38 msec after HMux failure. The delay reflects the time it takes for other switches to detect the failure, and for the routing to converge. The VIP was not available during this period, *i.e.*, there is no response to pings. (2) After 38 msec, pings to $VIP_3$ are successful again. (3) The VIPs assigned to other HMuxes and SMuxes are not affected; their latency is unchanged during HMux failure. These observations demonstrate the effectiveness of using SMux as a backstop in the DUET design.

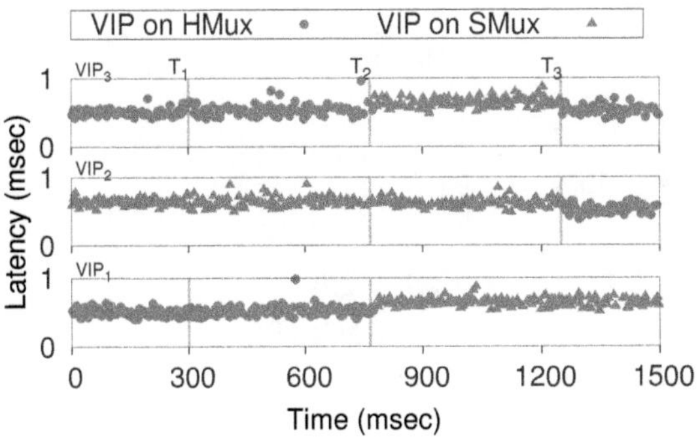


**Figure 13: VIP availability during migration.**

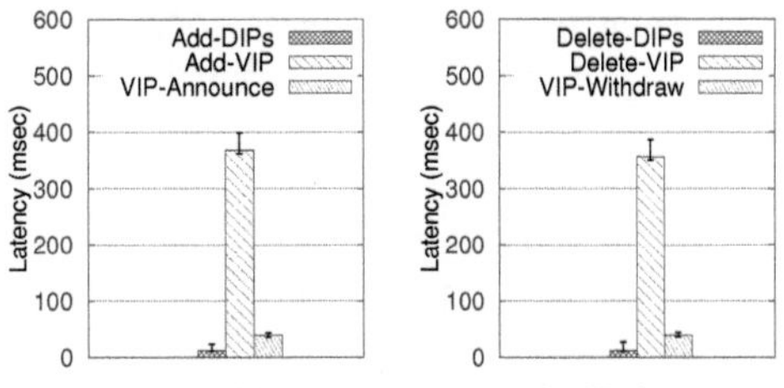


(a) Add (b) Delete

**Figure 14: Latency breakdown.**

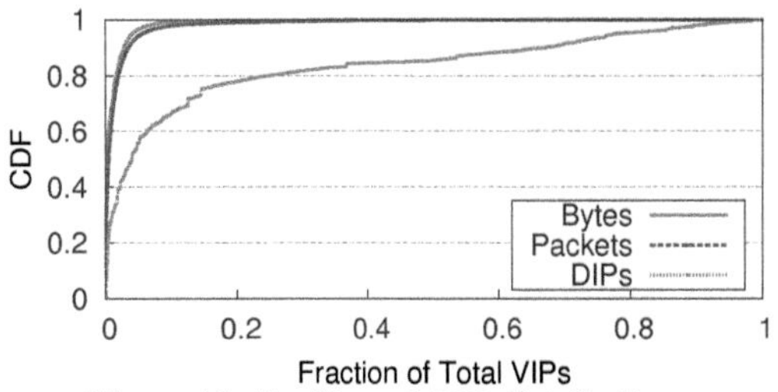


**Figure 15: Traffic and DIP distribution.**

## 7.3 VIP Migration

Recall that we also use SMux as a backstop during VIP migration. We now investigate the delays involved in this process. This delay is important because it places a lower bound on how quickly DUET can react to network conditions.

In this experiment, we assign 7 VIPs to the HMuxes and the remaining 3 VIPs to the SMuxes. We migrate a VIP from HMux-to-SMux ($VIP_1$), SMux-to-HMux ($VIP_2$), and HMux-to-HMux through SMux ($VIP_3$) at different times. We measure the VIP availability by monitoring the ping latency (every 3ms) to these VIPs, and we also measure the migration delay.

Figure 13 shows the ping latency. At time $T_1$, the controller starts the first wave of migration by sending the migrate command (migrate to SMuxes) to the corresponding switch agents for $VIP_1$ and $VIP_3$. It takes about 450ms for the migration to finish (time $T_2$), at which time, the controller sends another migrate command (migrate back to HMux) to $VIP_2$ and $VIP_3$, which takes about 400ms to take effect (time $T_3$). We see that that all three VIPs remain fully available during the migration process. The VIPs see a very slight increase in latency when they are on SMux, due to software processing of packets on SMux.

Note that unlike the failure scenario discussed earlier, during the migration process, there is no "failure detection" involved. This is why we see no ping packet loss in Figure 13.

Figure 14 shows the three components of the migration delay: (1) latency to add/delete a VIP as measured from the time the controller sends the command to the time other switches receive the BGP update for the operation, (2) latency to add/delete DIPs as measured similarly as the VIPs, (3) latency for the BGP update (routing convergence), measured as the time from the VIP is changed in the FIB on one switch till the routing is updated in the remaining switches, *i.e.,* BGP update time on those switches.

Almost all (80-90%) of the migration delay is due to the latency of adding/removing the VIP to/from the FIB. This is because our implementation of the switch agent is not fully optimized – improving it is part of our future work.

# 8. EVALUATION

In this section, we use large-scale simulations to show that: (1) DUET needs far fewer SMuxes than Ananta to load balance the same amount of VIP traffic; (2) Despite using fewer SMuxes (and hence being cheaper), DUET incurs low latency on load balanced traffic; (3) The VIP assignment algorithm is effective; (4) Network component failures do not cause significant congestion, even though DUET's VIP assignment algorithm is oblivious to network component failures; (5) The migration algorithm is effective.

## 8.1 Simulation Setup

**Network:** Our simulated network closely resembles that of a production datacenter, with a FatTree topology connecting 50k servers connected to 1600 ToRs located in 40 containers. Each container has 40 ToRs and 4 Agg switches, and the 40 containers are connected with 40 Core switches. The link and switch memory capacity were set with values observed in production datacenters: routing table and tunneling table sizes set to 16k and 512, respectively, and the link capacity set to 10Gbps between ToR and Agg switches, and 40 Gbps between Agg and Core switches.

**Workload:** We run the simulations using the traffic trace collected from one of our production datacenters. The trace consists of 30K VIPs, and the number of DIPs and the traffic distribution across the VIPs are shown in Figure 15. We divide the 3-hour trace into 10-minute intervals, and calculate the VIP assignment in each interval, based on the traffic demand matrix (the number of bytes sent and received between all sources and destinations), the topology and the forwarding tables.

## 8.2 SMux Reduction

We first compare the number of SMuxes needed in DUET and Ananta to load-balance same amount of traffic in the datacenter.

We calculate the number of SMuxes needed by Ananta such that no SMux receives traffic exceeding its capacity. We consider two SMux capacities: 3.6Gbps, as observed on the production SMuxes (§2), and 10Gbps, assuming the CPU will not be a bottleneck.

The number of SMuxes needed for DUET depends on the capacity of SMux, the traffic generated by VIPs that could not be assigned to HMuxes, and specifics of failure model, and migration probabilities (§3.3). In this experiment, we assign the VIPs to HMuxes using the algorithm described in §4, which tries to assign as many VIPs to HMuxes as it can, subject to switch memory and link bandwidth constraints. We have specified the memory and bandwidth details earlier.

Based on failure scenarios in [13, 21], we provision the number of SMuxes to handle the maximum traffic under either (1) entire container failure, or (2) three random switch failures. For example, if an entire container fails, the total traffic $T$ to all the VIPs assigned

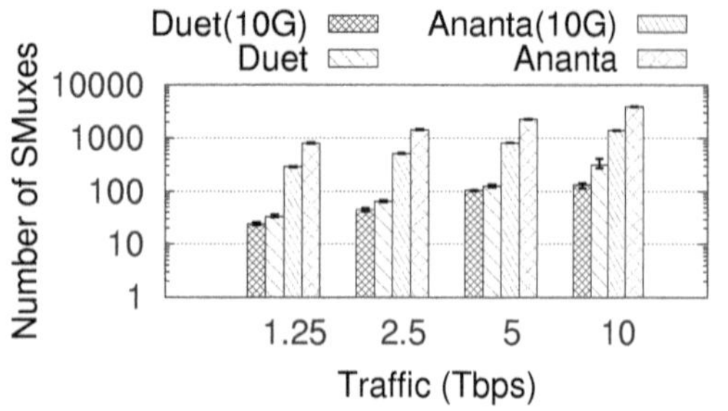

Figure 16: Number of SMuxes used in Duet and Ananta.

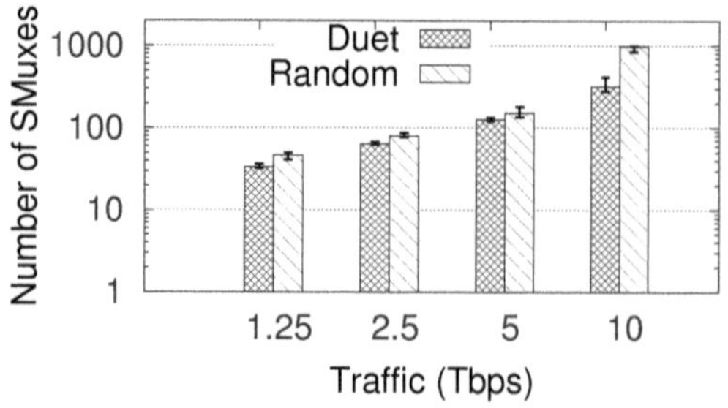

Figure 18: Number of SMuxes used by Duet and Random.

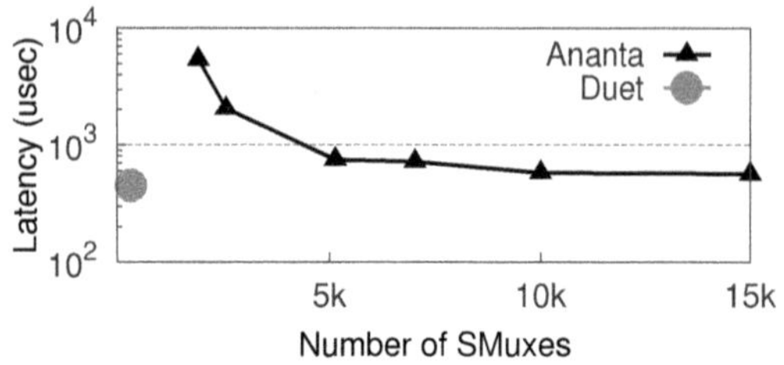

**Figure 17: Latency (microseconds) vs. number of SMuxes in Ananta and DUET.**

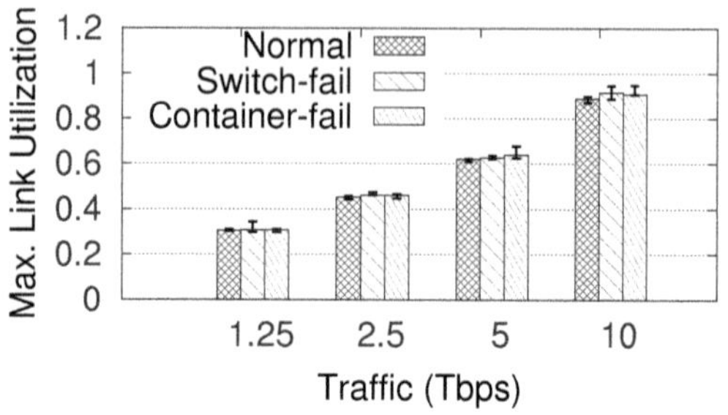

**Figure 19: Impact of failures on max. link utilization.**

to the switches inside need to fail over to SMuxes. Thus the number of SMuxes needed is $\frac{T}{C_{smux}}$ where $C_{smux}$ is SMux capacity.

We ignore migration – it is covered in §8.6.

Figure 16 shows that DUET requires far fewer SMuxes compared to Ananta at all traffic rates. *Note the log scale on Y axis.* For all the traffic rates, DUET was able to assign 16k VIPs to the HMuxes (routing table limit). Overall, compared to Ananta, DUET requires 12-24x times fewer SMuxes when the SMux capacity is 3.6 Gbps and 8-12x times fewer SMuxes when the SMux capacity is 10Gbps, across different traffic loads.

We note that for all traffic scenarios, majority of the SMuxes needed by DUET were needed to handle failure. The fraction of SMuxes needed to handle the traffic to the VIPs that could not be assigned to the HMux is small. This shows that the VIP assignment algorithm does a good job of "packing" VIPs into HMuxes.

## 8.3 Latency vs. SMuxes

Another way to look at the trade-off described in §8.2 is to hold the traffic volume constant, and see how many SMuxes Ananta needs to provide the same latency as DUET. This is shown in figure 17.

We hold the traffic at 10Tbps, and vary the number of SMuxes for Ananta from 2000 to 15,000. The black line shows median latency for Ananta. The red dot represents DUET. DUET used 230 SMuxes, and achieved median latency of 474 $\mu$sec.

We see that if Ananta were to use the same number of SMuxes as DUET (230), the median latency would be many times higher (over 6 ms). On the other hand, Ananta needs 15,000 SMuxes to achieve latency comparable to DUET.

The absolute latency numbers may appear small – however, recall that median DC RTTs are of the order of 381 $\mu$sec[6], and in many cases, to satisfy a single user request, an application like Search traverses load balancer multiple times. Any time lost in the network is *wasted* time – which could have otherwise been used by the application to improve user experience [8, 14, 19].

[6]Newer technologies such a RDMA lower this to 2-5 $\mu$sec!

## 8.4 Duet vs. Random

To understand the impact of assigning VIPs based on the maximum resource utilization, we compare the performance of DUET in terms of the number of SMuxes against a random strategy (Random) that selects the *first feasible* switch that does not violate the link or switch memory capacity. This assignment algorithm can be viewed as a variant of FFD (First Fit Decreasing) as the VIPs are assigned in the sorted order of decreasing traffic volume.

Figure 18 shows the total number of SMuxes needed by DUET and Random (note the log scale). We see that Random results in 120%–307% more SMuxes compared to DUET as the traffic load varies from 1.25 to 10 Tbps. This shows that by taking resource utilization into account, DUET ensures that only a small fraction of VIPs traffic is left to be handled by the SMuxes.

## 8.5 Impact of Failure

Microbenchmark results in §7.2 showed that DUET can handle HMux failures well – the VIPs fall back to SMux, and the disruption to the VIP traffic is minimal. In §8.2, we considered the number of SMuxes DUET needs to cope with failures. We now consider the bigger picture – what impact does failures of several switches, or even a container have on overall traffic?

We consider the same failure model as was used in §8.2 – a container or up to 3 switches can fail simultaneously. We evaluate failure resilience of DUET by measuring the maximum link utilization under these two scenarios: failure of a randomly selected container, or 3 randomly selected switches.

A random switch failure affects link traffic load in two ways. It causes the traffic of the VIPs assigned to the failed switch to be shifted to the backstop SMuxes, and other through traffic to be shifted to the alternative path. A container failure affects the traffic in more complicated ways: it not only causes all the switches inside to be disconnected, but also makes all the traffic with sources and destinations (DIPs) inside to disappear.

Figure 19 shows the measured maximum link utilization during the two failure scenarios in the 10 experiments. We see that as expected, link failures can result in transient congestion. However,

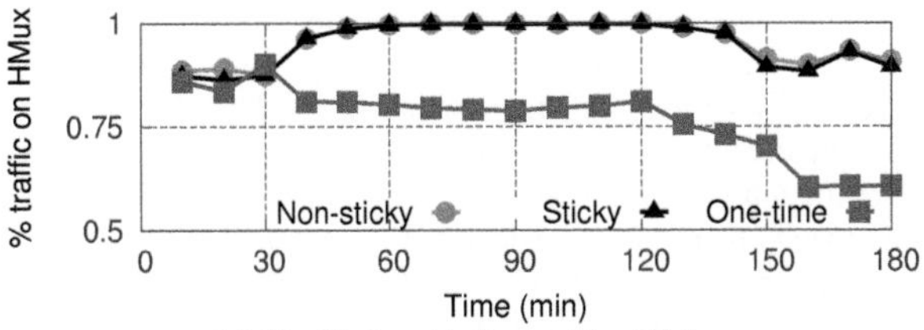

(a) Traffic load-balanced by HMux

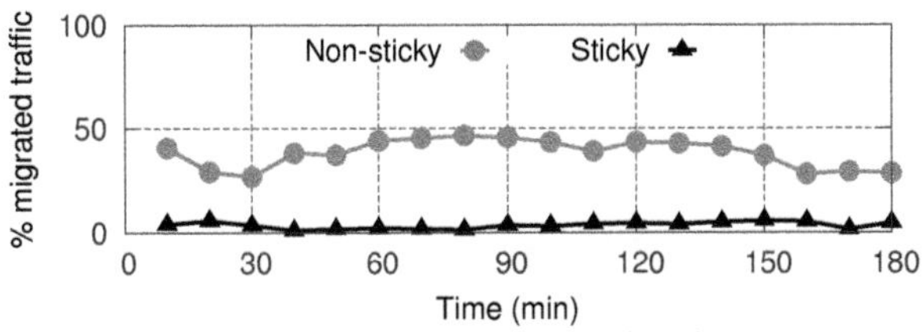

(b) Traffic shuffled during migration

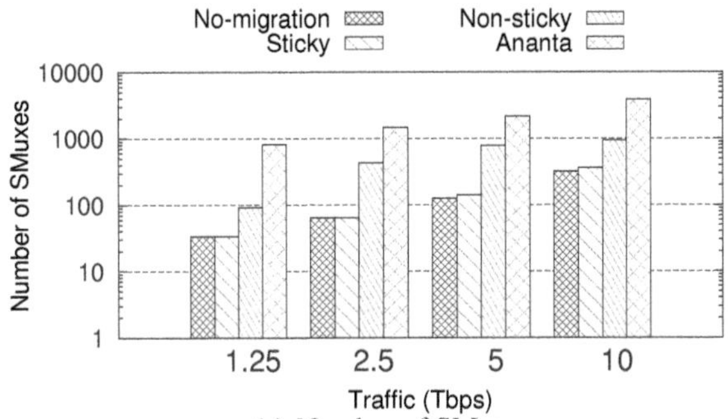

(c) Number of SMux

**Figure 20: Effectiveness of different migration algorithms.**

the utilization increase of any link in the network is no more than 16%, and hence is comfortably absorbed by the 20% bandwidth reservation made in the VIP assignment algorithm. Interestingly, the single container failure (with 44 switches inside) often results in less congestion than 3-switch failure. This can be explained by two reasons: (1) any traffic with source and sinks (DIPs) inside the container has disappeared, and (2) all the rest traffic which have sources or sinks outside the container are not shifted to other paths as their paths do not go through any switch inside the container.

## 8.6 VIP Migration

In this section, we evaluate the effectiveness of DUET's VIP migration algorithm, *Sticky* (§4.2). We set the threshold to be $\delta = 0.05$, *i.e.,* a VIP will migrate to a new assignment only if doing so reduces the MRU by 5%.

We compare *Sticky* with *Non-sticky*, which calculates the new assignment from scratch based on current traffic matrix (§4.1), but migrates all the VIPs at the same time through SMuxes to avoid the memory deadlock problem. We evaluate these two schemes by re-running the 3-hour traffic trace, where we reassign and migrate the VIPs for *Sticky* and *Non-sticky* every 10 minutes. The total VIP traffic varies between 6.2 to 7.1 Tbps in this trace.

**Effectiveness:** We first compare the portion of total traffic that are handled by the HMuxes under the two assignment schemes – the larger the portion, the more effective the assignment algorithm. Here, we also compare *Sticky* and *Non-sticky* against *One-time* algorithm, which assigns the VIPs at time 0 sec, and never change it. Figure 20(a) shows the results over the duration of the trace. First, as expected, while the portion of traffic handled by HMuxes started out the same, the initial assignment which is used by *One-time* throughout the trace, gradually loses its effectiveness, and results in only 60-89% (average 75.2%) of the total being handled by HMuxes. In contrast, *Sticky* and *Non-sticky* handle 86-99.9% (average 95.3%) of the traffic in HMuxes, from continuously adapting to the traffic dynamics. Second, even though *Sticky* only migrates VIPs that reduce the MRU by at least 5%, it is as effective as *Non-sticky* in maximizing the traffic assigned to HMuxes. In particular, it handles 86-99.7% traffic (average 95.1%) in HMuxes, which is almost identical to the 87-99.9% traffic (average 95.67%) handled by HMuxes under *Non-sticky*.

**Traffic shuffled:** Next, we compare the fraction of the total VIP traffic migrated under *Sticky* and *Non-sticky*– the less traffic are migrated, the fewer SMuxes need to be reserved as stepping stone. Figure 20(b) shows that migration using *Non-sticky* results in reshuffling almost 25-46% (average 37.4%) of the total VIP traffic each time throughout the trace duration, compared to only 0.7-4.4% (average 3.5%) under *Sticky*. Such a drastic reduction in the traffic shuffled under *Sticky* is attributed to its simple filtering scheme: a VIP is only migrated if it improves the MRU by 5%.

**Number of SMuxes:** Figure 20(c) shows the number of SMuxes needed by *Sticky* and *Non-sticky*. Additionally, we also calculate the SMuxes needed without migration (marked as No-migration) as well as number of SMuxes needed in Ananta considering the SMux capacity to 3.6Gbps. The number of SMuxes needed in *Sticky* and *Non-sticky* is calculated as maximum of SMuxes needed for VIP traffic, failure and transition traffic. It can be seen that, *Non-sticky* always requires more SMuxes compared to No-migration and *Sticky*, showing that *Sticky* does not increase the number of SMuxes to handle the traffic during migration.

# 9. DISCUSSION

**Why are there empty entries in switch tables?** DUET uses empty entries in the host table, ECMP table, and tunneling table in switches to implement HMux. Several reasons contribute to the abundance of such free resources in our production datacenter. The host table of ToR switches has only a few dozen entries for the hosts within each rack, and that of the rest of the switches is mostly empty. The ECMP table of switches is mostly empty because of the hierarchical DC network topology, where each switch has a small number of outgoing links among which all outgoing traffic is split via ECMP. The tunneling table is mostly free since few online services use encapsulation other than load balancing itself. We acknowledge that other DCs may have a different setup, but we believe that our design will be applicable in common cases.

**VIP assignment:** While the greedy VIP assignment algorithm described in §4 works well in our scenarios, we believe that it can be improved. The VIP assignment problem resembles bin packing problem, which has many sophisticated solutions. We plan to study them in future. Also, while we consider VIPs in order of traffic, other orderings are possible (*e.g.,* consider VIPs with latency sensitive traffic first).

**Failover and Migration:** DUET relies on SMuxes to simplify failover and migration. As hinted in §3.3, it may be possible to handle failover and migration by replicating VIP entries in multiple HMuxes. We continue to investigate this approach, although our initial exploration shows that the resulting design is far more complex than our current design.

# 10. RELATED WORK

To the best of our knowledge, DUET is a novel approach to building a performant, low-cost, organically scalable load balancer. We are not aware of any load balancing architecture that fuses switch-based load balancer with the software load balancers. However, there has been much work on load balancers, and we briefly review it here.

**Load balancer:** Traditional hardware load balancers [4, 1] are expensive and typically only provide 1+1 availability. DUET is much more cost effective, and provides enhanced availability by using SMuxes as a backstop. Importantly, compared to traditional load balancers, DUET gives us control over very important vantage point in our cloud infrastructure.

We have already discussed Ananta [17] software load balancer extensively. Other software-based load balancers [5, 6, 7] are also available, but they lack the scalability and availability of Ananta, as shown in [17]. Embrane [3] promises scalability, but suffers from the same fundamental limitations of the software load balancer.

**OpenFlow based load balancer:** Two recent proposals focus on using OpenFlow switches for load balancing. In [20], authors present a preliminary design for a load balancing architecture using OpenFlow switches. They focus on minimizing the number of wildcard rules. The paper, perhaps because it is a preliminary design, ignores many key issues such as handling switch failures. Plug-n-Serve [15] is another preliminary design that uses OpenFlow switches to load balance web servers deployed in unstructured, enterprise networks. DUET is very different from these approaches. DUET uses a combined hardware and software approach. DUET does not rely on OpenFlow support. DUET is designed for data center networks, and pays careful attention to handling numerous practical issues including various types of failures and VIP migration to adapt to network dynamics.

**Partitioning OpenFlow rules:** Researchers have also proposed using OpenFlow switches for a variety of other purposes. For example, DIFANE [22] uses some switches in the data center to cache rules, and act as authoritative switches. While a load balancing architecture can be built on top of DIFANE, the focus of the paper is very different from DUET. In vCRIB [16] authors propose to offload some of the traffic management rules from host agent to ToR switches, as well as to other host agents. Their goal is to ensure resource-aware and traffic-aware placement of rules. While vCRIB also faces problems such as managing network dynamics (*e.g.*, VM migration), their main focus is quite different than DUET.

**SDN architecture and middleboxes:** Similar to DUET, researchers have leveraged SDN architecture in the context of middleboxes to achieve policy enforcement and verification [18, 12], which is again a different goal than DUET.

**Improving single server performance:** Researchers have substantially improved packet processing capabilities on commodity servers [23, 11], which could potentially improve SMux performance. But, these improvements are unlikely to bridge the differences in packet processing capabilities between HMux and SMux for the load balancer workload.

Lastly, several algorithms for calculating flow hashes (*e.g.*, resilient hashing [2], cuckoo-hashing [23]) offer a wide variety of trade-offs. We do not review them here, although DUET can leverage any advances in this field.

## 11. CONCLUSION

DUET is a new distributed hybrid load balancer designed to provide high capacity, low latency, high availability, and high flexibility at low cost. The DUET design was motivated by two key observations: (1) software load balancers offer high availability and high flexibility but suffer high latency and low capacity per load balancer, and (2) commodity switches have ample spare resources and now also support programmability needed to implement load balancing functionality. The DUET architecture seamlessly integrates the switch-based load balancer design with a small deployment of software load balancer. We evaluate DUET using a prototype implementation and extensive simulations using traces from our production DC. Our evaluation shows that DUET provides 10x more capacity than a software load balancer, at a fraction of its cost, while reducing the latency by over 10x, and can quickly adapt to network dynamics including failures.

## Acknowledgements

We thank the members from Microsoft Azure team, especially Chao Zhang, for their help in shaping DUET. We also thank the reviewers and our shepherd Ali Ghodsi for their helpful feedback.

## 12. REFERENCES

[1] A10 networks ax series. http://www.a10networks.com.
[2] Broadcom smart hashing. http://http://www.broadcom.com/collateral/wp/StrataXGS_SmartSwitch-WP200-R.pdf.
[3] Embrane. http://www.embrane.com.
[4] F5 load balancer. http://www.f5.com.
[5] Ha proxy load balancer. http://haproxy.1wt.eu.
[6] Loadbalancer.org virtual appliance. http://www.load-balancer.org.
[7] Netscalar vpx virtual appliance. http://www.citrix.com.
[8] M. Alizadeh, A. Greenberg, D. A. Maltz, J. Padhye, P. Patel, B. Prabhakar, S. Sengupta, and M. Sridharan. Data center TCP (DCTCP). In *SIGCOMM*, 2010.
[9] P. Bodík, I. Menache, M. Chowdhury, P. Mani, D. A. Maltz, and I. Stoica. Surviving failures in bandwidth-constrained datacenters. In *SIGCOMM, 2012*.
[10] C. Chekuri and S. Khanna. On multi-dimensional packing problems. In *SODA, 1999*.
[11] M. Dobrescu, N. Egi, K. Argyraki, B.-G. Chun, K. Fall, G. Iannaccone, A. Knies, M. Manesh, and S. Ratnasamy. Routebricks: Exploiting parallelism to scale software routers. In *SOSP, 2009*.
[12] S. Fayazbakhsh, V. Sekar, M. Yu, and J. Mogul. Flowtags: Enforcing network-wide policies in the presence of dynamic middlebox actions. *Proc. HotSDN*, 2013.
[13] P. Gill, N. Jain, and N. Nagappan. Understanding network failures in data centers: measurement, analysis, and implications. In *ACM SIGCOMM CCR, 2011*.
[14] J. Hamilton. The cost of latency. http://perspectives.mvdirona.com/2009/10/31/TheCostOfLatency.aspx.
[15] N. Handigol, S. Seetharaman, M. Flajslik, N. McKeown, and R. Johari. Plug-n-serve: Load-balancing web traffic using openflow. *ACM SIGCOMM Demo*, 2009.
[16] M. Moshref, M. Yu, A. Sharma, and R. Govindan. Scalable rule management for data centers. In *NSDI*, 2013.
[17] P. Patel et al. Ananta: Cloud scale load balancing. In *SIGCOMM*, 2013.
[18] Z. A. Qazi, C.-C. Tu, L. Chiang, R. Miao, V. Sekar, and M. Yu. Simple-fying middlebox policy enforcement using sdn. In *SIGCOMM, 2013*.
[19] L. Ravindranath, J. padhye, R. Mahajan, and H. Balakrishnan. Timecard: Controlling User-Perceieved Delays in Server-based Mobile Applications. In *SOSP*, 2013.
[20] R. Wang, D. Butnariu, and J. Rexford. Openflow-based server load balancing gone wild. In *Usenix HotICE*, 2011.
[21] X. Wu, D. Turner, C.-C. Chen, D. A. Maltz, X. Yang, L. Yuan, and M. Zhang. Netpilot: automating datacenter network failure mitigation. *ACM SIGCOMM CCR, 2012*.
[22] M. Yu, J. Rexford, M. J. Freedman, and J. Wang. Scalable flow-based networking with difane. In *SIGCOMM*, 2010.
[23] D. Zhou, B. Fan, H. Lim, M. Kaminsky, and D. G. Andersen. Scalable, high performance ethernet forwarding with cuckooswitch. In *CoNext, 2013*.

# Guarantee IP Lookup Performance with FIB Explosion

Tong Yang,Gaogang Xie*
ICT, CAS, China.
yangtongemail@gmail.com,
*xie@ict.ac.cn

YanBiao Li
Hunan University, China
lybmath_cs@hnu.edu.cn

Qiaobin Fu
ICT, CAS, China
fuqiaobin@ict.ac.cn

Alex X. Liu
Department of Computer Science and Engineering, Michigan State University
alexliu@cse.msu.edu

Qi Li
ICT, CAS, China
liqi19872006@gmail.com

Laurent Mathy
University of Liege, Belgium
laurent.mathy@ulg.ac.be

## ABSTRACT

The Forwarding Information Base (FIB) of backbone routers has been rapidly growing in size. An ideal IP lookup algorithm should achieve constant, yet small, IP lookup time and on-chip memory usage. However, no prior IP lookup algorithm achieves both requirements at the same time. In this paper, we first propose SAIL, a Splitting Approach to IP Lookup. One splitting is along the dimension of the lookup process, namely finding the prefix length and finding the next hop, and another splitting is along the dimension of prefix length, namely IP lookup on prefixes of length less than or equal to 24 and IP lookup on prefixes of length longer than 24. Second, we propose a suite of algorithms for IP lookup based on our SAIL framework. Third, we implemented our algorithms on four platforms: CPU, FPGA, GPU, and many-core. We conducted extensive experiments to evaluate our algorithms using real FIBs and real traffic from a major ISP in China. Experimental results show that our SAIL algorithms are several times or even two orders of magnitude faster than well known IP lookup algorithms.

## Categories and Subject Descriptors

C.2.6 [**Internetworking**]: Routers; C.2.1 [**Computer-Communication Networks**]: Network Architecture and Design—*Store and forward networks*

## Keywords

IP Lookup; SAIL; Virtual Router Multi-FIB Lookup; LPM

## 1. INTRODUCTION

### 1.1 Background and Motivation

The growth of FIB sizes on backbone routers has been accelerating. According to the RIPE Network Coordination Centre, FIB sizes have become about half a million entries [3]. At the same time, cloud computing and network applications have driven the expectation on router throughput to the scale of 200 Gbps. The fast growth of FIB sizes and throughput demands bring significant challenges to IP lookup (*i.e.*, FIB lookup). An ideal IP lookup algorithm should satisfy the following two harsh requirements. First, *IP lookup time should meet wire speed yet remain constant as FIB sizes grow.* IP lookup time is per packet cost and should be optimized to the extreme to meet wire speed. Second, *on-chip memory usage should meet capacity constraints yet remain constant as FIB sizes grow.* On-chip memory (such as CPU cache and FPGA block RAM) is about 10 times faster than off-chip DRAM [9], but is limited in size (in the scale of a few MB) and much more expensive than DRAM; furthermore, as on-chip memory technologies advance, its sizes do not grow much as compared to DRAM. Without satisfying these two requirements, router performance will degrade as FIB grows, and router hardware will have to be upgraded periodically.

### 1.2 Summary and Limitations of Prior Art

IP lookup has long been a core networking issue and various schemes have been proposed. However, none of them satisfies the two requirements of both constant lookup time and constant on-chip memory usage. Some algorithms can achieve constant IP lookup time, such as TCAM based schemes [11,19] and FPGA based schemes [14,16], but their on-chip memory usage will grow quickly as FIB sizes grow. Some algorithms, such as full-expansion [31] and DIR-24-8 [13], can achieve constant memory usage by simply pushing all prefixes to levels 24 and 32, but even the lookup table for level 24 alone is too large to be stored in on-chip memory.

### 1.3 Proposed SAIL Approach

In this paper, we propose SAIL, a Splitting Approach to IP Lookup. We split the IP lookup problem along two dimensions as illustrated in Figure 1. First, we split the IP lookup problem into two sub-problems along the dimension of the lookup process: finding the prefix length (*i.e.*, finding the length of the longest prefix that matches the given IP address) and finding the next hop (*i.e.*, finding the next hop of this longest matched prefix). This splitting gives us the opportunity of solving the prefix length problem in on-chip memory and the next hop problem in off-chip memory. Furthermore, since on-chip and off-chip memory are


*SIGCOMM'14*, August 17–22, 2014, Chicago, IL, USA.

http://dx.doi.org/10.1145/2619239.2626297.

two entities, this splitting allows us to potentially pipeline the processes of finding the prefix length and the next hop.

| | Finding prefix length | Finding next hop |
|---|---|---|
| Prefix length 0~24 | On-Chip | Off-chip |
| Prefix length 25~32 | Off-chip | Off-chip |

**Figure 1: Two-dimensional splitting of IP lookup.**

Second, we split the IP lookup problem into two sub-problems along the dimension of prefix length: length $\leq 24$ and length $\geq 25$. This splitting is based on our key observation that on backbone routers, for almost all traffic, the longest matching prefix has a length $\leq 24$. This intuitively makes sense because typically backbone routers do not directly connect to small subnets whose prefixes are longer than 24. Our observation may not hold for edge routers; however, the FIBs for edge routers are significantly smaller that those for backbone routers. The scope of this paper is on backbone routers. The key benefit of this splitting is that we can focus on optimizing the IP lookup performance for traffic whose longest matching prefix length is $\leq 24$.

There is some prior work that performed splitting along the dimension of the lookup process or the dimension of prefix length; however, no existing work performed splitting along both dimensions. Dharmapurikar *et al.* proposed to split the IP lookup process into two sub-problems: finding the prefix length using Bloom filters and finding the next hop using hash tables [36]. Pierluigi *et al.* and Gupta *et al.* proposed to split IP prefixes into 24 and 32 based on the observation that 99.93% of the prefixes in a backbone router FIB has a length of less than or equal to 24 [13, 31]. Note that our IP prefix splitting criteria is different because our splitting is based on traffic distribution and their splitting is based on prefix distribution.

## 1.4 Technical Challenges and Solutions

The first technical challenge is to *achieve constant, yet small, on-chip memory usage for any FIB size.* To address this challenge, in this paper, we propose to find the longest matching prefix length for a given IP address using bit maps. Given a set of prefixes in a FIB, for each prefix length $i$ ($0 \leq i \leq 32$), we first build a bit map $B_i[0..2^i - 1]$ whose initial values are all 0s. Then, for each prefix $p$, we let $B_i[|p|] = 1$ where $|p|$ denotes the binary value of the first $i$ bits of $p$. Thus, for all prefixes of lengths 0~24 in any FIB, the total memory size for all bit maps is $\sum_{i=0}^{24} 2^i$ = 4MB, which is small enough to be stored in on-chip memory.

The second technical challenge is to *achieve constant, yet small, IP lookup time for any FIB size.* To address this challenge, in this paper, we classify the prefixes in the given FIB into two categories: those with length $\leq 24$ and those with length $\geq 25$. (1) For prefixes of length $\leq 24$, for each prefix length $i$ ($0 \leq i \leq 24$), we build a next hop array $N_i[0..2^i - 1]$ in off-chip memory so that for each prefix $p$ whose next hop is $n(p)$, we let $N_i[|p|] = n(p)$. Thus, given an IP address $a$, we first find its prefix length using bit maps in on-chip memory and find the next hop using one array lookup in off-chip memory. To find the prefix length using bit maps, for $i$ from 24 to 0, we test whether $B_i[a >> (32 - i)] = 1$; once we find the first $i$ so that $B_i[a >> (32 - i)] = 1$ holds, we know that the longest matching prefix length is $i$. Here $a >> (32 - i)$ means right shifting $a$ by $32 - i$ bits. In this step, the maximum number of on-chip memory accesses is 25. To find the next hop, suppose the longest matching prefix length for $a$ is $i$, we can find its next hop $N_i[a >> (32 - i)]$ by one off-chip memory access. (2) For prefixes of length $\geq 25$, many IP lookup schemes can be plugged into our SAIL framework. Possible schemes include TCAM (Ternary Content Addressable Memory), hash tables, and next-hop arrays. Choosing which scheme to deal with prefixes of length $\geq 25$ depends on design priorities, but have little impact on the overall IP lookup performance because most traffic hits prefixes of length $\leq 24$. For example, to bound the worst case lookup speed, we can use TCAM or next hop arrays. For next hop arrays, we can expand all prefixes of length between 25 and 31 to be 32, and then build a chunk ID (*i.e.*, offsets) array and a next hop array. Thus, the worst case lookup speed is two off-chip memory accesses.

The third technical challenge is to *handle multiple FIBs for virtual routers* with two even harsher requirements: (1) Multi-FIB lookup time should meet wire speed yet remain constant as FIB sizes and FIB numbers grow. (2) On-chip memory usage should meet capacity constraints yet remain constant as FIB sizes and FIB numbers grow. To address this challenge, we overlay all FIB tries together so that all FIBs have the same bit maps; furthermore, we overlay all next hop arrays together so that by the next hop index and the FIB index, we can uniquely locate the final next hop.

The remaining of the paper proceeds as follows. We first review related work in Section 2. In Section 3 and 4, we introduce our basic SAIL algorithm and optimization techniques, respectively. We then present our implementation details and experimental results in Section 5 and 6, respectively. We discuss the application of our SAIL framework to IPv6 lookup in Section 7. Finally, we give concluding remarks in Section 8.

## 2. RELATED WORK

As IP lookup is a core networking issue, much work has been done to improve its performance. We can categorize prior work into trie-based algorithms, Bloom filter based algorithms, range-based algorithms, TCAM-based algorithms, FPGA-based algorithms, GPU-based algorithms, and multi-FIB lookup algorithms.

**Trie-based Algorithms:** Trie-based algorithms use the trie structure directly as the lookup data structure or indirectly as an auxiliary data structure to facilitate IP lookup or FIB update. Example algorithms include binary trie [27], path-compressed trie [20], k-stride multibit trie [39], full expansion/compression [31], LC-trie [38], Tree Bitmap [40], priority trie [17], Lulea [28], DIR-24-8 [13], flashtrie [26], shapeGraph [15], and trie-folding [12]. A comprehensive survey of trie-based algorithms is in [27].

**Bloom Filter based Algorithms:** Dharmapurikar *et al.* proposed the PBF algorithm where they use Bloom filters to first find the longest matching prefix length in on-chip memory and then use hash tables in off-chip memory to find the next hop [36]. Lim *et al.* proposed to use one bloom filter to find the longest matching prefix length [22]. These Bloom filter based IP lookup algorithms cannot achieve constant lookup time because of false positives and hash collisions. Furthermore, to keep the same false positive rate, their on-chip memory sizes grow linearly with the increase of FIB size.

**Range-based Algorithms:** Range-based algorithms are based on the observation that each prefix can be mapped into a range in level 32 of the trie. Example such algorithms are binary search on prefix lengths [24], binary range search [27], multiway range trees [32], and range search using many cores [25].

**TCAM-based Algorithms:** TCAM can compare an incoming IP address with all stored prefixes in parallel in hardware using one cycle, and thus can achieve constant lookup time. However, TCAM has very limited size (typically a few Mbs like on-chip memory sizes), consumes a huge amount of power due to the parallel search capability, generates a lot of heat, is very expensive, and difficult to update. Some schemes have been proposed to reduce power consumption by enabling only a few TCAM banks to participate in each lookup [11]. Some schemes use multiple TCAM chips to improve lookup speed [19, 29, 34]. Devavrat *et al.* proposed to reduce the movement of prefixes for fast updating [8].

**FPGA-based Algorithms:** There are two main issues to address for FPGA-based IP lookup algorithms: (1) how to store the whole FIB in on-chip memory, and (2) how to construct pipeline stages. Some early FPGA-based algorithms proposed to construct compact data structures in on-chip memory [23, 33]; however, these compact data structures make the lookup process complex and therefore increase the complexity of FPGA logics. For FPGA in general, the more complex the logics are, the lower the clock frequency will be. To improve lookup speed, Hamid *et al.* proposed to only store a part of data structure in on-chip memory using hashing [14]. To balance stage sizes, some schemes have been proposed to adjust the trie structure by rotating some branches or exchanging some bits of the prefixes [7, 10, 16].

**GPU-based Algorithms:** Leveraging the massive parallel processing capability of GPU, some schemes have been proposed to use GPU to accelerate IP lookup [35, 42].

**Multi-FIB Lookup Algorithms:** The virtual router capability has been widely supported by commercial routers. A key issue in virtual routers is to perform IP lookup with multiple FIBs using limited on-chip memory. Several schemes have been proposed to compress multiple FIBs [18, 21, 37].

## 3. SAIL BASICS

In this section, we present the basic version of our SAIL algorithms. In the next section, we will present some optimization techniques. Table 1 lists the symbols used throughout this paper.

**Table 1: Symbols used in the paper**

| Symbol | Description |
|---|---|
| $B_i$ | bit map array for level $i$ |
| $N_i$ | next hop array for level $i$ |
| $C_i$ | chunk ID array for level $i$ |
| $BN_i$ | combined array of $B_i$ and $N_i$ |
| $BCN_i$ | combined array of $B_i, C_i$ and $N_i$ |
| $a$ | IP address |
| $v$ | trie node |
| $p$ | prefix |
| $\|p\|$ | value of the binary string in prefix $p$ |
| $p(v)$ | prefix represented by node $v$ |
| $n(v)$ | next hop of solid node $v$ |
| $l$ | trie level |
| SAIL_B | SAIL basic algorithm |
| SAIL_U | SAIL_B + updated oriented optimization |
| SAIL_L | SAIL_B + lookup oriented optimization |
| SAIL_M | SAIL_L extension for multiple FIBs |
| $a_{(i,j)}$ | integer value of bit string of $a$ from $i$-th bit to $j$-th bit |

### 3.1 Splitting Lookup Process

We now describe how we split the lookup process for a given IP address into the two steps of finding its longest matching prefix length and finding the next hop. Given a FIB table, we first construct a trie. An example trie is in Figure 2(b). Based on whether a node represents a prefix in the FIB, there are two types of nodes: *solid nodes* and *empty nodes*. A node is solid if and only if the prefix represented by the node is in the FIB. That is, a node is solid if and only if it has the next hop. A node is an empty node if and only if it has no next hop. Each solid node has a label denoting the next hop of the prefix represented by the node. For any node, its distance to the root is called its *level*. The level of a node locates a node vertically. Any trie constructed from a FIB has 33 levels. For each level $i$, we construct a bit map array $B_i[0..2^i-1]$ of length $2^i$, and the initial values are all 0*s*. At each level $i$ ($0 \leq i \leq 32$), for each node $v$, let $p(v)$ denote its corresponding prefix and $|p(v)|$ denote the value of the binary string part of the prefix (*e.g.*, $|11*| = 3$). If $v$ is solid, then we assign $B_i[|p(v)|] = 1$; otherwise, we assign $B_i[|p(v)|] = 0$. Here $|p(v)|$ indicates the horizontal position of node $v$ because if the trie is a complete binary tree then $v$ is the $|p(v)|$-th node on level $i$. Figure 2(c) shows the bit maps for levels 0 to 4 of the trie in 2(b). Taking bit map $B_3$ for level 3 as an example, for the two solid nodes corresponding to prefixes `001*/3` and `111*/3`, we have $B_3[1] = 1$ and $B_3[7] = 1$. Given the 33 bit maps $B_0, B_1, \cdots, B_{32}$ that we constructed from the trie for a FIB, for any given IP address $a$, for $i$ from 32 to 0, we test whether $B_i[a >> (32-i)] = 1$; once we find the first $i$ that $B_i[a >> (32-i)] = 1$ holds, we know that the longest matching prefix length is $i$. Here $a >> (32-i)$ means right shifting $a$ by $32-i$ bits. For each bit map $B_i$, we construct a next hop array $N_i[0..2^i-1]$, whose initial values are all 0s. At each level $i$, for each prefix $p$ of length $i$ in the FIB, denoting the next hop of prefix $p$ by $n(p)$, we assign $N_i[|p|] = n(p)$. Thus, for any given IP address $a$, once we find its longest matching prefix length $i$, then we know its next hop is $N_i[a >> (32-i)]$.

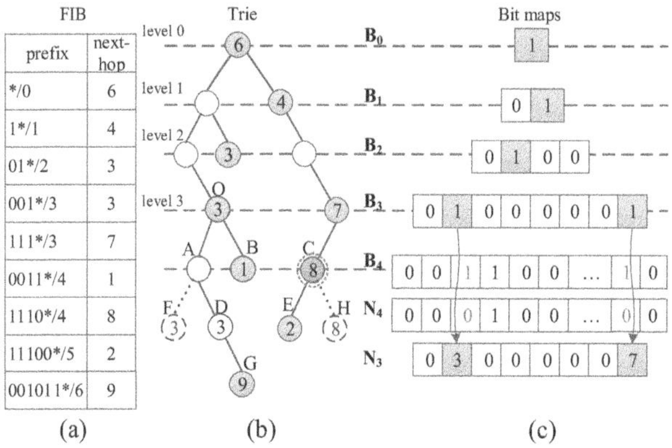


**Figure 2: Basic SAIL Algorithm.**

## 3.2 Splitting Prefix Length

Based on our observation that almost all the traffic of backbone routers has the longest matching prefix length $\leq 24$, we split all prefixes in the given FIB into prefixes of length $\leq 24$, which we call *short prefixes* and prefixes of length $\geq 25$, which we call *long prefixes*. By this splitting, we want to store the bit maps of prefixes of length $\leq 24$ in on-chip memory. However, given an IP address, because it may match a long prefix, it seems that we need to search among both short and long prefixes, which makes this splitting not much useful. In this paper, we propose a technique called *pivot pushing* to address this issue. Our basic strategy is that for a given IP address, we first test its longest matching prefix length is within $[0, 24]$ or $[25, 32]$; thus, after this testing, we continue to search among either short prefixes or long prefixes, but not both. We call level 24 the *pivot level*.

Given a trie and a pivot level, the basic idea of pivot pushing is two-fold. First, for each internal solid node on the pivot level, we push its label (*i.e.*, the next hop) to a level below the pivot level. Second, for each internal empty nodes on the pivot level, we let it inherit the label of its nearest solid ancestor node, *i.e.*, the next hop of the first solid node along the path from this empty node to the root, and then push this inherited label to a level below the pivot level. In this paper, we assume that the root always has a label, which is the default next hop. Thus, for any internal empty nodes on the pivot level, it always can inherit a label.

Given a trie and an IP address $a$, traversing $a$ from the root of the trie downward, for any internal or leaf node $v$ that the traversal passes, we say *$a$ passes $v$*. Based on the above concepts, we introduce Theorem 3.1.

THEOREM 3.1. *Given a trie constructed from a FIB, after pivot pushing, for any IP address $a$, $a$ passes a node on the pivot level if and only if its longest matching prefix is on the pivot level or below.*

PROOF. Given a trie and an IP address $a$ that passes a node $v$ on the pivot level, there are two cases: (1) $v$ is a leaf node, and (2) $v$ is an internal node. For the first case where $v$ is a leaf node, then $a$'s longest matching prefix is $p(v)$ (*i.e.*, the prefix represented by node $v$) and thus $a$'s longest matching prefix is on the pivot level. For the second case where $v$ is an internal node, because of pivot pushing, $a$ must pass a solid node on a level below the pivot level, which means that $a$'s longest matching prefix is below the pivot level. □

Based on Theorem 3.1, we construct the bit map for the pivot level $l$ as follows: for any node $v$ on level $l$, we assign $B_l[|p(v)|] = 1$; in other words, $B_l[i] = 0$ if and only if there is no node on level $l$ that corresponds to the prefix denoted by $i$. Thus, given an IP address $a$, $B_l[a >> (32 - l)] = 1$ if and only if its longest matching prefix is on the pivot level or below. In SAIL, we choose level 24 to be the pivot level. By checking whether $B_{24}[a >> 8] = 1$, we know whether the longest matching prefix length is $\leq 23$ or $\geq 24$, which will guide us to search either up or down. Consider the example in Figure 2(b), taking level 4 as the pivot level, node C on level 4 is an internal solid node, pushing C to level 5 results in a new leaf solid node H with the same next hop as C. Note that after pushing node C down, node C becomes empty.

Given a pivot pushed trie, we build a bit map array and a next hop array for each level of 0 to 24 as above. Note that for any $i$ $(0 \leq i \leq 23)$ and any $j$ $(0 \leq j \leq 2^i - 1)$, $B_i[j] = 1$ if and only if there is a solid node on level $i$ that corresponds to the prefix denoted by $j$; for level 24 and any $j$ $(0 \leq j \leq 2^{24} - 1)$, $B_{24}[j] = 1$ if and only if there is a node, no matter solid or empty, on level 24 that corresponds to the prefix denoted by $j$. Note that $B_{24}[j] = 1$ and $N_{24}[j] > 0$ if and only if there is a leaf node on level 24 that corresponds to the prefix denoted by $j$, which means that the longest matching prefix length is 24. Note that $B_{24}[j] = 1$ and $N_{24}[j] = 0$ if and only if there is an empty node on level that corresponds to the prefix denoted by $j$, which means that the longest matching prefix length is $\geq 25$. Thus, given an IP address $a$, if $B_{24}[a >> 8] = 0$, then we further check whether $B_{23}[a >> 9] = 1$, $B_{22}[a >> 10] = 1$, $\cdots$, $B_0[a >> 32] = 1$ until we find the first 1; if $B_{24}[a >> 8] = 1$, then we know $a$'s longest matching prefix length is $\geq 24$ and further lookup its next hop in off-chip memory. It is easy to compute that the on-chip memory usage is fixed as $\sum_{i=0}^{24} 2^i = 4MB$. Consider the example in Figure 2. Given an address `001010`, as the pivot level is 4, since $B_4[001010 >> 2] = B_4[0010] = B_4[2] = 1$ and $N_4[001010 >> 2] = N_4[0010] = N_4[2] = 0$, then we know that the longest matching prefix length is longer than 4 and we will continue the search on levels below 4.

The pseudocode for the above SAIL Basic, denoted by SAIL_B, is shown in Algorithm 1.

**Algorithm 1: SAIL_B**

**Input**: Bit map arrays: $B_0, B_1, \cdots, B_{24}$
**Input**: Next hop arrays: $N_0, N_1, \cdots, N_{24}$
**Input**: $a$: an IP address
**Output**: next hop of the longest matched prefix

```
if B24[a >> 8]=0 then
    for j = 23; j > 0; j -- do
        if Bj[a >> (32 - j)]=1 then
            return Nj[a >> (32 - j)]
        end
    end
end
else if N24[a >> 8]>0 then
    return N24[a >> 8];
end
else
    lookup on levels 25~32;
end
```

There are multiple ways to handle prefixes of length $\geq 25$. Below we give one simple implementation using next hop arrays. Let the number of internal nodes on level 24 be $n$. We can push all solid nodes on levels 25~31 to level 32. Afterwards, the number of nodes on level 32 is $256 * n$ because each internal node on level 24 has a complete subtree with 256 leaf nodes, each of which is called a *chunk*. As typically $256 * n$ is much smaller than $2^{32}$ based on our experimental results on real FIBs, constructing a next hop array of size $2^{32}$ wastes too much memory; thus, we construct a next hop array $N_{32}$ of size $256 * n$ for level 32. As we push all solid nodes on levels from 25 to 31 to level 32, we do not need bit maps $B_{25}, B_{26}, \cdots, B_{32}$. Now consider the nodes on level 24. For each leaf node, its corresponding entry in bit map $B_{24}$ is 1 and its corresponding entry in next hop array $N_{24}$ is the next hop of this node. For each internal node, its corresponding entry in bit map $B_{24}$ is 1 and its corresponding entry in next hop array $N_{24}$ is the chunk ID in $N_{32}$, multiplying which by 256 plus the last 8 bits of the given IP address locates the next hop in $N_{32}$. To distinguish these two cases, we let the next hop be a positive number and the chunk ID to be a negative number whose absolute value is the real chunk ID value. To have negative values, chunk IDs are named starting from 1. With our pivot pushing technique, looking up an IP address $a$ is simple: if $B_{24}[a >> 8] = 0$, then we know the longest matching prefix length is within $[0, 23]$ and further test whether $B_{23}[a >> 8] = 1$; if $B_{24}[a >> 8] = 1 \wedge N_{24}[a >> 8] > 0$, then we know that the longest matching prefix length is 24 and the next hop is $N_{24}[a >> 8]$; if $B_{24}[a >> 8] = 1 \wedge N_{24}[a >> 8] < 0$, then we know that the longest matching prefix length is longer than 24 and the next hop is $N_{32}[(|N_{24}[a >> 8]| - 1) * 256 + (a\&255)]$.

## 3.3 FIB Update for SAIL Basic

We now discuss how to adjust the lookup data structures when the given FIB changes. Note that the FIB update performance for levels 25~32 is less critical than that for levels 0~24. As most traffic hits levels 0~24, when the lookup data structures for levels 0~24 in on-chip memory change, no lookup can be performed before changes are finished and therefore may cause packet losses. For the lookup data structures in off-chip memory, one possible solution is to store two copies of the lookup data structures in two memory chips so that while one copy is being updated, the other copy can be used to perform lookups. Furthermore, many IP lookup schemes that can handle prefixes of length $\geq 25$ can be plugged into SAIL_B. Different IP lookup schemes have different FIB update algorithms. Therefore, in this paper, we focus on the update of data structures in on-chip memory.

For SAIL_B, updating the on-chip lookup data structures is simple: given an update prefix $p$ with length of $l$, whose next hop is denoted by $h$ where $h = 0$ means to withdraw prefix $p$ and $h > 0$ means to announce prefix $p$, if $l < 24$, we assign $B_l[|p|] = (h > 0)$ (*i.e.*, if $h > 0$, then we assign $B_l[|p|] = 1$; otherwise, we assign $B_l[|p|] = 0$). If $l = 24$, for the same update, we first locate the node in the trie, if it is an internal node, then $B_{24}$ is kept unchanged; otherwise, we assign $B_{24}[|p|] = (h > 0)$. Note that for one FIB update, we may need to update both the on-chip and off-chip lookup data structures. A router typically maintains the trie data structure on the control plane and uses it to compute the changes that need to be made to off-chip lookup data structures. Because little traffic hits the off-chip lookup data structures for levels 25~32, updating the off-chip lookup data structures often can be performed in parallel with IP lookups on the on-chip data structures.

# 4. SAIL OPTIMIZATION

In this section, we first present two optimization techniques of our SAIL algorithms, which favors the performance of FIB update and IP lookup, respectively. We use SAIL_U to denote SAIL_B with update oriented optimization, and SAIL_L to denote SAIL_B with lookup oriented optimization. Then, we extend SAIL_L to handle multiple FIBs.

## 4.1 Update Oriented Optimization

**Data Structures & Lookup Process:** In this optimization, by prefix expansion, we push all solid nodes on levels $0 \sim 5$ to level 6, all solid nodes on levels $7 \sim 11$ to level 12, all solid nodes on levels $13 \sim 17$ to level 18, and all solid nodes on levels $19 \sim 23$ to level 24. With this 4-level pushing, looking up an IP address $a$ is the same as without this pushing, except that if $B_{24}[a >> 8] = 0$, then we further check whether $B_{18}[a >> 14] = 1$, $B_{12}[a >> 20] = 1$, and $B_6[a >> 26] = 1$ till we get the first 1. This 4-level pushing brings two benefits to IP lookup. First, it reduces the maximum number of array lookups in on-chip memory from 24 to 4. Second, it reduces the on-chip memory usage by 49.2% because we do not need to store $B_0 \sim B_5$, $B_7 \sim B_{11}$, $B_{13} \sim B_{17}$, and $B_{19} \sim B_{23}$.

**FIB Update:** While improving lookup speed and reducing on-chip memory usage, this pushing incurs no extra cost to the update of on-chip data structures. With this pushing, we still achieve one on-chip memory access per FIB update because of three reasons. First, for any FIB update, it at most affects $2^6 = 64$ bits due to the above pushing. Second, typically by each memory access we can read/write 64 bits using a 64-bit processor. Third, as the lengths of the four bit maps $B_6$, $B_{12}$, $B_{18}$, and $B_{24}$ are dividable by 64, the 64 bits that any FIB update needs to modify align well with word boundaries in on-chip memory. We implement each of these four bit maps as an array of 64-bit unsigned integers; thus, for any FIB update, we only need to modify one such integer in one memory access.

## 4.2 Lookup Oriented Optimization

**Data Structures:** In SAIL_B and SAIL_U, the maximum numbers of on-chip memory accesses are 24 and 4, respectively. To further improve lookup speed, we need to push nodes to fewer number of levels. On one hand, the fewer number of levels means the fewer numbers of on-chip memory accesses, which means faster lookup. On the other hand, pushing levels $0 \sim 23$ to 24 incurs too large on-chip memory. To trade-off between the number of on-chip memory accesses and the data structure size at each level, we choose two levels: one is between 0~23, and the other one is 24. In our experiments, the two levels are 16 and 24. In this optimization, by prefix expansion, we first push all solid nodes on levels $0 \sim 15$ to level 16; second, we push all internal nodes on level 16 and all solid nodes on levels 17~23 to level 24; third, we push all internal nodes on level 24 and all solid nodes on levels $25 \sim 31$ to level 32. We call this *3-level pushing*. For level 16, our data structure has three arrays: bit map array $B_{16}[0..2^{16} - 1]$, next hop array $N_{16}[0..2^{16} - 1]$, and chunk ID array $C_{16}[0..2^{16} - 1]$, where the chunk ID starts from 1. For level 24, our data structure has three arrays: bit map array $B_{24}$, next hop array $N_{24}$, and chunk ID array $C_{24}$, where the size of each array is the number of internal nodes on level 16 times $2^8$. For level 32, our data structure has one array: next hop array $N_{32}$, whose size is the number of internal nodes on level 24 times $2^8$.

**Lookup Process:** Given an IP address $a$, using $a_{(i,j)}$ to denote the integer value of the bit string of $a$ from the $i$-th bit to the $j$-th bit, we first check whether $B_{16}[a_{(0,15)}] = 1$; if yes, then the $a_{(0,15)}$-th node on level 16 is a solid node and thus the next hop for $a$ is $N_{16}[a_{(0,15)}]$; otherwise, then the $a_{(0,15)}$-th node on level 16 is an empty node and thus we need to continue the search on level 24, where the index is computed as $(C_{16}[a_{(0,15)}] - 1) * 2^8 + a_{(16,23)}$. On level 24, denoting $(C_{16}[a_{(0,15)}] - 1) * 2^8 + a_{(16,23)}$ by $i$, the search process is similar to level 16: we first check whether $B_{24}[i] = 1$, if yes, then the $i$-th node on level 24 is a solid node and thus the next hop for $a$ is $N_{24}[i]$; otherwise, the $i$-th node on level 24 is an empty node and thus the next hop must be on level 32, to be more precise, the next hop is $(C_{24}[i] - 1) * 2^8 + a_{(24,31)}$. Figure 3 illustrates the above data structures and IP lookup process where the three pushed levels are 2, 4, and 6. The pseudocode for the lookup process of SAIL_L is in Algorithm 2, where we use the bit maps, next hop arrays, and the chunk ID arrays as separate arrays for generality and simplicity.

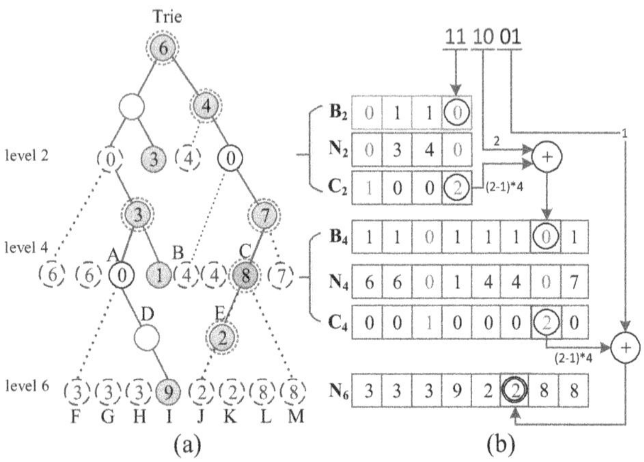


**Figure 3: Example data structure of SAIL_L.**

**Algorithm 2: SAIL_L**

**Input**: Bit map arrays: $B_{16}, B_{24}$
**Input**: Next hop arrays: $N_{16}, N_{24}, N_{32}$
**Input**: Chunk ID arrays: $C_{16}, C_{24}$
**Input**: $a$: an IP address
**Output**: the next hop of the longest matched prefix.

**if** $B_{16}[a >> 16]{=}1$ **then**
  **return** $N_{16}[a >> 16]$
**end**
**else if** $B_{24}[(C_{16}[a >> 16] - 1) << 8 + (a << 16 >> 24)]$ **then**
  **return** $N_{24}[(C_{16}[a >> 16] - 1) << 8 + (a << 16 >> 24)]$
**end**
**else**
  **return** $N_{32}[(C_{24}[a >> 8] - 1) << 8 + (a \& 255)]$
**end**

**Two-dimensional Splitting:** The key difference between SAIL_L and prior IP lookup algorithms lies in its two-dimensional splitting. According to our two-dimensional splitting methodology, we should store the three arrays $B_{16}$, $C_{16}$, and $B_{24}$ in on-chip memory and the other four arrays $N_{16}$, $N_{24}$, $C_{24}$, and $N_{32}$ in off-chip memory as shown in Figure 4. We observe that for $0 \leq i \leq 2^{16} - 1$, $B_{16}[i] = 0$ if and only if $N_{16}[i] = 0$, which holds if and only if $C_{16}[i] \neq 0$. Thus, the three arrays of $B_{16}$, $C_{16}$, and $N_{16}$ can be combined into one array denoted by $BCN$, where for $0 \leq i \leq 2^{16} - 1$, $BCN[i]_{(0,0)} = 1$ indicates that $BCN[i]_{(1,15)} = N_{16}[i]$ and $BCN[i]_{(0,0)} = 0$ indicates that $BCN[i]_{(1,15)} = C_{16}[i]$. Although in theory for $0 \leq i \leq 2^{16} - 1$, $C_{16}[i]$ needs 16 bits, practically, based on measurement from our real FIBs of backbone routers, 15 bits are enough for $C_{16}[i]$ and 8 bits for next hop; thus, $BCN[i]$ will be 16 bits exactly. For FPGA/ASIC platforms, we store $BCN$ and $B_{24}$ in on-chip memory and others in off-chip memory. For CPU/GPU/many-core platforms, because most lookups access both $B_{24}$ and $N_{24}$, we do combine $B_{24}$ and $N_{24}$ to $BN_{24}$ so as to improve caching behavior. $BN_{24}[i] = 0$ indicates that $B_{24}[i] = 0$, and we need to find the next hop in level 32; $BN_{24}[i] > 0$ indicates that the next hop is $BN_{24}[i] = N_{24}[i]$.

| | Finding prefix length | Finding next hop |
|---|---|---|
| Prefix length 0~24 | $B_{16}$, $C_{16}$, $B_{24}$ | $N_{16}$, $N_{24}$ |
| Prefix length 25~32 | $C_{24}$ | $N_{32}$ |

**Figure 4: Memory management for SAIL_L.**

**FIB Update:** Given a FIB update of inserting/deleting/modifying a prefix, we first modify the trie that the router maintains on the control plane to make the trie equivalent to the updated FIB. Note that this trie is the one after the above 3-level pushing. Further note that FIB update messages are sent/received on the control plane where the pushed trie is maintained. Second, we perform the above 3-level pushing on the updated trie for the nodes affected by the update. Third, we modify the lookup data structures on the data plane to reflect the change of the pushed trie.

SAIL_L can perform FIB updates efficiently because of two reasons, although one FIB update may affect many trie nodes in the worst case. First, prior studies have shown that most FIB updates require only updates on a leaf node [41]. Second, the modification on the lookup arrays (namely the bit map arrays, next hop arrays, and the chunk ID arrays) is mostly continuous, *i.e.*, a block of a lookup array is modified. We can use the `memcpy` function to efficiently write 64 bits in one memory access on a 64-bit processor.

## 4.3 SAIL for Multiple FIBs

We now present our SAIL_M algorithm for handling multiple FIBs in virtual routers, which is an extension of SAIL_L. A router with virtual router capability (such as Cisco CRS-1/16) can be configured to run multiple routing instances where each instance has a FIB. If we build independent data structures for different FIBs, it will cost too much memory. Our goal in dealing with multiple FIBs is to build one data structure so that we can perform IP lookup on it for each FIB. Note that our method below can be used to extend SAIL_B and SAIL_U to handle multiple FIBs as well, although for these two algorithms, the FIB update cost is no longer constant for the number of on-chip memory accesses.

**Data Structures:** Given $m$ FIBs $F_0, F_1, \cdots, F_{m-1}$, first, for each $F_i$ $(0 \leq i \leq m-1)$, for each prefix $p$ in $F_i$, we change its next hop $n_i(p)$ to a pair $(i, n_i(p))$. Let $F'_0, F'_1, \cdots,$ and $F'_{m-1}$ denote the resulting FIBs. Second, we build a trie for $F'_0 \cup F'_1 \cup \cdots \cup F'_{m-1}$, the union of all FIBs. Note that in this trie, a solid node may have multiple (FIB ID, next hop) pairs. Third, we perform leaf pushing on this trie.

Leaf pushing means to push each solid node to some leaf nodes [39]. After leaf pushing, every internal node is empty and has two children nodes; furthermore, each leaf node $v$ corresponding to a prefix $p$ is solid and has $m$ (FIB ID, next hop) pairs: $(0, n_0(p)), (1, n_1(p)), \cdots, (m-1, n_{m-1}(p))$, which can be represented as an array $\mathbb{N}$ where $\mathbb{N}[i] = n_i(p)$ for $0 \leq i \leq m-1$. Intuitively, we overlay all individual tries constructed from the $m$ FIBs, stretch all tries to have the same structure, and then perform leaf pushing on all tries. Based on the overlay trie, we run the SAIL_L lookup algorithm. Note that in the resulting data structure, in each next hop array $N_{16}$, $N_{24}$, or $N_{32}$, each element is further an array of size $m$. Figure 5 shows two individual tries and the overlay trie.

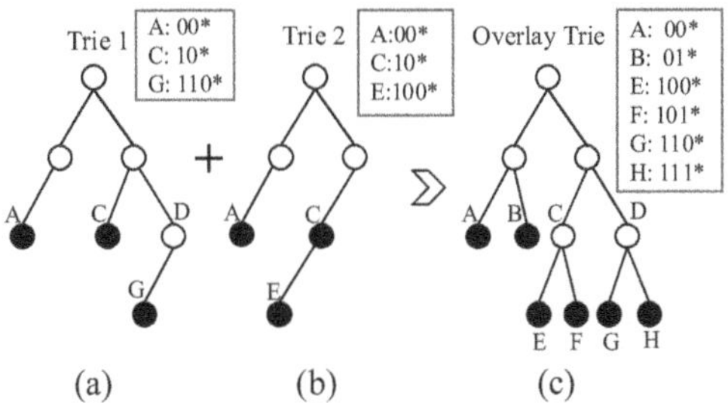


**Figure 5: Example of SAIL for multiple FIBs.**

**Lookup Process:** Regarding the IP lookup process for multiple FIBs, given an IP address $a$ and a FIB ID $i$, we first use SAIL_L to find the next hop array $\mathbb{N}$ for $a$. Then, the next hop for IP address $a$ and a FIB ID $i$ is $\mathbb{N}[i]$.

**Two-dimensional Splitting:** Regarding memory management, SAIL_M exactly follows the two-dimensional splitting strategy illustrated in Figure 4. We store $BC_{16}$, which is the combination of $B_{16}$ and $C_{16}$, and $B_{24}$ in on-chip memory, and store the rest four arrays $N_{16}$, $N_{24}$, $C_{24}$, and $N_{32}$ in off-chip memory. The key feature of our scheme for dealing with multiple FIBs is that the total on-chip memory needed is bounded to $2^{16} * 17 + 2^{24} = 2.13$MB *regardless of the sizes, characteristics and number of FIBs.* The reason that we store $BC_{16}$ and $B_{24}$ in on-chip memory is that given an IP address $a$, $BC_{16}$ and $B_{24}$ can tell us on which exact level, 16, 24, or 32 that we can find the longest matching prefix for $a$. If it is on level 16 or 24, then we need 1 off-chip memory access as we only need to access $N_{16}$ or $N_{24}$. If it is on level 32, then we need 2 off-chip memory access as we need to access $C_{24}$ and $N_{32}$. Thus, the lookup process requires 2 on-chip memory accesses (which are on $BC_{16}$ and $B_{24}$) and at most 2 off-chip memory accesses.

**FIB Update:** Given a FIB update of inserting/deleting/modifying a prefix, we first modify the overlay trie that the router maintains on the control plane to make the resulting overlay trie equivalent to the updated FIBs. Second, we modify the lookup data structures in the data plane to reflect the change of the overlay trie.

# 5. SAIL IMPLEMENTATION

In this section, we discuss the implementation of SAIL algorithms on four platforms: FPGA, CPU, GPU, and many-core.

## 5.1 FPGA Implementation

We simulated SAIL_B, SAIL_U, and SAIL_L using Xilinx ISE 13.2 IDE. We did not simulate SAIL_M because its on-chip memory lookup process is similar to SAIL_L. In our FPGA simulation of each algorithm, to speed up IP lookup, we build one pipeline stage for the data structure corresponding to each level.

We use Xilinx Virtex 7 device (model XC7VX1140T) as the target platform. This device has 1,880 block RAMs where each block has 36 Kb, thus the total amount of on-chip memory is 8.26MB [1]. As this on-chip memory size is large enough, we implement the three algorithms of SAIL_B, SAIL_U, and SAIL_L on this platform.

## 5.2 CPU Implementation

We implemented SAIL_L and SAIL_M on CPU platforms because their data structures have less number of levels as compared to SAIL_B and SAIL_U, and thus are suitable for CPU platform. For our algorithms on CPU platforms, the less number of levels means the less CPU processing steps. In contrast, in FPGA platforms, because we build one pipeline stage per level, the numbers of levels in our algorithms do not have direct impact on IP lookup throughput.

Our CPU experiments were carried out on an Intel(R) Core(TM) i7-3520M. It has two cores with four threads, each core works at 2.9 GHz. It has a 64KB L1 code cache, a 64KB L1 data cache, a 512KB L2 cache, and a 4MB L3 cache. The DRAM size of our computer is 8GB. The actual CPU frequency that we observe in our programs is 2.82GHz.

To obtain the number of CPU cycles of SAIL_L and SAIL_M, we reverse engineering our C++ code. The assembly code is shown in Table 2. This table shows that for SAIL_L, given an IP address $a$, if the next hop of $a$ can be found on level 16, then the lookup needs only 3 CPU instructions; if the next hop of $a$ can be found on level 24, then the lookup needs only 10 CPU instructions. Note that CPU could complete more than one instruction in one cycle. In comparison, for the Lulea algorithm, given an IP address $a$, if the next hop of $a$ can be found on level 16, then the lookup needs at least $17 \sim 22$ CPU cycles; if the next hop of $a$ can be found on level 24, then the lookup needs 148 CPU cycles. This explains why our algorithm is much faster than Lulea.

**Table 2: The disassembling code of lookup.**

| if((H=0 − $BCN_{16}[a \gg 16]$)>0); | | |
|---|---|---|
| 000000013F32589C | movzx | ecx,ax |
| 000000013F32589F | movzx | ebx,byte ptr[r10+rcx*2] |
| 000000013F3258A4 | neg | bl |
| 000000013F3258A6 | jne | sailtest+147h(013F3258D7h) |
| else if(H=$BN_{24}[(BCN[a \gg 16] \ll 8) + (a \ll 16 \gg 24)]$); | | |
| 000000013F3258A8 | movsx | ecx,word ptr[r10+rcx*2] |
| 000000013F3258AD | shl | ecx,8 |
| 000000013F3258B0 | movzx | eax,byte ptr [rdi+rdx*4+1] |
| 000000013F3258B5 | add | ecx,eax |
| 000000013F3258B7 | movzx | ebx,byte ptr [rcx+r9] |
| 000000013F3258BC | test | bl,bl |
| 000000013F3258BE | jne | sailtest+147h(013F3258D7h) |

## 5.3 GPU Implementation

We implemented SAIL_L in GPU platforms based on NVDIA's CUDA architecture [30]. In our GPU implementation, we store all data structures in GPU memory. Executing tasks on a GPU consists of three steps: (1) copy data from the CPU to the GPU, (2) execute multiple threads for the task, (3) copy the computing results back to the CPU; these three steps are denoted by *H2D, kernel execution, and D2H*, respectively. Thus, there is a natural communication bottleneck between the CPU and the GPU. To address this limitation, the common strategy is batch processing; that is, the CPU transfers a batch of independent requests to the GPU, and then the GPU processes them in parallel using many cores. In our GPU implementation, when packets arrive, the CPU first buffers them; when the buffer is full, the CPU transfers all their destination IP addresses to the GPU; when the GPU finishes all lookups, it transfers all lookup results back to the CPU. For our GPU based SAIL implementation, the data copied from the CPU to the GPU are IP addresses, and the computing results copied from the GPU to the CPU are the next hops for these IP addresses. In our GPU implementation, we employed two optimization techniques to speed up IP lookup performance: memory coalesce and multi-streaming.

The basic idea of memory coalesce is to let threads with continuous IDs read memory of continuous locations because GPU schedules its threads to access the main memory in the unit of 32 threads. In our GPU implementation, after the CPU transfers a batch of $32 * n$ IP addresses to the GPU's memory denoted as an array $A[0..32 * n - 1]$, if we assign threads $t_0, t_1, \cdots, t_{32*n-1}$ to process the IP addresses $A[0], A[1], \cdots, A[32*n-1]$, respectively, then all these $32*n$ IP addresses can be read in $n$ memory transitions by the GPU, instead of $32 * n$ memory accesses.

The basic idea of multi-streaming, which is available on INVIDA Fermi GPU architecture, is to pipeline the three steps of H2D, kernel execution, and D2H. According to the CUDA computing model, data transfers (*i.e.*, H2D and D2H) and kernel executions within different streams can be parallelized via page-locked memory. A stream is a sequence of threads that must be executed in order. In our GPU implementation, we assign each $32 * k$ ($k \geq 1$) threads to a unique stream. Thus, different streams of $32*k$ threads can be pipelined, *i.e.*, while one stream of $32 * k$ threads are transferring data from the CPU to the GPU, one stream of $32 * k$ threads are executing their kernel function, and another stream of $32*k$ threads are transferring data from the GPU to the CPU.

## 5.4 Many-core Implementation

We implemented SAIL_L on the many-core platform Telera TLR4-03680 [5], which has 36 cores and each core has a 256K L2 cache. Our experiments were carried out on a 64-bit operation system CentOS 5.9. One L2 cache access needs 9 cycles. In our many-core implementation, we let one core to serve as the main thread and all other cores to serve as lookup threads, where each lookup thread performs all steps for an IP address lookup.

# 6. EXPERIMENTAL RESULTS

In this section, we present the experimental results of our algorithms on the four platforms of FPGA, CPU, GPU, and many-core.

## 6.1 Experimental Setup

To obtain real FIBs, we used a server to establish a peer relationship with a tier-1 router in China so that the server can receive FIB updates from the tier-1 router but does not announce new prefixes to the tier-1 router; thus, gradually, the server obtained the whole FIB from the tier-1 router. Note that it is not practically feasible to dump the FIB of a tier-1 router to hard disk because of the unbearable overhead incurred on the router. On the server, we use the open source `Quagga` to dump the FIB every hour [2]. We captured real traffic in one of the tier-1 router's interfaces at the interval of 10 minutes per hour between October 22nd 08:00 AM 2013 to October 23rd 21:00 PM.

In addition, we downloaded 18 real FIBs from `www.ripe.net`. Six of them were downloaded at every 8:00 AM on January 1st of each year from 2008 to 2013, denoted by $FIB_{2008}, FIB_{2009}, \cdots, FIB_{2013}$. Twelve of them were downloaded from 12 routers on 08:00 AM August 8 2013, respectively, denoted by $rrc00, rrc01, rrc03, \cdots rrc07, rrc10, \cdots, rrc15$. We also generated 37 synthetic traffic traces. The first 25 traces contain packets with randomly chosen destinations. The other 12 traces were obtained by generating traffic evenly for each prefix in the 12 FIBs downloaded from the 12 routers on 08:00 AM August 8 2013; thus, we guarantee that each prefix has the same opportunity to be hit by the synthetic traffic. We call such traffic *prefix-based synthetic traffic*.

We evaluated our algorithms on four metrics: *lookup speed* in terms of pps (# of packets per second), *on-chip memory size* in terms of MB, *lookup latency* in terms of microsecond, and *update speed* in terms of the total number of memory accesses per update. For on-chip memory sizes, we are only able to evaluate the FPGA implementation of SAIL algorithms. For lookup latency, we evaluated our GPU implementation because the batch processing incurs more latency.

We compared our algorithms with four well-known IP lookup algorithms: PBF [36], LC-trie [38], Tree Bitmap [40], and Lulea [28]. We implemented our algorithms and these four prior algorithms using C++. We validated the correctness of all algorithms through exhaustive search: we first construct an exhaustive $2^{32} = 4G$ lookup table where the next hop of an IP address $a$ is the $a$-th entry in this table; second, for each IP address, we compare the lookup result with the result of this exhaustive table lookup, and all our implementations pass this validation.

## 6.2 Performance on FPGA

We evaluated the performance of our algorithm on FPGA platforms in comparison with PBF, which is best suitable for FPGA platforms among the four well known algorithms, because the other four algorithms did not separate their data structures for on-chip and off-chip memory.

We first evaluate SAIL_L for on-chip memory consumption in comparison with PBF. Note that PBF stores its Bloom filters in on-chip memory. We compute the on-chip memory usage of PBF as follows. In [36], it says that PBF needs 1.003 off-chip hash probes per lookup on average, given a routing table size of 116,819. To achieve 1.003 off-chip memory accesses per lookup assuming the best scenario of one memory access per hash probe, the overall false positive rate of the filters should be 0.003. Thus, each Bloom filter should have a false positive rate of $0.003/(32-8)$ since PBF uses 24 filters. Assuming that these Bloom filters always achieve the optimal false positive, then from $0.003/(32-8) = (0.5)^k$, we obtain $k = 13$ and $m/n = 18.755$, where $m$ is the total size of all Bloom filters and $n$ is the number of elements stored in the filter. Thus, given a FIB with $n$ prefixes, the total on-chip memory usage of PBF is $18.755 * n$.

*Our experimental results on on-chip memory usage show that within the upper bound of 2.13MB, the on-chip memory usage of SAIL_L grows slowly and the growth rate is slower than PBF, and that the on-chip memory usage of SAIL_L is smaller than PBF.* For on-chip memory usage, the fundamental difference between SAIL_L and PBF is that the on-chip memory usage of SAIL_L has an upper bound but that of PBF grows with the number of prefixes in the FIB linearly without a practical upper bound. Figure 6 shows the evolution of the on-chip memory usage for both SAIL_L and PBF over the past 6 years based on our results on the 6 FIBs: $FIB_{2008}, FIB_{2009}, \cdots$, and $FIB_{2013}$. Figure 7 shows the on-chip memory usage of the 12 FIBs $rrc00, rrc01$, $rrc03, \cdots rrc07$, $rrc10, \cdots, rrc15$. Taking FIB $rrc00$ with 476,311 prefixes as an example, SAIL_L needs only 0.759MB on-chip memory.

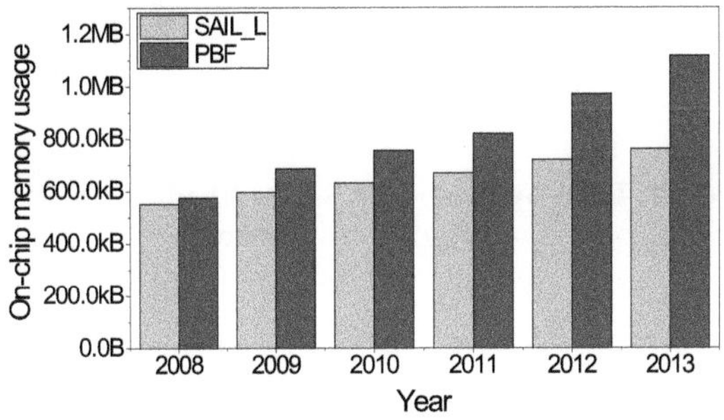


**Figure 6: On-chip memory usage over 6 years.**

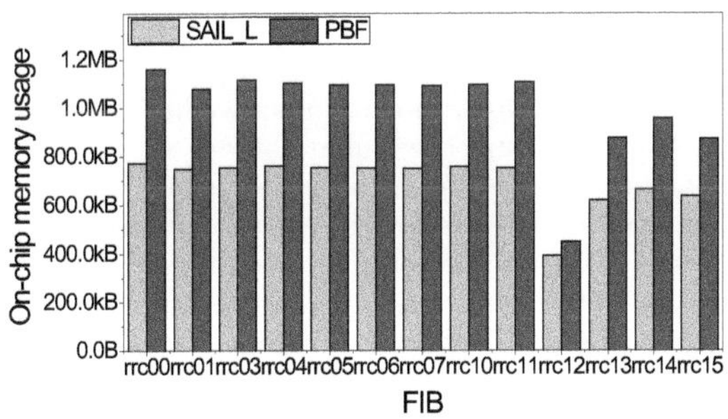


**Figure 7: On-chip memory usage of 12 FIBs.**

We next evaluate SAIL_L for lookup speed on FPGA platform Xilinx Virtex 7. We did not compare with PBF because [36] does not provide implementation details for its FPGA implementation. We focus on measuring the lookup speed on the data structures stored in on-chip memory because off-chip memory lookups are out of the FPGA chip. As we implement the lookup at each level as one pipeline stage, SAIL_B, SAIL_U, SAIL_L have 24, 4, 2 pipeline stages, respectively. The more stages our algorithms have, the more complex of the FPGA logics are, and the slower the FPGA clock frequency will be. Our experimental results show that SAIL_B, SAIL_U, SAIL_L have clock frequencies of 351MHz, 405MHz, and 479MHz, respectively. As each of our pipeline stage requires only one clock cycle, *the lookup speed of SAIL_B, SAIL_U, SAIL_L are 351Mpps, 405Mpps, and 479Mpps, respectively.*

Let us have a deeper comparison of SAIL_L with PBF. The PBF algorithm without pushing requires $25 * k$ hash computations and memory accesses in the worst case because it builds 25 Bloom filters, each of which needs $k$ hash functions. With pushing, PBF needs to build at least 1 Bloom filter because the minimum number of levels is 1 (by pushing all nodes to level 32), although which is impractical. Further we assume that PBF uses the Kirsch and Mitzenmacher's double hashing scheme based Bloom filters, which uses two hash functions to simulate multiple hash functions [6]. Although using the double hashing technique increases false positives, we assume it does not. Furthermore, suppose the input of hashing is 2 bytes, suppose PBF uses the well known CRC32 hash function, which requires 6.9 clock cycles per input byte. With these unrealistic assumptions, the number of cycles that PBF requires for searching on its on-chip data structures is $6.9 \times 2 \times 2$. In comparison, SAIL_L requires only 3~10 instructions as discussed in Section 5.2 and needs only 4.08 cycles per lookup based on Figure 8. In summary, even with many unrealistic assumptions that favor PBF, SAIL_L still performs better.

## 6.3 Performance on CPU

We evaluate the performance of our algorithm on CPU platforms in comparison with LC-trie, Tree Bitmap, and Lulea algorithms. We exclude PBF because it is not suitable for CPU implementation due to the many hashing operations.

*Our experimental results show that SAIL_L is several times faster than LC-trie, Tree Bitmap, and Lulea algorithms.* For real traffic, SAIL_L achieves a lookup speed of 673.22~708.71 Mpps, which is 34.53~58.88, 29.56~31.44, and 6.62~7.66 times faster than LC-trie, Tree Bitmap, and Lulea, respectively. For prefix-based synthetic traffic, SAIL_L achieves a lookup speed of 589.08~624.65 Mpps, which is 56.58~68.46, 26.68~23.79, and 7.61~7.27 times faster than LC-trie, Tree Bitmap, and Lulea, respectively. For random traffic, SAIL_L achieves a lookup speed of 231.47~236.08 Mpps, which is 46.22~54.86, 6.73~6.95, and 4.24~4.81 times faster than LC-trie, Tree Bitmap, and Lulea, respectively. Figure 8 shows the lookup speed of these 4 algorithms with real traffic on real FIBs. The 12 FIBs are the 12 FIB instances of the same router during the first 12 hours period starting from October 22nd 08:00 AM 2013. For each FIB instance at a particular hour, the real traffic that we experimented is the 10 minutes of real traffic that we captured during that hour. Figure 9 shows the lookup speed of these 4 algorithms with prefix-based synthetic traffic on the 12 FIBs downloaded from `www.ripe.net`. Figure 10 shows the lookup speed of these 4 algorithms with random traffic on $FIB_{2013}$. From these figures, we further observe that for each of these 4 algorithms, its lookup speed on real traffic is faster than that on prefix-based traffic, which is further faster than that on random traffic. This is because real traffic has the best IP locality, which results in the best CPU caching behavior, and random traffic has the worst IP locality, which results in the worst CPU caching behavior.

We now evaluate the FIB update performance of SAIL_L on the data plane. Figure 11 shows the variation of the number of memory accesses per update for 3 FIBs (rrc00, rrc01,

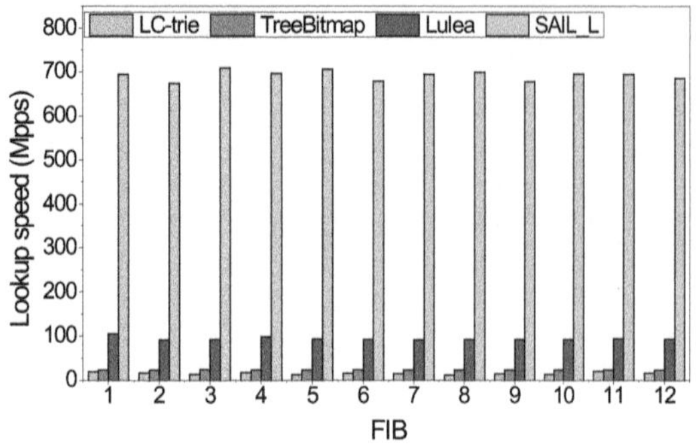


**Figure 8: Lookup speed with real traffic and FIBs.**

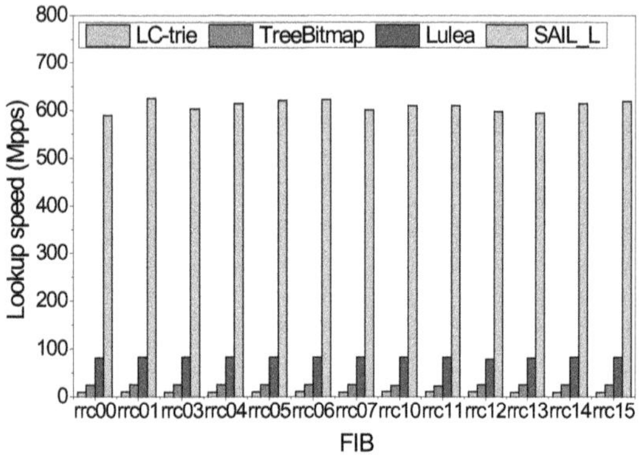


**Figure 9: Lookup speed with prefix-based traffic on 12 FIBs.**

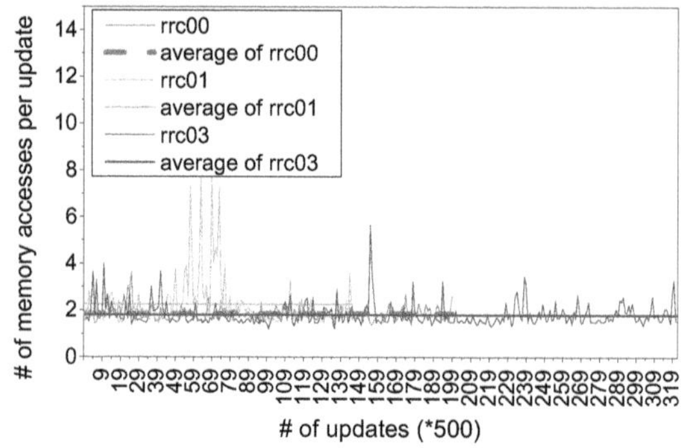


**Figure 11: # memory accesses per update.**

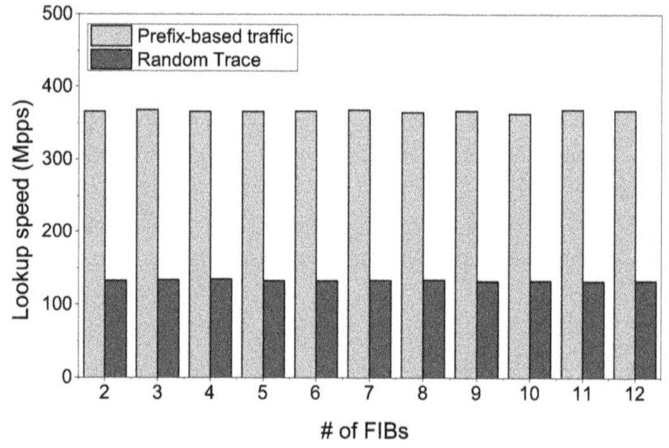


**Figure 12: Lookup speed of SAIL_M for 12 FIBs using prefix-based and random traffic.**

and rrc03) during a period with 319∗500 updates. The average numbers of memory accesses per update for these three FIBs are 1.854, 2.253 and 1.807, respectively. The observed worst case is 7.88 memory accesses per update.

We now evaluate the lookup speed of SAIL_M for virtual routers. Figure 12 shows the lookup speed of SAIL_M algorithm as the number of FIBs grows, where $x$ FIBs means the first $x$ FIBs in the 12 FIBs $rrc00, rrc01, rrc03, \cdots rrc07, rrc10, \cdots, rrc15$, for both prefix-based traffic and random traffic. This figure shows that on average SAIL_M achieves 132 Mpps for random traffic and 366 Mpps for prefix-based traffic.

## 6.4 Evaluation on GPU

We evaluate SAIL_L on GPU platform with CUDA 5.0. We carry out these experiments on a DELL T620 server with an Intel CPU (Xeon E5-2630, 2.30 GHz, 6 Cores) and

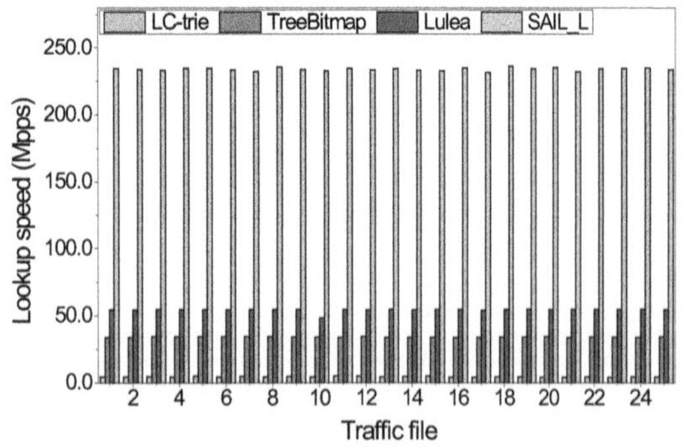


**Figure 10: Lookup speed with random traffic on $FIB_{2013}$.**

an NVIDIA GPU (Tesla C2075, 1147 MHz, 5376 MB device memory, 448 CUDA cores). These experiments use the 12 FIBs $rrc00, rrc01, rrc03, \cdots rrc07, rrc10, \cdots, rrc15$. We measure the lookup speed and latency with a range of CUDA configurations: the number of streams $(1, 2, \cdots, 24)$, the number of blocks per stream $(64, 96, \cdots, 512)$, and the number of threads per block $(128, 256, \cdots, 1024)$. The lookup speed is calculated as the total number IP lookup requests divided by the total lookup time. We use the Nvidia Visual Profiler tool to measure the lookup latency.

We evaluated the IP lookup speed versus traffic size (*i.e.*, the number of IP addresses in one batch of data sent from the CPU to the GPU). We generate 3 traffic traces of 3 different sizes 30K, 60K, 90K. Figure 13 shows our experimental results, from which we observe that larger traffic sizes lead to higher lookup speed. For the traffic size of 30K, SAIL_L achieves a lookup speed of 257∼322 Mpps. For the traffic size of 60K, SAIL_L achieves a lookup speed of 405∼447 Mpps. For the traffic size of 90K, SAIL_L achieves a lookup speed of 442∼547 Mpps.

We evaluated the IP lookup latency versus traffic size. Figure 14 shows our experimental results, from which we observe that larger traffic sizes lead to higher lookup latency. For the traffic size of 30K, SAIL_L has a lookup latency of 90∼124 $\mu s$. For the traffic size of 60K, SAIL_L has a lookup latency of 110∼152 $\mu s$. For the traffic size of 90K, SAIL_L has a lookup latency of 122∼185 $\mu s$.

## 6.5 Evaluation on Many-core Platform

We evaluated the lookup speed of SAIL_L versus the number of cores. We conducted our experiments on the many-core platform Telera TLR4-03680.

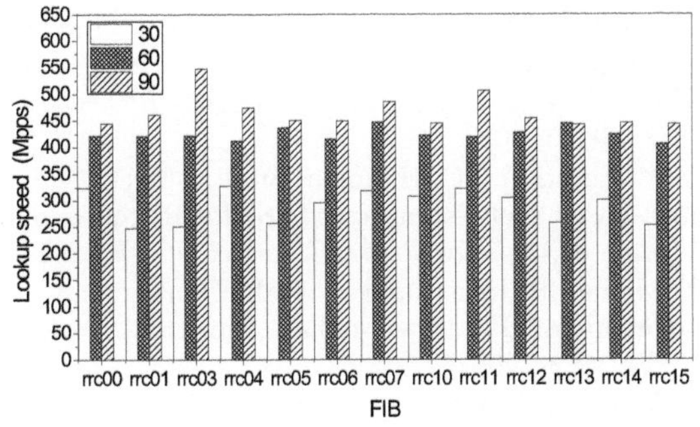


**Figure 13: Lookup speed VS. traffic size.**

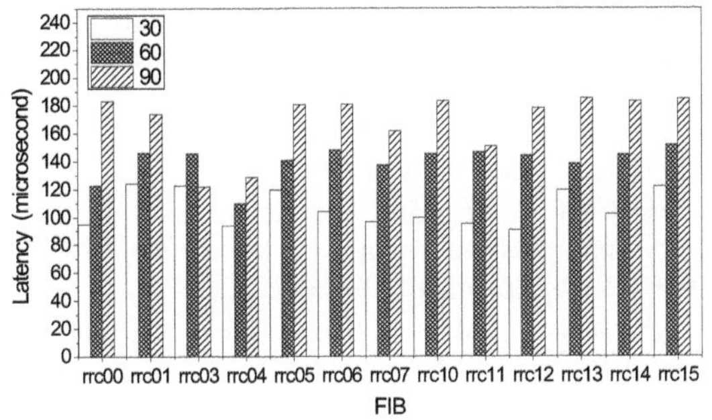


**Figure 14: Lookup latency VS. traffic size.**

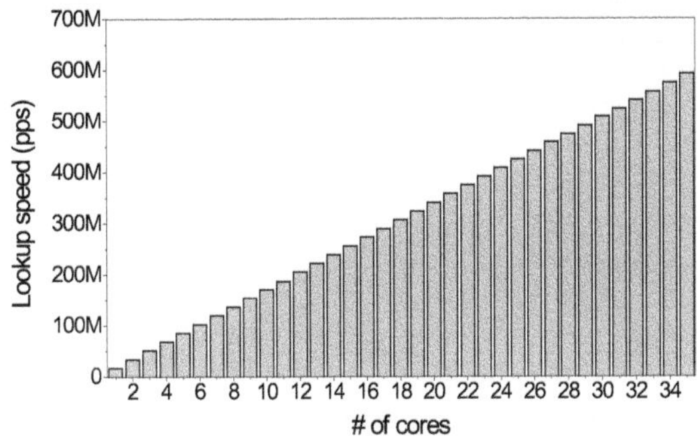


**Figure 15: Lookup speed VS. # of cores.**

*Our experimental results show that the lookup rate increases linearly as the number of cores grows.* Note that we only have the results of 35 cores, because one core is responsible for traffic distribution and results collection. Figure 15 shows the results on FIB *rrc*00 using prefix-based traffic. We have observed similar results for other FIBs.

# 7. DISCUSSION

Our SAIL framework is mainly proposed for IPv4 lookup; however, it can be extended for IPv6 lookup as well. An IPv6 address has 128 bits, the first 64 bits represent the network address and the rest 64 bits represent the host address. An IPv6 prefix has 64 bits. The real IPv6 FIBs in backbone routers from `www.ripe.net` only has around 14,000 entries, which are much smaller than IPv4 FIBs. To deal with IPv6 FIBs, we can push trie nodes to 6 levels of 16, 24, 32, 40, 48, and 64. To split along the dimension of prefix lengths, we perform the splitting on level 48. In other words, we store the bit map and chunk ID arrays of levels 16, 24, 32, 40, and bit map array of level 48 in on-chip memory. Our experimental results show that the on-chip memory for an IPv6 FIB is about 2.2MB. Although the on-chip memory usage for IPv6 is much larger than that for IPv4 in the worst case because IPv6 prefix length are much longer than IPv4, as IPv6 FIB sizes are orders of magnitude smaller than IPv4 FIB sizes, the one-chip memory usage for IPv6 is similar to that for IPv4.

# 8. CONCLUSION

We make three key contributions in this paper. First, we propose a two-dimensional splitting approach to IP lookup. The key benefit of such splitting is that we can solve the sub-problem of finding the prefix length $\leq 24$ in on-chip memory of bounded small size. Second, we propose a suite of algorithms for IP lookup based on our SAIL framework. One key feature of our algorithms is that we achieve constant, yet small, IP lookup time and on-chip memory usage. Another key feature is that our algorithms are cross platform as the data structures are all arrays and only require four operations of ADD, SUBTRACTION, SHIFT, and logical AND. Note that SAIL is a general framework where different solutions to the sub-problems can be adopted. The algorithms proposed in this paper represent particular instantiations of our SAIL framework. Third, we implemented our algorithms on four platforms (namely FPGA, CPU, GPU, and many-core) and conducted extensive experiments to evaluate our algorithms using real FIBs and traffic from a major ISP in China. Our experimental results show that our SAIL algorithms are several times or even two orders of magnitude faster than the well known IP lookup algorithms. Furthermore, we have open sourced our SAIL_L algorithm and three well known IP lookup algorithms (namely LC-trie, Tree Bitmap, and Lulea) that we implemented in [4].

# 9. ACKNOWLEDGEMENTS

We would like to thank Peng He for implementing the Tree Bitmap algorithm and Chunjing Han, Qinghua Wu and Taihua He for their valuable suggestions. We also would like to thank the anonymous reviewers and our shepherd, Andrew Moore, for their thoughtful suggestions. This work was supported in part by National Basic Research Program of China with Grant 2012CB315801, by National Natural Science Foundation of China (NSFC) with Grants (61133015, 61202489), and by Strategic Priority Research Program of CAS with Grant XDA06010303.

# 10. REFERENCES

[1] FPGA data sheet [on line]. Available: http://www.xilinx.com.

[2] Quagga routing suite [on line]. Available: http://www.nongnu.org/quagga/.

[3] RIPE network coordination centre [on line]. Available: http://www.ripe.net.

[4] SAIL webpage. http://fi.ict.ac.cn/firg.php?n=PublicationsAmpTalks.OpenSource.

[5] Tilera datasheet [on line]. Available: http://www.tilera.com/sites/default/files/productbriefs/TILE-Gx8036_PB033-02_web.pdf.

[6] K. Adam and M. Michael. Less hashing, same performance: Building a better bloom filter. In *Algorithms-ESA 2006*, pages 456–467. Springer, 2006.

[7] P. Derek, L. Ziyan, and P. Hang. IP address lookup using bit-shuffled trie. *IEEE Computer Communications*, 2014.
[8] S. Devavrat and G. Pankaj. Fast incremental updates on ternary-cams for routing lookups and packet classification. In *Proc. Hot Interconnects*, 2000.
[9] W. Feng and H. Mounir. Matching the speed gap between sram and dram. In *Proc. IEEE HSPR*, pages 104–109, 2008.
[10] B. Florin, T. Dean, R. Grigore, and S. Sumeet. A tree based router search engine architecture with single port memories. In *Proc. IEEE ISCA*, 2005.
[11] Z. Francis, N. Girija, and B. Anindya. Coolcams: Power-efficient tcams for forwarding engines. In *Proc. IEEE INFOCOM*, pages 42–52, 2003.
[12] R. Gábor, T. János, A. Korósi, A. Majdán, and Z. Heszberger. Compressing IP forwarding tables: Towards entropy bounds and beyond. In *Proc. ACM SIGCOMM*, 2013.
[13] P. Gupta, S. Lin, and N. McKeown. Routing lookups in hardware at memory access speeds. In *Proc. IEEE INFOCOM*, pages 1240–1247, 1998.
[14] F. Hamid, Z. M. Saheb, and S. Masoud. A novel reconfigurable hardware architecture for IP address lookup. In *Proc. ACM/IEEE ANCS*, pages 81–90, 2005.
[15] S. Haoyu, K. Murali, H. Fang, and L. TV. Scalable IP lookups using shape graphs. In *Proc. ACM/IEEE ICNP*, pages 73–82, 2009.
[16] L. Hoang, J. Weirong, and P. V. K. A sram-based architecture for trie-based IP lookup using fpga. In *Proc. IEEE FCCM*, pages 33–42, 2008.
[17] L. Hyesook, Y. Changhoon, and S. Earl. Priority tries for IP address lookup. *IEEE Transactions on Computers*, 59(6):784–794, 2010.
[18] F. Jing and R. Jennifer. Efficient IP-address lookup with a shared forwarding table for multiple virtual routers. In *Proc. ACM CoNEXT*. ACM, 2008.
[19] Z. Kai, H. Chengchen, L. Hongbin, and L. Bin. A tcam-based distributed parallel IP lookup scheme and performance analysis. *IEEE/ACM Transactions on Networking*, 14(4):863–875, 2006.
[20] S. Keith. A tree-based packet routing table for berkeley unix. In *USENIX Winter*, pages 93–99, 1991.
[21] L. Layong, X. Gaogang, S. Kavé, U. Steve, M. Laurent, and X. Yingke. A trie merging approach with incremental updates for virtual routers. In *Proc. IEEE INFOCOM*, pages 1222–1230, 2013.
[22] H. Lim, K. Lim, N. Lee, and K.-H. Park. On adding bloom filters to longest prefix matching algorithms. *IEEE Transactions on Computers (TC)*, 63(2):411–423, 2014.
[23] M. Mahmoud and M. Massato. A new hardware algorithm for fast IP routing targeting programmable routers. In *Network control and engineering for Qos, security and mobility II*, pages 164–179. Springer, 2003.
[24] W. Marcel, V. George, T. Jon, and P. Bernhard. Scalable high speed IP routing lookups. In *Proc. ACM SIGCOMM*, 1997.
[25] Z. Marko, R. Luigi, and M. Miljenko. Dxr: towards a billion routing lookups per second in software. *ACM SIGCOMM Computer Communication Review*, 42(5):29–36, 2012.
[26] B. Masanori and C. H. Jonathan. Flashtrie: hash-based prefix-compressed trie for IP route lookup beyond 100gbps. In *Proc. IEEE INFOCOM*, 2010.
[27] R. Miguel, B. Ernst, and D. Walid. Survey and taxonomy of IP address lookup algorithms. *Network, IEEE*, 15(2), 2001.
[28] D. Mikael, B. Andrej, C. Svante, and P. Stephen. Small forwarding tables for fast routing lookups. In *Proc. ACM SIGCOMM*, pages 3–14, 1997.
[29] A. Mohammad, N. Mehrdad, P. Rina, and S. Samar. A tcam-based parallel architecture for high-speed packet forwarding. *IEEE Transactions on Computers*, 56(1):58–72, 2007.
[30] NVIDIA Corporation. *NVIDIA CUDA C Best Practices Guide, Version 5.0*, Oct. 2012.
[31] C. Pierluigi, D. Leandro, and G. Roberto. IP address lookupmade fast and simple. In *Algorithms-ESA'99*, pages 65–76. Springer, 1999.
[32] W. Priyank, S. Subhash, and V. George. Multiway range trees: scalable IP lookup with fast updates. *Computer Networks*, 44(3):289–303, 2004.
[33] S. Rama, F. Natsuhiko, A. Srinivas, and S. Arun. Scalable, memory efficient, high-speed IP lookup algorithms. *IEEE/ACM Transactions on Networking*, 13(4):802–812, 2005.
[34] P. Rina and S. Samar. Reducing tcam power consumption and increasing throughput. In *Proc. High Performance Interconnects*, pages 107–112, 2002.
[35] H. Sangjin, J. Keon, P. KyoungSoo, and M. Sue. Packetshader: a gpu-accelerated software router. In *Proc. ACM SIGCOMM*, pages 195–206, 2010.
[36] D. Sarang, K. Praveen, and T. D. E. Longest prefix matching using bloom filters. In *Proc. ACM SIGCOMM*, pages 201–212, 2003.
[37] H. Song, M. Kodialam, F. Hao, and T. Lakshman. Building scalable virtual routers with trie braiding. In *Proc. IEEE INFOCOM*, 2010.
[38] N. Stefan and K. Gunnar. IP-address lookup using lc-tries. *Selected Areas in Communications, IEEE Journal on*, 17(6):1083–1092, 1999.
[39] S. Venkatachary and V. George. Fast address lookups using controlled prefix expansion. *ACM TOCS*, 17(1):1–40, 1999.
[40] E. Will, V. George, and D. Zubin. Tree bitmap: hardware/software IP lookups with incremental updates. *ACM SIGCOMM Computer Communication Review*, 34(2):97–122, 2004.
[41] T. Yang, Z. Mi, R. Duan, X. Guo, J. Lu, S. Zhang, X. Sun, and B. Liu. An ultra-fast universal incremental update algorithm for trie-based routing lookup. In *Proc. ACM/IEEE ICNP*, 2012.
[42] J. Zhao, X. Zhang, X. Wang, and X. Xue. Achieving O(1) IP lookup on gpu-based software routers. In *ACM SIGCOMM Computer Communication Review*, volume 40, pages 429–430. ACM, 2010.

# From the Consent of the Routed: Improving the Transparency of the RPKI

Ethan Heilman Danny Cooper Leonid Reyzin Sharon Goldberg
Dept. of Computer Science, Boston University, Boston, MA, USA
{heilman,dannyc}@bu.edu, {reyzin, goldbe}@cs.bu.edu

## ABSTRACT

The Resource Public Key Infrastructure (RPKI) is a new infrastructure that prevents some of the most devastating attacks on interdomain routing. However, the security benefits provided by the RPKI are accomplished via an architecture that empowers centralized authorities to *unilaterally* revoke any IP prefixes under their control. We propose mechanisms to improve the transparency of the RPKI, in order to mitigate the risk that it will be used for IP address takedowns. First, we present tools that detect and visualize changes to the RPKI that can potentially take down an IP prefix. We use our tools to identify errors and revocations in the production RPKI. Next, we propose modifications to the RPKI's architecture to (1) require any revocation of IP address space to receive *consent* from all impacted parties, and (2) detect when misbehaving authorities fail to obtain consent. We present a security analysis of our architecture, and estimate its overhead using data-driven analysis.

## 1. INTRODUCTION

The RPKI [38] is a new infrastructure for securing interdomain routing with BGP. BGP has traditionally operated as a "default-accept" architecture: any autonomous system (AS) can originate a BGP routing announcement (*i.e.*, claim to be the destination for) for any IP prefix, and other ASes will accept the BGP announcement by default. This has made BGP vulnerable to a number of routing attacks, the most common [19,21,41,50,51,56] and devastating [10,14,26,31] of which are prefix- and subprefix hijacks. In a prefix hijack, a hijacking AS originates BGP routes for IP prefixes that were not allocated to it, causing the traffic for those prefixes to be intercepted by the hijacker's AS.

The RPKI prevents these attacks by providing a trusted mapping from allocated IP prefixes to ASes authorized to originate them in BGP. To do this, the RPKI establishes a top-down hierarchy of *authorities*, rooted at the Regional Internet Registries (RIRs), that allocate and suballocate IP address space, as well as authorize its use in BGP by individual origin ASes; routers use the RPKI to distinguish between hijacked BGP routes and routes originated by a legitimate AS. The RPKI also turns out to be surprisingly effective against attacks it was not designed to prevent [26]; there is evidence [39] that more advanced secure routing solutions [32,37] provide limited benefits over what is already provided by the RPKI. The RPKI requires neither changes to BGP nor online cryptographic computations during routing. It is currently being rolled out by RIRs and adopted by individual network operators, and authorizes about 20,000 BGP routes as of January 2014 (Section 2.1).

**From default-accept to default-deny.** However, the security benefits of the RPKI are accompanied by a drastic shift from BGP's traditional "default accept" policies, to a new "default deny" mode: to prevent (sub)prefix hijacks, routers should only accept routes authorized by the RPKI, and discard all other routes by default (Section 3). Meanwhile, the RPKI's hierarchical architecture empowers centralized authorities to *unilaterally* revoke authorization (or *take down*) IP prefixes under their control. This shift has lead to concerns [7,17,43,44,61] that the RPKI creates powerful authorities with the technical means for taking down IP prefixes, and could be exploited by abusive authorities or governments to settle disputes or block undesirable content. This is a stark departure from the status quo, where these authorities (RIRs, National/Local Internet Registries, *etc.*) had the power to allocate IP address space, but not to impact routing to space that has been allocated [27,54].

**Transparency.** In light of the risk of takedowns, it would be useful to have mechanisms that can detect when RPKI authorities misbehave; this could create social (and possibly legal) pressure to motivate misbehaving authorities to fall in line. However, the architecture of the RPKI also makes it difficult to distinguish between revocations due to disputes or censorship, and those due to business arrangements that were agreed upon by all impacted parties (Section 3).

**Our contributions.** As RPKI deployment continues to gain traction, we present an investigation of the risk of RPKI takedowns, and propose technical solutions that mitigate this risk by improving the transparency of the RPKI. Our contributions are:

**1. Security audit (Section 3).** We untangle the often-unintuitive interactions between the RPKI and BGP, and explain why it is *not* always the case that a revocation in the RPKI can take down an IP prefix in BGP.

**2. Tools, measurement & modeling (Section 4).** We start by working within the current RPKI specifications, and


*SIGCOMM'14*, August 17–22, 2014, Chicago, IL, USA.

ACM 978-1-4503-2836-4/14/08 ...$15.00. http://dx.doi.org/10.1145/2619239.2626293.

build two tools that can increase its transparency by detecting and reacting to RPKI problems. Our *detector*, that identifies changes to the RPKI that can takedown IP prefixes, and a *visualizer*, that visualizes the results. We test our tools on the production RPKI and identify real-life errors and revocations (Sections 3,4.1). Since RPKI deployment is still in its infancy, we also develop models of a future full-deployment of the RPKI, based on routing data and RIR information (Section 5.7).

**3. Changes to the specifications (Section 5).** The current RPKI specifications still place power squarely in the hands of authorities. To remedy this, we propose modest modifications to the architecture of the RPKI. Our design ensures that once a route is authorized by the RPKI, it switches from "default-deny" to "default-accept"; that is, authorities that revoke IP address space must first obtain *consent* from all entities holding allocations (and suballocations) of that space. Our design also allow parties viewing RPKI information from different vantage points to detect when (1) their views are not *consistent*, and (2) authorities fail to properly obtain consent. We prove the security properties of our design. Because our design sometimes requires many entities to provide consent, we also estimate its extra overhead using data-driven analysis (Section 5.7).

## 2. RPKI PRIMER

We overview the RPKI's certificate hierarchy, explain how RPKI information determines route validity, and explain how the RPKI can limit threats to BGP.

### 2.1 The hierarchical structure of the RPKI.

The RPKI arranges authorities in a strict hierarchy that mirrors the IP address allocation hierarchy.[1] An authority may issue cryptographic objects for IP addresses that are *covered* by its own IP addresses. (An IP prefix $P$ *covers* prefix $\pi$ if $\pi$ is a proper subset of the address space in $P$ (*e.g.,* 63.160.0.0/12 covers 63.160.1.0/24) or if $P = \pi$. Also, prefix 63.160.0.0/12 has *length* 12.) Each authority has a *resource certificate (RC)*, a certificate that contains its cryptographic public key and its set of allocated IP addresses [40]. An authority may issue signed objects for IP addresses covered by its allocation, specifically: (1) an RC that suballocates a subset of its addresses to another authority, or (2) a *route origin authorization (ROA)*, that authorizes a specified AS to originate a set of prefixes, and its subprefixes up to a specified length called maxLength, in BGP [38]. ROAs protect BGP from routing attacks (Section 2.2).

**Model (Figure 1).** We show how an RIR (ARIN) uses its RC to suballocate a prefix to another authority (Sprint), which then issues RCs suballocating this prefix to other authorities (ETB S.A. ESP., Continental Broadband). (This is an excerpt of one of our models of the fully-deployed RPKI; see Section 5.7.) We say Sprint is the *parent* of Continental Broadband, and extend this to child, ancestor, *etc.*, in the obvious way. Sprint issues two ROAs that authorize a specified prefix and its subprefixes up to maxLength 24; the remaining ROAs shown authorize only a single prefix.

**Status of the RPKI (Table 2).** As of January 13, 2014, the production RPKI contains ROAs for about 20K

[1]The roots of the RPKI are the five RIRs (Table 2); in the future, IANA could be a single root [38, Section 2.4].

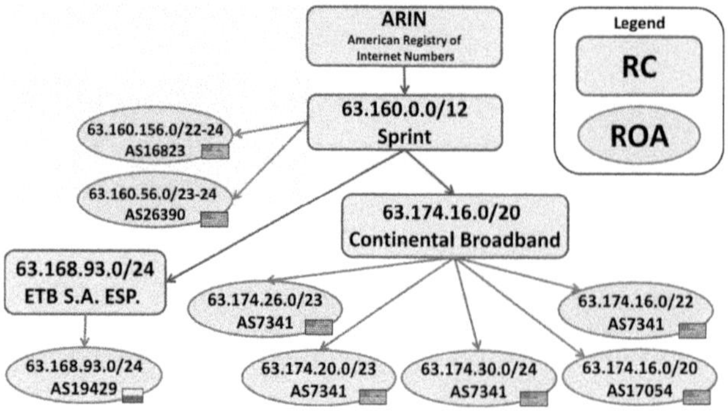


**Figure 1: Excerpt of a model RPKI**

prefix-to-origin-AS pairs. (About 488K prefixes were announced in BGP that day.) The RPKI's structure (Table 2) is slightly different than our models. At depth 0, there are trust anchors for each RIR (*e.g.,* ARIN). The trust anchors are long-lived certificates, who issue a handful of shorter-lived intermediate RCs to the RIRs (depth 1); our models and Figure 1 omit intermediate RCs. Intermediate RCs issue leaf RCs to organizations (*e.g.,* Sprint) who then issue ROAs. ARIN has an extra layer of intermediate RCs. RCs for suballocations like Continental Broadband and ETB in Figure 1 are absent; their ROAs could just be issued by Sprint. ROAs usually contain one AS and many prefixes (*e.g.,* all prefixes for AS 7341 could be issued in one ROA).

**Publication points.** The RPKI was designed to require minimal changes to BGP, and therefore operates entirely out-of-band. RPKI objects are stored in public repositories. Each RC has its own *publication point* (*i.e.,* directory in a file system) where it publishes every object it issued. Each RC also signs a *manifest* that logs the hash of every object present in its publication point. *Relying parties* download RPKI objects from publication points to their *local caches*, validate the objects, push information to their routers, and use it to inform routing decisions in BGP.

### 2.2 How the RPKI prevents threats to BGP.

BGP is especially vulnerable to subprefix hijacks because of longest-prefix-match routing: when a router learns BGP routes for a prefix and its subprefix, it always prefers the subprefix route. Subprefix hijackers exploit this by originating routes for subprefixes of a victim's prefix. This leads to a natural desideratum for the RPKI: a subprefix hijacker's route should be always be invalid when the legitimate route has a matching valid ROA.

**Origin authentication.** To achieve this desideratum, a relying party uses the RPKI for *origin authentication* as follows. For our purposes, a BGP *route* is an IP prefix $\pi$ and an origin AS $a$. Once a relying party has "access to a local cache of the complete set of valid ROAs" [29, Sec. 2], these valid ROAs are used to classify each route $(\pi, a)$ learned in BGP into one of three *route validation states* [29,42]:

- *Valid:* There is a valid *matching ROA*. A matching ROA has (1) a matching origin AS $a$, and (2) a prefix $P$ that covers prefix $\pi$, and (3) the specified maxLength no shorter than the length of $\pi$.
- *Unknown:* There is no valid *covering ROA*. A covering ROA is any ROA for a prefix that covers $\pi$.
- *Invalid:* The route is neither unknown or valid.

The rules above elegantly achieve the desideratum: if a le-

| Depth | 1 | 2 | 3 | 4 |
|---|---|---|---|---|
| RIPE | 4 RC | 1909 RC | 1512 ROA | |
| LACNIC | 4 RC | 282 RC | 282 ROA | |
| ARIN | 1 RC | 1 RC | 99 RC | 151 ROA |
| APNIC from IANA | 1 RC | 450 RC | 58 ROA | |
| AfriNIC | 1 RC | 27 RC | 48 ROA | |

**Table 2: Valid ROAs and RCs at each depth of the production RPKI on January 13, 2014.**

gitimate route in BGP has a matching valid ROA in the RPKI, a subprefix hijacker's route will always be "invalid" (because it is "covered" by the valid ROA). To stop subprefix hijacks, relying parties should *drop invalid routes*, *i.e.*, not select routes in BGP that are "invalid" per the RPKI.

# 3. AUDIT: THE RISK OF RPKI TAKEDOWNS

We explore RPKI threats that take down IP prefixes by causing legitimate BGP routes to be misclassified as "invalid".

**A trace of the production RPKI.** To aid our exposition, this section discusses real-life events that our tools detected in the production RPKI (described in Section 4). Events were observed in a trace we collected from 2013/10/23–2014/01/13. Each day, we used rcynic [2] to pull the state of the production RPKI to an empty local folder, and to cryptographically validate the result. The trace excludes a few days where our collector went down, and a few days where rcynic failed to properly sync to the repository (reporting <rsync_transfer_failed kind="bad">).

## 3.1 Tradeoff: BGP threats vs RPKI threats.

Now that we have understood how threats to BGP influenced the design of the RPKI, we look at how threats to the RPKI can impact routing with BGP. Specifically, to prevent subprefix hijacks on BGP, every route covered by ROA in the RPKI is classified as "invalid" *by default*, unless it has a matching valid ROA of its own. The RPKI is therefore a "default-deny" architecture,[2] and this comes with some risks; if a legitimate BGP route is wrongly classified as "invalid" by the RPKI, a relying party that *drops invalid routes* will lose connectivity to that route in BGP. As such, there have been concerns [7, 17, 43, 44, 61] that the RPKI creates a new technical means for IP-prefix takedowns.

Because moving to a default-deny regime is a drastic change for the routing infrastructure, relying parties are explicitly entitled to use their own "local policies" to decide what to do with "invalid" routes [29]. *Drop invalid routes* is the strictest local policy, and comes with the risk that threats to the RPKI can take down legitimate BGP routes. An more lenient policy suggested in RFC6483 [29] is to *depref "invalid" routes*: for a given prefix, a router should prefer "valid" routes over "invalid" routes. This policy implies that a router still selects an "invalid" route when there is no "valid" route for the *exact same* IP prefix. Thus, the router may still be able to reach routes that are wrongly classified as "invalid" as a result of problems with the RPKI. (However, availability of a route at one router can depend strongly on local policy used at other routers. For example, a router that uses the lenient *depref invalid* policy can lose connectivity to an "invalid" route if all its neighboring routers use the strict *drop invalid* policy.) On the other hand, this policy does *not* prevent subprefix hijacks [12, Section 5].

[2]The idea that the RPKI is a default-deny architecture is unintuitive, given the "unknown" route validity state. However, a BGP route without a matching valid ROA is "unknown" only when there is *no covering ROA*; see Section 2.2.

| policy | routing attack | RPKI manipulation |
|---|---|---|
| drop invalid | stops (sub)prefix hijacks | prefix goes offline |
| depref invalid | subprefix hijacks possible | prefix may stay online |

**Table 3: Impact of different local policies.**

Table 3 summarizes this difficult tradeoff; the local policy that is best at protecting against attacks on BGP is worst at protecting against problems with RPKI. While it is too early to tell what local policies will be adopted in the long run, better assurances about the trustworthiness of RPKI information are needed before relying parties can start enjoying the RPKI's full potential for protecting BGP from attack. Sections 4-5 focus on improving these assurances.

**A note on granularity.** While ROAs can have arbitrary prefix lengths, the longest IPv4 prefix length that is universally accepted by BGP routers is a /24. (Routers usually ignore longer prefixes to avoid bloating their routing tables.) Thus, our discussion on the RPKI's impact on IP prefix reachability should be thought of as having the granularity of a /24 (or shorter) IPv4 prefix, *i.e.*, no fewer than 256 IPv4 addresses; the RPKI, therefore, can be used for significantly coarser level of blocking than *e.g.*, the DNS [52, 53].

## 3.2 New threats created by the RPKI.

What threats to the RPKI can cause a legitimate BGP route to be classified as "invalid"? We consider two threat models: threats created by RPKI authorities themselves, and threats to the communication path between relying parties and the public RPKI repositories.

### 3.2.1 Threats created by RPKI authorities.

Because relying parties download RPKI objects from publication points that are *controlled by their issuer* [38, Section 8], the issuer can manipulate the contents of its publication points in any way it likes. There are two ways an issuer can cause a legitimate BGP route to be classified as "invalid":

**1. Adding a ROA.** If a new ROA added to the RPKI covers a legitimate BGP route without its own matching ROA, the legitimate BGP route will be wrongly classified as "invalid". Consider, for example, this incident:

■ **Case Study 1: ROA misconfiguration.** On December 13, a new ROA was added to the production RPKI rooted at ARIN, authorizing prefix 173.251.0.0/17 with maxlength 24 to AS 6128. This caused a large portion of the address space to downgrade from "unknown" to "invalid", including several legitimate /24 routes announced in BGP that did not have matching ROAs (AS 53725 originating 173.251.91.0/24, AS 13599 originating 173.251.54.0/24).

**2. Whacking a ROA.** Alternatively, missing information can cause the RPKI to misclassify a legitimate BGP route as "invalid". To see how, we first distinguish between route validity and RPKI object validity. An RPKI object (*i.e.*, an RC, ROA, *etc.*) is valid if it has a valid signature, is not malformed or corrupted, *etc.* Meanwhile, the validity of a route depends *exclusively* on the set of valid ROAs in a relying party's local cache. Thus, any action that prevents the delivery of a ROA object to a relying party has exactly the same effect — the corresponding BGP route becomes (a) "invalid" if the local cache contains some other valid covering ROA, or (b) "unknown" if there is no valid covering ROA. We therefore just say that a ROA is *whacked* whenever a relying party fails to receive the valid ROA object. There are many ways an authority can whack a descendant ROA:[3]

**a. Revoking.** An issuer can always revoke any object it issues using its certificate revocation list (CRL).

**b. Deleting or corrupting.** An authority can also delete or corrupt any object in its publication point. If the authority logs appropriate change in its manifest, relying parties will accept the change without complaint. For example:

■ **Case Study 2: Deleted ROA.** On December 19, 2013, a ROA for (79.139.96.0/24, AS 51813), for a network in Russia, was deleted from the production RPKI. Meanwhile, since at least November 21, the RPKI also had a covering ROA mapping 79.139.96.0/19-20 to another Russian ISP, AS 43782. (This is a covering ROA because the /19 prefix covers the /24 prefix.) The covering ROA caused the route corresponding to the whacked ROA to downgrade from valid to invalid (per Section 2.2). Both the whacked ROA and covering ROA were issued by the same RC.

**c. Overwriting.** Each RPKI object is identified by a uniform resource identifier (URI), and an authority may overwrite any RC it issued, so that modified objects can have persistent URIs (thus simplifying operations like certificate renewal and key rollover [30]). An authority can thus overwrite an RPKI object with one for a different set of IP addresses (or a different key, *etc.*); children of the overwritten RC can be whacked as a result, because they are no longer covered by the RC (or signed by the wrong key, *etc.*):

■ **Case Study 3: Overwritten parent RC.** On January 5, 2014, a ROA for (196.6.174.0/23, AS 37688) for a backbone connectivity network in Nigeria was whacked because its parent RC was overwritten. The incident occurred as follows: On January 4, the ROA's parent RC was allocated prefix 196.6.174.0/23. On January 5, the RC was overwritten with an RC with the same key but for an IPv6 prefix 2c0f:f668::/32. The ROA in question (which remained in the publication point) became invalid, because it was no longer covered by its parent. Interestingly, the RC had no valid descendants until January 6, when it issued ROAs covered by the IPv6 prefix to a different AS (AS 37600, in Mauritius).

Moreover, if an RC gets whacked, all its descendent objects also get whacked. Our earlier work [18] showed how an authority can whack distant descendant ROAs in a targeted manner that causes no collateral damage to other ROAs.

### 3.2.2 Threats that disrupt RPKI object delivery.

A third party, who disrupts the communication path from an RPKI repository to a relying party, can whack a ROA just by corrupting a single bit in the ROA. (This is because the ROA would fail cryptographic validation.) Fortunately, however, the RPKI has a mechanism for detecting lost/corrupted information:

**Manifests.** To provide assurance that no objects have been deleted from a publication point, a collision-resistant hash of the contents of every file issued by an RC is listed in a single file called a *manifest* [28, Section 2.1], which is digitally signed by the RC and stored at its publication point. The manifest must be updated whenever an RC issues, modifies, or revokes an object it issued. To prevent replay attacks and the propagation of stale information, manifests are short-lived; they usually expire and are renewed daily.

Of course, a third party can always corrupt or disrupt the delivery of the manifest itself. Consider the following:

■ **Case Study 4: Stale LACNIC manifests.** On December 20, 2013, an error at LACNIC whacked 4217 prefix-to-origin-AS pairs. The day before the incident, the RPKI rooted at LACNIC looked very similar to what is shown in Table 2. On December 20, the manifests and CRLs issued by all four of LACNIC's intermediate RCs (at depth 2) in our local cache all expired. The relying party software [2] raised an alarm and rejected all four of the intermediate RCs as invalid. All objects in subtree rooted at LACNIC became invalid; thus, there were no valid ROAs for any address space allocated by LACNIC, and BGP routes corresponding to LACNIC ROAs downgraded from "valid" to "unknown".

## 3.3 Transparency is (sometimes) difficult.

To mitigate risks created by the RPKI, a relying party should be able to detect when a problem with the RPKI has caused BGP route to be wrongly classified as "invalid". Fortunately, third-party attacks that disrupt object delivery are completely transparent – a relying party can always check that it received all the objects in a manifest, and that the manifest was valid and current. If not, relying parties should raise a *missing-information alarm*; RFC6486 [9, Sect 6.5] states that relying parties should react to such alarms at their own discretion.[4] Meanwhile, incidents where misconfigured or compromised RPKI authorities wrongly add or whack ROA are much less transparent; if the authority ensures that its manifest is consistent with the objects in its publication point, relying parties will not raise alarms.

**Alarms.** While the RPKI specifications do not focus on alarms, we think that they are crucial. While alarms alone cannot resolve problems, they do indicate that problems are present, and can trigger mitigation mechanisms. During a missing-information alarm, a relying party might try to reconnect the repository, search for missing objects in its local cache or at other relying parties, or search for unusual routing activity in the IP address space covered in the RC whose manifest triggered the alarm. Today, BGP misconfigurations are resolved by humans picking up the phone; RPKI alarms similarly provide guidance on when picking up the phone may be necessary. Indeed, in Section 5, alarms will be our primary tool for increasing transparency.

There is another important threat to transparency:

**Mirror world attacks.** In a mirror world attack, an (adversarial) RPKI authority presents one view of the RPKI to some relying parties, and a different view to others. (For example, the subject of an RC is shown a view containing the RC, but other relying parties are shown a view that omits the RC.) The current RPKI standard contains no mechanisms to prevent this attack. Our proposal in Section 5 builds in protections against mirror-world attacks.

## 4. TOOLS TO IMPROVE TRANSPARENCY

We now develop tools that can improve the trustworthiness of RPKI data, without requiring any modifications to the RPKI itself. Our *detector* tool detects when a change

[3]To be sure that the BGP route corresponding to the whacked ROA becomes "invalid", an authority can just issue a covering ROA, as in Case Study 2.

[4]The relying party software we used [2] in Case Study 4 rejected the stale manifest. Other policies are possible.

to the RPKI causes a route to *downgrade* from "valid" to "invalid/unknown", (or from "unknown" to "invalid"), and our *visualizer* visualizes these downgrades. We released the source for all our tools,[5] so they can be incorporated into professionally-maintained systems like [35, 46, 57].

## 4.1 A tool for detecting downgrades.

One way to detect inconsistencies between BGP and the RPKI is to take a BGP feed [3, 5], run the RPKI validation algorithm in Section 2.2 on each BGP route, and identify BGP routes that the RPKI classifies as "invalid"; indeed, this is done in [35, 46, 57]. Our goal, however, is to detect when a *change* to the RPKI (*i.e.*, an added or whacked ROA) causes a change in the validity status of a route; it can therefore act as alert system for potentially-harmful changes to the RPKI. Moreover, we do not want our tool to be limited to a view of BGP provided by a specific BGP feed; instead, our detector considers the space of *all* possible routes $(\pi, a)$, where $\pi$ is a prefix and $a$ is an origin AS, regardless of whether or not a particular route is visible to a particular BGP collector.

**Challenges.** The relationship between a single ROA and the validity of BGP routes is complex and dependent on the presence of other ROAs in the system. For example, a ROA giving an AS $a$ prefix $\pi$ of length 17 up to maxlength 22 actually makes $2^{(23-17)} - 1 = 63$ possible prefixes originated by AS $a$ in BGP become "valid". If the ROA gets whacked, BGP routes for these prefixes do not necessarily become "invalid": some may become "unknown" (if there is no covering ROA), while others may remain valid (if there is another ROA for AS $a$ and a super- or subprefix of $\pi$). Moreover, when such a ROA appears, it may downgrade "unknown" routes to "invalid" for any subprefix of $\pi$ of any length, depending on the other ROAs already in the RPKI.

**Data structures.** Naturally, representing the space of all possible routes $(\pi, a)$ requires an efficient data structure. Ours is based on the following observations. Consider the complete binary tree of all IP prefixes, with one IP address per leaf, and all possible prefixes as internal nodes. A ROA for prefix $\pi$, `maxLength` $m$, and origin AS $a$ makes a subtree of this tree "valid" for AS $a$ only; this subtree is rooted at $\pi$ and goes down to depth $m$. This ROA also makes "known" (*i.e.*, the complement of "unknown"), for other ASes, the subtree rooted at $\pi$ and going down to the bottom.

We call these subtrees *triangles* and we represent them using *interval trees*. A triangle has one interval per prefix length. The granularity of each interval depends on the prefix length; intervals at length $i$ have endpoints that are integer multiples of $2^{32-i}$. For each prefix length, the total number of intervals kept is bounded by the number of prefixes in ROAs in the RPKI. We can use interval trees to efficiently perform unions, intersections, and complements of sets of triangles. This gives us a "prefix-validity" data structure that stores the validity states for *all* possible routes, based on the ROAs in the RPKI; it can be created in time $O(n \log n)$ given ROAs for $n$ (prefix, AS, maxlength)-tuples.

Our tool uses this data structure to compare a current RPKI state $S_{\text{cur}}$ and a previous state $S_{\text{prev}}$. It processes each state once and creates its prefix-validity data structure. It then evaluates the impact of every single change from $S_{\text{prev}}$ to $S_{\text{cur}}$ in the context of other changes that occurred, by going through each (prefix, AS, maxlength)-tuple that appears or disappears from the RPKI (in the transition from$S_{\text{prev}}$ to $S_{\text{cur}}$), by extracting relevant information from the prefix-validity data structures.

[5] `https://github.com/BUSEC/RPKI_Downgrade_Detector`

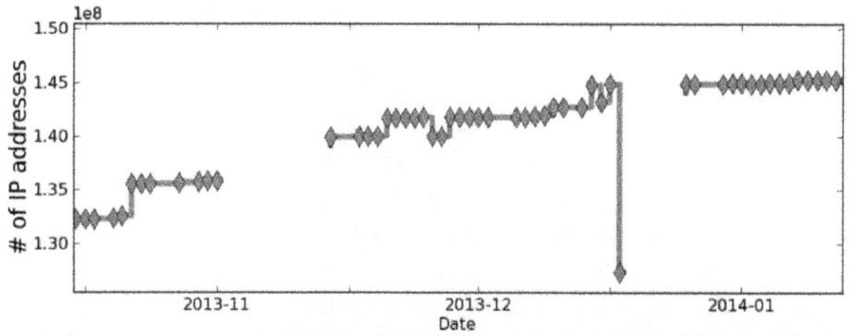


**Figure 4: # of invalid IP addresses over time.**

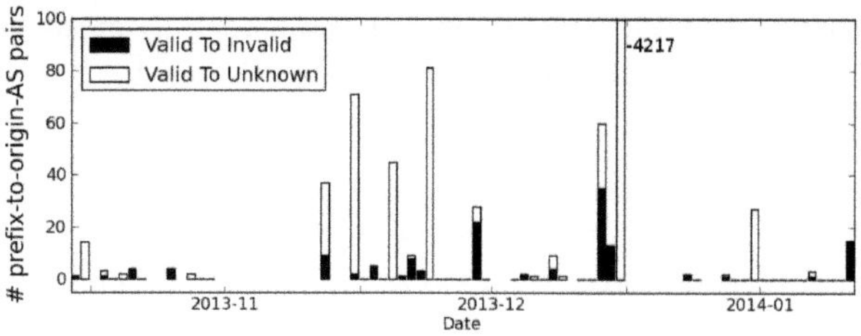


**Figure 5: Downgrades due to whacked ROAs.**

**Utilities for RPKI browsing.** Our detector identified all the events in our case studies, and we analyzed each using custom-built python utilities (available upon request) that parse RPKI objects and search RPKI trees based on URI, public key, prefix, and AS number fields.

We also used our detector to check for downgrades between consecutive entries in our trace of the production RPKI:

**Downgrades due to added ROAs (Figure 4).** Two things happen whenever a ROA is added to the RPKI: (1) routes for the AS authorized in the ROA become "valid", and (2) the IP address space covered by the ROA transitions to the default-deny state, *i.e.*, all the "unknown" address space it covers downgrades to "invalid", as in Case Study 1. Figure 4 shows the latter transition over the course of our trace. We show the number of IP addresses that are "invalid" for at least one AS over time, marking each entry in our trace with a diamond. The drop in the number of "invalid" addresses on December 20 was due to the the stale LACNIC manifests described in Case Study 4.

**Downgrades due to whacked ROAs (Figure 5).** We show the number of $(\pi, a)$ pairs that downgraded from "valid" to "invalid", and from "valid" to "unknown", for each consecutive entry in our trace that contained a successful pull of the RPKI. We show a value of zero if no downgrades occurred at some date, and a gap if our trace was missing an entry. To put these results in perspective, in January 2014, there were about 20,000 prefix-origin AS pairs authorized by ROAs in the RPKI. Most of the incidents in Figure 5 correspond to the whacking of a single ROA containing multiple prefixes; in many incidents, a new ROA appeared authorizing the prefix(es) in the whacked ROA to some other AS. Case Study 4 explains the dramatic event on December 20.

## 4.2 A tool for visualizing downgrades.

We present a new visualization of the effects of a single ROA on the validity states of multiple BGP routes, based on a modification of the Sierpiński triangle [59]. Our visualization takes in information from our detector and from a specific BGP feed [3, 5], and presents a binary tree that vi-

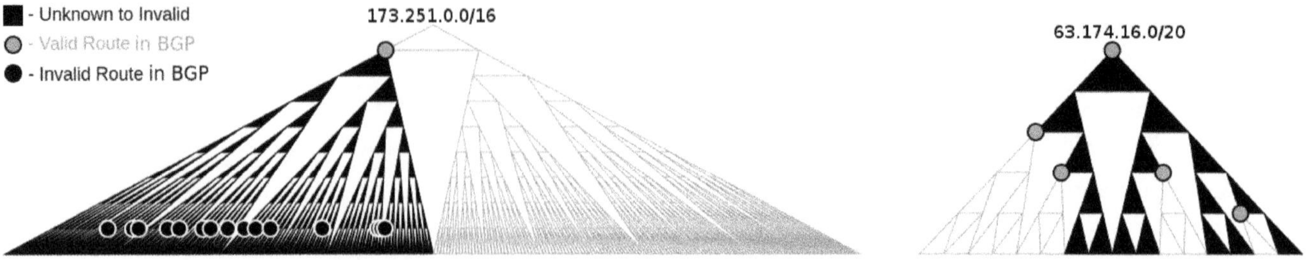


**Figure 6: (l) Visualization of downgrades in Case Study 1. (r) Downgrades when the ROA (63.174.16.0/20, AS 17054) is added to the RPKI in Figure 1.**

sualizes the triangles described above, as well as the validity state of specific routes announced in BGP.

**Figure 6(l)** We visualize Case Study 1. The tool outputs the prefix tree rooted at 173.251.0.0/16, and shows how the triangle rooted at 173.251.0.0/17 transitions from unknown to invalid. The valid route for prefix 173.251.0.0/17 is shown with a grey circle. The added ROA also caused a number of /24 routes in the BGP feed to transition to the "invalid" state; we show these with black circles.

**Figure 6(r).** Consider the prefixes covered by Continental Broadband in Figure 1, and suppose $S_{\text{prev}}$ has the all ROAs issued by Continental Broadband *except* the covering ROA for 63.174.16.0/20, and that the covering ROA is added in $S_{\text{cur}}$. We visualize downgrades from "unknown" to "invalid" in the transition from $S_{\text{prev}}$ to $S_{\text{cur}}$. Routes uncovered by the four ROAs in $S_{\text{prev}}$ are impacted during the transition; routes covered by the four ROAs in $S_{\text{prev}}$ were *already* "invalid" in $S_{\text{prev}}$, and do not appear as downgrades.

# 5. CHANGES TO RPKI SPECIFICATIONS

While our detector can alarm when changes to the RPKI cause routes in BGP to downgrade to "invalid", the RPKI still lacks mechanisms that can detect when such changes are legitimate, or when they result from abuse. Because the purpose of the RPKI is to secure routing, not to provide a new technical means for RPKI authorities to take-down IP address space, we now propose modifications to the RPKI specifications to restore the balance of power between RPKI authorities and the subjects of the RCs they issue. We start with our design goals (Section 5.1), overview our design (Section 5.2), and then discuss its details (Sections 5.3-5.4). We then justify our design by presenting its exact security guarantees (Section 5.5), explain why alternative designs would not suffice to provide these guarantees (Section 5.6), and estimate its overhead via data-driven analysis (Section 5.7). This paper overviews our proposal; details and security proofs are in our technical report.

## 5.1 Design goals.

The following goals have guided our design.

**Transparency through alarms.** Our overarching goal is to detect RPKI abuse. We want *provable* guarantees that relying parties will raise alarms when something goes wrong; as discussed in Section 3.3, alarms act as a trigger for relying parties to investigate and react to problems with the RPKI. As in the current RPKI specifications, we suppose that relying parties use their own local policies to decide how to resolve alarms [9, Section 6]; alarms could indicate that certain IP prefixes should be monitored for routing anomalies, or that a relying party should revert to an older ("stale") set of RPKI objects that did not raise alarms.

The problem of how relying parties should propagate and react to alarms is outside the scope of this paper. First, technical means alone will not able to resolve a business dispute that results a unilateral revocation of IP address space in the RPKI; was the issuer of the space at fault, or was it the holder of the address space? Moreover, even requiring different relying parties to agree on a consistent (let alone, correct) course of action to resolve an alarm requires solving the famously-difficult Byzantine agreement problem. We therefore assume that alarms will be resolved by out-of-band mechanisms (phone calls between network operators, social or even legal pressure), just like BGP misconfigurations are resolved today. Nevertheless, to discourage relying parties from raising false alarms, and to facilitate dispute resolution, our secondary goal is *accountability*; allowing relying parties to *provably* demonstrate, in as many situations as possible, (a) why they raised an alarm and (b) who is to blame.

**Consent from subjects of RCs.** Traditionally, routing has lacked a technical means for revoking IP address space; the RPKI changes this by allowing authorities to *unilaterally* revoke IP address space issued to their descendants. Our goal is to correct this power imbalance, so we require subjects of RCs to *consent* to RPKI modifications that can affect their address space. If consent is refused, this indicates that there is a dispute between the subject of the RC and its issuer, and relying parties should raise an alarm. During emergencies (disputes, lost/stolen keys) when it is impossible to obtain consent from the subject of the RC, the issuer can just unilaterally revoke the RC; these actions will be visible to relying parties, who will raise alarms and investigate the situation out-of-band. Theorem 5.1 formally states how we achieve this goal, and Section 5.7 analyzes the overhead of our consent mechanism.

**Consistency for relying parties.** We want different relying parties to see consistent views of the RPKI. Our goal is to prevent mirror-world attacks (Section 3.3) by allowing relying parties to compare their local views of the RPKI, and to raise an alarm whenever their views are inconsistent. Theorem 5.2 and 5.3 formally state this goal.

**Practicality.** Today, the RPKI specifications are still evolving [24, 33], since only a few authorities operate repositories (the five RIRs), and relying parties validate objects using a few evolving software packages like [2]. If our design is to be incorporated in the RPKI specifications, we need to achieve our goals with minimal changes to the current RPKI specifications. Thus, we cannot require synchronization between RPKI repositories or relying parties, and must retain most of the structure of the RPKI. Section 5.7 is a data-driven analysis of the practicality of our design.

## 5.2 Design overview.

To achieve our goals, we propose adding the following new elements to the RPKI. Some seem intuitively necessary; others may be less obvious, but we justify them in Section 5.6.

**Consent through `.dead` objects (Section 5.3.1).** Any action that *removes resources* (IP prefixes) or *invalidates* an RC requires the *consent* of the RC and all its impacted descendant RCs. To indicate its consent to having some/all of its resources taken away, an RC will sign a `.dead` object. The authority can then revoke (or remove resources from) the child by publishing the `.dead` object in its publication point and deleting (or overwriting) the child RC.[6] To simplify the exposition, we will not discuss consent from ROAs; instead we just suppose than any ROA that wishes to be entitled to consent is issued its own covering RC.[7]

**Consistency through manifests (Section 5.3.2).** In a default-deny architecture like the RPKI, a relying party must know that it has *all* the objects issued by an authority; otherwise, it might misclassify a legitimate BGP route as invalid because its ROA was missing. Fortunately, the RPKI's manifests contains the hash of every object the authority issues, and thus provide *positive attestation* to the authority's issued objects [9]. We therefore make manifests central to our design. Relying parties use them to check the consistency of their local caches, because if the manifests are equal, then (by the collision-resistance of the cryptographic hash) so are all the objects the authority issued. Because we cannot require relying parties to synchronize their interactions with the RPKI, we need to make sure they can still check consistency even if they are out of sync. To do this, we enable relying parties to be able to reconstruct all intermediate state of each publication point; to do this, we (1) maintain some extra state at each publication point, and (2) hash-chain manifests, so that each manifest contains the hash of the previous manifest.

**Strict checks to raise alarms (Section 5.4).** We design validation procedures that, in addition to validating RPKI objects, is also responsible for raising alarms. The procedure has two parts: a local consistency check (done by a single relying party to check consent) and a global consistency check (done by a pair of relying parties to check consistency). In a departure from current RPKI practice, where manifests play a secondary role, our local consistency check treats the manifest as the main cryptographic object, and validates one publication point and one manifest update at a time. Meanwhile, our global consistency check has relying parties compare hashes of the manifests in their local caches.

[6]Per Section 3.2, adding a ROA can also cause routes to downgrade from "unknown" to "invalid". However, we do not handle this because there is no way to obtain consent from entities originating "unknown" routes, since they do not participate in the RPKI. (If they did, they would already have ROAs, and their routes would not be "unknown".)

[7] Actually, each ROA's parent issues an X.509 end-entity (EE) certificate for an ephemeral one-time-use key, which is used to sign the ROA message [38, Section 2.3]. The ROA and EE cert are stored in a single `.roa` file, so we have treated them as one object. But a ROA could instead consent via its EE cert, instead of asking for its own RC.

## 5.3 Procedures for RPKI authorities.

We now detail our new `.dead` objects, and our modifications to the RPKI's specification of manifests [9].

### 5.3.1 Consent via `.dead` objects

Suppose an RC $A$ wants to revoke or modify a valid child RC $B$. (RC $B$ is "modified" if it is overwritten by a new RC $B'$ at the same URI.) $A$ needs the *consent* of $B$ and all the RCs that descend from $B$ that are whacked by the revocation/modification. Consent comes in the form of a `.dead` object, signed each consenting RC.

Revoking $B$ requires a `.dead` object from all the descendants of $B$. Modifications that remove IP address space from $B$ need `.dead` objects from each descendant of $B$ that overlap with the removed space. No `.dead` objects are required when a modification has no impact on descendants of $B$ (*e.g.*, modifying the parent pointer of $B$, or increasing the set of IP prefixes or AS numbers it certifies). All other modifications to $B$ must be accomplished by issuing a fresh RC at a different URI. We estimate the number of entities that must be involved in issuing `.dead` objects in Section 5.7.

**Constructing a `.dead`.** `.dead` objects are constructed recursively as follows: Let $D$ be a descendant of $B$ that needs to consent. Before $D$ can sign its own `.dead` object, $D$ first collects `.dead` objects from each of its own descendants. $D$ then signs its own `.dead` object, that includes (1) the hash of the `.dead` object issued by each *child* of $D$, (2) the hash of $m_D$, the manifest issued by $D$ at the time $D$ signs its own `.dead` object, and (3) the hash of the RC of $D$. $D$ then provides its own `.dead` object and the `.dead` objects for all its descendants to its issuer $C$. At this point, $D$ should no longer issue new objects or update its manifest. At the end of this process, $A$ has received the `.dead` objects from $B$ and all relevant descendants of $B$. (This recursive collection of `.dead` objects protects $A$, and its descendants, from being falsely accused of revoking a descendant without consent.)

RC $A$ then simultaneously (a) deletes RC $B$, (b) puts all the `.dead` objects in the publication point of $A$, and (c) logs all the `.dead` objects in the updated manifest of $A$.

**Key rollover.** Any PKI needs a mechanism for refreshing cryptographic keys. Adapting the RPKI's key rollover mechanism to our design, while still preserving transparency and consistency, requires some care. Details are in our tech report. Importantly, key rollover only requires consent from the RC whose key was rolled.

### 5.3.2 Manifests as positive attestations

We modify manifests [9] by (a) adding information, and (b) changing the semantics by which they are interpreted.

**Normative manifests.** We make manifests normative: any objects not logged in the issuer's current manifest are treated as nonexistent by relying parties. Once manifests become normative, we can simplify other aspects of the RPKI:

**1. Only manifests may expire.** In the current RPKI, manifest are "updated" when their issuer overwrites them with a fresh manifest with a higher "manifestNumber" [9]; manifests are therefore short-lived objects — most expire and updated with fresh versions within 24 hours. In our design, if a manifest expires before it is updated, then all objects logged in the manifest become "stale", rather than "invalid"; "stale" indicates that up-to-date information is unavailable, but does *not* indicate that the objects logged in the expired manifest have explicitly been revoked. A stale manifest (or any object logged in a current manifest but not obtained by a relying party) raises a *missing-information alarm* at the relying party (Section 5.4). Thus, we no longer require expiration dates on ROAs and RCs: any RC/ROA not logged in the current manifest is automatically invalid. This also prevents an authority from issuing short-lived ROAs/RCs so it can circumvent the need to obtain consent.

**2. Manifests must log only valid objects.** Any issuer that logs an invalid object in its manifest (*e.g.,* an object pointing to the wrong parent, has a prefix that not covered by the issuer's RC, *etc.*) risks the ire of relying parties, who raise alarms per Section 5.4. (This is necessary for our consistency mechanisms to work properly; see Counterexample 2.) By ensuring that manifests only attest to what is valid, we no longer need CRLs to attest to what is invalid. In fact, RCs/ROAs need not even be signed: signature on a manifest suffices, because the manifest contains the collision-resistant hash of every valid object (as in [25]).

These changes may seem unorthodox, but we note that the RPKI is different from the usual PKI where relying parties obtain and validate objects one-by-one; instead, all objects in a publication point are downloaded *en masse*, so it suffices just to validate the manifest. All these changes can be implemented without any modification to the RPKI object formats by having relying parties ignore CRLs, expiration times/signatures on RCs and ROAs.

**Hash chaining.** Manifests are hash-chained: each new manifest includes the hash of the contents (excluding the signature) of the manifest it supersedes. A *horizontal chain* is a sequence of consecutively issued manifests, each superseding the next. For each manifest $m$, hash chaining defines successor and predecessor manifests of manifest $m$ in the obvious way. We also require every manifest to include the hash of the manifest containing its issuer's RC ("parent manifest"), so that we can definitively determine the resources allocated to an RC at the time it signed its manifest. Thus, a *vertical chain* is a sequence of manifests, each containing the hash of the manifest above it and the hash of an RC that signed the manifest below it.

**Reconstructing intermediate states.** To prevent mirror world and other attacks (*e.g.,* Counterexample 1 in Section 5.6), relying parties must be able to reconstruct states that could have been seen by other relying parties. Thus, issuers must also provide relying parties with "hints" to enable reconstruction, between two syncs to a publication point, of every intermediate manifest along the horizontal hash chain along with its corresponding publication point state. Our technical report details the small amount of extra information maintained at each publication point for this purpose.

## 5.4 Validation procedures for relying parties.

The validation procedures for relying parties have three purposes: (1) to determine the set of valid RPKI objects, (2) to raise alarms when something goes wrong, and (3) whenever possible, to hold authorities accountable for causing alarms by proving that they violated procedures in Section 5.3. Since manifests are central to these procedures, we say that a manifest has been *obtained* if the relying party can (a) download a manifest that is validly signed by its issuer, OR (b) reconstruct the manifest as element in the horizontal hash chain that terminates in a manifest that is validly signed by its issuer, per Section 5.3.2.

| alarm | description |
|---|---|
| missing-information | manifest is stale/missing OR object logged in manifest is missing |
| bad key rollover | incorrect key rollover procedure |
| invalid syntax | RC issued malformed object |
| child too broad | RC issued object it does not cover |
| unilateral revocation | RC deleted/modified object without `.dead` |
| global inconsistency | manifest failed global consistency check |

**Table 7: Alarms**

**Initial sync.** The initial connection to the repository is as in the current RPKI: objects are downloaded and validated. If a relying party cannot obtain the valid current manifest of an RC $R$, or any object logged in the manifest, it raises a *missing information alarm.*

**Local consistency check.** In the current design of the RPKI, updates to a relying party's local cache are performed all at once. We, instead, require incremental processing of updates: a relying party updates its local cache one publication point and one consecutive manifest along the horizontal hash chain at a time. Updates are only performed for manifests issued by valid RCs. Incremental updates allow us to avoid race conditions that can occur when authorities update their manifests in parallel; see Counterexample 2. New RCs are an exception to this rule: the entire subtree rooted at a new RC should be downloaded and validated immediately to allow new RCs to quickly issue new objects.

Relying parties can sync to publication points in any order and parallelize updates of publication points that are not in an ancestor-descendant relationship. When a relying party Alice obtains an updated state of a publication point, she reconstructs all the intermediate states of the publication point along the horizontal hash-chain. Alice then compares pairs of consecutive states to check that (a) all new or modified objects are valid, and (b) all deletions and overwrites received proper consent. If not, she issues one of the middle alarms in Table 7. In some cases, the alarm is *accountable*, which means that Alice can specifically identify the RPKI authority that misbehaved, and can provide objects that will convince others of the authority's misbehavior (Section 5.5). Details are in our tech report.

**Global consistency check.** To defeat mirror-world attacks, relying parties can confirm that other relying parties see the same RPKI objects. A trivial, but unwieldy, solution has relying parties check consistency by synchronizing and exchanging their entire local caches. Our solution dispenses with synchronization and requires the exchange of much less information. We ask only that one party (Alice) is no more than time $t_g$ ("global consistency window") ahead of the other (Bob).

Bob sends Alice the hash $h$ of the contents (excluding the signature) of latest manifest that he *obtained* for each publication point in his local cache. For every hash value $h$ received from Bob, Alice checks that $h \in H_A$, where $H_A$ is the set that contains the hash of each manifest that Alice obtained, going back for time $t_g$. The check fails if $h \notin H_A$, and Alice raises a *global-inconsistency alarm* implicating the manifest corresponding to $h$.

A pairwise interactive protocol is not actually required here; Bob can just post his hash values in a public location for any other relying party to use.

## 5.5 Security analysis.

We now discuss the security properties of our design. We

only state theorems here; proofs are in our tech report.

**Threat model.** We suppose that the relying parties named in Theorems 5.1-5.3 are honest; everyone else can be arbitrarily malicious, but cannot break cryptography (*e.g.*, forge digital signatures, find hash collisions, steal keys, *etc.*). We therefore operate in the standard threat model used in *e.g.*, [20,36], where trusted auditors (relying parties) audit the behavior of a centralized authority (the RPKI).

We use the following definition: for an RC $R$ and relying party Alice, let the *immediate successor* of $R$ be an RC that (a) overwrites $R$, or (b) supersedes $R$ after a key rollover, whichever happens first from Alice's point of view. Define the set of *successors* of $R$ inductively as the set containing $R$ and immediate successors for each of its elements.

**Valid remains valid.** The following theorem tells us that once an honest relying party Alice sees a valid object, the object will remain valid for Alice until the object consents to revocation (or Alice raises an alarm):

THEOREM 5.1. *Suppose an RC $R$ was valid for a relying party Alice at time $t_1$. Consider some time $t_2 > t_1$. Then at time $t_2$, at least one of the following is true:*

1. *a successor of $R$ is valid in the local cache of Alice and has all the resources of $R$;*
2. *a successor of $R$ is valid in the local cache of Alice, is missing some resources that $R$ had, and Alice observed `.dead` object(s) signed successors of $R$ consenting to the revocation(s) of those resources;*
3. *at or before time $t_2$, Alice saw a `.dead` object signed by a successor of $R$, consenting to its revocation;*
4. *at or before time $t_2$, Alice raised a unilateral revocation alarm in response to a deleted or overwritten object; the alarm included a successor of $R$ as a victim, and blamed an ancestor (or a successor of the ancestor) of the deleted or overwritten certificate as the perpetrator.*

**No mirror worlds.** We prove robustness to mirror world attacks. Relying parties can be sure that if they see a valid RC in a manifest, and use this manifest in the global consistency check, others who successfully check against them also saw the same valid object:

THEOREM 5.2. *Suppose the local cache of a relying party Bob contains a valid RC $R$ and a manifest $m$ that was issued by the parent of $R$. Suppose that $R$ is not marked as stale; thus, the version of $R$ in Bob's local cache is same as the one logged in $m$. Suppose another relying party Alice performs a global consistency check against Bob; Bob sends the hash of $m$ to Alice, and Alice looks for it in her set $H_A$ of hashed manifests. Suppose the global consistency check does not raise the global-inconsistency alarm for $m$. Then either*

1. *Alice raised an alarm with $R$ as the victim when performing the local consistency check on a manifest in $H_A$, or*
2. *at any time $t_2$ after the global consistency check, at least one condition in Theorem 5.1 holds for $R$ and Alice.*

**No mirror worlds in the past.** Because manifests are hash-chained, a successful global consistency check also implies that parties were consistent in the past. We state the theorem only informally here:

THEOREM 5.3 (INFORMAL). *Suppose neither Alice nor Bob raised alarms for $k$ manifest updates in a row. Then if Alice passes a global consistency check against Bob, then for every RC $R$ seen as valid by Bob in any of the past $k$ manifests, at least one of the conditions specified in Theorem 5.1 holds for $R$ and Alice.*

**Alarms & accountability.** Our theorems assume that relying parties Alice and/or Bob are *honest*, and ensure that honest relying parties raise alarms when their local caches are missing/contain objects that violate our specifications. But we cannot, in general, prevent *dishonest* relying parties from raising false alarms, because it is impossible to prevent someone from falsely claiming they are missing information. As such, our alarms come in two categories: *accountable* and *unaccountable*.

If Alice raises an accountable alarm, then she is certain that some RPKI authority misbehaved, she can identify this authority (the "perpetrator"), and she can prove her knowledge to others (even those who do not trust Alice) by publishing the relevant objects from her local cache. Assuming that cryptography is not broken, even a malicious Alice cannot create an accountable alarm that is false.

Alice raises an unaccountable alarm when she is missing information — when, from Alice's point of view, there is not enough information to distinguish between an attack by an RPKI authority, and a disruption to the delivery of RPKI objects (*e.g.*, by a third-party that tampers with the communication path). While Alice will still raise an alarm in these cases, the alarm will not be provable to others, and even Alice herself cannot tell who perpetrated the alarm. If the missing information is found, then the alarm will either be resolved or become accountable.

To ensure that as many alarms as possible are accountable, we require authorities to commit (by means of hash values) to the context that is necessary to determine the validity of objects. For example, the validity of a `.dead` depends on its signer's manifest; thus, a `.dead` includes the hash of its signer's manifest (Section 5.3.1). Similarly, the validity of manifest $m$ depends on the validity of the manifest that logs the RC that issued $m$; thus, $m$ includes the hash of its parent's manifest (Section 5.3.2). An alarm is accountable if these objects are present in Alice's local cache, and unaccountable if they are missing. A missing information alarm is always unaccountable. Our tech report details when other alarms are accountable.

## 5.6 On the necessity of our modifications.

We give intuition for our design via two examples.

**Counterexample 1: Not checking intermediate state.** Suppose relying parties did not verify every consecutive manifest update. An authority $X$ could then launch a mirror world attack violating Theorems 5.2 and 5.3:

At time $t_1$, $X$ issues an RC $Y$; at time $t_2$, $X$ replaces $Y$ with a new valid RC $Y'$ that contains an additional IP prefix; and continues swapping between $Y$ (at odd-numbered times), and $Y'$ (at even-number times). Alice syncs to $X$'s publication point at odd-numbered times, and sees only $Y$; Bob syncs at even-numbered times and sees RC $Y'$. But, since Alice does not check full intermediate states (only manifest chains), she does not notice the transition from $Y'$ to $Y$, and does not realize that $X$ needs to get a `.dead` object from $Y'$. Thus, Alice and Bob live in mirror worlds.

**Counterexample 2: Race conditions.** A major challenge we faced was that relying parties can sync to different publication points at different times. This creates race conditions that complicate global consistency:

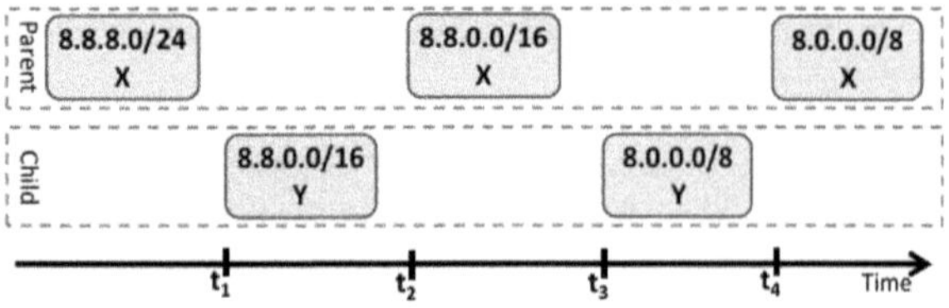


Suppose authority $X$ has small address block. At time $t_1$, $X$ issues a child RC $Y$ that is invalid because $Y$ contains more addresses than its parent $X$. At time $t_2$, parent $X$ is overwritten by an RC for those addresses, and its child $Y$ becomes valid. At time $t_3$, parent $X$ overwrites $Y$ with an RC that is invalid because it contains even more addresses. This process continues as above. Notice that from time $t_1$ to $t_2$, and from $t_3$ to $t_4$, the manifest of $X$ logs an invalid object. Suppose Alice syncs just after $t_1$ and just after $t_3$; she decides that $Y$ is invalid. Bob syncs just after $t_2$ and just after $t_4$; he decides that $Y$ is valid. Hence, mirror worlds!

This problem cannot be caught by checking for `.dead` objects for $Y$, since in Alice's view $Y$ is always invalid, and in Bob's view $Y$ just keeps getting more resources. Nor can it be caught by the global consistency check, because Alice and Bob see the same manifests. Our design eliminates this problem by requiring relying parties to alarm if invalid objects are logged in the manifest; in this example, Alice would raise an alarm. Theorems 5.2 and 5.3 would be false without this requirement.

## 5.7 Data-driven analysis of our design.

We discuss the impact of our changes on the RPKI.

**Less crypto.** One immediate improvement is that a single digital signature on the manifest needs to be issued and verified, rather than individual signatures on each RC, ROA, CRL, and manifest (Section 5.3.2). To put this perspective, on January 13, 2014 there were $\approx 10,400$ validly-signed objects in the RPKI; our changes require the validation of only $\approx 2,800$ manifests.

**No renewals.** RCs/ROAs do not expire in our design (Section 5.3.2); hence recipients of resources are no longer dependent on their issuers for routine renewals.

**Mandated interaction for obtaining consent.** However, issuers are dependent on recipients to provide consent (via `.dead` objects) for revocations and certain modifications (Section 5.3.1). To find out how often those events happen, we use our trace of the production RPKI for 2013/10/23–2014/01/21 (Section 3). The largest event we observed was in mid-November 2013, when RIPE removed 3,336 RCs/ROAs and issued new ones with new parent/child pointers and public keys, as part of repository restructuring. Our design would require RIPE to obtain `.dead` objects from all of them, which seems to impose a large burden on RIPE. However, unless RIPE holds the secret keys of its descendants (in which case it can just issue `.dead` objects by itself), interaction is needed even if `.dead` objects were not required, because RIPE's descendant RCs would need to reissue their objects in new publication points.

Besides this event, we saw 4,443 instances of modified/revoked RCs/ROAs. Of these, 3,569 (80%) were renewals, that are not needed in our design. Meanwhile, at most 230 (5%) would need a `.dead` object.

**How many parties need to consent?** Next, we consider how many parties need to be involved in signing a `.dead` when an RC is revoked. Our estimates, made from the production RPKI and a model of the RPKI, suggest that we do not require many `.dead` objects *on average*:

*1. Production RPKI.* **Table 2** shows the structure of the production RPKI on January 13, 2014. Suppose that ROAs were able to sign off on `.dead` objects (*e.g.*, because they had requested their own covering RCs, or via the mechanism in footnote 7). How many entities would need to sign a `.dead` object if we wanted to revoke a leaf RC in Table 2? We use ASes as a proxy for entities, and estimate this by counting the number of ASes in ROAs issued by each leaf RC; the results for the production RPKI are in **Table 8**, which shows that on average, only 1.6 ASes need to consent to revoking a leaf RC, and that 93% of leaf RCs can be revoked with the consent of no more than 3 ASes.

| # ASes | 1 | 2 | 3 | 4 | 5 | 6-10 | 10-30 | 98 |
|---|---|---|---|---|---|---|---|---|
| RIPE | 678 | 122 | 51 | 13 | 12 | 30 | 8 | 1 |
| LACNIC | 123 | 20 | 9 | 2 | 1 | 2 | 0 | 0 |
| APNIC | 26 | 8 | 2 | 0 | 2 | 0 | 0 | 0 |
| ARIN | 30 | 5 | 4 | 4 | 3 | 0 | 0 | 0 |
| AfriNIC | 9 | 2 | 1 | 1 | 0 | 0 | 0 | 0 |

**Table 8: # of leaf RCs issuing ROAs for $X$ ASes on January 13, 2014; $X$ is in the top row.**

| # ASes | 1-10 | 11-30 | 31-100 | 100-200 | 200 − 1073 |
|---|---|---|---|---|---|
| | 115,605 | 594 | 132 | 15 | 11 |

**Table 9: Similar to the distribution in Table 8, except for direct-allocation RCs in our model.**

*2. Model.* Because the RPKI is far from fully deployed, we also created a model for a full deployment of the RPKI using routing data for the week starting 2012/05/06. Our model has the RIRs sit at the highest layer of the hierarchy; they issues RCs to "direct allocations," *i.e.*, IP prefixes directly allocated by the RIRs (*e.g.*, Sprint in Figure 1). We obtained these top two layers of the hierarchy from files retrieved from the FTP site of each RIR. Our model omits intermediate RCs (since they are also held by RIRs). To model ROAs descended from each direct allocation, we extracted (prefix, origin AS)-tuples from BGP feeds [3,5] for the week starting 2012/05/06. (Any tuple not covered by a directly-allocated prefix was discarded as a bogon.)[8] We grouped tuples by AS and found that, on average, each direct allocation issues ROAs for only 1.5 ASes; the distribution is in **Table 9**.

**With great power comes great responsibility.** Tables 8, 9 indicate that there are a small percentage of outlier RCs that issue ROAs for many (even hundreds!) of ASes. (In our model, out of 116,357 total direct-allocation RCs, 26 (0.02%) have more than 100 ASes and 221 (0.18%) have more than 25 ASes.) Revoking these outliers requires a large number of `.dead` objects. However, we consider this to be a feature, not a bug: these RCs can impact routing to a large number of ASes, so revoking them should not be easy. Moveover, outright revocation may not be necessary if the goal is simply to change the resources given to them slightly, because we provide mechanisms for removing resources from RC that only require `.dead` objects from descendants that become invalid as a result (Section 5.3.1).

[8] Figure 1 is derived from this model. We built a subtree of RCs below each direct allocation RC, with one RC for every prefix with (prefix, AS)-tuple in the BGP feeds. The ancestor relationship corresponds to the cover relationship for prefixes, and we collapsed parent-child pairs of RCs generated for the same AS, ASes in the same organization per [16] or when if child was a "stub AS" per [63].

## 6. RELATED WORK

**Routing security.** The RPKI is a realization of a series of routing security proposals [6,32,48,64] for origin authentication (Section 2.2). A number of works [10,26,39] argue that origin authentication can significantly improve routing security. The RPKI is also the first step towards a comprehensive solution for securing the current routing system with BGPSEC [37] or other proposals surveyed in [14,31]. See also [65] for clean-slate architectures.

**Censorship.** Censorship is known to occur at all layers of the Internet's architecture; see *e.g.,* [45] for an overview. There is already evidence [8,56] of routing-based censorship with BGP; we explored the risk that the RPKI could also be used for this purpose.

**PKI design.** Our modified RPKI architecture (Section 5) is related to an long line of work on public key infrastructure (PKI) design, culminating in recent efforts to harden the web PKI [47]. The idea of validating the state of the RPKI over time is related to certificate pinning [23], and the idea of hash-chaining manifests is related to append-only-logs [58] (or see [20] and references therein) and ideas related to certificate transparency [22,34,36]. While these works suppose that a single logger tracks a stream of ordered events, we have to deal with the race conditions (Counterexample 2) that result from allowing individual RPKI authorities to maintain their own logs (*i.e.,* manifests). The idea of correcting power imbalances in a hierarchical system also appeared in work on distributing certificate authorities [66] and centralized systems like the DNS [1,15,55]; these works distribute the *issuance* of objects, but we only distribute *revocation* (since revocation can harm IP prefix reachability).

**The RPKI.** Research on the RPKI covers measurement [49, 62] and policy questions [17,43,44,61]. Our earlier HotNets paper [18] discusses the threat of misbehaving RPKI authorities, but does not provide solutions to any the threats it discusses; part of Section 3 overlap with [18], but the remainder of this paper presents new results.

Concurrently to our work, there have been efforts within the IETF to harden the RPKI against authorities that abuse their power [11,13,33]. Kent *et al.* [33] considers the threat of whacked ROAs and of "competing ROAs". A new ROA "competes" with an existing ROA if it contains prefixes covered by the older ROA; a competing ROA is a threat if BGP is attacked, since the AS in the competing ROA can perform a (sub)prefix hijack on the AS in the older ROA. Our architecture (Section 5) ignores this threat because we focus on the risk that the RPKI can take IP prefixes offline in the *absence* of an attack on BGP. Moreover, any authority that issues a competing ROA and then attacks BGP can be held accountable; the competing ROA itself is non-repudiable evidence of the attack. Both [33] and our design defend against whacked ROAs by comparing the state of the RPKI over time, but we also detect mirror world attacks and have a consent mechanism and exact security guarantees.

Systems have also been developed to monitor the RPKI [4, 35,46,57,60]; most use a snapshot of ROAs from the RPKI to determine the validity state of routes in publicly-available BGP route collectors [3,5]. Our detector (Section 4.1) is complementary because we detect when any *change* to the RPKI alters the validity state of *all* possible routes, not just the ones visible from a particular BGP vantage point at a specific time; it can therefore be used as an alert system (especially when RPKI deployment reaches steady state), even if a particular vantage point does not obtain a complete view of all routes announced in BGP. Our tools also provide a new way of visualizing downgrade events (Section 4.2).

## 7. CONCLUSION

We have explored a number of techniques to harden the RPKI against the risk of IP prefix takedowns. We have built tools for detecting takedowns within the existing RPKI specifications. We have also proposed changes to the specifications that (1) entitle parties to *consent* to revocations of their IP address space, and guarantee that relying parties can (2) detect misbehavior by RPKI authorities and (3) obtain a *consistent* view of information in the RPKI. Given the security improvements promised by the RPKI [10,26,39], we hope our work will catalyze further efforts to harden the RPKI against abusive authorities.

**Acknowledgements.** We thank Kyle Brogle for help with early stages of this work, Steve Kent for suggesting the term "ROA whacking", FCC CSRIC Working Group 6 - Secure BGP Deployment for inspiring this project, Tony Tauber, Ed Felten and various members of the IAB and the IETF SIDR working group for useful discussions, CAIDA for early access to their AS to organization mapping [16], and John Byers, Davide Proserpio, Ben Fuller, Phillipa Gill, Aanchal Malhotra, our shepherd Adrian Perrig, and the anonymous SIGCOMM reviewers for insightful comments on this draft. This work was supported by NSF awards 1017907, 1012798, and 1012910 and a gift from Cisco.

## 8. REFERENCES

[1] Github: namecoin repository. `https://github.com/namecoin/namecoin`.

[2] rcynic software. `http://trac.rpki.net`.

[3] RIPE RIS raw data. `http://www.ripe.net/data-tools/stats/ris/ris-raw-data`.

[4] Rpki spider. `http://rpkispider.verisignlabs.com/`.

[5] University of oregon route views project. `http://www.routeviews.org/`.

[6] W. Aiello, J. Ioannidis, and P. McDaniel. Origin authentication in interdomain routing. In *Proceedings of the 10th ACM conference on Computer and communications security*, pages 165–178. ACM, 2003.

[7] S. Amante. Risks associated with resource certification systems for internet numbers, 2012.

[8] D. Anderson. Splinternet behind the great firewall of china. *Queue*, 10(11):40, 2012.

[9] R. Austein, G. Huston, S. Kent, and M. Lepinski. *RFC 6486: Manifests for the Resource Public Key Infrastructure (RPKI)*. Internet Engineering Task Force (IETF), 2012. `http://tools.ietf.org/html/rfc6486`.

[10] H. Ballani, P. Francis, and X. Zhang. A study of prefix hijacking and interception in the Internet. In *SIGCOMM'07*, 2007.

[11] R. Bush. *Responsible Grandparenting in the RPKI*. Internet Engineering Task Force Network Working Group, 2012. `http://tools.ietf.org/html/draft-ymbk-rpki-grandparenting-02`.

[12] R. Bush. *RPKI-Based Origin Validation Operation*. Internet Engineering Task Force Network Working Group, 2012. `http://tools.ietf.org/html/draft-ietf-sidr-origin-ops-19`.

[13] R. Bush. *RPKI Local Trust Anchor Use Cases*. Internet Engineering Task Force (IETF), 2013. `http://www.ietf.org/id/draft-ymbk-lta-use-cases-00.txt`.

[14] K. Butler, T. Farley, P. McDaniel, and J. Rexford. A survey of BGP security issues and solutions. *Proceedings of the IEEE*, 2010.

[15] C. Cachin and A. Samar. Secure distributed dns. In *Dependable Systems and Networks, 2004 International Conference on*, pages 423–432. IEEE, 2004.

[16] CAIDA. AS to organization mapping. `http://as-rank.caida.org/?mode0=as-intro#as-org`.

[17] Communications Security, Reliability and Interoperability Council III (CSRIC). Secure bgp deployment. *Communications and Strategies.*

[18] D. Cooper, E. Heilman, K. Brogle, L. Reyzin, and S. Goldberg. On the risk of misbehaving RPKI authorities. *HotNets XII*, 2013.

[19] J. Cowie. Rensys blog: China's 18-minute mystery. http://www.renesys.com/blog/2010/11/chinas-18-minute-mystery.shtml.

[20] S. A. Crosby and D. S. Wallach. Efficient data structures for tamper-evident logging. In *USENIX Security Symposium*, pages 317–334, 2009.

[21] A. de Beaupre. ISC Diary: Multiple Banking Addresses Hijacked, 2013. http://isc.sans.edu/diary/BGP+multiple+banking+addresses+hijacked/16249.

[22] P. Eckersley. Sovereign key cryptography for internet domains. Technical report, EFF, 2011.

[23] C. Evans, C. Palmer, and R. Sleevi, editors. *Public Key Pinning Extension for HTTP.* IETF Web Security, Internet-Draft, November 27 2013. http://tools.ietf.org/html/draft-ietf-websec-key-pinning-09.

[24] R. Gagliano, T. Manderson, and C. M. Cagnazzo. *Multiple Repository Publication Points support in the Resource Public Key Infrastructure (RPKI).* Internet Engineering Task Force (IETF), 2013. http://tools.ietf.org/html/draft-ietf-sidr-multiple-publication-points-00.

[25] I. Gassko, P. Gemmell, and P. D. MacKenzie. Efficient and fresh cerification. In H. Imai and Y. Zheng, editors, *Public Key Cryptography*, volume 1751 of *Lecture Notes in Computer Science*, pages 342–353. Springer, 2000.

[26] S. Goldberg, M. Schapira, P. Hummon, and J. Rexford. How secure are secure interdomain routing protocols? In *SIGCOMM'10*, 2010.

[27] E. Goldman. Sex.com: An update. http://blog.ericgoldman.org/archives/2006/10/sexcom_an_updat.htm, 2006.

[28] G. Huston, R. Loomans, and G. Michaelson. *RFC 6481: A Profile for Resource Certificate Repository Structure.* Internet Engineering Task Force (IETF), 2012. http://tools.ietf.org/html/rfc6481.

[29] G. Huston and G. Michaelson. *RFC 6483: Validation of Route Origination Using the Resource Certificate Public Key Infrastructure (PKI) and Route Origin Authorizations (ROAs).* Internet Engineering Task Force (IETF), 2012. http://tools.ietf.org/html/rfc6483.

[30] G. Huston, G. Michaelson, and S. Kent. *RFC 6489: Certification Authority (CA) Key Rollover in the Resource Public Key Infrastructure (RPKI).* Internet Engineering Task Force (IETF), 2012. http://tools.ietf.org/html/rfc6489.

[31] G. Huston, M. Rossi, and G. Armitage. Securing BGP: A literature survey. *Communications Surveys & Tutorials, IEEE*, 13(2):199–222, 2011.

[32] S. Kent, C. Lynn, and K. Seo. Secure border gateway protocol (S-BGP). *J. Selected Areas in Communications*, 18(4):582–592, April 2000.

[33] S. Kent and D. Mandelberg. *Suspenders: A Fail-safe Mechanism for the RPKI.* Internet Engineering Task Force (IETF), 2013. http://tools.ietf.org/html/draft-kent-sidr-suspenders-00.

[34] T. H.-J. Kim, L.-S. Huang, A. Perrig, C. Jackson, and V. Gligor. Accountable Key Infrastructure (AKI): A Proposal for a Public-Key Validation Infrastructure. In *Proceedings of the International World Wide Web Conference (WWW)*, May 2013.

[35] LACNIC. RPKI looking glass. www.labs.lacnic.net/rpkitools/looking_glass/.

[36] B. Laurie, A. Langley, and E. Kasper. Certificate transparency. *Network Working Group Internet-Draft, v12, work in progress. http://tools. ietf. org/html/draft-laurie-pki-sunlight-12*, 2013.

[37] M. Lepinski, editor. *BGPSEC Protocol Specification.* IETF Network Working Group, Internet-Draft, July 2012. Available from http://tools.ietf.org/html/draft-ietf-sidr-bgpsec-protocol-04.

[38] M. Lepinski and S. Kent. *RFC 6480: An Infrastructure to Support Secure Internet Routing.* Internet Engineering Task Force (IETF), 2012. http://tools.ietf.org/html/rfc6480.

[39] R. Lychev, S. Goldberg, and M. Schapira. Is the juice worth the squeeze? BGP security in partial deployment. In *SIGCOMM'13*, 2013.

[40] T. Manderson, L. Vegoda, and S. Kent. *RFC 6491: Resource Public Key Infrastructure (RPKI) Objects Issued by IANA".* Internet Engineering Task Force (IETF), 1973. http://tools.ietf.org/html/rfc6491.

[41] S. Misel. "Wow, AS7007!". Merit NANOG Archive, apr 1997. www.merit.edu/mail.archives/nanog/1997-04/msg00340.html.

[42] P. Mohapatra, J. Scudder, D. Ward, R. Bush, and R. Austein. *RFC 6811: BGP prefix origin validation.* Internet Engineering Task Force (IETF), 2013. http://tools.ietf.org/html/rfc6811.

[43] M. Mueller and B. Kuerbis. Negotiating a new governance hierarchy: An analysis of the conflicting incentives to secure internet routing. *Communications and Strategies*, (81):125–142, 2011.

[44] M. Mueller, A. Schmidt, and B. Kuerbis. Internet security and networked governance in international relations. *International Studies Review*, 15(1):86–104, 2013.

[45] S. J. Murdoch and R. Anderson. *Access Denied: The Practice and Policy of Global Internet Filtering*, chapter Tools and technology of Internet filtering, pages 57–72. MIT Press, 2008.

[46] NIST. RPKI deployment monitor. http://www-x.antd.nist.gov/rpki-monitor/.

[47] NIST. Workshop on Improving Trust in the Online Marketplace, 2013. http://www.nist.gov/itl/csd/ct/ca-workshop-agenda2013.cfm.

[48] E. Osterweil, S. Amante, D. Massey, and D. McPherson. The great ipv4 land grab: resource certification for the ipv4 grey market. In *Proceedings of the 10th ACM Workshop on Hot Topics in Networks*, page 12. ACM, 2011.

[49] E. Osterweil, T. Manderson, R. White, and D. McPherson. Sizing estimates for a fully deployed rpki. Technical report, Verisign Labs Technical Report, 2012.

[50] A. Peterson. Researchers say u.s. internet traffic was re-routed through belarus. that's a problem. *Washington Post*, November 20 2013.

[51] A. Pilosov and T. Kapela. Stealing the internet, 2009.

[52] D. Piscitello. Guidance for preparing domain name orders, seizures & takedowns. Technical report, ICANN, March 2012.

[53] D. Piscitello. The value of assessing collateral damage before requesting a domain seizure. Technical report, ICANN, 2013.

[54] I. G. Project. In important case, RIPE-NCC seeks legal clarity on how it responds to foreign court orders, 2011. http://www.internetgovernance.org/2011/11/23/in-important-case-ripe-ncc-seeks-legal-clarity-on-how-it-responds-to-foreign-court-orders/.

[55] V. Ramasubramanian and E. G. Sirer. The design and implementation of a next generation name service for the internet. *ACM SIGCOMM Computer Communication Review*, 34(4):331–342, 2004.

[56] Rensys Blog. Pakistan hijacks YouTube. http://www.renesys.com/blog/2008/02/pakistan_hijacks_youtube_1.shtml.

[57] RIPE. RPKI validator. http://localcert.ripe.net:8088/trust-anchors.

[58] B. Schneier and J. Kelsey. Automatic event-stream notarization using digital signatures. In *Security Protocols*, pages 155–169. Springer, 1997.

[59] W. Sierpiński. Sur une courbe dont tout point est un point de ramification. *Comptes Rendus de l'Acadamie des Sciences*, 160:302–305, 1915.

[60] Surfnet. RPKI dashboard. http://rpki.surfnet.nl/validitytables.html.

[61] The President's National Security Telecommunications Advisory Committee. Nstac report to the president on communications resiliency, 2011.

[62] M. Wählisch, O. Maennel, and T. Schmidt. Towards detecting BGP route hijacking using the RPKI. In *Poster: SIGCOMM'12*, pages 103–104. ACM, 2012.

[63] L. Wang, J. Park, R. Oliveira, and B. Zhang. Internet topology collection. http://irl.cs.ucla.edu/topology/.

[64] R. White. Deployment considerations for secure origin BGP (soBGP). draft-white-sobgp-bgp-deployment-01.txt, June 2003, expired.

[65] X. Zhang, H.-C. Hsiao, G. Hasker, H. Chan, A. Perrig, and D. G. Andersen. SCION: scalability, control, and isolation on next-generation networks. In *IEEE Security and Privacy (SP)*, 2011.

[66] L. Zhou, F. B. Schneider, and R. Van Renesse. COCA: A secure distributed online certification authority. *ACM Transactions on Computer Systems (TOCS)*, 20(4):329–368, 2002.

# Network Neutrality Inference

Zhiyong Zhang[1,2]*, Ovidiu Mara[2], and Katerina Argyraki[2]
[1]UESTC, China
[2] EPFL, Switzerland

## ABSTRACT

When can we reason about the neutrality of a network based on external observations? We prove conditions under which it is possible to (a) detect neutrality violations and (b) localize them to specific links, based on external observations. Our insight is that, when we make external observations from different vantage points, these will most likely be inconsistent with each other if the network is not neutral. Where existing tomographic techniques try to form solvable systems of equations to infer network properties, we try to form *un*solvable systems that reveal neutrality violations. We present an algorithm that relies on this idea to identify sets of non-neutral links based on external observations, and we show, through network emulation, that it achieves good accuracy for a variety of network conditions.

## Categories and Subject Descriptors

C.2.3 [**Computer Communication Networks**]: Network monitoring

## Keywords

Network neutrality; network tomography

## 1. INTRODUCTION

Once a fundamental Internet property, network neutrality cannot be taken for granted today. There is evidence that Internet service providers (ISPs) differentiate against certain applications, typically BitTorrent [31], by deprioritizing [18], blocking [12], or shaping [11, 16] its traffic. More recently, there is evidence that ISPs are differentiating against traffic originating from specific content providers [1]. We are not saying that such differentiation should be illegal (although it is, in certain countries); our position is that—whether illegal or not—it should be transparent: if an ISP differentiates against specific end-hosts, protocols, or applications, that should be visible to the affected parties and regulators.

In this paper, we address two questions:

(a) Which neutrality violations can be detected based on external observations? There exist proposals for detecting specific kinds of neutrality violation. For instance, several systems can detect whether a network path differentiates based on transport- or application-layer information [18, 31, 15, 11]; however, they cannot detect differentiation based on source or destination IP address, even though end-users suspect that it does occur [1]. To the best of our knowledge, there exists no formal definition of which kinds of neutrality violation are detectable in the first place.

(b) Which neutrality violations can be localized to a specific link or sequence of links and how? Most existing systems can detect whether a *network path* violates neutrality, but they cannot localize it to a specific link or link sequence. An exception is NetPolice, which can determine whether a specific ISP violates neutrality by explicitly measuring the ISP's performance for different traffic flows using traceroute probes [31]. To the best of our knowledge, there exists no system that can localize a neutrality violation to a specific link sequence without explicitly measuring its performance.

Our approach is inspired by network performance tomography, whose goal is to infer performance properties of links (loss rate, latency, congestion status, or congestion probability) based on external observations, i.e., without monitoring these links directly. A tomographic technique typically forms a system of equations

$$\vec{y} = \mathbf{A} \cdot \vec{x},$$

where $\vec{y}$ is a given vector of external observations (end-to-end path measurements), $\mathbf{A}$ is a given matrix that specifies the relationships between links and paths, and $\vec{x}$ is the vector of link properties that we are trying to infer. It then estimates $\vec{x}$, either by solving this system of equations (when it has a unique solution [7, 8, 6, 22, 21, 14]) or by picking a solution that has some desirable property, e.g., assumes the smallest number of problematic links [23, 13, 26, 10] or occurs with the highest probability [22]. This approach fundamentally relies on the assumption that the network is neutral (each link treats traffic from all paths the same), otherwise it would be impossible to express path measurements as a function of link properties and form a solvable system of equations.

Our insight is that, if the network is not neutral, when we make external observations from different vantage points, these will most likely be "inconsistent" with each other, i.e., any system of equations that we form based on them will be unsolvable. So, in a sense, we turn network performance tomography on its head: where existing tomographic techniques assume network neutrality and try to form solvable systems of equations to infer network properties, we try to form *un*solvable systems that reveal neutrality violations. By applying this idea to carefully chosen "slices" of the network, we can reason not only about the neutrality of the entire network, but also that of link sequences or individual links.

One challenge in turning this insight into a practical algorithm is that, in practice, a network link that does not explicitly employ traffic differentiation (hence would be considered "neutral" by existing neutrality definitions) may behave "non-neutrally," e.g., it may appear to be congested to one traffic flow but non-congested to another, over the same time interval. Such network behavior may also lead to inconsistent external observations, and a naïve application of our theory would misinterpret these as willful neutrality violations. We present experimental evidence that we can avoid such

*This work was done at EPFL, when Zhiyong was a visiting PhD student in the Network Architecture Lab.


*SIGCOMM'14,* August 17–22, 2014, Chicago, IL, USA.

ACM 978-1-4503-2836-4/14/08 ...$15.00.
http://dx.doi.org/10.1145/2619239.2626308.

misleading inconsistencies by comparing observations of similarly sized traffic aggregates.

After describing our terminology and notation (Section 2), we make the following contribution: we prove conditions under which a neutrality violation is "observable," i.e., it manifests as a set of inconsistent external observations (Section 3), and a non-neutral link sequence is "identifiable," i.e., it causes inconsistent external observations that cannot be attributed to any other link sequence (Section 4). We also present an algorithm that takes as input a network graph and external observations, and it identifies all the non-neutral link sequences that are identifiable (Section 5). Finally, we present an initial experimental evaluation of our algorithm on small topologies, based on an open-source network emulator [2], and we show that it achieves good accuracy in a variety of network conditions (Section 6). We close with a discussion of open issues (Section 7), related work (Section 8), and conclusions (Section 9).

# 2. SETUP

In this section, we present our goal (Section 2.1), assumptions (Section 2.2), and theoretical model (Section 2.3).

## 2.1 Goal

Our goal is to design an algorithm that takes as input a network graph and external observations (end-to-end measurements), and it identifies non-neutral link sequences. Given that certain neutrality violations are infeasible to detect (Section 3), our algorithm will suffer some false-negatives, but, ideally, it should not suffer false-positives, i.e., a neutral link sequence should never be incorrectly identified as non-neutral.

Neutrality violation is typically informally defined as differentiation based on flow type, i.e., the contents of the IP header, transport-layer header, and/or payload. For example, a network link may throttle traffic coming from a specific content provider (based on IP addresses) or from a specific peer-to-peer (P2P) network (based on port numbers or deep-packet inspection). When a network link throttles a traffic flow, it upper-bounds the rate at which the flow can send traffic, typically below the rate at which the flow generates traffic; this results in a higher packet-loss rate and/or latency than the one experienced by unthrottled traffic. So, traffic differentiation results in different traffic flows experiencing different performance when traversing the same link(s).

We define "neutrality violation" as the situation where traffic from two different network paths experiences different performance when traversing the same network link (formal definition in Section 2.3). Hence, in our model, a flow type is represented by a set of paths. For example, suppose a network link throttles traffic coming from a specific content provider; we model this by saying that the network has two "performance classes," one class comprising all the paths that start at the content provider, and the other class comprising all the other paths. Similarly, suppose a network link throttles a specific kind of P2P traffic; again, we model this by saying that the network has two performance classes, one class comprising all the paths that carry this form of P2P traffic, and the other class comprising all the other paths. We will discuss the reason behind our choice of definition later in the paper, once we have presented our model and results.

We do not assume any knowledge on the network's differentiation criteria, the number of performance classes it distinguishes, or which network paths belong to the same class. If one does have such knowledge, it is possible to detect and localize neutrality violations with a simpler approach than ours. For example, suppose two parties connected to the same ISP suspect that the ISP throttles their P2P traffic; to test this, they can exchange first P2P traffic, then some other kind of traffic, and compare the achieved performance. On the other hand, this approach does not work when (a) the ISP throttles all traffic between the two parties and/or (b) the two parties communicate over more than one ISPs (in general, administrative domains), and any one of them could be throttling their traffic.

## 2.2 Assumptions

We make three assumptions:

1. We assume the existence of a measurement platform and knowledge of the network graph that interconnects the measurement points. A link in the network graph may correspond to an IP-level link, a domain-level link, or, in general, a sequence of consecutive physical links.

2. We assume that the status of each network link is independent from the status of any other network link.

3. Theorem 1 (Section 3.3) and Lemma 3 (Section 4.2) assume that: within any given time interval, if a non-neutral network link introduces non-negligible packet loss in its top-priority performance class (formal definition in Section 2.3), it introduces non-negligible packet loss in the other performance classes as well.

Assumptions #2 and #3 simplify our analysis and algorithm, but they are not fundamental to our approach; we discuss how we plan to relax them in our technical report [32].

## 2.3 Model

**Links and paths.**

We represent the network as a tuple $G = (V, L, P)$. $V$ and $L$ are, respectively, the nodes and links (edges) of the network graph. We distinguish two kinds of nodes: *end-hosts* and *relays* (the latter correspond to intermediate elements like switches or routers). A *path* is a loop-free sequence of consecutive links starting and ending at end-hosts, and $P$ is the set of all the paths in the network that are currently used.

We use $l$ to refer to some link in $L$, and $l_k$ to refer to the $k$-th link assuming an arbitrary ordering of all the $|L|$ links. We use $\lambda$ to refer to a loop-free sequence of consecutive links in $L$. We use $p$ to refer to some path in $P$, and $p_i$ to refer to the $i$-th path assuming an arbitrary ordering of all the $|P|$ paths.

A *pathset* is a set of paths, and we denote the set of all pathsets in the network with $P^*$ (the power set of $P$). We use $\pi$ to refer to some pathset. Given a set of pathsets $\Pi$, we use $\pi_i$ to refer to the $i$-th pathset assuming an arbitrary ordering of all the pathsets in $\Pi$.

We define the following helper functions: $Paths(l)$ is the set of all paths that traverse link $l$, $Paths(\lambda)$ is the set of all paths that traverse all the links in link sequence $\lambda$, $Links(p)$ is the set of all links traversed by path $p$, and $Links(\pi)$ is the set of all links traversed by at least one path in pathset $\pi$.

We say that link $l$ is *distinguishable* from link $l'$, when $Paths(l) \neq Paths(l')$.

**Performance classes and numbers.**

A *performance class* is a set of paths (that, as we will see below, are treated the "same" by the network), and we denote the set of all performance classes by $C$. We use $c_n$ to refer to the $n$-th class assuming an arbitrary ordering of all the $|C|$ classes.

A link is characterized by a set of performance numbers $\{x(n) \mid n = 1..|C|\}$. When traffic from a path that belongs to the $n$-th class traverses this link, it experiences performance $x(n)$. We use

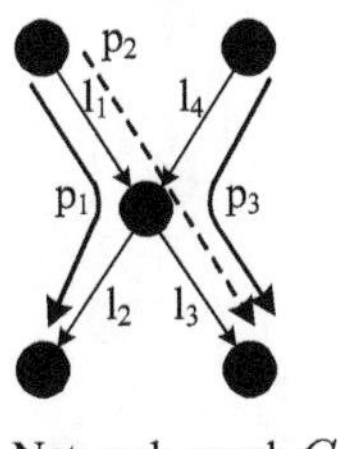


(a) Network graph $G$.

| | $l_1$ | $l_2$ | $l_3$ | $l_4$ |
|---|---|---|---|---|
| $\{p_1\}$ | 1 | 1 | 0 | 0 |
| $\{p_2\}$ | 1 | 0 | 1 | 0 |
| $\{p_3\}$ | 0 | 0 | 1 | 1 |
| $\{p_1, p_2\}$ | 1 | 1 | 1 | 0 |
| $\{p_1, p_3\}$ | 1 | 1 | 1 | 1 |
| $\{p_2, p_3\}$ | 1 | 0 | 1 | 1 |
| $\{p_1, p_2, p_3\}$ | 1 | 1 | 1 | 1 |

(b) A routing matrix $\mathbf{A}$.

**Figure 1: Example network with links $L = \{l_1, l_2, l_3, l_4\}$, paths $P = \{p_1, p_2, p_3\}$, and performance classes $C = \{\{p_1, p_3\}, \{p_2\}\}$. Link $l_1$ is non-neutral: it treats traffic from path $p_2$ worse than traffic from path $p_1$.**

$\{x_k(n) \mid n = 1..|C|\}$ to particularly denote the performance numbers of link $l_k$.

We say that a link is *neutral* when its performance number is the same for all performance classes: $x(n) = x, \; \forall n = 1..|C|$; otherwise, we say that the link is *non-neutral*. When there is only one performance class in the network, by definition, all links are neutral. We use $x_k$ to particularly denote the performance number of neutral link $l_k$. We denote all the neutral links in the network by $L_n$, and all the non-neutral links in the network by $L_{\bar{n}}$. The *top-priority class* of a non-neutral link is the class for which the link has the highest performance.

For example, in Figure 1(a), there are two performance classes, $\{p_1, p_3\}$ and $\{p_2\}$. Non-neutral link $l_1$ has performance numbers $\{x_1(1), x_1(2)\}$, while neutral link $l_3$ has performance number $x_3$. Traffic traversing $l_1$ experiences different performance, depending on which path it belongs to: traffic from path $p_1$ experiences performance $x_1(1)$, whereas traffic from path $p_2$ experiences performance $x_1(2)$. In contrast, all traffic traversing link $l_3$ experiences the same performance $x_3$.

Similarly, a link sequence is characterized by a set of performance numbers $\{\hat{x}(n) \mid n = 1..|C|\}$.

Finally, a pathset $\pi$ is characterized by a performance number $y$. Given a set of pathsets $\Pi$, we use $y_i$ to denote the performance number of pathset $\pi_i$.

**Performance metrics.**

In our experimental evaluation, we use the performance metric introduced in [22], which is defined as follows:

▷ Time is divided into intervals.

▷ We say that a link, link sequence, or path is *congestion-free* during a given time interval, when it introduces (or experiences, in the case of a path) negligible packet loss during that interval.

▷ The performance numbers of a link or link sequence $\lambda$ are $\{\hat{x}(n) \equiv \log(\mathbb{P}(\lambda, c_n)) \mid n = 1..|C|\}$, where $\mathbb{P}(\lambda, c_n)$ is the probability that $\lambda$ is congestion-free with respect to performance class $c_n$ during any given time interval.

▷ The performance number of pathset $\pi$ is $y \equiv \log(\mathbb{P}(\pi))$, where $\mathbb{P}(\pi)$ is the probability that all the paths in $\pi$ are congestion-free during any given time interval.

In general, we can use any metric that is "additive" in the following sense:

1. The performance of a link sequence $\lambda$ for class $c_n$ is equal to the sum of the performance of its member links for that class:
$$\hat{x}(n) = \sum_{k \mid l_k \in \lambda} x_k(n). \tag{1}$$
For example, in Figure 1(a), link sequence $\langle l_1, l_3 \rangle$ has performance numbers $\{\hat{x}(1) = x_1(1) + x_3, \hat{x}(2) = x_1(2) + x_3\}$.

2. In a neutral network, the performance of a pathset $\pi$ is equal to the sum of the performance of its member links:
$$y = \sum_{k \mid l_k \in Links(\pi)} x_k. \tag{2}$$
For example, if the network in Figure 1(a) was neutral, pathset $\{p_1, p_2\}$ would have performance number $y = x_1 + x_2 + x_3$.

We restrict ourselves to performance metrics that satisfy both Equations 1 and 2, because we have found that these reveal the largest number of neutrality violations. Not all intuitive metrics fall into this category; we discuss how to address this limitation in Section 7.

**Definition of network neutrality.**

A *neutral link sequence* is a sequence of neutral links and a *neutral network* is one that has only neutral links. Conversely, a *non-neutral* sequence or network is one that includes at least one non-neutral link.

**Neutrality inference.**

The input to our problem consists of: the network $G$ and the performance number of any pathset $\pi \in P^*$. The desired output is the set of non-neutral links $L_{\bar{n}}$.

**Generalized routing matrix.**

A *generalized routing matrix* represents the relationships between the links $L$ and a set of pathsets $\Pi$ (Figure 1(b)). More formally: Given a set of pathsets $\Pi$, a generalized routing matrix $\mathbf{A}(\Pi)$ is a $|\Pi| \times |L|$ matrix with
$$\mathbf{A}_{ik} = \begin{cases} 1, & \text{if at least one path in pathset } \pi_i \\ & \text{traverses link } l_k \\ 0, & \text{otherwise.} \end{cases}$$

**Systems of equations for a neutral network.**

Here are some of the equations we could write for the network in Figure 1, if it was neutral:
$$\begin{aligned} \{p_1\}: &\quad y_1 = x_1 + x_2 \\ \{p_2\}: &\quad y_2 = x_1 + x_3 \\ \{p_1, p_2\}: &\quad y_3 = x_1 + x_2 + x_3. \end{aligned}$$
Any such system of equations can be summarized as
$$\vec{y} = \mathbf{A}(\Pi) \cdot \vec{x}, \tag{3}$$
where $\vec{x} = \{x_k \mid k = 1..|L|\}$ and $\vec{y} = \{y_i \mid i = 1..|\Pi|\}$.

When the network is not neutral, the equations in System 3 are incorrect and—as we will see—the system is often unsolvable. This observation is the cornerstone of our work.

# 3. NETWORK NON-NEUTRALITY

In this section, we present a condition on the network $G$ and the location of the non-neutral links $L_{\bar{n}}$, which is necessary and sufficient for observing non-neutrality using our approach. When a non-neutral network meets this condition, we can observe that it is non-neutral; when it does not meet this condition, it appears neutral to our approach. We first define "observability" (Section 3.1) and the "equivalent neutral network," the basic construct that we use to formulate our result (Section 3.2), then state the condition and illustrate with examples (Section 3.3). The proof of the theorem is in our technical report [32].

## 3.1 Definition of Observability

LEMMA 1. *Consider a network with paths $P$. If there exists a set of pathsets $\Pi \subseteq P^*$ such that System 3 does not have a solution, then the network is non-neutral.*

The proof is trivial: When all the links are neutral, the routing matrix correctly captures the relationships between the link performance numbers $\vec{x} = \{x_k \mid k = 1..|L|\}$ and the external observations $\vec{y}$, so System 3 has at least one solution.

Lemma 1 says that, if System 3 has no solution, the only possible explanation is that the network is non-neutral. For example, consider the network shown in Figure 1 and the system of equations

$$\begin{aligned} \{p_1\}: &\quad y_1 = x_1 + x_2 \\ \{p_2\}: &\quad y_2 = x_1 + x_3 \\ \{p_3\}: &\quad y_3 = x_3 + x_4. \end{aligned}$$

Suppose we observe that (a) $y_1 = y_3 = 0$ (paths $p_1$ and $p_3$ are always congestion-free), whereas (b) $y_2 \neq 0$ (path $p_2$ is occasionally congested). These two observations are inconsistent: (a) indicates that $x_k = 0$ for all $k$ (all the links are always congestion-free), whereas (b) indicates that either $x_1 \neq 0$ or $x_3 \neq 0$ (either $l_1$ or $l_3$ is occasionally congested). The only possible explanation for this inconsistency is that $l_1$ and/or $l_3$ are non-neutral and treat traffic from path $p_2$ worse than the other traffic.

DEFINITION 1. *Consider a non-neutral network with paths $P$. We say that the network's neutrality violation is* observable, *when there exists a set of pathsets $\Pi \subseteq P^*$ such that System 3 does not have a solution.*

There exist neutrality violations that are not observable with our approach. For example, consider the network shown in Figure 2(a), where link $l_1$ is non-neutral, treating traffic from path $p_2$ worse than traffic from path $p_1$. In this particular network, there exists no unsolvable System 3. The intuition is that the worse treatment that $l_1$ inflicts on path $p_2$ can always be attributed to link $l_3$. As a result, any set of external observations can be explained through a neutral behavior of the links, which means that we cannot detect neutrality violation based on external observations.

## 3.2 Equivalent Neutral Network

From the point of view of the end-hosts, any non-neutral network with $|L_n|$ neutral links, $|L_{\bar{n}}|$ non-neutral links, and $|C|$ performance classes is equivalent to a neutral network with $|L_n| + |L_{\bar{n}}| \cdot |C|$ (neutral) links; by "equivalent" we mean that the two networks produce the same external observations. To generate an *equivalent neutral network*, we map each original non-neutral link $l$ into $|C|$ *virtual* neutral links, one of them modeling $l$'s common queue and the rest of them modeling $l$'s regulation of the lower-priority classes.

Figure 2 shows an example: in the original network, non-neutral link $l_1$ has performance numbers $x_1(1)$ and $x_1(2)$; in the neutral equivalent, $l_1$ is mapped to two virtual links:

a) Virtual link $l_1^+(1)$ models $l_1$'s common queue. It has performance number $x_1(1)$, and it is traversed by both paths. It captures any bad performance that link $l_1$ may inflict on $p_1$, which will necessarily also be inflicted on $p_2$ (since it is lower-priority).

b) Virtual link $l_1^+(2)$ models $l_1$'s regulation of performance class $c_2$. It has performance number $x_1(2) - x_1(1)$, and it is traversed only by path $p_2$. It captures any extra bad performance that link $l_1$ may inflict on $p_2$ due its regulation of performance class $c_2$.

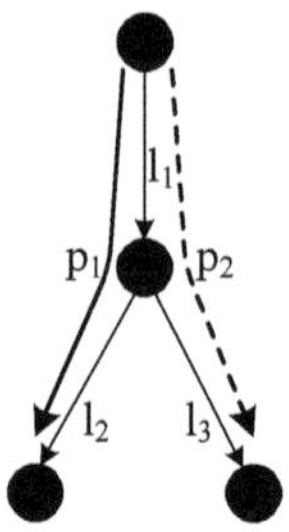


(a) Original network $G$.

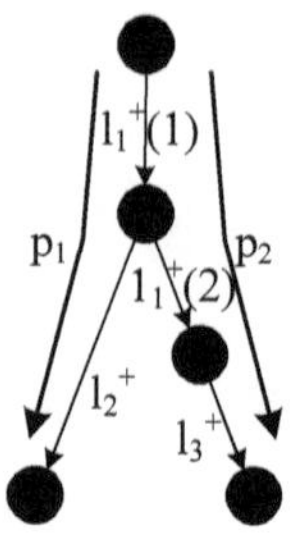


(b) Neutral equivalent $G^+$.

| | $l_1$ | $l_2$ | $l_3$ |
|---|---|---|---|
| $\{p_1\}$ | 1 | 1 | 0 |
| $\{p_2\}$ | 1 | 0 | 1 |

(c) A routing matrix $\mathbf{A}$.

| | $l_1^+(1)$ | $l_1^+(2)$ | $l_2^+$ | $l_3^+$ |
|---|---|---|---|---|
| $\{p_1\}$ | 1 | 0 | 1 | 0 |
| $\{p_2\}$ | 1 | 1 | 0 | 1 |

(d) A routing matrix $\mathbf{A}^+$.

**Figure 2: A non-neutral network (and its neutral equivalent) where neutrality violation is non-observable. There are two performance classes $C = \{\{p_1\}, \{p_2\}\}$. Link $l_1$ is non-neutral: it treats traffic from $p_2$ worse than traffic from $p_1$.**

An original non-neutral network $G = (V, L, P)$ and a neutral equivalent $G^+ = (V^+, L^+, P)$ are related as follows:

a) For each neutral link $l \in L_n$ with performance number $x$, there exists a link $l^+ \in L^+$ with the same performance number $x$ and $Paths(l^+) = Paths(l)$.

b) For each non-neutral link $l \in L_{\bar{n}}$ with performance numbers $\{x(n) \mid n = 1..|C|\}$ and top-priority class $c_{n^*}$, there exist $|C|$ links $\{l^+(n) \mid n = 1..|C|\} \in L^+$, where:

   i) $l^+(n^*)$ has performance number $x(n^*)$ and $Paths(l^+(n^*)) = Paths(l)$.

   ii) $l^+(n), \forall n \neq n^*$ has performance number $x(n) - x(n^*)$ and $Paths(l^+(n)) = Paths(l) \cap c_n$.

As a second example, Figure 3(a) shows the neutral equivalent for the network in Figure 1(a): neutral link $l_2$ is mapped to virtual link $l_2^+$, while non-neutral link $l_1$ is mapped to $l_1^+(1)$ and $l_1^+(2)$.

For any non-neutral network, there exists at least one neutral equivalent and potentially more. A neutral equivalent may include "loop links," which start and end at the same node; we show examples in our technical report. We use $\mathbf{A}^+$ to denote a generalized routing matrix of an equivalent neutral network.

## 3.3 Condition for Observability

THEOREM 1. *Consider a non-neutral network with links $L$, and its equivalent neutral network with links $L^+$. The network's neutrality violation is observable, if and only if there exists at least one virtual link $l^+(n) \in L^+$ that is distinguishable from any link in $L$.*

We illustrate with three examples:

**Non-observable violation.**

Consider again the non-neutral network in Figure 2(a) and its neutral equivalent in Figure 2(b). In this case, none of the two virtual links in the neutral equivalent satisfies the condition in Theorem 1: $l_1^+(1)$ is indistinguishable from $l_1$, and $l_1^+(2)$ is indistinguishable from $l_3$. Therefore, according to the theorem, this neutrality violation is not observable. Indeed, we said earlier that $l_1$'s worse effect on $p_2$ can always be attributed to $l_3$ (Section 3.1). This is an informal way of saying that $l_1^+(2)$ is indistinguishable from

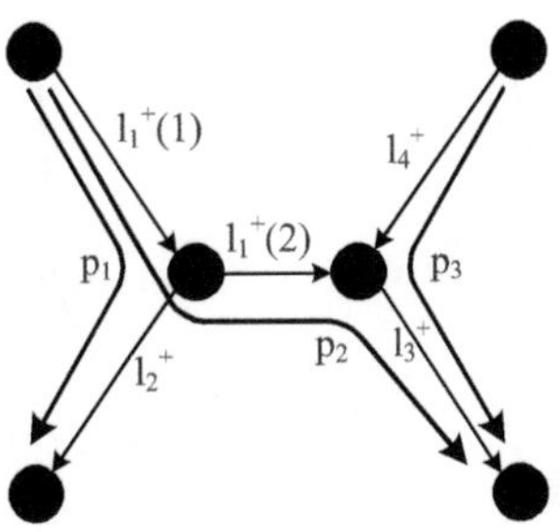


(a) Neutral equivalent $G^+$.

| | $l_1^+(1)$ | $l_1^+(2)$ | $l_2^+$ | $l_3^+$ | $l_4^+$ |
|---|---|---|---|---|---|
| $\{p_1\}$ | 1 | 0 | 1 | 0 | 0 |
| $\{p_2\}$ | 1 | 1 | 0 | 1 | 0 |
| $\{p_3\}$ | 0 | 0 | 0 | 1 | 1 |
| $\{p_1, p_2\}$ | 1 | 1 | 1 | 1 | 0 |
| $\{p_1, p_3\}$ | 1 | 0 | 1 | 1 | 1 |
| $\{p_2, p_3\}$ | 1 | 1 | 0 | 1 | 1 |
| $\{p_1, p_2, p_3\}$ | 1 | 1 | 1 | 1 | 1 |

(b) A routing matrix $\mathbf{A}^+$.

**Figure 3: Neutral equivalent for the network shown in Figure 1.**

$l_3$. Theorem 1 expresses this insight: if a virtual link $l^+(n)$ in the neutral equivalent is indistinguishable from some other link $l'$ in the original network, then the non-neutral behavior captured by $l^+(n)$ can be masked, because its effect can always be attributed to $l'$.

**Observable violation #1.**

Consider again the non-neutral network in Figure 1(a) and its neutral equivalent in Figure 3(a). In this case, virtual link $l_1^+(2)$ is distinguishable from any link in $L$. Therefore, according to the theorem, this neutrality violation is observable. Indeed, we said earlier that $l_1$'s effect on $p_2$ cannot be attributed to any set of neutral links (Section 3.1). Theorem 1 expresses this insight: if a virtual link $l^+(n)$ in the neutral equivalent is distinguishable from any link in the original network, then the non-neutral behavior captured by $l^+(n)$ cannot be masked, because it cannot be attributed to any other link(s).

**Observable violation #2.**

Consider the non-neutral network in Figure 4(a) and its neutral equivalent in Figure 4(b). Link $l_1$ introduces congestion into class-2 traffic with probability 0.5, while the rest of the network is congestion-free. In this case, virtual link $l_1^+(2)$ is distinguishable from any link in $L$. Therefore, according to the theorem, this neutrality violation is observable.

At first, it may seem counter-intuitive that this neutrality violation is observable, as it looks similar to the one in Figure 2 (which is not). However, a closer look reveals that, in this case, there does exist an unsolvable system of equations:

$$\begin{array}{ll} \{p_1\}: & y_1 = x_1 + x_2 \\ \{p_2\}: & y_2 = x_1 + x_3 \\ \{p_3\}: & y_3 = x_1 + x_4 \\ \{p_2, p_3\}: & y_4 = x_1 + x_3 + x_4. \end{array}$$

If we monitor this network, we observe that:

$$\begin{array}{ll} y_1 = 0 & p_1 \text{ is always congestion-free.} \\ y_2 = \log(0.5) & p_2 \text{ is congestion-free w.p. } 0.5. \\ y_3 = \log(0.5) & p_3 \text{ is congestion-free w.p. } 0.5. \\ y_4 = \log(0.5) & \{p_2, p_3\} \text{ is congestion-free w.p. } 0.5. \end{array}$$

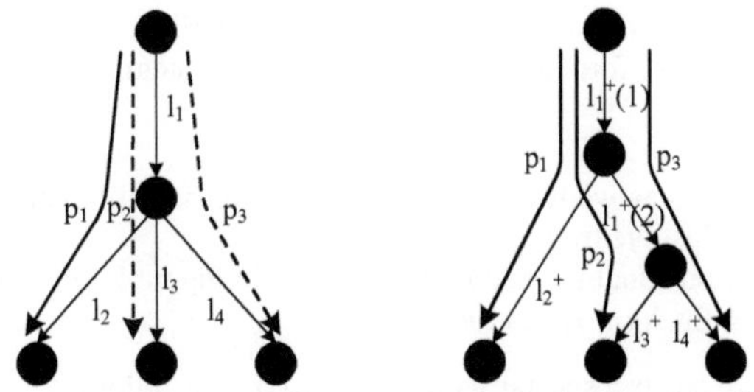


(a) Original network $G$. (b) Neutral equivalent $G^+$.

**Figure 4: A non-neutral network where neutrality violation is observable. There are two performance classes $C = \{\{p_1\}, \{p_2, p_3\}\}$. Link $l_1$ has performance numbers $\{x_1(1) = 0, x_1(2) = \log(0.5)\}$. The other links have performance numbers $x_2 = x_3 = x_4 = 0$.**

These observations are inconsistent: (a) $y_1$ indicates that $x_1 = x_2 = 0$, which means that link $l_1$ is always congestion-free. (b) $\{y_2, y_3, y_4\}$ form a system with unique solution:

$$\begin{array}{ll} x_1 = \log(0.5) & l_1 \text{ is congestion-free w.p. } 0.5. \\ x_3 = 0 & l_3 \text{ is always congestion-free.} \\ x_4 = 0 & l_4 \text{ is always congestion-free.} \end{array}$$

So, if we observe only path $p_1$, we conclude that link $l_1$ is always congestion-free, whereas if we observe only paths $\{p_2, p_3\}$, their congestion can only be attributed to link $l_1$. The only explanation is that link $l_1$ is non-neutral and treats traffic from paths $\{p_2, p_3\}$ worse than the rest.

As a side-note, this example illustrates the benefit of using performance metrics that can be defined and measured for pathsets, not only individual paths: The clue that gives away $l_1$'s non-neutrality is the fact that $p_2$ and $p_3$ always experience congestion *at the same time*; assuming that link statuses are independent (Section 2.2), this correlation can only be attributed to non-neutral behavior by $l_1$. This clue emerges only if we observe $p_2$ and $p_3$ as a pair and measure the probability that they are both congestion-free. Theorem 1 guarantees that, as long as there exists a distinguishable link $l^+(n)$ in the neutral equivalent, we can form an unsolvable system of equations; this system, however, may include equations on pathsets with more than one path, and we must be able to define and measure their performance.

# 4. LINK NON-NEUTRALITY

In this section, we present a condition on the paths $Paths(\lambda)$ that traverse a link sequence $\lambda$, which is sufficient for correctly inferring $\lambda$'s neutrality. We first define the "network slice," the basic construct that we use to formulate our result (Section 4.1), then state the condition and illustrate with examples (Section 4.2). The proofs of the lemmas are in our technical report [32].

## 4.1 Network Slice

Lemma 1 can help us reason not only about the neutrality of the entire network, but also about the neutrality of link sequences, even individual links. For example, consider the network shown in Figure 4(a), where the only link traversed by multiple paths is $l_1$. If we determine that this network is non-neutral, then the only possible explanation is that link $l_1$ is non-neutral, as it is the only link that handles traffic from multiple paths and can differentiate between them.

To reason about the neutrality of a link sequence $\lambda$, we apply Lemma 1 to a *network slice* $G_\lambda$, chosen such that any observable neutrality violation of this slice can only be attributed to $\lambda$. More specifically, we form a specialized version of System 3:

$$\vec{y} = \mathbf{A}_\lambda(\Pi_\lambda) \cdot \vec{x}. \quad (4)$$

We specify how we form this system in our technical report; here, we only illustrate by example.

To reason about the neutrality of link $l_1$ in Figure 5(a), we form System 4 for $\lambda = \langle l_1 \rangle$ as follows:

a) We create a special set of pathsets $\Pi_{\langle l_1 \rangle}$ as follows:

   i) We identify all path pairs whose only shared link is $l_1$: $\{p_1, p_4\}$, $\{p_2, p_4\}$, and $\{p_3, p_4\}$.

   ii) $\Pi_{\langle l_1 \rangle}$ consists of these path pairs plus their individual paths: $\Pi_{\langle l_1 \rangle} = \{\{p_1\}, \{p_2\}, \{p_3\}, \{p_4\}, \{p_1, p_4\}, \{p_2, p_4\}, \{p_3, p_4\}\}$.

b) We create network slice $G_{\langle l_1 \rangle}$ by abstracting away all individual links in the network other than $l_1$, as shown in Figure 5(b).

c) We form the system of equations that corresponds to generalized routing matrix $\mathbf{A}_{\langle l_1 \rangle}(\Pi_{\langle l_1 \rangle})$, shown in Figure 5(c).

There are two key points about System 4: First, it typically consists of a small number of equations, because $\Pi_\lambda$ tends to be small (for any link sequence $\lambda$, there are typically few path pairs whose *only* common link sequence is $\lambda$). Second, once we have created $\Pi_\lambda$, the topology of the overall network becomes irrelevant; the only factors that play a role in System 4 are the performance numbers of the paths and path pairs in $\Pi_\lambda$. This is different from existing tomography techniques, which typically combine large numbers of path measurements into a single large system of equations that is determined by the topology of the entire network.

## 4.2 Identifiability of Non-neutral Links

LEMMA 2. *Consider a link sequence $\lambda$ and its set of pathsets $\Pi_\lambda$. If System 4 does not have a solution, then $\lambda$ is non-neutral.*

System 4 is a special version of System 3 where the equations are picked for their particular relationship to link sequence $\lambda$. If System 4 does not have a solution, we already know from Lemma 1 that the network slice $G_\lambda$ is non-neutral; Lemma 2 tells us that link sequence $\lambda$ in particular is non-neutral. For example, if the system in Figure 5(c) does not have a solution, the only possible explanation is that link $l_1$ is not neutral. The intuition is related to our discussion on Observable Violation #2 in Section 3.3: pathsets $\{p_1\}$, $\{p_4\}$, $\{p_1, p_4\}$ will yield one estimate for $l_1$'s performance; pathsets $\{p_2\}$, $\{p_4\}$, $\{p_2, p_4\}$ will yield a second estimate; these can only be different (and the system in Figure 5(c) unsolvable), if link $l_1$ treats a subset of the involved paths differently.

DEFINITION 2. *Consider a non-neutral link sequence $\lambda$ and its set of pathsets $\Pi_\lambda$. We say that $\lambda$ is* identifiable, *when System 4 does not have a solution.*

There exist non-neutral links that are non-identifiable. For example, suppose we want to reason about the neutrality of link $l_2$ in Figure 5(a). To create $\Pi_{\langle l_2 \rangle}$, we first identify every path pair whose only shared link is $l_2$. There are no such path pairs, $\Pi_{\langle l_2 \rangle} = \emptyset$, and we cannot form System 4 for $\lambda = \langle l_2 \rangle$.

LEMMA 3. *Consider a non-neutral link sequence $\lambda$ with performance numbers $\{\hat{x}(n) \mid n = 1..|C|\}$ and top-priority class $c_{n^*}$. If the following conditions hold:*

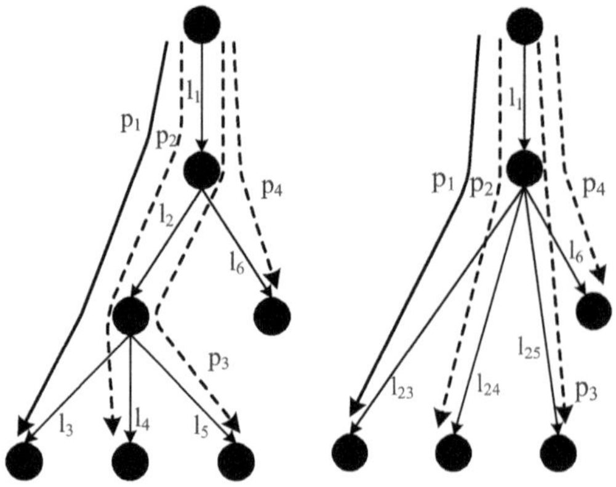


(a) Original network $G$. (b) Network slice $G_{\langle l_1 \rangle}$.

$$\begin{aligned}
\{p_1\}: &\quad y_1 = x_1 + x_{23} \\
\{p_2\}: &\quad y_2 = x_1 + x_{24} \\
\{p_3\}: &\quad y_3 = x_1 + x_{25} \\
\{p_4\}: &\quad y_4 = x_1 + x_6 \\
\{p_1, p_4\}: &\quad y_5 = x_1 + x_{23} + x_6 \\
\{p_2, p_4\}: &\quad y_6 = x_1 + x_{24} + x_6 \\
\{p_3, p_4\}: &\quad y_7 = x_1 + x_{25} + x_6.
\end{aligned}$$

(c) System 4 for $\lambda = \langle l_1 \rangle$.

**Figure 5: A non-neutral network where neutrality violation is observable. There are two performance classes $C = \{\{p_1\}, \{p_2, p_3, p_4\}\}$, where $\{p_1\}$ has top-priority. Link $l_1$ is non-neutral, identifiable. Link $l_2$ is non-neutral, non-identifiable.**

- *there exist at least two path pairs $\pi_i, \pi_j$ in $\Pi_\lambda$*
  $$(\exists\, \pi_i, \pi_j \in \Pi_\lambda);$$
- *and a lower-priority class $c_n$ $(\exists c_{n \neq n^*} \in C)$;*
- *such that $\pi_i$ is entirely in class $c_n$ and $\pi_j$ is not*
  $$(\pi_i \subset c_n,\ \pi_j \not\subset c_n);$$

*then $\lambda$ is identifiable.*

Informally, Lemma 3 says that a non-neutral link sequence is identifiable as long as it is traversed by a sufficiently diverse set of paths: We can determine that link sequence $\lambda$ is non-neutral, when it causes different path pairs in $\Pi_\lambda$ to experience inconsistent performance. This is guaranteed to happen for $l_1$ in Figure 5(a): on the one hand, path pair $\{p_2, p_4\}$ is entirely in performance class $c_2$, hence it will yield an estimate of $l_1$'s performance from the point of view of this performance class; on the other hand, path pair $\{p_1, p_4\}$ includes at least one path from performance class $c_1$, hence it will yield a different estimate of $l_1$'s performance. In contrast, there exist no path pairs at all that share only link $l_2$ in the same figure, hence we cannot identify it as a non-neutral link.

# 5. ALGORITHM

We will now present an algorithm that takes as input the network $G$ and the performance number of any pathset $\pi$, and it outputs a set of non-neutral link sequences $\Lambda_{\bar{n}}$. We will use three metrics to characterize the quality of the algorithm:

*False-negative rate*: It is the fraction of non-neutral links that do not participate in any link sequence present in $\Lambda_{\bar{n}}$. E.g., false-negative rate 10% means that 10% of the non-neutral links do not participate in any link sequence present in $\Lambda_{\bar{n}}$.

**Algorithm 1** Identification of non-neutral link sequences

Input: The links $L$ and paths $P$
Output: The set of identif. non-neutral link seqs $\Lambda_{\bar{n}}$

1: $\Lambda_n \leftarrow \emptyset$, $\Lambda_{\bar{n}} \leftarrow \emptyset$
2: **for** each path pair $\{p_i, p_j\} \in P^*$ **do**
3: $\quad \lambda = Links(p_i) \cap Links(p_j)$
4: $\quad$ **if** $\lambda \notin \Lambda_n$ **then**
5: $\quad\quad \Lambda_n \leftarrow \Lambda_n \cup \{\lambda\}$, $\Pi_\lambda \leftarrow \emptyset$
6: $\quad$ **end if**
7: $\quad \Pi_\lambda \leftarrow \Pi_\lambda \cup \{\{p_i\}, \{p_j\}, \{p_i, p_j\}\}$
8: **end for**
9: **for** each link sequence $\lambda \in \Lambda_n$ **do**
10: $\quad$ **if** $|\Pi_\lambda| < 5$ **then**
11: $\quad\quad \Lambda_n \leftarrow \Lambda_n \setminus \{\lambda\}$
12: $\quad$ **end if**
13: $\quad$ **if** system $\vec{y} = \mathbf{A}_\lambda(\Pi_\lambda) \cdot \vec{x}$ has no solution **then**
14: $\quad\quad \Lambda_n \leftarrow \Lambda_n \setminus \{\lambda\}$, $\Lambda_{\bar{n}} \leftarrow \Lambda_{\bar{n}} \cup \{\lambda\}$
15: $\quad$ **end if**
16: **end for**
17: **return** $\Lambda_{\bar{n}}$

*Granularity* is the average size of the link sequences in $\Lambda_{\bar{n}}$. Smaller granularity indicates higher-quality results. The ideal is 1, which means that we can localize each observable neutrality violation to a single link.

*False-positive rate*: It is the fraction of neutral links that participate in neutral link sequences incorrectly present in $\Lambda_{\bar{n}}$. E.g., false-positive rate 10% means that 10% of the neutral links participate in a neutral link sequence that is incorrectly in $\Lambda_{\bar{n}}$.

The core of our algorithm is Algorithm 1, which identifies all the non-neutral link sequences that are identifiable:

- Lines 1–12: We add to set $\Lambda_n$ every link sequence $\lambda$ for which $\Pi_\lambda$ contains at least 2 path pairs (which is equivalent to at least 5 pathsets).
- Lines 13–16: We move to set $\Lambda_{\bar{n}}$ any link sequence $\lambda \in \Lambda_n$ for which System 4 has no solution.

If we assume no measurement errors, Algorithm 1 suffers 0 false-positives and potentially a few false-negatives corresponding to the non-identifiable non-neutral link sequences. This is because its output consists exactly of all the identifiable non-neutral link sequences: (a) Every link sequence $\lambda \in \Lambda_{\bar{n}}$ is non-neutral. We have picked only link sequences for which System 4 does not have a solution. According to Lemma 2, any such link sequence is non-neutral. (b) Every non-neutral link sequence $\lambda \notin \Lambda_{\bar{n}}$ is non-identifiable. We have discarded only link sequences for which System 4 does have a solution. By Definition 2, any such link sequence is non-identifiable.

For example, consider the network in Figure 5(a), and suppose both links $l_1$ and $l_2$ are non-neutral. In this case, there are two non-neutral link sequences that are identifiable ($\langle l_1 \rangle, \langle l_1, l_2 \rangle$) and one non-neutral link sequence that is not ($\langle l_2 \rangle$). The algorithm correctly identifies the former: At line 8, $\Lambda_n = \{\langle l_1 \rangle, \langle l_1, l_2 \rangle\}$. Link sequence $\langle l_2 \rangle$ has not been added to $\Lambda_n$, because there exists no path pair such that $Links(p_i) \cap Links(p_j) = \{l_2\}$. At line 16, $\Lambda_{\bar{n}} = \{\langle l_1 \rangle, \langle l_1, l_2 \rangle\}$, because both $\langle l_1 \rangle$ and $\langle l_1, l_2 \rangle$ allow the formation of an unsolvable System 4. Hence, in this example, the algorithm's false-negative rate is 0 (both non-neutral links are present in $\Lambda_{\bar{n}}$) and the false-positive rate is also 0. The granularity is 1.5 (the average length of the identified non-neutral link sequences), which reflects our uncertainty about the neutrality of link $l_2$.

After running Algorithm 1, we remove from $\Lambda_{\bar{n}}$ all redundant link sequences. For example, suppose we have: $\Lambda_{\bar{n}} = \{\langle l_1, l_2 \rangle, \langle l_2, l_3 \rangle, \langle l_1, l_2, l_3 \rangle\}$; in this case, $\langle l_1, l_2, l_3 \rangle$ is redundant, because its presence in $\Lambda_{\bar{n}}$ does not add new information about the neutrality of the network. Formally, we consider a link sequence $\lambda \in \Lambda_{\bar{n}}$ *redundant*, if and only if:

$$\begin{aligned} \exists\{\lambda_i | i = 1..m\} \; : \; & \lambda_i \in \Lambda_n \cup \Lambda_{\bar{n}}, \; \forall i \in [1, m] \\ & \exists i \in [1, m] \; : \; \lambda_i \in \Lambda_{\bar{n}} \\ & \cup_{i=1}^{m} \lambda_i = \lambda. \end{aligned}$$

In words, there exists a set of link sequences $\{\lambda_i\}$ such that: all of them are either in $\Lambda_n$ or $\Lambda_{\bar{n}}$, at least one of them is in $\Lambda_{\bar{n}}$ (has been identified as non-neutral), and their union is equal to $\lambda$.

# 6. EXPERIMENTAL EVALUATION

In this section, we first describe our network emulator (Section 6.1) and how we process the measurements that we collect from it (Section 6.2). Then we present experimental results from two small topologies (Sections 6.3 and 6.4) and close with take-away points (Section 6.5).

## 6.1 Network Emulator

We perform our experiments within an open-source network emulator, where end-hosts generate actual TCP traffic and network links implement actual traffic-differentiation mechanisms. We do not simulate packet loss or queuing delay: traffic experiences actual packet loss and queuing delay depending on the queuing policies and the level of congestion it encounters in the network. We do not assume noise-free end-to-end measurements: end-hosts measure the performance of end-to-end paths based on the actual traffic they exchange.

Our emulator is similar to ModelNet [29], with the difference that the network is emulated by a user-level process, not a kernel module. We opted for a user-level implementation, because we found it easier to debug, and it avoids the overhead of porting between different operating systems. As in ModelNet, the role of end-hosts is played by virtual network interfaces that exchange real traffic. The role of the network (the relays) is played by a *network process* that implements network queues and policies. The size of each queue is set according to the maximum round-trip time (RTT) experienced by traffic traversing the queue. The only aspect of the network that is simulated is the propagation delay of links.

We implemented two traffic-differentiation mechanisms that are deployed in current network devices: policing and shaping. Both of them limit the fraction of a link's capacity that is consumed by a given performance class. Policing relies on a token bucket; the rate at which tokens are added to the bucket determines the maximum rate of the targeted performance class; the size of the bucket determines the maximum allowed burst; any excess traffic (that does not fit in the bucket) is immediately dropped. Shaping is similar, with the difference that any excess traffic is buffered in a dedicated queue.

In the experiments presented in this paper, the network either is neutral or implements $|C| = 2$ performance classes. When we say that a network link "implements policing," we mean that it passes all class-2 traffic through one policer, whose rate varies across experiments from 50% to 20% of link capacity. When we say that a network link "implements shaping," we mean that it passes all class-2 traffic through one shaper, whose rate $R$ varies across experiments from 50% to 20% of link capacity, while it passes all class-1 traffic through another shaper with rate $1-R$. Unless otherwise stated, link capacity and policing/shaping rate take the default values shown in Table 1.

In each experiment, the end-hosts generate TCP traffic for 10 minutes. Each pair of communicating end-hosts starts a number of parallel TCP flows with the transfer size following a Pareto distribution; when a TCP flow ends, a new one starts after an idle time that is governed by an exponential distribution. We chose this model, because there is evidence that it captures well the communication between pairs of Internet end-hosts [9], but it is not crucial to our results—it is just one way of generating dynamic traffic patterns. Across experiments, we vary the number of parallel flows per path, as well as the parameters of the Pareto and exponential distributions (that govern flow size and inter-flow idle time, respectively). Unless otherwise stated, these parameters take the default values shown in Table 1.

| Parameter | Value(s) |
|---|---|
| Bottleneck capacity (Mbps) | 100 |
| RTT (ms) | **50**, 80, 120, 200 |
| Policing/shaping rate (%) | 20, **30**, 40, 50 |
| Congestion-control algorithm | **CUBIC**, NewReno |
| Parallel TCP flows per path | 1, 12, **15**, 20, 70 |
| Mean TCP flow size (Mb) | 1, **10**, 40, 10000 |
| Mean inter-flow gap (s) | 10 |
| Loss threshold (%) | 1, **5**, 10 |
| Measurement interval (ms) | **100**, 200, 500 |

**Table 1: Experiment parameters. Default values are in bold.**

## 6.2 Measurement Processing

By our definition of neutrality, a neutral link $l$ inflicts congestion on any path $p \in Paths(l)$ with the same probability. In practice, we found that this may not hold, because packet loss is not uniform: if path $p_2$ carries more and/or larger TCP flows than path $p_1$, the same neutral link $l$ may drop a different fraction of packets from $p_2$ than $p_1$ during each time interval. As a result, even a neutral link may have different congestion probabilities for different performance classes.

To account for the above, we normalize our path measurements, such that they refer to traffic aggregates of the same rate. In particular, when we form System 4 for link sequence $\lambda$, we create the vector $\vec{y}$ as follows: (a) We discount certain packets from our measurements, such that: in each time interval, all paths in $Paths(\lambda)$ appear to have sent the same number of packets. (b) In each time interval, for each path $p \in Paths(\lambda)$, we count the fraction of packets that were lost; if this fraction is below a *loss threshold*, we decide that $p$ was congestion-free in this interval. (c) In each time interval, for each pathset $\pi \in \Pi_\lambda$, we decide that $\pi$ was congestion-free in this interval, when all its member paths were congestion-free. (d) We compute $\mathbb{P}(\pi)$ as the fraction of intervals in which $\pi$ was congestion-free. The exact process by which we create $\vec{y}$ is stated as Algorithm 2 in our technical report [32].

A key step of our algorithm is to determine whether various instances of System 4 "have a solution" (line 13 of Algorithm 1). In practice, none of these systems has a perfect solution, but some are significantly "more unsolvable" than others. We decide whether System 4 for link sequence $\lambda$ "has a solution" as follows: (a) We estimate $\lambda$'s performance number based on each path pair in $\Pi_\lambda$. We compute the system's *unsolvability* as the absolute difference between the minimum and the maximum estimate. (b) Based on this unsolvability, we assign the system to one of two clusters using standard clustering; we decide that the system "has a solution," when it belongs to the low-unsolvability cluster.

## 6.3 Results for Single Shared Link

We first consider a Dumbbell topology with a single shared link that (in some experiments) implements traffic differentiation. This could correspond to the scenario in Figure 6(a), where an ISP throttles all traffic from servers $S_3$ and $S_4$. In this case, the topology in Figure 6(b) is the network slice that we need to monitor in order to reason about the neutrality of the shared link $l_5$.

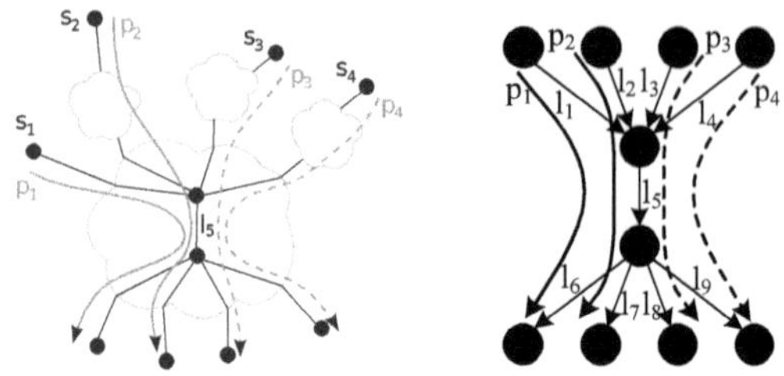


(a) Network. (b) Instantiated slice.

**Figure 6: Experiment topology $A$. In some experiments, link $l_5$ polices traffic from paths $p_3$ and $p_4$.**

| Set | Link $l_5$ behavior | Varying parameter | Value(s) $c_1$ | Value(s) $c_2$ |
|---|---|---|---|---|
| 1 | Neutral | Mean flow size (Mb) | 1 | 1, 10, 40, 10000 |
| 2 | Neutral | RTT (ms) | 50 | 50, 80, 120, 200 |
| 3 | Neutral | Congestion control | CUBIC | CUBIC, NewReno |
| 4 | Policing | Mean flow size (Mb) | 1, 10, 40, 10000 | |
| 5 | Policing | RTT (ms) | 50, 80, 120, 200 | |
| 6 | Policing | Policing rate (%) | – | 20, 30, 40, 50 |

**Table 2: Experiment parameters for topology $A$.**

**Experimental setup.**

We present six experiment sets, summarized in Table 2. We always refer to pathset $\{p_1, p_2\}$ as "class $c_1$" and to pathset $\{p_3, p_4\}$ as "class $c_2$." In experiments where the network is neutral, $c_1$ and $c_2$ do not constitute, strictly speaking, different performance classes, but we refer to them this way for simplicity.

In the first three experiment sets, the shared link does not implement any traffic differentiation. To make things difficult for our algorithm, we try to create network conditions that could be misinterpreted as non-neutrality. For instance, in experiment set #1, class $c_1$'s average flow size is 1Mb, while class $c_2$'s average flow size varies from 1Mb to 10Gb (a different value per experiment). Similarly, in sets #2 and #3, the two classes have different RTTs or use different congestion-control algorithms. As a result, in several of these experiments, the two classes exhibit dramatically different behavior, for instance, one class spends significantly more time in TCP slow start than the other.

In the last three experiment sets, the shared link polices the traffic in class $c_2$. Here, the difficult scenarios for our algorithm are the ones where all the paths carry the same kind of traffic. In each experiment set, we vary the average flow size, RTT, or policing rate of the shared link across experiments; however, in any single experiment, class-$c_1$ traffic and class-$c_2$ traffic have the same average flow size, RTT, and congestion-control algorithm.

In our technical report, we present three more experiment sets, where the shared link implements shaping. The results are similar to the ones of the policing experiments.

**Results.**

In all these experiments, our algorithm correctly decides whether the shared link is neutral or not.

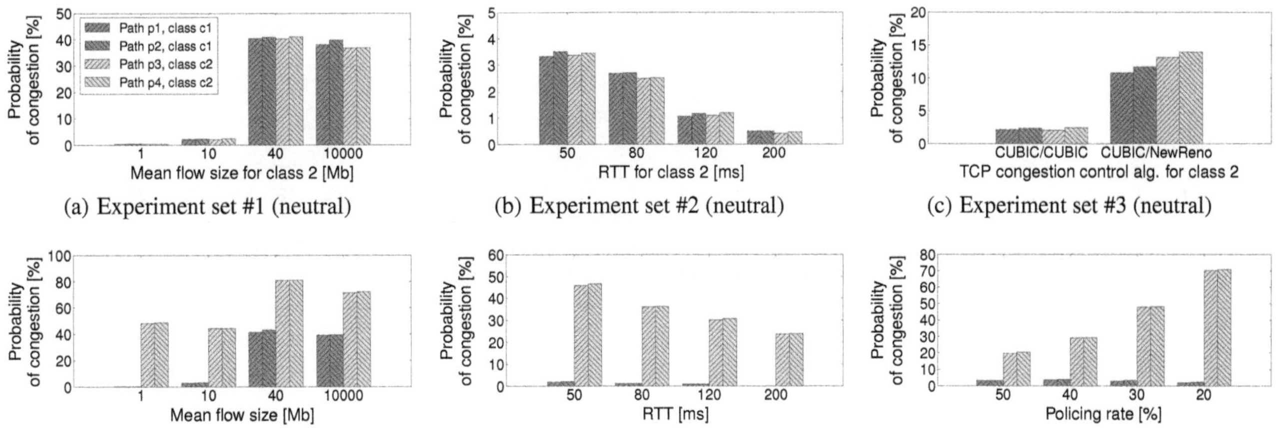


(a) Experiment set #1 (neutral) (b) Experiment set #2 (neutral) (c) Experiment set #3 (neutral)

(d) Experiment set #4 (policing) (e) Experiment set #5 (policing) (f) Experiment set #6 (policing)

**Figure 7: External observations for neutral and non-neutral network, topology $A$. Parameters in Table 2.**

Figure 7 shows the external observations for each experiment set. In each graph, the $y$-axis represents the probability that a path is congested, while the $x$-axis represents different experiments. For each $x$-axis value (each experiment), there are four data points, one for each of the four paths in our topology. For instance, in experiment set #1, when class $c_2$ has mean flow size 40Mb, each of the four paths is congested with probability 40% (Figure 7(a), third set of bars).

Figure 7 provides insight into how the algorithm works: When the shared link does not implement traffic differentiation, the 4 paths are congested with the same probability (top three graphs in Figure 7), which leads to consistent observations. When the shared link implements policing, the two paths in class $c_2$ are congested significantly more often than the two paths in class $c_1$ (bottom three graphs in Figure 7), which leads to inconsistent observations.

## 6.4 Results for Multiple Shared Links

Next, we consider the topology in Figure 8, which has multiple shared links. Links $l_5$, $l_{14}$, and $l_{20}$ implement policing, while the other links do not implement explicit traffic differentiation. This could correspond to the scenario where routers $R_1$ to $R_5$ form the backbone of a tier-1 ISP, while each of routers $R_6$, $R_7$, $R_{10}$, $R_{11}$, and $R_{12}$ belongs to a different tier-2 ISP or content provider. The tier-1 ISP uses policing on links $l_{14}$ and $l_{20}$ to throttle video or P2P traffic entering its network from routers $R_7$ and $R_{11}$, respectively; it uses policing on link $l_5$ to prevent internal P2P traffic from overloading its backbone network. We do not intend this to be a realistic topology, but to create a challenging scenario for our algorithm, with multiple shared links and bottlenecks.

**Experimental setup.**

We present an experiment where the network differentiates against long flows. There are three types of end-hosts: dark gray end-hosts with lines exchange short flows, light gray end-hosts with lines exchange long flows that are policed by links $l_5$, $l_{14}$, and $l_{20}$ (this is the class-$c_2$ traffic), and white end-hosts exchange a mix of short and long flows, but they do not participate in the measurements (they provide background traffic). Table 3 shows the exact parameters for each type.

**Results.**

In this experiment, our algorithm suffers no false-positives and no false-negatives (each of the three policing links appears in at least one link sequence that is classified as non-neutral). It achieves granularity 2.7.

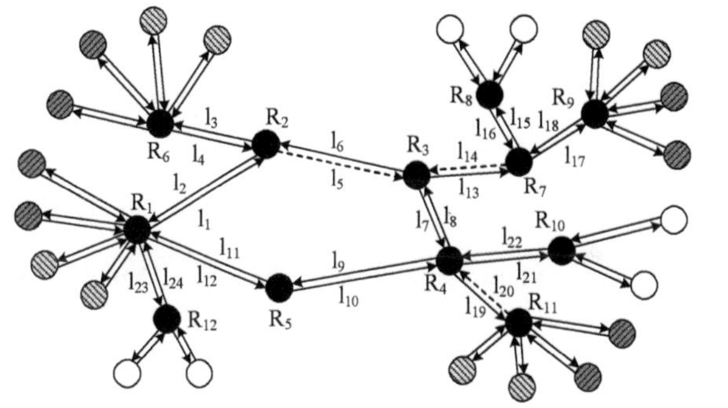


**Figure 8: Experiment topology $B$. Dark gray end-hosts with lines exchange short flows. Light gray end-hosts with lines exchange long flows, which are policed by links $l_5$, $l_{14}$, and $l_{20}$. White end-hosts exchange a mix of short and long flows, but do not participate in the measurements.**

| End-host group | Number and size of parallel TCP flows per path |
|---|---|
| Dark gray | 1 × 1Mb +1 × 10Mb +1 × 40Mb |
| Light gray | 1 × 10Gb |
| White | 1 × 1Mb +1 × 10Mb +1 × 40Mb +1 × 10Gb |

**Table 3: Traffic characteristics for topology $B$.**

Figure 9(a) summarizes the actual performance of each link with respect to each path. These numbers are ground truth, directly measured by the network; our algorithm does not use them in any way. For each link, we show two boxplots: the left one summarizes the link's actual performance for class $c_1$, and the right one summarizes its actual performance for class $c_2$. To create each boxplot, we measure the performance of the link with respect to every individual path traversing the link. For instance, consider link $l_{20}$: according to the figure, this link never introduces congestion into class-$c_1$ paths (left boxplot), while it introduces congestion on average 4% of the time into class-$c_2$ paths (right boxplot).

We see that, for links $l_5$, $l_{14}$, and $l_{20}$, the two boxplots are significantly further apart than for the rest of the links. This validates the basic premise of our model: links implementing traffic differentiation have significantly higher performance-number variability than the rest of the links.

Figure 9(b) summarizes the performance of different link sequences as inferred by our algorithm. In this network, there are 28

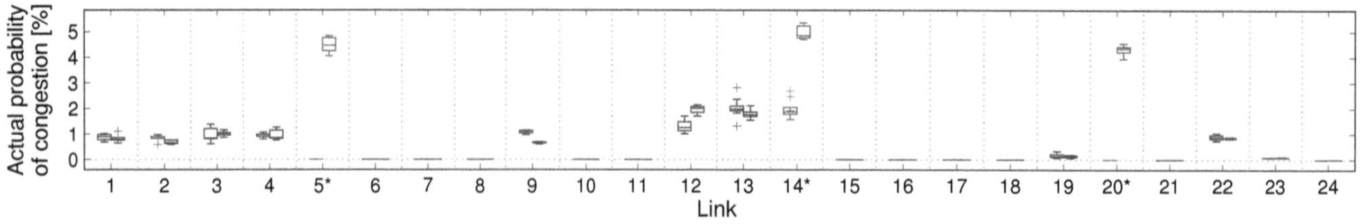


(a) Actual link performance. For each link, we show two boxplots: the left one summarizes the link's actual performance for class $c_1$, and the right one its actual performance for class $c_2$. Links marked with an asterisk implement policing.

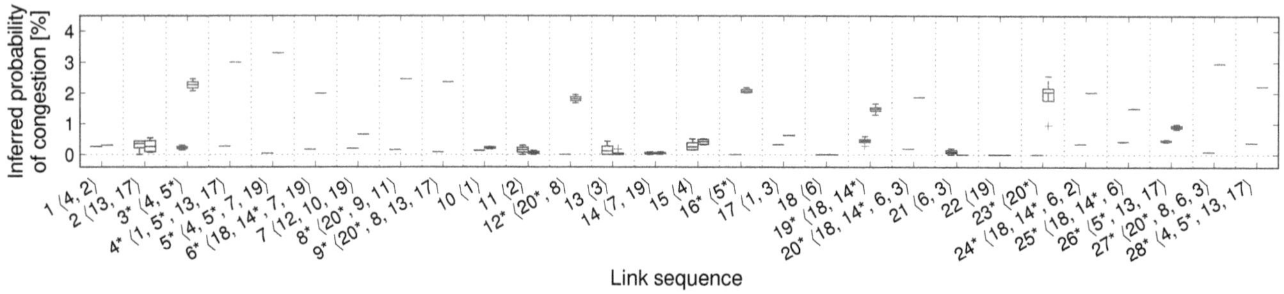


(b) Inferred link-sequence performance. For each link sequence, we show two boxplots: the left one summarizes its inferred performance for class $c_1$, and the right one its inferred performance for class $c_2$. Link sequences marked with an asterisk include at least one policing link.

**Figure 9: Ground truth and algorithm results for topology $B$. Parameters in Table 3.**

link sequences with two or more path pairs in $\Pi_\lambda$, 16 of them non-neutral and identifiable. For each such link sequence $\lambda$, we show two boxplots: the left one summarizes $\lambda$'s inferred performance for class $c_1$, and the right one summarizes its inferred performance for class $c_2$. To create each boxplot, we infer $\lambda$'s performance based on different path pairs (different subsets of equations of System 4). For instance, consider link sequence #28 $= \langle l_4, l_5, l_{13}, l_{17} \rangle$: according to the figure, if we monitor only path pairs in class $c_1$, we infer that this link sequence almost never introduces congestion (left boxplot); if we monitor only path pairs in class $c_2$, we infer that the same link sequence introduces congestion on average 2% of the time (right boxplot).

We see that, for the link sequences that include link $l_5$, $l_{14}$, or $l_{20}$, the two boxplots are significantly further apart than for the rest. This validates the basic premise of our algorithm: links implementing traffic differentiation result in significantly more inconsistent external observations than the rest of the links.

Our algorithm suffers no false-negatives in this experiment, even though it incorrectly classifies non-neutral link sequences #19, #25, and #26 as neutral. These three link sequences do introduce different levels of congestion into the two performance classes, however, the difference is small enough to confuse the clustering algorithm. In this particular experiment, these mistakes do not result in false-negatives, but they do worsen granularity. For instance, link sequence #19 $= \langle l_{18}, l_{14} \rangle$ is incorrectly classified as neutral. This does not lead to a false-negative, because non-neutral link $l_{14}$ is included in link sequence #20 $= \langle l_{18}, l_{14}, l_6, l_3 \rangle$, which is correctly classified as non-neutral. However, it worsens the algorithm's granularity, because it causes long link sequence #20 to remain in $\Lambda_{\bar{n}}$ (whereas it would have been discarded as redundant, had #19 been correctly classified as non-neutral).

## 6.5 Conclusions

Our algorithm did not misclassify a neutral link sequence as non-neutral in any of our experiments, even when half the paths traversing that link carried 1Mb flows and the other half carried 10Gb flows. This is because our performance metric is robust to TCP dynamics: The performance number of a path indicates *how often* it suffers non-negligible packet loss, not *how much* packet loss it suffers. TCP dynamics may cause the same link to introduce different amounts of packet loss during the same time interval; however, when the link does not explicitly differentiate between the two paths, it is unlikely to introduce non-negligible packet loss in one path and not in the other during the same time interval.

Congestion did not interfere with neutrality inference in any of our experiments. In the experiment on topology $B$, there exist both neutral and non-neutral, severely congested links. For instance, both links $l_{13}$ and $l_{14}$ operate close to capacity; if we look at packet loss and queue occupancy for these two links over time (shown in our technical report), there is no clue that $l_{14}$ applies traffic differentiation while $l_{13}$ does not. This does not affect the algorithm, because congestion on its own does not lead to significantly inconsistent external observations; only congestion that is preferentially inflicted on some paths does.

A key difference from network tomography is that we neither target nor require accurate inference of the performance of link sequences. For example, link $l_{20}$ has actual congestion probabilities 0 and 4% for the two classes (Figure 9(a)), whereas our algorithm infers that it has congestion probabilities 0 and 2% (Figure 9(b), link sequence #23). This is because the algorithm infers the link's congestion probabilities for normalized traffic aggregates (Section 6.2), which are conservative estimates of the link's congestion probabilities for the two performance classes. Despite this, our algorithm correctly classifies the link as non-neutral, because it uses clustering: a link sequence $\lambda$ is classified as non-neutral as long as its inferred performance numbers (in this case 0 and 2%) are sufficiently different that $\lambda$ is assigned to the high-unsolvability cluster (Section 6.2).

As a side-note, we found that modern TCP variants are designed to converge with minimal packet loss. This is detrimental to tomography algorithms that rely on packet-loss measurements, e.g., to identify bottleneck links. Our performance metric is robust to such cautious congestion control, because—as mentioned above—it is a function of the frequency, not severity of loss events. Cautious congestion control may enable all classes to converge with minimal packet loss; however, when a link implements traffic differentiation, it necessarily introduces more loss events into deprioritized traffic than the rest, even if each of these events is not severe.

We close by noting that we repeated our experiments with all the loss thresholds and measurement intervals stated in Table 1, and there was no significant change in the results.

# 7. DISCUSSION

In this section, we discuss open issues. We further discuss how to relax Assumptions #2 and #3 (Section 2.2) in our technical report [32].

**Measurement platform.**

We assume the existence of a measurement platform and knowledge of the network graph that interconnects the measurement points. The most realistic deployment option is to use an existing platform where coalitions of end-hosts periodically measure the performance of the paths between them and upload the results to a centralized location for processing [4, 3, 24].

To discover the network topology, we can leverage existing work like Rocketfuel [27], AS-level traceroute [20], and manually collected ISP topologies [5]. Many of these proposals rely on IP traceroute, and one may ask: if we can use traceroute for discovering topology, why not use it also for measuring link or ISP performance (Section 1)? One reason is that a link can treat traceroute probes differently from other traffic (purposefully or not). That said, when we do deploy our algorithm, we will have to compare it against probe-based algorithms [19, 31].

Another challenge is collecting (performance and topology) measurements from sufficiently diverse vantage points: Today, the end-hosts that participate in measurement platforms are typically located in University or residential networks. By measuring the performance of the one-way paths between these end-hosts, one can detect neutrality violations against P2P traffic [15, 11] or against particular end-hosts. However, if we want to detect neutrality violations against a content provider, we also need to know the performance and topology of the one-way paths from this provider to various end-hosts (which we cannot measure directly, assuming the provider does not participate in the measurement platform). One option we are exploring is to infer the performance of one-way paths from round-trip performance based on TCP semantics [25], and to infer the topology of the one-way paths using reverse traceroute [17].

**Path versus flow differentiation.**

We define a non-neutral link as one that differentiates between traffic from different paths, as opposed to one that differentiates by traffic type (which is the typical definition). What happens when the network does differentiate by traffic type, e.g., throttles BitTorrent traffic?

In a realistic scenario, we expect our algorithm to detect differentiation by traffic type without requiring any changes. Consider a scenario where each path carries a mix of traffic types, but different paths carry different mixes. For instance, any path from a content provider to an end-host carries only non-BitTorrent traffic, whereas any path between two end-hosts carries both BitTorrent and non-BitTorrent traffic. In this case, any link that differentiates against BitTorrent traffic also differentiates against paths that carry BitTorrent traffic (e.g., it drops packets from the these paths more often than from the rest); hence, differentiation by type results in differentiation by path, which is what our algorithm detects.

In the worst-case scenario, each path carries roughly the same mix of traffic types. To deal with this case, we need to redefine a non-neutral link as one that differentiates not between different paths, but between different traffic aggregates (where each traffic aggregate follows the same path, but there may be multiple traffic aggregates per path). This change of definition affects only the way we collect our external observations: in System 3, each element of the vector $\vec{y}$ corresponds to a different set of traffic aggregates (as opposed to a different pathset). We can create traffic aggregates as follows: for each path, we measure the end-to-end performance experienced by each UDP or TCP flow, and we classify flows that experience the same performance in every time interval into the same traffic aggregate.

**Performance metrics.**

We restrict ourselves to additive performance metrics that can be defined not only for paths, but also for pathsets. What happens when the network violates neutrality, but that results in inconsistent latency or jitter—in general, performance metrics that cannot be defined for pathsets?

A promising approach is to convert our desired performance metric into one that *can* be defined for pathsets. For instance, if we want to detect neutrality violations that result in inconsistent latency, we can define a link's performance as the probability that the link introduces latency below some pre-configured threshold; then we can define a pathset's performance as the probability that all the links traversed by the pathset introduce latency below some pre-configured threshold.

Defining performance as a probability of a congestion event means that our external observations are measurements of the frequency with which paths and pathsets are congested. The limitation of our approach is that we cannot detect a neutrality violation if it lasts for one (in practice, a small number of) measurement interval(s). However, our detection is not probabilistic: as long as a neutrality violation lasts for a significant number of intervals (and it is externally observable), our approach can detect it.

# 8. RELATED WORK

Several proposals detect traffic differentiation based on transport-layer headers or payload [18, 31, 15, 11]. The common theme of these proposals is to have two end-hosts exchange two different traffic flows (e.g., a BitTorrent flow and a flow that contains random bytes) over the same network path; if the treatment of the two flows is significantly different, then the network path between end-user and monitoring server must be non-neutral. Unlike our algorithms, these systems were not designed to detect traffic differentiation that affects all flows of an end-host, nor localize it to specific links.

NetPolice [31] belongs to the above body of work, but moreover detects whether an ISP treats traffic differently based on routing information, e.g., previous- or next-hop AS. The main idea is to use traceroute-like probes to measure the loss rate inflicted by an ISP on traffic associated with different neighboring ASes; if these loss rates are significantly different from each other, then the ISP must be non-neutral. We focus, instead, on the scenario where we cannot rely on traceroute-like probes (or any other mechanism) to directly measure the loss rates of links or link sequences (e.g., because there is no practical way of generating such probes, or probes are not treated the same as other traffic).

Nano [28] "detects whether an ISP causes performance degradation for a service when compared to performance for the same service through other ISPs." We view this work and ours as complementary: it detects whether two different ISPs inflict different performance on the same kind of traffic; we detect whether any particular link (or link sequence) inflicts different performance on different traffic.

ShaperProbe [16] and Packsen [30] detect whether a network path is shaping an end-user's traffic and also determine the parameters of the shaper. The main idea is to have the end-user send traffic to a monitoring server, while keeping track of the rate at which the server receives the user's traffic; the evolution of the receiving rate can reveal the presence of a shaper between end-user and server, as well as the shaper's properties. We view this work and ours as complementary: it detects whether any single flow is subjected to shaping and identifies the parameters of the shaper; we detect whether different traffic flows are subjected to different treatment (of any kind) and localize this differentiation to specific links.

# 9. CONCLUSION

We studied the problem of detecting network-neutrality violations and localizing them to specific links. We presented conditions under which neutrality violations are observable and non-neutral links are identifiable based solely on external observations. Based on our analysis, we proposed an algorithm that takes as input a network graph and end-to-end measurements, and it identifies non-neutral link sequences; we evaluated it using network emulation. Our results indicate that it is indeed possible to reason about network neutrality, even when we know nothing about the internal behavior of the network. We hope that this work is a small step toward making the Internet more transparent.

**Acknowledgments.** We would like to thank Constantine Dovrolis for encouraging us to pursue this work despite early difficulties; Udi Weinsberg, our shepherd Aditya Akella, and the 6 anonymous SIGCOMM reviewers, for their deep, thorough reviews; and Mihai Dobrescu, Jonas Fietz, Dimitri Melissovas, Pavlos Nikolopoulos, Patrick Thiran, for helping us improve the paper. This work was supported by the Swiss National Science Foundation (SNSF).

# 10. REFERENCES


[1] Is my ISP Throttling YouTube? http://productforums.google.com/forum/#!topic/youtube/fUig1oN9ce4.

[2] LINE Network Emulator. http://wiki.epfl.ch/line/.

[3] Measurement Lab. http://www.measurementlab.net/.

[4] PlanetLab: An Open Platform for Developing, Deploying, and Accessing Planetary-scale Services. http://www.planet-lab.org/.

[5] The Internet Topology Zoo. http://www.topology-zoo.org/.

[6] T. Bu, N. Duffield, F. L. Presti, and D. Towsley. Network Tomography on General Topologies. In *Proceedings of the ACM SIGMETRICS Conference*, 2002.

[7] R. Caceres, N. G. Duffield, J. Horowitz, and D. Towsley. Multicast-based Inference of Network-Internal Loss Characteristics. *IEEE Transactions on Information Theory*, 45:2462–2480, 1999.

[8] M. Coates and R. Nowak. Network Loss Inference Using Unicast End-to-End Measurement. In *Proceedings of the ITC Specialist Seminar on IP Traffic Measurement, Modeling and Management*, 2000.

[9] M. E. Crovella and A. Bestavros. Self-Similarity in World Wide Web Traffic: Evidence and Possible Causes. *IEEE/ACM Transactions on Networking*, 5(6):835–846, December 1997.

[10] A. Dhamdhere, R. Teixeira, C. Drovolis, and C. Diot. NetDiagnoser: Troubleshooting Network Unreachabilities Using End-to-end Probes and Routing Data. In *Proceedings of the ACM CoNEXT Conference*, 2007.

[11] M. Dischinger, M. Marcon, S. Guha, K. P. Gummadi, R. Mahajan, and S. Saroiu. Glasnost: Enabling End Users to Detect Traffic Differentiation. In *Proceedings of the USENIX Symposium on Networked Systems Design and Implementation (NSDI)*, 2010.

[12] M. Dischinger, A. Mislove, A. Haeberlen, and K. P. Gummadi. Detecting BitTorrent Blocking. In *Proceedings of the ACM Internet Measurement Conference (IMC)*, 2008.

[13] N. G. Duffield. Network Tomography of Binary Network Performance Characteristics. *IEEE Transactions on Information Theory*, 52(12):5373–5388, December 2006.

[14] D. Ghita, K. Argyraki, and P. Thiran. Network Tomography on Correlated Links. In *Proceedings of the ACM Internet Measurement Conference (IMC)*, 2010.

[15] P. Kanuparthy and C. Dovrolis. DiffProbe: Detecting ISP Service Discrimination. In *Proceedings of the IEEE INFOCOM Conference*, 2010.

[16] P. Kanuparthy and C. Dovrolis. ShaperProbe: End-to-end Detection of ISP Traffic Shaping Using Active Methods. In *Proceedings of the ACM Internet Measurement Conference (IMC)*, 2011.

[17] E. Katz-Bassett, H. V. Madhyastha, V. K. Adhikari, C. Scott, J. Sherry, P. van Wesep, T. Anderson, and A. Krishnamurthy. Reverse Traceroute. In *Proceedings of the USENIX Symposium on Networked Systems Design and Implementation (NSDI)*, 2010.

[18] G. Lu, Y. Chen, S. Birrer, F. E. Bustamante, C. Y. Cheung, and X. Li. End-to-end Inference of Router Packet Forwarding Priority. In *Proceedings of the IEEE INFOCOM Conference*, 2007.

[19] R. Mahajan, N. Spring, D. Wetherall, and T. Anderson. User-level Internet Path Diagnosis. In *Proceedings of the ACM Symposium on Operating Systems Principles (SOSP)*, 2003.

[20] Z. M. Mao, J. Rexford, J. Wang, and R. H. Katz. Towards an Accurate AS-Level Traceroute Tool. In *Proceedings of the ACM SIGCOMM Conference*, 2003.

[21] H. X. Nguyen and P. Thiran. Network Loss Inference with Second Order Statistics of End-to-End Flows. In *Proceedings of the IEEE Internet Measurement Conference (IMC)*, 2007.

[22] H. X. Nguyen and P. Thiran. The Boolean Solution to the Congested IP Link Location Problem: Theory and Practice. In *Proceedings of the IEEE INFOCOM Conference*, 2007.

[23] V. N. Padmanabhan, L. Qiu, and H. J. Wang. Server-based Inference of Internet Performance. In *Proceedings of the IEEE INFOCOM Conference*, 2003.

[24] M. Sanchez, J. Otto, Z. Bischof, D. Choffnes, F. Bustamante, B. Krishnamurthy, and W. Williger. Dasu: Pushing Experiments to the Internet's Edge. In *Proceedings of the USENIX Symposium on Networked Systems Design and Implementation (NSDI)*, 2013.

[25] S. Savage. Sting: a TCP-based Network Measurement Tool. In *Proceedings of the USENIX Symposium on Internet Technologies and Systems (USITS)*, 1999.

[26] H. H. Song, L. Qiu, and Y. Zhang. NetQuest: A Flexible Framework for Large-Scale Network Measurement. In *Proceedings of the ACM SIGMETRICS Conference*, 2006.

[27] N. Spring, R. Mahajan, D. Wetherall, and T. Anderson. Measuring ISP topologies with Rocketfuel. *IEEE/ACM Transactions on Networking*, 12(1):2–16, February 2004.

[28] M. B. Tariq, M. Motiwala, N. Feamster, and M. Ammar. Detecting Network Neutrality Violations with Causal Inference. In *Proceedings of the ACM CoNEXT Conference*, 2008.

[29] A. Vahdat, K. Yocum, K. Walsh, P. Mahadevan, D. Kostic, J. Chase, and D. Becker. Scalability and Accuracy in a Large-Scale Network Emulator. In *Proceedings of the USENIX Symposium on Operating Systems Design and Implementation (OSDI)*, 2002.

[30] U. Weinsberg, A. Soule, and L. Massoulie. Inferring Traffic Shaping and Policy Parameters using End Host Measurements. In *Proceedings of the IEEE INFOCOM Mini-Conference*, 2011.

[31] Y. Zhang, Z. M. Mao, and M. Zhang. Detecting Traffic Differentiation in Backbone ISPs with NetPolice. In *Proceedings of the ACM Internet Measurement Conference (IMC)*, 2007.

[32] Z. Zhang, O. Mara, and K. Argyraki. Network Neutrality Inference. Technical report, École Polytechnique Fédérale de Lausanne, 2014. Available at http://infoscience.epfl.ch/record/186414.

# Balancing Accountability and Privacy in the Network

David Naylor
Carnegie Mellon University
dnaylor@cs.cmu.edu

Matthew K. Mukerjee
Carnegie Mellon University
mukerjee@cs.cmu.edu

Peter Steenkiste
Carnegie Mellon University
prs@cs.cmu.edu

## ABSTRACT

Though most would agree that accountability and privacy are both valuable, today's Internet provides little support for either. Previous efforts have explored ways to offer stronger guarantees for one of the two, typically at the expense of the other; indeed, at first glance accountability and privacy appear mutually exclusive. At the center of the tussle is the source address: in an accountable Internet, source addresses undeniably link packets and senders so hosts can be punished for bad behavior. In a privacy-preserving Internet, source addresses are hidden as much as possible.

In this paper, we argue that a balance *is* possible. We introduce the Accountable and Private Internet Protocol (APIP), which splits source addresses into two separate fields — an *accountability address* and a *return address* — and introduces independent mechanisms for managing each. Accountability addresses, rather than pointing to hosts, point to *accountability delegates*, which agree to vouch for packets on their clients' behalves, taking appropriate action when misbehavior is reported. With accountability handled by delegates, senders are now free to mask their return addresses; we discuss a few techniques for doing so.

## Categories and Subject Descriptors

C.2.1 [**Computer-Communication Networks**]: Network Architecture and Design

## Keywords

accountability; privacy; source address

## 1. INTRODUCTION

Today's Internet is caught in a tussle [13] between service providers, who want accountability, and users, who want privacy. Each side has legitimate arguments: if senders cannot be held accountable for their traffic (e.g., source addresses are spoofable), stopping in-progress attacks and preventing future ones becomes next to impossible. On the other hand, there are legitimate anonymous uses of the Internet, such as accessing medical web sites without revealing personal medical conditions, posting to whistleblowing web sites, or speaking out against an oppressive political regime.

At the network layer, mechanisms for providing one or the other often boil down to either strengthening or weakening *source addresses*. In an accountable Internet, source addresses undeniably link packets and senders so miscreants can be punished for bad behavior, so techniques like egress filtering and unicast reverse path forwarding (uRPF) checks aim to prevent spoofing. In a private Internet, senders hide source addresses as much as possible, so services like Tor work by masking the sender's true source address.

We argue that striking a balance between accountability and privacy is fundamentally difficult because the IP source address is used both to to identify the sender (accountability) *and* as a return address (privacy). In fact, the function of the source address has evolved to be even more complex, serving a total of five distinct roles: packet sender, return address, error reporting (e.g., for ICMP), accountability (e.g., uRPF), and to calculate a flow ID (e.g., as part of the standard 5-tuple).

This paper asks the question, "What could we do if the accountability and return address roles were separated?" Our answer, the Accountable and Private Internet Protocol (APIP), does just that, creating an opportunity for a more flexible approach to balancing accountability and privacy in the network. APIP utilizes the accountability address in a privacy-preserving way by introducing the notion of *delegated accountability*, in which a trusted third party vouches for packets and fields complaints. With accountability handled by delegates, senders have more freedom to hide return addresses. We make the following contributions:

- An analysis of the roles of the source address in today's Internet.
- The definition of design options for an accountability address and the accompanying mechanisms for holding hosts accountable in a privacy-preserving way.
- An analysis of the impact of these design options on the privacy-accountability tradeoff.
- The definition and evaluation of two end-to-end instantiations of APIP.

The remainder of the paper is organized as follows. After teasing apart the various roles of the source address (§2), §3 discusses challenges in balancing accountability and privacy. §4 gives a high-level overview of APIP. §5 describes possible designs for delegated accountability while §6 analyzes their implications for privacy. §7 discusses real-world deployment


*SIGCOMM'14,* August 17–22, 2014, Chicago, IL, USA.

http://dx.doi.org/10.1145/2619239.2626306.

issues and presents two example end-to-end instantiations of APIP. We evaluate the feasibility of APIP in §8 and finish with a discussion of related work (§9) and conclusion (§10).

# 2. SOURCE ADDRESS OVERLOAD

We now investigate the roles of source addresses, since they play a key role in the seemingly fundamental conflict between accountability and privacy in the network. Source addresses today attempt to fulfill at least five distinct roles:

1) **Return Address** — This is a source address's most obvious role: the receiving application uses the source address as the destination for responses. (This is, for example, built into TCP connection establishment.)
2) **Sender Identity** — Historically, source addresses have been used as a crude (and ineffective) way of authenticating a sender or to link multiple sessions to a single "user".
3) **Error Reporting** — If a packet encounters a problem, the ICMP error message is directed to the source address.
4) **Flow ID** — Source addresses are one component of the 5-tuple used to classify packets into flows, both in the network (monitoring, traffic engineering) and at endpoints (demultiplexing).
5) **Accountability** — Techniques such as uRPF checks and egress filtering can be viewed as weak accountability mechanisms protecting against certain types of address spoofing. Recent work offers stronger protection than that offered by IP. For example, AIP [4] uses cryptographic identifiers as source addresses that can be used to verify that the host identified really did send the packet.

Somewhat to our surprise, many proposed architectures use source addresses for the same purposes. This includes proposals that are very different from IP, such as architectures that use paths or capabilities, rather than addresses, to identify a destination. For instance, SCION [37] headers include AS-level paths selected jointly by the ISPs and source and destination networks to specify how to reach the destination. However, each packet still has an AIP-style source identifier that fulfills the above roles. Also, in ICING [28] and capability-based architectures such as TVA [36], packets carry pre-approved router-level paths, but they also carry traditional source and destination addresses.

To understand the impact of repurposing the source address as an accountability address in APIP, we ask two questions about each role:

**(1) Is it needed by the network?** If not, it can be moved deeper in the packet, opening up more design options and simplifying the network header.

**(2) Is it needed in every packet?** If not, it could be stored elsewhere, e.g. on the routers or end-hosts that will use it. This simplifies the packet header, but may add complexity to protocols that have to maintain the state.

Table 1 summarizes the answers to these questions. Two high-level takeaways emerge: (1) not all roles involve the network, and (2) some information is not needed in every packet. The following observations are particularly relevant to the accountability versus privacy tussle:

1) **The accountability role is the network's primary use of source addresses.** Error reporting benefits the host, not the network. Hosts could choose to forgo error reports for the sake of privacy or have them sent to the accountability address. Flow ID calculation could use the accountability address.
2) **The return address role is not used by the network at all.** It could be moved deeper in the packet, encrypted end-to-end, and/or omitted after the first packet of a flow.

# 3. ACCOUNTABILITY VERSUS PRIVACY

A number of research efforts focus on improving either accountability or sender privacy in the network, but unfortunately this often comes at the price of weakening the other. To illustrate this point, we summarize one well-known technique for each and then elaborate on the goals of this paper.

## 3.1 Previous Work

**Accountability and Nothing But** The Accountable Internet Protocol (AIP) [4] is a network architecture whose primary objective is accountability. Each host's *endpoint identifier* (EID) is the cryptographic hash of its public key, and AIP introduces two mechanisms that use these "self-certifying" EIDs to hold hosts accountable.

First, first-hop routers in AIP prevent spoofing by periodically "challenging" a host by returning the hash of a packet it purportedly sent. Hosts maintain a cache of hashes of recently sent packets and respond affirmatively if they find the specified packet hash; the response is signed with the private key corresponding to the source EID. If a challenge elicits no response or the response has an invalid signature, the router drops the original packet. Second, AIP proposes a *shutoff* protocol: a victim under attack sends the attacking host a *shutoff packet*, prompting the attacker's NIC to install a filter blocking the offending flow. Shutoff packets contain the hash of an attack packet (to prove the host really sent something to the victim) and are signed with the victim's private key (to prove the shutoff came from the victim).

AIP suffers from three important limitations: first, cryptographically linking senders to their packets' source addresses precludes any possibility of privacy. Second, though bad behavior is always linkable to the misbehaving host, AIP does not facilitate a long-term fix—the shutoff protocol is only a stop-gap measure. Finally, AIP requires that well-intentioned owners install "smart NICs" that implement the challenge and shutoff protocols, since a compromised OS could ignore shutoffs. We draw heavily on ideas from AIP while addressing these limitations.

**Privacy and Nothing But** The best available solution for hiding a return address is using a mix net or onion routing service like Tor [12, 31, 32]. Observers in the network only see the identity of the two onion routers on that link in the Tor path. Of course, accountability is much more difficult to achieve since the identity of the sender is hidden inside the packet, behind one or more layers of encryption. Liu et al. propose an architecture that offers a high degree of privacy by baking Tor into the network itself [25]. However, in addition to the lack of accountability, the increased header overhead and latency make Tor unsuitable as a default, "always-on" solution.

| Role | Where Used | Layer | Comments |
|---|---|---|---|
| *Return Address* | Destination | Transport | Routers forward purely based on the destination address; the return address is used only by the destination. |
| *Sender Identity* | Destination | Application | No longer used to authenticate users, but may be used to, e.g., track "users" across sessions in web access logs. |
| *Error Reporting* | Routers<br>Destination | Network<br>Network | Destination for error messages. |
| *Flow ID* | Destination<br>Routers | Transport<br>Network | End-hosts need a way to demultiplex flows.<br>Routers distinguish flows for traffic monitoring/engineering. |
| *Accountability* | Routers | Network | In designs like AIP, routers may require a valid (challengeable) source address. |
| | Destination | Network | It must be possible to identify and shut down a malicious flow. |

Table 1: The roles a source address plays and where each is used.

## 3.2 Goals

The examples show that the source address represents a control point in the tussle between privacy and accountability. Unfortunately, it is a very crude one since there seem to be only two settings: privacy (x)or accountability. The high level goal of this paper is to redefine the source address so it can properly balance the accountability and privacy concerns of providers and users.

**Accountability** At the network layer, by accountability we mean that *hosts cannot send traffic with impunity: malicious behavior can be stopped and perpetrators can be punished.* Specifically, we would like our design to have the following three properties:

1) Anyone can verify that a packet is "vouched for" — someone is willing to take responsibility if the packet is malicious.
2) Malicious flows can be stopped quickly.
3) Future misbehavior from malicious hosts can be prevented (i.e., by administrative or legal action).

**Privacy** Our focus is on providing *the ability for a sender to hide its network address* so it can hide its identity from third-party observers in the source domain, from transit ISPs, and (optionally—see §6) from the destination. We assume these adversaries can observe all packets. Note that while our goal is to make it possible to hide the sender's address, APIP does not specify any one particular address hiding mechanism. We do not consider anonymity from the operator of the source domain itself (since it can identify the sender based on the physical "port" through which the packet entered the network).

Application-layer privacy concerns are outside the scope of this paper, nor are we concerned about hiding a packet's destination; senders wishing to make their packets unlinkable to the destination should use solutions such as Tor. Finally, though we do not introduce new techniques for flow anonymity, i.e., the inability of observers to link packets belonging to the same flow, we discuss how our solutions affect the linkability of packets in a flow.

# 4. BASIC DESIGN

The Accountable and Private Internet Protocol (APIP) ***separates accountability and return addresses.*** A dedicated accountability address allows us to address the limitations of an accountability-above-all-else approach like AIP by introducing ***delegated accountability***. Rather than identifying the sender, a packet's accountability address identifies an *accountability delegate*, a party who is willing to vouch for the packet. With accountability handled by delegates, senders are free to ***mask return addresses*** (e.g., by encrypting them end-to-end or using network address translation) without weakening accountability.

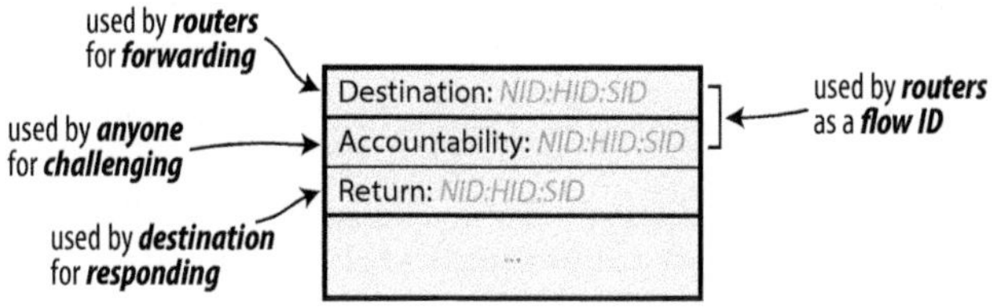


Figure 1: Packet carry a destination address (used by routers for forwarding), an accountability address (used to report malicious packets), and an optional return address (used by the receiving endpoint for responding).

**Addressing** We think APIP is applicable to many different network architectures, so as much as possible we avoid making protocol-specific assumptions. To discuss source addresses generally, we adopt three conventions.

First, each packet carries at least two addresses (Figure 1): (1) a *destination address* (used to forward the packet) and (2) an *accountability address* (identifying a party—not necessarily the sender—agreeing to take responsibility for the packet). It may also carry a *return address* (denoting where response traffic should be sent) as a separate field in the packet. Return addresses may not be present in all packets, e.g., they may be stored with connection state on the receiver. Also, as we discuss later, the return address may not always be part of the *network* header.

Second, an address consists of three logical pieces: (1) a *network ID* (NID), used to forward packets to the destination domain, (2) a *host ID* (HID), used within the destination domain to forward packets to the destination host, and (3) a *socket ID* (SID), used at the destination host to demultiplex packets to sockets. We write a complete address as *NID:HID:SID*. These logical IDs may be separate header

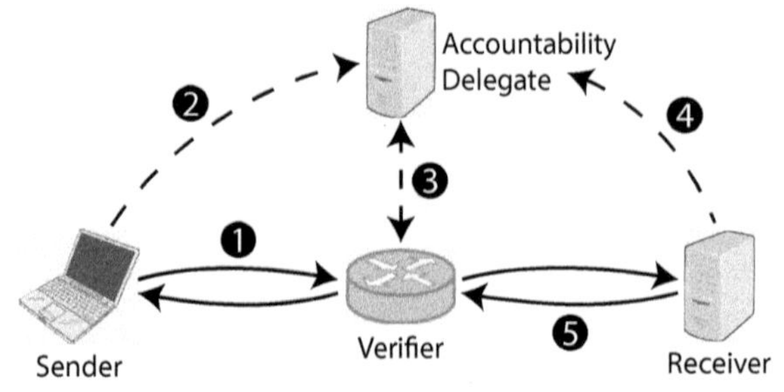


Figure 2: High-level overview of APIP.

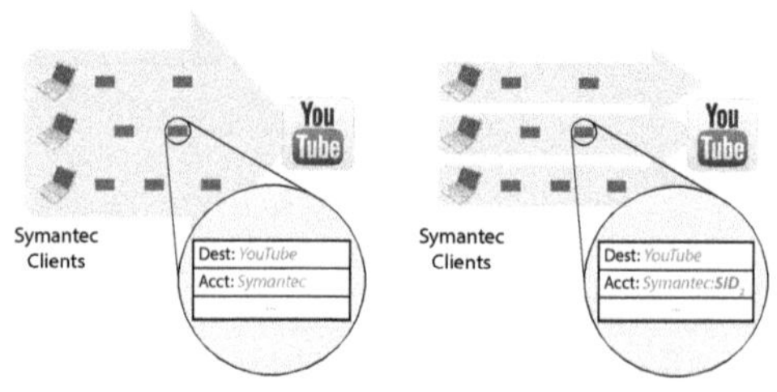


(a) Without *SIDs*. (b) Per-host *SIDs*.

Figure 3: Adding *SIDs* to accountability addresses for flow differentiation.

fields or could be combined (e.g., an IP address encodes both an NID and an HID; the port number serves as an SID).

Finally, to simplify our description of APIP, we initially assume that HIDs are *self-certifying*, as defined by AIP, to bootstrap trust in interactions with accountability delegates. We relax this assumption in §7.3

**Life of a Packet** Figure 2 traces the life of a packet through APIP.

1. The **sender** sends a packet with an *accountability address* identifying its **accountability delegate**. If a *return address* is needed, it can be encrypted or otherwise masked.
2. The **sender** "briefs" its **accountability delegate** about the packet it just sent.
3. A **verifier** (any on-path router or the receiver) can confirm with the **accountability delegate** that the packet is a valid packet from one of the delegate's clients. Packets that are not vouched for are dropped.
4. If the **receiver** determines that packets are part of a malicious flow, it uses the *accountability address* to report the flow to the **accountability delegate**, which stops verifying (effectively blocking) the flow and can pursue a longer term administrative or legal solution.
5. The **receiver** uses the *return address* in the request as the *destination address* in the response.

It is useful to identify the key differences between APIP and the AIP and Tor protocols discussed in Section 3. Delegated accountability offers two key benefits over AIP. First, it dramatically improves sender privacy: only the accountability delegate, not the whole world, knows who sent a packet. Second, it offers a more reliable way of dealing with malicious flows compared to a smart NIC. Third, it offers a clearer path to long-term resolution to bad behavior. For example, the delegate can contact the well-intentioned owner of a misbehaving host out-of-band (e.g., requiring them to run anti-virus tools). While Tor provides stronger privacy properties than APIP, by simply changing how source addresses are treated, APIP can provide sender privacy with much lower overhead since the return address can be hidden from the network. Techniques for doing so (§6) are lightweight enough to be viable options for "default on" use.

# 5. DELEGATING ACCOUNTABILITY

This section describes how accountability can be delegated. We will assume delegates can be trusted, e.g., their role is played by a reputable commercial company or source domain. We discuss the problem of rogue delegates in §7.1. APIP defines four aspects of delegate operation: the form of the address used to reach a delegate plus the three operations all delegates must support — the delegate "interface," so to speak. Delegates expose one operation to their clients:

> **brief(packet, clientID)**: Whenever a host sends a packet, it must "brief" its delegate — if the delegate is to vouch for the packet on behalf of the sender, it needs to know which packets its clients actually sent.

To the outside world, accountability delegates offer two operations, borrowed largely from AIP:

> **verify(packet)**: Anyone in the network can challenge a packet; its accountability delegate responds affirmatively if the packet was sent by a valid client and the flow has not been reported as malicious.

> **shutoff(packet)**: Given an attack packet, the victim can report the packet to the accountability delegate; in response, the delegate stops verifying (blocks) the flow in question and pursues a long term solution with the sender.

We now discuss options for constructing the accountability address and for implementing the delegate interface.

## 5.1 Accountability Addresses

Accountability addresses serve two related functions. First, the address is used to send verification requests and shutoffs to an accountability delegate. The NID:HID portion of the address is used to direct messages to the delegate server. Second, routers often need to identify flows, e.g., for traffic engineering (TE) or monitoring purposes, and today source addresses are often part of the flow ID. The granularity of this ID is even more important in APIP since traffic is verified (and blocked) per flow. In this section, we discuss the implications of replacing source addresses with accountability addresses for flow identification.

*Creating Flow IDs* Routers construct flow IDs using information available in the network and transport headers. However, in APIP, if an accountability address merely points to a delegate, packets from all clients of a particular delegate will be indistinguishable, robbing routers of the ability to distinguish flows at a finer granularity than *delegate↔destination* (Figure 3a). This may be too coarse-grained, especially since the flow ID is used for dropping packets from malicious flows. In effect, every flow that shares a delegate with a malicious flow will share its fate. (TE tends to work with coarser-grained flows, so destination addresses alone may be sufficiently granular.)

The simplest way to support finer-grain flow IDs is to include the delegate's SID in the calculation, similar to the

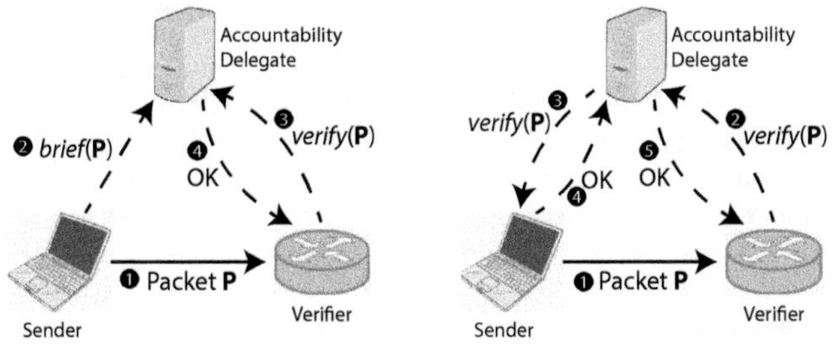


(a) Fingerprint Collection (b) Recursive Verification

Figure 4: Briefing Techniques

way port numbers are used today. For example, delegates could assign a group of SIDs to each client source domain, which it can use to define network-level flows as it sees fit (see below). Accountability delegates with many clients would require a large pool of SIDs to achieve fine granularity (e.g., at the host or TCP flow level). If the SID is not sufficient, it is possible to add a separate flow ID field to the packet header to improve granularity. In our discussion, we will use the term flow ID to refer to both the SID only and SID plus dedicated field approaches.

*Controlling Flow Granularity* How the flow ID is assigned affects both privacy and the amount of collateral damage caused when an aggregate flow containing a malicious sender is blocked. At one extreme, a delegate could use a single flow ID for all its customers, which provides the biggest possible anonymity set, but may result in a lot of legitimate traffic being dropped if any client sends malicious traffic. At the other extreme, assigning senders unique flow IDs (Figure 3b), or a separate flow ID per TCP flow, allows fine grain filtering, but allows sender/TCP flow linkability. The solution we propose is for delegates to assign each client a pool of flow IDs which it can assign to packets based on internal policies. Delegates check that clients are using flow IDs assigned to them as part of the verification process (§5.3).

*Source Domain Accountability Address Management* An interesting alternative to senders picking a flow ID for each packet (within boundaries set by their delegate) is to have flow IDs assigned at the level of the source domain. For example, individual hosts could send packets with a traditional source address. If a packet leaves the source domain, the gateway routers replace it with an accountability address and hide the return address (like a NAT; see § 6). This approach is especially attractive for source domains that act as the accountability delegate for their hosts (§7.4). Centralized management simplifies managing the pool of flow IDs, enforcing policies, and incremental deployment. The drawback is that individual users lose control over sender privacy.

## 5.2 Brief()

Accountability delegates need to know which packets their clients have sent if they are to vouch for them when challenged with a **verify()**. We consider two approaches in this section. Accountability delegates can choose any method, possibly on a per-client basis.

**Fingerprint Collection** The simplest solution is for senders to proactively send their delegates fingerprints of the packets they send (Figure 4a). The delegate stores the fingerprints (e.g., for 30 seconds), and when it receives a **verify()**, it searches for the fingerprint and returns `VERIFIED` if it finds it. For reasons explained in §5.3, a packet's fingerprint is actually more than just a simple hash:

$$F(P) = H\left(K_{SD_S} \mid\mid P_{header} \mid\mid H(P_{body})\right)$$

Here $H$ is a cryptographically secure hash function and $K_{SD_S}$ is a symmetric key established when sender $S$ signed up for service with delegate $D_S$. It is included in the fingerprint to prevent observers from linking $P$ to $F(P)$. Each brief includes a client ID, a fingerprint, and a message authentication code (MAC):

Sender transmits packet and brief:

$$\begin{aligned} S \rightarrow R: &\quad P \\ S \rightarrow D_S: &\quad \textbf{brief}(P) = \text{clientID} \mid\mid F(P) \\ &\quad \mid\mid \text{MAC}_{K_{SD_S}}(\text{clientID} \mid\mid F(P)) \end{aligned}$$

To reduce delegate storage requirements and network overhead, rather than sending full-sized fingerprints, hosts can instead periodically provide their delegate with a bloom filter of the fingerprints of all packets sent since the last brief. Accountability delegates keep the filters received in the last thirty seconds.

Note that in either case (fingerprints or bloom filters), the delegate can vouch for its clients' packets without knowing anything about their contents. Finally, if gateway routers assign accountability addresses, they can also take responsibility for briefing the delegate.

*Bootstrapping* Who vouches for briefs? That is, how do senders get briefs to their delegates if the packets carrying them cannot be verified? Clients include a special "token" in brief packet headers (e.g., as the SID in the destination address) proving to the delegate that the brief is from a valid client. Since verification requests include a copy of the unverified packet's header (see §5.3), the delegate can see that both the accountability *and destination* addresses point at the delegate, indicating the packet is a brief, cueing the delegate to check for the token. Delegates can use any scheme to select tokens. One possibility is using a hash chain based on a shared secret. Each brief uses the next hash in the chain, preventing replays. (This ensures the brief is from a valid client—we discuss "brief-flood" DoS attacks from malicious clients in §7.2.)

**Recursive Verification** The alternative to fingerprint collection is to have hosts store the fingerprints of recently sent packets. When a delegate receives a **verify()**, the delegate forwards the verification packet to the host that sent it. The host responds "yes" or "no" to the delegate, which passes the response on to the original challenger (Figure 4b). In this case, **brief()** is a NOP. Recursive verification reduces network and storage overhead, but the catch is that in order to work each verification request must carry enough information for the delegate to map the packet to a customer. This impacts the flow ID granularity (§5.1): when using recursive verification, delegate must ensure that no two clients share a flow ID (or it must be willing to forward a verification to multiple clients).

## 5.3 Verify()

**Verify()** is nearly identical to AIP's anti-spoofing challenge, the difference being that an AIP challenge asks, "Is this packet's source address spoofed?" whereas **verify()**

asks, "Do you vouch for this packet?" In AIP, first-hop routers periodically verify that packets purporting to be from a particular host are not spoofed. Likewise, in APIP routers periodically verify that flows are using valid accountability delegates and have not been reported for misbehavior. Verified flows are added to a whitelist whose entries expire at the end of each *verification interval* (e.g., 30 seconds); if a flow is still active, it is re-verified. Consider a sender $S$, a receiver $R$, and a router $V$ ("verifier"). If $V$ receives a packet $P$ from $S$ to $R$ and the flow $S \rightarrow R$ is not in the whitelist, $V$ sends a verification packet to $S$'s accountability delegate, $D_S$ (identified in the packet). To avoid buffering unverified packets, $V$ can drop $P$ and send an error message notifying $S$ that $P$ was dropped pending verification.

The verification packet includes $P$'s fingerprint plus a MAC computed with a secret key known only to $V$. $D_S$ now checks three things: (1) it has received a brief from $S$ containing $F(P)$, (2) the accountability address in $P$ is using an *SID* assigned to $S$, and (3) transmission from $S$ to $R$ has not been blocked via a shutoff (§5.4). If everything checks out, $D_S$ returns a copy of the verification packet signed with its private key to $V$, which adds $S \rightarrow R$ to its whitelist. The protocol, below, shows both fingerprint collection ($\star$) and recursive verification ($\blacklozenge$), though only one or the other would be used in practice. ($K_V$ is a secret known only to $V$; $K^+_{D_S}/K^-_{D_S}$ is the delegate's public/private keypair; $K_{SD_S}$ is the symmetric key shared by $S$ and $D_S$.)

Sender transmits packet and brief:

$S \rightarrow R: \quad P$

$\star \quad S \rightarrow D_S: \quad \textbf{brief}(P)$

Verifier sends error to sender and verification to delegate:

$V \rightarrow S: \quad \texttt{DROPPED (VERIFYING)} \,||\, F(P)$

$V \rightarrow D_S: \quad \textbf{verify}(P) = P_{header} \,||\, H(P_{body}) \,||\, \text{MAC}_{K_V}(P_{header} \,||\, H(P_{body}))$

Delegate verifies packet and responds:

$\blacklozenge \quad D_S \rightarrow S: \quad \{\textbf{verify}(P)\}_{K_{SD_S}}$

$\blacklozenge \quad S \rightarrow D_S: \quad \{\texttt{VERIFIED} \,||\, \textbf{verify}(P)\}_{K_{SD_S}}$

$D_S \rightarrow V: \quad \{\texttt{VERIFIED} \,||\, \textbf{verify}(P) \,||\, K^+_{D_S}\}_{K^-_{D_S}}$

$V: \quad$ add flow entry to whitelist

There are three points worth noting about this protocol. First, $D$ returns the original verification packet so $V$ does not have to keep state about pending verifications. $V$ uses the MAC to ensure that it originated the verification request, preventing attackers from filling $V$'s whitelist with bogus entries by sending it verifications it never asked for.

Second, the delegate needs to know the packet's destination address ($R$) so it can check if traffic $S \rightarrow R$ has been shut off. Since briefs only contain fingerprints, the delegate does not already have this information, so the verification request includes a copy of $P$'s header. It also includes a hash of the body so the delegate can finish computing the fingerprint of packet being verified to check that it matches a brief in its cache.

Third, the last line in the protocol adds the flow to the white list, identified by its accountability address, destination address, and flow ID, as described in §5.1.

**ISP Participation** Though *anyone* can verify a packet, APIP is most effective when routers closest to the source perform verification. An ISP that suspects a customer/peer might not be properly verifying its traffic can apply business pressure or possibly dissolve peering relationships if it finds an inordinate amount of unverified traffic. Another concern is that domains might verify traffic with a long verification interval (that is, after verifying a packet from a flow, the same flow is not verified again for an extended period of time). This allows malicious flows to do damage even if the flow's delegate receives a **shutoff()** since the flow will not be blocked until the next verification. The impact of long verification intervals could be mitigated if transit networks also verify traffic (see §8.1 for expected time-to-shutoff); after a **shutoff()**, the filter moves toward the sender as closer routers re-verify the flow. Also, even if routers are slow to react, APIP still facilitates a long-term fix eventually.

## 5.4 Shutoff()

Today, when hosts or routers identify a malicious flow, they can locally filter packets and work with neighboring ISPs to stop traffic. In APIP, they can also send a **shutoff()** request to the attacker's delegate. This is particularly useful for receivers, who should have the final say as to whether a flow is wanted or not. The protocol differs from AIP's shutoff protocol in two important ways. First, shutoffs are directed to accountability delegates, not to senders. Second a delegate can not only block the offending flow, but it can also pursue a long-term fix. The **shutoff()** protocol is shown below (between receiver $R$ and $S$'s delegate $D_S$ regarding packet $P$ from sender $S$):

Sender transmits packet and brief:

$S \rightarrow R: \quad P$

$S \rightarrow D_S: \quad \textbf{brief}(P)$

Receiver sends shutoff:

$R \rightarrow D_S: \quad \textbf{shutoff}(P) = \{P_{header} \,||\, H(P_{body}) \,||\, \textit{duration} \,||\, K^+_R\}_{K^-_R}$

Sender's delegate verifies shutoff and takes action:

$D_S: \quad$ check $H(K^+_R) == \textit{dest}(P_{header})$

$D_S: \quad$ block offending flow for *duration* sec

Receivers can *always* shut off traffic directed at them. When the delegate receives the **shutoff()**, it checks that the **shutoff()** was signed by the private key corresponding to the recipient of the packet in question (so the **shutoff()** contains both the victim's public key and the original packet's header; the delegate compares the hash of the public key to the packet's destination address). If the verifier is a router and the **shutoff()** is signed by an ISP's key, it might also be honored, but perhaps only with manual intervention—if a reputable ISP says one of your clients is attacking its network, chances are you should listen. After verifying a **shutoff()**, the attacker's delegate responds in two ways.

*Short-term fix:* To provide the victim immediate relief, the delegate blocks the offending flow by ceasing to verify packets from the attacker to the victim. Routers only save flow verifications in their whitelists temporarily; when a router on the path from $S$ to $R$ next tries to verify the attack flow, the delegate responds `DROP_FLOW`. This means the attack could last up to a router's verification interval—we discuss expected shutoff time in §8.1. If delegates work with ISPs, response time could be shortened by pushing verification revocations from delegates to routers. Alternatively, if we assume widespread shutoff support in NICs, delegates could send shutoffs to directly to attackers, as in AIP.

*Long-term fix:* Since clients sign contracts with their delegates, a delegate can contact the owner of misbehaving hosts out-of-band. Since most unwanted traffic comes from botnets of compromised hosts with well-intentioned owners [23], the owner will generally fix the problem, at which point the delegate can unblock flows from the host. If a client refuses to comply, the delegate can terminate service or report him to the authorities.

# 6. MASKING RETURN ADDRESSES

APIP separates accountability from other source address roles, allowing senders to hide the return address from observers in the network. APIP does not define any particular privacy mechanism, but rather enables various lightweight, "always-on" strategies for increasing the default level of privacy for all traffic without weakening accountability. We offer two examples: end-to-end return address encryption and network address translation. Since our focus is sender-flow unlinkability, our primary concern is the size of the sender anonymity set from the perspective of four possible adversaries: the source domain, observers in the source domain, transit networks, and the receiver (Table 2).

**End-to-end Encryption** Since the return address is used only by the receiver and not by routers, a simple idea is to encrypt it end-to-end (e.g., using IKE [18], à la IPsec); now only the destination and accountability addresses are visible in the network. We imagine two variants: one in which return address encryption is a network layer standard and can be performed end-to-end or gateway-to-gateway and one in which the return address is moved to a higher layer (e.g., transport or session layer).

Of course, though the return address is encrypted in the forward direction, it will plainly visible as the destination address in responses; determined attackers may be able to link the outbound and inbound traffic (e.g., with timing analysis). Still, even this simple strategy offers increased privacy against passive observers, e.g., reviewing logs from a core ISP.

**Network Address Translation** Encrypting the return address end-to-end hides it from the network, but not from the destination. For privacy from the network *and* the recipient, edge ISPs' border routers could perform address translation on outbound packets' return addresses by changing *NID:HID:SID* to *NID:HID':SID'*. (This can be done deterministically to avoid keeping large translation tables [30].) Note that in contrast to the encryption option, response packets sent by the destination will not reveal the identity of the original sender (in the destination address). The downside is that, in contrast to encrypted return addresses, the anonymity set shrinks closer to the source.

Today, increased use of NAT might be a controversial proposition, but cleaner thinking about source addresses mitigates some of the chief arguments against it. For example, in 2006 the entire nation of Qatar was banned from Wikipedia when one user vandalized an article because the country's sole ISP uses a NAT with one external IP address [3]; in APIP, all hosts could share one external return address while still being held individually accountable via the accountability address.

Second, NATs are traditionally deployed for address space separation—the privacy they provide is a side effect [35]. This is known to cause problems for servers or P2P applications. In contrast, we suggest NATing for privacy, which can be done selectively for outgoing connections. Incoming connections are not affected, so servers, for example, can publish their internal address to DNS and receive incoming connections without any kind of hole punching. Of course, NATing for incoming connections also has security benefits, but this is an orthogonal issue.

*Reducing Overhead* Not all packets need a return address. For connection oriented traffic, the return address needs to be sent to the destination only once during the establishment of the connection (and also when a mobile device switches networks). The destination can store it and reuse it for later packets. Doing so (1) ameliorates the header overhead introduced by splitting accountability and return addresses in the first place and (2) allows NATs to modify many fewer packets.

*Beyond the First Hop* No matter how far a packet travels, the sender anonymity set is still just the sender's source domain. Though this may be sufficient for most senders, the NAT approach can be extended by performing address translation at more border routers. Though core ISPs are unlikely to do this, if the first 2–3 domains in the path do, a packet's sender anonymity set grows significantly before reaching the core (and ultimately its destination).

# 7. IN THE REAL WORLD

## 7.1 Holding Delegates Accountable

Delegates have three responsibilities: protecting the privacy of their clients, verifying packets with fingerprints that match those sent by valid clients, and dropping invalid packets. We briefly discuss how malicious or compromised delegates can harm either their clients or allow their clients to harm others.

*(1) Releasing private information about clients.* Delegates can learn a lot about who their clients communicate with, information they could use for their own benefit or reveal to a third party. Upon discovering a leak, the client can terminate service, find a new delegate, and potentially pursue legal action for breach of contract. Note that delegates only see packet headers, *not* packet contents. (An interesting direction for future work is exploring anonymous briefing schemes, e.g., based on cryptography or the use of an intermediary.)

*(2) Failing to verify clients' packets.* Delegates can effectively perform a DoS attack on clients by failing to verify their packets. Senders can detect this due to the excessive number of `DROPPED (VERIFYING)` or `DROPPED (VERIFICATION FAILED)` error messages they will receive from verifiers. Again, the client can then terminate service.

*(3) Verifying invalid packets.* Delegates can support attacks by verifying packets for which they did not receive a brief from a client or which belong to flows that have been shut off. (Such a delegate may be compromised or misconfigured or may even be colluding with an attacker.) Victims can detect such malicious behavior (e.g., by observing that their shutoff requests have been ignored).

**Who Can be a Delegate?** The likelihood of any of the above problems occurring depends on *who can be a dele-*

| Adversary | End-to-end Encryption | Address Translation |
|---|---|---|
| *Source Domain* | Source domain always knows a packet's **sender**. | Source domain always knows a packet's **sender**. |
| *Observers in Source Domain* | Other **source domain customers**. | The **sender**. The sender's address is observable until the packet reaches the border router where NAT is performed. |
| *Transit Networks* | Starts as **source domain's customers** and **grows** the farther the packet travels. By the time it reaches the core, it could have come from anywhere. | **Source domain's customers**. |
| *Receiver* | The **sender**. The receiver decrypts the return address, which is the sender's address. If the sender is concerned with anonymity from the receiver, end-to-end encryption is not a viable option. | **Source domain's customers**. |

Table 2: Comparison of sender anonymity set, as seen by different adversaries, for end-to-end encryption and NAT.

*gate*. The issue of delegate oversight is complex; given space constraints, we can only hope to lay the groundwork for discussion and future work.

At one extreme, a single central authority could provide some form of oversight over delegates, similar to how ICANN accredits TLDs; verifiers would then only accept delegates on a whitelist published by this authority. This has the advantage that delegates can be monitored and misbehaving delegates can be immediately removed from the whitelist, creating an incentive for responsible delegate management. On the other hand, vetting all delegates is a huge burden for a single authority and the role (and power) of a single organization in charge of such a critical function is likely to raise political concerns.

The other extreme is a free-for-all: a host can pick any host to be its delegate. This flexibility opens the door for many deployment models. Besides commercial (third party) delegates, hosts can be their own delegates (similar to AIP), use their source domain as their delegate (§7.4), or form a peer-to-peer delegate network, in which hosts (or domains) vouch for one other. The critical drawback of this flexibility is weaker protection against attacks—bots in a botnet, for example, can vouch for one another's packets regardless how many **shutoff()**s they receive. It will clearly be harder to defend against such attacks compared to the case where there are only a limited number of vetted delegates.

Naturally, a pragmatic solution likely falls somewhere in between these extremes. For example, a set of well-known commercial "delegate authorities" could emerge, similar to today's certificate authority infrastructure, each publishing a delegate whitelist. Alternatively, various groups could maintain delegate blacklists based on historical incidents, similar to today's security companies' publishing malware signatures. Individual verifiers can then decide which delegates to accept, a decision that could depend on many factors, including their position in the network (tier 1 versus edge), local regulation, historical information, or the "trust domain" they belong to [37]. Many other forms of semi-structured self regulation are possible.

## 7.2 Attacking APIP

We need to ensure that hosts cannot use APIP mechanisms to undermine APIP itself; two potential such attacks are "verification-flooding" and "brief-flooding."

**Verification-Flooding** Attackers could attempt to overwhelm an accountability delegate with bogus verification requests—rendering it incapable of verifying honest hosts' packets—by sending a large number of dummy packets with accountability addresses pointing at the victim delegate. To these bogus verifications, the delegate could respond `DROP_HOST` (as opposed to `DROP_FLOW`). Source domains should track the number of `DROP_HOST`s their customers generate, taking action if it is too high.

**Brief-Flooding** Similar to verification flooding, malicious *clients* could target their own delegate by sending a flood of briefs. This attack is tricky, since it is hard to distinguish from an honest host that happens to send lots of packets. Delegates can enact their own policies (e.g.: will accept 1 brief per second; must use bloom filters), which should be agreed upon when the client initially signs up for service.

## 7.3 Bootstrapping Trust

We now relax our initial assumption that HIDs are self-certifying; doing so does not break APIP, but requires us to do a small amount of extra work in **brief()**, **verify()**, and **shutoff()**.

**brief()** Clients already encrypt **brief()**s using a symmetric key established when the client registered for service, so no change is required.

**verify()** Delegates use their private keys to sign verification responses. If keys are not bound to HIDs, a PKI can be used instead; verifiers now need to check a delegate's certificate before trusting a response.

**shutoff()** Victims sign **shutoff()** messages to convince the attacker's delegate that the shutoff truly came from the recipient of the offending packet. While we think it is reasonable to assume delegates register keys with a PKI for signing **verify()**s, there are many more hosts than delegates, so here we instead rely on verification. Upon receiving a **shutoff()**, the attacker's delegate sends a verification packet to the victim's delegate to check that the shutoff really came from the original packet's recipient:

$$\begin{aligned} R \rightarrow D_R &: \quad \textbf{brief}(\textbf{shutoff}(P)) \\ D_S \rightarrow D_R &: \quad X = \textbf{verify*}(\textit{shutoff}) \\ D_R \rightarrow D_S &: \quad \{\texttt{VERIFIED} \,||\, X\}_{K^-_{D_S}} \end{aligned}$$

When verifying a **shutoff()**, the delegate needs to look inside the shutoff packet, at the header of the original packet that prompted the shutoff, and check that its destination

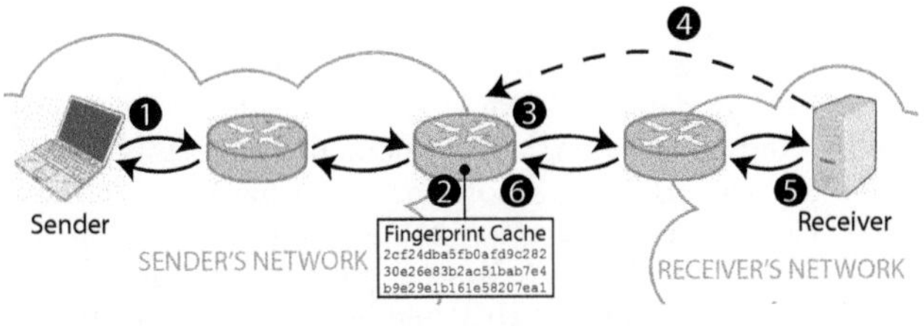


Figure 5: **Design 1:** ❶ Host sends packet using its own address as the source address. ❷ The ISP's border router saves a hash of the packet and ❸ performs address translation on the source address. ❹ If the packet is malicious, the receiver sends a **shutoff()** to the border router, otherwise ❺ it responds. ❻ The border router translates the response's destination address back to the original sender's address.

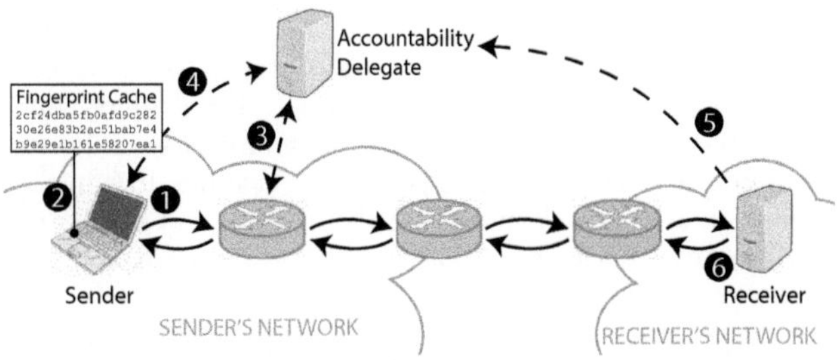


Figure 6: **Design 2:** ❶ Host sends packet and ❷ saves hash. ❸ First-hop router sends **verify()** to the packet's accountability delegate, which ❹ forwards the verification to the host. ❺ Using the accountability address, the receiver can send a **shutoff()**; otherwise ❻ it responds using the return address.

| | **Design 1** | **Design 2** |
|---|---|---|
| *Delegate* | Source domain | Third party |
| *Briefing* | Fingerprint collect. | Recursive ver. |
| *Source Addr.* | Single field | Separate fields |
| *Return Addr.* | NAT | NAT or encrypt |

Table 3: Two possible instantiations of APIP.

(the victim) sent the shutoff. (We denote **verify()** with this additional check **verify*()**.)

## 7.4 Concrete Designs

APIP is an architecture that allows routers and destinations to identify an entity that is willing to take responsibility for the packet, but properties of APIP depend on how it is deployed. For the sake of concreteness, we now sketch two end-to-end instantiations of APIP with very different properties. Table 3 summarizes the two designs.

**Design 1** In the first design (Figure 5), the source domain acts as the accountability delegate for its hosts. Hosts are not aware of APIP and send packets with traditional source addresses. The gateway routers for the domain use address translation to mask the return address, turning the source address into a combined accountability address and masked return address. They also collect packet fingerprints and respond to **verify()** and **shutoff()** requests. Gateway routers could either collectively act as a distributed accountability delegate and keep briefs locally, or they could periodically send briefs to a shared accountability server. This first design could be viewed as a variant of AIP, but implemented at the source domain level instead of individual senders.

This design offers a number of advantages. First, it is very efficient: gateway routers already naturally see all packets, eliminating the overhead of briefing a third party. Second, the source domain can immediately block malicious flows at the source in response to a shutoff, whereas external delegates can typically only stop flows indirectly. Third, hosts do not need to be modified.

Finally, this first design allows for incremental deployment of APIP over IP. Domains could implement accountability and address translation, as described. Packets would need to be marked to indicate whether the source domain supports APIP (e.g., by repurposing an ECN bit). Since both return traffic and **verify()**s/**shutoff()**s would arrive at the domain's border routers, **verify()** and **shutoff()** would each be assigned a new IP protocol number so the border router knows what to do with the packet. Since IP addresses are not cryptographic, external keys would have to be used to ensure the integrity of the **verify()** and **shutoff()** operations, as described in §7.3.

**Design 2** The second design (Figure 6) uses a commercial third party that offers accountability delegation as a service (perhaps as part of a bundle with antivirus or firewall software). In this design, senders insert both an accountability address and a return address in the packet; the return address can be masked either with encryption or a NAT. Since the delegate is off-site, recursive verification is attractive: rather than regularly sending briefs, hosts save packet hashes and the delegate challenges clients when it itself is challenged.

One advantage of this solution is that it allows companies, universities, or small domains to avoid the hassle of managing delegate servers themselves by outsourcing delegation. Another advantage is that it is harder for observers in the network to determine what source domain the sender belongs to. The drawback is that there is more overhead than in the first design.

# 8. EVALUATION

The primary question we consider in the section is: "is delegated accountability technically feasible?" Using a trace of NetFlow data from the border routers of a mid-sized university, we explore the costs of **brief()** and **verify()** and the efficacy of **shutoff()**. The five minute trace was taken on June 18, 2013 at noon and contains ten million flows. We then present a short privacy analysis.

## 8.1 Delegated Accountability

**Brief()** Briefing the delegate incurs computational overhead at the sender, storage overhead at the delegate, and bandwidth overhead in the network. In §5.2 we suggested that senders could report their traffic to their delegates by sending a list of packet fingerprints or by sending a bloom filter of recent fingerprints.

*Computational Overhead* Producing a packet fingerprint requires computing two hashes; we assume that computing the MAC of the fingerprint, in the worst case, costs one additional hash. Commodity CPUs can compute in the neighborhood of 5–20 MH/s [1], which translates to 0.9–3.4 Gbps (conservatively assuming 64B packets). This is more than reasonable for endhosts; for servers sending large volumes of traffic, we expect data centers could outsource briefing to an in-path appliance built with ASICs—current ASIC-based bitcoin miners perform 5–3,500 GH/s, translating to 0.9–600 Tbps.

*Storage Overhead* Next we consider the storage requirements at the delegate for saving briefs. Briefs are periodically purged from the cache; if a **verify()** arrives for a legitimate packet whose brief has been deleted, the sender must retransmit the packet. Assuming a single delegate serves all hosts in our trace, the first two series in Figure 7 show the size of the brief cache for different expiration intervals assuming the delegate stores individual fingerprints, each a 20 byte SHA-1 hash. The remaining series consider the space required if, instead of sending a fingerprint per packet, hosts send a bloom filter every second for each active flow[1]. We assume that hosts size each filter appropriately based on how many packets from the flow were sent during the past second. If briefs expire every $n$ seconds, we report brief cache sizes based on both the average and maximum number of packets seen across $n$-second bins in our trace.

*Bandwidth Overhead* Figure 8 shows the bandwidth required for the same briefing schemes discussed above. Sending fingerprints consumes an additional 2.5% of the original traffic volume, which was just under 10 Gbps; the bloom filter schemes consume 0.25%–0.5%. The bloom filter results assume a simple update scheme: every second, each host sends a bloom filter for packets sent in each flow[1] during the last 30 seconds; when the delegate gets a new filter for an existing flow, it replaces the old filter (using a bloom filter alternative that supports resizing is interesting future work). Note briefing overhead can be avoided entirely if (1) the ISP is the accountability delegate, so border routers save hashes directly, or (2) delegates use recursive verification (§5.2).

**Verify()** The magnitude of verification overhead is determined by the verification interval and flow granularity (fewer flows means fewer verifications; in our analysis, each "flow" is a TCP flow, so our numbers are an upper bound). There is a tradeoff between long and short verification intervals. The longer the interval, the more whitelist space is required at routers to remember which flows have been verified and the longer a malicious sender could transmit before being shut off. On the other hand, shorter intervals mean more work (more **verify()**s) for the delegate.

*Computational Overhead* Figure 9 shows how many **verify()**s per second an accountability delegate serving all the hosts in our trace would see at various verification intervals. A key observation here is that after 10 seconds, increasing the verification interval does not significantly decrease verification rate at the delegate since most flows are short. This knee suggests that 10 seconds might make a good interval for use in practice.

In our trace, a verification interval of 10 seconds generates a *maximum* of 78,000 **verify()**s per second, each causing a lookup in a table with 1.5 million entries (assuming delegates save briefs for 30 seconds) and one signature generation at the delegate. We think these numbers are reasonable and leave enough headroom to comfortably handle larger networks—CuckooFilter [38] achieves more than 180,000 lookups per second in a table with *one billion* entries and the Ed25519 signature system [8] can perform 109,000 signatures per second on a 2010 quad-core 2.4GHz Westmere CPU.

*Storage Overhead* As routers verify flows, they keep a whitelist of verified flows so that every single packet need not be verified. Whitelist entries expire at the end of each verification interval, at which point the flow is re-verified. We use our trace to estimate the size of this whitelist.

To account for network architectures with addresses significantly larger than IP's, we assume each address is 60 bytes—20 bytes each for the *NID*, *HID*, and *SID*. (Many research efforts explore self-certifying IDs [6, 27, 4, 17] which are typically the hashes of a name or public key; we choose 20 bytes since SHA-1 produces 20 byte digests.) Entries identify flows at a host-host granularity, so each one is 120 bytes (two 60 byte addresses).

Figure 10 shows the size of the whitelist as we vary the verification interval. For a given verification interval, we group the flows in our trace into bins the size of that interval; flows belong to a bin if they were active during that time period (so a flow could belong to multiple bins). The figure reports the whitelist size based on both the average number of flows across bins as well as the maximum seen in any bin. A 10 second interval requires a maximum of 94 MB of whitelist space.

**Shutoff()** After receiving a **shutoff()**, a delegate blocks malicious flows by ceasing to verify them. The next time a router on the path from the attacker to the victim verifies the flow, the delegate returns `DROP_FLOW` and the router blocks the flow. How quickly this happens after a **shutoff()** depends on how many on-path routers perform verification and how often they verify each flow. Figure 11 shows the expected delay before a shutoff takes effect for different verification intervals as a function of the number of participating routers.

## 8.2 Privacy

How much privacy does APIP buy? If a sender uses its source domain as a delegate, this depends on the size of that domain. Raghavan et. al. find that, if ISPs were to aggregate prefixes geographically, over half of the prefixes advertised by many popular last-mile ISPs would include more than 10 million IPs [30].

If a sender uses a third party delegate, the anonymity set grows the farther a packet travels from the source domain. To see how much, we use Route Views [2] data from January 1, 2014 to roughly estimate AS "fanout." For each AS, we track how many customer networks sit beneath it in the AS hierarchy. (To be conservative, we only count an AS as a customer if it originates a prefix. Transit networks with no hosts do not contribute to an anonymity set.) For each BGP announcement, we add the origin AS to its first- and second-hop providers' customer sets. Figure 12 shows a CDF of first- and second-hop anonymity set sizes. Notably, 50% of ASes originating prefixes have at least 180 first-hop "siblings" and 90% have over 900 second-hop siblings. Though

[1]In practice, we think hosts should send one bloom filter for *all* traffic each second, not one per flow. Unfortunately, for privacy reasons, our trace did not include local addresses, so we could not merge flows originating from the same sender.

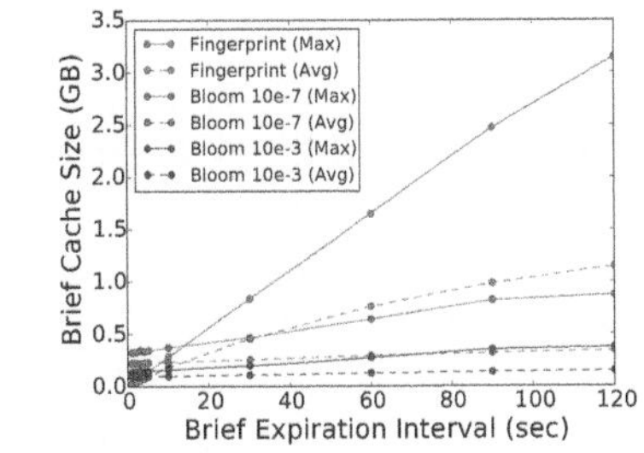


Figure 7: Brief cache size at delegate vs. fingerprint expiry interval.

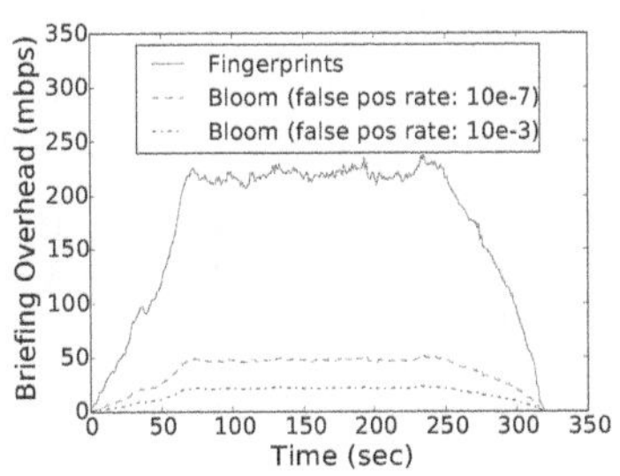


Figure 8: Briefing bandwidth overhead.

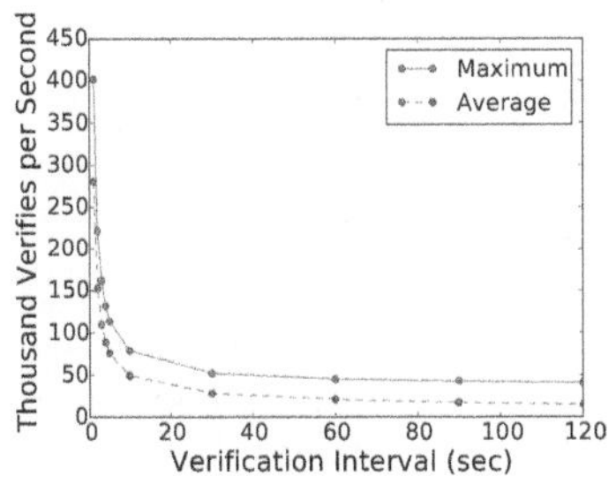


Figure 9: Verification rate at delegate vs. flow verification interval.

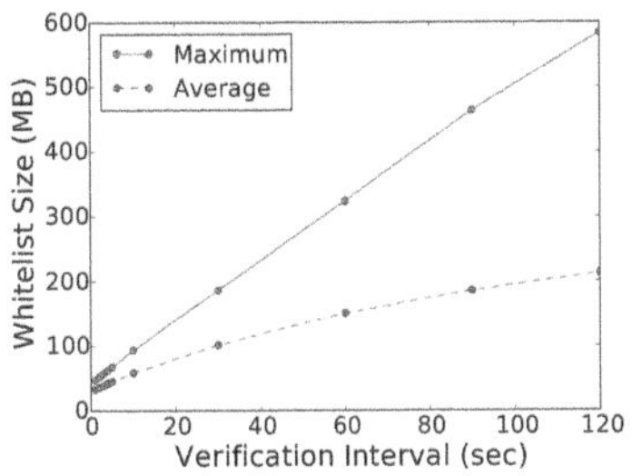


Figure 10: Size of whitelist of verified flows vs. flow verification interval.

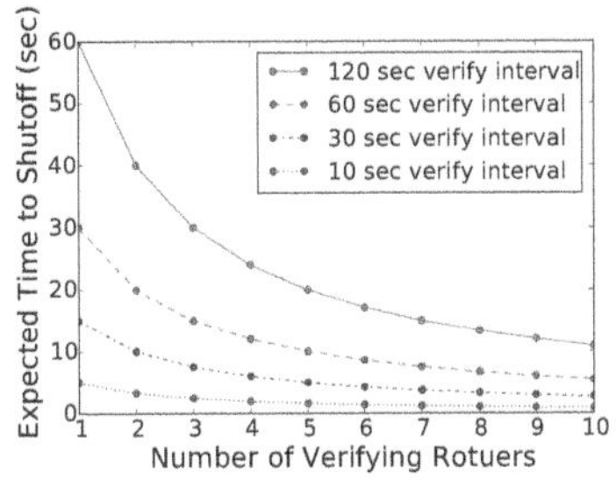


Figure 11: Expected time to shutoff vs. number of on-path verifiers.

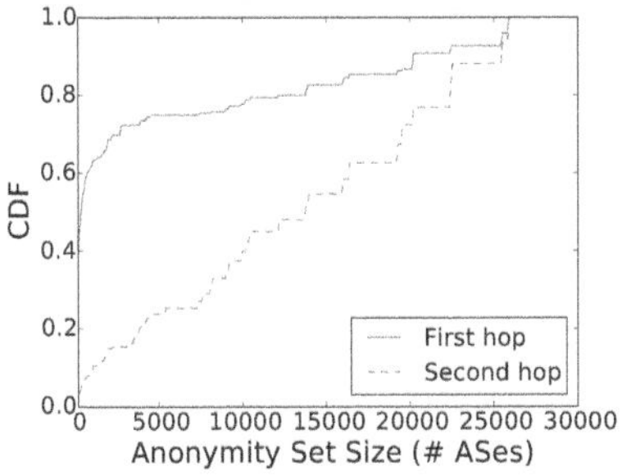


Figure 12: Anonymity Set Size

drawing conclusions about AS topology based on BGP announcements is imprecise, these ballpark figures give an idea of the anonymity benefits of delegated accountability.

# 9. RELATED WORK

**Privacy** Various techniques exist for hiding network source addresses, including crowds [32], mixes [12], and onion routing [31]. Real-world implementations based on these ideas include Anonymizer[2] and Tor[3]. Liu et al. consider building onion routing into the network architecture itself [25]. NDN [20] takes a more radical approach by eliminating source addresses altogether; data finds the sender by following "bread crumbs" left by the request. The drawback to all of these approaches is a complete lack of accountability; there is no easy way to link malicious traffic with senders.

Raghavan et. al. [30] describe ISPs offering NAT for privacy as a service but uses a single source address. LAP [19] is similar to (but more secure than) our "NAT-at-every-hop" approach but does not consider accountability.

**Accountability** Techniques like ingress/egress filtering [16, 24] aim to provide some degree of accountability by reducing the prevalence of source address spoofing; more sophisticated variants exist [29, 14, 21]. This class of approaches has limitations we address: (1) source addresses are only protected on a domain granularity, (2) filtering by itself provides no "shutoff" mechanism for misbehaving hosts who do not send spoofed packets, and (3) it is not compatible with schemes for hiding return addresses for the sake of anonymity.

As described in §3.1, our **verify()** and **shutoff()** mechanisms borrow heavily from AIP [4], which in turn based its mechanisms on ideas presented by Shaw [34] and in AITF [5]. By modifying these mechanisms to work with delegates, we make them privacy-preserving, enable long-term resolution, and avoid relying on self-certifying IDs.

Accountability delegates are described in [7], but the protocol is costly and is not evaluated; privacy receives only passing mention.

**Balancing Accountability and Privacy** The idea of identify escrow is not new (e.g., [10]). In particular, our notion of delegated accountability is similar in flavor to the *contractual anonymity* described in RECAP [33], in which a service provider (e.g., an online forum) offers its users anonymity which can be broken only if they violate a prearranged contract. The key difference is that RECAP provides contractual anonymity at the application layer while we balance anonymity and accountability at the network layer, which poses unique constraints (like requiring source addresses to be both routable and anonymizable).

**Addressing** The use of addresses that consist of separate network, host and socket IDs, creating separate identifiers and locators, has been widely proposed [15, 26, 22]. [11, 9] discuss the meaning of source addresses, though without our focus on privacy and accountability.

# 10. CONCLUSION

This paper attempts to show that a balance between accountability and privacy in the network *is* possible. By decoupling source addresses' roles as accountability addresses and return addresses, APIP strikes a balance between the two seemingly incompatible goals. Delegated accountability allows routers to verify that each packet they forward is vouched for and allows attack victims to report the abuse while at the same time permitting senders to hide their return addresses. Furthermore, the changes to traditional thinking about source addresses required to implement APIP

[2] `http://www.anonymizer.com/`
[3] `https://www.torproject.org/`

are not radical; though more exploration is clearly required, we think the ideas presented here could be applied to the current Internet.

## Acknowledgments

Many thanks to the reviewers and to our shepherd, John Wroclawski, for their insightful suggestions. This research was funded in part by NSF under award number CNS-1040801 and by DoD, Air Force Office of Scientific Research, National Defense Science and Engineering Graduate (NDSEG) Fellowship, 32 CFR 168a.

## 11. REFERENCES

[1] Mining Hardware Comparison. https://en.bitcoin.it/wiki/Mining_hardware_comparison.

[2] University of Oregon Route Views Project. http://www.routeviews.org.

[3] Wikipedia qatar ban 'temporary'. `http://news.bbc.co.uk/2/hi/technology/6224677.stm`, Jan. 2007.

[4] D. G. Andersen, H. Balakrishnan, N. Feamster, et al. Accountable internet protocol (AIP). SIGCOMM '08, pages 339–350, New York, NY, USA, 2008. ACM.

[5] K. J. Argyraki and D. R. Cheriton. Active internet traffic filtering: Real-time response to denial-of-service attacks. In *USENIX Annual Technical Conference, General Track*, pages 135–148, 2005.

[6] T. Aura. Cryptographically Generated Addresses (CGA). RFC 3972 (Proposed Standard), Mar. 2005. Updated by RFCs 4581, 4982.

[7] A. Bender, N. Spring, D. Levin, and B. Bhattacharjee. Accountability as a service. *SRUTI*, 7:1–6, 2007.

[8] D. J. Bernstein, N. Duif, T. Lange, P. Schwabe, and B.-Y. Yang. High-speed high-security signatures. *Journal of Cryptographic Engineering*, 2(2):77–89, 2012.

[9] M. B. Braun and J. Crowcroft. SNA: Sourceless Network Architecture. Technical Report UCAM-CL-TR-849, University of Cambridge, Computer Laboratory, Mar. 2014.

[10] J. Camenisch and A. Lysyanskaya. An efficient system for non-transferable anonymous credentials with optional anonymity revocation. In *Advances in Cryptology-EUROCRYPT 2001*, pages 93–118. Springer, 2001.

[11] C. Candolin and P. Nikander. IPv6 source addresses considered harmful. In *NordSec '01*, pages 54–68, 2001.

[12] D. Chaum. Untraceable electronic mail, return address, and digital pseudonyms. *Communications of the ACM*, 24(2):84–88, 1981.

[13] D. D. Clark, J. Wroclawski, K. R. Sollins, and R. Braden. Tussle in cyberspace: defining tomorrow's internet. SIGCOMM '02, pages 347–356, New York, NY, USA, 2002. ACM.

[14] Z. Duan, X. Yuan, and J. Chandrashekar. Constructing inter-domain packet filters to control ip spoofing based on bgp updates. In *INFOCOM*, 2006.

[15] D. Farinacci, V. Fuller, D. Meyer, and D. Lewis. The Locator/ID Separation Protocol (LISP). RFC 6830 (Experimental), Jan. 2013.

[16] P. Ferguson and D. Senie. Network Ingress Filtering: Defeating Denial of Service Attacks which employ IP Source Address Spoofing. RFC 2827 (Best Current Practice), May 2000. Updated by RFC 3704.

[17] D. Han, A. Anand, F. Dogar, et al. XIA: efficient support for evolvable internetworking. NSDI'12, pages 23–23, Berkeley, CA, USA, 2012. USENIX Association.

[18] D. Harkins and D. Carrel. The Internet Key Exchange (IKE). RFC 2409 (Proposed Standard), Nov. 1998. Obsoleted by RFC 4306, updated by RFC 4109.

[19] H.-C. Hsiao, T.-J. Kim, A. Perrig, et al. Lap: Lightweight anonymity and privacy. In *Security and Privacy (SP), 2012 IEEE Symposium on*, pages 506–520. IEEE, 2012.

[20] V. Jacobson, D. K. Smetters, J. D. Thornton, et al. Networking named content. CoNEXT '09, pages 1–12, New York, NY, USA, 2009. ACM.

[21] C. Jin, H. Wang, and K. G. Shin. Hop-count filtering: an effective defense against spoofed ddos traffic. In *CCS '03*, pages 30–41. ACM, 2003.

[22] V. Kafle, K. Nakauchi, and M. Inoue. Generic identifiers for id/locator split internetworking. In *K-INGN 2008.*, pages 299–306, 2008.

[23] S. Kandula, D. Katabi, M. Jacob, and A. Berger. Botz-4-sale: Surviving organized ddos attacks that mimic flash crowds. In *NSDI '05.*

[24] T. Killalea. Recommended Internet Service Provider Security Services and Procedures. RFC 3013 (Best Current Practice), Nov. 2000.

[25] V. Liu, S. Han, A. Krishnamurthy, and T. Anderson. Tor instead of ip. In *HotNets '11.*

[26] D. Meyer, L. Zhang, and K. Fall. Report from the IAB Workshop on Routing and Addressing. RFC 4984 (Informational), Sept. 2007.

[27] R. Moskowitz and P. Nikander. Host Identity Protocol (HIP) Architecture. RFC 4423 (Informational), May 2006.

[28] J. Naous, M. Walfish, A. Nicolosi, et al. Verifying and enforcing network paths with icing. CoNEXT '11, pages 30:1–30:12, New York, NY, USA, 2011. ACM.

[29] K. Park and H. Lee. On the effectiveness of route-based packet filtering for distributed dos attack prevention in power-law internets. In *SIGCOMM CCR*, volume 31, pages 15–26. ACM, 2001.

[30] B. Raghavan, T. Kohno, A. C. Snoeren, and D. Wetherall. Enlisting ISPs to improve online privacy: IP address mixing by default. PETS '09, pages 143–163, 2009.

[31] M. G. Reed, P. F. Syverson, and D. M. Goldschlag. Anonymous connections and onion routing. *IEEE Journal on Selected Areas in Communications*, 1998.

[32] M. K. Reiter and A. D. Rubin. Crowds: Anonymity for web transactions. *TISSEC*, 1(1):66–92, 1998.

[33] E. J. Schwartz, D. Brumley, and J. M. McCune. A contractual anonymity system. In *NDSS '10*, 2010.

[34] M. Shaw. Leveraging good intentions to reduce unwanted network traffic. In *Proc. USENIX Steps to Reduce Unwanted Traffic on the Internet workshop*, page 8, 2006.

[35] P. Srisuresh and K. Egevang. Traditional IP Network Address Translator (Traditional NAT). RFC 3022 (Informational), Jan. 2001.

[36] X. Yang, D. Wetherall, and T. Anderson. TVA: A DoS-limiting network architecture. *Networking, IEEE/ACM Transactions on*, 16(6):1267–1280, 2008.

[37] X. Zhang, H.-C. Hsiao, G. Hasker, et al. SCION: Scalability, control, and isolation on next-generation networks. In *Security and Privacy 2011(SP), 2011 IEEE Symposium on*, pages 212–227, 2011.

[38] D. Zhou, B. Fan, H. Lim, M. Kaminsky, and D. G. Andersen. Scalable, high performance ethernet forwarding with cuckooswitch. CoNEXT '13, pages 97–108, New York, NY, USA, 2013. ACM.

# Measuring IPv6 Adoption

Jakub Czyz
University of Michigan

Mark Allman
International Computer Science Institute

Jing Zhang
University of Michigan

Scott Iekel-Johnson
Arbor Networks, Inc.

Eric Osterweil
Verisign Labs

Michael Bailey
University of Michigan

## ABSTRACT

After several IPv4 address exhaustion milestones in the last three years, it is becoming apparent that the world is running out of IPv4 addresses, and the adoption of the next generation Internet protocol, IPv6, though nascent, is accelerating. In order to better understand this unique and disruptive transition, we explore twelve metrics using ten global-scale datasets to create the longest and broadest measurement of IPv6 adoption to date. Using this perspective, we find that adoption, relative to IPv4, varies by two orders of magnitude depending on the measure examined and that care must be taken when evaluating adoption metrics in isolation. Further, we find that regional adoption is not uniform. Finally, and perhaps most surprisingly, we find that over the last three years, the nature of IPv6 utilization—in terms of traffic, content, reliance on transition technology, and performance—has shifted dramatically from prior findings, indicating a maturing of the protocol into production mode. We believe IPv6's recent growth and this changing utilization signal a true quantum leap.

## Categories and Subject Descriptors

C.2.5 [**Local and Wide-Area Networks**]: Internet

## Keywords

Internet; IP; IPv4; IPv6; DNS; Measurement

## 1. INTRODUCTION

IPv4 is the common thread that has held the Internet together since its very early years, and, thus, it is both the most important and most widely-deployed networking protocol in existence. For basic end-to-end connectivity, devices need to have a unique IP address, but the world is rapidly running out of available IPv4 address space. Thus, if we want the Internet to continue growing and delivering its societal and economic benefits for the next generation, we have a challenge. In just the three years since February 2011, the organizations responsible for allocating IPv4 addresses, including the Internet Assigned Numbers Authority (IANA), as well as two of its five subordinate regional Internet registries (RIRs) have either completely exhausted address space or resorted to rationing their final address block. It appears that after years of both architecture changes and stop-gap measures forestalling IPv4 address exhaustion (e.g., classless interdomain routing [CIDR] [12], network address translation [NAT] [37]) the Internet has now begun its first core protocol change. Exhaustion is providing increased impetus for the network to finally adopt the next version of IP, IPv6. We show that, while raw IPv6 Internet traffic is still a small fraction (0.64%), the *nature* of its use and the *trajectory* of growth have shifted dramatically, and, consequently, IPv6 should no longer be dismissed by researchers as an uninteresting rarity.

In this paper, our aim is to empirically understand the adoption of IPv6. A once-in-a-lifetime opportunity to observe technological change on such a grand scale, this is both practically and scientifically important. However, with a handful of exceptions, most of the individual assessments of IPv6 that the community has produced, to date, are anecdotal (e.g., using one server's, campus's or Internet exchange point's perspective) and/or focus on only a single aspect of IPv6 adoption (e.g., route advertisement). No single existing perspective or study suffices to truly gauge the state of IPv6 in the large. We argue that, while this previous body of work has been invaluable at tracking aspects of adoption, a broader approach to measuring IPv6 deployment, which assembles a breadth of observations and compares existing datasets against each other, is needed to truly understand where we are. The goal is not to pick the "best" one, but to understand the *systemic* state of IPv6 deployment via all available measurements.

To achieve our goal we assemble a set of six publicly-accessible datasets that speak to one or more aspects of IPv6 adoption. We add four additional, previously-unpublished datasets, including a global Internet traffic dataset that includes traffic statistics from 260 providers and represents 16,200 petabytes/month, or approximately 33-50% of all Internet traffic—the largest traffic sample reported in an IPv6 study. In addition to the traffic data, we add DNS query data from several of the largest globally-distributed IPv4-based replicas of the .com and .net top-level domains (TLDs), as well as nearly all native IPv6 replicas for these TLDs.

To create a comprehensive view of IPv6 adoption, we enumerate and compare both previously-reported and novel metrics and weave them into a taxonomy. In applying these metrics to our datasets, we seek to reveal relationships and patterns not otherwise visible when studying any single metric in isolation. Further, we speculate that several recent IPv4 exhaustion events (IANA, APNIC, RIPE) and community IPv6 "flag days" (World IPv6 Day 2011 and Launch 2012) may have noticeably influenced the progression of adoption.

Through the lens of this comprehensive approach, we compose a picture of the current state of global IPv6 adoption. We find:


*SIGCOMM'14,* August 17–22, 2014, Chicago, IL, USA.

http://dx.doi.org/10.1145/2619239.2626295.

- **IPv6 is real.** Over the last three years, IPv6 has reached a significant developmental milestone and is finally being used natively and for normal, production traffic, on a non-trivial and accelerating scale. While IPv6 is still under 1% of Internet traffic, it has increased over 400% in each of the last two years, relies much less on transition technologies, and is used for similar applications to IPv4, with similar performance.
- **Measurements vary widely.** IPv6 adoption level differs by up to *two orders of magnitude* depending on the metric used. For instance, although IPv6 monthly address allocations are about 57% of IPv4, the percentage of IPv4 nameservers in .com that are IPv6-reachable is around 3%.
- **Geographic adoption differs.** Global regions are adopting IPv6 at different rates, but the relative level of adoption in the regions also varies by metric, suggesting that incentives and barriers to adopt the new protocol do not just vary globally, but across layers of the network within each region.

## 2. RELATED WORK

There are many papers in the literature that offer valuable data on the IPv6 adoption process from various perspectives. Several studies characterize IPv6 traffic from the perspective of one or more ISPs (e.g., [23, 34, 36]) and 6to4 relays (e.g., [18, 35]). On June 8, 2011, the Internet Society sponsored "IPv6 World Day" [22] and several pieces of work explore this event explicitly (e.g., [34]). Other work examines IPv6 adoption from the perspective of the World Wide Web (e.g., [7, 29]). Additionally, a variety of contributions explore the technical, economic, and social factors that influence adoption (e.g., [16, 20]). Finally, much previous work focuses on topology measurements and performance in IPv6 and their relationships to IPv4 (e.g., [5, 10, 13, 31, 39, 43, 44]). In contrast to much of these studies, our work sacrifices depth for breadth in order to understand the big picture of IPv6 adoption.

Claffy [6] discusses IPv6 evolution and observes that "we lack not only a comprehensive picture of IPv6 deployment, but also consensus on how to measure its growth, and what to do about it." Our paper is in part a response to this call, offering a possible way forward. Closest to our work in both spirit and substance is Karpilovsky *et al.* [23], who provide a snapshot of IPv6 adoption from three main perspectives (allocation data, routing data, and traffic from a tier-1 ISP). In comparison, our work broadens the traffic perspective to a large sample of global tier-1 ISPs and nearly 100 tier-2/regional ISPs (260 providers in total), includes large samples of .com and .net TLD data, and juxtaposes these datasets with seven additional (mostly public) datasets.

Our DNS packet analysis in § 5 extends work by researchers at Verisign [30, 40]. The key distinction of our contribution here over this previous work is that we examine DNS queries via both IPv4 and IPv6 traffic, we focus on IPv6 adoption, and the data presented is more recent; the earlier Verisign work contains longitudinal IPv4-only traffic analysis, though performed at greater detail.

## 3. OUR APPROACH

Since our aim is for a comprehensive picture of adoption, we must first decide what aspects to study. We start by thinking about the Internet Protocol from the perspective of the three major types of Internet stakeholders: content providers, service providers, and content consumers. Although there are notable entities that straddle or defy these labels (e.g. vendors and policy makers), these three categories encapsulate the key perspectives we believe should be considered to realistically assess deployment. We next divide the key aspects of IP itself into two classes. The first is the prerequisite functions that IP performs and that must be in place for nodes to communicate, including addressing, naming, routing, and end-to-end reachability. The second class is operational characteristics that are only evident once the network begins forwarding packets, these include transition technology use, traffic volume, application mix, and performance.

In Table 1 we propose one or more *metrics* that characterize the adoption of IPv6 from the key viewpoints sketched above. Some of these metrics cover more than one branch in the taxonomy. We admit that our use of the term "metric" is somewhat loose. Our aim is to point to many aspects of adoption that should be measured, but whose granularity and specificity varies. Thus, each metric could itself be thought of more as a category or issue for which specific measurements should be obtained. In this paper, we present one or several such measurements for each metric that we defined.

While we believe we have identified a sufficiently comprehensive set of metrics to provide a broad picture of adoption, we do not claim completeness. There are countless possible metrics that can tell a coherent and insightful story of the adoption process. Further, while a metric such as performance naturally breaks down into submetrics for assessing delay, loss, jitter, reordering, throughput, etc., the specific facets of IPv6 operation that are important in any given context are likely to vary by application. As such, we do not mean to discourage further assessment along different axes or granularities than we take in this paper. Rather, our goal is to set a course for developing a *high-level* and *comprehensive* understanding of the recent IPv6 adoption process. To this end, we bring to bear several large original datasets, as well as several public or previously published results, and use them to report measurements that align with our taxonomy. Table 2 summarizes the datasets we analyzed, separated into the public ones we reproduce and update, and the unique ones we contribute. We next discuss analyses of these data in detail, showing how adoption level differs and varies as we move from left to right in Table 1 and over time.

## 4. ADDRESSING

We first examine the initial steps for IPv6 deployment: address allocation and network advertisement.

### A1: Address Allocation

Before wide-scale IPv6 communication is possible, IPv6 addresses must be broadly available. Therefore, our first assessment is of the status of IPv6 address allocation. The allocation hierarchy begins with the Internet Assigned Numbers Authority (IANA) allocating address blocks to the five regional Internet registries (RIRs). In turn, the RIRs make allocations to various national and local registries and ISPs. Each RIR publishes a daily snapshot of the blocks of IP (v4 and v6) addresses (i.e., the number of prefixes) allocated to entities below it in the hierarchy. We have captured ten years of these snapshots, starting in January 2004. As a minor caveat, note that the size of a typical IPv6 prefix ($2^{96}$) is much larger than that of an IPv4 prefix ($2^{10}$), thus, prefix-based comparisons should be made with caution. However, address allocations typically correspond to network deployments, no matter the protocol; so, relative allocations do shed light on protocol deployment.

Figure 1 shows the aggregate number of prefixes allocated each month across all RIRs. There were less than 30 IPv6 prefixes allocated per month prior to 2007, generally increasing thereafter. In the past several years, we typically find more than 300 prefixes allocated per month, with a high point of 470 prefix allocations in February 2011. By January 2004 there had been 650 IPv6 prefix allocations, while at the end of December 2013 we observe 17,896 to-

**Table 1: IPv6 adoption metric taxonomy, showing the main three perspectives that Internet stakeholders occupy, the prerequisites for IPv6 to be used, as well as the operational characteristics of the protocol, once deployed.**

| | | Prerequisite IP Functions | | | | Operational Characteristics | |
|---|---|---|---|---|---|---|---|
| | | **Addressing** | **Naming** | **Routing** | **End-to-End Reachability** | **Usage Profile** | **Performance** |
| Perspective | **Content Provider** | | N1: Nameservers; R1: Server Readiness | | R1: Server Readiness | U3: Transition Technologies | |
| Perspective | **Service Provider** | A1: Address Allocation; A2: Address Advertisement | N2: Resolvers | A2: Address Advertisement; T1: Topology | | U1: Traffic Volume; U3: Transition Technologies | P1: Network RTT |
| Perspective | **Content Consumer** | | N3: Queries | | R2: Client Readiness | U2: Application Mix; N3: Queries | |

**Table 2: Dataset summary showing the time period, scale, and public or new status of the datasets we analyzed.**

| Dataset | Metrics | Time Period | Recent Scale | Public? |
|---|---|---|---|---|
| RIR Address Allocations | A1 | Jan 2004 – Jan 2014 | ≈18K allocation snapshots (5 daily) | Yes |
| Routing: Route Views | A2, T1 | Jan 2004 – Jan 2014 | 45,271 BGP table snapshots | |
| Routing: RIPE | A2, T1 | Jan 2004 – Jan 2014 | | |
| Google IPv6 Client Adoption | R2, U3 | Sep 2008 – Dec 2013 | millions of daily global samples | |
| Verisign TLD Zone Files | N1 | Apr 2007 – Jan 2014 | daily snapshots of ≈2.5 million A+AAAA glue records (.com & .net) | |
| CAIDA Ark Performance Data | P1 | Dec 2008 – Dec 2013 | ≈10 million IPs probed daily | |
| Arbor Networks ISP Traffic Data | U1, U2, U3 | Mar 2010 – Dec 2013 | ≈33-50% of global Internet traffic; 2013 daily median: 50 terabits/sec (avg.) | No |
| Verisign TLD Packets: IPv4 | N2, N3 | Jun 2011 – Dec 2013 | 4 global sites, 5 of 13 gTLD NS letters (.com/.net), ≈4.5Bn queries | |
| Verisign TLD Packets: IPv6 | N2, N3 | Jun 2011 – Dec 2013 | 15 global sites, both gTLD NS letters (.com/.net) w/IPv6, 647M queries | |
| Alexa Top Host Probing | R1 | Apr 2011 – Dec 2013 | 10,000 servers probed twice/month | |

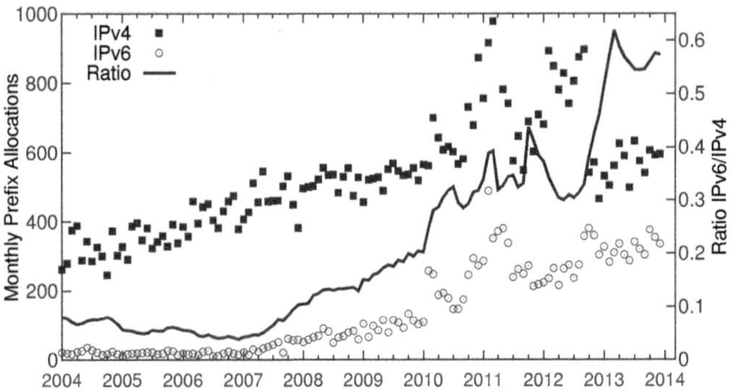


**Figure 1: Prefixes allocated. IPv4 and IPv6 allocations accelerate leading up to IANA exhaustion in early 2011. IPv4 dropped in 2012 and was flat in 2013, while IPv6 trended upward.**

tal prefix allocations—an increase of 27-fold. Finally, we note that at the end of our dataset the allocated IPv6 prefixes cover $2^{113}$ (i.e., $1.1\times10^{34}$) addresses.

To put the IPv6 allocation data in context, Figure 1 also shows IPv4 prefix allocations over the same period. The number of IPv4 prefix allocations grows from roughly 300 per month at the beginning of our observation period to a peak of 800–1000 per month at the start of 2011, after which it drops to around 500 per month in the last year, as the number of available addresses at RIRs has dwindled. [1] Overall, we find nearly 69K IPv4 prefix allocations at the beginning of our dataset and just over 136K at the end. This represents an increase of 67K prefixes—or, less than a doubling of the number of IPv4 prefix allocations over the course of the previous ten years. The figure contains a ratio line to show the relative allocation of IPv6 versus IPv4. We find that at the end of December 2013, on a monthly basis, the ratio of IPv6 to IPv4 prefix allocations is 0.57 and following a general upward trend. Thus, *although there are still significantly more allocated IPv4 prefixes (136k) than IPv6 prefixes (18k), and the monthly rate of IPv4 allocations is still about double, we see the IPv6 allocation rate continuing to grow while the IPv4 rate declines.* The ≈300 IPv6 versus ≈500 IPv4 allocations per month suggest *IPv6 is, for the first time, being deployed or planned on a majority of new networks.*

[1] We elide the April 2011 point such that the remainder of the plot is more readable. During that month, we find 2,217 IPv4 prefix allocations. This corresponds with APNIC's IPv4 pool dropping to a single remaining /8 and their "Final /8 Policy" being invoked, which caused a brief spike in allocated prefixes [3].

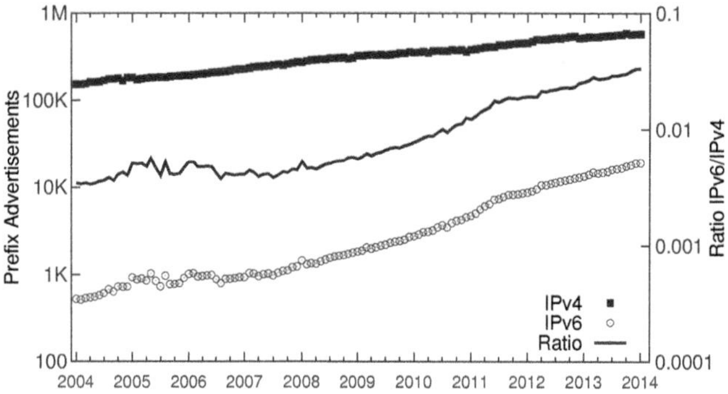


**Figure 2: Number of advertised prefixes. Over ten years, IPv6 prefixes increase 37-fold, while IPv4 increase four-fold.**

## A2: Network Advertisement

Address allocation is a start, but to be used for Internet traffic IP addresses must be advertised in the global routing table. Therefore, our second metric is the number of IPv6 prefixes found in the Internet's global routing table. The Route Views project [38] and RIPE [32] both have a number of routers used for data collection, each peering with production Internet routers to obtain the routing tables from those peers. Based on routing table snapshots made available by these collection efforts, we obtain the number of prefixes announced on the first day of each month from January 2004 to January 2014. While these routing datasets are known to have biases, as we elaborate in § 6, these biases are not expected to affect the view of *globally-reachable* network prefixes.

Figure 2 shows the number of announced prefixes over time. We find 526 IPv6 prefixes on January 1, 2004. In January 2014, 19,278 IPv6 prefixes were advertised—an increase of 37-fold over the course of ten years. For comparison, we also show the average number of IPv4 prefixes advertised per day; these increased four-fold from 153K in 2004 to 578K by 2014.

While total and monthly allocations and advertisements are both still higher for IPv4, the rate of IPv6 allocations is increasing at a faster pace than IPv4. This is expected since IPv4 has been an Internet reality for 30+ years now, and, hence, the need for additional addresses is, naturally, incremental. *The rate of IPv6 prefix allocations is now where IPv4 was 8 years ago.* What is more, in 2013 the monthly volume of allocations of IPv4 has dropped significantly, to 2009 levels, likely due to the exhaustion events starting in 2011. In sum, *the allocation and advertisement numbers and rates provide the basis for wide-scale Internet adoption of IPv6 from the addressing perspective.*

## 5. NAMING

Once IPv6 addresses are allocated and announced by routers, they must be used. The typical way addresses are referenced by Internet users and applications is via Domain Name System (DNS) names. Our next three metrics, therefore, focus on the prevalence of IPv6 support and use within the DNS ecosystem. A detailed description of DNS [28] is beyond the scope of this paper, but we remind the reader of some basic terminology. The authoritative groupings of names in the DNS hierarchy are called *zones*. DNS domain names map to IPv4 address via *A* records and to IPv6 addresses via *AAAA* ("quad a") records. DNS servers that manage zones and return records are called *authoritative nameservers*, while servers that execute queries on behalf of (usually many) users are broadly called *resolvers*.

### N1: DNS Authoritative Nameservers

Our first naming metric aims to understand the prevalence of authoritative nameservers that themselves can communicate via IPv6. While IPv6-addressed nameservers are not required for an organization to employ dual-stack IPv6 (i.e., it could serve AAAA records via IPv4 nameservers), we believe that the prevalence of such nameservers offers telling evidence on the adoption of IPv6, especially by content providers.

The top level of DNS has been IPv6-enabled since 2008, when root nameservers deployed AAAA records [21]. As of Jan. 2014, reports from Hurricane Electric show that 91% of the 381 top-level domains (TLDs) also have IPv6-enabled nameservers [25]. These include the largest TLDs, such as, .com, .net, .cn, etc. Of the thirteen .com and .net nameservers, all can serve AAAA but only two (a. and bmgtld-servers.net) are themselves IPv6-addressable. To understand the prevalence of IPv6 nameservers for second-level domains (e.g., example.com), we survey the .com and .net TLD zones. We analyzed sample .com and .net zone files between April 2007 and January 2014 to track the prevalence of DNS glue records for authoritative nameservers in the zones.

Figure 3 shows the number of A and AAAA glue records in the .com and .net zones over the last 7 years. IPv6-enabled nameservers (AAAA records) are dwarfed by IPv4 nameservers (A records), but both show long-term growth. Following the pattern of other metrics, the growth rate (second derivative) of IPv6-capable nameservers is higher than that of IPv4, and the ratio of AAAA to A is increasing. As of January 1, 2014, the ratio of AAAA to A glue records for .com is 0.0029. We also show the AAAA to A ratio from Hurricane Electric's published probing data, starting in 2009, wherein A and AAAA lookups for all domains in the zone are periodically performed [25]. Few nameservers in general have glue records in their zone, and IPv6-enabled ones seem to have this configuration even less often. The ratio of domains actually returning

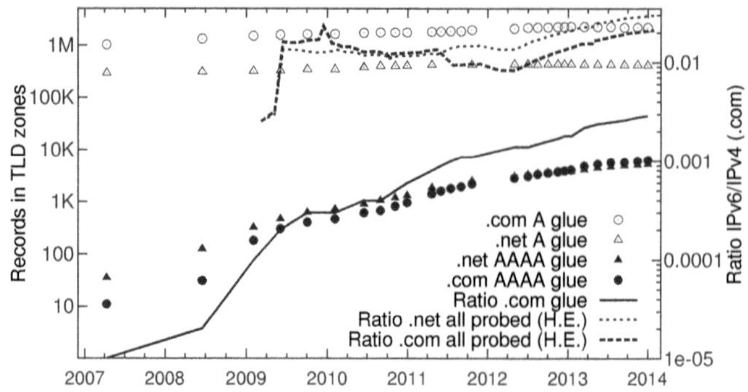


**Figure 3: IPv6 nameserver and domain readiness. We see a steady increase in the glue records and a general increase in the probed domain names.**

AAAA records via queries (vs. A) is an order of magnitude higher (0.02 for .com) than the glue record ratio.

In sum, *the authoritative nameserver data indicates low (0.0028 for .com glue, 0.02 for probed) but increasing (56% growth in 2013 for glue) support for IPv6 in the overall .com and .net zones.*

### N2: DNS Resolvers

A second naming metric we consider is the prevalence of resolvers requesting AAAA records. Due to caching within the DNS system, this is not a direct measure of demand; however, the number of resolvers looking up AAAA records indicates the breadth of the use of IPv6, and speaks to the basic capability of resolvers to issue AAAA queries as well as the existence of at least some clients within a resolver's pool making AAAA requests. Viewed over time, this can be used to gauge whether demand for IPv6 content is widespread or only from pockets of the network.

**Packet Datasets for .com and .net:** As an initial assessment, we examine two large datasets of packet-level DNS query traffic to the .com and .net TLD authoritative nameservers on five sample days between June 23, 2011 and December 23, 2013. One dataset consists of IPv4 packets, while the second contains IPv6 packets. Both are from Verisign, the registry operating the .com and .net zones. The IPv4 queries were captured at between three and five of the 17 largest globally-distributed .com and .net TLD server clusters (e.g., in Feb. 2013, from Dulles, VA; New York, NY; San Francisco, CA; and Amsterdam, NL). Our IPv4 data includes transactions with several instances of the lettered X.gtld-servers.net TLD nameservers. These 24-hour IPv4 datasets range from 2.3Bn to 4.2Bn queries (except for the first IPv4 sample, which only included 30 minutes of data and ≈110M queries). These same 17 global Verisign clusters support IPv6 traffic. The IPv6 samples analyzed were also each 24 hours and consisted of 420M–1,052M queries. While the packet collection apparatus for both datasets is known to be lossy, we performed analysis that suggests no systemic network effects that would skew the measurements we report [8].

We note that the IPv4 and IPv6 datasets shed light on slightly different aspects of adoption. The IPv4 data give us insight into behavior of networks that are not using IPv6 for their naming infrastructure but that happen to have clients and resolvers that make AAAA queries, which—given support by the resolver—is largely determined by operating system and application behavior. On the other hand, the IPv6 packet data represent networks where DNS resolvers are able to communicate via IPv6 to the .com and .net nameservers, which suggests a more advanced level of IPv6 adoption. Thus, the latter may be more representative of the behavior of fully-capable clients, whereas the former represents clients that

**Table 3: Percentage of resolvers making AAAA queries to .com and .net. While under a third of all IPv4 resolvers (N=3.5M in latest sample) make AAAA queries, most of the IPv6 packet population of resolvers (N=68K) does.**

| Resolvers | 2011-06-08 | 2012-02-23 | 2012-08-28 | 2013-02-26 | 2013-12-23 |
|---|---|---|---|---|---|
| IPv4 All | 33% | 28% | 26% | 30% | 31% |
| IPv4 Active | 90% | 93% | 83% | 93% | 94% |
| IPv6 All | 74% | 77% | 74% | 82% | 76% |
| IPv6 Active | 99% | 99% | 99% | 99% | 99% |

have software requesting AAAA records without the client necessarily having the ability to use them. For instance, Microsoft Windows XP clients that had a Teredo-configured [19] IPv6 addresses would, along with A, request AAAA records for names queried. However, these Teredo-based connections, either due to failure or preference, were found to be rarely completed by dual-stack hosts [41]. Windows Vista and later do not make AAAA queries when only a Teredo tunnel is available [9].

The resolver counts are, within an order of magnitude, stable over this period, with 3.5M seen in the most recent IPv4 sample and 68K in IPv6. Resolvers can service multiple, sometimes millions, of clients; so, this data represents the queries of many more than 3.5 million actual users. Although a single user or device can be configured to act as its own recursive resolver (e.g. by installing *bind*), we are more interested in the capabilities of resolvers serving multiple users. Therefore, in addition to aggregate results, we also report on a subset of the most active resolvers—e.g., enterprise or ISP-level—that send 10,000+ queries in a day.[2] There are 40K such active resolvers in the most recent IPv4 sample and 6K in IPv6.

In table 3 we show the percentage of resolvers in the two datasets that query for AAAA records. We see that nearly a third of all resolvers via IPv4 and three quarters via IPv6 make AAAA queries, as does the vast majority of active resolvers. Again, we stress this is not a measure of *use*, but an indication of *support* for IPv6 name resolution from within larger enterprises and networks. These numbers suggest that, *while AAAA records aren't in demand in every small corner of the network, at the organization or ISP level, IPv6 name resolution appears widely supported.*

## N3: DNS Queries

In addition to the numbers of IPv6-addressable nameservers and resolvers requesting IPv6 addresses measured above, a final naming component we consider is the distribution of actual IPv6-related DNS queries. This speaks to *how* naming is being used in IPv6. We first determine whether IPv6 users are interested in the same names as IPv4 users. This will inherently be influenced by user population differences (e.g., regional and sample effects), including client OS differences (which construct DNS requests). Therefore, differences are expected. To measure the agreement between queried domains via A and AAAA records in our two .com/.net packet samples, we calculated Spearman's rank correlation coefficient (ρ) between the top 100K domains by each of the four types (IPv4 sample A and AAAA, and IPv6 sample A and AAAA). We limited analysis to the most-queried 100K domains in order to avoid skewing results by rarely-queried domains, such as typos, but we wanted a large number in order to capture a diverse set of content.

Table 4 shows the results. As a preface, rank correlation is, by definition, lower than set intersection, and the intersection numbers (not shown) for the three sets of domain list pairs range from 55% to 84%. We see that the domain rank correlations between the

[2]This threshold is arbitrary. We certainly miss smaller organization-level resolvers, but the included ones are very active.

**Table 4: Spearman's ρ rank correlations for top 100K domains queried by A and by AAAA via IPv4 and IPv6 ($P < 0.0001$ in all cases). There is moderate to strong (darker grays) correlation between IPv4 and IPv6 domains for same record types.**

| Domain Lists | 2011-06-08 | 2012-02-23 | 2012-08-28 | 2013-02-26 | 2013-12-23 |
|---|---|---|---|---|---|
| 4.A : 6.A | 0.65 | 0.73 | 0.70 | 0.70 | 0.57 |
| 4.AAAA : 6.AAAA | 0.69 | 0.80 | 0.82 | 0.74 | 0.68 |
| 4.A : 4.AAAA | 0.32 | 0.32 | 0.35 | 0.34 | 0.42 |
| 6.A : 6.AAAA | 0.29 | 0.23 | 0.20 | 0.26 | 0.32 |

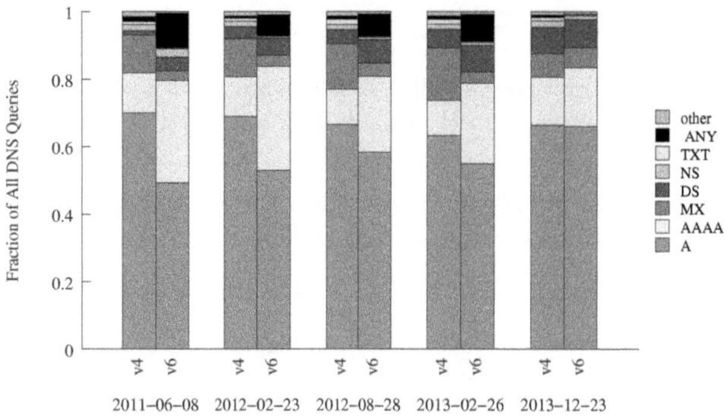


**Figure 4: Breakdown of query types across five IPv4 and IPv6 DNS samples between Jun. 2011 and Dec. 2013 (key is in stack order). The distribution of IPv4 and IPv6 query types within each day converges over time (p<0.05).**

IPv6 and IPv4 samples via the same record types are moderate to strong (ρ ≈ 0.70), indicating that *domain interest is similar between users of IPv4 naming infrastructure and those using IPv6*. Still, differences remain, and no clear trend is visible in this time period. Likewise, when we examine the within-packet-sample cross-type correlations (e.g., A vs. AAAA for IPv4), we see much less correlation. We suspect this is in part due to the fact that, whether an A or AAAA is requested by a given host is determined by applications and OSes in use, but there is greater similarity when examining the same application/OS patterns across protocol packet samples. Some of these differences may be accounted for by the differences in set sizes. Across the five samples, the median percentage of queries that the top 100K domains account for is 55% for A via IPv4 and 60% for A via IPv6; for AAAA, it is 77% for IPv4 and 42% for IPv6. No clear trend is evident. In sum, the data suggests *differences in application use of IPv6 (which is expected due to the N1 results) but marked overlap in the domains of interest to networks using IPv6 resolvers versus those using IPv4.*.

Turning from the names in the queries to the records, Figure 4 shows the top seven record types (plus all others under the "other" category) requested in the IPv4 and IPv6 packets on the five days of samples. We observe that, while there are still some differences in the distributions, *there is a statistically-significant convergence of query types over time (average monthly difference decrease of 1.65% with p<0.05), and the query types in IPv6 are now much more similar to IPv4 than just two and a half years ago.*

# 6. ROUTING

Once IPv6 addresses are allocated and advertised, as well as potentially being named, the next prerequisite for using the new protocol is routing. While routing itself has many components, and we have already discussed IPv6 prefix advertisement in section A2, a key aspect of routing that deserves careful measurement is topology. The richness of the IPv6 topology, in terms of the number

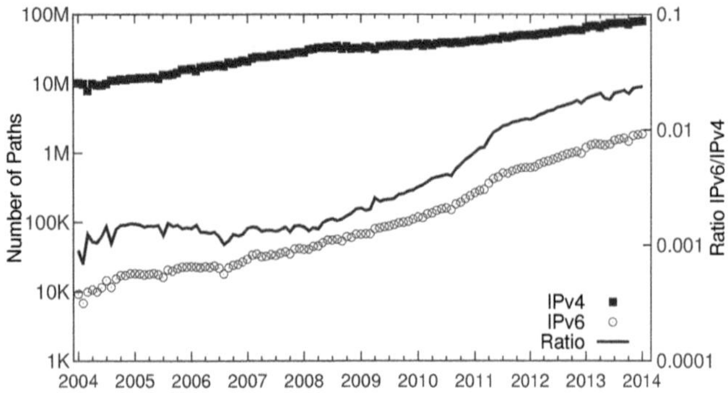


**Figure 5: Number of globally-seen IPv4 and IPv6 paths. There is a 110-fold increase in IPv6 paths over ten years.**

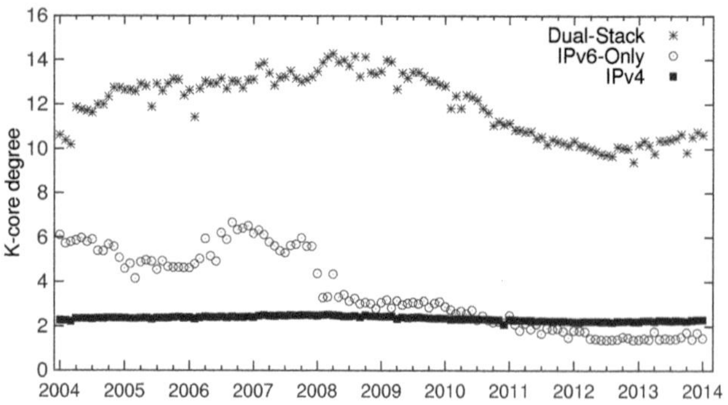


**Figure 6: AS centrality. Pure-IPv6 and dual-stack ASes are becoming more prevalent at the edge.**

and length of paths and the connectivity of ASes, speaks to the resilience, and, thus, production-readiness of the network.

## T1: Topology

The IPv4 topology has been studied in depth (e.g., [26, 42]), but we also need to understand the relationships between organizations with respect to external IPv6 routing capability and connectivity to understand the overall strength or brittleness of the network. As we did for the advertisement metric (A2) we use all of the routing table snapshots collected by Route Views [38] and RIPE-NCC RIS [33] between Jan. 2004 and Jan. 2014 in the following.

**Routing Table View Biases:** Before we delve into the insights that these data afford, it is important to understand possible bias. As noted by earlier studies (e.g., [15]) the global public routing datasets available (e.g., Route Views, RIS) suffer from at least two forms of bias. The first is geographic, in that global routing data is collected from a finite set of collectors, whose global distribution is not uniform, leading, for example, to fewer samples from the African continent. The second bias stems from most of the data in these collections coming from volunteer networks that turn out to generally be large top-tier ISPs. Therefore, many peer-to-peer paths between smaller ISPs are not visible in the data, since these routes are never propagated to the top-tier ISPs. These biases are a limitation of the data. However, we believe that even though imperfect the data still yields useful information about IPv6 adoption for the following reasons: *(i)* no substitute data lacking bias exists (e.g., traceroute also has bias); *(ii)* the view of the global routing infrastructure of ISPs whose routing data is represented is a real view from their perspective, and any path or AS counts observed are, at worst, lower bounds; *(iii)* we have no reason to believe that the bias present in these data for IPv6 differs systematically *relative* to that for IPv4, suggesting that looking at ratios of adoption, especially over time, is reasonable; and *(iv)* in the cases of counting globally-visible prefixes or ASes seen supporting IPv6, the fact that some local paths are missed does not speak to the *global* adoption state. Therefore, we present the data knowing full well it is a less-than-full statement on the routing state. We encourage the community to collect and refine our analysis using better data.

**AS Support and Connectivity:** We first examine the number of ASes supporting IPv6 globally as well as the number of unique globally-visible AS-paths (i.e., the paths with unique AS sequence). Both are indicators of IPv6 adoption, mostly at the service provider level. AS adoption is indicative of *support* for IPv6, while the number of AS-paths is an indicator of maturing *connectivity* between ASes. We omit the figure showing AS-level adoption in favor of Figure 5, which shows the number of unique IPv6 and IPv4 paths announced on the first day of each month. We observe that the number of IPv6 paths has a 110-fold increase from January 2004 to January 2014, while there is only an eight-fold increase in the number of IPv4 paths. However, the IPv6 to IPv4 ratio is only 0.02 in January 2014, indicating the IPv6 routing mesh is still at an early stage of maturity. AS-level support for IPv6 is not shown, but follows a faster upward trend, with an 18-fold increase (versus two-fold for IPv4) and the current ratio of IPv6 to IPv4 ASes is 0.19 – almost ten times the path count ratio. As expected, the indicator of ASes *supporting* IPv6 leads the measure of *connectivity*. Again, we note that, because of possible bias in the view afforded by this data, raw numbers of the IPv4 and IPv6 paths seen are less meaningful than is the overall ratio.

**AS Centrality:** To understand the topological position of IPv6 ASes, we next compute the *k-core degree* of each AS in the topology graph. A k-core of a graph is the maximal subgraph in which every node has at least degree k. A node has k-core degree of N if it belongs to the N-core but not to the $(N+1)$-core. As used in [17], this measure represents a natural notion of the *centrality* of ASes. In other words, ASes with a high k-core represent well-connected, typically large, ISPs, while those with low k-core represent edge or stub networks. We show the average k-core degree of ASes in Figure 6. We find that dual-stack ASes have a much higher degree of centrality than other ASes. In 2004, the pure IPv6 ASes were located in a relatively central position. However, we see pure-IPv6 ASes, a small fraction of all, becoming more prevalent at the edge after 2008. Our results are in accordance with those of CAIDA [10], who report that IPv6 is largely deployed at the core but lags in edge networks. Note [10] uses a deeper and more robust analysis of these same public datasets, wherein, notably, they filter out transient links. The numbers we find indicate *dual-stack becoming more widely deployed among well-connected central ISPs, while single-protocol networks are mostly those at the edge. In other words, the older edge networks are the laggards.*

We caution that studying native IPv6 topology is useful but insufficient. Transition from IPv4 to IPv6 introduces a co-dependence between the protocols. Therefore, unlike when studying IPv4 topology independently, when studying IPv6, we must consider the parts of IPv4 that glue together "islands" of IPv6. An in-depth analysis is beyond scope, but we point readers to recent work in [10].

# 7. END-TO-END REACHABILITY

Having dealt with the prerequisites of addressing, routing, and naming in the previous three sections, we now turn to the readiness of Internet end hosts to use IPv6. We split this into two metrics for the readiness of service-level devices and client-level devices.

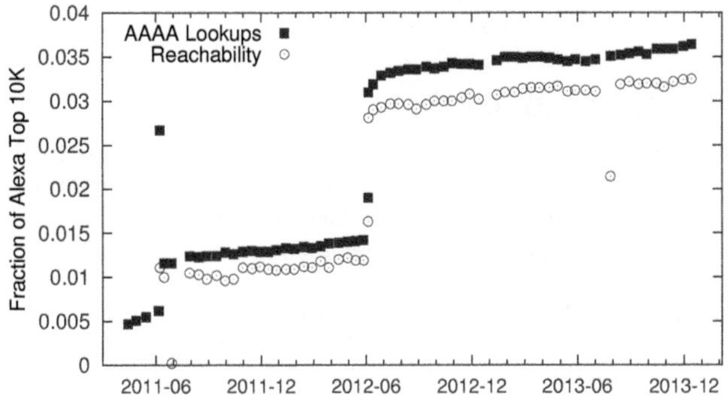


**Figure 7: Fraction of top 10K sites with AAAA records and reachable via IPv6. Two discontinuous jumps correspond to World IPv6 Day 2011 and World IPv6 Launch 2012.**

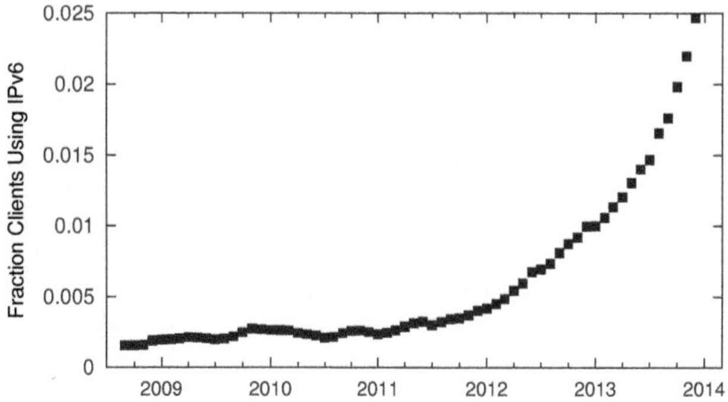


**Figure 8: Average monthly fraction of clients able to access Google over IPv6. 2.5% of clients use IPv6, but this number has been growing sharply. The most recent two-year annual growth rate averages 150%, a more than doubling each year.**

## R1: Server-Side Readiness

Obviously, wide-scale adoption requires services to be capable of handling IPv6 traffic; therefore, our first approach to end-host readiness involves assessing prevalence of IPv6-enabled services.

While not indicative of all services, one way to assess IPv6 service penetration is to measure popular web servers. Much like Nikkhah et al [29] and with congruent results we use Alexa [1] to determine the most popular web sites. We then determine which sites have a AAAA record in DNS, and, for those that do, we then test reachability of the web site via a tunnel to Hurricane Electric. Ideally, this metric tries to assess the server, but we have no way to do so without also assessing the path to the server. Hence, our measurements offer an approximation. We have been probing the top 10K web sites for AAAA records since April 2011 and for reachability since June 2011.[3] Figure 7 shows our results. We first note a jump in June 2011 that corresponds to World IPv6 Day. We find a roughly five-fold increase in AAAA records available at that point. However, we also see a nearly immediate fallback. This is understandable given that the stated goal of that day was merely to serve as a "test flight" of IPv6 capabilities, rather than to permanently enable IPv6 services [22]. Subsequent to this drop off, in spite of the limited goal, we find that World IPv6 Day 2011 is responsible for a sustained two-fold increase in the IPv6-capable web sites. In the following year, the June 2012 World IPv6 Launch Day also resulted in a sustained doubling of AAAA records. Further, aside from the two jumps, *we find a slowly growing trend across time with over 3.2% of the Alexa top 10K now being reachable via IPv6.* It is notable what an impact concerted community efforts, such as the two IPv6 readiness/launch days can have on IPv6 server readiness.

The second set of points on the plot show reachability. The data shows that most of the hosts for which we find AAAA records are also reachable. Further, the reachability trends generally mirror those for web servers having AAAA records. Our results generally agree with [29]. In conclusion, *while only about 3.5% of the top most popular websites are IPv6-ready, there has been significant growth in the last three years, and large jumps are possible.*

## R2: Client-Side Readiness

In addition to IPv6-capable services, clients need to be IPv6-enabled as well. This metric examines the ability of client systems to employ IPv6, subsuming all that is required on the client side (i.e., working IPv6 network transport, DNS, operating system, etc.).

Google makes aggregate data about client adoption of IPv6 available on an ongoing basis [14]. Their experiment consists of adding a JavaScript applet to search results from `www.google.com` for a randomly sampled set of users [29]. The script first performs a name lookup on one of two experimental host names and then sends a request to the IP address returned in the DNS response. In 90% of the cases the script chooses a name representing a dual-stacked server, while in the remaining cases a name representing a IPv4-only server is chosen for comparison purposes. The addresses point to 2–5 data centers (in Asia, the US, and Europe). The experiment is conducted millions of times per day. Note that, as with the R1 measurements, this data again conflates the client capabilities with those of the path from the client, and, therefore, this is an approximation of the ideal metric.

Figure 8 shows the average monthly fraction of clients that connect to Google via IPv6 over the last 5+ years. The plot shows a growth factor of 16 over the course of the dataset—from 0.15% in September 2008 to 2.5% in December 2013. Further, most of the growth comes in the last two years, where the ratio increased markedly, by 125% in 2012 and 175% in 2013, more than doubling each year. As discussed in section A3, this measure is probably somewhat optimistic; since Google has many direct private peerings to ISPs, some clients may be able to reach Google by IPv6 but not other content. However, these numbers are roughly in line with those reported in another large client study [41], which found that although 6% of a global sample of clients were IPv6-capable, only 1-2% of dual-stack preferred IPv6. In sum, *the data shows very strong growth in Google clients' ability to use IPv6, especially in the last two years.*

# 8. IPV6 USAGE PROFILE

While the metrics and data sketched in the previous sections set the stage for IPv6 adoption by measuring addressing, routing, naming, and end-host capabilities, in this section we aim to directly assess IPv6 traffic "in the wild". That is, we aim to understand the operational characteristics, or usage profile, of how IPv6 is actually employed by those that have adopted it.

## U1: Traffic Volume

Our first traffic-related metric simply aims to understand how much of Internet traffic is using IPv6. We begin by introducing the Internet traffic datasets we contribute.

**Arbor Internet Traffic Data:** We assembled two datasets describing the traffic traversing customer networks monitored by devices from Arbor Networks, a provider of traffic analytics and security devices for large networks. Arbor's customers include a signifi-

[3] Our probing data is available [2].

cant number of large ISPs in the world, and, in aggregate, they have visibility into nearly half of Interdomain (i.e., Internet) traffic. These two datasets consist of traffic summaries (daily netflow statistic aggregates, including protocol, port, and volume information), from peering, aggregation, and customer-facing routers at participating networks. The first, older, dataset tracked daily peak five-minute traffic volume for both IPv6 and IPv4, measured a sample of 12 Arbor customers providing anonymous data, and included data from the second quarter of 2010 through February 2013. The second Arbor dataset (for 2013) reports daily average volume, includes approximately 260 providers of anonymous data that together represent an *estimated 33-50% of global Internet traffic*, and collects data using the same methodology as Labovitz et al. [24] (now with more providers). We include the larger dataset starting in January 2013; however, even the smaller, 12-provider sample covers an aggregate of over 400 routers and 55K links, representing a cross-section of different-mission and varying-size Internet organizations. Both samples include global Tier 1 ISPs, national and regional Tier 2 ISPs, content/hosting providers, and universities. In the newer dataset, which represents 19 Tier-1 and 92 Tier-2 providers plus over 100 enterprises, content providers, etc., each continent is represented, as are both fixed-line and mobile Internet providers. We refer to the older (smaller) and newer (larger) datasets as $\mathcal{A}$, and $\mathcal{B}$, respectively. In the fourth quarter of 2013, the daily median Internet traffic in dataset $\mathcal{B}$ was 58 Tbps.

We normalized the traffic measurements by the number of Arbor Networks providers in the samples, to distinguish organic traffic growth from growth due to changes in the number of customers. Figure 9 shows the median daily peak and average traffic volume for each month in our two datasets, respectively. Since one set of points and line represent 5-minute peaks, and the other averages, we present the data as separate points. This difference helps explain the shift between the lines visible for the two months for which we had both datasets in January and February, 2013.

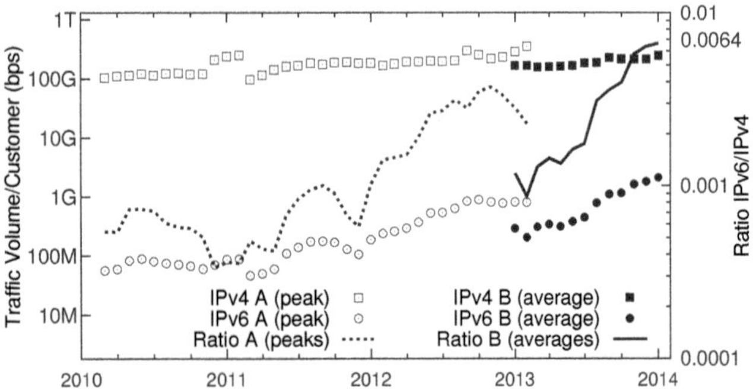


**Figure 9: Global Internet traffic data in two datasets: $\mathcal{A}$ for Mar. 2010–Feb. 2013, monthly median *peak* 5-minute volume for 12-provider sample; and $\mathcal{B}$ for 2013, the monthly median of daily *average* traffic volume for ≈260 providers. IPv6 is 0.6% of traffic, and 2-year growth relative to IPv4 is 451% annually.**

The figure shows that IPv6 is still dwarfed by IPv4 traffic (by roughly two orders of magnitude). However, both IPv4 and IPv6 peak traffic volumes are generally increasing, and IPv6 is on a strong upward trajectory. Over our measurement period we find roughly an order of magnitude increase in the median daily peak volume for both protocols. As the ratio line (representing the raw traffic, not normalized by customers) shows, we do find a significant rise in IPv6's relative contribution to Internet traffic. In March of 2010, the ratio of IPv6 to IPv4 is 0.0005, while in December 2013 it is 0.0064—a 13-fold increase. In sum, *while, overall, the proportion of IPv6 traffic on the Internet is still under one percent, it has grown, relative to IPv4, by 433% percent year-over-year in 2013, 469% in 2012, and 71% in 2011, a rapid pace.*

## U2: Application Mix

Another important metric when studying the IPv6 usage profile is what applications are used. This can, for instance, inform our understanding as to whether IPv6 is being used for typical user activity or for specialized use, as was reported in the past (e.g., [23]).

**Table 5: Application mix (%) between Dec. 2010 and 2013. HTTP/S increases from 6% to 95% for IPv6, surpassing IPv4, while back-end services (e.g., dns, ssh, rsync) decline significantly. IPv6 usage looks much more like IPv4 than in the past.**

| Application | Dec 2010 | Apr/May 2011 | Apr/May 2012 | | Apr–Dec 2013 | |
|---|---|---|---|---|---|---|
| | IPv6 | IPv6 | IPv6 | IPv4 | IPv6 | IPv4 |
| HTTP | 5.61 | 11.81 | 63.04 | 62.40 | 82.56 | 60.61 |
| HTTPS | 0.15 | 0.88 | 0.39 | 3.91 | 12.66 | 8.59 |
| DNS | 4.75 | 9.11 | 4.09 | 0.14 | 0.33 | 0.22 |
| SSH | 0.56 | 3.73 | 2.65 | 0.11 | 0.27 | 0.20 |
| Rsync | 20.78 | 5.11 | 2.65 | 0.00 | 0.13 | 0.00 |
| NNTP | 27.65 | 5.84 | 1.03 | 0.13 | 0.00 | 0.25 |
| RTMP | 0.00 | 0.05 | 0.11 | 2.39 | 0.00 | 2.74 |
| Other TCP | * | * | 18.72 | 3.20 | 1.66 | 4.08 |
| Other UDP | * | * | 1.73 | 11.90 | 0.27 | 2.82 |
| Non-TCP/UDP | * | * | 4.94 | 14.10 | 2.11 | 20.21 |

We have application information from Arbor Networks for the same traffic samples described earlier (although we are missing IPv4 data prior to 2012). The network flow monitors classify traffic by port number, and, hence, the categorization may not be completely accurate. For instance, we note that HTTP port 80 is often used for tunneling non-web applications, as it tends to be open in firewalls. However, we believe this categorization is useful as a first order analysis. Table 5 shows the proportion of traffic for each application that makes up at least 1% of either IPv6 or IPv4 traffic. We see in the 2012 and 2013 samples that HTTP dominates within both IPv6 and IPv4. In the 2013 sample, HTTPS has increased significantly in IPv6, surpassing even that in IPv4. Likewise, we see a dramatic uptick in HTTP/S traffic across the four years. The large fraction of likely web traffic now observed, at 95%, is a major departure from the patterns observed in earlier studies of IPv6 dating from 2008 and early 2009, which report HTTP traffic volume below one percent [23, 36]. Interestingly, Karpilovsky [23], Savola [35] and Hei [18] also report large amounts of DNS traffic (e.g., 80-90% in 2008 [23]), which continued to rank highly in our own data until 2012. Our 2013 sample is the first time we see DNS decreasing to IPv4 levels and actual content (HTTP/S) surpassing even what is seen for IPv4; this is a significant evolution. We note that one possible factor at play in the reduction of DNS traffic is the behavior of newer Windows operating systems (starting with Vista), which, as mentioned earlier, no longer make AAAA queries when their only IPv6 connection is via Teredo [9]. Likewise, we see a substantial reduction in IPv6 NNTP traffic [11]. We believe the previously large volume seen was related to (*i*) the fact that a large NNTP path is part of the traffic sample and (*ii*) NNTP was heavily used for piracy over IPv6 when several USENET services that otherwise required paid subscriptions offered free IPv6 access[4].

Additionally, in the 2013 sample, we find 4.04% and 27.11% of the traffic volume not ascribed to a particular application for IPv6 and IPv4, respectively, a large decline from 2012 for IPv6 and a smaller one for IPv4. However, the distribution of non-identified traffic is different between IPv6 and IPv4. For example, while most

[4] e.g., http://www.techjawa.com/2011/02/10/guide-get-free-usenet-access-with-ipv6/

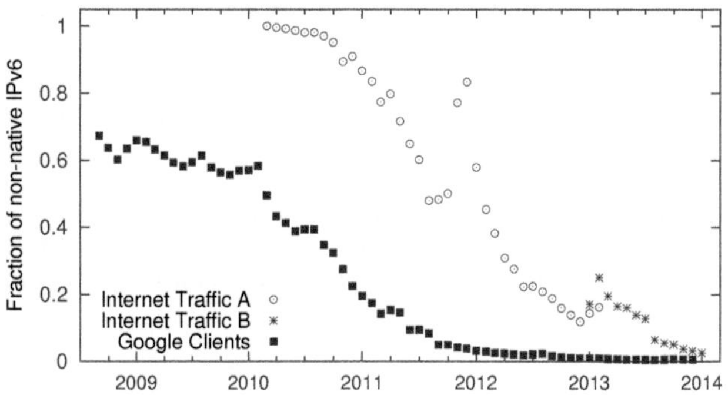


**Figure 10: Fraction of IPv6 traffic carried by the two most prevalent transition technologies in the Internet traffic and Google client samples. Non-native IPv6 traffic was the majority of packets 3-4 years ago, but currently represents less than three percent of traffic and one percent of Google clients.**

of the bytes in IPv4 are non-TCP/UDP at 20.21%, such traffic only contributes 2.11% of the overall bytes in IPv6. Although we were unable to investigate this "other" category more deeply, we speculate that the usage of peer-to-peer and similar popular non-well-known-port applications still differs between IPv4 and IPv6 in the TCP/UDP categories, while ICMP and tunneling protocol mix differ in the non-TCP/UDP category. The method of aggregation of untracked protocols for 2010 and 2011 does not allow comparison, unfortunately. To summarize, *over the last three years we see a dramatic evolution in IPv6 application use, wherein content packets now far outnumber infrastructure service packets (DNS, ICMP), and the profile now resembles IPv4.*

## U3: Transition Technologies

IPv4 and IPv6 coexistence is greatly complicated by the lack of backward compatibility. In what is now acknowledged as one of the most significant IPv6 design limitations, native IPv6 network devices cannot communicate with their IPv4 counterparts without an explicit network translation layer [27]. As a result, the success of any large-scale IPv6 transition depends on the complex interplay between the cost and scalability of translation technologies and the commercial incentives (or disincentives) motivating the transition to native IPv6 infrastructure. A common transition technology is tunneling. Tunneling technologies interconnect "islands" of IPv6 using encapsulation across IPv4 infrastructure, or vice versa. In addition to tunnels, Teredo [19] provides IPv6 connectivity to hosts behind IPv4-NATs using UDP-encapsulation. Our next metric aims to understand the prevalence of the most common transition technologies being used in the wild where end-to-end IPv6 addressing is not fully in place. As IPv6 matures, we expect a smaller fraction of its traffic to use these technologies and more of it to be native.

Both the Google client and Arbor Networks datasets described earlier include information on the prevalence of various transition technologies. The Google perspective provides a view on the capabilities of end hosts, while the Arbor view is an assessment of actual Internet traffic. Figure 10 shows the prevalence of non-native IPv6—which is defined as Teredo and IP protocol 41 traffic (used by 6to4 and 6in4). The two Internet traffic data points $\mathcal{A}$ and $\mathcal{B}$, refer to the Arbor Internet traffic datasets, $\mathcal{A}$ and $\mathcal{B}$, described earlier. The Google data shows that, while in 2008 only 30% of IPv6-enabled client end-hosts could use native IPv6, that number has increased to above 99% over the last four and a half years.

In 2010 we find the Internet traffic data shows nearly all IPv6 traffic using some tunneling technology. However, as of the end of December 2013, nearly 97% of the traffic is now native. We note that, of the tunneled IPv6 traffic in late 2013, IP protocol 41 dominates, contributing over 90% of the tunneled volume compared to less than 10% for Teredo. The Arbor numbers between mid-2011 and February 2012 correspond roughly to earlier measurements from that time, (e.g. [34] and [41]), while the Google numbers show much less transition technology used than those studies; this may be explained by the direct peerings phenomenon, described above. Overall, the data shows that *native traffic is now the vast majority of IPv6 traffic, a dramatic change from just three years ago. The Internet's IPv6 traffic is now real IPv6.*

# 9. PERFORMANCE

A crucial metric of IPv6 adoption is performance—which can mean different things depending on the measurement perspective we take (e.g., the speed of a site to load for a user, or, for an ISP, the bandwidth across peering links). Several works predating IPv4 address exhaustion offer initial results in the area of IPv6 performance (e.g., [5,7,39,44]). Further, there are some performance results since the exhaustion milestones [10,29]; both of these latter studies report that performance over IPv6 paths that align with IPv4 at the AS-level is similar for the two protocols but differs when paths diverge. More recent work exploring a methodology for passive measurement of IPv6 and IPv4 performance was contributed by Plonka and Barford [31], who found great variability in relative performance of the protocols in a campus traffic sample. The data we present here aims for a global and longitudinal, if less granular, examination of relative IPv6 network performance.

## P1: Network RTT

We suspect that hardware, software, and configuration differences could result in different quality of data transmission in IPv6 versus IPv4; indeed, previous measurements and ones we report here have shown differences. Although actual client-to-service network performance for large global sets of clients and services would be a more ideal metric, we use the approximation of average 10- and 20-hop round trip time (RTT), tested from dozens of global perspectives, as a proxy. This hides the details of path differences and heterogeneity of end points, allowing a simple apples-to-apples comparison of raw network performance over the same number of IPv4 versus IPv6 nodes. We don't claim that this is the only or the best IPv6 network performance metric, but it serves as a reasonable approximation of long-term performance evolution.

Our analysis is conducted on the traceroute-based performance data collected by CAIDA Archipelago Measurement Infrastructure (Ark) [4] to measure RTT in IPv4 and IPv6. Globally-distributed Ark monitors probe all IPv4 /24s and all announced IPv6 prefixes continuously. We analyze data from December 2008 to December 2013. While this dataset is also the basis of earlier work ( [10]), we re-analyze an updated longitudinal version to observe performance in the context of the other metrics we report.

Figure 11 shows the median RTT with hop distances 10 and 20 for each month. We find that in 2009 RTTs were roughly 1.5 times longer for IPv6 than for IPv4. While the IPv4 RTTs have increased slightly over this time period, IPv6 RTTs have decreased slightly. In 2013, the RTT for hop distance of 10 is almost identical for IPv4 and IPv6. IPv6 had better RTTs than IPv4 at 20 hops in 2012 through mid-2013. To compare relative performance, we show the IPv6 to IPv4 ratio for the 10-hop RTT, as it has been less favorable for IPv6. Since, the better the performance the smaller the RTT, we show the ratio of the reciprocal of RTT for each protocol. As noted in [10], the sample of IPv6 data is small and the results might be dominated by a few paths. Also, evolving tunnel use likely impacts

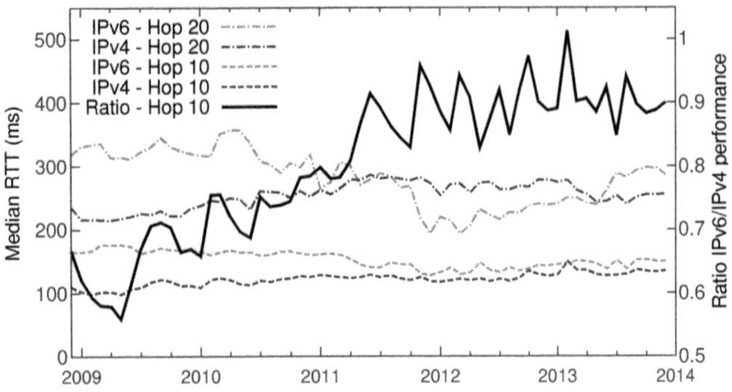


**Figure 11: Median Round Trip Time (ms) with hop distance 10 and 20 for IPv4 and IPv6. IPv6 showed poorer performance before 2010, but the last several years have seen performance converging to within about .90–.95 of IPv4.**

RTT and hop count. Thus, we cannot conclude that IPv6 has better RTT performance than IPv4, overall. However, *the long-term trend shows clear improvement for IPv6, and it has approached parity with IPv4 (≈95%), for the first time, in the last several years.*

# 10. IPV6 PRESENT AND FUTURE

We examined a set of twelve metrics for assessing the adoption of IPv6 based on a comprehensive set of ten longitudinal datasets—some original, some publicly available, most large and global. In some cases, we updated and replicated similar measures reported in years past (e.g. RIR allocation data, performance data); in others, we presented new large data samples (e.g. the Internet traffic data, the Verisign IPv6 .com and .net DNS packet data). Here, we first highlight what the current state of adoption looks like, when examined through the broad set of perspectives we consulted. After that, we provide rough estimates of where we expect adoption to be in five years, based on recent trends.

## 10.1 IPv6 Present

**The Value of a Broad Approach:** In Figure 13 we show five-year ratios of IPv6 relative to IPv4 for seven of our metrics. Most prominent is the result that different metrics give entirely different insight into the adoption of IPv6, and suggest orders of magnitude different progress. For instance, while roughly 36% of new monthly (and 12% of cumulative) allocated prefixes are IPv6, we find just 0.63% of average traffic is carried over IPv6—a two-order-of-magnitude difference. These differences across metrics serve to highlight that multiple viewpoints must be considered to fully understand the progression and true state of adoption. In addition to the differences seen when examining different types of data—i.e., different prerequisites or operational characteristics—differences within the same type, but from distinct perspectives, are also important to consider. For example, recall that the difference in non-native IPv6 traffic as seen by Arbor Networks versus that seen by Google in metric U3 has been noticeable. What is more, *the order of adoption, as reflected by the relative rank of metrics, generally follows the prerequisites for IPv6 deployment* (e.g., allocation precedes routing, which precedes clients, which precedes actual traffic).

**IPv6 is Now Real:** Compared to prior work and earlier data, *we see in our recent data a dramatic qualitative and quantitative evolution in the state of IPv6 adoption, indicating a major shift in how the protocol is being used in the last three years.* Table 6 summarizes the usage profile of IPv6, and how it has evolved over this time. Traffic data shows that IPv6, while just 0.63% of measured Internet packets, is growing at a rate of over 400% in each of the last two years; application mix data shows content packets now dominating traffic; transition technology data shows that virtually all IPv6 traffic and Google clients are now native; and, performance data shows IPv6 now nearly on par with IPv4. *IPv6 is finally being used natively, for production, and at a rapidly-increasing rate.*

**Table 6: Measures of actual operational characteristics of IPv6, recently and three years ago. These suggest that IPv6 is now mature. We contend that IPv6, as a real, production protocol, has finally come of age.**

| Metric: Operational Aspect Measured | IPv6 Status at End of: | |
|---|---|---|
| | 2010 | 2013 |
| U1: IPv6 Percent of Internet Traffic | 0.03% | 0.64% |
| U1: 1-yr. Growth vs. IPv4 (*Mar-2010 – Mar-2011) | −12%* | +433% |
| U2: Content's Portion of Traffic (HTTP+HTTPS) | 6% | 95% |
| U3: Native IPv6 Packets vs. All IPv6 | 9% | 97% |
| U3: Native IPv6 Google Clients | 78% | 99% |
| P1: Performance: 10-hop $RTT^{-1}$ vs. IPv4 | 75% | 95% |

**Inter and Intra-Regional Differences:** Our cross-metric analysis allows us to see stark regional differences in adoption. For example, when breaking down the cumulative allocation data by RIR (A1), we find RIPE responsible for 46% of allocations, while ARIN is responsible for 21%, and APNIC 18%. These three RIRs represent the most-connected portions of the Internet, and, therefore, it is not surprising that they allocate most of the new prefixes. We also observe that LACNIC and AFRINIC are responsible for 12% and 2% of the allocations, respectively. However, although the well-connected regions dominate the absolute number of prefixes, the *ratio* of IPv6 to IPv4 prefix allocation per region tells a slightly different story. Here, we find that LACNIC has, by far, the largest ratio at 0.280, followed by RIPE at 0.162, AFRINIC at 0.157, APNIC with 0.143, and we see only half as much IPv6 prefix allocation, 0.072, for ARIN. Part of the likely reason is that the ARIN region was an early adopter of IPv4, accumulating many prefixes before resources became constrained.

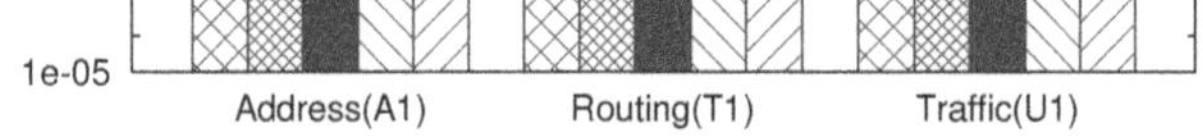


**Figure 12: IPv6 to IPv4 ratio for three metrics, broken down by region. We see that, not only do different regions have different levels of IPv6 adoption, but that the level of adoption varies by layer; i.e., the relative rank of regions differs across metrics.**

In Figure 12, we show an analysis of the IPv6 to IPv4 ratio for allocation (A1) as well as two additional metrics whose data allowed region differentiation (T1 [announced AS paths] and U1 [average traffic, $\mathcal{B}$]). Adoption level varies considerably across metrics for the regions (note the log scale), with the highest measured region for each metric at least three times higher than the lowest. We do not show its numbers, but the A2 metric ranks closely match T1, as they both track routing. While we might expect different

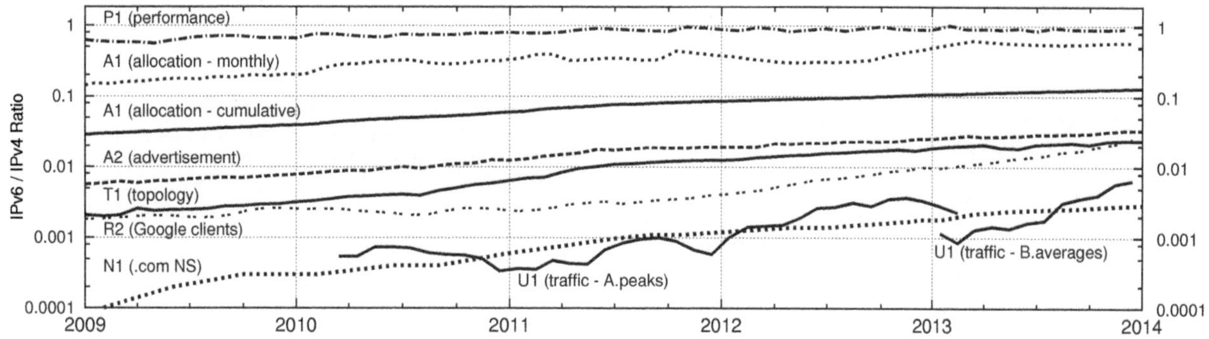


**Figure 13: The ratio of IPv6 to IPv4 for seven metrics over the last five years, showing adoption level ranges by two orders of magnitude depending on metric, and accelerated growth. For instance, the two traffic lines, 𝒜 (peak, through 2013-02) and ℬ (average, for 2013), show IPv6 traffic has increased over 400% in each of the last two years.**

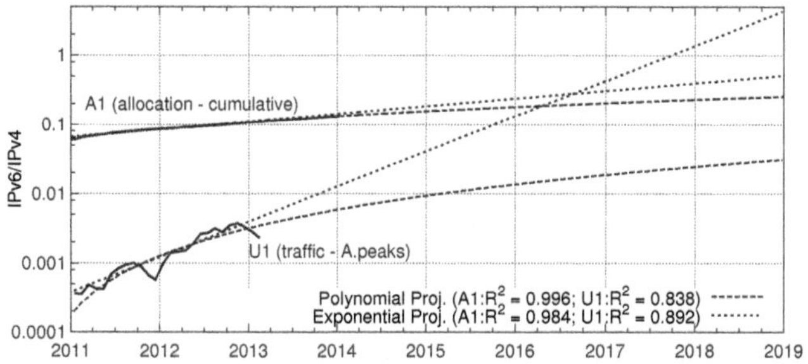


**Figure 14: Trends for Allocation and Traffic (using the older 𝒜 [peak] traffic data), starting with 2011, when IPv4 exhaustion pressure increased, and five-year projections. We caution that trends are volatile and prediction is hard.**

regions to adopt IPv6 at different rates, surprisingly, we also see that the same ordering of regions does not persist across metrics. For example, the Address Allocation metric shows that ARIN lags behind. However, ARIN performs much better on the other two metrics. First, this affirms our argument that a single metric cannot fairly reflect IPv6 adoption status. More surprisingly, this suggests that, *not only are different regions adopting IPv6 at different rates, but there are different incentives and obstacles (perhaps resource constraints, policy, etc.) that vary the rate for different layers of adoption (i.e., metrics) in any given region.* We intend to explore the cause of these varying pressures in future work.

## 10.2 IPv6 Future

We close by attempting to model how future IPv6 adoption may proceed. As a baseline, for the metrics for which we have four or more years of data, we have already seen that, over that time, nearly every measure of adoption of IPv6 relative to IPv4 has increased by an order of magnitude. In Figure 14 we show the IPv6 to IPv4 ratio for A1: Address Allocation (cumulative) and U1: Traffic (𝒜, peak), between 2011 and 2013 or 2014. We start with 2011, as this is when IPv4 exhaustion pressure became more acute and we began to see larger increases in several of our metrics, including traffic. We chose A1 and U1 as they bookend the gamut of adoption metrics, showing the highest and lowest level, respectively. These also represent the first and last step in deployment. We use the older traffic sample, which ends in 2013, instead of the newer, as the former is for a longer period (but is more conservative than the newer, whose rate of increase in 2013 was 433%). The figure also includes projections out to 2019 based on both polynomial and exponential fit functions ($R^2$ values as shown). Of course, it is possible that upcoming IPv4 exhaustion milestones or other events will lead to discontinuities in the adoption trends. Additionally the growth rate may shift for a number of reasons. Thus, we caution that, while these models represent predictions for where IPv6 adoption may be in five years based on recent trends, the same trends have been volatile in the past and even a small shift could result in much different outcomes. With those caveats in mind, according to the model's projections, *we expect that by 2019 the number of IPv6 prefixes allocated will be about .25–.50 of IPv4, while the IPv6 to IPv4 traffic ratio will be somewhere between .03 and 5.0. In other words, IPv6 appears headed to be a significant fraction of traffic.*

# 11. LIMITATIONS AND FUTURE WORK

In addition to the stated limitations of our datasets, we admit that our framework and proposed metrics are missing some notable perspectives. Social, behavioral, and economic factors are worthy of study, and there are also other technical aspects we did not look at. For instance, vendor support, including in software (e.g., operating system) and hardware (e.g., routers) is useful to understand. Characterizing the prevalence and motivations of actors that forego adopting IPv6 in favor of alternatives, such as carrier-grade NAT (CGN), is also a valuable tangential perspective on IPv6 deployment. Further, examining the factors that lead to differing incentives and obstacles to adoption across and within global regions would be a fascinating and useful endeavor. Even without such broadening of perspectives, the overall topic of IPv6 adoption is too large for any of us to tackle alone; we invite the community to continue contributing measurements and hope our own data and meta-analyses add to the community's understanding of the Internet's largest transition.

## Acknowledgments

This work was supported in part by the Department of Homeland Security Science and Technology Directorate under contract numbers FA8750-12-2-0314, and FA8750-12-2-0235; the National Science Foundation under contract numbers: (each CNS-) 0751116, 1111672, 1111699, 1213157, 1255153, 1330142, 08311174; and the Department of the Navy under contract N000.14-09-1-1042. The authors would like to also thank Arbor Networks, CAIDA, Google, RIPE-NCC, Route Views, and Verisign for making data available. We also thank Duane Wessels and Jared Mauch for supplying older zone files. Finally, we thank Matthew Luckie for insightful feedback on an earlier draft, our shepherd, Ellen Zegura, for help on the final version of the paper, and the anonymous reviewers for constructive critiques.

## 12. REFERENCES


[1] ALEXA. Alexa Top 1M Sites on 2012-10-02. http://www.alexa.com/topsites.

[2] ALLMAN, M. IPv6 DNS & Reachability Dataset. http://www.icir.org/mallman/data/ipv6-dns-data.tar.gz.

[3] APNIC PTY. LTD. APNIC's IPv4 Pool Usage, 2012. http://www.apnic.net.

[4] CAIDA. Archipelago Measurement Infrastructure. http://www.caida.org/projects/ark/.

[5] CHO, K., LUCKIE, M., AND HUFFAKER, B. Identifying IPv6 Network Problems in the Dual-stack World. In *Proceedings of the ACM SIGCOMM Workshop on Network Troubleshooting: Research, Theory and Operations Practice Meet Malfunctioning Reality* (2004).

[6] CLAFFY, K. Tracking IPv6 Evolution: Data We Have and Data We Need. *SIGCOMM Computer Communication Review* (2011).

[7] COLITTI, L., GUNDERSON, S. H., KLINE, E., AND REFICE, T. Evaluating IPv6 Adoption in the Internet. In *Proceedings of the 11th International Conference on Passive and Active Network Measurement*. 2010.

[8] CZYZ, J., ALLMAN, M., ZHANG, J., IEKEL-JOHNSON, S., OSTERWEIL, E., AND BAILEY, M. Measuring IPv6 Adoption. ICSI Technical Report TR-13-004, August 2013.

[9] DAVIES, J. Domain Name System Client Behavior in Windows Vista. http://technet.microsoft.com/en-us/library/bb727035.aspx, 2006.

[10] DHAMDHERE, A., LUCKIE, M., HUFFAKER, B., CLAFFY, K., ELMOKASHFI, A., AND ABEN, E. Measuring the Deployment of IPv6: Topology, Routing and Performance. In *Proceedings of the 12th ACM SIGCOMM Conference on Internet Measurement (IMC)* (2012).

[11] FEATHER, C. Network News Transfer Protocol (NNTP), 2006.

[12] FULLER, V., AND LI, T. RFC4632 - Classless Inter-domain Routing (CIDR): The Internet Address Assignment and Aggregation Plan, 2006.

[13] GIOTSAS, V., AND ZHOU, S. Detecting and Assessing the Hybrid IPv4/IPv6 AS Relationships. *SIGCOMM Computer Communication Review* (2011).

[14] GOOGLE. IPv6 Statistics. http://www.google.com/intl/en/ipv6/statistics/.

[15] GREGORI, E., IMPROTA, A., LENZINI, L., ROSSI, L., AND SANI, L. On the Incompleteness of the AS-level Graph: a Novel Methodology for BGP Route Collector Placement. In *Proceedings of the 12th ACM Conference on Internet Measurement (IMC)* (2012).

[16] GUÉRIN, R., AND HOSANAGAR, K. Fostering IPv6 Migration Through Network Quality Differentials. *SIGCOMM Computer Communication Review* (2010).

[17] GÜRSUN, G., RUCHANSKY, N., TERZI, E., AND CROVELLA, M. Inferring Visibility: Who's (Not) Talking to Whom? *SIGCOMM Computer Communications Review* (2012).

[18] HEI, Y., AND YAMAZAKI, K. Traffic Analysis and Worldwide Operation of Open 6to4 Relays for IPv6 Deployment. In *Proceedings of the International Symposium on Applications and the Internet* (2004).

[19] HUITEMA, S. RFC 4380: Teredo: Tunneling IPv6 over UDP through Network Address Translations (NATs), 2006.

[20] HUSTON, G. The Case for IPv6: Extinction, Evolution or Revolution? http://www.potaroo.net, 2006.

[21] IANA. IPv6 Addresses for the Root Servers. http://www.iana.org/reports/2008/root-aaaa-announcement.html, 2008.

[22] INTERNET SOCIETY. Internet Society - World IPv6 Day. http://www.worldipv6day.org/, 2011.

[23] KARPILOVSKY, E., GERBER, A., PEI, D., REXFORD, J., AND SHAIKH, A. Quantifying the Extent of IPv6 Deployment. In *Proceedings of the 10th International Conference on Passive and Active Network Measurement* (2009).

[24] LABOVITZ, C., IEKEL-JOHNSON, S., MCPHERSON, D., OBERHEIDE, J., AND JAHANIAN, F. Internet Inter-Domain Traffic. In *Proceedings of the 2007 Conference on Applications, Technologies, Architectures, and Protocols for Computer Communications (SIGCOMM)* (2010).

[25] LEBER, M. Global IPv6 Deployment Progress Report. http://bgp.he.net/ipv6-progress-report.cgi, 2014.

[26] MAHADEVAN, P., KRIOUKOV, D., FOMENKOV, M., DIMITROPOULOS, X., CLAFFY, K. C., AND VAHDAT, A. The Internet AS-level Topology: Three Data Sources and One Definitive Metric. *SIGCOMM Computer Communication Review* (2006).

[27] MARSAN, C. Biggest Mistake for IPv6: It's Not Backwards Compatible. http://www.networkworld.com/news/2009/032509-ipv6-mistake.html, 2009.

[28] MOCKAPETRIS, P., AND DUNLAP, K. J. Development of the Domain Name System. In *Proceedings of the 2007 Conference on Applications, Technologies, Architectures, and Protocols for Computer Communications (SIGCOMM)* (1988).

[29] NIKKHAH, M., GUÉRIN, R., LEE, Y., AND WOUNDY, R. Assessing IPv6 Through Web Access: A Measurement Study and Its Findings. In *Proceedings of the Seventh Conference on emerging Networking EXperiments and Technologies (CoNEXT)* (2011).

[30] OSTERWEIL, E., MCPHERSON, D., DIBENEDETTO, S., PAPADOPOULOS, C., AND MASSEY, D. Behavior of DNS' Top Talkers, a .com/.net View. In *Proceedings of the 13th International Conference on Passive and Active Network Measurement* (2012).

[31] PLONKA, D., AND BARFORD, P. Assessing Performance of Internet Services on IPv6. In *Proceedings of the IEEE Symposium on Computers and Communications (ISCC)* (2013).

[32] RIPE. RIPE Routing Information Service (RIS) Raw data Project. http://www.ripe.net/data-tools/stats/ris/ris-raw-data.

[33] RIPE NCC. Routing Information Service (RIS). http://www.ripe.net/ris/.

[34] SARRAR, N., MAIER, G., AGER, B., SOMMER, R., AND UHLIG, S. Investigating IPv6 Traffic - What Happened at the World IPv6 Day? In *Proceedings of the 13th International Conference on Passive and Active Network Measurement* (2012).

[35] SAVOLA, P. Observations of IPv6 Traffic on a 6to4 Relay. *SIGCOMM Computer Communication Review 35*, 1.

[36] SHEN, W., CHEN, Y., ZHANG, Q., CHEN, Y., DENG, B., LI, X., AND LV, G. Observations of IPv6 traffic. In *Proceedings of the International Colloquium on Computing, Communication, Control, and Management* (2009).

[37] SRISURESH, P., AND HOLDREGE, M. RFC2663 - IP Network Address Translator (NAT) Terminology and Considerations, 1999.

[38] UNIVERSITY OF OREGON. Route Views project. http://www.routeviews.org/.

[39] WANG, Y., YE, S., AND LI, X. Understanding Current IPv6 Performance: a Measurement Study. In *10th IEEE Symposium on Computers and Communications* (2005).

[40] WESSELS, D., LARSON, M., AND MANKIN, A. Analysis of Query Traffic to .com/.net Name Servers. http://www.apricot2013.net/__data/assets/pdf_file/0006/58884/130226-com-net-query-analysis-for-apricot-2013_1361840547.pdf, 2013. Slides of a talk given at APRICOT, Feb. 19–Mar. 1, Singapore.

[41] ZANDER, S., ANDREW, L. L., ARMITAGE, G., HUSTON, G., AND MICHAELSON, G. Mitigating Sampling Error When Measuring Internet Client IPv6 Capabilities. In *Proceedings of the 12th ACM Conference on Internet Measurement (IMC)* (2012).

[42] ZHANG, B., LIU, R., MASSEY, D., AND ZHANG, L. Collecting the Internet AS-level Topology. *SIGCOMM Computer Communication Review* (2005).

[43] ZHANG, G., QUOITIN, B., AND ZHOU, S. Phase Changes in the Evolution of the IPv4 and IPv6 AS-Level Internet Topologies. *Computer Communications 34*, 5 (Apr. 2011).

[44] ZHOU, X., AND VAN MIEGHEM, P. Hopcount and e2e Delay: IPv6 Versus IPv4. In *Proceedings of the 6th International Conference on Passive and Active Network Measurement* (2005).

# One Tunnel is (Often) Enough

Simon Peter, Umar Javed, Qiao Zhang, Doug Woos, Thomas Anderson, Arvind Krishnamurthy
University of Washington
{simpeter, ujaved, qiao, dwoos, tom, arvind}@cs.washington.edu

## ABSTRACT

A longstanding problem with the Internet is that it is vulnerable to outages, black holes, hijacking and denial of service. Although architectural solutions have been proposed to address many of these issues, they have had difficulty being adopted due to the need for widespread adoption before most users would see any benefit. This is especially relevant as the Internet is increasingly used for applications where correct and continuous operation is essential.

In this paper, we study whether a simple, easy to implement model is sufficient for addressing the aforementioned Internet vulnerabilities. Our model, called ARROW (Advertised Reliable Routing Over Waypoints), is designed to allow users to configure reliable and secure end to end paths through participating providers. With ARROW, a highly reliable ISP offers tunneled transit through its network, along with packet transformation at the ingress, as a service to remote paying customers. Those customers can stitch together reliable end to end paths through a combination of participating and non-participating ISPs in order to improve the fault-tolerance, robustness, and security of mission critical transmissions. Unlike efforts to redesign the Internet from scratch, we show that ARROW can address a set of well-known Internet vulnerabilities, for most users, with the adoption of only a single transit ISP. To demonstrate ARROW, we have added it to a small-scale wide-area ISP we control. We evaluate its performance and failure recovery properties in both simulation and live settings.

## Categories and Subject Descriptors

C.2.1 [**Network Architecture and Design**]: Packet-switching networks; C.2.2 [**Network Protocols**]: Routing protocols; C.2.5 [**Local and Wide-Area Networks**]: Internet

## Keywords

Internet; Source routing; Overlay networks; BGP; Reliability

## 1. INTRODUCTION

Increasingly, the Internet is being used for services where correct and continuous operation is essential: home health monitoring, active management of power sources on the electrical grid, 911 service, and disaster response are just a few examples. In these and other cases, outages are not just an inconvenience, they are potentially life threatening. Similarly, an economically important case is presented by the outsourcing of enterprise IT infrastructure to the cloud – connectivity outages to cloud servers can imply high costs due to disruptions of day-to-day business activities.

However, the present Internet is not up to the task. For example, router and link failures can trigger convergence delays in the Border Gateway Protocol (BGP). When combined with configuration errors on backup paths, outages can last for hours up to days [14]. Often these outages are partial or asymmetric, indicating that a viable path exists but the protocols and configurations are unable to find it. Other triggers of outages: required maintenance tasks such as software upgrades and policy reconfiguration, router misconfiguration, massive botnet denial-of-service attacks, router software bugs, ambiguities in complex protocols, and malicious behavior by competing ISPs. Even if the traffic is delivered, there are other vulnerabilities. Recently, intra-US traffic was intentionally re-routed through Belarus [6], and earlier, traffic from the US Department of Defense was routed through China [35]. The Internet lacks any protocol mechanism to prevent this type of event from recurring.

Because of its scale, the Internet is of necessity multi-provider, and routes often involve multiple organizations. While a number of research projects have proposed tools to diagnose problems (e.g., [14, 16]), and fixes to specific issues, such as prefix hijacking [5, 17,21,23], route convergence [13], and denial-of-service [7,26,38], there has been little progress towards deployment except in a few cases. Part of the problem is incentives. Many of the proposed solutions are only truly valuable if every ISP adopts; no one who adopts first will gain any advantage.

Another part of the problem is completeness. Is there a *set* of fixes that together would mean we could trust the Internet to reliably deliver packets with reasonable latency? For example, Secure BGP addresses some of the vulnerabilities surrounding spoofed routes, but it doesn't address denial of service or route convergence. The commercial case for deploying a partial defense is weak.

We note that reliability is not equally important for all traffic. Our goal is to design a system that will provide highly available communication for selected customers as long as there is a policy compliant physical path, without diverting the traffic to non-trustworthy ISPs. This property should hold despite node and link failures, software upgrades, byzantine behavior by neighboring networks, and denial-of-service attacks by third parties.

In this paper, we propose, implement, and evaluate a system called *Advertised Reliable Routing Over Waypoints* (ARROW) that allows ISPs to *sell* reliability and security *as a service*, without widespread adoption happening first. End users can obtain this service from any ISP offering it, including ISPs that do not face end-users and primarily serve the backbone of the Internet. At the core


*SIGCOMM'14*, August 17–22, 2014, Chicago, IL, USA.
ACM 978-1-4503-2836-4/14/08.
http://dx.doi.org/10.1145/2619239.2626318.

of our system is a protocol to provision a tunnel across a remote ISP; packets entering the tunnel are authenticated by the ISP, delivered to a specific exit PoP, and slightly re-written, e.g., to modify the destination address. In providing ARROW, an ISP promises only what it can guarantee itself: a high quality tunnel across its own network. The customer is responsible for stitching together ARROW into an end-to-end solution. Like local transit, ARROW is paid for by the requestor, arranged over the web in much the same way as one would purchase computing cycles in Amazon's EC2 cloud computing service.

ARROW shares similarities with Detour routing [29], the Internet Indirection Infrastructure [31], Nira [37], pathlet routing [10], and Platypus [27], among others. Unlike these earlier systems, the ARROW model takes into account resource exhaustion and byzantine attacks in addition to routing anomalies; experience has shown that these attacks are common. More importantly, a number of technology trends have converged to merit a fresh look at Detour-like systems for addressing Internet reliability:

- Large-scale ISPs have deployed sophisticated traffic and network management, making their own networks much more reliable. How can we best leverage this for end-to-end resilience?
- The Internet has become flatter and is more densely interconnected [20]. This has shortened BGP paths to the point that a single, well-placed tunnel is often sufficient to avoid a wide range of problems (as we show in §5).
- $5K PCs can cost-effectively process packets at Internet speeds (40Gbps), allowing for easy deployment of ARROW and the applications that build upon it.

In this paper, we present the design of ARROW, including how its main requirements, incremental deployability, high availability, and robustness, are achieved (§3). We present the ARROW API that can be used by ISPs and end-users to find, reserve, and establish paths on the Internet (§3.2). We present our implementation of ARROW and describe its deployment on a faux ISP that we control, including several applications we have built on top of this deployment (§4). Finally, we evaluate ARROW both in simulation and experimentally (§5). Our evaluation shows ARROW's resilience against transient routing problems, IP prefix-hijacking, inter-AS link failures, path performance problems, and ISP failures, with little overhead to Internet routing performance.

## 2. MOTIVATION

Consider the following example scenarios.

**Example 1:** Imagine a healthcare monitoring application that operates over the Internet. The patient wears a monitoring device sending measurements to a data center, where they are analyzed in real-time. Anomalies are forwarded to alert human experts who can ensure that no medical problem has occurred. To support such applications the network must provide high availability because the network may be part of a life-critical medical feedback loop with timeliness constraints. It must also provide desired levels of quality of service, i.e., provide high bandwidth streams with low loss rates. These services should not be disrupted by transient changes in underlying paths either due to cross-traffic or due to BGP dynamics.

**Example 2:** A large enterprise that is physically distributed across multiple sites, such as a Fortune 500 company, needs to use the Internet for inter-site communications, serving its customers, and accessing outsourced IT services in the cloud. It might have multiple requirements for its communications: traffic should be communicated reliably even in the presence of outages, there should be no information leakage due to traffic analysis, and traffic should be robust to security attacks such as prefix hijacking. To address these concerns, it wants to ensure that its traffic only traverses a set of pre-approved, trustworthy providers or a predictable set of ISPs that satisfy certain geographical/jurisdictional requirements. This is impossible to guarantee today. Near the source, an ISP can select BGP routes to a specific destination that obey certain restrictions. However, those routes can be changed by the downstream ISPs without pre-approval or prior notice; BGP will inform the upstream users only after the fact. Near the destination, the ISP has no standard way to signal that it should only be reached through pre-approved paths or through a predictable set of trusted ISPs.

The previous examples highlight just a few problems of Internet use for mission-critical services. A recent survey [32] enumerates other known security vulnerabilities of the Internet. A few examples include disruption of service by resource exhaustion attacks against network links and end hosts, prefix hijacks by malicious ISPs, and byzantine errors by neighboring ISPs (e.g., intentional disaggregation of addresses, causing router crashes).

Even without vulnerabilities to malicious attack, the Internet protocols are operationally fragile: Internet paths are often disrupted for short periods of time as BGP paths converge. Common operational changes, such as reboots or rewiring, and divergence between the control and data plane can also reduce availability. With today's protocols, an endpoint has no recourse in this case but to patiently wait for the problem to be repaired.

In our work, a key observation is that the amount of traffic for mission-critical applications can be quite small, especially compared to normal everyday Internet use. Yet this traffic is often very high value. Our proposal targets just these low-volume, high value applications. Most users find most of their Internet traffic works well enough most of the time, because much of the traffic on the Internet is for content delivery from nearby cached copies. For this type of traffic, the most critical factor is the reliability of the local ISP. Internet reliability is of course still an issue for many users, but it seems unlikely that this part of the problem requires an architectural fix beyond designing better tools for network operators to diagnose their own networks.

Our focus is thus on developing a system that can enhance the reliability and performance of mission-critical traffic using solutions that are incrementally deployable and provide benefits even when it is deployed by a small number of ISPs. Further, re-architecting the Internet from ground up seems overkill for such a small amount of traffic, no matter how important in human or commercial terms. Given the large number of known problems, it is unlikely that even a well-designed set of changes would fix every problem, and a massive change to the Internet protocol suite would run the risk of having unintended side effects.

## 3. ARROW DESIGN

We would like to develop a simple system that can be used to provide highly available communication in addition to the Internet's normal uses as long as there is a usable and policy-compliant physical path between a pair of endpoints. To this end, the key requirements of our solution are:

**Incremental Deployability:** In today's Internet, a provider ISP (or ISPs) mediates Internet service. This poses a chicken and egg problem: an ISP can't promise or charge for a new type of service unless all, or almost all, other ISPs already provide the service. We want to make it possible for end users, enterprises, and governments to leverage reliable intradomain paths made available by remote ISPs, *without* requiring global adoption of new protocols.

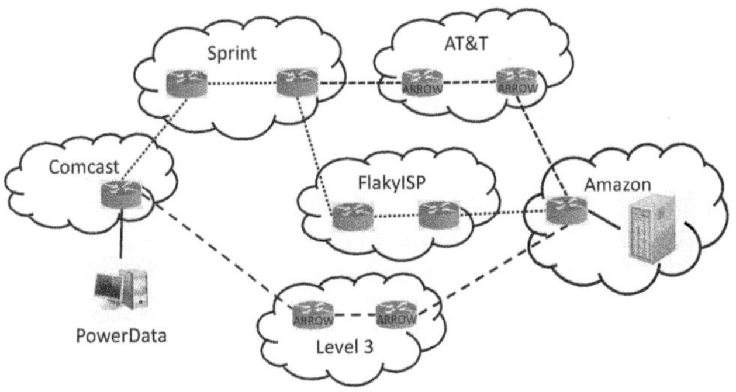


**Figure 1: Three example ARROW paths from PowerData to Amazon: the dotted lines represent the BGP path. The two dashed lines are ARROW paths.**

**High Availability:** We want endpoints to be able to establish one or more high quality paths across the Internet, provided a physical path exists through ISPs willing to be paid for the service. For availability, endpoints need the ability to route around persistent reachability problems, as well as to establish multiple paths to minimize disruptions due to transient routing loops and blackholes.

**Robustness:** Because security attacks against the Internet are a real threat, we need to provide endpoints the means to defend their routes, both by *proactive* installation of desirable paths and filters and *reactive* rerouting of traffic in response to degradation in packet delivery.

In this section, we provide a brief overview of our approach before describing the key components of our design.

## 3.1 Overview

We provide an overview of our approach using a simple example shown in Figure 1. A company called PowerData is using Amazon cloud services for its day-to-day data storage. Using BGP, traffic to Amazon would be routed via Comcast (PowerData's upstream ISP), Sprint, and either FlakyISP or AT&T. However, FlakyISP often drops packets and has caused PowerData's service to be slow whenever the path through FlakyISP is chosen by Sprint and Comcast. Note that, while PowerData can find out about the problem using various available Internet measurement technologies, it has limited or no control over the paths selected by Sprint (a remote ISP) and Comcast (the local transit provider).

To remedy this, PowerData buys ARROW transit from AT&T, which involves provisioning a path through AT&T and establishing the appropriate packet forwarding rules to transmit PowerData packets along to Amazon and received responses back to PowerData. This ensures that PowerData packets to and from Amazon are routed around FlakyISP since it does not appear on any of the paths between Comcast and AT&T nor does it appear on the paths between AT&T and Amazon. Note that PowerData does not have to provision paths across every ISP on its path to/from Amazon in order to avoid FlakyISP. Rather, a limited amount of route control at a remote ISP (AT&T in this example) suffices to achieve the desired paths.

To ensure that reconfigurations and temporary outages (for example, due to routing loops or misconfigurations) at Sprint and AT&T do not impact PowerData's service, PowerData also buys ARROW transit from Level 3 and can fail-over to this path in case of problems with the original path.

The example illustrates several properties of our proposed approach. First, the system is incrementally deployable by an ISP, with incremental incentives to that ISP. An ISP can provide ARROW even if none of its peer, customer or provider ISPs participate in the protocol. ARROW benefits from a network effect, but it still provides value to enterprises and data centers needing to control routes even if only a few ISPs have adopted the approach. In the example in Figure 1, ARROW is still useful to PowerData even if Sprint does not provide ARROW transit.

Second, ARROW aims to require only modest changes to the existing Internet infrastructure to facilitate deployment. We assume no changes to normal traffic, but we do require that mission critical traffic be specially encoded to simplify packet processing at the router. Redesigning services to work with ARROW requires minimal programmer effort, the costs of which should be outweighed by the benefits for mission-critical services. Alternately, we explain how a local ISP could offer an end to end service to its clients, by rebundling their mission critical traffic to use ARROW.

In the rest of this section, we present the ARROW design and outline the key components of our proposal including:

- the management interface for setting up transit through a remote ISP,
- the data plane operations required for supporting remote transit,
- the issues in setting up end-to-end paths, monitoring them, and responding to changes in path quality, and
- business considerations that affect the adoption of the proposed scheme.

## 3.2 Setting up Remote Transit

An ISP offering ARROW advertises its willingness to provide its transit, for a fee, via SSL, much as is currently done for cloud providers offering computer time. The control traffic (to find out about advertised ARROW tunnels, and to request the tunnel) can be carried over the existing Internet, or in turn use ARROW mechanisms to bootstrap more reliable routes that can be used for the contol traffic.

The ISP operates a portal that provides interested users with an interface for obtaining information regarding its ARROW service. If transit is granted for a fee, registering with an ISP's service would typically involve an exchange of the customer's credit card information. An ISP can exercise fine-grained control over its ARROW service, including between which of its peers to provide the service, and whether to attach Service Level Agreements (SLAs) to it that might provide bandwidth and latency guarantees. Other value-added services might also be offered, such as DoS protection.

The portal should provide at least the following:

- All offered transit paths and services from a specific ingress ISP (and optionally, ingress link) to a specific egress ISP (and optionally, egress link), including backup ingress router IP addresses in case of failures,
- the pricing model of the offered transit paths and services, and
- the SLAs provided, such as bandwidth, latency, and maximum packet loss rate guarantees.

In addition, the portal needs to provide the ability to obtain and relinquish a path by returning or accepting a corresponding identification token, which we call an *authenticator*. The authenticator is used in actual ARROW traffic to prove that the endpoint originating the packet is authorized to use the transit path. The router must check the authenticator and drop the packet if it does not match. If the authenticator is compromised, the only penalty is that the customer of the service is charged for extra unrelated traffic traversing the pipe. Techniques to safeguard the authenticator against eavesdropping, such as encoding it with the hash of the checksum of the packet, may be used. Attackers can then only replay entire packets, but they cannot use snooped authenticators for other packets.

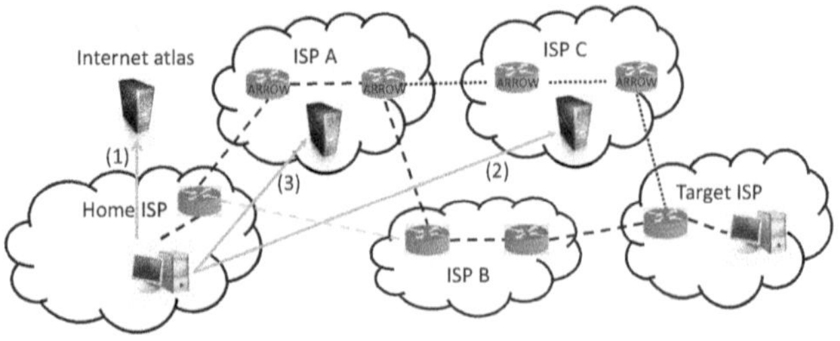


**Figure 2: Example ARROW transit setup process. Blue routers in ISPs A and C are ARROW-compatible, gray routers in ISP B are not. Dashed lines show the path chosen in case (a). Dotted lines show the detour taken via another ARROW ISP in case (b). The BGP path in this example is Home-B-Target.**

Finally, an RPC interface should be provided that allows clients to stitch together transit segments of multiple providers into an end-to-end path. The call may look like this:

```
chain_path(auth, nextHopAddr, nextHopAuth)
```

It causes the egress router of an existing ARROW tunnel segment (identified by its authenticator `auth`) to route tunnel traffic to the IP address `nextHopAddr` and set the ARROW authenticator of the next hop to `nextHopAuth`.

An end host contacts one or more of the ARROW ISPs on the route via this interface and requests provisioned paths through the individual networks. The ARROW customer then arranges for the routing of the packet by associating with each hop the address for each subsequent hop that needs to be traversed. We note that links within an ISP might run out of excess capacity, but that only prevents future ARROW tunnels from being set up; existing agreements can stay in place. Market prices can then signal a need for more capacity.

From the ISP-provided lists of ingress and egress points, endpoints are able to compile an atlas, which they can use to determine a path to a destination. Any shortest path discovery algorithm can be used on the atlas to determine which ISPs to use to create an end-to-end circuit. We envision that, eventually, another Internet webservice maintains the atlas and provides a path query interface, returning paths according to any of a number of these algorithms. Most of the information we require ISPs to advertise to potential customers is already advertised to their direct peers, and much of it is already publically available.

Figure 2 shows an example of an Internet endpoint arranging an ARROW circuit with a target endpoint, registering with a number of ISPs. It also shows how the circuit is maintained by each of the ISPs. Two cases are considered:

(a) A tier 1 **ISP A** that is the provider for our home ISP supports ARROW and a circuit is created via this ISP. Other traffic is routed via BGP through a non-ARROW supporting **ISP B** to the final destination. The path in this case is **Home-A-B-Target**.

(b) An additional ARROW-supporting **ISP C** is configured to avoid the non-ARROW **ISP B**. In this case, we configure **ISP A** to forward packets to **ISP C**, via ARROW. The path in this case is **Home-A-C-Target**.

In both cases, the endpoint first optionally contacts an Internet atlas service to determine which ISPs to contract for ARROW service (1). Then, the home endpoint contacts the portals of the appropriate ARROW ISPs on the circuit to create ARROW SLAs. This typically has to happen in reverse order (2 and then 3), from destination endpoint to source endpoint, so that next-hop information can be given.

ARROW paths are unidirectional. The reverse path can be provisioned either by the peer, or by the originator of the traffic. This

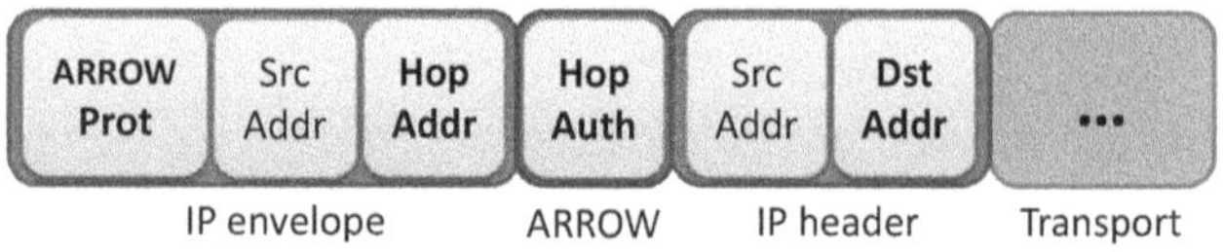


**Figure 3: Relevant fields of an ARROW packet (in bold). *Dst Addr* is the IP address of the final destination. Note that the source endpoint IP address and other IP header fields are duplicated by the envelope IP header.**

might depend upon the relationship of the peers. If the source party is a customer of a cloud service, it makes sense for the source to provision both paths. A peer-to-peer relationship can be provisioned by either peer individually.

## 3.3 Data Forwarding

To route traffic via ARROW, the source (or its proxy) encapsulates every IP data packet in a separate IP envelope, as shown in Figure 3. The envelope also contains the authenticator in a special field (Hop Auth). The envelope's destination is set to the next ARROW hop's IP address (Hop Addr) and its next-level protocol field is set to a value identifying ARROW (ARROW Prot).

The source then sends the packet normally through its local network. If the customer has a chain of ARROW providers, then each modifies the packet with the address and authenticator of the next hop, according to its local ARROW forwarding table; the last ISP in the chain removes the IP header encapsulation before forwarding. This model requires each ARROW router to have an appropriate entry per ARROW tunnel in its forwarding table, contributing to the growth of forwarding tables. Modern forwarding and table storage techniques [28], however, make routing table scalability less of a concern.

We do require some level of hardware support in routers, but it is minimal and similar to the hardware already in place: in many ISPs, ingress routers demux incoming traffic based on the destination address to a specific MPLS tunnel to route the traffic across their network. We can leverage similar hardware support in ARROW: the ingress router must be able to demux on the ARROW address (and if necessary the ARROW authenticator), route the packet using MPLS or other means, and then modify the header to insert the next hop address and authenticator. Alternatively, ISPs can operate high-speed software routers (e.g., RouteBricks [8], PacketShader [11]) at ingress/egress PoPs to perform the necessary tasks for ARROW traffic.

## 3.4 Failures and Performance Regressions

**Failures.** Most failures along an ARROW circuit can be handled by ISPs directly. Some failures require endpoints to cooperate, however. Specifically, in an ARROW circuit, failure can occur at several different levels:

- failure of a router internal to an ISP,
- failure of a router at the edge of an ISP, or
- failure of a whole ISP.

If an internal router fails, the ISP is responsible for detecting this failure and routing around it. ISPs today typically have multiple redundant paths between the ingress and egress PoPs, and can thus use MPLS mechanisms to configure backup paths and switch the intradomain paths in a seamless manner. For instance, MPLS Fast Reroute allows routers inside the ISP to redirect traffic onto a predetermined backup path when they detect failures in upstream routers [30].

Since edge routers correspond to boundaries between ISPs, edge routers belonging to different ISPs need to cooperatively handle failover. Thus, we have designed a failover protocol which must be implemented by each participating ISP. Our implementation does not perform failure detection, since we believe that in general the endpoint will be able to do a better job of determining whether its traffic is actually arriving at the server. Therefore, failover is an endpoint-driven process in this case.

When the endpoint detects a failure along an ARROW path (i.e., it detects that its traffic is not successfully arriving at the destination), it sends a special probe packet along the same path. Each ISP's router is required to respond to **the previous hop** of the probe packet and also forward it normally along the path. This is similar to what happens when an IP packet has reached its end of life, except that the packet is also forwarded and the response goes to the previous hop instead of the source of the packet.

If the endpoint does not receive an acknowledgment from the first ISP, it concludes that the first ISP is where the failure exists and fails over to another edge router in the same ISP. If the first ISP does receive the endpoint's probe, it first acknowledges it so that the endpoint doesn't assume it has failed, then forwards the probe to the second ISP. Thus, the probe is initiated by the endpoint but is actually performed at each non-failing ISP node in the circuit.

For example, assume a circuit has been established between an endpoint $E$, ISP $A$, ISP $B$, and a server $S$. Each ISP has three routing nodes; we call them $A_1$, $A_2$, $A_3$ and $B_1$, $B_2$, $B_3$. When the circuit is first established, it goes from $E$ to $A_1$ to $B_1$ to $S$. At some later time, $B_1$ fails. $E$ detects that $S$ isn't receiving its messages and initiates the failover process by sending a probe packet to $A_1$. $A_1$ receives and acknowledges the probe, then forwards it to $B_1$. $A_1$ does not receive an acknowledgment within a link-latency-determined timeout, and concludes (correctly) that $B_1$ has failed. $A_1$ then forwards the probe to $B_2$, which acknowledges it. In response, $A_1$ updates its local state so that packets on the circuit go to $B_2$ rather than $B_1$. Subsequent traffic is now routed through the new circuit and $E$ detects that the failover has succeeded.

If the ISP as a whole fails, the endpoint will need to provision an alternate route. An endpoint can establish multiple ARROW paths to the destination simultaneously and use them in conjunction with the original path for fast failover.

**Performance regressions.** To help endpoints investigate circuit performance, ISPs should provide a ping service at egress PoPs to arbitrary IP addresses and ARROW routers need to be able to respond to ICMP requests. Endpoints then have the ability to independently gather all required information to analyze the performance of each circuit segment.

## 3.5 Security

The design presented thus far has a few security issues: ARROW paths and their endpoints might be DoS-attacked, the availability of trusted ARROW ISPs might be spotty and traffic has to traverse non-ARROW ISPs, and ARROW users themselves might be malicious. We now address these issues.

**DoS attacks.** ARROW paths can be set up to resemble swarms of packet forwarders [7] in order to increase path availability in the face of DoS attacks. Figure 4 demonstrates how this can be achieved: multiple ARROW segments are configured within one ARROW supporting ISP to mitigate the effects of DoS attacks to ARROW ingress points. Since ARROW clients can migrate their traffic to another ingress PoP if their PoP is overloaded, attackers have to overwhelm all provided ingress points simultaneously in order to stop traffic to the destination. If the destination endpoint's

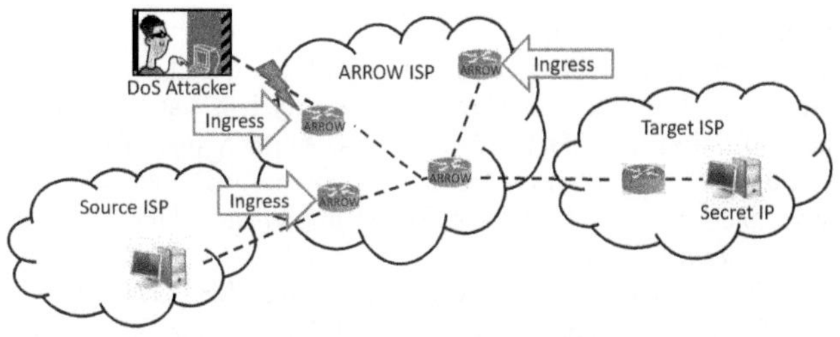


**Figure 4: DoS attack prevention using ARROW.**

IP address is kept secret, it does not matter whether the ARROW supporting ISP is the endpoint's local ISP or an arbitrary remote ISP. Otherwise, if the provider of the destination endpoint provides ARROW, the endpoint's ISP can drop all non-ARROW traffic and protect the endpoint in this way.

**Securing spotty ARROW routes.** To ensure that its packets traverse only trusted ISPs, an endpoint can set up ARROW circuits through each intermediate ISP in an end-to-end path. If some of the intermediate ISPs don't provide ARROW support, endpoints have to resort to normal Internet routing between the ARROW ISPs. This means that those hops are vulnerable to BGP effects such as prefix hijacking and rerouting of packets through untrusted ISPs. However, if the AS path lengths of the non-ARROW segments are small, then only those ASes that are within the local neighborhood of these segments would be able to mount an effective prefix hijacking attack. Additionally, in order to disrupt an ARROW route, the hijacking entity has to pollute the routing entry at a specific egress PoP as opposed to any arbitrary PoP inside the ARROW supporting ISP. Further, if an ARROW ISP is a provider of the non-participating ISP (e.g., the ARROW ISP is a tier 1 ISP), then also it is unlikely that prefix hijacking is effective—most ISPs in practice are configured to filter competing advertisements for addresses originating in their direct customers/providers, so the ARROW ISP would effectively filter out most forged announcements.

It is worth noting that if all we need is alternating compliant ISPs, the average number of ARROW hops we would need for an end to end path in today's Internet is very small, typically one or two. An endpoint can also constrain that all communications sent to it should be through ARROW tunnels by providing other endpoints with an ARROW address as opposed to its actual IP address.

In any case, it is important to know how many BGP hops are between the ARROW hops to gauge the vulnerability of the connection to attacks and failures. To figure out the number of intermediate hops, sources can initiate a traceroute to originate from the last ARROW supporting hop of the source end of the path, directed at the first ARROW hop of the destination end of the path. This can be done by sending a traceroute via ARROW from the source endpoint to the first ARROW hop of the destination end through the existing partial circuit.

**Misbehaving ARROW users.** We have thus far assumed that ARROW clients are well-behaved. A malicious or faulty client could repeatedly send false failover notices, or set up an ARROW circuit with a loop. An ARROW-supporting ISP would need to detect these scenarios (this is feasible because clients require strong identities to buy ARROW service) and ignore or rate-limit failover traffic from misbehaving customers.

## 3.6 Business issues

An ISP has an incentive to ensure correct forwarding of ARROW traffic across its network, because it is receiving revenue in addition to the price it is receiving for carrying the packet from its immediate neighbor. Also, since endpoints have the ability to switch over to pre-configured backup paths, it is in the ISP's interest to perform local fault recovery quickly if it wants to retain the traffic from the ARROW customers. Further, since ARROW would allow ISPs to attract traffic that they normally wouldn't receive, there is an incentive for ISPs to implement ARROW even when other ISPs don't.

An ISP might intentionally disrupt traffic to an ARROW provider, e.g., if it sees a packet destined for an ARROW address, it might drop it. While a sufficient number of such misbehaving ISPs will cause a problem regardless of the technology used, ARROW would allow customers to route around them, and provide further incentive (in the form of more potential customers) for other ISPs to adopt ARROW. As another option, ARROW destined packets could be encrypted when traversing non-cooperative ISPs, so that they appear to be SSL traffic.

Although ARROW will allow enterprises to contract for exactly the amount of route control, resilience, and DoS protection that they need, ISPs may also find it useful to leverage ARROW services on behalf of their customers. That is, a customer-facing ISP would arrange tunnels to important data services, and this would be (nearly) transparent to the ISP's customers, except that they would find their Internet service through the ISP to be highly reliable. This aggregation will be particularly valuable for thin devices that lack the ability to monitor routes and perform route control on their own.

# 4. IMPLEMENTATION

In this section, we describe our implementation of ARROW and its deployment. The deployment is a step toward building and running an ISP supporting ARROW, such that any Internet user will be able to try out ARROW for themselves. To this end we leverage the BGP Transit Portal [33] and PlanetLab VICCI clusters [34]. We have also built several services designed to enhance end-to-end performance and security on this deployment. These services include a DoS prevention system akin to the one described in §3.5, and a simple CDN.

## 4.1 Serval Implementation

We have integrated ARROW support into the Serval [25] protocol stack. Serval is a great fit for ARROW as it already supports client-side failover for connection failures and we can extend this support to failover among several ARROW paths. To extend Serval to support ARROW, we have added a new packet header extension (header extensions are a Serval feature), which contains the ARROW authenticator. This extension is included on every data packet. If the source endpoint's service access table contains a forward rule with an ARROW authenticator annotation, this header extension will be generated with the corresponding authenticator and all data packets forwarded to the specified next-hop service router. The service routers detect the ARROW extension and match it in a special ARROW authenticator table to the next-hop IP address, possibly with another ARROW annotation. Each packet's destination IP address and potentially ARROW authenticator is rewritten according to this table.

## 4.2 Internet Atlas

To provide the Internet atlas service, each ARROW ISP continuously performs measurements to generate and maintain a map of Internet paths from each of its PoPs to each routable prefix, with each path annotated with a rich set of attributes corresponding to the latency, available bandwidth, and loss rate of the path.

These collected measurements are made available through a *network atlas* service (with XMLRPC and SunRPC interfaces) so that they can be queried dynamically for metrics, such as reachability, latency and throughput performance, between an ARROW PoP and an arbitrary IP address. It is kept up-to-date with live active probe measurements, which are performed at regular intervals and also selectively reprobed based on passive observation of BGP feeds. As such, it can be used to determine the performance between any two PoPs, as well as the performance to any Internet prefix from an egress PoP. This is especially useful when choosing among multiple ARROW-offering ISPs.

```
require 'atlas'

egress = ARGV[0]
prefixes = Array.new
(1..ARGV.length-1).each { |i|
    prefixes.push(ARGV[i])
}

atlas = Atlas.new
prefixes.each{ |p|
    atlas.addPath(egress, p)
}
responses = atlas.queryPendingPaths
responses.each{ |r|
    if (r.latency < 300) # 300ms
        puts(r.path.join(" "))
    end
}
```

**Figure 5: A Ruby program that returns all ARROW paths with latency below 300 ms from a given egress PoP to a number of given IP addresses. Hops on a path are separated by spaces, paths are separated by newlines.**

To determine whether keeping the network atlas up-to-date is feasible, we have evaluated the average daily rate with which Internet paths change at the PoP-level. To do so, we count daily PoP-level changes in downstream paths from all tier-1 ASes to all prefixes within the entire year 2012 of historical iPlane traceroute measurements (cf. §5.4). We count in two ways: 1. also counting paths with IP-level changes where we have no IP-to-PoP mapping, and 2. where we ignore these changes. We arrive at an average rate of 10% and 1%, respectively, of paths changing daily, which can be processed efficiently at the atlas service.

The network atlas service expects a Ruby program on its input and provides the output of that program as its result. The Ruby program can make repeated queries to the database of collected measurements (using the call queryPendingPaths), filter out unnecessary results, and report back to the endpoint a pruned list of paths that match application-specific criteria. Figure 5 demonstrates a program that returns all paths with a latency below 300ms from a given egress PoP to a number of IP prefixes, given as a list of IP addresses living within each prefix, respectively.

## 4.3 Wide Area Deployment

We have deployed ARROW nodes in the wide area using the Transit Portal (TP) BGP testbed [33] and the VICCI set of geographically distributed compute clusters [34]. TP lets us announce /24 prefixes using six US universities as our providers: University of Washington (UW), University of Wisconsin (WISC), Georgia Tech (GATech), Princeton University, Clemson University and University of Southern California (USC). VICCI clusters are co-located with most of the TP sites, except for another VICCI cluster site at Stanford University that is not co-located. We envision each TP/VICCI site as a PoP for our ARROW ISP. An ARROW client simply addresses packets to a specific IP address in the TP prefix.

The Portal software router then redirects these packets to an ARROW software router via a VPN tunnel. We deploy the ARROW routers on a co-located VICCI cluster.

For redundancy, ARROW routers have replicas that are kept consistent via a distributed coordination service [12]. In a real deployment, router-specific protocols would be used to keep standby routers consistent with their primaries. Software routers run a Serval routing component in user space (kernel modifications are not allowed on VICCI); this is the data plane. Each router also runs an ARROW circuit creation daemon, a replica manager, and a failover management daemon; the control plane—implemented in Python.

## 4.4 ARROW Services

We have built several prototype services on our ARROW deployment, to demonstrate the value of additional services deployed with ARROW. We briefly describe two of these services in this section: a DoS protection service and a content distribution network.

**DoS Protection.** We have implemented the Phalanx [7] DoS protection scheme and deployed it at ARROW software router nodes at each Transit Portal PoP. The service can be offered to anyone on the Internet wishing to obtain a DoS protection layer for their own services. Phalanx achieves DoS protection by requiring clients to interleave packets to the server through a predetermined sequence of bandwidth-limiting proxy nodes (called mailboxes), each of which has a different IP address. Since the attacker does not know this sequence, they can affect only a fraction of the traffic exchanged. The client and server initially agree on the random sequence of mailboxes (through a secret key) before traffic can flow. The communication proceeds by the client sending a packet to the appropriate mailbox and the server requesting the packet from that mailbox. The router at the TP node forwards client packets and server requests to the ARROW VICCI nodes where client packets are stored until the server requests them.

**Content Distribution Network.** We have also implemented a simple CDN offering a traffic cache at each Transit Portal PoP. The CDN consists of a controller and a group of geo-replicated cache nodes. The controller is responsible for collecting content requests and directs them to the cache replica with the lowest latency to the requesting client. Each ISP offering CDN service is in a good position to know this information for its PoPs. In our prototype deployment, each replica stores a copy of each file. After receiving a client request, the controller instructs the cache nodes to measure their RTT latencies to the client and picks the one with the lowest RTT to serve the content to the client.

# 5. EVALUATION

We evaluate ARROW via simulation on AS and PoP-level Internet topology, as well as by measurement of our implementation, both when deployed on a local cluster of machines, as well as within our large-scale deployment. Specifically, we seek to answer the following questions:

- How are throughput and latency of Internet traffic affected when an ARROW path (of various lengths) is used?
- How nimble are the individual failover mechanisms that are deployed along an ARROW path?
- How quickly is ARROW able to re-establish end-to-end connectivity in the event of a link failure on the Internet?
- How resilient are various ARROW deployments to (potentially cascading) Internet link and AS failures and can we use ARROW to avoid untrusted ISPs?

| | RTT [$\mu s$] | Throughput [Gbits/s] |
|---|---|---|
| UDP/TCP | 44/96/107 | 9.05/9.36/9.68 |
| Serval | 73/81.23/154 | 9.35/9.52/9.74 |
| 1 ARROW hop | 113/131.96/290 | 9.37/9.55/9.85 |
| 2 ARROW hops | 158/191.38/444 | 8.19/8.49/8.72 |

**Table 1: RTT and throughput (min/avg/max) of different ARROW path lengths vs. UDP/TCP and Serval.**

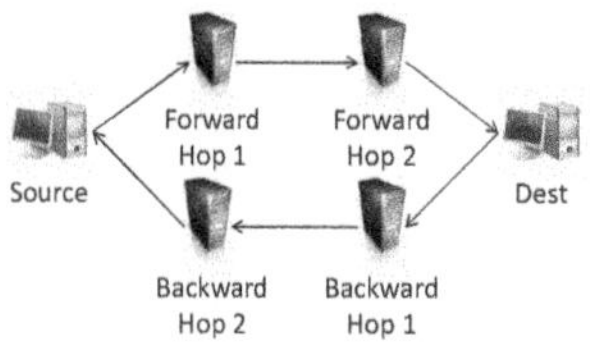


**Figure 6: ARROW 6-node cluster deployment.**

- How effectively do various ARROW deployments prevent IP prefix-hijacking attacks?
- Is the end-to-end latency of ARROW paths comparable to that of regular BGP paths?

We are especially concerned with evaluating whether a single tunnel (one ARROW hop) is enough to provide all of the benefits. Hence, with the exception of performance evaluation, we only evaluate one-hop tunnels within the experiments in this section (as opposed to the number of ARROW-supporting ASes, which we *do* vary).

## 5.1 Performance Overhead

To evaluate the latency and throughput overheads of our ARROW prototype, we have deployed it on a 6-node cluster. All nodes run Linux 3.2.0 on Intel Xeon E5-2430 processors at 2.2 GHz clock frequency, with 15 Mbytes total cache, 4 Gbytes memory, and Intel X520 dual-port 10 Gigabit Ethernet adapters, connected to a 10 Gigabit Ethernet switch. Figure 6 shows this setup.

In the cluster, one node acts as the source endpoint of a route and another one as the destination. The other nodes are used as ARROW routers. The deployment is symmetrical: Both forward and reverse ARROW paths are established between source and target, over distinct nodes in the cluster. We can construct up to 2 ARROW hops in this symmetrical fashion. We determine the latency along a path by measuring the average round-trip time (RTT) of 100 individual 64 byte UDP packets to the destination which echoes them back unmodified. We measure the average throughput over 5 TCP transfers of a data stream over 10 seconds each, using the iperf[1] bandwidth measurement tool.

Table 1 shows the measurement results of different lengths of ARROW routes compared to UDP/TCP and unmodified Serval. The TCP, UDP and Serval measurements measure direct bandwidth and RTT between two endpoints, without going through any intermediate hops. The ARROW measurements forward packets according to the experimental setup shown in Figure 6.

In terms of latency, ARROW adds an RTT overhead of 62% over the baseline Serval implementation and 37% over UDP. A 2-hop ARROW path has an overhead of 45% over the RTT latency of a 1-hop path. Throughput is not affected by adding ARROW to a 1-hop path. However, adding another ARROW hop impacts throughput by 10%. This might be due to our switch not being able to handle the bandwidth requirement.

We conclude that the overheads imposed by ARROW are small enough to merit the deployment of a wide-area prototype. In a pro-

[1] `http://iperf.sourceforge.net`

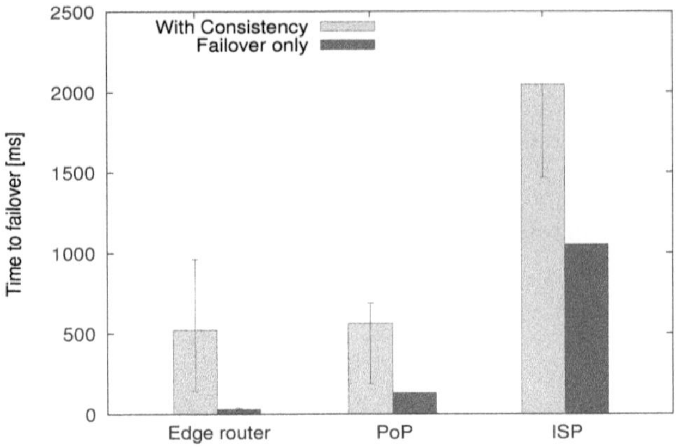


**Figure 7: Time to failover for various component failures along a ARROW path. The plot shows the median (min/max in error bars) over 5 measurements, each with Zookeeper and without.**

duction environment, purpose-built routers would likely be used. They already support the required features: MPLS tunnels can be used to forward packets among tunnel segments and Software Defined Networking (SDN) technology aids the setup and management of tunnel segments.

## 5.2 Path Failover Latency

For ARROW to provide significant benefit versus BGP, it is important that its own paths are not prone to long failover times itself. We examine the time taken to failover a complete path for each endpoint-observable failure along that path within our wide-area ARROW deployment.

The measured topology involves 3 PoPs (UW, Princeton, and Stanford), as well as 3 ASes: Home, Transit, and Dest. Home meets Transit at both UW and Princeton, and Transit meets Dest at Stanford. Using the VICCI cluster nodes, we "deploy" three redundant routers (one active, and two standby) of each AS at each PoP—six routers total at each PoP and 18 routers in the entire topology.

We then establish an ARROW path from Home via Transit to Dest. After the connection is established, we intentionally kill the software on a router node to simulate a failure. To simulate an edge router failure, we kill the active Transit ingress router at UW. For a PoP failure, we kill all routers at UW. Finally, for an ISP failure, we kill all Transit routers at both UW and Princeton.

Figure 7 shows the measured failover times over 5 measurements for each of the 3 failure cases, as observed from the endpoint, i.e. after the endpoint detected there is a failure until the connection is restored. This involves the execution of the entire failover protocol, as described in §3.4. Failover times increase with the scope of the failure. We also observe high failover times when the consistency service is used. While some consistency service is necessary, we believe that our choice of consistency service (Zookeeper [12]) could be optimized to remove some or all of this cost.

Edge routers exist within the same PoP and failure detection can be very aggressive. Hence, this is the shortest failover time of only 340ms (30ms without consistency service). If an entire PoP fails, none of the 3 edge router replicas are reachable and we have to re-route to another PoP, which can be far away. This is the case in our deployment (from UW to Princeton) and thus PoP failovers take slightly longer, roughly 414ms (128ms without consistency service). Finally, if an entire ISP fails, we have to probe several of its PoPs until we determine that the ISP is down. The endpoint then has to failover to a backup ARROW path. This takes on the order of 1.8 seconds (1 second without consistency service).

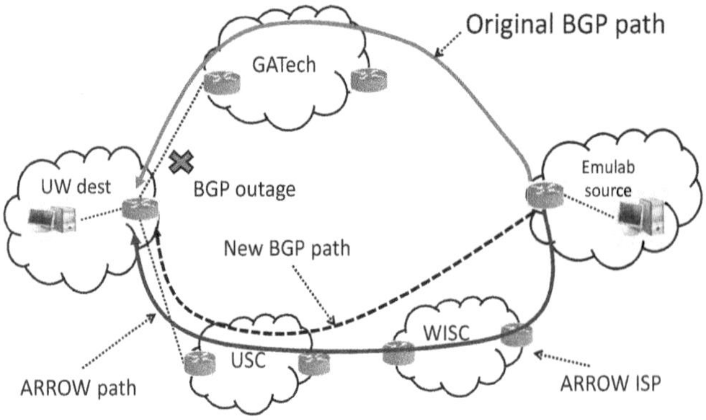


**Figure 8: Setup of the BGP outage experiment. We cause a failure at UW's upstream link with GATech. BGP will eventually failover to a path via USC. ARROW can use an alternative path via WISC.**

We conclude that most failures along an ARROW path can be addressed in a timespan that is hardly noticeable to most users, especially when router consistency is optimized. Only whole ISP failures take longer and might be noticeable at the endpoints. Compared to the time it takes for BGP to converge after such failures, ARROW still compares favorably in all of the cases.

## 5.3 End-to-end Recovery After BGP Outage

To examine how quickly end-to-end connectivity can be restored using an ARROW backup path in the event of a BGP outage, we conduct an experiment on our wide area deployment where we forcibly take down a BGP link, similar to an experiment conducted in RON [3]. The experiment setup is shown in Figure 8, where we have a multi-homed destination at the UW, by announcing a prefix through TP sites located at GATech and USC simultaneously. Our source is an Emulab [9] node, and its original path to the UW destination passes through GATech. We also have an ARROW deployment at WISC that is reachable using a prefix announced only through WISC. This provides us with a one-hop ARROW path through WISC to UW. We then establish a regular UDP connection from the source node to a destination within the UW prefix and continuously measure its throughput. We conduct this experiment twice, once with a failover using ARROW and once with a regular BGP failover.

The measured throughput over time is shown for both cases in Figure 9. 7 seconds into the experiment, we shut down the VPN tunnel between UW and GATech, resulting in a BGP session failure and an instantaneous loss of all packets along the path. The failure eventually causes BGP to withdraw the route through GATech and converge to the new route through USC (red line). This outage lasts for nearly 90 seconds until convergence to the new route takes place. In contrast, the ARROW deployment is able to detect and recover from the failure within a few hundred milliseconds (blue line). The source in this case detects the outage through a sequence of unacknowledged packets and immediately starts forwarding packets through the pre-established ARROW path.

We conclude that ARROW allows endpoints to failover an end-to-end path within a timespan of a typical TCP timeout, which is hardly noticeable at the endpoint and does not disrupt open connections, except for a short dip in throughput.

## 5.4 Simulation Dataset and Methodology

Next, we explore the potential reliability and performance properties of ARROW deployed at Internet-scale. For this purpose we examine BGP and ARROW routing on Internet topology. We do

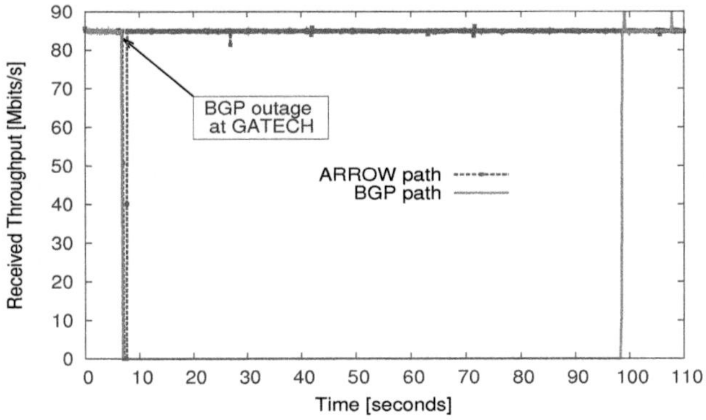


**Figure 9: Time-series showing throughput for a BGP failover and a ARROW failover for the experiment in Figure 8. The link fails at 7 seconds. BGP takes 90 seconds before convergence to a new path. ARROW failover is on the order of hundreds of milliseconds.**

this using two methodologies: 1. we simulate the effects of BGP routing decisions (§5.5 and §5.6) and 2. we use actual BGP routing measurements collected by iPlane[2] (§5.7, §5.8, and §5.9).

For the first method, we acquired the simulator used to evaluate Consensus Routing [13], which simulates routing decisions, BGP protocol control traffic, and link failures. We use the November 2013 CAIDA AS-level connectivity graph [1], gathered from RouteViews BGP tables [2], to simulate on a realistic Internet topology. This dataset has a total of 29,730 ASes and 159,049 unique AS-level links, annotated with the inferred business relationships of the linked ASes (customer-provider or peer-peer). The simulator uses standard route selection and advertisement policies of the Internet, such as "valley-free" export and "hot potato" routing. More detail about the simulator can be found in [13].

The iPlane dataset used in the second method is built using traceroutes from over 200 PlanetLab sites to more than 140,000 prefixes (almost every routable prefix on the Internet). The iPlane dataset also provides IP-to-AS mapping, IP-to-PoP mapping (where each PoP is a set of routers from a single AS co-located at a given geographic location), and the RTTs of inter-PoP links. We use the most recent iPlane snapshot collected in December 2013. This has a total of 27,075 ASes and 106,621 unique AS-AS links. At the PoP-level, it has 183,131 PoPs and 1,540,466 PoP-level links.

## 5.5 Resilience to Link Failures

We start by evaluating the resilience provided by ARROW in case of link failures. For this evaluation, we choose only provider links of multi-homed stub ASes in the topology. A multi-homed stub AS is an AS with more than one provider and no customers; our topology includes 20,338 such ASes. We focus on these because the stub AS has a valid physical route to the rest of the Internet even if a provider link L fails and we argue that this is also the worst possible case, as the Internet topology features much less redundancy towards its leaves (the stub ASes). Link failures closer to the core of the Internet would simply affect a much smaller fraction of ASes for both ARROW and BGP.

We arrive at a total number of 47,652 unique failures (the number of parent links over all multi-homed stub ASes), affecting an average of 4,404 AS paths for every multihomed AS. We fail each link L of each multi-homed stub AS A, successively. For each failure trial, we fail a link L, and see what fraction of ASes (on

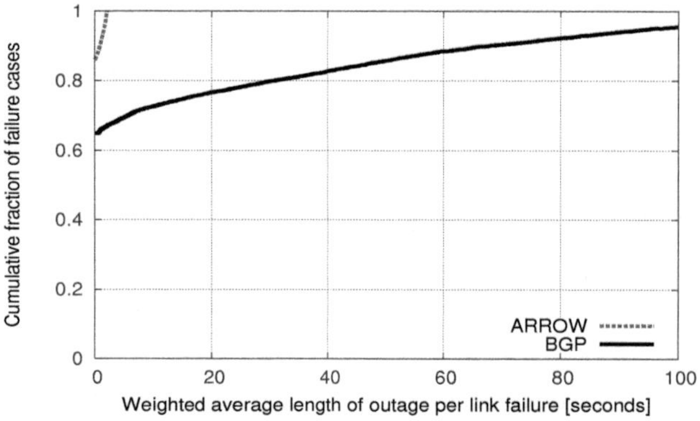


**Figure 10: CDF showing the fraction of link failures resulting in a certain amount of disconnectivity, weighted by the average duration of the disconnectivity event.**

the whole topology) are temporarily disconnected from the corresponding stub AS A, due to BGP convergence effects. In some cases, ASes become permanently disconnected, but we ignore these in our results (note that ARROW might still provide them with a valid route). We then also determine how long it takes, on average, for these ASes to become re-connected. For each failed link, we multiply the fraction of affected ASes by the length of the duration. This is the result we use for the BGP line in Figure 10.

To plot the ARROW line, we select one random tier-1 AS as our ARROW-supporting AS and fix it for all simulation runs. Then we conduct the same failure simulations, but in addition, we check for each affected AS whether it has a valid path to A via the chosen ARROW AS. For the failover duration we choose a fixed time of 2 seconds, which is a conservative estimate for ARROW, given the results in §5.3.

Figure 10 is a CDF plot of the results. The x-axis shows the fraction of disconnectivity in the topology as the result of the failure, weighted by the duration of the outage. For each such fraction $f$ on the x-axis we have the corresponding fraction of failures that resulted in at most $f$ disconnectivity on the y-axis. We crop the graph at 100 seconds. The tail of BGP outages goes on until a maximum of 418 seconds.

We can see that for 30% of link failures, BGP had an outage of at least 2 seconds, with a long tail: 12% of outages have a duration of at least a minute and 5% of outages last 100 seconds and longer. All outages are handled by a single ARROW tier-1 relay node within 2 seconds (and likely much shorter, according to §5.3). We conclude that a single tunnel is indeed enough to recover from link failure disconnectivities in a time-span significantly shorter than that of BGP in the worst possible case of a link failure to a parent of a multi-homed stub AS.

## 5.6 Resilience to AS Failures

The failure of an entire Autonomous System (AS) is a rare occurrence, but we would still like to gauge the effectiveness of ARROW routing around such catastrophic outages. To do this, we conduct a similar simulation to the previous one, but this time we simulate a simultaneous failure of all links of a particular AS. We picked 200 ASes at random from the set of all tier 2 and tier 3 transit ASes. Figure 11 is a CDF plot of the results. The x and y axes are the same as in Figure 10, except we crop the x-axis at 200 seconds.

We can see that around 60% of AS failures cause a BGP convergence period of at least 2 seconds. The tail is long again, with more than 50% of failures resulting in a convergence duration of at least 100 seconds. A single ARROW-supporting tier-1 AS provides instant failover for more than 55% of the failures. If ARROW were

[2] http://iplane.cs.washington.edu/data/data.html

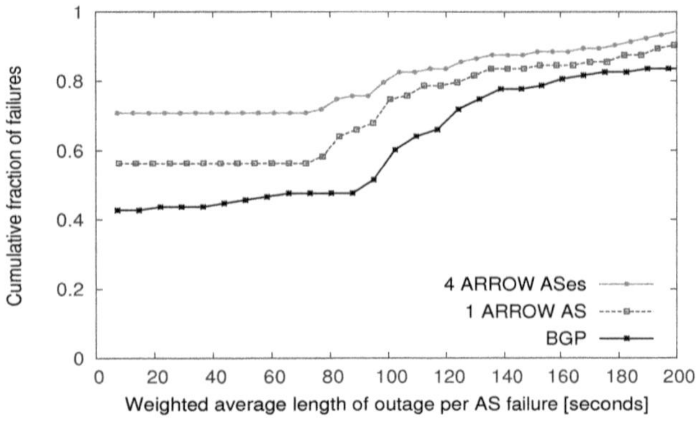


**Figure 11: CDF showing the fraction of AS failures resulting in a certain amount of disconnectivity, weighted by the average duration of the disconnectivity event.**

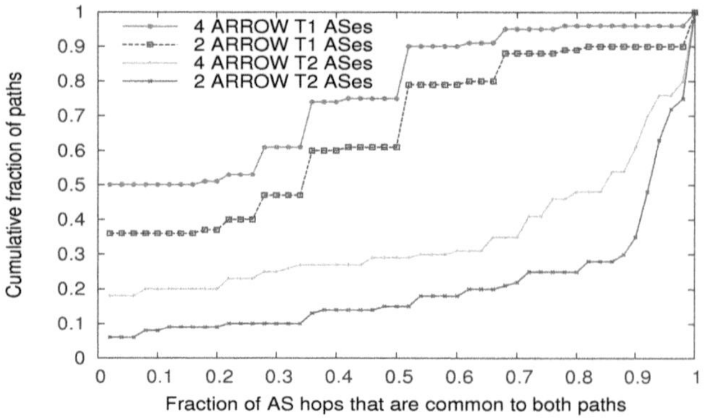


**Figure 12: CDF showing the number of common AS hops as a fraction of $p$'s length (x-axis) versus the cumulative fraction of paths with that amount of commonality (y-axis).**

deployed at 4 tier-1 sites, a single tunnel can provide failover for more than 70% of the failures. While a large number of failures can be circumvented this way, the number is not as encouraging as in Figure 10. This is because the interconnection density of tier-2 and tier-3 ASes is much higher than that of stub ASes and they are also closer to an ARROW supporting tier-1.

We conclude that ARROW enables us to route around a large number of transit AS failures. While a great improvement over BGP, a multi-hop ARROW path might be required to increase the number of preventable failures even further. We also note that these results can serve as an indicator of how likely it is that ARROW can be used to route around a transit AS that is otherwise not delivering traffic in the way we expect or that we simply do not trust, provided that it is not malicious. We will address one case of malicious ASes (prefix hijacking) in §5.8.

## 5.7 Path Redundancy

It is clear that ARROW can be used to route around single defective links and misbehaving ISPs. To reduce the risk of encountering a string of such misbehaviors, we ask if we can build an ARROW path with (near-)complete AS-level redundancy. We define a path $q$ to be completely redundant to path $p$ if the AS-hops in $q$ is disjoint from that of $p$, except for the source and destination ASes. We are interested in the number of common hops (disregarding source and destination) between the original path $p$ and the ARROW path $q$ with the highest disjointedness. Figure 12 shows this distribution over all paths in the iPlane dataset (approximately 5 million) for ARROW deployments on 2 and 4 tier-1 and tier-2 ASes.

In the tier-1 case, almost 40% of the paths for the 2-AS deployment, and 50% for the 4-AS deployment provide completely disjoint paths. Almost 80% of the paths in both cases have less than half of the ASes from the old path still present in the new ARROW path. The significant redundancy with a small ARROW deployment can be explained by the rich peering provided by tier-1 ISPs and the resulting high redundancy in the core of the Internet. This is confirmed by comparing with the tier-2 case, where significantly less redundancy is present.

We conclude that alternative ARROW paths ensure a high degree of redundancy between the old and new paths, making ARROW resilient even in the rare case of multiple cascading link and AS-level misbehaviors.

## 5.8 Protection Against Prefix Hijacking

IP prefix hijacking is a serious challenge to the reliability and security of the Internet. Since the Internet lacks any authoritative information on the ownership of prefixes, IP prefix hijacking is extremely hard to eliminate. ARROW can be used to mitigate the effects of prefix hijacking. We imagine a scenario where the prefix hijacking has already been detected. Specifically, given a standard ARROW deployment on a small number of tier-1s, we ask what fraction of sources still remain polluted (i.e., paths going through any of the polluted ASes) for a particular prefix hijacking attack.

To simulate prefix hijacks, we select a victim AS and an attacker AS, both stubs. We use all stubs in our iPlane topology as victims and average the results over a random selection of 20 attackers for each victim. This gives us a total of 16,160 victim ASes. For each attack, we determine the set of polluted ASes as follows: an AS is polluted if its BGP path to the attacker is shorter than its path to the victim [39]. For each attack and a given ARROW deployment we see what fraction of the sources remain unpolluted, i.e., able to send traffic to the victim through any of the ARROW path segments. Figure 13 shows the CCDF of the hijack attacks. The x-axis shows the fraction of sources remaining polluted as a result of the attack versus the corresponding fraction of attacks that resulted in at most $p$ pollution on the y-axis. We compare ARROW deployments of various sizes with BGP routing.

We observe that all three deployments of ARROW provide significant protection against prefix hijacks: For 75% of the attacks, a single ARROW AS cuts down pollution to 5% or less. Without ARROW the same scenario results in up to 30% pollution. An ARROW deployment on only four tier-1s eliminates almost all of the unreachability caused by prefix hijacks. We conclude that even a small ARROW deployment provides an effective means to combat prefix hijack attacks.

## 5.9 Reliable Performance

For redundant ARROW paths to be useful, it is important that the performance of these paths is not significantly worse than the original BGP path. We evaluate the performance of paths available in an ARROW deployment compared to the respective BGP path. For this purpose we use the PoP-level link latencies provided by the iPlane dataset. Using the same methodology as in previous subsections, we ask the question: what is the fraction of sources that have an alternative ARROW path with an end-to-end latency that is at most X% that of the original path?

We assume no overhead for ARROW routing in this simulation and solely look at the measured path latencies from the iPlane dataset. Hence, these results are slightly skewed towards ARROW and we expect an experimental evaluation on a real deployment to look slightly less encouraging for ARROW. Figure 14 shows a CDF of the ratio of the end-to-end latency achieved by an ARROW

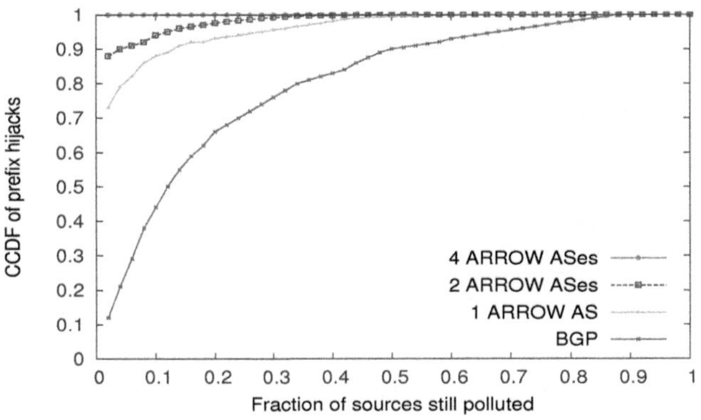


**Figure 13: CCDF showing the fraction of prefix hijack attacks resulting in a certain amount of pollution, as measured by the fraction of sources unable to reach the target as a result of the attack.**

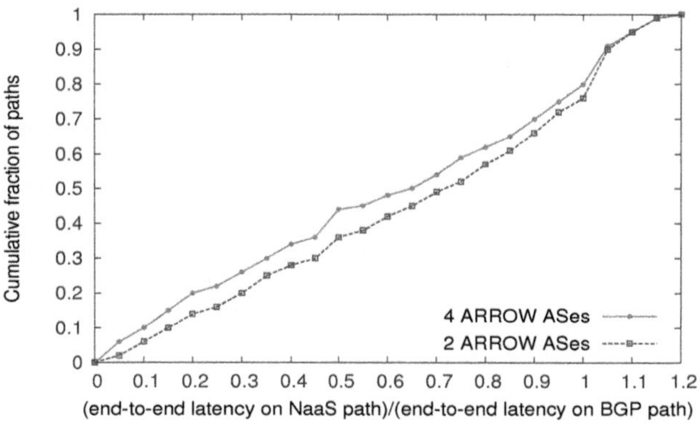


**Figure 14: CDF showing the ratio of end-to-end latency of an ARROW path between a source and destination PoP and the latency of the equivalent BGP path versus the cumulative fraction of paths with up to that ratio. Two ARROW deployments are shown.**

path and the latency of the equivalent BGP path between the same source and destination PoP for a total of 1,143,652 PoP-level paths.

We observe that in a deployment with 2 and 4 ARROW ASes, only 24% and 20% of ARROW paths have a latency slightly (up to 20%) worse than that of their equivalent BGP path, respectively. With 2 ARROW ASes, more than 76% of the sources actually experience an *improvement* in the end-to-end latency while using an ARROW path. As expected, the gains are even slightly higher for a deployment of 4 ARROW ASes.

We conclude that ARROW does not degrade the end-to-end latency for the vast majority of paths and, in fact, has the potential to *improve* their performance. This can serve as an important factor for ISPs in attracting traffic from the greater Internet. It also shows that using ARROW does not have to come at a performance tradeoff for most users.

# 6. RELATED WORK

Our goal in this work is to quantify the extent that a simple remote tunneling model such as ARROW can address a range of Internet vulnerabilities, particularly given the recent trend towards a flatter Internet topology [20] and very high-bandwidth servers.

Fifteen years ago, Detour [3, 29] observed that well-chosen indirect paths were often more reliable and higher performance than direct paths through the Internet, although it stopped short of suggesting this as a universal solution because processing costs would have been prohibitive at the time. The success of various Detour-like systems built by companies such as Akamai SureRoute and others have shown that better Internet reliability is commercially viable. Likewise the widespread move towards multihomed enterprises is proof of the value of improved reliability to end users.

Our work goes beyond earlier studies of Detour and multihoming to consider the range of attacks, both inadvertent and intentional, against the Internet. At an architectural level, a key distinction with Detour is that ARROW routes are composable. A sequence of ARROW circuits through participating providers will deliver packets at a given rate along the path, barring failure. Detour routes provide no such guarantee.

Source control over routing is an old idea. Loose source routing in the Internet is widely but not universally blocked [15] due to concerns about its possible use in denial-of-service attacks. This has led to a set of efforts that provide joint control over routes between the ISPs along the path and the endpoint. The most flexible of these is Icing [24]. Icing attempts to head off subversion of routing advertisements by asking every entity along the path to approve the use of the entire path; no traffic flows unless everyone agrees. Icing does not, however, attempt to address incremental or partial adoption. Yang el al. [37] propose a solution that allows both senders and receivers to choose AS-level routes to the Internet core, with the end-to-end path the concatenation of the two segments. Routing as a Service [22] recognized the conflict between users who want control over end-to-end paths and ISPs who desire control over how their infrastructure is used. To resolve this conflict, the authors introduce a separate entity that contracts with both ASes and customers and establishes paths that are acceptable to all entities.

Although ARROW is in many ways a simpler model, our results should apply to these other models as well. A goal of our work is to help answer whether a simpler model is sufficient for addressing known malicious and non-malicious errors, as well as to point a way towards incremental adoption of one of these more far-reaching solutions.

We also borrow a number of ideas from other proposals. Dynamic resolution of circuit ID's was introduced by ATM. Our topology announcements are similar to those in pathlet routing [10], although we assume users will want to bind traffic PoP to PoP rather than only ISP to ISP. By handing topology announcements out of band (that is, not via BGP), we make it easier for ISPs to add information such as price and expected performance to various prefixes. Using indirection as a method for addressing denial of service originated with the Internet Indirection Infrastructure (i3) [31]; packet authenticators for governing access to a tunnel was introduced by SOS and Mayday [4, 18].

Considerable effort has gone into incremental changes to BGP to address specific vulnerabilities. For example, MIRO [36] is a multi-path interdomain routing protocol that allows ISPs to negotiate alternate paths as needed. MIRO is designed to be an incrementally deployable extension to BGP. RBGP [19] proposes to use pre-computed backup paths to provide reliable delivery during periods where the network is adapting to failures. ARROW has similar goals, but obtains additional deployability benefits since it doesn't require changes to the inter-domain routing protocol. A single ISP can unilaterally provide ARROW service and obtain revenues directly from end users who would benefit from the service.

# 7. CONCLUSION

The Internet is increasingly being used for critical services, such as home health monitoring, management of the electrical grid, 911

IP service, and disaster response. The current Internet, however, is unable to meet the availability demands of these emerging and future uses. In this paper, we attempt to identify the minimal changes needed for the Internet to support such mission critical data transmissions.

This paper presents a mechanism to enable end users, enterprises, and governments to stitch together reliable end to end paths by leveraging highly reliable intradomain path segments. At the core is a protocol called *Advertised Reliable Routing Over Waypoints*, which allows users to provision a path across a remote ISP. We outlined the design of ARROW, examined how it can be used to enhance the robustness and security of end-to-end paths, and described an implementation of its key components. Our evaluations show that ARROW imposes only minor overheads to Internet routing infrastructure and can provide significant resiliency and performance benefits even when deployed by only a limited number of ISPs. Finally, ARROW provides the fabric for additional services that can be deployed on top of it. To show that this is feasible, we presented two of our own implementations: a DoS protection service and a content distribution network.

## Acknowledgments

We would like to thank AMS-IX and the universities that generously host the Transit Portal testbed. This work was funded by Cisco and NSF Grant CNS-1040663. Qiao Zhang was supported by a Wilma Bradley Endowed Fellowship.

## 8. REFERENCES

[1] http://www.caida.org/data/active/asrelationships/.

[2] http://www.routeviews.org.

[3] D. Andersen, H. Balakrishnan, F. Kaashoek, and R. Morris. Resilient overlay networks. In *SOSP*, 2001.

[4] D. G. Andersen. Mayday: Distributed filtering for internet services. In *USENIX Symposium on Internet Technologies and Systems*, 2003.

[5] D. G. Andersen, H. Balakrishnan, N. Feamster, T. Koponen, D. Moon, and S. Shenker. Accountable internet protocol (aip). In *SIGCOMM*, 2008.

[6] J. Cowie. The new threat: Targeted internet traffic misdirection. http://www.renesys.com/2013/11/mitm-internet-hijacking/. Retrieved 2014-05-20.

[7] C. Dixon, T. Anderson, and A. Krishnamurthy. Phalanx: Withstanding multimillion-node botnets. In *NSDI*, 2008.

[8] M. Dobrescu, N. Egi, K. Argyraki, B.-G. Chun, K. Fall, G. Iannaccone, A. Knies, M. Manesh, and S. Ratnasamy. Routebricks: exploiting parallelism to scale software routers. In *SOSP*, 2009.

[9] Emulab: A network emulation testbed. http://www.emulab.net.

[10] P. B. Godfrey, I. Ganichev, S. Shenker, and I. Stoica. Pathlet routing. In *SIGCOMM*, 2009.

[11] S. Han, K. Jang, K. Park, and S. Moon. Packetshader: a gpu-accelerated software router. In *SIGCOMM*, 2010.

[12] P. Hunt, M. Konar, F. P. Junqueira, and B. Reed. Zookeeper: Wait-free coordination for internet-scale systems. In *USENIX Annual Technical Conference*, 2010.

[13] J. John, E. Katz-Bassett, A. Krishnamurthy, T. Anderson, and A. Venkataramani. Consensus routing: the Internet as a distributed system. In *NSDI*, 2008.

[14] E. Katz-Bassett, H. Madhyastha, J. John, A. Krishnamurthy, D. Wetherall, and T. Anderson. Studying blackholes in the Internet with Hubble. In *NSDI*, 2008.

[15] E. Katz-Bassett, H. V. Madhyastha, V. K. Adhikari, C. Scott, J. Sherry, P. Van Wesep, T. Anderson, and A. Krishnamurthy. Reverse traceroute. In *NSDI*, 2010.

[16] E. Katz-Bassett, C. Scott, D. R. Choffnes, I. Cunha, V. Valancius, N. Feamster, H. V. Madhyastha, T. Anderson, and A. Krishnamurthy. LIFEGUARD: practical repair of persistent route failures. In *SIGCOMM*, 2012.

[17] S. Kent, C. Lynn, and K. Seo. Secure border gateway protocol (S-BGP). *IEEE Journal on Selected Areas in Communications*, 2000.

[18] A. Keromytis, V. Misra, and D. Rubenstein. SOS: An architecture for mitigating DDoS attacks. *IEEE Journal on Selected Areas in Communications*, 2003.

[19] N. Kushman, S. Kandula, and D. Katabi. R-BGP: Staying Connected in a Connected World. In *NSDI*, 2007.

[20] C. Labovitz, S. Iekel-Johnson, D. McPherson, J. Oberheide, and F. Jahanian. Internet inter-domain traffic. In *SIGCOMM*, 2010.

[21] M. Lad, D. Massey, D. Pei, Y. Wu, B. Zhang, and L. Zhang. PHAS: a Prefix Hijack Alert System. In *USENIX Security Symposium*, August 2006.

[22] K. Lakshminarayanan, I. Stoica, S. Shenker, and J. Rexford. Routing as a service. Technical Report UCB/EECS-2006-19, UC Berkeley, 2006.

[23] X. Liu, A. Li, X. Yang, and D. Wetherall. Passport: secure and adoptable source authentication. In *NSDI*, 2008.

[24] J. Naous, M. Walfish, A. Nicolosi, D. Mazières, M. Miller, and A. Seehra. Verifying and enforcing network paths with icing. In *CoNEXT*, 2011.

[25] E. Nordstrom, D. Shue, P. Gopalan, R. Kiefer, M. Arye, S. Ko, J. Rexford, and M. J. Freedman. Serval: An End-Host Stack for Service-Centric Networking. In *NSDI*, 2012.

[26] B. Parno, D. Wendlandt, E. Shi, A. Perrig, B. Maggs, and Y.-C. Hu. Portcullis: protecting connection setup from denial-of-capability attacks. In *SIGCOMM*, 2007.

[27] B. Raghavan and A. C. Snoeren. A system for authenticated policy-compliant routing. In *SIGCOMM*, 2004.

[28] G. Rétvári, J. Tapolcai, A. Kőrösi, A. Majdán, and Z. Heszberger. Compressing IP forwarding tables: Towards entropy bounds and beyond. In *SIGCOMM*, 2013.

[29] S. Savage, A. Collins, E. Hoffman, J. Snell, and T. Anderson. The end-to-end effects of internet path selection. In *SIGCOMM*, 1999.

[30] M. Shand and S. Bryant. IP Fast Reroute Framework. IETF Draft, 2007.

[31] I. Stoica, D. Adkins, S. Zhuang, S. Shenker, and S. Surana. Internet indirection infrastructure. In *SIGCOMM*, 2002.

[32] P. Trimintzios, C. Hall, R. Clayton, R. Anderson, and E. Ouzounis. Resilience of the Internet Interconnection Ecosystem. http://www.enisa.europa.eu/.

[33] V. Valancius, N. Feamster, J. Rexford, and A. Nakao. Wide-area route control for distributed services. In *USENIX Annual Technical Conference*, 2010.

[34] VICCI: A programmable cloud-computing research testbed. http://www.vicci.org.

[35] S. Waterman. Internet traffic was routed via chinese servers. http://www.washingtontimes.com/news/2010/nov/15/internet-traffic-was-routed-via-chinese-servers/. Retrieved 2014-05-20.

[36] W. Xu and J. Rexford. MIRO: multi-path interdomain routing. In *Proc. of SIGCOMM*, 2006.

[37] X. Yang, D. Clark, and A. W. Berger. NIRA: A New Inter-Domain Routing Architecture. *IEEE/ACM Transactions on Networking*, 2007.

[38] X. Yang, D. Wetherall, and T. Anderson. TVA: A DoS-limiting Network Architecture. *IEEE/ACM Transactions on Networking*, 2008.

[39] Z. Zhang, Y. Zhang, Y. C. Hu, Z. M. Mao, and R. Bush. iSPY: detecting IP prefix hijacking on my own. *IEEE/ACM Transactions on Networking*, 18(6):1815–1828, Dec. 2010.

# YouSlow: A Performance Analysis Tool for Adaptive Bitrate Video Streaming

Hyunwoo Nam, Kyung-Hwa Kim and Henning Schulzrinne
Columbia University
New York, NY
{hn2203, kk2515, hgs10}@columbia.edu

Doru Calin
Bell Laboratories, Alcatel-Lucent
Murray Hill, NJ
doru.calin@alcatel-lucent.com

## ABSTRACT

Adaptive bitrate (ABR) technologies are being widely used in today's popular HTTP-based video streaming such as YouTube and Netflix. Such a rate-switching algorithm embedded in a video player is designed to improve video quality-of-experience (QoE) by selecting an appropriate resolution based on the analysis of network conditions while the video is playing. However, a bad viewing experience is often caused by the video player having difficulty estimating transit or client-side network conditions accurately. In order to analyze the ABR streaming performance, we developed YouSlow, a web browser plug-in that can detect and report live buffer stalling events to our analysis tool. Currently, YouSlow has collected more than 20,000 of YouTube video stalling events over 40 countries.

## Categories and Subject Descriptors

D.2.8 [**Software Engineering**]: Metrics—*performance measures*

## Keywords

HTTP Video Streaming; Adaptive Bitrate Streaming (ABR); Video Quality of Experience

## 1. INTRODUCTION AND CHALLENGE

Today's over-the-top (OTT) video streaming services deliver video contents to clients over HTTP. In the early version of HTTP-based video streaming, a progressive download mechanism was used, where the server pushes the content as quickly as possible when a client requests a video. However, the major drawback is that all clients must download videos at the same bitrate [1], regardless of network conditions and performance of their devices. Several ABR technologies such as Apple HTTP Live Streaming (HLS), Microsoft IIS Smooth Streaming, Adobe HTTP Dynamic Streaming and Dynamic Adaptive Streaming over HTTP (DASH) have been introduced to resolve this issue. In ABR streaming, a video delivery node contains a set of segments that encode the same content at multiple bitrates, so a video player can adaptively select the appropriate bitrate based upon network conditions and CPU capacity of the clients' devices.

The self-adjusting mechanism aims to stream a video without interruption in the highest bitrate possible. Currently, video players select the best appropriate bitrates based on playout buffer size and its own bandwidth estimator [1]. The performance of ABR heuristic algorithm is directly related to user-perceived video quality. If the network capacity is overestimated, severe buffer stalling can occur by the video player requesting a higher bitrate than what is actually available. On the other hand, a low quality of video can play if the capacity is underestimated. Therefore, monitoring end-user's video QoE like the above is necessary for the analysis of ABR streaming performance.

Several researchers have been trying to analyze ABR streaming [2, 3]. Also, the performance study can be related to network neutrality issues [4, 5]. Most work has been done measuring video quality-of-service (QoS) metrics such as packet throughput, packet loss, jitter and delay. They collected the data from intermediate nodes (e.g., transit routers) between clients and video delivery nodes. These measurements are generally used to represent the impact on the video quality level from the network operator's point of view. Since they do not directly reflect the end-user's perceived video quality, we cannot simply use these metrics for ABR streaming performance test. In order to address this issue, we introduce YouSlow ("YouTube Too Slow!? - YouSlow"). This web browser plug-in is designed to monitor buffer stalling events while clients watch YouTube videos on Chrome browsers. When a buffer stalling is detected, YouSlow automatically reports the name of the local ISP the client is connected to, the duration, and approximate location of the event to our analysis tool. These collected data are then marked on Google maps (e.g., region, country and state) on our website for calculating statistics.

## 2. YOUSLOW OVERVIEW

Unlike the prior approaches, YouSlow obtains streaming status directly from a video player embedded in a web browser. Currently, YouSlow has been implemented in YouTube video players and published in the Chrome web store. The plug-in consists of Chrome extension content scripts [6] that allow our JavaScript codes to automatically activate when clients watch videos on YouTube's website. It uses the YouTube ActionScript 3.0 Player API [7] to access the video players


*SIGCOMM'14*, August 17–22, 2014, Chicago, IL, USA.
ACM 978-1-4503-2836-4/14/08.
http://dx.doi.org/10.1145/2619239.2631433.

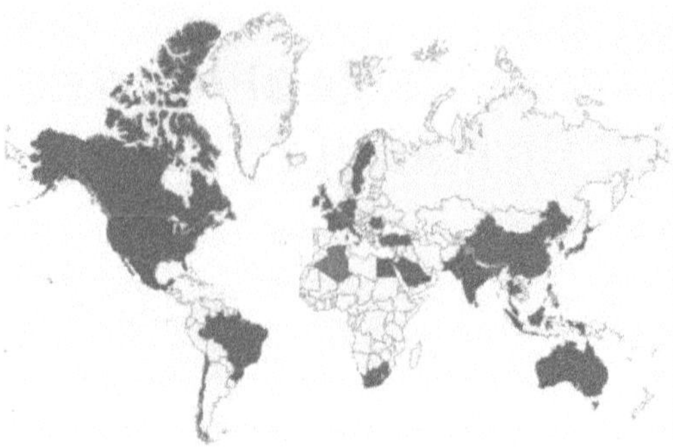

Country and avg. buffer stalling duration (sec)

| Country | Avg. duration |
|---|---|
| Algeria | 54 |
| Philippines | 25 |
| Bangladesh | 20 |
| Sweden | 18 |
| Indonesia | 12 |
| United Kingdom | 11 |
| South Korea | 5 |
| United States | 4 |

Table shows partial results

**Figure 1: Country maps and YouTube buffer stalling statistics on YouSlow website**

embedded in Chrome browsers. Using the player API, YouSlow dynamically monitors player status (e.g., `not started`, `ended`, `playing`, `paused`, `buffering` and `video cued`) and playback quality (e.g., `small`, `medium`, `large`, `hd720`, `hd1080` and `highres`) while a video is playing. We plan to extend our work to other popular video streaming services such as Netflix. YouSlow is designed to report the following objectives to our analysis tool.

- **Initial buffering time**: Measure start-up time from the instant a play button is clicked until it actually starts to play the video.
- **Requested bitrates**: Record bitrates requested from a video player. There are two cases: purposely changed by clients or automatically adjusted by ABR algorithms.
- **Buffer stalling duration**: Measure how long a client experiences buffer stalling during a download.
- **Approximate location of buffer stalling events and local ISP information**: An IP geolocation database[1] is used to pinpoint the approximate location of the event and the name of local ISP.

No other data is collected such as what videos are watched by clients or any account information. Through our website[2], clients can share their buffering experiences and compare local ISPs in their neighborhoods. It is also useful for network operators to analyze performance of their networks by monitoring buffer stalling events in real time. An introduction video can be found on YouTube[3].

# 3. EVALUATION OF ABR STREAMING

To analyze ABR streaming performance, we calculate 1) how long a buffer stalling event occurs for each bitrate during a download, 2) how long HD bitrates are played during a download, and 3) elapsed time from the instant a buffer stalling event occurs until playback rate changes. This indicates how well a video player adjusts bitrates without viewing interruption. For instance, if a video player changes a bitrate from HD to SD resolution before buffer stalling events occur, this means that the ABR heuristic algorithm is performing an appropriate rate-switching in timely manner.

[1]Maxmind GeoIP database - `http://dev.maxmind.com/`
[2]YouSlow - `http://dyswis.cs.columbia.edu/youslow/`
[3]`https://www.youtube.com/watch?v=9cdOoOkDIiO`

# 4. PRELIMINARY RESULTS

YouSlow has collected more than 20,000 YouTube buffer stalling events over 40 countries. According to the database, our key observations can be summarized as follows:

- Average watching duration per video session is 7 min 34 sec.
- Average buffer stalling duration as a fraction of the play time per video session is 6.86%. 85.2% of the total events experienced less than 5 sec of buffer stalling.
- Playback rate changes 2.25 times on average per video session. Average buffer stalling duration for each bitrate per video session is 2.59 sec.
- Playback rate statistics are `highres` (greater than 1080p - 0.017%), `hd1080p` (1.93%), `hd720p` (7.81%), `480p` (26.91%), `360p` (43.43%), `240p` (16.17%) and `tiny` (smaller than 240p - 3.72%).
- United States (4.91 sec), South Korea (5.17 sec) and England (11.28 sec) show shorter buffer stalling duration per video session, compared to Sweden (18.65 sec), Malaysia (22.56 sec) and Philippines (25.19 sec).

As more buffer stalling events are accumulated, we expect to conduct a more meaningful empirical investigation of ABR streaming.

# 5. REFERENCES


[1] S. Akhshabi, A. C. Begen, and C. Dovrolis, "An Experimental Evaluation of Rate-adaptation Algorithms in Adaptive Streaming over HTTP," in *Proceedings of the Second Annual ACM Conference on Multimedia Systems*, San Jose, CA, USA, Feb. 2011.

[2] Google Video Quality Report. [Online]. Available: http://www.google.com/get/videoqualityreport/

[3] R. Serral-Gracià, E. Cerqueira, M. Curado, M. Yannuzzi, E. Monteiro, and X. Masip-Bruin, "An Overview of Quality of Experience Measurement Challenges for Video Applications in IP Networks," in *Proceedings of the 8th International Conference on Wired/Wireless Internet Communications*, Lulea, Sweden, Jun. 2010.

[4] M. Dischinger, M. Marcon, S. Guha, K. P. Gummadi, R. Mahajan, and S. Saroiu, "Glasnost: Enabling End Users to Detect Traffic Differentiation," in *Proceedings of the 7th USENIX Conference on Networked Systems Design and Implementation*, San Jose, CA, Apr. 2010.

[5] Internet Tolls and the Case for Strong Net Neutrality. [Online]. Available: http://tinyurl.com/o4tpqz4

[6] Chrome Content Scripts. [Online]. Available: https://developer.chrome.com/extensions/content_scripts

[7] YouTube ActionScript 3.0 Player API. [Online]. Available: https://developers.google.com/youtube/flash_api_reference/

# RPKI vs ROVER
# Comparing the Risks of BGP Security Solutions*

Aanchal Malhotra
Boston University
aanchal4@bu.edu

Sharon Goldberg
Boston University
goldbe@cs.bu.edu

BGP, the Internet's interdomain routing protocol, is highly vulnerable to routing failures that result from unintentional misconfigurations or deliberate attacks. To defend against these failures, recent years have seen the adoption of the Resource Public Key Infrastructure (RPKI), which currently authorizes 4% of the Internet's routes. The RPKI is a completely new security infrastructure (requiring new servers, caches, and the design of new protocols), a fact that has given rise to some controversy [1]. Thus, an alternative proposal has emerged: Route Origin Verification (ROVER) [4, 7], which leverages the existing reverse DNS (rDNS) and DNSSEC to secure the interdomain routing system.

Both RPKI and ROVER rely on a hierarchy of authorities to provide trusted information about the routing system. Recently, however, [2] argued that the misconfigured, faulty or compromised RPKI authorities introduce new vulnerabilities in the routing system, which can take IP prefixes offline. Meanwhile, the designers of ROVER claim that it operates in a "fail-safe" mode, where "[o]ne could completely unplug a router verification application at any time and Internet routing would continue to work just as it does today". There has been debate in Internet community mailing lists [1] about the pros and cons of both approaches. This poster therefore compares the impact of ROVER failures to those of the RPKI, in a threat model that covers misconfigurations, faults or compromises of their trusted authorities.

## 1. ROVER AND RPKI PRIMER

The RPKI and ROVER each provide a trusted mapping from an IP prefix[1] to the Autonomous System(s) (ASes) authorized to originate (*i.e.,* claim to be the destination for) the prefixes in BGP. Both therefore protect against *prefix* and *subprefix hijacks*, where the hijacking AS originates routes for a victim IP prefix, that it is not authorized to originate. During the hijack, traffic destined for the victim IP prefix flows to the hijacker's AS instead.

**rDNS.** The rDNS is used to resolve IP addresses to hostnames. Zones in rDNS correspond to IP prefixes. Data in the reverse zone can be authenticated by standard DNSSEC signatures. Per Figure 1, the root for IPv4 is in-addr.arpa, maintained by IANA.[2] The root delegates 8.0.0.0/8 to Level3, which delegates 8.8.8.0/24 to Google and 8.34.114.0/24 to Metro Net. An rDNS zone is *authoritative* for its IP prefix and subprefixes, *excluding* those delegated to a child zone.

**ROVER.** ROVER introduces two new types of resource records to the rDNS: an *Secure Route Origin (SRO)* to authorize an IP prefix $\pi$ in the zone to be originated in BGP by an AS $a$, and a *Route Lock (RLOC)* to opt a zone in or out of ROVER. The presence of an RLOC in a zone means that an SRO is needed for every IP prefix for which the zone is authoritative. In Figure 1, Level3 has an RLOC and is authoritative for 8.0.0.0/9; thus, if AS 3356 wishes to originate 8.0.0.0/9 in BGP, a new SRO must be added to Level3's rDNS zone in Figure 1. Metro Net's zone does not have an RLOC, so the BGP routes for prefixes covered by 8.34.114.0/24 are opted-out of ROVER. SRO and RLOC records are validated in the usual DNSSEC manner.

**ROVER & route validity.** We say a *BGP route* is an IP prefix $\pi$ and the AS $a$ originating it in BGP. A router issues a ROVER query for *every* new route it learns in BGP. The response is (DNSSEC) validated and stored in a local cache, with standard DNS caching used to store responses. For example, if a router learns a BGP route for prefix 8.8.8.0/24 originated by AS 15169, it should query for *any* SRO corresponding to prefix 8.8.8.0/24; if no SRO is returned for the prefix, the router queries for the RLOC for the authoritative zone (Google). ROVER's SROs and RLOCs determine the validity of an advertised BGP route $(\pi, a)$ as:

- *Valid.* $(\pi, a)$ is *valid* if it has a matching valid SRO.
- *Unknown.* $(\pi, a)$ is *unknown* if both the RLOC for the zone that is authoritative for $\pi$, and the SRO for $(\pi, a)$ are absent or if either fails DNSSEC validation.
- *Invalid.* $(\pi, a)$ is *invalid* if (1) there are valid SROs for $\pi$ that do not match $a$, OR (2) there is no valid SRO for $\pi$ and there is a valid RLOC for $\pi$'s authoritative zone.

In Figure 1, a route for 8.0.0.0/8 originated by AS 3356 is *valid* (because of the matching valid SRO), and a route for 8.0.0.0/8 originated by AS 666 is *invalid* (because of the mismatched SRO). Any route for 8.34.114.0/24 is *unknown* (because Metro Net does not have an RLOC). Any route for 8.0.0.0/9 is *invalid* (because Level3 has an RLOC).

**RPKI.** RPKI has a similar hierarchy of authorities. Each

[1] IP prefix 8.0.0.0/8 has *length* 8 and *covers* 8.8.8.0/24.

[2] 8.0.0.0/8 is directly allocated by IANA. For non-legacy prefixes, RIRs are also a part of reverse zone hierarchy

*This is a partial summary of our results.
See http://eprint.iacr.org/2014/444 for a full version.


*SIGCOMM'14,* August 17–22, 2014, Chicago, IL, USA.
ACM 978-1-4503-2836-4/14/08 ...$15.00. http://dx.doi.org/10.1145/2619239.2631435.

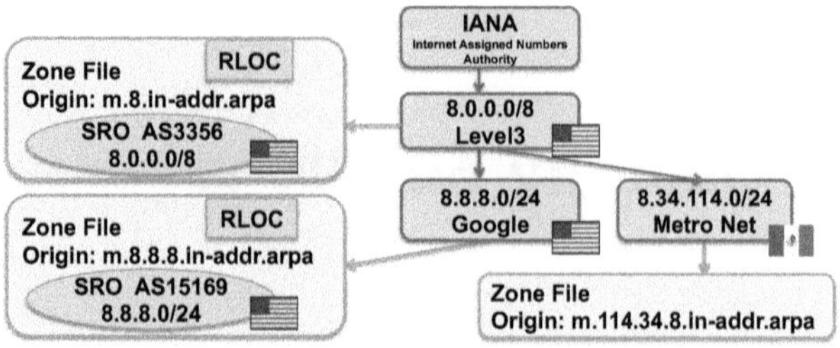


**Figure 1: Sample ROVER hierarchy**

authority has a *Resource Certificate (RC)*, signed by its parent, containing its allocated IP address space and cryptographic public key. An RC can sign (a) other RCs to suballocate address space, or (b) *Route Origin Authorizations (ROAs)* (the equivalent of SROs in ROVER) to authorize an IP prefix $\pi$ covered by the RC to be originated by an AS $a$. The RPKI has no equivalent to an RLOC.

**RPKI route validity.** In contrast to ROVER, where a new ROVER query is made each time a router learns a new route in BGP, an ISP that uses the RPKI downloads *all* objects in the public RPKI repositories to its local cache once per day. Objects are cryptographically verified, and the ISP pushes a list of valid ROAs to its routers. This list determines the validity states for a BGP route $(\pi, a)$, in a manner that is slightly different from that of ROVER:

- *Valid.* $(\pi, a)$ is *valid* if it has a matching valid ROA.
- *Unknown.* $(\pi, a)$ is *unknown* if there is no valid *covering ROA*; a covering ROA is any ROA for a prefix covering $\pi$.
- *Invalid.* $(\pi, a)$ is *invalid* if it is not *unknown* or *valid.*

**Routing policies.** A BGP router uses its own *local policies* to decide whether to discard, or assign lower preference to, *invalid* or *unknown* BGP routes. As discussed in [2], a router that discards *invalid/unknown* routes has the best possible protection against attacks on BGP, but can lose connectivity to routes that become *invalid/unknown* as a result of threats to the RPKI/ROVER. Here we assume the most plausible set of policies [2]: that a router discards *invalid* routes, and prefers *valid* routes over *unknown* routes. These local policies imply that a route will go offline if a threat to the RPKI/ROVER causes it to become *invalid*, but a route that becomes *unknown* will still be reachable.

## 2. ATTACKING PATHS TO ROVER/RPKI

We consider an attacker that disrupts the communication path to an RPKI/ROVER server but *cannot* forge signatures of RPKI/ROVER authorities.

**Blackholing BGP routes.** The assumed routing policies imply that a BGP route can be blackholed if the attacker can change its validity state from *valid* to *invalid.* [2] argues that an on-path RPKI attacker can do just that, by disrupting the delivery of ROAs from an RPKI repository during an ISP's daily update of its local cache. If an on-path attacker corrupts a single bit in the ROA for 8.8.8.0/24 during a bulk download of ROAs from the RPKI, then the corresponding route for 8.8.8.0/24 becomes *invalid* if there is a covering ROA authorizing AS 3356 to originate 8.0.0.0/8. Thus, the 8.8.8.0/24 route would no longer be reachable. (On the other hand, the RPKI uses *manifests* to indicate which objects it stores. Disrupting delivery of objects or manifests raises alarms at routers, making this attack more transparent; see discussion in [5].) With ROVER, however, the route would still be reachable; if an attacker disrupts the response to a ROVER query for 8.8.8.0/24, causing it to fail DNSSEC validation, then routes for 8.8.8.0/24 become *unknown.* This is a crucial manifestation of ROVER's "fail-safe" approach.

**Circumventing ROVER/RPKI protection of BGP.** Another concern is an attacker that disrupts communications with the RPKI (or ROVER) so that it may circumvent its protections against routing attacks. Suppose a subprefix hijacker at AS 666 originates 8.0.0.0/9, thus *sub*prefix hijacking 8.0.0.0/8 away from victim AS 3356. Per Figure 1, the hijacked route is *invalid* since it lacks a matching SRO but is opted into to ROVER with an RLOC. If an attacker can disrupt communications with RPKI/ROVER so that the hijacked route is marked as *unknown* instead of *invalid*, then routers will select the hijacked route, and fall victim to the hijack. (This follows because there is no *valid* BGP route for 8.0.0.0/9 that is preferred over the *unknown* hijacked route).

Suppose a router issues a ROVER query for the subprefix 8.0.0.0/9 that was hijacked in BGP; while there is no valid matching SRO in Figure 1, the on-path attacker will just inject a bogus, invalidly-signed SRO of its own for 8.0.0.0/9 and any AS. This SRO will fail DNSSEC validation, and the hijacked route therefore becomes *unknown.* Because ROVER issues a separate query for each route learned in BGP, this highly-targeted attack will affect only the hijacked prefix. Worse yet, advanced DNSSEC attacks [3, 6] mean that there is a risk that *off-path* attackers could launch such attacks; we will investigate these in future work.

Meanwhile, [2] argues that attacks of this form are less targeted with the RPKI. To transition a route $(\pi, a)$ from *invalid* to *unknown*, an on-path RPKI attacker needs to disrupt the delivery of *all* the ROAs that cover prefix $\pi$. However, this would cause all routes authorized by these ROAs to go from *valid* to *unknown*, making the attack easier to detect. Moreover, disrupting delivery of RPKI objects (or manifests) would also raise alarms at routers.

## 3. SUMMARY & OPEN QUESTIONS

We defer our analysis of misconfigurations and takedowns to the full version. Our analysis indicates that ROVER has several nice "fail-safe" characteristics, that are absent from the RPKI, to (1) protect BGP from ROVER misconfigurations and (2) prevent attackers that disrupt ROVER queries from blackholing BGP routes. However, these characteristics can be exploited by (3) attackers that disrupt ROVER queries in order to circumvent protection of BGP from (sub)prefix hijacks, and (4) authorities that take down routes authorized by their ROVER descendants. ROVER's use of point queries also makes targeted attacks easier, as compared to the RPKI. Our future work experimentally validates these threats to ROVER, and quantifies their impact on ROVER's ability to prevent routing attacks.

## 4. REFERENCES


[1] R. Austein. "Re: rpki vs. secure dns?", msg18. seclists NANOG Archive, June 2012. http://seclists.org/nanog/2012/Jun/18.

[2] D. Cooper, E. Heilman, K. Brogle, L. Reyzin, and S. Goldberg. On the risk of misbehaving rpki authorities. In *HotNets*, page 16, 2013.

[3] H. Duan, N. Weaver, Z. Zhao, M. Hu, J. Liang, J. Jiang, K. Li, and V. Paxson. Hold-on: Protecting against on-path dns poisoning. *SATIN*, 2012.

[4] J. Gersch and D. Massey. Rover: Route origin verification using dns. In *ICCCN*, pages 1–9, 2013.

[5] E Heilman, D Cooper, L Rezyin, and S Goldberg. From the consent of the routed: Improving the transparency of the rpki. In *SIGCOMM'14*, 2014.

[6] A. Herzberg and H. Shulman. Fragmentation considered poisonous. In *IEEE CNS*, pages 224–232, 2013.

[7] C. Olschanowsky J. Gersch, D. Massey and L. Zhang, editors. *DNS Resource Records for Authorized Routing Information*. IETF Internet-Draft, February 2013.

# CTE: Cost-Effective Intra-domain Traffic Engineering

Baobao Zhang[1,2] Jun Bi[1,2] Jianping Wu[1,2] Fred Baker[3]
zbb@netarchlab.tsinghua.edu.cn junbi@tsinghua.edu.cn jianping@cernet.edu.cn fred@cisco.com
1, Institute for Network Sciences and Cyberspace, Tsinghua University
2, Tsinghua National Laboratory for Information Science and Technology(TNList) ; 3, Cisco Systems Inc., USA

## Categories and Subject Descriptors

C.2.2 **[Computer-Communication Networks]:** Network Protocols

## Keywords

Traffic engineering, Access control list, static routes

## 1. PROBLEM STATEMENT

Internet Traffic Engineering (TE) is a very important research topic for production networks, where TE is typically formulated into minimizing the maximum link utilization (MLU). For example, with increasing IPv6 traffic, the backbone network of CERNET2[1] is suffering big traffic pressure on some critical long-haul links under the traditional shortest-path routing. Taking CERNET2 as an example, we develop a practical and cost-effective intra-domain TE method in this paper. Existing intra-domain TE proposals, such as MPLS-based proposal [2], OpenFlow-based proposal [3] and reactive-TE proposal [4], need to make great modifications to routers, and even have to replace existing routers with brand new routers, which makes the deployment be very high-cost. Other TE proposals, such as the work [5], optimize OSPF weights for the goal of TE. Although these methods have low deployment cost, they need to frequently change OSPF weights based on dynamically changed traffic matrices. Each change to OSPF weights may lead to transient routing loops or traffic disruption. Frequent routing loops or traffic disruption is intolerable for network operators. Therefore, in this paper, we propose a new intra-domain TE method named CTE. CTE works in an OSPF/IS-IS network, where shortest-path routing is run. The core idea of CTE is to use loop-free next hops [7] to route some traffic, which is realized by configuring some static routes and some access control list (ACL) rules. CTE does not make any modifications to existing routers. We only need to develop a remote control program that can configure static routes and ACL rules on routers. In addition, CTE can be incrementally deployed.

We now use an example to illustrate how CTE works. Figure 1 is a network topology composed a set of nodes and a set of links. The lowercase letters beside a node denote the prefixes associated with the node. We suppose that the capacity of each link is 100 units and the weight of each link is 1. We give the shortest-path tree towards the destination $F$ as shown in Figure 2. In Figure 2, the solid arrows direct the next hops towards the destination $F$ and the dash lines will not be used by the traditional shortest-path routing towards the destination $F$. Table 1 shows a prefix-granularity traffic matrix. Table 2 shows the corresponding node-granularity traffic matrix. Under this traffic matrix, the MLU

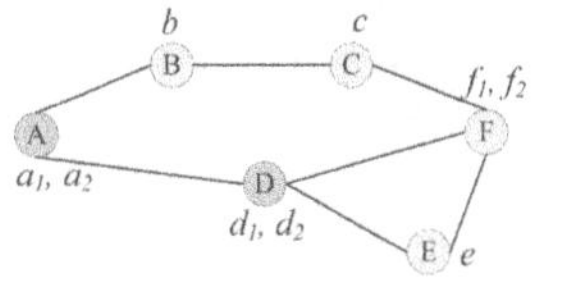


**Figure 1. Network topology**

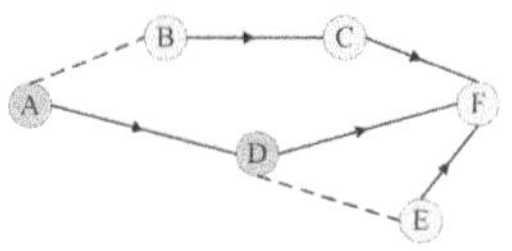


**Figure 2. Shortest-path tree to F**

**Table 1. Prefix-granularity traffic matrix**

| | |
|---|---|
| $a_1 \to f_2$: 10; | $a_2 \to f_2$: 10 |
| $a_2 \to f_1$: 30; | $d_1 \to f_1$: 10 |
| $d_2 \to f_1$: 40; | $c \to f_1$: 20 |

**Table 2. Node-granularity traffic matrix**

| |
|---|
| $A \to F$: 50 |
| $D \to F$: 50 |
| $C \to F$: 20 |

achieved by the traditional shortest-path routing is 1.0, which is high. We now show how CTE reduces the MLU. We suppose that Node $A$ and Node $D$ are two nodes that CTE can control. Node $B$ is a loop-free next hop of Node $A$ towards $F$. Node $E$ is a loop-free next hop of Node $D$ towards $F$. For CTE, the available next hops of Node $A$ towards $F$ are $\{D, B\}$ and the available next hops of Node $D$ towards $F$ are $\{F, E\}$. Based on the node-granularity traffic matrix and the shortest-path routing, we can calculate the optimal splitting ratios across the available next hops of each CTE node towards each destination. We will give the specific optimization model of this step in Section 2. In this example, the optimal splitting ratio across the available next hops $\{D, B\}$ of Node $A$ towards $F$ is 3:2 in order. The optimal splitting ratio across the available next hops $\{F, E\}$ of Node $D$ towards $F$ is *1:1*. Using these splitting ratios, the minimum MLU, which is 0.4, can be achieved. The next step of CTE is to configure static routes and ACL rules to realize the calculated splitting ratios as close as possible. In this example, to realize the calculated splitting ratios, we only need to configure a static route '*reaching the destination* $f_2$ *via B*' on Node $A$ and configure an ACL rule '*reaching the destination* $f_1$ *via E for the source* $d_2$' on Node $D$. Static routes and ACL rules have higher priority than OSPF routes. The MLU under the hybrid routers is 0.4, which the minimum. In addition, we design a mechanism of updating static routes and ACL rules to avoid routing loops and traffic disruption.

## 2. CTE APPROACH

We first develop an optimization model of calculating splitting ratios under a whole traffic matrix as shown in Table 3. This model is named TEW model for short. We now explain the TEW model. $V = \{1,2,\dots,|V|\}$ is the set of nodes. $E = \{1,2,\dots,|E|\}$ is the set of links. We use $c_e$ to denote the capacity of a link $e \in E$. $\{d_{ij}\}$ is a traffic matrix, where $d_{ij}$ denotes the size of traffic from Node $i$ to Node $j$. $\{g_{jk} \geq 0 \mid j \in V, k \in E\}$ is the set of routing variables, where $g_{jk}$ denotes the size of traffic destined to Node $j$ over Link $k$. The splitting ratio over Link $e$ on Node $i$ is $\frac{g_{je}}{\sum_{k \in OUT(i)} g_{jk}}$. $Ava(i,j)$ denotes the available next hops of Node $i$ towards Node $j$. If Node $i$ is a legacy node, the available next hops of Node $i$ are only the shortest-path next hops of Node $i$ towards Node $j$. If Node $i$ is a CTE node, the available next hops of Node $i$ are the shortest-path next hops and the loop-free next


*SIGCOMM'14*, August 17–22, 2014, Chicago, Illinois, USA.
ACM 978-1-4503-2836-4/14/08.
http://dx.doi.org/10.1145/2619239.2631438

**Table 3. TE model under a whole traffic matrix (TEW model)**

$$\min \alpha + \delta \sum_{j\in V, k\in E}\left(\frac{g_{jk}}{|E| * c_k}\right), \text{ subject to:}$$

$$\sum_{k\in OUT(i)} g_{jk} - \sum_{k\in IN(i)} g_{jk} = d_{ij} \quad \forall i \in V, j \in V, and\ i \neq j$$

$$\sum_{k\in OUT(i)-Ava(i,j)} g_{jk} = 0 \quad \forall i \in V, j \in V, and\ i \neq j$$

$$\sum_{j\in V}(g_{je}) \leq \alpha c_e \quad \forall e \in E$$

hops of Node $i$ towards Node $j$. $OUT(i)$ denotes the set of outgoing links of Node $i$. $IN(i)$ denotes the set of incoming links of Node $i$. α is the MLU variable. Note that only $\{g_{jk}\}$ and α are variables. All the other signs are constants. δ is a small enough constant. The traffic matrix can be collected by deploying NetFlow on each node. Inspired by the work [3], we develop a model of calculating optimal splitting ratios under the situation that NetFlow is only deployed on the routers that CTE can control. This model is named TEP model for short. We refer readers to our technical report [6] for the TEP model. We now give the performance gap between the TEW model and the TEP model.

**Theorem 1.** We suppose that the MLU achieved by splitting ratios calculated by the TEW model is $r_1$ and the MLU achieved by splitting ratios calculated by the TEP model is $r_2$. $r_1 \leq r_2 \leq \frac{1}{1-p} r_1$ must stand, where $p$ is the maximum packet loss rate among all the ingress-egress pairs.

**Proof.** See our technical report [6].

In the previous paragraphs, we have described how to compute proper splitting ratios across multiple next hops. We can configure static routes and ACL to implement calculated splitting ratios. In this paper, we mainly focus on how to update static routes and ACL rules without producing any transient routing loops and traffic disruption. For description simplicity, we use $f(S,L,D)$ to denote the fraction of traffic that is routed by the node $S$ via its neighbor $L$ towards the destination $D$. Some static routes and ACL rules will be configured to achieve the routing fraction $f(S,L,D)$. Our TEW and TEP models can guarantee that if $f(S,L,D) > 0$, $f(L,S,D) = 0$ must stand. If some static routes and ACL rules associated with $f(S,L,D) > 0$ are installed before the static routes and ACL rules associated with $f(L,S,D) > 0$ are completely removed, transient routing loops may occur. Therefore, we design a reliable update mechanism as follows.

**Reliable update mechanism:** (a) we should remove all the static routes and ACL rules associated with $f(S,L,D) > 0$ before we install some static routes and ACL rules associated with $f(L,S,D) > 0$. (b) if $f(L,S,D) = 0$, we can directly install or remove any static routes and ACL rules associated with $f(S,L,D)$.

**Theorem 2.** The reliable update mechanism will not produce any routing loops and traffic disruption. Using the reliable update mechanism, we can finish the updating in at most two steps.

**Proof.** See our technical report [6].

## 3. EVALUATIONS

All the routers in the CERNET2 backbone have deployed NetFlow. We collected a range of traffic matrices from 2013-02-19 22:10:00 to 2013-03-26 15:20:00 under the traditional OSPF routing. In addition, we collected the capacity of each link and the OSPF weight of each link. The traffic matrices are packaged per five minutes. In the simulations of this paper, we assume that our desired splitting ratios can be achieved by configuring static routes and ACL, which we will evaluate in the future. We applied splitting ratios computed by CTE based on the previous five-minute traffic matrix to the next five-minute traffic matrix and calculated the MLU reduction ratio, which is measured by the ratio of the MLU achieved by the optimized routing (such as CTE)

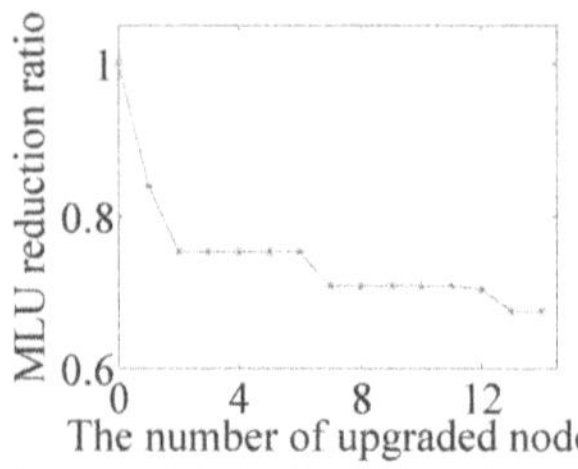


**Figure 3. Partially deployed results**

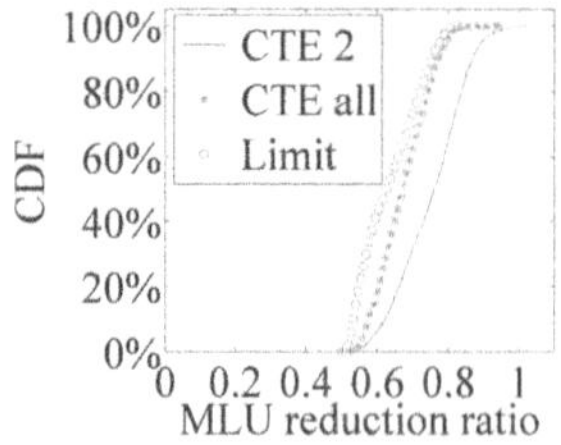


**Figure 4. CDF curves**

to the original MLU achieved by OSPF. Figure 3 shows results of the average MLU reduction ratio during all the five-minute time intervals with the number of nodes that CTE can control. We find that if we only upgrade two nodes to support CTE, the average MLU reduction ratio will be 0.75. In addition, we give the CDF curves of the MLU reduction ratios as shown in Figure 4. 'CTE 2' denotes the results of upgrading two routers. 'CTE all' denotes the results of upgrading all the routers. 'Limit' denotes the TE limit results, i.e. assuming that MPLS is universally deployed, desired splitting ratios can be realized and traffic matrices are known in advance. From Figure 4, we find that if CTE is universally deployed, the near optimal TE can be achieved.

## 4. CONCLUSIONS AND FUTURE WORK

In this paper, we propose a promising TE method named CTE. Without making any modifications to existing routers, CTE only needs a remote control program to configure static routes and ACL rules. Moreover, CTE is incrementally deployable. Our evaluation results show that CTE achieves near optimal TE performance when fully deployed, and achieves considerable TE performance when partially deployed. Some future work include: how to use minimum number of static routes and ACL rules to achieve the desired splitting ratios and how to incrementally update static routes and ACL rules.

## 5. ACKNOWLEDGMENTS


This research is supported by the National High-tech R&D Program ("863" Program) of China (No.2013AA013505), the National Science Foundation of China (No.61161140454), and Tsinghua-cisco joint lab research project. We also thank Kevin Yin, Zhiyan Zheng, Jiahai Yang, Lujing Sun and Chen Sun for their valuable comments, data collecting and processing. Jun Bi is the corresponding author.


## 6. REFERENCES


[1] Jianping Wu, et. al,, CNGI-CERNET2: an IPv6 deployment in China, ACM SIGCOMM Computer Communication Review, Vol.41, No.2, pp.48-52, 2011

[2] Hao Wang, et al., COPE: traffic engineering in dynamic networks, ACM SIGCOMM CCR, Vol. 36. No. 4., pp.99-100, 2006

[3] Sugam Agarwal, et al., Traffic engineering in software defined networks, INFOCOM13, pp. 2211-2219, 2013

[4] Amund Kvalbein, et al., Multipath load-adaptive routing: Putting the emphasis on robustness and simplicity, ICNP2009, pp.203-212, 2009

[5] Bernard Fortz, et al., Internet traffic engineering by optimizing OSPF weights, INFOCOM 00, Vol.2, pp.519-528, 2000

[6] Technical Report: http://netarchlab.tsinghua.edu.cn/~zbb/THU-NetArchLab-RTG-TR-CTE-20140515.pdf

[7] Alia K. Atlas, et al., Basic specification for IP fast-reroute: loop-free alternates, RFC 5286, 2008

# Traffic Statistics Collection with FleXam

Sajad Shirali-Shahreza
Department of Computer Science
University of Toronto, Canada
shirali@cs.toronto.edu

Yashar Ganjali
Department of Computer Science
University of Toronto, Canada
yganjali@cs.toronto.edu

## ABSTRACT

One of the limitations of wildcard rules in Software Defined Networks, such as OpenFlow, is losing visibility. FleXam is a flexible sampling extension for OpenFlow that allows the controller to define which packets should be sampled, what parts of each packet should be selected, and where they should be sent. Here, we present an interactive demo showing how FleXam enables the controller to dynamically adjust sampling rates and change the sampling scheme to optimally keep up with a sampling budget in the context of a traffic statistics collection application.

## Categories and Subject Descriptors

C.2.3 [**Communication Networks**]: Network Operations – *Network management, Network monitoring.*

## Keywords

OpenFlow; Sampling; SDN; Traffic Statistics.

## 1. Introduction

Software-Defined Networking (SDN) provides a centralized view of the network, simplifying programmatic manipulation and management of the network traffic. The ability to easily access and manage individual flows is a significant advantage of SDN in general, and OpenFlow specifically. This feature can be used to implement security and monitoring applications such as firewall [1] or anomaly detection [2] as control applications, eliminating the need for dedicated middleboxes.

While managing flows individually can be beneficial – *e.g.* for applications such as firewalls – fine-grained management of flows, especially short-lived ones, can lead to unacceptable side effects: increased flow setup delay (first packet waiting in a switch until the controller instructs the switch how to handle it), packet drops due to buffer size limitations (first packet of the flow needs to be buffered while waiting for the controller response), and flow evictions due to the limited size of flow tables in switches.

Coarse-grained handling of flows, *i.e.* dealing with flows as groups, is one way to overcome the aforementioned problems. OpenFlow provides this functionality using wildcard rules. There is a series of recent works that tackle the programming complexity of wildcard rules by enabling the user to implement the control applications in a high level language and abstraction, and then automatically compiling that into low level flow entries. A well-known example is NetCore [3] which is a high-level, declarative language to describe packet forwarding. There are other proposed programming languages built on NetCore such as Pyretic [4] and Flowlog [5].

Even the OpenFlow specifications seem to move in a direction that we will not have clear exact match rules anymore, and most rules will be wildcard rules instead. While a flow entry match in OpenFlow 1.0 specification is defined as a 12-tuple, it has been changed in newer revisions, and has been replaced with OpenFlow Extensible Match (OXM) in version 1.2. OXM allowing switches to support a variety of header fields (41 different types are defined in the latest version, OF 1.4).

Programming complexity is not the only challenge when using wildcard rules. Losing visibility in another important outcome of wildcard rules: the controller sees the packets matching any wildcard rule as one flow, and thus has limited (or no) knowledge of the individual flows that are aggregated. In reactive routing, each new flow in the network will trigger a Packet-In message that informs the controller of its existence. Furthermore, when a flow is finished, the associated flow entry in the switch will be expired after a predefined timeout, which triggers another Flow-Removed message to the controller. As a result, the controller can easily create and maintain a list of active flows in the network, which is essential for many network monitoring and management applications. However, the controller visibility over active flows is lost in proactive routing, and when we deal with wildcard rules.

We proposed FleXam [6] as a solution for this problem, and described how it could be used to implement security applications like port scan detection [7]. FleXam is a flexible sampling extension for OpenFlow that enables the controller to access packet-level information. Simply stated, the controller can define which packets should be sampled, what parts of each packet should be selected, and where they should be sent. Packets can be sampled stochastically (with a predetermined probability) or deterministically (based on a pattern), making it flexible for different types of applications. At the same time, it is simple enough to be done entirely in the data path. The controller can also request switches to only send parts of packets that are needed (e.g. headers only, payload, etc.) and define where they should be sent for analysis, making it possible to easily manage and distribute the load.

FleXam includes two types of sampling: (1) select each packet of the flow with a probability of $\rho$, and (2) select $m$ consecutive packets from each $k$ consecutive packets, skipping the first $\delta$ packets. The first case is the stochastic sampling. The second case is a generalized version of the deterministic sampling. For $m=1$, it is equivalent to the normal one out of $k$, or every $k^{th}$ packet sampling. If an application needs more than one consecutive sample, it can set $m$ to a value more than one. By choosing a very large $k$, an application can ensure it will only receive the first $m$ consecutive packets. This is usually what security applications,


*SIGCOMM'14*, August 17–22, 2014, Chicago, Illinois, USA.
ACM 978-1-4503-2836-4/14/08.
http://dx.doi.org/10.1145/2619239.2631441

such as intrusion detection, need. Finally, by changing the value of $\delta$, the application can skip the first few packets of each flow, *e.g.* to exclude small and short flows. Considering that sending full packets could impose a significant load on the network, and not all applications need full packet contents, the controller can define what parts of packets (e.g. IP header) should be sent.

## 2. Traffic Statistics Collection with FleXam

In this demo, we show how we can dynamically adjust sampling rates (and patterns) for various applications to optimally keep up with a sampling budget. More specifically, we use dynamic sampling to measure the amount of traffic exchanged between hosts inside our network and any destination IP outside. This data can be used for both security (*e.g.* to detect any suspicious activity) and routing (*e.g.* to select best possible ISPs).

The main idea here is that we sample packets that are sent to unidentified destinations with high rate (through a catch all wildcard rule). Whenever we see a new destination, we create a new rule to match all packets to that destination, and will sample them with a very low rate. So the majority of sampling budget is spent on finding new destinations.

The reason that we continue to sample packets that match rules for known destinations is to avoid sending stat collection queries to switches. By sampling from flows to known destinations, we automatically get updates as packets go through the system, without the need for continuously sending queries to switches. Also, with a fixed and low sampling rate the controller can optimize how frequently it should query statistics for a particular flow. For instance, it could query statistics after it received a specific number of samples, while decreasing the sampling rate if it receives too many samples or increasing that otherwise. This technique will ensure we will not incur a significant overhead for querying flows that are nearly or completely idle.

Furthermore, if we are only interested to know the number of packets that are sent to each destination, or if it is acceptable to estimate to the total byte count from size of sampled packets, then there is no need to query switches at all: we will use deterministic sampling, which enables the controller to count the number of matched packets based on sampling rate and received samples, and to estimate the total amount of transferred traffic based on the size of the sampled packets.

## 3. Implementation

We have implemented FleXam as a patch to Open vSwith[1] and the POX[2] controller. The controller application that installs rules, processes sampled packets, and collects information, is written as a Python program running as a POX module.

In the interactive demo, the user will surf the web through a web browser. As s/he visits different websites, new destinations are reached, which triggers new rule installations. At the same time, multiple connections may be created to known destinations.

Figure 1 shows the connectivity between the user and the Internet in our demo. There are four switches on the path. The first switch uses reactive routing, and installs an exact match rule for each new flow. We send repetitive queries to this switch to collect statistics about different flows. The second switch also uses reactive routing, but installs a wildcard rule matching all packets to a destination each time it receives a packet to a new destination. We send regular statistics queries to this switch as well. The third and fourth switches use FleXam sampling and wildcard rules, with the difference that the third switch queries switches to collect total transferred bytes, while the fourth switch will estimate this from the size of sampled packets and without any statistics queries sent to the switch.

The user will also see a live summary of data collected from each switch, including the top destinations, statistics about each of these destination (total packet count, total bytes transferred), number of installed rules, and network overhead (*e.g.* sampled packet count, switch statistics queries, packet-in messages). This enables the user to easily compare different approaches both from performance (collected statistics) and overhead perspectives.

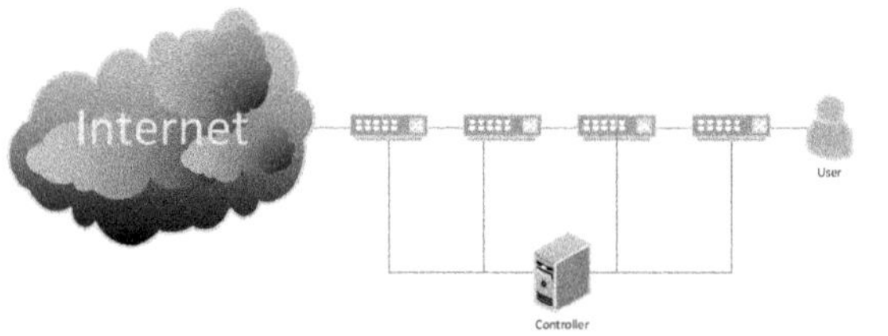


**Figure 1. Connectivity diagram of the demo.**

## 4. Conclusion

FleXam is designed to overcome the visibility loss of wildcard rules in OpenFlow. In this demo, we show how it could be used to efficiently collect traffic statistics about different destinations outside a given network that interact with internal hosts. Our demo allows users to interactively see how FleXam works in comparison with alternative approaches to collect flow level statistics.

## 5. Acknowledgement

This project was partially funded by NSERC SAVI strategic network grant.

## 6. REFERENCES

[1] Hu, H., et al. 2014. FlowGuard: Building Robust Firewalls for Software-Defined Networks. To appear in HotSDN 2014.

[2] Mehdi, S.A., Khalid, J., and Khayam, S.A. 2011. Revisiting traffic anomaly detection using software defined networking. In RAID'11. 161-180.

[3] Monsanto, C., et al. 2012. A compiler and run-time system for network programming languages. In POPL '12. 217-230.

[4] Monsanto, C., et al. 2013. Composing software-defined networks. In NSDI'13.

[5] Nelson, T., et al. 2014. Tierless Programming and Reasoning for Software-Defined Networks. In NSDI'14. 519-531.

[6] Shirali-Shahreza, S., and Ganjali, Y. 2013. FleXam: Flexible Sampling Extension for Monitoring and Security Applications in OpenFlow. In HotSDN 2013.

[7] Shirali-Shahreza, S. and Ganjali, Y. 2013. Efficient Implementation of Security Applications in OpenFlow Controller with FleXam. In HotI 2013. 49-54.

[1] http://openvswitch.org/

[2] http://www.noxrepo.org/

# Identifying Traffic Differentiation on Cellular Data Networks

Arash Molavi Kakhki[‡], Abbas Razaghpanah[⋆], Rajesh Golani[⋆]
David Choffnes[‡] , Phillipa Gill[⋆], Alan Mislove[‡]
[‡]Northeastern University, [⋆]Stony Brook University

## 1. INTRODUCTION

The goal of this research is to detect traffic differentiation in cellular data networks. We define traffic differentiation as any attempt to change the performance of network traffic traversing an ISP's boundaries. ISPs may implement differentiation policies for a number of reasons, including load balancing, bandwidth management, or business reasons. Specifically, we focus on detecting whether certain types of network traffic receive better (or worse) performance. As an example, a wireless provider might limit the performance of third-party VoIP or video calling services (or any other competing services) by introducing delays or reducing transfer rates to encourage users to use services provided by the provider. Likewise, a provider may allocate more bandwidth to preferred applications.

Previous work [1, 3, 5] explored this problem in limited environments. Glasnost focused on BitTorrent in the desktop/laptop environment, and used port/payload randomization to avoid differentiation. NetDiff covered a wide range of passively gathered traffic from a large ISP but likewise did not support targeted, controlled experiments. We address these limitations with *Mobile Replay*.

## 2. MOBILE REPLAY

We assume that ISPs will differentiate traffic based on properties such as hostname, IP addresses, ports, total number of connections, payload signatures, total bandwidth and time of day. Our system currently can detect all of these forms of differentiation with the exception of server-based differentiation.

### 2.1 Overview

Mobile Replay identifies service differentiation using two key components. First, it tests for differentiation by replaying real network traces generated from user interactions with apps. Meddle [4] facilitates capturing this information, and we develop new strategies for replaying arbitrary app traces. Second, Mobile Replay exploits the Meddle VPN to conduct controlled experiments. By alternately replaying traffic over tunneled and untunneled connections multiple times in rapid succession, we control ISP visibility into packet contents that may used to differentiate traffic.


*SIGCOMM'14*, August 17–22, 2014, Chicago, IL, USA.
ACM 978-1-4503-2836-4/14/08.
http://dx.doi.org/10.1145/2619239.2631445 .

Figure 1: Schematic view of how our project works. Traffic is sent unencrypted and through the Meddle VPN tunnel between the mobile client and a control server.

A key challenge is how to capture and replay the salient features of application traffic such that it will be subject to differentiation from middleboxes. To this end, we design a system that captures traffic generated by users' devices (via Meddle) and replays those flows from a replay server. Another challenge is how to establish ground truth as to whether the ISP is differentiating service for replay traffic. To address this, we exploit the VPN connection that Meddle provides as follows. When the VPN is enabled, the ISP cannot inspect flow contents and thus cannot differentiate based on the above factors except total bandwidth and time-of-day. We then compare this performance to the case when we send traffic untunneled. Using multiple successive trials of tunneled and untunneled replay experiments, we can determine the noise inherent in performance metrics in each type of experiment (tunneled vs not tunneled), then identify cases where there are statistically significant differences between them, indicating differentiation.

### 2.2 Replay and methodology

We support both UDP and TCP flows in our replay system, which consists of a client app running on the mobile device and a replay server written in Python in a event-driven fashion using Gevent [2], which performs efficiently with many concurrent clients. The server also performs UDP hole punching to support clients behind a NAT. The client and server coordinate to replay the original flows to reproduces packet timings, sequence of bytes, ports and client IPs. Since our replay is limited to using our own replay servers, we cannot detect differentiation based on arbitrary server IPs (a topic of ongoing work). Note, however, that if our replay servers are co-located with servers contacted in our traces, we do not suffer from this limitation. For example, if

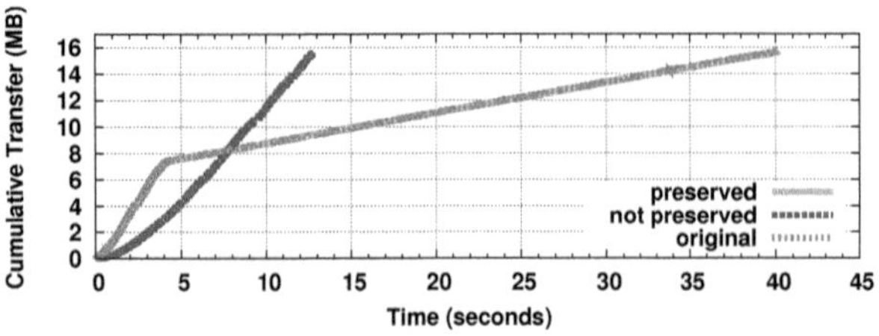


Figure 2: Cumulative byte-transfer plot of YouTube trace replays with inter-packet timing preserved vs. not preserved. The x-axis is time and y-axis is the total number of bytes transferred to that point. Observe that the original packet trace looks identical to the replay when timing is preserved.

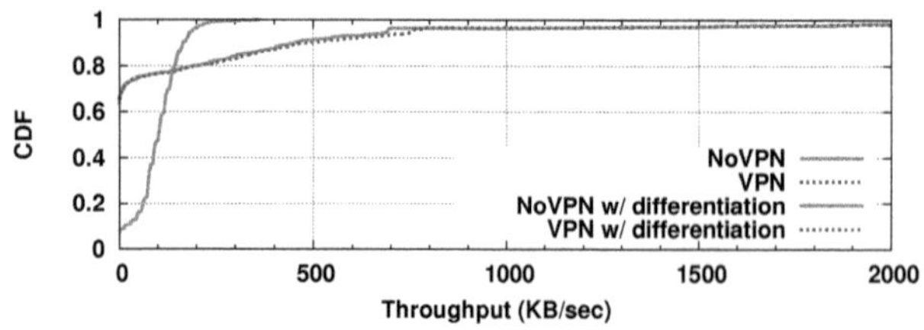


Figure 3: CDF of throughput over time, with and without extra delay and packet loss induced at the server. Our approach allows us to detect differences in throughput sample distributions when differentiation is applied.

we use EC2 servers and the tested app streams video from a server in the same data center (and/or same block of IP addresses), we may be able to trigger the same differentiation in our replays.

We detect differentiation according to the following metrics. First, we verify that the bytes sent/received at each endpoint during the replay are the same as the original trace. If not, we flag a case of content manipulation/blocking. Second, we compute summary statistics on throughput, loss, and RTT. Unlike manipulation/blocking, there are confounding factors other than differentiation that may causes changes in these statistics between the record and replay. To address this issue, we run multiple replay trials (10 total, though we are investigating dynamically adjusting the number of trials in response to observed noise), alternating between using a VPN connection ($R_T$) and an untunneled one ($R_U$). By computing statistics over multiple trials of one category ($R_T$ or $R_U$) we can quantify natural variations in performance that are not a result of differentiation. Having computed the variance over $R_T$ and $R_U$, we can compare the summary statistics (mean/median) of $R_T$ and $R_U$ and use the variance in each category to determine if the differences are statistically significant. Note that ISPs may apply differentiation to all VPN traffic, e.g., by throttling. To detect this, we group all $R_T$ samples and compare them to all $R_U$ samples across all applications and use the analysis described above.

## 2.3 Feasibility

We now demonstrate that our replay module performs as expected and can detect differentiation.

By preserving packet ordering and timing, our system produces very similar results to the original traffic. Figure 2 shows a YouTube trace replayed in both conditions side-by-side. Of course, a variety of factors can differ between record and replay, including network conditions and access technology. In particular, apps may change their behavior in response to network technology and available bandwidth. In such cases, we must ensure that we replay traffic that was originally captured over similar network conditions. In our experiments, YouTube was the only app that exhibited such behavior (due to adaptive bitrate streaming).

We next tested whether we can detect differentiation in a controlled environment. We ran a full replay test with YouTube in a test environment where we inject a simple form of differentiation by adding a 3% packet loss and 10ms of delay. Figure 3 shows CDFs of throughput during the replays, with and without differentiation. The effect of differentiation on the distribution is clear, indicating that our system and metrics allow us to distinguish between differentiation and noise. Last, we tested our approach using several application traces on Verizon in Boston. Figure 4 shows our replay results for two of those services, and we are able to confirm that there is no differentiation.

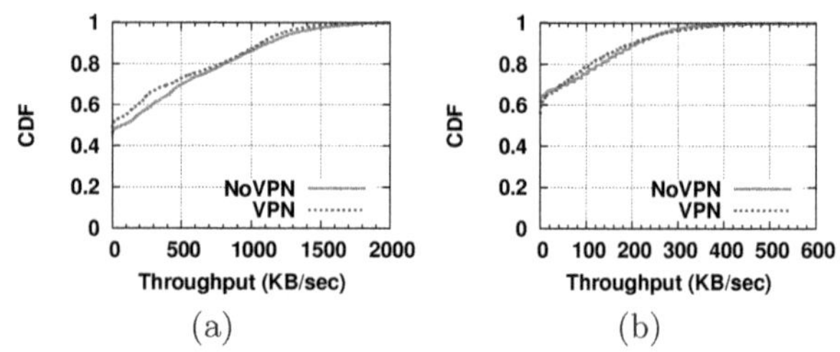


Figure 4: CDF of throughput over time for Verizon (left: Netflix, right: Spotify). Our tests show that Verizon does not differentiate traffic for these apps.

# 3. FUTURE WORK

To address the limitation that we cannot detect differentiation based on server ports, our future work includes leveraging source-spoofing such that the source IP in the server's packets are the same as in the original traces. Additionally, because the VPN itself may be subject to differentiation (or blocked), we are investigating using multiple differentiation detection approaches, including randomizing packet payloads and ports in the replay. We are also developing an app that allows average users to create and conduct tests from an mobile provider worldwide, and that efficiently uses scarce available data quota to run those tests. We plan to use the results to produce a Web site informing consumers of ISP policies.

# 4. REFERENCES


[1] M. Dischinger, M. Marcon, S. Guha, K. P. Gummadi, R. Mahajan, , and S. Saroiu. Glasnost: Enabling end users to detect traffic differentiation. In *NSDI*, 2010.

[2] `http://www.gevent.org`.

[3] M. B. Tariq, M. Motiwala, N. Feamster, and M. Ammar. Detecting network neutrality violations with causal inference. In *CoNEXT*, 2009.

[4] `http://www.meddle.mobi/papers/meddle-main.pdf`.

[5] Y. Zhang, Z. M. Mao, and M. Zhang. Detecting traffic differentiation in backbone isps with netpolice. In *SIGCOMM*, 2009.

# NIMBUS: Cloud-scale Attack Detection and Mitigation

Rui Miao
Univ. of Southern California
rmiao@usc.edu

Minlan Yu
Univ. of Southern California
minlanyu@usc.edu

Navendu Jain
Microsoft Research
navendu@microsoft.com

## Categories and Subject Descriptors

C.2.1 [**Computer-Communication Networks**]: Network Architecture and Design

## General Terms

Design, Experimentation

## Keywords

Cloud attack; Software-Defined Networking

## 1. INTRODUCTION

Cloud services are growing rapidly and their market is expected to reach $180 billion by 2015 [4]. Today, large cloud providers host tens of thousands of different services, so *inbound* attacks targeting the cloud can cause significant, and sometimes spectacular, collateral damage. A recent survey of datacenter operators indicates that half of them experienced DDoS attacks, with 94% of those experiencing regular attacks [2].

We highlight several unique features and evolution trend among those attacks [6, 1]: *(1) Large-scale.* These attacks have the volume up to hundreds of gigabits per second against a single cloud service. *(2) Diverse attacks.* The attacks range from network-layer (e.g. SYN flood, UDP flood) to application-layer (e.g. HTTP GET, SQL injection) with different characteristics on volume, number of connections, and packet header signatures (e.g., TCP flag, port). *(3) Fast ramp-up rate.* The attack traffic ramps up quickly and affects the target cloud service usually within one minute.

In response to the challenges above, the attack detection and mitigation system needs to 1) have sufficient capacity to accommodate attack volume, 2) support the detection of diverse range of attacks, and 3) have accurate and fast attack detection with low collateral damage to legitimate traffic.

To detect attacks, cloud operators commonly adopt commercial hardware boxes such as Firewalls, IDS, DDoS-protection appliances) in the network. There are three problems in these hardware boxes. First, these hardware boxes cannot scale up to handle attacks in cloud scale. For example, Firewall and IDS examine the detailed signatures and states of the traffic. So they cannot handle attacks with high volume. The DDoS-protection appliances check only significant traffic in network-layer. So they can handle larger attack volume but are still unable to accommodate extreme cloud-scale attacks with up to hundreds of gigabits per second. Second, these hardware boxes introduce unfavorable cost vs. capacity trade-offs. For example, the DDoS-protection appliance typically cost hundreds of thousands up to a few million dollars per box in each year [8]. Third, since these devices run proprietary software, they limit how operators can configure them to handle the increasing diversity of attacks today.

There have been some commercial attack prevention services (CloudFlare [3], Prolexic [1]) to redirect web service and enterprise traffic through a dedicated high-capacity scrubbing network for attack detection and mitigation. However, the cloud operator does not want tenant traffic to be re-routed given the private concerns.

In this paper, we propose a new paradigm of *attack-prevention-as-a-service* that leverages commodity VMs for attack detection and mitigation. We propose the NIMBUS service, which combines the elasticity of cloud computing resources with the kinds of programmability seen in software-defined networks (SDN). NIMBUS scales resource usage with traffic demands, is flexible to handle diverse attacks, and is relatively cheap and without the exposure of private tenant traffic.

## 2. NIMBUS DESIGN

There are several key challenges in designing and implementing NIMBUS:

**1.** Scaling to match datacenter traffic capacity at the order of hundreds of gigabits per second. The service should auto-scale to enable agility and cost-effectiveness.

**2.** Programmability to handle new and diverse types of network-based attacks, and flexibility to allow tenants/operators to configure policies specific to the traffic patterns and attack characteristics.

**3.** Fast and accurate detection and mitigation for attacks that ramp-up within one minute; once the attack subsides, we should revert the mitigation to avoid blocking legitimate traffic.

**4.** Robustness to prevent sophisticated attacks from a wise adversary, who knows our system well and want to attack either the NIMBUS service or individual cloud service.

In response to those design challenges, we design NIMBUS as an SDN-inspired framework, comprising a set of VM instances that analyze traffic for attack detection and an *auto-scale controller* that (a) does scale-out/in of VM instances to avoid overloading, (b) manages routing to traffic flows to them, and (c) dynamically instantiates anomaly detector and mitigation modules on them, as shown in Figure 2.


*SIGCOMM'14,* August 17–22, 2014, Chicago, IL, USA.
ACM 978-1-4503-2836-4/14/08.
http://dx.doi.org/10.1145/2619239.2631446 .

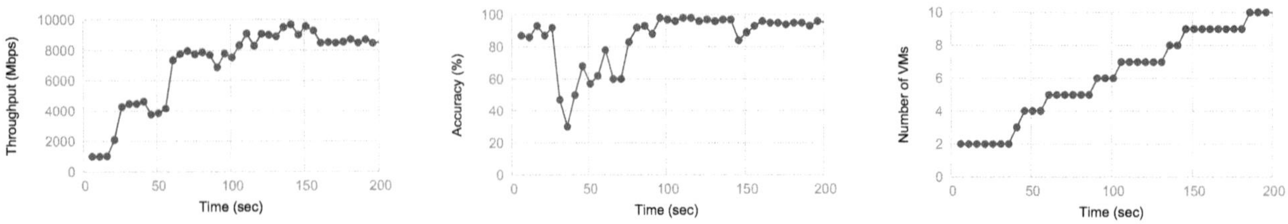


Figure 1: Timeline of attack burst. Starting with 1 Gbps and 2 VMs, and adding 9 Gbps attack traffic from 15th second.

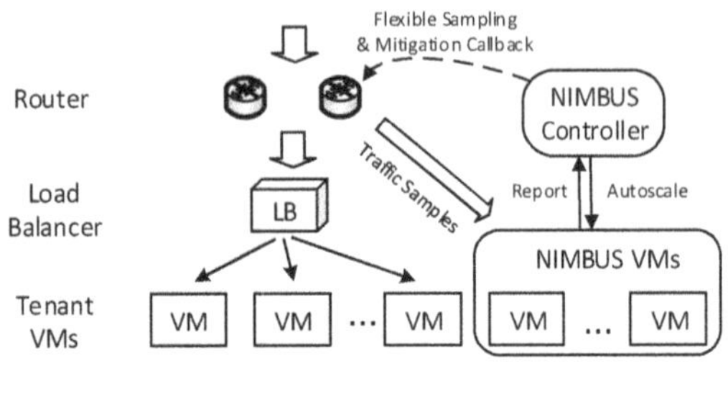


Figure 2: NIMBUS Architecture

**Flexible sampling.** NIMBUS supports flexible sampling configuration on different traffic flows, for the better accuracy of different attack detection applications. Since traffic monitoring in cloud data center typically employs uniform sampling with very low sample rate (e.g. 1 in 4000 packets), it is highly likely to miss median size DDoS attacks and other types of attacks (e.g. scan, Bruteforce). Biased sampling strategies have been proposed to have different sampling rate for different flow groups [9] or flow size [7], based on statistics over all packets in each flow group (e.g. sketch). However, those approaches need to change the hardware to support per-packet update for sampling rate. Here, we propose a flexible sampling strategy without hardware changes, where NIMBUS estimates traffic statistics from only traffic samples, and then adjusts the sampling rate for different flows accordingly. Finally, we would investigate an algorithm to allocate sampling resources to different flows to reduce the attack detection error for different attack types.

**Autoscale.** NIMBUS's central controller communicates with routers to direct traffic samples to different VMs, each of which detects attacks destined to different sets of cloud services. The VMs are allocated from available resources shared with other cloud tenant applications. When a VM is close to resource exhaustion under attack scenario, the controller can divert some of its traffic to other, possibly newly instantiated, VMs. By doing so, NIMBUS can maintain accurate attack detection with sufficient capacity provisioning.

One challenging is NIMBUS needs to manage the states of VMs in scale-up/down for consistent and responsive attack detection. Recent work [5] proposes to halt the packets of particular flows until state migration has completed. However, in an attack scenario, the traffic ramps up very fast and thus the VM is overloaded during the state migration. In this sense, NIMBUS needs to balance the traffic load immediately, even before the states have completely migrated. We need to investigate how to merge the new states and migrated states, and how to quantify the accuracy drop during the state migration. Further, in order to balance the cost (e.g. CPU, memory, bandwidth) of state migration and detection responsiveness, we need to investigate which flows to migrate and what associated states to migrate. In addition, we need to make NIMBUS robust to the wise adversary who may generate sophisticated attacks to degrade the effectiveness of autoscale system. For example, the adversary may generate on/off attack aligned with the auto-scale mechanism to waste NIMBUS resources and cause fluctuations of state migration.

**Detection and Mitigation.** NIMBUS supports flexible programmability for diverse and new attack detection using commodity VMs. For example, we may count throughput towards individual service to detect DoS-like attacks. In addition, we can also track the number of distinct IP sources to identify bot-like scan. Moreover, NIMBUS needs to be generic to support existing detection tools and algorithms (e.g., Deep Packet Inspection (DPI) [10]). One challenge is a wise adversary may generate attacks in a short burst that are hard to detect from the aggregated traffic statistics in a measurement epoch. Therefore, NIMBUS should dynamically change the aggregation time period to make it harder for the adversary to get around its detection while still saving cost. Once the attack characteristics (e.g., IP sources, header signature, payload) have been identified, NIMBUS controller can callback mitigation strategies to blacklist or rate-limit the attack traffic at the routers, prevent the attacks from hitting cloud infrastructure and tenant applications.

## 3. PRELIMINARY RESULTS

We build our prototype using three servers acting as the traffic generator, the host of NIMBUS VMs, and the NIMBUS controller, respectively. We connect them to a switch using 10G links. Our preliminary experiment is to detect flows with significant volume. The results are shown in Figure 1, where we add 9 Gbps attack burst from 15th second. As we can see, the accuracy decreases rapidly as the system drops lots of packets. As more VMs get started, the accuracy gradually recovers and the system throughput also increases to accommodate the attack traffic. In this experiment, The system has scaled-out to 10 VMs. With increasing number of active VMs, the system takes around 55 seconds to recover its measurement accuracy and 100 seconds to accommodate the 9 Gbps traffic burst.

## 4. REFERENCES

[1] Q4 2013 global ddos attack report. `http://goo.gl/1IyRmK`, 2013.

[2] Arbor Networks. Insight Into the Global Threat Landscape. `http://goo.gl/15oOx3`, February 2013.

[3] CloudFlare. `https://www.cloudflare.com/`.

[4] Gartner. `http://www.gartner.com/newsroom/id/2562415`. 2013.

[5] A. Gember, R. Viswanathan, C. Prakash, R. Grandl, J. Khalid, S. Das, and A. Akella. OpenNF: Enabling Innovation in Network Function Control. In *Sigcomm*, 2014.

[6] Google. Malware Distribution by Autonomous System. `http://goo.gl/mZQeG4`, 2013.

[7] A. Kumar and J. Xu. Sketch guided sampling - using on-line estimates of flow size for adaptive data collection. In *INFOCOM 2006. 25th IEEE International Conference on Computer Communications. Proceedings*, 2006.

[8] F. Networks. 2011 adc security survey global findings. In *http://goo.gl/A3b2Q*, 2011.

[9] A. Ramachandran, S. Seetharaman, N. Feamster, and V. Vazirani. Fast monitoring of traffic subpopulations. In *Proceedings of the 8th ACM SIGCOMM Conference on Internet Measurement*, IMC '08, 2008.

[10] Snort. `http://www.snort.org/`.

# A User Behavior based Cheat Detection Mechanism for Crowdtesting

Ricky K. P. Mok, Weichao Li, and Rocky K. C. Chang
Department of Computing
The Hong Kong Polytechnic University
{cskpmok|csweicli|csrchang}@comp.polyu.edu.hk

## ABSTRACT

Crowdtesting is increasingly popular among researchers to carry out subjective assessments of different services. Experimenters can easily assess to a huge pool of human subjects through crowdsourcing platforms. The workers are usually anonymous, and they participate in the experiments independently. Therefore, a fundamental problem threatening the integrity of these platforms is to detect various types of cheating from the workers.

In this poster, we propose cheat-detection mechanism based on an analysis of the workers' mouse cursor trajectories. It provides a jQuery-based library to record browser events. We compute a set of metrics from the cursor traces to identify cheaters. We deploy our mechanism to the survey pages for our video quality assessment tasks published on Amazon Mechanical Turk. Our results show that cheaters' cursor movement is usually more direct and contains less pauses.

## Categories and Subject Descriptors

H5.1 [**Information Interfaces And Presentation**]: Multimedia Information Systems—*Evaluation/methodology*

## Keywords

crowdsourcing, cheat-detection, cursor submovement

## 1. INTRODUCTION

Crowdtesting is increasingly popular among researchers to carry out subjective assessments. Through crowdsourcing platforms (e.g., Amazon Mechanical Turk, or AMT), they can evaluate the quality of experience (QoE) of different network services, such as video streaming, VoIP, and IPTV [1]. Experimenters can easily deploy their experiments by compiling the assessments as a website published in the crowdsourcing platform. After finishing the assessments, they can report to the platform to claim their payment.

The advantages of using crowdsourcing over traditional laboratory experiment are lower cost, and a larger and more diverse crowd of workers [3]. However, without any supervision, the quality of the works received from crowdtesting is questionable. Some cheaters only intend to maximize their payment with minimum effort by quickly submitting low-quality works. Therefore, identifying cheaters can help improve the reliability of a crowdtest-based assessment.

Existing anti-cheating methods can be categorized into two major approaches—cheater avoidance and cheater detection. The first approach can be achieved by a better experiment design or the use of CAPTCHAs. Cheater avoidance, however, can only avoid automatic answering program. On the other hand, cheater detection focuses on screening out outliers from the data collected. Comparing with gold standard data or checking the consistency of similar questions can help identify unreliable workers. But these methods cannot be applied to assessments with no absolute answers and can be easily spotted by (semi-) human cheaters. A summary of anti-cheating methods can be found in [3].

In this poster, we propose a novel cheat-detection mechanism which is based on the user behavior, such as cursor and click positions, on the survey page. We claim that these behaviors provide implicit measures for the reliability of workers. For example, their cursor would take a shorter and more direct path to the buttons as the cheaters aim at finishing the task quickly. Honest workers may click or highlight the questions which can assist them to read, whereas the cheaters may glance over the questions and then provide their answers quickly.

In particular, we apply submovement analysis [5] to systematically study the cursor trajectories. Submovement analysis is common in the human-computer interface area to investigate the performance and accuracy of pointing devices. Figure 1 shows an example of a cursor trajectory consisting of two submovements. The horizontal dotted line connects the start and end points. The first submovement is in upward direction away from the horizontal line. The second submovement changes to downward direction until reaching the end point. We compute cursor measures [4] with the user behavior data and flag the outliers as cheaters.

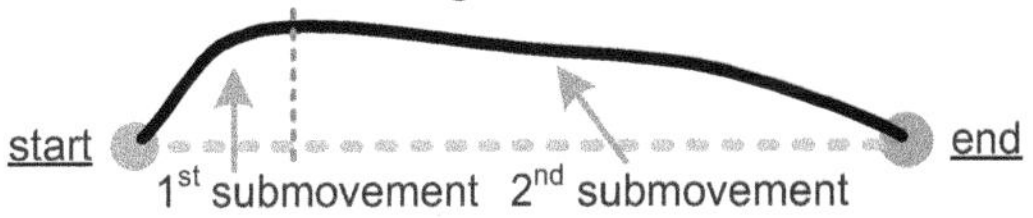


**Figure 1: A submovement example.**

We demonstrate our proposed method by using the user behavior dataset collected from our adaptive video quality assessment crowdsourced through the AMT. We insert a script written in jQuery to collect the user behavior in the background while they are rating the video quality by clicking the radio buttons. Our preliminary results show that


*SIGCOMM'14,* August 17–22, 2014, Chicago, IL, USA.
ACM 978-1-4503-2836-4/14/08.
http://dx.doi.org/10.1145/2619239.2631447.

3 workers consistently show abnormal behavior in multiple measures. Finally, we show the user behavior of a cheater to illustrate our proposed method.

## 2. METHODOLOGY

We have implemented a jQuery-based library to collect user behavior from the browser. Currently, these behaviors include cursor coordinates on the page, scrolling, and mouse click events. The library starts recording right after the page is loaded. All the events are time-stamped and periodically feedbacked to a dedicated web server using AJAX. The library can be deployed in the question page. Answering the questions must involve multiple mouse movements and clicks, such as using radio buttons to enter rating on a 5-point Likert scale.

### 2.1 Cursor measures

Our cheat-detection mechanism processes the user behavior offline after the tasks are completed. We first compute a set of cursor measures [4] for each trial and then apply the standard score to identify a set of outliers. Due to the page limitation, we introduce only three cursor measures below which are effective in screening out cheaters.

*1) Number of submovement.* This measure counts the total number of submovement on the whole question page. We expect cheaters to have less submovement than other workers. The number of submovement reveals whether the worker has read the questions before answering them, as cursor movements strongly correlate with the eye movement [2]. We parse the submovements by using zero-crossing of cursor velocity [5]. A new submovement is started when either the horizontal or the vertical velocity crosses 0.

*2) Mean cursor pause duration.* We compute the average duration of all the pauses recorded. This measure can infer the worker's think time between questions. Since cheaters usually answer questions quickly and continuously, the pause duration is expected to be shorter than honest workers.

*3) Number of cursor pause.* We count the number of cursor pauses which is longer than 50 ms. The mean pause duration above cannot handle cheaters mimicking an honest worker by using a single long pause. We design this pause count to differentiate pauses due to multiple thinking pauses from one long artificial wait. So, we expect that a cheater's behavior will have a smaller count in this measure.

## 3. RESULTS

We collected user behavior data from our crowdsourcing adaptive video streaming QoE assessments launched using the AMT. Each worker was required to rate the QoE of four 60-second video clips. After playing each video, they were prompted to answer 14 questions in a 5-point Likert scale by clicking radio buttons and answering one control question regarding the video content in the form of HTML select menu. Our library was run at the background and sent back the user behavior to our server every second.

Our assessments were completed by 127 workers, and 508 (=127 × 4) trials were conducted. Although all workers could correctly answer the control question, two of which were suspected to be cheaters after a manual inspection. Their works were subsequently rejected, and we did not receive any appeal from them.

We compute the three cursor measures and their Z-score for each trial. For each measure, a trial is considered an outlier if its Z-score is less than -1, and a worker is labeled as a suspect if he is involved in more than two outlying trials. If a worker is a suspect in more than one measure, he is flagged as a cheater.

With our mechanism, we found three workers matching our criteria for cheaters. One of which, labeled as Worker $C$, is also a rejected worker. We inspect the ratings received from Worker $C$. He simply chose 5 for all questions in all trials. Hence, we have high confidence that he is a cheater.

We further investigate the behavior of worker $C$ by comparing with an honest worker (Worker $R$). Figure 2(a) shows the cursor trajectories of both workers. The red dotted rectangle is the area for answering the questions. We can see that worker $C$ takes a much direct pathway to answer all the questions, but worker $R$ shows many submovements in between questions. Figure 2(b) plots the $x$ and $y$ velocity computed from the same trajectories. Worker $C$ finished the questions in less than 15 seconds, while worker R required more than 40 seconds. Besides, we can find a number of pauses for worker $R$ (two of them are indicated by arrows).

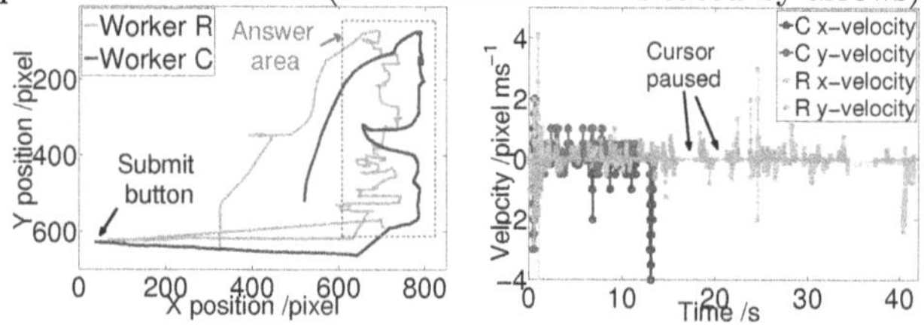


(a) Cursor trajectories. (b) Cursor velocity.

**Figure 2: Worker $C$'s and Worker $R$'s cursor data.**

## 4. CONCLUSION

This poster presented our user behavior based cheat-detection mechanism. Our preliminary results showed that cheaters show abnormal behavior when they are answering questions. We used three cursor measures to quantify the behaviors and detect the outliers. In the future, we will include more user behavior, such as click events and cursor location, to improve the accuracy and robustness of the mechanism.

**Acknowledgments:** This work is partially supported by an ITSP Tier-2 project grant (ref. no. GHP/027/11) from the Innovation Technology Fund in Hong Kong.

## 5. REFERENCES

[1] K.-T. Chen, C.-J. Chang, C.-C. Wu, Y.-C. Chang, and C.-L. Lei. Quadrant of euphoria: a crowdsourcing platform for QoE assessment. *IEEE Network*, 24(2):28–35, 2010.

[2] M. C. Chen, J. R. Anderson, and M. H. Sohn. What can a mouse cursor tell us more?: correlation of eye/mouse movements on web browsing. In *Proc. ACM CHI*, 2001.

[3] T. Hoßfeld, C. Keimel, M. Hirth, B. Gardlo, J. Habigt, K. Diepold, and P. Tran-Gia. Best practices for QoE crowdtesting: QoE assessment with crowdsourcing. *IEEE Trans. in Multimedia*, 16(2):541–558, 2014.

[4] F. Hwang, S. Keates, P. Langdon, and J. Clarkson. A submovement analysis of cursor trajectories. *Behaviour & Information Technology*, 24(3):205–217, 2005.

[5] D. E. Meyer, R. A. Abrams, S. Kornblum, C. E. Wright, and J. E. K. Smith. Optimality in human motor performance: Ideal control of repid aimed movements. *Psychological Review*, 95(3):340–370, 1988.

# ESCAPE: Extensible Service ChAin Prototyping Environment using Mininet, Click, NETCONF and POX


Attila Csoma, Balázs Sonkoly*, Levente Csikor*, Felicián Németh†, András Gulyás†
Budapest Univ. of Technology and Economics‡
{csoma,sonkoly,csikor,nemethf,gulyas}@tmit.bme.hu

Wouter Tavernier, Sahel Sahhaf
Ghent University – iMinds, Ghent, Belgium
{wouter.tavernier,sahel.sahhaf}@intec.ugent.be



## ABSTRACT

Mininet is a great prototyping tool which combines existing SDN-related software components (e.g., Open vSwitch, OpenFlow controllers, network namespaces, cgroups) into a framework, which can automatically set up and configure customized OpenFlow testbeds scaling up to hundreds of nodes. Standing on the shoulders of Mininet, we implement a similar prototyping system called ESCAPE, which can be used to develop and test various components of the service chaining architecture. Our framework incorporates Click for implementing Virtual Network Functions (VNF), NETCONF for managing Click-based VNFs and POX for taking care of traffic steering. We also add our extensible Orchestrator module, which can accommodate mapping algorithms from abstract service descriptions to deployed and running service chains.



## Categories and Subject Descriptors

C.2.3 [**Computer-Communication Networks**]: Network Operations—*Network management*

## Keywords

Service chain; Prototyping; SDN; Mininet; Click; NETCONF


## 1. INTRODUCTION

The concept of service chaining is not new but due to the networking revolution driven by SDN, it seems to re-magnetize the research/networking community [1]. A typical service consists of a series of service functions, traditionally implemented by middleboxes that have to be traversed in a given order by traffic flows. Service chain (or more generally service graph) is an abstraction to describe high level services in a generic way and to assemble processing flows for given traffic. Today's service deployment, service provisioning and service chaining have several limitations in terms of dynamics, flexibility, scalability, optimal usage of resources, as the built-in mechanisms are strongly coupled to the physical topology and the capabilities of special purpose, expensive hardware elements. As a consequence, configuring/deploying/operating service chains is a complex task and usually requires human interaction (the main problems are highlighted in [1]). In order to address these issues, different activities and research projects have been initiated. For instance, a dedicated working group (Service Function Chaining Working Group) has been established by the IETF dealing with several aspects of the service chaining architecture. The Network Functions Virtualization (NFV) group within ETSI aims at providing software-based telecommunication services, which can run in virtualized environment on a wide range of server hardwares instead of special purpose proprietary appliances. UNIFY (`http://www.fp7-unify.eu`) is an EU-funded FP7 project, which aims at unifying Cloud and carrier networks by developing an automated, dynamic service creation architecture based on a *dynamic fine-granular service chaining* model leveraging Cloud virtualization techniques and SDN.

In this demonstration, we present ESCAPE, our prototyping framework developed to the UNIFY architecture. Our system makes use of well-known, widely used tools, such as Mininet [2], Click [3], POX, and NETCONF, integrated into a common framework. An extensible Orchestrator module is also added, which makes our framework capable of setting up and configuring service chains on demand, mapping VNFs into physical resources, steering traffic according to chains' policies, and providing real-time management information on running VNFs.

## 2. ARCHITECTURE

The architecture proposed by UNIFY consists of three relevant layers enabling programmability at different abstraction levels. *Service layer* is aware of the service logic, handles service requests, and is responsible for SLAs. *Orchestrator layer* is the core of the framework. Based on a global network and resource view, it is responsible for mapping service requests to available resources and optimization. *Infrastructure layer* contains physical and virtual resources including compute, storage and networking resources, and components corresponding to local resource management. ESCAPE captures all these layers (Fig. 1) and provides a common plat-

*MTA-BME Future Internet Research Group
†MTA-BME Information systems research group

‡This work was conducted within the framework of the FP7 UNIFY project, which is partially funded by the Commission of the European Union.




*SIGCOMM'14,* August 17–22, 2014, Chicago, IL, USA.
ACM 978-1-4503-2836-4/14/08.
http://dx.doi.org/10.1145/2619239.2631448.

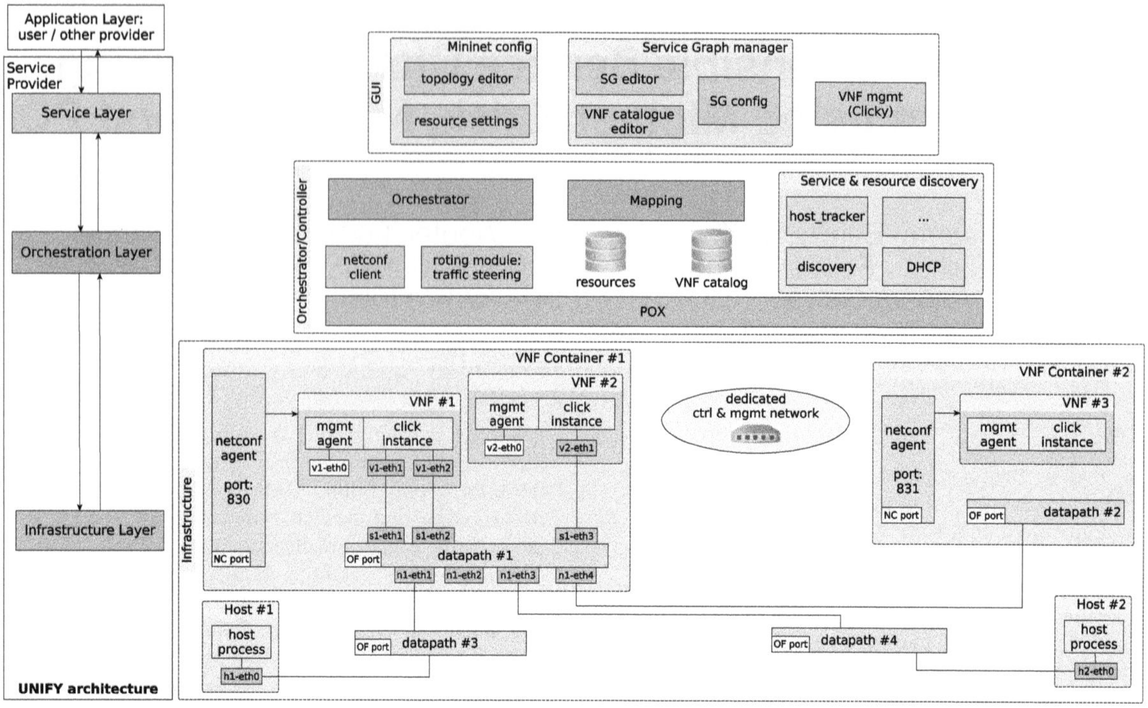


Figure 1: The main components of ESCAPE with the corresponding UNIFY architecture layers. The infrastructure layer is built on Mininet [2], which is a light-weight network emulation tool enabling agile prototyping.

form where the main steps of the service chaining process can be controlled, configured and further developed.

Our goal is to alleviate the developers' tedious task of setting up a whole service chaining environment and let them focus on their own work (e.g., developing a particular VNF, implementing an orchestration algorithm or a customized traffic steering). On the one hand, ESCAPE fosters VNF development by providing a simple, Mininet-based API where service graphs (SG), built from given VNFs, can be instantiated and tested automatically. ESCAPE also contains a VNF catalog, which is a built-in set of useful VNFs implemented in Click. The network infrastructure consists of OpenFlow switches (e.g., Open vSwitch) and a dedicated easy-to-configure controller application (implemented in the POX OpenFlow controller platform) is responsible for steering traffic between VNFs. Mininet is extended by the notion of VNFs that can be started as processes with configurable isolation models (based on cgroups in Linux). The establishment of dedicated control network is also possible where the management agents of the VNFs are connected to in order to be available from the service layer.

On the other hand, ESCAPE supports the development and the testing of orchestration components. Mininet is extended by NETCONF capability in order to support managed nodes (VNF containers) hosting VNFs. For this purpose, we integrate OpenYuma [4], an open-source NETCONF implementation, in the framework. A NETCONF agent is responsible for managing VNF containers and assigned switch(es). More specifically, the agent is able to start/stop VNFs and connect/disconnect VNFs to/from switches. The operation of the agent is described by the YANG data modeling language and implemented by low-level instrumentation codes. It is worth noting that the migration to real platforms require only the adaptation of the instrumentation part. The exposed RPCs of the agent are called from the orchestrator (NETCONF client module) to start/stop VNFs on demand. The paths are handled similarly by our traffic steering module. A dedicated component maps abstract service graphs into available resources based on different optimization algorithms (which can be easily changed or customized). Other components play a role in the automation of configuration processes. On top of these, a MiniEdit based GUI can be used to describe service graphs with given requirements (e.g., delay or bandwidth requirement on a sub-graph) and test topologies (resources and topology).

**During the demo**, we showcase every part of the architecture in a common GUI with the following steps[1]. The audience can (1) define VNF containers and the rest of the topology, (2) use the SG editor to create an abstract service graph where VNFs can be selected from a predefined list, (3) initiate the SG mapping to network resources and the deployment, (4) use standard tools to send and inspect live traffic, and (5) monitor the VNFs with Clicky.

# 3. REFERENCES

[1] P. Quinn and T. Nadeau. Service function chaining problem statement. IETF Draft, April 17, 2014.

[2] B. Lantz, B. Heller and N. McKeown. A network in a laptop: Rapid prototyping for software-defined networks. In *ACM HotNets 2010*.

[3] E. Kohler et al. The click modular router. *ACM Trans. Comput. Syst.*, 18(3):263–297, August 2000.

[4] OpenYuma. https://github.com/openclovis/openyuma.

[1]A screencast showing a simplified version of the demo is available: http://youtu.be/8ulstYXpHJA, http://sb.tmit.bme.hu/mediawiki/index.php/ESCAPE

# Sampling Online Social Networks: An Experimental Study of Twitter

Maksym Gabielkov
Inria
Sophia Antipolis, France
maksym.gabielkov@inria.fr

Ashwin Rao
Inria
Sophia Antipolis, France
ashwin.rao@inria.fr

Arnaud Legout
Inria
Sophia Antipolis, France
arnaud.legout@inria.fr

## ABSTRACT

Online social networks (OSNs) are an important source of information for scientists in different fields such as computer science, sociology, economics, etc. However, it is hard to study OSNs as they are very large. For instance, Facebook has 1.28 billion active users in March 2014 and Twitter claims 255 million active users in April 2014. Also, companies take measures to prevent crawls of their OSNs and refrain from sharing their data with the research community. For these reasons, we argue that sampling techniques will be the best technique to study OSNs in the future.

In this work, we take an experimental approach to study the characteristics of well-known sampling techniques on a full social graph of Twitter crawled in 2012 [2]. Our contribution is to evaluate the behavior of these techniques on a real directed graph by considering two sampling scenarios: (a) obtaining most popular users (b) obtaining an unbiased sample of users, and to find the most suitable sampling techniques for each scenario.

## Categories and Subject Descriptors

C.2.m [**Computer-communication Networks**]: Miscellaneous

## General Terms

Measurement, Experimentation

## Keywords

Twitter, social networks, sampling, social graph.

## 1. INTRODUCTION

The number of users of OSNs is constantly increasing. It will be harder to study OSNs as the data grows bigger. Indeed, companies take measures to prevent the crawls of their social networks, e.g., Twitter has discontinued the API 1.0 that supported anonymous requests and the use of already whitelisted machines, the new API 1.1 requires user authentication for each request making crawls harder and longer to perform.

Also, the Twitter social graph is very different from the graphs of classical social networks, e.g., Facebook, because it is directed. There is no notion of friendship on Twitter, users can only *follow* other users to subscribe for their tweets. The action of following does not require any confirmation from the person being followed. Directed graphs are harder to study than undirected ones.

In 2012 we collected the full graph of Twitter, resulting in a graph with 505 million nodes and 23 billion arcs [2]. We use this graph to see how the classical sampling techniques are working with a limited sampling budget, that is a limited number of nodes that can be sampled.

Our contribution is to show that classical sampling techniques have a large bias toward high degree nodes. So classical techniques can be used to identify such nodes, but not to perform a uniform sample of the directed social graph. We describe the techniques in Section 2 and present the result of the application of these techniques to our dataset in Section 3.

## 2. SAMPLING TECHNIQUES

For our experimental study, we considered two classical techniques of sampling. The social graph of Twitter is directed, therefore each technique can traverse the graph in three different directions (a) in the direction of *followers* (the arcs of the graph will be directed from followers to the users being followed), (b) in the direction of *followings* (the arcs will be directed in the opposite way), (c) *bidirectionaly* (arcs will be treated as edges).

**Breadth-first search (BFS)** is a natural way to sample social networks, because of the way the APIs of these networks are designed. Usually the APIs provide access to list of friends/followers/followings of a particular user of a social network, which corresponds to the adjacency list of the node in the graph. For example, Kwak *et al.* [3] used BFS with Perez Hilton as a seed to crawl the Twitter social graph in 2009. However, when the number of requests to the API is limited, the sample obtained with BFS will have a large bias.

**Random Walk (RW)** is a way of traversing the graph from node to node by picking a random neighbor. Random walks are known to visit the nodes with the probability proportional to the degree of the node. There is a large literature on random walks for undirected graph, but very few on directed ones.


*SIGCOMM'14,* August 17–22, 2014, Chicago, IL, USA.
ACM 978-1-4503-2836-4/14/08.
http://dx.doi.org/10.1145/2619239.2631452.

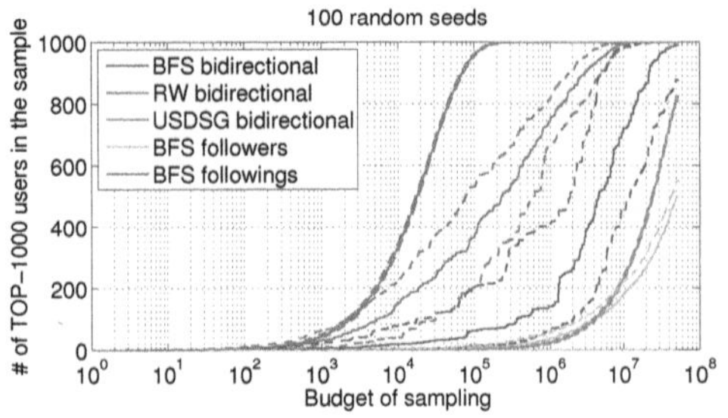


**Figure 1: Sampling high degree users.** The figure is based on 100 samples, solid line shows the median, dashed lines show the 25 and 75 percentiles.

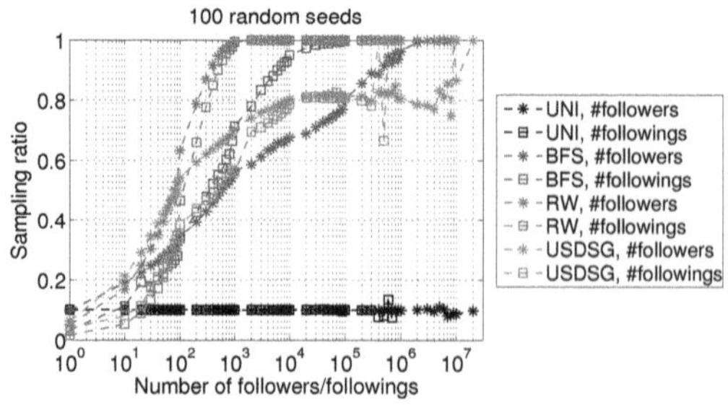


**Figure 2: Sampling ratio for the bins with different number of followers/followings.** The figure is based on 100 samples, lines show the median.

**Unbiased sampling method for directed social graphs (USDSG)** proposed by Wang *et al.* [4] is a modification of the random walk which discards a random jump to a node with a probability proportional to the degree of the node. The directed graph is treated as undirected, each arc is replaced by an edge.

## 3. RESULTS

We performed our experiments on the full Twitter social graph collected in 2012 that consists of 505 million accounts interconnected by 23 billion links [1]. For the purpose of this study, we took 100 random seeds and we performed each traversal 100 times starting from these seeds. We stopped the sampling when we sampled 10% of the graph (50.5 million nodes).

We do not present results of RW in the direction of followers and followings because RW stops when it encounters a node with no out-going arcs. In our experiments we observe such stops after sampling 50 nodes.

### 3.1 Popular users

To evaluate the ability of the techniques to sample popular users, we looked at the TOP 1000 most followed users in the sample, the result is presented on Figure 1. The best performance is achieved by RW, 342,000 nodes of the graph were crawled with RW to obtain all TOP 1000 most followed users. This behavior is explained by the fact that RW is biased towards high degree nodes. The BFS in all three directions has a high variance due to the position of the seed in the graph. Interestingly, BFS in the direction of followings can outperform RW when the budget is less than 2,000, because some of the Twitter users follow several popular accounts. So if we start the BFS from such a user, we can get with a limited budget a large number of popular users.

### 3.2 Unbiased sample

We now consider an unbiased sample in terms of the distribution of the number of followers and followings. To evaluate the quality of the distribution, we introduce a metric called *sampling ratio*. We distribute users in logarithmic bins based on the number of followers/followings they have. *Sampling ratio* is defined for each bin as the ratio of the number of sampled users in the bin to the total number of users in the bin. For the ground truth, we take a 10% uniform random sample of Twitter users (UNI on Figure 2).

Figure 2 presents the results for bidirectional versions of traversals. All the techiques we have tried have a high bias towards high degree nodes, including USDGS that fails to give an unbiased sample whereas it has been designed for that purpose.

We do not present BFS in the direction of followers and followings because some seeds do not have followers or followings resulting in an empty sample that can lead to the misinterpretation of the figure.

One may argue that the best way to obtain a uniform unbiased sample of the graph is to query the social network for randomly generated IDs (as shown in Figure 2 for UNI). However it is not always possible. For instance, the IDs on Facebook are assigned very sparsely, and only 75% of the account IDs in Twitter within the range $[0,\ 8 \times 10^8)$ correspond to valid accounts. Also companies may close the access to the IDs of the users to protect the privacy.

## 4. CONCLUSION

We have applied classical sampling techniques to the largest Twitter dataset ever collected. On the one hand, we showed that all classical sampling techniques introduce bias toward high degree nodes. This bias can completely change the results of the studies that rely on the partial crawl of the social graph. This motivates the need for a deeper study of the internal structure of social graphs to design an unbiased technique to sample directed OSNs.

On the other hand, the bias of these techniques towards high degree nodes gives a simple instrument to crawl high degree nodes, which correspond to popular users in the OSN.

More information about our study of Twitter can be found on our project page [1].

## 5. REFERENCES

[1] soTweet: Studying Twitter at Scale. `http://www-sop.inria.fr/members/Arnaud.Legout/Projects/sotweet.html`.

[2] M. Gabielkov, A. Rao, and A. Legout. Studying Social Networks at Scale: Macroscopic Anatomy of the Twitter Social Graph. In *Proc. of ACM Sigmetrics 2014*, Austin, TX, USA, Apr. 2014.

[3] H. Kwak, C. Lee, H. Park, and S. Moon. What is Twitter, a social network or a news media? In *Proc. of WWW'10*, Raleigh, NC, USA, May 2010.

[4] T. Wang, Y. Chen, Z. Zhang, P. Sun, B. Deng, and X. Li. Unbiased sampling in directed social graph. In *Proc. of SIGCOMM'10*, New Delhi, India, 2010.

# Mahimahi: A Lightweight Toolkit for Reproducible Web Measurement

Ravi Netravali, Anirudh Sivaraman, Keith Winstein,
Somak Das, Ameesh Goyal, and Hari Balakrishnan
MIT Computer Science and Artificial Intelligence Laboratory
{ravinet, anirudh, keithw, somakrdas, ameesh, hari}@csail.mit.edu

## ABSTRACT

This demo presents a measurement toolkit, Mahimahi, that records websites and replays them under emulated network conditions. Mahimahi is structured as a set of arbitrarily composable UNIX shells. It includes two shells to record and replay Web pages, *RecordShell* and *ReplayShell*, as well as two shells for network emulation, *DelayShell* and *LinkShell*. In addition, Mahimahi includes a corpus of recorded websites along with benchmark results and link traces (https://github.com/ravinet/sites).

Mahimahi improves on prior record-and-replay frameworks in three ways. First, it preserves the multi-origin nature of Web pages, present in approximately 98% of the Alexa U.S. Top 500, when replaying. Second, Mahimahi isolates its own network traffic, allowing multiple instances to run concurrently with no impact on the host machine and collected measurements. Finally, Mahimahi is not inherently tied to browsers and can be used to evaluate many different applications.

A demo of Mahimahi recording and replaying a Web page over an emulated link can be found at http://youtu.be/vytwDKBA-8s. The source code and instructions to use Mahimahi are available at http://mahimahi.mit.edu/.

## Categories and Subject Descriptors

C.4 [**Performance of Systems**]: Measurement Techniques; H.3.5 [**Information Storage and Retrieval**]: Online Information Services

## Keywords

Page Load Time; Record-and-Replay; Web Measurements

## 1. INTRODUCTION

Mahimahi is a toolkit that can be used to evaluate how effective techniques that aim to make the Web faster perform over different network conditions. This question is of interest to network protocol designers who seek to understand the application-level impact of new multiplexing protocols, Web developers who wish to speed up access to their websites, and browser developers who need to evaluate how changes to their DOM and JavaScript parsers impact page load times. Mahimahi is structured as a set of UNIX shells, each of which we describe below.


*SIGCOMM'14*, August 17–22, 2014, Chicago, IL, USA.
ACM 978-1-4503-2836-4/14/08.
http://dx.doi.org/10.1145/2619239.2631455.

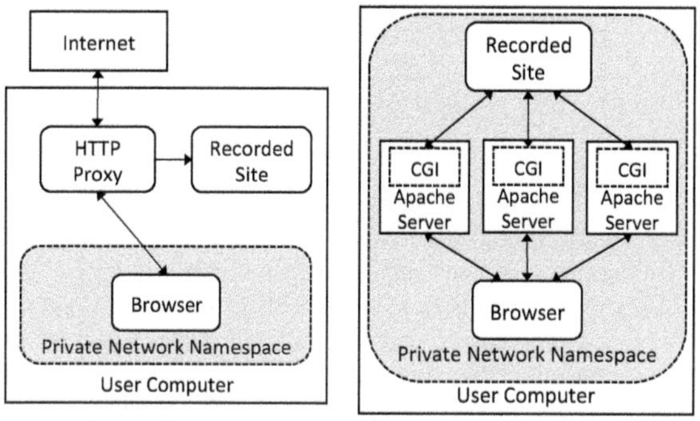


(a) RecordShell (b) ReplayShell

Figure 1: Arrows indicate direction of traffic

## 2. MAHIMAHI'S SHELLS

**RecordShell.** RecordShell (Figure 1a) records HTTP data sent during actual page loads and stores it on disk for subsequent replay. RecordShell spawns a man-in-the-middle proxy, equipped with an HTTP parser, on the host machine to store and forward all HTTP(S) traffic both to and from an application running within RecordShell.

At the end of a page load, a recorded folder contains a file for each request-response pair seen during that record session. RecordShell is compatible with any unmodified browser because recording is done transparently without modifying browser settings.

**ReplayShell.** ReplayShell (Figure 1b) mirrors a website using content recorded by RecordShell. ReplayShell accurately emulates the multi-origin nature of websites by spawning an Apache 2.4.6 Web server for each distinct IP/port pair seen while recording.

To operate transparently, ReplayShell binds its Apache Web servers to the same IP address and port number as their recorded counterparts. ReplayShell creates a separate virtual interface for each distinct server IP. All browser requests are handled by one of ReplayShell's servers, each of which can access the entire recorded content for the site. The Apache configuration redirects incoming requests to a CGI script which compares each request to the set of all recorded request-response pairs to locate a matching response.

**DelayShell.** DelayShell emulates a link with a fixed minimum one-way delay. All packets to and from an application running inside DelayShell are stored in a packet queue. A separate queue is maintained for packets traversing the link in each direction. Each packet is released from the queue after the user-specified one-way delay, enforcing a fixed per-packet delay.

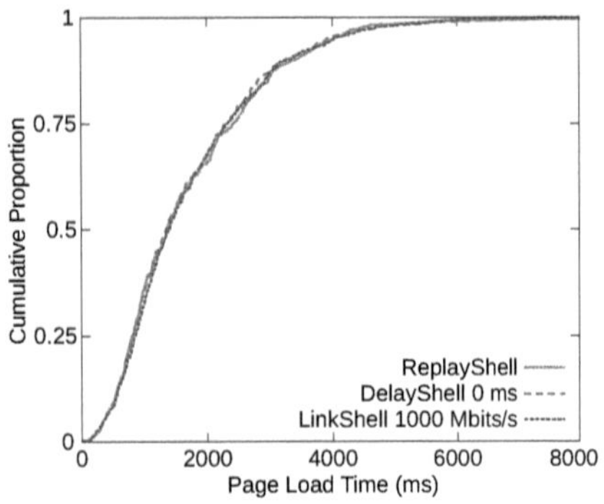


Figure 2: DelayShell's and LinkShell's low overhead

| | Machine 1 | Machine 2 |
|---|---|---|
| CNBC | $7584 \pm 120$ ms | $7612 \pm 111$ ms |
| wikiHow | $4804 \pm 37$ ms | $4800 \pm 37$ ms |

Table 1: Mean $\pm$ standard deviation for page load times across machines

**LinkShell.** LinkShell is used to emulate a link using packet-delivery traces. It is flexible enough to emulate both time-varying links such as cellular links and links with a fixed link speed. When a packet arrives into the link, it is directly placed into either the uplink or downlink packet queue. LinkShell releases packets from each queue based on the corresponding packet-delivery trace. Each line in the trace is a packet-delivery opportunity: the time at which an MTU-sized packet will be delivered in the emulation.

## 3. SUITABILITY FOR ACCURATE MEASUREMENT

**Low overhead.** Mahimahi imposes low overhead on page load time measurements. We illustrate this in Figure 2, which shows that when loading the 500 websites in our corpus, DelayShell with 0 ms imposes only a 0.15% overhead on median page load time compared to ReplayShell alone, while LinkShell with a 1000 Mbits/s trace adds 1.5% on top of ReplayShell.

**Reproducibility.** Table 1 shows a summary of the distribution of page load times when loading two Web pages, www.cnbc.com and www.wikihow.com, 100 times each on two separate host machines. The mean page load times for each site are less than 0.5% apart across the two machines, suggesting that Mahimahi produces comparable results on different host machines. Similarly, the standard deviations are all within 1.6% of their means, suggesting that Mahimahi produces consistent results on a single host machine.

## 4. NOVELTY

This section describes several new features in Mahimahi as compared with existing record-and-replay tools such as Google's web-page-replay [1].

**Multi-origin Web pages.** Unlike other tools, ReplayShell preserves the *multi-origin* nature of websites: websites today commonly include content belonging to several distinct origin servers. As we show below, preserving the multi-origin nature of websites is critical to the accurate measurement of page load times.

A non-trivial number of websites today are multi-origin. Using our corpus of recorded sites, we computed the distribution of physical servers per website in the Alexa U.S. Top 500. The median number of servers is 20 while the 95th percentile is 51. Only 9 Web pages use a single server.

To evaluate the impact of not capturing the multi-origin nature of websites, we modify ReplayShell to serve all content from a single Web server. Table 2 shows the median and 95th percentile difference in page load time between when multi-origin nature is and is not preserved, over nine different network configurations. Although the page load times are comparable over a 1 Mbit/s link, not capturing the multi-origin nature yields significantly worse performance at higher link speeds.

| | 30 ms | 120 ms | 300 ms |
|---|---|---|---|
| 1 Mbit/s | 1.6%, 27.6% | 1.7%, 10.8% | 2.1%, 9.7% |
| 14 Mbits/s | 19.3%, 127.3% | 6.2%, 42.4% | 3.3%, 20.3% |
| 25 Mbits/s | 21.4%, 111.6% | 6.3%, 51.8% | 2.6%, 15.0% |

Table 2: 50th, 95th percentile page load time difference without multi-origin preservation

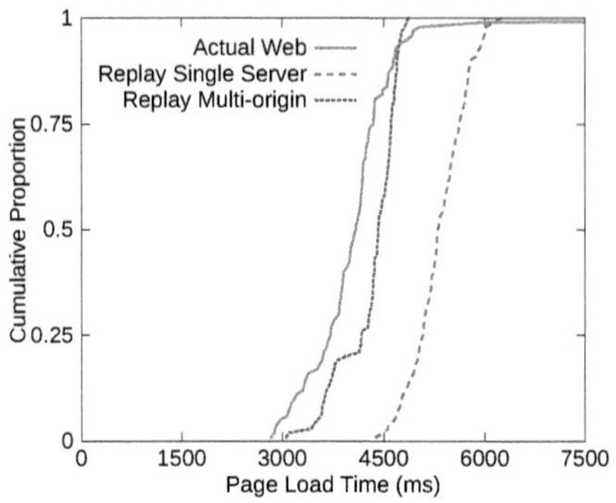


Figure 3: Multi-origin preservation yields measurements closer to the Web

We further illustrate the importance of multi-origin preservation by comparing measurements collected using ReplayShell to real page load times on the Web. Figure 3 shows the distribution of page load times when loading www.nytimes.com 100 times on the Web and inside ReplayShell with and without multi-origin preservation. For fair comparison, we record the minimum round trip time to www.nytimes.com for each page load on the Web and use DelayShell to emulate this for each page load with ReplayShell.

ReplayShell with multi-origin preservation yields page load times that more accurately resemble page load times collected on the Internet. The median page load time is 7.9% larger than the Internet measurements, which is less than the 29.6% discrepancy when the multi-origin nature is not preserved.

**Isolation.** Each namespace created by Mahimahi is separate from the host machine's default namespace and every other namespace. As a result, processes running inside the namespace of a Mahimahi tool are completely isolated from those running outside. This means that host machine traffic does not affect the measurements reported by Mahimahi, and Mahimahi's network emulation does not affect traffic outside of Mahimahi's network namespaces. This enables many different configurations to be concurrently tested on the same host machine, and in complete isolation from each other. In contrast, web-page-replay modifies DNS resolution on the host machine and affects all traffic from the host machine.

**Beyond browsers.** Although most existing record-and-replay frameworks only replay browser page loads, Mahimahi's design allows it to replay any application that uses HTTP. For instance, a mobile device emulator, such as for Android [2], can be used to analyze and measure mobile application performance.

## References


[1] http://code.google.com/p/web-page-replay.

[2] http://developer.android.com/tools/devices/emulator.html.

# A Time for Reliability – The Growing Importance of Being Always On

Zachary S. Bischof and Fabián E. Bustamante
Northwestern University
{zbischof, fabianb}@eecs.northwestern.edu

## Categories and Subject Descriptors

C.2.3 [**Communication Systems Organization**]: Computer Communication Networks—*Network Operations*; C.4 [**Performance of Systems**]: [Reliability, availability, and serviceability]

## Keywords

Access link reliability, Broadband access networks

## 1. INTRODUCTION

When a new technology reaches the market, we often focus on the want or need that it can fulfill. However, as the market for a technology matures, reliability often becomes a key differentiating factor between competing products. Examples of this abound, from cars to passenger flights, phones and televisions.

Broadband bandwidth capacities remain a challenge around the world. In the developed world, however, their rapid growth seems to have already passed current needs. Figure 1 shows how peak network usage (95th percentile hour) changes with growing bandwidth capacity (measured from over 7000 residential gateways in the US). We observe a law of diminishing returns in their relationship: the relative increase in demand is greater for lower capacity than for the larger capacity connections. At about 12 Mbps, most users 95th percentile usage remains below 15% of their capacity.

In this poster, we posit that in the developed world broadband reliability will soon become the dominant feature for service comparison. With increased capacity, a growing number of consumers switch their cable TV and landline phone subscription to video streaming or VoIP services over the Internet. For such users, service uptime becomes a serious concern. While previous outages resulted in mild inconveniences while browsing the web, today's network availability can determine the outcome of an emergency situation.

Previous works on broadband networks have focused on characterizing performance [1, 4], and works on reliability typically study wireless networks (cellular, WiFi, WiMax, etc). In this poster, we use data collected from residential gateways (via FCC/SamKnows) and end-hosts (via Namehelp) to study the availability and reliability of fixed-line broadband networks. We use traditional metrics (e.g. failure rate, MTBF, MTTR) to quantify each broadband service. We study the reliability of DNS, a service typically provided by ISPs. Using natural experiments, we look at the impact that increased network downtime has on user demand. Also, we note the severity of an outage largely depends on when it occurs (e.g. time of the day, day of the week). As a result, we use typical network usage patterns to design a new metric for service reliability, the average expected traffic lost (AETL), to quantify the impact of each service's outages.

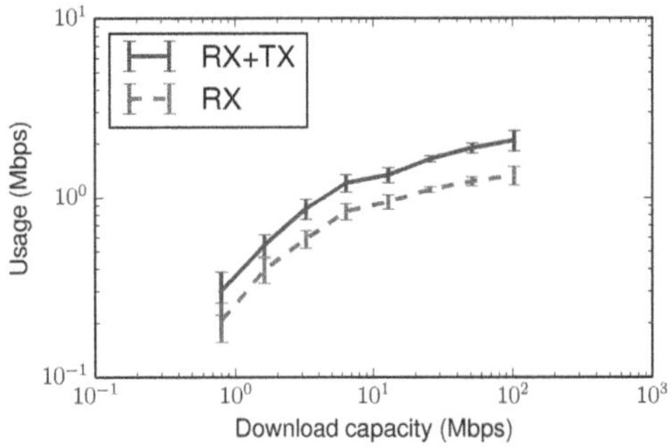


**Figure 1: Peak (95th percentile) network usage by download link capacity. The lines represent total traffic ($RX + TX$) and download traffic ($RX$).**

## 2. APPROACH

In this work, we leverage two datasets. First, we use data provided by the FCC [2], collected from gateways distributed to fixed-line broadband customers in the US. In our study, we use measurements of packet loss rates to M-Lab hosted measurement servers, DNS lookup failures, and byte counters of traffic over the WAN interface. Each of these are recorded at hour intervals. We consider an access link to be down when packet loss rates are above 10% for the hour.

Our end-host collected dataset comes from *namehelp* [3], a tool for improving DNS performance. We designed and deployed an extension for monitoring users' access links (at 30-second intervals) and ISP DNS servers, measuring service availability. In addition to providing more fine-grained information, this also gives us access to a diverse set of users (over 20,000 clients in 115 countries).


*SIGCOMM'14*, August 17–22, 2014, Chicago, IL, USA.
ACM 978-1-4503-2836-4/14/08.
http://dx.doi.org/10.1145/2619239.2631460 .

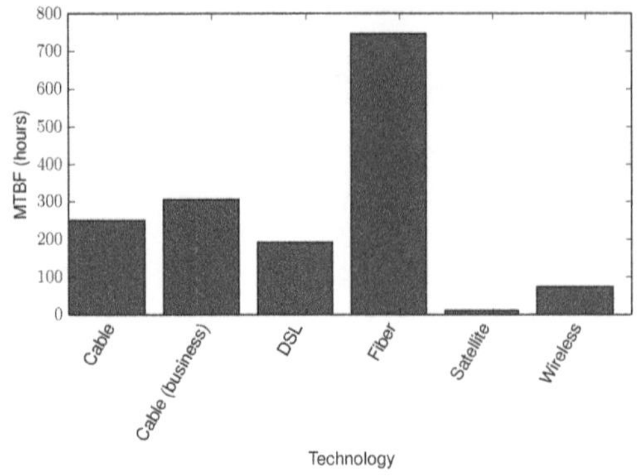


**Figure 2: Mean time between failure by technology.**

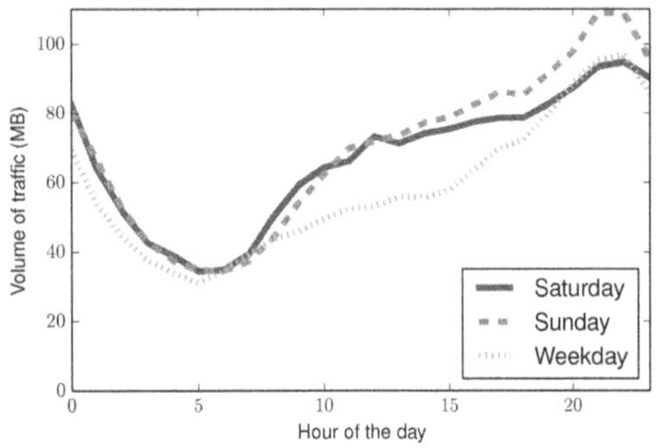


**Figure 3: Hourly usage by time of day for weekdays, Saturday, and Sunday.**

## 3. PRELIMINARY RESULTS

Our preliminary analysis has produced a number of interesting results. Below we provide a brief summary of our current findings.

First, we studied how service reliability was affected by the technology employed. Figure 2 shows the mean time between failure (MTBF), averaged for each technology. Overall, fiber services were by far the most reliable, with about 1600 hours (or about 67 days) between service outages. Next were DSL and cable services, with similar averages. Wireless services (such as Clearwire) and satellite services were the least reliable services, with less than 100 hours between failures.

Although DSL services had a higher MTBF than cable, we found that network outages in cable networks were typically more likely to occur during off-peak hours (i.e. in the middle of the night, between 2 and 4 am local time or in the early afternoon). In contrast, outages in DSL services were either uniformly distributed across the day or concentrated during peak usage hours.

With this in mind, we also want to compare services by the severity of their outages. To do this, we calculate the "typical" (median) demand at each hour of the day, for each day of the week, for all users, shown in Fig. 3 (Monday through Friday are grouped together as they showed similar usage patterns). This gives us an idea of how the impact of service outages differ on user traffic. For each service outage that we find, we use the "typical" number of bytes during that hour to estimate the volume of affected traffic.

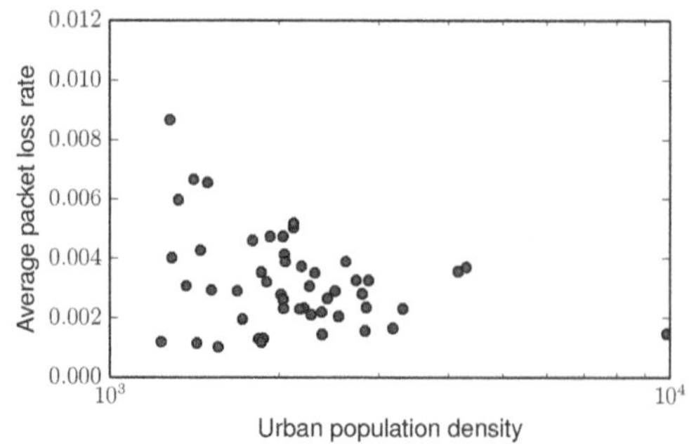


**Figure 4: Average packet loss rate in each state versus the average urban-area population density.**

We average this across all users to calculate the expected number of bytes of traffic lost, giving us an idea of the impact of each outage.

In this analysis, we found that outages on DSL services were typically more severe than in cable services. Also, we found that both cable and DSL services had similar mean times to recovery. The difference was largely due to differences in *when* the outages occurred. Therefore, despite the lower MTBF, we believe that cable networks in the US will tend to be perceived as more reliable.

We also investigated how service availability related to geographic settings. Since we only have course-grained (state) geographic information for users in the FCC/SamKnows dataset, we used census data from 2010 to find the fraction of the population in each state living in urban areas. Figure 4 shows the average packet loss rate in each state by the population density in urban regions of that state. For the most part, states with a lower urban population density tended to have higher packet loss rates rates. We expect that this is either due to the wider use of less reliable technologies, or that the implementations themselves are less reliable, as the have to cover greater distances. We are studying this, and other aspect of service reliability and availability in greater detail in our ongoing work.

## 4. ACKNOWLEDGEMENTS

The work was supported in part through NSF Awards CNS 1211375 and CNS 1218287, and a generous Google Faculty Award.

## 5. REFERENCES

[1] Z. S. Bischof, J. S. Otto, M. A. Sánchez, J. P. Rula, D. R. Choffnes, and F. E. Bustamante. Crowdsourcing ISP characterization to the network edge. In *Proc. of W-MUST*, 2011.

[2] FCC. Measuring broadband America. `http://www.fcc.gov/measuring-broadband-america`.

[3] J. S. Otto, M. A. Sánchez, J. P. Rula, and F. E. Bustamante. Content delivery and the natural evolution of DNS: Remote DNS trends, performance issues and alternative solutions. In *Proc. of IMC*, November 2012.

[4] S. Sundaresan, W. de Donato, N. Feamster, R. Teixeira, S. Crawford, and A. Pescapè. Broadband internet performance: a view from the gateway. In *Proc. of ACM SIGCOMM*, 2011.

# Vivisecting WhatsApp through Large-Scale Measurements in Mobile Networks

Pierdomenico Fiadino, Mirko Schiavone, Pedro Casas
FTW Vienna
surname@ftw.at

## ABSTRACT

WhatsApp, the new giant in instant multimedia messaging in mobile networks is rapidly increasing its popularity, taking over the traditional SMS/MMS messaging. In this paper we present the first large-scale characterization of WhatsApp, useful among others to ISPs willing to understand the impacts of this and similar applications on their networks. Through the combined analysis of passive measurements at the core of a national mobile network, worldwide geo-distributed active measurements, and traffic analysis at end devices, we show that: (i) the WhatsApp hosting architecture is highly centralized and exclusively located in the US; (ii) video sharing covers almost 40% of the total WhatsApp traffic volume; (iii) flow characteristics depend on the OS of the end device; (iv) despite the big latencies to US servers, download throughputs are as high as 1.5 Mbps; (v) users react immediately and negatively to service outages through social networks feedbacks.[1]

## Categories and Subject Descriptors

C.2 [**Computer-Communication Networks**]: Miscellaneous; C.4 [**Performance of Systems**]: Measurement Techniques

## Keywords

WhatsApp, Large-Scale Measurements, Mobile Networks.

## 1. MOTIVATION & METHODOLOGY

WhatsApp is doubtlessly the leading instant multimedia messaging service in mobile networks. It handles more than 64B messages per day, including 700M photos and 100M videos. With half a billion of active users, it has become the fastest-growing company in history in terms of users. The goal of this work is to provide the first large-scale characterization of the complete service, highly useful for mobile

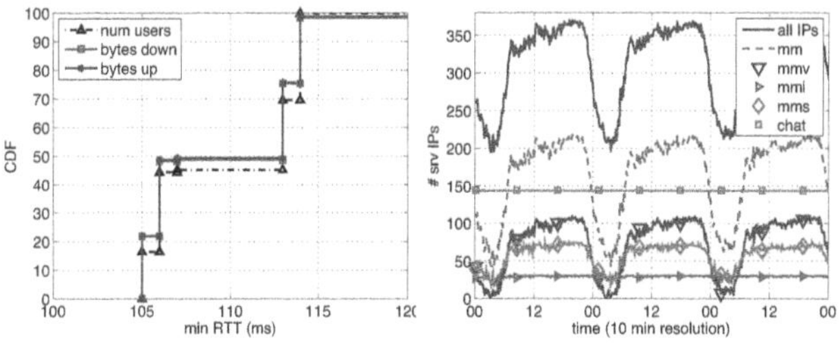


(a) min RTT to WhatsApp IPs. (b) WhatsApp daily active IPs.

**Figure 1: Characteristics of WhatsApp servers.**

operators and service providers, both to asses its impact on the network and to understand how to track its usage.

As WhatsApp traffic is encrypted, our study required a complex methodology to discover the traffic flows and the corresponding hosting servers: firstly, by analyzing WhatsApp traffic captures at end devices, and particularly focusing on the DNS requests, we identified the naming scheme used by the servers. Secondly, using this naming scheme on top of the HTTPTag traffic classification tool [1], and following a similar procedure to [2], we collected a week of WhatsApp flows at the core of a European national-wide mobile network (from 18.02 to 25.02), which were then analyzed through the DBStream large-scale analysis system [3]. In a nutshell, every time a user issues a DNS request for the fully qualified domain name **`*.whatsapp.net`**, HTTPTag creates an entry mapping this user to the server IPs provided in the DNS reply. Each entry is time stamped and expires after a time-out based on the TTL of the DNS reply. Using these mappings, all the subsequent flows between this user and the identified servers are assumed to be WhatsApp flows. To increase the robustness of the approach, the list of IPs is augmented by adding those servers signing the TLS/SSL certificates with the string **`*.whatsapp.net`**, as observed at the end device captures. Finally, by using the MaxMind GeoIP databases (**`http://www.maxmind.com`**), combined with geo distributed DNS active measurements using the RIPE Atlas monitoring network (**`https://atlas.ripe.net`**), we identified and characterized the WhatsApp hosting infrastructure.

## 2. ANALYSIS & FINDINGS

The complete dataset consists of more than 140M chat flows, 9M photo/audio content flows, and 5M video flows. Our main findings are the following:

**(i) WhatsApp uses a highly structured naming scheme to handle different message types:** servers are associated to different third-level domain names, de-

[1] This work has been done in the framework of the EU-IP project mPlane, funded by the EC under grant 318627. The work is partially funded by the DARWIN4 COMET project.


*SIGCOMM'14*, August 17–22, 2014, Chicago, IL, USA.
ACM 978-1-4503-2836-4/14/08.
http://dx.doi.org/10.1145/2619239.2631461.

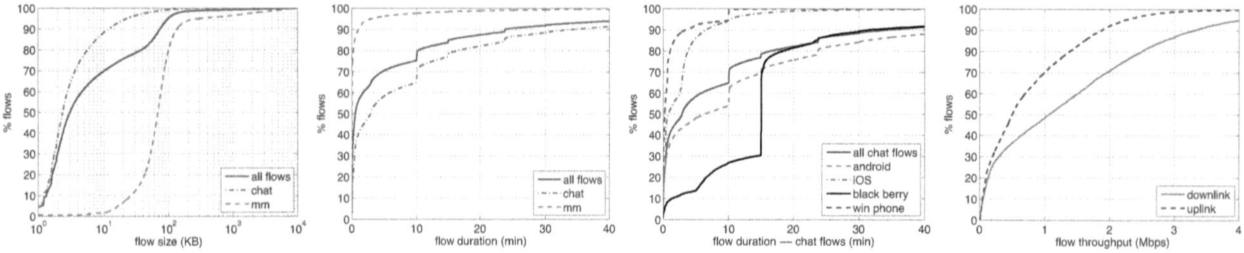


(a) Flow size. (b) Flow duration. (c) Flow duration per OS. (d) MM flow throughput.

**Figure 2: WhatsApp flow characteristics and performance.**

pending on the nature of the message (control, chat, media). Chat and control messages are handled by *chat servers* on ports 5222 (XMPP) or 443, identified by the domain names `e|c|dX.whatsapp.net` (`X` is a variable for load balancing). To allow a fast delivery of messages, chat connections are kept up while the application is active or in background. Transfers of photos, videos and audio are instead managed by HTTPS *multimedia servers* identified by `mms|mmi|mmvXYZ.whatsapp.net`, `mms|mmi` for audio and photos, and `mmv` for videos. Each HTTPS connection is dedicated to a single content, and closed on transfer completion.

**(ii) Despite its worldwide popularity, WhatsApp is a centralized service hosted by a single provider at servers located in the US:** 386 server IPs hosting WhatsApp are observed in the complete dataset, belonging to a single AS owned by the cloud provider SoftLayer (AS36351). To avoid biased conclusions about the set of IPs seen from a single Vantage Point (VP), we performed active measurements using RIPE Atlas: we analyzed which IPs were obtained resolving the same domain names from 600 boxes around the globe during multiple days. These measurements confirmed that the same set of IPs is always replied, regardless of the location of the requester. Using MaxMind, we observed that these IPs are mainly located in Dallas and Houston. We confirmed this through traceroutes and active RTT measurements. Fig. 1(a) plots the distribution of the min. RTT from the VP to the server IPs, weighted by the number of flows and traffic volume. The cdf shows that the service is evenly handled between two different yet potentially close locations at about 106ms and 114ms from the VP, which is compatible with our findings. To understand the dynamics of these IPs, fig. 1(b) shows the number of daily active IPs, split by message type. More than 350 IPs serve flows during peak hours, and 200 IPs are active even in the lowest load hours. Chat servers are constantly active to keep the state of active devices. Note that the `mmi` and `mms` IPs also seem to have a share of always-active IPs.

**(iii) Flow characteristics and performance:** Tab. 1 reports the downlink/uplink volume and flow shares. While the majority of the flows correspond to chat messages, media messages account for more than 76% of the total up/down traffic, with video covering almost 40%. In terms of flow size/duration, figs. 2(a-b) show that chat flows are small sized (6.7KB avg.) and long lasting (17' avg.), whereas media flows are bigger (225KB avg.) and shorter (2' avg.). The flow duration cdf additionally reveals some steps at exactly 10', 15' and 24', suggesting the usage of Time-Outs (TOs) to terminate idle connections. As shown in fig. 2(c), these values are dictated by the OS of the device. Different TOs are visible for Android at 10', 15' and 24'; iOS uses a TO

| features | chat (%) | mm (%) | mmv (%) | mmi (%) | mms (%) |
|---|---|---|---|---|---|
| $bytes_{down/up}$ | 17/30 | 83/70 | 40/36 | 13/16 | 30/18 |
| flows | 93.4 | 6.2 | 0.3 | 2.9 | 2.9 |

**Table 1: Volume and flows per traffic category.**

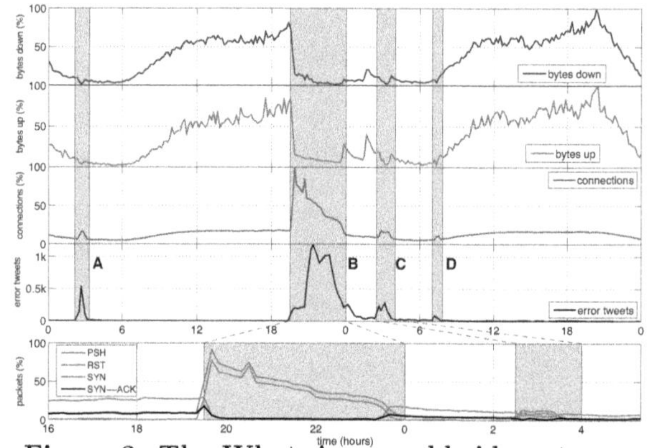


**Figure 3: The WhatsApp worldwide outage.**

of 3', BlackBerry has 15' TOs, whereas Win phones favors 10' TOs. When it comes to performance, fig. 2(d) indicates that, despite the big latencies to US servers, throughputs for multimedia flows bigger than 1MB are rather high, achieving an avg. down/up flow throughput of 1.5 Mbps/800 kbps.

**(iv) User reactions to WhatsApp outages are rapidly observed through social networks feeds**: fig. 3 depicts the volume and flow counts time series during 2 days around the major outage occurred in Feb. 22nd '14. The event is not only clearly visible from the traffic measurements, but can also be correlated with the user reactions on social networks. Through the `downdetector.com` application we collected the counts of Twitter feeds containing the keyword "whatsapp", coupled with keywords reflecting service impairments such as "outage", "is down" (i.e.*error tweets*). The main reported outage (event `B`) occurred at around 19:00CEST, but similar outages are observed in the error tweet counts which have the same network traffic signature (`A`, `C` and `D`), i.e., a traffic volume drop and an increase in the flows count. To better drill-down the outage, the figure also depicts a 12-hour-zoom of the TCP flags counters. A steeped increase of the SYN and RST packets indicates that devices were repeatedly trying to reconnect after the servers reset the connections, suggesting that the failure occurred at the application layer.

# 3. REFERENCES

[1] P. Fiadino, et al., "HTTPTag: A Flexible On-line HTTP Classification System for Operational 3G Networks", in *IEEE INFOCOM*, 2013.

[2] I. Bermudez, et al., "DNS to the rescue: Discerning Content and Services in a Tangled Web", in *ACM IMC*, 2012.

[3] A. Bär, et al., "DBStream: an Online Aggregation, Filtering and Processing System for Network Traffic Monitoring", in *TRAC*, 2014.

# Behind the Curtain

## The importance of replica selection in next generation cellular networks

John P. Rula Fabián E. Bustamante
Northwestern University

## 1. INTRODUCTION

Smartdevices are becoming the primary or only Internet point of access for an ever larger fraction of the population. Nearly a quarter of current web traffic is mobile, and recent industry studies have estimated a fourfold increase on global mobile data traffic by 2018, mainly driven by the content demands and growing number of smart phones and tablets [2]. The most recent CISCO VNI report estimates that by 2018, the majority of North America devices and connections will have 4G capability and, while 4G will be 15% of world-wide connections then, these connections will be responsible for 51% of traffic.

Cellular networks pose a challenge to content delivery networks (CDNs) given their opaque network structure, limited number of ingress points, and obfuscated DNS infrastructure. Previously, large cellular radio latencies meant CDN replica selection had little impact on the total end-to-end latency. However, the advancement of 4G networks such as LTE has lowered mobile device access latency to make it comparable with many existing broadband services, making the choice of content replica server a significant contributor to end-to-end performance.

In general, but particularly in cellular networks, CDNs have limited signals for locating clients. Mobile IPs have been shown to be dynamic for mobile end hosts [1], and external entities such as CDNs are prevented from probing their mobile clients or their infrastructure by NAT and firewall policies implemented by cellular operators.

In this poster, we present preliminary work looking at the impact of replica selection in next generation cellular networks. Using a collection of over 250 mobile end-hosts over a two-month period, we explore CDN replica selection in cellular networks measuring the latency to content replicas for a selection of popular mobile websites. We find that clients in next generation radio technologies can see up to 400% differences in latency to selected replicas. We discover that, in large part, these poor selections are due to current localization approaches employed by CDNs such as DNS redirection which, while fairly effective in wired hosts, performs rather poorly within cellular networks mainly due to cellular DNS behavior.


*SIGCOMM'14*, August 17–22, 2014, Chicago, IL, USA.
ACM 978-1-4503-2836-4/14/08.
http://dx.doi.org/10.1145/2619239.2631465.

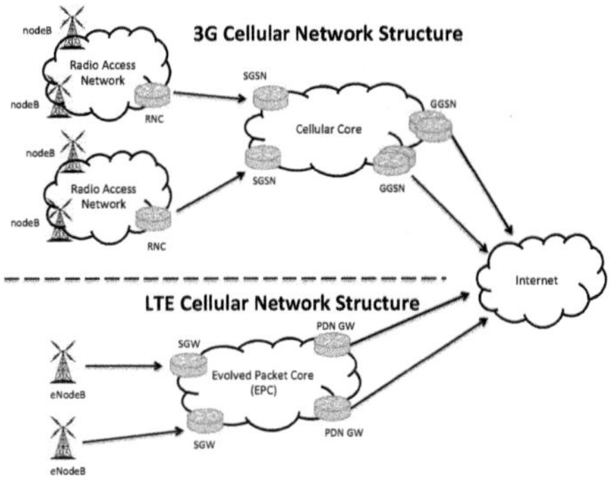


Figure 1: Network architecture evolution from 3G to LTE.

## 2. MOTIVATION

CDNs are responsible for delivering most of today's Internet content, replicating popular content on servers worldwide. CDNs direct users to "nearby" replicas based on the location of users' DNS resolver.

The significantly better performance of next generation cellular networks, like LTE, compared with 2G/3G networks have made content replica selection a significant factor of a mobile user's experience. When compared with 3G networks, 4G LTE offers a flatter network structure and significantly lower radio access latency and variance. For instance, median DNS resolution times for clients on LTE ranged from 30-50ms, while median resolution times for the same clients on 3G networks ranged from 100-200ms. Figure 1 illustrates the difference in network structures between 3G and 4G network architectures, including the elimination of the Radio Network Controller (RNC) which allows a direct link from each cellular tower to the network core.

We observe a wide range of performance diversity of content replicas seen by each client. We measured the HTTP time-to-first-byte to replicas for a collection of websites. By aggregating all replica servers seen by clients in our experiments, and taking the average client latency to each replica, we found the lowest latency replica for each website. All other replicas are shown as a percentage difference between their latency and the "best" seen replica. The cumulative distribution of these ratios is shown in Fig. 2.

While the degree of replica differential performance varies per operator, we consistently found replica latency increases ranging from 50% to 100% in all networks. In an extreme case, we observed replicas with 400% increased latency over the closest observed replica server for clients in Sprint.

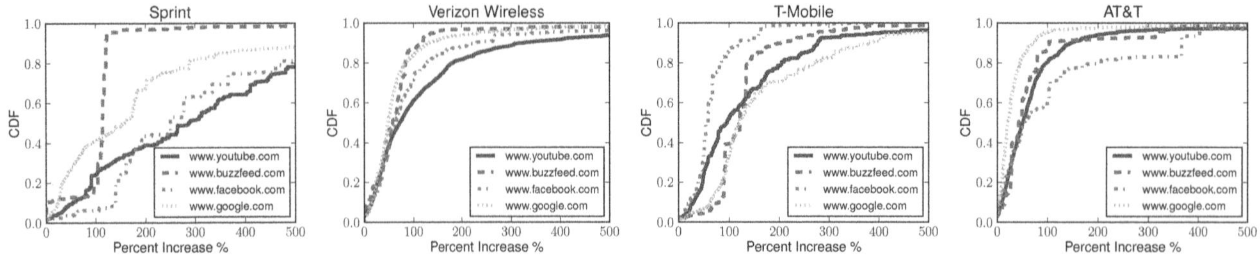


Figure 2: Performance comparison of HTTP time-to-first-byte for replica servers selected for mobile clients. We see cellular users directed toward a wide range of replica servers, with certain servers seeing 400% increased HTTP latency over the closest observed replica.

# 3. CELLULAR DNS BEHAVIOR

Many of the largest CDNs rely on DNS for client location/replica selection in cellular networks. Our results show that cellular DNS makes a poor indicator for client location, due to the opaqueness of cellular resolvers to external services, and the inconsistency between mobile clients and their visible LDNS resolvers.

CDNs typically aggregate client resolvers behind traceroute divergence points and map clients based on measurements to these points. Unlike the majority of DNS resolvers, cellular DNS resolvers are unable to be probed and measured by CDNs. The inability to traceroute the cellular DNS resolvers invalidates this approach.

We discovered inconsistency between mobile clients and their cellular DNS resolvers over time. In other words, a CDN will see the same client originating from different locations, and depending on the extent of DNS load balancing, users can see high variability in the quality and performance of selected content replicas.

The movement of a client's visible DNS resolver is shown in Fig. 3 for users in T-Mobile and AT&T. The figure plots the enumerated LDNS resolvers observed by mobile clients. The blue marks on the bottom plot represent individual IP addresses seen and the red marks on the top represent resolver /24 prefixes observed by the mobile client over time. Surprisingly, many of the different DNS resolvers observed exist in separate /24 prefixes. This shuffling between resolvers in different prefixes is important because we found several CDNs mapping replica servers to resolver /24 prefixes.

# 4. CELL NETWORKS HELP

Our work reveals several hurdles for cellular content delivery. Without the cooperation of cellular operators, CDNs have limited options for locating clients within cellular networks. Previous work has found the temporal inconsistency with cellular client IP addresses [1], and the previous section outlined our findings showing the inconsistency between mobile clients and their visible resolver. Additionally, our findings uncovered inconsistency in anycast addresses, limiting the appeal of anycast CDN services.

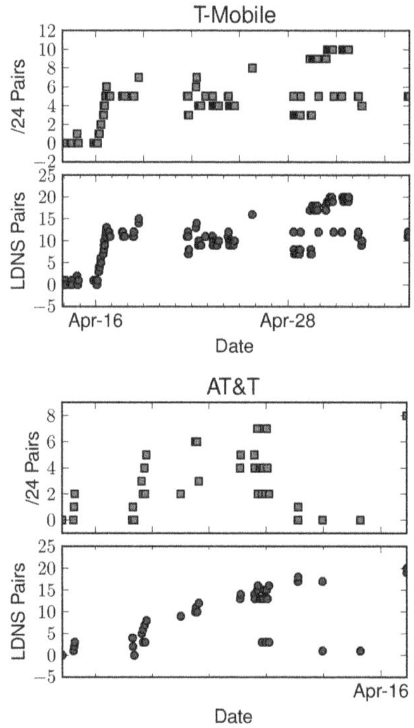


Figure 3: Number of external resolvers observed by a client in AT&T and T-Mobile. Bottom: number of external resolver IP addresses. Top: number of unique /24 prefixes observed by resolvers. Client DNS resolvers change not just within localized clusters, but span multiple /24 prefixes over time.

# 5. REFERENCES

[1] M. Balakrishnan, I. Mohomed, and V. Ramasubramanian. Where's that phone?: geolocating ip addresses on 3g networks. In *Proc. IMC*, 2009.
[2] CISCO. CISCO visual networking index: Global mobile data traffic forecast update 2013-2018. Technical report, CISCO Systems Inc., 2014.
[3] Q. Xu, J. Huang, Z. Wang, F. Qian, and A. G. Z. M. Mao. Cellular data network infrastructure characterization and implication on mobile content placement. In *Proc. ACM SIGMETRICS*, 2011.

# FlowInsight: Decoupling Visibility from Operability in SDN Data Plane

Yuliang Li, Guang Yao, and Jun Bi
Institute for Network Sciences and Cyberspace, Tsinghua University
Department of Computer Science, Tsinghua University
Tsinghua National Laboratory for Information Science and Technology (TNList)
liyuliang001@gmail.com, yaoguang@cernet.edu.cn, junbi@tsinghua.edu.cn

## 1. INTRODUCTION

In most designs of SDN scenarios, there is only one flow table in each switch, e.g. OpenFlow 1.0. Even with the adoption of multiple flow tables in later versions of OpenFlow, this feature is still not widely used.

In the current design of OpenFlow, a controller has two ways to get the view of a flow: 1) the controller passively learns a flow if the flow is mismatched in the flow table; 2) the controller proactively pulls the counters of each rule. If only one flow table is used, whether the controller can see a flow is wholly determined by the flow table, i.e. the visibility is coupled to the operability. However, the coupling has the following problems:

1. **Invisible flows**. The first packet of the flows may be required by some applications to learn the flows, but gets lost due to the limitation of the design. For example (Figure 1(a)), a wildcard rule installed by a forwarding application will mask all the matched micro-flows which should be visible to a firewall application. To ensure every micro-flow can be seen by the controller, Frenetic [2] installs an exact-match rule after each micro-flow's arrival instead of installing wildcard rules in advance, while introducing significant latency in forwarding.

2. **Unnecessary visibility**. The visibility of a part of flows may be unnecessary to any of the applications, but it is provided with extra resource cost or network performance degradation. For example (Figure 1(b)), whenever a load-balance application queries elephant flows from the flow table, all the mice flows are also unnecessarily got[1].

3. **Rule explosion**. Applications may query the counters of the flows, and the queries should be composed with the forwarding policy. However, the composition may cause rule explosion. For example (Figure 1(c)), in a single switch network where the forwarding behavior are only depend on the dstIP, the monitor wants to get the statistics from each srcIP. Separately, The number of rules needed by the forwarding APP and the monitor APP is respective O(n) and

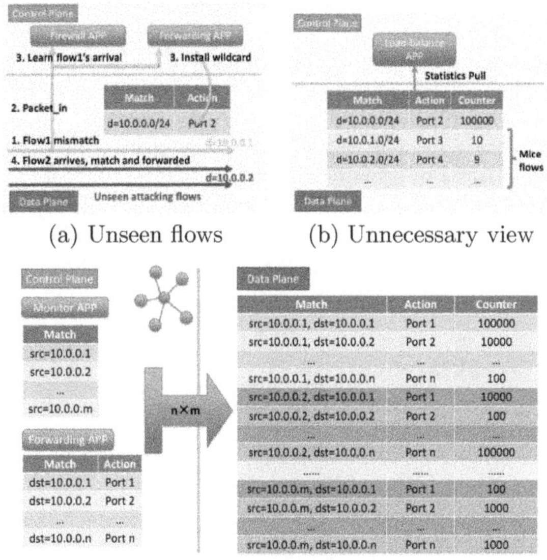


(a) Unseen flows (b) Unnecessary view

(c) Rule explosion

**Figure 1: The problems introduced by the coupling between the visibility and the operability**

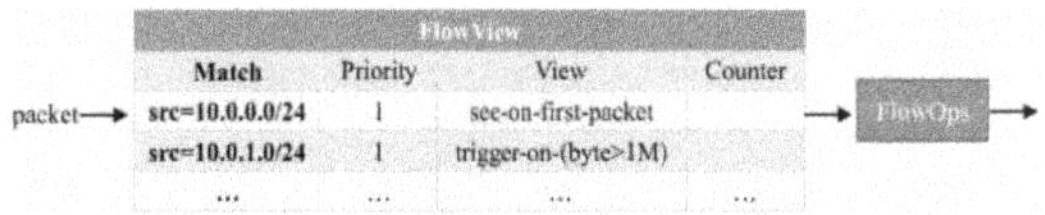


**Figure 2: The architecture of FlowInsight**

O(m). However, when they are composed into one flow table, the number becomes O(nm).

These problems originate from the coupling between the visibility and operability. In this demo, we propose FlowInsight, which separates the provision of visibility and operability. Moreover, we use a 2-stage pipeline of flow tables in OpenFlow 1.3 to implement a prototype, which can naturally solve the rule explosion problem.

## 2. FLOWINSIGHT

### 2.1 Architecture

In the data plane, there are two pipelined tables in FlowInsight: **FlowOps** and **FlowView**. Packets are processed by FlowView and FlowOps sequentially (Figure 2).


*SIGCOMM'14*, August 17–22, 2014, Chicago, IL, USA.
ACM 978-1-4503-2836-4/14/08.
http://dx.doi.org/10.1145/2619239.2631468 .

**FlowOps** determines the operations on each flow. It works the same as traditional flow table, i.e. matches against packets and applies forwarding to matching packets.

**FlowView** defines the flows that should be visibile to the controller. Basically, each rule in FlowView has a match field, a priority, a view field and counters. In the view field, one can specify what kinds of view of the match flow should be provided to the controller. There are two kinds of views:

1. **see-on-first-packet**. The first packet of each microflow which matches a rule with see-on-first-packet should be copied and sent to the controller. For example, in Figure 2, if two flows with respective src=10.0.0.1 and src=10.0.0.2 arrives, both their first packets should be copied and sent to the controller.

2. **trigger-on-condition**. As introduced by DevoFlow [1], the trigger-on-condition is specified with a threshold, and when the counter meets the threshold, the switch should notify the controller. However, in DevoFlow, the triggers are on the forwarding rules, so functionalities like triggers on the aggregate of several flows cannot be achieved, which can be easily achieved in FlowInsight with FlowView.

Additionally, there is another functionality called **query-by-condition**. Applications can query the FlowView with conditions. For example, applications can query flows whose total bytes reach 1M, or it can query the TCP flows whose destination port is 80.

## 2.2 Workflow

When a packet arrives, it is first matched against the rules in the FlowView. The rule with the highest priority updates its counter, and performs the functionalities specified in the view field. Then the packet is matched against the rules in the FlowOps, and is forwarded correspondingly.

The controller can send the query-by-condition to the switches proactively, and the switches should send all flows that meet the condition to the controller upon receiving the query.

## 2.3 How FlowInsight solves the problems

The see-on-first-packet directly solves the invisible flows problem. Because the forwarding action can be installed in FlowOps in advance without interfering the visibility, this will not introduce latency in the forwarding. The trigger-on-condition and query-by-condition together can solve the unnecessary visibility problem associated with flow size. Finally, since the FlowView is independent from FlowOps, the rule explosion problem is naturally solved, as shown in the next section.

# 3. IMPLEMENTATION AND DEMONSTRATION

We use the feature of multi-table pipeline in OpenFlow 1.3 to implement an experiment. Since see-on-first-packet and query-by-condition are not directly supported by OpenFlow 1.3, we leave them to our future work, only having a separate table with counters. Our experiment shows that it can significantly reduce the number of rules compared to the case where only one table is used, so it can solve the rule explosion problem.

In this demo, We perform a case study, where there is only one switch connecting 48 hosts. There are two applications. The first is a learning switch, which learns the <MAC,

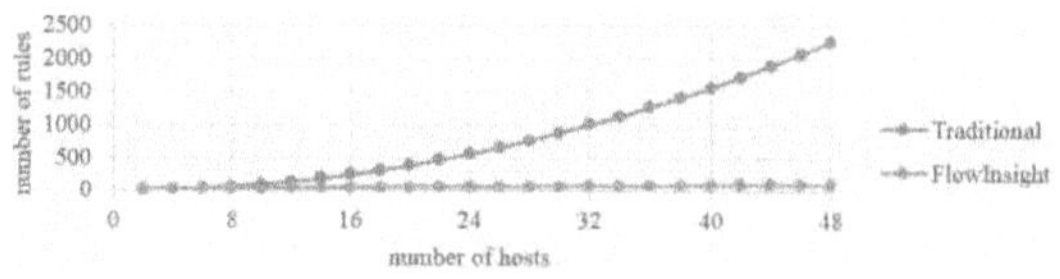


**Figure 3: Comparison of the number of rules between traditional method and FlowInsight**

port> mapping and forwards packets based on the destination MAC address. The second applications is a monitor, which monitors the traffic from each source MAC address every time unit.

In traditional implementation, for each packet <*src*, *dst*> sent to the controller, a corresponding rule with match field <src_MAC=*src*, dst_MAC=*dst*> should be installed. When monitor wants to get the statistics, it should pull all the counters, and groups them by their source addresses. In our implementation, for each packet <*src*, *dst*>, the monitor installs a rule with match field <src_MAC=*src*> in table 0, and the learning switch learns the *in_port* corresponding to the *src* and installs a rule with match field <dst_MAC=*src*> and action field <output_port=*in_port*> in table 1. When monitor wants to get the statistics, it should pull all the counters in table 0.

We tested the number of rules used with different number of hosts in mininet. The result is shown in Figure 3. The number of rules needed by traditional method grows quadratically with the number of hosts. Our methods reduces it down to linear growth.

# 4. CONCLUSION

Our contributions are, 1) presenting the problems introduced by the coupling between the visibility and the operability in the data plane, 2) proposing FlowInsight to solve the problems, and 3) implementing with OpenFlow 1.3 to show the feasibility and effectiveness of our method. In the future, we plan to add other functionalities to fully solve the problems.

## Acknowledgment


This work is supported by the National High-tech R & D Program ("863" Program) of China(No.2013AA013505), the National Science Foundation of China (No.61161140454), National Science & Technology Pillar Program of China (No.2012BAH01B01), the National Science Foundation of China (No. 61303194), and the China Postdoctoral Science Foundation (No.2013M530047). Jun Bi is the corresponding author.


# 5. REFERENCES


[1] A. R. Curtis, J. C. Mogul, J. Tourrilhes, P. Yalagandula, P. Sharma, and S. Banerjee. Devoflow: Scaling flow management for high-performance networks. In *Proc. SIGCOMM*, 2011.

[2] N. Foster, R. Harrison, M. J. Freedman, C. Monsanto, J. Rexford, A. Story, and D. Walker. Frenetic: A network programming language. In *ACM ICFP*, 2011.

# A Cliq of Content Curators

Angela H. Jiang
Northwestern University

Zachary S. Bischof
Northwestern University

Fabian E. Bustamante
Northwestern University

## ABSTRACT

A social news site presents user-curated content, ranked by popularity. Popular curators like Reddit, or Facebook have become effective way of crowdsourcing news or sharing for personal opinions. Traditionally, these services require a centralized authority to aggregate data and determine what to display. However, the trust issues that arise from a centralized system are particularly damaging to the "Web democracy" that social news sites are meant to provide.

In this poster, we present **cliq**, a decentralized social news curator. cliq is a P2P based social news curator that provides private and unbiased reporting. All users in cliq share responsibility for tracking and providing popular content. Any user data that cliq needs to store is also managed across the network. We first inform our design of cliq through an analysis of Reddit. We design a way to provide content curation without a persistent moderator, or usernames.

## Categories and Subject Descriptors

C.2.4 [**Communication Systems Organization**]: Distributed Systems

## Keywords

P2P systems, social news curation

## 1. MOTIVATION

Unlike other media, content shown on social media sites is determined by a "Web democracy", open to anyone. However, the trust issues that arise from a centralized system are particularly damaging to this goal. Users must accept that owners of these sites have the power to present content aligned with their own agenda. For example, BBC news recently reported that moderators of the subreddit "technology" were censoring posts that included banned words such as "bitcoin" or "net neutrality"[1].

[1] `http://www.bbc.com/news/technology-27100773`


*SIGCOMM'14,* August 17–22, 2014, Chicago, IL, USA.
ACM 978-1-4503-2836-4/14/08.
http://dx.doi.org/10.1145/2619239.2631470.

Further, centralized management of user data leads to concerns of personal information being sold or intruded upon. In recent years, citizens have learned of government programs in multiple countries that crawl the web and archive information off of such websites. In fact, there exist multiple public services that given a username, scrape reddit and analyze the user's behavior; even showing the topics most participated in and "Fun Guessed Data" such as if the user supports Occupy Wall Street[2]. Oppressive governments may act on such data, tracking individuals. Such a threat can affect a user's willingness to share content that is political or controversial.

An effective, fair and safe Web democracy should (*i*) present content that is relevant to the user's interests and (*ii*) popular, be (*iii*) resilience to biased reporting and (*iv*) to user data aggregation. Existing social news sites have provided an effective way to accomplish the first two goals. However, their centralized nature raises concerns about content bias and users privacy. cliq leverages the anonymity and autonomy that a decentralized systems provides to fulfill these additional requirements.

## 2. CLIQ ARCHITECTURE

We now present the design of cliq, a fully-distributed social news site. By using a P2P model, the responsibility of tracking content and popularity is randomly distributed among peers. We remove the need for a (potentially biased) dedicated moderator. To provide anonymity, Cliq users do not have usernames. Any user information collected is distributed among random nodes and will naturally expire as the network experiences churn. A fully decentralized user content curator, however, presents its own challenges.

### 2.1 Managing content

We organize content through cliq similarly to what is common in most social news sites; each post is associated with one or more category tags (e.g. politics, sports, or travel). We build cliq over Kademlia [1] a popular DHT. In the DHT, nodes use content tags as keys to store and find content in the network. For each tag, a subset of nodes with similar IDs are collectively responsible for managing its content. These duties include storing, ranking and disseminating links uploaded by users with that tag, as well as monitoring for malicious nodes.

[2] `http://www.redditinvestigator.com/`

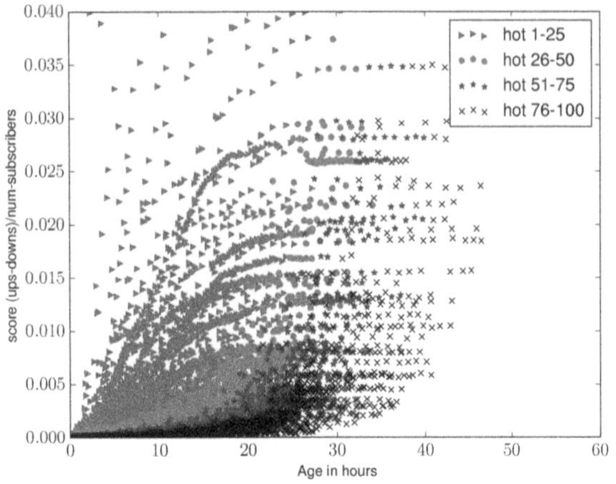


**Figure 1: Popular posts on Politics subreddit. Quartiles correspond to each of the first 4 pages of the subreddit.**

## 2.2 Load on users

As with any P2P system, we need to consider the potential load placed on cliq users. To do this, we monitor and measure activity on the social news site, reddit. We choose reddit because of its popularity (ranked 61 globally on Alexa) and very active user base.

Reddit is organized into user-created, topic-based "subreddit" communities. Subreddits serve a similar function that tags do in cliq. We look at the distribution of the sizes of the most popular subreddits. Among over 300,000 subreddits, only 212 have over 100,000 subscribers. 12 subreddits have over 1,000,000. Although the rate of activity is small compared to the number of subscribers, we find that average sized subreddits (>100,000 subscribers) can expect a popular post to gain thousands of votes within two days. We therefore expect to perform dynamic load balancing in cliq to account for a large variance in tag activity.

## 2.3 Determining popularity

In order to find an effective way for ranking content, we analyze popular posts of multiple subreddits. Here, popular posts refers to content on the first four pages (100 posts) of a subreddit. We find that popularity of reddit posts are strongly correlated with age of the post and it's voting score. Fig. 1 shows the age and score (normalized by the subreddit size) of popular posts of the "Politics" subreddit. Among the 100 most popular posts, we rarely see posts older than two days. This is fairly consistent among subreddits with over 100,000 subscribers.

However, ranking by score is not as straightforward, especially in cliq. Cliq tags differ from subreddits in that posts can be linked to multiple tags. However, we find that unnormalized scores of popular content vary drastically between subreddits. Therefore, a clliq node keeps track of a post's score and how many times it has shown this post to users. In effect, we rank posts by their "approval rate" rather than raw score to account for varying amounts of exposure. This feature will also be important to cliq's resilience to spam.

## 2.4 Resilience to spam

Without registered users or the vantage point of a centralized system, we cannot use traditional methods of detecting spammers. Instead, we take advantage of the fact that in the Kademlia P2P model, a node will be routed to a tag along the same nodes each time. Nodes along this path can collectively enforce good behavior from the users. For example, each node can store the set of IPs it has personally seen promote each link. If a user attempts to promote the same URL multiple times, the request will be dropped. Many of the randomly selected nodes along the path would need to be malicious to allow a single IP post many times. Promoters would not have to be shared among nodes but to further preserve privacy, storing promoters can be done probabilistically.

## 2.5 Replication

As we previously saw, nodes need to be able to dynamically offload responsibilities to other nodes. In cliq, a node can request a neighbor to replicate its most popular content. Therefore, when looking for content, a user is more likely to find popular posts. However, a malicious node could easily spam cliq with the ability to direct others to replicate arbitrary data. To account for this, if a node is asked to replicate data, it does not do so immediately. It first waits until it personally receives an upvote for the link to verify that it is indeed popular content.

Upon replicating, approval rating of the post starts back at 0. Therefore, even if enough nodes are colluding to induce replication, we would still not expect the post to get popular. Meanwhile, a post which is actually a trending will be able to regain its high ratio quickly.


# 3. ACKNOWLEDGEMENTS

This work is supported in part through NSF awards CNS 1211375 and CNS 1218287. The authors thank Andrew Kahn for his help implementing our first prototype of cliq.


# 4. REFERENCES


[1] P. Maymounkov and D. Mazieres. Kademlia: A peer-to-peer information system based on the xor metric. In *Proceeding IPTPS '01 Revised Papers from the First International Workshop on Peer-to-Peer Systems*, 2001.

# Native Actors: How to Scale Network Forensics

Matthias Vallentin
UC Berkeley
vallentin@cs.berkeley.edu

Dominik Charousset
HAW Hamburg
dcharousset@acm.org

Thomas C. Schmidt
HAW Hamburg
t.schmidt@ieee.org

Vern Paxson
ICSI / UC Berkeley
vern@icir.org

Matthias Wählisch
FU Berlin
waehlisch@ieee.org

## ABSTRACT

When an organization detects a security breach, it undertakes a forensic analysis to figure out what happened. This investigation involves inspecting a wide range of heterogeneous data sources spanning over a long period of time. The iterative nature of the analysis procedure requires an interactive experience with the data. However, the distributed processing paradigms we find in practice today fail to provide this requirement: the batch-oriented nature of MapReduce cannot deliver sub-second round-trip times, and distributed in-memory processing cannot store the terabytes of activity logs needed to inspect during an incident.

We present the design and implementation of Visibility Across Space and Time (VAST), a distributed database to support interactive network forensics, and `libcppa`, its exceptionally scalable messaging core. The extended actor framework `libcppa` enables VAST to distribute lightweight tasks at negligible overhead. In our live demo, we showcase how VAST enables security analysts to grapple with the huge amounts of data often associated with incident investigations.

## Keywords

Security, Network Forensics, Message-oriented Middleware

## 1. INTRODUCTION

Network forensics and incident response require prompt investigation and reaction to minimize the damage incurred by a security breach. When security analysts explore an incident, they typically need to access data from a large time span to determine scope and breadth of the attack.

The sheer volume of data to investigate during this process largely exceeds both storage and processing capacities of single-machine system architectures. In addition, analysts conducting forensics explore data in an extensive, iterative fashion, dynamically generating numerous queries as they work to pinpoint the salient evidence. Such an interactive process fits poorly to distributed approaches such as MapReduce architected around batch-oriented processing. Distributed in-memory cluster computing, which can provide quick response times, requires the entire data set to fit in memory—likewise infeasible when faced with the terabytes of data that logging at a large site produces every day.

Because no existing architecture suits the needs of this domain, we set out to design and implement a scalable, interactive platform. We compose our fully distributed system of lightweight, native actors embodied in the `libcppa` programming environment. The system, *visibility across space and time* (VAST), unifies in a single framework retrospective data analysis and proactive measures to automatically apply previously developed queries to events that may occur in the future [1].

Our demo showcases how VAST achieves the required performance and interactivity with real-world data. We give visitors the opportunity to see and interact with the system to better understand the nature of forensic network security analysis.

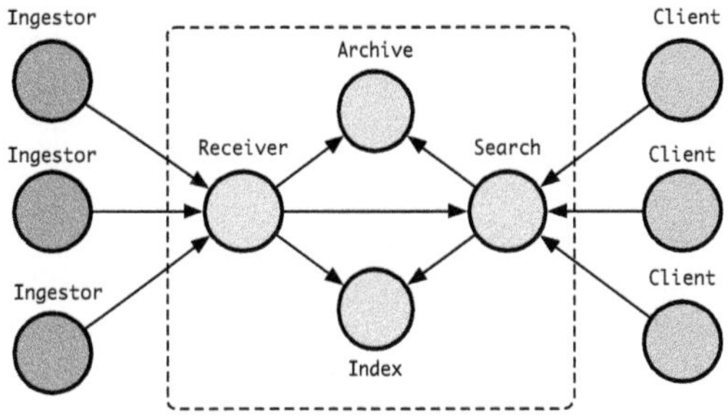


**Figure 1: VAST architecture based on actors (circles). Data enters the system through Ingestors and clients send queries to retrieve activities. Processing happens in the VAST core (dashed box) and scales over a cluster of commodity machines.**

## 2. SCALABLE FORENSICS

Scaling network forensics to terabyte volumes while retaining an interactive user experience requires a robust software infrastructure that proves highly scalable.

### 2.1 An Actor-based Architecture

Current heterogeneous compute environments can be fully exploited with a runtime abstraction that *(i)* harnesses available parallelism within a single machine, *(ii)* facilitates clus-


*SIGCOMM'14*, August 17–22, 2014, Chicago, Illinois, USA.
ACM 978-1-4503-2836-4/14/08.
http://dx.doi.org/10.1145/2619239.2631471.

ter deployments while providing a type-safe messaging layer with minimal memory usage, and *(iii)* can offload expensive computation to specialized hardware (such as GPUs). With `libcppa`,[1] we contribute an actor library that satisfies these needs. This C++ distribution layer is tailored to high-performance applications and has demonstrated superior performance [2]. The environment provides a programming paradigm based on the actor model [3]. In this model, concurrent entities—actors—execute independently and in parallel. Using unique, location-independent addresses, actors communicate asynchronously via message passing, and do not share state. The `libcppa` runtime system can distribute actors dynamically—even on GPUs—to balance work load. The actor model—originated in 1973—has gained momentum with the advent of multicore machines and cloud computing. Today, actor systems can be found in back-end software of large service providers such as eBay.[2] `libcppa` is the first native, open source framework that scales up to GPGPU-enhanced clusters and down to the IoT.

## 2.2 The VAST System

VAST employs `libcppa` as a central part of its design, and structures its logic entirely in terms of actors. Figure 1 shows a high-level overview of the system. Data arrives from a variety of different sources. The INGESTOR actor parses the input and transforms the data into VAST's internal event model before compressing it into *segments* and shipping it to VAST's core over the network. To allow for flexible deployment scenarios, the core may run on a single box as well as on a cluster of commodity machines, enabled by `libcppa`'s network-transparent messaging layer. The data segments arrive at the RECEIVER actor, which assigns the segment a unique identifier from a 64-bit ID space and then forwards it to ARCHIVE (a key-value store of compressed data segments) and INDEX (a horizontally partitioned array of type-specific bitmap indexes [4]). After decompressing the segment, the indexing process starts multiple worker actors, each of which process a slice of the contained events. Because `libcppa` uses copy-on-write semantics for intra-process messages, the workers can share the same (immutable) data safely. The high degree of concurrency enables single-machine ingestion rates of 100K events/sec and index construction rates of 50-200K events/sec, varying based on the data type to index (e.g., booleans vs. containers of values).

Clients request specific events by formulating boolean expressions. For example, the query

```
:addr in 10.0.0.0/8 && conn.proto == "udp"
```

would match all events containing an IP address from the subnet 10.0.0.0/8 with transport protocol UDP. Both predicates in this conjunction are strongly typed and the LHS and RHS must have compatible types. In the example above, the LHS of the first predicate represents a *type query* that applies to all events containing one or more values of type `address`. The LHS of the second predicate represents a *schema query* and refers to specific value (or set of values) that resolve according to `conn.proto`, where `conn` represents the event type and `proto` the name of the data value. VAST autogenerates schemas during data ingestion. In the future, we will allow operators to manually define their own schemas to perform explicit type conversions (e.g., to parse string values as IP addresses) and augment values with domain-specific semantics (e.g., label IP address values as connection originator and responder).

When a query enters the core, SEARCH performs syntactic and semantic checks against the schema and then forwards the parsed query AST to INDEX, which performs the query upon the relevant partitions. Each predicate yields a separate index hit, which INDEX combines asynchronously as they arrive. The index hits serve as pointers into the events located at ARCHIVE. A dedicated QUERY actor started by SEARCH receives hits, asks ARCHIVE for the corresponding segments, decompresses the received segments into events, checks for candidate matches (if the indexing cannot provide guaranteed matches for a given operator), and sends the matches back to CLIENT.

VAST currently comprises 25K lines code, available open-source under a BSD-style license.[3] In the near-term future, we plan to deploy and use VAST operationally at the Lawrence Berkeley National Laboratory.

# 3. DEMO

In our demonstration, we showcase how operators investigate security incidents in real time. Moreover, we allow attendees to interact with the system and ask their own queries.

Specifically, we illustrate typical workflows of security analysts. These often begin with a piece of intelligence (e.g., a sensitive URI, an IP address of a compromised machine, an MD5 hash of a file), which serves as starting point for an interactive, iterative search. Through refinement of search criteria, the analyst converges on a relevant set of events that isolate the activity germane to the incident.

Our VAST instance runs remotely and contains hundred of millions of events produced by the Bro network monitor [5], covering a time span of several months. We will show that interactive analysis with distributed actors is feasible for such numbers.

# 4. REFERENCES


[1] ALLMAN, M., KREIBICH, C., PAXSON, V., SOMMER, R., AND WEAVER, N. Principles for developing comprehensive network visibility. In *Proc. of Workshop on Hot Topics in Security (HotSec)* (July 2008).

[2] CHAROUSSET, D., SCHMIDT, T. C., HIESGEN, R., AND WÄHLISCH, M. Native Actors – A Scalable Software Platform for Distributed, Heterogeneous Environments. In *Proc. 4rd ACM SIGPLAN Conf. on Systems, Programming, and Applications (SPLASH '13), WS AGERE!* (Oct. 2013), ACM.

[3] HEWITT, C., BISHOP, P., AND STEIGER, R. A Universal Modular ACTOR Formalism for Artificial Intelligence. In *Proceedings of the 3rd IJCAI* (San Francisco, CA, USA, 1973), pp. 235–245.

[4] O'NEIL, P. E. Model 204 Architecture and Performance. In *Proceedings of the 2nd International Workshop on High Performance Transaction Systems* (London, UK, 1987), Springer-Verlag, pp. 40–59.

[5] PAXSON, V. Bro: A System for Detecting Network Intruders in Real-Time. *Computer Networks 31*, 23–24 (1999), 2435–2463.


[1] `http://libcppa.org`

[2] `http://www.ebaytechblog.com/2014/03/11`

[3] `https://www.github.com/mavam/vast`

# SOUP: An Online Social Network By The People, For The People

David Koll
University of Göttingen
Göttingen, Germany
koll@cs.uni-goettingen.de

Jun Li
University of Oregon
Eugene, USA
lijun@cs.uoregon.edu

Xiaoming Fu
University of Göttingen
Göttingen, Germany
fu@cs.uni-goettingen.de

## ABSTRACT

With increasing frequency, users raise concerns about data privacy and protection in centralized Online Social Networks (OSNs), in which providers have the unprecedented privilege to access and exploit every user's private data at will. To mitigate these concerns, researchers have suggested to decentralize OSNs and thereby enable users to control and manage access to their data themselves. However, previously proposed decentralization approaches suffer from several drawbacks. To tackle their deficiencies, we introduce the Self-Organized Universe of People (SOUP). In this demonstration, we present a prototype of SOUP and share our experiences from a real-world deployment.

## Categories and Subject Descriptors

C.2.4 [**Computer Systems Organization**]: Computer Communication Networks—*Distributed Systems*

## Keywords

DOSN; online social networks; decentralization

## 1. WHY DO WE NEED SOUP?

As online social network (OSN) providers deal with tremendous amounts of user information, they can obtain deep insights into their users' personal communication, interests, opinions, and social relationships, which raises severe privacy and security concerns. Facebook, for example, has passed the one billion user mark and controls data of roughly one sixth of the world's population. Still, the hunt for user data is not over, as showcased by the recent acquisitions of WhatsApp and Instagram in multi-billion dollar agreements.

While it remains to be seen whether OSN providers would give up a major source of income and grant comprehensive security and privacy means to their users, decentralized OSNs (DOSNs) pave a promising way for better user data security and privacy. Instead of relying on a central data repository, a DOSN can allow users to regain control over their data. For instance, they can encrypt their data and enforce access control to it according to their own need, and then distribute the data to specifically chosen storage sites.

However, recently proposed DOSNs introduce new shortcomings, ranging from limited success in providing high data availability to insufficient robustness, high management overhead, discrimination of users, a dependency on certain nodes, lack of data encryption, and deployability issues [3]. To address these drawbacks, we introduce a different DOSN approach called Self-Organized Universe of People (SOUP). In short, we provide the following contributions:

1) To achieve high data availability, we propose a new, generic approach to storing user data in a DOSN. In addition to enabling every user to store their data at their own machine, our mechanism selects other OSN participants as mirrors for the user's data to make the data highly available, even if the owner herself is offline. SOUP does not rely on permanently available storage, although it can make an opportunistic use of such resources as they become available by quickly spreading relevant information among users.

2) To provide a robust OSN, SOUP ensures that regardless of participants' social relations or online probabilities, data for *all* participants is highly available. Whereas previous works often limit a user in her mirror selection, we allow each user to select as many mirrors as required to make her data available. At the same time, SOUP ensures that there exist no more replicas than required to limit the overhead.

3) To achieve reliability and resiliency, SOUP is designed to be adaptive to the dynamics often seen in a DOSN. It can quickly respond to changes in the system and continue to provide high performance by favoring more recent observations in the network. Moreover, its operation is not significantly affected by malicious OSN users, as it can tolerate up to half of the links in the OSN being compromised.

4) To grant data privacy, SOUP offers effective encryption mechanisms based on Attribute Based Encryption [2], so that only eligible users can access (parts of) the data.

*A key component of SOUP that is critical to substantiate these contributions is how we select nodes as mirrors while addressing the critical challenges revealed by previous works. The selection process exploits recommendations and mirror feedback among friends to find the best suited mirrors for each user. We describe the procedure in detail in [3].*

## 2. SOUP IN A NUTSHELL

Nodes (or users) in SOUP form a structured overlay, as shown in Figure 1. The overlay acts as an information directory and is based on a distributed hash table (DHT). The DHT enables efficient publish and lookup operations


*SIGCOMM'14,* August 17–22, 2014, Chicago, IL, USA.
ACM 978-1-4503-2836-4/14/08.
http://dx.doi.org/10.1145/2619239.2631432 .

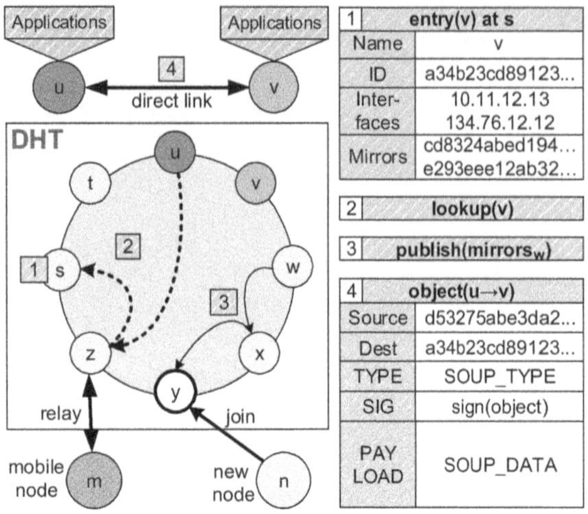


*Figure 1:* SOUP Design Overview

in a decentralized fashion, making a centralized information repository unnecessary. After joining the DHT via a bootstrapping node (e.g., $y$ in Fig. 1), every SOUP user can publish her directory entry at the node responsible for her ID in the DHT key space (e.g., $v$'s entry is published at $s$—Step 1 in Fig. 1), and any other node retrieve the entry (e.g., $u$ can look up $v$'s ID—Step 2). An entry contains a user's username, her unique SOUP ID, the interfaces via which she can currently be contacted, and the SOUP IDs of all the mirrors of her data.

Note, that a user only publishes a *pointer* (i.e., SOUP ID) to mirror nodes in the DHT (e.g., $w$ publishes the mirrors at $y$—Step 3), whereas her data—protected by encryption and access control—is stored among nodes themselves. Storing the data in the DHT would result in a high management overhead in the presence of OSN typical churn rates [1]. Instead, every user maintains its own data, and selects a small set of other nodes as mirrors to store a replica of its data, in order to keep its data available even when it is offline. Data replication is necessary, as SOUP does not rely on a central repository and users are not permanently online.

If a user wants to communicate with another user, she looks up the partner's entry and extracts the addressable interfaces to create a direct communication channel. The communication partners ($u$ and $v$ in Fig. 1) then exchange signed *SOUP objects*, which contain the OSN data (Step 4).

SOUP is also designed to be friendly to mobile nodes. As mobile nodes often experience high churn and long response times [1], SOUP exempts mobile nodes from the DHT and relays their DHT requests through relay nodes, which not only increases the stability of the DHT, but also saves resources at the mobile nodes.

On top of a SOUP node, applications will exploit the aforementioned features. SOUP provides a generic API to applications, and multiple applications can run concurrently on top of SOUP and share the same user data.

## 3. DEPLOYMENT EXPERIENCE

For both desktop and mobile Android devices we implemented (1) a SOUP middleware implementing the functionality shown in Figure 1 and (2) a demo application that uses SOUP and provides the user with a GUI. We show the interplay of the components in Figure 2. The demo application can create arbitrary application content, which is then encapsulated into SOUP objects before being transmitted to its destination, and thereby remains transparent to the

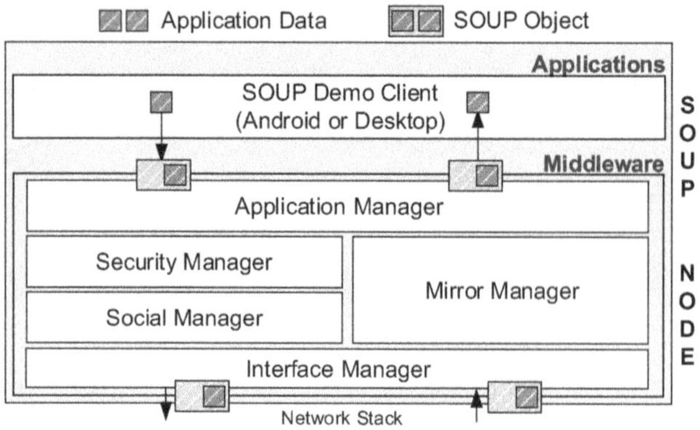


*Figure 2:* Implementation of a SOUP Node

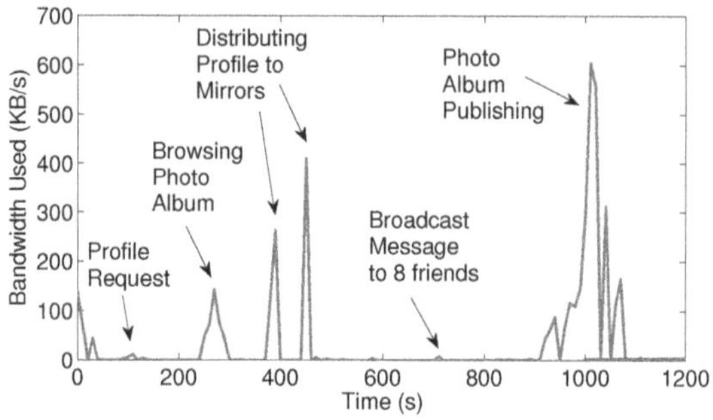


*Figure 3:* SOUP Bandwidth Consumption

middleware. Upon receiving application data, the reverse process is executed. As the underlying DHT, we use FreePastry.[1] Most of our code is available online.[2]

We have deployed our prototype in a real-world DOSN consisting of 31 devices of which four were Android devices. Figure 3 shows the most bandwidth-intense 20 minutes we observed for any user during multiple days of data collection. Messaging activities or simple profile requests are hardly distinguishable from an idle link. More intense features such as skipping through a photo album of a friend do not consume a regular user's bandwidth as well, as she takes her time to view the pictures. Note, that the traffic a user generates by *consuming* content is the same as in centralized OSNs, as the user needs to download the data in those systems as well. Only when *producing* content or acting as a mirror, SOUP generates additional traffic. As a consequence, in Figure 3, the link is most utilized is at the creation of a photo album, as the data has to be distributed to the mirrors as well.

## 4. REFERENCES

[1] BENEVENUTO, F., RODRIGUES, T., CHA, M., AND ALMEIDA, V. Characterizing User Behavior in Online Social Networks. In *IMC '09*.

[2] BETHENCOURT, J., SAHAI, A., AND WATERS, B. Ciphertext-Policy Attribute-Based Encryption. In *IEEE SP '07*.

[3] KOLL, D., LI, J., AND FU, X. With a Little Help From my Friends: Replica Placement in Decentralized Online Social Networks. *Technical Report IFI-TB-2013-01, Institute of Computer Science, University of Goettingen, Germany* (2013).

[1]http://www.freepastry.org

[2]http://soup.informatik.uni-goettingen.de/

# AI3: Application-Independent Information Infrastructure

Bo Zhang[1], Jinfan Wang[1], Xinyu Wang[1], Yingying Cheng[1], Xiaohua Jia[1], Jianfei He[2]
[1]City University of Hong Kong
[1]{bo.zhang, jfwang4, xinywang, yincheng, csjia}@cityu.edu.hk
[2]Huawei Technologies Co. Ltd.
[2]jeffrey.he@huawei.com

## ABSTRACT

In the current Internet architecture, application service providers (ASPs) own users' data and social groups information, which made a handful of ASP companies growing bigger and bigger and denied small and medium companies from entering this business. We propose a new architecture, called Application Independent Information Infrastructure (AI3). The design goals of AI3 are: 1) Decoupling users' data from ASPs and users' social relations from ASPs, such that ASPs become independent from users' data and social relations. 2) Open architecture, such that different ASPs can interoperate with each other. This demo is to show a prototype of AI3. The demo has four parts: 1) ASP-independent data management in AI3; 2) ASP-independent management of users' social relations in AI3; 3) inter-domain data transport and user roaming; 4) real-time communications by using AI3. The demo video can be watched at: `http://www.cs.cityu.edu.hk/~jia/AI3_DemoVideo.mp4`

## Categories and Subject Descriptors

C2.1 [**Network Architecture and Design**]: Network communications

## Keywords

Internet architecture, network infrastructure, storage system

## 1. INTRODUCTION

Fueled up by the explosive growth of social networks in recent years, User Generated Contents (UGC), such as videos, photos, and blogs, have become a dominant source of Internet traffic. The constant efforts of developing new Internet architectures have led to several projects for information dissemination, sharing and networking. The well-known projects [1, 2, 3, 4] include Information-centric networking (ICN), Named Data Networks (NDN), and PURSUIT. However, these systems focused on efficient content discovery and data transportation by using routing and caching technologies. The issues of ownership of UGC and management of UGC have been largely overlooked and not been addressed adequately. In the current setting, application service providers (ASPs), such as Facebook, Twitter, Tencent, etc., own users' data and manage the information about users' social groups, which made a handful of ASP companies growing bigger and bigger and denied small and medium companies from entering this business. There are several major problems with this structure of ASPs: 1) The ASPs use users' data and social relations to hijack the users to go with them, leaving users with little choice. 2) Users can only publish their data within the ASP that they registered with and the data cannot be shared by friends crossing different ASPs. 3) User's social groups are fragmented by ASPs and the members of a user's social group are often scattered among several ASPs.

We propose a new architecture, called Application Independent Information Infrastructure (AI3). There are two design goals of AI3:

1) Decoupling users' data and users' social relations from ASPs, such that ASPs become independent from users' data and social relations. The ownership of users' data and information of social groups are returned back to the users and managed by the AI3 architecture. ASPs become the ordinary applications on top of AI3, which breaks down the monopoly of a few giant ASPs and provides small companies a leveled ground to compete with them in business.

2) Open architecture, such that different ASPs can interoperate with each other. Users publish information no longer with a specific ASP, they publish information to their social groups. Once a user publishes a message to a social group through an ASP, all members in this social group can receive the message no matter which ASPs they registered with. The openness of the architecture also means the interoperation among different network domains, which facilitates roaming functions of users and automatic data migration across network domains.

## 2. AI3 ARCHITECTURE OVERVIEW

The overview of AI3 is described in Fig.1. There are two layers in the architecture, information layer and presentation layer.

Information layer is the core of AI3, which is responsible for data storage, access control and distribution. These functions are supported by a system called versatile storage system (VSS). In VSS system, each user has his own storage to store his data and social relations. Standard APIs are provided to the presentation layer, which allows the ASPs and user applications (APPs) to operate on user's social


*SIGCOMM'14*, August 17–22, 2014, Chicago, Illinois, USA.
ACM 978-1-4503-2836-4/14/08.
http://dx.doi.org/10.1145/2619239.2631424.

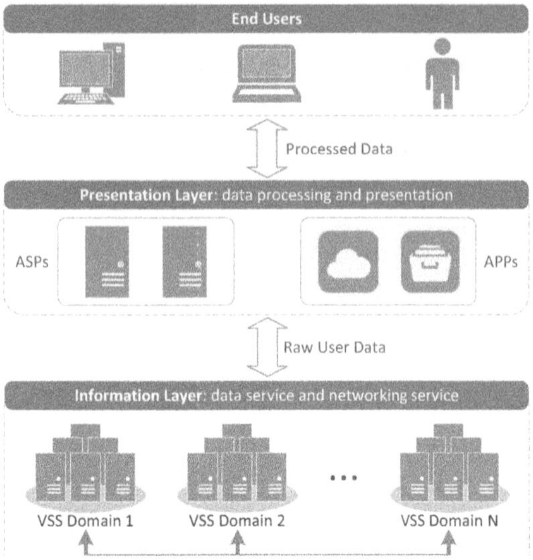


**Figure 1: The Architecture of AI3.**

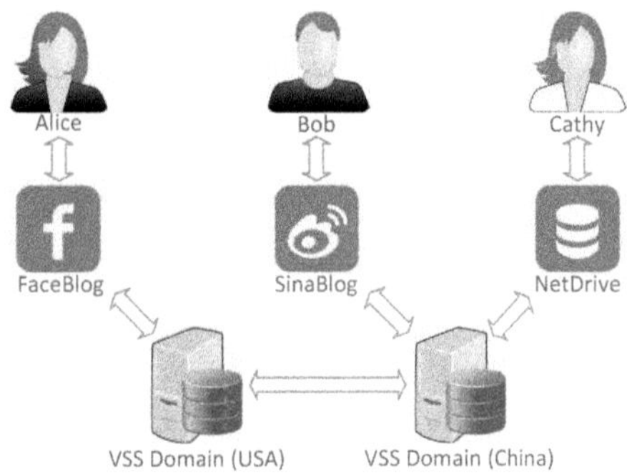


**Figure 2: The Demonstration Scenario.**

relations, and subscribe from and publish data to targeted social groups. To support the openness, AI3 also provides a standard inter-domain interface to allow interconnection between domains operated by different organizations. Users can move freely from one domain to another without affecting their data access experience and users from different domains can communicate seamlessly. Another design goal of AI3 is to make it as the infrastructure of data communication networks which support data transmission, inter-person real-time communication and data management. It integrates both data service and networking service into a versatile file service upon which various network applications can be built.

The presentation layer consists of the ASPs and APPs. These ASPs (or APPs) make use of the data obtained from the information layer, and provide a variety of services to the end users. Since users' data and social relations are decoupled from ASPs, all ASPs have to compete with each other to win users by providing high quality and innovative services.

# 3. DEMONSTRATION

Fig.2 shows the demonstration scenario. In this demo, there are three end users: Alice, Bob and Cathy, and three ASPs: FaceBlog, SinaBlog and NetDrive. We consider two VSS domains, one in USA and the other in China. There are four parts of the demo: 1) how AI3 decouples users' social relations from ASPs; 2) how AI3 decouples users' data from ASPs; 3) how AI3 enables the VSS systems operated by different organizations to cooperate with each other; and 4) how AI3 support real-time inter-person communication.

*A. ASP-Independent User Relations Management.* In this part of demo, Alice in FaceBlog follows Bob who uses a different ASP, say SinaBlog. Although Bob uses a different ASP from Alice, he can still see Alice becomes his fan from his own ASP. This is because all users' social relations are managed by AI3 and decoupled from the ASPs. ASPs use standard interface provided by AI3 to operate on users' social relations.

*B. ASP-Independent Data Management.* In this section of demo, Cathy shares a photo to public through a file management app - NetDrive. All her followers, say Alice and Bob, can see the photo in their own ASPs, such as FaceBlog and SinaBlog, even though they do not use NetDrive. This is because all users' data are managed by AI3 and are decoupled from the ASPs. These data are solely owned and controlled by the user. Once the user deletes the data, all references of the data that were published in multiple ASPs will be completely removed throughout the entire network.

*C. Inter-domain Data Transport and User Roaming.* In this subsection, we demonstrate that two users registered at different VSS domains communicate with each other, and roam to the other domains seamlessly without feeling performance degradation. The inter-domain communications are handled by AI3 inter-domain interface, and they are transparent to the end users. Data pre-caching technique is employed to ensure the seamless roaming of users across domains.

*D. Real-time Inter-person Communication.* In this part, we demonstrate real-time inter-person communications in AI3 architecture. Two users, Alice and Bob, make a video conference call by using the app VideoChat in presentation layer of AI3. The real-time video traffic is temporally stored at and relayed by a VSS system that is close to both users. The users can also archive the streaming data into their personal storage.

# 4. CONCLUSION

AI3 decouples ASPs from users' data and users' social relations. With AI3 architecture, ASPs can focus on developing more innovative applications and providing better quality services to win user groups. AI3 also integrates file services with traditional networking services. This is a good structure to support user's mobility and to implement architecture-wide information security.

# 5. REFERENCES


[1] PURSUIT: Publish subscribe internet technology. URL: http://www.fp7-pursuit.eu/PursuitWeb/.

[2] B. Ahlgren et al. Second NetInf architecture description. *4WARD EU FP7 Project, Deliverable D-6.2 v2. 0*, 2010.

[3] V. Jacobson et al. Networking named content. In *Proc. CoNEXT 09*, pages 1–12, New York, NY, USA, 2009.

[4] T. Koponen et al. A data-oriented (and beyond) network architecture. In *Proc. SIGCOMM 07*, pages 181–192, New York, USA, 2007.

# Robust Full Duplex Radio Link

Dinesh Bharadia
Stanford University
dineshb@stanford.edu

Kiran Raj Joshi
Stanford University
krjoshi@stanford.edu

Sachin Katti
Stanford University
skatti@stanford.edu

## ABSTRACT

This paper presents demonstration of a real-time full duplex point-to-point link, where transmission and reception occurs in the same spectrum band simultaneously between a pair of full-duplex radios. This demo first builds a full duplex radio by implementing self-interference cancellation technique on top of a traditional half duplex radio architecture. We then establish a point-to-point link using a pair of these radios that can transmit and receive OFDM packets. By changing the environmental conditions around the full-duplex radios we then demonstrate the robustness of the self-interference cancellation to adapt to the changing environment.

## Categories and Subject Descriptors

C.2.1 [**Computer Communication Networks**]: Network Architecture and Design—*Wireless communication*

**Keywords**: Full Duplex; Interference Cancellation; Non-linear Cancellation

## 1. INTRODUCTION

Full duplex radios have huge advantage over their half duplex counterparts. Several work on full duplex radios [5, 3, 7, 6, 4, 8] have proposed various hardware and algorithmic techniques to achieve different level of self-interference cancellation required for realization of full duplex radios. Yet, these works have failed to reduce the ingrained skepticism of both academia and industry alike regarding the feasibility of implementing these techniques and their adaptability to dynamic environmental conditions. This demo has two fold objectives; first, we implement a working full duplex radio using the architecture proposed in [5]. We then build full duplex radio link by using a pair of these full duplex radios and demonstrate that they can adapt to the changing environmental conditions around them [5].

In [5] they have shown that in order to achieve full duplex communication with regulatory power limit of existing half duplex WiFi radios, 110dB of self-interference cancellation is required. They have achieved this level of cancellation in two stages by designing analog cancellation and digital cancellation filters. After applying these two cancellations, the residue of the self-interference signal goes below the noise floor which enables the receiver to listen to the weak received signal. We demonstrate the cancellation of self-interference all the way to the noise floor by implementing analog and digital cancellation on WARP software radios and a host PC.

Using two such full duplex radios we build a full duplex point-to-point link, where each full duplex radio transmits data to and receives data from the other full duplex radio via the established link. In order to achieve stable full duplex link, it is necessary to achieve cancellation which adapts quickly to the changing environment. This paper demonstrates dynamically adaptive cancellation system, which achieves robust full duplex link even when the environmental condition changes frequently. In the rest of this paper, we first describe the implementation of the cancellation techniques used in our full duplex radio prototype. We then describe the full duplex point-to-point link.


*SIGCOMM'14,* August 17–22, 2014, Chicago, IL, USA.
ACM 978-1-4503-2836-4/14/08.
http://dx.doi.org/10.1145/2619239.2631425.

## 2. ADAPTIVE CANCELLATION

Let us see what are the major constituents of the self-interference signals that needs to be canceled to enable full duplex communication. In Figure 1a, T is the signal that is fed to the antenna for transmission, part of this signal is reflected back from the environment and a part is reflected from the antenna itself, and part of this signal leaks directly to the receive path via spurious path in the circulators. These reflected and leaked transmitted signal denoted by $aT$ in figure 1a are typically 15dB smaller that the signal $T$, therefore we still have to cancel 95 dB of the self-interference signal. The signal $T$ itself is composed of three parts as given in [5], first is linear form of the transmitted digital data that can be modeled, and the second is the non-linear distortion of the transmitted digital data that can be modeled, third is the transmitter noise which cannot be modeled (as noise is random). Since the transmit noise cannot be modeled in digital, the only way to cancel its effect is to take a copy of it and then cancel it from the received signal. This is best done in analog domain, and as given in [5] we need cancellation of the order of 70dB to eliminate all the self-interference due to the transmitter noise.

In addition to canceling the effect of the transmitter noise, the analog cancellation also cancels the effect of the environmental reflection from the near-field region of the antenna, as well as the reflection from the antenna itself arising due to impedance mismatch. After the analog cancellation, we are left with the residual signal $iT$, which consists of contribution from the linear and non-linear distortions due to power amplifier, mixer, and other analog components in the transmit chain as well as the contribution from the reflections coming from the far-field region of the antenna. This residual component is modeled adaptively using WiFi preamble to train the digital taps, which can then eliminate this residual signal.

In a typical radio operation, the environmental conditions in the near-field of the antenna is usually stable and does not vary that much over time. Whereas the far field region can experience very rapid changes, mainly due to the movement of persons in the surrounding. Because of this the taps used in analog cancellation of the full-duplex radio remains fairly constant for a given environment in which the radio is located, and consequently slower adaptation of these taps is sufficient. Since the far-field region of the antenna changes frequently, the taps used in the digital cancellation needs to be adjusted more frequently.

In order to demonstrate a dynamic robust full duplex radio, we have build the analog cancellation circuits and digital cancellation using WARP radios [2] as shown in figure 1b. We have accompa-

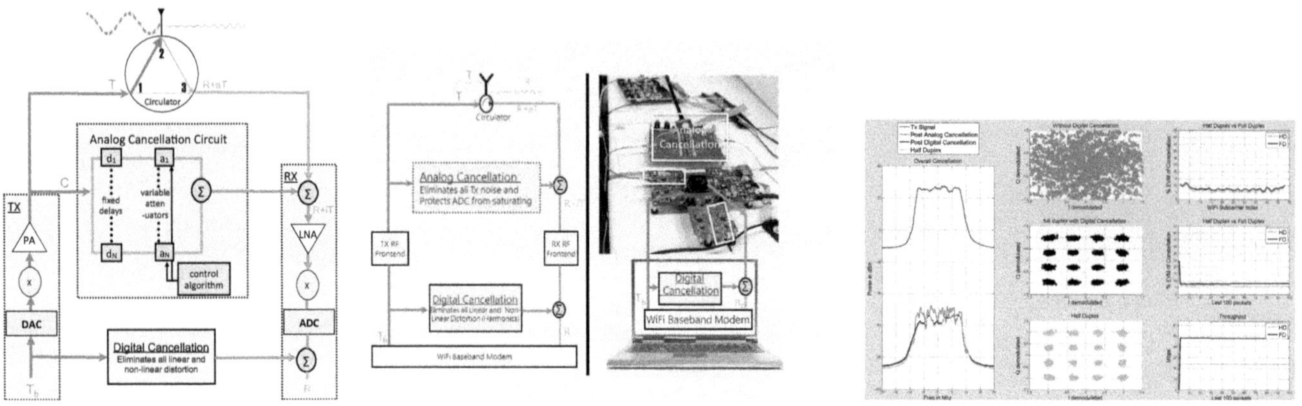


(a) Full duplex radio architecture

(b) Full duplex radio implementation

(c) User interface showing performance metric of full duplex link

Figure 1: **Demo of robust full duplex Link**

nied video of this demonstration in [1]. We see that even when the environment around the full duplex radio is not changing, the taps of the digital cancellation filters are frequently changing, to adapt to the changing condition in the far-field due to movement of people. The taps for analog cancellation remains fairly fixed, because the near field region and the reflection due to the mismatch are not varying over time. To demonstrate that the analog cancellation adapts to the changes in the near-field region, we introduce a metallic reflector very close to the antenna. This reflection adds strong self-interference in the near-field region which is then compensated for by adjusting the analog taps. We then move the reflector away, which will again cause the change in the near-field region of the antenna and the taps used for the analog cancellation adjusts back to the values that were there before the introduction of the metallic reflector.

# 3. POINT TO POINT FULL DUPLEX LINK

In this section we demonstrate the application of the full duplex radios by creating a full duplex point-to-point communication link. The setup for this link consists of two full-duplex radios that are trying to communicate with each other at the same time on the same spectrum (band). We implement standard 802.11n PHY based WiFi Modem for this demonstration. Figure 1c shows the user interface of the demo with various signals and evaluation metric for one of the radios. In order to compare the performance of the full duplex link to that of the half-duplex link, we alternate the operation between the full-duplex and half-duplex mode for every alternate packet and show the results together. First column in 1c shows the self-interference signals at different stages of the cancellation and the weak received signal after the self-interference cancellation. In the full-duplex mode after the self-interference cancellation, we want the received signal (black) to look exactly like the signal you would have received in the half duplex mode (green). The similarity of these two signals in the attached video indicates that the full-duplex link is operational.

The quality of a link can be visually evaluated by plotting the constellation of the received signal after demodulation. The second column of figure 1c shows the constellation at various stages of the full duplex link as well as that of the half duplex link. The top plot shows the constellation after only analog cancellation, here the constellation appears as a single blob instead of the 16 constellation points that was used for this demo. The middle plot shows the constellation after both the analog and the digital cancellations and we can clearly see that all the constellation points are tightly grouped around the true points, this tightness indicates the quality of the link. The bottom plot shows the constellation for the half duplex link and it looks very close to the full-duplex constellation points, which is yet another confirmation that the full-duplex link is operational.

A more quantitative metric to gauge the quality of a link is to measure % Error Vector Magnitude (EVM) of the constellation after demodulation. EVM measures the deviation of the constellation points in the received signals from the true constellation points. Therefore smaller the % EVM for a link higher is the quality of that link. The third column of the user interface shown in figure 1c plots the EVM of the links. As we can see the full-duplex link is slightly degraded compared to the half-duplex link, there is about 2% difference between the EVM of these two links. As reported in [5], the noise floor after the self-interference cancellation is roughly 1 dB more than the noise floor of a half-duplex radio, the difference in EVM is due to this marginal increase in the noise floor of the full duplex radio. The top plot show the EVM for each of the subcarriers and the middle plot shows the EVM of each packet for the last 100 packets. The occasional increase in EVM for full duplex link is due to sudden introduction of a reflector close to the radio 1. The taps in analog cancellation takes some time to adapt to this new change and hence the EVM increases momentarily, but once the taps have adapted the link quality increases again. This momentary degradation is an artifact of the current implementation and can be improved upon by performing adaptation using faster hardware support. Finally, the bottom plot shows the near doubling of the throughput via full-duplex link compared to its half-duplex counterpart.

# 4. REFERENCES


[1] *Robust Full-duplex Radio link*. https://vimeo.com/98308615.

[2] *WARP Project*. http://warpproject.org.

[3] E. Aryafar, M. A. Khojastepour, K. Sundaresan, S. Rangarajan, and M. Chiang. Midu: enabling mimo full duplex. In *Proceedings of the 18th annual international conference on Mobile computing and networking*, Mobicom '12, pages 257–268, New York, NY, USA, 2012. ACM.

[4] D. Bharadia and S. Katti. Full duplex mimo radios. In *11th USENIX Symposium on Networked Systems Design and Implementation (NSDI 14)*, pages 359–372, Seattle, WA, Apr. 2014. USENIX Association.

[5] D. Bharadia, E. McMilin, and S. Katti. Full duplex radios. In *Proceedings of the ACM SIGCOMM 2013 conference on SIGCOMM*, SIGCOMM '13, pages 375–386, New York, NY, USA, 2013. ACM.

[6] M. Duarte, C. Dick, and A. Sabharwal. Experiment-driven characterization of full-duplex wireless systems. *CoRR*, abs/1107.1276, 2011.

[7] Y. Hua, P. Liang, Y. Ma, A. Cirik, and Q. Gao. A method for broadband full-duplex mimo radio. *Signal Processing Letters, IEEE*, 19(12):793 –796, dec. 2012.

[8] M. Knox. Single antenna full duplex communications using a common carrier. In *Wireless and Microwave Technology Conference (WAMICON), 2012 IEEE 13th Annual*, pages 1–6, 2012.

# Demonstrating the Prospects of Dynamic Application-Aware Networking in a Home Environment

Florian Wamser, Thomas Zinner, Lukas Iffländer, Phuoc Tran-Gia
University of Würzburg, Institute of Computer Science
{wamser,zinner,ifflaender,trangia}@informatik.uni-wuerzburg.de

## Categories and Subject Descriptors

C.2.1 [**COMPUTER-COMMUNICATION NETWORKS**]: Network Architecture and Design—*Network communications*

## Keywords

Application-Aware Networking, Dynamic Resource Allocation, Home Networks, YouTube

## 1. INTRODUCTION

The success of tablet computers, game consoles, and Smart TVs reflects the increased user demand for Internet-based services at home. The users in the home network can access value-added services offered directly by the network provider, such as IPTV. Likewise, they also use Over-The-Top (OTT) services like YouTube, Netflix, or online gaming and browse the web or download files. All these services have specific requirements with respect to the network resources which have to be fulfilled to ensure a good Quality-of-Experience (QoE) for the users. Furthermore, multiple users may concurrently access different services via the central Internet access point in the home network, the home gateway, cf. Figure 1.

As stated by the Home Gateway Initiative (HGI) [1], the network at home and the broadband Internet access link may constitute a bottleneck. This may be due to the insufficient availability of broadband access, i.e., the network provider offers only smallband Internet access, or due to limitations within the home network, like the varying channel quality of the wireless networks.

Traffic in today's network structures is usually transmitted on a best effort basis. As a result, different services or applications with varying requirements and capabilities are treated equally on a per flow-basis, resulting in a unfairness in terms of QoE. Long lasting OS updates on a home computer may thus interfere with video streaming to a Smart TV which leads to video stallings and a degradation in the QoE of the user. In such a case, it is necessary to explicitly allocate the network resources unequally to the involved applications on network level to achieve a similar QoE across multiple applications.


*SIGCOMM'14*, August 17–22, 2014, Chicago, IL, USA.
ACM 978-1-4503-2836-4/14/08.
http://dx.doi.org/10.1145/2619239.2631450.

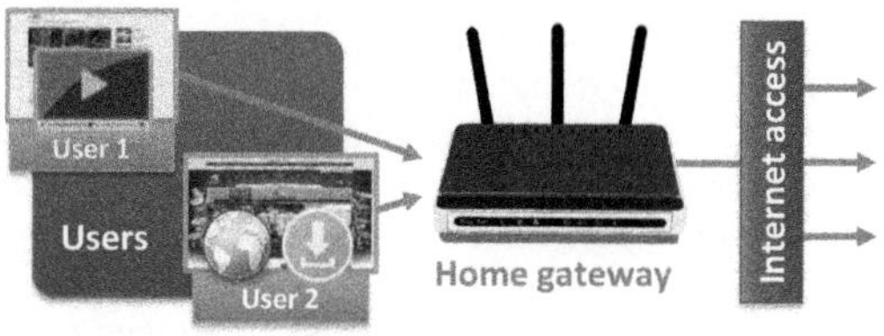


Figure 1: Illustration of a home network.

This explicit network resource control is known as Application-Aware Networking. Scalability issues hinder the implementation of such mechanisms within aggregation and wide area networks, but the small size of the home network makes it a promising candidate. Most of the traffic is forwarded in home networks via the home gateway, making it possible to control the network resources, and therewith the application quality, at this entity.

In this demonstration, we show the potential of flexibly allocating network resources to different applications. We focus on a two-application scenario where YouTube flows and a file download compete for resources via a shared bottleneck link. YouTube maintains a playback buffer to overcome resource limitations on a short time scale. We take advantage of this in order to provide an accurate reaction against video stallings. We implemented a network-based buffer estimator for YouTube which allows the accurate monitoring of the application buffer state. If the local video buffer runs empty, the IP flow is prioritized, if the buffer is sufficiently filled, the prioritization is turned off, or other applications like browsing are prioritized.

## 2. IMPLEMENTATION

This section highlights details of the monitoring and resource allocation mechanisms implemented on the home gateway, an AVM FRITZ!Box 3390 [2].

The user perceived quality of a service depends on a multitude of technical and non-technical factors. Some of the technical factors are application-specific indicators for the QoE, like the used video codec, the filling of the playback buffer, or the perceived delay on application level. For a targeted resource allocation in the network an accurate monitoring of the application state, i.e. of these indicators, is necessary. For YouTube video streaming, the buffered play-

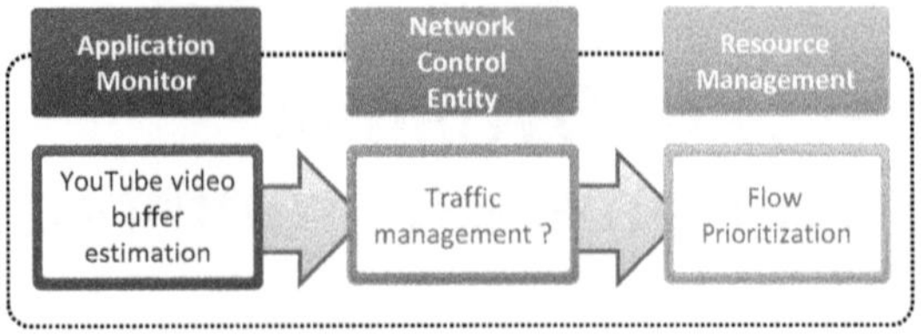


**Figure 2: Control loop taking application information into account.**

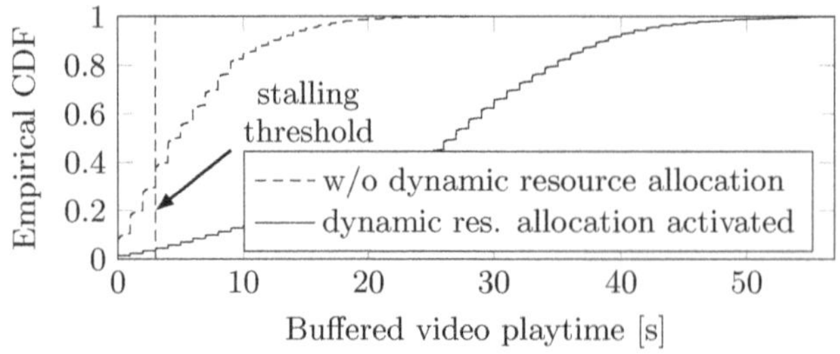


**Figure 3: CDF for YouTube buffer level.**

time is such a state parameter which has a high impact on the QoE [3]. If the buffer falls below a certain threshold, the video stalls and the QoE is affected.

To demonstrate a dynamic resource allocation of network capacity for two applications, namely YouTube video streaming and a parallel download, we implemented the necessary functionality on a FRITZ!Box running Freetz OS [4]:

(a) *YouTube video buffer estimation*, (b) *flow prioritization / flow de-prioritization* as resource management actions, and (c) *network control entity* that decides what value of application status leads to which resource management action, see Figure 2.

The resource management process is as follows: The application monitor detects a YouTube flow based on the HTTP GET URL of the YouTube video request [5]. For HTTP Secure (HTTPS) requests, a trusted man-in-the-middle proxy is installed. If a YouTube video and its corresponding IP flows are detected, the application monitor estimates the buffered playtime of the client by inspecting relevant data parts in the IP packets . Afterwards, the IP flow signature and the estimated buffered playtime is signaled to the network control entity. It decides whether the IP flows are prioritized or de-prioritized. The prioritization is performed with traffic control (tc) by setting up classful queueing disciplines in the standard Linux kernel of the home gateway.

To illustrate the prospects of this dynamic prioritization, we present results for an exemplary scenario. It consists of one YouTube video competing for bandwidth in a 3 Mbit/s IEEE 802.11b/g wireless access network with two file downloads. First, the YouTube video is started. Second, the downloads are started after 15 s. The YouTube video has an average video encoding rate of 2.9 Mbit/s.

Figure 3 shows the cumulative distribution function (CDF) of the buffered playtime in seconds at the client. The dashed line on the left in the figure corresponds to the stalling threshold where the playback at the YouTube player is restarted after buffering due to buffer underrun. In particular, this means that the buffer level should always exceed this threshold to avoid stalling and ensure a good QoE for this video [3]. In the first case, the buffered playtime is depicted without the proposed dynamic resource allocation. In 40 % of the time, the buffer is under the stalling threshold resulting in a bad QoE. In contrast, with the resource allocation activated, the buffer level can be maintained at a high level.

# 3. DEMONSTRATION SCENARIO AND PRESENTATION

To demonstrate the functionality of the dynamic resource allocation at the home gateway, as well as to foster an active discussion with the audience, we stick to the same scenario as described in the last section. Two Laptops are connected to the home gateway via wireless LAN, serving as end users which run the applications. Additionally, a detailed graphical user interface for YouTube has been developed to illustrate the functionality and to allow for a good presentation. As a consequence, viewers of the demonstration can follow the course of the buffer level of YouTube and see when the playback behavior is affected and when not.

We plan to show a predefined demonstration sequence, but any YouTube video or download can also be started manually at the request of viewers. The predefined sequence is as follows: (1) User 1 starts to watch a YouTube video. (2) After 15 s, User 2 is starting some downloads which overwhelm the access network. Consequently, the YouTube video experiences problems and the buffer level is decreasing, until the video stalls for several times. (3) Afterwards, we activate the resource allocation which detects the YouTube buffer level and adjusts the prioritization for the flows. In the end, this allows YouTube to download video data at the expense of the bandwidth for the downloads. The audience can see that YouTube is able to load the buffer up to a certain buffer level, while the downloads are automatically throttled if YouTube is below the particular buffer level. Consequently, the perceived quality of the YouTube user is good since stalling does not occur anymore. The downloads are throttled. From a QoE perspective, this however only affects the downloads to a minor extent.

That way, the demo's audience can observe the influence of the resource management mechanism for YouTube on the situation in the network as well as the improvements in QoE for the users. A screencast of this demonstration is available at `https://www.youtube.com/watch?v=Nk2Pjht6YVk`.

# 4. REFERENCES


[1] Home Gateway Initiative, "Home Gateway QoS Module requirements," whitepaper, Dec. 2012.

[2] AVM, "FRITZ!Box 3390," http://www.avm.de/en/Produkte/FRITZBox/FRITZ_Box_3390/.

[3] T. Hoßfeld, R. Schatz, E. Biersack, and L. Plissonneau, "Internet Video Delivery in YouTube: From Traffic Measurements to Quality of Experience." Springer's Computer Communications and Networks, 2013.

[4] Freetz Project, "Firmware image for home routers," http://freetz.org/.

[5] F. Wamser, D. Hock, M. Seufert, B. Staehle, R. Pries, and P. Tran-Gia, "Using Buffered Playtime for QoE-Oriented Resource Management of YouTube Video Streaming," *Transactions on Emerging Telecommunications Technologies*, vol. 24, Apr. 2013.

# A Middlebox-Cooperative TCP for a non End-to-End Internet

Ryan Craven
Naval Postgraduate School
rcraven@nps.edu

Robert Beverly
Naval Postgraduate School
rbeverly@nps.edu

Mark Allman
ICSI
mallman@icir.org

## ABSTRACT

Understanding, measuring, and debugging IP networks, particularly across administrative domains, is challenging. One particularly daunting aspect of the challenge is the presence of transparent middleboxes—which are now common in today's Internet. In-path middleboxes that modify packet headers are typically transparent to a TCP, yet can impact end-to-end performance or cause blackholes. We develop TCP HICCUPS to reveal packet header manipulation to both endpoints of a TCP connection. HICCUPS permits endpoints to cooperate with currently opaque middleboxes without prior knowledge of their behavior. For example, with visibility into end-to-end behavior, a TCP can selectively enable or disable performance enhancing options. This cooperation enables protocol innovation by allowing new IP or TCP functionality (e.g., ECN, SACK, Multipath TCP, Tcpcrypt) to be deployed without fear of such functionality being misconstrued, modified, or blocked along a path. HICCUPS is incrementally deployable and introduces no new options. We implement and deploy TCP HICCUPS across thousands of disparate Internet paths, highlighting the breadth and scope of subtle and hard to detect middlebox behaviors encountered. We then show how path diagnostic capabilities provided by HICCUPS can benefit applications and the network.

## Categories and Subject Descriptors

C.2.2 [**Computer-Communication Networks**]: Network Protocols—*TCP*; C.4 [**Computer-Communication Networks**]: Performance of Systems—*Measurement techniques*

## Keywords

TCP; Middlebox; Header Integrity; Header Modifications

## 1. INTRODUCTION

The traditional Internet architecture envisions intelligence at the ends and simplicity in the middle [13]. This traditional view, where the network focuses on forwarding packets, is long gone. Middleboxes now actively interpose on communication for a multitude of reasons [9], including implementing acceptable use policies, maintaining regulatory compliance, thwarting attacks, censoring or monitoring users, expanding address space, limiting or balancing resources, and generating revenue. However, the functional consequences of middlebox mechanisms, which are frequently decoupled from the end-to-end path, may be both intentional and unintentional. The prevalence of middleboxes, and the wide variety of behaviors they exhibit, is well-established by previous empirical research [18, 31, 36, 40, 46].

One side effect of middleboxes is that they make the task of debugging networks—already a difficult problem, especially across administrative domains—even harder by introducing a variety of unknowns [31]. Because of their privileged position in the network, it is important that middleboxes not adversely impact (e.g., block or degrade) the traffic of systems or users outside of their intended scope.

Unfortunately, middleboxes have been shown to induce not only the intended changes in traffic behavior, but also unintended side effects. Legacy equipment, non-standard implementations, and misconfigurations are known to interact with middleboxes to mutate critical packet fields, destroy semantics, create unintended protocol interactions, and violate the end-to-end nature of the Internet. For instance, previous measurements have shown that middleboxes frequently misconstrue and block new IP or transport functionality [6, 19, 25]. Thus, an important and often underappreciated class of network problems are the result of *non-malicious* and *unintentional* middlebox behavior.

While clean-slate designs (e.g., [45]) and software-defined management (e.g., [38, 41, 42]) attempt to more cohesively integrate middleboxes into the network, they depend on deployment and use; TCPs in the wild must continue to contend with a variety of middlebox behaviors. In contrast, we advocate for empowering TCP endpoints with awareness of middlebox packet header modifications along a path. Similar to how TCP currently infers end-to-end congestion state, a TCP host with knowledge of the end-to-end packet header modification state can better match its behavior to the capabilities of the path. By cooperatively adapting to middleboxes, TCP can improve performance. Perhaps more importantly, endpoints can realize the benefits of protocol innovation as new TCP or IP functionality can be more safely deployed and enabled in routers and operating systems.

We implement and deploy TCP HICCUPS (Handshake-based Integrity Check of Critical Underlying Protocol Se-


*SIGCOMM'14,* August 17–22, 2014, Chicago, IL, USA.
Copyright 2014 ACM 978-1-4503-2836-4/14/08 ...$15.00.
http://dx.doi.org/10.1145/2619239.2626321

mantics). HICCUPS permits endpoints to cooperate with currently opaque middleboxes without prior knowledge of their behavior. HICCUPS is incrementally deployable, backward compatible, introduces no new IP or TCP options, and adheres to all TCP/IP standards, i.e., will traverse the same paths as traditional TCP. HICCUPS provides bidirectional in-band measurement and feedback such that a TCP sender can infer the state of how her packet headers were received by the other end of the connection. With widespread deployment, HICCUPS would also enable a new general path diagnostic capability in the same way that `ping` (ICMP echo) can be used to test paths without prior endpoint coordination. We make the following primary contributions:

1. Design of TCP HICCUPS, an incrementally deployable improvement on TCP to reveal packet header manipulation to both ends of a TCP connection.
2. Real-world implementation and testing of TCP HICCUPS in the Linux kernel.
3. Deployment of, and measurements from, TCP HICCUPS across thousands of disparate Internet paths.
4. Demonstrable instances of degenerate middlebox behavior and the ways in which HICCUPS cooperation improves transfer performance.

# 2. BACKGROUND

Some Internet packet headers were designed to experience modification, for instance the IP time-to-live and checksum are decremented and recomputed respectively at each hop. Other fields such as the Differentiated Services Code Point (DSCP) [37] only have significance within each transiting network, having no guarantee to be constant along a path.

However, other fields have *end-to-end significance*, for example: source and destination addresses, transport ports, TCP flags, flow control window, and TCP options. Modifications to fields intended for interpretation only by endpoints can lead to subtle and unintentional problems. In the worst case, traffic can be blocked. In other instances, performance can suffer—sometimes dramatically. In this section, we first discuss some of the impacts resulting from the current environment of opaque middleboxes. We then examine prior work in providing integrity and diagnostics of packet manipulation. Lastly, we examine emerging research toward middlebox cooperation.

## 2.1 TCP/IP Misinterpretation

The unintended effects and architectural issues of middleboxes are well-documented. Medina et al. cataloged issues stemming from unexpected middlebox interactions [36]. Different behaviors were observed depending on the use of IP or TCP options and Explicit Congestion Notification (ECN).

Measurements from Honda et al. [25] discovered paths with middleboxes that strip both known and unknown TCP options, perform sequence numbers translation, and even exhibit port-dependent behavior, e.g., options removed from packets destined to a random transport port, but not port 80. At least 25% of the paths tested traversed a middlebox whose behavior depended on the packet's transport-layer. Not only is such interference detrimental to the validity of the protocol interactions, it is difficult to diagnose—making troubleshooting a complex endeavor.

We focus on *unintentional* and *unintended* middlebox behaviors. Several examples we find in the wild include:

- ***Sequence Number Translation:*** To mitigate security issues inherent in predictable TCP sequence numbers, some paths contain network elements that randomize and remap sequence numbers on behalf of a host [12] (the assumption being that hosts cannot be trusted to perform proper randomization). While investigating a performance problem at our own institution, we found that while sequence numbers were being remapped in the standard TCP header, they were not being remapped in SACK blocks—which appear in the options portion of the header. This renders selective acknowledgment information useless, impacting bulk transfer performance. Diagnosing this subtle error required trained engineers using cooperating endpoints.

- ***Options:*** TCP options—which convey information between endpoints that is not germane to the network itself—are frequently deleted, added, or modified, disrupting various protocol extensions. For example, some paths add a Maximum Segment Size (MSS) if not present, or rewrite MSS, impacting performance if the true path MSS is larger or smaller. Other paths modify or remove the Window Scaling option, causing a remote endpoint to misinterpret the receiver window and incorrectly apply flow control. Not only do these common options experience modification, newer options are often stripped or blocked. For example, legacy middleboxes that are unaware of Multipath TCP [20] may strip those options, impacting performance.

- ***Type of Service:*** The original IPv4 specification includes a byte for "type-of-service." That byte has long since been redefined to consist of two bits for Explicit Congestion Notification (ECN) and six bits of DSCP. Yet, a non-trivial fraction of devices and paths still use the previous definition and rewrite or zero the entire byte. This rewriting can prevent a TCP connection from utilizing router congestion signals, or more seriously, cause a TCP connection to falsely interpret congestion [6]. Managing congestion and improving TCP performance are critical to content providers and data centers. As one large content provider stated: "we want to enable ECN, but do not because enabling ECN may adversely affect some of our users." [3]

Such behavior by middleboxes can make it a challenge to diagnose the cause of various performance and connectivity issues. Even more troubling is the unintended effect middleboxes can have on protocol innovation and adoption: any new option, repurposed field, or otherwise unrecognized behavior is often misunderstood or blocked [19, 25].

## 2.2 Integrity

Most integrity mechanisms built into Internet communication protocols are intended solely for error detection, such as CRC and Internet checksums [43]. Such checksums must always match integrity for a packet to be accepted, lest a device assume the packet experienced some transmission error. By necessity, any middleboxes modifying the header must also recompute any error detection checksums.

A natural response to the middlebox-induced cases of misinterpretation cited above is to employ tamper-resistant mechanisms (i.e. cryptography to encrypt and sign traffic) to prevent alterations during transmission. Such mechanisms have been developed for the network [28, 29], transport [8, 32, 44] and application [21] layers. At the application layer, the use of encryption to protect payloads has been well-adopted and is pervasive throughout the Internet. However, at the lower layers the problems of key sharing between anonymous hosts hinder adoption while imposing unnecessary cost on higher layers. Furthermore, at lower layers users often desire properly functioning middlebox intervention—e.g., to share a single public IP address among multiple devices in their home—and therefore have a disincentive to utilize tamper-resistance. As we show in §3, we relax the requirements for tamper-resistance to implement a tamper-evident design that is more cooperative with modern middleboxes.

Tracebox is a diagnostic tool to detect changes made by middleboxes along the forward path [17]. Using a similar methodology as traceroute, tracebox progressively increments the TTL of packets while additionally inferring the presence of middleboxes by comparing ICMP time exceeded quotations [5] with the originally sent packets. One drawback to the method are the inconsistencies involved with ICMP router quotations [34]. Even though the approach works for a majority of paths—Detal et al. find that ≈80% of the paths they examined contained at least one full-quoting router—the paths that the method cannot test likely contain the most legacy equipment that could impact TCP.

While HICCUPS and tracebox share a common goal, there are key differences between the two approaches. Tracebox is a measurement tool that relies on the network to produce and respond with diagnostic feedback. Whereas HICCUPS is in-band, tracebox requires extra diagnostic packets, unblocked ICMP, and router response. Further, HICCUPS is tightly integrated into TCP, understands both the forward and reverse path, and allows TCP to make inferences about whether it is being misinterpreted.

## 2.3 Middlebox Cooperation

Middleboxes are an Internet reality. The middlebox market, estimated to reach more than $10B by 2016 [1], is ample evidence that middleboxes provide value. With the prevalence and reach of middleboxes increasing, several approaches seek explicit accommodation.

Walfish et al. propose a new architecture that gives all entities globally unique identifiers in a flat namespace while allowing for explicit intermediate packet processing [45]. More recent research seeks to reduce the sprawl of standalone, non-cohesive middleboxes and employ new software-defined approaches so they can be more easily managed [22, 38, 41, 42]. Meanwhile, multiple vendors have recognized the problem of middlebox cooperation and have added TCP options that allow middleboxes along a path to voluntarily participate in their transparent discovery [30]. While these schemes make it easier to manage middlebox deployments and keep them up-to-date, they depend on adoption and use. Software-defined management, for example, is confined to single administrative domains. However, TCP hosts in the wild must contend with a wide variety of middleboxes.

Each of the above schemes require some form of active cooperation by middleboxes or their operators. We emphasize that this is different from the manner in which HICCUPS is cooperative with middleboxes. We have designed HICCUPS so that it does not interfere with middlebox operation. It does not require active participation by middleboxes.

# 3. DESIGN SPACE

We aim to identify and address the class of problems involving misconfigured, non-standards conforming, and legacy in-path middleboxes impacting normal traffic behavior. In the same way that TCP currently infers end-to-end congestion state, a TCP instance aware of the end-to-end packet header modification state can better match its behavior to the capabilities of the path. For instance, TCP could improve path performance by selectively enabling or disabling extensions (e.g., ECN, SACK, Multipath TCP, etc.) when they are at risk of being misinterpreted on a given path.

At a high-level, we desire a TCP-based integrity check to detect in-network packet header modifications. Such modifications today are opaque, e.g., Medina [36] could not disambiguate between "a middlebox stripping or mangling the option or the web server not supporting [the option]"—our design must provide such visibility.

The space of possible solutions is large. While seemingly straightforward, no prior work accommodates all of the properties and functionality we require:

- ***In-band:*** Many paths block out-of-band traffic (e.g., ICMP) or treat it differently. By having both the detection and feedback mechanisms in-band, we hope to maximize the detection rate.
- ***Lightweight:*** The design should result in a minimal amount of overhead in terms of computation, communication, and RTTs.
- ***Symmetric feedback:*** It is important that hosts at each end of a connection know if and how their packets were modified in flight.
- ***Incrementally deployable:*** The design should not interfere with endpoints that have not been upgraded, nor require any updates to in-network elements.
- ***Improves TCP:*** The design should endow TCP endpoints with the information needed to reason about how the options and extensions they employ are interpreted by the remote endpoint.
- ***Middlebox-cooperative:*** The design should not impede or circumvent properly functioning middleboxes, and not exacerbate degenerate middlebox behaviors.
- ***End-to-end:*** Paths exhibiting modifications are the same paths most likely to block or strip any new instrumentation. Values should be properly communicated end-to-end.
- ***Granularity:***: Endpoints should be able to determine which packet header fields were changed.

In addition, our design should not enable any new attacks on the system (e.g., amplification, spoofing, flooding, etc.)

## 3.1 Meeting our Architectural Objectives

How well does our TCP HICCUPS (detailed in §4) meet the aforementioned requirements? We show the degree to which HICCUPS and other relevant prior works from §2 provide such functionality in Table 1. In particular, note that HICCUPS represents a unique point in the design space.

A key insight enabling our solution is the fresh point of view afforded by our security model of the inadvertent adversary, a non-malicious system in the middle of a connection that is corrupting critical packet semantics. Much of the prior research has focused on the edges of the spectrum: protecting integrity from either transmission errors or from strong adversaries (§2.2). When operating under the model of the misconfiguration adversary, such solutions either fail to expose problematic behaviors or make too many sacrifices in pursuit of strong cryptographic assurances.

Table 1: **HICCUPS in the context of existing and proposed integrity and middlebox cooperation schemes (● indicates that a scheme fully meets the criterion; ○ indicates a scheme does not meet the criterion).**

| Scheme | In-band | Light-weight | Symmetric feedback | Incrementally deployable | Improves TCP | Middlebox-cooperative | End-to-end | Granularity |
|---|---|---|---|---|---|---|---|---|
| Checksums [43] | ● | ● | ○ | ● | ○ | ● | ◔ | ○ |
| Tcpcrypt [8] | ● | ○ | ◑ | ◕ | ○ | ◔ | ◕ | ○ |
| Tracebox [17] | ○ | ◑ | ◑ | ◕ | ○ | ◕ | ◑ | ◕ |
| SIMPLE [38] | ○ | ◑ | ○ | ◔ | ◕ | ● | ◔ | ● |
| HICCUPS | ● | ● | ● | ● | ● | ● | ● | ● |

For example, standard checksums require middleboxes to recalculate them after changes and also provide no method to expose results of the integrity exchange to the endpoint initiating the connection. The lack of an explicit notification back to the sender when its packet arrives with a bad checksum has been a previously noted weak point [43].

HICCUPS allows both endpoints of a connection to receive feedback about the integrity of the (potentially asymmetric) paths taken by their traffic. Working within TCP makes checking bidirectional path integrity easier since the notion of a conversation is already clearly defined. By equipping the headers of the TCP 3WHS with integrity, we hope to capture the majority of performance-impacting modifications by middleboxes. While some issues with extensions would require covering the full connection to explicitly detect, protecting even just the 3WHS presents a large step toward making inferences that can improve performance. We present designs for protecting the full connection in [16].

Once a system is HICCUPS-enabled, it can perform integrity checks with other HICCUPS-enabled systems through any open remote TCP port. HICCUPS TCP stacks are interoperable with non-HICCUPS TCP stacks and its traffic appears no different to network devices from typical TCP traffic. If widely deployed, HICCUPS would provide a general diagnostic mechanism in a manner similar to `ping` and `traceroute`, wherein explicit endpoint cooperation is not required to measure a path. This "always on" property implies that utility to TCP will increase with the deployment of HICCUPS. Any HICCUPS-enabled system with an open service, e.g., a web server with TCP port 80 open, will support a HICCUPS measurement.

In contrast to `ping` and `traceroute` (as well as other middlebox detection tools like tracebox), we do not leverage out-of-band mechanisms (e.g., ICMP) in our design so as to avoid complications inherent in relying on external dependencies. In particular, note the difficulties with Path MTU Discovery as TCP operation is linked with ICMP traversal [33, 36]. A new method of PMTUD was later written that did not rely on receipt of the ICMP Packet Too Big (PTB) messages [35].

# 4. TCP HICCUPS

As a real-world instantiation of our architectural objectives, we develop the Handshake-based Integrity Check of Critical Underlying Protocol Semantics (HICCUPS), an enhancement to TCP. HICCUPS can assist TCP in determining the most appropriate set of end-to-end parameters that best fit the middleboxes along a particular path. In particular, HICCUPS would allow a TCP instance to reason about how the options and extensions it employs are interpreted by a remote endpoint, and subsequently make inferences about when it is safe to make use of new extensions. HICCUPS benefits TCP in two primary ways:

1. Equips TCP with critical path information that would allow it to more safely increase the use of performance-enhancing extensions relative to ultra conservative approaches where new extensions are disabled by default or left to run in "server-mode" *à la* ECN as deployed and configured in modern operating systems[1].

   **Examples:** ECN, Multipath TCP
2. Provides early warning of potential middlebox-induced issues with an extension that is enabled by default. TCP could proactively disable or ignore the extension to improve performance.

   **Examples:** SACK, Window Scaling

Our solution helps enable these performance benefits by monitoring the state of packet headers through an in-path integrity exchange, essentially creating a lightweight *tamper-evident* seal across the headers. The results of the exchange allow endhosts to work within the current path conditions to tailor the set of extensions they use to the middleboxes in the path between them.

## 4.1 Overview

Working within TCP to enable detection of in-path header modifications while maintaining interoperability with current network infrastructure and endhosts is a difficult systems problem. We first provide an overview of HICCUPS:

1. HICCUPS transmits packet header integrity information by *overloading* three header fields of the TCP 3-way handshake that can contain a flexible value: initial sequence numbers, initial IPIDs, and initial flow control windows. Doing so yields the highest degree of interoperability with the widest number of paths, but places tight constraints on the amount of information transmitted. See §4.2 for more.

2. When HICCUPS places integrity information in the sequence number, randomness is added for spoofing protection. See §4.2 for more.

3. The integrity information transmitted by HICCUPS includes three 12-bit hash fragments, each communicated through one of the overloaded fields in item 1. Spreading integrity across fields provides resilience to a single modification affecting any one of the three fields, e.g., sequence number translation. See §4.3 for more.

4. Reverse path integrity includes status values that enable a HICCUPS host to discover when modifications occur to just the forward path, just the reverse path, or to both paths. See §4.3 for more.

[1]In server-mode ECN, a TCP endpoint will not initiate ECN, but will negotiate ECN if initiated by the client.

5. HICCUPS supports granularity in its integrity checks. A set of coverage types allows endhosts to dynamically specify subsets of fields to be protected by HICCUPS. (§4.4)

6. As an additional protection, e.g., against middleboxes that might, in the future, actively attempt evasion, HICCUPS enables applications to optionally protect integrity with an *ephemeral secret* (§4.5). This secret limits false inferences of integrity in the event that a change is made and the integrity is recomputed. §4.6 provides a discussion of how we extend the Linux socket API to provide this feature.

## 4.2 Overloading Header Fields

To minimize interference from legacy and non-standard middleboxes, we avoid either redefining any field semantics or using any new IP or TCP options. New options and/or new semantics exacerbate middlebox incompatibility and we want to avoid being subject to the same issues we wish to detect. Furthermore, the TCP option space is already overcrowded [25] with many well-established extensions. By not competing for new space, we hope to avoid unintended interactions and facilitate easier adoption.

In order to integrate the integrity check within TCP/IP, we *overload* three specific fields in the headers that are allowed a certain degree of flexibility: the TCP initial sequence number (ISN), the initial IP Identification field (IPID), and the initial TCP flow control window (RCVWIN)[2]. Each end of the connection chooses its own 32-bit ISN, 16-bit IPID, and 16-bit RCVWIN resulting in a total of 64 bits at each end of the connection to be used by HICCUPS.

While HICCUPS adds meaning to the ISN, the ISN must remain unpredictable to thwart spoofing and off-path packet injection attacks. We therefore add randomness to our ISN integrity function. The bits of randomness, or salt, are sent in the clear to allow the remote host to verify the integrity. We place the random salt value in the lower half of the ISN and exclusive or (XOR)-encode the the integrity information in the upper half of the ISN with the same salt value.

Since the new ISN is created using a function of packet data, it will not be fully random, i.e., the probability of an off-path attacker being able to correctly guess the ISN is greater than $2^{-32}$. In the extreme worst case, the probability is $2^{-16}$, but that requires an attacker know: the flow tuple including the ephemeral port [2], the coverage type used (§4.4), and the exact contents of any packet header fields covered by that type. In practical use, an off-path adversary will not know the coverage type—two of which also cover the ephemeral port.

## 4.3 Integrity Exchange

Fundamental to HICCUPS is exchanging integrity and communication of the check results. Given a safe and reliable transmission mechanism (§4.2), we are able to exchange integrity, coverage, and status. Our objective is to utilize the 64 bits at our disposal in such a way as to be robust against paths that corrupt any of the three integrity exchange fields. In order to withstand a change to any single overloaded field, we place a portion of the integrity information, along with a copy of the coverage or status, in each of the three fields.

Figure 1 presents a simplified timing diagram illustrating the exchange of integrity between two HICCUPS-enabled

[2]Other works leverage these fields for steganographic covert channels [14]. In contrast, our goal is fundamentally different: the HICCUPS algorithm and field population is public.

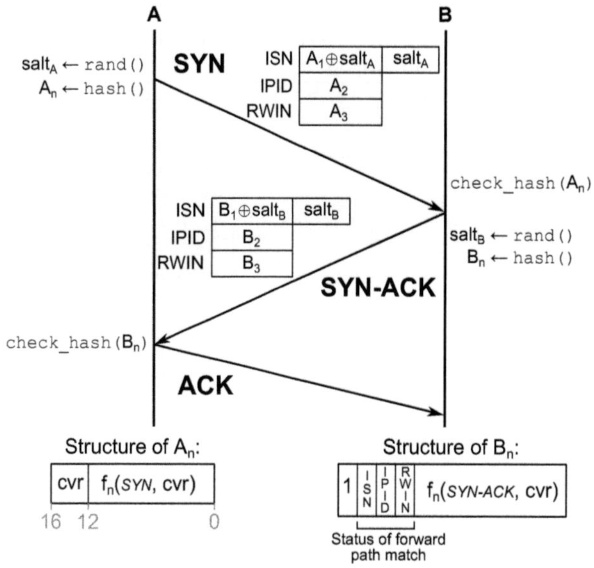


**Figure 1: HICCUPS integrity exchange: *A*'s SYN overloads random fields with integrity and coverage flags. *B*'s SYN-ACK encodes reverse path integrity and forward path status.**

hosts, $A$ and $B$. Unless otherwise noted, HICCUPS follows the TCP standard and uses standard congestion control algorithms (e.g., our implementation retains Linux CUBIC behavior). Host $A$ initiates the active open with $B$. Both SYNs of the three-way handshake (3WHS) utilize the ISN, IPID, and RCVWIN fields to transmit up to 16 bits each of integrity information, denoted in the figure as $A_n$ and $B_n$ where $n = 1...3$ and represents the ISN, IPID, and RCVWIN, respectively. Note that $A_1$ and $B_1$ are encoded with their respective 16-bit random salts.

The internal structure of each 16-bit integrity field $A_n$ and $B_n$ is shown below the timing diagram in Figure 1. Integrity values in the forward path from $A$ contain a 12-bit hash "fragment" and a 4-bit coverage type ($cvr$). The coverage type communicates which portions of the packet header are to be tested, and the same value is copied to each $A_n$. Coverage types are detailed in §4.4.

Similarly, integrity values sent from $B$ each contain a 12-bit hash fragment over packet header fields in the SYN-ACK, and 3 bits to return the forward path integrity results to $A$. $A$ examines these status bits in the received SYN-ACK to infer how its SYN arrived at $B$. To minimally impact the initial flow control window, the highest order bit of $B_3$ can be set to correspond to the true receive window. HICCUPS does not overload the window size field outside of the 3WHS.

In this paper, we abstract the integrity functions used to compute each 12-bit hash fragment as $f_n(\cdot)$. Thus $f_n(SYN, cvr)$ is the $n$'th integrity over the $cvr$ fields in the SYN packet. The integrity function must be public, allowing the host at the other end of the connection, $B$, to check the integrity value it receives. Our experimentally validated [16] implementation in Linux uses a combination of truncated CRC32 and Murmur3 [4]. However, HICCUPS could be standardized to use different functions in the future, based on diffusion and collision-resistance requirements.

Table 2 lists possible inferences $A$ and $B$ can make during connection establishment. When $B$ receives the SYN from $A$, it recomputes each $A'_n$ using the SYN header fields as re-

**Table 2: Possible knowledge gained by each host performing the integrity check**

| At $B$ after receiving SYN | Inference |
|---|---|
| $\lvert A'_n = A_n \rvert \geq 2\ \forall n$ | covered SYN fields unmodified |
| *else* | SYN modified or $A$ not capable |

| At $A$ after SYN-ACK recv'd | Inference |
|---|---|
| $\lvert B'_n = B_n \rvert \geq 2\ \forall n$ | SYN-ACK unmodified |
| $\sum status_i \geq 2\ \forall status \in B_n$ | SYN unmodified |
| Both cases above | SYN & SYN-ACK unmodified |
| *else* | SYN & SYN-ACK modified; or $B$ not capable |

ceived for each of the specified coverage types. The received integrity $A'_n$ matches the sent integrity if $A'_n = A_n$. If at least two of the three recalculated hashes match the received hashes, $B$ infers that the covered fields in $A$'s packet header were unmodified in transit.

Next, $B$ generates its own (different) salt and integrity values for the return SYN-ACK packet. $B$'s results from verifying each $A'_n$ are echoed back to $A$ by the inclusion of boolean flags for each of ISN, IPID, and RCVWIN in the SYN-ACK integrity $B_n$. When $A$ receives the SYN-ACK reply from $B$, it can also check the integrity values. $A$ examines the forward path status bits to determine whether the SYN experienced manipulations.

Using $n = 3$ integrity fields and a combination of hash functions is crucial given the size limits (12 bits each). HICCUPS infers a packet as HICCUPS-capable when any two integrity values match the locally computed integrity ($A'_n = A_n$). Thus, the probability of a pre-image other than the original generating the same hash with two different hash functions is $2^{-24}$, or approximately one in 16M. While this rate is non-negligible, it is low enough for practical use. Measurement instances requiring higher precision can run a HICCUPS integrity test multiple times.

## 4.4 What Header Field Was Modified

HICCUPS allows the connection initiator to specify which packet header field or subset of fields the handshake should check. For instance, a HICCUPS-enabled host opening a new connection could choose to only check the TCP MSS option, or it could focus on just the ECN flags. Each individual connection enabled with HICCUPS specifies which fields to check from a pre-defined list. HICCUPS currently supports the 16 coverage types shown in Table 3. A type that covers both the IP and TCP options blocks can be used to check other options. Our primary reasoning behind these design choices is directed by the highly constrained amount of space (we require the upper bits of $B_n$ for forward path status) and the initiator being the party that typically chooses which options to negotiate for the connection.

All header fields, except for those that are expected to change in transit (e.g., TTL) or fields used to carry integrity, can be covered by HICCUPS. These immutable fields are denoted with a solid gray background in Figure 2. The `HFULL` type is the broadest and covers all of the immutable fields. The remainder of the coverage types we have implemented are proper subsets of these fields.

In order to check multiple types, a progression of HICCUPS connections can be performed between two endpoints. In this progression, each individual connection uses one of the pre-defined coverage sets. The simplest approach is to check all possible coverages in order. Such an approach would require a separate connection for each, but could be done in parallel to reduce the latency of multiple RTTs waiting for results. Alternatively, the inferences might occur during the natural interaction and multiple connections between hosts. A smarter algorithm that could reduce the total number of connections required is described in §5.5.

**Table 3: Pre-defined coverage sets**

| | Coverage Type | Header fields that are covered |
|---|---|---|
| 0 | `HNONAT` | Everything, minus IPs and ports |
| 1 | `HFULL` | Everything |
| 2 | `HNAT` | IPs and ports |
| 3 | `HNOOPT` | `HNONAT` minus any IP or TCP options |
| 4 | `HONLYOPT` | IP and TCP options |
| 5 | `HECNIP` | ECN IP codepoint |
| 6 | `HECNTCP` | ECE and CWR TCP flags |
| 7 | `HLEN` | Length fields |
| 8 | `HMSS` | TCP MSS option |
| 9 | `HWINSCL` | TCP Window Scaling option |
| 10 | `HTSTAMP` | TCP Timestamp option |
| 11 | `HMPTCP` | TCP Multipath option |
| 12 | `HEXOPT` | An unused TCP option (kind = 99) |
| 13 | `HFLAGS` | IP_DF, non-ECN TCP flags, and TCP SACK_Permitted option |
| 14 | `HSAFE` | Reserved fields, protocol, and version |
| 15 | `HNULL` | Nothing (compatibility check) |

Selection of a coverage type for a given connection can be done manually by an application (§4.6) or automatically by the TCP stack. Once a type has been selected, we concatenate the covered packet header fields as input to the HICCUPS integrity functions $f_n(\cdot)$. The only exception is the two bits in the IP header that represent an ECN codepoint. For these two bits, we include their bitwise `OR` as input. Routers are allowed to modify this field, but only by turning an ECT0,1 codepoint into a CE codepoint. Nothing should set both bits to zero if either one was originally set high by an endpoint (an aberration observed in [6]).

Because a field carrying the integrity, $A_n$, could be modified, the endpoint analyzing the SYN must test all the coverage types it sees in the received $A'_n$. Ideally, none of $A_n$ will have been overwritten meaning all three coverage values are the same and only one check must be done. The worst case is that three checks must be done in the event that one or more of $A_n$ were overwritten. If the receiving endpoint finds a match, it must use the same coverage type when calculating $B_n$ for the SYN/ACK. Should the receiver fail to find a match (meaning part of the SYN was modified), a majority rule is used on the three coverage types listed in $A'_n$ to determine the coverage to use for $B_n$. If a majority is not found, a special coverage type is used in $B_n$ to indicate to host $A$ that at least two of $A_n$ were modified.

## 4.5 AppSalt Protection

HICCUPS is designed to be cooperative with middleboxes. Unlike with checksums, packets will not be rejected by a host due to incorrect HICCUPS integrity. Our primary goal is to allow TCP endpoints to choose their extensions based on whether the path will support their correct interpretation end-to-end. By not providing middleboxes with a reason to disrupt HICCUPS, overwriting and recomputation of the integrity fields by middleboxes should be uncommon.

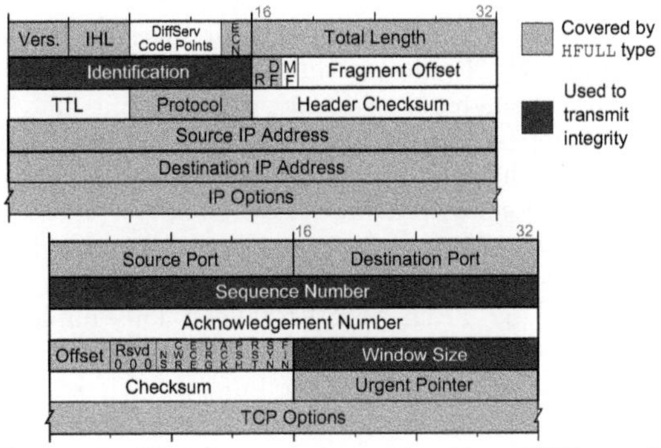


**Figure 2: Header coverage by the HFULL probe**

However, we recognize that future middleboxes, armed with knowledge of HICCUPS, may attempt to recompute hashes in an effort to induce endpoints into a false inference of path integrity. As a result, we designed HICCUPS with an optional, enhanced mode that we term "AppSalt."

AppSalt aims to make undetectable packet header manipulation expensive for a middlebox. With AppSalt, a middlebox must either (*i*) bear the cost of circumvention, (*ii*) reveal the modifications it makes to the endpoints or (*iii*) simply stop meddling in the communication. The value proposition of such a protocol is that (*i*) presents a high enough cost that the middlebox naturally chooses approach (*ii*) or (*iii*).

A middlebox, $M$, could disguise a packet header modification by rewriting the integrity values on SYNs from host $A$. Should $M$ also want to modify the SYN-ACK response, it would perform its changes and then recalculate new integrity for the SYN-ACK sent by $B$. This situation could lead to the reduced effectiveness of HICCUPS at detecting potential extension compatibility issues as middleboxes adjust to evade HICCUPS, but then either fail to properly support newer extensions or suffer from a future misconfiguration.

Since our design constraints preclude the use of a stronger construction, e.g., a keyed-HMAC, we cannot outright prevent $M$ from splitting the connection and recalculating valid integrity values for arbitrary packet header manipulations.

Instead, in AppSalt mode, HICCUPS protects integrity values by encoding them with a property of the connection that is only revealed *after* the 3WHS is complete. Such an "ephemeral secret" could be any property of a connection known only to the sender at the start of the connection.

From the perspective of the middlebox and receiver, the encoded integrity values in the three HICCUPS fields remain indistinguishable from random numbers until the ephemeral secret is revealed later in the connection. Thus, we are able to force a middlebox seeking to recompute our hashes to commit to a strategy *before* it even knows if the connection is HICCUPS-enabled. Since a HICCUPS-enabled TCP need not necessarily perform HICCUPS with every connection request, it is difficult for a middlebox to know when it should try to recompute new hashes. We thus add protection to the integrity while imposing as little of the increased burden as possible on the endhosts. The sending host only has to encode the integrity value and the receiving host only has to store the received integrity until the secret is revealed.

Both the future timing of packets and the number of packets in a flow are possible ephemeral secrets, yet those are difficult to control. Our HICCUPS implementation protects the SYN integrity values with future *application-layer content* from a data packet *yet to be sent*, an ephemeral secret

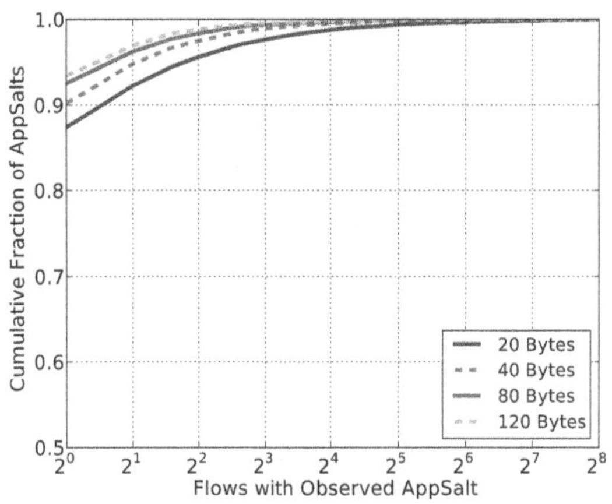


**Figure 3: Cumulative fraction of application-layer payloads ("AppSalts") of different lengths versus number of flows in which the AppSalt appears.**

that is difficult for a middlebox to reliably determine *a priori*. As in §4.3, the integrity values are placed in the ISN, IPID, and RCVWIN of the SYN, but now the receiving endhost, as well as any middleboxes, must know the contents of future application data in order to interpret the integrity.

For the ephemeral application-layer secret, we use a small portion of the data contained in the first data packet to make it simple for the receiver to locate and extract the AppSalt secret. We therefore examined the initial application payload of each flow in a full day of border traffic from our organization. Among application data payloads of 6,742,466 flows, we find 5,377,440 ($\approx$ 80%) where the first 40 bytes are unique. The 99th percentile of the distribution is that payloads appear twice, implying that 40 bytes of ephemeral secret is a reasonable lower-bound to prevent trivial guessing. Figure 3 shows the distributions for various lengths across a 30 minute capture.

To illustrate AppSalt operation, we present a scenario where a client connects to a webserver by performing the 3WHS and issues an HTTP GET request for a specific resource. Neither the remote server nor any in-path middleboxes can reliably determine the application data at the time the SYN is observed. Only the client knows with certainty the initial HTTP application data that will be sent. In this example, the application layer data might contain such items as the GET URL, the host parameter, and the user agent string as shown in the example of Figure 4.

Since the application data needed to properly decode the SYN's integrity is not available to $M$ at the time the SYN is received, it is difficult for $M$ to make an undetectable header modification or even just to check whether the connection is HICCUPS-enabled. The ephemeral secret forces $M$ to process the SYN packet before it can observe the application data. Otherwise, $M$ has two remaining options if its goal is to modify the packet headers and evade detection: make a best guess of the application data, or perform a man-in-the-middle (MITM) attack and fake a SYN-ACK response, inducing $A$ to expose the application data secret.

$M$ may attempt to guess the unseen application data, e.g., by using a profile of prior connections from $A$ to $B$. However, $M$ is unlikely to guess correctly for every connection between all pairs of hosts. If $M$ guesses incorrectly, integrity values will not validate and the manipulations can be detected. Of course, $M$ could later change the actual application data

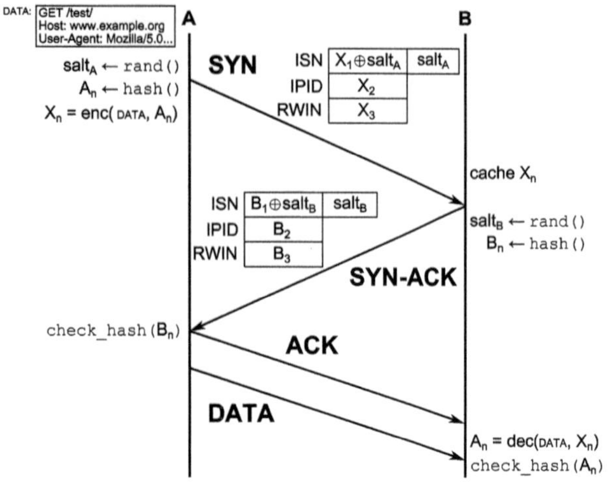


**Figure 4: HICCUPS AppSalt protection: the integrity values in the SYN are encoded with application-layer data *yet to be sent*, forming an ephemeral secret that raises the bar on middleboxes attempting to evade HICCUPS diagnostics.**

to match its guess, but doing so fundamentally alters the application-layer behavior of the connection.

In order to know the application data with certainty, $M$ must act as a TCP-terminating proxy, a behavior that is detectable based on timing and by issuing connections to known unreachable hosts as shown in [31]. This MITM behavior, whereby $M$ falsely claims to be $B$, spoofs the SYN-ACK and intercepts the resulting traffic, permits $M$ to rebuild the original SYN with an updated integrity value and forward it along to the true destination. The non-spoofed SYN-ACK from $B$ must be intercepted and the cached data from $A$ could be sent. This situation is more complicated than just rebuilding the integrity values; the middlebox has broken a connection and now has to marshal data between them, in addition to sending spoofed packets and buffering data. Further, the middlebox must do this for all connections, potentially representing many endpoints.

AppSalt represents our proactive approach to ensuring the continued effectiveness of HICCUPS once its algorithms and protocol become widely known. Another possible disruption technique is to perform a downgrade attack by arbitrarily overwriting all fields used by HICCUPS for integrity. This does not circumvent the tamper-evidence, however, and the downgrade fails when there is outside *a priori* knowledge that the remote end is performing HICCUPS.

## 4.6 API

We have implemented HICCUPS as a patch to Linux kernel 3.9 [15]. We allow applications to request a certain coverage via a `setsockopt()` call specifying their desired coverage type (§4.4). Similarly, applications can read results of a HICCUPS diagnostic from the kernel with `getsockopt()`.

The use of AppSalt mode requires a minor change to the sockets API. Traditionally, a client program issues a series of socket calls: `socket()`, `connect()`, and `send()`. However, with AppSalt, `connect()` cannot be called first as it will initiate the 3WHS and send the SYN before the kernel has the necessary application data over which to calculate integrity.

We therefore leverage the same socket API changes implemented by TCP Fast Open (TFO), a TCP modification that similarly requires data be known at the time of connection initiation [39]. Programs that use TFO initiate all connections using `sendto()` or `sendmsg()` with the `MSG_FASTOPEN` flag, as opposed to the typical `connect()` and `send()` sequence. In this way, the kernel can embed data in the SYN for connections with a valid TFO cookie.

To allow a client program to request AppSalt-mode HICCUPS, we add a new message flag within the framework established by TFO: "`MSG_HICCUPS`." This implementation style makes the addition of HICCUPS support trivial for applications that already support TFO, e.g., Google Chrome [23]. If application data cannot be used, i.e., a program does not use the new socket calls or it is a TFO connection with data in the SYN, plain HICCUPS is used instead (as in Figure 1).

# 5. RESULTS

This section details results from running HICCUPS in the wild. We examine the types, frequencies, and symmetry of HICCUPS-inferred modifications and give examples of how a TCP HICCUPS instance can adjust its behavior based on path inference to improve performance. Last, we discuss HICCUPS overhead, including the empirical number of RTTs for full-path characterization.

## 5.1 Controlled Environment

To test the validity of HICCUPS inferences, we validated against known ground truth in a controlled laboratory environment. Using NFQUEUE [10] and Scapy [7], we simulated a middlebox that makes a variety of packet header modifications [16]. On virtual machines running the HICCUPS kernel we performed 50,000 trials that established 3.2 million TCP connections—all traversing the middlebox simulator. Automated verification found that HICCUPS properly inferred the path behavior for 100% of the connections.

## 5.2 Overhead

We examined server-side overhead associated with HICCUPS using the Linux kernel's ftrace facility. Taking the average over 1000 connection attempts, we compared the total time spent processing a SYN/ACK between the HICCUPS-patched kernel and a vanilla kernel. We found that the average overhead added by our unoptimized implementation is about 8.5% of the compute time in the vanilla kernel.

Should a server begin to exhaust its resources (possibly due to a SYN flood or denial-of-service attack), mitigation methods are already available in the kernel to reduce this overhead. As the connection backlog fills, Linux can switch from processing HICCUPS checks on incoming SYNs to creating SYN cookies. While SYN cookies and HICCUPS cannot be used at the same time, they can still gracefully coexist since the situations where they perform best do not overlap.

## 5.3 Surveying Internet Paths with HICCUPS

While previous research (e.g., [6, 17, 25, 31, 36]) examined real Internet paths to catalog various forms of packet header modifications, these efforts required some degree of interaction external to the operating systems. To our knowledge, HICCUPS is the first solution to both capture measurements of packet header modifications within TCP and expose the results *directly through the operating system itself.* For example, the servers in our measurement infrastructure do not run any specialized server application. Instead, we simply start a standard HTTP daemon that listens on the desired

**Table 4: Top ASNs represented**

| Servers | | PlanetLab | | Ark | |
|---|---|---|---|---|---|
| AS16509 | 6 | AS680 | 13 | AS22773 | 3 |
| ... | 1 ea. | AS2200 | 6 | AS1213 | 2 |
| | | AS766 | 6 | ... | 1 ea. |
| | | ... | <6 ea. | | |
| Total | 7 | Total | 154 | Total | 53 |

**Table 5: Geographic distribution**

| Location | PlanetLab | Ark | Servers |
|---|---|---|---|
| Europe | 101 | 18 | 1 |
| N. America | 75 | 25 | 7 |
| Asia | 26 | 9 | 2 |
| S. America | 10 | 1 | 1 |
| Oceania | 6 | 0 | 1 |
| Africa | 0 | 3 | 0 |
| Total | 218 | 56 | 12 |

port(s). With a HICCUPS-enabled kernel, no extra support is required to perform HICCUPS and expose path behaviors to the operating system and applications.

Using HICCUPS-enabled hosts, we survey a diverse set of real Internet paths. We employ 218 Planetlab [11] nodes, 56 Archipelago (Ark) [26] nodes, and 12 distributed HICCUPS servers; the Autonomous System (ASN) and geographic distribution of our infrastructure is given in Tables 4 and 5. This infrastructure enables us to run HICCUPS between 3,288 pairs of distinct hosts, testing 26,304 directed path/port pairs.

### 5.3.1 *Experimental Infrastructure*

Our HICCUPS-enabled Linux kernel runs on 12 systems: four at the authors' institutions and one at each of the eight Amazon EC2 infrastructure sites. To run HICCUPS from PlanetLab (where installing a custom Linux kernel is not possible), we duplicate the connection initiation portion of TCP with HICCUPS into a user-space client that employs raw sockets to craft HICCUPS-enabled SYNs.

In selecting PlanetLab nodes, we used PlanetLab's management API to use a single node per site. Thus, all 218 Planetlab nodes we use represent distinct sites. The PlanetLab nodes were distributed both geographically and logically around the Internet. The Planetlab and Ark nodes reside in 207 distinct ASNs. Geographically, our Planetlab nodes are situated in five continents and 37 different countries, while the Ark nodes are spread across 28 countries.

### 5.3.2 *Experimental Parameters*

From each PlanetLab and Ark vantage point, we execute SYN exchanges with each server on four different TCP ports to capture port-specific behavior: 22, 80, 443, and 34343. The first three are common service ports; port 34343 is used for consistency with [25]. We send 16 SYNs to each of the four ports, with each SYN covering one of the different coverage types listed in Table 3. Note that not all paths require all 16 connections to fully ascertain the path conditions from HICCUPS; ~90% of paths can be fully characterized in two RTTs. We examine this aspect further in §5.5.

To make middlebox modification behaviors visible, we must enable different TCP and IP extensions during the connection setup. Table 6 lists the sets of options we use in our experiments, including MSS, SACK permitted, Window Scale, Timestamp [27], Multipath TCP MPCAPABLE [20], and a non-standard experimental option with a kind value of 99.

**Table 6: Experimental parameters for each trial**

| Trial | MSS | ECN | SACK Permit | Win Scale | Time stamp | MP-TCP | Exp |
|---|---|---|---|---|---|---|---|
| 1 | 1460 | | Y | 7 | Y | | Y |
| 2 | 1460 | | Y | 7 | Y | Y | |
| 3 | 1460 | | Y | 7 | Y | | |
| 4 | 1460 | Y | | | | | |
| 5 | 480 | | | | | | |
| 6 | 1460 | | | | | | |
| 7 | 1600 | | | | | | |
| 8 | None | | | | | | |

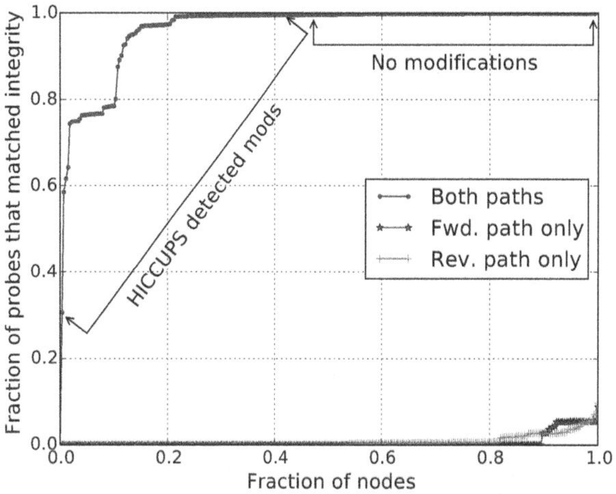


**Figure 5: Distribution of matching probes, by path direction. NAT modifications have been excluded.**

## 5.4 Detected Modifications

Following the inference procedure in §4.3 and Table 2, we use HICCUPS to detect a variety of packet header manipulations. If a probe passes integrity checks at the receiver and the forward path status bits return intact, the TCP initiator infers that its packets (on the forward path) arrive without modification. Similarly, if the integrity checks on the SYN-ACK match, the initiator infers that the reverse path does not modify headers. All data we present in this section comes from the clients on PlanetLab and Ark.

Figure 5 displays the cumulative fraction of probes per host with passing integrity versus the fraction of nodes (PlanetLab and Ark nodes combined with NAT results excluded). The common case is that both the forward and reverse paths experience no modifications. For approximately half of the nodes, all probes match integrity, while approximately 80% of the nodes have 99% of their probes match integrity. The distributions for the two asymmetrical integrity results are visible in the lower-right of the figure. Approximately 80% of nodes never experience this case.

Table 7 summarizes the probe results according to coverage type. The most common modification is paths that add or change MSS values. The HNAT—and consequently the inclusive HFULL probe—fails for the large majority of paths. This is unsurprising as address translation is performed near the server for 9 of our 12 servers. We verified that while our Amazon EC2 servers experienced NAT, they made no other header modifications. In the following subsections, we more closely examine specific modifications.

### 5.4.1 *ISN translation*

We find incidences of sequence number translation in tests from 24 of 218 Planetlab nodes (11.0%). The ISNs are trans-

**Table 7: Summary of results by coverage type**

| Coverage | Integrity Match | | | | |
|---|---|---|---|---|---|
| | Both | Fwd | Rev | Neither | Timeout |
| HFULL | 21867 | 597 | 985 | 80931 | 836 |
| HNAT | 25286 | 2 | 0 | 79129 | 799 |
| HNONAT | 91214 | 2397 | 2459 | 8329 | 817 |
| HNOOPT | 100535 | 71 | 2050 | 1732 | 828 |
| HONLYOPT | 92948 | 2542 | 1162 | 7736 | 828 |
| HECNIP | 102066 | 69 | 1693 | 572 | 816 |
| HECNTCP | 103777 | 10 | 47 | 585 | 797 |
| HLEN | 103451 | 17 | 359 | 574 | 815 |
| HMSS | 93365 | 2545 | 855 | 7632 | 819 |
| HWINSCL | 103685 | 16 | 5 | 690 | 820 |
| HTSTAMP | 103834 | 27 | 7 | 539 | 809 |
| HMPTCP | 103023 | 20 | 837 | 551 | 785 |
| HEXOPT | 102907 | 12 | 888 | 564 | 845 |
| HFLAGS | 102591 | 18 | 76 | 1719 | 812 |
| HSAFE | 103824 | 16 | 0 | 551 | 825 |
| HNULL | 103752 | 21 | 0 | 563 | 880 |
| Total | 1458125 | 8380 | 11423 | 192397 | 13131 |

lated in both directions on 20 nodes, while for four nodes, just the forward path translates sequence numbers. Only one of the Ark nodes is subject to ISN translation that occurs on forward path only.

The frequent occurrence of sequence number translation motivates in part our choice to use three hash fragments, as detailed in §4.3. If, for instance, the ISN alone carried integrity, HICCUPS would not work for 25 of our 274 nodes and we would be unable to detect any header modifications beyond ISN translation. In contrast, HICCUPS can withstand a single modification to any one of the three integrity-carrying fields (ISN, IPID, and RCVWIN).

However, should any pair of the three fields be modified, HICCUPS loses the capability to detect specific field modifications, only noting that a change occurred to at least one pair of the three integrity fields. Table 8 lists paths where this behavior occurs under the heading "HICCUPS not capable." 68 flows from PlanetLab (0.7%) and 4 flows from Ark (0.2%) saw two or more integrity fields overwritten. Since we control all the nodes, we performed post-mortem analysis of packet captures taken during measurement and see that the TCP receive window is artificially lowered in-path. In practical use, however, HICCUPS cannot obtain any fine-grained information for such paths.

### 5.4.2 ECN

We monitor behavior of the ECN fields in both the IP and TCP headers. Figure 6 shows the results of each probe arranged by host in the combined PlanetLab and Ark datasets. Each of the three plots in the figure represents the results from probing each of the 48 server ports from each of the 274 nodes. Each plot is sorted so that primary result types are grouped together. The first plot shows the behavior when ECN was disabled, while the lower two show behavior after ECN has been enabled. While ECE and CWR TCP flags are rarely affected (we only saw such mods on paths from one PlanetLab node), modifications to the IP codepoint are more common. We observed ~13% of paths on both PlanetLab and Ark would zero the codepoint if it were enabled.

### 5.4.3 Application Performance

An important consequence of HICCUPS is that knowledge of the end-to-end header modification state of a path can improve the performance of applications that depend on

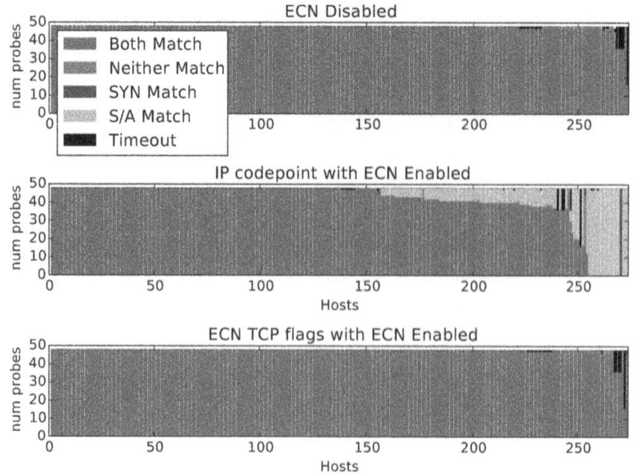


**Figure 6: Distribution of HICCUPS-inferred ECN path properties. For the IP codepoint, HICCUPS only notes a change to the OR of the bits (§4.4).**

TCP. For instance, in the case of sequence number translation that is SACK-naïve, performance suffers in proportion to loss rate [24]. For ECN, performance suffers when false congestion signals are inadvertently marked, experiencing dramatic performance impact if a congestion codepoint is added, or a TCP-layer congestion echo is added [6]. To highlight the potential impact on TCP performance, we examine a particular effect, observed in the wild, in detail.

We find a node where the forward communication transparently adds a TCP window scale value of 7 to the SYN, but the reverse path strips the window scale by replacing it with 4 NOP options in the returned SYN-ACK. The behavior is destination port-specific: it did not occur on connection attempts to ports 22 or 34343, only to 80 and 443. Ultimately, one end of the communication believes that window scaling negotiation has occurred, while the other does not.

We perform bulk transfer to the node performing window scaling and observe that the traffic is flow controlled—the receiver is sending scaled values in the receive window, but the sender interprets those values as unscaled. HICCUPS informs us of the option mangling and we disable window scaling. Our performance tests reveal a dramatic difference where the throughput more than doubles without window scaling since the congestion window can open more than one or two MSS. We alerted the operator of the node and they were unaware of the behavior. Further investigation revealed the issue was with a system in their provider's network.

## 5.5 Complete Path Knowledge

Given that only one coverage set from §4.4 is used per TCP 3WHS, a pair of TCP endpoints must develop fully granular knowledge of all header modifications over the course of multiple exchanges. When integrity matches for a coverage type that is a superset of other types, e.g., HFULL, no further information is gained from additional probing. However, if the integrity fails to match, more specific types can be used next to narrow down the source of the modification.

If integrity using HNULL does not match, then either one of two cases is occurring: (i) two or more of our three integrity fields are being modified, or (ii) the host with which we are interacting does not understand HICCUPS. Since HNULL is a diagnostic type that does not cover other fields, it should not fail unless the hash fragments are not present.

Table 8: **Summary of HICCUPS-inferred header modifications. Detection of ISN, IPID, and RCVWIN are mutually exclusive to HICCUPS. If two or three occurred, it registered as "HICCUPS not capable" instead.**

| | Planetlab | | | | | Ark | | | | |
|---|---|---|---|---|---|---|---|---|---|---|
| **Change** | **Both** | **Fwd** | **Rev** | **Flows** | **Affected** | **Both** | **Fwd** | **Rev** | **Flows** | **Affected** |
| HICCUPS not capable | 68 | 0 | 2 | 10360 | 0.68% | 4 | 0 | 0 | 2684 | 0.15% |
| NAT | 7704 | 0 | 0 | 10281 | 74.93% | 2114 | 0 | 0 | 2677 | 78.97% |
| ISN translation | 924 | 178 | 0 | 10290 | 10.71% | 0 | 48 | 0 | 2680 | 1.79% |
| IPID change | 0 | 0 | 0 | 10290 | 0.00% | 0 | 0 | 0 | 2680 | 0.00% |
| RCVWIN change | 0 | 0 | 0 | 10290 | 0.00% | 0 | 0 | 0 | 2680 | 0.00% |
| ECN IP add | 26 | 0 | 0 | 10270 | 0.25% | 2 | 0 | 0 | 2664 | 0.08% |
| ECN IP change | 16 | 1342 | 48 | 10283 | 13.67% | 11 | 342 | 0 | 2675 | 13.20% |
| ECN TCP add | 16 | 0 | 0 | 10261 | 0.16% | 6 | 0 | 0 | 2670 | 0.22% |
| ECN TCP change | 19 | 46 | 0 | 10285 | 0.63% | 16 | 0 | 0 | 2675 | 0.60% |
| MSS add | 119 | 47 | 1036 | 10258 | 11.72% | 10 | 96 | 140 | 2668 | 9.22% |
| MSS480 change | 21 | 0 | 1132 | 10281 | 11.21% | 5 | 0 | 139 | 2674 | 5.39% |
| MSS1460 change | 1113 | 0 | 0 | 10275 | 10.83% | 134 | 12 | 12 | 2678 | 5.90% |
| MSS1600 change | 1105 | 157 | 0 | 10294 | 12.26% | 140 | 154 | 12 | 2672 | 11.45% |
| SACK Permit changed | 1 | 24 | 0 | 10123 | 0.25% | 0 | 0 | 0 | 2667 | 0.00% |
| Timestamps add | 12 | 0 | 0 | 10267 | 0.12% | 9 | 0 | 0 | 2669 | 0.34% |
| Timestamps change | 26 | 2 | 0 | 10279 | 0.27% | 10 | 0 | 0 | 2672 | 0.37% |
| Window Scaling add | 45 | 0 | 0 | 10265 | 0.44% | 9 | 0 | 0 | 2665 | 0.34% |
| Window Scaling change | 24 | 0 | 0 | 10279 | 0.23% | 5 | 0 | 0 | 2669 | 0.19% |
| `MPCAPABLE` change | 24 | 837 | 0 | 10267 | 8.39% | 8 | 0 | 0 | 2673 | 0.30% |
| Exp. option change | 20 | 884 | 0 | 10266 | 8.81% | 13 | 0 | 0 | 2676 | 0.49% |

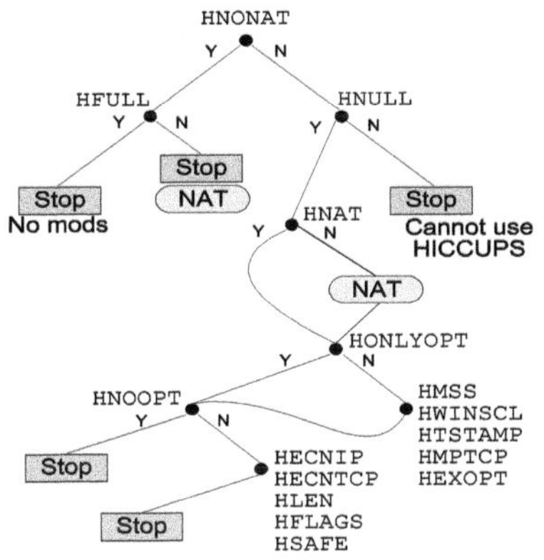


**Figure 7: HICCUPS Search Strategy**

Leveraging this information, we design a path interrogation strategy for HICCUPS. Using HICCUPS to determine the fully granular set of modifications along a path is similar in nature to a search problem. Our informed strategy is shown in Figure 7. We begin by checking coverages that are more comprehensive and then narrow the search, eventually checking a smaller sequence of types. Upon our first interaction with a TCP endpoint, we choose the `HNONAT` coverage type since it avoids fields modified by NATs, which are prevalent on the Internet [31]. If we find a match, we conclude the search. Subsequent connection attempts can retest using the `HNONAT` type in case the path conditions change.

Given that we expect regular interaction with non-HICCUPS TCP stacks, our strategy employs the `HNULL` type at the next opportunity. By doing so, we can terminate the search in the event that either the other endpoint (due to lack of capability) or middleboxes along the path (due to downgrading the integrity) prevent HICCUPS from being used. The remainder of the strategy searches for header modifications in either the options space or fixed-length fields, iterating through a series of more granular coverage types as needed.

### *5.5.1 Expected Interactions Required*

Across real paths in our PlanetLab and Ark datasets, we calculated the number of TCP interactions it would take for

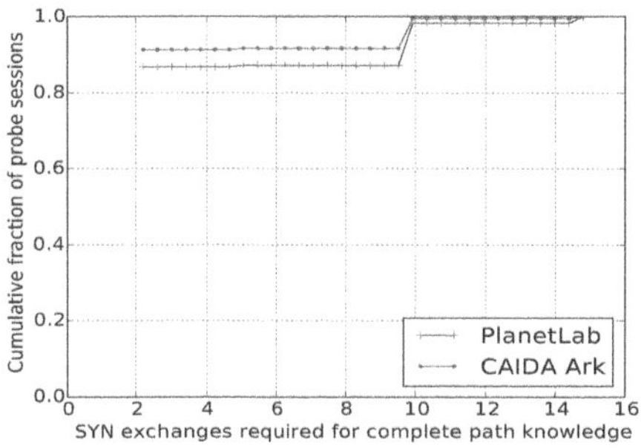


**Figure 8: Empirical HICCUPS RTTs required for complete path properties inference**

two HICCUPS hosts to fully ascertain the path header modification state. For PlanetLab, our dataset contained 83,712 flows with 261,185 total SYN exchanges required to fully explore the space of header modifications with HICCUPS. This amounts to an average of 3.1 SYN exchanges per flow. For Ark, we required 58,083 SYN exchanges across a total of 21,504 flows, for an average of 2.7 exchanges per flow.

Figure 8 shows that about 85% of flows were able to fully determine the modifications of their paths after checking just `HNONAT` and `HFULL`. Should NAT detection not be desired, the check for `HFULL` could be omitted from the strategy shown in Figure 7, further reducing the required number of probes.

## 6. CONCLUSIONS

Debugging IP network problems end-to-end is a difficult, often manual process exacerbated by the presence of currently opaque middleboxes. We present TCP HICCUPS, a backward-compatible and incrementally deployable extension to TCP that reveals packet header manipulation to both sides of a TCP connection, enabling endpoints to make the inferences needed to best adapt to middleboxes along their paths. For example, we show how HICCUPS helps achieve twice the throughput over a TCP naïve to paths that modify window scaling. HICCUPS can also help facilitate the safe deployment of new and experimental options.

Beyond improving TCP performance, widespread HICCUPS deployment could provide invaluable data to researchers, policy makers, and protocol designers. Measurements from running HICCUPS across a distributed and diverse set of paths discover a wide variety of (sometimes asymmetric) behaviors, including paths that modify, delete, or insert: sequence number, IPID or receive window, ECN, MSS, timestamps, window scaling, Multipath TCP, and an experimental option. Crucially, header modification behaviors are discovered by a HICCUPS-enabled TCP stack without prior coordination from the remote endpoint. Such a usage model also enables new diagnostic capabilities for network operators to help troubleshoot middlebox configurations on both forward and reverse data planes.

In future work, we wish to refine the efficient search strategy used by HICCUPS to granulate header modifications by field. We plan integration with response algorithms for TCP to automate the performance gains that HICCUPS inferences enable. To this end, we plan a more extensive performance characterization of selectively toggling extensions in response to behavior inferred by HICCUPS. Another approach we will pursue is to examine how some middleboxes, such as the array of proxy devices in mobile networks, could utilize and safely interact with HICCUPS integrity information. Last, we wish to continue our survey of Internet paths, analyzing header modifications and their impact over many more types of paths and investigating the potential to characterize middleboxes by the modifications they induce, e.g., TCP `NOP` options that are not required for alignment.

## Acknowledgments

We thank Geoff Xie, Nick Weaver, Mark Gondree, Justin Rohrer, and our shepherd Vivek Pai. Steve Bauer, Young Hyun, and Mark Richer provided infrastructure and testing. This work is supported in part by National Science Foundation (NSF) grants CNS-1213155, CNS-1213157, and CNS-1237265, and SPAWAR Systems Center Atlantic NISE. This material represents the position of the authors and does not reflect the official policy or position of the U.S. Government.

## 7. REFERENCES

[1] ABI. Enterprise network and data security spending shows remarkable resilience, Jan. 2011. http://goo.gl/E5Unmb.

[2] M. Allman. Comments on Selecting Ephemeral Ports. *SIGCOMM Comput. Commun. Rev.*, 39(2):13–19, Mar. 2009.

[3] Anonymous. Private communication, 2011.

[4] A. Appleby. MurmurHash 3.0, 2011.

[5] F. Baker. Requirements for IPv4 routers. RFC 1812, 1995.

[6] S. Bauer, R. Beverly, and A. Berger. Measuring the State of ECN Readiness in Servers, Clients, and Routers. In *Proceedings of the ACM SIGCOMM IMC*, pages 171–180, Nov. 2011.

[7] P. Biondi. Scapy. http://goo.gl/aTHPX8.

[8] A. Bittau, M. Hamburg, M. Handley, D. Mazières, and D. Boneh. The case for ubiquitous transport-level encryption. In *Proc. of the USENIX Security Symposium*, Aug. 2010.

[9] B. Carpenter and S. Brim. Middleboxes: Taxonomy and issues. RFC 3234, Feb. 2002.

[10] P. Chifflier. nfqueue-bindings. http://goo.gl/0OmFi9.

[11] B. Chun, D. Culler, T. Roscoe, A. Bavier, L. Peterson, M. Wawrzoniak, and M. Bowman. PlanetLab: an overlay testbed for broad-coverage services. *SIGCOMM Comput. Commun. Rev.*, 33(3):3–12, July 2003.

[12] Cisco Systems. Single TCP flow performance on firewall services module (FWSM), Oct. 2011. http://goo.gl/GktT8Z.

[13] D. Clark. The design philosophy of the DARPA internet protocols. *SIGCOMM CCR*, 18(4):106–114, Aug. 1988.

[14] E. Cole. *Hiding in Plain Sight: Steganography and the Art of Covert Communication.* Wiley Publishing Inc., 2003.

[15] R. Craven, R. Beverly, and M. Allman. Handshake-based Integrity Check of Critical Underlying Protocol Semantics (HICCUPS), 2014. http://tcphiccups.org.

[16] R. Craven, R. Beverly, and M. Allman. Techniques for the detection of faulty packet header modifications. Technical Report NPS-CS-14-002, Naval Postgraduate School, Mar. 2014.

[17] G. Detal, B. Hesmans, O. Bonaventure, Y. Vanaubel, and B. Donnet. Revealing Middlebox Interference with Tracebox. In *Proc. of the ACM SIGCOMM IMC*, pages 1–8, Oct. 2013.

[18] M. Dischinger, M. Marcon, S. Guha, P. K. Gummadi, R. Mahajan, and S. Saroiu. Glasnost: Enabling End Users to Detect Traffic Differentiation. In *USENIX NSDI*, 2010.

[19] R. Fonseca, G. Porter, R. Katz, S. Shenker, and I. Stoica. IP Options are not an option. Technical Report 2005-24, EECS UC Berkeley, Dec. 2005.

[20] A. Ford, C. Raiciu, M. Handley, and O. Bonaventure. TCP extensions for multipath operation with multiple addresses. RFC 6824, Jan. 2013.

[21] A. Freier, P. Karlton, and P. Kocher. The Secure Sockets Layer (SSL) Protocol Version 3.0. RFC 6101, Aug. 2011.

[22] A. Gember, P. Prabhu, Z. Ghadiyali, and A. Akella. Toward Software-Defined Middlebox Networking. In *Proc. of the ACM HotNets Workshop*, Oct. 2012.

[23] Google Inc. chromium code search, 2013. http://goo.gl/8PQrpG.

[24] B. Hesmans, F. Duchene, C. Paasch, G. Detal, and O. Bonaventure. Are TCP Extensions Middlebox-proof? In *Proc. of the HotMiddlebox Workshop*, pages 37–42, 2013.

[25] M. Honda, Y. Nishida, C. Raiciu, A. Greenhalgh, M. Handley, and H. Tokuda. Is it Still Possible to Extend TCP? In *Proc. of the ACM SIGCOMM IMC*, pages 181–194, 2011.

[26] Y. Hyun and k. claffy. Archipelago (Ark) measurement infrastructure. CAIDA, 2014. http://goo.gl/HY9AgZ.

[27] V. Jacobson, R. Braden, and D. Borman. TCP Extensions for High Performance. RFC 1323, May 1992.

[28] S. Kent. IP authentication header. RFC 4302, Dec. 2005.

[29] S. Kent and K. Seo. Security architecture for the Internet Protocol. RFC 4301, Dec. 2005.

[30] A. Knutsen, A. Ramaiah, and A. Ramasamy. TCP option for transparent Middlebox negotiation. Internet draft, Feb. 2013.

[31] C. Kreibich, N. Weaver, B. Nechaev, and V. Paxson. Netalyzr: Illuminating The Edge Network. In *SIGCOMM IMC*, 2010.

[32] A. Langley. Opportunistic Encryption Everywhere. *Web 2.0 Security and Privacy (W2SP)*, May 2009.

[33] M. Luckie and B. Stasiewicz. Measuring Path MTU Discovery Behaviour. In *Proc. of the ACM SIGCOMM IMC*, 2010.

[34] D. Malone and M. Luckie. Analysis of ICMP Quotations. In *Proc. of PAM Conference*. Apr. 2007.

[35] M. Mathis and J. Heffner. Packetization layer path MTU discovery. RFC 4821, Mar. 2007.

[36] A. Medina, M. Allman, and S. Floyd. Measuring the Evolution of Transport Protocols in the Internet. *SIGCOMM Comput. Commun. Rev.*, 35(2):37–52, Apr. 2005.

[37] K. Nichols, S. Blake, F. Baker, and D. Black. Definition of the differentiated services field (DS field) in the IPv4 and IPv6 headers. RFC 2474, Dec. 1998.

[38] Z. A. Qazi, C.-C. Tu, L. Chiang, R. Miao, V. Sekar, and M. Yu. SIMPLE-fying Middlebox Policy Enforcement Using SDN. In *Proc. of the ACM SIGCOMM Conference*, Aug. 2013.

[39] S. Radhakrishnan, Y. Cheng, J. Chu, A. Jain, and B. Raghavan. TCP Fast Open. In *Proc. of CoNEXT*, 2011.

[40] C. Reis, S. Gribble, T. Kohno, and N. Weaver. Detecting In-Flight Page Changes with Web Tripwires. In *Proc. of the USENIX Symposium on NSDI*, Apr. 2008.

[41] V. Sekar, S. Ratnasamy, M. K. Reiter, N. Egi, and G. Shi. The Middlebox Manifesto: Enabling Innovation in Middlebox Deployment. In *Proc. of the ACM HotNets Workshop*, 2011.

[42] J. Sherry, S. Hasan, C. Scott, A. Krishnamurthy, S. Ratnasamy, and V. Sekar. Making Middleboxes Someone Else's Problem: Network Processing as a Cloud Service. In *Proc. of the ACM SIGCOMM Conference*, pages 13–24, Aug. 2012.

[43] J. Stone and C. Partridge. When the CRC and TCP checksum disagree. *SIGCOMM CCR*, 30(4):309–319, 2000.

[44] J. Touch, A. Mankin, and R. Bonica. The TCP authentication option. RFC 5925, June 2010.

[45] M. Walfish, J. Stribling, M. Krohn, H. Balakrishnan, R. Morris, and S. Shenker. Middleboxes No Longer Considered Harmful. In *Proc. of the USENIX Symposium on OSDI*, Dec. 2004.

[46] Z. Wang, Z. Qian, Q. Xu, Z. Mao, and M. Zhang. An Untold Story of Middleboxes in Cellular Networks. In *Proc. of the ACM SIGCOMM Conference*, pages 374–385, Aug. 2011.

# OpenNF: Enabling Innovation in Network Function Control

Aaron Gember-Jacobson, Raajay Viswanathan, Chaithan Prakash, Robert Grandl,
Junaid Khalid, Sourav Das, and Aditya Akella
University of Wisconsin-Madison
{agember,raajay,cprakash,rgrandl,junaid,souravd,akella}@cs.wisc.edu
http://opennf.cs.wisc.edu

## ABSTRACT

Network functions virtualization (NFV) together with software-defined networking (SDN) has the potential to help operators satisfy tight service level agreements, accurately monitor and manipulate network traffic, and minimize operating expenses. However, in scenarios that require packet processing to be redistributed across a collection of network function (NF) instances, simultaneously achieving all three goals requires a framework that provides efficient, coordinated control of both internal NF state and network forwarding state. To this end, we design a control plane called OpenNF. We use carefully designed APIs and a clever combination of events and forwarding updates to address race conditions, bound overhead, and accommodate a variety of NFs. Our evaluation shows that OpenNF offers efficient state control without compromising flexibility, and requires modest additions to NFs.

## Categories and Subject Descriptors

C.2.1 [**Computer Communication Networks**]: Network Architecture and Design; C.2.3 [**Computer Communication Networks**]: Network Operations

## Keywords

Network functions, middleboxes, software-defined networking

## 1. INTRODUCTION

Network functions (NFs), or middleboxes, are systems that examine and modify packets and flows in sophisticated ways: e.g., intrusion detection systems (IDSs), load balancers, caching proxies, etc. NFs play a critical role in ensuring security, improving performance, and providing other novel network functionality [37].

Recently, we have seen a growing interest in replacing dedicated NF hardware with software-based NFs running on generic compute resources—a trend known as network functions virtualization (NFV) [12]. In parallel, software-defined networking (SDN) is being used to steer flows through appropriate NFs to enforce policies and jointly manage network and NF load [17, 20, 22, 26, 32].


*SIGCOMM'14*, August 17–22, 2014, Chicago, IL, USA.
Copyright 2014 ACM 978-1-4503-2836-4/14/08 ...$15.00.
http://dx.doi.org/10.1145/2619239.2626313.

Together, NFV and SDN can enable an important class of management applications that need to *dynamically redistribute packet processing across multiple instances of an NF*—e.g., NF load balancing [32] and elastic NF scaling [21]. In the context of such applications, "NFV + SDN" can help achieve three important goals: (**1**) satisfy tight service level agreements (SLAs) on NF performance or availability; (**2**) accurately monitor and manipulate network traffic, e.g., an IDS should raise alerts for *all* flows containing known malware; and (**3**) minimize NF operating costs. However, simultaneously achieving all three goals is not possible today, and fundamentally requires more control than NFV + SDN can offer.

To see why, consider a scenario where an IDS is overloaded and must be scaled out in order to satisfy SLAs on throughput (Figure 1). With NFV we can easily launch a new IDS instance, and with SDN we can reroute some in-progress flows to the new instance [17, 32]. However, attacks may go undetected because the necessary internal NF state is unavailable at the new instance. To overcome this problem, an SDN control application can wait for existing flows to terminate and only reroute new flows [22, 38], but this delays the mitigation of overload and increases the likelihood of SLA violations. NF accuracy may also be impacted due to some NF-internal state not being copied or shared.

In this example, the only way to avoid a trade-off between NF accuracy and performance is to allow a control application to *quickly and safely move the internal IDS state for some flows* from the original instance to the new instance, and *update network forwarding state alongside*. Similar needs arise in the context of other applications that rely on dynamic reallocation of packet processing: e.g., rapid NF upgrades and dynamic invocation of remote processing.

In this paper, we present OpenNF, a control plane architecture that *provides efficient, coordinated control of both internal NF state and network forwarding state* to allow quick, safe, and fine-grained reallocation of flows across NF instances. Using OpenNF, operators can create rich control applications that redistribute processing to optimally meet their performance, availability, security and cost objectives, thus avoiding the need to make undesirable trade-offs.

We address three major challenges in designing OpenNF:

**C1: Addressing race conditions.** This is the most basic issue that arises when reallocating in-progress flows: When some internal NF state is being moved, packets may arrive at the source instance after the move starts, or at the destination instance before the state transfer finishes. Unless care is taken, updates to NF state due to such packets may either be lost or happen out of order, violating move safety. Similarly, when state is copied across NF instances, updates occurring contemporaneously may cause state to become inconsistent. Depending on the NF, these issues may hurt its accuracy.

To account for race conditions, we introduce two novel constructs: (1) an event abstraction to externally observe and prevent

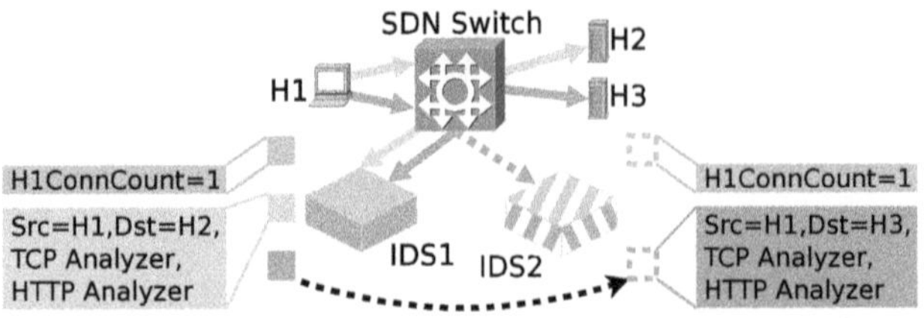


**Figure 1: A scenario requiring scale-out and load balancing to satisfy SLAs on throughput are and minimize operating expenses. The IDS [31] processes a copy of network traffic to detect port scans and malware in HTTP flows. For each active flow, the IDS maintains a connection object with src/dst IPs, ports, etc. and several analyzer objects with protocol-specific state (e.g., current TCP seq # or partially reassembled HTTP payloads). It also maintains host-specific connection counters. If the red (darker) flow is reassigned to the second IDS instance to avoid SLA violations, then the SDN switch's flow table must be updated, the flow-specific state must be moved, and the host-specific state must be copied or shared to ensure no attacks go undetected.**

local state changes inside NFs, and (2) a clever two-phase scheme for updating network forwarding state. We show how to combine the two to provably ensure state updates are not lost or reordered during state moves and shared state remains consistent.

**C2: Bounding overhead.** The second issue is ensuring that reallocation can be efficient. Moving and sharing state between NF instances consumes both NF CPU and network resources. Moreover, avoiding loss, reordering, and state inconsistency requires packet buffering, which introduces both latency and memory overhead. If these performance and resource overheads are unbounded, then we cannot satisfy tight SLAs or constrain operating costs.

To bound overhead, we propose a flexible *northbound API* that control applications use to *precisely* specify which state to move, copy, or share, and which guarantees to enforce (e.g., loss-free).

**C3: Accommodating a variety of NFs with minimal changes.** The final issue is ensuring that our framework is capable of accommodating a wide range of NFs in a largely non-intrusive fashion. Providing APIs for NFs to create/update state [34] is one approach, but it restricts how internal NF state is structured and may not accommodate the state allocation/access needs of some packet processing logic. Instead, we design a novel *southbound API* for NFs that allows a controller to request the export or import of NF state without changing how NFs internally manage state.

We have implemented our northbound API using Floodlight [6], and we have constructed several control applications that use this API. We have also augmented four NFs—Bro [31], Squid [15], iptables [9], and PRADS [13]—to support our southbound API (§7).

Our evaluation of OpenNF shows that: (1) OpenNF can eliminate spurious alerts and cut NF scale-in time by tens of minutes compared to using current control frameworks; (2) state can be moved, copied, and shared efficiently even when certain guarantees are requested—e.g., a loss-free move involving state for 500 flows takes only 215ms and imposes only 50ms of additional latency on packets received during the operation; and (3) additions to NFs to support OpenNF's southbound API increase code size by at most 9.8%, and packet processing time at NFs increases by less than 6% during state export or import.

## 2. WHY OpenNF?

When packet processing is being collectively handled by multiple instances of an NF, the NF deployment as a whole must typically meet three important goals: (1) satisfy tight NF service level agreements (SLAs) on performance or availability—e.g., aggregate throughput should exceed 1Gbps most of the time, and the time outdated/unpatched NFs are used to process flows should be less than 10 minutes per year; (2) accurately monitor and manipulate network traffic—e.g., an IDS should raise alerts for *all* HTTP flows containing known malware packages, and a redundancy elimination (RE) decoder should correctly restore redundancy removed by an RE encoder; and (3) operate with minimal cost—e.g., resources are shutdown when the extra capacity is not needed.

Simultaneously achieving all three goals is not possible today. In particular, we need additional control mechanisms, beyond those offered by combining NFV [12] and SDN [29]. Below, we describe several concrete examples and highlight how the aforementioned triumvirate of goals translate into control plane requirements. We also discuss how current NFV and SDN control frameworks, and simplistic enhancements to them, fall short in satisfying these needs.

### 2.1 Motivating Examples

**Always up-to-date NFs.** For maximum security, a cellular provider may want traffic to always be processed by the latest NF software. For example, an SLA may require that traffic is never processed by outdated NF instances for more than 10 minutes per year (goal #1). Fortunately, NFV allows us to launch an updated instance in a matter of milliseconds [28], and SDN allows us to reroute traffic to that instance just as quickly [17, 32]. However, this simple rerouting of traffic can compromise NF accuracy (goal #2) due to the absence of internal NF state at the new instance: e.g., rerouting active HTTP flows to a new IDS instance can cause the IDS to miss detecting some malware due to the lack of metadata for earlier packets in the flows. To overcome this issue, we can wait for existing flows to terminate and only reroute new flows [22, 38]. However, since flow durations are unbounded, this approach cannot guarantee the SLA will be satisfied: e.g., up to 40% of flows in cellular networks last longer than 10 minutes [36].[1] The only way to both satisfy the SLA and maintain NF accuracy is for the control plane to offer the ability to ***move NF state alongside updates to network forwarding state***. Furthermore, the ***operation must complete in bounded time***.

To guarantee NF accuracy (goal #2) during and after state transfer, it may be important that no packets or updates to state are lost and no re-ordering of updates happens. For example, IDS instances operating on a copy of traffic have no opportunity to request a packet retransmission if the copied traffic is dropped during state move; this can lead to missed alerts because only part of the data sent over a connection is checked for malware.[2] Likewise, the IDS may raise false alerts if it receives and processes SYN and data packets out of order. Thus, the control plane ***must offer support for key guarantees such as loss-freedom and order preservation.*** (We formally define *loss-freedom* and *order-preservation* in §5.1.)

**High performance network monitoring.** Performance is also a crucial concern for cellular providers. For example, an SLA may require NF deployment throughput to exceed 1Gbps most of the time. Meeting this SLA with a single NF instance can be challenging due to the complexity of packet processing. Fortunately, NFV enables NFs to be dynamically scaled-out as network load increases, and SDN enables flows to be rerouted to leverage the new capacity. However, as in the first scenario, flows must be rerouted *quickly*—waiting for flows to terminate can cause NF overload to persist and violate the SLA (goal #1)—and *safely*—rerouting flows without moving internal NF state (in a loss-free and order-preser-

[1] Prematurely terminating flows also violates SLAs.

[2] ***Is loss-free important given the network already can drop packets?*** Note that end points recover from network-induced drops using retransmissions, and the IDS can eventually get a copy; but the IDS can never recover packets dropped during state transfer. A similar argument applies to order-preserving.

ving manner) can compromise NF accuracy (goal #2). Similarly, when network load decreases the NF should be scaled-in, with flows rerouted quickly and safely beforehand, to minimize operating costs (goal #3). To achieve this, we again need the ability to move NF state alongside updates to network forwarding state, and the move must occur within bounded time and with key guarantees.

When rebalancing load, we must also account for the fact that NFs may depend on state that applies to more than one flow: e.g., an IDS maintains connection counters for each end-host. If traffic is balanced at the granularity of hosts or subnets, all flows for a host will traverse the same IDS instance, and the counters can be moved to that instance. However, when flows involving the same host are balanced to different instances, both instances must have the relevant counters. Furthermore, if one instance is later terminated and flows for a given host are re-routed to the same remaining instance, the counters from both instances should be merged. Thus, the control plane must offer the ability to ***move, copy or share, and combine NF state that applies to multiple flows***.

**Fast failure recovery with low resource footprint.** When an NF instance fails, we can minimize downtime (goal #1) by rerouting in-progress (and new) flows to a non-failed instance. For these flows to be accurately processed (goal #2), critical NF state must be available at the selected instance. One way to fulfil this is to periodically create a backup of all NF state; this consumes non-negligible CPU and memory bandwidth at the NF (violating goal #3), and the delay between copies will result in the backup containing significant amounts of stale state. A second approach would be to back up pieces of NF state as they are updated. This eliminates the stale state problem, and the resource footprint is proportional to the frequency of state updates and the amount of state being backed up. To support this, we need the ability to copy NF state, as well as the ability to ***track when/how state is updated***.

**Selectively invoking advanced remote processing.** Based on preliminary observations made by a local NF, an enterprise may want to employ deeper and more advanced processing of a subset of in-progress flows (variant of goal #2). For example, when an IDS detects that internal hosts are making HTTP requests for a blacklisted domain, the enterprise invokes additional packet processing to have the corresponding replies analyzed for malware. Due to limited resources at the local IDS instance, the enterprise may leverage a more powerful remote cloud-resident IDS. Further, to avoid the cost of redirecting all traffic to the cloud (goal #3), traffic from the remaining hosts should continue to be processed locally. This requires the support highlighted in earlier examples (e.g., moving flow-specific state with a loss-free guarantee). Additionally, more advanced processing typically requires maintaining more detailed state: e.g., the cloud-resident IDS may create additional state for the new flows to compare signatures to a large corpus of known attacks. Thus, the NF control plane ***should not restrict an NF's ability to create additional state***. Further, ***it should automatically capture this additional state*** if the processing of the flow is later transferred back to the original NF instance.

## 2.2 Related Work

Existing NF control planes such as PLayer [26], SIMPLE [32], Stratos [21], FlowTags [20], and connection acrobatics [30] only provide control over, and coordination of, traffic forwarding. As already discussed, forwarding changes alone are insufficient to satisfy multiple objectives without degrading NF accuracy.

VM [18] or process replication [5] only allows cloning of NF instances in their entirety. The additional, unneeded state included in a clone not only wastes memory, but more crucially can cause undesirable NF behavior: e.g., an IDS may generate false alerts (we

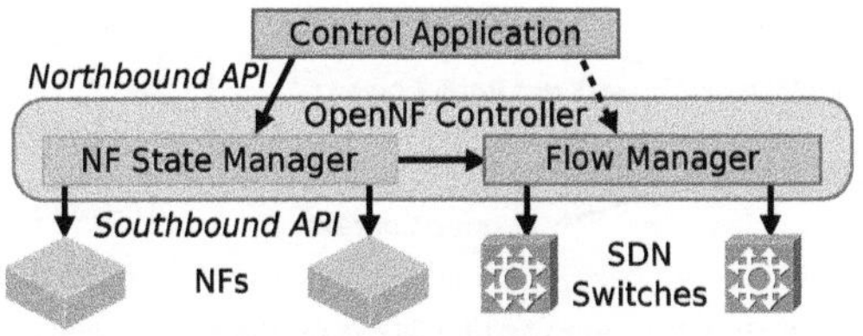


**Figure 2: OpenNF architecture**

quantify this in §8.4). Moreover, this approach prevents state from multiple NF instances from being moved and merged, precluding, e.g., fast elastic scale-down.[3] Because of their intrinsic limitations, combining existing control planes with techniques for VM migration/process replication does not address the above requirements.

Vendor-supplied controllers [4, 14] that move, copy, and share NF state between multiple NF instances can leverage knowledge about the internal workings of NFs. However, they cannot control network state in a way that fully satisfies all goals—e.g., it is hard to provide optimized load balancing across network links.

Split/Merge [34] and Pico Replication [33] are the only systems that provide some control over both internal NF state and network state. They provide a shared library that NFs use to create, access, and modify internal state through pre-defined APIs. In Split/Merge, an orchestrator is responsible for coordinating load balancing by invoking a simple *migrate (f)* operation that reroutes flow *f* and moves corresponding NF state. In Pico Replication, modules are added to an NF to manage the flow of packets in and out of each instance and to clone states at policy-defined frequencies.

Unfortunately, the migrate operation can cause lost or re-ordered NF state updates, since packets arriving at an NF instance after migrate is initiated are dropped, and a race exists between applying the network forwarding state update and resuming the flow of traffic (which is halted when migrate starts). Furthermore, the orchestrator and NF modules are targeted to specific problems, making them ill-suited to support other complex control applications. Finally, the API NFs must use to create and access states uses nondescript keys for non-flow-based state, making it difficult to know the exact states to move and copy when flows are rerouted, and the API only allows one state allocation per flow, requiring some internal NF state and packet processing logic to be significantly restructured. We discuss these issues in more detail later in the paper.

# 3. OpenNF OVERVIEW

OpenNF is a novel control plane architecture (Figure 2) that satisfies the aforementioned requirements and challenges. In this section, we outline our key ideas; §4 and §5 provide the details.

OpenNF allows control applications to closely manage the behavior and performance of NFs to satisfy high level objectives. Based on NF output or external input, control applications: (1) determine the precise sets of flows that specific NF instances should process, (2) direct the controller to provide the needed state at each instance, including both flow-specific state and state shared between flows, and (3) ask the controller to provide certain guarantees on state and state operations.

In turn, the OpenNF controller encapsulates the complexities of distributed state control and, when requested, guarantees loss-freedom, order-preservation, and consistency for state and state operations. We design two novel schemes to overcome underlying race conditions: (1) an *event abstraction* that the controller uses

[3]Basic scale-down can be supported by assigning new flows to the "combined" instance and waiting for flows at the "old" instance to terminate; but this can take a long time.

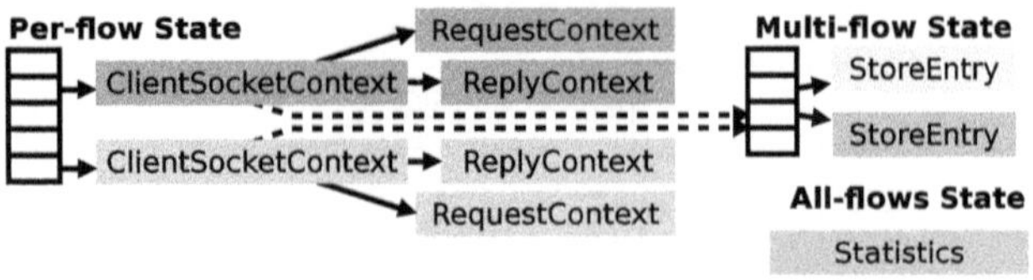


**Figure 3: NF state taxonomy, with state from the Squid caching proxy as an example**

to closely observe updates to state, or to prevent updates but know what update was intended, and (2) a *two phase forwarding state update* scheme. Using just the former, the controller can ensure move operations are loss-free, and state copies are eventually consistent. By carefully sequencing state updates or update prevention (scheme 1) with the phases of scheme 2, the controller can ensure move operations are loss-free and order-preserving; we provide a formal proof in our technical report [23]. Lastly, by buffering events corresponding to intended updates and handling them one at a time in conjunction with piece-meal copying of state, the controller can ensure state copies are strongly or strictly consistent.

OpenNF's southbound API defines a standard NF interface for a controller to request events or the export or import of internal NF state. We *leave it to the NFs to furnish all state matching a filter* specified in an export call, and to determine how to merge existing state with state provided in an import call. This requires modest additions to NFs and, crucially, does not restrict, or require modifications to, the internal state data structures that NFs maintain. Furthermore, we use the well defined notion of a flow (e.g., TCP connection) as the basis for specifying which state to export and import. This naturally aligns with the way NFs already create, read, and update state.

# 4. SOUTHBOUND API

In this section, we describe the design of OpenNF's southbound API. To ensure a variety of NFs can be easily integrated into OpenNF, we must address two challenges: (1) account for the diversity of NF state and (2) minimize NF modifications.

## 4.1 State Taxonomy

To address the first challenge, we must identify commonalities in how internal state is allocated and accessed across various NFs. To this end, we examined several types of NFs from a variety of vendors, including: NATs [9], IDSs [31], load balancers [1, 7], caching proxies [15], WAN optimizers [16], and traffic monitors [11, 13].

We observe that *state created or updated by an NF while processing traffic applies to either an individual flow (e.g., TCP connection) or a collection of flows.* As shown in Figure 1, the Bro IDS maintains connection and analyzer objects for each TCP/UDP/ICMP flow and state for each host summarizing observations relating to all flows involving that host. Similarly, as shown in Figure 3, the Squid caching proxy maintains socket context, request context, and reply context for each client connection and cache entries for each requested web object. Most NFs also have state which is updated for every packet or flow the NF processes: e.g., statistics about the number of packets/flows the NF processed.[4]

Thus, as shown in Figure 3, we classify NF state based on *scope*, or how many flows an NF-created piece of state applies to—one flow (*per-flow*), multiple flows (*multi-flow*), or all flows (*all-flow*). In particular, per-flow state refers to structures/objects that are read or updated only when processing packets from the same flow (e.g., TCP connection), while multi-flow state is read or updated when processing packets from multiple, but not all, flows.

Thinking about each piece of NF-created state in terms of its association with flows provides a natural way for reasoning about how a control application should move/copy/share state. For example, a control application that routes all flows destined for a host $H$ to a specific NF instance can assume the instance will need all per-flow state for flows destined for $H$ and all multi-flow state which stores information related to one or more flows destined for $H$. This applies even in the case of seemingly non-flow-based state: e.g., the fingerprint table in a redundancy eliminator is classified as all-flows state, and cache entries in a Squid caching proxy are multi-flow state that can be referenced by client IP (to refer to cached objects actively being served), server IP, or URL.

Prior works on NF state management either draw no association between state and flows [25], or they do not distinguish between multi-flow and all-flows state [34]. This makes it difficult to know the exact set of state to move, copy, or share when flows are rerouted. For example, in the Squid caching proxy, cached web objects (multi-flow states) that are currently being sent to clients must be copied to avoid disrupting these in-progress connections, while other cached objects may or may not be copied depending on the SLAs a control application needs to satisfy (e.g., high cache hit ratio vs. fast scale out).[5] We quantitatively show the benefits of granular, flow-based control in §8.1.2.

We also discovered during our examination of NFs that they tend to: (1) allocate state at many points during flow processing—e.g., when the Bro IDS is monitoring for malware in HTTP sessions, it allocates state when the connection starts, as protocols are identified, and as HTTP reply data is received—and (2) organize/label state in many different ways—e.g., the Squid caching proxy organizes some state based on a traditional 5-tuple and some state based on a URL. Prior works [34] assume NFs allocate and organize state in particular ways (e.g., allocate state once for each flow), which means NFs may need significant changes to use these frameworks.

## 4.2 API to Export/Import State

We leverage our taxonomy to design a simple API for NFs to export and import pieces of state; it requires minimal NF modifications. In particular, we leverage the well defined notion of a flow (e.g., TCP or UDP connection) and our definition of state scope to allow a controller to specify exactly which state to export or import. State gathering and merging is delegated to NFs which perform these tasks within the context of their existing internal architecture.

For each scope we provide three simple functions: get, put, and delete. More formally, the functions are:

```
multimap<flowid, chunk> getPerflow(filter)
void putPerflow(multimap<flowid, chunk>)
void delPerflow(list<flowid>)
multimap<flowid, chunk> getMultiflow(filter)
void putMultiflow(multimap<flowid, chunk>)
void delMultiflow(list<flowid>)
list<chunk> getAllflows()
void putAllflows(list<chunk>)
```

A *filter* is a dictionary specifying values for one or more standard packet header fields (e.g., source/destination IP, network protocol, source/destination ports), similar to match criteria in OpenFlow [29].[6] This defines the set of flows whose state to get/put/del-

[4]NFs also have configuration state. It is read but never updated by NFs, making it easy to handle; we ignore the details in this paper.

[5]NF-specific state sharing features, such as inter-cache protocols in Squid, can also be leveraged, but they do not avoid the need for per-flow state, and some multi-flow state, to be moved or copied.

[6]Some NFs may also support extended *filter*s and *flowid*s that include header fields for other common protocols: e.g., the Squid caching proxy may include the HTTP URL.

ete. Header fields not specified are assumed to be wildcards. The `getAllflows` and `putAllflows` functions do not contain a *filter* because they refer to state that applies to all flows. Similarly, there is no `delAllflows` function because all-flows state is always relevant regardless of the traffic an NF is processing.

A *chunk* of state consists of one or more related internal NF structures, or objects, associated with the same flow (or set of flows): e.g., a chunk of per-flow state for the Bro IDS contains a `Conn` object and all per-flow objects it references (Figure 1). A corresponding *flowid* is provided for each chunk of per-flow and multi-flow state. The *flowid* is a dictionary of header fields and values that describe the exact flow (e.g., TCP or UDP connection) or set of flows (e.g., host or subnet) to which the state pertains. For example, a per-flow *chunk* from the Bro IDS has a *flowid* that includes the source and destination IPs, ports, and transport protocol, while a multi-flow *chunk* containing a counter for an end-host has a *flowid* that only includes the host's IP.

When `getPerflow` or `getMultiflow` is called, the NF is responsible for identifying and providing all per-flow or multi-flow state that pertains to flows matching the *filter*. Crucially, *only fields relevant to the state are matched against the filter*; other fields in the *filter* are ignored: e.g., in the Bro IDS, only the IP fields in a *filter* will be considered when determining which end-host connection counters to return. This API design avoids the need for a control application to be aware of the way an NF internally organizes state. Additionally, by identifying and exporting state on-demand, we avoid the need to change an NF's architecture to conform to a specific memory allocation strategy [34].

The NF is also responsible for replacing or combining existing state for a given flow (or set of flows) with state provided in an invocation of `putPerflow` (or `putMultiflow`). Common methods of combining state include adding or averaging values (for counters), selecting the greatest or least value (for timestamps), and calculating the union or intersection of sets (for lists of addresses or ports). State merging must be implemented by individual NFs because the diversity of internal state structures makes it prohibitive to provide a generic solution.

## 4.3 API to Observe/Prevent State Updates

The API described above does not interpose on internal state creations and accesses. However, there are times when we need to prevent an NF instance from updating state—e.g., while state is being moved—or we want to know updates are happening—e.g., to determine when to copy state.

OpenNF uses two mechanisms to prevent and observe updates: (1) having NFs generate packet-received events for certain packets—the controller tells the NF which subset of packets should trigger events—and (2) controlling how NFs should act on the packets that generate events—process, buffer, or drop them.

Specifically, we add the following functions to the API:

`void enableEvents` (*filter*, *action*)
`void disableEvents` (*filter*)

The *filter* defines the set of packets that should trigger events; it has the same format as described in §4.2. The *action* may be `process`, `buffer`, or `drop`; any buffered packets are released to the NF for processing when events are disabled. The events themselves contain a copy of the triggering packet.

In the next section, we discuss how events are used to realize important guarantees on state and state operations.

# 5. NORTHBOUND API

OpenNF's northbound API allows control applications to flexibly move, copy, or share subsets of state between NF instances,

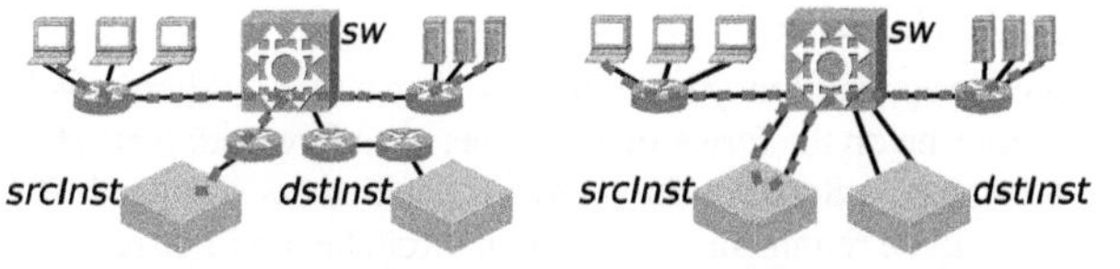


(a) Off-path NF (b) On-path NF

**Figure 4: Assumed topologies for move operation**

and to request important guarantees, including loss-freedom, order-preservation, and various forms of consistency. This API design appropriately balances OpenNF's generality and complexity: Not offering some guarantees would reduce complexity but make OpenNF insufficient for use with many NFs—e.g., a redundancy eliminator [16] will incorrectly reconstruct packets when re-ordering occurs (§5.1.2). Similarly, always enforcing the strongest guarantees would simplify the API but make OpenNF insufficient for scenarios with tight SLAs—e.g., a loss-free and order-preserving move is unnecessary for a NAT, and the latency increase imposed by these guarantees (§8.1) could cripple VoIP sessions.

The main challenge in supporting this API is designing suitable, low-overhead mechanisms to provide the necessary guarantees. In this section, we show how we use events together with fine-grained control over network forwarding to overcome this challenge. We first describe how we provide a loss-free and order-preserving `move` operation (we provide a formal proof of these guarantees in our technical report [23]), and what optimizations we use to improve efficiency. We then describe how OpenNF's `copy` and `share` operations provide eventual, strong, or strict consistency for state required by multiple NF instances.

## 5.1 Move Operation

OpenNF's `move` operation transfers both the state *and* input (i.e., traffic) for a set of flows from one NF instance (*srcInst*) to another (*dstInst*). Its syntax is:

`move` (*srcInst*, *dstInst*, *filter*, *scope*, *properties*)

As in the southbound API, the set of flows is defined by *filter*; a single flow is the finest granularity at which a move can occur. The *scope* argument specifies which class(es) of state (per-flow and/or multi-flow) to move, and the *properties* argument defines whether the move should be loss-free (§5.1.1) and order-preserving (§5.1.2).

In what follows, *sw* denotes the last SDN switch through which all packets matching *filter* will pass before diverging on their paths to reach *srcInst* and *dstInst* (Figure 4). We assume the SDN controller keeps track of *sw*. We also assume that loss and reordering does not occur on the network path from *sw* to *srcInst*; our technical report [23] includes a stronger version of order-preserving move (§5.1.2) that does not rely on this assumption.

For a move without guarantees, the controller (1) calls `getPerflow` and `delPerflow` on *srcInst*, (2) calls `putPerflow` on *dstInst*, and (3) updates the flow table on *sw* to forward the affected flows to *dstInst*. To move multi-flow state as well (or instead), the analogous multi-flow functions are also (instead) called. For the rest of this section, we assume the *scope* is per-flow, but our ideas can easily be extended to multi-flow state.

With the above sequence of steps, packets corresponding to the state being moved may continue to arrive at *srcInst* from the start of `getPerflow` until after the forwarding change at *sw* takes effect and all packets in transit to *srcInst* have arrived and been read from the NIC and operating system buffers. A simple approach of dropping these packets when *srcInst* receives them [34] prevents *srcInst* from establishing new state for the flows or failing due to missing state. But this is only acceptable in scenarios where an application is willing to tolerate the effects of skipped processing: e.g., scan detection in the Bro IDS will still function if some TCP packets are not processed, but it may take longer to detect scans. Alternatively, an NF may be on the forwarding path between flow endpoints (Figure 4(b)), e.g., a Squid caching proxy, in which case dropped TCP packets will be retransmitted, although throughput will be reduced.

### 5.1.1 Loss-free Move

In some situations loss is problematic: e.g., the Bro IDS's malware detection script will compute incorrect md5sums and fail to detect malicious content if part of an HTTP reply is missing; we quantify this in our technical report [23]. Thus, we need a move operation that satisfies the following property:

> **Loss-free:** *All state updates resulting from packet processing should be reflected at the destination instance, and all packets the switch receives should be processed.*

The first half of this property is important for ensuring all information pertaining to a flow (or group of flows) is available at the instance where subsequent packet processing for the flow(s) will occur, and that information is not left, or discarded, at the original instance. The latter half ensures an NF does not miss gathering important information about a flow.

In an attempt to be loss-free, Split/Merge halts, and buffers at the controller, all traffic arriving at *sw* while migrating per-flow state [34]. However, when traffic is halted, packets may already be in-transit to *srcInst*, or sitting in NIC or operating system queues at *srcInst*. Split/Merge drops these packets when they (arrive and) are dequeued at *srcInst*. This ensures that *srcInst* does not attempt to update (or create new) per-flow state after the transfer of state has started, guaranteeing the first half of our loss-free property. However, dropping packets at *srcInst* violates the latter half. While we could modify Split/Merge to delay state transfer until packets have drained from the network and local queues, it is impossible to know how long to wait, and extra waiting increases the delay imposed on packets buffered at the controller.

SDN consistency abstractions [27, 35] are also insufficient for guaranteeing loss-freedom. They can guarantee packets will be forwarded to *srcInst* or *dstInst*, but they do not provide any guarantees on what happens to the packets once they arrive at the NF instances. If *srcInst* processes the packets after state transfer has started, then the state installed at *dstInst* will not include some updates; if *srcInst* drops the packets instead, then some state updates will never occur.

What then should we do to ensure loss-freedom in the face of packets that are in-transit (or buffered) when the move operation starts? In OpenNF, we leverage events raised by NFs. Specifically, the controller calls `enableEvents` (*filter*, `drop`) on *srcInst* before calling `getPerflow`. This causes *srcInst* to raise an event for each received packet matching *filter*. The events are buffered at the controller until the `putPerflow` call on *dstInst* completes. Then, the packet in each buffered event is sent to *sw* to be forwarded to *dstInst*; any events arriving at the controller after the buffer has been emptied are handled immediately in the same way. Lastly, the flow table on *sw* is updated to forward the affected flows to *dstInst*.

Calling `disableEvents` (*filter*) on *srcInst* is unnecessary, because packets matching *filter* will eventually stop arriving at *srcInst* and no more events will be generated. Nonetheless, to eliminate the need for *srcInst* to check if it should raised events for incoming packets, the controller can issue this call after several minutes—i.e., after all packets matching *filter* have likely arrived or timed out.

### 5.1.2 Order-preserving Move

In addition to loss, NFs can be negatively affected by re-ordering. For example, the "weird activity" policy script included with the Bro IDS will raise a false "SYN_inside_connection" alert if the IDS receives and processes SYN and data packets in a different order than they were actually exchanged by the connection endpoints. Another example is a redundancy elimination decoder [16] where an encoded packet arriving before the data packet w.r.t. which it was encoded will be silently dropped; this can cause the decoder's data store to rapidly become out of synch with the encoders.

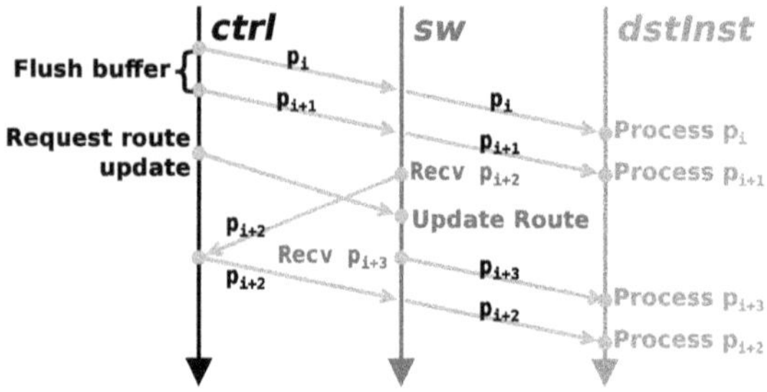


**Figure 5: Order-preserving problem in Split/Merge**

Thus, we need a move operation that satisfies the following:

> **Order-preserving:** *All packets should be processed in the order they were forwarded to the NF instances by the switch.*

This property applies within one direction of a flow (e.g., process SYN before ACK), across both directions of a flow[7] (e.g., process SYN before SYN+ACK), and, for moves including multi-flow state, across flows (e.g., process an FTP get command before the SYN for the new transfer connection).

Unfortunately, neither Split/Merge nor the loss-free move described above are order-preserving. The basic problem in both systems is a race between flushing packets buffered at the controller and changing the flow table at *sw* to forward all packets to *dstInst*. Figure 5 illustrates the problem in the context of Split/Merge. Even if all buffered packets ($p_i$ and $p_{i+1}$) are flushed before the controller requests a forwarding table update at *sw*, another packet ($p_{i+2}$) may arrive at *sw* and be forwarded to the controller before *sw* applies the forwarding table update. Once the update is applied, *sw* may start forwarding packets ($p_{i+3}$) to *dstInst*, but the controller may not have received the packet $p_{i+2}$ from *sw*. Thus, the packet $p_{i+2}$ will be forwarded to *dstInst* after a later packet of the flow ($p_{i+3}$) has already been forwarded to *dstInst*.

We use a clever combination of events and a two-phase forwarding state update to guarantee a loss-free *and* order-preserving move. Figure 6 has psuedo-code for the steps.

We start with the steps used for a loss-free move, through calling `putPerflow` on *dstInst*. After `putPerflow` completes we extract the packet from each buffered event, mark it with a special "do-not-buffer" flag, and send it to *sw* to be forwarded to *dstInst*; any events arriving at the controller after the buffer has been emptied are handled immediately in the same way. Then, we call `enableEvents` (*filter*, `buffer`) on *dstInst*, so that any packets forwarded directly to *dstInst* by *sw* will be buffered; note that the packets marked with "do-not-buffer" (discussed above) are not buffered.

Next, we perform the two phase forwarding state update. First, we update the forwarding entry for *filter* on *sw* to forward matching packets to both *srcInst* and the controller.[8] The controller waits

[7] If packets in opposite directions do not traverse a common switch before reaching the NF—e.g., a NAT is placed between two switches—then we lack a vantage point to know the total order of packets across directions, and we cannot guarantee such an order unless it is enforced by a flow's end-points—e.g., a server will not send SYN+ACK until the NAT forwards the SYN from a client.

[8] We use existing SDN consistency mechanisms [27, 35] to ensure the update is atomic and no packets are lost.

```
eventReceivedFromSrcInst (event)
    if shouldBufferEvents then
        eventQueue.enqueue (event.packet)
    else
        sw.forward (event.packet, dstInst)
packetReceivedFromSw (packet)
    if lastPacketFromSw== null then
        signal (GOT_FIRST_PKT_FROM_SW)    // wait @ 24
    lastPacketFromSw ← packet
eventReceivedFromDstInst (event)
    if event.packet == lastPacketFromSw then
        signal (DST_PROCESSED_LAST_PKT)  // wait @ 26
moveLossfreeOrderpreserve (srcInst, dstInst, filter)
    shouldBufferEvents ← true
    srcInst.enableEvents (filter, DROP)
    chunks ← srcInst.getPerflow (filter)
    srcInst.delPerflow (chunks.keys)
    dstInst.putPerflow (chunks)
    foreach event in eventQueue do
        sw.forward (event.packet, dstInst)
    shouldBufferEvents ← false
    dstInst.enableEvents (filter, BUFFER)
    sw.install (filter, {srcInst, ctrl}, LOW_PRIORITY)
    wait (GOT_FIRST_PKT_FROM_SW)
    sw.install (filter, dstInst, HIGH_PRIORITY)
    wait (DST_PROCESSED_LAST_PKT)
    dstInst.disableEvents (filter)
```

**Figure 6: Pseudo-code for loss-free and order-preserving move**

for at least one packet from *sw*, and always stores the most recent packet it receives. Second, we install a higher priority forwarding entry for *filter* on *sw* to forward matching packets to *dstInst*. Through this two phase update, the controller can become aware of the *last* packet sent to *srcInst*.[9]

Finally, we need to ensure that *dstInst* processes all packets forwarded to *srcInst* before processing any packets that *sw* directly forwards to *dstInst*. We achieve this with the following sequence of steps: (1) wait for an event from *srcInst* for the last packet sent to *srcInst*—this is the packet we stored during the two phase forwarding state update; (2) send the packet contained in the event to *sw* to forward to *dstInst*; (3) wait for an event from *dstInst* for the packet; and (4) call `disableEvents` (*filter*) on *dstInst* to release any packets that had already been sent to *dstInst* by *sw* and were buffered at *dstInst*.

In our technical report [23], we formally prove that this sequence of steps is loss-free and order-preserving.

The additional waiting required for order-preserving does come at a performance cost (we quantify this in §8.1.1). Thus, we offer applications three versions of move (loss-free and order-preserving, loss-free only, and no guarantees) so they can select the most efficient version that satisfies their requirements.

### *5.1.3 Optimizations*

Supporting the above guarantees may impose additional latencies on packets arriving during the move operation. In particular, when a move involves multiple flows, we halt the processing of those flows' packets from the time `enableEvents` is called until after `putPerflow` completes.

One way to reduce these latencies (and reduce drops in the case of a move without guarantees) is to reduce the total time taken to complete the move operation. To achieve this, an application could issue multiple pipelined moves that each cover a smaller portion of the flow space. However, this requires more forwarding rules in *sw* and requires the application to know how flows are divided among the flow space. Instead, we can leverage the fact that `getPerflow` and `putPerflow` operations can be, at least partially, executed *in parallel*. Rather than returning all requested states as a single result, the *srcInst* can return each *chunk* of per-flow state immediately, and the controller can immediately call `putPerflow` with just that *chunk*. The forwarding table update(s) at *sw* occurs after the `getPerflow` and all `putPerflow` calls have returned.

The additional latency imposed on redirected packets can be further reduced by following an *early release and late locking strategy*. For late-locking, the controller calls `getPerflow` on *srcInst* with a special flag instructing *srcInst* to enable events for each flow just before the corresponding per-flow state is prepared for export (avoiding the need to call `enableEvents` for all flows beforehand). Also, once `putPerflow` for a specific *chunk* returns, the controller can release any events pertaining to that *chunk*.[10]

The *parallelizing* optimization can be applied to any version of move, and the *early-release* optimization can be applied to a move of either per-flow or multi-flow state, but not a move involving both.

## 5.2 Copy and Share Operations

OpenNF's `copy` and `share` operations address applications' need for the same state to be readable and/or updateable at multiple NF instances and, potentially, for updates made at one instance to be reflected elsewhere. For example, in a failure recovery application (§2) a backup NF instance needs to keep an updated copy of all per-/multi-/all-flows state. Similarly, a load balancing application that distributes an end-host's flows among multiple IDS instances needs updates to the host connection counter at one instance to be reflected at the other instances to effectively detect port scans.

In particular, `copy` can be used when state consistency is *not required* or *eventual* consistency is desired, while `share` can be used when *strong* or *strict* consistency is desired. Note that eventual consistency is akin to extending our loss-free property to multiple copies of state, while strict consistency is akin to extending both our loss-free and order-preserving properties to multiple NF instances.

### *5.2.1 Copy Operation*

OpenNF's copy operation clones state from one NF instance (*srcInst*) to another (*dstInst*). Its syntax is:

`copy` (*srcInst*, *dstInst*, *filter*, *scope*)

The *filter* argument specifies the set of flows whose state to copy, while the *scope* argument specifies which class(es) of state (per-flow, multi-flow, and/or all-flows) to copy.

The `copy` operation is implemented using the get and put calls from the southbound API (§4.2). No change in forwarding state occurs as part of copy because state is not deleted from *srcInst*, allowing *srcInst* to continue processing traffic and updating its copy of state. It is up to control applications to separately initiate a change in forwarding state where the situation warrants (e.g., by directly interacting with the SDN controller, or calling `move` for some other class of state).

Eventual consistency can be achieved by occasionally re-copying the same set of state. As described in §4.2, an NF will automatically replace or combine the new and existing copies when `putPerflow`, `putMultiflow`, and `putAllflows` are called. Since there are many possible ways to decide when state should be re-copied—based on time, NF output, updates to NF state, or other

[9]The controller can check the counters on the first flow entry in *sw* against the number of packets it has received from *sw* to ensure the packet it currently has stored is in fact the last packet.

[10]Although state chunks get transferred and events get processed via the controller in our current system, they can also happen peer to peer.

external factors—we leave it to applications to issue subsequent copy calls. As a convenience, we do provide a function for control applications to become *aware* of state updates:

`void notify` (*filter*, *inst*, *enable*, *callback*)

When invoked with *enable* set to true, the controller calls `enableEvents` (*filter*, `process`) on NF instance *inst*, otherwise it calls `disableEvents` (*filter*) on *inst*. For each event the controller receives, it invokes the provided *callback* function.

### 5.2.2 *Share Operation*

Strong and strict consistency are more difficult to achieve because state reads and updates must occur at each NF instance in the same global order. For strict consistency this global order must match the order in which packets are received by *sw*. For strong consistency the global order may differ from the order in which packets were received by *sw*, but updates for packets received by a specific NF instance must occur in the global order in the order the instance received the packets.

Both cases require synchronizing reads/updates across all NF instances (`list`<*inst*>) that are using a given piece of state. OpenNF's `share` operation provides this:

`void share(list`<*inst*>, *filter*, *scope*, *consistency*)

The *filter* and *scope* arguments are the same as above, while *consistency* is set to `strong` or `strict`.

Events can again be used to keep state strongly consistent. The controller calls `enableEvents` (*filter*, `drop`) on each instance, followed by a sequence of get and put calls to initially synchronize their state. When events arrive at the controller, they are placed in a FIFO queue labeled with the *flowid* for the flow group to which they pertain; flows are grouped based on the coarsest granularity of state being shared (e.g., per-host or per-prefix).

For each queue, one event at a time is dequeued, and the packet it contains is marked with a "do-not-drop" flag and forwarded to the originating NF instance. The NF instance processes the packet and raises an event, which signals to the controller that all state reads/updates at the NF are complete. The controller then calls `getMultiflow` (or `getPerflow`, `getAllflows`) on the originating NF instance, followed by `putMultiflow` (or `putPerflow`, `putAllflows`) on all other instances in `list`<*inst*>. Then, the next event is dequeued and the process repeated.

Since events from different NFs may arrive at the controller in a different order than packets were received by *sw*, we require a slightly different approach for strict consistency. The controller must receive packets directly from the switch to know the global order in which packets should be processed. We therefore update all relevant forwarding entries in *sw*—i.e., entries that both cover a portion of the flow space covered by *filter* and forward to an instance in `list`<*inst*>—to forward to the controller instead. We then employ the same methodology as above, except we invoke `enableEvents` with *action* set to `process` and queue packets received from *sw* rather than receiving packets via events.

It is up to control applications to determine the appropriate consistency requirements for the situation, recognizing that strong or strict consistency comes at a significant performance cost (§8.1.1). Applications should also consider which multi-/all-flows state is required for accurate packet processing, and, generally, invoke copy or share operations on this state prior to moving per-flow state.

## 6. CONTROL APPLICATIONS

Using OpenNF, we have written control applications for several of the scenarios described in §2. The applications are designed for the environment shown in Figure 7. In all applications, we use the

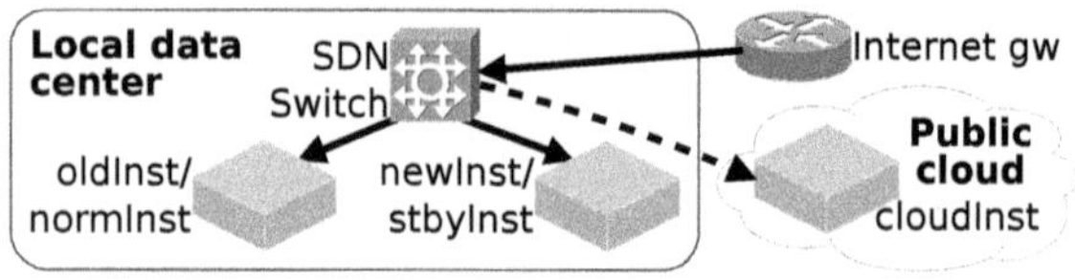


**Figure 7: The Bro IDS runs on VMs in both a local data center and a public cloud. An SDN switch in the local data center receives a copy of all traffic from the Internet gateway for the local network and routes it to an IDS instance. The local IDS instances monitor for port scans and HTTP requests from outdated web browsers. The cloud instances additionally check for malware in HTTP replies.**

```
movePrefix (prefix, oldInst, newInst)
    copy (oldInst, newInst, {nw_src: prefix}, MULTI)
    move (oldInst, newInst, {nw_src: prefix}, PER, LOSSFREE)
    while true do
        sleep (60)
        copy (oldInst, newInst, {nw_src: prefix}, MULTI)
        copy (newInst, oldInst, {nw_src: prefix}, MULTI)
```

**Figure 8: Load balanced network monitoring application**

Bro IDS, but different applications place different requirements on both the granularities of state operations and the guarantees needed; despite these differences, the applications are relatively simple to implement. We describe them below.

**High performance network monitoring.** The first application (Figure 8) monitors the CPU load on the local Bro IDS instances and calculates a new distribution of local network prefixes when load becomes imbalanced. If a subnet is assigned to a different IDS instance, the `movePrefix` function is invoked. This function calls `copy` to clone the multi-flow state associated with scan detection, followed by `move` to perform a loss-free transfer of the per-flow state for all active flows in the subnet.

We copy, rather than move, multi-flow state because the counters for port scan detection are maintained on the basis of ⟨external IP, destination port⟩ pairs, and connections may exist between a single external host and hosts in multiple local subnets. An order-preserving move is unnecessary because re-ordering would only potentially result in the scan detector failing to count some connection attempts, and, in this application, we are willing to tolerate moderate delay in scan detection. However, to avoid missing scans completely, we maintain eventual consistency of multi-flow state by invoking copy in both directions every 60 seconds.

**Fast failure recovery.** The second application (Figure 9) maintains a hot standby for each local IDS instance with an eventually consistent copy of all per-flow and multi-flow state. The `initStandby` function is invoked to initialize a standby (`stbyInst`) for an IDS instance (`normInst`). It notes which `normInst` the standby is associated with and requests notifications from `normInst` for packets whose corresponding state updates are important for scan detection and browser identification—TCP SYN, SYN+ACK, and RST packets and HTTP packets sent from a local client to an external server. The copy is made eventually consistent when these key packets are processed, rather than recopying state for every packet. In particular, events are raised by `normInst` for these packets and the controller invokes the `updateStandby` function. This function copies the appropriate per-flow state from `normInst` to the corresponding `stbyInst`. When a failure occurs, the forwarding table in the switch is updated to forward the appropriate prefixes to `stbyInst` instead of `normInst` (code not shown).

**Selectively invoking advanced remote processing.** The third application (code not shown) monitors for outdated browser alerts from each local Bro IDS instance, and uses the cloud to check for malware in connections triggering such alerts.

```
standbys ← {}
initStandby (normInst, stbyInst)
    standbys[normInst] ← stbyInst
    notify ({nw_proto: TCP, tcp_flags: SYN}, normInst, true,
    updateStandby)
    notify ({nw_proto: TCP, tcp_flags: RST}, normInst, true,
    updateStandby)
    notify ({nw_src: 10.0.0.0/8, nw_proto: TCP, tp_dst: 80},
    normInst, true, updateStandby)
updateStandby (event)
    normInst ← event.src
    stbyInst ← standbys[normInst]
    filter ← extractFlowId (event.pkt)
    copy (normInst, stbyInst, filter, PER)
```

**Figure 9: Fast failure recovery application**

When a local IDS instance (`locInst`) raises an alert for a specific flow (`flowid`), the application calls `move(locInst, cloudInst, flowid, perflow, lossfree)` to transfer the flow's per-flow state and forward the flow's packets to the IDS instance running in the cloud. The move must be loss-free to ensure all data packets contained in the HTTP reply are received and included in the md5sum that is compared against a malware database, otherwise malware may go undetected. Multi-flow state in this case, i.e., the set of scan counters at the local IDS instance, does not matter for the cloud instance's actions (i.e., malware signature detection), so it is not moved or copied.

# 7. IMPLEMENTATION

Our OpenNF prototype consists of a controller that implements our northbound API (§5) and several modified NFs—Bro, PRADS, Squid, and iptables–that implement our southbound API (§4).

The OpenNF controller is written as a module atop Floodlight [6] (≈4.7K lines of Java code). The controller listens for connections from NFs and launches two threads—for handling state operations and events—for each NF. The controller and NFs exchange JSON messages to invoke southbound functions, provide function results, and send events. Packets contained in events are forwarded to NFs by issuing OpenFlow packet-out control messages [29] to the SDN switch (*sw*); flow-mod messages are issued for route updates. The interface with control applications is event-driven.

We implemented NF-specific handlers for each southbound API functions. The NFs use a shared library for communicating with the controller. We discuss the NF-specific modifications below, and evaluate the extent of these modifications in §8.2.2.

**Bro IDS** [31] performs a variety of security analyses defined by policy scripts. The `get/putPerflow` handlers for Bro lookup (using linear search) and insert `Connection` objects into internal hash tables for TCP, UDP, and ICMP connections. The key challenge is serializing these `Connection` objects and the many other objects (>100 classes) they refer to; we wrote custom serialization functions for each of these objects using Boost [2]. We also added a *moved* flag to some of these classes—to prevent Bro from logging errors during `delPerflow`—and a mutex to the `Connection` class—to prevent Bro from modifying the objects associated with a flow while they are being serialized. Lastly, we added library calls to Bro's main packet processing loop to raise events when a received packet matches a filter on which events are enabled.

**PRADS asset monitor** [13] identifies and logs basic information about active hosts and the services they are running. The `get/putPerflow` and `get/putMultiflow` handlers for PRADS lookup and insert `connection` and `asset` structures, which store flow meta data and end-host operating system and service details, respectively, in the appropriate hash tables. If an `asset` object provided in a `putMultiflow` call is associated with the same end-host as an `asset` object already in the hash table, then the handler merges the contents of the two objects. The `get/putAllflows` handlers copy and merge, respectively, a global statistics structure.

**Squid caching proxy** [15] reduces bandwidth consumption by caching and serving web objects requested by clients. The per-flow state in Squid includes sockets, making it challenging to write `get/putPerflow` handlers. Fortunately, we are able to borrow code from CRIU [5] to (de)serialize sockets for active client and server connections. As with Bro, we wrote custom serialization functions, using Boost [2], for all objects associated with each connection. The `get/put/delMultiflow` handlers capture, insert, and remove entries from Squid's in-memory cache; entries are (de)serialized individually to allow for fine-grained state control.

**iptables** [9] is a firewall and network address translator integrated into the Linux kernel. The kernel tracks the 5-tuple, TCP state, security marks, etc. for all active flows; this state is read/written by iptables. We wrote an agent that uses libnetfilter_conntrack [10] to capture and insert this state when `get/putPerflow` are invoked. There is no multi-flow or all-flows state in iptables.

# 8. EVALUATION

Our evaluation of OpenNF answers the following key questions:

- Can state be moved, copied, and shared efficiently even when guarantees on state or state operations are requested by applications? What benefits do applications see from the ability to move, copy, or share state at varying granularities?
- How efficiently can NFs export and import state, and do these operations impact NF performance? How much must NFs be modified to support the southbound API?
- How is OpenNF's efficiency impacted by the scale of an NF deployment?
- To what extent do existing NF control planes hinder the ability to satisfy a combination of high-level objectives?

The testbed we used for our evaluation consists of an OpenFlow-enabled HP ProCurve 6600 switch and four mid-range servers (Quad-core Intel Xeon 2.8GHz, 8GB, 2 x 1Gbps NICs) that run the OpenNF controller and modified NFs and generate traffic. We use a combination of replayed university-to-cloud [24] and data-center [19] network traffic traces, along with synthetic workloads.

## 8.1 Northbound Operations

### 8.1.1 Efficiency with Guarantees

We first evaluate the efficiency of our northbound operations when guarantees are requested on state or state operations. We use two PRADS asset monitor instances ($PRADS_1$ and $PRADS_2$) and replay our university-to-cloud trace at 2500 packets/second. We initially send all traffic to $PRADS_1$. Once it has created state for 500 flows (≈80K packets have been processed), we `move` *all* flows and their per-flow state, or `copy` *all* multi-flow state, to $PRADS_2$; we evaluate finer granularity operations in §8.1.2. To evaluate sharing with strong consistency, we instead call `share` (for all multi-flow state) at the beginning of the experiment, and then replay our traffic trace. During these operations, we measure the number of dropped packets, the added latency for packets contained in events from $PRADS_1$ or buffered at $PRADS_2$, and the total operation time (for move and copy only). Although the specific values for these metrics vary based on the NF, scope, filter granularity (i.e., number of flows/states affected), and packet rate, the high-level takeaways still apply.

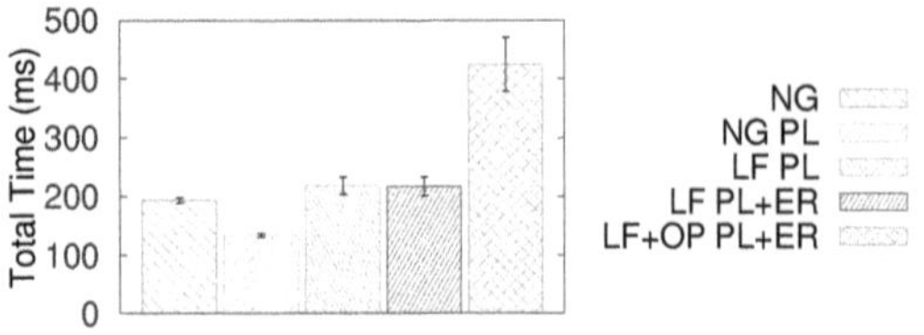


(a) Total `move` time

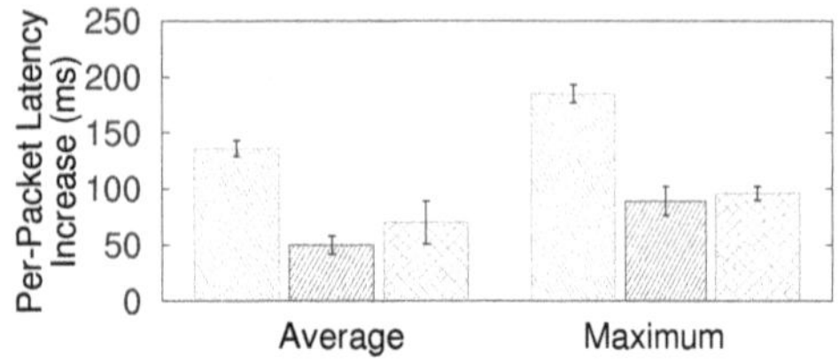


(b) Per-packet latency increase

**Figure 10: Efficiency of `move` with no guarantees (NG), loss-free (LF), and loss-free and order-preserving (LF+OP) with and without parallelizing (PL) and early-release (ER) optimizations; traffic rate is 2500 packets/sec; times are averaged over 5 runs and the error bars show 95% confidence intervals**

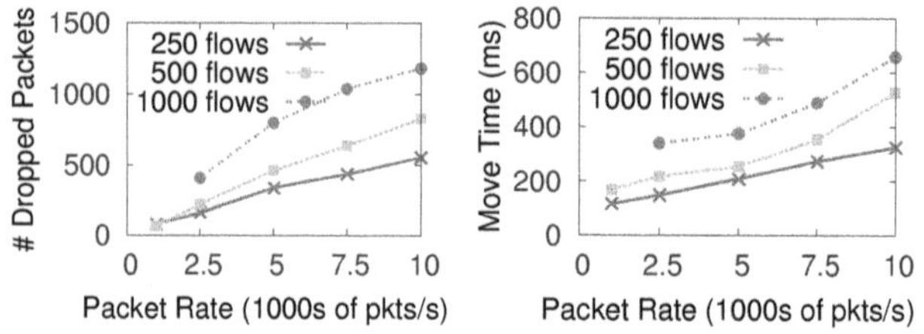


(a) Packet drops during a parallelized `move` with no guarantees (b) Total time for a parallelized loss-free `move`

**Figure 11: Impact of packet rate and number of per-flows states on parallelized `move` with and without a loss-free guarantee**

**Move.** Figure 10 shows our results for `move` with varying guarantees and optimizations.

A move without any guarantees or optimizations (NG) completes in 193ms. This time is primarily dictated by the time required for the NF to export (89ms) and import (54ms) state; we evaluate the southbound operations in detail in §8.2. The remaining 50ms is spent processing control messages from the NFs and performing the route update. Our parallelizing optimization (§5.1.3) can reduce the total time for the move operation (NG PL) to 134ms by exporting and importing state (mostly) in parallel. However, even this faster version of move comes at a cost: *225 packets are dropped!* Figure 11(a) shows how the number of drops changes as a function of the packet rate and the number of flows whose state is moved. We observe a linear increase in the number of drops as the packet rate increases, because more packets will arrive in the time window between the start of `move` and the routing update taking effect.

A parallelized loss-free move (LF PL) avoids drops by raising events. However, the 410 packets contained in events may each incur up to 185ms of additional latency. (Packets processed by $PRADS_1$ before the move or $PRADS_2$ after the move do not incur additional latency.) Additionally, the total time for the move operation increases by 62% (84ms). Figure 11(b) shows how the total move time scales with the number of flows affected and the packet rate. We observe that the total time for a parallelized loss-free move increases more substantially at higher packet rates. This is because more events are raised, and the rate at which the packets contained in these events can be forwarded to $PRADS_2$ becomes limited by the packet-out rate our OpenFlow switch can sustain. The average and maximum per-packet latency increase for packets contained in events also grows with packet rate for the same reason: e.g., the average (maximum) per-packet latency increase is 465ms (573ms) for a parallelized loss-free move of 500 flows at a packet rate of 10K packets/sec (graph not shown).

While we cannot decrease the total move time without using more rules in SDN switches, our early-release optimization (§5.1.3) can decrease the additional packet latency. At a rate of 2500 packets/sec, the average per-packet latency overhead for the 326 packets contained in events drops to 50ms (LF PL+ER in Figure 10(b)), a 63% decrease compared to LF PL; at 10K packets/sec this overhead drops to 201ms, a 99% decrease. Forwarding packets in events directly to $PRADS_2$, rather than sending packet-out commands to the OpenFlow switch, can likely reduce this latency even further.

In addition to added packet latency, a loss-free move also introduces re-ordering: 657 packets (335 from events + 322 received by $PRADS_2$ while packets from events are still arriving) are processed out-of-order with a parallelized loss-free move. However, this re-ordering can be eliminated with an order-preserving move.

A fully optimized loss-free and order-preserving move (LF+OP PL+ER in Figure 10) takes 96% (208ms) longer than a fully optimized loss-free-only move (LF PL+ER) due to the additional steps involved. Furthermore, packets buffered at $PRADS_2$ (100 packets on average), while waiting for all packets originally sent to $PRADS_1$ to arrive and be processed, each incur up to 96ms of additional latency (7% more than LF PL+ER). Thus, applications can benefit from choosing an alternative version of move if they do not require both guarantees.

**Copy and Share.** A parallelized copy takes 111ms, with no packet drops or added packet latency, as there is no interaction between forwarding state update and this operation. In contrast, a share operation that keeps multi-flow state strongly consistent adds at least 13ms of latency to every packet, with more latency incurred when a packet must wait for the processing of an earlier packet to complete. This latency stems from the need to call `getMultiflow` and `putMultiflow` on $PRADS_1$ and $PRADS_2$, respectively, after every packet is processed, because our events only provide hints as to whether state changed but do not inform us if the state update is significant. For example, every packet processed by the PRADS asset monitor causes an update to the last seen timestamp in the multi-flow state object for the source host, but only a handful of special packets (e.g., TCP handshake and HTTP request packets) result in interesting updates to the object. However, adding more PRADS asset monitor instances (we experimented with up to 6 instances) does not increase the latency because `putMultiflow` calls can be issued in parallel. In general, it is difficult to efficiently support strong consistency of state without more intrinsic support from an NF, e.g., information on the significance of a state update.

### 8.1.2 Benefits of Granular Control

Although the `move`, `copy`, and `share` operations above encompassed all flows, the northbound API allows applications to invoke these operations at any granularity, down to as fine as a single flow. We now examine the benefits this flexibility enables by using the `copy` operation with the Squid caching proxy. We generate 100 requests (drawn from a logarithmic distribution) for 40 unique URLs (objects are 0.5–4MB in size) from each of two clients at a rate of 5 requests/second. Initially, all requests are forwarded to $Squid_1$. After 20 seconds, we launch a second Squid instance ($Squid_2$) and take one of three approaches to handling multi-flow state: do nothing (*ignore*), invoke `copy` with the second client's

| Metric | Ignore | Copy Client | Copy All |
|---|---|---|---|
| Hits on $Squid_1$ | 117 | 117 | 117 |
| Hits on $Squid_2$ | Crashed | 39 | 50 |
| MB of multi-flow state transfered | 0 | 3.8 | 54.4 |

**Table 1: Effects of different ways of handling multi-flow**

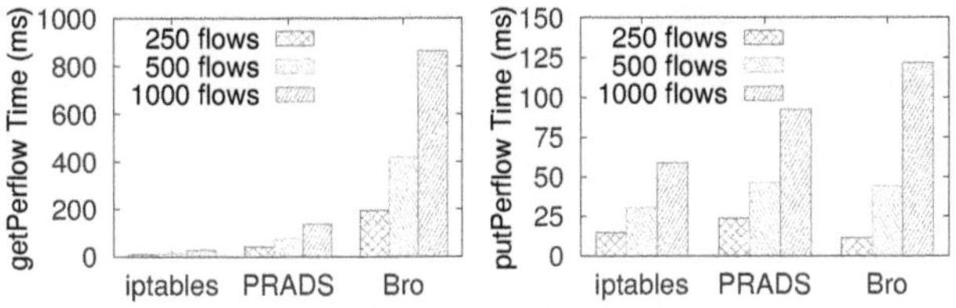


(a) Time for `getPerflow` (b) Time for `putPerflow`

**Figure 12: Efficiency of state export and import**

IP as the filter (*copy client*), or invoke `copy` for all flows (*copy all*). Then, we update routing to forward all in-progress and future requests from the second client to $Squid_2$.

Table 1 shows the number of cache hits at each instance, and the bytes of multi-flow state transfered, under the three different approaches for handling multi-flow state. In all three approaches, the number of cache hits for $Squid_1$ are the same because all the unique objects were cached before the copy. Ignoring multi-flow state entirely causes the second instance to *crash*, as the objects currently being served to the second client are not available. Copying multi-flow state for the second client's flows avoids the crash, but skipping the other multi-flow state results in a 28% lower cache hit ratio at $Squid_2$ compared to copying all multi-flow state (i.e, the entire cache). However, the latter requires a 14.2x larger state transfer. OpenNF's APIs allows each application to make the appropriate trade-offs in such respects when selecting the granularity at which to invoke operations.

## 8.2 Southbound API

The time required to export and import state at NFs directly impacts how quickly a `move` or `copy` operation completes and how much additional packet latency is incurred when `share` is used. We thus evaluate the efficiency of OpenNF's southbound operations for several of the NFs we modified. We also examine how much code was added to the NFs to support these operations.

### *8.2.1 API Call Processing*

Figures 12(a) and 12(b) show the time required to complete a `getPerflow` and `putPerflow` operation, respectively, as a function of the number of flows whose state is exported/imported. We observe a linear increase in the execution time of `getPerflow` and `putPerflow` as the number of per-flow state chunks increases. The time required to (de)serialize each *chunk* of state and send it to (receive it from) the controller accounts for the majority of the execution time. Additionally, we observe that `putPerflow` completes at least 2x faster than `getPerflow`; this is due to deserialization being faster than serialization. Overall, the processing time is highest for Bro because of the size and complexity of the per-flow state. The results for multi-flow state are qualitatively similar; we exclude them for brevity. We are working on techniques for further improving the efficiency of southbound API calls.

We also evaluate how NF performance is impacted by the execution of southbound operations. In particular, we measure average per-packet processing latency (including queueing time) during normal NF operation and when an NF is executing a `getPerflow` call. Among the NFs, the PRADS asset monitor has the largest relative increase—5.8% (0.120ms vs. 0.127ms), while the Bro IDS

| NF | LOC added for serialization | Total LOC added | Increase in NF code |
|---|---|---|---|
| Bro IDS | 2.9K | 3.3K | 4.0% |
| PRADS asset monitor | 0.1K | 1.0K | 9.8% |
| Squid caching proxy | 5.0K | 7.8K | 4.2% |
| iptables | 0.6K | 1.0K | n/a |

**Table 2: Additional NF code to implement OpenNF's southbound API**

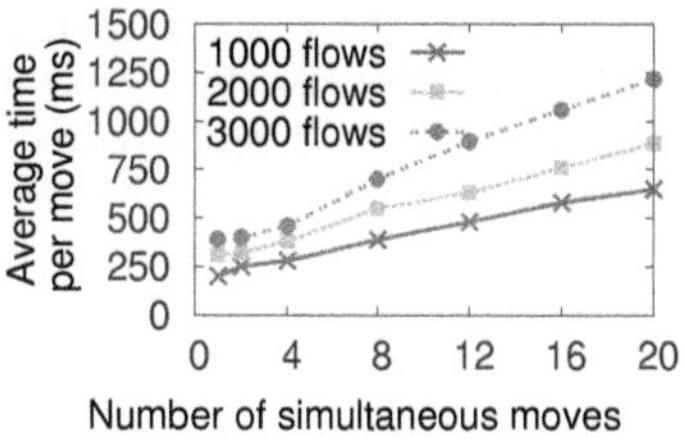


**Figure 13: Performance of concurrent loss-free `move` operations**

has the largest absolute increase—0.12ms (6.93ms vs. 7.06ms). In both cases, the impact is minimal, implying that southbound operations do not significantly degrade NF performance.

### *8.2.2 NF Changes*

To quantify the NF modifications required to support our southbound API, we counted the lines of code (LOC) that we added to each NF (Table 2). The counts do not include the shared library used with each NF for communication with the controller: ≈2.6K LOC. At most, there is a 9.8% increase in LOC[11], most of which is state serialization code that could be automatically generated [3]. Thus, the NF changes required to support OpenNF are minimal.

## 8.3 Controller Scalability

Since the controller executes all northbound operations (§5), its ability to scale is crucial. We thus measure the performance impact of conducting simultaneous operations across many pairs of NFs.

To isolate the controller from the performance of individual NFs, we use "dummy" NFs that replay traces of past state in response to `getPerflow`, simply consume state for `putPerflow`, and infinitely generate events during the lifetime of the experiment. The traces we use are derived from actual state and events sent by PRADS asset monitor while processing our cloud traffic trace. All state and messages are small (202 bytes and 128 bytes, respectively) for consistency, and to maximize the processing demand at the controller and minimize the impact due to network transfer.

Figure 13 shows the average time per loss-free `move` operation as a function of the number of simultaneous operations. The average time per operation increases linearly with both the number of simultaneous operations and the number of flows affected.

We profiled our controller using HPROF [8] and found that threads are busy reading from sockets most of the time. This bottleneck can be overcome by optimizing the size of state transfers using compression. We ran a simple experiment and observed that, for a `move` operation for 500 flows, state can be compressed by 38% improving execution latency from 110ms to 70ms.

## 8.4 Prior NF Control Planes

Lastly, we compare the ability to satisfy the objectives of an elastic/load balanced network monitoring application using OpenNF versus existing approaches [5, 18, 22, 26, 32] (§2.2). We start with one Bro IDS instance ($Bro_1$) and replay our data center traffic trace

[11]We do not calculate an increase for iptables because we wrote a user-level tool to export/import state rather than modifying the Linux kernel.

at a rate of 2500 packets/sec for 2 minutes. We then double the traffic rate, add a second Bro IDS instance ($Bro_2$), and rebalance all HTTP flows to $Bro_2$ (other flows remain at $Bro_1$); 2 minutes later we scale back down to one instance.

**VM Replication.** This approach takes a snapshot of the current state in an existing NF instance ($Bro_1$) and copies it to a new instance ($Bro_2$) as is. Since, VM replication does not do fine-grained state migration, we expect it to have unneeded states (§2.2) in all instances. We quantify unneeded state by comparing: a snapshot of a VM running the Bro IDS that has not yet received any traffic (*base*), a snapshot taken at the instant of scale up (*full*), and snapshots of VMs that have only received either HTTP or other traffic prior to scale up (*HTTP* and *other*). *Base* and *full* differed by 22MB. *HTTP* and *other* differed from *base* by 19MB and 4MB, respectively; these numbers indicate the overhead imposed by the unneeded state at the two Bro IDS instances. In contrast, the amount of state moved by OpenNF (i.e., per-flow and multi-flow state for all active HTTP flows) was 8.1MB. More crucial are the correctness implications of unneeded state: we found 3173 and 716 incorrect entries in conn.log at the two Bro IDS instances, arising because the migrated HTTP (other) flows terminate abruptly at $Bro_1$ ($Bro_2$).

**Scaling Without Re-balancing Active Flows.** Control planes that steer only new flows to new scaled out NF instances leave existing flows to be handled by the same NF instance [22]. Thus, $Bro_1$ continues to remain bottlenecked until some of the flows traversing it complete. Likewise, in the case of scale in, NFs are unnecessarily "held up" as long as flows are active. We observe that $\approx$9% of the HTTP flows in our cloud trace were longer than 25 minutes; this requires us to wait for more than 25 minutes before we can safely terminate $Bro_2$, otherwise we may miss detecting some attacks.

# 9. CONCLUSION

Fully extracting the combined benefits of NFV and SDN requires a control plane to manage both network forwarding state and internal NF state. Without such joint control, applications will be forced to make trade-offs among key objectives. Providing such control is challenging because we must address race conditions and accommodate a variety of application objectives and NF types. We presented a novel control plane architecture called OpenNF that addresses these challenges through careful API design informed by the ways NFs internally manage state today, and clever techniques that ensure lock-step coordination of updates to NF and network state. A thorough evaluation of OpenNF shows that: its joint control is generally efficient even when applications have certain stringent requirements; OpenNF allows applications to make suitable choices in meeting their objectives; and NFs need modest changes and incur minimal overhead when supporting OpenNF primitives.

# 10. ACKNOWLEDGEMENTS

We would like to thank Vivek Pai (our shepherd), Katerina Argyraki, Tom Anderson, David Cheriton, Vimalkumar Jeyakumar, Arvind Krishnamurthy, Ratul Mahajan, Jennifer Rexford, and the anonymous reviewers for their insightful feedback. This work is supported in part by a Wisconsin Alumni Research Foundation (WARF) Accelerator Award and National Science Foundation grants CNS-1302041, CNS-1314363 and CNS-1040757. Aaron Gember-Jacobson is supported by an IBM PhD Fellowship.

# 11. REFERENCES

[1] Balance. http://inlab.de/balance.html.

[2] Boost C++ libraries. http://boost.org.

[3] C++ Middleware Writer. http://webebenezer.net.

[4] Check Point Software: ClusterXL. http://checkpoint.com/products/clusterxl.

[5] CRIU: Checkpoint/Restore In Userspace. http://criu.org.

[6] Floodlight OpenFlow Controller. http://floodlight.openflowhub.org.

[7] HAProxy: The reliable, high performance TCP/HTTP load balancer. http://haproxy.1wt.eu/.

[8] HPROF. http://docs.oracle.com/javase/7/docs/technotes/samples/hprof.html.

[9] iptables. http://netfilter.org/projects/iptables.

[10] libnetfilter_conntrack project. http://netfilter.org/projects/libnetfilter_conntrack.

[11] nDPI. http://ntop.org/products/ndpi.

[12] Network functions virtualisation: Introductory white paper. http://www.tid.es/es/Documents/NFV_White_PaperV2.pdf.

[13] Passive Real-time Asset Detection System. http://prads.projects.linpro.no.

[14] RiverBed Steelhead Load Balancing. http://riverbed.com/products-solutions/products/wan-optimization-steelhead/wan-optimization-management.

[15] Squid. http://squid-cache.org.

[16] A. Anand, V. Sekar, and A. Akella. SmartRE: An architecture for coordinated network-wide redundancy elimination. In *SIGCOMM*, 2009.

[17] B. Anwer, T. Benson, N. Feamster, D. Levin, and J. Rexford. A slick control plane for network middleboxes. In *HotSDN*, 2013.

[18] P. Barham, B. Dragovic, K. Fraser, S. Hand, T. Harris, A. Ho, R. Neugebauer, I. Pratt, and A. Warfield. Xen and the art of virtualization. In *SOSP*, 2003.

[19] T. Benson, A. Akella, and D. Maltz. Network Traffic Characteristics of Data Centers in the Wild. In *IMC*, 2010.

[20] S. K. Fayazbakhsh, L. Chaing, V. Sekar, M. Yu, and J. C. Mogul. Enforcing network-wide policies in the presence of dynamic middlebox actions using FlowTags. In *NSDI*, 2014.

[21] A. Gember, R. Grandl, A. Anand, T. Benson, and A. Akella. Stratos: Virtual Middleboxes as First-Class Entities. Technical Report TR1771, University of Wisconsin-Madison, 2012.

[22] A. Gember, A. Krishnamurthy, S. St. John, R. Grandl, X. Gao, A. Anand, T. Benson, A. Akella, and V. Sekar. Stratos: A network-aware orchestration layer for middleboxes in the cloud. Technical Report arXiv:1305.0209, 2013.

[23] A. Gember, R. Viswanathan, C. Prakash, R. Grandl, J. Khalid, S. Das, and A. Akella. OpenNF: Enabling innovation in network function control. Technical report, University of Wisconsin-Madison, 2014.

[24] K. He, L. Wang, A. Fisher, A. Gember, A. Akella, and T. Ristenpart. Next stop, the cloud: Understanding modern web service deployment in EC2 and Azure. In *IMC*, 2013.

[25] D. Joseph and I. Stoica. Modeling middleboxes. *IEEE Network*, 2008.

[26] D. A. Joseph, A. Tavakoli, and I. Stoica. A policy-aware switching layer for data centers. In *SIGCOMM*, 2008.

[27] R. Mahajan and R. Wattenhofer. On consistent updates in software defined networks. In *HotNets*, 2013.

[28] J. Martins, M. Ahmed, C. Raiciu, V. Olteanu, M. Honda, R. Bifulco, and F. Huici. ClickOS and the art of network function virtualization. In *NSDI*, 2014.

[29] N. McKeown, T. Anderson, H. Balakrishnan, G. Parulkar, L. Peterson, J. Rexford, S. Shenker, and J. Turner. OpenFlow: Enabling innovation in campus networks. *ACM SIGCOMM CCR*, 38(2), 2008.

[30] C. Nicutar, C. Paasch, M. Bagnulo, and C. Raiciu. Evolving the internet with connection acrobatics. In *HotMiddlebox*, 2013.

[31] V. Paxson. Bro: a system for detecting network intruders in real-time. In *USENIX Security (SSYM)*, 1998.

[32] Z. A. Qazi, C.-C. Tu, L. Chiang, R. Miao, V. Sekar, and M. Yu. SIMPLE-fying middlebox policy enforcement using SDN. In *SIGCOMM*, 2013.

[33] S. Rajagopalan, D. Williams, and H. Jamjoom. Pico Replication: A high availability framework for middleboxes. In *SoCC*, 2013.

[34] S. Rajagopalan, D. Williams, H. Jamjoom, and A. Warfield. Split/Merge: System support for elastic execution in virtual middleboxes. In *NSDI*, 2013.

[35] M. Reitblatt, N. Foster, J. Rexford, C. Schlesinger, and D. Walker. Abstractions for network update. In *SIGCOMM*, 2012.

[36] M. Z. Shafiq, L. Ji, A. X. Liu, J. Pang, and J. Wang. A first look at cellular machine-to-machine traffic: Large scale measurement and characterization. In *SIGMETRICS*, 2012.

[37] J. Sherry, S. Hasan, C. Scott, A. Krishnamurthy, S. Ratnasamy, and V. Sekar. Making middleboxes someone else's problem: Network processing as a cloud service. In *SIGCOMM*, 2012.

[38] R. Wang, D. Butnariu, and J. Rexford. OpenFlow-based server load balancing gone wild. In *Hot-ICE*, 2011.

# Network Stack Specialization for Performance

Ilias Marinos
University of Cambridge
Ilias.Marinos@cl.cam.ac.uk

Robert N.M. Watson
University of Cambridge
Robert.Watson@cl.cam.ac.uk

Mark Handley
University College London
M.Handley@cs.ucl.ac.uk

## Abstract

Contemporary network stacks are masterpieces of generality, supporting many edge-node and middle-node functions. Generality comes at a high performance cost: current APIs, memory models, and implementations drastically limit the effectiveness of increasingly powerful hardware. Generality has historically been required so that individual systems could perform many functions. However, as providers have scaled services to support millions of users, they have transitioned toward thousands (or millions) of dedicated servers, each performing a few functions. We argue that the overhead of generality is now a key obstacle to effective scaling, making specialization not only viable, but necessary.

We present Sandstorm and Namestorm, web and DNS servers that utilize a clean-slate userspace network stack that exploits knowledge of application-specific workloads. Based on the netmap framework, our novel approach merges application and network-stack memory models, aggressively amortizes protocol-layer costs based on application-layer knowledge, couples tightly with the NIC event model, and exploits microarchitectural features. Simultaneously, the servers retain use of conventional programming frameworks. We compare our approach with the FreeBSD and Linux stacks using the nginx web server and NSD name server, demonstrating 2–10× and 9× improvements in web-server and DNS throughput, lower CPU usage, linear multicore scaling, and saturated NIC hardware.

## Categories and Subject Descriptors

C.2.1 [**Computer-Communication Networks**]: Network Architecture and Design — *Network communications*

## General Terms: Design, performance

## Keywords: Network stacks; network performance; network-stack specialization; clean-slate design

## 1. INTRODUCTION

Conventional network stacks were designed in an era where individual systems had to perform multiple diverse functions. In the last decade, the advent of cloud computing and the ubiquity of networking has changed this model; today, large content providers serve hundreds of millions of customers. To scale their systems, they are forced to employ many thousands of servers, with each providing only a single network service. Yet most content is still served with conventional general-purpose network stacks.

These general-purpose stacks have not stood still, but today's stacks are the result of numerous incremental updates on top of codebases that were originally developed in the early 1990s. Arguably, these network stacks have proved to be quite efficient, flexible, and reliable, and this is the reason that they still form the core of contemporary networked systems. They also provide a stable programming API, simplifying software development. But this generality comes with significant costs, and we argue that the overhead of generality is now a key obstacle to effective scaling, making specialization not only viable, but necessary.

In this paper we revisit the idea of specialized network stacks. In particular, we develop Sandstorm, a specialized userspace stack for serving static web content, and Namestorm, a specialized stack implementing a high performance DNS server. More importantly, however, our approach does not simply shift the network stack to userspace: we also promote tight integration and specialization of application and stack functionality, achieving cross-layer optimizations antithetical to current design practices.

Servers such as Sandstorm could be used for serving images such as the Facebook logo, as OCSP [20] responders for certificate revocations, or as front end caches to popular dynamic content. This is a role that conventional stacks should be good at: nginx [6] uses the `sendfile()` system call to hand over serving static content to the operating system. FreeBSD and Linux then implement zero-copy stacks, at least for the payload data itself, using scatter-gather to directly DMA the payload from the disk buffer cache to the NIC. They also utilize the features of smart network hardware, such as TCP Segmentation Offload (TSO) and Large Receive Offload (LRO) to further improve performance. With such optimizations, nginx does perform well, but as we will demonstrate, a specialized stack can outperform it by a large margin.

Namestorm is aimed at handling extreme DNS loads, such as might be seen at the root nameservers, or when a server is under a high-rate DDoS attack. The open-source state of the art here is NSD [5], which combined with a modern OS that minimizes data copies when sending and receiving UDP packets, performs well. Namestorm, however, can outperform it by a factor of nine.

Our userspace web server and DNS server are built upon FreeBSD's netmap [31] framework, which directly maps the NIC buffer rings to userspace. We will show that not only is it possible for a specialized stack to beat nginx, but on data-center-style networks when serving small files typical of many web pages, it can achieve


*SIGCOMM'14,* August 17–22, 2014, Chicago, Illinois, USA.

http://dx.doi.org/10.1145/2619239.2626311.

three times the throughput on older hardware, and more than six times the throughput on modern hardware supporting DDIO[1].

The demonstrated performance improvements come from four places. First, we implement a complete zero-copy stack, not only for payload but also for all packet headers, so sending data is very efficient. Second, we allow aggressive amortization that spans traditionally stiff boundaries – e.g., application-layer code can request pre-segmentation of data intended to be sent multiple times, and extensive batching is used to mitigate system-call overhead from userspace. Third, our implementation is synchronous, clocked from received packets; this improves cache locality and minimizes the latency of sending the first packet of the response. Finally, on recent systems, Intel's DDIO provides substantial benefits, but only if packets to be sent are already in the L3 cache and received packets are processed to completion immediately. It is hard to ensure this on conventional stacks, but a special-purpose stack can get much closer to this ideal.

Of course, userspace stacks are not a novel concept. Indeed, the Cheetah web server for MIT's XOK Exokernel [19] operating system took a similar approach, and demonstrated significant performance gains over the NCSA web server in 1994. Despite this, the concept has never really taken off, and in the intervening years conventional stacks have improved immensely. Unlike XOK, our specialized userspace stacks are built on top of a conventional FreeBSD operating system. We will show that it is possible to get all the performance gains of a specialized stack without needing to rewrite all the ancillary support functions provided by a mature operating system (e.g., the filesystem). Combined with the need to scale server clusters, we believe that the time has come to re-evaluate special-purpose stacks on today's hardware.

The key contributions of our work are:

- We discuss many of the issues that affect performance in conventional stacks, even though they use APIs aimed at high performance such as `sendfile()` and `recvmmsg()`.
- We describe the design and implementation of multiple modular, highly specialized, application-specific stacks built over a commodity operating system while avoiding these pitfalls. In contrast to prior work, we demonstrate that it is possible to utilize both conventional and specialized stacks in a single system. This allows us to deploy specialization selectively, optimizing networking while continuing to utilize generic OS components such as filesystems without disruption.
- We demonstrate that specialized network stacks designed for aggressive cross-layer optimizations create opportunities for new and at times counter-intuitive hardware-sensitive optimizations. For example, we find that violating the long-held tenet of data-copy minimization can increase DMA performance for certain workloads on recent CPUs.
- We present hardware-grounded performance analyses of our specialized network stacks side-by-side with highly optimized conventional network stacks. We evaluate our optimizations over multiple generations of hardware, suggesting portability despite rapid hardware evolution.
- We explore the potential of a synchronous network stack blended with asynchronous application structures, in stark contrast to conventional asynchronous network stacks supporting synchronous applications. This approach optimizes cache utilization by both the CPU and DMA engines, yielding as much as 2-10× conventional stack performance.

[1] Direct Data I/O. For more details, see Section 2.4

## 2. SPECIAL-PURPOSE ARCHITECTURE

What is the minimum amount of work that a web server can perform to serve static content at high speed? It must implement a MAC protocol, IP, TCP (including congestion control), and HTTP. However, their implementations do not need to conform to the conventional socket model, split between userspace and kernel, or even implement features such as dynamic TCP segmentation. For a web server that serves the same static content to huge numbers of clients (e.g., the Facebook logo or GMail JavaScript), essentially the same functions are repeated again and again. We wish to explore just how far it is possible to go to improve performance. In particular, we seek to answer the following questions:

- Conventional network stacks support zero copy for OS-maintained data – e.g., filesystem blocks in the buffer cache, but not for application-provided HTTP headers or TCP packet headers. Can we take the zero-copy concept to its logical extreme, in which received packet buffers are passed from the NIC all the way to the application, and application packets to be sent are DMAed to the NIC for transmission without even the headers being copied?
- Conventional stacks make extensive use of queuing and buffering to mitigate context switches and keep CPUs and NICs busy, at the cost of substantially increased cache footprint and latency. Can we adopt a bufferless event model that reimposes synchrony and avoids large queues that exceed cache sizes? Can we expose link-layer buffer information, such as available space in the transmit descriptor ring, to prevent buffer bloat and reduce wasted work constructing packets that will only be dropped?
- Conventional stacks amortize expenses internally, but cannot amortize repetitive costs spanning application and network layers. For example, they amortize TCP connection lookup using Large Receive Offload (LRO) but they cannot amortize the cost of repeated TCP segmentation of the same data transmitted multiple times. Can we design a network-stack API that allows cross-layer amortizations to be accomplished such that after the first client is served, no work is ever repeated when serving subsequent clients?
- Conventional stacks embed the majority of network code in the kernel to avoid the cost of domain transitions, limiting two-way communication flow through the stack. Can we make heavy use of batching to allow device drivers to remain in the kernel while colocating stack code with the application and avoiding significant latency overhead?
- Can we avoid any data-structure locking, and even cache-line contention, when dealing with multi-core applications that do not require it?

Finally, while performing all the above, is there a suitable programming abstraction that allows these components to be reused for other applications that may benefit from server specialization?

### 2.1 Network-stack Modularization

Although monolithic kernels are the *de facto* standard for networked systems, concerns with robustness and flexibility continue to drive exploration of microkernel-like approaches. Both Sandstorm and Namestorm take on several microkernel-like qualities:

**Rapid deployment & reusability**: Our prototype stack is highly modular, and synthesized from the bottom up using traditional dynamic libraries as building blocks (*components*) to construct a special-purpose system. Each component corresponds to a standalone service that exposes a well-defined API. Our specialized network stacks are built by combining four basic components:

- The netmap I/O (`libnmio`) library that abstracts traditional data-movement and event-notification primitives needed by higher levels of the stack.
- `libeth` component, a lightweight Ethernet-layer implementation.
- `libtcpip` that implements our optimized TCP/IP layer.
- `libudpip` that implements a UDP/IP layer.

Figure 1 depicts how some of these components are used with a simple application layer to form Sandstorm, the optimized web server.

Splitting functionality into reusable components does not require us to sacrifice the benefits of exploiting cross-layer knowledge to optimize performance, as memory and control flow move easily across API boundaries. For example, Sandstorm interacts directly with `libnmio` to preload and push segments into the appropriate packet-buffer pools. This preserves a service-centric approach.

**Developer-friendly**: Despite seeking inspiration from microkernel design, our approach maintains most of the benefits of conventional monolithic systems:

- Debugging is at least as easy (if not easier) compared to conventional systems, as application-specific, performance-centric code shifts from the kernel to more accessible userspace.
- Our approach integrates well with the general-purpose operating systems: rewriting basic components such as device drivers or filesystems is not required. We also have direct access to conventional debugging, tracing, and profiling tools, and can also use the conventional network stack for remote access (e.g., via SSH).
- Instrumentation in Sandstorm is a simple and straightforward task that allows us to explore potential bottlenecks as well as necessary and sufficient costs in network processing across application and stack. In addition, off-the-shelf performance monitoring and profiling tools "just work", and a synchronous design makes them easier to use.

## 2.2 Sandstorm web server design

Rizzo's netmap framework provides a general-purpose API that allows received packets to be mapped directly to userspace, and packets to be transmitted to be sent directly from userspace to the NIC's DMA rings. Combined with batching to reduce system calls, this provides a high-performance framework on which to build packet-processing applications. A web server, however, is not normally thought of as a packet-processing application, but one that handles TCP streams.

To serve a static file, we load it into memory, and *a priori* generate all the packets that will be sent, including TCP, IP, and link-layer headers. When an HTTP request for that file arrives, the server must allocate a TCP-protocol control block (TCB) to keep track of the connection's state, but the packets to be sent have already been created for each file on the server.[2]

The majority of the work is performed during inbound TCP ACK processing. The IP header is checked, and if it is acceptable, a hash table is used to locate the TCB. The offset of the ACK number from the start of the connection is used to locate the next prepackaged packet to send, and if permitted by the congestion and receive windows, subsequent packets. To send these packets, the destination address and port must be rewritten, and the TCP and IP checksums incrementally updated. The packet can then be directly fetched by the NIC using netmap. All reads of the ACK header and modifications to the transmitted packets are performed in a single pass, ensuring that both the headers and the TCB remain in the CPU's L1 cache.

Once a packet has been DMAed to the NIC, the packet buffer is returned to Sandstorm, ready to be incrementally modified again and sent to a different client. However, under high load, the same packet may need to be queued in the TX ring for a second client *before* it has finished being sent to the first client. The same packet buffer cannot be in the TX ring twice, with different destination address and port. This presents us with two design options:

- We can maintain more than one copy of each packet in memory to cope with this eventuality. The extra copy could be created at startup, but a more efficient solution would create extra copies on demand whenever a high-water mark is reached, and then retained for future use.
- We can maintain only one long-term copy of each packet, creating ephemeral copies each time it needs to be sent.

We call the former a *pre-copy* stack (it is an extreme form of zero-copy stack because in the steady state it never copies, but differs from the common use of the term "zero copy"), and the latter a *memcpy* stack. A pre-copy stack performs less per-packet work than a memcpy stack, but requires more memory; because of this, it has the potential to thrash the CPU's L3 cache. With the memcpy stack, it is more likely for the original version of a packet to be in the L3 cache, but more work is done. We will evaluate both approaches, because it is far from obvious how CPU cycles trade off against cache misses in modern processors.

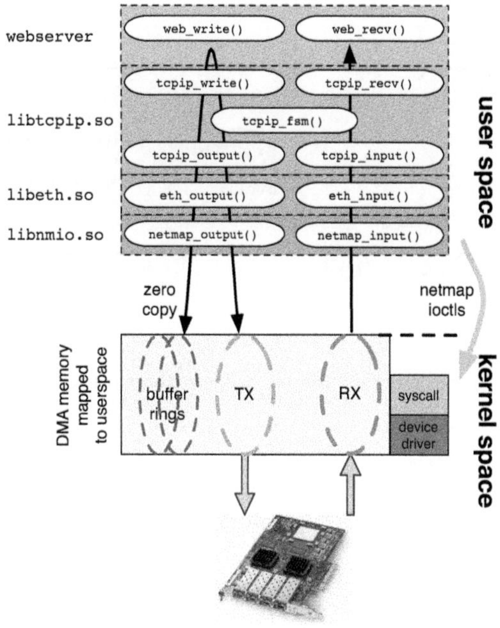


**Figure 1:** Sandstorm high-level architecture view.

[2]Our implementation packetizes on startup, but it could equally well do it on demand, the first time a file is requested, and the resulting packets retained to serve future requests, managed as an LRU cache.

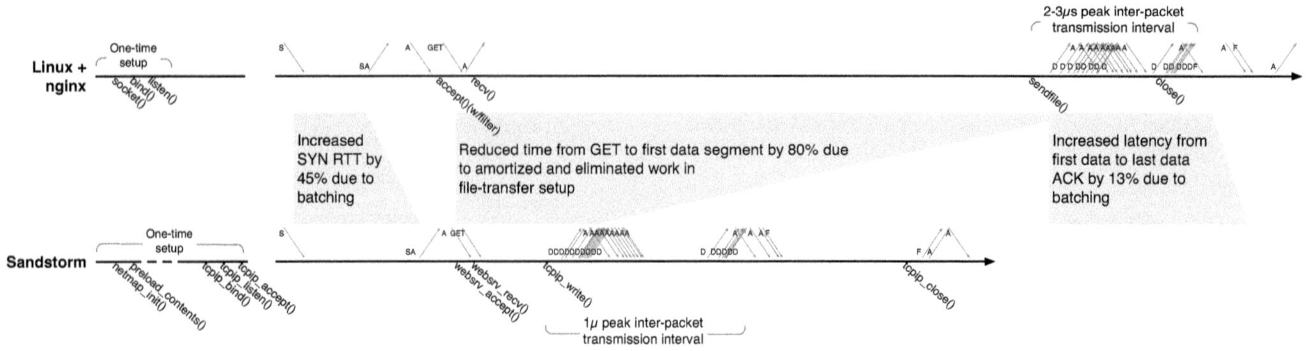


**Figure 2:** Several tradeoffs are visible in these packet traces taken on nginx/Linux and Sandstorm servers that are busy (but unsaturated).

Figure 2 illustrates tradeoffs through traces taken on nginx/Linux and pre-copy Sandstorm servers that are busy (but unsaturated). On the one hand, a batched design measurably increases TCP round-trip time with a relatively idle CPU. On the other hand, Sandstorm amortizes or eliminates substantial parts of per-request processing through a more efficient architecture. Under light load, the benefits are pronounced; at saturation, the effect is even more significant.

Although most work is synchronous within the ACK processing code path, TCP still needs timers for certain operations. Sandstorm's timers are scheduled by polling the Time Stamp Counter (TSC): although not as accurate as other clock sources, it is accessible from userspace at the cost of a single CPU instruction (on modern hardware). The TCP slow timer routine is invoked periodically (every ~500ms) and traverses the list of active TCBs: on RTO expiration, the congestion window and slow-start threshold are adjusted accordingly, and any unacknowledged segments are retransmitted. The same routine also releases TCBs that have been in *TIME_WAIT* state for longer than 2**MSL*. There is no buffering whatsoever required for retransmissions: we identify the segment that needs to be retransmitted using the oldest unacknowledged number as an offset, retrieve the next available prepackaged packet and adjust its headers accordingly, as with regular transmissions. Sandstorm currently implements TCP Reno for congestion control.

## 2.3 The Namestorm DNS server

The same principles applied in the Sandstorm web server, also apply to a wide range of servers returning the same content to multiple users. Authoritative DNS servers are often targets of DDoS attacks – they represent a potential single point of failure, and because DNS traditionally uses UDP, lacks TCP's three way handshake to protect against attackers using spoofed IP addresses. Thus, high performance DNS servers are of significant interest.

Unlike TCP, the conventional UDP stack is actually quite lightweight, and DNS servers already preprocess zone files and store response data in memory. Is there still an advantage running a specialized stack?

Most DNS-request processing is simple. When a request arrives, the server performs sanity checks, hashes the concatenation of the name and record type being requested to find the response, and sends that data. We can preprocess the responses so that they are already stored as a prepackaged UDP packet. As with HTTP, the destination address and port must be rewritten, the identifier must be updated, and the UDP and IP checksums must be incrementally updated. After the initial hash, all remaining processing is performed in one pass, allowing processing of DNS response headers to be performed from the L1 cache. As with Sandstorm, we can use pre-copy or memcpy approaches so that more than one response for the same name can be placed in the DMA ring at a time.

Our specialized userspace DNS server stack is composed of three reusable components, *libnmio*, *libeth*, *libudpip*, and a DNS-specific application layer. As with Sandstorm, Namestorm uses FreeBSD's netmap API, implementing the entire stack in userspace, and uses netmap's batching to amortize system call overhead. *libnmio* and *libeth* are the same as used by Sandstorm, whereas *libudpip* contains UDP-specific code closely integrated with an IP layer. Namestorm is an authoritative nameserver, so it does not need to handle recursive lookups.

Namestorm preprocesses the zone file upon startup, creating DNS response packets for all the entries in the zone, including the answer section and any glue records needed. In addition to type-specific queries for A, NS, MX and similar records, DNS also allows queries for ANY. A full implementation would need to create additional response packets to satisfy these queries; our implementation does not yet do so, but the only effect this would have is to increase the overall memory footprint. In practice, ANY requests prove comparatively rare.

Namestorm indexes the prepackaged DNS response packets using a hash table. There are two ways to do this:

- Index by concatenation of request type (e.g., A, NS, etc) and fully-qualified domain name (FQDN); for example, "`www.example.com`".
- Index by concatenation of request type and the wire-format FQDN as this appears in an actual query; for example, "*[3]*`www`*[7]*`example`*[3]*`com`*[0]*" where *[3]* is a single byte containing the numeric value 3.

Using the wire request format is obviously faster, but DNS permits compression of names. Compression is common in DNS answers, where the same domain name occurs more than once, but proves rare in requests. If we implement wire-format hash keys, we must first perform a check for compression; these requests are decompressed and then reencoded to uncompressed wire-format for hashing. The choice is therefore between optimizing for the common case, using wire-format hash keys, or optimizing for the worst case, assuming compression will be common, and using FQDN hash keys. The former is faster, but the latter is more robust to a DDoS attack by an attacker taking advantage of compression. We evaluate both approaches, as they illustrate different performance tradeoffs.

Our implementation does not currently handle referrals, so it can handle only zones for which it is authoritative for all the sub-zones. It could not, for example, handle the `.com` zone, because it would receive queries for `www.example.com`, but only have hash table entries for `example.com`. Truncating the hash key is trivial to do

| Function | Parameters | Description |
|---|---|---|
| `tcpip_init()` | *none* | Initialize TCP layer (timers, callbacks etc). |
| `tcp_bind()` | tcb, ip, port | Bind a specific TCB to an IP and port. |
| `tcp_listen()` | tcb | Set a TCB to LISTEN state. |
| `tcp_accept()` | tcb, accept_callback | Set an application-specific accept callback to allow the application to control which connections to accept. |
| `tcp_recv()` | tcb, receive_callback | Set an application-specific receive callback to be called when data from a connection is available for the application. |
| `tcp_sent()` | tcb, sent_callback | Set an application-specific sent callback to be called when data previously written to a connection has been successfully delivered. |
| `tcp_write()` | tcb, content, number of segments | Push data to a TCP connection. |
| `tcp_close()` | tcb | Close a TCP connection, equivalent to BSD socket `shutdown()`. |
| `netmap_init()` | interfaces | Initialize netmap I/O library for specific interfaces. |
| `netmap_input_set_cb()` | interface, callback function | Set a callback to push raw RX data to higher layers (e.g., Ethernet). |
| `netmap_input()` | interface | Start the input engine on a specific interface. |
| `netmap_output()` | nring, pktbuf pool, slot index, flags | Depending on flags, memory or zero copy a packet to the TX ring – this function also implements TX batching. |

**Table 1:** A selection of `libtcpip` and `libnmio` APIs.

1. Call RX poll to receive a batch of received packets that have been stored in the NIC's RX ring; block if none are available.
2. For each ACK packet in the batch:
   3. Perform Ethernet and IP input sanity checks.
   4. Locate the TCB for the connection.
   5. Update the acknowledged sequence numbers in TCB; update receive window and congestion window.
   6. For each new TCP data packet that can now be sent, or each lost packet that needs retransmitting:
      7. Find a free copy of the TCP data packet (or clone one if needed).
      8. Correct the destination IP address, destination port, sequence numbers, and incrementally update the TCP checksum.
      9. Add the packet to the NIC's TX ring.
      10. Check if $\delta t$ has passed since last TX poll. If it has, call TX poll to send all queued packets.
11. Loop back to step 1

**Figure 3:** Outline of the main Sandstorm event loop.

as part of the translation to an FQDN, so if Namestorm were to be used for a domain such as `.com`, the FQDN version of hashing would be a reasonable approach.

## 2.4 Main event loop

To understand how the pieces fit together and the nature of interaction between Sandstorm, Namestorm, and netmap, we consider the timeline for processing ACK packets in more detail. Figure 3 summarizes Sandstorm's main loop. SYN/FIN handling, HTTP, and timers are omitted from this outline, but also take place. However, most work is performed in the ACK processing code.

One important consequence of this architecture is that the NIC's TX ring serves as the sole output queue, taking the place of conventional socket buffers and software network-interface queues. This is possible because retransmitted TCP packets are generated in the same way as normal data packets. As Sandstorm is fast enough to saturate two 10Gb/s NICs with a single thread on one core, data structures are also lock free.

When the workload is heavy enough to saturate the CPU, the system-call rate decreases. The receive batch size increases as calls to RX poll become less frequent, improving efficiency at the expense of increased latency. Under extreme load, the RX ring will fill, dropping packets. At this point the system is saturated and, as with any web server, it must bound the number of open connections by dropping some incoming SYNs.

Under heavier load, the TX-poll system call happens in the RX handler. In our current design, $\delta t$, the interval between calls to TX poll in the steady state, is a constant set to $80\mu$s. The system-call rate under extreme load could likely be decreased by further increasing $\delta t$, but as the pre-copy version of Sandstorm can easily saturate all six 10Gb/s NICs in our systems for all file sizes, we have thus far not needed to examine this. Under lighter load, incoming packets might arrive too rarely to provide acceptable latency for transmitted packets; a 5ms timer will trigger transmission of straggling packets in the NIC's TX ring.

The difference between the pre-copy version and the memcpy version of Sandstorm is purely in step 7, where the memcpy version will simply clone the single original packet rather than search for an unused existing copy.

Contemporary Intel server processors support Direct Data I/O (DDIO). DDIO allows NIC-originated Direct Memory Access (DMA) over PCIe to access DRAM through the processor's Last-Level Cache (LLC). For network transmit, DDIO is able to pull data from the cache without a detour through system memory; likewise, for receive, DMA can place data in the processor cache. DDIO implements administrative limits on LLC utilization intended to prevent DMA from thrashing the cache. This design has the potential to significantly reduce latency and increase I/O bandwidth.

Memcpy Sandstorm forces the payload of the copy to be in the CPU cache from which DDIO can DMA it to the NIC without needing to load it from memory again. With pre-copy, the CPU only touches the packet headers, so if the payload is not in the CPU cache, DDIO must load it, potentially impacting performance. These interactions are subtle, and we will look at them in detail.

Namestorm follows the same basic outline, but is simpler as DNS is stateless: it does not need a TCB, and sends a single response packet to each request.

## 2.5 API

As discussed, all of our stack components provide well-defined APIs to promote reusability. Table 1 presents a selection of API functions exposed by `libnmio` and `libtcpip`. In this section we describe some of the most interesting properties of the APIs.

`libnmio` is the lowest-level component: it handles all interaction with netmap and abstracts the main event loop. Higher layers (e.g., `libeth`) register callback functions to receive raw incoming data as well as set timers for periodic events (e.g., TCP slow timer). The function `netmap_ouput()` is the main transmission routine: it enqueues a packet to the transmission ring either by memory or zero copying and also implements an adaptive batching algorithm.

Since there is no socket layer, the application must directly interface with the network stack. With TCP as the transport layer, it acquires a TCB (TCP Control Block), binds it to a specific IPv4 address and port, and sets it to *LISTEN* state using API functions. The application must also register callback functions to accept connections, receive and process data from active connections, as well as act on successful delivery of sent data (e.g., to close the connection or send more data).

# 3. EVALUATION

To explore Sandstorm and Namestorm's performance and behavior, we evaluated using both older and more recent hardware. On older hardware, we employed Linux 3.6.7 and FreeBSD 9-STABLE. On newer hardware, we used Linux 3.12.5 and FreeBSD 10-STABLE. We ran Sandstorm and Namestorm on FreeBSD.

For the old hardware, we use three systems: two clients and one server, connected via a 10GbE crossbar switch. All test systems are equipped with an Intel 82598EB dual port 10GbE NIC, 8GB RAM, and two quad-core 2.66 GHz Intel Xeon X5355 CPUs. In 2006, these were high-end servers. For the new hardware, we use seven systems; six clients and one server, all directly connected via dedicated 10GbE links. The server has three dual-port Intel 82599EB 10GbE NICs, 128GB RAM and a quad-core Intel Xeon E5-2643 CPU. In 2014, these are well-equipped contemporary servers.

The most interesting improvements between these hardware generations are in the memory subsystem. The older Xeons have a conventional architecture with a single 1,333MHz memory bus serving both CPUs. The newer machines, as with all recent Intel server processors, support Data Direct I/O (DDIO), so whether data to be sent is in the cache can have a significant impact on performance.

Our hypothesis is that Sandstorm will be significantly faster than nginx on both platforms; however, the reasons for this may differ. Experience [18] has shown that the older systems often bottleneck on memory latency, and as Sandstorm is not CPU-intensive, we would expect this to be the case. A zero-copy stack should thus be a big win. In addition, as cores contend for memory, we would expect that adding more cores does not help greatly.

On the other hand, with DDIO, the new systems are less likely to bottleneck on memory. The concern, however, would be that DDIO could thrash at least part of the CPU cache. On these systems, we expect that adding more cores would help performance, but that in doing so, we may experience scalability bottlenecks such as lock contention in conventional stacks. Sandstorm's lock-free stack can simply be replicated onto multiple 10GbE NICs, with one core per two NICs to scale performance. In addition, as load increases, the number of packets to be sent or received per system call will increase due to application-level batching. Thus, under heavy load, we would hope that the number of system calls per second to still be acceptable despite shifting almost all network-stack processing to userspace.

The question, of course, is how well do these design choices play out in practice?

## 3.1 Experiment Design: Sandstorm

We evaluated the performance of Sandstorm through a set of experiments and compare our results against the nginx web server running on both FreeBSD and Linux. Nginx is a high-performance, low-footprint web server that follows the non-blocking, event-driven model: it relies on OS primitives such as `kqueue()` for readiness event notifications, it uses `sendfile()` to send HTTP payload directly from the kernel, and it asynchronously processes requests.

Contemporary web pages are immensely content-rich, but they mainly consist of smaller web objects such as images and scripts. The distribution of requested object sizes for Yahoo! CDN, reveals that 90% of the content is smaller than 25KB [11]. The conventional network stack and web-server application perform well when delivering large files by utilizing OS primitives and NIC hardware features. Conversely, multiple simultaneous short-lived HTTP connections are considered a heavy workload that stresses the kernel-userspace interface and reveals performance bottlenecks: even with `sendfile()` to send the payload, the size of the transmitted data is not quite enough to compensate for the system cost.

For all the benchmarks, we configured nginx to serve content from a RAM disk to eliminate disk-related I/O bottlenecks. Similarly, Sandstorm preloads the data to be sent and performs its pre-segmentation phase before the experiments begin. We use *weighttp* [9] to generate load with multiple concurrent clients. Each client generates a series of HTTP requests, with a new connection being initiated immediately after the previous one terminates. For each experiment we measure throughput, and we vary the size of the file served, exploring possible tradeoffs between throughput and system load. Finally, we run experiments with a realistic workload by using a trace of files with sizes that follow the distribution of requested HTTP objects of the Yahoo! CDN.

## 3.2 Sandstorm Results

First, we wish to explore how file size affects performance. Sandstorm is designed with small files in mind, and batching to reduce overheads, whereas the conventional `sendfile()` ought to be better for larger files.

Figure 4 shows performance as a function of content size, comparing pre-copy Sandstorm and nginx running on both FreeBSD and Linux. With a single 10GbE NIC (Fig. 4a and 4d), Sandstorm outperforms nginx for smaller files by ~23–240%. For larger files, all three configurations saturate the link. Both conventional stacks are more CPU-hungry for the whole range of file sizes tested, despite potential advantages such as TSO on bulk transfers.

To scale to higher bandwidths, we added more 10GbE NICs and client machines. Figure 4b shows aggregate throughput with four 10GbE NICs. Sandstorm saturates all four NICs using just two CPU cores, but neither Linux nor FreeBSD can saturate the NICs with files smaller than 128KB, even though they use four CPU cores.

As we add yet more NICs, shown in Figure 4c, the difference in performance gets larger for a wider range of file sizes. With 6×10GbE NICs Sandstorm gives between 10% and 10× more throughput than FreeBSD for file sizes in the range of 4–256KB. Linux fares worse, experiencing a performance drop (see Figure 4c) compared to FreeBSD with smaller file sizes and 5–6 NICs. Low CPU utilization is normally good, but here (Figures 4f, 5b), idle time is undesirable since the NICs are not yet saturated. We have not identified any single obvious cause for this degradation. Packet traces show the delay to occur between the connection being accepted and the response being sent. There is no single kernel lock being held for especially long, and although locking is not negligible, it does not dominate, either. The system suffers one soft page fault for every two connections on average, but no hard faults, so data is already in the disk buffer cache, and TCB recycling is enabled. This is an example of how hard it can be to find performance problems with conventional stacks. Interestingly, this was an application-specific behavior triggered only on Linux: in benchmarks we conducted with other web servers (e.g., lighttpd [3], OpenLiteSpeed [7]) we did not experience a similar performance collapse on Linux with

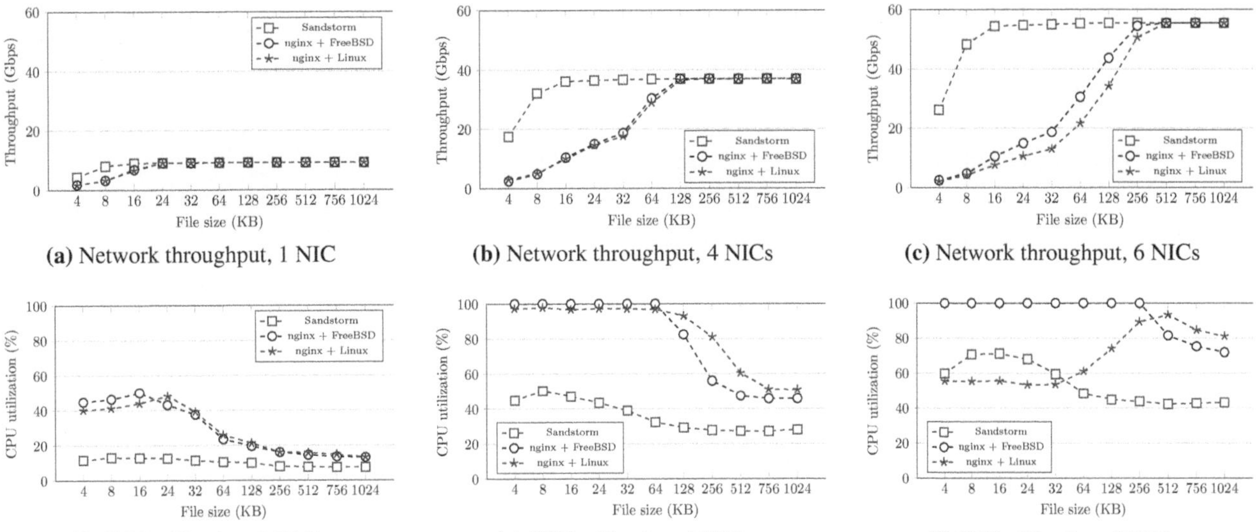


(a) Network throughput, 1 NIC (b) Network throughput, 4 NICs (c) Network throughput, 6 NICs

(d) CPU utilization, 1 NIC (e) CPU utilization, 4 NICs (f) CPU utilization, 6 NICs

**Figure 4:** Sandstorm throughput vs. file sizes and number of NICs.

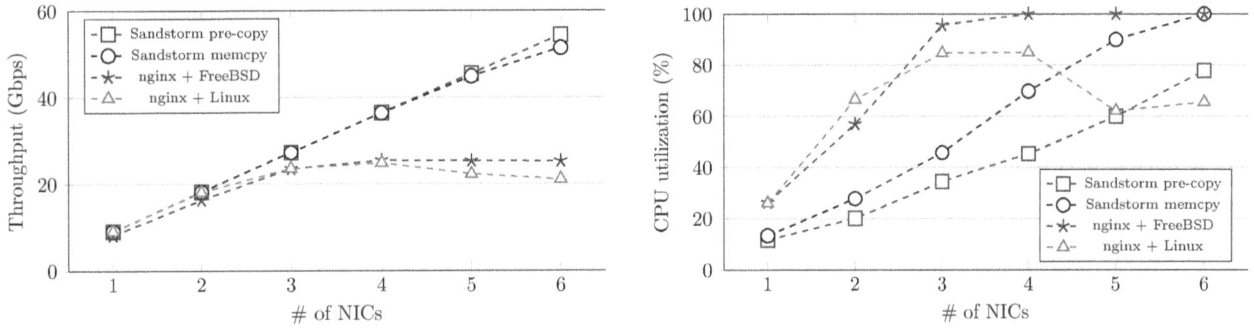


(a) Network throughput (b) CPU utilization

**Figure 5:** Network throughput and CPU utilization vs. number of NICs while serving a Yahoo! CDN-like workload.

more than four NICs. We have chosen, however, to present the nginx datasets as it offered the greatest overall scalability in both operating systems.

It is clear that Sandstorm dramatically improves network performance when it serves small web objects, but somewhat surprisingly, it performs better for larger files too. For completeness, we evaluate Sandstorm using a realistic workload: following the distribution of requested HTTP object sizes of the Yahoo! CDN [11], we generated a trace of 1000 files ranging from a few KB up to ~20MB which were served from both Sandstorm and nginx. On the clients, we modified *weighttp* to benchmark the server by concurrently requesting files in a random order. Figures 5a and 5b highlight the achieved network throughput and the CPU utilization of the server as a function of the number of the network adapters. The network performance improvement is more than 2× while CPU utilization is reduced.

Finally, we evaluated whether Sandstorm handles high packet loss correctly. With 80 simultaneous clients and 1% packet loss, as expected, throughput plummets. FreeBSD achieves approximately 640Mb/s and Sandstorm roughly 25% less. This is not fundamental, but due to FreeBSD's more fine-grained retransmit timer and its use of NewReno congestion control rather than Reno, which could also be implemented in Sandstorm. Neither network nor server is stressed in this experiment – if there had been a real congested link causing the loss, both stacks would have filled it.

Throughout, we have invested considerable effort in profiling and optimizing conventional network stacks, both to understand their design choices and bottlenecks, and to provide the fairest possible comparison. We applied conventional performance tuning to Linux and FreeBSD, such as increasing hash-table sizes, manually tuning CPU work placement for multiqueue NICs, and adjusting NIC parameters such as interrupt mitigation. In collaboration with Netflix, we also developed a number of TCP and virtual-memory subsystem performance optimizations for FreeBSD, reducing lock contention under high packet loads. One important optimization is related to `sendfile()`, in which contention within the VM subsystem occurred while TCP-layer socket-buffer locks were held, triggering a cascade to the system as a whole. These changes have been upstreamed to FreeBSD for inclusion in a future release.

### *To copy or not to copy*

The pre-copy variant of Sandstorm maintains more than one copy of each segment in memory so that it can send the same segment to multiple clients simultaneously. This requires more memory than nginx serving files from RAM. The memcpy variant only enqueues copies, requiring a single long-lived version of each packet, and

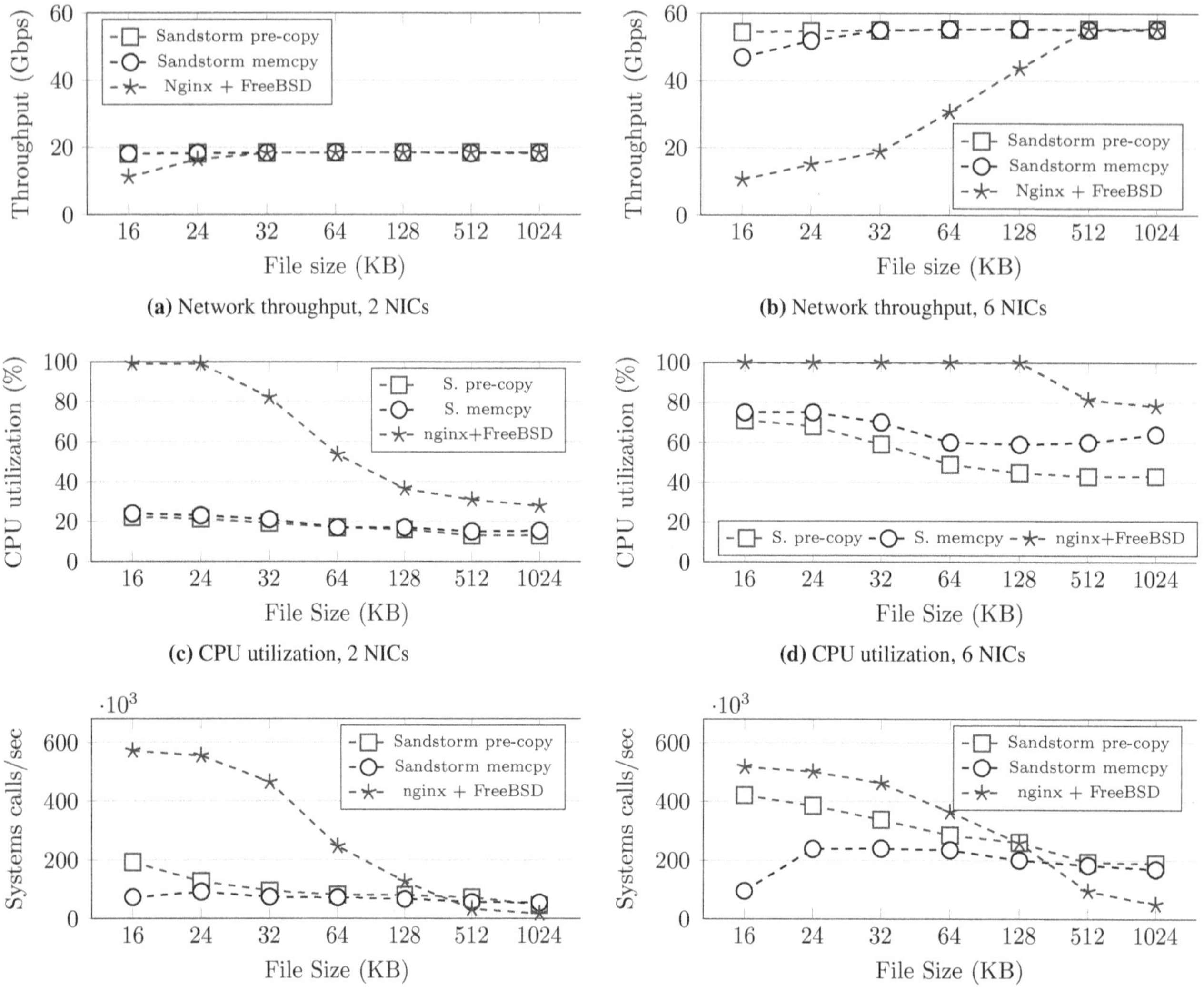


**(a)** Network throughput, 2 NICs

**(b)** Network throughput, 6 NICs

**(c)** CPU utilization, 2 NICs

**(d)** CPU utilization, 6 NICs

**(e)** System call rate, 2 NICs

**(f)** System call rate, 6 NICs

**Figure 6:** Sandstorm throughput and CPU utilization vs. variable number of NICs and file sizes.

uses a similar amount of memory to nginx. How does this `memcpy` affect performance? Figure 6 explores network throughput, CPU utilization, and system-call rate for two- and six-NIC configurations.

With six NICs, the additional `memcpy()` marginally reduces performance (Figure 6b) while exhibiting slightly higher CPU load (Figure 6d). In this experiment, Sandstorm only uses three cores to simplify the comparison, so around 75% utilization saturates those cores. The memcpy variant saturates the CPU for files smaller than 32KB, whereas the pre-copy variant does not. Nginx, using `sendfile()` and all four cores, only catches up for file sizes of 512KB and above, and even then exhibits higher CPU load.

As file size decreases, the expense of SYN/FIN and HTTP-request processing becomes measurable for both variants, but the pre-copy version has more headroom so is affected less. It is interesting to observe the effects of batching under overload with the memcpy stack in Figure 6f. With large file sizes, pre-copy and memcpy make the same number of system calls per second. With small files, however, the memcpy stack makes substantially fewer system calls per second. This illustrates the efficacy of batching: memcpy has saturated the CPU, and consequently no longer polls the RX queue as often. As the batch size increases, the system-call cost decreases, helping the server weather the storm. The pre-copy variant is not stressed here and continues to poll frequently, but would behave the same way under overload. In the end, the cost of the additional `memcpy` is measurable, but still performs quite well.

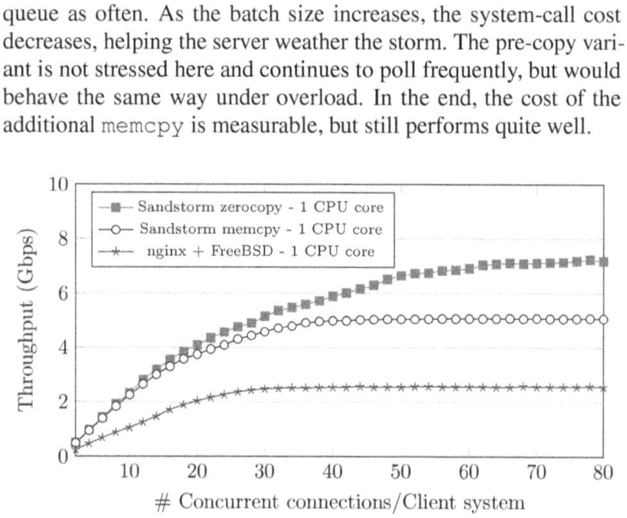


**Figure 7:** Network throughput, 1 NIC, ~23KB file, old hardware.

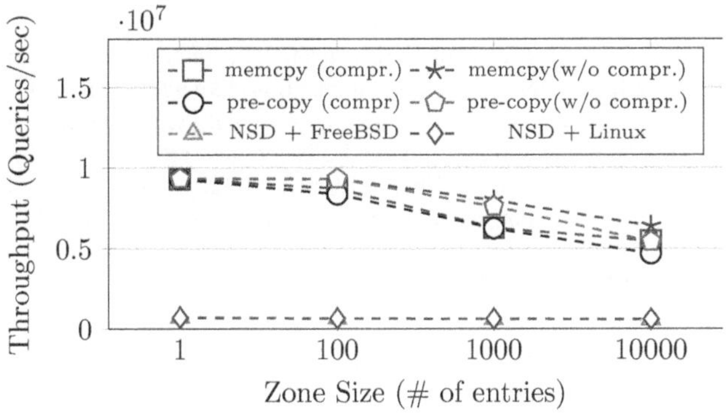


**(a)** Throughput, 1x10GbE NIC

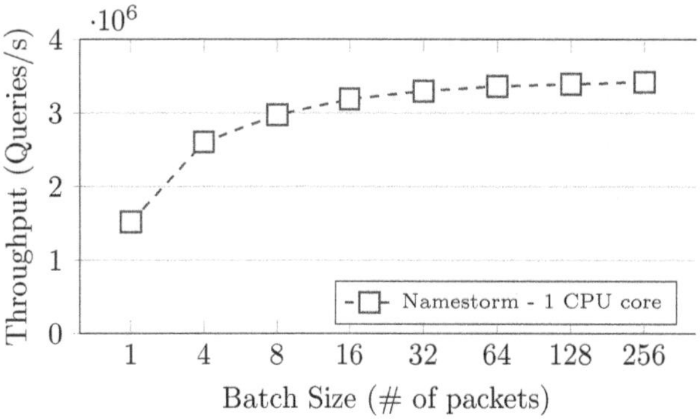


**(b)** Batching efficiency

**Figure 8:** Namestorm performance measurements.

Results on contemporary hardware are significantly different from those run on older pre-DDIO hardware. Figure 7 shows the results obtained on our 2006-era servers. On the older machines, Sandstorm outperforms nginx by a factor of three, but the memcpy variant suffers a 30% decrease in throughput compared to pre-copy Sandstorm as a result of adding a single `memcpy` to the code. It is clear that on these older systems, memory bandwidth is the main performance bottleneck.

With DDIO, memory bandwidth is not such a limiting factor. Figure 9 in Section 3.5 shows the corresponding memory read throughput, as measured using CPU performance counters, for the network-throughput graphs in Figure 6b. With small file sizes, the pre-copy variant of Sandstorm appears to do more work: the L3 cache cannot hold all of the data, so there are many more L3 misses than with memcpy. Memory-read throughput for both pre-copy and nginx are closely correlated with their network throughput, indicating that DDIO is not helping on transmit: DMA comes from memory rather than the cache. The memcpy variant, however, has higher network throughput than memory throughput, indicating that DDIO is transmitting from the cache. Unfortunately, this is offset by much higher memory write throughput. Still, this only causes a small reduction in service throughput. Larger files no longer fit in the L3 cache, even with memcpy. Memory-read throughput starts to rise with files above 64KB. Despite this, performance remains high and CPU load decreases, indicating these systems are not limited by memory bandwidth for this workload.

## 3.3 Experiment Design: Namestorm

We use the same clients and server systems to evaluate Namestorm as we used for Sandstorm. Namestorm is expected to be significantly more CPU-intensive than Sandstorm, mostly due to fundamental DNS protocol properties: high packet rate and small packets. Based on this observation, we have changed the network topology of our experiment: we use only one NIC on the server connected to the client systems via a 10GbE cut-through switch. In order to balance the load on the server to all available CPU cores we use four dedicated NIC queues and four Namestorm instances.

We ran Nominum's *dnsperf* [2] DNS profiling software on the clients. We created zone files of varying sizes, loaded them onto the DNS servers, and configured dnsperf to query the zone repeatedly.

## 3.4 Namestorm Results

Figure 8a shows the performance of Namestorm and NSD running on Linux and FreeBSD when using a single 10GbE NIC. Performance results of NSD are similar with both FreeBSD and Linux. Neither operating system can saturate the 10GbE NIC, however, and both show some performance drop as the zone file grows. On Linux, NSD's performance drops by ~14% (from ~689,000 to ~590,000 Queries/sec) as the zone file grows from 1 to 10,000 entries, and on FreeBSD, it drops by ~20% (from ~720,000 to ~574,000 Qps). For these benchmarks, NSD saturates all CPU cores on both systems.

For Namestorm, we utilized two datasets, one where the hash keys are in wire-format (*w/o compr.*), and one where they are in FQDN format (*compr.*). The latter requires copying the search term before hashing it to handle possible compressed requests.

With wire-format hashing, Namestorm memcpy performance is ~11–13× better, depending on the zone size, when compared to the best results from NSD with either Linux or FreeBSD. Namestorm's throughput drops by ~30% as the zone file grows from 1 to 10,000 entries (from ~9,310,000 to ~6,410,000 Qps). The reason for this decrease is mainly the LLC miss rate, which more than doubles. *Dnsperf* does not report throughput in Gbps, but given the typical DNS response size for our zones we can calculate ~8.4Gbps and ~5.9Gbps for the smallest and largest zone respectively.

With FQDN-format hashing, Namestorm memcpy performance is worse than with wire-format hashing, but is still ~9–13× better compared to NSD. The extra processing with FQDN-format hashing costs ~10–20% in throughput, depending on the zone size.

Finally, in Figure 8a we observe a noticeable performance overhead with the pre-copy stack, which we explore in Section 3.5.

### 3.4.1 *Effectiveness of batching*

One of the biggest performance benefits for Namestorm is that netmap provides an API that facilitates batching across the system-call interface. To explore the effects of batching, we configured a single Namestorm instance and one hardware queue, and reran our benchmark with varying batch sizes. Figure 8b illustrates the results: a more than 2× performance gain when growing the batch size from 1 packet (no batching) to 32 packets. Interestingly, the performance of a single-core Namestorm without any batching remains more than 2× better than NSD.

At a minimum, NSD has to make one system call to receive each request and one to send a response. Recently Linux added the new `recvmmsg()` and `sendmmsg()` system calls to receive and send multiple UDP messages with a single call. These may go some way to improving NSD's performance compared to Namestorm. They are, however, UDP-specific, and `sendmmsg()` requires the application to manage its own transmit-queue batching. When we implemented Namestorm, we already had *libnmio*, which abstracts

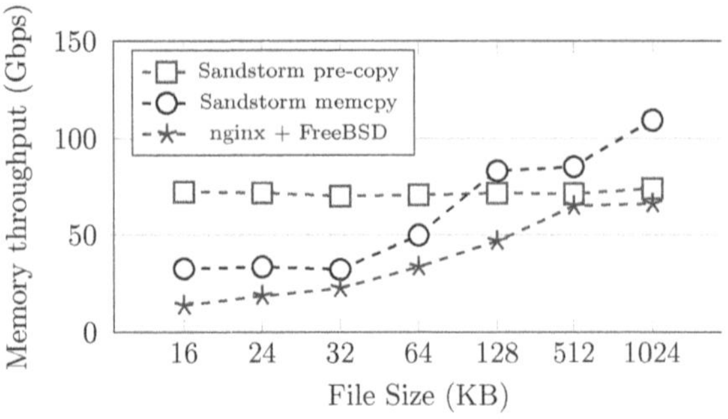


**Figure 9:** Sandstorm memory read throughput, 6 NICs.

and handles all the batching interactions with netmap, so there is no application-specific batching code in Namestorm.

## 3.5 DDIO

With DDIO, incoming packets are DMAed directly to the CPU's L3 cache, and outgoing packets are DMAed directly from the L3 cache, avoiding round trips from the CPU to the memory subsystem. For lightly loaded servers in which the working set is smaller than the L3 cache, or in which data is accessed with temporal locality by the processor and DMA engine (e.g., touched and immediately sent, or received and immediately accessed), DDIO can dramatically reduce latency by avoiding memory traffic. Thus DDIO is ideal for RPC-like mechanisms in which processing latency is low and data will be used immediately before or after DMA. On heavily loaded systems, it is far from clear whether DDIO will be a win or not. For applications with a larger cache footprint, or in which communication occurs at some delay from CPU generation or use of packet data, DDIO could unnecessarily pollute the cache and trigger additional memory traffic, damaging performance.

Intuitively, one might reasonably assume that Sandstorm's pre-copy mode might interact best with DDIO: as with `sendfile()` based designs, only packet headers enter the L1/L2 caches, with payload content rarely touched by the CPU. Figure 9 illustrates a therefore surprising effect when operating on small file sizes: overall memory throughput from the CPU package, as measured using performance counters situated on the DRAM-facing interface of the LLC, sees significantly less traffic for the memcpy implementation relative to the pre-copy one, which shows a constant rate roughly equal to network throughput.

We believe this occurs because DDIO is, by policy, limited from occupying most of the LLC: in the pre-copy cases, DDIO is responsible for pulling untouched data into the cache – as the file data cannot fit in this subset of the cache, DMA access thrashes the cache and all network transmit is done from DRAM. In the memcpy case, the CPU loads data into the cache, allowing more complete utilization of the cache for network data. However, as the DRAM memory interface is not a bottleneck in the system as configured, the net result of the additional memcpy, despite better cache utilization, is reduced performance. As file sizes increase, the overall footprint of memory copying rapidly exceeds the LLC size, exceeding network throughput, at which point pre-copy becomes more efficient. Likewise, one might mistakenly believe simply from inspection of CPU memory counters that nginx is somehow benefiting from this same effect: in fact, nginx is experiencing CPU saturation, and it is not until file size reaches 512K that sufficient CPU is available to converge with pre-copy's saturation of the network link.

By contrast, Namestorm sees improved performance using the memcpy implementation, as the cache lines holding packet data must be dirtied due to protocol requirements, in which case performing the memcpy has little CPU overhead yet allows much more efficient use of the cache by DDIO.

It is much more difficult to reason about the interaction between a conventional operating system, applications like nginx, and DDIO's effect on L3 cache behavior. Ideally, we would experiment by disabling DDIO and monitoring the L3 cache miss rate, but there is no way to disable it on the Xeon E5 CPUs we have used, nor modify the policy that controls the fraction of the cache used by DDIO.

# 4. DISCUSSION

We developed Sandstorm and Namestorm to explore the hypothesis that fundamental architectural change might be required to properly exploit rapidly growing CPU core counts and NIC capacity. Comparisons with Linux and FreeBSD appear to confirm this conclusion far more dramatically than we expected: while there are small-factor differences between Linux and FreeBSD performance curves, we observe that their shapes are fundamentally the same. We believe that this reflects near-identical underlying architectural decisions stemming from common intellectual ancestry (the BSD network stack and sockets API) and largely incremental changes from that original design.

Sandstorm and Namestorm adopt fundamentally different architectural approaches, emphasizing transparent memory flow within applications (and not across expensive protection-domain boundaries), process-to-completion, heavy amortization, batching, and application-specific customizations that seem antithetical to general-purpose stack design. The results are dramatic, accomplishing near-linear speedup with increases in core and NIC capacity – completely different curves possible only with a completely different design.

## 4.1 Current network-stack specialization

Over the years there have been many attempts to add specialized features to general-purpose stacks such as FreeBSD and Linux. Examples include `sendfile()`, primarily for web servers, `recvmmsg()`, mostly aimed at DNS servers, and assorted socket options for telnet. In some cases, entire applications have been moved to the kernel [13, 24] because it was too difficult to achieve performance through the existing APIs. The problem with these enhancements is that each serves a narrow role, yet still must fit within a general OS architecture, and thus are constrained in what they can do. Special-purpose userspace stacks do not suffer from these constraints, and free the programmer to solve a narrow problem in an application-specific manner while still having the other advantages of a general-purpose OS stack.

## 4.2 The generality of specialization

Our approach tightly integrates the network stack and application within a single process. This model, together with optimizations aimed at cache locality or pre-packetization, naturally fit a reasonably wide range of performance-critical, event-driven applications such as web servers, key-value stores, RPC-based services and name servers. Even rate-adaptive video streaming may benefit, as developments such as MPEG-DASH and Apple's HLS have moved intelligence to the client leaving servers as dumb static-content farms.

Not all network services are a natural fit. For example, CGI-based web services and general-purpose databases have inherently different properties and are generally CPU- or filesystem-intensive, deemphasizing networking bottlenecks. In our design, the control loop and transport-protocol correctness depend on the timely execution of application-layer functions; blocking in the application cannot be tolerated. A thread-based approach might be more suitable for such cases. Isolating the network stack and application into different threads still yields benefits: OS-bypass networking costs less, and saved CPU cycles are available for the application. However, such an approach requires synchronization, and so increases complexity and offers less room for cross-layer optimization.

We are neither arguing for the exclusive use of specialized stacks over generalized ones, nor deployment of general-purpose network stacks in userspace. Instead, we propose selectively identifying key scale-out applications where informed but aggressive exploitation of domain-specific knowledge and micro-architectural properties will allow cross-layer optimizations. In such cases, the benefits outweigh the costs of developing and maintaining a specialized stack.

### 4.3 Tracing, profiling, and measurement

One of our greatest challenges in this work was the root-cause analysis of performance issues in contemporary hardware-software implementations. The amount of time spent analyzing network-stack behavior (often unsuccessfully) dwarfed the amount of time required to implement Sandstorm and Namestorm.

An enormous variety of tools exist – OS-specific PMC tools, lock contention measurement tools, tcpdump, Intel vTune, DTrace, and a plethora of application-specific tracing features – but they suffer many significant limitations. Perhaps most problematic is that the tools are not *holistic*: each captures only a fragment of the analysis space – different configuration models, file formats, and feature sets.

Worse, as we attempted inter-OS analysis (e.g., comparing Linux and FreeBSD lock profiling), we discovered that tools often measure and report results differently, preventing sensible comparison. For example, we found that Linux took packet timestamps at different points than FreeBSD, FreeBSD uses different clocks for DTrace and BPF, and that while FreeBSD exports both per-process and per-core PMC stats, Linux supports only the former. Where supported, DTrace attempts to bridge these gaps by unifying configuration, trace formats, and event namespaces [15]. However, DTrace also experiences high overhead causing bespoke tools to persist, and is unintegrated with packet-level tools preventing side-by-side comparison of packet and execution traces. We feel certain that improvement in the state-of-the-art would benefit not only research, but also the practice of network-stack implementation.

Our special-purpose stacks are synchronous; after netmap hands off packets to userspace, the control flow is generally linear, and we process packets to completion. This, combined with lock-free design, means that it is very simple to reason about where time goes when handling a request flow. General-purpose stacks cannot, by their nature, be synchronous. They must be asynchronous to balance all the conflicting demands of hardware and applications, managing queues without application knowledge, allocating processing to threads in order to handle those queues, and ensuring safety via locking. To reason about performance in such systems, we often resort to statistical sampling because it is not possible to directly follow the control flow. Of course, not all network applications are well suited to synchronous models; we argue, however, that imposing the asynchrony of a general-purpose stack on all applications can unnecessarily complicate debugging, performance analysis, and performance optimization.

## 5. RELATED WORK

Web server and network-stack performance optimization is not a new research area. Past studies have come up with many optimization techniques as well as completely different design choices. These designs range from userspace and kernel-based implementations to specialized operating systems.

With the conventional approaches, userspace applications [1, 6] utilize general-purpose network stacks, relying heavily on operating-system primitives to achieve data movement and event notification [26]. Several proposals [23, 12, 30] focus on reducing the overhead of such primitives (e.g., KQueue, `epoll`, `sendfile()`). IO-Lite [27] unifies the data management between OS subsystems and userspace applications by providing page-based mechanisms to safely and concurrently share data. Fbufs [17] utilize techniques such as page remapping and shared memory to provide high-performance cross-domain transfers and buffer management. Pesterev and Wickizer [28, 14] have proposed efficient techniques to improve commodity-stack performance by controlling connection locality and taking advantage of modern multicore systems. Similarly, MegaPipe [21] shows significant performance gain by introducing a bidirectional, per-core pipe to facilitate data exchange and event notification between kernel and userspace applications.

A significant number of research proposals follow a substantially different approach: they propose partial or full implementation of network applications in kernel, aiming to eliminate the cost of communication between kernel and userspace. Although this design decision improves performance significantly, it comes at the cost of limited security and reliability. A representative example of this category is kHTTPd [13], a kernel-based web server which uses the socket interface. Similar to kHTTPd, TUX [24] is another noteworthy example of in-kernel network applications. TUX achieves greater performance by eliminating the socket layer and pinning the static content it serves in memory. We have adopted several of these ideas in our prototype, although our approach is not kernel based.

Microkernel designs such as Mach [10] have long appealed to OS designers, pushing core services (such as network stacks) into user processes so that they can be more easily developed, customized, and multiply-instantiated. In this direction, Thekkath et al [32], have prototyped capability-enabled, library-synthesized userspace network stacks implemented on Mach. The Cheetah web server is built on top of an Exokernel [19] library operating system that provides a filesystem and an optimized TCP/IP implementation. Lightweight libOSes enable application developers to exploit domain-specific knowledge and improve performance. Unikernel designs such as MirageOS [25] likewise blend operating-system and application components at compile-time, trimming unneeded software elements to accomplish extremely small memory footprints – although by static code analysis rather than application-specific specialization.

OS-bypass and userspace network processing is another technique explored by the academic community with several studies such as Arsenic [29], U-Net [33], Linux PF_RING [16], as well as netmap [31]. lwIP [4] is a lightweight general-purpose network stack which was designed for low-end, embedded devices; although performance and specialization are not their primary goals, we have borrowed several ideas for our TCP API. mTCP [22] is another recent effort in userspace networking that demonstrates significant performance improvements: likewise, this work is related, but differs from ours in that it offers a general-purpose stack aiming to minimize integration effort for existing applications, while our proposal sacrifices backward compatibility in favor of specialization and performance. Finally, Solarflare OpenOnload [8] is one of the most sophisticated commercial proposals: it is a hybrid stack, capable of operating both in usermode and kernel, minimizing interrupts, data copies, and context switches. It requires, however, vendor-specific hardware (NIC) and likewise retains the BSD sockets API rather than exploiting domain-specific knowledge and cross-layer optimizations.

## 6. CONCLUSION

In this paper, we have demonstrated that specialized userspace stacks, built on top of netmap framework, can vastly improve the performance of scale-out applications. These performance gains sacrifice generality by adopting design principles at odds with contemporary stack design: application-specific cross-layer cost amortizations, synchronous and buffering-free protocol implementations, and an extreme focus on interactions between processors, caches, and NICs. This approach reflects a widespread adoption of scale-out computing in data centers, which deemphasizes multifunction hosts in favor of increased large-scale specialization. Our performance results are compelling: a 2–10× improvement for web service, and a roughly 9× improvement for DNS service. Further, these stacks have proven easier to develop and tune than conventional stacks, and their performance improvements are portable over multiple generations of hardware.

General-purpose operating system stacks have been around a long time, and have demonstrated the ability to transcend multiple generations of hardware. We believe the same should be true of special-purpose stacks, but that tuning for particular hardware should be easier. We examined performance on servers manufactured seven years apart, and demonstrated that although the performance bottlenecks were now in different places, the same design delivered significant benefits on both platforms.

## 7. ACKNOWLEDGMENTS

We thank Peter Tsonchev, Arvind Jadoo and Cristian Petrescu for their help in the genesis of this work, and Luigi Rizzo for his feedback on the ideas in this paper. We also gratefully acknowledge Scott Long, Adrian Chadd, and Lawrence Stewart at Netflix, and Jim Harris from Intel's Storage Division, for their assistance in performance measurement, analysis, and optimization. Finally, we thank David Chisnall, Nikola Gvozdiev, Charalampos Rotsos, Malte Schwarzkopf, Bjoern Zeeb, our anonymous reviewers, and our shepherd Paul Barford for their insightful comments.

This work was supported by the Defense Advanced Research Projects Agency (DARPA) and the Air Force Research Laboratory (AFRL), under contracts FA8750-10-C-0237 and FA8750-11-C-0249, by EMC/Isilon, by Google, Inc, and by the EU CHANGE FP7 project. The views, opinions, and/or findings contained in this report are those of the authors and should not be interpreted as representing the official views or policies, either expressed or implied, of DARPA or the Department of Defense.

## 8. REFERENCES

[1] Apache http server. `http://httpd.apache.org/`.

[2] DNSPerf. `http://nominum.com/measurement-tools/`.

[3] Lighttpd. `http://www.lighttpd.net/`.

[4] lwIP. `http://savannah.nongnu.org/projects/lwip/`.

[5] Name Server Daemon. `http://www.nlnetlabs.nl/nsd/`.

[6] Nginx web server. `http://nginx.org/`.

[7] OpenLiteSpeed. `http://open.litespeedtech.com/`.

[8] Solarflare OpenOnload. `http://www.openonload.org/`.

[9] weighttp: a lightweight benchmarking tool for webservers. `http://redmine.lighttpd.net/projects/weighttp/wiki`.

[10] M. Accetta, R. Baron, W. Bolosky, D. Golub, R. Rashid, A. Tavanian, and M. Young. Mach: A new kernel foundation for Unix development. In *Proceedings of the 1986 USENIX Annual Technical Conference*, ATC '86. USENIX, June 1986.

[11] M. Al-Fares, K. Elmeleegy, B. Reed, and I. Gashinsky. Overclocking the Yahoo!: CDN for faster web page loads. In *Proceedings of the 2011 Internet Measurement Conference*. ACM, 2011.

[12] G. Banga, J. C. Mogul, and P. Druschel. A scalable and explicit event delivery mechanism for UNIX. In *Proceedings of the 1999 USENIX Annual Technical Conference*, ATC '99. USENIX, 1999.

[13] M. Bar. Kernel Korner: kHTTPd, a Kernel-Based Web Server. *Linux Journal*, 2000(76), Aug. 2000.

[14] S. Boyd-Wickizer, A. T. Clements, Y. Mao, A. Pesterev, M. F. Kaashoek, R. Morris, and N. Zeldovich. An analysis of Linux scalability to many cores. In *Proceedings of the 2010 USENIX Conference on Operating Systems Design and Implementation*, OSDI '10. USENIX, 2010.

[15] B. M. Cantrill, M. W. Shapiro, and A. H. Leventhal. Dynamic instrumentation of production systems. In *Proceedings of the 2004 USENIX Annual Technical Conference*, ATC '04. USENIX, 2004.

[16] L. Deri et al. Improving passive packet capture: Beyond device polling. In *Proceedings of SANE 2004*. NLUUG, 2004.

[17] P. Druschel and L. L. Peterson. Fbufs: A High-Bandwidth Cross-Domain Transfer Facility. In *Proceedings of the Fourteenth ACM Symposium on Operating Systems Principles*, SOSP '93. ACM, 1993.

[18] N. Egi, A. Greenhalgh, M. Handley, M. Hoerdt, F. Huici, and L. Mathy. Towards high performance virtual routers on commodity hardware. In *Proceedings of the 2008 ACM CoNEXT Conference*. ACM, 2008.

[19] D. R. Engler, M. F. Kaashoek, and J. O'Toole, Jr. Exokernel: An operating system architecture for application-level resource management. In *ACM SIGOPS Operating Systems Review*, volume 29, pages 251–266. ACM, 1995.

[20] S. Galperin, S. Santesson, M. Myers, A. Malpani, and C. Adams. X. 509 Internet Public Key Infrastructure Online Certificate Status Protocol-OCSP. 2013.

[21] S. Han, S. Marshall, B.-G. Chun, and S. Ratnasamy. MegaPipe: a new programming interface for scalable network I/O. In *Proceedings of the 2012 USENIX Conference on Operating Systems Design and Implementation*, OSDI '12. USENIX, 2012.

[22] E. Jeong, S. Woo, M. Jamshed, H. Jeong, S. Ihm, D. Han, and K. Park. mTCP: a highly scalable user-level TCP stack for multicore systems. In *Proceedings of the 2014 USENIX Symposium on Networked Systems Design and Implementation*, NSDI '14. USENIX, 2014.

[23] J. Lemon. KQueue: A Generic and Scalable Event Notification Facility. In *Proceedings of the 2001 USENIX Annual Technical Conference, FREENIX track*. USENIX, June 2001.

[24] C. Lever, M. A. Eriksen, and S. P. Molloy. An Analysis of the TUX Web Server. Technical Report 00-8, Center for Information Technology Integration (CITI), University of Michigan, Ann Arbor, MI, Nov. 2000.

[25] A. Madhavapeddy, R. Mortier, C. Rotsos, D. Scott, B. Singh, T. Gazagnaire, S. Smith, S. Hand, and J. Crowcroft. Unikernels: library operating systems for the cloud. In *Proceedings of the 2013 International Conference on Architectural support for Programming Languages and Operating Systems*, ASPLOS '13. ACM, 2013.

[26] M. K. McKusick and G. V. Neville-Neil. *The Design and Implementation of the FreeBSD Operating System*. Addison-Wesley Professional, Reading, MA, USA, April 2004.

[27] V. S. Pai, P. Druschel, and W. Zwaenepoel. IO-Lite: a unified I/O buffering and caching system. *ACM Transactions on Computer Systems (TOCS)*, 18(1), 2000.

[28] A. Pesterev, J. Strauss, N. Zeldovich, and R. T. Morris. Improving network connection locality on multicore systems. In *Proceedings of the 7th ACM European Conference on Computer Systems*, EuroSys '12. ACM, 2012.

[29] I. Pratt and K. Fraser. Arsenic: A user-accessible gigabit Ethernet interface. In *INFOCOM 2001. Twentieth Annual Joint Conference of the IEEE Computer and Communications Societies*. IEEE, 2001.

[30] N. Provos and C. Lever. Scalable Network I/O in Linux. In *Proceedings 2000 USENIX Annual Technical Conference*, ATC '00. USENIX, 2000.

[31] L. Rizzo. netmap: A novel framework for fast packet I/O. In *Proceedings of the 2012 USENIX Annual Technical Conference*, ATC '12. USENIX, 2012.

[32] C. A. Thekkath, T. D. Nguyen, E. Moy, and E. D. Lazowska. Implementing network protocols at user level. *IEEE/ACM Transactions on Networking (TON)*, 1(5):554–565, 1993.

[33] T. von Eicken, A. Basu, V. Buch, and W. Vogels. U-Net: a user-level network interface for parallel and distributed computing. In *Proceedings of the 1995 ACM Symposium on Operating Systems Principles*, SOSP '95. ACM, 1995.

# A Buffer-Based Approach to Rate Adaptation: Evidence from a Large Video Streaming Service

Te-Yuan Huang, Ramesh Johari, Nick McKeown, Matthew Trunnell*, Mark Watson*
Stanford University, Netflix*
{huangty,rjohari,nickm}@stanford.edu, {mtrunnell,watsonm}@netflix.com

## ABSTRACT

Existing ABR algorithms face a significant challenge in estimating future capacity: capacity can vary widely over time, a phenomenon commonly observed in commercial services. In this work, we suggest an alternative approach: rather than presuming that capacity estimation is required, it is perhaps better to begin by using *only* the buffer, and then ask *when* capacity estimation is needed. We test the viability of this approach through a series of experiments spanning millions of real users in a commercial service. We start with a simple design which directly chooses the video rate based on the current buffer occupancy. Our own investigation reveals that capacity estimation is unnecessary in steady state; however using simple capacity estimation (based on immediate past throughput) is important during the startup phase, when the buffer itself is growing from empty. This approach allows us to reduce the rebuffer rate by 10–20% compared to Netflix's then-default ABR algorithm, while delivering a similar average video rate, and a higher video rate in steady state.

## Categories and Subject Descriptors

C.2.0 [**Computer Systems Organization**]: Computer-Communication Networks—*General*

## Keywords

HTTP-based Video Streaming; Video Rate Adaptation Algorithm

## 1. INTRODUCTION

During the evening peak hours (8pm–1am EDT), well over 50% of US Internet traffic is video streamed from Netflix and YouTube [16, 17]. Unlike traditional video downloads that must complete fully before playback can begin, streaming video starts playing within seconds. Each video is encoded at a number of different rates (typically 235kb/s standard definition to 5Mb/s high definition) and stored on servers as separate files. The video client—running on a home TV, game console, web browser, DVD player, etc.—chooses which video rate to stream by monitoring network conditions and estimating the available network capacity. This process is referred to as *adaptive bit rate selection* or ABR.


*SIGCOMM'14*, August 17–22, 2014, Chicago, Illinois, USA.

ACM 978-1-4503-2836-4/14/08 ...$15.00.
http://dx.doi.org/10.1145/2619239.2626296.

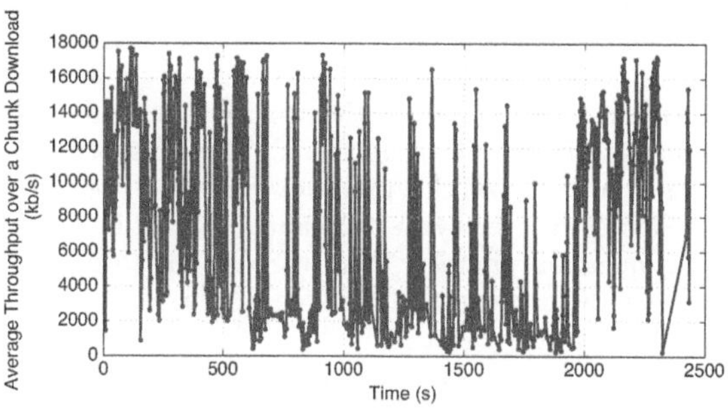


**Figure 1: Video streaming clients experience highly variable end-to-end throughput.**

ABR algorithms used by such services balance two overarching goals. On one hand, they try to maximize the video quality by picking the highest video rate the network can support. On the other hand, they try to minimize *rebuffering events* which cause the video to halt if the client's playback buffer goes empty.

It is easy for a streaming service to meet either one of the objectives on its own. To maximize video quality, a service could just stream at the maximum video rate $R_{\max}$ all the time. Of course, this would risk extensive rebuffering. On the other hand, to minimize rebuffering, the service could just stream at the minimum video rate $R_{\min}$ all the time—but this extreme would lead to low video quality. The design goal of an ABR algorithm is to *simultaneously* obtain high performance on both metrics in order to give users a good viewing experience [7].

One approach is to pick a video rate by estimating future capacity from past observations. In an environment with constant throughput, past observations are reliable to predict future capacity. However, in an environment with highly variable throughput, although past observations still provide valuable ballpark figures, accurate estimation of future capacity becomes challenging. Figure 1 is a sample trace reported by a Netflix video player, showing how the measured throughput varies wildly from 17Mb/s to 500kb/s. Each point in the figure represents the average throughput when downloading a video chunk. This variation has a significant impact on customers: approximately 10% of our sessions experience at least this much variation, and 22% of sessions experience at least half as much variation.[1] Variation can be caused by many factors, such as WiFi interference, congestion in the network, congestion in the client (e.g. anti-virus software scanning incoming http traffic), or congestion at an overloaded video server.

In part due to highly variable throughput, current ABR algorithms often augment their capacity estimation with an "adjustment" based on the current level of the playback buffer [6, 20]. Informally, the idea is that this adjustment should make the rate selection more conservative when the buffer is at risk of underrunning, and more aggressive when the buffer is close to full. As we will see in Section 2, designing an optimal adjustment in a highly variable throughput environment is challenging; it is very hard to find an adjustment function that prevents rebuffering without being overly conservative. However, the notion of buffer-based adjustment used in current schemes is quite suggestive: note that the occupancy of the playback buffer is the primary state variable we are trying to manage. This inspires the following question: namely, can we take the design to its logical extreme, and choose the video rate based *only* on the playback buffer occupancy?

In this paper, we consider using *only* the buffer to choose a video rate, and then ask *when* capacity estimation is needed. We observe two separate phases of operation: a *steady-state* phase when the buffer has been built up, and a *startup* phase when the buffer is still growing from empty. Our analysis and experiments show that capacity estimation is not needed during the steady state. We can rely only on the current buffer occupancy to pick a video rate, allowing for a simple function to map current buffer occupancy to video rate. On the other hand, as we will see in Section 6, during the startup phase—just like the slow-start algorithm in TCP—the buffer occupancy carries little or no information about current network conditions. As a result, crude capacity estimation is helpful to quickly ramp up the video rate and drive the algorithm into the steady state.

In this paper, we show—both formally and through a deployment in the commercial Netflix service—that our algorithms can avoid unnecessary rebuffering events and yet achieve a high average video rate. We test this approach in a Netflix browser-based video player, a popular commercial streaming service, and present results from two A/B tests with over half a million real users each, on three continents, over two weekends during May-September 2013. Our experiments allow us to evaluate the viability of the buffer-based design. We find that *this design approach can reduce the rebuffer rate by 10–20% compared to Netflix's then-default ABR algorithm, while improving the steady-state video rate.*

In Section 2, we first dig into the implication of highly variable throughput on ABR algorithm design. This discussion motivates the buffer-based approach. In Section 3, we introduce the broad class of buffer-based algorithms (BBA), and identify the criteria to achieve our design goals in the ideal setting. In Section 4, we design a very simple baseline algorithm to test the viability of this approach in the steady-state. The baseline algorithm reduces the rebuffer rate by a promising 10–20% relative to a production algorithm. Nevertheless, the rebuffer rate is still larger than our empirical lower bound and delivers a lower average video rate than the control algorithm.

We identify two reasons for the lower performance. First, our baseline algorithm does not address variable bit-rate (VBR) video encoding; we adapt our algorithm with a simple fix to handle VBR in Section 5. Second, and more importantly, our baseline algorithm is optimized for steady-state. During the startup phase (the first few minutes of viewing), the buffer is close to empty and contains less information while in a transient phase. Although the performance of the baseline buffer-based algorithm suggests capacity estimation is not necessary in steady state, simple capacity estimation is useful in the startup phase. In Section 6, we validate this hypothesis by implementing techniques to improve video quality in the startup phase by estimating the immediate past throughput. Together, our two improvements maintain the reduction in rebuffer rate by approximately 10–20%, while improving the video rate during steady state, and leaving the average video rate essentially unchanged. Finally, in Section 7, we propose mechanisms to minimize rate switching while providing some protections against temporary network outages.

[1] We define variation to be the ratio of 75th to 25th percentile throughput; which is 5.6 for this trace.

# 2. THE CHALLENGES OF A HIGHLY VARIABLE ENVIRONMENT

In an environment with stable capacity, past observations yield good estimates of future capacity. But if capacity is varying widely, estimating future capacity is much harder. Many techniques have been proposed to leverage the buffer occupancy to work with inaccurate capacity estimates. In this section, we first look into the dynamics of the playback buffer and understand how the buffer occupancy encodes the relation between the selected video rate and the system capacity. We then consider how the buffer occupancy is used to adjust inaccurate capacity estimates: essentially, the algorithm becomes more "aggressive" when the buffer is close to full, and more "conservative" when the buffer is close to empty. While appealing, we find that if capacity is *highly* variable (as we find it to be in practice), it is hard to prevent rebuffering events with only an adjustment to the capacity estimate.

However, the design of buffer-based adjustments is suggestive, and motivates our design. In particular, our design begins by using *only* the buffer occupancy to pick a video rate, and then considers *when* capacity estimation is needed. The pure buffer-based approach is sufficient when the buffer contains enough information about the past capacity trace, i.e., in steady state. On the other hand, simple capacity estimation proves valuable when the buffer contains little information, i.e., when the buffer is still growing from empty a few minutes after the session starts.

## 2.1 Dynamics of the Playback Buffer

Figure 2 shows the dynamics of the playback buffer in the client. The buffer occupancy is generally tracked in *seconds of video*. Every second, one second of video is removed from the buffer and played to the user. The buffer drains at unit rate (since one second is played back every second of real time). The client requests *chunks* of video from the server, each chunk containing a fixed duration of video (four seconds per chunk in our service). The higher the video rate, the larger the chunk (in bytes).

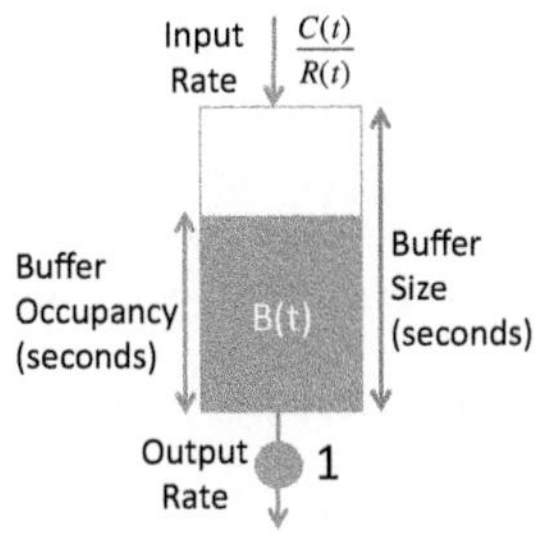


**Figure 2: The relationship between system capacity, $C(t)$, and video rate, $R(t)$, in a video playback buffer.**

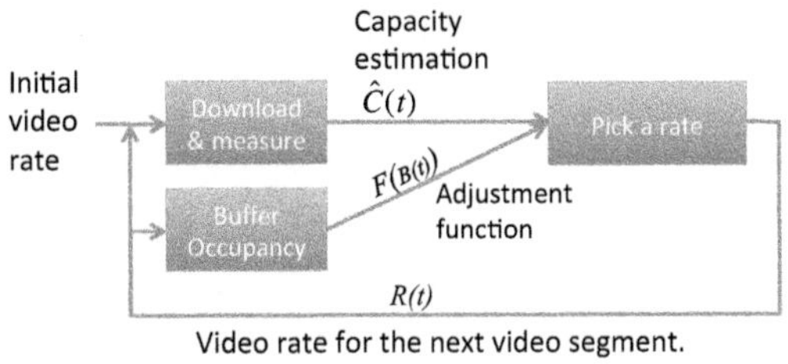


**Figure 3: Current practice adjusts the estimation based on the buffer occupancy.**

If the ABR algorithm *overestimates* the capacity and picks a video rate, $R(t)$, that is greater than the system capacity, $C(t)$, then new data is put into the buffer at rate $C(t)/R(t) < 1$ and so the buffer decreases. Put another way, if more than one chunk is played before the next chunk arrives, then the buffer is depleted. If the ABR algorithm keeps requesting chunks that are too big for the network to sustain (i.e., the video rate is too high), eventually the buffer will run dry, playback freezes and we see the familiar "Rebuffering..." message on the screen.

## 2.2 Working with Inaccurate Estimates

Many techniques have been proposed to work with inaccurate estimates, by incorporating information about the playback buffer. Some leverage control theory to adjust the capacity estimation based on the buffer occupancy [6, 20], some smooth the quality degradation according to the buffer occupancy [15], and some randomize chunk scheduling depending on the buffer occupancy to have better samples of the channel [10].

At a high level, we can capture existing approaches using the abstract design flow in Figure 3. The client measures how fast chunks arrive to estimate capacity, $\hat{C}(t)$. The estimate is optionally supplemented with knowledge of the buffer occupancy, which we represent by an *adjustment* factor $F(B(t))$, a function of the playback buffer occupancy. The selected video rate is $R(t) = F(B(t))\hat{C}(t)$; different designs use different adjustment functions $F(\cdot)$.

When the buffer contains many chunks, $R(t)$ can safely deviate from $C(t)$ without triggering a rebuffer. The client can "aggressively" try to maximize the video quality by picking $R(t) = \hat{C}(t)$.

But when the buffer is low, the client should be more "conservative", deliberately underestimating capacity so as to pick a lower video rate and quickly replenish the buffer. In

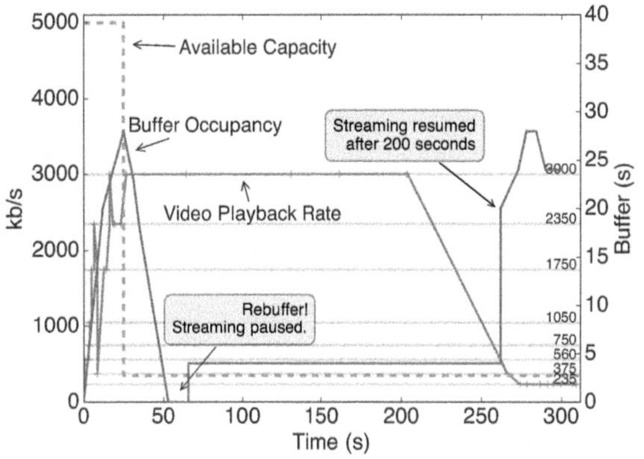


**Figure 4: *Being too aggressive*: A video starts streaming at 3Mb/s over a 5Mb/s network. After 25s the available capacity drops to 350 kb/s. Instead of switching down to a lower video rate, e.g., 235kb/s, the client keeps playing at 3Mb/s. As a result, the client rebuffers and does not resume playing video for 200s. Note that the buffer occupancy was not updated during rebufferings.**

this case, designing the adjustment function is much harder, as the following analysis shows. Consider the case when there is only one chunk in the buffer. The requested chunk ($V$ seconds) must arrive before the current chunk plays, else the buffer will run dry. In other words, we require $VR(t)/C(t) < B(t)$, where $VR(t)$ is the chunk size in bytes. Thus, the selected video rate $R(t)$ needs to satisfy:

$$R(t) < \left(\frac{B(t)}{V}\right) C(t)$$

to prevent rebuffers. Replacing the selected video rate $R(t)$ with $F(B(t))\hat{C}(t)$ in the above inequality, we get the following requirement on $F(B(t))$ to avoid rebuffers:

$$F(B(t)) < \left(\frac{B(t)}{V}\right)\left(\frac{C(t)}{\hat{C}(t)}\right) \text{ for all } t. \quad (1)$$

This tells us we must pick $F(V)$ to be smaller than the *worst case ratio* of $C(t)$ to $\hat{C}(t)$. Unfortunately, $C(t)/\hat{C}(t)$ is tiny if the throughput is varying wildly; and since we have to choose $F$ without knowing the actual capacity that will be observed, it leads to a very conservative algorithm. For example, in Figure 1, the ratio $C(t)/\hat{C}(t)$ can be as small as 0.03 (500 kb/s $< C(t) <$ 17 Mb/s). In other words, for this session, we need to pick $F(V) \leq 0.03$ to prevent rebuffers, and the video rate will be just 3% of the rate we could pick with an accurate estimate. Worse, if $F(.)$ makes us pick a rate lower than the minimum video rate available, the constraint becomes impossible to meet.

In practice, large throughput variation within a session is not uncommon. A random sample of 300,000 Netflix sessions shows that roughly 10% of sessions experience a median throughput *less than half of the 95th percentile throughput.* When designing an ABR algorithm, the service provider needs to choose a $F(\cdot)$ that works well for *all* customers, with both stable and variable throughput.

An example from a Netflix session illustrates the problem. Figure 4 shows an ABR algorithm that is not conservative enough; it keeps requesting video at too high a rate after the capacity has dropped. The client rebuffers and freezes playback for 200 seconds. But notice that the rebuffer is entirely unnecessary because the available capacity $C(t)$ is above $R_{\min}$ for the entire time series. In fact, if the network capacity is always greater than the lowest video rate $R_{\min}$, i.e., $C(t) > R_{\min}, \forall t > 0$, there *never* needs to be a rebuffering event — the algorithm can simply pick $R(t) = R_{\min}$ so that $C(t)/R(t) > 1, \forall t > 0$ and the buffer keeps growing. The main reason the client does not switch is that it overestimates the current capacity, and the adjustment function is not small enough to offset the difference. As a result, despite the fact that capacity is sufficient to sustain $R_{\min}$, the client does not find its way to that video rate in time.

## 2.3 The Buffer-Based Approach

The discussion above is suggestive. Despite the challenge of finding the right adjustment, using buffer-based adjustments in algorithms is quite appealing, because the playback buffer is the exact state variable an ABR algorithm is trying to control. For example, the easiest way to ensure that the algorithm never unnecessarily rebuffers is to simply request rate $R_{\min}$ when the buffer approaches empty, allowing the buffer to grow as long as $C(t) > R_{\min}$. Note in particular that in the scenario in the preceding section, this approach would have avoided a rebuffering event. On the other hand, as the buffer grows, it is safe to increase $R(t)$ up to the maximum video rate as the buffer approaches full. This motivates our design: our starting point is a simple algorithm design that chooses the video rate based only on the playback buffer.

Inspired by this discussion, we design our algorithms as follows. First, we focus on a pure buffer-based design: we select the video rate directly as a function of the current buffer level. As we find, this approach works well when the buffer adequately encodes information about the past history of capacity. However, when the buffer is still growing from empty (during the first few minutes of a session), it does not adequately encode information about available capacity. In this phase, the pure buffer-based design can be improved by leveraging a capacity estimate.

We call this design the *buffer-based approach.* This design process leads to two separate phases of operation: During the steady-state phase, when the buffer encodes adequate information, we choose the video rate based only on the playback buffer. During the startup phase, when the buffer contains little information, we augment the buffer-based design with capacity estimation. In this way, our design might be thought of as an "inversion" of Figure 3: namely, we begin by using only the playback buffer, and then "adjust" this algorithm using capacity estimation where needed.

# 3. BUFFER-BASED ALGORITHMS

We say that an ABR algorithm is *buffer-based* if it picks the video rate as a function of the current buffer occupancy, $B(t)$. The design space for this class of algorithms is expressed by a buffer-rate plane where the buffer-axis is buffer occupancy and the rate-axis is video rate. The region between $[0, B_{\max}]$ on the buffer-axis and $[R_{\min}, R_{\max}]$ on the rate-axis defines the feasible region. Any curve $f(B)$ on the plane within the feasible region defines a *rate map*, a function that produces a video rate between $R_{\min}$ and $R_{\max}$ given the current buffer occupancy.

## 3.1 Theoretical Criteria for Design Goals

From this feasible region, our goal is to find a class of mapping functions that can: (1) avoid unnecessary rebufferings, and (2) maximize average video rate.

To start with, we make the following simplifying assumptions:

1. The chunk size is infinitesimal, so that we can change the video rate continuously.
2. *Any* video rate between $R_{\min}$ and $R_{\max}$ is available.
3. Videos are encoded at a constant bit-rate (CBR).
4. Videos are infinitely long.

We can show that any rate maps that are (1) *continuous* functions of the buffer occupancy $B$; (2) *strictly increasing* in the region $\{B : R_{\min} < f(B) < R_{\max}\}$; and (3) pinned at both ends, i.e., $f(0) = R_{\min}$ and $f(B_{\max}) = R_{\max}$, will meet the two design goals. In other words, we can achieve our goal by picking any rate map that increases the video rate from lowest to highest as the buffer increases from empty to full. We leave the formal proof in our technical report [9], and we summarize the proof here:

**No unnecessary rebuffering:** As long as $C(t) \geq R_{\min}$ for all $t$ and we adapt $f(B) \to R_{\min}$ as $B \to 0$, we will never unnecessarily rebuffer because the buffer will start to grow before it runs dry.

**Average video rate maximization:** As long as $f(B)$ is (1) increasing and (2) eventually reaches $R_{\max}$, the average video rate will match the average capacity when $R_{\min} < C(t) < R_{\max}$ for all $t > 0$.

Next, we explore how to remove the assumptions above, then validate the approach with the Netflix deployments in Section 4, 5 and 6.

## 3.2 Real World Challenges

In practice, the chunk size is finite ($V$ seconds long) and a chunk is only added to the buffer after it is downloaded. To avoid interruption, we always need to have at least one chunk available in the buffer. To handle the finite chunk size, as well as some degree of variation in the system, we shift the rate map to the right and create an extra *reservoir*, noted as $r$. When the buffer is filling up the reservoir, i.e., $0 \leq B \leq r$, we request video rate $R_{\min}$. Once the reservoir is reached, we then increase the video rate according to $f(B)$. Also because of the finite chunk size, the buffer does not stay at $B_{\max}$ even when $C(t) \geq R_{\max}$; thus, we should allow rate map to reach $R_{\max}$ before $B_{\max}$. We call the buffer between the reservoir and the point where $f(B)$ first reaches $R_{\max}$ the *cushion*, and the buffer after the cushion the *upper reservoir*.

Since many video clients have no control over TCP sockets and they cannot cancel an ongoing video chunk download, we can only pick a new rate when a chunk *finishes* arriving. If the network suddenly slows down while we are in the middle of downloading a chunk, the buffer might run dry before we get the chance to switch to a lower rate. Thus, we need to aim to maintain the buffer level to be above the reservoir $r$, so that there is enough buffer to absorb the variation caused both by the varying capacity and by the finite chunk size. As a result, $f(B)$ should be designed to ensure a chunk can always be downloaded before the buffer shrinks into the reservoir area. Based on these observations, we say $f(B)$ operates in the *safe* area if it always picks chunks that will finish downloading before the buffer runs below $r$, when $C(t) \geq R_{\min}$ for all $t$. In other words, $Vf(B)/R_{\min} \leq (B - r)$. Otherwise, $f(B)$ is in the

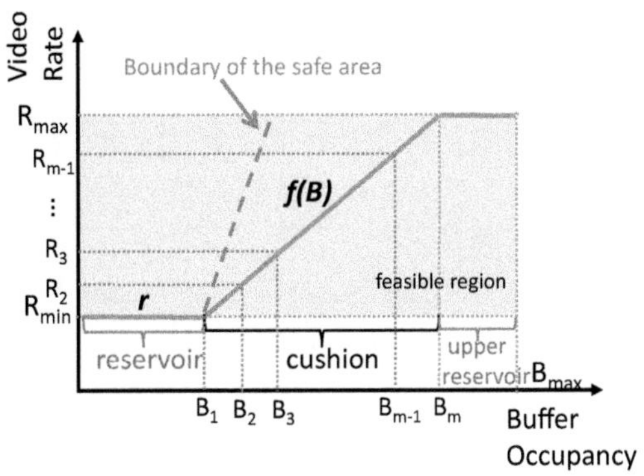


**Figure 5: The rate map used in the BBA-0 buffer-based algorithm.**

*risky* area. Overall, the class of functions that we consider take the piecewise form described in Figure 5. We illustrate there the reservoir, the cushion, and the upper reservoir. We also illustrate the notion of safety described in the previous paragraph: we plot the boundary of the safe area as the red dashed line in the figure. Any $f(B)$ below the boundary will be a safe choice.

In Section 4, we test this concept by deploying a baseline algorithm with fixed-size reservoir and cushion.

# 4. THE BASELINE ALGORITHM

To test the buffer-based approach, we first construct a baseline algorithm with a relatively simple and naive rate map. We implement the algorithm in Netflix's browser-based player, which has a 240 second playback buffer and downloads the ABR algorithm at the start of the video session. Although this player enjoys a bigger buffer (240s) than players on embedded devices, it does not have visibility into, or control of, the network layer.

As a baseline algorithm, we first set the size of reservoir to be 90s (a value we thought would be big enough to handle VBR). To maximize the buffer distance between neighboring rates while leaving some room for the upper reservoir, we then set the $f(B)$ to be a linear function that reaches $R_{max}$ when the buffer is 90% full (216 seconds). Note that a rate map by itself does not fully define the algorithm: the rate map is continuous, while streamed video rates are discrete, $R_{\min}, R_2, R_3...R_{m-1}, R_{\max}$. We therefore adapt the rate following a simple rule: stay at the current video rate as long as the rate suggested by the rate map does not cross the next higher ($\text{Rate}_+$) or lower ($\text{Rate}_-$) discrete video rate. If either "barrier" is hit the rate is switched up or down (respectively) to a new discrete value suggested by the rate map. In this way, the buffer distance between the adjacent video rates provides a natural cushion to absorb rate oscillations, making the video rate a little "sticky". This algorithm, together with the rate map we just defined, constructs our first buffer-based algorithm. We call this algorithm *BBA-0* since it is the simplest of our buffer-based algorithms. The detailed pseudo-code can be found in our technical report [9].

## 4.1 Experiments

We randomly picked three groups of Netflix users around the world to take part in the experiments between September 6th (Friday) and 9th (Monday), 2013.

Group 1 is our *Control* group and they use Netflix's then-default ABR algorithm.[2] The *Control* algorithm has steadily improved over the past five years to perform well under many conditions. The *Control* algorithm directly follows the design in Figure 3: it picks a video rate primarily based on capacity estimation, with buffer occupancy as a secondary signal. It is representative of how video streaming services work; e.g. Hulu [8] and YouTube [21] are based on capacity estimation. Netflix traffic represents 35% of the US peak Internet traffic and they serve 40 million users world-wide. For these reasons, we believe the Netflix *Control* algorithm is a reasonable algorithm to compare against.

Group 2 always stream at $R_{\min}$, and we call this degenerate algorithm $R_{\min}$ *Always*. Always operating at the lowest video rate minimizes the chances of rebuffering, giving us a lower bound on the rebuffer rate to compare new algorithms against. For most sessions $R_{\min} = 560kb/s$, but in some cases it is $235kb/s$.[3]

Group 3 uses our new BBA-0 algorithm.

All three user groups are distributed similarly across ISPs, geographic locations, viewing behaviors and devices. The only difference between the three groups of clients is the rate selection algorithm; they share the same code base for other mechanisms, such as prebuffering, CDN selection, and error handling. As a result, all three groups share similar join delay and error rate, allowing us to concentrate on the quality metrics during playback.

Even though testing against a range of other complex algorithms would not be possible in this testing environment, it's unprecedented to be able to report video performance results from a huge commercial service, such as Netflix, and we believe the insight it offers into a real system is invaluable. During our experiments each group of users viewed roughly 120,000 hours of video. To compare their performance, we measure the overall number of rebuffers per playhour and the average delivered video rate in each group.

## 4.2 Results

**Rebuffer Rate.** Figure 6(a) plots the number of rebuffers per playhour throughout the day. Figure 6(b) simplifies a visual comparison between algorithms by normalizing the average rebuffer rate to the *Control* group in each two-hour period. Peak viewing hours for the USA are highlighted in yellow. Error bars represent the variance of rebuffer rates from different days in the same two-hour period. The $R_{\min}$ *Always* algorithm provides an empirical lower bound on the rebuffer rate. Note that because the users in the three groups are different and their environments are not exactly the same, $R_{\min}$ *Always* only approximates the lower bound for the other groups. The first thing to notice from the figure is that $R_{\min}$ *Always* and BBA-0 always have a lower rebuffer rate than the *Control* algorithm. The difference between the *Control* algorithm and the $R_{\min}$ *Always* algorithm suggests that 20–30% of the rebuffers might be caused by poor choice of video rate.

[2]The ABR algorithm in commercial services keeps evolving, and so Netflix's current algorithm is now different.

[3]In our service, $R_{min}$ is normally $235kb/s$. However, most customers can sustain 560kb/s, especially in Europe. If a user historically sustained 560kb/s we artificially set $R_{min} = 560kb/s$ to avoid degrading the video experience too far. The mechanism to pick $R_{\min}$ is the same across all three test groups.

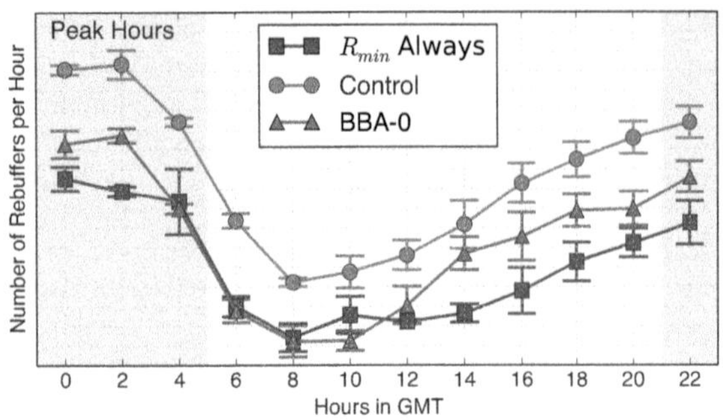


(a) Number of rebuffers per playhour.

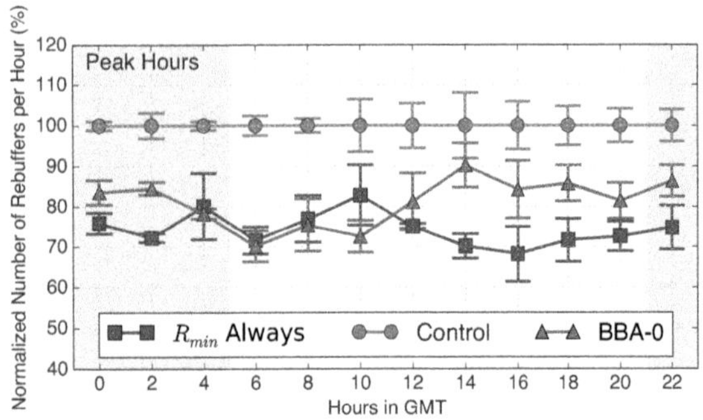


(b) Normalized number of rebuffers per playhour.

**Figure 6: Number of rebuffers per playhour for the *Control*, $R_{\min}$ *Always*, and BBA-0 algorithms.**

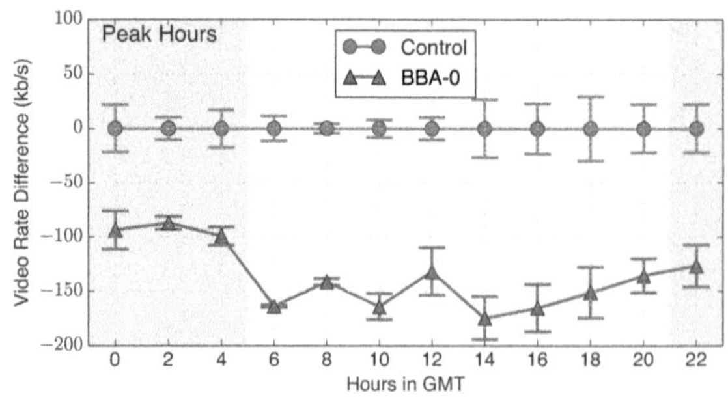


**Figure 7: Comparison of video rate between *Control* and BBA-0.**

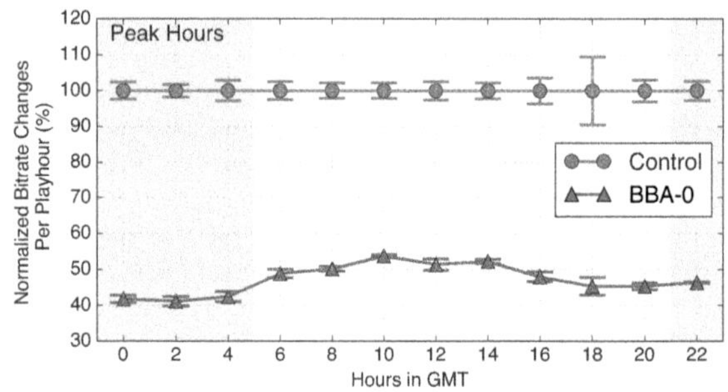


**Figure 8: Average video switching rate per two hour window for the *Control* and *BBA-0* algorithms.**

During the middle-of-night period in the USA just after peak viewing (6am–12pm GMT), BBA-0 matches the $R_{\min}$ *Always* lower bound very closely. At 10am GMT, even though BBA-0 has a lower average rebuffer rate than $R_{\min}$ *Always*, the difference is not statistically significant.[4] These two algorithms perform equally during this off-peak period, because the viewing rate is relatively low, overall Internet usage is low, and the network capacity for individual sessions does not change much. The rebuffer rate during these hours is dominated by random local events, such as WiFi interference, instead of congested networks.

During peak hours, the performance with BBA-0 is significantly worse than with the $R_{\min}$ *Always* algorithm. Nevertheless, the BBA-0 algorithm consistently has a 10–30% lower rebuffer rate than the *Control* algorithm. This performance difference is encouraging given the extremely simple nature of the BBA-0 algorithm. Still, we hope to do better. In Section 5 and 6, we will develop techniques to improve the rebuffer rate of buffer-based algorithms.

**Video Rate.** Figure 7 shows the difference in the delivered video rate between *Control* and BBA-0. The daily average bitrate for the *Control* algorithm for each ISP can be found in the Netflix ISP Speed Index [18]. Since $R_{\min}$ *Always* always streams at $R_{\min}$ (except when rebuffering), its delivered video rate is a flat line and is excluded from the figure. The BBA-0 algorithm is roughly 100kb/s worse than the *Control* algorithm during peak hours, and 175kb/s worse during off-peak hours. There are two main reasons for the degradation in video quality. First, our BBA-0 algorithm uses a large and fixed-size reservoir to handle VBR, while the size of reservoir should be adjusted to be just big enough to absorb the variation introduced by VBR. Second, and more significantly, while the reservoir is filling up during the startup period, our BBA-0 algorithm always requests video at rate $R_{\min}$. Given that we picked a 90s reservoir, it downloads 90 seconds worth of video at rate $R_{\min}$, which is a non-negligible fraction of the average session length. We will address both issues in Section 5 and 6.

**Video Switching Rate.** For buffer-based algorithms, the video rate fluctuates as the buffer occupancy changes. However, as mentioned in Section 3, our algorithm uses the buffer distance between adjacent video rates to naturally cushion and absorb rate oscillations. Figure 8 compares BBA-0 with the *Control* algorithm. Note the numbers are normalized to the average switching rate of the Control group for each two-hour period. The BBA-0 algorithm reduces the switching rate by roughly 60% during peak hours, and by roughly 50% during off-peak hours.

In summary, BBA-0 confirms that the buffer-based approach can reduce rebuffer rate and video switching rate. However, BBA-0 performs worse on video rate compared to the *Control* algorithm. In the next section, we will develop techniques to improve both rebuffer rate and video rate by considering the VBR encoding scheme.

# 5. HANDLING VARIABLE BITRATE (VBR)

In Section 4, the BBA-0 algorithm attempts to handle VBR by setting the reservoir size to a large and somewhat arbitrary value. Although BBA-0 reduces the rebuffer rate significantly compared to the *Control*, there is still room

[4]The hypothesis of BBA-0 and $R_{\min}$ *Always* share the same distribution is not rejected at the 95% confidence level (p-value = 0.25).

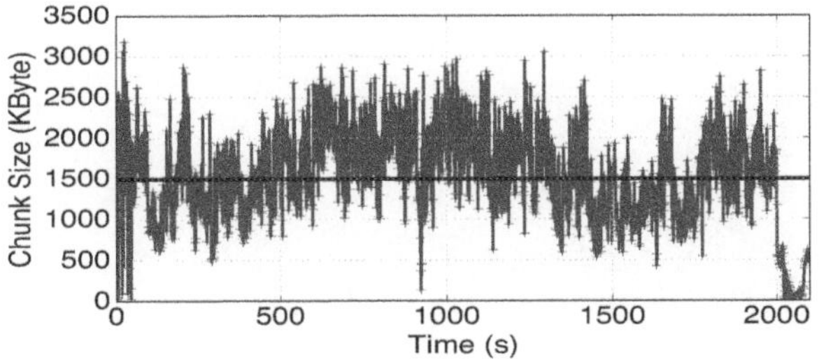


**Figure 9: The size of 4-second chunks of a video encoded at an average rate of 3Mb/s. Note the average chunk size is 1.5MB (4s times 3Mb/s).**

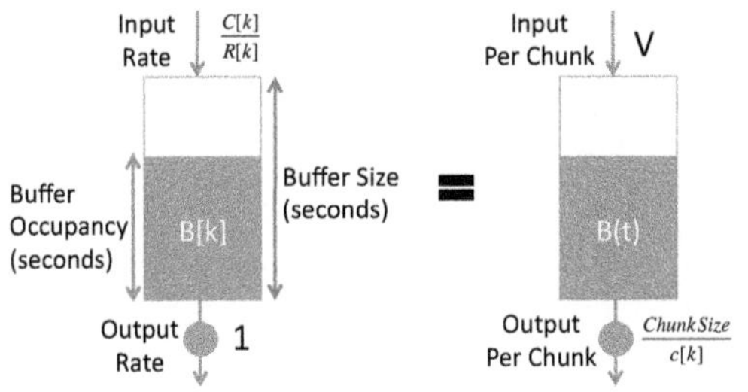


**Figure 10: Two equivalent models of the streaming playback buffer.**

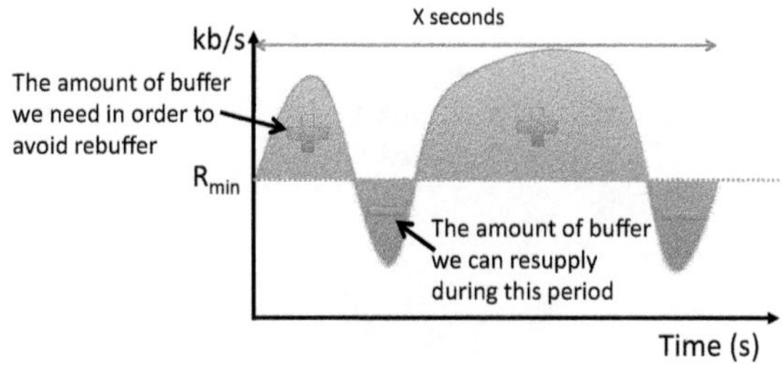


**Figure 11: Reservoir calculation: We calculate the size of the reservoir from the chunk size variation.**

to improve when comparing to the empirical lower bound. In addition, the average video rate achieved by the BBA-0 algorithm is significantly lower than the *Control* algorithm. In this section, we will discuss techniques to improve both rebuffer rate and video rate by taking the encoding scheme into consideration. A key advance is to *design* the reservoir based on the instantaneous encoding bitrate.

In practice, most of the video streaming services encode their videos in variable bitrate (VBR). When a video is encoded in VBR at a nominal video rate, the nominal rate represents the *average* video rate, and the instantaneous video rate varies around the average value. As a result, the chunk size will not be uniformly identical in a stream of a given rate. Figure 9 shows the size of 4-second chunks over time from a production video (*Black Hawk Down*) encoded at 3 Mb/s. The black line represents the average chunk size. As we can see from the figure, the variation on chunk size can be significant within a single video rate.

Given the variation on chunk size, we need to take the size of each chunk into consideration and re-consider the buffer dynamics under VBR. Because we can only select video rates on a chunk-by-chunk basis, it is useful to consider the buffer dynamics when observed *at the time points when a chunk finishes*, as shown in Figure 10. Let $r[k]$ be the video rate selected for the $k$-th chunk and $c[k]$ be the average system capacity during the download of the $k$-th chunk. For the $k$-th chunk from the stream of nominal video rate $r$, we denote the chunk size as $Chunk[r][k]$. Since each chunk still contains $V$ seconds of video, the buffer now drains $Chunk[r][k]/c[k]$ seconds while it fills with $V$ seconds of video.

## 5.1 Reservoir Calculation

Since the instantaneous video rate can be much higher than the nominal rate in VBR, we could still encounter a rebuffer event even when the capacity $c[k]$ is exactly equal to $R_{\min}$, unless we have enough buffer to absorb the buffer oscillation caused by the variable chunk size. Thus, the size of reservoir should be big enough to ensure the client can continue playing at $R_{\min}$ when $c[k] = R_{\min}$.

Assuming $c[k] = R_{\min}$, when the chunk size is larger than the average, $VR_{\min}$, the video client will consume more video in the buffer than the input. On the other hand, when the chunk size is lower than the average, the buffer is consumed more slowly than the input and the buffer occupancy will increase. Thus, by summing up the amount of buffer the client will consume minus the amount it can resupply during the next $X$ seconds, we can calculate the amount of reservoir we need. We dynamically adjust the reservoir based on this prospective calculation over the lifetime of the stream. Figure 11 summarizes how the calculation is done. In the implementation, we set $X$ as twice of the buffer size, i.e., 480 seconds. The calculated reservoir size depends highly on the specific video and the playing segment. As a practical matter, we bound the size of reservoir to be between 8 seconds to 140 seconds.

## 5.2 Chunk Map

Since the buffer dynamics now depend on the chunk size instead of the video rate, we can generalize the rate-axis of Figure 5 to the chunk-axis and map the buffer occupancy to the chunk size directly. Each curve in the figure now defines a *chunk map*, which maps the current buffer occupancy to the maximal chunk size that the algorithm can download. In the design space, the feasible region is now defined between $[0, B_{\max}]$ on the buffer-axis and $[Chunk_{\min}, Chunk_{\max}]$ on the chunk-axis, where $Chunk_{\min}$ and $Chunk_{\max}$ represent the average chunk size in $R_{\min}$ and $R_{\max}$, respectively.

Our algorithm can be generalized to use the chunk map: the algorithm stays at the current video rate as long as the chunk size suggested by the map does not pass the size of the next upcoming chunk at the next highest available video rate (Rate$_+$) or the next lowest available video rate (Rate$_-$). If either of these "barriers" are passed, the rate is switched up or down, respectively. Note that by using the chunk map, we no longer have a fixed mapping between buffer levels and video rates. This could result in a higher frequency of video rate switches. We will address this issue in Section 7.

## 5.3 Results

We use the same setup as in Section 4 and select the same number of users to use our VBR-enabled buffer-based algorithm. We will refer to this algorithm as *BBA-1*, as it is our second iteration of the buffer-based algorithm. This experi-

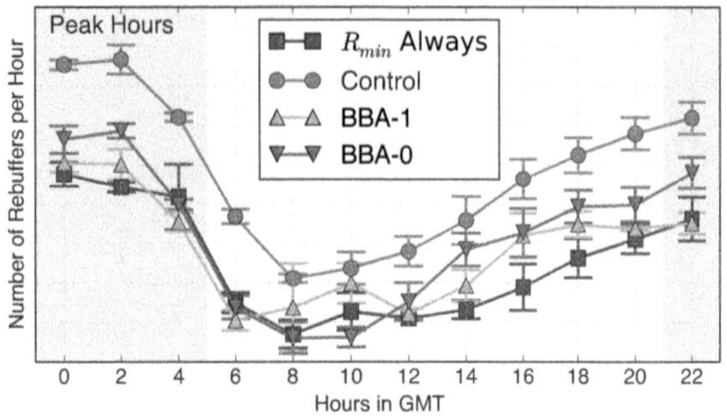


(a) Number of rebuffers per playhour.

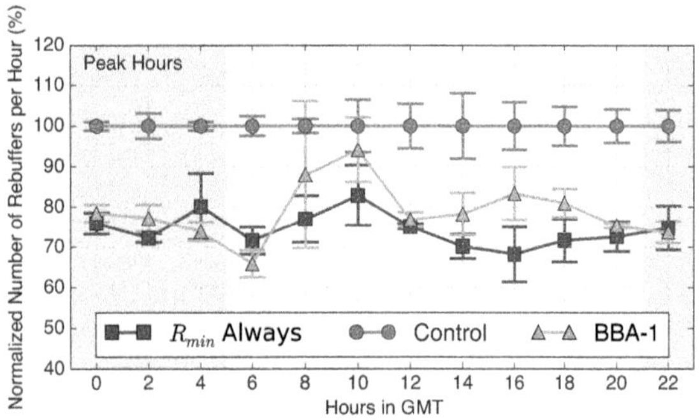


(b) Normalized number of rebuffers per playhour.

**Figure 12: The BBA-1 algorithm achieves close-to-optimal rebuffer rate, especially during the peak hours.**

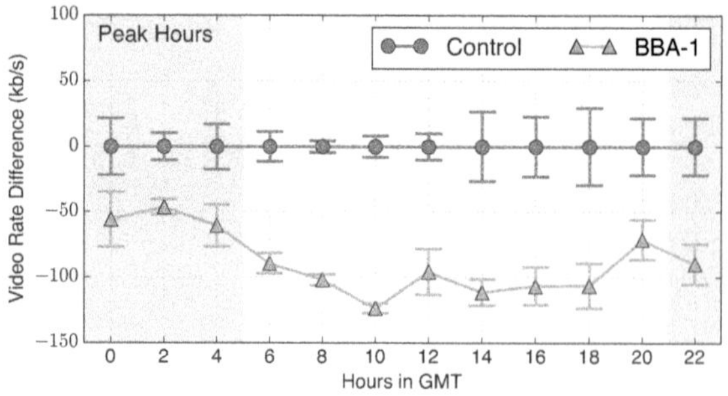


**Figure 13: The BBA-1 algorithm improved video rate by 40–70 kb/s compare to BBA-0, but still 50–120 kb/s away from the *Control*.**

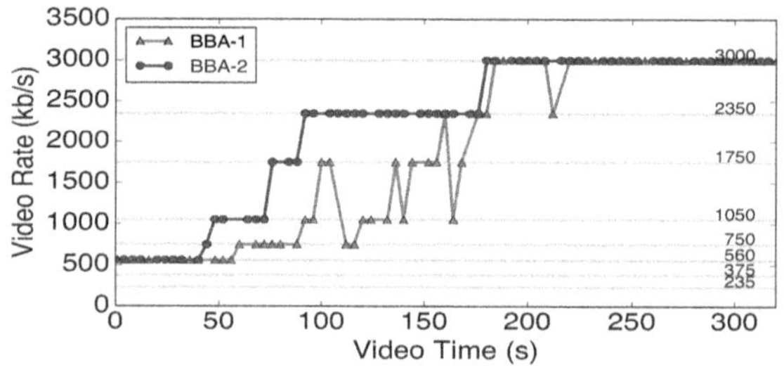


**Figure 14: Typical time series of video rates for BBA-1 (red) and BBA-2 (blue). BBA-1 follows the chunk map and ramps slowly. BBA-2 ramps faster and reaches the steady-state rate sooner.**

ment was conducted along with the experiment in Section 4 between September 6th (Friday) and 9th (Monday), 2013.

Figure 12(a) shows the rebuffer rate in terms of number of rebuffers per playhour, while Figure 12(b) normalizes to the average rebuffer rate of the *Control* in each two-hour period. We can see from the figure that BBA-1 comes close to the optimal line and performs better than BBA-0. The improvement over the *Control* is especially clear during peak hours, where BBA-1 provides a 20–28% improvement in rebuffer rate. Note that although BBA-1 has a lower average rebuffer rate than $R_{min}$ *Always* during 4–6am GMT, the difference is not statistically significant.[5]

Figure 13 shows the difference in average video rate between *Control*, BBA-0, and BBA-1. As shown in Figure 13, BBA-1 also improves the video rate compared to BBA-0 by 40–70kb/s on average, although it is still 50–120kb/s away from the *Control*. This discrepancy in video rate comes from the startup period, when the buffer is still filling up. If we compare the average video rate of the first 60 seconds between BBA-1 and *Control*, BBA-1 achieves 700kb/s less than the *Control*. Before the client builds up its buffer to the size of the reservoir, BBA-1 always requests for $R_{\min}$, as it is the only *safe* rate given the buffer occupancy. In the next section, we will further improve the video rate by entering into the *risky* area and develop techniques to minimize the risk.

[5]The hypothesis of BBA-1 and $R_{\min}$ *Always* share the same distribution is not rejected at the 95% confidence level (p-value = 0.74).

# 6. THE STARTUP PHASE

Most of the differences in video rate between BBA-1 and *Control* can be accounted for by the startup phase, i.e., after starting a new video or seeking to a new point.[6] During the startup phase, the playback buffer starts out empty and carries no useful information on available capacity. BBA-1 follows the usual chunk map, starting out with a low video rate since the buffer level is low. It gradually increases the rate as the buffer fills, as shown by the red line in Figure 14. BBA-1 is too conservative during startup. The network can sustain a much higher video rate, but the algorithm is just not aware of it yet.

In this section, we test the following hypothesis. During the startup, we can improve the video rate by entering into the risky area; in the steady state, we can improve both video rate and rebuffer rate by using a chunk map. Our next algorithm, BBA-2, tries to be more aggressive during the startup phase, by incorporating a simple capacity estimation into the startup behavior. When possible, BBA-2 ramps up quickly and fills the buffer with a much higher rate than what the map suggests.

This two phases of operation can be found in many network protocols, such as the slow-start and congestion avoidance phases in TCP. For TCP, when a connection starts, the congestion control algorithm knows nothing about network conditions from the sending window, and the window is quickly opened to use available capacity until packet losses

[6]Note that the startup phase does not refer to the join delay. The startup phase refers to the first few minutes *after* the video has started.

are induced. Similar to TCP, ABR algorithms get little or no information from the playback buffer at the beginning of a session. However, while ABR algorithms also ramp up the video rate quickly, unlike TCP, they need to do it in a controlled manner to prevent unnecessary rebuffers.

From Figure 10, we know that the change of the buffer, $\Delta B = V - (ChunkSize/c[k])$, captures the difference between the instantaneous video rate and system capacity. Now, assuming the current video rate is $R_i$, to safely step up a rate, $c[k]$ needs to be at least $R_{i+1}$ to avoid rebuffers. In other words, we require $\Delta B \geq V - (ChunkSize/R_{i+1})$. Further, since videos are encoded in VBR, the instantaneous video rate can be much higher than the nominal rate. Let the max-to-average ratio in a VBR stream be $e$, so that $eR_{i+1}$ represents the maximum instantaneous video rate in $R_{i+1}$. When the player first starts up, since there is no buffer to absorb the variation, $c[k]$ needs to be at least larger than $eR_{i+1}$ in order to safely step up a rate. In other words, when considering VBR and the buffer is empty, $\Delta B$ needs to be larger than $V - (ChunkSize/(eR_{i+1}))$ for the algorithm to safely step up from $R_i$ to $R_{i+1}$. According to Figure 9, the max-to-average ratio $e$ is around 2 in our system. Since $e = 2$, $R_i/R_{i+1} \sim 2$, and a chunk size can be smaller than half the average chunk size ($ChunkSize \leq 0.5VR_i$), $\Delta B$ needs to be larger than $0.875V$s to safely step up a rate when the buffer is empty in our system.

Based on the preceding observation, BBA-2 works as follows. At time $t = 0$, since the buffer is empty, BBA-2 only picks the next highest video rate, if the $\Delta B$ increases by more than $0.875V$s. Since $\Delta B = V - ChunkSize/c[k]$, $\Delta B > 0.875V$ also means that the chunk is downloaded *eight times* faster than it is played. As the buffer grows, we use the accumulated buffer to absorb the chunk size variation and we let BBA-2 increase the video rate faster. Whereas at the start, BBA-2 only increases the video rate if the chunk downloads *eight times* faster than it is played, by the time it fills the cushion, BBA-2 is prepared to step up the video rate if the chunk downloads *twice* as fast as it is played. The threshold decreases linearly, from the first chunk until the cushion is full. The blue line in Figure 14 shows BBA-2 ramping up faster. BBA-2 continues to use this startup algorithm until (1) the buffer is decreasing, or (2) the chunk map suggests a higher rate. Afterwards, we use the $f(B)$ defined in the BBA-1 algorithm to pick a rate.

Note that BBA-2 is using $\Delta B$ during startup, which encodes a simple capacity estimate: the throughput of the last chunk. This design helps make the algorithm more aggressive at a point when the buffer has not yet accumulated enough information to accurately determine the video rate to use. Nevertheless, note that our use of capacity estimation is restrained. We only look at the throughput of the last chunk, and crucially, once the buffer is built up and the chunk map starts to suggest a higher rate, BBA-2 becomes buffer-based—it picks a rate from the chunk map, instead of using $\Delta B$. In this way, BBA-2 enables us to enjoy the improved steady-state performance of the buffer-based approach, without sacrificing overall bitrate due to a slow startup ramp.

## 6.1 Results

We ran our experiments during the same time period and with the same pool of users as the previously described experiments, which all occurred between September 6th (Friday) and 9th (Monday), 2013. Figure 15 shows the difference in the average video rate between *Control*, BBA-1, and BBA-2. From the figures, we see that BBA-2 does indeed increase the video rate. With a faster startup-phase ramp, the video rate with BBA-2 is almost indistinguishable from the *Control* algorithm. This supports our hypothesis that the lower video rates seen by BBA-0 and BBA-1 were due to their conservative rate selection during startup. Furthermore, if we exclude the first two minutes as an approximation of the steady state, the average video rate of BBA-2 is mostly higher than *Control*, as shown in Figure 16. This observation verifies our discussion in Section 3: The buffer-based approach is able to better utilize network capacity and achieve higher average video rate in the steady state.

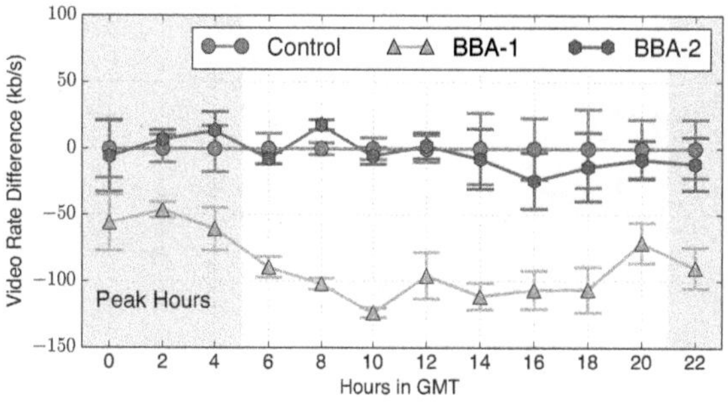


**Figure 15: BBA-2 achieved a similar video rates to the *Control* algorithm overall.**

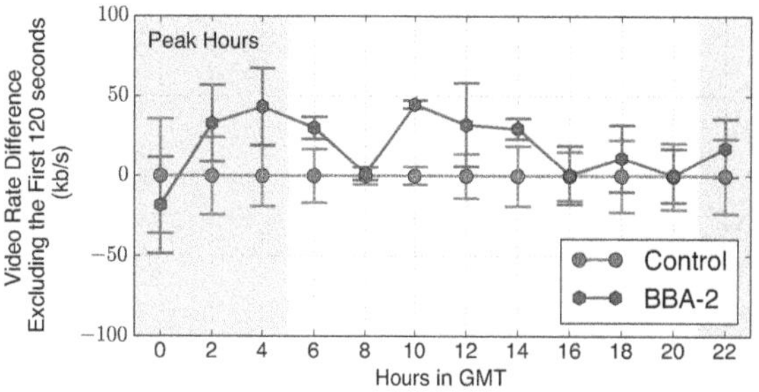


**Figure 16: BBA-2 achieved better video rate at the steady state. The steady state is approximated as the period after the first two minutes in each session.**

Figure 17 shows absolute and normalized rebuffer rate. BBA-2 slightly increases the rebuffer rate. BBA-2 operates in the *risky* zone of Figure 5 and therefore will inevitably rebuffer more often than BBA-1, which only operates in the *safe* area. Nevertheless, the improvements are significant relative to *Control*: BBA-2 maintains a *10–20% improvement in rebuffer rate* compared to *Control* during peak hours.

So far, we have successfully relaxed the four idealized assumptions made in Section 3. In BBA-0, we handle the finite chunk size and discrete available video rates through a piecewise mapping function. In BBA-1, we handle the VBR encoding through a variable reservoir size and a chunk map. In BBA-2, we further handle the finite video length by dividing each session into two phases. BBA-2 still follows the buffer-based approach in the steady state, but it uses a simple capacity estimation to ramp up the video rate during the startup. The results demonstrate that by focusing

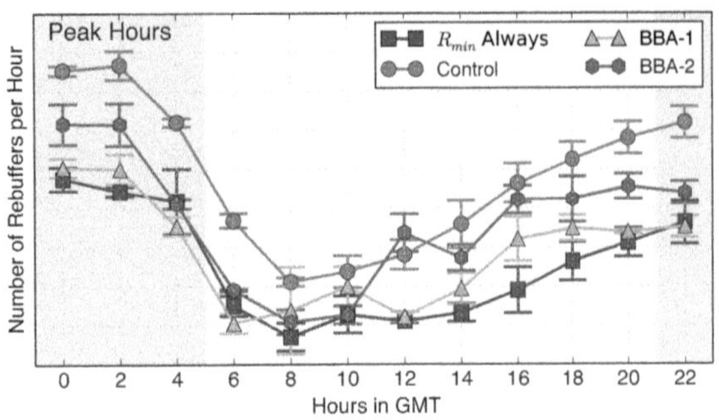


(a) Number of rebuffers per playhour.

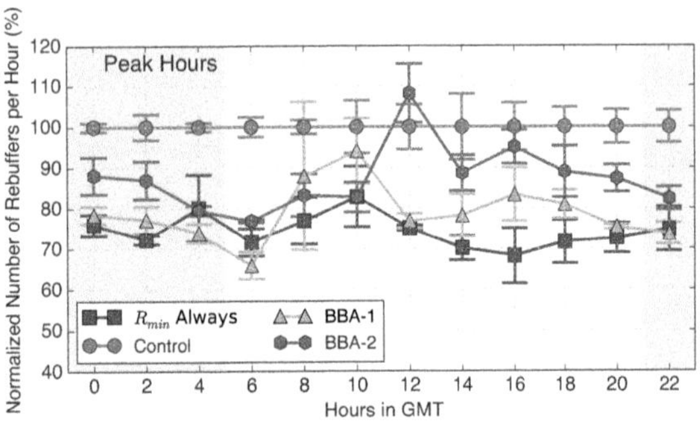


(b) Normalized number of rebuffers per playhour.

**Figure 17: BBA-2 has a slightly higher rebuffer rate compared to BBA-1, but still achieved 10–20% improvement compared to the *Control* algorithm during peak hours.**

on the buffer, we can reduce the rebuffer rate without compromising the video rate. In fact, the buffer-based approach improves the video rate in the steady state.

In the following, we will further discuss how to extend the buffer-based approach to tackle other practical concerns.

# 7. OTHER PRACTICAL CONCERNS: RATE SWITCHES AND OUTAGES

In Section 5, we have shown that we can improve the video rate by using a chunk map and dynamic reservoir calculation. However, this choice makes the video rate change frequently, as shown in Figure 18. Note that it is debatable as to whether video switching rate really matters to the viewer's quality of experience. For example, if a service offers closely spaced video rates, the viewer might not notice a switch. Nevertheless, in the following we will revise the dynamic reservoir calculation and introduce a modified algorithm, *BBA-Others*, to reduce the switching rate. We will see that by smoothing the changes, we can at least match the switching rate of the *Control* algorithm. *BBA-Others* will also converge to a higher buffer occupancy than before, providing some protection against temporary network outage.[7]

There are two main reasons our buffer-based algorithms increase the frequency of video-rate switches. First, when we

[7]Temporary network outages of 20–30s are not uncommon; e.g., when a DSL modem retrains or a WiFi network suffers interference.

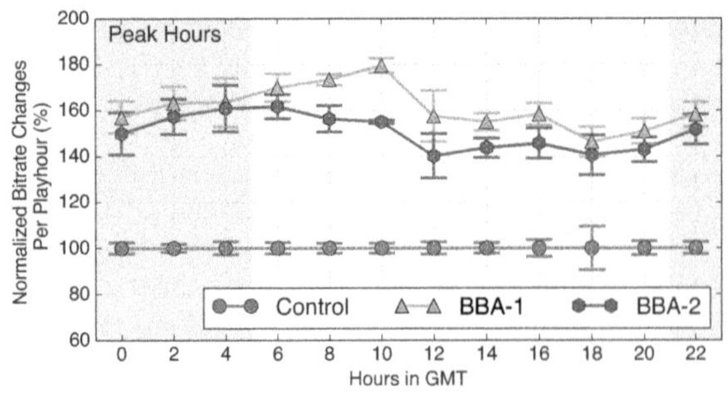


**Figure 18: After switching to chunk map, the video switching rate of BBA-1 and BBA-2 is much higher than the *Control* algorithm.**

use the chunk map, there is no longer a fixed mapping function between buffer levels and video rates. Instead, buffer levels are mapped to chunk sizes, and the nominal rate might change every time we request a new chunk. Even if the buffer level remains constant, the chunk map will cause BBA-1 to frequently switch rates, since the chunk size in VBR encoding varies over time. We can reduce the chance of switching to a new rate—and then switching quickly back again—by looking ahead to future chunks. When encountering a small chunk followed by some big chunks, even if the chunk map tells us to step up a rate, our new algorithm *BBA-Others* will not do so to avoid a likely step down in the near future. The further this modified algorithm looks ahead, the more it can smooth out rate changes. If, in the extreme, we look ahead to the end of the movie, it is the same as using a rate map instead of a chunk map. In the implementation of BBA-Others, we look ahead the same number of chunks as what we have in the buffer. When the buffer is empty, we pick a rate by only looking at the next chunk; when the buffer is full, we look ahead for the next 60 chunks.[8] Note that BBA-Others only smooths out *increases* in video rate. It does not smooth decreases so as to avoid increasing the likelihood of rebuffering.

Figure 11 helps to explain the second reason. The reservoir size is calculated from the chunk size variation in the next 480 seconds. Thus, the reservoir will shrink and expand depending on the upcoming chunks. If large chunks are coming up, the chunk map will be right-shifted; if small chunks are coming up, the chunk map will be left-shifted. Even if the buffer level remains constant, a shifted chunk map might cause the algorithm to pick a new video rate. We reduce the number of changes by only allowing the chunk map to shift to the right, never to the left, i.e., the reservoir expands but never shrinks. Since the reservoir cannot be shrunk, the reservoir grows faster than it needs to, allowing us to allocate the excess to protect against temporary network outage.

## 7.1 Results

As before, we randomly pick three groups of real users for our experiment. One third are in the *Control* group, one third always stream at $R_{\min}$, giving us an approximation of the lower bound on rebuffer rate, and one third run the BBA-Others algorithm, which smooths the switching rate by looking ahead and by only allowing the chunk map to

[8]Our buffer size is 240 seconds and each chunk is 4 seconds.

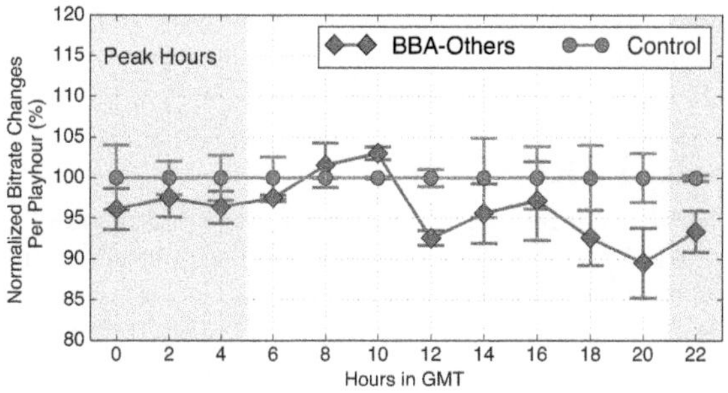


**Figure 19: BBA-Others smoothes the frequency of changes to the video rate, making it similar to the *Control* algorithm.**

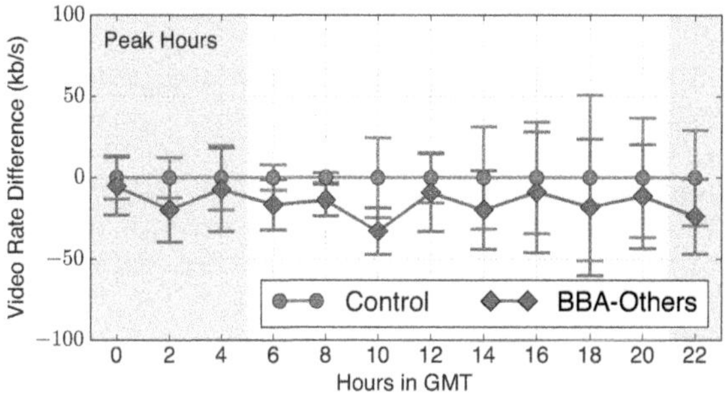


**Figure 20: BBA-Others achieves a similar video rate during the peak hours but reduces the video rate by 20–30kb/s during the off-peak.**

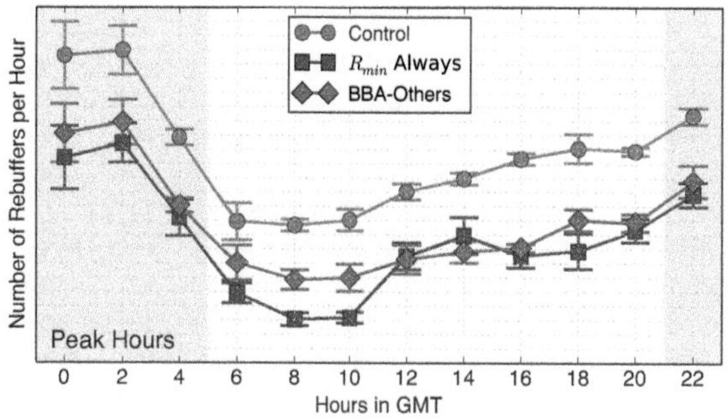


(a) Number of rebuffers per playhour.

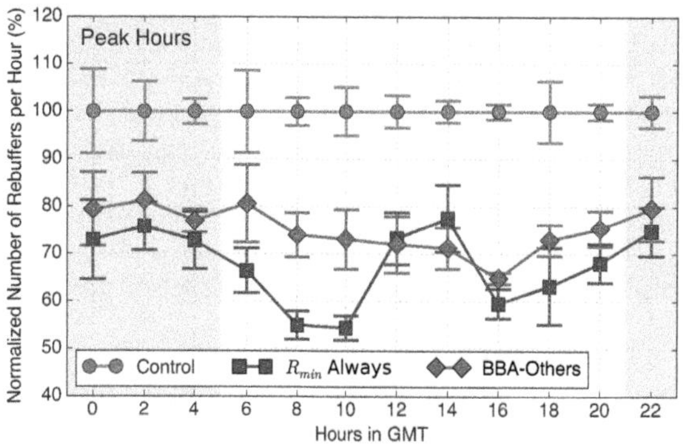


(b) Normalized number of rebuffers per playhour.

**Figure 21: BBA-Others reduces rebuffer rate by 20–30% compared to the *Control* algorithm.**

be right-shifted. The experiment was conducted between September 20th (Friday) and 22nd (Sunday), 2013.

Figure 19 shows that the video rate changes much less often with BBA-Others than with BBA-1 or BBA-2 (Figure 18). In fact, BBA-Others is almost indistinguishable from *Control*—sometimes higher, sometimes lower.[9] Figure 20 shows the video rate for BBA-Others. Since we does not allow the chunk map to be left-shifted, BBA-Others switches up more conservatively than BBA-2. Although the video rate is almost the same as *Control*, we trade about 20kb/s of video rate compared to BBA-2 in Figure 15.[10] As other buffer-based algorithms, BBA-Others improves the rebuffer rate, since we do not change the frequency of switches to a lower rate. As shown in Figure 21, BBA-Others improves the rebuffer rate by 20–30% compares to the *Control*.

## 8. RELATED WORK

**Understanding the Impact of Inaccurate Estimates.** Prior works have shown that sudden changes in available network capacity confuse existing ABR algorithms, causing the algorithms to either overestimate or underestimate the available network capacity [1, 2, 5, 10, 12].

The overestimation leads to unnecessary rebuffers [1, 5]. In this paper, we show that 20–30% of rebuffers in a production system are unnecessary. This observation motivates the buffer-based approach. The underestimation not only fills the buffer with lower quality video, but also leads to the ON-OFF traffic pattern: when the playback buffer is full, the client pauses the download until there is space. When competing with other TCP flows, the ON-OFF pattern can trigger a bad interaction between TCP and the ABR algorithm, causing a further underestimate of capacity and a downward spiral in video quality [8]. When competing with other video players, overlapping ON-OFF periods can confuse capacity estimation, leading to oscillating quality and unfair link share among players [2, 10, 12].

In our work, since we request only $R_{max}$ when the buffer approaches full, the ON-OFF traffic pattern appears only when the available capacity is higher than $R_{max}$. When competing with a long-lived TCP flow, our algorithm continues to request $R_{max}$ when the ON-OFF pattern occurs, avoiding the downward spiral. When competing with other video players, if the buffer is full, all players have reached $R_{max}$, and so the algorithm is fair.

**Buffer-aware ABR Algorithms.** Others have proposed using buffer level to adjust capacity estimation. Tian et al. [20] uses a buffer and a PID controller to compute the adjustment function applied to capacity estimates, balancing responsiveness and smoothness. Elastic [6] first measures the network capacity through a harmonic filter, then drives the buffer to a set-point through a controller. These prior works reveal that buffer occupancy provides important information for selecting a video rate. In this paper, we observe that buffer occupancy is in fact the primary state variable that an ABR algorithm should control. This motivates a

[9]The numbers are normalized to the average switching rate in *Control* for each two-hour window.

[10]This is only an approximation, since the tests in Figure 15 and 20 ran in two different weekends in September, 2013.

design that directly chooses the video rate according to the current buffer occupancy, and uses simple capacity estimation only when the buffer itself is growing from empty.

**Quality Metrics and User Engagement.** User engagement and quality of experience (QoE) are known to depend on rebuffering rate and video rate [7, 11, 14], as well as the delay before playing and how often the video rate changes [7, 19]. Modeling user engagement is complex and on-going [4, 14]. In this work, we focus on the tradeoff between rebuffer events and video bitrate (with some consideration for switching rate). The buffer-based approach can serve as a foundation when considering other metrics.

**Improving QoE through Other System Designs.** Although the distributed nature of client-side ABR algorithms yields system scalability, the decisions of these algorithms are reactive and optimize only the performance of a single client. Thus, a centralized control plane is proposed to optimize the global performance through aggregating measurements [13]. The potential benefits from CDN augmentation mechanisms, such as CDN federation and peer-assisted CDN-P2P hybrid model, are also investigated [3]. Our work is complementary to these efforts and will benefit from them.

# 9. CONCLUSION

Existing ABR algorithms face a significant challenge in environments where the capacity is rapidly varying (as is observed in practice). In response, ABR algorithms often adjust the capacity estimate based on the buffer occupancy, becoming more conservative (resp., aggressive) as the buffer falls (resp., grows). Motivated by the observation that accurate estimation is challenging when capacity is highly variable, we take this design to an extreme: we directly choose the video rate based on the current buffer occupancy and only use estimation when necessary. Our own investigation reveals that capacity estimation is unnecessary in steady state; however using (simple) capacity estimation (based on immediate past throughput) is important during the startup phase, when the buffer occupancy is growing from empty. We test the viability of this approach through a deployment in Netflix, and the results show that our algorithm can achieve a significant performance improvement.

More generally, our work suggests an alternative roadmap for the development of ABR algorithms: rather than presuming that capacity estimation is required, it is perhaps better to begin by using *only* the buffer, and then ask *when* capacity estimation is needed. Similar to the observations we make in this paper, we might expect that in settings where the startup phase is a significant fraction of the overall video playback, estimation may be valuable (e.g., for short videos). However, in all such cases, the burden of proof is on the algorithm designer to ensure the additional complexity is necessary.

# Acknowledgment

We are grateful to our shepherd Krishna Gummadi and the anonymous reviewers for their valuable comments and feedback, which greatly improved the final version. The authors would also like to thank Yiannis Yiakoumis, Greg Wallace-Freedman, Daniel Ellis, Kevin Morris, Wei Wei, Siqi Chen, and many other colleagues in both Stanford and Netflix for helpful discussions that shaped the paper. This work was supported by Google U.S./Canada PhD Student Fellowship and the National Science Foundation under grants CNS-0832820, CNS-0904609, and CNS-1040593.

# 10. REFERENCES


[1] S. Akhshabi et al. An Experimental Evaluation of Rate Adaptation Algorithms in Adaptive Streaming over HTTP. In *ACM MMSys*, 2011.

[2] S. Akhshabi et al. What Happens When HTTP Adaptive Streaming Players Compete for Bandwidth? In *ACM NOSSDAV*, 2012.

[3] A. Balachandran et al. Analyzing the Potential Benefits of CDN Augmentation Strategies for Internet Video Workloads. In *ACM IMC*, October 2013.

[4] A. Balachandran et al. Developing a Predictive Model of Quality of Experience for Internet Video. In *ACM SIGCOMM*, 2013.

[5] L. D. Cicco et al. An Experimental Investigation of the Akamai Adaptive Video Streaming. In *USAB*, 2010.

[6] L. D. Cicco et al. ELASTIC: a Client-side Controller for Dynamic Adaptive Streaming over HTTP (DASH). In *IEEE Packet Video Workshop*, 2013.

[7] F. Dobrian et al. Understanding the Impact of Video Quality on User Engagement. In *ACM SIGCOMM*, 2011.

[8] T.-Y. Huang et al. Confused, Timid, and Unstable: Picking a Video Streaming Rate is Hard. In *ACM IMC*, November 2012.

[9] T.-Y. Huang et al. A Buffer-Based Approach to Video Rate Adaptation. Technical report, 2014. `http://yuba.stanford.edu/~huangty/bba_report.pdf`.

[10] J. Jiang et al. Improving fairness, efficiency, and stability in http-based adaptive video streaming with festive. In *ACM CoNEXT*, 2012.

[11] S. S. Krishnan et al. Video Stream Quality Impacts Viewer Behavior: Inferring Causality Using Quasi-Experimental Designs. In *ACM IMC*, 2012.

[12] Z. Li et al. Probe and adapt: Rate adaptation for http video streaming at scale. In *http://arxiv.org/pdf/1305.0510*.

[13] X. Liu et al. A Case for a Coordinated Internet Video Control Plane. In *ACM SIGCOMM*, 2012.

[14] Y. Liu et al. User Experience Modeling for DASH Video. In *IEEE Packet Video Workshop*, 2013.

[15] R. Mok et al. QDASH: a QoE-aware DASH system. In *ACM MMSys*, 2012.

[16] Sandvine: Global Internet Phenomena Report 2012 Q2. `http://tinyurl.com/nyqyarq`.

[17] Sandvine: Global Internet Phenomena Report 2013 H2. `http://tinyurl.com/nt5k5qw`.

[18] Netflix ISP Speed Index. `http://ispspeedindex.netflix.com/`.

[19] H. Sundaram, W.-C. Feng, and N. Sebe. Flicker Effects in Adaptive Video Streaming to Handheld Devices. In *ACM MM*, November 2011.

[20] G. Tian and Y. Liu. Towards Agile and Smooth Video Adaptation in Dynamic HTTP Streaming. In *ACM CoNEXT*, December 2012.

[21] Private conversation with YouTube ABR team.

# FastForward: Fast and Constructive Full Duplex Relays

Dinesh Bharadia
Stanford University
dineshb@stanford.edu

Sachin Katti
Stanford University
skatti@stanford.edu

## ABSTRACT

This paper presents, **FastForward** (FF), a novel full-duplex relay that constructively forwards signals such that wireless network throughput and coverage is significantly enhanced. FF is a Layer 1 in-band full-duplex device, it receives and transmits signals directly and simultaneously on the same frequency. It cleanly integrates into existing networks (both WiFi and LTE) as a separate device and does not require changes to the clients. FF's key invention is a constructive filtering algorithm that transforms the signal at the relay such that when it reaches the destination, it constructively combines with the direct signals from the source and provides a significant throughput gain. We prototype FF using off-the-shelf software radios running a stock WiFi PHY and show experimentally that it provides a 3$\times$ median throughput increase and nearly a 4$\times$ gain at the edge of the coverage area.

## Categories and Subject Descriptors

C.2.1 [**Computer Communication Networks**]: Network Architecture and Design—*Wireless communication*
**Keywords**: Full Duplex Relay; Cancellation; Full Duplex ; low-latency cancelation

## 1. INTRODUCTION

We have all often experienced perplexingly poor wireless performance. For example, it's not uncommon to find that one's connection is flaky and offers very low throughput even when one is the only user of the WiFi AP in a home. Similarly, for LTE networks, even at nights when the network is lightly loaded, performance can be poor indoors or in urban concrete jungles, with raw link speeds varying between a few hundred Kbps to a couple of Mbps. This is despite continuous evolution of wireless standards over the last few years to provide very high link bitrates. For example, the 802.11ac WiFi standard promises bitrates of up to 1.3Gbps, while LTE downlink speeds are expected to be up to 300Mbps [5, 1]. These gains are coming from two factors: use of higher modulation (up to 256QAM for both LTE and WiFi) and higher MIMO spatial multiplexing (up to 4 parallel streams for both LTE and WiFi). Both these features should work well when there is little to no contention/interference and a single or a few users are connected to the WiFi AP or the LTE basestation. Yet often users don't realize these benefits in practice, experiencing raw speeds that are one to two orders of magnitude less than the advertised speeds.

There are two fundamental reasons for the poor performance described above: propagation loss and MIMO rank degradation. Propagation loss is a natural and expected cause of the drop in link rates. Fig. 1 shows a typical 2000 sq. ft. home with a WiFi AP at one corner of the house in the living room. We model propagation and other effects using commercial grade wireless ray propagation modeling software [21, 4] that is used for planning wireless deployments. As we can see, except for the immediate area around the AP, most of the coverage area in the middle of the home experiences SNRs between 10-15dB (as seen in Fig. 1), and at the edge the performance is worse, with SNRs between 0-6dB. This cuts down the highest modulation that can be used to QAM/16-QAM from 256-QAM, a 4$\times$ reduction in bitrate. An analogous argument can be made for LTE networks where the coverage area is larger, and signals often have to propagate through large buildings in urban areas which further cause signal loss due to shadowing effects.

The second fundamental reason is MIMO rank degradation as seen in Fig. 2. To send multiple data streams via MIMO spatial multiplexing, the channel between the AP and the client needs to have several independent strong propagation paths available (in other words, the MIMO channel matrix needs to be full rank and have strong eigenvalues [9]). But in most indoor and urban scenarios, often we find that only a single strong path exists between the AP and the client, and the rest are weak or non-existent. This happens because of the geometry of homes, offices and hotels which typically have a single or few corridors with rooms off the corridors. The corridor acts like an RF pinhole [9, 17] since it is typically the only strong path available between the AP and the client, and focuses all the signals to go through a single path which makes all of the paths correlated at the destination. The consequence is that the MIMO channel rank is reduced, and the AP cannot send multiple independent streams, reducing the bitrate significantly. LTE signals behave analogously, in that the only path indoors for the signal is through windows or doors (walls tend to block signals almost completely), and the doors/windows acts as RF pinholes. Combined with the propagation loss described above, this results in nearly a 6-10x reduction in bitrate in the middle and edge of the coverage from the AP.

Our goal in this paper is to design a general, practical and easily deployable system that provides high-throughput uniform wireless coverage. By general, we mean the fundamental technique should be applicable to any OFDM based standard. By practical and easily deployable, we mean that the system should require minimal to no changes to the existing infrastructure of APs , clients and/or standards.

We design and implement a novel system called **FastForward** (FF) that achieves the above goals. FF's core operation is simple to describe. It is a single device that operates independently listening to the signal from the source, digitizing it to IQ samples, processing it by passing the IQ stream through a filter (in both digital and RF domains), and up-converting and amplifying the processed IQ stream to RF signals that are then transmitted to the destination on the same frequency. The filtering and amplification are done in such a way that the SNR of the signal at the destination is signifi-


*SIGCOMM'14*, August 17–22, 2014, Chicago, Illinois, USA.

ACM 978-1-4503-2836-4/14/08...$15.00.
http://dx.doi.org/10.1145/2619239.2626327 .

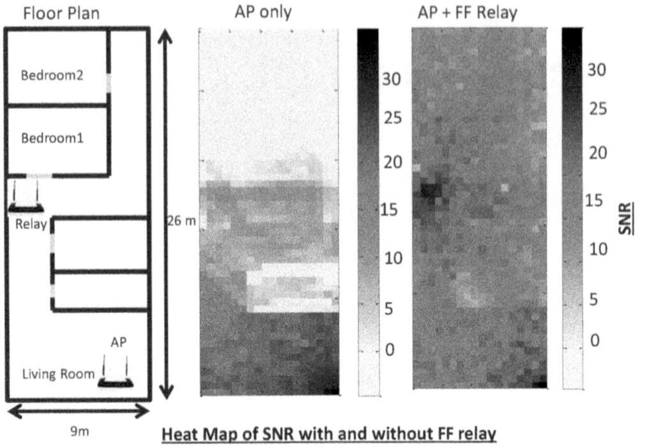


Figure 1: Heatmap of SNR with AP alone and with AP and FF relay. A majority of the home has poor SNR due to propagation loss in the AP only scenario.

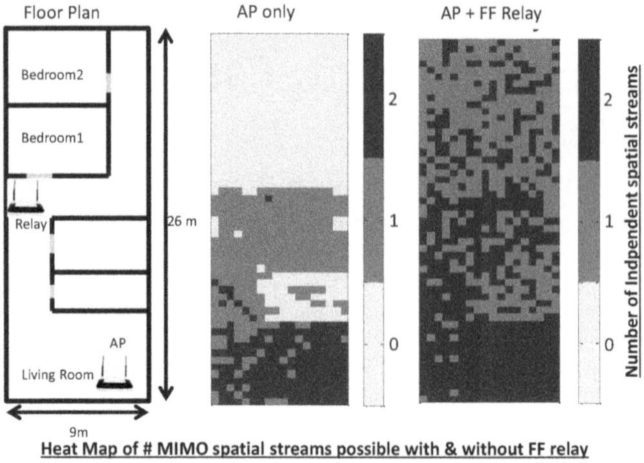


Figure 2: Heatmap of number of MIMO spatial streams possible with AP alone and with AP and FF relay. A majority of the home has poor MIMO channel rank due to pinhole effects and poor link propagation through walls.

cantly increased and the number of independent MIMO paths at the destination is also increased, enabling a significantly higher bitrate. Thus it acts as a controlled strong multi-path creator of the signals that is completely transparent to the AP and the client, they do not even realize that an FF device exists. A glimpse of its performance is shown in the heatmaps (Figs. 1,2).

The key insight behind FF is a novel technique that we invent called **construct-and-forward full-duplex relaying**. The basic idea is best described in terms of a single SISO transmission from the AP to the client. With a simple full-duplex amplify-and-forward relay that has been discussed in the literature [20], the client would receive two signals: one directly from the AP and the other amplified version from the relay. A naive implementation of the relay will result in both these signals acting as destructive interference to each other, and the relay potentially amplifying noise. FF's innovation is to control the properties of the relayed multi-path signal to in fact turn such potential interference into a constructive SNR gain. The design relies on the fact that if an OFDM receiver receives multiple reflected copies of a signal, then as long as the reflections are within the OFDM cyclic prefix (CP) interval (around 400ns for WiFi and $4.69\mu s$ for LTE), they do not cause inter-symbol interference (ISI) to each other. If we can ensure that the processing delay through the FF relay is minimized so that the relayed signal does not fall outside the OFDM CP interval at the receiver, we can achieve no inter symbol interference. FF's low latency cancellation technique achieve this purpose. Thus, FF's relay acts as an amplified multi-path component at the receiver.

While limiting the processing delay ensures that inter-symbol interference is avoided, it still does not provide a constructive SNR gain. The second aspect of construct-and-forward relaying is to intelligently process the received signal at the relay before transmission such that the relayed signal adds up constructively with the other signals that the destination is directly receiving from the source to significantly enhance the effective SNR. The basic idea is that the relay first collects the channel state information about three links: source-relay, relay-destination and source-destination. Now, when it receives the transmission from the source, it passes the signal through a filter such that cumulative effect for the received signal at the destination (which has now gone through the channel from the AP to the FF relay, the filter at the relay and the channel from the relay to the client) is such that it adds coherently (in almost complete alignment) at the destination with the direct signal received by the destination from the source. Fig. 5 shows the effect visually, the relay rotates the incoming signal such that it aligns up with the vector representing the channel between the source and the destination. The constructive addition significantly increases the SNR at the destination (client), enabling a higher bitrate to be used by the source (AP). A similar effect happens when the FF relay is combating the pinhole effect, it computes a filter that increases the number of spatial streams and the SNR at the destination (client), enabling the source (AP) to use a higher level of spatial multiplexing and therefore higher bitrates. Note that the relay can be used to improve the link from the client to the AP as well.

The challenge in realizing such construct-and-forward relaying while ensuring that processing delays is much smaller than the OFDM CP is the full duplex nature of the relay. The FF relay is transmitting and receiving signals at the same time on the same frequency. Further, the transmitted signal is essentially a slightly delayed and amplified version of the received signal. To receive the signal from the AP, the FF relay has to cancel the transmitted signal. The amount of cancellation puts a limit on the amount of amplification that we can apply at the relay, since if we amplify more than the cancellation, residual signal is left over and is recycled for transmission, creating an unstable positive feedback loop. Maximizing the amount of cancellation is therefore crucial to maximizing amplification. However, unlike prior work on full duplex, the cancellation has to be performed within a time budget as small as possible (e.g. within 100ns for WiFi since the CP is only 400ns long) to ensure that the relayed signal can take advantage of FF's constructive relaying capability. A second key contribution of this paper is a novel cancellation technique for relays that achieves nearly 110dB of cancellation while operating within a processing time budget of 100ns.

We design and implement FF on the WARP radio platform [8] and by designing our own self-interference cancellation RF boards. We evaluate FF in an indoor testbed and show that FF provides a $3\times$ median increase in throughput and nearly $4\times$ at the edge of the coverage area. The gains come from different aspects for different clients. For clients with decent SNR already, the gains come from MIMO rank expansion. For clients at the edge of the coverage area where the SNR is already quite poor, the gains come from the SNR gain constructive relaying provides. We also compare against the half duplex packet-level relay (e.g. the Apple Airport Express) and show than FF provides at least $2\times$ better throughput and coverage.

## 2. RELATED WORK

A natural question is whether there are other approaches that can be used to solve the problem of coverage and capacity that FF aims

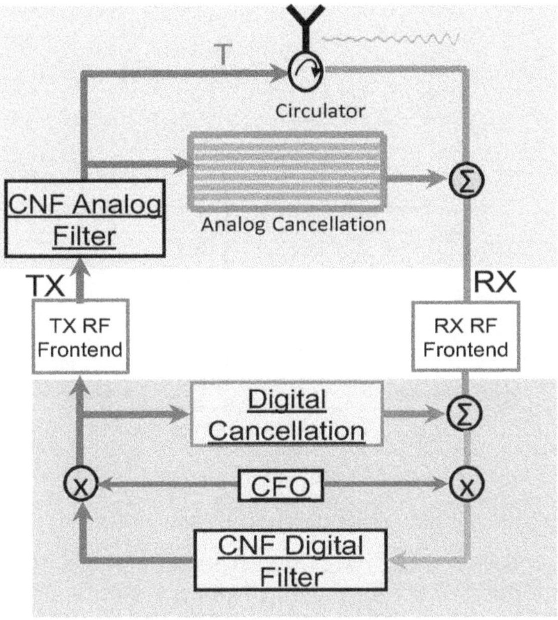


Figure 3: Overall Block Diagram of a FF relay. There are two key pieces: construct-and-forward (CNF) analog and digital filters, and self-interference cancellation.

to? There has been of course a large body of work in recent years that have proposed several PHY and MAC layer enhancements to increase network capacity and robustness, FF however is operating on signals directly and is therefore orthogonal to those approaches.

However there is one approach that could help and is immediately deployable: a half-duplex mesh router like the Apple Airport Express. These devices help extend WiFi coverage by connecting to the AP as a client, and then turning around and transmitting to the actual client in the next slot (hence the name half duplex router). Theoretical literature on relaying refers to such techniques as **decode-and-forward** relaying. However, as we show in Sec. 5 these devices do not provide capacity gains except in the edge of the coverage area. This is because they essentially require close to twice the number of time slots for transmitting the same amount of traffic. Further for clients with decent SNRs to the AP, the half-duplex mesh router is a bad option, it is better to have a single-hop medium-SNR link rather than using two hops over high-SNR links.

There are several products in the market that are called repeaters. These devices are simple **amplify-and-forward** relays. They receive a signal, and then immediately amplify it and transmit it. Such devices are available for both WiFi and LTE networks. However these devices cannot amplify too much, they are severely limited by the amount of isolation between the signals they are receiving and relaying as we show in Sec. 3.5. Second, since they are blindly amplifying signals, they amplify noise and often hurt performance as we show in Sec. 5.5. FF also belongs to the class of **amplify-and-forward** relays, however this paper makes three novel contributions:

- FF is selective and smart about relaying, it exploits the knowledge of channel state information to intelligently filter and amplify signals such that they appear as a constructive multipath component at the destination, rather than increase noise and/or add up destructively like a standard repeater would.
- FF designs a novel low-latency self-interference cancellation technique which ensures that relayed signals fall within the CP for OFDM signals and do not cause inter-symbol interference. The technique is applicable to standard repeaters too and they can benefit from being able to use a higher amplification factor due to the increased amount of cancellation.
- This paper also provides a full design, implementation and evaluation of full-duplex relays, to the best of our knowledge we are not aware of prior work that provides an experimental characterization of how well other kinds of relays work in practice.

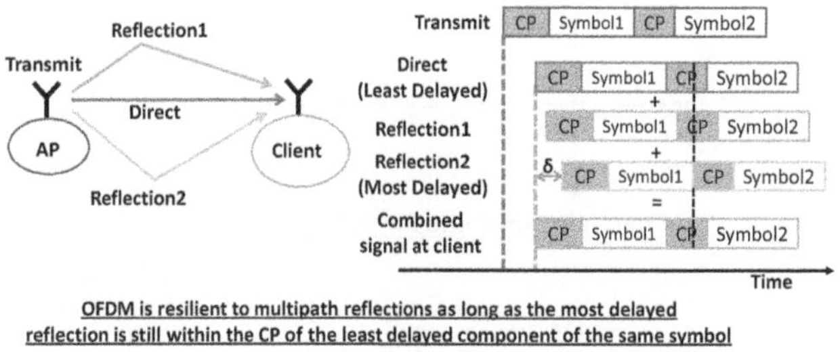


Figure 4: OFDM is resilient to multipath reflections as long as the extra delay experienced by the slowest reflection compared to the quickest arriving signal at the destination is less than the cyclic prefix (CP).

Finally, there is a large body of theoretical work on relays in the information theory literature [24, 14, 27]. Starting from early work by Shannon, there have been several proposals on relaying [13, 22, 12, 26]. Apart from the amplify-and-forward and decode-and-forward relaying techniques; a third well known class of techniques is **compress-and-forward**: this is an intermediate version between the above two relays. Here the relay may not decode the entire packet, but only the symbols and re-encodes them in a more efficient way [30, 16, 29, 19]. The destination has to combine the relayed information with the direct transmission from the source to recover the original packet. This method is typically quite complex to implement since it requires changes at the client with techniques such as soft interference cancellation and combining, as well as sophisticated processing at the relay.

# 3. DESIGN

FF is a layer 1 full-duplex relay, i.e. it receives signals from the source, processes them both in the analog and digital domains, and then converts them back to RF signals and transmits them on the same channel they were received on. Fig. 3 shows the high-level block diagram of an FF single-antenna relay. Note that an FF relay can have multiple antennas and can relay MIMO signals, however we use the single-antenna SISO FF relay for describing the key ideas in a concise manner. However the techniques and algorithms naturally translate to a MIMO relay implementation.

As we can see there are three main components in the design: cancellation, constructive filtering (CNF) and amplification. The insight underpinning these components is exploiting the structure of OFDM such that relaying can produce a constructive SNR gain at the receiver. We start by describing first the basics of OFDM.

## 3.1 OFDM Background

OFDM was introduced to combat the negative effects of multipath and inter-symbol interference. The basic idea is widely known and described in textbooks [15], but we include it here because it helps explain some of FF's algorithmic design choices later.

The basic idea of OFDM is to divide the available bandwidth $B$ into $N$ smaller subcarriers (e.g. 802.11ac with 80MHz bandwidth is divided into 512 subcarriers whereas LTE divides into subcarriers of width 15KHz). Each subcarrier can be conceptually treated as an independent orthogonal channel carrying independent symbols. Hence the symbol time is $N/B$, i.e. the symbol is $N$ times longer, as compared to a typical communication system transmitting symbol at $1/B$, for bandwidth $B$. Further to each symbol, a

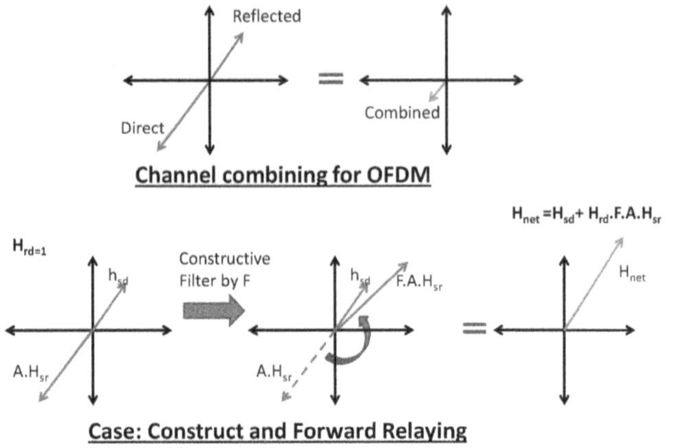


Figure 5: FF's construct-and-forward relaying rotates the relayed signal such that it aligns with the direct signal from the source to the destination and provides a constructive SNR gain. The top figure shows what happens with normal OFDM where instead of the relay there is a normal reflection of the same delay. The channel gains add up destructively and reduce SNR at the destination.

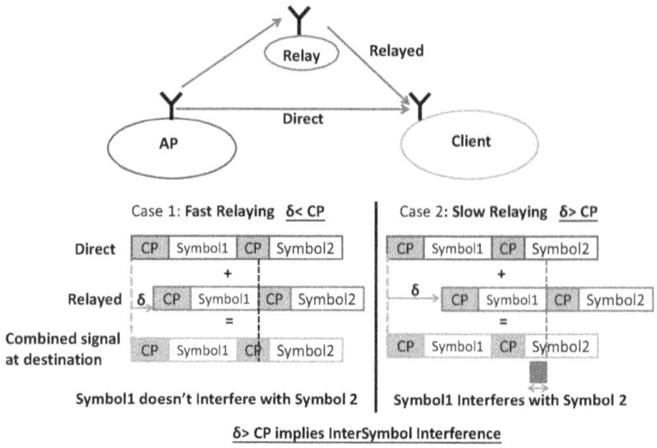


Figure 6: Low latency processing at the FF relay is critical. If the delay of processing in the FF relay is greater than the OFDM CP, then the relayed signal will cause inter-symbol interference at the destination [15].

guard period known as the cyclic prefix (CP) (typically 25% of the symbol time) is added. Hence as long as the extra delay of a multipath reflection of an OFDM symbol w.r.t. the first arriving version at the destination is less than the CP length, no inter-symbol interference is caused as seen in Fig.4. The length of the cyclic prefix is 400ns in WiFi and 4.69$\mu$s in LTE. Hence in WiFi there is tolerance for a distance spread of 400 feet whereas for LTE its almost 5000 feet, which is expected since WiFi is designed for covering homes whereas LTE is designed for covering larger outdoor areas.

Given the above fact, how does the effective channel look at the receiver? In other words how do the multipath reflections add up if they are not causing ISI with each other? To visualize this, consider Fig. 5. We are plotting the channel gains for a single OFDM subcarrier (i.e. the attenuation and phase shift applied by the direct path channel to any signal on that subcarrier). Now suppose there is another multipath reflection with a slightly longer path and higher attenuation. The channel gain for this second path shows up as a second vector that is rotated w.r.t the first channel gain. Assuming the extra delay is within the CP, the overall channel perceived by the receiver is the sum of these two channel gains. The effective SNR at the client therefore depends on the relative orientation and gains of the direct and reflected channel paths, if they are aligned with each other in the same direction SNR increases, if they are in opposite directions SNR decreases.

## 3.2 Construct-and-Forward Relaying

FF's construct-and-forward relaying builds on top of OFDM. Our basic insight is to make FF look like another strong multipath reflector, albeit with the ability to amplify and modify the signals. Since FF operates at the signal level, at the receiver the signal from the relay looks like yet another multipath component, albeit a strong one. As long as the extra delay of this component is within the CP, the receiver will not perceive any inter-symbol interference. The constraint then is that the overall delay of the signal going through the FF relay has to be as low as possible, and definitely well within the CP interval. Since we still have to account for normal propagation delay from the source to the relay and then from the relay to the destination, ideally we want to completely minimize the processing delay in the FF relay.

As we see in Fig. 6, by minimizing the relative delay below cyclic prefix between direct and reflected (or relayed) path we can avoid inter-symbol interference. However, depending on the relative phase of the channel gains from the relay to the destination (relayed) and from the source to the destination (direct), we might hurt overall SNR at the receiver as shown in of Fig. 5.a. So might FF be hurting the SNR by relaying ?

FF's key invention is a novel technique that leverages its relaying capability in a way to actually significantly enhance the SNR at the client. Remember that the relay has the opportunity to modify the signal before it amplifies and sends it to the destination. FF's novel idea is to apply a filter before amplifying and relaying the signal such that it adds up *constructively* at the destination to maximize the SNR gain. Mathematically, let us say the channel from the source to the destination is $h_{sd}$, and from the source to the relay is $h_{sr}$ and from the relay to the destination is $h_{rd}$, for a particular subcarrier. Further the noise at the destination is $n_d$, and at the relay is $n_r$. The relay would amplify the signal by a factor $A$ and then pass the signal through a constructive filter whose response is $F$ at that subcarrier. The SNR at the destination for that subcarrier, is given by

$$SNR_d = \left| \frac{h_{sd} + h_{rd} F A h_{sr}}{N_o} \right|^2 \tag{1}$$

where $N_o = n_d + h_{rd} F A n_r$. The second term in $N_o$ is small, since the amplification ($A$) is controlled as described in Sec. 3.5, which makes sure that noise is not amplified at the destination. For now we will assume the controlled amplification is represented by, $A < A_{max}$ and we will ignore $N_o$ in optimization of Eq. 1. Visually this is demonstrated in Fig. 5.

Note that the constructive filter can introduce additional processing delay, however as before the overall delay still has to be well within the CP so that we can take advantage of OFDM. Further constructive relaying assumes that the relay knows all three channels. The channels from the source to the relay and from the relay to the destination are easy to measure by the relay itself. However the channel from the source to the destination cannot be measured by the relay and has to be explicitly fed to it. We discuss in Sec. 4.2 how this can be done in both WiFi and LTE using existing mechanisms in the standards.

The above discussion has focused on the SISO case. However the same arguments hold for the MIMO case. In effect the relay adds a separate independent strong MIMO path which increases the rank of the MIMO matrix. For constructive relaying, instead of optimizing the above equation, the relay would perform the following optimization

$$\max_{F,A} \quad \det(H_{sd} + H_{rd} F A H_{sr}) \tag{2}$$

$$\text{subject to} \qquad A < A_{max}$$

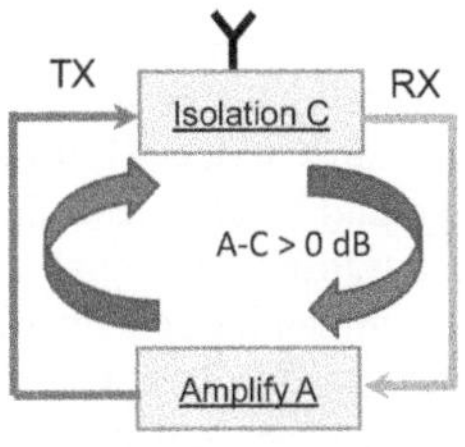


Figure 7: Amplification $A$ is limited by the amount of isolation $C$. Amplifying more than the isolation implies there is still some residual left over after isolation by $C$ dB, which is then again amplified and relayed in the next time instant and so on. This creates an unstable positive feedback loop.

where $H_{sd}$ is an $N \times M$ channel matrix where the source and destination have $M$ and $N$ antennas respectively, $H_{sr}$ is a $K \times M$ channel matrix to the relay (the relay has $K$ antennas) and $H_{rd}$ is an $N \times K$ matrix, $A$ is again the scalar amplification factor (power) and $F$ is the constructive filter which is a $K \times K$ rotation matrix in this case. Intuitively, the path through the relay acts as a strong independent MIMO path and adds rank to the overall matrix. Since a $K$ antenna relay has only $K$ dimensions, it can increase the MIMO rank at the destination at most by $K$. The filter again in this case acts as a mechanism to maximize the SNR. The optimization problem described in Eqn. 2 is non-convex and is solved using non-linear optimization technique. Note that it can be solved for $F.A$ as a single variable, and only needs to be solved whenever any of the three channels are updated, and not for every packet. The solution to this problem is referred to as $H_c(f_i)$ in the later sections, overall filter response is referred as $H_c$.

The takeaway from the above algorithm is that FF needs to implement two key blocks: **amplification** and **constructive filtering**. Note that both these blocks need to be as low latency as possible, ideally within a 100ns budget given that the WiFi CP is 400ns. If we can design it with that delay then the techniques will work for LTE too since it has a longer CP. We turn to the design and implementation of these blocks next.

## 3.3 FF: Low-Latency Amplification

As we saw in the previous section, FF enables constructive relaying by applying an amplification $A$ and a filter $F$ to the received signal at the relay. As expected the relay cannot receive a signal if it is also transmitting an amplified signal at the same time on the same frequency. Hence to build a relay we need to isolate the received signal from the transmitted signal, i.e. remove the transmitted signal from the received signal. Further, the amount of isolation directly dictates how much amplification the relay can apply on the received signal, which in turn dictates how much the relay expands the range and capacity of the network.

To see why, consider what happens if we amplify beyond the achievable isolation as seen in Fig. 7. In effect this means that some of the signal that is being transmitted is still left over in the received signal after isolation since amplification is greater than isolation. But remember that the transmitted signal is simply a delayed version of the received signal. So in the next instant the transmitted signal would contain a copy of the transmitted signal that was left over in the previous instant. This iteratively accumulates and creates a positive feedback loop where ultimately the relayed signal simply consists of leftover copies of the same signal from previous time instants. The positive feedback loop is unstable and ultimately leads to poor performance. On the other hand if the amplification is lower than the isolation, then all of the transmitted signal is removed from the received signal, and the relay operation proceeds smoothly.

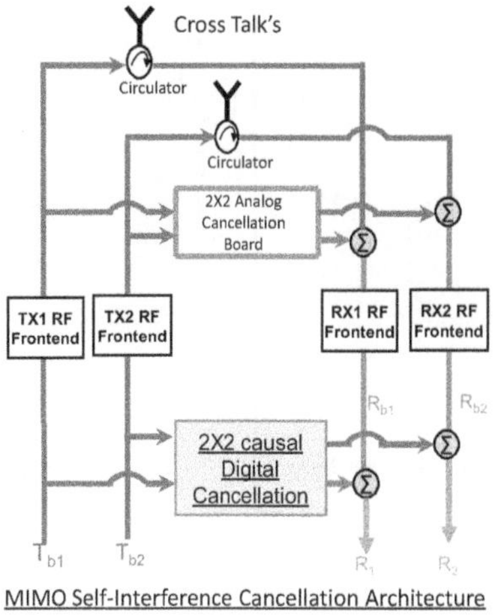


Figure 8: Self-interference cancellation architecture for a $2 \times 2$ MIMO FF relay.

Our goal therefore is to maximize the isolation from the TX to the RX. We turn to recent work on self-interference cancellation for full duplex radios [11, 10] to provide the isolation between RX and TX signals. These techniques enable a radio to almost completely cancel the transmitted signal and enable clean reception of the received signal. However there is a catch which prevents us from being able to directly apply the cancellation techniques, the self-interference cancellation has to be performed with as little latency as possible (e.g. much smaller than 400ns for WiFi signals). Self-interference cancellation in the prior work has two components, an analog and a digital cancellation stage. Analog cancellation has negligible delay (around 10ns). However the digital cancellation stage (including the ADC and DAC delays) has a delay of nearly 400ns which would put us out of range for the relay requirements for WiFi. The ADCs and the DACs contribute around 50ns of delay, hence the digital cancellation stage adds nearly 350ns of delay.

We invent a novel self-interference cancellation technique that performs the cancellation with a near-zero delay (excluding than the latency of implementation, which is a few ns or lesser). In prior work on cancellation, the delay is primarily due to the fact that digital cancellation is non-causal [11]. In other words, the digital cancellation filters like to peek ahead into the future of the signal and use that information to cancel the signal at the present. In this relay, we could do this by buffering the received signal, so when we are canceling the self-interference signal at any instant, we know the future of the transmitted signal is going to be. However buffering means delay, for example buffering even 5 digital IQ samples at a 100Msps sampling rate means a delay of 50ns. Hence in FF, we invent a digital cancellation technique that is causal, i.e. it only uses information about what has been already transmitted to cancel the self-interference and does not do any buffering of the received signal before transmission. So received samples are passed in a streaming fashion to the transmit side without any delay. However causal cancellation results in digital cancellation filters which are slightly longer, they need to use more taps to recreate the self-interference for cancellation. However these taps do not add delay, they are for signal samples that have already been transmitted.

Fig. 8 shows the cancellation architecture for a $2 \times 2$ MIMO FF relay. Analog cancellation is implemented as discussed in prior work [11, 10] using a tunable FIR analog filter. Digital cancellation is slightly different, it uses a FIR filter like before but there is no buffering and delay, it is a causal filter as shown in Fig. 9.a. The samples that are used for cancellation are only the samples that are

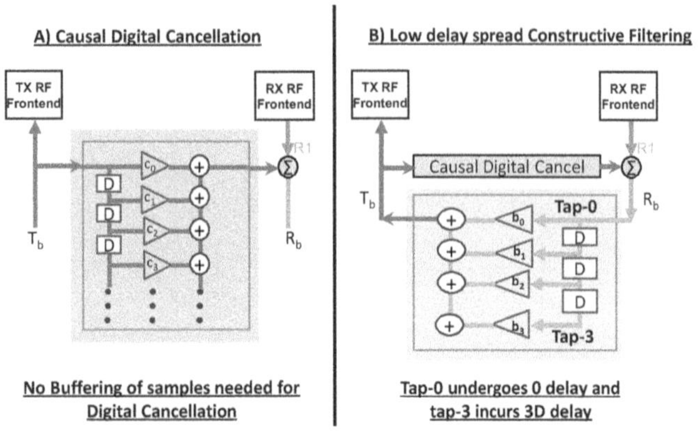


Figure 9: a) Digital cancellation in FF is causal, i.e. the cancellation is performed only using the current and past transmitted samples. No buffering of received samples is performed, which minimizes processing delay through the relay. b) The larger the number of tap delay, higher is the probability that it would cause inter-symbol interference at the destination.

currently being or have already been transmitted, indicating causality.

The coefficients for both the analog and digital cancellation filter are dynamically tuned to maximize cancellation. However, dynamically tuning cancellation in a full duplex relay is more complex than standard full duplex. The reason is that the signal that is being transmitted is a slightly delayed version of the signal being received. To see how this impacts the tuning algorithm, we can look at what happens during analog cancellation. The cancellation problem is given by:

$$\begin{aligned} y(t) &= x_R(t) + h(t) * x_T(t) - \widehat{h}(t) * x_T(t) \\ &= x_T(t+\tau) + h(t) * x_T(t) - \widehat{h}(t) * x_T(t) \end{aligned}$$

where $x_R(t)$ is the signal relay is receiving from the source, $x_T(t)$ is the signal the relay is transmitting to the destination, $h(t)$ is the time domain transformation applied by the channel before the transmitted signal from the relay causes self-interference to the received signal, $\widehat{h}(t)$ represents the filter that is being used by the analog cancellation block to approximate $H$ and implement cancellation, and $y(t)$ is the combined signal that is being received by the relay. Clearly cancellation is maximized when $h(t) = \widehat{h}(t)$. In the second part of the above equation we substitute $x_R(t)$ with $x_T(t+\tau)$ because the relayed signal is a future version of the received signal, where the delay is represented by $\tau$.

Prior work on analog cancellation solve the above estimation problem in the frequency domain. So the above problem can be rewritten in the frequency domain as:

$$\begin{aligned} Y(f) &= X_R(f) + H(f)X_T(f) - \widehat{H}(f)X_T(f) \\ &= \alpha(f)X_T(f) + H(f)X_T(f) - \widehat{H}(f)X_T(f) \\ &= \{\alpha(f) + H(f)\}X_T(f) - \widehat{H}(f)X_T(f) \end{aligned}$$

Where $\alpha(f) = exp(j2\pi f\tau)$ The above equation shows why correlation is a problem, in effect its quite likely that the tuning algorithm adapts $\widehat{H}(f)$ to approximate $\alpha(f) + H(f)$ which will end up canceling the received signal from the source too! We may end up with no received signal at the relay in this case.

To solve this challenge, we invent a novel cancellation tuning mechanism: we artificially inject Gaussian noise at a very low power, which is similar to the transmitter noise of the transmission, only this is known to us (30dB below the transmitted signal or 80dB above the noise floor in the worst case). Gaussian noise only undergoes the channel $H(f)$, as it is not part of received signal. Hence to figure out the response $H(f)$, i.e. the tuning parameters, we compute the correlation of the received signal with the Gaussian noise that was transmitted, and estimate the self-interference channel parameters. However once cancellation is tuned, we know that analog cancellation provides around 70dB of cancellation, and digital cancellation takes both the transmitted signal and Gaussian noise as input to eliminate all the remaining self-interference. So as soon as the cancellation is turned on, all of the Gaussian noise is canceled and is not left over in the canceled signal. Finally this injected noise doesn't affect the client data rate (since the maximum SNR required is 28dB for the highest data rate) and very likely by the time the relayed signal reaches it, the injected noise is quite likely attenuated to below the receiver noise floor of the client's receiver.

**Experimental Results**: We prototype the above cancellation design using WARP software radios with setup similar to the one used in [10], which is used in the evaluation Sec. 5. We experimentally evaluated the amount of cancellation when the FF relay node is placed at different locations in our indoor testbed, while its receiving the signal from another and re-transmitting the same signal after the constructive filtering. We observe that our design consistently achieves between 108-110dB of cancellation. Note that the maximum cancellation expected is 110dB, since the maximum transmit power is 20dBm and the noise floor is -90dBm.

## 3.4 FF: Low-delay Constructive Filter

As noted before, the relay can apply a filter such that the relayed signal adds up constructively at the receiver, as seen in Sec. 3.2. A typical implementation of this filter consists of a series of delay lines, each with its own gain, as shown in Fig. 9.b. Note that the signal at Tap-N of the filter ($N = 3$ in Fig. 9.b.) has an $ND$ extra delay with respect to the signal at Tap-0, where $D$ is the delay introduced by each tap. It is important to note that we have a constraint on the number of taps we can employ in our filter because the filter delay $ND$ (which dominantly dictates the maximum delay at the relay) needs to be such that the relayed signal does not fall outside the cyclic prefix at the destination. This section describes how the ideal filter $H_c$ can be implemented with as less filter delay as possible.

Recall that the basic intuition behind this filter is to rotate (i.e., change the phase of) the relayed signal such that it aligns with the direct signal at the destination, as we saw in Fig. 5. For example, to rotate a relayed signal at 2.45GHz by 90 degrees, the constructive filter needs to introduce a 100ps delay (400 ps is the time period of one wave at 2.45GHz which corresponds to 360 degrees, hence 100ps corresponds to 90 degrees). It is extremely hard to implement such fine-grained delays on the order of a hundred picoseconds in the digital domain. For example, if we have a sampling bandwidth of 100MHz, successive digital IQ samples are spaced 10ns apart, in other words two orders of magnitude greater than the delay resolution desired. Figuring out the minute variation in the signal that is delayed by 100ps (which is an intermediate point between two consecutive digital samples) is possible, but extremely complex [28, 18] and defeats our filter delay requirement. The reason is that figuring out the value that an analog signal will take at an intermediate point between digital samples requires us to use sinc interpolation that spans many more future and past digital samples. Using a large number of past digital samples implies that our filter needs to have a large number of taps, which in turn increases the filter delay and thus increases the chances that the relayed signal falls outside the OFDM CP at the destination.

To tackle this problem, FF therefore designs a programmable analog filter that can provide the fine-grained delay adjustment constructive filtering needs as seen in Fig.10, without introducing significantly delay multi-path. We design a tunable analog FIR filter structure with four fixed delays and tunable gains on each delay.

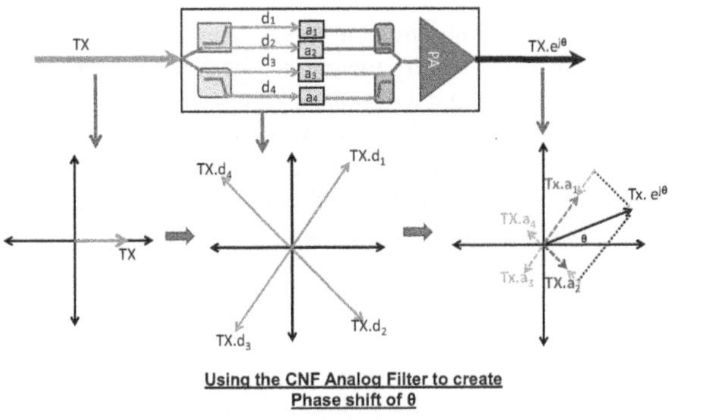


Figure 10: FF's constructive analog filter. The filter enables us to rotate the input signal TX by a fixed angle $\theta$ by appropriately adjusting the gains on the four taps of the analog filter. The four taps are placed 90 degrees apart, which at 2.45GHz implies that the tap delays are in increasing multiples of 100 picoseconds.

The delays are spaced 100 picoseconds apart (quarter wavelength of center frequency). To delay a signal by some intermediate value (between 0 to 400ps), the signal is split and passed through all the taps and the gains applied on each tap are adjusted such that the eventual signal has the right phase. Fig. 10 shows the basic idea with four delay lines separated by 100 ps and tunable gains on each line. The incoming signal is at 2.45GHz, hence the two copies of the signal after going through the filter have a relative phase shift of 90 degrees. Now, by adjusting the gain on each delay line, we can rotate the vector to any intermediate phase between 0 and 90 degrees. FF's constructive analog filter applies the same idea using 4 delay lines and spans the entire 360 degrees.

However the above discussion applies to only a single subcarrier, but the signals we are relaying are wider band and have multiple subcarriers. The challenge is that typically each subcarrier needs a different phase shift because channels are frequency selective. The analog filter applies the same delays to all subcarriers, so almost all of them will be rotated by the different phase shift and which wont lead to constructive filtering on all the subcarriers.

To tackle this challenge, we use a pre-filter that is implemented in the digital domain as seen in block diagram Fig. 3 (called as CNF Digital Filter). The intuition is that this pre-filter pre-rotates the phase in each subcarrier by different amounts such that after the analog rotation occurs, all the subcarrier phases are almost lined up for constructive relaying. Note that this rotation in digital is coarse on the order of a few nanoseconds and hence is much less complex to implement, the analog CNF filter is still responsible for the fine-grained rotation necessary for constructive filtering.

However the pre-filter is limited in the number of taps it can use because each tap adds delay (e.g. for a 80Msps sampling rate, each extra tap adds 12.5ns of delay). To build a reasonable low-delay spread filter, we therefore allow only a delay budget of 50ns which would imply a 4-tap filter at 80Msps. To compute the optimal values of the coefficients for this limited pre-filter, we solve the following optimization problem:

$$\min_{h_D(n),H_A(f_i)} \left| H_A(f_i).\left\{ \sum_{n=0}^{4} h_D(n)e^{j2\pi f_i n} \right\} - H_c(f_i) \right|^2$$

where, $H_A(f_i)$ is the response of the analog constructive filter, $h_D(n)$ represents the pre-filter as described above and $H_c(f_i)$ is the desired overall constructive filter response as computed in Sec. 3.2. The above problem is essentially trying to divide up the work of rotation for constructive filtering between the digital and analog CNF filter stages in an optimal manner so as to best approximate the desired constructive filtering response. We omit the details of how to solve this optimization problem for brevity, we use a standard convex optimization technique called sequential convex programming (SCP) to solve it [7].

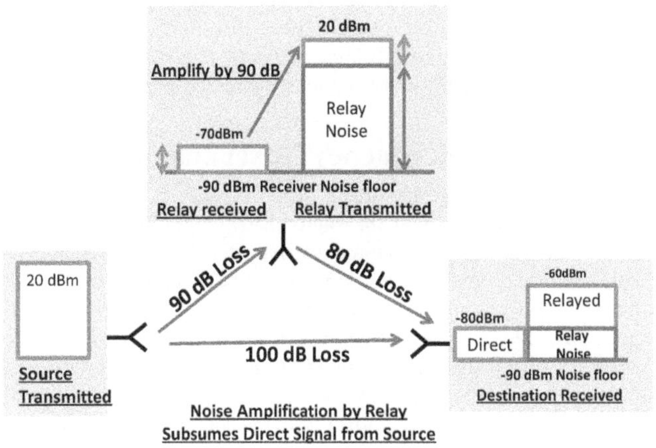


Figure 11: Naive amplification at relay can amplify and relay noise to the destination, which can subsume the direct signal from the source to the destination and negate the benefits of construct-and-forward relaying.

At this point the constructive filtering is complete. We incur a 50ns delay in the digital domain, and a negligible delay (3ns) in the analog constructive filter. Fig. 3 shows the overall block diagram.

## 3.5 Does the relay amplify noise?

A natural concern is whether the relay amplifies noise. For example, let's say the relay is receiving a signal at 20dB SNR. If the actual noise floor is -90dBm, the signal received is at -70dBm. Lets say it applies the 90dB amplification and transmits a 20dBm signal, in that 20dBm signal, noise is at 0dBm. If the path from the relay to the destination attenuates the signal by 80dB, then even at the receiver the noise from the relay is at -80dBm. This can overwhelm any signal directly received by the destination from the source if the SNR on that direct link is less than 10dB. So in effect the direct signal from the source is drowned out by the noise that is amplified by the relay. Fig. 11 shows how this visually.

Our key insight is that this can be prevented by smartly leveraging the relay's knowledge of the channels. The idea is to compute the amplification factor that ensures that the noise from the relay, by the time it is attenuated by the relay-destination channel, is well below the destination's noise floor. To accomplish this, let's say the attenuation applied by the channel from the relay to the destination is $a$ dB, the maximum amplification factor is given by $(a-3)$ dB (the 3dB is extra margin for safety). In other words amplification is dictated by how much the signal is attenuated from the relay to the destination, the higher the attenuation, the higher the amplification that can be applied. Remember however that amplification is limited at the top by the amount of cancellation achievable.

In the above example where the relay-destination channel attenuation is 80dB, if we use a maximum amplification of 77dB, the relay would transmit a 7dBm signal, and noise would be at -13dBm. This signal after being attenuated by the channel would be received at the destination at -73dBm and noise would be -93dBm. Since the destination's own noise floor is at -90dBm, higher than the noise received in the relayed signal, it doesn't hurt performance. Now the direct signal from the source is not washed out, and assuming constructive and forward filtering has been applied, it should add up to provide a SNR gain.

# 4. IMPLEMENTATION

A full design of FF has to grapple with several engineering challenges, we describe a few prominent ones below. Note that we defer the discussion of how the relay knows the identity of the source and destination of the packet it is relaying to Sec. 6, it needs this information to use the right CNF filter. For now, we assume that the FF relay knows the identities of the source and destination to simplify description.

## 4.1 Carrier Frequency Offset and other issues

As with any radio, inevitably there is a carrier frequency offset between the radios at the source and the destination. Relaying should not introduce another carrier offset into the relayed signal, this would break the assumption of it being another multi-path from the source and can confuse the receiver's CFO correction algorithms. Ideally to avoid confusion, the receiver should get the relayed signal also with the same CFO as the signal it is receiving from the source. So the relay should in fact try to relay the signal such that the original CFO offset from the source is preserved.

This would be easy to achieve if the relay itself did not need to process the signal. However for the relay's own processing and constructive filtering, the CFO w.r.t the source has to be removed. Hence the relay applies the following trick: It computes its CFO wrt to the source. When it receives a signal from the source, it first corrects for that CFO [23]. After that it performs its processing, including digital cancellation and constructive filtering. Before transmission however, it applies the reverse of the CFO correction it applied earlier. In effect it restores the CFO that existed in the signal from the source.

## 4.2 How does the relay know the channels for construct and forward relaying?

For construct and forward relaying, the relay needs to know the channel from the source to the destination which it cannot directly measure, as well as channels from the source to itself and from itself to the destination. The channel between itself and the source can be easily measured using received signals, and the channel from the destination to the relay can be measured by snooping on ACK packets and estimating the channel. However the direct channel between the source and destination cannot be measured by the relay, it needs to be explicitly informed of it.

**Direct Channel**: In cellular systems such as LTE, clients measure the channel from the basestation to themselves and feed it back explicitly to help with scheduling [6], our relay can snoop on this feedback and learn the channel. However WiFi has historically been passive, there is no explicit channel feedback from the receiver to the source. To obtain this information for WiFi at the relay, we use recent enhancements in the WiFi standards. Specifically 802.11n/ac implements an explicit channel sounding phase [25, 2, 3] where the AP sends a pre-defined packet which each client uses to measure their channels from the AP. The clients respond with the compressed channel state measurement later when polled by the AP. This is known as the Very High Throughput (VHT) beacon packet [2] in the 802.11ac standard. When FF relays are deployed, we make the corresponding AP send out the HT sounding packet every 50ms.

FF relays then take advantage of this mechanism to obtain the channel estimates from the source to each destination in the network. We make the FF relay spoof the AP and send a polling packet to all clients in the network periodically (every 50ms). The relay then listens to the replies from the clients which contain the channel estimates of the channel from the AP to themselves. Further the relay uses these packets to also measure the channel between the relay and each client in the network. The relay also keeps track of the channel between itself and the AP whenever it receives a packet from the AP.

Note that once the relay computes the constructive filter to use in the downlink direction for a particular AP-client pair, it can use the same filter in the uplink direction for the same client-AP pair. The reason is that by reciprocity the environment between the AP and the client is the same in the reverse direction. Further, the cumulative effect of the channel from the AP to the relay, the constructive filter and from the relay to the client is the same even if the order of channels and filter is permuted and multiplied in a different order by commutativity. Hence the same constructive filter can be used in both directions[1].

## 4.3 Hardware Prototype

We have built a prototype of the FF relay using the WARP software radio boards [8]. We build on prior full duplex radio implementations [10], but modify them appropriately to implement the relaying functionality. For all our experiments, we have built a MIMO full duplex $2 \times 2$ FF relay building on the self-interference cancellation design from [11, 10]. The prototype has 2 antennas and uses the MIMO analog cancellation design described in recent work [10]. The analog cancellation circuit has 8 taps that are spaced around 100-200ps apart as well as taps for canceling the cross-talk between MIMO antennas. Each tap has tunable digital step attenuators [11] which can be adjusted in increments of 0.25dB from 0 to 31.75dB. The couplers get a copy of the signal from the transmit side, and couple it back in to cancel it on the receive side as seen in Fig.8. The cancellation circuit is tuned from baseband after observing the residual using the algorithm described in Sec. 3.3.

The baseband implementation is relatively simple. We implement a 4 tap digital construct and forward filter, as well as implement digital cancellation using a 120 tap causal filter. Further CFO correction and re-distortion blocks are also located in baseband. The overall extra delay introduced by baseband process is less than 100ns in our prototype, of which nearly 50ns is from the digital CNF pre-filter and the rest are ADC and DAC delays, the digital cancellation itself doesn't introduce any delay because its causal. Finally, the signature technique identifying the source destination discussed in Sec. 6 is implemented which lets the relay know the source and the destination of the packet and allows the right constructive filter to use for relaying.

All of our experiments are run with a standard 20MHz OFDM PHY that is based on the WiFi PHY. The PHY uses 56 subcarriers and a 400ns cyclic prefix interval (this is the faster version of WiFi which uses a smaller CP). The numbers we report in our evaluation are all PHY layer throughputs and do not include MAC layer effects. Since the relay is operating at Layer 1, we are orthogonal to any MAC layer effects, so we expect the relative gains should carry over.

# 5. EVALUATION

We evaluate the performance of FF using experiments in an indoor setting. We place the AP and a FF relay in *various different indoor* settings, those are, open wide office space, L-shaped corridor and a wide room, two large wide room and including the one shown in the Fig. 1. The AP is a $2 \times 2$ MIMO AP, and the relay and the client are also equipped with two antennas can $2 \times 2$ MIMO. We were limited to 2-antenna devices primarily because of the availability of analog cancellation boards at the relay, we require four of them for implementing MIMO full duplex. We also require four RF analog construct-and-forward boards. However the qualitative conclusions from the experiments apply to any MIMO setup since the constructive filtering technique for improving SNR and MIMO

[1]Note that, the amplification applied is different in both direction, as the noise introduced at the relay receiver, is asymmetric in uplink and downlink directions.

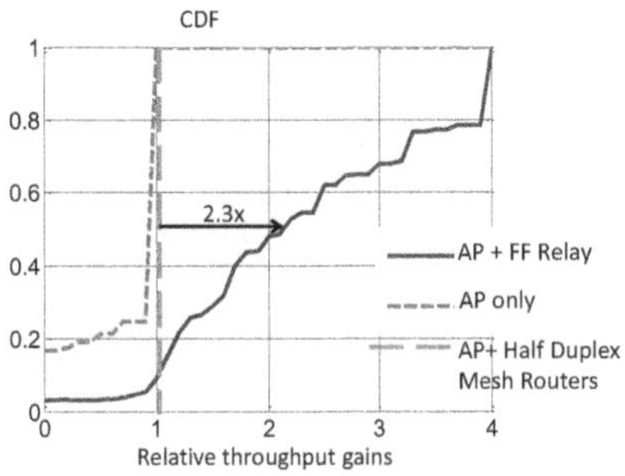


Figure 12: FF's overall throughput gains. FF provides a $3\times$ increase in median throughput, and nearly a $4\times$ gain in dead spot scenarios. Further, it significantly outperforms half duplex mesh routers, almost by a factor of $2.3\times$.

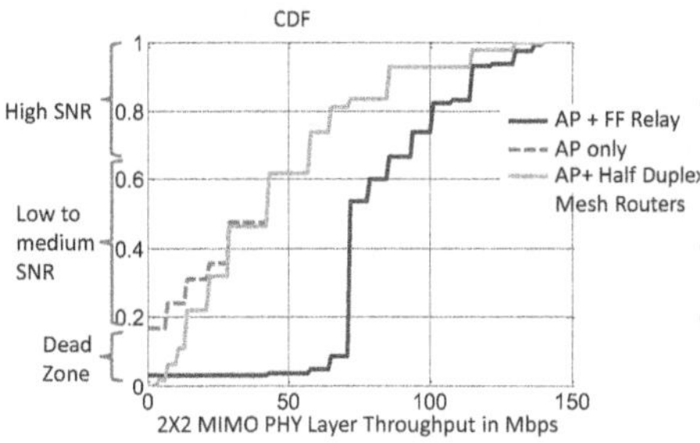


Figure 13: PHY Layer absolute throughputs achieved by different schemes. FF provides a significant throughput for nodes that were previously almost getting no connectivity or very low throughput.

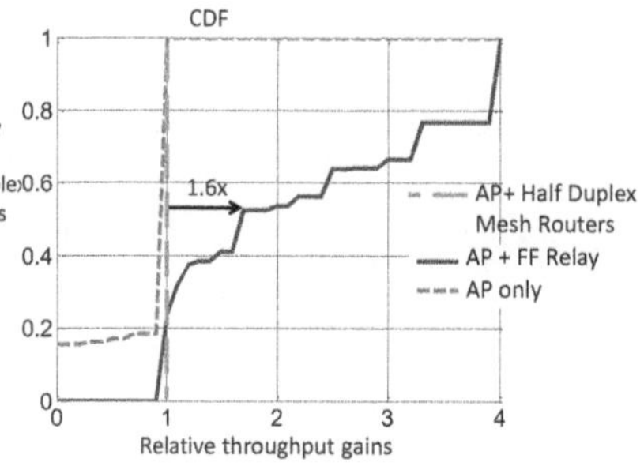


Figure 14: FF's throughput gains due to SNR amplification from construct-and-forward relaying for a SISO AP, FF relay and client. FF provides a median gain if $1.6\times$ even without the benefit of MIMO rank expansion.

rank is independent of the number of antennas. We assume relay knows the source and destination for every transmission.

We compare the following three approaches:

- **AP only**: In this approach we only assume that an AP is deployed without any relays.
- **AP + Half-Duplex Mesh Routers**: This is akin to the approach where we have an AP and a half duplex router such as the Apple Airport Express. To make sure the gains are reported correctly, we assume that the AP and the mesh router are perfectly synchronized and transmit in alternative time slots to eliminate any MAC layer contention effects. Hence the numbers reported are PHY layer throughputs assuming perfect MAC coordination. The half-duplex mesh router also has two antennas. Also, AP is smart enough to figure out when it should use the half-duplex router and when not to use it.
- **AP + FF Relay**: This is the design proposed in this paper. We place it at the same location as the half duplex mesh node. Here too we pick the optimal bitrate to use at the AP assuming the construct-and-forward relaying is in place.

The metric we use is PHY layer throughput which is defined as the optimal bitrate that can be used at any location given the SNR and the MIMO rank. Hence we eliminate any impact of bitrate adaptation algorithms, MAC layer artifacts etc and the experiments purely quantify the impact of relaying. Further to make relative comparisons across the compared approaches, we use a relative throughput gain metric where the baseline scenario is the AP and the half duplex mesh router case. We do not use the AP only scenario because we have dead spots in this scenario where the throughput is zero and we cannot compute relative gain. So all relative gain numbers are wrt to the throughput achieved by using the AP and half duplex mesh router.

Our experiments show that:

- FF provides a median throughput gain of $3\times$ in our experiments wrt to the AP only case. For the bottom 20th percentile of the locations, the throughput gain is as high as $4\times$.
- FF's gains from MIMO rank increase and SNR gains affect different nodes. For clients that had a decent SNR but low MIMO rank, the majority of the gains are from the addition of a separate independent MIMO path. For clients that are located in dead spots or with very low SNRs, the big gains are from the SNR gain.
- Construct-and-forward relaying has significant benefits, especially for clients with low SNRs. An amplify-and-forward relay without FF's constructive filtering capability performs worse, the median gain wrt to the AP only scenario drops to $1.5\times$.
- Low latency cancellation and constructive filtering are critical, without them relaying can actually hurt overall performance due to inter-symbol interference, in some cases the performance is worse than no relaying.

## 5.1 Overall Performance Gains

We begin with the basic question: how much does the FF relay help in improving throughput and coverage. We conduct the experiment as follows. We place clients at different locations in the testbed relative to the AP and relay placement as shown before. We measure the channels from the AP to the client and feed it to the relay. We also measure the channel between the AP to the relay and from the relay to the destination. These measurements are all made available to the relay and the measurements are repeated every 50ms. The relay uses these measurements to compute the construct-and-forward filter. We then conduct an experiment where the AP transmits directly to the client without any assistance from the relay. We then repeat this experiment assuming the relay is a half duplex mesh router, and then with the FF relay. We compute the relative throughput gain and plot the two CDFs in Fig. 12.

The FF relay provides a $3\times$ increase in median throughput over the AP alone, and a $2.3\times$ increase over half duplex relays. The reasons are as expected, the SNR gain we get from construct-and-forward relaying, as well as the increase in MIMO rank due to the additional independent path from the relay. Consequently the AP is able to use very high bitrates. Further at the edge of the coverage area where performance is typically poor, a FF relay improves performance by a factor of $4\times$. Compared to the half duplex router, the gains are primarily because a full duplex relay does not need an additional time slot to relay. The half duplex relay definitely helps in the edge of the coverage area, where the direct channel from the AP to the client is so poor, that it is better to take the extra hop with the half duplex mesh node.

A natural question is how much of the gains are coming from the SNR gain due to construct and forward, and how much are due to MIMO rank enhancement. We evaluate this question next.

## 5.2 Performance gain with SISO

We conduct this experiment by using a SISO WiFi AP, a SISO client and a SISO relay (both for the HD and the FF cases). The rest of the experiment is conducted the same way as above. We plot the CDFs of the relative throughput gains in Fig. 14. The gains in this experiment should be purely from the SNR gain from construct-

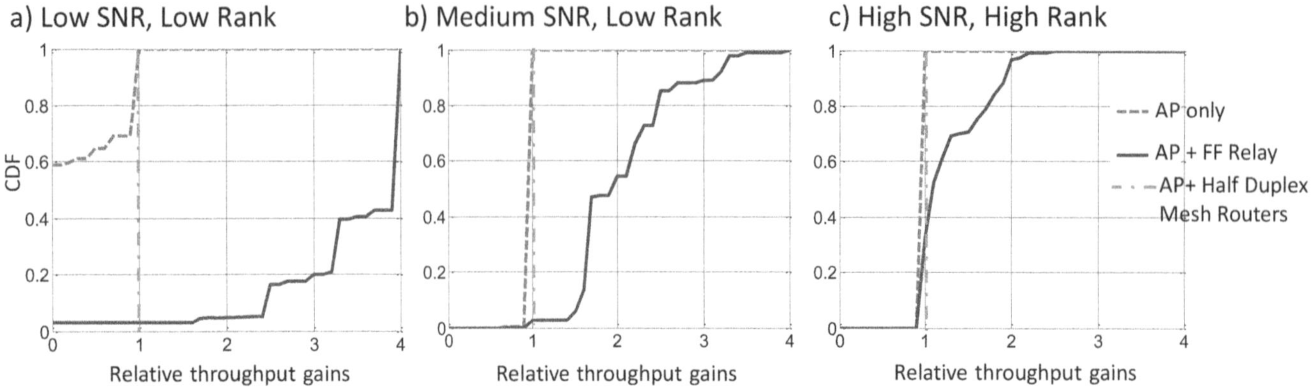


Figure 15: FF's performance gains in different scenarios. In low SNR and low MIMO rank scenario (figure a) the gains are significant because FF provides both a SNR gain as well as MIMO rank expansion, leading to a 4× increase in throughput. FF's performance gains in medium SNR and low MIMO rank scenarios (figure b) leads to a 1.7× increase in throughput. FF's gains in the scenarios where the clients already had high SNR and good MIMO rank (figure c) are minor as expected.

and-forward relaying since there is no MIMO. As we can see, the median gain is 1.6× and the gain at the tail is 4×. The experiment demonstrates the fact that in this case the clients at the edge of the coverage area benefit the most. This is expected, since without the AP these clients probably have an SNR in the range of 2-8dB. The relay significantly improves the SNR to about 15-20dB. This translates to allowing the AP to use a 64-256QAM modulation compared to BPSK or QAM before, leading to a $3 - 4\times$ increase in throughput. On the other hand clients that had medium to high SNR with the AP already don't benefit as much, the gains for them are marginal. The reason is that going from 64QAM to 256QAM doesn't help much, it only increases the bitrate by 33%. The intuitive reason is that the Shannon capacity curve is concave with SNR, there are diminishing returns in terms of capacity as SNR increases. For example, going from 64QAM to 256QAM requires a 6dB increase in SNR, but it only increases the bitrate by 33%.

## 5.3 Performance gains due to MIMO rank expansion

Next we turn to evaluating the impact of FF's ability to expand MIMO rank. We conduct the same experiment as in Sec. 5.1. However we divide the results into three classes according to how the MIMO channel matrix looked between the AP and the client without any relaying. The first category is when the SNR and the MIMO channel rank are both low, this corresponds to clients at the edge of the coverage area where both propagation losses and MIMO rank degradation are severe. The second category is when the SNR is medium to good, but the MIMO channel rank is low. This corresponds to clients which are suffering from the pinhole effect, they only have one strong path to the AP which reduces MIMO rank but the SNR is still decent. Finally, the last category is high SNR and full MIMO rank, this of course corresponds to clients which are close to the AP and enjoy strong, multiple independent links to the AP. Fig. 15 plots the CDFs of throughput gains in those categories.

Fig. 15.c shows that the benefits from FF for the last scenario (high rank, strong SNR) are small, only around 15%. This is as expected, since FF cant increase rank any more and benefits from SNR gains are small. For the second category Fig. 15.b, where there is good SNR but low rank due to pinholes, the benefits are substantial from using the FF relay. In effect these relays end up providing an additional strong MIMO path and increase the rank to full rank for MIMO, thus providing close to a 1.7× increase in throughput.

The last category shows the (Fig. 15.a) maximum gains, because the relays end up providing a rank of at least two between the AP and the client, as well as enhancing SNR. Given the low baseline these clients are starting from, the gains are therefore significant, showing a 4× increase in throughput.

## 5.4 Impact of Processing Latency

As we discussed earlier, processing latency at the FF relay has a significant impact. In this experiment we quantify the impact. We artificially introduce some buffering to vary the processing delay at the FF relay from 100ns to 400ns. We then repeat the same throughput experiments as before and plot the median throughput gain as a function of processing latency at the relay in Fig. 16. As we can see, the median throughput gains drop significantly and is in fact worse than having no relay when the processing latency exceeds 300ns. The reason is as expected, above a certain latency we hinder OFDM's ability to absorb highly delayed multipath reflections into the current symbol and avoid inter-symbol interference.

## 5.5 Impact of No Construct-and-Forward Relaying

In this experiment, we turn off construct-and-forward filtering at the relay and let it simply amplify the received signal to the maximum extent, i.e. as much as the amount of cancellation we obtain. The rest of the throughput experiment is the same as before. We plot the CDF in Fig. 17. As we can see, there are still significant gains at the tail. These correspond to client which were at the edge of the coverage area of the AP, and benefit significantly from the amplified relaying. However the median gain is small to non-existent. This is because for the clients that have medium to good SNRs, blind amplification ends up amplifying noise and washing out the direct signal from the AP to the client. Hence the gains are limited and in some cases are worse than before because of the enhanced noise.

## 5.6 Impact of Reduced Cancellation

We conduct an experiment where we vary the amount of cancellation at the relay. Remember that cancellation sets an upper limit on the amount of amplification that the relay could use. We plot the median throughput gain as a function of the amount of cancellation obtained in Fig. 18. As expected, with reduced cancellation, overall median throughput gains drop significantly. The reason is that at the edge of the coverage area, being able to use high amplification factors is crucial. A reduced amount of cancellation means the

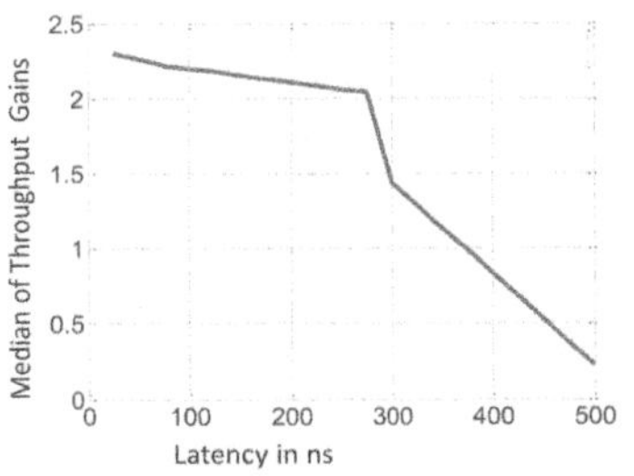


Figure 16: Relaying performance suffers as processing latency increases at the relay. Higher latency means that the relayed OFDM symbol falls outside the CP of the quickest arriving OFDM symbol at the destination, leading to inter-symbol interference and poor performance.

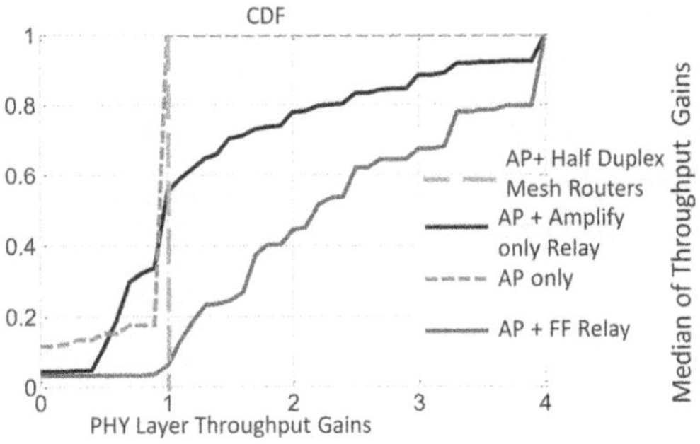


Figure 17: FF's construct-and-forward relaying is crucial for obtaining good performance. If we disable it and implement simple amplify-and-forward relaying, sometimes the performance is worse than no relaying because noise gets amplified.

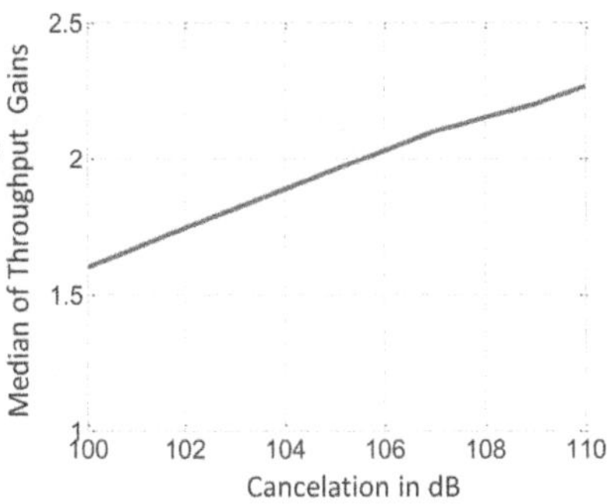


Figure 18: Reduced cancellation means reduced amplification, which leads to significantly reduced throughput gains for FF relays.

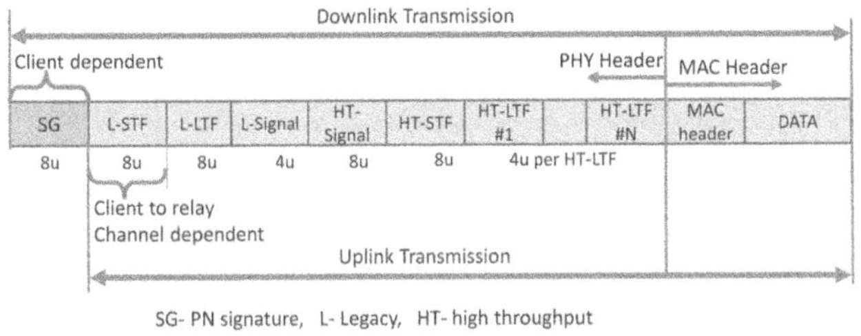


Figure 19: WiFi Header with the amendment on the downlink and for uplink we use standard WiFi header, but we use the STF to find the source of the uplink.

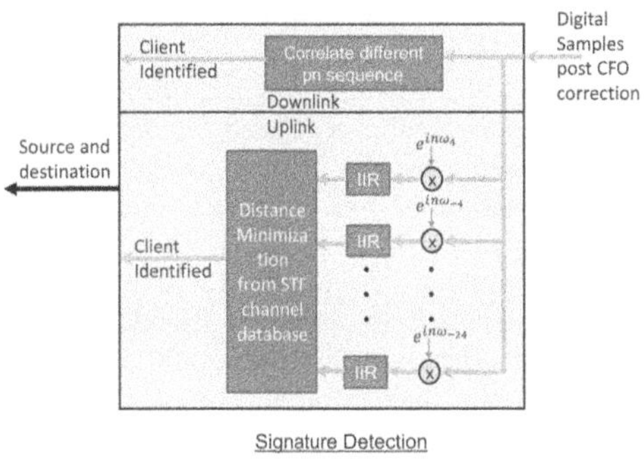


Figure 20: Signature Detection technique showing both uplink and Downlink. For Downlink we use correlation based client identifier. For uplink we extract the 10 subcarriers of STF (using the complex exponent and low latency IIR filters) to run distance minimizing on the database of client estimation, which is simply finding minimum distance vector with a phase compensation.

relay's amplification factor is reduced and consequently clients in dead spots see reduced throughput.

# 6. HOW CAN WE DEPLOY FF?

A final implementation question is how selective is the FF relay. Should it relay any packet it detects? Further, which construct and forward filter should it apply? If it did just an amplify and forward, the FF device might relay packets from a different network and AP (neighbor's WiFi for example) and cause destructive multi-path. Even within the network, if the channel between source and destination is strong, relaying may hurt performance by adding noise. Hence we make a conscious design decision that FF should only constructively relay the packets from its own network.

Further to achieve construct and forward filtering, the relay needs to learn the identities of the source and destination pair to apply the correct constructive filter. In the last section, relay knew the identity of source and destination to know whether to relay or not, and which filter to apply. In scheduled systems such as LTE, this information is known in advance to the AP and can be communicated to the relay explicitly, hence this isn't an issue in LTE. However systems such as WiFi are random access and at any point of time any of the clients or the AP could be transmitting.

One approach could be for the relay to just decode the MAC header (as seen in Fig. 19 )it is receiving, identify the source and destination and use that to then apply the right constructive filter. However this won't work in practice, because the MAC header is after the PHY header and channel estimation at the destination is performed using the PHY header. Hence the destination would use an incorrect channel estimate in decoding, if relay waits for MAC header to start construct and forward relaying. Therefore in WiFi, we need to find a mechanism for the relay to start applying the right constructive filter before the PHY header itself.

To do so, we make each AP explicitly prepend a pseudo-random sequence of length $4\mu s$, repeated twice, to each packet they transmit. A separate pseudo-random sequence is used for each associated client, and these sequences are learned by the relay on the fly, as AP transmits packets to these clients. The relay continuously looks for these sequences via simple correlation as seen in Fig. 20, and whenever it finds a match, picks up the right constructive filter and applies it to the rest of the packet. The pseudo-random sequence at the start of the packet does not affect the client since its decoding kicks in only after it recognizes the standard WiFi preamble. Fig. 19 shows the structure of the downlink packet.

The above technique clearly requires the APs to change, and we believe thats reasonable to expect since its relatively easier to upgrade them. However, we cannot use this technique at the clients, since it will be far harder to expect them all to be upgraded with this new feature. Therefore the above technique only works in the downlink. So, what could we do about the uplink?

We make a key observation here, unlike the downlink, on the uplink the identity of the destination is fixed, its the AP. All we need to do is identify the source, i.e. the transmitting client. To do so, we design a fingerprinting technique as seen in Fig. 20. The idea is that every WiFi packet has a short preamble at the start of the packet that is known in advance and when it is transmitted it undergoes a transformation governed by the channel between the client and the relay. Remember that the relay already knows the channel between every client in the network to itself, so it can try and match the received preamble to a set of pre-transformed preambles

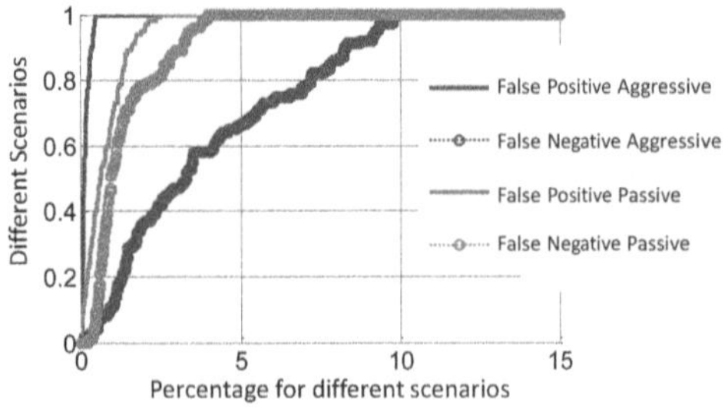


Figure 21: Performance of two channel fingerprinting technique, the aggressive one is more suitable.

corresponding to all the clients. This is once again similar to the pseudo-random sequence correlation idea used in the downlink, but in this case we are simply using the transformed standard preambles itself as the sequences to correlate against. Note that this technique does not require any changes to the clients.

This technique will have false positives , since the WiFi preamble even after transformations corresponding to different channels does not have the same differentiating properties as a set of carefully designed pseudo-random sequences. In Sec. 6.1 we evaluate the false negative and positive rates of this technique. A false negative is relatively harmless, since it just means that no constructive filtering will be applied and the situation will be no worse than a standard WiFi network. A false positive (defined as mistaking one client for another) could in some cases worsen the SNR by applying the wrong filter. Hence we tune our identification thresholds to have nearly a zero false positive rate at the expense of a higher false negative rate.

## 6.1 Sender Identity from Channel Fingerprints

We evaluate how well our correlation based technique to identify the identity of the sender in the uplink direction as described in Sec. 6 works in practice. We place 4 different client in 100 different locations in our testbed, and for each location calculate the accuracy of sender identification over a time period of five minutes and atleast 1000 packets per client. The extended time period allows us to also account for any channel fluctuations over time. Fig. 21 plots the CDF of false positive and negative rates. A false negative means that no sender is identified, whereas a false positive means that some other sender from the actual sender is identified. We see that the technique does have a 5% false negative rate, but essentially a zero false positive rate. The reason for the false negatives is the aggressive threshold applied for identification, sometimes legitimate senders are missed because of these stringent requirement. The conservative trade-off does ensure a zero false positive rate however and prevents the relay from doing any harm.

# 7. CONCLUSION

This paper demonstrated how we can design powerful yet simple relaying techniques that can greatly improve throughput and coverage, yet are minimally invasive and do not require sophisticated changes to clients. FF operates within the framework of the current network architecture and design, and we believe can be easily deployed.

**Acknowledgments**: We would like to thank Brad Karp, Manu Bansal, Rakesh Misra, Aaron Schulman and the Stanford Networked Systems Group members and anonymous reviewers for their insightful comments. This work was supported by a Thomas and Sarah Kailath Stanford Graduate Fellowship.

# 8. REFERENCES

[1] *LTE Advanced Speeds.* http://en.wikipedia.org/wiki/4G#LTE_Advanced.

[2] *802.11ac: The Fifth Generation of Wi-Fi.* http://www.cisco.com/en/US/prod/collateral/wireless/ps5678/ps11983/white_paper_c11-713103.pdf.

[3] *Meraki White Paper: 802.11n Technology.* https://meraki.cisco.com/lib/pdf/meraki_whitepaper_802_11n.pdf.

[4] *Modeling Indoor Propagation.* http://www.remcom.com/examples/modeling-indoor-propagation.html.

[5] *Next Generation Gigabit WiFi - 802.11ac.* http://www.netgear.com/landing/80211ac/images/wp_netgear_802_11ac_wifi.pdf.

[6] *Physical layer procedures(FDD).* http://www.qtc.jp/3GPP/Specs/25214-890.pdf.

[7] *Sequential Convex Programming.* http://www.stanford.edu/class/ee364b/lectures/seq_slides.pdf.

[8] *WARP Project.* http://warpproject.org.

[9] P. Almers, F. Tufvesson, and A. Molisch. Keyhole effect in mimo wireless channels: Measurements and theory. *Wireless Communications, IEEE Transactions on*, 5(12):3596–3604, December 2006.

[10] D. Bharadia and S. Katti. Full duplex mimo radios. In *11th USENIX Symposium on Networked Systems Design and Implementation (NSDI 14)*, pages 359–372, Seattle, WA, Apr. 2014. USENIX Association.

[11] D. Bharadia, E. McMilin, and S. Katti. Full duplex radios. *SIGCOMM '13: To appear in the Proceedings of the ACM SIGCOMM 2013 conference*, 2013.

[12] A. Carleial. Multiple-access channels with different generalized feedback signals. *Information Theory, IEEE Transactions on*, 28(6):841–850, Nov 1982.

[13] T. Cover and A. Gamal. Capacity theorems for the relay channel. *Information Theory, IEEE Transactions on*, 25(5):572–584, Sep 1979.

[14] M. Duarte, A. Sengupta, S. Brahma, C. Fragouli, and S. Diggavi. Quantize-map-forward (qmf) relaying: An experimental study. In *Proceedings of the Fourteenth ACM International Symposium on Mobile Ad Hoc Networking and Computing*, MobiHoc '13, pages 227–236, New York, NY, USA, 2013. ACM.

[15] A. Goldsmith. *Wireless Communications.* Cambridge University Press, New York, NY, USA, 2005.

[16] D. Gunduz, A. Goldsmith, and H. Poor. Mimo two-way relay channel: Diversity-multiplexing tradeoff analysis. In *Signals, Systems and Computers, 2008 42nd Asilomar Conference on*, pages 1474–1478, Oct 2008.

[17] V. V. Khang and N. D. Thong. Rank-deficiency in indoor mimo. In *TENCON 2007 - 2007 IEEE Region 10 Conference*, pages 1–4, Oct 2007.

[18] T. Laakso, V. Valimaki, M. Karjalainen, and U. Laine. Splitting the unit delay [fir/all pass filters design]. *Signal Processing Magazine, IEEE*, 13(1):30–60, Jan 1996.

[19] S.-H. Lee and S.-Y. Chung. When is compress-and-forward optimal? In *Information Theory and Applications Workshop (ITA), 2010*, pages 1–3, Jan 2010.

[20] A. Lo and P. Guan. Performance of in-band full-duplex amplify-and-forward and decode-and-forward relays with spatial diversity for next-generation wireless broadband. In *Information Networking (ICOIN), 2011 International Conference on*, pages 290–294, Jan 2011.

[21] P. Mededovic, M. Veletic, and Z. Blagojevic. Wireless insite software verification via analysis and comparison of simulation and measurement results. In *MIPRO, 2012 Proceedings of the 35th International Convention*, pages 776–781, May 2012.

[22] E. C. V. D. Meulen. Three-terminal communication channels. *Advances in Applied Probability*, 3(1):pp. 120–154, 1971.

[23] P. Murphy and A. Sabharwal. Design, implementation and characterization of a cooperative communications system. *CoRR*, abs/1102.0485, 2011.

[24] A. Ozgur and S. Diggavi. Approximately achieving gaussian relay network capacity with lattice codes. In *Information Theory Proceedings (ISIT), 2010 IEEE International Symposium on*, pages 669–673, June 2010.

[25] R. Porat, E. Ojard, N. Jindal, M. Fischer, and V. Erceg. Improved mu-mimo performance for future 802.11 systems using differential feedback. In *Information Theory and Applications Workshop (ITA), 2013*, pages 1–5, Feb 2013.

[26] B. Rankov and A. Wittneben. Achievable rate regions for the two-way relay channel. In *Information Theory, 2006 IEEE International Symposium on*, pages 1668–1672, July 2006.

[27] S. Simoens, O. Muñoz Medina, J. Vidal, and A. Del Coso. Compress-and-forward cooperative mimo relaying with full channel state information. *Trans. Sig. Proc.*, 58(2):781–791, Feb. 2010.

[28] V. VÃď limÃď ki and T. I. Laakso. Principles of fractional delay filters. In *PROCEEDINGS OF THE IEEE INTERNATIONAL CONFERENCE ON ACOUSTICS, SPEECH AND SIGNAL PROCESSING*, pages 5–9, 2000.

[29] M. Yuksel and E. Erkip. Diversity-multiplexing tradeoff in cooperative wireless systems. In *Information Sciences and Systems, 2006 40th Annual Conference on*, pages 1062–1067, March 2006.

[30] M. Yuksel and E. Erkip. Multiple-antenna cooperative wireless systems: A diversity x2013;multiplexing tradeoff perspective. *Information Theory, IEEE Transactions on*, 53(10):3371–3393, Oct 2007.

# LTE Radio Analytics Made Easy and Accessible

Swarun Kumar[†] Ezzeldin Hamed[†] Dina Katabi[†] Li Erran Li[⋆]
[†]Massachusetts Institute of Technology
{swarun, ezz, dk}@mit.edu
[⋆]Bell Labs, Alcatel-Lucent
erranlli@research.bell-labs.com

## ABSTRACT

Despite the rapid growth of next-generation cellular networks, researchers and end-users today have limited visibility into the performance and problems of these networks. As LTE deployments move towards femto and pico cells, even operators struggle to fully understand the propagation and interference patterns affecting their service, particularly indoors. This paper introduces LTEye, the first open platform to monitor and analyze LTE radio performance at a fine temporal and spatial granularity. LTEye accesses the LTE PHY layer without requiring private user information or provider support. It provides deep insights into the PHY-layer protocols deployed in these networks. LTEye's analytics enable researchers and policy makers to uncover serious deficiencies in these networks due to inefficient spectrum utilization and inter-cell interference. In addition, LTEye extends synthetic aperture radar (SAR), widely used for radar and backscatter signals, to operate over cellular signals. This enables businesses and end-users to localize mobile users and capture the distribution of LTE performance across spatial locations in their facility. As a result, they can diagnose problems and better plan deployment of repeaters or femto cells. We implement LTEye on USRP software radios, and present empirical insights and analytics from multiple AT&T and Verizon base stations in our locality.

**Categories and Subject Descriptors** C.2.2 [**Computer Systems Organization**]: Computer-Communications Networks

**Keywords** LTE; Cellular; Analytics; PHY; Wireless

## 1. INTRODUCTION

Cellular service has become an integral part of our life. Yet as users and researchers, we have little visibility into the performance and real problems of these networks. Even the little information we have is primarily from trace analysis sanctioned by mobile operators [15, 16]. The lack of open and transparent access into the operation and inefficiencies of the cellular physical layer limits our ability as researchers to contribute effectively to the development of these networks. It also limits the ability of policy makers to independently verify operators' claims of spectrum needs, and make informed decisions on licensed vs. unlicensed spectrum.


*SIGCOMM'14*, August 17–22, 2014, Chicago, IL, USA.

ACM 978-1-4503-2836-4/14/08
http://dx.doi.org/10.1145/2619239.2626320 ...$15.00.

The need for increased visibility into the cellular PHY-layer is further emphasized by three recent trends. First, cellular deployment is moving towards small, femto, and pico cells [26], many of which will be deployed by a user to cover her home or small business. As a result, cellular operators no longer have full control over their LTE deployments, and struggle to understand the propagation and interference patterns affecting their service, particularly in indoor settings. Open, cheap, and ubiquitous radio monitoring can help deal with the challenging propagation patterns introduced by small cells. Second, the rise of LTE-based M2M applications motivates a more open access to LTE signal-based analytics. For example, Walmart, Home Depot, or Disneyland may leverage LTE signals and recent RF-based localization techniques to track how clients navigate their space and obtain business analytics. Also, oil and gas companies that deploy LTE-supported seismic sensors [7] can leverage access to LTE radio propagation to better plan their sensor network and debug connectivity problems. Third, the FCC plans to repurpose certain bands (e.g., 3.5 GHz) for multi-tier spectrum sharing, including LTE small cell deployments [10]. Operating in a shared spectrum naturally fits with an open model for signal monitoring and analysis, where all the entities sharing the spectrum can better understand the problems and cooperate to find solutions.

All of these reasons motivate a more open access to the cellular PHY layer, particularly LTE. In this paper, we ask the following question: Can we access the cellular PHY-layer of today's LTE deployments, without support from mobile operators? Specifically, can we do this without requiring access to private user data or encrypted LTE channels? If such a service exists, it could enable better deployment of femto cells and repeaters, more businesses built over LTE networks, better informed spectrum policies, more efficient sharing of newly released bands, and an overall rise in transparency in an industry that is a major part of the world economy.

We introduce LTEye, an open platform for monitoring and analyzing the LTE PHY layer. LTEye is a passive sniffer that runs on off-the-shelf software radios (e.g. USRPs). It does not require provider support, and hence can serve end users, researchers, policy makers, or mobile broadband providers. LTEye extracts per-user analytics purely from the LTE control channels that contain meta-deta on uplink and downlink transmissions, without accessing private data or system parameters from encrypted data channels. Specifically, it tracks individual users based on their temporal PHY-layer IDs, without requiring or exposing their private information. It then intelligently links these IDs across control messages to generate transmission records for each user. Each record reports the transmission's resource utilization, modulation and coding rate, and frame loss rate. LTEye also records the wireless channel it perceives from base stations and mobile users within radio range. These channels are used to accurately monitor the 3-dimensional physical location of the users. LTEye maintains these records in a database called LTEyeDB. It processes the records to generate two dimensions of fine-grained analytics: temporal analytics, to track LTE performance over time, and spatial analytics, to characterize LTE service across spatial locations.

We implemented LTEye on USRP software radios [8]. We deployed LTEye in four locations in our campus to compare the temporal performance of two major LTE providers: AT&T and Verizon. Our results revealed several inefficiencies in these networks. First, both providers deploy a Frequency Division Duplexing scheme, which uses independent equally sized frequency bands for uplink and downlink traffic. However, LTEye reported that for both providers, the average utilization of downlink resources (25.2% - AT&T, 58.2% - Verizon) far exceeded that of uplink resources (0.6% - AT&T, 2.6% - Verizon). While it is expected that the downlink is higher in demand, our results reveal that the LTE uplink is a remarkable 20 to 40 times less utilized than the downlink. LTEye's analytics can therefore help policy makers encourage operators to adopt revised LTE standards that allow more prudent allocation of resources to the uplink and downlink[1], without relying on data from providers themselves to make the case.

Second, LTEye localized certain spots in our campus, where Verizon cellphones suffer poor link quality and often switch to 3G, despite reporting high signal power from the LTE base station. To investigate this, we moved our LTEye sniffers to these spots and found that they experienced high inter-cell interference (about 27 dB) from as many as five different base stations. To make matters worse, many of these base stations used overlapping channel estimation pilots, significantly impacting the decodability of these transmissions. These results help end-users identify poor placement of femto cells that cause such interference. Further, they benefit cellular providers themselves because they reveal interference problems that end-users face in indoors, hitherto inaccessible to providers. Interestingly, some of these PHY-layer inefficiencies may be unknown even to the operators as they are part of the PHY-layer implementations adopted by the base station vendors.[2]

LTEye also benefits researchers by providing deep insights into the PHY-layer protocols deployed by cellular providers. While the LTE standard spells out much of the PHY layer, the choice of rate adaptation algorithm is still left to individual operators. To gain insights into this algorithm, we analyzed LTEyeDB records of an AT&T base station in our locality. We found that even for static users with completely coherent channels and stable SNRs, the modulation and coding scheme changes significantly even between adjacent transmissions. More interestingly, the average modulation and coding of frames sent to a user changes, based not only on her wireless channels, but also on the network state as a whole. Specifically, if the network is scarcely utilized, the base station transmits to the user conservatively at low modulation on average, even if the wireless link is stable and supports much higher modulation. In contrast, as network utilization increases, under identical SNRs, the base station steadily increases its modulation to support more aggressive data rates to the user. Such analytics on the performance and design choices of today's cellular operators help researchers design better LTE protocols.

LTEye enables businesses and network administrators to continuously monitor the spatial locations of mobile users, and build a geographic heatmap of LTE coverage and performance within their facility. However, accurately localizing mobile users purely based on their LTE signals is a challenging task. This is because past work on accurate indoor localization proposes two classes of solutions that are ill-suited to LTE networks: First, localization using antenna arrays [30, 18] requires large bulky arrays, owing to the relatively low frequencies of LTE signals. Second, recent localization techniques using synthetic aperture radar (SAR) are less bulky, but are limited to signals transmitted and received by the same node (e.g. radar [12] or RFID backscatter [29] systems) and therefore do not apply to LTE signals. LTEye provides the best of both these solutions by extending SAR localization techniques to operate over communication signals as opposed to backscatter or radar signals. It also introduces a novel technique to handle errors due to multipath by identifying the shortest (or most direct) path.

Our evaluation of LTEye's spatial analytics in large indoor environments reveals a median accuracy in 3D localization of mobile users of 61 cm in line-of-sight and 85 cm in non-line-of-sight settings. Further, we visualize the LTE performance of the mobile users across locations, helping building managers find optimal locations for relays or femtocells.

**Contributions:** This paper contributes the following:

- The paper presents LTEye, the first open platform to monitor and analyze per-user LTE PHY performance at fine temporal and spatial granularity.
- LTEye employs a new technique to identify and track individual users at the LTE PHY layer in a robust manner, without help from operators, and without requiring or exposing private user information.
- LTEye develops an innovative technique for accurate localization of users based on their LTE signals. This involves extending synthetic aperture radar (SAR) to operate over communication signals as opposed to backscatter and radar signals, and a novel technique for identifying the shortest and most direct path in the presence of multipath.
- LTEye's evaluation on AT&T and Verizon LTE deployments reveal deep insights on the inefficiencies, utilization patterns, and differences between these providers. LTEye also provides heat maps to characterize LTE performance across indoor locations, without GPS support.

## 2. RELATED WORK

**(a) LTE Sniffing Equipment:** Devices such as Wavejudge, ThinkRF and IntelliJudge [25, 28] are wireless protocol sniffers to capture RF signals. They are mainly tools for wireless development and interoperability testing that provide visibility into the interaction between the PHY and protocol layers. Unlike LTEye, these devices need inputs from the cellular provider and do not perform localization or provide spatial analytics.

**(b) Open LTE Implementations:** There have been efforts in developing open source implementations of LTE protocols, notably OpenAirInterface [9], and OSLD [13]. These initiatives enable running LTE base stations on software radios; they do not extract spatial or temporal analytics.

**(c) LTE Measurement Studies:** Many recent LTE studies have been conducted using traces collected on participating smartphones or from inside LTE networks. Findings from these studies include: (1) The available bandwidth of LTE networks is highly variable and TCP is not able to fully utilize the bandwidth [16]; (2) LTE is significantly less power efficient than Wi-Fi [15]; (3) LTE latency is more consistent (less variable) than Wi-Fi [27]. Such studies focus on the higher layers of the stack, e.g., TCP throughput, transfer delay, and power usage. In contrast, LTEye focuses on the LTE radio layer; it provides fine-grained temporal and spatial information and does not require traces from the provider.

[1]E.g. Asymmetric Carrier Aggregation [19] in LTE Advanced (3GPP Release 10) allows downlink resources to exceed the uplink.
[2]We confirmed this privately with some base station vendors.

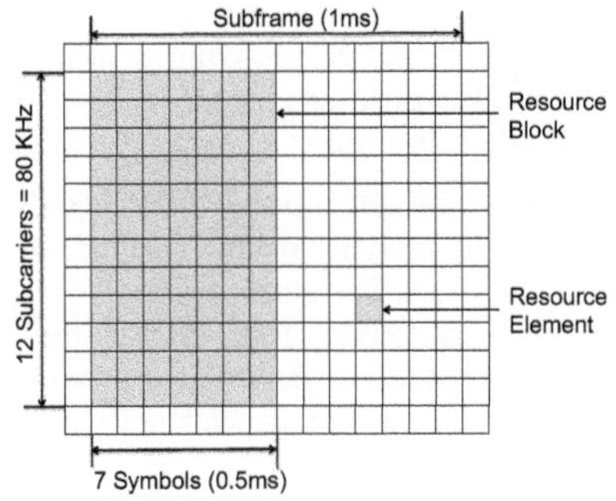


Figure 1: The Resource Grid is divided into multiple Resource Blocks.

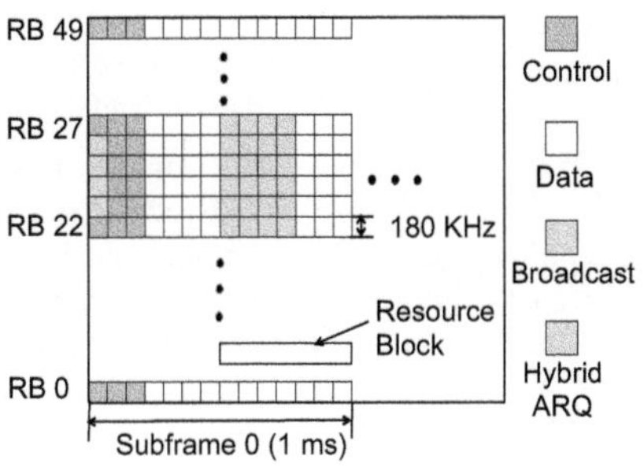


Figure 2: Physical Channels are mapped to well defined Resource Elements in the Grid.

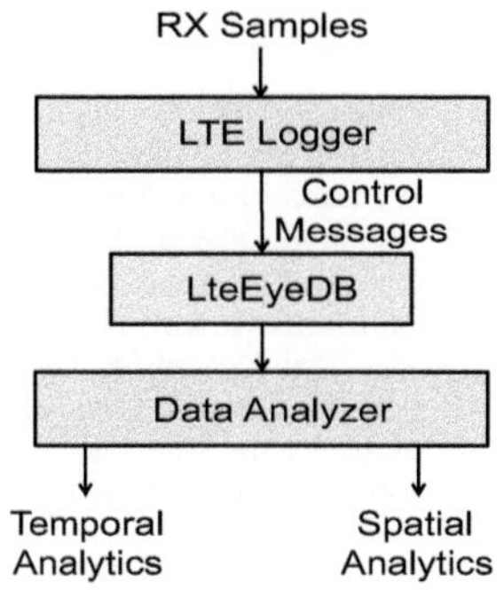


Figure 3: **LTEye's Architecture**: Contains the LTE Logger and Data Analyzer.

**(d) Cellular Location-Specific RF Measurements:** Cellular operators need location-specific RF measurements to troubleshoot performance problems and plan future deployments. They typically obtain coarse location information by mapping a user to her serving cell. Operators then rely on drive tests to refine the spatial measurements. Drive tests are costly and constitute a big part of the network operating expenditure [17]. Further, they are increasingly inadequate as operators move toward femto cells, and need indoor coverage data. To reduce the cost and improve the spatial measurements, recent LTE releases propose mechanisms known as MDT [2]. MDT techniques localize a mobile phone either using in-network time measurement or by collecting location information using the phone's GPS. It is well-known however that in-network localization in cellular networks is not accurate (at hundreds of meters [22]) as time-delay measurements are only available for the serving cell of a mobile user. Even the E911 service using positioning reference signals can only guarantee 150m accuracy 95% of the time [21]. GPS measurements cannot be invoked often as they drain the user's battery. They also cannot capture indoor location.

**(e) RF-based Localization Techniques:** Our work is related to past work on RF-based localization. This problem has received much recent interest resulting in highly accurate systems. ArrayTrack [30] and PinPoint [18] are an antenna-array based indoor location systems that tracks wireless clients at fine granularity. Chen et. al.[14] build antenna arrays using software radios synchronized with a reference signal. PinIt [29] is an RFID localization system that combines SAR with a deployment of reference RFIDs to achieve highly accurate localization.

Our design builds on this past work but differs in that it introduces two innovative localization techniques. First, we extend SAR to operate over communication signals exchanged between a transmitter and a receiver. This contrasts with the current approach for SAR, which is limited to backscatter and radar signals, where the transmitter and receiver are a single node with no Carrier Frequency Offset (CFO) or Sampling Frequency offset (SFO). Second, we introduce a new technique that when combined with SAR or standard antenna arrays, estimates the delay difference between the various paths traversed by the signal to identify the shortest path. In particular, we measure these delays in time based on phase offsets in the frequency domain. Hence, LTEye can resolve differences in delay below one time sample, unlike past work that estimates these delays via correlation in time [18].

## 3. LTE PRIMER

In this section, we briefly introduce LTE concepts relevant to this paper. LTE networks are divided into multiple geographical regions called cells. Each cell contains a cellular base station that serves multiple mobile users. We focus on Frequency Division Duplexing, the mode of LTE most widely used by cellular operators. This LTE mode uses different dedicated carrier frequency bands for uplink and downlink transmissions. Hence, each base station uses a pair of frequency bands to communicate with users in its cell.

**(a) Radio Resources.** LTE's uplink and downlink transmissions are based on OFDM. While medium access and resource sharing is largely distributed in typical OFDM-based systems such as Wi-Fi, LTE centralizes much of resource allocation at the base station. Specifically, base stations divide radio resources into multiple frames over time, each containing ten subframes, spanning 1 ms each. Resources in each sub-frame are divided both along time and frequency as a 2-D time-frequency grid, as in Fig. 1. Each cell in the grid, called a resource element corresponds to one OFDM subcarrier (15 KHz) over the duration of one OFDM symbol (66.7 $\mu$s).

The key task of an LTE base station is to allot both uplink and downlink resources between different users along both time and frequency. It allocates resources to users at the granularity of *resource blocks*, each spanning 0.5 ms (i.e., half a sub-frame) by 180 kHz (i.e., 12 sub-carriers). To combat frequency-selective fading, the assignment of resource blocks to users both on the uplink and downlink is not fixed, but hops from transmission to transmission.

**(b) Physical Layer Channels.** As LTE centralizes PHY-layer control, base stations need to transmit both data and control information to the users. To this end, LTE partitions network resources into well defined channels, each responsible for different types of information. These channels are mapped to well-known resource elements of the grid, as shown in Fig. 2.

Broadly, LTE base stations use four main channels on the downlink: (1) A data channel to send users their downlink data. (2) A control channel to allocate network resources. (3) A broadcast channel for new users to learn system parameters. (4) A hybrid-ARQ channel to send ACKs to the users. Similarly, the mobile users on the uplink are allocated data and control channels to transmit their uplink data and control messages. Table 1 describes these channels in greater detail.

We point out here that the downlink control channel bears rich information on the LTE PHY-layer. Specifically, it contains multiple *downlink control information messages* in which the base station allocates resource blocks to specific users for every transmission on either the uplink or downlink. In addition, the control information also specifies the modulation and coding to be used in these blocks. Upon hearing a control message, a user accesses the relevant data channel to send (receive) her uplink (downlink) transmission.

**(c) PHY User Identifier.** The LTE PHY refers to each mobile user using a temporary unique ID called the Cell Radio Network Temporary Identifier (C-RNTI). The C-RNTI reveals no private information about the user. It is local to the users's serving cell, and

| Downlink LTE Channels | |
|---|---|
| *Name* | *Description* |
| PBCH | Physical Broadcast Channel: Carries general information about the cell, like number of antennas on the base station and total bandwidth. |
| PDCCH | Physical Downlink Control Channel: Sends downlink control messages, e.g. for resource allocation on uplink/downlink. |
| PDSCH | Physical Downlink Shared Channel: Holds downlink data meant for users in resource blocks indicated by the PDCCH. |
| PHICH | Physical Hybrid-ARQ Channel: Contains positive or negative acknowledgments for uplink data. |
| **Uplink LTE Channels** | |
| PUCCH | Physical Uplink Control Channel: Holds control information from users to base stations, e.g. ACKs, channel reports and uplink scheduling requests. |
| PUSCH | Physical Uplink Shared Channel: Mainly carries uplink data in resource blocks indicated by the PDCCH. |

Table 1: **LTE Channels.** Details the name and function of PHY-layer channels, as defined in LTE standards [3].

is assigned when she enters the cell via a higher-layer connection establishment procedure[4].

A user continues to have the same C-RNTI as long as she is in the same cell and is not idle for more than the pre-configured tail timer value. The timer value is typically a few seconds to tens of seconds (12 sec in the measurement result of [15]). Hence, the C-RNTI assigned to a user may change quite often if it transmits sporadically.

## 4. LTEYE

LTEye is an open platform to analyze LTE radio performance. Its design aims to satisfy the following key attributes:

- *Provider-Independent:* LTEye does not require any information or support from mobile providers. Thus, LTEye allows end-users, policy makers and third parties to make a fair assessment and comparison of the service quality of different providers, without relying on information furnished by the providers themselves.
- *Off-the-Shelf:* LTEye must be built on low-end off-the-shelf components, such as standard laptops and software radios. This makes LTEye more accessible to end-users and easy to be deployed in large numbers.

### 4.1 System Architecture

LTEye operates as a passive 2-antenna MIMO receiver. LTEye's architecture is a pipeline of two components: (1) the LTE Logger, and (2) the Data Analyzer. (see Fig. 3)

**(a) LTE Logger:** The LTE Logger sniffs on the LTE control channels to generate transmission records. The logger begins by listening to the broadcast channel to gather system parameters. It then sniffs the downlink control channel and performs LTE decoding, i.e., it demodulates the OFDM symbols, applies de-interleaving, descrambling and convolutional decoding to extract the actual bits of the downlink control messages.

The logger reads each of these control messages to populate LTEyeDB, a database of LTE information records tagged with their transmission time. Each transmission record consists of several fields retrieved from the control messages, as listed in Table 2. Many of these fields help characterize network performance and utilization, both for the user over time, and for the network as a whole, if viewed in aggregate. In addition, notice two important fields in the records: (1) Each record is indexed by the user's C-RNTI (i.e. her PHY-layer user ID), which are key to link multiple records belonging to the same user. (2) Records maintain the uplink channels seen by the LTEye sniffer over time. In §6, we show how these channels are essential to localize users.

**(b) Data Analyzer:** The data analyzer processes the records in LTEyeDB to extract fine-grained analytics on both cellular base-stations and individual mobile users. It extracts two types of analytics: temporal analytics which describe LTE PHY metrics as functions of time (e.g., the per-user resource allocation over time), and spatial analytics which describe position-dependent RF metrics (e.g., the user location and the observed multipath effects). Sections §5 and §6 discuss both types of analytics in detail.

## 5. ENABLING TEMPORAL LTE ANALYTICS

In this section, we describe some of the challenges in obtaining temporal analytics, without access to private user information or system parameters in encrypted data channels.

**Uniquely Identifying Users:** To extract per-user temporal analytics, LTEye needs to uniquely identify each user (i.e mobile device) served by the base station. We do not know the phone numbers of users, but can instead use the series of C-RNTIs (i.e. PHY-layer user IDs) assigned to them. One option is to require LTEye to sniff the LTE channel continuously for an extended time to catch each user at the time she joins the cell and capture her C-RNTI assignment. Unfortunately this option has two limitations: First, the C-RNTI assignment is often transmitted from higher layers in the encrypted downlink data channel [4]. Second, low-end off-the-shelf equipment is unlikely to be able to continuously monitor and decode the LTE channel in real-time [6]. Instead, LTEye sniffers should be able to periodically sniff the channel and obtain representative snapshots of the system. Hence, we need LTEye to uniquely identify all users, including those who joined the cell even when LTEye is not sniffing (i.e., LTEye did not hear their C-RNTI assignment).

To address this problem, we observe that a user's C-RNTI is used to scramble her control information on the downlink control channel. Specifically, recall from §3 that the control channel transmitted by the base station consists of multiple downlink control information messages, for different users. At the end of each message is a 16-bit sequence, which is the XOR of the checksum of the control message with the user's C-RNTI. Traditionally, a user de-scrambles this sequence by her C-RNTI to retrieve the checksum and validate correctness of the control information. In contrast, LTEye performs the *opposite* operation to retrieve the C-RNTI: It decodes each control message in the log including their corresponding scrambled checksums. For each of these packets, LTEye reconstructs the expected checksum and XORs them with the scrambled checksum to recover the C-RNTI. Of course, it is important to verify if the control messages and C-RNTIs that are decoded are actually correct. To do this, LTEye convolutionally re-encodes the retrieved control information message and compares it against the original coded control message to obtain the number of bit errors. It then discards control messages and C-RNTIs that report bit errors beyond a few bits.[3] Hence, our solution enables LTEye to map a C-RNTI to a user even if it was assigned when LTEye is not sniffing the channel.

**Tracking User IDs:** LTEye's second challenge is to map C-RNTIs between logs. Recall from §3 that a user's C-RNTI may be reassigned if she is idle beyond a few seconds. Further, the same C-RNTI can map to multiple users over time. Hence, while the C-RNTI is a natural PHY-layer user ID, LTEye must recognize when a user's C-RNTI changes to find the list of C-RNTIs mapped to her.

[3] In our experiments, LTEye correctly retrieved 99.5% of C-RNTIs across locations.

| Field | Description | Format |
|---|---|---|
| Time | Transmission Time | 32-bit timestamp |
| C-RNTI | PHY-layer ID | 16-bit Sequence |
| UL/DL | Uplink or Downlink | 0/1 |
| nrb | Number of Resource Blocks | 0 to $N_{RB}$ |
| alloc | Bit-Map of Resource Blocks | $N_{RB}$ bits |
| MCS | Modulation and Coding Scheme | 5 bits |
| isAcked | Acknowledgment | $\pm1$ (ACK/NACK) |
| UE-channel | Channel from user (if U/L) | $N_{sc}N_{rx}$ Complex Floats |
| BS-channel | Channel from Base Station | $N_{sc}N_{tx}N_{rx}$ Complex Floats |
| SNR, SINR | SNR and SINR of Base Station | Floating Point |

Table 2: **Fields of LTEyeDB.** Where $N_{RB}$: Number of resource blocks, $N_{tx}$: Number of base-station antennas, $N_{rx}$: Number of sniffer antennas, $N_{sc}$: Number of OFDM sub-carriers.

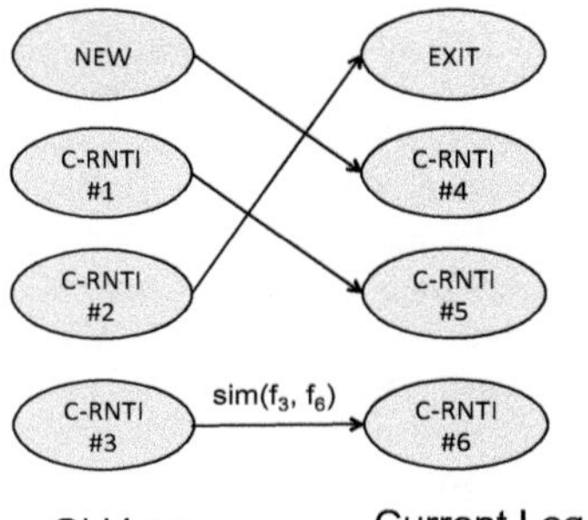


Figure 4: **Mapping C-RNTI.** Mapping C-RNTI from old logs to the current log.

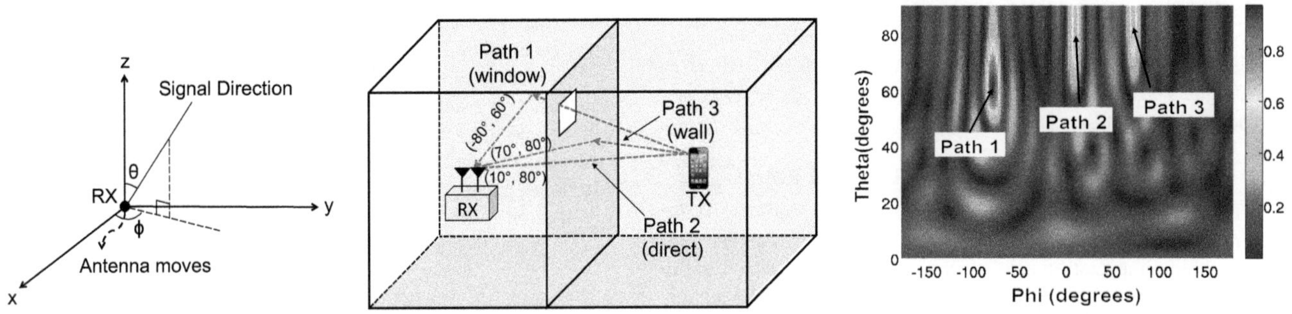


(a) Signal Direction Notation (b) Multipath (Layout) (c) Multipath Profile

Figure 5: (a) Definition of $(\phi, \theta)$ in 3-D space. (b) Depicts an example layout of a transmitter and receiver in two rooms separated by a wall. The signal has three main paths: Path 1 is the strongest, and reflects from the ceiling through a window. Path 2 is the direct path penetrating a wall. Path 3 is the weakest reflecting at the farthest wall. The figure labels $(\phi, \theta)$ for each path. (c) Simulated multipath profile for (b) has peaks for each path at expected $(\phi, \theta)$. The height of the peaks (in shades of red) corresponds to the relative power of the corresponding paths.

LTEye addresses this challenge by formulating it as a matching problem. The goal of this problem is to map C-RNTIs in the current (most recent) log produced by the LTE logger with the C-RNTIs in prior logs as shown in the bi-partite graph in Fig. 4. In addition, the graph has two additional nodes: EXIT and NEW, which account for C-RNTIs in the old log that have "exit" the system, and C-RNTIs in the current log that are "new" to the cell, respectively. The weights in this graph must capture the similarity between the users associated with each pair of C-RNTIs. Specifically, we associate with each C-RNTI #$i$ an RF fingerprint $f_i$ that includes metrics such as the user's location (extracted by our localization method described in §6), its SNR and multi-path characteristics. We can then assign a weight to each edge $(i,j)$ in the graph by the similarity metric between these fingerprints $sim(f_i,f_j)$. In §6.3, we design effective RF fingerprints and similarity metrics based on spatial analytics.

Given the graph and weights, we can now solve this matching problem using the standard Hungarian Algorithm[20].[4] The resulting matching either maps a C-RNTI to a user in a prior log, or identifies her as a new user.

**Extracting System Parameters:** LTEye needs to *reverse-engineer* several PHY parameters, otherwise available to users via encrypted data channels. For e.g., the LTE standard allows several possible formats for downlink control information, each spanning multiple lengths [5]. Exhaustively searching for each of the possible format-length pairs in all downlink control messages is highly expensive. Fortunately, operational LTE base stations use only a small subset of these formats for all users (only three possible formats for AT&T and Verizon). As a result, LTEye learns the possible list of formats and lengths using the first few control messages to greatly reduce the search-space of formats for subsequent control information.

[4]We modify the algorithm to allow multiple C-RNTIs to map to NEW/EXIT simply by replicating these nodes. Edges at NEW/EXIT are weighted by a minimum threshold similarity.

## 6. ENABLING SPATIAL LTE ANALYTICS

The core of LTEye's spatial analytics is the ability to localize an LTE source. To this end, LTEye performs the following functions:

- *Extracts the multipath profile of an LTE signal:* First, LTEye extracts the multipath profile of a signal, which measures the power received along each spatial angle, i.e., along each signal path. Fig. 5(c) is an example multipath profile, where the signal traverses three paths causing three local maxima in the graph.
- *Identifies the direct path from the source:* Once LTEye has the multipath profile, it is natural to try to identify which path is in direct line of sight to the source (e.g., path 2 in Fig. 5(b)). Finding the direct path is an important step in localizing the source. Note that in some cases the direct path may be completely blocked and absent from the multipath profile. Our objective is to identify the direct path provided it exists in the multipath profile.
- *Localizes the source of the LTE signal:* Once LTEye finds the direct path to the source, it can localize the source to within a specific spatial direction. We can then deploy multiple LTEye sniffers to locate the source at the intersection of the direct paths as seen from these sniffers.

Past work on RF-based localization takes two approaches to build multipath profiles: The first approach, shown for Wi-Fi, uses an antenna array to steer its beam spatially and identify the power along each spatial direction [30]. However, LTE runs at much lower frequencies than Wi-Fi (700 MHz as opposed to 2.4 GHz), and hence an LTE antenna array will be 4 to 5 times more bulky than a comparable Wi-Fi array. The second approach uses synthetic aperture radar (SAR) [29], which uses a single movable antenna to emulate a virtual array of many antennas. As the antenna moves, it traces the locations of antenna elements in a virtual array.

SAR has traditionally been used in radar and RFID localization as it assumes backscatter signals where the transmitter and receiver are the same node and therefore have no carrier frequency offset (CFO) relative to each other. Hence, changes in the channel as the antenna moves are a function only of the antenna's location. In contrast, LTE signals are exchanged between an independent transmitter and receiver, with non-zero CFO. As the antenna moves, the channel changes both due to CFO and antenna movement. One option is to estimate and correct the CFO. Unfortunately this solution is fragile since any residual error in CFO estimation accumulates over the duration of movement and causes large localization errors. In the following section, we explain how we perform SAR over LTE signals without CFO estimation to realize the three functions in the beginning of this section.

### 6.1 SAR over LTE Signals Using Channel Ratios

LTEye operates as a 2-antenna MIMO receiver, with one static antenna and another movable antenna. The movable antenna may be mounted on a rotating arm attached to the device, which is the approach taken in our implementation (see Fig. 6(a)). The advantage of this approach is that it provides the 3-D spatial direction (i.e. both the azimuthal angle $\phi$ and polar angle $\theta$) of the various signal paths as shown in Fig. 5(a). Alternatively, the antenna may slide back and forth on an arm fixed to the body of the device.

LTEye uses its MIMO capability to perform SAR over communication signals, but without frequency offset estimation. Our key idea is that instead of applying the SAR equations to the wireless channel of the moving antenna [12], we apply SAR equations to the *ratio* between the channel of the moving antenna to that of the static antenna. Taking the ratio of the two channels eliminates any effect of frequency offset since both MIMO antennas experience the same offset relative to the sender. However, since the ratio is between two antennas, one moving and the other static, it preserves how antenna displacement changes the channel of the moving antenna. This allows SAR to safely retrieve the multipath profile of the signal from the ratio, modulo frequency offsets.

Next, we mathematically show the validity of the above technique. Suppose that the receiver, placed at the origin, wants to measure the power of the signal $P(\theta,\phi)$ received from an independent transmitter along a spatial direction specified by the polar angle $\theta$ and azimuthal angle $\phi$ (see Fig. 5(a)). According to the SAR formulation, this quantity can be measured as: [11, 23]:

$$P(\theta,\phi) = |h(\theta,\phi)|^2, \text{ where } h(\theta,\phi) = \sum_t a_f(t,\theta,\phi)h(t) \quad (1)$$

Here, $h(t)$ is the wireless channel to the moving antenna at time $t$, assuming zero frequency offset between the transmitter and receiver. The quantity $a_f(t,\theta,\phi)$ captures the relative motion of the transmitter and receiver, and is independent of the wireless channels. For e.g., if the antenna moves along a straight line (i.e., linear SAR) $a_f(t,\theta,\phi)$ is defined as: $a_f(t,\theta,\phi) = e^{-j\frac{2\pi f}{c}x(t)cos(\phi)}$, where $x(t)$ is the antenna location at time $t$, and $f$ is the frequency of the signal [29]. Similarly, if the antenna rotates with radius $r$ (i.e., circular SAR) $a_f(t,\theta,\phi) = e^{-j\frac{2\pi f}{c}rcos(\phi-\phi_0(t))}$, where $\phi_0(t)$ is the angular position of the antenna at time $t$ (see Fig. 6(b)).

Past work on SAR require both transmitters and receivers to share a common reference clock. For e.g., SAR devices on airplanes or satellites both transmit signals and receive their reflections to image the topography of the ground[12]. Consequently, the measured channel $\tilde{h}(t)$ at the moving antenna is independent of frequency offset, i.e., $\tilde{h}(t) = h(t)$.

Unfortunately, when performing SAR between *independent* transmitters and receivers, the measured wireless channel $\tilde{h}(t)$ varies both due to position and due to carrier and sampling frequency offset between the transmitter and receiver, as well as any phase noise. In particular, we denote:

$$\tilde{h}(t) = h(t)e^{j\psi(t)} \quad (2)$$

Where $\psi(t)$ denotes the phase accumulated due to any carrier frequency offset, sampling frequency offset or phase noise between the reference clocks of the transmitter and receiver until time $t$. Thus, the key challenge to measure the power of the signal along any spatial direction, $P(\theta,\phi)$, as in the SAR Eqn. 1, is to eliminate this accumulated phase.

To resolve this challenge, LTEye is built on receivers that have at least two antennas: a static antenna, and a mobile antenna that moves along a known path. Let $\tilde{h}_1(t)$ and $\tilde{h}_2(t)$ denote the measured wireless channels from a given transmit antenna to a mobile and static antennas respectively (see Fig. 6(c)). As both antennas are connected to the same reference clock, they both accumulate the same phase $\psi(t)$ until time $t$. Hence, from Eqn. 2, we have:

$$\tilde{h}_1(t) = h_1(t)e^{j\psi(t)}, \qquad \tilde{h}_2(t) = h_2(t)e^{j\psi(t)} \quad (3)$$

where $h_2(t) \approx h_2$ is relatively constant over a short duration since antenna-2 is static. Hence, the ratio of the wireless channels is: $\tilde{h}_r(t) = \frac{\tilde{h}_1(t)}{\tilde{h}_2(t)} = \frac{1}{h_2}h_1(t)$ ; that is, the channel ratio is a constant multiple of the moving antenna channel without the phase accumulation from frequency offset or phase noise. Thus, we can perform SAR as in Eqn. 1 by substituting the channel ratio $\tilde{h}_r(t)$ for the value of $h(t)$. Hence, LTEye allows a wireless receiver to perform SAR over LTE signals without frequency offset or phase noise estimation.
Finally, we make a few important observations:

- The above approach readily extends to OFDM / OFDMA. Specifically, let $h(\theta,\phi) = \sum_f \sum_t a_f(t,\theta,\phi)h_{r,f}(t)/h_{r,f}(0)$ in Eqn. 1, where the quantity $\tilde{h}_{r,f}(t)$ on subcarrier $f$ of the OFDM signal is the ratio of the frequency (Fourier) Domain channels $\tilde{h}_1(t)$ and $\tilde{h}_2(t)$ measured on that subcarrier.[5]
- Our solution is resilient to movement of the transmitter that can be neglected relative to the movement of the rotating antenna. LTEye's rotation speed is chosen to deal with typical dynamism in indoor settings, e.g. walking speeds. However, one can easily detect and exclude fast moving transmitters by checking if the channel of the static antenna $\tilde{h}_2(t)$ is coherent over a rotation of the moving antenna, using the coherence metric in §8.3.
- While this paper applies our solution to LTE, our technique can be extended to apply to Wi-Fi and other such technologies.

### 6.2 Identifying the Direct Signal Path

In this section, we describe how LTEye separates the direct path from the reflected paths in a multipath profile reported by SAR so as to localize the transmitter. Intuitively, the direct path is the shortest path among all paths traversed by the signal (even if the direct path is completely blocked, the shortest path is the path closest to the direct path). Thus, one may identify the direct path (or the path closest to the direct path) by measuring the delay difference between the various paths in the multipath profile of the signal.

Directly measuring time delays (e.g. by correlating with known pilot signals), however is not sufficiently accurate. Specifically,

[5]Note that this is robust to frequency hopping by LTE users.

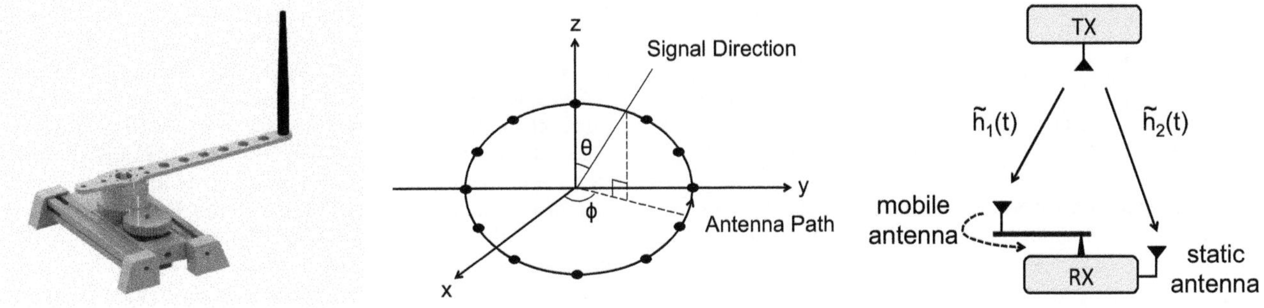


(a) LTEye Sniffer Prototype (b) Circular SAR (c) Channel Notation

Figure 6: (a) Prototype of the rotating antenna on a LTEye sniffer. (b) Circular Synthetic Aperture Radar (c) Depicts $\tilde{h}_1(t)$ and $\tilde{h}_2(t)$, the measured wireless channels from a transmit antenna to the mobile and static antennas respectively

LTE receivers have a channel bandwidth of 10 MHz. However, electromagnetic waves travel at the speed of light. Hence an error of even one time sample for a 10 MHz sampling rate (i.e., each time sample spans $0.1\mu s$) translates to an error in path lengths of 30 m.

Below we explain how LTEye can measure *sub-sample delay differences* between the signal paths. The key idea is to exploit that delay in time translates into phase rotation in the frequency domain. Since LTE signals use OFDM, a time delay of the signal translates into phase rotation in the OFDM subcarriers. Yet, different OFDM subcarrier rotate at different speeds – i.e., higher OFDM frequencies rotate faster than lower frequencies. In fact, the phase rotation of a particular OFDM subcarrier $f_i$ as a result of a delay $\tau$ is $\psi_i = 2\pi f_i \tau$. Thus, for each subcarrier, the difference in delay between two paths, $p$ and $q$, for a particular subcarrier is:

$$\tau = \frac{\psi_{p,i} - \psi_{q,i}}{2\pi f_i} \tag{4}$$

One may also average across subcarriers to improve robustness to noise. Multiple sub-carriers can also resolve ambiguity if $|\psi_{p,i} - \psi_{q,i}| > 2\pi$ by correcting discontinuities in $\psi_{p,i} - \psi_{q,i}$ across frequencies. Thus, to identify the shortest path in a multipath profile, LTEye does the following:

- First, it computes the phase of the channel for each subcarrier for each path separately. This can be done using the fact that the SAR formulation defines $h(\theta, \phi)$, which provides not just the power, but also the phase of the channel component along each spatial direction (see Eqn. 1). Hence, we can simply measure the phase of this path as $\psi = arg[h(\theta, \phi)]$, for each OFDM subcarrier.
- Second, it computes the delay difference between each pair of paths using the Eqn. 4 above. It then identifies the shortest path as the one with least delay.

Once the direct path is found, the source is localized along this path. Complete localization can be performed using multiple LTEye receivers and intersecting their direct paths. If the direct paths do not intersect, the best estimate is the point minimizing total distance (or equivalently, delay) to all LTEye receivers. This point can be found using a simple geometric optimization omitted for brevity.

Next, we show how the multipath profile reported by SAR allows us to compute unique RF fingerprints for the users.

### 6.3 Measuring RF Fingerprints with Multipath Profiles

As described in §5, LTEye tracks the different C-RNTIs (PHY-layer user IDs) assigned to mobile users between logs. To this end, LTEye employs RF fingerprints [31, 29] to map C-RNTIs between logs. LTEye defines a user's fingerprint as the set of observed multipath profiles at each LTEye sniffer (See §6.1). The key advantage of this fingerprint is that it captures the user's location, multipath, and SNR, as perceived from LTEye sniffers. To measure similarity of two fingerprints, we employ dynamic time warping (DTW[24]), a technique that has recently been applied to capture similarity of two multipath profiles[29]. Given any two multipath profiles, DTW returns a cost function that varies inversely with their similarity. Hence, LTEye defines the similarity metric between two RF fingerprints as the inverse of the total DTW cost function[29] between each pair of profiles in the fingerprints.

One might wonder if LTEye's fingerprint matching algorithm scales, given that a cell may serve a large number of users. Fortunately, while LTE cells can serve hundreds of users, we observed that only a small fraction of these users (about 4%) are re-assigned C-RNTIs between two logs.[6] Further, while capturing C-RNTI re-assignments is essential to track individual users over time, it does not alter aggregate radio analytics in a statistically significant way, given that 96% of users in a cell retain their C-RNTI between logs.

## 7. IMPLEMENTATION

We implemented LTEye on USRP N210 software radios[8] and WBX daughter-boards. The USRPs receive in the 700MHz frequency range at a bandwidth of 10 MHz on uplink and downlink channels corresponding to either AT&T (734-744MHz) or Verizon (746-756MHz). We implement an OFDMA receiver for LTE signals that interfaces directly with the USRP Hardware driver (UHD).

To obtain temporal analytics, we decode the downlink control channel in a pipeline of two modules: The first module in C++ performs synchronization, channel estimation and QPSK demodulation. It logs the demodulated soft bits received over one second into a file, and repeats this process every three seconds. The second module in MEX (C++) and Matlab reads the file and performs descrambling, de-interleaving and convolutional decoding. It validates the downlink control information messages by only admitting those passing the convolutional decoder with very high confidence, as described in §5. It then processes the control messages to get per-user LTEyeDB records for uplink and downlink traffic, as in §4.1.

To obtain spatial analytics, we build prototype LTEye sniffers, each containing two USRPs connected to an external clock. We mount the antenna of one of the USRPs on a light-weight rotating arm fabricated by a 3D printer, with an adjustable radius of 15-30 inches, as shown in Fig. 6. The arm is driven by an off-the-shelf stepper motor rotate at 30-120 rotations per minute.[7] We use an Arduino UNO board to rotate the stepper motor accurately at a constant speed and provide real-time feedback on the position

[6] This is on average 1-2 users for AT&T and 3-4 users for Verizon.
[7] We plan to support higher torque in future iterations of the device.

| Metric | AT&T | | Verizon | |
|---|---|---|---|---|
| | Mean | Std-dev | Mean | Std-dev |
| Number of Users | 23.37 | 7.90 | 87.66 | 44.75 |
| % Downlink Utilization | 25.20 | 17.35 | 58.18 | 20.58 |
| % Uplink Utilization | 0.59 | 0.47 | 2.60 | 1.06 |
| Downlink MCS (bits/RE) | 4.56 | 0.26 | 5.23 | 0.30 |
| Uplink MCS (bits/RE) | 3.25 | 0.22 | 3.61 | 0.18 |

Table 3: **Aggregate Statistics**. Tabulates mean and standard deviation of statistics over four locations for AT&T and Verizon.

of the rotating antenna. We implement a C++ module to use these positions and channel measurements, as in §6, to localize the users.

We evaluate LTEye's spatial analytics using five LTEye sniffers in multiple indoor testbeds, in both line-of-sight and non-line-of-sight settings. We employ ten Samsung Galaxy Note LTE smart phones as users. Unless specified otherwise, each user communicates over LTE with a mix of varying traffic patterns including browsing activity, file transfer, Skype calls, and video streaming.

# 8. RESULTS ON RADIO ANALYTICS

In this section, we perform an extensive evaluation of LTEye's temporal and spatial analytics:

- We compare temporal analytics of two LTE providers and highlight their PHY-layer inefficiencies in §8.1 and §8.2.
- We provide insights on the LTE rate adaptation algorithm in §8.3.
- We apply LTEye's spatial analytics to two applications: detecting cheaters in an exam hall in §8.4 and visualizing a spatial heatmap of LTE performance in §8.5.
- We perform micro-benchmarks to evaluate the accuracy of LTEye's localization and RF fingerprints in §8.6 and §8.7.

## 8.1 Comparing Temporal Analytics of Providers

End-users can deploy LTEye sniffers to compare the providers in their locality in terms of usage patterns, quality of service and congestion. In this experiment, we compare aggregate temporal analytics of two providers in our campus: AT&T and Verizon.

**Setup.** We place LTEye sniffer in four locations in the MIT campus, each listening to the AT&T and Verizon base stations that serve that location. We populate LTEyeDB over the duration of a representative weekday from 9:00am to 9:00pm. To reduce processing overhead, LTEye's logger collects traces for a duration of one second, every three seconds. It validates these traces by only accepting control information with low bit error rate as reported by the convolutional decoder. We then measure the following metrics for each one-second trace: (1) Number of Active Users; (2) Mean Utilization of the Uplink and Downlink; (3) Mean Link Quality measured as the number of bits per resource element (bits/RE) in the uplink and downlink. We average each of these quantities over one minute intervals and plot them over time of day at a representative location (Fig. 7). We also estimate the mean value of these metrics across locations over one week to infer aggregate trends (Table 3).

**Number of Active Users.** Fig. 7(a) measures the number of active mobile users in a representative AT&T and Verizon cell over different times of the day. We observe that for both providers, the number of users in the morning increases steadily, and peaks at around 12:00 pm, after which the number begins to decrease. The increase in activity at around noon may be attributed to a greater number of subscribers who access LTE outdoors as they leave for lunch. Across locations, we observe that Verizon has a greater number of active users on average at 87.7, while AT&T has 23.4 active users through the day (see Table 3).

**Network Utilization.** Fig. 7(b) plots the utilization of a representative AT&T and Verizon cell, over different times of the day. Specifically, we measure the percentage of resource elements used by uplink and downlink traffic. Two trends emerge: First, both providers often achieve high downlink utilization (over 80%) through the day. AT&T achieves such high utilization sporadically through the day (for 2% of the day), while Verizon is heavily utilized for a more significant fraction of the day (for 18% of the day). Second, the utilization of the uplink is significantly lower than the utilization of the downlink, both for AT&T and Verizon.

Specifically, the mean downlink utilization (25.2% - AT&T, 58.2% - Verizon), far exceeds uplink utilization (0.6% - AT&T, 2.6% - Verizon) even when averaged across locations. While it is expected that the downlink is higher in demand, our results reveal that the LTE uplink is an unprecedented 20 to 40 times less utilized than the downlink. This exposes the practical limits of Frequency Division Duplexing mode of the LTE standard used by both AT&T and Verizon, which provides independent equally sized uplink and downlink frequency bands. Hence, our results can help policy makers encourage operators to adopt revised LTE Advanced standards that permit unequal allocation of resources to the uplink and downlink (e.g., via asymmetric carrier aggregation[19]) without relying on data from providers themselves to make the case.

**Link Quality.** Fig. 7(c) measures the average quality of channels in the network for a representative AT&T And Verizon cell measured over different times of the day. In particular, we measure the mean number of bits transmitted per resource element (bits/RE), capturing the modulation and coding scheme (MCS) on the uplink and downlink. Our results show that the mean quality on the downlink (5.2 - Verizon, 4.6 - AT&T) exceeds that of the uplink (3.6 - Verizon, 3.3 - AT&T). As mentioned earlier, this is because users are limited in transmit power and number of MIMO antennas, when compared to the base station. Further, the mean link quality of Verizon is marginally higher when compared to AT&T.

## 8.2 Identifying PHY-Layer Problems and Inefficiency

Cellular Providers and independent researchers can use LTEye to diagnose problems and inefficiencies at the LTE-PHY layer. In this experiment, we identify such deficiencies by analyzing the LTEyeDB database populated for both AT&T and Verizon. In particular, we consider the traces gathered over four locations in our campus served by different base stations over one week, as explained in §8.1. Interestingly, many of these PHY-layer inefficiencies may be unknown even to the operators as they are part of the PHY-layer implementations adopted by the base station vendors.[8]

**Unnecessary Control Overhead.** As explained in §3, the LTE resource grid on the downlink is divided into three main PHY-layer channels: the broadcast channel, the control channel and the data channel. The control channel occupies the first 1-3 symbols of each LTE sub-frame resulting in a control overhead ranging from 7% to 21% of all downlink resources. Ideally, an LTE base station should adapt the number of control symbols used in each sub-frame depending on the amount of control traffic that is required to be sent.

In practice, we discovered that the control overhead of AT&T base-stations was 10%, while that of Verizon base-stations was 21%. This is because, unlike AT&T, Verizon always uses three control symbols in each sub-frame, regardless of the amount of control traffic they contain. One might wonder if this is because Verizon's control channels are significantly more utilized, warranting the additional overhead. Fig. 8(a) plots the control overhead of both AT&T and Verizon, as well as how much of this overhead is

[8]We confirmed this privately with some base station vendors.

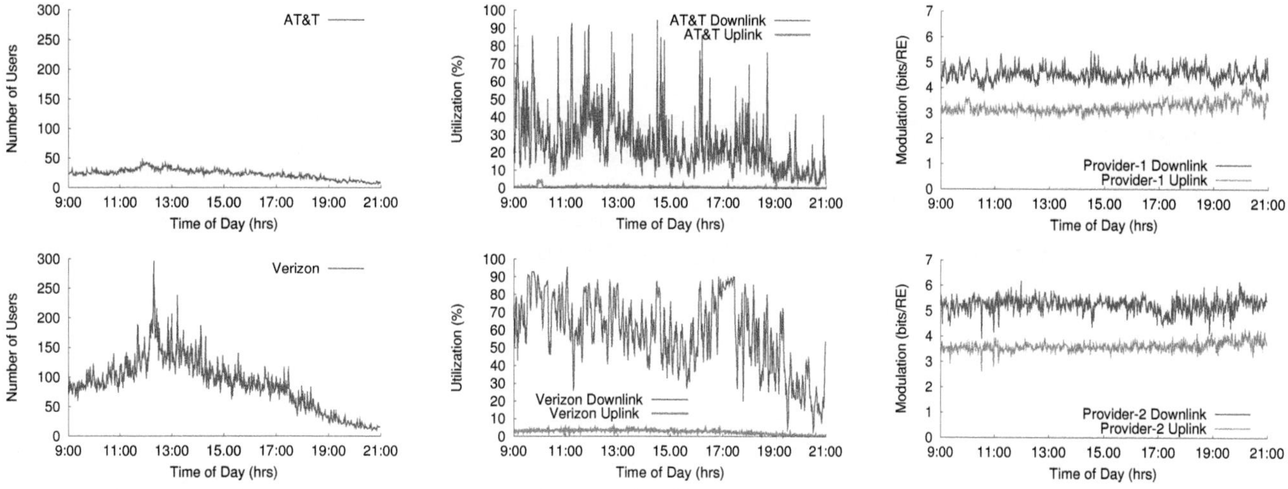


(a) Number of Users (b) Network Utilization (c) Link Quality

Figure 7: The plots show the following metrics for AT&T (above) and Verizon (below), measured every minute over a typical working day from a representative base station: (a) Number of Active Users per second; (b) Percentage of Utilized Resource Elements on the Uplink (red) and Downlink (blue); (c) Mean Number of Bits per Resource Element on the Uplink (red) and Downlink (blue).

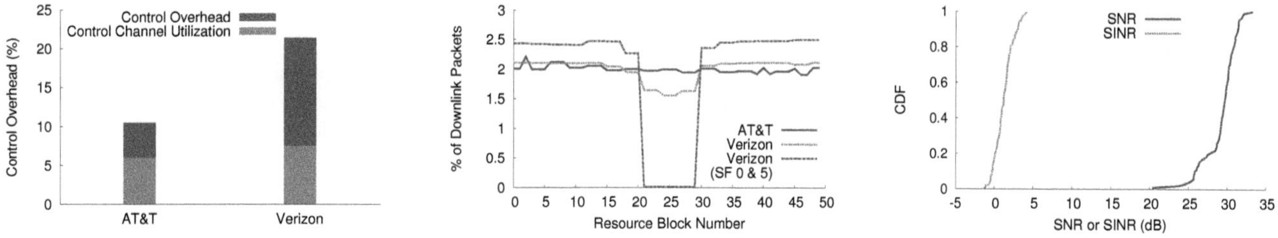


(a) Unnecessary Control Overhead (b) Inefficient Resource Allocation (c) Inter-Cell Interference

Figure 8: **PHY-Layer Inefficiencies**: (a) Measures the utilization of the control channel for AT&T and Verizon, across different number of symbols allotted to the control channel. (b) Plots the percentage of data allotted to different downlink resource blocks for AT&T and Verizon. (c) CDF of measured Signal-to-Noise Ratio (SNR) and Signal to Interference Plus Noise Ratio (SINR) at spots of high inter-cell interference.

utilized. Clearly, the overhead of Verizon is significantly larger, despite having only a marginally higher control traffic (7.5%) than AT&T (6.1%). As a result, we estimate that Verizon can gain as much as 10% of additional downlink resources for data, just by adapting its control overhead to control-traffic demand.

**Inefficient Resource Allocation.** In this experiment, we analyze the downlink resource allocation mechanism of LTE base-stations during periods of high network utilization (over 80%). Fig. 8(b) plots the percentage of downlink data transmitted in each resource block across users, measured for both AT&T and Verizon. For AT&T, the graph remains flat across resource blocks, indicating that on average, a user is equally likely to get any of the downlink resource blocks. For Verizon however, we observe a peculiar dip around resource blocks 22-27. To investigate this, we noticed that Verizon avoids these resource blocks completely on subframes 0 and 5. This is because a few symbols in these resource blocks are dedicated for the broadcast channel. As a result, Verizon avoids allocating these resource blocks completely, leading the remaining symbols in these resource blocks to lie completely unused, even during peak hours of demand.

**Inter-Cell Interference.** One of the key benefits of LTEye is to provide insight into why users obtain poor performance. During the course of our experiments, LTEye localized users at certain spots that achieved poor link quality on the downlink (the lowest QPSK rate), but high quality on the uplink. To investigate this, we moved our LTEye sniffers and testbed mobile phones to these locations. Surprisingly, our phones at these spots reported very high RSSI[9] from the base station, yet often switched to 3G. We then used our LTEye sniffers at these spots to measure the signal-to-noise ratio (SNR) as well as the signal-to-interference plus noise ratio (SINR) on the downlink. Fig. 8(c) reports the CDF of these quantities across these locations. The figure demonstrates that these locations suffer from significant interference, with a mean SINR of 1.3 dB and a minimum of -1.2 dB, despite a high mean SNR of 29 dB. We realized the source of about 27 dB of interference is from neighboring Verizon base stations sharing same downlink spectrum. Specifically, our sniffer could sense as many as five distinct base station cell IDs at a single location. This is problematic as it affects pilot reference signals (known as cell-specific reference signals) that are critical for channel estimation. Base stations transmit these pilots in one of three different subsets of resource elements depending on their cell ID.[10] Given that five base stations are observed at a given location, some of these pilots will inevitably collide, significantly impacting the decodability of signals from those base-

[9]The phone reported a receive signal strength (RSSI) of around -85 to -95 dBm, where the noise floor is at -120 dBm.

[10]For 2-antenna base stations, reference signals on both antennas occupy one of three subsets of REs, based on cell ID modulo 3 [3].

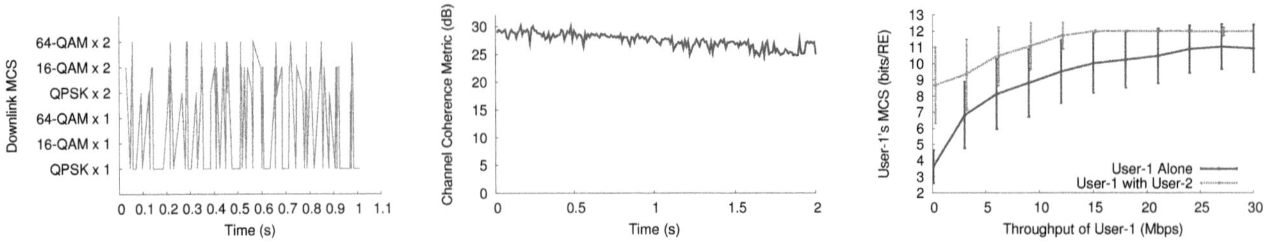


(a) Downlink MCS (b) Channel Coherence (c) MCS vs. Demand

Figure 9: **Insights into Rate Adaptation**: (a) Trace of Downlink MCS for a user over time; (b) Channel Coherence metric of a USRP placed at the user's location over time; (c) Mean downlink MCS (bits/resource element) across demand, with and without another high-demand user.

stations. Hence, these observations emphasize the need for effective placement and power control of base stations and small cells. They further highlight the importance of careful assignment of cell IDs to neighboring cells, to avoid interference between their pilots.

## 8.3 Insights into LTE Rate Adaptation

While the LTE standard describes much of the PHY-layer protocol and procedures, the rate adaptation algorithm is still left to the choice of individual operators. In this section, we show how LTEye can shed light on some interesting aspects of this algorithm for an AT&T base-station in our locality.

We consider a single user device that downloads a random bitfile over a 1 Mbps TCP link from a server (we control TCP rate by throttling the bandwidth at the server using tc[1]). We conduct our experiment during periods of low network utilization, where the mobile device in our testbed is the sole active user of the network. The user device is placed at a static high SNR location, which should support the highest modulation and coding on the downlink.

Fig. 9(a) plots the user's modulation and coding scheme for one second on the downlink. Surprisingly, the graphs indicate that the rate adaptation algorithm hops over a wide range of modulation, during the experiment. One possible explanation is that the base station is responding to loss of downlink packets. However, the control channel indicated no packet loss on the downlink over the entire experiment. A second explanation is that the wireless channel is not actually coherent over the duration of one second, even though the phone is static. To investigate this, we place a USRP at the user's location and estimate a channel coherence metric[11] capturing the base station's SNR over two seconds, assuming the channel was estimated only once at time 0 (see Fig. 9(b)). We observe that the channel is indeed coherent throughout the experiment. Hence, the rate adaptation algorithm is fairly complex, involving aggressive modulation exploration.

Next, we repeat the above experiment for different downlink demands (i.e. TCP throughput) under identical SNR, and plot the mean downlink modulation (in bits per resource element) as shown by the blue line in Fig. 9(c). Interestingly, as the downlink demand increases, the observed modulation also increases as well. In other words, the base station avoids transmitting packets to the user at high modulation (i.e. avoids risking higher loss probability), unless it is forced to, since the user demands high throughput.

Finally, we repeat the above experiment, this time adding a second user device (User-2) to the network, while first user (User-1) downloads a file at different TCP throughputs, as before. We allow User-2 to download a large bitfile containing random strings via six simultaneous TCP connections so as to saturate the LTE downlink demand. Interestingly, we now observe that packets to User-1 are sent at higher modulation, across demands (see the red line in Fig. 9(c)). To understand why this is the case, note that by sending data to User-1 at higher modulation, the base station consumes less downlink resources per bit for User-1's data. This relieves more network resources that the base station can now assign to User-2 to serve its high demand. Therefore, base stations transmit packets at conservative modulation, only when this does not impact overall network throughput.

## 8.4 Detecting Cheaters in a Large Exam Hall

LTEye can enable new applications customized to the need of a particular community of users. For example, many modern exams follow an open book/material policy and allow students access to computers during the exams. However, students are asked to abstain from using the Internet to chat and collude online. Enforcing this policy over Wi-Fi is relatively easy by monitoring the Wi-Fi channels, turning the access point off, or even jamming the signal. However cheaters can still use their cellular service to chat with an accomplice. In this experiment, we demonstrate how LTEye's spatial analytics can help localize such cheaters in a large exam hall that accommodates up to 300 students.

**Setup.** We consider a large 24m $\times$ 17m exam hall as shown in Fig. 10(a) that seats up to 300 students. The exam hall has multiple chairs on a platform that slopes upwards from the podium. We place two LTEye sniffers on ledges close to the walls, as shown by the blue squares in the figure. The sniffers localize the 3-D location of ten LTE cellphones, corresponding to ten active cheaters accessing the Internet, placed among twenty randomly chosen locations (the red circles in the figure).

**Results.** Fig. 10(b) plots a CDF of the error in each dimension of the estimated 3D-location of each cellphone. We observe a mean error in localization of 34 cm along each dimension and 61 cm in 3D displacement between the measured and actual location. Note that our errors are in 3-D space unlike past work [30, 29] and the experiments were performed in a large 24m $\times$ 17m area. LTEye identified the cheater's seat among the 300 seats in the room with 95% accuracy. Note that a random guess has an accuracy of just 1/300. Even when LTEye makes an error, it reports a seat adjacent to the cheater, which is sufficient to visually identify the cheater in most proctored situations. Note that the cellphones are predominantly in line-of-sight to the LTEye sniffers, due to the nature of the exam hall. In §8.5, we estimate the error in localization for non-line-of-sight scenarios as well.

## 8.5 Visualizing LTE Performance over Space

As end-users, we have limited visibility into how LTE performance varies in different parts of our home or work place. In this

[11]Given an initial channel $h(0)$ and current CFO-adjusted channel $h(t)$, channel coherence metric is $10\log_{10}|h(t)|^2/|h(t)-h(0)|^2$

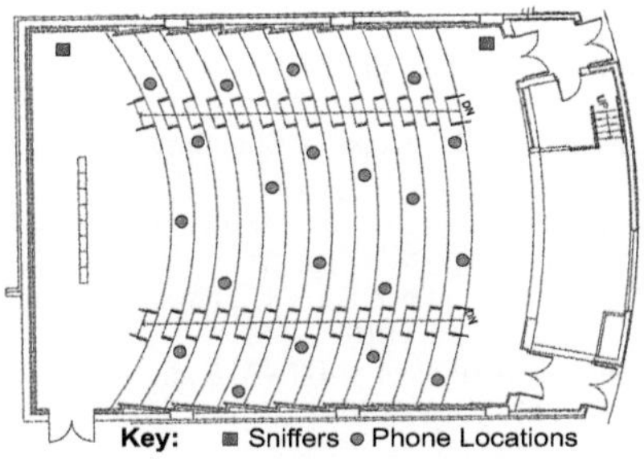


(a) Classroom Testbed

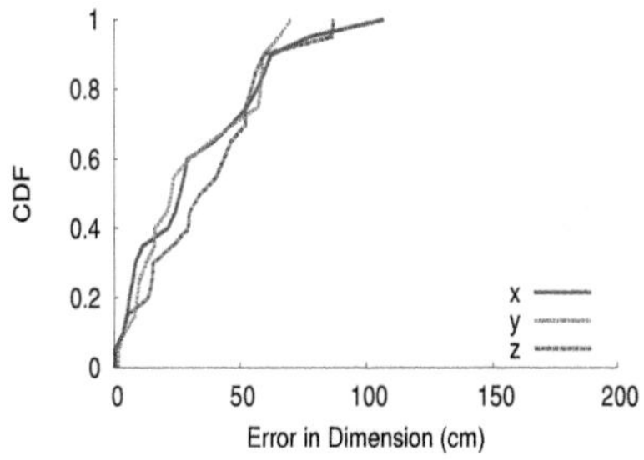


(b) LOS Localization Error

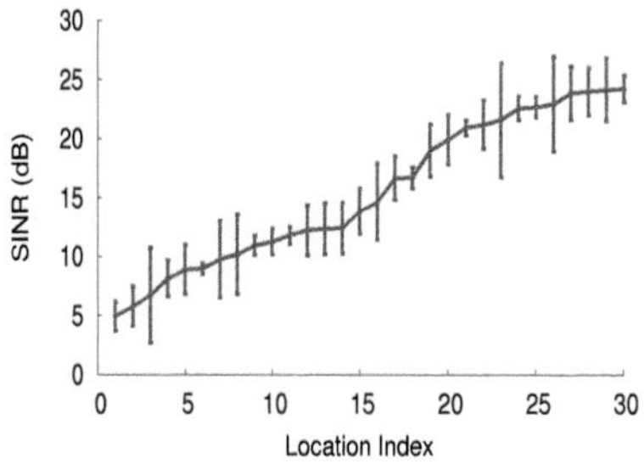


(c) SINR across Locations

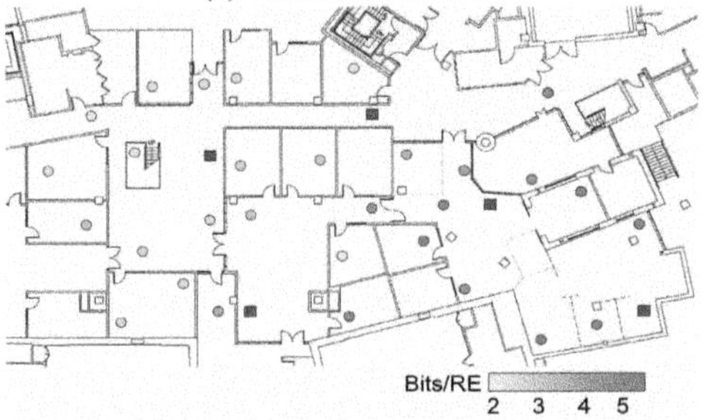


(d) NLOS Testbed & Heatmap

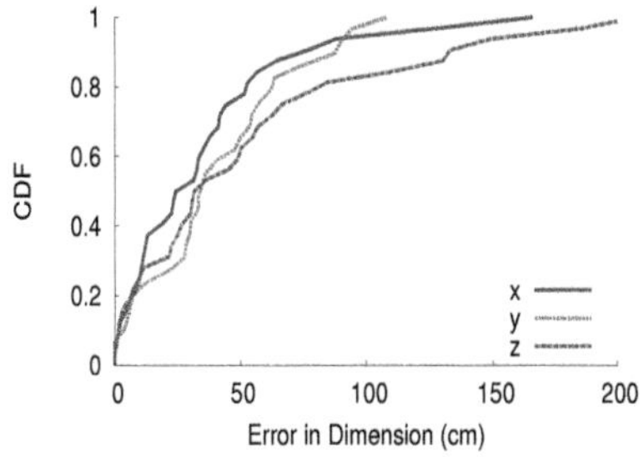


(e) NLOS Localization Error

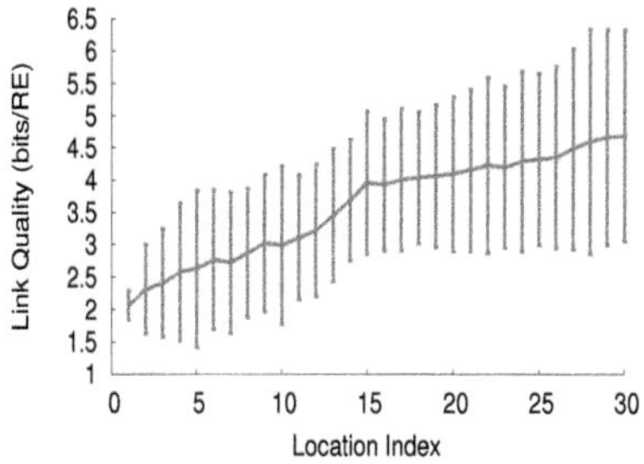


(f) Link Quality across Locations

Figure 10: (a),(d): Depicts our two testbeds a large exam hall and a floor of a large building. LTEye sniffers are denoted as blue squares and candidate phone locations as red circles. Further, the red circles in (d) are colored in shades of red, based on observed link quality from the base station; (b),(e): CDF of the error in 3D localization on each dimension in line-of-sight and non-line-of-sight scenarios respectively; (c),(f): Plots the measured SINR using USRPs and observed link quality from the downlink control channel across phone locations.

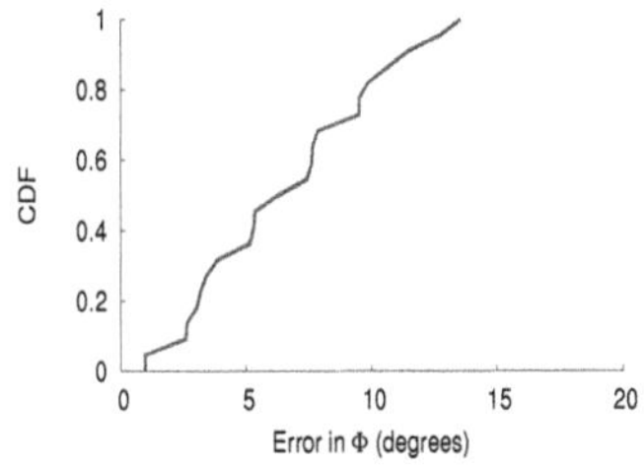


(a) $\phi$ Accuracy in LOS

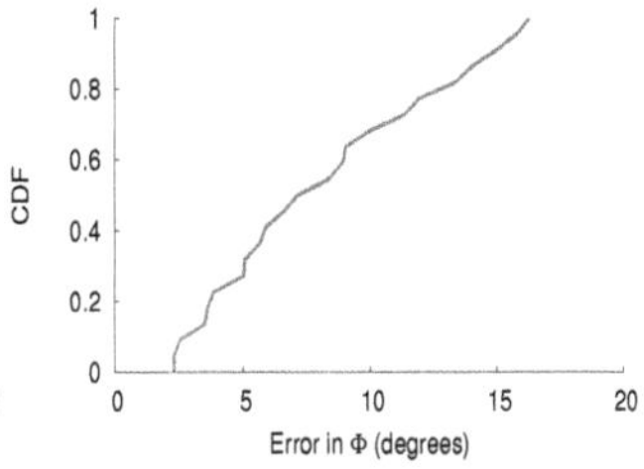


(b) $\phi$ Accuracy in NLOS

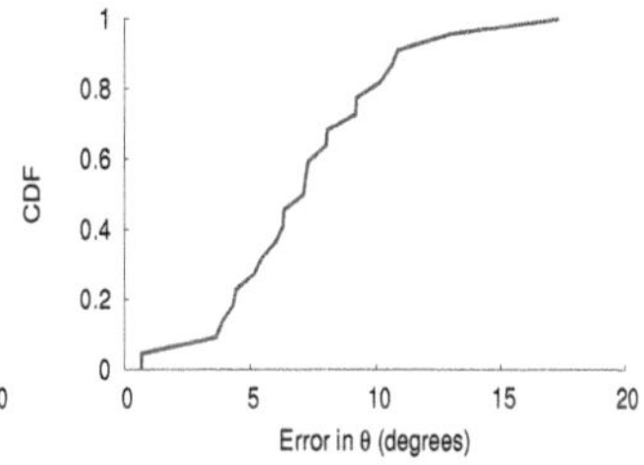


(c) $\theta$ Accuracy in LOS

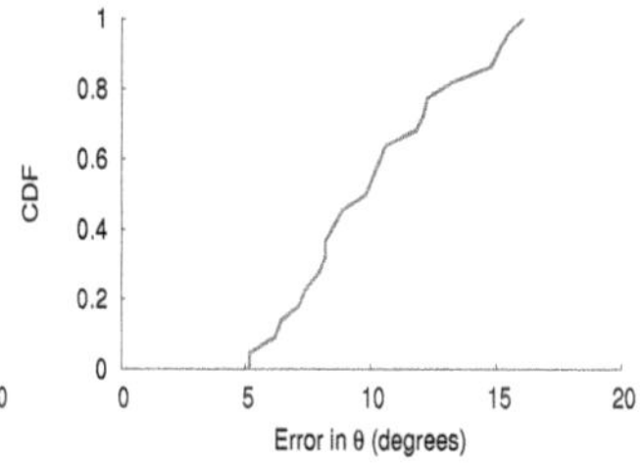


(d) $\theta$ Accuracy in NLOS

Figure 11: **Accuracy of $\theta$ and $\phi$:** Plots CDF of error in measured spatial angles in line-of-sight (LOS) and non-line-of-sight (NLOS).

experiment, we address this issue by synergizing LTEye's temporal and spatial analytics to visualize the performance of a cellular provider across spatial locations.

**Setup.** We deploy five LTEye sniffers on a 60m×34m floor of a large building, denoted by the blue squares in Fig. 10(d). We place ten phones in each of thirty randomly chosen locations shown as red circles in the figure. Note that several phones are in non-line-of-sight relative to all LTEye sniffers. We emphasize that for each client device, 3D-localization is performed using the spatial angles from at most three LTEye sniffers. The localization error can be further improved by incorporating spatial angles from additional LTEye sniffers.

**Results.** Fig. 10(e) plots the CDF of localization error along each of the three dimensions for phones that are in non-line-of-sight relative to all LTEye sniffers. Our results show a mean error in localization of 43.7 cm along each dimension and 84.6 cm in net 3-D displacement. Our algorithm to identify the direct line-of-sight path from §6.2 is crucial to localize phones in non-line-of-sight. Of course, the algorithm hinges on the fact that the line of sight path is, at the very least, observable in the multipath profile produced by SAR (See §6.1), even if it is not the most dominant path. Our experiments revealed that the line-of-sight path was always observed in the multipath profile of every phone in our large indoor testbed, including those furthest away from each LTEye sniffer in Fig. 10(d). Of course, while this may not generalize to every environment, our observations show the benefits of better penetration of signals in the 700 MHz frequency range through walls and obstacles, compared to Wi-Fi signals at 2.4 GHz or 5 GHz, and the higher transmit power of LTE devices in general.

Fig. 10(c) measures the mean and variance of Signal to Interference plus Noise Ratio (SINR) observed by a USRP placed in each of the thirty phone locations. The locations are sorted by mean SINR for ease of visualization. Fig. 10(f) plots the mean and variance of link quality for each phone (as bits per resource element) at the same locations, measured from LTEyeDB based on the downlink control channels. We observe that the link quality and SNR follow similar trends, showing that LTEye can effectively characterize the performance of the LTE network across spatial locations.

Fig. 10(d) visualizes the spatial distribution of link quality across phone locations, denoting positions of high quality as circles with darker shades of red, and low quality with lighter shades of red. The figure indicates that the link quality is strongest at locations to the bottom right, and weakest along locations to the top left. In fact, we found that placing an LTE relay at the top-left part of the floor significantly improves LTE service across the floor.

### 8.6 Measuring Accuracy of Observed Spatial Angles

In this experiment, we measure the accuracy of the polar angle $\theta$ and azimuthal angle $\phi$, that are key primitives to LTEye's localization algorithm in §6, across spatial locations.

**Setup.** We consider an LTEye sniffer placed in one of five possible locations (denoted by blue squares) in a floor of a large building, as in Fig. 10(d). The LTEye sniffers are elevated on ledges close to the walls.[12] We place ten phones in several randomly chosen locations in both line-of-sight and non-line-of-sight, spanning the full range of spatial angles. We find the ground truth of the spatial angles by noting the actual 3D positions of the phones and the sniffer on a scaled high-resolution building floorplan.

**Results.** Fig.11(a)-(d) plot the CDF of error in $\theta$ and $\phi$ in line-of-sight (LOS) and non-line of sight (NLOS) locations. The figures show a low median error in both $\phi$ (LOS: 6.9°, NLOS: 7.8°) and $\theta$ (LOS: 7.2°, NLOS: 9.9°) across locations. Note that the accuracy can be further improved with multiple LTEye sniffers, particularly, in cases where the deviation in angles is large. Note that our algorithm to find the path of minimum delay was crucial for the accuracy of spatial angles in non-line-of-sight.

### 8.7 Tracking C-RNTIs using RF Fingerprints

In this section, we evaluate LTEye's RF fingerprinting to map C-RNTIs assigned to the same phone. We consider the setup in §8.6 above and populate LTEyeDB across several experiments spanning ten minutes each. We track the correct C-RNTI mapping by constantly listening on the uplink from multiple USRPs placed close to each phone to recognize the high power signals that are sent during connection establishment. We also measure the inferred C-RNTI mapping from RF-fingerprints (See §5 and §6.3).

**Results.** We measure two quantities: (1) Precision: The percentage of new C-RNTIs which were correctly mapped to old C-RNTIs. (2) Recall: The percentage of correctly retrieved C-RNTIs-mappings among all actual C-RNTI mappings. Our algorithm achieves a high mean precision of $98.4 \pm 1.3\%$ and mean recall of $96.7 \pm 1.4\%$, demonstrating the effectiveness of LTEye's C-RNTI matching algorithm. Note that we leveraged RF fingerprints to track C-RNTIs of users in §8.4 and §8.5 above.

## 9. CONCLUSION

We presented LTEye, the first open platform to provide fine-grained temporal and spatial analytics on LTE radio performance, without private user information or provider support. LTEye employs a novel extension of synthetic aperture radar to communication signals to accurately localize mobile users, despite the presence of multipath. We empirically evaluate LTEye on software radios and provide deep insights on the LTE PHY and highlight shortcomings such as inter-cell interference and inefficient spectrum utilization.

**Acknowledgments:** We are grateful to John Romanishin for fabricating the rotating arm used in our experiments. We thank Vimalkumar Jeyakumar, Srinivas N.G., Arthur Berger, the NETMIT group and our reviewers for their insightful comments. This work is funded by NSF. We thank members of the MIT Center for Wireless Networks and Mobile Computing: Amazon, Cisco, Google, Intel, Mediatek, Microsoft, ST Microelectronics and Telefonica for their interest and support.

[12] LTEye cannot tell apart up from down as the rotating antenna path is symmetric. Placing sniffers on ledges removes this ambiguity.

## 10. REFERENCES


[1] Linux Advanced Routing and Traffic Control. http://lartc.org.
[2] 3gpp. Radio Measurement Collection for Minimization of Drive Tests (MDT). http://www.etsi.org/deliver/etsi_ts/137300_137399/137320/11.03.00_60/ts_137320v110300p.pdf.
[3] 3rd Generation Partnership Project. E-UTRA, Physical Channels and Modulation, TS 36.211, v8.9.0. 2010.
[4] 3rd Generation Partnership Project. E-UTRA, Radio Resource Control, TS 36.331, v8.9.0. Apr 2010.
[5] 3rd Generation Partnership Project. E-UTRA, v8.8.0, Multiplexing and Channel Coding, TS 36.212. 2010.
[6] B. Ayvazian. LTE Deployment Strategies: Network Overlay vs. Single RAN. *White Paper: UBM Tech*, 2013.
[7] B. Conley. M2M Implications of the 4G LTE Buildout. *Remote Magazine*, 2013.
[8] USRP N210. http://www.ettus.com. Ettus Inc.
[9] Eurecom. OpenAirInterface. http://www.openairinterface.org/.
[10] Federal Communications Commission. Enabling Innovative Small Cell Use In 3.5 GHZ Band NPRM & Order. FCC 12-148, 2012.
[11] R. Fenby. Limitations on Directional Patterns of Phase-Compensated Circular Arrays. *Radio and Electronic Engineer*, 1965.
[12] P. J. Fitch. *Synthetic Aperture Radar*. Springer-Verlag, 1988.
[13] FlexNets Group. Open-Source Long-Term Evolution (LTE) Deployment (OSLD). https://sites.google.com/site/osldproject/.
[14] C. Hsieh-Chung et al. Determining RF Angle of Arrival using COTS Antenna Arrays: A Field Evaluation. In *MILCOM*, 2012.
[15] J. Huang, F. Qian, A. Gerber, Z. M. Mao, S. Sen, and O. Spatscheck. A Close Examination of Performance and Power Characteristics of 4G LTE Networks. MobiSys, 2012.
[16] J. Huang, F. Qian, Y. Guo, Y. Zhou, Q. Xu, Z. M. Mao, S. Sen, and O. Spatscheck. An In-depth Study of LTE: Effect of Network Protocol and Application Behavior on Performance. SIGCOMM, 2013.
[17] Huawei. SingleSON Whitepaper. http://www.huawei.com/en/static/SingleSON-75714-1-127574.pdf, 2012.
[18] K. Joshi, S. Hong, and S. Katti. PinPoint: Localizing Interfering Radios. NSDI, 2013.
[19] Y. Kakishima, T. Kawamura, Y. Kishiyama, H. Taoka, and T. Nakamura. Experimental Evaluation on Throughput Performance of Asymmetric Carrier Aggregation in LTE-Advanced. In *VTC Spring*, 2011.
[20] H. W. Kuhn. The Hungarian Method for the Assignment Problem. *NRL Quarterly*, 1955.
[21] C. Laurendeau and M. Barbeau. Centroid Localization of Uncooperative Nodes in Wireless Networks Using a Relative Span Weighting Method. *EURASIP Journal on Wireless Communications and Networking*, 2010.
[22] V. Loscri et al. Carrier Independent Localization Techniques for GSM Terminals. In *PIMRC*, 2008.
[23] S. J. Orfanidis. Electromagnetic Waves and Antennas. http://www.ece.rutgers.edu/ orfanidi/ewa/.
[24] S. Salvador and P. Chan. Toward Accurate Dynamic Time Warping in Linear Time and Space. *IDA*, 2007.
[25] Sanjole. The WaveJudge Wireless Test System. http://www.sanjole.com/our-products/wavejudge-test-system/.
[26] M. Solutions. White Paper: Femtocells - The Gateway to the Home. 2010.
[27] J. Sommers and P. Barford. Cell vs. WiFi: On the Performance of Metro Area Mobile Connections. IMC, 2012.
[28] ThinkRF. Product Concept Brief for Distributed and Remote LTE Analysis. http://thinkrf.com/.
[29] J. Wang and D. Katabi. Dude, Where's My Card?: RFID Positioning That Works with Multipath and Non-line of Sight. SIGCOMM, 2013.
[30] J. Xiong and K. Jamieson. ArrayTrack: A Fine-grained Indoor Location System. NSDI, 2013.
[31] J. Xiong and K. Jamieson. SecureArray: Improving WiFi Security with Fine-grained Physical-layer Information. MobiCom, 2013.

# Control-Plane Protocol Interactions in Cellular Networks

Guan-Hua Tu[†*], Yuanjie Li[†*], Chunyi Peng[‡], Chi-Yu Li[†], Hongyi Wang[†], Songwu Lu[†]
[†]University of California, Los Angeles [‡]The Ohio State University, Columbus
[†]{ghtu, yuanjie.li, lichiyu, hywang, slu}@cs.ucla.edu [‡]chunyi@cse.ohio-state.edu

## ABSTRACT

Control-plane protocols are complex in cellular networks. They communicate with one another along three dimensions of cross layers, cross (circuit-switched and packet-switched) domains, and cross (3G and 4G) systems. In this work, we propose signaling diagnosis tools and uncover six instances of problematic interactions. Such control-plane issues span both design defects in the 3GPP standards and operational slips by carriers. They are more damaging than data-plane failures. In the worst-case scenario, users may be out of service in 4G, or get stuck in 3G. We deduce root causes, propose solutions, and summarize learned lessons.

## Categories and Subject Descriptors

C.2.1 [**Computer-Communication Networks**]: Network Architecture and Design—*Wireless Communication*; C.4 [**Performance of Systems**]: *Design Studies, Modeling Techniques*

## Keywords

Cellular networks; control-plane; protocol verification

## 1. INTRODUCTION

The cellular network serves as a large-scale wireless infrastructure to support mobile data and voice services. A salient feature of its design has been its control-plane protocols. Compared with the Internet, these components provide more complex signaling functions. They follow the layered protocol architecture (see Figure 1 for an illustration), and run at both the network infrastructure and the end device. Together, they provide control utilities vital to 3G/4G networks, including mobility support, radio resource control, session management for data and voice, *etc*..

In this paper, we examine protocol interactions in cellular networks. We focus on a set of critical components on the control plane (see Table 2 for the list). Our goal is to uncover problems during inter-protocol communications. Although each signaling protocol may be well designed individually, proper interactions among them in the networked environment are not guaranteed.

There are two challenges. First, compared with the Internet, cellular networks are still closed systems. Signaling exchanges are not readily accessible from carriers, nor from devices during normal operations. Second, patterns of inter-protocol communication on the control plane are much richer than their Internet counterparts. In addition to the inter-layer case, they exhibit in both cross-domain and cross-system scenarios in cellular networks. Since both data and carrier-grade voice are indispensable services, both packet switching (PS) and circuit switching (CS) are used. Signaling protocols thus regulate both PS and CS domains. Moreover, Inter-system switching between 3G and 4G is also common due to hybrid deployment, user mobility, or CSFB (CS Fallback)-based calls. Signaling protocols consequently need to work cross 3G and 4G systems. In a nutshell, interactions among control-plane protocols are common in 3G/4G systems. They span three dimensions: between layers of the protocol stack (cross-layer[1]), between CS and PS domains (cross-domain), and between 3G and 4G systems (cross-system).

In this work, we devise *CNetVerifier*, a tool to analyze all such cases (§3). Our tool adapts model-checking methods with cellular-specific heuristics. It further instruments the device to collect protocol traces for validation. We apply the tool and delve into all above three dimensions. Our study yields interesting findings (§4). We show two classes of problematic interactions among signaling protocols. They are exemplified using six concrete instances, spanning cross-layer, cross-domain, and cross-system dimensions (see Table 1). In the first class (§5), we show that some inter-protocol communications are necessary yet troublesome. The necessity of signaling synergy is partly driven by the requirement for carrier-grade voice support, partly by inter-system switching in hybrid 3G/4G deployments, and partly by mobility management. However, interactions among signaling protocols are not always designed and operated right: (S1) a user device is temporarily out of service because its vital context in 4G is shared but not well protected (being deleted after inter-system switching); (S2) Users are denied network access right after being accepted because higher-layer protocols make unrealistic assumptions on lower layers; (S3) 4G users get stuck in 3G because inconsistent policies are used for CS and PS domains in 3G and 4G. The second class (§6) concerns independent operations by protocols. We discover that, some are unnecessarily coupled and have unexpected consequence: (S4) outgoing calls are delayed for unjustified location updates because cross-layer actions are "improperly" correlated and prioritized; (S5) PS data sessions suffer from rate reduction (51% − 96% drop observed) when traffic in both domains shares the same channel; (S6) User devices are out of service when the failure is propagated to another system. We validate most instances with traces collected from our tool when running tests over two US carriers. We further conduct a two-week user study to assess their real-world impact (§7). We propose and evaluate solutions that help to resolve above issues (§8 and §9).

## 2. BACKGROUND

The cellular network architecture consists of base stations (BSes) and a core network. The BSes provide radio access to user devices (*e.g.*, phones), whereas the core network connects them to the wired Internet or the public telephony network. Figure 1 illustrates the network architecture and main protocols for both 3G and 4G.

The 4G LTE network offers PS data service only. It has three core elements: (1) MME (Mobility Management Entity) to manage

*The first two authors contribute equally to this work. The correspondence faculty author is C. Peng.


*SIGCOMM'14,* August 17–22, 2014, Chicago, IL, USA.

http://dx.doi.org/10.1145/2619239.2626302.

[1]We use inter-layer and cross-layer interchangeably in this paper, for a slight abuse of definition.

| Category | Problems | Type | Protocols | Dimension | Root Causes |
|---|---|---|---|---|---|
| Necessary but problematic cooperations | **S1:** User device is temporarily *"out-of-service"* during 3G→4G switching. | Design | SM/ESM, GMM/EMM | Cross-system | States are shared but unprotected between 3G and 4G; States are deleted during inter-system switching (§5.1). |
| | **S2:** User device is temporarily *"out-of-service"* during the attach procedure. | Design | EMM, 4G-RRC | Cross-layer | MME assumes reliable transfer of signals by RRC; RRC cannot ensure it (§5.2). |
| | **S3:** User device gets stuck in 3G. | Design | 3G-RRC, CM, SM | Cross-domain; Cross-system | RRC state change policy is inconsistent for inter-system switching (§5.3). |
| Independent but coupled operations | **S4:** Outgoing call/Internet access is delayed. | Design | CM/MM, SM/GMM | Cross-layer | Location update does not need to be, but is served with higher priority than outgoing call/data requests (§6.1). |
| | **S5:** PS rate declines (*e.g.*, 96.1% in OP-II) during ongoing CS service. | Operation | 3G-RRC, CM, SM | Cross-domain | 3G-RRC configures the shared channel with a single modulation scheme for both data and voice (§6.2). |
| | **S6:** User device is temporarily *"out-of-service"* after 3G→4G switching. | Operation | MM, EMM | Cross-system | Information and action on location update failure in 3G are exposed to 4G (§6.3). |

**Table 1: Finding summary.**

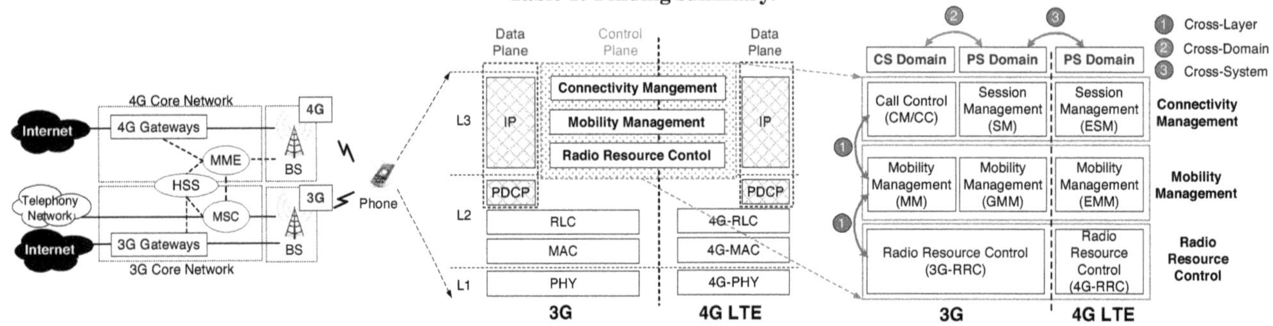


**Figure 1: 4G/3G network architecture and control-protocol interactions in three dimensions.**

user mobility (*e.g.*, location update or paging), (2) 4G gateways that route PS packets between the Internet and the 4G BSes, and (3) HSS (Home Subscriber Server), which stores user subscription information. In contrast, the 3G network supports both CS and PS services. Its core network consists of: (1) MSC (Mobile Switching Center), which pages and establishes CS services (*i.e.*, voice calls) with mobile devices, (2) 3G Gateways, which forward PS data packets, and (3) HSS, which is similar to its counterpart in 4G.

Similar to the Internet, cellular network protocols have adopted the layered structure. The protocol family spans both data and control planes. The data plane is responsible for actual data and voice transfer. The control plane provides a variety of signaling functions to facilitate the data-plane operations. Specifically, three major functions are provisioned at three sub-layers: (1) Connectivity Management (CM), which is responsible for creating and mandating voice calls and data sessions; (2) Mobility Management (MM), which provides location update and mobility support for call/data sessions; (3) Radio Resource Control (RRC), which controls radio resources and helps to route signaling messages.

We next introduce major procedures in cellular networks.

**Attach/detach cellular networks.** The mobile device must *attach* to the cellular networks before using any cellular network service[2] (*e.g.*, data or voice service). It happens when the device powers on. The attach procedure is mandated by Mobility Management control protocols (*i.e.*, MM, GMM and EMM) running on mobile devices, 3G MSC, 3G Gateways and 4G MME, respectively. Once it completes, the mobile device is *"registered"* until being detached. The *detach* procedure can be triggered either by the device (*e.g.*, the phone powers off) or the network (*e.g.*, under resource constraints). Once detached, the device enters the *"deregistered"* (*i.e.*, "out-of-service") state and cannot access any cellular service.

**Data and voice services.** Both are essential services offered by cellular networks. To enable any *data* service, the mobile device has to first establish a bearer with the core network. This procedure is done via "EPS Bearer activation" in 4G or "PDP Context activation" in 3G, which is mandated by Evolved Session Management (ESM in 4G) or Session Management (SM in 3G). Once it succeeds, the core network assigns an IP address, reserves resources to meet QoS requirements and establishes the routing path for the device. In fact, the information vital to data sessions (*e.g.*, IP address and QoS parameters) is stored at both the device and the 3G/4G gateways via the 3G PDP (or 4G EPS bearer) context.

In 3G, the voice service is supported via CS and handled by the Call Control (CC) protocol at the mobile device and MSC. In 4G, the voice service is designed to run over PS via Voice-over-LTE (VoLTE) [2]. However, due to the high deployment cost and complexity of VoLTE, most 4G operators adopt another voice solution, Circuit-Switched Fallback (CSFB), which switches 4G users to legacy 3G and accesses CS voice service in 3G [5].

**Radio resource control (RRC).** RRC is responsible for controlling radio resources between the device and the BS. An established RRC connection is the prerequisite for any communication (data, voice or signaling) between the device and the core network. A RRC state machine is used for this purpose. Two states of `IDLE` and `CONNECTED` denote whether the RRC connection has been established or not. For goals of optimization and energy efficiency, 3G and 4G also offer multiple connected sub-states. Specifically, 3G uses `FACH` and `DCH`. The former supports low-rate communication with less radio resource and power consumption, whereas the latter consumes more but sends packets at higher speed. In contrast, 4G supports three modes of continuous reception, short and long discontinuous reception.

**Mobility management.** The cellular network supports two types of mobility: (1) intra-system handover, where the user stays within 3G or 4G only and updates its location during roaming. It is done by one of the following procedures: location area update via MSC (3G CS), routing area update via 3G Gateways (3G PS) or tracking area update via MME (4G); (2) inter-system switch, where the user device switches between 3G and 4G. Once the switch succeeds, the device updates its location to the new serving network via the above procedure. For signaling protocols, mobility support is realized through MM, GMM, and EMM in 3G CS, 3G PS and 4G PS (see Figure 1), respectively. The underlying radio access switch (*e.g.*, radio channel setup/teardown) is handled by 3G/4G RRC .

[2]The only exception is to make emergency calls.

# 3. METHODOLOGY

We develop *CNetVerifier*, a tool that conducts two-phase protocol diagnosis, as shown in Figure 2. It helps to uncover two types of issues: *(i) design problems* originated from the 3GPP standards, and *(ii) operational slips* originated from the carrier practice.

## 3.1 CNetVerifier Overview

*CNetVerifier* takes a two-phase approach. During the *screening* phase, *CNetVerifier* first explores *possible* logical design defects in control-plane protocols via model-checking techniques, and produces counterexamples due to design defects. Once they are found, we move to the *validation* phase. For each counterexample, we set up the corresponding experimental scenario and conduct measurements over operational networks for validation.

We use the two-phrase approach since both phases are necessary. The issues discovered during the first phase are implementation- and measurement-independent ones, since they come from the 3GPP design standards. Moreover, its outputs (*i.e.*, these counterexamples) offer us hints to configure the experiments to validate possible design problems. The second phase alone may not uncover all problematic issues since it is measurement dependent. This phase is needed for validating the design problems and studying their impact. Moreover, it helps to identify operational slips or implementation bugs. For example, S5 and S6 are found during the S3's validation experiments.

Before elaborating techniques for each phase, we rush to point out several downsides of *CNetVerifier*. First, it focuses on the control-plane protocol interactions, thus simplifying data-plane operations (*e.g.*, ignoring packet communication time and call durations). Second, the defined properties are from the user's perspective. It may not uncover all issues at base stations and in the core network which operators are interested in. Third, using random sampling for usage scenarios, some parameter-sensitive defects may not be exposed. The impact could be alleviated by increasing sampling rates. Fourth, due to limited access to cellular networks, some findings may not be validated by experiments. For example, S2 is discovered by protocol screening but not observed through phone-based experiments. We cannot confirm whether it rarely happens or it is not a real defect. Finally, we mainly conduct experiments according to those counterexamples reported during the *screening* phase. Not all operational slips may be identified.

## 3.2 Domain-Specific Protocol Screening

During protocol screening, we discover the issues originated from cellular network design. To this end, we develop a cellular-specific model-checking tool, which is written in Spin [12]. It works as follows. First, we model signaling protocol interactions, and define cellular-oriented properties. Second, given these inputs, *CNetVerifier* checks whether a set of desired properties are satisfied. It thus generates a counterexample for each concrete instance of property violation, which indicates a possible design defect. To make the above idea work in the cellular context, we address three domain-specific issues: (1) How to model cellular networks? (2) How to define the desired properties? (3) How to check the property given the cellular network model?

### 3.2.1 Modeling

Our modeling effort covers both parts of 3G/4G protocol stacks and usage scenarios. The protocol interactions occur between protocols in the stack, and are driven by usage scenarios.

**Modeling 3G/4G protocol stacks.** The modeling of cellular protocols is derived from the 3GPP standards [3,6–8], which specify the operations for each protocol. Table 2 lists the studied cellular protocols, including PS/CS services, mobility management and

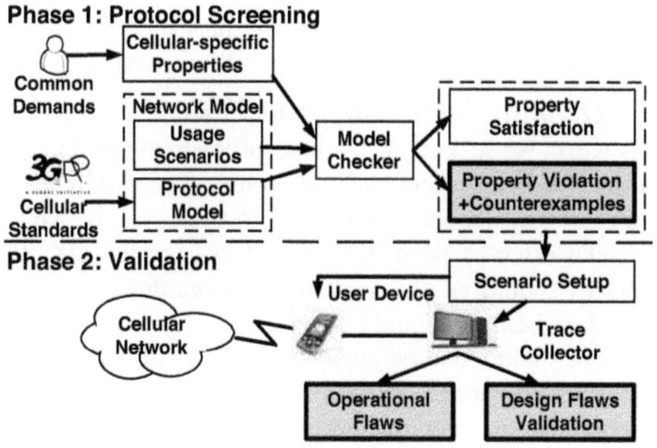


**Figure 2: *CNetVerifier* Overview**

| Function | Name | System | Net. Element | Standard | Description |
|---|---|---|---|---|---|
| PS/CS | CM/CC | 3G | MSC | TS24.008 | CS Connectivity Management |
| | SM | 3G | 3G Gateways | TS24.008 | PS Session Management |
| | ESM | 4G | MME | TS24.301 | 4G Session Management |
| Mobility | MM | 3G | MSC | TS24.008 | CS Mobility Management |
| | GMM | 3G | 3G Gateways | TS24.008 | PS Mobility Management |
| | EMM | 4G | MME | TS24.301 | 4G Mobility Management |
| Radio | 3G-RRC | 3G | 3G BS | TS25.331 | Radio Resource Control |
| | 4G-RRC | 4G | 4G BS | TS36.331 | Radio Resource Control |

**Table 2: Studied protocols on network elements and devices.**

radio resource control. We model each cellular protocol as two Finite State Machines (FSMs), one running at the user device and the other operating in the specific network element (for instance, CM/MM, SM/GMM, ESM/EMM are operated at MSC, 3G Gateways and MME, respectively).

**Modeling usage scenarios.** Modeling usage scenarios is more challenging. They are not formally defined by the 3GPP standards, and largely depend on user demands and operation policies. Ideally, we should test all combinations of usage scenarios, so that all possible design defects can be found. However, some usage scenarios may have unlimited choices. Enumeration is thus deemed unrealistic. Consequently, we take the random sampling approach. We assign each usage scenario with certain probability, and randomly sample all possible usage scenarios. Specifically, for scenarios with limited options (*e.g.*, device switch on/off, all types of accept/reject requests, all inter-system switch techniques), we enumerate all possible combinations. For scenarios with unbounded options (*e.g.*, user mobility at various speed, traffic arrival patterns of PS/CS services), we implement a run-time signal generator that randomly activates these options at any time. Last, each customizable parameter is initialized with a random value. By increasing the sampling rate, we expect that more defects can be revealed. Specifically, we model user demands and operator responses as follows.

∘ *User demands* In our model, the phone device uses at most one network at a time, and cannot concurrently access both 3G and 4G networks. This is the default practice for most smartphones in reality. Once the device powers on, it randomly attaches to 3G or 4G. Afterwards, a run-time signal generator randomly creates user-specific events, such as starting voice or data service, location change or user-initiated detach (*i.e.*, switch off). These events thus trigger relevant protocol entities at the device to respond accordingly and further activate procedures towards the network.

∘ *Operator responses* Upon receiving a user request, the network accepts or rejects it. We equally test with all the possibilities, including the reject with various error causes. For example, more than 30 error causes are defined in the 4G attach procedure [8]. In the meantime, the run-time signal generator randomly produces network-specific events, *e.g.*, inter-system switch and network-oriented detach. Similarly, corresponding procedures towards the user device are triggered. Note that all options for network-specific events are stipulated by the standards and will be enumerated in our model. More details will be given later.

### 3.2.2 Defining Desirable Properties

In this work, we seek to check those problematic protocol interactions that incur user-perceived problems. The properties to be checked represent the services offered to users. Thus, we define three cellular-oriented properties: (1) *PacketService_OK*: Packet data services should be always available once device attached to 3G/4G, unless being explicitly deactivated. (2) *CallService_OK*: Call services should also be always available. In particular, each call request should not be rejected or delayed without any explicit user operation (*e.g.*, hanging up at the originating device). (3) *MM_OK*: inter-system mobility support should be offered upon request. For example, a 3G↔4G switch request should be served if both 3G/4G are available. We consider inter-system mobility only because intra-system mobility is seamlessly supported in practice. Note that *PacketService_OK* and *CallService_OK* represent the expected behaviors for network services, while *MM_OK* is for mobility support. In *CNetVerifier*, these properties act as logical constraints on the PS/CS/mobility states.

### 3.2.3 Property Checking

We perform the formal model checking procedure. First, the model checker creates the entire state space by interleaving all FSMs for each individual protocol. With the constraints of three properties, some states will be marked with "error." Then we run the depth-first algorithm to explore the state transitions from the initial state (*i.e.*, the device attempting to attach to 3G/4G networks) under various usage scenarios. Once an error state is hit, a counterexample is generated for the property violation. The model checker finally generates all counterexamples and their violated properties for further experimental validation.

## 3.3 Phone-based Experimental Validation

Given counterexamples for design defects, the validation phase needs to conduct experiments, collect protocol traces from real networks and compare them with the anticipated operations. The main challenge is trace collection. The core cellular network is operated as a black box, so it is not easy to obtain protocol traces from cellular network operators. Therefore, we seek to retrieve protocol traces from user devices. Fortunately, most cellular modem vendors (*e.g.*, QualComm or Mediatek) allow for developers to power on the debugging mode and obtain protocol traces[3]. Based on this, we collect five types of information: (1) timestamp of the trace item using the format of hh:mm:ss.ms(millisecond), (2) trace type (*e.g.*, STATE), (3) network system (*e.g.*, 3G or 4G), (4) the module generating the traces (*e.g.*, MM or CM/CC), and (5) the basic trace description (*e.g.*, a call is established).

To facilitate PS and CS signaling exchanges, we further devise automatic test tools on the phone. One is to automatically dial out, answer and terminate an incoming voice call. The other is to keep turning on and off data services. We use Speedtest [1] to measure the uplink and downlink speed of the Internet access on the phone. Each experiment has 10 runs unless explicitly specified.

We conduct experiments over two major US operators, denoted as OP-I and OP-II, for privacy concerns. They together serve more than 140M subscribers. We use five smartphone models that support dual 3G and 4G LTE operations: HTC One, LG Optimus G, Samsung Galaxy S4 and Note 2, and Apple iPhone5S. They cover both Android and iOS. All phones are used in all validation experiments. The experimental settings are constructed based on the counterexamples from the screening phase. We also test with common use scenarios to explore whether any operational slip is observed to break three properties in practice.

[3]For example, both QXDM (http://www.qualcomm.com/qxdm) and XCAL-Mobile (http://www.accuver.com) support this mode.

# 4. OVERVIEW OF FINDINGS

We uncover signaling interaction problems in both design and operations through *CNetVerifier*. We examine standards specification to identify design issues, and collect protocol traces to infer improper operational practice. Our findings are summarized in Table 1. They are grouped into two classes. The first class, *necessary yet problematic cooperations*, refers to the protocol interactions that are required but misbehave. The second class, *independent yet unnecessarily coupled operations*, refers to the protocol interactions that are not necessary but indeed occur and result in negative impact. The troubling inter-protocol signaling each leads to functional incorrectness or performance penalty. Not all the issues are operational slips, so they cannot be fully fixed by simply updating their implementations. For design problems, 3GPP standards should be revised to address them. Specifically, we first identify four instances S1-S4 in the screening phrase and then uncover two more operational issues S5 and S6 in the validation phrase. In fact, other issues are revealed by *CNetVerifier*, but they are not reported here because they do not belong to problematic protocol interactions. Both classes of issues are found in all three dimensions.

• **Cross-layer** Protocols in the upper-layer and low-layer directly interact with each other via the interfaces between them. Two representative instances are found in this category. In both cases, the principle of protocol layering is not properly honored. In the first case (§5.2), the low-layer RRC protocol fails to offer reliable and in-sequence signal delivery required by the upper-layer EMM protocol. EMM thus should have implemented its own end-to-end mechanism but does not. Subsequently, the signaling exchange between the device and the network can be lost or delayed, triggering wrong reactions from EMM. It denies user's network access right after accepting the access request. In the second case (§6.1), CM/SM and MM/GMM protocols, running on different layers in 3G, should act on outgoing call/data requests and location updates independently and concurrently. However, they prioritize location updates over call/data requests. The head of line blocking is experienced, and the outgoing calls and data are unnecessarily delayed.

• **Cross-domain** In cross-domain protocol interactions, protocol variants are developed for different domains and indirectly coupled over the common lower-layer protocols (*e.g.*, RRC). The cross-domain category also has two cases. In principle, the CS-domain voice and the PS-domain data have distinct requirements. Data prefers high throughput whereas voice values timely delivery. They should be treated differentially. However, in both cases, identical operations are performed on traffic from both domains. In the first case (§5.3), RRC keeps its state for the aggregated CS and PS data traffic. When the CS traffic terminates, the PS data may get stuck in 3G without returning to 4G networks. In the second case (§6.2), carriers use RRC to assign PS and CS sessions on a shared channel, using a single modulation scheme for both voice and data. The PS data rate may drop significantly over the shared channel.

• **Cross-system** Cross-system interactions occur with an 3G↔4G switch. Two instances are further uncovered in this category. In this scenario, both systems may be motivated to share or even act on certain state information. On one hand, correct information should be properly protected and shared during the cross-system operations. This is exemplified by the first case (§5.1). To enable data services, the user and the network must keep the PDP context in 3G and the EPS bearer context in 4G. However, such states are not well protected during inter-system switching. 3G may delete the PDP context, and then the 4G network cannot recover its EPS bearer context. The user device is thus out of service in 4G after the inter-system handover. In the second case (§6.1), 3G and 4G share information on location update failures. The actions on such failures should be confined between 3G and 4G networks. However, 4G takes action on the user device when handling failure signals from 3G. The user consequently loses its network access.

In following §5 and §6, we elaborate on each problematic case. Given each instance, we describe its concrete procedure, deduce its root cause, validate and assess its negative impact over US carriers.

# 5. IMPROPER COOPERATION

We describe three instances S1-S3 that exhibit troubling interactions in cross-system, cross-layer, and cross-domain settings.

## 5.1 Unprotected Shared Context in 3G/4G

The first is on *cross-system* signaling interactions between 3G and 4G. When the user device switches from 4G to 3G during mobility or CSFB calls, the data service is indeed migrated accordingly. However, under certain conditions, when the user switches back to the 4G network (*e.g.*, after completing a CSFB call or roaming back to a 4G BS), the device might be temporarily *out of service*. Our experiments validate its existence, and show that this out-of-service status may last from several to tens of seconds in operational networks. It is also quite common in reality. The root cause lies in improper cross-system interactions, and the involved protocols are SM/GMM in 3G and ESM/EMM in 4G, running at two signaling layers of session control and mobility support. These protocols should interact, because they need to support seamless PS data sessions when user devices switch between 3G and 4G. They thus share contexts in 3G and 4G. However, 4G mandates such shared states but 3G may have deleted them, thus causing state recovery failure after successful inter-system handover.

### 5.1.1 Inter-System Switch

The inter-system switch is commonly observed between 3G and 4G in practice. It occurs in three popular usage settings. First, in hybrid 3G/4G deployment, the mobile user leaves the coverage of current system, enters the cell of another system, and then roams back to the old system. Second, a user makes a CSFB-based call in 4G LTE networks, which triggers two handoffs, *i.e.*, one from 4G to 3G to start the voice call in 3G, and one from 3G to 4G after the call completes. Third, carriers may initiate such switching for users for load balancing or better resource availability. In case PS data access is enabled (when the mobile data network is ON), a 3G↔4G information migration will be performed accordingly. Note that, critical information and states are stored in PDP or EPS bearer context in 3G or 4G before the switching. To ensure smooth migration, the PDP context in 3G and the EPS bearer context in 4G are translated and kept consistent. For example, the IP address, *etc.*. remains the same before and after the switching.

Figure 3 shows how signaling protocols interact during 4G→3G switching[4] [4]. There are three steps. First, 4G RRC at the device receives the command from the 4G base station, disconnects the RRC connection between the device and the base station, and informs EMM. Second, 3G RRC at the device connects to the 3G base station using the information carried in the above command. It informs MM and GMM of such an inter-system switching for both CS and PS domains. MM and GMM subsequently initiate the location update procedure in both 3G CS and PS domains. If any data service was initiated when the device was in 4G, the gateways and MME (in Figure 1) collaborate to transfer the 4G EPS bearer

[4]The scenario shown here is "*RRC connection release with redirect*", which is a typical inter-system switching mechanism.

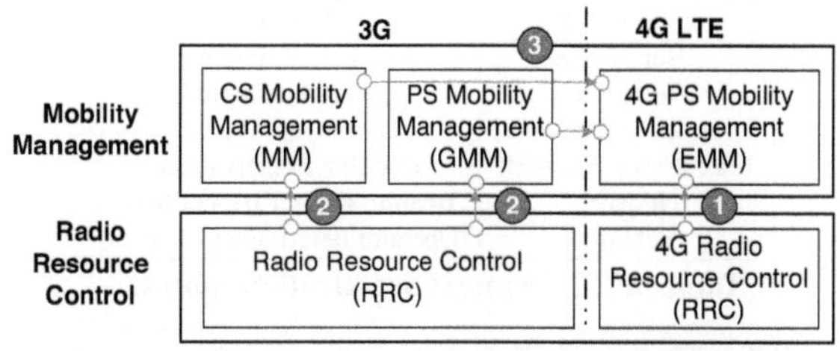


**Figure 3: The 4G→3G inter-system switching flow.**

context into the 3G PDP context during the location update procedure. After the conversion, the resources reserved for the 4G EPS bearer will be released. Third, MM/GMM in 3G informs EMM in 4G regarding the successful switching. The procedure for 3G→4G switching is similar. The 3G PDP context is migrated to the 4G EPS bearer context during the location update performed in 4G.

### 5.1.2 Issues and Root Causes

In the instance S1, our tool reports that the above protocols violate the property of *PacketService_OK*. We find that the user becomes *out-of-service* after an inter-system switching.

The scenario is as follows. The user device is initially in 4G and has its EPS bearer context activated. It then switches to 3G in one of the three usage scenarios. The EPS bearer context is subsequently deleted from 4G to release resource reservation. While in 3G, the PDP context can also be deactivated for various reasons (listed in Table 3). However, when later switching back to 4G, the device cannot register to the 4G network, since 4G only supports PS services and EPS bearer context is required. It detaches itself and becomes out of service in 4G. We next understand the root cause and the impact in three aspects.

We first see why the PDP context is deleted in 3G. The EPS bearer context or the PDP context is essential to enabling PS services. Since 4G only supports PS, its EPS bearer context is *mandatory* for data service and signaling exchange. Whenever it cannot be constructed, no service access is available based on the 4G standards [8]. On the other hand, the PDP context in 3G is allowed to be deactivated. It is *not mandatory* in 3G. Since 3G supports both CS and PS, a user can still use the CS voice service without the PDP context. Deactivation of the PDP context is common in 3G. Both the network and the user device can initiate it. It can also be triggered by various reasons (listed in Table 3).

We next look into whether it is a serious issue and how bad its negative impact is. Note that most smartphones do not support dual radios for both 3G and 4G. Each phone thus access one network at any time. Once being detached by 4G, the device has access to neither 4G nor 3G. This can last a few seconds. Of course, the device may immediately seek to re-register to 4G. It leaves the "*out-of-service*" state once registration succeeds. Otherwise, it keeps trying until the maximum retry count is reached. When all retries fail, the device may start to try 3G.

We finally see whether the above problem can be eliminated. The issue can be fully addressed since it stems from a design defect. First, the 3G PDP context does not need to be deactivated in all cases. Therefore, the 4G EPS bearer context can be re-constructed and the device obtains data access after switching from 3G to 4G. For example, the reason "QoS not accepted" in Table 3 states that the QoS cannot be satisfied at the user device. If so, the PDP context can be kept while changing to a lower QoS policy at the phone. The factor "Incompatible PDP context" implies that the active PDP context is not compatible for all PS services, *e.g.*, MMS and Internet. The PDP context can also be modified rather than being deleted. The cause "Regular deactivation" is triggered by the user (*e.g.*, when turning off the mobile data) or by the network. The

| Originator | Cause |
|---|---|
| User device | Insufficient resources |
| User device | **QoS not accepted** |
| User device/Network | Low layer failures |
| User device/Network | **Regular deactivation** |
| Network | **Incompatible PDP context** |
| Network | Operator determined barring |

**Table 3: PDP context deactivation causes.**

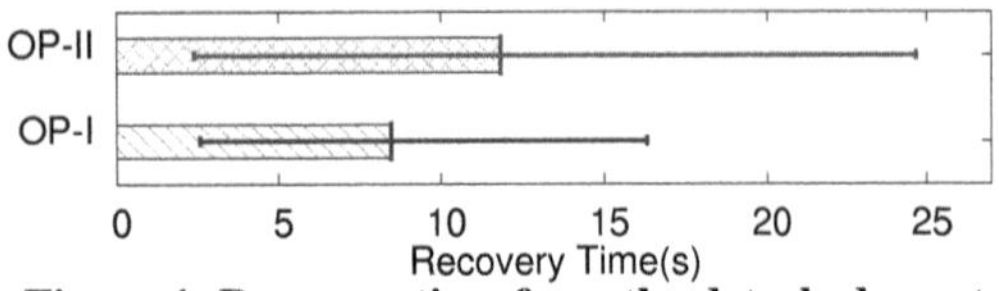


**Figure 4: Recovery time from the detached event.**

PDP context can also be kept until the switching to 4G succeeds. Second, even the PDP context has to be deactivated in 3G for compelling reasons, the user device can still avoid out-of-service after the inter-system switching. The reason is that, now the user device is still in registered state in 4G, it can reactivate a EPS bearer rather than being detached. This way, the device recovers from the PDP context deactivation.

### *5.1.3 Experimental Validation*

We next conduct experiments to validate and assess the above issue. We run tests to switch phones between 3G and 4G networks and collect protocol traces at the phone. The switching is done through two methods: (1) by CSFB call, and (2) by driving back and forth between two areas covered by 3G and 4G networks. We verify the instance in both OP-I and OP-II in our tested phones. When the device switches to 3G, the PDP context is deactivated by the network. After migrating back to 4G, the phone is detached by 4G due to *"No EPS Bearer Context Activated"* error.

We also observe the same issue when users disable cellular data services or switch to WiFi networks. For most smartphones, they will disable the mobile data service whenever a local WiFi network is accessible. While staying in 3G, some (here, HTC One and LG Optimus G) deactivate all PDP contexts. As a result, when users later switch to 4G, they become out of service for the same error.

We further observe an implementation issue that is complementary to S1. The tested phone may stay in the *out-of-service* state longer than expected. When no PDP context is found during switching to 4G, the phone does not detach immediately by following the 3GPP standards. Instead, it initiates the attach procedure until receiving the message of location update reject from networks. Note that it is not designed in 3GPP standards but observed in our tested phones. Figure 4 plots the median, minimum and maximum recovery time measured on Samsung S4 over more than 50 runs in both carriers. The recovery time is the one from the time when the tracking area update reject is received to the time when re-attach succeeds. We see that the device takes 2.4s to 24.7s to complete the attach procedure. Similar results are observed at other phones (median gap $< 0.5$s). It is because the re-attach is mainly controlled by operators. The phone is unreachable (*i.e.*, out of service) during the recovery time.

**Insight 1:** *For the contexts shared between different systems, the actions and policies shall be consistent across systems. Otherwise, cross-system issues may arise.*

## 5.2 Out-of-Sequenced Signaling in Inter-Protocol Communications

The instance S2 appears during cross-layer protocol interactions in 4G networks. The two involved protocols are EMM and RRC. We find that, the user device may temporarily be *"out-of-service"* and lose 4G access. It is induced by the improper action taken by

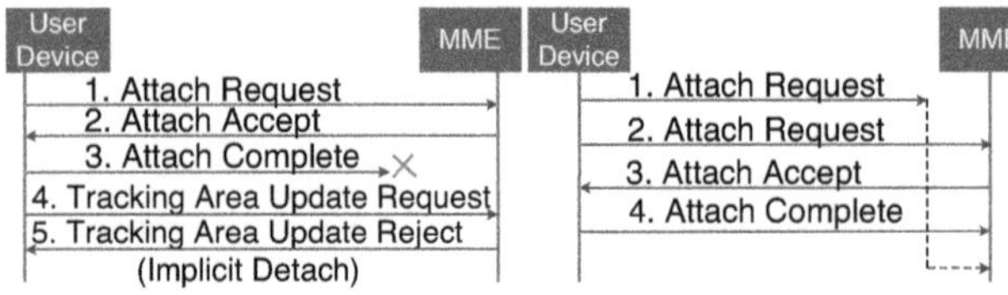


(a) Lost signal (b) Duplicate signal

**Figure 5: Device is detached by lost/duplicate signals.**

EMM when communicating with RRC. The EMM protocol relies on RRC to transfer signals, but assumes reliable, in-sequence signaling messages. The underlying RRC protocol does not provide it. Even worse, the design of EMM does not anticipate any lost or delayed signaling exchange. This leads to unexpected consequence. The user is detached from 4G right after successful attach.

### *5.2.1 Issues and Root Causes*

We find that the above protocol interaction violates the property of *PacketService_OK*. The device enters the *"deregistered"* state (*i.e.*, out of service in 4G), after receiving error signals of either attach reject or location update reject. There are two cases.

○ *Lost signaling messages.* The first case happens when the attach request message is lost. Figure 5(a) plots the signaling sequence during the attach procedure. Initially, EMM at the device sends an attach request to MME in the core network (Step 1), which replies an attach accept (Step 2). The device establishes the EPS bearer , and responds to MME with an attach complete signal (Step 3). However, this signal may be lost when invoking the RRC protocol for transmission to the base station, which further relays it to MME. According to the standards [7], RRC does not always ensure reliable delivery and the signal can be lost (*e.g.*, over the air). Since MME does not receive the attach complete message, inconsistent EMM states exist between the device and MME.

On the user side, he believes the attach procedure succeeds, while MME does not think so. Once the tracking area update (*i.e.*, location update in 4G) is triggered , the problem worsens. During this operation, the user sends the tracking area update request to MME (Step 5). However, upon receiving it, the EMM protocol at MME does not process it since it believes the attach procedure has not completed yet. EMM thus rejects it with error type *"implicitly detach"* and deregisters (*i.e.*, detaches) the device from 4G, which subsequently deletes the EPS bearer context. When receiving this reject message, the user device has to detach itself from the network after the prior attach success.

○ *Duplicate signaling messages.* The second case is observed when duplicate attach requests are received at MME (shown in Figure 5(b)). After sending the attach request (Step 1) through BS1, the mobile user roams to BS2. However, BS1 is under heavy load and defers the delivery of this signal to MME. Since it does not receive the reply message on time, the device retransmits the request signal (Step 2) via BS2 and receives the attach accept from MME. This completes the attach procedure at both the device and MME. However, the duplicated attach request finally arrives at MME via BS1. Given this duplicate signal, standards [8] stipulate that the EPS bearer context is deleted and MME processes the duplicate attach request. Two outcomes are possible. One is that the duplicate request is rejected. The device becomes *"out-of-service"*. The other is that it is accepted. The EPS bearer has to be re-constructed, and packet service is unavailable during the transition.

The EMM protocol at MME seems to have valid reasons to take above actions. Whenever it observes incomplete attach (in the first case), EMM has no reason to retain the EPS bearer context for the device. When receiving a new attach request at the registered state for the device, EMM has to reprocess it. Otherwise, it may lead to inconsistent states (*i.e.*, registered or deregistered) at MME and the user device. EMM indeed needs to reprocess the request to resolve inconsistency in other settings. Assume that the device is suddenly out of battery and cannot notify MME. MME still keeps the device in the registered state, thus leading to inconsistency between the device and MME. When the device later powers on after recharge and sends attach request to MME, EMM should process it to recover consistency.

There are two causes rooted in improper cross-layer interaction. First, EMM protocol itself is not prepared for out-of-sequenced signaling exchange. It makes the assumption that the underlying protocols ensure reliable, in-sequence signal delivery. Its design does not consider cases of lost and duplicate signals. Second, end-to-end (*i.e.*, from the device to MME through intermediate base stations) reliable delivery for signals is not readily ensured. This holds true even when reliable delivery is assured between user device and base station, as well as between the base station and MME. The exception arises during user mobility. Signals can be relayed by two different base stations, and the signals may still lose their original sequencing when arriving at MME.

### 5.2.2 *Experimental Validation*

In the experiments, we use three approaches to trigger the attach/reattach procedure in 4G: (1) power on and off the 4G-only devices, (2) manually change the network type between 3G-only and 4G-only on the device, and (3) reuse the experiments conducted in §5.1. To make signals lost in the air, we conduct experiments in the areas with weak signal coverage (*i.e.*, RSSI is below -110dBm).

Our tests indeed show that EMM signaling messages are lost when the radio transmission is bad. However, we do not observe the implicit detach due to lost signals. The most common scenario we observe is that user device keeps retransmitting the attach requests, while no attach accept message is received. It is because cellular networks are still closed systems, we are unable to drop or delay specific EMM signals from 4G base stations/MME to validate this design detect. In the future work, we plan to cooperate with operators to investigate network elements at the validation phase.

**Insight 2:** *During cross-layer protocol interactions, the key functionality of upper layer protocols should not merely rely on the non-always-guaranteed features in lower layer protocols. Otherwise, they are operating at the risk of failures.*

## 5.3 Inconsistent Cross-Domain/Cross-System Protocol State Transition

The third instance S3 is both cross-domain (between 3G CS and 3G PS ) and cross-system (between 3G and 4G). We find that, a 4G user device may get stuck in 3G, thus losing its 4G connectivity and high-speed access, after completing a CSFB voice call. This occurs when the device still carries a high-rate data session, regardless of whether the user is roaming or not. Note that this is against the design of CSFB, which should move the device back to 4G after the call. This scenario complements our recent study [27], which only uncovers similar problems but when the device uses low-rate data service. The root cause lies in inconsistent state transition for the RRC protocol when handling both CS-domain voice and PS-domain data in the process of inter-system switching.

### 5.3.1 *Issues and Root Causes*

Both instance S3 and that in [27] violate the property *MM_OK* (*i.e.*, inter-system mobility support). The device thus gets stuck in 3G, and cannot go back to 4G after the CSFB call. It happens when a CSFB call has terminated. Specifically, when making the call, the 4G user switches to 3G but still uses data service in the PS domain. Once the call completes, the device intends to switch back to 4G.

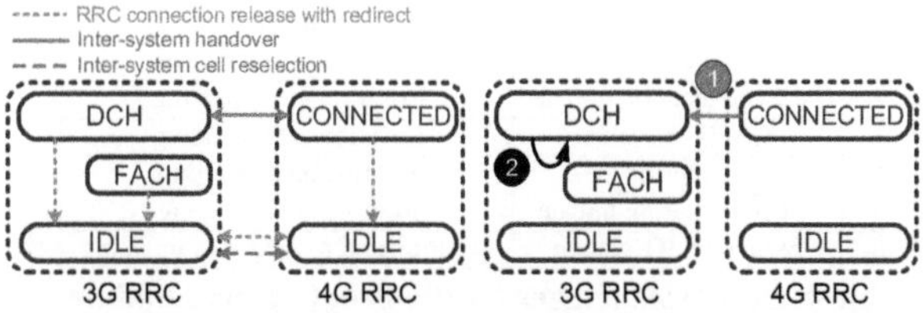

(a) Inter-system switch options (b) High-rate data + CSFB

**Figure 6: RRC states in various inter-system switching options.**

However, this inter-system switching cannot be activated (the property *MM_OK* is violated). We have two observations. First, there is an ongoing PS data session since the PDP context is active. Second, the 3G RRC state is at either `FACH` or `DCH` (*i.e.*, `CONNECTED`).

The root cause lies in the RRC protocol, which regulates both the CS domain and the PS domain during the inter-system switching between 3G and 4G. Figure 6(a) illustrates RRC transitions in three inter-system switching options. The first option, "RRC connection release with redirect", starts with RRC non-IDLE state and forces an RRC connection release before the inter-system switching. It migrates the device back to 4G but disrupts the ongoing high-rate data session. Second, an inter-system handover is invoked. It supports the direct transition between 3G `DCH` and 4G `CONNECTED`. It mitigates interruption of data session but incurs operation overhead for carriers (*e.g.*, buffering and relaying packets during the handover). The third option is "inter-system cell selection". It works for RRC IDLE state and it is triggered by the mobile device to look for better 3G/4G cells for subsequent switching.

The standard gives the carriers freedom to choose these switching options. However, the state transition for inter-system switching has design defects. Figure 6(b) shows the simplified RRC state transition in this CSFB case. When the CSFB call starts, the RRC state migrates from 4G to 3G `DCH` (Step 1) due to the high-rate data service. When the CSFB call in the 3G CS domain completes, RRC remains at the `DCH` state since the high-rate data is still ongoing. It is stuck in 3G if inter-system cell selection option is selected by operators. We see that the RRC state is determined by both CS-domain voice and PS-domain data. Although PS and CS domains do not interact directly, both domains rely on RRC for control. They share the same RRC state. This shows that, signaling interaction between CS and PS domains is done through the RRC protocol. The cross-domain signaling is needed because CS and PS domains are dependent. As long as the CS-based call is ongoing, data session in the PS domain has to stay in 3G. It may move to 4G only after the call terminates.

Carriers should not be held responsible for the deadlock. They do follow the standards. It is understandable for carriers to use "inter-system cell selection" to switch back to 4G after the CSFB call ends. First, it reduces the network loading to monitor and respond to each CSFB call state, since it is triggered by mobile device. Second, it does not interrupt current data sessions. However, the fundamental problem is that, 3G/4G standards fail to design the bullet-proof RRC protocol, which should handle all cross-domain, cross-system scenarios.

### 5.3.2 *Experimental Validation*

We start a 60-min UDP uplink/downlink data session at high rate (200kbps) in both OP-I and OP-II. We make a CSFB call from the LTE phone and hang it upon after the call starts. We confirm that the RRC state at the phone remains at `DCH` after the call hangs up. In OP-I, the phone switches to 4G in a few seconds through the option of *RRC Connection Release and Redirect*. Its data session is disrupted. In OP-II, the device gets stuck in 3G. It is the same as the duration of data sessions (about 60 minutes in our experiments).

| No | Scenario | Category |
|---|---|---|
| 1 | Cross location area | Location area updating |
| 2 | Periodic location update | Location area updating |
| 3 | CSFB call ends | Location area updating |
| 4 | Cross routing area | Routing area updating |
| 5 | Periodic routing update | Routing area updating |
| 6 | Switch to 3G system | Location and routing area updating |

**Table 4: Scenarios trigger location/routing area update.**

**Insight 3:** *The original well-designed features can become error-prone as new functions are enabled. Design options should be prudently justified, tested and regulated. Otherwise, the desirable benefit may be compromised by various unregulated option choices.*

# 6. PROBLEMATIC COUPLED ACTIONS

We now report three problematic coupling instances, discuss the root causes, and evaluate their impact on users.

## 6.1 HOL Blocking for Independent Updates

The instance S4 is on unnecessary coupling between cross-layer protocols in 3G. Both voice and data services may suffer from Head of Line (HOL) Blocking and thus extra latency due to independent, yet unnecessarily prioritized location update at underlaying layers. The involved protocols are CM/MM and SM/GMM for the CS domain and the PS domain, respectively.

### 6.1.1 Issues and Root Causes

The network needs to know the location of the device. Without it, the network cannot route *incoming* calls to the user. Table 4 lists various usage scenarios that may trigger location update. This update is performed for roaming users, and it is also used for periodic refresh without mobility or after inter-system switching. In 3G CS domain, the *location update* is initiated by MM protocol on user device, and sent to MSC. In 3G PS domain, the location update is performed by GMM via *routing area update*, and 3G gateway is responsible for accepting/rejecting it.

*CNetVerifier* reports that outgoing CS/PS service requests from the CM/SM layer can be delayed while the MM/GMM layer is doing location/routing area update. In CS, the issue arises when an outgoing call is initiated and CM sends the request[5] to MM. However, the CM service request is delayed (or even rejected based on the standards [6]) when MM is running the location update. Similar results can be observed on the cross-layer interaction of GMM and SM in the PS domain. Note that both the outgoing call request and the location update are initiated by the user device in S4 here.

At first sight, the above decision seems to be plausible. Two requests are waiting to be served. One is the CS/PS service request at CM/SM, while the other is the location update request at MM/GMM. The service request should be deferred and yield to the location update. Without correct location information updated at the network, the device is not reachable by others. Location updates should be processed with high priority.

However, this is not well grounded. Note that the call/data request is *outbound*. The device can always send it out. If this call request is served first, MSC also *implicitly* updates the location for the device as a byproduct of call serving. Therefore, *inbound* services are not affected by whether the location update request or the call request is served first. There is no need to serve the location update request in the expedited manner. Implicit update can be realized without any extra resource. The service requests on upper-layer CM/SM protocols are independent of the location updates at lower-layer MM/GMM. Artificially correlating and prioritizing them incur unnecessary latency to user service requests.

[5]It is used to establish the signaling connection between the device and MSC for call setup.

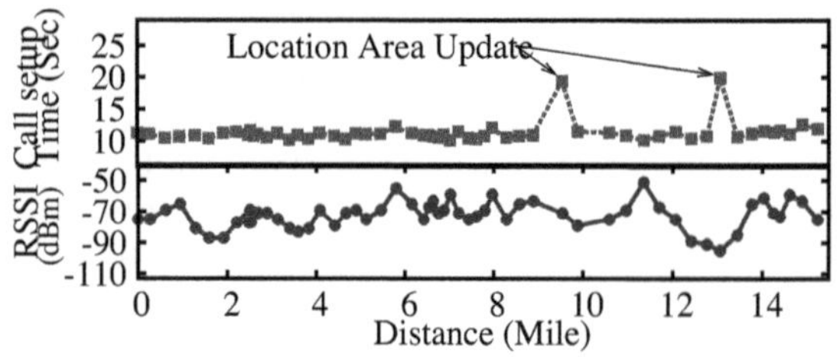


**Figure 7: Call setup time and RSSI on Route-1 in OP-I.**

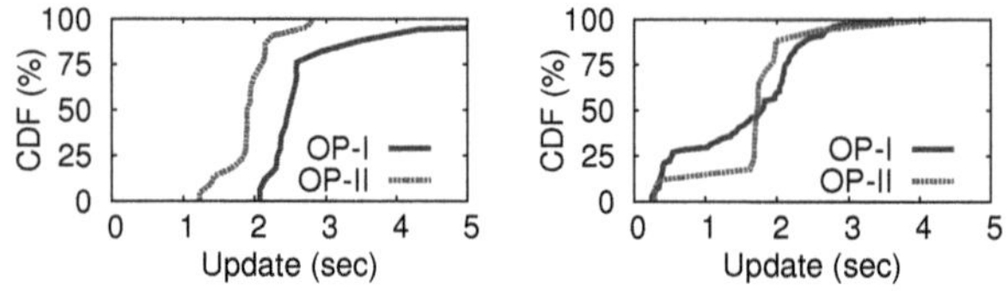


(a) Location area update (CS) (b) Routing area update (PS)

**Figure 8: CDF of location update durations in OP-I and OP-II.**

### 6.1.2 Experimental Validation

**Call service.** In the experiment, the caller repeatedly dials the callee, and immediately dials again once the callee hangs up. It is done when we drive along two routes: Route-1 (15-mile freeway) and Route-2 (28.3-mile freeway+local), in both OP-I and OP-II. The observed phenomenon is similar between carriers and across test runs. We show results in OP-I only. We indeed see that phones delay the call request until location update is completed. Figure 7 plots the call setup time on Route-1 (*i.e.*, from dialing to connected call) and the measured signal strength (RSSI). The average setup time is around 11.4 seconds, and RSSI varies within the good-signal range [-51dBm, -95dBm]. We observe two location updates at two spots of the route, 9.5 mile (RSSI:-73dBm) and 13.2 mile (RSSI:-87dBm). When the call is initiated during location update, the call setup time increases to 19.7 seconds, about 8.3 seconds longer than the average. Since the measured RSSI is strong, we infer that the extra time is caused by the location update. Figure 8(a) plots the CDF of duration for location area update. In OP-I, all updates take longer than 2 seconds, and the average is about 3 seconds. In OP-II, 72% of routing area updates take 1.2–2.1 seconds, and the average is 1.9 seconds.

We also notice a chain effect for delayed call services. The call requests are delayed for 8.3 seconds, whereas location update takes 4 seconds. It turns out, the extra 4.3 second gap is incurred by MM while it process both cross-layer MM and RRC related commands in the state "*MM-WAIT-FOR-NET-CMD*" [6] after the location update. In this state, all the call requests will be unnecessarily delayed until new commands from network arrive.

**Internet data service.** In this test, we first turn on the data service and transfer data packets to an Internet server, and then disable the PS service. Our experiments show that, the SM data requests are not immediately processed during the routing area update. Figure 8(b) plots the CDF of duration for routing area update. In OP-I, around 75% of updates take 1-3.6 seconds. In OP-II, 90% of routing area updates take from 1.6 seconds to 4.1 seconds. Therefore, the impact of routing area update in the PS domain is a little bit smaller than location update in the CS domain. This is because GMM does not process RRC related functions, whereas MM has to. However, routing area update is performed more frequently than location update. The user is more likely to experience delayed data service than a deferred outgoing call.

**Insight 4:** *Some procedures in upper and lower layers seem independent but are coupled by their execution order. Without prudent design, HOL blocking may happen.*

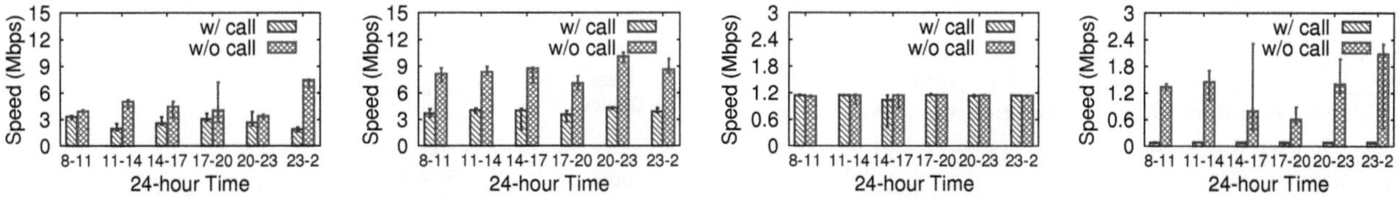


(a) Downlink (OP-I) (b) Downlink (OP-II) (c) Uplink (OP-I) (d) Uplink (OP-II)

**Figure 9: Downlink and uplink data speed (maximum, median and minimum) with/without CS calls in both carriers.**

```
10:22:48.056 EVENT 3G RRC    64QAM, set data rate = 21 Mbps   ON
10:22:48.379 EVENT 3G RRC    64QAM, Active

10:22:50.692 EVENT 3G CM/CC  Call is connecting
10:22:51.732 EVENT 3G RRC    64QAM, Inactive                  OFF
10:22:53.033 EVENT 3G CM/CC  Call is connected
10:22:56.067 EVENT 3G RRC    64QAM, Inactive

10:22:56.195 EVENT 3G CM/CC  Call is disconnected
10:22:58.212 EVENT 3G RRC    64QAM, set data rate = 21 Mbps   ON
10:22:58.627 EVENT 3G RRC    64QAM, Active
```

**Figure 10: An example protocol trace (64QAM is disabled during CS voice call, OP-I).**

## 6.2 Fate Sharing for Voice and Data

The instance S5 is an operational problem in dual-domain operations. In our experiments, we keep observing fate-sharing on transmission rates between PS and CS domains. When both PS and CS are accessing the 3G network on the phone, the PS data rate decreases significantly, compared with the case of accessing 3GPS only. This is due to improper cross-domain (CS/PS) coupling between PS and CS in 3G. It is implemented by carriers, and does not appear to be a design slip in the standards.

Figure 9 plots the downlink and uplink speed when the PS service is enabled with/without the CS call at different hours of a day. When both services are concurrently enabled, downlink and uplink data rates (expect the uplink rate in OP-I) decrease. It seems reasonable since PS and CS are competing for the shared radio resource. However, given that the best 3G CS voice is 12.2kbps [11], the actual PS data rate degrades beyond expectation (a small or mild drop expected). The downlink decline is up to 3.5-5.8 Mbps, about 73.9% in OP-I and 74.8% in OP-II. The uplink speed drop in OP-II reaches 96.1% (for OP-I, one 51.1% drop observed).

We figure out that, the large rate drop in PS is due to the inappropriate cross-domain channel sharing. In general, CS voice and PS data have different requirements. The CS traffic requires high resilience and low loss to ensure timely delivery and reduce voice message retransmission. It thus prefers the more robust, low-rate modulation scheme (*e.g.*, 16QAM). In contrast, PS traffic prefers high data rate for faster access. It thus prefers high-rate modulation (*e.g.*, 64QAM). Our protocol trace analysis shows that, both carriers configure the phone via the RRC protocol. The phone transfers both CS and PS traffic over the shared channel and apply the same modulation scheme. The modulation scheme is chosen so that the CS traffic is satisfied first, at the cost of PS rate degradation. Figure 10 gives an example trace collected in OP-I. We see that, before the voice call is made, the used modulation scheme is 64QAM, thus offering downlink speed up to 21Mbps. Once the voice call starts, both OP-I and OP-II disable 64QAM. The highest-rate modulation turns 16QAM, thus reducing the theoretical downlink speed to 11Mbps. The user thus suffers from large rate drop in its data service. Certainly, a tradeoff between performance and radio resource control exists. Sending CS and PS traffic over the shared channel may reduce carriers' resource waste [23]. However, it is achieved at the cost of large PS rate decline. The above measurements indicate that current tradeoff is not a good practice from users' perspective.

A different sharing scheme may yield better results. Consider each shared channel used by multiple users allow each to adopt his own modulation scheme; The modulation scheme may change over time due to varying signal strength. Also, one device can use multiple channels. Instead of coupling the CS and PS traffic from the same device on the shared channel, we can cluster PS sessions from multiple devices and let them share the same channel while CS sessions are grouped together and sent over the shared channel using the same modulation scheme. An alternative approach is to allow CS and PS to adopt their own modulation scheme. This way, diverse requirements of CS and PS traffic can both be met.

**Insight 5:** *When two domains have different goals and properties, their services should be decoupled as possible. Otherwise at least one domain's demands can be sacrificed.*

## 6.3 3G Failures Propagated to 4G System

S6 is a cross-system coupling case found from our experiments. The involved protocols are MM in 3G and EMM in 4G. The usage scenario is to make phone calls in 4G from the LTE phone. In this setting, CSFB is again used. The 4G carrier thus uses its legacy 3G system for the call. During the inter-system changes due to CSFB, location updates are performed in both 3G and 4G. However, such updates may fail. In both OP-I and OP-II, the error message on location area update failure in 3G is propagated to 4G. The 4G user may consequently become out of service, and the operator gains no benefit. Note that, location update is triggered during periodic refresh or CSFB calls, in addition to user mobility. The problem appears to be partly due to improper operational practice, and partly due to the standards that fail to specify the procedure.

Two location updates in 3G are performed when using CSFB for voice calls. The first update is needed after the 4G→3G switching once the call starts. It is initiated by the device. The standards state that this update action can be deferred until the call completes [5]; this helps to reduce the latency when serving the call in 3G. When the call completes, the second location update in 4G is done after the device switches back to 4G. It is done by the network. The update is first processed by MME in 4G, which relays the update request to MSC in 3G. Therefore, based on the standards, two location updates in 3G are activated.

Among the two location updates, one is deemed redundant. It yields no benefit, but incurs penalty. Which specific update does harm depends on the carrier. In OP-I, the first update hurts. The reason is that the delayed update is done once the call terminates. Since the inter-system switching back to 4G is fast, the device-initiated first update is disrupted. This incomplete update status is propagated from 3G to 4G, which sends the device a message with error type "*implicitly detach*". Upon receiving the error, the device enters the "*out-of-service*" state. Note that the 3G system already completes the second update, and the first one is unnecessary. In OP-II, the second update causes damage. The first update is completed first, since it takes more time for the carrier to switch from 3G back to 4G. The success of the first update may trigger MSC in 3G to refuse the second update that is relayed by MME to 3G. It thus replies to 4G MME with an error type "*MSC temporarily not reachable*". A detach request is sent by 4G to the device, and user enters the "*out-of-service*" state.

| Problem | S1 | S2 | S3 | S4 | S5 | S6 |
|---|---|---|---|---|---|---|
| **Observed** | √ | × | √ | √ | √ | √ |
| **Occurrence Prob.** | 3.1% (4/129) | 0.0% (0/30) | 62.1% (64/103) | 7.6% (6/79) | 77.4% (113/146) | 2.6% (5/190) |

**Table 5: Summary of user-based study on S1-S6.**

| Operator | Min | Median | Max | 90th percentile | Avg |
|---|---|---|---|---|---|
| OP-I | 1.1s | 2.3s | 52.6s | 13.7s | 6.2s |
| OP-II | 14.7s | 24.3s | 253.9s | 34.7s | 39.6s |

**Table 6: Duration in 3G after the CSFB call ends (S3).**

Note that both carriers make their decision with plausible excuses. If location update in 3G fails, it does harm the 4G LTE user. The user may miss *incoming* calls. Such incoming calls cannot reach the mobile user if its location update fails. This is why both carriers share and act on the error messages regarding location update failures in 3G and 4G. However, this error-handling process should be confined between 3G MSC and 4G MME inside the network infrastructure. Indeed, they can collaborate to resolve the failures. The error-handling actions should not be directed and exposed to the device. This malpractice can be avoided.

**Insight 6:** *For the same functions in different networks, they should be coordinated to reduce the conflict. Particularly, the internal failure from one network should not be propagated to another network.*

# 7. USER STUDY

To assess the real-world impact, we conduct two-week user study with 20 volunteers, including students, faculty members, engineers and technology-unsavvy people. 12 people use 4G-capable phones, while others use 3G-only phones. We observe 190 CSFB calls, 146 CS calls in 3G, 436 inter-system switches (380 switches are caused by 190 CSFB calls), and 30 attaches induced by (re)starting user devices or auto recovery from the *out-of-service* state. Table 5 summarizes the results for six instances S1-S6.

**S1 (§5.1):** In S1, a user in 3G fails to switch to 4G if its PDP context is deactivated. In our study, we observe 218 4G→3G switches due to CSFB calls (190), user mobility (10) and carrier operations[6] (8). 129 of them are made while mobile data is ON, and 4 S1 events are observed. This results in about 3.1% (4/129) for S1 events in case of 4G→3G switches with enabled mobile data.

**S2 (§5.2):** S2 results in the attach failure. 30 attaches are observed but none of them fails. It implies that S2 rarely occurs. This can be due to that all are performed in the area with good coverage (the weakest signal strength is -95dBm).

**S3 (§5.3):** In S3, users do not immediately return to 4G when a CSFB call ends. Among 190 CSFB calls, 103 (39 in OP-I and 64 in OP-II) are made while mobile data is enabled. Table 6 shows the duration in 3G after their CSFB calls end. OP-I users usually switch back to 4G within 3 seconds. It is because OP-I uses "*RRC Connection Release with redirect*," which can be triggered at RRC Non-IDLE state. However, OP-II users get stuck in 3G much longer because OP-II performs "*inter-system cell selection*," which occurs only at RRC IDLE state. We note that all are shorter than that in validation experiments. This is because the duration of getting stuck in 3G depends on the lifetime of ongoing data sessions.

**S4 (§6.1):** We mainly consider the HOL blocking for 3G CS calls. We check whether there is any location area update done in 1.2 s right after the outgoing call starts, because this update takes at least 1.2 s to complete (§6.1). We observe 79 outgoing calls out of 146 CS calls in 3G. Six (*i.e.*, 7.6%) are affected. In case of longer location area updates (>1.2 s), the ratio is larger.

[6]Note that it may be still triggered by user mobility. However, we cannot justify it since GPS is not always turned on by participants.

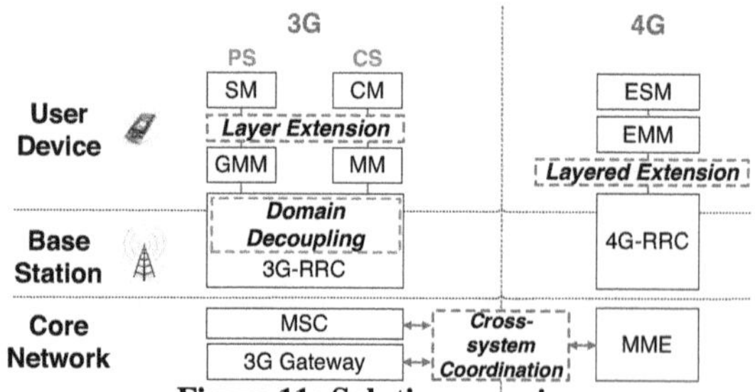

**Figure 11: Solution overview.**

**S5 (§6.2):** We examine how often CS calls affect PS data traffic and how much data is affected during a call. It is observed that 77.4% 3G CS calls (113 out of 146) happen while data traffic is ongoing. For these calls, the average duration is 67s, and the average affected data volume is 368KB. Most calls (109/113) affect the data volume less than 550KB, whereas the remaining four calls have impact on more than 4MB data (the largest one is 18.5MB).

**S6: (§6.3):** In addition to S1, the failure of location update required by CSFB calls make the users fail to switch back to 4G after a CSFB call. It turns out to happen in 5 out of 190 calls (2.6%).

This study with small samples may not accurately quantify the real-world impact and can be further improved with more participants. The result partly confirms that current cellular networks are largely successful. However, it also shows that the found issues do occur in our daily life and affect our real mobile usage. Moreover, though some issues arise with small or negligible probability during normal usage, they may be manipulated and inflated if malicious exploits are launched against cellular networks or users.

# 8. SOLUTION

We now present our solution, as shown in Figure 11. It has three modules of layer extension, domain decoupling and cross-system coordination. We next elaborate on each component.

**Layer Extension.** We propose a slim layer with reliable transfer for the out-of-sequence signaling in §5.2 at the EMM, and then parallelize independent operations in §6.1. In the former, the slim layer is inserted between EMM and RRC. Its reliable transfer ensures the end-to-end in-order signal exchange between the phone and MME. To be compatible with the current system, it bridges the interfaces between EMM and RRC and encapsulates the information of reliable transfer function. For the latter, location update should be decoupled from the CS or PS service request for MM and GMM, respectively. Each of MM/GMM maintains two parallel threads. One is for the location update, whereas the other is for remaining functions including the outgoing CS/PS service request. The outgoing CS/PS service request is given higher priority than location update, since the former procedure implicitly does the latter.

**Domain Decoupling.** Two domains are coupled at the RRC layer. Therefore, we propose a domain decoupling module in RRC. It aims to eliminate the unnecessary interference (*e.g.*, triggered events in §5.3, modulation downgrade in §6.2) from one domain to another. For the triggered events, one domain should not be constrained by another domain. That is, when CSFB is triggered in the CS domain, it should perform 3G→4G switch when the call ends. If the switch condition is satisfied (*e.g.*, 4G is available), the switch will be executed, not blocked by the operations in the PS domain. To this end, the base station adds a CSFB tag to assist the subsequent inter-system switching.

To avoid the modulation downgrade, the 3G RRC can decouple PS and CS services by assigning different channels. Therefore, PS and CS services can be transmitted with different modulation schemes (*e.g.*, 64QAM for PS and 16QAM for CS). To enable the decoupling, we distinguish CS/PS traffic and assign radio resource independently. Both can be satisfied within the current standard and system. First, Radio Link Control (RLC, refer to Figure 1) can exploit the source of traffic (different modules and interfaces used for CS and PS) to differentiate voice and data traffic. Second, the standard allows to assign one device multiple radio channels, each of which can be configured separately.

**Cross-system Coordination.** The similar functions in different systems should be coordinated because they seek to serve the similar purpose, despite using (slightly) different system-specific approaches. The key is to (1) share the information with each other and (2) collaborate to enforce proper operation. Specifically, 4G EPS bearer context and PDP context are equivalently critical to enable data services. Two systems should enforce the proper transition when the user device switches across 3G and 4G. We recommend that one detach condition should be removed in the standard. It is triggered when the user device without active PDP context switches from 3G to 4G. Instead of detaching itself, the device should immediately activate EPS bearer after inter-system 3G→4G switching. Thus seamless system change can be ensured (§5.1).

In case of failures in one system, the other system should help on recovery if possible. For example, in the second issue (§6.3), the 4G MME should not detach the user device upon the failure of location update in the 3G. Instead, it should recover the devices' location update with the 3G MSC on behalf of the device. In the standard, it is not stipulated that the MME should detach the user device upon the 3G failure. We suggest the operators abolish it.

# 9. PROTOTYPE AND EVALUATION

We describe the solution prototype and assess its effectiveness.

**Prototype of Control Plane.** We prototype the control plane functions at three major components, user device, base station, and core network in the cellular network. The user device uses a programmable Android phone. We use two commercial machines (both Lenovo X230) to emulate the base station and the core network. Note that our prototype is based on our own proof-of-concept 3G/4G stacks, since the operational stacks are not accessible.

We implement the modules of connectivity management (CC/SM/ESM) and mobility management (MM/GMM/EMM) at both the user device and the core network. For connectivity management, there are two functions: CS/PS service establishment/release, and the activation/deactivation of PDP context/EPS bearer. The mobility management module provides three functions: attach/detach, location update, and signaling establishment of SM/CM/ESM. We also implement the RRC layer at the device and the base station. Since the transmission at the RRC layer is not reliable, we use UDP to emulate it. We use TCP to forward (relay) RRC payloads between the base station and the core network, since their transmission is assumed to be reliable. All functions are implemented in the application layer.

## 9.1 Layer Extension

We show that our reliable shim layer in §8 prevents the detach caused by the duplicate or the lost EMM signaling messages. To emulate the lost of EMM messages, the RRC at the base station drops the message according to a given drop rate. For each test, user device does both attach and tracking area update for 100 times. Figure 12 (left) shows that the number of detach varies with the given drop rate with/without our solution. Note that the detach times linearly increase with the drop rate when no solution is used. With our solution, there is no detach while the drop rate increases.

To decouple the location update from the CS service, both the device and core network's MM create two threads to handle them

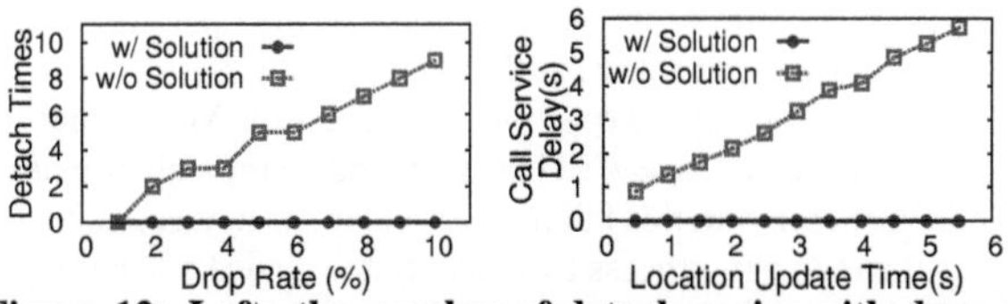


**Figure 12: Left: the number of detach varies with drop rate. Right: the call delay call varies with the location update time.**

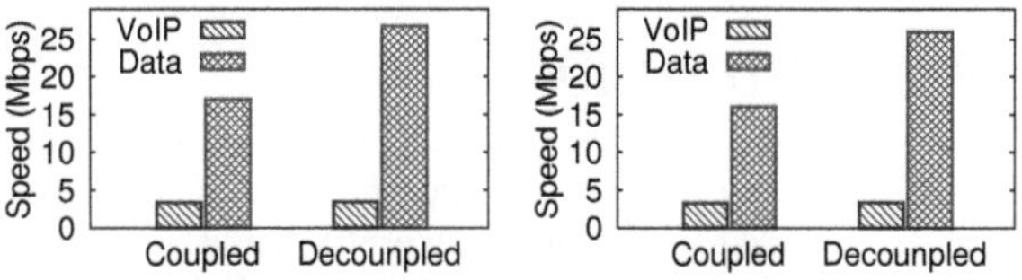


**Figure 13: The data speeds vary with/without the coupled data and voice: downlink (Left) and uplink (Right).**

concurrently. The location update and the PS service for GMM are also decoupled in the same way. We examine the CS/PS service delay incurred by the location update in MM/GMM. We show only the result of the CS service, and PS service's result is similar. The MM function is configured to do location update every 30 seconds. When the location update is triggered, CM at the user device immediately triggers a call service through MM. Figure 12 (right) shows that the call service delay at MM varies with the processing time of location update. Note that the processing time may vary with the loading of signalling at the core network. Without enabling our solution, the service delay linearly increases with the processing time. However, our solution does not have delay since MM has two threads to deal with location update and call service concurrently.

## 9.2 Domain Decoupling

We decouple the CS/PS service with two actions. First, we apply different modulations (channels) to CS and PS traffic. Since we have no BS access, we use WiFi Rate Adaptation (RA) module to emulate 16QAM and 64QAM modulation in the CS/PS decoupling case. This can be approximated by using two 48 Mbps and 24 Mbps rates in 802.11a. Note that the overhead could be different between 3G and WiFi, but the result is similar. Figure 13 shows the speed for voice and data in both coupled and decoupled cases. Voice traffic is generated by Skype's VOIP calls. It is observed that the speed of data traffic at the decoupling can be improved by about 1.6 times for both downlink and uplink. In the mean time, the voice can still be carried by a robust modulation. The difference between the speeds of voice and data at the coupling, comes from the voice's small packet size. It incurs more overhead on transmission.

Second, to prevent the CSFB inter-system switching from being blocked in the PS domain, we add a new function into the BS's RRC. It asks the user device to switch its RRC state to a proper state for inter-system switching, once the switching is used to complete the CSFB procedure. It is verified that the user device's CSFB switching is never blocked, by enabling our solution.

## 9.3 Cross-system Coordination

We prototype two remedies for the cross-system coordination between 3G and 4G. First, the user device always activates the EPS bearer if it does not have active PDP context, after inter-system 3G→4G switching. We test it in the scenario that the user device without PDP context switches from 3G to 4G. The remedy can prevent the device from being detached, so the switch takes only 0.1-0.4s (median is 0.27s). Without the remedy, it takes 0.3-1.3s (median is 0.9s) since the device has to re-attach to 4G network after being detached. This delay may be much larger due to more complicated procedure or the heavy loading at the operator's core network. It is observed as large as 24.7s (§5.1).

In the second remedy, two actions are taken by MME once it receives the failure message of 3G location update for a user device. First, it does not forward this failure message to the device. Second, it triggers the recovery process by updating the device's location to the 3G MSC. It is verified that the MME does not detach the user device upon the failure of location update in the 3G, and further recover it by updating device's location with the MSC later.

# 10. RELATED WORK

Cellular networking has been an active research area in recent years. Some interesting findings on inappropriate cellular network operations are reported, including the interplay between applications and cellular infrastructure [9, 14], TCP over cellular data forwarding [13], mutual interference between data and voice [27], and misbehaviors in cellular functions [21, 22, 26], to name a few. Our work differs from all such early studies. They focus on packet transmission on the data plane while we work on the control plane. Moreover, they study protocols at the end hosts whereas our entities are at both the devices and the infrastructure elements.

Protocol verification has been investigated for the Internet protocols [12, 17, 19, 24]. New techniques have been recently developed for more complex scenarios. For example, [18] presents SAT-based data-plane debugging; [10] enhances the OpenFlow application debugging with symbolic execution of event handlers; header space analysis is applied for testing complex interactions between various Internet protocols [15]. Our study is orthogonal to these efforts. We focus on protocol verification for cellular networks.

In cellular networks, formal model analysis has been applied to individual protocols. [20] verifies the 2G handover protocol using a generic mobility model with $\pi$-calculus. [25] models the authentication protocol and identifies several security loopholes. Our work differs in both the problem and the solution approach. We study protocol interactions and employ two-phrase verification.

# 11. CONCLUSION

In 3G/4G cellular networks, control-plane protocols are more complex than their counterparts over the Internet. They have to work in more diversified usage settings, e.g., between CS and PS domains, and across 3G and 4G systems. They also support additional functions, including mobility, data and carrier-grade voice, fine control over radio resources. Consequently, inter-protocol signaling is widespread along all three dimensions of cross-layer, cross-domain, and cross-system scenarios.

We show that, some interactions are not well designed, whereas others are not properly operated. The inter-dependent signaling protocols may not take concerted actions. The independent ones are unnecessarily coupled. The incurred damages include both functional incorrectness and performance degradation. The penalty is more pronounced than data-plane faults in data transfer. They may get mobile users stuck in 3G, or deny them 4G access.

Three domain-specific lessons in cellular networks are learnt from our work. First, in the cross-layer case, the well-tested layering rule from the Internet should be honored. If the lower layer does not provide certain functions, the higher layer has to do so, or to be prepared to work without those functions. Coupling inter-layer actions is also not a good practice unless properly justified. Second, in the cross-domain case, signaling design should recognize the inter-domain difference. Treating domains identically seems to reduce design and operational complexity, but makes it overly simplistic and error prone. Third, in the cross-system case, failure messages can be shared and even acted upon between systems. However, it is better not to expose such failure-handling operations outside the system unless absolutely needed.

In the broader scope, research on control-plane protocols in cellular networks warrants more efforts. 3G/4G is a large-scale infrastructure on a par with the wired Internet. There is no competing wireless technology for universal coverage and wide-area mobility support on the horizon. Given such a critical system indispensable to smartphones and tablets, more research is needed. The control-plane research in cellular networks also complements the study on the Internet counterpart. While the Internet seeks to enhance its control plane (*e.g.*, [16]), the cellular system needs to simplify its signaling design. Both can benefit from each other in the process.

# 12. ACKNOWLEDGMENTS

We greatly appreciate our shepherd, Dr. Ratul Mahajan, and the SIGCOMM reviewers for their valuable feedback. We also thank all participants in the user study. This project at its early stage was partially supported by NSF Grant CSR-1017127.

# 13. REFERENCES

[1] Speedtest.net - Ookla. http://www.SpeedTest.net.
[2] Voice over LTE. http://www.gsma.com/technicalprojects/volte.
[3] 3GPP. TS25.331: Radio Resource Control (RRC), 2006.
[4] 3GPP. TS23.401: GPRS Enhancements for E-UTRAN Access, 2011.
[5] 3GPP. TS23.272: CSFB in EPS, 2012.
[6] 3GPP. TS24.008: Mobile Radio Interface Layer 3, 2012.
[7] 3GPP. TS36.331: Radio Resource Control (RRC), 2012.
[8] 3GPP. TS24.301: Non-Access-Stratum (NAS) for EPS; , Jun. 2013.
[9] N. Balasubramanian, A. Balasubramanian, and A. Venkataramani. Energy Consumption in Mobile Phones: A Measurement Study and Implications for Network Applications. In *IMC*, 2009.
[10] M. Canini, D. Venzano, P. Peresini, D. Kostic, and J. Rexford. A NICE Way to Test OpenFlow Applications. In *NSDI*, 2012.
[11] H. Holma and A. Toskala. *WCDMA for UMTS - HSPA Evolution and LTE*. Wiley, 2007.
[12] G. J. Holzmann. *Design and Validation of Computer Protocols*. Bell Laboratories, 1991.
[13] J. Huang, F. Qian, Y. Guo, Y. Zhou, Q. Xu, Z. M. Mao, S. Sen, and O. Spatscheck. An in-depth study of LTE: Effect of network protocol and application behavior on performance. In *SIGCOMM'13*.
[14] U. Javed, D. Han, R. Caceres, J. Pang, S. Seshan, and A. Varshavsky. Predicting Handoffs in 3G Networks. *SIGOPS Oper. Syst. Rev.*, 45(3):65–70, Jan. 2012.
[15] P. Kazemian, G. Varghese, and N. McKeown. Header Space Analysis: Static Checking for Networks. In *NSDI*, 2012.
[16] T. Koponen, M. Casado, N. Gude, et al. Onix: A distributed control platform for large-scale production networks. In *OSDI*, 2010.
[17] B. T. Loo, J. M. Hellerstein, I. Stoica, et al. Declarative routing: Extensible routing with declarative queries. In *SIGCOMM'05*.
[18] H. Mai, A. Khurshid, R. Agarwal, et al. Debugging the data plane with anteater. *SIGCOMM Comp. Comm. Rev.*, 41(4):290–301, 2011.
[19] M. Musuvathi and D. R. Engler. Model checking large network protocol implementations. In *NSDI*, 2004.
[20] F. Orava and J. Parrow. An algebraic verification of a mobile network. *Formal Aspects of Computing*, 4(6):497–543, 1992.
[21] C. Peng, C. Li, G. Tu, S. Lu, and L. Zhang. Mobile Data Charging: New Attacks and Countermeasures. In *CCS*, 2012.
[22] C. Peng, G. Tu, C. Li, and S. Lu. Can We Pay for What We Get in 3G Data Access? In *MobiCom*, 2012.
[23] Qualcomm. Circuit-Switched Voice Services over HSPA.
[24] M. A. Smith. Formal Verification of Communication Protocols. In *FORTE*, pages 129–144, 1996.
[25] C. Tang. *Modeling and Analysis of Mobile Telephony Protocols*. PhD thesis, Stevens Institute of Technology, 2013.
[26] G. Tu, C. Peng, C. Li, et al. Accounting for Roaming Users on Mobile Data Access: Issues and Root Causes. In *MobiSys*, 2013.
[27] G. Tu, C. Peng, H. Wang, C. Li, and S. Lu. How Voice Calls Affect Data in Operational LTE Networks. In *MobiCom*, 2013.

# RF-IDraw: Virtual Touch Screen in the Air Using RF Signals

Jue Wang, Deepak Vasisht, and Dina Katabi
Massachusetts Institute of Technology
{jue_w,deepakv,dk}@mit.edu

## ABSTRACT

Prior work in RF-based positioning has mainly focused on discovering the absolute location of an RF source, where state-of-the-art systems can achieve an accuracy on the order of tens of centimeters using a large number of antennas. However, many applications in gaming and gesture based interface see more benefits in knowing the detailed shape of a motion. Such trajectory tracing requires a resolution several fold higher than what existing RF-based positioning systems can offer.

This paper shows that one can provide a dramatic increase in trajectory tracing accuracy, even with a small number of antennas. The key enabler for our design is a multi-resolution positioning technique that exploits an intrinsic tradeoff between improving the resolution and resolving ambiguity in the location of the RF source. The unique property of this design is its ability to precisely reconstruct the minute details in the trajectory shape, even when the absolute position might have an offset. We built a prototype of our design with commercial off-the-shelf RFID readers and tags and used it to enable a virtual touch screen, which allows a user to interact with a desired computing device by gesturing or writing her commands in the air, where each letter is only a few centimeters wide.

## 1. INTRODUCTION

RF-based positioning has become the next frontier for innovation in mobile computing, business analytics, and human-computer interaction [16, 29, 17]. The topic has attracted much interest from both the industry [30, 14, 23, 3] and the research community, which translated to many advanced RF-localization systems [41, 19, 39]. So far, however, the literature has mainly focused on the problem of discovering the exact location of an RF source on a building floor [41, 19, 13, 28]. Many applications, on the other hand, care more about the detailed trajectory of a target as opposed to its exact location; for example, in gesture-based user interfaces, it is more important to be able to precisely track the shape of a gesture with high resolution and fidelity, while the actual position may still have an offset. For such applications, existing schemes cannot reproduce an accurate version of the trajectory shape to satisfy the applications' needs.

This paper introduces RF-IDraw, a system that can accurately trace the trajectory of an RF source, particularly an RFID. RF-IDraw's trajectory tracing is so accurate that it enables a *virtual touch screen* based on RF signals. Today, a user can write, scroll, or swipe on a touch screen of a smart phone or tablet. Taking this a step further, RF-IDraw allows a user to input her commands by writing, scrolling, swiping, etc., without being in physical touch with a screen – the user can write in the air any word or command using an RFID attached to a pen or a finger splint, as shown in Fig. 1(a). RF-IDraw would reconstruct the RFID's trajectory and interpret the user's writing and gestures as input to the desired computing device. Essentially, RF-IDraw can transform any plane or surface in space into a virtual touch screen. Fig. 1(b) shows an example of RF-IDraw's output which was entered by writing in the air using an RFID on the user's finger. Such a virtual touch screen can be used to realize a variety of applications. For example, it can be used to interact with a remote screen, to send commands to a cell phone without touching it, or to interface with small devices (e.g., sensors) that do not have space for a keyboard.

RF-IDraw's technology is based on the realization that a different design principle for leveraging multiple antennas can lead to a significant improvement in both tracing and localization accuracy. Specifically, state-of-the-art RF-based positioning systems typically use an antenna array, and leverage its beamsteering capability to detect the direction of the source [41, 39, 12, 21]. The location of the source can then be computed by intersecting the beams of multiple such arrays. Hence, to obtain a high accuracy, they need an array with a narrow beam, which requires a large number of antennas. For example, Fig. 2 compares the beam width of 2-antenna and 4-antenna arrays; both have the default antenna spacing of $\frac{\lambda}{2}$,


*SIGCOMM'14*, August 17–22, 2014, Chicago, IL, USA.

ACM 978-1-4503-2836-4/14/08 ...$15.00.
http://dx.doi.org/10.1145/2619239.2626330 .

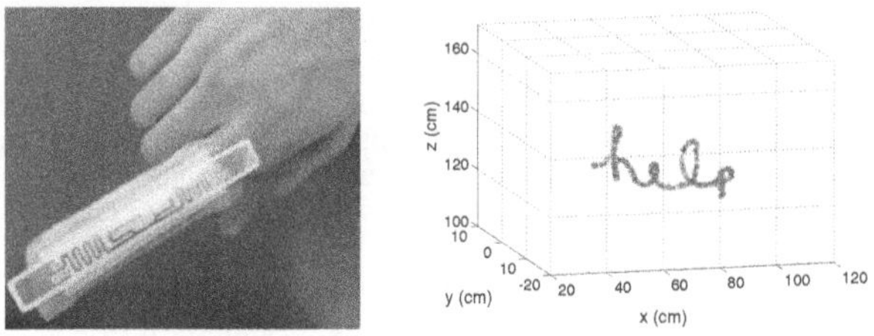


(a) RFID (b) Reconstructed Word

**Figure 1—Enabling Virtual Touch Screen:** By accurately tracing the trajectory shape of an RFID on the user's finger, RF-IDraw can transform any plane or surface into a virtual touch screen, allowing the user to input her commands in the air using RF signals.

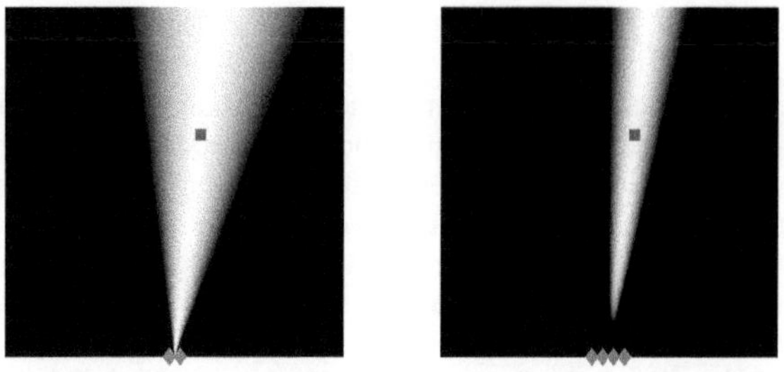

(a) 2-Antenna Array Beam (b) 4-Antenna Array Beam

**Figure 2—Antenna Array Beam Resolution:** The figure shows an RF source in blue, and the beams of two antenna arrays with 2 and 4 antenna elements each. The more antennas in the array, the narrower its beam, and the tighter it can bound the source direction.

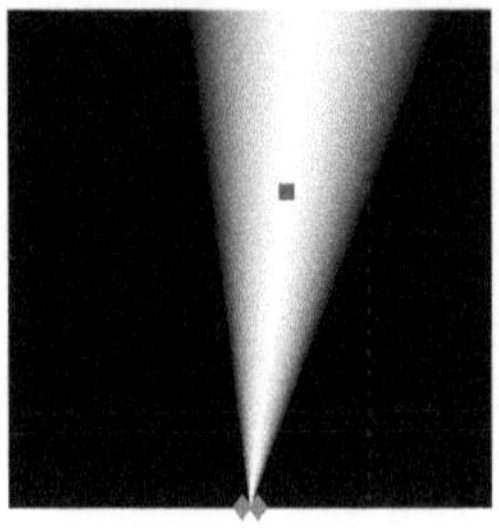
(a) $\frac{\lambda}{2}$ Separation

(b) $\lambda$ Separation

(c) $8\lambda$ Separation

**Figure 3—Tradeoff Between Improving Resolution and Removing Ambiguity:** As the separation of the antenna pair (marked in red) increases, the number of beams increases accordingly, causing ambiguity in localizing the source (marked in blue). On the other hand, each beam gets narrower, leading to a higher resolution.

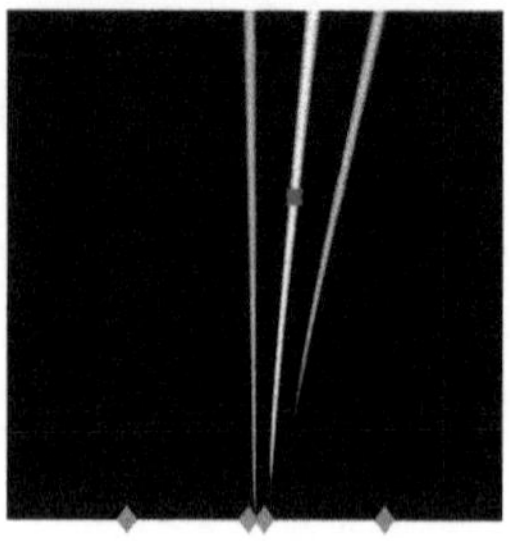

**Figure 4—Multi-Resolution Design:** The wide beam in Fig. 3(a) acts as a filter on Fig. 3(c), removing ambiguity while maintaining the high resolution.

where $\lambda$ is the wavelength. Clearly, the more antennas on the array, the narrower its beam and the higher the resolution it provides in identifying the direction of the source. Thus, a standard approach in RF positioning systems is to increase the number of antennas in the array in order to achieve higher accuracy [41, 39].

In contrast, in designing RF-IDraw, we realize that for any number of antennas, there is always a tradeoff between *resolution* and *unambiguity*. Specifically, let us fix the number of antennas to be 2, and consider the beam patterns of this pair of antennas when they are separated by $\frac{\lambda}{2}$, $\lambda$, and $8\lambda$ respectively, as shown in Fig. 3(a), (b) and (c). As we can see, when the antenna separation is $\frac{\lambda}{2}$, the array has a single beam; yet the beam is wide and does not pinpoint the direction of the source, i.e., low resolution. As the antenna separation increases, the beam becomes narrower and more tightly bounds the direction of the source. However, instead of a single beam, we start to see multiple beams, despite the fact that there is a single direction along which the actual signal arrives, which causes ambiguity. Thus, there is a tradeoff in antenna spacing, between localizing with high resolution and localizing with no ambiguity.

Past work uses arrays with a maximum antenna spacing of $\lambda/2$ [41, 39, 19], hence avoiding ambiguity, but also sacrificing the potential of higher resolution. In contrast, in RF-IDraw, we leverage our understanding of the structure of the ambiguity to increase localization accuracy. In particular, RF-IDraw uses a few antenna pairs with different separations. The pairs with larger separation have very narrow beams and hence define the resolution of the positioning system. The pairs with small separation operate as filters to eliminate the ambiguity introduced by the widely separated antenna pairs, while maintaining the high resolution. Fig. 4 shows the result after applying the wide beam in Fig. 3(a) as a filter on Fig. 3(c). As we can see, most of the unintended beams have been filtered out and there is one distinctive narrow beam (whiter means higher likelihood) that bounds the correct direction of the source. Note that, both Fig. 2(b) and Fig. 4 are produced using a total of 4 antennas, yet the latter offers significantly higher resolution (i.e., much narrower beam) than the standard 4-antenna array, and thus demonstrates a more effective way of arranging the antennas.

A key characteristic of RF-IDraw's design is its ability to trace the detailed shape of an RF source's trajectory, even when the actual position has some offset. The tracing accuracy is due to the use of the fine beams in Fig. 3(c). Recall that tracking with an antenna array means that the beam of the array rotates to follow the source direction. When we have multiple beams as in Fig. 3(c), the correct beam rotates to track the source, but the wrong beams also rotate with it. Thus, even if one mistook the correct beam, the shape of the trajectory would continue to match the performed gesture, as further explained in §4.

We have built a prototype of RF-IDraw using commercial RFID readers and used it to track off-the-shelf UHF RFIDs. Further, we integrated RF-IDraw with the handwriting recognition functionality in the MyScript Stylus [36] Android app to evaluate RF-IDraw's function as a virtual touch screen. We run our experiments with five users in both line-of-sight and non-line-of-sight, 2–5 meters away from the reader antennas.[1] Our experiments lead to the following findings:

- RF-IDraw can track the detailed trajectory shape of the users' writing with a median accuracy of 3.7 cm, 11× more accurate than the state-of-the-art antenna array based technique using the same number of antennas. Note that, this accuracy number does not fully capture the power of RF-IDraw's trajectory tracing. In particular, even with a median 3.7 cm error on points along the trajectory, the shape of the overall trajectory is still preserved, because this error only reflects the coherent stretching or squeezing of the trajectory. Therefore, the handwritten characters reconstructed by RF-IDraw are correctly recognized by MyScript Stylus in 97.5% of the cases, and the words reconstructed by RF-IDraw are correctly recognized in 92% of the cases. In contrast, for the trajectories reproduced by the antenna array based technique using the same number of antennas as RF-IDraw, the character recognition success rate is less than 4%, which is equivalent to a random guess, and the word recognition success rate is 0%.
- RF-IDraw's trajectory tracing accuracy holds in non-line-of-sight scenarios, where the median accuracy is 4.9 cm, and the character recognition success rate is 96.8%.
- Even when identifying the exact location, as opposed to tracing, RF-IDraw's accuracy is 2.2× higher than the baseline that uses antenna arrays with the same number of antennas as RF-IDraw.

To our knowledge, RF-IDraw is the first RF-based system that can transform any plane or surface into a virtual touch screen, which opens up an entirely new range of applications in user interaction interfaces.

## 2. RELATED WORK

Prior work on RF-based positioning has primarily relied on RSSI (Received Signal Strength) [13, 28] or AoA (Angle of Arrival) information [41, 19, 22]. State-of-the-art systems use antenna arrays or synthetic aperture radar (SAR) to extract AoA of an RF signal and can achieve a positioning accuracy on the order of tens of centimeters [41, 19]. Using a dense, surveyed grid of reference sources,

[1]Unlike WiFi based localization work that aims to locate users on an office floor (e.g., [41]), RF-IDraw operates at a shorter range since it is based on RFID. §9.3 discusses the prospect of applying RF-IDraw's techniques to WiFi systems.

several schemes can achieve a higher accuracy of a few centimeters by identifying the nearest references [39, 37]. For example, the work in [37] leverages the motion of a robot equipped with reference RFIDs to enable centimeter-scale accuracy in grasping an object tagged with RFIDs. RF-IDraw differs from these past schemes in both techniques and capabilities. By effectively exploiting the high resolution of antenna pairs with large separations, RF-IDraw offers unmatched accuracy in tracking an RF device's detailed trajectory without the use of references. As such, it enables a whole new class of applications which are previously infeasible using RF signals, such as virtual touch screen in the air.

The conception and design of RF-IDraw are inspired by astronomical interferometry, where telescopes are used to image the sky and search for planets [20, 34, 2]. In particular, in astronomy, pairs of telescopes with large separation are used to produce high-resolution fringes. One can consider these telescopes as antennas. The narrow beams produced by RF-IDraw's antenna pairs with large separation and the fringes in interferometry are similar in nature, i.e., both offer high resolution at the cost of ambiguity. Ambiguity in interferometry is resolved using delay lines which effectively orient each telescope pair towards a particular part of the sky, whereas in RF-IDraw, we use a pair of antennas with small separation to focus on a particular region in the area of interest. Furthermore, in astronomy, the rotation of the Earth/sky is exploited to facilitate better coverage and accuracy. In RF-IDraw, although we do not have a known motion like the rotation of the Earth to leverage, we integrate information gathered throughout the trajectory of the RF device to improve the elimination of ambiguity, which has a similar flavor. However, while the underlying intuition is transferable between the two, RF-IDraw's algorithms, signal processing techniques, and applications significantly differ from astronomical interferometry.

In the context of RF antenna arrays, recently there is a growing interest in exploring the use of sparse arrays to estimate the angle of arrival [31, 25, 18]. For example, [31, 25] propose the use of coprime sampling in a large uniform linear array to reduce the number of antennas needed; [18] evaluates the use of compressive sensing in sampling the antenna positions. By virtue of emulating very large arrays, these schemes show asymptotic improvement over the naive AoA approach through theoretical analyses. However, for a small number of antennas available to our application of interest (i.e., 8 in total), the asymptotic analysis does not lead to any meaningful gain, and hence these proposals cannot achieve the resolution enabled by RF-IDraw. Furthermore, they focus on estimating a single measurement of angle of arrival, as opposed to tracing the trajectory shape as RF-IDraw does.

Systems such as [7] and [32] make use of depth sensors (e.g., Kinect) and infrared cameras (e.g., Wii) to turn a projector screen or wall into a touch screen and allow a user to interact with the display using a specially designed pen. RF-IDraw is the first RF-based virtual touch screen; unlike solutions based on depth imaging or infrared, it does not require line-of-sight to work. Further, since RF sources have unique IDs (e.g., RFID EPC ID [15]), it is easy to scale to a larger number of users simultaneously interacting through the virtual touch screen without causing confusion.

Finally, RF-IDraw's application is inspired by recent work on motion tracking [27, 10, 9] which uses RF signals to enable a user to interact with the environment. Differing from these systems, RF-IDraw is the first RF-based solution that can accurately reconstruct the detailed trajectory of a user's writing or gesturing in the air, where each letter or gesture is only a few centimeters wide. Such capability is not supported by prior work in RF-based gesture recognition. For example, [27] presents a state-of-the-art WiFi-based interface, yet it only supports the detection and classification of a predefined set of nine gestures. Further, past work on RF-based gesture recognition requires modified hardware [27, 10, 9]. In contrast, RF-IDraw is a software patch that can be added to today's standard RFID readers, and does not require any hardware modification.

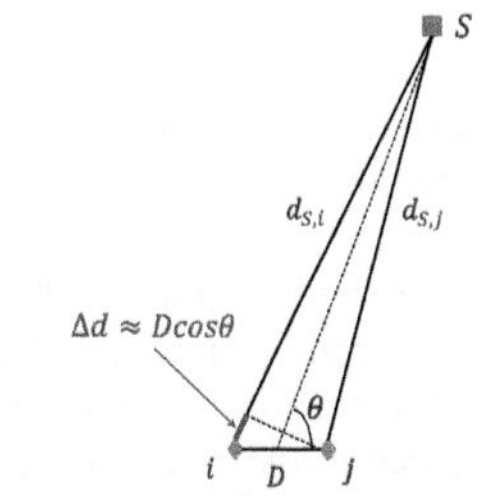


**Figure 5—Angle of Arrival at Antenna Pair:** Based on the signal phase difference measured between a pair of antennas, one can estimate the spatial direction along which the source's signal arrives.

## 3. Multi-Resolution Positioning

### 3.1 Primer

In RF-based positioning, the Angle of Arrival (AoA) of an RF source is computed by comparing the phases of the received signals at multiple antennas [24]. Underlying the AoA computation is the widely known principle that the phase of an RF signal rotates by $2\pi$ for every $\lambda$ distance the signal travels [35], where $\lambda$ is the wavelength. Specifically, let us consider a signal source at position $S$, and a pair of receive antennas $i$ and $j$ separated by $D$ in Fig. 5. $d_{S,i}$ and $d_{S,j}$ denote the distances from $S$ to the two antennas respectively, and $\phi_i$ and $\phi_j$ are the phases of the received signal that we measure at the two antennas. $\phi_i, \phi_j \in [0, 2\pi)$. The distances and the received signal phases have the following known relations due to the phase rotation [35]:

$$\begin{aligned} \phi_i &= -mod(\frac{2\pi}{\lambda}d_{S,i}, 2\pi) \\ \phi_j &= -mod(\frac{2\pi}{\lambda}d_{S,j}, 2\pi) \end{aligned} \tag{1}$$

Hence, the phase difference between the received signals at the two antennas, $\Delta\phi_{j,i} = \phi_j - \phi_i$, relates to the difference in their distances from the source, $\Delta d_{i,j} = d_{S,i} - d_{S,j}$, as follows:

$$\frac{\Delta d_{i,j}}{\lambda} = \frac{\Delta\phi_{j,i}}{2\pi} + k, \tag{2}$$

where $k$ can be any integer in $[-\frac{D}{\lambda} - \frac{\Delta\phi_{j,i}}{2\pi}, \frac{D}{\lambda} - \frac{\Delta\phi_{j,i}}{2\pi}]$.

When $S$ is relatively far from the antenna pair, as Fig. 5 shows, $\frac{\Delta d_{i,j}}{\lambda}$ can be approximated as $\frac{D\cos\theta}{\lambda}$ where $\theta$ is the angle of arrival. Thus, in this case we can rewrite Eq. 2 as

$$\frac{D\cos\theta}{\lambda} = \frac{\Delta\phi_{j,i}}{2\pi} + k \tag{3}$$

We note that Equations 2 and 3 are the same except for the approximation $\frac{\Delta d_{i,j}}{\lambda} \approx \frac{D\cos\theta}{\lambda}$, which is satisfied when the receive antennas are at some distance from the source. Eq. 3 is more intuitive since it directly articulates the spatial angle to the source, $\theta$. Hence, we use this form in the rest of the section for our explanation. However, Eq. 2 is more accurate at close distances from the source and could be used directly in the implementation to avoid unnecessary approximation noise. Indeed, the precise formulation in Eq. 2 is a standard equation representing one or a set of hyperbolas. When the distance is large, a hyperbola reduces to a ray pointing towards a specific spatial direction.

### 3.2 Grating Lobes

There is a tradeoff between increasing the resolution and removing the ambiguity in detecting a signal's angle of arrival. As Fig. 3 shows, when the separation between the two antennas is greater than $\lambda/2$, the beam pattern exhibits multiple beams, although there is only one direction along which the signal arrives. The additional beams are often referred to as *grating lobes* [24].

Here we explain the cause and characteristics of grating lobes in the context of angle of arrival. For a particular phase difference measured $\Delta\phi_{j,i}$, there are one or a set of spatial angles $\theta$ that satisfy Eq. 3. Specifically, since $\cos\theta \in [-1, 1]$, when $D \leq \lambda/2$, $k$ can take only one value which is 0. Thus, in this case, we can derive a unique angle of arrival $\theta = \arccos(\frac{\lambda}{D}\frac{\Delta\phi_{j,i}}{2\pi})$, which means we will observe a single beam in the antenna pair's beam pattern.

As $D$ increases, the number of possible $k$ values increases. For $D = K\frac{\lambda}{2}$, the number of possible values $k$ can take is $K$. Hence, there are $K$ different values of $\theta$ that will satisfy Eq. 3: $\theta = \arccos(\frac{\lambda}{D}\frac{\Delta\phi_{j,i}}{2\pi} + \frac{k\lambda}{D})$, only one of which refers to the actual angle of arrival. This is where ambiguity arises. We will see multiple beams (i.e., grating lobes) in the antenna pair's beam pattern corresponding to the multiple spatial angles. In summary, each grating lobe corresponds to one spatial direction $\theta$, and the number of grating lobes increases linearly with the antenna separation $D$.

### 3.3 Resolution and Robustness to Noise

Since grating lobes cause ambiguity in deciding the actual angle of arrival, they are typically considered detrimental and past RF localization systems try to avoid them by imposing the constraint that adjacent antennas must be separated by no more than $\frac{\lambda}{2}$ [41, 39]. However, while grating lobes introduce ambiguity, there are two properties about grating lobes that are highly desirable in the context of localization: high resolution and robustness to noise.

**Resolution:** Let us first look at the resolution of the spatial angle of arrival as computed by an antenna pair with $D$ separation. We can rewrite Eq. 3 as

$$\cos\theta = \frac{\lambda}{D}\frac{\Delta\phi_{j,i}}{2\pi} + \frac{k\lambda}{D}. \tag{4}$$

Recall that the value we can measure is the signal's phase difference, $\Delta\phi_{j,i}$, and the value we intend to compute is the signal's spatial angle of arrival $\theta$. Any hardware has some resolution, $\delta$, for how it expresses $\phi_{j,i}$ and hence $\Delta\phi_{j,i}$. The value of $\delta$ defines the minimum measurable change in $\Delta\phi_{j,i}$, and hence the finest quantization of $\cos\theta$, i.e., its resolution. In particular, the finest quantization we have in computing $\cos\theta$ is $\frac{\lambda}{D}\frac{\delta}{2\pi}$. As the antenna separation $D$ increases (i.e., more grating lobes), the minimum quantization level for expressing $\cos\theta$ decreases, leading to a finer resolution in estimating the spatial angle $\theta$.

**Robustness to Noise:** In addition to providing high resolution, grating lobes of antenna pairs with a large separation also prove to be more robust to wireless noise. Eq. 4 represents the noise-free case. Now let us take into consideration a phase noise term $\phi_n$ in the measured phase difference:

$$\cos\theta = \frac{\lambda}{D}\frac{\Delta\phi_{j,i} + \phi_n}{2\pi} + \frac{k\lambda}{D} \tag{5}$$

Eq. 5 shows that as $D$ increases, $\cos\theta$'s sensitivity to phase noise $\phi_n$ decreases linearly. To put this into perspective, when the phase difference measurement has a $\phi_n = \frac{\pi}{5}$ noise, that translates into 0.2 additive error in $\cos\theta$ if $D = \frac{\lambda}{2}$. But if we increase the separation to $D = 8\lambda$, the same signal phase noise of $\phi_n = \frac{\pi}{5}$ would only lead to 0.0125 additive error in $\cos\theta$, which is minimal. Thus, the larger the antenna pair separation is, the less effect wireless noise has on the spatial angle of arrival, i.e., the more resilient the system is.

### 3.4 Intersecting Grating Lobes for Positioning

The discussion above shows that grating lobes of a widely separated antenna pair offer high resolution and noise resilience in detecting the spatial angle of a signal source. To actually localize an RF source, we need to translate knowledge about the spatial angle of the source into information about the source position. To do so, we can intersect the grating lobes of multiple antenna pairs.

Consider the example in Fig. 6(a) with antennas 1, 2, 3, and 4 placed at the four corners of a square of size $8\lambda \times 8\lambda$.[2] The goal here is to localize the RF source marked in blue based on the phases measured at the antennas. The 4 antennas form a total of 6 pairs as indicated by the red lines in Fig. 6(a). Based on the phase difference measured at each antenna pair, we can obtain a set of grating lobes for each antenna pair. We can then intersect these grating lobes to identify candidate point locations for the source as indicated by the white dots in Fig. 6(a). One of these candidate locations matches the exact location of the source (the white dot is covered by the blue dot in the figure).

### 3.5 Resolving Ambiguity

Although each dot in Fig. 6(a) is very fine (i.e., high resolution), there are a number of them and we cannot tell which one includes the actual position of the source. The challenge is to resolve the ambiguity in positioning while maintaining the high resolution.

**Multi-Resolution Filtering:** One interesting observation is that in Fig. 6(a), the intersections (i.e., white dots) are fairly sparse, i.e., they are far away from each other. This means that if we can apply a *coarse* spatial filter to them, we will be able to eliminate the undesired intersections and resolve ambiguity.

Thus, our design of RF-IDraw adopts a multi-resolution approach – we create coarse spatial filters by leveraging the unique, low-resolution beams of antenna pairs with small separation to resolve the position ambiguity caused by the high-resolution grating lobes of the widely-separated antenna pairs. Specifically, in addition to the widely spaced antennas, we use a second set of antenna pairs that are spaced by $\lambda/2$. Our implementation uses four additional antennas organized in two pairs <5,6> and <7,8>. Since the spacing is $\lambda/2$, each pair produces one unique wide beam. Intersecting the two wide beams leads to a coarse spatial filter indicated as the white region in Fig. 6(b). We can further refine this filter to Fig. 6(c) by also utilizing all other antenna pairs, namely <5,7>, <5,8>, <6,7>, and <6,8>. Finally, when we overlay Fig. 6(c) as a filter on Fig. 6(a), ambiguity is resolved and the correct position of the RF source is uncovered, as shown in Fig. 6(d) (again, the white dot is covered by the blue mark representing the source).

This demonstrates how RF-IDraw's multi-resolution design leverages the unambiguous coarse filter produced by antenna pairs with small separation to effectively reduce the ambiguity caused by the high-resolution grating lobes.

We note that our implementation of RF-IDraw uses two RFID readers each equipped with 4 antennas. The first reader is used for the widely spaced antenna pairs, while the second reader is used for the tightly spaced antenna pairs. We only measure the AoA using antenna pairs that belong to the same reader. While using antenna pairs across the two readers could further improve the resolution of the system, in practice that would add complexity and potential

[2] Today's commercial RFID reader typically has four antenna ports and there is no phase offset between the received signals on these ports. Hence, one can properly compare the phases measured at any pair of antennas on the same reader.

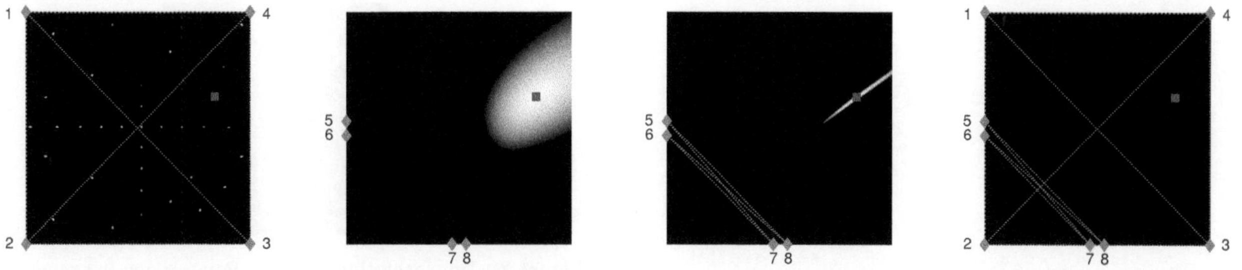


(a) Intersecting grating lobes to provide high resolution

(b) Coarse spatial filter obtained by intersecting wide beams

(c) Finer spatial filter

(d) Removing ambiguity while maintaining high resolution

**Figure 6—Multi-Resolution Positioning:** This figure shows an example of using RF-IDraw's multi-resolution positioning to localize a signal source marked in blue. The red dotted lines represent which antenna pairs are used in each subplot. (a) shows the common intersections of different antenna pairs' grating lobes, which offer high resolution in positioning yet causing ambiguity. (b) shows a coarse spatial filter formed by intersecting the wide beams of two tightly spaced antenna pairs. (c) shows the finer filter obtained when four more antenna pairs with larger separation are used to refine (b). Applying the filter in (c) on (a) eliminates ambiguity and uncovers the correct position as (d) shows.

errors because the phase offset between the two readers will need to be calibrated or removed. Hence, in our implementation, we only use antenna pairs within the same reader.

# 4. THE POWER OF GRATING LOBES FOR TRAJECTORY TRACING

Instead of just localizing a static device, many applications in gaming, smart homes, and healthcare are more interested in tracking the trajectory of an RF source as it moves. The unique property of RF-IDraw's grating lobe based approach is its ability to accurately detect the shape of a trajectory. In fact, this is true even in the case where there are errors in the absolute positioning along the trajectory. For example, one may get the initial point of where the trajectory starts wrong by a small offset, yet the shape of RF-IDraw's reconstructed trajectory will still match the actual shape of the trajectory with very high fidelity. This property is desirable for many applications, such as gesture recognition and virtual touch screen. In these applications, it is important to recognize the gesture or writing of the user, while a small offset in the exact location of the gesture is tolerable.

To provide an intuition for why RF-IDraw's design has this property, let us start with the basic case of a standard antenna array. Consider the scenario where the RF source is moving along a continuous trajectory. In the case of an antenna array, tracing the trajectory of this source means that the antenna array's beam will rotate accordingly with the movement of the source such that it keeps pointing towards the source. Now consider what happens when we have grating lobes. The actual source will be on one of these grating lobes. As the source moves, the correct grating lobe will rotate such that it continues to track the source direction. However, since all grating lobes rotate together, they will all follow the movement of the source. Hence, even if one makes the wrong assumption that the source lies on a particular grating lobe which differs from the correct one, this wrong grating lobe's motion (i.e., rotation in particular) does not fundamentally differ from the motion of the correct grating lobe as it tracks the source direction.

To illustrate this property, Fig. 7(a) shows what happens when we pick the correct grating lobe and also for the cases where we pick wrong grating lobes adjacent to the correct one. Specifically, this figure shows a trajectory that follows the handwriting of the letter 'q', the ground truth of which is shown in black. Fig. 7(a) shows the reconstructed trajectories for nine different sets of grating lobes. The trajectory in the center is reconstructed by tracking the motion of the correct set of grating lobes. The other eight trajectories are reconstructed by using wrong grating lobes adjacent to the correct ones. As we can see, although the absolute positions have an offset, the shapes of the trajectories remain accurate and the letter 'q' can still be easily recognized. This demonstrates the point that even if we end up tracking the motion of a wrong grating lobe, which is not too far away from the correct one, the shape of the reconstructed trajectory will still remain similar to the ground truth.

It is important to note that, the further the correct grating lobe is from the one we pick, the more distortion there is in the shape of the reconstructed trajectory. The reason is as follows. While all grating lobes rotate together, (i.e., if the correct one turns with the source, the others will turn accordingly), they do not have exactly the same forms. Let us refer to the grating lobes in Fig. 3(c) again to better understand this point. There we can see that the grating lobes close to each other tend to have similar forms, while further apart grating lobes' forms are more different. Thus, although all grating lobes rotate together, their form differences will introduce distortion to the shape of the reconstructed trajectory, and this distortion increases as we pick a grating lobe further away from the correct one. For instance, Fig. 7(b) shows the reconstructed trajectory of the handwritten 'q' by using a set of grating lobes far away from the correct ones. As we can see, the shape of this reconstructed trajectory is less similar to the ground truth than the trajectories in Fig. 7(a).

This emphasizes the importance of using the multi-resolution system in §3. Although it may not completely eliminate the ambiguity among grating lobes in certain cases, it helps confine us to a region very close to the correct set of grating lobes, which ensures good shape fidelity.

# 5. ALGORITHM

In this section, we describe the algorithm behind RF-IDraw's multi-resolution positioning and trajectory tracing.

## 5.1 Multi-Resolution Positioning Algorithm

RF-IDraw's multi-resolution positioning design is implemented as a two-stage voting algorithm to identify the position of an RF source. In stage 1, each antenna pair with small separation casts one vote on each point in space, based on its belief that the RF source is at that position. Then, the points with high total votes from all antenna pairs with small separation will form the candidate region to be used in stage 2. In stage 2, each antenna pair with large separation casts one vote on each point within the candidate region, based on its belief that the RF source is at this position. Then the points with higher total votes from all antenna pairs will be considered as the more likely positions for the RF source.

Now the only question is how to define the vote. First, let us consider the vote cast by each antenna pair with $\frac{\lambda}{2}$ separation. Recall

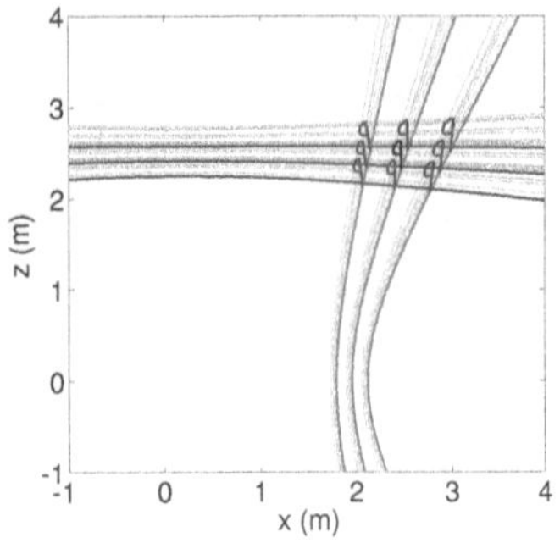


(a) Reconstructed trajectories using grating lobes adjacent to the correct ones

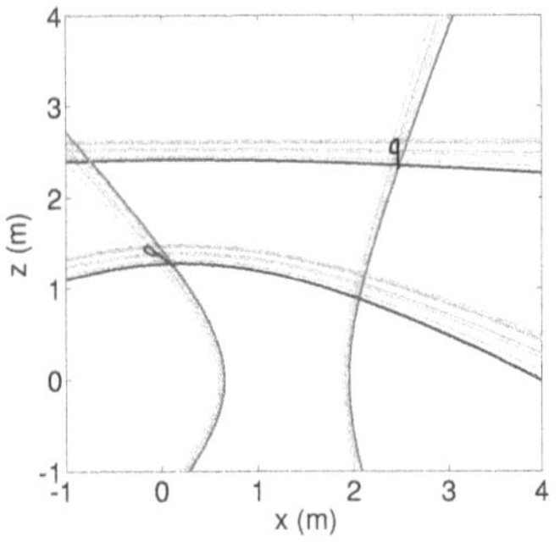


(b) Reconstructed trajectories using grating lobes far away from the correct ones

**Figure 7—Effect of Choosing Wrong Grating Lobes in Trajectory Tracing:** The ground truth trajectory is a handwritten 'q' as shown in black. When we pick a wrong grating lobe adjacent to the correct one to track, the reconstructed trajectory has a very similar shape as the actual shape, despite the absolute position offset, as (a) shows. However, if we end up tracking a wrong set of grating lobes far away from the correct ones, the distortion in the shape will be large, rendering the letter difficult to recognize, as (b) shows.

that an antenna pair with $\frac{\lambda}{2}$ separation has one beam. We let the antenna pair vote on a point in space based on how far the point is from the antenna pair's beam center. In particular, the vote is designed to be less or equal to 0. When the point lies along the direction of the center of the beam, the vote is 0; as it gets further away from the beam center, the vote becomes lower (i.e., more negative).

For example, consider the beam of an antenna pair in Fig. 8, whose center is shown as the red solid line. This antenna pair's votes on $P_1$ and $P_2$ will both be 0 because they lie along the beam center, while $P_3$ and $P_4$ will have a lower vote because they are further away from the beam center.

Formally, the direction of antenna pair $<i,j>$'s beam is defined by Eq. 3 with $k = 0$. In the more precise formulation, the center of the beam is defined by Eq. 2 also for $k = 0$. Hence, antenna pair $<i,j>$'s vote on point $P$ is calculated as:

$$V_{i,j}(P) = -\|\frac{\Delta d_{i,j}}{\lambda} - \frac{\Delta \phi_{j,i}}{2\pi}\|^2, \quad (6)$$

when the two antennas are separated by $\frac{\lambda}{2}$.

Now let us extend this vote to the case of antenna pairs with large separation. For an antenna pair with large separation, the only difference is that instead of one beam, it will have multiple grating lobes. Thus, instead of voting based on how far the point is from one beam center, a widely spaced antenna pair votes based on how far the point is from the grating lobe closest to it. Specifically, the vote will be:

$$V_{i,j}(P) = -\min_k \|\frac{\Delta d_{i,j}}{\lambda} - \frac{\Delta \phi_{j,i}}{2\pi} - k\|^2, \quad (7)$$

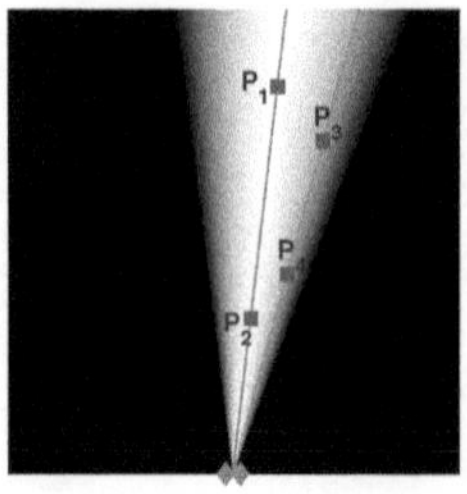

**Figure 8—Interpretation of Vote:** Points along the same spatial direction have the same vote from the antenna pair, e.g., $P_1$ and $P_2$, $P_3$ and $P_4$ have the same votes. Points closer to the beam center have higher votes than the ones further away from the center, e.g., $P_1$, $P_2$ have higher votes than $P_3$ and $P_4$.

where the minimization over $k$ captures the distance to the closest grating lobe among all grating lobes.

Now we have the votes from all antenna pairs, we combine them to identify the intersections of the antenna pairs' beams or grating lobes. The higher the total vote $V(P) = \sum_{i,j} V_{i,j}(P)$ is, the more likely $P$ is the actual position of the RF source.

## 5.2 Trajectory Tracing Algorithm

For the purpose of trajectory tracing, recall the discussion in §4 which shows that even if we start from a wrong initial position and track a wrong grating lobe (not too far away from the correct one), the shape of the reconstructed trajectory will still be quite accurate. Aside from this insight, from a slightly different perspective, Fig. 7 also reveals another important point: to achieve shape fidelity, we are better off tracking the continuous rotation of a grating lobe, as opposed to switching grating lobes in the middle of a trajectory.

Based on this idea, we develop RF-IDraw's trajectory tracing algorithm exploring the continuity of the RF source's motion and the continuous rotation of the grating lobes, as described below:

- RF-IDraw selects a few candidate initial positions with the highest total votes as calculated in §5.1 using the initial phase measurements.
- For each candidate initial position, RF-IDraw identifies the grating lobe of each antenna pair that is closest to this position, and keeps tracking the continuous rotation of this grating lobe.
- To estimate the next position, RF-IDraw evaluates the votes for all points within the vicinity of the current position. In computing each antenna pair's vote, RF-IDraw also enforces the rule to rotate with the same grating lobe, which is done by fixing $k$ and unwrapping $\Delta\phi_{i,j}$ in Eq. 7, i.e., ensuring continuity when angles wrap around $[0, 2\pi]$.
- RF-IDraw iteratively estimates the consecutive positions to reconstruct the entire trajectory.
- After having reconstructed one trajectory for each candidate initial position, RF-IDraw picks the one whose sum of votes across all points on the trajectory is the highest as its final estimate.

The reason for choosing the trajectory with the highest overall vote is as follows. Recall that we have an over-constrained system, i.e., there are more antenna pairs than needed to specify a point in space (using their grating lobes). In this over-constrained system, if we start from the correct initial position, the set of grating lobes (one from each widely spaced antenna pair) we track will move coherently and hence always intersect, because they all agree on the actual trajectory of the RF source. This means their total vote will be high always. In contrast, for a wrong initial position, the associated wrong grating lobes will not move coherently, and hence do not consistently intersect throughout the trajectory. Therefore, their total vote will drop later on. In other words, with an over-constrained system, we can detect incohesive rotations of

**Figure 9—Commercial UHF RFID Used in Experiments:** Alien Squiggle General Purpose UHF RFID

these grating lobes. Thus, by choosing the reconstructed trajectory with the highest overall trajectory vote, RF-IDraw further refines the initial position estimate, as demonstrated in §7.

## 6. IMPLEMENTATION

We built a prototype of RF-IDraw using commercial off-the-shelf UHF RFID readers to locate and trace the trajectories of EPC Gen-2 [15] UHF RFIDs.

**Readers and Software Implementation:** We use two ThingMagic M6e 4-port UHF RFID readers [33], each connected with four AN-900LH 900 MHz omni-directional antennas [1]. We program the readers to continuously query the RFIDs using a carrier frequency of 922 MHz and return the signal phase for every RFID reply. We implemented RF-IDraw's multi-resolution positioning and trajectory tracing algorithms in MATLAB and ran them in real-time.

**RFIDs:** We use the Alien Squiggle tag [11] shown in Fig. 9, which is a commercial off-the-shelf passive UHF RFID widely used in supply chain and asset tracking applications. Each of them costs 5-10 cents. We also experimented with the Omni-ID Exo 800 tag [5] to verify RF-IDraw's design across different types of RFIDs.

**Ground Truth:** We use the VICON motion capture system [8] to measure the ground truth trajectory of the RFID. In a $5 \times 6$ m$^2$ room instrumented with a grid of infrared cameras, the VICON system can provide sub-centimeter accuracy in tracking an object tagged with infrared reflective markers. For experiments in the VICON room, we measure the ground truth by putting infrared reflective markers on the user's hand, around the RFID. For experiments outside the VICON room in an office lounge, we let the user write along a specific set of trajectories for which the ground truth has been measured manually in advance.

**Compared Schemes:** We compare RF-IDraw with the state-of-the-art antenna array AoA-based approach [12] using the same number of antennas as RF-IDraw. In particular, both RF-IDraw and the antenna array AoA-based systems employ 8 antennas connected to two RFID readers. RF-IDraw's 8 antennas are deployed as shown in Fig. 6(d). Since RFIDs communicate by backscattering the reader signal [38], the signal phase reading returned by the reader reflects the round trip distance instead of the one-way distance. Hence, each tightly spaced antenna pair (i.e., <5, 6>, <7, 8>) has a separation of $\frac{\lambda}{4}$ (as opposed to $\frac{\lambda}{2}$) to ensure there is only one beam.[3] The widely spaced antenna pairs (i.e., each edge) have separation of $8\lambda$ (i.e., 2.6 m). The antenna array AoA-based scheme uses two antenna arrays, each with 4 antennas spaced by $\frac{\lambda}{4}$ (to account for the backscattering round trip also). One antenna array is placed along the left edge of the square in Fig. 6(d), the other is placed along the bottom edge.

**Application Evaluation:** We interface RF-IDraw with the MyScript Stylus app [36] on an Android phone using the MonkeyRunner Android API [4]. This API allows developers to send specified sequences of events to an Android device. We use this API to convert the reconstructed trajectory of the RFID to touch screen input sequences on an Android phone. The MyScript Stylus app, then, interprets the input as text. We let the users write words randomly sampled from the top 5000 most commonly used words in the Corpus of Contemporary American English [6]. Some examples include: "*play*", "*clear*", "*import*", etc. Then, we evaluate the character and word recognition success rates of the reconstructed trajectories as recognized by the MyScript Stylus app.

[3]The equations in this paper apply to the general case of an RF transmitter. To account for the special case of RFID backscattering, one needs to add a 2 factor to all the $\Delta d_{j,i}$ and $\cos\theta$ in the equations.

## 7. MICROBENCHMARK

We start with a microbenchmark experiment to provide insights into the working of the system. In particular, to better understand the capabilities and properties of RF-IDraw's trajectory tracing, we let a user write the word "*clear*" using the RFID on his hand, in the $5 \times 6$ m$^2$ VICON room. RF-IDraw uses a total of 8 antennas connected to two RFID readers. All reader antennas are deployed on a wall at one side of the VICON room. The user stands 2 m away. Fig. 6 presents the side view of the room, facing the wall of antenna deployment. Antenna separations and placement are chosen based on the application's needs and room size. Fig. 10(a) shows the ground truth trajectory of the user's handwriting measured by the VICON motion capture system. Now let us see how RF-IDraw's tracing works in practice.

### 7.1 Granularity of Tracing

In this experiment, RF-IDraw's multi-resolution positioning algorithm (described in §5.1) returned two candidate initial positions. Fig. 10(b) and Fig. 10(c) show the trajectories reconstructed from these positions using RF-IDraw's trajectory tracing algorithm, described in §5.2. As we can see, RF-IDraw is able to trace every minute change in the RFID position during the user's writing. For example, the letter 'e' in the middle is only about 5 cm wide, yet RF-IDraw is able to reproduce the details in its shape by tracking the rotation of the high-resolution grating lobes.

### 7.2 Choosing the Correct Initial Position

In order to decide which trajectory to choose out of the two (as the final output), as §5.2 describes, RF-IDraw looks at the total vote from all antenna pairs for each position on the trajectory and picks the trajectory whose overall vote (summing up total votes from all antenna pairs for all positions along the trajectory) is the highest. Fig. 10(f) shows the evolution of the total vote from all antenna pairs as the blue and red reconstructed trajectories progress. As we can see, initially, both the blue and the red have high total votes (i.e., close to 0). That is exactly why their starting points have been identified by the multi-resolution positioning algorithm as the candidate initial positions. However, as the two reconstructed trajectories progress, the red one's total vote quickly drops, significantly deviating from 0, while the blue one's vote stays fairly stable and close to 0, having only occasional deviation. This is because the grating lobes of the antenna pairs closest to the red initial position do not consistently agree throughout the trajectory, leading to no common intersection later in the trace, which results in their poor total vote later on. The detection of this is made possible by the over-constrained system where we have more antenna pairs than needed to specify a single point in space, as explained in §5.2.

Comparing the overall votes throughout the trajectories, RF-IDraw picks the blue trajectory as its final output. Fig. 10(d) shows the ground truth, RF-IDraw's final output, and the red trajectory on the same plot. As we can see, the blue trajectory which RF-IDraw picks indeed better matches the ground truth than the red one, and the blue initial position is also closer to the ground truth than the red candidate. This demonstrates RF-IDraw's power in leveraging its trajectory tracing to further refine its positioning.

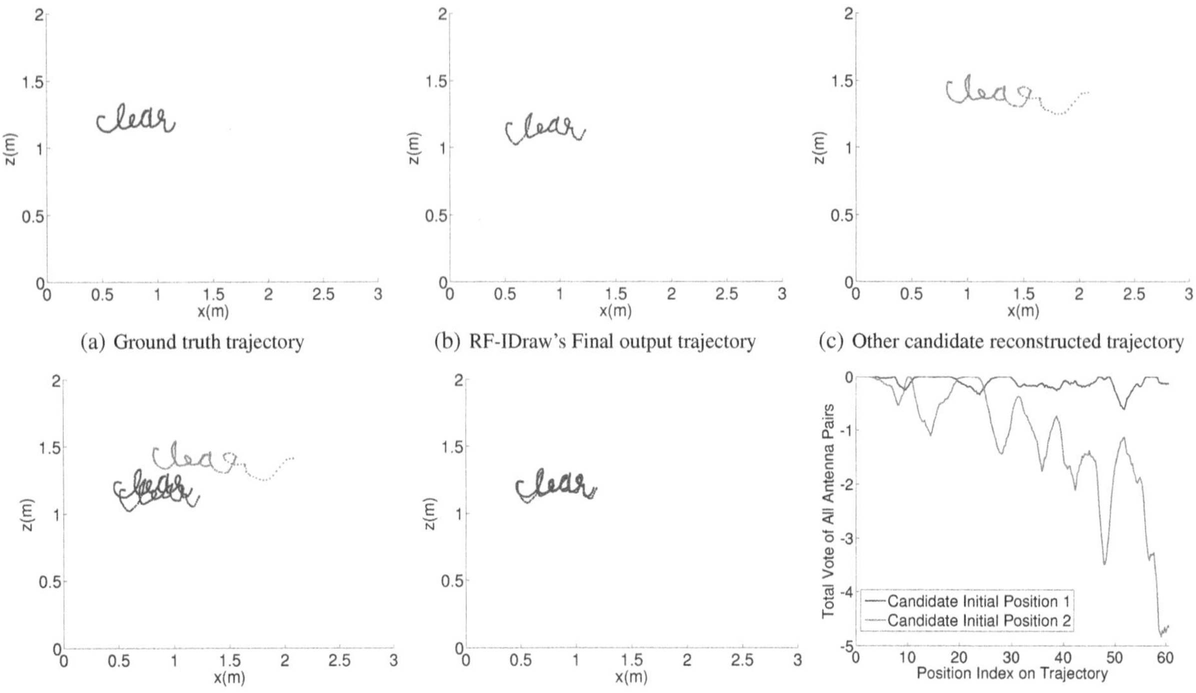


(a) Ground truth trajectory (b) RF-IDraw's Final output trajectory (c) Other candidate reconstructed trajectory

(d) Comparing the three trajectories (e) RF-IDraw's Final output trajectory shifted (f) Evolution of vote throughout trajectory

**Figure 10—Tracing a User's Writing in the Air:** (a) shows the actual trajectory of the RFID as the user writes the word "*clear*" in the air, as measured by the infrared VICON motion capture system. (b) and (c) show two trajectories reconstructed by RF-IDraw, starting from two candidate initial positions provided by the multi-resolution positioning algorithm. Both reproduce all the detailed turns in the trajectory shape and can be recognized as the correct word. Based on the overall trajectory votes in (f), RF-IDraw chooses the blue one as its final output, which is indeed closer to the ground truth position, as shown in (d), demonstrating RF-IDraw's capability to refine positioning through trajectory tracing. Finally, (e) shows the comparison between the actual trajectory and RF-IDraw's output after removing the initial offset. The similarity between the two curves proves the unique shape resilience property of RF-IDraw's trajectory tracing.

### 7.3 Shape Resilience

Finally, these figures also demonstrate the unique property of RF-IDraw's trajectory tracing design, which is that, the *shape* will be well preserved in the reconstructed trajectory, even if the initial position estimate has an offset.

Let us first look at the comparison between the blue reconstructed trajectory and the ground truth. The blue initial position is about 7 cm away from the ground truth initial position.[4] In Fig. 10(e), we show the blue reconstructed trajectory after removing this 7 cm initial position offset from it. As we can see, this shifted version of the reconstructed trajectory closely matches the ground truth, accurately preserving the shape of the writing. Furthermore, even in the red reconstructed trajectory, whose initial position is off by 41 cm, the shape of the word is still roughly preserved.

As §4 explains, shape fidelity can be achieved despite initial position offset because all grating lobes of an antenna pair rotate together, and hence picking a wrong grating lobe's rotation to track only results in a transform of the trajectory. Furthermore, if the grating lobe picked is fairly close to the correct one, the reconstructed shape will be very similar to the correct shape, and the distortion in shape increases as we pick a grating lobe further away from the correct one. Indeed, as compared with the blue reconstructed trajectory, the red one is less similar to the green ground truth's shape, because its initial position is off by more.

[4] Our further analysis reveals that, given the phase difference measurements, the grating lobes intersecting at the blue initial position are indeed the ones closest to the ground truth initial position as well. In other words, the initial positioning error is due to the error in the measurements of the signal phases, which are likely caused by random wireless noise and the multipath effect [22, 35].

This demonstrates the shape resilience property of RF-IDraw's trajectory tracing, while also underscoring the value of finding an initial position reasonably close to the correct one. This property can be particularly useful in applications where recognizing the trajectory of a motion offers high value. In this trace, in fact all three trajectories in Fig. 10(d) have been correctly identified as the word "*clear*" by the handwriting recognition app RF-IDraw interfaces with. In §9, we validate the robustness of RF-IDraw's trajectory tracing through the evaluation of character and word recognition success rates.

## 8. EVALUATION

We evaluate our prototype of RF-IDraw by having five users write 150 words randomly sampled from the 5000 most frequently used words in the Corpus of Contemporary American English [6]. The users write in the air with a UHF RFID on their hands as shown in Fig. 1(a). The average width of each letter written is around 10 cm. We conduct experiments in both LOS and NLOS settings, in the $5\times6$ m$^2$ VICON room as well as a large office lounge of size $8\times12$ m$^2$ divided into cubicles.

We compare the performance of RF-IDraw with state-of-the-art antenna array based approach [12] using the same number of antennas. Both RF-IDraw and the antenna array based system employ 8 antennas connected to two RFID readers. The details of the antenna setup for both schemes are described in §6. The users stand 2–5 meters away from the reader antennas in our experiments.[5] RF-

[5] The commercial RFID reader's range limits the range of our current prototype. Beyond 5 meters, we start to see significant message loss because the RFID cannot harvest enough energy to wake up.

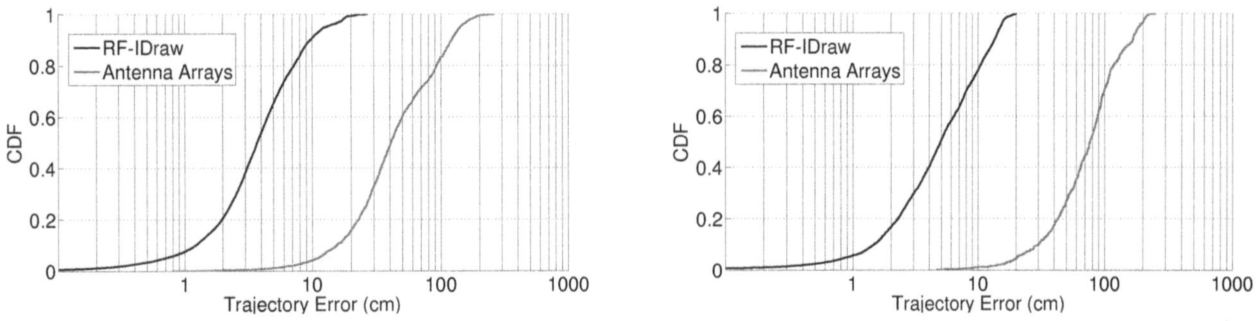


(a) CDF of Trajectory Error Distance in LOS

(b) CDF of Trajectory Error Distance in NLOS

**Figure 11—CDF of Trajectory Error Distance in LOS and NLOS:** The median point-by-point error distance for RF-IDraw's reconstructed trajectory after removing the initial offset is 3.7 cm and 4.9 cm in LOS and NLOS respectively, 11× and 16× lower than the median errors (after removing the offset) for the antenna array based scheme in LOS and NLOS, significantly improving the accuracy of trajectory tracing. Furthermore, the errors for RF-IDraw are due to the coherent stretching and squeezing of the trajectory shape, rather than being random. Hence, despite this error, RF-IDraw's reconstructed trajectories of letters a few centimeters wide can still be successfully recognized in 97.5% of the cases by a handwriting recognition app, as we show in §9.1.

IDraw uses the multi-resolution positioning and trajectory tracing algorithms described in §5 to reconstruct the trajectory and estimate the initial position of the RFID. In the antenna array based system, each 4-antenna array measures an angle of arrival of the RFID, then the beams of the arrays are intersected to estimate the RFID position for each point on the trajectory, reproducing the trajectory.

In this section, we focus on analyzing the trajectory tracing and positioning accuracy of RF-IDraw and the antenna array based scheme. In §9, we further assess the capabilities of the two systems in the virtual touch screen application.

## 8.1 Trajectory Accuracy

Let us start by evaluating the accuracy of the two systems in reconstructing the RFID trajectory.

**Metric:** To focus on how much the reconstructed trajectory shape deviates from the actual trajectory shape, we remove a fixed offset between the reconstructed and the ground truth trajectories. The trajectory error for RF-IDraw is computed by removing the initial position offset from its reconstructed trajectory, and calculating the point-by-point position difference between its shifted reconstructed trajectory and the ground truth. For example, the trajectory error for the reconstructed trajectory in Fig. 10(b) would be the point-by-point differences between the two curves in Fig. 10(e). For the antenna array based scheme, since the errors along the trajectory are random and independent from each other, removing the initial position offset results in even larger error distances for other points on the trajectory. Hence, instead we compute the average position difference (a vector in space) between the reconstructed trajectory and the ground truth. We remove this average position difference from the reconstructed trajectory, then calculate the point-by-point differences between the shifted reconstructed trajectory and the ground truth. Note that, removing the average position difference essentially removes the DC offset and thus is favorable to the compared scheme.

**Trajectory Accuracy Results in LOS:** Fig. 11(a) shows the CDF of the trajectory errors for the two systems in LOS. The median error for RF-IDraw is 3.7 cm (point-by-point difference) and the 90th percentile is 9.7 cm. For the antenna array based system using the same number of antennas, the median error is 40.8 cm and the 90th percentile is 121.1 cm. Hence, RF-IDraw's trajectory tracing is 11× more accurate than the antenna array approach in LOS.

- Note that, the 3.7 cm accuracy does not fully capture the capability of RF-IDraw's trajectory tracing. Specifically, despite this error, RF-IDraw's reconstructed trajectory of letters a few centimeters wide can still be successfully recognized by a simple handwriting recognition app in 97.5% of the cases, as we evaluate in the virtual touch screen application in §9. This is because the point-by-point errors along RF-IDraw's reconstructed trajectory are not independent random errors. Instead, they have a structure and reflect coherent stretching, squeezing, and enlarging in the trajectory shape. Thus, although the trajectory error as defined here is a few centimeters, in most cases, the distortion does not affect the recognition of the letter or word (e.g., Fig. 10(c)).
- RF-IDraw's 11× trajectory accuracy improvement over the antenna array based scheme is enabled by mainly two levers. First, the high-resolution and robustness to noise features of grating lobes allow RF-IDraw to trace the details of the RFID trajectory. Second, RF-IDraw's trajectory tracing algorithm tracks the continuous rotation of the grating lobes, resulting in shape resilience.
- Using the same number of antennas as RF-IDraw, the standard antenna arrays will have much wider beams which fail to provide the resolution or robustness needed to track the shape of a word written by a user in the air. Also, as opposed to the coherent deviations on RF-IDraw's trajectory, the errors the antenna array based scheme has are random and scattered all over the place, resulting in completely unrecognizable trajectories as §9 reveals.

**Trajectory Accuracy Results in NLOS:** We also evaluate the two systems' performance in non-line-of-sight experiments. The NLOS setup is in an office lounge area ($8\times12$ m$^2$) divided into cubicles by 2.5 m tall, 20 cm thick separators made of two layers of wood. The reader setup is deployed behind these separators and we ensure that there is no LOS path from any of the reader antennas to the RFID on the user's hand. Similar to the literature on RFIDs [39, 37, 22, 12], we cannot do cross-room evaluation because the RFID reader cannot power an RFID from a different room.

Fig. 11(b) shows the trajectory error for both RF-IDraw and the antenna array based solution in NLOS. The median error of RF-IDraw is 4.9 cm and the 90th percentile is 13.6 cm, similar to LOS. In comparison, the antenna array based system's median trajectory error in NLOS is 76.9 cm and the 90th percentile is 166.7 cm.

- The degradation in trajectory accuracy caused by NLOS is more severe for the antenna array based scheme (40.8 cm in LOS v.s. 76.9 cm in NLOS) than for RF-IDraw (3.7 cm in LOS v.s. 4.9 cm in NLOS)). This is likely due to the different effects multipath [22, 35] has on the two methods. In NLOS, the direct path

As RFID manufacturers compete to increase the range, it is constantly growing and we expect RF-IDraw to benefit from that trend.

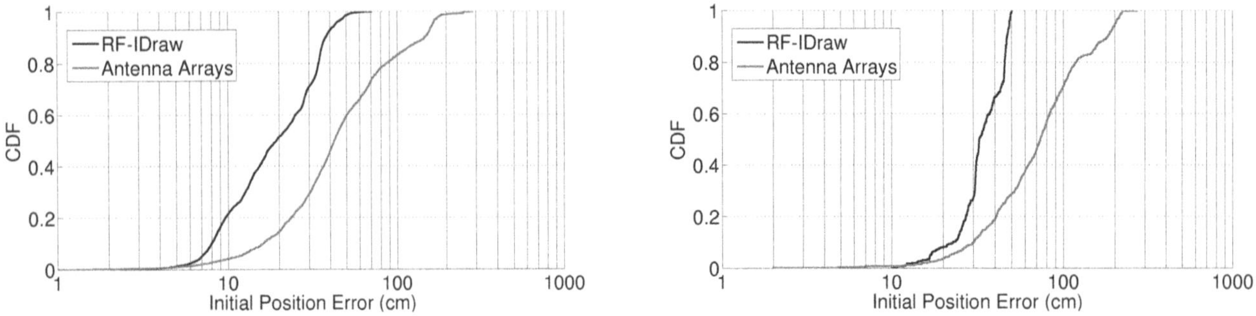


(a) CDF of Initial Position Error Distance in LOS

(b) CDF of Initial Position Error Distance in NLOS

**Figure 12—CDF of Initial Position Error Distance in LOS and NLOS:** The median initial position error of RF-IDraw is 19 cm and 32 cm in LOS and NLOS respectively, 2.2× and 2.3× lower than the median initial position error for the antenna array based scheme in LOS and NLOS. This localization accuracy improvement comes from RF-IDraw's use of trajectory tracing votes to refine its initial position estimate.

is attenuated and the dominant path may differ from the direct path. In this case, estimating the absolute position becomes challenging, as past work has shown [19, 39, 41]. As a result, the antenna arrays' performance significantly worsens. Yet the trajectory shape of RF-IDraw is more robust, because as long as there is a dominant path, the shape will still be discovered by following the dominant path.

In conclusion, RF-IDraw enables accurate trajectory tracing in both LOS and NLOS, outperforming the antenna array based technique using the same number of antennas by 11× and 16× in LOS and NLOS respectively. Note that, while several past RF localization techniques have also achieved centimeter scale accuracy [41, 39, 9], they either require a dense deployment of reference sources and/or a large number of antennas, or GHz of bandwidth. In contrast, RF-IDraw shows that, for the first time, one can trace the trajectory shape of an RF source with centimeter accuracy with a small number of antennas, without reference sources, and using commercial narrowband devices.

## 8.2 Initial Position Accuracy

Next, we evaluate the initial position estimation accuracy. Fig. 12 shows the CDF for initial position error for RF-IDraw and the antenna array based system. In LOS, the median initial position error of the antenna array based system is 42 cm and its 90th percentile is 148 cm; RF-IDraw's median initial position error is 19 cm, 2.2× better than AoA, and its 90th percentile is 38 cm, 3.9× better than AoA. In NLOS, the accuracy for both systems degrades, because of the attenuation of the direct path from the reader antennas to the RFID as well as the multipath caused by structures in the office lounge. The median initial position error for RF-IDraw in NLOS is 32 cm and the 90th percentile is 47 cm. For the antenna array based scheme, the median and 90th percentile accuracy is 74 cm and 183 cm respectively.

- It is worth noting that, the initial position accuracy for the antenna array based scheme is similar to its trajectory accuracy discussed in the previous section. This is because the antenna array based system estimates each position along the trajectory independently using the same method as it estimates the initial position. Therefore, the errors along the trajectory are random and independent from each other, and hence the trajectory error will be similar to the absolute position error.
- Using the same number of antennas, in both LOS and NLOS, RF-IDraw improves the initial position accuracy over the antenna array based technique by over 2.2×. This improvement stems from the fact that the overall trajectory vote is used to identify the best initial position, which refines RF-IDraw's accuracy, as shown in §7.2.

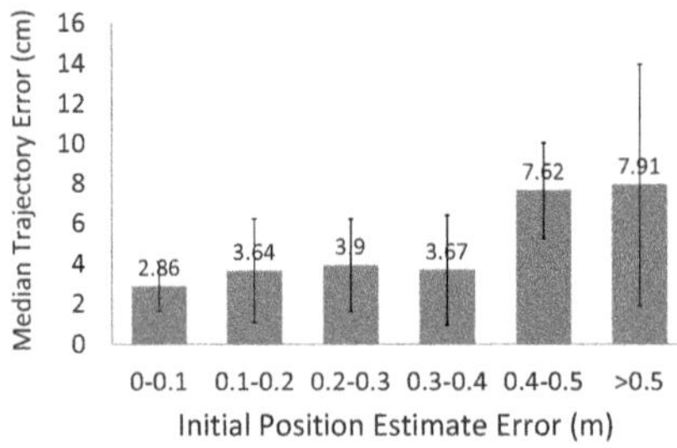


**Figure 13—Initial Position Accuracy v.s. Trajectory Accuracy in RF-IDraw:** When the initial position picked by RF-IDraw is within 40 cm of the actual initial position, this initial offset has minimal effect on the trajectory accuracy, due to the similarity between closeby grating lobes. If the initial position has a fairly large offset, the trajectory reconstructed will be more distorted, resulting in a higher trajectory error. Yet this higher error is mainly due to the enlarging of certain parts in the trajectory, and hence does not translate into high recognition error (e.g., red curve in Fig. 10(d)).

## 8.3 The Effect of Initial Position Accuracy on Trajectory Accuracy in RF-IDraw

As we have demonstrated through the microbenchmark experiment in §7, even when the initial position estimate has some offset, the shape of RF-IDraw's reconstructed trajectory is still preserved. Here let us further analyze the relationship between the trajectory accuracy and the initial position accuracy of RF-IDraw. Specifically, for each word written, we remove the initial position offset from RF-IDraw's reconstructed trajectory, then compute the median error for all the positions throughout the trajectory. Then we group the traces according to their initial position error, and study the trajectory error for each initial position error range.

Fig. 13 shows the trajectory error as a function of the initial position error.

- When the initial position error is below 40 cm, RF-IDraw's trajectory accuracy almost remains the same, i.e., around 3 cm. Hence, a reasonably small initial position offset does not affect the shape resilience of RF-IDraw.
- When the initial offset is fairly large, the trajectory error also increases, to a median of around 7–8 cm. To understand why this happens, recall the microbenchmark trace in §7, in particular Fig. 10(d). As we can see, if the initial position is off by a fairly large amount, while the shape of the reconstructed word is recognizable, the end of the trajectory is enlarged. Intuitively, this is due to the fact that we end up tracking a wrong grating lobe further away from the correct one, whose motion has the same trend as the correct one yet leads to a larger distortion in the shape as the RFID moves more. Indeed, in many cases where we observe

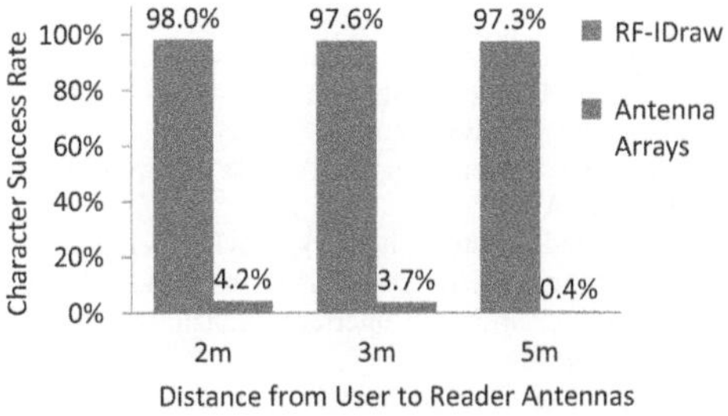


**Figure 14—Character Recognition Success Rate:** RF-IDraw's reconstructed trajectories for letters can be correctly recognized in 97.5% of the cases by the handwriting recognition Android app, whereas the character trajectories reproduced by the antenna array based system can only be recognized in less than 4% of the cases, equivalent to a random guess.

a high median trajectory error, it is due to the enlarging of the shape towards the end of the trace.

# 9. VIRTUAL TOUCH SCREEN APPLICATION

We use our prototype of RF-IDraw to demonstrate the feasibility of an RF-based virtual touch screen, which allows a user to input her commands to a desired computing device (e.g., an Android phone) by writing in the air. In particular, we feed each reconstructed trajectory as a set of instructions to an Android phone and the instructions emulate a sequence of touch screen events. Then we let the handwriting recognition function in the MyScript Stylus app [36] interpret it as text. We evaluate success rates for recognizing the character and word trajectories as reconstructed by RF-IDraw and the antenna array based system respectively.

## 9.1 Character Recognition Success Rates

The average width of a user's handwritten character is around 10 cm. Fig. 14 shows the success rate of correctly recognizing the character, as a function of the distance from the user to the reader antennas. As we can see, the character error rate almost remains the same at around 97%-98% when the user is 2 m, 3 m, and 5 m away from the reader antennas. The overall character recognition success rate for RF-IDraw's reconstructed trajectory is 97.5%, while the success rate for the antenna array based scheme is less than 4%.

The following points are worth noting:

- One may be wondering, with the 3–4 cm median trajectory accuracy as shown in Fig. 11(a) and Fig. 11(b), how can the trajectories reconstructed by RF-IDraw be successfully recognized for characters each of only a few centimeters wide. This is because the errors on the trajectory are not random errors from point to point. Instead, they are mostly due to the transform/distortion (e.g., stretching and squeezing) in the shape of the trajectory, as opposed to independent positioning errors. For example, the blue reconstructed trajectory (after removing initial position offset) in Fig. 10(e) deviates from the ground truth in the lower part of letter "c", resulting in trajectory error of a few centimeters. Yet because it is only a slight distortion instead of random errors, it does not affect the character recognition. In fact, different users write the same letter differently, and hence such type of distortion is naturally taken care of by the handwriting recognition app.
- The errors on the antenna array based scheme's reconstructed trajectory are random and incohesive. As a result, they lead to significant errors in recognizing the letters. In fact, even in the very rare cases where the trajectory is interpreted as the correct letter, the decision is more like a random guess by the software, because even a human could not recognize the letter.

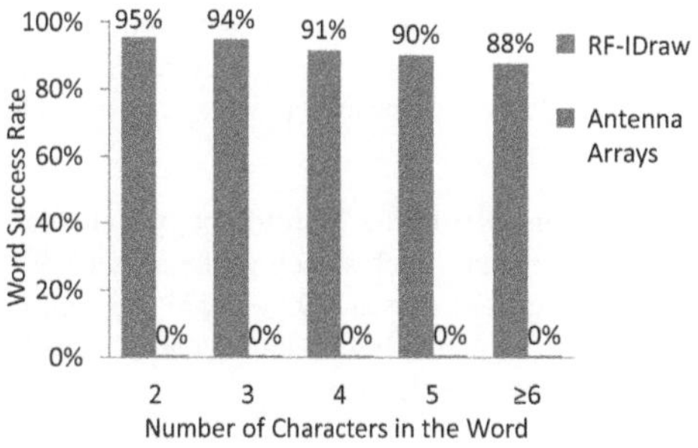


**Figure 15—Word Recognition Success Rate:** RF-IDraw's reconstructed trajectories for words can be correctly recognized in 92% of the cases by the Android app, enabling an effective virtual touch screen interface, far exceeding the capability of existing RF-based positioning system using the same number of antennas. None of the word trajectories reproduced by the antenna array based scheme is correctly recognized.

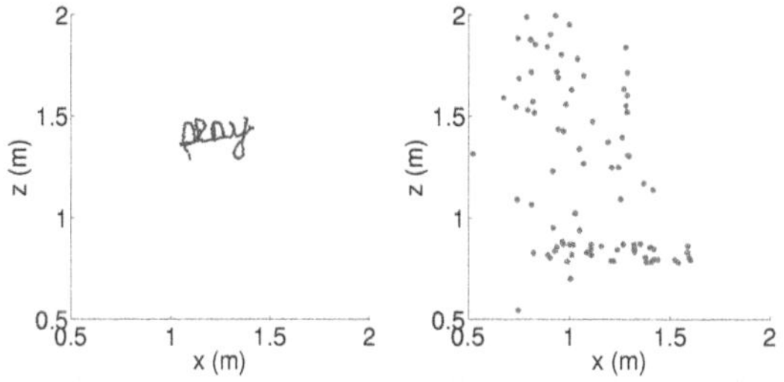


(a) RF-IDraw (b) Antenna Array Based Scheme

**Figure 16—Reconstructed Trajectories of "play" Written 5 m Away:** RF-IDraw's reconstructed trajectory reproduces all the details in the user's writing. The antenna array based scheme's reconstructed trajectory is scattered all over the place, due to the antenna arrays' low-resolution beams and their high sensitivity to noise.

- Finally, the character recognition success rate of RF-IDraw's reconstructed trajectories holds similar for different distances. The reason for this is that the trajectory error at larger distances in many cases is due to the enlarging of certain part of the trajectory, which has fairly little effect on the recognition of a letter, and thus does not affect the recognition success rate.

## 9.2 Word Recognition Success Rates

Next, we study the success rate of recognizing the reconstructed trajectories for words. Overall, 92% of the word trajectories reconstructed by RF-IDraw were correctly recognized by the handwriting recognition app.

- Fig. 15 shows the word recognition success rate as a function of the number of characters in the word. It is expected that as the word gets longer, it is more difficult to recognize it correctly. Yet the word recognition success rate for RF-IDraw holds above 88% even for words consisting of 6 letters or more. Note that, the simple Android app that we use has only a basic handwriting recognition function suitable for a mobile phone. To enable a larger, full-fledged virtual touch screen, one could use advanced techniques in natural language processing to improve the success rate, especially for longer words, the dictionary of which is more confined and can be leveraged for better inference [40].
- None of the word trajectories reconstructed by the antenna array based scheme can be recognized correctly, i.e., 0% success rate. This is not surprising given its low character success rate above.
- Fig. 16 shows the trajectories for the same word "play" written by a user 5 m away from the reader antennas, as reconstructed by RF-IDraw and by the antenna array based system respectively.

While RF-IDraw is able to reconstruct the whole word, the antenna array based scheme's output fails to form any meaningful shape, because of its wide beams' low resolution and high sensitivity to noise.

In summary, using RF-IDraw's prototype, we enable a first-of-its-kind RF-based virtual touch screen in the air with 97.5% character recognition success rate and 92% word recognition success rate, far exceeding the capability of antenna array based technique with the same number of antennas.

### 9.3 Discussion

Finally, a few points are worth elaborating on, regarding the application of RF-IDraw:

- One could distinguish between two classes of in-the-air user interfaces. One class is based on a priori defining a few gestures like forward/backward motion [27], then using a machine learning approach to learn patterns and classify gestures into the learned categories. The alternative is an interface that is similar to having a pen for tablets. This interface does not require training or learning different user's motions. Yet it can trace a much richer set of gestures: one can create any command by drawing or writing, e.g., people can annotate slides in a meeting, draw icons/signs which would be interpreted by different computing devices, etc. While classification of a limited set of simple gestures may be sufficient for certain applications, we believe many emerging applications will benefit from an interface that can interpret a rich set of commands and does not rely on training, which is the approach we adopt in RF-IDraw.
- For applications that require selecting and manipulating items on a display, one can use RF-IDraw in a manner similar to operating a mouse to control a cursor on the screen. The user sees the cursor's position in real time and will naturally adjust her motion to reach the desired position based on the visual feedback.
- A limitation of our current implementation of RF-IDraw's virtual touch screen is that we manually segment the user's writing into words. We believe this can be addressed by using standard segmentation methods [26] in natural language processing, which would allow us to build a full-fledged virtual touch screen that can automatically process continuous streams of input.
- Finally, we note that the key idea of using grating lobes in RF-IDraw is transferable to other RF systems beyond RFID, such as WiFi and bluetooth. For example, one can potentially implement RF-IDraw on WiFi access points to trace the trajectories of nearby cellphones, which is one of our ongoing efforts. We acknowledge that the operating assumptions, constraints, and requirements of WiFi and bluetooth systems propose new challenges for applying RF-IDraw, which we plan to explore and address in future work.

## 10. CONCLUSION

This paper presents RF-IDraw, an accurate RFID-based trajectory tracing system that can transform any plane or surface into a virtual touch screen, allowing a user to interact with a desired computing device by writing her commands in the air. We believe RF-IDraw opens up a whole new class of applications in gaming and user interaction interface.

**Acknowledgments:** We thank Haitham Hassanieh, Fadel Adib, Zach Kabelac, the reviewers and our shepherd, Brad Karp for their insightful comments. This research is funded by Lincoln Laboratory and the U.S. Air Force. We thank the members of the MIT Center for Wireless Networks and Mobile Computing, including Amazon.com, Cisco, Google, Intel, MediaTek, Microsoft, ST Microelectronics, and Telefonica, for their interest and support.

## 11. REFERENCES

[1] AN-900LH 900MHz antenna. rf-links.com/newsite/pdf/an900lh.pdf.
[2] Atacama Large Millimeter/submillimeter Array(ALMA). alma.mtk.nao.ac.jp/e/aboutalma/.
[3] Google Acquires Indoor/Outdoor Wireless Location Patents.
[4] MonkeyRunner API. developer.android.com/tools/help/MonkeyRunner.html.
[5] Omni-id exo 800. http://www.omni-id.com/products/.
[6] The corpus of contemporary american english. www.wordfrequency.info/.
[7] Ubi interactive. www.ubi-interactive.com.
[8] Vicon t-series. www.vicon.com/products/documents/Tseries.pdf.
[9] F. Adib, Z. Kabelac, D. Katabi, and R. C. Miller. 3d tracking via body radio reflections. NSDI, 2014.
[10] F. Adib and D. Katabi. See through walls with WiFi! SIGCOMM'13.
[11] Alien Technology Inc. ALN-9640 Squiggle Inlay. www.alientechnology.com.
[12] S. Azzouzi et al. New measurement results for the localization of uhf rfid transponders using an angle of arrival (aoa) approach. In *IEEE RFID 2011*.
[13] K. Chintalapudi, A. Padmanabha Iyer, and V. N. Padmanabhan. Indoor localization without the pain. MobiCom '10.
[14] Cisco. Cisco Announces Acquisition of ThinkSmart.
[15] EPCglobal Inc. EPCglobal Class 1 Generation 2.
[16] Forbes. Microsoft, Motorola, Nokia And RIM To Battle Google Over Indoor Location Market.
[17] Frost and Sullivan. Breakthrough Innovations in Indoor GPS, 2013.
[18] M. Hawes and W. Liu. Robust sparse antenna array design via compressive sensing.
[19] K. Joshi, S. Hong, and S. Katti. Pinpoint: Localizing interfering radios. NSDI, 2013.
[20] C. U. Keller. Interferometers. ATI 2010.
[21] R. Miesen et al. Holographic localization of passive uhf rfid transponders. In *IEEE RFID 2011*.
[22] P. Nikitin et al. Phase based spatial identification of uhf rfid tags. In *IEEE RFID 2010*.
[23] NOKIA. Accurate Mobile Indoor Positioning Industry Alliance, called In-Location, to promote deployment of location-based indoor services and solutions.
[24] S. J. Orfanidis. *Electromagnetic Waves and Antennas*. Macmillan Publishing Co., New York, 2010.
[25] P. Pal and P. Vaidyanathan. Coprime sampling and the music algorithm. 2011.
[26] R. Plamondon and S. N. Srihari. On-line and off-line handwriting recognition: A comprehensive survey. *IEEE Trans. Pattern Anal. Mach. Intell.*, 2000.
[27] Q. Pu, S. Gupta, S. Gollakota, and S. Patel. Whole-home gesture recognition using wireless signals. MobiCom, 2013.
[28] A. Rai, K. K. Chintalapudi, V. N. Padmanabhan, and R. Sen. Zee: zero-effort crowdsourcing for indoor localization. Mobicom '12.
[29] M. T. Review. The Indoor Positioning System Era.
[30] SlashGear. Qualcomm Gimbal takes on Apple iBeacon for Micro-Location.
[31] Z. Tan, Y. Eldar, and A. Nehorai. Direction of arrival estimation using co-prime arrays: A super resolution viewpoint. 2013.
[32] TED. Free or cheap wii remote hacks.
[33] ThingMagic. Mercury6e rfid reader module. www.thingmagic.com/embedded-rfid-readers.
[34] A. R. Thompson, J. M. Moran, and G. W. Swenson. *Interferometry and Synthesis in Radio Astronomy*. Wiley-Interscience, 2001.
[35] D. Tse and P. Vishwanath. *Fundamentals of Wireless Communications*. Cambridge University Press, 2005.
[36] VisionObjects. Myscript stylus. www.visionobjects.com/en/myscript/.
[37] J. Wang, F. Adib, R. Knepper, D. Katabi, and D. Rus. Rf-compass: Robot object manipulation using rfids. MobiCom, 2013.
[38] J. Wang, H. Hassanieh, D. Katabi, and P. Indyk. Efficient and reliable low-power backscatter networks. SIGCOMM, 2012.
[39] J. Wang and D. Katabi. Dude, where's my card?: Rfid positioning that works with multipath and non-line of sight. SIGCOMM, 2013.
[40] W. Wang, A. Brakensiek, and G. Rigoll. Combination of multiple classifiers for handwritten word recognition. ICFHR'02.
[41] J. Xiong and K. Jamieson. Arraytrack: A fine-grained indoor location system. NSDI '13, 2013.

# A Global Name Service for a Highly Mobile Internetwork

Abhigyan Sharma Xiaozheng Tie Hardeep Uppal Arun Venkataramani
David Westbrook Aditya Yadav *
{abhigyan, xztie, hardeep, arun, westy, ayadav}@cs.umass.edu

School of Computer Science, University of Massachusetts Amherst

## ABSTRACT

Mobile devices dominate the Internet today, however the Internet rooted in its tethered origins continues to provide poor infrastructure support for mobility. Our position is that in order to address this problem, a key challenge that must be addressed is the design of a massively scalable global name service that rapidly resolves identities to network locations under high mobility. Our primary contribution is the design, implementation, and evaluation of Auspice, a next-generation global name service that addresses this challenge. A key insight underlying Auspice is a *demand-aware* replica placement engine that intelligently replicates name records to provide low lookup latency, low update cost, and high availability. We have implemented a prototype of Auspice and compared it against several commercial managed DNS providers as well as state-of-the-art research alternatives, and shown that Auspice significantly outperforms both. We demonstrate proof-of-concept that Auspice can serve as a complete end-to-end mobility solution as well as enable novel context-based communication primitives that generalize name- or address-based communication in today's Internet.

## Categories and Subject Descriptors

C.2.4 [**Computer Systems Organization**]: COMPUTER-COMMUNICATION NETWORKS—*Distribtued Systems*

## Keywords

Mobility; distributed systems; network architecture

## 1. INTRODUCTION

"Mobile" has long arrived, but the Internet remains unmoved. Today, there is roughly one cellphone per human; the number of smartphones sold last year alone roughly equals the number of wired hosts on the Internet [28]; and the total traffic originated by mobiles is poised to approach that by wired devices [18]. However, the current Internet continues to operate as it did when dominated by tethered hosts, simply ignoring frequent endpoint mobility.

Today, an application developer can not easily initiate communication with a smartphone even when it has a public IP address as there is no global infrastructure support for locating it. Applications like smartphone notification systems, playback video, or cloud storage have to develop application-level support to enable a seamless experience for their users even as they change addresses several times a day, or let connections break (as popular VoIP apps do today). The lack of intrinsic support for mobility means that developers are forced to redundantly develop and maintain common-case functionality. Furthermore, we are paying an unknowable price in terms of long-term growth and innovation by strait-jacketing communication initiation to be unidirectional.

Many before us have criticized the Internet architecture's poor support for mobility as well as multihoming [33, 8, 24, 54]. A common criticism is the Internet's so-called conflation of identity and location, i.e., the use of an IP address both to represent the identity of an interface as well as its network location, which is problematic for mobility (same identity, changing locations) and multihoming (single identity, multiple locations). It is commonly accepted wisdom that a cleaner separation of identity and location is instrumental to fixing these problems. However, the Internet does separate identities (domain-names) from network locations (IP addresses) through DNS. Most high-level programming languages also provide syntactic sugar to `connect` to names remaining oblivious to IP addresses; and techniques from a long line of work on connection migration could be employed to seamlessly handle mid-connection mobility.

But a key missing element from this package today is a distributed name resolution infrastructure that can scale to orders of magnitude higher update rates than envisioned when DNS was created. To appreciate the envisioned scale, consider tens of billions of mobile identifiers changing network addresses at least tens of times per day. DNS's heavy reliance on TTL-based caching, a key strength recognized by its creators, researchers, and operators alike, poses a significant handicap by increasing update propagation delays, load on name servers, and overall client-perceived latency. It is not uncommon for DNS update propagation to take a day or more, resulting in long outage times when online services have to be moved unexpectedly, prompting cries for help on operator forums [7, 47]. A less widely noted limitation of DNS is its reliance on hierarchical names for scaling via federation and its single root of trust, which constrains mobile applications from selecting arbitrary application-specific names (as elaborated in §2.2 and §3.2).

*Authors ordered alphabetically by last name.


*SIGCOMM'14*, August 17–22, 2014, Chicago, IL, USA.

ACM 978-1-4503-2836-4/14/08 ...$15.00.
http://dx.doi.org/10.1145/2619239.2626331.

Our position is that seamless support for mobility requires a logically centralized global name service that rapidly translates identities to locations irrespective of how exactly identities and locations are individually represented. Our primary contribution is the design, implementation, and evaluation of Auspice, a distributed system that helps address this challenge. Compared to today's ICANN/DNS-based approach, our approach cleanly separates name resolution from adjudication and certification issues (§3.2). Auspice is also deployable as a managed DNS provider in today's Internet; compared to them, a key strength of Auspice is a *demand-aware* replica placement engine that significantly reduces the *time-to-connect* to mobile destinations in a cost-effective manner. Under light load, Auspice's demand-aware replica placement aggressively uses available resources to massively replicate name records, while under heavy load, it carefully controls the number and choice of replica locations based on the read-write patterns and pockets of high demand for each name.

We have implemented a prototype of Auspice as a geo-distributed key-value store to serve as a flexible name resolution service for the current Internet as well as several "future" Internet or endpoint architectures such as MobilityFirst[54], HIP[33], or XIA[31]. We have extensively evaluated Auspice using a combination of Planetlab, emulation clusters, and Amazon EC2. Our contributions are as follows.

1. A case for a global name service as an indispensable part of any Internetwork design with intrinsic support for high mobility (§2).
2. Auspice, a scalable, geo-distributed, federated global name service that significantly reduces the time-to-connect under any given resource constraints despite high mobility and arbitrary endpoint identifiers (§3,§4).
3. A proof-of-concept demonstration of intrinsic support for—*(i)* all four types of endpoint mobility; *(ii)* novel context-aware delivery primitives that generalize name- or address-based communication—over the current Internet as well as MobilityFirst [54] (§4.3).
4. Comparison against several best-of-breed managed DNS services showing that Auspice's demand-aware approach significantly lowers time-to-connect and/or update cost even for today's (hardly mobile) domain names (§4.4).

To provide a historical perspective, until the early 80s, the Internet relied on a system called `HOSTS.TXT` for name resolution, which was simply a centrally maintained text file distributed to all hosts. The current Internet's distributed DNS arose in response to the rapidly increasing file size and distribution costs. Mockapetris and Dunlap [43] point to TTL-based caching to reduce load and response times as a key strength, noting that "*the XEROX system* [Grapevine [51]] *was then ... the most sophisticated name service in existence, but it was not clear that its heavy use of replication, light use of caching ... were appropriate*". We have since come a full circle, turning to active replication (§2.2) in Auspice in order to address the challenges of mobility, a concern that wasn't particularly pressing in the 80s. Compared to classical systems like Grapevine or ClearingHouse, Auspice enables support for automated *demand-aware* replica placement for *arbitrary names* (using several modern design elements such as consensus, the key-value abstraction, self-certifying names, consistent hashing, etc). Auspice, through its support for context-aware delivery, is also a step towards addressing some of the challenges to which Lampson alludes on representing "descriptive names" [40].

# 2. CASE FOR A GLOBAL NAME SERVICE

Given the huge body of prior work specifically on mobility as well as more broadly on Internet architecture, it is natural to begin by asking: Is a global name resolution service critical to handling mobility if we had the luxury of refactoring Internet naming and routing from a clean slate?

## 2.1 Internet mobility background

Despite a staggering diversity of proposals re-architecting Internet naming and routing, we find that they explicitly or implicitly embed one of three broad approaches to handling mobility–*indirection-based routing, global name-to-address resolution*, or *name-based routing*–based on how they go from the name of an endpoint to the endpoint itself.

**Indirection-based routing** schemes are simple as an endpoint remains oblivious to the mobility of other endpoints. No name-to-address[1] lookup is needed at connection initiation time as a human-readable name maps to a *home address* (an IP address in Mobile IP [48] or a flat identifier's consistent-hash location in i3 [53]) that rarely changes by design. Mid-connection mobility, even when both endpoints move concurrently, is seamless to endpoints. However, the data plane pays the price for this simplicity—every data packet must be routed via an indirection agent at the home address, potentially causing significant routing stretch, e.g., two participants at a conference may in each direction need to detour packets halfway across the world despite being in the same room. Furthermore, indirection-based schemes require widespread deployment of indirection agents across different domains, posing a barrier to immediate adoption.

**Global name-to-address resolution** schemes rely on a distributed service to resolve names to addresses as the first step in connection establishment. The current Internet's DNS as well as a number of designs addressing the Internet's so-called identity-location conflation problem also need such a resolution infrastructure, e.g., to translate a self-certifying host identifier in HIP [33], AIP[12], XIA[31], or MobilityFirst[4]) or an identifier in LISP [8] or HAIR [24] to either an IP address [33], a self-certifying network identifier [12, 31, 4], or a hierarchical locator [24] that encodes routing information. Global name-to-address resolution schemes also subsume DHT-based Internet architectures such as LNA [14, 56] as well as resolution systems like CoDoNS [49] that present a DHT-based drop-in replacement for DNS.

Global name-to-address resolution schemes need explicit support at endpoints to handle mid-connection mobility. There is a general consensus [52, 13, 26] that end-to-end connection migration, i.e., bilaterally without relying on an external service, suffices to migrate connections efficiently when endpoints move one at a time, but an external resolution service is needed to support concurrent mobility. Although the latter is seen as a rare case in most connection migration work, it can be common in disconnection-tolerant, mobile application scenarios, e.g., when a user closes her laptop at home and opens it at a coffee shop to continue watching a movie, by which time the cloud-hosted virtual server may have been migrated for load balancing.

[1] We use the terms *name* and *identifier* interchangeably; likewise for the terms *address* and *location*.

**Name-based routing** schemes in the ideal have a tantalizing intellectual lure—to seamlessly handle mobility by routing directly over names with no resolution step—but are marred by several fundamental and practical challenges. First, name-based routing approaches can support seamless mobility only if routing update propagation delays are on the order of milliseconds, a daunting challenge given that interdomain routing can take several minutes to converge today. Second, theoretical results on compact routing [36] suggest discouraging fundamental trade-offs between the size of forwarding tables at routers and path stretch even without any mobility or multihoming, e.g., routing over N flat identifiers entails a prohibitive $\Omega(N)$ forwarding table size per router in order to ensure a small constant stretch factor ($\approx$3) compared to shortest-path routing. Simulation-based studies of flat-label routing strategies (e.g., ROFL [17]) reaffirm pessimistic conclusions about its scalability.

Although it may appear that the scalability limitations of name-based routing can be alleviated by adding a hierarchical structure to names [29, 35, 32] (e.g., NDN-style [32] names such as `/umass/phone42/call3/frame7`), frequent mobility still poses a challenge as routers would have to maintain special forwarding entries for "displaced names", i.e., names that move from their hierarchically organized namespace (say, from `/umass` to `/comcast` in this example) for longest-prefix matching to work correctly. That is, high mobility effectively makes routing directly over structured names as hard as routing over flat names unless indirection or a name resolution infrastructure is used, a conjecture that has recently been empirically reinforced by Gao et al. [27].

**Summary.** Our position is that a global name-to-address resolution service is critical for handling high mobility in any network architecture as it offers the best combination of trade-offs: (1) a constant update overhead per mobility event to the name service, (2) a modest connection establishment overhead and rapid mid-connection mobility, (3) no data path inflation beyond underlying policy routing, and (4) small forwarding table sizes in conjunction with aggregatable addresses (IP prefixes like today or self-certifying network addresses [4, 31]). Perhaps the most compelling argument for global name-to-address resolution is our decades of familiarity with DNS and the Internet; handling mobility would be a drop-in replacement to DNS provided we address the challenge of building a distributed system that scales to billions of devices making many updates a day and yet returns up-to-date responses within milliseconds.

## 2.2 Limitations of DNS

What specific design traits of DNS make it poorly suited for mobile applications? The first two traits below limit its scalability with respect to the rate of endpoint mobility, and the third limits its scalability with respect to the size of the namespace if applications were to have the luxury of using arbitrary (but fixed) names.

(1) *TTL-based caching:* TTL-based caching is the single-most important mechanism for DNS's scalability; caching not only helps DNS sustain essentially arbitrarily high *lookup load* but also dramatically reduces client-perceived *lookup latency* for cache hits. However, caching is ineffective when TTLs are near-zero, as would have to be the case under high mobility, causing both increased load on name servers and higher client-perceived latencies. Caching is also less effective if lookups are distributed relatively uniformly, as could be the case with mobile device names, unlike lookups for today's domain names that are highly skewed [34, 45].

(2) *Static placement:* Authoritative DNS servers are essentially rendezvous points that allow a mobile endpoint to inform potential correspondents of its current location(s). In order to reduce the time-to-connect, authoritative servers must be located close to potential correspondents. However, authoritative server locations today are static, either close to a mobile endpoint's "home" location or a pre-packaged set of geo-distributed locations provided by a managed DNS provider. Engineering a scalable geo-distributed system that can dynamically move object replicas in a demand-aware manner is nontrivial and real-world examples of such systems have only recently begun to emerge [19].

(3) *Hierarchical names:* The hierarchical structure of DNS names is key to leveraging *federation* to scale to an arbitrary number of names by delegating different portions of the name space (or zones) to different organizations. For example, root name servers today only have to maintain state for a small number of top-level domain names. In contrast, arbitrary or flat names, e.g., "`JohnSmith3142's watch`" can not be supported in DNS while retaining the scaling benefits of federation as the root name servers would have to maintain nonzero state, e.g., at least the authoritative name server(s) and the DNSSEC key of a name, for essentially all names. Our position is that the design of a general-purpose global name service must not restrict the structure of names as names carry application-specific semantics; in §4.3.3, we show examples of novel context-aware communication primitives that are feasible with unrestricted names.

Our approach to address the first two issues above relies on *active* and *demand-aware* replication: (1) Active replication significantly reduces (but does not eliminate) the reliance on passive caching; (2) Demand-aware replication ensures that active replicas of a name record are accessible close to clients querying the name, so as to reduce the overall time-to-connect. A glib but pedagogically helpful way to highlight the difference from DNS is that, in the extreme case, our approach can create an active replica of a name record near every DNS local name server that stores a passively cached copy today. Our approach addresses the third issue above by cleanly separating resolution of names from adjudication and certification. We explain our approach in detail next.

# 3. Auspice DESIGN & IMPLEMENTATION

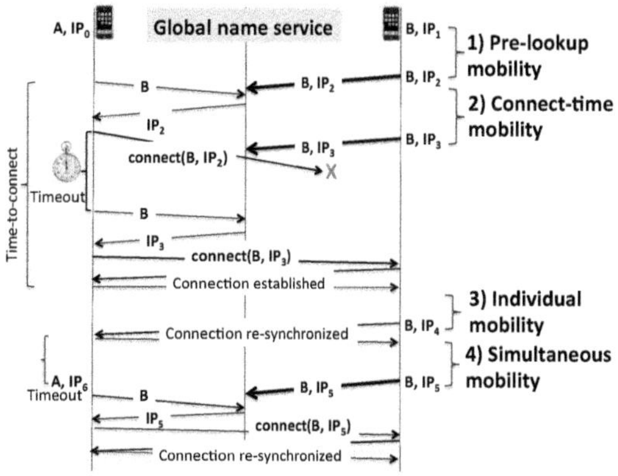


**Figure 1: Four kinds of mobility—(1) *pre-lookup*, (2) *connect-time*, (3) *individual*, (4) *simultaneous*—three of which require a global name service.**

Our envisioned GNS enables endpoint mobility as shown in Figure 1. An endpoint A initiates communication with another endpoint B by querying the GNS for B's current addresses and connecting to one of them, thereby enabling *prelookup* mobility. If B moves after A's query but before before a connection has been mutually established via a three-way handshake (*connect-time* mobility), A times out and reverts back to the GNS. After a connection has been established, if either endpoint moves one at a time (*individual* mobility), it can re-synchronize the connection with a bilateral three-way handshake without relying upon the GNS (noting however that router-level late-binding proposals relying on a GNS-like infrastructure have also been proposed [44, 4]). If an endpoint moves mid-connection after the other endpoint has moved but before it could re-synchronize the connection (*simultaneous* mobility), one or both endpoint(s) eventually query the GNS and re-synchronize the connection.

## 3.1 Design goals

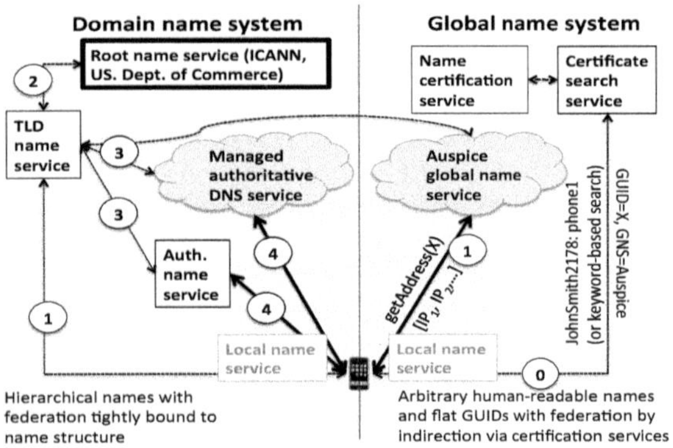


**Figure 2: DNS vs. GNS: Auspice can be deployed as a managed DNS provider today (left) or as a GNS provider that provides resolution service for its customer GUIDs (right). Name certification services bind a human-readable name to a GUID and its GNS provider, and certificate search services can help index and distribute certificates from all certification services. Solid (dotted) lines represent frequent (infrequent) query paths for a given mobile destination. Except for the tightly controlled DNS root service, all services above are designed to be purveyed competitively.**

Much of the envisioned functionality of a GNS as above boils down to one over-arching distributed systems challenge: *any principal–endpoint or router–should get the look and feel of a high-availability name service that is nearby (≈ few milliseconds) and rapidly returns up-to-date responses.* A more precise breakdown of goals is as follows.

**(1) Time-to-connect performance**: The design must ensure low latencies for name lookups to return up-to-date values, which determines the *time to connect* to a destination when the value being queried for is an address like above.

**(2) Resource cost**: The design must ensure low replication cost. A naive way to minimize lookup latencies is to replicate every name record at every possible location, however high mobility means high update rates, so the cost of pushing each update to every replica would be prohibitive. Worse, load hotspots can actually degrade lookup latencies.

**(3) High availability**: The design must ensure resilience to node failures including outages of entire datacenters; by consequence, it should also prevent crippling load hotspots.

**(4) Security**: The design must be robust to malicious users attempting to hijack or corrupt name records. The design must support flexible access control policies to ensure the desired level of privacy of name records.

**(5) Federation**: The design must allow different name service providers to co-exist and for users to freely choose one or more preferred providers.

**(6) Extensibility**: The design must be agnostic to how names, addresses, and resolution policies are represented by a future Internetwork. In particular, it should support flat names and a rich set of attributes and resolution policies for multi-homed mobility (e.g.,"prefer WiFi to cellular"), etc.

## 3.2 Design overview

To address the above goals, the Auspice GNS is designed as a massively geo-distributed key-value store. The geo-distribution is essential to the latency and availability goals while the key-value API enables extensibility. Each *name record* in Auspice is associated with a globally unique identifier (GUID) that is the record's primary key. A name record contains an associative array of key-value pairs, wherein each key $K_i$ is a string and the value $V_i$ may be a string, a primitive type, or recursively a key-value pair, as shown below.

GUID $\mid K_1, V_1 \mid K_2, V_2 \mid \cdots$

The GUID is a self-certifying identifier computed as a compact one-way hash of a public key. Each name record is aliased to one or more globally unique human-readable names that are bound to the GUID by a certificate supplied by one or more *name certification service(s)* (NCS). Loosely speaking, the human-readable name is analogous to a DNS domain name and a name record to a zone file, but with the following important differences.

**Security.** As shown in Fig. 2, to initiate communication with a destination Y, an endpoint X must first obtain a certificate of the form [`JohnSmith2178:Phone1`, $Y, P]_{K^-}$ that binds the human-readable name to the GUID Y and its GNS provider P, and is signed by the private key $K^-$ of an NCS that X trusts. A certificate search service (e.g., a search engine or ISP) can help index certificates from different NCSes, and help X find a certificate from a trusted NCS, and even find the human-readable name based on keywords.

**Federation.** Unlike ICANN and root DNS servers that respectively act as a single name adjudication authority and root of trust for certification, our approach decentralizes trust across different NCS providers, potentially allowing endpoints to use quorum-based approaches to resolve conflicting name certificates. More importantly, our federation approach allows endpoints to select arbitrary human-readable names and NCS providers unlike DNS that restricts domain names to be hierarchical and federation and the DNSSEC keychain to strictly follow the name structure. An inevitable implication of decentralizing trust is that two endpoints can communicate securely only if they share a trusted NCS provider, but this change we argue is preferable to and a strict generalization of the single-root-of-trust model that some perceive as arbitrary [10, 9].

**Extensibility.** Our design cleanly separates the GNS provider's resource-intensive responsibility of name resolution under high mobility from the slow-changing certification process. It also allows for the GNS provider to be deployed today as a managed authoritative DNS provider (Fig. 2) with the DNSSEC key deriving the GUID. Finally, the key-value store API enables an extensible name record represen-

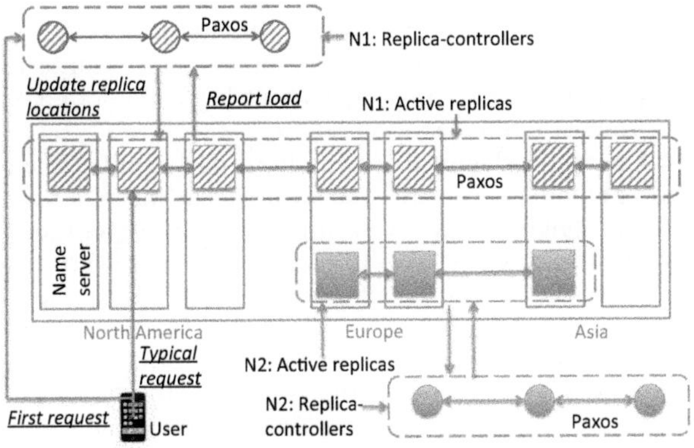


**Figure 3: Geo-distributed name servers in Auspice. Replica-controllers (logically separate from active replicas) decide placement of active replicas and active replicas handle requests from end-users. N1 is a globally popular name and is replicated globally; name N2 is popular in select regions and is replicated in those regions.**

tation. By default, each top-level key has associated read and write ACLs that could either be a blacklist or whitelist of GUIDs that respectively have read or write access. For example, a name record for GUID X that helps context-aware delivery or multihoming policies (detailed in §4.3.3) is below.

```
{X: {IPs:[{IP: 23.55.66.43, plan: Unlimited}, {IP:
62.44.65.75, plan: Limited}], geoloc: {[lat,long],
readWhitelist:[Y,Z]}, multihome_policy: Unlimited}}
```

## 3.3 Auspice's geo-distributed design

Next, we explain how Auspice achieves the first three design goals. At the core of Auspice is a placement engine that achieves the latency, cost, and availability goals by adapting the number and locations of replicas of each name record in accordance with (1) the lookup and update request rates for the name, (2) the geo-distribution of requests for the name, and (3) the aggregate request load across all names.

Figure 3 illustrates the placement engine. Each name is associated with a fixed number, $F$, of *replica-controllers* and a variable number of *active replicas* of the corresponding name record. The name's replica-controllers are computed using consistent hashing to select $F$ consecutive or otherwise deterministic nodes along the ring *onto* which the hash function maps names and nodes. The replica-controllers are responsible only for determining the number and locations of the active replicas, and the actives replicas are responsible for maintaining the actual name record and processing client requests. The replica-controllers implement a replicated state machine using Paxos [38] in order to maintain a consistent view of the current set of active replicas.

A name's replica-controllers compute its active replica locations in a *demand-aware* manner. This computation proceeds in epochs as follows. At creation time, the active replicas are chosen to be physically at the same locations as the corresponding replica-controllers. In each epoch, the replica-controllers obtain from each active replica a summarized load report that contains the request rates for that name from different regions as seen by that replica. Here, *regions* partition users into non-overlapping groups that capture locality, e.g., IP prefixes or a geographic partitioning based on cities; and the *load report* is a spatial vector of request rates as seen by the replica. The replica-controllers aggregate these load reports to obtain a concise spatial distribution of all requests for the name.

### *3.3.1 Demand-aware replica placement*

In each epoch, the replica-controllers use a placement algorithm that takes as input the aggregated load reports and capacity constraints at name servers to determine the number and locations of active replicas for each name so as to minimize client-perceived latency. We have formalized this *global* optimization problem as a mixed-integer program and shown it to be computationally hard. As our focus is on simple, practical algorithms, we defer the details of the optimization approach [1], using it only as a benchmark in small-scale experiments with Auspice's heuristic algorithm

Auspice's placement algorithm is a simple heuristic and can be run *locally* by each replica-controller. The placement algorithm computes the number of replicas using the lookup-to-update ratio of a name in order to limit the update cost to within a small factor of the lookup cost. The number of replicas is always kept more than the minimum number needed to meet the availability objective under failures. The location of these replicas are decided to minimize lookup latency by placing a fraction of replicas close to pockets of high demand for that name while placing the rest randomly so as to balance the potentially conflicting goals of reducing latency and balancing load among name servers.

Specifically, the placement algorithm computes the number of replicas for a name as $(F + \beta r_i/w_i)$, where $r_i$ and $w_i$ are the lookup and update rates of name $i$; $F$ is the minimum number of replicas needed to meet the availability goal (§3.1); and $\beta$ is a replication control parameter that is automatically determined by the system so as to trade off latency benefits of replication against update costs given capacity constraints as follows. In each epoch, the replica-controllers recompute $\beta$ so that the aggregate load in the system corresponds to a preset threshold utilization fraction $\mu$. For simplicity of exposition, suppose read and write operations impose the same load, and the total capacity across all name servers (in reads/sec) is $C$. Then, $\beta$ is set so that

$$\mu C = \sum_i r_i + \sum_i (F + \beta \frac{r_i}{w_i}) w_i \qquad (1)$$

where the right hand side represents the total load summed across all names. The first term in the summation above is the total read load and the second is the total write load.

Having computed $\beta$ as above, replica-controllers compute the locations of active replicas for name $i$ as follows. Out of the $F + \beta r_i/w_i$ total replicas, a fraction $\nu$ of replicas are chosen based on locality, i.e., replica-controllers use the spatial vector of load reports to select $\nu(F + \beta r_i/w_i)$ name servers that are respectively the closest to the top $\nu(F + \beta r_i/w_i)$ regions sorted by demand for name $i$. The remaining $(1-\nu)(F + \beta r_i/w_i)$ are chosen randomly without repetition. The locality-based replicas above are chosen as the *closest* with respect to round-trip latency plus load-induced latency measured locally at each name server. An earlier design chose them based on round-trip latency alone, but we found that adding load-induced latencies in this step (in addition to choosing the remaining replicas randomly) ensures better load balance and lowers overall client-perceived latency. Our current prototype and system experiments fix the random perturbation knob $\nu$ to 0.5. We have since developed a slightly modified placement scheme that relieves the administrator from setting $\nu$ manually, automatically balancing locality-awareness and load to ensure low latencies [1]. Thus, an administrator need only specify F and $\mu$ based on fault tolerance and aggressiveness of capacity utilization.

### 3.3.2 *Client request routing*

A client request is routed from an end-host to a suitable name server as follows. The set of all name servers in an Auspice instance is known to each member name server and can be obtained from a well-known location. End-hosts can either directly send requests to a name server or channel them through a local name server like today. When a local name server encounters a request for a name for the first time, it uses the known set of all name servers and consistent hashing to determine the replica-controllers for that name and sends the request to the closest replica-controller. The replica-controller returns the set of active replicas for the name and the client resends the request to the closest active replica. In practice, we expect replica-controllers to be contacted infrequently as the set of active replicas can be cached and reused until they change in some future epoch.

Network latency as well as server-load-induced latency help determine the closest replica at a local name server. Each local name server maintains an estimate of the round-trip latency to all name servers using infrequent pings; an (as yet unimplemented) optimization to reduce the overhead of all-to-all pings is to use coordinate embedding, geo-IP, or measurement-driven techniques [42]. To incorporate load-induced latency, the latency estimate to a name server is passively measured as a moving average over lookups sent to that name server. The local name server also maintains a timeout value based on the moving average and variance of the estimates. If a lookup request sent to a name server times out, the local name server infers that either the server or network route is congested, and it multiplicatively increases its latency estimate to that name server by a fixed factor. Thus, if multiple lookups sent to a name server time out, the estimated latency shoots up and the local name server stops sending requests to that name server, which effectively acts as a more agile load-balancing policy in the request routing plane (complementing the replica placement plane above that operates in coarser-grained epochs).

### 3.3.3 *Consistency with static replication*

As a global name-to-address resolution service, Auspice must at least ensure this eventual consistency property: *all active replicas must eventually return the same value of the name record and, in a single-writer scenario, this value must be the last update made by the (only) client*; "eventually" means that there are no updates to a name record and no replica failures for sufficiently long. Violating this property means that a mobile client may be persistently unreachable even though it is no longer moving (updating addresses).

With a static set of replicas, it is straightforward to support this property. A replica receiving a client update need only record the write in a persistent manner locally, return a commit to the client, and lazily propagate the update to other active replicas for that record. Lazy propagation is sufficient to ensure that all replicas eventually receive every update committed at any replica, and a deterministic reconciliation policy, e.g., as in Dynamo [21], suffices to ensure that concurrent updates are consistently applied across all replicas. Temporary divergence across replicas under failures can be shortened by increasing durability, i.e., by recording the update persistently at more replicas before returning a commit to the client. The additional "single-writer" clause is satisfied simply by incorporating a client-local timestamp in the deterministic reconciliation policy.

**Total write ordering.** As Auspice is designed to be an expressive name service with sophisticated attributes, it may be useful in some scenarios to ensure that update operations (like appending to or deleting from a list) to a name are applied in the same order by all active replicas. Ensuring a total ordering of all updates to a name is a stronger property than eventual consistency, calling for a state-machine approach, which Auspice supports as an option.

To this end, active replicas for a name participate in a Paxos instance maintained separately for each name (distinct from Paxos used by replica-controllers to compute active replicas for that name). Each update is forwarded to the active replica that is elected as the Paxos coordinator that, under graceful execution, first gets a majority of replicas to accept the update number and then broadcasts a commit. Total write ordering of course implies that updates can make progress only when a majority of active replicas can communicate with each other while maintaining safety (consistent with the so-called CAP dilemma).

### 3.3.4 *Consistency with replica reconfiguration*

With a dynamic set of replicas as in Auspice, achieving eventual consistency is straightforward, as it suffices if a replica recovering from a crash lazily propagates all pending writes to a name to its *current* set of active replicas as obtained from any of the consistently-hashed replica-controllers for the name. However, satisfying the (optional) total write order property above is nontrivial.

To this end, we have designed a two-tier reconfigurable Paxos system that involves explicit coordination between the consensus engines of the replica-controllers and active replicas. Reconfiguration is accomplished by a replica-controller issuing and committing a stop request that gets committed as the last update of the current active replica group. The replica-controller subsequently initiates the next group of active replicas that can obtain the current record value from any member of the previous group. This design shares similarities with Vertical Paxos [39], however we were unable to find existing implementations or even reference systems using similar schemes, so we had to develop it from scratch. The details of the reconfiguration protocol are here [1].

### 3.3.5 *Scalability: A performance-cost analysis*

**Cost.** Auspice's replica placement scheme (Eq. 1) is designed to use a fraction $\mu$ of system-wide resources so as to make at least $F$ and at most $M$ replicas of each name, where $M$ is the total number of name server locations. Thus, at light load, Auspice may replicate every name at every location, while under heavy load, it may create exactly $F$ replicas for all but the most popular names. In the common case, a lookup involves one request and response between a local name server and an active replica; an update involves $\approx$ thrice (twice) as many messages as the number of active replicas with total write ordering (eventual) consistency.

**Performance.** The worst-case time-to-connect latency for a name $i$ depends on the lookup latency $l_i$, the update rate $w_i$, the worst-case update propagation latency $d_i$, i.e., the time for all active replicas to receive an update, and the connect timeout $T$ (Fig. 1), as follows [1].

$$\text{TTC}_i = l_i[1 + (e^{w_i d_i} - 1)(1 + \frac{T}{l_i})] \qquad (2)$$

Thus, the time-to-connect increases with (1) the lookup latency $l_i$ that in turn improves with demand-aware replication; (2) the update rate $w_i$ and update propagation delay $d_i$ that in combination determine the likelihood of obtaining a stale response, noting that the latter increases with more aggressive replication; and (3) the connect timeout $T$ that is at most the default transport-layer timeout (e.g., a few seconds for TCP) and potentially as low as the round-trip delay between the connecting client and the destination being connected to if the destination network is capable of generating an "no route to host" error message.

**TTLs.** The above analysis implicitly assumes near-zero TTLs. With a nonzero $\text{TTL}_i$ for name $i$, the worst-case time-to-connect can be approximated as [1].

$$\begin{aligned}\text{TTC}_i \simeq\ & \tau_i \frac{(r_i + w_i + 1/\text{TTL}_i + r_i w_i \text{TTL}_i)}{(1 + r_i\text{TTL}_i)(r_i + w_i + 1/\text{TTL}_i)} \\ & + \frac{T\ r_i\ w_i}{(r_i + 1/\text{TTL}_i)(r_i + w_i + 1/\text{TTL}_i)}\end{aligned} \qquad (3)$$

where $\tau_i$ above is $\text{TTC}_i$ (with a 0 TTL) as in Eq 2. Thus, a long TTL is meaningful only if the update rate $w_i$ is low; if so, a carefully chosen TTL can reduce the load on the system as well as the client-perceived time-to-connect; if not, a long TTL can inflate the time-to-connect by the connect timeout $T$ ( = the second term above for $w_i \gg r_i$ and high $\text{TTL}_i$).

**Comparison to DNS.** All of the above analyses are applicable also to geo-replicated managed DNS providers were they to employ Auspice's demand-aware replication approach. The main difference between Auspice and today's managed DNS providers that rely on simplistic static replica placement schemes is in the lookup latency $l_i$ achieved for any given resource cost; we evaluate this performance-cost tradeoff extensively in our experiments (§4.2 and §4.4).

### 3.3.6 *Implementation status*

We have implemented Auspice as described in Java with 28K lines of code. We have been maintaining an alpha deployment for research use for many months across eight EC2 regions. We have implemented support for two pluggable NoSQL data stores, MongoDB (default) and Cassandra, as persistent local stores at name servers. We do not rely on any distributed deployment features therein as the coordination middleware is what Auspice provides.

We have developed a simple NCS as a proof of concept, which through a web portal (`http://gns.name`) or a command-line console allows a user to bind a self- or system-selected GUID to a human-readable name that is simply an email address, i.e., our proof-of-concept NCS is a trivial CA that relies on email-based identity verification. Clients currently have to use a custom Auspice developer library to perform lookups and updates or custom socket library, msocket (§4.3), for end-to-end mobility features. We have also developed a simple proxy to translate between BIND and Auspice's wire-line protocol so as to interoperate with DNS.

## 4. EVALUATION

Our evaluation seeks to answer the following questions: (1) How well does Auspice's design meet its performance, cost, and availability goals compared to state-of-the-art alternatives under high mobility? (2) Can Auspice serve as a complete, end-to-end solution for mobility and enable novel communication abstractions? (3) How does Auspice's cost-performance tradeoff compare to best-of-breed managed DNS services for today's (hardly mobile) domain name workloads?

### 4.1 Experimental setup

**Testbeds:** We use geo-distributed testbeds (Amazon EC2 or Planetlab) or local emulation clusters (EC2 or a departmental cluster) depending upon the experiment's goals.

**Workload:** There is no real workload today of clients querying a name service in order to communicate with mobile devices frequently moving across different network addresses, both because such a name service does not exist and mobile devices do not have publicly visible IP addresses. So we conduct an evaluation using synthetic workloads for device names (§4.2), but to avoid second-guessing future workload patterns, we conduct a comprehensive sensitivity analysis against all of the relevant parameters such as the read rate, write rate, popularity, and geo-locality of demand [1].

The following are default experimental parameters for *device names*. The ratio of the total number of lookups across all devices to the total number of updates is 1:1, i.e., devices are queried for on average as often as they change addresses. The lookup rate of any single device name is uniformly distributed between 0.5–1.5× the average lookup rate; the update rate is similarly distributed and drawn independently.

How requests are geographically distributed is clearly important for evaluating a replica placement scheme. We define the *geo-locality* of a name as the fraction of requests from the top-10% of regions where the name is most popular. This parameter ranges from 0.1 (least locality) to 1 (high locality). For a device name with geo-locality of $g$, a fraction $g$ of the requests are assumed to originate from 10% of the local name servers, the first of which is picked randomly and the rest are the ones geographically closest to it. We pick the geo-locality $g = 0.75$ for device names, i.e., the top 10% of regions in the world will account for 75% of requests, an assumption that is consistent with the finding that communication and content access exhibits a high country-level locality [37], and is consistent with the measured geo-locality (below) of service names today.

In addition to device names, *service names* constitute a small fraction (10%) of names and are intended to capture domain names like today with low mobility. Their lookup rate (or popularity) distribution and geo-distribution are used directly from the Alexa dataset [2]. Using this dataset, we calculated the geo-locality exhibited by the top 100K websites to be 0.8. Updates for service names are a tiny fraction (0.01%) of lookups as web services can be expected to be queried much more often than they are moved around. The lookup rate of service names is a third of the total number of requests (same as the lookup or update rates of devices).

**Replication schemes compared:** **Auspice** uses the replica placement strategy as described in §3 with the default parameter values $F = 3, \mu = 0.7, \nu = 0.5$. We compare Auspice against the following: (1) **Random-M** replicates each name at three random locations; (2) **Replicate-All** replicates all names at all locations; (3) **DHT+Popularity** replicates names using consistent hashing with replication similar to Codons[49]. The number of replicas is chosen based on the popularity ranking of a name and the location of replicas is decided by consistent hashing. The average hop count in Codons's underlying Beehive algorithm is set so that it creates the same average number of replicas as

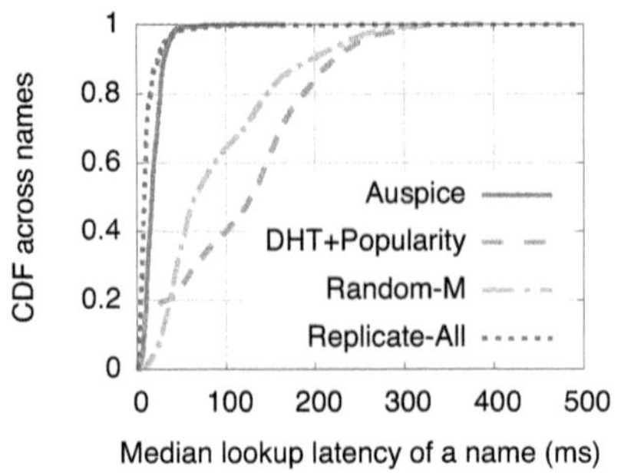

(a) Lookup latencies (load = 0.3)

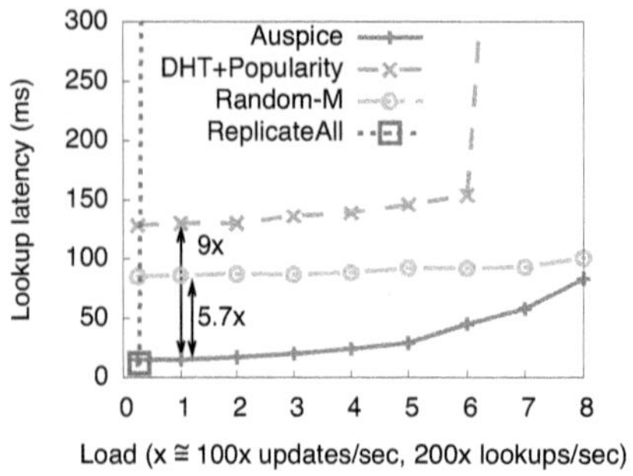

(b) Lookup latency vs. load

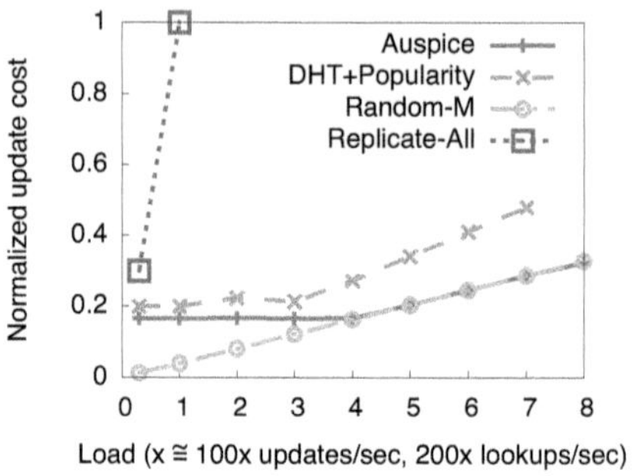

(c) Update cost vs. load

**Figure 4: Auspice has up to 5.7× to 9× lower latencies than Random-M and DHT+Popularity reps. (4(b)). A load of 1 means 200 lookups/sec and 100 updates/sec per name server. Replicate-All peaks out at a load of 0.3 while Auspice can sustain a request load of up to 8 as it carefully chooses between 3 and 80 replicas per name.**

Auspice for a fair comparison. All schemes direct a lookup to the closest available replica after the first request.

## 4.2 Evaluating Auspice's replica placement

We conduct experiments in this subsection on a 16-node (each with Xeon 5140, 4-cores, 8 GB RAM) departmental cluster, wherein each machine hosts 10 instances of either nameservers or local nameservers so as to emulate an 80-nameserver Auspice deployment. We instrument the instances so as to emulate wide-area latencies between any two instances that correspond to 160 randomly chosen Planetlab nodes. We choose emulation instead of a geo-distributed testbed in this experiment in order to obtain reproducible results while stress-testing the load-vs.-response time scaling behavior of various schemes given identical resources.

### *4.2.1 Lookup latency and update cost*

How well does Auspice use available resources for replicating name records? To evaluate this, we compare the lookup latency of schemes across varying load levels. A machine running 10 name servers receives on average 2000 lookups/sec and 1000 updates/sec at a load = 1. For each scheme, load is increased until 2% of requests fail, where a failed request means no response is received within 10 sec. The experiment runs for 10 mins for each scheme and load level. To measure steady-state behavior, both Auspice and DHT+Popularity pre-compute the placement at the start of the experiment based on prior knowledge of the workload.

Figure 4(a) shows the distribution of median lookup latency across names at the smallest load level (load = 0.3). Figure 4(b) shows load-vs-lookup latency curve for schemes, where "lookup latency" refers to the mean of the median lookup latencies of names. Figure 4(c) shows the corresponding mean of the distribution of update cost across names at varying loads; the update cost for a name is the number of replicas times the update rate of that name.

*Replicate-All* gives low lookup latencies at the smallest load level, but generates a very high update cost and can sustain a request load of at most 0.3. This is further supported by Figure 4(c) that shows that the update cost for Replicate-All at load = 0.4 is more than the update cost of Auspice at load = 8. In theory, Auspice can have a capacity advantage of up to N/M over Replicate-All, where N is the total number of name servers and M is the minimum of replicas Auspice must make for ensuring fault tolerance (resp. 80 and 3 here). *Random-M* can sustain a high request load (Fig. 4(b)) due to its low update costs, but its lookup latencies are higher as it only creates 3 replicas randomly.

*Auspice* has 5.7×−9× lower latencies over Random-M and DHT+Popularity respectively (Figure 4(b), load=1). This is because it places a fraction of the replicas close to pockets of high demand unlike the other two. At low to moderate loads, servers have excess capacity than the minimum needed for fault tolerance, so Auspice creates as many replicas as it can without exceeding the threshold utilization level (Eq. 1), thereby achieving low latencies for loads≤4. At loads ≥ 4, servers exceed the threshold utilization level even if Auspice creates the minimum number of replicas needed for fault tolerance. This explains why Auspice and Random-M have equal update costs for loads ≥ 4 (Figure 4(c)). Reducing the number of replicas at higher loads allows Auspice to limit the update cost and sustain a maximum request load that is equal to Random-M.

*DHT+Popularity* has higher lookup latencies as it replicates based on lookup popularity alone and places replicas using consistent hashing without considering the geo-distribution of demand. Further, it answers lookups from a replica selected enroute the DHT route. Typically, the latency to the selected replica is higher than the latency to the closest replica for a name, which results in high latencies. DHT+Popularity replicates 22.3% most popular names at all locations. Lookups for these names go to the closest replica and achieve low latencies; lookups for remaining 77.7% of names incur high latencies.

DHT+Popularity incurs higher update costs than Auspice even though both schemes create nearly equal numbers of replicas at every load level. This is because DHT+Popularity decides the number of replicas of a name only based on its popularity, i.e., lookup rates, while Auspice decides the number of replicas based on lookup-to-update ratio of names. Due to its higher update costs, DHT+Popularity can not sustain as high a request load as Auspice.

### *4.2.2 Update latency, update propagation delay*

The *client-perceived update latency*, i.e., the time from when when a client sends an update to when it receives a confirmation. These numbers are measured from the experiment in §4.2.1 for load=0.3. The median and 90th percentile update latency for Auspice with total write ordering is 284ms and is comparable to other schemes. A request, after arriving an active replica, takes four one-way network delays (two rounds) to be committed by Paxos. The median update latency is a few hundred milliseconds for all schemes as it is dominated by update propagation delays.

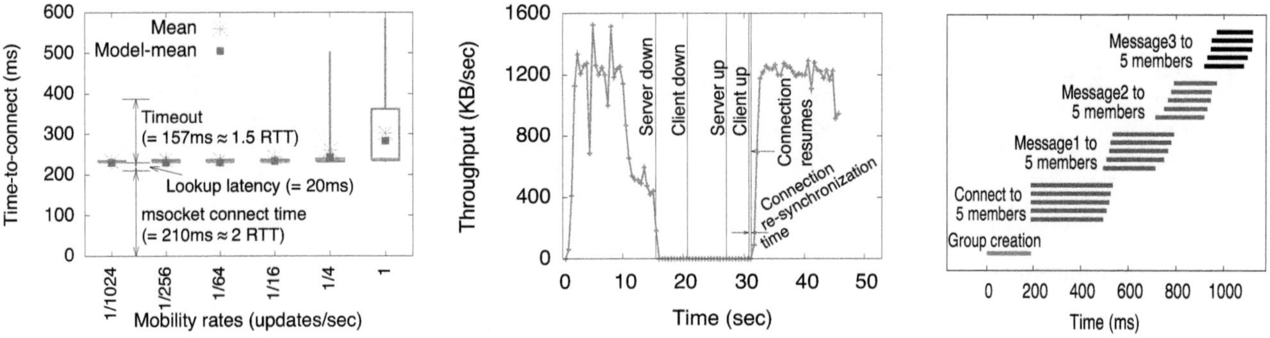


(a) E2E time-to-connect (b) Simultaneous mobility (c) Context-aware delivery

**Figure 5: (a) Time-to-connect≈lookup latency for moderate mobility rates ($< \frac{1}{10s}$) as Auspice returns up-to-date responses w.h.p., but sharply rises thereafter (Eq. 2); (b) Simultaneous mobility recovery in ≈2 RTTs after both endpoints resurface; (c) Context-aware delivery showing 3 messages geo-cast to 5 members.**

The *update propagation delay*, i.e., the time from when a client issued a write till the last replica executes the write, is a key determiner of the time-to-connect. As shown in §3.3.5, with eventual consistency, update propagation takes one round, while with total write ordering, update propagation takes two rounds and 50% more messages.

The measured update propagation delay is consistent with expectations. With eventual consistency, this delay is 154 ms, while with total write ordering, it is 292ms. Thus. the cost of the stronger consistency provided by total write ordering compared to eventual is that it can increase the time-to-connect latency by up to 2×. Note that the 2× inflation is a worst-case estimate, i.e., it will impact the time-to-connect latency only if a read request arrives at a replica while a write is under propagation to that replica, as we show below.

## 4.3 End-to-end mobility case studies

Can Auspice serve as the basis of a complete end-to-end mobility solution? To address this question, we have developed msocket, a user-level socket library that interoperates with Auspice, and supports all four types of endpoint mobility. The details of msocket's design and implementation is the subject of a separate paper [6]. Here, we *use* msocket to show proof-of-concept of some of Auspice's capabilities.

### *4.3.1 Time-to-connect to "moving" endpoints*

We evaluate the time-to-connect to a moving destination as a function of the mobility (or update) rate. The *end-to-end time-to-connect* here is measured as the latency to look up an up-to-date address of the destination (or the time-to-connect as defined in §3.2) plus the time for msocket to successfully establish a TCP connection between the client and the mobile destination. This e2e-time-to-connect also incorporates the impact of timeouts and retried lookups if the client happens to have obtained a stale value (as in Fig. 1). The experiment is conducted on PlanetLab and consists of a single msocket client and a single mobile msocket server that is "moving" by changing its listening port number on a remote machine, and updating the name record replicated on three Auspice name servers accordingly. A successful connection setup delay using msocket is takes 2 RTTs (2 × 105 ms) [6]. As defined in Eq. 2, the values of the update propagation latency $d_i$ and the lookup latency $l_i$ are 250 ms and 20 ms respectively, and the update rate $w_i$ varies from 1/1024/s to 1/s. The timeout value ($T$) in our experiment is dependent on the RTT between the client and the server. If the client attempts to connect to the server on a port which the server is not listening on, the server immediately returns an error response to the client. Specifically, the timeout value is either 1 or 2 RTTs with equal probability depending on whether the connection failed during the first or the second round-trip of msocket's connection setup. The client sends lookups at a rate of 10/s (but this rate does not affect the time-to-connect), and both lookups and updates inter-arrival times are exponentially distributed.

Figure 5(a) shows the distribution of the time-to-connect with update propagation delays entailed by eventual consistency. For low-to-moderate mobility rates ($< \frac{1}{64s}$), we find that all time-to-connect values are close to 230 ms, of which 20ms is the lookup latency, and 210ms is msocket's connection setup latency. The reason the client is able to obtain the correct value upon first lookup in all cases is that the update propagation latency of 250ms is much smaller than the average inter-update interval (64s). The update propagation delay becomes a non-trivial fraction of the inter-update interval at high mobility rates of ≈1/sec that results in 26% of lookups returning stale values. The mean e2e-time-to-connect increases to 302 ms for an update rate of 1/sec, which suggests that Auspice's time-to-connect is limited by network propagation delays in this regime. Nevertheless, once a connection is successfully established, individual migration can quickly resynchronize the connection in ≈two round-trips between the client and the mobile without relying on Auspice (not shown here).

Figure 5(a) also shows that the time-to-connect as predicted by our analytical model (Eq. 2) are close to those observed in the experiment, thereby re-affirming our design.

### *4.3.2 Simultaneous endpoint mobility*

Figure 5(b) shows an experiment involving simultaneous mobility. The client is an Android phone using msocket via a WiFi interface to connect to a publicly addressable Planetlab machine at time 0. The server and client shut down their interfaces respectively around 15 and 20 sec. Subsequently, the server restarts its interface and starts listening on a different port and updates Auspice accordingly. After that, the client restarts its interface and attempts to re-synchronize the connection. This re-synchronization time is roughly 300ms as shown and consists of the following delays. The client performs a query to Auspice to resolve the

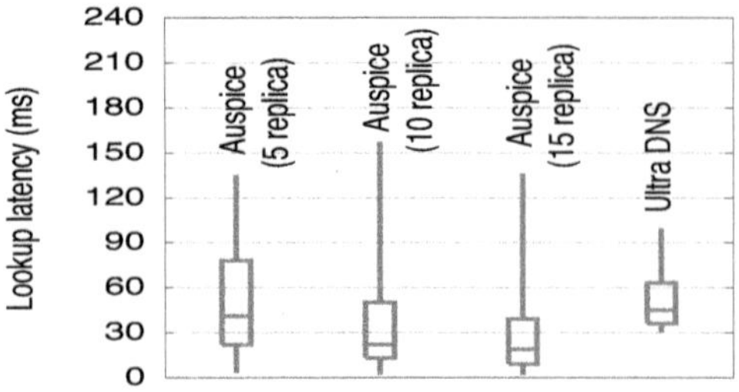


**Figure 6: Lookup latency: Auspice with 5 replicas is comparable to UltraDNS (16 replicas); Auspice with 15 replicas has 60% lower latency than UltraDNS.**

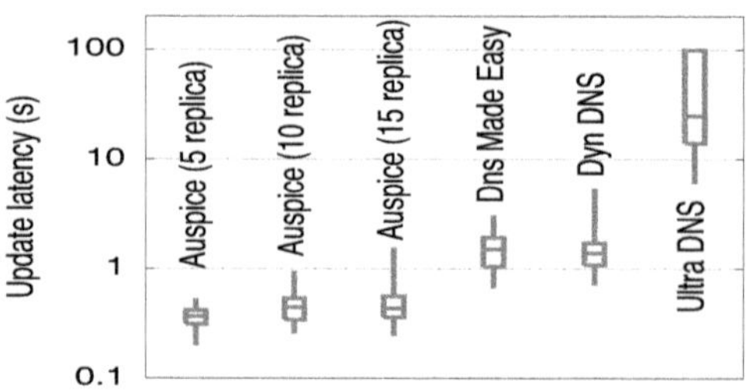


**Figure 7: Update propagation delay: Auspice with 5 replicas is 1.0 to 24.7 secs lower than three top-tier managed DNS service providers.**

server's GUID to its new socket address (IP, port), which takes roughly 50ms and mostly corresponds to the round-trip delay between the client and the Auspice nameserver. The remaining 250ms roughly correspond to 2 RTTs of delay between the client and the server that are separated by a round-trip delay of 120ms.

### *4.3.3 Context-aware delivery*

Next, we show a proof of concept of context-aware communication, a novel communication primitive enabled by Auspice's extensible key-value API. Auspice allows applications to bind an msocket not only to human-readable names or GUIDs, but also to abstract context descriptors as in `msocket.bind("[geoloc: [lat,long],radius]")`. Writes to this msocket are reliably delivered to all GUIDs in the geo-fence created by this descriptor. Underneath the covers, msocket invokes Auspice to create on-demand a group GUID, i.e., a GUID with a membership field consisting of a set of member GUIDs, and obtains this member set. msocket internally resolves each member GUID to its socket address and establishes an msocket connection for reliably delivery.

Figure 5(c) shows an experiment involving a group creator (also the message sender) on an Android phone and a number of potential members on PlanetLab nodes, 5 of which fake-register their coordinates in Auspice so as to appear to be within the created geo-fence. The RTT between the group creator and members is 125ms. The figure shows that group creation, a single call to Auspice that returns all member GUIDs, takes roughly 200ms. Subsequently, an internal msocket connect to each member involves another Auspice lookup to resolve the GUID to a socket address and connect in parallel to all 5 members, which takes 250-280ms. After this, the creator sends 3 short messages back-to-back that each take roughly 1 RTT to be reliably delivered.

More details of optimizing context-aware queries in Auspice, reducing membership staleness, the connection migration protocol, etc. are outside the scope of this paper [6]. This experiment seeks only to exemplify a powerful, new communication primitive enabled by context descriptors compared to strictly hierarchical DNS names, as argued in §2.2.

## 4.4 Auspice vs. managed DNS providers

Can demand-aware replication benefit commercial managed DNS providers that largely rely on statically replicating today's (hardly mobile) domain names? To investigate this, we compare Auspice against three top-tier providers, UltraDNS, DynDNS, and DNSMadeEasy that offer geo-replicated authoritative DNS services widely used by enterprises (e.g., Dyn provides DNS service for Twitter).

### *4.4.1 Lookup latency*

We compare Auspice to UltraDNS for a workload of lookups for domain names serviced by the provider. We identify 316 domain names among the top 10K Alexa websites serviced by this provider, and determine the geo-distribution of lookups for each name from their data [2]. For each name, we measure the latency for 1000 lookups from across 100 PlanetLab nodes. We ensure that lookups are served from the name servers maintained by the provider by requesting the address for a new random sub-domain name each time, e.g, `xqf4p.google.com` instead of `google.com`, that is unlikely to exist in a cache and requires an authoritative lookup. Auspice name servers are deployed across a total of 80 PlanetLab locations while UltraDNS has 16 known server locations [50]. We evaluate Auspice for three configurations with 5, 10, and 15 replicas of a name respectively.

Figure 6 shows the lookup latencies of names for Auspice and for UltraDNS. UltraDNS incurs a median latency of 45 ms with 16 replicas, while Auspice incurs 41 ms, 22 ms, and 18 ms respectively with 5, 10, and 15 replicas. With 5 replicas, Auspice's performance is comparable to UltraDNS with one-third the replication cost. With 15 replicas, Auspice incurs 60% lower latency for a comparable cost. The comparison against the other two, Dyn and DNSMadeEasy, is qualitatively similar [1]. Thus, Auspice's demand-aware replication achieves a better cost–performance tradeoff compared to static replication.

### *4.4.2 Update propagation delay*

To measure update propagation delays, we purchase DNS service from three providers for separate domain names. All providers replicate a name at 5 locations across US and Europe for the services we purchased. We issue address updates for the domain name serviced by that provider and then immediately start lookups to the authoritative name servers for our domain name. These authoritative name servers can be queried only via an anycast IP address, i.e., servers at different locations advertise the same externally visible IP address. Therefore, to maximize the number of provider locations queried, we send queries from 50 random PlanetLab nodes. From each location, we periodically send queries until all authoritative name server replicas return the updated address. The update propagation latency at a node is the time between when the node starts sending lookup to when it receives the updated address. The latency of an update is the the maximum update latency measured at any of the nodes. We measure latency of 100 updates for each provider.

To measure update latencies for Auspice, we replicate 1000 names at a fixed number of PlanetLab nodes across

US and Europe. The number of nodes is chosen to be 5, 10, and 20 across three experiments. A client sends an update to the nearest node and waits for update confirmation messages from all replicas. The latency of an update is the time difference between when the client sent an update and when it received the update confirmation message from all replicas (an upper bound on the update propagation delay). We show the distribution of measured update latencies for Auspice and for three managed DNS providers in Figure 7.

Auspice incurs lower update propagation latencies than all three providers for an equal or greater number of replica locations for names. We were unable to ascertain from UltraDNS why their update latencies are an order of magnitude higher than network propagation delays, but this finding is consistent with a recent study [50] that has shown latencies of up to tens of seconds for these providers. Indeed, some providers even distinguish themselves by advertising shorter update propagation delays than competitors [50].

*Sensitivity analyses and other results.*

We have conducted a comprehensive evaluation of the sensitivity of Auspice's performance-cost trade-offs to workload and system parameters across scales varying by several orders of magnitude. These include workload parameters such as geo-locality, read-to-write rate ratio, ratio of device-to-service names, etc. and system parameters such as the fault-tolerance threshold, capacity utilization, perturbation knob, the tunable overhead of replica reconfiguration, etc. using a combination of simulation and system experiments. These results do not qualitatively change the findings in this paper, and are deferred to the technical report [1].

## 5. RELATED WORK

Our work draws on lessons learned from an enormous body of prior work on network architecture as well as distributed systems, as described in §1 and §2.1. We discuss related work not covered elsewhere in the paper here.

**DNS.** Many have studied issues related to performance, scalability, load balancing, or denial-of-service vulnerabilities in DNS's resolution infrastructure [46, 49, 16, 22]. Several DHT-based alternatives have been put forward [49, 20, 45] and we compare against one representative proposal, Codons [49]. In general, DHT-based designs are ideal for balancing load across servers, but are less well-suited to scenarios with a large number of service replicas that have to coordinate upon updates, and are at odds with scenarios requiring placement of replicas close to pocket of demand. In comparison, Auspice uses a planned placement approach.

Vu et al. describe DMap [55], an in-network DHT scheme that is similar in spirit to Random-M as evaluated in our experiments (§4) (with a more direct comparison in [1]), showing that demand-aware placement can dramatically outperform randomized placement. A more important qualitative distinction is that DMap ties federation to the interconnection structure between ISPs, which entails commensurate lookup latency penalties and potential incentive mismatches by mapping GUIDs to non-provider ISPs. In comparison, the Auspice approach decouples the federation structure between GNS providers from that between ISPs.

**Server selection.** Many prior systems have addressed the server selection problem with data or services replicated across a wide-area network. Examples include anycast services [25, 15, 57] to map users to the best server based on server load or network path characteristics. These systems as well as CDNs and cloud hosting providers share our goals of proximate server selection and load balance given a fixed placement of server replicas. Auspice differs in that it additionally considers replica placement itself as a degree of freedom in achieving latency or load balance.

**Dynamic placement.** We were unable to find prior systems that *automatically* reconfigure the *geo-distributed* replica locations of frequently *mutable objects* while preserving *consistency* (i.e., those satisfying all four italicized properties). However, reconfigurable placement has been studied for static or slow changing content [30] or within a single datacenter, or without replication. For example, Volley [11] optimizes the placement of mutable data objects based on the geo-distribution of accesses and is similar in spirit to Auspice in this respect, however it implicitly assumes a single replica for each object, so it does not have to worry about high update rates or replica coordination overhead.

Auspice is related to many distributed key-value stores [5, 23, 3], most of which are optimized for distribution within, not across, data centers. Some (e.g., Cassandra) support a geo-distributed deployment using a fixed number of replica sites. Spanner [19] is a geo-distributed data store that synchronously replicates data ("directories") across datacenters with a semi-relational database abstraction. Compared to Spanner, Auspice does not provide any guarantees on operations spanning multiple records, but unlike Spanner's geographic placement of replicas that "administrators control" by creating a "menu of named options", Auspice automatically reconfigures the number and placement of replicas so as to reduce lookup latency and update cost. Furthermore, Spanner assigns a large number of directory objects to a much smaller number of fixed Paxos groups; Auspice supports an arbitrarily reconfigurable Paxos group per object based on principles in recent theoretical work on reconfigurable consensus, e.g., Vertical Paxos [39] and the more recent report on Viewstamped Replication Revisited [41].

## 6. CONCLUSIONS

In this paper, we presented the design, implementation, and evaluation of Auspice, a scalable, geo-distributed, federated global name service for any Internetwork where high mobility is the norm. The name service can resolve flexible identifiers (human-readable names, self-certifying identifiers, or arbitrary strings) to network locations or other attributes that can also be defined in a flexible manner. At the core of Auspice is a placement engine for replicating name records to achieve low lookup latency, low update cost, and high availability. Our evaluation shows that Auspice's placement strategy can significantly improve the performance-cost tradeoffs struck both by commercial managed DNS services employing simplistic replication strategies today as well as previously proposed DHT-based replication alternatives with or without high mobility. Our case studies confirm that Auspice can form the basis of an end-to-end mobility solution and also enable novel context-aware communication primitives that generalize name- or address-based communication. A pre-release version of Auspice on EC2 can be accessed through the developer portal at `http://gns.name`.

**Acknowledgments.** This research was funded in part by CNS-1040781 and CNS-0845855. We thank the rest of the MobilityFirst team, the paper's past and recent reviewers, our shepherd Ellen Zegura, Anand Seetharam, Emmanuel Cecchet, Jim Kurose, Marvin Sirbu, and NSF-FIA meeting participants for their feedback.

## 7. REFERENCES


[1] A Global Name Service for a Highly Mobile Internetwork. UMass SCS Technical Report, 2013 and 2014. https://web.cs.umass.edu/publication.

[2] Alexa Web Information Service. http://www.alexa.com.

[3] Cassandra. http://cassandra.apache.org.

[4] MobilityFirst Future Internet Architecture Project. http://mobilityfirst.cs.umass.edu/.

[5] mongoDB. http://www.mongodb.org/.

[6] msocket: System Support for Developing Seamlessly Mobile, Multipath, and Middlebox-Agnostic Applications. UMass SCS Technical Report, 2014. https://web.cs.umass.edu/publication.

[7] Server fault: DNS - Any way to force a name server to update the record of a domain? http://serverfault.com/questions/41018.

[8] The Locator/ID Separation Protocol (LISP). RFC 6830.

[9] ICANN Hears Concerns about Accountability, Control, October 2008. http://www.infoworld.com/t/networking/icann-hears-concerns-about-accountability-control-216.

[10] Debate Rages over who Should Control ICANN. *Processor*, 31(16), June 2009.

[11] S. Agarwal, J. Dunagan, N. Jain, S. Saroiu, A. Wolman, and H. Bhogan. Volley: Automated Data Placement for Geo-Distributed Cloud Services. In *USENIX NSDI*, 2010.

[12] D. G. Andersen, H. Balakrishnan, N. Feamster, T. Koponen, D. Moon, and S. Shenker. Accountable Internet Protocol. In *ACM SIGCOMM*, 2008.

[13] M. Arye, E. Nordstrom, R. Kiefer, J. Rexford, and M. J. Freedman. A Formally-Verified Migration Protocol For Mobile, Multi-Homed Hosts. In *ICNP*, 2012.

[14] H. Balakrishnan, K. Lakshminarayanan, S. Ratnasamy, S. Shenker, I. Stoica, and M. Walfish. A Layered Naming Architecture for the Internet. In *ACM SIGCOMM*, 2004.

[15] S. Bhattacharjee and et al. Application-Layer Anycasting. In *IEEE INFOCOM*, 1997.

[16] N. Brownlee, K. Claffy, and E. Nemeth. DNS Measurements at a Root Server. In *GLOBECOM*, 2001.

[17] M. Caesar, T. Condie, and J. Kannan et al. ROFL: Routing on Flat Labels. In *ACM SIGCOMM*, 2006.

[18] Cisco. Visual Networking Index: Global Mobile Data Traffic Forecast Update, 2012-2017. http://ciscovni.com.

[19] J. C. Corbett and J. Dean et al. Spanner: Google's Globally Distributed Database. *USENIX OSDI*, 2012.

[20] R. Cox, A. Muthitacharoen, and R. Morris. Serving DNS Using a Peer-to-Peer Lookup Service. In *IPTPS*, 2002.

[21] G. DeCandia and et al. Dynamo: Amazon's Highly Available Key-value Store. In *ACM SOSP*, 2007.

[22] DNSSEC. DNS Threats & Weaknesses of the Domain Name System, 2012. http://www.dnssec.net/dns-threats.php.

[23] R. Escriva, B. Wong, and E. G. Sirer. HyperDex: A Distributed, Searchable Key-value Store. In *ACM SIGCOMM*, 2012.

[24] A. Feldmann and et al. HAIR: Hierarchical Architecture for Internet Routing. In *ReArch Workshop*, 2009.

[25] M. J. Freedman, K. Lakshminarayanan, and D. Mazières. OASIS: Anycast for Any Service. In *USENIX NSDI*, 2006.

[26] D. Funato, K. Yasuda, and H. Tokuda. TCP-R: TCP mobility support for continuous operation. In *ICNP*, 1997.

[27] Z. Gao, A. Venkataramani, and J. F. Kurose. Towards a quantitative comparison of location-independent network architectures. In *ACM SIGCOMM*, 2014.

[28] Gartner. Sales of Android Phones to Approach One Billion in 2014. http://www.gartner.com/newsroom/id/2665715.

[29] M. Gritter and D. R. Cheriton. An Architecture for Content Routing Support in the Internet. In *USITS*, 2001.

[30] J. Gwertzman and M. Seltzer. The case for geographical push caching. In *IEEE HotOS Workshop*, May 1995.

[31] D. Han, A. Anand, F. Dogar et al., B. Li, H. Lim, and M. et al. XIA: Efficient Support for Evolvable Internetworking. In *USENIX NSDI*, 2012.

[32] V. Jacobson and et al. Networking Named Content. In *ACM SIGCOMM CoNEXT*, 2009.

[33] P. Jokela, P. Nikander, J. Melen, J. Ylitalo, and J. Wall. Host Identity Protocol, Extended Abstract. In *Wireless World Research Forum*, 2004.

[34] J. Jung, E. Sit, H. Balakrishnan, and R. Morris. DNS Performance and the Effectiveness of Caching. *IEEE/ACM Transactions on Networking*, October 2002.

[35] T. Koponen, M. Chawla, B.-G. Chun, A. Ermolinskiy, K. H. Kim, S. Shenker, and I. Stoica. A Data-Oriented (and Beyond) Network Architecture. In *ACM SIGCOMM*, 2007.

[36] D. Krioukov and et al. On Compact Routing for the Internet. *ACM SIGCOMM CCR*, 2007.

[37] H. Kwak, C. Lee, H. Park, and S. Moon. What is Twitter, a Social Network or a News Media? In *WWW*, 2010.

[38] L. Lamport. The Part-Time Parliament. *ACM Transactions on Compututer Systems*, 16(2):133–169, May 1998.

[39] L. Lamport, D. Malkhi, and L. Zhou. Vertical Paxos and Primary-Backup Replication. In *ACM PODC*, 2009.

[40] B. W. Lampson. Designing a Global Name Service. In *ACM PODC*, 1986.

[41] B. Liskov and J. Cowling. Viewstamped replication revisited. Technical Report MIT CSAIL-TR-2012-021, 2012.

[42] H. V. Madhyastha and et al. iPlane: An Information Plane for Distributed Services. In *USNIX OSDI*, 2006.

[43] P. Mockapetris and K. J. Dunlap. Development of the domain name system. ACM SIGCOMM, 1988.

[44] E. Nordstrom and et al. Serval: An End-Host Stack for Service-Centric Networking. In *USENIX NSDI*, 2012.

[45] V. Pappas, D. Massey, A. Terzis, and L. Zhang. A Comparative Study of the DNS Design with DHT-Based Alternatives. In *IEEE INFOCOM*, 2006.

[46] V. Pappas, Z. Xu, S. Lu, D. Massey, A. Terzis, and L. Zhang. Impact of Configuration Errors on DNS Robustness. In *ACM SIGCOMM*, 2004.

[47] M. Parwez and et al. DNS propagation delay: An effective and robust solution using authoritative response from non-authoritative server. In *ICIME*, 2010.

[48] C. Perkins. RFC 3220: IP Mobility Support for IPv4, 2002.

[49] V. Ramasubramanian and E. G. Sirer. The Design and Implementation of a Next Generation Name Service for the Internet. In *ACM SIGCOMM*, 2004.

[50] J. Read. Comparison and Analysis of Managed DNS Providers, Aug 2012. Cloud Harmony Inc.

[51] M. D. Schroeder, A. D. Birrell, and R. M. Needham. Experience with Grapevine: the Growth of a Distributed System. *ACM Trans. Comput. Syst.*, 1984.

[52] A. C. Snoeren and H. Balakrishnan. An End-to-End Approach to Host Mobility. In *ACM MobiCom*, 2000.

[53] I. Stoica, D. Adkins, S. Zhuang, S. Shenker, and S. Surana. Internet Indirection Infrastructure. In *SIGCOMM*, 2002.

[54] A. Venkataramani, J. Kurose, D. Raychaudhuri, K. Nagaraja, M. Mao, and S. Banerjee. MobilityFirst: A Mobility-Centric and Trustworthy Internet Architecture. *ACM SIGCOMM CCR*, 2014.

[55] T. Vu and et al. DMap: A Shared Hosting Scheme for Dynamic Identifier to Locator Mappings in the Global Internet. In *IEEE ICDCS*, 2012.

[56] M. Walfish, J. Stribling, M. Krohn, H. Balakrishnan, R. Morris, and S. Shenker. Middleboxes No Longer Considered Harmful. In *OSDI*, 2004.

[57] P. Wendell, J. W. Jiang, M. J. Freedman, and J. Rexford. DONAR: Decentralized Server Selection for Cloud Services. In *ACM SIGCOMM*, 2010.

# Towards a Quantitative Comparison of Location-Independent Network Architectures

Zhaoyu Gao Arun Venkataramani James Kurose Simon Heimlicher
{gaozy, arun, kurose, heimlicher}@cs.umass.edu
School of Computer Science, University of Massachusetts Amherst

## ABSTRACT

This paper presents a quantitative methodology and results comparing different approaches for *location-independent* communication. Our approach is empirical and is based on real Internet topologies, routing tables from real routers, and a measured workload of the mobility of devices and content across network addresses today. We measure the extent of network mobility exhibited by mobile devices with a home-brewed Android app deployed on hundreds of smartphones, and measure the network mobility of Internet content from distributed vantage points. We combine this measured data with our quantitative methodology to analyze the different cost-benefit tradeoffs struck by location-independent network architectures with respect to routing update cost, path stretch, and forwarding table size. We find that more than 20% of users change over 10 IP addresses a day, suggesting that mobility is the norm rather than the exception, so intrinsic and efficient network support for mobility is critical. We also find that with purely name-based routing approaches, each event involving the mobility of a device or popular content may result in an update at up to 14% of Internet routers; but, the fraction of impacted routers is much smaller for the long tail of unpopular content. These results suggest that recent proposals for *pure* name-based networking may be suitable for highly aggregateable content that moves infrequently but may need to be augmented with addressing-assisted approaches to handle device mobility.

## Categories and Subject Descriptors

C.4.3 [**Computer Systems Organization**]: COMPUTER-COMMUNICATION NETWORKS—*Network Architecture and Design*

## Keywords

Location-independence; mobility; network architecture


*SIGCOMM'14*, August 17–22, 2014, Chicago, IL, USA.

ACM 978-1-4503-2836-4/14/08 ...$15.00.
http://dx.doi.org/10.1145/2619239.2626333 .

## 1. INTRODUCTION

Providing an abstraction of *location-independent communication*—enabling communication using fixed names without concern for changing network locations—has been a long-time goal of networking research. For example, proposals designed to provide seamless host mobility [36] target an abstraction of the form `connect(host_id)`; a number of proposals for information-centric networking [28, 13, 22, 16, 19] target an abstraction of the form `get(content_name)`.

Why is the current TCP/IP Internet seen as falling short of this goal? A common criticism is the so-called location-identity conflation problem [42]. The Internet uses an IP address to identify an interface as well as its network location. As a result, connections break when an endpoint changes network addresses, requiring application-layer workarounds to provide a semblance of seamless mobility. Advocates of information-centric networking argue that the Internet, having inherited a century-old, tethered, device-to-device communication abstraction from the wired telephony world, is poorly-suited for an Internet dominated by content traffic and a communication abstraction requiring endpoints to first obtain the network location of a host serving the requested content instead of simply procuring a copy from *any* convenient location. In response, researchers have proposed a number of designs to refactor naming, addressing, and routing in order to enable location-independent communication [22, 12, 36, 11, 28, 13, 22, 16, 19].

Our work is motivated by the observation that, although many architectural proposals share location-independence as a key design goal, there has been little prior research quantitatively comparing the different cost-benefit tradeoffs struck by these architectures in achieving that goal. One reason for the paucity of cross-architectural comparisons may be that network architecture is considered by some as part science and in good part *art* [51]. Another is that until recently, most Internet architecture efforts rarely went beyond paper designs, so a lack of a reasonably complete design specification and protocol-level implementation made it hard to justify investing research effort comparing them; however programs such as GENI[4], FIA[6], and FIRE [3] are changing this state of affairs. We believe that a quantitative comparison of different approaches for location-independent communication is timely and indeed critical for gaining a deeper understanding of cross-cutting architectural principles.

Our contribution is a quantitative methodology and empirical results comparing different location-independent architectures based on a common set of metrics, namely, routing update cost, path stretch, and forwarding table size, in a context where both devices and content may be mobile. We find that a number of existing approaches for location independence can be categorized into one of three "puristic" classes (§2): *indirection routing* (e.g., Mobile IP or GSM), *name-to-address resolution* (e.g., DNS and IP), and *name-based routing* (e.g., TRIAD [22], ROFL [12] or NDN [28]). Our methodology is empirical, comparing these three pure approaches using realistic Internet topologies, routing tables from real routers, and a measured workload of content and device mobility across addresses in today's Internet (§3).

To measure *device mobility* across network locations, we have developed an Android app, NomadLog, deployed on over 372 Android devices and has been collecting device mobility data for over 14 months (§4). To measure *content mobility,* we deployed a system across distributed Planetlab nodes to estimate the rate of change of network addresses of popular content domain names (including those delegated to CDNs) as well as unpopular content domain names. Combining this measured mobility workload with our evaluation methodology, we arrive at the following key findings.

1. Pure name-based routing entails a prohibitively high router update cost to handle device mobility today, e.g., some routers may be impacted by up to 14% of all device mobility events today.
2. Over 20% of users change network addresses over 10 times a day, suggesting that high mobility is the norm rather than the exception. The median user spends around 25% of a day at ASes at least two AS hops away from the dominant AS, implying a commensurate path stretch for indirection routing approaches.
3. Pure name-based routing imposes a much lower update cost for content mobility today, e.g., with best-port forwarding, routers are impacted by at most 6% of popular content mobility events, and are hardly impacted by mobility of the long tail of unpopular content.

A key implication of our findings is that name-based routing approaches in their puristic form may be better suited for content alone, but need to be augmented with addressing-assisted approaches such as DNS, Mobile IP, or a next-generation name resolution service [49] in order to serve as a general-purpose replacement for the TCP/IP Internet. Our findings also show the important differences between device and content mobility, as well as the emerging importance of the strategy layer [28, 55] in content-oriented architectures.

The remainder of this paper is structured as follows. We begin with a discussion of background and related work (§2) followed by a detailed description of our evaluation methodology (§3); the NomadLog app to measure network mobility of devices (§4); an expository analytical model for the path stretch vs. update cost trade-off (§5); the results of our empirical evaluation of the cost-benefit trade-offs of different approaches for location independence in the context of device (§6) and content (§7) mobility; a confession of limitations and open questions (§8); and conclusions (§9).

## 2. BACKGROUND AND RELATED WORK

Despite the enormous body of work on refactoring naming, addressing, and routing so as to enable location-independent communication, most known approaches fundamentally take one of just three different approaches: (1) indirection routing; (2) name resolution; (3) name-based routing.

The fact that there are not too many different approaches to enable location independence should not be surprising – in order to enable a communication abstraction of the form `connect(B,A)` where B and A are fixed names of endpoint principals (e.g., hosts, content, or services), each of which could be simultaneously multi-homed at different locations at any point in time and the set of these locations could suddenly change, endpoint B must resort to one of three options in order to send the first packet to A—(1) send the packet to one (or a small number of) network router(s) that know(s) A's current location; (2) acquire knowledge of A's current location through an extra-network service and send the packet to that location; or (3) send the packet stamped with the name A to any router, trusting a coordinated routing and forwarding strategy across routers to deliver the packet to A's current location. These three approaches are illustrated in Figure 1. Let us next consider how a number of proposed network architectures embody these approaches.

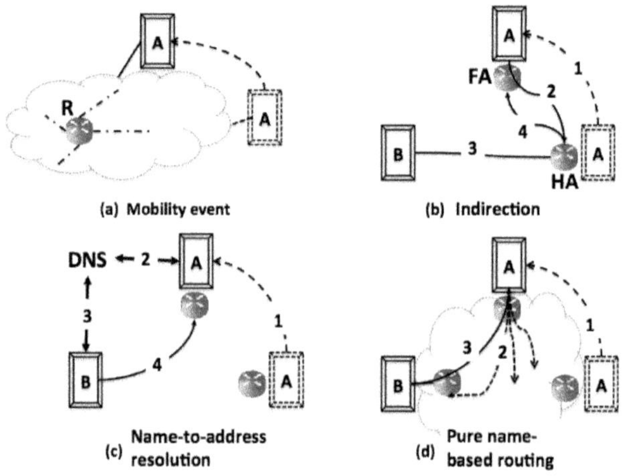


**Figure 1: A mobility event (a) and three purist approaches (b, c, d) to handle them.**

**Indirection routing** translates the problem of fixed-name routing to fixed-address routing as the first step. A name resolution infrastructure may be infrequently queried to translate an endpoint's name to a *home* address that rarely changes by design. A home agent in the home network as in GSM, Mobile IP and other architectures (e.g., [30]) or a randomly chosen rendezvous location in i3 [46] is responsible for maintaining up-to-date *visited* addresses of its subscribers and detouring packets to them. The main strength of indirection is simplicity – an endpoint remains completely oblivious to endpoint mobility. The downside is path stretch – in order to remain oblivious, a sender must detour all packets through the destination's home agent [41], even if the two endpoints happen to be in the same local network. The update cost of indirection routing is minimal because an endpoint only needs to update its home agent upon each mobility event. The forwarding table size at routers remains unchanged and is equal to the number of disaggregated prefixes (e.g., ≈400K at core routers in today's Internet).

**Name resolution** approaches rely on an extra-network service like DNS as the first step in all network communication in order to resolve a destination's name to its current address. A name resolution service is an integral part of the Internet as well as a number of network architectures such as HIP, AIP, LISP, Nimrod, MobilityFirst, and XIA. As in indirection routing, the update cost of handling a mobility event is minimal because it suffices to make a single update at a logically centralized service like DNS. Network routing is based on structured addresses, so the forwarding table size at routers depends on the "aggregateability" of endpoint IP addresses, e.g., if all endpoints move randomly, then routers would have to store on the order of 4B IP addresses instead of 400K prefixes today. The path stretch depends only upon the underlying network routing; a shortest-path routing network has no stretch by definition while policy-driven interdomain routing as in the Internet can incur significant path inflation [44]. Enabling location-independence through name resolution only adds a lookup latency at connection setup time, but does not add additional data path stretch compared to underlying network routing.

**Name-based routing**, unlike both approaches above, routes directly over names without using addresses at all. Examples include flat-label routing architectures such as ROFL [12] or SEATTLE [29] (for a single enterprise network) or information-centric routing architectures such as TRIAD [22] and NDN [28]. From an endpoint's perspective, eliminating addresses is a silver bullet as the network comes with intrinsic support for location-independent communication. However, achieving this abstraction purely at the network layer without inducing significant stretch or long outage times upon mobility events is nontrivial. Quantifying this trade-off is an important focus of our work.

All three broad approaches above have a number of other advantages and disadvantages (e.g., incremental deployability, manageability, security, handoff outage times, etc.). We have omitted a discussion of these in line with our goal of a nuanced analysis of the cost-benefit tradeoffs with respect to quantitative metrics such as path stretch, update cost, and forwarding table size. An explicit non-goal of our work is to determine the "best" among existing location-independent architectures or to propose yet another new one.

## 2.1 Related work

The contributions of our paper lie at the intersection of network measurement—empirically characterizing the changing connectivity of both devices and content to the Internet—and network architecture–analyzing the cost-benefit tradeoffs with respect to several metrics for different approaches for location-independence). Consequently, there is related past research in several areas.

**Network mobility measurement.** Many studies have empirically characterized physical human mobility among access points or base stations and discussed the impact of physical user mobility patterns on network performance and design. Human mobility traces have been collected from diverse access networks such as WLANs [31, 25, 14], Bluetooth networks [14], and cellular networks [23, 39, 26]. Some [23, 39, 15] have related human mobility patterns to AP and base station resource use, and have found [23, 39] that the extent of users' physical mobility is low and concentrated among a small number base stations within a provider's network with infrequent visits to other base stations in that network. Zarifis et al. [57] characterize metro-level path inflation (rather than mobility itself) experienced by mobile users accessing Google, identifing inter-domain routing, peering, and carrier topology as possible causes. Similarly, other studies have focused on the measured performance (throughput or delay) of WiFi or cellular connections in the wild [37, 43, 18] but focus on connection performance rather than on mobility itself. Acculoc [53] and CelloScope [9] describe applications that take measurements capturing location-specific information about cellular connections, but do not focus on mobility across locations or access networks as in our work.

Individual WiFi and cellular measurements include data from a single type of network, and more importantly characterize *physical* user/content mobility among access points or base stations, rather than changing points of attachment to the Internet (i.e., as characterized by changing IP addresses and AS numbers). Our NomadLog measurements characterize this latter aspect of mobility *across* networks, rather than physical mobility in space—a critical distinction. For example, a physically mobile user might maintain the same IP address as they move among base stations in a provider network; for our purposes, this user is considered stationary as their IP address does not change despite physical mobility. Conversely, a user may "move" from one network (cellular) to another (WiFi) while hardly moving physically.

**In-network name resolution.** A number of studies have considered the performance of in-network name resolution. [55] compares the performance of an instantiated NDN forwarding plane [28] with traditional IP forwarding, with an emphasis on security and congestion mitigation. [10] compares the performance of network-based name resolution in an instantiated NDN context versus a logically centralized approach as in MobilityFirst's GNS approach [49], considering forwarding table size as a function of an abstract, parameterized model of name aggregation. Neither of these works consider either content or device mobility—the key consideration in our present paper.

Several recent efforts have considered name-based content retrieval in a mobile environment. [50] considers information dissemination in a linear V2V network using NDN, focusing primarily on the impact of protocol timer values on performance; our present paper focuses on mobility among multiple networks with general topologies and is aimed at a broad comparison between different location-independent network architectures. Proxies and/or indirection points (such as the HLR in cellular networks and home agent in Mobile IP) have been a common feature of many architectures supporting mobility, including recent proposals for NDN-like architectures. [33, 24] both adopt a proxy-based approach and rely on underlying tunneling or the existence of IP addresses to deliver content. Most recently, Kim [30] proposes the use of an indirection point where mobile content publishers and subscribers can register (content publishers) mobility-related name changes or query (content subscribers) for new names associated with a mobile publisher. [30] presents a protocol for NDN-like architectures for real-time, single-sender-single-receiver scenarios, conjecturing that "*... content providers, and their locations are relatively stable. Hence, the mobility problem for the 'stored contents' is limited to the scope of user-side mobility*". Our measurement results (§7) suggest otherwise. Further, our focus here is on pure name-based routing (or in-network name resolution), rather than proxies or indirection points.

**Mobile IP and indirection.** Much of the analysis of Mobile IP [40] has focused on analyzing proposed enhancements that improve handoff performance (e.g., [17]) or minimize signaling overhead (e.g., [58, 52]). Our goal, instead, is to empirically characterize location update rates as nodes change their point of attachment to the Internet, and the average "distance" from their home network—two key performance considerations for any architecture with a home-agent-like component. As noted above, there are many measurement studies of mobility among individual access points and base stations, but none of these characterize the rate at which users change their IP address or AS-affiliation, and it is this latter aspect of mobility (not intra-network mobility that is "invisible" outside that network) that determines update rates at home agents.

The triangle routing problem in Mobile IP [41], which results in longer paths between a sender and receiver when routed through an indirection point (the home agent) is well known, and enhancements to allow direct routing have been proposed [41]. The tradeoff between providing shortest-path routes versus the overhead entailed (e.g., in forwarding table size) is characterized by compact routing results [32, 47]. For example, with N flat identifiers, to be within 3x stretch of shortest-path, each router needs to maintain $\Omega(N)$ forwarding entries.; for up to 5x stretch, it is $\Omega(\sqrt(N))$. These lines of work, that seek to either develop new protocols to minimize path stretch due to indirection or theoretically characterize path stretch versus table-size tradeoffs, address different challenges than our work that empirically characterizes a mobile device's distance from "home."

# 3. EVALUATION METHODOLOGY

In this section, we explain our methodology to evaluate the cost-benefit tradeoffs struck by different location-independent approaches to handle mobility. The metrics of interest are routing update cost, forwarding table size, and path stretch for mobility of devices as well as content.

## 3.1 Intradomain device or content mobility

Consider a simple shortest-path routing network as shown in Figure 1(a) and a singly-homed endpoint A that changes its address from 22.33.44.55 belonging to the 22.33.44.0/24 subnet to 22.33.88.55 belonging to the 22.33.0.0/16 subnet. With name-to-address resolution (indirection routing), A simply needs to update DNS (its home agent) and data traffic can subsequently flow directly (indirectly) to A's new location. With a purely network-layer approach, some routers such as R may need to update their forwarding behavior in order to continue routing packets correctly to A. Whether R needs to update its forwarding table depends on whether R's shortest-path forwarding entries for 22.33.44.0/24 and 22.33.0.0/16 point to different output ports. If they do, say to ports 5 and 3 respectively, then R must introduce another entry `[22.33.44.55/32, 3]` in its forwarding table so that longest-prefix matching continues to route correctly to A. More generally, a router needs to update its forwarding table if an endpoint moves from one longest-matching prefix to another in its forwarding table, each pointing to different output ports. We refer to such mobility events as an endpoint A being *displaced* with respect to router R.

Displaced content names induce an update at name-based routers by moving across hierarchical name spaces in a manner analogous to endpoints moving across IP address spaces. An example is shown in Figure 2(b), wherein say `/20thCenturyFox/StarWars-EpisodeIV` moves to `/Disney/StarWars-EpisodeIV` because of a distribution rights transfer. Router Q must update its forwarding table if Q maintained different output ports for the corresponding longest-matching prefixes `/20thCenturyFox/*` and `/Disney/*`, i.e., if `StarWars-EpisodeIV` is displaced with respect to Q.

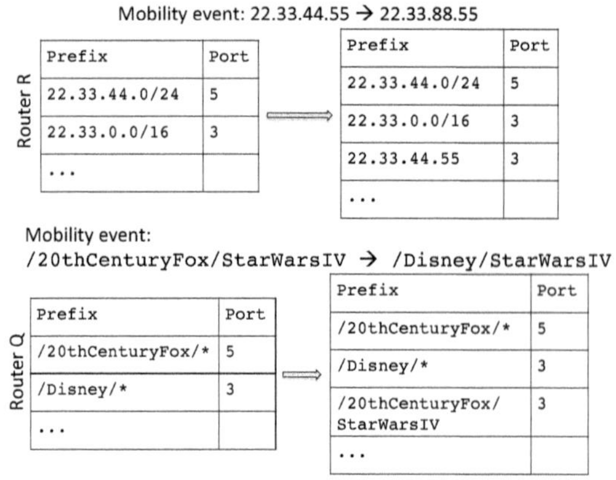


**Figure 2: Example of a device or content *displaced* w.r.t. a router's forwarding table.**

## 3.2 Interdomain mobility

From the example above, it is clear that the *update cost* of mobility depends on at least three factors: (1) the nature of network mobility patterns of endpoints; (2) the physical topology of the network; and (3) route selection policy. The policy used to select routes, e.g., shortest-path routing or BGP-style policy-driven route selection, matters because that is what determines the forwarding table at a router. Unlike shortest-path intradomain routing for which it is straightforward to answer whether or not a mobility event causes an update at any given router, it is much harder to answer this question in an interdomain network like the Internet driven primarily by policy routing.

One strawman is to use publicly available intradomain [35] and interdomain [2] topologies and combine them with a simple model of Internet routing, namely, prefer customers over peers over providers, then use AS path length to break ties, then use early-exit routing to further break ties, and so on. Unfortunately, given that even our knowledge of the Internet's physical AS-level as well as intradomain topology is incomplete [38], these models serve as a poor substitute for real Internet routing that is messier, e.g., prior studies [34] have found that interdomain routes predicted by such a model had barely 30% predictive accuracy.

Consequently, in this work, we work with a small set of real Internet routers whose RIBs (route information bases) and some route preference metrics are available to us. These RIBs already incorporate the global impact of the Internet's physical topology and import and export policy decisions made by other routers. We use these RIBs to derive the corresponding FIBs and ask, in a manner analogous to intradomain routing above, whether or not the router would update its forwarding table in response to a mobility event without having to simulate global Internet routing.

## 3.3 Multihomed device or content mobility

The methodology above implicitly assumed a singly-homed device or content principal. We next extend it to model the impact of mobility of multihomed principals on the update cost and forwarding table size at routers. For ease of exposition, we explain the model in the context of content mobility, but note that it applies to both device and content mobility.

### 3.3.1 Update cost

In order to assess the update cost of a mobility event, we begin with a *mobility workload* consisting of domain names and the set of all IP addresses to which they resolve (as measured for content in §7 from distributed vantage points). Consider a domain $d$, e.g., `graphics.nytimes.com`, and let $Addrs(d, t_1)$ denote the set of all IP addresses to which it resolves at time $t_1$. A mobility event refers to a change in the set to $Addrs(d, t_2)$ at a future time $t_2$. Does this mobility event cause a content router $R$ to update its forwarding behavior? That is, is there a difference between the sets $FIB(R, d, t_1)$ and $FIB(R, d, t_2)$, where $FIB(R, d, t)$ denotes the set of all eligible output ports to which router R could choose to forward packets destined to $d$ at time $t$?

To answer the above question, we distinguish between two *forwarding strategies— best-port forwarding* and *controlled flooding* —that respectively forward packets on at most a single best output port (like today) and forward packets to more than one eligible output port. The set of all eligible ports, $F(R, d, t)$, is determined as the set of output ports at $R$ corresponding to the set of IP addresses $Addrs(d, t)$ at that time, each of which in turn is computed using $R$'s FIB as for interdomain mobility above (§3.2). Best-port forwarding picks a single output port denoted as $best(FIB(R, d, t)$. The update cost depends on which of the two forwarding strategies is in use and is defined as follows.

The *update cost* of a mobility event at a router is 1 for best-port forwarding if there is a change in its best forwarding port, i.e., $best(FIB(R, d, t_1)) \neq best(FIB(R, d, t_2))$ for the mobility event $Addrs(d, t_1)$ to $Addrs(d, t_2)$; otherwise it is 0. The update cost is 1 for controlled flooding if there is a change in the set of all eligible output ports, i.e., $FIB(R, d, t_1) \neq FIB(R, d, t_2)$ for the mobility event $Addrs(d, t_1)$ to $Addrs(d, t_2)$; otherwise it is 0.

### 3.3.2 Forwarding table size and aggregateability

The forwarding table size at a content router depends on two factors: (1) forwarding strategy (as defined above) and (2) *aggregateability*, a metric that captures the extent to which forwarding tables can be compacted by relying on longest-prefix matching and inherent network locality in the content name space. To formally define this metric, we introduce some notation. Consider a set S of hierarchically organized domain names such as `yahoo.com, cnn.com, mit.edu, travel.yahoo.com`, etc. and a router R employing some forwarding strategy to route to these domains. For each domain $d \in S$, let $FIB(R, d)$ denote the (set of) forwarding output port(s). We refer to the set of forwarding entries $\{[d, FIB(R, d)]\}_{d \in S}$ as the *complete forwarding table.* Let $d_1 \prec d_2$ mean that $d_1$ is a strict subdomain of $d_2$, e.g., `travel.yahoo.com` $\prec$ `yahoo.com`. If $d_1 \prec d_2$ and $FIB(R, d_2) = FIB(R, d_1)$, then we say that the forwarding entry for $d_1$ is *subsumed* by $d_2$ with longest-prefix matching. For example, as shown in Figure 3, the entry `[travel.yahoo.com, 2]` is subsumed by the entry `[yahoo.com, 2]` as longest-prefix matching obviates storing an entry explicitly for the former, but a separate entry is needed for `[sports.yahoo.com, 5]`. We refer to the forwarding table consisting of the subset of entries in the complete forwarding table that excludes all subsumed entries as the *LPM forwarding table.*

We define *aggregateability* at a router as the ratio of the size of the complete forwarding table to the size of the corresponding LPM forwarding table.

| **Prefix** | **Port** |
|---|---|
| yahoo.com | 2 |
| ~~travel.yahoo.com~~ | ~~2~~ |
| sports.yahoo.com | 5 |
| cnn.com | 2 |
| mit.edu | 4 |
| ... | |

**Figure 3: Example of a content forwarding entry subsumed because of longest-prefix matching.**

### 3.3.3 Limitations and extensions

Our simple model of controlled flooding implicitly focuses on control plane costs, not on forwarding traffic. In particular, it implies that the update cost of controlled flooding increases with the rate of mobility events and is at least as high as that of best-port forwarding. However, there exist forwarding strategies that trade off update cost against increased traffic in the forwarding plane for which neither implication is true. For example, consider a hypothetical strategy wherein a router $R$ computes $FIB(R, d, t)$ based on the union of all past addresses observed for destination $d$, i.e., $\bigcup\{Addrs(d, t_i)\}_{t_i < t}$ instead of just $Addrs(d, t)$. In this case, the update cost at $R$ attributable to $d$ will soon approach 0 if $d$ rarely visits completely new network locations no matter how frequently it flits across previously visited locations. $R$'s controlled flooding strategy could simply forward across all of the corresponding output ports in $FIB(R, d, t)$, ensuring that at least one copy reaches $d$.

The strategy above reduces update cost (and, potentially, path stretch) but increases the costs of forwarding traffic and forwarding table size. Recognizing the fungibility of these costs—update cost, forwarding table size, and forwarding traffic—allows for other intriguing architectural combinations that have not been considered in this paper. Extending our evaluation to incorporate more general trade-offs including forwarding traffic is an interesting line of future research.

## 4. NETWORK MOBILITY MEASUREMENT

In this section, we describe an Android app, NomadLog [5], a development effort we undertook motivated both by the intractable or simplistic nature of purely theoretical analyses (refer §5) as well as the lack of public data on *network mobility* (unlike geographic mobility) of mobile devices.

**Figure 4: Screenshots of the NomadLog app.**

NomadLog is a lean app explicitly designed to measure the changing IP addresses of Android devices and does little else. The value proposition for potential downloaders is that they get cool visualizations of their network mobility statistics on a map, but realistically we expect people with a bent for citizen science or personal analytics to be more likely to install the app. The app runs in the background and attempts to record the public-facing IP address upon each connectivity event. A *connectivity event* is when either network interface wakes up and successfully connects to a cellular or WiFi network or disconnects from a network. Upon a connectivity event, the app contacts a server we maintain in order to determine its public-facing IP address, so addresses are logged only if they are usable for Internet connectivity, so automatic connects to WiFi APs blocked by a paywall or authentication page will not be logged unless successful.

The app is designed to be as inconspicuous as possible and is conservative in using battery power and data traffic as follows. First, its event-driven design obviates polling the network interfaces. Second, except for a single small message to infer its public-facing IP address, the app stores all data logs locally until it is both connected to power and WiFi; at this point, it attempts to transfer previously untransferred log files to a postgresql database that we maintain. Each entry logged in the database is in the following format.

*device_id* | *time* | *ip_addr* | *net_type* | *(lat, long)* ···

*device_id* is the hashed device identifier used to track the user while providing limited privacy; *time* is the event's timestamp; *net_type* indicates the type of the connected network, WiFi or cellular; and *(lat, long)* is the geolocation.

The user's geolocation is recorded only with user permission at install time and is collected only if the GPS is already on and has obtained a recent reading on behalf of some other app, i.e., NomadLog itself does not consume GPS resources. Users can either visualize their mobility statistics through the app or use their device identifier in order to access their data from the app's website from any device. Except for the (hashed) *device_id*, we do not maintain any other information directly identifying a user in our database.

We have acquired 372 users, mostly from the United States, Europe, and South America through word-of-mouth publicity alone. The user recruitment and data collection spanned over 14 months from Mar 2013 to May 2014. Because different users downloaded the app at different times and a small fraction uninstalled the app quickly (a learning experience that helped us engineer the resource and data usage optimizations), we removed users who ran the app for less than a day. Our analysis is based on daily statistics of network mobility, so our conclusions are unlikely to be biased significantly by the differing measurement period across users.

# 5. PATH STRETCH VS. UPDATE COST: AN EXPOSITORY ANALYTIC MODEL

In this section, we develop a simple analytic model to quantify the tradeoff between path stretch and update cost with two goals. The first is expository and helps us better appreciate the fundamental nature of the tradeoffs evaluated empirically in this paper. The second is to suggest that anything beyond simple toy topologies is difficult to analyze theoretically, making a stronger case for empirical analysis.

Our model and results are similar in spirit to theoretical work on compact routing (see [32] for a survey) that has focused on path stretch vs. forwarding table size tradeoffs, but the difference is that we model endpoint mobility and its update costs. Informally, compact routing results say that in order to achieve small stretch over shortest-path routing in a network with arbitrary (or flat) endpoint identifiers, roughly all routers must maintain an entry for roughly all endpoint identifiers. The question we ask is: in order to achieve small stretch over shortest-path routing, how many routers need to be updated when endpoints move across routers?

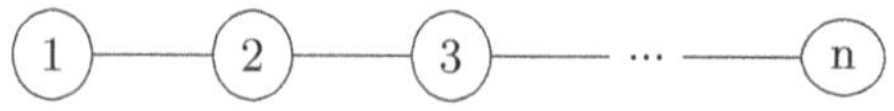

**Figure 5: A simple chain network topology.**

Intuitively, if every router is updated upon every mobility event, then the path stretch could be minimized. Also intuitively, if updates are restricted to at most one router (like a home agent) per mobility event, the path stretch could be as high as the diameter of the network as packets to the mobile endpoint must go through the only router that knows its whereabouts. We formally model these tradeoffs for several toy topologies and explain one of these in detail below.

## 5.1 Chain topology

Consider a chain network topology as shown in Figure 5 with routers numbered from 1 to $n$, and a user $u$ that randomly hops from one router to another. This mobility can be modeled using a discrete-time Markov process as follows. Let $L_t(u)$ be a random variable representing $u$'s location at time slot $t$. If the transition probability $P(L_{t+1}(u) = j|L_t(u) = i) = \frac{1}{n}$, then the steady-state distribution of $L_t(u)$ is uniform, i.e., $P(L_t(u) = i) = \frac{1}{n}$.

### 5.1.1 Indirection routing

Let $H(u)$ denote $u$'s home agent that keeps track of its current location. We define $path\_stretch_t$ as the hop-count distance from the home agent to an endpoint's location at time $t$. If $H(u)$ were chosen randomly (as would be the case in a network where different nodes were equally likely to be homed at any router and moved around randomly), the stretch is derived as follows. Below $dist(u, v)$ refers to the hop count distance between $u$ and $v$.

$$E[path\_stretch_t] = E[dist(H(u), L_t(u))]$$
$$= \sum_{i=1}^{n} P(H(u) = i) \sum_{j=1}^{n} P(L_t(u) = j)|i - j|$$
$$= \sum_{i=1}^{n} \frac{1}{n} \sum_{j=1}^{n} \frac{1}{n}|i - j|$$
$$= \frac{n^2-1}{3n} \simeq \frac{n}{3} \qquad \text{(refer [21] for details)}$$

Thus, with indirection, the expected path stretch is $\frac{n}{3}$ and the update cost is 1 per mobility event. Note that we define path stretch as the additive distance over the shortest-path length (as opposed to a multiplicative factor) as this matches what we are able to measure empirically (§6.3).

### 5.1.2 Name-based routing

With name-based routing, the path stretch is 0 if we assume that routers are designed to always maintain forwarding tables corresponding to shortest-path routing. What is the *aggregate update cost*, i.e., the fraction of routers that must be updated, to achieve this minimal stretch? We derive it as follows. Suppose each router has three ports, a left (right) port connecting to the leftwise (rightwise) adjacent router, and a local port connected to the local subnet. Then a router $i$ must update its forwarding table whenever an endpoint either moves from any leftward router to a rightward router or vice-versa, or moves from any router other than $i$ to $i$ or vice-versa. The expected update cost at router $k$ is

$$E[update\_cost_k] = P(L(u) < k) \cdot P(L(u) \geq k)$$
$$+ P(L(u) = k) \cdot P(L(u) \neq k) + P(L(u) > k) \cdot P_k(L(u) \leq k)$$
$$= \frac{k-1}{n}\frac{n-k+1}{n} + \frac{1}{n}\frac{n-1}{n} + \frac{n-k}{n}\frac{k}{n}$$

The expected aggregate update cost across all $n$ routers is

$$E[update\_cost] = \frac{1}{n}\sum_{k=1}^{n} E[update\_cost_k]$$
$$= \frac{n^3+3n^2-n}{3n^3} \simeq \frac{1}{3} \qquad \text{(refer [21] for details)}$$

Thus, for name-based routing, the aggregate update cost per mobility event is 1/3 and the path stretch is 0.

### 5.1.3 *Summary of results*

We have similarly quantified the aggregate update cost vs. path stretch tradeoff for other toy topologies and the simplistic random mobility model. The proofs are deferred to a technical report [21]. Note that we have omitted the analysis for a DNS-based approach above as the data path stretch is 0 (ignoring a constant lookup overhead in the connection initiation step) and the expected update cost is simply $O(1)$ (to the DNS), irrespective of topology.

| Topology | Indirection | | Name-based routing | |
|---|---|---|---|---|
| | stretch | update cost | stretch | update cost |
| Chain | $n/3$ | $1/n$ | 0 | $1/3$ |
| Clique | 1 | $1/n$ | 0 | 1 |
| Binary tree | $2\log_2 n$ | $1/n$ | 0 | $\frac{2\log_2 n}{n-1}$ |
| Star | 2 | $1/n$ | 0 | $\frac{1}{n+1}$ |

**Table 1: Path stretch vs. aggregate update cost.**

## 6. DEVICE MOBILITY

In this section, we combine the measured NomadLog data in §4 with the methodology in §3 to evaluate the cost-benefit tradeoffs of different approaches to handle mobility of devices across networks. We begin by analyzing the extent of network mobility across devices in the NomadLog data.

### 6.1 Extent of device mobility across networks

Figure 6 shows the distribution across users of the average number of distinct network locations per day visited by a user[1]. The trace consists of 372 users each of which is present for at least one day in our trace. The median number of ASes, IP prefixes, and IP addresses visited per day are 2, 2, and 3 respectively. This observation is consistent with the expectation that users typically move across a cellular, home, and work address in the course of a day.

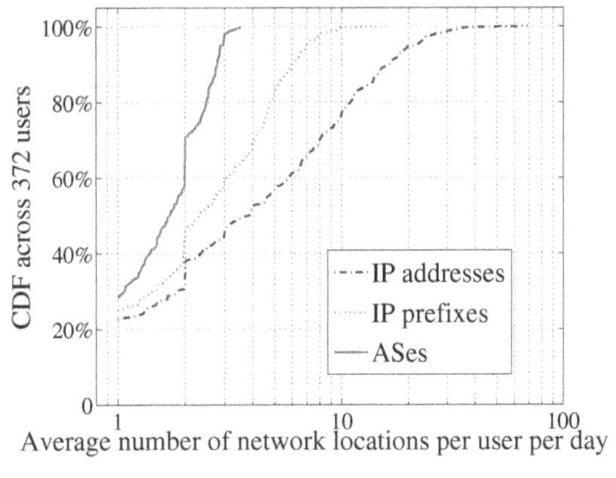


**Figure 6: Average number of distinct network locations per day visited by users.**

Figure 7 shows the distribution of the average number of transitions across network locations per day by a user. The number of AS transitions shows a lot more variation compared to the number of distinct ASes in Figure 6, which is because a user can switch many times between a small number of ASes. The number of transitions depends upon the user's physical mobility, network performance or outage patterns, and behavioral patterns, e.g., some users may prefer to use WiFi for some apps but use LTE for others or make these choices depending on current network quality. The maximum and minimum numbers of average AS transitions per day are 31.6 and 0.25 respectively. The median user transitions across roughly one AS and three IP addresses.

[1]We use the terms *user* and *device* interchangeably.

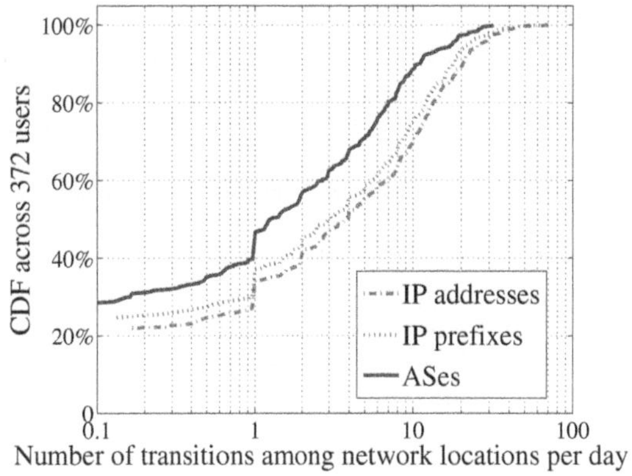


**Figure 7: Average number of transitions across network locations per day made by users.**

### 6.2 Update cost of device mobility

To provide the abstraction of location-independence communication, a device must update its changing network addresses *somewhere*, either in DNS, or at its home agent(s), or at routers. For the first two cases, the update cost is straightforward and directly corresponds to the rate of address transitions as shown above. For the third case, we estimate the update cost using the methodology described in §3.1 and §3.2 respectively.

#### 6.2.1 *Using Routeviews data*

To this end, we use RIBs from 12 BGP-speaking Routeviews routers [8]. The set of routers includes four in Oregon (labeled Oregon-1 to Oregon-4) and one each in Virginia, California, Georgia, Mauritius, London, Tokyo, Sydney and Sao Paulo. A single entry in a router's RIB lists several attributes of a single inter-domain route towards a given prefix. Typically, there are several routes to any given prefix and the set of all prefixes covers the entire IP address space.

ip_prefix | next_hop | local_pref. | metric | AS path | ··· |

To construct the FIB from a router's RIB, we need to compute a rank ordering of all of the routes for a single prefix. We apply the following rules in priority order based on typical BGP policies and the priority order suggested [8].

1. A route with a higher local_preference value is preferred. As local preference values are not available for most of the router dumps, we simply rely on the customer > peer > provider policy using standard techniques for inferring AS relationships [20].
2. A route with a shorter AS path is preferred.
3. A route with a smaller MED value is preferred.

Note that the above rules approximate typical BGP policies. The numerical value of `local_preference` is uniformly 0 in these RIBs, so we use AS relationships instead in the first rule. The RIBs also do not have sufficient information to implement early- or late-exit policies that are typically of higher priority than multi-exit discriminator values.

### 6.2.2 Update cost of name-based routing

To determine if the movement of a user from one address to another results in a change in a router's forwarding behavior, we must determine whether the the mobility event induces a change in the output port corresponding to the highest ranked route for the user's address. We use the next_hop AS path attribute as a proxy for the output port, implicitly assuming that the forwarding output port changes if and only if the next_hop attribute changes, an assumption believed to hold more often than not [45]. In practice, different next_hop addresses can correspond to the same output port, and the same next_hop can correspond to different output ports at different times because of intradomain concerns, so we may under- or over-estimate the actual update cost.

Figure 8 shows the update cost at all of the routers using the RIB data published on Mar 31, 2014. The update cost is shown as the fraction of all mobility events that induce a forwarding update at the router, also referred to as the *update rate*. The results show that the update rate can be as high as 14% at some routers. The routers at Mauritius and Tokyo experience hardly any updates, which is unsurprising as most of our users are located in the USA, Europe, and South America, so their mobility is less likely to impact distant routers. We verified that the Georgia router has a much lower next-hop degree compared to the Oregon routers, which could plausibly explain its lower update rate.

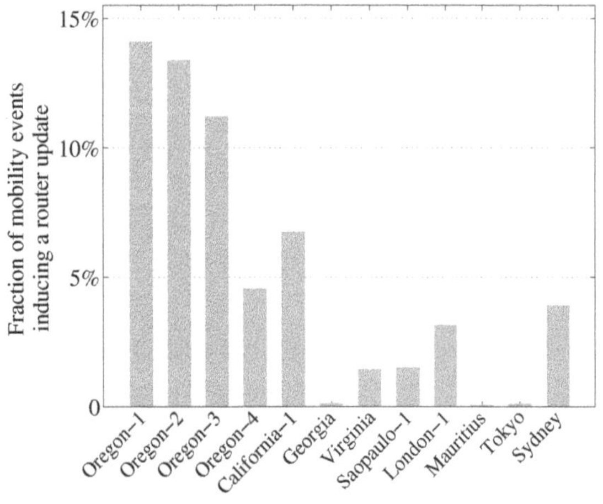


**Figure 8: Fraction of device mobility events inducing a routeviews router update.**

**Sensitivity analysis.** We further investigated the sensitivity of the above results to: (1) time, (2) the set of routers, and (3) the mobility workload. For the first, we repeated the experiment for 20 different days and found that, at every router, the standard deviation of the update rate is less than 0.005 (or 0.5%). For the second, we repeated the experiment using 13 RIPE routers [7] located in 13 different cities, 10 of which are distinct from the RouteViews set, and found qualitatively similar conclusions: the update rate at the median (most affected) router in the RouteViews and RIPE sets were 3.15% (14%) and 2.74% (11.3%) respectively.

For the third, we resorted to a significantly larger dataset [54] consisting of 7137 users from UMass IMAP servers that recently became available to us. These traces measure *user* mobility in a sense distinct from *device* mobility (an exception to the footnote in §6.1) as observed from a specific (but universally used) application's perspective, so the two traces are not directly comparable. Our preliminary analysis as above, using user mobility as a proxy for device mobility, shows that the update rates observed at all 25 RouteViews and RIPE routers are highly correlated with those for the NomadLog data, with a correlation coefficient of 0.88 (with more details deferred to the technical report [21]).

*Back-of-the-envelope calculations.*

*Update cost:* Combining the above results with the results in the previous section, we can arrive at a crude estimate of the absolute rate of updates induced at routers because of user mobility today. For example, if 2 billion smartphones change network addresses three (seven) times per day like our median (mean) user, and 3% of these mobility events induce an update at a router, the corresponding update rate is 2.1K/sec (4.8K/sec). These numbers are prohibitively high for even high-end routers today. Although it is possible to redesign router control planes to handle such high update rates using more compute resources and a software-defined control plane, it is difficult to justify this computation cost and the bandwidth cost of propagating these updates to a large number of Internet routers. In comparison, it is straightforward to handle this aggregate load by distributing it across a large number of DNS servers or home agents.

*Forwarding table size:* Combining the typical update rate of 3% with the fact that users typically spend 30% of a day away from the dominant IP address (see §6.3 below) suggests that a typical router would have to maintain extra forwarding entries for ≈1% of all devices that are *displaced* (as defined in §3.1) with respect to it at any given time.

## 6.3 Data path stretch with device mobility

The update cost analysis above induces no data path stretch (over underlying Internet routing) for name-based routing or for a DNS-based approach. However, indirection routing inflates the data path because of triangle routing via the home agent. Next, we quantify this path stretch overhead.

### 6.3.1 Displacement from dominant location

We introduce the notion of a *dominant location*, i.e., the network location where a user spends the largest fraction of time compared to all other locations in the course of a single day. Figure 9 shows the distribution across all days and all users of the percentage of time spent in the dominant location. For example, the plot shows that over 40% of users spend around 70% of their day at the dominant IP address and around 85% of their day at the dominant AS.

The dominant location is a natural candidate for a home agent in an indirection routing architecture. In order to compute path stretch, we need to determine C→H→M/C→M, where C→H→M is the sum of the network latency from a correspondent C to the home agent H and that from H to the mobile M, and C→M is the network latency of routing directly from C to M. We do not have a dataset of correspondents initiating communication with mobile devices (because it is largely not possible today to initiate communication to mobile devices), so instead we simply quantify the displacement of mobile users from their home agents in network distance, i.e., the latency of the path from H→M.

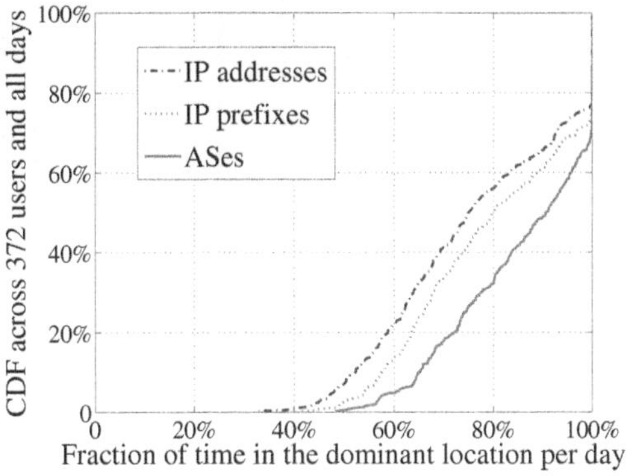


**Figure 9: The CDF of time that each user spends in the dominant location.**

### 6.3.2 *Path stretch of indirection routing*

In order to determine the network distance from a user's dominant location (or home) to their current location in the NomadLog trace, we rely on iPlane, a system that uses daily traceroute measurements from a large number of distributed vantage points to stub networks in order to predict the route (and its latency) between an arbitrary pair of IP addresses. Although using iPlane is convenient, it comes with two severe caveats for our analysis. First, iPlane returns valid responses for only 5% of the dominant and current IP address pairs in our trace; this is because it is designed to return responses only if it has sufficient traceroutes that enable it to constructed a predicted route using segments of measured routes. Second, even when iPlane returns a response, the predicted route may be inaccurate.

Figure 10 shows the distribution of network latencies across the dominant-to-current IP address pairs for which iPlane returned a predicted route. The median displacement delay from the dominant location is around 50ms and the corresponding AS hop count is 4. Recognizing the limitations of the estimates obtained using iPlane, we use a different technique to estimate a lower bound on the AS hop count of the displacement from home. We compute the length of the shortest AS path from the home to the current location using the Internet's AS-level physical topology [2] (even if this route may not exist in the AS-level routing topology). The median AS hop count of this shortest AS path is 2, suggesting that mobile users typically wander two or more ASes away from the home AS.

## 7. CONTENT MOBILITY

In this section, we evaluate the cost-benefit tradeoffs in terms of update cost, forwarding table size, and path stretch for content mobility. We begin by describing the procedure used to measure content mobility today.

### 7.1 Content mobility measurement

We begin with two sets of content domain names: a *popular* set and an *unpopular* set. The former is the set of the top 500 domains ranked according to popularity by Alexa [1] and the set of all of their subdomains. The latter is the least popular 500 domains and their subdomains in a

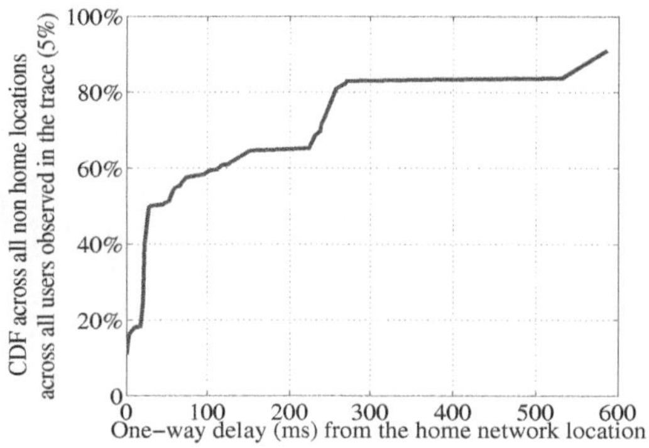


**Figure 10: Distribution of delay for the IP addresses pairs that get response from iPlane.**

list of the top 1 million domain names also ranked by popularity. We explicitly obtain a list of subdomains because Alexa ranks "websites" or top-level enterprise domains, e.g., `nytimes.com` or `yahoo.com`, but not their subdomains like `graphics.nytimes.com` or `travel.yahoo.com`. More importantly, the distribution of popular, bulky content that is ideally suited to name-based routing techniques is often outsourced to CDNs, and a common technique to achieve this is to CNAME-alias subdomains, e.g., `graphics.nytimes.com` is aliased to the canonical name `static.nytimes.com.edgesuite.net` that is in turn aliased to `a1158.g1.akamai.net` that finally gets dynamically resolved to one or more IP addresses close to the querying client or its local name server.

The dynamic nature of resolution of domain names to IP addresses (either because they are resolved by a CDN delegate in a locality-aware manner or because of DNS-based load balancing employed by the origin server) means that any single vantage point will see only a subset of all IP addresses from where a domain's content may be potentially served. Our methodology to assess content mobility (in §3.3) relies on monitoring any changes to the set of all IP addresses corresponding to a domain name. This methodology implicitly assumes that a purely name-based routing network will announce a content domain name from all of the locations (including CDN locations) where it resides today.

In order to measure a reasonably complete set of IP addresses to which each domain name maps, we conduct a measurement distributed across 74 Planetlab nodes that are chosen from as many different countries as possible and all continents (except Africa where Planetlab nodes were unavailable). We conducted the measurements for a three week period from May 1 to May 22, 2014. Each node resolves each domain name once every hour, thereby observing a subset of the domain's IP addresses at that time. A central controller node collects measurements obtained from all of the vantage points and merges them in time so that for each domain name for each hour, the set of IP addresses is the union of all IP addresses obtained from all vantage points for that domain. As the measurement interval once per hour, precise time synchronization is not necessary. The measurement is done just once per hour per domain because our list of subdomains corresponding to the 500 most popular Alexa domains contains 12,342 entries, so a much higher rate would overwhelm some nodes or trigger security alarms.

### 7.2 Update cost of content mobility

Figure 11(a) shows the extent of daily mobility of popular content (i.e., the 12,342 subdomains obtained from the most

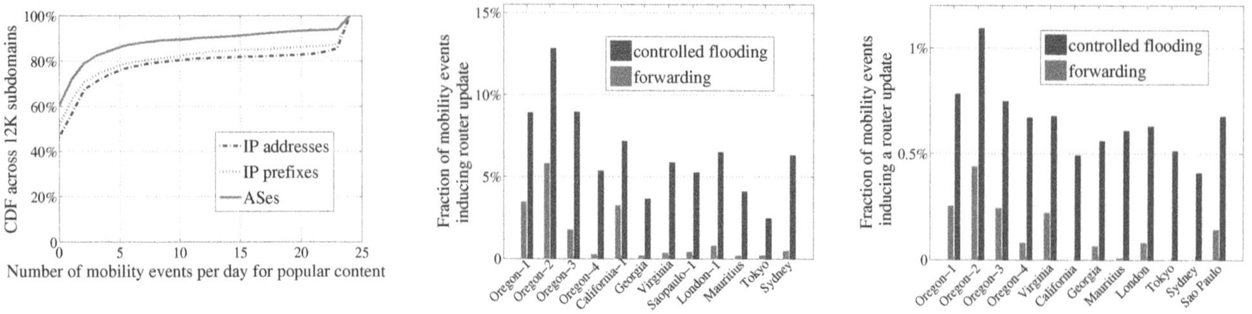


(a) The average number of transitions for popular content mobility events (b) Fraction of popular content mobility events inducing a router update (c) Fraction of unpopular content mobility events inducing a router update

**Figure 11: Results on the extent of content mobility and its impact on the update cost at routers.**

popular 500 domains). The median number of changes in the set of IP addresses per day is 2 (the similarity to device mobility being just coincidental) and the maximum is bounded at 24 because of our hourly measurement procedure.

Figure 11(b) shows the update rate at each of the twelve routers because of mobility events involving popular content. The plot shows that up to 13% of content mobility events can induce an update at some routers when controlled flooding (i.e., forwarding on all ports matching any of the domain's IP addresses) is used. However, at most 6% of the mobility events induce an update at any of the routers in our dataset when best-port forwarding is used. The reason is that although there may be some flux in the set of addresses corresponding to a domain name, the address that is the closest to any given router rarely changes because most of the addresses in the set remain unchanged, i.e., unlike devices that jump seemingly randomly from one address to an unrelated address, content locations do not change arbitrarily.

Figure 11(c) shows the corresponding result for unpopular content or the least popular 500 domains and their subdomains with a popularity rank of near about one million. The update cost for unpopular content is dramatically lower than that for popular content; at most 1% of updates induce an update at any of the routers even with controlled flooding. With best-port forwarding, almost none of the routers experience any update during the course of our measurement period (the median is 0.08%). This result is not surprising as unpopular content is unlikely to be delegated to CDNs and is probably served only from a small number of network locations that rarely change; these multiple locations if at all are chosen mainly for fault-tolerance or load balancing purposes rather than proximity to clients, so they rarely change. We further explicitly estimated [21] the fraction of domains delegated to CDNs in our trace for unpopular content to be only 1.6% compared to 24.5% for popular content.

## 7.3 Forwarding table size

Figure 12 shows the aggregateability (as defined in §3.3.2) for the 500 most popular domain names on 12 routeviews routers by using the best-port forwarding strategy. We see that the aggregateability at different routers varies between 2× to 16×, which suggests a commensurate reduction in the forwarding table sizes at these routers compared to the total number of popular content domain names. Unpopular content domain names in our dataset have hardly any sub-

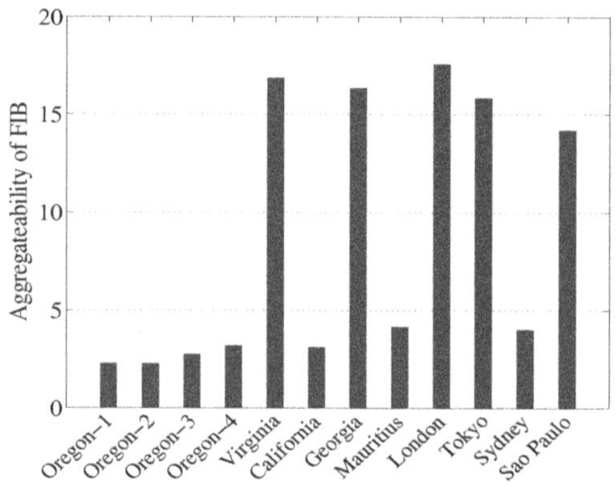


**Figure 12: FIB aggregateability of popular content.**

domains, which implies that content routers would have to nominally store one entry each for the long tail of unpopular content domain names, unless a different ontological structure that helps compact routing information is used to rename them. With respect to forwarding table size, unpopular content domain names present a challenge similar to device names, i.e., they both entail one forwarding entry per principal at a router unless a location-aware scheme (like IP addresses or geo-location) is used to "rename" them.

*Back-of-the-envelope calculations.*

Performing a calculation similar to that at the end of §6, if we assume 1B content domain names (noting that DNS has ≈150M domains), an update rate of 2/day, and a 0.5% likelihood of inducing an update at a router, the router would receive at most 100 updates/sec. Furthermore, for the vast majority of long-tail domains ranked below 1M, the update cost is likely to be even lower even if controlled flooding is used as the forwarding strategy. Finally, with best-port forwarding, the router update cost due to the mobility for vast majority of (unpopular) content is near-zero.

# 8. LIMITATIONS AND OPEN ISSUES

We began with an ambitious goal but have only managed to scratch the surface. Below, we list the limitations of our evaluation, caveats attached to our findings, and open issues.

The hundreds of users in our device mobility dataset may not be a representative sample of smartphone users even today, leave alone in a future Internetwork. However, given the lack of existing datasets on network mobility (unlike physical mobility) of devices, we believe our measurements are an important and necessary first step for developing meaningful mobility datasets in order to compare different architectures. An alternative might have been to develop an abstract model (e.g., the equivalent of a random-waypoint model [56] for network mobility of devices or content), but this abstract model would hardly be any more convincing unless validated through measurements (such as those presented here).

The unrepresentativeness critique applies also to other aspects of the data in our evaluation including the use of today's routing topologies, routing policies, access network diversity, content locations, etc. that may be radically different in the future and may indeed be influenced by the very architectures we seek to evaluate, were they to be widely adopted. The empirical nature of our evaluation comes with the necessary caveat that our findings are limited to network environments like today's Internet; but we do note that our findings are unlikely to change qualitatively if the extent of device or content mobility were perturbed by large factors.

Our characterization of content mobility by measuring the change in resolved IP addresses associated with domain names implicitly assumes that a purely name-based routing network will announce content domain names from all of the locations—including CDN locations—where they resides today. It is possible, even likely, that popular content will be announced from far fewer primary locations with commensurately less flux in a name-based architecture that can leverage on-path caching (as in NDN). However, that would only strengthen our favorable assessment of name-based routing for handling the update cost of content mobility. What was not clear to us when we began this work was whether routing directly over a hierarchical domain name space would scale even in today's Internet; our findings lean towards the affirmative (unlike analyses based on abstract models [10]).

Our scope of evaluation as well as goals suffer from some limitations. First, we have evaluated three pure strategies for location-independence but not the many possible combinations of these strategies in a network architecture (e.g., exploiting indirection points within a name-based routing system [27]). Second, network architecture itself is indeed part science and part art. Not everything may be easily quantifiable; what is easily quantifiable may not be the most pressing concern. Nevertheless, our position is that pushing the envelope of what is quantifiable is valuable for scientific discourse, and our work is a first step towards that goal.

Even within the confines of the three purist approaches, our empirical focus constrained the nature of the trade-offs we could evaluate. For name-based routing, we could empirically evaluate metrics such as update cost and forwarding table size, but not other control plane metrics such as routing convergence delays or data plane metrics such as forwarding traffic or user-perceived path stretch with on-path caching. We note however that on-path content caching can benefit most architectures, including ones based on name resolution like the Internet (e.g., transparent caching today) or MobilityFirst [48], but does not suffice to ensure reachability to at least one copy of the requested content.

Our methodology considers one class of controlled flooding strategies that generalize routing and forwarding strategies used in today's Internet. However, as noted in §3.3.3, the fungibility of costs between update cost, forwarding table size, and forwarding traffic allows for other exotic architectural alternatives whose cost-benefit trade-offs are harder to analyze. Investigating these more sophisticated forwarding strategies is an interesting avenue of future research, as also alluded to by calls for a stateful forwarding plane [55].

# 9. CONCLUSIONS

The intellectual pursuit of a location-independent communication abstraction has long intrigued networking researchers, and has in no small part influenced the design of many clean-slate Internet architectures. However, despite sharing this common goal, there has been little prior work on quantitatively comparing the different cost-benefit tradeoffs struck by these architectures in accomplishing this goal.

As a first step towards addressing this gap, we have developed a quantitative methodology to empirically evaluate three puristic approaches that drive the designs of a number of location-independent network architectures. We combine this methodology with measured traces of device mobility and content mobility on the Internet using realistic physical and routing topologies. Based on measured network mobility patterns of hundreds of devices of NomadLog, an Android app we developed explicitly for this goal, and hundreds of content domains including those delegated to content distribution networks, we find that pure name-based routing induces a prohibitively high update cost at routers because of device mobility, but induces a far lower update cost in conjunction with simple forwarding strategies for most of today's content that happens to exhibit high locality. Taken together, our results suggest that recent proposals for name-based networking in their puristic form are better suited for content distribution alone, but may need to be augmented with addressing-assisted approaches like DNS or Mobile IP in order to handle device mobility, so as to serve as a general-purpose replacement for the TCP/IP Internet.

**Acknowledgments.** This research was funded in part by CNS-1040781. We thank the paper's reviewers, the shepherd Scott Shenker, and Antonio Rocha, Dave Oran, Lixia Zhang, and participants at NSF FIA meetings for their feedback.

# 10. REFERENCES

[1] Alexa: `http://www.alexa.com/`.

[2] CAIDA: `http://www.caida.org`.

[3] FIRE: Future Internet Research and Experimentation: `http://cordis.europa.eu/fp7/ict/fire/`.

[4] GENI: `http://www.geni.net`.

[5] Nomad Log: `https://nomadlog.net/`.

[6] NSF Future Internet Project: `http://www.nets-fia.net/`.

[7] RIPE: `http://www.ripe.net/`.

[8] RouteViews: `http://www.routeviews.org/`.

[9] Celloscope: `http://celloscope.net`, 2014.

[10] A. Baid, T. Vu, and D. Raychaudhuri. Comparing Alternative Approaches for Networking of Named Objects in the Future Internet. In *IEEE INFOCOM NOMEN Workshop*, 2012.

[11] H. Balakrishnan, K. Lakshminarayanan, S. Ratnasamy, S. Shenker, I. Stoica, and M. Walfish. A Layered Naming Architecture for the Internet. In *ACM SIGCOMM*, 2004.

[12] M. Caesar, T. Condie, J. Kannan, K. Lakshminarayanan, I. Stoica, and S. Shenker. ROFL: Routing on Flat Labels. In *ACM SIGCOMM*, 2006.

[13] A. Carzaniga and A. L. Wolf. Content-Based Networking: A New Communication Infrastructure. In *NSF Workshop on Developing an Infrastructure for Mobile and Wireless Systems*. Springer-Verlag, 2002.

[14] A. Chaintreau, P. Hui, J. Crowcroft, C. Diot, R. Gass, and J. Scott. Impact of Human Mobility on Opportunistic Forwarding Algorithms. *IEEE Trans. on Mobile Computing*, 6(6):606–620, 2007.

[15] Y.-C. Chen, J. Kurose, and D. Towsley. A Mixed Queueing Network Model of Mobility in a Campus Wireless Network. In *IEEE INFOCOM*, 2012.

[16] C. Dannewitz. NetInf: An Information-centric Networking Architecture. *Computer Communications*, 36(7), 2013.

[17] S. Das, A. Misra, and P. Agrawal. TeleMIP: Telecommunications-enhanced Mobile IP Architecture for Fast Intradomain Mobility. *IEEE Personal Communications*, 7(4):50–58, Aug 2000.

[18] P. Deshpande, X. Hou, and S. Das. Performance Comparison of 3G and Metro-Scale WiFi for Vehicular Network Access. In *ACM SIGCOMM IMC*, 2010.

[19] N. Fotiou, P. Nikander, D. Trossen, and G. C. Polyzos. Developing Information Networking Further: From PSIRP to PURSUIT. In *Broadband Communications, Networks, and Systems*, pages 1–13. Springer, 2012.

[20] L. Gao. On Inferring Autonomous System Relationships in the Internet. *IEEE/ACM Trans. on Networking*, 9(6), 2001.

[21] Z. Gao, A. Venkataramani, J. Kurose, and S. Heimlicher. Towards a Quantitative Comparison of Location-Independent Network Architectures. *UMass SCS Technical Report, 2014*. `http://web.cs.umass.edu/publication/`.

[22] M. Gritter and D. R. Cheriton. An architecture for content routing support in the internet. In *USENIX Symposium on Internet Technologies and Systems (USITS)*, 2001.

[23] E. Halepovic and C. Williamson. Characterizing and Modeling User Mobility in a Cellular Data Network. In *ACM Workshop on Performance Evaluation of Wireless Ad Hoc, Sensor, and Ubiquitous Networks*, 2005.

[24] F. Hermans, E. Ngai, and P. Gunningberg. Global Source Mobility in the Content Centric Networking Architecture. In *ACM Workshop on Emerging Name-Oriented Mobile Networking Design - [...] (NoM)*, 2012.

[25] W. Hsu, D. Dutta, and A. Helmy. Structural Analysis of User Association Patterns in University Campus Wireless LANs. *IEEE Trans. on Mobile Computing*, 11(11):1734–1748, Nov. 2012.

[26] S. Isaacman, R. Becker, R. Cáceres, M. Martonosi, J. Rowland, A. Varshavsky, and W. Willinger. Human Mobility Modeling at Metropolitan Scales. In *ACM SIGMOBILE MobiSys*, 2012.

[27] V. Jacobson and R. L. Braynard et al. Custodian-based Information Sharing. *IEEE Communications Magazine*, 50(7):38–43, 2012.

[28] V. Jacobson, D. K. Smetters, J. D. Thornton, M. F. Plass, N. H. Briggs, and R. L. Braynard. Networking Named Content. In *ACM SIGCOMM CoNEXT*, 2009.

[29] C. Kim, M. Caesar, and J. Rexford. Floodless in Seattle: A Scalable Ethernet Architecture for Large Enterprises. In *ACM SIGCOMM*, 2008.

[30] D.-h. Kim, J.-h. Kim, Y.-s. Kim, H.-s. Yoon, and I. Yeom. Mobility Support in Content Centric Networks. In *ACM Workshop on Information-Centric Networking*, 2012.

[31] M. Kim, D. Kotz, and S. Kim. Extracting a Mobility Model from Real User Traces. In *IEEE INFOCOM*, 2006.

[32] D. Krioukov, K. Fall, A. Brady, et al. On Compact Routing for the Internet. In *ACM SIGCOMM*, 2007.

[33] J. Lee, D. Kim, M. wuk Jang, and B.-J. Lee. Proxy-based Mobility Management Scheme in Mobile Content Centric Networking (CCN) Environments. In *IEEE International Conference on Consumer Electronics*, 2011.

[34] H. V. Madhyastha, E. Katz-Bassett, T. E. Anderson, A. Krishnamurthy, and A. Venkataramani. iPlane Nano: Path Prediction for Peer-to-Peer Applications. In *USENIX NSDI*, 2009.

[35] R. Mahajan, N. Spring, D. Wetherall, and T. Anderson. Inferring Link Weights Using End-to-end Measurements. In *ACM Sigcomm Workshop on Internet Measurment*, 2002.

[36] R. Moskowitz, P. Nikander, P. Jokela, and T. Henderson. RFC 5201: Host Identity Protocol, Apr 2008.

[37] A. Nikravesh, D. R. Choffnes, E. Katz-Bassett, Z. M. Mao, and M. Welsh. Mobile Network Performance from User Devices: A Longitudinal, Multidimensional Analysis. In *Passive and Active Measurement Conference (PAM)*, 2014.

[38] R. Oliveira, D. Pei, W. Willinger, B. Zhang, and L. Zhang. The (in) completeness of the observed internet as-level structure. *IEEE/ACM Trans. on Networking*, 18(1), 2010.

[39] U. Paul, A. Subramanian, M. Buddhikot, and S. Das. Understanding Traffic Dynamics in Cellular Data Networks. In *IEEE INFOCOM*, 2011.

[40] C. Perkins. RFC 3220: IP Mobility Support for IPv4, 2002.

[41] C. Perkins and D. Johnson. Route Optimization for Mobile IP. *Cluster Computing*, 1(2):161–176, 1998.

[42] J. Saltzer. RFC 1498: On the Naming and Binding of Network Destinations, Aug. 1993.

[43] J. Sommers and P. Barford. Performance Comparison of 3G and Metro-Scale WiFi for Vehicular Network Access. In *ACM SIGCOMM Internet Measurement Conference*, 2012.

[44] N. Spring, R. Mahajan, and T. Anderson. The Causes of Path Inflation. In *ACM SIGCOMM*, 2003.

[45] N. Spring, R. Mahajan, and D. Wetherall. Measuring ISP Topologies with Rocketfuel. In *ACM SIGCOMM*, 2002.

[46] I. Stoica, D. Adkins, S. Zhuang, S. Shenker, and S. Surana. Internet Indirection Infrastructure. In *ACM SIGCOMM'02*.

[47] M. Thorup and U. Zwick. Compact Routing Schemes. In *ACM Symposium on Parallel Alg. and Arch. (SPAA)*, 2001.

[48] A. Venkataramani, J. Kurose, D. Raychaudhuri, K. Nagaraja, M. Mao, and S. Banerjee. MobilityFirst: A Mobility-Centric and Trustworthy Internet Architecture. *ACM SIGCOMM Computer Comm. Review (CCR)*, 2014.

[49] A. Venkataramani, A. Sharma, X. Tie, H. Uppal, D. Westbrook, J. Kurose, and D. Raychaudhuri. Design Requirements of a Global Name Service for a Mobility-Centric, Trustworthy Internetwork. In *COMSNETS*, 2013.

[50] L. Wang, A. Afanasyev, R. Kuntz, and R. Vuyyuru et al. Rapid Traffic Information Dissemination Using Named Data. In *ACM Workshop on Emerging Name-Oriented Mobile Networking Design - [...] (NoM)*, 2012.

[51] J. Wroclawski. All Hat No Answers: Some Issues Related to the Evaluation of Architecture. In *Spring 2013 NSF FIA PI meeting, Salt Lake City, http://www.nets-fia.net/Meetings/Spring13/FIA-Arch-Eval-JTW.pptx*.

[52] J. Xie and I. Akyildiz. A Novel Distributed Dynamic Location Management Scheme for Minimizing Signaling Costs in Mobile IP. *IEEE Trans. on Mobile Computing*, 1(3):163–175, 2002.

[53] Q. Xu, A. Gerber, Z. M. Mao, and J. Pang. AccuLoc: Practical Localization of Performance Measurements in 3G Networks. In *ACM SIGMOBILE MobiSys*, 2011.

[54] S. Yang, S. Heimlicher, J. Kurose, and A. Venkataramani. User Transitioning Among Networks-a Measurement and Modeling Study. *UMass SCS Technical Report*, 2014. `http://web.cs.umass.edu/publication/`.

[55] C. Yi, A. Afanasyev, I. Moiseenko, L. Wang, B. Zhang, and L. Zhang. A Case for Stateful Forwarding Plane. *Elsevier Computer Communication*, 36(7):779–791, Apr. 2013.

[56] J. Yoon, M. Liu, and B. Noble. Random Waypoint Considered Harmful. In *IEEE INFOCOM*, 2003.

[57] K. Zarifis, T. Flach, S. Nori, D. Choffnes, R. Govindan, E. Katz-Bassett, Z. M. Mao, and M. Welsh. Diagnosing Path Inflation of Mobile Client Traffic. In *Passive and Active Measurement Conference (PAM)*, 2014.

[58] X. Zhang, J. G. Castellanos, and A. T. Campbell. P-MIP: Paging Extensions for Mobile IP. *Kluwer Academic Mobile Networks and Applications*, 7(2):127–141, 2002.

# Lightweight Source Authentication and Path Validation

Tiffany Hyun-Jin Kim
CyLab, CMU
hyunjin@cmu.edu

Cristina Basescu
ETH Zürich
cba@inf.eth.ch

Limin Jia
CyLab, CMU
liminjia@cmu.edu

Soo Bum Lee
Qualcomm
soobuml@qti.qualcomm.com

Yih-Chun Hu
UIUC
yihchun@uiuc.edu

Adrian Perrig
ETH Zürich
perrig@inf.eth.ch

## ABSTRACT

In-network source authentication and path validation are fundamental primitives to construct higher-level security mechanisms such as DDoS mitigation, path compliance, packet attribution, or protection against flow redirection. Unfortunately, currently proposed solutions either fall short of addressing important security concerns or require a substantial amount of router overhead. In this paper, we propose lightweight, scalable, and secure protocols for shared key setup, source authentication, and path validation. Our prototype implementation demonstrates the efficiency and scalability of the protocols, especially for software-based implementations.

## Categories and Subject Descriptors

C.2.0 [**Computer-Communication Networks**]: Security and protection; C.2.1 [**Network Architecture and Design**]: Circuit-switching networks, Packet-switching networks

## Keywords

Source Authentication, Path Validation, Retroactive Key Setup

## 1. INTRODUCTION

Source authentication and path validation are useful primitives to help mitigate various network-based attacks, such as DDoS, address spoofing, and flow redirection attacks [7]. Path validation, in particular, provides a way to enforce path compliance according to the policies of ISPs, enterprises, and datacenters. Endhosts and ISPs desire to validate service level agreement compliance regarding data delivery in the network: Did the packet truly originate from the claimed client? Did the client select a path that complies with the service provider's policy? Did the packet indeed travel through the path selected by the client?

Unfortunately, the current Internet provides almost no means for source authentication and path validation by routers or endhosts, opening up numerous attack surfaces. For example, a malicious ISP may forward a packet on an inferior path while claiming to its client that it forwarded the packet on the premium path. Alternatively, a malicious router may inject packets with a spoofed source address to incriminate a victim source node into having sent an excessive number of packets. A malicious router may simply alter the contents of received packets as well. The inability to detect such attacks near the point of deviation wastes downstream resources. Furthermore, an adversary may exploit the routing protocol to divert traffic to traverse a point of eavesdropping it controls—a serious issue in particular for sensitive information.

End-to-end encryption and authentication mechanisms, such as TLS, do not solve any of the above issues, since they are agnostic to which path the packet takes. A stronger approach is needed, which enables routers and destinations to perform source authentication and path validation. As we discuss in the related work, existing solutions either require extensive overhead, or only partially address fundamental problems, affecting both feasibility and practicality in the existing network. For example, ICING [26] addresses both source authentication and path validation, but it requires each intermediate router on a path to store and look up keys shared with other routers; ICING requires 42 bytes per verifying router in the packet header. Furthermore, ICING requires each router to calculate a Message Authentication Code (MACs) for *all other routers on the path.* In contrast, our protocol does not require any per-client state on routers; it requires only 16 bytes per hop (which can be reduced to 2 bytes for a lower level of security), and only a single MAC and a single PRF computation per router *irrespectively of the path length.* Moreover, one of our protocol instantiations prevents against coward attacks [20], where an adversary only attacks when it knows that the attack will not be detected. Our protocol, however, offers reduced security in the case of a malicious sender colluding with a malicious router on the path, which we describe in detail in the related work section. Since in the common case, sender and receiver trust each other, the performance gain of $O(1)$ MAC operation per router instead of $O(n)$ is worth the tradeoff.

**Contributions.** In this paper, we present *Dynamically Recreatable Key* (DRKey) protocols that enable routers to (re-)create symmetric keys shared with the endhosts on the fly. The stateless operation of DRKey on routers prevents state exhaustion DoS attacks and simplifies router architecture. We further enrich DRKey with a new notion called *retroactive key setup* that provides the following desirable properties: (1) in contrast to previous protocols, source and destination can start the communication without needing to wait for the expensive key setup to complete, providing *efficiency*; (2) if misbehavior is suspected, endhosts set up keys retroactively to verify previous packets, *defending against coward attacks.*

Based on the dynamically (re-)creatable keys through DRKey protocols, we present *Origin and Path Trace* (OPT)—lightweight, scalable, and secure protocols for source authentication and path validation. We introduce an extension called *Retroactive-PathTrace* that supports the destination to perform path validation with retroac-


*SIGCOMM'14,* August 17–22, 2014, Chicago, IL, USA.

http://dx.doi.org/10.1145/2619239.2626323.

tive key setup and to detect coward attackers with small, constant overhead in the packet header. Our OPT protocols enable implementation on SW routers with minimal performance impact.

# 2. PROBLEM DEFINITION

## 2.1 Desired Security Properties

**Source authentication and data authentication.** The destination and each intermediate router should be able to determine whether the packet indeed originated from the claimed source and whether the packet content has not been altered en route. In this paper, source authentication includes data authentication.

**Path validation.** The source, intermediate routers, and the destination should be able to validate that the packet indeed traversed the path known to (or selected by) the source. Successful path validation ensures that the packet traversed each honest router on the path in the correct order. Unfortunately, no scheme can provide any guarantees for malicious routers: if malicious router $R_m$ publishes its secret keys, another malicious router $R_{m'}$ could perform cryptographic operations on a packet without traversing $R_m$.

## 2.2 Elided Security Properties

**No packet delivery guarantee.** Routers generally have the freedom to decide whether or not to forward packets. Hence, it is not the purpose of path validation to guarantee that packets will be delivered to the specified destination.

**No detection of packet siphoning.** Misbehaving router $R_m$ on the source-selected path can siphon packets and send them over a separate channel to a remote entity. Since $R_m$ still forwards the packet to $R_{m+1}$, this attack is not detected. We consider $R_m$ as obeying the protocol as long as it performs protocol-compliant operations with the packet.

**No locating of packet altering and dropping routers.** Locating routers that alter or drop packets is the goal of fault-localization mechanisms—another challenging problem especially in inter-domain settings [39]. Since path validation is a simpler problem, the goal is to achieve a more efficient protocol than heavy-weight fault localization.

## 2.3 Adversary Model

We consider a computationally-bounded network attacker that deviates from the protocol and violates its security goals as we describe next.

**Packet alteration.** A malicious router alters any part of the packet, such as source address, header information, or payload data.

**Packet injection.** A malicious router fabricates a packet and sends it towards a destination of its choice. A packet replay attack is a special case of packet injection.

**Path deviation.** A malicious router may perform *path deviation attacks*, which cause packets to be forwarded along a path other than the path previously selected by the source. We subdivide this attack as follows:

- **Path detour:** Malicious router $R_m$ causes a packet to deviate from the intended forwarding path, but later the packet returns to the correct downstream router $R_{m+1}$ to resume traversal of *all* routers on the intended path.
- **Router skipping:** A malicious router redirects the packet and skips other router(s) on the path. Thus, some routers on the intended path does not forward the packet.
- **Out-of-order traversal:** An adversary causes path deviations such that routers on the intended path are not traversed in the right order.

**Coward attack.** An adversary launches a coward attack [20] only when the adversary believes that the attack cannot be detected. For example, an attacker diverts traffic only when the protocol is inactive (e.g., required keys for validation have not been established).

**Denial-of-Service (DoS).** As part of DoS attacks, we consider memory and computation exhaustion attacks on routers performing source authentication and path validation.

**Collusion.** Protocol participants may collude to carry out any of the attacks listed above. For example, two or more intermediate routers may collude to claim the use of an expensive path for monetary profit, or the source may collude with an intermediate router to spoof authenticators for its downstream routers if the destination prefers/trusts skipped routers. Also, both the source and the destination could collude with some intermediate routers to frame another router on the path by not forwarding packets to it.

In Section 6, we explore potential attacks against our protocols that violate the desired properties and discuss how OPT defends against these attacks.

# 3. OPT DESIGN OVERVIEW

We consider a setting in which source $S$ sends a packet to destination $D$ along a sequence of routers $R_i$. We refer to $S$, $D$, and $R_i$'s as *tracing entities*. At a very high level, the main insights for achieving source authentication and path validation without requiring routers to maintain per-source or per-path-length state are as follows: (1) In the packet header, source $S$ includes $H(P)$, which is the hash of the packet payload to help receiving entities identify the packet while avoiding expensive hash computation at each router; (2) On demand, each router $R_i$ generates key $K_i$ using a symmetric cryptographic operation, and requires only router's local secret $SV_{R_i}$ and a special value called SESSIONID in the packet header as inputs. Consequently, generating deterministic keys is stateless and faster than storing or retrieving secrets. (3) Each router performs source authentication using a MAC computed over $H(P)$; (4) Each router $R_i$ extends a special authentication field called PVF by performing a MAC operation. Hence, path validation is achieved through a chain consisting of nested MACs.

## 3.1 Assumptions

For the communication properties of the network, we assume that the source knows the path that the packet will traverse at the AS- or router-level granularity to enable path validation, and that the source knows which entities in that path desire to perform the validations. This information can stem from (1) the BGP protocol where the source can learn the AS path that the packet is expected to traverse, (2) Pathlet routing [11] or SCION [40] where the source can specify the path in the packet header, or (3) i3 [33] or Platypus [29] where the source can define a sequence of servers to traverse. Alternatively, an ISP may provide the premium path information to clients as an extra service (e.g., transatlantic cable for financial transactions [28]), in which case a client can validate that the traversed path is indeed the premium path paid for.

For the cryptographic key setup, the source and the destination need to be able to authenticate the router's cryptographic materials (i.e., validate a signature that binds an entity to some cryptographic materials). In the case of AS-level tracing, the AS needs to be authenticated, and such authentication can be achieved through RPKI [4], which is already operational. RPKI provides a PKI that enables authentication of AS certificates, each of which binds an AS number to its public key, given the correct RPKI public root key. In case of router-level tracing, we assume that each AS in turn creates certificates for each router using the AS's private key—enabling the tracing entity to verify via the AS certificate using RPKI.[1]

[1]Alternatively, OPT can authenticate entities based on mechanisms

Table 1: Notation.

| | |
|---|---|
| $(PK_E, PK_E^{-1})$ | Entity $E$'s public-private key pair |
| $Cert_{PK_E}$ | Entity $E$'s public-key Certificate |
| $\hat{K}_{SD}$ | Long-term symmetric key between $S$ and $D$, which is valid over multiple sessions |
| $K_E$ | Symmetric key among $S$, $D$, and entity $E$ for a single session |
| $K_{E_1E_2}$ | Symmetric key between entities $E_1$ and $E_2$ for a single session |
| $K_{E_1E_2\sigma}$ | Symmetric key for $E_1$ and $E_2$ in session $\sigma$ for $E_1$-initiated packets |
| $SV_E$ | Entity $E$'s local secret value |
| $P$ | Network packet payload |
| $(PK_\sigma, PK_\sigma^{-1})$ | Public-private key pair of session $\sigma$ |
| $PATH_\sigma$ | Session $\sigma$'s path information |
| $T_\sigma$ | Time when $S$ initiates session $\sigma$ |
| SESSIONID | Hash of session $\sigma$'s public key, path, session initiation time |
| $AUTH_\sigma$ | Authenticated and encrypted SESSIONID and private key for session $\sigma$ |
| $SignKEY_{PK_E^{-1},\sigma}$ | Signature on a symmetric key for session $\sigma$ using entity $E$'s private key |
| $EncKEY_{K,\sigma}$ | Encryption of a symmetric key for session $\sigma$ using key $K$ |
| $KEYS_\sigma$ | Set of shared keys between routers and $S$ for session $\sigma$ |
| DATAHASH | Hash of the packet's payload |
| PVF | Field enabling $D$ to verify the path |
| $\text{PVF}^S$ | Field enabling $R_i$ and $D$ to verify the path |
| $\text{PVF}^D$ | Field enabling $D$ to confirm the actual path |
| $\text{OV}_i$ | Field enabling $R_i$ to validate the packet sender |
| $\text{OPV}_i$ | Field enabling $R_i$ to verify both the packet sender and path |
| $Sign_{PK_E^{-1}}(\cdot)$ | Signature using entity $E$'s private key |
| $CheckSig_{PK_E^{-1}}(\cdot)$ | Signature verification using entity $E$'s private key |
| $Enc_K(\cdot)$, $Dec_K(\cdot)$ | Encryption, decryption using key $K$ |
| $AuthEnc_K(\cdot)$ | Authenticated encryption using key $K$ |
| $AuthDec_K(\cdot)$ | Authenticated decryption using key $K$ |
| $F_K(\cdot)$ | Pseudo-random function using key $K$ |
| $MAC_K(\cdot)$ | Message Authentication Code using key $K$ |
| $H(\cdot)$ | Cryptographic hash operation |

We also assume that the source and destination entities that perform the tracing of the intermediate routers can establish a secret key between each other. In case the tracing entities are AS infrastructure hosts such as edge routers, firewalls, or a middlebox at a service provider, either RPKI can be used as described above or an administrator can set up trusted public keys between entities that need path verification. If endhosts perform tracing, then a shared key can be set up through SSL or TLS if one of the endhosts is a HTTPS server, through IPsec or SSH. The public keys can be verified through a regular PKI, administrator-based set up of trusted keys, TOFU (Trust On First Use) in SSH, TOFU with Perspectives [35], RPKI with domain-certified host keys, self-certifying IDs as public keys [1,23,24,34], or self-validation using an anonymous service [10]. We assume that one of these approaches is used to set up symmetric key $\hat{K}_{SD}$ between source $S$ and destination $D$.

## 3.2 Main Insights

One of OPT's crucial insights is our approach to avoid storing per-flow state on routers; unlike prior approaches that require each router to maintain a secret key for each flow, our design enables routers to derive the secret keys on the fly using only local secrets stored at the routers and an efficient pseudo-random function. Thus, we avoid storing all the keys.

More precisely, OPT runs in *sessions*. In each session $\sigma$, source $S$ sends packets to destination $D$ on path $PATH_\sigma$. $S$ and $D$ leverage long-term symmetric key $\hat{K}_{SD}$ to set up keys with each router in $PATH_\sigma$. DRKey, the details of which is explained in Section 4, is instrumental in achieving OPT's efficiency properties. In particular, the source prepares and inserts a special field in the packet header called SESSIONID such that intermediate routers $R_i$ on $PATH_\sigma$ dynamically compute the shared symmetric key with $S$ and $D$ ($R_i$ only needs to look up its local secret $SV_{R_i}$ for computation).

that use self-certifying IDs as public keys [1,23,24,34] as assumed in ICING. However, such mechanisms have issues with key revocations. Hence, we prefer to use RPKI.

Our key establishment mechanism does not require any per-flow state on the routers. Consequently, OPT is robust against DoS attacks based on state exhaustion. Moreover, computing pseudo-random function (PRF) $F$ is faster than performing a cache access; for instance, a key derivation using AESni takes 32 cycles, whereas a L3 cache read operation requires approximately 40 cycles (on Intel "Sandy-Bridge"-based Xeon architecture).

OPT includes the hash of the packet payload $H(P)$ in the header, which enables an important optimization: routers can either parallelize the computations of MAC and the hash of the packet, or probabilistically validate $H(P)$.

## 3.3 OPT Protocol Overview

**DRKey for path selection and key setup.** When source $S$ initiates session $\sigma$ at time $T_\sigma$, $S$ selects path $PATH_\sigma$ to destination $D$, generates asymmetric public/private key pair $(PK_\sigma, PK_\sigma^{-1})$, and creates a session identifier, where $\text{SESSIONID} = H(PK_\sigma \| PATH_\sigma \| T_\sigma)$. After preparing some values that support source authentication and path validation for other entities on $PATH_\sigma$, $S$ forwards the OPT packet to its downstream router on $PATH_\sigma$. If $T_\sigma$ is recent (i.e., within some predefined interval by the AS), each intermediate router $R_i$ sets up shared symmetric key $K_i$ using its local secret $SV_{R_i}$ and SESSIONID. Detailed DRKey protocols are explained in Section 4.

**Generation of verification fields.** $S$ uses the path information to pre-compute verification fields, one for each router $R_i$ on $PATH_\sigma$, and a special field called PVF such that routers can perform source authentication and path validation.

**Verification and update by intermediate routers.** Upon receiving a packet, $R_i$ first regenerates the shared symmetric key $K_i$ and recomputes the verification field based on PVF. When the computed value matches what is present in the packet header for $R_i$, it successfully authenticates the source and the content of the packet, and validates the traversed path. $R_i$ then updates PVF, by applying a MAC operation using $K_i$ to the field. This process helps downstream routers and the destination to validate that each router on the path has indeed seen the packet.

**Verification by destination.** The destination finally recomputes the verification fields using all the symmetric keys shared with other entities on the path. Successful verification indicates source and packet content authentication as well as path validation.

# 4. DYNAMICALLY RECREATABLE KEYS

This section introduces the DRKey protocols that enable routers to set up shared keys with source $S$ and destination $D$. Section 4.1 describes the case when both $S$ and $D$ trust each other. Section 4.2 relaxes this assumption and describes the case when $S$ and $D$ do not trust each other. Section 4.3 describes how $S$ and $D$ retroactively set up shared keys with intermediate routers to enable path validation of *prior* packets.

## 4.1 DRKey for Benign Source and Destination

When both $S$ and $D$ trust each other, each entity on the source-selected path needs to pre-establish only one symmetric key that is shared with both $S$ and $D$. Figure 1 shows the key setup steps and the associated cryptographic operations.

$S$ creates a fresh public/private key pair $(PK_\sigma, PK_\sigma^{-1})$ for each session such that routers encrypt session symmetric key $K_i$'s. Since $S$ and $D$ trust each other, they share private key $PK_\sigma^{-1}$, the encrypted and authenticated value of which is sent to $D$. The public key is used to derive the SESSIONID as follows: $\text{SESSIONID} = H(PK_\sigma \| PATH_\sigma \| T_\sigma)$, where $PATH_\sigma$ is the source-selected path and $T_\sigma$ is when $S$ initiates session $\sigma$. Note that $T_\sigma$ prevents replay attacks since routers can drop expired packets based on loose time synchronization.

**Initialization by Source $S$**

0. Assume long-term symmetric key $\hat{K}_{SD}$ shared with $D$

(Optional) Assume public/private key pair $(PK_S, PK_S^{-1})$, and $Cert_{PK_S}$

1. Initiate new session $\sigma$ and pick random session key $(PK_\sigma, PK_\sigma^{-1})$
2. Obtain $PATH_\sigma = \langle S, R_1, R_2, D \rangle$
3. Measure current time $T_\sigma$
4. Compute $\text{SESSIONID} = H(PK_\sigma \| PATH_\sigma \| T_\sigma)$

(Optional) Authenticate session: $Sign_{PK_S^{-1}}(\text{SESSIONID})$

5. Compute $K_{SD\sigma} = F_{\hat{K}_{SD}}(S\|D\|\text{SESSIONID})$
$K_{DS\sigma} = F_{\hat{K}_{SD}}(D\|S\|\text{SESSIONID})$
6. Compute $AUTH_\sigma = AuthEnc_{K_{SD\sigma}}(\text{SESSIONID}\|PK_\sigma^{-1})$

$S \rightarrow R_1$

7. Forward $\{PK_\sigma, PATH_\sigma, T_\sigma, AUTH_\sigma,$ (optional) $Sign_{PK_S^{-1}}(\text{SESSIONID})$ $\}$

**Pairwise Key Derivation by $R_1$**

8. Compute $K_1 = F_{SV_{R_1}}(\text{SESSIONID})$
9. Encrypt $K_1$: $EncKEY_{R_1,\sigma} = Enc_{PK_\sigma}(K_1)$
Sign: $SignKEY_{R_1,\sigma} = Sign_{PK_{R_1}^{-1}}(K_1\|PK_\sigma)$

$R_1 \rightarrow R_2$

10. Forward $\{PK_\sigma, PATH_\sigma, T_\sigma, AUTH_\sigma,$ (optional) $Sign_{PK_S^{-1}}(\text{SESSIONID})$, $EncKEY_{R_1,\sigma}$, $SignKEY_{R_1,\sigma}$ $\}$

**Pairwise Key Derivation by $R_2$**

11. Computes $K_2 = F_{SV_{R_2}}(\text{SESSIONID})$
12. Encrypt $K_2$: $EncKEY_{R_2,\sigma} = Enc_{PK_\sigma}(K_2)$
Sign: $SignKEY_{R_2,\sigma} = Sign_{PK_{R_2}^{-1}}(K_2\|PK_\sigma)$

$R_2 \rightarrow D$

13. Forward $\{PK_\sigma, PATH_\sigma, T_\sigma, AUTH_\sigma,$ (optional) $Sign_{PK_S}(\text{SESSIONID})$, $EncKEY_{R_1,\sigma}$, $SignKEY_{R_1,\sigma}$, $EncKEY_{R_2,\sigma}$, $SignKEY_{R_2,\sigma}\}$

**Key Retrieval by Destination $D$**

14. Already has $\hat{K}_{SD}$, which is the long-term shared symmetric key with $S$
15. Check that $D$ is the last entity on $PATH_\sigma$
16. Compute $\text{SESSIONID} = H(PK_\sigma\|PATH_\sigma\|T_\sigma)$ and check the integrity
17. Compute $K_{SD\sigma} = F_{\hat{K}_{SD}}(S\|D\|\text{SESSIONID})$
$K_{DS\sigma} = F_{\hat{K}_{SD}}(D\|S\|\text{SESSIONID})$
18. Decrypt $AUTH_\sigma$ and authenticate $PK_\sigma^{-1}$: $AuthDec_{K_{SD\sigma}}(AUTH_\sigma)$
19. Decrypt $K_1$ and $K_2$ and check their signatures:
$Dec_{PK_\sigma^{-1}}(EncKEY_{R_1,\sigma}), CheckSig_{PK_{R_1}}(SignKEY_{R_1,\sigma})$
$Dec_{PK_\sigma^{-1}}(EncKEY_{R_2,\sigma}), CheckSig_{PK_{R_2}}(SignKEY_{R_2,\sigma})$
$K_1$ and $K_2$ become shared symmetric keys between each router and $D$
20. Compute $K_D = F_{SV_D}(\text{SESSIONID})$

$D \rightarrow S$

21. Forward authenticated and encrypted shared keys:
$KEYS_\sigma = AuthEnc_{K_{DS\sigma}}(K_1\|K_2\|K_D\|AUTH_\sigma)$

**Key Retrieval by Source $S$**

22. Decrypt and authenticate the keys received from $D$: $AuthDec_{K_{DS\sigma}}(KEYS_\sigma)$
$K_1$, $K_2$ and $K_D$ become shared keys between $S$ and $R_1$, $R_2$, and $D$

**Figure 1: A session key setup for path $S \rightarrow R_1 \rightarrow R_2 \rightarrow D$.**

**Path Agreement and Key Setup Initialization by Source S**

1. Initiate new session $\sigma$and pick random session key $(PK_{S\sigma}, PK_{S\sigma}^{-1})$
$R_i$ uses this key to authenticate $S$'s packets
2. Obtain $PATH_\sigma = \langle S, R_1, R_2, D\rangle$
3. Measure current time $T_\sigma$
4. Compute $\text{SESSIONID}_S = H(PK_{S\sigma}\|PATH_\sigma\|T_\sigma)$

(Optional) Authenticate session: $Sign_{PK_S^{-1}}(\text{SESSIONID}_S)$

$S \rightarrow D$

5. Forward $\{PK_{S\sigma}, PATH_\sigma, T_\sigma, Sign_{PK_S^{-1}}(PK_{S\sigma}\|PATH_\sigma\|T_\sigma)\}$

**Path Agreement and Key Setup Initialization by Destination D**

6. Pick random session key $(PK_{D\sigma}, PK_{D\sigma}^{-1})$ that $R_i$ uses with $D$
7. Compute $\text{SESSIONID}_D = H(PK_{D\sigma}\|PATH_\sigma\|T_\sigma)$

(Optional) Authenticate session: $Sign_{PK_D^{-1}}(\text{SESSIONID}_D)$

$D \rightarrow S$

8. Forward $\{PK_{D\sigma}, PATH_\sigma, T_\sigma, Sign_{PK_D^{-1}}(PK_{S\sigma}\|PK_{D\sigma}\|PATH_\sigma)$, $\text{SESSIONID}_D$, (optional) $Sign_{PK_D^{-1}}(\text{SESSIONID}_D)$ $\}$

**Initialization by S**

$S \rightarrow R_1$

9. Forward $\{PK_{S\sigma}, PK_{D\sigma}, PATH_\sigma, T_\sigma,$ (optional) $Sign_{PK_S^{-1}}(\text{SESSIONID}_S), Sign_{PK_D^{-1}}(\text{SESSIONID}_D)$ $\}$

**Pairwise Key Derivation by $R_1$**

10. Compute $K_{S1} = F_{SV_{R_1 S}}(\text{SESSIONID}_S))$
$K_{D1} = F_{SV_{R_1 D}}(\text{SESSIONID}_D))$
11. Encrypt $K_{S1}$: $EncKEY_{R_1 S,\sigma} = Enc_{PK_{S\sigma}}(K_{S1})$
$K_{S2}$: $EncKEY_{R_1 D,\sigma} = Enc_{PK_{D\sigma}}(K_{D1})$
12. Sign: $SignKEY_{R_1 S,\sigma} = Sign_{PK_{R_1}^{-1}}(K_{S1}\|PK_{S\sigma}\|S)$
$SignKEY_{R_1 D,\sigma} = Sign_{PK_{R_1}^{-1}}(K_{D1}\|PK_{D\sigma}\|D)$

$R_1 \rightarrow R_2$

13. Forward $\{PK_{S\sigma}, PK_{D\sigma}, PATH_\sigma, T_\sigma,$ (optional) $Sign_{PK_S^{-1}}(\text{SESSIONID}_S), Sign_{PK_D^{-1}}(\text{SESSIONID}_D)$, $EncKEY_{R_1 S,\sigma}, SignKEY_{R_1 S,\sigma}, EncKEY_{R_1 D,\sigma}, SignKEY_{R_1 D,\sigma}\}$

**Pairwise Key Derivation by $R_2$**

14. Compute $K_{S2} = F_{SV_{R_2 S}}(\text{SESSIONID}_S))$
$K_{D2} = F_{SV_{R_2 D}}(\text{SESSIONID}_D))$
15. Encrypt $K_{S2}$: $EncKEY_{R_2 S,\sigma} = Enc_{PK_{S\sigma}}(K_{S2})$
$K_{S2}$: $EncKEY_{R_2 D,\sigma} = Enc_{PK_{D\sigma}}(K_{D2})$
16. Sign: $SignKEY_{R_2 S,\sigma} = Sign_{PK_{R_2}^{-1}}(K_{S2}\|PK_{S\sigma}\|S)$
$SignKEY_{R_2 D,\sigma} = Sign_{PK_{R_2}^{-1}}(K_{D2}\|PK_{D\sigma}\|D)$

$R_2 \rightarrow D$

17. Forward $\{PK_{S\sigma}, PK_{D\sigma}, PATH_\sigma, T_\sigma,$ (optional) $Sign_{PK_S^{-1}}(\text{SESSIONID}_S), Sign_{PK_D^{-1}}(\text{SESSIONID}_D)$, $EncKEY_{R_1 S,\sigma}, SignKEY_{R_1 S,\sigma}, EncKEY_{R_1 D,\sigma}, SignKEY_{R_1 D,\sigma}$, $EncKEY_{R_2 S,\sigma}, SignKEY_{R_2 S,\sigma}, EncKEY_{R_2 D,\sigma}, SignKEY_{R_2 D,\sigma}\}$

**Key Retrieval by D**

18. Check that $D$ is the last entry in $PATH_\sigma$
19. Decrypt $K_{D1}$ and $K_{D2}$ and check their signatures
$Dec_{PK_{D\sigma}^{-1}}(EncKEY_{R_1 D,\sigma}), CheckSig_{PK_{R_1}}(SignKEY_{R_1 S,\sigma})$
$Dec_{PK_{D\sigma}^{-1}}(EncKEY_{R_2 D,\sigma}), CheckSig_{PK_{R_2}}(SignKEY_{R_2 S,\sigma})$
$K_{D1}$ and $K_{D2}$ become shared symmetric key between each router and $D$
20. Compute $K_D = F_{SV_D}(\text{SESSIONID}_S))$
21. Encrypt $K_D$: $EncKEY_{D,\sigma} = Enc_{PK_{S\sigma}}(K_D)$
22. Sign: $SignKEY_{D,\sigma} = Sign_{PK_D^{-1}}(K_D\|PK_{S\sigma}\|S)$

$D \rightarrow S$

23. Forward $\{EncKEY_{R_1 S,\sigma}, SignKEY_{R_1 S,\sigma}, EncKEY_{R_2 S,\sigma}, SignKEY_{R_2 S,\sigma}$, $EncKEY_{D,\sigma}, SignKEY_{D,\sigma}\}$

**Key Retrieval by Source $S$**

24. Decrypt and authenticate keys received from $D$
$K_{S1}$, $K_{S2}$ and $K_D$ become shared keys between $S$ and $R_1$, $R_2$, and $D$.

**Figure 2: A modified session key setup when $S$ and $D$ do not trust each other. The path is: $S \rightarrow R_1 \rightarrow R_2 \rightarrow D$.**

Each intermediate router $R_i$ generates shared key $K_i$ using an efficient PRF keyed with a secret $SV_i$ only known to $R_i$. The PRF takes SESSIONID as an input. For high efficiency, we compute our PRF from a pseudo-random permutation using AES. The overhead of the key setup is negligible to affect the on-going traffic (see Section 8). Resulting key $K_i$ is encrypted with public key $PK_\sigma$, and digitally signed to enable verification that (encrypted) $K_i$ indeed originates from the correct router (as any entity could have performed the public-key encryption on an arbitrary key).

To prevent reflection attacks (i.e., replaying message in the opposite order of communication), communication between $S$ and $D$ uses different symmetric keys for each direction: $K_{SD\sigma}$ and $K_{DS\sigma}$ for $S$-initiated and $D$-initiated packets, respectively.

The optional operations in Figure 1 are used only if the router also needs to authenticate $S$, in which case $S$ also signs the SESSIONID, and certificates needed for routers to verify $S$'s public key are included in the message.

## 4.2 Extended-DRKey for Distrusting Source and Destination

When we assume that the source $S$ and the destination $D$ trust each other and that they share the same public-private key pair for the session, then each intermediate router needs to set up only one shared key with both $S$ and $D$. However, $S$ and $D$ may not necessarily trust each other, or they may collude. To strengthen the security guarantees under such circumstances, we introduce *Extended-DRKey* , which requires each intermediate router to set up two keys, $K_{Si}$ and $K_{Di}$, where $K_{Si}$ is the shared symmetric key between $S$ and $R_i$ and $K_{Di}$ is the shared symmetric key between $R_i$ and $D$. Figure 2 describes the Extended-DRKey protocol and its cryptographic operations.

Unlike DRKey in Section 4.1, Extended-DRKey does not require $AUTH_\sigma$ since $R_i$ shares different keys with $S$ and $D$. For creating shared keys (i.e., $K_{Si}$ and $K_{Di}$), $R_i$ and $D$ use distinct local secrets to encode the directionality of the keys.

## 4.3 Retroactive-DRKey

The key setup protocols as presented in Figures 1 and 2 run *once* before the session starts. However, the key setup process incurs the following extra latency and computational overhead: (1) Key setup itself requires an extra round trip between the source and the destination; and (2) Key setup requires each intermediate router to encrypt and sign its shared key. Furthermore, running an independent key setup protocol *a priori* allows routers to launch a coward attack, since the key setup protocol warns possibly misbehaving routers to start behaving correctly and to avoid detection. Consequently, achieving path validation without the apparent key setup process is desirable.

We introduce Retroactive-DRKey that enables entities to set up shared keys at any time *after* the first packet in a session reaches the destination. Note that Retroactive-OPT is invoked only if the source or the destination wishes to perform source authentication or path validation (i.e., there could be sessions during which the source or the destination performs *no* retroactive key setup).

To support such a feature, we still assume that source $S$ and destination $D$ establish a shared symmetric key $\hat{K}_{SD}$ in advance, and $S$ derives a session key pair $(PK_\sigma, PK_\sigma^{-1})$ before the session starts. Unlike DRKey or Extended-DRKey, Retroactive-DRKey utilizes that $S$ creates $K_D$—a shared symmetric key with $D$ for the session (i.e. $K_D = F_{SV_S}(\text{SESSIONID})$)—and includes encrypted and authenticated $K_D$in $AUTH_\sigma$ in the data packets of the forwarding protocol header. In this way, $S$ can already use $K_D$ to compute some fields such that $D$ can check. When a forwarding protocol is used with Retroactive-DRKey, the routers use some keys for OPT during a session, and only reveal them at a later time (Section 5.2.1).

Retroactive-DRKey is very similar to the key setup protocol in Figure 1. The only difference is that $D$ does not derive $K_D$, because it is already included in each forwarded packet. Retroactive-DRKey runs *at most once* during or after a session ends. We observe that $S$ can set $T_\sigma$ to a future time when $S$ may want to trigger source and path validation if $S$ of $D$ detect an anomaly.

# 5. OPT PROTOCOL DESCRIPTION

The DRKey protocols described in Section 4 and the techniques we introduce in this section span a protocol family of source authentication and path validation with varying assumptions and properties. Unfortunately, exploring the entire design space is out of scope for this paper, and we will present several protocol instantiations: (1) *OriginValidation* for source authentication (S and D trust each other), (2) *PathTrace* for path validation (S and D trust each other), and (3) *Origin and Path Trace (OPT)* for source authentication and path validation (S and D may not trust each other).

## 5.1 OriginValidation for Source Authentication

OriginValidation enables each intermediate router and the destination to perform source authentication using MACs computed over the hash of the packet. For efficient authentication, the source includes the following fields in the packet header:

- DATAHASH: Hash of the packet's payload $H(P)$;
- SESSIONID: Hash of the session public key, path, and session initiation time $H(PK_\sigma \| PATH_\sigma \| T_\sigma)$;
- $\text{OV}_i$: Origin Verification field. $\text{OV}_i$ is a Message Authentication Code computed over DATAHASH using key $K_i$ that $R_i$ shares with $S$ (i.e., $\text{OV}_i = MAC_{K_i}(H(P))$). Similarly, $\text{OV}_D = MAC_{K_D}(H(P))$. The source creates an OV field for each intermediate router and the destination.

OriginValidation provides efficient MAC verification using the DATAHASH field without requiring each intermediate router to compute the hash over the entire packet. Figure 3 represents the packet header, and only DATAHASH, SESSIONID and OV fields are needed for OriginValidation.

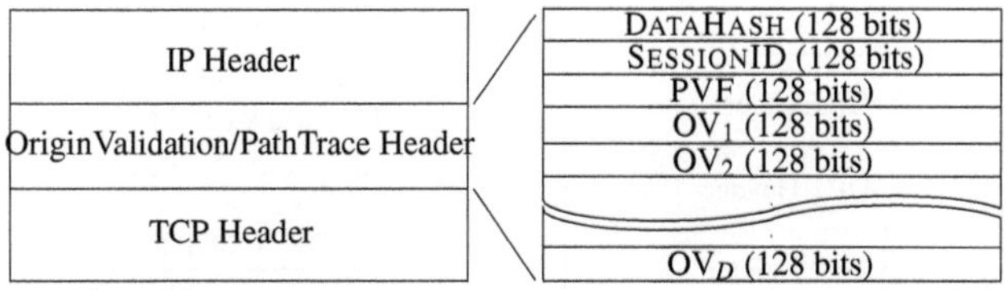


**Figure 3: The packet header format for OriginValidation and PathTrace. DATAHASH, SESSIONID, and OVs help intermediate routers and the destination authenticate the source (OriginValidation), and DATAHASH, SESSIONID, and PVF help the destination validate the path (PathTrace).**

When intermediate router $R_1$ receives a packet from the source $S$, $R_1$ computes the symmetric key $(K_1)$ it shares with $S$ using $R_1$'s local secret and SESSIONID from the packet header. Then $R_1$ generates a MAC as follows: $\text{OV}'_1 = MAC_{K_1}(\text{DATAHASH})$. If $\text{OV}'_1$ is the same as $\text{OV}_1$ in the packet header, $R_1$ is assured that the packet indeed originated from the claimed source $S$, and forwards the packet to $R_2$. $R_2$ and $D$ perform the same operations as $R_1$.

Although we present the protocol with OV fields of size 128, the size can be altered to reflect the desired level of security. In general, assuming a secure MAC function, the success probability of a forged $n$-bit MAC is $2^{-n}$, which already results in a low rate at $n = 16$. Thus, for many applications, 2 byte long OV fields suffice, as a router would only let 1 in 65536 packets pass on average.

## 5.2 PathTrace

PathTrace is to help the source and destination validate that a received packet traversed the source-selected path. This main objective is achieved by Path Validation Field (PVF), which is a nested MAC that intermediate routers update in the packet header as they forward the packet. In Figure 3, only DATAHASH, SESSIONID, and PVF fields are used for PathTrace, thus, the packet overhead is irrespective of the path length. Next we describe how PathTrace supports the source and the destination to validate the path.

**PathTrace for destination.** To enable *only* the destination to validate the path, the source generates $\text{PVF}_0$—the initial PVF value which is a MAC of DATAHASH using the shared symmetric key between the source and the destination. Then the source initializes the PVF field in the header with $\text{PVF}_0$:

$$\text{PVF} \leftarrow \text{PVF}_0 = MAC_{K_D}(\text{DATAHASH}). \tag{1}$$

Any intermediate router $R_i$ on the path generates $\text{PVF}_i$ and updates the PVF field in the header as follows:

$$\text{PVF} \leftarrow \text{PVF}_i = MAC_{K_i}(\text{DATAHASH}\|\text{PVF}_{i-1}). \tag{2}$$

The shared symmetric key $K_i$ is shared with *both* the source and the destination according to the key setup protocol in Section 4.1. Hence, upon receiving a packet, the destination first re-creates the nested MACs (here shown for a path of 2 routers):

$$\begin{aligned}\text{PVF}' &= MAC_{K_2}(\text{DATAHASH}\| \\ &\quad MAC_{K_1}(\text{DATAHASH}\|MAC_{K_D}(\text{DATAHASH}))).\end{aligned} \tag{3}$$

If $\text{PVF}'$ is the same as PVF in the packet header, the destination is assured that the packet was indeed delivered on the source-selected path. Otherwise, the destination drops the packet.

**PathTrace for source.** To help the source authenticate that its packet is delivered to the intended destination using the source-selected path, the destination forwards the PVF from the received

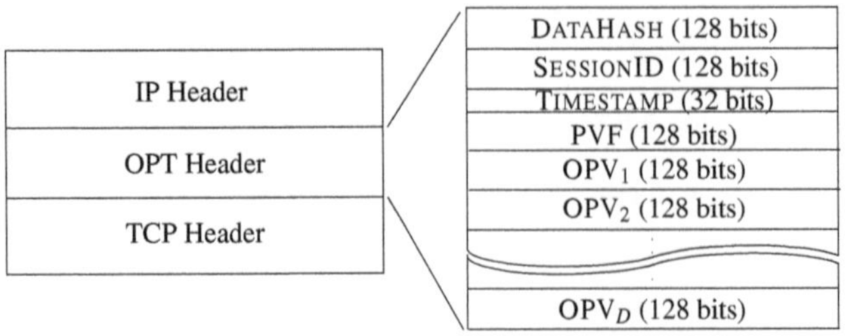


**Figure 4: OPT header. The source $S$ initializes all the fields. Intermediate routers only update the PVF field.**

packet header back to the source as follows:

$$D \rightarrow S : Enc_{K_D}(\text{PVF} \| \text{DATAHASH}). \quad (4)$$

Upon receiving this information, the source first decrypts the message using $K_D$ and then performs the validation by re-constructing the nested MACs using DATAHASH as shown in Eq. (3) and comparing it with PVF. A successful validation indicates that the packet was indeed delivered on the source-selected path.

### 5.2.1 *Retroactive-PathTrace*

Retroactive-PathTrace supports path validation without the apparent key setup process in advance. Instead, it utilizes Retroactive-DRKey that runs after the session ends. Unlike PathTrace, in Retroactive-PathTrace the source cannot pre-compute the $\text{OPV}_i$ fields; hence no OPV fields can be used in the packet header. Instead, under the assumption that the source and the destination trust each other, Retroactive-PathTrace requires that the source creates $K_D$—the session-specific shared key with the destination, and the source additionally includes $K_D$ and its authenticated encryption in the packet header. The source uses $K_D$ to compute $\text{PVF}_0$ and the routers derive their shared key and update the PVF field accordingly.

Retroactive-PathTrace requires the destination to store per-packet information for later checking. However, the benefit of defending against coward attacks overcomes such a disadvantage. Namely, the destination stores for each packet the tuple (SESSIONID, DATAHASH,PVF). When the destination wants to validate the path, it requests the source to initiate Retroactive-DRKey such that intermediate routers reveal the key that was used for the received packets. Then the destination can check the PVF fields and detect coward attacks. The source can independently initiate the retroactive process as well.

## 5.3 OPT: Origin and Path Trace

In this section, we introduce OPT that combines OriginValidation and PathTrace such that all entities (including intermediate routers) on the path can perform both source authentication and path validation when they trust the source. We assume that all the routers in a session are loosely time synchronized (within a few milliseconds, e.g., using NTP).[2]

Figure 4 illustrates the OPT header format. In addition to DATAHASH, SESSIONID, and PVF, an OPT header includes the following additional fields to enable each intermediate router to perform path validation.

- TIMESTAMP: Time when $S$ creates the OPT packet to mitigate timing-based attacks, such as replay attacks.
- $\text{OPV}_i$: Origin and Path Verification field. $\text{OPV}_i$ is a MAC that enables all entities on the path to perform path validation.

[2]http://www.ntp.org/

**Algorithm 1** OPT header initialization and validation pseudo code. An arrow represents the header field initialization.

**function** SOURCE INITIALIZATION
**Require:** $K_i$ and $K_D$ that $R_i$'s and $D$ share with $S$, respectively after running key setup protocol in Figure 1
  DATAHASH $\leftarrow H(P)$
  SESSIONID $\leftarrow H(PK_\sigma \| PATH_\sigma \| T_\sigma)$
  PVF $\leftarrow \text{PVF}_0 = MAC_{K_D}(\text{DATAHASH})$
  $l$ = source-selected path length
  **for** each intermediate router $R_i$, where $1 \leq i < l$ **do**
    $\text{PVF}_i = MAC_{K_i}(\text{PVF}_{i-1})$
    $\text{OPV}_i \leftarrow MAC_{K_i}(\text{PVF}_{i-1} \| \text{DATAHASH} \| R_{i-1} \| \text{TIMESTAMP})$
  **end for**
  **for** destination $D$ **do**
    $\text{OPV}_D \leftarrow MAC_{K_D}(\text{PVF}_{l-1} \| \text{DATAHASH} \| R_{l-1} \| \text{TIMESTAMP})$
  **end for**
  TIMESTAMP $\leftarrow$ current time
**end function**

**function** VALIDATION AND UPDATE BY $R_i$
  (Note PVF in OPT header = $\text{PVF}_{i-1}$)
  Compute $\text{OPV}'_i = MAC_{K_i}(\text{PVF}_{i-1} \| \text{DATAHASH} \| R_{i-1} \| \text{TIMESTAMP})$
  **if** $\text{OPV}'_i == \text{OPV}_i$ **then**
    PVF $\leftarrow \text{PVF}_i = MAC_{K_i}(\text{PVF}_{i-1})$
    Forward the packet to $R_{i+1}$
  **else**
    Drop the packet
  **end if**
**end function**

**function** DESTINATION VALIDATION
  (Note PVF in OPT header = $\text{PVF}_{l-1}$)
  $l$ = source-selected path length
  Compute $\text{PVF}' = MAC_{K_{l-1}}(\ldots(MAC_{K_1}(MAC_{K_D}(\text{DATAHASH}))))$
  Compute $\text{OPV}'_D = MAC_{K_D}(\text{PVF}_{l-1} \| \text{DATAHASH} \| R_{l-1} \| \text{TIMESTAMP})$
  **if** ($\text{PVF}' == \text{PVF}$) && ($\text{OPV}'_D == \text{OPV}_D$) **then**
    Validation succeeds
    Prepare packet using Eq. (4) and forward to source
  **else**
    Drop the packet
  **end if**
**end function**

The SOURCE INITIALIZATION pseudo code in Algorithm 1 describes how the source initializes the OPT header fields. Each OPV field includes the following as inputs.

**Previous PVF:** Including $\text{PVF}_{i-1}$ in the $\text{OPV}_i$ computation supports the detection of a malicious intermediate router that forwards the packet to a benign router, which is not specified by the source but follows the protocol.

**Previous router address:** PVF by itself cannot support entities to detect the packet injection attack. Hence, we include the address of the previous router from which each entity receives the packet.

**TIMESTAMP:** This field mitigates authenticator cloning attacks. Consider an example where packet $P_{crt}$ is expected to be sent along the source-selected path $PATH_{crt}$, the source previously sent packet $P_{old}$ on $PATH_{old}$, and $P_{crt}$ and $P_{old}$ have the same payload. Consider router $R_{bad}$ that is in both $PATH_{crt}$ and $PATH_{old}$ such that $PATH_{crt} = \{R_1, R_2, \ldots, R_{bad}, R_{bad+1}, \ldots, R_n\}$ and $PATH_{old} = \{R'_1, R'_2, \ldots, R_{bad}, R'_{bad+1}, \ldots, R_m\}$. In this scenario, $R_{bad}$ can replace $\{R_{bad+1}, \ldots, R_n\}$ with $\{R'_{bad+1}, \ldots, R_m\}$ in $PATH_{crt}$ and all the corresponding fields in the $P_{crt}$ header with those in $P_{old}$. Therefore, without TIMESTAMP, the destination cannot detect the misbehavior and ends up validating path $\{R_1, R_2, \ldots, R_{bad}, R'_{bad+1}, \ldots, R_m\}$ for $P_{crt}$. By setting the TIMESTAMP field when the source sends out a packet, authenticator cloning attacks are mitigated with loose time synchronization between the source and other entities on the path.

VALIDATION AND UPDATE BY $R_i$ and DESTINATION VALIDATION functions in Algorithm 1 describe the OPT procedure that intermediate router $R_i$ and the destination performs, respectively.

### 5.3.1 Distrusting source and destination

The previous protocols assumes that the source and the destination are honest and trust each other. We now relax this assumption and present an extension that handles distrusting entities. In OPT, the source can generate all PVFs by itself since it knows all $K_i$'s. Consequently, a malicious source can collude with an intermediate router (e.g., $R_2$) and forward the packet on a path $S \rightarrow R_2 \rightarrow D$ without going through $R_1$ in Figure 1.

To prevent such an attack and address the problem of a distrusting source and destination, we use the key setup protocol in Section 4.2 such that intermediate routers generate two separate shared keys for the source and the destination. Unlike OPT, the Extended-OPT header requires two PVF fields: $\text{PVF}^S$ that enables intermediate routers and the destination to validate the source, and $\text{PVF}^D$ that enables the destination to confirm the *actual* path, even if the source is malicious and colludes with (at least) one intermediate router.

## 6. SECURITY ANALYSIS

We prove that OPT has origin authenticity and path validation properties when both the source and the destination are trusted. This property holds on any network configuration, including ones that have malicious routers. Extended-OPT offers stronger properties: the router's origin and path validation property assumes that only the source is honest; and the destination's path validation property does not assume the source is honest.

We describe how OPT and its variants defend against the adversary model described in Section 2.3. OPT's security properties have been formally verified using the Coq interactive theorem prover; details can be found in our technical report [17].

**Packet alteration.** Without the secret keys ($K_D$ and $K_i$), a malicious router cannot compute valid $\text{PVF}_i$ and $\text{OPV}_i$. Consequently, in OPT, a successful verification of $\text{PVF}_{i-1}$ ($\text{PVF}_n$) based on $\text{OPV}_i$ ($\text{OPV}_D$) implies that there can be no packet alteration attacks to router $R_i$ (the destination), provided that the source and destination are trusted. A malicious destination can carry out the packet alteration attack, as it can generate all the necessary PVF and OPV fields. Extended-OPT provides similar protections for intermediary routers except that only the source needs to be trusted.

**Packet injection attack.** OPT routers can check that an incoming packet does come from an intended AS, as such information is included in OPV. Therefore, a malicious router $A$ can only inject packet to a router $B$ if $A$ is $B$'s neighbor and the link $AB$ is on the intended path. We will revisit this attack when discussing collusion attacks.

In order to inject a packet with a valid header, an attacker can replay a previously seen packet, which is only possible when the same payload has been sent on that path before. Such replay attacks can be mitigated by including a timestamp in the packet. OPT is also vulnerable to packet injection when the destination colludes with the injecting router.

**Path deviation attack.** OPT ensures that a successful verification of $\text{PVF}_{i-1}$ ($\text{PVF}_n$) against $\text{OPV}_i$ ($\text{OPV}_D$) implies that the payload $R_i$ (the destination) received has traversed all the honest routers in the source-intended path in the correct order, assuming that both source and destination are honest. OPT provides this guarantee because the attacker does not possess the secret keys required to compute $\text{PVF}_i$ and $\text{OPV}_i$, and thus cannot generate valid $\text{PVF}_i$ or $\text{OPV}_i$. As a result, malicious routers cannot mount router skipping or out-of-order traversal attacks.

This indicates that if a malicious router selects a path not intended by the source, an honest intermediary router will reject the packet. However, a malicious router can mount a path detour attack and send the payload to other routers that are not on the intended path.

In Extended-OPT, even if the destination is malicious, it cannot select the unauthorized path that drops or reorders honest routers. Extended-OPT also assures the destination that neither the malicious routers nor the malicious source can select a path that drops or reorders honest routers on the source-intended path.

**Coward attack.** Retroactive-OPT can mitigate coward attacks by requiring all forwarding routers to compute relevant PVF and OPV fields for probabilistic auditing. As a router cannot reliably guess when audits will happen, it does not know when to carry out an attack. We are unaware of any other path validation protocols that can defend against the coward attack, including ICING.

**DoS attack.** We consider attacks aiming to exhaust memory and computational resources on routers (Section 2.3). Each OPT router stores only a secret value ($SV_{R_i}$), regardless of the number of sources sending traffic and the number of flows transiting the router. For this reason, memory exhaustion attacks are not possible under OPT. OPT routers perform very few symmetric cryptographic operations per packet during forwarding, which run at line speed (Section 7). Therefore, OPT is more resilient to computation resource exhaustion attacks than existing schemes such as ICING that provide similar security guarantees.

**Collusion.** The path and source validation are conditioned upon whether a router is honest, i.e., correctly runs the protocol. When no two malicious routers are adjacent to each other on the intended path before $R_i$, malicious routers can redirect the packet to any routers as it chooses. However, all preceding links on the desired path are still traversed in the correct sequence for this packet to be accepted by $R_i$. Similarly, a malicious router could replace the path in the packet and trick its neighbor into forwarding the packet to a router outside the intended path. Again, this packet will be dropped when it reaches an honest router.

When there are multiple adjacent malicious routers on the intended path ($R_{j1}$ to $R_{jn}$), a wormhole is present: an honest router down the path can only conclude that the packet has entered into the hole via $R_{j1}$ and exited the hole from $R_{jn}$, but has no knowledge as to where the packet has been to in between these two points. In particular, when the source colludes with $R_i$, $R_{i+1}$ can be tricked into accepting and forwarding any packet.

## 7. IMPLEMENTATION AND EVALUATION

We implemented OPT in Section 5.3 with DRKey as a user-level application that performs source authentication and path validation.

The cryptographic operations performed by a router during packet forwarding are purely symmetric cryptographic operations, which we instantiate with the AES block cipher. We list the cryptographic functions used in the implementation. To compute MACs, we used CBC-MAC based on AES, since it requires a single AES operation to authenticate a 128-bit value. For computing the PRF, we also use the same CBC-MAC. We implement AES using AESni, a new CPU instruction set provided by recent Intel and AMD CPUs to speed up AES operations. AESni is fast: According to Intel, executing an encryption using AES-128 in CBC mode takes 4.15 cycles per byte to encrypt a 1 KB buffer [13]. While this number bounds the processing latency per byte, router throughput can be increased, as we can process 4 blocks in parallel on a single core in AES-128 in CBC mode, resulting in 1.33 cycles per byte. We implemented authenticated encryption using Galois/Counter Mode (GCM) with AES.

We use SHA-3 for computing hashes on long strings, such as the hash of the payload DATAHASH. We truncate the hash from

**Table 2: Per-session storage ($\sigma$), long-term storage (LT) related to the key setup, and communication overhead of DRKey's and ICING's key setup for a path of length $n$.**

| | | Router | Source | Destination |
|---|---|---|---|---|
| **Storage [#items]** | DRKey ($\sigma$) | 0 | $n+2$ | $n+2$ |
| | ICING ($\sigma$) | 2 | $n+1$ | $2*n+1$ |
| | DRKey (LT) | 1 | 1 | 2 |
| | ICING (LT) | $\leq$ 400,000 | 0 | 0 |
| **Key setup [#packets]** | DRKey | 2 | | |
| | ICING | $4*n+4$ | | |

a 256-bit value to a 128-bit value. For computing hashes on short strings, such as $H(PK_\sigma)$, we use the Merkle-Damgard construction with a Matyas-Meyer-Oseas AES-based compression function that makes use of the fast hardware AESni instructions. We choose a single-block-length compression function that outputs 128-bit hash values. We use 128-bit hash values to obtain a smaller OPT header size. Nevertheless, this decision does not pose security concerns: an adversary besides the source needs to perform a second-pre-image collision attack, which is still in the order of $O(2^{128})$ for SHA-3 and close to $O(2^{128})$ for Matyas-Meyer-Oseas.

For signatures, we use Ed25519 [6], providing high efficiency and security, and small signatures. For a security level of $2^{128}$ operations, Ed25519 signature generation and verification on a 3.4GHz Core i7 takes $20us$ and $60us$, respectively. Public keys and signatures are only 32 and 64 bytes, respectively. Certificates can thus be as small as 128 bytes, enabling routers to add their certificate to the key setup message. As explained in Section 3, router certificates can be generated by an AS and signed with the AS's private key. The AS's public key can be obtained and verified through RPKI.

For encrypting routers' keys in DRKey, we use RSA-2048, which offers fast encryption. Although decryption is an order of magnitude slower, it is performed by the endhost which is less performance critical.

**ICING implementation and configuration.** We compare OPT with ICING, the code of which we obtained from their website[3]. To ensure the fairness of our comparison, we implemented ICING that also uses AESni. In ICING, the source obtains a proof of consent (PoC) from the consent server of each node on the path. A PoC certifies that the node consents to the full path. Furthermore, each node has an associated tag that describes a set of actions that the source can take for packets. The authors describe an optimization for computing the tag keys needed for the PoCs [25], which can diminish the number of required PRF rounds to 0. In our ICING implementation, we favor ICING and consider that computing these keys has no computational or memory lookup overhead.

Another important concept in ICING is the proofs of provenance (PoPs)—proofs to the nodes that the packet originates from the sender. Computing PoPs requires shared symmetric keys between each pair of ICING nodes on the path. These keys can be either derived on demand, using non-interactive Diffie-Hellman, or cached once computed. Since non-interactive Diffie-Hellman is expensive and impractical on the fast path, PoP keys are always retrieved from the cache in our ICING implementation.

## 7.1 DRKey Evaluation

DRKey enables the design of low-overhead protocols in terms of router resources, such as OPT. In OPT, we use DRKey for key setup, which is executed once per session. Thus, the key setup cost is amortized over an OPT session.

Table 2 provides an analysis of *storage overhead* at the source, destination, and intermediate routers for DRKey and ICING. We also compare the *communication overhead* for setting up keys.

[3]`http://www.cs.utexas.edu/icing/`

**Table 3: Packet latency during DRKey processing.**

| Entity | Path length | Latency |
|---|---|---|
| Router | Irrelevant | 381 $\mu s$ |
| Source | 2 | 621 $\mu s$ |
| | 4 | 609 $\mu s$ |
| | 8 | 628 $\mu s$ |
| Destination | 2 | 3820 $\mu s$ |
| | 4 | 5520 $\mu s$ |
| | 8 | 14814 $\mu s$ |

Given a path of length $n$ (excluding the source and the destination), DRKey requires the source and the destination to store, per session, $n+1$ symmetric keys and a public-private session key pair. The long-term storage of the source and the destination, which outlives multiple sessions, consists of their shared symmetric key and the destination's secret value. The OPT routers do not store any per-session information. Instead, the routers merely store a single local secret each.

In contrast, ICING's source and destination need to store $n+1$ symmetric keys. Each ICING router needs to store pairwise keys with every router in the Internet, which, according to the ICING authors, is within 400,000. The source also stores PoCs of all entities in the path.

Regarding the communication overhead of the key setup in DRKey, the source and the destination send one message each, resulting in 2 messages per session *regardless of the path length.* In ICING, however, the source contacts the PoC server of every node on the path (routers and destination), which leads to $2*(n+1)$ messages for a path of length $n$. The source also sets up pairwise shared keys with each entity on the path, requiring at least a round trip (2 messages) per entity, resulting in at least $2*(n+1)$ messages. We do not count the messages that are necessary to set up pairwise shared keys between ICING routers, because these keys are set up once between all entities in the Internet and then stored at each entity.

To prove the efficiency of DRKey, we evaluate the *per-packet computation overhead* at the source, destination and intermediate routers. Our experiment measures the latency of key setup packets while they transit the network entities. For the experiment, we use a traffic generator that initiates key setup operations and connects to a server that performs the key setup operations of the source, router, or destination. After the key setup, the server forwards the packets back to the traffic generator, which measures the receive rate.

Table 3 presents the latency of DRKey packets at the source, routers, and the destination. The results show that our cryptographic algorithm choices optimize router performance, which is in any case independent of path length.

For the source and the destination, a longer path increases the amount of computation. In the case of the source, this is hardly noticeable, because the source does not perform public-key cryptography operations that depend on the path length. In contrast, the destination performs per-hop public-key decryption using RSA-2048 to obtain the shared keys, which is expensive and considerably affects the latency. Nevertheless, the results satisfy our objectives: since the source and the destination have a significantly lower traffic throughput than routers, they can spend more cycles on performing key setup.

## 7.2 OPT Evaluation

We evaluate OPT with respect to the desired performance proper-

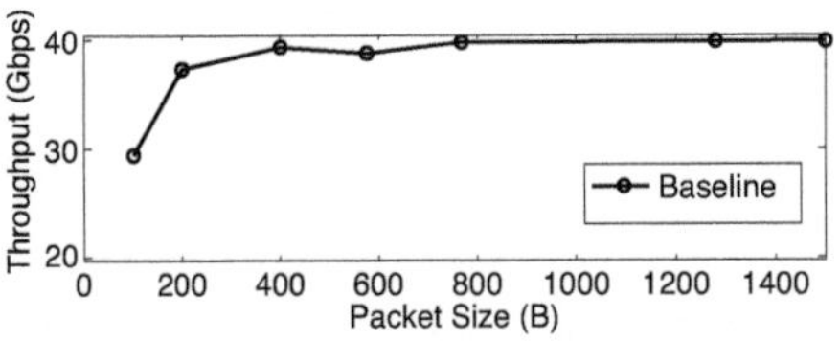


**Figure 5: Throughput of I/O Engine. Since our experiments use I/O Engine for traffic delivery, I/O engine represents our baseline.**

ties for source and path validation, namely *efficient forwarding* and *scalable state*, and the cost associated with meeting them. Specifically, we examine (1) OPT's overhead in terms of per-packet processing by measuring both the *throughput* (the bandwidth utilized by whole packets including the Ethernet header)[4] and *goodput* (the bandwidth used to transmit the payload of the packets, excluding the OPT protocol header); and (2) scalability with respect to the path length. For our evaluation, we set up a software router that validates the source and the path of the incoming packets before forwarding them. Our comparison is with ICING [26], which we discuss in more detail in Section 9 since both provide similar security guarantees. We experiment with OPT and ICING to perform source and path validations and we use PacketShader's I/O Engine [15] to send/receive packets to/from the NICs.

A central aspect of our work is the forwarding speed of a router. Since OPT does not keep any per-source or per-flow state, an OPT router's forwarding speed is not influenced by varying the number of sources sending packets or the number of flows transiting a router. In contrast, we analyze the impact of (1) cryptographic operations and (2) memory lookup of cryptographic keys, because the forwarding overhead of path validation protocols that use cryptography depends on these metrics.

**Evaluation system.** Our testbed consists of two routers A and B. Both are equipped with two Intel Ethernet Server Adapter X520-T2 NICs, and they both run Ubuntu Linux Kernel version 3.2.0-3. System A runs a traffic generator featuring 6 x 2GB DDR3 RAM and two Xeon L5640 2.26GHz (6 cores) processors. System B runs our software router code featuring 16 x 4GB DDR3 RAM and two Intel Xeon E5-2680 2.70GHz (8 cores) processors. The traffic generator generates traffic at a rate of $40Gbps$, which is processed on the software router and sent back for measurement.

## 7.3 Experiment setup

We first describe how packets are forwarded from one router to the other. Then we describe the software router implementation for source authentication and path validation for OPT and ICING.

We use PacketShader's I/O Engine [15], a high-speed open source implementation to send/receive packets to/from the NICs. On the sending router, I/O Engine takes the packets generated by the user-level traffic generator and sends them to the NIC. When the packets arrive at the second router's NIC, I/O Engine takes the packets from the NIC and delivers them to the user-level application, where they are processed according to the protocol (OPT or ICING). The last step is to send these packets back to the first router. In the remainder of this section we consider the packet processing that takes place at the second router from the moment I/O Engine delivers the packets to the user-level application and until the packets are ready to be sent back.

**Experiments.** We measure the forwarding speed of the software router for OPT and ICING. Our experiments consider AS-level path validation scenarios, where path validation is performed at a single router (e.g., ingress router) within an AS. Since an AS is administered by a single authority and its internal routing topology is confidential, redundant path verifications are unlikely to happen inside an AS in practice. Consequently, we perform tests with a maximum path length of 10 hops (without counting the source). The minimum path length is 2 hops, corresponding to the case of a source, an intermediate hop, and a destination.

To measure the forwarding overhead at a router, which includes the memory overhead for storing keys and for retrieving them, we consider a network where each node has $\alpha$ neighbors. The parameter $\alpha$ is important only if the router performs work that depends on the number of neighbors. This is not the case for OPT, because the router merely computes the key it shares with the source to verify its OPV field, then computes the hash of the payload and finally updates the PVF field. These operations do not depend on the number of neighbors the router has nor on the path length.

However, in ICING the router has to look up the shared symmetric keys with each node on the path in a table that contains the keys of all the nodes the router had previously seen on a path. For a path of maximum length $n$, these nodes are located within $n$-hop distance away from the router. Our choice for the parameter $\alpha = 3$ and the maximum path length of 10 hops gives $\frac{(3^{11}-1)}{2} = 9841$ as a maximum key table size, which is within ICING's maximum key table size of 400,000 [25].

The router receives packets at a line rate of $40Gbps$. To quantify the throughput and goodput with respect to the overhead of OPT and ICING, we perform tests with payload sizes of $20B$, $256B$, $576B$, $768B$, and $1024B$. We add to these values the OPT and ICING header overhead, respectively, whose size corresponds to the tested path length. The $20B$ of the smallest payload size correspond to the TCP header size to simulate TCP/ICING and TCP/OPT. We note that TCP/OPT includes the IP header since OPT runs over the IP network; whereas TCP/ICING does not include the IP header since ICING is designed to replace IP. Hence, the goodput computation favors ICING.

The biggest payload size is computed by subtracting from the MTU the header size of ICING for the longest tested path (10 hops), as ICING has a higher header overhead than OPT. More precisely, ICING has a per-hop overhead of $42B$ plus $24B$ for the source identifier and $13B$ of common fields, which gives a header length of $457B$ for a 10-hop path. The computation is $1500B - 457B = 1043B$, which explains our choice of $1024B$ of the maximum payload. In case of OPT, $52B$ common fields, $16B$ per-hop overhead and $40B$ TCP/IP header result in $252B$. As a result, the maximum payload size is dictated by the size of the ICING header for the longest path considered.

**Method.** We generate traffic for 10 seconds at a rate of $40Gbps$, which is forwarded to the router running the protocol for source authentication and path validation, and then forwarded back to the source. To measure the throughput, we employ I/O Engine's scripts, which operate as follows. These scripts read the RX and TX counter values of the NIC at the beginning of the experiment and then read the values again every second to compute the number of packets sent and received. Consequently, we obtain the throughput values every second, which we then average to compute the final throughput value. For goodput results we subtract the OPT or ICING header, respectively, from the packet size.

## 7.4 Forwarding Overhead

We evaluate the most computationally intensive protocol version of OPT described in Section 5.3. The evaluation results show that OPT outperforms ICING by a significant margin. Since the other versions of OPT feature smaller packet headers and less computa-

[4] We add 20B Ethernet overhead in computing the throughput.

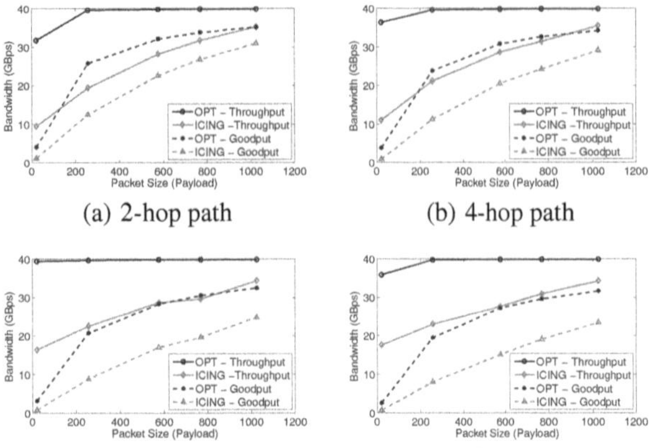


(a) 2-hop path (b) 4-hop path

(c) 8-hop path (d) 10-hop path

**Figure 6: Throughput and goodput (i.e., throughput obtained only for the payload part of the packet) of OPT and ICING for different packet sizes expressed in bytes and path lengths varying from 2 to 10 hops.**

tional overhead, they would outperform ICING with an even larger margin.

Figure 6 depicts the results for throughput and goodput for OPT and ICING. We performed experiments for different path lengths and packet sizes described in Section 7.3, and the numbers we obtained show consistent results over all experiments, as explained in the next paragraphs.

A first observation is that throughput registers higher values than goodput, as expected, due to the OPT or ICING header overhead that adds to the packet size, yet is not accounted for when measuring goodput. We also notice that, for all path lengths, OPT's throughput is close to $40Gbps$ except for the smallest packet size (i.e., 20B). We note that OPT's throughput for small packets is mainly limited by I/O Engine's throughput as shown in Figure 5. As the path length grows, I/O Engine's bottleneck becomes released because of the reduced number of packet copies between the NIC and the user-level packet processing engine[5]; and as a consequence, OPT's throughput becomes close to $40Gbps$. This result is consistent with Figure 5.

For each path length, the goodput of both OPT and ICING increase as the packet size increases, because the protocol header represents a smaller fraction of the total packet size as the payload size increases. Even though ICING's throughput also increases with the packet size, its value is much smaller than OPT's throughput. Given the choices for our ICING implementation, as explained earlier, this result is mainly due to the key table lookup for the PoP keys. Instead, OPT uses AESni operations to derive the keys shared with the source, on the fly. This choice in protocol design therefore proves to be decisive in obtaining a higher forwarding speed in OPT as much as $10Gbps$ in comparison to ICING.

## 7.5 Path Length Scalability

In order to analyze the protocols' scalability with respect to the path length, we depict in Figure 7 the ratio between the goodput and the throughput (named *goodput ratio*) for 256B and 1024B packets. We vary the path length from 2 to 10 hops.

The goodput ratios of 256B packets are lower those of than 1024B packets since small packets have higher header overhead (see previous section). Path length increase adds more overhead to the packet header, resulting in goodput degradation for both OPT and ICING.

[5]The increased header size reduces the number of packets needed to saturate the link bandwidth.

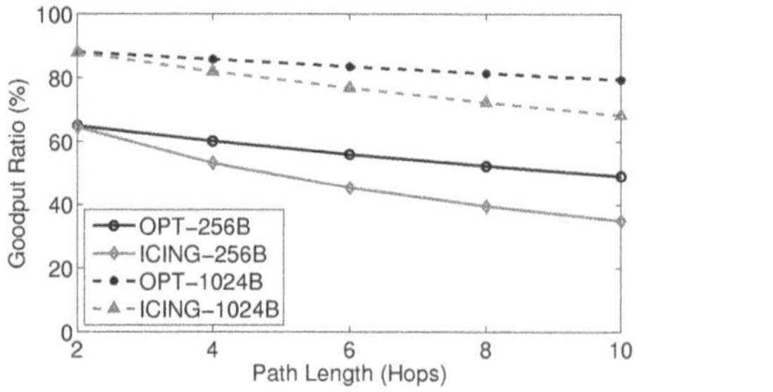


**Figure 7: The goodput ratio (i.e., goodput/throughput) of OPT and ICING for small and large packets, in the context of path lengths varying from 2 to 10 hops.**

The figure shows that OPT has better path length scalability than ICING since the goodput ratio of OPT decreases slower than that of ICING as the path length increases. Specifically, when the 2-hop path is used as a baseline, for 256B packets, OPT's average per-hop goodput degradation ratio is $\frac{(64.7-49.0)}{64.7\cdot 8} = 3.03\%$, while ICING's is $\frac{(64.5-34.9)}{64.5\cdot 8} = 5.74\%$; for 1024B packets, OPT's goodput degradation ratio per hop is $\frac{(88.1-79.3)}{88.1\cdot 8} = 1.25\%$, while ICING's is $\frac{(87.9-68.2)}{87.9\cdot 8} = 2.80\%$.

## 8. DISCUSSION

**Key lifetime.** The keys associated with a session $\sigma$ are valid as long as (1) $PATH_\sigma$ between $S$ and $D$ in the session $\sigma$ does not change, and (2) $S$ or $D$ do not terminate the session due to application-driven session lifetime requirement.

According to the first point, the maximum key lifetime is determined by route stability. Recent end-to-end route stability analyses reveal that most of network routes are stable from tens of minutes to days, even when ISPs apply traffic engineering techniques [9, 18, 22]. Although many routes are still short-lived, entities send packets over long-lived routes (longer than 6 hours) for 96% of the times [9]. In particular, considering the fact that the load balancing within an ISP causes most route variations (i.e., up to 82%), OPT running at AS-level uses more stable routes than router-level OPT. Furthermore, when routers perform per-flow or per-destination load balancing, paths used in OPT are not affected.

Yet an attacker could cause changes in network routes, as demonstrated by numerous incidents such as Man-in-the-Middle BGP route hijacking [8]. In this case, the network routes could flap as the attacker wishes. Yet, some future Internet architecture proposals (Nebula [2], Pathlets [12], SCION [40], XIA [14]) relieve this pain point by having packets carry forwarding information in the packet header, so that the source is always aware of the path and would set up a new session if the path changes.

We expect paths to be stable on the order of at least tens of minutes. Similarly, we expect that applications re-key sessions at the earliest at a granularity of tens of minutes. Thus, the key setup overhead represents a tiny fraction of the total computation and communication overhead of a long-lived high-bandwidth connection.

**Efficient packet content authentication.** As described in Section 5.3, each intermediate router uses the DATAHASH field in the OPT header when it verifies its OPV field. Such a verification does not authenticate the packet content since a malicious intermediate router could alter the data without changing DATAHASH. To mitigate such an attack, a router can verify the DATAHASH field in parallel while the packet is being scheduled for transmission.

As an alternative, probabilistic verification schemes [16] can be applied such that every router decreases the verification probability if the DATAHASH verification succeeds. However, if a router detects a packet with a bogus hash value, the probability to run hash verification increases. Furthermore, as soon as a router receives multiple mismatching hash values, it immediately performs hash verification on all subsequent packets. As a result, the routers neighboring a malicious router would verify all hashes of packets incoming on interfaces arriving from the malicious router. With such a probabilistic verification approach, we can further improve the efficiency and practicality while providing data authentication.

**OPT in the current Internet.** OPT could be incrementally deployed in the current Internet. An AS could announce its OPT functionality within BGP update messages (as a transitive attribute) or as extension to RPKI certificates, enabling the selection and construction of end-to-end OPT paths at source ASes. Endhosts could obtain OPT path information from a local route server which collects BGP and RPKI information.

To carry OPT-based information in packets, the simplest approach would be an IPv6 extension header. In IPv4, spare IP header bits would need to be used to indicate the presence of an extra OPT header or trailer, but an extra header after the IP header may disrupt processing at legacy firewalls or other middleboxes. With the increasing support for IPv6, we prefer incremental deployment via the IPv6 extension header. Since the DRKey information is larger than the 256 bytes that fit into an IPv6 extension header, we propose to use a new protocol number for DRKey packets, which routers would check for and process in the slow path. Alternatively, ASes could specify addresses of DRKey servers that would handle DRKey packets to set up the keys for the routers and thus would share the secret keys $K_{R_i}$ of routers. An endhost could then place a sequence of DRKey server addresses (similar to a loose source routing option in IPv4) into the DRKey packet, which would be sequentially processed and forwarded until the destination. This latter approach avoids routers from analyzing the IP protocol field.

# 9. RELATED WORK

The most closely related work for source authentication and path validation is **ICING** by Naous et al. [26]. In a nutshell, the source pre-computes a verifier MAC ($V_i$) for each intermediate router $R_i$ using the respective shared secret key as well as the hash value of the path and the static content in the header. For each packet, $R_i$ first reconstructs and XORs the MAC for the source and each upstream router, and verifies if the XORed MACs are equivalent to what is stored in $V_i$. Then $R_i$ (1) computes a MAC for each downstream router on the path using the shared secret key, the hash of the path, and the data, and (2) XORs the MAC for each downstream router with each $V_j$ ($j \geq i$).

ICING is more heavy-weight than OPT. ICING requires each $R_i$ to derive a Diffie-Hellman (DH) key with each router $R_j$ on the path, which requires routers to cache keys to avoid the heavy-weight DH computation during packet forwarding. For the case the keys are not cached any more, ICING suggests adding the 20-byte public key of each router into each packet, resulting in a high per-packet overhead. Also, ICING requires each node to insert a MAC for each subsequent verifier, requiring each node to compute $n+1$ MAC operations per packet. In contrast, OPT does not require routers to store keys shared with sources or other routers, nor perform a MAC computation for each router on the path. In terms of security, even ICING intermediate routers can detect colluding path deviation attacks mounted by the source and a malicious router to another intermediary router. In contrast, Extended-OPT supports the destination to detect such attacks. More specifically, the origin and path validation property of the routers still depends on the correct behavior of the source, but not on the destination. Consequently, Extended-OPT offers the same security guarantee as ICING for the destination. In other words, if the source is malicious, an illegitimate packet travels longer in Extended-OPT than ICING, but will be rejected by the destination. Beside the malicious source collusion attack, OPT and ICING provide the same kind of source and path authenticity properties for the destination. On the other hand, retroactive key setup OPT with path tracing (which only enables the destination to verify the path) can mitigate the coward attack, which ICING fails to mitigate.

Liu et al. propose **Passport** for intermediate routers to perform source authentication [21]. Passport proposes that BGP route advertisements carry Diffie-Hellman public keys, which enables any two ASes to compute a shared secret based on Diffie-Hellman key exchange. Using the respective shared secret key with each downstream AS, the source AS computes a MAC for each AS on the path, and inserts it in the Passport header. Each intermediate AS authenticates the source AS by recomputing the MAC using the shared key and confirming that it matches the MAC in the Passport header. Similar to Passport, **the accountability service** by Bender et al. [5] requires the source AS to embed an authenticator for subsequent ASes. In **SNAPP**, the sender sets up keys with routers through a key derivation mechanism that is similar to DRKey (although it cannot provide retroactive key setup) and uses these keys for embedded source authenticators. Passport and the accountability service provide weaker security guarantees than OPT, as they provide only source AS authentication, and fail to defend against source and data spoofing, as well as path deviation attacks. While SNAPP does prevent against source and data spoofing, it does not prevent path deviation attacks.

**Other source and path validation schemes.** In IP traceback, researchers proposed mechanisms that require routers carry per-packet state [19, 31], perform packet marking [30, 32], or active path interrogation [27]. Pi suggests a path identifier to detect source IP address spoofing [36]. Unfortunately, these schemes are susceptible to attacks listed in Section 2.3, because they were designed for a different purpose. Similarly, network capability mechanisms [3, 29, 37, 38] cannot provide source authentication or path validation as the capability can be easily copied and inserted by the last AS.

# 10. CONCLUSION

Despite the importance of network-based source authentication and path validation, these primitives have not been implemented so far, perhaps because of the lack of an efficient protocol that does not burden the router. This paper introduces (1) DRKeys as efficient and dynamically recreatable key setup protocols, and (2) OPT as an extremely lightweight, scalable, and secure protocol that provides source authentication and path validation. Compared with currently proposed solutions, OPT achieves performance improvements with minimal latency and computational overhead on routers regardless of the path length. Moreover, OPT does not require routers to maintain per-source or per-flow state, further improving its practicality. We also introduce a retroactive key setup process that protects against coward attacks, as routers cannot know in advance which paths are being monitored subsequently. We anticipate that OPT's security and performance properties will bring source authentication and path validation into the realm of practicality.

# 11. ACKNOWLEDGMENTS

We thank George Danezis, Yue-Hsun Lin, Raphael Reischuk, members of the XIA team, our shepherd Ratul Mahajan, and the anonymous reviewers for their insightful feedback and suggestions.

We gratefully acknowledge funding support for this research from CyLab at Carnegie Mellon, NSF under award CNS-1040801, European Research Council under the European Union's Seventh Framework Programme (FP7/2007-2013) / ERC grant agreement 617605, and a gift from KDDI.

## 12. REFERENCES

[1] D. G. Andersen, H. Balakrishnan, N. Feamster, T. Koponen, D. Moon, and S. Shenker. Accountable Internet Protocol (AIP). In *Proceedings of ACM SIGCOMM*, 2008.

[2] T. Anderson, K. Birman, R. Broberg, M. Caesar, D. Comer, C. Cotton, M. Freedman, A. Haeberlen, Z. Ives, A. Krishnamurthy, W. Lehr, B. Loo, D. Mazières, A. Nicolosi, J. Smith, I. Stoica, R. van Renesse, M. Walfish, H. Weatherspoon, and C. Yoo. The nebula future internet architecture. In A. Galis and A. Gavras, editors, *The Future Internet*, volume 7858 of *Lecture Notes in Computer Science*, pages 16–26. Springer Berlin Heidelberg, 2013.

[3] T. Anderson, T. Roscoe, and D. Wetherall. Preventing Internet Denial-of-Service with Capabilities. In *Proceedings of Hotnets-II*, 2003.

[4] ARIN. Resource Public Key Infrastructure (RPKI). `https://www.arin.net/resources/rpki/`.

[5] A. Bender, N. Spring, D. Levin, and B. Bhattacharjee. Accountability as a Service. In *Proc. of USENIX SRUTI*, 2007.

[6] D. J. Bernstein, N. Duif, T. Lange, P. Schwabe, and B.-Y. Yang. High-speed high-security signatures. In *Proc. of CHES*, 2011.

[7] J. Cowie. The new threat: Targeted internet traffic misdirection. `http://www.renesys.com/2013/11/mitm-internet-hijacking/`, Nov. 2013.

[8] J. Cowie. The New Threat: Targeted Internet Traffic Misdirection. Popular Mechanics, `http://www.renesys.com/2013/11/mitm-internet-hijacking/`, Nov 2013.

[9] I. Cunha, R. Teixeira, and C. Diot. Measuring and characterizing end-to-end route dynamics in the presence of load balancing. In *Proc. of PAM'11*, 2011.

[10] Y. Gilad and A. Herzberg. Plug-and-Play IP Security: Anonymity Infrastructure Instead of PKI. In *Proceedings of ESORICS*, 2013.

[11] B. Godfrey, S. Shenker, and I. Stoica. Pathlet Routing. In *Proc. of SIGCOMM*, 2009.

[12] P. B. Godfrey, I. Ganichev, S. Shenker, and I. Stoica. Pathlet routing. In *Proceedings of the ACM SIGCOMM 2009 Conference on Data Communication*, 2009.

[13] S. Gueron. Intel Advanced Encryption Standard (AES) New Instructions Set, Mar. 2010. white paper 323641-001, Revision 3.

[14] D. Han, A. Anand, F. Dogar, B. Li, H. Lim, M. Machado, A. Mukundan, W. Wu, A. Akella, D. G. Andersen, J. W. Byers, S. Seshan, and P. Steenkiste. XIA: Efficient support for evolvable internetworking. In *Proceedings of USENIX Conference on Networked Systems Design and Implementation*, 2012.

[15] S. Han, K. Jang, K. Park, and S. Moon. PacketShader: a GPU-accelerated software router. *ACM SIGCOMM Computer Communication Review*, Aug. 2010.

[16] H.-C. Hsiao, A. Studer, C. Chen, A. Perrig, F. Bai, B. Bellur, and A. Iyer. Flooding-Resilient Broadcast Authentication for VANETs. In *Proc. of MobiCom*, 2011.

[17] L. Jia, C. Basescu, T. H.-J. Kim, A. Perrig, Y.-C. Hu, and F. Zhang. Mechanized network origin and path authenticity proofs. Technical Report CMU-CyLab-14-007, Carnegie Mellon University, 2014.

[18] M. S. Kang, S. B. Lee, and V. D. Gligor. The Crossfire Attack. In *Proc. of IEEE Security and Privacy*, 2013.

[19] J. Li, M. Sung, J. Xu, and L. Li. Large-Scale IP Traceback in High-Speed Internet: Practical Techniques and Theoretical Foundation. In *Proc. of IEEE Security and Privacy*, 2004.

[20] B. Liu, J. T. Chiang, J. J. Haas, and Y.-C. Hu. Coward Attacks in Vehicular Networks. *Mobile Computing and Communications Review*, 2010.

[21] X. Liu, A. Li, X. Yang, and D. Wetherall. Passport: Secure and Adoptable Source Authentication. In *Proc. of NSDI*, 2008.

[22] H. V. Madhyastha, E. Katz-Bassett, T. Anderson, A. Krishnamurthy, and A. Venkataramani. iPlane Nano: Path Prediction for Peer-to-peer Applications. In *Proc. of NSDI*, 2009.

[23] D. Mazieres, M. Kaminsky, M. F. Kaashoek, and E. Witchel. Separating Key Mangement from File System Security. In *Proceedings of SOSP*, 1999.

[24] R. Moskowitz and P. Nikander. *Host Identity Protocol (HIP) Architecture*, May 2006. `http://tools.ietf.org/html/rfc4423`.

[25] J. Naous. Path-policy Compliant Networking and a Platform for Heterogeneous IAAS management. In *PhD thesis*, 2011.

[26] J. Naous, M. Walfish, A. Nicolosi, D. Mazieres, M. Miller, and A. Seehra. Verifying and Enforcing Network Paths with ICING. In *Proceedings of ACM CoNEXT*, 2011.

[27] V. N. Padmanabhan and D. R. Simon. Secure Traceroute to Detect Faulty or Malicious Routing. *ACM SIGCOMM Computer Communications Review*, January 2003.

[28] J. Pappalardo. New Transatlantic Cable Built to Shave 5 Miliseconds off Stock Trades. Popular Mechanics, `http://www.popularmechanics.com/technology/engineering/infrastructure/a-transatlantic-cable-to-shave-5-milliseconds-off-stock-trades`, Oct 2011.

[29] R. Raghavan and A. C. Snoeren. A system for authenticated policy-compliant routing. In *Proc. of ACM SIGCOMM*, 2004.

[30] S. Savage, D. Wetherall, A. Karlin, and T. Anderson. Practical Network Support for IP Traceback. In *Proc. of SIGCOMM*, 2000.

[31] A. C. Snoeren, C. Partridge, L. A. Galindo, C. E. Jones, F. Tchakounito, S. T. Kent, and W. T. Strayer. Hash-Based IP Traceback. In *Proceedings of ACM SIGCOMM*, 2001.

[32] D. X. Song and A. Perrig. Advanced and Authenticated Marking Schemes for IP Traceback. In *Proceedings of IEEE INFOCOM*, 2001.

[33] I. Stoica, D. Adkins, S. Zhaung, S. Shenker, and S. Surana. Internet indirection infrastructure. In *Proc. of SIGCOMM*, 2002.

[34] M. Walfish, J. Stribling, M. Krohn, H. Balakrishnan, R. Morris, and S. Shenker. Middleboxes No Longer Considered Harmful. In *Proceedings of OSDI*, 2004.

[35] D. Wendlandt, D. G. Andersen, and A. Perrig. Perspectives: Improving SSH-style host authentication with multi-path probing. In *Proceedings of USENIX Annual Technical Conference*, June 2008.

[36] A. Yaar, A. Perrig, and D. Song. Pi: A Path Identification Mechanism to Defend against DDoS Attacks. In *Proc. of IEEE Security and Privacy*, 2003.

[37] A. Yaar, A. Perrig, and D. Song. An Endhost Capability Mechanism to Mitigate DDoS Flooding Attacks. In *Proc. of the IEEE Security and Privacy*, May 2004.

[38] X. Yang, D. Wetherall, and T. Anderson. A DoS-limiting Network Architecture. In *Proc. of SIGCOMM*, 2005.

[39] X. Zhang. *Secure and Efficient Network Fault Localization.* PhD thesis, Carnegie Mellon University, 2012.

[40] X. Zhang, H.-C. Hsiao, G. Hasker, H. Chan, A. Perrig, and D. G. Andersen. SCION: Scalability, control, and isolation on next-generation networks. In *Proceedings of the IEEE Symposium on Security and Privacy (Oakland)*, May 2011.

# Quartz: A New Design Element for Low-Latency DCNs

Yunpeng James Liu
University of Waterloo
y493liu@uwaterloo.ca

Peter Xiang Gao
UC Berkeley
petergao@berkeley.edu

Bernard Wong
University of Waterloo
bernard@uwaterloo.ca

Srinivasan Keshav
University of Waterloo
keshav@uwaterloo.ca

## ABSTRACT

Most datacenter network (DCN) designs focus on maximizing bisection bandwidth rather than minimizing server-to-server latency. We explore architectural approaches to building low-latency DCNs and introduce Quartz, a design element consisting of a full mesh of switches. Quartz can be used to replace portions of either a hierarchical network or a random network. Our analysis shows that replacing high port-count core switches with Quartz can significantly reduce switching delays, and replacing groups of top-of-rack and aggregation switches with Quartz can significantly reduce congestion-related delays from cross-traffic. We overcome the complexity of wiring a complete mesh using low-cost optical multiplexers that enable us to efficiently implement a logical mesh as a physical ring. We evaluate our performance using both simulations and a small working prototype. Our evaluation results confirm our analysis, and demonstrate that it is possible to build low-latency DCNs using inexpensive commodity elements without significant concessions to cost, scalability, or wiring complexity.

## Categories and Subject Descriptors

C.2.1 [**Network Architecture and Design** ]: Network topology

## Keywords

Optical Technologies; WDM; Datacenter; Latency

## 1. Introduction

Network latency is a critical factor in determining the performance of many datacenter-scale, distributed applications. For example, in most distributed realtime computation frameworks such as MPI [24] and Storm [13], network latency manifests as a substantial component of coordination delay and is therefore on the critical path. In realtime or interactive applications such as search engines, social networks, and high frequency financial trading, a wide-area request may trigger hundreds of message exchanges inside a datacenter. For example, in a measurement study from Facebook, servicing a remote HTTP request can require as many as 88 cache lookups, 35 database lookups, and 392 backend remote procedure calls [23]. Therefore, there is an urgent, market-driven need for reducing network latency.


*SIGCOMM'14*, August 17–22, 2014, Chicago, IL, USA.

http://dx.doi.org/10.1145/2619239.2626332 .

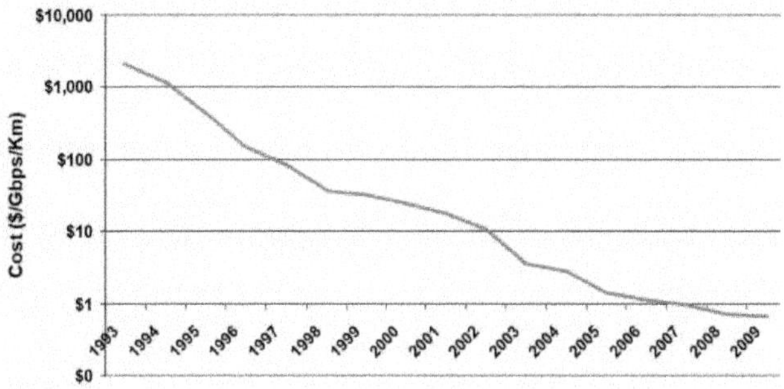


*Figure 1: Backbone DWDM per-bit, per-km cost improvements over time [20].*

Past work on low-latency datacenter networks (DCNs) has primarily focussed on reducing packet processing delays in the OS network stack [31], network interface card (NIC) [32] and network switches [3], and avoiding network congestion through bandwidth reservations [29] or congestion-aware flow scheduling [19, 27, 40, 41, 43]. Combining these techniques can, in theory, result in an order of magnitude reduction in end-to-end network latency.

However, there are a number of limitations with current techniques. For example, state-of-the-art low-latency cut-through switches are limited in scale ($\leq$ 64 ports) compared to standard store-and-forward switches ($\leq$ 1024 ports). Large DCNs must choose to deploy either standard switches in their core-switching tier or introduce an additional switching tier, which not only increases the number of switching hops but also creates additional congestion points.

In this paper, we explore an *architectural approach* to reducing network latency that is complementary to previous efforts. Our key insight is that switching latency is minimized by interconnecting top-of-rack (ToR) switches with a full mesh instead of a high-port count core switch or an aggregation layer of switches. Unfortunately, a full mesh topology is a wiring nightmare and does not scale well. We overcome wiring complexity by exploiting commodity photonics in the form of optical wavelength division multiplexers (WDMs) to implement a complex O($n^2$) mesh as a simple O($n$) optical ring. Similar techniques have been used to construct wide-area optical mesh networks [11, 34]. We show that implementing a full mesh in an optical ring is equally applicable in a datacenter. Using commodity photonics allows our solution, *Quartz* to ride the cost reduction curve in WDM equipment, which is driven by the large-scale roll out of fiber-to-the-home (see Figure 1 [20]).

To deal with the limited scalability of a mesh topology, we envision that Quartz can be used to replace *portions* of traditional DCNS:

| Component | Standard | State of Art |
|---|---|---|
| OS Network Stack | 15$\mu$s [36] | 1 - 4 $\mu$s [31] |
| NIC | 2.5 - 32$\mu$s [36] | 0.5$\mu$s [32] |
| Switch | 6 $\mu$s [5] | 0.5$\mu$s [3] |
| Congestion | 50$\mu$s [31] | |

*Table 2: Network latencies of different network components.*

- Replacing large top-of-rack (ToR) switches in single-tier networks with a single Quartz mesh to reduce latency and allow incremental upgrades.
- Replacing both ToR and aggregation switches in a standard 3-tier network with a single Quartz tier to significantly reduce the impact of cross-traffic.
- Replacing core switches to provide a large-scale, low-latency, and incrementally upgradable core switching tier.
- Replacing sets of switches in a randomized DCN [37,38] to provide lower latency for traffic with strong locality.

We evaluate Quartz through both simulations using a packet-level simulator and experiments on a working prototype consisting of four switches and six WDM muxes/demuxes. Our results demonstrate that Quartz can significantly reduce both switching and queuing latencies on various application workloads. We evaluate the cost of Quartz and show that it is cost competitive for many deployment scenarios. Moreover, we expect the cost of our solution to diminish over time as WDM shipping volumes rise.

Overall, our work makes three contributions:

- We present a novel use of commodity photonics in DCNs to build Quartz, a WDM-based design element for reducing communication latency.
- We show how Quartz can be used in different topologies to reduce latency and congestion.
- We evaluate performance using both simulations and a small working prototype and find that Quartz can reduce latency by 50% in many scenarios.

# 2. Background and Related Work

This section describes the different sources of network latency and the previous work to address each source. It also introduces the optical network technologies used in Quartz.

## 2.1 Sources of Latency

There are many sources of latency in DCNs (see Table 2 for a summary). We discuss each in turn.

### 2.1.1 Network Stack

Packets often need to wait for one or more context switches before they are received by a user-space application. Techniques such as kernel bypass and zero-copy processing can reduce this latency. In recent work, the Chronos [31] system uses these techniques to significantly reduce the operating system kernel latency for datacenter applications.

### 2.1.2 Network Interface Cards

Commodity Network Interface Cards (NICs) can introduce tens of microseconds of latency from performing basic buffering and packet processing. Recent work shows that by offloading packet processing to a FPGA and optimizing the communication between the FPGA and the host processor, NIC latency can be reduced to hundreds of nanoseconds [32]. Alternatively, RDMA over Infiniband or Ethernet [28] can reduce latency by eliminating communication between the NIC and the host processor for certain operations.

### 2.1.3 Switch Latency

Switching delay is a significant source of network latency. For example, the Cisco Catalyst 4948 10 Gigabit Ethernet Switch, which is commonly used in modern datacenters, has a switching latency of at least 6$\mu$s. In a typical three-tier network architecture, switching delay can therefore be as high as 30$\mu$s. Switching delay can be reduced by having fewer network tiers, and adopting low-latency cut-through switches. Unlike store-and-forward switches, cut-through switches start to send a frame before fully receiving it. Low-latency switches, such as the Arista 7100 [3], have a switching delay of approximately 500 ns. Cut-through switches command only a small price premium over the same port density store-and-forward switches [2, 6]. Unfortunately, they are currently limited to 64 ports, compared to more than 1000 ports for standard switches, and are therefore mainly used as ToR or aggregation switches.

### 2.1.4 Congestion

Although current datacenter networks support high bisection bandwidths, bursty traffic can still increase queuing delay over short time scales adding tens of microseconds to end-to-end latency. Recent work has identified several techniques for reducing network congestion. For example, DCTCP [19] utilizes Explicit Congestion Notifications (ECN) as congestion signals. However, DCTCP is only partially effective at reducing congestion delays over time scales shorter than a few round-trip-times. Recent proposals such as $D^2$TCP [40] and PDQ [27] use distributed congestion avoidance algorithms to manage flows at end-hosts and switches respectively.

DeTail [43] reduces network latency by detecting congestion and selecting alternative uncongested paths to reduce queuing delay. Deadline Driven Delivery ($D^3$) [41] is deadline-driven protocol where the sender requests the amount of bandwidth equal to the total amount of data divided by the time to the deadline. $D^3$ does not coexist with legacy TCP and requires that the user application knows the size and deadline of each of its flows, which in practice can lead to significant underutilization.

These protocol-based techniques require significant changes to the application, are unable to scale to a large number of short flows, and are limited by the amount of path diversity in the underlying network topology.

### 2.1.5 Topology

Topology is a critical factor in determining a network's equipment and deployment cost, wiring complexity, scalability, and performance characteristics (bisection and end-to-end latency). We outline the latency characteristics of different topologies next.

**Tree Networks:** Tree topologies, such as the standard multi-root tree structure [1] and Fat-Tree [17], organize the network into multiple switch tiers. Switches in each tier are only connected to switches in adjacent tiers, with the lowest tier of ToR switches connected to servers. This topology is scalable and, at least for the standard multi-root tree structure, has relatively low wiring complexity. However, each tier increases the maximum hop-count by two. The additional switching tiers also create focal points for congestion because the path diversity is very low. Even for Fat-Tree, where there is significant path diversity, congestion due to cross-traffic from different racks is still possible unless every flow is scheduled to use completely independent paths, which is difficult for short flows.

**Server-Centric Networks:** DCell [26], BCube [25] and CamCube [16] are networks that use servers as switches to assist in packet for-

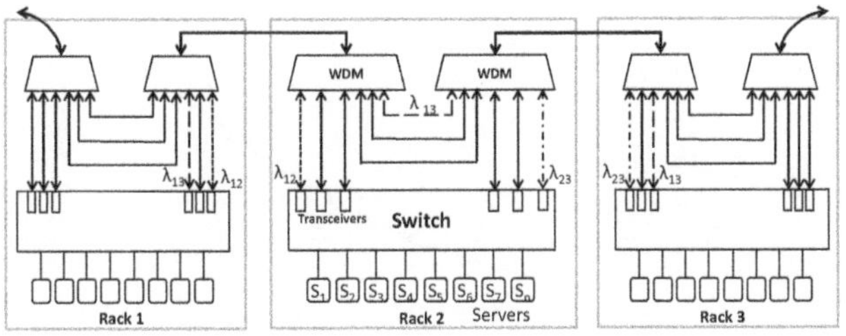


*Figure 3: Quartz switches with $n = 8$ and $k = 6$. Each switch is only physically connected to two nearby switches by an optical cable. Switch 1 and switch 2 are connected using channel $\lambda_{12}$. Switch 1 and switch 3 are connected using wavelength channel $\lambda_{13}$.*

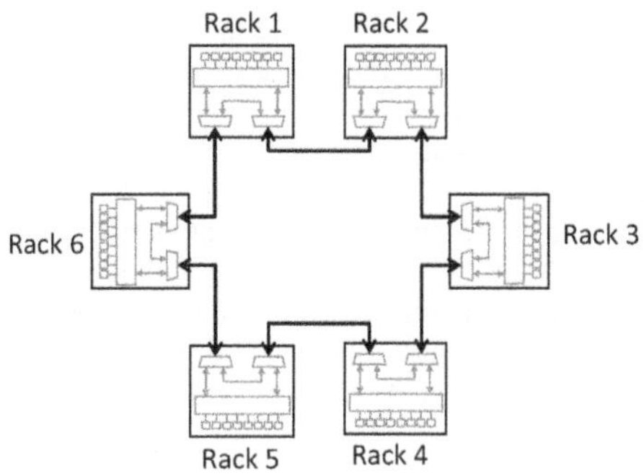


*Figure 4: Quartz ring of size 6. The logical topology is equivalent to a mesh structure where any two switches are directly connected. By using WDM, only adjacent switches are connected with a optical fiber.*

warding. These are scalable networks with high bisection bandwidth and path diversity. However, using servers to perform packet forwarding can introduce substantial delays in the OS network stack. Furthermore, server-centric networks can reduce the performance of computationally-intensive jobs, because high-bandwidth packet forwarding requires a significant number of CPU cycles [16, 37].

**Randomized Networks:** SWDC [37] and Jellyfish [38] propose to randomly connect servers or switches in a datacenter network. Random topologies usually have high path diversity and high bisection bandwidth. However, the worst case network diameter is typically much larger than a similar size tree network, even if the average path length is smaller. Randomized networks are also difficult to deploy and manage as they have very high wiring complexity.

**Mesh Networks:** Mesh networks directly connect every node to every other node, where a node can either be a server or a switch. A full mesh network provides the lowest possible network diameter and eliminates congestion arising from cross-traffic from other nodes. These properties make mesh networks an attractive option for low-latency DCNs. However, mesh topologies are rarely used in DCNs because the $O(n^2)$ connections requirement greatly limits scalability and increases wiring complexity.

## 2.2 Optical Network Technologies

Our work takes advantage of optical multiplexers and demultiplexers (mux/demux) to reduce the wiring complexity of mesh networks. An optical mux/demux uses Wavelength Division Multiplexing (WDM) to carry multiple network connections using different wavelengths in a single optical cable. Through judicious selection of wavelengths, it is possible to implement a full mesh network as a small set of optical rings that share a single physical ring. Importantly, unlike packet switching approaches, optical multiplexing and demultiplexing does not introduce additional switching or queuing latency.

It is also important to distinguish between a WDM and an optical switch. A WDM is a low-cost commodity photonic element that is deployed at mass-scale to build fiber-to-the-home networks. Figure 1 (taken from [20]) shows that the cost of DWDMs (Dense WDMs) have fallen at an exponential rate since 1993. Assuming this trend continues to hold, Quartz will only become more cost-competitive over time. In contrast, optical switches are complex, low-volume, and expensive to build due to the use of custom ASICs.

# 3. Quartz

Quartz is a *WDM-ring network* that implements a full mesh as a single physical ring. We now describe it in more detail.

Each Quartz switch has, in addition to $n$ standard ports, $k$ *optical transceivers*[1]. These devices convert electrical signals to and from optical signals. Transceivers can be tuned to specific wavelengths of light. Two transceivers connected by an optical cable must be tuned to the same wavelength to communicate.

Each switch on a Quartz ring is also associated with an *add/drop multiplexer*. The multiplexer portion combines optical signals of different wavelengths (also called 'channels') onto a single *multiplexed optical signal* for transmission on a single optical cable. Conversely, the demultiplexer portion splits a multiplexed optical signal into its constituent channels, with each channel placed on a separate optical cable.

Direct connection between switches $s$ and $t$ on the Quartz ring requires allocating them a dedicated channel denoted $\lambda_{st}$. Moreover, one of the transceivers on each switch is tuned to this channel. Switch $s$ uses the demultiplexer to remove ('drop') all channels of the form $\lambda_{*s}$ from the ring and to add channels of the form$\lambda_{s*}$ to the ring. Thus implementing a full mesh requires only *two* physical cables to connect to each Quartz switch.

Figure 3 shows a small Quartz ring. In this example, switch 1 and switch 2 are directly connected and they communicate using channel $\lambda_{12}$. Switch 1 and switch 3 communicate with each other using channel $\lambda_{13}$. At switch 2, the $\lambda_{13}$ channel in the multiplexed optical signal essentially passes through to switch 3. Therefore, there is an optical connection between switch 1 and switch 3, even through they are not physically connected.

Quartz allows for a flexible tradeoff between cost and network oversubscription. As shown in Figure 3, the switches in Quartz have two parameters $n$ (# ports to server) and $k$ (# ports to other switches), where $n : k$ is the server-to-switch ratio, and $n+k$ is the port density of a switch. A DCN designer can reduce the number of required switches in the network by increasing the server-to-switch ratio at the cost of higher network oversubscription.

## 3.1 Channel Assignment

Note that communication between switch $s$ and switch $t$ in Quartz requires them to have exclusive ownership of channel $\lambda_{st}$. If an optical cable could support an infinite number of channels, we could build an optical ring of arbitrarily large size that supports pairwise communication between switches. However, current technology can only multiplex 160 channels in an optical fiber and commodity Wavelength Division Multiplexers can only support about 80 chan-

[1] Most 10GigE and all future 40/100GigE ToR switches already use optical transceivers due to their lower power consumption and higher signal quality.

nels. Therefore, we need to determine the optimal way to assign channels such that we can build a ring of size $K$ using the minimum number of channels.

Quartz attempts to assign $\Lambda$ available channels to each pair of switches in a ring of size $M$ using two principles: (1) For any two switches $s$, $t$ in the ring, there exists an optical path between them using wavelength $\lambda_{st}$. (2) For all optical links on the path between $s$ and $t$, there is no other channel using the same wavelength $\lambda_{st}$. For example, in Figure 4 if switch 1 and switch 3 are using wavelength $\lambda_{13}$, then using $\lambda_{13}$ between rack 2 and rack 4 should be avoided, because $\lambda_{13}$ would be used twice on the link between switch 2 and switch 3.

Given these constraints, the wavelength assignment problem can be formulated as an Integer Linear Program (ILP) similar to [42]. The ILP problem is known to be NP-Complete. However, for a small ring, we can still find the optimal solution by ILP. We also introduce a greedy packing algorithm to calculate the minimum number of wavelengths needed for building such a ring for larger ring sizes. The ILP Formulation and our greedy algorithm are as follows:

Let $C_{s,t,i}$ denote the clockwise path from $s$ to $t$ using channel $i \in \{1, ..., \Lambda\}$ and let $C_{t,s,i}$ denote the anti-clockwise path. Variable $C_{s,t,i}$ is set to 1 if channel $i$ is used for communication between $s$ and $t$. Each $s$, $t$ switch pair should use one channel for their communication on either clockwise or counter-clockwise direction (Eq. 2).

Variable $L_{s,t,i,m}$ is the indicator variable of whether link $m$, the link between switch $m$ and $(m+1)\ mod\ M$, is using channel $i$ for the path between switch $s$ and $t$. We define static value $P_{s,t,m} = 1$ if the clockwise path between $s$ and $t$ passes through link $m$. If link $m$ is on the path between switch $s$ and switch $t$, and wavelength $i$ is used for their communication $L_{s,t,i,m}$. This is guaranteed by Eq. 3.

On each link $m$, a single channel $i$ should be only used at most once. We ensure this set of constraints by Eq. 4. To count the total number of channels used, variable $\lambda_i$ is created to show whether channel $i$ is used in the ring. Eq. 5 makes sure that $\lambda_i$ equals 1 if channel $i$ is used in the ring.

$$\text{minimize: } \sum_i \lambda_i \tag{1}$$

subject to:

$$\forall s < t, \sum_i C_{s,t,i} + \sum_i C_{t,s,i} = 1 \tag{2}$$

$$\forall s, t, i, m,\ L_{s,t,i,m} = P_{s,t,m} C_{s,t,i} \tag{3}$$

$$\forall m,\ i, \sum_{s,t} L_{s,t,i,m} \le 1 \tag{4}$$

$$\forall i, \sum L_{s,t,i,m} \le M\lambda_i \tag{5}$$

$$\forall\ variable \in \{0, 1\} \tag{6}$$

The goal is to minimize the total number of used channels. If the ILP is solvable, it means all switch pairs can communicate with each other. The optimization result is the minimum number of channels required for the given ring size.

### 3.1.1 Greedy Channel Assignment

We outline a simple, greedy algorithm to solve the channel assignment problem. For all the paths between switch pairs $(s, t)$, they are first sorted by their length. For a ring with $M$ nodes, the maximum path length between two switches is $\lfloor M/2 \rfloor$, so there are $\lfloor M/2 \rfloor$ sets of path lengths. Consider an algorithm with $\lfloor M/2 \rfloor$ iterations, where paths in each set is assigned in one iteration. Our heuristic is to give priority to long paths to avoid fragmenting the available channels on the ring. Shorter paths are assigned later because short path are less constrained on channels that are available on consecutive links. In each iteration, starting from a random location, the channels are greedily assigned to the paths until all paths are assigned or the channels are used up.

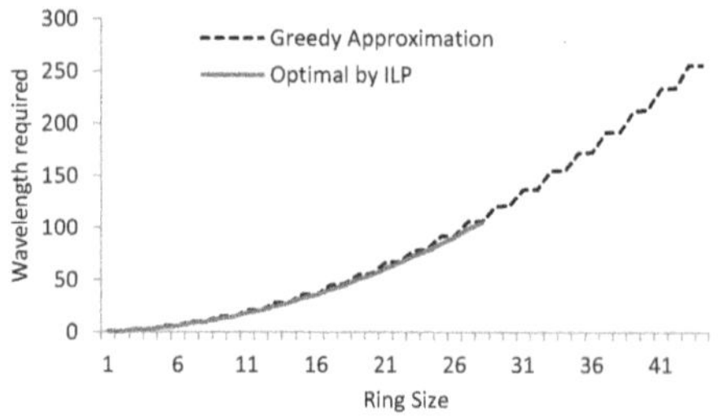


*Figure 5: Optimal wavelength assignment*

To evaluate the greedy algorithm, we compare the results with the ILP solution. Figure 5 illustrates the results of this evaluation, and shows that our greedy heuristic performs nearly as well as the optimal solution. Furthermore, it shows that the maximum ring size is 35 since current fiber cables can only support 160 channels at 10 Gbps. Note that wavelength planning is a one-time event that is done at design time. Quartz does not need to dynamically reassign wavelengths at runtime. Since we can use a fixed wavelength plan for all Quartz rings of the same size, wavelength planning and switch to DWDM cabling can be performed by the device manufacturer at the factory. Moreover, our greedy heuristic only requires seconds to compute on a standard workstation even for a ring size of 35. Therefore, we believe our greedy algorithm is fast enough for practical use.

## 3.2 Scalability

Because of its full mesh structure, the maximum size of a Quartz network is, in part, limited by the port count of the switches. Using low-latency 64-port switches, where each switch connects each one of 32 of its ports to a different switch, this configuration mimics a 1056 (32×33) port switch. This relatively small maximum network size suggests that Quartz should be used as a component in new DCN designs, rather than as a replacement for existing DCNs. We explore using Quartz as a network design element in Section 4.

For deployment scenarios where a larger Quartz network is necessary, one can increase the size of the network by connecting each server to more than one ToR switch. For example, for a configuration where (1) each server has two NICs, (2) there are two top-of-rack switches in each rack, (3) each server is connected to both switches in its rack, and (4) each rack has a direct connection to every other rack, the longest path between any two servers is still two switches. This configuration can support up to 2080 ($32 \times 65$) ports at the cost of an additional switch per rack, and a second optical ring since wavelength restrictions limit the number of switches per ring to 35. In theory, even larger Quartz networks can be constructed by adding more switches per rack and more optical rings. However, we believe this approach to scalability is cost prohibitive in practice. For most deployment scenarios that require more than 1056 ports, Quartz should instead be used as a component in a large DCN.

## 3.3 Insertion Loss

Although an optical hop between switches does not introduce any discernible amount of latency, it does degrade the optical signal due to insertion loss from the WDMs. Quartz compensates for this signal degradation by adding pump laser-based signal amplifiers as needed between optical hops.

To determine the feasibility of this approach, we evaluate the cost of adding signal amplifiers in a 24-node Quartz ring. In this example, we use 10Gbps DWDM transceivers [7], and 80 channel DWDMs [8]. The transceiver has a maximum output power of 4 dBm and a receiver sensitivity of -15 dBm. A typical 80 channel DWDM has an insertion loss of 6 dB. Therefore, the number of DWDMs that a channel can pass through without amplification is:

$$(4dBm - (-15dBm))/6dB = 3.17$$

In this configuration, we need to add a signal amplifier [12] after every sequence of three DWDMs. Since each optical hop in the ring requires traversing two DWDMs, we need one amplifier for every two switches. This only increases the cost of a 24-node Quartz ring by three percent. To avoid overloading the amplifiers and transceivers, we also need to add optical attenuators to the ring. However, attenuators [10] are simple passive devices that do not meaningfully affect the cost of the network.

## 3.4 Routing in Quartz

We now discuss the integration of Quartz into link layer addressing and routing. A naïve approach to routing in Quartz would be to treat all servers as being in the same L2 Ethernet network. However, because Ethernet creates a single spanning tree to determine the forwarding path of packets, it can only utilize a small fraction of the links in the network. To utilize all direct paths between switches, we advocate using ECMP routing in the Quartz's mesh. Since there is a single shortest path between any pair of switches in a full mesh, ECMP always selects the direct one-hop path, which minimizes hop count and interference from cross-traffic.

A possible problem with only using the direct paths in Quartz is the amount of bandwidth oversubscription between each pair of switches. In a Quartz configuration using 64-port switches where 32 ports from each switch are connected to servers, there is a 32:1 oversubscription between racks, which can be a problem for certain workloads. However, workloads that spread traffic across different racks, such as standard scatter/gather workloads in large-scale computational platforms such as MPI [24] and MapReduce [21], are unaffected by this kind of independent, rack-to-rack bandwidth oversubscription.

For workloads that concentrate traffic between two racks, one can significantly reduce rack-to-rack oversubscription by using Valiant Load Balancing (VLB) [22,33] to make use of two-hop routes. We configure each switch to send $k$ fraction of the traffic through the $n - 2$ two-hop paths and the remaining fraction through the direct path. For instance, if there is a large amount of traffic from rack 6 to rack 3 in Figure 7(b), VLB will send $k$ fraction of this traffic through Rack 1, 2, 4, and 5 over two-hop paths. The parameter $k$ can be adaptive depending on the traffic characteristics. We provide a detailed bandwidth analysis of Quartz and different tree topologies in Section 5.1. Quartz not only reduces transmission delay, it also reduces queuing delay by reducing congestion due to cross-traffic. We evaluate the impact of cross-traffic on latency in Section 6.1.

## 3.5 Fault Tolerance

Rings are well known to be less fault tolerant than a multi-rooted tree: two link failures in a ring partition the network. However, by using multiple physical optical fibers to interconnect switches and multi-hop paths, we can significantly reduce the likelihood of partitioning the network. For example, if a Quartz network with 33

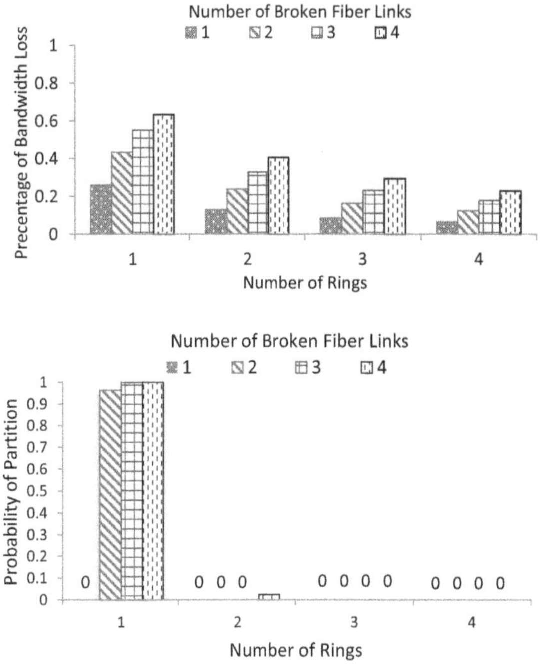


*Figure 6: The top graph shows the percentage of bandwidth loss from broken fibre links with different ring sizes. The bottom figure shows the probability of network partitioning. With two rings, four link failures can partition the network at a very low probability of 0.0024.*

switches requires 137 channels, we can use two 80-channel WDM muxes/demuxes instead of a single mux/demux at each switch. In this configuration, there will be two optical links between any two nearby racks, forming two optical rings, and link failures are less likely to partition the network. Of course, this resilience comes at an additional cost.

Since combinatorial analysis of multi-hop path reachability is complex, we use simulations to evaluate the performance of Quartz with one to four physical rings under random link failures. Figure 6 shows the average bandwidth loss and probability of the network partitioning in a 33-switch Quartz network. The top figure shows the percentage of aggregate bandwidth loss. With only one ring, a physical optical link failure results in a 20% reduction of the network bandwidth. Using 4 rings, the average bandwidth reduction is only 6%. The network partition probability for two or more link failures in a single-link network is more than 90%. Surprisingly, by adding a single additional physical ring, the probability of the network partitioning is less than 0.24% even when four physical links fail at the same time.

# 4. Quartz as a Design Element

A Quartz mesh has low latency, high path diversity with VLB, and the same wiring complexity as ring networks. Yet its scalability is limited by the size of low-latency cut-through switches. A Quartz network built using 64-port switches and a single switch per rack provides 1056 server ports, which, as a DCN, is only sufficient for small datacenters.

Larger datacenters can instead use Quartz as a design element to, for instance, replace portions of their DCNs in order to reduce switching or congestion delays for traffic between servers in nearby racks. In the following sections, we explore using Quartz in the edge as a replacement for both the ToR and aggregation tiers in

| Datacenter Size | Network Utilization | Sample Topologies | Latency Reduction using Quartz | Cost/Server |
|---|---|---|---|---|
| Small (500 Servers) | Low | Two-tier tree | 33% | $589 |
| | | Single Quartz ring | | $633 |
| | High | Two-tier tree | 50% | $589 |
| | | Single Quartz ring | | $633 |
| Medium (10K Servers) | Low | Three-tier tree | 20% | $544 |
| | | Quartz in edge | | $612 |
| | High | Three-tier tree | 40% | $544 |
| | | Quartz in edge | | $612 |
| Large (100K Servers) | Low | Three-tier tree | 70% | $525 |
| | | Quartz in core | | $525 |
| | High | Three-tier tree | 74% | $525 |
| | | Quartz in edge and core | | $614 |

*Table 8: Approximate cost and latency comparison. Costs include all the hardware expenses except servers. Costs of Quartz include a single ring of switches.*

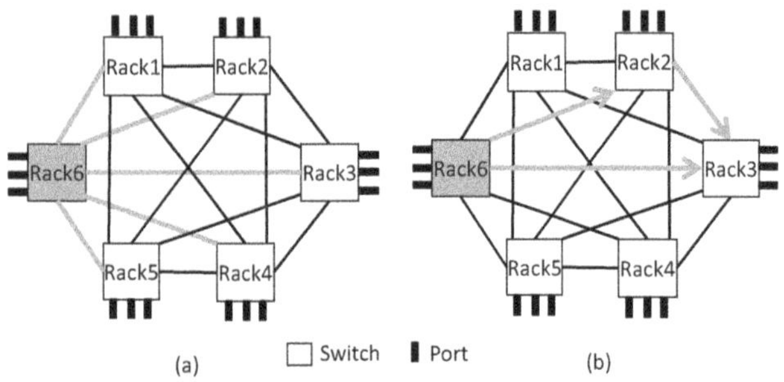


*Figure 7: A flat mesh network where ToR switches are directly connected. (a) direct routing (b) two-hop routing.*

a 3-tier tree network, in the core tier as a replacement for large, high-latency core switches, and in randomized networks to reduce switching and congestion delays for traffic with strong locality.

## 4.1 Quartz in the Edge

Current DCNs typically employ either a 2 or 3-tier tree topology [17]. Figure 15(a) illustrates a 3-tier tree network in which each ToR switch in the edge tier is connected to one or more switches in the aggregation tier, each of which is in turn connected to the switches in the core tier. Although a 3-tier tree network is highly scalable and easy to deploy, it has significant switching and queuing delays due to its high hop count and the congestion points in its top two tiers. Furthermore, because of the low path diversity in tree topologies, applications running in a 3-tier tree network cannot avoid congestion points even when they are generating traffic with strong locality (i.e., between nearby racks).

We can significantly reduce the latency of a 3-tier tree network by replacing a portion of the edge and aggregation tiers with a Quartz tier, as illustrated in Figure 15(c). This configuration reduces the maximum hop count from five to three and the number of congestion points by effectively eliminating a tier from the network. Moreover, unlike in a 2-tier tree network, localized traffic that span multiple racks can be grouped into a single Quartz ring and can therefore avoid the large switching delay of the core switch. The full connectivity of the Quartz network also provides more freedom for application specific locality optimizations, which is important given that most datacenter traffic patterns show strong locality [30].

## 4.2 Quartz in the Core

Large DCNs that connect hundreds of thousands of servers require core switches with port count in excess of a thousand ports because of the need to interconnect several hundred aggregation switches. These switches are based on slower but more scalable store-and-forward designs, and have switching latencies that are an order of magnitude more than low-latency cut-through switches. Furthermore, they are generally very expensive, with a significant portion of the cost being the large chassis that connects the switch line cards. Therefore, although these switches provide modular scalability, the large upfront cost of the chassis means incorrect growth prediction is very costly.

To avoid the high latency and poor price scalability of current core switches, we explore a configuration that replaces core switches with Quartz, as illustrated in Figure 15(b). A Quartz network using low-latency switches has significantly lower switching delays than core switches. It also does not require an expensive upfront investment; switches and WDMs can be added as needed. A potential problem with replacing core switches with Quartz is that, unlike core switches, Quartz does not offer full bisection bandwidth. We evaluate the impact of this limitation using a pathological traffic pattern in Section 7.2.

## 4.3 Quartz in Random Topology Networks

Random topology networks, such as Jellyfish [38] and SWDC [37], offer an exciting new design point in DCNs. However, without any network structure, it is difficult for applications running in random topology networks to take advantage of traffic locality. Furthermore, much like mesh networks, random topology networks have high wiring complexity, which limits their scale.

To address these issues, we propose an alternative design to Jellyfish that, instead of creating a random graph of switches, creates a random graph of Quartz networks. This configuration enables applications to take advantage of traffic locality in the same way as we discussed in Section 4.1. Furthermore, by grouping nearby switches together into a Quartz network before connecting the Quartz networks together into a random graph, this configuration reduces the number of random connections and therefore greatly simplifies the DCN's wiring complexity.

## 4.4 Configurator

Datacenter providers must balance the gain from reducing end-to-end latency with the cost of using low-latency hardware. Unfortunately, as we have discussed earlier, latency arises from numerous factors, including datacenter size, network topology, traffic load, and switch type. Therefore, it is possible to only give approximate guidelines regarding the gain from introducing low-latency components into a DCN.

We make a 'best-effort' attempt to quantify the cost-benefit tradeoff of using Quartz in Table 8, which summarizes the cost of using

Quartz in various network configurations. We consider different datacenter sizes, ranging from 500 servers to 100,000 servers. For all of the tree-based configurations, we use cut-through switches [4] in the edge and aggregation tiers, and high-port density store-and-forward switches [9] in the core tier. We also use commercially available amplifiers [12], DWDMs [8], and transceivers [7]. To simplify the evaluation, the prices include all the hardware expenses except for the cost of the servers.

We take into account (at a very high level) the network utilization of a datacenter; we consider when the network's utilization is 'high,' which corresponds to a mean link utilization of 70%, and 'low,' which corresponds to a mean link utilization of 50%. We also investigate various network topologies including a two-tier tree, three-tier tree, a single Quartz ring, and the use of Quartz in the edge or core layer (or both). We present the approximate packet latency reduction from using Quartz based on our simulation results in Section 7 and the cost per server for these various network configurations.

We first analyse the use of Quartz for small datacenters, which have approximately 500 servers. We observe that the use of Quartz increases the cost per server by 7% compared to a two-tier tree structure. However, we can achieve a latency reduction of at least 33% in an environment with low network utilization and more than 50% with high network utilization.

In the case for medium-sized datacenters, which consists of 10,000 servers, we find that the use of Quartz increases the cost of the datacenter by 13% and reduces the datacenter's latency by 20% with low traffic, and more than 40% with high traffic. The cost of using Quartz is higher in a medium-sized datacenter than a small-sized datacenter because of the larger size of the Quartz ring needed to serve more servers; thus, more optical hardware is required.

Finally, we consider a large datacenter that contains 100,000 servers. We find that using Quartz at the core layer does not increase cost per server since the three-tier tree requires a high port density switch. As high port density switches are also expensive, their cost is similar to the optical hardware that is found in a Quartz ring. By replacing high port density switches with Quartz rings, we see a 70% improvement in latency with low traffic. We also consider the use of Quartz at the both edge and core layer in an environment with high network utilization. We see that the cost increases by 17% and latency is reduced by more than 74%.

To summarize, we realize that it is impossible to give exact cost-benefit tradeoffs due to the numerous sources of network latency. We demonstrate however that (a) Quartz can be used as a design element in many different standard DCNs (b) the additional (one-time) cost due to introducing Quartz is fairly small and (c) in all cases, using Quartz significantly reduces end-to-end latency.

# 5. Analysis

We analyze the properties of five representative network topologies (2-tier tree, Fat-Tree [17], BCube [25], Jellyfish [38] and mesh) and determine their suitability as a low-latency network design element. In this analysis, we configure each topology to mimic a single switch with approximately 1000 ports. We compute the path diversity of each topology using the metric defined in [39]. Note that Jellyfish's path diversity depends on both the chosen routing algorithm (k-shortest-path or ECMP) and the number of switch-to-switch links. We define wiring complexity as the number of cross-rack links. Table 9 shows a summary of their key properties.

Out of the five network topologies, the 2-tier tree structure requires the fewest switches to provide 1k usable ports and therefore has the lowest relative equipment cost. It is also the simplest structure to wire; each ToR switch only has a small constant number of connections to each of the second tier switches. However, as established by previous work [17], providing high bisection bandwidth in a tree network requires high port count second tier switches that are both expensive and, more importantly, have high latency. This problem, combined with its low path diversity, which can result in significant congestive delays, make 2-tier tree networks a poor choice for a low-latency design element.

By increasing path diversity, Fat-Tree, BCube, and Jellyfish have lower congestive delays and offer significantly more bisection bandwidth than 2-tier tree networks without requiring high port count switches. Fat-tree is the most expensive of the three structures, but provides full bisection bandwidth without requiring server-side packet switching. BCube's use of server-side packet switching results in the highest latency of the five topologies. All three systems have relatively high wiring complexity.

Finally, a mesh network offers the highest path diversity, lowest hop count and latency when using direct routing, and relatively high bisection bandwidth when using indirect routing with VLB. It also has relatively high wiring complexity, but by implementing it using a WDM ring, the wiring complexity can be simplified to be as low as a 2-tier tree network.

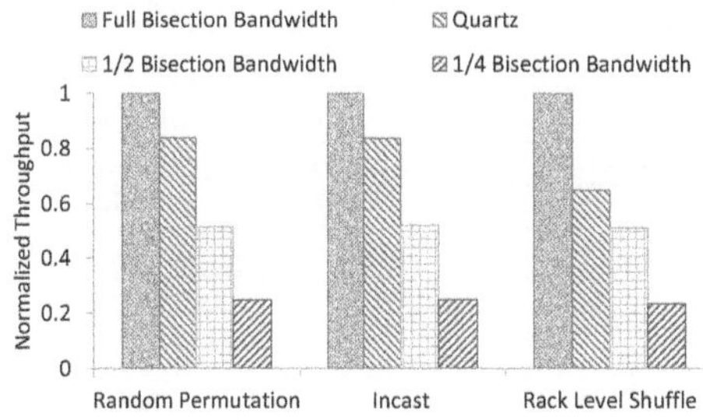


*Figure 10: Normalized throughput for three different traffic patterns*

## 5.1 Bisection Bandwidth

Given Quartz's high path diversity, it is difficult to analytically calculate its bisection bandwidth. Instead, we use simulations to compare the aggregate throughput of a Quartz network using both one- and two-hop paths to that of an ideal (full bisection bandwidth) network for typical DCN workloads. We also compare Quartz's throughput with reduced capacity networks with 1/2 and 1/4 bisection bandwidth. We use the following common datacenter communication patterns in our comparison:

1. **Random Permutation Traffic**. Each server sends traffic to one randomly selected server, while at the same time, it receives traffic from a different randomly selected server.
2. **Incast Traffic**. Each server receives traffic from 10 servers at random locations of the network, which simulates the shuffle stage in a MapReduce workload.
3. **Rack Level Shuffle Traffic**. Servers in a rack send traffic to servers in several different racks. This represents traffic when the administrator is trying to balance the load between racks through VM migration. This load pattern is common in elastic datacenters, where servers are turned off at off peak hours.

Figure 10 shows the normalized throughput for three traffic patterns. The normalized throughput equals to 1 if every server can send traffic at its full rate. For random permutation traffic and incast traffic, Quartz throughput is about 90% of a full bisection bandwidth network. For rack level shuffle traffic, the normalized

| | Network Latency without Congestion | # of 64-port Switches | Wiring Complexity | Path Diversity |
|---|---|---|---|---|
| 2-Tier Tree | 1.5$\mu$s (3 Switch Hops) | 17 | 16 | 1 |
| Fat-Tree | 1.5$\mu$s (3 Switch Hops) | 48 | 1024 | 32 |
| BCube | 16$\mu$s (2 Switch Hops & 1 Server Hop) | 32 | 960 | 2 |
| Jellyfish | 1.5$\mu$s (3 Switch Hops) | 24 | 240 | $\leq$32 |
| Mesh | 1.0$\mu$s (2 Switch Hops) | 33 | 528<br>32 (with WDMs) | 32 |

*Table 9: Summary of different network structures with 1k servers*

*Figure 11: Quartz with 4 switches, connected by WDMs*

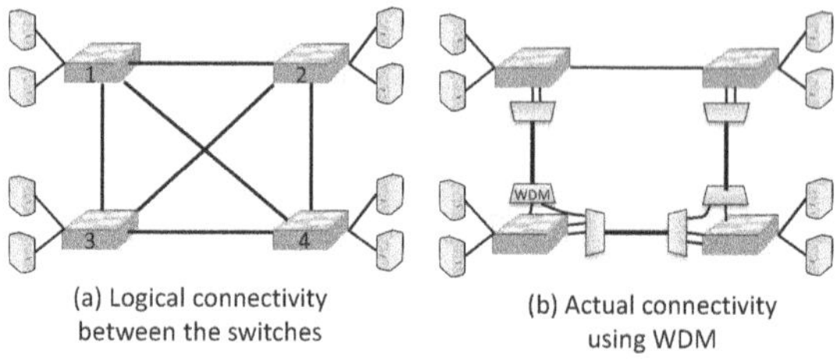


*Figure 12: Topology of our testbed.*

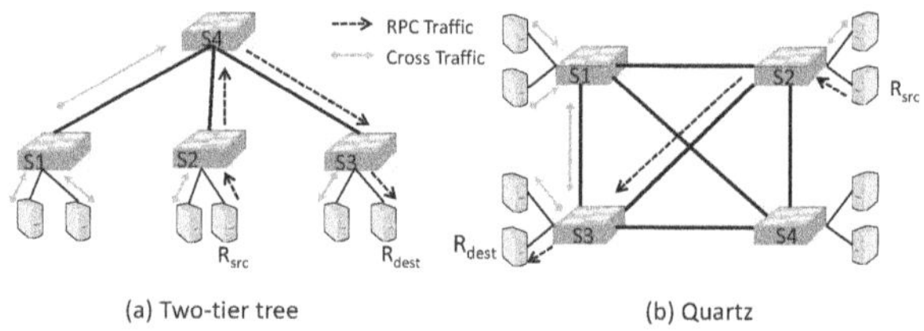


*Figure 13: Traffic flows of cross-traffic experiment*

throughput is about 0.75. We conclude that Quartz's bisection bandwidth is less than full bisection bandwidth but greater than 1/2 bisection bandwidth. Overall, Quartz provides significantly higher throughput than the other oversubscribed network topologies for all three traffic patterns.

# 6. Prototype

In this section, we validate the Quartz design by building a small prototype, and determine the relative performance difference between Quartz and a 2-tier tree in a simple cross-traffic experiment. Our prototype consists of 4 commodity switches and 8 servers, as illustrated in Figure 11. Three of the switches are Nortel 5510-48T, and the fourth is a Cisco Catalyst 4948. All four are 1 Gbps managed switches with 48 ports. Figure 12(a) shows the logical connectivity between the switches. By using WDM muxes/demuxes, we can simplify the network cabling to Figure 12(b), where there are only optical links between nearby switches in a ring. The network has 8 servers in total and 4 links between any bisection of the network, which means it can provide full bisection bandwidth. Our prototype has 12 CWDM SFP transceivers which support 1.25Gbps bidirectional communications. Among the transceivers, 8 of them use the 1470nm wavelength band, 2 of them use the 1490nm band, and the remaining 2 use the 1510nm band. We also use 4-channel CWDM muxes/demuxes in our prototype to multiplex different channels into one optical fibre cable. Signal amplifiers are unnecessary in this small testbed. We actually need to use attenuators to protect the receivers from overloading.

Each server is equipped with a 1 Gbps Intel Pro/1000 GT Desktop Adapter and is running Ubuntu 11.10 without any low-latency OS or network stack changes. In order to isolate the impact of the network architecture on latency, we present relative rather than absolute performance results while maintaining the same software and hardware configurations throughout our experiments.

To precisely control the traffic paths in our experiments, we use the technique introduced in SPAIN [35] to expose alternative network paths to the application. We create 4 virtual interfaces on each server, where each virtual interface sends traffic using a specific VLAN and the spanning trees for the VLANs are rooted at different switches. Therefore, an application can select a direct two-hop path or a specific indirect three-hop path by sending data on the corresponding virtual interface.

## 6.1 Impact of Cross-Traffic

We evaluate the performance of Quartz and a 2-tier tree topology using a cross-traffic workload. In order to ensure a fair comparison, we use the prototype described in Section 6 for evaluating Quartz, and rewired the switches from the Quartz prototype into a 2-tier tree (1 aggregation and 3 ToR switches) to perform our 2-tier tree experiments. Each ToR switch is connected to two servers and we use six total servers in our experiments.

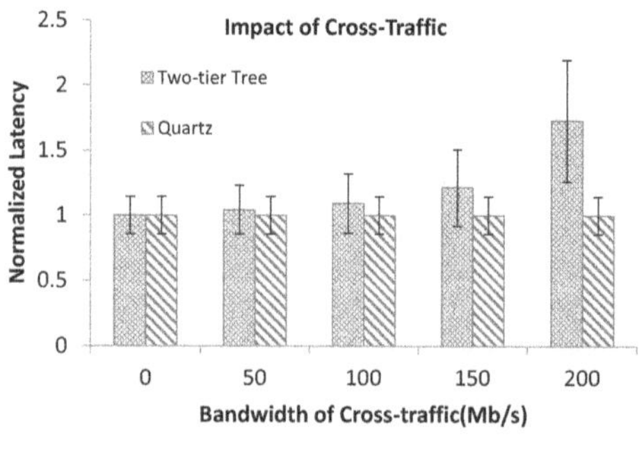


*Figure 14: Impact of cross-traffic on different topologies*

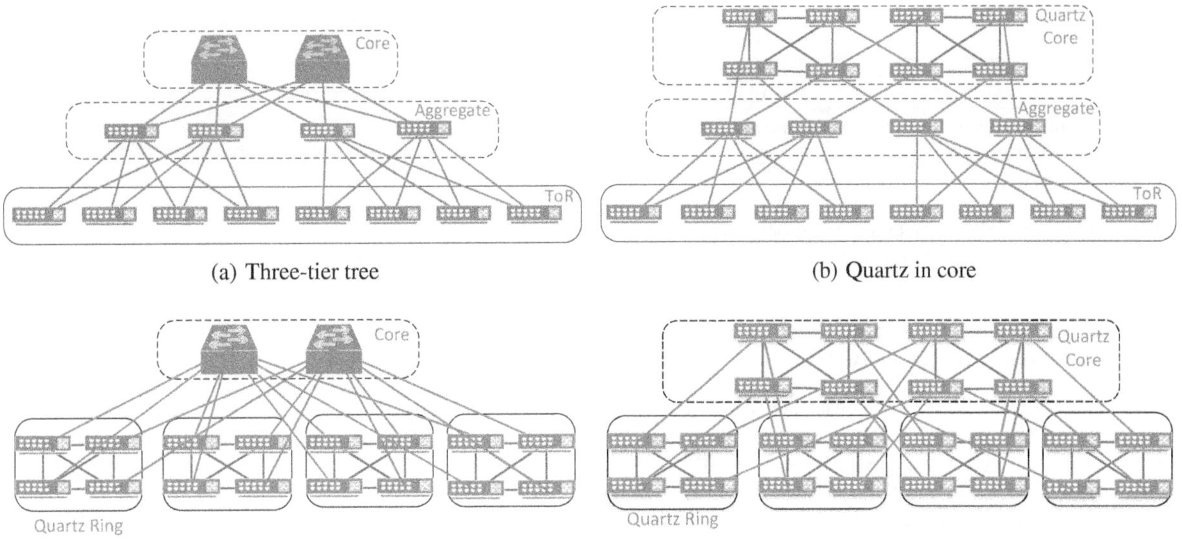


(a) Three-tier tree

(b) Quartz in core

(c) Quartz in edge

(d) Quartz in edge and core

*Figure 15: Simulated network topologies. Jellyfish and Quartz in Jellyfish topologies are not shown..*

Our cross-traffic workload consists of a "Hello World" RPC written in Apache Thrift [14] between two servers ($R_{src}$ and $R_{dst}$) connected to different ToR switches ($S_2$ and $S_3$), which represents a latency sensitive flow, and additional bursty traffic generated using Nuttcp [15] from three servers connected to $S_1$ and $S_2$ to a server connected to $S_3$. Figure 13 illustrates the topologies and the different flows. Note that we only use direct paths and we do not use the servers connected to $S_4$ in this experiment. To minimize OS scheduling related uncertainties, each server is only involved with one flow. The RPC application executes $10,000$ RPC calls one at a time for each experiment, and the bursty cross-traffic consist of 20 packet bursts that are separated by idle intervals, the duration of which is selected to meet a target bandwidth. The bursty traffic from the three servers are not synchronized. We perform 100 runs of each experiment and show the 95% confidence interval as error bars.

Figure 14 shows that, as we increase the cross-traffic from 0 to 200 Mbps (0 to 20% of the link bandwidth), the RPC latency rapidly increases for the tree topology due to congestion. At 200 Mbps, the RPC latency for the tree topology increases by more than 70% compared to its latency without cross-traffic. In contrast, the RPC latency is unaffected by cross-traffic with Quartz. These results corroborate with our analysis in Section 5, and demonstrate the impact of the network topology on reducing network congestion from cross-traffic.

## 7. Simulation Study

In order to evaluate the performance of Quartz and other topologies at scale, we implemented our own packet-level discrete event network simulator that we tailored to our specific requirements. We have performed extensive validation testing of our simulator to ensure that it produces correct results that match queuing theory. We make the simplifying assumptions that servers send 400-byte packets according to a Poisson process. We model two state-of-the-art switches in our simulator:

- Cisco Nexus 7000 core switch (CCS)
- Arista 7150 ultra low latency switch (ULL)

The specifications of these switches are summarized in Table 16. In our simulated architectures, we use ULL for both ToR switches and aggregation switches, and CCS as core switches. We use ULL exclusively in Quartz. Each simulated Quartz ring consists of four switches; the size of the ring does not affect performance and only affects the size of the DCN. We implement the following network architectures in our simulator:

1. **Three-tier Tree (Figure 15(a)):** A basic three-tier tree structure with each ToR switch connected to two aggregation switches over 40Gbps links, and each aggregation switch connected to two core switches over 40Gbps links.
2. **Quartz in Core (Figure 15(b)):** Each core switch is replaced with a Quartz ring. The aggregation switches connect to the Quartz ring over 40 Gbps links.
3. **Quartz in Edge (Figure 15(c)):** The ToR and aggregation switches are replaced with Quartz rings. Servers connect to the Quartz rings using 10 Gbps links, and the Quartz rings connect to the core switches using 40 Gbps links.
4. **Quartz in Edge and Core (Figure 15(d)):** Both core and edge layers are replaced with Quartz rings.
5. **Jellyfish:** A random topology consisting of 16 ULL, with each switch dedicating four 10 Gbps links to connect to other switches.
6. **Quartz in Jellyfish:** A random topology consisting of four Quartz rings, with each Quartz ring dedicating a total of four 10 Gbps links to connect to switches in the other rings.

### 7.1 Results

We evaluate the performance of the different topologies using three common traffic patterns:

- **Scatter:** One host is the sender and the others are receivers. The sender concurrently sends a flow of packets to the receivers.

| Switch | Latency | Port Count |
|---|---|---|
| Cisco Nexus 7000 (CCS) | 6 us | 768 10Gbps or 192 40Gbps |
| Arista 7150S-64 (ULL) | 380 ns | 64 10Gbps or 16 40Gbps |

*Table 16: Specifications of switches used in our simulations.*

- **Gather:** One host is the receiver and the others are senders. The senders concurrently send a flow of packets to the receiver.
- **Scatter/Gather:** One host sends packets to all the other hosts, then all the receivers send back reply packets to the sender.

These traffic patterns are representative of latency sensitive traffic found in social networks and web search [19], and are also common in high-performance computing applications, with MPI [24] providing both scatter and gather functions as part of its API. With these workloads, we are primarily interested in determining the impact of cross-traffic on latency, where cross-traffic is generated by running multiple instances of these traffic patterns at the same time. Note that we do not show Quartz using ECMP and VLB separately. This is because there is negligible performance difference between the two protocols when using these traffic patterns.

Figure 17 shows the average latency of each scatter, gather, or scatter/gather operation in which the senders and receivers are randomly distributed across servers in the network. Both the scatter and the gather workloads show that the three-tier tree introduces significant latency even with only a single task where there is minimal congestion. Most of this latency is from the high-latency core switch. There is also an approximately linear increase in latency with additional tasks for the three-tier tree. Performing both scatter and gather exacerbates the problem with the three-tier tree exhibiting both a higher linear increase in latency with additional tasks, and a substantial jump in latency going from three to four tasks. This latency jump is due to link saturation from an oversubscribed link.

Using Quartz in the edge reduces the absolute latency compared to the three-tier tree even with only one task. This is due to the additional paths between servers in the same ring that avoid the core switch. More importantly, latency is mostly unaffected by adding additional scatter or gather tasks, which can be attributed to the high path diversity of the Quartz ring. Introducing additional scatter/gather task does increase the latency of Quartz in the edge, although at a lower rate than the three-tier tree.

As we had expected, the main performance benefit from using Quartz in the core is a reduction in the absolute latency of the core tier. There is more than a three microsecond reduction in latency by replacing the core switches in a three-tier tree with Quartz rings.

Using Quartz in both the edge and core reduces latency by nearly half compared to the three-tier tree. The latency reduction comes from a combination of a reduction in hop-count, and a significantly lower latency core tier.

Jellyfish and Quartz in Jellyfish perform almost identically for these traffic patterns. Therefore, we omit the Quartz in Jellyfish line to improve the clarity of the graphs. These random networks exhibit low latency due to their relatively low average path length and high path diversity. They have a similar response to an increase in cross-traffic as Quartz in the core, with a slightly lower absolute latency. However, these results are, in part, due to the small simulated network size. For networks that are one or two orders of magnitude larger, we would expect a small increase in path length that would increase the absolute latency by a few microseconds. In

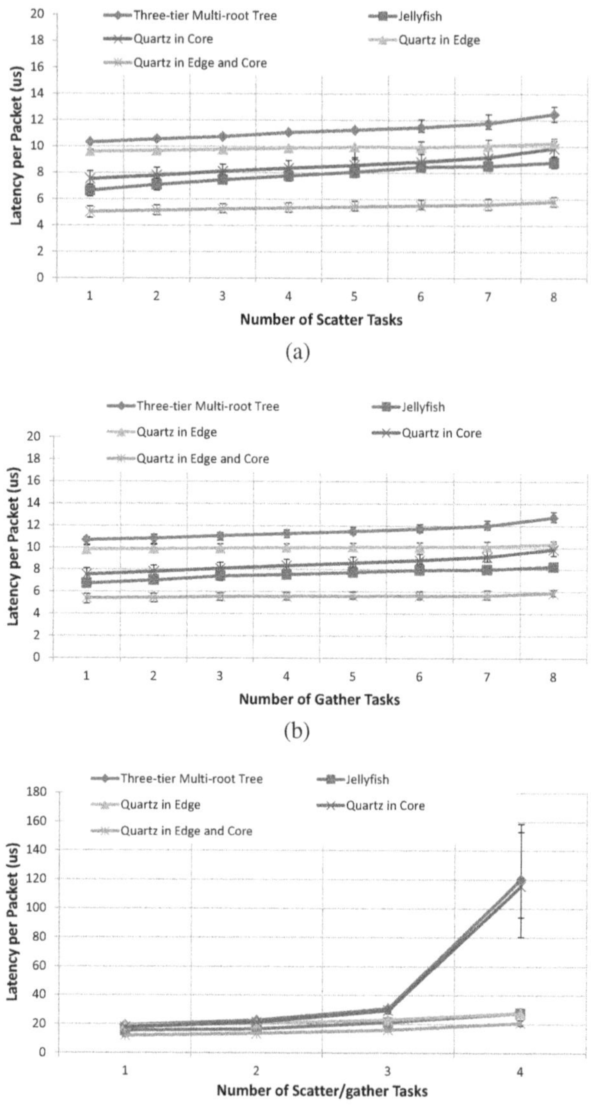


*Figure 17: Average latency comparison for global traffic pattern. This graph is best viewed in colour.*

contrast, the other network topologies can support these larger network sizes without an increase to their path lengths. Furthermore, Jellyfish's random topology is especially well-suited for handling globally distributed traffic patterns. Therefore, we next look at traffic patterns that exhibit strong locality.

Figure 18 shows the average latency of a local task, that is, a task that only performs scatter, gather, or scatter/gather operations between servers in nearby racks. There is only one local task per experiment; the remaining tasks are have randomly distributed senders and receivers and are used to generate cross-traffic. The three-tier tree has significantly lower latency as the local task traffic does not have to traverse the core tier. However, it still exhibits a linear increase in latency with additional tasks.

Jellyfish has the highest latency for these traffic patterns because it is unable to take advantage of the traffic locality. Note that in our experiments, the local task performs scatter, gather, operations to fewer targets than the non-local tasks. This accounts for the slight

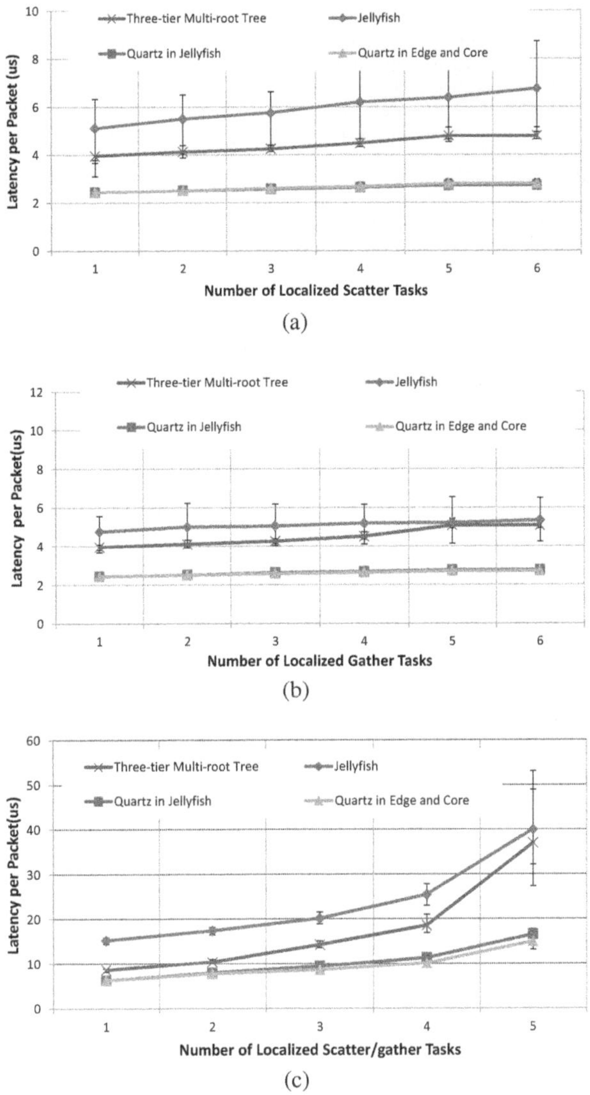


*Figure 18: Average latency comparison for localized traffic pattern. This graph is best viewed in colour.*

reduction in latency for Jellyfish's local task compared to its non-local tasks.

By using Quartz in the edge or as part of Jellyfish, there is a significant reduction in latency for the local task. Traffic from the local task remain within the Quartz ring, and because of Quartz's high path diversity, these topologies are mostly unaffected by cross-traffic. We only see an increase in latency when increasing the number of scatter/gather tasks.

## 7.2 Pathological Traffic Pattern

Replacing a core switch with a Quartz ring significantly reduces latency and, for smaller networks with plans for growth, avoids the upfront cost of purchasing a large, expensive, and mostly empty core switch chassis. However, a Quartz ring does not provide full bisection bandwidth, which can impact performance for certain workloads. In this section, we compare the performance of a non-blocking core switch to that of using Quartz in the core. We use a simple pathological traffic pattern that, when used on Quartz, sends multiple flows of traffic from different ports on switch $S_1$ to

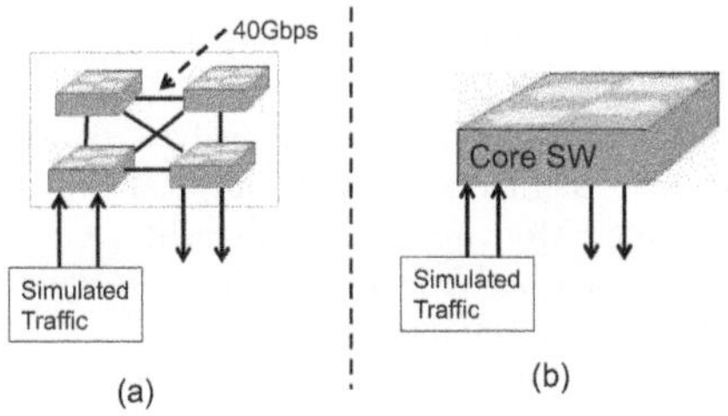


*Figure 19: Pathological traffic pattern.*

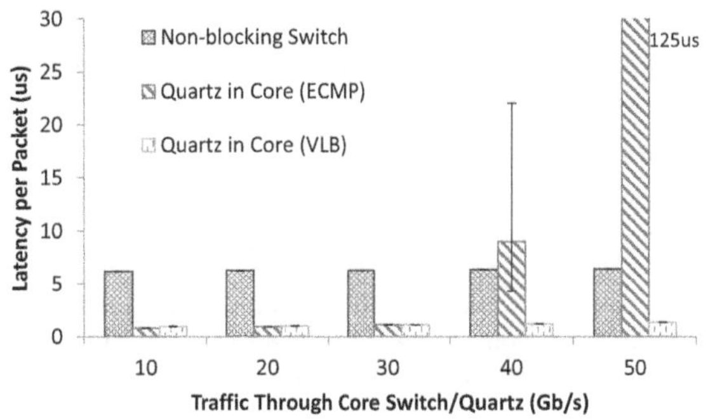


*Figure 20: Average latency comparison for pathological pattern.*

multiple receivers connected to switch $S_2$, which stresses switch-to-switch bandwidth. Our Quartz ring consists of four $40GbE$ switches logically connected as shown in Figure 19(a) and we use a standard non-blocking core switch as shown in Figure 19(b) for comparison.

Figure 20 shows the packet latency of these flows as we increase the aggregate flow bandwidth. As expected, the non-blocking core switch is unaffected by the competing flows, but introduces a significant amount of switch latency because of its store-and-forward design. Using Quartz in the core with ECMP routing, which only uses direct paths, offers significantly lower latency than the core switch until it saturates the link bandwidth between the source and destination switch. Beyond saturation, the packet latency of these flows becomes unbounded. Using Quartz in the core with VLB routing, which uses both direct and indirect paths, the latency is essentially equivalent to using ECMP routing for the low traffic experiments. Even with 50 Gbps aggregate traffic, there is no noticeable increase in packet latency when performing VLB routing.

# 8. Discussion

Our work is motivated by the requirements of latency-sensitive applications in DCNs. Existing approaches to reduce latency are primarily based on protocol changes, such as using explicit congestion signals to reduce the number of dropped packets [19, 43], perform network-wide flow scheduling [18], or offer strict resource reservations [29]. Instead, we make the observation that, similar to optical mesh networks in the wide area, commodity WDMs allow an O($n^2$) mesh to be implemented as an O($n$) physical ring in a datacenter.

This observation could not be put into practice earlier due to the high cost of optical WDMs. However, due to the recent large-scale rollout of fiber-to-the-home, optical part costs have been dropping exponentially, making their use feasible as replacements for electronic switches. Although Quartz still carries a price premium over traditional DCNs, we expect the price difference will diminish as WDM shipping volumes continue to rise. Some DCN operators may prefer to invest the price premium into higher bisection bandwidth instead of lower network latency. However, for applications that require ultra low latency, our analysis shows that there is no cost-effective alternative that can realistically be deployed in a modern datacenter. More importantly, we believe our work paves the way for future innovative architectures that integrate low-cost commodity WDM hardware into DCNs.

The main limitation of a WDM mesh ring is its limited scalability. We have turned this limitation into an advantage by making Quartz a design element that can replace *portions* of current DCNs. Quartz, by design, is completely backwards compatible with existing DCNs. It can be incrementally deployed as needed to cut latency in portions of DCNs, or to allow incremental deployment of a core switch. Moreover, if port count of low-latency cut-through switches increase, Quartz becomes more scalable.

# 9. Conclusions

Drawing on the requirements of latency-sensitive applications such as high-performance computing, we present an *architectural approach* to latency reduction. Our key breakthrough is to present Quartz, a logical O($n^2$) mesh implemented as a physical O($n$) ring using inexpensive commodity Wavelength Division Multiplexers. Although current port counts of low-latency switches limit the scale of a single Quartz network, we demonstrate that Quartz can be used to incrementally replace latency-sensitive portions of standard DCN topologies to cut end-to-end latency between 33% to 50%.

Compared to existing topologies, Quartz has three advantages: (a) least possible hop count, so minimal latency (b) elimination of queuing latency due to cross traffic and (c) if necessary, the ability to use two-hop paths to achieve high bisection bandwidths, at the expense of slightly higher latency. Quartz is completely legacy-compatible: its benefits can be obtained *without* having to replace current DCNs.

We have evaluated our ideas using analysis, simulations, and a small prototype. We find that Quartz can significantly reduce latency. In particular, we found that using Quartz in both the core and edge can reduce latency by 50% in typical scenarios.

# Acknowledgment

We thank our shepherd Jitendra Padhye and the anonymous reviewers for their insightful comments. This work is supported by the Natural Sciences and Engineering Research Council of Canada, and the Canada Research Chairs Program.

# 10. References

[1] Data Center Multi-Tier Model Design. *Cisco Data Center Infrastructure 2.5 Design Guide*, December 2007. http://bit.ly/1lusMXi.

[2] Acmemicro - Arista 7148SX, December 2013. http://bit.ly/14xquvm.

[3] Arista 7100 Series. December 2013. http://bit.ly/VBolLl.

[4] Arista 7150 Series. December 2013. http://bit.ly/PUH7uD.

[5] Cisco Catalyst 4948 Switch. December 2013. http://bit.ly/VtlIbf.

[6] Quanta T3048-LB8, December 2013. http://bit.ly/173tPpz.

[7] 10Gbps 10GHz DWDM SFP Single Mode 40km Optical Transceivr, May 2014. http://bit.ly/1hAwCXP.

[8] 80 channels, 2RU Rack Mount, Duplex, Athermal AWG, DWDM Mux & Demux, May 2014. http://bit.ly/1iaUSzG.

[9] Cisco Nexus 7700 Switches. May 2014. http://bit.ly/SZGzs2.

[10] Fixed Flange E2000/APC Fiber Optic Attenuator 1 to 30dB optional, May 2014. http://bit.ly/1r0skSW.

[11] Optical Impairment-Aware WSON Control Plane for Cisco ONS 15454 MSTP Data Sheet, May 2014. http://bit.ly/RC8Ljo.

[12] OpticTrans DWDM 80 Channel Amplifier / EDFA / Fiber Optic Amplifier, June 2014. http://bit.ly/TxiMjg.

[13] Storm: Distributed and fault-tolerant realtime computation, January 2014. http://storm-project.net/.

[14] Website for Apache Thrift, January 2014. http://thrift.apache.org/.

[15] Website for Nuttcp, January 2014. http://bit.ly/1bDluG9.

[16] H. Abu-Libdeh, P. Costa, A. Rowstron, G. O'Shea, and A. Donnelly. Symbiotic routing in future data centers. In *Proceedings of SIGCOMM*, New Delhi, India, August 2010.

[17] M. Al-Fares, A. Loukissas, and A. Vahdat. A scalable, commodity data center network architecture. In *Proceedings of SIGCOMM*, Seattle, Washington, August 2008.

[18] M. Al-Fares, S. Radhakrishnan, B. Raghavan, N. Huang, and A. Vahdat. Hedera: Dynamic flow scheduling for data center networks. In *Proceedings of NSDI*, San Jose, California, April 2010.

[19] M. Alizadeh, A. Greenberg, D. Maltz, J. Padhye, P. Patel, B. Prabhakar, S. Sengupta, and M. Sridharan. Data center TCP (DCTCP). In *Proceedings of SIGCOMM*, New Delhi, India, August 2010.

[20] J. E. Berthold. Optical Networking for Data Center Interconnects Across Wide Area Networks. In *Proceedings of the Symposium on High-performance Interconnects*, New York, New York, August 2009.

[21] J. Dean and S. Ghemawat. MapReduce: simplified data processing on large clusters. *Communications of the ACM Magazine*, January 2008.

[22] M. Dobrescu, N. Egi, K. Argyraki, B.-G. Chun, K. Fall, G. Iannaccone, A. Knies, M. Manesh, and S. Ratnasamy. Routebricks: Exploiting parallelism to scale software routers. In *Proceedings of SOSP*, Big Sky, Montana, October 2009.

[23] N. Farrington and A. Andreyev. Facebook's data center network architecture. 2013. http://bit.ly/1mABW01.

[24] I. Foster. *Designing and Building Parallel Programs: Concepts and Tools for Parallel Software Engineering*. Boston, MA, Feburary 1995.

[25] C. Guo, G. Lu, D. Li, H. Wu, X. Zhang, Y. Shi, C. Tian, Y. Zhang, and S. Lu. BCube: a high performance, server-centric network architecture for modular data centers. In *Proceedings of SIGCOMM*, Barcelona, Spain, August 2009.

[26] C. Guo, H. Wu, K. Tan, L. Shi, Y. Zhang, and S. Lu. DCell: a scalable and fault-tolerant network structure for data centers. In *Proceedings of SIGCOMM*, Seattle, Washington, August 2008.

[27] C. Hong, M. Caesar, and P. Godfrey. Finishing flows quickly with preemptive scheduling. In *Proceedings of SIGCOMM*, Helsinki, Finland, August 2012.

[28] N. S. Islam, M. W. Rahman, J. Jose, R. Rajachandrasekar, H. Wang, H. Subramoni, C. Murthy, and D. K. Panda. High performance rdma-based design of hdfs over infiniband. In *Proceedings of the International Conference on High Performance Computing, Networking, Storage and Analysis*, Salt Lake City, Utah, November 2012.

[29] N. Jiang, D. Becker, G. Michelogiannakis, and W. Dally. Network congestion avoidance through speculative reservation. In *Proceedings of the HPCA*, New Orleans, Louisiana, Feburary 2012.

[30] S. Kandula, S. Sengupta, A. Greenberg, P. Patel, and R. Chaiken. the nature of data center traffic: Measurements & analysis. In *Proceedings of the IMC*, Chicago, Illinois, November 2009.

[31] R. Kapoor, G. Porter, M. Tewari, G. Voelker, and A. Vahdat. Chronos: predictable low latency for data center applications. In *Proceedings of the Symposium on Cloud Computing(SoCC)*, San Jose, CA, October 2012.

[32] H. Litz, H. Froning, M. Nuessle, and U. Bruning. A HyperTransport Network Interface Controller for Ultra-low Latency Message Transfers. *Hyper Transport Consortium*, Feburary 2008.

[33] H. Liu and R. Zhang-Shen. On direct routing in the valiant load-balancing architecture. In *Proceedings of the GLOBECOM*, St. Louis, Missouri, November 2005.

[34] S. Miller. *Optical fiber telecommunications*. Elsevier, 1979.

[35] J. Mudigonda, P. Yalagandula, M. Al-Fares, and J. C. Mogul. Spain: Cots data-center ethernet for multipathing over arbitrary topologies. In *Proceedings of NSDI*, San Jose, CA, April 2010.

[36] S. M. Rumble, D. Ongaro, R. Stutsman, M. Rosenblum, and J. K. Ousterhout. It's time for low latency. In *Proceedings of HotOS*, Napa, California, May 2011.

[37] J.-Y. Shin, B. Wong, and E. G. Sirer. Small-world datacenters. In *Proceedings of the ACM Symposium on Cloud Computing*, Cascais, Portugal, October 2011.

[38] A. Singla, C. Hong, L. Popa, and P. Godfrey. Jellyfish: Networking data centers randomly. In *Proceedings of NSDI*, San Jose, California, April 2012.

[39] R. Teixeira, K. Marzullo, S. Savage, and G. M. Voelker. Characterizing and measuring path diversity of internet topologies. June 2003.

[40] B. Vamanan, J. Hasan, and T. Vijaykumar. Deadline-aware datacenter tcp (D2TCP). In *Proceedings of SIGCOMM*, Helsinki, Finland, August 2012.

[41] C. Wilson, H. Ballani, T. Karagiannis, and A. Rowtron. Better never than late: meeting deadlines in datacenter networks. In *Proceedings of SIGCOMM*, Toronto, Canada, August 2011.

[42] H. Zang and J. P. Jue. A review of routing and wavelength assignment approaches for wavelength-routed optical WDM networks. *Springer's Optical Networks Magazine*, January 2000.

[43] D. Zats, T. Das, P. Mohan, D. Borthakur, and R. Katz. DeTail: Reducing the flow completion time tail in datacenter networks. In *Proceedings of SIGCOMM*, Helsinki, Finland, August 2012.

# Using RDMA Efficiently for Key-Value Services

Anuj Kalia Michael Kaminsky† David G. Andersen
Carnegie Mellon University †Intel Labs
{akalia,dga}@cs.cmu.edu michael.e.kaminsky@intel.com

## ABSTRACT

This paper describes the design and implementation of HERD, a key-value system designed to make the best use of an RDMA network. Unlike prior RDMA-based key-value systems, HERD focuses its design on reducing network round trips while using efficient RDMA primitives; the result is substantially lower latency, and throughput that saturates modern, commodity RDMA hardware.

HERD has two unconventional decisions: First, it does not use RDMA reads, despite the allure of operations that bypass the remote CPU entirely. Second, it uses a mix of RDMA and messaging verbs, despite the conventional wisdom that the messaging primitives are slow. A HERD client writes its request into the server's memory; the server computes the reply. This design uses a single round trip for all requests and supports up to 26 million key-value operations per second with 5 µs average latency. Notably, for small key-value items, our full system throughput is similar to native RDMA read throughput and is over 2X higher than recent RDMA-based key-value systems. We believe that HERD further serves as an effective template for the construction of RDMA-based datacenter services.

## Keywords

RDMA; InfiniBand; RoCE; Key-Value Stores

## 1. INTRODUCTION

This paper explores a question that has important implications for the design of modern clustered systems: What is the best method for using RDMA features to support remote hash-table access? To answer this question, we first evaluate the performance that, with sufficient attention to engineering, can be achieved by each of the RDMA communication primitives. Using this understanding, we show how to use an unexpected combination of methods and system architectures to achieve the maximum performance possible on a high-performance RDMA network.

Our work is motivated by the seeming contrast between the fundamental time requirements for cross-node traffic vs. CPU-to-memory lookups, and the designs that have recently emerged that use multiple RDMA (remote direct memory access) reads. On one hand, going between nodes takes roughly 1-3 µs, compared to 60-120 ns for a memory lookup, suggesting that a multiple-RTT design as found in the recent Pilaf [21] and FaRM [8] systems should be fundamentally slower than a single-RTT design. But on the other hand, an RDMA read bypasses many potential sources of overhead, such as servicing interrupts and initiating control transfers, which involve the host CPU. In this paper, we show that there is a better path to taking advantage of RDMA to achieve high-throughput, low-latency key-value storage.

A challenge for both our and prior work lies in the lack of richness of RDMA operations. An RDMA operation can only read or write a remote memory location. It is not possible to do more sophisticated operations such as dereferencing and following a pointer in remote memory. Recent work in building key-value stores [21, 8] has focused exclusively on using RDMA reads to traverse remote data structures, similar to what would have been done had the structure been in local memory. This approach invariably requires multiple round trips across the network.

Consider an ideal RDMA read-based key-value store (or cache) where each `GET` request requires only 1 small RDMA read. Designing such a store is as hard as designing a hash-table in which each `GET` request requires only one random memory lookup. We instead provide a solution to a simpler problem: we design a key-value cache that provides performance similar to that of the ideal cache. However, our design does not use RDMA reads at all.

In this paper, we present HERD, a key-value cache that leverages RDMA features to deliver low latency and high throughput. As we demonstrate later, RDMA reads cannot harness the full performance of the RDMA hardware. In HERD, clients transmit their request to the server's memory using RDMA writes. The server's CPU polls its memory for incoming requests. On receiving a new request, it executes the `GET` or `PUT` operation in its local data structures and sends the response back to the client. As RDMA write performance does not scale with the number of outbound connections, the response is sent as a SEND message over a datagram connection.

Our work makes three main contributions:

- A thorough analysis of the performance of RDMA verbs and expose the various design options for key-value systems.
- Evidence that "two-sided" verbs are better than RDMA reads for key-value systems, refuting the previously held assumption [21, 8].
- Describing the design and implementation of HERD, a key-value cache that offers the maximum possible performance of RDMA hardware.

The following section briefly introduces key-value stores and RDMA, and describes recent efforts in building key-value stores using RDMA. Section 3 discusses the rationale behind our design decisions and demonstrates that messaging verbs are a better choice than RDMA reads for key-value systems. Section 4 discusses the design and implementation of our key-value cache. In Section 5, we evaluate our system on a cluster of 187 nodes and compare it against FaRM [8] and Pilaf [21].


*SIGCOMM'14*, Aug 17-22 2014, Chicago, IL, USA
ACM 978-1-4503-2836-4/14/08.
http://dx.doi.org/10.1145/2619239.2626299

## 2. BACKGROUND

This section provides background information on key-value stores and caches, which are at the heart of HERD. We then provide an overview of RDMA, as is relevant for the rest of the paper.

### 2.1 Key-Value stores

DRAM-based key-value stores and caches are widespread in large-scale Internet services. They are used both as primary stores (e.g., Redis [4] and RAMCloud [23]), and as caches in front of backend databases (e.g., Memcached [5]). At their most basic level, these systems export a traditional `GET`/`PUT`/`DELETE` interface. Internally, they use a variety of data structures to provide fast, memory-efficient access to their underlying data (e.g., hash table or tree-based indexes).

In this paper, we focus on the communication architecture to support both of these applications; we use a cache implementation for end-to-end validation of our resulting design.

Although recent in-memory object stores have used both tree and hash table-based designs, this paper focuses on hash tables as the basic indexing data structure. Hash table design has a long and rich history, and the particular flavor one chooses depends largely on the desired optimization goals. In recent years, several systems have used advanced hash table designs such as Cuckoo hashing [24, 17, 9] and Hopscotch hashing [12]. Cuckoo hash tables are an attractive choice for building fast key-value systems [9, 31, 17] because, with $K$ hash functions (usually, $K$ is 2 or 3), they require only $K$ memory lookups for `GET` operations, plus an additional pointer dereference if the values are not stored in the table itself. In many workloads, `GET`s constitute over 95% of the operations [6, 22]. This property makes cuckoo hashing an attractive backend for an RDMA-based key-value store [21]. Cuckoo and Hopscotch-based designs often emphasize workloads that are read-intensive: `PUT` operations require moving values within the tables. We evaluate both balanced (50% `PUT`/`GET`) and read-intensive (95% `GET`) workloads in this paper.

To support both types of workloads without being limited by the performance of currently available data structure options, HERD internally uses a *cache* data structure that can evict items when it is full. Our focus, however, is on the network communication architecture—our results generalize across both caches and stores, so long as the implementation is fast enough that a high-performance communication architecture is needed. HERD's cache design is based on the recent MICA [18] system that provides both cache and store semantics. MICA's cache mode uses a lossy associative index to map keys to pointers, and stores the values in a circular log that is memory efficient, avoids fragmentation, and does not require expensive garbage collection. This design requires only 2 random memory accesses for both `GET` and `PUT` operations.

### 2.2 RDMA

Remote Direct Memory Access (RDMA) allows one computer to directly access the memory of a remote computer without involving the operating system at any host. This enables zero-copy transfers, reducing latency and CPU overhead. In this work, we focus on two types of RDMA-providing interconnects: InfiniBand and RoCE (RDMA over Converged Ethernet). However, we believe that our design is applicable to other RDMA providers such as iWARP, Quadrics, and Myrinet.

InfiniBand is a switched fabric network widely used in high-performance computing systems. RoCE is a relatively new network protocol that allows direct memory access over Ethernet. InfiniBand and RoCE NICs achieve low latency by implementing several layers of the network stack (transport layer through physical layer) in hardware, and by providing RDMA and kernel-bypass. In this section, we provide an overview of RDMA features and terminology that are used in the rest of this paper.

#### *2.2.1 Comparison with classical Ethernet*

To distinguish from RoCE, we refer to non-RDMA providing Ethernet networks as "classical Ethernet." Unlike classical Ethernet NICs, RDMA NICs (RNICs) provide reliable delivery to applications by employing hardware-based retransmission of lost packets. Further, RNICs provide kernel bypass for all communication. These two factors reduce end-to-end latency as well as the CPU load on the communicating hosts. The typical end-to-end ($\frac{1}{2}$RTT) latency in InfiniBand/RoCE is 1 $\mu$s while that in modern classical Ethernet-based solutions [2, 18] is 10 $\mu$s. A large portion of this gap arises because of differing emphasis in the NIC design. RDMA is increasing its presence in datacenters as the hardware becomes cheaper [21]. A 40 Gbps ConnectX-3 RNIC from Mellanox costs about $500, while a 10 Gbps Ethernet adapter costs between $300 and $800. The introduction of RoCE will further boost RDMA's presence as it will allow sockets applications to run with RDMA applications on the same network.

#### *2.2.2 Verbs and queue pairs*

Userspace programs access RNICs directly using functions called *verbs*. There are several types of verbs. Those most relevant to this work are RDMA read (READ), RDMA write (WRITE), SEND, and RECEIVE. Verbs are posted by applications to queues that are maintained inside the RNIC. Queues always exist in pairs: a *send queue* and a *receive queue* form a *queue pair* (QP). Each queue pair has an associated *completion queue* (CQ), which the RNIC fills in upon completion of verb execution.

The verbs form a semantic definition of the interface provided by the RNIC. There are two types of verbs semantics: memory semantics and channel semantics.

**Memory semantics**: The RDMA verbs (READ and WRITE) have memory semantics: they specify the remote memory address to operate upon. These verbs are *one-sided*: the responder's CPU is unaware of the operation. This lack of CPU overhead at the responder makes one-sided verbs attractive. Furthermore, they have the lowest latency and highest throughput among all verbs.

**Channel semantics**: SEND and RECEIVE (RECV) have channel semantics, i.e., the SEND's payload is written to a remote memory address that is specified by the responder in a pre-posted RECV. An analogy for this would be an unbuffered sockets implementation that required `read()` to be called before the packet arrived. SEND and RECV are *two-sided* as the CPU at the responder needs to post a RECV in order for an incoming SEND to be processed. Unlike the memory verbs, the responder's CPU is involved. Two-sided verbs also have slightly higher latency and lower throughput than one sided verbs and have been regarded unfavorably for designing key-value systems [21, 8].

Although SEND and RECV verbs are technically RDMA verbs, we distinguish them from READ and WRITE. We refer to READ and WRITE as *RDMA verbs*, and refer to SEND and RECV as *messaging verbs*.

Verbs are usually posted to the send queue of a QP (except RECV, which is posted to the receive queue). To post a verb to the RNIC, an application calls into the userland RDMA driver. Then, the driver prepares a Work Queue Element (WQE) in the host's memory and

| Verb | RC | UC | UD |
|---|---|---|---|
| SEND/RECV | ✓ | ✓ | ✓ |
| WRITE | ✓ | ✓ | ✗ |
| READ | ✓ | ✗ | ✗ |

**Table 1: Operations supported by each connection type.** UC does not support READs, and UD does not support RDMA at all.

rings a doorbell on the RNIC via Programmed IO (PIO). For ConnectX and newer RNICs, the doorbell contains the entire WQE [27]. For WRITE and SEND verbs, the WQE is associated with a payload that needs to be sent to the remote host. A payload up to the maximum PIO size (256 in our setup) can be *inlined* in the WQE, otherwise it can be fetched by the RNIC via a DMA read. An inlined post involves no DMA operations, reducing latency and increasing throughput for small payloads.

When the RNIC completes the network steps associated with the verb, it pushes a completion event to the queue pair's associated completion queue (CQ) via a DMA write. Using completion events adds extra overhead to the RNIC's PCIe bus. This overhead can be reduced by using *selective signaling*. When using a selectively signaled send queue of size $S$, up to $S-1$ consecutive verbs can be *unsignaled*, i.e., a completion event will not be pushed for these verbs. The receive queue cannot be selectively signaled. As $S$ is large ($\sim$ 128), we use the terms "selective signaling" and "unsignaled" interchangeably.

### 2.2.3 *Transport types*

RDMA transports can be connected or unconnected. A connected transport requires a connection between two queue pairs that communicate exclusively with each other. Current RDMA implementations support two main types of connected transports: Reliable Connection (RC) and Unreliable Connection (UC). There is no acknowledgement of packet reception in UC; packets can be lost and the affected message can be dropped. As UC does not generate ACK/NAK packets, it causes less network traffic than RC.

In an unconnected transport, one queue pair can communicate with any number of other queue pairs. Current implementations provide only one unconnected transport: Unreliable Datagram (UD). The RNIC maintains state for each active queue in its queue pair context cache, so datagram transport can scale better for applications with a one-to-many topology.

InfiniBand and RoCE employ lossless link-level flow control, namely, credit-based flow control and Priority Flow Control. *Even with unreliable transports (UC/UD), packets are never lost due to buffer overflows.* Reasons for packet loss include bit errors on the wire and hardware failures, which are extremely rare. Therefore, our design, similar to choices made by Facebook and others [22], sacrifices transport-level retransmission for fast common case performance at the cost of rare application-level retries.

Some transport types support only a subset of the available verbs. Table 1 lists the verbs supported by each transport type. Figure 1 shows the DMA and network steps involved in posting verbs.

## 2.3 Existing RDMA-based key-value stores

**Pilaf** [21] is a key-value store that aims for high performance and low CPU use. For GETs, clients access a cuckoo hash table at the server using READs, which requires 2.6 round trips on average for single GET request. For PUTs, clients send their requests to the server using a SEND message. To ensure consistent GETs in the presence of concurrent PUTs, Pilaf's data structures are *self-verifying*: each hash table entry is augmented with two 64-bit checksums.

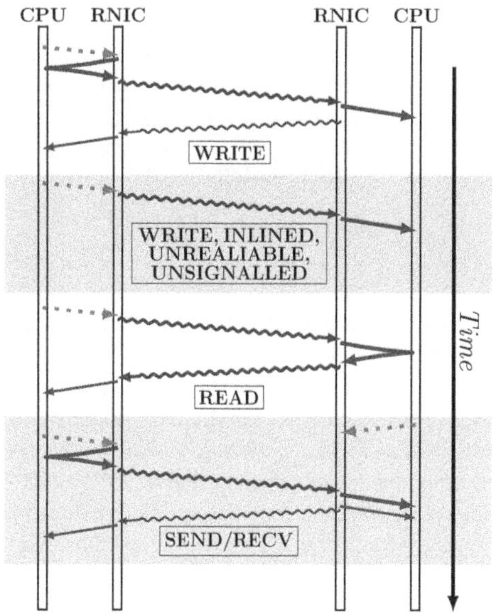


**Figure 1: Steps involved in posting verbs.** The dotted arrows are PCIe PIO operations. The solid, straight arrows are DMA operations: the thin ones are for writing the completion events. The thick wavy arrows are RDMA data packets and the thin ones are ACKs.

The second key-value store we compare against is based upon the store designed in **FaRM** [8]. It is important to note that FaRM is a more general-purpose distributed computing platform that exposes memory of a cluster of machines as a shared address space; we compare *only* against a key-value store implemented on top of FaRM that we call FaRM-KV. Unlike the client-server design in Pilaf and HERD, FaRM is symmetric, befitting its design as a cluster architecture: each machine acts as both a server and client.

FaRM's design provides two components for comparison. First is its key-value store design, which uses a variant of Hopscotch hashing [12] to create a locality-aware hash table. For GETs, clients READ several consecutive Hopscotch slots, one of which contains the key with high probability. Another READ is required to fetch the value if it is not stored inside the hash table. For PUTs, clients WRITE their request to a circular buffer in the server's memory. The server polls this buffer to detect new requests. This design is not specific to FaRM—we use it merely as an extant alternative to Pilaf's Cuckoo-based design to provide a more in-depth comparison for HERD.

The second important aspect of FaRM is its symmetry; here it differs from both Pilaf and HERD. For small, fixed-size key-value pairs, FaRM can "inline" the value with the key. With inlining, FaRM's RDMA read-based design still achieves lower maximum *throughput* than HERD, but it uses less CPU. This tradeoff may be right for a cluster where all machines are also busy doing computation; we do not evaluate the symmetric use case here, but it is an important consideration for users of either design.

## 3. DESIGN DECISIONS

Towards our goal of supporting key-value servers that achieve the highest possible throughput with RDMA, we explain in this section the reasons we choose to use—and not use—particular RDMA features and other design options. To begin with, we present an analysis of the performance of the RDMA verbs; we then craft a

| Name | Nodes | Hardware |
|---|---|---|
| Apt | 187 | Intel Xeon E5-2450 CPUs. ConnectX-3 MX354A (56 Gbps IB) via PCIe 3.0 x8 |
| Susitna | 36 | AMD Opteron 6272 CPUs. CX-3 MX353A (40 Gbps IB) and CX-3 MX313A (40 Gbps RoCE) via PCIe 2.0 x8 |

**Table 2: Cluster configuration**

communication architecture using the fastest among them that can support our application needs.

As hinted in Section 1, one of the core decisions to make is whether to use memory verbs (RDMA read and write) or messaging verbs (SEND and RECV). Recent work from the systems and networking communities, for example, has focused on RDMA reads as a building block, because they bypass the remote network stack and CPU entirely for `GET`s [21, 8]. In contrast, however, the HPC community has made wider use of messaging, both for key-value caches [14] and general communication [16]. These latter systems scaled to thousands of machines, but provided low throughput—less than one million operations per second in memcached [14]. The reason for low throughput in [14] is not clear, but we suspect application design that makes the system incapable of leveraging the full power of the RNICs.

There remains an important gap between these two lines of work, and to our knowledge, HERD is the first system to provide the best of both worlds: throughput even higher than that of the RDMA-based systems while scaling to several hundred clients.

HERD takes a hybrid approach, using both RDMA and messaging to best effect. RDMA reads, however, are unattractive because of the need for multiple round trips. In HERD, clients instead write their requests to the server using RDMA writes over an Unreliable Connection (UC). This write places the `PUT` or `GET` request into a per-client memory region in the server. The server polls these regions for new requests. Upon receiving one, the server process executes in conventional fashion using its local data structures. It then sends a reply to the client using messaging verbs: a SEND over an Unreliable Datagram.

To explain why we use this hybrid of RDMA and messaging, we describe the performance experiments and analysis that support it. Particularly, we describe why we prefer using RDMA writes instead of reads, not taking advantage of hardware retransmission by opting for unreliable transports, and using messaging verbs despite conventional wisdom that they are slower than RDMA.

## 3.1 Notation and experimental setup

In the rest of this paper, we refer to an RDMA read as READ and to an RDMA write as WRITE. In this section, we present microbenchmarks from Emulab's [29] Apt cluster, a large, modern testbed equipped with 56 Gbps InfiniBand. Because Apt has only InfiniBand, in Section 5, we also use the NSF PRObE's [11] Susitna cluster to evaluate on RoCE. The hardware configurations of these clusters are shown in Table 2.

These experiments use one server machine and several client machines. We denote the server machine by $M_S$ and its RNIC by $RNIC_S$. Client machine $i$ is denoted by $C_i$. The server and client machines may run multiple server and client processes respectively. We call a message from client to server a *request*, and the reply from server to client, a *response*. The host issuing a verb is the *requester* and the destination host *responder*. For unsignaled SEND and WRITE over UC, the destination host does not actually send a response, but we still call it a responder.

For throughput experiments, processes maintain a window of several outstanding verbs in their send queues. Using windows allows us to saturate our RNICs with fewer processes. In all of our throughput experiments, we manually tune the window size for maximum aggregate throughput.

## 3.2 Using WRITE instead of READ

There are several benefits to using WRITE instead of READ. WRITEs can be performed over the UC transport, which itself confers several performance advantages. Because the responder does not need to send packets back, its RNIC performs less processing, and thus can support higher throughput than with READs. The reduced network bandwidth similarly benefits both the server and client throughput. Finally, as one might expect, the latency of an unsignaled WRITE is about half that ($\frac{1}{2}$ RTT) of a READ. This makes it possible to replace one READ by two WRITEs, one client-to-server and one server-to-client (forming an application-level request-reply pair), without increasing latency significantly.

### 3.2.1 *WRITEs have lower latency than READs*

Measuring the latency of an unsignaled WRITE is not straightforward as the requester gets no indication of completion. Therefore, we measure it indirectly by measuring the latency of an *ECHO*. In an ECHO, a client transmits a message to a server and the server relays the same message back to the client. If the ECHO is realized by using unsignaled WRITEs, the latency of an unsignaled WRITE is at most one half of the ECHO's latency.

We also measure the latency of signaled READ and WRITE operations. As these operations are signaled, we use the completion event to measure latency. For WRITE, we also measure the latency with payload inlining.

Figure 2 shows the average latency from these measurements. We use inlined and unsignaled WRITEs for ECHOs. On our RNICs, the maximum size of the inlined payload is 256 bytes. Therefore, the graphs for WR-INLINE and ECHO are only shown up to 256 bytes.

**Unsignaled verbs**: For payloads up to 64 bytes, the latency of ECHOs is close to READ latency, which confirms that the one-way WRITE latency is about half of the READ latency. For larger ECHOs, the latency increases because of the time spent in writing to the RNIC via PIO.

**Signaled verbs**: The solid lines in Figure 2 show the latencies for three signaled verbs—WRITE, READ, and WRITE with inlining (WR-INLINE). The latencies for READ and WRITE are similar because the length of the network/PCIe path travelled is identical. By avoiding one DMA operation, inlining reduces the latency of small WRITEs significantly.

### 3.2.2 *WRITEs have higher throughput than READs*

To evaluate throughput, it is first necessary to observe that with many client machines communicating with one server, different verbs perform very differently when used at the clients (talking to one server) and at the server (talking to many clients).

**Inbound throughput:** First, we measured the throughput for *inbound* verbs, i.e., the number of verbs that multiple remote machines (the clients) can issue to one machine (the server). Using the notation introduced above, $C_1, ..., C_N$ issue operations to $M_S$ as shown in Figure 3a. Figure 3b shows the cumulative throughput observed across the active machines. For up to 128 byte payloads, WRITEs achieve 35 Mops, which is about 34% higher higher than

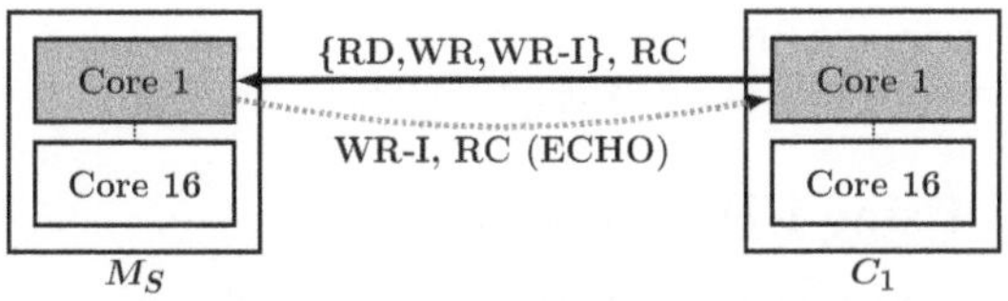


**(a)** Setup for measuring verbs and ECHO latency. We use one client process to issue operations to one server process

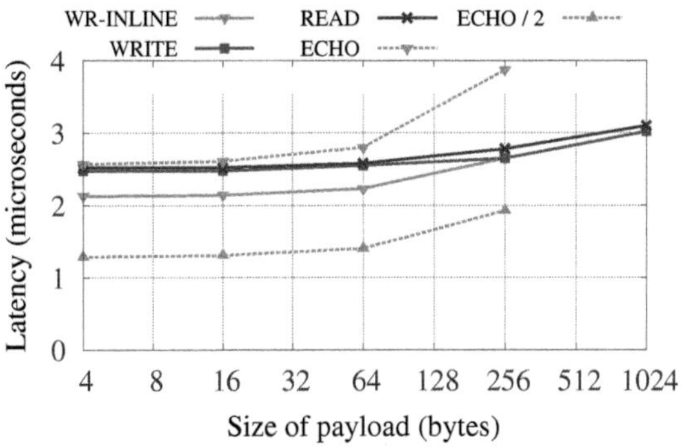


**(b)** The one-way latency of WRITE is half of the ECHO latency. ECHO operations used unsignaled verbs.

**Figure 2: Latency of verbs and ECHO operations**

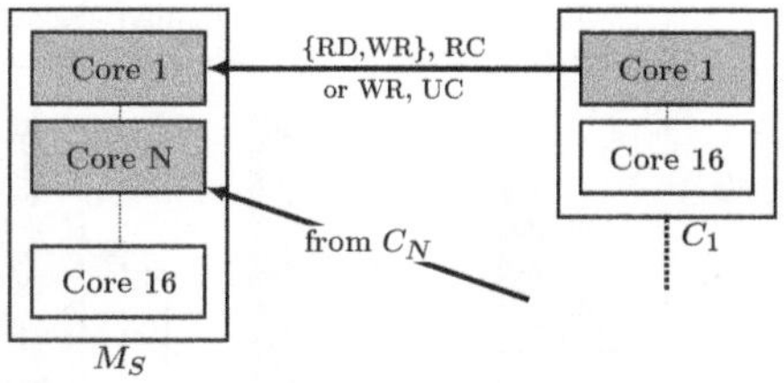


**(a)** Setup for measuring inbound throughput. Each client process communicates with only one server process

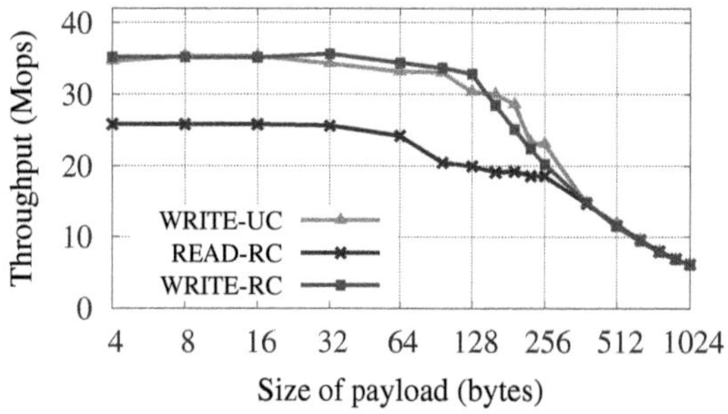


**(b)** For moderately sized payloads, WRITE has much higher inbound throughput than READs.

**Figure 3: Comparison of inbound verbs throughput**

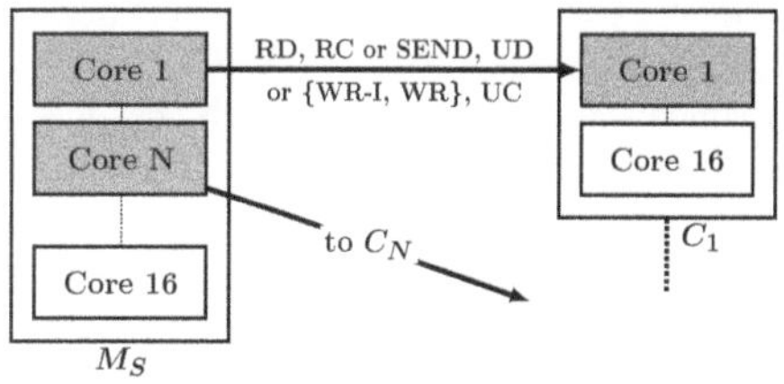


**(a)** Setup for measuring outbound throughput. Each server process communicates with only one client process.

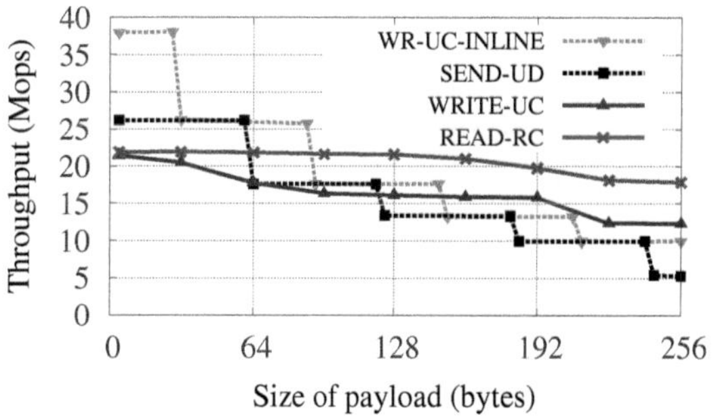


**(b)** For small payloads, WRITE with inlining has a higher outbound throughput than READ.

**Figure 4: Comparison of outbound verbs throughput**

the maximum READ throughput (26 Mops). Interestingly, reliable WRITEs deliver significantly higher throughput than READs despite their identical InfiniBand path. This is explained as follows: writes require less state maintainance both at the RDMA and the PCIe level because the initiator does not need to wait for a response. For reads, however, the request must be maintained in the initiator's memory till a response arrives. At the RDMA level, each queue pair can only service a few outstanding READ requests (16 in our RNICs). Similarly, at the PCIe level, reads are performed using non-posted transactions, whereas writes use cheaper, posted transactions.

Although the inbound throughput of WRITEs over UC and RC is nearly identical, using UC is still beneficial: It requires less processing at $RNIC_S$, and HERD uses this saved capacity to SEND responses.

**Outbound throughput**: We next measured the throughput for *outbound* verbs. Here, $M_S$ issues operations to $C_1, ..., C_N$. As shown in Figure 4a, there are $N$ processes on $M_S$; the $i^{th}$ process communicates with $C_i$ only (the scalability problems associated with all-to-all communication are explained in Section 3.3). Apart from READs, WRITEs, and inlined WRITEs over UC, we also measure the throughput for inlined SENDs over UD for reasons outlined in Section 3.3. Figure 4b plots the throughput achieved by $M_S$ for different payload sizes. For small sizes, inlined WRITEs and SENDs have significantly higher outbound throughput than READs. For large sizes, the throughput of all WRITE and SEND variants is less than for READs, but it is never less than 50% of the READ throughput. Thus, even for these larger items, using a single WRITE (or SEND) for responses remains a better choice than using multiple READs for key-value items.

**ECHO throughput** is interesting for two reasons. First, it provides an upper bound on the throughput of a key-value cache based on one round trip of communication. Second, ECHOs help characterize the processing power of the RNIC: although the advertised message rate of ConnectX-3 cards is 35 Mops, bidirectionally, they can process many more messages.

An ECHO consists of a request message and a response message. Varying the verbs and transport types yield several different implementations of ECHO. Figure 5 shows the throughput for some of the possible combinations and for 32 byte payloads. The figure also shows that using inlinining, selective signaling, and UC transport increases the performance significantly.

ECHOs achieve maximum throughput (26 Mops) when both the request and the response are done as RDMA writes. However, as shown in Section 3.3, this approach does not scale with the number of connections. HERD uses RDMA writes (over UC) for requests and SENDs (over UD) for responses. *An ECHO server using this hybrid also achieves 26 Mops—it gives the performance of WRITE-based ECHOs, but with much better scalability.*

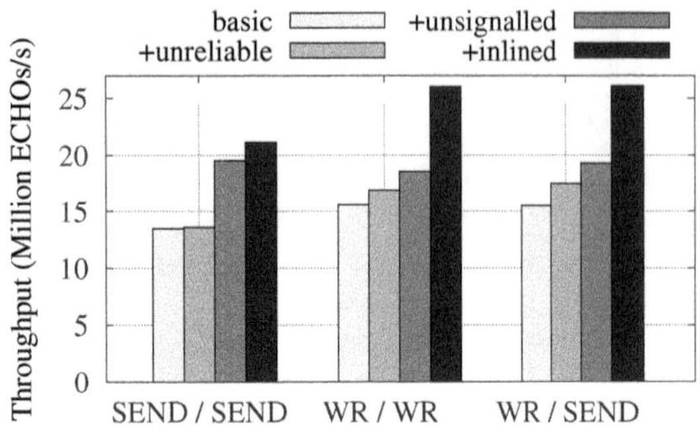


**Figure 5: Throughput of ECHOs with 32 byte messages.** In WR-SEND, the response is sent over UD.

By avoiding the overhead of posting RECVs at the server, our method of WRITE based requests and SEND-based responses provides better throughput than purely SEND-based ECHOs. Interestingly, however, after enabling all optimizations, the throughput of purely SEND-based ECHOs (with no RDMA operations) is 21 Mops, which is more than three-fourths of the peak inbound READ throughput (26 Mops). Both Pilaf and FaRM have noted that RDMA reads vastly outperform SEND-based ECHOs, which our results agree with *if our optimizations are removed.* With these optimizations, however, SENDs significantly outperform READs in cases where a single SEND-based ECHO can be used in place of multiple READs per request.

Our experiments show that several ECHO designs, with varying degrees of scalability, can perform better than multiple-READ designs. *From a network-centric perspective, this is fortunate: it also means that designs that use only one cross-datacenter RTT can potentially outperform multiple-RTT designs both in throughput and in latency.*

**Discussion of verbs throughput**: The ConnectX-3 card is advertised to support 35 million messages per second. Our experiments show that the card can achieve this rate for inbound WRITEs (Figure 3b) and slightly exceed it for very small outbound WRITEs (Figure 4b). All other verbs are slower than 30 Mops regardless of operation size. While the manufacturer does not specify bidirectional message throughput, we know empirically that $RNIC_S$ can service 30 million ECHOs per second (WRITE-based ECHOs achieve 30 Mops with 16 byte payloads; Figure 5 uses 32 byte payloads), or at least 60 total Mops of inbound WRITEs and outbound SENDs.

The reduced throughputs can be attributed to several factors:

- For outbound WRITEs larger than 28 bytes, the RNIC's message rate is limited by the PCIe PIO throughput. The sharp decreases in the WR-UC-INLINE and SEND-UD graphs in Figure 4b at 64 byte intervals are explained by the use of write-combining buffers for PIO acceleration. With the write-combining optimization, the unit of PIO writes is a cache line instead of a word. Due to the larger datagram header, the throughput for SEND-UD drops for smaller payload sizes than for WRITEs
- The maximum throughput for inbound and outbound READs is 26 Mops and 22 Mops respectively, which is considerably smaller than the advertised 35 Mops message rate. Unlike WRITEs, READs are bottlenecked by the RNIC's processing power. This is as expected. Outbound READs involve a PIO operation, a packet transmission, a packet reception, and a DMA write, whereas outbound WRITEs (inlined and over UC) avoid the last two steps. Inbound READs require a DMA read by the RNIC followed by a packet transmission, whereas inbound WRITEs only require a DMA write.

## 3.3 Using UD for responses

Our previous experiments did not show that as the number of connections increases, connected transports begin to slow down. To reduce hardware cost, power consumption, and design complexity, RNICs have very little on-chip memory (SRAM) to cache address translation tables and queue pair contexts [26]. A miss in this cache requires a PCIe transaction to fetch the data from host memory. When the communication fan-in or fan-out exceeds the capacity of this cache, performance begins to suffer. This is a potentially important effect to avoid both for cluster scaling, but also because it interacts with the cache or store architectural decisions. For example, the cache design we build on in HERD partitions the keyspace between several server processes in order to achieve efficient CPU and memory utilization. Such partitioning further increases the fan-in and fan out of connections to a single machine.

To evaluate this effect, we modified our throughput experiments to enable *all-to-all* communication. We use $N$ client processes (one process each at $C_1,...,C_N$) and $N$ server processes at $M_S$. For measuring inbound throughput, client processes select a server process at random and issue a WRITE to it. For outbound throughput, a server process selects a client at random and issues a WRITE to it. The results of these experiments for 32 byte messages are presented in Figure 6. Several results stand out:

**Outbound WRITEs scale poorly**: for $N = 16$, there are 256 active queue pairs at $RNIC_S$ and the server-to-clients throughput degrades to 21% of the maximum outbound WRITE throughput (Figure 4b). With many active queue pairs, each posted verb can cause a cache miss, severely degrading performance.

**Inbound WRITEs scale well**: Clients-to-server throughput is high even for $N = 16$. The reason for this is that queueing of outstanding verbs operations is performed at the requesting RNIC and very little state is maintained at the responding RNIC. Therefore, the responding RNIC can support a much larger number of active queue pairs without incurring cache misses. The higher requester overhead is amortized because the clients outnumber the server.

In a different experiment, we used 1600 client processes spread over 16 machines to issue WRITEs over UC to one server process. HERD uses this many-to-one configuration to reduce the number of active connections at the server (Section 4.2). This configuration also achieves 30 Mops.

Outbound WRITEs scale poorly only because $RNIC_S$ must manage many connected queue pairs. This problem cannot be solved if we use connected transports (RC/UC/XRC) because they require at least as many queue pairs at $M_S$ as the number of client machines. Scaling outbound communication therefore mandates using datagrams. UD transport supports one-to-many communication, i.e., a single UD queue can be used to issue operations to multiple remote UD queues. The main problem with using UD in a high performance application is that it only supports messaging verbs and not RDMA verbs.

Fortunately, messaging verbs only impose high overhead at the receiver. Senders can directly transmit their requests; only the receiver must pre-post a RECV before the SEND can be handled. For the sender, the work done to issue a SEND is identical to that required to post a WRITE. Figure 6 shows that, when performed over Unreliable Datagram transport, SEND side throughput is high and scales well with the number of connected clients.

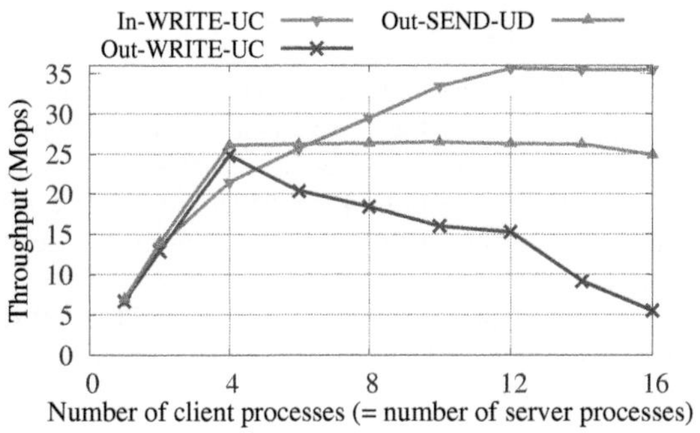


**Figure 6: Comparison of UD and UC for all-to-all communication with 32 byte payloads.** Inbound WRITEs over UC and outbound SENDs over UD scale well up to 256 queue pairs. Outbound WRITEs over UC scale poorly. All operations are inlined and unsignaled.

The slight degradation of SEND throughput beyond 10 connected clients happens because the SENDs are unsignaled, i.e., server processes get no indication of verb completion. This leads to the server processes overwhelming *RNICs* with too many outstanding operations, causing cache misses inside the RNIC. As HERD uses SENDs for responding to requests, it can use new requests as an indication of the completion of old SENDs, thereby avoiding this problem.

# 4. DESIGN OF HERD

To evaluate whether these network-driven architectural decisions work for a real key-value application, we designed and implemented an RDMA-based KV cache, called HERD, based upon recent high-performance key-value designs. Our HERD setup consists of one server machine and several client machines. The server machine runs $N_S$ server processes. $N_C$ client processes are uniformly spread across the client machines.

## 4.1 Key-Value cache

The fundamental goal of this work is to evaluate our networking and architectural decisions in the context of key-value systems. We do not focus on building better back-end key-value data structures but rather borrow existing designs from MICA [18].

MICA is a near line-rate key-value cache and store for classical Ethernet. We restrict our discussion of MICA to its cache mode. MICA uses a lossy index to map keys to pointers, and stores the actual values in a circular log. On insertion, items can be evicted from the index (thereby making the index lossy), or from the log in a FIFO order. In HERD, each server process creates an index for 64 Mi keys, and a 4 GB circular log. We use MICA's algorithm for both `GET`s and `PUT`s: each `GET` requires up to two random memory lookups, and each `PUT` requires one.

MICA shards the key space into several partitions based on a keyhash. In its "EREW" mode, each server core has exclusive read and write access to one partition. MICA uses the Flow Director [3] feature of modern Ethernet NICs to direct request packets to the core responsible for the given key. HERD achieves the same effect by allocating per-core request memory at the server, and allowing clients to WRITE their requests directly to the appropriate core.

### *4.1.1 Masking DRAM latency with prefetching*

To service a `GET`, a HERD server must perform two random memory lookups, prepare the SEND response (with the key's value inlined in the WQE), and then post the SEND verb using the `post_send()` function. The memory lookups and the `post_send()` function are the two main sources of latency at the server. Each random memory access takes 60-120 *ns* and the `post_send()` function takes about 150 *ns*. While the latter is unavoidable, we can mask the memory access latency by overlapping memory accesses of one request with computation of another request.

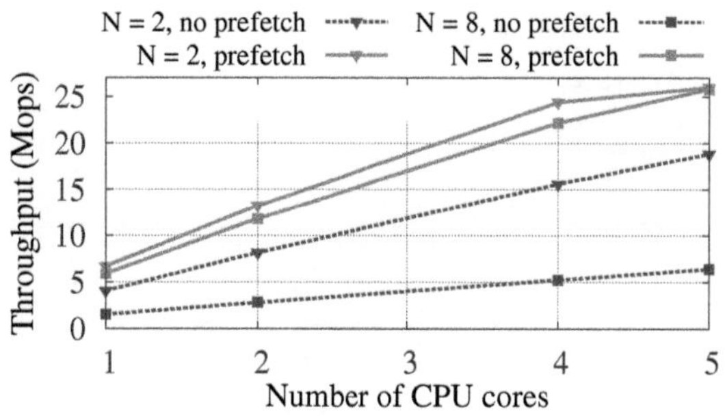


**Figure 7: Effect of prefetching on throughput**

MICA and CuckooSwitch [18, 31] mask latency by overlapping memory fetches and prefetches, or request decoding and prefetches. HERD takes a different approach: we overlap prefetches with the `post_send()` function used to transmit replies. To process multiple requests simultaneously in the absence of a driver that itself handles batches of packets [2, 18, 31]), HERD creates a pipeline of requests at the application level.

In HERD, the maximum number of memory lookups for each request is two. Therefore, we create a request pipeline with two stages. When a request is in stage $i$ of the pipeline, it performs the $i$-th memory access for the request and issues a prefetch for the next memory address. In this way, requests only access memory for which a prefetch has already been issued. On detecting a new request, the server issues a prefetch for the request's index bucket, advances the old requests in the pipeline, pushes in the new request, and finally calls `post_send()` to SEND a reply for the pipeline's completed request. The server process expects the issued prefetches to finish by the time `post_send()` returns.

Figure 7 shows the effectiveness of prefetching. We use a WRITE/SEND-based ECHO server but this time the server performs $N$ random memory accesses before sending the response. Prefetching allows fewer cores to deliver higher throughput: 5 cores can deliver the peak throughput even with $N = 8$. We conclude that there is significant headroom to implement more complex key-value applications, for instance, key-value stores, on top of HERD's request-reply communication mechanism.

With a large number of server processes, this pipelining scheme can lead to a deadlock. A server does not advance its pipeline until it receives a new request, and a client does not advance its request window until it gets a response. We avoid this deadlock as follows. While polling for new requests, if a server fails for 100 iterations consecutively, it pushes a no-op into the pipeline.

## 4.2 Requests

Clients WRITE their `GET` and `PUT` requests to a contiguous memory region on the server machine which is allocated during initialization. This memory region is called the *request region* and is shared among all the server processes by mapping it using `shmget()`. The request region is logically divided into 1 KB slots (the maximum size of a key-value item in HERD is 1 KB).

Requests are formatted as follows. A `GET` request consists only of a 16-byte keyhash. A `PUT` request contains a 16-byte keyhash, a 2-byte LEN field (specifying the value's length), and up to 1000 bytes for the value. To poll for incoming requests, we use the left-

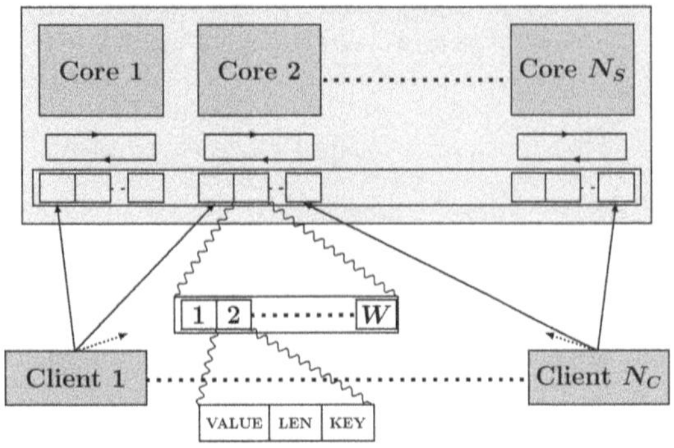


**Figure 8: Layout of the request region at the server**

to-right ordering of the RNIC's DMA writes [16, 8]. We use the keyhash field to poll for new requests; therefore, the key is written to the rightmost 16 bytes of the 1 KB slot. A non-zero keyhash indicates a new request, so we do not allow the clients to use a zero keyhash. The server zeroes out the keyhash field of the slot after sending a response, freeing it up for a new request.

Figure 8 shows the layout of the request region at the server machine. It consists of separate chunks for each server process which are further sub-divided into per-client chunks. Each per-client chunk consists of $W$ slots, i.e., each client can have up to $W$ pending requests to each server process. The size of the request region is $N_S \cdot N_C \cdot W$ KB. With $N_C$ = 200, $N_S$ = 16 and $W$ = 2, this is approximately 6 MB and fits inside the server's L3 cache. Each server process polls the per-client chunks for new requests in a round robin fashion. If server process $s$ has seen $r$ requests from client number $c$, it polls the request region at the request slot number $s \cdot (W \cdot N_c) + (c \cdot W) + r \; mod \; W$.

A network configuration using bidirectional, all-to-all, communication with connected transports would require $N_C \cdot N_S$ queue pairs at the server. HERD, however, uses connected transports for only the request side of communication, and thus requires only $N_C$ connected queue pairs. The configuration works as follows. An initializer process creates the request region, registers it with $RNIC_S$, establishes a UC connection with each client, and goes to sleep. The $N_S$ server processes then map the request region into their address space via `shmget()` and do not create any connections for receiving requests.

### 4.3 Responses

In HERD, responses are sent as SENDs over UD. Each client creates $N_S$ UD queue pairs (QPs) whereas each server process uses only one UD QP. Before writing a new request to server process $s$, a client posts a RECV to its $s$-th UD QP. This RECV specifies the memory area on the client where the server's response will be written. Each client allocates a *response region* containing $W \cdot N_S$ response slots: this region is used for the target addresses in the RECVs. After writing out $W$ requests, the client starts checking for responses by polling for RECV completions. On each successful completion, it posts another request.

The design outlined thus far deliberately shifts work from the server's RNIC to the client's, with the assumption that client machines often perform enough other work that saturating 40 or 56 gigabits of network bandwidth is not their primary concern. The servers, however, in an application such as Memcached, are often dedicated machines, and achieving high bandwidth is important.

## 5. EVALUATION

We evaluate HERD on two clusters: Apt and Susitna (Table 2). Due to limited space, we restrict our discussion to Apt and only present graphs for RoCE on Susitna. A detailed discussion of our results on Susitna may be found in [15]. Although Susitna uses similar RNICs as Apt, the slower PCIe 2.0 bus reduces the throughput of all compared systems. Despite this, our results on Susitna remain interesting: just as ConnectX-3 cards overwhelm PCIe 2.0 x8, we expect the next-generation Connect-IB cards to overwhelm PCIe 3.0 x16. Our evaluation shows that:

- HERD uses the full processing power of the RNIC. A single HERD server can process up to 26 million requests per second. For value size up to 60 bytes, HERD's request throughput is *greater than native READ throughput* and is much greater than that of READ-based key-value services: it is over 2X higher than FaRM-KV and Pilaf.
- HERD delivers up to 26 Mops with approximately 5 $\mu$s average latency. Its latency is over 2X lower than Pilaf and FaRM-KV at their peak throughput respectively.
- HERD scales to the moderately sized Apt cluster, sustaining peak throughput with over 250 connected client processes.

We conclude the evaluation by examining the seeming drawback of the HERD design relative to READ-based designs—its higher server CPU use—and put this in context with the *total* (client + server) CPU required by all systems.

### 5.1 Experimental setup

We run all our throughput and latency experiments on 18 machines in Apt. The 17 client machines run up to 3 client processes each. With at most 4 outstanding requests per client, our implementation requires at least 36 client processes to saturate the server's throughput. We over-provision slightly by using 51 client processes. The server machine runs 6 server processes, each pinned to a distinct physical core. The machine configuration is described in Table 2. The machines run Ubuntu 12.04 with Mellanox's OFED v2.2 stack.

**Comparison against stripped-down alternatives**: In keeping with our focus on understanding the effects of network-related decisions, we compare our (full) HERD implementation against simplified implementations of Pilaf and FaRM-KV. These simplified implementations use the same communication methods as the originals, but *omit* the actual key-value storage, instead returning a result instantly. We made this decision for two reasons. First, while working with Pilaf's code, we observed several optimization opportunities; we did not want our evaluation to depend on the relative performance tuning of the systems. Second, we did not have access to the FaRM source code, and we could not run Windows Server on our cluster. Instead, we created and evaluated emulated versions of the two systems which do not include their backing data structures. This approach gives these systems the maximum performance advantage possible, so the throughput we report for both Pilaf and FaRM-KV may be higher than is actually achievable by those systems.

Pilaf is based on 2-level lookups: a hash-table maps keys to pointers. The pointer is used to find the value associated with the key from flat memory regions called *extents*. FaRM-KV, in its default operating mode, uses single-level lookups. It achieves this by inlining the value in the hash-table. It also has a two-level mode, where the value is stored "out-of-table." Because the out-of-table mode is necessary for memory efficiency with variable length keys, we compare HERD against both modes. In the following two subsections, we denote the size of a key, value, and pointer by $S_K$, $S_V$, and $S_P$ respectively.

### 5.1.1 *Emulating Pilaf*

In *K*-*B* cuckoo hashing, every key can be found in *K* different buckets, determined by *K* orthogonal hash functions. For associativity, each bucket contains *B* slots. Pilaf uses 3-1 cuckoo hashing with 75% memory efficiency and 1.6 average probes per `GET` (higher memory efficiency with fewer, but slightly larger, average probes is possible with 2-4 cuckoo hashing [9]). When reading the hash index via RDMA, the smallest unit that must be read is a bucket. A bucket in Pilaf has only one slot that contains a 4 byte pointer, two 8 byte checksums, and a few other fields. We assume the bucket size in Pilaf to be 32 bytes for alignment.

**`GET`**: A `GET` in Pilaf consists of 1.6 bucket READs (on average) to find the value pointer, followed by a $S_V$ byte READ to fetch the value. It is possible to reduce Pilaf's latency by issuing concurrent READs for both cuckoo buckets. As this comes at the cost of decreased throughput, we wait for the first READ to complete and issue the second READ only if it is required.

**`PUT`**: For a `PUT`, a client SENDs a $S_K + S_V$ byte message containing the new key-value item to the server. This request may require relocating entries in the cuckoo hash-table, but we ignore that as our evaluation focuses on the network communication only.

In emulating Pilaf, we enable all of our RDMA optimizations for both request types; we call the resulting system Pilaf-em-OPT.

### 5.1.2 *Emulating FaRM-KV*

FaRM-KV uses a variant of Hopscotch hashing to locate a key in approximately one READ. Its algorithm guarantees that a key-value pair is stored in a small neighborhood of the bucket that the key hashes to. The size of the neighborhood is tunable, but its authors set it to 6 to balance good space utilization and performance for items smaller than 128 bytes. FaRM-KV can inline the values in the buckets, or it can store them separately and only store pointers in the buckets. We call our version of FaRM-KV with inlined values FaRM-em and without inlining FaRM-em-VAR (for variable length values).

**`GET`**: A `GET` in FaRM-em requires a 6 * $(S_K + S_V)$ byte READ. In FaRM-em-VAR, a `GET` requires a 6 * $(S_K + S_P)$ byte READ followed by a $S_V$ byte READ.

**`PUT`**: FaRM-KV handles `PUT`s by sending messages to the server via WRITEs, similar to HERD. The server notifies the client of `PUT` completion using another WRITE. Therefore, a `PUT` in FaRM-em (and FaRM-em-VAR) consists of one $S_K + S_V$ byte WRITE from a client to the server, and one WRITE from the server to the client. For higher throughput, we perform these WRITEs over UC unlike the original FaRM paper that used RC (Figure 5).

## 5.2 Workloads

Three main workload parameters affect the throughput and latency of a key-value system: relative frequency of `PUT`s and `GET`s, item size, and skew.

We use two types of workloads: *read-intensive* (95% `GET`, 5% `PUT`) and *write-intensive* (50% `GET`, 50% `PUT`). Our workload can either be *uniform* or *skewed*. Under a uniform workload, the keys are chosen uniformly at random from the 16 byte keyhash space. The skewed workload draws keys from a Zipf distribution with parameter .99. This workload is generated offline using YCSB [7]. We generated 480 million keys once and assigned 8 million keys to each of the 51 client processes.

## 5.3 Throughput comparison

We now compare the end-to-end throughput of HERD against the emulated versions of Pilaf and FaRM.

Figure 9 plots the throughput of these system for read-intensive and write-intensive workloads for 48-byte items ($S_K$ = 16, $S_V$ = 32). We chose this item size because it is representative of real-life workloads: an analysis of Facebook's general-purpose key-value store [6] showed that the 50-th percentile of key sizes is approximately 30 bytes, and that of value sizes is 20 bytes. To compare the READ-based `GET`s of Pilaf and FaRM with Pilaf's SEND/RECV-based `PUT`s, we also plot the throughput when the workload consists of 100% `PUT`s.

In HERD, both read-intensive and write-intensive workloads achieve 26 Mops, which is slightly larger than the throughput of native RDMA reads of a similar size (Figure 3b). For small key-value items, there is very little difference between `PUT` and `GET` requests at the RDMA layer because both types of requests fit inside one cacheline. Therefore, the throughput does not depend on the workload composition.

The `GET` throughput of Pilaf-em-OPT and FaRM-em(-VAR) is directly determined by the throughput of RDMA READs. A `GET` in Pilaf-em-OPT involves 2.6 READs (on average). Its `GET` throughput is 9.9 Mops, which is about 2.6X smaller than the maximum READ throughput. For `GET`s, FaRM-em requires a single 288 byte READ and delivers 17.2 Mops. FaRM-em-VAR requires a second READ and has throughput of 11.4 Mops for `GET`s.

Surprisingly, the `PUT` throughput in our emulated systems is much larger than their `GET` throughput. This is explained as follows. In FaRM-em(-VAR), `PUT`s use small WRITEs over UC that outperform the large READs required for `GET`s. Pilaf-em-OPT uses SEND/RECV-based requests and replies for `PUT`. Both Pilaf and FaRM assume that messaging-based ECHOs are much more expensive than READs. (Pilaf reports that for 17 byte messages, the throughput of RDMA reads is 2.449 Mops whereas the throughput of SEND/RECV-based ECHOs is only 0.668 Mops.) If SEND/RECV can provide only one fourth the throughput of READ, it makes sense to use multiple READs for `GET`.

However, we believe that these systems do not achieve the full capacity of SEND/RECV. After optimizing SENDs by using unreliable transport, payload inlining, and selective signaling, SEND/RECV based ECHOs, as shown in Figure 5, achieve 21 Mops, which is considerably more than half of our READ throughput (26 Mops). Therefore, we conclude that SEND/RECV-based communication, when used effectively, is more efficient than using multiple READs per request.

Figure 10 shows the throughput of the three systems with 16 byte keys and different value sizes for a read-intensive workload. For up to 60-byte items, HERD delivers over 26 Mops, which is slightly greater than the peak READ throughput. Up to 32-byte values, FaRM-em also delivers high throughput. However, its throughput declines quickly with increasing value size because the size of FaRM-em's READs grow rapidly (as 6 * $(S_V + 16)$). This problem is fundamental to the Hopscotch-based KV design which amplifies the READ size to reduce round trips. FaRM-KV quickly saturates link bandwidths (PCIe or InfiniBand/RoCE) with smaller items than HERD, which conserves network bandwidth by transmitting only essential data. Figure 10 illustrates this effect. FaRM-em saturates the PCIe 2.0 bandwidth on Susitna with 4 byte values, and the 56 Gbps InfiniBand bandwidth on Apt with 32 byte values. HERD achieves high performance for up to 32 byte values on Susitna, and

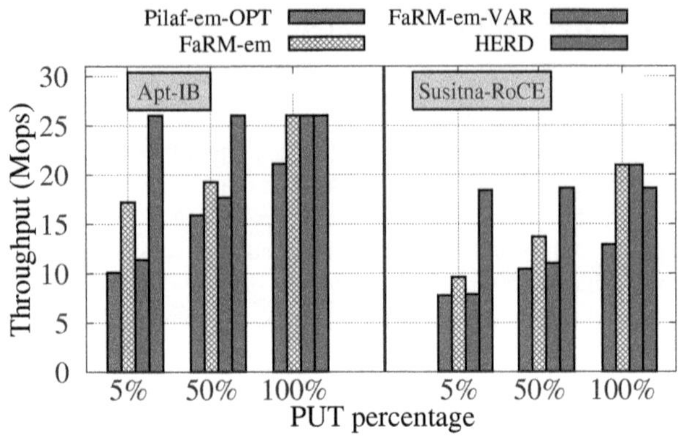


**Figure 9: End-to-end throughput comparison for 48 byte key-value items**

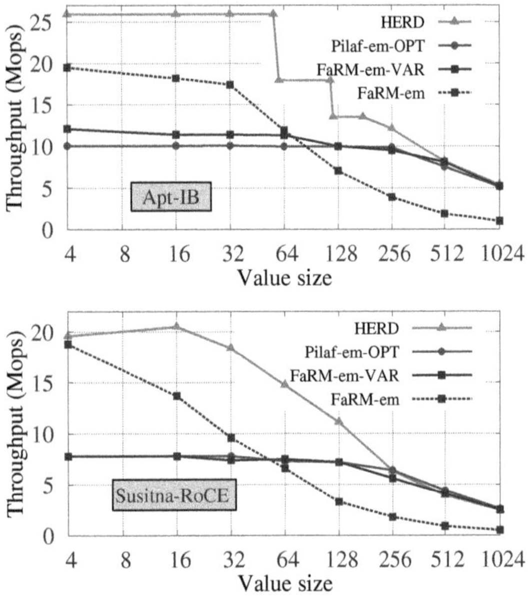


**Figure 10: End-to-end throughput comparison with different value sizes**

60 bytes values on Apt, and is bottlenecked by the smaller PCIe PIO bandwidth.

With large values (144 bytes on Apt, 192 on Susitna), HERD switches to using non-inlined SENDs for responses. The outbound throughput of large inlined messages is less than non-inlined messages because DMA outperforms PIO for large payloads (Figure 4b). For large values, the performance of HERD, FaRM-em, and Pilaf-em-OPT are within 10% of each other.

## 5.4 Latency comparison

Unlike FaRM-KV and Pilaf, HERD uses only one network round trip for any request. FaRM-KV and Pilaf use one round trip for `PUT` requests but require multiple round trips for `GET`s (except when FaRM-KV inlines values in the hash-table). This causes their `GET` latency to be higher than the latency of a single RDMA READ.

Figure 11 compares the average latencies of the three systems for a read-intensive workload; the error bars indicate the 5th and 95th percentile latency. To understand the dependency of latency on throughput, we increase the load on the server by adding more

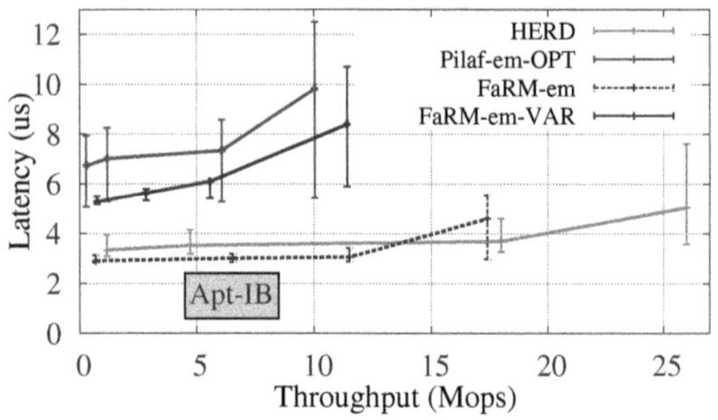


**Figure 11: End-to-end latency with 48 byte items and read-intensive workload**

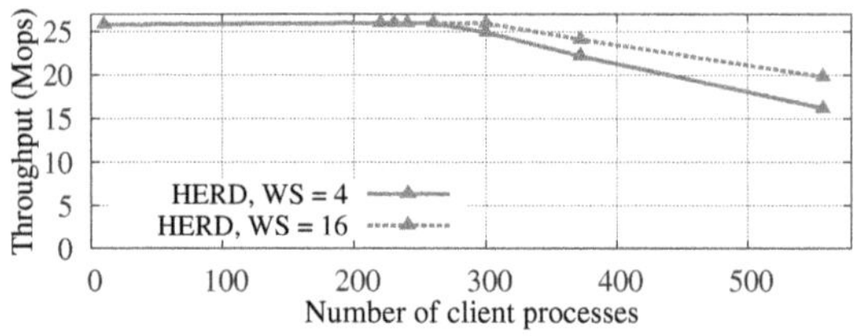


**Figure 12: Throughput with variable number of client processes and different window sizes**

clients until the server is saturated. When using 6 CPU cores at the server, HERD is able to deliver 26 million requests per second with approximately 5 $\mu$s average latency. For fixed-length key-value items, FaRM-em provides the lowest latency among the three systems because it requires only one network round trip (unlike Pilaf-em-OPT) and no computation at the server (unlike HERD). For variable length values, however, FaRM's variable length mode requires two RTTs, yielding worse latency than HERD.

The `PUT` latency for all three systems (not shown) is similar because the network path traversed is the same. The measured latency for HERD was slightly higher than that of the emulated systems because it performed actual hash table and memory manipulation for inserts, but this is an artifact of the performance advantage we give Pilaf-em and FaRM-em.

## 5.5 Scalability

We conducted a larger experiment to understand HERD's number-of-clients scalability. We used one machine to run 6 server processes and the remaining 186 machines for client processes. The experiment uses 16 byte keys and 32 byte values.

Figure 12 shows the results from this experiment. HERD delivers its maximum throughput for up to 260 client processes. With even more clients, HERD's throughput starts decreasing almost linearly. The rate of decrease can be reduced by increasing the number of outstanding requests maintained by each client, at the cost of higher request latency. Figure 12 shows the results for two window sizes: 4 (HERD's default) and 16. This observation suggests that the decline is due to cache misses in *RNICs*, as more outstanding verbs in a queue can reduce cache pressure. We expect this scalability limit to be resolved with the introduction of Dynamically Connected Transport in the new Connect-IB cards [1, 8].

Another likely scalability limit of our current HERD design is the round-robin polling at the server for requests. With thousands of clients, using WRITEs for inbound requests may incur too much CPU overhead; mitigating this effect may necessitate switching to a SEND/SEND architecture over Unreliable Datagram transport.

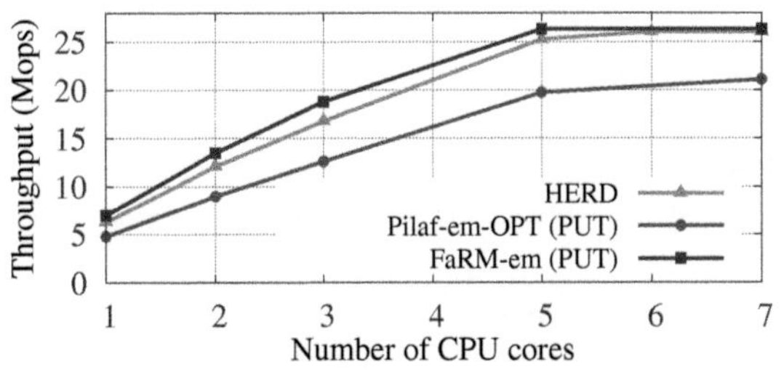


**Figure 13: Throughput as a function of server CPU cores**

Figure 5 shows there is a 4-5 Mops decrease to this change, but once made, the system should scale up to many thousands of clients, while still outperforming an RDMA READ-based architecture.[1] We expect the performance of the SEND/SEND architecture relative to WRITE-SEND to increase with the introduction of inlined RECVs in Connect-IB cards. This will reduce the load on RNICs by encapsulating the RECV payload in the RECV completion.

## 5.6 HERD CPU Use

The primary drawback of not using READs in HERD is that `GET` operations require the server CPU to execute requests, in exchange for saving one cross-datacenter RTT. While at first glance, it might seem that HERD's CPU usage should be higher than Pilaf and FaRM-KV, we show that in practice these two systems also have significant sources of CPU usage that reduce the extent of the difference.

First, issuing extra READs adds CPU overhead at the Pilaf and FaRM-KV clients. To issue the second READ, the clients must poll for the first READ to complete. HERD shifts this overhead to the server's CPU, making more room for application processing at the clients.

Second, handling `PUT` requests requires CPU involvement at the server. Achieving low-latency `PUT`s requires dedicating server CPU cores that poll for incoming requests. Therefore, the exact CPU use depends on the fraction of `PUT` throughput that server is *provisioned* for, because this determines the CPU resources that must be allocated to it, not the dynamic amount actually used. For example, our experiments show that, even ignoring the cost of updating data structures, provisioning for 100% `PUT` throughput in Pilaf and FaRM-KV requires over 5 CPU cores. Figure 13 shows FaRM-em and Pilaf-em-OPT's `PUT` throughput for 48 byte key-value items and different numbers of CPU cores at the server. Pilaf-em-OPT's CPU usage is higher because it must post RECVs for new `PUT` requests, which is more expensive than FaRM-em's request-region polling.

In Figure 13, we also plot HERD's throughput for the same workload by varying the number of server CPU cores. HERD is able to deliver over 95% of its maximum throughput with 5 CPU cores. The modest gap to FaRM-em arises because the HERD server in this experiment is handling hash table lookups and updates, whereas the emulated FaRM-KV is handling only the network traffic.

We believe, therefore, that HERD's higher throughput and lower latency, along with the significant CPU utilization in Pilaf and FaRM-KV, justifies the architectural decision to have the CPU involved on the `GET` path for small key-value items. For a 50% `PUT` workload, for example, the moderate extra cost of adding a few more cores—or using the already-idle cycles on the cores—is likely worthwhile for many applications.

[1] Figure 5 uses SENDs over UC, but we have verified that similar throughput is possible using SENDs over UD.

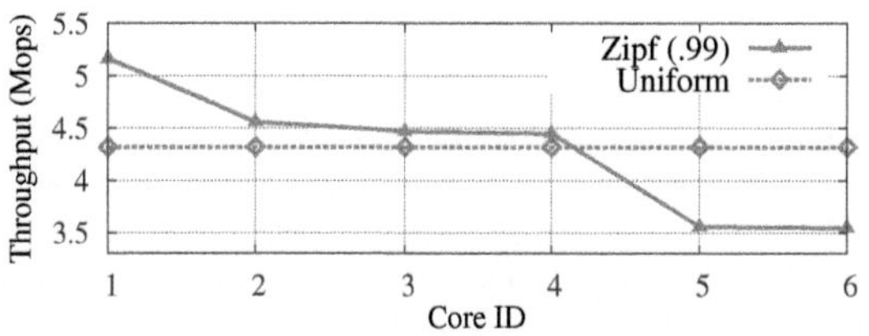


**Figure 14: Per-core throughput under skewed and uniform workloads.** Note that the y-axis does not begin at 0.

## 5.7 Resistance to skew

To understand how HERD's behavior is impacted by skew, we tested it with a workload where the keys are drawn from a Zipf distribution. HERD adapts well to skew, delivering its maximum performance even when the Zipf parameter is .99. HERD's resistance to skew comes from two factors. First, the back-end MICA architecture [18] that we use in HERD performs well under skew; a skewed workload spread across several partitions produces little variation in the partitions' load compared to the skew in the workload's distribution. Under our Zipf-distributed workload, with 6 partitions, the most loaded CPU core is only 50% more so than the least loaded core, even though the most popular key is over $10^5$ times more popular than the average.

Second, because the CPU cores share the RNIC, the highly loaded cores are able to benefit from the idle time provided by the less-used cores. Figure 13 demonstrates this effect: with a *uniform* workload and using only a single core, HERD can deliver 6.3 Mops. When the system is configured to use 6 cores—the minimum required by HERD to deliver its peak throughput—the system delivers 4.32 Mops *per core*. The per-core performance reduction is not because of a CPU bottleneck, but because the server processes saturate the PCIe PIO throughput. Therefore, even if the workload is skewed, there is ample CPU headroom on a given core to handle the extra requests.

Figure 14 shows the per-core throughput of HERD for a skewed workload. The experimental configuration is: 48-byte items, read-intensive, skewed workload, 6 total CPU cores. The per-core throughput for a uniform workload is included for comparison.

# 6. RELATED WORK

**RDMA-based key-value stores:** Other than Pilaf and FaRM, several projects have designed memcached-like systems over RDMA. Panda et al. [14] describe a memcached implementation using a hybrid of UD and RC transports. It uses SEND/RECV messages for all requests and avoids the overhead of UD transport (caused by a larger header size than RC) by actively switching connections between RC and UD. Although their cluster (ConnectX, 32 Gbps) is comparable to Susitna (ConnectX-3, 40 Gbps), their request rate is less than 1.5 Mops. Stuedi et al. [25] describe a SoftiWARP [28] based version of memcached targeting CPU savings in wimpy nodes with 10GbE.

**Accelerating systems with RDMA:** Several projects have used verbs to improve the performance of systems such as HBase, Hadoop RPC, PVFS [30, 13, 20]. Most of these use only SEND/RECV verbs as a fast alternative to socket-based communication. In a PVFS implementation over InfiniBand [30], `read()` and `write()` operations in the filesystem use both RDMA and SEND/RECV. They favor WRITEs over READs for the same reasons as in our work, suggesting that the performance gap has existed over several generations of InfiniBand hardware. There have been several versions of MPI over InfiniBand [16, 19]. MPICH2 uses RDMA writes for one-sided messaging: the server polls the head of a circular buffer that is written to by a client. HERD extends this messaging in a scalable fashion for all-to-all request-reply communication. While [30, 13, 20, 16, 19] have benchmarked verbs performance before, it has been for large messages in the context of applications like NFS and MPI. Our work exploits the performance differences that appear only for small messages and are relevant for message rate-bound applications like key-value stores.

**User level networking:** Taken together, we believe that one conclusion to draw from the union of HERD, Pilaf, FaRM, and MICA [18] is that the biggest boost to throughput comes from bypassing the network stack and avoiding CPU interrupts, *not* necessarily from bypassing the CPU entirely. All four of these systems use mechanisms to allow user-level programs to directly receive requests or packets from the NIC: the userlevel RDMA drivers for HERD, Pilaf, and FaRM, and the Intel DPDK library for MICA. As we discuss below, the *throughput* of these systems is similar, but the batching required by the DPDK-based systems confers a latency advantage to the hardware-supported InfiniBand systems. These lessons suggest profitable future work in making user-level classical Ethernet systems more portable, easier to use, and lower-latency. One ongoing effort is NIQ [10], an FPGA-based low-latency NIC which uses cacheline-sized PIOs (without any DMA) to transmit and receive small packets. Inlined WRITEs in RDMA use the same mechanism at the requesters's side.

**General key-value stores:** MICA [18] is a recent key-value system for classical Ethernet. It assigns exclusive partitions to server cores to minimize memory contention, and exploits the NIC's capability to steer requests to the responsible core [3]. A MICA server delivers 77 Mops with 4 dual-port, 10 Gbps PCIe 2.0 NICs, with 50 μs average latency (19.25 Gbps with one PCIe 2.0 card). This suggests that, comparing the state-of-the-art, classical Ethernet-based solutions can provide comparable throughput to RDMA-based solutions, although with much higher latency. RAMCloud [23] is a RAM-based, persistent key-value store that uses messaging verbs for low latency communication.

# 7. CONCLUSION

This paper explored the options for implementing fast, low-latency key-value systems atop RDMA, arriving at an unexpected and novel combination that outperforms prior designs and uses fewer network round-trips. Our work shows that, contrary to widely held beliefs about engineering for RDMA, single-RTT designs with server CPU involvement can outperform the "optimization" of CPU-bypassing remote memory access when the RDMA approaches require multiple RTTs. These results contribute not just a practical artifact—the HERD low-latency, high-performance key-value cache—but an improved understanding of how to use RDMA to construct future DRAM-based storage services.

**Acknowledgements** We thank our shepherd Chuanxiong Guo and the anonymous reviewers for their feedback that helped improve the paper. We also thank Miguel Castro and Dushyanth Narayanan for discussing FaRM with us, Kirk Webb and Robert Ricci for getting us early access to the Apt cluster, and Hyeontaek Lim for his valuable insights. This work was supported by funding from the National Science Foundation under awards CNS-1314721 and CCF-0964474, and Intel via the Intel Science and Technology Center for Cloud Computing (ISTC-CC). The PRObE cluster [11] used for many experiments is supported in part by NSF awards CNS-1042537 and CNS-1042543 (PRObE).

# References

[1] Connect-IB: Architecture for Scalable High Performance Computing. URL http://www.mellanox.com/related-docs/applications/SB_Connect-IB.pdf.

[2] Intel DPDK: Data Plane Development Kit. URL http://dpdk.org.

[3] Intel 82599 10 Gigabit Ethernet Controller: Datasheet. URL http://www.intel.com/content/www/us/en/ethernet-controllers/82599-10-gbe-controller-datasheet.html.

[4] Redis: An Advanced Key-Value Store. URL http://redis.io.

[5] memcached: A Distributed Memory Object Caching System, 2011. URL http://memcached.org.

[6] B. Atikoglu, Y. Xu, E. Frachtenberg, S. Jiang, and M. Paleczny. Workload Analysis of a Large-Scale Key-Value Store. In *SIGMETRICS*, 2012.

[7] B. F. Cooper, A. Silberstein, E. Tam, R. Ramakrishnan, and R. Sears. Benchmarking Cloud Serving Systems with YCSB. In *SoCC*, 2010.

[8] A. Dragojevic, D. Narayanan, O. Hodson, and M. Castro. FaRM: Fast Remote Memory. In *USENIX NSDI*, 2014.

[9] B. Fan, D. G. Andersen, and M. Kaminsky. MemC3: Compact and Concurrent MemCache with Dumber Caching and Smarter Hashing. In *USENIX NSDI*, 2013.

[10] M. Flajslik and M. Rosenblum. Network Interface Design for Low Latency Request-Response Protocols. In *USENIX ATC*, 2013.

[11] G. Gibson, G. Grider, A. Jacobson, and W. Lloyd. PRObE: A Thousand-Node Experimental Cluster for Computer Systems Research.

[12] M. Herlihy, N. Shavit, and M. Tzafrir. Hopscotch Hashing. In *DISC*, 2008.

[13] J. Huang, X. Ouyang, J. Jose, M. W. ur Rahman, H. Wang, M. Luo, H. Subramoni, C. Murthy, and D. K. Panda. High-Performance Design of HBase with RDMA over InfiniBand. In *IPDPS*, 2012.

[14] J. Jose, H. Subramoni, K. C. Kandalla, M. W. ur Rahman, H. Wang, S. Narravula, and D. K. Panda. Scalable Memcached Design for InfiniBand Clusters Using Hybrid Transports. In *CCGRID*. IEEE, 2012.

[15] A. Kalia, D. G. Andersen, and M. Kaminsky. Using RDMA Efficiently for Key-Value Services. In *Technical Report CMU-PDL-14-106*, 2014.

[16] J. Li, J. Wu, and D. K. Panda. High Performance RDMA-Based MPI Implementation over InfiniBand. *International Journal of Parallel Programming*, 2004.

[17] H. Lim, B. Fan, D. G. Andersen, and M. Kaminsky. SILT: A Memory-efficient, High-performance Key-value Store. In *SOSP*, 2011.

[18] H. Lim, D. Han, D. G. Andersen, and M. Kaminsky. MICA: A Holistic Approach to Fast In-Memory Key-Value Storage. In *USENIX NSDI*, 2014.

[19] J. Liu, W. Jiang, P. Wyckoff, D. K. Panda, D. Ashton, D. Buntinas, W. Gropp, and B. Toonen. Design and Implementation of MPICH2 over InfiniBand with RDMA Support. In *IPDPD*, 2004.

[20] X. Lu, N. S. Islam, M. W. ur Rahman, J. Jose, H. Subramoni, H. Wang, and D. K. Panda. High-Performance Design of Hadoop RPC with RDMA over InfiniBand. In *ICPP*, 2013.

[21] C. Mitchell, Y. Geng, and J. Li. Using One-Sided RDMA Reads to Build a Fast, CPU-Efficient Key-Value Store. In *USENIX ATC*, 2013.

[22] R. Nishtala, H. Fugal, S. Grimm, M. Kwiatkowski, H. Lee, H. C. Li, R. McElroy, M. Paleczny, D. Peek, P. Saab, D. Stafford, T. Tung, and V. Venkataramani. Scaling Memcache at Facebook. In *USENIX NSDI*, 2013.

[23] D. Ongaro, S. M. Rumble, R. Stutsman, J. Ousterhout, and M. Rosenblum. Fast Crash Recovery in RAMCloud. In *SOSP*, 2011.

[24] R. Pagh and F. F. Rodler. Cuckoo Hashing. *J. Algorithms*, 2004.

[25] P. Stuedi, A. Trivedi, and B. Metzler. Wimpy Nodes with 10GbE: Leveraging One-Sided Operations in Soft-RDMA to Boost Memcached. In *USENIX ATC*, 2012.

[26] S. Sur, A. Vishnu, H.-W. Jin, W. Huang, and D. K. Panda. Can Memory-Less Network Adapters Benefit Next-Generation InfiniBand Systems? In *HOTI*, 2005.

[27] S. Sur, M. J. Koop, L. Chai, and D. K. Panda. Performance Analysis and Evaluation of Mellanox ConnectX Infiniband Architecture with Multi-Core Platforms. In *HOTI*, 2007.

[28] A. Trivedi, B. Metzler, and P. Stuedi. A Case for RDMA in Clouds: Turning Supercomputer Networking into Commodity. In *APSys*, 2011.

[29] B. White, J. Lepreau, L. Stoller, R. Ricci, S. Guruprasad, M. Newbold, M. Hibler, C. Barb, and A. Joglekar. An Integrated Experimental Environment for Distributed Systems and Networks. In *OSDI*, 2002.

[30] J. Wu, P. Wyckoff, and D. K. Panda. PVFS over InfiniBand: Design and Performance Evaluation. In *Ohio State University Tech Report*, 2003.

[31] D. Zhou, B. Fan, H. Lim, M. Kaminsky, and D. G. Andersen. Scalable, High Performance Ethernet Forwarding with CuckooSwitch. In *CoNEXT*, 2013.

# Fastpass: A Centralized "Zero-Queue" Datacenter Network

Jonathan Perry, Amy Ousterhout, Hari Balakrishnan, Devavrat Shah, Hans Fugal
M.I.T. Computer Science & Artificial Intelligence Lab Facebook
http://fastpass.mit.edu/

## ABSTRACT

An ideal datacenter network should provide several properties, including low median and tail latency, high utilization (throughput), fair allocation of network resources between users or applications, deadline-aware scheduling, and congestion (loss) avoidance. Current datacenter networks inherit the principles that went into the design of the Internet, where packet transmission and path selection decisions are distributed among the endpoints and routers. Instead, we propose that each sender should delegate control—to a centralized arbiter—of when each packet should be transmitted and what path it should follow.

This paper describes Fastpass, a datacenter network architecture built using this principle. Fastpass incorporates two fast algorithms: the first determines the time at which each packet should be transmitted, while the second determines the path to use for that packet. In addition, Fastpass uses an efficient protocol between the endpoints and the arbiter and an arbiter replication strategy for fault-tolerant failover. We deployed and evaluated Fastpass in a portion of Facebook's datacenter network. Our results show that Fastpass achieves high throughput comparable to current networks at a 240× reduction is queue lengths (4.35 Mbytes reducing to 18 Kbytes), achieves much fairer and consistent flow throughputs than the baseline TCP (5200× reduction in the standard deviation of per-flow throughput with five concurrent connections), scalability from 1 to 8 cores in the arbiter implementation with the ability to schedule 2.21 Terabits/s of traffic in software on eight cores, and a 2.5× reduction in the number of TCP retransmissions in a latency-sensitive service at Facebook.

## 1. INTRODUCTION

Is it possible to design a network in which: (1) packets experience *no queueing delays* in the network, (2) the network achieves *high utilization*, and (3) the network is able to support *multiple resource allocation objectives* between flows, applications, or users?

Such a network would be useful in many contexts, but especially in datacenters where queueing dominates end-to-end latencies, link rates are at technology's bleeding edge, and system operators have to contend with multiple users and a rich mix of workloads. Meeting complex service-level objectives and application-specific goals would be much easier in a network that delivered these three ideals.


*SIGCOMM'14*, August 17–22, 2014, Chicago, IL, USA.

ACM 978-1-4503-2836-4/14/08...$15.00.
http://dx.doi.org/10.1145/2619239.2626309.

Current network architectures distribute packet transmission decisions among the endpoints ("congestion control") and path selection among the network's switches ("routing"). The result is strong fault-tolerance and scalability, but at the cost of a loss of control over packet delays and paths taken. Achieving high throughput requires the network to accommodate bursts of packets, which entails the use of queues to absorb these bursts, leading to delays that rise and fall. Mean delays may be low when the load is modest, but tail (e.g., 99th percentile) delays are rarely low.

Instead, we advocate what may seem like a rather extreme approach to exercise (very) tight control over when endpoints can send packets and what paths packets take. We propose that *each* packet's timing be controlled by a logically centralized *arbiter*, which also determines the packet's path (Fig. 1). If this idea works, then flow rates can match available network capacity over the time-scale of individual packet transmission times, unlike over multiple round-trip times (RTTs) with distributed congestion control. Not only will persistent congestion be eliminated, but packet latencies will not rise and fall, queues will never vary in size, tail latencies will remain small, and packets will never be dropped due to buffer overflow.

This paper describes the design, implementation, and evaluation of *Fastpass*, a system that shows how centralized arbitration of the network's usage allows endpoints to burst at wire-speed while eliminating congestion at switches. This approach also provides *latency isolation*: interactive, time-critical flows don't have to suffer queueing delays caused by bulk flows in other parts of the fabric. The idea we pursue is analogous to a hypothetical road traffic control system in which a central entity tells every vehicle when to depart and which path to take. Then, instead of waiting in traffic, cars can zoom by all the way to their destinations.

Fastpass includes three key components:

1. A fast and scalable **timeslot allocation algorithm** at the arbiter to determine when each endpoint's packets should be sent (§3). This algorithm uses a fast maximal matching to achieve objectives such as max-min fairness or to approximate minimizing flow completion times.
2. A fast and scalable **path assignment algorithm** at the arbiter to assign a path to each packet (§4). This algorithm uses a fast edge-coloring algorithm over a bipartite graph induced by switches in the network, with two switches connected by an edge if they have a packet to be sent between them in a timeslot.
3. A **replication strategy for the central arbiter** to handle network and arbiter failures, as well as a reliable control protocol between endpoints and the arbiter (§5).

We have implemented Fastpass in the Linux kernel using high-precision timers (hrtimers) to time transmitted packets; we achieve sub-microsecond network-wide time synchronization using the IEEE1588 Precision Time Protocol (PTP).

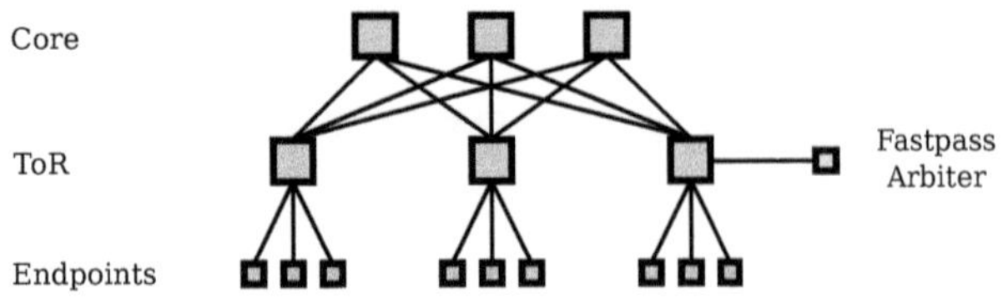

Figure 1: Fastpass arbiter in a two-tier network topology.

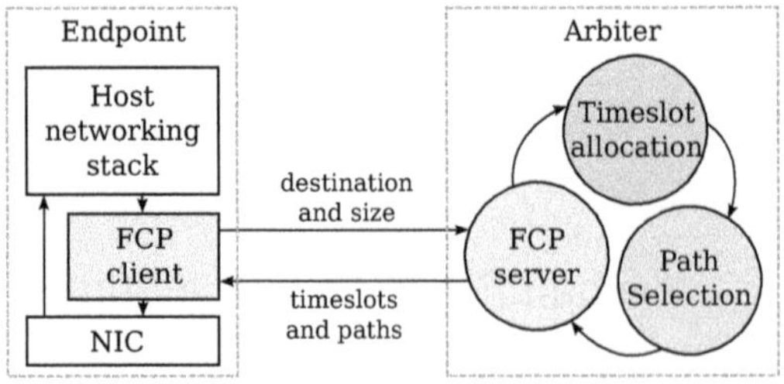

Figure 2: Structure of the arbiter, showing the timeslot allocator, path selector, and the client-arbiter communication.

We conducted several experiments with Fastpass running in a portion of Facebook's datacenter network. Our main findings are:

1. High throughput with nearly-zero queues: On a multi-machine bulk transfer workload, Fastpass achieved throughput only 1.6% lower than baseline TCP, while **reducing the switch queue size from a median of 4.35 Mbytes to under 18 Kbytes**. The resulting RTT reduced from 3.56 ms to 230 µs.
2. Consistent (fair) throughput allocation and fast convergence: In a controlled experiment with multiple concurrent flows starting and ending at different times, Fastpass **reduced the standard deviation of per-flow throughput by a factor over 5200**× compared to the baseline with five concurrent TCP connections.
3. Scalability: Our implementation of the arbiter shows nearly linear scaling of the allocation algorithm from one to eight cores, with the **8-core allocator handling 2.21 Terabits/s**. The arbiter responds to requests within tens of microseconds even at high load.
4. Fine-grained timing: The implementation is able to synchronize time accurately to within a few hundred nanoseconds across a multi-hop network, sufficient for our purposes because a single 1500-byte MTU-sized packet at 10 Gbits/s has a transmission time of 1230 nanoseconds.
5. Reduced retransmissions: On a real-world latency-sensitive service located on the response path for user requests, **Fastpass reduced the occurrence of TCP retransmissions by** 2.5×, from between 4 and 5 per second to between 1 and 2 per second.

These experimental results indicate that Fastpass is viable, providing a solution to several specific problems observed in datacenter networks. First, reducing the tail of the packet delay distribution, which is important because many datacenter applications launch hundreds or even thousands of request-response interactions to fulfill a single application transaction. Because the longest interaction can be a major part of the transaction's total response time, reducing the 99.9th or 99.99th percentile of latency experienced by packets would reduce application latency.

Second, avoiding false congestion: packets may get queued behind other packets headed for a bottleneck link, delaying non-congested traffic. Fastpass does not incur this delay penalty.

Third, eliminating incast, which occurs when concurrent requests to many servers triggers concurrent responses. With small router queues, response packets are lost, triggering delay-inducing retransmissions [26], whereas large queues cause delays to other bulk traffic. Current solutions are approximations of full control, based on estimates and assumptions about request RTTs, and solve the problem only partially [28, 37].

And last but not least, better sharing for heterogeneous workloads with different performance objectives. Some applications care about low latency, some want high bulk throughput, and some want to minimize job completion time. Supporting these different objectives within the same network infrastructure is challenging using distributed congestion control, even with router support. By contrast, a central arbiter can compute the timeslots and paths in the network to jointly achieve these different goals.

## 2. FASTPASS ARCHITECTURE

In Fastpass, a logically centralized arbiter controls all network transfers (Fig. 2). When an application calls send() or sendto() on a socket, the operating system sends this *demand* in a request message to the Fastpass arbiter, specifying the destination and the number of bytes. The arbiter processes each request, performing two functions:

1. **Timeslot allocation**: Assign the requester a set of *timeslots* in which to transmit this data. The granularity of a timeslot is the time taken to transmit a single MTU-sized packet over the fastest link connecting an endpoint to the network. The arbiter keeps track of the source-destination pairs assigned each timeslot (§3).
2. **Path selection**. The arbiter also chooses a path through the network for each packet and communicates this information to the requesting source (§4).

Because the arbiter knows about all current and scheduled transfers, it can choose timeslots and paths that yield the "*zero-queue*" property: the arbiter arranges for each packet to arrive at a switch on the path just as the next link to the destination becomes available.

The arbiter must achieve high throughput and low latency for both these functions; a single arbiter must be able to allocate traffic for a network with thousands of endpoints within a few timeslots.

Endpoints communicate with the arbiter using the Fastpass Control Protocol (FCP) (§5.3). FCP is a reliable protocol that conveys the demands of a sending endpoint to the arbiter and the allocated timeslot and paths back to the sender. FCP must balance conflicting requirements: it must consume only a small fraction of network bandwidth, achieve low latency, and handle packet drops and arbiter failure without interrupting endpoint communication. FCP provides reliability using timeouts and ACKs of aggregate demands and allocations. Endpoints aggregate allocation demands over a few microseconds into each request packet sent to the arbiter. This aggregation reduces the overhead of requests, and limits queuing at the arbiter.

Fastpass can recover from faults with little disruption to the network (§5). Because switch buffer occupancy is small, packet loss is rare and can be used as an indication of component failure. Endpoints report packet losses to the arbiter, which uses these reports to isolate faulty links or switches and compute fault-free paths. The arbiter itself maintains only soft state, so that a secondary arbiter can take over within a few milliseconds if the primary arbiter fails.

To achieve the ideal of zero queueing, Fastpass requires precise timing across the endpoints and switches in the network (§6.3). When endpoint transmissions occur outside their allocated timeslots, packets from multiple allocated timeslots might arrive at a switch at the same time, resulting in queueing. Switch queues allow the network to tolerate timing inaccuracies: worst-case queueing is no larger than the largest discrepancy between clocks, up to 1.5 Kbytes for every 1.2 μs of clock divergence at 10 Gbits/s.

Fastpass requires no switch modifications, nor the use of any advanced switch features. Endpoints require some hardware support in NICs that is currently available in commodity hardware (§6.3), with protocol support in the operating system. Arbiters can be ordinary server-class machines, but to handle very large clusters, a number of high-speed ports would be required.

### 2.1 Latency experienced by packets in Fastpass

In an ideal version of Fastpass, endpoints receive allocations as soon as they request them: the latency of communication with the arbiter and the time to compute timeslots and paths would be zero. In this ideal case, the end-to-end latency of a packet transmission would be the time until the allocated timeslot plus the time needed for the packet to traverse the path to the receiver with empty queues at all egress ports.

In moderately-loaded to heavily-loaded networks, ideal allocations will typically be several timeslots in the future. As long as the Fastpass arbiter returns results in less than these several timeslots, Fastpass would achieve the ideal minimum packet latency in practice too.

In lightly-loaded networks, Fastpass trades off a slight degradation in the mean packet latency (due to communication with the arbiter) for a significant reduction in the tail packet latency.

### 2.2 Deploying Fastpass

Fastpass is deployable incrementally in a datacenter network. Communication to endpoints outside the Fastpass boundary (e.g., to hosts in a non-Fastpass subnet or on the Internet) uses Fastpass to reach the boundary, and is then carried by the external network. Incoming traffic either passes through gateways or travels in a lower priority class. Gateways receive packets from outside the boundary, and use Fastpass to send them within the boundary. Alternatively, incoming packets may use a lower-priority class to avoid inflating network queues for Fastpass traffic.

This paper focuses on deployments where a single arbiter is responsible for all traffic within the deployment boundary. We discuss larger deployments in §8.1.

## 3. TIMESLOT ALLOCATION

The goal of the arbiter's timeslot allocation algorithm is to choose a *matching* of endpoints in each timeslot, i.e., a set of sender-receiver endpoint pairs that can communicate in a timeslot. For a simpler exposition, we assume here that all endpoint links run at the same rate. The demand for any given link in the network can exceed its capacity; the arbiter selects sender-receiver pairs and assigns a path to packets (described in §4) to ensure that traffic issued in a given timeslot will not exceed any link's bandwidth.

Networks are often organized into tiers, with each tier providing network transport to components below it: top-of-rack switches connect servers in a rack, aggregation switches connect racks into clusters, core routers connect clusters. Fastpass requires that tiers be *rearrangeably non blocking* (RNB) [14], networks where any traffic that satisfies the input and output bandwidth constraints of the network can be routed such that no queuing occurs.

The RNB property allows the arbiter to perform timeslot allocation separately from path selection: as long as the allocated matching satisfies the bandwidth constraints in and out of each tier, path selection is guaranteed to successfully assign paths on the physical topology. Consequently, each tier can be abstracted as a single switch for the purpose of timeslot allocation.[1] The result is a tree topology on which it is easy for timeslot allocation to check bandwidth constraints, even when the physical network is oversubscribed and has many paths between endpoints. Non-oversubscribed (full-bisection bandwidth) topologies [4, 18, 27, 38] can be abstracted further: we can view the entire network as a single switch.

Because the arbiter has knowledge of all endpoint demands, it can allocate traffic according to global policies that would be harder to enforce in a distributed setting. For instance, the arbiter can allocate timeslots to achieve max-min fairness, to minimize flow completion time, or to limit the aggregate throughput of certain classes of traffic. When conditions change, the network does not need to converge to a good allocation – the arbiter can change the allocation from one timeslot to the next. As a result, the policy (e.g., fairness) can be achieved even over short time scales.

How fast must a viable allocation algorithm be? At first glance, endpoint link speeds determine the allowed allocator runtime, since the arbiter's processing rate must match endpoint link speed. This is about one timeslot per microsecond for 10 Gbits/s links with 1500-byte timeslots. However, parallelism can enable longer runtimes: if the allocation of multiple timeslots can be run in parallel, allocation of each timeslot can take longer while still maintaining the arbiter's processing rate.

A long runtime (compared to the minimum RTT between the endpoints) is acceptable with some workloads, but not others. On heavily-loaded endpoints, the time until the first available timeslot can be tens to hundreds of microseconds, so traffic will observe the ideal end-to-end latency (§2.1), even if allocation takes many microseconds. On the other hand, traffic on lightly-loaded networks doesn't enjoy this masking of allocation latency; the algorithm must finish promptly if a small end-to-end latency increase is desired.

Complete knowledge of all network demands thus becomes a double-edged sword; in order to meet these latency and throughput requirements, the timeslot allocator requires very fast algorithms.

Finding an allocation with the largest possible number of pairs (a *maximum matching*) is expensive; switch algorithms (e.g., [34, 9, 24]) generally use heuristics to find good, but not maximum, matchings. Fastpass uses a similar approach: as the arbiter processes demands, it greedily allocates a source-destination pair if allocating the pair does not violate bandwidth constraints.[2] When the arbiter finishes processing all demands, it has a *maximal matching*, a matching in which none of the unallocated demands can be allocated while maintaining the bandwidth constraints.

### 3.1 A pipelined allocator

The allocator takes a list of all network demands (how many timeslots are waiting to be sent between each pair of endpoints), and computes the allocated matching and the remaining demands after the allocation. Figure 3 shows how Fastpass allocators are arranged into a pipeline: the input to the allocator processing timeslot $t$ is the remaining demand after allocating timeslot $t-1$.

The arbiter implements different allocation policies by changing the order in which demands are processed. For max-min fairness, the arbiter orders demands by the last timeslot that was allocated to the source-destination pair, "least recently allocated first"; for minimizing flow completion time (min-FCT), the arbiter tracks the

[1]A switch where port capacity reflects the aggregate bandwidth in and out of the tier to that component.

[2]In a non-oversubscribed network, the arbiter checks that neither the source nor the destination have already been allocated to a different pair. Oversubscribed topologies require the arbiter to additionally check bandwidth constraints in and out of each network tier.

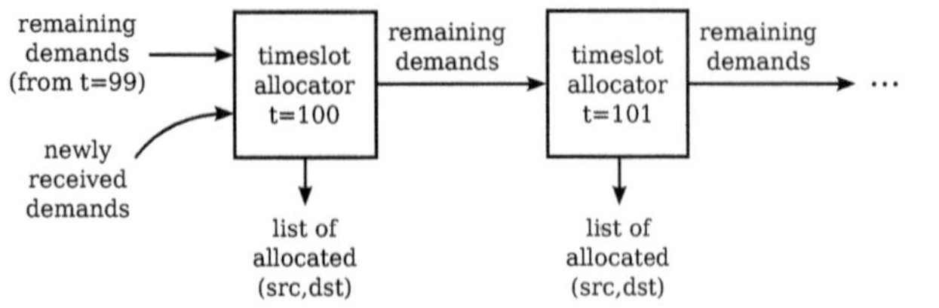


Figure 3: Pipelined timeslot allocation. The allocator for timeslot $t$ processes the demands not fully satisfied by the allocator for $t-1$

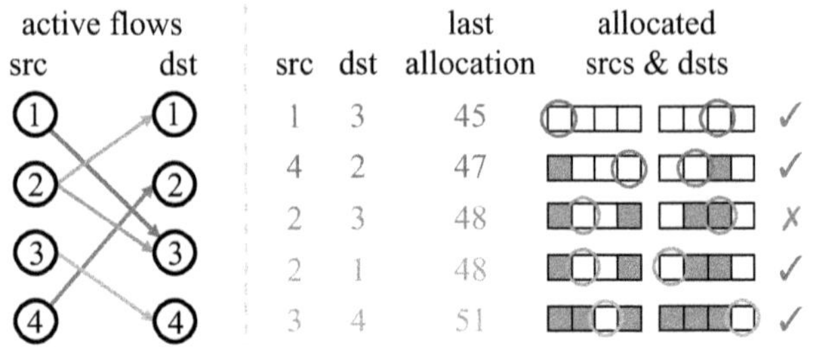


Figure 4: Timeslot allocation for the max-min fairness allocation objective.

number of pending bytes (measured in MTU-sized chunks) and performs "fewest remaining MTUs first".

Figure 4 demonstrates the allocation of one timeslot in a simple network with four endpoints. The allocator orders the demands by the last timeslot allocated to each pair, and processes them in that order. On the right is the state used to track bandwidth constraints: one bit for each source and for each destination. The first two demands can be allocated because both the source and destination are available, but the third demand cannot be allocated because destination 3 has already been allocated. The remaining two demands can be allocated, yielding a maximal matching.

Each allocator in the pipeline receives a stream of demands. Ideally, an allocator could process each demand as soon as it is produced by the previous allocator. If demands can appear out of the desired order, however, the allocator must reorder them first. In a worst-case scenario, the last demand from the previous allocator should be processed first. The allocator would have to wait until the previous allocator produced all demands in the stream before it could start processing, eliminating the concurrency gained by pipelining.

Fortunately, with both max-min fairness and min-FCT (and other such objectives), demands can be kept in roughly the correct order with only limited reordering. For example, in max-min fairness, the allocator of timeslot $t$ only changes the last allocated timeslot of a source-destination pair if that pair is allocated, and will only change it to $t$. Therefore, an allocator for timeslot $t+1$ can process all demands with last allocated timeslot strictly less than $t$ immediately. Only demands with last allocated timeslot equal to $t$ need to be kept until all demands are received.

To reduce the overhead of processing demands, the allocator allocates a batch of 8 timeslots in one shot using a fast data structure, the *bitmap table*. This table maintains a bitmap for each sender-receiver pair in the network, with one bit per timeslot. A "1" in the bitmap signifies that the pair is not scheduled to communicate in that timeslot, while a "0" indicates otherwise. To find the first available timeslot for a given packet, the allocator computes the bitwise AND of the source and destination bitmaps, and then uses the "find first set" operation (the `bsf` instruction on x86). Modern processors perform this operation fast [2]. Pairs that have been allocated and have remaining demand are kept, and the arbiter will attempt to allocate more batch timeslots to them; pairs that cannot be allocated in this batch are sent to the next allocator in the pipeline.

### 3.2 Theoretical guarantees

We prove in the appendix that in those topologies where timeslot allocation and path selection can be separated, the average latency with Fastpass is no worse than 2× the average latency of an optimal scheduler with half as much network capacity on its worst-case workload. The result upper-bounds the latency cost of using Fastpass over any other solution. The bound, however, is not tight: Fastpass achieves low latency even at much higher network loads (§7).

## 4. PATH SELECTION

Path selection assigns packets that have been allocated timeslots to paths through the network that avoid queueing. Common datacenter topologies (e.g., multi-rooted trees) include redundant paths between endpoints. If the timeslot allocator admits traffic that utilizes the full network bandwidth, and more packets attempt to traverse a link than that link can sustain, queueing will result. To utilize the full network bandwidth without queueing, path selection must balance packet load across all available links.

Existing approaches for load balancing all have significant disadvantages. Equal-cost multi-path (ECMP, RFC 2992) routing can result in multiple flows hashing onto the same path, causing significant skew over short time scales. Hedera [5] is able to re-route "elephant" flows for better load balance, but focuses only on such flows; the load generated by small flows at finer scales is left unbalanced, and that could be substantial in practice.

The goal of path selection is to assign packets to paths such that no link is assigned multiple packets in a single timeslot; this property guarantees that there will be no queueing within the network. Timeslot allocation guarantees that this property holds for the links directly connected to each endpoint; path selection must provide this guarantee for the remainder of the network. In a network with two tiers, ToR and core, with each ToR connected directly to a subset of core switches (Fig. 1) each path between two ToRs can be uniquely specified by a core switch. Thus path selection entails assigning a core switch to each packet such that no two packets (all of which are to be sent in the same timeslot) with the same source ToR or destination ToR are assigned the same core switch.

**Edge-coloring.** This assignment can be performed with *graph edge-coloring* [21]. The edge-coloring algorithm takes as input a bipartite graph and assigns a color to each edge such that no two edges of the same color are incident on the same vertex. We model the network as a bipartite graph where the vertices are ToR switches, edges are the allocated packets, and colors represent core switches/paths. The edge-coloring of this graph provides an assignment of packets to paths such that no link is assigned multiple packets.

Figure 5 shows an example. The matching of packets to be transmitted in a given timeslot (a) is transformed into a bipartite multi-

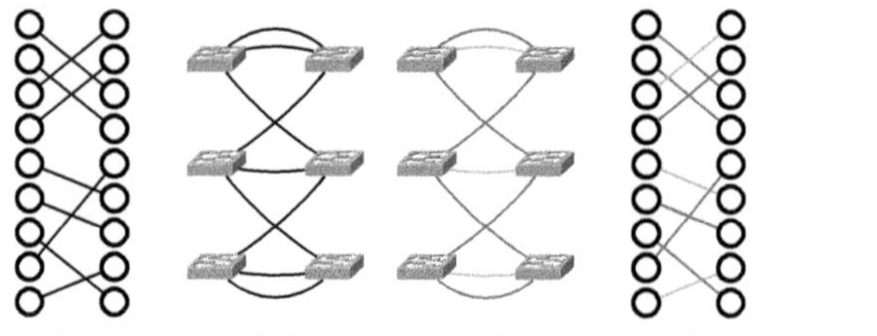


Figure 5: Path selection. (a) input matching (b) ToR graph (c) edge-colored ToR graph (d) edge-colored matching.

graph of ToRs (b), where the source and destination ToRs of every packet are connected. Edge-coloring colors each edge ensuring that no two edges of the same color are incident on the same ToR (c). The assignment guarantees that at most one packet occupies the ingress, and one occupies the egress, of each port (d).

Edge-coloring requires uniform link capacities; in networks with heterogeneous link capacities, we can construct a virtual network with homogeneous link capacities on which to assign paths. Here, we replace each physical switch with high-capacity links with multiple switches with low capacity links that connect to the same components as the physical switch (e.g., one switch with 40 Gbits/s links would be replaced by four switches with 10 Gbits/s links). All packets assigned a path through the duplicate switches in the virtual topology would be routed through the single high-capacity switch on the physical topology.

Edge-coloring also generalizes to oversubscribed networks and networks with multiple tiers. Only traffic that passes through a higher network tier is edge-colored (e.g., in a two-tier network, only inter-rack traffic requires path selection). For a three-tier datacenter with ToR, Agg, and Core switches (and higher-tier ones), paths can be assigned hierarchically: the edge-coloring of the ToR graph assigns Agg switches to packets, then an edge-coloring of the Agg graph chooses Core switches [21, §IV].

**Fast edge-coloring.** A network with $n$ racks and $d$ nodes per rack can be edge-colored in $O(nd \log d)$ time [12, 23]. Fast edge-coloring algorithms invariably use a simple and powerful building block, the *Euler-split*. An Euler-split partitions the edges of a regular graph where each node has the same degree, $2d$, into two regular graphs of degree $d$. The algorithm is simple: (1) find an Eulerian cycle (a cycle that starts and ends at the same node, and contains every edge exactly once, though nodes may repeat) of the original graph, (2) assign alternate edges of the cycle to the two new graphs, (3) repeat.

An Euler-split divides the edges into two groups that can be colored separately. $d-1$ Euler-splits can edge-color a graph with power-of-two degree $d$ by partitioning it into $d$ perfect matchings, which can each be assigned a different color. Graphs with non-power-of-two degree can be edge-colored using a similar method that incorporates one search for a perfect matching, and has only slightly worse asymptotic complexity [23].

The Fastpass path selection implementation maintains the bipartite graph in a size-optimized bitmap-based data structure that can fit entirely in a 32 KB L1 cache for graphs with up to 6,000 nodes. This data structure makes the graph walks needed for Euler-split fast, and yields sufficiently low latencies for clusters with a few thousand nodes (§7.3).

# 5. HANDLING FAULTS

Three classes of faults can render a Fastpass network ineffective: failures of in-network components (nodes, switches and links), failures of the Fastpass arbiter, and packet losses on the communication path between endpoints and the arbiter.

## 5.1 Arbiter failures

Fastpass runs multiple arbiters, one primary and a few secondaries. The arbiters all subscribe to a pre-determined IP multicast destination address to which all requests from endpoints are sent (responses are unicast to the endpoint). All the arbiters receive all requests (modulo packet loss), but only the designated primary responds to all requests; the secondaries drop the requests and generate no allocations.

The secondaries detect the failure of the primary as follows. The primary sends out tiny watchdog packets on the multicast group every $T_w$ microseconds. If a secondary receives no watchdog packets during an interval of time $T_d$, that secondary assumes that the primary has failed, and starts responding to client requests. If there is more than one secondary, a pre-defined rank order determines the order in which secondaries attempt to take over as the primary. Our current implementation uses only one secondary.

In practice, arbiters can be aggressive about detecting and reacting to failure, allowing recovery within 1–2 ms. An implementation can use $T_w = 100$ microseconds and $T_d = 1$ millisecond to achieve fast failover, consuming under 10 Mbits/s.

Upon an arbiter failover, the new arbiter must obtain an updated snapshot of all endpoint demands, so it can start allocating timeslots. The Fastpass Control Protocol (described below) assumes only soft-state at the arbiter, allowing endpoints to re-synchronize with the new arbiter in 1–2 round-trip times.

The transition period between old and new arbiters needs careful handling to prevent persistent queues from building up. For example, if the old arbiter tells $A$ to send to $C$ at some timeslot, and the new arbiter tells $B$ to send to $C$ at the same time, a queue will form at $C$'s ingress until encountering a free timeslot.

Conservative timing can ensure that by the time an arbiter failure is detected and the secondary takes over, no allocations made by the failed arbiter remain in the network. In our implementation, the arbiter allocates each timeslot 65 μs before the timeslot's start time to leave enough time for notifications to reach the endpoints; this number is much smaller than the 1 millisecond before the secondary takes over.

As a result, the old and new arbiters do not have to share information to make the failover possible, simplifying the implementation: the new arbiter just resynchronizes with endpoints and starts allocating.

## 5.2 Network failures

Arbiters need to know the network topology under their control, so packets can successfully traverse the network in their allotted timeslots. If links or switches become unavailable undetected, the arbiter would continue to allocate traffic through them, causing packet loss.

Because Fastpass maintains low queue occupancies, it can use packet drops to detect network faults. Sporadic packet losses due to bit flips in the physical layer still occur, but persistent, correlated packet loss is almost surely due to component failure. The path each packet traverses is known to the endpoints, which helps localize the fault.

A network service performs fault isolation, separate from the arbiter. Endpoints report packet drops to this fault isolation service, which correlates reports from multiple endpoints to identify the malfunctioning component. The faulty component is then reported to the arbiter, which avoids scheduling traffic through the component until the fault is cleared. Since packet errors can be detected quickly, failure detection and mitigation times can be made extremely short, on the order of milliseconds.

## 5.3 Fastpass Control Protocol (FCP)

Communication between endpoints and the arbiter is not scheduled and can experience packet loss. FCP must protect against such loss. Otherwise, if an endpoint request or the arbiter's response is dropped, a corresponding timeslot would never be allocated, and some packets would remain stuck in the endpoint's queue.

TCP-style cumulative ACKs and retransmissions are not ideal for FCP. At the time of retransmission, the old packet is out of date: for a request, the queue in the endpoint might be fuller than it was; for an allocation, an allocated timeslot might have already passed.

FCP provides reliability by communicating aggregate counts; to inform the arbiter of timeslots that need scheduling, the endpoint sends the sum total of timeslots it has requested so far for that destination. The arbiter keeps a record of each endpoints' latest demands; the difference from the kept record and the new aggregate demands specifies the amount of new timeslots to be allocated.

The counts are idempotent: receiving the same count multiple times does not cause timeslots to be allocated multiple times. Idempotency permits aggressive timeouts, leading to low allocation latency even in the face of occasional packet loss. Endpoints detect the loss of allocated timeslots using aggregate counts sent by the arbiter, triggering a request for more timeslots.

**Handling arbiter failure.** When a secondary arbiter replaces a failed primary, its aggregate counts are out of sync with the endpoints. The mismatch is detected using a random nonce established when the arbiter and endpoint synchronize. The nonce is incorporated into the packet checksum, so when an arbiter is out of sync with an endpoint, it observes a burst of failed checksums from an endpoint that triggers a re-synchronization with that endpoint.

Upon re-synchronization, the arbiter resets its aggregate counts to zeros, and the endpoint recomputes fresh aggregate counts based on its current queues. The process takes one round-trip time: as soon as the endpoint processes the RESET packet from the arbiter, it can successfully issue new requests to the arbiter.

# 6. IMPLEMENTATION

We implemented the arbiter using Intel DPDK [1], a framework that allows direct access to NIC queues from user space. On the endpoints, we implemented a Linux kernel module that queues packets while requests are sent to the arbiter. Our source code is at `http://fastpass.mit.edu/`

## 6.1 Client

FCP is implemented as a Linux transport protocol (over IP). A Fastpass *qdisc* (queueing discipline) queues outgoing packets before sending them to the NIC driver, and uses an FCP socket to send demands to and receive allocations from the arbiter.

The Fastpass qdisc intercepts each packet just before it is passed to the NIC, and extracts the destination address from its packet header.[3] It does not process transport protocol headers (e.g., TCP or UDP).

The Fastpass arbiter schedules network resources, obviating the need for TCP congestion control. TCP's congestion window (cwnd) could needlessly limit flow throughput, but packet loss is rare, so cwnd keeps increasing until it no longer limits throughput. At this point, TCP congestion control is effectively turned off.

The current implementation does not modify TCP. The evaluated system maintains long-lived flows, so flows are not cwnd-limited, and we preferred not to deal with the complexities of TCP. Nevertheless, modifying TCP's congestion control would be worthwhile for improving short-lived TCP flow performance.

The client is not limited to sending exactly one packet per timeslot. Instead, it greedily sends packets while their total transmission time is less than the timeslot length. This aggregation reduces the amount of potentially wasted network bandwidth caused by many small packets destined to the same endpoint.

## 6.2 Multicore Arbiter

The arbiter is made up of three types of cores: *comm-cores* communicate with endpoints, *alloc-cores* perform timeslot allocation, and *pathsel-cores* assign paths.

The number of cores of each type can be increased to handle large workloads: each comm-core handles a subset of endpoints, so endpoints can be divided among more cores when protocol handling becomes a bottleneck; alloc-cores work concurrently using pipeline parallelism (§3); and pathsel-cores are "embarrassingly parallel", since path assignments for different timeslots are independent.

[3]On a switched network, MAC addresses could be used. However, in the presence of routing, IP addresses are required.

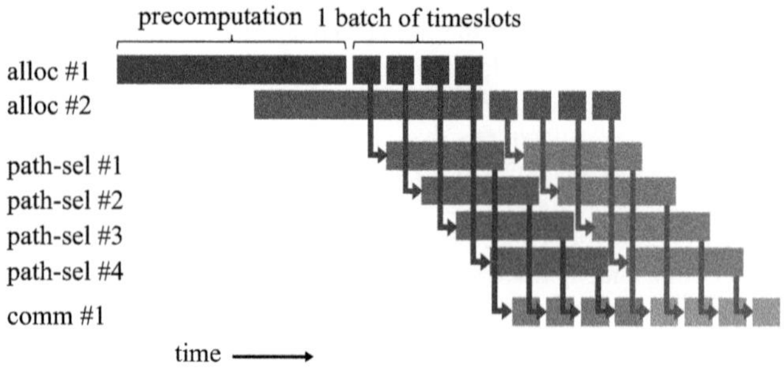


Figure 6: Multicore allocation: (1) allocation cores assign packets to timeslots, (2) path selection cores assign paths, and (3) communication cores send allocations to endpoints.

Fig. 6 shows communication between arbiter cores. Comm-cores receive endpoint demands and pass them to alloc-cores (not shown). Once a timeslot is completely allocated, it is promptly passed to a pathsel-core. The assigned paths are handed to comm-cores, which notify each endpoint of its allocations.

Performance measurements of each core type are presented in §7.

## 6.3 Timing

To keep queue occupancy low, end-node transmissions should occur at the times prescribed by the arbiter. Otherwise, packets from multiple endpoints might arrive at a switch's egress port together, resulting in queueing.

The amount of queueing caused by time-jitter is determined by the discrepancy in clocks. For example, if all clocks are either accurate or one timeslot fast, at most two packets will arrive at any egress: one from an accurate node, the other from a fast node.

**Clock synchronization.** The deployment synchronizes end-node time using the IEEE1588 Precision Time Protocol (PTP), which achieves sub-microsecond clock synchronization by carefully mitigating causes of time-synchronization jitter. PTP-capable NICs timestamp synchronization packets in hardware [29], thus avoiding jitter due to operating system scheduling. NICs with PTP support are widely available; the experiment used Intel 82599EB NICs.

Variable queueing delays inside the network also cause synchronization inaccuracies, and PTP-supported switches report their queueing delays so endpoints can compensate. However, Fastpass keeps queue-length variability low, enabling high quality time synchronization without PTP switch support.

**Client timing.** The client uses Linux high-resolution timers (hrtimers), previously demonstrated to achieve microsecond-scale precision when shaping flow throughput [33].

The client uses locks to synchronize access to the qdisc queues and to allocation state. Because waiting for these locks when transmitting packets causes variable delays, we allow the qdisc to send packets after their scheduled times, up to a configurable threshold. Endpoints re-request overly late allocations from the arbiter.

# 7. EVALUATION

The goal of Fastpass is to simultaneously eliminate in-network queueing, achieve high throughput, and support various inter-flow or inter-application resource allocation objectives in a real-world datacenter network. In this section, we evaluate how well Fastpass meets these goals, compared to a baseline datacenter network running TCP.

| Summary of Results | |
|---|---|
| §7.1 | **(A)** Under a bulk transfer workload involving multiple machines, Fastpass reduces median switch queue length to 18 KB from 4351 KB, with a 1.6% throughput penalty.<br>**(B)** Interactivity: under the same workload, Fastpass's median ping time is 0.23 ms vs. the baseline's 3.56 ms, 15.5× lower with Fastpass. |
| §7.2 | **(C)** Fairness: Fastpass reduces standard deviations of per-sender throughput over 1 s intervals by over 5200× for 5 connections. |
| §7.3 | **(D)** Each comm-core supports 130 Gbits/s of network traffic with 1 μs of NIC queueing.<br>**(E)** Arbiter traffic imposes a 0.3% throughput overhead.<br>**(F)** 8 alloc-cores support 2.2 Terabits/s of network traffic.<br>**(G)** 10 pathsel-cores support >5 Terabits/s of network traffic. |
| §7.4 | **(H)** In a real-world latency-sensitive service, Fastpass reduces TCP retransmissions by 2.5×. |

**Experimental setup.** We conducted experiments on a single rack of 32 servers, with each server connected to a top-of-rack (ToR) switch with a main 10 Gbits/s Ethernet (GbE) network interface card (NIC). Servers also have a 1 Gbit/s NIC meant for out-of-band communication. The 10 GbE top-of-rack switch has four 10 GbE uplinks to the four cluster switches [16]. Each server has 2 Intel CPUs with 8 cores each (16 hyper-threads per CPU, for a total of 32 hyper-threads) and 148 GB RAM. One server is set aside for running the arbiter. We turn off TCP segmentation offload (TSO) to achieve better control over the NIC send queues.

## 7.1 Throughput, queueing, and latency

**Experiment A: throughput and queueing.** Our first experiment compares the throughput and switch queue occupancy of Fastpass to the baseline network. Four rack servers run `iperf` to generate traffic (20 TCP flows per sender) to a single receiver. The experiment lasts 20 minutes and is run twice—once with the baseline and once with Fastpass.

Fastpass achieves throughput close to the baseline's: 9.43 Gbits/s in the baseline run versus 9.28 Gbits/s with Fastpass. At the same time, Fastpass reduces the median switch queue occupancy from 4.35 Megabytes in the baseline to just 18 kilobytes with Fastpass, a reduction of a factor of 242× (Fig. 7).

It isn't just the median but also the tails of the queue-occupancy distribution that are a lot lower, as shown here:

| | Median | 90th %ile | 99th | 99.9th |
|---|---|---|---|---|
| Baseline (Kbytes) | 4351 | 5097 | 5224 | 5239 |
| Fastpass (Kbytes) | 18 | 36 | 53 | 305 |

Most of the 1.6% difference in throughput can be attributed to Fastpass reserving about 1% of the achieved throughput for FCP traffic. The remainder is due to the client re-requesting timeslots when packet transmissions were delayed more than the allowed threshold (§6.3).

Switch queues are mostly full in the baseline because TCP continues to increase the sending rate until a packet is dropped (usually due to a full queue). In contrast, Fastpass's timeslot allocation keeps queues relatively empty: the 99.9th percentile occupancy was 305 KB over the entire experiment. Although the design intends queues to be strictly 0, the implementation does not yet achieve it because of jitter in endpoint transmission times. We believe that queueing

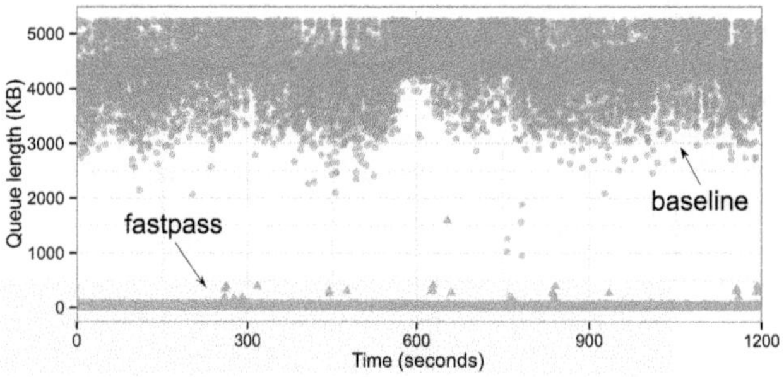


Figure 7: Switch queue lengths sampled at 100ms intervals on the top-of-rack switch. The diagram shows measurements from two different 20 minute experiments: baseline (red) and Fastpass (blue). Baseline TCP tends to fill switch queues, whereas Fastpass keeps queue occupancy low.

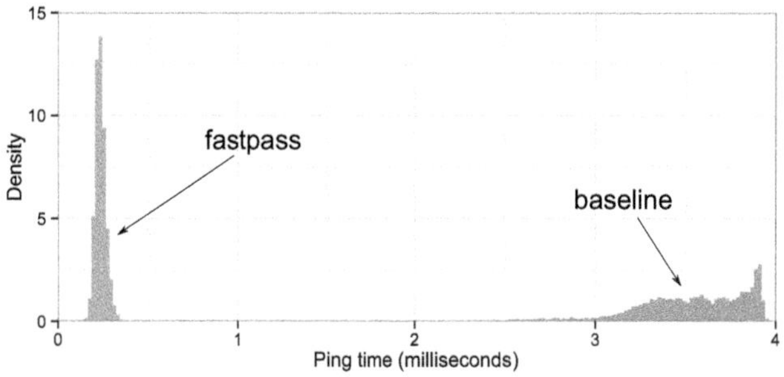


Figure 8: Histogram of ping RTTs with background load using Fastpass (blue) and baseline (red). Fastpass's RTT is 15.5× smaller, even with the added overhead of contacting the arbiter.

can be further reduced towards the zero ideal by using finer-grained locking in the kernel module.

**Experiment B: latency.** Next, we measure the round-trip latency of interactive requests under high load. This experiment uses the same setup as Experiment A, augmented with a fifth machine that sends a small request to the receiving server every 10 ms, using ping.

Fastpass reduces the end-to-end round-trip time (RTT) for interactive traffic when the network is heavily loaded by a factor of 15.5×, from a median of 3.56 ms to 230 μs (Fig. 8). The tail of the distribution observes significant reductions as well:

| | Median | 90th %ile | 99th | 99.9th |
|---|---|---|---|---|
| Baseline (ms) | 3.56 | 3.89 | 3.92 | 3.95 |
| Fastpass (ms) | 0.23 | 0.27 | 0.32 | 0.38 |

Note that with Fastpass ping packets are scheduled in both directions by the arbiter, but even with the added round-trips to the arbiter, end-to-end latency is substantially lower because queues are much smaller. In addition, Fastpass achieves low latency for interactive traffic without requiring the traffic to be designated explicitly as "interactive" or "bulk," and without using any mechanisms for traffic isolation in the switches: it results from the fairness properties of the timeslot allocator.

## 7.2 Fairness and convergence

**Experiment C: fairness and convergence.** Here we examine how fairly Fastpass allocates throughput to multiple senders, and how quickly it converges to a fair allocation when a sender arrives or departs. Five rack servers each send a bulk TCP flow to a sixth receiving server. The experiment begins with one bulk flow; every

30 seconds, a new bulk flow arrives until all five are active for 30 seconds, and then one flow terminates every 30 seconds. The entire experiment therefore lasts 270 seconds.

We calculate each connection's throughput over 1-second intervals. The resulting time series for the baseline TCP and for Fastpass are shown in Figure 9.

The baseline TCPs exhibit much larger variability than Fastpass. For instance, when the second connection starts, its throughput is about 20-25% higher than the first connection throughout the 30-second interval; similarly, when there are two senders remaining between time 210 to 240 seconds, the throughputs "cross over" and are almost never equal. With more connections, the variation in throughput for TCP is more pronounced than with Fastpass.

To quantify this observation, we calculate the standard deviation of the per-connection throughputs achieved in each 1-second interval, in Mbits/s, when there are 3, 4, and 5 concurrent connections each for the baseline TCP and Fastpass. We then compute the median over all standard deviations for a given number of connections (a median over 60 values when there are 3 or 4 connections and over 30 values when there are 5 connections). The results are:

| #connections | Baseline | Fastpass | Improvement |
|---|---|---|---|
| 3 | 543.86 | 15.89 | 34.2× |
| 4 | 628.49 | 0.146 | 4304.7× |
| 5 | 459.75 | 0.087 | 5284.5× |

These results show that Fastpass exhibits significantly lower variability across the board: its standard deviation of throughput is over 5200 **times** lower than the baseline when there are five concurrent connections.

Fastpass's pipelined timeslot allocation algorithm prioritizes flows based on their last transmission time, so when a new flow starts, it is immediately allocated a timeslot. From that point on, all flows contending for the bottleneck will be allocated timeslots in sequence, yielding immediate convergence and perfect fairness over intervals as small as 1 MTU per flow (for 5 flows on 10 Gbits/s links, this yields fairness at the granularity of 6 μs).

The benchmark shows low total throughput for one and two senders because of packet processing overheads, which are usually reduced by TSO. (In contrast, Experiments A and B use many more connections, so they achieve high utilization). Fastpass senders also require additional processing in the Fastpass qdisc, which is limited to using one core; NIC support (§8.3) or a multicore implementation will alleviate this bottleneck.

## 7.3 Arbiter performance

**Experiment D: request queueing.** To estimate how long requests queue at the arbiter before they are processed, we measure the NIC polling rate of the comm-core under increasing amounts of network traffic. Every 10 seconds, a rack server starts a TCP transfer to an unloaded server.

As the load increases, the arbiter spends more time processing requests, the NIC polling rate decreases (Fig. 10), and requests are delayed in the arbiter's NIC queues. A deployment can control this queueing delay by limiting the amount of traffic each comm-core handles: 130 Gbits/s for 1 μs queueing, 170 Gbits/s for 10 μs, etc.

**Experiment E: communication overhead.** To determine the network capacity requirements at the arbiter, we measure the total amount of control traffic the arbiter receives and transmits in experiment D. The network overhead of communication with the arbiter is 1-to-500 for request traffic and 1-to-300 for allocations for the tested workload (Fig. 11): to schedule as much as 150 Gbits/s, the comm core receives less than 0.3 Gbits/s of requests and sends out 0.5 Gbits/s of allocations. When the NIC polling rate decreases

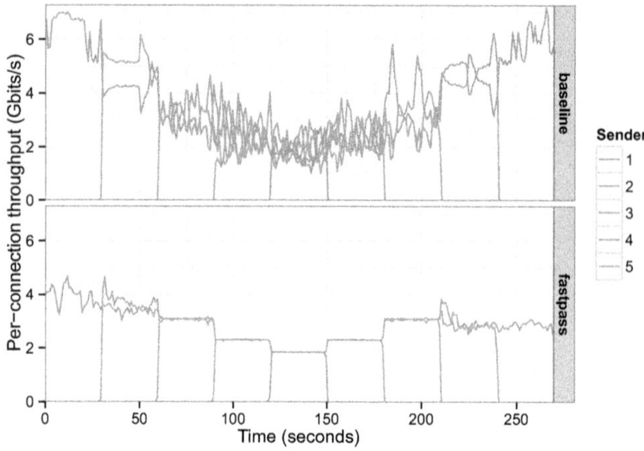


Figure 9: Each connection's throughput, with a varying number of senders. Even with 1s averaging intervals, baseline TCP flows achieve widely varying rates. In contrast, for Fastpass (bottom), with 3, 4, or 5 connections, the throughput curves are on top of one another. The Fastpass max-min fair timeslot allocator maintains fairness at fine granularity. The lower one- and two-sender Fastpass throughput is due to Fastpass qdisc overheads (§7.2).

sufficiently, incoming request packets start getting dropped (seen around 160 Gbits/s). The arbiter is still able to allocate all traffic because FCP retransmissions summarize aggregate demands; hence, not every demand packet needs to be received.

**Experiment F: timeslot allocation cores.** To determine the number of arbiter cores necessary for timeslot allocation, we measure the throughput of the max-min fair timeslot allocation implementation. Requests are generated by a synthetic stress-test-core, rather than received from a comm-core. The workload has Poisson arrivals, senders and receivers chosen uniformly at random from 256 nodes, and requests are for 10 MTUs. We vary the mean inter-arrival time to produce different network loads.

| | **2 cores** | **4 cores** | **6 cores** | **8 cores** |
|---|---|---|---|---|
| Throughput (Gbits/s) | 825.6 | 1545.1 | 1966.4 | 2211.8 |

Eight alloc-cores support over 2.21 Terabits/s of network traffic, or 221 endpoints transmitting at a full 10 Gbits/s. This corresponds to over 86% network utilization.

**Experiment G: path selection cores.** To determine the number of arbiter cores needed for path selection, we measure the average processing time per timeslot as load increases. We use the synthetic workload described above with exponentially distributed request sizes (with a mean of 10 MTUs). The chosen topology has 32 machines per rack and four paths between racks, with no over-subscription (motivated in part by the "4-post" cluster topology [16]). Note that non-oversubscribed topologies could be considered worst-case topologies for path selection: over-subscription reduces the amount of traffic leaving each rack and thus simplifies path-selection.

Fig. 12 shows that the processing time increases with network utilization until many of the nodes reach full degree (32 in the tested topology), at which point the cost of pre-processing[4] the graph decreases, and path selection runs slightly faster.

Because path-selection can be parallelized by having a different core select paths for each timeslot, these measurements indicate how many pathsel-cores are required for different topologies. For exam-

[4]Path selection adds dummy edges to the graph until all nodes have the same degree (i.e., number of packets).

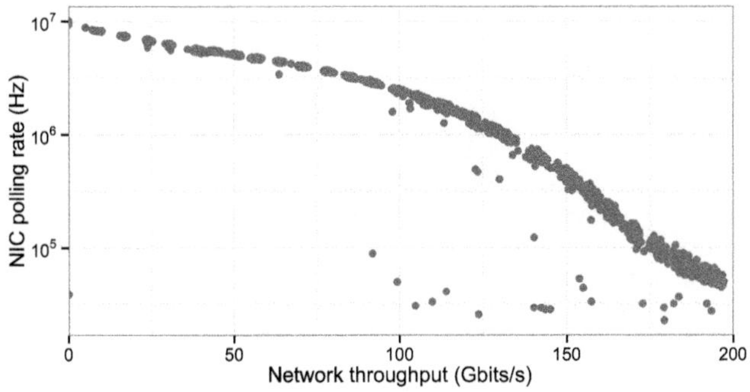


Figure 10: As more requests are handled, the NIC polling rate decreases. The resulting queueing delay can be bounded by distributing request-handling across multiple comm-cores.

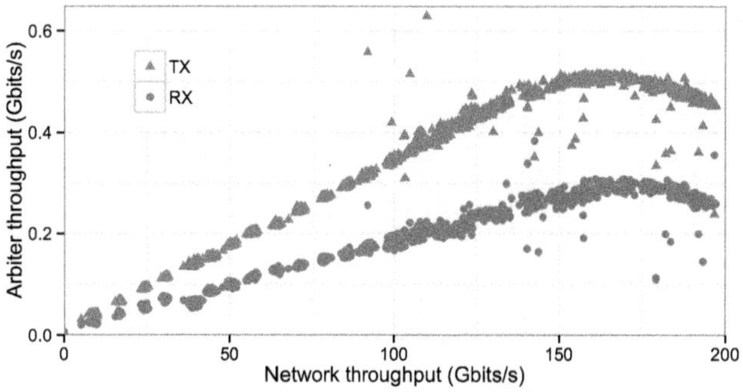


Figure 11: The arbiter requires 0.5 Gbits/s TX and 0.3 Gbits/s RX bandwidth to schedule 150 Gbits/s: around 0.3% of network traffic.

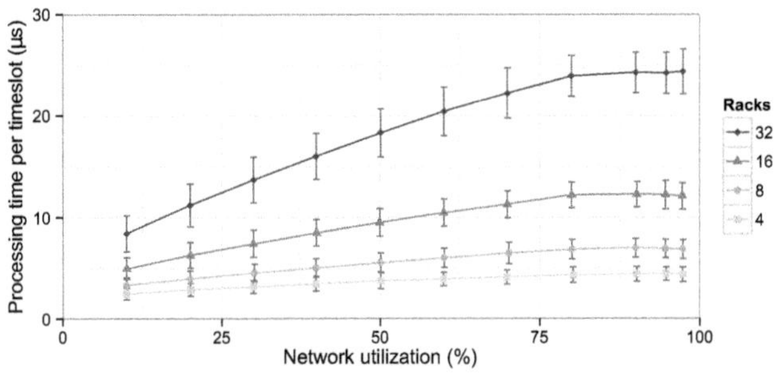


Figure 12: Path selection routes traffic from 16 racks of 32 endpoints in <12 µs. Consequently, 10 pathsel-cores would output a routing every <1.2 µs, fast enough to support 10 Gbits/s endpoint links. Error bars show one standard deviation above and below the mean.

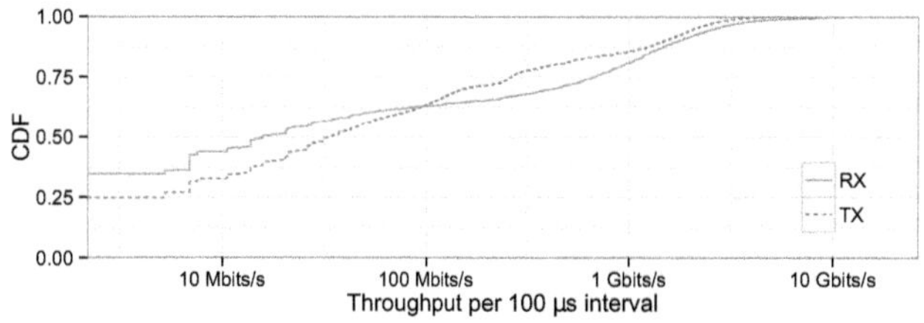


Figure 13: Distribution of the sending and receiving rates of one production server per 100 microsecond interval over a 60 second trace.

ple, path selection of 16 racks can be done in under 12 microseconds; hence, for 1.2 microsecond timeslots, 10 pathsel-cores suffice.

## 7.4 Production experiments at Facebook

**Workload.** We deployed Fastpass on a latency-sensitive service that is in the response path for user web requests. This service has a partition-aggregate workload similar to common search workloads [10]. Each server runs both an aggregator and a leaf; when an aggregator receives a query from a web server, it requests relevant data from several leaves, processes them, and returns a reduced result. Each rack of 30–34 aggregator-leaf servers works independently.

To maintain acceptable latency as traffic load changes during the day, the service adjusts the number of internal queries generated by each request; in aggregate, a rack handles between 500K and 200M internal queries per second. When load is low, the aggregator considers more items and produces higher quality results. In times of heavy load, when the 99th percentile latency increases, the number of items considered per web request is reduced aggressively.

Cluster traffic is bursty, but most of the time utilizes a fraction of network capacity (Fig. 13). We measure throughput over 100 µs time intervals on one production server. 25% of these intervals have no ingress traffic, 25% have no egress traffic, and only 10% of these intervals have aggregate traffic exceeding 2 Gbits/s.

The production workload changes gently over time scales of tens of minutes, enabling comparative testing when schemes are applied in sequence. The live experiment ran for 135 minutes: the rack started in baseline mode, switched to Fastpass at 30 minutes, and back to baseline at 110 minutes.

**Experiment H: production results.** Fig. 14 shows that the 99th percentile web request service time using Fastpass is very similar to the baseline's. The three clusters pertain to groups of machines that were assigned different load by the load-balancer. Fig. 15 shows the cluster's load as the experiment progressed, showing gentle oscillations in load. Fastpass was able to handle the load without triggering the aggressive load-reduction.

Fastpass reduced TCP retransmissions by 2–2.5× (Fig. 16). We believe the remaining packet loss is due to traffic exiting the rack, where Fastpass is not used to keep switch queues low. Extending the Fastpass scheduling boundary should further reduce this packet loss.

# 8. DISCUSSION

## 8.1 Large deployments

A single arbiter should be able to handle hundreds to thousands of endpoints. At larger scales, however, a single arbiter's computational and network throughput become bottlenecks, and several arbiters would need to cooperate.

A hierarchical approach might be useful: an arbiter within each cluster would send its demands for intra-cluster traffic to a core-arbiter, which would decide which timeslots each cluster may use, and what paths packets at these timeslots must follow. The cluster arbiters would then pass on these allocations to endpoints.

A core arbiter would have to handle a large volume of traffic, so allocating at MTU-size granularity would not be computationally feasible. Instead, it could allocate timeslots in bulk, and trust cluster arbiters to assign individual timeslots fairly among endpoints.

An alternative for large deployments could be the use of specialized hardware. An FPGA or ASIC implementation of timeslot allocation and path selection algorithms would likely allow a single arbiter to support much larger clusters.

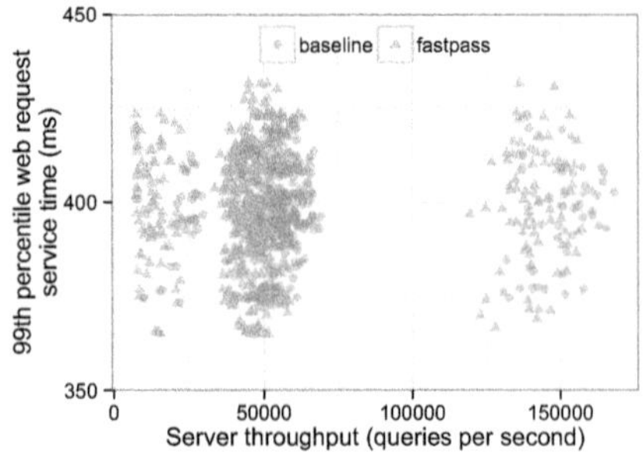


Figure 14: 99th percentile web request service time vs. server load in production traffic. Fastpass shows a similar latency profile as baseline.

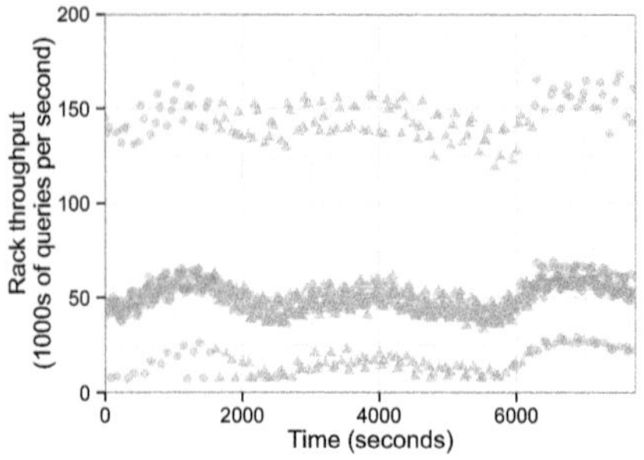


Figure 15: Live traffic server load as a function of time. Fastpass is shown in the middle with baseline before and after. The offered load oscillates gently with time.

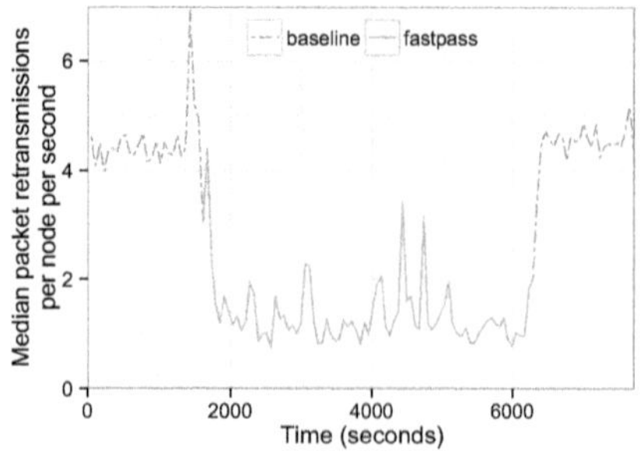


Figure 16: Median server TCP retransmission rate during the live experiment. Fastpass (middle) maintains a 2.5× lower rate of retransmissions than baseline (left and right).

## 8.2 Routing packets along selected paths

Packets must be made to follow the paths allocated to them by the arbiter. Routers typically support IP source routing only in software, if at all, rendering it too slow for practical use. Static routing [38] and policy based routing using VLANs are feasible, but could interfere with existing BGP configurations, making them less suitable for existing clusters. Tunneling (e.g. IP-in-IP or GRE) entails a small throughput overhead, but is supported in hardware by many switch chipsets making it a viable option [18].

Finally, routing along a specific path can be achieved by what we term *ECMP spoofing*. ECMP spoofing modifies fields in the packet header (e.g., source port) to specific values that will cause each switch to route the packet to the desired egress, given the other fields in the packet header and the known ECMP hash function. The receiver can then convert the modified fields to their original values, stored elsewhere in the packet.

## 8.3 Scheduling support in NICs

Fastpass enqueues packets into NIC queues at precise times, using high resolution timers. This frequent timer processing increases CPU overhead, and introduces operating-system jitter (e.g., due to interrupts). These timers would not be necessary if NICs implement support for precise packet scheduling: packets could be enqueued when Fastpass receives an allocation. A "send-at" field in the packet descriptor would indicate the desired send time.

## 8.4 Small packet workloads

A current limitation of Fastpass is that it allocates at the granularity of timeslots, so if an endpoint has less than a full timeslot worth of data to send, network bandwidth is left unused. This waste is reduced or eliminated when an endpoint sends many small packets to the same destination, which are batched together (§6.1). Workloads that send tiny amounts of data to a large number of destinations still waste bandwidth. A possible mitigation is for the arbiter to divide some timeslots into smaller fragments and allocate these fragments to the smaller packets.

# 9. RELATED WORK

Several systems use centralized controllers to get better load balance and network sharing, but they work at "control-plane" granularity, which doesn't provide control over packet latencies or allocations over small time scales.

Hedera [5] discovers elephant flows by gathering switch statistics, then reroutes elephants for better load balancing. It aims for high throughput, and has no mechanism to reduce network latency.

Datacenter TDMA [35] and Mordia [17] use gathered statistics to estimate future demand, then compute a set of matchings that are applied in sequence to timeslots of duration on the order of 100 μs. Both schemes target elephant flows; short flows are delegated to other means.

Orchestra [11] coordinates transfers in the shuffle stage of MapReduce/Dryad so all transfers finish roughly together, by assigning weights to each transfer. Orchestra is an application-level mechanism; the actual transfers use TCP.

SWAN [19] frequently reconfigures the network's data plane to match demand from different services. All non-interactive services coordinate with the central SWAN controller, which plans paths and bandwidth and implements those paths by updating forwarding tables in network devices.

Distributed approaches usually set out to solve a restricted datacenter problem: minimizing Flow Completion Time (FCT), meeting deadlines, balancing load, reducing queueing, or sharing the network. To our knowledge, no previous scheme provides a general platform to support all these features, and some schemes perform sub-optimally because they lack complete knowledge of network conditions.

DCTCP [6] and HULL [7] reduce switch queueing, but increase convergence time to a fair-share of the capacity, and do not eliminate queueing delay.

In MATE [15] and DARD [38], ingress nodes reroute traffic selfishly between paths until converging to a configuration that provides good load balance across paths.

In multi-tenant datacenters, Seawall [32] provides weighted fair sharing of network links, and EyeQ [22] enforces traffic constraints.

Schemes such as pFabric [8] and PDQ [20] modify the switches to reduce flow completion time, while $D^3$ [36] and PDQ minimize flow completion times to meet deadlines. These switch modifications raise the barrier to adoption because they need to be done across the network. PDQ and pFabric use a distributed approximation of the *shortest remaining flow first* policy, which Fastpass can implement in the arbiter.

Differentiated Services (DiffServ, RFC2474) provides a distributed mechanism for different classes of traffic to travel via distinct queues in routers. The number of DiffServ Code Points available is limited, and in practice operational concerns restrict the number of classes even further. Most commonly, there are classes for bulk traffic and latency-sensitive traffic, but not a whole lot more.

## 10. CONCLUSION

We showed how to design and implement a datacenter network in which a centralized arbiter determines the times at which each packet should be transmitted and the path it should take. Our results show that compared to the baseline network, the throughput penalty is small but queueing delays reduce dramatically, flows share resources more fairly and converge quickly, and the software arbiter implementation scales to multiple cores and handles an aggregate data rate of 2.21 Terabits/s.

Even with such a seemingly heavy-handed approach that incurs a little extra latency to and from the arbiter, tail packet latencies and the number of retransmitted packets reduce compared to the status quo, thanks to the global control exerted by the arbiter. Our results show that Fastpass opens up new possibilities for high-performance, tightly-integrated, predictable network applications in datacenters, even with commodity routers and switches.

We hope we have persuaded the reader that centralized control at the granularity of individual packets, achieved by viewing the entire network as a large switch, is both practical and beneficial.

## Acknowledgements

We are grateful to Omar Baldonado and Sanjeev Kumar of Facebook for their enthusiastic support of this collaboration, Petr Lapukhov and Doug Weimer for their generous assistance with the Facebook infrastructure, Garrett Wollman and Jon Proulx at MIT CSAIL for their help and efforts in setting up environments for our early experiments, and David Oran of Cisco for his help. We thank John Ousterhout, Rodrigo Fonseca, Nick McKeown, George Varghese, Chuck Thacker, Steve Hand, Andreas Nowatzyk, Tom Rodeheffer, and the SIGCOMM reviewers for their insightful feedback. This work was supported in part by the National Science Foundation grant IIS-1065219. Ousterhout was supported by a Jacobs Presidential Fellowship and a Hertz Foundation Fellowship. We thank the industrial members of the MIT Center for Wireless Networks and Mobile Computing for their support and encouragement.

## 11. REFERENCES

[1] Packet processing on intel architecture. http://www.intel.com/go/dpdk.

[2] *Intel 64 and IA-32 Architectures Optimization Reference Manual*. Number 248966-029. March 2014.

[3] M. Ajmone Marsan, E. Leonardi, M. Mellia, and F. Neri. On the stability of input-buffer cell switches with speed-up. In *INFOCOM*, 2000.

[4] M. Al-Fares, A. Loukissas, and A. Vahdat. A Scalable, Commodity Data Center Network Architecture. In *SIGCOMM*, 2008.

[5] M. Al-Fares, S. Radhakrishnan, B. Raghavan, N. Huang, and A. Vahdat. Hedera: Dynamic Flow Scheduling for Data Center Networks. In *NSDI*, 2010.

[6] M. Alizadeh, A. Greenberg, D. A. Maltz, J. Padhye, P. Patel, B. Prabhakar, S. Sengupta, M. Sridharan, C. Faster, and D. Maltz. DCTCP: Efficient Packet Transport for the Commoditized Data Center. In *SIGCOMM*, 2010.

[7] M. Alizadeh, A. Kabbani, T. Edsall, B. Prabhakar, A. Vahdat, and M. Yasuda. Less is More: Trading a Little Bandwidth for Ultra-Low Latency in the Data Center. In *NSDI*, 2012.

[8] M. Alizadeh, S. Yang, S. Katti, N. McKeown, B. Prabhakar, and S. Shenker. Deconstructing Datacenter Packet Transport. In *HotNets*, 2012.

[9] T. E. Anderson, S. S. Owicki, J. B. Saxe, and C. P. Thacker. High-Speed Switch Scheduling for Local-Area Networks. *ACM Trans. on Comp. Sys.*, 11(4):319–352, 1993.

[10] L. A. Barroso, J. Dean, and U. Holzle. Web Search for a Planet: The Google Cluster Architecture. *IEEE Micro*, 23(2):22–28, 2003.

[11] M. Chowdhury, M. Zaharia, J. Ma, M. Jordan, and I. Stoica. Managing Data Transfers in Computer Clusters with Orchestra. In *SIGCOMM*, 2011.

[12] R. Cole, K. Ost, and S. Schirra. Edge-Coloring Bipartite Multigraphs in $O(E \log D)$ Time. *Combinatorica*, 21(1):5–12, 2001.

[13] J. Dai and B. Prabhakar. The throughput of data switches with and without speedup. In *INFOCOM*, 2000.

[14] J. Duato, S. Yalamanchili, and L. Ni. *Interconnection Networks*. Morgan Kaufmann, 2003.

[15] A. Elwalid, C. Jin, S. Low, and I. Widjaja. MATE: MPLS Adaptive Traffic Engineering. In *INFOCOM*, 2001.

[16] N. Farrington and A. Andreyev. Facebook's Data Center Network Architecture. In *IEEE Optical Interconnects Conf.*, 2013.

[17] N. Farrington, G. Porter, Y. Fainman, G. Papen, and A. Vahdat. Hunting Mice with Microsecond Circuit Switches. In *HotNets*, 2012.

[18] A. Greenberg, J. R. Hamilton, N. Jain, S. Kandula, C. Kim, P. Lahiri, D. A. Maltz, P. Patel, and S. Sengupta. VL2: A Scalable and Flexible Data Center Network. In *SIGCOMM*, 2009.

[19] C.-Y. Hong, S. Kandula, R. Mahajan, M. Zhang, V. Gill, M. Nanduri, and R. Wattenhofer. Achieving High Utilization with Software-Driven WAN. In *SIGCOMM*, 2013.

[20] Hong, C. Y. and Caesar, M. and Godfrey, P. Finishing Flows Quickly with Preemptive Scheduling. *SIGCOMM*, 2012.

[21] F. Hwang. Control Algorithms for Rearrangeable Clos Networks. *IEEE Trans. on Comm.*, 31(8):952–954, 1983.

[22] V. Jeyakumar, M. Alizadeh, D. Mazieres, B. Prabhakar, and C. Kim. EyeQ: Practical Network Performance Isolation for the Multi-Tenant Cloud. In *HotCloud*, 2012.

[23] A. Kapoor and R. Rizzi. Edge-coloring bipartite graphs. *Journal of Algorithms*, 34(2):390–396, 2000.

[24] N. McKeown. The iSLIP Scheduling Algorithm for Input-Queued Switches. *IEEE/ACM Trans. on Net.*, 7(2):188–201, 1999.

[25] N. McKeown, A. Mekkittikul, V. Anantharam, and J. Walrand. Achieving 100% Throughput in an Input-Queued Switch. *IEEE Trans. Comm.*, 47(8):1260–1267, 1999.

[26] D. Nagle, D. Serenyi, and A. Matthews. The Panasas ActiveScale Storage Cluster: Delivering Scalable High Bandwidth Storage. In *Supercomputing*, 2004.

[27] R. Niranjan Mysore, A. Pamboris, N. Farrington, N. Huang, P. Miri, S. Radhakrishnan, V. Subramanya, and A. Vahdat. PortLand: A Scalable Fault-Tolerant Layer 2 Data Center Network Fabric. In *SIGCOMM*, 2009.

[28] R. Nishtala, H. Fugal, S. Grimm, M. Kwiatkowski, H. Lee, H. C. Li, R. McElroy, M. Paleczny, D. Peek, P. Saab, et al. Scaling memcache at facebook. In *NSDI*, 2013.

[29] P. Ohly, D. N. Lombard, and K. B. Stanton. Hardware Assisted Precision Time Protocol. Design and Case Study. In *LCI Intl. Conf. on High-Perf. Clustered Comp.*, 2008.

[30] D. Shah. Maximal matching scheduling is good enough. In *GLOBECOM*, 2003.

[31] D. Shah, N. Walton, and Y. Zhong. Optimal Queue-Size Scaling in Switched Networks. In *SIGMETRICS*, 2012.

[32] A. Shieh, S. Kandula, A. Greenberg, C. Kim, and B. Saha. Sharing the Data Center Network. In *NSDI*, 2011.

[33] R. Takano, T. Kudoh, Y. Kodama, and F. Okazaki. High-Resolution Timer-Based Packet Pacing Mechanism on the Linux Operating System. *IEICE Trans. on Comm.*, 2011.

[34] Y. Tamir and H.-C. Chi. Symmetric crossbar arbiters for VLSI communication switches. *IEEE Trans. Par. Dist. Sys.*, 4(1):13–27, 1993.

[35] B. C. Vattikonda, G. Porter, A. Vahdat, and A. C. Snoeren. Practical TDMA for Datacenter Ethernet. In *EuroSys*, 2012.

[36] C. Wilson, H. Ballani, T. Karagiannis, and A. Rowtron. Better Never Than Late: Meeting Deadlines in Datacenter Networks. In *SIGCOMM*, 2011.

[37] H. Wu, Z. Feng, C. Guo, and Y. Zhang. ICTCP: Incast Congestion Control for TCP in Data Center Networks. In *CoNext*, 2010.

[38] X. Wu and X. Yang. DARD: Distributed Adaptive Routing for Datacenter Networks. In *ICDCS*, 2012.

## Appendix: Theoretical Properties of the Timeslot Allocator

**System model.** We consider a network with $N$ endpoints denoted by $1,\ldots,N$, with each endpoint potentially having requests for any other endpoint. Time is slotted; in a unit timeslot each endpoint can transmit at most one MTU-sized packet to any other endpoint and receive at most one packet from any other endpoint. New requests arrive at an endpoint $i$ for endpoint $j$ with probability $p_{ij}$ in each timeslot. An arriving request brings a random number of packets, distributed according to a distribution $G_{ij}$ and independent of everything else.

Let $\mathbb{E}[G_{ij}] = g_{ij}$. Thus, on average $\lambda_{ij} = p_{ij}g_{ij}$ packets arrive at endpoint $i$ for endpoint $j$ per timeslot. The matrix $\Lambda = [\lambda_{ij}]$ denotes the net average data traffic between endpoints arriving in each timeslot. We assume a non-oversubscribed (also called full bisection bandwidth) network: the network can support any traffic where each node is paired to at most one other node per timeslot.

In the above setup, all traffic matrices, $\Lambda$, that can be served by any system architecture, must be *doubly sub-stochastic*. That is,

$$\sum_{k=1}^{N} \lambda_{ik} < 1, \text{ for all } i \text{ and } \sum_{k=1}^{N} \lambda_{kj} < 1, \text{ for all } j. \tag{1}$$

By the celebrated result of Birkhoff and von Neumann, all doubly stochastic matrices can be decomposed as a weighted sum of permutation matrices (i.e., matchings) with the sum of the weights being at most 1. Therefore, non-oversubscribed networks can support all doubly stochastic traffic matrices. A traffic matrix $\Lambda$ is called *admissible* if and only if $\rho(\Lambda) < 1$ where, the system *load* $\rho(\Lambda)$ is defined as

$$\rho(\Lambda) = \max_{i,j}\Big(\sum_{k=1}^{N}\lambda_{ik}, \sum_{k=1}^{N}\lambda_{kj}\Big). \tag{2}$$

Finally, let $Q_{ij}(t)$ denote the total number of packets (potentially across different requests) waiting to be transferred from endpoint $i$ to endpoint $j$ at time $t$. This setup is similar to that used in literature on input-queued switches [25], enabling us to view the network as a big input-queued switch with $Q_{ij}(t)$ the Virtual Output Queue sizes.

**Main result.** The arbiter's timeslot allocation algorithm of §3 is equivalent to the following: each queue $(i,j)$ has a "priority score" associated with it. In the beginning of each timeslot, the arbiter starts processing queues in non-decreasing order of these priority scores. While processing, the arbiter allocates a timeslot to queue $(i,j)$ if the arbiter has not already allocated another packet starting from $i$ or destined to $j$ in this timeslot. Therefore, at the end of processing the timeslot, the allocations correspond to a *maximal matching* between endpoints in the bipartite graph between endpoints, where an edge is present between $(i,j)$ if there are packets waiting at endpoint $i$ destined for $j$. From the literature on input-queued switches, it is well-known that any maximal matching provides 50% throughput guarantees [13, 3]. Building upon these results as well as [30], we state the following property of our algorithm.

THEOREM 1. *For any $\rho < 1$, there exists $\Lambda$ with $\rho(\Lambda) = \rho$ such that for* any *allocator,*

$$\liminf_{t} \mathbb{E}\Big[\sum_{ij} Q_{ij}(t)\Big] \geq \frac{N\rho}{2(1-\rho)}. \tag{3}$$

*Further, let $V \geq 1$ be such that $\mathbb{E}[G_{ij}^2] \leq V\mathbb{E}[G_{ij}]$ for all $i,j$ (bounded $G_{ij}$); if we allow the Fastpass arbiter to schedule (as well as transmit through the network) twice per unit timeslot,[5] then the induced average queue-size*

$$\limsup_{t} \mathbb{E}\Big[\sum_{ij} Q_{ij}(t)\Big] \leq \frac{N\rho(\rho+V)}{2(1-\rho)}. \tag{4}$$

*Proof Sketch.* To establish the lower bound (3) for any scheduling algorithm, it is sufficient to consider a specific scenario of our setup. Concretely, let the traffic matrix be uniform, i.e., $\Lambda = [\lambda_{ij}]$ with $\lambda_{ij} = \frac{\rho}{(N-1)}$ for all $i \neq j$ and 0 when $i = j$; $p_{ij} = 1$ for all $i \neq j$; and let $G_{ij}$ be Poisson variables with parameter $\lambda_{ij}$. The network can be viewed as unit-sized packets arriving at each endpoint according to a Poisson arrival process of rate $\rho$ and processed (transferred by the network) at unit rate. That is, the queue-size for each endpoint $j$ is bounded below by that of an $M/D/1$ queue with load $\rho$, which is known to be bounded below by $\frac{\rho}{(2(1-\rho))}$ [31]. Therefore, the network-wide queue-size is bounded below by $\frac{N\rho}{(2(1-\rho))}$.

To establish an upper bound, we use the fact that the algorithm effectively achieves a maximal matching in the weighted bipartite graph between endpoints in each timeslot. Given this fact, and under the assumption that Fastpass can schedule as well as transfer data at twice the speed, this is effectively a *speedup* of 2 in the classical terminology of switch scheduling. Therefore, for the Lyapunov function (cf. [13]),

$$L(t) = \sum_{i,j} Q_{ij}(t)[Q_{i\cdot}(t) + Q_{\cdot j}(t)]$$

it can be shown using calculations similar to [30] that

$$\mathbb{E}[L(t+1) - L(t)|Q(t)] \leq 4(\rho-1)\big(\sum_{i,j} Q_{ij}(t)\big) + 2N\rho^2 + 2VN\rho.$$

Telescoping this inequality for $t \geq 0$ and using the fact that the system reaches equilibrium due to ergodicity, we obtain the desired result. ■

*Implications.* Equation (3) says that there is some (worst case) input workload for which any allocator will have an expected aggregate queue length at least as large as $\frac{N\rho}{2(1-\rho)}$. Equation (4) says that with a speedup of 2 in the network fabric, for every workload, the expected aggregate queue length will be no larger than $\frac{N\rho(\rho+V)}{2(1-\rho)}$. Here $V$ is effectively a bound on burst size; if it is small, say 1, then it is within a factor of 2 of the lower bound! There is, however, a gap between theory and practice here, as in switch scheduling; many workloads observed in practice seem to require only small queues even with no speedup.

[5] Equivalent to having to double the network fabric bandwidth.

# FireFly: A Reconfigurable Wireless Data Center Fabric Using Free-Space Optics

Navid Hamedazimi,[†] Zafar Qazi,[†] Himanshu Gupta,[†] Vyas Sekar,[*] Samir R. Das,[†] Jon P. Longtin,[†]
Himanshu Shah,[†] and Ashish Tanwer[†]
[†]Stony Brook University [*]Carnegie Mellon University

## ABSTRACT

Conventional *static* datacenter (DC) network designs offer extreme cost vs. performance tradeoffs—simple leaf-spine networks are cost-effective but oversubscribed, while "fat tree"-like solutions offer good worst-case performance but are expensive. Recent results make a promising case for *augmenting* an oversubscribed network with reconfigurable inter-rack wireless or optical links. Inspired by the promise of reconfigurability, this paper presents *FireFly*, an inter-rack network solution that pushes DC network design to the extreme on three key fronts: (1) all links are reconfigurable; (2) all links are wireless; and (3) non top-of-rack switches are eliminated altogether. This vision, if realized, can offer significant benefits in terms of increased flexibility, reduced equipment cost, and minimal cabling complexity. In order to achieve this vision, we need to look beyond traditional RF wireless solutions due to their interference footprint which limits range and data rates. Thus, we make the case for using free-space optics (FSO). We demonstrate the viability of this architecture by (a) building a proof-of-concept prototype of a steerable small form factor FSO device using commodity components and (b) developing practical heuristics to address algorithmic and system-level challenges in network design and management.

## Categories and Subject Descriptors

C.2.1 [Computer-Communication Networks]: Network Architecture and Design

## Keywords

Data Centers; Free-Space Optics; Reconfigurablility

## 1 Introduction

A robust *data center (DC) network* must satisfy several goals: high throughput [13, 23], low equipment and management cost [13, 40], robustness to dynamic traffic patterns [14, 26, 48, 52], incremental expandability [18, 45], low cabling complexity [37], and low power and cooling costs. With respect to cost and performance, conventional designs are either (i) overprovisioned to account for worst-case traffic patterns, and thus incur high cost (e.g., fat-trees or Clos networks [13, 16, 23]), or (ii) oversubscribed (e.g., simple trees or leaf-spine architectures [1]) which incur low cost but offer poor performance due to congested links.


*SIGCOMM'14*, August 17–22, 2014, Chicago, IL, USA.

ACM 978-1-4503-2836-4/14/08 ...$15.00.
http://dx.doi.org/10.1145/2619239.2626328.

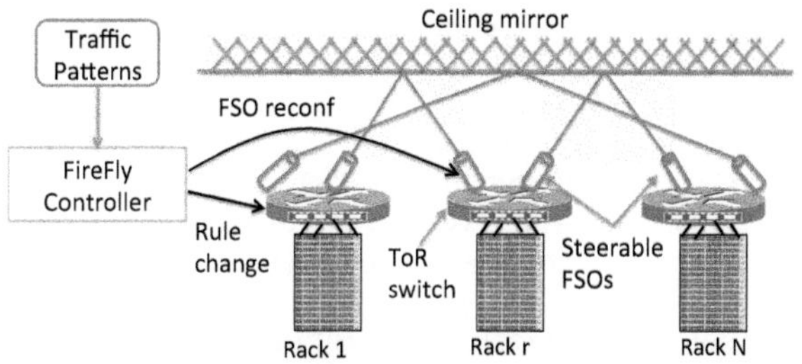


**Figure 1: High-level view of the FireFly architecture. The only switches are the Top-of-Rack (ToR) switches.**

Recent work suggests a promising middleground that augments an oversubscribed network with a few reconfigurable links, using either 60 Ghz RF wireless [26, 52] or optical switches [48]. Inspired by the promise of these flexible DC designs,[1] we envision a radically different DC architecture that pushes the network design to the *logical extreme* on three dimensions: (1) All inter-rack links are flexible; (2) All inter-rack links are wireless; and (3) we get rid of the *core* switching backbone.

This extreme vision, if realized, promises unprecedented qualitative and quantitative benefits for DC networks. First, it can reduce infrastructure cost without compromising on performance. Second, flexibility increases the effective operating capacity and can improve application performance by alleviating transient congestion. Third, it unburdens DC operators from dealing with cabling complexity and its attendant overheads (e.g., obstructed cooling) [37]. Fourth, it can enable DC operators to experiment with, and benefit from, new topology structures that would otherwise remain unrealizable due to cabling costs. Finally, flexibly turning links on or off can take us closer to the vision of energy proportionality (e.g., [29]).

This paper describes *FireFly*,[2] a first but significant step toward realizing this vision. Figure 1 shows a high-level overview of FireFly. Each ToR is equipped with reconfigurable wireless links which can connect to other ToR switches. However, we need to look beyond traditional radio-frequency (RF) wireless solutions (e.g., 60GHz) as their interference characteristics limit range and capacity. Thus, we envision a new use-case for *Free-Space Optical communications* (FSO) as it can offer high data rates (tens of Gbps) over long ranges using low transmission power and with zero interference [31]. The centralized FireFly controller reconfigures the topology and forwarding rules to adapt to changing traffic patterns.

While prior work made the case for using FSO links in DCs [19, 28], these fail to establish a viable hardware design and also do not address practical network design and management challenges that

[1]We use the terms *flexible* and *reconfigurable* interchangeably.
[2]FireFly stands for Free-space optical Inter-Rack nEtwork with high FLexibilitY.

arise in reconfigurable designs. Our work bridges this gap along three dimensions:

- **Practical steerable FSO devices (§3):** Commodity FSO designs are bulky, power hungry, and offer fixed point-to-point links. Our vision imposes new form-factor, cost, and steerability requirements which are fundamentally different w.r.t. traditional FSO use-cases. To this end, we establish the viability for a small-form factor FSO design using commodity optical devices. We demonstrate two promising *steering* technologies using switchable mirrors [4] and Galvo mirrors [2].
- **Network provisioning (§4):** Given the budget and physical constraints, the FireFly network hardware must be provisioned to handle unforeseen traffic patterns. We argue that flexible network designs should strive to optimize a new notion of *dynamic bisection bandwidth.* While it is hard to analytically reason about topologies that optimize this metric, we show that random regular graphs are surprisingly good in practice.
- **Network management (§5,§6):** The FireFly controller needs fast and efficient topology selection and traffic engineering algorithms to adapt to changing traffic conditions. However, state-of-art off-the-shelf solvers fail to scale beyond 32-rack DCs. Thus, we develop fast heuristics that achieve near-optimal performance (§5). In addition, the FireFly controller must ensure that performance is not adversely impacted during reconfigurations. We design simple but effective mechanisms that ensure that the network always remains connected, there are no black holes, and that the per-packet latency is bounded.

We evaluate our FSO prototype using a range of controlled lab experiments and a longitudinal study in a real DC setting. We find that the links are robust to real environmental disturbances and achieve wireline-equivalent throughput, and the steering mechanisms are fast, precise, and accurate. We evaluate the end-to-end performance of FireFly using a combination of detailed packet-level simulations [3], large scale flow-level simulations, and virtual emulation platforms [7]. We compare FireFly against state-of-art augmented designs and overprovisioned DC architectures. Overall, we find that FireFly can achieve performance close to a full bisection bandwidth network but at 40-60% of the cost.

We acknowledge that there are several operational concerns, especially related to maintenance, reliability, and reluctance of operators to adopt dynamic network designs. (We discuss some of these in §9). We also note that other cost factors may dominate deployment considerations; e.g., server vs. network vs. management costs. In spite of these valid concerns, we believe that there is value in exploring an FSO-based all-wireless design since it could lead to unprecedented benefits. In particular, pursuing such a vision could open up other avenues amenable to more incremental adoption (e.g., hybrid/augmented networks) and inspire other novel use cases for FSO in DCs.

# 2 Motivation and Overview

We begin with motivating key aspects of our vision: *full flexibility*, *wireless links*, and use of *free-space optics*.

## 2.1 Case for Full Flexibility

A key intuition behind FireFly's design is that a *fully-flexible inter-rack network can yield near-optimal bisection bandwidth even without any core (non-ToR) switches.*

To provide the basis for this intuition, we consider an abstract model of a DC network with $n$ racks (and hence $n$ ToR switches). We consider two abstract DC designs: (a) *FBB:* a full-bisection bandwidth network, and (b) *Flexible($f$):* an architecture with only

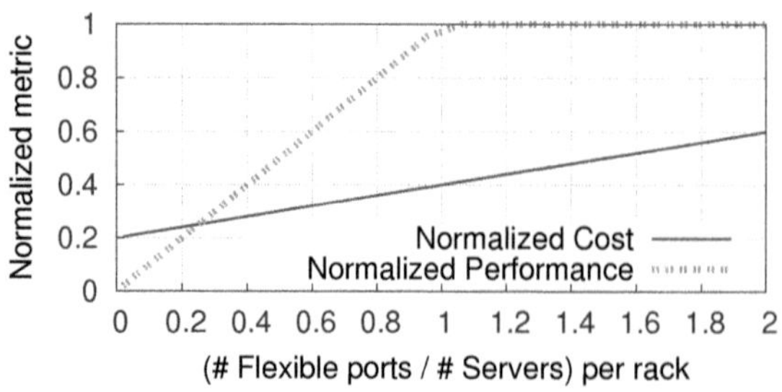


**Figure 2: A fully-flexible network can offer optimal (full-bisection) performance at a fraction of the cost. Here, the *normalized* performance and costs are that of the flexible architecture w.r.t. a full-bisection bandwidth network.**

ToR switches, each of which has $f$ flexible ports that can be rewired, whenever needed, to connect to another ToR switch. (The flexible ports are in addition to the ports connected to the servers.)

The performance metric of interest here is the *evacuation time* of satisfying the demands in a given inter-rack traffic matrix. Computing evacuation time for FBB is straightforward as there is no congestion. For Flexible($f$) too, we can compute evacuation time by computing a near-optimal sequence of reconfigurations (see [27] for details). Note that, for a given traffic matrix, Flexible($f$) can reconfigure the topology multiple times; we restrict the number of reconfigurations to be at most the number of non-zero entries in the given traffic matrix.

In Figure 2, we plot the normalized performance and cost of Flexible($f$) w.r.t. FBB, for varying *ratio* of number of flexible ports and number of servers on each rack. Here, we model the cost as simply a (constant) multiple of the total number of ports in the architecture. The normalized performance is the average ratio of evacuation times of the two architectures, over many random traffic matrices. The key takeaway is that the coreless fully-flexible Flexible($f$) architecture yields near-optimal performance when the number of flexible ports ($f$) is equal to the number of servers per rack, and at this point, its cost is only 40% of FBB (assuming FBB to be a *complete* FatTree [13]). We note that this result is independent of the number of racks or the number of servers per rack.[3]

Of course, any actual realization of Flexible($f$) will be less optimal because of limited flexibility, non-zero reconfiguration latency, and other system inefficiencies. We show that our instantiation of Flexible($f$) via FireFly results in only a minimal degradation in this cost-performance tradeoff.

## 2.2 Case for Wireless via Free-Space Optics

To realize a Flexible($f$)-like network, conceptually we need a "patch-panel" between racks. Of course, this is infeasible on several fronts: (1) it requires very high fanout and backplane capacity (potentially nullifying the cost benefits), (2) the cabling complexity would be high [37], and (3) it introduces a single-point of failure [14, 20]. Thus, we look toward *reconfigurable wireless* links between the ToR switches.

The seemingly natural solution is RF-based wireless (e.g., 60GHz) [26, 52]. However, since we seek to remove the wired core entirely rather than just augment it, we need a large number of high-bandwidth links to be active simultaneously. This makes the interference management problem much more challenging than prior work (e.g., using interference alignment and cancellation [22]). Alternatively, one could *eliminate* interference by enabling laser-like

[3] We can show that the normalized performance of Flexible($f$) w.r.t. FBB is $\approx \min(f/l, 1)$ where $l$ is the number of servers per rack [27].

directionality in RF links, but this would require antennas or antenna arrays that are a few meters wide [39].[4] Fundamentally, the hardness here is due to the large wavelengths of RF for commonly used RF bands. Finally, regulations over RF bandwidth and transmit power further limit achievable data rates.

These limitations can be circumvented if we use a different part of the EM spectrum with much smaller wavelengths. In particular, free-space optics (FSO) is a relatively established technology[5] that uses modulated visible or infrared (IR) laser beams transmitted through free space [31]. Laser beams can be very narrow, thus automatically eliminating interference and minimizing path loss. Further, optical spectrum is unregulated and has no bandwidth limitations. Thus, FSO links can easily offer Gbps–Tbps bitrates at long distances (several kms) using relatively low transmit power [15,31].

## 2.3 FireFly System Overview

Building on the previous insights, FireFly uses a fully-flexible inter-rack fabric enabled by wireless FSO links (Figure 1). FireFly uses traditional wires for intra-rack connections. We assume an out-of-band control network to configure the ToR switches and the FSO devices (e.g., [8]).

**FSO Links.** Each ToR is equipped with a number of *steerable* FSO devices. We assume that the FSO devices export APIs to the controller for reconfiguration. We exploit the space above the racks to establish an obstruction-free optical path. To ensure that the FSO devices do not obstruct each other, we use ceiling mirrors [52] as shown in Figure 1. The requirements of such mirrors are quite minimal so long as they reflect IR and many conventional mirrors work sufficiently well (§3). The ceiling mirror need not be a single piece, and small unevenness in the mirrors is unlikely to be an issue due to the misalignment tolerance of the FSO links (§3.1).

**Network Provisioning.** In the limit, we would like to have a very large number of FSO devices per ToR. In practice, however, there are physical and geometric constraints. For instance, FSO devices will have a finite size that constrains the number of such devices per ToR. Thus, we need to provision or *preconfigure* the network so that it is robust to future (and unforeseen) traffic patterns.

**Network Management.** The FireFly controller dynamically selects the *runtime topology* and configures forwarding paths, based on prevailing traffic demands and events. Following prior work, we leverage software-defined networking (SDN) capabilities for data plane reconfiguration [12, 17, 38]. Each SDN-capable ToR switch also reports observed traffic demands to the controller. FireFly can use other demand estimation algorithms; e.g., host buffer sizes [12] or new switch features [17]. Since our focus is on FireFly-specific aspects, we do not discuss these extensions.

In the following sections, we describe the design of a viable steerable FSO link, network preconfiguration, and run-time network management.

# 3 Practical Steerable FSO Design

In order for the FireFly vision to deployed in a DC, the FSO devices must ideally have a small form factor (e.g., so we can pack several devices on each ToR), be low-cost commodity devices (e.g., as we envision thousands of these in a DC), with low power footprint relative to switches, and be steerable to enable flexibility.

At first glance, these requirements are at odds with the trajectory of today's commercial FSO devices—they are bulky, expensive, and power-intensive [5]. The main challenge is that achieving robust links at high data-rates and long ranges (a requirement in both traditional deployments and FireFly) is hard. It has typically required powerful lasers and expensive mechanisms for dynamic alignment for outdoor use. Furthermore, conventional FSO deployments provide fixed point-to-point links and do not focus on steerability.

In this section, we demonstrate (perhaps surprisingly) that (a) it is viable to repurpose commodity DC-centric optical networking gear to establish robust and sufficiently long FSO links in a DC, and (b) we can leverage existing commodity optical technologies to steer the FSO beam with high precision and low latency.

## 3.1 FSO Link Engineering

As a first step, we demonstrate that it is possible to engineer an FSO optical link using commodity DC-grade optical networking equipment that can achieve high data rates, at ranges sufficient for DC-scale deployment, and with sufficient (mis)alignment tolerance. In particular, we can avoid the additional overheads in commercial FSO devices as concerns about outdoor environmental factors largely disappear in the indoor controlled DC setting. However, we do need to carefully design the *optical path* to balance the tradeoff between the laser beam divergence and misalignment tolerance, as we discuss below.

We engineer the FSO system by coupling two optical fiber end points directly with a free-space link without any opto-electric conversion thus saving on both power and cost. This Fiber–FSO–Fiber link connects to standard optical interconnect technology widely used in DCs (e.g., 10GBASE-SR). A typical example of this interface is optical SFP (small form-factor pluggable) or its variants such as SFP+.

This approach requires optical designs on both ends: (i) on the transmit side, where the fiber 'launches' the laser beam in free space, and (ii) on the receive side, where the laser beam is received into the fiber (Figure 3(a)). Normally, when the laser beam comes out of the fiber into free space it diverges with a significantly large angle. To minimize divergence, we collimate the beam using a suitably designed lens located at its focal length from the transmitting fiber endpoint.[6] A similar lens near the receiving fiber end point focuses the beam back to the fiber.

The above optical design is done carefully to ensure that the laser beam maintains a sufficient width [46] so that it can tolerate minor misalignments due to rack vibrations and other effects. However, this presents a tradeoff: wider beams can tolerate misalignments better, but suffer from a poorer power density at the receiving end. The design we develop shows that a good balance is indeed possible using optical SFPs used for long range fiber communications (e.g., 10GBASE-LR can go up to 10 km). They use highly sensitive detectors that can work with very little received power. Our current prototype has been tested for 20m. (20m is a limitation of our lab set up; the general design can extend to 100 m [27].)

This approach satisfies all the design requirements except steering. The lens is small (about 3 cm diameter) with focal length about the same. Even considering additional hardware (e.g., mounts or adapters), the footprint of the assembly is only 5 cm across. The costs are also modest when procured in volume: ≈ \$50 for the lens and \$50 for the assembly. We acknowledge that there might be an additional cost of using optical SFP (≈\$100), if optical wired links are not already used. Finally, there is no additional power burden

[4]In effect, we need RF beams with angular divergence ≈ 1 milliradian to create a small interference footprint at 50-100m range.

[5]TeraHertz wireless technology may be a good alternative, but it is much less mature at this time.

[6]For brevity, we skip the details of the optical design. We only state the basic approach and relevant tradeoffs. We refer readers to a similar approach that has been used in a different context [51].

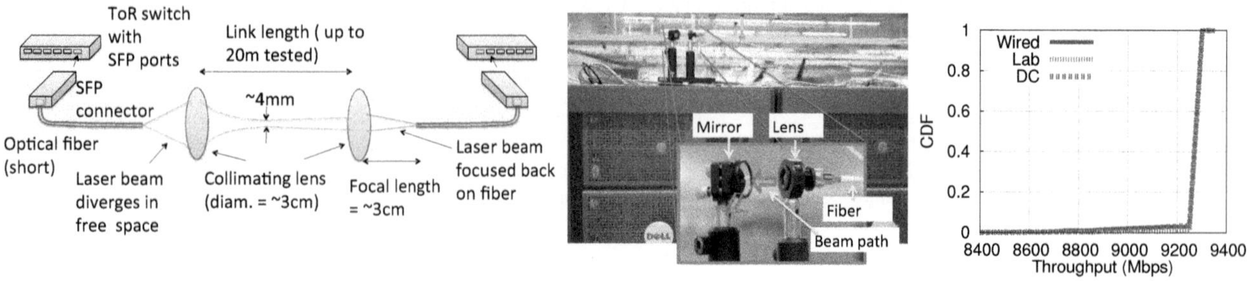


(a) FSO link design (b) DC set up (c) TCP throughput

**Figure 3: FSO link design, prototype and performance. (a) Optical path and networking gear (not drawn to scale). (b) One end point of the 10 Gbps link prototype running in a DC over $\approx$ 20m); the inset shows a zoomed in version. The FSO link connects to a similar set up on the other end. (c) Distribution of per-sec TCP throughputs on a 10 Gbps FSO link over $\approx$ 20m on optical bench (Lab) and DC racks (DC), over days of continuous runs. Throughput distribution on wired optical fiber is used for comparison.**

beyond the SFP power consumption as the design does not add any new opto-electronic conversion.

**Prototype.** We have developed a proof-of-concept prototype following the above design. We have successfully used both 1 Gbps and 10 Gbps links with very similar optical setups. The prototype links use 1000BASE-LX (1GBASE-LR) SFP (SFP+) for the 1 Gbps (10 Gbps) case and multi-mode fibers for their larger diameter. We first use standard optical bench set up to validate the design using controlled experiments and then test the link in a production DC. Figure 3(a) shows the general setup.[7] For the current design the collimated laser beam maintains a $\approx$4 mm diameter after it converges. To get up to a 20 m length on a small optical bench, we use a standard technique used in optics: the beam path is reflected multiple times via mirrors. This also validates use of mirrors on the optical path and shows that optical loss due to reflections is low.

**Link Performance.** We test the link by running continuous TCP transfers over the FSO link for several days at a time for several selected link lengths with the set up on the optical bench. The results are very similar for different lengths. For brevity we only report the results for the longest tested case ($\approx$20m) for the 10 Gbps link. See Figure 3(c). Note that the distribution of TCP throughputs is almost identical to that observed over regular fiber links, demonstrating no additional loss in the FSO links. To study misalignment tolerance, we shift the transmit side set up in tiny incremental steps (using a translating mount) perpendicular to the beam axis keeping the receive side fixed. We see no throughput loss until 6 mm shift, beyond which the link becomes unstable. As we will see below, this 6 mm tolerance is sufficient to handle minor misalignments due to rack vibrations and environmental issues in a DC.

To understand the link performance "in the wild," we set up the link in a production (university run) DC environment. Unlike the optical bench, this real environment has several key differences that can produce mis-alignments: (1) racks experience vibrations due to several factors (e.g., server fans, discs, HVAC and UPS units [47]) and (2) the beam could 'wander' due to fluctuating air density caused by temperature variations. We set up the FSO link with the optical components placed on top of the rack using magnetic bases. Two racks are used at $\approx$20 m apart. See Figure 3(b). We use mirrors on the beam path - one on each end - for ease of alignment. The reader can view these mirrors as proxies for mirrors to be used in steering (next subsection). Alignment is done manually with the help of an infra-red viewer (more on this in §9). The TCP transfer experiment is run continuously over several days as before. The statistics of per-sec TCP throughput is almost identical again to the optical bench and wired cases (Figure 3(c)). This establishes the potential of our design. The average TCP throughput is $\approx$ 9.3 Gbps — note that no commodity RF technology exists in small-form factor that can deliver such throughput at 20 m range.

The above design provides a basis for a low-cost, commoditizable, and small-form factor FSO link at high data rates over ranges sufficient for DC scale. Our experiments suggest that the link is likely robust to realistic (mis)alignment concerns due to environmental effects in DCs.

## 3.2 Developing Steering Mechanisms

Having established the viability of a point-to-point FSO link using commodity optics, next we focus on making the beam steerable to enable flexibility. Our goal is to establish a design roadmap that is *commoditizable*. We explore two promising solutions: switchable mirrors and Galvo mirrors. We do not claim these are optimal in any sense or that these are the only alternatives. Our choice is pragmatic in that we want to establish a feasible roadmap using off-the-shelf components. (There are a variety of other beam steering approaches [35], but they are not off-the-shelf technologies.) Both solutions offer different tradeoffs w.r.t. latency, degree of flexibility, and cost/power, and at this time, no one solution is strictly better. Thus, we believe it is instructive to understand and evaluate the promise of both alternatives and the tradeoffs they offer.

**Switchable Mirrors (SMs).** Switchable mirrors (SM) are made from a special liquid crystal material that can be electrically controlled to rapidly switch between reflection (mirror) and transparent (glass) states at millisecond timescales [4]. While the intended use cases are different (e.g., rear-view mirrors that switch between a regular mirror and a back-up camera display), we can use them for beam steering as shown Figure 4(a).

Each FSO device has multiple SMs, with each SM aligned (during a pre-configuration step as discussed in §4) to target a point on a ceiling mirror and thus, a receiving FSO. The link is established by switching one of the SMs to the mirror state, while leaving the rest in the transparent state. (This is done at both ends, but we only show transmit side for clarity.)

SMs directly satisfy our design requirements. It can be miniaturized as it only needs to be slightly larger than the beam diameter: 1 $cm^2$ is sufficient. A SM of this size is expected to have low cost (< \$5) at volume [33]. Power consumption is also low: only 40 mW for the stated size [4]. We have evaluated the reconfigu-

[7]Note that typical optical SFPs require two fibers and thus two optical paths for duplex communication. However, single fiber SFPs [9] that use WDM principles to multiplex both links on a single fiber are beginning to be available. For 1 Gbps experiments we use such SFPs. Due to unavailability of such devices for 10 Gbps, we use fiber for the return path for the 10 Gbps experiments; all reported performance measurements are from the FSO path.

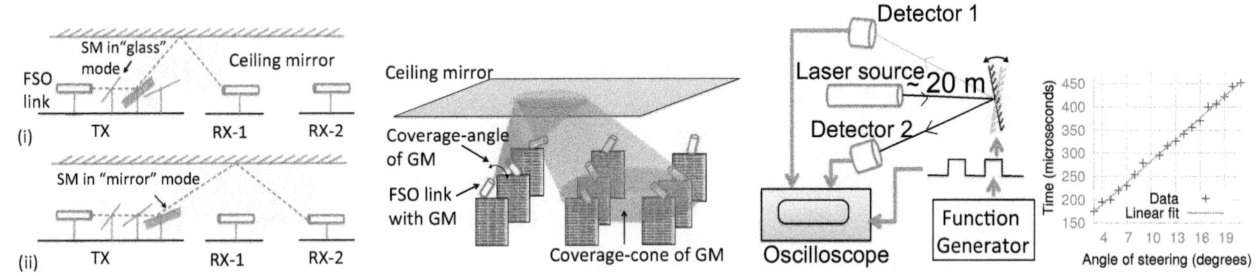


Experimental set up Response time

(a) Switchable mirror operation (b) Galvo mirror operation (c) Galvo mirror response

**Figure 4: (a) Using switchable mirrors (SMs) with FSOs: (i) 2nd SM is in mirror mode to steer the beam to RX-1; (ii) 3rd SM is in mirror mode, steering the beam to RX-2. RX-s also have aligned SMs to direct the beam to its detector (not shown for clarity). (b) Galvo mirror (GM) on an FSO device can steer the beam within its coverage-cone. (c) Evaluating Galvo mirror response.**

ration latency using an off-the-shelf 12" x 15" SM [4], and it is ≈250 msec. The switching latency decreases with the decrease in the surface area, and is estimated [33] to be ≈10-20 msec latency for the 1 $cm^2$ SM size we envision.

**Galvo Mirrors (GMs).** Galvo mirrors (GMs) [2] are typically used in laser scanning applications. Here, a small mirror, few mm across, rotates (up to specific angular limits) around an axis on the plane of the mirror in response to an electrical signal. The laser beam is made to reflect from this mirror. The mirror rotation deflects the reflected beam by a specified angle depending on the signal. Using a pair of such mirrors at right angles, we can steer the beam within a desired rectangular cone. In our context, equipping an FSO device with a GM enables us to target any receiver within a pre-configured rectangular cone chosen offline. See Figure 4(b).

As proof of concept, we evaluate the response parameters of GMs using an off-the-shelf GM [10] using the setup shown in Figure 4(b). The mirror rotation is controlled programmatically changing the applied voltage. Here, two detectors receive the reflected beam from the mirror alternately as the mirror is fed by a square wave (100 Hz) from a function generator. We measure the time between the instant the voltage trigger is initiated (via the square wave generator) and the time the mirror settles to its new position. Figure 4(c) shows that the steering latency is linear w.r.t. the steering angle and $\leq$ 0.5 ms even for angles up to about $\pm 20°$. We measured the pointing error to be $\leq 10\,\mu$rad, which translates into ≈1 mm positioning error at 100 m, which is well within the 6 mm tolerance of the FSO link.

The GM is inexpensive (≈$100) and small (few inches across). But, off-the-shelf GMs have a somewhat higher average power consumption (7 W measured) due to the use of an electro-mechanical system. That said, MEMS-based scanning mirrors that provide the same functionality as GMs are already being commoditized [6] and can reduce the power to a few milliWatts.

## 3.3 Design Summary

In summary, the device roadmap we outlined will have: (1) a rough form factor of 3"x6"; (2) a range of ≈100m and a misalignment tolerance of 6mm; (3) a power footprint of 3W (most of this is in SFP, assuming MEMS-based GMs); and (4) an estimated per-port cost of $300 ($100 for the SFP and $200 for the FSO+steering when produced in volume). The two steering mechanisms impose different constraints and tradeoffs for the FireFly network design (discussed in §4). In particular, having $k$ SMs at an FSO can switch the FSO beam between a set of $k$ arbitrarily chosen but pre-aligned receivers, while a GM on an FSO can steer the beam to any receiver within the coverage-cone that the GM has been pre-oriented to target.

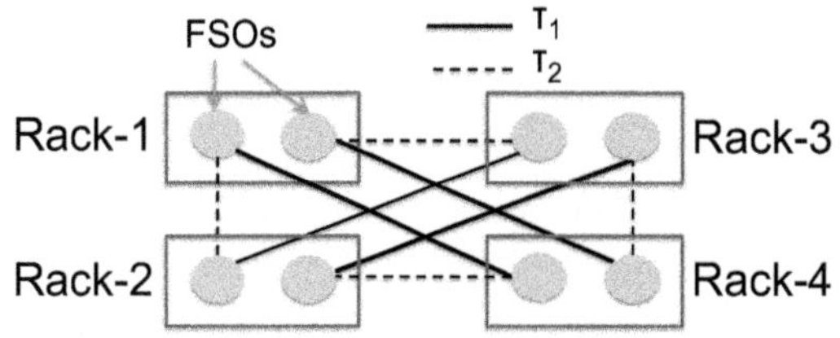


**Figure 5: A PCFT with candidate links (solid and dashed). The set of solid links represents one possible realizable topology ($\tau_1$), and the set of dashed lines represents another ($\tau_2$).**

# 4 Network Preconfiguration

At a high level, there are two network design problems in FireFly that occur at different timescales:

- First, we need to provision the network hardware (e.g., how many FSOs) and also pre-align/pre-orient the SMs/GM at each FSO. This is done offline in a *pre-configuration* phase.
- Second, given a pre-configured network, we need to *reconfigure* the network in near real-time to implement a *runtime* topology suited for the current traffic.

We address the first problem of preconfiguration in this section, and defer the second problem to the next section. Ideally, we want to create a dense preconfigured network by placing a large number of FSO devices on each rack, with each FSO device equipped with several SMs or high-coverage GMs. In practice, we have physical limitations, e.g., the size/cost of the FSO devices, size of SM, angle of GMs etc. Our goal is to design a high performance DC network working within these size and cost constraints.

## 4.1 Preliminaries and Objective

Consider a FireFly network, i.e., a set of FSOs on each rack with pre-aligned SMs or pre-oriented GMs. We can establish a *candidate (bi-directional) link* between a pair of FSOs $a$ and $b$ if (i) $a$ has an SM aligned towards $b$ and vice-versa or (ii) $a$ is located in the coverage-cone of the GM at $b$ and vice-versa. At any instant, only one candidate link per FSO can be an *active link*. For example, in Figure 4(a), links (TX, RX-1) and (TX, RX-2) are candidate links, and link (TX, RX-1) is active in Figure 4(a)(i) while (TX, RX-2) is active in Figure 4(a)(ii). We refer to the set of all candidate links as the *pre-configured flexible topology (PCFT)*. Given a PCFT, we refer to a set of candidate links that can be active simultaneously as a *realizable topology*. Note that the only constraint on a set of links to be active simultaneously is that each FSO has at most one active candidate link incident on it, due to lack of wireless interference. Thus, any realizable topology is a matching in the PCFT graph over FSOs (Figure 5) and vice-versa.

**Metric of Goodness.** If we knew the expected set of traffic demands, then we can design a customized PCFT that is optimal for this set. However, DC workloads are variable and unpredictable [23]. Thus, we want a metric to quantify the performance of a PCFT that is analogous to the traditional notion of high bisection bandwidth that captures the throughput of a network for arbitrary traffic patterns [32]. More formally, given a topology $t$ and considering all possible partitions $P$ of $t$ into two equi-sized sets of racks, the *bisection bandwidth* is defined as $\min_{p \in P} \text{BW}(t,p)$, where $BW(t,p)$ is the cut-size in $t$ corresponding to $p$. However, bisection bandwidth only applies to a *static* topology, and is not meaningful for a flexible network. With flexible designs such as FireFly, the topology $t$ itself can be changed on demand, which the bisection bandwidth metric fails to capture.

We introduce a new notion of *dynamic bisection bandwidth (DBW)* as the metric of goodness to evaluate a PCFT. The dynamic bisection bandwidth of a PCFT $\Pi$ is defined as follows. Let $T$ be the set of realizable topologies of a given PCFT $\Pi$. Then, the *dynamic bisection bandwidth* (DBW) for a PCFT $\Pi$ is defined as: $\min_{p \in P} \max_{t \in T} \text{BW}(t,p)$. Note that this reflects the ability to choose the best realizable topology $t$ for each given partition $p$.

To illustrate this, consider the PCFT in Figure 5 again. If we consider $\tau_1$ (solid lines) as a static topology, its bisection bandwidth is zero due to the partition $\{(2,3), (1,4)\}$ of racks. Similarly, we can see that the bisection bandwidth of $\tau_2$ (dashed lines) is 2. However, the DBW of the overall PCFT is 4, since $\tau_1$ yields a bandwidth of 4 for all equi-partitions except for $\{(2,3), (1,4)\}$, for which $\tau_2$ yields a bandwidth of 4.

**Constrained Optimization.** Our goal is to design a PCFT that operates within the given cost and physical constraints and optimizes the DBW. For clarity, we focus on the SM and GM problems independently and defer hybrid SM-GM combinations for future work. In each case, we solve the overall budgeted PCFT selection problem in two steps. First, we develop techniques to design a PCFT with maximum DBW for a fixed configuration (i.e., fixing #FSOs, coverage angle, and #SMs per FSO). Then, given the price/size constraints, we exhaustively search the space of *feasible* combinations of these network parameters and pick a feasible PCFT with the highest DBW. Since preconfiguration runs offline, this brute force step is reasonable.

## 4.2 SM-PCFT Design Problem

**Problem Formulation.** Given the number of racks $n$, number of FSOs $m$ per rack, and the number of SMs $k$ per FSO, the SM-PCFT problem is determine the *alignments* of each SM such that the resulting PCFT has maximum dynamic bisection bandwidth.

Said differently, we want a PCFT with maximum DBW, under the constraint that the number of candidate links at each FSO is at most $k$. From this view, the SM-PCFT problem falls in the class of network design problems [25], but is different from prior work due to the novel DBW objective. For instance, even the special case of $k = 1$, the SM-PCFT problem reduces to constructing an $m$-regular graph over $n$ nodes with maximum (static) bisection bandwidth. Even this simple case is harder than the well-studied problem of determining an upper-bound on the bisection bandwidth of $m$-regular graphs of size $n$, for which approximate results are known only for very small values of $m$ and $n$ [36]

**Random Graphs for SM-PCFT.** One promising approach to constructing a SM-PCFT solution is to consider random regular graphs. This is based on the intuition that graphs with (static) bisection bandwidth are likely to have high DBW. (Because random graphs have near-optimal spectral gap [21], they are good "expanders" and have high static bisection bandwidth.) We can construct an $n$-node regular graph of degree $mk$, and then group the $mk$ edges on each node into $m$ sets of $k$ edges each (corresponding to each of the $m$ FSOs). For every edge connecting a pair of FSOs $(a, b)$, we align one SM each of $a$ and $b$ towards each other. Because of the randomness, there is a small chance of some random instance performing poorly; thus, we generate many different solutions, and pick the one with the best DBW.[8]

## 4.3 GM-PCFT Design Problem

**Problem Formulation.** Given the DC layout, the number of racks $n$, number of FSOs per rack $m$, and uniform coverage-angle (see Figure 4(b)) of GMs, the GM-PCFT problem is to determine the *orientation* of the GM on each FSO such that the resulting PCFT has the maximum dynamic bisection bandwidth.

Note that we cannot directly use a random graph as a GM-PCFT solution, since an FSO $a$'s neighbors in a PCFT must be colocated in a coverage-cone of the GM at $a$. Thus, this problem imposes certain geometric constraints. In particular, for a pair $(a, b)$ to form a (bi-directional) candidate link in the resulting PCFT, the coverage-cone of GM at $a$ must cover $b$ and vice-versa. A naive approach is to iteratively pick a pair of FSOs $(a, b)$ at a time and orient their GMs towards each other. However, this approach may create only one candidate link per FSO/GM, and hence, could result in a sparse PCFT with poor DBW.

**Block-based Heuristic.** To address the shortcomings of the above strawman approach, we use a "block"-based approach. The intuition here is to create a random graph at a coarser *block* granularity, where each block is a group of nearby FSOs that fall within a GM's coverage cone.

The approach runs in $m$ iterations, and in each iteration we fix the orientation of the GM on the $i^{th}$ FSO of each rack, as described below. (The numbering of FSOs is arbitrary; we just need some ordering.) In each iteration, we randomly partition the set of racks into disjoint *blocks*. The only requirement here is that each block of racks is colocated and small enough to be covered by a GM (when oriented appropriately) on any FSO in the DC. That is, for each block $B$ and FSO $a \notin B$, there exists an orientation of GM at $a$ such that all racks in $B$ fall within its coverage cone. At first glance, this partitioning requirement may seem complex, but we observe that a simple grid-based partitioning scheme is sufficient in practice. Next, we create a random block-level matching $M_i$ over the blocks. Now, for each edge $(B_1, B_2) \in M_i$, we orient the GM on each $i$-FSO in each rack within block $B_1$ (correspondingly $B_2$) towards $B_2$ ($B_1$). By construction, the partitioning algorithm guarantees that a GM on any $i$-FSO in $B_1$ can cover (with some orientation) all $i$-FSOs on racks in $B_2$.

The partitioning in each iteration $i$ can be different. In particular, we can create random partitioning schemes: starting from the basic grid, we can do a random offset to create a new partitioning scheme. Finally, as in the case of SM-PCFT, we generate many randomized GM-PCFT solutions, and pick the best.

# 5 Real-time Reconfiguration

We consider two types of reconfigurations in FireFly: (1) *periodically* optimizing the network based on estimated demands; and (2) *triggered* by certain network events (e.g., planned migrations or elephant flows).

[8]One subtle issue is even computing DBW is hard. To estimate the DBW for a given random instance, we extend the Kernighan-Lin [32] heuristic for estimating the bisection bandwidth. Our experiments suggest this is within 5-7% of the true DBW. Due to space constraints, we do not discuss the DBW estimation in depth.

$$\max \sum_{i,j} T_{i,j}, \ subject\ to: \quad (1)$$

$$\forall b: \sum_{a\ s.t\ (a,b)\in\kappa} l_{a,b} \leq 1; \ \forall a: \sum_{b\ s.t.\ (a,b)\in\kappa} l_{a,b} \leq 1 \quad (2)$$

$$\forall a,b: \sum_{i,j} f_{a,b}^{i,j} \leq l_{ab} \times C \times E \quad (3)$$

$$\forall i,j,k: \sum_{a} \sum_{b\in FSOs(k)} f_{a,b}^{i,j} = \sum_{b\in FSOs(k)} \sum_{d} f_{b,d}^{i,j} \quad (4)$$

$$\forall i,j: \sum_{a\in FSOs(i)} \sum_{b} f_{a,b}^{i,j} = \sum_{a} \sum_{b\in FSOs(j)} f_{a,b}^{i,j} = T_{i,j} \quad (5)$$

$$\forall i,j: T_{i,j} \leq D_{i,j} \quad (6)$$

$$\forall (a,b)\in\kappa: l_{a,b}\in\{0,1\}; \ \forall i,j,a,b: f_{a,b}^{i,j} \geq 0 \quad (7)$$

**Figure 6: ILP formulation for periodic reconfiguration.**

## 5.1 Periodic Reconfiguration

Given a PCFT and the prevailing traffic load, the *periodic reconfiguration problem* is to optimally select a runtime (i.e., some realizable) topology and set up routes for the current traffic flows.

This constrained optimization is captured by the integer linear program (ILP) shown in Figure 6.[9] Let $\kappa$ be the set of candidate links in the PCFT, $C$ be the (uniform) link capacity, $E$ be the given epoch size (say a few seconds), and $D_{i,j}$ be the estimated traffic demand (volume) between a pair of racks $(i, j)$. This demand can be obtained by using the measurement counters from the SDN switches from previous epoch(s). We use the subscripts $a$, $b$, $c$, $d$ to refer to FSOs, and $i, j, k$ to refer to racks, and $FSOs(k)$ to denote the set of FSOs on the top of rack $k$.

There are two key sets of control variables: (i) The binary variable $l_{a,b}$ models *topology selection* and is 1 iff a candidate link $(a, b)$ is chosen to be active; and (ii) $f_{a,b}^{i,j}$ captures the *traffic engineering* (TE) strategy in terms of the volume of inter-rack traffic between $i$ and $j$ routed over the link $(a, b)$. Let $T_{i,j}$ be the total traffic volume satisfied for the flow $(i, j)$.

For clarity, we consider a simple objective function that maximizes the total demand satisfied across all rack pairs as shown in Eq (1). Eq (2) ensures that each FSO can have at most 1 active link. Eq (3) ensures that the total flow on each link (on average) does not exceed the capacity. Eq (4) are flow conservation constraints for each flow $(i, j)$ and a rack $k$. Eq (5) captures the volume of the demand satisfied using a constraint over the ingress and egress racks. Eq (6) ensures that the volume satisfied for each rack pair is at most the demand. Finally, we have bounds on the control variables.

Unfortunately, even state-of-art solvers like `Gurobi` or `CPLEX` take several hours to solve this ILP (§8.4). Hence, we follow a heuristic strategy and decouple the optimization into two stages. First, we solve the "integer" problem to select the active links. Then, given this runtime topology, we compute the flow routes.

**Greedy Matching for Topology Selection.** Recall from §4 that a realizable topology is essentially a matching over FSOs in the PCFT graph. Thus, a simple starting point is to select the maximum-weighted matching, where each candidate link $(a, b)$ is weighted by the inter-rack traffic demand $D_{i,j}$ between the racks $i$ and $j$. In effect, this maximizes the total demand that can be served using direct links. However, this can be very inefficient if the given PCFT does not have direct links between racks with high traffic demands.

[9]This problem is harder than the optimization problem considered in §2.1, since we were assuming arbitrary flexibility.

The high-level idea behind our heuristic is to extend the traditional Blossom algorithm for computing the maximum matching to incorporate multi-hop traffic. Recall that the Blossom algorithm improves the matching by computing an alternating path at each stage. We define a new utility function that captures multi-hop traffic and then pick the path with the highest benefit. Specifically, we use the intuition that shorter inter-rack paths imply lower resource usage and higher network throughput [45]. Thus, we define the *benefit* of an alternating path $L$ as the decrease in the weighted-sum of inter-rack distances if $L$ were used to modify the current matching. Formally, given a current matching $\tau$, the benefit of an alternating path $L$ that would modify the matching from $\tau$ to $\tau'$, is the total reduction in the network footprint: $\sum_{ij} D_{i,j}(h_{i,j} - h'_{i,j})$, where $h_{i,j}$ and $h'_{i,j}$ are the inter-rack distances between racks $(i, j)$ in $\tau$ and $\tau'$ respectively (when seen as graphs over racks).

We run this extended Blossom algorithm until there is no alternating path that can improve the network footprint and then output the final topology at this stage.

**Flow Routing.** Given a specific runtime topology (i.e., values of $l_{a,b}$), the residual TE problem is theoretically solvable in polynomial time as a multi-commodity flow (MCF) problem. However, even this takes hundreds of seconds for 256/512 racks §8.4), which is not acceptable as a near real-time solution. To address this, we use a greedy algorithm to compute the values of these flow variables. Essentially, we extend the traditional augmenting-path approach for max-flow algorithms and greedily pick an augmenting path for a currently unsatisfied commodity. We run the algorithm until no more augmenting paths can be picked; i.e., the network is saturated. From this solution, we use the "path stripping" idea [42] to convert the values of the $f_{a,b}^{i,j}$ variables into end-to-end paths.

## 5.2 Triggered Reconfigurations

In addition to periodically reconfiguring the network, FireFly can also run localized reconfigurations triggered by traffic events. Such reconfigurations may be frequent but likely require minimal topology and flow-route changes. We currently support two types of triggers. First, if we detect elephant flows that have sent more than 10 MB of aggregate data [17], then we activate links to create a shorter or less-congested path for this flow. Second, if traffic between a particular pair of racks exceeds some configurable threshold, then we create a direct link between them, if this does not require deactivating recently activated or high utilization links.

# 6 Correctness During Reconfigurations

A reconfiguration in FireFly entails: (i) addition and/or deletion of (candidate) links from the given runtime topology, and (ii) corresponding changes to the network forwarding tables (NFTs). This flux raises natural concerns about correctness and performance during reconfigurations. Our goal is to ensure that: (i) network remains connected at all times, (ii) there are no black holes (e.g., all forwarding table entries refer to available/usable links), and (iii) packet latency remains bounded (and thus, delivery is guaranteed).

The main challenges in designing a correct data plane strategy stem from two factors: (i) Activation or deactivation of candidate links incur a non-zero latency (few msecs); and (ii) We may need to execute reconfigurations concurrently if the triggers occur frequently (e.g., for every elephant flow arrival). At a high level, these are related to the problem of consistent updates [34, 43]. The key difference is that we can engineer simpler requirement-specific solutions rather than use more general-purpose solutions proposed in prior work.

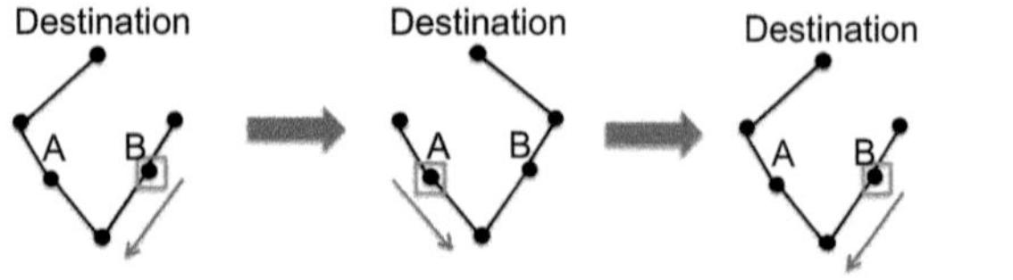


**Figure 7: Packet (in-flight location shown by a square) continues to "swing" from $B$ to $A$ and back, due to a rapid sequence of reconfigurations.**

## 6.1 Handling sequential reconfigurations

We begin by focusing on correctness when we execute reconfigurations serially and defer concurrent execution to the next subsection.

### *6.1.1 Avoiding Black Holes*

To see why "black holes" may arise, consider a reconfiguration that changes the network's runtime topology by steering FSOs $a$ and $b$ towards each other, and in the process activating the link $(a, b)$ and deactivating some link $(a, c)$. Suppose the NFTs change from $\mathcal{F}$ to $\mathcal{F}'$. Now, there is a period of time (when GM/SMs at $a$ is changing state) during which neither $(a, b)$ nor $(a, c)$ is available. During this period, irrespective of when the NFTs get updated (say, even atomically) from $\mathcal{F}$ to $\mathcal{F}'$, some entries in the NFTs may refer to either $(a, b)$ or $(a, c)$, inducing black holes in the network.

**Our Solution.** To avoid black holes, we split a reconfiguration into multiple steps such that: (i) link deletion is reflected in the NFTs *before* their deactivation is initiated, and (ii) link addition is reflected only *after* the activation is complete. Thus, a reconfiguration that involves deactivation (activation) of a set of links $\bigtriangledown$ ($\varDelta$) is translated to the following sequence of steps:

**S1**: Update the NFTs to reflect deletion of $\bigtriangledown$.
**S2**: Deactivate $\bigtriangledown$ and activate $\varDelta$.
**S3**: Update the NFTs to reflect addition of links $\varDelta$.

One additional invariant we maintain is that every switch has a default low priority rule at all times to reach every destination rack via *some* active outgoing link. We do so to explicitly ensure that packets can reach their destination, possibly on sub-optimal paths, as long as the network is connected (see below).

### *6.1.2 Maintaining Connectivity*

To ensure network connectivity at all times, we simply reject reconfigurations that might result in a disconnected network in step **S1** above. That is, we add a step S0 before the three steps above.

**S0**: Reject the reconfiguration, if deletion of links $\bigtriangledown$ disconnects the network.

To reduce the chance of such rejections, we also extend our reconfiguration algorithms to retain a connected subnetwork from the prior topology. The high-level idea here is to construct a rack-level spanning tree using the current graph, and explicitly remove these links/FSOs from consideration during the greedy matching step.

### *6.1.3 Bounded Packet Latency*

If reconfigurations occur at a very high frequency, then we may see unbounded packet latency. Figure 7 shows a simple example where a packet can never reach its destination because the links/routes are being reconfigured quite rapidly.

**Our Solution.** The example also suggests a natural strategy to avoid such cases—we can delay or reject reconfigurations to allow the in-flight packets to use one of the intermediate topologies to reach its destination. We introduce a small delay of $x$ units between two consecutive NFTs-updates, where $x$ is the maximum packet latency in a fixed realizable topology. This ensures that each packet "sees" at most two configurations during its entire flight. This, bounds the packet latency by $(2x + z)$ where $z$ is the total NFTs-update time.

## 6.2 Handling Concurrent Reconfigurations

Computing and executing a reconfiguration can take a few tens of msecs in a large DC. To achieve good performance, we may need to reconfigure the network frequently; e.g. for every elephant flow arrival in the network, which may happen every msec or less. Thus, we need mechanisms that allow reconfigurations to be executed concurrently. We could batch reconfigurations, but that merely delays the problem rather than fundamentally solving it because a batch may not finish before the next set of reconfigurations arrive.

We observe that to handle concurrent reconfigurations, we need to extend the approach from §6.1 to handle two concerns.

- *Connectivity:* One concern is that each reconfiguration in isolation may not disconnect the network but combining them might. Thus, to ensure network connectivity, the controller maintains an atomic global topology variable $\mathcal{G}$, and uses this variable to accept/reject in step S0. ($\mathcal{G}$ is also updated by accepted reconfigurations in S1 and S3.)
- *Conflicting reconfigurations:* In step S0, we also reject any reconfiguration that "conflicts" (in terms of link activations or deactivations) with already-accepted but yet-unfinished reconfigurations. That is, we follow a non pre-emptive strategy of allowing outstanding reconfigurations to complete.

We note that no other changes are required to §6.1 to handle concurrency. Black holes are still avoided since only non-conflicting reconfigurations are executed concurrently and packet latency is bounded since a minimum time-interval already precludes concurrent processing of different NFTs-updates.

## 6.3 Overall Scheme

Based on the previous building blocks, our overall scheme is as follows. Each reconfiguration $\rho$ that deletes and adds a set of links $\bigtriangledown$ and $\varDelta$, is translated into the following four steps. Here, $\mathcal{G}$ is as described in §6.2.

C0: Accept $\rho$ if (i) deletion of links $\bigtriangledown$ does not disconnect $\mathcal{G}$, and (ii) $\rho$ doesn't conflict with any unfinished reconfigurations.
C1: Update $\mathcal{G}$ and NFTs to reflect deletion of $\bigtriangledown$.
C2: Deactivate $\bigtriangledown$ and activate $\varDelta$.
C3: Update $\mathcal{G}$ and NFTs to reflect addition of links $\varDelta$.

In addition, as discussed in §6.1, we ensure (a) default path rules, and (b) a minimum time-interval (= maximum packet latency) units between consecutive NFTs-updates.

We can analytically prove that the above overall scheme ensures that (i) there are no black holes, (ii) network remains connected, and (iii) packet latency is bounded by $(2x + z)$, where $z$ is the NFTs-update time. This claim holds irrespective of how the NFTs are updated across the network; i.e., we do not require atomic updates. We refer readers to our technical report for the proof [27].

# 7 FireFly Controller Implementation

We implement the FireFly controller as modules atop the POX controller. We chose POX/OpenFlow primarily for ease of prototyping. We use custom C++ modules for the PCFT generation and reconfiguration optimization algorithms. For reconfiguration, we implement heuristics to "dampen" reconfigurations by checking if there is a significant (e.g., more than 10%) improvement in the objective function from Figure 6. We use a simple translation logic to convert the output of the optimization solver to OpenFlow rules where the "flow" variables are mapped to prefix-range based forwarding entries [49]. For elephant flows, we set up exact match flow rules [12]. We use existing OpenFlow measurement capabilities to estimate the inter-rack demands and use the observed traffic from the previous epoch as the input to the controller. Our prototype does not implement elephant flow detection [12, 17]; we currently assume this information is available out of band.

# 8 Evaluation

We established the performance of individual steerable FSO links in §3. In this section, we focus on:

1. Performance w.r.t. other DC architectures (§8.1);
2. Impact on performance during reconfigurations (§8.2);
3. Optimality of the preconfiguration algorithms (§8.3);
4. Optimality and scalability of reconfiguration (§8.4);
5. Sensitivity analysis w.r.t. degree of flexibility and reconfiguration latency (§8.5); and
6. Cost comparison w.r.t. prior DC architectures (§8.6).

For (1), we use a combination of detailed packet-level simulations using `htsim` and augment it with larger-scale flow-level simulations using a custom flow-level simulator. For (2), we use a detailed system-level emulation using MiniNet. For (3) and (4), we use offline trace-driven evaluations. For (5), we use the flow-level simulation. Finally, for (6) we use public cost estimates and projections from §3.

## 8.1 System Performance

**Setup and Workloads.** We consider three classes of architectures: (1) FireFly (both SM and GM) with 10Gbps links, (2) (wired) 10Gbps full-bisection bandwidth networks such as FatTree [13], and (3) augmented architectures such as c-Through [48] and 3D-Beamforming (3DB) [52] with a 5Gbps (i.e., 1:2 oversubscribed) core.[10] (We do not compare Flyways [26] since it is subsumed by 3D-Beamforming.) By default, FireFly has 48 FSOs per rack with each equipped with 10 SMs; we assume a rack size of $4' \times 2'$, which is sufficient to easily hold 48 FSO devices (§3.3). We also evaluated Jellyfish [45], but do not show this for ease of visualization since the result was close to FatTree ($\approx$ 10% lower). We assume an overall reconfiguration latency of 20 msecs for FireFly, and conservatively use zero latency for c-Through/3DB. We use ECMP routing for FatTree and backbone cores of 3dB and c-Through, and route the "overflow" traffic to their augmented links [52]. Finally, for FireFly, we use the routing strategies described in §5.

Following prior work, we use synthetic traffic models based on DC measurements [23,52]. As a baseline, we consider a `Uniform` model where flows between pairs of racks arrive independently with a Poisson arrival-rate $\lambda$/s, with an empirically-derived flow size distribution [23]. We use $\lambda$ as the knob to tune the level of network saturation. Based on prior observations, we also consider the `Hotspot` model [23], where in addition to the `Uniform` baseline, a subset of rack pairs have a higher arrival rate $\lambda_2$ and a fixed large flow size of 128MB [52]. For `Uniform` loads, we use the label `Uniform X` where $X$ is average load per server (in Gbps) by choosing suitable $\lambda$. For `Hotspot` loads, we use the label `Hotspot(Y,X)` where $Y$ is the % of racks that are hotspots and $X$ is the *additional* average load on each hotspot server; all `Hotspot` workloads use `Uniform 5` as the background traffic.

**Performance Comparison.** There are two key metrics here: (1) the average throughput per server, and (2) flow completion time

[10]While a lower oversubscription would improve c-Through's performance, the cost increases almost proportionally—eventually becoming equal to FatTree at 1:1 oversubscription.

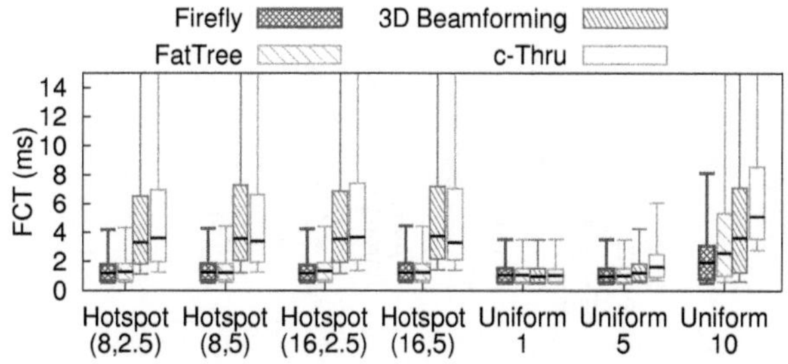


(a) Flow completion for long flows

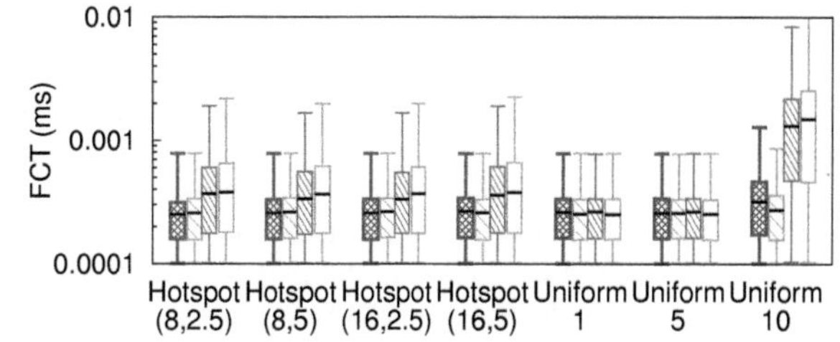


(b) Flow completion for short flows

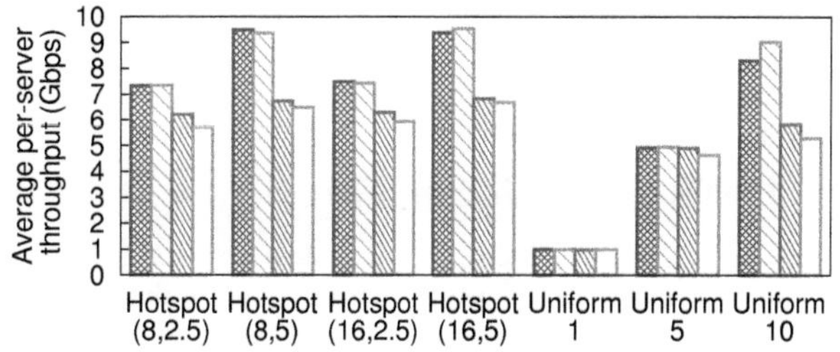


(c) Average throughput per server (Gbps)

**Figure 8: Flow completion times (FCT) and average throughput per-server using the `htsim` simulator on a 64-node topology for different workloads**

(FCT). For ease of visualization, we do not show error bars over multiple runs, since the results were consistent across multiple runs. We also do not show FireFly-GM (with 40° coverage-angle GMs) results, since they are similar to the default FireFly-SM.

As a starting point, we use `htsim` for a detailed packet-level simulation. We extended `htsim` to support short flows, arbitrary traffic matrices, and route reconfigurations. Due to scaling limitations of `htsim`, even on a high-end server (2.6GHz, 64 GB RAM), we could only scale to a 64-rack DC at our 10 Gbps workloads. Figure 8(a) and 8(b) show a box-and-whiskers plot (showing maximum, minimum, median, 25%iles, and 75%iles) of the FCT for long/short flows respectively for a 30 secs run. The result shows that FireFly's performance is close to the full-bisection bandwidth network in both cases. c-Through and 3DB do not perform as well because their augmented network is not sufficient to compensate for the oversubscription. Thus, their tail performance for long flows suffers. We also see that the FCT for short flows is similar across FireFly and FatTree.

Figure 8(c) shows the effective average per-server throughput in the 64-rack setup for different workloads. For the `Uniform` the average is over all servers whereas for `Hotspot` the average is over the hotspot servers. In short, we see that FireFly's performance is close to the full-bisection bandwidth network and roughly 1.5$\times$ better than the augmented architectures.

To scale to larger DCs, we use a custom flow-level simulator. We do so after confirming that these simulations roughly match the packet-level simulations. In general, the flow-level simula-

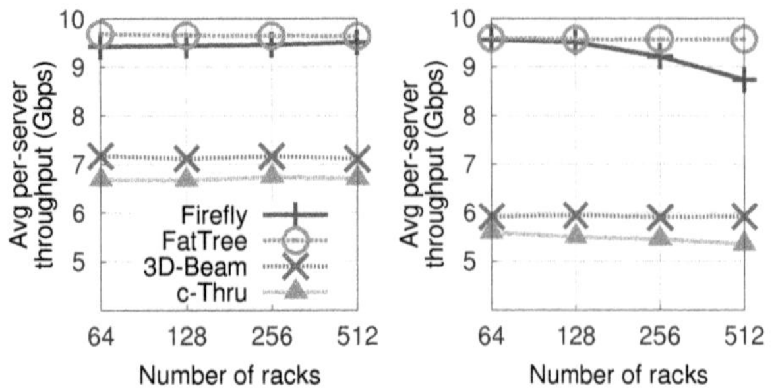


(a) Hotspot(16,5) (b) Uniform10

**Figure 9: Scalability evaluation using a flow-level simulator**

tions overestimates the throughput 5-7% *for all* architectures since it does not model packet-level effects. Since our goal is to compare the relative performance of these architectures, these simulations are still instructive. Figure 9 shows that the earlier performance results continue to hold for the most saturating workloads even at larger scales. The only drop is at 512 racks for `Uniform10`; here the number of SMs/FSO is slightly sub-optimal as the number of racks grows. We revisit this in §8.5.

We also measured the packet latency (number of hops) statistics and found that the average latency were 3.91 (FireFly), 4.81 (FatTree), and 3.9 (3dB, c-Through), while the maximum was 5 for FireFly and 6 for the rest.

## 8.2 Performance during Flux

Because packet- or flow-level simulations do not give us a detailed replay of the events at the FireFly controller and in the network, we use `Mininet` for this evaluation [7]. Due to scaling limitations, we scale down the DC size to 32 racks and the link rates to 10 Mbps, and correspondingly scale the workload down. Since our goal is to understand the *relative* impact of reconfigurations w.r.t. the steady state behavior, we believe this setup is representative. In particular, note that the relative "penalty" of the reconfiguration latency remains the same since we also scale down the workload with the link rates.

For the following result, we consider a `HotSpot` workload, with seven distinct reconfigurations as elephant flows arrive. We poll the virtual switches to obtain link utilization and loss rates and use a per-rack-pair ping script to measure inter-rack latency. We divide these measurements into two logical bins: (a) *During reconfigurations* and (b) *Steady state* (i.e., no active reconfiguration). Figure 10 shows the distribution link utilization, loss rate, and inter-rack latency for each bin. While there is a small increase in the tail values, the overall distributions are very close. This suggests that the impact on the network during reconfigurations is quite small and that our mechanisms from §6 work as expected.

## 8.3 Preconfiguration Efficiency

| #Racks | Normalized DBW w.r.t. upper bound | |
|---|---|---|
| | SM-PCFT | GM-PCFT |
| 64 | 0.96 | 0.84 |
| 128 | 0.93 | 0.84 |
| 256 | 0.91 | 0.85 |
| 512 | 0.94 | 0.88 |

**Table 1: Efficiency of the PCFT algorithms**

As before, we use 48 FSOs per rack and 10 SMs per FSO for SM-PCFT, and assume GMs with an coverage-angle of 40° for GM-PCFT. We generate $\approx 15n$ ($n$ is the number of racks) random instances and pick the best. We normalize the estimated DBW w.r.t an upper bound of $\frac{nm}{2}$.[11] Table 1 shows that the SM-PCFT and GM-PCFT solutions achieve $\geq$ 91% and $\geq$84% of the upper bound across different DC sizes. The lower performance of GM-PCFT is likely because of less randomness due to a block-level construction. (This does not however impact the performance of the runtime topology in practice for the workloads we consider.)

We also evaluate an incremental expansion scenario where we want to retain most existing PCFT as we add new racks similar to Jellyfish [45]. We find that incrementally constructed PCFTs perform nearly identical w.r.t. a PCFT computed from scratch (not shown). We posit that this stems from the incremental expandability of random graphs [45].

## 8.4 Reconfiguration Efficiency

| # Racks | Time (ms) | | | Optimality Gap |
|---|---|---|---|---|
| | Full-LP | Greedy-LP | FireFly two-step | (%) |
| 32 | 138 | 110 | 27 | 2.8% |
| 128 | 4945 | 208 | 54 | 2.6% |
| 256 | $1.7\times10^6$ | $3.3\times10^4$ | 60 | 1.3% |
| 512 | $6.4\times10^8$ | $1.9\times10^7$ | 68 | 2.8% |

**Table 2: Scalability and optimality of the FireFly reconfiguration algorithm.**

Table 2 shows the computation time and optimality gap of the FireFly two-step heuristic from §5.1. We consider two points of comparison: (a) *Full-LP*, a LP relaxation of Figure 6, which also yields an upper-bound on the optimal, and (b) *Greedy-LP* which uses greedy topology selection but solves the flow routing LP using `Gurobi`. Our approach is several orders of magnitude faster—Full-LP and Greedy-LP simply do not scale for $\geq$ 32 racks. This is crucial as the FireFly controller may need to periodically reoptimize the network every few seconds. Moreover, the (upper bound) on the optimality gap is $\leq$ 2.8%. Finally, we note that triggered reconfigurations (§5.2) incur only 5-10 msec (not shown). Most of the time is actually spent in route computation, which can be run in parallel to allow a high rate of concurrent reconfigurations.

## 8.5 Sensitivity Analysis

| | # FSOs per rack | | | |
|---|---|---|---|---|
| | 36 | 40 | 44 | 48 |
| # SMs per FSO = 10 | 5.14 | 6.07 | 7.47 | 8.83 |
| # SMs per FSO = 13 | 6.21 | 7.27 | 8.20 | 9.17 |
| # SMs per FSO = 15 | 6.45 | 7.54 | 8.31 | 9.25 |
| $GM$-based network | 6.87 | 7.84 | 8.66 | 9.24 |

**Table 3: Average throughput per-server on `Uniform10` for varying network parameters.**

Given that we are considering a new technology, we evaluate the sensitivity w.r.t. key parameters: number of FSOs, number of SMs, and the reconfiguration latency. Table 3 shows the average per-server throughput on a range of FireFly instantiations. As before, we use the configuration of 512 racks with 48 servers each. As expected from the insights from §2.1, the performance decreases almost linearly with decrease in the number of FSOs (i.e., flexible ports) per rack. The performance degradation in GM-based networks is comparatively better. Note that the networks with fewer FSOs also have almost-proportionally lower cost. However, increasing the number of SMs per FSO does counter the degradation to some extent, due to increase in flexibility. If FSO size is the limiting concern, one way to get higher performance is to simply

[11] Any equi-sized partition of $n$ racks with $m$ FSOs can have at most $nm/2$ active links (one per FSO) in a "cut".

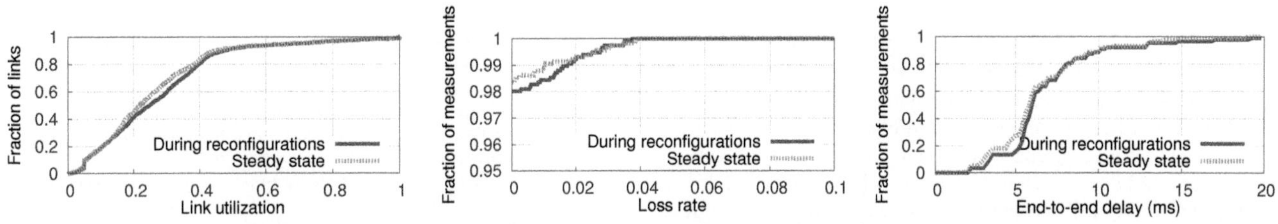


**Figure 10: Comparing network performance during reconfigurations and in steady state**

| | Equip | | Cable | | Power | | Total | |
|---|---|---|---|---|---|---|---|---|
| | Fiber | Cu | Fiber | Cu | Fiber | Cu | Fiber | Cu |
| FatTree | 22 | 15 | 8 | 2 | 1 | 2 | 31 | 20 |
| 3DB | 13 | 9 | 5 | 2 | 1 | 1 | 19 | 12 |
| cThru | 13 | 9 | 5 | 2 | 1 | 1 | 19 | 12 |
| FireFly | 12 | | 0 | | 1 | | 13 | |

**Table 4: Cost (in USD millions) of equipment, power, and cabling assuming 512 racks with 48 servers/rack. Since these are estimates, we round to the nearest million.**

decrease the number of servers per rack; i.e., increase number of racks for a fixed total number of servers (not shown).

Finally, with respect to reconfiguration latency, we observe that varying the latency from 10msec to 50 msec has minimal (< 5%) impact on FireFly's performance (not shown). This is a positive result that we can achieve pretty good performance even with unoptimized steering delays and network update times.

## 8.6 Cost Comparison

As an instructive case, we consider a DC with 512 racks and 48 servers/rack to compute the equipment, power, and cabling costs of different architectures in Table 4. We consider both copper- and fiber-based realizations for the wired architectures.

We conservatively estimate the "bulk" price of 10GbE network switches to be $100 per port [11, 50] and that of 10GbE SFPs at $50 each; these estimates are roughly 50% of their respective retail costs. Thus, fiber-based architectures (including FireFly) incur a cost of $150 per-port, while copper-based architecture incur a cost of only $100 per-port. FireFly uses a 96-port (10G) ToR switch on each rack with 48 FSOs, the full-bisection FatTree needs 1536 96-port (10G) switches, while the 1:2 oversubscribed cores of c-Through/3DB use roughly half the ports of FatTree. FireFly has an additional cost for FSO devices (on *half* the ports), which we estimate to be $200 per device including SMs or a GM (§3). For 3DB, we assume there are 8 60 GHz radios per rack with each assembly costing $100. For c-Through, we conservatively assume the 512-port optical switch to be $0.5M. We assume ceiling mirrors in FSO and 3DB have negligible cost. For cabling, we use an average cost of $1 and $3 per meter for copper and optical-fiber respectively, and use an average per-link length of 30m [40]. We estimate the 5-yr energy cost using a rate of 6.5cents/KWHr, and per-port power consumption of 3W (fiber) and 6W (copper). We ignore the negligible energy cost of SMs, 60GHz radios, and the optical switches.

Overall, the total cost of FireFly is 40-60% lower than FatTree and is comparable (or better) than the augmented architectures. Note that the augmented architectures have worse performance compared to FireFly, and copper wires have length limitations.

# 9 Discussion

Given our radical departure from conventional DC designs, we discuss a sampling of potential operational concerns and possible mechanisms to address some of these issues. We acknowledge that there might be other unforeseen concerns that require further investigation over pilot long-term deployments.

**Pre- and re-alignment.** We will need external tools for pre-aligning SMs/GMs. Fortunately, as this will be done infrequently, this mechanism does not need the stringent cost/size requirements and we can repurpose existing mechanical assemblies. While our design tolerates minor misalignment (§3), long term operation may need occasional alignment corrections. Here, we can use the feedback from the digital optical monitoring support available on optical SFPs; GMs can directly use such feedback, but SMs may need additional micro-positioning mechanisms (e.g., piezoelectrics).

**Operational Concerns.** Some recurrent concerns we have heard include dust settling on optics, light scattering effects, reliability of mechanical parts, and human factors (e.g., need for protective eyewear for operators). We believe that these are not problematic. Specifically, dust/scattering may reduce the signal but our design has sufficiently high link margins (15dB), and the devices can be easily engineered to minimize dust (e.g., non-interfering lids or blowing filtered air periodically). While we studied an electro-mechanical GM here, future MEMS-based scanning mirrors [6] are expected to be very robust. Finally, the lasers we use are infra-red and very low power which are not harmful to human eye.

**Beyond 10 Gbps.** Current long-range connector standards for 40/100 Gbps (e.g., 40 or 100GBASE-LR4) use WDM to multiplex lower rate channels on the same fiber, one in each direction. However, just like the 10 GbE standard that we have used, there are still two optical paths (with two fibers) for duplex links. Single-fiber solutions (as we have used for 1 GbE [9]) are not commodity yet at these speeds as the market is still nascent. We expect, however, this to change in future. Otherwise, we will need two optical paths or custom single-path solutions.

# 10 Related Work

**Static Wired Topologies.** Early DCs used tree-like structures, which have poor performance due to *oversubscription*. This motivated designs providing full bisection bandwidth [13, 16, 45], which are overprovisioned to handle worst-case patterns. In addition to high cost, such networks are not incrementally expandable [45]. In contrast, FireFly is flexible, eliminates cabling costs, and amenable to incremental expansion. Other efforts proposed architectures where servers act as relay nodes (e.g., [24]). However, they are not cost competitive [40] and raise concerns about isolation and CPU usage.

**Optical Architectures.** High traffic volumes coupled with the power use of copper-based Ethernet, has motivated the use of optical links. Early works such as c-Through [48] and Helios [20] suggested hybrid electric/optical switch architectures, while recent efforts consider all-optical designs [14,41]. The use of free-space optics avoids the cabling complexity that such optical designs incur. Furthermore, by using multiple FSOs per rack, FireFly can create richer topologies (at the rack level) than simple matchings [14,20,41,48]. Moreover, FireFly doesn't need optical switching, thus eliminating concerns about cost/scalability. Finally, optical switching can disconnect substantial portions of the optical network during reconfiguration. While FireFly also has transient link-off periods, these are localized—which enables us to avoid black holes and disconnections using simpler data plane strategies (§6).

**Wireless in DCs.** The FireFly vision is inspired by Flyways [26] and 3D-Beamforming [52]. However, RF wireless technology suffers from high interference and range limitations and limits performance. The use of free-space optics in FireFly eliminates interference concerns. Shin et al. consider a static all-wireless (not only inter-rack) DC architecture using 60 Ghz links [44]. However, this requires restructuring DC layout and has poor bisection bandwidth due to interference.

**Consistency during Reconfigurations.** Recent work identified the issue of consistency during network updates [34, 43]. FireFly introduces unique challenges because the topology changes as well. While these techniques can also apply to FireFly, they are more heavyweight for the specific properties (no black holes, connectivity, and bounded packet latency) than the domain-specific solutions we engineer. Other work minimizes congestion during updates [30]. While FireFly's mechanisms do not explicitly address congestion, our results (§8.2) suggest that this impact is quite small.

## 11 Conclusions

In this work, we explore the vision of a fully-flexible, all-wireless, coreless DC network architecture. We identified free-space optics as a key enabler for this vision and addressed practical hardware design, network provisioning, network management, and algorithmic challenges to demonstrate the viability of realizing this vision in practice. Our work is by no means the final word. There remains significant room for improvement in various aspects of our design, viz., cost and form-factor of hardware elements, algorithmic techniques for network provisioning and management, which should further improve the cost-performance tradeoff.

## Acknowledgments

We thank Yuvraj Agarwal, Daniel Halperin, and our shepherd Jitendra Padhye for their feedback, and Hanfei Chen for GM measurements. This research was supported in part by NSF grants CNS-1117719 and CNS-0831791.

## 12 References


[1] A Simpler Data Center Fabric Emerges . http://tinyurl.com/kaxpotw.

[2] Galvo mirrors. http://www.thorlabs.us/NewGroupPage9.cfm?ObjectGroup_ID=3770.

[3] htsim simulator. http://nrg.cs.ucl.ac.uk/mptcp/implementation.html.

[4] Kent optronics, inc. http://kentoptronics.com/switchable.html.

[5] Lightpointe flightstrata g optical gigabit link. http://tinyurl.com/k86o2vh.

[6] Mems scanning mirror. http://www.lemoptix.com/technology/mems-scanning-mirrors.

[7] Mininet. http://yuba.stanford.edu/foswiki/bin/view/OpenFlow/Mininet.

[8] OpenGear out of band management. http://tinyurl.com/n773hg3.

[9] Single-fiber sfp. http://www.championone.net/products/transceivers/sfp/single-fiber-single-wavelength/.

[10] Xinyu laser products. http://www.xinyulaser.com/index.asp.

[11] 10GBASE-T vs. GbE cost comparison. *Emulex white paper*, 2012. Available at http://www.emulex.com/artifacts/cdc1a1d3-5d2d-4ac5-9ed8-5cc4a72bd561/elx_sb_all_10gbaset_cost_comparison.pdf.

[12] M. Al-Fares et al. Hedera: Dynamic flow scheduling for data center networks. In *NSDI*, 2010.

[13] M. Al-Fares, A. Loukissas, and A. Vahdat. A scalable, commodity data center network architecture. In *ACM SIGCOMM*, 2008.

[14] K. Chen et al. OSA: An optical switching architecture for data center networks with unprecedented flexibility. In *NSDI*, 2012.

[15] E. Ciaramella et al. 1.28-Tb/s (32 × 40 Gb/s) free-space optical WDM transmission system. *IEEE Photonics Technology Letters*, 21(16), 2009.

[16] C. Clos. A study of non-blocking switching networks. *Bell System Technical Journal*, 32, 1953.

[17] A. Curtis et al. DevoFlow: Scaling flow management for high-performance networks. In *ACM SIGCOMM*, 2011.

[18] A. Curtis, S. Keshav, and A. Lopez-Ortiz. LEGUP: Using heterogeneity to reduce the cost of data center network upgrades. In *CoNEXT*, 2010.

[19] H. L. Davidson et al. Data center with free-space optical communications. US Patent 8,301,028, 2012.

[20] N. Farrington et al. Helios: A hybrid electrical/optical switch architecture for modular data centers. In *ACM SIGCOMM*, 2010.

[21] J. Friedman. On the second eigenvalue and random walks in random $d$-regular graphs. *Combinatorica*, 11(4), 1991.

[22] S. Gollakota, S. D. Perli, and D. Katabi. Interference alignment and cancellation. In *ACM SIGCOMM*, 2009.

[23] A. Greenberg et al. VL2: A scalable and flexible data center network. In *ACM SIGCOMM*, 2009.

[24] C. Guo et al. BCube: A high performance, server-centric network architecture for modular data centers. In *ACM SIGCOMM*, 2009.

[25] A. Gupta and J. Konemann. Approximation algorithms for network design: A survey. *Surveys in Operations Research and Management Science*, 16, 2011.

[26] D. Halperin et al. Augmenting data center networks with multi-gigabit wireless links. In *ACM SIGCOMM*, 2011.

[27] N. Hamedazimi et al. FireFly: A reconfigurable wireless data center fabric using free-space optics (full version). http://www.cs.stonybrook.edu/~hgupta/ps/firefly-full.pdf.

[28] N. Hamedazimi, H. Gupta, V. Sekar, and S. Das. Patch panels in the sky: A case for free-space optics in data centers. In *ACM HotNets*, 2013.

[29] B. Heller et al. ElasticTree: Saving energy in data center networks. In *NSDI*, 2010.

[30] C.-Y. Hong et al. Achieving high utilization with software-driven WAN. In *ACM SIGCOMM*, 2013.

[31] D. Kedar and S. Arnon. Urban optical wireless communication networks: The main challenges and possible solutions. *IEEE Communications Magazine*, 2004.

[32] B. Kernighan and S. Lin. An efficient heuristic procedure for partitioning graphs. *The Bell Systems Technical Journal*, 49(2), 1970.

[33] L. Li. CEO, KentOptronics. Personal communication.

[34] R. Mahajan and R. Wattenhofer. On consistent updates in software defined networks (extended version). In *ACM HotNets*, 2013.

[35] P. F. McManamon et al. A review of phased array steering for narrow-band electrooptical systems. *Proceedings of the IEEE*, 2009.

[36] B. Monien and R. Preis. Upper bounds on the bisection width of 3- and 4-regular graphs. *Journal of Discrete Algorithms*, 4, 2006.

[37] J. Mudigonda, P. Yalagandula, and J. C. Mogul. Taming the flying cable monster: A topology design and optimization framework for data-center networks. In *USENIX ATC*, 2011.

[38] N. McKeown et al. OpenFlow: enabling innovation in campus networks. *ACM SIGCOMM CCR*, 38(2), 2008.

[39] S. Orfanidis. Electromagnetic waves and antennas; Chapter 15, 19. http://www.ece.rutgers.edu/~orfanidi/ewa/.

[40] L. Popa et al. A cost comparison of datacenter network architectures. In *CoNEXT*, 2010.

[41] G. Porter et al. Integrating microsecond circuit switching into the data center. In *ACM SIGCOMM*, 2013.

[42] P. Raghavan and C. D. Thompson. Randomized rounding: a technique for provably good algorithms and algorithmic proofs. *Combinatorica*, 7(4), 1987.

[43] M. Reitblatt et al. Abstractions for network update. In *ACM SIGCOMM*, 2012.

[44] J. Shin, E. G. Sirer, H. Weatherspoon, and D. Kirovski. On the feasibility of completely wireless datacenters. In *ANCS*, 2012.

[45] A. Singla, C.-Y. Hong, L. Popa, and P. B. Godfrey. Jellyfish: Networking data centers randomly. In *NSDI*, 2012.

[46] O. Svelto. *Principles of Lasers*. Plenum Press, New York, Fourth edition, 1998.

[47] J. Turner. Effects of data center vibration on compute system performance. In *SustainIT*, 2010.

[48] G. Wang et al. c-Through: Part-time optics in data centers. In *ACM SIGCOMM*, 2010.

[49] R. Wang, D. Butnariu, and J. Rexford. Openflow-based server load balancing gone wild. In *Hot-ICE*, 2011.

[50] Y. Yang, S. Goswami, and C. Hansen. 10GBASE-T ecosystem is ready for broad adoption. *Commscope/Intel/Cisco White Paper*, 2012. Available at http://www.cisco.com/en/US/prod/collateral/switches/ps9441/ps9670/COM_WP_10GBASE_T_Ecosystem_US4.pdf.

[51] K. Yoshida, K. Tanaka, T. Tsujimura, and Y. Azuma. Assisted focus adjustment for free space optics system coupling single-mode optical fibers. *IEEE Trans. on Industrial Electronics*, 60(11), 2013.

[52] X. Zhou et al. Mirror mirror on the ceiling: Flexible wireless links for data centers. In *ACM SIGCOMM*, 2012.

# A "Hitchhiker's" Guide to Fast and Efficient Data Reconstruction in Erasure-coded Data Centers

K. V. Rashmi[1], Nihar B. Shah[1], Dikang Gu[2], Hairong Kuang[2], Dhruba Borthakur[2], and Kannan Ramchandran[1]

[1]UC Berkeley [2]Facebook

{rashmikv, nihar, kannanr}@eecs.berkeley.edu, {dikang, hairong, dhruba}@fb.com

## ABSTRACT

Erasure codes such as Reed-Solomon (RS) codes are being extensively deployed in data centers since they offer significantly higher reliability than data replication methods at much lower storage overheads. These codes however mandate much higher resources with respect to network bandwidth and disk IO during reconstruction of data that is missing or otherwise unavailable. Existing solutions to this problem either demand additional storage space or severely limit the choice of the system parameters.

In this paper, we present *Hitchhiker*, a new erasure-coded storage system that reduces both network traffic and disk IO by around 25% to 45% during reconstruction of missing or otherwise unavailable data, *with no additional storage*, the same fault tolerance, and arbitrary flexibility in the choice of parameters, as compared to RS-based systems. Hitchhiker "rides" on top of RS codes, and is based on novel encoding and decoding techniques that will be presented in this paper. We have implemented Hitchhiker in the Hadoop Distributed File System (HDFS). When evaluating various metrics on the data-warehouse cluster in production at Facebook with real-time traffic and workloads, during reconstruction, we observe a 36% reduction in the computation time and a 32% reduction in the data read time, in addition to the 35% reduction in network traffic and disk IO. Hitchhiker can thus reduce the latency of degraded reads and perform faster recovery from failed or decommissioned machines.

## 1. INTRODUCTION

Data centers storing multiple petabytes of data have become commonplace today. These data centers are typically built out of individual components that can be unreliable, and as a result, the system has to deal with frequent failures. Various additional systems-related issues such as software glitches, machine reboots and maintenance operations also contribute to machines being rendered unavailable from time to time. In order to ensure that the data remains reliable and available despite frequent machine unavailability, data is replicated across multiple machines, typically across multiple racks as well. For instance, the Google File System [10] and the Hadoop Distributed File System (HDFS) [28] store three copies of all data by default. Although disk storage seems inexpensive for small data sizes, this assumption is no longer true when storing multiple copies at the massive scales of operation of today's data centers. As a result, several large-scale distributed storage systems [4,10] now deploy erasure codes, that provide higher reliability at significantly lower storage overheads, with the most popular choice being the family of Reed-Solomon (RS) codes [23].


*SIGCOMM'14*, August 17–22, 2014, Chicago, USA

http://dx.doi.org/10.1145/2619239.2626325

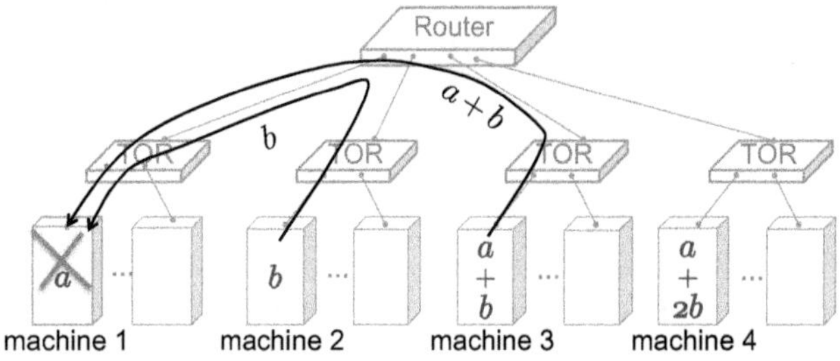


**Figure 1: High network usage during reconstruction of erasure-coded data: reconstructing a single missing unit '$a$' in this example requires transfer of twice the amount of data through the top-of-rack (TOR) switches.**

An RS code is associated with two parameters: $k$ and $r$. A $(k,\ r)$ RS code encodes $k$ units of data into $r$ *parity* units, in a manner that guarantees the recoverability of all the $k$ data units from *any* $k$ out of these $(k + r)$ units. It thus allows for tolerating unavailability of *any* $r$ of its $(k + r)$ units. This collection of $(k+r)$ units is called a *stripe*. In a system deploying an RS code, the $(k+r)$ units belonging to a stripe are stored on distinct machines in order to maximize diversity and tolerate maximum machine unavailability. In addition, these machines are chosen from distinct racks in order to maximize tolerance to rack failures. An example of such a setting is depicted in Fig. 1, with an RS code having parameters $(k = 2, r = 2)$. Here $\{a,\ b\}$ are the two data units, which are encoded to generate two parity units, $(a+b)$ and $(a+2b)$. The figure depicts these four units stored across four machines on different racks. The data-warehouse cluster at Facebook employs an RS code with parameters $(k = 10, r = 4)$, thus resulting in a $1.4\times$ storage overhead. In contrast, for similar levels of reliability, a replication-based system would require a $3\times$ storage overhead.

We posit that the primary reason that makes RS codes particularly attractive for large-scale distributed storage systems is its two following properties:

***P1: Storage optimality.*** A $(k,\ r)$ RS code entails the minimum storage overhead among all $(k,\ r)$ erasure codes that tolerate any $r$ failures.[1] This property is particularly relevant for large-scale storage systems since disk space usage is quickly becoming the dominant factor in these systems.

***P2: Generic applicability.*** RS codes can be constructed for arbitrary values of the parameters ($k$, $r$), thus allowing complete flexibility in the design of the system.

Although RS codes improve storage efficiency in data centers, they cause a *significant increase in the disk and network traffic.* This is due to the heavy download requirement during reconstruction of any missing or otherwise unavailable unit, as elaborated below. In a system that performs replication, a data unit can be reconstructed simply by copying it from another existing replica. However, in an RS-coded system, there is no such replica. To see the reconstruction operation under an RS code, let us first consider the example of a ($k = 2$, $r = 2$) RS code as in Fig. 1. The figure depicts the reconstruction of the first data unit "$a$" (machine 1) from machines 2 and 3. Observe that this reconstruction operation requires transfer of two units across the network. In general, under a ($k$, $r$) RS code, reconstruction of a single unit involves the download of $k$ of the remaining units. An amount equal to the logical size of the data in the stripe is thus read from the disks and downloaded through the network, from which the missing unit is reconstructed. *This is $k$ times the size of the data to be reconstructed.*

We have performed extensive measurements on Facebook's data-warehouse cluster in production, which consists of multiple thousands of nodes, and which stores multiple Petabytes of RS-encoded data. These measurements reveal that a median of more than 50 machine-unavailability events occur per day, and a median of 95,500 blocks of RS-encoded data are recovered each day (the typical size of a block is 256 Megabytes (MB)). The reconstruction operations for RS-encoded data consume a large amount of disk and cross-rack bandwidth: a median of more than 180 Terabytes (TB) of data is transferred through the top-of-rack switches every day for this purpose. For more details, the reader is referred to our earlier work [20].

In addition to the increased toll on network and disk resources, the significant increase in the amount of data to be read and downloaded during reconstruction affects RS-based storage systems in two ways. First, it *drastically hampers the read performance of the system in "degraded mode"*, i.e., when there is a read request for a data unit that is missing or unavailable. Serving such a request is called a 'degraded read'. In a replication based system, degraded reads can be performed very efficiently by serving it from one of the replicas of the requisite data. On the other hand, the high amount of data read and downloaded as well as the computational load for reconstructing any data block in an RS-based system *increases the latency of degraded reads.* Second, it *increases the recovery time of the system*: recovering a failed machine or decommissioning a machine takes significantly longer than in a replication-based system. Based on conversations with teams from multiple enterprises that deploy RS codes in their storage systems, we gathered that *this increased disk and network traffic and its impact on degraded reads and recovery is indeed a major concern*, and is one of the bottlenecks to erasure coding becoming more pervasive in large-scale distributed storage systems.

[1]In the parlance of coding theory, an RS code has the property of being 'Maximum Distance Separable (MDS)' [16].

Storage optimality and generic applicability:

| | |
|---|---|
| Storage requirement | Same (optimal) |
| Supported parameters | All |
| Fault tolerance | Same (optimal) |

Data reconstruction:

| | |
|---|---|
| Data downloaded (i.e., network traffic) | 35% less |
| Data read (i.e., disk traffic) | 35% less |
| Data read time (median) | 31.8% less |
| Data read time (95$^{th}$ percentile) | 30.2% less |
| Computation time (median) | 36.1% less |

Encoding:

| | |
|---|---|
| Encoding time (median) | 72.1% more |

**Table 1: Performance of *Hitchhiker* as compared to Reed-Solomon-based system for default HDFS parameters.**

The problem of decreasing the amount of data required to be downloaded for reconstruction in erasure-coded systems has received considerable attention in the recent past both in theory and practice [7,11–14,17,19,21,22,26,27,29,30,32]. However, all existing practical solutions either demand additional storage space [7, 12, 17, 21, 26, 27]), or are applicable in very limited settings [11, 15, 30, 32]. For example, [7,12,17] add at least 25% to 50% more parity units to the code, thereby increasing the storage overheads, [21,27] necessitate a high redundancy of $r \geq (k-1)$ in the system, while [11,15,30,32] operate in a limited setting allowing only two or three parity units.

In this paper, we present *Hitchhiker*, an erasure-coded storage system that fills this void. *Hitchhiker reduces both network and disk traffic during reconstruction by 25% to 45% without requiring any additional storage and maintaining the same level of fault-tolerance as RS-based systems.*[2] Furthermore, Hitchhiker can be used with any choice of the system parameters $k$ and $r$, thus retaining both the attractive properties of RS codes described earlier. Hitchhiker accomplishes this with the aid of two novel components proposed in this paper: (i) a new encoding and decoding technique that builds on top of RS codes and reduces the amount of download required during reconstruction of missing or otherwise unavailable data, (ii) a novel disk layout technique that ensures that the savings in network traffic offered by the new code is translated to savings in disk traffic as well.

In proposing the new storage code, we make use of a recently proposed theoretical framework [22] called the 'Piggybacking framework'. In this paper, we employ this theoretical framework of piggybacking to design a novel erasure code that reduces the amount of data required during reconstruction while maintaining the storage optimality and generic applicability of RS codes. Our design offers the choice of either using it with only XOR operations resulting in significantly faster computations or with finite field arithmetic for a greater reduction in the disk and network traffic during reconstruction. Interestingly, we also show that the XOR-only design can match the savings of non-XOR design if the underlying RS code satisfies a certain simple condition.

The proposed storage codes reduce the amount of download required for data reconstruction, and this directly trans-

[2]It takes a free-ride on top of the RS-based system, retaining all its desired properties, and hence the name 'Hitchhiker'.

lates to reduction in network traffic. In the paper, we then propose a novel disk layout which ensures that the savings in network resources are also translated to savings in disk resources. In fact, this technique is applicable to a number of other recently proposed storage codes [11,15,19,21,26,27,29] as well, and hence may be of independent interest. The proposed codes also help reduce the computation time during reconstruction as compared to the existing RS codes.

Hitchhiker optimizes reconstruction of a single unit in a stripe without compromising any of the two properties of RS-based systems. Single unit reconstruction in a stripe is the most common reconstruction scenario in practice, as validated by our measurements from Facebook's data-warehouse cluster which reveal that 98.08% of all recoveries involve recovering a single unit in a stripe (see §6.5). Moreover, at any point in time, Hitchhiker can alternatively perform the (non-optimized) reconstruction of single or multiple units as in RS-based systems by connecting to *any* $k$ of the remaining units. It follows that any optimization or solution proposed outside the erasure coding component of a storage system (e.g., [3, 5, 18]) can be used in conjunction with Hitchhiker by simply treating Hitchhiker as functionally equivalent to an RS code, thereby allowing for the benefits of both solutions.

We have implemented Hitchhiker in the Hadoop Distributed File System (HDFS). HDFS is one of the most popular open-source distributed file systems with widespread adoption in the industry. For example, multiple tens of Petabytes are being stored via RS encoding in HDFS at Facebook, a popular social-networking company.

We evaluated Hitchhiker on two clusters in Facebook's data centers, with the default HDFS parameters of ($k = 10, r = 4$). We first deployed Hitchhiker on a test cluster comprising 60 machines, and verified that the savings in the amount of download during reconstruction is as guaranteed by theory. We then evaluated various metrics of Hitchhiker on the data-warehouse cluster in production consisting of multiple thousands of machines, in the presence of ongoing real-time traffic and workloads. We observed that Hitchhiker reduces the time required for reading data during reconstruction by 32%, and reduces the computation time during reconstruction by 36%. Table 1 details the comparison between Hitchhiker and RS-based systems with respect to various metrics for ($k = 10, r = 4$).[3] Based on our measurements [20] of the amount of data transfer for reconstruction of RS-encoded data in the data-warehouse cluster at Facebook (discussed above), employing Hitchhiker would save close to 62TB of disk and cross-rack traffic every day while retaining the same storage overhead, reliability, and system parameters.

In summary, we make the following contributions:

- Introduce *Hitchhiker*, a new erasure-coded storage system that reduces both network and disk traffic during reconstruction of missing or otherwise unavailable data by 25% to 45% without requiring any additional storage and maintaining same level of fault-tolerance as RS-based systems. It can be used with any choice of the system parameters $k$ and $r$. To the best of our knowledge, this is the first practical solution available in literature that reduces the disk and network traffic during reconstruction without increasing the storage overhead or (severely) limiting the system design.
- Propose a new storage code built on top of RS that makes use of the theoretical framework of piggybacking to reduce the amount of data required for reconstruction.
- Propose a novel disk layout technique that ensures that the savings in network traffic are translated to savings in disk traffic as well. This technique is general and can also be used to save disk resources in other storage codes.
- Implement Hitchhiker in HDFS, and test it by deploying it on a test cluster with 60 machines in a data center at Facebook and verify the theoretical guarantees of 35% savings in network and disk traffic during reconstruction.
- Evaluate the read time and compute time metrics of Hitchhiker on *the data-warehouse cluster in production at Facebook consisting of multiple thousands of machines with ongoing real-time traffic and workloads*, showing a 32% reduction in time to read data and a 36% reduction in computation time during reconstruction. This establishes that Hitchhiker can reduce the latency of degraded reads, and also perform faster recovery from machine failures and decommissioning.

[3]More specifically, these numbers are for the 'Hitchhiker-XOR+' version of Hitchhiker.

# 2. THEORETICAL BACKGROUND

## 2.1 Reed-Solomon (RS) codes

As discussed briefly in §1, a ($k$, $r$) RS code [23] encodes $k$ data bytes into $r$ parity bytes. The code operates on each set of $k$ bytes independently and in an identical fashion. Each such set on which independent and identical operations are performed by the code is called a *stripe*. Fig. 2 depicts ten units of data encoded using a ($k = 10$, $r = 4$) RS code that generates four parity units. Here, $a_1, \ldots, a_{10}$ are one byte each, and so are $b_1, \ldots, b_{10}$. Note that the code is operating independently and identically on the two columns, and hence each of the two columns constitute a stripe of this code.

We use the notation $\boldsymbol{a} = [a_1 \cdots a_{10}]$ and $\boldsymbol{b} = [b_1 \cdots b_{10}]$. Each of the functions $f_1$, $f_2$, $f_3$ and $f_4$, called *parity functions*, operate on $k = 10$ data bytes to generate the $r = 4$ parities. The output of each of these functions comprises one byte. These functions are such that one can reconstruct $\boldsymbol{a}$ from any 10 of the 14 bytes $\{a_1, \ldots, a_{10}, f_1(\boldsymbol{a}), \ldots, f_4(\boldsymbol{a})\}$. In general, a ($k$, $r$) RS code has $r$ parity functions generating the $r$ parity bytes such that all the $k$ data bytes are recoverable from any $k$ of the ($k + r$) bytes in a stripe.

In the above discussion, each unit is considered indivisible: all the bytes in a unit share the same fate, i.e., all the bytes are either available or unavailable. Hence, a reconstruction operation is always performed on one or more entire units. A unit may be the smallest granularity of the data handled by a storage system, or it may be a data chunk that is always written onto the same disk block.

Reconstruction of any unit is performed in the following manner. Both the stripes of any 10 of the remaining 13 units are accessed. The RS code guarantees that any desired data can be obtained from any 10 of the units, allowing for reconstruction of the requisite unit from this accessed data. This reconstruction operation in the RS code requires accessing a total of 20 bytes from the other units.

## 2.2 Theoretical Framework of Piggybacking

In this section, we review a theoretical framework proposed in [22] for the construction of erasure codes, called the

| | | 1 byte (stripe) | 1 byte (stripe) |
|---|---|---|---|
| Data | unit 1 | $a_1$ | $b_1$ |
| | $\vdots$ | $\vdots$ | $\vdots$ |
| | unit 10 | $a_{10}$ | $b_{10}$ |
| Parity | unit 11 | $f_1(\boldsymbol{a})$ | $f_1(\boldsymbol{b})$ |
| | unit 12 | $f_2(\boldsymbol{a})$ | $f_2(\boldsymbol{b})$ |
| | unit 13 | $f_3(\boldsymbol{a})$ | $f_3(\boldsymbol{b})$ |
| | unit 14 | $f_4(\boldsymbol{a})$ | $f_4(\boldsymbol{b})$ |

**Figure 2: Two stripes of a ($k$=10, $r$=4) Reed-Solomon (RS) code. Ten units of data (first ten rows) are encoded using the RS code to generate four parity units (last four rows).**

| 1 byte (1st substripe) | 1 byte (2nd substripe) |
|---|---|
| $a_1$ | $b_1+g_1(\boldsymbol{a})$ |
| $\vdots$ | $\vdots$ |
| $a_{10}$ | $b_{10}+g_{10}(\boldsymbol{a})$ |
| $f_1(\boldsymbol{a})$ | $f_1(\boldsymbol{b})+g_{11}(\boldsymbol{a})$ |
| $f_2(\boldsymbol{a})$ | $f_2(\boldsymbol{b})+g_{12}(\boldsymbol{a})$ |
| $f_3(\boldsymbol{a})$ | $f_3(\boldsymbol{b})+g_{13}(\boldsymbol{a})$ |
| $f_4(\boldsymbol{a})$ | $f_4(\boldsymbol{b})+g_{14}(\boldsymbol{a})$ |

stripe

**Figure 3: The theoretical framework of Piggybacking [22] for parameters ($k$= 10, $r$=4). Each row represents one unit of data.**

| 1 byte (1st substripe) | 1 byte (2nd substripe) |
|---|---|
| $a_1$ | $b_1$ |
| $\vdots$ | $\vdots$ |
| $a_{10}$ | $b_{10}$ |
| $f_1(\boldsymbol{a})$ | $f_1(\boldsymbol{b})$ |
| $f_2(\boldsymbol{a})$ | $f_2(\boldsymbol{b})\oplus a_1\oplus a_2\oplus a_3$ |
| $f_3(\boldsymbol{a})$ | $f_3(\boldsymbol{b})\oplus a_4\oplus a_5\oplus a_6$ |
| $f_4(\boldsymbol{a})$ | $f_4(\boldsymbol{b})\oplus a_7\oplus a_8\oplus a_9\oplus a_{10}$ |

stripe

**Figure 4: Hitchhiker-XOR code for ($k$=10, $r$=4). Each row represents one unit of data.**

Piggybacking framework. The framework operates on pairs of stripes of an RS code (e.g., the pair of columns depicted in Fig. 2). The framework allows for arbitrary functions of the data pertaining to one stripe to be added to the second stripe. This is depicted in Fig. 3 where arbitrary functions $g_1, \ldots, g_{14}$ of the data of the first stripe of the RS code $\boldsymbol{a}$ are added to the second stripe of the RS code. Each of these functions outputs values of size one byte.

The Piggybacking framework performs independent and identical operations on pairs of columns, and hence a stripe consists of two columns. The constituent columns of a stripe will be referred to as *substripes* (see Fig. 3).

Irrespective of the choice of the Piggybacking functions $g_1, \ldots, g_{14}$, the code retains the fault tolerance and the storage efficiency of the underlying RS code. To see the fault tolerance, recall that RS codes allow for tolerating failure of any $r$ units. In our setting of ($k=10$, $r=4$), this amounts to being able to reconstruct the entire data from any 10 of the 14 units in that stripe. Now consider the code of Fig. 3, and consider any 10 units (rows). The first column of Fig. 3 is identical to the first stripe (column) of the RS code of Fig. 2, which allows for reconstruction of $\boldsymbol{a}$ from these 10 units. Access to $\boldsymbol{a}$ now allows us to compute the values of the functions $g_1(\boldsymbol{a}), \ldots, g_{14}(\boldsymbol{a})$, and subtract the respective functions out from the second columns of the 10 units under consideration. What remains are some 10 bytes out of $\{b_1, \ldots, b_{10}, f_1(\boldsymbol{b}), \ldots, f_4(\boldsymbol{b})\}$. This is identical to the second stripe (column) of the RS code in Fig. 2, which allows for the reconstruction of $\boldsymbol{b}$. It follows that the code of Fig. 3 can also tolerate the failure of any $r$ = 4 units. We will now argue storage efficiency. Each function $g_i$ outputs one byte of data. Moreover, the operation of adding this function to the RS code is performed via "finite field arithmetic", and hence the result also comprises precisely one byte.[4] Thus the amount of storage is not increased upon performing these operations. It is easy to see that each of these arguments extend to any generic values of the parameters $k$ and $r$.

The theoretical framework of Piggybacking thus provides a high degree of flexibility in the design of the erasure code by allowing for an arbitrary choice of the functions $g_i$'s. When using this framework for constructing codes, this choice must be made in a manner that imparts desired features to the erasure code. In this paper we design these functions to increase the efficiency of reconstruction.

[4]We do not employ any special properties of finite field arithmetic in the paper, and do not assume the reader to be conversant of the same.

# 3. HITCHHIKER'S ERASURE CODE

One of the main components of Hitchhiker is the new erasure code proposed in this paper. The proposed code reduces the amount of data required during reconstruction, without adding any additional storage overhead. Furthermore, the code can be used for any values of the system parameters $k$ and $r$, thus maintaining both (P1) storage optimality and (P2) generic applicability properties of RS codes. This code is based on the recently proposed theoretical framework of piggybacking ([22];§2).

The proposed code has three versions, two of which require only XOR operations in addition to encoding of the underlying RS code. The XOR-only feature of these erasure codes significantly reduces the computational complexity of decoding, making degraded reads and failure recovery faster (§6.3). Hitchhiker's erasure code optimizes only the reconstruction of data units; reconstruction of parity units is performed as in RS codes.

The three versions of Hitchhiker's erasure code are described below. Each version is first illustrated with an example for the parameters ($k$ = 10, $r$ = 4), followed by the generalization to arbitrary values of the parameters. Without loss of generality, the description of the codes' operations considers only a single stripe (comprising two substripes). Identical operations are performed on each stripe of the data.

## 3.1 Hitchhiker-XOR

As compared to a ($k$ = 10, $r$ = 4) RS code, Hitchhiker-XOR saves 35% in the amount of data required during the reconstruction of the first six data units and 30% during the reconstruction of the remaining four data units.

### 3.1.1 Encoding

The code for ($k$ = 10, $r$ = 4) is shown in Fig. 4. The figure depicts a single stripe of this code, comprising two substripes. The encoding operation in this code requires only XOR operations in addition to the underlying RS encoding.

### 3.1.2 Reconstruction

First consider reconstructing the first unit. This requires reconstruction of $\{a_1, b_1\}$ from the remaining units. Hitchhiker-XOR accomplishes this using only 13 bytes from the other units: the bytes belonging to both the substripes of units $\{2,3\}$ and the bytes belonging to only the second substripe of units $\{4,\ldots,12\}$. These 13 bytes are $\{a_2, a_3, b_2, b_3 \ldots, b_{10}, f_1(\boldsymbol{b}), f_2(\boldsymbol{b}) \oplus a_1 \oplus a_2 \oplus a_3\}$. The decoding procedure comprises three steps. Step 1: observe that the 10 bytes $\{b_2, \ldots, b_{10}, f_1(\boldsymbol{b})\}$ are identical to the corresponding 10 bytes in the RS encoding of $\boldsymbol{b}$ (Fig. 2). RS decoding of these 10 bytes gives $\boldsymbol{b}$ (and this includes one of the desired bytes $b_1$). Step 2: XOR $f_2(\boldsymbol{b})$ with the second byte ($f_2(\boldsymbol{b}) \oplus a_1 \oplus a_2 \oplus a_3$) of the $12^{\text{th}}$ unit. This gives $(a_1 \oplus a_2 \oplus a_3)$. Step 3: XORing this with $a_2$ and $a_3$ gives $a_1$. Thus both $a_1$ and $b_1$ are reconstructed by using only 13 bytes, as opposed to 20 bytes in RS codes, resulting in a saving of 35%.

Let us now consider the reconstruction of any unit $i \in \{1,\ldots,10\}$, which requires reconstruction of $\{a_i, b_i\}$. We shall first describe what data (from the other units) is required for the reconstruction, following which we describe the decoding operation. Any data unit $i \in \{1,2,3\}$ is reconstructed using the following 13 bytes: the bytes of both the substripes of units $\{1,2,3\}\backslash\{i\}$, and the bytes belonging to only the second substripe from units $\{4,\ldots,12\}$.[5] Any data unit $i \in \{4,5,6\}$ is also reconstructed using only 13 bytes: the bytes belonging to both the substripes of units $\{4,5,6\}\backslash\{i\}$, and the bytes belonging to only the second substripe of units $\{1,2,3,7,\ldots,11,13\}$. Any data unit $i \in \{7,8,9,10\}$ is reconstructed using 14 bytes: both substripes of units $\{7,8,9,10\}\backslash\{i\}$, and only the second substripe of units $\{1,\ldots,6,11,14\}$.

**Three-step decoding procedure:**

**Step 1**: The set of 10 bytes $\{b_1,\ldots,b_{10}, f_1(\boldsymbol{b})\}\backslash\{b_i\}$ belonging to the second substripe of the units $\{1,\ldots,11\}\backslash\{i\}$ is identical to the 10 corresponding encoded bytes in the RS code. Perform RS decoding of these 10 bytes to get $\boldsymbol{b}$ (which includes one of the desired bytes $b_i$).

**Step 2**: In the other bytes accessed, subtract out all components that involve $\boldsymbol{b}$.

**Step 3**: XOR the resulting bytes to get $a_i$.

Observe that during the reconstruction of any data unit, the remaining data units *do not* perform any computation. In the parlance of coding theory, this property is called 'repair-by-transfer' [26]. This property carries over to all three versions of Hitchhiker's erasure code.

## 3.2 Hitchhiker-XOR+

Hitchhiker-XOR+ further reduces the amount of data required for reconstruction as compared to Hitchhiker-XOR, and employs only additional XOR operations. It however requires the underlying RS code to possess a certain property. This property, which we term the *all-XOR-parity* property, requires at least one parity function of the RS code to be an XOR of all the data units. That is, a $(k,\ r)$ RS code satisfying all-XOR-parity will have one of the $r$ parity bytes as an XOR of all the $k$ data bytes. For $(k = 10,\ r = 4)$, Hitchhiker-XOR+ requires 35% lesser data for reconstruction of any of the data units as compared to RS codes.

[5] For any set $\mathcal{A}$ and any element $i \in \mathcal{A}$, the notation $\mathcal{A}\backslash\{i\}$ denotes all elements of $\mathcal{A}$ except $i$.

### 3.2.1 Encoding

The $(k = 10,\ r = 4)$ Hitchhiker-XOR+ code is shown in Fig. 5. The Hitchhiker-XOR+ code is obtained by performing one additional XOR operation on top of Hitchhiker-XOR: in the second parity of Hitchhiker-XOR, the byte of the second substripe is XORed onto the byte of the first substripe to give Hitchhiker-XOR+. The underlying RS code in this example satisfies the all-XOR-parity property with its second parity function $f_2$ being an XOR of all the inputs.

We now argue that this additional XOR operation does not violate the fault tolerance level and storage efficiency. To see fault tolerance, observe that the data of the second parity unit of Hitchhiker-XOR+ can always be converted back to that under Hitchhiker-XOR by XORing its second substripe with its first substripe. It follows that the data in any unit under Hitchhiker-XOR+ is equivalent to the data in the corresponding unit in Hitchhiker-XOR. The fault tolerance properties of Hitchhiker-XOR thus carry over to Hitchhiker-XOR+. Storage efficiency is retained because the additional XOR operation does not increase the space requirement.

### 3.2.2 Decoding

The recovery of any unit $i$ requires 13 bytes from the other units. The choice of the bytes to be accessed depends on the value of $i$, and is described below. The bytes required for the reconstruction of any data unit $i \in \{1,\ldots,6\}$ are identical to that in Hitchhiker-XOR. Any data unit $i \in \{7,8,9\}$ is reconstructed using the following 13 bytes: the bytes of both substripes of units $\{7,8,9\}\backslash\{i\}$, and the bytes of only the second substripes of units $\{1,\ldots,6,10,11,14\}$. The tenth unit is also reconstructed using only 13 bytes: the bytes of only the second substripes of units $\{1,\ldots,9,11,13,14\}$, and the byte of only the first substripe of unit 12. The decoding procedure that operates on these 13 bytes is identical to the three-step decoding procedure described in §3.1.2.

## 3.3 Hitchhiker-nonXOR

We saw that Hitchhiker-XOR+ results in more savings as compared to Hitchhiker-XOR, but requires the underlying RS code to have the all-XOR-parity property. Hitchhiker-nonXOR presented here guarantees the same savings as Hitchhiker-XOR+ even when the underlying RS code does not possess the all-XOR-parity property, but at the cost of additional finite-field arithmetic. Hitchhiker-nonXOR can thus be built on top of any RS code. It offers a saving of 35% during the reconstruction of any data unit.

### 3.3.1 Encoding

The code for $(k = 10,\ r = 4)$ is shown in Fig. 6. As in Hitchhiker-XOR, in the second parity, the first byte is XORed with the second byte. The final value of the second parity as shown in Fig. 6 is a consequence of the fact that $f_2(\boldsymbol{a}) \oplus f_2(a_1, a_2, a_3, 0, \ldots, 0) = f_2(0,0,0,a_4,\ldots,a_{10})$ due to the linearity of RS encoding (this is discussed in greater detail in §5.2.2).

### 3.3.2 Decoding

Recovery of any unit requires only 13 bytes from other units. This set of 13 bytes is the same as in Hitchhiker-

| | | |
|---|---|---|
| unit 1 | $a_1$ | $b_1$ |
| $\vdots$ | $\vdots$ | $\vdots$ |
| unit 10 | $a_{10}$ | $b_{10}$ |
| unit 11 | $f_1(\boldsymbol{a})$ | $f_1(\boldsymbol{b})$ |
| unit 12 | $\bigoplus_{i=4}^{10} a_i \oplus \bigoplus_{i=1}^{10} b_i$ | $\bigoplus_{i=1}^{10} b_i \oplus \bigoplus_{i=1}^{3} a_i$ |
| unit 13 | $f_3(\boldsymbol{a})$ | $f_3(\boldsymbol{b}) \oplus \bigoplus_{i=4}^{6} a_i$ |
| unit 14 | $f_4(\boldsymbol{a})$ | $f_4(\boldsymbol{b}) \oplus \bigoplus_{i=7}^{9} a_i$ |

**Figure 5: Hitchhiker-XOR+ for $(k=10, r=4)$. Parity 2 of the underlying RS code is all-XOR.**

| | |
|---|---|
| $a_1$ | $b_1$ |
| $\vdots$ | $\vdots$ |
| $a_{10}$ | $b_{10}$ |
| $f_1(\boldsymbol{a})$ | $f_1(\boldsymbol{b})$ |
| $f_2(0,0,0,a_4,\ldots,a_{10}) \oplus f_2(\boldsymbol{b})$ | $f_2(\boldsymbol{b}) \oplus f_2(a_1,a_2,a_3,0,\ldots,0)$ |
| $f_3(\boldsymbol{a})$ | $f_3(\boldsymbol{b}) \oplus f_2(0,0,0,a_4,a_5,a_6,0,\ldots,0)$ |
| $f_4(\boldsymbol{a})$ | $f_4(\boldsymbol{b}) \oplus f_2(0,\ldots,0,a_7,a_8,a_9,0)$ |

**Figure 6: Hitchhiker-nonXOR code for $(k=10, r=4)$. This can be built on any RS code. Each row is one unit of data.**

XOR+. The decoding operation is a three-step procedure. The first two steps are identical to the first two steps of the decoding procedure of Hitchhiker-XOR described at the end of §3.1.2. The third step is slightly different, and requires an RS decoding operation (for units 1 to 9), as described below.

During reconstruction of any unit $i \in \{1,2,3\}$, the output of the second step is the set of three bytes $\{a_1, a_2, a_3, f_1(a_1, a_2, a_3, 0, \ldots, 0)\} \backslash \{a_i\}$. This is equivalent to having some 10 of the 11 bytes of the set $\{a_1, a_2, a_3, 0, \ldots, 0, f_1(a_1, a_2, a_3, 0, \ldots, 0)\}$. Now, this set of 11 bytes is equal to the set of first 11 bytes of the RS encoding of $\{a_1, a_2, a_3, 0, \ldots, 0\}$. An RS decoding operation thus gives $\{a_1, a_2, a_3\}$ which contains the desired byte $a_i$. Recovery of any other unit $i \in \{4, \ldots, 9\}$ follows along similar lines.

During the reconstruction of unit 10, the output of the second step is $f_1(0, \ldots, 0, a_{10})$. Hence the third step involves only a single (finite-field) multiplication operation.

### 3.4 Generalization to any $(k,\ r)$

The encoding and decoding procedures for the general case follow along similar lines as the examples discussed above, and are formally described in the Appendix. In each of the three versions, the amount of data required for reconstruction is reduced by 25% to 45% as compared to RS codes, depending on the values of the parameters $k$ and $r$. For instance, $(k = 6, r = 3)$ provides a saving of 25% with Hitchhiker-XOR and 34% with Hitchhiker-XOR+ and Hitchhiker-nonXOR; $(k = 20, r = 5)$ provides a savings of 37.5% with Hitchhiker-XOR and 40% with Hitchhiker-XOR+ and Hitchhiker-nonXOR.

## 4. "HOP-AND-COUPLE" FOR DISK EFFICIENCY

The description of the codes in §2 and §3 considers only two bytes per data unit. We now move on to consider the more realistic scenario where each of the $k$ data units to be encoded is larger (than two bytes). In the encoding process, these $k$ data units are first partitioned into stripes, and identical encoding operations are performed on each of the stripes. The RS code considers one byte each from the $k$ data units as a stripe. On the other hand, Hitchhiker's erasure code has two substripes within a stripe (§3) and hence *couples* pairs of bytes within each of the $k$ data units to form the substripes of a stripe. We will shortly see that the choice of the bytes to be coupled plays a crucial role in determining the efficiency of disk reads during reconstruction.

A natural strategy for forming the stripes for Hitchhiker's erasure code is to couple adjacent bytes within each unit, with the first stripe comprising the first two bytes of each of the units, the second stripe comprising the next two bytes, and so on. Fig. 7a depicts such a method of coupling for $(k = 10, r = 4)$. In the figure, the bytes accessed during the reconstruction of the first data unit are shaded. This method of coupling, however, results in highly discontiguous reads during reconstruction: alternate bytes are read from units 4 to 12 as shown in the figure. This high degree of discontinuity is detrimental to disk read performance, and forfeits the potential savings in disk IO during data reconstruction. The issue of discontiguous reads due to coupling of adjacent bytes is not limited to the reconstruction of the first data unit - it arises during reconstruction of any of the data units.

In order to ensure that the savings offered by Hitchhiker's erasure codes in the amount of data read during reconstruction are effectively translated to gains in disk read efficiency, we propose a coupling technique for forming stripes that we call *hop-and-couple*. This technique aims to minimize the degree of discontinuity in disk reads during the reconstruction of data units. The hop-and-couple technique couples a byte with another byte within the same unit that is a certain distance ahead (with respect to the natural ordering of bytes within a unit), i.e., it couples bytes after "hopping" a certain distance. We term this distance as the *hop-length*. This technique is illustrated in Fig. 7b, where the hop-length is chosen to be half the size of a unit.

The hop-length may be chosen to be any number that divides $\frac{B}{2}$, where $B$ denotes the size of each unit. This condition ensures that all the bytes in the unit are indeed coupled. Coupling adjacent bytes (e.g., Fig. 7a) is a degenerate case where the hop-length equals 1. The hop-length significantly affects the contiguity of the data read during reconstruction of the data units, in that the data is read as contiguous chunks of size equal to the hop-length. For Hitchhiker's erasure codes, a hop-length of $\frac{B}{2}$ minimizes the total number of discontiguous reads required during the reconstruction of data units. While higher values of hop-length reduces the number of discontiguous reads, it results in bytes further apart being coupled to form stripes. This is a trade-off to be considered when choosing the value of the hop-length, and is discussed further in §7.

We note that the reconstruction operation under RS codes reads the entire data from $k$ of the units, and hence trivially, the reads are contiguous. On the other hand, any erasure code that attempts to make reconstruction more efficient by downloading *partial* data from the units (e.g., [11, 15, 19, 21, 26, 27, 29]) will encounter the issue of discontiguous

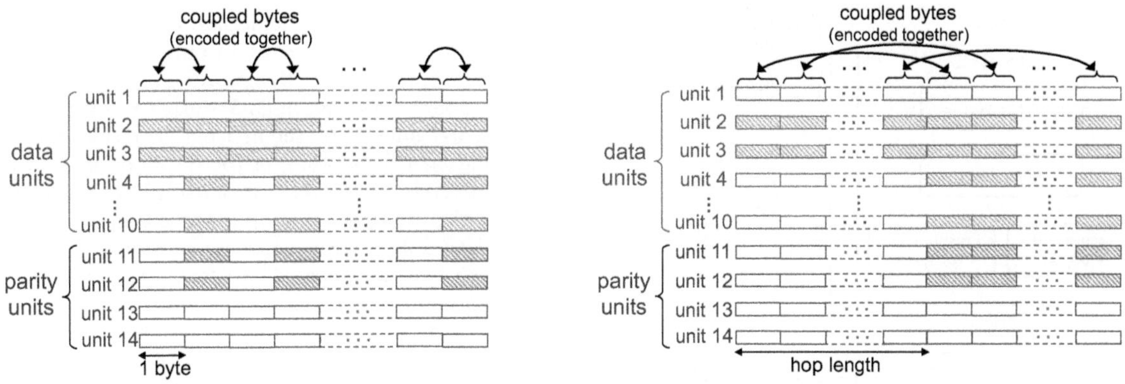


(a) coupling adjacent bytes to form stripes (b) hop-and-couple

**Figure 7: Two ways of coupling bytes to form stripes for Hitchhiker's erasure code. The shaded bytes are read and downloaded for the reconstruction of the first unit. While both methods require the same amount of data to be read, the reading is discontiguous in (a), while (b) ensures that the data to be read is contiguous.**

reads, as in Hitchhiker's erasure code. Any such erasure code would have multiple (say, $\alpha$) substripes in every stripe and would read a subset of these substripes from each of the units during reconstruction. The hop-and-couple technique can be applied to any such erasure code to translate the network savings to disk savings as well. The hop-length can be chosen to be any number that divides $\frac{B}{\alpha}$. As in the case of Hitchhiker's erasure codes (where $\alpha = 2$), this condition ensures that all the bytes are indeed coupled. If the bytes to be coupled are chosen with hop-length equal to $B/\alpha$, then the hop-and-couple technique would ensure that all the bytes of a substripe are contiguous within any unit. Reading a substripe from a unit would then result in a contiguous disk read, thereby minimizing the total degree of discontiguity in disk reads during reconstruction.

# 5. IMPLEMENTATION

We have implemented Hitchhiker in the Hadoop Distributed File System (HDFS). HDFS-RAID [1] is a module in HDFS that deals with erasure codes and is based on [8]. This module forms the basis for the erasure-coded storage system employed in the data-warehouse cluster at Facebook, and is open sourced under Apache. HDFS-RAID deployed at Facebook is based on RS codes, and we will refer to this system as RS-based HDFS-RAID. Hitchhiker builds on top of RS codes, and the present implementation uses the RS encoder and decoder modules of RS-based HDFS-RAID as its building blocks.

## 5.1 Brief description of HDFS-RAID

HDFS stores each file by dividing it into *blocks* of a certain size. By default, the size of each block is 256MB, and this is also the value that is typically used in practice. In HDFS, three replicas of each block are stored in the system by default. HDFS-RAID offers RS codes as an alternative to replication for maintaining redundancy.

The relevant modules of HDFS-RAID and the execution flows for relevant operations are depicted in Fig. 8. The *RAID-Node* manages all operations related to the use of erasure codes in HDFS. It has a list of files that are to be converted from the replicated state to the erasure-coded state, and periodically performs encoding of these files via MapReduce jobs. Sets of $k$ blocks from these files are encoded to generate $r$ parity blocks each.[6] Once the $r$ parity blocks of a set are successfully written into the file system, the replicas of the $k$ data blocks of that set are deleted. The MapReduce job calls the *Encoder* of the erasure code to perform encoding. The Encoder uses the *Parallel-Reader* to read the data from the $k$ blocks that are to be encoded. The Parallel-Reader opens $k$ parallel streams, issues HDFS read requests for these blocks, and puts the data read from each stream into different buffers. Typically, the buffers are 1MB each. When one buffer-sized amount of data is read from each of the $k$ blocks, the Encoder performs the computations pertaining to the encoding operation. This process is repeated until the entire data from the $k$ blocks are encoded.

The RAID-Node also handles recovery operations, i.e., reconstructing missing blocks in order to maintain the reliability of the system. The RAID-Node has a list of blocks that are missing and need to be *recovered.* It periodically goes through this list and reconstructs the blocks by executing a MapReduce job. The MapReduce job calls the *Decoder* of the erasure code to perform the reconstruction operation. The Decoder uses the Parallel-Reader to read the data required for reconstruction. For an RS code, data from $k$ blocks belonging to the same set as that of the block under reconstruction is read in parallel. As in the encoding process, data from the $k$ blocks are read into buffers, and the computations are performed once one buffer size amount of data is read from each of the $k$ blocks. This is repeated until the entire block is reconstructed.

HDFS directs any request for a *degraded read* (i.e., a read request for a block that is unavailable) to the *RAID File System.* The requested block is reconstructed on the fly by the RAID-Node via a MapReduce job. The execution of this reconstruction operation is identical to that in the reconstruction process discussed above.

## 5.2 Hitchhiker in HDFS

We implemented Hitchhiker in HDFS making use of the new erasure code (§3) and the hop-and-couple technique (§4) proposed in this paper. We implemented all three versions of the proposed storage code: Hitchhiker-XOR, Hitchhiker-XOR+, and Hitchhiker-nonXOR. This required implementing new Encoder, Decoder and Parallel-Reader

[6]In the context of HDFS, the term block corresponds to a unit and we will use these terms interchangeably.

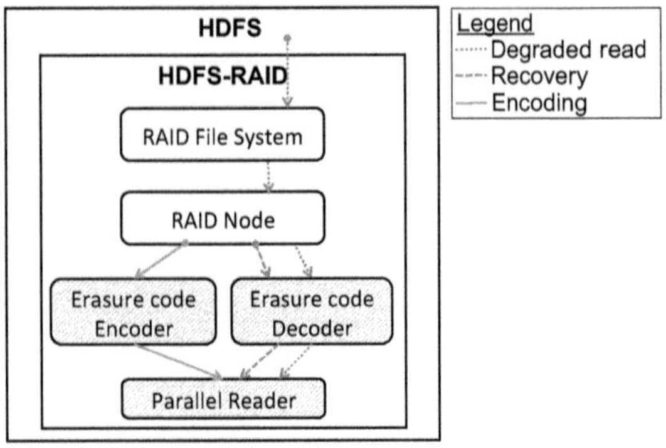


**Figure 8: Relevant modules in HDFS-RAID. The execution flow for encoding, degraded reads and reconstruction operations are shown. Hitchhiker is implemented in the shaded modules.**

modules (shaded in Fig. 8), entailing 7k lines of code. The implementation details described below pertain to parameters ($k = 10$, $r = 4$) which are the default parameters in HDFS. We emphasize that, however, Hitchhiker is generic and supports all values of the parameters $k$ and $r$.

### 5.2.1 Hitchhiker-XOR and Hitchhiker-XOR+

The implementation of these two versions of Hitchhiker is exactly as described in §3.1 and §3.2 respectively.

### 5.2.2 Hitchhiker-nonXOR

Hitchhiker-nonXOR requires finite field arithmetic operations to be performed in addition to the operations performed for the underlying RS code. We now describe how our implementation executes these operations.

***Encoder:*** As seen in Fig. 6, in addition to the underlying RS code, the Encoder needs to compute the functions $f_2(a_1,a_2,a_3,0...,0)$, $f_2(0,...,0,a_4,a_5,a_6,0...,0)$, and $f_2(0,...,0,a_7,a_8,a_9,0)$, where $f_2$ is the second parity function of the RS code. One way to perform these computations is to simply employ the existing RS encoder. This approach, however, involves computations that are superfluous to our purpose: The RS encoder uses an algorithm based on polynomial computations [16] that inherently computes *all* the four parities $f_1(\boldsymbol{x})$, $f_2(\boldsymbol{x})$, $f_3(\boldsymbol{x})$, and $f_4(\boldsymbol{x})$ for any given input $\boldsymbol{x}$. On the other hand, we require only one of the four parity functions for each of the three distinct inputs $(a_1,a_2,a_3,0...,0)$, $(0,...,0,a_4,a_5,a_6,0...,0)$ and $(0,...,0,a_7,a_8,a_9,0)$. Furthermore, these inputs are sparse, i.e., most of the input bytes are zeros.

Our Encoder implementation takes a different approach, exploiting the fact that RS codes have the property of *linearity*, i.e., each of the parity bytes of an RS code can be written as a linear combination of the data bytes. Any parity function $f_\ell$ can thus be specified as $f_\ell(\boldsymbol{x}) = \bigoplus_{j=1}^{10} c_{\ell,j}x_j$ for some constants $c_{\ell,1},\ldots,c_{\ell,10}$. We first inferred the values of these constants for each of the parity functions (from the existing "black-box" RS encoder) in the following manner. We first fed the input $[1\ 0\ \cdots\ 0]$ to the encoder. This gives the constants $c_{1,1},\ldots,c_{4,1}$ as the values of the four parities respectively in the output from the encoder. The values of the other constants were obtained in a similar manner by feeding different unit vectors as inputs to the encoder. Note that obtaining the values of these constants from the "black-box" RS encoder is a one-time task. With these constants, the encoder computes the desired functions simply as linear combinations of the given data units (for example, we compute $f_2(a_1,a_2,a_3,0\ldots,0)$ simply as $c_{2,1}a_1 \oplus c_{2,2}a_2 \oplus c_{2,3}a_3$).

***Decoder:*** As seen in §3.3, during reconstruction of any of the first nine units, the first byte is reconstructed by performing an RS decoding of the data obtained in the intermediate step. One straightforward way to implement this is to use the existing RS decoder for this operation. However, we take a different route towards a computationally cheaper option. We make use of two facts: (a) Observe from the description of the reconstruction process (§3.3) that for this RS decoding operation the data is known to be 'sparse', i.e., contains many zeros, and (b) the RS code has the linearity property, and furthermore, any linear combination of zero-valued data is zero. Motivated by this observation, our Decoder simply inverts this sparse linear combination to reconstruct the first substripe in a more efficient manner.

### 5.2.3 Hop-and-couple

Hitchhiker uses the proposed hop-and-couple technique to couple bytes during encoding. We use a hop-length of half a block since the granularity of data read requests and recovery in HDFS is typically an entire block. As discussed in §4, this choice of the hop-length minimizes the number of discontiguous reads. However, the implementation can be easily extended to other hop-lengths as well.

When the block size is larger than the buffer size, coupling bytes that are half a block apart requires reading data from two different locations within a block. In Hitchhiker, this is handled by the Parallel-Reader.

### 5.2.4 Data read patterns during reconstruction

During reconstruction in Hitchhiker, the choice of the blocks from which data is read, the seek locations, and the amount of data read are determined by the identity of the block being reconstructed. Since Hitchhiker uses the hop-and-couple technique for coupling bytes to form stripes during encoding, the reads to be performed during reconstruction are always contiguous within any block (§4).

For reconstruction of any of the first nine data blocks in Hitchhiker-XOR+ or Hitchhiker-nonXOR or for reconstruction of any of the first six data blocks in Hitchhiker-XOR, Hitchhiker reads and downloads two full blocks (i.e., both substripes) and nine half blocks (only the second substripes). For example, the read patterns for decoding blocks 1 and 4 are as shown in Fig. 9a and 9b respectively. For reconstruction of any of the last four data blocks in Hitchhiker-XOR, Hitchhiker reads and downloads three full blocks (both substripes) and nine half blocks (only the second substripes). For recovery of the tenth data block in Hitchhiker-XOR+ or Hitchhiker-nonXOR, Hitchhiker reads half a block each from the remaining thirteen blocks. This read pattern is shown in Fig. 9c.

# 6. EVALUATION

## 6.1 Evaluation Setup and Metrics

We evaluate Hitchhiker using two HDFS clusters at Facebook: (i) the data-warehouse cluster in production comprising multiple thousands of machines, with ongoing real-time traffic and workloads, and (ii) a smaller test cluster comprising around 60 machines. In both the clusters, machines are connected to a rack switch through 1Gb/s Ether-

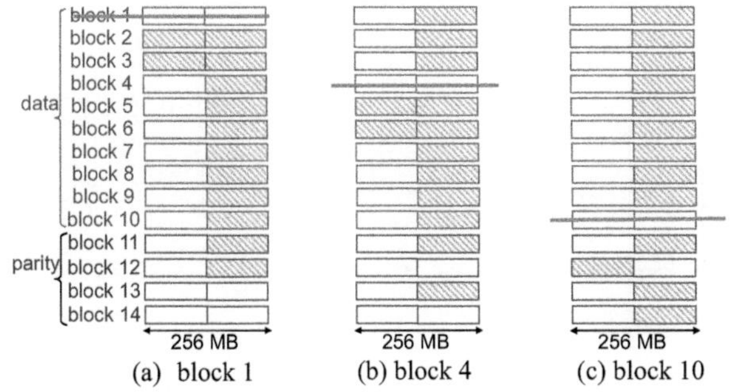


**Figure 9: Data read patterns during reconstruction of blocks 1, 4 and 10 in Hitchhiker-XOR+: the shaded bytes are read and downloaded.**

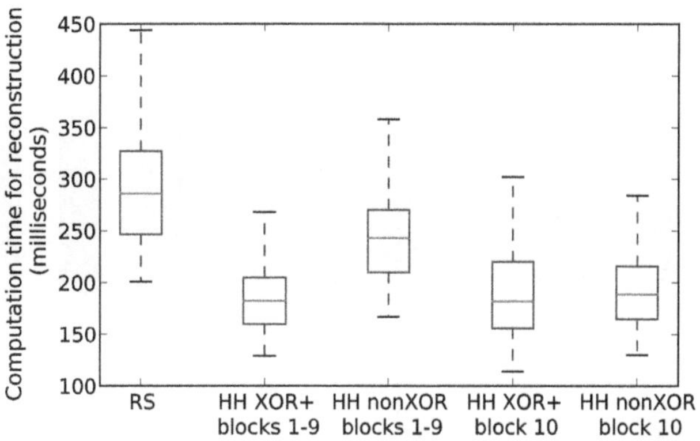


**Figure 10: A box plot comparing the computation time for reconstruction of 1MB (buffer size) from 200 runs each on Facebook's data-warehouse cluster with real-time production traffic and workloads. (HH = Hitchhiker.)**

net links. The higher levels of the network tree architecture have 8Gb/s Ethernet connections.

We compare Hitchhiker and RS-based HDFS-RAID in terms of the time taken for computations during encoding and reconstruction, the time taken to read the requisite data during reconstruction, and the amount of data that is read and transferred during reconstruction.[7] Note that in particular, the computation and the data read times during reconstruction are vital since they determine the performance of the system during degraded reads and recovery.

## 6.2 Evaluation Methodology

The encoding and reconstruction operations in HDFS-RAID, including those for degraded reads and recovery, are executed as MapReduce jobs. The data-warehouse cluster does not make any distinction between the MapReduce jobs fired by the RAID-Node and those fired by a user. This allows us to perform evaluations of the timing metrics for encoding, recovery, and degraded read operations by running them as MapReduce jobs on the production cluster. Thus evaluation of all the timing metrics is performed in the presence of real-time production traffic and workloads.

We deployed Hitchhiker on a 60-machine test cluster in one of the data centers at Facebook, and evaluated the end-to-end functionality of the system. Tests on this cluster verified that savings in network and disk traffic during reconstruction are as guaranteed in theory by Hitchhiker's erasure code.

For all the evaluations, we consider the encoding parameters ($k = 10$, $r = 4$), a block size of 256MB (unless mentioned otherwise), and a buffer size of 1MB. These are the default parameters in HDFS-RAID. Moreover, these are the parameters employed in the data-warehouse cluster in production at Facebook to store multiple tens of Petabytes.

In the evaluations, we show results of the timing metrics for *one buffer size.* This is sufficient since the same operations are performed repeatedly on one buffer size amount of data until an entire block is processed.

## 6.3 Computation time for degraded reads & recovery

Fig. 10 shows the comparison of computation time during data reconstruction (from 200 runs each). Note that (i) in both Hitchhiker-XOR+ and Hitchhiker-nonXOR, reconstruction of any of the first nine data blocks entails same amount of computation, (ii) reconstruction of any data block in Hitchhiker-XOR is almost identical to reconstruction of block 1 in Hitchhiker-XOR+. Hence, for brevity, no separate measurements are shown.

We can see that Hitchhiker's erasure codes perform faster reconstruction than RS-based HDFS-RAID for any data block. This is because (recall from §3) the reconstruction operation in Hitchhiker requires performing the resource intensive RS decoding only for *half* the substripes as compared to RS-based HDFS-RAID. In Hitchhiker, the data in the other half of substripes is reconstructed by performing either a few XOR operations (under Hitchhiker-XOR and Hitchhiker-XOR+) or a few finite-field operations (under Hitchhiker-nonXOR). One can also see that Hitchhiker-XOR+ has 25% lower computation time during reconstruction as compared to Hitchhiker-nonXOR for the first nine data blocks; for block 10, the time is almost identical in Hitchhiker-XOR+ and Hitchhiker-nonXOR (as expected from theory (§3)).

## 6.4 Read time for degraded reads & recovery

Fig. 11a and Fig. 11b respectively compare the median and the 95th percentile of the read times during reconstruction for three different block sizes: 4MB, 64MB, and 256MB in Hitchhiker-XOR+. The read patterns for reconstruction of any of the first nine blocks are identical (§3.2).

In the median read times for reconstruction of blocks 1-9 and block 10 respectively, in comparison to RS-based HDFS-RAID, we observed a reduction of 41.4% and 41% respectively for 4MB block size, 27.7% and 42.5% for 64MB block size, and 31.8% and 36.5% for 256MB block size. For the $95th$ percentile of the read time we observed a reduction of 35.4% and 48.8% for 4MB, 30.5% and 29.9% for 64MB, and 30.2% and 31.2% for 256MB block sizes.

The read pattern of Hitchhiker-nonXOR is identical to Hitchhiker-XOR+, while that of Hitchhiker-XOR is the same for the first six blocks and almost the same for the remaining four blocks. Hence for brevity, we plot the statistics only for Hitchhiker-XOR+.

Although Hitchhiker reads data from more machines as compared to RS-based HDFS-RAID, we see that it gives a superior performance in terms of read latency during reconstruction. The reason is that Hitchhiker reads only *half* a block size from most of the machines it connects to (recall from §5) whereas RS-based HDFS-RAID reads entire blocks.

[7]Both systems read the same data during encoding, and are hence trivially identical on this metric.

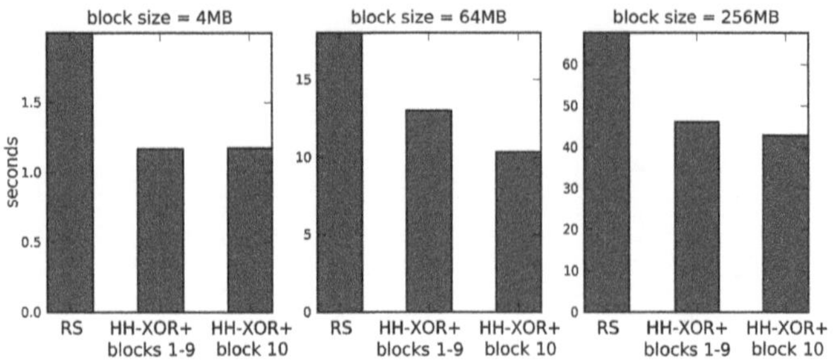


(a) Median

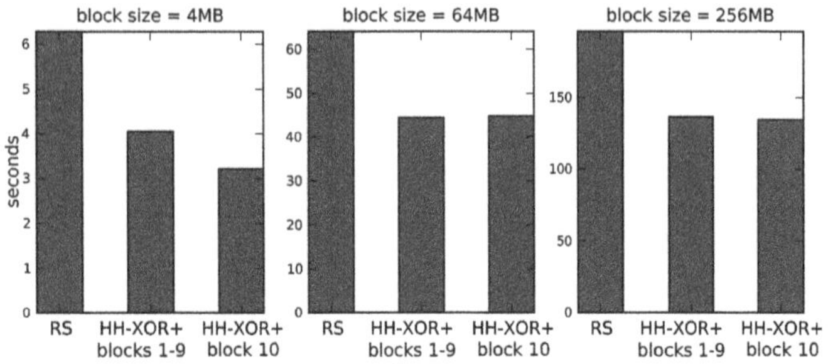


(b) 95$^{\text{th}}$ percentile

**Figure 11: Total read time (in seconds) during reconstruction from 200 runs each on Facebook's data-warehouse cluster with real-time production traffic and workloads. (HH = Hitchhiker.)**

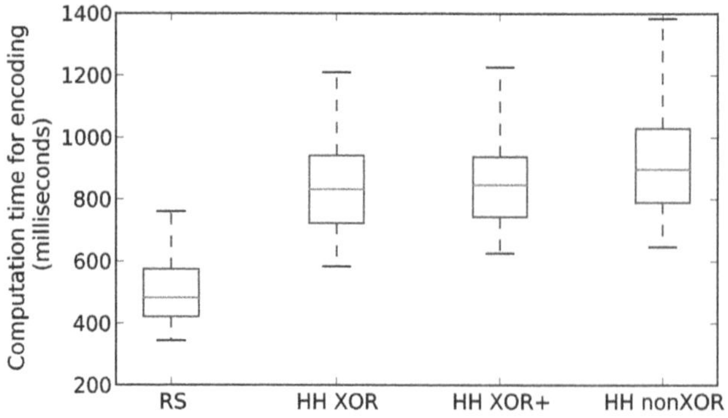


**Figure 12: A box plot comparing the computation time for encoding of 1MB (buffer size) from 200 runs each on Facebook's data-warehouse cluster with real-time production traffic and workloads. (HH = Hitchhiker.)**

## 6.5 Computation time for encoding

Fig. 12 compares the computation time for the encoding operation. Hitchhiker entails higher computational overheads during encoding as compared to RS-based systems, and Hitchhiker-XOR+ and Hitchhiker-XOR are faster than the Hitchhiker-nonXOR. This is expected since Hitchhiker's encoder performs computations in addition to those of RS encoding. §7 discusses the tradeoffs between higher encoding time and savings in other metrics.

## 6.6 Statistics of single block reconstruction

Hitchhiker optimizes data reconstruction in scenarios when only one block of a stripe is unavailable. If multiple blocks belonging to a stripe are unavailable, Hitchhiker performs reconstruction in a manner identical to RS-based HDFS-RAID, by reading and downloading 10 entire blocks. We collected measurements of the number of missing blocks per stripe across six months in the data-warehouse cluster in production at Facebook, which stores multiple Petabytes of RS-coded data. We observed that among all the stripes that had at least one block to be reconstructed, 98.08% of them had exactly one such block missing, 1.87% had two blocks missing, and the number of stripes with three or more such blocks was 0.05%. The measurements thus reveal single block reconstructions to be by far the most common scenario in the system at hand.

One might alternatively think of *lazily* performing reconstruction by waiting for multiple blocks in a stripe to fail and then reconstructing them all at once, in order to amortize the cost of disk reads and download during reconstruction. However, such a waiting approach may not be feasible when read performance is key: a failed systematic block must be repaired quickly to serve future read requests. Furthermore, degraded reads are performed on a single block in real time, and there is no equivalent of waiting for more failures.

## 6.7 Deployment and testing

We deployed HDFS-RAID with both Hitchhiker and the RS-based system on a 60-machine test cluster at Facebook in order to verify Hitchhiker's end-to-end functionality. We created multiple files with a block size of 256MB, and encoded them separately using Hitchhiker and RS-based HDFS-RAID. The block placement policy of HDFS-RAID ensures that the 14 blocks of an encoded stripe are all stored on different machines. We then forced some of these machines to become unavailable by stopping HDFS related scripts running on them, and collected the logs pertaining to the MapReduce jobs that performed the reconstruction operations. We verified that all reconstruction operations were successful. We also confirmed that the amount of data read and downloaded in Hitchhiker was 35% lower than in RS-based HDFS-RAID, as guaranteed by the proposed codes. We do not perform timing measurements on the test cluster since the network traffic and the workload on these machines do not reflect the real (production) scenario. Instead, we evaluated these metrics directly on the production cluster itself (as discussed earlier).

# 7. DISCUSSION ON TRADE-OFFS

*a) Three versions of the code:* During encoding and reconstruction, Hitchhiker-XOR requires performing only XOR operations in addition to the operations of the underlying RS code. Hitchhiker-XOR+ allows for more efficient reconstruction in terms of network and disk resources in comparison to Hitchhiker-XOR, while still using only XOR operations in addition to the RS code's operations. Hitchhiker-XOR+, however, requires the underlying RS code to satisfy the all-XOR-parity property (§3.2). Hitchhiker-nonXOR provides the same efficiency in reconstruction as Hitchhiker-XOR+ without imposing the all-XOR-parity requirement on the RS code, but entails additional finite-field arithmetic during encoding and reconstruction.

*b) Connecting to more machines during reconstruction:* Reconstruction in RS-coded systems requires connecting to exactly $k$ machines, whereas Hitchhiker entails connecting to more than $k$ machines. In certain systems, depending on the setting at hand, this may lead to an increase in the read latency during reconstruction. However, in our experiments on the production data-warehouse cluster at Facebook, we saw no such increase in read latency. On the contrary, we consistently observed a significant reduction in the latency due to the significantly lower amounts of data required to be read and downloaded in Hitchhiker (see Fig. 11).

*c) Option of operating as an RS-based system:* The storage overheads and fault tolerance of Hitchhiker are identical to RS-based systems. Moreover, a reconstruction operation in Hitchhiker can alternatively be performed as in RS-based systems by downloading any $k$ entire blocks. Hitchhiker thus provides an option to operate as an RS-based system when necessary, e.g., when increased connectivity during reconstruction is not desired. This feature also ensures Hitchhiker's compatibility with other alternative solutions proposed outside the erasure-coding component (e.g., [3, 5, 18]).

*d) Choice of hop-length:* As discussed in §4, a larger hop-length leads to more contiguous reads, but requires coupling of bytes that are further apart. Recall that reconstructing any byte also necessitates reconstructing its coupled byte. In a scenario where only a part of a block may need to be reconstructed, all the bytes that are coupled with the bytes of this part must also be reconstructed even if they are not required. A lower hop-length reduces the amount such frivolous reconstructions.

*e) Higher encoding time vs. improvement in other metrics:* Hitchhiker trades off a higher encoding time for improvement along other dimensions (Table 1). Encoding of raw data into erasure-coded data is a one time task, and is often executed as a background job. On the other hand, reconstruction operations are performed repeatedly, and degraded read requests must be served in real time. For these reasons, the gains in terms of other metrics achieved by Hitchhiker outweigh the additional encoding cost in the systems we consider.

# 8. RELATED WORK

Erasure codes have many pros and cons over replication [25, 31]. The most attractive feature of erasure codes is that while replication entails a minimum of 2× storage redundancy, erasure codes can support significantly smaller storage overheads for the same levels of reliability. Many storage systems thus employ erasure codes for various application scenarios [2, 3, 9, 24]. Traditional erasure codes however face the problem of inefficient reconstruction. To this end, several works (e.g., [3, 5, 18]) propose system level solutions that can be employed to reduce data transfer during reconstruction operations, such as caching the data read during reconstruction, batching multiple recovery operations in a stripe, or delaying the recovery operations. While these solutions consider the erasure code as a black-box, Hitchhiker modifies this black box, employing the new erasure code of this paper to address the reconstruction problem. Note that Hitchhiker retains all the properties of the underlying RS-based system. Hence any solution proposed outside of the erasure-code module can be employed in conjunction with Hitchhiker to benefit from both the solutions.

The problem of reducing the amount of data accessed during reconstruction through the design of new erasure codes has received much attention in the recent past [7, 11, 12, 17, 19, 21, 22, 27, 30, 32]. However, all existing practical solutions either require the inclusion of additional parity units, thereby increasing the storage overheads [7, 12, 17, 21, 27], or are applicable in very limited settings [11, 15, 30, 32].

The idea of connecting to more machines and downloading smaller amounts of data from each node was proposed in [6] as a part of the 'regenerating codes model'. However, all existing practical constructions of regenerating codes necessitate a high storage redundancy in the system, e.g., codes in [21] require $r \geq (k-1)$. Rotated-RS [15] is another class of codes proposed for the same purpose. However, it supports at most 3 parities, and moreover, its fault tolerance is established via a computer search. Recently, optimized recovery algorithms [30, 32] have been proposed for EVEN-ODD and RDP codes, but they support only 2 parities. For the parameters where [15, 30, 32] exist, Hitchhiker performs at least as good, while also supporting an arbitrary number of parities. An erasure-coded storage system which also optimizes for data download during reconstruction is presented in [11]. While this system achieves minimum possible download during reconstruction, it supports only 2 parities. Furthermore, [11] requires decode operation to be performed for every read request since it cannot reconstruct an identical version of a failed unit but only reconstruct a functionally equivalent version.

The systems proposed in [7, 12, 17] employ another class of codes called local-repair codes to reduce the number blocks accessed during reconstruction. This, in turn, also reduces the total amount of data read and downloaded during reconstruction. However, these codes necessitate addition of at least 25% to 50% more parity units to the code, thereby increasing the storage space requirements.

# 9. CONCLUSION

We have introduced a systematically-designed, new and novel storage system called *Hitchhiker* that "rides" on top of existing Reed-Solomon based erasure-coded systems. *Hitchhiker* retains the key benefits of RS-coded systems over replication-based counterparts, namely that of (i) optimal storage space needed for a targeted level of reliability, as well as (ii) fine-grained flexibility in the design choice for the system. We show how Hitchhiker can *additionally* reduce both network traffic and disk traffic by 25% to 45% over that of RS-coded systems during reconstruction of missing or otherwise unavailable data. Further, our implementation and evaluation of Hitchhiker on two HDFS clusters at Facebook also reveals savings of 36% in the computation time and 32% in the time taken to read data during reconstruction.

As we look to scale next-generation data centers and cloud storage systems, a primary challenge is that of sustaining this massive growth in the volume of data needing to be stored and retrieved reliably and efficiently. Replication of data, while ideal from the viewpoint of flexible access and efficient reconstruction when faced with missing or unavailable nodes, is clearly not a sustainable option for all but a small fraction of the massive volume of data needing to be stored. Specifically, replication of data costs a redundancy factor of at least 2×. Not surprisingly, therefore, RS-coded systems, which can offer near-arbitrary fine-grained redundancy factors between 1× and 2×, have received more traction in data centers, despite their shortcomings with regard to large network and disk traffic requirements when faced with reconstruction of missing or unavailable data. This underscores the importance of Hitchhiker which aims at getting the best of both worlds in a systematic and scalable manner.

# 10. REFERENCES


[1] HDFS-RAID. http://wiki.apache.org/hadoop/HDFS-RAID.

[2] Seamless reliability. http://www.cleversafe.com/overview/reliable, Feb. 2014.

[3] R. Bhagwan, K. Tati, Y. C. Cheng, S. Savage, and G. Voelker. Total recall: System support for automated availability management. In *NSDI*, 2004.

[4] D. Borthakur. HDFS and Erasure Codes (HDFS-RAID). http://hadoopblog.blogspot.com/2009/08/hdfs-and-erasure-codes-hdfs-raid.html, Aug. 2009.

[5] B.-G. Chun, F. Dabek, A. Haeberlen, E. Sit, H. Weatherspoon, M. F. Kaashoek, J. Kubiatowicz, and R. Morris. Efficient replica maintenance for distributed storage systems. In *NSDI*, 2006.

[6] A. G. Dimakis, P. B. Godfrey, Y. Wu, M. Wainwright, and K. Ramchandran. Network coding for distributed storage systems. *IEEE Trans. Inf. Th.*, Sept. 2010.

[7] K. Esmaili, L. Pamies-Juarez, and A. Datta. CORE: Cross-object redundancy for efficient data repair in storage systems. In *IEEE International Conf. on Big data*, 2013.

[8] B. Fan, W. Tantisiriroj, L. Xiao, and G. Gibson. Diskreduce: RAID for data-intensive scalable computing. In *Proceedings of the 4th Annual Workshop on Petascale Data Storage*, pages 6–10. ACM, 2009.

[9] B. Fan, W. Tantisiriroj, L. Xiao, and G. Gibson. Diskreduce: RAID for data-intensive scalable computing. In *ACM Workshop on Petascale Data Storage*, 2009.

[10] S. Ghemawat, H. Gobioff, and S. Leung. The Google file system. In *ACM SOSP*, 2003.

[11] Y. Hu, H. C. Chen, P. P. Lee, and Y. Tang. Nccloud: Applying network coding for the storage repair in a cloud-of-clouds. In *USENIX FAST*, 2012.

[12] C. Huang, H. Simitci, Y. Xu, A. Ogus, B. Calder, P. Gopalan, J. Li, and S. Yekhanin. Erasure coding in Windows Azure storage. In *USENIX ATC*, 2012.

[13] S. Jiekak, A. Kermarrec, N. Scouarnec, G. Straub, and A. Van Kempen. Regenerating codes: A system perspective. *arXiv:1204.5028*, 2012.

[14] G. Kamath, N. Silberstein, N. Prakash, A. Rawat, V. Lalitha, O. Koyluoglu, P. Kumar, and S. Vishwanath. Explicit MBR all-symbol locality codes. In *ISIT*, 2013.

[15] O. Khan, R. Burns, J. Plank, W. Pierce, and C. Huang. Rethinking erasure codes for cloud file systems: minimizing I/O for recovery and degraded reads. In *FAST*, 2012.

[16] S. Lin and D. Costello. *Error control coding.* Prentice-hall Englewood Cliffs, 2004.

[17] S. Mahesh, M. Asteris, D. Papailiopoulos, A. G. Dimakis, R. Vadali, S. Chen, and D. Borthakur. Xoring elephants: Novel erasure codes for big data. In *VLDB*, 2013.

[18] J. Mickens and B. Noble. Exploiting availability prediction in distributed systems. In *NSDI*, 2006.

[19] D. Papailiopoulos, A. Dimakis, and V. Cadambe. Repair optimal erasure codes through hadamard designs. *IEEE Trans. Inf. Th.*, May 2013.

[20] K. V. Rashmi, N. B. Shah, D. Gu, H. Kuang, D. Borthakur, and K. Ramchandran. A solution to the network challenges of data recovery in erasure-coded distributed storage systems: A study on the Facebook warehouse cluster. In *Proc. USENIX HotStorage*, June 2013.

[21] K. V. Rashmi, N. B. Shah, and P. V. Kumar. Optimal exact-regenerating codes for the MSR and MBR points via a product-matrix construction. *IEEE Trans. Inf. Th.*, 2011.

[22] K. V. Rashmi, N. B. Shah, and K. Ramchandran. A piggybacking design framework for read-and download-efficient distributed storage codes. In *IEEE International Symposium on Information Theory*, 2013.

[23] I. Reed and G. Solomon. Polynomial codes over certain finite fields. *Journal of SIAM*, 1960.

[24] S. Rhea, P. Eaton, D. Geels, H. Weatherspoon, B. Zhao, and J. Kubiatowicz. Pond: The OceanStore prototype. In *USENIX FAST*, 2003.

[25] R. Rodrigues and B. Liskov. High availability in DHTs: Erasure coding vs. replication. In *IPTPS*, 2005.

[26] N. Shah, K. Rashmi, P. Kumar, and K. Ramchandran. Distributed storage codes with repair-by-transfer and non-achievability of interior points on the storage-bandwidth tradeoff. *IEEE Trans. Inf. Theory*, 2012.

[27] N. B. Shah. On minimizing data-read and download for storage-node recovery. *IEEE Communications Letters*, 2013.

[28] K. Shvachko, H. Kuang, S. Radia, and R. Chansler. The Hadoop distributed file system. In *IEEE MSST*, 2010.

[29] I. Tamo, Z. Wang, and J. Bruck. Zigzag codes: MDS array codes with optimal rebuilding. *IEEE Trans. Inf. Th.*, 2013.

[30] Z. Wang, A. Dimakis, and J. Bruck. Rebuilding for array codes in distributed storage systems. In *ACTEMT*, 2010.

[31] H. Weatherspoon and J. D. Kubiatowicz. Erasure coding vs. replication: A quantitative comparison. In *IPTPS*, 2002.

[32] L. Xiang, Y. Xu, J. Lui, and Q. Chang. Optimal recovery of single disk failure in RDP code storage systems. In *ACM SIGMETRICS*, 2010.


# APPENDIX

***Hitchhiker-XOR:*** The encoding procedure of Hitchhiker-XOR first divides the $k$ data units into $(r-1)$ disjoint sets of roughly equal sizes. For instance, in the $(k=10, r=4)$ code of Fig. 4, the three sets are units $\{1,2,3\}$, units $\{4,5,6\}$ and units $\{7,8,9,10\}$. For each set $j \in \{1,\ldots,r-1\}$, the bytes of the first substripe of all units in set $j$ are XORed, and the resultant is XORed with the second substripe of the $(j+1)^{\text{th}}$ parity unit.

Reconstruction of a data unit belonging to any set $j$ requires the bytes of both the substripes of the other data units in set $j$, only the second byte of all other data units, and the second bytes of the first and $(j+1)^{\text{th}}$ parity units. The decoding procedure for reconstruction of any data unit $i$ is executed in three steps:

*Step 1*: The $k$ bytes $\{b_1,\ldots,b_k,f_1(\boldsymbol{b})\}\backslash\{b_i\}$ belonging to the second substripe of the units $\{1,\ldots,k+1\}\backslash\{i\}$ are identical to the $k$ corresponding encoded bytes in the underlying RS code. Perform RS decoding of these $k$ bytes to get $\boldsymbol{b}$ (which includes one of the desired bytes $b_i$).

*Step 2*: In the other bytes accessed, subtract out all components that involve $\boldsymbol{b}$.

*Step 3*: XOR the resulting bytes to get $a_i$.

If the size of a set is $s$, reconstruction of any data unit in this set requires $(k+s)$ bytes (as compared to $2k$ under RS).

***Hitchhiker-XOR+:*** Assume without loss of generality that, in the underlying RS code, the all-XOR property is satisfied by the second parity. The encoding procedure first selects a number $\ell \in \{0,\ldots,k\}$ and partitions the first $(k-\ell)$ data units into $(r-1)$ sets of roughly equal sizes. On these $(k-\ell)$ data units and $r$ parity units, it performs an encoding identical to that in Hitchhiker-XOR. Next, in the second parity unit, the byte of the second substripe is XORed onto the byte of the first substripe.

Reconstruction of any of the first $(k-\ell)$ data units is performed in a manner identical to that in Hitchhiker-XOR. Reconstruction of any of the last $\ell$ data units requires the byte of the first substripe of the second parity and the bytes of the second substripes of all other units. The decoding procedure remains identical to the three-step procedure of Hitchhiker-XOR stated above.

For any of the first $(k-\ell)$ data units, if the size of its set is $s$ then reconstruction of that data unit requires $(k+s)$ bytes (as compared to $2k$ under RS). The reconstruction of any of the last $\ell$ units requires $(k+r+\ell-2)$ bytes (as compared to $2k$ under RS). The parameter $\ell$ can be chosen to minimize the average or maximum data required for reconstruction as per the system requirements.

***Hitchhiker-nonXOR:*** The encoding procedure is identical to that of Hitchhiker-XOR+, except that instead of XORing the bytes of the first substripe of the data units in each set, these bytes are encoded using the underlying RS encoding function considering all other data units that do not belong to the set as zeros.

The collection of data bytes required for the reconstruction of any data unit is identical to that under Hitchhiker-XOR+. The decoding operation for reconstruction is a three-step procedure. The first two steps are identical to the first two steps of the decoding procedure of Hitchhiker-XOR described above. The third step requires an RS decoding operation (recall the (10, 4) case from §3.3). In particular, the output of the second step when reconstructing a data unit $i$ will be equal to $k$ bytes that would have been obtained from the RS encoding of the data bytes in the units belonging to that set with all other data bytes set to zero. An RS decoding operation performed on these bytes now gives $a_i$, thus recovering the $i^{\text{th}}$ data unit (recall that $b_i$ is reconstructed in Step 1 itself.) The data access patterns during reconstruction and the amount of savings under Hitchhiker-nonXOR are identical to that under Hitchhiker-XOR+.

# Enabling Near Real-time Central Control for Live Video Delivery in CDNs

Matthew K. Mukerjee*, JungAh Hong†, Junchen Jiang*, David Naylor*, Dongsu Han†, Srinivasan Seshan*, Hui Zhang*

*Carnegie Mellon University †KAIST

{mukerjee, junchenj, dnaylor, srini, hzhang}@cs.cmu.edu
{hja2508, dongsu_han}@kaist.ac.kr

## Categories and Subject Descriptors

C.2.4 [**Computer-Communication Networks**]: Distributed Systems—*Distributed applications*

## Keywords

live video; CDNs; central optimization; hybrid control

## 1. INTRODUCTION

Internet video delivery is experiencing a dramatic change. Live video dominates on-demand video in user engagement—PC viewers watch live video 11x more than VoD [2]. Live streaming services like Twitch, YouTube Live, and Ustream support many workloads: from mega-events (e.g., sporting events) viewed by tens of millions of users, to thousands of popular channels (>1,000 viewers), to many more less popular channels in the "long-tail". However, the addition of user-created live content is causing a fundamental shift towards unpredictable popularity dynamics.

Provisioning a video delivery network for such workloads is challenging. The CDN needs to maximize video-specific quality metrics (e.g., high bitrate and low join time) for both popular and unpopular streams while simultaneously coping with unexpected shifts in popularity/network conditions. Failures in addressing these challenges result in difficulties broadcasting live TV shows [3, 8] and effective blackouts during mega-events such as the Oscars [11]. These service disruptions, which are apparent to end-users, will only get worse as user-created live channels with rapidly shifting popularity (virality) increase in number.

These issues are a direct result of a few underlying problems. Today, we rely on CDNs that were originally designed to support Web page delivery to deliver most Internet video traffic [1]. Thus, CDNs face many challenges in live video delivery: 1) CDNs are already responsible for a significant fraction of video quality problems for both live and VoD (including 20% of join failures and 22% of bitrate degradation) [6], 2) unlike VoD, live video cannot benefit from prefetching or caching, requiring content to be sent through the internal delivery network in real-time, 3) live video is shifting to viral user-created streams, and 4) CDNs are shifting to higher bitrate streams (e.g., 15+Mbps 4K streams [10]). With multiple encodings for different devices (e.g., desktop, mobile, set-top boxes) and a variety of bitrates, a single video channel could easily consume 150+Mbps.

Many techniques exist to improve video delivery from CDNs' edge servers to users, including placing edge servers closer to the users, bolstering last mile links, and choosing better CDNs and edge servers (or multiplexing them) [7]. However, we argue that dynamic fine-grained control over the *internal delivery network* is needed to overcome these underlying problems, rather than traditional DNS-based redirection [9]. To be successful, a live video delivery system must provide:

- **Quality:** It must optimize for application-specific quality metrics (e.g., high bitrate). Note that more throughput does not always mean higher bitrate and may even reduce other metrics.
- **Dynamic provisioning and scalability:** It must support the workload of today's largest CDNs by scaling to thousands of live video streams and millions of users, using thousands of CDN distribution clusters, while provisioning for individual videos on-the-fly.
- **Responsiveness:** It must respond to user- and network-induced events with low latency (less than a second).

Existing solutions do not satisfy all three requirements. Traffic engineering schemes (e.g., SWAN [4], B4 [5]) do not optimize for video-specific metrics and traditional DNS-based solutions are too coarse to react to quick shifts in popularity at a per-video granularity, especially in long-lived live video sessions [9].

For this, significant innovations in the CDN's control plane are required. We present Video Delivery Network (VDN), a new CDN architecture designed specifically for live video. We believe that the two fundamental challenges to achieve these goals are: (1) video-specific global optimization and (2) a scalable and robust control plane that operates at a very fine timescale.

## 2. SYSTEM OVERVIEW AND RESULTS

VDN reuses the current CDN infrastructure as much as possible but redesigns its control plane to overcome the challenges of live video distribution by using application-specific global coordination and local adaptation. We make two major contributions:


*SIGCOMM'14,* August 17–22, 2014, Chicago, IL, USA.
ACM 978-1-4503-2836-4/14/08.
http://dx.doi.org/10.1145/2619239.2631444.

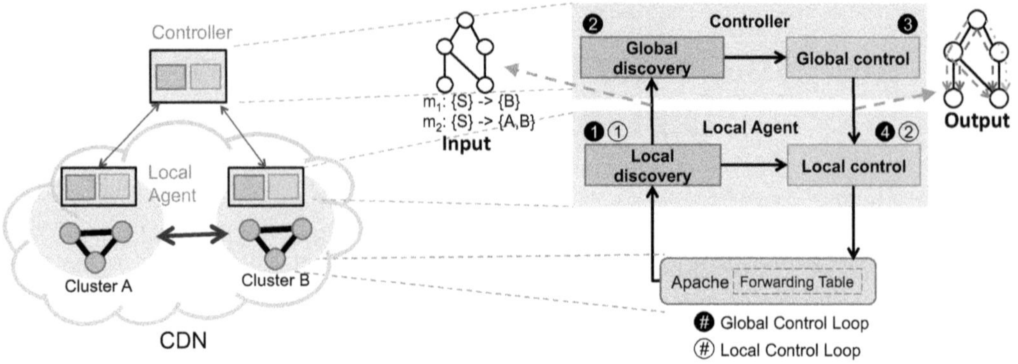


**Figure 1: *VDN System Overview***

- A **centralized coordination algorithm** that optimizes for live-video-specific objectives at the stream level using an approximate linear optimization. It carefully picks the most efficient combination of *distribution trees* out of many possible trees to maximize video-specific metrics (e.g., highest supported bitrate). The algorithm can scale to the workload of today's largest CDNs (1000s of concurrent live video streams delivered via 1000-2000 clusters) while delivering close-to-optimal results.
- A **hybrid control** approach where individual clusters safely deviate from the central algorithm to respond to changes in network conditions and/or viewership at the timescale of 100s of milliseconds. We show that this approach meets the strict responsiveness requirements of live video while providing sustained quality at Internet scale.

Figure 1 shows our design. A *local agent* in each cluster discovers link and viewership information ❶ which it forwards to the *central controller* as a network graph ❷. The central controller computes the globally optimal distribution trees for the current video channels over this network graph using a linear program ❸, the result of which it sends to the clusters ❹. This is the *global control loop*. If the local agent discovers a new user-/network-event (e.g., new channel request, link failure, etc.) ①, then it responds to this event in a purely local fashion ② (subject to certain restrictions). We refer to this as the *local control loop*. We omit the details due to space, but we take care to ensure these two control loops do not work against each other.

**Summary of results:** In Figure 2(a), we compare different algorithms for building distribution trees. *Local* is a greedy algorithm using local information to construct distribution trees by recursively looking for parents that have the best available bandwidth. *Best-Tree* greedily constructs distribution trees using a global view of the remaining network bandwidth. Our application-specific centralized coordination algorithm *VDN* provides a 2x improvement in average *video bitrate* over traditional CDN deployments while simultaneously scaling to 600 video channels and 1,000 CDN distribution clusters.

Figure 2(b) shows VDN's response time in a 10 machine deployment on Amazon EC2. Our hybrid control plane allows VDN to react to network and viewership changes at a timescale of 100s of milliseconds and with much less variation than a purely local approach.

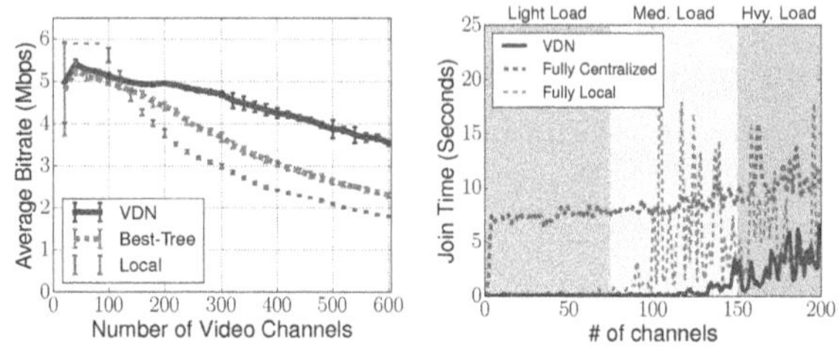


(a) Quality comparison (b) Join time

**Figure 2: *VDN's quality and responsiveness***


## Acknowledgments

This work is supported in part by NSF Grant #1040801, NDSEG Fellowship 32 CFR 168a, the National Research Foundation of Korea (NRF-2013R1A1A1076024), and the ICT R&D Program 2014 of MSIP, Korea.


## 3. REFERENCES


[1] Cisco visual networking index: Forecast and methodology, 2012-2017. http://www.cisco.com/en/US/solutions/collateral/ns341/ns525/ns537/ns705/ns827/white_paper_c11-481360_ns827_Networking_Solutions_White_Paper.html.

[2] Ooyala global video index q3 2013. http://go.ooyala.com/rs/OOYALA/images/Ooyala-Global-Video-Index-Q3-2013.pdf.

[3] Forbes. Game of thrones premier brings hbo more customers despite episode crash. http://www.forbes.com/sites/brandindex/2014/05/06/game-of-thrones-premier-brings-hbo-more-customers-despite-episode-crash/, May 2014.

[4] Hong, C.-Y., Kandula, S., Mahajan, R., Zhang, M., Gill, V., Nanduri, M., and Wattenhofer, R. Achieving high utilization with software-driven wan. In *Proc. ACM SIGCOMM* (2013).

[5] Jain, S., Kumar, A., Mandal, S., Ong, J., Poutievski, L., Singh, A., Venkata, S., Wanderer, J., Zhou, J., Zhu, M., et al. B4: Experience with a globally-deployed software defined wan. In *Proc. ACM SIGCOMM* (2013), pp. 3–14.

[6] Jiang, J., Sekar, V., Stoica, I., and Zhang, H. Shedding light on the structure of internet video quality problems in the wild. In *Proc. of the ACM CoNEXT* (2013).

[7] Liu, X., Dobrian, F., Milner, H., Jiang, J., Sekar, V., Stoica, I., and Zhang, H. A case for a coordinated internet video control plane. In *Proc. ACM SIGCOMM* (2012), pp. 359–370.

[8] Reporter, T. H. Hbo go crashes during 'true dective' finale. http://www.hollywoodreporter.com/live-feed/hbo-go-crashes-true-detective-687087, March 2014.

[9] Su, A.-J., and Kuzmanovic, A. Thinning akamai. In *Proc. ACM IMC* (2008).

[10] Time. Netflix rolls out 4k tv support, for the extreme minority that have it. http://time.com/53882/netflix-rolls-out-4k-tv-support-for-the-extreme-minority-that-have-it/, April 2014.

[11] Variety. Abc's live oscar internet stream suffers nationwide outage. http://variety.com/2014/digital/news/abcs-live-internet-oscar-stream-suffers-nationwide-outage-1201124215/, March 2014.

# NetAssay: Providing New Monitoring Primitives for Network Operators

Sean Donovan
Georgia Institute of Technology
sdonovan@cc.gatech.edu

Nick Feamster
Georgia Institute of Technology
feamster@cc.gatech.edu

## ABSTRACT

Home and business network operators have limited network statistics available over which management decisions can be made. Similarly, there are few triggered behaviors, such as usage or bandwidths cap for individual users, that are available. By looking at sources of traffic, based on Domain Name System (DNS) cues for content of particular web addresses or source Autonomous System (AS) of the traffic, network operators could create new and interesting rules for their network. NetAssay is a Software-Defined Networking (SDN)-based, network-wide monitoring and reaction framework. By integrating information from Border Gateway Protocol (BGP) and the Domain Name System, NetAssay is able to integrate formerly disparate sources of control information, and use it to provide better monitoring, more useful triggered events, and security benefits for network operators.

## Keywords

Network monitoring, network management, software-defined networking

## 1. INTRODUCTION

Network management is a complex area. On stub networks, where the network is only a client to other networks, monitoring user behavior is limited. Bandwidth monitoring at the port or address level is among the more complex operations that are available. Similarly, triggered behaviors such as usage caps are limited. More complex behavior is available, primarily in highly specialized security appliances, however these are not general purpose devices.

What is needed is a generalized system that can monitor network activity and produce behaviors based on high level policies. For instance, a network operator would like to know how much video traffic each user is consuming. Right now, there is no easy way of doing this.

NetAssay is being developed to make it easy for network operators to implement such policies. In the video bandwidth example, NetAssay needs to decide what network flows are video traffic. Traffic coming from googlevideo.com will be classified as video, as could any traffic associated with AS 2906, Netflix's AS. Identifying the user, at least on a stub network, can be done a number of ways, such as statically assigned IPs or MAC addresses. A policy for this could be expressed as:

```
video-count-Bob = count_bytes(3600,['src-ip'])
video-count-Bob.register_callback(check_video_count)
video-from-Bob = match(srcip = 198.51.100.8) &
                 (matchAS(2906) | matchClass('video'))
pol = video-from-Bob >> video-count-Bob
```

More interesting triggered behaviors are also possible. Continuing the above example, being able to react to Bob's excessive video consumption is desirable. For instance, being able to redirect Bob's video traffic through a rate limited link could be a useful policy to implement.

As a further, more security oriented example, a network operator has blacklists of ASes and domains that are associated with malicious behavior, but do host some legitimate content that should still be accessible. In this case, if a connection was destined for an IP associated with a potentially malicious AS, the network could automatically redirect traffic to a virus scanning appliance, rather than needing to send all traffic through the appliance. Another use would be to set a limit for amount of data that would be sent to a blacklisted AS before blocking connections, due to suspected bad behavior.

Similar triggered behaviors have been described in prior works [5][1], however this has been limited to network security security devices.

## 2. DESIGN

NetAssay is SDN-based system running on Pyretic [3], an easy to use and extend SDN programming language. NetAssay is divided into two sections, as can be seen in Figure 1. These are the monitoring modules, two of which are described below, that provide traffic identification and monitoring information to the main control module (MCM). The MCM is responsible for combining the results from the monitoring modules, and triggering the reactive policies defined by the network operator.

### 2.1 Monitoring Modules

The monitoring modules perform two major functions: identifying flows that belong to a particular category and monitoring information related to that category. To identify flows, the modules can use information gleamed from


*SIGCOMM'14,* August 17–22, 2014, Chicago, IL, USA.
ACM 978-1-4503-2836-4/14/08.
http://dx.doi.org/10.1145/2619239.2631451.

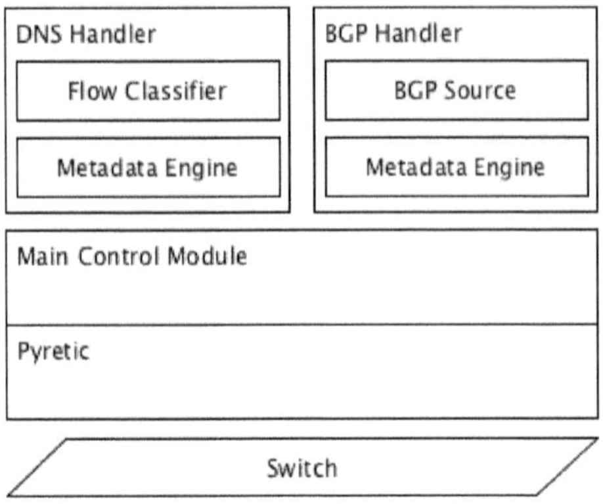


**Figure 1: NetAssay architecture**

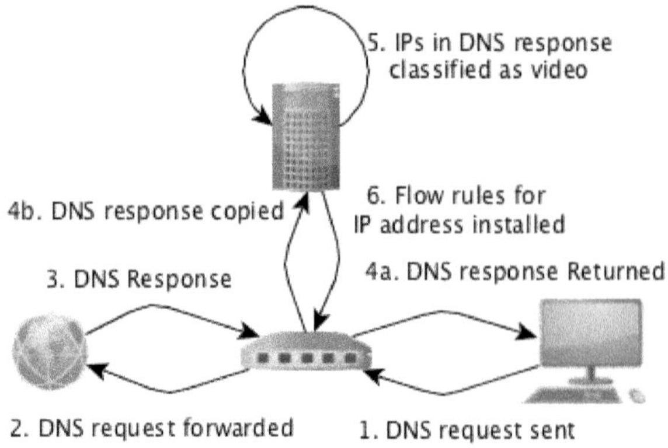


**Figure 2: Behavior of NetAssay's DNS handler classifying a video flow.**

monitoring network flows or from external data sources. The monitoring modules are designed such that new modules can be added in the future.

## 2.2 DNS and BGP Handlers

For the initial implementation, there are two modules being developed. Both are similar in design, but use different sources of information. The first, a DNS-based handler, will be described in detail, while the BGP-based handler will be quickly described.

The DNS handler which contains two parts, a flow classifier based on part of FlowQoS [4] and a metadata engine. To perform flow classification, two pieces of information are needed: URL-to-classification mapping and IP-to-URL mapping. The URL-to-classification mapping is mentioned above where `googlevideo.com` maps to 'video'. This is a manual lookup, implemented as regular expression matching. The IP-to-URL mapping is based on monitoring DNS responses. At initialization, rules are installed at all ingress network devices to make a copy of DNS responses, forward one to the actual destination, and forward the second to the DNS handler. The flow classifier then extracts the domains and associated IP addresses, and uses the URL-to-classification mapping to determine what type of traffic is associated with a particular IP address. The metadata engine handles policy implementation for DNS-based classification. The metadata engine is responsible for breaking down the high-level policies passed from the MCM into the constituent components, and handling any changes that my occur dynamically (*i.e.*, when a new DNS response comes in, or DNS response time-to-live (TTL) is reached). It is also responsible for aggregating data, such as aggregating the number of bytes transferred by video sources.

To go over the example above, if during the example above a DNS response from `googlevideo.com` with associated IP of 198.51.100.8 was seen, the URL will be classified as video, and, as such, traffic coming from 198.51.100.8 would be classified as video. This will cause the `matchClass` policy to generate a new `match` action to run in parallel with any preexisting actions associated with video traffic.

To allow for rules based on traffic related to a particular AS, BGP information is necessary. NetAssay uses an external source of BGP information. This could be a connection to a local BGP server, or could be a static database of known routes. The BGP information source plays a similar role to the Flow Classifier in the DNS handler: it provides a lookup source for AS routes, and, more importantly, ranges of addresses controlled by a particular AS.

## 3. PROGRESS AND FUTURE WORK

Work on NetAssay is ongoing. Design work on the two handlers is complete, with implementation and testing ongoing. Triggered behaviors is the current area of focus. Further simplification to reduce the policy in the introduction to be a single line, is desired.

Future work, beyond finishing implementation and testing, primarily focuses on optimization. Proactive DNS look ups from various public DNS sources provides a broader data set. Additionally, handling conflicts between handlers' policies needs to be addressed, both with data flows and potential 'double counting' between multiple handlers.

Further work incorporating this system into an Internet Exchange Point, particularly in the form of SDX [2], is a natural next step

## 4. REFERENCES

[1] J. R. Ballard, I. Rae, and A. Akella. Extensible and scalable network monitoring using opensafe. *Proceedings of USENIX Internet Network Management Workshop/Workshop on Research on Enterprise Networking*, 2010.

[2] A. Gupta, L. Vanbever, M. Shahbaz, S. Donovan, B. Schlinker, N. Feamster, J. Rexford, S. Shenker, R. Clark, and E. Katz-Bassett. Sdx: A software defined internet exchange. *Proceedings of the ACM SIGCOMM 2014 conference*, 2014. To Appear.

[3] J. Reich, C. Monsanto, N. Foster, J. Rexford, and D. Walker. Modular sdn programming with pyretic. *USENIX ;login,*, 38(5):128–134.

[4] M. S. Seddiki, M. Shahbaz, S. Donovan, S. Grover, M. Park, N. Feamster, and Y.-Q. Song. Flowqos: Qos for the rest of us. *HotSDN 2014*, 2014. To Appear.

[5] S. Shin and G. Gu. Cloudwatcher: Network security monitoring using openflow in dynamic cloud networks. *20th IEEE International Conference on Network Protocols*, 2012.

# OpenSAN: A Software-defined Satellite Network Architecture

Jinzhen Bao, Baokang Zhao, Wanrong Yu, Zhenqian Feng, Chunqing Wu, Zhenghu Gong
College of Computer
National University of Defense Technology
Changsha, Hunan, China
jzbao89@gmail.com, {bkzhao, wlyu, zqfeng, wuchunqing, gong}@nudt.edu.cn

## ABSTRACT
In recent years, with the rapid development of satellite technology including On Board Processing (OBP) and Inter Satellite Link (ISL), satellite network devices such as space IP routers have been experimentally carried in space. However, there are many difficulties to build a future satellite network with current terrestrial Internet technologies due to the distinguished space features, such as the severely limited resources, remote hardware/software upgrade in space. In this paper, we propose OpenSAN, a novel architecture of software-defined satellite network. By decoupling the data plane and control plane, OpenSAN provides satellite network with high efficiency, fine-grained control, as well as flexibility to support future advanced network technology. Furthermore, we also discuss some practical challenges in the deployment of OpenSAN.

## Categories and Subject Descriptors
C.2.1 [**Network Architecture and Design**]: Centralized networks, Network communications

## Keywords
Satellite Network, Software-Defined Network

## 1. INTRODUCTION
In recent years, the development of satellite technologies such as OBP and ISL has greatly promoted the development of satellite network [1]. The traditional approach of satellite network is bent pipe, which means that all the packets are transmitted from transmission terminal to an intermediate station, and then relayed to the reception terminal. This approach simplifies the architecture of satellite payload, but leads to a long latency because of two-hop communication. The OBP indicates that the satellite payload has the capabilities to support signal regeneration, packet switching and so on. Compared with Bent Pipe, OBP enhances the utilization of resources and decreases the communication time. There are two types of OBP according to its orbits. One is GEO, such as IRIS. The IRIS JCTD placed an IP router payload on a Geostationary Earth Orbit (GEO) satellite to accelerate network-centric capabilities in space [2]. It has a great improvement in the delay compared with bent pipe technology. The other one is Low Earth Orbit (LEO)/ Medium Earth Orbit (MEO), such as Teledesic. Teledesic is a constellation of Low Earth Orbit (LEO) communication satellites connected by ISL. The advantage of LEO with OBP is small delay and full connectivity, but it makes the management and routing more complex [3]. Since the OBP supports on-board switching and the satellites connect with each other by ISL, applying the mature and future advanced technologies of terrestrial Internet to satellite network become possible.

However, there are many difficulties to build a future satellite network with current terrestrial Internet technologies. (1) The resources of satellite nodes are severely limited. (2) The satellite network is closed and scheduled, so the maintenance, upgrade and expansion of satellite network are difficult. (3) As the topology changes frequently, it is difficult to maintain the stability of satellite network. The static routing algorithm used in satellite network which is called snapshot is inflexible and lacks the ability of fault tolerance. However, the dynamic routing algorithm is resource-consuming. Therefore, it requires a mechanism to balance the flexibility and cost. (4) The number of new services and applications increases fast, but the satellite payload cannot identify various kinds of new services.

To address the above issues, we propose OpenSAN, a novel architecture of software-defined satellite network. By decoupling the data plane and control plane of each satellite [4], OpenSAN provides satellite network with efficiency, fine-grained control, as well as flexibility to support future advanced network technology.

## 2. AN OVERVIEW OF OPENSAN
The overview of our software-defined satellite network architecture is shown in Fig. 1. It contains three parts: Data Plane (Satellite infrastructure, terminal router), Control Plane (GEO Group) and Management Plane (Network Operations and Control Center).

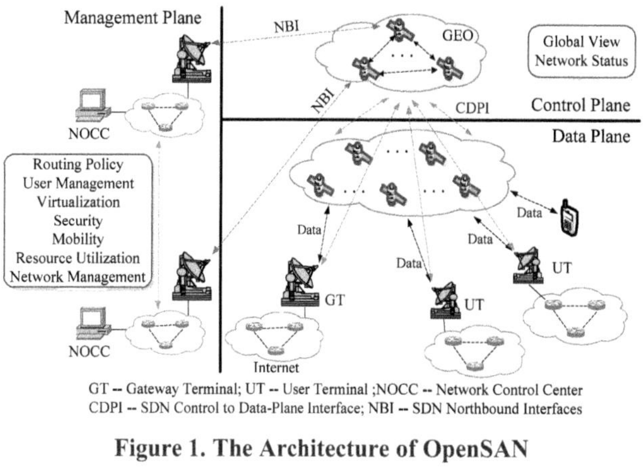


**Figure 1. The Architecture of OpenSAN**


*SIGCOMM'14*, August 17–22, 2014, Chicago, Illinois, USA.
ACM 978-1-4503-2836-4/14/08.
http://dx.doi.org/10.1145/2619239.2631454

## 2.1 Data Plane: Satellite infrastructure

The data plane consists of the terminal router distributed around the world and the multi-layered satellite infrastructure (such as GEO, MEO, LEO). The satellites and routers run flow table "match-action" protocol and focus on packets forwarding. The protocol matches the header of each packet such as IP address, port and user-defined segment to support forwarding, multicast, virtual network, access management, IPv6 and so on. The multi-layered satellite network has distinguished features. For example, the GEO satellite has a long delay but its link is reliable. On the contrary, the delay of LEO satellite is short. Therefore by choosing different routes, the multi-layered satellite network can guarantee the QoS of various services.

Since OpenSAN decouples the satellite and router from the control plane, the data plane is more flexible and controllable based on fine-grained flow table. And it also makes the device tend to be standard and decreases the cost.

## 2.2 Control Plane: GEO Group

Due to the ability of reliable link, wide coverage, broadcasting and stationary to the ground, the GEO satellite is suitable to control the data plane. As three GEO satellites can cover the earth, the GEO Group consists of at least three GEO satellites to cover the whole data plane. GEO Group is a logically centralized entity which focuses on 1) translating the rules from management plane to the data plane, 2) monitoring the satellite network's status (link status, network traffic, different flow status) information through CDPI interface, and then sending to the management plane for an abstract view of the satellite network. Compared with the traditional satellite monitoring and control system, OpenSAN reduces the number of ground stations and simplifies the process of control flow.

As shown in Fig. 2, there are three topologies of GEO Group distinguished by reliability and complexity. In Fig. 2(a), the GEO controllers communicate with NOCC via a primary GEO, this topology is suited to a small scale of data plane. In Fig. 2(b), the topology chooses a primary Ground Station to centralized relay the packets, which reduces the burden of primary GEO. And in Fig. 2(c), the topology increases the reliability by distributed NOCCs, but it requires a protocol to keep the consistency of satellite network.

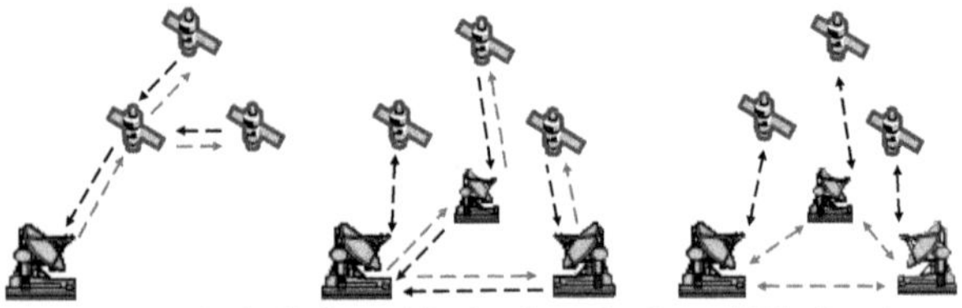


**Figure 2. The topology of GEO controller**

## 2.3 Management Plane: NOCC

NOCC is the management plane of the multi-layered satellite network. It runs different modules for various kinds of applications, such as routing policy calculation, virtualization, security, resources utilization and mobility management. The applications depend on the satellite network's status provided by GEO Group. For example, when a mobile terminal joins the network, NOCC has to recalculate routing policy and translate the new flow table down to data plane.

# 3. PRELIMINARY ANALYSIS

The centralized topology of OpenSAN has a significant progress in decreasing the link bandwidth compared with the traditional dynamic routing protocols. For example, OSPF routing protocol sends $O(n^2)$ packets, $n$ is the number of routers. All link states are broadcasted to every router and each of them calculates the route based on the Dijkstra algorithm. In OpenSAN, the GEO Group needs to collect the status of data plane, and the NOCC performs routing calculation. Then it broadcasts the route updates to the data plane leading to a $O(n)$ cost.

# 4. DYNAMIC SDN CONTROL STRATEGY

Different from traditional fixed or mobile networks, the satellites (mainly LEO) in the Data Plane run quickly around the earth, which makes the topology of the whole network change frequently. And another problem is that the user traffic changes with the time and location. All these characteristics of satellite network pose challenges to the present SDN control strategy.

Fortunately, the satellite is regular and predictable. So the applications and controller can predict the status of the whole network. In OpenSAN, we can use prediction-based algorithm such as neural network to aware the change of the whole network. Combining with back-up flow table, it can avoid the disruption of service. And we will further explore the design of NBI and CDPI to achieve a reliable and efficient control path.

# 5. ACKNOWLEDGMENTS

The work described in this paper is supported by the project of National Science Foundation of China under grant No.61202488, No.61103182, No.61379147 the program for Changjiang Scholars and Innovative Research Team in University (No.IRT1012).

# 6. REFERENCES

[1] AJIBESIN, A.A., BANKOLE, F.O., and ODINMA, A.C., 2009. A review of next generation satellite networks: Trends and technical issues. In Proc. AFRICON, 2009, 1-7.

[2] FLORIO, M.A., FISHER, S.J., MITTAL, S., YAGHMOUR, S., JANSSON, G., HEUSER, D., MURRAY, P.L., WORTHEN, A.P., and CUEVAS, E.G., 2007. Internet Routing in Space: Prospects and Challenges of the IRIS JCTD. In Proc. MILCOM 2007. IEEE, 1-6.

[3] Satellite Orbits for Communications Satellites. In Handbook of Satellite Applications, Springer New York, 93-114.

[4] MCKEOWN, N., ANDERSON, T., BALAKRISHNAN, H., PARULKAR, G., PETERSON, L., REXFORD, J., SHENKER, S., and TURNER, J., 2008. OpenFlow: enabling innovation in campus networks. SIGCOMM Comput. Commun. Rev. 38, 2, 69-74.

# SENSS: Observe and Control Your Own Traffic in the Internet

Abdulla Alwabel
USC/ISI

Minlan Yu
USC

Ying Zhang
Ericsson Research

Jelena Mirkovic
USC/ISI

## ABSTRACT

We propose a new software-defined security service – SENSS – that enables a victim network to request services from remote ISPs for traffic that carries source IPs or destination IPs from this network's address space. These services range from statistics gathering, to filtering or quality of service guarantees, to route reports or modifications. The SENSS service has very simple, yet powerful, interfaces. This enables it to handle a variety of data plane and control plane attacks, while being easily implementable in today's ISP. Through extensive evaluations on realistic traffic traces and Internet topology, we show how SENSS can be used to quickly, safely and effectively mitigate a variety of large-scale attacks that are largely unhandled today.

## Categories and Subject Descriptors

C.0 [**Computer-Communication Networks**]: General—*security and protection*; C.2.3 [**Network Operations**]: Network Management,Network Monitoring

## General Terms

Security,Design

## Keywords

Security, Privacy, SDN, Design, Management

## 1. INTRODUCTION

With a rapidly growing number of critical as well as business applications deployed on the Internet today, network attacks have both become more lucrative for the attackers and more damaging to the victims. Data plane attacks, such as distributed denial-of-service (DDoS), can render the victim unoperational for days [5], and can impact Internet services such as routing infrastructure. Control plane misconfigurations and attacks on the interdomain routing protocol BGP [2, 4] can also have dire implications for victim networks, leading to traffic rerouting, sniffing, modification or dropping.


*SIGCOMM'14*, August 17–22, 2014, Chicago, IL, USA.
ACM 978-1-4503-2836-4/14/08.
http://dx.doi.org/10.1145/2619239.2631459 .

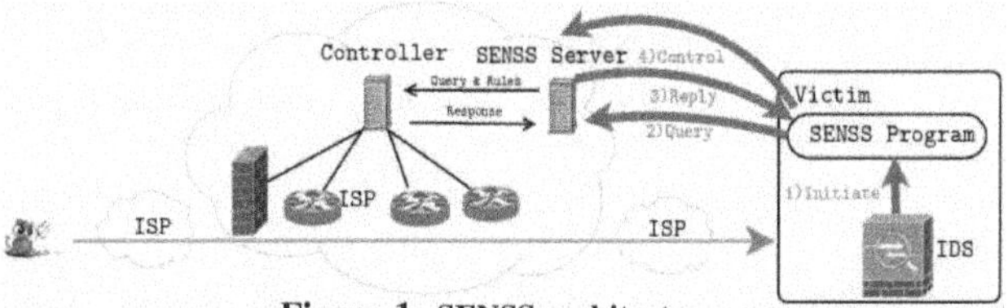


**Figure 1: SENSS architecture.**

Many solutions have been proposed to detect and mitigate *individual* attacks in data plane and control plane at the victim or at the victim's ISP. While many attack instances can be handled by the victim and its ISP, there will always exist attacks that cannot be diagnosed or mitigated without help from remote networks.Today's Internet lacks such *wide-scale, general service for automated multi-ISP collaboration on security problem diagnosis and mitigation.*

There have been numerous research works security solutions that require inter-ISP collaboration. However, these proposals are still not deployed today because of three reasons: (1) Focus on detection or mitigation of one attack type or variant; (2) Requirement for complex changes of the data plane or new router functionalities, which are difficult to achieve; (3) Lack of proper incentives for ISPs to collaborate with each other.

## 2. SENSS

Inspired by software-defined networking, which provides a simple interface (flow-based rules) to facilitate the advancement of networking protocols, we propose SENSS – Software dEfiNed Security Service. SENSS enables an end network to request help from remote ISPs to observe and control its traffic and routes, to diagnose and mitigate a variety of Internet attacks. SENSS has three key features:

**Simple and expressive interfaces at ISPs:** SENSS introduces simple interfaces for victims to request services from remote ISPs including traffic query, traffic control, route query, and route control. These interfaces are expressive to support the detection/mitigation of a variety of attacks.

**Victim oriented programming for diverse attacks:** The victim can make strategic decisions on which actions to take and where, based on the information it gathers from SENSS, combined with the victim's knowledge of its network, business and priorities.

**Incentives for SENSS adoptions.** End networks have every incentive to use SENSS, since they receive much needed help and they pay only when they use the service. It is economically appealing for ISPs because they can charge the victims for the services they provide. Also, the information and services exposed by SENSS interfaces are similar to those that today's ISPs already perform for their direct customers.

We give an overview of the SENSS architecture in Figure 1. A SENSS-deploying AS (called *SENSS AS*) provides SENSS service

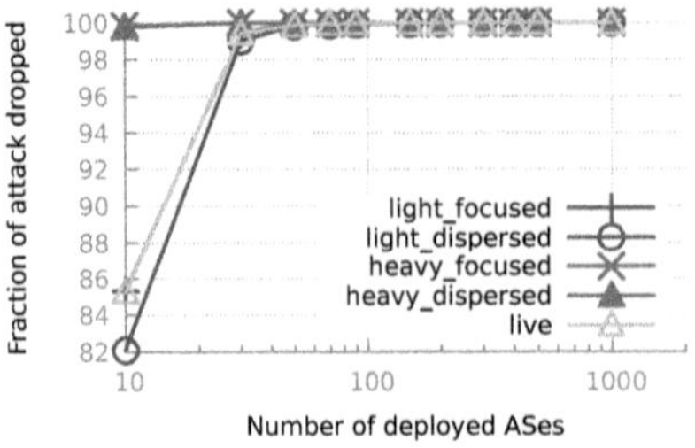


**Figure 2: Attack bandwidth eliminated.**

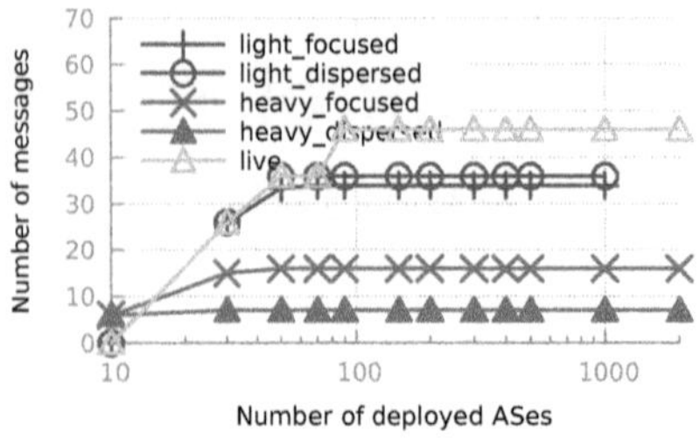


**Figure 3: #queries to drop 95% attack.**

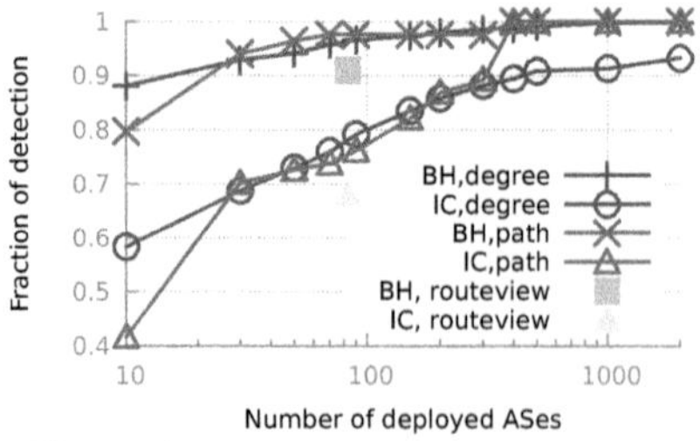


**Figure 4: Accuracy in partial deployment**

| Attack | Query | Control |
|---|---|---|
| DDoS w/ signature | Traffic queries | Traffic filter based on signatures at identified ASes |
| DDoS w/o signature | Traffic queries to get and compare traffic distribution | Non-specific traffic filters at identified ASes |
| DDoS reflection | Reduces to DDoS w/ or w/o signature, depending on attack details | |
| Crossfire | Traffic queries to identify bottlenecks | Bandwidth guarantees at identified ASes |
| Blackholing | Route queries to detect the bogus route | Route demotion to reduce the false route's propagation |
| Interception | Route queries to obtain control plane routes; Traffic queries to obtain data plane paths | Route modification to change the false path segment at polluted ASes |

**Table 1: Example SENSS Applications**

by exposing query and control interfaces. The victim first detects it is under attack through local observations, and initiates attack diagnosis. It queries multiple ASes about its traffic or about the AS's routes to victim prefixes. Then, the victim analyzes the replies to its queries locally, to identify best action to take and best locations for remediation. Finally, it issues control messages to chosen SENSS ASes to mitigate the attack. The communications between the victim and ASes are authenticated and encrypted.

In reality, there will be only a few ASes deploying SENSS at the beginning. We assume that Tier 1 and Tier 2 ASes are more likely to be the first to deploy SENSS. We show some example applications in Table 1.

# 3. EVALUATION

We developed a simulator in C++ to simulate both the DDoS attacks and the prefix hijacking attacks on AS-level Internet topology. We also implemented different victim programs for different attacks. These programs interact with SENSS ASes by sending queries to the ASes, making decisions based on the replies, and sending more queries or control commands. To simulate DDoS attacks, we setup up some attack and legitimate traffic flows on our AS topology. To simulate prefix hijacking, each time, we select one attacker and one victim, and let the attacker hijacks the victim's route by announcing the victim's prefix either as its origin AS (blackholing) or as an immediate next hop to the neighbor AS (interception).

## 3.1 Data plan attacks

For brevity, we focus on several variants of DDoS attacks and describe how to use SENSS to diagnose and mitigate them. Real victims are likely to deploy their own decision process when handling real attacks, that may not resemble what we describe here.

The victim seeks to deploy filters at enough remote SENSS ASes to drop most of the attack traffic. To achieve this, the victim first sends traffic queries the attack signature to identify the ASes with high attack traffic, and then installs traffic filters at these ASes.

In some DDoS attacks the victim cannot identify a useful signature. The victim install filters at points carried little traffic before attack that carry a lot in the attack. In Figure 2 we show the median percentage of attack traffic eliminated. With light attacker distribution we need 30 deployment points to eliminate more than 95% of the attack, while with heavy attacker distribution we can achieve this with 10 deployment points. Figure 3 show the number of messages (queries and filters, together) required to achieve 95% attack filtering. For all traffic distributions less than 36 messages are needed.

## 3.2 Control Plane Attacks

In the control plane, attackers leverage prefix hijacking either to absorb the victim's traffic (*i.e.,* blackholing) or to divert the traffic (*i.e.,* interception), to inspect it or to modify it, before sending it to the victim. In both blackholing and interception attacks, victim communicates with the small number of chosen ASes, sending *route queries* to obtain the control plane routing information and *traffic queries* to identify the victim's traffic distribution. To identify best SENSS ASes to query the victim first builds an AS-level Internet topology, e.g., from sources like Routeviews [1], and annotates it with AS relationships, e.g., using algorithm [3]. Blackholing is mitigated by either downgrades the malicious route or promotes the victim's route, by sending route demotion messages to a number of SENSS ASes. To mitigate interception attacks, the victim modifies the control plane to match the data plane by asking a few ASes to correct their route to the victim.

For mitigation, the victim may ask all the deployed ASes to perform the *route control*, which will correct as many polluted ASes as possible. However, to minimize the number of control requests, it may also try to select a small set of SENSS ASes to perform mitigation.

Figure 4 shows that with 30 ASes deployed, the detection accuracy can reach 90% for BH and 70% for IC. After that, the accuracy increases slower with more deploying ASes.

# 4. REFERENCES

[1] University of Oregon Route Views Archive Project. www.routeviews.org.

[2] V. J. Bono. 7007 Explanation and Apology. NANOG 97-04.

[3] L. Gao. On Inferring Autonomous System Relationships in the Internet. In *Proc. IEEE Global Internet Symposium*, 2000.

[4] M. Lad, R. Oliveira, B. Zhang, and L. Zhang. Understanding resiliency of internet topology against prefix hijack attacks. In *DSN*, 2007.

[5] T. N. Y. Times. How the Cyberattack on Spamhaus Unfolded. http://www.nytimes.com/interactive/2013/03/30/technology/how-the-cyberattack-on-spamhaus-unfolded.html.

# Locating Throughput Bottlenecks in Home Networks

Srikanth Sundaresan[†], Nick Feamster[†], Renata Teixeira[‡]
[†]Georgia Tech [‡]INRIA

## Abstract

We present a demonstration of *WTF (Where's The Fault?)*, a system that localizes performance problems in home and access networks. We implement WTF as custom firmware that runs in an off-the-shelf home router. WTF uses timing and buffering information from passively monitored traffic at home routers to detect both access link and wireless network bottlenecks.

**Categories and Subject Descriptors:** C.2.3 [Computer-Communication Networks] *Network Operations*: Network Management; C.2.3 [Computer-Communication Networks] *Network Operations*: Network Monitoring

**General Terms:** Measurement, Performance

**Keywords:** bottleneck location; home networks; performance diagnosis; troubleshooting

## 1 Introduction

We develop an algorithm and tool that determines whether network performance bottlenecks lie inside or outside the home network. *WTF (Where's The Fault?)* runs on commodity home routers and detects access link and wireless bottlenecks in a home network. WTF uses timing and buffering information from passively monitored traffic to design two maximum likelihood detectors: one detects access link bottlenecks and the other detects wireless network bottlenecks. Together, these detectors allow us to infer properties of the network and the most likely location of performance problems. These detectors can be easily measured from resource-constrained home routers. Although WTF does not determine *why* a particular bottleneck or problem exists, it takes an important first step in helping users and ISPs determine *where* the problem exists, at least to the granularity of whether the problem is inside or outside the home.

To deploy WTF in as many homes as possible, we implemented it as custom firmware that runs on a commodity home router. Although this approach allows us to collect measurements on a low-cost device that users are familiar with (and hence, more than willing and able to install), it introduces a unique set of challenges because the device is resource constrained. This environment makes it difficult to apply existing bottleneck detection and wireless analysis tools [1, 2], since they typically require additional affordances (*e.g.*, multiple wireless vantage points, significant trace collection). WTF works within these constraints and only collects lightweight passive measurements and conducts lightweight data processing on the home router.


*SIGCOMM'14*, August 17–22, 2014, Chicago, IL, USA.
Copyright 2014 ACM 978-1-4503-2836-4/14/08
http://dx.doi.org/10.1145/2619239.2631440

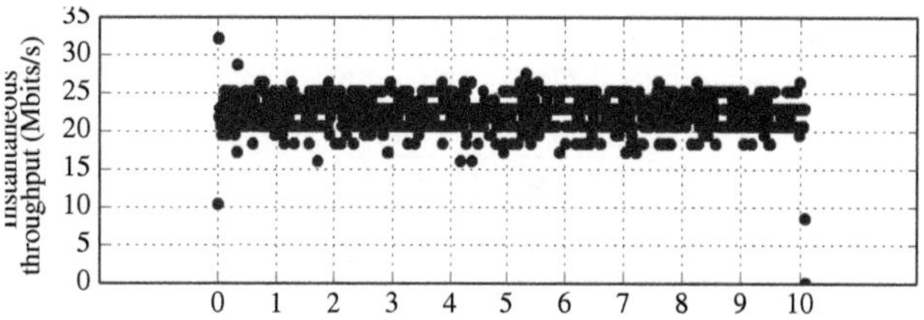


**(a) Access link is not the bottleneck.** *Instantaneous throughput at the WAN interface varies at short time scales due to high variance in packet inter-arrival times.*

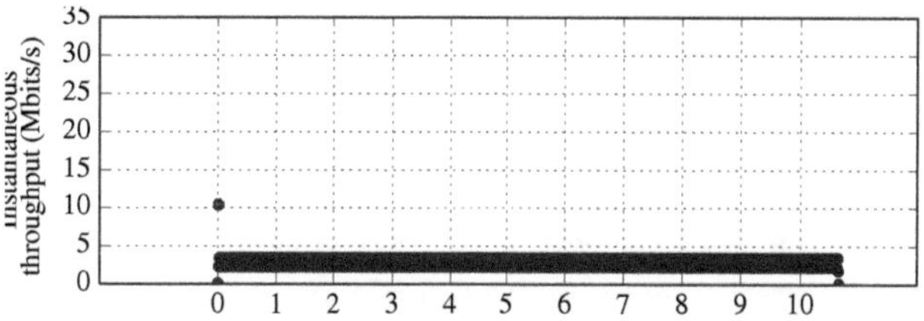


**(b) Access link is the bottleneck.** *Instantaneous throughput at the WAN interface is steady, due relatively uniform packet interarrival times caused by upstream shaping.*

**Figure 1:** *Behavior of packet inter-arrival times.*

## 2 Detection Algorithm

We exploit a fundamental property of bottleneck links: *packets buffer at the head of the bottleneck queue.* This property manifests itself in two ways from the point of view of the access point depending on the location of the bottleneck.

**Access link bottleneck.** *We use the intuition that bottleneck links smooth packet arrival rates.* Because a bottleneck link services packets at a rate slower than they arrive, queues build up at the link, and the link paces packets at an even rate. Packets upstream of the bottleneck will arrive according to the natural variation induced by TCP congestion control, but packets are more evenly spaced downstream of the bottleneck link. We assume that the most likely bottleneck upstream of the home network is the access link, so *all* flows are buffered, which allows us to use the overall packet distribution for detection.

We expect to see high variance in packet interarrival times before the bottleneck link due to congestion control, but significantly lower variance after the bottleneck link itself because the buffer smoothes packet arrivals. Figure 1 shows this effect: It shows the instantaneous TCP throughput at a granularity of 10 ms, as measured from the gateway. In Figure 1a, the access link throughput is 100 Mbit-s/s; the wireless link is the bottleneck because the maximum TCP throughput it can support is about 21 Mbits/s. In Figure 1b, we shape the access link to 3 Mbits/s, significantly lower than the wireless capacity. In this case, throughput is less variable. Indeed, the coefficient of variation for packet interarrival times, $c_v$, when the

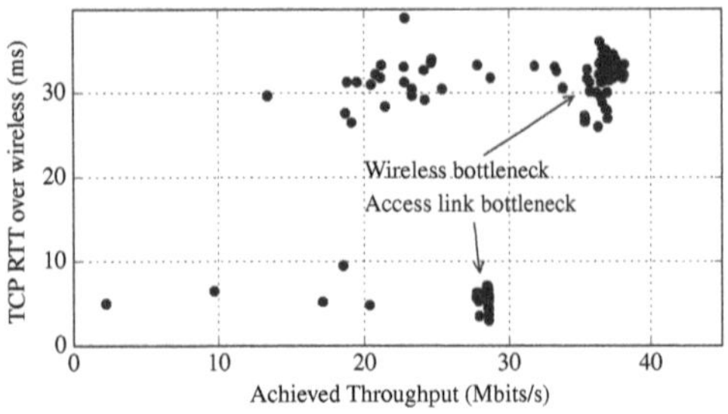


**Figure 2:** *TCP RTT between client and gateway. RTT is significantly higher when the wireless link is the bottleneck; this is caused by buffering.*

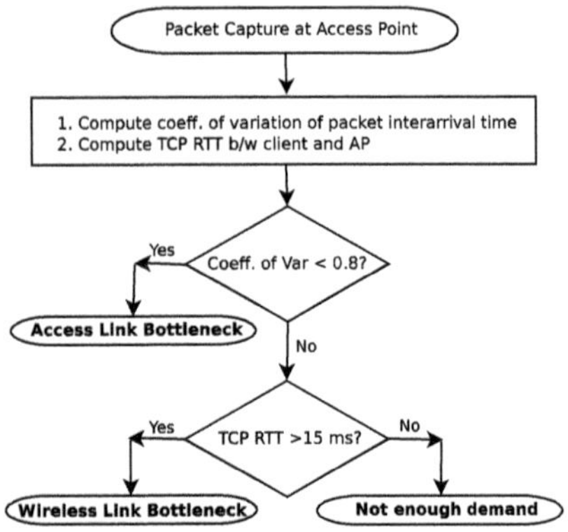


**Figure 3:** *Combining the two bottleneck detectors to create a single combined detection algorithm for access link bottlenecks (event B) and wireless bottlenecks (event W).*

access link is the bottleneck for this example is 0.05; in contrast, when it is *not* the bottleneck, $c_v$ is 0.88.

**Wireless bottleneck.** *We use the intuition that TCP round-trip time from the wireless router to the client is high if the wireless link is the bottleneck.* Queues build up at the head of a bottleneck link. Because we cannot view the wireless buffer directly without instrumenting the driver, we look at the impact of buffering on TCP flows. We run `tcptrace` on the traces we collect on the router to obtain the RTT of TCP flows, $\tau$, between the router and the clients in the local network. If the wireless link is not the bottleneck, the RTT is expected to be low, as the packet will dispatched without delay. Even though the wireless link is not work-conserving, the delays caused by medium access control are low compared to buffering delays.

Figure 2 illustrates this effect with an example. We run two tests in a setting where the wireless link capacity is about 40 Mbits/s (obtained by repeated measurements). In the first case, the access link is throttled to 30 Mbits/s, so it is always the bottleneck. In the second case, the access link is throttled to 70 Mbits/s so that the wireless link becomes the bottleneck. We see that there is a significant disparity in the TCP RTT in these two cases; when the wireless link is the bottleneck, the RTT is about 25–30 ms, while when the access link is the bottleneck, the RTT is about 5 ms. This effect does not depend on the achieved throughput; it depends solely on the occurrence of buffering.

**Putting it together.** We combine the access link and the wireless link bottleneck detectors using a simple algorithm. Figure 3 shows the algorithm. Both the detectors are simple threshold based; therefore there are four scenarios. When either the access link threshold or the wireless threshold is breached, we deem the corresponding link to be the bottleneck. When neither thresholds are breached, we

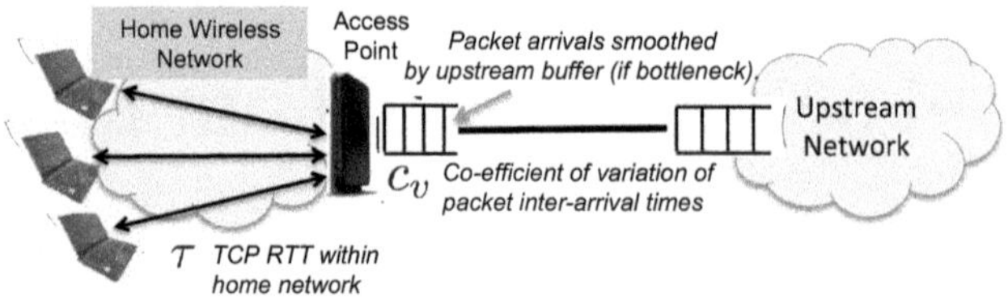


**Figure 4:** *WTF runs on the gateway between the home network and the access link, thus offering a unique vantage point for observing pathologies on either side.*

deem the bottleneck to be elsewhere, or the application demand to be insufficient. In our experiments, we model this by introducing latency or loss in the path so that TCP throughput is less than the access link and the wireless throughput—neither are the bottlenecks. The case when both the thresholds are breached is likely to happen only when the access link and the wireless link throughputs are closely matched, as there can only be one throughput bottleneck in the end-to-end path. We test all the above cases rigorously with controlled experiments. We obtained robust thresholds for both $c_v$ and $\tau$. We saw that testing for $c_v$ with a threshold of 0.8 and $\tau$ with a threshold of 15 ms produced more than a 95% true positive detection rate and less than a 5% false negative rate for all the cases (the algorithm produces similar results over a broad range of thresholds; we use the above values).

## 3 Demonstration Details

In our demo, we will show WTF working on a commodity home router. We will use an experiment setup as shown in Figure 4. We will use traffic controllers to vary the bandwidth, latency, and loss in the end-to-end path with wireless clients, and show how WTF accurately detects cases where there are throughput bottlenecks — both access link and wireless bottlenecks — and also cases where there are no throughput bottlenecks. The tool front-end will be a simple web page hosted on the router that is constantly refreshed with the current state of the access link and the wireless clients. We will also provide detailed information about the wireless network performance that each client gets (bitrates, retransmission rates, *etc.* ); this will allow us to better understand client performance. While we can conduct the demo without an upstream Internet connection, the demo will be enhanced with an Internet connection, especially as it will be easier to get more people to associate with our router wireless, and therefore emulate realistic scenarios.

## Acknowledgments

We thank Dina Papagiannaki and Yan Grunenberger for early discussions that led to development of Where's the Fault. This project is supported by NSF Award CNS-1059350, a Google Focused Research Award, and the European Community's Seventh Framework Programme (FP7/2007-2013) no. 258378 (FIGARO).

## References

[1] R. Mahajan, M. Rodrig, D. Wetherall, and J. Zahorjan. Analyzing the mac-level behavior of wireless networks in the wild. In *In Proc. ACM SIGCOMM*, pages 75–86, 2006.

[2] Y. Zhang, L. Breslau, V. Paxson, and S. Shenker. On the characteristics and origins of internet flow rates. In *Proc. ACM SIGCOMM*, Pittsburgh, PA, Aug. 2002.

# OpenANFV: Accelerating Network Function Virtualization with a Consolidated Framework in OpenStack


Xiongzi Ge[†], Yi Liu[§], David H.C. Du[†], Liang Zhang[‡], Hongguang Guan[‡], Jian Chen[‡], Yuping Zhao[‡] and Xinyu Hu[‡]

[†]Department of Computer Science and Engineering, University of Minnesota
[§]Shenzhen Institutes of Advanced Technology, Chinese Academy of Sciences
[‡]Huawei Corporation

xiongzi@cs.umn.edu, liuyi@siat.ac.cn, du@cs.umn.edu, zhangliang1@huawei.com



## Categories and Subject Descriptors

C.2.3 [**Network Operations**]: Network management

## Keywords

Network Function Virtualization; Middlebox; OpenStack; FPGA


## 1. INTRODUCTION

Specified appliances or *middleboxes* (MBs) have been explosively used to satisfy a various set of functions in operational modern networks, such as enhancing security (e.g. firewalls), improving performance (e.g. WAN optimized accelerators), providing QoS (e.g. Deep Packet Inspection (DPI)), and meeting the requisite others [3]. Network Function Virtualization (NFV) recently has been proposed to optimize the deployment of multiple network functions through shifting the MB processing from customized MBs to software-controlled inexpensive and commonly used hardware platforms (e.g. Intel standard x86 servers) [4]. However, for some functions (e.g. DPI and Network Deduplication (Dedup), Network Address Translation (NAT)), the commodity shared hardware substrate remain limited performance. For a standard software based Dedup MB (Intel E5645, 2.4GHZ, 6 cores, exclusive mode), we can only achieve 267Mbps throughput in each core at most. Therefore, the resources of dedicated accelerators (e.g. FPGA) are still required to bridge the gap between software-based MB and the commodity hardware.

To consolidate various hardware resources in an elastic, programmable and reconfigurable manner, we design and build a flexible and consolidated framework, OpenANFV, to support virtualized acceleration for MBs in the cloud environment. OpenANFV is seamlessly and efficiently put into Openstack to provide high performance on top of commodity hardware to cope with various virtual function requirements. OpenANFV works as an independent component to manage and virtualize the acceleration resources (e.g. *cinder* manages block storage resources and *nova* manages computing resources). Specially, OpenANFV mainly has the following three features.

- **Automated Management.** Provisioning for multiple VNFs is automated to meet the dynamic requirements of NFV environment. Such automation alleviates the time pressure of the complicated provisioning and configuration as well as reduces the probability of manually induced configuration errors.
- **Elasticity.** VNFs are created, migrated, and destroyed on demand in real time. The reconfigurable hardware resources in pool can rapidly and flexibly offload the corresponding services to the accelerator platform in the dynamic NFV environment.
- **Coordinating with OpenStack.** The design and implementation of the OpenANFV APIs coordinate with the mechanisms in OpenStack to support required virtualized MBs for multiple tenancies.



*SIGCOMM'14*, August 17–22, 2014, Chicago, IL, USA.
ACM 978-1-4503-2836-4/14/08.
http://dx.doi.org/10.1145/2619239.2631426.


## 2. ARCHITECTURE AND IMPLEMENTATION

Figure 1 briefly shows the architecture of OpenANFV. From the top-to-down prospective view, when a specific MB is needed, its required resources are orchestrated by OpenStack. There are sufficient northbound APIs in this open platform. Each VNF of MB is instantiated by a Virtual Machine (VM) node, running on the common x86 platform. Once deployed, these MBs aim to provide services as well as the original appliances. The role of *VNF controller* is to leverage the resource demand of VMs associated with underlying virtual resource pools.

*NFV Infrastructure* (NFVI) comes from the concept of *IaaS* to virtualize corresponding hardware resources. In NFVI, the *Network Functions Acceleration Platform* (NFAP) provides a heterogeneous PCIe based FPGA card which supports isolated *Partial Reconfigure* (PR) [5]. PR can virtualize and reconfigure the acceleration functions shortly in the same FPGA without affecting the exiting virtualized accelerators. Using PR, different accelerators are placed and routed in special regions.

The FPGA is divided into static and partially reconfigurable regions (PR). When the network requirements are changed, the function of PR could be replaced with a new

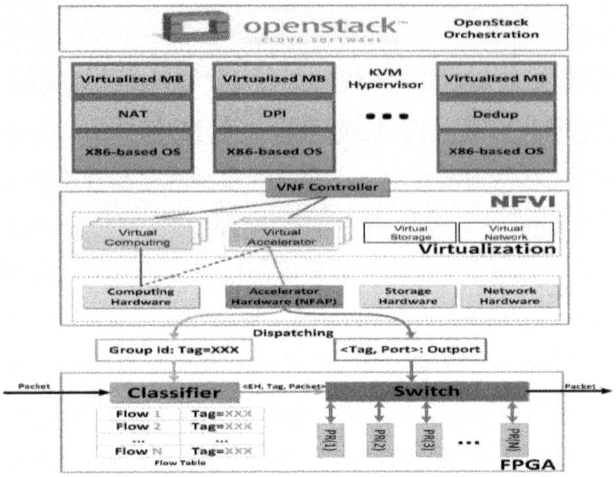


Figure 1: Brief OpenANFV architecture.

one. The PR is implemented to support different accelerators, and controlled by one VM exclusively. When one accelerator is reloading without affecting the other accelerators are not affected. The PR and VM can communicate through PCIe SR-IOV efficiently. The static region contains the shared resources (e.g. the storage and network interfaces).

The responsibility of NFAP is dispatching the rules to the two modules of FPGA, the *classifier* and the *switch*. The *classifier* identifies the flow where the rule format conforms to $\langle$*group id, tag*$\rangle$, when the flow matches the condition *group id*, classifier will add an item to the flow table in the classifier. Based on the flow table, the classifier could divide the traffic into different NFs. The switch get the MB chain configuration [$\langle$*Tag,Port*$\rangle$:*Outport*], and forward the encapsulated head (EH) based packet combining with the tag and income port. The packets are redirected to the MB in the chain in sequence until to the last one. The encapsulated packet with its tag can transfer more than one PRs, moreover, the tag could also support the load balancing between the NFs. Compared with FlowTags [2], we use the tag in the encapsulation to expand flexibly without affecting the field of the original packet header.

We have implemented the prototype of integrating NFAP into OpenStack following the methodology which is proposed by the ETSI standards group [1]. The K-V pair of <*vAccelerator, number of running vAccelerators*> is ued to track the current status of NFAP. *vAccelerator* is the aliased key to identify the PCIe device and *number of running vAccelerators* is to identify the current virtual accelerators. The scheduler has been finished in the *VNF controller* which is followed by the standard *nova scheduler*. Finally, the extended *VM.xml generation* includes allocation of a PCIe device virtual function to a VM.

# 3. EVALUATION AND CONCLUSION

We evaluate the prototype of NFAP in a demo FPGA cards (Altera FPGA Stratix A7, 8GB DDR3, 8M QDR, 4 SPF+). The experimental environment consists of one x86-based server (2.3GHz 8Core Intel Xeon E5, 96GB RAM, 40G NIC) with Altera FPGA card, two x86-based servers running the controller and OpenStack, respectively. The

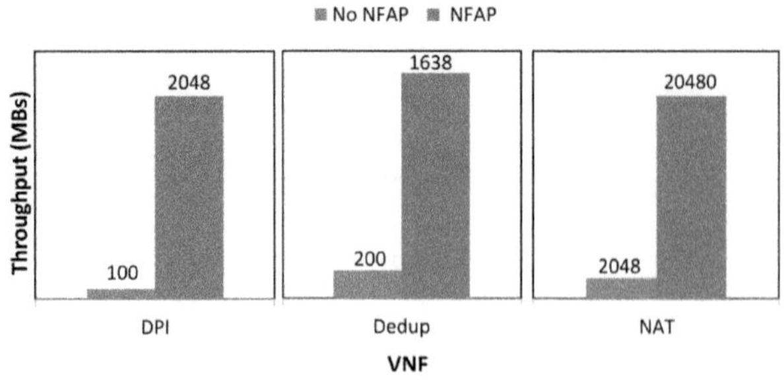


Figure 2: Performance results on throughput with or without adopting NFAP.

IXIA XM2(with NP8 board) is used as the source and the sink of packets. The server with the NFAP runs KVM hypervisor, and each NFAP could provide three empty PRs for the server. The VMs used for the test have the same configuration (1 vCPU, 16G RAM and 1TB Disk).

Our tests include three VNFs, NAT, DPI, and Dedup. Each VNF has two versions, with and without adopting NFAP. Without NFAP, the computing resources of VNFs are completely provided by *nova* in OpenStack. For NFAP assisted NAT, the software in the VM has an Openflow-like API with the NFV controller and configures the policy using a hardware abstract API. The hardware part in the NFAP offloads the flow table, the header replacement, and the checksum calculation from the VM. The packet will be merely processed in the NFAP, if the flow is matched in the flow table. For NFAP assisted DPI, we offload all the string match (Mutihash Algorithm and Bloomfilter), regular match, and the rules table in the NFAP, and the VM keeps the rule compiler and the statistics which are needed by the controller. The rule compiler compiles perl compatible regular expression to Deterministic Finite Automata (DFA) rule. For NFAP assisted Dedup, we offload the rabin hash, Marker select algorithm and chunk hash (Murmur hash). As the TCP is too complex to implement in the FPGA, the tcp-stack is still in the VM and the packets are received and sent out via the software tcp-stack. We still do some optimizations like using the Data Plane Development Kit (DPDK) driver and use space tcp-stack. As shown in Figure 2, the performance of DPI, Dedup, and NAT with adopting NFAP in OpenANFV outperforms the scheme without NFAP by 20X, 8.2X, and 10X, respectively.

# 4. REFERENCES

[1] Enhanced platform awareness for pcie devices. https://wiki.openstack.org/wiki/Enhanced-platform-awareness-pcie.

[2] Fayazbakhsh, S. K., Chiang, L., Sekar, V., Yu, M., and Mogul, J. C. Enforcing network-wide policies in the presence of dynamic middlebox actions using flowtags. In *Proc. 11th USENIX NSDI* (2014), USENIX Association, pp. 543–546.

[3] Gember, A., Grandl, R., Khalid, J., and Akella, A. Design and implementation of a framework for software-defined middlebox networking. In *Proceedings of the ACM SIGCOMM 2013* (2013), ACM, pp. 467–468.

[4] Martins, J., Ahmed, M., Raiciu, C., Olteanu, V., Honda, M., Bifulco, R., and Huici, F. Clickos and the art of network function virtualization. In *Proceedings of the 11th NSDI* (2014), USENIX, pp. 459–473.

[5] Yin, D., Unnikrishnan, D., Liao, Y., Gao, L., and Tessier, R. Customizing virtual networks with partial fpga reconfiguration. *ACM SIGCOMM Computer Communication Review 41*, 1 (2011), 125–132.

# Towards the Super Fluid Cloud

Filipe Manco, Joao Martins, Felipe Huici
NEC Europe Ltd.

## ABSTRACT

Traditionally, the number of VMs running on a server and how quickly these can be migrated has been less than optimal mostly because of the memory and CPU requirements imposed on the system by the full-fledged OSes that the VMs run. More recently, work towards VMs based on minimalistic or specialized OSes has started pushing the envelope of how reactive or fluid the cloud can be. In this demo we will demonstrate how to concurrently execute thousands of Xen-based VMs on a single inexpensive server. We will also show instantiation and migraion of such VMs in tens of milliseconds, and transparent, wide area migration of virtualized middleboxes by combining such VMs with the multi-path TCP (MPTCP) protocol.

## Keywords

cloud; performance; server consolidation; virtualization; xen

## 1. INTRODUCTION

In recent years, cloud and data centers deployments have become pervasive, largely as a result of the availability of inexpensive commodity servers, higher capacity network links and ever improving virtualization technologies. Services such as Amazon EC2 [1], Rackspace [11], and Microsoft Azure [9] are now commonplace, and even network operators are looking to get into the game by deploying so call micro-data centers at Points-of-Presence sites [5] in order to run applications such as CDN caches or virtualized middlebox processing [4] close to end users.

Traditionally, the number of VMs running on each server has been low, in the order of ten or so, mostly because of the memory and CPU requirements imposed on the system by the full-fledged OSes that the VMs run. Further, while it is commonplace to speak of clouds being elastic because such VMs can be easily instantiated, suspended and migrated, their size and complexity means that performing such operations can take in the order of seconds or worse (e.g., when migrating a VM hundreds of megabytes or bigger in size).


*SIGCOMM'14*, August 17–22, 2014, Chicago, IL, USA.
ACM 978-1-4503-2836-4/14/08.
http://dx.doi.org/10.1145/2619239.2631449.

More recently, work towards VMs based on minimalistic or specialized OSes (e.g., OSv [10], ClickOS [8], Mirage [7], Erlang on Xen [3], HalVM [6], etc.) has started pushing the envelope of how reactive or fluid the cloud can be. These VMs' small CPU and memory footprints (as little as a few megabytes) enable a number of scenarios that are not possible with traditional VMs.

First, such VMs have the potential be instantiated and suspended in tens of milliseconds. This means that they can be deployed on-the-fly, even as new flows arrive in a network, and can be used to effectively cope with flash crowds. Second, the ability to quickly migrate the VM and its state would allow operators to run their servers at "hotter" load levels without fear of overload, since processing could be near instantaneously moved to a less loaded server. Finally, these VMs' small memory footprints could potentially allow thousands or even more such VMs to run on a single, inexpensive server; this would lead to important investment and operating savings, and would allow for fine granularity, virtualized network processing (e.g., per-customer firewalls or CPEs, to name a couple).

Realizing such a super fluid cloud, however, poses a number of important challenges, since the virtualization technologies that these VMs run on (e.g., Xen or KVM) were never designed to run this large number of concurrent VMs. In the case of Xen [2], the system that this demo is based on, attempts to tackle *some* of the issues such as limited number of event channels or memory grants are under way, but these are still in their infancy and are not necessarily aiming to run the huge number of VMs we are envisioning.

In this demo we will demonstrate how to concurrently execute thousands of MiniOS-based guests [1] on a single inexpensive server. We will also show instantiation and migration of such VMs in tens of milliseconds, and transparent, wide area migration of virtualized middleboxes by combining such VMs with the multi-path TCP (MPTCP) protocol.

## 2. SYSTEM DESCRIPTION

We base our demo on Xen, a type 1 hypervisor (see figure 1). In order to keep the hypervisor efficient and secure, device drivers and the system's control plane are offloaded to a special virtual machine commonly running a standard Linux distribution and called the *control domain* or dom0 for short.

The control plane is based around the XenStore, a proc-like filesystem that keeps system and per-VM information

[1]MiniOS is a minimalistic, paravirtualized operating system distributed with the Xen sources.

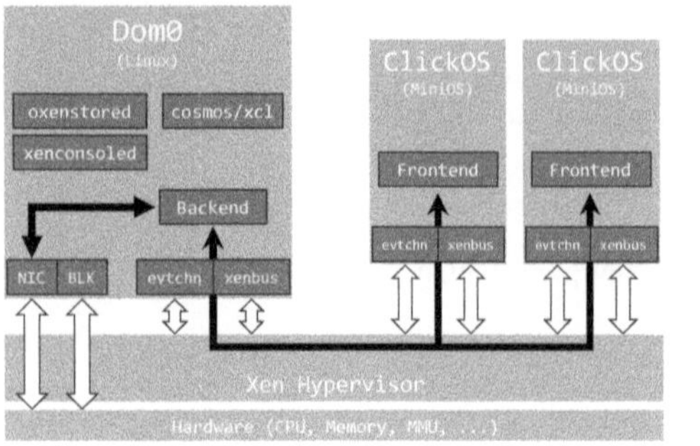


**Figure 1: System architecture.**

such as virtual CPUs, virtual interfaces and memory assignments. Users control Xen (e.g., to create VMs) by means of its *toolstack*: the `xl` command line tool, which in turn uses the `libxl` library to interact with Xen components. In terms of network I/O, Xen uses a split-driver model: a virtualized *netfront* driver resides in the VMs, and a complimentary *netback* driver sits in dom0. dom0 further includes a backend software switch to direct traffic from network drivers to the netback driver. Finally, event channels are essentially virtual interrupts used to signal the availability of packets.

For the actual virtual machine (also called a guest), we rely on MiniOS. More specifically, we use ClickOS virtual machines, which are basically guests running the Click modular router software on top of MiniOS (please see [8]).

**Our contribution:** Our work uses these guests to analyze bottlenecks when attempting to run large numbers of VMs, and implements and configures a number of improvements to the Xen ecosystem. These include (1) a lean version of the `libxl` library called `libxcl` which reduces the number of write operations to the XenStore from 37 to 17 per VM and contains less generic code (e.g., it removes code that handles full virtualization guests); (2) a new command line tool called `cosmos` to make use of `libxcl`; (3) a simplified virtual interface hotplug script for attaching interfaces to bridges; (4) placement of all relevant files (hotplug scripts, VM config files, VM images) on a RAM disk; (5) pinning of all vCPUs and reservation of one for the XenStore and another one for the XenConsole process; (6) addressing guests by ID rather than name (the latter causes toolstack code to sequentially go through all existing VM names); (7) use of multiple backend switches to overcome a maximum number of interfaces per switch limitation; and (8) increasing the maximum number of open files and virtual terminals in Linux in order to support the VMs' consoles. Finally, we implement support for suspending and resuming MiniOS guests which enables migration scenarios.

## 3. DEMO DESCRIPTION

In the demo we will show our early work towards booting large number of Xen-based guests on a single inexpensive x86 server, as well as quick migration of these VMs. Figure 2 plots the individual boot times of up to 10,000 ClickOS guests on a system with 4 AMD Opteron 6376@2.3GHz CPUs and 64GB of memory (costing about $3,500). As shown, the initial VMs take only tens of milliseconds to start, while the last ones still take under one second. The cumulative time to start all 10,000 VMs was about two hours, and we test the VMs by having them respond to a ping.

In greater detail, we will show (1) between 1K-2K ClickOS VMs booting and running; (2) operation times (create, suspend, resume, migrate) when large numbers of VMs are already running; and (3) transparent and quick migration of ClickOS middleboxes in a WAN by leveraging MPTCP. As future work we are looking into how to improve the Xen networking back-end to be able to cope with the potentially large traffic that so many VMs might generate or receive.

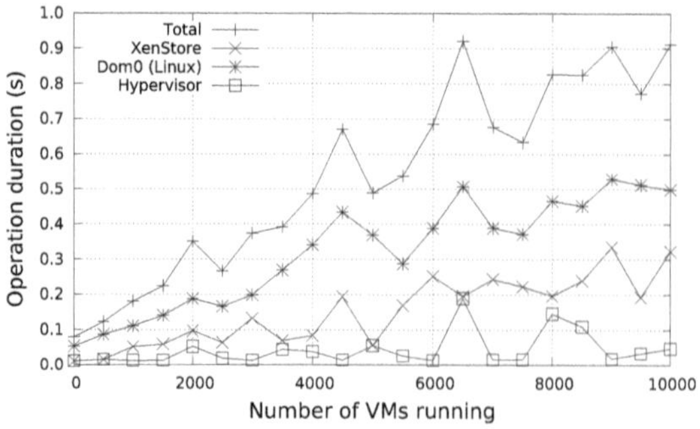


**Figure 2: Individual boot times for 10,000 ClickOS virtual machines on a single x86 server.**

## 4. REFERENCES

[1] Amazon. Amazon Elastic Compute Cloud (EC2). `https://aws.amazon.com/ec2/`, May 2014.

[2] P. Barham, B. Dragovic, K. Fraser, S. Hand, T. Harris, A. Ho, R. Neugebauer, I. Pratt, and A. Warfield. Xen and the Art of Virtualization. In *Proc. ACM SOSP, 2003*, New York, NY, USA, 2003. ACM.

[3] Erlang on Xen. Erlang on Xen. `http://erlangonxen.org/`, May 2014.

[4] ETSI Portal. Network Functions Virtualisation: An Introduction, Benefits, Enablers, Challenges and Call for Action. `http://portal.etsi.org/NFV/NFV_White_Paper.pdf`, October 2012.

[5] B. Frank, I. Poese, Y. Lin, G. Smaragdakis, A. Feldmann, B. Maggs, J. Rake, S. Uhlig, and R. Weber. Pushing cdn-isp collaboration to the limit. *SIGCOMM Comput. Commun. Rev.*, 43(3):34–44, July 2013.

[6] HalVM. The Haskell Lightweight Virtual Machine Source Archive. `https://github.com/GaloisInc/HaLVM`, May 2014.

[7] A. Madhavapeddy, R. Mortier, C. Rotsos, D. Scott, B. Singh, T. Gazagnaire, S. Smith, S. Hand, and J. Crowcroft. Unikernels: Library operating systems for the cloud. *SIGPLAN Not.*, 48(4):461–472, Mar. 2013.

[8] J. Martins, M. Ahmed, C. Raiciu, V. Olteanu, M. Honda, R. Bifulco, and F. Huici. ClickOS and the Art of Network Function Virtualization. In *Proc. USENIX NSDI*, April 2014.

[9] Microsoft Corporation. Azure: Microsoft's Cloud Platform. `azure.microsoft.com/`, May 2014.

[10] OSv. OSv - The Operating System Designed for the Cloud. `http://osv.io`, May 2014.

[11] Rackspace. Public Cloud Hosting, Computing, Storage and Networking. `http://www.rackspace.com`, May 2014.

# Ziria: Language for Rapid Prototyping of Wireless PHY

Gordon Stewart [1]
Princeton
gstew5@gmail.com

Mahanth Gowda [1]
UIUC
gowda2@illinois.edu

Geoffrey Mainland [2]
Drexel
mainland@cs.drexel.edu

Božidar Radunović
Microsoft Research
bozidar@microsoft.com

Dimitrios Vytiniotis
Microsoft Research
dimitris@microsoft.com

Doug Patterson
Microsoft
dougpatt@microsoft.com

## ABSTRACT

Software-defined radios (SDR) have the potential to bring major innovation in wireless networking design. However, their impact so far has been limited due to complex programming tools. Most of the existing tools are either too slow to achieve the full line speeds of contemporary wireless PHYs or are too complex to master. In this demo we present our novel SDR programming environment called Ziria. Ziria consists of a novel programming language and an optimizing compiler. The compiler is able to synthesize very efficient SDR code from high-level PHY descriptions written in Ziria language. To illustrate its potential, we present the design of an LTE-like PHY layer in Ziria. We run it on the Sora SDR platform and demonstrate on a test-bed that it is able to operate in real-time.

## 1. INTRODUCTION

The past few years have witnessed tremendous innovation in the design and implementation of wireless protocols, both in industry and academia ([7, 4, 2]). Much of the work has occurred at the physical (PHY) layer of the protocol stack, which manages the translation between radio hardware signals and protocol packets. The numerous new signal processing algorithms and novel coding schemes that have resulted—many of which were first implemented using software-defined radio (SDR) platforms—have greatly increased the efficiency of existing radio communication channels.

However, SDRs have not yet reached the mainstream of wireless research. The main impediment is implementation complexity. Wireless PHY algorithms have to be very fast and efficient to meet line rate requirements. Software has to process tens of millions of complex samples per second, which is equivalent to a processing rate of close to a gigabit per second. To cope with these speeds a programmer has to have a good understanding of the underlying SDR hardware architecture and the effects of her design choices on performance.

[1]This work was done during an internship with Microsoft Research.

[2]Part of the work was done while the author was with Microsoft Research.



*SIGCOMM'14*, August 17–22, 2014, Chicago, IL, USA.
ACM 978-1-4503-2836-4/14/08.
http://dx.doi.org/10.1145/2619239.2631427.

In order to design wireless algorithms, an SDR programmer has to have a profound understanding of signal processing and wireless networking, and in order to efficiently implement them she has to be an expert in computer architecture and system design. An average graduate student finds it quite hard to master all these areas, which is why only very few research groups have found enough resources to pursue this line of research.

To illustrate this complexity we consider two popular SDR designs. The first example is FPGA-based platforms, such as Warp [5] and Lyrtech [6]. A typical state-of-the-art SDR programming tool for FPGA platforms is based on Matlab, Simulink and an FPGA compiler. One of the main benefits of this environment is a rich set of DSP bulding blocks (such as basic fixed-point arithmetics, FFT, encoders, decoders, etc.). Further, being integrated in Matlab, this environment provides a programmer with powerful tools for debugging input and output signals, and for simulating different real-world effects using readily available libraries. However, the programming model is essentially the same as hardware design in VHDL or Verilog. A programmer has to have a fundamental understanding of how FPGAs operate. She has to be aware of different propagation delays and their effects on the system performance. One misplaced delay element can easily lead to a week of debugging!

Recently, several SDR platforms, such as GnuRadio [3] and Sora [8], allow programmers to design SDR code on general-purpose CPU processors. The hardware part of the platform performs analog-to-digital and digital-to-analog conversion of the baseband signals and supplies these signals to a CPU, where a programmer can further process it as desired.

Signal processing on a CPU provides great flexibility and permits rapid experimentation, but often at the price of decreased performance. Writing fast, real-time PHY code on a CPU can be equally, if not more complex than programming FPGAs. In fact, most of the recent academic works on SDR do not even attempt to process signals in real-time. They only use SDR platforms to capture signals. Post-processing is later done offline at much smaller processing rates than required by PHY. This approach clearly precludes any real-world networking experiments on SDR platforms.

One of the first CPU-based SDR platforms that has managed to process wireless baseband signals at a line rate is Sora [8]. It has demonstrated interoperability with commodity WiFi cards. But this performance comes with increased complexity. The code for Sora has to be written in C/C++ and a programmer needs to manually optimize the code to achieve the required speeds. The Sora project has put substantial effort into designing a C++ template library that eases the programming pain. However, the use of templates imposes several limitations, in particular on state sharing and dynamic reconfigurability of the dataflow graphs. It is worth noting that GnuRadio has a similar architecture based on C++ templates and similar limitations. We next overview the architecture of Ziria and we explain how it addresses these issues.

## 2. ZIRIA

Ziria is a new wireless programming platform. It consists of the Ziria language and an optimizing compiler. Ziria has a 2-layer design. The lower layer is an imperative language. It can be seen as a mix of C and Matlab code, with features of the two selectively choosen to guarantee efficient compilation. The higher layer is the language used to specify and stage stream processors.

The Ziria optimizing compiler consists of two parts. It has a front-end which parses a Ziria program and stores it in an abstract representation, and then performs several optimization passes on it. It also has a back-end which compiles the optimized abstract representation into a low-level execution model optimized for a target architecture. Our current back-end targets a low-level execution model in C for the Sora SDR platform, but it can easily be extended to other platforms, such as GnuRadio.

There are several benefits of this approach when compared to the existing approaches:

- *Dynamic staging of the control graph:* Ziria language for staging data flows allows for a dynamic reconfiguration of the control graph. This reconfiguration is very flexible, so for example a downstream component can reconfigure an upstream component or any other part of the graphs (for example using parameter passing and the repeat construct). This is in contrast with Sora and GnuRadio C++ templates that allow limited downstream reconfigurability using the multiplexing block.

- *No need for shared state:* Ziria dynamic reconfigurability and parameter passing between blocks eliminate the need for share states. Instead, a state is passed explicitly between components and all the dependencies are checked at the compile time. This is in contrast with Sora and GnuRadio which heavily rely on shared states. One example of a negative consequence is that an unitialized state cannot be detected by the compiler and causes program misbehaviour.

- *Code optimization:* Ziria compiler's optimization phase can optimize jointly the imperative part of the language and the data-flow graph. It can merge data-flow blocks, change input and output widths, inline expressions and unroll loops. One example of a useful code optimization are look-up tables. Ziria compiler can automatically identify blocks of code that operate on small bit inputs (e.g. scrambler and encoder) and convert them into lookup tables, which execute much faster on a CPU than bit operations. All this is in contrast to Sora and GnuRadio C++ template libraries where C compiler does not have an explicit understanding of the control flow graph and can perform far fewer optimizations. Lookup tables have to be implemented and tuned manually.

Overall, Ziria code is much more concise. For example, an implementation of a WiFi scrambler in Sora takes 90 lines of C++ code. The same code can be implemented in Ziria in 13 lines. It is easier to understand and has very similar performance to the hand-tuned Sora code.

## 3. DEMO DESCRIPTION

In the demo we present a Ziria implementation of an LTE-like PHY layer. The demo consists of two Sora SDR nodes. One node transmits a video transmission over the air and the other node receives it and plays it on the screen. All PHY code is developed entirely in Ziria. A real-time video transmission is a proof-of-concept of the real-time performance of Ziria.

Ziria is released as an open-source project. Further information about the project as well as a link to the code, examples and documentation can be found on [1].

## 4. REFERENCES


[1] Ziria. `http://research.microsoft.com/en-us/projects/ziria/`.

[2] T. Bansal et al. Symphony: Cooperative packet recovery over the wired backbone in enterprise WLANs. In *MOBICOM*, 2013.

[3] E. Blossom. GNURadio: tools for exploring the radio frequency spectrum. *Linux Journal*, 2004(122):4, 2004.

[4] T. Li et al. CRMA: Collision-resistant multiple access. In *MOBICOM*, 2011.

[5] P. Murphy, A. Sabharwal, and B. Aazhang. Design of WARP: a wireless open-access research platform. In *ESPC*, 2006.

[6] Nutaq. Zeptosdr. `http://nutaq.com/en/products/zeptosdr`.

[7] S. Sen, R. R. Choudhury, and S. Nelakuditi. No time to countdown: Migrating backoff to the frequency domain. In *MOBICOM*, 2011.

[8] K. Tan et al. Sora: High performance software radio using general purpose multi-core processors, 2009.

# Demonstrating the Optimal Placement of Virtualized Cellular Network Functions in Case of Large Crowd Events


Steffen Gebert, David Hock, Thomas Zinner, Phuoc Tran-Gia
University of Würzburg, Germany

Marco Hoffmann, Michael Jarschel, Ernst-Dieter Schmidt
Nokia
Munich, Germany

Ralf-Peter Braun
Deutsche Telekom T-Labs
Berlin, Germany

Christian Banse
Fraunhofer AISEC
Garching, Germany

Andreas Köpsel
BISDN
Berlin, Germany


## Categories and Subject Descriptors

C.2.3 [**Computer Systems Organization**]: Computer-Communication Networks—*Network Operations*


## Keywords

function placement, network functions virtualisation


## 1. INTRODUCTION

This demonstration highlights how Network Functions Virtualization (NFV) [1] can be used by a mobile network operator to dynamically provide required mobile core network functions for a large "Mega" event like a football game or a concert. Economic reasons may not justify the deployment or continuous maintenance of expensive dedicated hardware at the event site, which is necessary to cope with the extra load temporarily generated by the visitors.

The Evolved Packet Core (EPC) in nowadays' mobile LTE networks consists of several, specialized components: first, pure control plane elements like Mobility Management Entities (MME), which can be installed on virtualized IT hardware in the cloud. Second, gateways which are a mixture of control and user plane. Such a component is the Serving Gateway (SGW), which switches GTP (GPRS Tunneling Protocol) tunnels in LTE networks. Usually, per $\approx 10$ mio. subscribers, 10 SGW devices are in use and statically placed with respect to normal traffic demand. In case of "Mega" events, however, the spatial distribution of the traffic demand changes, resulting in the need to dynamically attach new SGWs to the LTE network for the duration of the event. This needed flexibility and on-demand behavior can be provided by virtualized network functions.



*SIGCOMM'14*, August 17–22, 2014, Chicago, IL, USA.
ACM 978-1-4503-2836-4/14/08
http://dx.doi.org/10.1145/2619239.2631428 .


To successfully deploy NFV-based EPC components, several challenges have to be addressed [2]. These include the deployment, interconnection, and configuration of LTE components in the cloud. Therefore, entities that instantiate and orchestrate the virtualized functions are required.

The presented demonstration illustrates a dynamic attachment of virtualized SGWs to an LTE network to support additional users, cf., Figure 1. New SGWs are placed in the network according to the varying traffic demands. This is achieved by reprogramming SDN-enabled network elements (NE+). Figure 1(a) shows the normal configuration of the LTE network with the static SGW and the NE+ that can be turned into virtual SGWs on demand. For better readability, non-reprogrammable network elements (NE) and base stations omitted. Figure 1(b) shows the situation with dynamic function placement. Large crowd events, indicated by stars of different sizes, lead to increased traffic demand. By reprogramming several NE+, additional demands can be handled. Depending on the number, size, and location of the events, an adequate number of NE+ has to be selected.

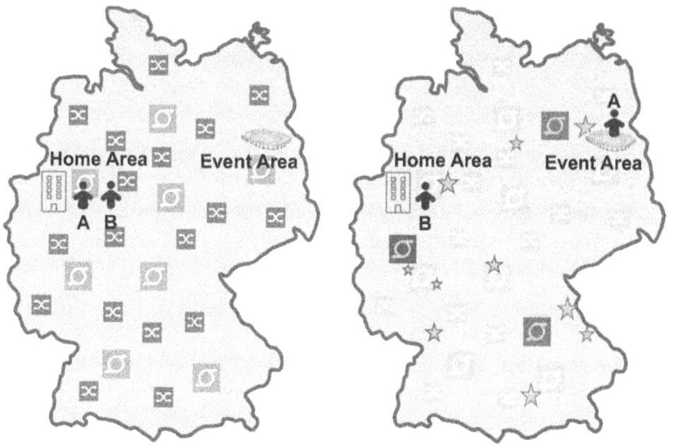


(a) Normal configuration. (b) Adaptive configuration using virtualized SGWs.

SGWs Reprogrammable NE+ Virtual SGWs ☆Crowd Events

**Figure 1: Dynamic function attachment to the LTE core network.**

In the following, the steps of the function placement are described and the involved tools introduced. Then, a sketch of the planned demonstration at SIGCOMM as well as the demonstration setup is provided.

## 2. DYNAMIC FUNCTION PLACEMENT

Figure 2 indicates the different steps of the dynamic capacity addition and gives an overview of the involved components. First, the SGW placement has to be optimized. In this demo, this step is performed by an extension of the POCO tool [3, 4]. POCO allows the consideration of trade-offs between different metrics, such as the number of additional SGWs, the maximum latency to the gateways, their processing capabilities, or load balancing on the SGWs. As second and third step, the dynamically added applications are deployed, interconnected, monitored, and configured. This is done by NOKIA's Cloud Application Manager (CAM) [5] based on OpenStack. For network operations and the triggering of CAM and POCO an NOKIA orchestration tool called Network Utilization Controller (NUC) is used.

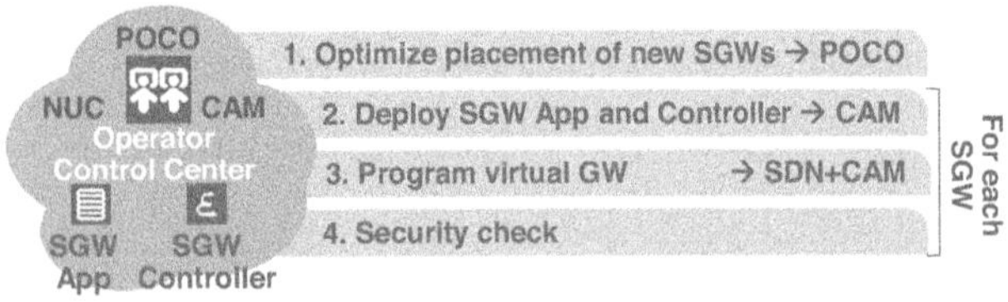


**Figure 2: Steps of dynamic capacity addition.**

## 3. SCENARIO AND DEMO PRESENTATION

In the presented demonstration, a "Mega" event use case is shown. Ann and Ben are living in a so-called home area and are subscribers to an LTE network. Together with many others, Ann is traveling to the event area, a stadium. Ben stays in the home area. This is indicated by the locations of the icons representing Ann and Ben in Figure 1. Figure 3 illustrates the considered scenario, including the normal situation Figure 3(a) and the event situation Figure 3(b).

The home area is a typical LTE network including base stations, an evolved packet core, and data centers. OpenStack is used to manage the mobile operator's cloud (data centers). The mobile network operator is aware of the situation that subscribers in the event area will extensively share pictures or videos and will make video calls resulting in a higher network load. Therefore, the operator will activate additional base stations that are installed in the event area, but inactive during normal operations. Additionally, base stations, e.g. mounted on vans, can be set up and connected to the network. POCO selects optimal NE+ locations for additional SGW, which will be activated using CAM by installing an SDN GTP controller and an SGW application in a data center best located in relation to the network element.

After deployment, configuration, and activation of the network element the event area is ready for the "Mega" event, as illustrated by Figure 3(b). Then all visitors, including Ann, enter the stadium, the "Mega" event starts, and Ann places a video call to Ben who is still in the home area. After the end of the "Mega" event, all visitors leave the event area and the operator releases the deployed resources.

The demo emulates a real LTE network as closely as possible. All LTE network components are realized through an

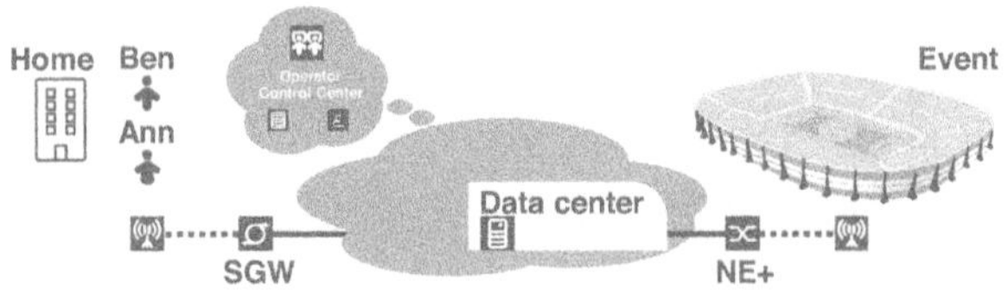


(a) Normal situation. Ann is at home.

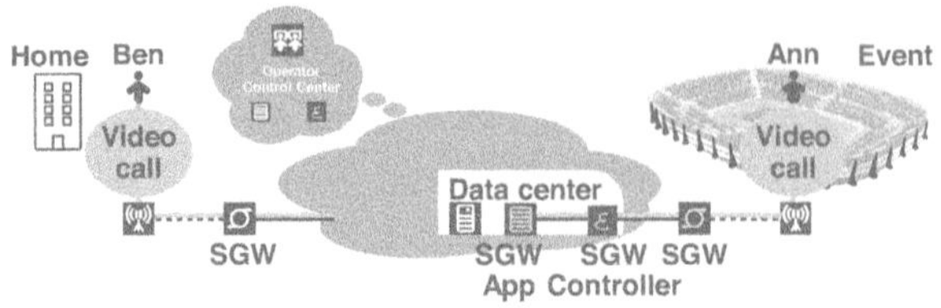


(b) Event situation. Ann is visiting a "Mega" event.

**Figure 3: Demonstration scenario.**

LTE emulator provided by Nokia, except the SGW. It is an SDN-based gateway consisting of Ethernet/IP/GTP enabled NE, SDN Ethernet/IP/GTP controllers, and an SGW application. The LTE emulator establishes a 3GPP compliant user and control plane communication in which the SGW is integrated. Furthermore, base stations and user equipments are part of the emulator. The components are realized in software and are installed in the cloud environment of Deutsche Telekom T-Labs. The cloud is managed by OpenStack and the CAM is used for application management. To show the video call, two tablets are connected via a WiFi access point to the user equipment (endpoints) of the emulator and WiFi traffic is translated into 3GPP compliant traffic. CAM, NUC and POCO have their own graphical user interfaces that are integrated into a demo control GUI.

## 4. ACKNOWLEDGMENTS

This work has been performed in the framework of the CELTIC EUREKA project SASER-SIEGFRIED (Project ID CPP2011/2-5), and it is partly funded by the BMBF (Project ID 16BP12308). The authors alone are responsible for the content of the paper.

## 5. REFERENCES

[1] "Network Functions Virtualisation - Introductory White Paper," 2012.

[2] A. Basta, W. Kellerer, H. J. Morper, and M. Hoffmann, "Applying NFV and SDN to LTE Mobile Core Gateways; The Functions Placement Problem," in *Accepted for ACM SIGCOMM 2014 Workshop All Things Cellular*, Chicago, USA, 2014.

[3] D. Hock, M. Hartmann, S. Gebert, M. Jarschel, T. Zinner, and P. Tran-Gia, "Pareto-Optimal Resilient Controller Placement in SDN-based Core Networks," in *ITC*, Shanghai, China, 2013.

[4] D. Hock, M. Hartmann, S. Gebert, T. Zinner, and P. Tran-Gia, "POCO-PLC: Enabling Dynamic Pareto-Optimal Resilient Controller Placement in SDN Networks," in *INFOCOM*, Toronto, Canada, 2014.

[5] NOKIA FutureWorks, "SDN in Mobile Networks," in *Mobile World Congress*, Barcelona, Spain, 2014.

# Tracing Multipath TCP Connections

B. Hesmans, O. Bonaventure
ICTEAM, Université Catholique de Louvain
Louvain-La-Neuve – Belgium
firstname.name@uclouvain.be

## 1. INTRODUCTION

Multipath TCP [2] is a major extension to the TCP protocol. Multipath TCP enables a host to send packets belonging to one connection over different interfaces and IP addresses. This is a major change to TCP where one connection is always bound to one four-tuple (source and destination addresses and ports). To understand the basics of Multipath TCP, let us consider the simple and important use case of a smartphone[1] using WiFi and 3G to connect to a server. To start a Multipath TCP connection, the smartphone initiates a three-way handshake with the server over the 3G interface. This handshake includes specific options to negotiate the utilisation of Multipath TCP. Once this TCP connection has been established, it becomes the first subflow of the Multipath TCP connection. To use the WiFi interface, the smartphone starts another three-way handshake over this interfaces and indicates that TCP connection is the second subflow of the Multipath TCP connection. The number of subflows associated to one Multipath TCP connection can vary over time.

Once the subflows have been established, data can be transmitted over anyone of them. If there are losses, data transmitted initially on one subflow can be retransmitted over another one. For this, Multipath TCP uses two levels of sequence numbers. The regular TCP sequence number ensures that the data sent over one subflow are in sequence. The Multipath TCP sequence number enables the receiver to reorder the data received over subflows having different delays.

During the last years, various researchers have analyzed the performance of Multipath TCP [1, 4] and proposed various improvements [5]. Unfortunately, analyzing Multipath TCP performance remains difficult given the lack of flexible tools. We fill this gap with `mptcptrace`[3] that converts a Multipath TCP packet trace in various graphs and metrics that can be used by researchers. We illustrate a few of the capabilities of `mptcptrace` in this paper.

[1]As of this writing, there are already hundreds of millions of Apple smartphones that use Multipath TCP.


*SIGCOMM'14*, August 17–22, 2014, Chicago, IL, USA.
ACM 978-1-4503-2836-4/14/08
http://dx.doi.org/10.1145/2619239.2631453.

## 2. ANALYZING MULTIPATH TCP TRACES

`tcptrace` [2], written by S. Ostermann, is a flexible packet trace analysis software. It extracts a wide range of metrics from a TCP packet trace and has been used by many researchers who analyze TCP performance. When confronted with performance problems, the first reaction of a Multipath TCP researcher will probably be to explore a packet trace with `tcptrace` to understand the problem. `tcptrace` is very convenient for such analysis since it provides both an interactive visualisation and summary statistics about each TCP connection.

As an example, we captured two long Multipath TCP connections between two virtual machines in distant Amazon EC2 datacenters. Each connection was configured to use four TCP subflows and a window of 1.2 MB. The goodput of these two connections was very different. The first one reached 21 Mbps while the second managed to achieve 40 Mbps.

`tcptrace` cannot be used directly on these traces because it cannot link the subflows together. This link can be extracted from the Multipath TCP options used in the three-way handshake. If we do this manually, we can compare the round-trip-times of the four subflows of each Multipath TCP connection. On the worse performing Multipath TCP connection, we observe a large deviation of the round-trip-time values. On the other hand, the best connection has stable round-trip-times, but the subflows achieve different throughputs. On this connection, the subflow with the lowest average round-trip-time reaches the highest throughput.

What is the reason for large deviation in the round-trip times of the low performing connection ? Figure 1 provides a CDF of the round-trip times measured over each subflow. The right part of the figure confirms the stable round-trip-times of high goodput connection. The left part shows that for the low-performing connection, three subflows have two clusters of round-trip times. One cluster arounds 200 msec and another around 400 msec. This indicates a rerouting even during the lifetime of this connection that forced those three subflows to follow a longer path. This rerouting did not affect the other subflow.

[2]`http://www.tcptrace.org/`

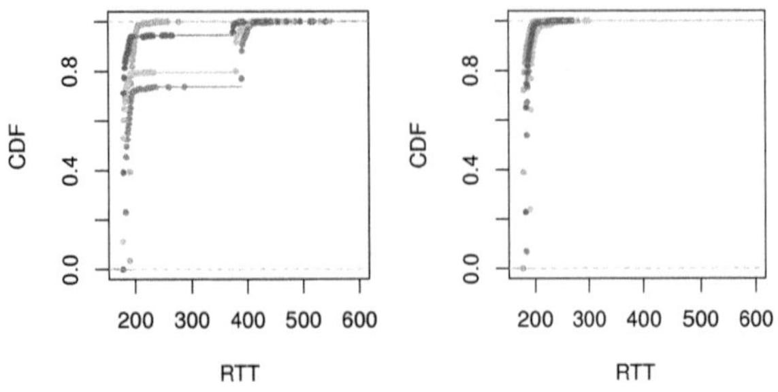


**Figure 1: Per flow RTT CDF**

## 2.1 Measuring Reordering

A regular TCP receiver reorders the data received out-of-sequence before delivering them to the application. In today's networks, reordering mainly happens after a packet loss. With Multipath TCP, reordering becomes normal. Since Multipath TCP uses subflows with different round-trip times, data is not always received in sequence at the receiver. These out-of-sequence data consume both memory and CPU time and furthermore increase the end-to-end delay perceived by the application.

Measuring and understanding when reordering occurs is major issue when analyzing Multipath TCP performance. `mptcptrace` can help such analysis by parsing all the Multipath TCP options and understanding their semantics.

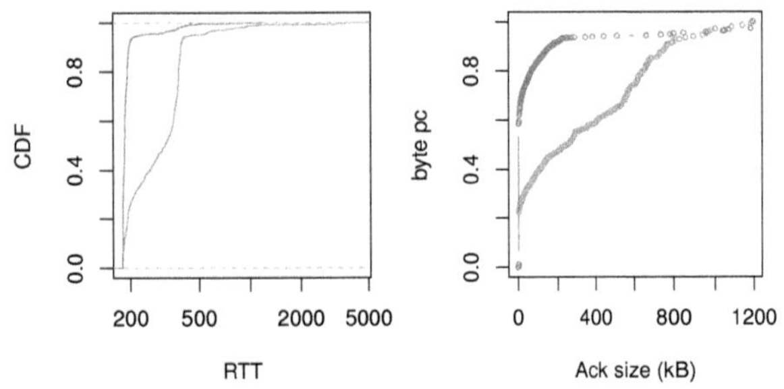


**Figure 2: MPTCP rtt CDF and Ack size**

The left part of figure 2 analyzes the round-trip times at the Multipath TCP level on each connection. For this, `mptcptrace` computes a round-trip time for each data successfully transmitted by analyzing the Multipath TCP sequence numbers and acknowledgements. The high performing connection is characterized by small end-to-end round-trip times while they are much larger with the low performing connection. Note that compared with figure 1, for this connection, the Multipath TCP round-trip times are much larger than the per-subflow round-trip times. This indicates additional delays at the receiver side.

Another angle to analyze this problem are the Multipath TCP acks. With regular TCP, when data is received in sequence, it is immediately acknowledged and each ack acknowledges one packet's worth of data. With Multipath TCP, data is sent over different subflows. Even if there are no losses, data can be out-of-order at the Multipath TCP level when subflows have different delays. The right part of figure 2 shows that the cumulative percentage of the bytes that are acknowledged by acks of size $x$. On the high performing connection, 70 % of the traffic is acknowledged by acks that acknowledge less than 10 KBytes. 90 % of the traffic is acknowledged by acks of size less than 200 KBytes. This indicates a small reordering queue. For the low performing subflow, the situation is different. We observe that a large fraction of the traffic is acknowledged in bursts. This indicates a large occupancy of the reordering queue.

Figure 3 highlights the impact of this problem on the performance of the Multipath TCP connection. Three curves are plotted. The green curve is the receive window advertised by the receiver. The read lines show the sum the amount of unacknowledged data over each of the four subflows. The orange lines show the data that has been sent by Multipath TCP (over any subflow) and not yet acknowledged by a Multipath TCP acknowledgement. The gap between the red and the orange curves corresponds to the size of the reordering queue at the Multipath TCP level.

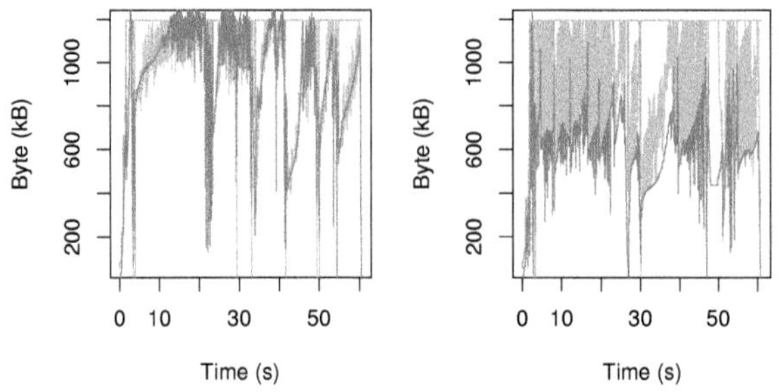


**Figure 3: TCP and MPTCP unacknowledged data**

The goodput of a Multipath TCP connection is not simply the sum of the goodput of the underlying subflows because the same data can be transmitted over several subflows. This can happen when losses occur, subflows terminate or when a subflow is underperforming [5]. By parsing all Multipath TCP options, `mptcptrace` detects all these retransmissions. In our example traces, 0.53% of the bytes were transmitted on more than one subflow for the low performing connection. For the high performing connection, 0.11% of the bytes were transmitted on more than one subflow. `mptcptrace` detected that 0.01% of the bytes were transmitted over three of the four subflows. This was likely due to the reinjection algorithm explained in [5].

## Acknownledgements

This work was supported by FNRS under project T.0128.13.

## 3. REFERENCES

[1] Y.-C. Chen et al. A Measurement-based Study of Multipath TCP Performance over Wireless Networks. In *ACM IMC*, 2013.

[2] A. Ford et al. TCP Extensions for Multipath Operation with Multiple Addresses. RFC6824, Jan. 2013.

[3] B. Hesmans. MPTCP traces analysis tool. `http://mptcptrace.multipath-tcp.org/`.

[4] C. Raiciu, S. Barre, C. Pluntke, A. Greenhalgh, D. Wischik, and M. Handley. Improving Datacenter Performance and Robustness with Multipath TCP. In *ACM SIGCOMM*, 2011.

[5] C. Raiciu et al. How hard can it be? Designing and Implementing a Deployable Multipath TCP. In *USENIX NSDI*, 2012.

# Demo: A Virtualized Lab Testbed with Physical Network Outlets for Hands-on Computer Networking Education

Mark Schmidt Florian Heimgaertner Michael Menth
{mark-thomas.schmidt,florian.heimgaertner,menth}@uni-tuebingen.de
University of Tuebingen, Dept. of Computer Science, Tuebingen, Germany

## ABSTRACT

This demo presents a testbed for computer networking education. It leverages hardware virtualization to accommodate 6 PCs and 2 routers on a single testbed host to reduce costs, energy consumption, space requirements, and heat emission. The testbed excels by providing dedicated physical Ethernet and USB interfaces for virtual machines so that students can interconnect them with cables and switches like in a non-virtualized testbed.

## Categories and Subject Descriptors

K.3.2 [**Computers and Education**]: Computer and Information Science Education; C.2.3 [**Computer-Communication Networks**]: Network Operations

## Keywords

Computer networking education; virtual machines; VLAN

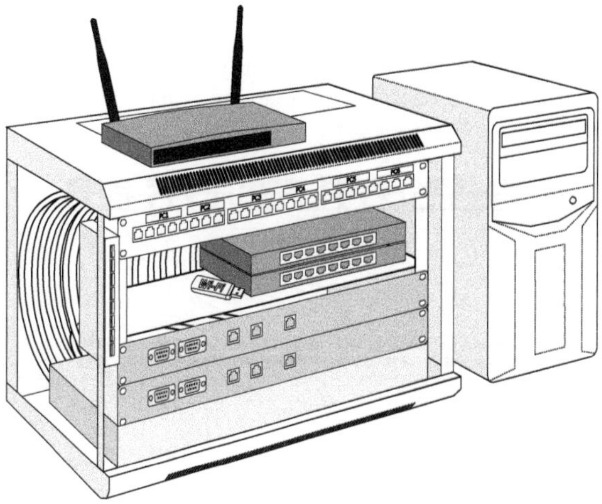

**Figure 1: Networking cabinet and testbed host.**

## 1. INTRODUCTION

Hands-on labs are essential for computer networking education. At the University of Tuebingen, two hands-on networking courses are offered. An undergraduate course based on [3] comprises networking basics, routing, DHCP, DNS, Transport Layer, and Email. The graduate course includes networking and security technologies like TLS, Firewalls, Virtual Private Networks, WiFi Security, and Voice over IP.

An existing lab setup featured 3 physical testbeds, each consisting of 6 PCs and 2 Cisco 2514 routers. Aging and degradation of hardware, along with limited lab capacity, excessive power consumption, and emission of heat and noise led to a re-design of the testbed setup. The goal was to provide testbeds for more participants and to overcome the issues of the old setup. Another objective was to keep hardware costs low and reuse the new equipment as workstations if not needed for lab exercises. These requirements called for a virtualization solution. Existing approaches include replacing physical computers and routers by virtual machines (VMs) on a testbed host, or even multiple testbeds on a single server. However, physical hands-on experience, i.e., connecting the VMs with cables and switches, should be preserved as well as interoperability with physical devices.

Our solution consists of PCs and routers running as VMs on a testbed host. Physically accessible ports for Ethernet devices of the virtualized PCs and routers are provided on an extra panel so that the same hands-on experience is possible as with an entirely physical testbed. The passthrough of interfaces from the VMs to the physical outlets was achieved by unconventional use of advanced networking and virtualization concepts on commodity hardware.

## 2. TESTBED ARCHITECTURE

The nodes (6 Linux PCs and 2 routers) of the testbeds are realized as VMs. The physical computer (testbed host) is running the virtualization platform built by the Linux Kernel based Virtual Machine (KVM) [1], libvirt and QEMU.

To enable efficient virtualization and device passthrough, hardware support is required. Intel-VT [5] is used to enable hardware accelerated virtualization of x86 systems. Single-Root I/O Virtualization (SR-IOV) [4] supports advanced device virtualization by providing multiple virtual functions (VF) per physical function (PF). A PF is a full-featured PCI device whereas VFs are lightweight PCI devices that are managed by a PF.

Figure 1 shows a lab testbed. The networking hardware is placed in a standard 19-inch wall mount cabinet. At the bot-


*SIGCOMM'14,* August 17–22, 2014, Chicago, IL, USA.
ACM 978-1-4503-2836-4/14/08. http://dx.doi.org/10.1145/2619239.2631429.

tom a managed switch is mounted facing backwards. Above the switch, two front panels with DB9 and RJ45 outlets represent the virtual routers. Unmanaged desktop switches and other networking devices for use in the lab exercises are placed on a rack-mount shelf. The topmost rack unit contains a labeled patch panel providing Ethernet ports for the virtualized PCs.

For experiments involving IEEE 802.11 technology, a wireless access point is available as a physical device. WiFi adapters for the PCs are provided as USB devices that can be passed through to the VMs.

To enable the students to physically interact with the VMs, e.g., interconnect them with real cables and switches, we provide physical access to the virtual interfaces. We achieve this objective for Ethernet interfaces by using VLAN technology [2] and a VLAN-capable managed switch. IEEE 802.1Q supports insertion of *tags* into the header of Ethernet frames which enables multiplexing several VLANs over a single physical link or port.

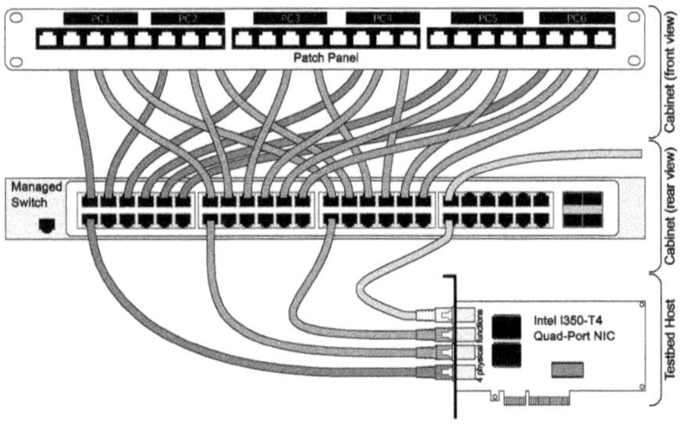


**Figure 2: A managed switch connects the quad-port NIC of the testbed host to the patch panel.**

Figure 2 shows an SR-IOV capable quad-port NIC, a managed switch, a patch panel, and twisted pair cables to connect them. Each of the four ports is implemented as a separate PF providing 7 VFs. Interfaces of the router VMs are omitted in the figure. The VF devices are separately passed through to the VMs and serve as their Ethernet interfaces. We use dedicated VLANs with unique IDs for each VF. The PFs act as an Ethernet bridge and forward data for the VFs as tagged VLANs. Those VLANs are then demultiplexed by the managed switch, stripped of their tags, and diverted via separate switch ports to the patch panel.

The Intel I350 network adapter used in our setup provides a feature called *PF loopback*. It allows to bypass an external switch when source and destination are VFs of the same PF. While PF loopback can improve performance for data center applications, it breaks our setup because the patch panel and the cables placed by the students would be bypassed as well. This issue was solved by setting the internal bridge of the PF to Virtual Ethernet Port Aggregator (VEPA) mode.

In addition to Ethernet interfaces, we make physical USB devices like WiFi adapters available in the VMs. They are passed through to the VMs, which works slightly different than the passthrough mechanism for PCI devices. USB devices are identified by their address on the bus and a unique identifier. The passthrough is realized by mapping the entire address into the VM. This can be achieved by libvirt with the help of special udev rules.

To retain the look and feel of real routers that provide a Cisco IOS like user interface, we use the routing software suite Quagga. Quagga provides a CLI called `vtysh` that behaves similar to the text-based interface of IOS. To not only keep the user interface impression, but also the physical one, we designed a special front panel for the cabinet that provides the typical look of a Cisco router. The serial link between different routers is implemented by a PPP connection, a null modem RS-232 serial cable, and USB/Serial converters. However, PPP by default provides flow control for its connections which has a bad effect: packets are not dropped if the physical link is broken but are queued until the link becomes available again and then sent at once. This results in the measured round-trip-time (RTT) being dominated by the downtime of the link and not being the real delay. Therefore, we explicitly disable flow control to get the desired behavior.

## 3. DEMONSTRATION

Our demonstration shows parts of a lab experiment adapted from [3] for our undergraduate course. A video[1] giving a short impression is available at our webserver.

First, we provide a glimpse of the lab and then focus on one testbed where we present the graphical user interface to interact with the VMs. After starting and connecting to the VMs, we show the topology for a dynamic routing experiment created by plugging cables. Integrating an additional serial link between the two routers triggers changes in the routing tables, pointing out the shortcomings of the hop-count metric for routing. This can be seen by an increased RTT for ICMP messages between two VMs, while the packets take a shorter path (3 instead of 4 hops) using the slower serial link.

Afterward we demonstrate how to switch the testbed from testbed mode to workstation mode running a regular desktop Linux installation. This way, the testbed resources can be used for programming and simulation courses while no hands-on networking course is running.

## 4. ACKNOWLEDGEMENTS

The authors would like to thank W. Braun, M. Hoefling, A. Stockmayer, and S. Veith for support in assembling the testbeds and preparing the demo.

The authors acknowledge the funding by the Deutsche Forschungsgemeinschaft (DFG) under grant ME2727/1-1. The authors alone are responsible for the content of the paper.

## 5. REFERENCES

[1] A. Kivity et al. kvm: the Linux virtual machine monitor. In *Linux Symposium*, 2007.

[2] LAN/MAN Standards Committee of the IEEE Computer Society. *IEEE 802.1Q: Virtual Bridged Local Area Networks*, 2003.

[3] J. Liebeherr and M. E. Zarki. *Mastering networks – an internet lab manual.* Pearson Education, 2003.

[4] PCI SIG. Single Root I/O Virtualization and Sharing Specification 1.1, 2010.

[5] R. Uhlig et al. Intel Virtualization Technology. *IEEE Computer*, 38(5):48–56, 2005.

[1] `http://kn.inf.uni-tuebingen.de/demos/sigcomm14`

# Rethinking Congestion Control Architecture: Performance-oriented Congestion Control

Mo Dong
University of Illinois at Urbana-Champaign

Qingxi Li
University of Illinois at Urbana-Champaign

Doron Zarchy
Hebrew University of Jerusalem

Brighten Godfrey
University of Illinois at Urbana-Champaign

Michael Schapira
Hebrew University of Jerusalem

## ABSTRACT

After more than two decades of evolution, TCP and its end host based modifications can still suffer from severely degraded performance under real-world challenging network conditions. The reason, as we observe, is due to TCP family's fundamental architectural deficiency, which hardwires packet-level events to control responses and ignores emprical performance. Jumping out of TCP lineage's architectural deficiency, we propose Performance-oriented Congestion Control (PCC), a new congestion control architecture in which each sender controls its sending strategy based on empirically observed performance metrics. We show through preliminary experimental results that PCC achieves consistently high performance under various challenging network conditions.

## Categories and Subject Descriptors

C.2.1 [**Computer-Communication Networks**]: Network Architecture and Design—*Network Communication*

## Keywords

congestion control

## 1. INTRODUCTION

In the roughly 25 years since its deployment, TCP's congestion control architecture has been notorious for degraded performance in numerous real-world scenarios. TCP performs poorly on lossy links, penalizes high-RTT flows, has difficulty utilizing high bandwidth-delay product (BDP) connections, can collapse in an incast [3] scenario and incurs bufferbloat [4].

Two broad avenues of research have been pursued to improve the performance of TCP. The first is for network devices to give end-hosts explicit feedback. However, because these designs require hardware and configuration changes and (for [6]) packet header changes, in-network solutions have rarely seen widespread deployment.


*SIGCOMM'14*, August 17–22, 2014, Chicago, IL, USA.
ACM 978-1-4503-2836-4/14/08.
http://dx.doi.org/10.1145/2619239.2631456 .

In the second avenue of research, end-host-based modifications have addressed problems in specific network conditions, resulting in an innumerably long string of designs tweaking TCP. These include using latency rather than just loss as a signal of congestion [8], sophisticated window expansion algorithms [5] for high bandwidth-delay produce link, coordinated adjustment of the receive window across connections at the receiver to mitigate incast [10], viewing a certain amount of packet loss as unrelated to congestion [7] for lossy wireless networks, expanding the window quicker by setting up a reference RTT [2] to speed up TCP on satellite links and so on.

Although they use distinct congestion control algorithms, all end-host-based TCP variants inherit the very same TCP-based congestion control architecture: hardwiring certain packet-level events (e.g. packet-loss) directly to certain control responses (e.g. halving the window size) like a ***mapping function***. New TCP variants change the mapping function, but the *mapping*-based design itself has not changed.

Unfortunately, two critical problems remain unsolved. First, the very fact that there are such a large number of modifications indicates that each is only a point solution: they yield better performance in certain cases, but break in others, i.e. ***consistently high performance*** is not achieved. Second, and actually worse, we found through real-world experiments that in many cases the performance of these modifications is still far from optimal even in the network conditions towards which they are specially engineered.

We believe these two problems are due to the fundamental deficiency in the TCP-based congestion control architecture. The design rationale behind the mapping function architecture is to make assumptions about the packet-level events. When seeing a packet-level event, TCP *assumes* the network is in a certain state and thus tries to optimize the performance by triggering a predefined control behavior as response to that *assumed* network state. However, in real networks, it is very common that the observed packet-level events were not a result of the assumed network condition. When this assumed link breaks, TCP still mechanically carries out the mismatched control response without even being aware of the severely degraded performance. Take an event-control pair from textbook TCP for example: a packet loss halves the congestion window size. TCP assumes that the packet loss event indicates congestion in the network. If the assumptions about this packet loss event are valid, halving the window size will result in reduced loss rate and may improve performance. However, this assumption can be easily violated: packet loss can be random and unrelated to congestion and thus halving the window size will cause

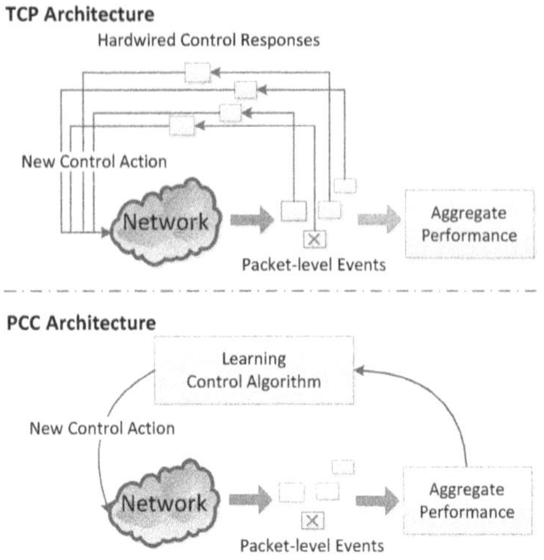


**Figure 1:** ***The TCP and PCC architectures compared.***

severe performance and fairness degradation. Even the recently proposed TCP exMachina [9] still follows TCP's architecture: in a computationally-intensive offline optimization, it generates a TCP-like event-control mapping function optimized for a set of assumed network conditions. This helps improve performance when the network conforms to the assumptions, but when underlying network condition become different from the input model (e.g. the number of concurrent senders exceeds the expected value), performance still degrades. Therefore, achieving consistently high performance across a range of challenging network conditions ***within the 25-year-old TCP based mapping architecture*** is fundamentally hard.

To solve these problems, we rethink congestion control architecture design and propose Performance-oriented Congestion Control (PCC). PCC *makes control decisions directly based on empirically observed performance outcomes* and we show through preliminary but large scale experiments that it is a promising path towards a congestion control architecture that achieves consistently high performance over a range of challenging network scenarios.

## 2. ARCHITECTURE OVERVIEW

Unlike the TCP family's congestion control architecture, PCC does not use any predefined packet-level event to trigger certain control behavior. Instead, PCC, as shown in Fig. 1, optimizes applications' performance objectives based on real performance metrics: it picks a sending rate, continuously observes the resulting effect on its performance such as loss rate, throughput, and RTT; and feeds these performance values into a utility function to produce a numerical performance value reflecting the application's objective such as "high throughput and low loss rate". The sender then runs an online learning control algorithm to selfishly adjust its sending rate to maximize this utility over time. Intuitively, this performance oriented congestion control architecture is more robust than traditional TCP's event-control design because it makes fewer assumptions. Rather than using packet-level events to trigger hardwired responses, PCC *observes meaningful performance* and *learns the empirically best strategy* to optimize this performance.

Though PCC has no notion of fairness in its design, it turns out that PCC's selfish optimization need not equate to loss of stability, convergence, or fairness. When choosing a certain kind of utility function expressing the widely-applicable goal of *high throughput and low loss rate*, competing PCC senders will provably converge to a fair share point (unique Nash Equlibrium).

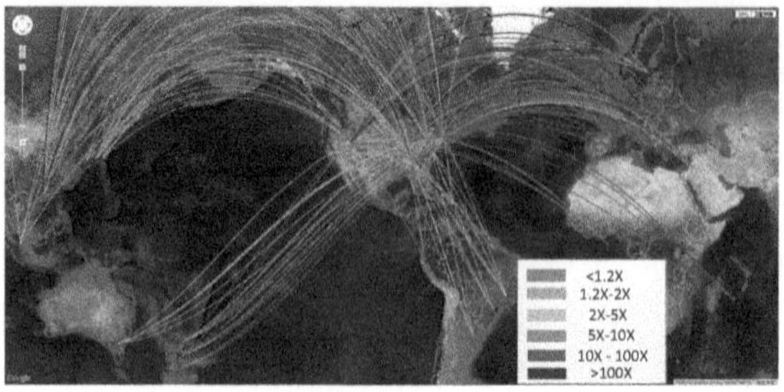


**Figure 2:** ***Large scale Internet experiment demonstrating PCC's performance improvement over TCP CUBIC***

## 3. IMPLEMENTATION AND EVALUATION

We built a PCC prototype on top of UDP and evaluated it in experiments spanning PlanetLab, the GENI network, Emulab, and a local testbed. These experiments, ***carried out without any tweaking of control algorithm***, show PCC significantly beating or at least matching specially engineered TCPs on challenging network environments: **a.** provisioned very high capacity backbone networks for scientific data transfer, **b.** incast in data center networks, **c.** lossy satellite links, **d.** links with tiny buffers, **e.** links with bufferbloat, **f.** unfairness of RTT, **g.** the wild and complex conditions of the real Internet, **h.** unusually high loss rate and **i.** latency sensitive applications requiring high throughput and low latency. We also show that PCC's convergence is more stable than TCP even though it has no explicit concern for fairness in its design. Due to the space limit, we only briefly expand two interesting examples here.

**High performance satellite communication:** satellite links serve critical missions but have packet loss and excessively high latency. State-of-the-art solutions use relay nodes [1] and the purpose-built TCP Hybla [2]. PCC achieves $17\times$ higher throughput than Hybla on links with satellite characteristics, reaching 90% capacity.

**5X faster data delivery over Internet:** In our global-scale evaluation over 480 sender-receiver pairs across the commercial Internet (Fig. 2), PCC outperforms high BDP optimized TCP CUBIC by $5.52\times$ in the median and achieves $\geq 10\times$ for 41% of source-destination pairs.

**Acknowledgement:** This work was supported by National Science Foundation grant CNS 1149895.

## 4. REFERENCES

[1] TCP accelarate on satellite link. `http://goo.gl/E6q6Yf`.

[2] C. Caini and R. Firrincieli. TCP Hybla: a tcp enhancement for heterogeneous networks. *International Journal of Satellite Communications and Networking*, 2004.

[3] Y. Chen, R. Griffith, J. Liu, R. H. Katz, and A. D. Joseph. Understanding tcp incast throughput collapse in datacenter networks. *Proc. ACM SIGCOMM Workshop on Research on Enterprise Networking*, 2009.

[4] J. Gettys and K. Nichols. Bufferbloat: Dark buffers in the internet. December 2011.

[5] S. Ha, I. Rhee, and L. Xu. CUBIC: a new TCP-friendly high-speed TCP variant. *Proc. ACM SIGOPS*, 2008.

[6] D. Katabi, M. Handley, and C. Rohrs. Congestion control for high bandwidth-delay product networks. *Proc. ACM SIGCOMM*, August 2002.

[7] S. Liu, T. Başar, and R. Srikant. Tcp-illinois: A loss-and delay-based congestion control algorithm for high-speed networks. *Performance Evaluation*, 65(6):417–440, 2008.

[8] D. Wei, C. Jin, S. Low, and S. Hegde. FAST TCP. *IEEE/ACM Trans. Networking*, December 2006.

[9] K. Winstein and H. Balakrishnan. Tcp ex machina: Computer-generated congestion control. *Proc. ACM SIGCOMM*, 2013.

[10] H. Wu, Z. Feng, C. Guo, and Y. Zhang. ICTCP: Incast congestion control for TCP in data center networks. *Proc. CoNEXT*, 2010.

# DOT: Distributed OpenFlow Testbed

Arup Raton Roy, Md. Faizul Bari, Mohamed Faten Zhani,
Reaz Ahmed, and Raouf Boutaba
David R. Cheriton School of Computer Science, University of Waterloo
{ar3roy, mfbari, mfzhani, r5ahmed, rboutaba}@uwaterloo.ca

## Keywords

Testbed; Emulator; Software Defined Networking

## 1. INTRODUCTION

With the growing adoption of Software Defined Networking (SDN) technology, there is a compelling need for an SDN emulator that can facilitate experimenting with new SDN solutions. In this context, Mininet [1] has been proposed as an emulator for prototyping a network on a single machine. It allows users to create, control, and customize an emulated network on which they can run and test new control applications like routing, traffic engineering, *etc.* However, Mininet cannot scale for large networks and high traffic volumes [3].

To address these limitations, we developed *Distributed OpenFlow Testbed* (DOT), a highly scalable emulator for SDN. DOT distributes the emulated network across multiple physical machines to scale with network size and traffic volume. It also provides guaranteed compute and network resources for the emulated components (i.e., switches, hosts and links). Moreover, DOT can emulate a wider range of network services compared to other publicly available SDN emulators and simulators.

Our demonstration will illustrate several features of DOT including: (i) how easy it is to setup the emulator, (ii) how to deploy a topology using a single configuration file, (iii) how to run a connectivity test to ensure that the emulated network is properly deployed, and (iv) how to control and monitor the emulated components from a centralized location. We will also showcase DOT by emulating two applications: (i) policy based traffic steering through middleboxes [2] and (ii) traffic monitoring [5]. Our goal is to encourage researchers to use DOT for their SDN-related experiments and gather feedback to further improve its design and performance.

## 2. DESIGN

DOT provisions an emulated topology across a cluster of physical machines (Fig. 1(c)). One of these machines orchestrates the whole emulation process. We call this physical machine the `DOT Manager`. The other machines are called `DOT Nodes`. These machines contain virtual switches and hosts used to build the emulated topology.

Our embedding algorithm (detailed in [4]) considers the resource capacity of each `DOT node` and finds an embedding that minimizes physical bandwidth usage and the number of physical machines. The embedding algorithm partitions the emulated network and maps each partition to a particular physical machine. When the algorithm embeds virtual links, two cases may arise due to partitioning. First, if the virtual link connects two virtual switches embedded in the same physical machine, then this link is provisioned inside that machine (link `b` in Fig. 1(a)), and hence we call it an *intra-host virtual link*. Second, a virtual link connecting two virtual switches residing at different physical machines (hereafter called a *cross-host virtual link*) is mapped onto a path passing through the physical network (link `e` in Fig. 1(a)).

An intra-host virtual link is emulated by instantiating two virtual Ethernet interfaces (`veth(s)`) within the same physical machine (using Linux `add ip link` command). The virtual link bandwidth and delay are emulated using the `tc` and `netem` commands, respectively.

To forward traffic passing through a cross-host virtual link, we create a specialized switch called the *Gateway Switch* (GS) in each physical machine (`GS1` and `GS2` in Fig. 1(b)). GSs are connected through pair-wise `GRE` tunnels. Then we create two segments (using Linux `add ip link` command) for a cross-host link in each physical machine where its end points reside (in Fig. 1(b), `e` has two segments $e'$ and $e''$). Each segment connects one of its end points to the GS in the physical machine. A unique identifier is assigned to each cross-host link, *i.e.*, both segments have the same identifier.

Whenever a GS receives a packet from one of the segments, it encapsulates the packet within a `GRE` header, tags this packet with the identifier of the segment, and unicasts it to the destination physical machine. The receiving GS (at the other end of the tunnel) decapsulates the packet, inspects the tag, and forwards the packet to the corresponding segment. We pre-install forwarding rules in the GSs to enable this mechanism. It is worth noting that GSs are completely transparent to the DOT users and are used to hide the fact that different portions of the emulated network are distributed across a cluster of physical machines. Moreover, DOT does not install any forwarding rules in the virtual switches of the emulated topology.

For emulating the end hosts, DOT supports both OS level (`Linux Container`) and full virtualization (`Kernel Virtual`


*SIGCOMM'14*, August 17–22, 2014, Chicago, Illinois, USA.
ACM 978-1-4503-2836-4/14/08.
http://dx.doi.org/10.1145/2619239.2631457.

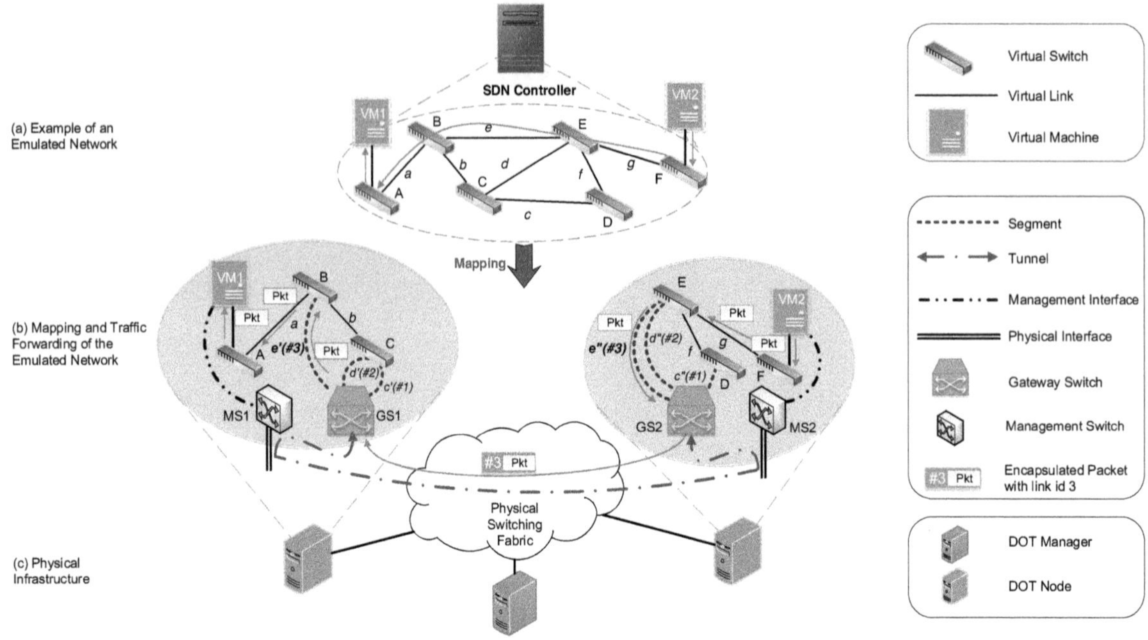


**Figure 1: Emulated network embedding and traffic forwarding in DOT**

`Machine (KVM)`). Moreover, `tiny core Linux` (a minimalistic flavor of Linux) is used as guest OS to minimize resource footprint of the Virtual Machines (VMs).

An emulated network in DOT also includes a separate (out-of-band) management network. Each VM/container is equipped with a virtual management interface. This interface is attached to a management switch (`MS1` and `MS2` in Fig. 1(b)) of the respective physical host. The management network allows direct access (using `ssh`) to the VMs/containers and ensures that management traffic does not interfere with emulation traffic in any way to affect the outcome of an experiment.

## 3. FEATURES

The key features of DOT are as follows:

- **Scalability:** DOT can be deployed across multiple physical machines. It can be scaled to meet the requirements of the emulated topology. This feature provides DOT an edge over other emulators.
- **Transparency:** The specialized components required for distributed deployment are kept hidden from the users' controller(s). As a result, intra-host and cross-host links appear indistinguishable to the controller(s).
- **Guaranteed performance:** Our embedding algorithm provides resource guarantee for all emulated components (*i.e.*, switches, links, and hosts). Thus, the performance of the emulated network is close to that of a real network.
- **Flexibility:** DOT supports both OS-level and full virtualization. Full virtualization enables DOT to use heterogeneous (different versions of kernel) end hosts. It also provides opportunities to emulate a larger class of network services, *e.g.*, managing middleboxes [2].
- **Multi-tenancy:** DOT can be easily extended to provide access to multiple users to run simultaneously their emulations on the same physical infrastructure.
- **Hybrid networks:** Non-OpenFlow switches can be deployed in DOT. A user can use DOT for emulating a network that includes both OpenFlow and non-OpenFlow switches.
- **Physical switch integration:** Physical switches can be included in an emulated network in DOT. This feature enables flexible experimental setup to aid gradual rollout of SDN technology in the production network by emulating one part of the network in DOT while keeping the other parts running on actual hardware.

## 4. IMPLEMENTATION

DOT is available as an open source software at `www.dothub.org`. We have deployed networks with different sizes and resource requirements to test our current implementation. Almost all publicly available OpenFlow controller can be used with DOT. We have tested DOT with Floodlight, OpenDaylight, NOX, and POX.

## 5. ACKNOWLEDGMENTS

This work was supported by the Natural Science and Engineering Council of Canada (NSERC) under the Smart Applications on Virtual Infrastructure (SAVI) Research Network.

## 6. REFERENCES


[1] Handigol, N., Heller, B., Jeyakumar, V., Lantz, B., and McKeown, N. Reproducible network experiments using container-based emulation. In *ACM CoNEXT 2012*.

[2] Qazi, Z. A., Tu, C.-C., Chiang, L., Miao, R., Sekar, V., and Yu, M. SIMPLE-fying middlebox policy enforcement using SDN. In *ACM SIGCOMM 2013*.

[3] Roy, A., Yocum, K., and Snoeren, A. C. Challenges in the emulation of large scale software defined networks. In *APSYS 2013*.

[4] Roy, A. R., Bari, M. F., Zhani, M. F., Ahmed, R., and Boutaba, R. Design and Management of DOT: A Distributed OpenFlow Testbed. In *IEEE/IFIP NOMS 2014*.

[5] Yu, M., Jose, L., and Miao, R. Software defined traffic measurement with OpenSketch. In *USENIX NSDI 2013*.

# Evaluating the Effect of Centralization on Routing Convergence on a Hybrid BGP-SDN Emulation Framework


Adrian Gämperli
ETH Zurich
Zurich, Switzerland
gaadrian@student.ethz.ch

Vasileios Kotronis
ETH Zurich
Zurich, Switzerland
vkotroni@tik.ee.ethz.ch

Xenofontas Dimitropoulos
FORTH
Heraklion, Greece
fontas@ics.forth.gr


## 1. MOTIVATION

A lot of applications depend on reliable and stable Internet connectivity. These characteristics are crucial for mission-critical services such as telemedical applications. An important factor that can affect connection availability is the convergence time of BGP, the de-facto inter-domain routing (IDR) protocol in the Internet. After a routing change, it may take several minutes until the network converges and BGP routing becomes stable again [13]. Kotronis *et al.* [8,9] propose a novel Internet routing approach based on SDN principles that combines several Autonomous Systems (AS) into groups, called clusters, and introduces a logically centralized routing decision process for the cluster participants. One of the goals of this concept is to stabilize the IDR system and bring down its convergence time. However, testing whether such approaches can improve on BGP problems requires hybrid SDN and BGP experimentation tools that can emulate multiple ASes. Presently, there is a lack of an easy to use public tool for this purpose. This work fills this gap by building a suitable emulation framework and evaluating the effect that a proof-of-concept IDR controller has on IDR convergence time.


## Categories and Subject Descriptors

C.2.2 [**Network Protocols**]: Routing Protocols
; C.2.3 [**Network Operations**]: Network Management

## Keywords

BGP; Software Defined Networks; Emulation


## 2. OBJECTIVES

Our primary objective is to support hybrid BGP-SDN experiments with multiple ASes using real router software. This is needed since when deploying a new IDR approach one cannot change the whole infrastructure at once. The framework should take care of configuration management such as IP prefixes and BGP policy templates and the user should be able to actively control the experiments, e.g., dynamically changing the topology and verifying the effects of changes. Furthermore, it should be possible to easily create topologies based on measured Internet data or theoretical models. This way an experimenter should be able to concentrate more on the experiments and her concept rather than bothering with configuration and management.

Our second objective is to demonstrate the effect of centralization on IDR convergence time. We designed and implemented a proof-of-concept IDR SDN controller that exploits centralization to improve IDR convergence time based on the following design goals. First, the controller should inter-operate with legacy BGP routers. Moreover, the cluster network is transparent to the legacy BGP world, therefore ASes within the cluster maintain their AS identity. In addition, we want to support disjoint AS sub-clusters controlled by the same controller, so that an intra-cluster link failure does not isolate the controlled ASes: paths over the legacy Internet could still connect the sub-clusters.

## 3. HYBRID SDN & BGP EMULATION FRAMEWORK

The framework is based on a slightly modified version of Mininet [10] that supports the functionality of Quagga [3] – a popular BGP software. The topologies can be either artificial or built from the iPlane Inter-PoP links [12] and the CAIDA AS Relationship [11] datasets. The framework automatically assigns IP addresses and configures network devices, including customer-to-provider and peer-to-peer relationships. To isolate the effects of inter-domain from intra-domain routing every AS is emulated by a single network device. This abstraction is useful for use-cases such as ours.

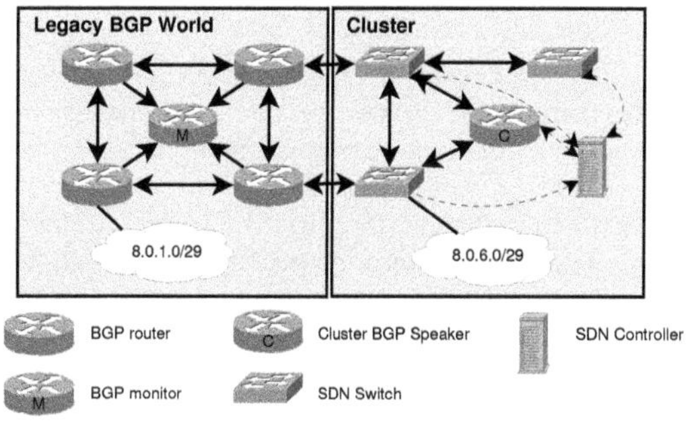


**Figure 1: The different components of an example hybrid BGP/SDN emulation experiment.**



*SIGCOMM'14,* August 17–22, 2014, Chicago, IL, USA.
ACM 978-1-4503-2836-4/14/08.
http://dx.doi.org/10.1145/2619239.2631458.

In Fig. 1 we show the components of an example experiment. On the left side, we see the legacy BGP part of the emulated network, whereas on the right side we illustrate an SDN cluster, composed of OpenFlow switches. BGP routers and SDN switches can originate prefixes. It is also possible to add hosts with IP addresses within a particular prefix for monitoring end-to-end connectivity with tools like ping, etc. All BGP routers peer with a BGP route collector, which collects routing updates for monitoring purposes. Moreover, within the SDN cluster we have a special BGP speaker, called *cluster BGP speaker*, which relays routing information between external BGP routers and the SDN controller. The cluster BGP speaker is implemented with ExaBGP [6]. For every BGP peering there is a link from the cluster BGP speaker to the border SDN switch, so as to relay control plane information over the switches.

Experimental setups can be written in Python. We implemented several additional Mininet-BGP commands to announce prefixes, wait until BGP has converged, etc. Additionally, the framework supports tools for automatic log file analysis, network graph creation, convergence time and loss measurement, and route change visualization. For example, to facilitate experiments on IDR stability, the framework detects when the network has converged and whether there is stable connectivity between all hosts. Other compatible tools can be added as Mininet is an extensible platform.

We built an IDR SDN controller over the cluster BGP speaker (using POX [2]), to evaluate the effect of IDR centralization on convergence time. More details on the design and implementation of the IDR controller can be found at [7]. An important insight that we gained is that we can not naively use the same loop avoidance mechanism as BGP, due to the differences between the distributed path selection of BGP and the centralized routing control of SDN. We therefore introduce two graphs for the route selection process: the *Switch graph*, representing the physical topology of the switches in the cluster and the *AS topology graph*, which is a transformation of the switch graph per destination prefix. The transformation is restructuring the graph taking carefully into account paths that cross the legacy world and the SDN cluster so as to avoid loops. Best path calculations are based on the Dijkstra algorithm, running on the AS topology graph. AS routes are then compiled to flow rules on the SDN switches. Another design insight we gained is the need for a delayed recomputation of best paths on the controller's side, so as to improve overall stability and rate-limit route flaps due to bursts in external BGP input.

# 4. DEMO AND RESULTS

The demonstration will show the framework and our usecase. One part of the demo will focus on how researchers can use the framework to run and manage experiments [1]. Secondly, we will demonstrate the effect of SDN centralization on IDR convergence time showing visually how it affects an end-to-end video application under different scenarios. Our experiments on a clique topology [7] show that IDR centralization can improve the convergence time even with small SDN cluster deployments. In Fig. 2 we show how the convergence time can be linearly reduced in a route withdrawal experiment with different percentages of SDN deployment in a 16-node clique. On the other hand, route fail-over and announcement experiments did not show this linear improvement, but smaller reductions.

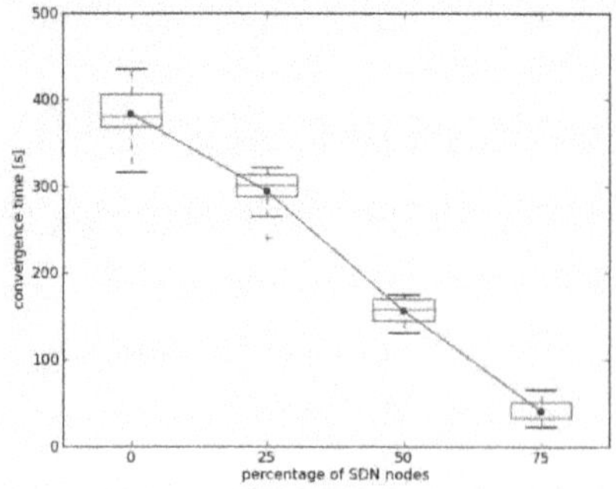


**Figure 2: IDR convergence time of route withdrawal on a 16-AS clique topology versus fraction of ASes with centralized route control. The remaining ASes use standard BGP. We show boxplots over 10 runs.**

# 5. RELATED WORK

MiniNext [4] is a hybrid SDN - legacy routing emulator based on Mininet and Quagga. However, while MiniNext aims at emulating operational environments and focuses on low-level APIs, our framework focuses on multi-AS IDR experiments and provides a high-level API for experiment lifecycle orchestration. The Open Network Operating System (ONOS) [14] is built to be production ready for large-scale networks. Our approach is better suited for rapid prototyping. Due to simplifications such as cooperative multitasking, we can focus more on research questions than on state consistency and concurrency issues. Finally, RouteFlow [5] is a platform where the controller application mirrors the SDN topology to a virtual network and runs a legacy routing protocol on top of it. Our controller however does not rely on routing decisions of legacy protocols but runs its own algorithms, enabling better integration with SDN concepts.

**Acknowledgements:** This work was partly funded by European Research Council Grant Agreement n. 338402.

# 6. REFERENCES


[1] http://youtu.be/Cbc8XlIp_CO.
[2] POX. http://www.noxrepo.org/pox/about-pox/.
[3] Quagga Routing Software Suite. http://www.nongnu.org/quagga/.
[4] B. Schlinker et al. Try Before you Buy: SDN Emulation with (Real) Interdomain Routing. In *Proc. of ONS*, 2014.
[5] C. E. Rothenberg et al. Revisiting Routing Control Platforms with the Eyes and Muscles of Software-defined Networking. In *Proc. of ACM HotSDN*, 2012.
[6] Exa Networks. Exa-Networks/exabgp. https://github.com/Exa-Networks/exabgp.
[7] A. Gämperli. Evaluating the Effect of SDN Centralization on Internet Routing Convergence. Master's thesis, ETH Zürich, 2014.
[8] V. Kotronis, X. Dimitropoulos, and B. Ager. Outsourcing the Routing Control Logic: Better Internet Routing Based on SDN Principles. In *Proc. of ACM HotNets-XI*, 2012.
[9] V. Kotronis, X. Dimitropoulos, and B. Ager. Outsourcing Routing using SDN: The Case for a Multi-Domain Routing Operating System. In *Poster Proc. of ONS*, 2013.
[10] B. Lantz, B. Heller, and N. McKeown. A Network in a Laptop: Rapid Prototyping for Software-defined Networks. In *Proc. of ACM HotNets-IX*, 2010.
[11] CAIDA. As relationships dataset. http://www.caida.org/data/as-relationships/.
[12] University of Washington. iPlane: Datasets. http://iplane.cs.washington.edu/data/data.html.
[13] Oliveira, Ricardo et al. Quantifying Path Exploration in the Internet. In *Proc. of ACM IMC*, 2006.
[14] ON.Lab. What is ONOS? http://tools.onlab.us/onos.html.

# Droid-Sec: Deep Learning in Android Malware Detection

Zhenlong Yuan[‖‡] Yongqiang Lu[†] Zhaoguo Wang[≀] and Yibo Xue[‡*]
[†]Baidu Inc., Beijing, China
[‖]Department of Automation, Tsinghua University, Beijing, China
[‡]Research Institute of Information Technology, Tsinghua University, Beijing, China
[*]Tsinghua National Lab for Information Science and Technology, Beijing, China
[≀]School of Computer Science and Technology, Harbin Institute of Technology, Harbin, China
yuanzl11@mails.tsinghua.edu.cn, luyongqiang@baidu.com, {wangzhaoguo, yiboxue}@tsinghua.edu.cn

## ABSTRACT

As smartphones and mobile devices are rapidly becoming indispensable for many network users, mobile malware has become a serious threat in the network security and privacy. Especially on the popular Android platform, many malicious apps are hiding in a large number of normal apps, which makes the malware detection more challenging. In this paper, we propose a ML-based method that utilizes more than 200 features extracted from both static analysis and dynamic analysis of Android app for malware detection. The comparison of modeling results demonstrates that the deep learning technique is especially suitable for Android malware detection and can achieve a high level of 96% accuracy with real-world Android application sets.

## Categories and Subject Descriptors

C.2.0 [**Computer Communication Networks**]: General—*Security and protection*

## Keywords

Android malware, deep learning, detection

## 1. INTRODUCTION

A recent report from Gartner[1] shows that Android tablet sales grew 127 percent and reached the No.1 position in 2013. Application market such as Google Play Store is playing an important role in the popularity of Android devices and drive the economy of Android applications. However, the openness of the Android market also makes it a hot target for malware attacks, which is a serious threat for network users' security and privacy. Consequently, there is an urgent need to pick up the malware from normal apps.

Currently, the main defense mechanism for Android to fight against malware is a risk communication mechanism, which will warn users about the permissions an app requires before the user installs it. This approach is indeed ineffective as it presents the permissions of an app in a "stand-alone" fashion and requires too much technical knowledge for a general user to distinguish malware. Note that a normal app and a malicious app may require the same permissions and thus it is hard for users to make a right decision. In fact, more users tend to know directly whether it is a malware or not, without concerning too much on the risk assessment.

Deep learning [1], as a new area of machine learning research, has gained increasing attentions in artificial intelligence (AI) and motivated a great number of successful applications in speech and image recognition. In this paper, we first extract more than 200 features[2] from both static analysis and dynamic analysis of each Android app, and then apply the deep learning technique to classify the malware from normal apps. In addition, our comparison of modeling results demonstrates that the deep learning technique is far more suitable than some other machine learning techniques, includes Naïve Bayes, SVM, C4.5, Logistic Regression (LR) and Multi-layer Perceptron (MLP).

## 2. STATIC AND DYNAMIC ANALYSIS

In order to systematically characterize Andorid apps (i.e. normal and malicious apps), we employ both static and dynamic analysis to extract 202 features from each app. In particular, these features will fall into three types: required permission, sensitive API and dynamic behavior. Among them, required permission and sensitive API are extracted through static analysis while dynamic behavior is extracted through dynamic analysis, as shown in Table 1. Note that some other types of features can also be added in our model to make it better for characterizing Android apps [3]. Here our main goal is to demonstrate that deep learning can achieve a high level of accuracy with a set of key features.

In the case of static analysis, all we need is the .apk file of an Android app. After uncompressing the apk file with the '`7-Zip`' tool, we mainly focus on parsing the two files 'AndroidManifest.xml' and 'classes.dex' respectively. By parsing the 'AndroidManifest.xml' file with the tool '`AXMLPrinter2`' and the parser '`TinyXml`', we can know what permissions an app indeed requires, e.g. permission '`android.permission.call_phone`' stands for permitting an app to make a phone call. Actually, we totally search for 120 permissions in this part. Besides, by parsing 'classes.dex' file with the disassembler '`baksmali`', we can know what sensitive API will be called, e.g. function '`ContentResolver;->delete`' stands for a sensitive API and might be used for

[*]Corresponding author.

[1]`http://www.gartner.com/newsroom/id/2674215`

[2]More details can be found at http://www.droid-sec.com.


*SIGCOMM'14*, August 17–22, 2014, Chicago, IL, USA.
ACM 978-1-4503-2836-4/14/08.
http://dx.doi.org/10.1145/2619239.2631434.

Table 1: Features from Analysis

| Static Analysis | | Dynamic Analysis |
|---|---|---|
| **Required Permission** | **Sensitive API** | **Dynamic Behavior** |
| ACCESS_FINE_LOCATION | IActivityManager*Stub*Proxy;->shutdown | ACTION_DEXCLASS_LOAD |
| ACCESS_COARSE_LOCATION | ActivityManager;->killBackgroundProcesses | ACTION_RECVNET |
| ACCESS_MOCK_LOCATION | ActivityManagerNative;->restartPackage | ACTION_SERVICESTART |
| ...... | ...... | ...... |

deleting users' messages or contacts. Totally, we search for 64 sensitive APIs in this part.

In the case of dynamic analysis, we run the .apk file of an app in the 'DroidBox[3]'. DroidBox is a kind of sandbox that is developed based on TaintDroid [2]. After running an app for a fixed period of time, DroidBox can generate some information log which includes the dynamic behaviors that happened from the app, such as '`action_sendnet`' which stands for an action that sends data over the network. Totally, we search for 18 dynamic behaviors in the part.

# 3. DEEP LEARNING MODEL

Traditional machine learning models, such as SVM etc. that has less than three layers of computation units, are considered to have shallow architectures. Fortunately, deep learning with a deep architecture changed that. In reality, deep learning model actually can be trained in various ways with different approaches or algorithms. In this paper, due to the space limitation, we mainly present our framework on building model for Android malware detection as shown in Figure 1.

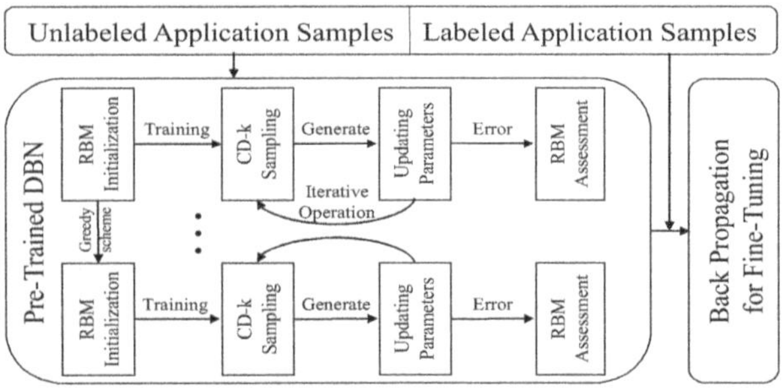


Figure 1: Framework of Deep Learning Model

As a semi-supervised training algorithm, deep learning consists of two phases, the 'unsupervised pre-training phase' and the 'supervised back-propagation phase'. In the pre-training phase, we adopt the deep belief network (DBN) [1] for pre-training. The DBN is hierarchically built by stacking a number of restricted Boltzmann machines (RBM) with regarding the deep neural network as a latent variable model, which is beneficial for better characterizing Android apps. In the back-propagation phase, the pre-trained neural network is to be fine-tuned with labeled value in a supervised manner. After that, the whole deep learning model is built completely. Besides, more details will be presented in Section 4.

# 4. EVALUATION

To validate our deep learning model in Android malware detection, we experiment on public application sets (mixed with malware apps and normal apps). The malware set (250 samples) is downloaded from the famous *contagio mobile*[4] and the normal app set is crawled from the top 250 apps in *Google Play Store*. Note that the number of malware and the number of normal apps are always mixed equally in the training or test sets.

Table 2: Accuracy with Different Constructions

| Num of Layers | Num of Neurons | Accuracy |
|---|---|---|
| 6 | [150,150,150,150,150,150] | 94.0% |
| 5 | [150,150,150,150,150] | 95.0% |
| 4 | [150,150,150,150] | 94.5% |
| 3 | [170,170,170] | 93.0% |
| **3** | [150,150,150] | 96.5% |
| 3 | [130,130,130] | 95.0% |
| 2 | [150,150] | 89.5% |

Significantly, there are two key parameters while building the deep learning model, one is the number of layers in DBN and the other is the number of neurons in each layer. Table 2 shows the accuracy changes with different model constructions. In addition, we conduct a comparison between the deep learning model and other five typical machine learning models as shown in Table 3. The five machine learning models are all optimized for the best accuracy by using the grid search technique.

Table 3: The Comparison of Modeling Results

| Model | Training Set | Test Set | Accuracy |
|---|---|---|---|
| SVM | 300 | 200 | 80.0% |
| C4.5 | 300 | 200 | 77.5% |
| Naïve Bayes | 300 | 200 | 79.0% |
| LR | 300 | 200 | 78.0% |
| MLP | 300 | 200 | 79.5% |
| **Deep Learning** | 300 | 200 | 96.5% |

To better mitigate mobile malware threats, we plan to automate the deep learning based tool for online Android malware detection in our future work, you can follow up our ongoing project at http://www.droid-sec.com.

# 5. ACKNOWLEDGEMENT

This work was supported by the National Key Technology R&D Program of China under Grant No.2012BAH46B04.

# 6. REFERENCES

[1] Y. Bengio. Learning deep architectures for ai. *Foundations and trends in Machine Learning*, 2(1):1–127, 2009.

[2] W. Enck, P. Gilbert, B.-G. Chun, L. P. Cox, J. Jung, P. McDaniel, and A. Sheth. Taintdroid: An information-flow tracking system for realtime privacy monitoring on smartphones. In *OSDI'10*, volume 10, pages 1–6, 2010.

[3] Y. Zhou and X. Jiang. Dissecting android malware: characterization and evolution. In *IEEE S&P'12*, pages 95–109, 2012.

[3] `https://code.google.com/p/droidbox`

[4] `http://contagiominidump.blogspot.com`

# Accelerating Incast and Multicast Traffic Delivery for Data-intensive Applications using Physical Layer Optics

Payman Samadi, Varun Gupta, Berk Birand, Howard Wang, Gil Zussman, Keren Bergman
Department of Electrical Engineering, Columbia University, New York, NY, 10027
[ps2805@, vg2297@, berk@ee, howard@ee., gil@ee., bergman@ee.]columbia.edu*

## ABSTRACT

We present a control plane architecture to accelerate multicast and incast traffic delivery for data-intensive applications in cluster-computing interconnection networks. The architecture is experimentally examined by enabling physical layer optical multicasting on-demand for the application layer to achieve non-blocking performance.

**Categories and Subject Descriptors:** C.2.1 [Computer-Communication Networks]: Network Architecture and Design Network communications, Circuit-switching networks
**Keywords:** Hybrid Data Center Networks; Optics; Incast; Multicast.

## 1. INTRODUCTION

With the enormous increase in the generation and complexity of Big Data, new opportunities and challenges related to its storage and processing on cluster-computing platforms arise. The interconnection networks of such platforms are generally over-subscribed, due to the switching cost and cabling complexity. Designing these interconnection networks based on the traffic patterns of the applications running on clusters can improve the overall performance of the system. In general, these applications use distributed file systems for storage and MapReduce type of algorithms for data processing. In analyzing these applications and the interconnection network, we found that large flows with traffic patterns that include multiple nodes result in heavy network congestion.

For example, in GoogleFileSystem, when storing and requesting data, blocks of 64MB are sent from one node to multiple nodes (point-to-multipoint: Multicast) or one node receives data from multiple nodes (many-to-one: Incast). Similar processes exist in HadoopFileSystem and in the shuffle stage of the MapReduce algorithm. Additionally, in other data center applications such as virtual machine provisioning or in-cluster software updating, there is a multicast of 300-800MB among 100-1000 nodes. Moreover, in parallel database join operation, there is multicast of several 100MB. Furthermore, in the Broadcast phase of Orchestra controlled by Spark [1], 300MB is multicast on 100 iterations. In current platforms, these patterns are managed either by sequence of unicast transmissions or software solutions such as peer-to-peer methods. These methods are naturally inefficient since multiple copies of the same data are transmitted on the network. For instance, the Orchestra system transmits 12 copies of the same data.

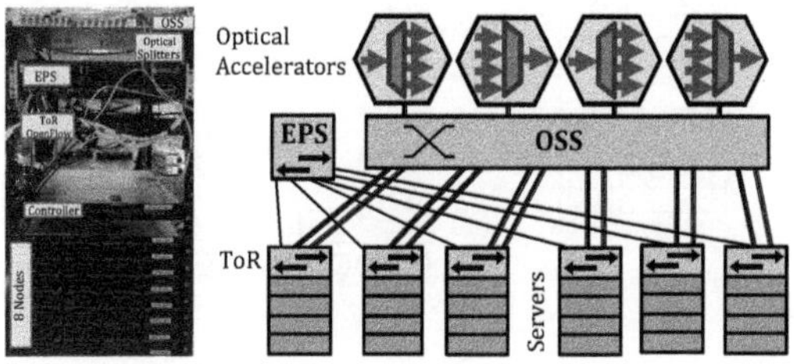


**Figure 1: Optical accelerators in the hybrid arch.**

Traditionally, electrical packet switching (EPS) networks in Fat-tree or multi-tier architecture are used for the interconnection networks of cluster-computing platforms. Recently, hybrid network architecture that combine EPS and optical circuit switching have been proposed to offload larger flows to the optical network [2, 3]. The switching of the optical network is implemented by optical space switches (OSS). The OSS, that performs point-to-point circuit switching can also serve as a substrate to connect optical modules as accelerators. For example, passive optical splitters can be used to provide a significantly more efficient multicasting [4]. In this method, data is optically replicated in the physical layer and transmitted by setting up a multicast tree between the source and the destinations. This operation sends only one copy of data and all the nodes receive the data simultaneously at the line-rate (non-blocking performance). Incast traffic delivery can also be optically accelerated using passive optical combiners and time-sharing the circuit between the senders. In both cases, the OSS that has slow switching time (25ms) is reconfigured once and this results in lower latency compared to the point-to-point architectures. These accelerators can potentially offload heavy data from the over-subscribed packet switching network and make them smaller and cheaper. The passive nature of these accelerators, can also reduce the networking power consumption. The main challenge in utilizing optical accelerator is the integration of

*This work was supported in part by CIAN NSF ERC under grant EEC-0812072.


*SIGCOMM'14*, August 17–22, 2014, Chicago, IL, USA.
ACM 978-1-4503-2836-4/14/08.
http://dx.doi.org/10.1145/2619239.2631436.

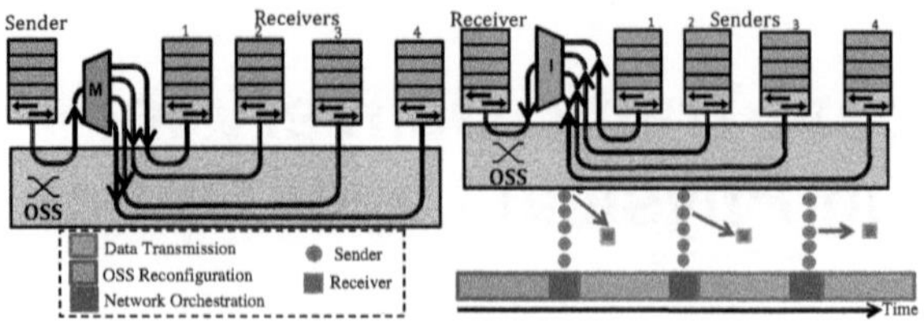


**Figure 2: Left: Optical multicasting by passive optical splitter, Right: Optical incast using passive optical combiner and the time-sharing orchestration.**

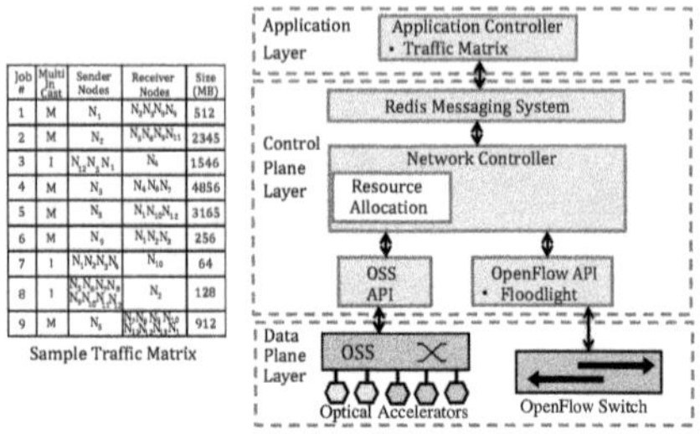


**Figure 3: Network Orchestration Architecture.**

optics with current network architectures due to the complexities in configuring optical devices and the circuit-based nature of optics. Cross-layer architectures can potentially overcome these complexities and provide optical functionalities more seamlessly to the application layer.

In this work, we present a control plane architecture that accelerates multicast and incast data delivery using passive optical modules. The architecture is experimentally examined on our 10G hybrid cluster-computing testbed with a demonstration of physical layer optical multicasting. The implemented control plane employs a messaging system, a resource allocation algorithm, and APIs to control the optical and electrical switching network.

## 2. IMPLEMENTATION AND RESULT

Fig. 1 shows the hybrid network architecture with optical accelerators. Top-of-Rack (ToR) switches are aggregated by an electrical packet switching network and an optical circuit switching network. An OSS is used to provide switching in the optical network and also as a substrate to connect optical accelerators. Physical layer optical multicast can be addressed using passive optical splitters that transparently duplicate the optical signal. Fig. 2 (left) shows the hardware configuration to generate multiple copies of data at the line rate. The incast traffic can be addressed by passive optical combiner with an orchestration system running on the packet switching network (Fig. 2 (right)). Optical splitters and combiners are data rate transparent, passive, and commercially available in high port counts. Also the OSS can be configured in a way to cascade multiple modules. Fig. 3 demonstrates the network orchestration architecture consisting of the Application, Control, and Data Plane layers. The Control Plane has a central network controller that manages the network and includes a resource allocation algorithm. The network controller communicates with the Data Plane layer via southbound APIs including Floodlight for the OpenFlow switches and OSS API, which is a python-based API developed in-house. For the northbound API of

**Table 1: Completion time of 50 multicast jobs (seconds) Proposed optical Multicast and non-blocking Internet Protocol Multicast**

| | Group Size | |
|---|---|---|
| | 7 | 4 |
| Proposed | 226.179 | 187.348 |
| Non-blocking | 218.517 | 191.680 |

the Control Plane, we have developed a pub/sub messaging system using Redis. Byte size messages are transmitted on the EPS network between the nodes and the central controllers. We observed the latency by sending 200 messages of 20 bytes among nodes and measured average latency of 300 $\mu s$.

For optical multicasting, the general algorithm of the network controller is as followings: The application controller submits the traffic matrix of the jobs that require optical resources to the network controller via the Redis messaging system. The traffic matrix includes the source, destinations, and the size of the multicast job. The resource allocation algorithm tries to schedule the optical splitters across the multicast requests by maximizing the obtained throughput. We model this problem as an Integer Program (IP) and solve using the GLPK solver that implements a branch-and-bound method. Using the solution of IP, the network controller generates the network configuration for the next job. Then, the ToR switches are configured using Floodlight, and the OSS connections are applied using our API. For optical multicasting, the network controller first notifies the receivers using the Redis messaging system. Then, the senders are notified to begin the transmission. Each receiver sends a message to the controller, notifying the completion of the job. Once the controller receives these messages from all the receivers for a given job, it updates the traffic matrix and reruns the algorithm. We evaluated the performance of our architecture for multicasting in comparison with Internet Protocol (IP) multicast over a non-blocking EPS network on our 8-node hybrid cluster-computing test-bed (Fig. 1). Two sets of 50 multicast jobs (500MB-5GB) with the maximum group size of 4 and 7 were generated. The former involves maximum half of the nodes and one splitter. The latter can involve the whole network and requires cascading of splitters. Table 1 shows the completion time in seconds. Our proposed optical multicast performs similar to the ideal fully non-blocking network. This means that our architecture provides line rate non-blocking multicast between the nodes that is not possible in practical interconnection networks. Additionally, it can potentially decongest the over-subscribed EPS network by offloading the multi/in-cast traffic to the optical network.

## 3. REFERENCES

[1] M. Chowdhury, M. Zaharia, J. Ma, M. I. Jordan, and I. Stoica. Managing data transfers in computer clusters with orchestra. In *ACM SIGCOMM*, 2011.

[2] N. Farrington, G. Porter, S. Radhakrishnan, H. H. Bazzaz, V. Subramanya, Y. Fainman, G. Papen, and A. Vahdat. Helios: A hybrid electrical/optical switch architecture for modular data centers. In *ACM SIGCOMM*, 2010.

[3] G. Wang, D. G. Andersen, M. Kaminsky, K. Papagiannaki, T. E. Ng, M. Kozuch, and M. Ryan. c-through: Part-time optics in data centers. In *ACM SIGCOMM*, 2010.

[4] H. Wang, Y. Xia, K. Bergman, T. E. Ng, S. Sahu, and K. Sripanidkulchai. Rethinking the physical layer of data center networks of the next decade: Using optics to enable efficient *-cast connectivity. *SIGCOMM Com. Comm. Rev.*, July 2013.

# Social SDN: Online Social Networks Integration in Wireless Network Provisioning


Arjuna Sathiaseelan
University of Cambridge
Cambridge, UK
as2330@cam.ac.uk

M. Said Seddiki
Georgia Tech / Lorraine University
Atlanta,USA / Nancy, France
seddiki.said@gatech.edu

Stoyan Stoyanov
University of Cambridge
Cambridge, UK
sis26@cam.ac.uk

Dirk Trossen
InterDigital Europe Ltd
London, UK
dirk.trossen@interdigital.com



## Categories and Subject Descriptors

C.2.2 [**Computer Systems Organization**]: Network Operations—*Network management*

## Keywords

Software Defined Networking; Online Social Networks.


## 1. INTRODUCTION

The recent advances in Software Defined Networking (SDN) have demonstrated more flexibility in controlling and managing access networks by the different stakeholders, such as users, infrastructure providers, or virtual network operators (see [3]). SDN is a natural evolution that brings programmability to network elements by merging datacoms with telecoms where the need for higher programmability of the data plane has been pushed from data centres into wider area networks. Network operators are making sure to leave no stone unturned to take advantage of the flexibility offered by the SDN paradigm to manage and make time and cost critical traffic engineering decisions, thus avoiding/reducing the costs incurred to the different stakeholders that use and operate the network. Network operators perform large scale data analytics on *internal* network and traffic data which is then fed back to network applications that utilise specific control plane functions to reconfigure and manage the network. The integration of Big Data with SDN is seen as an important strategy by the network operators.

In this paper, we propose the idea of integrating *external* data (such as information from Facebook, Twitter, news feeds etc.) with SDN to enable operators to make intelligent traffic engineering decisions with their networks. Such integration would pave the way for novel ways of identifying not only the internal network and traffic characteristics (as currently carried out by operators) but also external/user needs (engineering the network dynamically to support the needs of the users). Imagine a scenario where data from Online Social Networks (OSN) could be used to predict the need for allocation for resources: for e.g. based on twitter trends the network operator understanding/predicting flash crowds in an area and allocating resources dynamically to satisfy the need or network operators understanding trends in OSN for certain TV programs and estimating the demand that will be placed on the network and allocating the capacity. Such integration will also be very useful during emergencies, such as natural disasters or terrorist activities, where networks could be opened up to the public to communicate.

We define **Social SDN**, a SDN architecture that enables integration of OSN with wireless networks. The architecture defines the necessary northbound APIs that interface data from OSNs to the appropriate control functions that make the necessary traffic engineering decisions. These decisions are then pushed to the network via south bound APIs by the controller. We will demonstrate a use case of this architecture by developing a new application that enables home owners to express their home network sharing policies based on online social relationships. These policies are then translated into traffic engineering decisions providing varying Quality of Service (QoS) levels to users who use the sharer's wireless network based on their OSN relationship with the sharer.

## 2. ARCHITECTURE

In our proposed architecture (Fig. 1), the control plane exposes a minimal northbound RESTful API, through which third party applications access the different control functions provided by the control plane for queue/QoS management, traffic redirection etc. Specific applications can be developed that utilise the policies expressed by the different stakeholders as well as the data mined data from OSNs to use specific control plane functions to orchestrate new rules within the network. These control functions are distributed across the network and we demonstrate one such function in the next section. The Access Point Manager (APM) resides in home broadband access points exposing to the controller a configuration API for traffic shaping queues, access point QoS management and an Openflow control interface. The Slice Manager enables creation



*SIGCOMM'14,* August 17–22, 2014, Chicago, IL, USA.
ACM 978-1-4503-2836-4/14/08.
http://dx.doi.org/10.1145/2619239.2631437.

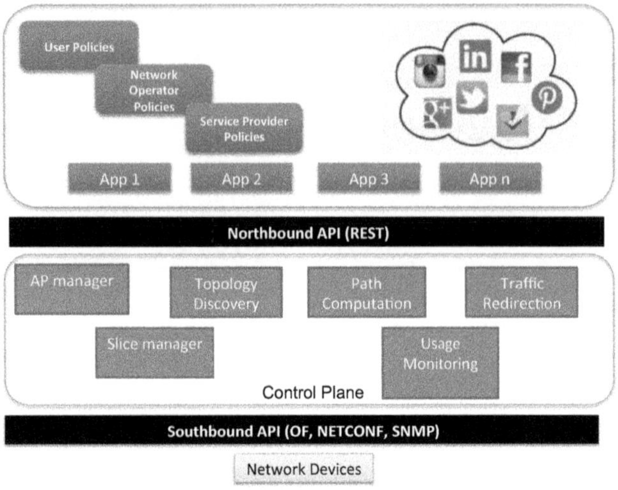


**Figure 1: Social SDN: Proposed Architecture.**

and management of individual network slices, providing strict traffic isolation and traffic guarantees. For this, the information provided by the Topology Discovery provides a global view of individual node resource availability. Such view in turn being utilized to provide Path Computation and Traffic Redirection functions within the individual slices, complemented with the appropriate accounting functionality based on the Usage Monitoring function. All network control decisions (new rules) are pushed to the data plane via the south bound APIs that support both OpenFlow as well as legacy protocols such as NETCONF, SNMP etc.

# 3. USE CASE: EXPLOITING ONLINE SOCIAL RELATIONSHIPS TO ENABLE HOME BANDWIDTH MANAGEMENT

The proposed use case demonstrates how online social relationships can be translated into network sharing decisions. In our use case, we developed an application that enables home owners to express network sharing policies based on online social relationships. These policies are then translated into traffic engineering decisions providing varying QoS levels to users who use the network based on their OSN relationship with the sharer. The sharing policies are based on the concept of social relationships, or "friendships" in Facebook, between the sharer and other users of the network classified through the different classes of relationships represented in Facebook (e.g., close friends, family, acquaintances or not in the friend's list). These classes are very intuitive for users and users would be able to easily translate from this Facebook classification scheme to the concept of different classes of users within a network which may receive different resource allocations. For e.g. a group of people who are members of the network owner's "close friends" group on Facebook may receive a higher bandwidth on the owner's network than users who are not friends or 'close friends' might receive priority over any non-friends. The use of OSN for making networking related decisions is not new. Openwifi [5], FON [2] and Cisco Meraki [1] have recently deployed solutions that allow users to log into the wireless network using their Facebook credentials. However, these solutions do not support any procedures for

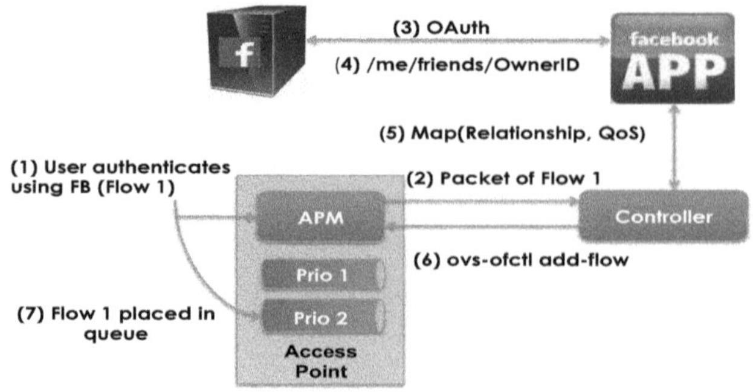


**Figure 2: Mapping social relationships to network resource provisioning.**

a network owner to create a customised sharing policy or control how capacity is granted to connected users.

Figure 2 presents the control flow diagram of our proposed use case. Whenever, an user tries to use a WiFi network that is shared by a network owner (for e.g. in a crowdshared network such as FON), our application daemon (Facebook APP) running on the home access point checks if the user has been authenticated. If not authenticated, the user is immediately redirected to a Facebook login page. Upon successful authentication, the web page obtains the user identification data plus an access token, an opaque string that identifies the user, application or web page, information about when the token will expire and which application generated the token. Using this information our application uses the Facebook Graph API to obtain a list of the friends of the recently-authenticated user. The data from this API is returned in a JSON format. The application then uses the data returned from the Graph API to determine the social relationship between the user and the network owner and categorize the user into the appropriate class. This data is then used to create a mapping between the specific user and the QoS. The controller then pushes the specific OpenFlow rule to the APM and the user is granted access and capacity based on the sharing policies created by the network' owner. **Ongoing Work**: We have built a prototype of the use case by integrating a kernel module of Open vSwitch on OpenWRT. The controller was developed by extending the functionality of the Floodlight controller (v0.9). The code is publicly available at [4]. More work is being carried out to develop new applications that will demonstrate the benefits of our proposed architecture. Performance benchmarking of the control plane functions will also be carried out.

# 4. REFERENCES


[1] Cisco Meraki. `http://meraki.cisco.com/`.

[2] Fon. `http://www.fon.com`.

[3] A. Sathiaseelan, C. Rotsos, C. Sriram, D. Trossen, P. Papadimitriou, and J. Crowcroft. Virtual public networks. In *Second European Workshop on Software Defined Networks (EWSDN)*, pages 1–6, 2013.

[4] Virtual Public Networks code. `https://github.com/sarjuna/vpun`.

[5] K.-K. Yap, Y. Yiakoumis, M. Kobayashi, S. Katti, G. Parulkar, and N. McKeown. Separating authentication, access and accounting: A case study with openwifi. *Open Networking Foundation, Tech. Rep*, 2011.

# Flow-level State Transition as a New Switch Primitive for SDN

Masoud Moshref, Apoorv Bhargava, Adhip Gupta, Minlan Yu, Ramesh Govindan
University of Southern California

## Categories and Subject Descriptors

C.2.0 [**Computer-Communication Networks**]; C.2.1 [**Network Architecture and Design**]; C.2.4 [**Distributed Systems**]: Network operating systems

## Keywords

Software-defined Network; State Machine

## 1. INTRODUCTION

Software-defined networking has changed networking by separating the control plane from the data plane. While there have been many innovations on the controller applications for different network management needs, most of these applications still rely on flow-based rules in the data plane. These flow-based rules often match on multiple packet header fields (e.g., source/destination IP addresses), take predefined actions on the matching packets (e.g., dropping the packet, forwarding it to an outgoing port), or maintain counters (e.g., the number of packets or bytes).

The controller saves flow-based rules to the switches in two modes: proactive and reactive. In the *proactive* approach, the controller populates rules in switches ahead of time for all the flows coming to the switch. However, the proactive approach requires a priori knowledge of events at switches, and how to handle these events.

The *reactive* approach supports more dynamic applications, but has poor performance. In the reactive approach, switches often send the events (e.g. the first packet of each flow) to the controller, and the controller installs flow-based rules based on these events. However, this introduces significant overhead (CPU, memory, etc.) at the switch, high performance overhead (i.e., delay and throughput), and scalability problems due to the limited communication channel between the switches and the controller [1]. For example, consider a stateful firewall that denies unsolicited inbound traffic if it cannot find a corresponding outbound flow in established state. The controller becomes aware of the state of outbound flows by receiving the TCP signals (e.g., SYN, FIN) from the switch and denies the unsolicited inbound flows and installs forwarding rules for others upon receiving their first packet. This means that switches have to send *multiple* packets of the same flow to the controller, and


*SIGCOMM'14*, August 17–22, 2014, Chicago, IL, USA.
ACM 978-1-4503-2836-4/14/08.
http://dx.doi.org/10.1145/2619239.2631439.

1) Task:=(StateMachine,InstanceMapping)
2) StateMachine:=({State},{Transition},{Action},Filter)
3) State:=(name,{Variable})
4) Variable:=(name,#bits)
5) Transition:=(StartState,Condition,TargetState,$\mathcal{F}$)
6) Condition:=$f_1$(StartState.Variables,Packet)$\rightarrow$True|False
7) $\mathcal{F}$:=$f_2$(State.Variables,Packet)$\rightarrow$TargetState.Variables
8) Action:=(State,Condition,Instruction,Priority)
9) Filter:=$f_3$(Packet)$\rightarrow$True|False
10) InstanceMapping:=$f_4$(Packet)$\rightarrow$Index

Table 1: FAST abstraction

the controller has to reactively change the flow-level rules based on these incoming packets.

To reduce the controller's involvement in many dynamic applications, many works recognize the limitations of flow-based rules and have proposed specific optimizations in the data plane. DevoFlow [1] reduces the controller overhead by introducing rule cloning and measurement triggers. OpenFlow 1.3 supports rate limiting by allowing switches to track flow rates and tag/drop excess traffic without the controller involvement. Open vSwitch adopts learn actions for software switches that can install new rules when traffic matches an old one.

Instead of proposing yet another specific optimization, we aim at identifying a new generic data-plane abstraction to replace flow-based rules. We observe that many networking tasks can be expressed as local state machines over a flow or an aggregate of flows. For example, to implement the stateful firewall, the controller may install a state machine on the switch to keep track of TCP states. The associated action on each state can allow/deny inbound traffic based on the TCP state.

We propose FAST (Flow-level State Transitions) as a new switch abstraction. FAST allows the controller to proactively program state transitions, and allows the switches to run *dynamic* actions based on local information. FAST supports a wide range of dynamic applications and can be easily implemented with today's commodity switch components.

## 2. DESIGN & EVALUATION

FAST includes three parts: (1) an abstraction that allows operators to program their state machines for a variety of applications; (2) a FAST controller that translates state machines to the data plane API and manages the interaction of local state machines with network-wide tasks; (3) a FAST data plane that includes a pipeline of tables to support state machines with commodity switch components. The detail of each component comes next.

**Abstraction:** Table 1 describes how a task is defined in FAST using state machines. The parentheses represent a tuple, curly brackets show a set, and right arrows define the output of a function. We now highlight the important aspects of the task definition: States may require storing counters that represent many states over the

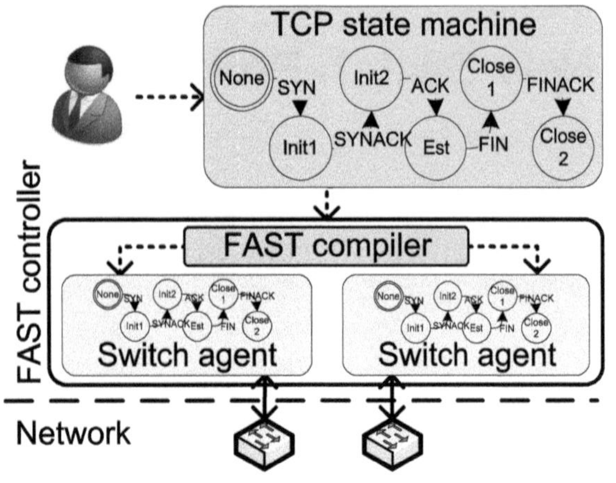


Figure 1: FAST architecture

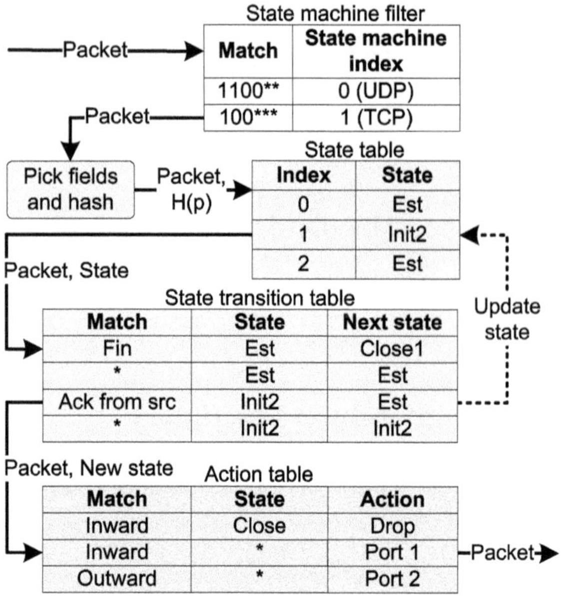


Figure 2: Implementing TCP state machine in FAST data plane

| Approach | Mean | $5^{th}$ | $95^{th}$ |
|---|---|---|---|
| Proactive | 1.85 | 1.45 | 3.68 |
| Reactive | 84.8 | 57.84 | 109.7 |
| FAST | 3.02 | 1.34 | 5.93 |

Table 2: Comparing flow completion delay (ms) for 100 experiments

variable values. Later, the controller can map the state names and their variables to a bit string representing an extended set of states where each counter value makes a new state. Transitions leverage a guard condition which can match on state variables. Actions execute a standard OpenFlow instructions. The programmer can also filter the traffic going through a set of state machines, and finally the abstraction includes a state mapping function over packet headers to map a packet to the right state machine instance.

**Controller:** The FAST compiler translates user's state machine definitions to the actual code (switch agents) that can run state machines at individual switches (Figure 1). It uses the knowledge of topology and switch constraints to make switch agents specific to the switch capabilities and configures them to install the state machines only on a subset of switches (e.g., ingress). A switch agent has three responsibilities: (1) It converts state machines to the switch API. (2) If the switch does not support a required feature to implement a state machine, the switch agent falls back to the reactive approach and performs part of the state machine by receiving packet-ins. (3) If a network-wide task (e.g., traffic engineering) requires to be informed of a local event (state change), the switch agent programs the switch to send packet-ins to report to the task.

**Data-plane:** Figure 2 describes FAST data plane on top of the current flow-based multi-table architecture. While this is not the only architecture to support state machines, especially, in the software switches, we believe it is a transition step from the flow-based rules to a state-machine based data plane. We use TCP state machine as a running example to illustrate the components of state machines, which can be implemented with hardware currently available on commodity switches. The design contains four tables. The state machine filter table is shared among multiple types of state machines, but the other three are specific to each state machine definition. The state table keeps track of state machine instances and is implemented as a hash-table. We decouple actions from state transitions for two reasons. First, it can be more compact: a single entry in action table can cover the actions in multiple states. For example, regardless of whether the state machine is in the Established or Init1 state, one can specify the same action (e.g., forward to port 1). More important, however, is that we *need* this decoupling for our problem domain. While there is one instance of a TCP state machine, the action corresponding to a flow being in a specific state may depend on the flow itself (e.g. output port). The switch agent installs a state machine on data plane by adding a rule in the filter table, specifying the hash fields and the initial state for the state table, and installing state transition rules and action rules in the corresponding tables.

We have implemented a FAST prototype with POX and Open vSwitch. At the controller side, a switch agent proactively installs state machines using OpenFlow protocol. We have instantiated the state machines and changed their states leveraging the Open vSwitch learn action. We use TCP state machine as an example. The state machine transits on SYN, SYNACK, ACK, FIN, and FINACK flags; thus we added the matching on TCP signals in Open vSwitch and OpenFlow commands. Table 2 compares the delay of going through the TCP state machine for a flow as the time between initiating a connection with only one data packet until terminating it. FAST has much smaller delay comparing to the reactive approach because there is no need to send the signals to the controller. However, due to the overhead of calculating the hashes and updating the state table, its delay is larger than simple proactive approach. Note that the proactive approach cannot track TCP state machine. We also compared the throughput of an iperf connection in FAST vs. proactive approach. As the iperf connection remains in the Established state, this shows the overhead of only hashing and checking the current state. The throughput of FAST is very close to proactive approach (7.8 Gbps vs 8.2 Gbps, respectively with standard deviation of 0.2Gbps over 30 tries).

To summarize, compared to the primitive of flow-based rules, FAST can support more flexible networking tasks, improves the performance and scalability of the SDN controller, and can be easily implemented with commodity switch components. The future work at the controller side includes partially installing, consistent installing, verifying, and composing state machines. At the data plane, we plan to use richer set of features at switches such as flexibly parsing the packet header and to optimize memory usage of state machines to fit in switches with limited resources.

# 3. REFERENCES

[1] A. R. Curtis, J. C. Mogul, J. Tourrilhes, P. Yalagandula, P. Sharma, and S. Banerjee. Devoflow: Scaling flow management for high-performance networks. In *SIGCOMM*, 2011.

# T-DNS: Connection-Oriented DNS to Improve Privacy and Security (poster abstract)

Liang Zhu[1] Zi Hu[1] John Heidemann[1]
Duane Wessels[2] Allison Mankin[2] Nikita Somaiya[1]
1: University of Southern California 2: Verisign Labs

**Categories and Subject Descriptors:** C.2.2 [**Computer-Communication Networks**]: Network Protocols—*Applications*; C.2.3 [**Computer-Communication Networks**]: Network Operations—*Public networks*; C.2.5 [**Computer-Communication Networks**]: Local and Wide-Area Networks—*Internet*

**Keywords:** Domain Name System (DNS), Transport Layer Security (TLS), privacy, security, network protocols, performance

## 1. INTRODUCTION

DNS is the canonical protocol for connectionless UDP. Yet DNS today is challenged by eavesdropping that compromises privacy, source-address spoofing that results in denial-of-service (DoS) attacks on the server and third parties, injection attacks that exploit fragmentation, and size limitations that constrain policy and operational choices. We propose *T-DNS* to address these problems. It uses TCP to smoothly support large payloads and to mitigate spoofing and amplification for DoS. T-DNS uses transport-layer security (TLS) to provide privacy from users to their DNS resolvers and optionally to authoritative servers. Expectations about DNS suggest connections will balloon client latency and overwhelm servers with state, but our evaluation shows costs are modest: end-to-end latency from *TLS to the recursive resolver is only about 9% slower* with UDP to the authoritative server, and 22% slower with TCP to the authoritative. With diverse traces we show that frequent connection reuse is possible (60–95% for stub and recursive resolvers, although half that for authoritative servers), and after connection establishment, we show TCP and TLS latency is equivalent to UDP. With conservative timeouts (20 s at authoritative servers and 60 s elsewhere) and conservative estimates of connection state memory requirements, we show that *server memory requirements match current hardware*: a large recursive resolver may have 24k active connections requiring about 3.6 GB additional RAM. We identify the key design and implementation decisions needed to minimize overhead: query pipelining, out-of-order responses, TLS connection resumption, and plausible timeouts.

Here we summarize our approach and poster, and expand on evaluation, alternatives, and deployment elsewhere [17];

## 2. PROBLEM STATEMENT

Our goal is to reduce the limitations that result from DNS' current optimization around a single-packet exchange.


*SIGCOMM'14*, August 17–22, 2014, Chicago, IL, USA.
ACM 978-1-4503-2836-4/14/08.
http://dx.doi.org/10.1145/2619239.2631442.

**Need for DNS Privacy:** Traditionally, privacy of Internet traffic has not been seen as critical. However, recent trends in DNS use, deployment and documentation of widespread eavesdropping increase the need for query privacy [3]. First, end-user queries are increasingly exposed to possible eavesdropping, through use of third-party DNS services such as OpenDNS and Google Public DNS, and through open networks such as WiFi hotspots. Second, the presence of widespread eavesdropping and misdirection is now well documented, for government espionage [7], censorship [1], and criminal gain [12]. Finally, ISPs have recognized the opportunity to monetize DNS typos, redirecting non-existing domain responses (NXDOMAIN hijacking), a practice widespread since 2009 (for example [13]).

**Need for Sender Validation:** *Uncertainty about the source address of senders* is a problem affecting DNS servers and others on the Internet. Today source IP addresses are easy to spoof, allowing botnets to mount denial-of-service (DoS) attacks on DNS servers directly [10], and to leverage DNS servers in amplification attacks [16] against third parties. Specific work-arounds to DNS' role in DoS attacks exist, and rate-limiting helps. T-DNS would greatly reduce the vulnerability of DNS to DoS in a general way. Well established techniques protect DNS servers from TCP-based DoS attacks [6, 15], and TCP's connection establishment precludes source address spoofing, eliminating amplification attacks, and webservers developed solutions for TCP-specific risks [17].

**Avoiding Arbitrary Limits to Response Size:** *Limitation in payload size* is an increasing problem as DNS evolves to improve security. Without EDNS, UDP DNS messages are limited to 512 B. With EDNS, clients and servers may increase this limit (4096 B is typical), although this can lead to IP fragmentation raising its own problems [11]. UDP packet limitations expose DNS to fragmentation attacks and security problems [8]. Of greater concern, UDP size constraints have a corrosive effect on policy decisions. Three examples include limits to the number of root servers, limits to sizes of DNSSEC keys and raising concerns about key rollover. By replacing current 1024-bit RSA signatures with longer ones in a trace captured at one server for `.com`, over the 13.5M DNSSEC enabled responses, we find that with a 2048-bit Zone Signing Key (ZSK), 5% of DNSSEC responses, almost *all* NXDomain responses, and some DNSKEYs during rollover will suffer IP fragmentation.

## 3. DESIGN AND IMPLEMENTATION

T-DNS uses in-band TLS negotiation (our addition). We identify implementation choices needed for good performance.

**Upwards TLS Negotiation:** IETF encourages in-band upgrade to TLS (not new ports); this approach is the current preference for many protocols, including IMAP and SMTP. We therefore propose [9] a new EDNS0 extension [5] to negotiate the use of TLS. We suggest a new "TLS OK" (TO) bit as an EDNS0 option. A client requests TLS by setting this bit and sending a DNS query. A server that supports TLS responds with the same bit set, then both client and server transition to a TLS handshake. The DNS query made to start TLS negotiation is sent without encryption so it should not disclose information. We recommend a distinguished query for name "STARTTLS," type TXT, class CH, analogous to current support queries.

**Implementation choices** are critical to good performance. *Pipelining* is the ability to send several queries before the responses arrive. It avoids round-trip delays by the stop-and-wait alternative. Batches of queries are common: recursive resolvers with many clients will have concurrent queries to popular authoritative servers like `.com`, and 62% of web pages have 4 or more unique domain names.

*Out-of-order processing* (OOOP) at recursive resolvers avoids head-of-line blocking in pipelines. OOOP is defined and explicitly allowed by RFC-5966 [2]. Without OOOP, queries to even a small percentage of distant servers will stall a strictly-ordered queue, unnecessarily delaying all subsequent queries. Without connections, concurrent UDP queries are naturally independent and all major DNS servers process them concurrently. We know of no DNS server today that supports out-of-order processing of TCP queries; `BIND` and `Unbound` instead resolve each query for a TCP connection before considering the next.

Two protocol optimizations can speed re-opening of closed connections. *TCP fast open* [4] allows data to be exchanged in the three-way handshake packets, saving one round-trip time (RTT) in the TCP handshake. With *TLS resumption* [14], a sever gives the client all state needed to securely re-create a TLS connection, saving one RTT in TLS setup.

We describe strategies for gradual deployment elsewhere [17].

# 4. T-DNS PERFORMANCE EVALUATION

The main contribution of our work is a careful performance study of T-DNS to show that TCP and TLS have reasonable cost. We show that connection reuse works well, that servers require a reasonable amount of state, and that clients have only modest latency improvements.

**Connection reuse and server state:** Connection caching poses a fundamental trade-off: clients prefer long-lived connections (they have resources and hate latency), but servers prefer short-lived connections (they share resources over may clients). We examine this trade-off, varying connection timeout to measure the *connection hit fraction*, how often an existing connection can be reused without setup, and *concurrent connections*, how many connections are active on a server at any time. We recommend timeouts of 60 s for recursive resolvers and 20 s for authoritative servers based on analysis of traces and conservative choices. Trace analysis with these values shows 85% connection hit rates, and Figure 1 shows the number of concurrent connections. If we assume 150 kB memory per connection, the 75%iles suggest the Level 3 recursive resolver requires 3.6 GB RAM, and the B-Root authoritative resolver requires about 7.4 GB. These values are well within current, commodity server hardware.

**End-to-end Latency:** For clients, the primary cost of T-DNS is the additional latency due to connection setup. We experimentally evaluate the stub-to-recursive and recursive-to-authoritative latency with TCP and TLS respectively in prototyped implementations. These results show that connection setup latency is dominated by protocol RTT requirements, and that connection reuse can completely remove setup latency in the 85% of connection hits.

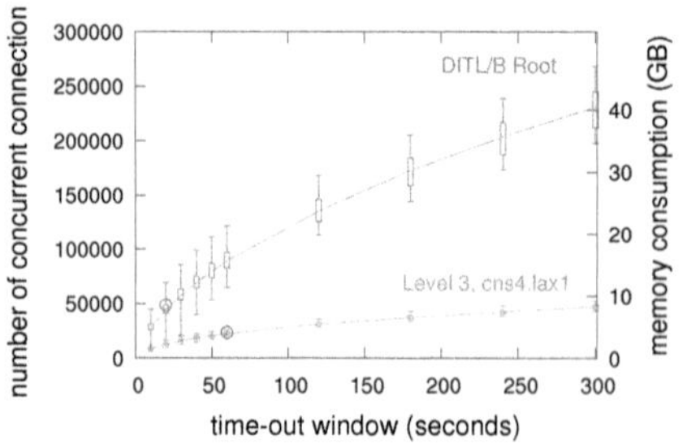


Figure 1: Median and quartiles of numbers concurrent connections. Datasets: Level 3/cns4.lax1 and B-Root

We model the expected (average) *end-to-end* latency for DNS users. We see that *use of TCP and TLS to the local resolver adds moderate latency*: TLS is only 9% slower with UDP upstream. Second, we see that use of connections between recursive and authoritative is very expensive: with TLS stub-to-recursive, adding TCP to the authoritative is 22% slower and adding TLS to the authoritative is more than 170% slower. This cost follows because a single stub-to-recursive query can lead to multiple recursive-to-authoritative queries, at large RTTs with a lower connection-hit fraction.

# 5. REFERENCES


[1] Anonymous. The collateral damage of internet censorship by DNS injection. *SIGCOMM CCR*, June 2012.

[2] R. Bellis. DNS Transport over TCP - Implementation Requirements. RFC 5966, Aug. 2010.

[3] S. Bortzmeyer. DNS privacy problem statement. Internet draft, Dec. 2013.

[4] Y. Cheng, J. Chu, S. Radhakrishnan, and A. Jain. TCP fast open, Dec. 2011. Work in progress (Internet draft draft-cheng-tcpm-fastopen-02).

[5] J. Damas, M. Graff, and P. Vixie. Extension mechanisms for DNS (EDNS(0)). RFC 6891, Apr. 2013.

[6] W. Eddy. TCP SYN flooding attacks and common mitigations. RFC 4987, Aug. 2007.

[7] G. Greenwald. NSA collecting phone records of millions of Verizon customers daily. *The Guardian*, June 2013.

[8] A. Herzberg and H. Shulmanz. Fragmentation considered poisonous. IEEE-CNS, Oct. 2013.

[9] Z. Hu, L. Zhu, J. Heidemann, A. Mankin, and D. Wessels. Starting TLS over DNS. Internet draft, Jan. 2014.

[10] ICANN. Root server attack on 6 February 2007. Technical report, Mar. 2007.

[11] C. A. Kent and J. C. Mogul. Fragmentation considered harmful. In *SIGCOMM*, pages 390–401, Aug. 1987.

[12] W. Meng, R. Duan, and W. Lee. DNS Changer remediation study. Talk at M3AAWG 27th, Feb. 2013.

[13] C. Metz. Comcast trials (domain helper service) DNS hijacker. The Register, July 2009.

[14] J. Salowey, H. Zhou, P. Eronen, and H. Tschofenig. Transport Layer Security (TLS) Session Resumption without Server-Side State. RFC 5077, Jan. 2008.

[15] W. Simpson. TCP cookie transactions, Jan. 2011.

[16] R. Vaughn and G. Evron. DNS amplification attacks. `http://isotf.org/news/DNS-Amplification-Attacks.pdf`, Mar. 2006.

[17] L. Zhu, Z. Hu, J. Heidemann, D. Wessels, A. Mankin, and N. Somaiya. T-DNS: Connection-oriented DNS to improve privacy and security (extended). Technical Report ISI-TR-2014-693, USC/ISI, June 2014.

# Extending the Software-defined Network Boundary

Oliver Michel
University of Colorado Boulder
oliver.michel@colorado.edu

Michael Coughlin
University of Colorado Boulder
michael.coughlin@colorado.edu

Eric Keller
University of Colorado Boulder
eric.keller@colorado.edu

## ABSTRACT

Given that Software-Defined Networking is highly successful in solving many of today's manageability, flexibility, and scalability issues in large-scale networks, in this paper we argue that the concept of SDN can be extended even further. Many applications (esp. stream processing and big-data applications) rely on graph-based inter-process communication patterns that are very similar to those in computer networks. To our mind, this network abstraction spanning over different types of entities is highly suitable for and would benefit from central (SDN-inspired) control for the same reasons classical networks do. In this work, we investigate the commonalities between such intra-host networks and classical computer networking. Based on this, we study the feasibility of a central network controller that manages both network traffic and intra-host communication over a custom bus system.

## Categories and Subject Descriptors

C.2.1 [**Computer-Communication Networks**]: Network Architecture and Design—*packet-switching networks, network topology*; C.2.4 [**Computer-Communication Networks**]: Distributed Systems—*distributed applications*

## General Terms

Design, Performance, Reliability

## 1. INTRODUCTION

Software-Defined Networking (SDN) has been highly successful in solving many of today's manageability, flexibility, and scalability issues in large-scale networks. In the years since SDN was introduced we have seen the software-defined network boundary extended from the physical network into the hypervisor. We argue that the concept of SDN can be extended even further. We believe that certain systems benefit from SDN-inspired control of all their communication which includes inter-process and inter-thread communication.


*SIGCOMM'14*, August 17–22, 2014, Chicago, IL, USA.
ACM 978-1-4503-2836-4/14/08.
http://dx.doi.org/10.1145/2619239.2631443.

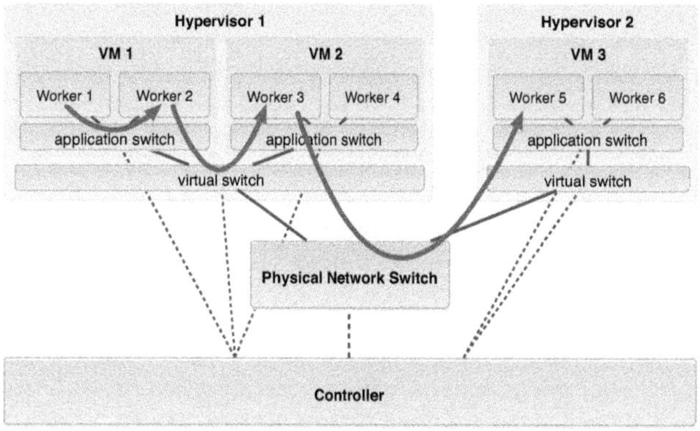


**Figure 1: System Architecture**

Many applications (*esp.* stream processing and big-data applications) rely on graph-based communication patterns that are very similar to those in computer networks. This network abstraction spanning over different types of entities (threads, processes, virtual hosts, and physical hosts) is highly suitable for and would benefit from central control for the same reasons classical networks do.

In this work, we investigate the commonalities between such intra-host networks and classical computer networking. Based on this, we study the feasibility of a central network controller that manages both network traffic and intra-host communication over a custom or modified bus or message queue system, as illustrated in figure 1. We believe that also in this scenario, central control can be beneficial to system performance, flexibility and elasticity as it allows for dynamic demand-driven re-wiring and re-balancing of graph-based systems regardless whether a given edge is spanning across hosts or is local to a single host.

## 2. SOFTWARE-DEFINED INTRA-HOST COMMUNICATION

### 2.1 Stream Processing

While there are several use-cases for extending central communication control into the host, this work is highly motivated by stream processing systems. While existing well-known frameworks like Hadoop focus on batch-style processing and analytics of data, a more recent trend focuses on processing of data generated in real-time [3]. Examples for such systems are Storm, Samza, and S4. In these systems, data-streams traverse a graph consisting of worker instances.

While nodes in this graph may correspond to actual virtual or physical hosts, this is not necessarily the case. Subsequently, edges in such a graph may stay within the boundaries of one host or span across the network.

Despite the fact that most stream processing frameworks have some notion of dynamically re-balancing the processing topology, this functionality is still generally inflexible, is not designed to dynamically respond to processing demand and, most importantly, does not support the dynamic introduction of new classes of workers (*e.g.,* an additional monitoring layer) at runtime. These limitations make it difficult for systems to respond automatically to changes in demand or introduce new functionality without halting the entire system. This is mainly due to static placement of message queue systems like RabbitMQ or Kafka in between workers.

Furthermore, a major challenge that arises with such systems is the influence network performance can have on the rate of processing obtainable. Much research has examined the impact network performance can have on Hadoop-style computation ([4] among others), especially in multi-tenant clouds, and proposed solutions to improve performance [1, 2]. Yet, little work has been done with regard to stream-processing frameworks.

### 2.2 The case for central control

In order to provide stream processing systems with an ability to change a running data processing graph, improve flexibility and elasticity, we elaborate on the idea of using SDN-inspired control of both network communication and inter-worker communication on a single host. Even though we have fine grained control over the communication between nodes, typically only local and low-level configuration options are available for all communication that stays within the boundaries of a host. We propose extending the software-defined network boundary into the operating system and even applications. The SDN controller can then be used to create network abstractions for particular applications and change properties of the communication graph to react to application's needs.

We believe that a central controller may handle both network communication and communication local to a host. Thereby, we provide a general abstraction for communication patterns independent of whether communication partners are placed on the same host or not. In fact, our system may provide a very similar API to the one used by the most prominent SDN wire protocol OpenFlow. That is a flow abstraction to specify data streams across the network. With this abstraction (which would also seamlessly work with existing SDN technology), it does not matter if a flow between nodes or across the topology is local to a single host or spreads across an entire datacenter.

Going one step further, this abstraction also allows tenants in a datacenter to specify their data-flow graph and the controller may allocate bandwidth, place, and migrate virtual machines to provide the requested topology and characteristics.

Through central control, optimized placement across the entire administrative domain (potentially saving resources and money by giving their placement logic to the datacenter operator) is possible.

### 2.3 Prototype

Instead of directly integrating this idea into existing stream processing frameworks, we started by implementing a very limited custom prototype of a stream processing framework incorporating central control of the topology and its properties. Our prototype consists of skeleton code for workers, a so-called application switch and the central controller. The controller controls both OpenFlow switches deployed throughout the network and application switches, our messaging mechanism leverages Linux' D-Bus message bus system to pass data between workers. If the next processing worker of a given tuple is not local to the application switch, the data is sent to the appropriate host where it is again handled by an application switch instance.

Based on our early evaluations, our system is able to dynamically (at runtime) migrate workers between hosts, change network properties based on application demands, and insert and remove workers and classes of workers. We believe that this approach may significantly improve flexibility and elasticity of such and other systems that highly rely on intra- and inter-host communication. Furthermore, given that applications are able to dynamically dictate their needs to the network, and more quickly react to increased demand, we expect overall processing performance to increase in many cases.

## 3. FUTURE DIRECTIONS

In the future, we propose investigating three major areas along the lines of this project. First, we believe it is imperative to extend an existing stream-processing framework such as Storm or Samza with our technology. This would allow us to perform case studies and performance evaluations using typical workloads for these systems. Also, consequences of dynamic, feedback-based reconfiguration and placement such as optimized resource utilization can be explored. Second, we would like to explore which other types of applications may benefit from our idea. We believe that operating systems could directly expose an API to control messaging and communication flows between processes. Third, leveraging the flexibility that our system provides, it is possible to centrally control scheduling, shuffling and partitioning behavior of stream processing applications.

## 4. REFERENCES


[1] H. Ballani, P. Costa, T. Karagiannis, and A. Rowstron. Towards Predictable Datacenter Networks. In *Procesdings of SIGCOMM 2011.*

[2] A. D. Ferguson, A. Guha, C. Liang, R. Fonseca, and S. Krishnamurthi. Participatory Networking: An API for Application Control of SDNs. In *Proceedings of SIGCOMM 2013.*

[3] K. Goodhope, J. Koshy, and J. Kreps. Building LinkedIn's Real-time Activity Data Pipeline. *IEEE Data Eng. ...*, 2012.

[4] J. Schad, J. Dittrich, and J.-A. Quiané-Ruiz. Runtime measurements in the cloud: Observing, analyzing, and reducing variance. *Proc. VLDB Endow.*, Sept. 2010.

# Diagnosing Missing Events in Distributed Systems with Negative Provenance

Yang Wu
University of Pennsylvania

Mingchen Zhao
University of Pennsylvania

Andreas Haeberlen
University of Pennsylvania

Wenchao Zhou
Georgetown University

Boon Thau Loo
University of Pennsylvania

## ABSTRACT

When debugging a distributed system, it is sometimes necessary to explain the *absence* of an event – for instance, why a certain route is *not* available, or why a certain packet did *not* arrive. Existing debuggers offer some support for explaining the *presence* of events, usually by providing the equivalent of a backtrace in conventional debuggers, but they are not very good at answering "Why not?" questions: there is simply no starting point for a possible backtrace. In this paper, we show that the concept of *negative provenance* can be used to explain the absence of events in distributed systems. Negative provenance relies on counterfactual reasoning to identify the conditions under which the missing event *could have* occurred. We define a formal model of negative provenance for distributed systems, and we present the design of a system called Y! that tracks both positive and negative provenance and can use them to answer diagnostic queries. We describe how we have used Y! to debug several realistic problems in two application domains: software-defined networks and BGP interdomain routing. Results from our experimental evaluation show that the overhead of Y! is moderate.

## Categories and Subject Descriptors

C.2.3 [**Network operations**]: Network management; D.2.5 [**Testing and debugging**]: Diagnostics

## Keywords

Diagnostics, Debugging, Provenance

## 1. INTRODUCTION

Finding problems in complex distributed systems has always been challenging, as the substantial literature on network debugging and root-cause analysis tools [5, 9, 12, 13, 18] can attest. The advent of software-defined networking (SDN) has added a new dimension to the problem: forwarding can now be controlled by programs, and, like all other programs, these programs can have bugs. Finding such bugs can be difficult because, in a complex network of hosts, routers, switches, and middleboxes, they can manifest in subtle ways that have no obvious connection with the root cause.


*SIGCOMM'14*, August 17–22, 2014, Chicago, Illinois, USA.

ACM 978-1-4503-2836-4/14/08 ...$15.00.
http://dx.doi.org/10.1145/2619239.2626335.

It would be useful to have a "network debugger" that can assist the network operator with this task, but existing techniques tend to be protocol-specific and cannot necessarily be applied to arbitrary distributed applications, or SDNs with arbitrary control programs. Hence, as others [8,9] have observed, a more powerful debugger is needed.

Existing solutions, such as NetSight [9] or SNP [35], approach this problem by offering a kind of "backtrace", analogous to a stack trace in a conventional debugger, that links an observed effect of a bug to its root causes. For instance, suppose the administrator notices that a server is receiving requests that should be handled by another server. The administrator can then trace the requests to the last-hop switch, where she might find a faulty flow entry; she can trace the faulty entry to a statement in the SDN controller program that was triggered by a certain condition; she can trace the condition to a packet from another switch; and she can continue to recursively explain each effect by its direct causes until she reaches a set of root causes. The result is the desired "backtrace": a causal chain of events that explains how the observed event came to pass. We refer to this as the *provenance* [1] of the event.

Provenance can be a useful tool for debugging complex interactions, but there are cases that it cannot handle. For instance, suppose that the administrator observes that a certain server is *no longer receiving any requests* of a particular type. The key difference to the earlier scenario is that the observed symptom is not a positive event, such as the arrival of a packet, that could serve as a "lead" and point the administrator towards the root cause. Rather, the observed symptom is a negative event: the *absence* of packets of a certain type. Negative events can be difficult to debug: provenance does not help, and even a manual investigation can be difficult if the administrator does not know where the missing packets would normally come from, or how they would be generated.

Nevertheless, it is possible to construct a similar "backtrace" for negative events, using the concept of *negative provenance* [10,32]. The key insight is to use counterfactual reasoning, that is, to examine all possible causes that *could have* produced the missing effect. For instance, it might be the case that the missing packets could only have reached the server through one of two upstream switches, and that one of them is missing a flow entry that would match the packets. Based on the controller program, we might then establish that the missing entry could only have been installed if a certain condition had been satisfied, and so on, until we either reach a positive event (such as the installation of a conflicting flow entry with higher priority) that can be traced with normal provenance, or a negative root cause (such as a missing entry in a configuration file).

Negative provenance could be a useful debugging tool for networks and distributed systems in general, but so far it has not been explored very much. A small number of papers from the database

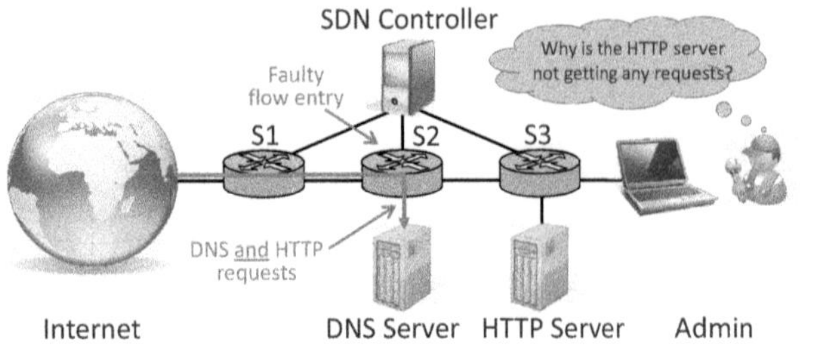


**Figure 1: Negative event scenario: Web requests from the Internet are no longer reaching the web server because a faulty program on the controller has installed an overly general flow entry in the switch in the middle (S2).**

community [3, 10, 19] have used negative provenance to explain why a given database query did *not* return a certain tuple, but, other than our earlier workshop paper that made a case for negative provenance [32], we are not aware of any previous applications in the networking domain.

In Section 2, we provide an overview of positive and negative provenance. We then make the following contributions:

- A formal model of positive and negative provenance in distributed systems, as well as a concrete algorithm for tracking such provenance (Section 3);
- A set of heuristics for simplifying the resulting provenance graphs and for making them more readable to a human investigator (Section 4);
- The design of Y! (pronounced "Why not?"), a system for tracking positive and negative provenance and for answering queries about it (Section 5);
- Two case studies of Y!, in the context of software-defined networks and BGP (Section 6); and
- An experimental evaluation of an Y! prototype, based on Mininet, Trema [29] and RapidNet [24] (Section 7).

We discuss related work in Section 8 and conclude the paper in Section 9.

# 2. OVERVIEW

In this section, we take a closer look at negative provenance, and we discuss some of the key challenges.

## 2.1 Scenario: Network debugging

Figure 1 shows a simple example scenario that illustrates the problem we are focusing on. A network administrator manages a small network that includes a DNS server, a web server, and a connection to the Internet. At some point, the administrator notices that the web server is no longer receiving any requests from the Internet. The administrator strongly suspects that the network is somehow misconfigured, but the only observable symptom is a *negative event* (the absence of web requests at the server), so there is no obvious starting point for an investigation.

Today, the only way to resolve such a situation is to manually inspect the network until some positive symptom (such as requests arriving at the wrong server) is found. In the very simple scenario in Figure 1, this is not too difficult, but in a data center or large corporate network, it can be a considerable challenge. It seems preferable for the administrator to directly ask the network for an explanation of the negative event, similar to a "backtrace" in a conventional debugger. This is the capability we seek to provide.

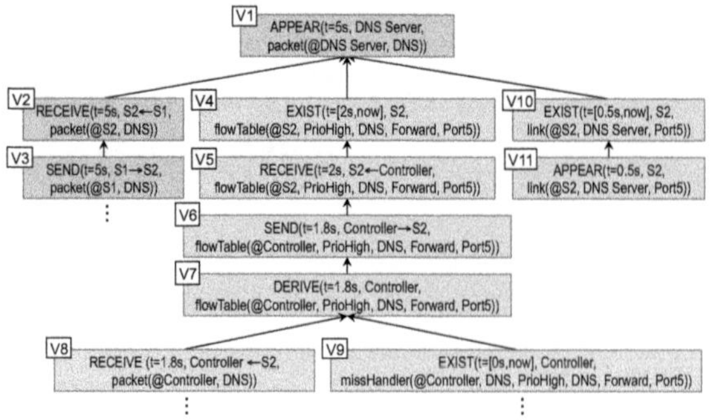


**Figure 2: *Positive* provenance example, explaining how a DNS packet made its way to the DNS server.**

## 2.2 Positive provenance

For *positive* events, there is a well-understood way to generate such a "backtrace": whenever an event occurs or some new state is generated, the system keeps track of its causes, and when an explanation is requested, the system recursively explains each event with its direct causes, until it reaches a set of "base events" (such as external inputs) that cannot be explained further. The result can be represented as a DAG, in which each vertex represents an event and each edge indicates a direct causal relationship. In the database literature, this is called the *provenance* [1] of the event; to distinguish it from negative provenance, we will refer to it as *positive provenance*.

Figure 2 shows an example that explains why a DNS request appeared at the DNS server at time $t = 5$ (V1). The DNS server had received the packet from switch S2, which in turn had received it from S1, and ultimately from the Internet (V2–V3); the switch was connected to the DNS server via port #5 (V10–V11) and had a flow entry that directed DNS packets to that port (V4). The flow entry had been installed at $t = 2$ (V5–V7) because the switch had forwarded an earlier DNS packet to the controller (V8), which had generated the flow entry based on its configuration (V9).

Positive provenance is an active research area, but some solutions for distributed systems are already available, such as ExSPAN [37] or SNP [35]. Provenance is often a useful debugging tool, just like the "backtraces" that many debuggers are offering.

## 2.3 Case study: Broken flow entry

We now return to the scenario in Figure 1. One possible reason for this situation is that the administrator has configured the controller to produce a generic, low-priority flow entry for DNS traffic and a specific, high-priority flow entry for HTTP traffic. If both entries are installed, the system works as expected, but if the low-priority entry is installed first, it matches HTTP packets as well; thus, these packets are not forwarded to the controller and cannot trigger the installation of the high-priority entry. This subtle race condition might manifest only at runtime, e.g., when both entries expire simultaneously during an occasional lull in traffic; thus, it could be quite difficult to find.

Positive provenance is not helpful here because, as long as requests are still arriving at the HTTP server, their provenance contains only the high-priority entry, and when the requests stop arriving, there is no longer anything to generate the provenance *of*!

## 2.4 How common are negative symptoms?

To get a sense of how common this situation is, we surveyed diagnostics-related posts on three mailing lists. We chose lists that cover a mix of different diagnostic situations, including NANOG-user and Outages [23] (for faults and misconfigurations), and

| Mailing list | Posts related to diagnostics | Initial symptoms | |
|---|---|---|---|
| | | Positive | Negative |
| NANOG-user | 29/144 | 14 (48%) | 15 (52%) |
| floodlight-dev | 19/154 | 5 (26%) | 14 (74%) |
| Outages [23] | 46/60 | 8 (17%) | 38 (83%) |

**Table 1: Survey of networking problems and their symptoms, as discussed on three mailing lists over a two-month period, starting on November 22, 2013.**

floodlight-dev (for software bugs). To get a good sample size, we examined a two-month period for each list, starting on November 22, 2013. In each post, we looked for the description of the initial symptoms and classified them as either positive (something bad happened) or negative (something good failed to happen).

Table 1 shows our results. While the proportion of positive and negative symptoms varies somewhat between lists, we find that the negative symptoms are consistently *in the majority* – that is, it seems more common for problems to initially manifest as the absence of something (e.g., a route, or a response to a probe packet) than as the presence of something (e.g., high latencies on a path, or a DDoS attack).

Many of the problems we surveyed were eventually diagnosed, but we observe that the process seems comparatively harder: there were significantly more (and lengthier) email threads where negative symptoms resulted in inconclusive identification of root causes. Moreover, troubleshooting negative symptoms often required exploratory "guesswork" by the mailing list participants. Since this trial-and-error approach requires lots of time and effort, it seems useful to develop better tool support for this class of problems.

## 2.5 Negative provenance

Our approach towards such a tool is to extend provenance to negative events. Although these cannot be explained directly with positive provenance, there is a way to construct a similar "backtrace" for negative events: instead of explaining how an actual event *did* occur, as with positive provenance, we can simply find all the ways in which a missing event *could have* occurred, and then show, as a "root cause", the reason why each of them did not come to pass.

Intuitively, we can use a kind of counterfactual reasoning to recursively generate the explanations, not unlike positive provenance: for a web request to arrive at the web server, a request would have had to appear at the rightmost switch (S3), which did not happen. Such a request could only have come from the switch in the middle (S2), and, eventually, from the switch on the left (S1). But S2 would only have sent the request if there had been 1) an actual request, 2) a matching flow entry with a forward action to S3, and 3) no matching higher-priority flow entry. Conditions 1) and 2) were satisfied, but condition 3) was not (because of the DNS server's flow entry). We can then ask where the higher-priority flow entry came from, which can be answered with positive provenance. We refer to such a counterfactual explanation as *negative provenance*.

## 2.6 Challenges

To explain the key challenges, we consider two strawman solutions. First, it may seem that there is a simpler way to investigate the missing HTTP requests from Section 2.3: why not simply compare the system state before and after the requests stopped arriving, and return any differences as the likely cause? This approach may indeed work in some cases, but in general, there are way too many changes happening in a typical system: even if we could precisely pinpoint the time where the problem appeared, chances are that most of the state changes at that time would be unrelated. Moreover, if the problem was caused by a *chain* of events, this method would return only the last step in the chain. To identify the relevant events reliably, and to trace them back to the root cause, we must have a way to track *causality*, which is, in essence, what provenance represents.

Second, it may seem that, in order to track negative provenance, we can simply take an existing provenance system, like ExSPAN or SNP, and associate each positive provenance vertex with a negative "twin". However, the apparent similarity between positive and negative provenance does not go very deep. While positive provenance considers only *one specific* chain of events that led to an observed event, negative provenance must consider *all possible* chains of events that *could have* caused the observed event. This disparity between existential and universal quantifiers has profound consequences: for instance, negative provenance graphs are often infinite and cannot be materialized, and responses to negative queries tend to be a lot more complex, and thus need more sophisticated post-processing before they can be shown to a human user. These are some of the challenges we address in Y!.

# 3. BASIC NEGATIVE PROVENANCE

In this section, we show how to derive a simple provenance graph for both positive and negative events. For ease of exposition, we will assume that the distributed system is written in Network Datalog (NDlog) [16], since this representation makes provenance particularly easy to see. However, our approach is not specific to NDlog, or even to declarative languages; indeed, our case studies in Section 6.1 apply it to Pyretic [21], an existing imperative programming language for SDNs, as well as to BGP debugging.

## 3.1 Background: Network Datalog

We begin by briefly reviewing the features of NDlog that are relevant here. In NDlog, the state of a node (switch, controller, or server) is modeled as a set of *tables*. Each table contains a number of *tuples*. For instance, an SDN switch might contain a table called `flowTable`, and each tuple in this table might represent a flow entry, or a SDN controller might have a table called `packetIn` that contains the packets it has received from the switches. Tuples can be manually inserted, or they can be programmatically derived from other tuples; the former are called *base tuples*, and the latter are referred to as *derived tuples*.

NDlog programs consist of *rules* that describe how tuples should be derived from each other. For instance, the rule `A(@X,P):-B(@X,Q),Q=2*P` says that a tuple `A(@X,P)` should be derived on node X whenever there is also a `B(@X,Q)` tuple on that node, and `Q=2*P`. Here, P and Q are variables that must be instantiated with values when the rule is applied; for instance, a `B(@X,10)` tuple would create an `A(@X,5)` tuple. The `@` operator specifies the node on which the tuple resides. (NDlog supports other operators – e.g., arithmetic or aggregation operators – as well as user-defined functions, but we do not consider these here.) A key advantage of a declarative formulation is that causality is very easy to see: if a tuple `A(@X,5)` was derived using the rule above, then `A(@X,5)` exists simply because `B(@X,10)` exists, and because `10=2*5`.

Rules may include tuples from different nodes; for instance, `C(@X,P):- C(@Y,P)` says that tuples in the C-table on node Y should be sent to node X and inserted into the C-table there. We write $+\tau$ to denote a message saying that the recipient should insert a tuple $\tau$, and $-\tau$ to denote a message saying that the recipient should remove $\tau$. To avoid redundancy, we write $\pm\tau$ when a statement applies to both types of messages. When a tuple can be derived in more than one way, $+\tau$ is only sent when the first derivation appears, and $-\tau$ only when the last derivation disappears.

## 3.2 Goals

Before we define our provenance graph, we first state, somewhat informally, the properties we would like to achieve. One way to describe what "actually happened" in an execution of the system is by means of a *trace*: a sequence of message transmissions and arrivals, as well as base tuple insertions and deletions. (Other events, such as derivations, follow deterministically from these.) Following [36], we can then think of the provenance $G(e, \mathcal{E})$ of an event $e$ in a trace $\mathcal{E}$ as describing a series of trace properties, which, in combination, cause $e$ to appear – or, in the case of a negative event, prevent $e$ from appearing. We demand the following properties:

- **Soundness:** $G(e, \mathcal{E})$ must be consistent with $\mathcal{E}$;
- **Completeness:** There must not be another execution $\mathcal{E}'$ that is also consistent with $G(e, \mathcal{E})$ but does not contain the event $e$; and
- **Minimality:** There must not be a subset of $G(e, \mathcal{E})$ that is also sound and complete.

Informally, soundness means that $G(e, \mathcal{E})$ must describe events that actually happened in $\mathcal{E}$ – we cannot explain the absence of a tuple with the presence of a message that was never actually sent. Completeness means that $G(e, \mathcal{E})$ must be sufficient to explain $e$, and minimality means that all events in $G(e, \mathcal{E})$ must actually be relevant (though there could be more than one provenance that is minimal in this sense). We will state these properties formally in Section 3.8.

## 3.3 The provenance graph

Provenance can be represented as a DAG in which the vertices are events and the edges indicate direct causal relationships. Thanks to NDlog's simplicity, it is possible to define a very simple provenance graph for it, with only ten types of event vertices (based on [35]):

- EXIST($[t_1, t_2], N, \tau$): Tuple $\tau$ existed on node $N$ from time $t_1$ to $t_2$;
- INSERT($t, N, \tau$), DELETE($t, N, \tau$): Base tuple $\tau$ was inserted (deleted) on node $N$ at time $t$;
- DERIVE($t, N, \tau$), UNDERIVE($t, N, \tau$): Derived tuple $\tau$ acquired (lost) support on $N$ at time $t$;
- APPEAR($t, N, \tau$), DISAPPEAR($t, N, \tau$): Tuple $\tau$ appeared or disappeared on node $N$ at time $t$;
- SEND($t, N \rightarrow N', \pm\tau$), RECEIVE($t, N \leftarrow N', \pm\tau$): $\pm\tau$ was sent (received) by node $N$ to/from $N'$ at $t$; and
- DELAY($t, N \rightarrow N', \pm\tau, d$): $\pm\tau$, sent from node $N$ to $N'$ at time $t$, took time $d$ to arrive.

The edges between the vertices correspond to their intuitive causal connections: tuples can appear on a node because they a) were inserted as base tuples, b) were derived from other tuples, or c) were received in a message from another node (for cross-node rules). Messages are received because they were sent, and tuples exist because they appeared. Note that vertices are annotated with the node on which they occur, as well as with the relevant time; the latter will be important for negative provenance because we will often need to reason about past events.

This model can be extended to support negative provenance by associating each vertex with a negative "twin" [32]:

- NEXIST($[t_1, t_2], N, \tau$): Tuple $\tau$ never existed on node $N$ in time interval $[t_1, t_2]$;
- NINSERT($[t_1, t_2], N, \tau$), NDELETE($[t_1, t_2], N, \tau$): Tuple $\tau$ was never inserted (removed) on $N$ in $[t_1, t_2]$;
- NDERIVE($[t_1, t_2], N, \tau$), NUNDERIVE($[t_1, t_2], N, \tau$): $\tau$ was never derived (underived) on $N$ in $[t_1, t_2]$;
- NAPPEAR($[t_1,t_2],N, \tau$), NDISAPPEAR($[t_1,t_2],N, \tau$): Tuple $\tau$ never (dis)appeared on $N$ in $[t_1, t_2]$;
- NSEND($[t_1, t_2], N, \tau$), NRECEIVE($[t_1, t_2], N, \tau$): $\tau$ was never sent (received) by node $N$ in $[t_1, t_2]$; and
- NARRIVE($[t_1, t_2], N_1 \rightarrow N_2, t_3, \tau$): $\tau$ was sent from $N_1$ to $N_2$ at $t_3$ but did not arrive within $[t_1, t_2]$.

Again, the causal connections are the intuitive ones: tuples never existed because they never appeared, they never appeared because they were never inserted, derived, or received, etc. However, note that, unlike their positive counterparts, *all* negative vertices are annotated with time intervals: unlike positive provenance, which can refer to specific events at specific times, negative provenance must explain the *absence* of events in certain intervals.

## 3.4 Handling multiple explanations

Sometimes the absence of an event can have more than one cause. For instance, suppose there is a rule `A:-B,C,D` and, at some time $t$, none of the tuples B, C, or D exist. How should we explain the absence of A in this case? One possible approach would be to include the absence of all three tuples; this would be useful, for instance, if our goal was recovery – i.e., if we wanted to find a way make A appear. However, for diagnostic purposes, the resulting provenance is somewhat verbose, since the absence of each individual tuple is already sufficient to explain the absence of A. For this reason, we opt to include only a *sufficient reason* in our provenance trees.

In cases where there is more than one sufficient reason, the question arises which one we should choose. Since we aim for compact provenance trees, *we try to find the reason that can be explained with the fewest vertices.* For instance, if B and D are derived tuples whose absence is due to a complex sequence of events on several other nodes, whereas C is a base tuple that simply was never inserted, we would choose the explanation that is based on C, which only requires a single NINSERT vertex. In practice, it is not always easy to see which explanation is simplest (at least not without fully expanding the corresponding subtree), but we can use heuristics to find a good approximation, e.g., based on a look-ahead of a few levels down the tree.

## 3.5 Graph construction

Provenance systems like ExSPAN [37] rely on a materialized provenance graph: while the distributed system is executing, they build some representation of the vertices and edges in the graph, and they respond to queries by projecting out the relevant subtree. This approach does not work for negative provenance because the provenance graph is typically infinite: for instance, it contains NEXIST vertices for every tuple that could *potentially* exist, and, for each vertex with that contains a time interval $I$, it also contains vertices with intervals $I' \subseteq I$.

For this reason, we adopt a top-down procedure for constructing the provenance of a given (positive or negative) event "on demand", without materializing the entire graph. We define a function QUERY(v) that, when called on a vertex $v$ in the provenance graph, returns the immediate children of $v$. Thus, the provenance of a negative event $e$ can be found by constructing a vertex $v_e$ that describes $e$ (e.g., a NEXIST vertex for an absent tuple) and then calling QUERY recursively on $v_e$ until leaf vertices are reached. The

```
function QUERY(EXIST([t1, t2],N,τ))
    S ← ∅
    for each (+τ,N,t,r,c) ∈ Log:   t1 ≤ t ≤ t2
        S ← S ∪ { APPEAR(t,N,τ,r,c) }
    for each (−τ,N,t,r,c) ∈ Log:   t1 ≤ t ≤ t2
        S ← S ∪ { DISAPPEAR(t,N,τ,r,c) }
    RETURN S
function QUERY(APPEAR(t,N,τ,r,c))
    if BaseTuple(τ) then
        RETURN { INSERT(t,N,τ) }
    else if LocalTuple(N,τ) then
        RETURN { DERIVE(t,N,τ,r) }
    else RETURN{RECEIVE(t,N ← r.N,τ)}
function QUERY(INSERT(t,N,τ))
    RETURN ∅
function QUERY(DERIVE(t,N,τ,τ:-τ1,τ2...))
    S ← ∅
    for each τi: if (+τi,N,t,r,c) ∈ Log:
        S ← S ∪ { APPEAR(t,N,τi,c) }
    else
        tx ← max t' < t: (+τ,N,t',r,1) ∈ Log
        S ← S ∪ { EXIST([tx,t],N,τi,c) }
    RETURN S

function QUERY(RECEIVE(t,N1 ← N2,+τ))
    ts ← max t' < t: (+τ,N2,t',r,1) ∈ Log
    RETURN { SEND(ts,N1 → N2,+τ),
        DELAY(ts,N2 → N1,+τ,t − ts) }
function QUERY(SEND(t,N → N',+τ))
    FIND (+τ,N,t,r,c) ∈ Log
    RETURN { APPEAR(t,N,τ,r) }
function QUERY(NEXIST([t1,t2],N,τ))
    if ∃t < t1 : (-τ,N,t,r,1) ∈ Log then
        tx ← max t < t1: (-τ,N,t,r,1) ∈ Log
        RETURN { DISAPPEAR(tx,N,τ),
            NAPPEAR((tx,t2],N,τ) }
    else RETURN { NAPPEAR([0,t2],N,τ) }
function QUERY(NDERIVE([t1,t2],N,τ,r))
    S ← ∅
    for (τi, Ii) ∈ PARTITION([t1,t2],N,τ,r)
        S ← S ∪ { NEXIST(Ii,N,τi) }
    RETURN S
function QUERY(NSEND([t1,t2],N,+τ))
    if ∃t1 < t < t2 : (-τ,N,t,r,1) ∈ Log then
        RETURN { EXIST([t1,t],N,τ),
            NAPPEAR((t,t2],N,τ) }
    else RETURN { NAPPEAR([t1,t2],N,τ) }

function QUERY(NAPPEAR([t1,t2],N,τ))
    if BaseTuple(τ) then
        RETURN { NINSERT([t1,t2],N,τ) }
    else if LocalTuple(N,τ) then
        RETURN ⋃_{r∈Rules(N):Head(r)=τ}
            { NDERIVE([t1,t2],N,τ,r) }
    else RETURN {NRECEIVE([t1,t2],N,+τ)}
function QUERY(NRECEIVE([t1,t2],N,+τ))
    S ← ∅, t0 ← t1 − Δmax
    for each N' ∈ SENDERS(τ,N):
        X ← {t0 ≤ t ≤ t2 | (+τ,N',t,r,1) ∈ Log}
        tx ← t0
        for (i=0; i< |X|; i++)
            S ← S ∪ {NSEND((tx,Xi),N',+τ),
          NARRIVE((t1,t2),N' → N,Xi,+τ)}
            tx ← Xi
        S ← S ∪ { NSEND([tx,t2],N',+τ) }
    RETURN S
function Q(NARRIVE([t1,t2],N1 → N2,t0,+τ))
    FIND (+τ,N2,t3,(N1,t0),1) ∈ Log
    RETURN { SEND(t0,N1 → N2,+τ),
        DELAY(t0,N1 → N2,+τ,t3 − t0) }
```

**Figure 3: Graph construction algorithm. Some rules have been omitted; for instance, the handling of $+\tau$ and $-\tau$ messages is analogous, and the rules for INSERT/DELETE, APPEAR/DISAPPEAR, and DERIVE/UNDERIVE are symmetric.**

interval in $v_e$ can simply be some interval in which $e$ was observed; it does not need to cover the entire duration of $e$, and it does not need to contain the root cause(s).

QUERY needs access to a log of the system's execution to date. We assume that the log is a sequence of tuples $(\pm\tau, N, t, r, c)$, which indicate that $\tau$ was derived $(+\tau)$ or underived $(-\tau)$ on node $N$ at time $t$ via rule $r$. Since some tuples can be derived in more than one way, we include a derivation counter $c$, which is 1 when a tuple first appears, and is increased by one for each further derivation. For tuples that node $N$ received from another node $N'$, we set $r = N'$, and for base tuples, we set $r = \perp$ and $c = 1$.

Figure 3 shows part of the algorithm we use to construct positive and negative provenance. There are several points worth noting. First, the algorithm uses functions BaseTuple($\tau$) and LocalTuple(N,$\tau$) to decide whether a missing tuple $\tau$ is a base tuple that was not inserted, a local tuple on node $N$ that was not derived, or a remote tuple that was not received. The necessary information is a byproduct of the compilation of any NDlog program and is thus easily obtained. Second, to account for propagation delays, the algorithm uses a constant $\Delta$max that denotes the maximum time a message can spend in the network and still be accepted by the recipient; this is used to narrow down the time interval during which a missing message could have been sent. Third, the algorithm can produce the same vertex more than once, or semantically identical vertices with adjacent or overlapping intervals; in these cases, it is necessary to coalesce the vertices using the union of their intervals in order to preserve minimality. Finally, the algorithm uses two functions PARTITION and SENDERS, which we explain next.

## 3.6 Explaining nonderivation

The PARTITION function encodes a heuristic for choosing among several possible explanations of a missing derivation. When explaining why a rule with multiple preconditions did not derive a certain tuple, we must consider a potentially complex parameter space. For instance, if `A(@X,p):-B(@X,p,q,r),C(@X,p,q)` did not derive `A(@X,10)`, we can explain this with the absence of `B(@X,10,q,r)`, `C(@X,10,q,r)`, or a combination of both – e.g., by dividing the possible $q$ and $r$ values between the two preconditions. Different choices can result in explanations of dramatically different sizes once the preconditions themselves have been explained; hence, we would prefer a partition of the parameter space (here, $Q \times R$) that results in an explanation that is as small as possible. In general, finding the optimal partition is at least as hard as the SETCOVER problem, which is NP-hard; hence the need for a heuristic. In our experiments, we use a simple greedy heuristic that always picks the largest available subspace; if there are multiple subspaces of the same size, it explores both for a few steps and then picks the one with the simplest subgraph.

## 3.7 Missing messages

The SENDERS($\pm\tau$,N) function is used to narrow down the set of nodes that could have sent a specific missing message $\pm\tau$ to node $N$. One valid choice is to simply return the set of all nodes in the system that have a rule for deriving $\tau$; however, the resulting provenance can be complex, since it must explain why *each* of these nodes did not send $\pm\tau$. Hence, it is useful to enhance SENDERS with other information that may be available. For instance, in a routing protocol, communication is restricted by the network topology, and messages can come only from direct neighbors.

In some cases, further nodes can be ruled out based on the specific message that is missing: for instance, a BGP message whose AS path starts with 7 should come from a router in AS 7. We do not pursue this approach here, but we hypothesize that static analysis of the NDlog program could be used for inferences of this type.

## 3.8 Formal properties

We now briefly present the key definitions from our formal model [33]. An *event* $d@n = (m, r, t, c, m')$ represents that rule $r$ was triggered by message $m$ and generated a set of (local or remote) messages $m'$ at time $t$, given the precondition $c$ (a set of tuples that existed on node $n$ at time $t$). Specifically, we write $d@n_{recv} = (m@n_{send}, -, t, 1, m@n_{recv})$ to denote a message $m$ (from $n_{send}$ is delivered at $n_{recv}$ at $t$). A *trace* $\mathcal{E}$ of a system execution is an ordered sequence of events from an initial state $\mathcal{S}_0$, $\mathcal{S}_0 \xrightarrow{d_1@n_1} \mathcal{S}_1 \xrightarrow{d_2@n_2} \ldots \xrightarrow{d_x@n_x} \mathcal{S}_x$. We say a trace $\mathcal{E}$ is *valid*, if (a) for all $\tau_k \in c_i$, $\tau_k \in \mathcal{S}_{i-1}$, and (b) for all

$d_i@n_i = (m_i, r_i, t_i, c_i, m'_i)$, either $m_i$ is a base message from an external source, or there exists $d_j@n_j = (m_j, r_j, t_j, c_j, m'_j)$ that precedes $d_i@n_i$ and $m_i \in m'_j$. We say that $\mathcal{E}'$ is a *subtrace* of $\mathcal{E}$ (written as $\mathcal{E}' \subseteq \mathcal{E}$) if $\mathcal{E}'$ consists of a subset of the events in $\mathcal{E}$ in the same order. In particular, we write $\mathcal{E}|n$ to denote the subtrace that consists of all the events on node $n$ in $\mathcal{E}$. We say that $\mathcal{E}'$ and $\mathcal{E}$ are equivalent (written as $\mathcal{E}' \sim \mathcal{E}$) if, for all $n$, $\mathcal{E}'|n = \mathcal{E}|n$.

To properly define minimality, we use the concept of a *reduction*: given negative provenance $G(e, \mathcal{E})$, if there exist vertices $v_1, v_2 \in V(G)$, where the time interval of $v_1$ and $v_2$ ($t(v_1)$ and $t(v_2)$ respectively) are adjacent, and $v_1$ and $v_2$ have the same dependencies, then $G$ can be reduced to $G'$ by combining $v_1$ and $v_2$ into $v \in V(G')$, where $t(v) = t(v_1) \cup t(v_2)$. Given two negative provenance $G(e, \mathcal{E})$ and $G'(e, \mathcal{E})$, we say $G'$ is *simpler* than $G$ (written as $G' < G$), if any of the following three hold: (1) $G'$ is a subgraph of $G$; (2) $G'$ is reduced from $G$ (by combining $v_1$ and $v_2$); or (3) there exists $G''$, such that $G' < G''$ and $G'' < G$.

Using these definitions, we can formally state the three properties from Section 3.2 as follows:

**Property (Soundness):** *Negative provenance $G(e, \mathcal{E})$ is sound iff (a) it is possible to extract a valid subtrace $\mathcal{E}_{sub} \subseteq \mathcal{E}'$, such that $\mathcal{E}' \sim \mathcal{E}$ and (b) for all vertices in $G(e, \mathcal{E})$, their corresponding predicates hold in $\mathcal{E}$.*

**Property (Completeness):** *Negative provenance $G(e, \mathcal{E})$ is complete iff there exists no trace $\mathcal{E}'$ such that a) $\mathcal{E}'$ assumes the same external inputs as $G(e, \mathcal{E})$, and b) e exists in $\mathcal{E}'$.*

**Property (Minimality):** *Negative provenance $G(e, \mathcal{E})$ is minimal, if no $G' < G$ is sound and complete.*

We have proven that our provenance graph has all three properties. The proofs are available in [33].

# 4. ENHANCING READABILITY

So far, we have explained how to generate a "raw" provenance graph. This representation is correct and complete, but it is also extremely detailed: for instance, simple and common events, such as message exchanges between nodes, are represented with many different vertices. This "clutter" can make the provenance difficult to read. Next, we describe a post-processing technique that can often simplify the provenance considerably, by pruning unhelpful branches, and by summarizing common patterns into higher-level vertices.

## 4.1 Pruning unhelpful branches

**Logical inconsistencies:** Some explanations contain logical inconsistencies: for instance, the absence of a tuple $\tau_1$ with parameter space $S_1$ might be explained by the absence of a tuple $\tau_2$ with parameter space $S_2 \subseteq S_1$. If we can recognize such inconsistencies early, there is no need to continue generating the provenance until a set of base tuples is reached – the precondition is clearly unsatisfiable. Thus, we can safely truncate the corresponding branch of the provenance tree.

**Failed assertions:** Some branches explain the absence of events that the programmer has already ruled out. For instance, if a branch contains a vertex NEXIST($[t_1, t_2]$,N,P(5)) and it is known that P can only contain values between 0 and 4, the subtree below this vertex is redundant and can be removed. We use programmer-specified assertions (where available) to recognize situations of this type. The assertions do not have to be provenance-specific – they can be the ones that a good programmer would write anyway.

**Branch coalescing:** A naïve execution of the algorithm in Figure 3 would result in a provenance *tree*, but this tree would contain many duplicate vertices because many events have more than one effect. To avoid redundancy, we combine redundant vertices whenever possible, which turns the provenance tree into a DAG. If two vertices have overlapping time intervals but are otherwise identical, we use the union of the two intervals. (Note that a smart implementation of PARTITION could take the multiplicity of shared subtrees into account.)

**Application-specific invariants:** Some explanations may be irrelevant for the particular SDN that is being debugged. For instance, certain data – such as constants, topology information, or state from a configuration file – changes rarely or never, so the absence of changes, or the presence of a specific value, do not usually need to be explained. One simple way to identify constant tables is by the absence of derivation rules in which the table appears at the head. Optionally, the programmer can use a special keyword to designate additional tables as constant.

## 4.2 Different levels of detail

Another way to make negative provenance graphs more useful for the human investigator is to display the provenance at different levels of detail. For instance, if a message fails to appear at node $N_1$ but could only have originated at node $N_2$ several hops away, the basic provenance tree would show, for each node on the path from $N_1$ to $N_2$, that the message was not sent from there, because it failed to appear there, because it was not received from the next-hop node, etc. We can improve readability by summarizing these (thematically related) vertices into a single *super-vertex*. When the graph is first shown to the human investigator, we include as many super-vertices as possible, but the human investigator has the option to expand each super-vertex into the corresponding fine-grained vertices if necessary.[1]

We have identified three situations where this summarization can be applied. The first is a chain of transient events that originates at one node and terminates at another, as in the above example; we replace such chains by a single super-vertex. The second is the (common) sequence NEXIST($[t_1, t_2], N, \tau$) $\leftarrow$ NAPPEAR($[t_1, t_2], N, \tau$) $\leftarrow$ NDERIVE($[t_1, t_2], N, \tau$), which basically says that a tuple was never derived; we replace this with a single ABSENCE($[t_1, t_2], N, \tau$) super-vertex; its positive counterpart EXISTENCE($[t_1, t_2], N, \tau$) is used to replace a positive sequence. The third situation is a derivation that depends on a small set of triggers – e.g., flow entries can only be generated when a packet $p$ is forwarded to the controller $C$. In this case, the basic provenance will contain a long series of NAPPEAR($[t_i, t_{i+1}], C, p$) vertices that explain the *common* case where the trigger packet $p$ *does not* exist; we replace these with a single super-vertex ONLY-EXIST($\{t_1, t_2, \ldots\}$ $in$ $[t_{\text{start}}, t_{\text{end}}], C, p$) that initially focuses attention on the *rare* cases where the trigger *does* exist.

# 5. THE Y! SYSTEM

In this section, we describe the design of Y! (for "Why not?"), a system for capturing, storing, and querying both positive and negative provenance.

## 5.1 Overview

Like any debugger, Y! is meant to be used in conjunction with some other application that the user wishes to diagnose; we refer to this as the *target application*. Y! consists of four main components: The *provenance extractor* (Section 5.2) monitors the target

[1] More generally, visualization and interactive exploration are useful strategies for working with large provenance graphs [17].

application and extracts relevant events, such as state changes or message transmissions. These events are passed to the *provenance storage* (Section 5.3), which appends them to an event log and also maintains a pair of indices to enable efficient lookups of negative events. When the user issues a provenance query, the *query processor* uses the stored information to construct the relevant subtree of the provenance graph, simplifies the subtree using the heuristics from Section 4, and then sends the result to the *frontend*, so that the user can view, and interactively explore, the provenance. We now explain some key components in more detail.

### 5.2 Provenance extractor

Recall from Section 3 that the input to the graph construction algorithm is a sequence of entries $(\pm\tau, N, t, r, c)$, which indicate that the $c$.th derivation of tuple $\tau$ appeared or disappeared on node $N$ at time $t$, and that the reason was $r$, i.e., a derivation rule or an incoming message. The purpose of the provenance extractor is to capture this information from the target application. This functionality is needed for all provenance systems (not just for negative provenance), and it should be possible to use any of the several approaches that have been described in the literature. For instance, the target application can be annotated with calls to a special library whenever a relevant event occurs [22], the runtime that executes the target application (e.g., an NDlog engine or a virtual machine) can report the relevant events [37], or a special proxy can reconstruct the events from the sequence of messages that each node sends and receives [35]. Note that the latter two approaches can be applied even to legacy software and unmodified binaries.

### 5.3 Provenance storage

The provenance storage records the extracted events in an append-only log and makes this log available to the query processor. A key challenge is efficiency: with positive provenance, it is possible to annotate each event with pointers to the events that directly caused it, and, since there is a fairly direct correspondence between events and positive vertices in the provenance graph, these pointers can then be used to quickly navigate the graph. With negative provenance, however, it is frequently necessary to evaluate range queries over the time domain ("Did tuple $\tau$ ever exist during interval $[\tau_1, \tau_2]$"). Moreover, our PARTITION heuristic requires range queries over other domains, e.g., particular subspaces of a given table ("Are there any `X(a,b,c)` tuples on this node with $5 \leq b \leq 20$?") to decide which of several possible explanations might be the simplest. If Y! evaluated such range queries by scanning the relevant part of the log, performance would suffer greatly.

Instead, Y! uses R-trees [7] to efficiently access the log. R-trees are tree data structures for indexing multi-dimensional data; briefly, the key idea is to group nearby objects and to represent each group by its minimum bounding rectangle at the next-higher level of the tree. Their key advantage in our setting is that they can efficiently support multidimensional range queries.

On each node, Y! maintains two different R-trees for each table on that node. The first, the *current tree*, contains the tuples that currently exist in the table; when tuples appear or disappear, they are also added or removed from the current tree. The second, the *historical tree*, contains the tuples that have existed in the past. State tuples are added to the historical tree when they are removed from the current tree; event tuples, which appear only for an instant, are added directly to the historical tree.

The reason for having two separate trees is efficiency. It is known that the performance of R-trees degrades when elements are frequently inserted and removed because the bounding rectangles will no longer be optimal and will increasingly overlap. By separating the historical tuples (where deletions can no longer happen) from the current tuples, we can obtain a more compact tree for the former and confine fragmentation to the latter, whose tree is much smaller. As an additional benefit, since tuples are appended to the historical tree in timestamp order, splits in that tree will typically occur along the time dimension; this creates a kind of "time index" that works very well for our queries.

### 5.4 Pruning the historical tree

Since the historical tree is append-only, it would eventually consume all available storage. To avoid this, Y! can reclaim storage by deleting the oldest tuples from the tree. For instance, Y! can maintain a cut-off time $T_{cut}$; whenever the tree exceeds a certain pre-defined size limit, Y! can slowly advance the cut-off time and keep removing any tuples that existed before that time until enough space has been freed. To enable the user to distinguish between tuples that were absent at runtime and tuples that have been deleted from the tree, the graph construction algorithm can, whenever it accesses information beyond $T_{cut}$, annotate the corresponding vertex as potentially incomplete.

### 5.5 Limitations

Like other provenance systems, Y!'s explanations are limited by the information that is available in the provenance graph. For instance, Y! could trace a misconfiguration to the relevant setting, but not to the person who changed the setting (unless that information were added to the provenance graph). Y! also has no notion of a program's *intended* semantics: for instance, if a program has a concurrency bug that causes a negative event, a query for that event will yield a detailed explanation of how the given program produced that event. Only the operator can determine that the program was supposed to do something different.

## 6. CASE STUDIES

In this section, we describe how we have applied Y! to two application domains: software-defined networks (SDN) and BGP routing. We chose these domains partly because they yield interesting debugging challenges, and partly because they do not already involve declarative code (applying Y! to NDlog applications is straightforward!). We illustrate two different implementation strategies: automatically extracting declarative rules from existing code (for SDN) and writing a declarative description of an existing implementation (for BGP). We report results from several specific debugging scenarios in Section 7.

### 6.1 SDN debugging

Our first case study is SDN debugging: as others [8] have pointed out, better debugging support for SDNs is urgently needed. This scenario is challenging for Y! because SDNs can have almost arbitrary control programs, and because these programs are typically written in non-declarative languages. Provenance can be extracted directly from imperative programs [22], but switching to a different programming model would require some adjustments to our provenance graph. Hence, we use automated program transformation to extract declarative rules from existing SDN programs.

**Language: Pyretic** We chose to focus on the Pyretic language [21]. We begin by briefly reviewing some key features of Pyretic that are relevant here. For details, please see [21].

Pyretic programs can define a mix of *static* policies, which are immutable, and *dynamic* policies, which can change at runtime based on system events. Figure 4 shows a summary of the relevant syntax. A static policy consists of *actions*, e.g., for forwarding packets to a specific port (`fwd(port)`), and *predicates* that

**Primitive actions:**

```
A ::= drop | passthrough | fwd(port) | flood |
      push(h=v) | pop(h) | move(h1=h2)
```

**Predicates:**

```
P ::= all_packets | no_packets | match(h=v) |
      ingress | egress | P & P | (P | P) | ~P
```

**Query policies:**

```
Q ::= packets(limit,[h]) | counts(every,[h])
```

**Policies:**

```
C ::= A | Q | P[C] | (C|C) | C>>C | if_(P,C,C)
```

**Figure 4: Static Pyretic syntax (from [21])**

```
def learn(self):
  def update(pkt):
    self.P = if_(match(dstmac=pkt['srcmac']),
    switch=pkt['switch']),
      fwd(pkt['inport']), self.P)
    q = packets(1,['srcmac','switch'])
    q.when(update)
    self.P = flood | q
def main():
  return dynamic(learn)()
```

**Figure 5: Self-learning switch in Pyretic (from [21])**

restrict these actions to certain types of packets, e.g., to packets with certain header values (`match(h=v)`). Two policies `a` and `b` can be combined through *parallel composition* (`a|b`), meaning that `a` and `b` should be applied to separate copies of each packet, and/or through *sequential composition* (`a>>b`), meaning that `a` should be applied to incoming first, and `b` should then be applied to any packet(s) that `a` may produce. For instance, `match(inport=1)>>(fwd(2)|fwd(3))` says that packets that arrive on port 1 should be forwarded to both ports 2 and 3.

Dynamic policies are based on *queries*. A query describes packets or statistics of interest – for instance, packets for which no policy has been defined yet. When a query returns new data, a callback function is invoked that can modify the policy. Figure 5 (taken from [21]) shows a simple self-learning switch that queries for packets with unknown MAC addresses; when a packet with a new source MAC $m$ is observed on port $p$, the policy is updated to forward future packets with destination MAC $m$ to port $p$.

Pyretic has other features besides these, and providing comprehensive support for them is beyond the scope of our case study. Here, our goal is to support an interesting subset, to demonstrate that our approach is feasible.

**Translation to NDlog:** Our Pyretic frontend transforms all static policies into a "normal form" that consists of groups of parallel "atoms" (with a sequence of matches and a single action) that are arranged sequentially. This form easily translates to OpenFlow wildcard entries: we can give the highest priority to the atoms in the first group, and assign further priorities to the following groups in descending order. To match Pyretic's behavior, we do not install the wildcard entries in the switch directly, but rather keep them as base tuples in a special `MacroRule` table in the controller. A second stage then matches incoming packets from the switches against this table, and generates the corresponding microflow entries (without wildcards), which are then sent to the switch.

For each query policy, the frontend creates a separate table and a rule that sends incoming packets to this table if they match the query. The trigger is evaluated using NDlog aggregations; for instance, waiting for a certain number of packets is implemented with NDlog's `count<>` operator.

Our frontend supports one type of dynamic policies: policies that append new logic in response to external events. These are essentially translated to a single NDlog rule that is triggered by the relevant external event (specified as a query policy) and computes

```
MacroRule(@C,sw,inPort0,dstMAC0,act,Prio0) :-
  UpdateEvent(@C,sw,srcMac), HighestP(@C,Prio),
  PktIn(@sw,inPort1,srcMAC,dstMAC1), inPort0=*,
  dstMAC0=srcMAC, act=fwd(inPort1),
  Prio0=Prio1+10
```

**Figure 6: NDlog translation of the self-learning switch.**

and installs the new entry. The self-learning switch from Figure 5 is an example of such a policy; Figure 6 shows the rule that it is translated to. The rule directly corresponds to the `if-then` part in Figure 5, which forwards packets to newly observed MAC addresses to the correct port, and otherwise (in the `else` branch) falls back on the existing policy. Once translated in this way, it is easy to see the provenance of a dynamic policy change: it is simply the packet that triggered the change.

## 6.2 BGP debugging

Our second case study focuses on BGP. There is a rich literature on BGP root-cause analysis, and a variety of complex real-world problems have been documented. Here, we focus exclusively on the question whether Y! can be used to diagnose BGP problems with negative symptoms, and we ignore many other interesting questions, e.g., about incentives and incremental deployment. (Briefly, we believe that the required infrastructure and the privacy implications would be roughly comparable to those of [27]; in a partial deployment, some queries would return partial answers that are truncated at the first vertex from a network outside the deployment.)

To apply Y!, we follow the approach from [35] and write a simple declarative program that describes how the BGP control plane makes routing decisions. Our implementation is based on an NDlog encoding of a general path vector protocol provided by the authors of [30]; since this code was generic and contained no specific policies, we extended it by adding simple routing policies that respect the Gao-Rexford guidelines and import/export filters that implements the valley-free constraint. This yielded essentially a declarative specification of an ISP's routing behavior. With this, we could capture BGP message traces from unmodified routers, as described in [35], and infer the provenance of the routing decisions by replaying the messages to our program.

# 7. EVALUATION

In this section, we report results from our experimental evaluation of Y! in the context of SDNs and BGP. Our experiments are designed to answer two high-level questions: 1) is negative provenance useful for debugging realistic problems? and 2) what is the cost for maintaining and querying negative provenance?

We ran our experiments on a Dell OptiPlex 9020 workstation, which has a 8-core 3.40 GHz Intel i7-4770 CPU with 16 GB of RAM. The OS was Ubuntu 13.04, and the kernel version was 3.8.0.

## 7.1 Prototype implementation

For our experiments, we built a prototype of Y! based on the RapidNet declarative networking engine [24]. We instrumented RapidNet to capture provenance for the NDlog programs it executes, and we added provenance storage based on the R-tree implementation from [14]. To experiment with SDNs, we set up networks in Mininet [20]. Since NDlog is not among the supported controllers, we wrote a simple proxy for Trema [29] that translates controller messages to NDlog tuples and vice versa. To capture the provenance of packets flowing through the network, we set up port mirroring on the virtual switches and used `libpcap` to record packet traces on the mirrored ports. Since Y!'s provenance graphs only use the packet headers, we capture only the first 96 bytes of header and its timestamp.

| | | |
|---|---|---|
| Q1 | SDN1 | NAPPEAR($[t_1,t_2]$, packet($@D$, PROTO=HTTP)) |
| Q2 | SDN2 | NAPPEAR($[t_1,t_2]$, packet($@D$, PROTO=ICMP)) |
| Q3 | SDN3 | NAPPEAR($[t_1,t_2]$, packet($@D$, PROTO=SQL)) |
| Q4 | SDN2 | APPEAR ($t_3$, packet($@D$, PROTO=ICMP)) |
| Q5 | SDN3 | APPEAR ($t_3$, packet($@D$, PROTO=SQL)) |
| Q6 | BGP1 | NAPPEAR($[t_1,t_2]$, bestroute($@AS2$, TO=AS7)) |
| Q7 | BGP2 | NAPPEAR($[t_1,t_2]$, packet($@AS7$, SRC=AS2)) |
| Q8 | BGP3 | NAPPEAR($[t_1,t_2]$, bestroute($@AS2$, TO=AS7)) |
| Q9 | BGP4 | NAPPEAR($[t_1,t_2]$, bestroute($@AS2$, TO=AS7)) |

**Table 2: Queries we used in our experiments**

To demonstrate that our approach does not substantially affect throughput and latency, we also built a special Trema extension that can capture the provenance directly, without involving RapidNet. This extension was used for some of experiments in Section 7.5, as noted there. Other than that, we focused more on functionality and complexity than on optimizing performance; others have already shown that provenance can be captured at scale [15], and the information Y! records is not substantially different from theirs – Y! merely uses it in a different way.

## 7.2 Usability: SDN debugging

For our SDN experiments, we used Mininet to create the following three representative SDN scenarios:

- **SDN1: Broken flow entry.** A server receives no requests because an overly general flow entry redirects them to a different server (taken from Section 2.3).
- **SDN2: MAC spoofing.** A host, which is connected to the self-learning switch from Figure 5, receives no responses to its DNS lookups because another machine has spoofed its MAC address.
- **SDN3: Incorrect ACL.** A firewall, intended to allow Internet users to access a web server $W$ and internal users a database $D$, is misconfigured: Internet users can access only $D$, and internal users only $W$.

Each scenario consists of four hosts and three switches. For all three scenarios, we use Pyretic programs that have been translated to NDlog rules (Section 6.1) and are executed on RapidNet; however, we verified that each problem also occurs with the original Pyretic runtime. Note that, in all three scenarios, positive provenance cannot be used to diagnose the problem because there is no state whose provenance could be queried.

The first three queries we ask are the natural ones in these scenarios: in SDN1, we ask why the web server is not receiving any requests (Q1); in SDN2, we ask why there are no responses to the DNS lookups (Q2); and in SDN3, we ask why the internal users cannot get responses from the database (Q3). To exercise Y!'s support for positive provenance, we also ask two positive queries: why a host in SDN2 *did* receive a certain ICMP packet (Q4), and why the internal database is receiving connections from the Internet (Q5). To get a sense of how useful negative provenance would be for debugging realistic problems in SDNs, we ran diagnostic queries in our three scenarios and examined the resulting provenance. The first five rows in Table 2 show the queries we used. The full responses are in the long version of this paper [33], but we do not have the space to discuss all of them here; hence, we focus on Q1 from scenario SDN1, which asks why HTTP requests are no longer appearing at the web server.

Figure 7 shows the provenance generated by Y! for Q1. The explanation reads as follows: HTTP requests did not arrive at the HTTP server (V1) because there was no suitable flow entry at the

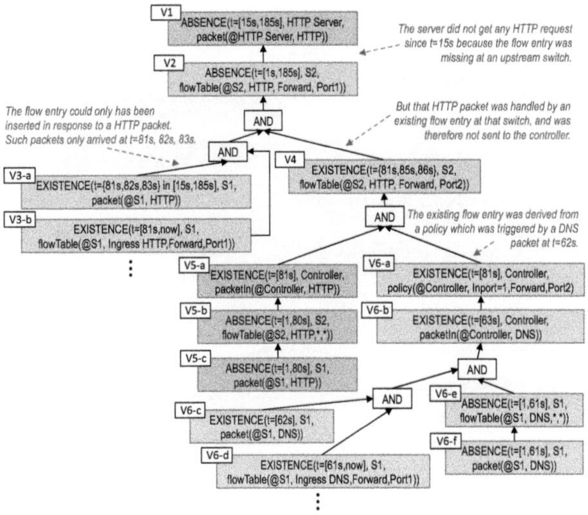


**Figure 7: Answer to Q1, as returned by Y!**

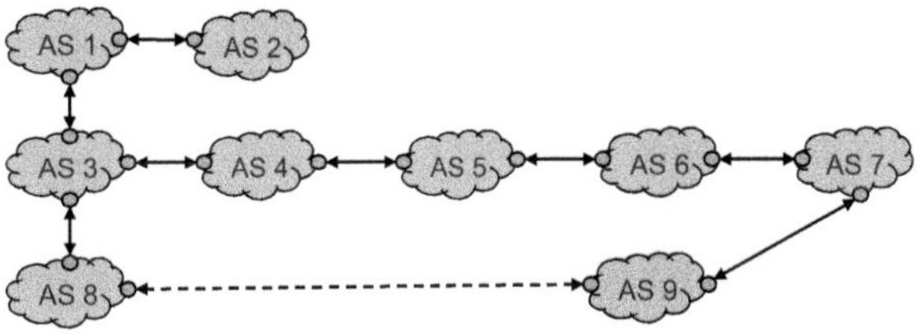


**Figure 8: Topology for the BGP1 scenario.**

switch (V2). Such an entry could only have been installed if a HTTP packet had arrived (V3a+b) and caused a table miss, but the latter did not happen because there already was an entry – the low-priority entry (V4) – that was forwarding HTTP packets to a different port (V5a-c), and that entry had been installed in response to an earlier DNS packet (V6a-f). We believe that "backtraces" of this kind would be useful in debugging complex problems.

## 7.3 Usability: BGP debugging

For our BGP experiments, we picked four real BGP failure scenarios from our survey (Section 2.4):

- **BGP1: Off-path change.** In the topology from Figure 8, AS 2 initially has a route to AS 7 via AS 1,3,4,5,6, but loses that route when a new link is added between AS 8 and AS 9 (neither of which is on the path). This is a variant of a scenario from [27].
- **BGP2: Black hole.** A buggy router advertises a spurious /32 route to a certain host, creating a "black hole" and preventing that host from responding to queries.
- **BGP3: Link failure.** An ISP temporarily loses connectivity, due to a link failure at one of its upstream ASes.
- **BGP4: Bogon list.** A network cannot reach a number of local and federal government sites from its newly acquired IP prefix because that prefix was on the bogon list earlier.

We set up small BGP topologies, using between 4 and 18 simulated routers, to recreate each scenario. In each scenario, we then asked one query: why AS 2 in scenario BGP1 has no route to AS 7 (Q6), why a host in scenario BGP2 cannot reach the black-holed host (Q7), why the ISP in scenario BGP3 cannot reach a certain

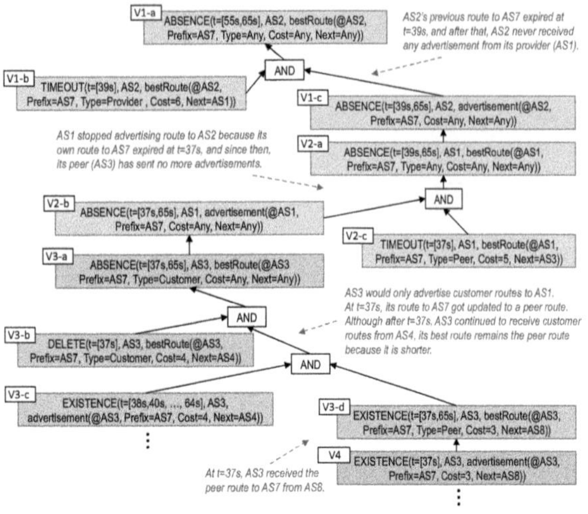


**Figure 9: Answer to Q6, as returned by Y!**

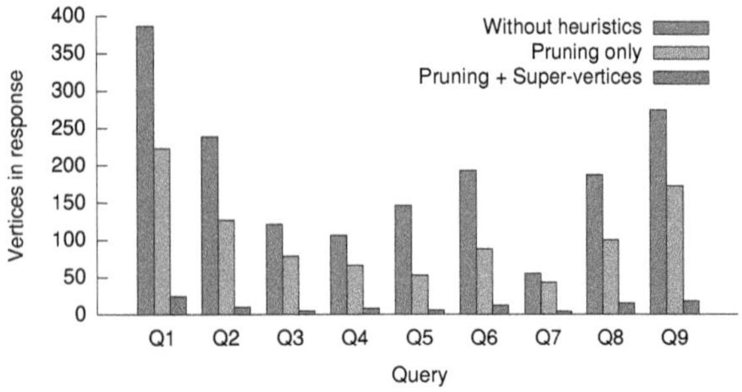


**Figure 10: Size of the provenance with some or all heuristics disabled.**

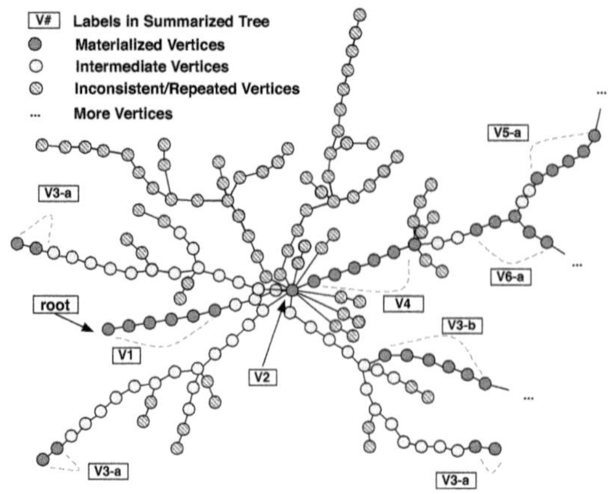


**Figure 11: Raw provenance for query Q1 before post-processing.**

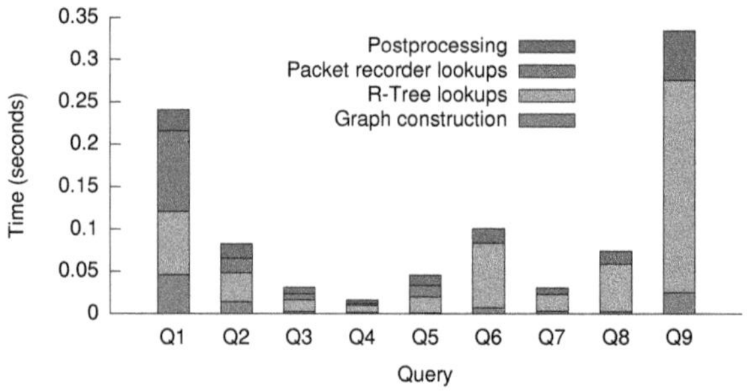


**Figure 12: Turnaround time for the queries in Table 2.**

AS (Q8), and why the network in scenario BGP4 cannot connect to a particular site (Q9). Table 2 shows the specific queries. As expected, Y! generated the correct response in all four scenarios; here, we focus on one specific query (Q6/BGP1) due to lack of space. The other results (available in [33]) are qualitatively similar.

Figure 9 shows the provenance generated by Y! for query Q6. The explanation reads as follows: AS 2 has no route to AS 7 (V1-a) because its previous route expired (V1-b) and it has not received any new advertisements from its provider AS 1 (V1-c). This is because AS 1 itself has no suitable route: its peer AS 3 stopped advertising routes to AS 7 (V2a-c) because AS 3 only advertises customer routes to AS 7 due to the valley-free constraint (V3-a). AS 3 previously had a customer route but it disappeared (V3-b). Although AS 3 continues to receive the customer route from AS 4 (V3-c), the peer route through AS 8 (V4) is preferred because it has a shorter AS path (V3-d). The provenance of the peer route could be further explored by following the graph beyond V4.

## 7.4 Complexity

Recall from Section 4 that Y! uses a number of heuristics to simplify the provenance before it is shown to the user. To quantify how well these heuristics work, we re-ran the queries in Table 2 with different subsets of the heuristics disabled, and we measured the size of the corresponding provenance graphs.

Figure 10 shows our results. Without heuristics, the provenance contained between 55 and 386 vertices, which would be difficult for a human user to interpret. The pruning heuristics from Section 4.1 generally remove about half the vertices, but the size of the provenance remains substantial. However, the super-vertices from Section 4.2 are able to shrink the provenance considerably, to between 4 and 24 vertices, which should be much easier to interpret.

To explain where the large reduction comes from, we show the raw provenance tree (without the heuristics) for Q1 in Figure 11. The structure of this tree is typical of the ones we have generated: a "skeleton" of long causal chains, which typically correspond to messages and events propagating across several nodes, and a large number of small branches. The pruning heuristics remove most of the smaller branches, while the super-vertices "collapse" the long chains in the skeleton. In combination, this yields the much-simplified tree from Figure 7.

## 7.5 Run-time overhead

**Disk storage:** Y! maintains two data structures on disk: the packet traces and the historical R-tree. The size of the former depends on the number of captured packets; each packet consumes 120 bytes of storage. To estimate the size of the latter, we ran a program that randomly inserted and removed `flowEntry` tuples, and we measured the number of bytes per update. We found that, for trees with $10^3$ to $10^6$ updates, each update consumed about 450 byte of storage on average.

These numbers allow us to estimate the storage requirements in a production network. We assume that there are 400 switches that each handle 45 packets per second, and that the SDN controller generates 1,200 flow entries per second. Under these assumptions, a commodity hard disk with 1TB capacity could easily hold the provenance for the most recent 36 hours. If necessary, the storage cost could easily be reduced further, e.g., by compressing the data, by storing only a subset of the header fields, and/or by removing redundant copies of the headers in each flow.

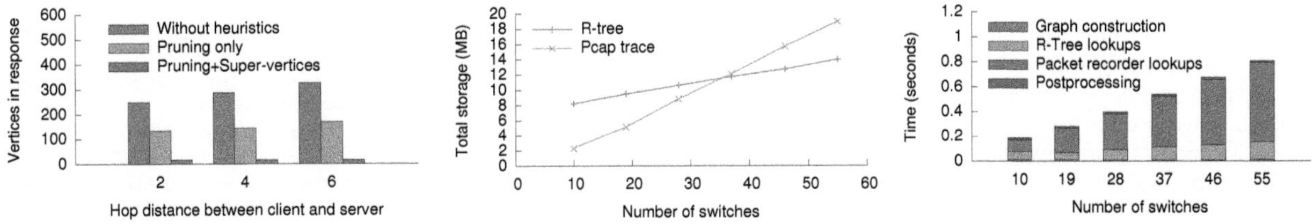


(a) Size of query results (b) Use of storage space (c) Query turnaround time

**Figure 13: Scalability results**

**Latency and throughput:** Maintaining provenance requires some additional processing on the SDN controller, which increases the latency of responses and decreases throughput. We first measured this effect in our prototype by using `Cbench` to send streams of PacketIn messages, which is a current standard in evaluating OpenFlow controllers [4]. We found that the 95th percentile latency increased by 29%, from 48.38 ms to 62.63 ms, when Y! was enabled; throughput dropped by 14%, from 56.0 to 48.4 requests per second.

However, these results are difficult to generalize because RapidNet's performance as an SDN controller is not competitive with state-of-the-art controllers, even without Y!. We therefore repeated the experiment with our Y! extension for native Trema (Section 7.1); here, adding Y! increased the average latency by only 1.6%, to 33 microseconds, and decreased the average throughput by 8.9%, to 100,540 PacketIn messages per second. We note that this comparison is slightly unfair because we manually instrumented a specific Trema program to work with our extension, whereas the RapidNet prototype can work with any program. However, adding instrumentation to Trema programs is not difficult and could be automated. More generally, our results suggest that capturing provenance is not inherently expensive, and that an optimized RapidNet could potentially do a lot better.

## 7.6 Query processing speed

When the user issues a provenance query, Y! must recursively construct the response using the process from Section 3.5 and then post-process it using the heuristics from Section 4. Since debugging is an interactive process, a quick response is important. To see whether Y! can meet this requirement, we measured the turnaround time for the queries in Table 2, as well as the fraction of time consumed by Y!'s major components.

Figure 12 shows our results. We make two high-level observations. First, the turnaround time is dominated by R-tree and packet recorder lookups. This is expected because the graph construction algorithm itself is not very complex. Second, although the queries vary in complexity and thus their turnaround times are difficult to compare, we observe that none of them took more than one second; the most expensive query was Q9, which took 0.33 seconds to complete.

## 7.7 Scalability

We do not yet have experience with Y!, or negative provenance, in a large-scale deployment. However, we have done a number of experiments to get an initial impression of its scalability. Due to lack of space, we report only a subset of our results here.

**Complexity:** In our first experiment, we tested whether the complexity of the provenance increases with the number of possible traffic sources. We simulated a four-layer fat-tree topology with 15 switches, and we placed the client and the server on different leaves, to vary the hop distance between them from 2 to 6. Our results for running the learning-switch query (Q1) are shown in Figure 13a (the bars are analogous to Figure 10). As expected, the size of the raw provenance for Q1 grew substantially – from 250 to 386 vertices – because 1) there number of possible sources for the missing traffic increased, because each additional hop brings additional branches on the backtrace path and 2) each additional hop required extra vertices to be represented in the provenance. But the first effect was mitigated by our pruning heuristics, since the extra sources were inconsistent with the network state, and the second effect was addressed by the summarization, which merged the vertices along the propagation path into a single super-vertex. Once all the heuristics had been applied, the size of the provenance was 16 vertices, independent of the hop count.

**Storage:** In our second experiment, we simulated three-layer fat-tree topologies of different sizes (i.e., with different node degrees); each edge switch was connected to a fixed number of active hosts that were constantly sending HTTP requests to the server. Figure 13b shows how Y!'s storage requirements grew with the number of switches in the network. As expected, the size of both the `pcap` trace and the R-tree was roughly proportional to the size of the network; this is expected because a) each new switch added a fixed number of hosts, and b) the depth of the tree, and thus the hop count between the server and its clients, remained constant. Generally, the storage requirement depends on the rate at which events of interest (packet transmissions, routing changes, etc.) are captured, as well as on the time for which these records are retained.

**Query speed:** Our third experiment is analogous to the second, except that we issued a query at the end and measured its turnaround time. Figure 13c shows our results. The dominant cost was the time it took to find packets in the `pcap` trace; the R-tree lookups were much faster, and the time needed to construct and post-process the graph was so small that it is difficult to see in the figure. Overall, the lookup time was below one second even for the largest network we tried.

**Possible optimizations:** Since our implementation has not been optimized, some of the costs could grow quickly in a large-scale deployment. For instance, in a data center with 400 switches that handle 1 Gbps of traffic each, our simple approach of recording `pcap` traces at each switch would consume approximately 30 GB of storage *per second* for the date center, or about 75 MB for each switch. Packet recorder lookups, which compromise a major portion of query latency, in such a large trace would be limited by disk read throughput, and could take minutes. However, we note that there are several ways to reduce these costs; for instance, techniques from the database literature – e.g., a simple time index – could be used to speed up the lookups, and the storage cost could be reduced by applying filters.

## 7.8 Summary

Our results show that Y! – and, more generally, negative provenance – can be a useful tool for diagnosing problems in networks: the provenance of the issues we looked at was compact and readable, and Y! was able to find it in less than a second in each case. Our results also show that the readability is aided considerably by Y!'s post-processing heuristics, which reduced the number of vertices by more than an order of magnitude. Y!'s main run-time cost is the storage it needs to maintain a history of the system's past states, but a commodity hard-drive should be more than sufficient to keep this history for more than a day.

# 8. RELATED WORK

**Network debugging:** Many tools and techniques for network debugging and root cause analysis have been proposed, e.g., [5, 9, 18, 26], but most focus on explaining positive events. These tools can be used to (indirectly) troubleshoot negative symptoms, but the results from our survey in Section 2.4 suggest that the lack of direct support for negative queries makes this significantly more difficult. Hubble [12] uses probing to find AS-level reachability problems but is protocol-specific; header space analysis [13] provides finer-grain results but relies on static analysis and thus cannot explain complex, dynamic interactions like the ones we consider here. ATPG [34] tests for liveness, reachability, and performance, but cannot handle dynamic nodes like the SDN controller. NICE [2] uses model checking to test whether a given SDN program has specific correctness properties; this approach is complementary to ours, which focuses on diagnosing unforeseen problems at runtime. We are not aware of any protocol-independent systems that can explain negative events in a dynamic distributed system.

**Negative provenance:** There is a substantial literature on tracking provenance in databases [1, 6, 11, 25, 31] and in networks [35, 37], but only a few papers have considered negative provenance. Huang et al. [10] and Meliou et al. [19] focus on instance-based explanations for missing answers, that is, how to obtain the missing answers by making modifications to the value of base instances (tuples); Why-Not [3] and ConQueR [28] provide query-based explanations for SQL queries, which reveal over-constrained conditions in the queries and suggest modifications to them. None of these papers considers distributed environments and networks, as we do here. In the networking literature, there is some prior work on *positive* provenance, including our own work on ExSPAN [37], SNP [35], and DTaP [36], but none of these systems can answer (or even formulate) negative queries. To our knowledge, the only existing work that does support such queries is our own workshop paper [32], on which this paper is based.

# 9. CONCLUSION

In this paper, we have argued that debuggers for distributed systems should not only be able to explain why an unexpected event *did* occur, but also why an expected event *did not* occur. We have shown how this can be accomplished with the concept of *negative provenance*, which so far has received relatively little attention. We have defined a formal model of negative provenance, we have presented an algorithm generating such provenance, and we have introduced Y!, a practical system that can maintain both positive and negative provenance in a distributed system and answer queries about it. Our evaluation in the context of software-defined networks and BGP suggests that negative provenance can be a useful tool for diagnosing complex problems in distributed systems.

**Acknowledgments:** We thank our shepherd Nate Foster and the anonymous reviewers for their comments and suggestions. We also thank Behnaz Arzani for helpful comments on earlier drafts of this paper. This work was supported by NSF grants CNS-1065130, CNS-1054229, CNS-1040672, and CNS-0845552, as well as DARPA contract FA8650-11-C-7189.

# 10. REFERENCES

[1] P. Buneman, S. Khanna, and W. C. Tan. Why and where: A characterization of data provenance. In *Proc. ICDT*, Jan. 2001.

[2] M. Canini, D. Venzano, P. Perešíni, D. Kostić, and J. Rexford. A NICE way to test OpenFlow applications. In *Proc. NSDI*, Apr. 2012.

[3] A. Chapman and H. V. Jagadish. Why not? In *Proc. SIGMOD*, June 2009.

[4] D. Erickson. The Beacon OpenFlow controller. In *Proc. HotSDN*, Aug. 2013.

[5] A. Feldmann, O. Maennel, Z. M. Mao, A. Berger, and B. Maggs. Locating Internet routing instabilities. In *Proc. SIGCOMM*, Aug. 2004.

[6] T. J. Green, G. Karvounarakis, N. E. Taylor, O. Biton, Z. G. Ives, and V. Tannen. ORCHESTRA: Facilitating collaborative data sharing. In *Proc. SIGMOD*, June 2007.

[7] A. Guttman. R-trees: A dynamic index structure for spatial searching. In *Proc. SIGMOD*, June 1984.

[8] N. Handigol, B. Heller, V. Jeyakumar, D. Mazières, and N. McKeown. Where is the debugger for my software-defined network? In *Proc. HotSDN*, Aug. 2012.

[9] N. Handigol, B. Heller, V. Jeyakumar, D. Mazières, and N. McKeown. I know what your packet did last hop: Using packet histories to troubleshoot networks. In *Proc. NSDI*, Apr. 2014.

[10] J. Huang, T. Chen, A. Doan, and J. F. Naughton. On the provenance of non-answers to queries over extracted data. *Proc. VLDB Endow.*, 1(1):736–747, Aug. 2008.

[11] R. Ikeda, H. Park, and J. Widom. Provenance for generalized map and reduce workflows. In *Proc. CIDR*, Jan. 2011.

[12] E. Katz-Bassett, H. V. Madhyastha, J. P. John, A. Krishnamurthy, D. Wetherall, and T. Anderson. Studying black holes in the Internet with Hubble. In *Proc. NSDI*, Apr. 2008.

[13] P. Kazemian, G. Varghese, and N. McKeown. Header space analysis: static checking for networks. In *Proc. NSDI*, Apr. 2012.

[14] libspatialindex. `http://libspatialindex.github.io/`.

[15] D. Logothetis, S. De, and K. Yocum. Scalable lineage capture for debugging DISC analysis. Technical Report CSE2012-0990, UCSD.

[16] B. T. Loo, T. Condie, M. Garofalakis, D. E. Gay, J. M. Hellerstein, P. Maniatis, R. Ramakrishnan, T. Roscoe, and I. Stoica. Declarative networking. *Commun. ACM*, 52(11):87–95, Nov. 2009.

[17] P. Macko and M. Seltzer. Provenance Map Orbiter: Interactive exploration of large provenance graphs. In *Proc. TaPP*, June 2011.

[18] H. Mai, A. Khurshid, R. Agarwal, M. Caesar, P. B. Godfrey, and S. T. King. Debugging the data plane with Anteater. In *Proc. SIGCOMM*, Aug. 2011.

[19] A. Meliou and D. Suciu. Tiresias: the database oracle for how-to queries. In *Proc. SIGMOD*, May 2012.

[20] Mininet. `http://mininet.org/`.

[21] C. Monsanto, J. Reich, N. Foster, J. Rexford, and D. Walker. Composing software-defined networks. In *Proc. NSDI*, Apr. 2013.

[22] K.-K. Muniswamy-Reddy, D. A. Holland, U. Braun, and M. Seltzer. Provenance-aware storage systems. In *Proc. USENIX ATC*, May 2006.

[23] Outages mailing list. `http://wiki.outages.org/index.php/Main_Page#Outages_Mailing_Lists`.

[24] RapidNet. `http://netdb.cis.upenn.edu/rapidnet/`.

[25] C. Ré, N. Dalvi, and D. Suciu. Efficient top-k query evaluation on probabilistic data. In *Proc. ICDE*, Apr. 2007.

[26] A. Singh, P. Maniatis, T. Roscoe, and P. Druschel. Using queries for distributed monitoring and forensics. In *Proc. EuroSys*, Apr. 2006.

[27] R. Teixeira and J. Rexford. A measurement framework for pin-pointing routing changes. In *Proc. Network Troubleshooting workshop (NetTS)*, Sept. 2004.

[28] Q. T. Tran and C.-Y. Chan. How to ConQueR why-not questions. In *Proc. SIGMOD*, June 2010.

[29] Trema. `http://trema.github.io/trema/`.

[30] A. Wang, L. Jia, W. Zhou, Y. Ren, B. T. Loo, J. Rexford, V. Nigam, A. Scedrov, and C. L. Talcott. FSR: Formal analysis and implementation toolkit for safe inter-domain routing. *IEEE/ACM ToN*, 20(6):1814–1827, Dec. 2012.

[31] J. Widom. Trio: A system for integrated management of data, accuracy, and lineage. In *Proc. CIDR*, Jan. 2005.

[32] Y. Wu, A. Haeberlen, W. Zhou, and B. T. Loo. Answering Why-Not queries in software-defined networks with negative provenance. In *Proc. HotNets*, 2013.

[33] Y. Wu, M. Zhao, A. Haeberlen, W. Zhou, and B. T. Loo. Diagnosing missing events in distributed systems with negative provenance. Technical Report MS-CIS-14-06, University of Pennsylvania, 2014.

[34] H. Zeng, P. Kazemian, G. Varghese, and N. McKeown. Automatic test packet generation. In *Proc. CoNEXT*, Dec. 2012.

[35] W. Zhou, Q. Fei, A. Narayan, A. Haeberlen, B. T. Loo, and M. Sherr. Secure network provenance. In *Proc. SOSP*, Oct. 2011.

[36] W. Zhou, S. Mapara, Y. Ren, Y. Li, A. Haeberlen, Z. Ives, B. T. Loo, and M. Sherr. Distributed time-aware provenance. In *Proc. VLDB*, Aug. 2013.

[37] W. Zhou, M. Sherr, T. Tao, X. Li, B. T. Loo, and Y. Mao. Efficient querying and maintenance of network provenance at Internet-scale. In *Proc. SIGMOD*, 2010.

# Troubleshooting Blackbox SDN Control Software with Minimal Causal Sequences

Colin Scott[◇] Andreas Wundsam[†⋆] Barath Raghavan[⋆] Aurojit Panda[◇]
Andrew Or[◇] Jefferson Lai[◇] Eugene Huang[◇] Zhi Liu[ø] Ahmed El-Hassany[⋆]
Sam Whitlock[♯⋆] H.B. Acharya[⋆] Kyriakos Zarifis[‡⋆] Scott Shenker[◇⋆]
[◇]UC Berkeley [†]Big Switch Networks [⋆]ICSI [ø]Tshinghua University [♯]EPFL [‡]USC

## ABSTRACT

*Software bugs are inevitable in software-defined networking control software, and troubleshooting is a tedious, time-consuming task. In this paper we discuss how to improve control software troubleshooting by presenting a technique for automatically identifying a minimal sequence of inputs responsible for triggering a given bug, without making assumptions about the language or instrumentation of the software under test. We apply our technique to five open source SDN control platforms—Floodlight, NOX, POX, Pyretic, ONOS—and illustrate how the minimal causal sequences our system found aided the troubleshooting process.*

## Categories and Subject Descriptors

C.2.4 [**Computer-Communication Networks**]: Distributed Systems—*Network operating systems*; D.2.5 [**Software Engineering**]: Testing and Debugging—*Debugging aids*

## Keywords

Test case minimization; Troubleshooting; SDN control software

## 1. INTRODUCTION

Software-defined networking (SDN) proposes to simplify network management by providing a simple logically-centralized API upon which network management programs can be written. However, the software used to support this API is anything but simple: the SDN control plane (consisting of the network operating system and higher layers) is a complicated distributed system that must react quickly and correctly to failures, host migrations, policy-configuration changes and other events. All complicated distributed systems are prone to bugs, and from our first-hand familiarity with five open source controllers and three major commercial controllers we can attest that SDN is no exception.

When faced with symptoms of a network problem (*e.g.* a persistent loop) that suggest the presence of a bug in the control plane software, software developers need to identify which events are triggering this apparent bug before they can begin to isolate and fix it. This act of "troubleshooting" (which precedes the act of debugging the code) is highly time-consuming, as developers spend hours poring over multigigabyte execution traces.[1] Our aim is to reduce effort spent on troubleshooting distributed systems like SDN control software, by automatically eliminating events from buggy traces that are not causally related to the bug, producing a "minimal causal sequence" (MCS) of triggering events.

Our goal of minimizing traces is in the spirit of delta debugging [58], but our problem is complicated by the distributed nature of control software: our input is not a single file fed to a single point of execution, but an ongoing sequence of events involving multiple actors. We therefore need to carefully control the interleaving of events in the face of asynchrony, concurrency and non-determinism in order to reproduce bugs throughout the minimization process. Crucially, we aim to minimize traces without making assumptions about the language or instrumentation of the control software.

We have built a troubleshooting system that, as far as we know, is the first to meet these challenges (as we discuss further in §8). Once it reduces a given execution trace to an MCS (or an approximation thereof), the developer embarks on the debugging process. We claim that the greatly reduced size of the trace makes it easier for the developer to figure out which code path contains the underlying bug, allowing them to focus their effort on the task of fixing the problematic code itself. After the bug has been fixed, the MCS can serve as a test case to prevent regression, and can help identify redundant bug reports where the MCSes are the same.

Our troubleshooting system, which we call STS (SDN Troubleshooting System), consists of 23,000 lines of Python, and is designed so that organizations can implement the technology within their existing QA infrastructure (discussed in §5); over the last year we have worked with a commercial SDN company to integrate STS. We evaluate STS in two ways. First and most significantly, we use STS to troubleshoot seven previously unknown bugs—involving concurrent events, faulty failover logic, broken state machines, and deadlock in a distributed database—that we found by fuzz testing five controllers (Floodlight [16], NOX [23], POX [39], Pyretic [19], ONOS [43]) written in three different languages (Java, C++, Python). Second, we demonstrate the boundaries of where STS works well by finding MCSes for previously known and synthetic bugs that span a range of bug types. In our evaluation, we quantitatively show that STS is able to minimize (non-synthetic) bug traces by up to 98%, and we anecdotally found that reducing traces to MCSes made it easy to understand their root causes.

[1]Software developers in general spend roughly half (49% according to one study [21]) of their time troubleshooting and debugging, and spend considerable time troubleshooting bugs that are difficult to trigger (the same study found that 70% of the reported concurrency bugs take days to months to fix).


*SIGCOMM'14*, August 17–22, 2014, Chicago, Illinois, USA.

ACM 978-1-4503-2836-4/14/08 ...$15.00.
http://dx.doi.org/10.1145/2619239.2626304.

## 2. BACKGROUND

Network operating systems, the key component of SDN software infrastructure, consist of control software running on a replicated set of servers, each running a controller instance. Controllers coordinate between themselves, and receive input events (*e.g.* link failure notifications) and statistics from switches (either physical or virtual), policy changes via a management interface, and possibly dataplane packets. In response, the controllers issue forwarding instructions to switches. All input events are asynchronous, and individual controllers may fail at any time. The controllers either communicate with each other over the dataplane network, or use a separate dedicated network, and may become partitioned.

The goal of the network control plane is to configure the switch forwarding entries so as to enforce one or more invariants, such as connectivity (*i.e.* ensuring that a route exists between every endpoint pair), isolation and access control (*i.e.* various limitations on connectivity), and virtualization (*i.e.* ensuring that packets are handled in a manner consistent with the specified virtual network). A bug causes an invariant to be violated. Invariants can be violated because the system was improperly configured (*e.g.* the management system [2] or a human improperly specified their goals), or because there is a bug within the SDN control plane itself. In this paper we focus on troubleshooting bugs in the SDN control plane after it has been given a policy configuration.[2]

In commercial SDN development, software developers work with a team of QA engineers whose job is to find bugs. The QA engineers exercise automated test scenarios that involve sequences of external (input) events such as failures on large (software emulated or hardware) network testbeds. If they detect an invariant violation, they hand the resulting trace to a developer for analysis.

The space of possible bugs is enormous, and it is difficult and time consuming to link the symptom of a bug (*e.g.* a routing loop) to the sequence of events in the QA trace (which includes both external events and internal monitoring data), since QA traces contain a wealth of extraneous events. Consider that an hour long QA test emulating event rates observed in production could contain 8.5 network error events per minute [22] and 500 VM migrations per hour [49], for a total of $8.5 \cdot 60 + 500 \approx 1000$ inputs.

## 3. PROBLEM DEFINITION

We represent the forwarding state of the network at a particular time as a configuration $c$, which contains all the forwarding entries in the network as well as the liveness of the various network elements. The control software is a system consisting of one or more controller processes that takes a sequence of external network events $E = e_1 \rightarrow e_2 \rightarrow \cdots e_m$ (*e.g.* link failures) as inputs, and produces a sequence of network configurations $C = c_1, c_2, \ldots, c_n$.

An invariant is a predicate $P$ over forwarding state (a safety condition, *e.g.* loop-freedom). We say that configuration $c$ violates the invariant if $P(c)$ is false, denoted $\overline{P}(c)$.

We are given a log $L$ generated by a centralized QA test orchestrator.[3] The log $L$ contains a sequence of events

$$\tau_L = e_1 \rightarrow i_1 \rightarrow i_2 \rightarrow e_2 \rightarrow \cdots e_m \rightarrow \cdots i_p$$

which includes external events $E_L = e_1, e_2 \cdots e_m$ injected by the orchestrator, and internal events $I_L = i_1, i_2 \cdots i_p$ triggered by the control software (*e.g.* OpenFlow messages). The events $E_L$ include timestamps $\{(e_k, t_k)\}$ from the orchestrator's clock.

A replay of log $L$ involves replaying the external events $E_L$, possibly taking into account the occurrence of internal events $I_L$ as observed by the orchestrator. We denote a replay attempt by $replay(\tau)$. The output of $replay$ is a sequence of configurations $C_R = \hat{c}_1, \hat{c}_2, \ldots, \hat{c}_n$. Ideally $replay(\tau_L)$ reproduces the original configuration sequence, but this does not always hold.

If the configuration sequence $C_L = c_1, c_2, \ldots, c_n$ associated with the log $L$ violated predicate $P$ (*i.e.* $\exists_{c_i \in C_L}.\overline{P}(c_i)$) then we say $replay(\cdot) = C_R$ reproduces that violation if $C_R$ contains an equivalent faulty configuration (*i.e.* $\exists_{\hat{c}_i \in C_R}.\overline{P}(\hat{c}_i)$).

The goal of our work is, when given a log $L$ that exhibited an invariant violation,[3] to find a small, replayable sequence of events that reproduces that invariant violation. Formally, we define a minimal causal sequence (MCS) to be a sequence $\tau_M$ where the external events $E_M \in \tau_M$ are a subsequence of $E_L$ such that $replay(\tau_M)$ reproduces the invariant violation, but for all proper subsequences $E_N$ of $E_M$ there is no sequence $\tau_N$ such that $replay(\tau_N)$ reproduces the violation. Note that an MCS is not necessarily *globally* minimal, in that there could be smaller subsequences of $E_L$ that reproduce this violation, but are not a subsequence of this MCS.

We find approximate MCSes by deciding which external events to eliminate and, more importantly, when to inject external events. We describe this process in the next section.

## 4. MINIMIZING TRACES

Given a log $L$ generated from testing infrastructure,[3] our goal is to find an approximate MCS, so that a human can examine the MCS rather than the full log. This involves two tasks: searching through subsequences of $E_L$, and deciding when to inject external events for each subsequence so that, whenever possible, the invariant violation is retriggered.

### 4.1 Searching for Subsequences

Checking random subsequences of $E_L$ would be one viable but inefficient approach to achieving our first task. We do better by employing the delta debugging algorithm [58], a divide-and-conquer algorithm for isolating fault-inducing inputs. We use delta debugging to iteratively select subsequences of $E_L$ and $replay$ each subsequence with some timing $T$. If the bug persists for a given subsequence, delta debugging ignores the other inputs, and proceeds with the search for an MCS within this subsequence. The delta debugging algorithm we implement is shown in Figure 1.

The input subsequences chosen by delta debugging are not always valid. Of the possible inputs sequences we generate (shown in Table 2), it is not sensible to replay a recovery event without a preceding failure event, nor to replay a host migration event without modifying its starting position when a preceding host migration event has been pruned. Our implementation of delta debugging therefore prunes failure/recovery event pairs as a single unit, and updates initial host locations whenever host migration events are pruned so that hosts do not magically appear at new locations.[4] These two heuristics account for validity of all network events

[2]This does not preclude us from troubleshooting misspecified policies so long as test invariants [31] are specified separately.

[3]We discuss how these logs are generated in §5.

[4]Handling invalid inputs is crucial for ensuring that the delta debugging algorithm finds a minimal causal subsequence. The algorithm we employ [58] makes three assumptions about inputs: monotonicity, unambiguity, and consistency. An event trace that violates monotonicity may contain events that "undo" the invariant violation triggered by the MCS, and may therefore exhibit slightly inflated MCSes. An event trace that violates unambiguity may exhibit multiple MCSes; delta debugging will return one of them. The most important assumption is consistency, which requires that the test outcome can always be determined. We guarantee neither monotonicity nor unambiguity, but we guarantee consistency by ensuring that subsequences are always semantically valid by applying the two heuristics described above. Zeller wrote a follow-on

shown in Table 2. We do not yet support network policy changes as events, which have more complex semantic dependencies.[5]

## 4.2 Searching for Timings

Simply exploring subsequences $E_S$ of $E_L$ is insufficient for finding MCSes: the timing of when we inject the external events during $replay$ is crucial for reproducing violations.

**Existing Approaches.** The most natural approach to scheduling external events is to maintain the original wall-clock timing intervals between them. If this is able to find all minimization opportunities, *i.e.* reproduce the violation for all subsequences that are a supersequence of some MCS, we say that the inputs are isolated. The original applications of delta debugging [6,47,58,59] make this assumption (where a single input is fed to a single program), as well as QuickCheck's input "shrinking" [12] when applied to blackbox systems like synchronous telecommunications protocols [4].

We tried this approach, but were rarely able to reproduce invariant violations. As our case studies demonstrate (§6), this is largely due to the concurrent, asynchronous nature of distributed systems; consider that the network can reorder or delay messages, or that controllers may process multiple inputs simultaneously. Inputs injected according to wall-clock time are not guaranteed to coincide correctly with the current state of the control software.

We must therefore consider the control software's internal events. To deterministically reproduce bugs, we would need visibility into every I/O request and response (*e.g.* clock values or socket reads), as well as all thread scheduling decisions for each controller. This information is the starting point for techniques that seek to minimize thread interleavings leading up to race conditions. These approaches involve iteratively feeding a single input (the thread schedule) to a single entity (a deterministic scheduler) [11, 13, 28], or statically analyzing feasible thread schedules [26].

A crucial constraint of these approaches is that they must keep the inputs fixed; that is, behavior must depend uniquely on the thread schedule. Otherwise, the controllers may take a divergent code path. If this occurs some processes might issue a previously unobserved I/O request, and the replayer will not have a recorded response; worse yet, a divergent process might deschedule itself at a different point than it did originally, so that the remainder of the recorded thread schedule is unusable to the replayer.

Because they keep the inputs fixed, these approaches strive for a subtly different goal than ours: minimizing thread context switches rather than input events. At best, these approaches can indirectly minimize input events by truncating individual thread executions.

With additional information obtained by program flow analysis [27, 34, 50] however, the inputs no longer need to be fixed. The internal events considered by these program flow reduction techniques are individual instructions executed by the programs (obtained by instrumenting the language runtime), in addition to I/O responses and the thread schedule. With this information they can compute program flow dependencies, and thereby remove input events from anywhere in the trace as long as they can prove that doing so cannot possibly cause the faulty execution path to diverge.

While program flow reduction is able to minimize inputs, these techniques are not able to explore alternate code paths that still trigger the invariant violation. They are also overly conservative in removing inputs (*e.g.* EFF takes the transitive closure of all possible dependencies [34]) causing them to miss opportunities to remove dependencies that actually semantically commute.

paper [59] that removes the need for these assumptions, but incurs an additional factor of $n$ in complexity in doing so.

[5]If codifying the semantic dependencies of policy changes turns out to be difficult, one could just employ the more expensive version of delta debugging to account for inconsistency [59].

| Internal Message | Masked Values |
|---|---|
| OpenFlow messages | xac id, cookie, buffer id, stats |
| packet_out/in payload | all values except src, dst, data |
| Log statements | varargs parameters to printf |

Table 1: Internal messages and their masked values.

**Allowing Divergence.** Our approach is to allow processes to proceed along divergent paths rather than recording all low-level I/O and thread scheduling decisions. This has several advantages. Unlike the other approaches, we can find shorter alternate code paths that still trigger the invariant violation. Previous *best-effort* execution minimization techniques [14, 53] also allow alternate code paths, but do not systematically consider concurrency and asynchrony.[6] We also avoid the performance overhead of recording all I/O requests and later replaying them (*e.g.* EFF incurs ~10x slowdown during replay [34]). Lastly, we avoid the extensive effort required to instrument the control software's language runtime, needed by the other approaches to implement a deterministic thread scheduler, interpose on syscalls, or perform program flow analysis. By avoiding assumptions about the language of the control software, we were able to easily apply our system to five different control platforms written in three different languages.

**Accounting for Interleavings.** To reproduce the invariant violation (whenever $E_S$ is a supersequence of an MCS) we need to inject each input event $\textcircled{e}$ only after all other events, including internal events, that precede it in the happens-before relation [33] from the original execution ($\{i \mid i \rightarrow \textcircled{e}\}$) have occurred [51].

The internal events we consider are (a) message delivery events, either between controllers (*e.g.* database synchronization messages) or between controllers and switches (*e.g.* OpenFlow messages), and (b) state transitions within controllers (*e.g.* a backup node deciding to become master). Our replay orchestrator obtains visibility into (a) by interposing on all messages within the test environment (to be described in §5). It optionally obtains partial visibility into (b) by instrumenting controller software with a simple interposition layer (to be described in §5.2).

Given a subsequence $E_S$, our goal is to find an execution that obeys the original happens-before relation. We do not control the occurrence of internal events, but we can manipulate when they are delivered through our interposition layer,[7] and we also decide when to inject the external events $E_S$. The key challenges in choosing a schedule stem from the fact that the original execution has been modified: internal events may differ syntactically, some expected internal events may no longer occur, and new internal events may occur that were not observed at all in the original execution.

**Functional Equivalence.** Internal events may differ syntactically (*e.g.* sequence numbers of control packets may all differ) when replaying a subsequence of the original log. We observe that many internal events are *functionally equivalent*, in the sense that they have the same effect on the state of the system with respect to triggering the invariant violation. For example, `flow_mod` messages may cause switches to make the same change to their forwarding behavior even if their transaction ids differ.

We apply this observation by defining masks over semantically extraneous fields of internal events.[8] We show the fields we mask

[6]PRES explores alternate code paths in best-effort replay of multithreaded executions, but does not minimize executions [45].

[7]In this way we totally order messages. Without interposition on process scheduling however, the system may still be concurrent.

[8]One consequence of applying masks is that bugs involving masked fields are outside the purview of our approach.

Input: $T_{\text{✗}}$ s.t. $T_{\text{✗}}$ is a trace and $test(T_{\text{✗}}) = \text{✗}$. Output: $T'_{\text{✗}} = ddmin(T_{\text{✗}})$ s.t. $T'_{\text{✗}} \subseteq T_{\text{✗}}$, $test(T'_{\text{✗}}) = \text{✗}$, and $T'_{\text{✗}}$ is minimal.

$$ddmin(T_{\text{✗}}) = ddmin_2(T_{\text{✗}}, \emptyset) \quad \text{where}$$

$$ddmin_2(T'_{\text{✗}}, R) = \begin{cases} T'_{\text{✗}} & \text{if } |T'_{\text{✗}}| = 1 \text{ ("base case")} \\ ddmin_2(T_1, R) & \text{else if } test(T_1 \cup R) = \text{✗} \text{ ("in } T_1\text{")} \\ ddmin_2(T_2, R) & \text{else if } test(T_2 \cup R) = \text{✗} \text{ ("in } T_2\text{")} \\ ddmin_2(T_1, T_2 \cup R) \cup ddmin_2(T_2, T_1 \cup R) & \text{otherwise ("interference")} \end{cases}$$

where $test(T)$ denotes the state of the system after executing the trace $T$, ✗ denotes an invariant violation, $T_1 \subset T'_{\text{✗}}$, $T_2 \subset T'_{\text{✗}}$, $T_1 \cup T_2 = T'_{\text{✗}}$, $T_1 \cap T_2 = \emptyset$, and $|T_1| \approx |T_2| \approx |T'_{\text{✗}}|/2$ hold.

Figure 1: Automated Delta Debugging Algorithm from [58]. $\subseteq$ and $\subset$ denote subsequence relations.

| Input Type | Implementation |
|---|---|
| Switch failure/recovery | TCP teardown |
| Controller failure/recovery | `SIGKILL` |
| Link failure/recovery | `ofp_port_status` |
| Controller partition | `iptables` |
| Dataplane packet injection | Network namespaces |
| Dataplane packet drop | Dataplane interposition |
| Dataplane packet delay | Dataplane interposition |
| Host migration | `ofp_port_status` |
| Control message delay | Controlplane interposition |
| Non-deterministic TCAMs | Modified switches |

Table 2: Input types currently supported by STS.

```
procedure PEEK(input subsequence)
  inferred ← [ ]
  for e_i in subsequence
    checkpoint system
    inject e_i
    Δ ← |e_{i+1}.time − e_i.time| + ε
    record events for Δ seconds
    matched ← original events & recorded events
    inferred ← inferred + [e_i] + matched
    restore checkpoint
  return inferred
```

Figure 2: PEEK determines which internal events from the original sequence occur for a given subsequence.

in Table 1. Note that these masks only need to be specified once, and can later be applied programmatically.

We then consider an internal event $i'$ observed in $replay$ equivalent (in the sense of inheriting all of its happens-before relations) to an internal event $i$ from the original log if and only if all unmasked fields have the same value and $i$ occurs between $i'$'s preceding and succeeding inputs in the happens-before relation.

**Handling Absent Internal Events.** Some internal events from the original log that "happen before" some external input may be absent when replaying a subsequence. For instance, if we prune a link failure, the corresponding notification message will not arise.

To avoid waiting forever we infer the presence of internal events before we $replay$ each subsequence. Our algorithm (called PEEK()) for inferring the presence of internal events is depicted in Figure 2. The algorithm injects each input, records a checkpoint[9] of the network and the control software's state, allows the system to proceed up until the following input (plus a small time $\epsilon$), records the observed events, and matches the recorded events with the functionally equivalent internal events observed in the original trace.[10]

[9]We discuss the implementation details of checkpointing in 5.3.

[10]In the case that, due to non-determinism, an internal event occurs during PEEK() but does not occur during $replay$, we time out on internal events after $\epsilon$ seconds of their expected occurrence.

**Handling New Internal Events.** The last possible induced change is the occurrence of new internal events that were not observed in the original log. New events present multiple possibilities for where we should inject the next input. Consider the following case: if $i_2$ and $i_3$ are internal events observed during $replay$ that are both in the same equivalence class as a single event $i_1$ from the original run, we could inject the next input after $i_2$ or after $i_3$.

In the general case it is always possible to construct two state machines that lead to differing outcomes: one that only leads to the invariant violation when we inject the next input *before* a new internal event, and another only when we inject *after* a new internal event. In other words, to be guaranteed to traverse any state transition suffix that leads to the violation, we must recursively branch, trying both possibilities for every new internal event. This implies an exponential worst case number of possibilities to be explored.

Exponential search over these possibilities is not a practical option. Our heuristic is to proceed normally if there are new internal events, always injecting the next input when its last expected predecessor either occurs or times out. This ensures that we always find state transition suffixes that contain a subsequence of the (equivalent) original internal events, but leaves open the possibility of finding divergent suffixes that lead to the invariant violation.

**Recap.** We combine these heuristics to replay each subsequence chosen by delta debugging: we compute functional equivalency for all internal events intercepted by our test orchestrator's interposition layer (§5), we invoke PEEK() to infer absent internal events, and with these inferred causal dependencies we $replay$ the input subsequence, waiting to inject each input until each of its (functionally equivalent) predecessors have occurred while allowing new internal events through the interposition layer immediately.

## 4.3 Complexity

The delta debugging algorithm terminates after $\Omega(\log n)$ invocations of $replay$ in the best case, and $O(n)$ in the worst case, where $n$ is the number of inputs in the original trace [58]. Each invocation of $replay$ takes $O(n)$ time (one iteration for PEEK() and one iteration for the replay itself), for an overall runtime of $\Omega(n \log n)$ best case and $O(n^2)$ worst case replayed inputs. The runtime can be decreased by parallelizing delta debugging: speculatively replaying subsequences in parallel, and joining the results. Storing periodic checkpoints of the system state throughout testing can also reduce runtime, as it allows us to $replay$ starting from a recent checkpoint rather than the beginning of the trace.

# 5. SYSTEMS CHALLENGES

Thus far we have assumed that we are given a faulty execution trace. We now provide an overview of how we obtain traces, and then describe our system for minimizing them.

**Obtaining Traces.** All three of the commercial SDN companies

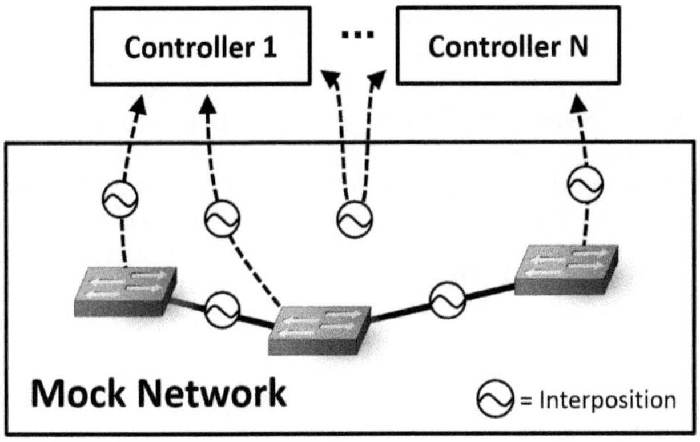


Figure 3: STS runs mock network devices, and interposes on all communication channels.

that we know of employ a team of QA engineers to fuzz test their control software on network testbeds. This fuzz testing infrastructure consists of the control software under test, the network testbed (which may be software or hardware), and a centralized test orchestrator that chooses input sequences, drives the behavior of the testbed, and periodically checks invariants.

We do not have access to such a QA testbed, and instead built our own. Our testbed mocks out the control plane behavior of network devices in lightweight software switches and hosts (with support for minimal dataplane forwarding). We then run the control software on top of this mock network and connect the switches to the controller(s). The mock network manages the execution of events from a single location, which allows it to record a serial event ordering. This design is similar to production software QA testbeds, and is depicted in Figure 3. One distinguishing feature of our design is that the mock network interposes on all communication channels, allowing it to delay or drop messages to induce failure modes that might be seen in real, asynchronous networks.

We use our mock network to find bugs in control software. Most commonly we generate random input sequences based on event probabilities that we assign (*cf.* §6.8), and periodically check invariants on the network state.[11] We also run the mock network interactively so that we can examine the state of the network and manually induce event orderings that we believe may trigger bugs.

**Performing Minimization.** After discovering an invariant violation, we invoke delta debugging to minimize the recorded trace. We use the testing infrastructure itself to *replay* each intermediate subsequence. During *replay* the mock network enforces event orderings as needed to maintain the original happens-before relation, by using its interposition on message channels to manage the order (functionally equivalent) messages are let through, and waiting until the appropriate time to inject inputs. For example, if the original trace included a link failure preceded by the arrival of a heartbeat message, during *replay* the mock network waits until it observes a functionally equivalent ping probe to arrive, allows the probe through, then tells the switch to fail its link.

STS is our realization of this system, implemented in more than 23,000 lines of Python in addition to the Hassel network invariant checking library [31]. STS also optionally makes use of Open vSwitch [46] as an interposition point between controllers. We have made the code for STS publicly available at ucb-sts.github.com/sts.

**Integration With Existing Testbeds.** In designing STS we aimed to make it possible for engineering organizations to implement the technology within their existing QA test infrastructure. Organizations can add delta debugging to their test orchestrator, and optionally add interposition points throughout the testbed to control event ordering during replay. In this way they can continue running large scale networks with the switches, middleboxes, hosts, and routing protocols they had already chosen to include in their QA testbed.

We avoid making assumptions about the language or instrumentation of the software under test in order to facilitate integration with preexisting software. Many of the heuristics we describe below are approximations that might be made more precise if we had more visibility and control over the system, *e.g.* if we could deterministically specify the thread schedule of each controller.

## 5.1 Coping with Non-Determinism

Non-determinism in concurrent executions stems from differences in system call return values, process scheduling decisions (which can even affect the result of individual instructions, such as x86's interruptible block memory instructions [15]), and asynchronous signal delivery. These sources of non-determinism can affect whether STS is able to reproduce violations during *replay*.

The QA testing frameworks we are trying to improve do not mitigate non-determinism. STS's main approach to coping with non-determinism is to *replay* each subsequence multiple times. If the non-deterministic bug occurs with probability $p$, we can model[12] the probability[13] that we will observe it within $r$ replays as $1-(1-p)^r$. This exponential works strongly in our favor; for example, even if the original bug is triggered in only 20% of replays, the probability that we will not trigger it during an intermediate replay is approximately 1% if we replay 20 times per subsequence.

## 5.2 Mitigating Non-Determinism

When non-determinism is acute, one might seek to prevent it altogether. However, as discussed in §4.2, deterministic replay techniques [15, 20] force the minimization process to stay on the original code path, and incur substantial performance overhead.

Short of ensuring full determinism, we place STS in a position to record and replay all network events in serial order, and ensure that all data structures within STS are unaffected by randomness. For example, we avoid using hashmaps that hash keys according to their memory address, and sort all list return values.

We also optionally interpose on the controller software itself. Routing the `gettimeofday()` syscall through STS helps ensure timer accuracy.[14][15] When sending data over multiple sockets, the operating system exhibits non-determinism in the order it schedules I/O operations. STS optionally ensures a deterministic order of messages by multiplexing all sockets onto a single true socket. On the controller side STS currently adds a shim layer atop the control software's socket library,[16] although this could be achieved transparently with a libc shim layer [20].

STS may need visibility into the control software's internal state transitions to properly maintain happens-before relations during *replay*. We gain visibility by making a small change to the control

[11] We currently support the following invariants: (a) all-to-all reachability, (b) loop freeness, (c) blackhole freeness, (d) controller liveness, and (e) POX ACL compliance.

[12] See §6.5 for an experimental evaluation of this model.

[13] This probability could be improved by guiding the thread schedule towards known error-prone interleavings [44, 45].

[14] When the pruned trace differs from the original, we make a best-effort guess at what the return values of these calls should be. For example, if the altered execution invokes `gettimeofday()` more times than we recorded in the initial run, we interpolate the timestamps of neighboring events.

[15] Only supported for POX and Floodlight at the moment.

[16] Only supported for POX at the moment.

software's logging library[15]: whenever a control process executes a log statement, which indicates that an important state transition is about to take place, we notify STS. Such coarse-grained visibility into internal state transitions does not handle all cases, but we find it suffices in practice.[17] We can also optionally use logging interposition as a synchronization barrier, by blocking the process when it executes logging statements until STS unblocks it.

## 5.3 Checkpointing

To efficiently implement the PEEK() algorithm depicted in Figure 2 we assume the ability to record checkpoints (snapshots) of the state of the system under test. We currently implement checkpointing for the POX controller[18] by telling it to `fork()` itself and suspend its child, transparently cloning the sockets of the parent (which constitute shared state between the parent and child processes), and later resuming the child. This simple mechanism does not work for controllers that use other shared state such as disk. To handle other shared state one could checkpoint processes within lightweight Unix containers [1]. For distributed controllers, one would also need to implement a consistent cut algorithm [9], which is available in several open source implementations [3].

If developers do not choose to employ checkpointing, they can use our implementation of PEEK() that replays inputs from the beginning rather than a checkpoint, thereby increasing replay runtime by a factor of $n$. Alternatively, they can avoid PEEK() and solely use the event scheduling heuristics described in §5.4.

Beyond its use in PEEK(), snapshotting has three advantages. As mentioned in §4.3, only considering events starting from a recent checkpoint rather than the beginning of the execution decreases the number of events to be minimized. By shortening the replay time, checkpointing coincidentally helps cope with the effects of non-determinism, as there is less opportunity for divergence in timing. Lastly, checkpointing can improve the runtime of delta debugging, since many of the subsequences chosen throughout delta debugging's execution share common input prefixes.

## 5.4 Timing Heuristics

We have found three heuristics useful for ensuring that invariant violations are consistently reproduced. These heuristics may be used alongside or instead of PEEK().

**Event Scheduling.** If we had perfect visibility into the internal state transitions of control software, we could replay inputs at precisely the correct point. Unfortunately this is impractical.

We find that keeping the wall-clock spacing between replay events close to the recorded timing helps (but does not alone suffice) to ensure that invariant violations are consistently reproduced. When replaying events, we `sleep()` between each event for the same duration that was recorded in the original trace, less the time it takes to replay or time out on each event.

**Whitelisting keepalive messages.** We observed during some of our experiments that the control software incorrectly inferred that links or switches had failed during *replay*, when it had not done so in the original execution. Upon further examination we found in these cases that LLDP and OpenFlow echo packets periodically sent by the control software were staying in STS's buffers too long during *replay*, such that the control software would time out on them. To avoid these differences, we added an option to always pass through keepalive messages. The limitation of this heuristic is that it cannot be used on bugs involving keepalive messages.

[17]We discuss this limitation further in §5.6.

[18]We only use the event scheduling heuristics described in §5.4 for the other controllers.

**Whitelisting dataplane events.** Dataplane forward/drop events constitute a substantial portion of overall events. However, for many of the controller applications we are interested in, dataplane forwarding is only relevant insofar as it triggers control plane events (*e.g.* host discovery). We find that allowing dataplane forward events through by default, *i.e.* never timing out on them during *replay*, can greatly decrease skew in wall-clock timing.

## 5.5 Root Causing Tools

Throughout our experimentation with STS, we often found that MCSes alone were insufficient to pinpoint the root causes of bugs. We therefore implemented a number of complementary root causing tools, which we use along with Unix utilities to finish the debugging process. We illustrate their use in §6.

**OFRewind**. STS supports an interactive replay mode similar to OFRewind [56] that allows troubleshooters to query the network state, filter events, check additional invariants, and even induce new events that were not part of the original event trace.

**Packet Tracing**. Especially for controllers that react to flow events, we found it useful to trace the path of individual packets through the network. STS includes tracing instrumentation similar to NetSight [25] for this purpose.

**OpenFlow Reduction**. The OpenFlow commands sent by controller software are often redundant, *e.g.* they may override routing entries, allow them to expire, or periodically flush and later repopulate them. STS includes a tool for filtering out such redundant messages and displaying only those commands that are directly relevant to triggering invalid network configurations.

**Trace Visualization**. We often found it informative to visualize the ordering of message deliveries and internal state transitions. We implemented a tool to generate space-time diagrams [33], as well as a tool to highlight ordering differences between multiple traces, which is especially useful for comparing intermediate delta debugging replays in the face of acute non-determinism.

## 5.6 Limitations

Having detailed the specifics of our approach we now clarify the scope of our technique's use.

**Partial Visibility.** Our event scheduling algorithm assumes that it has visibility into the occurrence of relevant internal events. For some software this may require substantial instrumentation beyond preexisting log statements, though as we show in §6, most bugs we encountered can be minimized without perfect visibility.

**Non-determinism.** Non-determinism is fundamental in networks. When non-determinism is present STS (i) replays multiple times per subsequence, and (ii) employs software techniques for mitigating non-determinism, but it may nonetheless output a non-minimal MCS. In the common case this is still better than the tools developers employ in practice. In the worst case STS leaves the developer where they started: an unpruned log.

**Lack of Guarantees.** Due to partial visibility and non-determinism, we do not provide guarantees on MCS minimality.

**Bugs Outside the Control Software.** Our goal is not to find the root cause of individual component failures in the system (*e.g.* misbehaving routers, link failures). Instead, we focus on how the distributed system as a whole reacts to the occurrence of such inputs.

**Interposition Overhead.** Performance overhead from interposing on messages may prevent STS from minimizing bugs triggered by high message rates.[19] Similarly, STS's design may prevent it from minimizing extremely large traces, as we evaluate in §6.

[19]Although this might be mitigated with time warping [24].

**Correctness vs. Performance.** We are primarily focused on correctness bugs, not performance bugs.

# 6. EVALUATION

We first demonstrate STS's viability in troubleshooting real bugs. We found seven new bugs by fuzz testing five open source SDN control platforms: ONOS [43] (Java), POX [39] (Python), NOX [23] (C++), Pyretic [19] (Python), and Floodlight [16] (Java), and debugged these with the help of STS. Second, we demonstrate the boundaries of where STS works well and where it does not by finding MCSes for previously known and synthetic bugs that span a range of bug types encountered in practice.

Our ultimate goal is to reduce effort spent on troubleshooting bugs. As this is difficult to measure,[20] since developer skills and familiarity with code bases differs widely, we instead quantitatively show how well STS minimizes logs, and qualitatively relay our experience using MCSes to debug the newly found bugs.

We show a high-level overview of our results in Table 3. Interactive visualizations and replayable event traces for all of these case studies are publicly available at ucb-sts.github.com/experiments.

## 6.1 New Bugs

**Pyretic Loop.** We discovered a loop when fuzzing Pyretic's `hub` module, whose purpose is to flood packets along a minimum spanning tree. After minimizing the execution (runtime in Figure 4a), we found that the triggering event was a link failure at the beginning of the trace followed some time later by the recovery of that link. After roughly 9 hours over two days of examining Pyretic's code (which was unfamiliar to us), we found what we believed to be the problem in its logic for computing minimum spanning trees: it appeared that down links weren't properly being accounted for, such that flow entries were installed along a link even though it was down. When the link recovered, a loop was created, since the flow entries were still in place. The loop seemed to persist until Pyretic periodically flushed all flow entries.

We filed a bug report along with a replayable MCS to the developers of Pyretic. They found after roughly five hours of replaying the trace with STS that Pyretic told switches to flood out all links before the entire network topology had been learned (including the down link). By adding a timer before installing entries to allow for links to be discovered, the developers were able to verify that the loop no longer appeared. A long term fix for this issue is currently being discussed by the developers of Pyretic.

**POX Premature PacketIn.** During a POX fuzz run, the `l2_multi` routing module failed unexpectedly with a `KeyError`. The initial trace had 102 input events, and STS reduced it to an MCS of 2 input events as shown in Figure 4b.

We repeatedly replayed the MCS while adding instrumentation. The root cause was a race condition in POX's handshake state machine. The OpenFlow standard requires a 2-message handshake. POX, however, requires an additional series of message exchanges before notifying applications of its presence via a *SwitchUp* event.

The switch was slow in completing the second part of the handshake, causing the *SwitchUp* to be delayed. During this window, a *PacketIn* (LLDP packet) was forwarded to POX's `discovery` module, which in turned raised a *LinkEvent* to `l2_multi`, which then failed because it expected *SwitchUp* to occur first. We verified with the lead developer of POX that is a true bug.

This case study demonstrates how even a simple handshake state machine can behave in a manner that is hard to understand without being able to repeat the experiment with a minimal trace. Making heavy use of the MCS replay, a developer unfamiliar with the two subsystems was able to root-cause the bug in ~30 minutes.

**POX In-Flight Blackhole.** We found a persistent blackhole while POX was bootstrapping its discovery of link and host locations. There were initially 27 inputs. The initial trace was affected by non-determinism and only replayed successfully 15/20 times. We were able to reliably replay it by employing multiplexed sockets, overriding `gettimeofday()`, and waiting on logging messages. STS returned a 11 input MCS (runtime shown in Figure 4c).

We provided the MCS to the lead developer of POX. Primarily using the console output, we were able to trace through the code and identify the problem within 7 minutes, and were able to find a fix for the race condition within 40 minutes. By matching the console output with the code, he found that the crucial triggering events were two in-flight packets (set in motion by prior traffic injection events): POX first incorrectly learned a host location as a result of the first in-flight packet showing up immediately after POX discovered that port belonged to a switch-switch link—apparently the code had not accounted for the possibility of in-flight packets directly following link discovery—and then as a result the second in-flight packet POX failed to return out of a nested conditional that would have prevented the blackhole from being installed.

**POX Migration Blackhole.** We noticed after examining POX's code that there might be some corner cases related to host migrations. We added host migrations to the randomly generated inputs and checked for blackholes. Our initial input size was 115 inputs. STS produced a 3 input MCS (shown in Figure 4d): a packet injection from a host ('A'), followed by a packet injection by another host ('B') towards A, followed by a host migration of A. This made it immediately clear what the problem was. After learning the location of A and installing a flow from B to A, the routing entries in the path were never removed after A migrated, causing all traffic from B to A to blackhole until the routing entries expired.

**NOX Discovery Loop.** Next we tested NOX on a four-node mesh, and discovered a routing loop between three switches within roughly 20 runs of randomly generated inputs.

Our initial input size was 68 inputs, and STS returned an 18 input MCS (Figure 4e). Our approach to debugging was to reconstruct from the minimized trace how NOX should have installed routes, then compare how NOX actually installed routes. This case took us roughly 10 hours to debug. Unfortunately the final MCS did not reproduce the bug on the first few tries, and we suspect this is due to the fact NOX chooses the order to send LLDP messages randomly, and the loop depends crucially on this order. We instead used the console output from the shortest subsequence that did produce the bug (21 inputs, 3 more than the MCS) to debug this trace.

The order in which NOX discovered links was crucial: at the point NOX installed the 3-loop, it had only discovered one link towards the destination. Therefore all other switches routed through the one known neighbor switch. The links adjacent to the neighbor switch formed 2 of the 3 links in the loop.

The destination host only sent one packet, which caused NOX to initially learn its correct location. After NOX flooded the packet though, it became confused about its location. One flooded packet arrived at another switch that was currently not known to be attached to anything, so NOX incorrectly concluded that the host had migrated. Other flooded packets were dropped as a result of link failures in the network and randomly generated packet loss. The loop was then installed when the source injected another packet.

**Floodlight Loop.** Next we tested Floodlight's routing application. In about 30 minutes, our fuzzing uncovered a 117 input sequence that caused a persistent 3-node forwarding loop. In this case, the

[20]We discuss this point further in §7.

| | Bug Name | Topology | Runtime (s) | Input Size | MCS Size | MCS WI | MCS Helpful? |
|---|---|---|---|---|---|---|---|
| Newly Found | Pyretic Loop | 3 switch mesh | 266.2 | 36 | 1 | 2 | Yes |
| | POX Premature PacketIn | 4 switch mesh | 249.1 | 102 | 2 | NR | Yes |
| | POX In-Flight Blackhole | 2 switch mesh | 1478.9 | 27 | 11 | NR | Yes |
| | POX Migration Blackhole | 4 switch mesh | 1796.0 | 29 | 3 | NR | Yes |
| | NOX Discovery Loop | 4 switch mesh | 4990.9 | 150 | 18 | NR | Indirectly |
| | Floodlight Loop | 3 switch mesh | 27930.6 | 117 | 13 | NR | Yes |
| | ONOS Database Locking | 2 switch mesh | N/A | 1 | 1 | 1 | N/A |
| Known | Floodlight Failover | 2 switch mesh | - | 202 | 2 | - | Yes |
| | ONOS Master Election | 2 switch mesh | 2746.0 | 20 | 2 | 2 | Yes |
| | POX Load Balancer | 3 switch mesh | 2396.7 | 106 | 24 (N+1) | 26 | Yes |
| Synthetic | Delicate Timer Interleaving | 3 switch mesh | N/A | 39 | NR | NR | No |
| | Reactive Routing Trigger | 3 switch mesh | 525.2 | 40 | 7 | 2 | Indirectly |
| | Overlapping Flow Entries | 2 switch mesh | 115.4 | 27 | 2 | 3 | Yes |
| | Null Pointer | 20 switch FatTree | 157.4 | 62 | 2 | 2 | Yes |
| | Multithreaded Race Condition | 10 switch mesh | 36967.5 | 1596 | 2 | 2 | Indirectly |
| | Memory Leak | 2 switch mesh | 15022.6 | 719 | 32 (M+2) | 33 | Indirectly |
| | Memory Corruption | 4 switch mesh | 145.7 | 341 | 2 | 2 | Yes |

Table 3: Overview of Case Studies. 'WI' denotes 'Without Interposition', and 'NR' denotes 'Not Replayable'.

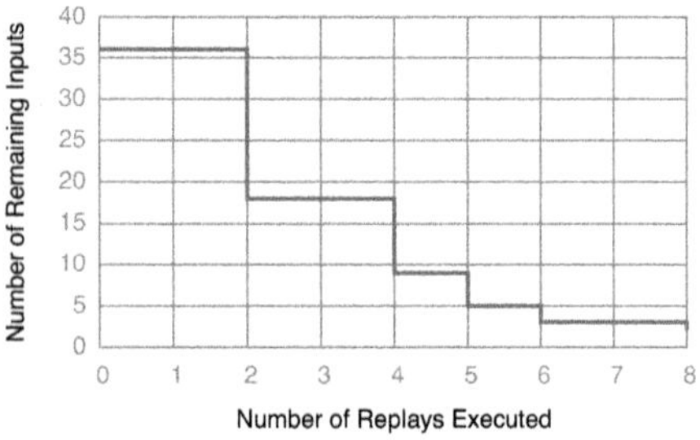


(a) Pyretic Loop.

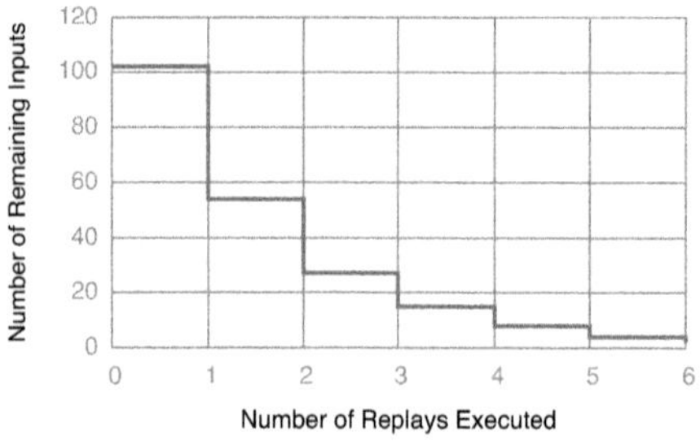


(b) POX Premature PacketIn.

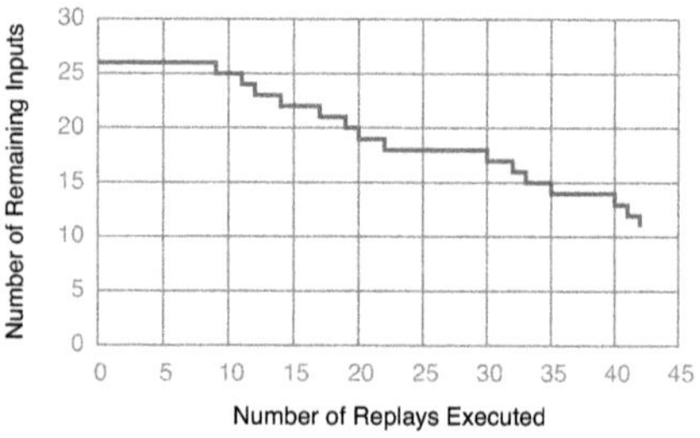


(c) POX In-Flight Blackhole.

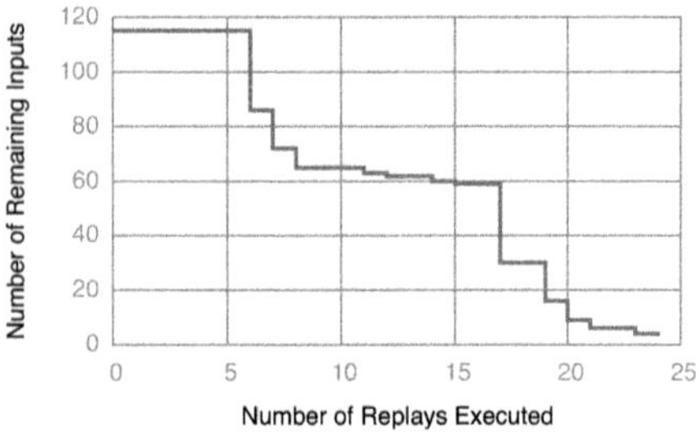


(d) POX Migration Blackhole.

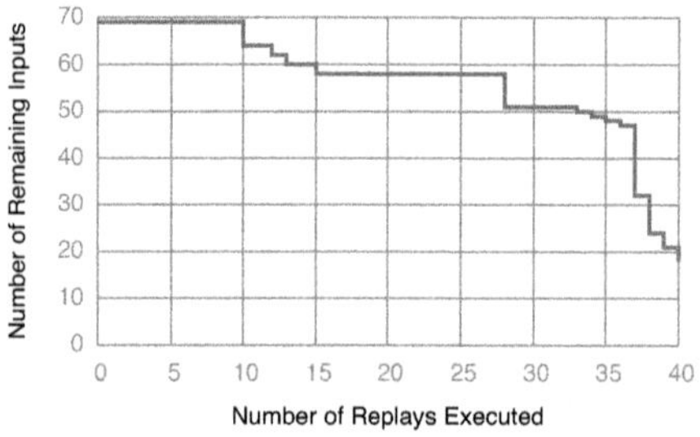


(e) NOX Discovery Loop.

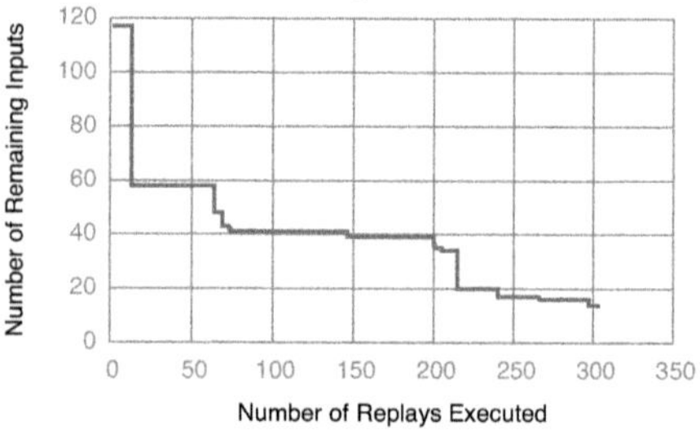


(f) Floodlight Loop.

Figure 4: Minimization runtime behavior.

controller exhibited significant non-determinism, which initially precluded STS from efficiently reducing the input size. We worked around this by increasing the number of replays per subsequence to 10. With this, STS reduced the sequence to 13 input events in 324 replays and 8.5 hours (runtime shown in Figure 4f).

We repeatedly replayed the 13 event MCS while successively adding instrumentation and increasing the log level each run. After 15 replay attempts, we found that the problem was caused by interference of end-host traffic with ongoing link discovery packets. In our experiment, Floodlight had not discovered an inter-switch link due to dropped LLDP packets, causing an end-host to flap between perceived attachment points.

While this behavior cannot strictly be considered a bug in Floodlight, the case-study nevertheless highlights the benefit of STS over traditional techniques: by repeatedly replaying the MCS, we were able to diagnose the root cause—a complex interaction between the LinkDiscovery, Forwarding, and DeviceManager modules.

**ONOS Database Locking.** When testing ONOS, a distributed open-source controller, we noticed that ONOS controllers would occasionally reject switches' attempts to connect. The initial trace was already minimized, as the initial input was the single event of the switches connecting to the controllers with a particular timing. When examining the logs, we found that the particular timing between the switch connects caused both ONOS controllers to encounter a "failed to obtain lock" error from their distributed graph database. We suspect that the ONOS controllers were attempting to concurrently insert the same key, which causes a known error. We modified ONOS's initialization logic to retry when inserting switches, and found that this eliminated the bug.

## 6.2 Known bugs

**Floodlight Failover.** We were able to reproduce a known problem [17] in Floodlight's distributed controller failover logic with STS. In Floodlight switches maintain one hot connection to a master controller and several cold connections to replica controllers. The *master* holds the authority to modify the configuration of switches, while the other controllers are in *backup* mode and do not change the switch configurations. If a link fails shortly after the master controller has died, all live controllers are in the backup role and will not take responsibility for updating the switch flow table. At some point when a backup notices the master failure and elevates itself to the master role it will proceed to manage the switch, but without ever clearing the routing entries for the failed link, resulting in a persistent blackhole.

We ran two Floodlight controller instances connected to two switches, and injected 200 extraneous link and switch failures, with the controller crash and switch connect event[21] that triggered the blackhole interleaved among them. We were able to successfully isolate the two-event MCS: the controller crash and the link failure.

**ONOS Master Election.** We reproduced another bug, previously reported in earlier versions and later fixed, in ONOS's master election protocol. If two adjacent switches are connected to two separate controllers, the controllers must decide between themselves who will be responsible for tracking the liveness of the link. They make this decision by electing the controller with the higher ID as the master for that link. When the master dies, and later reboots, it is assigned a new ID. If its new ID is lower than the other controllers', both will incorrectly believe that they are not responsible for tracking the liveness of the link, and the controller with the prior higher ID will incorrectly mark the link as unusable such that no routes will traverse it. This bug depends on initial IDs chosen at random, so we modified ONOS to hardcode ID values. We were able to successfully minimize the trace to the master crash and recovery event, although we were also able to do so without any interposition on internal events.

**POX Load Balancer.** We are aware that POX applications do not always check error messages sent by switches rejecting invalid packet forwarding commands. We used this to trigger a bug in POX's load balancer application: we created a network where switches had only 25 entries in their flow table, and proceeded to continue injecting TCP flows into the network. The load balancer application proceeded to install entries for each of these flows. Eventually the switches ran out of flow entry space and responded with error messages. As a result, POX began randomly load balancing each subsequent packet for a given flow over the servers, causing session state to be lost. We were able to minimize the MCS for this bug to 24 elements (there were two preexisting flow entries in each routing table, so 24 additional flows made the 26 (N+1) entries needed to overflow the table). A notable aspect of this MCS is that its size is directly proportional to the flow table space, and developers would find across multiple fuzz runs that the MCS was always 24 elements.

## 6.3 Synthetic bugs

**Delicate Timer Interleaving.** We injected a crash on a code path that was highly dependent on internal timers firing within POX. This is a hard case for STS, since we have little control of internal timers. We were able to trigger the code path during fuzzing, but were unable to reproduce the bug during replay after five attempts. This is the only case where we were unable to replay the trace.

**Reactive Routing Trigger.** We modified POX's reactive routing module to create a loop upon receiving a particular sequence of dataplane packets. This case is difficult for two reasons: the routing module's behavior depends on the (non-deterministic) order these links are discovered in the network, and the triggering events are multiple dataplane packet arrivals interleaved at a fine granularity. We found that the 7 event MCS was inflated by at least two events: a link failure and a link recovery that we did not believe were relevant to triggering the bug. We noticed that after PEEK() inferred expected internal events, our event scheduler still timed out on some link discovery messages–those that happened to occur during the PEEK() run but did not show up during replay due to non-determinism. We suspected that these timeouts were the cause of the inflated MCS, and confirmed our intuition by turning off interposition on internal events altogether, which yielded a 2 event MCS (although this MCS was still affected by non-determinism).

**Overlapping Flow Entries.** We ran two modules in POX: a capability manager in charge of providing upstream DoS protection for servers, and a forwarding application. The capabilities manager installed drop rules upstream for servers that requested it, but these rules had lower priority than the default forwarding rules in the switch. We were able to minimize 27 inputs to the two traffic injection inputs necessary to trigger the routing entry overlap.

**Null Pointer.** On a rarely used code path we injected a null pointer exception, and were able to successfully minimize a fuzz trace of 62 events to the expected triggering conditions: control channel congestion followed by decongestion.

**Multithreaded Race Condition.** We created a race condition between multiple threads that was triggered by any packet I/O, regardless of input. With 5 replays per subsequence, we were able to minimize a 1596 input in 10 hours to a replayable 2 element failure/recovery pair. The MCS itself though may have been somewhat misleading to a developer (as expected), as the race condition was triggered randomly by any I/O, not just these two inputs events.

**Memory Leak.** We created a case that would take STS very long to minimize: a memory leak that eventually caused a crash in POX. We artificially set the memory leak to happen quickly after allocating 30 (M) objects created upon switch handshakes, and interspersed 691 other input events throughout switch reconnect events. The final MCS found after 4 hours 15 minutes was exactly 30 events, but it was not replayable. We suspect this was because STS was timing out on some expected internal events, which caused POX to reject later switch connection attempts.

**Memory Corruption.** We created a case where the receipt of a link failure notification on a particular port causes corruption to one of POX's internal data structures. This causes a crash much later when the data structure is accessed during the corresponding port up. These bugs are hard to debug, because considerable time can pass between the event corrupting the data structure and the event triggering the crash, making manual log inspection or source level debugging ineffective. STS proved effective in this case, reducing a larger trace to exactly the 2 events responsible for the crash.

## 6.4 Overall Results & Discussion

We show our overall results in Table 3. We note that with the exception of Delicate Timer Interleaving and ONOS Database Locking, STS was able to significantly reduce input traces.

The MCS WI column, showing the MCS sizes we produced when ignoring internal events entirely, indicates that our techniques for interleaving events are often crucial. In one case however—Reactive Routing Trigger—non-determinism was particularly acute, and STS's interposition on internal events actually made minimization worse due to timeouts on inferred internal events that did not occur after PEEK(). In this case we found better results by simply turning off interposition on internal events. For all of the other case studies, either non-determinism was not problematic, or we were able to counteract it by replaying multiple times per subsequence and adding instrumentation.

The cases where STS was most useful were those where a developer would have started from the end of the trace and worked back-

[21] We used a switch connect event rather than a link failure event for logistical reasons, but both can trigger the race condition.

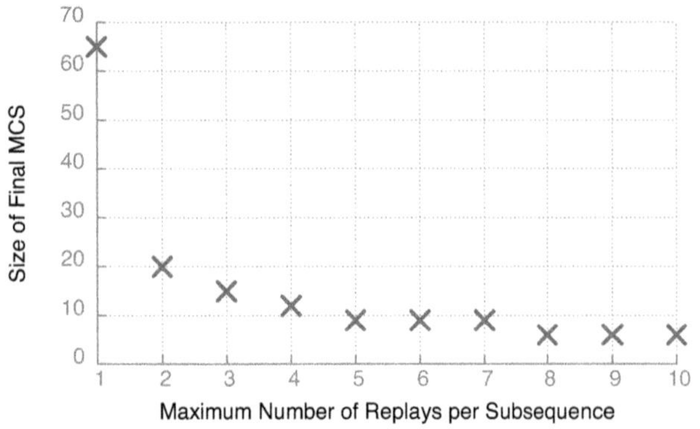


Figure 5: Effectiveness of replaying subsequences multiple times in mitigating non-determinism.

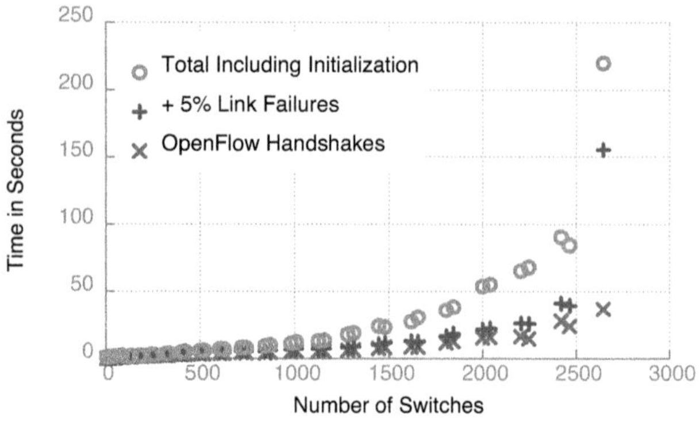


Figure 6: Runtime for bootstrapping FatTree networks, cutting 5% of links, and processing the controller's response.

wards, but the actual root cause lies many events in the past (as in Memory Corruption). This requires many re-iterations through the code and logs using standard debugging tools (*e.g.* source level debuggers), and is highly tedious on human timescales. In contrast, it was easy to step through a small event trace and manually identify the code paths responsible for a failure.

Bugs that depend on fine-grained thread-interleaving or timers inside of the controller are the worst-case for STS. This is not surprising, as they do not directly depend on the input events from the network, and we do not directly control the internal scheduling and timing of the controllers. The fact that STS has a difficult time reducing these traces is itself indication to the developer that fine-grained non-determinism is at play.

## 6.5 Coping with Non-determinism

Recall that STS optionally replays each subsequence multiple times to mitigate the effects of non-determinism. We evaluate the effectiveness of this approach by varying the maximum number of replays per subsequence while minimizing a synthetic non-deterministic loop created by Floodlight. Figure 5 demonstrates that the size of the resulting MCS decreases with the maximum number of replays, at the cost of additional runtime; 10 replays per subsequence took 12.8 total hours, versus 6.1 hours without retries.

## 6.6 Instrumentation Complexity

For POX and Floodlight, we added shim layers to the control software to redirect `gettimeofday()`, interpose on logging statements, and demultiplex sockets. For Floodlight we needed 722 lines of Java, and for POX we needed 415 lines of Python.

## 6.7 Scalability

Mocking the network in a single process potentially prevents STS from triggering bugs that only appear at large scale. We ran STS on large FatTree networks to see where these scaling limits lie. On a machine with 6GB of memory, we ran POX as the controller, and measured the time to create successively larger FatTree topologies, complete the OpenFlow handshakes for each switch, cut 5% of links, and process POX's response to the link failures. As shown in Figure 6, STS's processing time scales roughly linearly up to 2464 switches (a 45-pod FatTree). At that point, the machine started thrashing, but this limitation could easily be removed by running on a machine with >6GB of memory.

Note that STS is not designed for high-throughput dataplane traffic; we only forward what is necessary to exercise the controller software. In proactive SDN setups, dataplane events are not relevant for the control software, except perhaps for host discovery.

## 6.8 Parameters

We found throughout our experimentation that STS leaves open several parameters that need to be set properly.

**Setting fuzzing parameters.** STS's fuzzer allows the user to set the rates different event types are triggered at. In our experiments with STS we found several times that we needed to set these parameters such that we avoided bugs that were not of interest to developers. For example, in one case we discovered that a high dataplane packet drop rate dropped too many LLDP packets, preventing the controller from discovering the topology. Setting fuzzing parameters remains an important part of experiment setup.

**Differentiating persistent and transient violations.** In networks there is a fundamental delay between the initial occurrence of an event and the time when other nodes are notified of the event. This delay implies that invariant violations such as loops or blackholes can appear before the controller(s) have time to correct the network configuration. In many cases such transient invariant violations are not of interest to developers. We therefore provide a threshold parameter in STS for how long an invariant violation should persist before STS reports it as a problem. In general, setting this threshold depends on the network and the invariants of interest.

**Setting $\varepsilon$.** Our algorithm leaves an open question as to what value $\varepsilon$ should be set to. We experimentally varied $\varepsilon$ on the POX In-Flight Blackhole bug. We found that the number of events we timed out on while isolating the MCS became stable for values above 25 milliseconds. For smaller values, the number of timed out events increased rapidly. We currently set $\varepsilon$ to 100 milliseconds.

# 7. DISCUSSION

**How much effort do MCSes really save?** Based on conversations with engineers and our own industrial experience, two facts seem to hold. First, companies dedicate a substantial portion of their best engineers' time on troubleshooting bugs. Second, the larger the trace, the more effort is spent on debugging, since humans can only keep a small number of facts in working memory [41]. As one developer puts it, "Automatically shrinking test cases to the minimal case is immensely helpful" [52].

**Why do you focus on SDN?** SDN represents both an opportunity and a challenge. In terms of a challenge, SDN control software—both proprietary and open source—is in its infancy, which means that bugs are pervasive.

In terms of an opportunity, SDN's architecture facilitates the implementation of systems like STS. The interfaces between components (*e.g.* OpenFlow for switches [40] and OpenStack Neutron for management [2]) are well-defined, which is crucial for codifying functional equivalencies. Moreover, the control flow of SDN control software repeatedly returns to a quiescent state after processing inputs, which means that many inputs can be pruned.

Although we focus on SDN control software, we are currently evaluating our technique on other distributed systems, and believe it to be generally applicable.

**Enabling analysis of production logs.** STS does not currently support minimization of production (as opposed to QA) logs. Production systems would need to include Lamport clocks on each message [33] or have sufficiently accurate clock synchronization to obtain a happens-before relation. Inputs would also need to need to be logged in sufficient detail for STS to replay a synthetic version. Finally, without care, a single input event may appear multiple times in the distributed logs. The most robust way to avoid redundant input events would be to employ perfect failure detectors [8], which log a failure iff the failure actually occurred.

# 8. RELATED WORK

Our primary contribution, techniques for interleaving events, made it possible to apply input minimization algorithms (*cf.* Delta Debugging [58, 59] and domain-specific algorithms [12, 47, 55]) to blackbox distributed systems. We described the closest work to us, thread schedule minimization and program flow reduction, in §4.2.

We characterize the other troubleshooting approaches as (i) instrumentation (tracing), (ii) bug detection (invariant checking), (iii) replay, and (iv) root cause analysis (of network device failures).

**Instrumentation.** Unstructured log files collected at each node are the most common form of diagnostic information. The goal of tracing frameworks [5, 10, 18, 25, 48] is to produce structured logs that can be easily analyzed, such as DAGs tracking requests passing through the distributed system. An example within the SDN space is NetSight [25], which allows users to retroactively examine the paths dataplane packets take through OpenFlow networks. Tools like NetSight allow developers to understand how, when, and where the dataplane broke. In contrast, we focus on making it easier for developers to understand why the control software misconfigured the network in the first place.

**Bug Detection.** With instrumentation available, it becomes possible to check expectations about the system's state (either offline [36] or online [37]), or about the paths requests take through the system [48]. Within the networking community, this research is primarily focused on verifying routing tables [30–32, 38] or forwarding behavior [60, 61]. We use bug detection techniques (invariant checking) to guide delta debugging's minimization process.

It is also possible to infer performance anomalies by building probabilistic models from collections of traces [5, 10]. Our goal is to produce exact minimal causal sequences, and we are primarily focused on correctness instead of performance.

Model checkers [7, 42] seek to proactively find safety and liveness violations by analyzing all possible code paths. After identifying a bug with model checking, finding a minimal code path leading to it is straightforward. However, the testing systems we aim to improve do not employ formal methods such as model checking, in part because model checking usually suffers from exponential state explosion when run on large systems,[22] and because large systems often comprise multiple (interacting) languages, which may not be amenable to formal methods. Nonetheless, we are currently exploring the use of model checking to provide provably minimal MCSes.

[22] For example, NICE [7] took 30 hours to model check a network with two switches, two hosts, the NOX MAC-learning control program (98 LoC), and five concurrent messages between the hosts.

**Replay.** Crucial diagnostic information is often missing from traces. Record and replay techniques [20, 35] instead allow users to step through (deterministic) executions and interactively examine the state of the system in exchange for performance overhead. Within SDN, OFRewind [56] provides record and replay of OpenFlow channels between controllers and switches. Manually examining long system executions can be tedious, and our goal is to minimize such executions so that developers find it easier to identify the problematic code through replay or other means.

**Root Cause Analysis.** Without perfect instrumentation, it is often not possible to know exactly what events are occurring (*e.g.* which components have failed) in a distributed system. Root cause analysis [29, 57] seeks to reconstruct those unknown events from limited monitoring data. Here we know exactly which events occurred, but seek to identify a minimal sequence of events.

It is worth mentioning another goal outside the purview of distributed systems, but closely in line with ours: program slicing [54] is a technique for finding the minimal subset of a program that could possibly affect the result of a particular line of code. This can be combined with delta debugging to automatically generate minimal unit tests [6]. Our goal is to slice the temporal dimension of an execution rather than the code dimension.

# 9. CONCLUSION

SDN aims to make networks easier to manage. SDN does this, however, by pushing complexity into SDN control software itself. Just as sophisticated compilers are hard to write, but make programming easy, SDN control software makes network management easier, but only by forcing the developers of SDN control software to confront the challenges of asynchrony, partial failure, and other notoriously hard problems inherent to all distributed systems.

Current techniques for troubleshooting SDN control software are primitive; they essentially involve manual inspection of logs in the hope of identifying the triggering inputs. Here we developed a technique for automatically identifying a minimal sequence of inputs responsible for triggering a given bug, without making assumptions about the language or instrumentation of the software under test. While we focused on SDN control software, we believe our techniques are applicable to general distributed systems.

**Acknowledgments.** We thank our sheperd Nate foster and the anonymous reviewers for their comments. We also thank Shivaram Venkataraman, Sangjin Han, Justine Sherry, Peter Bailis, Radhika Mittal, Teemu Koponen, Michael Piatek, Ali Ghodsi, and Andrew Ferguson for providing feedback on earlier versions of this text. This research is supported by NSF CNS 1040838, NSF CNS 1015459, and an NSF Graduate Research Fellowship.

# 10. REFERENCES

[1] Linux kernel containers. `linuxcontainers.org`.

[2] OpenStack Neutron. `http://tinyurl.com/qj8ebuc`.

[3] J. Ansel, K. Arya, and G. Cooperman. DMTCP: Transparent Checkpointing for Cluster Computations and the Desktop. IPDPS '09.

[4] T. Arts, J. Hughes, J. Johansson, and U. Wiger. Testing Telecoms Software with Quviq QuickCheck. Erlang '06.

[5] P. Barham, A. Donnelly, R. Isaacs, and R. Mortier. Using Magpie for Request Extraction and Workload Modelling. OSDI '04.

[6] M. Burger and A. Zeller. Minimizing Reproduction of Software Failures. ISSTA '11.

[7] M. Canini, D. Venzano, P. Peresini, D. Kostic, and J. Rexford. A NICE Way to Test OpenFlow Applications. NSDI '12.

[8] T. Chandra and S. Toueg. Unreliable Failure Detectors for Reliable Distributed Systems. JACM '96.

[9] K. M. Chandy and L. Lamport. Distributed Snapshots: Determining Global States of Distributed Systems. ACM TOCS '85.

[10] M. Y. Chen, E. Kiciman, E. Fratkin, A. Fox, O. Fox, and E. Brewer. Pinpoint: Problem Determination in Large, Dynamic Internet Services. DSN '02.

[11] J. Choi and A. Zeller. Isolating Failure-Inducing Thread Schedules. SIGSOFT '02.

[12] K. Claessen and J. Hughes. QuickCheck: a Lightweight Tool for Random Testing of Haskell Programs. ICFP '00.

[13] K. Claessen, M. Palka, N. Smallbone, J. Hughes, H. Svensson, T. Arts, and U. Wiger. Finding Race Conditions in Erlang with QuickCheck and PULSE. ICFP '09.

[14] J. Clause and A. Orso. A Technique for Enabling and Supporting Debugging of Field Failures. ICSE '07.

[15] G. W. Dunlap, S. T. King, S. Cinar, M. A. Basrai, and P. M. Chen. ReVirt: Enabling Intrusion Analysis Through Virtual-Machine Logging and Replay. OSDI '02.

[16] Floodlight Controller. `http://tinyurl.com/ntjxa6l`.

[17] Floodlight FIXME comment. Controller.java, line 605. `http://tinyurl.com/af6nhjj`.

[18] R. Fonseca, G. Porter, R. Katz, S. Shenker, and I. Stoica. X-Trace: A Pervasive Network Tracing Framework. NSDI '07.

[19] N. Foster, R. Harrison, M. J. Freedman, C. Monsanto, J. Rexford, A. Story, and D. Walker. Frenetic: A Network Programming Language. ICFP '11.

[20] D. Geels, G. Altekar, S. Shenker, and I. Stoica. Replay Debugging For Distributed Applications. ATC '06.

[21] P. Godefroid and N. Nagappan. Concurrency at Microsoft - An Exploratory Survey. CAV '08.

[22] A. Greenberg, J. R. Hamilton, N. Jain, S. Kandula, C. Kim, P. Lahiri, D. A. Maltz, P. Patel, and S. Sengupta. VL2: A Scalable and Flexible Data Center Network, Sec. 3.4. SIGCOMM '09.

[23] N. Gude, T. Koponen, J. Pettit, B. Pfaff, M. Casado, N. McKeown, and S. Shenker. NOX: Towards an Operating System For Networks. CCR '08.

[24] D. Gupta, K. Yocum, M. Mcnett, A. C. Snoeren, A. Vahdat, and G. M. Voelker. To Infinity and Beyond: TimeWarped Network Emulation. NSDI '06.

[25] N. Handigol, B. Heller, V. Jeyakumar, D. Maziéres, and N. McKeown. I Know What Your Packet Did Last Hop: Using Packet Histories to Troubleshoot Networks. NSDI '14.

[26] J. Huang and C. Zhang. An Efficient Static Trace Simplification Technique for Debugging Concurrent Programs. SAS '11.

[27] J. Huang and C. Zhang. LEAN: Simplifying Concurrency Bug Reproduction via Replay-Supported Execution Reduction. OOPSLA '12.

[28] N. Jalbert and K. Sen. A Trace Simplification Technique for Effective Debugging of Concurrent Programs. FSE '10.

[29] S. Kandula, R. Mahajan, P. Verkaik, S. Agarwal, J. Padhye, and P. Bahl. Detailed Diagnosis in Enterprise Networks. SIGCOMM '09.

[30] P. Kazemian, M. Change, H. Zheng, G. Varghese, N. McKeown, and S. Whyte. Real Time Network Policy Checking Using Header Space Analysis. NSDI '13.

[31] P. Kazemian, G. Varghese, and N. McKeown. Header Space Analysis: Static Checking For Networks. NSDI '12.

[32] A. Khurshid, W. Zhou, M. Caesar, and P. Godfrey. VeriFlow: Verifying Network-Wide Invariants in Real Time. NSDI '13.

[33] L. Lamport. Time, Clocks, and the Ordering of Events in a Distributed System. CACM '78.

[34] K. H. Lee, Y. Zheng, N. Sumner, and X. Zhang. Toward Generating Reducible Replay Logs. PLDI '11.

[35] C.-C. Lin, V. Jalaparti, M. Caesar, and J. Van der Merwe. DEFINED: Deterministic Execution for Interactive Control-Plane Debugging. ATC '13.

[36] X. Liu. WiDs Checker: Combating Bugs in Distributed Systems. NSDI '07.

[37] X. Liu, Z. Guo, X. Wang, F. Chen, X. Lian, J. Tang, M. Wu, M. F. Kaashoek, and Z. Zhang. $D^3S$: Debugging Deployed Distributed Systems. NSDI '08.

[38] H. Mai, A. Khurshid, R. Agarwal, M. Caesar, P. B. Godfrey, and S. T. King. Debugging the Data Plane with Anteater. SIGCOMM '11.

[39] J. Mccauley. POX: A Python-based OpenFlow Controller. `http://www.noxrepo.org/pox/about-pox/`.

[40] N. McKeown, T. Anderson, H. Balakrishnan, G. Parulkar, L. Peterson, J. Rexford, S. Shenker, and J. Turner. OpenFlow: Enabling Innovation in Campus Networks. SIGCOMM CCR '08.

[41] G. A. Miller. The Magical Number Seven, Plus or Minus Two: Some Limits on Our Capacity for Processing Information. Psychological Review '56.

[42] M. Musuvathi, S. Qadeer, T. Ball, G. Basler, P. A. Nainar, and I. Neamtiu. Finding and Reproducing Heisenbugs in Concurrent Programs. SOSP '08.

[43] ON.Lab. Open Networking Operating System. `http://onlab.us/tools.html`.

[44] S. Park, S. Lu, and Y. Zhou. CTrigger: Exposing Atomicity Violation Bugs from their Hiding Places. ASPLOS '09.

[45] S. Park, Y. Zhou, W. Xiong, Z. Yin, R. Kaushik, K. H. Lee, and S. Lu. PRES: Probabilistic Replay with Execution Sketching on Multiprocessors. SOSP '09.

[46] B. Pfaff, J. Pettit, K. Amidon, M. Casado, T. Koponen, and S. Shenker. Extending Networking into the Virtualization Layer. HotNets '09.

[47] J. Regehr, Y. Chen, P. Cuoq, E. Eide, C. Ellison, and X. Yang. Test-case Reduction for C Compiler Bugs. PLDI '12.

[48] P. Reynolds, C. Killian, J. L. Winer, J. C. Mogul, M. A. Shah, and A. Vadhat. Pip: Detecting the Unexpected in Distributed Systems. NSDI '06.

[49] V. Soundararajan and K. Govil. Challenges in Building Scalable Virtualized Datacenter Management. OSR '10.

[50] S. Tallam, C. Tian, R. Gupta, and X. Zhang. Enabling Tracing of Long-Running Multithreaded Programs via Dynamic Execution Reduction. ISSTA '07.

[51] G. Tel. *Introduction to Distributed Algorithms*. Thm. 2.21. Cambridge University Press, 2000.

[52] A. Thompson. `http://tinyurl.com/qgc387k`.

[53] J. Tucek, S. Lu, C. Huang, S. Xanthos, and Y. Zhou. Triage: Diagnosing Production Run Failures at the User's Site. SOSP '07.

[54] M. Weiser. Program Slicing. ICSE '81.

[55] A. Whitaker, R. Cox, and S. Gribble. Configuration Debugging as Search: Finding the Needle in the Haystack. SOSP '04.

[56] A. Wundsam, D. Levin, S. Seetharaman, and A. Feldmann. OFRewind: Enabling Record and Replay Troubleshooting for Networks. ATC '11.

[57] S. Yemini, S. Kliger, E. Mozes, Y. Yemini, and D. Ohsie. A Survey of Fault Localization Techniques in Computer Networks. Science of Computer Programming '04.

[58] A. Zeller. Yesterday, my program worked. Today, it does not. Why? ESEC/FSE '99.

[59] A. Zeller and R. Hildebrandt. Simplifying and Isolating Failure-Inducing Input. IEEE TSE '02.

[60] H. Zeng, P. Kazemian, G. Varghese, and N. McKeown. Automatic Test Packet Generation. CoNEXT '12.

[61] H. Zeng, S. Zhang, F. Ye, V. Jeyakumar, M. Ju, J. Liu, N. McKeown, and A. Vahdat. Libra: Divide and Conquer to Verify Forwarding Tables in Huge Networks. NSDI '14.

# Planck: Millisecond-scale Monitoring and Control for Commodity Networks

Jeff Rasley[†] Brent Stephens[‡] Colin Dixon[◇] Eric Rozner[*] Wes Felter[*]
Kanak Agarwal[*] John Carter[*] Rodrigo Fonseca[†]

[†]Brown University [‡]Rice University [*]IBM Research–Austin,TX [◇]Brocade

## ABSTRACT

Software-defined networking introduces the possibility of building self-tuning networks that constantly monitor network conditions and react rapidly to important events such as congestion. Unfortunately, state-of-the-art monitoring mechanisms for conventional networks require hundreds of milliseconds to seconds to extract global network state, like link utilization or the identity of "elephant" flows. Such latencies are adequate for responding to persistent issues, e.g., link failures or long-lasting congestion, but are inadequate for responding to transient problems, e.g., congestion induced by bursty workloads sharing a link.

In this paper, we present Planck, a novel network measurement architecture that employs oversubscribed port mirroring to extract network information at 280 µs–7 ms timescales on a 1 Gbps commodity switch and 275 µs–4 ms timescales on a 10 Gbps commodity switch, *over 11x and 18x faster than recent approaches*, respectively (and up to 291x if switch firmware allowed buffering to be disabled on some ports). To demonstrate the value of Planck's speed and accuracy, we use it to drive a traffic engineering application that can reroute congested flows in milliseconds. On a 10 Gbps commodity switch, Planck-driven traffic engineering achieves aggregate throughput within 1–4% of optimal for most workloads we evaluated, even with flows as small as 50 MiB, an improvement of up to 53% over previous schemes.

## Categories and Subject Descriptors

C.2.3 [**Computer-Communication Networks**]: Network Operations—*Network monitoring*; C.4 [**Performance of Systems**]: Measurement techniques

## Keywords

Networking Measurement; Software-Defined Networking; Traffic Engineering

## 1. INTRODUCTION

Modern data center networks operate at speeds and scales that make it impossible for human operators to respond to transient problems fast enough, e.g., congestion induced by workload dynamics. Gone are the days of monitoring and tuning networks at the granularity of days, hours, and minutes [4]. Even reacting in seconds can cause significant disruption, so data center networks are frequently constructed to have full bisection bandwidth to avoid congestion [1, 13]. This brute force approach adds substantial cost, results in poorly utilized networks, and only reduces the likelihood of issues [14]. Instead, if done quickly enough, detecting congestion and routing traffic to avoid it could both reduce costs and improve performance.

Software-defined networking (SDN) allows for this kind of autonomous, self-tuning network that constantly monitors network conditions and reacts rapidly to problems. Previous work has demonstrated that routes can be installed by an SDN controller in tens of milliseconds [11, 39], but state-of-the-art network measurement systems typically spend hundreds of milliseconds or more collecting statistics [2, 4, 6, 10, 41], which limits the minimum latency of any autonomous measurement-decision-actuation network management control loop. In modern 10 Gbps and 40 Gbps networks, this is too slow to react to any but the largest network events, e.g., link failures, VM migrations, and bulk data movement. Problems induced by transient conditions, e.g., conflicting small-to-medium flows, cannot be identified fast enough to respond before they disappear, resulting in frequent bursts of congestion. To support future autonomous SDNs, a much lower latency network monitoring mechanism is necessary.

This paper introduces Planck, a network measurement architecture that extracts network information at 280 µs–7 ms timescales on a 1 Gbps commodity switch and 275 µs–4 ms timescales on a 10 Gbps commodity switch, *over an order of magnitude (11–18x) faster than state-of-the-art*, see Table 1. Planck achieves this level of performance through a novel use of the *port mirroring* mechanism.

Port mirroring is supported by most modern switches to enable a variety of network monitoring and security applications. When port mirroring is enabled, traffic destined for a *single* port is mirrored to a monitoring port that is connected to a monitoring or intrusion detection system. Planck repurposes this existing port mirroring capability to support an extremely high rate of packet sampling. In Planck, *multiple* (or all) ports are mirrored to a single monitoring port, which introduces a problem: the total traffic flowing through the switch, and thus mirrored to the monitoring port, often will exceed the capacity of the monitoring port. When this happens, the switch mirrors as much as it can and drops the rest, in effect providing a sample of the monitored traffic. In our experimentation, the buffering and drop behaviors of two different commercial switches (IBM RackSwitch G8264 and Pronto 3290) did not persistently fail to sample specific flows and provided samples that allowed for accurate estimates of link utilization and flow rates.


*SIGCOMM'14*, August 17–22, 2014, Chicago, IL, USA.

ACM 978-1-4503-2836-4/14/08 ...$15.00.
http://dx.doi.org/10.1145/2619239.2626310.

| System | Speed | Slowdown vs 10 Gbps Planck |
|---|---|---|
| Planck 10 Gbps minbuffer | 275–850 µs | 1/15–1/5x |
| Planck 1 Gbps minbuffer | 280–1150 µs | 1/15–1/4x |
| **Planck 10 Gbps** | **< 4.2 ms** | **1x** |
| Planck 1 Gbps | < 7.2 ms | 1.7x |
| Helios [10] | 77.4 ms | 18x |
| sFlow/OpenSample [41] | 100 ms | 24x |
| Mahout Polling† [5] (implementing Hedera) | 190 ms | 45x |
| DevoFlow Polling† [6] | 500 ms–15 s | 119–3570x |
| Hedera [2] | 5 s | 1190x |

**Table 1: A comparison of measurement speed and slowdown to gather accurate per-flow throughput information at each link compared to Planck on a 10 Gbps switch. Planck is 11–18x faster than Helios, the next fastest scheme. The "minbuffer" rows show how fast Planck could be on switches that were configured with minimal buffering for mirror ports, a feature our firmware does not expose. A † indicates the value is not the primary implementation proposed in the corresponding work, but is a reported value or estimate. For more details see § 5.5.**

Each monitoring port is connected to a *collector* running on a separate server that uses netmap [30] to process traffic sent by a monitoring port at line-rate. A single server hosts many collectors. Planck collectors can record the stream of sampled packets and perform lightweight analysis of the stream to extract information of interest. Collectors export a number of capabilities, including sFlow-style sampling, extremely low latency link utilization and flow rate estimation, and the ability to capture and dump raw packet samples of any traffic in the network. Applications can query the collector for statistics or subscribe and respond to notifications from the collector, e.g., when a specific level of congestion is detected. To support these capabilities, Planck requires as little as one port per switch and one server per fourteen switches to handle samples.

To demonstrate the value of Planck's speed and accuracy, we built a traffic engineering application that (i) uses Planck to monitor the network, (ii) decides when conditions warrant reconfiguring the network, and, (iii) when so, executes the preferred reconfiguration. This Planck-driven traffic engineering achieves aggregate throughput within 1–4% of optimal for most workloads we evaluated on a 10 Gbps commodity switch, even with flows as small as 50 MiB, an improvement of up to 53% over previous schemes.

This paper makes four main contributions:

1. We present a novel measurement platform, Planck, that uses oversubscribed port mirroring and high speed packet processing to provide millisecond-scale network monitoring.
2. We provide a detailed analysis of switch packet drop and buffering policies and their impact on monitoring latency.
3. We develop an algorithm to accurately estimate a flow's throughput within a 200–700 µs timescale, using samples obtained from an unknown sampling function.
4. We demonstrate the feasibility of millisecond timescale traffic engineering on commercial 10 Gbps switches using a combination of Planck and an SDN application that responds to congestion using ARP messages to switch rapidly between pre-installed alternate routes.

The remainder of this paper is organized as follows. In Section 2 we present background on low-latency network measurement. Sections 3 and 4 describe the design and implementation of Planck. Section 5 evaluates Planck including the impact of oversubscribed port mirroring on network traffic and the nature of Planck's samples. Section 6 describes two applications that use Planck, a vantage point monitor and traffic engineering tool. We evaluate our Planck-based traffic engineering application in Section 7 and then discuss related work in Section 8. Finally, we provide a retrospective discussion in Section 9 and conclude in Section 10.

# 2. BACKGROUND

Network measurement is too broad a field to fully characterize here. We focus on measurement techniques that are useful in discovering either link utilization or the most significant flows crossing each link at fine time granularities, i.e., seconds or faster. We omit a discussion of probe-based measurement techniques. While they can discover network conditions, e.g., congestion, they typically cannot determine the specific traffic causing those conditions.

## 2.1 Packet Sampling

In packet sampling, switches forward one-in-N packets they receive, along with metadata, such as the packet's input port, to a *collector*. The collector then estimates the traffic on the network by multiplying the packet and byte counts from the samples by N [29].

Sampling forms the core of the sFlow [32] standard that many switches implement. sFlow typically strips off the packet payload and adds metadata such as a switch ID, the sampling rate used when this packet was selected, and the output port(s) selected for this packet. Sampled packets are then sent out via the control plane CPU of the switch. Figure 1(a) shows the path samples take when using sFlow with the dashed line labeled 'sFlow'.

Recent work [41] has reported that involving the switch control plane CPU and the PCI bus connecting them limits the achievable sampling rate. In the case of the IBM RackSwitch G8264 [16], the maximum rate is about 300 samples per second. This low sample rate results in high estimation error unless samples are aggregated over long periods of time, i.e, a second or more. The error for a throughput estimate from s samples is approximately $196 \cdot \sqrt{1/s}$ [29], so even if all 300 samples in a second come from a single link, that link's estimated load will be off by about 11%. In more realistic scenarios the error will be noticeably worse: the collector will have to wait longer than a second to report information.

## 2.2 Port Counters

Switches usually maintain counters that track the number of bytes and packets that are sent and received for each port. While these counters provide little direct insight into the flows crossing each link[1], they can be periodically polled to infer link utilization over time. Port counters can be read via most existing switch interfaces including SNMP [38], OpenFlow [26], and sFlow [32].

## 2.3 Flow Counters

Many switches track the number of packets and bytes handled by individual match-action table entries, which can be used to track individual flows. When available, these counters are exported by querying so-called "ACL rules", OpenFlow rules, and/or NetFlow [3].

Flow-based counters have a number of limitations. First, ACL/OpenFlow tables are typically small, e.g., the IBM Rackswitch G8264 supports only about 1,000 flow-granularity rules. Also, many switches do not support fast flow counter polling—it can take seconds to read all of them [6]. More recent work indicates that it takes 75–200 ms [5, 10] to extract flow counters, as shown in Table 1.

[1] The field of network tomography provides some insights into how one might deduce flows from port counters. These approaches are usually time-intensive and at best give probabilistic information at host-pair granularity [22].

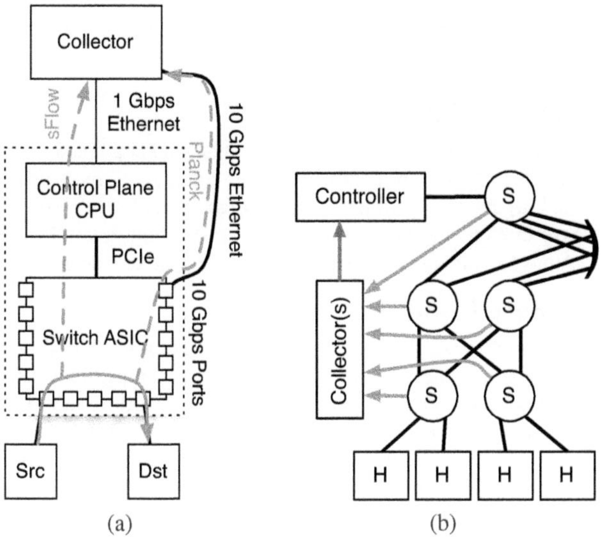


**Figure 1: Planck architecture: (a) Switch architecture illustrating the fast (Planck) and slow (sFlow) paths. (b) Network architecture showing one pod of a fat tree consisting of hosts (H), switches (S), collector(s), and the SDN controller. Traffic from hosts is forwarded by the switches to the collector(s), where they are processed. The collector(s) send events to the controller, which can send messages to the switches to reconfigure routes.**

NetFlow takes a slightly different approach—it maintains a cache of information on active TCP and UDP flows. Whenever a switch receives a packet, NetFlow checks to see if the packet belongs to a cached flow. If so, it increments the associated flow counters. If not, it creates a new cache entry. If the cache is full, an older entry is evicted and sent to the collector. This approach uses the collector like a backing store for information about layer-4 flows crossing a given device. Cache entries also can be configured to time out periodically, giving the collector a more up-to-date view of the network, but the timeouts are on the order of seconds [3], which provides little or no advantage over counter polling.

# 3. DESIGN

Figure 1 illustrates Planck's three main components: (i) switches configured to provide samples at high rates, (ii) a set of collectors that process those samples and turn them into events and queryable data, and (iii) a controller that can act on the events and data. The remainder of this section discusses each of those elements in turn.

## 3.1 Fast Sampling at Switches

As previously discussed, current mechanisms for extracting switch measurements leave much to be desired. Even sFlow [32], which is designed to provide samples in real time, can only generate hundreds of samples per second on a modern 10 Gbps switch. At that rate, it takes seconds to infer network state with accuracy. We overcome this limitation by leveraging the port mirroring feature found in most commodity switches. Port mirroring enables non-disruptive traffic monitoring by *replicating* all—or a subset of—traffic destined for a given output port to a designated *monitor port*.

We repurpose this functionality to support high sampling rates by oversubscribing the monitor port(s), i.e., configuring the switch such that traffic destined to multiple output ports is replicated to each monitor port. When the total traffic flowing through the mirrored ports is light, all traffic is forwarded out the monitor port(s). However, when incoming traffic exceeds the capacity of the monitor port(s), congestion ensues and mirrored packets get buffered. If congestion persists, eventually the buffer fills up, at which time the switch starts dropping mirrored packets. This effect constrains the rate of samples that Planck can capture to the aggregate bandwidth of the monitor port(s). In general, we can subdivide a given switch's N ports in to k monitor ports and $N - k$ normal data ports. In the common case, we expect that $k = 1$ will provide more than enough visibility into the network at the cost of giving up only a single port per switch. In Section 5 we show that this approach is feasible.

One complication of this design is that the sampling rate, the fraction of packets passing through the switch that are mirrored, varies as traffic load changes. When traffic flowing through the switch is light, 100% of packets are mirrored. Once traffic exceeds the capacity of the monitor port(s), Planck is limited to receiving as many packets as the monitor port(s) can carry. The instantaneous sampling rate is unknown because it dynamically scales proportional to the rate of traffic being mirrored divided by the bandwidth of the output port(s). We compensate for this uncertainty by using sequence numbers to compute throughput (see Section 3.2.2) rather than requiring a known sampling rate.

## 3.2 Collector

The collector has four major goals: (i) process sampled packets at line rate, (ii) infer the input and output ports for each packet, (iii) determine flow rates and link utilization, and (iv) answer relevant queries about the state of the network.

The collector uses netmap [30] for line-rate processing and borrows from a substantial body of work on line-rate packet processing on commodity servers [18, 19, 24, 28], so only the last three goals are discussed in detail here. Without monitor port buffer latency, the collector can determine reasonably stable global network statistics every few hundred microseconds, which is on par with an RTT in our network. While the collector determines utilization statistics on shorter time periods, these statistics are not stable due to the on/off nature of Ethernet and the bursty behavior of TCP.

### *3.2.1 Determining Input and Output Ports*

Traditional network sampling techniques append metadata, e.g., input and output ports, to each packet sample. This metadata is important for determining if a given port (link) is congested. Mirrored packets do not include metadata, so the collector must infer input and output ports from the packet alone. To solve this problem, the SDN controller shares the topology of the network and the rules embedded in each switch's forwarding tables with the Planck collector. As long as the network employs deterministic routing, which includes ECMP if the hash function is known, the collector can infer the full path that a packet follows based on the packet header, and thus determine the input and output port the packet traversed through a particular switch. Keeping the forwarding table information consistent between the controller, switches, and collector(s) requires care, but in practice it does not vary quickly. Alternately, the collectors can infer the path any given flow takes, and thus the input and output ports on each switch, based on samples from multiple switches. However, depending on the sampling rate and the length of a flow, the information about paths could be incomplete.

### *3.2.2 Determining Flow Rates and Link Utilization*

The Planck collector parses packet headers to maintain a NetFlow-like flow table that tracks information about individual TCP flows, including their throughputs and paths through the network. Traditionally, sampling-based measurements determine flow rates and link utilization by multiplying the throughput of samples received for a given flow or port by the sampling rate. However, port mirroring does not provide a fixed sampling rate.

To determine the throughput of TCP flows, the collector tracks byte counts over time by using the TCP sequence numbers, which are byte counters in and of themselves. If the collector receives a TCP packet A with sequence number $S_A$ at time $t_A$, and a TCP packet B with sequence number $S_B$ at time $t_B$ from the same flow, such that $t_A < t_B$, the collector is able to recover an estimate of the throughput of that flow. Upon receiving such a packet B, the collector can infer the flow's throughput information by computing $(S_B - S_A)/(t_B - t_A)$. To compute link utilization, the controller sums the throughput of all flows traversing a given link.

By itself, this approach tends to produce jittery rate estimates due to TCP's bursty behavior, especially during slow start. To reduce jitter, Planck clusters packets into *bursts* (i.e. collections of packets sent in quick succession) separated from other bursts by sizable time gaps[2]. This behavior is common, for example, during TCP slow start. Bandwidth estimates are done on bursts. Once a flow hits steady state, the gaps between packets shrink as TCP settles into a continuous stream of packets clocked by received ACKs. Planck limits a burst to at most 700 µs to get regular rate estimates from flows once they are in steady state.

If the collector sees an out of order packet, i.e., $t_A < t_B$ and $S_A > S_B$, it cannot determine if this is due to reordering or retransmission, and thus ignores the packet when it comes to throughput estimation. In practice, out of order packets are uncommon enough in data center networks that ignoring them does not affect accuracy significantly. A collector could infer the rate of retransmissions based on the number of duplicate TCP sequence numbers it sees, but we leave this to future work.

While the discussion thus far has focused on TCP, many other types of traffic contain sequence numbers, and the previously described method is general enough to apply to any packet type that places sequence numbers in packets. If the sequence numbers represent packets rather than bytes, then they need to be multiplied by the average packet size seen in samples as well, but this shouldn't significantly hurt rate estimation. We leave developing a model for throughput of flows without sequence numbers to future work.

## 3.3 Controller

The SDN controller performs two Planck-specific functions: (i) install mirroring rules in the switches and (ii) keep the collector(s) informed of the network topology and forwarding rules. It also exports functionality to network applications: (iii) the ability to query for link and flow statistics and (iv) the ability to subscribe to collector events.

The simplest Planck-specific SDN controller extension is to forward statistics requests to the collectors. This acts as a drop-in replacement for most, if not all, SDN controller statistics APIs and typically results in a much lower latency statistics capability than provided by SDN controllers, e.g., using OpenFlow counters.

Perhaps a more interesting new feature of Planck is that it allows SDN applications to subscribe to events generated by the collector(s). This allows SDN controller applications to start reacting to network events within milliseconds of when they are detected by the collector(s). Currently, the only events exported by the collector(s) are when link utilizations cross a specified threshold, but it would be straightforward to add others. Events include context annotations, e.g., the link congestion event includes the flows using the link and their current estimated rates. Annotations are intended to help an application better respond to the event, e.g., reroute an individual flow to deal with the congestion.

[2] At 10 Gbps, we find 200 µs works well as a minimum gap size.

# 4. IMPLEMENTATION

Planck's implementation consists of a fast packet collector and an extended OpenFlow controller. The collector is built using netmap [30] and the controller is built on Floodlight [12]. We detail the base implementation in this section; in Section 6 we discuss extensions for vantage point monitoring and traffic engineering.

## 4.1 Base Controller

The Planck controller is a modified and extended Floodlight OpenFlow controller [12]. Its main features are (i) a modified routing module that adds actions to the switch forwarding tables to mirror traffic and (ii) a module that communicates installed and alternate routes to the collector(s) for traffic input-output port inference. The former involved modifying Floodlight's routing module to dynamically add a second OpenFlow output action to each rule that replicates traffic to the appropriate monitor port. The latter involved extending the controller to broadcast updates to the collector(s) whenever it modifies existing routes or installs new ones. The controller also refrains from using new or modified routes for a short period of time after installing them to give the collector(s) time to process the new route information and thus infer input and output ports correctly.

## 4.2 Collector

In our current design, each monitor port is associated with a separate collector process and is connected directly to the server on which this process executes, i.e., mirrored traffic does not traverse intermediate switches. Numerous collector instances are run on a single physical machine. Each collector instance runs in user space and connects to the netmap [30] Linux kernel module to receive samples. Because the collector knows the current state of its switch's forwarding tables and because we route on MAC addresses, it can uniquely identify an arbitrary packet's output port based solely on the destination MAC address of the packet. Further, it can uniquely identify the input port based only on the source-destination MAC address pair.

Our current implementation supports three queries: (i) link utilization, (ii) rate estimation of flows crossing a given link, and (iii) a raw dump of a configurable number of the last packet samples. Additionally, it allows for subscription to link utilization events. We leave the development and support for more queries to future work.

# 5. PLANCK EVALUATION

In this section, we describe microbenchmarks we ran to: (i) determine the impact of oversubscribed port mirroring on switch traffic, (ii) characterize sampled traffic, and (iii) evaluate the accuracy of Planck's throughput estimation scheme. All the microbenchmarks are performed on a single switch—testbed details can be found in Section 7.1.

## 5.1 Impact of Mirroring on Switch Traffic

To accommodate transient output port congestion, modern switches dedicate a modest amount of memory for buffering packets waiting to be forwarded. For example, the Broadcom Trident switch ASIC contains 9 MB of buffer space shared between its 64 ports, of which a small amount is dedicated to each output port while most is allocated dynamically. A single congested port can consume up to 4 MB of buffer space, which for a 10 Gbps switch adds 3.5 ms of queueing latency. Counterintuitively, latency induced by congestion

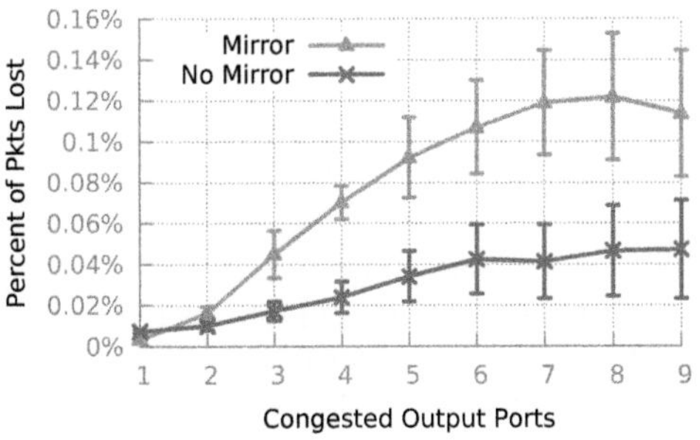


**Figure 2: Drops of non-mirrored packets, as logged on the switch, as the number of congested output ports is varied.**

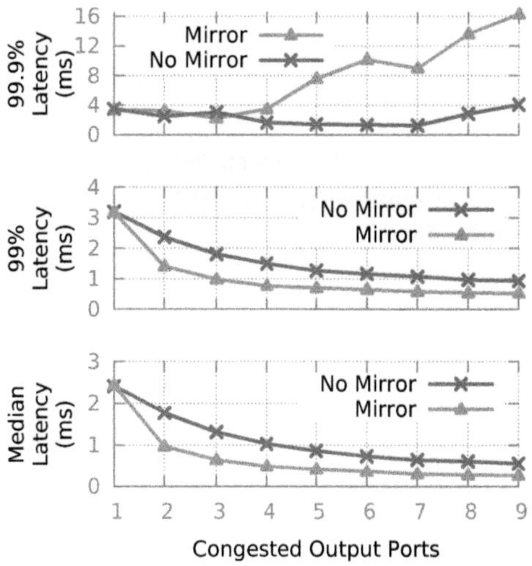


**Figure 3: Latency of non-mirrored traffic as the number of congested output ports is varied.**

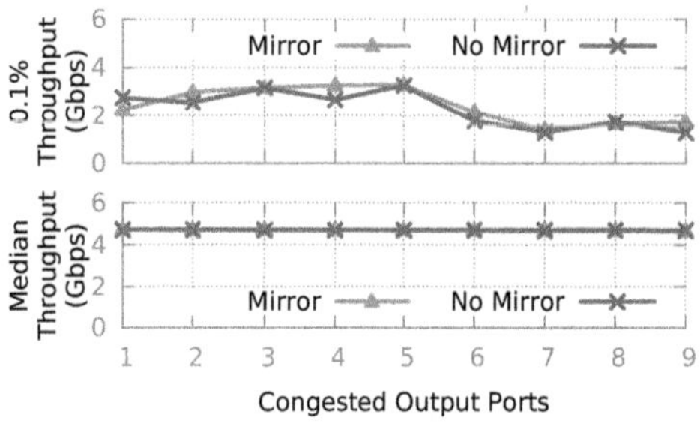


**Figure 4: Flow throughput, averaged over 1 second intervals, as the number of congested output ports is varied.**

decreases as more ports become congested because each port receives a smaller share of the shared buffer. Since Planck deliberately oversubscribes mirror ports, mirrored traffic is frequently buffered, which has two negative effects: (i) samples are delayed and (ii) any buffer space used to buffer samples is not available to handle bursts on other (non-mirror) ports.

To understand the impact of oversubscribed port mirroring on the non-mirrored (original) traffic passing through the switch, we conduct a series of tests to measure the loss, latency, and throughput of non-mirrored traffic under a variety of network conditions when mirroring is enabled and disabled. We vary the number of *congested ports*, ones where two hosts saturate TCP traffic to the same destination, from one (three hosts) to nine (27 hosts) to stress the shared switch buffers. All graphs are generated over 15 runs.

Port mirroring uses some of the shared buffer space on the switch, and thus there is less buffer space available to the other ports. Figure 2 shows that port mirroring can increase non-mirrored traffic loss due to decreased buffer space, but the absolute drop rates are very small, with average loss less than 0.12%. Figure 3 shows the latency of non-mirrored traffic as we vary the number of congested ports. Decreased buffer space at the switch manifests itself in *lower* latencies for the average (not shown), median, and $99^{th}$-percentile cases when mirroring is enabled. Also shown in the figure is the $99.9^{th}$-percentile latency, which shows the effect of retransmission delays from extra loss incurred due to buffer space contention. Note that since loss rates are low, we only see latency affected in the $99.9^{th}$-percentile. Finally, Figure 4 shows that the median and tail ($0.1^{th}$-percentile) flow throughput for non-mirrored traffic is unaffected by mirroring. As discussed in Section 9.2, limiting the buffer space made available to sampling ports should mitigate the already small impacts of our scheme.

## 5.2 Undersubscribed Sample Latency

Ideally, to measure the sample latency, we would measure the time from when the first bit of a packet arrived on the wire toward a switch, i.e., when the packet started consuming network resources, to when the packet arrived at the collector and could be processed. Unfortunately, we were not able to measure this precisely because our testbed did not provide a way to get an accurate timestamp for when a packet was placed on the wire. Instead, we measured the time between when `tcpdump` reported the packet being sent to when the collector received the packet. This includes some delay at the sender as the packet traverses the lower parts of the kernel and the NIC, which is not technically sample delay. As a result our measurements are strict overestimates of true sample latency.

To eliminate clock skew, we used separate NICs on the same physical server as both the sender and the collector. In an otherwise idle network, we observed sample latencies of 75–150 $\mu$s on our 10 Gbps network and 80–450 $\mu$s on our 1 Gbps network.

## 5.3 Analysis of Sampled Data

We then investigated the characteristics of sample data by varying the number of max-rate flows with unique source-destination pairs mirrored to the same monitor port on the switch. All flows have dedicated ports on the switches, so in the absence of congestion, each flow saturates its links. We analyze two metrics on the sampled data: *burst length*, the number of packets from a given flow received consecutively by the collector, and *inter-arrival length*, the number of packets from other flows received between two bursts of a given flow. In an idealized setting where each flow has identical offered (max) load and the switch performs perfect round-robin scheduling, burst length would be one and inter-arrival length would be NUMFLOWS − 1.

Figure 5 shows a CDF of burst length, in MTUs (i.e., 1500 bytes), for 13 concurrent flows on the switch. Over 96% of the time, burst length is less than or equal to one MTU, which indicates the scheduler on the monitor port typically samples one packet at a time from each flow under saturated conditions. Figure 6 shows average inter-arrival length, in MTUs, for a varying number of flows. For more than four flows in the network, inter-arrival length increases linearly, as predicted. In this case we omitted error bars because they are large, e.g., the standard deviation for 13 flows is roughly 28. The red (top) line in Figure 7 shows the CDF of inter-arrival lengths, in MTUs, for 13 flows. Over 85% of the time the inter-arrival time

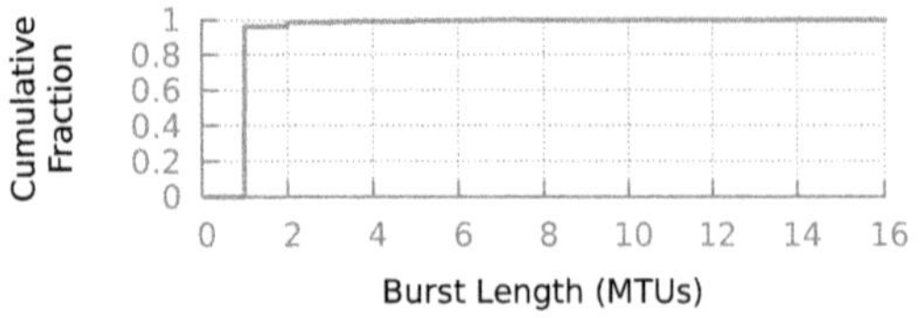


**Figure 5: CDF of burst lengths, in MTUs, for 13 concurrent flows on sampled data.**

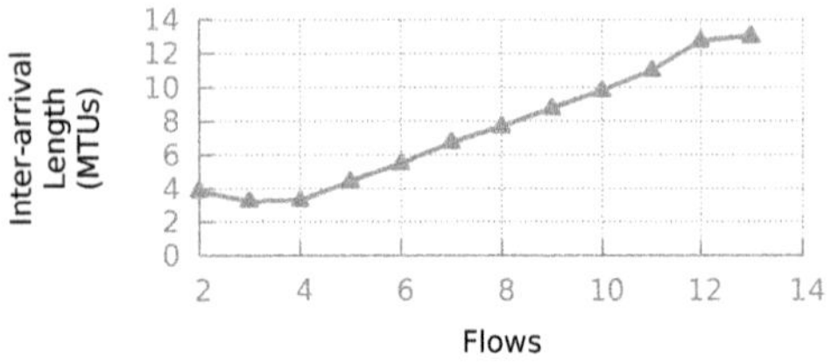


**Figure 6: Inter-arrival lengths, in MTUs, for varying number of flows on sampled data.**

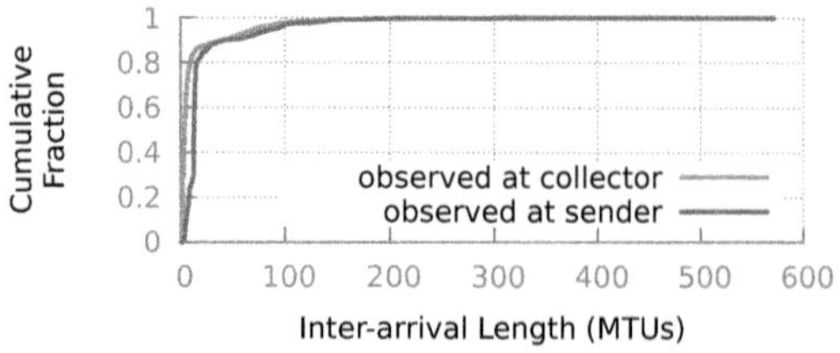


**Figure 7: CDF of inter-arrival lengths, in MTUs, for 13 concurrent flows. The red line shows the inter-arrival lengths on the sampled data, and the blue line shows the length of bursts that could fit between a sender's non-transmitting periods.**

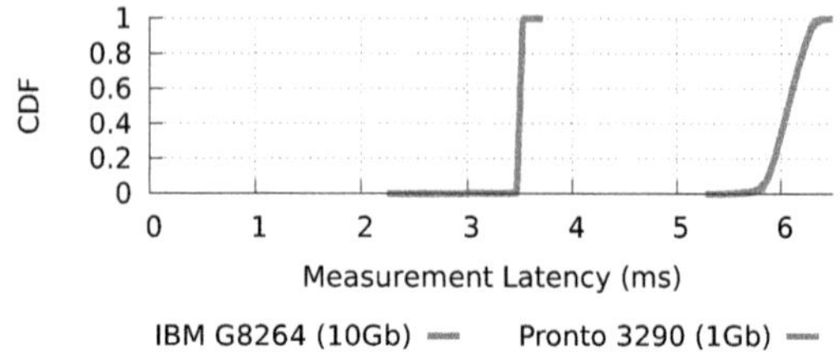


**Figure 8: An experiment showing the latency between when a packet is sent and received by the collector on 10 Gbps and 1 Gbps switches during high congestion.**

is less than or equal to 13 MTUs, but there is a long tail. Sender burstiness is a known problem [23] and the blue (bottom) line in Figure 7 quantifies this burstiness by showing the number of MTUs that could be sent in the gaps between packet departure times at a flow source in our testbed. The fact that the gaps observed at the sender closely match the gaps observed at the collector indicates, that the large inter-arrival times are an artifact of TCP and not Planck.

Finally, we examine the latency induced on mirrored traffic due to oversubscription. Figure 8 presents a CDF of the latency between when a packet is sent and the collector receiving it. Three hosts send saturated TCP traffic to a unique destination to oversubscribe the monitor port. We measure the latency imposed on mirrored data for an IBM G8264 10 Gbps switch and a Pronto 3290 1 Gbps switch, and observe a median latency of roughly 3.5 ms on the 10 Gbps network and just over 6 ms on the 1 Gbps network. Figure 9 shows the average sample latency as we vary the *oversubscription factor* on the 10 Gbps switch. The oversubscription factor indicates how many more times traffic we are sending to the monitor port than its capacity. The roughly constant observed latency indicates that the IBM switch likely allocates a fixed amount of buffer space to the mirrored port.

## 5.4 Throughput Estimation

Figure 10(a) shows the collector's throughput estimate of a single TCP flow as it starts, using a 200 µs rolling average. These results illustrate the perils of estimating throughput at microsecond scales. During slow start, TCP sends short bursts of packets at line rate followed by periods of nearly an RTT of no packets. As the RTT on our network varies from about 180 µs to 250 µs during the run, the rolling window usually captures one burst, but sometimes includes either zero or two bursts, which causes substantial variation in the instantaneous throughput estimates.

As pointed out in prior work [23], bursty behavior is common in 10 Gbps environments. To get accurate measurements, Planck uses the window-based rate estimation mechanism described in Section 3.2.2 using 200 µs gaps to separate bursts. This results in more stable estimates, as seen in Figure 10(b).

We further investigate the performance of Planck rate estimation in Figure 11. As the throughput across the entire switch increases, the sampling rate of our measurements decreases, which could reduce accuracy. In this experiment we increase the oversubscription rate and measure the mean relative error of the rate estimates. We obtained ground truth sending rates by using the rate estimation described in Section 3.2.2 on the full `tcpdump` traces from the sender and compared them with Planck's throughput estimate which resulted in a roughly constant error rate of 3%.

## 5.5 Latency Breakdown

In order to better understand all of the events that contribute to measurement latency we broke down the events a sample packet sees into a timeline, seen in Figure 12.

This timeline shows the events we were able to directly measure, such as when a packet is sent (seen via `tcpdump`), when our collector sees it (via netmap) and when our collector has an accurate estimate of the flow's throughput (via our rate estimator).

On a 10 Gbps network with minimum buffering on the monitoring port we see a total measurement delay of 275–850 µs, which comes from 75–150 µs (§5.2) until our collector sees the sample and 200–700 µs (§5.4) until we have a stable rate estimate of the flow. We see similar results on a 1 Gbps network, where the total measurement latency is 280–1150 µs coming from a sample delay of 80–450 µs (§5.2) and the same rate estimation delay.

In terms of prior measurement work presented in Table 1, we see a 291x speed-up when comparing this minimum-buffering case against the reported measurement latency of Helios [10]. As our switch's firmware did not allow us to minimize the monitor port's buffering, we report our worst-cast measurement latency of 4.2 ms at 10 Gbps, or an 18x speed-up.

# 6. APPLICATIONS

In addition to the core Planck architecture, we have built two applications that exemplify ways that Planck can be extended.

## 6.1 Vantage Point Monitoring

While there are exceedingly good tools for capturing traffic from end hosts, most notably `tcpdump`, there are far fewer tools for capturing high-fidelity traffic traces from switches short of port-

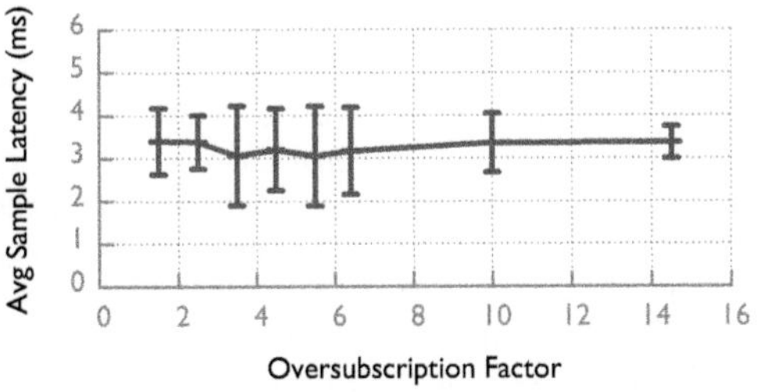


**Figure 9: Planck's latency between when a packet is sent and received by the collector on 10 Gbps with various oversubscription factors. As an example, an oversubscription factor of 1.5 means we sent 15 Gbps worth of traffic through a 10 Gbps monitor port.**

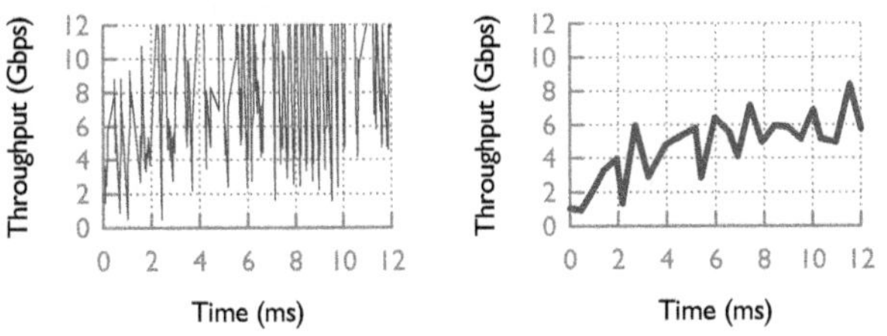


(a) (b)

**Figure 10: Planck's estimate of throughput as a TCP flows starts using (a) a 200 µs rolling average and (b) Planck's smoothed rate estimator.**

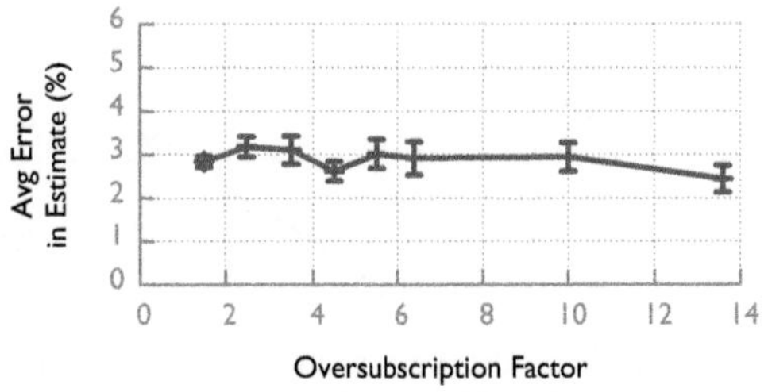


**Figure 11: Planck's error in estimating throughput with various oversubscription factors stays around 3%.**

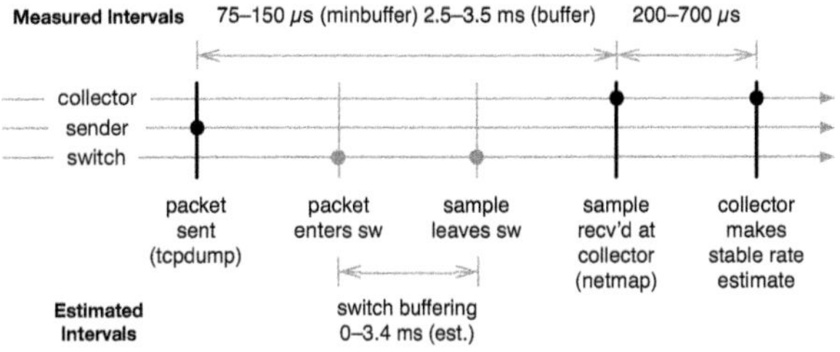


**Figure 12: Timeline of measured and estimated sample latency events on a 10 Gbps network. Black vertical bars indicate accurately measured events. Blue vertical bars indicate estimates.**

mirroring one port at a time to a monitoring port and running `tcpdump` on an attached machine.

Instead, our vantage point monitoring application runs inside the collector and stores as many recently received samples from each switch as is possible and writes them to a `tcpdump`-compatible pcap [27] file when asked. While this doesn't provide a full trace due to sampling, it provides a high fidelity view of what the switch is actually seeing while only giving up a single output port to monitor the full switch. Planck's input and output port information can also be included by creating a pcap file for each port.

These pcap files can then be used with normal network monitoring and measurement tools like wireshark [43] and `tcpdump`. We also note that this application provides the data for much of our evaluation as it provides data at finer time scales and with more consistent timestamps than other techniques we tried.

As future work we intend to provide options to infer missed packets for TCP to provide more complete traces as well as explore how to use this application to create network traces at the switch level for use in creating realistic workloads and other research efforts.

## 6.2 Traffic Engineering

To show Planck's value when running realistic workloads, we built a traffic engineering application on top of our base controller (see Section 4.1) which uses link congestion events produced by the collector, combined with the other features of the platform, to quickly reroute flows from congested paths to more lightly-loaded ones. They key benefit of using Planck for this application is its very fast control loop, which, as we show in Section 7, greatly improves the achieved aggregate throughput.

With network events being triggered in hundreds of microseconds, for a controller to keep pace, its decisions about how to alter forwarding behavior must be based on simple calculations. Our approach is to pre-install alternate paths between each source and destination. Thus, the controller only needs to decide which of the alternate paths to use, if any, when reacting to an event. In effect this splits path selection into two parts: first selecting a good set of possible paths offline and second selecting among them in an online setting. This drastically reduces the online computation required.

Our application has three main components that extend the base Planck infrastructure, and which we describe below: (i) the ability to find and pre-install multiple paths in the network, (ii) an algorithm for selecting new paths in the event of congestion, and (iii) a mechanism to quickly install route changes in the network.

**Alternate Forwarding Paths** Our controller application, implemented as an additional module on our Floodlight-based controller, uses layer-2 Per-Address Spanning Trees (PAST) for multipath routing [39]. PAST provides similar functionality and performance as Equal-Cost Multipath (ECMP) routing does at layer-3. Lastly, we chose PAST for its scalability and because, unlike ECMP, our testbed supports it.

In addition to installing standard PAST routes, a destination-oriented spanning tree for every reachable MAC address, the controller installs three additional spanning trees per host. Each alternate path is provisioned with its own unused, unique destination MAC address, which we term a *shadow MAC address*. We install four paths in total, but this number is not fundamental. However, four carefully chosen alternate paths are sufficient for traffic engineering on our topology.

An example of shadow MAC addresses can bee seen in Figure 13. Using destination MAC addresses that differ from host MAC address can be problematic for the destination host because, by default, hosts do not accept packets not destined for them. However, this problem is easily resolved by installing MAC rewrite rules at the destination's egress switch. Even in physical switches, these extra rules only require TCAM state proportional to the number of alternate routes and hosts per switch.

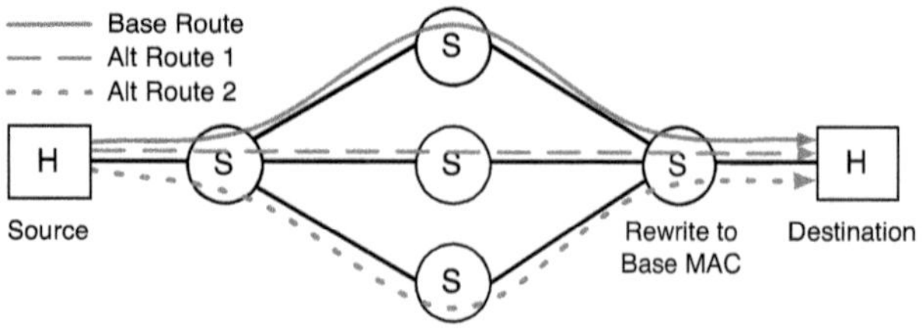


**Figure 13: Example of alternate routes between a source and destination using shadow MAC addresses.**

**Algorithm 1** – Traffic Engineering Application

*Input:* A flow congestion notification (congn), the application's view of the network (net), and a flow timeout (ftimeout)
*Output:* Route control notifications

```
process_cong_ntfy(congn, net, ftimeout):
  flows = get_congn_flows(congn, net)
  paths = get_flow_paths(congn, net, flows)
  net_update_state(congn, net, flows, paths)
  remove_old_flows(net, ftimeout)
  for flow in flows:
    greedy_route_flow(net, flow)

greedy_route_flow(net, flow):
  bestpath = net_rem_flow_path(net, flow)
  bestbtlneck = find_path_btlneck(net, bestpath)
  for path in flow.altpaths:
    if find_path_btlneck(net, path) > bestbtlneck:
      bestpath = path
      bestbltneck = find_path_btlneck(net, path)
  net_add_flow_path(net, flow, bestpath)
  send_route_control(flow, bestpath)
```

Choosing alternate paths with sufficient path diversity is necessary for traffic engineering. Consequently, choosing paths with many common links can lead to an inability to avoid congestion. Currently, our routing implementation uses the fact that finding edge-disjoint spanning trees in fat trees is trivial as each core switch defines a unique spanning tree. However, this computation is done offline, and more complex algorithms for different topologies or applications are possible. We leave optimizing the set of pre-installed paths for other metrics and determining how many alternate paths are required to future work.

**Reacting to Congestion** The controller subscribes to link utilization events from the collector(s). The core design for traffic engineering is to, for every congestion notification, greedily route each flow in the notification to a less congested path, if possible, by quickly changing routing labels. The greedy routing of flows, presented in Algorithm 1, which uses Algorithm 1 from DevoFlow [6] to implement `find_path_btlneck`, considers each flow independently and finds the alternate path of a flow with the largest expected bottleneck capacity, which, for a constant number of alternate paths of length P, is only expected to be an O(P) operation.

When selecting alternate paths, flow rerouting must consider flows on other links that it has heard of in the past. In order to avoid using stale information, flow entries in the controller are expunged after a specified timeout and thus traffic engineering does not consider them when calculating available bandwidth along routes.

**Fast Rerouting** In addition to implementing Algorithm 1 and to leverage shadow-MAC-address-based alternate routes, a mechanism for dynamically changing a flow's destination MAC address is required. We implemented two different mechanisms to switch a flow's destination MAC address, both requiring a single message: (i) using an OpenFlow rule to rewrite the destination MAC address at the source host's ingress switch and (ii) using spoofed ARP messages to update the ARP cache of the source host.

The OpenFlow-based rerouting mechanism is straightforward, but the TCAM rule state requirements of this method at each switch can be proportional to the number of hosts in the network. To address this problem, we developed MAC address rewriting through ARP spoofing, which requires no switch state, and thus no OpenFlow rule installation to reroute a flow. If the controller sends an ARP message pretending to be from the destination IP but using the alternate shadow MAC address, the source will update its ARP cache to the new address and almost immediately send packets using the new route. Although this may seem unsafe at first, since this is essentially ARP poisoning, in many SDN environments the controller intercepts all ARP messages from hosts, so the controller is the only entity capable of sending ARP messages.

Two caveats to the ARP-based rerouting mechanism are that some operating systems, e.g., Linux, ignore spurious ARP replies and in addition lock an ARP cache entry for a period of time after changing. The first problem is solved by sending unicast ARP requests which, on Linux, still performs MAC learning for the request and thus updates its ARP cache. The second method requires setting a `sysctl` to enable faster ARP cache updates.

## 7. APPLICATION EVALUATION

We evaluate our Planck-based traffic engineering application with a series of synthetic and realistic workloads based on similar tests done in previous related work [2, 6, 10].

### 7.1 Methodology

**Testbed** All experiments were conducted on a physical testbed consisting of 16 workload generator servers, five collector servers and five 64-port, 10 Gbps IBM RackSwitch G8264 top-of-rack switches [16]. The workload generators are IBM x3620 M3s with six-core Intel Westmere-EP 2.53 GHz CPUs and Mellanox ConnectX 10 Gbps NICs. The collector machines are IBM x3650 M4s with two eight-core Intel Sandy Bridge-EP 2.4 GHz CPUs and seven two-port Intel 82599 10 Gbps NICs. We used Linux 3.5. Note that our experiments use only a fraction of the resources of these servers.

**Topology** To evaluate Planck and its applications, we wanted a network topology that provided high path diversity. We chose to build a three-tier fat-tree [1] with 16 hosts.

We built the 16-host fat-tree topology by subdividing four 64-port switches into 20 five-port logical switches using OpenFlow. Due to limited TCAM size we place only five logical switches on each physical switch, leaving many ports unused. Four ports of the subswitch were wired up to build the fat-tree, the final port was used for sampling and connected directly to a collector interface.

**Workloads** We evaluate the traffic engineering schemes on our testbed with a set of synthetic and realistic workloads, similar to previous related work [2, 6, 10]. A brief description of the workloads follows. As in the prior work, host indices used in the descriptions are contiguous within pods.

*Stride(8)*: The node with index x sends a flow to the node with index $(x+8) \mod (num\_hosts)$. Stride(8) is a taxing workload because all flows traverse the core.

*Shuffle*: Each node sends a large amount of data to every other node in the network in random order. This workload mimics Hadoop/MadReduce workloads commonly encountered in real data center networks. In our evaluation, each node sends to two other nodes at a time, and the shuffle completes when all nodes finish.

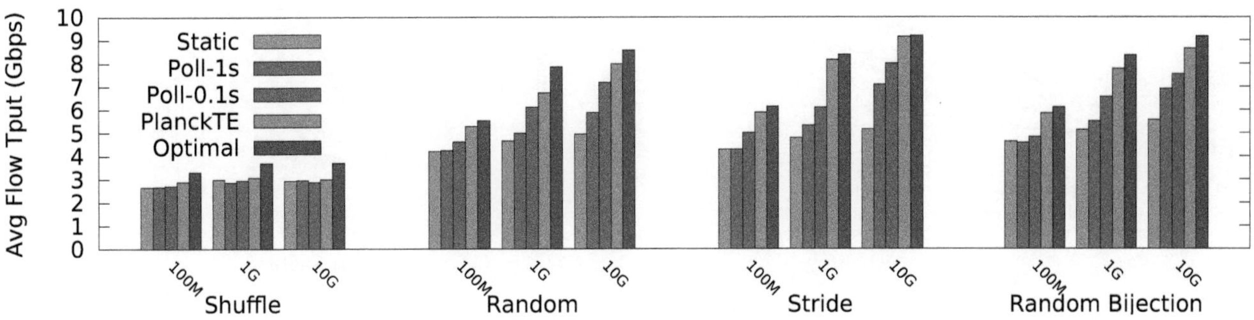


**Figure 14: Average flow throughput in each workload.**

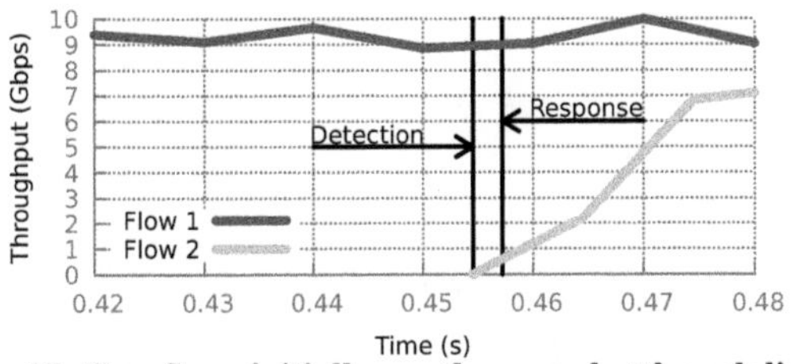


**Figure 15: Two flows initially use the same bottleneck link and are then rerouted, demonstrating the latency to detect congestion and reroute one of the flows. Flow 1 does not reduce its sending rate because the detection and rerouting occurs *faster than the switch's buffer fills*, so it sees no loss.**

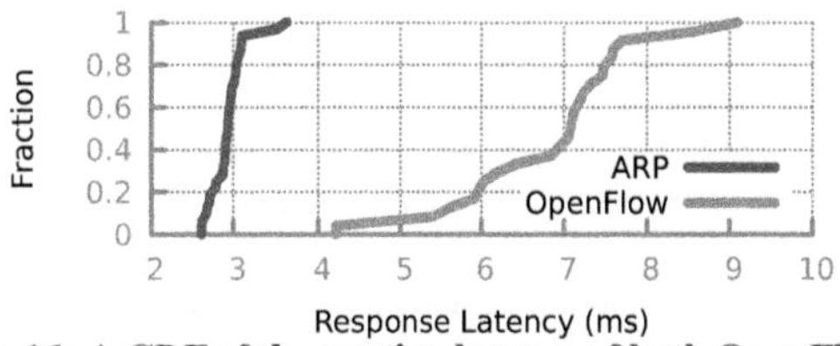


**Figure 16: A CDF of the routing latency of both OpenFlow rule control and ARP-based control.**

*Random Bijection*: Every node is exactly the source of one flow and the destination of another flow. Each run in our experiment represents a different random bijection mapping.

*Random*: Every node picks a destination not equal to itself from a uniform distribution. Each run is a different mapping. These runs allow for hotspots to form in the network.

For each of the above workloads, we perform experiments with 100 MiB, 1 GiB, and 10 GiB flow sizes, unless otherwise noted. A flow size in the shuffle workload represents the amount of data each host needs to send to another host, so a 1 GiB workload represents a 240 GiB shuffle. We tried different configurations of shuffle and stride, and also other workloads such as Staggered Prob (as in [2]), but we found the trends to be consistent, so we omit those results for brevity. All experiments are run using TCP and we run all <workload, flow size> combinations over 15 runs.

We run four different routing algorithms for each of the workloads. As an upper bound, all 16 hosts connect to one of our 64-port 10 Gbps Ethernet switches. This topology is used to represent an optimal non-blocking network, referenced by the name *Optimal*. To provide a baseline, we use PAST [39], a static multipath routing algorithm with performance comparable to ECMP, which is referenced by the name *Static*. To emulate previous traffic engineering projects that rely on polling [2, 6], we implement a global first fit routing algorithm that greedily reroutes every flow either once a second, which is referenced by the name *Poll-1s*, or once every 100 ms, which is called *Poll-0.1s*. Lastly, the traffic engineering algorithm described in Section 6.2 uses a 3 ms flow timeout, approximately the latency of rerouting a flow, and is referenced by the name *PlanckTE*.

## 7.2 Planck Control Loop Latency

Figure 15 demonstrates the full control loop of our system when ARP messages are used for fast control. In this experiment, we show the throughput over time of two flows, *Flow 1* and *Flow 2*. The flows use initial routes that collide, and *Flow 2* is started after *Flow 1* has reached steady state. The labels *Detection* and *Response* mark the times when congestion is detected and the flow is rerouted, respectively. The latency between detecting the first packet that causes congestion and sending a congestion notification was between 25–240 µs across runs, and the difference between detection and response is 2.6 ms in this figure. Because the throughput of *Flow 1* never decreases, we can see that the switch had sufficient buffer capacity to avoid dropping a packet during the time in which both flows were active but before a flow was rerouted.

Figure 16 further characterizes the control loop of our system by presenting a CDF of the response latency of both OpenFlow- and ARP-based control, where response latency is defined as the time from when the congestion notification was sent to the time at which a collector sees a packet with the updated MAC address. We see that ARP-based control takes around 2.5 ms to 3.5 ms, while the latency for OpenFlow-based control varies from about 4 ms to 9 ms, with the median control time taking over 7 ms. As in Section 5.3, the majority of this latency can be attributed to switch buffering.

## 7.3 Traffic Engineering

In this section, we evaluate the effectiveness of a traffic engineering scheme designed to work within our monitoring framework. We analyze the performance of this scheme by comparing it against other traffic engineering schemes under various workloads.

**Varying Flow Sizes** We first investigate the performance of each traffic engineering scheme under a variety of flow sizes. If PlanckTE can operate on fine-grained timescales, then its performance should track the performance of Optimal for smaller flow sizes. We vary the flow sizes in a stride(8) workload from 50 MiB up to 100 GiB and plot the average throughput achieved by each flow in the network in Figure 17. We use average flow throughput as a metric because fine-grained traffic engineering can impact the initial stages of a flow's throughput and capturing these effects are important.

We note the following trends in the figure. First, PlanckTE can effectively route on small time scales, given its performance relative to Optimal. PlanckTE and Optimal have similar performance for flows as small as 50 MiB, which theoretically can take as little as

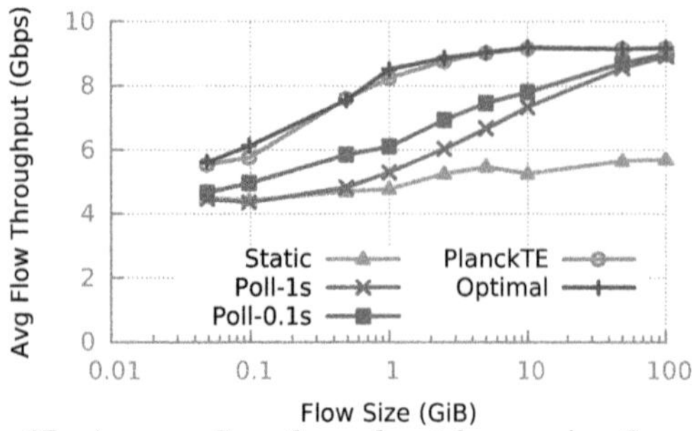


**Figure 17: Average flow throughput for varying flow sizes in stride(8), shown at log-scale, for flow sizes ranging from 50 MiB to 100 GiB.**

4.2 ms to transfer. Poll-1s can only engineer flows larger than 1 GiB because these are the first flow sizes whose stride(8) workload takes longer than one second to complete, whereas Poll-0.1s can optimize 100 MiB flows. The performance of Poll-1s and Poll-0.1s eventually approach Optimal's performance as the flow size increases. With 100 GiB flows, all schemes but static provide similar performance.

**Varying Workloads** Figure 14 presents the performance of different traffic engineering schemes for each of the workloads detailed in Section 7.1. As in the previous section, the average throughput of an individual flow is used as the metric. For each workload, the performance of three different flow sizes (100 MiB, 1 GiB and 10 GiB) are presented for the traffic engineering schemes.

We notice the following trends in the figure. First, PlanckTE can closely track the performance of Optimal for all flow sizes. Even under the smallest flow size of 100 MiB, PlanckTE typically comes within 1–4% of Optimal's performance (with the exception of the shuffle workload, where PlanckTE comes within a worst case of 12.3% to Optimal). Second, for both Poll schemes, the performance increases as the flow size increases with Poll-0.1s performing better as expected. Finally, PlanckTE provides benefits over both Poll schemes. The improvement is small for the shuffle workloads where traffic is distributed across many links, and we saw similar trends for Staggered Prob (not shown) where traffic is typically isolated near the network edges. However, in the other workloads, the improvement of PlanckTE over Poll-1s ranges from 24.4% (random) to 53% (stride), and the improvement over Poll-0.1s ranges from 11% (random) to 33% (random bijection).

Lastly, we examine the performance of two different workloads with 100 MiB flow sizes in more detail. Figure 18(a) presents a CDF comparing shuffle completion times for each host in each engineering scheme. The median host completion times are 3.31 seconds for Poll-1s, 3.01 seconds for Poll-0.1s, 2.86 seconds for PlanckTE, and 2.52 seconds for Optimal.

Figure 18(b) contains a CDF of the individual flow throughputs for the stride(8) workload. PlanckTE and Poll-0.1s obtain median flow throughputs of 5.9 Gbps and 4.9 Gbps respectively, and we can see that the performance of PlanckTE closely tracks that of Optimal.

## 8. RELATED WORK

The work most related to Planck consists of low-latency network measurement techniques and dynamic routing mechanisms for traffic engineering. Traffic engineering is a broad field, but we focus on the recent work predominantly aimed at fine-grained traffic engineering for the data center supported by SDN.

A few recent efforts have focused on how to implement counters and measurement in switches. OpenSketch [44] proposes adding reconfigurable measurement logic to switches and exposing an in-

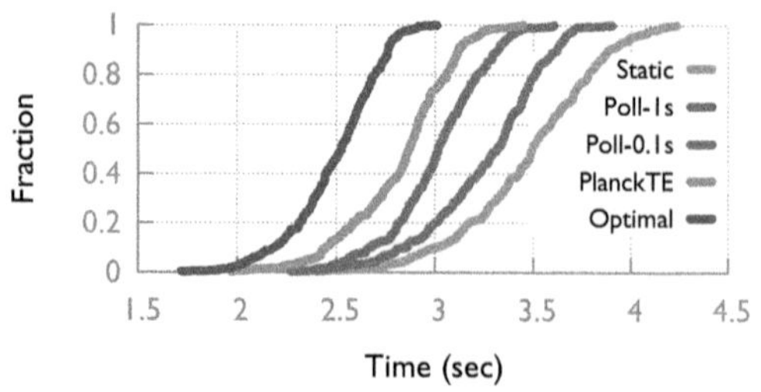


(a) Shuffle

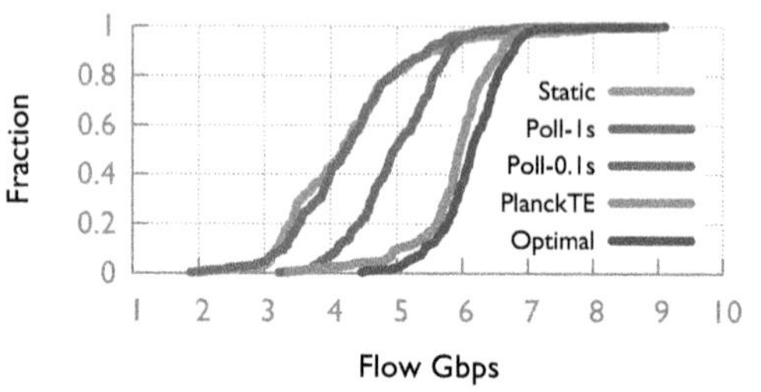


(b) Stride

**Figure 18: CDFs for 100 MiB flow workloads. The first figure shows host completion times for their shuffle and the second figure shows the flow throughputs for a stride(8) workload.**

terface to program it in much the same way that OpenFlow allows for programming forwarding behavior. Other work [25] looks at software-defined counters with a hybrid implementation across the switching ASIC and control plane CPU that might provide better trade-offs in terms of how quickly counters can be read. Additionally, future switching ASICs could provide the ability for fast data-plane only sampling without involving the control plane CPU. Planck provides similar benefits, i.e., comprehensive low-latency measurements, today and this paper uses it to demonstrate how such measurements could be used if and when such new hardware arrives.

A separate related line of work looks at improving network measurements in terms of accuracy and coverage [7, 8, 9]. Unlike our work, which focuses on obtaining flow-level throughput measurements at very tight time-scales, they focus on accurately monitoring transit networks at coarser time-scales.

Our traffic engineering application draws inspiration from Hedera [2] and MicroTE [4] and takes a similar approach of measuring the network and rerouting flows based on measurements. However, Hedera and MicroTE use five second and one second control loops, respectively. Further, they both use 1 Gbps links and would need to be noticeably faster to get similar results on 10 Gbps links.

Mahout [5] gets low-latency measurements by modifying end-hosts to detect elephant flows in 1.5–5.5 ms. We expect that using these detections to infer global network state would take notably longer. Planck detects more than just elephant flows without end-host modifications at the same or smaller time-scales.

LocalFlow [31] shows the benefit of a faster traffic engineering control loop in simulation, but does not consider implementing it.

B4 [20] and SWAN [15] monitor and shape traffic at the edge of the network, but these projects operate on the order of seconds or minutes. Similarly, Seawall [35] and EyeQ [21] monitor and shape traffic at the edge, but do not monitor switches.

Additional work has looked at integrating optical links in data centers [10, 40, 42]. This work typically leverages optical networks by building hybrid networks that contain both optical circuit switches and traditional electrical packet switches and needs fast measurements to quickly predict a traffic matrix and then schedule optical circuits to carry the largest components. Despite this, they can only measure the network every 75–100 ms at minimum. Planck could be used to inform such schemes at much smaller time-scales.

SideCar [36], like Planck, directly attaches servers, called SideCars, to switches with the goal of observing and modifying network behavior. While Planck's collectors are similar, we attach multiple switches to each and use them to monitor and change the behavior of a network of unmodified end-hosts. By contrast, SideCar attaches one server per switch and uses end-host (hypervisor) modifications to invoke them to assist in more general tasks including multicast.

Closely related to Planck is the work of OpenSample [41] and sFlow-RT [33]. OpenSample leverages traditional sFlow [32] samples to detect elephant flows and reroute them to avoid congestion. They also use TCP sequence numbers to improve the accuracy of their samples but do not use them in the presence of a dynamic sampling rate. Additionally, OpenSample operates with a 100 ms control loop and is only evaluated on 10 Mbps links and in simulation.

InMon sFlow-RT [33] also uses sampling to measure the network with the intent of using SDN controllers, but anecdotally takes hundreds of milliseconds to seconds to detect large flows [34].

# 9. DISCUSSION

## 9.1 Scalability

While our testbed is insufficient to evaluate Planck at scale, we use measurements and calculations to estimate scalability as switch port counts and the resources required to monitor a network increase.

First, as switch port counts increase, Planck's sampling rate will decrease if only one port is used for samples. However, monitor ports can be added at additional cost to increase the sampling rate.

Second, while collectors are completely independent and thus scale out well, the number of collector instances that can fit on a single server and thus the resources required to monitor a network are worth considering. This depends primarily on the packet processing system used, the number of NICs that can fit in a server, and the number of cores on the server. Our implementation uses netmap [30], and a given collector instance stays below 90% utilization of a single core when processing 10 Gbps at line rate. Recent results from Intel show that it is possible to route 50-60 Gbps per socket [17], so 100 Gbps should be possible on a 2-socket server. We were able to build fourteen 10 Gbps Ethernet ports on a single 2U, 16-core server, so such a server should be able to collect samples from 10-14 switches depending on memory and PCIe bandwidth constrains. In our experiments, we only ran eight collector instances per server due to an unresolved memory bug in netmap for Linux.

Assuming 14 collector instances per server, Planck results in a modest addition to the overall cost for real networks. If 64-port switches are used, with one port being dedicated to monitoring, a full-bisection-bandwidth $k = 62$ three-level fat-tree can be built to support 59,582 hosts from 4,805 switches, which would require 344 collectors, resulting in about 0.58% additional machines. Other topologies that use fewer switches per host, e.g., Jellyfish [37], would require many fewer collectors. For example, a full-bisection-bandwidth Jellyfish with the same number of hosts requires only 3,505 switches and thus only 251 collectors, representing 0.42% additional machines. Using a monitor port also causes the network to support a smaller number of hosts for a given number of switches. For the same number of switches, a fat-tree with monitor ports only supports 1.4% fewer hosts than without monitor ports, and a Jellyfish supports 5.5% fewer hosts than without monitor ports.

Given the performance gains that Planck can offer when coupled with traffic engineering, its possible that networks with lower bisection bandwidths could still see better performance. By tolerating a lower bisection bandwidth, networks could recover extra ports to add more hosts.

Because the volume of network events is far smaller than the volume of samples, we expect that a reasonable network controller will be able to handle the notifications produced by this number of collectors, but we leave that evaluation to future work.

## 9.2 Implications for Future Switch Design

In building Planck, we have encountered several challenges which we feel point to opportunities to improve the design and implementation of switches and their firmware in the future.

**Data Plane Sampling** Support for sampling in the data plane to remove the control plane bottleneck is the most obvious addition that future switches could make to enable Planck-like functionality. It would enable much higher sampling rates while also maintaining the metadata which Planck is forced to recover including input port, output port, and sampling rate.

**Sampling Rate vs. Rate of Samples** Traditional sampling-based network monitoring [32] allows a user (or monitoring system) to set a *sampling rate* where statistically one in N packets are sampled. While this is easy to configure and understand, we have found that it causes suboptimal trade-offs. The sampling rate can cause a switch to exceed the rate of samples it can actually send, making the sampling rate inaccurate. To avoid this problem, sampling rates must be set conservatively so that even with high traffic volumes, the switches do not exceed their sampling rate. The result is that when there are low traffic volumes, very few samples are gathered.

Instead, we propose that future sampling-based network monitoring center around a desired *rate of samples* and switches should vary their sampling rates to approximate this rate. This is useful not just to avoid overrunning switch capabilities, but also to match the capacity of the system processing the samples. Planck does this by constraining samples to the link speed of the monitoring port, but future switches should provide ways to do this for arbitrary rates.

**Minimized sample buffering** One of the biggest challenges we found in Planck was that the oversubscribed monitor ports became congested and samples were buffered. This buffering both increases the latency to receive samples and uses buffer space that the rest of the switch could be using for burst tolerance. Reducing the buffering for samples to a minimum would eliminate both of these issues.

Reducing the buffer space allocated to a monitor port should be possible with simple firmware changes to existing switches.

**Clear Sampling Model** Our experiments have shown that oversubscribed monitor ports don't exhibit an obvious model that explains the sampling rate across flows or ports. This means that we can only infer the sampling rate for traffic with sequence numbers. Having a clear model for what traffic will be sampled at what rate under what circumstances, especially given that we believe sampling rates should be dynamic, will be essential.

**Preferential Sampling of Special Traffic** Certain packets are more important than others. For instance, packets with TCP SYN, FIN, and RST flags mark the beginning and end of flows. Sampling these packets at a higher rate, perhaps even sampling all of them, would aid in providing accurate measurements and faster knowledge of these network events.

We had hoped to achieve this effect by matching on these flags and using OpenFlow to put these packets in a higher priority queue on the monitor ports, but OpenFlow does not currently allow for matching on TCP flags. However, types of traffic OpenFlow can match on could be given higher priority sampling with this method.

Further, it is important to limit what fraction of the total samples are allowed to be sampled from higher priority packet classes to avoid allowing an attacker to suppress all normal samples by sending a high rate of traffic in the priority classes, e.g., a SYN flood.

**In-switch Collectors** Lastly, while we believe there will always be places in which the flexibility of sampling-based measurement will be useful, there may be common information and events that the switch could produce based on it's own samples without needing to commit network resources to the samples themselves. In effect, this would be like running the collector for a switch on the switch itself.

## 9.3 Future Work

We believe that there is significant future work to be done with Planck. We have shown many ideas about how we build networks, certainly software-defined networks need to be rethought if we want to capitalize on millisecond-scale (or faster) measurements. For example, with careful engineering Planck can allow a network to react to congestion faster than switch buffers fill meaning TCP would not see losses from congestion in the common case.

Going forward, we would also like to turn Planck into a more extensible measurement platform and define the relevant APIs to plug modules into key places. For example, many of the techniques described in OpenSketch [44] could be implemented as streaming operators on the samples Planck receives.

# 10. CONCLUSION

This paper presented Planck, a novel network measurement system that uses oversubscribed port mirroring to provide measurements every 4.2 ms–7.2 ms—*more than an order of magnitude (11–18x) improvement* over the current state-of-the-art (and up to 291x if switch firmware allowed buffering to be disabled on mirror ports). To demonstrate that this increased speed translates to improved performance, we built a traffic engineering application designed to operate at similar speeds which is able to detect congestion and reroute flows in about 3 milliseconds. Doing so provides near-optimal throughput even for small flow sizes, e.g., 50 MiB, and even at 10 Gbps link speeds. Further, this granularity of measurement radically changes how we should be thinking about network control loops and how we build SDN controllers.

**Acknowledgements:** We thank our shepherd Amin Vahdat and the anonymous reviewers for their helpful comments. We also thank Andrew Ferguson for his feedback and discussions. Brent Stephens is supported by an IBM Fellowship. Jeff Rasley is supported by an NSF Graduate Research Fellowship (DGE-1058262).

# References

[1] M. Al-Fares, A. Loukissas, and A. Vahdat. A Scalable, Commodity Data Center Network Architecture. In *SIGCOMM*, 2008.

[2] M. Al-fares, S. Radhakrishnan, B. Raghavan, N. Huang, and A. Vahdat. Hedera: Dynamic Flow Scheduling for Data Center Networks. In *NSDI*, 2010.

[3] B. Claise, Ed. Cisco Systems NetFlow Services Export Version 9. RFC 3954. http://www.ietf.org/rfc/rfc3954.txt, October 2004.

[4] T. Benson, A. Anand, A. Akella, and M. Zhang. MicroTE: Fine Grained Traffic Engineering for Data Centers. In *CoNEXT*, 2011.

[5] A. Curtis, W. Kim, and P. Yalagandula. Mahout: Low-Overhead Datacenter Traffic Management using End-Host-Based Elephant Detection. In *INFOCOM*, 2011.

[6] A. R. Curtis, J. C. Mogul, J. Tourrilhes, P. Yalagandula, P. Sharma, and S. Banerjee. DevoFlow: Scaling Flow Management for High-Performance Networks. In *SIGCOMM*, 2011.

[7] N. Duffield, C. Lund, and M. Thorup. Learn More, Sample Less: Control of Volume and Variance in Network Measurement. *IEEE Transactions on Information Theory*, 51(5):1756–1775, 2005.

[8] C. Estan, K. Keys, D. Moore, and G. Varghese. Building a Better NetFlow. In *SIGCOMM*, 2004.

[9] C. Estan and G. Varghese. New Directions in Traffic Measurement and Accounting. In *SIGCOMM*, 2002.

[10] N. Farrington, G. Porter, S. Radhakrishnan, H. H. Bazzaz, V. Subramanya, Y. Fainman, G. Papen, and A. Vahdat. Helios: A Hybrid Electrical/Optical Switch Architecture for Modular Data Centers. In *SIGCOMM*, 2010.

[11] A. D. Ferguson, A. Guha, C. Liang, R. Fonseca, and S. Krishnamurthi. Participatory Networking: An API for Application Control of SDNs. In *SIGCOMM*, 2013.

[12] Floodlight OpenFlow Controller. http://floodlight.openflowhub.org/.

[13] A. Greenberg, J. R. Hamilton, N. Jain, S. Kandula, C. Kim, P. Lahiri, D. A. Maltz, P. Patel, and S. Sengupta. VL2: A scalable and flexible data center network. In *SIGCOMM*, 2009.

[14] D. Halperin, S. Kandula, J. Padhye, P. Bahl, and D. Wetherall. Augmenting Data Center Networks with Multi-Gigabit Wireless Links. In *SIGCOMM*, 2011.

[15] C.-Y. Hong, S. Kandula, R. Mahajan, M. Zhang, V. Gill, M. Nanduri, and R. Wattenhofer. Achieving High Utilization with Software-driven WAN. In *SIGCOMM*, 2013.

[16] IBM BNT RackSwitch G8264. http://www.redbooks.ibm.com/abstracts/tips0815.html.

[17] Intel® Data Plane Development Kit (Intel® DPDK) Overview Packet Processing on Intel® Architecture. http://goo.gl/qdg3rZ, December 2012.

[18] Intel® DPDK: Data Plane Development Kit. http://www.dpdk.org.

[19] V. Jacobson. Van Jacobson's Network Channels. http://lwn.net/Articles/169961/, January 2006.

[20] S. Jain, A. Kumar, S. Mandal, J. Ong, L. Poutievski, A. Singh, S. Venkata, J. Wanderer, J. Zhou, M. Zhu, J. Zolla, U. Hölzle, S. Stuart, and A. Vahdat. B4: Experience with a Globally-deployed Software Defined WAN. In *SIGCOMM*, 2013.

[21] V. Jeyakumar, M. Alizadeh, D. Mazières, B. Prabhakar, C. Kim, and A. Greenberg. EyeQ: Practical Network Performance Isolation at the Edge. In *NSDI*, 2013.

[22] S. Kandula, S. Sengupta, A. Greenberg, and P. Patel. The Nature of Datacenter Traffic: Measurements and Analysis. In *IMC*, 2009.

[23] R. Kapoor, A. C. Snoeren, G. M. Voelker, and G. Porter. Bullet Trains: A Study of NIC Burst Behavior at Microsecond Timescales. In *CoNEXT*, 2013.

[24] E. Kohler, R. Morris, B. Chen, J. Jannotti, and M. F. Kaashoek. The Click Modular Router. *ToCS*, 18(3):263–297, August 2000.

[25] J. C. Mogul and P. Congdon. Hey, You Darned Counters! Get Off My ASIC! In *HotSDN*, 2012.

[26] Openflow-switch. https://www.opennetworking.org/standards/openflow-switch.

[27] Libpcap File Format. http://wiki.wireshark.org/Development/LibpcapFileFormat.

[28] PF_RING: High-speed Packet Capture, Filtering and Analysis. http://www.ntop.org/products/pf_ring/.

[29] P. Phaal and S. Panchen. Packet Sampling Basics. http://www.sflow.org/packetSamplingBasics/index.htm.

[30] L. Rizzo. Netmap: A Novel Framework for Fast Packet I/O. In *USENIX ATC*, 2012.

[31] S. Sen, D. Shue, S. Ihm, and M. J. Freedman. Scalable, Optimal Flow Routing in Datacenters via Local Link Balancing. In *CoNEXT*, 2013.

[32] sFlow. http://sflow.org/about/index.php.

[33] sFlow-RT. http://inmon.com/products/sFlow-RT.php.

[34] Large Flow Detection Script. http://blog.sflow.com/2013/06/large-flow-detection-script.html, June 2013.

[35] A. Shieh, S. Kandula, A. Greenberg, C. Kim, and B. Saha. Sharing the Data Center Network. In *NSDI*, 2011.

[36] A. Shieh, S. Kandula, and E. G. Sirer. SideCar: Building Programmable Datacenter Networks without Programmable Switches. In *HotNets*, 2010.

[37] A. Singla, C.-Y. Hong, L. Popa, and P. B. Godfrey. Jellyfish: Networking Data Centers Randomly. In *NSDI*, 2012.

[38] Version 2 of the Protocol Operations for the Simple Network Management Protocol (SNMP). RFC 3416. http://www.ietf.org/rfc/rfc3416.txt.

[39] B. Stephens, A. Cox, W. Felter, C. Dixon, and J. Carter. PAST: Scalable Ethernet for Data Centers. In *CoNEXT*, 2012.

[40] G. P. R. Strong, N. Farrington, A. Forencich, P. Chen-Sun, T. Rosing, Y. Fainman, G. Papen, and A. Vahdat. Integrating Microsecond Circuit Switching into the Data Center. In *SIGCOMM*, 2013.

[41] J. Suh, T. T. Kwon, C. Dixon, W. Felter, and J. Carter. OpenSample: A Low-latency, Sampling-based Measurement Platform for SDN. In *ICDCS*, 2014.

[42] G. Wang, D. G. Andersen, M. Kaminsky, K. Papagiannaki, T. S. E. Ng, M. Kozuch, and M. Ryan. c-Through: Part-time Optics in Data Centers. In *SIGCOMM*, 2010.

[43] Wireshark. http://www.wireshark.org/.

[44] M. Yu, L. Jose, and R. Miao. Software Defined Traffic Measurement with OpenSketch. In *NSDI*, 2013.

# DREAM: Dynamic Resource Allocation for Software-defined Measurement

Masoud Moshref† Minlan Yu† Ramesh Govindan† Amin Vahdat*
†University of Southern California *Google and UC San Diego

## ABSTRACT

Software-defined networks can enable a variety of concurrent, dynamically instantiated, measurement tasks, that provide fine-grain visibility into network traffic. Recently, there have been many proposals to configure TCAM counters in hardware switches to monitor traffic. However, the TCAM memory at switches is fundamentally limited and the accuracy of the measurement tasks is a function of the resources devoted to them on each switch. This paper describes an adaptive measurement framework, called DREAM, that dynamically adjusts the resources devoted to each measurement task, while ensuring a user-specified level of accuracy. Since the trade-off between resource usage and accuracy can depend upon the type of tasks, their parameters, and traffic characteristics, DREAM does not assume an a priori characterization of this trade-off, but instead dynamically searches for a resource allocation that is sufficient to achieve a desired level of accuracy. A prototype implementation and simulations with three network-wide measurement tasks (heavy hitter, hierarchical heavy hitter and change detection) and diverse traffic show that DREAM can support more concurrent tasks with higher accuracy than several other alternatives.

## Categories and Subject Descriptors

C.2.0 [**Computer-Communication Networks**]; C.2.3 [**Network Operations**]: Network monitoring; C.2.4 [**Distributed Systems**]: Network operating systems

## Keywords

Software-defined Measurement; Resource Allocation

## 1. INTRODUCTION

Today's data center and enterprise networks require expensive capital investments, yet provide surprisingly little visibility into traffic. Traffic measurement can play an important role in these networks, by permitting traffic accounting, traffic engineering, load balancing, and performance diagnosis [7, 11, 13, 19, 8], all of which rely on accurate and timely measurement of time-varying traffic at all switches in the network. Beyond that, tenant services in a multi-tenant cloud may need accurate statistics of their traffic, which requires collecting this information at all relevant switches.

Software-defined measurement [39, 25, 31] has the potential to enable concurrent, dynamically instantiated, *measurement tasks*. In this approach, an SDN controller orchestrates these measurement tasks at multiple spatial and temporal scales, based on a global view of the network. Examples of measurement tasks include identifying flows exceeding a given threshold and flows whose volume changes significantly. In a cloud setting, each tenant can issue distinct measurement tasks. Some cloud services have a large number of tenants [1], and cloud providers already offer simple per-tenant measurement services [2].

Unlike prior work [39, 35, 31, 29], which has either assumed specialized hardware support on switches for measurement, or has explored software-defined measurements on hypervisors, our paper focuses on TCAM-based measurement in switches. TCAM-based measurement algorithms can be used to detect heavy hitters and significant changes [31, 41, 26]. These algorithms can leverage existing TCAM hardware on switches and so have the advantage of immediate deployability. However, to be practical, we must address a critical challenge: TCAM resources on switches are fundamentally limited for power and cost reasons. Unfortunately, measurement tasks may require multiple TCAM counters, and the number of allocated counters can determine the accuracy of these tasks. Furthermore, the resources required for accurate measurement may change with traffic, and tasks may require TCAM counters allocated on multiple switches.

**Contributions.** In this paper, we discuss the design of a system for TCAM-based software-defined measurement, called DREAM. Users of DREAM can dynamically instantiate multiple concurrent measurement tasks (such as heavy hitter or hierarchical heavy hitter detection, or change detection) at an SDN controller, and additionally specify a *flow filter* (e.g., defined over 5-tuples) over which this measurement task is executed. Since the traffic for each task may need to be measured at multiple switches, DREAM needs to allocate switch resources to each task.

To do this, DREAM first leverages two important observations. First, although tasks become more accurate with more TCAM resources, there is a point of diminishing returns: beyond a certain accuracy, significantly more resources are necessary to increase the accuracy of the task. Moreover, beyond this point, the *quality* of the retrieved results, say heavy hitters is marginal (as we quantify later). This suggests that it would be acceptable to maintain the accuracy of measurement tasks above a high (but below 100%) user-specified *accuracy bound*. Second, tasks need TCAM resources only on switches at which there is traffic that matches the specified flow filter, and the number of resources required depends upon the traffic volume and the distribution. This suggests that allocat-


*SIGCOMM'14*, August 17–22, 2014, Chicago, Illinois, USA.
Copyright 2014 ACM 978-1-4503-2836-4/14/08 ...$15.00.
http://dx.doi.org/10.1145/2619239.2626291.

ing just enough resources to tasks at switches and over time might provide *spatial and temporal statistical multiplexing benefits*.

DREAM uses both of these observations to permit more concurrent tasks than is possible with a static allocation of TCAM resources. To do this, DREAM needs to estimate the TCAM resources required to achieve the desired accuracy bound. Unfortunately, the relationship between resource and accuracy for measurement tasks cannot be characterized *a priori* because it depends upon the traffic characteristics. If this relationship could have been characterized, an optimization-based approach would have worked. Instead, DREAM contains a novel resource adaptation strategy for determining the right set of resources assigned to each task at each switch. This requires measurement algorithm-specific estimation of task accuracy, for which we have designed *accuracy estimators* for several common measurement algorithms. Using these, DREAM increases the resource allocated to a task at a switch when its global estimated accuracy is below the accuracy bound and its accuracy at the switch is also below the accuracy bound. In this manner, DREAM decouples resource allocation, which is performed locally, from accuracy estimation, which is performed globally. DREAM continuously adapts the resources allocated to tasks, since a task's accuracy and resource requirements can change with traffic. Finally, if DREAM is unable to get enough resources for a task to satisfy its accuracy bound, it *drops* the task.

DREAM is at a novel point in the design space: it permits multiple concurrent measurements without compromising their accuracy, and effectively maximizes resource usage. We demonstrate through extensive experiments on a DREAM prototype (in which multiple concurrent tasks three different types are executed) that it performs significantly better than other alternatives, especially at the tail of important performance metrics, and that these performance advantages carry over to larger scales evaluated through simulation. DREAM's satisfaction metric (the fraction of task's lifetime that its accuracy is above the bound) is 2× better at the tail for moderate loads than an approach which allocates equal share of resources to tasks: in DREAM, almost 95% of tasks have a satisfaction higher than 80%, but for equal allocation, 5% have a satisfaction less than 40%. At high loads, DREAM's average satisfaction is nearly 3× that of equal allocation. Some of these relative performance advantages also apply to an approach which allocates a fixed amount of resource to each task, but drops tasks that cannot be satisfied. However, this fixed allocation rejects an unacceptably high fraction of tasks: even at low load, it rejects 30% of tasks, while DREAM rejects none. Finally, these performance differences persist across a broad range of parameter settings.

# 2. RESOURCE-CONSTRAINED SOFTWARE-DEFINED MEASUREMENT

In this section, we motivate the fundamental challenges for real-time visibility into traffic in enterprise and data center networks. Software-defined Measurement (SDM) provides this capability by permitting a large amount of dynamically instantiated network-wide *measurement tasks*. These tasks often leverage flow-based counters in TCAM in OpenFlow switches. Unfortunately, the number of TCAM entries are often limited. To make SDM more practical, we propose to dynamically allocate measurement resources to tasks, by leveraging the diminishing returns in the accuracy of each task, and temporal/spatial resource multiplexing across tasks.

## 2.1 TCAM-based Measurement

In this paper, we focus on TCAM-based measurement tasks on hardware switches. Other work has proposed more advanced measurement primitives like sketches [39], which are currently not available in commercial hardware switches and it is unclear when they will be available. For this reason, our paper explicitly focuses on TCAM-based measurement, but many of the techniques proposed in this paper can be extended to sketch-based measurement (we leave such extensions to future work). In more constrained environments like data centers, it may be possible to perform measurement in software switches or hypervisors (possibly even using sketches), but this approach (a) can be compromised by malicious code on end-hosts, even in data-center settings [37, 9], (b) does not generalize to wide-area deployments of SDN [24], and (c) introduces additional constraints (like hypervisor CPU usage) [22].

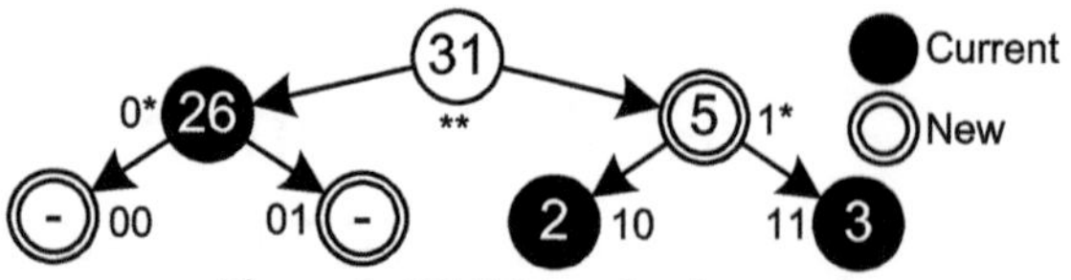

**Figure 1: TCAM-based task example**

To understand how TCAM memory can be effectively used for measurement, consider the heavy hitter detection algorithm proposed in [26]. The key idea behind this (and other TCAM-based algorithms) is, in the absence of enough TCAM entries to monitor every flow in a switch, to selectively monitor *prefixes* and drill down on prefixes likely to contain heavy hitters. Figure 1 shows a prefix trie of two bits as part of source IP prefix trie of a task that finds heavy hitter source IPs (IPs sending more than, say, 10Mbps in a measurement epoch). The number inside each node is the volume of traffic from the corresponding prefix based on the "current" set of monitored prefixes. The task reports source IPs (leaves) with volume greater than threshold.

If the task cannot monitor every source IP in the network because of limited TCAM counters, it only monitors a subset of leaves trading off some accuracy. It also measures a few internal nodes (IP prefixes) to guide which leaves to monitor next to maximize accuracy. For example in Figure 1, suppose the task is only allowed to use 3 TCAM counters, it first decides to monitor 11, 10 and 0*. As prefix 0* sends large traffic, the task decides to drill down under prefix 0* in the next epoch to find heavy hitters hoping that they will remain active then. However, to respect the resource constraint (3 TCAM counters), it must free a counter in the other sub-tree by monitoring prefix 1* instead of 10 and 11.

## 2.2 Task Diversity and Resource Limitations

While the previous sub-section described a way to measure heavy hitters at a single switch, the focus of our work is to design an SDM system that (a) permits multiple types of TCAM-based measurement tasks across multiple switches that may each contend for TCAM memory, and (b) adapts the resources required for concurrent tasks without significantly sacrificing accuracy.

SDM needs to support a large number of concurrent tasks, and dynamic instantiation of measurement tasks. In an SDN-capable WAN, network operators may wish to track traffic anomalies (heavy hitters, significant changes), and simultaneously find large flows to effect preferential routing [7], and may perform each of these tasks on different traffic aggregates. Operators may also instantiate tasks dynamically to drill down into anomalous traffic aggregates. In an SDN-capable multi-tenant data center, individual tenants might each wish to instantiate multiple measurement tasks. Modern cloud services have a large number of tenants; for example, 3 million domains used AWS in 2013 [1]. Per-tenant measurement services are already available — Amazon CloudWatch provides tenant operators very simple network usage counters per VM [2]. In the future, we anticipate tenants instantiating many measurement tasks to achieve distinct goals such as DDoS detection or better bandwidth provisioning [10, 38].

Each measurement task may need hundreds of TCAM entries for sufficient accuracy [31, 26, 41], but typical hardware switches have only a limited number of TCAMs. There are only 1k-2k TCAM entries in switches [19, 23], and this number is not expected to increase dramatically for commodity switches because of their cost and power usage. Moreover, other management tasks such as routing and access control need TCAMs and this can leave fewer entries for measurement.

## 2.3 Dynamic Resource Allocation for SDM

Given limited resources and the need to support concurrent measurement tasks, it is important to efficiently allocate TCAM resources for measurement.

**Leverage: Diminishing returns in accuracy for measurement.** The *accuracy* of a measurement task depends on the resources allocated to it [31, 39]. For example, for heavy hitter (HH) detection, *recall*, the fraction of true HHs that are detected, is a measure of accuracy. Figure 2 shows the result of our HH detection algorithm on a CAIDA traffic trace [3] with a threshold of 8 Mbps (See Section 5 for implementation details).

The figure shows that more counters leads to higher recall. For example, doubling counters from 512 to 1024 increases recall from 60% to 80% (Figure 2(a)). There is a point of diminishing returns for many measurement tasks [17, 30, 28, 27] where additional resource investment does not lead to proportional accuracy improvement. The accuracy gain becomes smaller as we double the resources; it only improves from 82% to 92% when doubling the number of counters from 1024 to 2048, and even 8K counters are insufficient to achieve an accuracy of 99%. Furthermore, the precise point of diminishing returns depends on the task type, parameters (e.g., heavy hitter threshold) and traffic [31].

Another important aspect of the relationship between accuracy and resource usage of TCAM-based algorithms is that, beyond the point of diminishing returns, additional resources yield less significant outcomes, on average. For example, the heavy hitters detected with additional resources are intuitively "less important" or "smaller" heavy hitters and the changes detected by a change detection algorithm are smaller, by nearly a factor of 2 on average (we have empirically confirmed this).

This observation is at the core of our approach: *we assert that network operators will be satisfied with operating these measurement tasks at, or slightly above, the point of diminishing returns, in exchange for being able to concurrently execute more measurement tasks.*[1] At a high-level, our approach permits operators to dynamically instantiate three distinct kinds of measurement tasks (discussed later) and to specify a target accuracy for each task. It then allocates TCAM counters to these tasks to enable them to achieve the specified accuracy, adapts TCAM allocations as tasks leave or enter or as traffic changes. Finally, our approach performs admission control because the accuracy bound is inelastic and admitting too many tasks can leave each task with fewer resources than necessary to achieve the target accuracy.

**Leverage: Temporal and Spatial Resource Multiplexing.** The TCAM resources required for a task depends on the properties of monitored traffic. For example, as the number of heavy hitters increases, we need more resources to detect them. This presents an opportunity to *statistically multiplex* TCAM resources across tasks on a single switch: while a heavy hitter task on a switch may see many heavy hitters at a given time, a concurrent change detection task may see fewer anomalies at the same instant, and so may need fewer resources. This dependence on TCAM resources with traffic is shown in Figure 2(a), where the recall of the HH detection task with 256 entries decreases in the presence of more HHs and we need more resources to keep its recall above 50%. If we allocate fixed resources to each task, we would either over-provision the resource usage and support fewer tasks, or under-provision the resource usage and obtain low accuracy.

Measurement tasks also permit *spatial statistical multiplexing*, since the task may need resources from multiple switches. For example, we may need to find heavy hitter source IPs on flows of a prefix that come from multiple switches. Figure 2(b) shows the *recall* of heavy hitters found on two switches monitoring different traffic: the recall at each switch is defined by the portion of detected heavy hitters on this switch over true heavy hitters. The graph shows that with the same amount of resources, the switches exhibit different recall; conversely, different amounts of resources may be needed at different switches.

These leverage points suggest that it may be possible to efficiently use TCAM resources to permit multiple concurrent measurement tasks by (a) permitting operators[2] to specify desired accuracy bounds for each task, and (b) adapting the resources allocated to each task in a way that permits temporal and spatial multiplexing. This approach presents two design challenges.

**Challenge: Estimating resource usage for a task with a desired accuracy.** Given a task and target accuracy, we need to determine the resources to allocate to the task. If we knew the dependence of accuracy on resources, we could solve the resource allocation problem as an optimization problem subject to resource constraints. However, it is impossible to characterize the resource-accuracy dependence a priori because it depends on the traffic, the task type, the measurement algorithms, and the parameters [31]. Furthermore, if we knew the current accuracy, we could then compare it with the desired accuracy and increase/decrease the resource usage correspondingly. Unfortunately, it is also impossible to know the current accuracy because we may not have the ground truth during the measurement. For example, when we run a heavy hitter detection algorithm online, we can only know the heavy hitters that the algorithm detects (which may have false positives/negatives), but require offline processing to know the real number of heavy hitters. To address this challenge, we need to *estimate* accuracy and then dynamically increase or decrease resource usage until the desired accuracy is achieved. For example, to estimate recall (a measure of accuracy) for heavy hitter detection, we can compute the real number of heavy hitters by estimating the number of missed heavy hitters using the collected counters. In Figure 1, for example, the task cannot miss more than two heavy hitters by monitoring prefix 0* because there are only two leaves under node 0* and its total volume is less than three times the threshold. In Section 5, we use similar intuitions to describe accuracy estimators for other measurement tasks.

**Challenge: Spatial and Temporal Resource Adaptation.** As traffic changes over time, or as tasks enter and leave, an algorithm that continually estimates task accuracy and adapts resource allocation to match the desired accuracy (as discussed above) will also be able to achieve temporal multiplexing. In particular, such an

[1] Indeed, under resource constraints, less critical measurement tasks might well return very interesting/important results even well below the point of diminishing returns. We have left an exploration of this point in the design space to future work.

[2] Operators may not wish to express and reason about accuracy bounds. Therefore, a deployed system may have reasonable defaults for accuracy bounds, or allow priorities instead of accuracy bounds, and translate these priorities to desired accuracy bounds. We have left an exploration of this to future work.

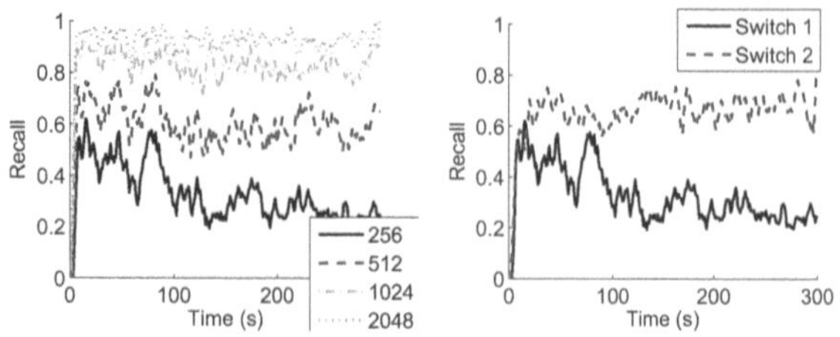

(a) Resource change (b) Spatial diversity

**Figure 2: Accuracy of HH detection**

algorithm will allocate minimal resources to measurement tasks whose traffic does not exhibit interesting phenomena (e.g., heavy hitters), freeing up resources for other tasks that may incur large changes, for example. However, this algorithm alone is not sufficient to achieve spatial multiplexing, since, for a given task, we may need to allocate different resources on different switches to achieve a desired *global* accuracy. For example, a task may wish to detect heavy hitters within a prefix $P$, but traffic for that prefix may be seen on switch $A$ and $B$. If the volume of prefix $P$'s traffic on $A$ is much higher than on $B$, it may suffice to allocate a large number of TCAM resources on $A$, and very few TCAM resources on $B$. Designing an algorithm that adapts network-wide resource allocations to achieve a desired global accuracy is a challenge, especially in the presence of traffic shifts between switches. DREAM leverages both the global estimated accuracy and a measure of accuracy estimated for each switch to decide on which switch a task needs more resources in order to achieve the desired global accuracy.

# 3. DREAM OVERVIEW

DREAM enables resource-aware software-defined measurement. It supports dynamic instantiation of measurement tasks with a specified accuracy, and automatically adapts TCAM resources allocated to each task across multiple switches. DREAM can also be extended to other measurement primitives (like sketches) and tasks for which it is possible to estimate accuracy.

**Architecture and API.** DREAM implements a collection of algorithms (defined later) running on an SDN controller. Users of DREAM submit *measurement tasks* to the system. DREAM periodically reports measurement results to users, who can use these results to reconfigure the network, install attack defenses, or increase network capacity. A DREAM user can be a network operator, or a software component that instantiates tasks and interprets results.

Our current implementation supports three *types* of measurement tasks, each with multiple parameters:

**Heavy Hitter (HH)** A heavy hitter is a traffic aggregate identified by a packet header field that exceeds a specified volume. For example, heavy hitter detection on source IP finds source IPs contributing large traffic in the network.

**Hierarchical Heavy Hitter (HHH)** Some fields in the packet header (such as the source/destination IP addresses) embed hierarchy, and many applications such as DDoS detection require aggregates computed at various levels within a hierarchy [33]. Hierarchical heavy hitter (HHH) detection is an extension of HH detection that finds longest prefixes that exceed a certain threshold even after *excluding* any HHH descendants in the prefix trie [15].

**Change Detection (CD)** Traffic anomalies such as attacks often correlate with significant changes in some aspect of a traffic aggregate (e.g., volume or number of connections). For example, large changes in traffic volume from source IPs have been used for anomaly detection [41].

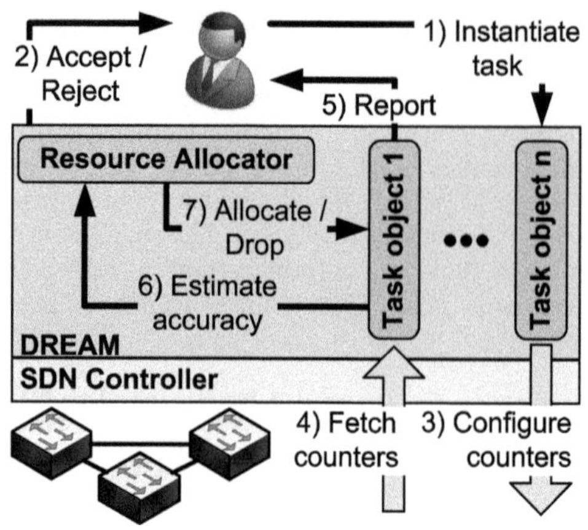


**Figure 3: DREAM System Overview**

Each of these tasks takes four parameters: a *flow filter* specifying the traffic aggregate to consider for the corresponding phenomenon (HH, HHH or CD); a *packet header field* on which the phenomenon is defined (e.g., source IP address); a *threshold* specifying the minimum volume constituting a HH or HHH or CD; and a user-specified *accuracy bound* (usually expressed as a fraction). For example, if a user specifies, for a HH task a flow filter $< 10/8, 12/8, *, *, * >$, source IP as the packet header field, a threshold of 10Mb and an accuracy of 80%, DREAM measures, with an accuracy higher than 80%, heavy hitters in the source IP field on traffic from 10/8 to 12/8, where the heavy hitter is defined as any source IP sending more than 10Mb traffic in a measurement epoch. The user does not specify the switch to execute the measurement task; multiple switches may see traffic matching a task's flow filter, and it is DREAM's responsibility to install measurement rules at all relevant switches.

**Workflow.** Figure 3 shows the DREAM workflow, illustrating both the interface to DREAM and the salient aspects of its internal operation. A user instantiates a task and specifies its parameters (step 1). Then, DREAM decides to accept or reject the task based on available resources (step 2). For each accepted task, DREAM initially configures a default number of counters at one or more switches (step 3). DREAM also creates a *task object* for each accepted task: this object encapsulates the resource allocation algorithms run by DREAM for each task.

Periodically, DREAM retrieves counters from switches and passes these to task objects (step 4). Task objects compute measurement results and report the results to users (step 5). In addition, each task object contains an *accuracy estimator* that measures current task accuracy (step 6). This estimate serves as input to the *resource allocator* component of DREAM, which determines the number of TCAM counters to allocate to each task and conveys this number to the corresponding task object (step 7). The task object determines how to use the allocated counters to measure traffic, and may reconfigure one or more switches (step 3). If a task is dropped for lack of resources, DREAM removes its task object and de-allocates the task's TCAM counters.

**DREAM Generality.** These *network-wide* measurement tasks have many applications in data centers and ISP networks. For example, they are used for multi-path routing [7], optical switching [12], network provisioning [21], threshold-based accounting [20], anomaly detection [42, 41, 26] and DDoS detection [33].

Furthermore, DREAM can be extended to more general measurement primitives beyond TCAMs. Our tasks are limited by TCAM capabilities because TCAM counters can only measure traffic volumes for specific prefixes. Moreover, TCAM-based tasks need a few epochs to drill down to the exact result. However, DREAM's key ideas — using accuracy estimators to allocate resources, and spatially multiplexing resource allocation — can be extended to other measurement primitives not currently available on commodity hardware, such as sketches. Sketches do not require controller involvement to detect events and can cover a wider range of measurement tasks than TCAMs (volume and connection-based tasks such as Super-Spreader detection) [39]. We can augment DREAM to use sketches, since sketch accuracy depends on traffic properties and it is possible to estimate this accuracy [17]. We leave discussion of these extensions to future work.

There are two main challenges in DREAM, discussed in subsequent sections: the design of the resource allocator, and the design of task-specific accuracy estimators.

# 4. DYNAMIC RESOURCE ALLOCATION

DREAM allocates TCAM resources to measurement tasks on multiple switches. Let $r_{i,s}(t)$ denote the amount of TCAM resources allocated to the $i$-th task on switch $s$ at time $t$. Each task is also associated with an instantaneous global accuracy $g_i(t)$. Recall that the accuracy of a task is a function of the task type, parameters, the number of its counters per switch and the traffic matching its flow filter on each switch.

DREAM allocates TCAM resources to maintain high average task *satisfaction*, which is the fraction of time where a task's accuracy $g_i(t)$ is greater than the operator specified bound. More important, at each switch, DREAM must respect switch capacity: the sum of $r_{i,s}(t)$ for all $i$ must be less than the total TCAM resources at switch $s$, for all $t$.

To do this, DREAM needs a *resource allocation* algorithm to allocate counters to each task (i.e., the algorithm determines $r_{i,s}(t)$). DREAM also needs an *admission control* algorithm; since the accuracy bound is inelastic (Section 2), admitting tasks indiscriminately can eventually lead to zero satisfaction as no task receives enough resources to achieve an accuracy above the specified bound.

*Strawman approaches.* One approach to resource allocation is to apply a convex optimization periodically, maximizing the number of satisfied tasks by allocating $r_{i,s}(t)$ subject to switch TCAM constraints. This optimization technique requires a characterization of the resource-accuracy curve, a function that maps target accuracy to TCAM resources needed. The same is true for an optimization technique like simulated annealing which requires the ability to predict the "goodness" of a neighboring state. As discussed in Section 2.3, however, it is hard to characterize this curve a priori, because it depends upon traffic characteristics, and the type of task.

An alternative approach is to perform this optimization iteratively: jointly (for all tasks across all switches) optimize the increase or decrease of TCAM resources, measure the resulting accuracy, and repeat until all tasks are satisfied. However, this joint optimization is hard to scale to large numbers of switches and tasks because the combinatorics of the problem is a function of product of the number of switches and the number of tasks.

If the total resource required for all tasks exceeds system capacity, the first approach may result in an infeasible optimization, and the second may not converge. These approaches may then need to *drop* tasks after having admitted them, and in these algorithms admission control is tightly coupled with resource allocation.

*Solution Overview.* DREAM adopts a simpler design, based on two key ideas. First, compared to our strawman approaches, it loosely decouples resource allocation from admission control. In most cases, DREAM can reject new tasks by carefully estimating spare TCAM capacity, and admitting a task only if sufficient spare capacity (or *headroom*) exists. This headroom accommodates variability in aggregate resource demands due to traffic changes. Second, DREAM decouples the decision of *when* to adapt a task's resources from *how* to perform the adaptation. Resource allocation decisions are made when a task's accuracy is below its target accuracy bound. The *task accuracy computation* uses global information. However, in DREAM, a *per-switch resource allocator* maps TCAM resources to tasks on each switch, which increases/decreases TCAM resources locally at each switch step-wise until the overall task accuracy converges to the desired target accuracy. This decoupling avoids the need to solve a joint optimization for resource allocation, leading to better scaling.

Below, we discuss three components of DREAM's TCAM resource management algorithm: the task accuracy computation, the per-switch resource allocator, and the headroom estimator. We observe that these components are generic and do not depend on the types of tasks (HH, HHH, or CD) that the system supports.

**Task Accuracy Computation.** As discussed above, DREAM allocates additional resources to a task if its current accuracy is below the desired accuracy bound. However, because DREAM tasks can see traffic on multiple switches, it is unclear what measure of accuracy to use to make this decision per switch. There are two possible measures: *global* accuracy and *local* accuracy on each switch. For example, if a HH task has 20 HHs on switch $A$ and 10 HHs on switch $B$, and we detect 5 and 9 true HHs on each switch respectively, the global accuracy will be 47% and the local accuracy will be 25% for $A$ and 90% for $B$.

Let $g_i$ be the global accuracy for task $i$, and $l_{i,s}$ be its local accuracy at switch $s$. Simply using $g_i$ to make allocation decisions can be misleading: at switch $s$, $l_{i,s}$ may already be above the accuracy bound, so it may be expensive to add additional resources to task $i$ at switch $s$. This is because many measurement tasks reach a point of diminishing returns in accuracy as a function of assigned resources. In the above example, we do not want to increase resources on switch $B$ when the accuracy bound is 80%. Conversely, $l_{i,s}$ may be low, but adding measurement resources to $i$ at switch $s$ may be unnecessary if $g_i$ is already above the accuracy bound. For the above example, we do not want to increase resources on switch $A$ when the accuracy bound is 40%.

This discussion motivates the use of an *overall accuracy* $a_{i,s} = max(g_i, l_{i,s})$ to decide when to make resource allocation decisions. Of course, this quantity may itself fluctuate because of traffic changes and estimation error. To minimize oscillations due to such fluctuations, we smooth the overall accuracy using an EWMA filter. In what follows, we use the term overall accuracy to refer to this smoothed value. The overall accuracy for a task is calculated by its task object in Figure 3.

**The Per-switch Resource Allocator.** The heart of DREAM is the per-switch resource allocator (Figure 3), which runs on the controller and maps TCAM counters to tasks for each switch.[3] It uses the overall accuracy $a_{i,s}(t)$ to redistribute resources from *rich tasks* (whose overall accuracy are above the accuracy bound) to *poor tasks* (whose overall accuracy is below the accuracy bound) to ensure all tasks are above the accuracy bound. DREAM makes allocation decisions at the granularity of multiple measurement epochs, an *allocation epoch.* This allows DREAM to observe the effects of its allocation decisions before making new allocations.

*Ensuring Fast Convergence with Adaptive Step Sizes:* The allocator does not a priori know the number of necessary TCAM counters for a task to achieve its target accuracy (we call this the *resource*

[3] In practice, an operator might reserve a fixed number of TCAM counters for important measurement tasks, leaving only a pool of dynamically allocable counters. DREAM operates on this pool.

*target*, denoted by $R_{i,s}$). The resource target for each task may also change over time with changing traffic. The key challenge is to quickly converge to $R_{i,s}(t)$; the longer $r_{i,s}(t)$ is below the target, the less the task's satisfaction.

Because $R_{i,s}$ is unknown and time-varying, at each allocation epoch, the allocator iteratively increases or decreases $r_{i,s}(t)$ in *steps* based on the overall accuracy (calculated in the previous epoch) to reach the right amount of resources. The size of the step determines the convergence time of the algorithm and its stability. If the step is too small, it can take a long time to move resources from a rich task to a poor one; on the other hand, larger allocation step sizes enable faster convergence, but can induce oscillations. For example, if a satisfied task needs 8 TCAMs on a switch and has 10, removing 8 TCAMs can easily drop its accuracy to zero. Intuitively, for stability, DREAM should use larger step sizes when the task is far away from $R_{i,s}(t)$, and smaller step sizes when it is close.

Since $R_{i,s}$ is unknown, DREAM estimates it by determining when a task changes its status (from poor to rich or from rich to poor) as a result of a resource change. Concretely, DREAM's resource allocation algorithm works as follows. At each measurement epoch, DREAM computes the sum of the step sizes of all the poor tasks $s_P$, and the sum of the step sizes of all the rich tasks $s_R$.[4] If $s_P \leq s_R$, then each rich task's $r_{i,s}$ is reduced by its step size, and each poor task's $r_{i,s}$ is increased in proportion to its step size (i.e., $s_R$ is distributed proportionally to the step size of each poor task). The converse happens when $s_P > s_R$. If we increase or decrease $r_{i,s}$ during one allocation epoch, and this does not change the task's rich/poor status in the next epoch, then, we increase the step size to enable the task to converge faster to its desired accuracy. However, if the status of task changes as a result of a resource change, we return TCAM resources (but use a smaller step size) to converge to $R_{i,s}$.

Figure 4 illustrates the convergence time to $R_{i,s}(t)$ for different increase/decrease policies for the step size. Here, multiplicative (M) policies change step size by a factor of 2, and additive (A) policies change step size by 4 TCAM counters every epoch. We ran this experiment with other values and the results for those values are qualitatively similar. Additive increase in AM and AA has slow convergence when $R_{i,s}(t)$ changes since it takes a long time to increase the step size. Although MA reaches the goal fast, it takes long for it to decrease the step size and converge to the goal. Therefore, we use multiplicative increase and decrease (MM) for changing the step size; we have also experimentally verified its superior performance.

As an aside, note that our problem is subtly different from fair bandwidth allocation (e.g., as in TCP). In our setting, different tasks can have different $R_{i,s}$, and the goal is to keep their allocated resources, $r_{i,s}$, above $R_{i,s}$ for more tasks, but fairness is a non-goal. By contrast, TCP attempts to converge to a target fair rate that depends upon the bottleneck bandwidth. Therefore, some of the intuitions about TCP's control laws do not apply in our setting. In the language of TCP, our approach is closest to AIAD, since our step size is independent of $r_{i,s}$. In contrast to AIAD, we use large steps when $r_{i,s}$ is far from $R_{i,s}$ for fast convergence, and we use small step sizes otherwise for saving resources by making $r_{i,s}$ close to $R_{i,s}$.

*Spare TCAM capacity, or* headroom. Since $R_{i,s}$ can change over time because of traffic changes, running the system close to the capacity can result in low task satisfaction. Therefore, DREAM maintains *headroom* of TCAM counters (5% of the total TCAM capacity in our implementation), and immediately rejects a new task if the headroom is below a target value on any switch for the task. This permits the system to absorb fluctuations in total resource usage, while ensuring high task satisfaction.

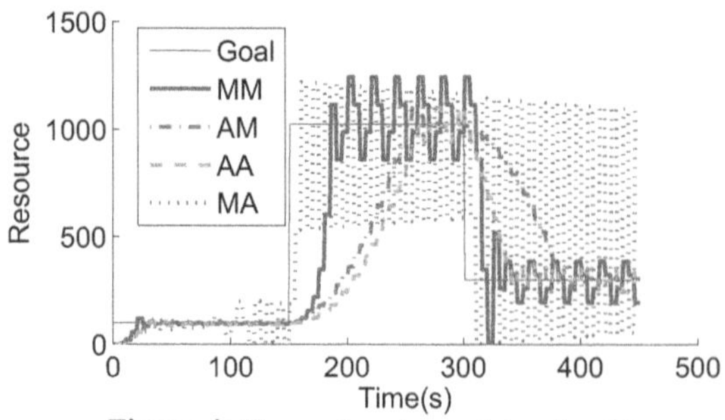

**Figure 4: Comparing step updates algorithms**

However, because it is impossible to predict traffic variability, DREAM may infrequently drop tasks when headroom is insufficient.[5] In our current design, operators can specify a *drop priority* for tasks. DREAM lets the poor tasks with low drop priority (i.e., those that should be dropped last) steal resources from those tasks with high drop priority (i.e., those that can be dropped first). When tasks with high drop priority get fewer and fewer resources on some switches, and remain poor for several consecutive epochs, DREAM drops them, to ensure that they release resources on *all* switches.

DREAM does not literally maintain a pool of unused TCAM counters as headroom. Rather, it always allocates enough TCAM counters to all tasks to maximize accuracy in the presence of traffic changes, but then calculates *effective headroom* when a new task arrives. One estimate of effective headroom is $s_R - s_P$ (the sum of the step sizes of the rich tasks minus that of the poor tasks). However, this can under-estimate headroom: a rich task may have more resources than it needs, but its step size may have converged to a small value and may not accurately reflect how many resources it can give up while still maintaining accuracy. Hence, DREAM introduces a *phantom* task on each switch whose resource requirement is equal to the headroom. Rich tasks are forced to give up resources to this phantom task, but, when a task becomes poor due to traffic changes, it can steal resources from this phantom task (this is possible because the phantom task is assigned the lowest drop priority). In this case, if $r_{ph}$ is the phantom task's resources, the effective headroom is $r_{ph} + s_R - s_P$, and DREAM uses this to determine if the new task should be admitted.

# 5. TASK OBJECTS AND ACCURACY ESTIMATION

In DREAM, task objects implement individual task instances. We begin by describing a generic algorithm that captures task object functionality. An important component of this algorithm is a *task-independent* iterative algorithm for configuring TCAM counters across multiple switches. This algorithm leverages TCAM properties, and does not depend upon details of each task type (i.e., HH, HHH or CD). We conclude the section with a discussion of the *task-dependent* components of the generic algorithm, such as the *accuracy estimator*.

This deliberate separation of functionality between generic, task-independent, and task dependent parts enables easier evolution of DREAM. To introduce a new task type, it suffices to design new algorithms for the task-dependent portion, of which the most complicated is the accuracy estimator.

[4] In our implementation, a task is considered rich only if $a_{i,s} > A + \delta$, where $A$ is the target accuracy bound. The $\delta$ is a hysteresis threshold that prevents a task from frequently oscillating between rich and poor states.

[5] Here, we assume that perimeter defenses are employed (e.g., as in data centers), so malicious traffic cannot trigger task drops. In future work, we plan to explore robustness to attack traffic.

**Algorithm 1**: DREAM task object implementation

```
1 foreach measurement iteration do
2 |   counters=fetchCounters(switches);
3 |   report = createReport(counters);
4 |   (global, locals) = t.estimateAccuracy(report, counters);
5 |   allocations = allocator.getAllocations(global, locals);
6 |   counters = configureCounters(counters, allocations);
7 |   saveCounters(counters,switches);
8 end
```

## 5.1 A Generic Algorithm for Task Objects

A DREAM task object implements Algorithm 1; each task object runs on the SDN controller. This algorithm description is generic and serves as a design pattern for any task object independent of the specific functionality it might implement (e.g., HH, HHH or CD).

Each newly admitted task is initially allocated one counter to monitor the prefix defined by the task's flow filter (Section 3). Task object structure is simple: at each *measurement interval*, a task object performs six steps. It fetches counters from switches (line 2), creates the report of task (line 3) and estimates its accuracy (line 4). Then, it invokes the per-switch allocator (line 5, Section 4) and allows the task to update its counters to match allocations and to improve its accuracy (line 6). Finally, the task object installs the new counters (line 7).

Of these six steps, one of them `configureCounters()` can be made *task-independent*. This step relies on the capabilities of TCAMs alone and not on details of how these counters are used to measure HHs, HHHs or significant changes. Two other steps are *task-dependent*: `createReport`, and `estimateAccuracy`.

## 5.2 Configuring Counters for TCAMs

**Overview.** After the resource allocator assigns TCAM counters to each task object on each switch, the tasks must decide how to *configure* those counters, namely which traffic aggregates to monitor on which switch using those counters (`configureCounters()` in Algorithm 1). A measurement task cannot monitor every flow in the network because, in general, it will not have enough TCAM counters allocated to it. Instead, it can measure traffic aggregates, trading off some accuracy. For example, TCAM-based measurement tasks can count traffic matching a traffic aggregate expressed as a wild-card rule (e.g., traffic matching an IP prefix).

The challenge then becomes choosing the right set of prefixes to monitor for a sufficiently accurate measurement while bounding resource usage. A task-independent iterative approach works as follows. It starts by measuring an initial set of prefixes in the prefix trie for the *packet header field* (source or destination IP) that is an input parameter to our tasks. Figure 5 shows an example prefix trie for four bits.

Then, if the count on one of the monitored prefixes is "interesting" from the perspective of the specific task (e.g., it reveals the possibility of heavy hitters within the prefix), it *divides* that prefix to monitor its children and use more counters. Conversely, if some prefixes are "uninteresting", it *merges* them to free counters for more useful measurements.

While this approach is task-independent, it depends upon a task-dependent component: a prefix *score* that estimates how "interesting" the prefix is for the specific task. Finally, DREAM can only measure network phenomena that last long enough for this iterative approach to complete (usually, on the order of several seconds).

**Divide-and-Merge.** Algorithm 2 describes this *divide-and-merge* algorithm in detail. The input to this algorithm includes (a) the current configuration of counters allocated to the task and (b) the new resource allocation. The output of this algorithm is a new configuration describing the prefixes to be monitored in the next measurement interval.

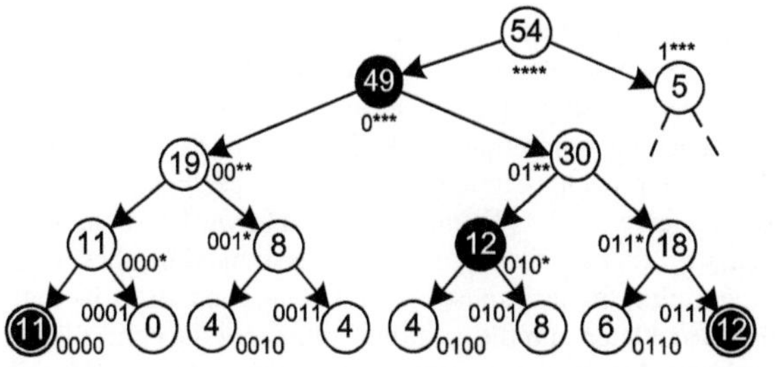


**Figure 5: A prefix trie of source IPs where the number on each node shows the bandwidth used by the associated IP prefix in Mb in an epoch. With threshold 10, the nodes in double circles are heavy hitters and the nodes with shaded background are hierarchical heavy hitters.**

In the first step, the algorithm invokes a task-dependent function that returns the score associated with each prefix currently being monitored by the task object (line 1). We describe prefix scoring later in this section, but scores are non-negative, and the *cost* of merging a set of prefixes is the sum of their score. Now, if the new TCAM counter allocation at some switches is lower than the current allocation (we say that these switches are *overloaded*), the algorithm needs to find prefixes to merge. It iteratively finds a set of prefixes with minimum cost that can be merged into their ancestors, thereby freeing entries on overloaded switches (lines 2-4). We describe how to find such candidate prefixes (`cover()` function) below. After merging, the score of the new counter will be the total score of merged counters.

Next, the algorithm iteratively divides and merges (lines 5-16). First, it picks the counter with maximum score to divide (line 6) and determines if that results in overloaded switches, designated by the set $F$ (line 7). If $F$ is empty, for example, because the resource allocator increased the allocation on all switches, no merge is necessary, so the merge cost is zero. Otherwise, we use the `cover()` function to find the counters to merge (line 10). Next, if the score of the counter is worth the cost, we apply divide and merge (lines 12-15). After dividing, the score of children will be half of the parent's score [42]. The algorithm loops over all counters until no other counter is worth dividing.

A similar algorithm has been used for individual measurement tasks (e.g., HH [26], HHH [31], and traffic changes [41]). In this paper, we provide a general task-independent algorithm, ensuring that the algorithm uses bounded resources and adapting to resource changes on multiple switches.

**Algorithm 2**: Divide and Merge

```
1  computeScores(counters);
2  while F = {over-allocated switches} ≠ Φ do
3  |   merge(cover(F, counters, allocations));
4  end
5  repeat
6  |   m = maxIndex(counters.score);
7  |   F = toFree(m, allocations);
8  |   solution.cost=0;
9  |   if F ≠ Φ then
10 |   |   solution=cover(F, counters, allocations);
11 |   end
12 |   if solution.cost<m.score then
13 |   |   divide(m);
14 |   |   merge(solution);
15 |   end
16 until no counter to divide;
```

**On multiple switches.** We now explain how divide-and-merge works across multiple switches. We consider tasks that measure phenomena on a single packet header field, and we leave to future work extensions to multiple fields. For ease of exposition, we describe our approach assuming that the user specifies the source IP field for a given task. We also assume that we know the ingress switches for each prefix that a task wishes to monitor; then to monitor the prefix, the task must install a counter on all of its ingress switches and later sum the resulting volumes at the controller.

Dividing a prefix may need an additional entry on *multiple* switches. Formally, if two sibling nodes in the prefix trie, $A$ and $B$, have traffic on switch sets $S_A$ and $S_B$, monitoring $A$ and $B$ needs one entry on each switch in $S_A$ and one on each switch in $S_B$, but monitoring the parent $P$ needs one entry on $S_P = S_A \cup S_B$ switches. Therefore, merging $A$ and $B$ and monitoring the parent prefix frees one entry on $S_A \cap S_B$. Conversely, dividing the parent prefix needs one additional entry on switches in $S_A \cap S_B$. For example, suppose that $S_{0000} = \{1,2\}$ and $S_{0001} = \{2,3\}$ in Figure 5 where set elements are switch ids. Merging $S_{0000}$ and $S_{0001}$ saves an entry on 2.

The challenge is that we may need to merge more than two sibling prefixes to their ancestor prefix to free an entry in a switch. For example, suppose that $S_{0010} = \{3,4\}$ and $S_{0011} = \{4,1\}$. To free an entry on switch 3, we must merge $S_{0001}$ and $S_{0010}$. Therefore, we merge all four counters to their common ancestor $00**$. [6]

To generalize, suppose that for each internal node $j$ in the prefix trie (ancestor of counters), we know that merging all its descendant counters would free entries on a set of switches, say $T_j$. Furthermore, let the cost for node $j$ be the sum of the scores of the descendant monitored prefixes of $j$. The function `cover()` picks those $T_j$ sets that cover the set of switches requiring additional entries, $F$, with minimum total cost. There are fast greedy approximation algorithms for Minimum Subset Cover [36].

Finally, we describe how to compute $T_j$ for each internal node. For each node $j$, we keep two sets of switches, $S_j$ and $T_j$. $S_j$ contains the switches that have traffic on $j$ and is simply $S_{j_{left}} \cup S_{j_{right}}$ when $j$ has two children $j_{left}, j_{right}$. $T_j$ contains the switches that will free at least one entry if we merge all its descendant counters to $j$. Defining it recursively, $T_j$ includes $T_{j_{left}}$ and $T_{j_{right}}$, and contains (by the reasoning described above) the common entries between the switches having traffic on the left and right children, $S_{j_{left}} \cap S_{j_{right}}$. $T_j$ is empty for prefixes currently being monitored.

## 5.3 Task-Dependent Algorithms

Beyond these task-independent algorithms, each task object implements three task-dependent algorithms. We present the task-dependent algorithms for HH, HHH, and CD tasks. A key task-dependent component is accuracy estimation, and we consider two task accuracy metrics: *precision*, the fraction of retrieved items that are true positives; and *recall*, the fraction of true positives that are retrieved. For these definitions, an item refers to a HH, HHH or change detection. Depending on the type of measurement task, DREAM estimates one of these accuracy measures to determine TCAM resource allocation.

The task-dependent algorithms for these tasks are summarized in Table 1, but we discuss some of the non-trivial algorithms below.

**Heavy hitters:** A heavy hitter is a traffic aggregate that exceeds a specified volume. For example, we can define heavy hitters as the source IPs whose traffic exceeds a threshold $\theta$ over a measurement epoch. Figure 5 shows an example of bandwidth usage for each IP prefix during an epoch. With a threshold of $\theta = 10Mb$, there are a

| Task | Create report | Estimate accuracy | Score |
|---|---|---|---|
| HH | Report exact counters with $volume > \theta$ | Estimate recall by estimating missed HHs | $\frac{volume}{\#wildcards+1}$ |
| HHH | Traverse prefix trie bottom-up and report a prefix $h$ if $volume_h - \sum_i volume_i > \theta$ where $i$ is a descendant detected HHH of $h$ [15] | Estimate precision by finding if a detected HHH is a true one | $volume$ |
| CD | Report exact counters with $\lvert volume - mean \rvert > \theta$ | Estimate recall by estimating missed changes | $\frac{\lvert volume-mean \rvert}{\#wildcards+1}$ |

**Table 1: Task dependent methods**

total of two leaf heavy-hitters shown in double circles. Our divide-and-merge approach iteratively drills-down to these two leaves.

*Accuracy Estimation:* For our TCAM-based algorithm, all detected HHs are true, which means the precision is always one in this algorithm. For this reason, we use recall as a measure of accuracy for HH detection. Doing so requires an estimate of the number of true HHs the algorithm misses. We use the smaller of the following two bounds to estimate the missed heavy hitters under a non-exact prefix. First, a prefix with $b$ wildcard bits cannot miss more than $2^b$ heavy hitters. For example, prefix $0***$ in Figure 5 has 8 heavy hitters at most. Second, if the volume of the prefix is $v$, there can only be $\lfloor \frac{v}{\theta} \rfloor$ missed heavy hitters. This bound for prefix $0***$ will be 4.

Finally, we need to estimate both local and global recall (Section 4). We compute the local recall for a switch based on detected HHs, and we estimate missed HHs from prefixes that have traffic on the switch. However, there are cases where only a subset of switches are bottlenecked (i.e., they have used all available counters, so it is not possible to further divide prefixes). In this case, we only consider missed HHs on these switches.

**Hierarchical heavy hitters:** A variant of heavy hitters, called *Hierarchical Heavy Hitters (HHHs)* [15] is useful for anomaly detection [42] and DDoS detection [33]. A HHH is (recursively) defined by the longest IP prefixes that contribute traffic exceeding a threshold $\theta$ of total traffic, after *excluding* any HHH descendants in the prefix trie. For example in Figure 5, prefix 010* is a HHH as IPs 0100 and 0101 *collectively* have large traffic, but prefix 01** is not a HHH because excluding descendent HHHs (010* and 0111), its traffic is less than the threshold.

*Accuracy Estimation:* For HHHs, our algorithm estimates precision by determining whether a detected HHH is a true positive or a false positive. Our algorithm assigns a precision value to each detected HHH: the value is either 0 if it is a false positive, 1 if a true positive, or fractional if there is ambiguity in the determination, as discussed below. The overall accuracy estimate is an average of these values. The method for making these value assessments is different for HHHs without and with detected descendant HHHs.

If a detected HHH $h$ has no detected descendant HHHs (e.g., 0000, 010*, 0111 in Figure 5), it is a false positive HHH if it has been detected instead of one of its descendants. So, for it to be a true positive HHH, we need to ensure that none of its descendants could have been a HHH. There are three cases. (1) $h$ is an exact IP. (2) We monitored the descendants of $h$ and their volume is below the threshold $\theta$. For example, if we monitor 0100 and 0101, we can confirm that the detected HHH 010* is a true one. In these two cases, it is easy to tell $h$ is a true HHH. (3) We only monitored $h$ and do not know about its descendants. If $h$ has a count larger than $2\theta$, then $h$ cannot be a true HHH, because the volume of at least one of its children must be above $\theta$. If the volume is smaller than $2\theta$, either the detected prefix or one of its sub-prefixes is HHH, so we set its precision value to 0.5.

For an HHH $h$ with detected descendant HHHs, the error in the detected descendant HHHs can make $h$ a false HHH. For example

[6] Although we could just merge those two to $00**$, this creates overlapping counters that makes the algorithm more complex and adds delay in saving rules at switches.

in Figure 5, suppose that we report 0000, 010* and 011* as HHHs. Now, the volume for 0*** excluding descendant HHHs will be 8 because of false detection of 011*. Therefore, instead of 0***, we detect **** as HHH. In this scenario, we have over-approximated the traffic from descendant HHHs of ****. In the worst case, the over-approximated traffic has been excluded from a child of the detected HHH. Thus, for each child prefix, we find if adding up these over-approximations could make them a HHH. If any child with a new volume becomes HHH, the parent cannot be, so as a heuristic, we halve the precision weight of $h$. The over-approximation for a HHH confirmed to be true is 0, and the over-approximation for other HHHs can be at most $volume - \theta$.

The global precision is the average precision value of detected HHHs. To compute the local precision per switch, we compute the average precision value of HHH prefixes from each switch. If a HHH has traffic from multiple switches, we give the computed precision value only to bottleneck switches, and precision 1 to other switches.

For HHH tasks, recall can be calculated similar to HH tasks. We have experimentally found that, for HHH, recall is correlated with precision.

**Change detection:** A simple way to define the traffic change of a prefix is to check if the difference between its current volume and a moving average of its volume exceeds a specified threshold. In this sense, change detection is similar to HH detection: a change is significant if $|volume - mean| > \theta$. Thus, for change detection, reporting, prefix scoring, and accuracy estimation are similar to those for HH tasks (Table 1): wherever volume is used in HH tasks, $|volume - mean|$ is used for CD.

# 6. EVALUATION

We have implemented a complete prototype of DREAM, and use this to evaluate our approach and compare it with alternatives. We then use simulations to explore the performance of DREAM on larger networks, and also study its parameter sensitivity.

## 6.1 Evaluation Methodology

**DREAM Implementation:** We have implemented the DREAM resource allocator and the task objects in Java on the Floodlight controller [4]. Our implementation interfaces both with hardware OpenFlow switches, and with Open vSwitch [5]. We have also implemented alternative resource allocation strategies, described below. Our total implementation is nearly 20,000 lines of code.

**DREAM Parameter Settings:** We use a one second measurement interval and a two second allocation interval. We set the headroom to 5% of the switch capacity and drop tasks if their global accuracy is below the bound for 6 consecutive allocation iterations. The sensitivity of DREAM to these parameters is explored in Section 6.4.

**Tasks:** Our workload consists of the three types of tasks, HH, HHH and CD, both individually and in combination. We choose 80% as the default accuracy bound for all tasks since we have empirically observed that to be the point of diminishing returns for many tasks, but also explore DREAM's performance for other choices of accuracy bounds. We smooth the local and global accuracies using EWMA with history weight of $\alpha = 0.4$. The flow filters for the tasks are chosen randomly from prefixes with 12 wildcard bits to fit all our tasks. The default threshold for the above tasks is 8Mb, and for change detection we also use the history weight of $\alpha = 0.8$. Our default drop priority is to drop the most recent task first.

By controlling the mapping of prefixes to switches, we create different scenarios of tasks on switches. For example, a tenant can own a subnet of /12, and its virtual machines in this subnet can be located on different switches. If we assign multiple /10 prefixes to switches (i.e., each switch sees traffic from many tenants), each task will have traffic from one switch. However, if we assign /15 prefixes to switches (i.e., one tenant sends traffic from many switches), each task monitors traffic from 8 switches at most.

Tasks run for an average of 5 minutes. For evaluations on our prototype, 256 tasks having traffic from 8 switches arrive based on a Poisson process during 20 minutes. For the large-scale simulation, 4096 tasks having traffic from 8 out of 32 switches arrive during 80 minutes. We note that these are fairly adversarial settings for task dynamics, and are designed to stress test DREAM and other alternatives.

Finally, we use a 5-hour CAIDA packet trace [3] from a 10Gbps link with an average 2Gbps load. We divide it into 5-min chunks, each of which contains 16 /4 prefixes, of which only prefixes with >1% total traffic are used. Each task randomly picks a /4 prefix which is mapped to its /12 filter

**Evaluation metrics:** We evaluate DREAM and other alternatives using three metrics. The *satisfaction* of a task is the percentage of time a task has an accuracy above the bound when the task was active. In results from our prototype, we use *estimated* accuracy because delays in installing TCAM counters in the actual experiment make it difficult for us to assess the ground-truth in the traffic seen by a switch. We have found in our evaluations that the estimated accuracy consistently under-estimates the real accuracy by 5-10% on average, so our prototype results are a conservative estimate of the actual satisfaction that tasks would see in practice. In our simulation results, we use the real accuracy.

We show both the average and $5^{th}$ percentile for this metric over all tasks. The latter metric captures the tail behavior of resource allocation: a 5-th percentile of 20 means that 95% of tasks had an accuracy above the bound for 20% of their lifetime. The *drop* and *rejection* ratios measure the percentage of tasks that are dropped and rejected, respectively. While the rejection ratios can be a function of the workload and can be high in highly overloaded conditions, we expect drop ratios to be small for a viable scheme (i.e., it is desirable that a task, once admitted, is not dropped, but may be rejected before admission).

**Alternative Strategies:** One alternative we explore is to reserve a *Fixed* fraction of counters on each switch for a task, and reject tasks for which this fixed allocation cannot be made. While we evaluated fixed allocation with different fractions, here we only show the results for the scenario that allocates $\frac{1}{32}$ of the resources on a switch per task. Larger allocations result in higher satisfaction for fewer tasks and a higher rejection ratio, and smaller fixed allocations accept more tasks at the expense of lower satisfaction. A more complex algorithm is to give *Equal* amounts of resources to each task. When a task joins, it gets an equal share of counters as other tasks on the switches it has traffic from. The allocations are also updated when a task leaves, and *Equal* does not reject tasks.

**Experimental setup:** We replay the CAIDA traffic on 8 switches. We attempted to evaluate DREAM on a modern hardware switch (the Pica8 3290 [6]) but its delay for rule installation is unacceptably high: 256 rules take 1 second, and 512 rules take 10 seconds. We believe better engineering will result in improved installation times in the future; indeed, for applications with tight control loops like ours, it is essential to improve installation times in hardware switches. Our evaluations are conducted on software switches [5] that can delete and save 512 rules in less than 20ms. We also reduce control loop delay by using *incremental update* of TCAM counters and associated rules, updating at each epoch only the rules that have changed from the previous epoch. We show below that this strategy results in acceptable rule installation performance (Section 6.5). In our experiments, the DREAM prototype runs on a Floodlight controller [4] on a quad core 2.4 Ghz Xeon processor connected to the switches through a 1Gbps shared link with ping delay of 0.25ms.

## 6.2 Results from Prototype

Figure 6 shows, for different switch capacities, the $5^{th}$ percentile and mean satisfaction of tasks for HHH, HH, and CD separately, as well as a combined workload that runs a mixture of these tasks. *The mean value is the upper end of each vertical bar, and the $5^{th}$ percentile is the lower end.* These figures demonstrate DREAM's superior performance compared to the alternatives, both in terms of the mean and the $5^{th}$ percentile.

*Large capacity switches.* For large switches, DREAM can keep almost all tasks satisfied by temporally and spatially multiplexing TCAM resources without rejecting or dropping any task (Figure 7). For example, Figure 6(b) shows that 95% of tasks were satisfied for more than 94% of their lifetime. By contrast, a high mean and a dramatically lower $5^{th}$ percentile (about 40%, or nearly 2× less than DREAM) for Equal indicate that this scheme has undesirable tail behavior: it keeps tasks that require fewer resources satisfied, but leaves large tasks unsatisfied. This is undesirable in general: larger tasks are where the action happens, in a manner of speaking, and cannot be left dissatisfied. The Fixed approach achieves high average satisfaction, but has two drawbacks: poor tail performance, and a high rejection ratio of about 30%.

*Highly resource-constrained switches.* For smaller switches, where our workload overloads the resources on switches, DREAM leverages rejection to limit the load and keep active tasks satisfied by multiplexing resources. For example, in Figure 6(a) for a switch with 512 counters, DREAM rejects about 50% of tasks, but can keep 95% of tasks satisfied for more than 70% of their lifetime. By contrast, in this setting, Equal performs pathologically worse: its average satisfaction is 20% and 5% of tasks under Equal get nearly zero satisfaction. This is because Equal does not perform admission control and it under-provisions resources in small switches and thus gets low satisfaction. We emphasize that this is an adversarial workload and represents a high degree of overload: DREAM has to reject nearly 50% of the tasks, and drop about 10% in order to satisfy the remaining tasks. Also, DREAM's mean and $5^{th}$ percentile satisfaction is a little lower than for the larger switch capacity case, mostly because the adaptation required to fit tasks into the smaller switch requires more allocation epochs to converge.

Across different task types, the results are qualitatively consistent, save for two exceptions. First, the drop ratio for HH detection (Figure 7(a)) increases from switch capacity of 512 to 1024, which is likely because of a decrease in the rejection ratio. Moreover, its drop rate is higher than other tasks, which we believe is because we under-estimate the accuracy of tasks. Remember that to calculate the number of missed HHs under a prefix we used the bound of $\frac{volume}{\theta}$. However, the missed HHs could have larger volumes than $\theta$ and make this upper bound loose. This loose upper bound ensures better $5^{th}$ percentile performance than other schemes we have tried, so it seems a better design choice: it drops more tasks to favor satisfying more. Second, the average satisfaction of Equal and Fixed is higher than other task types for change detection (but the tail performance is poor). This is because, in our dataset, not all epochs have a significant change, thus the tasks are satisfied in those epochs even with very small resources.

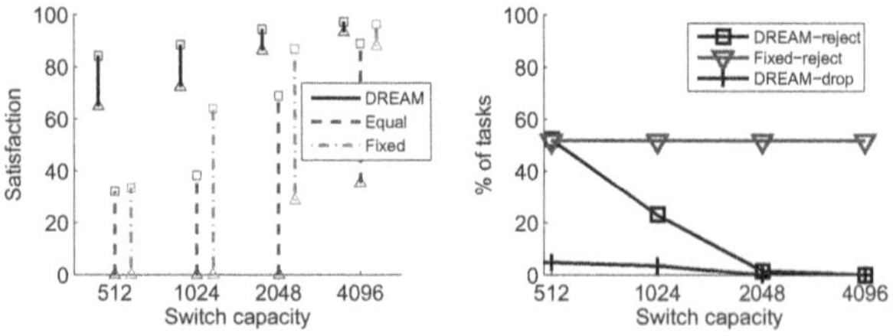

(a) Satisfaction (b) Rejection and drop

**Figure 8: Large scale simulation (combined workload)**

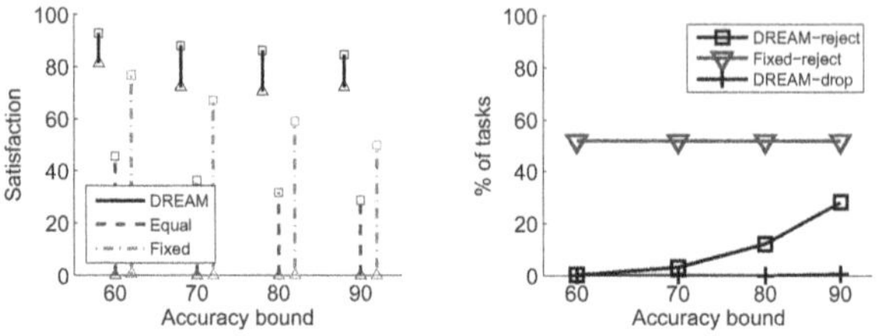

(a) Satisfaction (b) Rejection and drop

**Figure 9: Accuracy bound paramter sensitivity analysis**

## 6.3 Results from Simulation at Scale

We use simulation to study the performance of DREAM and other alternatives at larger scale. Our simulator uses the same code base as the prototype and is validated for the same setting [32].

DREAM's superior performance is also evident in larger networks. Figure 8 compares the satisfaction and rejection ratio of the combined workload on 32 switches with 4096 tasks (results for individual task types are quantitatively similar). In this much larger setting, the superior tail satisfaction of DREAM at low load (high capacity) and the superior average satisfaction at high load (low capacity) are strikingly evident. As with smaller networks, DREAM has a small drop ratio (less than 5%) at high load.

## 6.4 Parameter Sensitivity Analysis

To understand how sensitive our results are to changes in various parameters, we conduct several experiments with a switch capacity of 1024 TCAM entries, but vary several other parameters. We note that for our baseline workload, 1024 TCAM entries represent a constrained setting. For this set of results, we show results for a specific type of task (HHH), rather than using results from a combined workload, as this makes it easier to interpret the results (Figures 9). A companion report [32] evaluates sensitivity to HHH threshold, number of switches per task, task duration and task arrival rate. The qualitative behavior of other tasks is similar.

**DREAM keeps tasks satisfied for different accuracy bounds.** With higher accuracy bounds the allocation becomes harder, since tasks in general need more resources, but DREAM can keep more tasks satisfied with a smaller rejection rate compared to Fixed allocation (Figure 9). DREAM is also uniformly better than Equal allocation because it effectively multiplexes resources across tasks.

**Headroom is important to keep drop rate low.** If DREAM does not reject tasks a priori, many tasks will starve just after joining the system. For example, Figure 10(b) shows a drop rate of 30% for DREAM when there is no headroom at an allocation interval of 2s. Interestingly, the level of headroom does not seem to make a significant difference in the statistics of satisfaction, but can affect drop rates. With a 5% and 10% headroom, drop rates are negligible.

Other DREAM parameters include allocation interval, drop threshold, and the MM algorithm multiplicative factor. Figure 10(a) shows

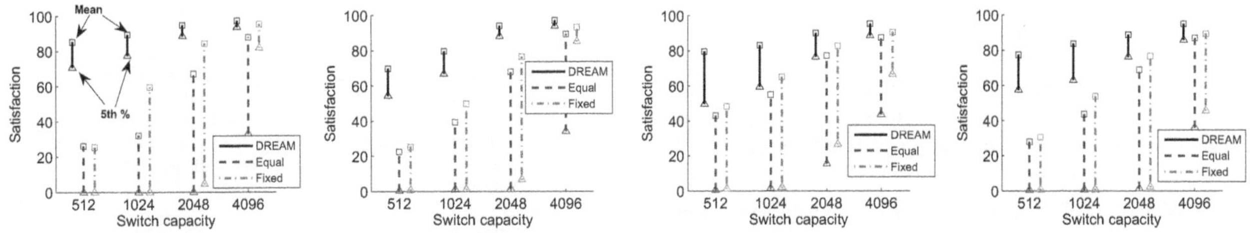

(a) HH (b) HHH (c) CD (d) Combined workload

**Figure 6: Satisfaction in prototype**

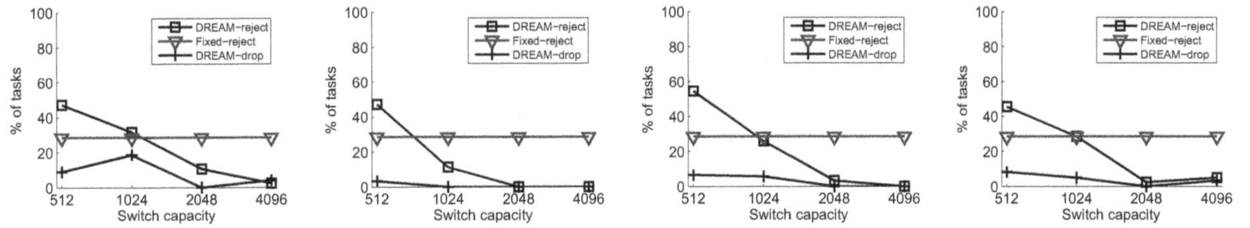

(a) HH (b) HHH (c) CD (d) Combined workload

**Figure 7: Rejection and drop in prototype**

that allocating resources infrequently with a larger allocation interval results in lower satisfaction because DREAM cannot adapt resources quickly enough. Smaller drop threshold increases the drop rate and satisfaction, and increasing the multiplicative factor of the MM algorithm causes higher rejection rate because poor tasks overshoot their goal by large change step sizes and thereby reduce headroom. Note that a smaller multiplication factor requires a larger drop threshold to avoid unnecessary drops in under-loaded cases.

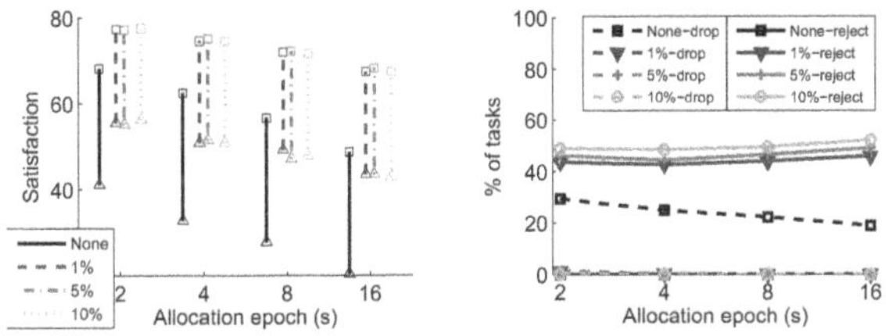

(a) Satisfaction (b) Rejection and drop

**Figure 10: Headroom and allocation epoch (combined workload)**

## 6.5 Control Loop Delay

The delay of the control loop – the process of configuring counters and updating rules in TCAMs – can affect the accuracy of real prototypes because important events can be missed while these counters are being updated. We calculate the control loop delay by calculating the average delay between fetching the counters from the switches to receiving the OpenFlow barrier reply from all switches after installing incremental rules on the prototype.

Figure 11(a) breaks down the delay of control loop into: saving the incremental rules, fetching the counters, allocating resources, creating the report and estimating its accuracy, configuring counters through divide and merge algorithm and the runtime overhead for combining counter statistics from multiple switches and creating a counter on multiple switches for all tasks. The interesting points are: (1) the allocation delay (the overhead of computing new allocations) is negligible compared to other delays; (2) the average ($95^{th}\%$) allocation delay decreases with increasing switch size from 0.65 (3.1) ms to 0.5 (1.3) ms, because for larger switches, fewer tasks are dissatisfied although more tasks have been admitted; (3) fetch times dominate save times (although it takes longer to save or delete a counter than to fetch one) because we fetch all counters, but only delete and save incrementally. For example, for the case of switches with 1024 TCAM capacity, on average in each epoch 90% of the counters did not change. This number increases for larger switch capacities as tasks need to configure their counters less frequently because (a) they already have an accurate view of network (b) their allocations changes rarely as more tasks are satisfied with more resources.

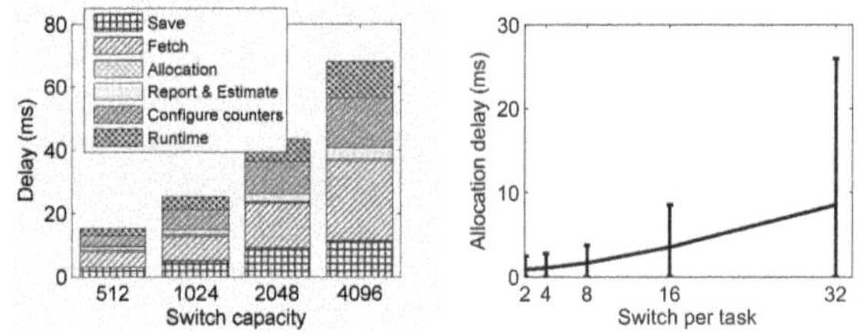

(a) Prototype delay (b) Allocation delay

**Figure 11: Control loop delay (combined workload)**

Finally, the DREAM controller scales to many tasks because it is highly parallelizable; each task can run on a core and each per-switch allocator can run separately. The per-switch resource allocator does more work as we increase the number of switches per task, since each switch sees more tasks. Figure 11(b) shows that the mean, and $95^{th}$ percentile of allocation delay in the large scale simulation environment (on a 32 core machine) increases for larger number of switches per task, but the mean is still less than 10ms and the control loop delay is still dominated by other (unavoidable) latencies in the system.

# 7. RELATED WORK

**Software-defined measurement and programmable measurement:** Prior work has explored different measurement primitives [20, 35], but, unlike DREAM, assumes *offline* analysis of collected measurement data, and thus cannot dynamically change their measurement resource usage when traffic changes or more measurement tasks come.

Previous work on software-defined measurement [39, 31, 25] and programmable measurement [18, 40] has shown the benefits of allowing operators or cloud tenants to customize the measurement for their traffic with different measurement primitives. Amazon CloudWatch [2] also provides simple customized measurement interface for tenants. Like these, DREAM allows measurement tasks to specify the flows and traffic characteristics to measure, but, beyond prior work, provides dynamic resource allocation solutions to enable more and finer-grained measurement tasks.

**Resource allocation of measurement tasks:** OpenSketch [39] uses *worst case* theoretical bounds of sketches to allocate resources on a single switch to measurement tasks. CSAMP [34] uses consistent sampling to distribute flow measurement on multiple switches for a single measurement task and aims at maximizing the flow coverage. Volley [29] uses a sampling-based approach to monitor state changes in the network, with the goal of minimizing the number of sampling operations. Payless [14] decides the measurement frequency for concurrent measurement tasks to minimize the controller bandwidth usage, but does not provide any guarantee on accuracy or bound on switch resources. In contrast, DREAM focuses on flow-based rules in TCAM. DREAM dynamically allocates network-wide resources to multiple measurement tasks to achieve their given accuracy bound.

**TCAM-based measurement and accuracy estimators:** Previous TCAM-based algorithms for specific measurement tasks either only work on a single switch [31, 26, 25] or do not adjust counters for bounded resources at switches [41, 26]. We designed a generic divide-and-merge measurement framework for multiple switches with resource constraints. Previous work has proved the theoretical bounds for the *worst case* resource usage for only hash-based measurements [17, 16]. We proposed heuristics for estimating the accuracy of TCAM-based measurement algorithms by exploiting relationships between counters already collected.

# 8. CONCLUSIONS

Measurement is fundamental for network management systems. DREAM enables operators and cloud tenants to flexibly specify their measurement tasks in a network, and dynamically allocates TCAM resources to these tasks based on the resource-accuracy tradeoffs for each task. DREAM ensures high accuracy for tasks, while taking network-wide resource constraints as well as traffic and task dynamics into account.

# 9. ACKNOWLEDGEMENTS

We thank our shepherd Rodrigo Fonseca and SIGCOMM reviewers for their helpful feedback. This paper is partially supported by Software R&D Center at Samsung Electronics, Cisco, Google, and USC Zumberge.

# 10. REFERENCES

[1] http://news.netcraft.com/archives/2013/05/20/amazon-web-services-growth-unrelenting.html.

[2] Amazon CloudWatch. http://aws.amazon.com/cloudwatch/.

[3] CAIDA Anonymized Internet Traces 2012. http://www.caida.org/data/passive/passive_2012_dataset.xml.

[4] Floodlight. http://www.projectfloodlight.org/floodlight/.

[5] Open vSwitch. http://openvswitch.org/.

[6] Pica8 P-3290 switch. http://www.pica8.com/documents/pica8-datasheet-48x1gbe-p3290-p3295.pdf.

[7] M. Al-Fares, S. Radhakrishnan, B. Raghavan, N. Huang, and A. Vahdat. Hedera: Dynamic Flow Scheduling for Data Center Networks. In *NSDI*, 2010.

[8] M. Alizadeh, S. Yang, M. Sharif, S. Katti, N. McKeown, B. Prabhakar, and S. Shenker. pFabric: Minimal Near-optimal Datacenter Transport. In *SIGCOMM*, 2013.

[9] A. M. Azab, P. Ning, and X. Zhang. SICE: A Hardware-level Strongly Isolated Computing Environment for x86 Multi-core Platforms. In *CCS*, 2011.

[10] H. Ballani, P. Costa, T. Karagiannis, and A. I. Rowstron. Towards Predictable Datacenter Networks. In *SIGCOMM*, 2011.

[11] T. Benson, A. Anand, A. Akella, and M. Zhang. MicroTE: Fine Grained Traffic Engineering for Data Centers. In *CoNEXT*, 2011.

[12] K. Chen, A. Singla, A. Singh, K. Ramachandran, L. Xu, Y. Zhang, X. Wen, and Y. Chen. OSA: An Optical Switching Architecture for Data Center Networks With Unprecedented Flexibility. In *NSDI*, 2012.

[13] Y. Chen, R. Griffith, J. Liu, R. H. Katz, and A. D. Joseph. Understanding TCP Incast Throughput Collapse in Datacenter Networks. In *WREN*, 2009.

[14] S. R. Chowdhury, M. F. Bari, R. Ahmed, and R. Boutaba. PayLess: A Low Cost Network Monitoring Framework for Software Defined Networks. In *IEEE/IFIP NOMS*, 2014.

[15] G. Cormode, F. Korn, S. Muthukrishnan, and D. Srivastava. Finding Hierarchical Heavy Hitters in Data Streams. In *VLDB*, 2003.

[16] G. Cormode and S. Muthukrishnan. An Improved Data Stream Summary: The Count-Min Sketch and its Applications. *Journal of Algorithms*, 55(1), 2005.

[17] G. Cormode and S. Muthukrishnan. Summarizing and Mining Skewed Data Streams. In *SIAM Conference on Data Mining (SDM)*, 2005.

[18] C. Cranor, T. Johnson, O. Spataschek, and V. Shkapenyuk. Gigascope: a Stream Database for Network Applications. In *SIGMOD*, 2003.

[19] A. Curtis, J. Mogul, J. Tourrilhes, P. Yalagandula, P. Sharma, and S. Banerjee. DevoFlow: Scaling Flow Management for High-Performance Networks. In *SIGCOMM*, 2011.

[20] C. Estan and G. Varghese. New Directions in Traffic Measurement and Accounting. *SIGCOMM Computer Communication Review*, 32(4):323–336, 2002.

[21] A. Feldmann, A. Greenberg, C. Lund, N. Reingold, J. Rexford, and F. True. Deriving Traffic Demands for Operational IP Networks: Methodology and Experience. *Transactions on Networking*, 9(3), 2001.

[22] R. Gandhi, H. Liu, Y. Hu, G. Lu, J. Padhye, L. Yuan, and M. Zhang. Duet: Cloud Scale Load Balancing with Hardware and Software. In *SIGCOMM*, 2014.

[23] D. Y. Huang, K. Yocum, and A. C. Snoeren. High-fidelity Switch Models for Software-defined Network Emulation. In *HotSDN*, 2013.

[24] S. Jain, A. Kumar, S. Mandal, J. Ong, L. Poutievski, A. Singh, S. Venkata, J. Wanderer, J. Zhou, M. Zhu, et al. B4: Experience with a Globally-deployed Software Defined WAN. In *SIGCOMM*, 2013.

[25] L. Jose, M. Yu, and J. Rexford. Online Measurement of Large Traffic Aggregates on Commodity Switches. In *Hot-ICE*, 2011.

[26] F. Khan, N. Hosein, C.-N. Chuah, and S. Ghiasi. Streaming Solutions for Fine-Grained Network Traffic Measurements and Analysis. In *ANCS*, 2011.

[27] A. Kumar, M. Sung, J. J. Xu, and J. Wang. Data Streaming Algorithms for Efficient and Accurate Estimation of Flow Size Distribution. In *SIGMETRICS*, 2004.

[28] A. Lall, V. Sekar, M. Ogihara, J. Xu, and H. Zhang. Data Streaming Algorithms for Estimating Entropy of Network Traffic. In *SIGMETRICS/Performance*, 2006.

[29] S. Meng, A. K. Iyengar, I. M. Rouvellou, and L. Liu. Volley: Violation Likelihood Based State Monitoring for Dataceners. *ICDCS*, 2013.

[30] M. Mitzenmacher, T. Steinke, and J. Thaler. Hierarchical Heavy Hitters with the Space Saving Algorithm. *arXiv:1102.5540*, 2011.

[31] M. Moshref, M. Yu, and R. Govindan. Resource/Accuracy Tradeoffs in Software-Defined Measurement. In *HotSDN*, 2013.

[32] M. Moshref, M. Yu, R. Govindan, and A. Vahdat. DREAM: Dynamic Resource Allocation for Software-defined Measurement. Technical Report 14-945, Computer Science, USC, 2014. http://www.cs.usc.edu/assets/007/91037.pdf.

[33] V. Sekar, N. G. Duffield, O. Spatscheck, J. E. van der Merwe, and H. Zhang. LADS: Large-scale Automated DDoS Detection System. In *ATC*, 2006.

[34] V. Sekar, M. K. Reiter, W. Willinger, H. Zhang, R. R. Kompella, and D. G. Andersen. CSAMP: A System for Network-Wide Flow Monitoring. In *NSDI*, 2008.

[35] V. Sekar, M. K. Reiter, and H. Zhang. Revisiting the Case for a Minimalist Approach for Network Flow Monitoring. In *IMC*, 2010.

[36] V. V. Vazirani. *Approximation Algorithms*. Springer-Verlag New York, Inc., 2001.

[37] Z. Wang and X. Jiang. Hypersafe: A Lightweight Approach to Provide Lifetime Hypervisor Control-flow Integrity. In *SP*, 2010.

[38] D. Xie, N. Ding, Y. C. Hu, and R. Kompella. The Only Constant is Change: Incorporating Time-varying Network Reservations in Data Centers. *SIGCOMM Computer Communication Review*, 42(4), 2012.

[39] M. Yu, L. Jose, and R. Miao. Software Defined Traffic Measurement with OpenSketch. In *NSDI*, 2013.

[40] L. Yuan, C.-N. Chuah, and P. Mohapatra. ProgME: Towards Programmable Network MEasurement. *Transactions on Networking*, 19(1), 2011.

[41] Y. Zhang. An Adaptive Flow Counting Method for Anomaly Detection in SDN. In *CoNEXT*, 2013.

[42] Y. Zhang, S. Singh, S. Sen, N. Duffield, and C. Lund. Online Identification of Hierarchical Heavy Hitters: Algorithms, Evaluation, and Applications. In *IMC*, 2004.

# Decentralized Task-Aware Scheduling for Data Center Networks

Fahad R. Dogar, Thomas Karagiannis, Hitesh Ballani, and Antony Rowstron
Microsoft Research
{fdogar, thomkar, hiballan, antr}@microsoft.com

## ABSTRACT

Many data center applications perform rich and complex tasks (e.g., executing a search query or generating a user's news-feed). From a network perspective, these tasks typically comprise multiple flows, which traverse different parts of the network at potentially different times. Most network resource allocation schemes, however, treat all these flows in isolation – rather than as part of a task – and therefore only optimize flow-level metrics.

In this paper, we show that task-aware network scheduling, which groups flows of a task and schedules them together, can reduce both the average as well as tail completion time for typical data center applications. To achieve these benefits in practice, we design and implement Baraat, a *decentralized* task-aware scheduling system. Baraat schedules tasks in a FIFO order but avoids head-of-line blocking by dynamically changing the level of multiplexing in the network. Through experiments with Memcached on a small testbed and large-scale simulations, we show that Baraat outperforms state-of-the-art decentralized schemes (e.g., pFabric) as well as centralized schedulers (e.g., Orchestra) for a wide range of workloads (e.g., search, analytics, etc).

**Categories and Subject Descriptors:** C.2.5 [Computer-Communication Networks]: Network Protocols
**Keywords:** datacenter; transport; scheduling; response time

## 1. INTRODUCTION

Today's data center applications perform rich and complex *tasks*, such as answering a search query or building a user's social news-feed. These tasks involve hundreds and thousands of components, *all* of which need to finish before a task is considered complete. This has motivated efforts to allocate data center resources in a "task-aware" fashion. Examples include task-aware allocation of caches [6], network bandwidth [11], and CPUs and network [7].

In recent work, Coflow [10] argues for tasks (or Coflows) as a first-order abstraction for the network data plane. This allows applications to expose their semantics to the network, and the network to optimize for application-level metrics. For example, allocating network bandwidth to tasks in a FIFO fashion, such that they are scheduled over the network one at a time, can improve the average task completion time as compared to per-flow fair sharing (e.g., TCP) [11]. While an exciting idea with important architectural ramifications, we still lack a good understanding of the performance implications of task-aware network scheduling in data centers– (i). How should tasks be scheduled across the network?, (ii). Can such scheduling only improve average performance?, and (iii). Can we realize these gains for small (sub-second) tasks common in data centers? In this paper, we answer these questions and make the following three contributions.

First, *we study policies regarding the order in which tasks should be scheduled.* We show that typical data center workloads include some fraction of heavy tasks (in terms of their network footprint), so obvious scheduling candidates like FIFO and size-based ordering perform poorly. We thus propose FIFO-LM or FIFO with *limited multiplexing*, a policy that schedules tasks based on their arrival order, but dynamically changes the level of multiplexing when heavy tasks are encountered. This ensures small tasks are not blocked behind heavy tasks that are, in turn, not starved.

Second, *we show that task-aware policies like FIFO-LM (and even FIFO) can reduce both the average and the tail task completion times.* They do so by smoothing bursty arrivals and ensuring that a task's completion is only impacted by tasks that arrive before it. For example, data center applications typically have multiple *stages* where a subsequent stage can only start when the previous stage finishes. In such scenarios, FIFO scheduling can smooth out a burst of tasks that arrive at the first stage. As a result, tasks observe less contention at the later stages, thereby improving the tail completion times.

Third, *we design Baraat, a decentralized task-aware scheduling system for data centers.* Baraat avoids the problems associated with centralized scheduling (i.e., scalability, fault-tolerance, etc) while addressing the challenges of decentralized scheduling i.e., making coordinated scheduling decisions while incurring low coordination overhead. To achieve this, Baraat uses a simple heuristic. Each task has a globally unique priority – *all* flows within the task use this priority, irrespective of *when* these flows start or *which* part of the network they traverse. This leads to consistent treatment for all flows of a task across time and space, and improves the chances that all flows of a task make progress together.

By generating flow priorities in a task-aware fashion, Baraat transforms the task-aware scheduling problem into the rel-


*SIGCOMM'14,* August 17–22, 2014, Chicago, IL, USA.

http://dx.doi.org/10.1145/2619239.2626322.

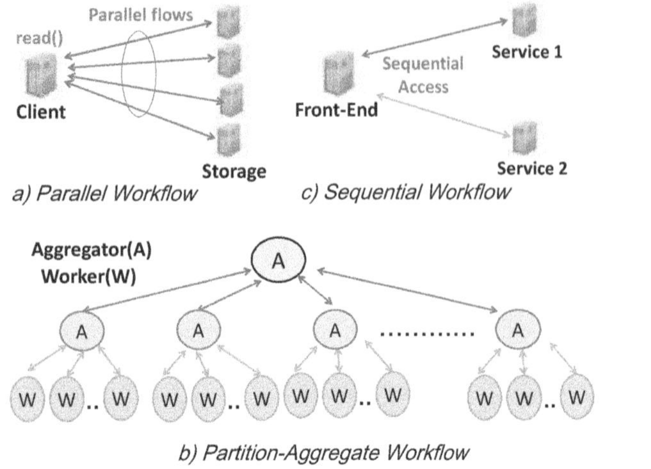


**Figure 1: Common workflows.**

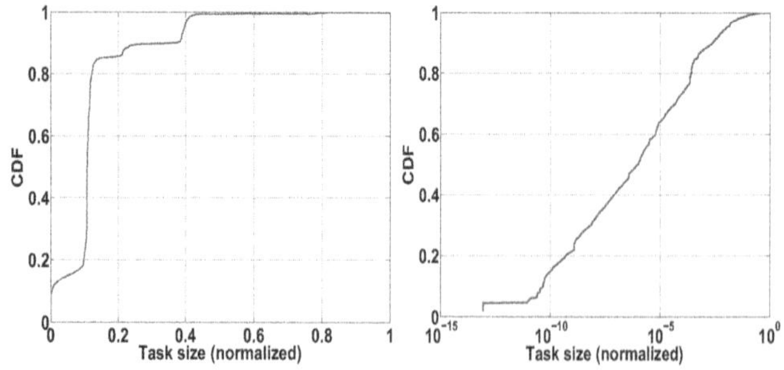


**Figure 2: Normalized distribution of task sizes for search (left), data analytics (right) workflows. For data analytics we use the input size of a MapReduce job as a proxy for its size.**

atively well-understood flow prioritization problem. While many flow prioritization mechanisms exist (e.g., priority queues, PDQ [17], $D^3$ [28], pFabric [5]), we show that they do not meet all the requirements of supporting FIFO-LM. Thus, Baraat introduces Smart Priority Class (SPC), which combines the benefits of priority classes and explicit rate protocols [17, 13, 28]. It also deals with on-the-fly identification of heavy tasks and changes the level of multiplexing accordingly. Finally, like traditional priority queues, SPC supports work-conservation which ensures that Baraat does not adversely impact the utilization of non-network resources in the data center.

To demonstrate the feasibility and benefits of Baraat, we evaluate it on three platforms: a small-scale testbed for validating our proof-of-concept prototype; a flow based simulator for conducting large-scale experiments based on workloads from Bing [18] and data-analytics applications [9]; the ns-2 simulator for conducting micro-benchmarks. We have also integrated the popular in-memory caching application, Memcached [2], with Baraat. We compare Baraat against the state-of-the-art decentralized network scheduling scheme (i.e., pFabric [5]) as well as centralized schedulers which target MapReduce style workloads (e.g., Orchestra [11]). Our results show that for the Bing-like workload, Baraat reduces the $95^{th}$ percentile task completion time by 70% compared to pFabric and by 27% compared to Orchestra. For the data-analytics workload, Baraat reduces the $95^{th}$ percentile task completion time by 43% and 93% compared to pFabric and Orchestra, respectively.

## 2. A CASE FOR TASK-AWARENESS

Baraat's design is based on scheduling network resources at the unit of a task. To motivate the need for task-aware scheduling policies, we start by studying typical application workflows, which leads us to a formal definition of a task. We then examine task characteristics of real applications and show how flow-based scheduling policies fail to provide performance gains given such task characteristics.

### 2.1 Task-Oriented Applications

The distributed nature and scale of data center applications results in rich and complex workflows. Typically, these applications run on many servers that, in order to respond to a user request, process data and communicate across the internal network. Despite the diversity of such applications, the underlying workflows can be grouped into a few common categories which reflect their communication patterns (see Figure 1).

All these workflows have a common theme. The "application task" being performed can typically be linked to a waiting user. Examples of such tasks include a read request to a storage server, a search query, the building of the user's social news-feed or even a data analytics job. Thus, we define *a task as the unit of work for an application that can be linked to a waiting user*. Further, *completion time of tasks* is a critical application metric as it directly impacts user satisfaction. In this paper, we aim to minimize task completion time focusing at both the average and the tail ($95^{th}$ percentile and beyond).

As highlighted by the examples in Figure 1, a typical application task has another important characteristic: it generates multiple flows across the network. A task's flows may traverse different parts of the network and not all of them may be active at the same time. When *all* these flows finish, the task finishes and the user gets a response or a notification.

**Task characterization.** We use data from past studies to characterize two features of application tasks in today's data centers: 1) the task size and 2) the number of flows per task. Both are critical when considering task-aware scheduling for the network; the first influences the scheduling policy, while the latter governs when task-aware scheduling outperforms flow-based scheduling, as we will later discuss.

(1) A task's size is its network footprint, i.e. the sum of the sizes of network flows involved in the task. We examine two popular applications, namely web search and data analytics. Figure 2 (left) presents the normalized distribution of task sizes for the query-response workflow at Bing. For each query, the task size is the sum of flows sizes across all workers involved in the query. The figure reflects the analysis of roughly 47K queries based on datasets collected in [18]. While most tasks have the same size, approximately 15% of the tasks are significantly heavier than others. This is due to the variability in the number of the responses or iterations [4]. By contrast, Figure 2 (right) presents the distribution of the input size across MapReduce jobs at Facebook (based on the datasets used in [9]). This represents the task size distribution for a typical data analytics workload. The figure shows that the task sizes follow a heavy-tailed distribution, which agrees with previous observations [9, 8,

| Application | Flows/task | Notes |
|---|---|---|
| Web search [4] | 88 (lower-bound) | Each aggregator queries 43 workers. Number of flows per search query is much larger. |
| MapReduce [6] | 30 (lower-bound) | Job contains 30 mappers/reducers at the median, 50000 at the maximum. |
| Cosmos [26] | 55 | 70% of tasks involve 30-100 flows, 2% involve more than 150 flows |

**Table 1: Tasks in data centers comprise multiple flows.**

6]. Similar distributions have been observed for the other phases of such jobs.

Overall, we find that the distribution of task sizes depends on the application. For some applications, all tasks can be similarly sized while others may have a heavy tailed distribution. In § 3.2, we show that heavy-tailed task distributions rule out some obvious scheduling candidates. Hence, *a general task-aware scheduling policy needs to be amenable to a wide-range of task size distributions, ranging from uniform to heavy-tailed.*

(2) For the number of flows per task, it is well accepted that most data center applications result in a complex communication pattern. Table 1 summarizes the number of flows per task for three production data center applications. Flows per task can range from a few tens to hundreds, and as discussed earlier, subsets of flows can be active at different times and across different parts of the network.

**Implications for the data center network.** Some of the above task characteristics (e.g., large number of concurrent flows) also contribute towards network congestion (and losses), which in turn, results in increased response times for the users. This has even been observed in production data centers (e.g., Bing [4, 18], Cosmos [7], Facebook [22]) which typically have modest average data center utilization. Thus, the network, and its resource allocation policy, play an important role in providing good performance to data center applications. In the following section, we show why today's flow-based resource allocation approaches are a misfit for typical task-oriented workloads.

## 2.2 Limitations of Flow-based Policies

Traditionally, allocation of network bandwidth has targeted per-flow fairness. Protocols like TCP and DCTCP [4] achieve fair-sharing by apportioning an equal amount of bandwidth to all the flows. This increases the completion time of flows and thus, the task completion time too. Because latency is the primary goal for many data center applications, recent proposals give up on per-flow fairness, and optimize *flow-level* metrics like meeting flow deadlines and minimizing flow completion time [28, 5]. For example, PDQ [17] and pFabric [5] can support a scheduling policy like shortest flow first (*SFF*), which minimizes flow completion times by assigning resources based on flow sizes. However, as we have shown, typical data center application tasks can have many flows, potentially of different sizes. SFF considers flows in isolation, so it will schedule the shorter flows of every task first, leaving longer flows to the end. This can hurt application performance by delaying completion of tasks.

We validate this through a simple simulation that compares fair sharing (e.g., TCP/DCTCP/RCP) with SFF in terms of task completion times, for a simple single stage partition-aggregate workflow scenario with 40 tasks comprising flows uniformly chosen from the range [5, 40]KB. Figure 3 shows SFF's improvement over fair-sharing as a function of the number of flows in a task. We also compare it with the performance of a straw-man task-aware scheme, where flows for the same task are grouped and scheduled together. If a task has just a single flow, SFF reduces the task completion time by almost 50%. However, as we increase the number of flows per task, the benefits reduce. Most tasks in data centers involve tens and hundreds of flows. The figure shows that in such settings, SFF performs similar to fair-sharing proposals. While this is a simple scenario, this observation extends to complex workflows as shown in our evaluation (§5). In contrast, the benefits are stable for the task-aware scheme.

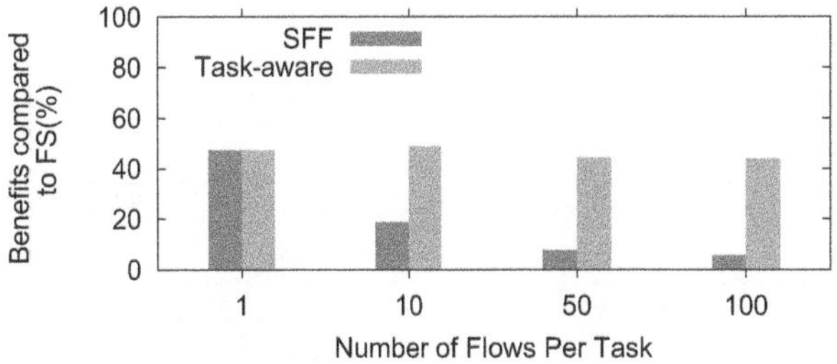


**Figure 3: SFF fails to improve over fair sharing (in terms of task completion time) for realistic number of flows per task while a straw-man task-aware policy provides consistent benefits.**

# 3. SCHEDULING POLICY

The scheduling policy determines the order in which tasks are scheduled across the network. Determining an ordering that minimizes task completion time is NP-hard; flow-shop scheduling [14, 25], a well known NP-hard problem in production systems, can be reduced to task-aware scheduling. Flow-shop scheduling is considered as one of the hardest NP-hard problems, with exact solutions not known for even small instances of the problem [15]. Thus, we need to consider heuristic scheduling policies.

The heuristic policy should meet two objectives. First, it should help reduce both the average as well as tail task completion time. Most scheduling policies optimize for one of these, but not both. Second, it should be amenable to decentralized implementation, i.e., it should facilitate scheduling decisions to be made locally (at the respective end-points and switches) without requiring any centralized coordination. While decentralization may appear at odds with the recent trend towards a centralized control plane [3], it is crucial for supporting applications with small (sub-second) tasks (e.g., search, social networking, etc) [23]. This class of applications is the most challenging to handle because of their flow dynamics, but also benefits the most from any improvement in task completion time due to their user-facing nature.

## 3.1 Task Serialization

The space of heuristics to allocate bandwidth in a task-aware fashion is large. Guided by flow-based policies that schedule flows one at a time [17], we consider serving tasks

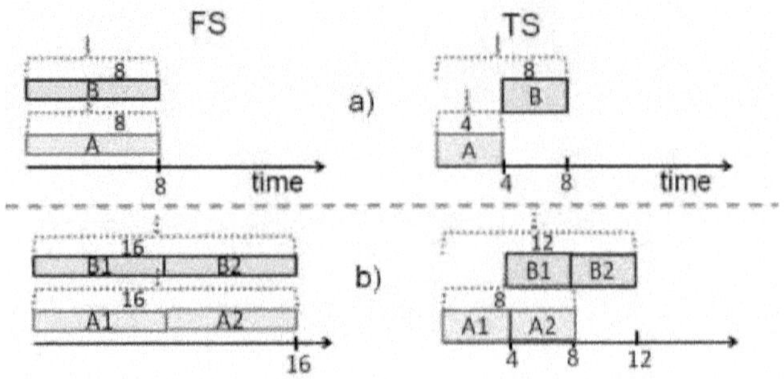


**Figure 4: Distilling the Benefits of Task Serialization (TS) over Fair Sharing (FS) for single stage (a) and multi-stage transfers. In case of multiple stages, we assume that each stage has a different network bottleneck.**

one at a time. This can help finish tasks faster by reducing the amount of contention in the network. Consequently, we define *task serialization* as the set of policies where an entire task is scheduled before moving to the next.

Through simple examples, we illustrate the benefits of task serialization (TS) over fair sharing (FS). The first example illustrates the most obvious benefit of TS (Fig 4a). There are two tasks, A and B, which arrive at the same time (t = 0) bottlenecked at the same resources. FS assigns equal bandwidth to both the tasks, increasing their completion times. In contrast, TS allocates all resources to A, finishes it, and then schedules B. Compared to FS, A's completion time is reduced by half, but B's completion time remains the same.

Orchestra [11] confirms the above benefits of task serialization in improving the average task completion time for batched workloads. However, the question that still remains unanswered is: *can task serialization also provide gains in tail task completion time?*

One scenario where task serialization can improve the tail task completion time is shown in Fig 4b. There is an application with two stages, as in the partition-aggregate workflow of search. Each stage has a different network bottleneck, which is the case for an application like search, where downlink to the mid-level aggregator is the bottleneck in the first stage and downlink to the top-level aggregator is the bottleneck in the second stage.

There are two tasks, A and B, which arrive in the system at the same time (t = 0). With FS, both tasks get the same amount of resources and thus make similar progress: they finish the first stage at the same time, then move together to the second stage, and finally finish at the same time. TS, in contrast, enables efficient pipelining of these tasks. Task A gets the full bandwidth in the first stage, finishes early, and then moves to the second stage. In parallel, B makes progress in the first stage. By the time B reaches the second stage, A is already finished. This reduces the completion times of both the tasks. In the next section, we show how choosing the right ordering of tasks (scheduling policy), can also result in improving the tail task completion time, even for single stage workloads.

## 3.2 Task Serialization Policies

We begin with two obvious policies for task serialization: FIFO which schedules tasks in their arrival order and STF

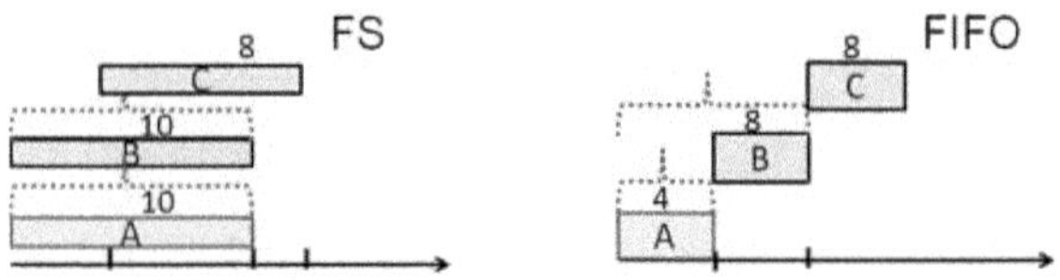


**Figure 5: FIFO ordering can reduce tail completion times compared to fair sharing (FS).**

(shortest task first) that schedules tasks based on their size. STF can provide good average performance but can lead to high tail latency, or even starvation, for large sized tasks. Moreover, it requires knowledge about task sizes up front, which is impractical for many applications.

FIFO is attractive for many reasons. In addition to being simple to implement, FIFO also limits the maximum time a task has to wait, as a task's waiting time depends only on the tasks that arrive *before* it. This is illustrated in Figure 5 which compares a FIFO policy with fair sharing (FS). While tasks A and B arrive at t = 0, task C arrives later (t = 4). With FS, C's arrival reduces the bandwidth share of existing tasks as all three tasks need to share the resources. This increases the completion times of both A and B and they both take 10 units of time to finish. In contrast, with TS, C's arrival does not affect existing tasks and none of the tasks take more than 8 units of time to finish. *This example illustrates that in an online setting, even for single stage workflows, a FIFO task serialization policy can reduce both the average and tail task completion times compared to FS.*

In fact under simple settings, FIFO is proven to be optimal for minimizing the tail completion time, if task sizes follow a light tailed distribution. i.e., task sizes are fairly homogeneous and do not follow a heavy-tailed distribution [27]. However, if task sizes are heavy-tailed, FIFO may result in blocking small tasks behind a heavy task. As discussed earlier in §2.1, data center applications do have such heavy tasks. For such applications, we need a policy that can separate out these "elephants" from the small tasks.

## 3.3 FIFO-LM

We propose to use FIFO-LM[1], which processes tasks in a FIFO order, but can dynamically vary the number of tasks that are multiplexed at a given time. If the degree of multiplexing is one, it performs exactly the same as FIFO. If the degree of multiplexing is $\infty$, it works similar to fair sharing. This policy is attractive because it can perform like FIFO for the majority of tasks (the small ones), but when a large task arrives, we can increase the level of multiplexing and allow small tasks to make progress as well.

An important question is how to determine that a task is heavy i.e., how big is a heavy task. We assume that the data center has knowledge about task size distribution based on historically collected data. Based on this history, we need to identify a threshold (in terms of task size) beyond which we characterize a task as heavy. For applications with bimodal task size distribution or resembling the Bing workload in Figure 2, identifying this threshold is relatively straightforward. As soon as the task size enters the second mode, we classify it as heavy and increase the level of multiplexing.

[1]typically referred to as limited processor sharing in scheduling theory [21].

For heavy-tailed distributions, our experimental evaluation with a number of heavy-tailed distributions such as Pareto or Lognormal with varying parameters (shape or mean respectively), shows that a threshold in the range of $80^{th}$-$90^{th}$ percentile provides the best results.

# 4. BARAAT

Baraat is a decentralized task-aware scheduling system for data center networks. It aims to achieve FIFO-LM scheduling in a decentralized fashion, without any explicit coordination between network switches.

In Baraat, each task is assigned a globally unique identifier (*task-id*) based on its arrival (or start) time. Tasks with lower ids have a higher priority over ones with a higher id. Network flows carry the identifier of the task they belong to and inherit its priority. Based on this identifier switches can make *consistent* decisions without any coordination. If two switches observe flows of two different tasks, both make the same decision in terms of flow prioritization (consistency over space). If a switch observes flows of two tasks at different times, it makes the same decision (consistency over time). Such consistent resource allocation increases the likelihood that flows of a task get "similar" treatment across the network and hence, tasks actually progress in a serial fashion. Finally, switches *locally* decide when to increase the level of multiplexing through on-the-fly identification of heavy tasks.

In the next section, we discuss how the task priorities are generated. We then discuss how switches act on these priorities and why existing mechanisms are insufficient. Finally, we present the Smart Priority Class mechanism, and discuss how it meets our desired prioritization goals.

## 4.1 Generating Task Identifiers

Baraat uses monotonically increasing counter(s) to keep track of incoming tasks. We only need a single counter when all incoming tasks arrive through a common point. Examples of such common points include the load balancer (for user-facing applications like web search), the job scheduler (for data parallel and HPC applications), the meta-data manager (for storage applications), and so on.

The counter is incremented on a task's arrival and is used as the task's *task-id*. We use multiple counters when tasks arrive through multiple load balancers. Each counter has a unique starting value and an increment value, i, which represents the number of counters in the system. For example, if there are two counters, they can use starting values of 1 and 2 respectively, with i = 2. As a result, one of them generates odd *task-ids* (1, 3, 5,...) while the other generates even *task-ids* (2, 4, 6...). We highlight such a setting, which approximates a FIFO ordering in a distributed scenario, in one of our testbed experiments in §5. These counters can be loosely synchronized and any inconsistency between them could be controlled and limited through existing techniques [29].

The generation of task identifiers should also account for background services (e.g., index update) that are part of most production data centers. Tasks of such services often involve long flows which can negatively impact tasks of online services, if not properly handled. In Baraat, we assign strictly lower priority to such background tasks by assigning them *task-ids* that do not overlap with the range of *task-ids* reserved for the high priority online service. For example, *task-ids* less than $n$ could be reserved for the online service while *task-ids* greater than $n$ could be used for the background service.

**Propagation of task identifiers.** A flow needs to carry the identifier for its parent task. Thus, all physical servers involved in a task need to know its *task-id*. Applications can propagate this identifier along the task workflow; for example, for a web-search query, aggregators querying workers inform them of the *task-id* which can then be used for the response flows from the workers back to the aggregators.

| | Strict Priority | Fair Sharing | Heavy Task Support | Work Conservation | Preemption |
|---|---|---|---|---|---|
| DCTCP | No | Yes | No | Yes | No |
| RCP | No | Yes | No | Yes | No |
| $D^3$ | Partial | Yes | No | Yes | No |
| pFabric / Priority Queues | Yes | Yes | No | Partial | Yes |
| PDQ | Yes | No | No | Yes | Yes |

**Table 2: Desired properties and whether they are supported in existing mechanisms.**

## 4.2 Prioritization Mechanism - Requirements

Baraat's task-aware assignment of flow priorities, in the form of *task-ids*, opens up the opportunity to use existing flow prioritization mechanisms (e.g., priority queues, pFabric [5], PDQ [17], etc) at the switches and end-points. While these mechanisms provide several attractive properties, they do not meet all the requirements of supporting FIFO-LM. Table 2 lists the desired properties and whether they are supported in existing mechanisms.

The first three properties, *strict priority*, *fair-sharing* and *heavy task support*, are the basic building blocks for FIFO-LM: we should be able to strictly prioritize flows of one task over another; likewise, if the need arises (e.g., heavy task in the system), we should be able to do fair-sharing of bandwidth amongst a set of flows. Finally, the system should on-the-fly identify heavy tasks and then change the level of multiplexing accordingly.

The last two properties, *work-conservation* and *preemption*, are important for system efficiency. Work conservation ensures that a lower priority task is scheduled if the highest priority task is unable to saturate the network – for example, when the highest priority task is too small to saturate the link or if it is bottlenecked at a subsequent link. Finally, preemption allows a higher priority task to grab back resources assigned to a lower priority task. Thus, preemption *complements* work conservation – the latter lets lower priority tasks make progress when there is spare capacity, while the former allows higher priority tasks to grab back the resources if they need to. These two properties also prove crucial in supporting background services; such services can continue to make progress whenever there are available resources while high priority tasks can always preempt them.

**Limitations of existing mechanisms.** As the table highlights, no existing mechanism supports all these five properties. Support for handling heavy tasks is obviously missing as none of these mechanisms targets a policy like FIFO-LM. PDQ [17] does not support fair-sharing of bandwidth, so two flows having the same priority are scheduled in a serial fashion. Similarly, pFabric [5] and priority queues do not support work-conservation in a multi-hop setting because end-hosts always send at the maximum rate, so flows continue to send data even if they are bottlenecked at a subsequent hop. In such scenarios, work-conservation would mean that these flows back-off and let a lower priority flow, which is not bottlenecked at a subsequent hop, send data. Protocols like PDQ avoid this problem with the help of explicit feedback from the switches, but they have other limitations, as we discussed earlier.

These limitations of existing mechanisms motivate Smart Priority Class (SPC), which we describe next.

## 4.3 Smart Priority Class

We propose Smart Priority Class (SPC), which is *logically* similar to priority queues used in switches: flows mapped to a higher priority class get strict preference over those mapped to a lower priority class, and flows mapped to the same class share bandwidth according to max-min fairness. However, compared to traditional priority queues, SPC has two additional *smarts*:

- To provide work-conservation in multi-hop settings, SPC supports *explicit feedback* from switches. We leverage prior work on explicit rate control protocols to communicate this feedback between the switches and the end-hosts [17, 13]. However, unlike prior work, we only keep aggregate, per-task counters at the switches, instead of per-flow state.
- SPC supports *dynamic mapping* of flows to priority queues — this is required to support FIFO-LM as a flow's mapping may change during its lifetime, if a heavy task is identified in the system. We implement a light-weight *classifier* in each switch, which uses the per-task counters to identify heavy tasks and maps tasks to priority classes accordingly.

Figure 6a provides an overview of SPC functionality, which comprises support at the switches and an end-host transport.[2] The figure shows the key steps in sending a block of data from a sender to a receiver: i) Applications pass the *task-id* and data to the SPC transport, which computes the flow *demand* based on the size of data. ii) The *task-id* and demand are passed to the next-hop switch in a packet header. iii) Each switch adds its feedback to the packet header. The feedback is calculated based on the flow's priority class and aggregate task information stored locally at each switch (such as the total demand of the task and the number of flows in the task). iv) The receiver piggybacks the consolidated feedback on the acknowledgment packets that are sent back to the sender. v) Finally, each sender uses this feedback to decide the rate at which it should send data. The process is repeated once every round trip time, until the sender has no more data to send. Other senders who are part of the task also follow the same steps without explicitly coordinating with each another.

While Baraat requires changes to both end-hosts and switches, we believe that such changes are worthwhile given the performance benefits of Baraat. Further, the changes required at the switches are practically feasible, as demonstrated by prior proposals [28, 17] and our software-switch implementation. Specifically, in terms of switch state, PDQ [17] shows that switches only need 10KB memory to keep per-flow state (Baraat stores even less information i.e. per-task only). In §6, we also discuss how recent work may further simplify introducing Baraat-like functionality in future data centers.

We now elaborate on the most important parts of SPC—the classifier and how explicit feedback is calculated. Finally, we describe the rate control transport protocol that is used between end-hosts and switches.

### 4.3.1 Classifier

As shown in Figure 6b, the classifier maps flows to appropriate priority classes. It maintains a mapping between *task-id* and priority classes, so flows are first mapped to tasks (based on their *task-id*) and then to the relevant priority class. By default, the classifier maintains a *one-to-one* mapping between tasks and priority classes. The highest priority task maps to the highest priority class and so on. This achieves the standard FIFO scheduling where tasks are scheduled one by one based on their priority (*task-id*).

To support FIFO-LM, the classifier also does *on-the-fly* identification of heavy tasks (hence tasks need not know their size *upfront*). The classifier queries per-task counters to check whether a task is heavy or not. We maintain a counter that keeps track of the total bytes reserved by flows of a task, which we use as proxy for the task's size. If the task size exceeds a pre-determined threshold, the task is marked as heavy.[3] Subsequently, the heavy task and the task immediately next in priority to the heavy task share the same class. For example, as shown in the figure, if task 1 is identified as heavy, it shares the top priority class with task 2. This enables small tasks to make progress, so when task 2 finishes, task 3 is moved to the top priority queue.

In addition to supporting FIFO-LM, our classifier design provides two key advantages. First, it maps all flows of a task to the *same* class, which ensures that flows of the same task are active simultaneously, instead of being scheduled one-by-one (e.g., as in [17]), thereby reducing the overhead of flow switching. Second, it decouples classification from feedback computation and rate control protocol, which makes it easier to support other scheduling policies in the system. By just changing the way flows are mapped to classes, we can support policies like fair sharing, flow level prioritization, etc.

### 4.3.2 Explicit Feedback

After mapping a flow to its appropriate class, the next step is to compute the feedback, which corresponds to the rate that the switch can support for the given flow. As shown in Figure 6b, feedback is computed based on the flow's priority class and aggregate task counters.

The feedback provided to each flow roughly corresponds to the rate that the flow would get with standard priority queues. Thus, the entire link capacity is allocated to the highest priority class; any leftover is given to the next class, and so on. Whether the highest priority class is able to use the entire link capacity depends on its total demand, which in turn depends on how many tasks are mapped to

[2]We assume that end-hosts and switches are protocol compliant, a reasonable assumption for production data center environments. Further, compared to FIFO or sized based scheduling, FIFO-LM limits the impact of non-confirming sources (if any) by increasing the level of multiplexing.

[3]A heavy task on one switch may not be identified as heavy in some other part of the network (where it will not be causing head-of-line blocking).

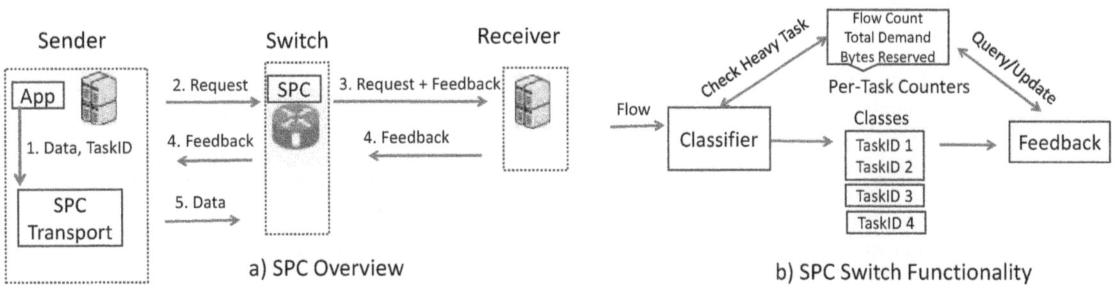


**Figure 6: Overview of SPC and its switch functionality.**

this class, and the aggregate demand of each of these tasks (stored in the per-task counters)[4]. If the total demand of the highest priority class is more than the available capacity[5], we assign a max-min fair bandwidth allocation. To this end, we maintain another per-task counter, which keeps track of the number of flows in the task.

**Algorithm 1** Explicit Feedback Calculation

**Require:** TaskID, Demand for flow, $D$, and the allocation for the previous interval.
**Output:** AR, NR.
Link capacity is C; A reflects current allocations across all flows; $D_k$ is the sum of flow demands belonging to class k; $F_k$ is the number of flows belonging to class k.

```
Return Previous Allocation and Demand by subtracting from relevant counters
k = Classifier(TaskID)
ClassAvlBW = max(0, C − Σ_{i=1}^{k−1} D_i)
AvailShare = max(0, ClassAvlBW − D_k)
if AvailShare ≥ D then
    NR ← D
else
    NR ← ClassAvlBW/F_k
end if
AR ← min(NR, C − A)
Update Packet with AR and NR
Update counters and A
```

Algorithm 1 lists all the steps followed in computing feedback for a flow. A key aspect of our design is that unlike prior explicit feedback protocols that maintain per-flow state (e.g., PDQ [17]), we only use aggregate, per-task counters to compute feedback. Given the typical large number of flows per task, this can provide an order of magnitude or more reduction in the amount of state kept at the switches. However, without per-flow state, providing work-conservation becomes challenging, as switches no longer keep track of the bottleneck link of each flow.

We address this challenge by providing *two* rates to sources through the switch feedback. An *actual rate* (AR) at which senders should send data in the next RTT and a *nominal rate* (NR), which is the maximum share of the flow based on its priority. NR might differ from AR due to flow dynamics — the switch might have already assigned bandwidth to a lower priority flow which needs to be preempted before NR is available. NR essentially allows senders to identify their current nominal bottleneck share, which they use to adjust their demand, thus allowing other switches along the path to free up unused bandwidth and allocate it to lower-priority flows (i.e., work conservation). In the next section, we describe how end-host transport precisely calculates this demand.

[4]total demand corresponds to the *current* aggregate demand of a task while bytes-reserved is the sum of *all* prior reservations for the task.

[5]We adjust for over and under utilization of a link by using the notion of virtual capacity, which is increased or decreased depending on link utilization and queuing [13, 28].

### *4.3.3 End-host Transport*

As shown in Figure 6a, SPC end-host transport logic leverages prior work on explicit rate based protocols [13, 17, 28]. The key difference is in the way senders calculate their *demand*. In SPC, demand calculation is more *accurate* and reflects not only how much data the sender can send (as is the case in prior work), but also how much data the bottleneck link on the path can support. A more accurate demand ensures that non-bottleneck switches only reserve what is required by the flow, which leads to work conservation in multi-hop settings, without requiring per-flow state at the switches.

**Algorithm 2** Sender – Calculating Demand

```
1: MinNR - minimum NR returned in the previous RTT
2: Demand_{t+1} ← min(NIC_Rate, DataInBuffer/RTT)
   //if flow already setup
3: if MinNR < Demand_t then
4:     Demand_{t+1} ← min(Demand_{t+1}, MinNR + δ)
5: end if
```

Algorithm 2 provide details on how senders calculate demand. The initial demand is set to the sender's NIC rate (e.g., 1Gbps) or lower if the sender has only a small amount of data to send (Step 2). Based on the earlier feedback from switches (the NR and AR vectors), the sender identifies the bottleneck rates: it transmits data at the minimum of the rates specified in the AR vector as discussed earlier, and uses the NR vector to determine how much it should demand in the next RTT. If the flow is bottlenecked on a network link (i.e., the minimum of the NR vector is less than the previously requested demand), the sender lowers its demand for the next RTT and sets it equal to $NR + \delta$. Lowering the demand allows other links to only allocate the necessary bandwidth that will actually be used by the flow, using the rest for lower priority flows (i.e., work conservation). Adding a small value ($\delta$) ensures that whenever the bottleneck link frees up, the sender recognizes this and is able to again increase its demand to the maximum level.

In addition to rate control, the SPC transport also implements other transport functionality, such as reliability and flow control. Note that due to the explicit nature of our protocol, loss should be rare, but end-hosts still need to provide reliability. Our reliability mechanism is similar to TCP. Each data packet has a sequence number, receivers send acknowledgments, and senders keep timers and retransmit, if they do not receive a timely acknowledgment.

## 4.4 Implementation

We have built a proof-of-concept switch and end-host implementation and have deployed it on a 25 node testbed. Both the switch and end-host are implemented on server-grade machines. We have also integrated Baraat with Memcached application. Both the end-host and switch implementations run in user-space and leverage zero-copy support between the kernel and user-space to keep the overhead low. At end-hosts, applications use an extended Sockets-like API to convey *task-id* information to the transport protocol. This information is passed when a new socket is created. The application also ensures that all flows per task use the same *task-id*. Our switch implementation is also efficient. On a server-grade PC, we can saturate four links at full duplex line rate. To keep SPC header processing overhead low in switches, we use integer arithmetic for rate calculations. Overall, the average SPC processing time was indistinguishable from normal packet forwarding. Thus, we believe that it will be feasible to implement Baraat's functionality in commodity switches.

**Header:** The SPC header requires 26 bytes. Each *task-id* is specified in 4 bytes. We encode rates as $Bytes/\mu s$. This allows us to a use a single byte to specify a rate – for example, 1Gbps has a value of 128. We use a scale factor byte that can be used to encode higher ranges. Most of the header space is dedicated for feedback from the switches. Each switch's response takes 2 bytes (one for NR and one for AR). Based on typical diameter of data center networks, the header allocates 12 bytes for the feedback, allowing a maximum of 6 switches to provide feedback. The sender returns its previous ARs assigned by each switch using 6 bytes. We also need an additional byte to keep track of the switch index – each switch increments it before forwarding the packet and uses 2 bytes to specify the current and previous demands.

# 5. EVALUATION

We evaluate Baraat across three platforms: our small scale testbed, an ns-2 implementation and a large-scale data center simulator. Our data center simulator allows us to implement a range of schemes, including the state-of-the-art flow-based protocol (i.e., pFabric), a prior task-aware centralized scheduler (i.e., Orchestra), idealized schemes (e.g., centralized scheduler with complete task size information), and compare their performance with Baraat. We use the ns-2 simulator to verify the basic properties of Baraat (e.g., work conservation, preemption, etc) and to quantify the overheads. Finally, our testbed allows us to evaluate Baraat with a real application (Memcached) and to cross validate the results of our simulator platforms. Here, we only present the key results from our testbed and large scale simulator experiments. Detailed results, including ns-2 micro-benchmarks, are available in the accompanying technical report [12].

| | Avg | $95^{th}$ perc. | $99^{th}$ perc. |
|---|---|---|---|
| RCP | 40ms | 72ms | 120ms |
| Baraat | 29ms | 41ms | 68ms |
| Improvement | 27% | 43% | 43.3% |

**Table 3: Performance comparison of Baraat against RCP in a Memcached usage scenario.**

In our evaluation, we consider three varied workloads: search, data analytics, and applications with homogeneous network footprint. We also analyze Baraat's performance across three different workflows – partition-aggregate, storage retrieval and data parallel. In all our experiments, the primary metric for comparison is the *task completion time*. We consider both the average as well as the tail ($95^{th}$ percentile and beyond) task completion time.

Below is a summary of our key results.

- Against decentralized schemes: Baraat reduces the $95^{th}$ percentile of the task completion time by 70%, 43% and 66% compared to the best known decentralized scheme (pFabric) for search, data-analytics and uniform workloads respectively.

- Against centralized schedulers: In a hypothetical scenario where centralized schedulers like Orchestra are made to handle search-like workloads, we show that Baraat's FIFO-LM policy reduces tail ($95^{th}$ percentile) task completion time by 27% compared to Orchestra and by 84% compared to a size-aware scheduler. For data-analytics workloads, tail completion time reduces by 93% and 37% over Orchestra and size-aware schedulers respectively.

## 5.1 Testbed experiments

We evaluate Baraat on our testbed and demonstrate its use with Memcached. Our testbed has five racks with four nodes each. The racks are connected through a two level tree topology: each rack has a top-of-rack (TOR) switch and the TOR switches are connected through a root switch. All end-hosts and switches are Dell Precision T3500 servers with a quad core Intel Xeon 2.27GHz processor, 4GB RAM and 1 Gbps interfaces.

In addition to Baraat, we have also implemented an optimized version of RCP [13] on our testbed.[6] For the testbed experiments, we compare Baraat against RCP for a storage retrieval scenario whereby a client reads data from multiple storage servers in parallel. This represents a parallel workflow.

**Online Data Retrieval with Memcached.** Our Memcached setup mimics a typical web-service scenario. We have one rack dedicated to the front-end nodes (i.e., Memcached clients) while the four other racks are used as the Memcached caching back-end. The front-end comprises of four clients; each client maintains a separate counter that is used to assign a *task-id* to incoming requests. Each counter is

[6] We have introduced a number of optimizations to account for data center environments, such as information about the exact number of active flows at the router (RCP uses algorithms to approximate this). With our RCP implementation sources know exactly the rate they should transmit at, whereas probe-based protocols like TCP/DCTCP need to discover it. Hence, our RCP implementation can be considered as an upper-bound for fair-share protocols.

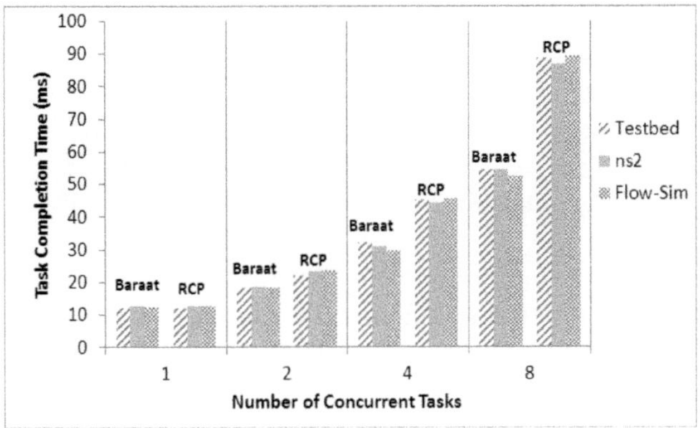


**Figure 7: Baraat's performance against RCP for a parallel workflow scenario across all experimental platforms.**

initialized to a unique value and is incremented by four for every incoming request. This models a scenario where requests arrive through multiple load-balancers (see §4.1).

For the experiment, we consider an online scenario where each client independently receives requests based on a Poisson arrival process. Each request (or task) corresponds to a multi-get that involves fetching data from three randomly chosen memcached servers. Table 3 compares Baraat with RCP for an experiment with 1000 requests, task size of 800KB, and an average client load of 50%. In this case, Baraat reduces average task completion time by 27% compared to RCP. We observe more gains at high percentiles where Baraat provides around 43% improvement over RCP.

**Batched Requests.** We now evaluate the impact of varying the number of concurrent tasks in the system and also use this experiment to cross-validate our testbed results (without Memcached) with the simulation platforms. This experiment is inspired by similar workloads considered in prior work to show incast in storage retrieval scenarios [24]. For this experiment, one node acts as a client while the other three nodes in the rack act as storage servers. All data is served from memory. For the request, the client retrieves 400 KB chunks from each of the three servers. The request finishes when data is received from all servers.

Figure 7 compares the performance of Baraat against RCP as we vary the number of concurrent tasks (i.e., read requests) in the system. Our results ignore the overhead of requesting the data which is the same for both Baraat and RCP. The first bar in each set shows testbed results. For a single task, Baraat and RCP perform the same. However, as the number of concurrent tasks increases, Baraat starts to outperform RCP. For 8 concurrent tasks, Baraat reduces the average task completion time by almost 40%. The experiment also shows that our implementation is able to saturate the network link — a single task takes approximately 12msec to complete, which is equal to the sum of the task transmission time ($\frac{1.2MB}{1Gbps}$) and the protocol overhead (2 RTTs of 1msec in our testbed).

**Cross-validation and comparison with optimal.** We repeated the same experiment in the ns-2 and large-scale simulators. Figure 7 also shows that the results are similar across the three platforms; absolute task completion times across our testbed and simulation platforms differ at most by 5%. This establishes the fidelity of our simulators which we use for more detailed evaluation in the following sections. We also used simple brute-force approach for this experiment and found that Baraat's schedules are optimal. In general, this is a strong NP-hard problem [15], so computing optimal for even modest-sized experiments is infeasible.

## 5.2 Large-scale performance

To evaluate Baraat at large scale, we developed a simulator that coarsely models a typical data center. The simulator uses a three-level tree topology with no path diversity, where racks of 40 machines with 1Gbps links are connected to a Top-of-Rack (ToR) switch and then to an aggregation switch. By varying the connectivity and the bandwidth of the links between the switches, we vary the over-subscription of the physical network. We model a data center with 36,000 physical servers organized in 30 pods, each comprising 30 racks.

Each simulated task involves workers and one or more layers of aggregators. The simulator can thus model different task workflows and task arrival patterns. We evaluate Baraat's performance under three different workloads. The first two workloads are based on the Bing and Facebook traces discussed earlier (§2) while the third one models a more homogeneous application with flow sizes that are uniformly distributed across [2KB, 50KB] (as suggested in prior work [4, 28, 17]). For single-stage workloads, the aggregator queries all other nodes in the rack, so each task comprises 40 flows. For two-stage workloads, the top-level aggregator queries 30 mid-level aggregators located in separate racks, which in turn query 40 workers each, resulting in 1200 flows per task. Top-level aggregators are located in a separate rack, one per pod. We use network over-subscription of 2:1 at the ToR switch and a selectivity of 3% (data input-to-output ratio for aggregator nodes), which is consistent with observations of live systems for data aggregation tasks [9]. We examine other configurations towards the end of the section.

Over the following sections, we first compare Baraat's performance against various decentralized and centralized solutions. We then dive into Baraat's performance for various workflows and explore a series of parameters that affect performance.

### 5.2.1 Comparison against Existing Solutions

We first compare Baraat against decentralized solutions – such solutions can handle scenarios involving short flows but are not task-aware. We then compare against centralized solutions – while these solutions are task-aware, they are not amenable to handling short flow scenarios.

**Comparison against Decentralized Solutions.** We consider two flow-based schemes: i) pFabric [5], which is the state-of-the-art transport protocol with the best reported performance. Our simulator models the best-case performance of pFabric because it implements the shortest flow first scheduling policy with no protocol overhead; and ii) RCP [13], which represents the best case performance of any fair sharing scheme (i.e., TCP/DCTCP, etc). Fair sharing schemes present a good baseline for comparison and can also surprisingly do quite well under certain scenarios. Like Baraat, both these schemes are decentralized, and hence suitable for scenarios involving small tasks (e.g., search).

Figure 8 highlights the reduction in tail task completion time ($95^{th}$ percentile) with Baraat relative to pFabric and

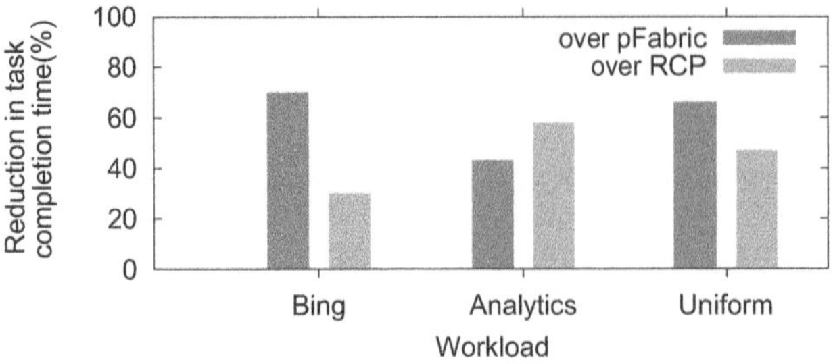


**Figure 8: Reduction in tail task completion time with Baraat against decentralized schemes.**

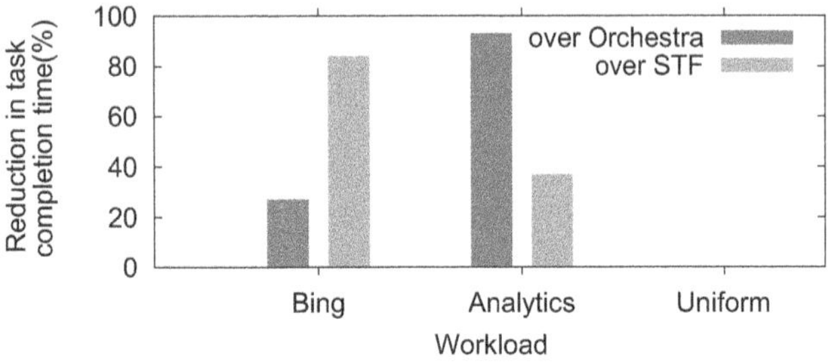


**Figure 9: Reduction in tail task completion time with Baraat against centralized schemes.**

RCP for the three workloads. The results reflect the execution of 10,000 tasks for 80% data center load, which captures the average load of bottlenecked network links. We examine how load and other parameters affect results in the following section. For all workloads, Baraat significantly improves task completion times compared to the other two decentralized solutions: The $95^{th}$ percentile task completion time reduces by 70%, 43% and 66% over pFabric for Bing, data-analytics and uniform workloads respectively (30%, 58% and 47% over RCP).

**Comparison against Centralized Solutions.** While making centralized solutions work for short tasks is still an open problem, we consider the hypothetical scenario in which this is feasible and evaluate their performance. We compare Baraat against two centralized, task-aware solutions: Orchestra [11], which schedules tasks in a FIFO order, and ii) Shortest Task First (STF), which determines the ordering of tasks based on their sizes (assuming an idealized scenario where the centralized scheduler has the whole task size information upfront).

We use the previous experiment settings and again compare performance at the $95^{th}$ percentile task completion time. Figure 9 shows that even though Baraat is decentralized, it is able to outperform centralized schedulers – compared to Orchestra, it provides 27% and 93% reduction in task completion completion for the Bing and data-analytics workloads, respectively. Similar gains of 84% and 37% are achieved for the same workloads in comparison with STF. For uniform workloads, all centralized solutions perform the same, as they all schedule tasks in a task-aware fashion and for this workload all tasks are similar in size.

**Detailed Analysis.** To understand the gains of Baraat against both centralized and decentralized solutions, we now examine the results in more detail. Table 4 reports the median, $95^{th}$ percentile, and $99^{th}$ percentile task completion time reduction with Baraat compared to all other schemes.

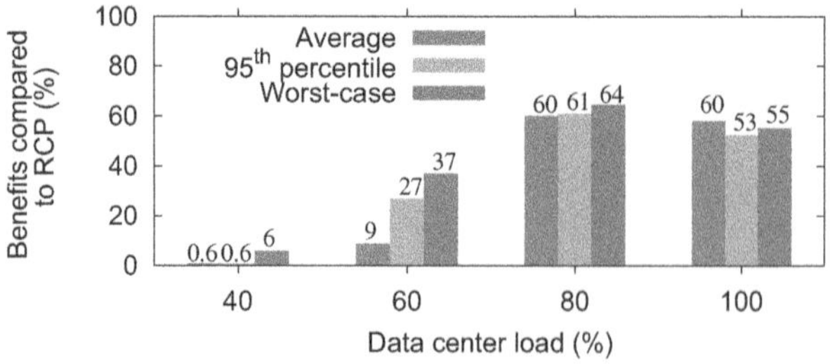


**Figure 10: Reduction in task completion time for the partition-aggregate workflow.**

For the Bing-like workload, we observe that Baraat outperforms Orchestra at both the median and higher percentiles. This is because of head-of-line blocking with Orchestra's FIFO based scheduling. Other schemes (pFabric, RCP) perform close to Baraat at the median (or even slightly better in the case of RCP) because they allow small tasks to finish quicker while Baraat may give only a fixed fraction of link bandwidth to small tasks (i.e., limited multiplexing). However, the difference in performance is small and at higher percentiles Baraat provides significant gains over these schemes.

For data analytics workloads exhibiting heavy-tailed distributions (Table 4), Orchestra again suffers from head-of-line blocking. In this case, size-based policies (pFabric, STF) do result in reduction of completion time compared to fair-sharing policies like RCP, especially beyond the median up to the $95^{th}$ percentile. However, even in this case, Baraat's FIFO-LM policy results in improved performance of roughly 60% relative to RCP and 36% over size-based policies at the $95^{th}$ percentile.

For uniform workloads, Baraat and task-aware policies (Orchestra and STF) have similar performance. Note that due to the absence of heavy tasks in this workload, Baraat and Orchestra collapse to the same policy. However, compared to pFabric, Baraat provides reduction of 66% and 75% at the $95^{th}$ and $99^{th}$ percentiles, respectively.

In summary, our results highlight that compared to existing solutions, Baraat can reduce the task completion time both at the median and at the tail, and for a wide range of workloads (uniform, bi-modal, heavy-tailed, etc).

### *5.2.2 Varying Workflows*

We now look at Baraat's performance under the different workflows described in Figure 1 in §2. In particular, we examine three workflows – (i) a two-level partition aggregate workflow where requests arrive in an online fashion, (ii) the storage retrieval scenario used for our testbed experiments where tasks have parallel workflows and request arrival is online, and (iii) a data-parallel application where tasks have a parallel workflow and there is a batch of jobs to execute. For this set of experiments, our focus is on the different workflows, so we keep the workload static (i.e., homogeneous workload described in the previous section) and use RCP as the baseline for comparison.

Figure 10 plots the reduction in the task completion time with Baraat compared to RCP for the partition-aggregate workflow. As expected, the benefits increase with the load – at 80% load, the worst case task completion time reduces by 64%, while the average and $95^{th}$ percentile by 60% and 61% respectively. In all cases, the confidence intervals for the values provided are less than 10% within the mean, and

| Policy | Bing | | | Data-analytics | | | Uniform | | |
|---|---|---|---|---|---|---|---|---|---|
| | median | $95^{th}$ perc. | $99^{th}$ perc. | median | $95^{th}$ perc. | $99^{th}$ perc. | median | $95^{th}$ perc. | $99^{th}$ perc. |
| RCP | -5% | 30% | 34% | 25% | 58% | 62% | 7% | 37% | 40% |
| pFabric | 4% | 70% | 76% | 4% | 43% | 61% | 38% | 66% | 75% |
| STF | -8% | 84% | 97% | 0 | 37% | 64% | 0 | 1% | 6% |
| Orchestra | 28% | 27% | 16% | 94% | 93% | 84% | 0 | 0 | 0 |

**Table 4: Reduction in task completion time with Baraat relative to other policies.**

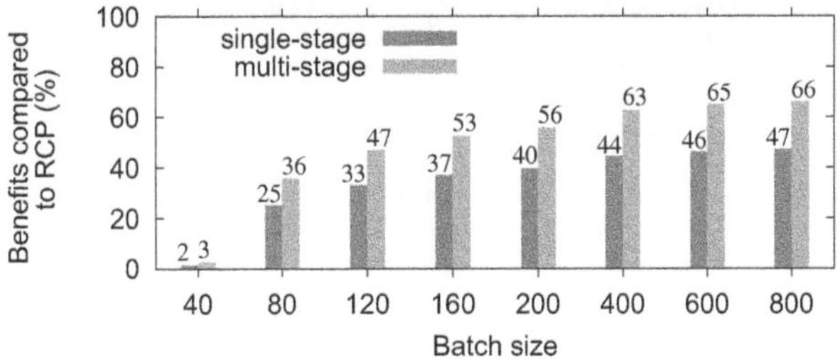


**Figure 11: Reduction in mean task completion time for data-parallel jobs.**

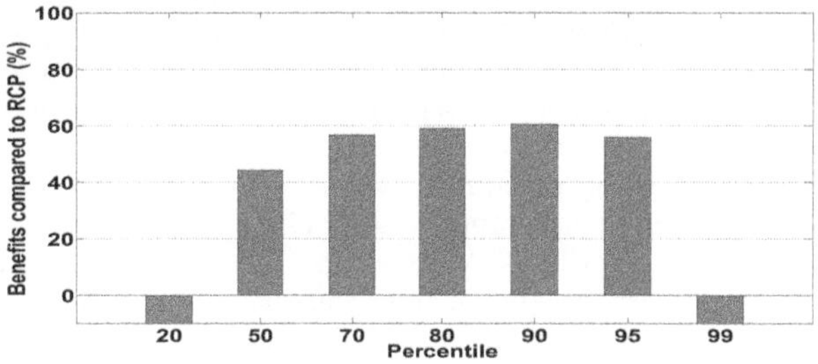


**Figure 12: Performance of Baraat when varying the heavy-task identification threshold for the data analytics workload.**

are not plotted for clarity. For the storage retrieval scenario, the worst case completion time reduces by 36% compared to RCP at 80% load (35% and 16% reduction at $95^{th}$ percentile and the average respectively). The reduced benefit results from the fact that tasks here involve a single stage.

Figure 11 presents Baraat's benefits for the scenario involving a batch of data-parallel jobs. For batch sizes of 400 jobs, average task completion time is reduced by 44% and 63% for single-stage and multi-stage jobs respectively. As discussed in §2, batch execution scenarios involving single-stage jobs only provide benefits at the average. For multiple stages, worst case completion time also drops beyond batch sizes of 40; for batch sizes of 400, worst case completion time reduces by 32%.

### 5.2.3 *Varying parameters*

We now examine how varying the experiment parameters affect performance. We will focus on the partition-aggregate workflow at 80% load. We present only an overview of our observations, which are based on Baraat's performance in comparison with RCP. Detailed results are available in the technical report [12].

**Adding computation.** While our paper focuses on network performance, we now consider tasks featuring both network transfers and computation. We extend the simulator to model computation for worker machines as an exponentially distributed wait time. As expected, as computation time increases as a fraction of the total task completion time, the benefits of Baraat drop. However, overall Baraat still provides significant benefits. For example, at 80% load and when computation comprises 50% of the task, the worst case completion time reduces by 25% and the average completion time reduces by 14% (50% reduction when computation comprises 25% of the task completion time).

**Heavy task identification.** As discussed in §4, classification is threshold-based in Baraat. For heavy-tailed distributions (e.g., Pareto or Log-normal), we found that a threshold in the range between the $80^{th}$ and the $90^{th}$ percentile provides the best performance. Figure 12 highlights this for the data analytics workload. Note that while Baraat shows robust performance under a wide range of thresholds, a significant mis-estimation of the threshold can severely affect performance: if the threshold is too low, the policy will converge to fair-sharing (RCP) and if the threshold is too high, it will converge to Orchestra.

## 6. DISCUSSION

The notion of task-aware scheduling underlying Baraat is both affected by and has implications for various aspects of data center network design. We briefly discuss some important issues here.

**Changes to the Network Fabric.** While Baraat's mechanism (SPC) requires light-weight changes to the network switches, recent work may make it feasible to support task-aware scheduling in a more non-intrusive manner. For example, PASE [20] supports flow-based scheduling using existing data plane functionality (i.e., priority queues and ECN) but cannot support other Baraat requirements such as heavy task identification. Similarly, proposals for programmable switches[19] may make it easier to introduce Baraat-like functionality in future.

**Incremental Deployment.** This paper focused on the scenario where applications and network elements are both Baraat compliant. We believe that there are potential benefits of incrementally rolling-out the system. From an applications perspective, Baraat can be incrementally deployed by considering non-Baraat traffic as background traffic on a link. From a network perspective, Baraat can be deployed on a subset of switches (e.g., close to the aggregators) to gain partial benefits. We leave the exploration of these benefits for future work.

**Non-network resources.** Baraat reduces network contention through task serialization. However, it still retains pipelined use of other data center resources. Consider a web search example scenario where an aggregator receives responses from a few workers. Today, either the CPU or the network link at the aggregator will be the bottleneck resource. Baraat is work conserving, so it will ensure the fewest number of simultaneously active tasks that can ensure that either the aggregator's network link is fully utilized or the CPU at the aggregator is the bottleneck. Thus, Baraat does not adversely impact the utilization of non-network resources. While additional gains can be had from coordinated task-aware scheduling across multiple resources, we leave this to future work.

# 7. RELATED WORK

We briefly discuss work that is most relevant to Baraat.

**Task-Aware Schedulers and Network Abstractions.** Proposals that most closely relate to Baraat include Orchestra [11] and CoFlow [10] which also argue for bringing task-awareness in data centers. Orchestra focuses on how task-awareness could provide benefits for MapReduce style workloads. Baraat differs from Orchestra in three ways. First, Baraat makes the scheduling decisions in a *decentralized* fashion rather than through a centralized controller. Second, Baraat uses FIFO-LM which has not been considered in prior network scheduling proposals including Orchestra. Third, while Orchestra focuses on improvement in the average task completion time for batched workload, we show that we can also improve the tail completion time, for dynamic scenarios and multi-stage workloads.

CoFlow [10] focuses on a new abstraction that can capture rich task semantics, which is orthogonal to Baraat's focus on scheduling policy and the underlying mechanism. However, beyond the abstraction, CoFlow does not propose any new scheduling policy or mechanism to achieve task-awareness.

**Cluster Schedulers and Resource Managers.** There is a large body of work on *centralized* cluster schedulers and resource managers [16, 23, 11, 1]. Some of these proposals use policies similar to FIFO-LM to balance fairness and performance in their systems. For example, the Hadoop fair scheduler [1] allows limited multiplexing, although the limit is set by the user/administrator. However, the above proposals focus on scheduling jobs on machines and not on decentralized scheduling of flows (or tasks) over the network, which requires new mechanisms.

**Straggler Mitigation Techniques.** Many prior proposals attempt to improve task completion times through various straggler mitigation techniques (e.g., re-issuing the request) [7, 18]. These techniques are orthogonal to our work as they focus on non-scheduling delays, such as delays caused by slow machines or failures, while we focus on the delays due to the resource sharing policy.

# 8. CONCLUSIONS

Baraat is a decentralized system for task-aware network scheduling. It provides a consistent treatment to all flows of a task, both across space and time. This allows active flows of the task to be loosely synchronized and make progress at the same time. By changing the level of multiplexing, Baraat effectively deals with the presence of heavy tasks and thus provides benefits for a wide range of workloads. Our experiments show that Baraat can significantly reduce the average as well as tail task completion time.

**Acknowledgements:** We thank our shepherd, Amin Vahdat, and the SIGCOMM reviewers for their feedback. We are also grateful to the Kwiken [18] team, especially Ishai Menache and Virajith Jalaparti, for sharing their Bing traces.

# 9. REFERENCES

[1] The Hadoop Fair Scheduler. https://hadoop.apache.org/docs/r1.2.1/fair_scheduler.html.

[2] Memcached. http://memcached.org/.

[3] M. Al-Fares, S. Radhakrishnan, B. Raghavan, N. Huang, and A. Vahdat. Hedera: Dynamic flow scheduling for data center networks. In *Proc. of NSDI*, pages 19–19, 2010.

[4] M. Alizadeh, A. G. Greenberg, D. A. Maltz, J. Padhye, P. Patel, B. Prabhakar, S. Sengupta, and M. Sridharan. Data center TCP (DCTCP). In *Proc. of SIGCOMM*, 2010.

[5] M. Alizadeh, S. Yang, M. Sharif, S. Katti, N. McKeown, B. Prabhakar, and S. Shenker. pfabric: Minimal near-optimal datacenter transport. In *ACM SIGCOMM*, 2013.

[6] G. Ananthanarayanan, A. Ghodsi, A. Wang, D. Borthakur, S. Kandula, S. Shenker, and I. Stoica. PACMan: coordinated memory caching for parallel jobs. In *Proc. of NSDI*, 2012.

[7] G. Ananthanarayanan, S. Kandula, A. G. Greenberg, I. Stoica, Y. Lu, B. Saha, and E. Harris. Reining in the outliers in map-reduce clusters using mantri. In *Proc. of OSDI*, 2010.

[8] R. Appuswamy, C. Gkantsidis, D. Narayanan, O. Hodson, and A. Rowstron. Scale-up vs scale-out for hadoop: Time to rethink? In *Proc. of SOCC*, 2013.

[9] Y. Chen, A. Ganapathi, R. Griffith, and R. Katz. The case for evaluating mapreduce performance using workload suites. In *Proc. of MASCOTS*, 2011.

[10] M. Chowdhury and I. Stoica. Coflow: An application layer abstraction for cluster networking. In *ACM Hotnets*, 2012.

[11] M. Chowdhury, M. Zaharia, J. Ma, M. Jordan, and I. Stoica. Managing data transfers in computer clusters with orchestra. In *Proc. of ACM SIGCOMM*, 2011.

[12] F. R. Dogar, T. Karagiannis, H. Ballani, and A. Rowstron. Decentralized Task-aware Scheduling for Data Center Networks. Technical Report MSR-TR-2013-96, Microsoft Research, September 2013. http://research.microsoft.com/apps/pubs/?id=201494.

[13] N. Dukkipati. *Rate Control Protocol (RCP): Congestion control to make flows complete quickly*. PhD thesis, Stanford University, 2007.

[14] M. Garey and D. Johnson. Computers and intractability. 1979.

[15] L. Hall. Approximability of flow shop scheduling. *Mathematical Programming*, 82(1):175–190, 1998.

[16] B. Hindman, A. Konwinski, M. Zaharia, A. Ghodsi, A. D. Joseph, R. Katz, S. Shenker, and I. Stoica. Mesos: A platform for fine-grained resource sharing in the data center. In *Proc. of NSDI*, pages 22–22. USENIX Association, 2011.

[17] C. Hong, M. Caesar, and P. Godfrey. Finishing flows quickly with preemptive scheduling. *ACM SIGCOMM Computer Communication Review*, 42(4):127–138, 2012.

[18] V. Jalaparti, P. Bodik, S. Kandula, I. Menache, M. Rybalkin, and C. Yan. Speeding up distributed request-response workflows. In *Proc. of SIGCOMM*, 2013.

[19] V. Jeyakumar, M. Alizadeh, C. Kim, and D. Mazières. Tiny packet programs for low-latency network control and monitoring. In *Proceedings of Hotnets*, HotNets-XII. ACM, 2013.

[20] A. Munir, G. Baig, S. Irteza, I. Qazi, I. Liu, and F. Dogar. Friends, not foes — synthesizing existing transport strategies for data center networks. In *Proc. of SIGCOMM*, 2014.

[21] J. Nair, A. Wierman, and B. Zwart. Tail-robust scheduling via limited processor sharing. *Performance Evaluation*, 67(11):978–995, 2010.

[22] R. Nishtala, H. Fugal, S. Grimm, M. Kwiatkowski, H. Lee, H. C. Li, R. McElroy, M. Paleczny, D. Peek, P. Saab, et al. Scaling memcache at facebook. In *Proc. of NSDI*, 2013.

[23] K. Ousterhout, P. Wendell, M. Zaharia, and I. Stoica. Sparrow: distributed, low latency scheduling. In *Proc. of SOSP*, 2013.

[24] A. Phanishayee, E. Krevat, V. Vasudevan, D. G. Andersen, G. R. Ganger, G. A. Gibson, and S. Seshan. Measurement and analysis of tcp throughput collapse in cluster-based storage systems. In *FAST*, volume 8, pages 1–14, 2008.

[25] H. Röck. The three-machine no-wait flow shop is np-complete. *Journal of the ACM*, 31(2):336–345, 1984.

[26] A. Shieh, S. Kandula, A. Greenberg, C. Kim, and B. Saha. Sharing the data center network. In *Proc. of NSDI*, 2011.

[27] A. Wierman and B. Zwart. Is tail-optimal scheduling possible? *Operations Research*, 60(5):1249–1257, 2012.

[28] C. Wilson, H. Ballani, T. Karagiannis, and A. Rowstron. Better never than late: Meeting deadlines in datacenter networks. In *Proc. of ACM SIGCOMM*, 2011.

[29] H. Yu, A. Vahdat, et al. Efficient numerical error bounding for replicated network services. In *Proc. of VLDB*, 2000.

# Efficient Coflow Scheduling with Varys

Mosharaf Chowdhury[1], Yuan Zhong[2], Ion Stoica[1]
[1]UC Berkeley, [2]Columbia University
{mosharaf, istoica}@cs.berkeley.edu, yz2561@columbia.edu

## ABSTRACT

Communication in data-parallel applications often involves a collection of parallel flows. Traditional techniques to optimize flow-level metrics do not perform well in optimizing such collections, because the network is largely agnostic to application-level requirements. The recently proposed coflow abstraction bridges this gap and creates new opportunities for network scheduling. In this paper, we address inter-coflow scheduling for two different objectives: decreasing communication time of data-intensive jobs and guaranteeing predictable communication time. We introduce the *concurrent open shop scheduling with coupled resources* problem, analyze its complexity, and propose effective heuristics to optimize either objective. We present Varys, a system that enables data-intensive frameworks to use coflows and the proposed algorithms while maintaining high network utilization and guaranteeing starvation freedom. EC2 deployments and trace-driven simulations show that communication stages complete up to 3.16× faster on average and up to 2× more coflows meet their deadlines using Varys in comparison to per-flow mechanisms. Moreover, Varys outperforms non-preemptive coflow schedulers by more than 5×.

## Categories and Subject Descriptors

C.2 [**Computer-communication networks**]: Distributed systems—*Cloud computing*

## Keywords

Coflow; data-intensive applications; datacenter networks

## 1 Introduction

Although many data-intensive jobs are network-bound [7,9,15,23], network-level optimizations [7, 8, 12, 25] remain agnostic to job-specific communication requirements. This mismatch often hurts application-level performance, even when network-oriented metrics like flow completion time (FCT) or fairness improve [15].

Despite the differences among data-intensive frameworks [3, 4, 18,26,29,37,41], their communication is structured and takes place between groups of machines in successive computation stages [16].


*SIGCOMM'14,* August 17–22, 2014, Chicago, IL, USA.

ACM 978-1-4503-2836-4/14/08 ...$15.00.
http://dx.doi.org/10.1145/2619239.2626315.

Often a communication stage cannot finish until all its flows have completed [15, 19]. The recently proposed coflow abstraction [16] represents such collections of parallel flows to convey job-specific communication requirements – for example, minimizing completion time or meeting a deadline – to the network and enables application-aware network scheduling (§2). Indeed, optimizing a coflow's completion time (CCT) decreases the completion time of corresponding job [15].

However, jobs from one or more frameworks create multiple coflows in a shared cluster. Analysis of production traces shows wide variations in coflow characteristics in terms of total size, the number of parallel flows, and the size of individual flows (§4). Simple scheduling mechanisms like FIFO and its variants [15, 19], which are attractive for the ease of decentralization, do not perform well in such an environment – one large coflow can slow down many smaller ones or result in many missed deadlines.

Simply applying a shortest- or smallest-first heuristic, the predominant way to solve most scheduling problems, is not sufficient either (§5). Inter-coflow scheduling is different from scheduling individual flows [8, 25], because each coflow involves multiple parallel flows. It also differs from related problems like scheduling parallel tasks [9, 40] or caching parallel blocks [10]; unlike CPU or memory, the network involves *coupled resources* – each flow's progress depends on its rates at both source and destination. We show that these coupled constraints make *permutation schedules* – scheduling coflows one after another without interleaving their flows – suboptimal. Consequently, centralized scheduling becomes impractical, because the scheduler might need to preempt flows or recalculate their rates at arbitrary points in time even when no new flows start or complete.

In this paper, we study the inter-coflow scheduling problem for arbitrary coflows and focus on two objectives: improving application-level performance by minimizing CCTs and guaranteeing predictable completions within coflow deadlines. We prove this problem to be strongly NP-hard for either objective and focus on developing effective heuristics. We propose a coflow scheduling heuristic that – together with a complementary flow-level rate allocation algorithm – makes centralized coflow scheduling feasible by rescheduling only on coflow arrivals and completions.

In the presence of coupled constraints, the bottleneck endpoints of a coflow determine its completion time. We propose the *Smallest-Effective-Bottleneck-First* (SEBF) heuristic that greedily schedules a coflow based on its bottleneck's completion time. We then use the *Minimum-Allocation-for-Desired-Duration* (MADD) algorithm to allocate rates to its individual flows. The key idea behind MADD is to *slow down all the flows in a coflow to match the completion time of the flow that will take the longest to finish.* As a result, other coexisting coflows can make progress and the average

CCT decreases. While the combination of SEBF and MADD is not necessarily optimal, we have found it to work well in practice.

For guaranteed coflow completions, we use admission control; i.e., we do not admit any coflow that cannot meet its deadline without violating someone else's. Once admitted, we use MADD to *complete all the flows of a coflow exactly at the coflow deadline* for guaranteed completion using the minimum amount of bandwidth.

We have implemented the proposed algorithms in a system called Varys[1] (§6), which provides a simple API that allows data-parallel frameworks to express their communication requirements as coflows with minimal changes to the framework. User-written jobs can take advantage of coflows *without* any modifications.

We deployed Varys on a 100-machine EC2 cluster and evaluated it (§7) by replaying production traces from Facebook. Varys improved CCTs both on average (up to 3.16×) and at high percentiles (3.84× at the 95th percentile) in comparison to per-flow fair sharing. Hence, end-to-end completion times of jobs, specially the communication-heavy ones, decreased. The aggregate network utilization remained the same, and there was no starvation. In trace-driven simulations, we found Varys to be 3.66× better than fair sharing, 5.53× better than per-flow prioritization, and 5.65× better than FIFO schedulers Moreover, in EC2 experiments (simulations), Varys allowed up to 2× (1.44×) more coflows to meet their deadlines in comparison to per-flow schemes; it marginally outperformed resource reservation mechanisms [11] as well.

We discuss current limitations of Varys and relevant future research in Section 8 and compare Varys to related work in Section 9.

# 2 Background and Motivation

This section overviews the coflow abstraction (§2.1) and our conceptual model of the datacenter fabric (§2.2), and illustrates the advantages of using coflows (§2.3).

## 2.1 The Coflow Abstraction

A coflow [16] is a collection of flows that share a common performance goal, e.g., minimizing the completion time of the latest flow or ensuring that flows meet a common deadline. We assume that the amount of data each flow needs to transfer is known before it starts [8, 15, 19, 25]. The flows of a coflow are independent in that the input of a flow does not depend on the output of another in the same coflow, and the endpoints of these flows can be in one or more machines. Examples of coflows include the shuffle between the mappers and the reducers in MapReduce [18] and the communication stage in the bulk-synchronous parallel (BSP) model [37].

Coflows can express most communication patterns between successive computation stages of data-parallel applications (Table 1) [16]. Note that traditional point-to-point communication is still a coflow with a single flow.

## 2.2 Network Model

In our analysis, we consider a network model where the entire datacenter fabric is abstracted out as one non-blocking switch [8, 11, 27, 33] interconnecting all the machines (Figure 1), and we focus only on its ingress and egress ports (e.g., machine NICs). This abstraction is attractive because of its simplicity, yet it is practical because of recent advances in full bisection bandwidth topologies [22, 32] and techniques for enforcing edge constraints into the network [11, 21]. Note that we use this abstraction to simplify our analysis, but we do not enforce it in our experiments (§7).

In this model, each ingress port has some flows from one or more coflows to various egress ports. For ease of exposition, we organize them in Virtual Output Queues [31] at the ingress ports as shown in Figure 1. In this case, there are two coflows $C_1$ and $C_2$; $C_1$ has three flows transferring 1, 2, and 4 units of data, while $C_2$ has two flows transferring 2 data units each.

[1] Pronounced \'vä-ris\.

| Communication in Data-Parallel Apps | Coflow Structure |
|---|---|
| Comm. in dataflow pipelines [3,4,26,41] | Many-to-Many |
| Global communication barriers [29,37] | All-to-All |
| Broadcast [3,26,41] | One-to-Many |
| Aggregation [3,4,18,26,41] | Many-to-One |
| Parallel read/write on dist. storage [13,14,17] | Many One-to-One |

**Table 1:** Coflows in data-parallel cluster applications.

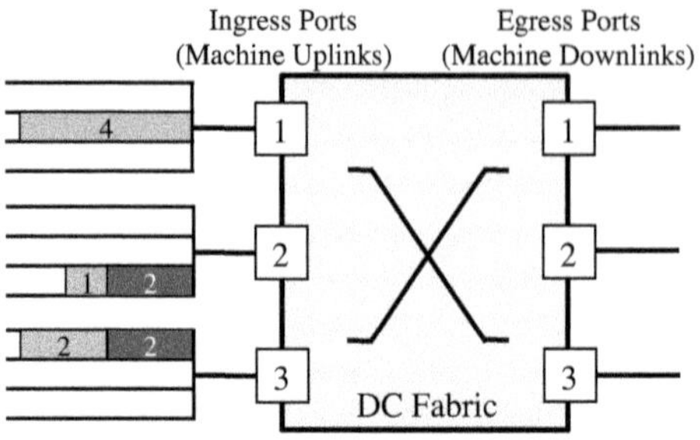


**Figure 1:** Coflow scheduling over a × datacenter fabric with three ingress/egress ports. Flows in ingress ports are organized by destinations and color-coded by coflows – $C_1$ in orange/light and $C_2$ in blue/dark.

## 2.3 Potential Benefits of Inter-Coflow Scheduling

While the network cares about flow-level metrics such as FCT and per-flow fairness, they can be suboptimal for minimizing the time applications spend in communication. Instead of improving network-level metrics that can be at odds with application-level goals, coflows improve performance through application-aware management of network resources.

Consider Figure 1. Assuming both coflows to arrive at the same time, Figure 2 compares four different schedules. Per-flow fairness (Figure 2a) ensures max-min fairness among flows in each link. However, fairness among flows of even the same coflow can increase CCT [15]. WSS (Figure 2c) – the optimal algorithm in homogeneous networks – is up to 1.5× faster than per-flow fairness for individual coflows [15]; but for multiple coflows, it minimizes the completion time across all coflows and increases the average CCT. Recently proposed shortest-flow-first prioritization mechanisms [8, 25] (Figure 2b) decrease average FCT, but they increase the average CCT by interleaving flows from different coflows. Finally, the optimal schedule (Figure 2d) minimizes the average CCT by finishing flows in the coflow order ($C_2$ followed by $C_1$). The FIFO schedule [15, 19] would have been as good as the optimal if $C_2$ arrived before $C_1$, but it could be as bad as per-flow fair sharing or WSS if $C_2$ arrived later.

**Deadline-Sensitive Communication** Assume that $C_1$ and $C_2$ have the same deadline of 2 time units – $C_1$ would never meet its deadline as its minimum CCT is 4. Using per-flow fairness or WSS, both $C_1$ and $C_2$ miss their deadlines. Using earliest-deadline-first (EDF) across flows [25], $C_2$ meets its deadline only 25% of the time. However, the optimal coflow schedule does not admit $C_1$, and $C_2$ always succeeds.

Note that egress ports do not experience any contention in these examples; when they do, coflow-aware scheduling can be even more effective.

# 3 Varys Overview

Varys is a coordinated coflow scheduler to optimize either the performance or the predictability of communication in data-intensive applications. In this section, we present a brief overview of Varys

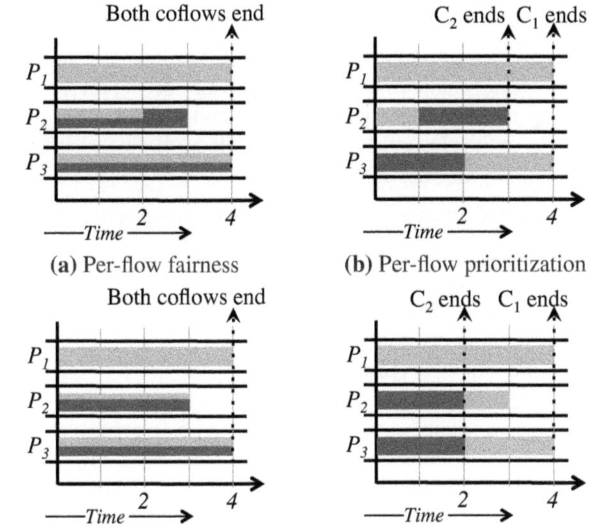


(a) Per-flow fairness (b) Per-flow prioritization (c) WSS [15] (d) The optimal schedule

**Figure 2:** Allocation of *ingress* port capacities (vertical axis) using different mechanisms for the coflows in Figure 1. Each port can transfer one unit of data in one time unit. The average FCT and CCT for (a) per-flow fairness are . and time units; (b) per-flow prioritization are . and . time units; (c) Weighted Shuffle Scheduling (WSS) are . and time units; and (d) the optimal schedule are and time units.

to help the reader follow the measurements of coflows in production clusters (§4), analysis and design of inter-coflow scheduling algorithms (§5), and Varys's design details (§6).

### 3.1 Problem Statement

When improving performance, given a coflow with information about its individual flows, their size, and endpoints, Varys must decide *when to start* its flows and *at what rate* to serve them to minimize the average CCT of the cluster. It can preempt existing coflows to avoid head-of-line blocking, but it must also avoid starvation. Information about a coflow is unknown prior to its arrival.

When optimizing predictability, Varys must *admit a new coflow* if it can be completed within its deadline without violating deadline guarantees of the already-admitted ones.

Irrespective of the objective, the inter-coflow scheduling problem is NP-hard (§5). Varys implements a scheduler that exploits the variations in coflow characteristics (§4) to perform reasonably well in realistic settings.

### 3.2 Architectural Overview

Varys master schedules coflows from different frameworks using global coordination (Figure 3). It works in two modes: it either tries to minimize CCT or to meet deadlines. For the latter, it uses admission control, and rejected coflows must be resubmitted later. Frameworks use a client library to interact with Varys to register and define coflows (§6.1). The master aggregates all interactions to create a global view of the network and determines rates of flows in each coflow (§6.2) that are enforced by the client library.

Varys daemons, one on each machine, handle *time-decoupled* coflows, where senders and receivers are not simultaneously active. Instead of hogging the CPU, sender tasks (e.g., mappers) of data-intensive applications often complete after writing their output to the disk. Whenever corresponding receivers (e.g., reducers) are ready, Varys daemons serve them by coordinating with the master. Varys daemons use the same client library as other tasks. Additionally, these daemons send periodic measurements of the network usage at each machine to Varys master. The master aggregates them

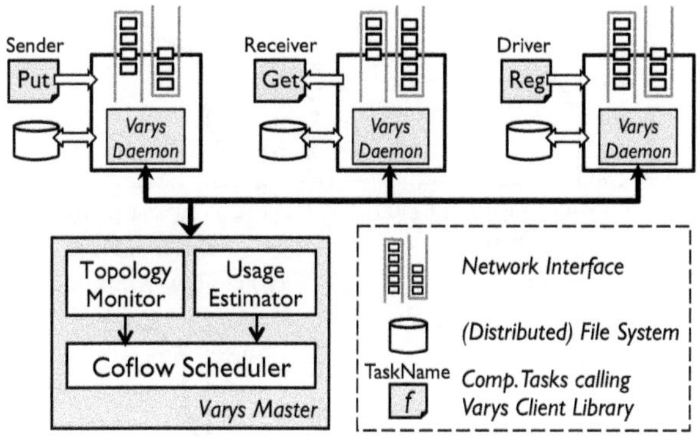


**Figure 3:** Varys architecture. Computation frameworks interact with Varys through a client library.

using existing techniques [17] to estimate current utilizations and use remaining bandwidth ($Rem(.)$) during scheduling (§5.3).

We have implemented Varys in the application layer out of practicality – it can readily be deployed in the cloud, while providing large improvements for both objectives we consider (§7).

**Fault Tolerance** Failures of Varys agents do not hamper job execution, since data can be transferred using regular TCP flows in their absence. Varys agents store soft states that can be rebuilt quickly upon restart. In case of task failures and consequent restarts, corresponding flows are restarted too; other flows of the same coflow, however, are not paused.

**Scalability** Varys reschedules only on coflow arrival and completion events. We did not observe the typical number of concurrent coflows (tens to hundreds [15, 33]) to limit its scalability. Varys batches control messages at $O(100)$ milliseconds intervals to reduce coordination overheads, which affect small coflows (§7.2). Fortunately, most traffic in data-intensive clusters are from large coflows (§4). Hence, we do not use Varys for coflows with bottlenecks smaller than 25 MB in size.

## 4 Coflows in Production

The impact of coflows on job durations and their network footprint have received extensive attention [15, 17, 33, 35, 39]. We focus on understanding their structural characteristics by analyzing traces from a 3000-machine, 150-rack Hive/MapReduce data warehouse at Facebook [17]. We highlight two attributes – wide variety in coflow structures and disproportionate footprint of few large coflows – that motivate and guide Varys's design.

### 4.1 Diversity of Coflow Structures

Because a coflow consists of multiple parallel flows, it cannot be characterized just by its size. We define the *length* of a coflow to be the size of its largest flow in bytes, its *width* to be the number of parallel flows, and its *size* to be the sum of all its flows in bytes. Furthermore, we consider *skew*, i.e., the coefficient of variation of its flows in terms of their size.

The key takeaway from the CDF plots in Figure 4 is that coflows vary widely in all four characteristics. We observe that while more than 40% coflows are short ($\leq$1 MB in length), flows in some coflows can be very large. Similarly, more than 60% narrow coflows (with at most 50 flows) reside with coflows that consist of millions of flows. Furthermore, we see variations of flow sizes within the same coflow (Figure 4c), which underpins the possible improvements from inter-coflow scheduling – e.g., the optimal schedule in Figure 2 outperforms the rest, primarily because it exploits the skew in $C_1$. Note that we rounded up flow sizes to 1 MB to calculate skew in Figure 4c to ignore small variations.

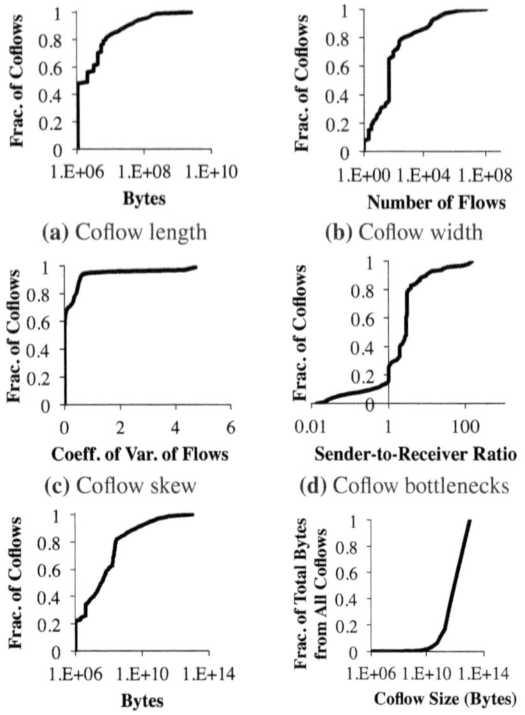


(a) Coflow length (b) Coflow width (c) Coflow skew (d) Coflow bottlenecks (e) Coflow size (f) Coflow footprint

**Figure 4:** Coflows in production vary widely in (a) length, (b) width, (c) skew of flow sizes, (c) bottleneck locations, and (e) total size. Moreover, (f) numerous small coflows have tiny network footprint.

Identifying bottlenecks and exploiting them is the key to improvements. Figure 4d shows that the ratio of sender and receiver ports/machines[2] can be very different across coflows, and senders can be bottlenecks in almost a third of the coflows.

We found that length and width of a coflow have little correlation; a coflow can have many small flows as well as few large flows. However, as Figure 4b and Figure 4c suggest, width and skew are indeed correlated – as width increases, the probability of variations among flows increases as well. We also observed large variation in coflow size (Figure 4e).

### 4.2 Heavy-Tailed Distribution of Coflow Size

Data-intensive jobs in production clusters are known to follow heavy-tailed distributions in terms of their number of tasks, size of input, and output size [10, 17]. We observe the same for coflow size as well. Figure 4f presents the fraction of total coflows contributed by coflows of different size. Comparing it with Figure 4e, we see that almost all traffic are generated by a handful of large coflows – 98% (99.6%) of the relevant bytes belong to only 8% (15%) of the coflows that are more than 10 GB (1 GB) in size. This allows Varys to focus only on scheduling large coflows, where gains significantly outweigh coordination overheads.

## 5 Coflow Scheduling: Analytical Results

The inter-coflow scheduling problem is NP-hard. In this section, we provide insights into its complexity (§5.1) and discuss desirable properties of an ideal scheduler along with associated tradeoffs (§5.2). Based on our understanding, we develop two inter-coflow scheduling algorithms: one to minimize CCTs (§5.3) and another to guarantee coflow completions within their deadlines (§5.4).

Detailed analysis and proofs can be found in the appendix.

[2]One machine can have multiple tasks of the same coflow.

### 5.1 Problem Formulation and Complexity

We consider two objectives for optimizing data-intensive communication: either *minimizing* the average CCT or improving predictability by *maximizing* the number of coflows that meet deadlines (§A). Achieving either objective is NP-hard, even when

1. all coflows can start at the same time,
2. information about their flows are known beforehand, and
3. ingress and egress ports have the same capacity.

We prove it by reducing the concurrent open-shop scheduling problem [34] to inter-coflow scheduling (**Theorem A.1**).

The online inter-coflow scheduling problem is even harder because of the following reasons:

1. *Capacity constraints.* Ingress and egress ports of the datacenter fabric have finite, possibly heterogeneous, capacities. Hence, the optimal solution must find the best *ordering* of flows to dispatch at each ingress port and simultaneously calculate the best *matching* at the egress ports. Furthermore, when optimizing predictability, it must decide whether or not to *admit* a coflow.
2. *Lack of future knowledge.* Arrival times and characteristics of new coflows and their flows cannot be predicted.

Because the rate of any flow depends on its allocations at both ingress and egress ports, we refer to the inter-coflow scheduling problem as an instance of the concurrent open shop scheduling *with coupled resources* (**Remark A.2**). To the best of our knowledge, this variation of the problem – with ordering and matching requirements – has not appeared in the literature prior to this work.

### 5.2 Desirable Properties and Tradeoffs

Efficient scheduling (minimizing completion times) and predictable scheduling (guaranteeing coflow completions within their deadlines) are inherently conflicting. The former requires *preemptive* solutions to avoid *head-of-line* blocking. Shortest-remaining-time-first (SRTF) for optimally scheduling flows on a single link is an example [25]. Preemption, in the worst case, can lead to starvation; e.g., SRTF starves long flows. The latter, on the contrary, requires admission control to provide guarantees.

We expect an ideal scheduler to satisfy the following goals in addition to its primary objective.

1. *Starvation freedom.* Coflows, irrespective of their characteristics, should not starve for arbitrarily long periods.
2. *Work-conserving allocation.* Available resources should be used as much as possible.

The former ensures eventual completion of coflows irrespective of system load. The latter avoids underutilization of the network, which intuitively should result in lower CCTs and higher admissions. However, both are at odds with our primary objectives (§B).

Predictable scheduling has an additional goal.

3. *Guaranteed completion.* If admitted, a coflow must complete within its deadline.

In the following, we present algorithms that achieve high network utilization, and ensure starvation freedom when minimizing CCT (§5.3) and guarantees completion of admitted coflows when maximizing predictability (§5.4).

### 5.3 Inter-Coflow Scheduling to Minimize CCT

Given the complexity, instead of finding an optimal algorithm, we focus on understanding what an offline optimal schedule might look like under simplifying assumptions. Next, we compute the minimum time to complete a single coflow. We use this result as a building block to devise a scheduling heuristic and an iterative

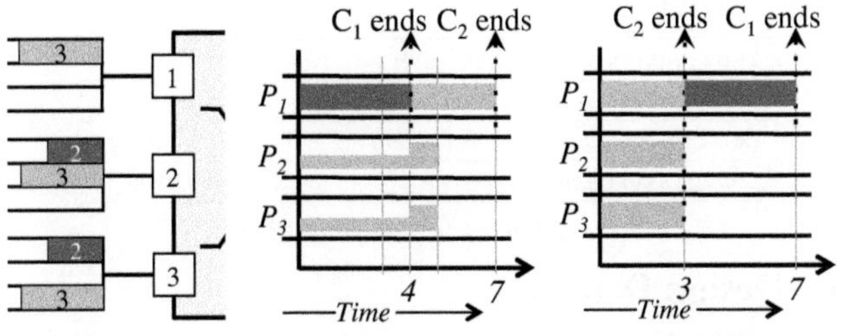


**(a)** Input **(b)** SCF/NCF/TCF **(c)** SEBF

**Figure 5:** Allocations of *egress* port capacities (vertical axis) for the coflows in (a) on a × fabric for different coflow scheduling heuristics (§5.3.2).

bandwidth allocation algorithm. We conclude by presenting the necessary steps to transform our offline solution to an online one with guarantees for starvation freedom and work conservation.

#### 5.3.1 Solution Approach

Consider the offline problem of scheduling $|\mathbb{C}|$ coflows ($\mathbb{C} = \{C_1, C_2, \ldots, C_{|\mathbb{C}|}\}$) that arrived at time 0. The optimality of the shortest-processing-time-first (SPTF) heuristic on a single link suggests that shortest- or smallest-first schedules are the most effective in minimizing completion times [8, 25]. However, in the multi-link scenario, links can have different schedules. This makes the search space exponentially large – there are $((|\mathbb{C}|P)!)^P$ possible solutions when scheduling $|\mathbb{C}|$ coflows with $P^2$ flows each on a $P \times P$ fabric!

If we remove the capacity constraints from either ingress or egress ports, under the assumptions of Section 5.1, the coflow scheduling problem simplifies to the traditional concurrent open shop scheduling problem, which has optimal *permutation schedules* [30]; meaning, scheduling coflows one after another is sufficient, and searching within the $|\mathbb{C}|!$ possible schedules is enough. Unfortunately, permutation schedules can be suboptimal for coupled resources (**Theorem C.1**), which can lead to flow preemptions at arbitrary points in time – not just at coflow arrivals and completions (**Remark C.2**). To avoid incessant rescheduling, we restrict ourselves to permutation schedules.

#### 5.3.2 The Smallest-Effective-Bottleneck-First Heuristic

Once scheduled, a coflow can impact the completion times of all other coflows scheduled after it. Our primary goal is to minimize the opportunity lost in scheduling each coflow.

Given the optimality of the shortest- or smallest-first policy in minimizing the average FCT [8, 25], a natural choice for scheduling coflows would be to approximate that with a *Shortest-Coflow-First (SCF)* heuristic. However, SCF does not take into account the width of a coflow. A width-based alternative to SCF is the *Narrowest-Coflow-First (NCF)* heuristic, but NCF cannot differentiate between a short coflow from a long one. A *smallesT-Coflow-First (TCF)* heuristic is a better alternative than the two – while SCF can be influenced just by a single long flow (i.e., coflow length) and NCF relies only on coflow width, TCF responds to both.

However, the completion time of coflow actually depends on its bottleneck. A coflow $C$ must transfer $\sum_j d_{ij}$ amount of data through each ingress port $i$ ($P_i^{\text{in}}$) and $\sum_i d_{ij}$ through each egress port $j$ ($P_j^{\text{out}}$), where $d_{ij}$ is the amount of data to transfer from $P_i^{\text{in}}$ to $P_j^{\text{out}}$ at rate $r_{ij}$. The minimum CCT ($\Gamma$) becomes

$$\Gamma = \max\left(\max_i \frac{\sum_j d_{ij}}{Rem(P_i^{\text{in}})}, \max_j \frac{\sum_i d_{ij}}{Rem(P_j^{\text{out}})}\right) \tag{1}$$

where $Rem(.)$ denotes the remaining bandwidth of an ingress or egress port estimated by Varys measurements. The former argument of Equation (1) represents the minimum time to transfer $\sum_{ij} d_{ij}$ ($= Size(C)$) amount of data through the input ports, and the latter is for the output ports.

**Pseudocode 1** Coflow Scheduling to Minimize CCT

```
1:  procedure ALLOCBANDWIDTH(Coflows ℂ, Rem . , Bool cct)
2:      for all C ∈ ℂ do
3:          τ = Γ^C (Calculated using Equation (1))
4:          if not cct then
5:              τ = D^C
6:          end if
7:          for all d_ij ∈ C do                                  ▷ MADD
8:              r_ij = d_ij/τ
9:              Update Rem P_i^in and Rem P_j^out
10:         end for
11:     end for
12: end procedure

13: procedure MINCCTOFFLINE(Coflows ℂ, C, Rem . )
14:     ℂ' = SORT_ASC ℂ ∪ C using SEBF
15:     allocBandwidth(ℂ', Rem . , true)
16:     Distribute unused bandwidth to C ∈ ℂ'   ▷ Work conserv. (§5.3.4)
17:     return ℂ'
18: end procedure

19: procedure MINCCTONLINE(Coflows ℂ, C, Rem . )
20:     if timeSinceLastDelta() < T then      ▷ T-interval: Decrease CCT
21:         ℂ' = minCCTOffline(ℂ, C, Rem . )
22:         Update ℂzero, the set of starved coflows
23:     else                                   ▷ δ-interval: Starvation freedom
24:         C* = ⋃C for all C ∈ ℂzero
25:         Apply MADD on C*
26:         Schedule a call to minCCTOnline(.) after δ interval
27:     end if
28: end procedure
```

We propose the *Smallest-Effective-Bottleneck-First (SEBF)* heuristic that considers a coflow's length, width, size, and skew to schedule it in the smallest-$\Gamma$-first order. Figure 5 shows an example: although $C_2$ (orange/light) is bigger than $C_1$ in length, width, and size, SEBF schedules it first to reduce the average CCT to 5 time units from 5.5. While no heuristic is perfect, we found SEBF to be 1.14×, 1.36×, and 1.66× faster than TCF, SCF, and NCF, respectively, in trace-driven simulations and even more in synthetic ones. Additionally, SEBF performs ≥5× better than non-preemptive coflow schedulers (§7.4).

#### 5.3.3 Minimum-Allocation-for-Desired-Duration

Given a schedule of coflows $\mathbb{C}' = (C_1, C_2, \ldots, C_{|\mathbb{C}|})$, the next step is to determine the rates of individual flows. While single-link optimal heuristics would allocate the entire bandwidth of the link to the scheduled flow, we observe that completing a flow faster than the bottleneck does not impact the CCT in coflow scheduling.

Given $\Gamma$, *the minimum completion time of a coflow can be attained as long as all flows finish at time* $\Gamma$. We can ensure that by setting the rates ($r_{ij}$) of each flow to $d_{ij}/\Gamma$. We refer to this algorithm (lines 7–10 in Pseudocode 1) as MADD; this generalizes WSS [15], which works only for homogeneous links. *MADD allocates the least amount of bandwidth to complete a coflow in minimum possible time.*

We use MADD as a building block to allocate rates for the given schedule. We apply MADD to each coflow $C_i \in \mathbb{C}'$ to ensure its fastest completion using minimum bandwidth, and we iteratively distribute (line 15) its unused bandwidth to coflows $C_j$ ($i < j \leq |\mathbb{C}|$). Once $C_i$ completes, the iterative procedure is repeated to complete $C_{i+1}$ and to distribute its unused bandwidth. We stop after $C_{|\mathbb{C}|}$ completes.

**Pseudocode 2** Coflow Scheduling to Guarantee Completion

```
1: procedure MEETDEADLINE(Coflows ℂ, C, Rem . )
2:     allocBandwidth(ℂ, Rem . , false)   ▷ Recalc. min rates for C ∈ ℂ
3:     if Γ^C ≤ D^C then                  ▷ Admission control
4:         ℂ′ = Enqueue C to ℂ            ▷ Add C in the arrival order
5:         allocBandwidth(ℂ′, Rem . , false)
6:         Distribute unused bandwidth to C ∈ ℂ′   ▷ Work conservation
7:         return true
8:     end if
9:     Distribute unused bandwidth to C ∈ ℂ
10:    return false
11: end procedure
```

#### 5.3.4 From Offline to Online

**Work-Conserving Allocation** Letting resources idle – as the offline iterative MADD might do – can hurt performance in the online case. We introduce the following backfilling pass in MINCCTOFFLINE (line 16 of Pseudocode 1) to utilize the unallocated bandwidth throughout the fabric as much as possible. For each ingress port $P_i^{\text{in}}$, we allocate its remaining bandwidth to the coflows in $\mathbb{C}'$; for each active coflow $C$ in $P_i^{\text{in}}$, $Rem(P_i^{\text{in}})$ is allocated to $C$'s flows in their current $r_{ij}$ ratios, subject to capacity constraints in corresponding $P_j^{\text{out}}$.

**Avoiding Perpetual Starvation** Preemption to maintain an SEBF schedule while optimizing CCT may lead to starvation. To avoid perpetual starvation, we introduce the following simple adjustment to the offline algorithm.

We fix tunable parameters $T$ and $\delta$ ($T \gg \delta$) and alternate the overall algorithm (MINCCTONLINE) between time intervals of length $T$ and $\delta$. For a time period of length $T$, we use MINCCTOFFLINE to minimize CCT. At the end of time $T$, we consider all coflows in the system which have not received any service during the last $T$-interval ($\mathbb{C}_{\text{zero}}$). We treat all of them as one collective coflow, and apply MADD for a time period of length $\delta$ (lines 24–26 in Pseudocode 1). All coflows that were served during the last $T$-interval do not receive any service during this $\delta$-interval. At the end of the $\delta$-interval, we revert back, and repeat.

The adjustments ensure that *all* coflows receive non-zero service in every $(T + \delta)$ interval and eventually complete. This is similar to ensuring at least one ticket for each process in lottery scheduling [38]. Avoiding starvation comes at the cost of an increased average CCT. At every $(T + \delta)$ interval, the total CCT increases by at most $|\mathbb{C}|\delta$, and it depends on the ratio of $T$ and $\delta$ (§6.2).

### 5.4 Inter-Coflow Scheduling to Guarantee Deadline

To guarantee a coflow's completion within deadline ($D^C$), completing its bottlenecks as fast as possible has no benefits. *A coflow can meet its deadline using minimum bandwidth as long as all flows finish exactly at the deadline.* We can achieve that by setting $r_{ij} = d_{ij}/D^C$ using MADD.

To provide guarantees in the online scenario, we introduce admission control (line 3 in Pseudocode 2). We admit a coflow $C$, if and only if it can meet its deadline without violating that of any existing coflow. Specifically, we recalculate the minimum bandwidth required to complete all existing coflows within their deadlines (line 2 in Pseudocode 2) and check if the minimum CCT of $C$, $\Gamma^C \leq D^C$. Otherwise, $C$ is rejected. An admitted coflow is never preempted, and a coflow is never rejected if it can safely be admitted. Hence, there is no risk of starvation. We use the backfilling procedure from before for work conservation.

| `VarysClient` Methods | Caller |
|---|---|
| `register`(*numFlows*, [*options*]) ⟹ *coflowId* | Driver |
| `put`(*coflowId*, *dataId*, *content*, [*options*]) | Sender |
| `get`(*coflowId*, *dataId*) ⟹ *content* | Receiver |
| `unregister`(*coflowId*) | Driver |

**Table 2:** The Coflow API

## 6 Design Details

We have implemented Varys in about 5,000 lines of Scala with extensive use of Akka [1] for messaging and the Kryo serialization library [5]. This section illustrates how frameworks interact with Varys (§6.1) and discusses how Varys schedules coflows (§6.2).

### 6.1 Varys Client Library: The Coflow API

Varys client library provides an API similar to DOT [36] to abstract away the underlying scheduling and communication mechanisms. Cluster frameworks (e.g., Spark, Hadoop, or Dryad) must create `VarysClient` objects to invoke the API and interact with Varys. User jobs, however, do *not* require any modifications.

The coflow API has four primary methods (Table 2). Framework drivers initialize a coflow through `register()`, which returns a unique *coflowId* from Varys master. *numFlows* is a hint for the scheduler on when to consider the coflow READY to be scheduled. Additional information or hints (e.g., coflow deadline or dependencies) can be given through *options* – an optional list of key-value pairs. The matching `unregister()` signals coflow completion.

A sender initiates the transfer of a *content* with an identifier *dataId* using `put()`. A *content* can be a file on disk or an object in memory. For example, a mapper would `put()` $r$ pieces of *content* for $r$ reducers in a MapReduce job, and the Spark driver would `put()` a common piece of data to be broadcasted from memory to its workers (we omit corresponding `put()` signatures for brevity). The *dataId* of a *content* is unique within a coflow. Any flow created to transfer *dataId* belongs to the coflow with the specified *coflowId*.

A receiver indicates its interest in a *content* using its *dataId* through `get()`. Only after receiving a `get()` request, the scheduler can create and consider a flow for scheduling. Receiver tasks learn the *dataIds* of interest from respective framework drivers. Varys scheduler determines when, from where, and at what rate to retrieve each requested *dataId*. `VarysClient` enforces scheduler-determined rates at the application layer and notifies the master upon completion of `get()`.

**Usage Example** Consider shuffle – the predominant communication pattern in cluster frameworks. Shuffle transfers the output of each task (mapper) in one computation stage to the tasks (reducers) in the next. The following example shows how to enable a $3 \times 2$ shuffle (with 3 mappers and 2 reducers) to take advantage of inter-coflow scheduling. Assume that all entities interacting with Varys have their own instances of `VarysClient` objects named `client`.

First, the driver registers the shuffle indicating that Varys should consider it READY after receiving `get()` for all six flows.

```
val cId = client.register(6)
```

When scheduling each task, the driver passes along the `cId` for the shuffle. Each mapper $m$ uses `cId` when calling `put()` for each reducer $r$.

```
// Read from DFS, run user-written map method,
// and write intermediate data to disk.
// Now, invoke the coflow API.
for (r <- reducers)
  client.put(cId, dId-m-r, content-m-r)
```

**Pseudocode 3** Message Handlers in Varys Scheduler

```
procedure ONCOFLOWREGISTER(Coflow C)
    Mark C as UNREADY
    ℂcur = ℂcur ∪ {C}                     ▷ ℂcur is the set of all coflows
end procedure

procedure ONCOFLOWUNREGISTER(Coflow C)
    ℂcur = ℂcur \ {C}
    ℂready = ℂ.filter(READY)
    Call appropriate scheduler from Section 5
end procedure

procedure ONFLOWPUT(Flow f, Coflow C)
    Update Size C  and relevant data structures
end procedure

procedure ONFLOWGET(Flow f, Coflow C)
    Update relevant data structures
    Mark C as READY after get() is called numFlows times
    if C is READY then
        ℂready = ℂ.filter(READY)
        Call appropriate scheduler from Section 5
    end if
end procedure
```

In the snippet above, `dId-m-r` is an application-defined unique identifier for individual pieces of data and `content-m-r` is the corresponding path to disk. This is an example of time-decoupled communication.

Reducers use `cId` to retrieve the shuffled pieces of content by the mappers (served by Varys daemons).

```
// Shuffle using the coflow API.
for (m <- mappers)
  content-m-r = client.get(cId, dId-m-r)
// Now, sort, combine, and write to DFS.
```

Once all reducers are done, the driver terminates the coflow.

```
client.unregister(cId)
```

Note that the example abstracts away some details – e.g., the pipelining between shuffle and sort phases in reducers, which can be handled by providing a `VarysInputStream` implementation.

Replacing the communication layer of a data-intensive framework with just the aforementioned changes can enable *all* its user jobs to take advantage of inter-coflow scheduling.

### 6.2 Inter-Coflow Scheduling in Varys

Varys implements the algorithms in Section 5 for inter-coflow scheduling, which are called upon coflow arrival and completion events. $Rem(.)$ is calculated from the aggregated measurements collected by Varys daemons. Pseudocode 3 lists the key event handlers in Varys. Initially, all coflows are marked UNREADY (ONCOFLOWREGISTER). The size of a coflow is updated as `VarysClient` instances periodically notify flow-related events using ONFLOWPUT and ONFLOWGET. A coflow is considered READY to be scheduled after *numFlows* `get()` calls (ONFLOWGET). Varys master groups the new allocations calculated by the scheduler by respective `VarysClients` and sends the changes asynchronously.

**Choice of $T$ and $\delta$ Values** A smaller $\delta$ in Pseudocode 1 ensures a lower impact on the average CCT. However, too small a $\delta$ can cause the underlying transport protocol (e.g., TCP) to behave erratically due to significant variation of available bandwidth over short time intervals. We suggest $\delta$ to be $O(100)$ milliseconds and $T$ to be $O(1)$ seconds.

| **Shuffle Dur.** | < | – | – | ≥ |
|---|---|---|---|---|
| **% of Jobs** | | | | |

**Table 3:** Jobs binned by time spent in communication.

| **Coflow Bin** | **1 (SN)** | **2 (LN)** | **3 (SW)** | **4 (LW)** |
|---|---|---|---|---|
| **Length** | Short | Long | Short | Long |
| **Width** | Narrow | Narrow | Wide | Wide |
| **% of Coflows** | | | | |
| **% of Bytes** | . | . | . | . |

**Table 4:** Coflows binned by width and length.

## 7 Evaluation

We evaluated Varys through a set of experiments on 100-machine EC2 [2] clusters using a Hive/MapReduce trace collected from a large production cluster at Facebook. For a larger scale evaluation, we used a trace-driven simulator that performs a detailed replay of task logs from the same trace. The highlights are:

- For communication-dominated jobs, Varys improves the average (95th percentile) CCT and job completion time by up to $3.16\times$ $(3.84\times)$ and $2.5\times$ $(2.94\times)$, respectively, over per-flow fairness. Across all jobs, the improvements are $1.85\times$ $(1.74\times)$ and $1.25\times$ $(1.15\times)$ (§7.2).
- Simulations show that Varys improves the average (95th percentile) CCT by $5.53\times$ $(5.8\times)$ over per-flow prioritization mechanisms (§7.2).
- Varys enables almost $2\times$ more coflows to meet their deadlines in EC2 experiments (§7.3).
- All coflows eventually complete using Varys without starvation, and simulations show Varys to be $5.65\times$ faster than a non-preemptive solution ($7.7\times$ at the 95th percentile) (§7.4).

### 7.1 Methodology

**Workload** Our workload is based on a Hive/MapReduce trace at Facebook that was collected on a 3000-machine cluster with 150 racks. The original cluster had a $10:1$ core-to-rack oversubscription ratio with a total bisection bandwidth of 300 Gbps. We scale down jobs accordingly to match the maximum possible 100 Gbps bisection bandwidth of our deployment. During the derivation, we preserve the original workload's communication characteristics.

We consider jobs with non-zero shuffle and divide them into bins (Table 3) based on the fraction of their durations spent in shuffle. Table 4 divides the coflows in these jobs into four categories based on their characteristics. Based on the distributions of coflow lengths and widths (Figure 4), we consider a coflow to be *short* if its longest flow is less than 5 MB and *narrow* if it involves at most 50 flows.

For deadline-constrained experiments, we set the deadline of a coflow to be its minimum completion time in an empty network ($\Gamma_{empty}$) multiplied by $(1 + \mathsf{U}(0, x))$, where $\mathsf{U}(0, x)$ is a uniformly random number between 0 and $x$. Unless otherwise specified, $x = 1$. The minimum deadline is 200 milliseconds.

**Cluster** Our experiments use extra large high-memory EC2 instances, which appear to occupy entire physical machines and have enough memory to perform all experiments without introducing disk overheads. We observed bandwidths close to 800 Mbps per machine on clusters of 100 machines. We use a compute engine similar to Spark [41] that uses the coflow API. We use $\delta = 200$ milliseconds and $T = 2$ seconds as defaults.

**Simulator** We use a trace-driven simulator to gain more insights into Varys's performance at a larger scale. The simulator performs a detailed task-level replay of the Facebook trace. It preserves input-

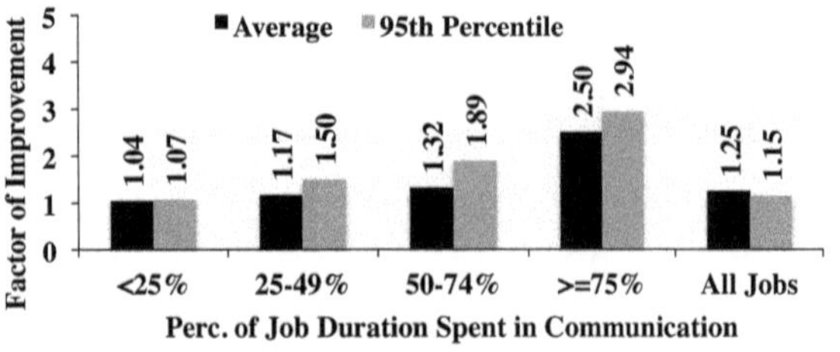


(a) Improvements in job completion times

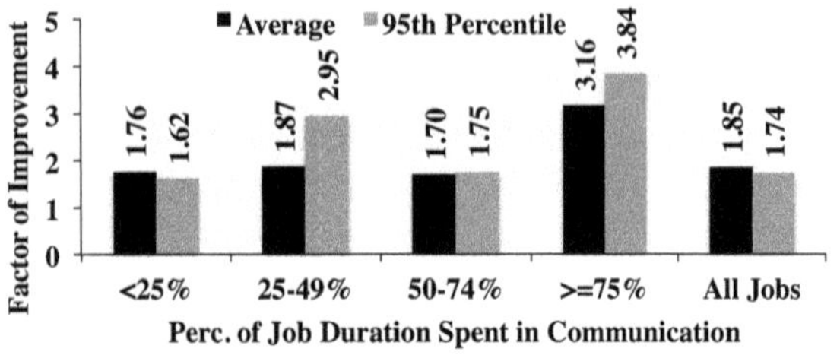


(b) Improvements in time spent in communication

**Figure 6:** [EC2] Average and th percentile improvements in job and communication completion times over per-flow fairness using Varys.

to-output ratios of tasks, locality constraints, and inter-arrival times between jobs. It runs at $10s$ decision intervals for faster completion.

**Metrics** Our primary metric for comparison is the improvement in average completion times of coflows and jobs (when its last task finished) in the workload, where

$$\text{Factor of Improvement} = \frac{\text{Current Duration}}{\text{Modified Duration}}$$

For deadline-sensitive coflows, the primary metric is the percentage of coflows that meet their deadlines.

The baseline for our deployment is TCP fair-sharing. We compare the trace-driven simulator against per-flow fairness as well. Due to the lack of implementations of per-flow prioritization mechanisms [8, 25], we compare against them only in simulation.

### 7.2 Varys's Performance in Minimizing CCT

Figure 6a shows that inter-coflow scheduling reduced the average and 95th percentile completion times of communication-dominated jobs by up to $2.5\times$ and $2.94\times$, respectively, in EC2 experiments. Corresponding average and 95th percentile improvements in the average CCT (CommTime) were up to $3.16\times$ and $3.84\times$ (Figure 6b). Note that varying improvements in the average CCT in different bins are not correlated, because it depends more on coflow characteristics than that of jobs. However, as expected, jobs become increasingly faster as the communication represent a higher fraction of their completion times. Across all bins, the average end-to-end completion times improved by $1.25\times$ and the average CCT improved by $1.85\times$; corresponding 95th percentile improvements were $1.15\times$ and $1.74\times$.

Figure 7 shows that Varys improves CCT for diverse coflow characteristics. Because bottlenecks are not directly correlated with a coflow's length or width, pairwise comparisons across bins – specially those involving bin-2 and bin-3 – are harder. We do observe more improvements for coflows in bin-1 than bin-4 in terms of average CCT, even though their 95th percentile improvements contradict. This is due to coordination overheads in Varys – recall that Varys does not handle small coflows to avoid fixed overheads.

Figure 8a presents comparative CDFs of CCTs for all coflows. Per-flow fairness performs better – $1.08\times$ on average and $1.25\times$ at the 95th percentile – only for some of the tiny, sub-second (<500 milliseconds) coflows, which still use TCP fair sharing. As coflows

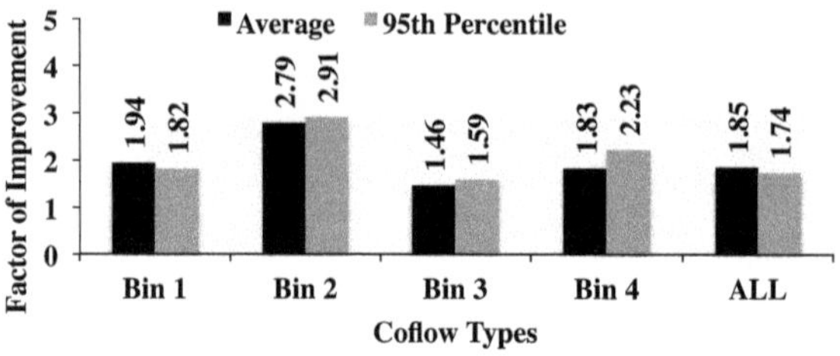


**Figure 7:** [EC2] Improvements in the average and th percentile CCTs using coflows w.r.t. the default per-flow fairness mechanism.

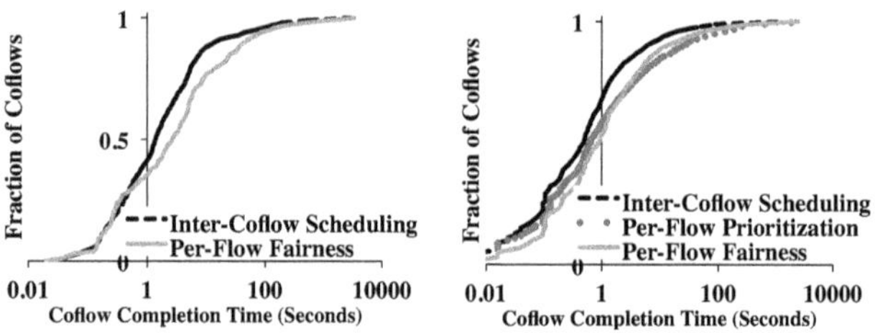


(a) EC2 (b) Simulation

**Figure 8:** CCT distributions for Varys, per-flow fairness, and per-flow prioritization schemes (a) in EC2 deployment and (b) in simulation. Note that the X-axes are in logarithmic scale.

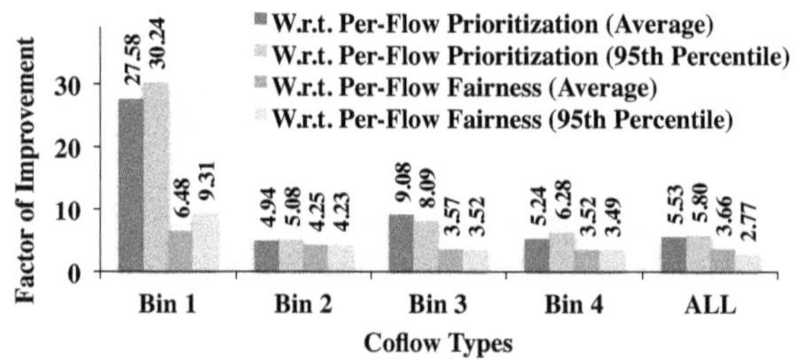


**Figure 9:** [Simulation] Improvements in the average and th percentile CCTs using inter-coflow scheduling.

become larger, the advantages of coflow scheduling becomes more prominent. We elaborate on Varys's overheads next; later, we show simulation results that shed more light on the performance of small coflows in the absence of coordination overheads.

**Overheads** Control plane messages to and from the Varys master are the primary sources of overheads. Multiple messages from the same endpoint are batched whenever possible. At peak load, we observed a throughput of 4000+ messages/second at the master. The scheduling algorithm took 17 milliseconds on average to calculate new schedules on coflow arrival or departure. The average time to distribute new schedules across the cluster was 30 milliseconds.

An additional source of overhead is the synchronization time before a coflow becomes READY for scheduling. Recall that a coflow waits for *numFlows* `get()` calls; hence, a single belated `get()` can block the entire coflow. In our experiments, the average duration to receive all `get()` calls was 44 milliseconds with 151 milliseconds being the 95th percentile.

A large fraction of these overheads could be avoided in the presence of in-network isolation of control plane messages [21].

**Trace-Driven Simulation** We compared the performance of inter-coflow scheduling against per-flow fairness and prioritization schemes in simulations. Without coordination overheads, the improvements are noticeably larger (Figure 9) – the average and 95th percentile CCTs improved by $3.66\times$ and $2.77\times$ over per-flow fairness and by $5.53\times$ and $5.8\times$ over per-flow prioritization.

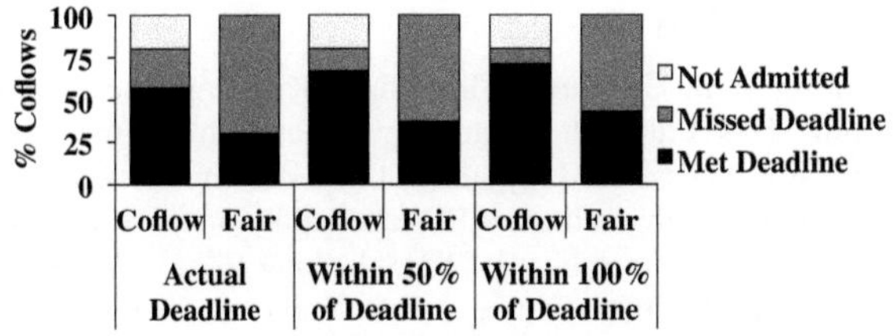


**Figure 10:** [EC2] Percentage of coflows that meet deadline using Varys in comparison to per-flow fairness. Increased deadlines improve performance.

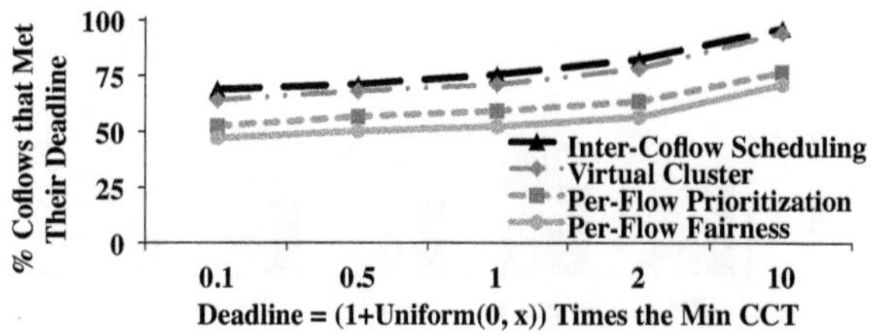


**Figure 11:** [Simulation] More coflows meet deadline using inter-coflow scheduling than using per-flow fairness and prioritization schemes.

| | # Coflows | %SN | %LN | %SW | %LW |
|---|---|---|---|---|---|
| Mix-N | | 48 | 40 | | |
| Mix-W | | | | 24 | 39 |
| Mix-S | | 50 | | 10 | |
| Mix-L | | | 27 | | 31 |

**Table 5:** Four extreme coflow mixes from the Facebook trace.

Note that comparative improvements for bin-1 w.r.t. other bins are significantly larger than that in experiments because of the absence of scheduler coordination overheads. We observe larger absolute values of improvements in Figure 9 in comparison to the ones in Figure 7. Primary factors for this phenomenon include instant scheduling, zero-latency setup/cleanup/update of coflows, and perfectly timed flow arrivals (i.e., coflows are READY to be scheduled upon arrival) in the simulation. In the absence of these overheads, we see in Figure 8b that Varys can indeed outperform per-flow schemes even for sub-second coflows.

**What About Per-Flow Prioritization?** Figure 9 highlights that per-flow prioritization mechanisms are even worse (by 1.52×) than per-flow fairness provided by TCP when optimizing CCTs. The primary reason is indiscriminate interleaving across coflows – while all flows make some progress using flow-level fairness, per-flow prioritization favors only the small flows irrespective of the progress of their parent coflows. However, as expected, flow-level prioritization is still 1.08× faster than per-flow fairness in terms of the average FCT. Figure 8b presents the distribution of CCTs using per-flow prioritization in comparison to other approaches.

**How Far are We From the Optimal?** While finding the optimal schedule is infeasible, we tried to find an optimistic estimation of possible improvements by comparing against an *offline* 2-approximation combinatorial ordering heuristic for coflows *without* coupled resources [30]. We found that the average CCT did not change using the combinatorial approach. For bin-1 to bin-4, the changes were 1.14×, 0.96×, 1.46×, and 0.92×, respectively.

### 7.3 Varys's Performance for Deadline-Sensitive Coflows

Inter-coflow scheduling allowed almost 2× more coflows to complete within corresponding deadlines in EC2 experiments (Figure 10) – 57% coflows met their deadlines using Varys as opposed to 30% using the default mechanism. Coflows across different bins experienced similar results, which is expected because Varys does not differentiate between coflows when optimizing for deadlines.

Recall that because the original trace did not contain coflow-specific deadlines, we introduced them based on the minimum CCT of coflows (§7.1). Hence, we did not expect 100% admission rate. However, a quarter of the admitted coflows failed to meet their deadlines. This goes back to the lack of network support in estimating utilizations and enforcing Varys-determined allocations: Varys admitted more coflows than it should have had, which themselves missed their deadlines and caused some others to miss as well. Trace-driven simulations later shed more light on this.

To understand how far off the failed coflows were, we analyzed if they could complete with slightly longer deadlines. After doubling the deadlines, we found that almost 94% of the admitted coflows succeeded using Varys.

**Trace-Driven Simulation** In trace-driven simulations, for the default case ($x$=1), Varys admitted 75% of the coflows and *all* of them met their deadlines (Figure 11). Note that the admission rate is lower than that in our experiments. Prioritization schemes fared better than per-flow fairness unlike when the objective was minimizing CCT: 59% coflows completed within their deadlines in comparison to 52% using fair sharing.

As we changed the deadlines of all coflows by varying $x$ from 0.1 to 10, comparative performance of all the approaches remained almost the same. Performance across bins were consistent as well.

**What About Reservation Schemes?** Because the impact of admission control is similar to reserving resources, we compared our performance with that of the Virtual Cluster (VC) abstraction [11], where all machines can communicate at the same maximum rate through a virtual non-blocking switch. The VC abstraction admitted and completed slightly fewer coflows (73%) than Varys (75%), because reservation using VCs is more conservative.

### 7.4 Impact of Preemption

While minimizing CCT, preemption-based mechanisms can starve certain coflows when the system is overloaded. Varys takes precautions (§5.3.4) to avoid such scenarios. As expected, we did not observe any perpetual starvation during experiments or simulations.

**What About a Non-Preemptive Scheduler?** Processing coflows in their arrival order (i.e., FIFO) avoids starvation [15]. However, simulations confirmed that head-of-line blocking significantly hurts performance – specially, the short coflows in bin-1 and bin-3.

We found that processing coflows in the FIFO order can result in 24.64×, 5.44×, 34.2×, and 5.03× slower completion times for bin-1 to bin-4. The average (95th percentile) CCT became 5.65× (7.7×) slower than that using Varys.

### 7.5 Impact on Network Utilization

To understand Varys's impact on network utilization, we compared the ratios of *makespans* in the original workload as well as the ones in Table 5. Given a fixed workload, a change in makespan means a change in aggregate network utilization.

We did not observe significant changes in makespan in our EC2 experiments – the exact factors of improvements were 1.02×, 1.06×, 1.01×, 0.97×, and 1.03× for the five workloads. This is expected because while Varys is not work-conserving at every point in time, its overall utilization is the same as non-coflow approaches.

Makespans for both per-flow fairness and coflow-enabled schedules were the same in the trace-driven simulation.

### 7.6 Impact of Coflow Mix

To explore the impact of changes in the coflow mix, we selected four extreme hours (Table 5) from the trace and performed hour-long experiments on EC2. These hours were chosen based on the

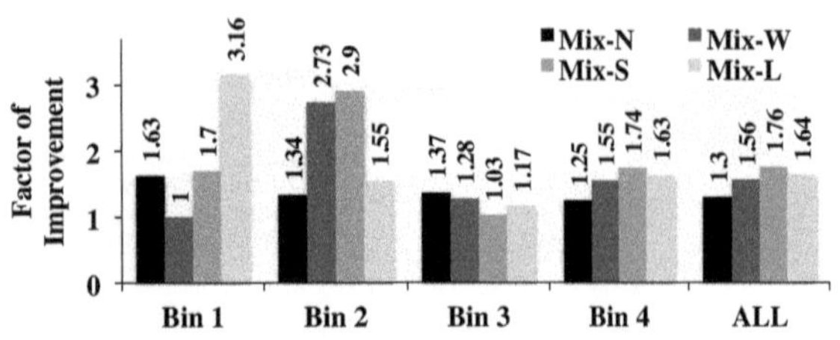


**Figure 12:** [EC2] Improvements in the average CCT using coflows for different coflow mixes from Table 5.

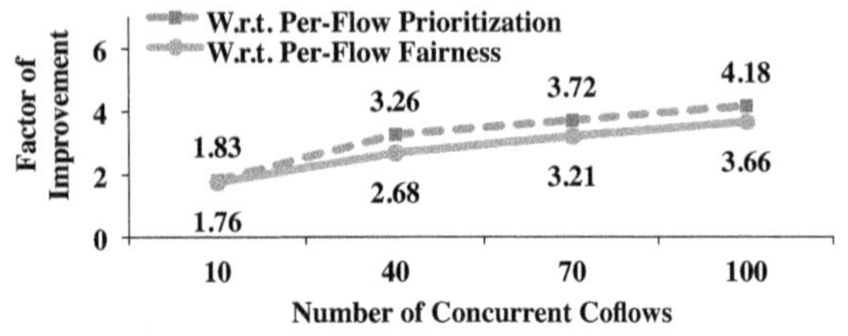


**Figure 13:** [Simulation] Improvements in the average CCT for varying numbers of concurrent coflows.

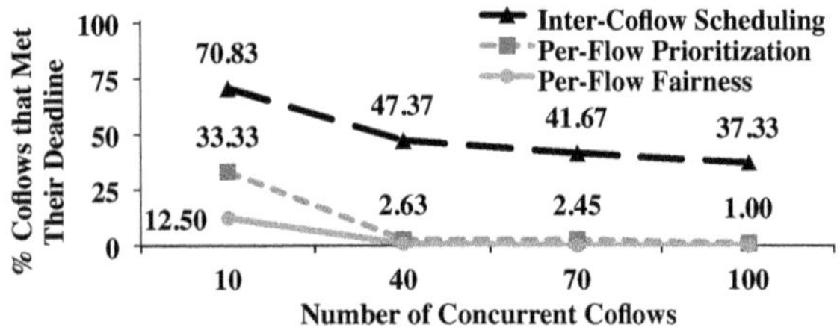


**Figure 14:** [Simulation] Changes in the percentage of coflows that meet deadlines for varying numbers of concurrent coflows.

high percentage of certain types of coflows (e.g., narrow ones in Mix-N) during those periods.

Figure 12 shows that the average CCT improves irrespective of the mix, albeit in varying degrees. Observations made earlier (§7.2) still hold for each mix. However, identifying the exact reason(s) for different levels of improvements is difficult. This is due to the online nature of the experiments – the overall degree of improvement depends on the instantaneous interplay of concurrent coflows. We also did not observe any clear correlation between the number of coflows or workload size and corresponding improvements.

### 7.7 Impact of Cluster/Network Load

So far we have evaluated Varys's improvements in online settings, where the number of concurrent coflows varied over time. To better understand the impact of network load, we used the same coflow mix as the original trace but varied the number of concurrent coflows in an offline setting. We see in Figure 13 that Varys's improvements increase with increased concurrency: per-flow mechanisms fall increasingly further behind as they ignore the structures of more coflows. Also, flow-level fairness consistently outperforms per-flow prioritization mechanisms in terms of the average CCT.

**Deadline-Sensitive Coflows** We performed a similar analysis for deadline-sensitive coflows. Because in this case Varys's performance depends on the arrival order, we randomized the coflow order across runs and present their average in Figure 14. We observe that as the number of coexisting coflows increases, a large number of coflows (37% for 100 concurrent coflows) meet their deadlines using Varys; per-flow mechanisms completely stop working even before. Also, per-flow prioritization outperforms (however marginally) flow-level fairness for coflows with deadlines.

## 8 Discussion

**Scheduling With Unknown Flow Sizes** Knowing or estimating exact flow sizes is difficult in frameworks that push data to the next stage as soon as possible [26], and without known flow sizes, preemption becomes impractical. FIFO scheduling can solve this problem, but it suffers from head-of-line blocking (§7.4). We believe that coflow-level fairness can be a nice compromise between these two extremes. However, the definition and associated properties of fairness at the coflow level is an open problem.

**Decentralized SEBF+MADD** Varys's centralized design makes it less useful for small coflows (§3); however, small coflows contribute less than 1% of the traffic in data-intensive clusters (§4). Furthermore, in-network isolation of control plane messages [21] or faster signaling channels like RDMA [20] can reduce Varys's application-layer signaling overheads (§7.2) to support even smaller coflows. We see a decentralized approximation of our algorithms as the most viable way to make Varys useful for low-latency coflows. This requires new algorithms and possible changes to network devices, unlike our application-layer design.

**Handling Coflow Dependencies** While most jobs require only a single coflow, dataflow pipelines (e.g., Dryad, Spark) can create multiple coflows with dependencies between them [16]. A simple approach to support coflow dependencies would be to order first by ancestry and then breaking ties using SEBF. Some variation of the Critical-Path Method [28] might perform even better. We leave it as a topic of future work. Note that dependencies can be passed along to the scheduler through *options* in the `register()` method.

**Multi-Wave Coflows** Large jobs often schedule mappers in multiple waves [10]. A job can create separate coflows for each wave. Alternatively, if the job uses its wave-width (i.e., the number of parallel mappers) as *numFlows* in `register()`, Varys can handle each wave separately. Applications can convey information about wave-induced coflows to the scheduler as dependencies.

**In-Network Bottlenecks** Varys performs well even when the network is not a non-blocking switch (§7). If likely bottleneck locations are known, e.g., rack-to-core links are typically oversubscribed [17], Varys can be extended to allocate rack-to-core bandwidth instead of NIC bandwidth. When bottlenecks are unknown, e.g., due to in-network failures, routing, or load imbalance, Varys can react based on bandwidth estimations collected by its daemons. Nonetheless, designing and deploying coflow-aware routing protocols and load balancing techniques remain an open challenge.

## 9 Related Work

**Coflow Schedulers** Varys improves over Orchestra [15] in four major ways. First, Orchestra primarily optimizes individual coflows and uses FIFO among them; whereas, Varys uses an efficient coflow scheduler to significantly outperform FIFO. Second, Varys supports deadlines and ensures guaranteed coflow completion. Third, Varys uses a rate-based approach instead of manipulating the number of TCP flows, which breaks if all coflows do not share the same endpoints. Finally, Varys supports coflows from multiple frameworks like Mesos [24] handles non-network resources.

Baraat [19] is a FIFO-based decentralized coflow scheduler focusing on small coflows. It uses fair sharing to avoid head-of-line blocking and does not support deadlines. Furthermore, we formulate the coflow scheduling problem and analyze its characteristics.

**Datacenter Traffic Management** Hedera [7] manages flows using a centralized scheduler to increase network throughput, and MicroTE [12] adapts to traffic variations by leveraging their short-term predictability. However, both work with flows and are unsuitable for optimizing CCTs. Sinbad [17] uses endpoint flexible transfers for load balancing. Once it makes network-aware placement decisions, Varys can optimize cross-rack write coflows.

**High Capacity Networks** Full bisection bandwidth topologies [22,32] do not imply contention freedom. In the presence of skewed data and hotspot distributions [17], managing edge bandwidth is still necessary. Inter-coflow scheduling improves performance and predictability even in these high capacity networks.

**Traffic Reduction Techniques** Data locality [18], both disk [9,40] and memory [10], reduces network usage only during reads. The amount of network usage due to intermediate data communication can be reduced by pushing filters toward the sources [6, 23]. Our approach is complementary; i.e., it can be applied to whatever data traverses the network after applying those techniques.

**Network Sharing Among Tenants** Fair sharing of network resources between multiple tenants has received considerable attention [11, 33, 35, 39]. Our work is complementary; we focus on optimizing performance of concurrent coflows within a single administrative domain, instead of achieving fairness among competing entities. Moreover, we focus on performance and predictability as opposed to the more debated notion of fairness.

**Concurrent Open Shop Scheduling** Inter-coflow scheduling has its roots in the concurrent open shop scheduling problem [34], which is strongly NP-hard for even two machines. Even in the offline scenario, the best known result is a 2-approximation algorithm [30], and it is inapproximable within a factor strictly less than $6/5$ if P≠NP [30]. Our setting is different as follows. First, machines are not independent; i.e., links are coupled because each flow involves a source and a destination. Second, jobs are not known a priori; i.e., coflows arrive in an online fashion.

# 10 Concluding Remarks

The coflow abstraction [16] effectively enables application-aware network scheduling. We have implemented coflows in a system called Varys and introduced the *concurrent open shop scheduling with coupled resources* problem. To minimize coflow completion times (CCT), we proposed the SEBF heuristic to schedule coflows and the MADD algorithm to allocate bandwidth to their flows. Together, they decrease the average CCT without starving any coflow and maintain high network utilization. Through EC2 deployments and trace-driven simulations, we showed that Varys outperforms per-flow mechanisms by up to $3.16\times$ and non-preemptive coflow schedulers by more than $5\times$. Furthermore, by applying MADD in conjunction with admission control, Varys allowed up to $2\times$ more coflows to meet their deadlines in comparison to per-flow schemes.

In conclusion, this paper is only a first step in understanding the intricacies of inter-coflow scheduling and opens up a variety of exciting research problems, which include scheduling without knowing flow sizes, exploring the notion of coflow fairness, decentralizing the proposed algorithms, and handling coflow dependencies.

# Acknowledgments

We thank Mohammad Alizadeh, Justine Sherry, Rachit Agarwal, Peter Bailis, Ganesh Ananthanarayanan, Tathagata Das, Ali Ghodsi, Gautam Kumar, David Zats, Matei Zaharia, the AMPLab members, our shepherd Nandita Dukkipati, and the anonymous reviewers of NSDI'14 and SIGCOMM'14 for useful feedback. This research is supported in part by NSF CISE Expeditions Award CCF-1139158, LBNL Award 7076018, and DARPA XData Award FA8750-12-2-0331, and gifts from Amazon Web Services, Google, SAP, The Thomas and Stacey Siebel Foundation, Apple, Inc., Cisco, Cloudera, EMC, Ericsson, Facebook, GameOnTalis, Guavus, HP, Huawei, Intel, Microsoft, NetApp, Pivotal, Splunk, Virdata, VMware, WANdisco and Yahoo!.

# 11 References

[1] Akka. http://akka.io.
[2] Amazon EC2. http://aws.amazon.com/ec2.
[3] Apache Hadoop. http://hadoop.apache.org.
[4] Apache Hive. http://hive.apache.org.
[5] Kryo serialization library. https://code.google.com/p/kryo.
[6] S. Agarwal et al. Reoptimizing data parallel computing. In *NSDI'12*.
[7] M. Al-Fares et al. Hedera: Dynamic flow scheduling for data center networks. In *NSDI*. 2010.
[8] M. Alizadeh et al. pFabric: Minimal near-optimal datacenter transport. In *SIGCOMM*. 2013.
[9] G. Ananthanarayanan et al. Reining in the outliers in mapreduce clusters using Mantri. In *OSDI*. 2010.
[10] G. Ananthanarayanan et al. PACMan: Coordinated memory caching for parallel jobs. In *NSDI*. 2012.
[11] H. Ballani et al. Towards predictable datacenter networks. In *SIGCOMM*. 2011.
[12] T. Benson et al. MicroTE: Fine grained traffic engineering for data centers. In *CoNEXT*. 2011.
[13] D. Borthakur. The Hadoop distributed file system: Architecture and design. Hadoop Project Website, 2007.
[14] R. Chaiken et al. SCOPE: Easy and efficient parallel processing of massive datasets. In *VLDB*. 2008.
[15] M. Chowdhury et al. Managing data transfers in computer clusters with Orchestra. In *SIGCOMM*. 2011.
[16] M. Chowdhury et al. Coflow: A networking abstraction for cluster applications. In *HotNets-XI*, pages 31–36. 2012.
[17] M. Chowdhury et al. Leveraging endpoint flexibility in data-intensive clusters. In *SIGCOMM*. 2013.
[18] J. Dean et al. MapReduce: Simplified data processing on large clusters. In *OSDI*, pages 137–150. 2004.
[19] F. Dogar et al. Decentralized task-aware scheduling for data center networks. Technical Report MSR-TR-2013-96, 2013.
[20] A. Dragojević et al. FaRM: Fast remote memory. In *NSDI*. 2014.
[21] A. D. Ferguson et al. Participatory networking: An API for application control of SDNs. In *SIGCOMM*. 2013.
[22] A. Greenberg et al. VL2: A scalable and flexible data center network. In *SIGCOMM*. 2009.
[23] Z. Guo et al. Spotting code optimizations in data-parallel pipelines through PeriSCOPE. In *OSDI*. 2012.
[24] B. Hindman et al. Mesos: A Platform for Fine-Grained Resource Sharing in the Data Center. In *NSDI*. 2011.
[25] C.-Y. Hong et al. Finishing flows quickly with preemptive scheduling. In *SIGCOMM*. 2012.
[26] M. Isard et al. Dryad: Distributed data-parallel programs from sequential building blocks. In *EuroSys*, pages 59–72. 2007.
[27] N. Kang et al. Optimizing the "One Big Switch" abstraction in Software-Defined Networks. In *CoNEXT*. 2013.
[28] J. E. Kelley. Critical-path planning and scheduling: Mathematical basis. *Operations Research*, 9(3):296–320, 1961.
[29] G. Malewicz et al. Pregel: A system for large-scale graph processing. In *SIGMOD*. 2010.
[30] M. Mastrolilli et al. Minimizing the sum of weighted completion times in a concurrent open shop. *Operations Research Letters*, 38(5):390–395, 2010.
[31] N. McKeown et al. Achieving 100% throughput in an input-queued switch. *IEEE Transactions on Communications*, 47(8), 1999.
[32] R. N. Mysore et al. PortLand: A scalable fault-tolerant layer 2 data center network fabric. In *SIGCOMM*, pages 39–50. 2009.
[33] L. Popa et al. FairCloud: Sharing the network in cloud computing. In *SIGCOMM*. 2012.
[34] T. A. Roemer. A note on the complexity of the concurrent open shop problem. *Journal of Scheduling*, 9(4):389–396, 2006.
[35] A. Shieh et al. Sharing the data center network. In *NSDI*. 2011.
[36] N. Tolia et al. An architecture for internet data transfer. In *NSDI'06*.
[37] L. G. Valiant. A bridging model for parallel computation. *Communications of the ACM*, 33(8):103–111, 1990.
[38] C. A. Waldspurger et al. Lottery scheduling: Flexible proportional-share resource management. In *OSDI*. 1994.

[39] D. Xie et al. The only constant is change: Incorporating time-varying network reservations in data centers. In *SIGCOMM*. 2012.
[40] M. Zaharia et al. Delay scheduling: A simple technique for achieving locality and fairness in cluster scheduling. In *EuroSys*. 2010.
[41] M. Zaharia et al. Resilient distributed datasets: A fault-tolerant abstraction for in-memory cluster computing. In *NSDI*. 2012.

# APPENDIX

## A Problem Formulation and Complexity

Each coflow $C(\mathbf{D})$ is a collection of flows over the datacenter backplane with $P$ ingress and $P$ egress ports, where the $P \times P$ matrix $\mathbf{D} = [d_{ij}]_{P \times P}$ represents the structure of $C$. For each non-zero element $d_{ij} \in \mathbf{D}$, a flow $f_{ij}$ transfers $d_{ij}$ amount of data from the $i$th ingress port ($P_i^{\text{in}}$) to the $j$th egress port ($P_j^{\text{out}}$) across the backplane at rate $r_{ij}$, which is determined by the scheduling algorithm.

If $C_k$ represents the time for all flows of the $k$th coflow to finish and $r_{ij}^k(t)$ the bandwidth allocated to $f_{ij}$ of the $k$th coflow at time $t$, the objective of minimizing CCT ($\mathsf{O}(.)$) in the offline case can be represented as follows.

$$\text{Minimize} \sum_{k=1}^{K} C_k \tag{2}$$

$$\text{Subject to} \sum_{j',k} r_{ij'}^k(t) \le 1 \qquad \forall t, \forall i; \tag{3}$$

$$\sum_{i',k} r_{i'j}^k(t) \le 1 \qquad \forall t, \forall j; \tag{4}$$

$$\sum_{t=1}^{C_k} r_{ij}^k(t) \ge d_{ij}^k \qquad \forall i, j, k. \tag{5}$$

The first two inequalities are the capacity constraints on ingress and egress ports. The third inequality ensures that all flows of the $k$th coflow finish by time $C_k$.

By introducing a binary variable $U_k$ to denote whether a coflow finished within its deadline $D_k$, we can express the objective of maximizing the number of coflows that meet their deadlines ($\mathsf{Z}(.)$) in the offline case as follows.

$$\text{Maximize} \sum_{k=1}^{K} U_k \tag{6}$$

Subject to inequalities (3), (4), and (5);

$$\text{Where } U_k = \begin{cases} 1 & C_k \le D_k \\ 0 & C_k > D_k \end{cases}$$

Optimizing either objective ($\mathsf{O}$ or $\mathsf{Z}$) is NP-hard.

**Theorem A.1** *Even under the assumptions of Section 5.1, optimizing* $\mathsf{O}$ *or* $\mathsf{Z}$ *in the offline case is NP-hard for all* $P \ge 2$.

**Proof Sketch** We reduce the NP-hard concurrent open shop problem [34] to the coflow scheduling problem. Consider a network fabric with only 2 ingress and egress ports ($P = 2$) and all links have the same capacity (without loss of generality, we can let this capacity be 1). Since there are only 2 ports, all coflows are of the form $C(\mathbf{D})$, where $\mathbf{D} = (d_{ij})_{i,j=1}^2$ is a $2 \times 2$ data matrix. Suppose that $n$ coflows arrive at time 0, and let $\mathbf{D}^k = (d_{ij}^k)_{i,j=1}^2$ be the matrix of the $k$th coflow. Moreover, assume for all $k$, $d_{ij}^k = 0$ if $i = j$. In other words, every coflow only consists of 2 flows, one sending data from ingress port $P_1^{\text{in}}$ to egress port $P_2^{\text{out}}$, and the other sending from ingress port $P_2^{\text{in}}$ to egress port $P_1^{\text{out}}$.

Consider now an equivalent concurrent open shop scheduling problem with 2 identical machines (hence the same capacity). Suppose $n$ jobs arrive at time 0, and the $k$th job has $d_{12}^k$ amount of work for machine 1 and $d_{21}^k$ for machine 2. Since this is NP-hard [34], the coflow scheduling problem described above is NP-hard as well. ■

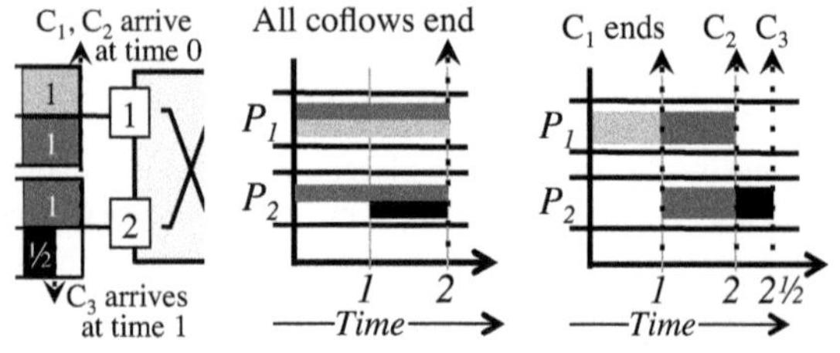


**Figure 15:** Allocation of *ingress* port capacities (vertical axis) for the coflows in (a) on a × datacenter fabric for (b) a work-conserving and (c) a CCT-optimized schedule. While the former is work-conserving and achieves higher utilization, the latter has a lower average CCT.

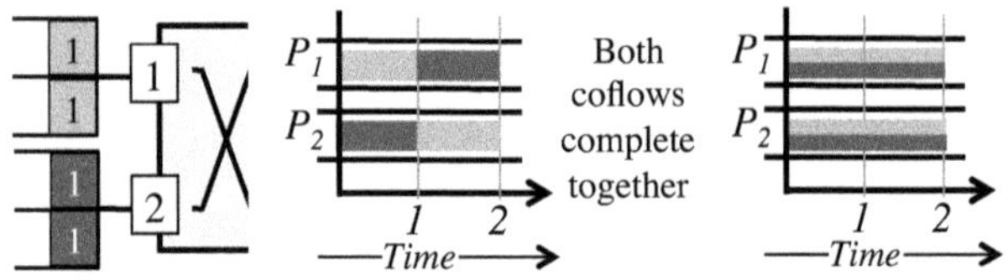


**Figure 16:** Flow-interleaved allocation of *ingress* port capacities (vertical axis) for the coflows in (a) for CCT-optimality (b).

**Remark A.2** Given the close relation between concurrent open shop scheduling and coflow scheduling, it is natural to expect that techniques to express concurrent open shop scheduling as a mixed-integer program and using standard LP relaxation techniques to derive approximation algorithms [30, 34] would readily extend to our case. However, they do not, because the coupled constraints (3) and (4) make permutation schedules sub-optimal (**Theorem C.1**). We leave the investigation of these topics as future work.

## B Tradeoffs in Optimizing CCT

**With Work Conservation** Consider Figure 15a. Coflows $C_1$ and $C_2$ arrive at time 0 with one and two flows, respectively. Each flow transfers unit data. $C_3$ arrives one time unit later and uses a single flow to send 0.5 data unit. Figure 15b shows the work-conserving solution, which finishes in 2 time units for an average CCT of 1.67 time units. The optimal solution (Figure 15c), however, takes 2.5 time units for the *same* amount of data (i.e., it lowers utilization); still, it has a $1.11\times$ lower average CCT (1.5 time units).

**With Avoiding Starvation** The tradeoff between minimum completion time and starvation is well-known for flows (tasks) on individual links (machines) – longer flows starve if a continuous stream of short flows keep arriving. The same tradeoff holds for coflows, because the datacenter fabric and coflows generalize links and flows, respectively.

## C Ordering Properties of Coflow Schedules

**Theorem C.1** *Permutation schedule is not optimal for minimizing the average CCT.*

**Proof Sketch** Both permutation schedules – $C_1$ before $C_2$ and $C_2$ before $C_1$ – would be suboptimal for the example in Figure 16a. ■

**Remark C.2** In Varys, SEBF would schedule $C_1$ before $C_2$ (arbitrarily breaking the tie), and iterative MADD will allocate the minimum bandwidth to quickly finish $C_1$ and then give the remaining bandwidth to $C_2$ (Figure 16c). The average CCT will be the same as the optimal for this example.

# Multi-Resource Packing for Cluster Schedulers

Robert Grandl[1,2] Ganesh Ananthanarayanan[1,3] Srikanth Kandula[1]
Sriram Rao[1] Aditya Akella[1,2]
Microsoft[1], Univ. of Wisconsin, Madison[2], Univ. of California, Berkeley[3]

**Abstract**– Tasks in modern data-parallel clusters have highly diverse resource requirements along CPU, memory, disk and network. We present Tetris, a multi-resource cluster scheduler that *packs* tasks to machines based on their requirements of all resource types. Doing so avoids resource *fragmentation* as well as *over-allocation* of the resources that are not explicitly allocated, both of which are drawbacks of current schedulers. Tetris adapts heuristics for the multidimensional bin packing problem to the context of cluster schedulers wherein task arrivals and machine availability change in an online manner and wherein task's resource needs change with time and with the machine that the task is placed at. In addition, Tetris improves average job completion time by preferentially serving jobs that have less remaining work. We observe that fair allocations do not offer the best performance and the above heuristics are compatible with a large class of fairness policies; hence, we show how to simultaneously achieve good performance and fairness. Trace-driven simulations and deployment of our Apache YARN prototype on a 250 node cluster show gains of over 30% in makespan and job completion time while achieving nearly perfect fairness.

## Categories and Subject Descriptors

C.2.4 [Computer-Communication Networks]: Distributed Systems

## Keywords

Cluster schedulers; multi-dimensional packing; makespan; completion time; fairness

## 1. INTRODUCTION

To analyze large datasets, it has become typical to use clusters of machines to execute *jobs* consisting of many *tasks*. Jobs of many applications coexist on these clusters and their tasks have *diverse resource demands*. For instance, machine learning tasks are CPU-intensive while sort tasks are memory-intensive. Often, tasks are constrained on *multiple* resources, e.g., reduce tasks that are both memory- as well as network-intensive.

Given such diversity, we seek to build a cluster scheduler that *packs* tasks to machines based on their requirements on all the resources. Our objective in packing is to maximize the task throughput (or minimize makespan [1]) and speed up job completion. Packing is important in today's clusters due to *balanced* machine specifications (e.g., enough memory to be able to use all available disk drives and enough cross-rack network bandwidth [8, 13, 15] to use all the available CPU cores). Therefore, *any* of the resources—cores, memory, disk or network—can become fully used on a machine and prevent further tasks from being scheduled there.

Current schedulers neither pack tasks nor consider all their relevant resource demands. This results in *fragmentation* and *over-allocation* of resources, respectively. (*i*) Schedulers divide resources into slots (corresponding to some amount of memory and cores [5]) and offer the slots greedily to the job that is furthest from its *fair* share [3, 4, 12]. Such scheduling results in resource fragmentation, the magnitude of which increases with the number of resources being allocated [20].[2] (*ii*) Schedulers also ignore disk and network requirements of tasks [5, 12, 18]. When assigning tasks to machines, they only check that tasks' CPU and memory needs are satisfiable. Hence, they can schedule many network or disk-intensive tasks on the same machine. Such *over-allocation* leads to interference–disk seeks or network incast– that can sharply lower throughput. Also, over-allocation wastes resources. For example, when two tasks that can both use all of the available network bandwidth on a machine are scheduled together, they will take twice as long to finish. In doing so, they hold to their cores and memory and prevent other tasks that do not need the network from using them. Our analysis shows that, due to fragmentation and over-allocation of resources, the state-of-the-art schedulers in Facebook's and Bing's analytics clusters delay job completions and increase makespan by over 45%.

Multi-resource packing of tasks is analogous to multi-dimensional bin packing. Given balls and bins with sizes in $\mathcal{R}^d$, where $d$ is the number of resources to be allocated, multi-dimensional bin packing assigns the balls to the fewest number of bins. Doing so maximizes the number of simultaneously scheduled tasks, thus minimizing makespan and improving job completion time. Even though multi-dimensional bin packing is known to be APX-Hard [27],[3] several heuristics exist [20]. However, they do not directly apply to our scenario. Whereas the heuristics consider balls of a fixed size, the resource demands of tasks (a) vary with time and based on the machine that they are placed at, and (b) are elastic, as in, tasks can function with less than their peak demand. Further, whereas the heuristics assume all balls are known apriori, a cluster scheduler has to cope with *online* arrivals of jobs, the *dependencies* between tasks, and cluster activity such as evacuation and ingestion of new data which compete for resources with tasks.

This paper presents Tetris, a cluster scheduler that packs tasks to machines based on their requirements along multiple resources. Tetris adaptively learns task requirements $t_r$ and monitors available resources at machines $m_r$. The packing heuristic projects $t_r$ and $m_r$ into a euclidean space and picks the ⟨task, machine⟩ pair with the highest dot product value. Task requirements are adjusted to reflect placement at the given machine; only tasks whose requirements are satisfiable are considered; and the dot product prefers large tasks and those that use resources in proportions similar to what is available; for e.g., if machine has network free, other things being equal,

[1] Makespan = time to finish a set of jobs

[2] With $d$ resources, the packing efficiency can be $(\frac{1}{2d})^{\text{th}}$ of optimal.

[3] APX-Hard means that there is no asymptotic polynomial time approximation unless P=NP; it is a strict subset of NP-hard.


*SIGCOMM'14*, August 17–22, 2014, Chicago, IL, USA.
Copyright 2014 ACM 978-1-4503-2836-4/14/08 ...$15.00.
http://dx.doi.org/10.1145/2619239.2626334.

a network-intensive task has a higher dot product. This heuristic prevents over-allocation and reduces resource fragmentation.

Achieving good packing efficiency improves makespan but does not necessarily speed up individual jobs. Preferentially offering resources to the job with the *smallest remaining time* (SRTF) will minimize average job completion time [16]. However, the job with the least remaining work may not have tasks that pack well and hence a strict job time ordering can slow down everyone. Tetris develops a multi-resource version of SRTF for jobs which are DAGs of dependent tasks and combines both heuristics – best packing and shortest remaining job time – to reduce average job completion time.

While we have focused on performance metrics thus far, *fairness* is an important tool to ensure predictable performance. Prior work has developed multi-resource versions of fairness [12]. We show by counter-example as well as our evaluation that fair allocations, even when *pareto efficient* [4] and *work conserving*, do not yield the best job completion time and makespan. We also find that the best-performing schedule is not incompatible with the most-fair schedule. In particular, typical fair schedulers operate by offering resources to the job (or group of jobs) that is currently furthest from fair share. Using Tetris to pick the best-for-packing task from among this constrained subset will improve performance without compromising on fairness. Tetris offers a natural generalization— use the packing and job time heuristics to pick the best task from the $(1 - f)$ fraction of running jobs (or groups) that are furthest from their fair share. Choosing $f = 0$ leads to best makespan and completion time, while $f \rightarrow 1$ offers *strict* fairness. We will show that for $f \in [.25, .5]$, Tetris offers nearly the best performance and the impact on jobs due to the resulting unfairness is negligibly small.

We believe our work makes the following advancements.

- We identify the importance of scheduling and packing *all relevant resources.* Otherwise, resources get fragmented and can be over-allocated, significantly affecting performance.
- We present a heuristic solution to the APX-hard problem of *packing* tasks along multiple resources in cluster schedulers.
- We show how to combine heuristics that improve packing efficiency with those that lower average job completion time.
- We show that pareto-efficient fair allocations do not yield best performance. Whereas performance and fairness are often unacheivable together, we show that in the context of cluster schedulers much better performance can be achieved with just a little unfairness and expose the trade-off with a knob.

We have built Tetris, the first data-parallel cluster scheduler to explicitly consider multi-resource packing, as a modification to the scheduler in YARN [5]. Tetris estimates task demands from previous executions of the same job and from completed tasks of the current job. Tetris uses a resource tracker to independently monitor the utilizations at the machines, thus allowing it to account for any errors in demand estimations and to adjust scheduling around unforeseen hotspots and misbehaving nodes. Tetris has been evaluated in simulations over production traces and using a deployment on a 250 machine cluster. Compared to state-of-the-art scheduling policies (slot-based [3, 4] as well as multi-resource fair (DRF) [12]), Tetris improves makespan and job completion by 30% in deployment and up to 40% in simulations over Facebook traces. These gains are 80% of the estimated gains from a simple upper-bound (not a true upper-bound since computing that is intractable). Further, Tetris offers a smooth trade-off between fairness and performance; we use $f = 0.25$ to achieve the above gains and fewer than 6% of the jobs slow down compared to a fair allocation; the average (max) slowdown is 6 (10)%.

[4]no job can increase share without decreasing the share of another

## 2. MOTIVATION

We motivate multi-resource packing of tasks using examples and production workloads. By devising an approximate upper bound on the potential gains from packing, we show that production jobs could speed up by 45% compared to existing schedulers.

### 2.1 Limitations of Existing Schedulers

Current schedulers are limited in their ability to pack tasks because they define slots based on only one resource (e.g., memory) and they allot slots to tasks based only on fairness. Job completion times and packing efficiency suffer as a consequence.

**Slots:** Analytics frameworks typically define slots based on only one resource (commonly, memory) [3, 4, 5, 18]. It is easy to see that statically sizing the slots leads to wastage and fragmentation when task requirements vary. While dynamic sizing of slots avoids wastage of the resource on which the slots are defined, other resources end up being *over-allocated.*

Take the example of intermediate tasks of a job (e.g., reduce tasks in MapReduce). These tasks read data from multiple machines and have high network requirements. Scheduling them based on only their memory footprint can cause needless contention for the network (and the disk if they write a lot of output). When tasks contend for a resource, the total effective throughput is lowered due to systemic reasons such as buffer overflows on switches (incast), disk seek overheads, and processor cache misses. Further, tasks delayed due to contention hold the memory for much longer and prevent other tasks from being scheduled at that machine.

**Fairness:** As mentioned earlier, a commonly used scheduling approach is to pick tasks from the job that is farthest from its fair share. A common problem with fairness based schedulers is that they do not *pack* the different resources. We use examples of Dominant Resource Fairness (DRF) [12] to illustrate this.

Consider a cluster with 18 cores, 36GB of memory and 3Gbps of network. Three jobs A, B and C have two phases each that are separated by a barrier; the "map" phase consists of 18, 6, and 6 tasks respectively and the "reduce" phase has 3 tasks for all jobs. Map tasks of job A require 1 core and 2GB of memory, while those for jobs B and C require 3 cores and 1GB of memory. All reduce tasks need 1Gbps of network and very little CPU or memory. Assume that all tasks run for $t$ time units. Note that this example resembles map-reduce; map tasks are CPU and memory intensive while reduce tasks are network-intensive.

DRF will schedule 6 map tasks of job A and 2 map tasks each of jobs B and C, at a time, giving each job a dominant resource share of $\frac{1}{3}$ (A's dominant resource is memory whereas for B and C it is CPU cores). Hence, all of the map phases finish at $3t$. Such an allocation, however, leaves 20GB of cluster memory idle. For the reduce phase, DRF will run 1 reduce task from each of the jobs (network is the dominant resource for all jobs now) for a dominant resource share of $\frac{1}{3}$ per job. All jobs finish at 6t.

Consider a packing scheduler instead. Scheduling all 18 map tasks of A would fully use up the cluster's memory. Then, reduce tasks of A become runnable and have *complementary* resource demands to the mappers, allowing the cluster to schedule all 6 maps of B along with the 3 reducers of A. Such a schedule is shown in Figure 1. The jobs now finish at times 2t, 3t and 4t. Average completion time reduces by 50% over DRF (6t → 3t); the cluster's makespan reduces by 33% (6t → 4t) and every job finishes earlier compared to the fair schedule!

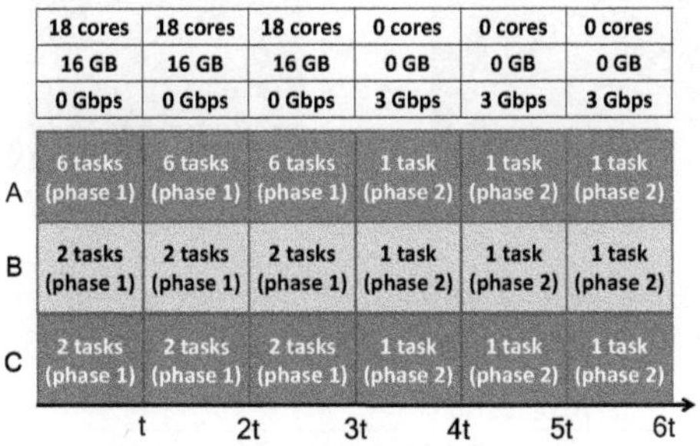


(a) Job schedule under DRF allocation

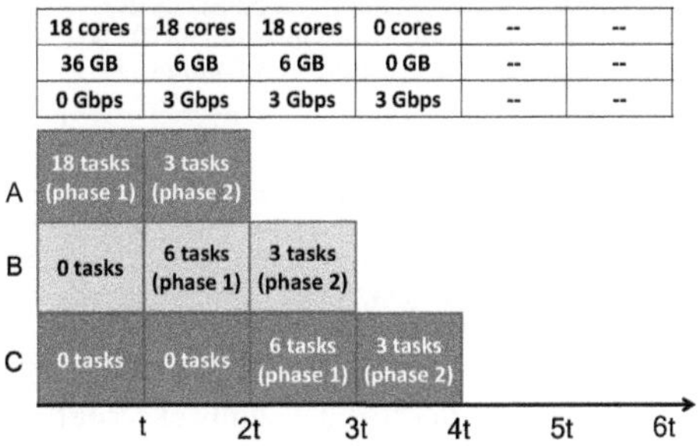


(b) Job schedule with multi-resource Packing

**Figure 1: Comparing schedules for DAGs of tasks that result from fairness based allocation (e.g., DRF [12]) with alternatives. Each job has two phases with a strict barrier between them. The tables on top (in white) show resource utilization. Packing can avoid resource fragmentation and leverage complementarity of task requirements.**

Observe that these gains hold if the packing schedule is used for any permutation among jobs A, B and C. Second, we implicitly extended DRF to also consider the network above; if DRF only considers CPU and memory, after the map phase phases, it would schedule all of the reduce tasks simultaneously since reducers have insignificant CPU and memory needs. Each reduce task then gets only $\frac{1}{3}$Gbps due to contention, causing tasks to run for 3t each and potentially longer if incast happens. Third, note that treating the cluster as one big bag of resources hides the impact of fragmentation. If instead the cluster consists of three machines with one-third cluster resources each, then with DRF all of the jobs will finish at 7t[5]. This is 43% worse makespan and 57% worse avg. completion time. Finally, the gains for the packing schedule accrue from avoiding fragmentation, preferring jobs with less remaining work and by exploiting complementarity in tasks' resource demands; we will show how Tetris show can do all of these.

The above examples highlight that fairness-based schedulers do not optimize job completion time. We have also discussed how slot-based scheduling causes fragmentation and wastage. And, disregarding relevant resources leads to their over-allocation and detrimental interference.

## 2.2 Workload Analysis

We build upon the aspects highlighted in the previous section to analyze their impact on production workloads.

[5]Here is the DRF schedule for the map phases; read it as the first map task of job A, $A_m^1$, scheduled at machine $M_1$ for the first $t$ units. The reduce phases take an extra 3t similar to the case of Fig. 1(a).

| | $t$ | $2t$ | $3t$ | $4t$ |
|---|---|---|---|---|
| $M_1$ | $A_m^1 A_m^2 B_m^2 A_m^7$ | $C_m^2 A_m^{10} A_m^{11} A_m^{12}$ | $A_m^{13} A_m^{14} B_m^6$ | $C_m^6$ |
| $M_2$ | $B_m^1 A_m^3 A_m^5 A_m^8$ | $B_m^3 B_m^4$ | $B_m^5 A_m^{15} A_m^{17}$ | |
| $M_3$ | $C_m^1 A_m^4 A_m^6 A_m^9$ | $C_m^3 C_m^4$ | $C_m^5 A_m^{16} A_m^{18}$ | |

| | Bing | Facebook |
|---|---|---|
| Dates | 12/2013, two days | 1/2012, 1month |
| Cluster Size | Thousands | 3000 |
| Framework | Dryad [17] | Hadoop [1] |
| Script | Scope [30] | Hive [24] |
| DAG Depth | Large | 2 |
| File System | Cosmos | HDFS |
| Network Links | 10Gbps | 1Gbps |
| Oversubscription | <2 | 4 |

**Table 1: Summary of datasets.**

| | Cores | Memory | Disk | Network |
|---|---|---|---|---|
| Cores | — | 0.33, 0.41 | 0.22, 0.12 | 0.29, 0.23 |
| Memory | — | — | −0.11, 0.28 | 0.04, −0.1 |
| Disk | — | — | — | 0.26, −0.07 |
| Network | — | — | — | — |

**Table 2: Correlation matrix of task resource demands; each table entry shows the numbers for {Bing, Facebook}. There is little correlation across demands for various resources.**

### 2.2.1 *Production Clusters*

We analyze production traces from Facebook's Hadoop and Bing's Cosmos clusters. These clusters consist of thousands of machines that are well provisioned in the number of cores, memory, disks and network connectivity. The clusters co-locate computation and storage. Table 1 lists some details. Both traces contain task-level information: start and end times, size of input and output, the machine on which it executed, along with tasks' resource requirements of CPU cycles, memory, disk IOPS and network bandwidth usage.

The computation frameworks in these clusters define slots based on cores and memory and *allot* slots to jobs based on fairness, i.e., distributing proportionally the slots between the running jobs. Both clusters preferentially place tasks close to their input data.

### 2.2.2 *Task Profiles*

Tasks are significantly diverse in their requirements. Figure 2 shows the variation of resource requirements of tasks across resources. CPU usage varies all the way from only 2% of a core to over 6 cores. Similarly, memory usage ranges from 100MB to nearly 17GB. While some tasks are IO-intensive, others are less so. Overall, the minimum values of resource requirements are 5−10× lower than the median, which in turn is 20× lower than the maximum values. The coefficient-of-variations among tasks in their requirements for CPU, memory, disk and network bandwidths are high at 1.42, 1.26, 2.24 and 2.05, respectively.

Demands for different resources are not correlated. Table 2 lists the correlation coefficients between pairs of resources. Even the highest correlation, between cores and memory, is only moderate. This is because the variety of specialized applications using these frameworks have focused requirements, e.g., compute- or IO-intensive. Hence overall, the tasks have *complementary* demands.

As a result of the diversity of resource demands and lack of correlation between them, utilization of different resources peaks at different times. Table 3 quantifies the fraction of times when the utilizations are "tight" (defined as, usage being higher than a certain fraction of capacity). Multiple resources become tight, albeit at different machines and times, thus calling for a packing solution that dynamically accounts for contended resources.

### 2.2.3 *Upper bounding potential gains*

How much can a scheduler that considers varying task requirements and resource usages help? Finding the optimal packing solution, especially considering dynamic job arrivals, is a daunting task (APX-hard). Instead, we solve a related but much simplified prob-

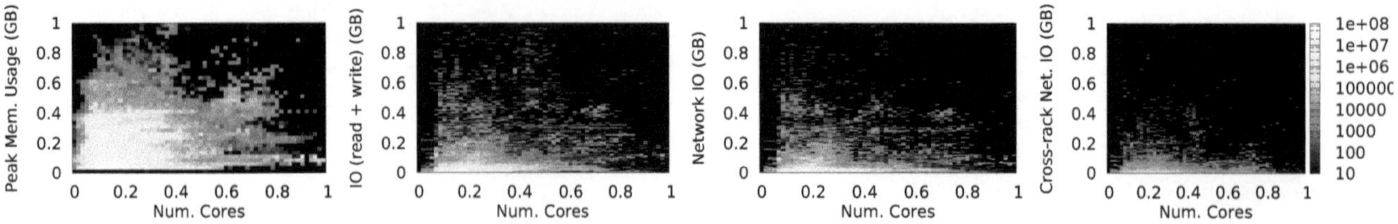


**Figure 2: Heatmap of task requirements. Note the significant variation in the number of cores, memory, network and disk usage of tasks. The axes are normalized; the color of a point indicates the number of tasks, in logarithmic scale, having the corresponding resource demands.**

| | > 75% used | > 90% used | > 95% used |
|---|---|---|---|
| CPU | 0.58 | 0.35 | 0.28 |
| Memory | 0.68 | 0.41 | 0.22 |
| Disk in | 0.11 | 0.02 | 0.003 |
| Disk out | 0.26 | 0.04 | 0.006 |
| Network in | 0.22 | 0.01 | 0.008 |
| Network out | 0.44 | 0.28 | 0.05 |

**Table 3: Tightness of resources. Probability that a type of resource is used at above a certain fraction of its capacity in the Facebook cluster.**

| Term | Explanation |
|---|---|
| $d_j^{\text{cpu}}, f_j^{\text{cpu}}$ | CPU demand (i.e., cores) ($d$) and cpu cycles ($f$) |
| $d_j^{\text{mem}}$ | Peak memory used by task |
| $d_j^{\text{diskR}}, d_j^{\text{diskW}}, f_{ij}^{\text{diskR}}, f_j^{\text{diskW}}$ | Peak disk read/write bandwidth of the task ($d$), bytes to be read from machine $i$ and output ($f$) |
| $d_j^{\text{netIn}}, d_j^{\text{netOut}}$ | Peak network bandwidth in/out of a machine that the task can use ($d$) |

**Table 4: Resource demands of task $j$. Note that the demands for network resource depend on task placement.**

lem and hope that the optimal solution to the actual problem will not be better. In particular, this loose upper bound has these simplifying assumptions. First, it is offered an aggregated view of the cluster across each of its resources, i.e., one large bin per time rather than a bin per machine per time; hence, it does not have to worry about resource fragmentation at machine-level. Second, it assumes that tasks of a job (or phase) have the same resource requirements, thus reducing the search space; this assumption is mostly true (§4.1). Third, it avoids over-allocation explicitly by scheduling a task only when enough resources are available to meet its demands. We believe that gains for this simpler problem are an upper bound on the gains from optimal packing.

Our analysis shows that packing could reduce makespan (average job completion time) by 49% (46%) compared to slot-based fair scheduling and 38% (41%) compared to DRF. But, the gains are lopsided— 16% of the jobs slow down by 26%; the overall gains were calculated including the slowed-down jobs.

Motivated by the gains, we seek to design an online scheduler that packs tasks based on their requirements to improve cluster throughput and job completion times, while limiting the fallout due to any unfairness in the allocations.

## 3. Tetris SCHEDULER

In this section, we describe Tetris's scheduling heuristic, assuming complete knowledge of the resource requirements of tasks and resource availabilities at machines; we explain how to estimate these in §4. We begin with an analytical model that explains the computational complexity of our problem (§3.1). We then develop heuristics that match tasks to machines so as to reduce makespan (§3.2) and average job completion time (§3.3). Finally, we combine these heuristics with a large class of fairness algorithms (§3.4).

### 3.1 Analytical model

To connect the task scheduling problem with prior theoretical work, we cast it into a general optimization framework.

**Notations:** We consider demands of tasks along four resources: CPU, memory, disk, and network bandwidth (see Table 4). For every resource $r$, we denote ($i$) the capacity of that resource on machine $i$ as $c_i^r$, and ($ii$) the demand of task $j$ on resource $r$ as $d_j^r$.

Next, we define variables that encode the task schedule and resource allocation. Note that allocation happens across machines (spatial) and over time (temporal). Let $Y_{ij}^t$ be an indicator variable that is 1 if task $j$ is allocated to machine $i$ at time $t$ (time is discretized). Also, task $j$ is allocated $X_{ij}^{r,t}$ units of resource type $r$ on machine $i$, at time $t$. Let $i_j^*$ denote the machine that task $j$ is scheduled at and $\text{start}_j$ and $\text{duration}_j$ denote the corresponding aspects of task $j$.[6] We do not model preemption here for simplicity. Note that a task may need network and other resources at multiple machines in the cluster due to remote reads.

**Constraints:** First, the cumulative resource usage on a machine $i$ at any given time cannot exceed its capacity:

$$\sum_j X_{ij}^{r,t} \leq c_i^r, \forall i, t, r. \tag{1}$$

Second, tasks need no more than their peak requirements and no resources are allocated when tasks are inactive.

$$0 \leq X_{ij}^{r,t} \leq d_j^r, \forall r, i, j, t. \tag{2}$$

$$\forall_{i,r,t}\ X_{ij}^{r,t} = 0 \text{ if } t \notin [\text{start}_j, \text{start}_j + \text{duration}_j]. \tag{3}$$

Third, to avoid costs of preemption, schedulers may prefer to uninterruptedly allot resources until the task completes.

$$\sum_{t=\text{start}_j}^{\text{start}_j+\text{duration}_j} Y_{ij}^t = \begin{cases} \text{duration}_j & \text{machine } i = i_j^* \\ 0 & \text{other machines} \end{cases} \tag{4}$$

Fourth, the duration of a task depends on task placement and resource allocation:

$$\text{duration}_j = \max \left( \begin{array}{l} \frac{f_j^{\text{cpu}}}{\sum_t X_{i_j^* j}^{\text{cpu},t}}, \frac{f_j^{\text{diskW}}}{\sum_t X_{i_j^* j}^{\text{diskW},t}}, \\ \forall i\ \frac{f_{ij}^{diskR}}{\sum_t X_{ij}^{\text{diskR},t}}, \\ \frac{\sum_{i \neq i_j^*} f_{ij}^{diskR}}{\sum_t X_{i_j^* j}^{\text{netIn},t}}, \\ \forall i \neq i_j^*,\ \frac{f_{ij}^{diskR}}{\sum_t X_{ij}^{\text{netOut},t}} \end{array} \right) \tag{5}$$

[6]Though we use $\text{start}_j$ and $i_j^*$ in the constraints below for convenience, note that they are unknown apriori. Hence, all their occurrences need to be replaced with equivalent terms using the indicator variables $Y_{ij}^t$. For example $X_{i_j^* j}^{r,t} = \sum_i Y_{ij}^t X_{ij}^{r,t}$.

| Term | Explanation |
|---|---|
| $c_i^{\text{cpu}}, c_i^{\text{mem}}$ | Number of cores, Memory size |
| $c_i^{\text{diskR}}, c_i^{\text{diskW}}$ | Disk read and write bandwidth |
| $c_i^{\text{netIn}}, c_i^{\text{netOut}}$ | Network bandwidth in/out of machine |

**Table 5: Resources measured at machine $i$. Note that the availability of these resources changes as tasks are scheduled on the machine.**

In each term, the numerator(f) is the total resource requirement (e.g., cpu cycles or bytes), while the denominator is the allocated resource rate (e.g., cores or bandwidth). From top to bottom, the terms correspond to cpu cycles, writing output to local-disk, reading from (multiple) disks containing the input, network bandwidth into the machine that runs the task and network bandwidth out of other machines that have task input. Note here that cores and memory are only allocated at the machine that the task is placed at but the disk and network bandwidths are needed at every machine that contains task input. We assumed here for simplicity that task output just goes to local disk and that the bandwidths are provisioned at each time so as to not bottleneck transfers, i.e.,

$$\forall t, j, i \neq i_j^* \;\; X_{ij}^{\text{netOut},t} \geq X_{ij}^{\text{diskR},t} \text{ and } X_{i_j^* j}^{\text{netIn},t} \geq \sum_{i \neq i^*} X_{ij}^{netOut,t}.$$

We also assumed that the task is allocated its peak memory size since unlike the above resources, tasks' runtime can be arbitrarily worse (due to thrashing) if it were allocated less than its peak required, i.e., $\forall t \;\; X_{i_j^* j}^{\text{mem},t} = d_j^{\text{mem}}$.

**Objective function:** Our setup lends itself to various objective functions of interest to distributed clusters including minimizing *makespan* [7] and *job completion time* [8]. Minimizing makespan is equivalent to maximizing packing efficiency. Further, we can pose fairness as an additional constraint to be meet at all times.[9]

**Takeaways:** The above analytical formulation is essentially a hardness result. Regardless of the objective, several of the constraints are non-linear. Resource malleability (eqn:2), task placement (eqn:5) and how task duration relates to the resources allocated at multiple machines (eqn:5) are some of the complicating factors. Fast solvers are only known for a few special cases with non-linear constraints (e.g., the quadratic assignment problem). Finding the optimal allocation, therefore, is computationally expensive. Note that these non-linearities remain *inspite* of ignoring the dependencies between tasks (e.g., the DAG) and the several simplifications used throughout (e.g., no task preemption). In fact, scheduling theory shows that even when placement considerations are eliminated, the problem of packing multi-dimensional balls to minimal number of bins is APX-Hard [27]. Worse, re-solving the problem whenever new jobs arrive requires online scheduling. For the online case, recent work also shows that no polynomial time approximation scheme is possible with competitive ratio of the number of dimensions unless NP=ZPP [9].

Given this computational complexity, unsurprisingly, cluster schedulers deployed in practice do not attempt to pack tasks. All known research proposals rely on heuristics. We discuss them in further detail later, but note here that we are unaware of any that considers multiple resources and simultaneously considers improving makespan, average job completion time and fairness considerations. Next, we develop heuristics for packing efficiency (§3.2), job completion time (§3.3) and incorporate fairness (§3.4).

[7] Makespan = $\max_{\text{job } J} \max_{\text{task } j \in J} \max_{\text{time } t} (Y_{ij}^t > 0)$

[8] Job $J$'s finish time is $\max_{\text{task } j \in \text{ job } J} \max_{\text{time } t} (Y_{ij}^t > 0)$

[9] Dominant resource share of $J$ at time $t$ = $\max_{\text{resource } r} \frac{\sum_{i, j \in J} X_{ij}^{r,t}}{\sum_i c_i^r}$.

## 3.2 Packing Efficiency for Makespan

Packing tasks to machines is analogous to the multi-dimensional bin packing referred above. To develop an efficient heuristic, we draw an analogy with the solution in a one-dimensional space (both balls and bins). An effective heuristic proceeds by repeatedly matching the largest ball that fits in the current bin; when no more balls fit, a new bin is opened. Intuitively, this approach reduces the unused space in each bin (i.e., reduces fragmentation) and therefore, reduces the total number of bins used. In one-dimensional space, this heuristic requires no more than $(\frac{11}{9})$OPT+1 bins, where OPT is the optimal number of bins [25].

**Alignment:** We extend the above heuristic by defining *alignment* of a task relative to a machine across multiple dimensions. Similar to the one-dimensional case, the larger the alignment the lower the fragmentation. We considered many options for defining the alignment. Among them, the best packing efficiency was obtained using the dot product between task requirements and resource availabilities on machines.

Our allocation operates as follows. When resources on a machine become available, the scheduler first selects the set of tasks whose peak usage of each resource can be accommodated on that machine. For each task in this set, Tetris computes an *alignment score* to the machine. The alignment score is a weighted dot product between the vector of machine's available resources and the task's peak usage of resources. The task with the *highest* alignment score is scheduled and allocated its peak resource demands. This process is repeated recursively until the machine cannot accommodate any further tasks.

Picking tasks as above has these properties. First, only tasks' whose peak demands are satisfiable are considered; so over-allocation is impossible. Under-utilization of resources is possible, however, we discuss how to mitigate that using a resource tracker in §4.1. Second, the alignment score is largest for the task that uses the most resources on the machine along every resource type. Third, if a particular resource is abundant on a machine, then tasks that require that resource will have higher scores compared to tasks that use the same amount of resources overall. Together, this reduces fragmentation; loosely, bigger balls are placed first and machine resources that are currently abundant are used up before those that are currently scarce by choosing tasks appropriately.

When computing the dot product, Tetris normalizes the task requirements as well as available resources on the machine by the machine's overall capacity. This ensures that the numerical range of a machine's resource (e.g., 16 cores vs. 96GB of RAM) and tasks' demands (e.g., 4 cores vs. 1 Gbps network) do not affect the alignment score. All the resources are weighed equally.

**Incorporating task placement:** A subtle aspect in calculating the alignment score is to appropriately adjust the disk and network demands based on task placement. Recall that while CPU and memory allotment are primarily local, disk and network resources may be needed at multiple machines if data is read (or written) remotely. For remote reads, Tetris checks before placing a task on a machine that sufficient disk read and network-out bandwidth are available at each of the remote machines that contain task input and that sufficient network-in bandwidth is available at the local machine. Including these remote resources in the alignment score computation (dot product) is problematic. The vectors become as large as the number of machines in the cluster. Also, since the score is higher for tasks that use more resources overall, remote placement is preferred! Instead, Tetris computes the alignment score with only the local resources and imposes a remote penalty (of, say, 10%) to penalize use of remote resources. We run sensitivity analysis on the value of this remote penalty in §5.3.3. Together, this ensures that over-allocation is still impossible, fragmentation is reduced and using local resources is preferred. Consequently, the network and remote disks are free for tasks that compulsively need them.

## 3.3 Average Completion Time

Achieving packing efficiency does not necessarily improve job completion time. Consider two jobs running on a two machine cluster. Machines have 2 cores and 4GB of memory. The first job has six tasks each requiring ⟨2 cores, 3 GB⟩ while the second job has two tasks requiring ⟨1 cores, 2 GB⟩. Tasks of the first job have higher alignment score. Hence, the above packing efficiency heuristic schedules all tasks of the first job before the second job's tasks. Assuming all the tasks have the same duration, it is easy to see that swapping the order lowers average job completion time.

A useful starting point to reduce average job completion time is the shortest-remaining-time-first (SRTF) algorithm [16]. SRTF schedules jobs in ascending order of their remaining time. While one can extend SRTF to consider multiple resource requirements of tasks, its greedy scheduling approach nonetheless leads to resource fragmentation [20]. The consequent loss in packing efficiency delays the scheduling of other waiting jobs, thus inflating their durations. Therefore, the challenge in improving job completion time is to *balance prioritization of jobs that have less remaining work against loss in packing efficiency.*

### 3.3.1 Shortest Remaining Time

We first extend the SRTF scheduling algorithm to incorporate multiple resources. Consider scheduling jobs in increasing order of their number of remaining tasks. The fewer tasks remaining in a job, the lower is its remaining duration. However, tasks can have different durations. Worse, tasks can have varying requirements for different resources. Scheduling a job with high resource requirements, even if it has the smallest duration, incurs the opportunity cost of not scheduling other jobs simultaneously. Intuitively, favoring jobs that have the least remaining work improves average completion time the most with the least effort.

**Scoring job's remaining work:** We calculate the total resource requirements of all remaining tasks of the job across all dimensions. To be immune to variations in numerical ranges of the different resources, we normalize the various resources as before. The resource consumption of a task is the sum across all the (normalized) resource dimensions multiplied by the task duration. We estimate task duration based on earlier runs of the same or similar jobs as well as the completed tasks of the same phase. The score for a job is the total resource consumption of its remaining tasks.

Scheduling jobs with lower scores first reduces average completion time the most. The score prefers jobs with low duration mimicing the SRTF heuristic. In addition, favoring jobs that need less resources has smaller opportunity cost since more resources are available for other jobs.

### 3.3.2 Combining with Packing Efficiency

Recall that we need to combine the above score with the packing efficiency heuristic since using only the above score can fragment resources which delays jobs and inflates cluster makespan.

We combine the two metrics —remaining resource usage and alignment score—using a weighted sum. Denoting the alignment score by $a$ and the remaining resource usage as $p$, we pick the task with the highest value of $(a + \varepsilon \cdot p)$. To ensure that the expression is not dominated by either, we recommend $\varepsilon = (\bar{a}/\bar{p})$, where $\bar{a}$ and $\bar{p}$ denote the average scores for alignment and remaining work. Note that $a$ is per-task, whereas $p$ is per-job. While the best choice of $\varepsilon$ depends on the workload, our evaluation shows that the gains from packing efficiency are only moderately sensitive to $\varepsilon$ since most jobs have pending tasks with similar resource profiles. Improving average job completion time, however, requires non-zero values of $\varepsilon$ though the gains stabilize quickly. We will show in §5.3 that the above combination significantly improves over alternatives.

## 3.4 Incorporating fairness

As described so far, Tetris matches tasks to machines to improve cluster efficiency and job completion time without considering fairness. Fairness is a useful tool in shared clusters. Conversations with cluster operators indicate that proportional allocations improve performance predictability. However, it is not an absolute requirement and deviations in fairness for better performance are acceptable. Other properties such as strategy-proofness, envy freedom and sharing incentive are less important in private clusters since the organization can mandate sharing and audit jobs post facto. Here, we describe how Tetris balances performance with fair allocations.

A common property to many fairness based schedulers is to keep track of the allocations of running jobs and offer the next available resource to the job that is farthest from its fair share. Slot based fairness [3, 4] has this property: the next slot is allocated to the job that occupies the fewest slots relative to its fair share. Likewise, DRF [12] offers resources to the job whose dominant resource's allocation is furthest from its fair share. Similar to DRR scheduling, long-running or resource-hungry tasks (alt: large packets) cause short-term unfairness during such allocation. However, bounded task sizes (as in our clusters) limits the unfairness and, in practice, the above method offers fairness at meaningful timescales.

Tetris uses a *fairness knob* to trade-off fairness for performance. The knob $f$ takes values in the range of $[0, 1)$ and intuitively quantifies the extent to which Tetris adheres to fair allocations. When resources become available, Tetris sorts the jobs (set $J$) in decreasing order of how far they are from their fair share. Note that most fair schedulers already maintain such a list. It then looks for the best task (as before) among the runnable tasks belonging to the first $\lceil (1 - f)\ J \rceil$ jobs in the sorted list. Setting $f = 0$ results in the most efficient scheduling choice, whereas $f \rightarrow 1$ yields perfect fairness. In this way, Tetris can incorporate most policies for fairness.

The trade-off between fairness and performance is rarely smooth. However, in scheduling tasks in data-parallel clusters, we find that the above knob lets Tetris achieve schedules that are both reasonably fair and reasonably efficient. For knob values in the range [0.25,0.5], Tetris's makespan is within 10% of the most-efficient (and most-unfair) schedule while delaying jobs by no more than 10% compared to the fair schedulers. This is because though the fairness constraint restricts which jobs (or queues) the available resources can be offered to, there are many tasks pending in a job or queue and from among these many choices it is still possible to pick a task that aligns well with the resources on the machine to be allocated, leading to nearly the same packing efficiency.

## 3.5 Discussion

**DAG Awareness:** The last few tasks before a barrier (e.g., sometimes, no reduce task can start before all maps finish) present a low-cost high-gain opportunity. For the purpose of this discussion, the end of a job can also be considered a barrier. Delay in scheduling these tasks directly impacts job completion time. However, scheduling just these last few tasks preferentially has little impact on other jobs since it is taking away only a small amount of resources. Tetris uses knowledge of the job's DAG to preferentially schedule the last few tasks before a barrier. Given a barrier knob value $b \in [0, 1)$, whenever resources are available Tetris preferentially offers them to tasks that remain after $b$ fraction of tasks in the stage preceding a

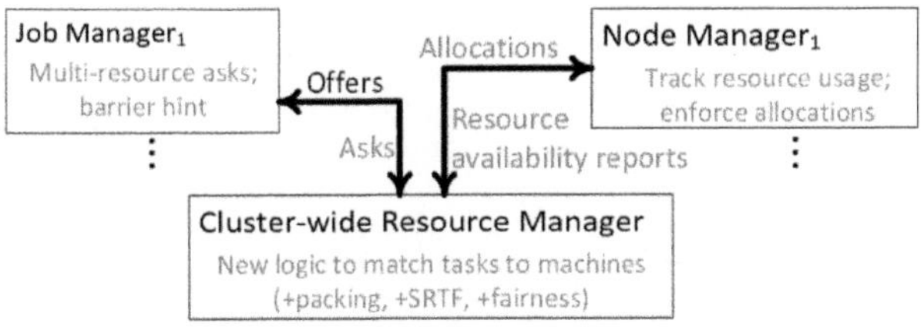


**Figure 3: Typical Architecture of a Data-Parallel Cluster Scheduler and the changes to add Tetris (shown in red).**

barrier have finished. Among these tasks, Tetris still ensures that sufficient resources are available and chooses based on alignment score. Results in §5.3.3 show that values of $b \in [.85, .95]$ improve both job completion time and makespan.

**Starvation Prevention:** Initially, we were concerned that the above solution can *starve* tasks that have large resource demands. Since the scheduler assigns resources on a machine as soon as they are available, it could take a long time to accommodate large tasks. Note that DAG awareness kicks in only for the last few tasks of a job, and hence may not help. However, in practice, we do not encounter such starvation due to two reasons. First, recall from Figure 2 that most tasks have demands within one order of magnitude of one another. As a result, it is likely that the machine resources that become free when one or a small number of tasks finish suffice to fit even the larger tasks. Second, machines report resource availability to the scheduler periodically (§4.4). The intended goal was to keep the scheduler load low. But, doing so also causes the scheduler to learn about all the resources freed up by the tasks that finish in the preceding period together. A more principled solution that reserves machine resources for *starved* tasks is left to future work.

**Future Demands:** While our solution is online, we point out that (imperfect) knowledge of the future is already available. Since each job manager knows its DAG, it knows the future tasks. The scheduler can also estimate when future machine resources become available; each job manager can estimate when an assigned task will finish similar to how they estimate tasks' resource demands. Using such future knowledge, the scheduler can better mimic the offline solution. We leave to future work how to extend the scheduler to use such future knowledge.

# 4. SYSTEM DESIGN

In this section, we describe how Tetris estimates task requirements and resource availability at machines, and how to add Tetris to cluster schedulers.

## 4.1 Estimating task demands and available resources

Recall from Tables 4 and 5 that Tetris considers the following resources for scheduling: CPU, memory, disk and the network. Since clusters today have small over-subscription factors in the core [13], a simplification is to only consider the network bandwidth on the last hop, i.e., the link between the machine and the ToR switch.

Per resource, Tetris has to estimate their dynamic availability at machines. To do so, Tetris employs a resource tracker process that runs at every node in the cluster; the tracker observes aggregate resource usages from operating system counters and periodically reports to a cluster-wide resource manager that handles scheduling.

Also, per-resource Tetris has to estimate tasks' peak demands (e.g., rate of reading in Gbps). Here, Tetris uses these ideas. First, the size and location of inputs of tasks are known before their execution. Second, *recurring jobs* are fairly common in clusters [7]; analytics jobs repeat hourly (or daily) to do the same computation on newly arriving data. For such jobs, Tetris uses task statistics measured in prior runs of the job. Third, since tasks in a phase perform the same computation on different partitions of data, their resource use is statistically similar. Hence, Tetris estimates the demands of later tasks in a phase using the measured statistics from the first few tasks. In our traces we find that the coefficient-of-variation in resource use among tasks in a phase is 0.13, 0.022, 0.25 and 0.41 for CPU, memory, disk and network bandwidths respectively at median. Many phases with large CoV have only a small number of tasks. Other phases have greater variation on the low-end, e.g., tasks placed locally do not use network bandwidth. Fourth, when none of the above methods are available, such as for the first few tasks in a phase, Tetris over-estimates their task demands. Over-estimation is better than under-estimation which needlessly slows down tasks. However, resources can remain idle due to such over-estimates. Tetris relies on the resource tracker to report unused resources and allocates them to new tasks. In its reports, the tracker provides allowance for newly assigned tasks to "ramp up" their usages. It does so by increasing the observed usage by a small amount per task; the amount decreases over the task's lifetime and goes to zero after a threshold (we use 30*s*). Finally, there has been recent work on static program analysis to estimate resource demands [14]. The techniques are not yet applicable to arbitrary programs but represent a potential solution for the future.

## 4.2 Enforcing allocations

Due to arbitrariness in the user code, tasks' actual resource use may not conform to their allocations. For e.g., a TCP flow can ramp up to use all the available network bandwidth. To guard against this, Tetris explicitly *enforces* allocations.[10] For disk and network usage, Tetris intercepts all calls to read or write from the filesystem, including remote reads. Each call is routed to a corresponding token bucket that allows the call to go through if enough tokens remain, or queues it otherwise. Tokens arrive at the allocated rate, the size of the bucket determines the maximum burst size, and each call deducts a corresponding number of tokens when it goes through.

## 4.3 Ingest, evac., and other cluster activity

The resource tracker also helps the scheduler to be aware of other activities in the cluster. In addition to executing jobs, data ingestion and maintenance operations can use up a lot of cluster resources. Ingestion refers to storing incoming data for later analytics; some clusters report volumes of up to 10TB per hour [2, 6]. Prior to maintenance operations on machines, their data is evacuated and re-replicated to ensure that availability is unchanged. By using the tracker's reports, the scheduler can avoid contention between its tasks and these activities.

## 4.4 Adding Tetris to cluster schedulers

Figure 3 depicts the core pieces of typical cluster schedulers today and shows in red the new functionality to be added to each piece for Tetris. For scale, performance and reliability, today's data-parallel cluster schedulers, as well as earlier grid computing schedulers [23], breakdown cluster scheduling into three parts. A node manager runs on every node in the cluster, responsible for running tasks and reporting node liveness. Per job, a job manager process runs on some node in the cluster and holds job context such as task progress and dependencies (e.g., DAG). A cluster-wide resource arbiter receives *asks* from various job managers for their pending tasks; an ask

[10] For memory and CPU cores, Tetris relies on existing support in Yarn; it uses OS mechanisms for the latter and explicitly tracks the total memory used by the task and its child processes for the former.

encodes preferences for data locality etc., and in turn *offers* guidance as to where the tasks can run.

We incorporated Tetris into the Yarn framework (Hadoop 2.4).[11] To do so, we made these modifications:

1. Matching tasks to machines, at the cluster-wide resource manager, now implements the ideas in §3 (packing, multi-resource SRTF, fairness knob, barrier hints).
2. The job manager estimates task demands from historical jobs and from earlier tasks in the phase (§4.1); asks from the job manager report task demands across multiple resource types and also identify the last few tasks before a barrier (§3.5).
3. The node manager now observes dynamic resource availability across various resources and enforces task allocations.

These changes do not impact the underlying complexity and hence the scheduler's scalability with two exceptions. First, since task placement changes its demands for disk and network, e.g., losing data locality adds need for network bandwidth, how can the job manager specify demands in its ask before the task is placed? If the ask were to contain task demands for each possible placement, it would be too large. Tetris keeps the asks succinct by observing that given the locations and sizes of a task's inputs, its resource demands can be inferred for any potential placement. Second, the new logic to match tasks to machines is more complex; we report overhead measured using our prototype in §5.2.2.

# 5. EVALUATION

We evaluate Tetris using our prototype implementation on a 250 machine cluster. To understand performance at larger scale, we do trace-driven simulations using traces from production clusters.

## 5.1 Setup

**Cluster:** On the larger, 250 server, cluster each machine has 32 cores, 96GB of memory, 8 1TB 7200RPM disk drives, a 10Gbps NIC and runs Linux 2.6.32. The machines are 40 to a rack connected in a folded CLOS with 1.25X over-subscription between racks. We also report experiments on a smaller, 7 server, cluster. Here each machine has 6 cores, 12GB of memory, 3 1TB disks and a 1Gbps NIC.

**Baselines:** We compare Tetris to state-of-the-art scheduling algorithms implemented in Hadoop 2.4. The Fair and Capacity Schedulers [3] are deployed in production clusters at Facebook and Yahoo! respectively. Conceptually, both schedulers allocate slots (defined on memory) to jobs based on fairness; we use a slot size of 2GB similar to the Facebook cluster. Dominant Resource Fairness (DRF) [12] is a recent multi-resource fairness algorithm that is available with YARN. DRF considers memory and CPU requirements. To the best of our knowledge, none of the existing schedulers consider disk or network bandwidths in their allocations. Further, the schedulers try to place map tasks on local slots [29] and reduce tasks on any available slot. Finally, we also compare Tetris's gains to the simple upper bound described in §2.2.

**Trace-driven Simulator:** To evaluate Tetris at a larger scale and under many more parameter choices, we built a trace-driven simulator that replays logs from Facebook's production clusters. The simulator mimics these aspects from the original trace: job arrival times, task resource requirements, the input and output sizes of tasks, the location of inputs in HDFS and the probabilities of failures. Further, we use the same machine profile as the original cluster: 12 cores, 32GB memory, 4 disks operating at 50MBps each for read/write and a 1Gbps NIC.

[11] In Yarn's terminology, the Job Manager in Fig. 3 is referred to as the application master (AM), the Cluster-wide resource manager is called the RM and the node manager is NM.

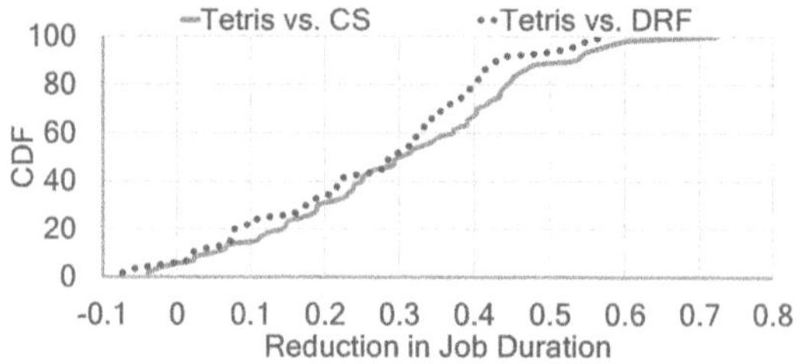


(a) CDF of change in Job Completion Time

| | Avg. | Stdev. |
|---|---|---|
| Tetris vs. CS | 29% | 2.94% |
| Tetris vs. DRF | 27.5% | 3.50% |

(b) Makespan Reduction

**Figure 4: Comparing Tetris vs. baselines. The results are from running a workload of over 100 jobs on a 250 server cluster running Yarn 2.4. Each experiment run takes > 10 hours; repeat five times.**

**Workload:** To test our prototype, we constructed a workload suite of over 100 jobs by picking uniformly at random from the following choices. Job size (number of tasks) and the selectivity of map and reduce tasks are chosen from one of four choices: large & highly-selective, medium & inflating, medium & selective and, small & selective. The ratios of input to output are: 1:2 for inflating, 1:0.5 for selective and 1:0.2 for highly selective. The sizes are: couple 1000 tasks for large, 1000 for medium, 100s for small. A map- or reduce- stage could either have tasks of high-mem (8GB) or low-mem (2GB). Similarly the stage could either have tasks with high-cpu or low-cpu; the former indicates that tasks do substantial computation per data read or written and hence have low peak I/O demands. Job arrival time is uniformly picked at random between [0:3600]s. Each experiment run takes about five hours and we repeat five times.

**Metrics:** Our figures of merit are improvements in job completion time, makespan and the extent of unfairness. For the first two metrics, we compute the percentage improvement (or reduction) as $100 \times \frac{baseline - tetris}{baseline}$. 25% improvement means Tetris is 1.33X better. We report the changes at the average as well as the distribution across jobs. To quantify unfairness, we report the fraction of jobs that slow down (and by how much) compared to a fair allocation.

**Highlights:** The highlights of our evaluation are as follows.

1. Tetris improves cluster makespan and average job completion time by about 30% in our deployment and by up to 40% when replaying Facebook traces in simulation. We estimate that these gains are 80% of the simple upper bound §2.2.3. The gains accrue from avoiding fragmentation and over-allocation and from exploiting complementary demands for better packing.
2. Tetris offers the above efficiency gains with only a slight loss in fairness. These gains use fairness knob $f = 0.25$ and fewer than 6% of jobs are delayed by no more than 10% compared to a fair allocation. Setting $f = 0$, the most efficient and unfair schedule, improves makespan by up to 50% but the ensuing unfairness delays more jobs. Surprisingly $f = 1$, the most fair schedule, also offers sizable improvements in efficiency.
3. We compare against several alternatives and perform a detailed sensitivity analysis on parameters.

## 5.2 Deployment Results

Figure 4 compares the performance of Tetris with baseline schemes. Each experiment runs our workload (described above) on the cluster. We see that Tetris improves job completion time, at median, by 30%. The top fifth of jobs improve by over 40%. Gains are

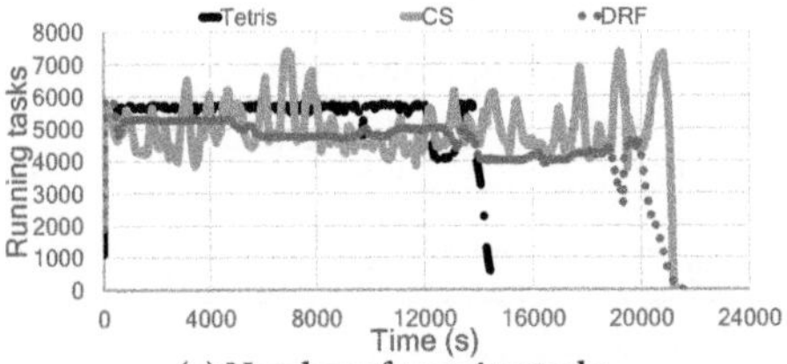


(a) Number of running tasks

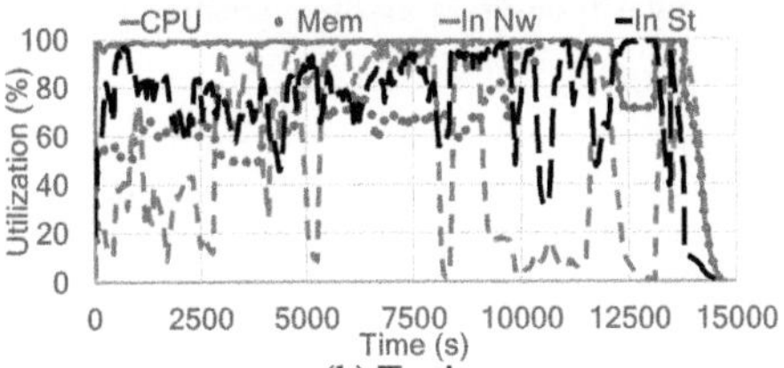


(b) Tetris

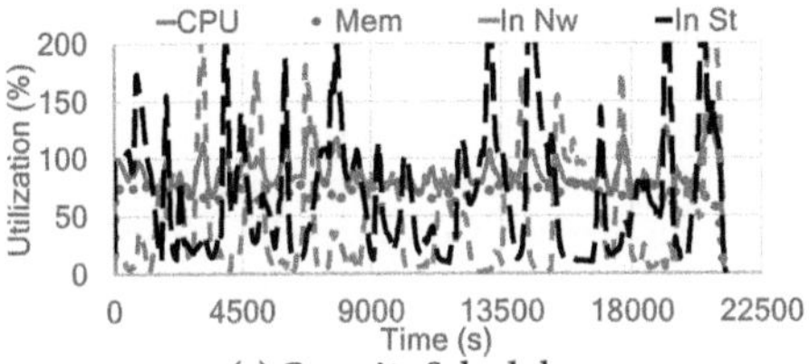


(c) Capacity Scheduler

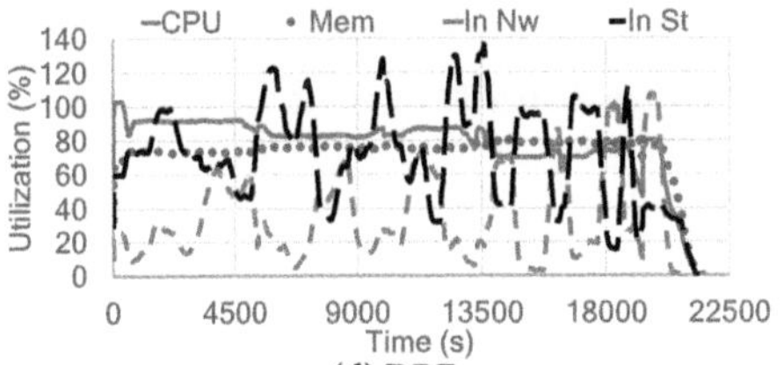


(d) DRF

**Figure 5: Number of running tasks and total resources used during an example experiment run.**

| | CPU | Memory | Disk | Network |
|---|---|---|---|---|
| Tetris | .90, .82, – | .47, .31, – | .41, .24, – | .55, .30, – |
| CS | .87, .33, .18 | .38, –, – | .29, .19, .13 | .42, .34, .28 |
| DRF | .53, .13, – | .56, –, – | .12, .07, .05 | .40, .27, .20 |

**Table 6: Probability that a machine is highly using a type of resource at above a certain fraction (> 75%, > 90%, > 100%) of its capacity.**

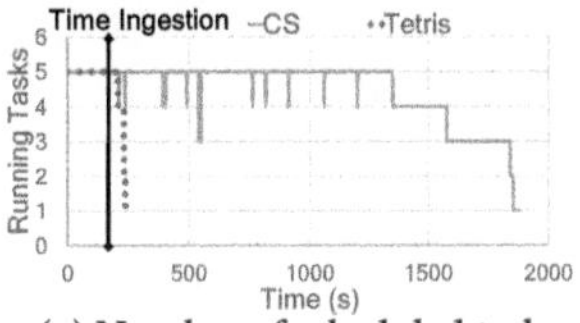


(a) Number of scheduled tasks

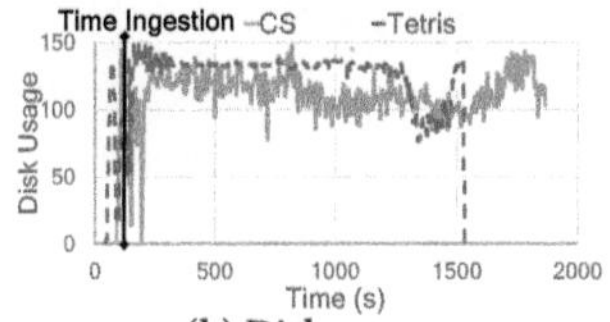


(b) Disk usage

**Figure 6: On a machine overloaded by data ingestion, Tetris stops scheduling further tasks. CS does not react; the resulting contention lowers disk throughput slowing down both tasks and ingestion.**

| Time to process | CS 15K (45K) tasks | Tetris 15K (45K) tasks |
|---|---|---|
| NM heartbeat | .06ms (.12ms) | .06ms (.07ms) |
| AM heartbeat | .2ms (.2ms) | .15ms (.15ms) |

**Table 7: Overheads: Average time to process heartbeats from the NM and the AM with and without Tetris; vary tasks pending; 250 servers.**

slightly larger compared to the capacity scheduler (CS) than with DRF. Makespan also improves by about 30%.

To understand in a bit more detail, Figure 5 shows the details for one example run. A couple of points stand out. First, we see from Fig. 5a that Tetris keeps consistently high numbers of running tasks in the cluster. DRF, at all times, has scheduled fewer tasks. Capacity scheduler (CS) has slightly higher throughput but is less consistent. Partly, this is because neither DRF nor CS explicitly avoid resource fragmentation. Further, DRF is not pareto-efficient when allocating resources spread across multiple machines; it uses a simpler one-machine model [12]. More importantly, pareto efficient fair allocations do not lead to the best performance, as we saw in the example; partly, this is due to the DAG structure of jobs and tasks having different resource profiles. Second, Fig. 5b shows the (estimated) usage of resources across the cluster. We see that, with Tetris, the cluster is bottlenecked on different resources at different times. Comparatively, we see in Fig. 5c that the capacity scheduler is unable to fully use even the resources that it considers explicitly for scheduling (memory and CPU). This is due to fragmentation. Worse, it over-allocates the other resources (network and disk cross 100% at several times). DRF is slightly better but qualitatively similar. Third, we observe that due to efficient packing, not only is the bottleneck resource fully utilized at all times but also the utilization of other resources increases. For example, the network and disk usages are markedly higher with Tetris compared to the baselines. We summarize that avoiding fragmentation and over-allocation by explicitly packing on all the relevant resources improves efficiency. The gains accrue from (a) increase in the number of simultaneously running tasks, (b) reduced task duration (by not over-allocating) and (c) improved usage of all cluster resources.

Table 6 depicts aspects of machine-level resource usage during an example run. It measures the likelihood of a machine to have a certain usage for each resource. We confirm that Tetris is able to use more of all resources (by avoiding fragmentation). Baseline schemes under-use due to fragmentation and occasionally over-allocate the disk and network.

### 5.2.1 *Micro-benchmark: resource tracker*

We use micro-benchmarks to highlight aspects that are not as easy to see from the large workload runs above.

To evaluate how Tetris adapts to cluster activity, we mimic ingestion on a machine in our small cluster. Fig. 6 shows the number of running tasks on that machine as well as the disk load of the machine; ingestion begins at $t = 125s$. We see that the resource tracker used by Tetris observes the rising disk usage and schedules no more tasks on that machine. Tasks already scheduled complete at $t = 250s$. In contrast, the capacity scheduler proceeds unaware; the resulting contention lowers disk throughput leading to both straggler tasks and delays in ingestion.

### 5.2.2 *Overheads and Scalability*

Recall from our prototype description (§4.4) that Tetris's logic to match tasks to machines is more complex than that in Yarn. To estimate overheads, we ran experiments with different cluster sizes and different numbers of jobs and pending tasks. We find that the additional network overhead, due to expanding the size of the *asks* is negligible. Further, the memory usage at the cluster-wide resource manager increases very slightly; the timeline graphs (not shown) are dominated by when garbage collection happens. For the computational overhead, we observe the time taken by the cluster-wide resource manager (RM) to process a *heartbeat* from the node manager (NM) and from the job manager (AM). Yarn's RM does the actual allocation during the NM heartbeat; AM asks are cumulative, so at an AM heartbeat, the RM simply updates the cumulative ask and responds with any tasks in the (past) asks that have been

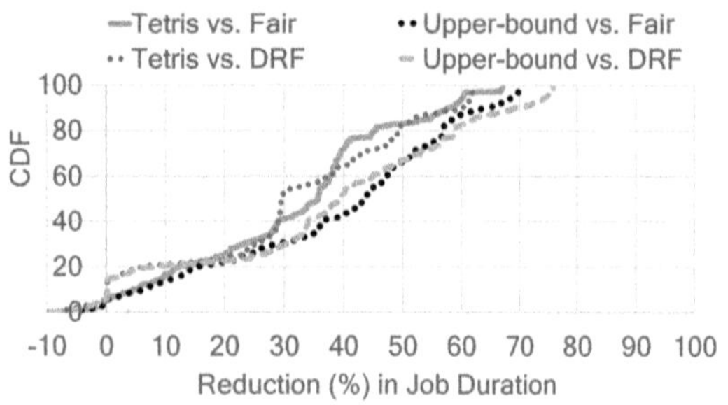


**Figure 7: CDF of improvement in job completion time. The top 20% of jobs improve by over 50%.**

matched (during the NM heartbeats) since the AM's previous ask. We see from Table 7 that Tetris takes about the same time for an AM heartbeat, but is slightly faster on the NM heartbeat esp: when more tasks are pending. This is because default Yarn RM does some extra work per heartbeat that is not needed given Tetris. Despite the fact that our prototype is not optimized, we estimate that an RM using Tetris scales similarly to the default Yarn. Recall that scalability was a key reason behind our choice to avoid more complex solutions based on flow-networks and integer linear programming [18].

## 5.3 Trace-driven Simulations

Here, we mimic scheduling in a several thousand server facebook cluster. Unless otherwise specified, results use Tetris's default parameter values (fairness knob $f = 0.25$, barrier knob $b = 0.9$, $\varepsilon = \frac{\bar{a}}{\bar{p}}$). We measure sensitivity to parameters in §5.3.2 and §5.3.3.

### 5.3.1 *Efficiency*

**Job Completion Time:** Compared to the fair scheduler and DRF, Tetris speeds up jobs by 40% and 35% on average. Figure 7 shows the CDF of the improvement in job completion time over jobs in the trace. We see that the top fifth of jobs speed-up by over 50%. The gains at the median are over 30%. Tetris's gains are slightly more relative to the fair-scheduler in Hadoop than in DRF but not markedly so. Further, Tetris's average gains are 81% of those from the simple upper-bound scheduler. Recall that the simple upper-bound ensures minimal fragmentation and avoids over-allocation but is not a true upper bound; the true upper bound is intractable to compute. A few jobs slow down– fewer than 6% of jobs by less than 10% each. These slow downs are because Tetris trades off fairness for efficiency.

Where do the gains come from? We find that task durations improve by about 25%. Since resource fragmentation has no impact on task duration, we believe task durations improve because of avoiding over-allocation. Reduce tasks improve more than the map tasks. Recall that the baseline schedulers do not consider disk- or network-bandwidths when scheduling tasks and can over-allocate these resources causing tasks to contend needlessly for disk and network while holding on to the other resources. If Tetris were modified to consider only CPU and memory (i.e., it also over-allocates disk and network bandwidths), the average gains drop from 40% to 15% for Tetris vs. Fair and 35% to 13% for Tetris vs. DRF. Hence, nearly two-thirds of the gains are due to avoiding over-allocation, and one-third due to avoiding fragmentation.

Further, we find that while jobs of all sizes see speed-up in completion time, large jobs ($\geq$ 1000 tasks) see a greater benefit; over 50% (not shown). This is likely because avoiding fragmentation allows Tetris to schedule more of their tasks early. Gains for small jobs ($\leq$ 25 tasks), however, are still significant at 35% due largely to our use of SRTF heuristic. Using *only* the SRTF heuristic lowers the improvement in average completion time to 27% and 26% over the fair scheduler and DRF, respectively. The corresponding numbers from using *only* the packing efficiency heuristic are 31% and 28%. We conclude that Tetris's combination of the two heuristics is better than using either individually.

| Alignment Heuristic | Avg. Gain in Job Completion Time (%) | Gain in Makespan (%) |
|---|---|---|
| *Cosine Similarity* | 40% | 41% |
| *L2-Norm-Diff* | 30% | 40% |
| *L2-Norm-Ratio* | 33% | 36% |
| *FFD-Prod* | 25% | 24% |
| *FFD-Sum* | 26% | 31% |

**Table 8: Cosine similarity outperforms the alternatives for calculating the alignment score.**

**Makespan:** To analyze the change in makespan, we assume that all jobs arrived at the beginning of the trace and measure the time until the last job finishes. Tetris reduces makespan by 33% and 24% compared to the fair scheduler and DRF. These gains are less than the simple upper bound scheduler's makespan reductions of 49% and 38%, respectively. The main reason is that Tetris's preference for jobs with less remaining work loses some of the makespan gains in favor of reducing average job completion time. In fact, just using the packing heuristic ($\varepsilon = 0$) improves makespan by a bit more, 41% and 29% respectively. We believe $\varepsilon = \frac{\bar{a}}{\bar{p}}$ to be a reasonable compromise; we evaluate sensitivity on $\varepsilon$ in §5.3.3.

**Alternative Packing Heuristics:** Tetris's use of cosine similarity to calculate the alignment score performed the best among several alternatives proposed in literature [20, 25]. For a task with demands $d$ to be scheduled on a machine with available resources $a$, cosine similarity is $a \cdot d$ where both the $a$ and $d$ vectors are normalized to the machine's capacity. To compare, L2-Norm-Diff is $\sum_i (d_i - a_i)^2$, L2-Norm-Ratio is $\sum_i \left(\frac{d_i}{a_i}\right)^2$, FFD-Prod is $\prod_i d_i$ and FFD-Sum is $\sum_i d_i$ [20]. Table 8 has our findings. Gains in both completion time as well as makespan are clearly better with cosine similarity; L2-Norm-Diff does well on makespan but lags behind in speeding up jobs. We conclude by noting that better heuristics may exist.

### 5.3.2 *Fairness vs. Efficiency*

Recall from §3.4 that Tetris offers a trade-off between fairness ($f \to 1$) and efficiency ($f = 0$). Figure 8 shows job completion and makespan for different values of this knob $f$.

Couple points stand out. First, even with $f \to 1$, wherein available resources are always allocated to the job that is furthest from fair share, Tetris offers sizable gains. Makespan improves by 10% and average job duration improves by 23%. This is because even when restricted to the subset of allocations that are fair (e.g., which job(s) to give resources to) there are many choices (e.g., which of the pending tasks in those job(s) to schedule). By picking a suitable task from the constrained set of jobs, Tetris improves efficiency while being fair. Second, knob values around 0.25 achieve most of the gains. Job completion time gains plateau beyond $f = 0.5$. While makespan continuously improves by reducing $f$, $f = 0.25$ is less than 10% away from the best possible gains.

Finally, we report the impact of unfairness on jobs. Whereas most jobs finish faster under Tetris, some jobs slow down. We can measure the impact of Tetris's unfairness through the prevalence and magnitude of job slow-down. Figure 9 shows the fraction of jobs that slow-down and the average (error-bars=worst) per-job slow-down due to unfairness compared to the fair scheduler and DRF. Whereas $f = 0$ can slowdown up to 15% of jobs, $f = 0.25$ has nearly the same impact as choosing $f \to 1$; about 5% of jobs slow down by

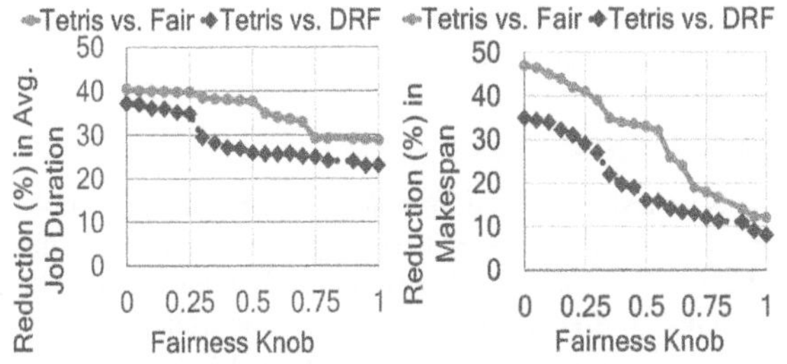


(a) Job Duration (b) Makespan

**Figure 8: Impact of varying the fairness knob. We see that setting a knob value around 0.75 offers nearly the best possible efficiency.**

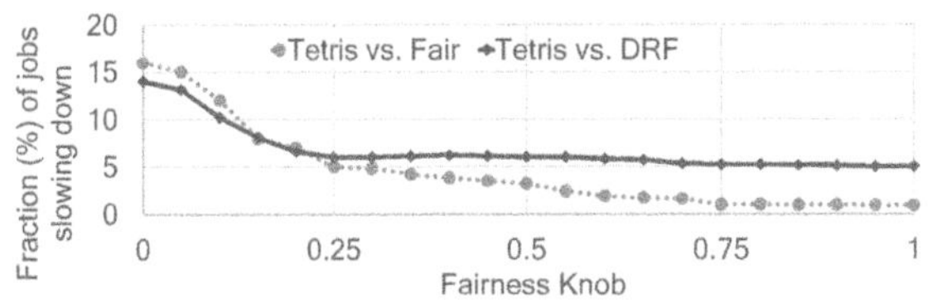


(a) % jobs slowing down

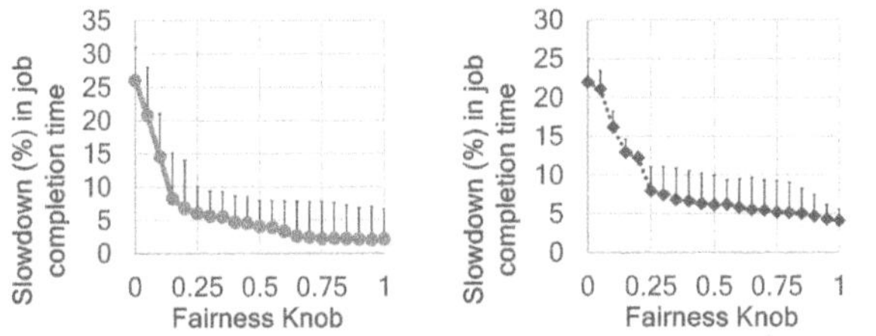


(b) Baseline: Fair (c) Baseline: DRF

**Figure 9: Job Slowdown. For fairness knob values $\in [0.25, 0.5]$, only a few jobs slow down and only by a small amount.**

about 5% each. Notice that even $f \to 1$ slows-down some jobs; some of this is statistical noise; some of it is because even with $f \to 1$, Tetris picks tasks from the job in an order that is appropriate for packing which may not be the best for job's runtime (for example if a long-running task is scheduled later).

**Relative Integral Unfairness:** We now employ a stricter metric to quantify unfairness: if $a(t)$ and $f(t)$ are the actual allocation received by a job at time $t$ and its purported fair allocation, we measure $\left(\int_t \frac{a(t)-f(t)}{f(t)} dt\right)$ where the integral runs over the job's runtime. We call this the relative integral unfairness. Jobs that have a value below zero have received worse service due to Tetris than they would have in a fair scheme; value above zero implies job was treated better by Tetris. We find only a few jobs have negative values (about 5%) and the average negative value is small (about 5%). This hints that Tetris's violations of fair allocation are *transient*; when measured across the lifetime of a job the net violation (and hence, slowdown) are small.

### 5.3.3 *Sensitivity Analysis*

Here, we evaluate Tetris under different conditions.

**Barrier Knob:** Recall from §3.5 that Tetris preferentially schedules the last few tasks in a stage preceding a barrier after a $b$ fraction of tasks finish. Figure 10 shows the impact of changing $b$. When $b = 1$, no tasks are preferentially treated. Lower the value of $b$, the larger the fraction of tasks that receive preference. Doing so will speed up the corresponding job but can delay other jobs since it takes resources away from them. Figure 10 shows that $b < 0.75$ is worse than not using the barrier promotion at all (i.e., $b = 1$). However, setting $b$ around .9 is net positive. For e.g., Tetris vs. DRF, makespan reduction increases from 22% to 30%. Across different subsets of jobs

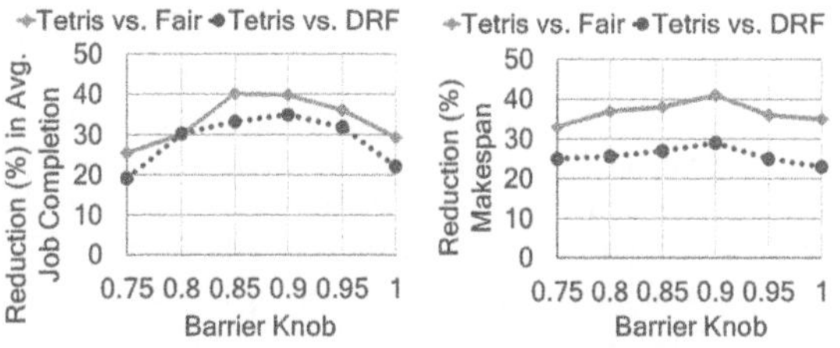


(a) Job Duration (b) Makespan

**Figure 10: Barrier threshold value of 0.9 balances stagnation-avoidance with the loss from not picking the best task for packing.**

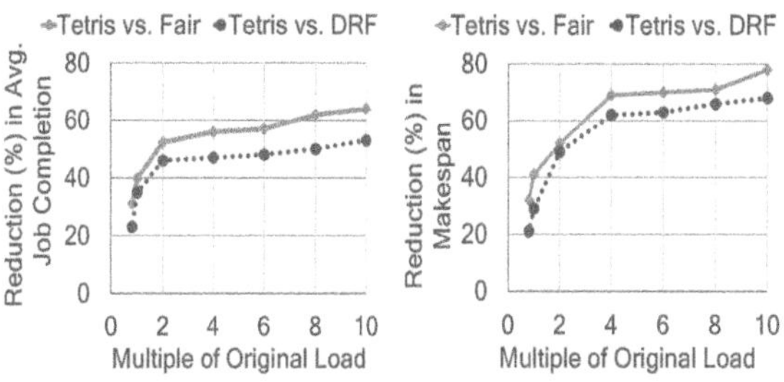


(a) Job Duration (b) Makespan

**Figure 11: Tetris's gains increase as the cluster load increases.**

and traces from different days, we found $b \in [.85, .95]$ to be a good choice for the Facebook cluster.

**Remote Penalty:** Tetris uses a penalty in its alignment score (of 10%) when remote resources are used by a task. The penalty is a simple way to prefer local placement whenever possible. Our analysis shows that both completion time and makespan change little when the penalty value is between 6% and 15%. On either side of this range, gains drop moderately due to over-using remote resources or being too conservative and letting them lie fallow.

**Weighting Alignment vs. SRTF:** Recall that we combine alignment score ($a$) and remaining work ($p$) using a weighted sum, $(a + \varepsilon \cdot p)$ (§3.3.2). Our default choice of $\varepsilon$ is $\bar{a}/\bar{p}$ where $\bar{x}$ is the average value of $x$. Here we evaluate the sensitivity of $\varepsilon$. Let $m = \varepsilon\bar{p}/\bar{a}$. While gains in completion time drop by about 10% for $m = 0$, they do not improve beyond $m = 1.5$. Gains in makespan are higher by 8% for $m = .5$ and do not drop much beyond $m = 1.5$. Thus, using a value of $m$ close to 1 is appropriate.

**Cluster Load:** Utilization of a cluster impacts the possible gains from better packing/ scheduling. For example, if the load is one task at a time, packing is not required. The cluster whose trace we replay is only moderately loaded. Figure 11 examines the performance of Tetris under different cluster load. We vary load by changing the number of servers; half as many servers leads to twice the load. As expected, the figure shows that the gains due to Tetris improve with cluster load. At 4× the current load, Tetris improves makespan by well over 60% and average completion time by over 50%. Several studies show that faster job completion cause more jobs to be submitted to the cluster [6, 21]. Hence, techniques such as Tetris could be more useful in the future.

## 6. RELATED WORK

Tetris's contributions are, ($a$) multi-resource packing of tasks to machines, and ($b$) simultaneous support for complementary objectives of fairness, minimizing job completion time and minimizing cluster makespan. We contrast these contributions with some existing work. We did relate to well-known algorithmic results on bin packing earlier (§3.1); we mention a few more here.

**Cluster Schedulers:** Early cluster schedulers [3, 18, 4] focused primarily on maximizing data locality, scale and fairness. Dominant Resource Fairness [12] allocates multiple resources in a manner that is pareto-efficient, strategy-proof, envy-free and incentivizes sharing. Available implementations of DRF and the earlier schedulers only consider CPU and memory. We show that the focus on fairness detracts considerably from performance; that ignoring disk and network leads to harmful over-allocation; and posit multi-dimensional packing to be a key aspect of cluster scheduling.
**Network Optimizations:** Allocating IO is not a simple extension to multi-resource schedulers. Unlike CPU and memory which are purely local resources, the IO demands of a task depend on its placement relative to its input locations. Some prior work focuses on fair network allocation even when the applications are uncooperative [22], as well as better ways to schedule network transfers [10] and to steer around network hotspots [11]. Here, Tetris shows how to seamlessly choose between local and remote task placements and to allocate network and disk bandwidths to tasks so as to improve job and cluster performance.
**Fairness vs. Cluster Efficiency vs. Job completion time:** We are hardly the first to explore this trade-off. There is notable performance analysis on the impact of preferring short jobs [28] and on the unfairness of schedulers [26]. While less analytical, our key contribution here is a practical system that reaches a good operating point in this trade-off space. We also notice how in data-parallel clusters the tradeoff is smoother since one can be fair to jobs and still improve packing by scheduling an appropriate task.
**Bin Packing:** We build upon algorithmic work on multi-dimensional bin packing. Their goal translates directly to minimizing cluster makespan. We rely on them to understand the computational complexity of our problem [9, 27] and use their heuristics [20, 25] as a starting point. We extend to handle practical concerns (placement, resource malleability) and add support for complementary objectives (minimize job completion time; fairness).
**Virtual Machine Packing:** A related problem involves consolidating VMs, with multi-dimensional resource requirements, on to the fewest number of servers [19]. The best work there focuses on different challenges and is not applicable to task packing. For e.g., they balance load across servers, ensure VM availability inspite of failures, allow for quick software and hardware updates etc. They have no corresponding entity to a job and hence job completion time is unexpressible. Explicit resource requirements (e.g., small VM) makes VM packing simpler but since VMs last for much longer than tasks mistakes in packing substantially reduce gains.

## 7. CONCLUSION

In the context of multi-resource schedulers, we show that the focus on fairness and not allocating IO lead to significantly worse performance. We present heuristics that efficiently pack along multiple resources and prefer jobs with less "remaining work". As a result both cluster efficiency (makespan) and average job completion time improve. Both these aspects are novel in the context of cluster schedulers. Devising an optimal solution to the core problem of scheduling tasks with diverse resource demands is hard; just packing to minimize makespan is APX-Hard. Our approach here is towards finding a practical solution, which requires, in addition to the above, the ability to incorporate fairness. We do not offer new notions of fairness but rather show how achieving desired amounts of fairness can coexist with improving cluster performance through packing. We note that our methods to avoid starvation and properly use the DAG structure of jobs are rather ad-hoc. However, we believe this to be a first substantial step in the right direction. We have implemented our heuristics inside the YARN framework; trace-driven simulations and deployment show encouraging initial results.

## Acknowledgements

We thank our shepherd Andrew Moore and the anonymous reviewers for their feedback. Chris Douglas and Carlo Curino offered help and suggestions that significantly improved our prototype. Ganesh was supported in part by NSF grants CCF-1139158, the DARPA XData Award FA8750-12-2-0331 and gifts from various companies. Robert and Aditya were supported in part by NSF grants CNS-1302041, CNS-1314363 and CNS-1040757.

## References

[1] Apache Hadoop. `http://hadoop.apache.org`.
[2] Facebook Data Grows By Over 500 TB Daily. `http://bit.ly/1p5EV3c`.
[3] Hadoop MapReduce - Capacity Scheduler. `http://bit.ly/1tGpbDN`.
[4] Hadoop MapReduce - Fair Scheduler. `http://bit.ly/1p7sJ1I`.
[5] Hadoop YARN Project. `http://bit.ly/1iS8xvP`.
[6] Petabyte Storage at Half Price with QFS. `http://bit.ly/1x4A6vF`.
[7] S. Agarwal et al. Re-optimizing data parallel computing. In *NSDI*, 2012.
[8] M. Al-Fares et al. A Scalable, Commodity Data Center Network Architecture. In *SIGCOMM*, 2008.
[9] Y. Azar et al. Tight Bounds for Online Vector Bin Packing. In *STOC*, 2013.
[10] M. Chowdhury et al. Managing Data Transfers in Computer Clusters with Orchestra. In *SIGCOMM*, 2011.
[11] M. Chowdhury et al. Leveraging Endpoint Flexibility in Data-Intensive Clusters. In *SIGCOMM*, 2013.
[12] A. Ghodsi et al. Dominant Resource Fairness: Fair Allocation Of Multiple Resource Types. In *NSDI*, 2011.
[13] A. Greenberg et al. A Scalable and Flexible Datacenter Network . In *SIGCOMM*, 2009.
[14] S. Gulwani et al. SPEED: Precise And Efficient Static Estimation Of Program Computational Complexity. In *POPL*, 2009.
[15] C. Guo et al. BCube: A High Performance, Server-centric Network Architecture for Modular Data Centers . In *SIGCOMM*, 2009.
[16] M. Harchol-Balter et al. Connection Scheduling in Web Servers. In *USITS*, 1999.
[17] M. Isard et al. Dryad: Distributed Data-Parallel Programs From Sequential Building Blocks. In *EuroSys*, 2007.
[18] M. Isard et al. Quincy: Fair Scheduling For Distributed Computing Clusters. In *SOSP*, 2009.
[19] L. Lu et al. Predictive VM Consolidation on Multiple Resources: Beyond Load Balancing. In *IWQoS*, 2013.
[20] R. Panigrahy et al. Heuristics for Vector Bin Packing. In *MSR TR*, 2011.
[21] A. Rasmussen et al. Themis: An I/O-Efficient MapReduce. In *SoCC*, 2012.
[22] A. Shieh et al. Sharing the Data Center Network. In *NSDI*, 2011.
[23] T. Tannenbaum et al. Condor – A Distributed Job Scheduler. In *Beowulf Cluster Computing with Linux*. MIT Press, 2001.
[24] A. Thusoo et al. Hive: A Warehousing Solution Over A Map-Reduce Framework. *Proc. VLDB Endow.*, 2009.
[25] V. V. Vazirani. Approximation Algorithms. In *Springer-Verlag*, 2001.
[26] A. Wierman et al. Classifying Scheduling Policies with Respect to Unfairness in an M/GI/1 . In *SIGMETRICS*, 2003.
[27] G. J. Woeginger. There Is No Asymptotic Ptas For Two-Dimensional Vector Packing. In *Information Processing Letters*, 1997.
[28] C.-W. Yang et al. Tail Asymptotics For Policies Favoring Short Jobs In A Many-Flows Regime. In *SIGMETRICS*, 2006.
[29] M. Zaharia et al. Delay Scheduling: A Technique For Achieving Locality And Fairness In Cluster Scheduling. In *EuroSys*, 2010.
[30] J. Zhou et al. SCOPE: Parallel Databases Meet MapReduce. *Proc. VLDB Endow.*, 2012.

# Application-Driven Bandwidth Guarantees in Datacenters

Jeongkeun Lee Yoshio Turner Myungjin Lee* Lucian Popa+ Sujata Banerjee
Joon-Myung Kang Puneet Sharma
HP Labs, *University of Edinburgh, +Databricks

## ABSTRACT

Providing bandwidth guarantees to specific applications is becoming increasingly important as applications compete for shared cloud network resources. We present *CloudMirror*, a solution that provides bandwidth guarantees to cloud applications based on a new network abstraction and workload placement algorithm. An effective network abstraction would enable applications to easily and accurately specify their requirements, while simultaneously enabling the infrastructure to provision resources efficiently for deployed applications. Prior research has approached the bandwidth guarantee specification by using abstractions that resemble physical network topologies. We present a contrasting approach of deriving a network abstraction based on application communication structure, called *Tenant Application Graph or TAG*. CloudMirror also incorporates a new workload placement algorithm that efficiently meets bandwidth requirements specified by TAGs while factoring in high availability considerations. Extensive simulations using real application traces and datacenter topologies show that CloudMirror can handle 40% more bandwidth demand than the state of the art (e.g., the Oktopus system), while improving high availability from 20% to 70%.

**Categories and Subject Descriptors:** C.2.3 [Computer-Communication Networks]: Network Operations
**Keywords:** Datacenter; Bandwidth; Availability; Cloud; Virtual Network; Application

## 1. INTRODUCTION

A growing trend is the consolidation of computing infrastructure and applications into large datacenters, including virtualized cloud environments. Many of these emerging cloud applications are complex combinations of multiple services and require predictable performance, high availability, and high intra-datacenter bandwidth; e.g., Facebook "experiences 1000 times more traffic inside its data centers than it sends to and receives from outside users", and the internal traffic has increased much faster than Internet-facing bandwidth [1]. Meanwhile, many datacenter networks are oversubscribed, as high as 40:1 in some Facebook datacenters [2], causing the intra-datacenter traffic to contend for core bandwidth. Hence, *providing bandwidth guarantees* to specific applications is highly desirable, in order to preserve their response-time predictability when they compete for bandwidth with other applications.


*SIGCOMM'14,* August 17–22, 2014, Chicago, IL, USA.

http://dx.doi.org/10.1145/2619239.2626326.

Today, it is easy to share and virtualize compute and storage resources effectively. In contrast, implementing network virtualization with bandwidth guarantees on a shared network infrastructure is an inherently complex and challenging task [3–7, 18, 45], which requires three key technologies: 1) An easy-to-use *network abstraction model* for tenants to accurately express their bandwidth requirements; 2) A workload *placement algorithm* that efficiently allocates datacenter resources to meet the tenant requests, and 3) A scalable *runtime mechanism to enforce the bandwidth guarantees* and utilize unused bandwidth efficiently. In this paper, we propose *CloudMirror*, a solution that combines a new network abstraction with a new workload placement algorithm, while leveraging an existing mechanism [7] for enforcing guarantees.

An effective network abstraction model serves two purposes. One purpose is for tenants to specify their network requirements in a simple and intuitive yet accurate manner. The other purpose is to facilitate easy translation of these requirements to an efficient deployment on the low level infrastructure components. Most prior work, e.g., [4–9], has designed abstractions for specifying bandwidth guarantees that can be expressed as idealized physical network models, e.g., non-blocking switch (hose) [8] or two-level tree (hierarchical hose) [4, 6]. This is a natural approach since, for example, in cloud computing, tenants want to have the illusion of running their applications on dedicated hardware; with such a model, tenants would have the illusion of running their application over a dedicated physical network.

In contrast to these prior approaches, our approach is *to derive the network abstraction model based on application communication structure, and not a given underlying physical network topology.* We show that not only is such an abstraction easier to understand and reason about by tenants, but it can also be significantly more efficient in reserving bandwidth than the commonly proposed abstractions, such as the hose model. The intuition for its efficiency is that our abstraction accurately captures the bandwidth requirements of an application rather than imposing a pre-defined and perhaps a poor fit network abstraction (e.g., hose) for applications to map their requirements to.

To instantiate the bandwidth guarantees, the high-level abstraction must be mapped onto the low level physical topology via a job (VM) placement mechanism. We describe a new algorithm that exploits our refined network abstraction to more efficiently utilize datacenter resources. Efficient bandwidth utilization is often achieved by colocating application VMs in a single server or rack, which hurts availability; our placement algorithm provides high availability (HA) while efficiently guaranteeing bandwidth.

Finally, a runtime mechanism must enforce the virtual network abstraction for any traffic matrix in the datacenter. Our network abstraction can be easily supported through minor changes to existing frameworks for enforcing hose guarantees, such as those proposed in [4, 5, 7].

In this paper, we make the following contributions, building on our prior work [10].

1. A new tenant network abstraction model – *Tenant Application Graphs or TAGs* (§3). Deriving application structures from empirical datasets, we show that TAGs can be easier to use and more efficient in reserving bandwidth than the existing abstractions. We also develop a methodology to generate TAG models automatically from raw communication traces.
2. A new fast VM placement algorithm that resource-efficiently maps TAGs onto a tree-shaped physical network, satisfying the bandwidth requirements and also any specified high availability (HA) goals (§4). Bandwidth efficiency and HA can be conflicting goals [11]. We mathematically derive conditions that determine when colocating VMs would save bandwidth resource. When the conditions are violated, i.e., no bandwidth savings from colocation, our VM placement adopts anti-colocation to improve HA and to achieve balanced utilization of bandwidth with other types of resources.
3. Demonstration of the benefits of the TAG model and of our placement algorithm through extensive simulations using real application traces and datacenter topologies (§5). With a simple prototype, we show that the TAG model can be easily implemented on top of an existing mechanism [7] that enforces the hose model.

We next describe the current state of the art in providing bandwidth guarantees in cloud datacenter networks. Through examples of real applications, we show how existing network abstractions fall short and thus motivate the need for our new TAG model.

# 2. BACKGROUND AND RELATED WORK

Prior cloud networking research has primarily focused on supporting network requirements for Hadoop and Pregel like batch processing applications. Obviously, many applications are not similar in structure to Hadoop or Pregel exhibiting simple all-to-all communication patterns. In this paper we focus on other application types such as interactive applications (e.g., web and OLTP) hosted in today's cloud environments [12–14]. These applications have complex and tiered structures, and are not well represented using the prior models (§2.2). Moreover, unlike batch applications that can tolerate network bottlenecks, *interactive applications have very stringent performance requirements, and demand predictable throughput and tail latencies* [13]. Amazon has reported incurring e-commerce sales loss of 1% for every 100 msec increase in response latency [15]. Parley [16] demonstrated that adequate bandwidth is critical for applications to maintain low tail latencies. In our tests with Wikipedia benchmark [17], we also observed a sharp increase in web response time (from 250 to 900 msec) when the network bandwidth between the web and database VMs was throttled, only for 10 seconds, to 10% below bottleneck-free capacity.[1] This demonstrates the severe impact of insufficient bandwidth on web applications and a strong need for guaranteeing bandwidth for interactive applications.

Our private conversations with cloud users/operators as well as various benchmark reports confirm that *non-batch, interactive workloads often have similar or higher bandwidth requirements relative to more CPU-bound batch workloads.* Fig. 1(a) plots the ratio of aggregate application throughput (Mbps) to aggregate CPU consumption (GHz) for various cloud workloads.[2] From

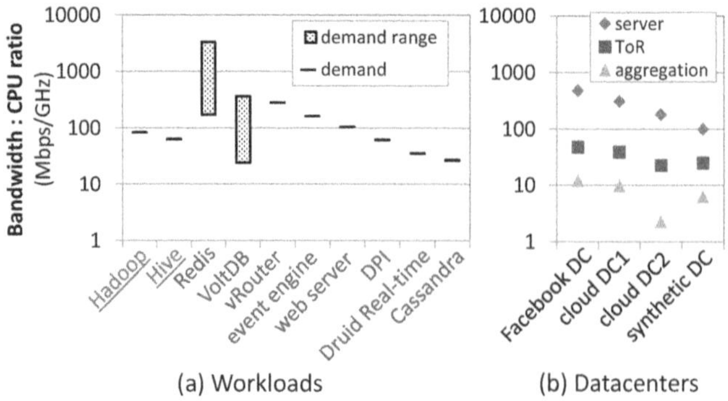


**Figure 1: Bandwidth-to-CPU ratio for 10 workloads and 4 datacenters. Batch jobs in red; interactive applications in blue.**

Fig. 1(a), we observe that the interactive workloads (Redis to Cassandra [19–24]) have similar or higher ratios of network-to-CPU compared to the batch jobs (Hadoop and Hive [18]).

Meanwhile, today's datacenters (DCs) are often oversubscribed and lack enough bandwidth to avoid contention between applications. Fig. 1(b) plots the provisioned ratio of bandwidth-to-CPU resources of four cloud datacenter environments at different tree topology levels.[3] We consider two production cloud DCs, Facebook DC [2,25] and the synthetic DC topology simulated in [4,18]. Comparing Figs. 1(a) and 1(b), we find that most datacenters are well provisioned to meet network demands of the workloads at the server level, but not at the ToR or aggregation level due to network oversubscription. Despite a recent trend toward less oversubscription, provisioning full-bisection bandwidth remains costly for large-scale datacenters. Bandwidth contention on oversubscribed core links is worsened by the need to spread VMs of an application across multiple servers and racks to increase robustness to single-point-of-failure. Even for non-oversubscribed networks, an efficient tenant network abstraction coupled with bandwidth guarantees benefits applications and operators, because extra bandwidth can facilitate lossless/fast network updates [26] and fault-resiliency [27].

While some cloud providers start to guarantee bandwidth [28, 29], they do so at specific fixed bandwidth-to-vCPU ratios, which limits flexibility in serving applications with diverse bandwidth-to-CPU demand ratios (Fig 1(a)). Their models, typically simplified from the hose model, also fail to capture bandwidth demands in an accurate or resource-efficient way, as we describe next.

## 2.1 Example Application Structure

Let us consider two illustrative applications to highlight the shortcomings of prior models for abstracting and provisioning network bandwidth.

Many user-facing applications and sophisticated enterprise applications are composed of multiple tiers with complex traffic interactions [11,12,14]. Fig. 2(a) shows a simple example of a three-tiered web application with a frontend web tier, a business logic tier, and a backend database tier. Each tier contains multiple VMs and the edges of the communication graph are annotated with the bandwidth requirements between tiers. The second example is a real-

[1] In contrast, [18] observed only marginal increase (<5%) of completion times of various batch jobs when their per-VM bandwidths were capped at 33% below bottleneck-free capacity.

[2] CPU consumption: # of vCPUs × core speed × CPU busy %. BW/CPU likely understate BW usage; i) reported CPU% ranges [50,100] and ii) we treat it as 100% when not reported to make sure we do not over estimate the ratio. Redis [19] and VoltDB [20] benchmarks report transactions-per-second; we converted them to ranges of network throughput by assuming data size ranges [100,1500] bytes.

[3] At the server level, we compute the ratio of the server's NIC bandwidth and the aggregate server CPU cycles. At the Top-of-Rack (ToR) and aggregate switch levels, we compute the same ratio as the uplink bandwidth normalized by the total CPU cycles of servers under the ToR/aggregate switch.

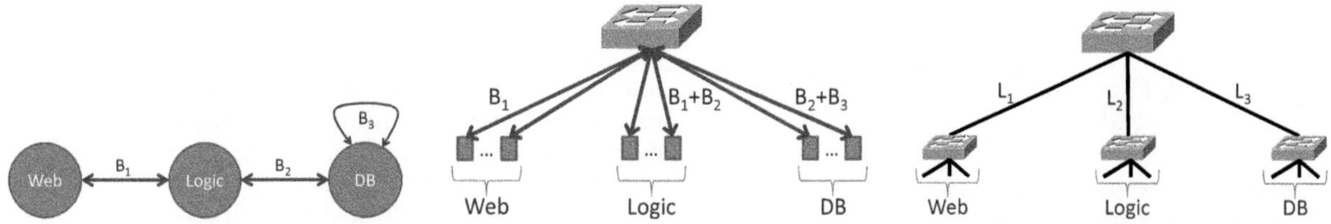


(a) 3-tier web application (b) Hose modeling (c) Physical deployment example

**Figure 2: Three tiered application example deployed using the hose model.**

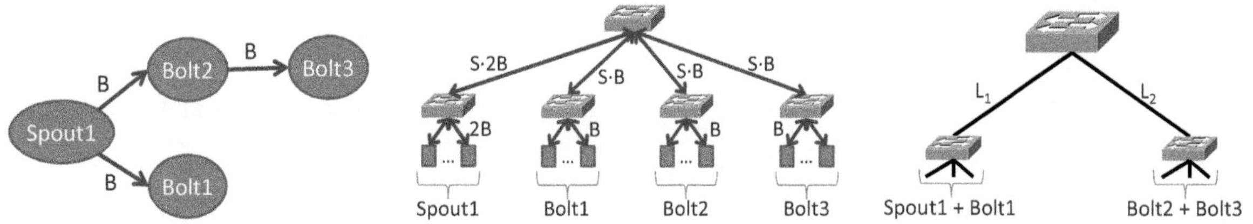


(a) Storm example (b) VOC Modeling (c) Physical deployment example

**Figure 3: Storm [30] application example deployed using the VOC model.**

time data analytics application shown in Fig. 3(a), implemented using Storm [30]. Storm is a popular platform for online machine learning, continuous computation on data streams, etc. Storm applications have two types of components, implemented using Java threads: "spouts", which are similar to mappers in MapReduce, and "bolts", which represent both a mapper and a reducer.

## 2.2 Shortcomings of Prior Models

The most commonly used abstractions are variants of the hose model and the pipe model. These are often a poor fit for modeling many applications, as we describe next.

• **Hose Model:** In the hose model abstraction [4,7,8], all VMs are connected to a central (virtual) switch by a dedicated link (hose) having a minimum bandwidth guarantee. We consider a generalized hose model [8] where each VM can have a heterogeneous bandwidth guarantee (unlike [4,28]) to better match application requirements. While the hose model well describes batch applications with homogeneous all-to-all communication patterns [18], it does not accurately express the requirements for applications composed of multiple tiers with complex traffic interactions. It can also be severely inefficient in terms of resource utilization. Consider the example of Fig. 2(a) and assume that $B_1$ represents the typical bandwidth demand between one VM of the web tier and one VM of the business logic tier. $B_2$ is the bandwidth demand between one VM of the business logic tier and one VM of the database tier, while $B_3$ is the bandwidth demand between two database VMs representing traffic for maintaining database consistency. For simplicity, we assume an equal number of VMs in each tier and equal bandwidth requirements in both directions of each edge while ignoring bandwidth requirements for Internet access.

Fig. 2(b) presents the hose model guarantees for the example in Fig. 2(a). The fundamental problem is that the hose model *aggregates* the demands for multiple different communications – e.g., logic-DB ($B_2$) and DB-DB ($B_3$) for a database VM – into one hose. This prevents the cloud operator from accurately computing the required bandwidth on physical links and leads to inefficient bandwidth consumption. Suppose that each application tier is deployed on a separate subtree of the physical network as shown in Fig. 2(c). To satisfy the hose model representation, the bandwidth that must be reserved on link $L_3$ for each database VM would be $B_2$+$B_3$.[4] The hose model hides the fact that $B_3$ is intended for the communication within the DB tier rather than for communication with other tiers. The tenant does not actually need the full guarantee of ($B_2$+$B_3$) indicated by the hose model on link $L_3$, thus wasting $B_3$ on $L_3$.

In addition to being inefficient, the hose model also *fails to guarantee the required bandwidth in case of congestion.* In the 3-tier example of Fig. 4, simplified from Fig. 2(a), suppose $B_1 = 500$, $B_2 = 100$ (in Mbps) and that all the tiers are placed under the same switch with each VM in a separate server. The hose guarantee for the business logic VM would be the sum of the requirements $500 + 100 = 600$ Mbps. Suppose the bottleneck bandwidth towards the business logic VM is also 600 Mbps. If the business logic VM momentarily receives an aggregate of 500 Mbps traffic from web VMs and also another 500 Mbps from DB VMs, the total 1000 Mbps traffic exceeds the available bandwidth and the hose guarantee (both 600 Mbps). Because the hose model aggregates the requirements for two different communications (from web and DB), the model is agnostic to the actual guarantees that the business logic VM needs for different sources. Existing solutions would partition the 600 Mbps hose guarantee by TCP-like max-min fairness [7] and yield 300:300 (Mbps), assuming equal number of sending VMs from each tier, but fail to provide the 500 Mbps guarantee for the communication with the web tier.

• **Virtual Oversubscribed Cluster (VOC):** This model proposed in [4, 6] enhances the hose model by organizing VMs into clusters, each with a hose model guarantee. Clusters are then connected together with per-cluster hoses with capacity of $B \cdot S/O$, where $B$ is the guarantee of each VM inside the cluster, $S$ is the size of the cluster (number of VMs) and $O$ is the oversubscription factor [4]. Again, to better suit applications, we consider a generalized VOC model that accommodates different guarantees, sizes and oversubscription factors for each cluster, unlike the more constrained homogeneous model in [4].

The VOC model is also not well suited to represent most applications. Consider the Storm example in Fig. 3(a), where for simplicity we assume that each component has the same number of VMs $S$, and the outgoing bandwidth of each VM to a communicating component is $B$. Even for this simple example it is non-trivial to derive a good VOC model representation from many possible representations. Fig. 3(b) presents one possible mapping where each application component is represented as a VOC cluster. The resulting model is a relaxed VOC model with no oversubscription of

[4]We assume here that $B_2 + B_3 < B_1 + B_1 + B_2$, and so the minimum that needs to be reserved on $L_3$ is $B_2$+$B_3$ rather than $2B_1$+$B_2$.

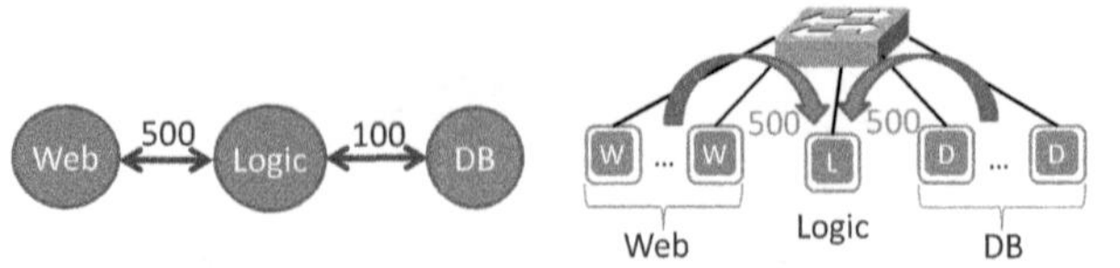


**Figure 4: Hose fails to separately guarantee traffic to Logic from Web and DB in case of congestion.**

the clusters. This model also fails to accurately capture the application's communication pattern as the Storm components do not communicate internally using that bandwidth.

The goal behind the VOC model is to isolate highly connected application tiers and place them in better connected topology subtrees. Having clusters that are not oversubscribed and that do not communicate among their VMs defeats the purpose of the VOC model, and, in fact, has an adverse effect. The placement algorithm may place the VMs of each Storm component in separate subtrees in an attempt to localize intra-component traffic, as Oktopus [4] does. This wastes bandwidth as the Storm threads communicate only between components.

Fig. 3(c) shows a potential deployment where two Storm components are placed in one branch of the physical tree while the other two are in a different branch. In this case, the bandwidth reservation on links $L_1$ and $L_2$ should be $S \cdot B$ given the communication pattern (since only "Spout1" communicates with "Bolt2" between the two branches). However, VOC will reserve twice this bandwidth since VOC is agnostic to actual inter-component communication pattern and requires $\min(3S \cdot B, 2S \cdot B) = 2S \cdot B$.

In essence, the VOC model also *aggregates* bandwidth requirements towards different components into a single hose and a single oversubscribed hose. This aggregation prevents: 1) determining the actual inter-component bandwidth needed at physical links, and 2) guaranteeing the required bandwidth in case of congestion (similar to Fig. 4). Recently, Hadrian [6] extended VOC by enabling each component X to list the components that X communicates with, e.g., Spout1: {Bolt1, Bolt2}, but this still aggregates requirements towards the listed components into a single oversubscribed hose and does not spell out the actual inter-component patterns.[5]

To see the significance of inter-component traffic, we analyzed the component-to-component traffic matrix from the `bing.com` datacenter, provided by the authors of [11]. In this example, we found that *most application components have high inter-component communications.* The inter-component traffic fraction of each component averages 91% over 500+ components. The total inter-component traffic constituted 65% of the entire datacenter traffic.Excluding traffic from management and common services, the *total* inter-component traffic becomes 37% of the entire non-management traffic; VOC model is still ineffective since the *per-component* ratio of inter-component traffic is still high at 85% on average.

Gatekeeper [9] tried to better model inter-component guarantees by allowing the composition of multiple hoses for each VM. In the example of Fig. 4, the business logic VM would be connected to two hoses: one for 500 Mbps guarantee towards the web tier and the other for 100 Mbps towards the DB tier. However, the hoses unnecessarily include intra-component traffic, wasting physical bandwidth to provide the unnecessary guarantees or failing to meet the intended guarantee: e.g., DB-DB traffic can hog the bandwidth intended for logic-DB traffic.

• **Pipe Model:** Another alternative is to specify bandwidth guarantees between pairs of VMs [3, 31, 32] as virtual pipes. While this model can precisely capture the application's traffic needs, it is too rigid and *it lacks statistical multiplexing*. Typically, the VMs belonging to different tiers that exchange data are selected by run-time load balancers, which do not guarantee perfectly uniform load distribution to every destination. Thus, load to each destination can vary over time even when the aggregate load is constant. Inability to update each pipe rapidly to tightly track their time-varying demand likely requires worst case reservations of peak load for each pipe [8]. For instance, the pipe model might force 2X overprovisioning based on a benchmark report for Amazon's Elastic Load Balancer that shows that the sum of the peak loads to each destination is at least double the peak aggregate traffic [33]. The pipe model is also tedious to use as the tenants can have hundreds and even thousands of VMs, leading to tens of thousands of pairwise guarantees, *hurting scalability* in placing tenant VMs (§5).

In summary, as opposed to the hose model and its variants that aggregate (or reduce) various communication patterns into a single hose guarantee, we need a new abstraction that spells out the actual communication pattern between pairs of components, similar to the pipe model, but without suffering from being tedious and slow like the pipe model.

[5] In addition, Hadrian's extension to VOC is meant to model inter-tenant requirements instead of inter-component requirements.

# 3. TENANT APPLICATION GRAPH (TAG)

We propose the Tenant Application Graph (TAG), a new model that tenants can use to describe bandwidth requirements for applications. Unlike hose and VOC abstractions, which present models resembling physical networks, the TAG abstraction aims to model the actual communication patterns of applications. The TAG model leverages the tenant's knowledge of an application's structure to yield a concise yet flexible representation of the application's communication pattern.

A TAG model is *a graph, where each vertex represents an application component* (or *tier*, we use the two terms interchangeably to indicate the set of VMs performing the same function). Since most applications are conceptually composed of multiple tiers [12], a tenant can simply map each tier onto a TAG vertex. For example, for the application in Fig. 2(a) the tenant would identify three tiers: web, business logic, and database. One or more special components are used to model nodes external to the TAG tiers, e.g., the Internet, a storage service, another tenant, etc. Each component $u$ has a 'size' attribute, $N^u$, denoting the number of VMs in that component, which is optional for the special components.

Tenants request bandwidth guarantees between tiers by placing directed edges between the corresponding vertices in the TAG model. Each directed edge $e = (u, v)$ from tier $u$ to tier $v$ is labeled with an ordered pair $< S_e, R_e >$ that represents per-VM bandwidth guarantees. Specifically, each VM in tier $u$ is guaranteed bandwidth $S_e$ for sending traffic to VMs in tier $v$, and each VM in tier $v$ is guaranteed bandwidth $R_e$ to receive traffic from VMs in tier $u$.

Having two values (sending and receiving) instead of a single bandwidth guarantee for each edge is useful when the sizes of the two tiers are different. If tiers $u$ and $v$ have sizes $N^u$ and $N^v$, respectively, then the total bandwidth that TAG guarantees for traffic sent from tier $u$ to tier $v$ is $B_{u \to v} = \min(S_e \cdot N^u, R_e \cdot N^v)$ because the total outgoing traffic from tier $u$ cannot exceed the total incoming traffic to tier $v$, and vice versa.

To model communication among VMs within tier $u$, the TAG model allows a self-loop edge of the form $e = (u, u)$ that is labeled with a single bandwidth guarantee $SR_e$, which represents both the sending and the receiving guarantee for each individual VM in that tier (or vertex). A self-loop edge is equivalent to a conventional hose model; each VM in tier $u$ can be considered to be attached to

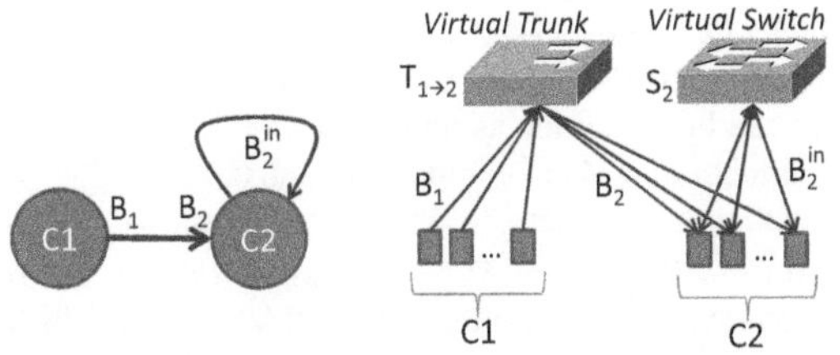


**Figure 5: TAG model (a) example, (b) explained.**

a virtual switch via a transmission hose of rate $SR_e$ and a receive hose of rate $SR_e$.

Fig. 5(a) shows a TAG model for a simple example application with two tiers $C1$ and $C2$. In this example, a directed edge from $C1$ to $C2$ is labeled $< B_1, B_2 >$. Thus, each VM in $C1$ is guaranteed to be able to send at rate $B_1$ to the set of VMs in $C2$. Similarly, each VM in $C2$ is guaranteed to be able to receive at rate $B_2$ from the set of VMs in $C1$.

To better understand the TAG model, Fig. 5(b) shows an alternative way of visualizing the guarantees expressed in Fig. 5(a). The directional guarantees between C1 and C2 is represented by the *virtual trunk* $T_{1\to2}$. Each VM in $C1$ is connected to $T_{1\to2}$ by a dedicated directional link of capacity $B_1$; and $T_{1\to2}$ is connected through a directional link of capacity $B_2$ to each VM in $C2$. Thus, a virtual trunk can be seen as a *directional* hose model between the VMs of the two communicating tiers; $T_{1\to2}$ captures one-to-many/many-to-one send/receive bandwidth for each VM in $C1/C2$. This differs from two alternatives in modeling inter-tier guarantees: 1) guaranteeing the aggregate bandwidth between $C1$ and $C2$ through a tier-to-tier pipe, and 2) provisioning every send-receive VM pair with a pipe [31]. The alternatives lack the efficiency and flexibility benefits of using TAG that we will describe soon.

The TAG model example in Fig. 5(a) has a self-loop edge for tier $C2$, describing the bandwidth guarantees for traffic where both source and destination are in $C2$, e.g., the traffic between database servers in Fig. 2(a). A self-loop edge is equivalent to a hose model between the VMs of that tier. For example, in Fig. 5(b), each VM in $C2$ is connected through a bidirectional link of capacity $B_2^{in}$ to a *virtual switch* $S_2$.

Note that hose and pipe models are special cases of TAG: a TAG with one component and a self-loop is the hose model, and a TAG with exactly one VM per component and no self-loops is the pipe model.

**Benefits:** Because the TAG abstraction mirrors real application structure, it is *intuitive, descriptive and easy to use*. Mirroring application structure enables the TAG model to be *efficient*, describing the bandwidth needs of complex structured applications accurately unlike hose or VOC models that often lead to over-allocation of bandwidth (§2.2).

Furthermore, the TAG model is *flexible*. Like the hose model, TAG presents per-VM guarantees, enabling it to take advantage of statistical multiplexing by specifying a guarantee based on the peak of the sum of VM-to-VM demands instead of the (typically larger) sum of peak demands needed by the pipe model. TAG is also flexible to dynamic re-sizing of tiers (known as *"auto-scaling"* [34]); per-VM bandwidth guarantees $S_e$ and $R_e$ typically do not need to change when tier sizes are changed by scaling. For example, Netflix's benchmark on AWS exhibited stable per-VM bandwidth while scaling up the number of VMs from 48 to 288 [24]. This is unlike a VM-to-VM pipe model [31, 32] where *per-pipe* bandwidth guarantees need to be recomputed whenever dynamic load-balancing or auto-scaling takes place, or else bandwidth must be heavily overprovisioned. This is also unlike guaranteeing an aggregate total bandwidth between components, which would have to change when components scale up/down.

Finally, grouping VMs by component in the TAG model enables tenants to specify a much smaller number of values than for the pipe model.[6]

**Producing TAG Models:** Users who understand the structure of their distributed applications can specify a matching TAG model and tune the component bandwidth guarantees to their needs. Alternatively, cloud orchestration systems like OpenStack Heat and AWS CloudFormation could be extended to generate TAG models automatically along with their current ability to automate application deployment and control application scaling. These systems use application templates, possibly provided as a library for users, that explicitly describe application components and their configuration and could be extended with bandwidth guarantee information for each component.

For users who do not know the structure and bandwidth demands of their applications, the provider or the user can try to infer an appropriate TAG model. We are exploring an approach that clusters VMs that exhibit similarity in their communication pattern, e.g., VMs that share a common set of destinations. For each VM, a feature vector is constructed based currently only on the VM-to-VM bandwidth weighted traffic matrix. The feature vector includes the VM's row and column entries, i.e., both outgoing and incoming traffic, and similarity is computed as the angular distance between vectors. A projection graph is formed containing one vertex for each VM and edges with weight set to the similarity between the VMs for the two incident vertices. Known algorithms [35, 36] that maximize graph modularity are applied to the projection graph to identify clusters of VMs with high edge weight within the cluster, indicating high similarity among the VMs. The TAG model is formed by treating each cluster as a component and using the traffic matrix bandwidths to identify all hose and trunk guarantees. When identifying these guarantees, we use a time series of traffic matrices to factor in savings from statistical multiplexing.

We applied this approach to the `bing.com` dataset to determine how well it could infer the known component structure given only the VM-to-VM traffic matrix. Using the metric of adjusted mutual information ranging from 0 (independent) to 1 (identical) clustering [37], we obtained on average 0.54 over 80 applications using Louvain clustering [35], indicating substantial commonality between the ground truth clustering and the inferred clusters, but also the need for further improvement.

**Component-Level Graph Models:** Graph models have been proposed to describe generic topologies between service components and desirable communication policies (security, priority, forwarding) between components, e.g., in Service-Oriented Architecture [38], Group-based Policy [31, 39] and Network Functions Virtualisation [40]. Our TAG model can be viewed as extending these models by explicitly representing *bandwidth guarantees* between communicating components.

# 4. DEPLOYING TAG

TAGs capture tenant application structures rather than physical network topologies. We present a VM placement algorithm that bridges the gap between the high level TAG to the low level physical infrastructure. As most cloud datacenter topologies are tree structures, we aim to efficiently deploy TAG instances on tree-

[6]To be even simpler for users, two edges in opposite directions between two tiers can be combined into a single undirected edge when the incoming/outgoing values for the tiers are the same (i.e., $S_{(u,v)} = R_{(v,u)}$ and $R_{(u,v)} = S_{(v,u)}$).

shaped physical topologies. For simplicity, we describe our algorithm assuming a single-rooted tree, however our algorithm can similarly be applied to a multi-rooted tree.

Existing network-aware approaches have focused on reducing bandwidth usage by localizing network traffic into a small region/sub-tree: thus colocating VMs that incur high network traffic between them [4, 11, 32]. In this section, we first derive the key conditions that enable bandwidth reduction through colocation. Next, we show that bandwidth reduction through colocation is often infeasible or undesirable due to high availability (HA) and other requirements. Finally, we present our VM placement algorithm that uses the bandwidth reduction conditions to efficiently deploy TAG models and also to improve high availability.

## 4.1 Bandwidth Required by TAG

To deploy an application that is described by a TAG model, the cloud provider must allocate sufficient bandwidth on physical links to support the bandwidth guarantees specified in the TAG model. For a given TAG model, we calculate the amount of bandwidth that must be allocated on the uplink of a particular subtree of a datacenter tree topology, when the subtree contains a subset of the TAG VMs. The subtree could be at any level of the topology, e.g., server, ToR switch, or aggregation switch; and the uplink connects the subtree to the rest of the datacenter topology.

Let $X$ denote the set of TAG components placed in the subtree of interest, and $\overline{X}$ denote the set of all components that are outside this subtree. A component can be a member of both sets if it has some VMs in the subtree and the other VMs outside the subtree. Let $N_X^t$ represent the number of VMs of component $t$ that reside in the subtree, and let $N_{\overline{X}}^{t'}$ represent the number of VMs of component $t'$ that reside outside the subtree.

For the TAG model, the bandwidth $C_{X,\text{out}}$ that must be allocated for outgoing transmission from $X$ to $\overline{X}$ is given by summing up the requirement for each pair of components where the first component ($t$) has at least one VM in the subtree and the second component ($t'$) has at least one VM outside the subtree. Define $B_{\text{snd}}^{t\to t'}$ as the bandwidth needed for each VM in component $t$ for transmission to component $t'$, and $B_{\text{rcv}}^{t\to t'}$ as the bandwidth needed for each VM in component $t'$ for reception from component $t$. These values are obtained directly from the TAG model. Then, we have

$$\begin{aligned} C_{X,\text{out}} &= \sum_{t\in X}\sum_{t'\in\overline{X}} \min(N_X^t B_{\text{snd}}^{t\to t'}, N_{\overline{X}}^{t'} B_{\text{rcv}}^{t\to t'}) \\ &= B_{\text{trunk}} + B_{\text{hose}}. \\ B_{\text{trunk}} &= \sum_{t\in X}\sum_{\substack{t'\in\overline{X}\\ t'\neq t}} \min(N_X^t B_{\text{snd}}^{t\to t'}, N_{\overline{X}}^{t'} B_{\text{rcv}}^{t\to t'}). \\ B_{\text{hose}} &= \sum_{t\in X\cap\overline{X}} \min(N_X^t B_{\text{snd}}^{t\to t}, N_{\overline{X}}^t B_{\text{rcv}}^{t\to t}). \end{aligned} \quad (1)$$

$B_{\text{trunk}}$ is the inter-component requirement (i.e., virtual trunk) and $B_{hose}$ is the intra-component requirement (i.e., hose).[7] The TAG bandwidth requirement in the opposite direction from $\overline{X}$ to $X$, say $C_{X,\text{in}}$, is calculated similarly.

## 4.2 Bandwidth Savings by Colocation

We derive key conditions that enable bandwidth savings through colocation from Eq. 1. Consider $B_{hose}$ that defines the outgoing *hose bandwidth* needed at the subtree uplink. The min() term for $B_{hose}$ defines each $t$'s hose bandwidth across the subtree uplink. This term can be re-written as $\min(N_X^t, N^t - N_X^t)B_{\text{snd}}^{t\to t}$ where $N^t$ is the total number of VMs of component $t$ and because $B_{\text{snd}}^{t\to t} = B_{\text{rcv}}^{t\to t}$. As $N_X^t$ increases from zero to $N^t$, the hose bandwidth increases from zero to $\frac{N^t}{2}B_{\text{snd}}^{t\to t}$ when $N_X^t = \frac{N^t}{2}$ and then decreases to zero. The hose bandwidth is zero either when all VMs of $t$ reside in $X$ or $\overline{X}$. From the standpoint of $t$ in the subtree, hose bandwidth saving due to increasing degree of colocation happens only when

$$N_X^t > \frac{N^t}{2}. \quad (2)$$

*Thus, the necessary and sufficient condition to achieve hose bandwidth saving is that more than half the VMs of t must be colocated in the subtree.*

The min() term for $B_{trunk}$ in Eq. 1 defines the *virtual trunk bandwidth* from $t$ to $t'$ (where $t' \neq t$) across the subtree uplink, for outgoing traffic. Let $N^{t'}$ denote the total number of VMs of $t'$. Then the outgoing trunk bandwidth, denoted by $B1$, is computed as

$$B1 = \min(N_X^t B_{\text{snd}}^{t\to t'}, (N^{t'} - N_X^{t'})B_{\text{rcv}}^{t\to t'}). \quad (3)$$

We next derive the worst-case trunk bandwidth requirement, $B2$, and compute the amount of trunk bandwidth saving as $B2 - B1$. The worst-case trunk bandwidth is incurred when all VMs of $t'$ are placed outside of the subtree ($N_X^{t'} = 0$), in which case no bandwidth is saved and $B2 = \min(N_X^t B_{\text{snd}}^{t\to t'}, N^{t'} B_{\text{rcv}}^{t\to t'})$. For simplicity, we assume that the total sending rate from $t$ is equal to the total receiving rate of $t'$, i.e., $N^t B_{\text{snd}}^{t\to t'} = N^{t'} B_{\text{rcv}}^{t\to t'}$; we have $B2 = N_X^t B_{\text{snd}}^{t\to t'}$ since $N_X^t \le N^t$. Then, the bandwidth that can be saved by (partial) colocation is:

$$B2 - B1 = \max(N_X^t B_{\text{snd}}^{t\to t'} - (N^{t'} - N_X^{t'})B_{\text{rcv}}^{t\to t'}, 0). \quad (4)$$

The condition to have non-zero trunk bandwidth saving, $B2 - B1 > 0$, is given as

$$N_X^t B_{\text{snd}}^{t\to t'} + N_X^{t'} B_{\text{rcv}}^{t\to t'} > N^{t'} B_{\text{rcv}}^{t\to t'}. \quad (5)$$

It is clear that the bandwidth saving increases as $N_X^t$ and $N_X^{t'}$ increase, i.e., as more VMs of $t$ and $t'$ are colocated. The required uplink bandwidth is zero when hosting all VMs of $t$ and $t'$ in the subtree: $N_X^t = N^t$ and $N_X^{t'} = N^{t'}$. Again assuming that the total sending rate from $t$ is equal to the total receiving rate of $t'$, i.e., $N^t B_{\text{snd}}^{t\to t'} = N^{t'} B_{\text{rcv}}^{t\to t'}$, Eq. 5 becomes $N^{t'} N_X^t + N^t N_X^{t'} > N^t N^{t'}$; its *necessary* condition is easily proven to be:

$$N_X^t > \frac{N^t}{2} \text{ or } N_X^{t'} > \frac{N^{t'}}{2}. \quad (6)$$

*Thus, to achieve trunk bandwidth saving, more than half of the VMs of t or those of t′ need to be colocated in the subtree*, similar to the hose saving condition Eq. 2. Since Eq. 6 is a necessary but not sufficient condition for trunk savings, our placement algorithm verifies savings using Eq. 4 before colocating multiple tiers.

## 4.3 Disadvantages of Colocation

A naive approach to deploy a TAG would be to identify a set of TAG tiers that heavily communicate with each other and colocate them on the same subtree to save bandwidth, while ensuring valid placements by satisfying the requirement of Eq. 1. This is the approach taken by existing network-aware placement solutions [3, 4, 31] though they use different abstractions: hose, VOC, or pipe.

However, bandwidth saving by VM colocation can lead to single-point-of-failure and conflict with High Availability (HA) requirements. In addition, colocation can cause unbalanced utilization of the different types of resources available on each host (bandwidth, CPU, memory); in turn, this may increase the number of

[7] $C_{X,\text{out}}$ for the VOC model is similarly defined as $\min\left(\sum_{t\in X}\sum_{\forall t'\neq t} N_X^t B_{\text{snd}}^{t\to t'}, \sum_{t'\in\overline{X}}\sum_{\forall t\neq t'} N_{\overline{X}}^{t'} B_{\text{rcv}}^{t\to t'}\right) + B_{\text{hose}}$. From this, one can easily prove that the TAG model always requires a bandwidth allocation that is less or equal to that needed with the VOC model.

hosts and potentially the network bandwidth allocation needed to support a given application demand. We next elaborate on these two disadvantages of colocation.

**Colocation vs. High Availability (HA).** Colocation increases the chance for applications to experience downtime with a single server or switch failure. Thus, HA requirements may conflict with bandwidth-saving goals. An HA requirement is often expressed as anti-affinity (anti-colocation): the VMs of the same tier/service must reside on multiple servers or switches to retain service availability in case of a server/switch failure. Anti-affinity improves HA but depletes bandwidth saving from colocation. Anti-affinity also increases the need for bandwidth saving in oversubscribed datacenter networks: e.g., anti-affinity enforced at the tree level $L_{AA}$ increases the chance for tenant traffic to consume the bandwidth of level $L_{AA}+1$ subtrees, which have smaller aggregate bandwidth than level $L_{AA}$.

Previous work addressing HA requirements for workload placement (for example [11, 41, 42]) has not, to our knowledge, also provided bandwidth guarantees. Some, notably Bodik et al. [11], have presented techniques to jointly maximize bandwidth savings and HA but without providing guarantees. Our placement algorithm provides both bandwidth guarantees as well as optional HA guarantees on a per-tenant basis. Even for tenants without HA requirements, we can opportunistically increase survivability when bandwidth is not the bottleneck.

**Colocation vs. Efficient Resource Utilization.** Colocation can reduce the efficiency of resource utilization when there are disproportionate demands for different resource types, e.g., network vs. CPU (Fig. 1). In Fig. 6, we consider an example of placing three hose components under a rack that has enough resources to accommodate the request. The placement in Fig. 6(c) localizes 16 Mbps bandwidth demands from components A and B under the two leftmost servers but cannot provide requested guarantees to component C. If there is no available VM slot outside this rack, this request will be rejected and this rack will be underutilized. Previous network-aware VM placement algorithms would blindly colocate A's VMs and B's VMs and yield this inefficient allocation. The alternative allocation in Fig. 6(d) does not save the total bandwidth at the server uplinks but efficiently utilizes both slot and bandwidth resources while providing the guarantees. The key to achieving this balanced and efficient utilization is *placing high-bandwidth and low-bandwidth demanding VMs together, even though they do not communicate with each other.* Note that this placement also improves HA.

**Algorithm 1:** VM scheduler (simplified)

```
1  def AllocTenant(TAG g):
2      st = FindLowestSubtree(g, 0);
3      while st:
           /* Pass g's copy to Alloc.  map:  server
              locations of placed VMs                       */
4          map = Alloc(g, st);
5          if entire g in map:
               /* Reserve bandwidth for map upto root       */
6              ReserveBW(map, root); return map;
7          Dealloc(map, st);
8          if st is root: return False;
9          st = FindLowestSubtree(g, level(st)+1);
10     return False;
11 def Alloc(g, st):
12     map = {} ;
13     if level(st)==0: /* st is a server.  reserve its
       slots and uplink BW.                                 */
14         map[st] += g; ReserveBW(map,st);
15         return map;
       /* First, minimize BW usage by colocation            */
16     if BwSavingsFeasible():
17         map = Colocate(g, st);
18         g.Subtract(map);
       /* Second, balance resource utilization              */
19     if g.size > 0:
20         map += Balance(g, st);
21     if map:
22         if ReserveBW(map, st) is False:
23             Dealloc(map, st);
24             map = {};
25     return map;
26 def Colocate(g, st):
27     amap = {};
28     (g_sub, child) = FindTiersToColoc(g, st);
29     while g_sub.size > 0:
30         map = Alloc(g_sub, child);
31         amap += map; g.Subtract(map);
32         (g_sub, child) = FindTiersToColoc(g, st);
33     return amap;
34 def Balance(g, st):
35     amap = {};
36     (g_sub, child) = MdSubsetSum(g, st);
37     while g_sub.size >0:
38         map = Alloc(g_sub, child);
39         amap += map; g.Subtract(map);
40         (g_sub, child) = MdSubsetSum(g, st);
41     return amap;
```

## 4.4 VM Placement Algorithm

We aim to maximize the datacenter resource utilization by accepting as many TAG requests as possible while guaranteeing requested bandwidth. This problem is NP-hard similar to optimally placing hose models [8]. We first present our main heuristic in Algorithm 1, and extend it to support HA in §4.5. For brevity, we sketch the steps in the algorithm and define only major functions in the pseudocode. We assume identical VM types and slots; extending for heterogeneous cases is straightforward.

The algorithm starts with `AllocTenant`, which takes a TAG graph **g** as an input; **g** lists application components (vertices), communication edges, and their attributes (component size and bandwidth demand). In order to localize the traffic between the VMs in **g**, `FindLowestSubtree` in line **2** searches for a valid lowest-level subtree, `st`, under which the entire **g** is likely to fit. The search starts from the server level (0) and moves upward. **g**'s demands for 1) VM slots and 2) bandwidth for communication with its external entities are validated against 1) the total number of VM slots available in the servers under `st` and 2) the available uplink bandwidth from `st` to the tree `root`.

`AllocTenant` in line **4** attempts to deploy **g** on `st` by calling `Alloc`, which reserves slot and bandwidth resources in the subtree below `st` and returns a `map` of allocated VMs and their server locations. If `map` covers all VMs of **g**, the algorithm successfully returns after reserving slot and bandwidth resources from `st` up to `root` and the cloud provider will launch VMs on the specified servers in `map`. `Alloc` may fail to allocate the entire **g** under `st`, because the bandwidth availability of the links below `st` is not guaranteed by `FindLowestSubtree`; the actual requirements on those links are unknown until we know the exact number of VMs of each tier that will be placed in each server under `st`. In case of such failure, `Dealloc` in line **7** releases the resources reserved for the VMs in `map`. The algorithm next tries to allocate **g** under a new subtree at `st`'s parent level (line **9**). When moving to the parent level of `st`, the siblings of `st` will be considered for placement of **g** either in its entirety or split across multiple siblings. The algorithm continues

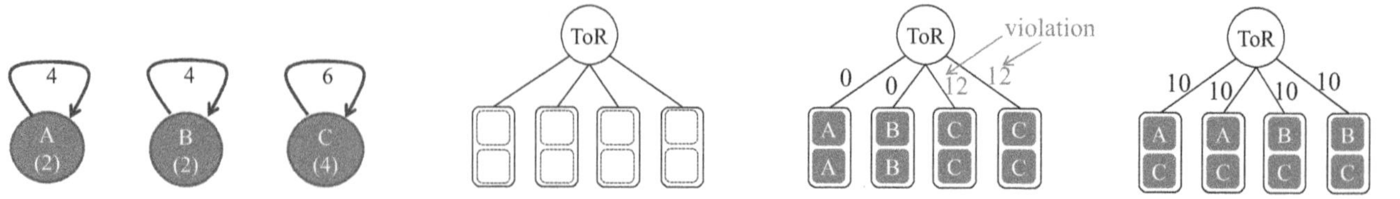


(a) Request for 3 hose components, total 8 VMs and 40 Mbps demand.

(b) Rack with 4 servers, each with 2 slots and 10 Mbps NIC.

(c) Colocation for saving bandwidth of A and B.

(d) No saving but efficient resource utilizations.

**Figure 6: Colocation for bandwidth saving can hurt efficient resource utilization.**

to move to higher levels of the tree until either placement succeeds or else placement finally fails at the tree `root` (line **8**).

`Alloc` (line **11**) is a recursive function, invoked by its two subroutines: `Colocate` and `Balance`. (We describe `Alloc` and the subroutines in a depth-first manner.) Before reaching the subroutines, `Alloc` first checks if the target `st` is a server: if so, it allocates `g`'s VMs on the server and returns; we assume sufficient bandwidth is always available for communication between VMs in the same server. If `st` is a ToR or higher level switch, `Alloc` strategically allocates `g`'s VMs over `st`'s child nodes by `Colocate` and `Balance`.

`Colocate` is invoked only when bandwidth saving through colocation is feasible (line **16**), determined by the size conditions (Eqs. 2 and 6) and the HA requirement (§4.5). As the algorithm recurses down the tree by subsequent invocations of `Alloc`, the number of VMs of a hose tier (or a pair of trunk tiers) in `g` may become less than 50% of the original tier size(s); bandwidth saving thus becomes infeasible. Likewise, if anti-affinity is required at level $L_{AA}$ with 50% or higher worst case survivability ($R_{WCS}$, defined in §4.5), it is impossible to place >50% of a tier under a subtree at level-$L_{AA}$ or lower.

`FindTiersToColoc` in `Colocate` identifies a set of VMs $g_{sub}$ ($\subset$ `g`) that provide (hose, trunk or both) bandwidth saving through colocation by using the size conditions of Eqs. 2-6. It excludes from $g_{sub}$ low-bandwidth tiers (e.g., A and B in Fig. 6) that can subsequently be placed together with high bandwidth tiers (e.g., C in Fig. 6) to increase resource utilization across different resource types, e.g., network and CPU. The idea is to identify tiers having low per-VM bandwidth demand compared to the per-slot available bandwidth of `st`'s child nodes, and then place VMs of these low-bandwidth tiers together with VMs of higher bandwidth tiers, where the VMs of each higher bandwidth tier are not themselves colocated (due to the size or HA constraints tested on algorithm line **16**).[8] Note that this strategy places low-bandwidth VMs and high-bandwidth VMs together even when the two types of VMs do not communicate with each other.

To achieve this balance of slot and bandwidth utilization, `Balance` is invoked (line **20**) to deploy the VMs, remaining in `g` after `Colocate`, for which bandwidth saving is infeasible. `MdSubsetSum` in `Balance` tries to find the best `child` node of `st` and the best set of VMs $g_{sub}$ ($\subset$`g`) that will lead both slot and uplink utilization of `child` to approach 100%; this is similar to a known Multi-Dimensional Subset-Sum problem. We extended the standard one-dimensional greedy algorithm [43] to three dimensions (slot, in BW, out BW) by using the utilization ratio of each resource as a common metric. We also improved its speed by iterating over `g`'s tiers, instead of every VM, as the VMs in the same tier have the same demands.

**Algorithm Complexity:** We compare asymptotic complexity of Algorithm 1 with that of Oktopus and two pipe-based algorithms [3, 32]. All four algorithms recurse over the hierarchical datacenter structure; we analyze the complexity of each recursion. We fix the datacenter tree degrees as constant. The complexity for `Alloc` to find a valid placement of a TAG graph `g` in each recursion is $O(T^2)$, where $T$ is the number of tiers in a tenant, because `FindTiersToColoc` iterates over the tier-to-tier edges in `g` to find tiers with large bandwidth saving. Oktopus's complexity at each recursion is $O(K)$; $K$ is a mean tier size. But Oktopus deploys each tier of a VOC separately and every tier invokes a separate top-level recursion; per-recursion complexity becomes $O(KT)$. We found CloudMirror and Oktopus runtimes are comparable, their difference within an order of magnitude: CloudMirror is faster for some tenants and vice versa. The work in [32] performs a min-cut over a VM-to-VM graph at each recursion with $O(N^4)$ complexity; $N$ is the number of VMs of a tenant ($N = KT$). SecondNet [3] reduced the complexity to $O(N^3)$ at the cost of optimality but it is still >1000 times slower than CloudMirror or Oktopus when $K \cong 10$, $T \cong 5$ (from the `bing` dataset excluding the management services).

## 4.5 Providing High-Availability

We next extend the main VM placement algorithm to support two approaches in meeting HA goals in addition to providing bandwidth guarantees: 1) guaranteeing anti-affinity for scenarios with strict HA requirements and 2) opportunistic anti-affinity for scenarios that do not have strict HA requirements but would still benefit from increasing HA.

**Guaranteeing Anti-Affinity.** Guaranteeing network bandwidth for predictable performance and achieving high availability are both first class goals for many applications. We found cloud providers tend to deploy fault-resilient networking [44], especially at core switches, but there is no such mechanism for server failures. Thus, anti-affinity – placing VMs of a tier under multiple subtrees – is more desired at server level to increase worst-case survivability (WCS) of the tier. WCS is defined as the smallest fraction of VMs of the same tier that remain functional during a failure of a single subtree at level-$L_{AA}$ in a datacenter [11].[9] In this paper we use servers as default fault isolation domains and set default $L_{AA}$ to server level. To guarantee a required WCS, $R_{WCS}$, we extend the main algorithm and set an upper bound for $N_X^t$, the number of VMs placed under a subtree of $L_{AA}$ or lower level:

$$N_X^t <= \max(1, \text{int}(N^t * (1 - R_{WCS}))), \qquad (7)$$

Our evaluations will show that guaranteeing WCS may decrease datacenter utilization while increasing fault tolerance.

**Opportunistic Anti-Affinity.** For tenants not paying for HA

[8] This could be a poor strategy if subsequently arriving tiers/tenants require large bandwidth allocations. To obtain needed bandwidth, the algorithm would have to reverse its earlier decisions and choose locality maximization for previously placed tiers, a capability we currently do not consider for simplicity.

[9] Ref. [11] modeled fault-domain also considering powerline failures, which our algorithm can be extended to incorporate.

guarantees, we still opportunistically improve HA by distributing their VMs across servers when bandwidth saving is infeasible (from the size conditions of Eqs. 2-6) or *undesirable*, a new property we now introduce to capture relative difference between bandwidth availability and bandwidth demand. For example, bandwidth saving could be less desirable at server level because server uplink bandwidth can support the demand of most applications (Fig. 1). Formally, we determine bandwidth saving *desirability* by comparing the available bandwidth averaged over unallocated slots under `st` against the average per-VM bandwidth demand of input `g`, factoring in the expected contributions of future tenant VMs (predicted based on previous arrivals). If the former is smaller than the latter, bandwidth saving is deemed desirable.

To implement the opportunistic approach, we make three modifications to the main algorithm. We modify line **16** to consider also the desirability such that `Colocate` is invoked only when it is both *feasible* and *desirable*. Similarly, `FindLowestSubtree` starts searching from the lowest level where bandwidth saving is desirable, instead of blindly starting from the server level, to facilitate VM placements across multiple servers. The third modification goes to `MdSubsetSum`, which originally returned as many VMs as possible in $\texttt{g}_{\texttt{sub}}$ (line **36**) to fill in the chosen `child` node (in a resource-balanced way) and leaved more sibling child nodes with more slots available for future tenants to do colocation. We modify `MdSubsetSum` to return only one VM in $\texttt{g}_{\texttt{sub}}$ and to select the best `child` for that VM when bandwidth saving is *not* desirable. This encourages distributed VM allocations over **all** child nodes while still achieving balanced slot and bandwidth utilization of the child nodes. Our evaluation will show that this opportunistic approach can greatly improve average WCS at the cost of marginally decreased datacenter utilization while preserving all bandwidth guarantees. The decrease is due to the imperfect estimation of future demands and thus suboptimal desirability decision.

# 5. EVALUATION

We next evaluate the benefit of our TAG model and the performance of our proposed CloudMirror placement algorithm (CM). We evaluate 1) their efficiency in (a) *reserving less network bandwidth* and (b) *accepting more tenant requests* compared to other models and placement algorithms. Our evaluation isolates the separate impacts of the TAG model and the CM placement algorithm on these efficiency metrics. We also evaluate 2) the ability of our placement algorithm to *guarantee and improve availability*, while providing bandwidth guarantees. Finally, we verify 3) the feasibility of deploying our solution on a real testbed.

To evaluate 1) and 2), we wrote a simulator in Python that implements CM to deploy TAG models, and Oktopus [4] to deploy virtual cluster (VC) – hose with homogeneous bandwidth – and VOC models. We found VC always performed worse than VOC and TAG. Thus, we omit the VC results and use VOC as a baseline. We substantially improved the Oktopus algorithm [4] by: handling the case when "Alloc" fails to allocate the requested slots, placing clusters of the same VOC under a common subtree to localize inter-cluster traffic, and relaxing the VOC model to allow arbitrary sizes, cluster bandwidth and core bandwidth for different clusters.

**Simulation Setup:** We simulate a tree-shaped 3-level network topology inspired by a real cloud datacenter, with 2048 servers. For simplicity, we assume all VMs have identical CPU and memory requirements, and each server can host 25 VMs.

Each simulation run consists of 10,000 Poisson tenant arrivals and departures. Arriving tenants are uniformly sampled at random from a pool of 80 tenants, described below. We vary the mean arrival rate ($\lambda$) to control the *load* on a datacenter while keeping tenant dwell time ($T_d$) fixed; the load is $\frac{T_s \lambda T_d}{2048 \times 25}$, where the mean tenant size (#VMs) is $T_s$ and the denominator is the total VM slots.

| Algorithm | Server | ToR | Agg |
|---|---|---|---|
| CM+TAG | 3209.0 | 1006.8 | 0.7 |
| CM+VOC | 3266.5 (1.02) | 1230.1 (1.22) | 1.7 (2.55) |
| OVOC | 2978.8 (0.93) | 1299.7 (1.29) | 14.7 (22.08) |

**Table 1: Reserved bandwidth (Gbps) for `bing` workload. Values in () report bandwidth ratio compared to CM+TAG.**

Each tenant arrival has a single TAG or VOC request. Experiments draw arrivals from one of three workloads: empirical datasets from `bing.com` [11] and `hpcloud.com` [29], and a synthetic workload. Due to space constraints, we primarily present results from the `bing` workload. The `bing` workload consists of a set of services, the service size ranging from one to a few hundred VMs. The services constitute a diverse range of job types (interactive web services or batch data-processing) and communication patterns (e.g., linear, star, ring, mesh; shown in Fig. 7 in [11]), and some have large intra-service demands (similar to MapReduce). A set of central management and logging services communicates with every other service, but mostly at low bandwidth. We remove the common management/logging services and their traffic, as similar to [11], to create a set of isolated tenants which our experiments randomly sample to simulate arrivals. In total there are 80 tenants in the pool: their mean size $T_s$ is 57, with some large tenants over 200 VMs in size; the largest tenant has 732 VMs. We consider each service as corresponding to a component/tier in the TAG model and to a cluster in the VOC model.

## 5.1 Simulation Results

We first evaluate the main CloudMirror algorithm (CM) that does not consider HA.

**Bandwidth Reserved:** Table 1 lists the aggregate bandwidth reserved on uplinks from the server, ToR, and agg switch network levels, for three combinations of model and placement algorithm – CM+TAG, CM+VOC and Oktopus+VOC (OVOC). Since CM is not designed to place VOC models, CM+VOC uses the placement obtained by CM+TAG but reports the bandwidth allocation resulting from modeling the tenants using VOC. For fair comparison, we simulate an ideal network topology with unlimited network capacity; all three combinations deploy the same set of tenants. We simulate only tenant arrivals (no departure) and measure the aggregate bandwidth usage of the deployed tenants when the first tenant rejection happens due to lack of VM slots.

Table 1 shows results for the `bing.com` workload containing both intra- and inter-component traffic. Comparing VOC and TAG models with the same CM placement, VOC consumes more bandwidth than TAG at all three network levels, because the VOC model lacks inter-component traffic pattern information and, thus, reserves unnecessary bandwidth (§2.2). However, the bandwidth advantage of TAG over VOC is small at server level. This is because the services (components) in the `bing` workload are either smaller or $> 2\times$ larger than the server size (25 VM slots), leaving no trunk bandwidth savings advantage for TAG through colocation (Eq. 6) at server level. Trunk bandwidth saving is possible at ToR and agg levels resulting in a greater difference between TAG and VOC models. Comparing placement algorithms, CM+VOC consumes more server-level bandwidth than Oktopus+VOC (OVOC) because CM avoids colocation for low-bandwidth components, instead spreading their VMs across servers to achieve balanced resource utilization (as in Fig. 6(d)); we demonstrate the benefits of resource balancing below where we introduce bandwidth capac-

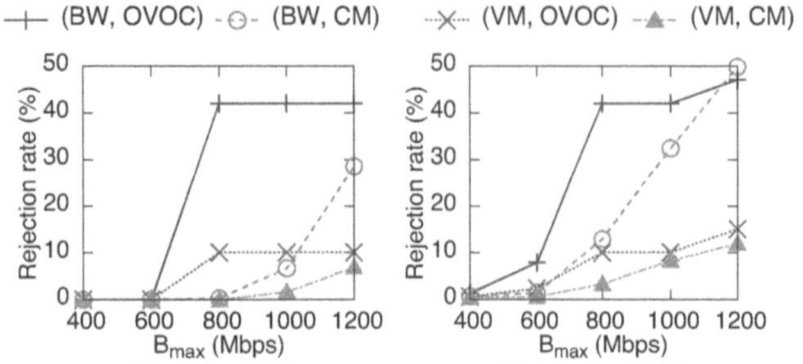


(a) Load = 50%    (b) Load = 90%

**Figure 7: Rejection rates with various bandwidth scaling. Legend format: (metric, algorithm).**

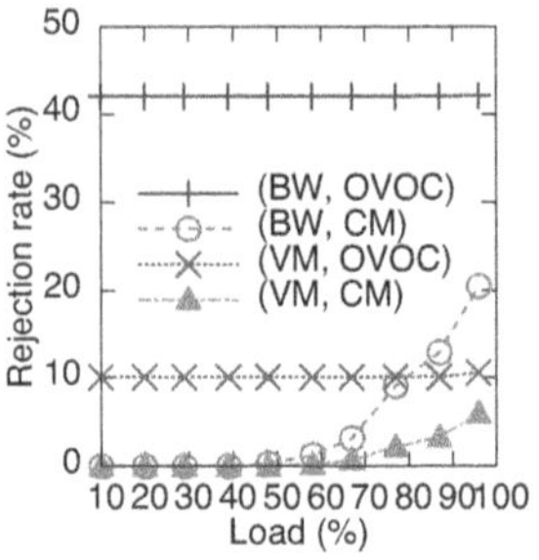


**Figure 8: Rejection rates with varying loads. $B_{max}$ = 800Mbps.**

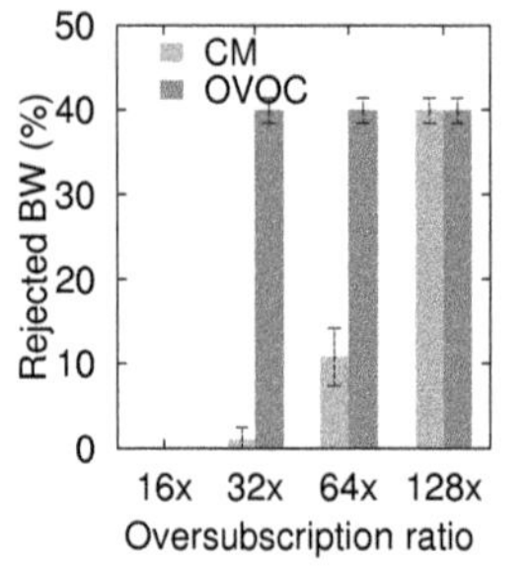


**Figure 9: Bandwidth rejection rate across different oversubscription ratios.**

ity constraints into the network topology. At ToR and agg switch levels, CM+VOC allocates less bandwidth than OVOC. CM placement can achieve savings through its strategy of colocating components with high inter-component traffic in the same subtree, unlike Oktopus which places components independently.

Experiments (not shown) using a synthetic workload, formed by artificially mixing different application sizes and types (e.g., three tier web services and MapReduce jobs) and experiments using the `hpcloud` workload yielded results similar to Table 1.

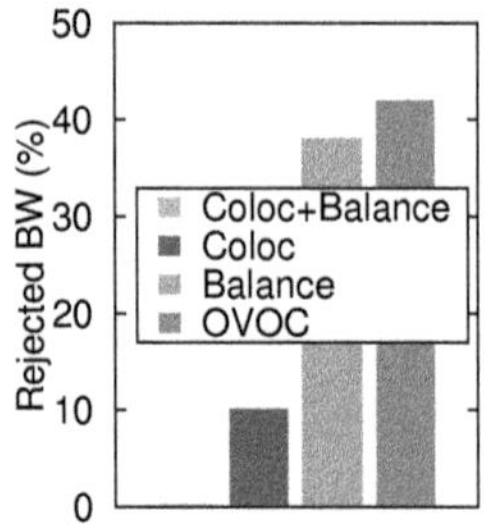


**Figure 10: Micro-benchmarking of CM.**

**Workload Rejection Rate:** We extend the experiment to a topology with constrained bandwidth capacity and we simulate tenant arrivals and departures while varying the mean arrival rate. Now some tenant requests may be rejected due to lack of network capacity, and thus we compare the rate of rejected tenant requests. We assume each server has a 10G uplink to its ToR switch; and ToR-aggregation and aggregation-core links are oversubscribed by a 32:8:1 ratio, mimicking real datacenters [2].

Fig. 7 plots the ratios of rejected tenants' #VMs and aggregate bandwidth relative to those of the total tenant arrivals. Rejection of a tenant can happen due to insufficient available bandwidth and/or CPU/memory resources (slots). The bandwidth values in the `bing.com` workload dataset are relative, not absolute. We scale the bandwidth values such that the average per-VM demand ($B_{vm}$) of the tenant with the largest $B_{vm}$ becomes the target per-VM bandwidth ($B_{max}$). Fig. 7(a) shows that for some $B_{max}$, CM (=CM+TAG) can deploy almost all requests while OVOC rejects up to 40% of bandwidth requests. Fig. 7(b) also shows a substantial difference between CM and OVOC for a different target load. In

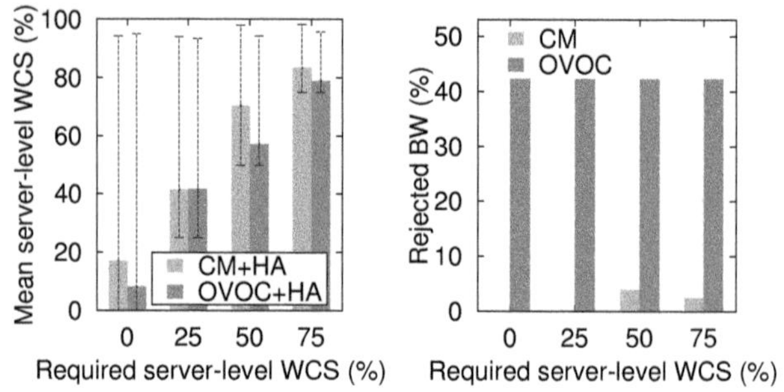


(a) Achieved WCS    (b) Rejected BW

**Figure 11: Impact of guaranteeing WCS. The error bar denotes max and min achieved WCS.**

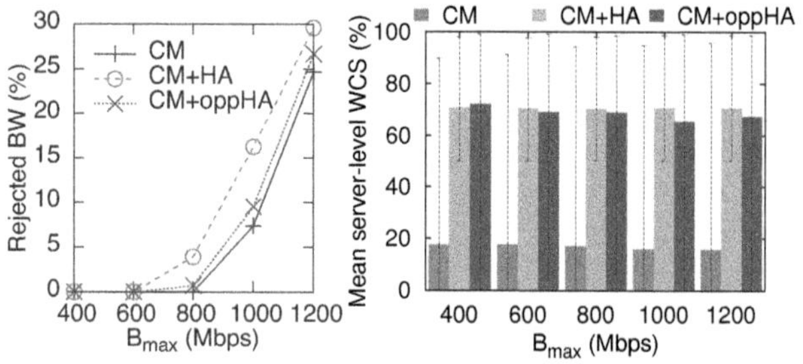


(a) Rejected BW    (b) Achieved WCS

**Figure 12: Comparison of different HA mechanisms. CM: default approach w/o any HA. CM+HA: guarantee 50% WCS. CM+oppHA: opportunistic HA.**

all experiments, tenant rejection rate is less than 2.2%, but rejected tenants tend to have unusually large VM/bandwidth requirements.

The results with varying load are shown in Fig. 8. OVOC fails to deploy a set of tenants having large slot or bandwidth demands even at low loads while CM efficiently places most of them. We stress-test CM and OVOC by increasing the network topology oversubscription ratio. Fig. 9 illustrates that CM is resilient to highly bandwidth-constrained network environments while OVOC is quickly incapable of deploying tenants.

To evaluate the impact of two subroutines of the CM algorithm – `Coloc` and `Balance` – we deactivate each subroutine one by one and plot the TAG bandwidth rejection rate of each case (`Coloc` only and `Balance` only) with that of the original CM (`Coloc+Balance`) and, just for reference, OVOC in Fig. 10. Colocation is clearly the main factor in accepting more resource requests but `Balance` also contributes by preventing a subtree from leaving its compute resource heavily underutilized while its network is maxed out and vice versa (Fig. 6). Even without `Coloc`, which seeks colocation benefits between components, the `Balance`-only approach performed close to OVOC in Fig. 10.

**High Availability (HA):** Some tenants need guaranteed HA as much as guaranteed bandwidth. Our HA extension, CM+HA, can place VMs while guaranteeing bandwidth and worst-case survivability (WCS) at a specified tree level, $L_{AA}$. For comparison, we also extended Oktopus to implement WCS-guarantees. Fig. 11 shows that the required WCS ($R_{WCS}$, x-axis) is achieved with both algorithms when $L_{AA}$=SERVER. CM+HA achieves higher average WCS across the deployed application components than OVOC because CM tries a balanced resource utilization by colocating VMs with opposite resource requirements (high bandwidth VM and low bandwidth VM) instead of blindly colocating VMs from the same component. Guaranteeing HA with a higher WCS requirement increases the bandwidth rejection rate. The increase is small in Fig 11(b) because bandwidth is not a bottleneck at the server level; we observed higher increases when we set $L_{AA}$ to higher-levels.

We next evaluate the opportunistic anti-affinity enhancement to CM described in §4.5. Fig. 12 shows that the opportunistic HA (CM+oppHA) can achieve high average WCS comparable with the guaranteed HA approach, while yielding bandwidth rejection rates as low as the default CM algorithm (see the points where $B_{\max} = 1000$ in Fig. 12(a)). With its opportunistic non-guaranteed approach, CM+oppHA may achieve high or low WCS values close to zero (see error bars in Fig. 12(b)). We also tested when $L_{AA}$=TOR and observed very similar patterns with Fig. 12, except that CM+HA rejected more BW than in Fig. 12(a)).

**Algorithm runtime:** CM, implemented in Python (single-thread), typically runs within 200 msec for tenants of up to 100s of VMs and up to a few seconds for tenants of up to 1000 VMs, demonstrating its scalability. Our CM and Oktopus implementations have similar runtimes. We ran the simulations on Standard-type compute instances in HP Public Cloud.

We also implemented the SecondNet [3] algorithm that places pipe models, using C++ for core libraries. We converted the `bing` TAG models to idealized pipe models by dividing each hose and trunk guarantee uniformly across the corresponding pipes (instead of planning realistically for worst-case as described in §2.2). SecondNet is faster than another pipe model algorithm [32] but still slow to deploy the `bing` workload especially at high datacenter utilization, taking tens of minutes to place one large tenant. Assuming ideal placement, idealized pipe models are fundamentally more bandwidth-efficient than the more flexible TAG models. However, SecondNet produced less efficient resource allocations than CM+TAG leading to higher tenant rejection and also much longer execution time. This demonstrates the sheer complexity of placing VM-VM pipes rendering the pipe model less practical. Since pipe is a special case of TAG, we were able to evaluate running CM to deploy the idealized `bing` pipe models, and observed CM+pipe consuming 8% less bandwidth than SecondNet. CM+pipe runtime, while slower than CM+TAG, was comparable to that of SecondNet; note that CM is implemented in Python while SecondNet in C++ and Python.

## 5.2 Guarantee Enforcement Prototype

Enforcement of TAG model guarantees can be implemented as a straightforward patch to most prior solutions for enforcing hose-model bandwidth guarantees, such as [4, 5, 7, 9]. The intuition is that all these frameworks rate-limit pairs of source-destination VMs (the rate-limit is based on the two VMs' bandwidth guarantees, their current communication pattern, the degree of congestion, etc.). Since the TAG model can be seen as being composed from a set of (directional) hose models, the only conceptual change to be made to these frameworks is to identify to which hose a particular source-destination VM pair belongs. We have implemented a proof of concept based on this approach in ElasticSwitch, a recent proposal for enforcing work-conserving hose-model bandwidth guarantees [7]. This patch consists of 30 lines of code.

Fig. 13(a) shows a simple experiment scenario and topology. We aim to show that the two bandwidth guarantees of VM $Z$ from tier $C2$ are isolated from each other (one guarantee for traffic from $C1$ and one for $C2$ intra-tier traffic). For simplicity we set $B_1 = B_2 = B_2^{in} = 450$ Mbps; the bottleneck link towards VM $Z$ is 1 Gbps and we leave 10% of the bandwidth unreserved. In our experiment, VM $Z$ receives TCP traffic from VMs in both tiers $C1$ and $C2$. We use a single sender, VM $X$, in tier $C1$, and we vary the number of senders in tier $C2$. Fig. 13(b) plots application-level

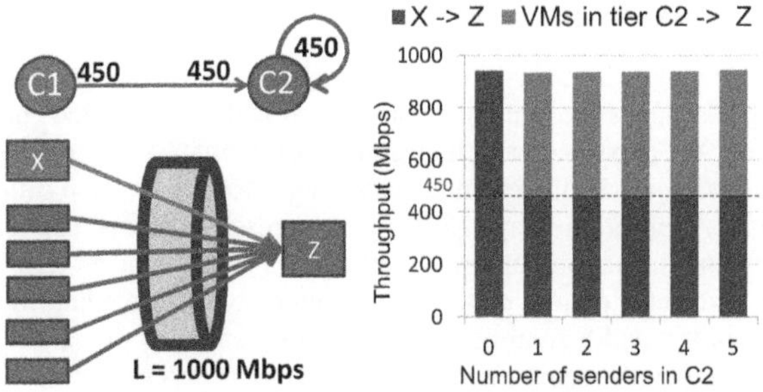


(a) Experiment setup (b) TCP throughput of VM Z

**Figure 13: TAG guarantees using ElasticSwitch.**

throughput of VM $Z$ between the senders in tiers $C1$ and $C2$ as we increase the number of senders in tier $C2$. Traffic from VM $X$ of tier $C1$ is protected from the larger intra-tier traffic.

# 6. DISCUSSION AND FUTURE WORK

Here we briefly discuss several extensions of the TAG model and the overall CloudMirror system design.

Large-scale variations in load will trigger tenants to scale up or down by "auto-scaling", which is flexibly handled by the TAG model. We plan to extend our placement algorithm to better support auto-scaling. Smaller-scale load variations, which do not trigger scaling, can vary bandwidth requirements over time; CloudMirror can adopt existing approaches, such as workload profiling [18] or history-based prediction [45], to be even more efficient.

We believe that the TAG model is versatile and could potentially express other requirements and policies besides bandwidth, including latency, security, access control, reliability, and auto-scaling. Generalizing the TAG concept with additional application level requirements is a potential topic for follow-on work.

Automatic generation of TAG requirements is another ripe area of research. We have sketched a measurement-based system to automatically identify application components and their bandwidth requirements from raw VM-VM level traffic. We plan to conduct a rigorous evaluation of the outlined techniques.

Cloud operators often provide popular application components as infrastructure services (e.g., block storage, front-end web cluster). Tenants can use TAG to express their bandwidth demands between those infrastructure service components and the other components they bring in. When every tenant component is an infrastructure service (e.g., Platform-as-a-Service), TAG can be used internally by the cloud provider to capture the bandwidth demands between the components.

We expect that TAG and CM placement principles can be applied to future datacenters and workloads. For example, next-generation resource-disaggregated datacenters [46, 47] will likely interconnect pools of compute capacity with pools of non-volatile memory (NVRAM) in a hierarchical network. The NVRAM will have throughput and access times orders of magnitude faster than the rotating storage media it displaces, thus imposing much higher bandwidth demands on future datacenter-wide interconnect. This challenge further strengthens the need for efficient and balanced resource allocation, as provided by CloudMirror. We envision extending the TAG model to capture bandwidth guarantees between compute elements and NVRAM; each TAG component currently defining a set of similar VMs can be split into one component that defines a set of similar compute elements, and one component that defines a set of NVRAM, with virtual trunks added to specify bandwidth guarantees between these components.

## 7. CONCLUSION

Migrating mission critical applications to cloud environments demands a network virtualization solution with performance guarantees. We introduced an efficient network virtualization solution, *CloudMirror*, with three components – a network abstraction called Tenant Application Graph (TAG) that represents the true application communication pattern, an efficient VM placement strategy that efficiently utilizes datacenter resources while providing high availability, and a runtime mechanism that enforces the application bandwidth requirements. Our simulation experiments using real application traces demonstrate significantly improved datacenter resource efficiency over existing solutions.

**Acknowledgments:** We thank Peter Bodik and the other authors of [11] for providing us with the data we used in the presented experiments. We also thank the anonymous reviewers and our shepherd, Chuanxiong Guo, for their guidance on the paper.

## 8. REFERENCES

[1] "Facebook Future-Proofs Data Center With Revamped Network." http://tinyurl.com/6v5pswv.

[2] N. Farrington and A. Andreyev, "Facebook's Data Center Network Architecture," IEEE Optical Interconnects, 2013.

[3] C. Guo, G. Lu, H. J. Wang, S. Yang, C. Kong, P. Sun, W. Wu, and Y. Zhang, "SecondNet: a Data Center Network Virtualization Architecture with Bandwidth Guarantees," ACM CoNEXT, 2010.

[4] H. Ballani, P. Costa, T. Karagiannis, and A. Rowstron, "Towards Predictable Datacenter Networks," ACM SIGCOMM, 2011.

[5] V. Jeyakumar, M. Alizadeh, , D. Mazières, B. Prabhakar, C. Kim, and A. Greenberg, "EyeQ: Practical Network Performance Isolation at the Edge," USENIX NSDI, 2013.

[6] H. Ballani, K. Jang, T. Karagiannis, C. Kim, D. Gunawardena, and G. O'Shea, "Chatty Tenants and the Cloud Network Sharing Problem," USENIX NSDI 2013.

[7] L. Popa, P. Yalagandula, S. Banerjee, J. C. Mogul, Y. Turner, and J. R. Santos, "ElasticSwitch: Practical Work-Conserving Bandwidth Guarantees for Cloud Computing," ACM SIGCOMM, 2013.

[8] N. G. Duffield, P. Goyal, A. Greenberg, P. Mishra, K. K. Ramakrishnan, and J. E. van der Merive, "A Flexible Model for Resource Management in Virtual Private Networks," ACM SIGCOMM, 1999.

[9] H. Rodrigues, J. R. Santos, Y. Turner, P. Soares, and D. Guedes, "Gatekeeper: Supporting Bandwidth Guarantees for Multi-tenant Datacenter Networks," USENIX WIOV, 2011.

[10] J. Lee, M. Lee, L. Popa, Y. Turner, S. Banerjee, P. Sharma, and B. Stephenson, "CloudMirror: Application-Aware Bandwidth Reservations in the Cloud," USENIX HotCloud, 2013.

[11] P. Bodík, I. Menache, M. Chowdhury, P. Mani, D. A. Maltz, and I. Stoica, "Surviving Failures in Bandwidth-Constrained Datacenters," ACM SIGCOMM, 2012.

[12] M. Hajjat, X. Sun, Y.-W. E. Sung, D. Maltz, S. Rao, K. Sripanidkulchai, and M. Tawarmalani, "Cloudward Bound: Planning for Beneficial Migration of Enterprise Applications to the Cloud," ACM SIGCOMM, 2010.

[13] J. Dean and L. A. Barroso, "The Tail at Scale," *Communications of The ACM*, vol. 56, Feb 2013.

[14] "AWS Architecture Center." http://aws.amazon.com/architecture/.

[15] "Amazon - Every 100ms delay costs 1% of sales." http://tinyurl.com/k635quz.

[16] V. Jeyakumar, A. Kabbani, J. C. Mogul, and A. Vahdat, "Flexible Network Bandwidth and Latency Provisioning in the Datacenter," in *arXiv:1405.0631*, 2014.

[17] "WikiBench: Web hosting benchmark." http://www.wikibench.eu/.

[18] D. Xie, N. Ding, Y. C. Hu, and R. Kompella, "The Only Constant is Change: Incorporating Time-varying Network Reservations in Data Centers," ACM SIGCOMM, 2012.

[19] "Redis Benchmark & Rackspace Performance VMs." http://tinyurl.com/omyzyax.

[20] "877,000 TPS with Erlang and VoltDB." http://tinyurl.com/naoakwl.

[21] "Testing Vyatta 6.5 R1 under VMware." http://tinyurl.com/l7u9gfa.

[22] J.-C. Huang, M. Monchiero, Y. Turner, and H.-H. Lee, "Ally: OS-transparent packet inspection using sequestered cores," ACM/IEEE ANCS, 2011.

[23] J. Summers, T. Brecht, D. Eager, and B. Wong, "Methodologies for Generating HTTP Streaming Video Workloads to Evaluate Web Server Performance," ACM SYSTOR, 2012.

[24] Netflix Tech Blog, "Benchmarking Cassandra Scalability on AWS." http://tinyurl.com/3ogo79c.

[25] H. Li and A. Michael, "Intel Motherboard Hardware v2.0," tech. rep., Open Compute Project.

[26] X. Jin, H. H. Liu, R. Gandhi, S. Kandula, R. Mahajan, J. Rexford, R. Wattenhofer, and M. Zhang, "Dionysus: Dynamic Scheduling of Network Updates," ACM SIGCOMM, 2014.

[27] H. H. Liu, S. Kandula, R. Mahajan, M. Zhang, and D. Gelernter, "Traffic Engineering with Forward Fault Correction," ACM SIGCOMM, 2014.

[28] "Rackspace: Welcome to Performance Cloud Servers; Have Some Benchmarks!." http://tinyurl.com/pam57uy.

[29] K. LaCurts, S. Deng, A. Goyal, and H. Balakrishnan, "Choreo: Network-aware task placement for cloud applications," ACM IMC, 2013.

[30] "Storm: Distributed and fault-tolerant realtime computation." http://storm-project.net/.

[31] T. Benson, A. Akella, A. Shaikh, and S. Sahu, "CloudNaaS: A Cloud Networking Platform for Enterprise Applications," ACM SOCC, 2011.

[32] X. Meng, V. Pappas, and L. Zhang, "Improving the scalability of data center networks with traffic-aware virtual machine placement," IEEE INFOCOM, 2010.

[33] Brian Adler, "Load Balancing in the Cloud: Tools, Tips, and Techniques." RightScale Technical Whitepaper.

[34] "Amazon Web Services - Auto Scaling." http://aws.amazon.com/autoscaling/.

[35] V. D. Blondel, J.-L. Guillaume, R. Lambiotte, and E. Lefebvre, "Fast unfolding of communities in large networks," *J. Stat. Mech.*, 2008.

[36] M. Rosvall and C. T. Bergstrom, "Maps of random walks on complex networks reveal community structure," *PNAS 2008.*

[37] N. X. Vinh, J. Epps, and J. Bailey, "Information Theoretic Measures for Clusterings Comparison: Variants, Properties, Normalization and Correction for Chance," *Journal of Machine Learning Research*, vol. 11, pp. 2837–54, 2010.

[38] A. Klein, F. Ishikawa, and S. Honiden, "Towards Network-aware Service Composition in the Cloud," ACM WWW, 2012.

[39] "OpenDaylight, Group-based Policy project." http://tinyurl.com/n42h3ju.

[40] "ETSI, Network Functions Virtualisation." http://tinyurl.com/maaqnng.

[41] F. Hermenier, J. Lawall, and G. Muller, "BtrPlace: A Flexible Consolidation Manager for Highly Available Applications," *IEEE TDSC*, vol. 10, no. 5, 2013.

[42] E. Bin, O. Biran, O. Boni, E. Hadad, E. K. Kolodner, Y. Moatti, and D. H. Lorenz, "Guaranteeing high availability goals for virtual machine placement," ICDCS, 2011.

[43] B. Przydatek, "A fast approximation algorithm for the subset-sum problem," 1999.

[44] "Cisco Virtual Switching Systems (VSS)." http://tinyurl.com/yqg97w.

[45] K. LaCurts, J. Mogul, H. Balakrishnan, and Y. Turner, "Cicada: Introducing Predictive Guarantees for Cloud Networks," USENIX HotCloud, 2014.

[46] S. Han, N. Egi, A. Panda, S. Ratnasamy, G. Shi, and S. Shenker, "Network Support for Resource Disaggregation in Next-Generation Datacenters," ACM HotNets, 2013.

[47] K. Asanovic, "FireBox: A Hardware Building Block for 2020 Warehouse-Scale Computers," USENIX FAST 2014 Keynote.

# An Experimental Study of the Learnability of Congestion Control

Anirudh Sivaraman, Keith Winstein, Pratiksha Thaker, and Hari Balakrishnan
Computer Science and Artificial Intelligence Laboratory
Massachusetts Institute of Technology, Cambridge, Mass.
{anirudh, keithw, prthaker, hari}@mit.edu

## ABSTRACT

When designing a distributed network protocol, typically it is infeasible to fully define the target network where the protocol is intended to be used. It is therefore natural to ask: How faithfully do protocol designers really need to understand the networks they design for? What are the important signals that endpoints should listen to? How can researchers gain confidence that systems that work well on well-characterized test networks during development will also perform adequately on real networks that are inevitably more complex, or future networks yet to be developed? Is there a tradeoff between the performance of a protocol and the breadth of its intended operating range of networks? What is the cost of playing fairly with cross-traffic that is governed by another protocol?

We examine these questions quantitatively in the context of congestion control, by using an automated protocol-design tool to approximate the best possible congestion-control scheme given imperfect prior knowledge about the network. We found only weak evidence of a tradeoff between operating range in link speeds and performance, even when the operating range was extended to cover a thousand-fold range of link speeds. We found that it may be acceptable to simplify some characteristics of the network—such as its topology—when modeling for design purposes. Some other features, such as the degree of multiplexing and the aggressiveness of contending endpoints, are important to capture in a model.

## CATEGORIES AND SUBJECT DESCRIPTORS

C.2.2 [**Computer-Communication Networks**]: Network Protocols

## KEYWORDS

Protocol; Machine Learning; Congestion Control; Learnability; Measurement; Simulation

## 1. INTRODUCTION

Over the last 30 years, Internet congestion control has seen considerable research interest. Starting with seminal work in the 1980s [24, 15, 7], the Transmission Control Protocol (TCP) has adopted a series of end-to-end algorithms to share network resources among contending endpoints [14, 6, 12, 27]. Another line of work has explored the use of in-network algorithms running at bottleneck routers to help perform this function more efficiently [11, 10, 9, 18, 23, 21, 16].


*SIGCOMM'14,* August 17–22, 2014, Chicago, IL, USA.

ACM 978-1-4503-2836-4/14/08 ...$15.00.
http://dx.doi.org/10.1145/2619239.2626324.

As the Internet grows and evolves, it appears likely that new network protocols will continue to be developed to accommodate new subnetwork behaviors and shifting application workloads and goals. Some of these may be intended for specialized environments—e.g., inside a centrally-managed datacenter—while some will be for broad use across the wide-area Internet, or over cellular network paths.

In practice, however, it is challenging to guarantee that a distributed system's performance on well-characterized test networks will extend to real networks, which inevitably differ from those envisioned in development and will continue to evolve over time. This uncertain generalizability presents an obstacle to any new protocol's deployment.

In this paper, we formalize the design process for generating end-to-end congestion-control protocols to quantify: *how easy is it to "learn" a network protocol to achieve desired goals, given a necessarily imperfect model of the networks where it will ultimately be deployed?*

Under this umbrella, we examine a series of questions about what knowledge about the network is important when designing a congestion-control protocol and what simplifications are acceptable:

1. **Knowledge of network parameters.** Is there a tradeoff between the performance of a protocol and the breadth of its intended operating range of network parameters [30]? Will a "one size fits all" protocol designed for networks spanning a broad range of link speeds (§4.1), degrees of multiplexing (§4.2), or propagation delays (§4.3) necessarily perform worse than one targeted at a narrower subset of networks whose parameters can be more precisely defined in advance?

2. **Structural knowledge.** How faithfully do protocol designers need to understand the topology of the network? What are the consequences of designing protocols for a simplified network path with a single bottleneck, then running them on a network with two bottlenecks (§4.4)?

3. **Knowledge about other endpoints.** In many settings, a newly-designed protocol will need to coexist with traffic from other protocols. What are the consequences of designing a protocol with the knowledge that some endpoints may be running incumbent protocols whose traffic needs to be treated fairly (e.g. the new protocol needs to divide a contended link evenly with TCP), versus a clean-slate design (§4.5)? Similarly, what are the costs and benefits of designing protocols that play nicely with traffic optimized for other

objectives—e.g., a protocol that aims for bulk throughput but wants to accommodate the needs of cross-traffic that may prioritize low delay (§4.6)?

4. **Knowledge of network signals.** What kinds of congestion signals are important for an endpoint to listen to? How much information can be extracted from different kinds of feedback, and how valuable are different congestion signals toward the protocol's ultimate goals? (§3.4)

### 1.1 Tractable attempts at optimal (Tao) protocols

Each of the above areas of inquiry is about the effect of a protocol designer's imperfect understanding of the future network that a decentralized congestion-control protocol will ultimately be run over.

In principle, we would quantify such an effect by evaluating, on the actual network, the performance of the "best possible" congestion-control protocol designed for the imperfect network *model*, and comparing that with the best-possible protocol for the actual network itself.

In practice, however, we know of no tractable way to calculate the optimal congestion-control protocol for a given network.[1] Instead, throughout this study we use the Remy automatic protocol-design tool [29], a heuristic search procedure that generates congestion-control protocols, as a proxy for the optimal solution.

We refer to these automatically generated congestion-control protocols as "tractable attempts at optimal" (Tao) end-to-end congestion-control protocols for a given network. Tao protocols represent a practically realizable tilt at developing an optimal protocol for an imperfect model of a real network.

Constructing a Tao for a complex network model requires searching a huge space, an intensive task even using Remy's search optimizations. In most cases, the protocol stopped improving within a CPU-year of processing time (five days on our 80-core machine), though there were a few cases where improvements continued to occur.

We emphasize that there can be no assurance that the Tao actually comes close to the optimal congestion-control protocol, except to the extent that it approaches upper bounds on performance, such as the ideal fair allocation of network resources. To characterize how close the Tao protocols come to the bound, we formalize the notion of a hypothetical "omniscient" protocol. This is a centralized protocol that knows the topology of the network, the link speeds, the locations of senders and receivers, and the times at which they turn on or off. Each time a sender turns on or off, the omniscient protocol computes the proportionally fair throughput allocation [17] for all senders that are on. Each sender then transmits at its proportionally fair throughput allocation, and no flow builds up a standing queue at any bottleneck. For a particular node, the long-term average throughput of the omniscient protocol is the expected value of its throughput allocation, with no queueing delay.

As a calibration experiment to validate the Tao approach, we design a Tao protocol with parameters shown in Table 1 (where the buffer size of 5 BDP refers to 5 times the bandwidth-delay product: the network link speed times the minimum round trip time (RTT)). We summarize the performance of a protocol using a throughput-delay graph as shown in Figure 1. For each protocol, we plot the

[1] The problem can be formulated as a search procedure for an optimal policy for a decentralized partially observable Markov decision process or Dec-POMDP [29]. However, the search for an optimal policy under a general Dec-POMDP is known to be NEXP-complete [4], and no faster search procedure for the particular problem of network-protocol design has been found.

| | |
|---|---|
| Link speed | 32 Mbits/sec |
| Minimum RTT | 150 ms |
| Topology | Dumbbell |
| Senders | 2 |
| Workload | 1 sec ON/OFF times |
| Buffer size | 5 BDP |
| Objective | $\sum log(tpt) - log(delay)$ |

Table 1: Network parameters for the calibration experiment.

median throughput and delay (small white circle) and an ellipse representing one standard deviation of variation. The Tao protocols are considerably better than two human-designed protocols: Cubic [12] (the default end-to-end congestion-control algorithm on Linux) and Cubic over sfqCoDel (Cubic coupled with sfqCoDel [2], a recent proposal for queue management and scheduling that runs on the gateway nodes) on both throughput and delay. Furthermore, they come within 5% of the omniscient protocol on throughput and 10% on delay.

The calibration experiment does not prove that the Tao protocols will continue to approach omniscient performance when there is uncertainty about the network scenario at runtime, or when the network scenarios are more complex. It also does not demonstrate the relationship between the Tao protocols and the true "optimal" solution, which (unlike the omniscient protocol) is one that will be realizable in an end-to-end algorithm when endpoints have only partial information about the true network state.

However, the results do give confidence that the Tao protocols can be used as tractable proxies for an optimal protocol. In this study, we compare human-designed protocols to various Tao protocols and the omniscient protocol, generally finding that Tao protocols can approach the omniscient protocol and can outperform the existing human-designed protocols that have been designed to date (Figures 2, 3, 4, and 6).

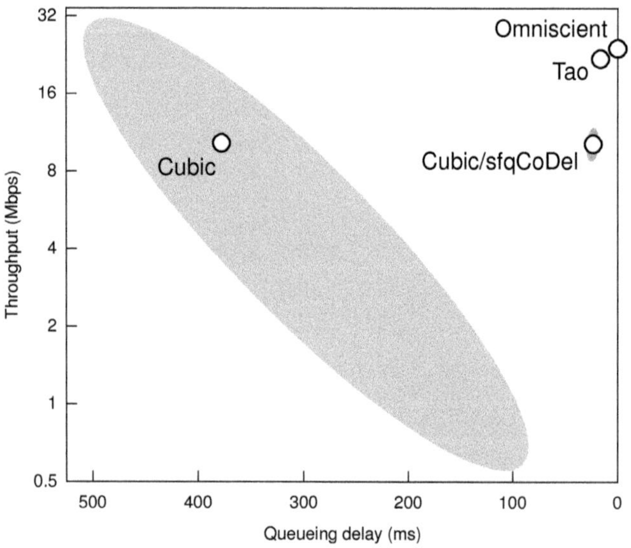


Figure 1: In the calibration experiment, the Tao protocol approached the performance of the omniscient protocol.

### 1.2 Summary of results

Here are the principal findings of this study:

**Modeling a two-bottleneck network as a single bottleneck hurt performance only mildly.** On the two-hop network illustrated by Figure 5, on average we find that a protocol designed for a simplified, single-bottleneck model of the network underperformed by **only 17%** (on throughput) a protocol that was designed with full knowledge of the network's two-bottleneck structure (Figure 6). Furthermore, the simplified protocol also outperformed TCP Cubic by a factor of 7.2× on average throughput and outperformed Cubic-over-sfqCoDel by 2.75× on average throughput.

Thus, in this example, full knowledge of the network topology during the design process was not crucial.

**Weak evidence of a tradeoff between link-speed operating range and performance.** We created a Tao protocol designed for a range of networks whose link speeds spanned a thousand-fold range between 1 Mbps and 1000 Mbps, as well as three other protocols that were more narrowly-targeted at hundred-fold, ten-fold, and two-fold ranges of link speed (Figure 2).

The "thousand-fold" Tao achieved close to the peak performance of the "two-fold" Tao. Between link speeds of 22–44 Mbps, the "thousand-fold" Tao achieved **within 3% of the throughput** of the "two-fold" protocol that was designed for this exact range. However, the queueing delay of the "thousand-fold" protocol was **46% higher**, suggesting some benefit from more focused operating conditions. It also takes a lot longer to compute (offline) a "thousand-fold" Tao compared to a two-fold Tao; in run-time operation, though, the computational cost of the two algorithms is similar.

Over the full range of 1 Mbps to 1000 Mbps, the "thousand-fold" Tao protocol matched or outperformed TCP Cubic and Cubic-over-sfqCoDel over the entire range (Figure 2).

The results suggest that highly optimized protocols may be able to perform adequately over a broad range of actual networks. Broad operating range had only a weak effect on peak performance, suggesting that "one size fits all" congestion-control protocols that perform considerably better than TCP—as well as TCP plus in-network assistance, in the case of sfqCoDel—may be feasible.

**Performance at high degrees of multiplexing may be in opposition with performance when few flows share a bottleneck.** We created five Tao protocols for a range of networks with varying degrees of multiplexing: 1–2 senders, 1–10, 1–20, 1–50, and 1–100 (Figure 4.2 and Table 3a).

We found that a Tao protocol designed to handle between 1 and 100 senders came close to the performance achieved by an omniscient protocol over most of that range. However, this came at the cost of diminished throughput at lower degrees of multiplexing. Conversely, a protocol trained to handle between 1 and 2 senders suffered large queuing delays (when the link never dropped packets) or repeated packet drops (on a link with finite buffering) when run on a network with 100 senders.

These results suggest that—unlike with link speed—prior knowledge of the expected degree of multiplexing over bottleneck links may be beneficial when designing a congestion-control protocol.

**TCP-awareness hurt performance when TCP cross-traffic was absent, but helped dramatically when present.** We measured the costs and benefits of "TCP-awareness"—designing a protocol with the explicit knowledge that it may be competing against other endpoints running TCP, compared with a "TCP-naive" protocol for a network where the other endpoints only run the same TCP-naive protocol.

When contending only with other endpoints of the same kind, the "TCP-naive" protocol achieved **55% less queueing delay** than the TCP-aware protocol. In other words, "TCP-awareness" has a cost measured in lost performance when TCP cross-traffic is not present (Figure 7).

But when contending against TCP, the "TCP-naive" protocol was squeezed out by the more aggressive cross-traffic presented by TCP. By contrast, the "TCP-aware" protocol achieved **36% more throughput** and **37% less queueing delay** than the "TCP-naive" protocol, and claimed its fair share of the link capacity from TCP.

Instructions to reproduce the results in this paper, along with the congestion-control protocols produced by Remy in the process are available at http://web.mit.edu/remy/learnability.

## 2. RELATED WORK

This section discusses closely related work on congestion control and explains how our work has an analogy with theoretical notions of learnability.

### 2.1 Congestion control

Congestion control over packet-switched networks has been a productive area of research since the seminal work of the 1980s, including Ramakrishnan and Jain's DECBit scheme [24] and Jacobson's TCP Tahoe and Reno algorithms [15]. End-to-end algorithms typically compute a congestion window or a paced transmission rate using the stream of acknowledgments (ACKs) arriving from the receiver. In response to congestion, inferred from packet loss or, in some cases, rising delays, the sender reduces its window or rate; conversely, when no congestion is perceived, the sender increases its window or rate.

In this paper, we use the Remy [29] protocol-design tool to generate end-to-end Tao congestion-control schemes from first principles. The Remy work showed that such an approach can produce schemes whose performance is competitive with or outperforms human-generated schemes, including most varieties of TCP congestion control, on intended target networks.

By contrast, this paper uses the Remy program as a tool for understanding the nature of the problem of protocol design without being able to fully define the intended target networks. We use the program's output as a proxy for the "best possible" Tao congestion-control protocol intended for a particular imperfect network model, and then ask how that protocol performs on a different set of networks that varies from the model in some respect (topology, link speed, behavior of contending endpoints, etc.).

For reference, we also compare with existing congestion-control protocols in wide use, including Linux's TCP Cubic [12], and the less-aggressive NewReno algorithm [14]. End-to-end congestion control may be assisted with explicit router participation; we also measure Cubic in conjunction with sfqCoDel [2]. sfqCoDel runs at the bottleneck gateways and uses the CoDel [21] queue management algorithm along with the stochastic fair queueing [20] scheduling algorithm.

### 2.2 Learnability

TCP congestion control was not designed with an explicit objective function in mind. Kelly et al. present an interpretation of TCP congestion-control variants in terms of the implicit goals they attempt to optimize [17]. This line of work is known as Network Utility Maximization (NUM); more recent work has modeled stochastic NUM problems [31], where a stochastic process dictates how flows enter and leave the network over time.

We extend this problem by examining the difficulty of designing a network protocol given an *imperfect* model of the network where it will be deployed, in order to understand the inherent difficulties of the problem of congestion control.

Formally speaking, designing such a protocol is a problem in sequential decision-making under uncertainty and can be modeled as a decentralized partially observable Markov decision process [4] (Dec-POMDP). In that context, the purpose of this paper is to ask: how well can a protocol designer "learn" the optimal policy (protocol) for one Dec-POMDP on a given set of networks and successfully apply the learned policy to a different set of networks?

In doing so, we draw an explicit analogy to the concept of "learnability" employed in machine learning [28, 25]. A canonical machine-learning task attempts to design a classifier for a large population of data points, supplied with only a smaller (and possibly skewed) "training set" meant to teach the classifier about the full population of data. Subsequently, the performance of the resulting classifier is evaluated in how well it correctly classifies points in a "test set", generally drawn from the actual population. Learnability theory measures the difficulty of inferring an accurate classifier for the test set, given a training set.

Just as a classifier-design procedure may minimize the error rate or maximize the width of the margin [5] over the training set as a proxy for maximizing predictive performance on unseen inputs, the Remy tool uses an objective function in terms of throughput and delay, averaged over the design model, as a proxy for performance on as-yet-unseen networks.

In our work, we envision a protocol designer working to generate a congestion-control protocol for a large set of real networks (e.g., the Internet), supplied with only an imperfect model of the range of variation and behavior of those networks. The imperfect model is the "training scenarios"—a model of the target networks used for design purposes. The "testing scenarios" are drawn from the population of actual target networks. In contrast with theoretical notions of learnability that rigorously demonstrate the learnability of entire families of functions [28], this study assesses learnability experimentally: we measure the difficulty (in terms of lost performance) of designing an adequate protocol for a network *model*, and then deploying it on target networks that cannot be perfectly envisioned at the time of design.

## 3. EXPERIMENTAL SETUP

We describe our experimental procedure below. First, we specify a set of *training scenarios*: a set of network configurations (§3.1) that express the designer's imperfect model of the network. Next, we specify an *objective function* (§3.2). The protocol-design process (§3.3) synthesizes a congestion-control protocol that maximizes the value of this function, averaged over the set of training scenarios. Finally (§3.6), we specify the *testing scenarios* of network configurations, which may be similar or dissimilar to the training scenarios.

We evaluate the synthesized congestion-control protocol on the testing scenarios to assess the questions of this study—how easy is it to "learn" a network protocol to achieve desired goals, given an imperfect model of the networks where it will ultimately be deployed?

### 3.1 Training scenarios

The training scenarios specify the set of network configurations that the protocol-design process is given access to. Formally, a network configuration specifies:

1. The topology: the link speed and propagation delay of each link in the network along with a graph representing the interconnections between nodes.

2. The locations of senders and receivers within the topology, and the paths connecting the senders to the receivers.

3. A model of the workload generated by the application running at each endpoint. We use an on/off model for the workload, where a sender turns "on" for a certain duration drawn from an exponential distribution, then turns "off" for an amount of time drawn from another exponential distribution before turning on again.

4. The buffer size and queueing discipline at each gateway. For all training scenarios in this paper, we model a FIFO queue. For testing scenarios, we model a FIFO queue except in the case of Cubic-over-sfqCoDel, which runs sfqCoDel at the gateway nodes.

### 3.2 Objective function

The objective function expresses the protocol designer's figure of merit for the goodness of a congestion-control protocol. Many such metrics have been proposed, including alpha-fair throughput [26], flow completion time [8], throughput-over-delay [22], or measures based on a subjective opinion score [13].

In this study, we specifically considered objective functions of the form:

$$\log(\text{throughput}) - \delta \log(\text{delay}) \qquad (1)$$

Here, "throughput" is the average information transmission rate of a sender-receiver pair, defined as the total number of bytes successfully delivered divided by the total time the sender was "on" and hence had offered load. The "delay" is the average per-packet delay of packets in the connection, including propagation delay and queueing delay. The $\delta$ factor expresses a relative preference between high throughput and low delay.

The protocol-design process works to maximize the *sum* of the objective function across all connections. The log in the objective function expresses a preference for "proportionally fair" resource allocation [17]—for example, it is worthwhile to cut one connection's throughput in half, as long as this allows another connection's throughput to be more-than-doubled.

### 3.3 Protocol-design process

We outline the Remy protocol-design tool briefly here, following the treatment of [29]. Remy models a congestion-control protocol as a set of match-action rules, mapping between the state maintained by the sender and an action to be executed. The "state" tracks a small set of congestion signals, updated on every acknowledgment from the receiver. The "action" specifies changes in the behavior of the congestion-control protocol.

To simplify learning, Remy assumes a piecewise-constant mapping, and searches for the mapping that maximizes the average value of the objective function across the training scenarios. The mapping is initialized to prescribe a default action for all memory values. Remy then simulates the protocol on the training scenarios and uses the simulation results—and the resulting value of the objective function—to gradually refine the mapping.

For the experiments in this paper, the sender tracks four congestion signals:

1. `rec_ewma`: An exponentially-weighted moving average, or EWMA, of the interarrival times between acks with a weight of 1/8 for new samples.

2. `slow_rec_ewma`: The same as `rec_ewma`, but with a weight of 1/256 for new samples, producing an average taken over a longer history.

3. send_ewma: A moving average of the intersend time between sender timestamps echoed in the received ACKs, with a weight of 1/8 for new samples.

4. rtt_ratio: The ratio of the most recent round-trip-time measurement and the minimum RTT seen so far.

### 3.4 Value of the congestion signals

We performed a measurement study to evaluate the value of each of these four signals on the ultimate performance of a congestion-control protocol. We selectively "knocked out" each signal in turn and designed a new congestion-control protocol from scratch (missing that signal), in order to observe the effect of losing the signal on the protocol's ultimate behavior.

In our measurements, we found that each of these congestion signals independently brought value to a congestion-control protocol. No three-signal subset was as strong as using all four signals. The most valuable signal—by which we mean the signal whose removal caused the greatest harm to the ultimate performance—was the rec_ewma. This suggests that these protocols may gain considerable value from understanding the short-term packet-arrival dynamics at the receiver.

### 3.5 The congestion response

The action uses a window-based congestion-control protocol that caps the number of packets in flight, with pacing to regulate the rate at which an end host meters packets into the network. The action for any value of the memory is a triplet that specifies:

1. A multiplier $m$ to the current value of the congestion window.

2. An increment $b$ to the current value of the congestion window.

3. A lower bound $\tau$ on the pacing interval between outgoing packet transmissions.

To emphasize that the resulting protocol is a brute-force approximation of the best algorithm for a given set of training scenarios and objective function, we refer to such protocols as "tractable attempts at optimal" congestion control, or Tao protocols.

### 3.6 Evaluation procedure

To measure the difficulty of learning a congestion-control protocol with an imperfect model of the eventual network, we choose a testing scenario of network configurations and evaluate the Tao protocol on it. All evaluations are performed in the ns-2 simulator. Using a different simulator for training and testing helps build confidence that the congestion-control protocols learned are robust to quirks in a simulator implementation.

We compare the performance of Tao protocols optimized for "accurate" models of the network against Tao protocols optimized for various kinds of imperfect models, in order to measure how faithfully protocol designers need to understand the network they are designing for. In the interest of reproducibility, for each experiment that we run, we tabulate the training and testing scenarios (for e.g. Tables 3a and 3b).

For reference, we also compare the Tao protocols with two common schemes in wide use today:

1. TCP Cubic [12], the default congestion-control protocol in Linux

2. Cubic over sfqCoDel [2], an active-queue-management and scheduling algorithm that runs on bottleneck routers and assists endpoints in achieving a fairer and more efficient use of network resources

### 3.7 Caveats and non-goals

We view this work as a first step towards answering questions under the broad umbrella of the "learnability" of congestion control. The simulation experiments are deliberately simplistic, favoring scenarios that explore foundational questions over simulations that are representative of deployed networks. We use Remy-generated protocols as a proxy for the optimal solutions, which means that the results may change when better protocol-design tools are developed, or when these protocols are tested on real physical networks outside of simulation. It is not our goal here to reverse-engineer the per-node, microscopic behavior of Tao protocols—we are interested in using measurements of their varying performance to characterize the learnability of the protocol-design problem itself.

## 4. INVESTIGATING THE LEARNABILITY OF CONGESTION CONTROL

### 4.1 Knowledge of link speed

We evaluated the difficulty of designing a congestion-control protocol, subject to imperfect knowledge of the parameters of the network.

Some congestion-control protocols have been designed for specific kinds of networks [3, 19] or require explicit knowledge of the link speed *a priori* [16]. Others are intended as a "one size fits all," including most variants of TCP.

We set out to answer a question posed in [30]: are "one size fits all" protocols inherently at a disadvantage, because of a tradeoff between the "operating range" of a protocol and its performance?

To quantify this, we designed four Tao protocols for training scenarios encompassing a thousand-fold variation in link speeds, a hundred-fold variation, a ten-fold variation, and a two-fold variation. Each range was centered on the geometric mean of 1 and 1000 Mbps (32 Mbps), and each set of training scenarios sampled 100 link speeds logarithmically from the range. The training and testing scenarios are shown in Table 2.

| Tao | Link speeds | RTT | Number of senders |
|---|---|---|---|
| 1000x | 1–1000 Mbps | 150 ms | 2 |
| 100x | 3.2–320 Mbps | 150 ms | 2 |
| 10x | 10–100 Mbps | 150 ms | 2 |
| 2x | 22–44 Mbps | 150 ms | 2 |

(a) Tao protocols designed for breadth in link speed

| Link speeds | RTT | Number of senders |
|---|---|---|
| 1–1000 Mbps | 150 ms | 2 |

(b) Testing scenarios to explore breadth in link speed

Table 2: Scenarios for "knowledge of link speed" experiment, showing the effect of varying the intended link-speed operating range. Each Tao was designed for a network with a single bottleneck, and each sender had a mean "on" and "off" time of 1 s.

We tested these schemes in ns-2 by sweeping the link speed between 1 and 1000 Mbps, keeping the other details of the simulated network identical to the training scenario. The results are shown Figure 2.

We find evidence of a weak tradeoff between operating range and performance—optimizing for a smaller range did help modestly over that range. However, the improvements in objective from narrowing down the operating range were modest, and each Tao

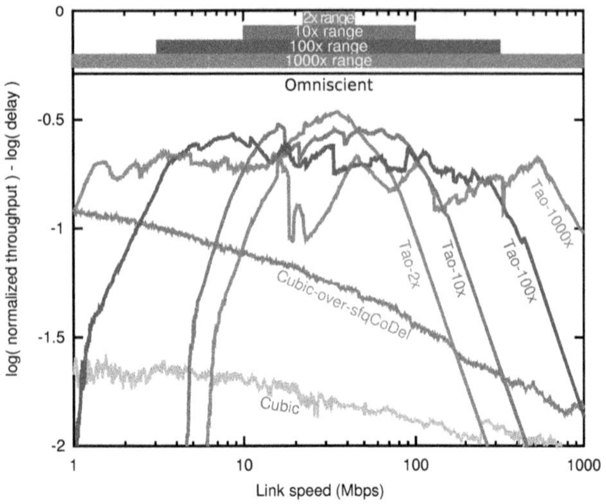


Figure 2: Evidence of a weak tradeoff between operating range in link speed of a congestion-control protocol and performance. The Tao protocols designed with more specific network models (Tao-2x and Tao-10x) performed modestly better—within their design ranges—than protocols designed for a broader range of networks (Tao-100x and Tao-1000x), at a cost of deterioration when the actual network did not fall within the training scenarios. The four Tao protocols outperformed Cubic and Cubic-over-sfqCoDel over their design ranges.

(including the Tao-1000x) outperformed existing algorithms over its full design range.

## 4.2 Knowledge of the degree of multiplexing

Congestion-control protocols have to cope with uncertainty in the degree of multiplexing from one use to the next even when running on a network with a fixed and known topology. The number of users on the network could change as could the number of flows generated by these users. Here, we evaluate whether it is possible to learn a protocol that is robust to such uncertainty.

Specifically, we designed five Tao protocols, each for a fixed dumbbell topology, but with increasing degrees of multiplexing as described in Table 3a. We then test all five protocols on the testing scenarios in Table 3b. Figure 3 shows the results for two cases: one with a buffer size of five times the bandwidth-delay product and an extreme case where the link doesn't drop any packet. In both cases, we see that it is possible to train a protocol to perform well across a wide range of multiplexing, but at the cost of diminished performance at very low degrees of multiplexing. On the flip side, designing for a much smaller range in the degree of multiplexing degrades performance dramatically outside that range.

Put differently, there is a tradeoff between good performance at high and low degrees of multiplexing. A high degree of multiplexing requires a protocol to be conservative in grabbing spare bandwidth and good performance at low degrees of multiplexing needs a protocol to quickly grab spare bandwidth. As a result, protocols trained for low degrees of multiplexing are too aggressive at higher degrees, causing either large queuing delays, when the buffer never drops a packet, or diminished throughput, when the buffer drops packets and causes more retransmissions than transmissions[2]. In either case, the result is a degradation in the objective function when such low-degree protocols are tested outside their training range. Conversely, a protocol trained for a wide range in the degree of multiplexing is unduly conservative at lower degrees of multiplexing leading to lost throughput and a degradation in the objective function.

[2]This is similar to the congestion collapse that triggered the development of TCP congestion control [15].

| Tao | Link speeds | On avg. | Off avg. | min-RTT | # senders |
|---|---|---|---|---|---|
| Tao-1–2 | 15 Mbps | 1 sec | 1 sec | 150 ms | 2 |
| Tao-1–10 | 15 Mbps | 1 sec | 1 sec | 150 ms | 10 |
| Tao-1–20 | 15 Mbps | 1 sec | 1 sec | 150 ms | 20 |
| Tao-1–50 | 15 Mbps | 1 sec | 1 sec | 150 ms | 50 |
| Tao-1–100 | 15 Mbps | 1 sec | 1 sec | 150 ms | 100 |

(a) Tao protocols designed for breadth in multiplexing

| Link speeds | On avg. | Off avg. | min-RTT | # senders | Buffer |
|---|---|---|---|---|---|
| 15 Mbps | 1 sec | 1 sec | 150 ms | 1–100 | 5 BDP, no drop |

(b) Testing scenarios to explore breadth in multiplexing

Table 3: Scenarios for "knowledge of the degree of multiplexing" experiment

## 4.3 Knowledge of propagation delays

Today, some specialized congestion-control protocols are tailored for networks with either large propagation delays (e.g., the Aspera [1] file transfer protocol over long-distance links) or short delays (such as DCTCP [3] within the data center). Here, we ask whether it is possible to design a single congestion-control protocol with good performance without making strong assumptions about the propagation delay *a priori*.

We designed four Tao protocols for varying ranges of the minimum round trip time of the network as shown in Table 4a and tested it on the scenarios shown in Table 4b. Figure 4 shows that training for exactly one minimum RTT (150 ms) results in a protocol with good performance over the 50–250 ms range, but its performance degrades drastically below 50 ms.

| Tao | Link speeds | On avg. | Off avg. | min-RTT | # senders |
|---|---|---|---|---|---|
| rtt-150 | 33 Mbps | 1 sec | 1 sec | 150 ms | 2 |
| rtt-145–155 | 33 Mbps | 1 sec | 1 sec | 145–155 ms | 2 |
| rtt-140–160 | 33 Mbps | 1 sec | 1 sec | 140–160 ms | 2 |
| rtt-50–250 | 33 Mbps | 1 sec | 1 sec | 50–250 ms | 2 |

(a) Tao protocols designed for breadth in propagation delay.

| Link speeds | On avg. | Off avg. | min-RTT | # senders |
|---|---|---|---|---|
| 33 Mbps | 1 sec | 1 sec | 1, 2, 3 . . . 300 ms | 2 |

(b) Testing scenarios to explore breadth in propagation delay.

Table 4: Scenarios for "knowledge of propagation delay" experiment

On the other hand, adding a little diversity to the training — by looking at minimum RTTs from 145 to 155 ms instead — results in performance over the 1–300 ms range that is commensurate with a protocol trained for the much broader range of 50 to 250 ms.

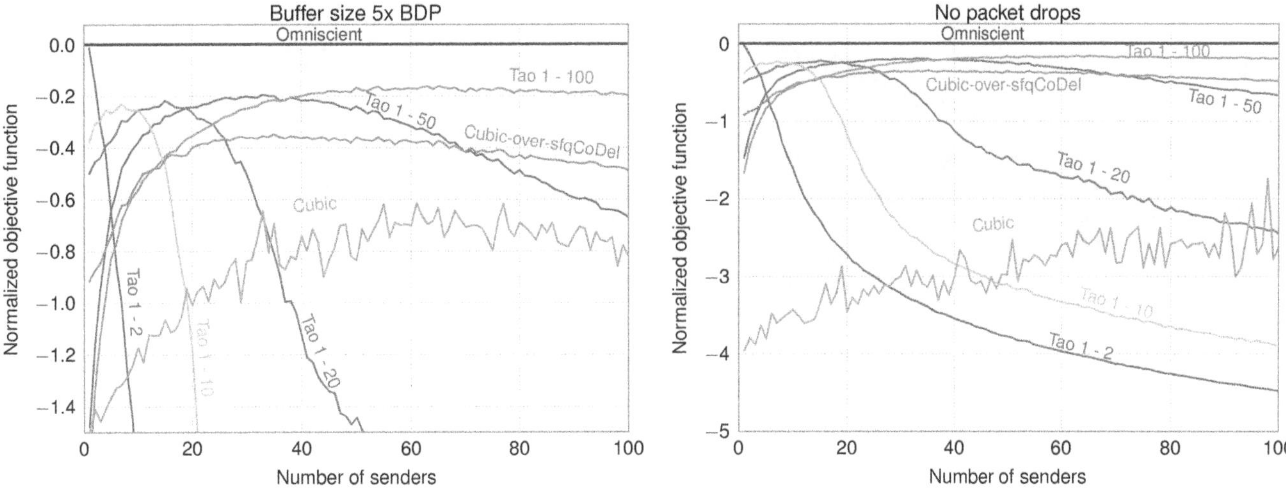


Figure 3: Tao protocols perform well across a wide range of multiplexing, but at the cost of diminished performance when there are very few senders. However, training to accommodate lower degrees of multiplexing degrades performance at higher degrees of multiplexing.

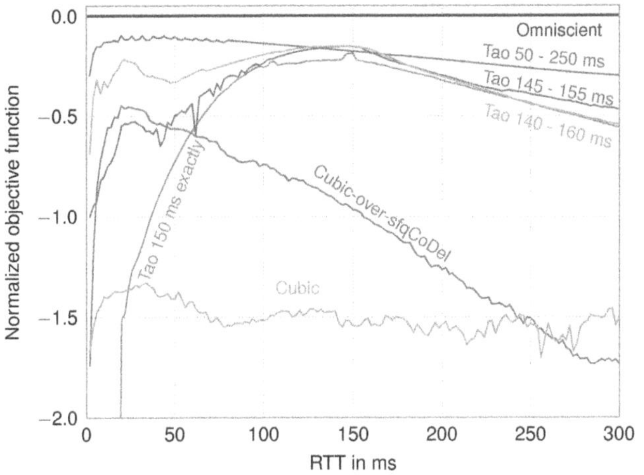


Figure 4: Training for a little diversity in propagation delays results in good performance over a much wider range of propagation delays.

These results suggest that prior knowledge of the propagation delay of a target network may not be particularly necessary or valuable to the protocol designer.

## 4.4 Structural knowledge

We evaluated the difficulty of designing a congestion-control protocol, subject to imperfect knowledge of the network's structure or topology.

It is an understatement to say that the Internet is a vast network whose full structure is known to nobody and which no model can accurately capture. Nonetheless, researchers regularly develop new distributed protocols for the Internet, which are deployed based on tests in example network paths that imperfectly capture the Internet's true complexity.

In practice, protocol designers expect that they can reason about the performance of a distributed network algorithm by modeling the network as something simpler than it is. We worked to capture that intuition rigorously by studying quantitatively how difficult it is to learn a congestion-control protocol for a more-complicated network, given a simplified model of that network's structure.

In ns-2, we simulated a network with two bottlenecks in a "parking-lot" topology, shown in Figure 5. Flow 1 crosses both links and encounters both bottlenecks. It contends with Flow 2 for access to the bottleneck queue at node A, and contends with Flow 3 for access to the bottleneck queue at node B.

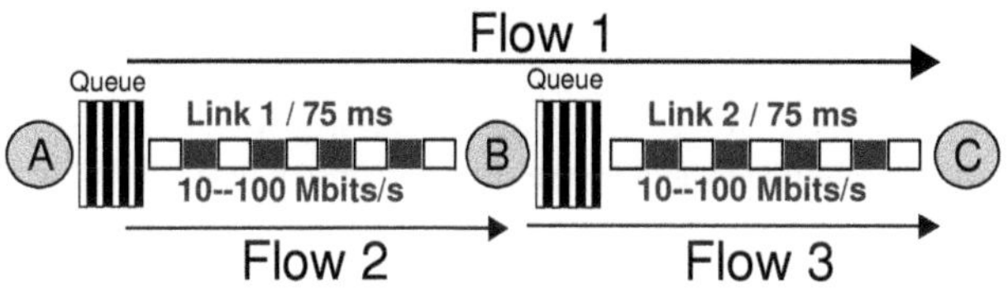


Figure 5: Parking-lot topology used to measure the consequences of imperfect knowledge of the network's structure.

| Tao | Links modeled | Num. senders |
|---|---|---|
| one-bottleneck | one, 150 ms delay | 2 |
| full two-bottleneck | two, 75 ms delay each | 3 |

Table 5: Training scenarios used to measure the consequences of imperfect knowledge of the network structure. Both protocols were designed for link speeds distributed log-uniformly between 10 and 100 Mbps, and for flows with mean "on" and "off" time of 1 second.

The results for Flow 1 (the flow that crosses both links) are shown in Figure 6.[3] The experiment sweeps the rate of each of the two links between 10 and 100 Mbps, and the shaded area in the figure shows the full locus of throughputs seen by Flow 1. For each pair of rates (for link 1 and link 2), we also calculate the ideal proportionally fair throughput allocation, and plot the locus of these allocations as the throughput achievable by the omniscient protocol.

The results suggest that a congestion-control protocol designed for a simplified model of the network's structure will experience

[3]Results for Flow 2 and Flow 3 (flows crossing only a single link) were nearly identical between the schemes.

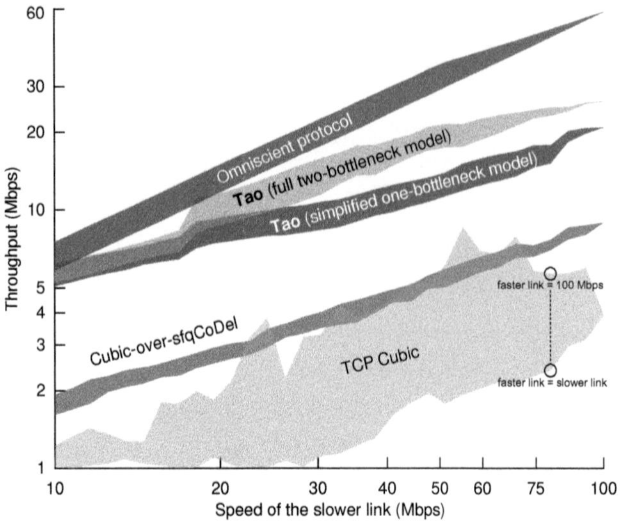


Figure 6: How well do endpoints need to understand the network around them? To assess this, we measure the throughput of four congestion-control schemes across a simulated two-hop network path, as the speed of each link is swept between 10 and 100 Mbps, with 75 ms of delay per hop. A tractable attempt at optimal (Tao) congestion control for a simplified one-bottleneck model of the network performs only a little worse than a protocol designed with knowledge of the network's full two-bottleneck structure.

a small, but quantifiable, penalty to its performance, indicated on the figure as the gap between the two Tao protocols. Results from Cubic and Cubic-over-sfqCoDel are shown for comparison.

These results give some rigorous support to a protocol designer's intuition that understanding the true network in all its complexity may not be crucial.

### 4.5 Knowledge about incumbent endpoints

We investigated the consequences of designing a congestion-control protocol with the knowledge that some cross-traffic may be the product of pre-existing incumbent protocols.

This question has considerable practical relevance; in practice, the developer of a new network protocol will rarely be able to arrange a "flag day" when all endpoints switch to the new protocol.[4]

On the broad Internet today, cross-traffic will typically be the product of traditional loss-triggered TCP congestion-control protocols, such as NewReno or Cubic. This status quo presents a serious problem for new protocols that seek to perform differently or that try to avoid building up standing queues inside the network.

Some protocols, such as Vegas [6], perform well when contending only against other flows of their own kind, but are "squeezed out" by the more-aggressive cross-traffic produced by traditional TCP. Conventional wisdom is that any "delay-based" protocol will meet a similar fate. This has contributed to a lack of adoption of Vegas and other delay-based protocols.

Ideally, a newly-designed protocol would perform well (e.g. high throughput, low delay) when interacting with other endpoints running the same protocol, **and** would appropriately share a network with incumbent endpoints running traditional TCP. But what are the actual consequences of building this "TCP-awareness" into a protocol?

[4]There has not been a "flag day" on the Internet since the switch to IP in 1983!

| Tao | Link rates | RTT | Senders | ON/OFF time |
|---|---|---|---|---|
| TCP-aware | 9–11 Mbps | 100 ms | 2 Tao | 5 sec ON/OFF |
| | | | 1 Tao, 1 AIMD | 5 sec ON, 10 ms OFF |
| TCP-naive | 9–11 Mbps | 100 ms | 2 Tao | 5 sec ON/OFF |
| | | | | 5 sec ON, 10 ms OFF |

(a) Tao protocols with and without TCP awareness, dumbbell network with buffer size 2 BDP

| Link rates | RTT | Senders | ON/OFF time |
|---|---|---|---|
| 10 Mbps | 100 ms | 2 TCP-aware | 5 sec ON, 10 ms OFF |
| 10 Mbps | 100 ms | 2 TCP-naive | 5 sec ON, 10 ms OFF |
| 10 Mbps | 100 ms | TCP-aware, AIMD | 5 sec ON, 10 ms OFF |
| 10 Mbps | 100 ms | TCP-naive, AIMD | 5 sec ON, 10 ms OFF |
| 10 Mbps | 100 ms | 2 AIMD | 5 sec ON, 10 ms OFF |

(b) Testing scenarios for "knowledge about incumbent endpoints" experiment, dumbbell network with buffer size 2 BDP

Table 6: Scenarios for "knowledge about incumbent endpoints" experiment

We studied this by designing two Tao protocols, *TCP-Naive* and *TCP-Aware*, for a simple network—one whose model specified that the cross-traffic would be from the same protocol, and one whose model included a training scenario where the cross-traffic was from traditional TCP half the time (Table 6a). Remy uses an AIMD protocol similar to TCP NewReno to simulate TCP cross-traffic.

The results are shown in Figure 7. In the left panel, protocols compete only with cross-traffic from the same protocol. In this homogeneous setting, adding TCP-awareness to a Tao protocol builds up standing queues, more than doubling the queueing delay without affecting throughput.

But in a mixed setting (Figure 7, right panel) where a Tao competes against TCP NewReno, the TCP-naive Tao is squeezed out and does not get its fair share of the link. In the shaded region showing the results when NewReno competes with the TCP-aware Tao, TCP-awareness allows the Tao to claim its fair share of the link and reduces the queueing delay experienced both by itself and by TCP NewReno.

To further understand the differing performance of TCP-naive and TCP-aware Tao protocols, we inspect their transmissions in the time domain, when contending with a contrived model of TCP cross-traffic (Figure 8) that turns on exactly at time t=5 seconds and turns off exactly at t=10 seconds. The results show that TCP-awareness is a complicated phenomenon, which yields higher delays in isolation but smaller delays when contending with TCP. It is not simply a question of "more aggressive" or "less aggressive" congestion-control.

The results suggest that new delay-minded protocols *can* avoid being squeezed out by traditional loss-triggered TCP, but building in this behavior comes at a cost to performance in the absence of TCP cross-traffic.

### 4.6 The price of sender diversity

We further generalize the notion of TCP-awareness by asking whether it is possible to design multiple new congestion-control protocols to simultaneously achieve differing objectives when contending on the same bottleneck link.

We consider two extreme cases: a throughput-sensitive sender that weighs throughput ten times over delay ($\delta = 0.1$, *Tpt. Sender*), and a delay-sensitive sender that weighs delay ten times over

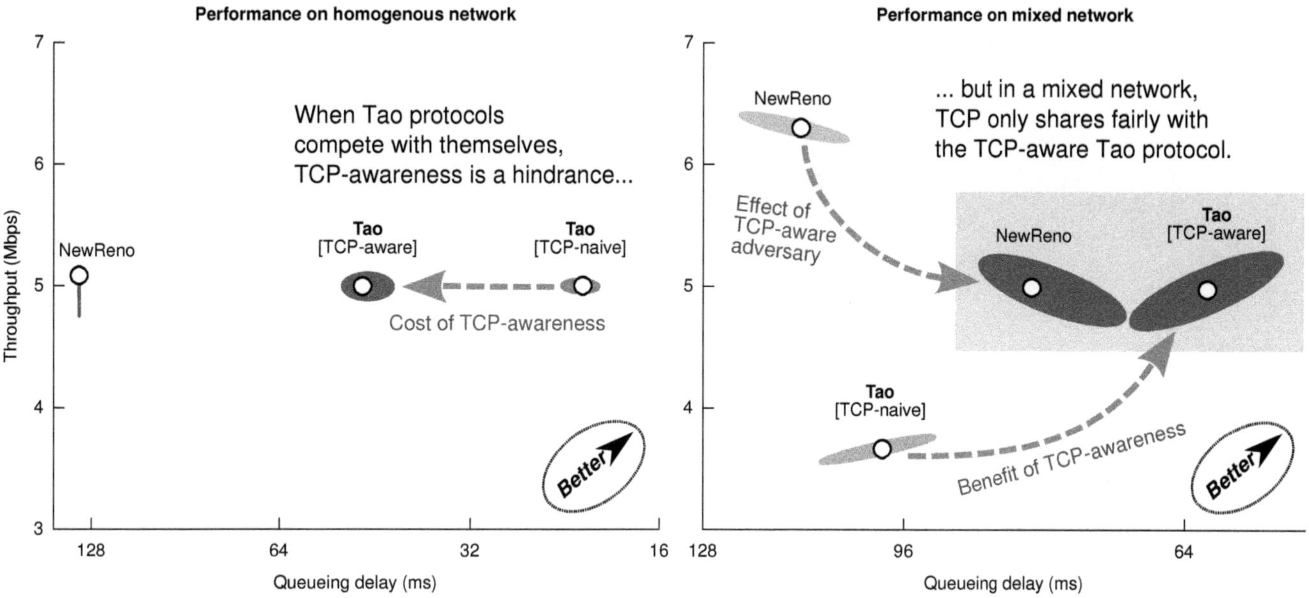


Figure 7: Tao protocols designed with and without TCP-awareness, competing against themselves or against TCP. Shown here, two endpoints contending for a 10 Mbps link with 100 ms RTT, 250 kB of buffer capacity (200 ms maximum queueing delay), and almost-continuous offered load. The fair share of throughput is 5 Mbps per endpoint. Ellipses show 1-$\sigma$ range of results.

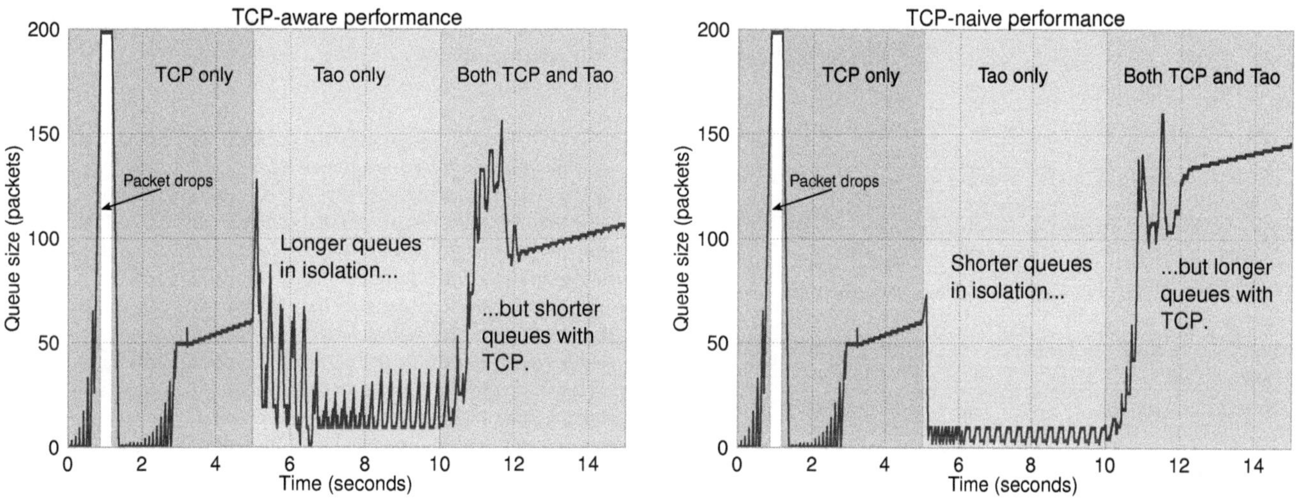


Figure 8: In isolation, a TCP-aware Tao protocol is more aggressive than required, leading to higher delays. But when competing with TCP cross-traffic, the Tao protocol achieves the reverse situation—lower queueing delay, and higher throughput, than the TCP-naive Tao protocol.

throughput ($\delta = 10.0$, *Del. Sender*). Tables 7a and 7b list the training and testing scenarios for this experiment.

We suspected that achieving diversity in this manner may not be possible, reasoning that endpoints that share the same bottleneck link will necessarily experience the same queueing delay, and therefore endpoints that achieve an optimal throughput-to-delay tradeoff will experience the same overall performance on both throughput and delay.

However, contrary to this hypothesis, our findings are that it is possible to co-optimize congestion-control algorithms such that they each try to obtain a different objective, and yet—because of variable duty cycles—are able to coexist. Even when running together (Figure 9b), the delay-sensitive sender sees lower delay than the throughput-sensitive sender, while the opposite is true with throughput. When congestion-control protocols are co-optimized, but each sender runs homogeneously (Figure 9a), each sender receives higher throughput or lower delay, as the case they may be.

However, coexistence does come at a price to the throughput-sensitive sender, which suffers a loss in throughput by being "nice" to the delay-sensitive sender, both when run with the delay-sensitive sender and when running by itself . By comparison, the performance of the delay-sensitive sender is affected only modestly.

## 5. CONCLUSION

This study represents an early step towards a rigorous understanding of the tradeoffs and compromises of network protocol design. We asked: *how easy is it to "learn" a network protocol to achieve desired goals, given a necessarily imperfect model of the networks where it will ultimately be deployed?*

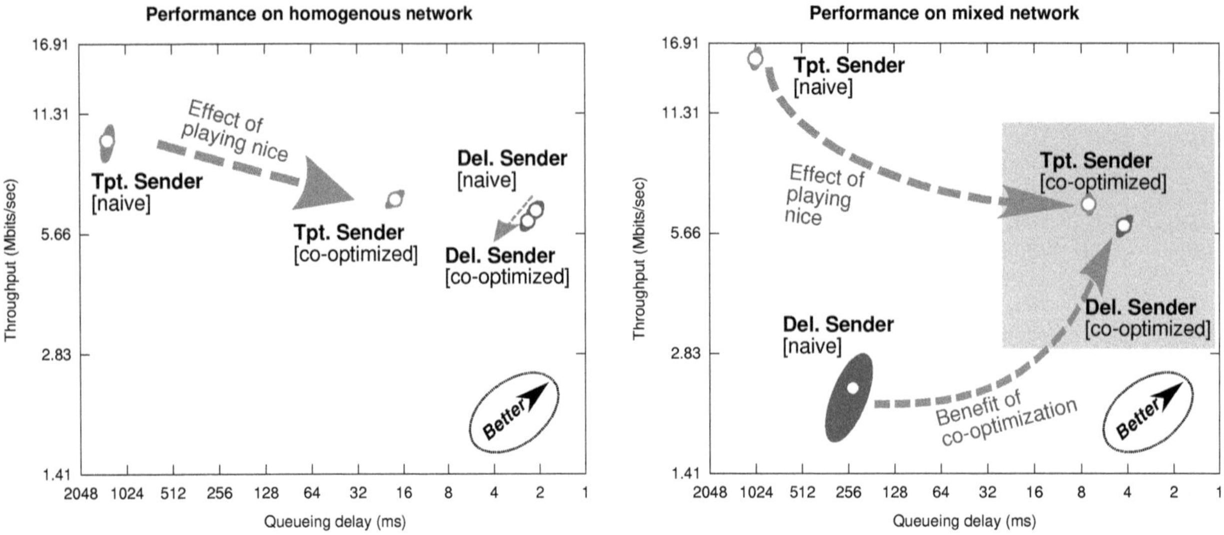


(a) When senders with different preferences run by themselves, training to coexist hurts the throughput of the throughput-sensitive sender. The delay-sensitive sender isn't materially affected.

(b) When senders that are independently optimized for different preferences run on the same network, the delay-sensitive sender experiences much higher delays (compared with the case where it runs by itself). In contrast, co-optimizing the senders hurts the throughput-sensitive sender, but allows the delay-sensitive sender to achieve both lower delay and higher throughput.

Figure 9: The cost and benefits of sender diversity.

| Tao | Link rates | RTT | Senders | ON/OFF time | $\delta$ | Buffer |
|---|---|---|---|---|---|---|
| Del. Sender | 10 Mbps | 100 ms | 0, 1, or 2 of each type | 1 sec ON/OFF | 10.0 | No drop |
| Tpt. Sender | 10 Mbps | 100 ms | 0, 1, or 2 of each type | 1 sec ON/OFF | 0.1 | No drop |

(a) Tao protocols for diverse senders: one favors throughput, the other delay

| Link rates | RTT | Senders | ON/OFF time | Buffer |
|---|---|---|---|---|
| 10 Mbps | 100 ms | 1 Del. Sender<br>1 Tpt.Sender | 1 sec ON/OFF | No drop |

(b) Testing scenarios for "price of sender diversity" experiment

Table 7: Scenarios for "price of sender diversity" experiment

We investigated several questions under this umbrella by using Remy as a design tool to produce a tractable-attempt-at-optimal (Tao) protocol under various prior assumptions about the network environment. We found only weak evidence of a tradeoff between operating range and performance, even when the operating range covered a thousand-fold range of link speeds. We found that it may be acceptable to simplify some characteristics of the network—such as its topology—when modeling for design purposes. In contrast, features such as the degree of multiplexing and the aggressiveness of contending endpoints were important to capture.

Much remains to be understood about the protocol-design problem before computer-generated protocols will be practically deployable across the broad Internet. For example, can we tractably synthesize a single computer-generated protocol that outperforms human-generated incumbents over a wide range of topologies, link speeds, propagation delays, and degrees of multiplexing simultaneously? Does such a protocol still perform well on networks more complicated than the two-hop parking lot? While our experimental results suggest qualitatively that Remy-generated protocols do not carry a substantial risk of catastrophic congestion collapse, can a protocol optimizer maintain and verify this requirement mechanistically, as part of the design process? Our findings from this study suggest that optimization tools may be able to tackle these kinds of questions in the near future.

Our formalization of the protocol-design process rests on asking the Remy tool to construct a congestion-control scheme, given stated assumptions about the network and an objective function. By contrast, for a human-designed protocol (e.g., existing flavors of TCP), it is usually not possible to describe exactly the implicit underlying assumptions about the network or the intended objective. For that reason, it cannot be guaranteed that our conclusions are truly applicable to the problem of protocol design generally, rather than simply to Remy and similar computer-generated protocol-design methods.

Nonetheless, we do qualitatively observe that the performance of human-designed protocols can depend strongly on network parameters. The single-peaked performance of Cubic-over-sfqCoDel in Figure 4 and the declining performance in Figure 2 suggest that this protocol rests on assumptions about the network parameters—assumptions that may hold more or less well in practice. We therefore believe that our results, and our method generally, can provide useful insights to network protocol designers about what factors are important to model accurately and what factors may be simplified as part of a design process.

In the future, we envision network protocols will be developed mechanistically from first principles: with human designers documenting the objectives and assumptions that a new protocol will have, and automatic processes synthesizing the resulting protocol itself. Such a methodology would allow for a more agile network architecture, because changing requirements or subnetwork behaviors could be accommodated simply by changing the inputs to an automatic process.

While it may have been more straightforward in the past and present for human designers to create protocols directly, based on intuitive design guidelines, the experience of other fields of engineering—mechanical, electrical, civil—suggests to us that protocol design will eventually also adopt a more structured foundation. We will need answers to questions like the ones in this study to make such a transition successful.

## 6. ACKNOWLEDGMENTS

This work has benefited immensely from discussions with many people, including Scott Shenker, John Wroclawski, Leslie Kaelbling, Chris Amato, Dina Katabi, Frans Kaashoek, Hariharan Rahul, Jonathan Perry, Eugene Wu, and Arun Chaganty. Our shepherd, Aditya Akella, and the anonymous SIGCOMM reviewers gave many helpful comments. We thank Frans Kaashoek, Nickolai Zeldovich, and Li-Shiuan Peh for the use of multicore machines at MIT, and the members of the MIT Center for Wireless Networks and Mobile Computing (Wireless@MIT), including Amazon.com, Cisco, Google, Intel, Mediatek, Microsoft, ST Microelectronics, and Telefonica, for their support. This work was also supported in part by NSF grant CNS-1040072.

## REFERENCES

[1] Aspera - High-speed File Transfer Technology - Asperasoft. http://asperasoft.com/technology/.

[2] sfqCoDel. http://www.pollere.net/Txtdocs/sfqcodel.cc.

[3] M. Alizadeh, A. Greenberg, D. A. Maltz, J. Padhye, P. Patel, B. Prabhakar, S. Sengupta, and M. Sridharan. Data Center TCP (DCTCP). In *SIGCOMM*, 2010.

[4] D. S. Bernstein, R. Givan, N. Immerman, and S. Zilberstein. The Complexity of Decentralized Control of Markov Decision Processes. *Mathematics of Operations Research*, 27(4):819–840, Nov. 2002.

[5] B. E. Boser, I. M. Guyon, and V. N. Vapnik. A training algorithm for optimal margin classifiers. In *Proceedings of the Fifth Annual Workshop on Computational Learning Theory*, COLT '92, pages 144–152, New York, NY, USA, 1992. ACM.

[6] L. S. Brakmo, S. W. O'Malley, and L. L. Peterson. TCP Vegas: New Techniques for Congestion Detection and Avoidance. In *SIGCOMM*, 1994.

[7] D.-M. Chiu and R. Jain. Analysis of the Increase and Decrease Algorithms for Congestion Avoidance in Computer Networks. *Computer Networks and ISDN Systems*, 17:1–14, 1989.

[8] N. Dukkipati and N. McKeown. Why flow-completion time is the right metric for congestion control. *SIGCOMM Comput. Commun. Rev.*, 36(1):59–62, Jan. 2006.

[9] W. Feng, K. Shin, D. Kandlur, and D. Saha. The BLUE Active Queue Management Algorithms. *IEEE/ACM Trans. on Networking*, Aug. 2002.

[10] S. Floyd. TCP and Explicit Congestion Notification. *CCR*, 24(5), Oct. 1994.

[11] S. Floyd and V. Jacobson. Random Early Detection Gateways for Congestion Avoidance. *IEEE/ACM Trans. on Networking*, 1(4), Aug. 1993.

[12] S. Ha, I. Rhee, and L. Xu. CUBIC: A New TCP-Friendly High-Speed TCP Variant. *ACM SIGOPS Operating System Review*, 42(5):64–74, July 2008.

[13] O. Habachi, Y. Hu, M. van der Schaar, Y. Hayel, and F. Wu. Mos-based congestion control for conversational services in wireless environments. *Selected Areas in Communications, IEEE Journal on*, 30(7):1225–1236, August 2012.

[14] J. C. Hoe. Improving the Start-up Behavior of a Congestion Control Scheme for TCP. In *SIGCOMM*, 1996.

[15] V. Jacobson. Congestion Avoidance and Control. In *SIGCOMM*, 1988.

[16] D. Katabi, M. Handley, and C. Rohrs. Congestion Control for High Bandwidth-Delay Product Networks. In *SIGCOMM*, 2002.

[17] F. P. Kelly, A. Maulloo, and D. Tan. Rate Control in Communication Networks: Shadow Prices, Proportional Fairness and Stability. *Journal of the Operational Research Society*, 49:237–252, 1998.

[18] S. Kunniyur and R. Srikant. Analysis and Design of an Adaptive Virtual Queue (AVQ) Algorithm for Active Queue Management. In *SIGCOMM*, 2001.

[19] S. Mascolo, C. Casetti, M. Gerla, M. Sanadidi, and R. Wang. TCP Westwood: Bandwidth Estimation for Enhanced Transport over Wireless Links. In *MobiCom*, 2001.

[20] P. E. McKenney. Stochastic Fairness Queueing. In *INFOCOM*, 1990.

[21] K. Nichols and V. Jacobson. Controlling Queue Delay. *ACM Queue*, 10(5), May 2012.

[22] K. Nichols and V. Jacobson. Controlled Delay Active Queue Management. Technical report, Internet-draft draft-nichols-tsvwg-codel-01, 2013.

[23] R. Pan, B. Prabhakar, and K. Psounis. CHOKe—A Stateless Active Queue Management Scheme for Approximating Fair Bandwidth Allocation. In *INFOCOM*, 2000.

[24] K. K. Ramakrishnan and R. Jain. A Binary Feedback Scheme for Congestion Avoidance in Computer Networks. *ACM Trans. on Comp. Sys.*, 8(2):158–181, May 1990.

[25] R. E. Schapire. The strength of weak learnability. *Machine learning*, 5(2):197–227, 1990.

[26] R. Srikant. *The Mathematics of Internet Congestion Control*. Birkhauser, 2004.

[27] K. Tan, J. Song, Q. Zhang, and M. Sridharan. A Compound TCP Approach for High-speed and Long Distance Networks. In *INFOCOM*, 2006.

[28] L. G. Valiant. A Theory of the Learnable. *CACM*, 27(11):1134–1142, Nov. 1984.

[29] K. Winstein and H. Balakrishnan. TCP ex Machina: Computer-Generated Congestion Control. In *SIGCOMM*, Hong Kong,, August 2013.

[30] J. Wroclawski. TCP ex Machina. http://www.postel.org/pipermail/end2end-interest/2013-July/008914.html, 2013.

[31] Y. Yi and M. Chiang. Stochastic Network Utility Maximisation. *European Transactions on Telecommunications*, 19(4):421–442, 2008.

# Friends, not Foes – Synthesizing Existing Transport Strategies for Data Center Networks

Ali Munir[1]*, Ghufran Baig[2], Syed M. Irteza[2], Ihsan A. Qazi[2],
Alex X. Liu[1], Fahad R. Dogar[3]
[1]Michigan State University, [2]LUMS, [3]Microsoft Research
{munirali, alexliu}@cse.msu.edu, {ghufran.baig, syed.irteza, ihsan.qazi}@lums.edu.pk,
fdogar@microsoft.com

## ABSTRACT

Many data center transports have been proposed in recent times (e.g., DCTCP, PDQ, pFabric, etc). Contrary to the common perception that they are *competitors* (i.e., protocol A vs. protocol B), we claim that the underlying strategies used in these protocols are, in fact, *complementary*. Based on this insight, we design PASE, a transport framework that *synthesizes* existing transport strategies, namely, self-adjusting endpoints (used in TCP style protocols), in-network prioritization (used in pFabric), and arbitration (used in PDQ). PASE is deployment friendly: it does not require any changes to the network fabric; yet, its performance is comparable to, or better than, the state-of-the-art protocols that require changes to network elements (e.g., pFabric). We evaluate PASE using simulations and testbed experiments. Our results show that PASE performs well for a wide range of application workloads and network settings.

**Categories and Subject Descriptors:** C.2.2 [Computer-Communication Networks]: Network Protocols
**Keywords:** datacenter; transport; scheduling

## 1. INTRODUCTION

Popular data center applications (e.g., search) have many distributed components that interact via the internal data center network. Network delays, therefore, inflate application response times which, in turn, affects user satisfaction. Thus, several recent data center transport proposals focus on providing low latency for user-facing services. These proposals optimize for specific application goals, such as minimizing flow completion times (FCT) or meeting flow deadlines, and use a variety of underlying techniques to achieve their objective, from the more traditional TCP-style approaches (e.g., DCTCP [11]) to those that use an explicit rate control protocol (e.g., PDQ [18]) or a new prioritized network fabric (e.g., pFabric [12]).

*Part of the work was done while the author was an intern at Microsoft Research.


*SIGCOMM'14*, August 17–22, 2014, Chicago, IL, USA.
Copyright 2014 ACM 978-1-4503-2836-4/14/08 ...$15.00.
http://dx.doi.org/10.1145/2619239.2626305.

All these techniques have their own strengths and weaknesses: some provide good performance, but require changes to the network fabric [12, 18, 24], while others are deployment friendly, but have inferior performance [22, 23]. In this paper, we take a clean slate approach towards designing a data center transport that provides good performance while also being deployment friendly. To this end, we take a step back and ask the following question: *how can we design a data center transport from scratch while leveraging the insights offered by existing proposals?*

As a first step towards answering this question, we distill the three underlying strategies used in data center transports: *i) self adjusting endpoints*, where senders independently make their rate increase/decrease decision based on the observed network conditions (used in DCTCP [11] style protocols), *ii) arbitration*, where a common network entity (e.g., a switch) allocates rates to each flow (used in $D^3$ [24], PDQ [18], etc), and *iii) in-network prioritization*, where switches schedule and drop packets based on their priority (used in pFabric [12]).

We observe that each strategy has its own role. It works best when it is fulfilling its role and encounters problems otherwise. Unfortunately, existing protocols only use *one* of the above strategies and try to make it work under *all* scenarios. In this paper, we make a case that these transport strategies should be used *together* as they nicely complement each other. For example, approaches that rely on arbitration alone have high flow switching overhead because flows need to be explicitly paused and unpaused [18]. With in-network prioritization, switching from a high priority flow to the next is seamless [12]. Conversely, arbitration can also help in-network prioritization approaches. For example, in-network prioritization mechanisms typically need to support a large number of priority levels whereas existing switches only have a limited number of priority queues. An arbitrator can address this problem by *dynamically* changing the mapping of flows to queues — flows whose turn is far away can all be mapped to the lowest priority queue while flows whose turn is about to come can be mapped to the high priority queues.

To demonstrate the benefits of using these strategies together, we design PASE, a transport framework for private data center environments. PASE employs distributed arbitrators that decide the share (priority) of a flow given other flows in the system. A TCP-like end-host transport uses this information for its rate control and loss recovery. Within the network, PASE uses existing priority queues to prioritize the scheduling of packets over network links. This appropriate division of responsibilities among the three strategies makes PASE outperform state-of-the-art transport protocols while also being *deployment friendly* i.e., no changes to the network fabric are required.

A key aspect of PASE is a scalable control plane for arbitration. For every link in the data center topology, a dedicated arbitrator is responsible for arbitration. This functionality can be implemented at the end-hosts themselves (e.g., for their own links to the switch) or on dedicated nodes within the data center. We exploit the typical tree based data center topology features to make the arbitration decisions in a bottom up fashion, starting from the endpoints and going up to the core. This has several performance and scalability benefits. First, for intra-rack communication, which can constitute a sizeable share of data center traffic [11], only the source and destination are involved, obviating the need to communicate with any other entity. Second, lower level arbitrators (those closer to the leaf nodes) can do *early pruning* by discarding flows that are unlikely to become part of the top priority queue. Third, higher level arbitrators (those closer to the root) can *delegate* their arbitration decisions to lower level arbitrators. Both early pruning and delegation reduce the arbitration overhead (at the cost of potentially less accurate decisions).

The outcome of arbitration is the *priority queue* and *reference rate* for the flow – this information is used by PASE's end-host transport for rate control and loss recovery. Compared to traditional transport protocols (e.g., TCP/DCTCP), our rate control is more *guided*. For example, instead of slow start, the transport uses the reference rate as its starting point. However, loss recovery in PASE is more challenging because packets can be delayed in a lower priority queue for a long time, which may trigger spurious timeouts if we use today's timeout mechanisms. Thus, for lower priority flows, instead of retransmitting the data packet, PASE uses small *probe* packets which help in determining whether the packet was lost, or waiting in a lower priority queue.

We implement PASE on a small testbed and in the ns2 simulator [6]. We compare PASE with the best performing transport protocol (pFabric [12]) as well as deployment friendly options ($D^2$TCP [23]). Compared to deployment friendly options, PASE improves the average FCT (AFCT) by 40% to 60% for various scenarios. PASE also performs within 6% of pFabric in scenarios where pFabric is close to optimal while in other scenarios (all-to-all traffic pattern or under high network load), PASE outperforms pFabric by up to 85% both in terms of the AFCT as well as the $99^{th}$ percentile FCT.

This paper makes the following key contributions.

- We distill the underlying strategies used in data center transport protocols and highlight their strengths and weaknesses.

- We design PASE, a data center transport framework which synthesizes existing transport strategies. PASE includes two new components: a scalable arbitration control plane for data center networks, and an end-host transport protocol that is explicitly aware of priority queues and employs a guided rate control mechanism.

- We conduct a comprehensive evaluation of PASE, which includes macro-benchmarks that compare PASE's performance against multiple existing transport protocols, and micro-benchmarks that focus on the internal working of the system.

PASE shows the promise of combining existing transport strategies in a single transport framework. We view it as a first step towards a more holistic approach for building the next generation data center transport protocols.

# 2. TRANSPORT STRATEGIES

To achieve high performance,[1] existing data center transports use one of the three following transport strategies: (a) *Self-Adjusting Endpoints*, (b) *Arbitration*, or (c) *In-network Prioritization*. We first describe these strategies and discuss their limitations when they are employed in isolation. We then discuss how these limitations can be addressed if these strategies are used together.

## 2.1 Transport Strategies in Isolation

Each transport strategy has its own advantages and disadvantages as shown in Table 1. We now describe the basic working of each strategy, discuss its advantages, and highlight their key limitations through simulation experiments.

**Self-Adjusting Endpoints:** Traditional transport protocols like TCP use this strategy. Under this transport strategy, endpoints *themselves* decide the amount of data to send based on network congestion. The state of network congestion is determined through a congestion signal that could be implicit (e.g., packet loss) or explicit (i.e., ECN). In case of congestion, the window size is reduced by the same factor for all flows, if fairness is the objective [11], or the factor could depend on other parameters (e.g., remaining flow size [22] or deadline [23]), if flow prioritization is the objective.

Protocols in this category are easy to deploy because they do not require any changes to the network infrastructure or depend on any entity except the endpoints. However, when considering flow prioritization, their performance is inferior to the state-of-the-art data center transport protocols (e.g., pFabric [12], PDQ [18]). One reason for their poor performance is that they do not provide strict priority scheduling – even low priority flows, which should be paused, continue to send at least one packet per RTT. This hurts performance, especially at high loads when multiple flows are active.

To illustrate this behavior, we consider two protocols that follow the self-adjusting endpoint strategy: DCTCP [11] and $D^2$TCP [23] (a deadline-aware version of DCTCP), and compare their performance with pFabric [12], the state-of-the-art data center transport with the best reported performance. We replicate a deadline oriented scenario in ns2[2]. Figure 1 shows the fraction of deadlines met (or *application throughput*) as a function of load for the three schemes. While at low loads, $D^2$TCP is able to meet deadlines (i.e., achieve prioritization), at higher loads its performance approaches its fair-sharing counterpart, DCTCP. Moreover, both these

[1]In the context of data center transports, *high performance* usually refers to minimizing completion times, maximizing throughput, or reducing the deadline miss rate [11, 18].

[2]This corresponds to Experiment 4.1.3 in the $D^2$TCP paper [23] – it represents an intra-rack scenario, where the source and destination of each flow is picked randomly and the flow sizes are uniformly distributed between [100 KB, 500 KB] in the presence of two background long flows. The deadlines are uniformly distributed from 5 ms-25 ms.

| Transport Strategy | Pros | Cons | Examples |
|---|---|---|---|
| Self-Adjusting Endpoints | Ease of deployment | Lack of support for strict priority scheduling | DCTCP [11], $D^2$TCP [23], $L^2$DCT [22] |
| Arbitration | 1) Supports strict priority scheduling<br>2) Fast convergence | 1) High flow switching overhead<br>2) Hard to compute precise rates | $D^3$ [24], PDQ [18]. |
| In-network Prioritization | 1) Work conservation<br>2) Low flow switching overhead | 1) Limited number of priority queues in existing switches<br>2) Switch-local decisions | pFabric [12] |

**Table 1: Comparison of different transport strategies.**

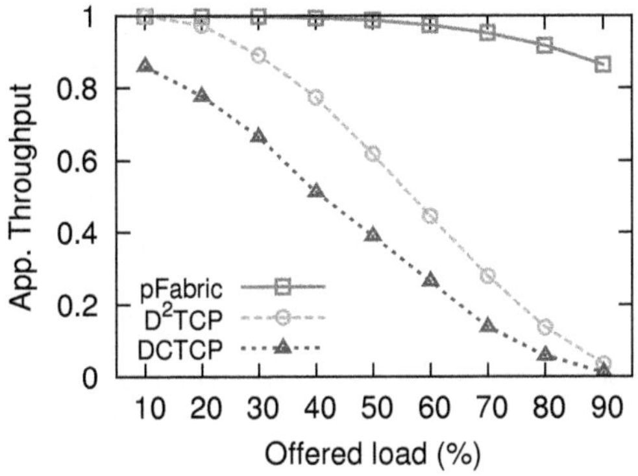


**Figure 1: Comparison of two self-adjusting endpoint based protocols ($D^2$TCP and DCTCP) with the state-of-the-art data center transport (pFabric).**

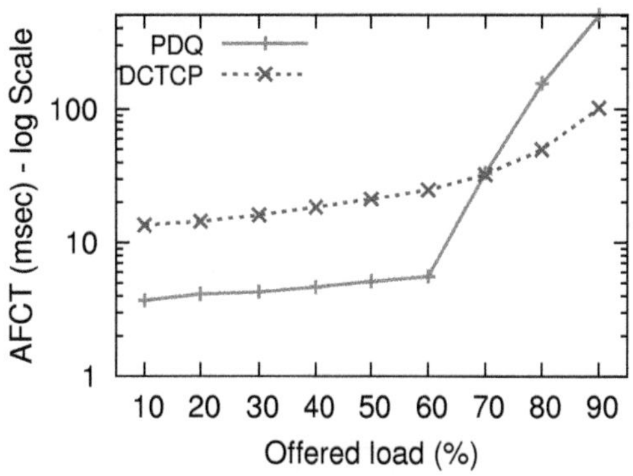


**Figure 2: Comparison of PDQ (an arbitration based approach) with DCTCP. At high loads, PDQ's high flow switching overhead leads to poor performance.**

protocols perform much worse than pFabric at high loads, highlighting their limitations in achieving priority scheduling across a wide range of network loads.

**Arbitration:** Explicit rate protocols, like PDQ [18], use arbitration as their underlying transport strategy. Instead of endpoints making decisions on their own, arbitration based approaches [18, 24] require the switches to make the scheduling decision, keeping in view all network flows and their individual priorities (e.g., deadline, flow size). The scheduling decision is communicated as a *rate* at which flows should send data. The rate could be zero, if the flow needs to be paused because of its low priority, or it could be the full link capacity, if the flow has the highest priority. While a centralized problem in general, prior work [18, 24] shows that arbitration can be done in a decentralized fashion – each switch along the path of a flow adds its rate to the packet header and the minimum rate is picked by the sender for transmitting data.

The explicit nature of arbitration based approaches ensures that flows achieve their desired rate quickly (typically in one RTT). Moreover, the ability to pause and unpause flows enables strict priority scheduling of flows: the highest priority flow gets the full link capacity (if it can saturate the link) while other flows are paused. However, this explicit rate assignment comes with its own set of problems. For example, calculating accurate rates for flows is challenging as flows could be bottlenecked at non-network resources (e.g., source application, receiver). Another important issue is the *flow switching overhead*, which refers to the overhead of pausing and unpausing flows. This overhead is typically ~1-2 RTTs, which can be significant in scenarios involving short flows (when flows last for a small duration) and at high loads (when flows need to be frequently preempted).

We illustrate the impact of flow switching overhead in a practical scenario through a simulation experiment. We consider PDQ [18][3], which is considered the best performing arbitration based scheme, and compare its performance with DCTCP [11]. The scenario is a repeat of the previous intra-rack, all-to-all experiment, except the metric here is AFCT. Figure 2 shows the AFCT as a function of network load. At low loads, PDQ outperforms DCTCP because of its fast convergence to the desired rate. However, at high loads, the flow switching overhead becomes significant as more flows contend with each other, thereby requiring more preemptions in the network. As a result, PDQ's performance degrades and the completion time becomes even higher than that of DCTCP.

**In-network Prioritization:** In transport protocols that use in-network prioritization (e.g., pFabric [12]), packets carry flow priorities, such as the flow deadline or size, and switches use this priority to decide which packet to schedule or drop (in case of congestion). This behavior ensures two desirable properties: *work conservation*, a lower priority packet is scheduled if there is no packet of higher priority, and *preemption*, when a higher priority packet arrives, it gets precedence over a lower priority packet.

The well-known downside to in-network prioritization is the limited number of priority queues available in switches – typically ~4-10 [24] (see Table 2). For most practical scenarios, this number is much smaller than the number of unique flow priorities in the system. Proposals that support a large number of *priority levels* require changing the network fabric [12], which makes them hard to deploy.

Another shortcoming of this strategy is that switches make local decisions about prioritization which can lead to sub-optimal performance in multi-link scenarios. This is shown in Figure 3 through a simple toy example involv-

[3]Based on the simulator code obtained from the PDQ authors. It supports all the optimizations that reduce the flow switching overhead.

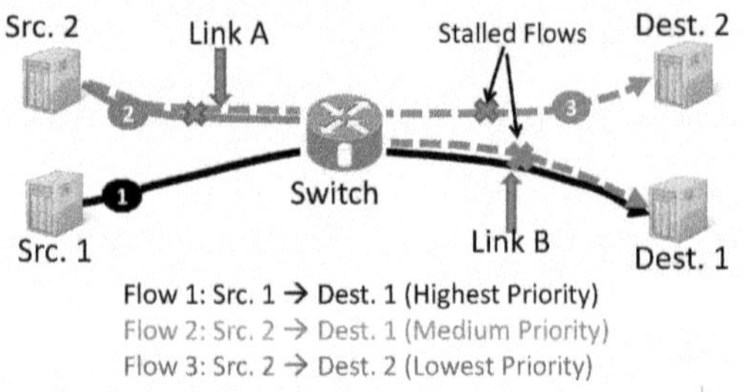


**Figure 3: Toy example illustrating problem with pFabric.**

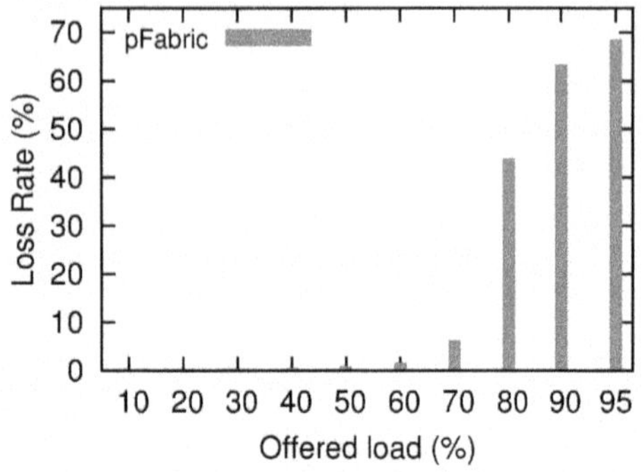


**Figure 4: Loss rate for pFabric with varying load. Local prioritization leads to losses at high loads.**

ing three flows. Flow 1 has the highest priority; Flow 2 has medium priority and flow 3 has the lowest priority. Flows 1 and 2 share link B, so only flow 1 can progress while flow 2 should wait. A protocol like pFabric continues to send packets of flow 2 on link A even though these packets are later dropped at link B. These unnecessary transmissions stall flow 3, which could have run in parallel with flow 1 as both flows do not share any link.

The above toy example highlights a common use case present in all-to-all traffic patterns (e.g., MapReduce [16], Search) where a node typically has data to send to many other nodes. To quantify this problem under such practical settings, we simulate the interaction between workers and aggregators within a single rack of a search application. Each worker-aggregator flow is uniformly distributed between [2-198] KB. We focus on the loss rate of pFabric when the network load is increased. As shown in Figure 4, loss rate shoots up as the load on network links is increased. For a load of 80%, more than 40% packets are dropped. These lost packets translate into loss of throughput as we could have used these transmissions for packets belonging to other flows. In Section 4, we show how this high loss rate results in poor FCT for pFabric.

## 2.2 Transport Strategies in Unison

We now discuss how *combining* these transport strategies offers a simple solution to the problems identified earlier.

**In-network Prioritization complementing arbitration:** The high flow switching overhead of arbitration-only approaches can be avoided with the help of in-network prioritization. As today's arbitration-only approaches, like PDQ [18], assume no prioritization within the network, they have to achieve priority scheduling by communicating explicit rates to end-hosts, which takes time, and thus results in a high flow switching overhead. If we have in-network prioritization, the arbitrator can just assign *relative* priorities to the flows (e.g., high priority flow vs low priority flow), leaving it up to the switches to *enforce* this relative priority through a suitable scheduling and dropping mechanism. The current in-network prioritization mechanisms (e.g., priority queues) provide seamless switching between flows of different priorities, so there is no flow switching overhead and link utilization remains high during this period.

A simple example illustrates this benefit. Assume we have two flows – $F_1$ (higher priority) and $F_2$ (lower priority). With arbitration-only approaches, $F_1$ is initially assigned the entire link capacity while $F_2$ is paused during this time. When $F_1$ finishes, we have to explicitly signal $F_2$ to unpause. With in-network prioritization, we can just assign these flows to different priority classes – $F_1$ is mapped to the high priority class while $F_2$ is mapped to the low priority class. The switch ensures that as soon as there are no more packets of $F_1$ in the high priority queue, it starts scheduling packets of $F_2$ from the lower priority queue.

**Arbitration aiding In-network Prioritization:** The small number of priority queues cause performance degradation when multiple flows get mapped to the high priority queue [12]. This results in multiplexing of these flows instead of strict priority scheduling (i.e., one flow at a time). This problem can be avoided with the help of arbitration. Instead of statically mapping flows to queues, an arbitrator can do a *dynamic* mapping. So a flow's priority queue keeps on changing during it's lifetime. A flow whose "turn" is far away is mapped to lower priority queue. As a flow's turn is about to come, it moves up to a higher priority queue.

We explain this idea through a simple two queue example. Suppose queue A ($Q_A$) is the high priority queue and queue B ($Q_B$) is the lower priority queue. We have four flows to schedule ($F_1$, $F_2$, $F_3$, and $F_4$, with $F_1$ having the highest priority and $F_4$, the lowest) — as the number of flows is more than the number of queues, any static mapping of flows to queues will result in sub-optimal performance. With the help of arbitration, we can initially map $F_1$ to $Q_A$ and the other three flows to $Q_B$. When $F_1$ finishes, we can change the mapping of $F_2$ from $Q_B$ to $Q_A$ while flows $F_3$ and $F_4$ are still mapped to $Q_B$. A similar process is applied when $F_2$ (and later on, $F_3$) finishes. In short, the highest priority queue is used for the active, high priority flow while the lower priority queue is used primarily to keep link utilization high (i.e., work-conservation). The example shows how arbitration can help leverage the limited number of priority queues without compromising on performance.

**Arbitration helping Self-Adjusting Endpoints :** With arbitration-only approaches, calculating precise flow rates can be hard because the arbitrator may not have accurate information about all the possible bottlenecks in the system [18, 24]. Thus, we can end up underestimating or overestimating the available capacity. Unfortunately, in arbitration-only approaches, endpoints – which typically have a better idea of path conditions – are dumb: they always transmit at the rate assigned by the arbitrator, so even if they are in a position to detect congestion or spare capacity in the network, they cannot respond.

The self-adjusting endpoint strategy naturally addresses this problem as it constantly probes the network: if there is any spare capacity, it will increase its rate, and if there is congestion, it will back off. For example, suppose there

| Switch | Vendor | Num. Queues | ECN |
|---|---|---|---|
| BCM56820 [2] | Broadcom | 10 | Yes |
| G8264 [4] | IBM | 8 | Yes |
| 7050S [1] | Arista | 7 | Yes |
| EX3300 [5] | Juniper | 5 | No |
| S4810 [3] | Dell | 3 | Yes |

**Table 2: Priority Queues and ECN support in popular commodity top-of-rack switches. The numbers are per interface.**

are two flows in the system with different priorities. The higher priority flow is assigned the full link capacity but it is unable to use it. The lower priority flow will remain paused if we do not use self-adjusting endpoints. However, if the endpoint uses a self-adjusting policy, it will detect spare capacity and increase its rate until the link is saturated. Note that arbitration also helps the self-adjusting endpoint strategy: instead of just blindly probing the network for its due share, a flow can use information from the arbitrator to "bootstrap" the self-adjusting behavior.

# 3. PASE

PASE is a transport framework that synthesizes the three transport strategies, namely in-network **P**rioritization, **A**rbitration, and **S**elf-adjusting **E**ndpoints. The underlying design principle behind PASE is that each transport strategy should focus on what it is best at doing, such as:

- Arbitrators should do inter-flow prioritization at coarse time-scales. They should not be responsible for computing precise rates or for doing fine-grained prioritization.
- Endpoints should probe for any spare link capacity on their own, without involving any other entity. Further, given their lack of global information, they should not try to do inter-flow prioritization (protocols that do this have poor performance, as shown in Section 2).
- In-network prioritization mechanism should focus on per-packet prioritization at short, sub-RTT timescales. The goal should be to obey the decisions made by the other two strategies while keeping the data plane simple and efficient.

Given the above roles for each strategy, the high-level working of PASE is as follows. Every source periodically contacts the arbitrator to get its *priority queue* and *reference rate*. The arbitration decision is based on the flows currently in the system and their priorities (e.g., deadline, flow-size). As the name suggests, the reference rate is not binding on the sources, so depending on the path conditions, the sources may end up sending at higher or lower than this rate (i.e., self-adjusting endpoints). A key benefit of PASE is that we do not require any changes to the data plane: switches on the path use existing priority queues to schedule packets and employ explicit congestion notification (ECN) to signal congestion. As shown in Table 2, most modern switches support these two features.

To achieve high performance while being deployment friendly, PASE incorporates two key components: a control plane arbitration mechanism and an end-host transport protocol. While existing arbitration mechanisms operate in the data plane (and hence require changes to the network fabric), we implement a separate control plane for performing arbitration in a scalable manner. To this end, we introduce optimizations that leverage the typical tree structure of data center topologies to reduce the overhead of arbitration. Finally, PASE's transport protocol has an explicit notion of reference rate and priority queues, which leads to new rate control and loss recovery mechanisms.

In the following sections, we describe the control plane and the end-host transport protocol of PASE, followed by the details of its implementation.

## 3.1 Arbitration Control Plane

While a centralized arbitrator is an attractive option for multiple reasons, making it work in scenarios involving short flows is still an open problem [10, 15]. Prior work [18] shows that the problem of flow arbitration can indeed be solved in a distributed fashion: each switch along the path of a flow independently makes the arbitration decision and returns the allocated rate for its own link, and the source can pick the minimum rate. While prior work implements arbitration as part of the data plane, PASE supports this as part of the control plane because experiences with prior protocols (e.g., XCP [20]) show that even small changes to the data plane are hard to deploy.

We first describe the basic arbitration algorithm used in PASE and the key sources of overhead that limit the scalability of the arbitration process. We then present two optimizations that reduce the arbitration overhead by exploiting the characteristics of typical data center topologies.

**Algorithm 1** Arbitration Algorithm

**Input:** $< FlowSize, FlowID, demand(optional) >$
**Output:** $< PrioQue, R_{ref} >$
Arbitrator locally maintains a sorted list of flows
**Step#1:** Sort/update flow entry based on the $FlowSize$
**Step#2:** Compute $PrioQue$ and $R_{ref}$ of the flow.
//Link capacity is $C$, and AggregateDemandHigher ($ADH$) is the sum of demands of flows with priority higher than current flow.
1: Assign rate:
**if** $ADH < C$ **then**
$R_{ref} = min(demand, C - ADH)$;
**else**
$R_{ref} = baserate$;
**end if**
2: Assign $PrioQue$:
$PrioQue = \lceil ADH/C \rceil$;
**if** $PrioQue > LowestQueue$ **then**
$PrioQue = LowestQueue$;
**end if**
3: return $< PrioQue, R_{ref} >$;

### 3.1.1 Basic Arbitration Algorithm

For each link in the data center topology, there is an arbitrator that runs the arbitration algorithm and makes decisions for all flows that traverse the particular link. The arbitrator can be implemented on any server in the data center or on dedicated controllers that are co-located with the switches. The arbitration algorithm works at the granularity of a flow, where a flow could be a single RPC in a typical client-server interaction, or a long running TCP-like connection between two machines.

The interaction between a flow's source and the arbitrator(s) is captured in Algorithm 1. The source provides the arbitrator(s) with two pieces of information: i) the flow size (*FlowSize*), which is used as the criterion for scheduling (i.e., shortest flow first). To support other scheduling techniques, the *FlowSize* can be replaced by deadline [24] or task-id for task-aware scheduling [17]. ii) demand, this represents the maximum rate at which the source can send data. For long flows that can saturate the link, this is equal to the NIC rate, while for short flows that do not have enough data to saturate the link, this is set to a lower value. Demand and flow size are inputs to the arbitration algorithm whereas the output is the reference rate ($R_{ref}$) and a priority queue (*PrioQue*) of the flow.

To compute $R_{ref}$ and *PrioQue*, the arbitrator locally maintains a sorted list of flows based on their sizes. This list is updated based on the latest *FlowSize* information of the current flow. The flow's priority queue and reference rate depend on the aggregate demand (AggregateDemandHigher - or ADH) of flows that have higher priority compared to the current flow. An ADH value less than the link capacity $C$ implies that there is some spare capacity on the link and the flow can be mapped to the top queue. Thus, if the flow's demand is less than the spare capacity, we set the reference rate equal to the demand. Otherwise, we set the reference rate equal to the spare capacity.

The other case is when the ADH exceeds link capacity. This happens when a link is already saturated by higher priority flows, so the current flow cannot make it to the top queue. In this case, the flow's reference rate is set to a base value, which is equal to one packet per RTT. This allows such low priority flows to make progress in case some capacity becomes available in the network, and to even increase their rate in the future based on self-adjusting behavior.

Finally, if the current flow cannot be mapped to the top queue, it is either mapped to the lowest queue (if ADH exceeds the aggregate capacity of intermediate queues) or is mapped to one of the intermediate queues. Thus, each intermediate queue accommodates flows with an aggregate demand of $C$ and the last queue accommodates all the remaining flows.

**Challenges.** While the above design provides a simple distributed control plane for arbitration, it has three sources of overhead that limit its scalability.

- Communication Latency. The communication latency between the source and the arbitrator depends on their physical distance within the data center. This delay matters the most during flow setup time as it can end up increasing the FCT, especially for short flows. To keep this delay small, arbitrators must be placed carefully, such that they are located as close to the sources as possible.

- Processing Overhead. The second challenge is the processing overhead of arbitration messages, which can potentially add non-negligible delay, especially under high load scenarios.

- Network Overhead. Due to a separate control plane, each arbitration message is potentially processed as a separate packet by the switches which consumes link capacity. We need to ensure that this overhead is kept low and that it does not cause network congestion for our primary traffic.

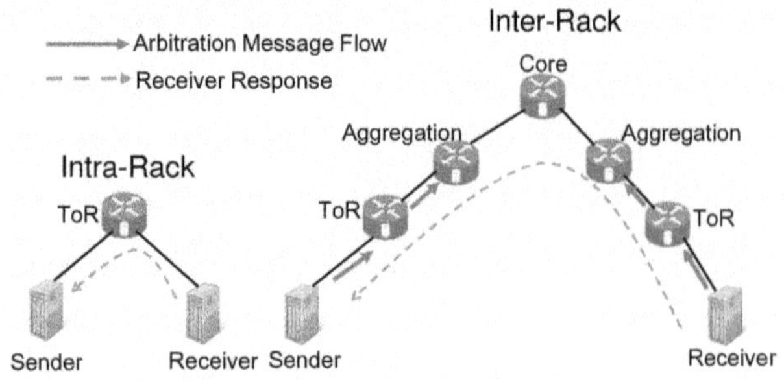


**Figure 5: The bottom-up approach employed by PASE for intra-rack and inter-rack scenarios.**

To reduce these overheads, we extend the basic PASE design by introducing a bottom-up approach to arbitration, which we describe next.

### *3.1.2 Bottom Up Arbitration*

We exploit the typical tree structure of data center topologies. Sources obtain information about the *PrioQue* and $R_{ref}$ in a bottom-up fashion, starting from the leaf nodes up to the core as shown in Figure 5. For this purpose, the end-to-end path between a source and destination is divided into two halves – one from the source up to the root and the other from the destination up to the root.

For each half, the respective leaf nodes (i.e., source and destination) initiate the arbitration. They start off with their link to the ToR switch and then move upwards. The arbitration request messages move up the arbitration hierarchy until it reaches the top level arbitrator. The responses move downwards in the opposite direction.

This bottom-up approach ensures that for intra-rack communication, arbitration is done solely at the endpoints, without involving any external arbitrator. Thus, in this scenario, flows incur no additional network latency for arbitration. This is particularly useful as many data center applications have communication patterns that have an explicit notion of rack affinity [11, 13].

For the inter-rack scenario, the bottom up approach facilitates two other optimizations, *early pruning* and *delegation*, to reduce the arbitration overhead and latency. Both early pruning and delegation exploit a trade-off between low overhead and high accuracy of arbitration. As our evaluation shows, by giving away some accuracy, they can significantly decrease the arbitration overhead.

**Early Pruning.** The network and processing overheads can be reduced by limiting the number of flows that contact the arbitrators for *PrioQue* and $R_{ref}$ information. In early pruning, only flows that are mapped to the highest priority queue move upwards for arbitration. Thus, in Algorithm 1 a lower level arbitrator only sends the arbitration message to its parent if the flow is mapped to the top queue(s). This results in lower priority flows being pruned at lower levels, as soon as they are mapped to lower priority queues (see Figure 6). The intuition behind this is that a flow mapped to a lower priority queue on one of its links will never make it to the highest priority queue irrespective of the arbitration decision on other links. This is because a flow always uses the lowest of the priority queues assigned by all the arbitrators (i.e., bottleneck in the path). Thus, we should avoid the overhead of making arbitration decisions for the flows mapped to lower priority queues.

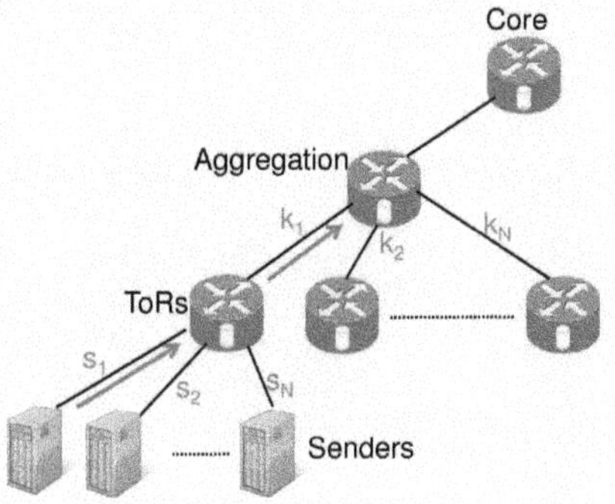


**Figure 6: The *early pruning* optimization used by PASE for reducing the arbitration overhead. Note that $s_i$ and $k_i$ represent flows that are mapped to the highest priority queue at the senders and the ToR arbitrators, respectively.**

There are two key benefits of early pruning. First, it reduces the network overhead as arbitration messages for only high priority flows propagate upwards. Second, it reduces the processing load on higher level arbitrators. In both cases, the reduction in overhead can be significant, especially in the more challenging heavy load scenarios, where such overhead can hurt system performance.

In general, early pruning makes the overhead independent of the total number of flows in the system. Instead, with early pruning, the overhead depends on the number of children that a higher level arbitrator may have because each child arbitrator only sends a limited number of flows (the top ones) upwards. Due to limited port density of modern switches (typically less than 100), the number of children, and hence the overhead, is quite small. This leads to significant reduction in the overhead compared to the non-pruning case where the overhead is proportional to the total number of flows traversing a link, which can be in thousands (or more) for typical data center settings [11, 13]. However, the above overhead reduction comes at the cost of less precise arbitration. As we only send the top flows to the higher level arbitrators, flows that are pruned do not get the complete and accurate arbitration information. Our evaluation shows that sending flows belonging to the top two queues upwards (rather than just the top queue), provides the right balance: there is little performance degradation while reduction in overhead is still significant.

**Delegation.** Delegation is specially designed to reduce the arbitration latency. While early pruning can significantly reduce the arbitration processing overhead as well as the network overhead, it does not reduce the latency involved in the arbitration decision because top flows still need to go all the way up to the top arbitrator.

In delegation, a higher level link (i.e., closer to the core) is divided into smaller "virtual" links of lower capacity – each virtual link is delegated to one of the child arbitrators who then becomes responsible for all arbitration decisions related to the virtual link. Thus, it can make a local decision about a higher level link without going to the corresponding arbitrator. On each virtual link, we run the same arbitration algorithm i.e., Algorithm 1 as we do for normal links.

As a simple example, the aggregation-core link of capacity $C$ shown in Figure 7 can be divided into $N$ virtual links of capacity $a_iC$ each (where $a_i$ is the fraction of capacity allocated to virtual link $i$) and then delegated to one of the child

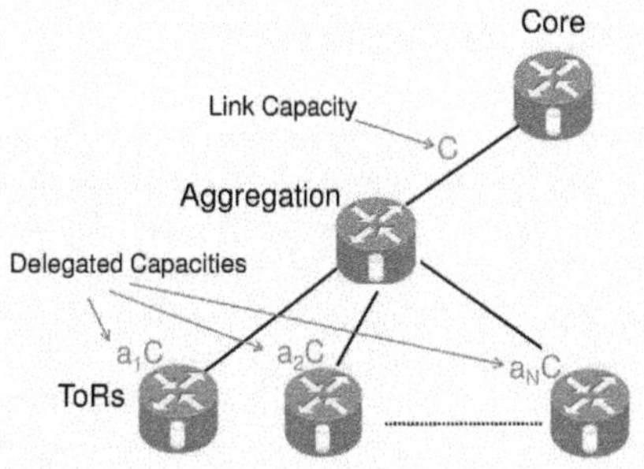


**Figure 7: The *delegation* optimization used by PASE for reducing the setup latency and control overhead.**

arbitrators. The capacity of each virtual link is updated periodically, reflecting the *PrioQue* of flows received by each child arbitrator. For example, one child that is consistently observing flows of higher priorities can get a virtual link of higher capacity.

Delegation provides two benefits. First, it reduces the flow setup delay because arbitration decisions for higher level links are made at lower level arbitrators, which are likely to be located close to the sources (e.g., within the rack). Second, it reduces the control traffic destined towards higher level arbitrators. Note that this happens because only *aggregate* information about flows is sent by the child arbitrators to their parents for determining the new share of virtual link capacities.

The impact on processing load has both positive and negative dimensions. While it reduces the processing load on higher level arbitrators, it ends up increasing the load on lower level arbitrators as they need to do arbitration for their parents' virtual links too. However, we believe this may be acceptable as lower level arbitrators typically deal with fewer flows compared to top level arbitrators.

Like early pruning, delegation also involves the overhead-accuracy trade-off. The capacity assigned to a specific virtual link may not be accurate which may lead to performance degradation. For example, we may have assigned a lower virtual capacity to a child who may suddenly start receiving higher priority flows. These flows would need to wait for an update to the virtual link capacity before they can get their due share. On the other hand, there could be cases where the virtual capacity may remain unused if the child does not have enough flows to use this capacity. This is especially true in scenarios where a link is delegated all the way to the end-host and the end-host may have a bursty flow arrival pattern.

Given the above trade-off, PASE only delegates the Aggregation-Core link capacity to its children (TOR-Aggregation arbitrators). These child arbitrators should be typically located within the rack of the source/destination (or co-located with the TOR switch). Thus, for any inter-rack communication within a typical three level tree topology, the source and destination only need to contact their TOR-aggregation arbitrator, who can do the arbitration all the way up to the root. In fact, flows need not wait for the feedback from the other half i.e., destination-root. Thus, in PASE, a flow starts as soon as it receives arbitration information from the child arbitrator. This approach is reasonable in scenarios where both halves of the tree are likely to have similar traffic patterns. If that is not true then PASE's self-adjusting behavior ensures that flows adjust accordingly.

### 3.2 End-host Transport

PASE's end-host transport builds on top of existing transports that use the self-adjusting endpoints strategy (e.g., DCTCP). Compared to existing protocols, the PASE transport has to deal with two new additional pieces: (a) a priority queue (*PrioQue*) on which a flow is mapped and (b) a reference sending rate ($R_{ref}$). This impacts two aspects of the transport protocol: rate control and loss recovery. Rate control in PASE is more guided and is closely tied to the $R_{ref}$ and the *PrioQue* of a flow. Similarly, the transport requires a new loss recovery mechanism because flows mapped to lower priority queues may experience spurious timeouts as they have to wait for a long time before they get an opportunity to send a packet. We now elaborate on these two aspects.

**Rate Control:** A PASE source uses the $R_{ref}$ and the *PrioQue* assigned by the arbitrators to guide its transmission rate. The rate control uses congestion window (*cwnd*) adjustment, based on the $R_{ref}$ and the flow RTT, to achieve the average reference rate at RTT timescales.

Algorithm 2 describes the rate control mechanism in PASE. For the flows mapped to the top queue, the congestion window is set to $R_{ref} \times RTT$ in order to reflect the reference rate assigned by the arbitrator. For all other flows, the congestion window is set to one packet. Note that for flows belonging to the top queue, the reference rate $R_{ref}$ is generally equal to the access link capacity unless flows have smaller sizes.

For the flows mapped to lower priority queues (except the bottom queue), the subsequent increase or decrease in congestion window *cwnd* is based on the well-studied control laws of DCTCP [11]. In particular, when an unmarked ACK is received, the window size is increased as

$$cwnd = cwnd + 1/cwnd. \quad (1)$$

When a marked ACK (i.e., with ECN-Echo flag set) is received, the window size is reduced as

$$cwnd = cwnd \times (1 - \alpha/2) \quad (2)$$

where $\alpha$ is the weighted average of the fraction of marked packets. This self-adjusting behavior for higher priority queues is important for ensuring high fabric utilization at all times because the $R_{ref}$ may not be accurate and there may be spare capacity or congestion along the path.

For the flows mapped to the bottom queue, the window size always remains one. This is because under high loads all flows that cannot make it to the top queues are mapped to the bottom queue, so the load on the bottom queue can be usually high.

**Loss Recovery:** For flows belonging to the top queue, we use existing loss recovery mechanisms (i.e., timeout based retransmissions). However, flows that get mapped to the lower priority queues can timeout for two reasons: (a) their packet(s) could not be transmitted because higher priority queues kept the link fully utilized and (b) a packet was lost. In case of scenario (a), a sender should avoid sending any new packets into the network as it increases the buffer occupancy and the likelihood of packet losses especially at high network loads. In case of scenario (b), a sender should retransmit the lost packet as early as it is possible so that the flows can make use of any available capacity without under-utilizing the network. However, differentiating between these two scenarios is a challenging task without incurring any additional overhead.

**Algorithm 2** Rate Control

```
Input: < PrioQue, R_ref >
Output: < cwnd > // congestion window
// Priority queues q_1, q_2,.., q_k where q_1 is the highest priority queue and q_2, q_3, and q_{k-1} are intermediate queues
// if an ACK with the ECN-Echo flag set is received
if ACK_marked == 1 then
cwnd = cwnd × (1 − α/2); // Use DCTCP decrease law
else
if PrioQue == q_1 then
cwnd = R_ref × RTT;
isInterQueue = 0; // not an intermediate queue
else if PrioQue ∈ {q_2, q_3, .., q_{k-1}} then
// if already mapped to an intermediate queue
if isInterQueue == 1 then
cwnd = 1 + 1/cwnd; // Use DCTCP increase law
else
isInterQueue = 1; cwnd = 1;
end if
else if PrioQue == q_k then
cwnd = 1; isInterQueue = 0;
end if
end if
```

We use small probe packets instead of retransmitting the entire packet whenever a flow, mapped to one of the lower priority queues, times out. If we receive an ACK for the probe packet (but not the original packet), it is a sign that the data packet was lost, so we retransmit the original data packet. If the probe packet is also delayed (no ACK received), we increase our timeout value (and resend another probe) just like we do this for successive losses for data packets. An alternative approach is to set suitable timeout values: smaller values for flows belonging to the top queue and larger values for the other flows.

Finally, a related issue is that of *packet reordering*. When a flow from a low priority queue gets mapped to a higher priority queue, packet re-ordering may occur as earlier packets may be buffered at the former queue. This can lead to unnecessary backoffs which degrades throughput. To address this, we ensure that when a flow moves to a higher priority queue, we wait for the ACKs of already sent packets to be received before sending packets with the updated priority.

### 3.3 Implementation

We implement PASE on a small-scale Linux testbed as well as in the ns2 simulator. Our ns2 implementation supports all the optimizations discussed in Section 3 whereas our testbed implementation only supports the basic arbitration algorithm (described in Section 3.1.1). For the testbed evaluation, we implement the transport protocol and the arbitration logic as Linux kernel modules. The Linux transport module, which is built on top of DCTCP, communicates with the arbitration module to obtain the packet priority and the reference rate. It then adds the PASE header on outgoing packets. For the desired switch support, we use the PRIO [7] queue and CBQ (class based queueing) implementation, on top of the RED queue implementation in Linux and ns2. We use eight priority queues/classes and

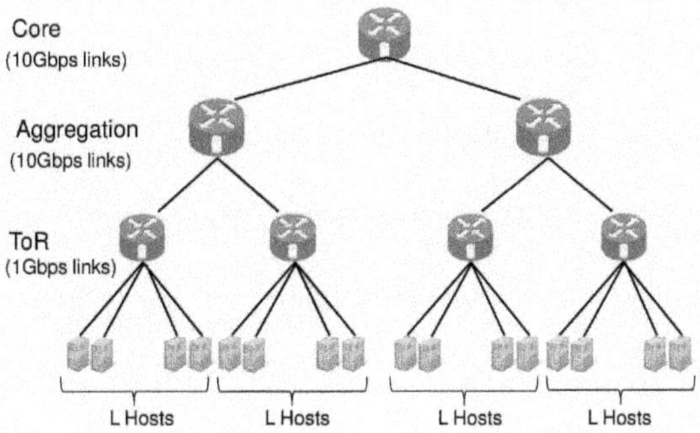


**Figure 8: Baseline topology used in simulations. Note that $L = 40$ hosts.**

classify packets based on the ToS field in the IP header. Out of these eight queues, a separate, strictly lower priority queue is maintained for background traffic. For the RED queue, we set the low and high thresholds of RED queue to $K$ and perform marking based on the instantaneous rather than the average queue length as done in DCTCP [11].

# 4. EVALUATION

In this section we evaluate the performance of PASE using the ns2 simulator [6] as well as through small-scale testbed experiments. First, we conduct macro-benchmark experiments in ns2 to compare PASE's performance against existing data center transports. We compare PASE against both deployment-friendly protocols including DCTCP [11], D$^2$TCP [23], and L$^2$DCT [22] (§4.2.1) as well as the best performing transport, namely, pFabric [12] (§4.2.2). Second, we micro-benchmark the internal working of PASE (e.g., benefits of arbitration optimizations, use of reference rate, etc) using simulations (§4.3). Finally, we report evaluation results for our testbed experiments (§4.4).

## 4.1 Simulation Settings

We now describe our simulation settings including the data center topology, traffic workloads, performance metrics, and the protocols compared.

**Data center Topology:** We use a 3-tier topology for our evaluation comprising layers of ToR (Top-of-Rack) switches, aggregation switches, and a core switch as shown in Figure 8. This is a commonly used topology in data centers [9, 23, 24]. The topology interconnects 160 hosts through 4 ToR switches that are connected to 2 aggregation switches, which in turn are interconnected via a core switch. Each host-ToR link has a capacity of 1 Gbps whereas all other links are of 10 Gbps. This results in an oversubscription ratio of 4:1 for the uplink from the ToR switches. In all the experiments, the arbitrators are co-located with their respective switches. The end-to-end round-trip propagation delay (in the absence of queueing) between hosts via the core switch is 300$\mu$s.

**Traffic Workloads:** We consider traffic workloads that are derived from patterns observed in production data centers. Flows arrive according to a Poisson process and flow sizes are drawn from the interval [2 KB, 198 KB] using a uniform distribution, as done in prior studies [18, 24]. This represents query traffic and latency sensitive short messages in data center networks. In addition to these flows, we generate two long-lived flows in the background, which represents the 75$^{th}$ percentile of multiplexing in data centers [11]. Note that we always use these settings unless specified otherwise.

| Scheme | Parameters |
|---|---|
| DCTCP<br>D$^2$TCP<br>L$^2$DCT | qSize = 225 pkts<br>markingThresh = 65<br>minRTO = 10 ms |
| pFabric | qSize = 76 pkts (= 2×BDP)<br>initCwnd = 38 pkts (= BDP)<br>minRTO = 1 ms (∼3.3×RTT) |
| PASE | qSize = 500 pkts<br>minRTO (flows in top queue) = 10 ms<br>minRTO (flows in other queues) = 200 ms<br>numQue = 8 |

**Table 3: Default simulation parameter settings.**

We consider two kinds of flows: *deadline-constrained flows* and *deadline-unconstrained flows*. They cover typical application requirements in today's data centers [23].

**Protocols Compared:** We compare PASE with several data center transports including DCTCP [11], D$^2$TCP [23], L$^2$DCT [22], and pFabric [12]. We implemented DCTCP, D$^2$TCP and L$^2$DCT in ns2 and use the source code of pFabric provided by the authors to evaluate their scheme. The parameters of these protocols are set according to the recommendations provided by the authors, or reflect the best settings, which we determined experimentally (see Table 3).

**Performance Metrics:** For traffic without any deadlines, we use the FCT as a metric. We consider the AFCT as well as the 99$^{th}$ percentile FCT for small flows. For deadline-constrained traffic, we use application throughput as our metric which is defined as the fraction of flows that meet their deadlines. We use the control messages per second to quantify the arbitration overhead.

## 4.2 Macro-benchmarks

### 4.2.1 *Comparison with Deployment Friendly Schemes*

PASE is a deployment friendly transport that does not require any changes to the network fabric. Therefore, we now compare PASE's performance with deployment friendly data center transports, namely, DCTCP and L$^2$DCT. DCTCP [11] is a *fair sharing* protocol that uses ECN marks to infer the degree of congestion and employs adaptive backoff factors to maintain small queues. The goal of L$^2$DCT [22] is to minimize FCT – it builds on DCTCP by *prioritizing* short flows over long flows through the use of adaptive control laws that depend on the size of the flows.

**Deadline-unconstrained flows:** We consider an inter-rack communication scenario (termed as *left-right*) where 80 hosts in the left subtree of the core switch generate traffic towards hosts in the right subtree. This is a common scenario in user-facing web services where the front-end servers and the back-end storage reside in separate racks [25]. The generated traffic comprises flows with sizes drawn from the interval [2 KB, 198 KB] using a uniform distribution. In addition, we generate two long-lived flows in the background.

Figure 9(a) shows the improvement in AFCT as a function of network load. Observe that PASE outperforms L$^2$DCT and DCTCP by at least 50% and 70%, respectively across a wide range of loads. At low loads, PASE performs better primarily because of its quick convergence to the correct rate for each flow. At higher loads, PASE ensures that shorter flows are *strictly* prioritized over long flows, whereas with L$^2$DCT, all flows, irrespective of their priorities, continue to send at least one packet into the network. This lack

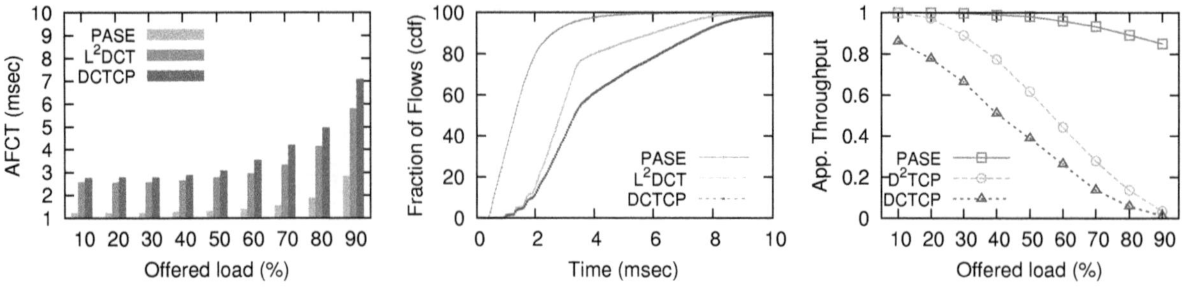


(a) AFCT (b) CDF of FCTs (c) Application Throughput

**Figure 9: (a) Comparison of PASE with $L^2$DCT and DCTCP in terms of AFCTs under the (*left-right*) inter-rack scenario, (b) shows the CDF of FCTs at 70% load in case of (a), and (c) Deadline-constrained flows: Comparison of application throughput for PASE with $D^2$TCP and DCTCP under the intra-rack scenario.**

of support for strict priority scheduling in $L^2$DCT leads to larger FCTs for short flows. DCTCP does not prioritize short flows over long flows. Thus, it results in worst FCTs across all protocols.

Figure 9(b) shows the CDF of FCTs at 70% load. Observe that PASE results in better FCTs for almost all flows compared to $L^2$DCT and DCTCP.

***Deadline-constrained flows:*** We now consider latency-sensitive flows that have specific deadlines associated with them. Thus, we compare PASE's performance with $D^2$TCP, a deadline-aware transport protocol. We replicate the $D^2$TCP experiment from [23] (also described earlier in §2) which considers an intra-rack scenario with 20 machines and generate short query traffic with flow sizes drawn from the interval [100 KB, 500 KB] using a uniform distribution. Figure 9(c) shows the application throughput as a function of network load. PASE significantly outperforms $D^2$TCP and DCTCP, especially at high loads because of the large number of active flows in the network. Since each $D^2$TCP and DCTCP flow sends at least one packet per RTT, these flows consume significant network capacity which makes it difficult for a large fraction of flows to meet their respective deadlines. PASE, on the other hand, ensures that flows with the earliest deadlines are given the desired rates and are strictly prioritized inside the switches.

### *4.2.2 Comparison with Best Performing Scheme*

We now compare the performance of PASE with pFabric, which achieves close to optimal performance in several scenarios but requires changes in switches. With pFabric, packets carry a priority number that is set independently by each flow. Based on this, pFabric switches perform priority-based scheduling and dropping. All flows start at the line rate and backoff only under persistent packet loss.

PASE performs better than pFabric in two important scenarios: (a) multi-link (single rack) scenarios with all-to-all traffic patterns and (b) at high loads (generally $>80\%$) whereas it achieves similar performance ($<6\%$ difference in AFCTs) compared to pFabric in the following two cases: (a) single bottleneck scenarios and (b) when the network load is typically less than 80%.

We first consider the *left-right* inter-rack scenario where the aggregation-core link becomes the bottleneck. Figure 10(a) shows the $99^{th}$ percentile FCT as a function of load. Observe that pFabric achieves smaller FCT for up to 50% load and PASE achieves comparable performance. However, at $\geq 60\%$ loads, PASE results in smaller FCT than pFabric. At 90% load, this improvement is more than 85%. This happens due to high and persistent loss rate with pFabric at high loads. Figure 10(b) shows the CDF of FCT at 70% load for the same scenario.

Next we consider an all-to-all intra-rack scenario, which is common in applications like web search where responses from several worker nodes within a rack are combined by an aggregator node before a final response is sent to the user. Moreover, any node within a rack can be an aggregator node for a user query and the aggregators are picked in a round robin fashion to achieve load balancing [8].

Figure 10(c) shows that PASE provides up to 85% improvement in AFCT over pFabric and results in lower AFCTs across *all* loads. This happens because with pFabric multiple flows sending at line rate can collide at a downstream ToR-host link. This causes a significant amount of network capacity to be wasted on the host-ToR links, which could have been used by other flows (as this is an all-to-all scenario). With PASE, flows do not incur any arbitration latency in the intra-rack scenario as new flows start sending traffic at line rate based on the information (priority and reference rate) from their local arbitrator. After one RTT, all flows obtain their global priorities which helps in avoiding any persistent loss of throughput in case the local and global priorities are different.

## 4.3 Micro-benchmarks

In this section, we evaluate the basic components of PASE with the help of several micro-benchmarks. Our results show that PASE optimizations significantly reduce the control traffic overhead and the number of messages that arbitrators need to process. In addition, we find that other features of PASE such as its rate control are important for achieving high performance.

### *4.3.1 Arbitration Optimizations*

PASE introduces early pruning and delegation for reducing the arbitration overhead of update messages. We now evaluate the overhead reduction brought about by these optimizations as well as study their impact on the performance of PASE. Figure 11(b) shows the overhead reduction that is achieved by PASE when all its optimizations are enabled. Observe that these optimizations provide up to 50% reduction in arbitration overhead especially at high loads. This happens because when these optimizations are enabled, higher-level arbitrators delegate some portion of the bandwidth to lower level arbitrators, which significantly reduces

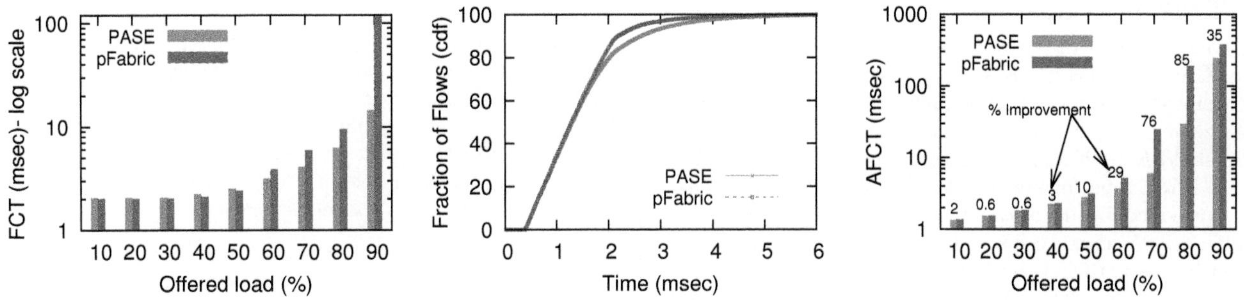


(a) *left-right* inter-rack (b) *left-right* inter-rack (c) all-to-all intra-rack

**Figure 10: Comparison of PASE with pFabric under (a) $99^{th}$ percentile FCT in the *left-right* inter-rack scenario, (b) CDF of FCTs under the *left-right* scenario at 70% load, and (c) all-to-all intra-rack scenario.**

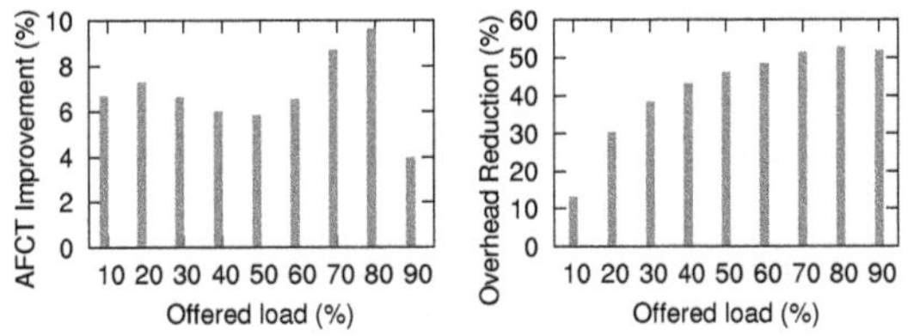


(a) AFCT (b) Overhead

**Figure 11: AFCT improvement and overhead reduction as a function of load for PASE with its optimizations in the *left-right* scenario.**

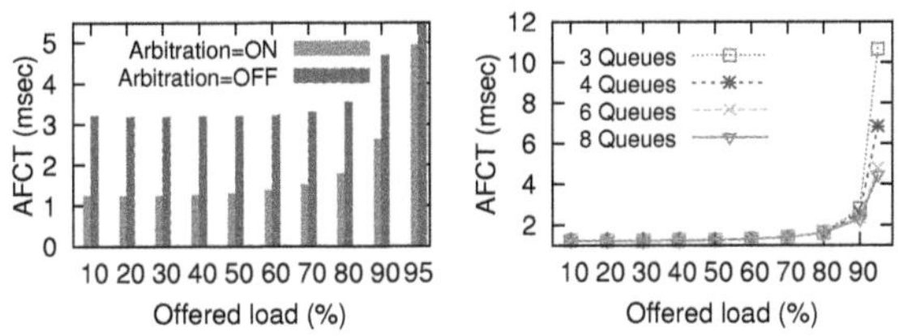


(a) AFCT (b) Priority Queues

**Figure 12: (a) Comparison of AFCT with and without end-to-end arbitration and (b) PASE with varying number of priority queues (*left-right* scenario).**

the control overhead on ToR-Aggregation links. In addition, updates of only those flows are propagated that map to the highest priority queues due to early pruning. Figure 11(a) shows that these optimizations also improve the AFCT by 4-10% across all loads. This happens because of delegation, which reduces the arbitration delays.

**Benefit of end-to-end arbitration:** PASE enables global prioritization among flows through its scalable end-to-end arbitration mechanism. This arbitration, however, requires additional update messages to be sent on the network. It is worth asking if most of the benefits of PASE are realizable through only local arbitration, which can be solely done by the endpoints. Thus, we now compare the performance of end-to-end arbitration and local arbitration in the *left-right* inter-rack scenario. Figure 12(a) shows that end-to-end arbitration leads to significant improvements (up to 60%) in AFCTs across a wide range of loads. This happens because local arbitration cannot account for scenarios where contention does not occur on the access links, thus leading to sub-optimal performance.

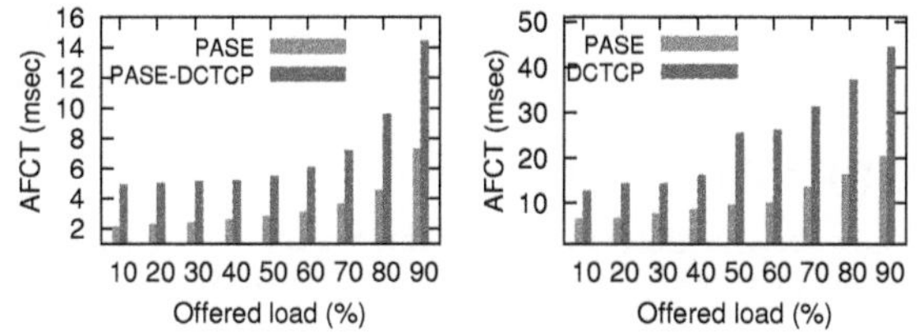


(a) PASE vs PASE-DCTCP (b) Testbed Evaluation

**Figure 13: (a) Comparison of PASE with PASE-DCTCP in the intra-rack scenario with 20 nodes and uniformly distributed flow sizes from [100 KB, 500 KB] and (b) Testbed Evaluation: Comparison of AFCT for PASE with DCTCP.**

### 4.3.2 *In-network Prioritization and Transport Micro-benchmarks*

**Impact of number of priority queues:** We now evaluate the impact of changing the number of priority queues in the switches. To test this scenario we repeat the *left-right* inter-rack scenario with different number of queues. Figure 12(b) shows that using 4 queues provide significant improvement in AFCT at loads $\geq 70\%$. However, increasing the number of queues beyond this provides only marginal improvement in AFCT. These results further reinforce the ability of PASE to achieve high performance with existing switches that support a limited number of priority queues.

**Reference Rate:** We now evaluate the benefit of using the reference rate information. We compare PASE with PASE-DCTCP, where *all* flows (including the ones mapped to the top queue as well as the lowest priority queue) behave as DCTCP sources and do not use the reference rate. However, these flows are mapped to different priority queues through the normal arbitration process. As shown in Figure 13(a), leveraging reference rate results in AFCTs of PASE to be 50% smaller than the AFCTs for PASE-DCTCP.

**Impact of RTO and Probing:** Flows that are mapped to the lower priority queues may experience large number of timeouts, which can affect performance. We implemented probing in which flows mapped to the lowest priority queue send a header-only probe packet every RTT rather than a full-sized packet. We found that using probing improves performance by $\approx 2.4\%$ and $\approx 11\%$ at 80% and 90% loads, respectively in the all-to-all intra-rack scenario. Note that unlike pFabric, PASE does not require small RTOs which forgoes the need to have high resolution timers.

### 4.4 Testbed Evaluation

We now present a subset of results from our testbed evaluation. Our testbed comprises of a single rack of 10 nodes (9 clients, one server), with 1 Gbps links, 250 $\mu$sec RTT and a queue size of 100 packets on each interface. We set the marking threshold $K$ to 20 packets and use 8 priority queues. We compare PASE's performance with the DCTCP implementation (provided by its authors). To emulate data center like settings, we generate flows sizes that are uniformly distributed between 100 KB and 500 KB, as done in [23]. We start 1000 short flows and vary the flow arrival rate to generate a load between 10% to 90%. In addition, we also generate a long lived background flow from one of the clients. We compare PASE with DCTCP and report the average of ten runs. Figure 13(b) shows the AFCT for both the schemes. Observe that PASE significantly outperforms DCTCP: it achieves ≈50%-60% smaller AFCTs compared to DCTCP. This also matches the results we observed in ns2 simulations.

## 5. RELATED WORK

We now briefly describe and contrast our work with the most relevant research works. We categorize prior works in terms of the underlying transport strategies they use.

**Self-Adjusting Endpoints:** Several data center transports use this strategy [11, 14, 22, 23]. DCTCP uses an adaptive congestion control mechanism based on ECN to maintain low queues. $D^2$TCP and $L^2$DCT add deadline-awareness and size-awareness to DCTCP, respectively. MCP [14] improves performance over $D^2$TCP by assigning more precise flow rates using ECN marks. These rates are based on the solution of a stochastic delay minimization problem. These protocols do not support flow preemption and in-network prioritization, which limits their performance.

**Arbitration:** PDQ [18] and $D^3$ [24] use network-wide arbitration but incur high flow switching overhead. PASE's bottom up approach to arbitration has similarities with EyeQ [19], which targets a different problem of providing bandwidth guarantees in multi-tenant cloud data centers. PASE's arbitration mechanism generalizes EyeQ's arbitration by dealing with scenarios where contention can happen at links other than the access links.

**In-network Prioritization:** pFabric [12] uses in-network prioritization by doing priority-based scheduling and dropping of packets. DeTail [25], a cross layer network stack, focuses on minimizing the *tail* latency but does not target the average FCT. In [21], authors propose virtual shapers to overcome the challenge of limited number of rate limiters. While both DeTail and virtual shapers use in-network prioritization, they do not deal with providing mechanisms for achieving network-wide arbitration.

In general, prior proposals target one specific transport strategy, PASE uses all these strategies in unison to overcome limitations of individual strategies and thus achieves high performance across a wide range of scenarios while being deployment friendly.

## 6. CONCLUSION

We proposed PASE, a transport framework that synthesizes existing transport strategies. PASE is deployment friendly as it does not require any changes to the network fabric and yet, its performance is comparable to, or better than the state-of-the-art protocols that require changes to network elements. The design of PASE includes a scalable arbitration control plane which is specifically tailored for typical data center topologies, and an end-host transport that explicitly uses priority queues and information from arbitrators. We believe that PASE sets out a new direction for data center transports, where advances in specific techniques (e.g., better in-network prioritization mechanisms or improved control laws) benefit everyone.

**Acknowledgements:** We thank our shepherd, Nandita Dukkipati, and the SIGCOMM reviewers for their feedback. We also thank Thomas Karagiannis and Zafar Ayyub Qazi for their useful comments.

## 7. REFERENCES


[1] Arista 7050s switch. http://www.aristanetworks.com/docs/Manuals/ConfigGuide.pdf.

[2] Broadcom bcm56820 switch. http://www.broadcom.com/collateral/pb/56820-PB00-R.pdf.

[3] Dell force10 s4810 switch. http://www.force10networks.com/CSPortal20/KnowledgeBase/DOCUMENTATION/CLIConfig/FTOS/Z9000_CLI_8.3.11.4_23-May-2012.pdf.

[4] Ibm rackswitch g8264 application guide. http://www.bladenetwork.net/userfiles/file/G8264_AG_6-8.pdf.

[5] Juniper ex3300 switch. http://www.juniper.net/us/en/products-services/switching/ex-series/ex3300/.

[6] The network simulator - ns-2. http://www.isi.edu/nsnam/ns/.

[7] Prio qdisc linux. http://linux.die.net/man/8/tc-prio, 2006.

[8] D. Abts and B. Felderman. A guided tour of data-center networking. *Commun. ACM*, 55(6):44–51, June 2012.

[9] M. Al-Fares, A. Loukissas, and A. Vahdat. A Scalable, Commodity Data Center Network Architecture. In *SIGCOMM'08*.

[10] M. Al-Fares, S. Radhakrishnan, B. Raghavan, N. Huang, and A. Vahdat. Hedera: dynamic flow scheduling for data center networks. In *NSDI'10*.

[11] M. Alizadeh, A. G. Greenberg, D. A. Maltz, J. Padhye, P. Patel, B. Prabhakar, S. Sengupta, and M. Sridharan. Data center TCP (DCTCP). In *SIGCOMM'10*.

[12] M. Alizadeh, S. Yang, M. Sharif, S. Katti, N. McKeown, B. Prabhakar, and S. Shenker. pfabric: Minimal near-optimal datacenter transport. In *SIGCOMM'13*.

[13] T. Benson, A. Akella, and D. A. Maltz. Network traffic characteristics of data centers in the wild. In *IMC'10*.

[14] L. Chen, S. Hu, K. Chen, H. Wu, and D. H. K. Tsang. Towards minimal-delay deadline-driven data center tcp. In *Hotnets'13*.

[15] A. Curtis, J. Mogul, J. Tourrilhes, P. Yalagandula, P. Sharma, and S. Banerjee. Devoflow: scaling flow management for high-performance networks. In *SIGCOMM'11*.

[16] J. Dean and S. Ghemawat. MapReduce: Simplified Data Processing on Large Clusters. In *OSDI'04*.

[17] F. R. Dogar, T. Karagiannis, H. Ballani, and A. Rowstron. Decentralized Task-aware Scheduling for Data Center Networks. In *SIGCOMM'14*.

[18] C. Hong, M. Caesar, and P. Godfrey. Finishing flows quickly with preemptive scheduling. In *SIGCOMM'12*.

[19] V. Jeyakumar, M. Alizadeh, D. Mazieres, B. Prabhakar, C. Kim, and A. Greenberg. EyeQ: Practical Network Performance Isolation at the Edge. In *NSDI'13*.

[20] D. Katabi, M. Handley, and C. Rohrs. Congestion Control for High Bandwidth-Delay Product Networks. In *SIGCOMM'02*.

[21] G. Kumar, S. Kandula, P. Bodik, and I. Menache. Virtualizing traffic shapers for practical resource allocation. In *HotCloud'13*.

[22] A. Munir, I. A. Qazi, Z. A. Uzmi, A. Mushtaq, S. N. Ismail, M. S. Iqbal, and B. Khan. Minimizing Flow Completion Times in Data Centers. In *INFOCOM'13*.

[23] B. Vamanan, J. Hasan, and T. Vijaykumar. Deadline-aware datacenter tcp ($d^2$tcp). In *SIGCOMM'12*.

[24] C. Wilson, H. Ballani, T. Karagiannis, and A. Rowstron. Better never than late: Meeting deadlines in datacenter networks. In *SIGCOMM'11*.

[25] D. Zats, T. Das, P. Mohan, D. Borthakur, and R. Katz. Detail: Reducing the flow completion time tail in datacenter networks. In *SIGCOMM'12*.

# CONGA: Distributed Congestion-Aware Load Balancing for Datacenters

Mohammad Alizadeh, Tom Edsall, Sarang Dharmapurikar, Ramanan Vaidyanathan, Kevin Chu, Andy Fingerhut, Vinh The Lam (Google), Francis Matus, Rong Pan, Navindra Yadav, George Varghese (Microsoft)
Cisco Systems

## ABSTRACT

We present the design, implementation, and evaluation of CONGA, a network-based distributed congestion-aware load balancing mechanism for datacenters. CONGA exploits recent trends including the use of regular Clos topologies and overlays for network virtualization. It splits TCP flows into flowlets, estimates real-time congestion on fabric paths, and allocates flowlets to paths based on feedback from remote switches. This enables CONGA to efficiently balance load and seamlessly handle asymmetry, without requiring any TCP modifications. CONGA has been implemented in custom ASICs as part of a new datacenter fabric. In testbed experiments, CONGA has 5× better flow completion times than ECMP even with a single link failure and achieves 2–8× better throughput than MPTCP in Incast scenarios. Further, the Price of Anarchy for CONGA is provably small in Leaf-Spine topologies; hence CONGA is nearly as effective as a centralized scheduler while being able to react to congestion in microseconds. Our main thesis is that datacenter fabric load balancing is best done in the network, and requires global schemes such as CONGA to handle asymmetry.

**Categories and Subject Descriptors:** C.2.1 [Computer-Communication Networks]: Network Architecture and Design
**Keywords:** Datacenter fabric; Load balancing; Distributed

## 1. INTRODUCTION

Datacenter networks being deployed by cloud providers as well as enterprises must provide large bisection bandwidth to support an ever increasing array of applications, ranging from financial services to big-data analytics. They also must provide agility, enabling any application to be deployed at any server, in order to realize operational efficiency and reduce costs. Seminal papers such as VL2 [18] and Portland [1] showed how to achieve this with Clos topologies, Equal Cost MultiPath (ECMP) load balancing, and the decoupling of endpoint addresses from their location. These design principles are followed by next generation overlay technologies that accomplish the same goals using standard encapsulations such as VXLAN [35] and NVGRE [45].

However, it is well known [2, 41, 9, 27, 44, 10] that ECMP can balance load poorly. First, because ECMP randomly hashes flows to paths, hash collisions can cause significant imbalance if there are a few large flows. More importantly, ECMP uses a purely *local* decision to split traffic among equal cost paths without knowledge of potential downstream congestion on each path. Thus ECMP fares poorly with *asymmetry* caused by link failures that occur frequently and are disruptive in datacenters [17, 34]. For instance, the recent study by Gill *et al.* [17] shows that failures can reduce delivered traffic by up to 40% despite built-in redundancy.

Broadly speaking, the prior work on addressing ECMP's shortcomings can be classified as either centralized scheduling (e.g., Hedera [2]), local switch mechanisms (e.g., Flare [27]), or host-based transport protocols (e.g., MPTCP [41]). These approaches all have important drawbacks. Centralized schemes are too slow for the traffic volatility in datacenters [28, 8] and local congestion-aware mechanisms are suboptimal and can perform even worse than ECMP with asymmetry (§2.4). Host-based methods such as MPTCP are challenging to deploy because network operators often do not control the end-host stack (e.g., in a public cloud) and even when they do, some high performance applications (such as low latency storage systems [39, 7]) bypass the kernel and implement their own transport. Further, host-based load balancing adds more complexity to an already complex transport layer burdened by new requirements such as low latency and burst tolerance [4] in datacenters. As our experiments with MPTCP show, this can make for brittle performance (§5).

Thus from a philosophical standpoint it is worth asking: Can load balancing be done in the network without adding to the complexity of the transport layer? Can such a network-based approach compute globally optimal allocations, and yet be implementable in a realizable and distributed fashion to allow rapid reaction in microseconds? Can such a mechanism be deployed today using standard encapsulation formats? We seek to answer these questions in this paper with a new scheme called CONGA (for *Cong*estion *A*ware Balancing). CONGA has been implemented in custom ASICs for a major new datacenter fabric product line. While we report on lab experiments using working hardware together with simulations and mathematical analysis, customer trials are scheduled in a few months as of the time of this writing.

Figure 1 surveys the design space for load balancing and places CONGA in context by following the thick red lines through the design tree. At the highest level, CONGA is a distributed scheme to allow rapid round-trip timescale reaction to congestion to cope with bursty datacenter traffic [28, 8]. CONGA is implemented within the network to avoid the deployment issues of host-based methods and additional complexity in the transport layer. To deal with asymmetry, unlike earlier proposals such as Flare [27] and LocalFlow [44] that only use local information, CONGA uses global congestion information, a design choice justified in detail in §2.4.


*SIGCOMM'14*, August 17–22, 2014, Chicago, IL, USA.
Copyright 2014 ACM 978-1-4503-2836-4/14/08 ...$15.00.
http://dx.doi.org/10.1145/2619239.2626316 .

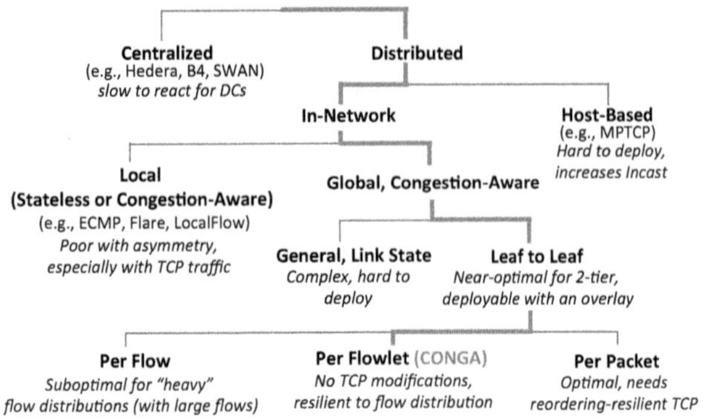


**Figure 1: Design space for load balancing.**

Next, the most general design would sense congestion on every link and send generalized link state packets to compute congestion-sensitive routes [16, 48, 51, 36]. However, this is an N-party protocol with complex control loops, likely to be fragile and hard to deploy. Recall that the early ARPANET moved briefly to such congestion-sensitive routing and then returned to static routing, citing instability as a reason [31]. CONGA instead uses a 2-party "leaf-to-leaf" mechanism to convey path-wise congestion metrics between pairs of top-of-the-rack switches (also termed leaf switches) in a datacenter fabric. The leaf-to-leaf scheme is provably near-optimal in typical 2-tier Clos topologies (henceforth called *Leaf-Spine*), simple to analyze, and easy to deploy. In fact, it is deployable in datacenters today with standard overlay encapsulations (VXLAN [35] in our implementation) which are already being used to enable workload agility [33].

With the availability of very high-density switching platforms for the spine (or core) with 100s of 40Gbps ports, a 2-tier fabric can scale upwards of 20,000 10Gbps ports.[1] This design point covers the needs of the overwhelming majority of enterprise datacenters, which are the primary deployment environments for CONGA.

Finally, in the lowest branch of the design tree, CONGA is constructed to work with flowlets [27] to achieve a higher granularity of control and resilience to the flow size distribution while not requiring any modifications to TCP. Of course, CONGA could also be made to operate per packet by using a very small flowlet inactivity gap (see §3.4) to perform optimally with a *future* reordering-resilient TCP.

In summary, our major contributions are:

- We design (§3) and implement (§4) CONGA, a distributed congestion-aware load balancing mechanism for datacenters. CONGA is immediately deployable, robust to asymmetries caused by link failures, reacts to congestion in microseconds, and requires no end-host modifications.

- We extensively evaluate (§5) CONGA with a hardware testbed and packet-level simulations. We show that even with a single link failure, CONGA achieves more than 5× better flow completion time and 2× better job completion time respectively for a realistic datacenter workload and a standard Hadoop Distributed File System benchmark. CONGA is at least as good as MPTCP for load balancing while outperforming MPTCP by 2–8× in Incast [47, 12] scenarios.

- We analyze (§6) CONGA and show that it is nearly optimal in 2-tier Leaf-Spine topologies using "Price of Anarchy" [40] analysis. We also prove that load balancing behavior and the effectiveness of flowlets depends on the coefficient of variation of the flow size distribution.

[1]For example, spine switches with 576 40Gbps ports can be paired with typical 48-port leaf switches to enable non-blocking fabrics with 27,648 10Gbps ports.

## 2. DESIGN DECISIONS

This section describes the insights that inform CONGA's major design decisions. We begin with the desired properties that have guided our design. We then revisit the design decisions shown in Figure 1 in more detail from the top down.

### 2.1 Desired Properties

CONGA is an in-network congestion-aware load balancing mechanism for datacenter fabrics. In designing CONGA, we targeted a solution with a number of key properties:

1. **Responsive:** Datacenter traffic is very volatile and bursty [18, 28, 8] and switch buffers are shallow [4]. Thus, with CONGA, we aim for rapid round-trip timescale (e.g., 10s of microseconds) reaction to congestion.

2. **Transport independent:** As a network mechanism, CONGA must be oblivious to the transport protocol at the end-host (TCP, UDP, etc). Importantly, it should not require any modifications to TCP.

3. **Robust to asymmetry:** CONGA must handle asymmetry due to link failures (which have been shown to be frequent and disruptive in datacenters [17, 34]) or high bandwidth flows that are not well balanced.

4. **Incrementally deployable:** It should be possible to apply CONGA to only a subset of the traffic and only a subset of the switches.

5. **Optimized for Leaf-Spine topology:** CONGA must work optimally for 2-tier *Leaf-Spine* topologies (Figure 4) that cover the needs of most enterprise datacenter deployments, though it should also benefit larger topologies.

### 2.2 Why Distributed Load Balancing?

The distributed approach we advocate is in stark contrast to recently proposed centralized traffic engineering designs [2, 9, 23, 21]. This is because of two important features of datacenters. First, datacenter traffic is very bursty and unpredictable [18, 28, 8]. CONGA reacts to congestion at RTT timescales ($\sim$100$\mu$s) making it more adept at handling high volatility than a centralized scheduler. For example, the Hedera scheduler in [2] runs every 5 seconds; but it would need to run every 100ms to approach the performance of a distributed solution such as MPTCP [41], which is itself outperformed by CONGA (§5). Second, datacenters use very regular topologies. For instance, in the common Leaf-Spine topology (Figure 4), all paths are exactly two-hops. As our experiments (§5) and analysis (§6) show, distributed decisions are close to optimal in such regular topologies.

Of course, a centralized approach is appropriate for WANs where traffic is stable and predictable and the topology is arbitrary. For example, Google's inter-datacenter traffic engineering algorithm needs to run just 540 times per day [23].

### 2.3 Why In-Network Load Balancing?

Continuing our exploration of the design space (Figure 1), the next question is *where* should datacenter fabric load balancing be implemented — the transport layer at the end-hosts or the network?

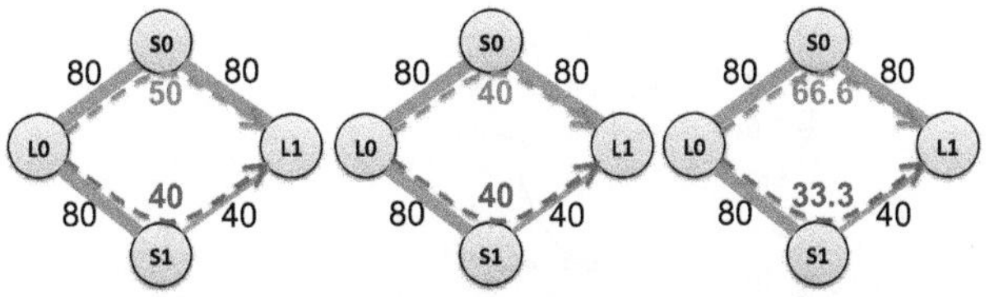

(a) Static (ECMP) (b) Congestion-Aware: Local Only (c) Congestion-Aware: Global (CONGA)

**Figure 2: Congestion-aware load balancing needs non-local information with asymmetry. Here, L0 has 100Gbps of TCP traffic to L1, and the (S1, L1) link has half the capacity of the other links. Such cases occur in practice with link-aggregation (which is very common), for instance, if a link fails in a fabric with two 40Gbps links connecting each leaf and spine switch.**

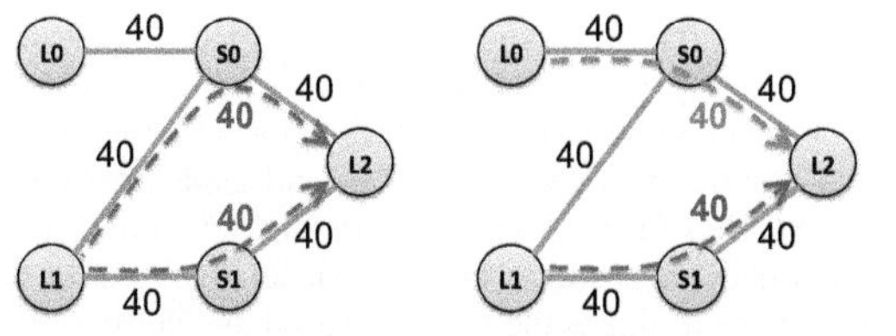

(a) L0➔L2=0, L1➔L2=80 (b) L0➔L2=40, L1➔L2=40

**Figure 3: Optimal traffic split in asymmetric topologies depends on the traffic matrix. Here, the L1→L2 flow must adjust its traffic through S0 based on the amount of L0→L2 traffic.**

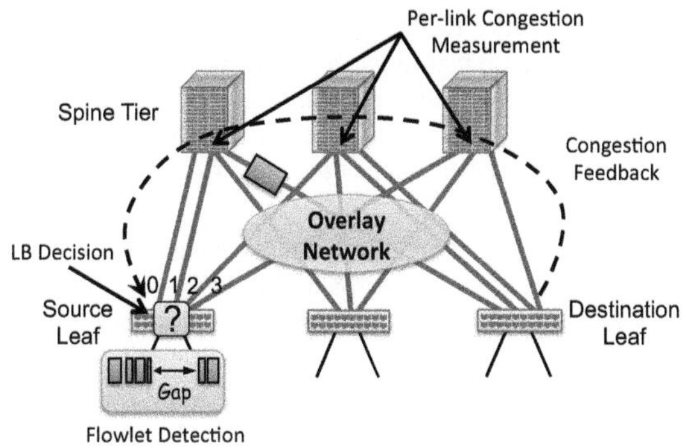


**Figure 4: CONGA architecture. The source leaf switch detects flowlets and routes them via the least congested path to the destination using congestion metrics obtained from leaf-to-leaf feedback. Note that the topology could be asymmetric.**

The state-of-the-art multipath transport protocol, MPTCP [41], splits each connection into multiple (e.g., 8) sub-flows and balances traffic across the sub-flows based on perceived congestion. Our experiments (§5) show that while MPTCP is effective for load balancing, its use of multiple sub-flows actually increases congestion at the edge of the network and degrades performance in Incast scenarios (Figure 13). Essentially, MPTCP increases the burstiness of traffic as more sub-flows contend at the fabric's access links. Note that this occurs despite MPTCP's coupled congestion control algorithm [50] which is designed to handle shared bottlenecks, because while the coupled congestion algorithm works if flows are in steady-state, in realistic datacenter workloads many flows are short-lived and transient [18].

The larger architectural point however is that datacenter fabric load balancing is too specific to be implemented in the transport stack. Datacenter fabrics are highly-engineered, homogenous systems [1, 34]. They are designed from the onset to behave like a giant switch [18, 1, 25], much like the internal fabric within large modular switches. Binding the fabric's load balancing behavior to the transport stack which already needs to balance multiple important requirements (e.g., high throughput, low latency, and burst tolerance [4]) is architecturally unappealing. Further, some datacenter applications such as high performance storage systems bypass the kernel altogether [39, 7] and hence cannot use MPTCP.

## 2.4 Why Global Congestion Awareness?

Next, we consider local versus global schemes (Figure 1). Handling asymmetry essentially requires *non-local* knowledge about downstream congestion at the switches. With asymmetry, a switch cannot simply balance traffic based on the congestion of its local links. In fact, this may lead to even worse performance than a static scheme such as ECMP (which does not consider congestion at all) because of poor interaction with TCP's control loop.

As an illustration, consider the simple asymmetric scenario in Figure 2. Leaf L0 has 100Gbps of TCP traffic demand to Leaf L1. Static ECMP splits the *flows* equally, achieving a throughput of 90Gbps because the flows on the lower path are bottlenecked at the 40Gbps link (S1, L1). Local congestion-aware load balancing *is actually worse* with a throughput of 80Gbps. This is because as TCP slows down the flows on the lower path, the link (L0, S1) appears *less* congested. Hence, paradoxically, the local scheme shifts more traffic to the lower link until the throughput on the upper link is also 40 Gbps. This example illustrates a fundamental limitation of any local scheme (such as Flare [27], LocalFlow [44], and packet-spraying [10]) that strictly enforces an equal traffic split without regard for downstream congestion. Of course, global congestion-aware load balancing (as in CONGA) does not have this issue.

The reader may wonder if asymmetry can be handled by some form of oblivious routing [32] such as weighted random load balancing with weights chosen according to the topology. For instance, in the above example we could give the lower path half the weight of the upper path and achieve the same traffic split as CONGA. While this works in this case, it fails in general because the "right" traffic splits in asymmetric topologies depend also on the traffic matrix, as shown by the example in Figure 3. Here, depending on how much L0→L2 traffic there is, the optimal split for L1→L2 traffic changes. Hence, static weights cannot handle both cases in Figure 3. Note that in this example, the two L1→L2 paths are symmetric when considered in isolation. But because of an asymmetry in another part of the network, the L0→L2 traffic creates a *bandwidth asymmetry* for the L1→L2 traffic that can only be detected by considering non-local congestion. Note also that a local congestion-aware mechanism could actually perform worse than ECMP; for example, in the scenario in part (b).

## 2.5 Why Leaf-to-Leaf Feedback?

At the heart of CONGA is a leaf-to-leaf feedback mechanism that conveys real-time path congestion metrics to the leaf switches. The leaves use these metrics to make congestion-aware load balancing decisions based on the global (fabric-wide) state of congestion (Figure 4). We now argue (following Figure 1) why leaf-to-leaf congestion signaling is simple and natural for modern data centers.

**Overlay network:** CONGA operates in an overlay network consisting of "tunnels" between the fabric's leaf switches. When an endpoint (server or VM) sends a packet to the fabric, the source leaf, or source tunnel endpoint (TEP), looks up the destination endpoint's address (either MAC or IP) to determine to which leaf (destination TEP) the packet needs to be sent.[2] It then encapsulates the packet — with outer source and destination addresses set to the source and destination TEP addresses — and sends it to the spine. The spine switches forward the packet to its destination leaf based entirely on the outer header. Once the packet arrives at the destination leaf, it decapsulates the original packet and delivers it to the intended recipient.

Overlays are deployed today to virtualize the physical network and enable multi-tenancy and agility by decoupling endpoint identifiers from their location (see [38, 22, 33] for more details). However, the overlay also provides the ideal conduit for CONGA's leaf-to-leaf congestion feedback mechanism. Specifically, CONGA leverages two key properties of the overlay: (i) The source leaf knows the ultimate destination leaf for each packet, in contrast to standard IP forwarding where the switches only know the next-hops. (ii) The encapsulated packet has an overlay header (VXLAN [35] in our implementation) which can be used to carry congestion metrics between the leaf switches.

**Congestion feedback:** The high-level mechanism is as follows. Each packet carries a congestion metric in the overlay header that represents the extent of congestion the packet experiences as it traverses through the fabric. The metric is updated hop-by-hop and indicates the utilization of the most congested link along the packet's path. This information is stored at the destination leaf on a per source leaf, per path basis and is opportunistically fed back to the source leaf by piggybacking on packets in the reverse direction. There may be, in general, 100s of paths in a multi-tier topology. Hence, to reduce state, the destination leaf *aggregates* congestion metrics for one or more paths based on a generic identifier called the *Load Balancing Tag* that the source leaf inserts in packets (see §3 for details).

## 2.6 Why Flowlet Switching for Datacenters?

CONGA also employs *flowlet switching*, an idea first introduced by Kandula *et al.* [27]. Flowlets are bursts of packets from a flow that are separated by large enough gaps (see Figure 4). Specifically, if the idle interval between two bursts of packets is larger than the maximum difference in latency among the paths, then the second burst can be sent along a different path than the first without reordering packets. Thus flowlets provide a higher granularity alternative to flows for load balancing (without causing reordering).

### *2.6.1 Measurement analysis*

Flowlet switching has been shown to be an effective technique for fine-grained load balancing across Internet paths [27], but how does it perform in datacenters? On the one hand, the very high bandwidth of internal datacenter flows would seem to suggest that the gaps needed for flowlets may be rare, limiting the applicability of flowlet switching. On the other hand, datacenter traffic is known to be extremely bursty at short timescales (e.g., 10–100s of microseconds) for a variety of reasons such as NIC hardware offloads designed to support high link rates [29]. Since very small flowlet gaps suffice in datacenters to maintain packet order (because the network latency is very low) such burstiness could provide sufficient flowlet opportunities.

We study the applicability of flowlet switching in datacenters using measurements from actual production datacenters. We instrument a production cluster with over 4500 virtualized and bare metal hosts across ~30 racks of servers to obtain packet traces of traffic flows through the network core. The cluster supports over 2000 diverse enterprise applications, including web, data-base, security, and business intelligence services. The captures are obtained by having a few leaf switches mirror traffic to an analyzer without disrupting production traffic. Overall, we analyze more than 150GB of compressed packet trace data.

[2] How the mapping between end-point identifiers and their locations (leaf switches) is obtained and propagated is beyond the scope of this paper.

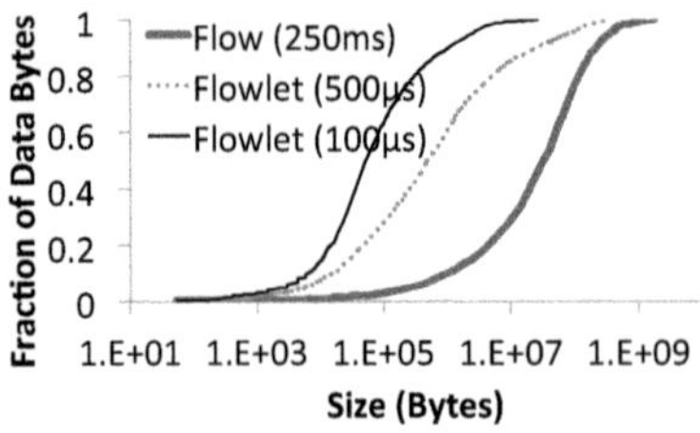


**Figure 5: Distribution of data bytes across transfer sizes for different flowlet inactivity gaps.**

**Flowlet size:** Figure 5 shows the distribution of the data bytes versus flowlet size for three choices of flowlet inactivity gap: 250ms, 500$\mu$s, and 100$\mu$s. Since it is unlikely that we would see a gap larger than 250ms in the same application-level flow, the line "Flow (250ms)" essentially corresponds to how the bytes are spread across flows. The plot shows that balancing flowlets gives significantly more fine-grained control than balancing flows. Even with an inactivity gap of 500$\mu$s, which is quite large and poses little risk of packet reordering in datacenters, we see nearly two orders of magnitude reduction in the size of transfers that cover most of the data: 50% of the bytes are in flows larger than ~30MB, but this number reduces to ~500KB for "Flowlet (500$\mu$s)".

**Flowlet concurrency:** Since the required flowlet inactivity gap is very small in datacenters, we expect there to be a small number of concurrent flowlets at any given time. Thus, the implementation cost for tracking flowlets should be low. To quantify this, we measure the distribution of the number of distinct 5-tuples in our packet trace over 1ms intervals. We find that the number of distinct 5-tuples (and thus flowlets) is small, with a median of 130 and a maximum under 300. Normalizing these numbers to the average throughput in our trace (~15Gbps), we estimate that even for a very heavily loaded leaf switch with say 400Gbps of traffic, the number of concurrent flowlets would be less than 8K. Maintaining a table for tracking 64K flowlets is feasible at low cost (§3.4).

# 3. DESIGN

Figure 6 shows the system diagram of CONGA. The majority of the functionality resides at the leaf switches. The source leaf makes load balancing decisions based on per uplink congestion metrics, derived by taking the maximum of the local congestion at the uplink and the remote congestion for the path (or paths) to the destination leaf that originate at the uplink. The remote metrics are stored in the Congestion-To-Leaf Table on a per destination leaf, per uplink basis and convey the maximum congestion for all the links along the path. The remote metrics are obtained via feedback from the destination leaf switch, which opportunistically piggybacks values in its Congestion-From-Leaf Table back to the source leaf. CONGA measures congestion using the Discounting Rate Estimator (DRE), a simple module present at each fabric link.

Load balancing decisions are made on the *first packet* of each flowlet. Subsequent packets use the same uplink as long as the flowlet remains active (there is not a sufficiently long gap). The source leaf uses the Flowlet Table to keep track of active flowlets and their chosen uplinks.

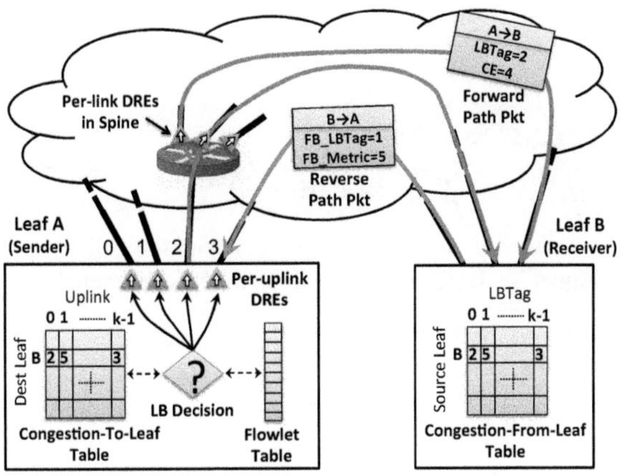


**Figure 6: CONGA system diagram.**

## 3.1 Packet format

CONGA leverages the VXLAN [35] encapsulation format used for the overlay to carry the following state:

- **LBTag (4 bits):** This field partially identifies the packet's path. It is set by the source leaf to the (switch-local) port number of the uplink the packet is sent on and is used by the destination leaf to aggregate congestion metrics before they are fed back to the source. For example, in Figure 6, the LBTag is 2 for both blue paths. Note that 4 bits is sufficient because the maximum number of leaf uplinks in our implementation is 12 for a non-oversubscribed configuration with $48 \times$ 10Gbps server-facing ports and $12 \times$ 40Gbps uplinks.
- **CE (3 bits):** This field is used by switches along the packet's path to convey the extent of congestion.
- **FB_LBTag (4 bits) and FB_Metric (3 bits):** These two fields are used by destination leaves to piggyback congestion information back to the source leaves. FB_LBTag indicates the LBTag the feedback is for and FB_Metric provides its associated congestion metric.

## 3.2 Discounting Rate Estimator (DRE)

The DRE is a simple module for measuring the load of a link. The DRE maintains a register, $X$, which is incremented for each packet sent over the link by the packet size in bytes, and is decremented periodically (every $T_{dre}$) with a multiplicative factor $\alpha$ between 0 and 1: $X \leftarrow X \times (1 - \alpha)$. It is easy to show that $X$ is proportional to the rate of traffic over the link; more precisely, if the traffic rate is $R$, then $X \approx R \cdot \tau$, where $\tau = T_{dre}/\alpha$. The DRE algorithm is essentially a first-order low pass filter applied to packet arrivals, with a $(1 - e^{-1})$ rise time of $\tau$. The congestion metric for the link is obtained by quantizing $X/C\tau$ to 3 bits ($C$ is the link speed).

The DRE algorithm is similar to the widely used Exponential Weighted Moving Average (EWMA) mechanism. However, DRE has two key advantages over EWMA: (i) it can be implemented with just one register (whereas EWMA requires two); and (ii) the DRE reacts more quickly to traffic bursts (because increments take place immediately upon packet arrivals) while retaining memory of past bursts. In the interest of space, we omit the details.

## 3.3 Congestion Feedback

CONGA uses a feedback loop between the source and destination leaf switches to populate the remote metrics in the Congestion-To-Leaf Table at each leaf switch. We now describe the sequence of events involved (refer to Figure 6 for an example).

1. The source leaf sends the packet to the fabric with the LBTag field set to the uplink port taken by the packet. It also sets the CE field to zero.
2. The packet is routed through the fabric to the destination leaf.[3] As it traverses each link, its CE field is updated if the link's congestion metric (given by the DRE) is larger than the current value in the packet.
3. The CE field of the packet received at the destination leaf gives the maximum link congestion along the packet's path. This needs to be fed back to the source leaf. But since a packet may not be immediately available in the reverse direction, the destination leaf stores the metric in the Congestion-From-Leaf Table (on a per source leaf, per LBTag basis) while it waits for an opportunity to piggyback the feedback.
4. When a packet is sent in the reverse direction, *one* metric from the Congestion-From-Leaf Table is inserted in its FB_LBTag and FB_Metric fields for the source leaf. The metric is chosen in round-robin fashion while, as an optimization, favoring those metrics whose values have changed since the last time they were fed back.
5. Finally, the source leaf parses the feedback in the reverse packet and updates the Congestion-To-Leaf Table.

It is important to note that though we have described the forward and reverse packets separately for simplicity, every packet *simultaneously* carries both a metric for its forward path and a feedback metric. Also, while we could generate explicit feedback packets, we decided to use piggybacking because we only need a very small number of packets for feedback. In fact, all metrics between a pair of leaf switches can be conveyed in at-most 12 packets (because there are 12 distinct LBTag values), with the average case being much smaller because the metrics only change at network round-trip timescales, not packet-timescales (see the discussion in §3.6 regarding the DRE time constant).

**Metric aging:** A potential issue with not having explicit feedback packets is that the metrics may become stale if sufficient traffic does not exit for piggybacking. To handle this, a simple aging mechanism is added where a metric that has not been updated for a long time (e.g., 10ms) will gradually decay to zero. Note that this also guarantees that a path that appears to be congested will eventually be probed again.

## 3.4 Flowlet Detection

Flowlets are detected and tracked in the leaf switches using the Flowlet Table. Each entry of the table consists of a port number, a valid bit, and an age bit. When a packet arrives, we lookup an entry based on a hash of its 5-tuple. If the entry is valid ($valid\_bit ==1$), the flowlet is active and the packet is sent on the port indicated in the entry. If the entry is not valid, the incoming packet starts a new flowlet. In this case, we make a load balancing decision (as described below) and cache the result in the table for use by subsequent packets. We also set the valid bit.

Flowlet entries time out using the age bit. Each incoming packet resets the age bit. A timer periodically (every $T_{fl}$ seconds) checks the age bit before setting it. If the age bit is set when the timer

[3] If there are multiple valid next hops to the destination (as in Figure 6), the spine switches pick one using standard ECMP hashing.

checks it, then there have not been any packets for that entry in the last $T_{fl}$ seconds and the entry times out (the valid bit is set to zero). Note that a single age bit allows us to detect gaps between $T_{fl}$ and $2T_{fl}$. While not as accurate as using full timestamps, this requires far fewer bits allowing us to maintain a very large number of entries in the table (64K in our implementation).

**Remark 1.** Although with hashing, flows may collide in the Flowlet Table, this is not a big concern. Collisions simply imply some load balancing opportunities are lost which does not matter as long as this does not occur too frequently.

### 3.5 Load Balancing Decision Logic

Load balancing decisions are made on the first packet of each flowlet (other packets use the port cached in the Flowlet Table). For a new flowlet, we pick the uplink port that minimizes the maximum of the local metric (from the local DREs) and the remote metric (from the Congestion-To-Leaf Table). If multiple uplinks are equally good, one is chosen at random with preference given to the port cached in the (invalid) entry in the Flowlet Table; i.e., a flow only moves if there is a strictly better uplink than the one its last flowlet took.

### 3.6 Parameter Choices

CONGA has three main parameters: (i) $Q$, the number of bits for quantizing congestion metrics (§3.1); (ii) $\tau$, the DRE time constant, given by $T_{dre}/\alpha$ (§3.2); and (iii) $T_{fl}$, the flowlet inactivity timeout (§3.4). We set these parameters experimentally. A control-theoretic analysis of CONGA is beyond the scope of this paper, but our parameter choices strike a balance between the stability and responsiveness of CONGA's control loop while taking into consideration practical matters such as interaction with TCP and implementation cost (header requirements, table size, etc).

The parameters $Q$ and $\tau$ determine the "gain" of CONGA's control loop and exhibit important tradeoffs. A large $Q$ improves congestion metric accuracy, but if too large can make the leaf switches over-react to minor differences in congestion causing oscillatory behavior. Similarly, a small $\tau$ makes the DRE respond quicker, but also makes it more susceptible to noise from transient traffic bursts. Intuitively, $\tau$ should be set larger than the network RTT to filter the sub-RTT traffic bursts of TCP. The flowlet timeout, $T_{fl}$, can be set to the maximum possible leaf-to-leaf latency to guarantee no packet reordering. This value can be rather large though because of worst-case queueing delays (e.g., 13ms in our testbed), essentially disabling flowlets. Reducing $T_{fl}$ presents a compromise between more packet reordering versus less congestion (fewer packet drops, lower latency) due to better load balancing.

Overall, we have found CONGA's performance to be fairly robust with: $Q = 3$ to 6, $\tau = 100\mu s$ to $500\mu s$, and $T_{fl} = 300\mu s$ to 1ms. The default parameter values for our implementation are: $Q = 3$, $\tau = 160\mu s$, and $T_{fl} = 500\mu s$.

## 4. IMPLEMENTATION

CONGA has been implemented in custom switching ASICs for a major datacenter fabric product line. The implementation includes ASICs for both the leaf and spine nodes. The Leaf ASIC implements flowlet detection, congestion metric tables, DREs, and the leaf-to-leaf feedback mechanism. The Spine ASIC implements the DRE and its associated congestion marking mechanism. The ASICs provide state-of-the-art switching capacities. For instance, the Leaf ASIC has a non-blocking switching capacity of 960Gbps in 28nm technology. CONGA's implementation requires roughly 2.4M gates and 2.8Mbits of memory in the Leaf ASIC, and consumes negligible die area ($< 2\%$).

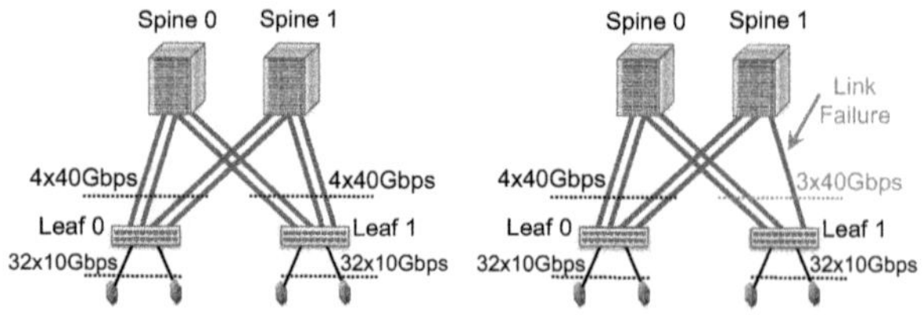


(a) Baseline (no failure) (b) With link failure

**Figure 7: Topologies used in testbed experiments.**

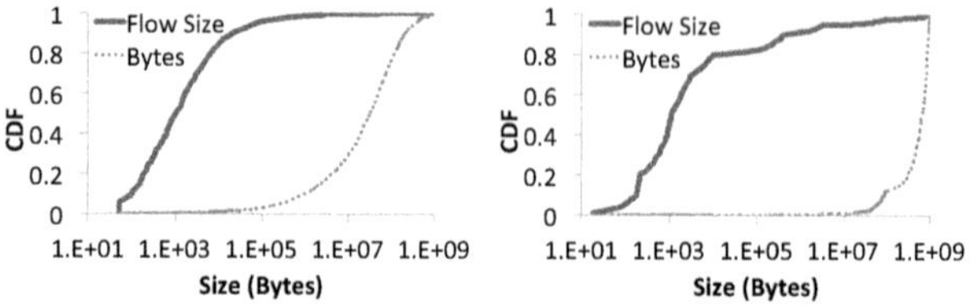


(a) Enterprise workload (b) Data-mining workload

**Figure 8: Empirical traffic distributions. The Bytes CDF shows the distribution of traffic bytes across different flow sizes.**

## 5. EVALUATION

In this section, we evaluate CONGA's performance with a real hardware testbed as well as large-scale simulations. Our testbed experiments illustrate CONGA's good performance for realistic empirical workloads, Incast micro-benchmarks, and actual applications. Our detailed packet-level simulations confirm that CONGA scales to large topologies.

**Schemes compared:** We compare **CONGA**, **CONGA-Flow**, **ECMP**, and **MPTCP** [41], the state-of-the-art multipath transport protocol. CONGA and CONGA-Flow differ only in their choice of the flowlet inactivity timeout. CONGA uses the default value: $T_{fl} = 500\mu s$. CONGA-Flow however uses $T_{fl} = 13$ms which is greater than the maximum path latency in our testbed and ensures no packet reordering. CONGA-Flow's large timeout effectively implies one load balancing decision per flow, similar to ECMP. Of course, in contrast to ECMP, decisions in CONGA-Flow are informed by the path congestion metrics. The rest of the parameters for both variants of CONGA are set as described in §3.6. For MPTCP, we use MPTCP kernel v0.87 available on the web [37]. We configure MPTCP to use 8 sub-flows for each TCP connection, as Raiciu *et al.* [41] recommend.

### 5.1 Testbed

Our testbed consists of 64 servers and four switches (two leaves and two spines). As shown in Figure 7, the servers are organized in two racks (32 servers each) and attach to the leaf switches with 10Gbps links. In the baseline topology (Figure 7(a)), the leaf switches connect to each spine switch with two 40Gbps uplinks. Note that there is a 2:1 oversubscription at the Leaf level, typical of today's datacenter deployments. We also consider the *asymmetric* topology in Figure 7(b) where one of the links between Leaf 1 and Spine 1 is down. The servers have 12-core Intel Xeon X5670 2.93GHz CPUs, 128GB of RAM, and 3 2TB 7200RPM HDDs.

### 5.2 Empirical Workloads

We begin with experiments with realistic workloads based on empirically observed traffic patterns in deployed datacenters. Specifically, we consider the two flow size distributions shown in Figure 8. The first distribution is derived from packet traces from our own datacenters (§2.6) and represents a large enterprise workload. The second distribution is from a large cluster running data mining

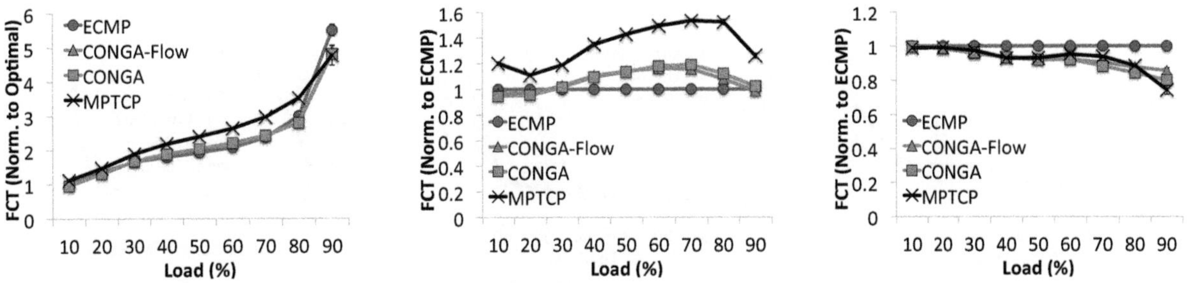


(a) Overall Average FCT (b) Small Flows (<100KB) (c) Large Flows (> 10MB)

**Figure 9: FCT statistics for the enterprise workload with the baseline topology. Note that part (a) is normalized to the optimal FCT, while parts (b) and (c) are normalized to the value achieved by ECMP. The results are the average of 5 runs.**

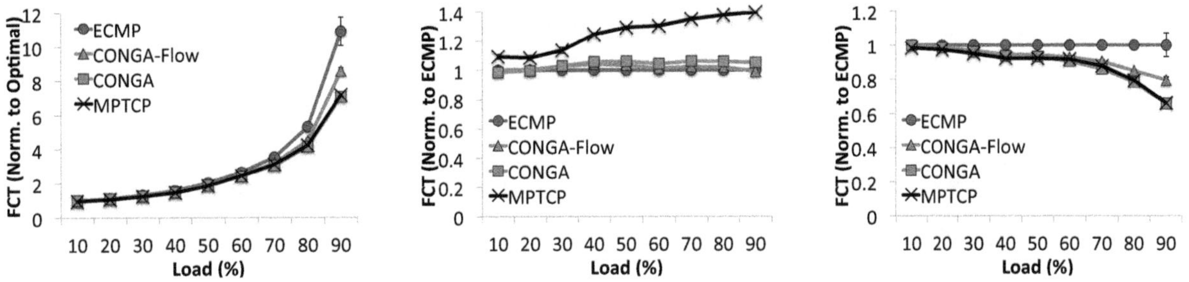


(a) Overall Average FCT (b) Small Flows (< 100KB) (c) Large Flows (> 10MB)

**Figure 10: FCT statistics for the data-mining workload with the baseline topology.**

jobs [18]. Note that both distributions are heavy-tailed: A small fraction of the flows contribute most of the data. Particularly, the data-mining distribution has a very heavy tail with 95% of all data bytes belonging to ∼3.6% of flows that are larger than 35MB.

We develop a simple client-server program to generate the traffic. The clients initiate 3 long-lived TCP connections to each server and request flows according to a Poisson process from randomly chosen servers. The request rate is chosen depending on the desired offered load and the flow sizes are sampled from one of the above distributions. All 64 nodes run both client and server processes. Since we are interested in stressing the fabric's load balancing, we configure the clients under Leaf 0 to only use the servers under Leaf 1 and vice-versa, thereby ensuring that all traffic traverses the Spine. Similar to prior work [20, 5, 13], we use the flow completion time (FCT) as our main performance metric.

### *5.2.1 Baseline*

Figures 9 and 10 show the results for the two workloads with the baseline topology (Figure 7(a)). Part (a) of each figure shows the overall average FCT for each scheme at traffic loads between 10–90%. The values here are normalized to the optimal FCT that is achievable in an idle network. In parts (b) and (c), we break down the FCT for each scheme for small (< 100KB) and large (> 10MB) flows, normalized to the value achieved by ECMP. Each data point is the average of 5 runs with the error bars showing the range. (Note that the error bars are not visible at all data points.)

**Enterprise workload:** We find that the overall average FCT is similar for all schemes in the enterprise workload, except for MPTCP which is up to ∼25% worse than the others. MPTCP's higher overall average FCT is because of the small flows, for which it is up to ∼50% worse than ECMP. CONGA and similarly CONGA-Flow are slightly worse for small flows (∼12–19% at 50–80% load), but improve FCT for large flows by as much as ∼20%.

**Data-mining workload:** For the data-mining workload, ECMP is noticeably worse than the other schemes at the higher load levels. Both CONGA and MPTCP achieve up to ∼35% better overall average FCT than ECMP. Similar to the enterprise workload, we find a degradation in FCT for small flows with MPTCP compared to the other schemes.

**Analysis:** The above results suggest a tradeoff with MPTCP between achieving good load balancing in the core of the fabric and managing congestion at the edge. Essentially, while using 8 sub-flows per connection helps MPTCP achieve better load balancing, it also increases congestion at the edge links because the multiple sub-flows cause more burstiness. Further, as observed by Raiciu *et al.* [41], the small sub-flow window sizes for short flows increases the chance of timeouts. This hurts the performance of short flows which are more sensitive to additional latency and packet drops. CONGA on the other hand does not have this problem since it does not change the congestion control behavior of TCP.

Another interesting observation is the distinction between the enterprise and data-mining workloads. In the enterprise workload, ECMP actually does quite well leaving little room for improvement by the more sophisticated schemes. But for the data-mining workload, ECMP is noticeably worse. This is because the enterprise workload is less "heavy"; i.e., it has fewer large flows. In particular, ∼50% of all data bytes in the enterprise workload are from flows that are smaller than 35MB (Figure 8(a)). But in the data mining workload, flows smaller than 35MB contribute only ∼5% of all bytes (Figure 8(b)). Hence the data-mining workload is more challenging to handle from a load balancing perspective. We quantify the impact of the workload analytically in §6.2.

### *5.2.2 Impact of link failure*

We now repeat both workloads for the asymmetric topology when a fabric link fails (Figure 7(b)). The overall average FCT for both workloads is shown in Figure 11. Note that since in this case the bisection bandwidth between Leaf 0 and Leaf 1 is 75% of the original capacity (3 × 40Gbps links instead of 4), we only consider offered loads up to 70%. As expected, ECMP's performance drastically deteriorates as the offered load increases beyond 50%. This is because with ECMP, half of the traffic from Leaf 0 to Leaf 1

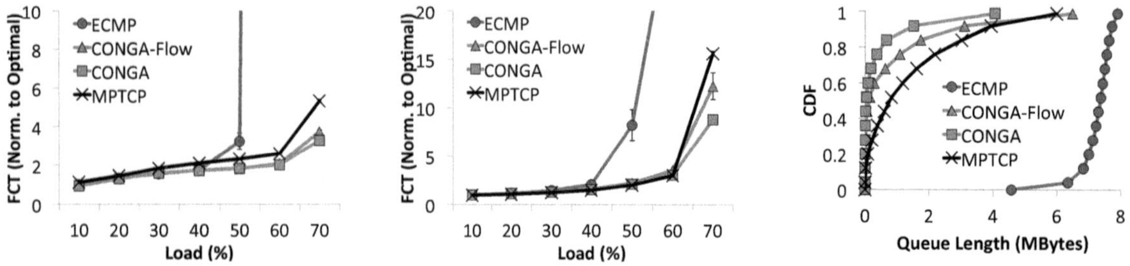


(a) Enterprise workload: Avg FCT (b) Data-mining workload: Avg FCT (c) Queue length at hotspot

**Figure 11: Impact of link failure. Parts (a) and (b) show that overall average FCT for both workloads. Part (c) shows the CDF of queue length at the hotspot port [Spine1→Leaf1] for the data-mining workload at 60% load.**

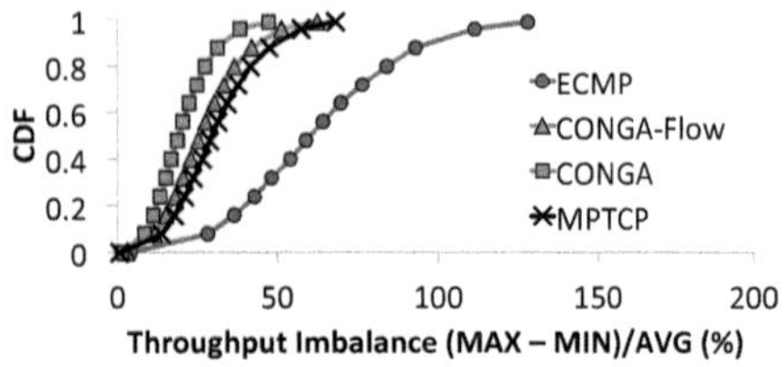


(a) Enterprise workload

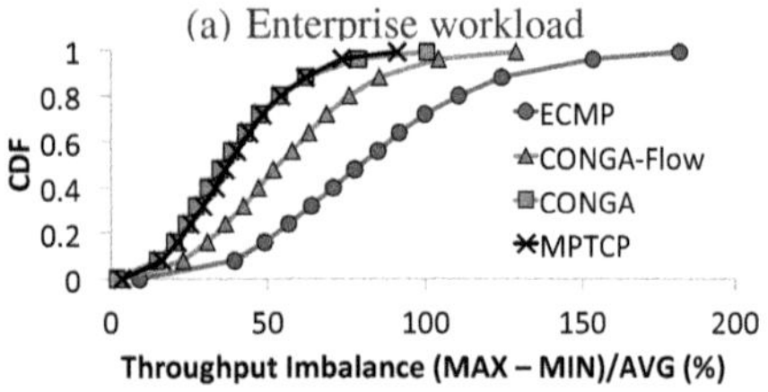


(b) Data-mining workload

**Figure 12: Extent of imbalance between throughput of leaf uplinks for both workloads at 60% load.**

is sent through Spine 1 (see Figure 7(b)). Therefore the single [Spine1→Leaf1] link must carry twice as much traffic as each of the [Spine0→Leaf1] links and becomes oversubscribed when the offered load exceeds 50%. At this point, the network effectively cannot handle the offered load and becomes unstable.

The other *adaptive* schemes are significantly better than ECMP with the asymmetric topology because they shift traffic to the lesser congested paths (through Spine 0) and can thus handle the offered load. CONGA is particularly robust to the link failure, achieving up to ~30% lower overall average FCT than MPTCP in the enterprise workload and close to 2× lower in the data-mining workload at 70% load. CONGA-Flow is also better than MPTCP even though it does not split flows. This is because CONGA *proactively* detects high utilization paths before congestion occurs and adjusts traffic accordingly, whereas MPTCP is *reactive* and only adjusts when sub-flows on congested paths experience packet drops. This is evident from comparing the queue occupancy at the hotspot port [Spine1→Leaf1] for the different schemes. This is shown for example for the data-mining workload at 60% load in Figure 11(c). We see that CONGA controls the queue occupancy at the hotspot much more effectively than MPTCP, for instance achieving a 4× smaller 90th percentile queue occupancy.

### *5.2.3 Load balancing efficiency*

The FCT results of the previous section show end-to-end performance which is impacted by a variety of factors, including load balancing. We now focus specifically on CONGA's load balancing efficiency. Figure 12 shows the CDF of the *throughput imbalance* across the 4 uplinks at Leaf 0 in the baseline topology (without link failure) for both workloads at the 60% load level. The throughput imbalance is defined as the maximum throughput (among the 4 uplinks) minus the minimum divided by the average: $(MAX - MIN)/AVG$. This is calculated from synchronous samples of the throughput of the 4 uplinks over 10ms intervals, measured using a special debugging module in the ASIC.

The results confirm that CONGA is at least as efficient as MPTCP for load balancing (without any TCP modifications) and is significantly better than ECMP. CONGA's throughput imbalance is even lower than MPTCP for the enterprise workload. With CONGA-Flow, the throughput imbalance is slightly better than MPTCP in the enterprise workload, but worse in the data-mining workload.

## 5.3 Incast

Our results in the previous section suggest that MPTCP increases congestion at the edge links because it opens 8 sub-flows per connection. We now dig deeper into this issue for Incast traffic patterns that are common in datacenters [4].

We use a simple application that generates the standard Incast traffic pattern considered in prior work [47, 12, 4]. A client process residing on one of the servers repeatedly makes requests for a 10MB file striped across $N$ other servers. The servers each respond with 10MB/$N$ of data in a synchronized fashion causing Incast. We measure the effective throughput at the client for different "fan-in" values, $N$, ranging from 1 to 63. Note that this experiment does not stress the fabric load balancing since the total traffic crossing the fabric is limited by the client's 10Gbps access link. The performance here is predominantly determined by the Incast behavior for the TCP or MPTCP transports.

The results are shown in Figure 13. We consider two minimum retransmission timeout ($minRTO$) values: 200ms (the default value in Linux) and 1ms (recommended by Vasudevan *et al.* [47] to cope with Incast); and two packet sizes ($MTU$): 1500B (the standard Ethernet frame size) and 9000B (jumbo frames). The plots confirm that MPTCP significantly degrades performance in Incast scenarios. For instance, with $minRTO = 200$ms, MPTCP's throughput degrades to less than 30% for large fan-in with 1500B packets and just 5% with 9000B packets. Reducing $minRTO$ to 1ms mitigates the problem to some extent with standard packets, but even reducing $minRTO$ does not prevent significant throughput loss with jumbo frames. CONGA +TCP achieves 2–8× better throughput than MPTCP in similar settings.

## 5.4 HDFS Benchmark

Our final testbed experiment evaluates the end-to-end impact of CONGA on a real application. We set up a 64 node Hadoop cluster (Cloudera distribution hadoop-0.20.2-cdh3u5) with 1 NameNode and 63 DataNodes and run the standard TestDFSIO benchmark included in the Apache Hadoop distribution [19]. The benchmark tests the overall IO performance of the cluster by spawning

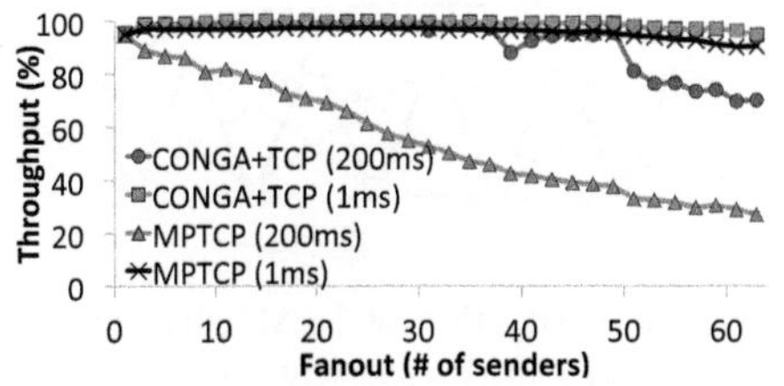


(a) MTU = 1500B

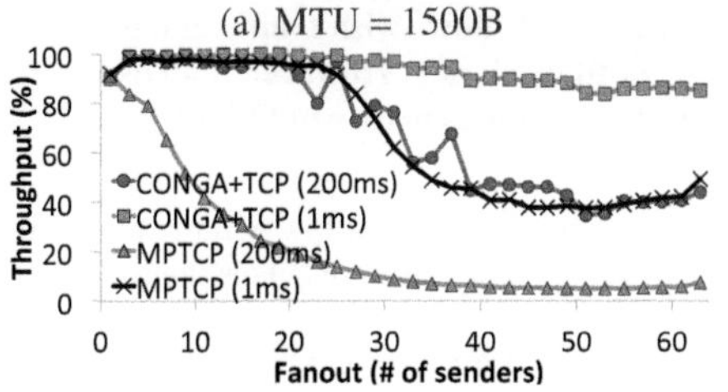


(b) MTU = 9000B

**Figure 13: MPTCP significantly degrades performance in Incast scenarios, especially with large packet sizes (MTU).**

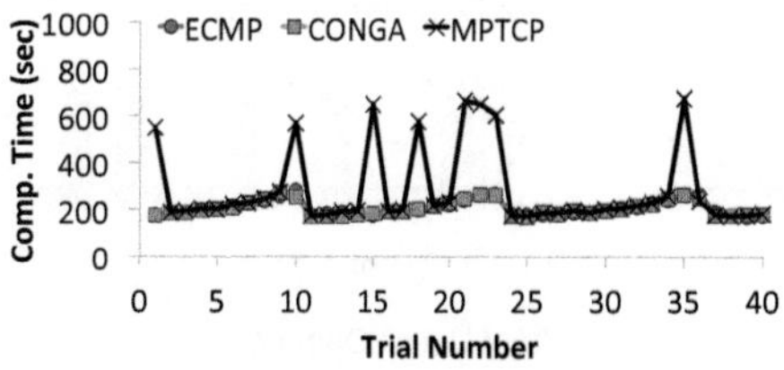


(a) Baseline Topology (w/o link failure)

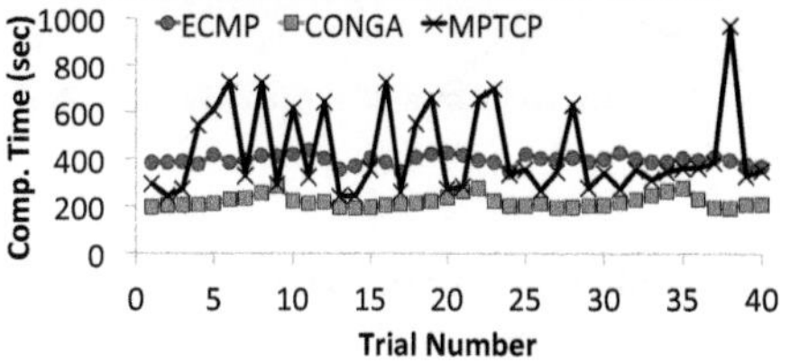


(b) Asymmetric Topology (with link failure)

**Figure 14: HDFS IO benchmark.**

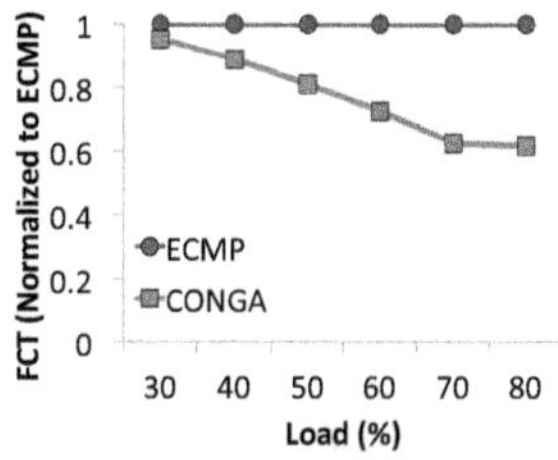


(a) 10Gbps access links

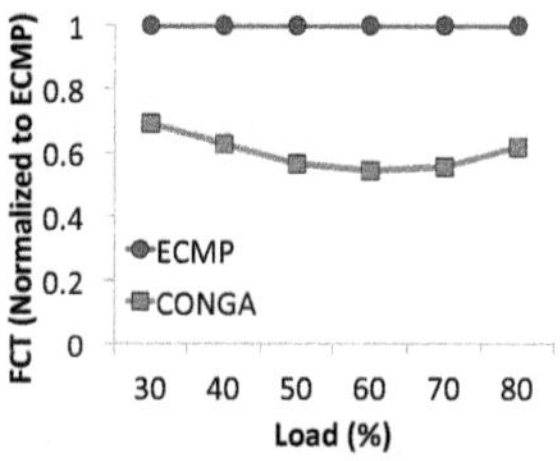


(b) 40Gbps access links

**Figure 15: Overall average FCT for a simulated workload based on web search [4] for two topologies with 40Gbps fabric links, 3:1 oversubscription, and: (a) 384 10Gbps servers, (b) 96 40Gbps servers.**

a MapReduce job which writes a 1TB file into HDFS (with 3-way replication) and measuring the total job completion time. We run the benchmark 40 times for both of the topologies in Figure 7 (with and without link failure). We found in our experiments that the TestDFSIO benchmark is *disk-bound* in our setup and does not produce enough traffic on its own to stress the network. Therefore, in the absence of servers with more or faster disks, we also generate some background traffic using the empirical enterprise workload described in §5.2.

Figure 14 shows the job completion times for all trials. We find that for the baseline topology (without failures), ECMP and CONGA have nearly identical performance. MPTCP has some outlier trials with much higher job completion times. For the asymmetric topology with link failure, the job completion times for ECMP are nearly twice as large as without the link failure. But CONGA is robust; comparing Figures 14 (a) and (b) shows that the link failure has almost no impact on the job completion times with CONGA. The performance with MPTCP is very volatile with the link failure. Though we cannot ascertain the exact root cause of this, we believe it is because of MPTCP's difficulties with Incast since the TestDFSIO benchmark creates a large number of concurrent transfers between the servers.

## 5.5 Large-Scale Simulations

Our experimental results were for a comparatively small topology (64 servers, 4 switches), 10Gbps access links, one link failure, and 2:1 oversubscription. But in developing CONGA, we also did extensive packet-level simulations, including exploring CONGA's parameter space (§3.6), different workloads, larger topologies, varying oversubscription ratios and link speeds, and varying degrees of asymmetry. We briefly summarize our main findings.

*Note:* We used OMNET++ [46] and the Network Simulation Cradle [24] to port the actual Linux TCP source code (from kernel 2.6.26) to our simulator. Despite its challenges, we felt that capturing exact TCP behavior was crucial to evaluate CONGA, especially to accurately model flowlets. Since an OMNET++ model of MPTCP is unavailable and we did experimental comparisons, we did not simulate MPTCP.

**Varying fabric size and oversubscription:** We have simulated realistic datacenter workloads (including those presented in §5.2) for fabrics with as many as 384 servers, 8 leaf switches, and 12 spine switches, and for oversubscription ratios ranging from 1:1 to 5:1. We find qualitatively similar results to our testbed experiments at all scales. CONGA achieves ~5–40% better FCT than ECMP in symmetric topologies, with the benefit larger for heavy flow size distributions, high load, and high oversubscription ratios.

**Varying link speeds:** CONGA's improvement over ECMP is more pronounced and occurs at lower load levels the closer the access link speed (at the servers) is to the fabric link speed. For example, in topologies with 40Gbps links everywhere, CONGA achieves 30% better FCT than ECMP even at 30% traffic load, while for topologies with 10Gbps edge and 40Gbps fabric links, the improvement at 30% load is typically 5–10% (Figure 15). This is because in the latter case, each fabric link can support multiple (at least 4) flows without congestion. Therefore, the impact of hash collisions in ECMP is less pronounced in this case (see also [41]).

**Varying asymmetry:** Across tens of asymmetrical scenarios we simulated (e.g., with different number of random failures, fabrics with both 10Gbps and 40Gbps links, etc) CONGA achieves near optimal traffic balance. For example, in the representative scenario shown in Figure 16, the queues at links 10 and 12 in the spine (which are adjacent to the failed link 11) are ~10× larger with ECMP than CONGA.

# 6. ANALYSIS

In this section we complement our experimental results with analysis of CONGA along two axes. First, we consider a game-theoretic model known as the *bottleneck routing game* [6] in the context of CONGA to quantify its Price of Anarchy [40]. Next, we consider a stochastic model that gives insights into the impact of the traffic distribution and flowlets on load balancing performance.

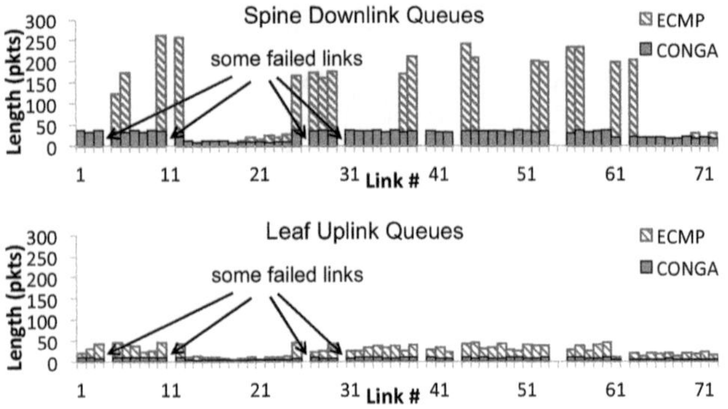


**Figure 16: Multiple link failure scenario in a 288-port fabric with 6 leaves and 4 spines. Each leaf and spine connect with 3 × 40Gbps links and 9 randomly chosen links fail. The plots show the average queue length at all fabric ports for a web search workload at 60% load. CONGA balances traffic significantly better than ECMP. Note that the improvement over ECMP is much larger at the (remote) spine downlinks because ECMP spreads load equally on the leaf uplinks.**

## 6.1 The Price of Anarchy for CONGA

In CONGA, the leaf switches make independent load balancing decisions to minimize the congestion for their own traffic. This uncoordinated or "selfish" behavior can potentially cause inefficiency in comparison to having centralized coordination. This inefficiency is known as the Price of Anarchy (PoA) [40] and has been the subject of numerous studies in the theoretical literature (see [43] for a survey). In this section we analyze the PoA for CONGA using the bottleneck routing game model introduced by Banner *et al.* [6].

**Model:** We consider a two-tier Leaf-Spine network modeled as a complete bipartite graph. The leaf and spine nodes are connected with links of arbitrary capacities $\{c_e\}$. The network is shared by a set of users $U$. Each user $u \in U$ has a traffic demand $\gamma_u$, to be sent from source leaf, $s_u$, to destination leaf, $t_u$. A user must decide how to split its traffic along the paths $P^{(s_u,t_u)}$ through the different spine nodes. Denote by $f_p^u$ the flow of user $u$ on path $p$. The set of all user flows, $f = \{f_p^u\}$, is termed the *network flow*. A network flow is *feasible* if $\sum_{p \in P^{(s_u,t_u)}} f_p^u = \gamma_u$ for all $u \in U$. Let $f_p = \sum_{u \in U} f_p^u$ be the total flow on a path and $f_e = \sum_{p|e \in p} f_p$ be the total flow on a link. Also, let $\rho_e(f_e) = f_e/c_e$ be the utilization of link $e$. We define the *network bottleneck* for a network flow to be the utilization of the most congested link; i.e., $B(f) \triangleq \max_{e \in E} \rho_e(f_e)$. Similarly, we define the bottleneck for user $u$ to be the utilization of the most congested link it uses; i.e., $b_u(f) \triangleq \max_{e \in E | f_e^u > 0} \rho_e(f_e)$.

We model CONGA as a non-cooperative game where each user selfishly routes its traffic to minimize its own bottleneck; i.e., it only sends traffic along the paths with the smallest bottleneck available to it. The network flow, $f$, is said to be at *Nash equilibrium* if no user can improve its bottleneck given the choices of the other users. Specifically, $f$ is a Nash flow if for each user $u^* \in U$ and network flow $g = \{g_p^u\}$ such that $g_p^u = f_p^u$ for each $u \in U \backslash u^*$, we have: $b_{u^*}(f) \leq b_{u^*}(g)$. The game above always admits at least one Nash flow (Theorem 1 in [6]). Note that CONGA converges to a Nash flow because the algorithm rebalances traffic (between a particular source/destination leaf) if there is a path with a smaller bottleneck available.[4] The PoA is defined as the worst-case ratio of the network bottleneck for a Nash flow and the minimum network bottleneck achievable by any flow. We have the following theorem.

[4]Of course, this is an idealization and ignores artifacts such as flowlets, quantized congestion metrics, etc.

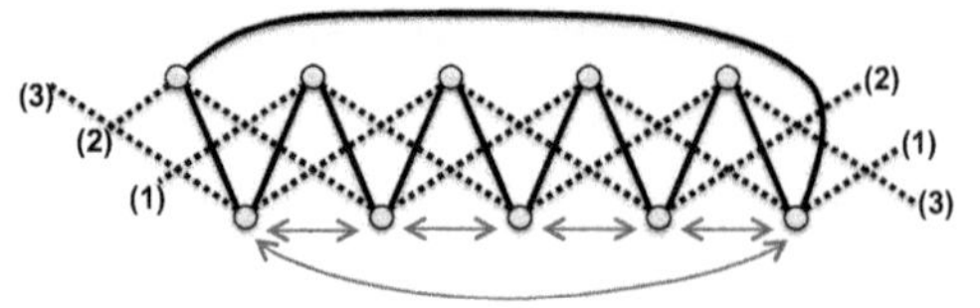


**Figure 17: Example with PoA of 2. All edges have capacity 1 and each pair of adjacent leaves send 1 unit of traffic to each other. The shown Nash flow (with traffic along the solid edges) has a network bottleneck of 1. However, if all users instead used the dashed paths, the bottleneck would be $1/2$.**

**Theorem** 1. *The PoA for the CONGA game is 2.*

PROOF. An upper bound of 2 can be derived for the PoA using a similar argument to that of Corollary 2 (Section V-B) in Banner *et al.* [6]. The proof leverages the fact that the paths in the Leaf-Spine network have length 2. The corresponding lower bound of 2 for the PoA follows from the example shown in Figure 17. Refer to the longer version of this paper for details [3]. □

Theorem 1 proves that the network bottleneck with CONGA is at most twice the optimal. It is important to note that this is the *worst-case* and can only occur in very specific (and artificial) scenarios such as the example in Figure 17. As our experimental evaluation shows (§5), in practice the performance of CONGA is much closer to optimal.

**Remark 2.** If in addition to using paths with the smallest congestion metric, if the leaf switches also use only paths with *the fewest number* of bottlenecks, then the PoA would be 1 [6], i.e., optimal. For example, the flow in Figure 17 does not satisfy this condition since traffic is routed along paths with two bottlenecks even though alternate paths with a single bottleneck exist. Incorporating this criteria into CONGA would require additional bits to track the number of bottlenecks along the packet's path. Since our evaluation (§5) has not shown much potential gains, we have not added this refinement to our implementation.

## 6.2 Impact of Workload on Load Balancing

Our evaluation showed that for some workloads ECMP actually performs quite well and the benefits of more sophisticated schemes (such as MPTCP and CONGA) are limited in symmetric topologies. This raises the question: *How does the workload affect load balancing performance?* Importantly, *when are flowlets helpful?*

We now study these questions using a simple stochastic model. Flows with an arbitrary size distribution, $S$, arrive according to a Poisson process of rate $\lambda$ and are spread across $n$ links. For each flow, a random link is chosen. Let $N^k(t)$ and $A^k(t)$ respectively denote the number of flows and the total amount of traffic sent on link $k$ in time interval $(0,t)$; i.e., $A^k(t) = \sum_{i=1}^{N^k(t)} s_i^k$, where $s_i^k$ is the size of $i^{th}$ flow assigned to link $k$. Let $Y(t) = \min_{1 \leq k \leq n} A^k(t)$ and $Z(t) = \max_{1 \leq k \leq n} A^k(t)$ and define the *traffic imbalance*:

$$\chi(t) \triangleq \frac{Z(t) - W(t)}{\frac{\lambda \mathrm{E}(S)}{n} t}.$$

This is basically the deviation between the traffic on the maximum and minimum loaded links normalized by the expected traffic on each link. The following theorem bounds the expected traffic imbalance at time $t$.

**Theorem** 2. *Assume* $\mathrm{E}(e^{\theta S}) < \infty$ *in a neighborhood of zero:* $\theta \in (-\theta_0, \theta_0)$. *Then for t sufficiently large:*

$$\mathrm{E}(\chi(t)) \leq \frac{1}{\sqrt{\lambda_e t}} + o(\frac{1}{t}), \quad (1)$$

*where:*

$$\lambda_e = \frac{\lambda}{8n \log n \left(1 + (\frac{\sigma_S}{\mathrm{E}(S)})^2\right)}. \quad (2)$$

*Here* $\sigma_S$ *is the standard deviation of S.*

*Note:* Kandula *et al.* [27] prove a similar result for the deviation of traffic on *a single link* from its expectation while Theorem 2 bounds the traffic imbalance *across all links.*

The proof follows standard probabilistic arguments and is given in the longer version of this paper [3]. Theorem 2 shows that the traffic imbalance with randomized load balancing vanishes like $1/\sqrt{t}$ for large $t$. Moreover, the leading term is determined by the *effective arrival rate*, $\lambda_e$, that depends on two factors: (i) the *per-link flow arrival rate*, $\lambda/n$; and (ii) the *coefficient of variation* of the flow size distribution, $\sigma_S/\mathrm{E}(S)$. Theorem 2 quantifies the intuition that workloads that consists mostly of small flows are easier to handle than workloads with a few large flows. Indeed, it is for the latter "heavy" workloads that we can anticipate flowlets to make a difference. This is consistent with our experiments which show that ECMP does well for the enterprise workload (Figure 9), but for the heavier data mining workload CONGA is much better than ECMP and is even notably better than CONGA-Flow (Figure 10).

# 7. DISCUSSION

We make a few remarks on aspects not covered thus far.

**Incremental deployment:** An interesting consequence of CONGA's resilience to asymmetry is that it does not need to be applied to *all* traffic. Traffic that is not controlled by CONGA simply creates *bandwidth asymmetry* to which (like topology asymmetry) CONGA can adapt. This facilitates incremental deployment since some leaf switches can use ECMP or any other scheme. Regardless, CONGA reduces fabric congestion to the benefit of all traffic.

**Larger topologies:** While 2-tier Leaf-Spine topologies suffice for most enterprise deployments, the largest *mega* datacenters require networks with 3 or more tiers. CONGA may not achieve the optimal traffic balance in such cases since it only controls the load balancing decision at the leaf switches (recall that the spine switches use ECMP). However, large datacenter networks are typically organized as multiple *pods*, each of which is a 2-tier Clos [1, 18]. Therefore, CONGA is beneficial even in these cases since it balances the traffic within each pod optimally, which also reduces congestion for inter-pod traffic. Moreover, even for inter-pod traffic, CONGA makes better decisions than ECMP at the first-hop.

A possible approach to generalizing CONGA to larger topologies is to pick a sufficient number of "good" paths between each pair of leaf switches and use leaf-to-leaf feedback to balance traffic across them. While we cannot cover all paths in general (as we do in the 2-tier case), the theoretical literature suggests that simple path selection policies such as periodically sampling a random path and retaining the best paths may perform very well [30]. We leave to future work a full exploration of CONGA in larger topologies.

**Other path metrics:** We used the *max* of the link congestion metrics as the path metric, but of course other choices such as the *sum* of link metrics are also possible and can easily be incorporated in CONGA. Indeed, in theory, the sum metric gives a Price of Anarchy (PoA) of 4/3 in *arbitrary* topologies [43]. Of course, the PoA is for the worst-case (adversarial) scenario. Hence, while the PoA is better for the sum metric than the max, like prior work (e.g., TeXCP [26]), we used max because it emphasizes the bottleneck link and is also easier to implement; the sum metric requires extra bits in the packet header to prevent overflow when doing additions.

# 8. RELATED WORK

We briefly discuss related work that has informed and inspired our design, especially work not previously discussed.

Traditional traffic engineering mechanisms for wide-area networks [15, 14, 42, 49] use centralized algorithms operating at coarse timescales (hours) based on long-term estimates of traffic matrices. More recently, B4 [23] and SWAN [21] have shown near optimal traffic engineering for inter-datacenter WANs. These systems leverage the relative predictability of WAN traffic (operating over minutes) and are not designed for highly volatile datacenter networks. CONGA is conceptually similar to TeXCP [26] which dynamically load balances traffic between ingress-egress routers (in a wide-area network) based on path-wise congestion metrics. CONGA however is significantly simpler (while also being near optimal) so that it can be implemented directly in switch hardware and operate at microsecond time-scales, unlike TeXCP which is designed to be implemented in router software.

Besides Hedera [2], work such as MicroTE [9] proposes centralized load balancing for datacenters and has the same issues with handling traffic volatility. F10 [34] also uses a centralized scheduler, but uses a novel network topology to optimize failure recovery, not load balancing. The Incast issues we point out for MPTCP [41] can potentially be mitigated by additional mechanisms such as explicit congestion signals (e.g., XMP [11]), but complex transports are challenging to validate and deploy in practice.

A number of papers target the coarse granularity of flow-based balancing in ECMP. Besides Flare [27], LocalFlow [44] proposes spatial flow splitting based on TCP sequence numbers and DRB [10] proposes efficient per-packet round-robin load balancing. As explained in §2.4, such local schemes may interact poorly with TCP in the presence of asymmetry and perform worse than ECMP. DeTail [52] proposes a per-packet adaptive routing scheme that handles asymmetry using layer-2 back-pressure, but requires end-host modifications to deal with packet reordering.

# 9. CONCLUSION

The main thesis of this paper is that datacenter load balancing is best done in the network instead of the transport layer, and requires global congestion-awareness to handle asymmetry. Through extensive evaluation with a real testbed, we demonstrate that CONGA provides better performance than MPTCP [41], the state-of-the-art multipath transport for datacenter load balancing, without important drawbacks such as complexity and rigidity at the transport layer and poor Incast performance. Further, unlike local schemes such as ECMP and Flare [27], CONGA seamlessly handles asymmetries in the topology or network traffic. CONGA's resilience to asymmetry also paid unexpected dividends when it came to incremental deployment. Even if some switches within the fabric use ECMP (or any other mechanism), CONGA's traffic can work around bandwidth asymmetries and benefit all traffic.

CONGA leverages an existing datacenter overlay to implement a leaf-to-leaf feedback loop and can be deployed without any modifications to the TCP stack. While leaf-to-leaf feedback is not always the best strategy, it is near-optimal for 2-tier Leaf-Spine fabrics that suffice for the vast majority of deployed datacenters. It is also simple enough to implement in hardware as proven by our implementation in custom silicon.

In summary, CONGA senses the distant drumbeats of remote congestion and orchestrates flowlets to disperse evenly through the fabric. We leave to future work the task of designing more intricate rhythms for more general topologies.

**Acknowledgments:** We are grateful to Georges Akis, Luca Cafiero, Krishna Doddapaneni, Mike Herbert, Prem Jain, Soni Jiandani, Mario Mazzola, Sameer Merchant, Satyam Sinha, Michael Smith, and Pauline Shuen of Insieme Networks for their valuable feedback during the development of CONGA. We would also like to thank Vimalkumar Jeyakumar, Peter Newman, Michael Smith, our shepherd Teemu Koponen, and the anonymous SIGCOMM reviewers whose comments helped us improve the paper.

## 10. REFERENCES

[1] M. Al-Fares, A. Loukissas, and A. Vahdat. A scalable, commodity data center network architecture. In *SIGCOMM*, 2008.

[2] M. Al-Fares, S. Radhakrishnan, B. Raghavan, N. Huang, and A. Vahdat. Hedera: Dynamic Flow Scheduling for Data Center Networks. In *NSDI*, 2010.

[3] M. Alizadeh et al. CONGA: Distributed Congestion-Aware Load Balancing for Datacenters. `http://simula.stanford.edu/~alizade/papers/conga-techreport.pdf`.

[4] M. Alizadeh et al. Data center TCP (DCTCP). In *SIGCOMM*, 2010.

[5] M. Alizadeh et al. pFabric: Minimal Near-optimal Datacenter Transport. In *SIGCOMM*, 2013.

[6] R. Banner and A. Orda. Bottleneck Routing Games in Communication Networks. *Selected Areas in Communications, IEEE Journal on*, 25(6):1173–1179, 2007.

[7] M. Beck and M. Kagan. Performance Evaluation of the RDMA over Ethernet (RoCE) Standard in Enterprise Data Centers Infrastructure. In *DC-CaVES*, 2011.

[8] T. Benson, A. Akella, and D. A. Maltz. Network Traffic Characteristics of Data Centers in the Wild. In *SIGCOMM*, 2010.

[9] T. Benson, A. Anand, A. Akella, and M. Zhang. MicroTE: Fine Grained Traffic Engineering for Data Centers. In *CoNEXT*, 2011.

[10] J. Cao et al. Per-packet Load-balanced, Low-latency Routing for Clos-based Data Center Networks. In *CoNEXT*, 2013.

[11] Y. Cao, M. Xu, X. Fu, and E. Dong. Explicit Multipath Congestion Control for Data Center Networks. In *CoNEXT*, 2013.

[12] Y. Chen, R. Griffith, J. Liu, R. H. Katz, and A. D. Joseph. Understanding TCP Incast Throughput Collapse in Datacenter Networks. In *WREN*, 2009.

[13] N. Dukkipati and N. McKeown. Why Flow-completion Time is the Right Metric for Congestion Control. *SIGCOMM Comput. Commun. Rev.*, 2006.

[14] A. Elwalid, C. Jin, S. Low, and I. Widjaja. MATE: MPLS adaptive traffic engineering. In *INFOCOM*, 2001.

[15] B. Fortz and M. Thorup. Internet traffic engineering by optimizing OSPF weights. In *INFOCOM*, 2000.

[16] R. Gallager. A Minimum Delay Routing Algorithm Using Distributed Computation. *Communications, IEEE Transactions on*, 1977.

[17] P. Gill, N. Jain, and N. Nagappan. Understanding Network Failures in Data Centers: Measurement, Analysis, and Implications. In *SIGCOMM*, 2011.

[18] A. Greenberg et al. VL2: a scalable and flexible data center network. In *SIGCOMM*, 2009.

[19] Apache Hadoop. `http://hadoop.apache.org/`.

[20] C.-Y. Hong, M. Caesar, and P. B. Godfrey. Finishing Flows Quickly with Preemptive Scheduling. In *SIGCOMM*, 2012.

[21] C.-Y. Hong et al. Achieving High Utilization with Software-driven WAN. In *SIGCOMM*, 2013.

[22] R. Jain and S. Paul. Network virtualization and software defined networking for cloud computing: a survey. *Communications Magazine, IEEE*, 51(11):24–31, 2013.

[23] S. Jain et al. B4: Experience with a Globally-deployed Software Defined Wan. In *SIGCOMM*, 2013.

[24] S. Jansen and A. McGregor. Performance, Validation and Testing with the Network Simulation Cradle. In *MASCOTS*, 2006.

[25] V. Jeyakumar et al. EyeQ: Practical Network Performance Isolation at the Edge. In *NSDI*, 2013.

[26] S. Kandula, D. Katabi, B. Davie, and A. Charny. Walking the Tightrope: Responsive Yet Stable Traffic Engineering. In *SIGCOMM*, 2005.

[27] S. Kandula, D. Katabi, S. Sinha, and A. Berger. Dynamic Load Balancing Without Packet Reordering. *SIGCOMM Comput. Commun. Rev.*, 37(2):51–62, Mar. 2007.

[28] S. Kandula, S. Sengupta, A. Greenberg, P. Patel, and R. Chaiken. The nature of data center traffic: measurements & analysis. In *IMC*, 2009.

[29] R. Kapoor et al. Bullet Trains: A Study of NIC Burst Behavior at Microsecond Timescales. In *CoNEXT*, 2013.

[30] P. Key, L. Massoulié, and D. Towsley. Path Selection and Multipath Congestion Control. *Commun. ACM*, 54(1):109–116, Jan. 2011.

[31] A. Khanna and J. Zinky. The Revised ARPANET Routing Metric. In *SIGCOMM*, 1989.

[32] M. Kodialam, T. V. Lakshman, J. B. Orlin, and S. Sengupta. Oblivious Routing of Highly Variable Traffic in Service Overlays and IP Backbones. *IEEE/ACM Trans. Netw.*, 17(2):459–472, Apr. 2009.

[33] T. Koponen et al. Network Virtualization in Multi-tenant Datacenters. In *NSDI*, 2014.

[34] V. Liu, D. Halperin, A. Krishnamurthy, and T. Anderson. F10: A Fault-tolerant Engineered Network. In *NSDI*, 2013.

[35] M. Mahalingam et al. VXLAN: A Framework for Overlaying Virtualized Layer 2 Networks over Layer 3 Networks. `http://tools.ietf.org/html/draft-mahalingam-dutt-dcops-vxlan-06`, 2013.

[36] N. Michael, A. Tang, and D. Xu. Optimal link-state hop-by-hop routing. In *ICNP*, 2013.

[37] MultiPath TCP - Linux Kernel implementation. `http://www.multipath-tcp.org/`.

[38] T. Narten et al. Problem Statement: Overlays for Network Virtualization. `http://tools.ietf.org/html/draft-ietf-nvo3-overlay-problem-statement-04`, 2013.

[39] J. Ousterhout et al. The case for RAMCloud. *Commun. ACM*, 54, July 2011.

[40] C. Papadimitriou. Algorithms, Games, and the Internet. In *Proc. of STOC*, 2001.

[41] C. Raiciu et al. Improving datacenter performance and robustness with multipath tcp. In *SIGCOMM*, 2011.

[42] M. Roughan, M. Thorup, and Y. Zhang. Traffic engineering with estimated traffic matrices. In *IMC*, 2003.

[43] T. Roughgarden. *Selfish Routing and the Price of Anarchy*. The MIT Press, 2005.

[44] S. Sen, D. Shue, S. Ihm, and M. J. Freedman. Scalable, Optimal Flow Routing in Datacenters via Local Link Balancing. In *CoNEXT*, 2013.

[45] M. Sridharan et al. NVGRE: Network Virtualization using Generic Routing Encapsulation. `http://tools.ietf.org/html/draft-sridharan-virtualization-nvgre-03`, 2013.

[46] A. Varga et al. The OMNeT++ discrete event simulation system. In *ESM*, 2001.

[47] V. Vasudevan et al. Safe and effective fine-grained TCP retransmissions for datacenter communication. In *SIGCOMM*, 2009.

[48] S. Vutukury and J. J. Garcia-Luna-Aceves. A Simple Approximation to Minimum-delay Routing. In *SIGCOMM*, 1999.

[49] H. Wang et al. COPE: Traffic Engineering in Dynamic Networks. In *SIGCOMM*, 2006.

[50] D. Wischik, C. Raiciu, A. Greenhalgh, and M. Handley. Design, Implementation and Evaluation of Congestion Control for Multipath TCP. In *NSDI*, 2011.

[51] D. Xu, M. Chiang, and J. Rexford. Link-state Routing with Hop-by-hop Forwarding Can Achieve Optimal Traffic Engineering. *IEEE/ACM Trans. Netw.*, 19(6):1717–1730, Dec. 2011.

[52] D. Zats, T. Das, P. Mohan, D. Borthakur, and R. H. Katz. DeTail: Reducing the Flow Completion Time Tail in Datacenter Networks. In *SIGCOMM*, 2012.

# Calendaring for Wide Area Networks

Srikanth Kandula Ishai Menache Roy Schwartz Spandana Raj Babbula

Microsoft

**Abstract**– Datacenter WAN traffic consists of high priority transfers that have to be carried as soon as they arrive, alongside large transfers with preassigned *deadlines* on their completion. The ability to offer guarantees to large transfers is crucial for business needs and impacts overall cost-of-business. State-of-the-art traffic engineering solutions only consider the current time epoch or minimize maximum utilization and hence cannot provide pre-facto *promises* to long-lived transfers. We present Tempus, an online temporal planning scheme that appropriately *packs* long-running transfers across network paths and future timesteps, while leaving capacity slack for future changes. Tempus builds on a tailored approximate solution to a mixed packing-covering linear program, which is parallelizable and scales well in both running time and memory usage. Consequently, Tempus can quickly and effectively update the promised future flow allocation when new transfers arrive or unexpected changes happen. Our experiments on traces from a large production WAN show, Tempus can offer and keep promises to long-lived transfers well in advance of their actual deadlines; the promise on minimal transfer size is comparable with an *offline* optimal solution and outperforms state-of-the-art solutions by 2-3X.

## Categories and Subject Descriptors

C.2.1 [Computer-Communication Networks]: Network Architecture and Design

## Keywords

Inter-datacenter; wide area networks; software-defined networking; deadlines; mixed packing covering

## 1. INTRODUCTION

Calendaring, colloquially, refers to setting aside future resources so that long term objectives are met in spite of short-term demands for resources.

Several large cloud companies operate geo-distributed datacenters connected through a Wide Area Network (WAN). The WANs carry traffic on the order of terabits/sec; are expensive and business critical [11, 13].

Traffic on the inter-datacenter WAN can be roughly characterized as a mix of two types. The first, called *highpri* traffic, comprises of instantaneously arriving demands due to customer facing traffic. These demands are somewhat unpredictable but are in general much smaller than the total capacity and need to be fully met. The second comprises of large transfers between datacenters that require WAN capacity over extended periods of time (see, e.g., [11, 13]). These make up the bulk of traffic on the WAN. Examples include moving a new search index generated at one datacenter to all the other distribution datacenters or moving datasets collected at one datacenter for later analysis on a big data cluster at another datacenter.

Long-running transfers are often time-critical. Delaying them may directly impact service quality and customer revenue. For example, delays in transferring the search index reduce response quality. Delays in onboarding datasets into Azure or AWS reduce revenue. In addition, transfer delays increase cost by wasting other resources, e.g., servers and developers are idle waiting for datasets to arrive. The time-sensitivity of the long-running transfers can be modeled in the form of a *deadline*. Some deadlines are hard, i.e., transfers are useless if late; however, many are "soft"; the transfer still needs to be completed however its "value" reduces past the deadline.

Ideally, a network provider should serve both types of traffic well. That is, the network should at all times be able to support the instantaneous demands. In addition, enough resources should be assigned to the longer term traffic so that these transfers have a predictable completion time. The objective of this paper is to design a solution to the calendaring problem, with the following characteristics:

1. No delays and zero loss rate for high-priority traffic.
2. When not limited by network capacity, long-running requests are fully met before the deadline.
3. When demands exceed network capacity, continue to offer guarantees such as maximizing the minimal fraction of transfers that finish before deadline (fairness), or maximizing a specified total utility function.

Satisfying all these goals is hard. Prior TE schemes minimize the maximum link utilization; some are dynamic [14] whereas others can be oblivious to the actual demands and network topology [1, 9]. With inter datacenter WANs, maximizing return on the investment requires operating at nearly full utilization; hence prior work does not apply. More recently, TE schemes have been proposed for inter-datacenter WANs [11, 13]. While they do operate at high utilizations, for reasons that we will explain below, these schemes only plan for a single future timestep (e.g., five minutes). Any transfers that last longer receive no guarantees. Further, such one-timestep TE has poor practical performance since (a) it cannot differentiate which of the large transfers to serve before the others, and along which network paths and (b) a current high transfer rate does not guarantee high transfer rates in the future. Scheduling transfers in earliest deadline first (EDF) order is also far from optimal primarily because it does not carefully spread transfers across the network. By scheduling strictly on deadline order, EDF can miss opportunities to simultaneously schedule non overlapping transfers. Also, EDF is unfair and performs poorly when all of the deadlines cannot be met.

To understand why calendaring is hard, consider the simpler *offline* scenario in which all requests and their requirements are known ahead of time. Satisfying all of the demands before the corresponding deadlines, or getting as close as possible to that goal,


*SIGCOMM'14,* August 17–22, 2014, Chicago, IL, USA.

http://dx.doi.org/10.1145/2619239.2626336.

requires optimally spreading traffic not just along all the available network paths but also along future times. This optimization problem can be formulated as a linear program (LP) but the size, as we will show, is typically huge (millions of variables and constraints).

The *online* version is harder still. Clearly the problem evolves with time; new long-running requests may arrive; links may fail or the volume of high-priority traffic can change. So the (offline) optimization problem described above has to now *run repeatedly*, e.g., once every few minutes or whenever substantial changes happen. This increases the computational cost. Worse, the cumulative effect of running a sequence of optimizations, each of which has only a limited knowledge of the future, can be very poor compared to the offline oracle solution above. For example, requests arriving later will be treated unfairly if all future network capacity has been promised to prior requests. Also, by not being able to *jointly optimize* over requests that arrive at different times, the solution quality will be poor (as we show later). Reneging on promises made to prior requests does help improve solution quality, i.e., more requests can be finished before deadline, but doing so significantly reduces the value of calendaring; no promises are "for sure" and hence, programmer's and customer's overall plans are disrupted.

Calendaring requires *online temporal* planning; *temporal* implies network resource has to be allocated far into the future to offer and meet guarantees to long-running transfers; *online* implies having to do this with imperfect future knowledge. To the best of our knowledge, no prior solution exists to this problem.

We present Tempus, a solution to the calendaring problem that meets these goals. Flows are allocated far into the future. Traffic is spread across network paths and time so as to maximize the minimal fraction of requests served before deadline as well as to maximize a utility function overall. Current network capacity is fully allocated. Future network capacity is systematically under-allocated so as to (a) offer high promises to requests that are currently in the system and (b) leave room open for future arrivals and other changes.

We achieve all of the above with an appropriate sequence of linear programs to be solved at each timestep. Tempus uses our novel mixed-packing covering solvers, which have the following distinctive features: (a) they have smaller memory footprint compared to running an LP solver at each timestep, and perhaps more importantly, (b) they conserve computation. That is, since the cumulative effect of the online optimization across all timesteps allocates only as much network flow as the offline LP, the total computational cost should be similar; i.e., the running time when added up across all timesteps equals the runntime of the offline LP; and hence the per timestep running time is much smaller. Our main algorithmic contribution is in showing how the packing-covering solver at each timestep proceeds by editing the flow allocation from the previous timestep rather than having to begin from scratch. In general, this is harder to achieve in an LP solver. Finally, we also show how to parallelize our mixed packing-covering solver.

We evaluate Tempus by measuring its ability to schedule large transfers that resemble those observed on a production WAN across a wide range of load factors. Compared to the offline optimal scheme, we see that Tempus achieves nearly the same minimum guarantee on transfer satisfaction, and nearly finishes the same fraction of flows before their deadlines. Along both these metrics, Tempus improves on top of the best performing variants of greedy (one timestep) schemes. Further, Tempus offers a promise to each transfer that is nearly the best possible as soon as the transfer arrives or soon after. Greedy heuristics, in contrast, can offer no guarantees beyond the fraction that has already been served. Tempus's parallelized version appears comparable to top-of-the-shelf LP solver on running time.

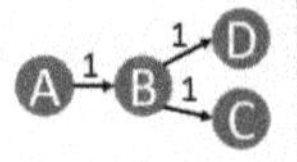


$a$: arrival, $D$: demand, $d$: deadline

| Request | $a$ | $D$ | $d$ |
|---|---|---|---|
| $R_1$: A → B | 1 | 4 | 6 |
| $R_2$: A → C | 1 | 2 | 8 |
| $R_3$: A → D | 1 | 2 | 7 |
| $R_4$: B → C | 4 | 5 | 9 |

| | $R_1$ | $R_2$ | $R_3$ | $R_4$ |
|---|---|---|---|---|
| Offline | [2,5] | 1,8 | [6,7] | [4,7], 9 |
| EDF | [1,4] | [7,8] | [5,6] | [4,6][9,10] |
| Greedy | [1,8] | [1,6] | [1,6] | [4,9] |
| Online | [1,4] | [7,8] | [5,6] | [4,6][9,10] |
| Tempus | [1,6] | [1,8] | [1,7] | [4,9] |

**Figure 1: An example illustrating online temporal planning. On the left are the network and request requirements. On the right are the schedules output by various schemes; some schedules have multiple requests active at the same time on the same edge, assume then that each request gets a fair share. The shares due to Tempus are uneven as we describe later.**

# 2. INTER-DC CALENDARING MODEL

In this section we describe characteristics of inter-datacenter traffic, motivate the need for online temporal planning and observe some key requirements for a calendaring solution.

## 2.1 Inter-DC WAN Traffic

**Heterogeneous traffic types/ deadlines.** As described earlier, traffic on the WAN is a mix of high priority traffic and large long-running transfers. The former has to be served fully with no delays whereas the latter can be served more flexibly. We use the term *request* to denote an application-desired transfer that the logically centralized traffic engineering algorithm has to manage (as in [11, 13]). Source and destination for requests are typically groups of servers (10s-1000s) in different datacenters. Consequently, requests can achieve high cumulative rate. The request specifies a begin time, the bytes to move within a deadline, optionally a set of paths through the network that the request's traffic should be sent over and optionally a peak traffic rate. We assume that the scheduling epochs are much coarser than TCP time-scales, (e.g., minutes vs. RTT of 100ms). Typical request sizes range from tens of terabytes to petabytes; deadlines range from an hour to a couple days.

**Need to highly utilize the WAN and to offer service guarantees to traffic.** The WAN between datacenters is an expensive resource; one study estimates amortized annual cost of 100s of millions of dollars [11]. Hence, fully utilizing the WAN maximizes return on cost. Prior work on managing inter-DC traffic designs an application-network interface to learn application requirements and runs an optimal traffic allocation per timestep. The resultant allowed rates are conveyed to each app and desired routes programmed into the network [11, 13]. Tempus uses a similar architecture. However, prior work either allocates traffic one time-step at a time [11, 13] or minimizes the maximum link utilization [1, 9, 14, 22] and cannot offer deadline SLAs to transfers.

**Estimating volume of high-priority traffic:** We observe that source servers can mark traffic type (e.g., using the IP ToS field). Our analysis of DC-WAN traces (taken from Microsoft's inter-DC WAN) indicates that high-priority traffic is estimatable: the per DC-pair time series of the volume of high priority traffic, over a period of a day exhibits a coefficient-of-variation, ranging from 0.06 to 0.48. A scheduling framework can plan based on the statistical averages of highpri demand but has to be robust to their variations.

## 2.2 Guidelines for Online Temporal Planning

In view of the above observations, there is a crucial need to spread the long-running requests over network paths and time so as to maximize deadline satisfaction as well as network utilization. However, such planning should be able to incorporate future request arrivals as well as the variability in the volume of high-priority traffic. Here, we observe some guidelines for such a solution.

**The "offline" calendaring problem can be formulated as a linear program (LP).** When the details of all requests and the precise volume of highpri transfers are known in advance, calendaring can be written as an LP. The details are deferred to §3. Table 1 lists the sizes of this LP. We note that a typical problem consists of networks with hundred datacenter sites, thousand links ($m$), tens of thousands of requests ($R$), i.e., a handful of requests per datacenter pair, and hundreds of time units ($T$) (e.g., corresponding to a five minute resolution, where the overall time horizon is a single day). The LP then has millions of variables and constraints. Such large LPs can in principle by solved by state-of-the-art LP solvers running on powerful machines but the space and running-time complexities are substantial. Here, we consider whether simpler *combinatorial* solutions exist for the core problem.

**Planning in the midst of dynamically evolving conditions.** Certainly, the calendaring problem evolves: new long-running requests arrive, the network can change etc. Simply re-running the above offline optimization problem, whenever a change happens or a short period later is computationally challenging. Worse, if the optimizations at each timestep run with no *context* of the others, the resultant allocations can be extremely poor.

We use a simple example to illustrate the important aspects that an online optimizer has to get right so as to approximate the offline oracle in spite of operating at each timestep without future knowledge. Figure 1 depicts a simple network and four requests. When requests are known a-priori, i.e., the offline case, observe that there exists a schedule that finishes all requests within their deadlines.

Let us first consider online strategies that look one timestep at a time. Earliest deadline first (*EDF*), at each timestep, schedules the requests in order of their deadlines. EDF does not finish $R_4$ before its deadline. EDF's key weakness is that picking requests strictly on deadline order prevents it from finding beneficial schedules that simultaneously schedule requests on different parts of the network (e.g., schedule $R_2$ early so that $R_1$ and $R_4$ can run simultaneously). Observe that in the above example, each request has exactly one usable path; EDF would have a harder time when traffic has to be spread across multiple paths. *Greedy* corresponds to schedulers proposed by prior work [11] that at each timestep allocate traffic evenly and are work-conserving; it cannot finish $R_1$ on time. The primary weakness here is the inability to plan into the future; fair share at each timestep does not translate to meeting deadlines, esp: if the deadlines are short. *Online* corresponds to a scheduler that does plan into the future for all the requests that it is currently aware of; it cannot finish $R_4$ on time. The primary weakness is that the schedule chosen at $t = 1$ offers promises to the first three requests without knowing what would arrive in the future; hence, very likely it picks a schedule that is not compatible. Re-scheduling at $t = 4$ does not help either because flow allocations in the past cannot be revisited. Reneging on promises can help the online scheduler meet deadlines of new requests but they counteract the value of calendaring. TEMPUS, as we show later is able to meet all deadlines. TEMPUS only allocates a small fraction of the capacity of edges in future timesteps. Since TEMPUS plans well into the future and attempts to finish as many requests as possible before their deadline, requests $R_1$, $R_2$, $R_3$ are "safe" with TEMPUS because there is enough capacity to finish them all before their deadlines even after under-allocating future edges. Further, due to the under-allocation TEMPUS retains enough capacity on future edges, e.g., the $B \to C$ edge for timesteps after 4, so as to finish request $R_4$.

**Promises.** As we saw above, a good calendaring solution has these properties: (a) offer to each request a promise on the fraction that will be satisfied before deadline; it is better to offer large promises early in the request lifetime; (b) do not renege on promises; (c) ensure promises are fair (or proportionally fair) in spite of online changes and (d) maintain high network utilization. In essence, the cumulative effect of the online optimizations should mimic closely the offline (impractical) scheme. Simply repeating the offline optimization at each timestep does not offer these properties.

| Scheme | Num. Equations | Num. Variables |
|---|---|---|
| Optimal Offline (flow) | $\approx n\text{RT} + m\text{T} + \text{R}$ | $m$RT |
| Optimal Offline (path) | $\approx m\text{T} + \text{R}$ | PRT |
| Online LP | above, at each timestep | |
| Greedy [11, 13] | per timestep, above with T set to 1 | |

**Table 1: Estimating the size of LPs to be solved for the calendaring problem; for a network graph with $n$ nodes, $m$ edges; planning $T$ timesteps into the future; and $R$ requests. Optionally, each request can require to be routed only along given paths (say $P$ per request).**

**Conservation of computation.** Notice that the online optimizations done at each timestep allocate all together a similar amount of flow as the single offline LP. Hence, it is natural to ask whether the total computation cost of the online optimizations can be about the same as the cost of running the single offline LP. For typical LP solvers, this does not hold; in fact, the cost of the optimization in each timestep can be as much as that of the offline LP.

In the rest of this paper, we will describe TEMPUS, an online temporal planner, that satisfies both the above requirements on solution quality and computation cost.

# 3. OVERVIEW OF TEMPUS

The goal of TEMPUS is to accommodate the long-term requests, while leaving enough capacity for ad-hoc high-priority requests. The system uses available information on long-running requests to efficiently *pack* these requests over time and network paths. Our goal here is to identify some key aspects, we defer the details to §4.

**Preliminaries.** The input for our problem consists of a graph $G = (V, E)$ where $|V| = n$ and $|E| = m$, and non-negative edge capacities $c : E \to \mathcal{R}^+$. Each long-term request $i$ with strict deadline is defined by the tuple $(a_i, b_i, d_i, D_i, s_i, t_i, \mathcal{P}_i)$ where: $a_i$ is the *aware time* in which TEMPUS becomes aware of the request; $b_i$ is the *begin time* from which the request can be scheduled; $d_i$ is the *deadline* after which the request cannot be scheduled anymore; $D_i$ is the *demand* of the request; $s_i$ is the *source* node the request needs to be routed from; $t_i$ is the *target* node the request needs to be routed to; $\mathcal{P}_i$ is the collection of admissible paths from $s_i$ to $t_i$ of the request. Requests with soft deadlines are defined similarly, with a value function replacing the strict deadline $d_i$; the details are deferred to §4. Additionally, the algorithm has an estimate $\chi_{e,t}$ for the fraction of the capacity $c_e$ of edge $e$ that will be needed by the high priority requests at time $t$; only the remaining $(1 - \chi_{e,t})$ fraction can be allocated to long-term requests.

## 3.1 Offline version

**Formulating offline calendaring as an optimization problem:** TEMPUS uses variables $f_{i,p,t}$ to denote the amount of flow allocated for request $i$ on path $p \in \mathcal{P}_i$ in time $t$. Using these variables, linear inequalities can be formulated to assert the allocation's feasibility: in every time and for every edge the total flow allocated on it does not exceed the available capacity. Further the traffic for request $i$, can only be routed when it is available $t \in [b_i, d_i]$ and totals no more than demand $D_i$ (and is at least $\alpha_i D_i$). Goals include maximizing the minimum fraction of request traffic routed before deadline ($\max \min_i \alpha_i$). The offline problem assumes perfect future knowledge of all requests and hence is not a practical solution.

**Adding utility.** While maximizing the smallest fraction $\alpha_i$ corresponds to a *fairness* objective, some parts of the network might remain under-utilized, i.e., more flow can be allocated but the request with the least $\alpha$ cannot be improved further. To fully use the network, we introduce a supplementary utility function, e.g., $\delta = \text{avg}_i \alpha_i$. We defer the precise definition of utility to later (§4), however, we note that several forms of utility can be specified as linear functions. After maximizing $\alpha$, we execute a second optimization problem to maximize the total utility.

Note that TEMPUS does not directly maximize how many transfers finish before their deadline. The *all-or-nothing* nature of the metric makes it hard to optimize; e.g., it cannot be captured with a linear constraint. However, maximizing $\alpha$ and then utility, as TEMPUS does, is a close approximation. In particular, when all deadlines are satisfiable TEMPUS will find such a flow allocation. Further, due to utility maximization, TEMPUS will finish some transfers before their deadline even when it cannot finish all transfers.

## 3.2 Online temporal planning

The main challenge is to solve the above optimization problem in an online manner, since new long-term requests can arrive at any time and other changes may happen. As discussed before, repeatedly applying the above offline optimization problem is computationally expensive because it has to plan far into the future. Further, it can lead to a substantially worse solution. Here, we discuss how to solve the latter; speeding-up the computation is in §3.3.

Rerunning the above optimization problem at each timestep treats requests that arrive later unfairly. Maximizing the minimum $\alpha_i$ and then, maximizing the total utility, can use up all of the available capacity on edges causing later requests to receive a very small $\alpha$. As we saw before, it also reduces how many requests finish before their deadlines because it cannot jointly optimize over all requests.

To retain fairness and improve solution quality, TEMPUS **systematically under-allocates future edges**. When planning at time $\tau$, the fraction of edge capacity that is available for allocation at times $t > \tau$ is denoted by $\beta_{e,t,\tau}$. We choose $\beta$ to be a function that decreases with $t - \tau$. Intuitively, the further an edge is into the future the less its capacity can be used up during the current timestep. At each consecutive timestep, more of the capacity becomes available ensuring that later arriving requests can be allocated on that {edge, time}. This helps with fairness. Solution quality also improves because TEMPUS allocates more capacity on timesteps in the near future for which it understands the requirements more completely. Due to the progressive release of capacity, TEMPUS's promise to long-term requests $\alpha_i$ increases with time; TEMPUS aims to offer large promises early in the lifetime of the request.

Another concern is that whereas capacity can be set aside on future edges for highpri traffic ($\chi_{e,t}$), the actual highpri traffic may require more or less capacity. If more is needed, some flow that has been promised to long-term requests has to be lowered causing promises to be reneged. TEMPUS **corrects the solution for actual usages of high-priority requests.** Edges that are under-used by highpri traffic need no special consideration since TEMPUS uses the spare capacity to increase the flow for requests that are not fully satisfied. To correct over-usage, TEMPUS reduces the pre-promised flows $f_{i,p,\tau}$ of a carefully chosen set of long-term requests such that (a) the total flow on every edge remains below capacity, while (b) having minimal effect on promises $\alpha_i$ as well as the total utility. We use an LP for this correction; the LP is small since it only considers the current timestep $\tau$. Intuitively, the LP chooses requests that have later deadlines or other less constrained paths, and hence decreases in $f_{i,p,\tau}$ can be made up for at other times or along other paths.

Observe that link and switch failures can also be handled similarly because a link failure can be mimicked as if a highpri request with demand equal to link capacity appears for that timestep.

A side-effect of the above is that TEMPUS can renege upon a promise. In practice, however, we see that this occurs rarely; because TEMPUS preferentially lowers the flows of requests that can be made up for later. Further, when TEMPUS reneges, we find that the fraction served by TEMPUS is close to the fraction served by the optimal offline scheme (which has perfect future knowledge).

Lengthy requests, i.e., with a large $d_i - a_i$, will slow down any temporal planner by forcing each timestep to plan far into the future (up to $\max d_i$ time). To ensure a fast solution, TEMPUS optionally employs a **sliding window** approach; i.e., it only plans for a fixed number of time steps into the future. Requests whose deadline lies beyond the sliding window's length are *broken* into a smaller request and their demand is scaled accordingly.

## 3.3 Approximate packing-covering solvers

We have a **choice of solvers**; whereas the overall framework described so far leads to a novel solution for the online temporal planning problem, how the optimization at each timestep is solved crucially impacts the practicality of the solution. We offer a brief background on iterative solvers for mixed packing covering problems and then comment on how TEMPUS extends them for calendaring.

**Background on Packing-Covering Solvers:** Given a variable vector $\mathbf{x}$, a *packing* matrix $\mathbf{P}$ and a *covering* matrix $\mathbf{C}$, a mixed packing covering problem finds a feasible solution for these inequalities:

$$\{\mathbf{Px} \le 1,\ \ \mathbf{Cx} \ge 1,\ \ \mathbf{x} \ge 0\}, \tag{1}$$

where $\mathbf{x} \in \mathcal{R}_n$, $\mathbf{P} \in \mathcal{R}^+_{m\times n}$, $\mathbf{C} \in \mathcal{R}^+_{\ell\times n}$; $\mathcal{R}^+$ indicates that all entries in $\mathbf{P}$ and $\mathbf{C}$ are non-negative.

It is easy to see that any mixed packing covering problem is a linear program (LP). While it can be solved using typical LP solvers, its special structure allows for iterative solutions that have some useful properties. Intuitively, a common approach in the design of iterative solvers is the following. First, let $\mathbf{x} = 0$ be the starting zero solution; all packing constraints are trivially satisfied but none of the covering constraints are met. Second, inductively, suppose there exists an increment $\Delta\mathbf{x}$ to the variables that satisfies:

$$\max \mathbf{P}(\mathbf{x} + \Delta\mathbf{x}) - \max \mathbf{Px} \le \min \mathbf{C}(\mathbf{x} + \Delta\mathbf{x}) - \min \mathbf{Cx}. \tag{2}$$

Here, max (min) is taken over the $m$ ($l$) packing (covering) constraints. In words, the above equation ensures that the smallest covering constraint improves by more than the largest packing constraint. Incrementing the variables by such a $\Delta\mathbf{x}$ is helpful since it moves the solution closer towards satisfying all covering constraints while giving up a smaller amount on the packing constraints. Finally, observe that repeating the above step until all covering constraints are satisfied would yield a feasible solution.

Translating the above intuition into a solution is challenging because (a) it is not apriori clear how to search for such a $\Delta\mathbf{x}$ and (b) more importantly, it is unclear that a solution for every feasible mixed packing-covering problem could be found by summing up increments that satisfy (2).

Young's method [24], among several other methods, adopts the above approach. First, since min and max are not smooth functions, Young replaces them with:

$$\min_{1\le i\le n} \{\mathbf{x}_i\} \ge lmin(\mathbf{x}) \triangleq -\ln\left(\sum_{i=1}^{n} e^{-\mathbf{x}_i}\right),$$

$$\max_{1\le i\le n} \{\mathbf{x}_i\} \le lmax(\mathbf{x}) \triangleq \ln\left(\sum_{i=1}^{n} e^{\mathbf{x}_i}\right).$$

Second, Young restricts the increment per iteration to a small amount and to one variable $\mathbf{x}_i$ in $\mathbf{x}$. Then, condition (2) becomes:

$$\frac{\partial lmax\,(\mathbf{Px})}{\partial \mathbf{x}_i} \leq \frac{\partial lmin\,(\mathbf{Cx})}{\partial \mathbf{x}_i}. \quad (3)$$

In words, for variable $\mathbf{x}_i$, the rate of change of the maximum over packing constraints should be smaller than the rate of change of the minimum over covering constraints. Equipped with this new condition, Young [24] proved that if the packing-covering problem is feasible, then for any current value assignment to variables $\mathbf{x}$ there is a variable $\mathbf{x}_i$ that satisfies (3). The solver starts with $\mathbf{x} = 0$, repeatedly makes increments satisfying (3) and terminates when no such increment can be found or when all covering constraints are met.

**Extending mixed packing covering solvers to online temporal planning:** Here, we mention how iterative solvers for mixed packing covering problems are more suitable for the calendaring problem and show how TEMPUS extends the theoretical work.

For the online step in the calendaring problem, we observe that the solution to the mixed packing-covering problem in a timestep can be *edited* into a feasible starting point for the problem of the next timestep. Observe that edge capacity translates to a packing constraint, request satisfaction translates to a covering constraint and that the variable vector $\mathbf{x}$ contains flow allocations. To wit, in the online step, the constraints change as follows (precise details are in §4.2): for each newly arriving request and {edge, time} that is to be newly considered, new constraints on their respective deadline satisfaction and capacity are added. Some existing constraints are edited, for example, to release more capacity for allocation. The solution to the previous packing-covering problem is expanded by adding flow variables for newly arriving requests and on new edges and setting them to zero. Crucially, observe that none of the packing constraints are violated (new edges have flow 0 and every old edge has strictly larger capacity to allocate). The old covering constraints are unchanged whereas the new covering constraints are unmet (flow for new requests is 0). Hence, the old solution is a feasible searching point for the new problem. Further, as we show later by extending Young's proof that if the new problem is feasible, increments that satisfy condition (3) will continue to exist.

This is incredibly useful because: (a) all of the previously promised allocations are retained and (b) none of the work that has been done by the previous steps, in terms of allocating flow, needs to be redone which speeds-up the computation as we prove later.

We also observe that solving calendaring with a mixed packing-covering solver requires less memory. Table 1 describes the problem size for different approaches. Notice that in the calendaring problem, the most numerous are the flow variables; per request, per time and per path (or per edge) they record how much flow has been allocated. We assert that the iterative solver above need not maintain all of the flow variables. In fact it suffices to keep per-packing and covering constraint (edge and request), the current state of $\mathbf{Px}$ or $\mathbf{Cx}$ respectively, i.e., available capacity and unmet demand. Upon allocating some flow along a path to a request, the effect to these constraints is recorded. The precise flow variables are needed only for the current time instance, so as to push appropriate routes into the network, and can be computed by solving a small LP for the current timestep that takes as input the total that has been allocated to requests in that timestep. Consequently, the memory overhead reduces by at least one order of magnitude (see §5.1 and §6.3).

Similarly to [24], we note that the iterative solver can be parallelized since typically many feasible increments $\Delta\mathbf{x}$ exist. Young describes how to parallelize the search process. However, we observe some additional aspects of our problem that make searching for a feasible increment much faster (§5.3). Consequently, the bottleneck shifts to applying the increment for which we design a novel parallelization technique (§5.2).

Finally, we note that a packing-covering solver only outputs an *approximate* solution to a *feasibility* problem. They guarantee that: (a) if the packing-covering equations are infeasible, the solver would report infeasibility; (b) if the packing-covering equations are feasible, the solver reports feasibility but the solution can violate the packing constraints by a small amount. We extend TEMPUS to cope with the imprecision and yet obtain the desired objective by solving a small number of feasibility problems (§4.2).

## 3.4 Takeaways

We have described how to design appropriate optimization problems to solve at each timestep such that their cumulative effect avoids unfairness and provides a good quality solution; close to that from the offline oracle (§3.2). The per-timestep optimization can also be posed as a packing-covering problem. And, we develop a new *online* version of Young's algorithm to solve sequences of packing-covering problems (§3.3). This solution has some nice properties compared to a general LP solver. We emphasize that unlike greedy approaches (e.g., [11]), our online algorithm schedules flows far in the future, and can thus provide *promises* $\alpha_i$ on the fraction of the demand that each request $i$ would be able to transfer. Since inter-DC WANs operate at nearly full utilization, prior efforts to minimize network congestion do not apply [1, 9, 14, 22]. Further, inter-DC WANs have less statistical multiplexing than ISP networks - few large requests contribute most of the bytes - and hence, deadline SLAs to large requests is an important part of the overall traffic management problem. We proceed to the details.

# 4. DESIGN OF TEMPUS

In this section, we present details of TEMPUS including provable guarantees on its runtime. For clarity, we first examine the offline case (§4.1) and then build our novel formulation for the online case (§4.2). In either case, we first describe the optimization problem, which can be solved using an LP, and then present the TEMPUS algorithm that builds on Young's method [24].

Recall from §3 that the input for our problem is a graph $G = (V, E)$ with edge capacities $c_e$; requests defined by their parameter tuple $(a_i, b_i, d_i, D_i, s_i, t_i, \mathcal{P}_i)$ (see §3 for definitions of parameters). Additionally, unless otherwise specified, we assume that there is an absolute size $T$ that upper bounds all request deadlines.

## 4.1 (Impractical) Offline Case

In the offline case, note that the algorithm is aware of all (future) requests. Given the input graph $G$ and all $k$ requests, we first wish to find the largest $\alpha$, $0 \leq \alpha \leq 1$, such that a fraction of at least $\alpha$ of the demand of each request can be routed before its deadline while respecting the capacity constraints. Maximizing $\alpha$ corresponds to a *fairness* objective. This is the well-known *Concurrent Multi-commodity Flow* problem. Suppose $f_{i,p,t}$ denotes the flow variable associated with request $i$ at time $t$ on path $p \in \mathcal{P}_i$ and $\mathbf{f}$ denotes the vector of all flow variables. Consider these quantities,

$$h_{e,t}(\mathbf{f}) \triangleq \sum_{i:b_i \leq t \leq d_i} \sum_{p \in \mathcal{P}_i : e \in p} f_{i,p,t} \qquad \text{(capacity usage)}$$

$$\ell_i(\mathbf{f}) \triangleq \sum_{t=b_i}^{d_i} \sum_{p \in \mathcal{P}_i} f_{i,p,t} \qquad \text{(satisfied demand)}$$

$$g(\mathbf{f}) \triangleq \sum_{i=1}^{k} \sum_{p \in \mathcal{P}_i} \sum_{t=b_i}^{d_i} u_{i,p,t} \cdot f_{i,p,t} \qquad \text{(utility)},$$

where $h_{e,t}(\mathbf{f})$ corresponds to the total flow on edge $e$ at time $t$, $\ell_i(\mathbf{f})$ corresponds to the demand of request $i$ satisfied by its deadline, and $g(\mathbf{f})$ corresponds to the value of the secondary utility function. Recall that we add a secondary *utility function* such that maximizing utility would increase the network utilization even when the request with the worst $\alpha$ cannot be further improved. We restrict utility to functions having $u_{i,p,t} \geq 0$ so that $g(\mathbf{f})$ would correspond to a covering constraint. We emphasize that $u_{i,p,t}$ are inputs to the solver and are *not* variables for the optimization problem. Note that the $\delta$ = average $\alpha$ mentioned earlier is a special case with $u_{i,p,t} = \frac{1}{k \cdot D_i}$.

We seek to maximize utility $g(\mathbf{f})$ among all the optimal solutions of the fairness objective (maximizing $\min_i \alpha_i$). If $\alpha$ and $U$ are the target values for each of these goals, two LPs could be formulated to maximize each of them in sequence with the following constraints:

$$LP(\alpha, U) = \Big\{ \begin{array}{lll} h_{e,t}(\mathbf{f}) \leq c_e & \forall e \in E, \forall t \in [0, T], & \text{(capacity)} \\ \ell_i(\mathbf{f}) \leq D_i & \forall 1 \leq i \leq k, & \text{(demand)} \\ \ell_i(\mathbf{f}) \geq \alpha D_i & \forall 1 \leq i \leq k, & \text{(fairness)} \\ g(\mathbf{f}) \geq U, & & \text{(utility)} \\ \mathbf{f} \geq 0 \Big\} & & \end{array}$$

### 4.1.1 Applying mixed packing-covering solvers

Observe that $LP(\alpha, U)$ is exactly in the form of (1), as we can normalize the constraints so that their right hand side is all 1s. Directly maximizing $\alpha$ and then $U$ is not possible however since the iterative solver only checks the feasibility for given values of each. Hence, we start with $U = 0$ and conduct a search to find the largest $\alpha$ for which $LP(\alpha, 0)$ is feasible. The resulting $\alpha$ is then kept fixed and we search for the largest $U$ for which $LP(\alpha, U)$ is feasible.

Next, we describe how to use Young's algorithm to determine given some values for $\alpha$ and $U$ whether a flow vector $\mathbf{f}$ exists that satisfies $LP(\alpha, U)$? Figure 2 shows the pseudo-code for the algorithm. It follows the intuition described in §3.3. We use these internal variables, each corresponding to a constraint of $LP(\alpha, U)$:

$$\begin{array}{ll} y_{e,t} \triangleq e^{\frac{N}{\varepsilon \cdot c_e} \cdot h_{e,t}(\mathbf{f})} & \text{(capacity)} \\ q_i \triangleq e^{\frac{N}{\varepsilon \cdot D_i} \cdot \ell_i(\mathbf{f})} & \text{(demand - packing)} \\ z_i \triangleq e^{-\frac{N}{\varepsilon \cdot \alpha \cdot D_i} \cdot \ell_i(\mathbf{f})} & \text{(fairness)} \\ r \triangleq e^{-\frac{N}{\varepsilon \cdot U} \cdot g(\mathbf{f})} & \text{(utility),} \end{array}$$

where $\varepsilon$ is an accuracy parameter and $N$ is a scaling factor to be specified later. The algorithm begins with an all 0s solution. In every iteration a specific variable $f_{i^*,p^*,t^*}$ in $\mathbf{f}$ is increased by a small amount. This variable is chosen according to condition $(*)$, which is equivalent to condition (3) from Section 3.3. However, we simplify by including only the unsatisfied covering constraints in $(*)$, i.e., requests $i$ for which $\ell_i(\mathbf{f}) < \alpha D_i$ and possibly the utility constraint if $g(\mathbf{f}) < U$. One can verify the equivalence between $(*)$ and (3) by calculating the appropriate partial derivatives of the following two functions that correspond to $lmax(\mathbf{Px}), lmin(\mathbf{Cx})$ respectively:

$$\ln\left(\sum_{e \in E}\sum_{t=0}^{T} y_{e,t} + \sum_{i=1}^{k} q_i\right), -\ln\left(\sum_{i=1}^{k} 1_{\{\ell_i(\mathbf{f})<\alpha D_i\}} z_i + 1_{\{g(\mathbf{f})<U\}} r\right).$$

Here, $1_A$ refers to the indicator function of the event $A$, i.e., $1_A = 1$ if $A$ is true and 0 otherwise.

### 4.1.2 Analysis

The following two theorems summarize the correctness of the algorithm and bound its runtime (proofs are deferred to [15]).

---

**initialization**

$$\begin{array}{ll} y_{e,t} \leftarrow 1 & \forall e \in E, \forall 0 \leq t \leq T \\ q_i \leftarrow 1 & \forall 1 \leq i \leq k \\ z_i \leftarrow 1 & \forall 1 \leq i \leq k \\ r \leftarrow 1, \mathbf{f} \leftarrow 0 & \end{array}$$

**while** $\exists 1 \leq i \leq k$ *s.t.* $\ell_i(\mathbf{f}) < \alpha D_i$ *or* $g(\mathbf{f}) < U$ **do**

Find $1 \leq i^* \leq k$, $b_{i^*} \leq t^* \leq d_{i^*}$, and $p^* \in \mathcal{P}_{i^*}$ s.t.:

$$\frac{\sum_{e \in p^*} \frac{y_{e,t^*}}{c_e} + \frac{q_{i^*}}{D_{i^*}}}{\sum_{e \in E}\sum_{t=0}^{T} y_{e,t} + \sum_{i=1}^{k} q_i} \leq \frac{1_{\{\ell_{i^*}(\mathbf{f})<\alpha D_{i^*}\}} \frac{z_{i^*}}{\alpha D_{i^*}} + 1_{\{g(\mathbf{f})<U\}} \frac{u_{i^*,p^*,t^*}}{U} r}{\sum_{i=1}^{k} 1_{\{\ell_i(\mathbf{f})<\alpha D_i\}} z_i + 1_{\{g(\mathbf{f})<U\}} r} \quad (*)$$

**if** *there is no such* $i^*$, $t^*$ *and* $p^*$ **then**

abort and return there is no feasible solution;

**else**

// choosing step size parameter $\gamma$

$\gamma \leftarrow \varepsilon \cdot \min\{D_{i^*}, \min_{e \in p^*}\{c_e\}\}$;

**if** $\ell_{i^*}(\mathbf{f}) < \alpha D_{i^*}$ **then**

$\gamma \leftarrow \min\{\gamma, \varepsilon \alpha D_{i^*}\}$;

**if** $g(\mathbf{f}) < U$ **then**

$\gamma \leftarrow \min\left\{\gamma, \varepsilon \frac{U}{u_{i^*,p^*,t^*}}\right\}$;

// updating internal variables

$y_{e,t^*} \leftarrow y_{e,t^*} \cdot e^{\frac{\gamma}{c_e}}, \forall e \in p^*$;

$q_{i^*} \leftarrow q_{i^*} \cdot e^{\frac{\gamma}{D_{i^*}}}$;

$z_{i^*} \leftarrow z_{i^*} \cdot e^{-\frac{\gamma}{\alpha \cdot D_{i^*}}}$;

$r \leftarrow r \cdot e^{-\frac{u_{i^*,p^*,t^*} \cdot \gamma}{U}}$;

// updating $\mathbf{f}$ [a]

$f_{i^*,p^*,t^*} \leftarrow f_{i^*,p^*,t^*} + \frac{\varepsilon}{N} \cdot \gamma$;

**return f**;

---

**Figure 2: Pseudo-Code for Feasibility Check of $LP(\alpha, U)$**

[a] If the increase in $f_{i^*,p^*,t^*}$ causes a covering constraint to change from being violated to satisfied, the algorithm chooses the smallest $\gamma$ value such that this covering constraint is satisfied with equality.

**Theorem 1.** *For any* $0 \leq \alpha \leq 1$ *and* $U \geq 0$, *if* $LP(\alpha, U)$ *is feasible then for every* $0 < \varepsilon \leq 1/2$ *and*

$$N \geq \ln\left((m(T+1)+k) \cdot (k+1)^{\frac{1+\varepsilon}{1-\varepsilon/2}}\right)$$

*the output* $\mathbf{f}$ *of Algorithm 2 satisfies:*

$$\begin{array}{ll} h_{e,t}(\mathbf{f}) \leq (1+3\varepsilon)c_e & \forall e \in E, \forall 0 \leq t \leq T \\ \ell_i(\mathbf{f}) \leq (1+3\varepsilon)D_i & \forall 1 \leq i \leq k \\ \ell_i(\mathbf{f}) \geq \alpha D_i & \forall 1 \leq i \leq k \\ g(\mathbf{f}) \geq U. & \end{array}$$

**Theorem 2.** *For every* $0 < \varepsilon \leq 1/2$, *Algorithm 2 terminates within* $\frac{N}{\varepsilon^2}[(1+3\varepsilon)(m(T+1)+k)+(k+1)]+(k+2)$ *iterations.*

Note that Theorem 1 proves that for any feasible set of packing-covering constraints, the pseudocode shown will find a feasible solution with the caveat that the packing constraints can be violated by a small amount of $(1+3\varepsilon)$. Smaller the value of $\varepsilon$, the less the violation. Note also that $N \approx \ln(mTk)$. From Theorem 2, we see that the number of iterations is at most $O\left(\varepsilon^{-2}(mT+k)\ln(mTk)\right)$; so smaller $\varepsilon$ increases running time. We use $\varepsilon = .1$ in TEMPUS.

## 4.2 Online Temporal Planning

Here, we present a novel formulation that copes with online arrival of requests and the TEMPUS algorithm. The algorithm has two main properties: it sets the $\alpha_i$ in a fair manner; and it makes only *incremental* changes to the solution at each subsequent time-step.

We index the online model with the current time-step $\tau$. Let $R(\tau)$ denote the requests that are relevant at time $\tau$, i.e., requests that the algorithm is aware of (those with $a_i \le \tau$) and whose deadline did not expire yet (those with $d_i \ge \tau$). Analogous to §4.1, for a time-step $\tau$, we consider the following quantities:

$$h^{\tau}_{e,t}(\mathbf{f}) \triangleq \sum_{i\in R(\tau):\max\{\tau,b_i\}\le t\le d_i} \sum_{p\in\mathcal{P}_i:e\in p} f_{i,p,t}$$

$$\ell^{\tau}_i(\mathbf{f}) \triangleq \sum_{t=\max\{\tau,b_i\}}^{d_i} \sum_{p\in\mathcal{P}_i} f_{i,p,t}$$

$$g^{\tau}(\mathbf{f}) \triangleq \sum_{i\in R(\tau)} \sum_{p\in\mathcal{P}_i} \sum_{t=\max\{\tau,b_i\}}^{d_i} u_{i,p,t}\cdot f_{i,p,t}\,.$$

As before, the online problem can be formulated as two linear optimization problems at each time-step $\tau$: first maximize $\min_i \alpha_i$ and then maximize $U$, with the following constraints:

$$\begin{aligned} LP^{\tau}(\boldsymbol{\alpha},U) = \{ & h^{\tau}_{e,t}(\mathbf{f}) \le c_e && \forall e\in E, \forall \tau\le t\le T,\\ & \ell^{\tau}_i(\mathbf{f}) \le D_i - F_{i,\tau-1} && \forall i\in R(\tau),\\ & \ell^{\tau}_i(\mathbf{f}) \ge \alpha_i D_i - F_{i,\tau-1} && \forall i\in R(\tau),\\ & g^{\tau}(\mathbf{f}) \ge U - U_{\tau-1},\\ & \mathbf{f}\ge 0\}. \end{aligned}$$

Here $F_{i,\tau-1}$ denotes the total flow of request $i$ routed *prior* to time step $\tau$, i.e., up to time step $\tau-1$ including. Similarly, $U_{\tau-1}$ denotes the total utility obtained *prior* to time step $\tau$. Formally,

$$F_{i,\tau-1} \triangleq \sum_{t=b_i}^{\tau-1} \sum_{p\in\mathcal{P}_i} f_{i,p,t}$$

$$U_{\tau-1} \triangleq \sum_{i=1}^{k} \sum_{p\in\mathcal{P}_i} \sum_{t=b_i}^{\tau-1} u_{i,p,t}\cdot f_{i,p,t}\,.$$

It is important to notice the following. First, $\boldsymbol{\alpha}$ given as input to $LP^{\tau}(\boldsymbol{\alpha},U)$ is a *vector* since different requests can have different promises based in part on when they are made aware to the optimization problem. Second, coordinates $f_{i,p,t}$ of $\mathbf{f}$ are variables of $LP^{\tau}(\boldsymbol{\alpha},U)$ only if the request is relevant and the time has not yet passed, i.e., $t\ge\tau$ and $i\in R(\tau)$. Flow variables from the past are fixed constants and cannot be changed by the algorithm.

### 4.2.1 *The basic* TEMPUS *algorithm*

First, we describe how to check whether a feasible flow assignment $\mathbf{f}$ exists that satisfies $LP^{\tau}(\boldsymbol{\alpha},U)$ given some values for $\boldsymbol{\alpha}$ and $U$. Observe that, to check feasibility, one can apply Algorithm 2 with syntactic changes that follow from the definition of $LP^{\tau}(\boldsymbol{\alpha},U)$. Specifically, replace $D_i$ by $(D_i - F_{i,\tau-1})$, replace $\alpha D_i$ by $(\alpha_i D_i - F_{i,\tau-1})$ and replace $U$ by $(U - U_{\tau-1})$. Further, the range of search for a satisfactory increment $i^*, t^*$ should be restricted to flows that are relevant and time that is in the future, i.e., $i\in R(\tau), t\ge\tau$. Similarly, the denominators of condition $(*)$ are changed to include only the relevant edges $(t\ge\tau)$ and requests $(i\in R(\tau))$.

Second, it is more interesting to examine how the solution from the current time-step $\mathbf{f}$ is usable as a starting point in the subsequent time-step.[1] All requests $i$ that are not new, i.e., $a_i<\tau$, already have a promised $\alpha_i$ value from the previous time step. Newly aware requests are initialized to a promise of 0; all their flow variables are also set to 0. All flow variables on edges in time-steps that have not been allocated before are also set to 0. Additionally let $U$ be the guarantee on the secondary utility from the previous time step. Our online algorithm conducts a *water filling* process, in which the lowest promise values are increased as long as $LP^{\tau}(\boldsymbol{\alpha},U)$ is feasible, while keeping $U$ from the previous time step fixed. Once the water filling process cannot proceed anymore, the resulting $\boldsymbol{\alpha}$ is fixed and a search for the largest possible $U$ value is conducted.

We note that by using the previous solution $\mathbf{f}$ as a starting point in each time-step, the *total* network capacity that TEMPUS allocates across all steps is the same as the offline optimization; bar a few cases where pre-promised flows are moved elsewhere. Hence, intuitively, the work done by the algorithm and its running time are amortized over time-steps; i.e., the per time-step running time is very small. General LP solvers do not behave similarly.

### 4.2.2 *Analysis*

Similar to Section 4.1.2, one can prove that if $LP^{\tau}(\boldsymbol{\alpha},U)$ is feasible, then the online algorithm, regardless of the $\mathbf{f}$, will find an $i^*\in R(\tau)$, $t^*\in[\max\{\tau,b_{i^*}\},d_{i^*}]$ and $p^*\in\mathcal{P}_{i^*}$ that satisfy $(*)$.

We will focus though on bounding the number of iterations that the online algorithm executes per time-step. Let $K$ be an upper bound on the number of relevant requests in any time step $\tau$, namely $|R(\tau)|\le K$ for all $0\le\tau\le T$.

**Theorem 3.** *The number of iterations in the rth* successful *execution of the algorithm that decides whether $LP^{\tau}(\boldsymbol{\alpha},U)$ is feasible, is upper bounded by*

$$K+1+\frac{N}{\varepsilon^2}\left[X_r+(K+1)\right]\,,$$

*where the summation of $X_r$ over all successful executions is at most* $(1+3\varepsilon)(m(T+1)+K)$.[2]

Note that as before $N\approx\ln(mTK)$ and the number of iterations per timestep is at most $O\left(\varepsilon^{-2}(X_r+K)\ln(mTK)\right)$, where $X_r = O(mT+K)$. Comparing this with Theorem 2 shows that the total number of iterations used by TEMPUS are similar in the offline and online cases; the proof can be found in [15].

### 4.2.3 *Additional Features in* TEMPUS

We now discuss additional aspects in TEMPUS that build upon the above basic algorithm (§4.2.1). Throughout this discussion, $\tau$ refers to the current time-step while $t$ refers to a general time-step.

**Traffic Smoothening:** Recall that to retain fairness when requests arrive online, TEMPUS systematically under-allocates future edges. Otherwise, early arrivals can use up all of the capacity resulting in poor promises to later arrivals and low fairness.

Intuitively, our goal with *traffic smoothening* is to limit the capacity that is allocated at any one time-step to leave room for future arrivals. Formally, we denote by $\beta_{e,t,\tau}$ the fraction of the capacity of edge $e$ in future time $t$ that can be allocated by online TEMPUS at time step $\tau$. This changes the capacity constraint of $LP^{\tau}(\boldsymbol{\alpha},U)$ as follows: $h^{\tau}_{e,t}(\mathbf{f})\le\beta_{e,t,\tau}c_e$. Given an edge $e\in E$ and a time $t$, $\beta_{e,t,\tau}$ is a function defined for $t\ge\tau$ with a non-decreasing value in $[0,1]$. We require that $\beta_{e,\tau,\tau}=1$, since the entire capacity of an edge that belongs to the current time-step can be safely used. In our experiments, we use $\beta_{e,t,\tau} = exp\left(-(t-\tau)/c\right)$ for some constant $c$.

[1]Note that $\mathbf{f}$ also determines the initial values of $y_{e,t}$, $q_i$, $z_i$ and $r$ as per their definition in §4.1.

[2]Choose $N\ge\ln\left((m(T+1)+K)K^{(1+\varepsilon)/(1-\varepsilon/2)}\right)$.

Note that this function depends only on $t - \tau$, i.e., how much further into the future the edge is. An important side-effect is that the promises offered by the online allocation rely more on network capacity in the immediate future than on network capacity that is far into the future; this reduces the risk of reneging on promises since unpredictability increases the further one looks into the future.

**Bounded Horizon:** In order to speed up the running time, TEMPUS optionally uses a *sliding window* approach - given window size $W$, TEMPUS only plans up to $W$ time steps into the future. Accordingly, $LP^\tau(\boldsymbol{\alpha}, U)$ can be edited to include only time-steps $t \in [\tau, \tau + W]$. We replace active requests whose deadline falls outside the window, with equivalent smaller ones that fits within the window. That is, the smaller request has deadline $\tau + W$ and has demand proportional (according to time) to its current unmet demand. When $W$ is large, the fraction of total demand from such requests is small and there is little net impact on solution quality.

**Capacity Grace:** As stated in Theorem 1 and §3 when discussing their applicability, iterative packing covering solvers can produce solutions that violate the packing constraints (esp: edge capacities) by a small multiplicative factor of at most $(1+3\varepsilon)$. Normally, this is not an issue due to the above under-allocation, i.e., $(1+3\varepsilon)\beta_{e,t,\tau} \cdot c_e$ can be smaller than $c_e$. Hence, then, we set the $\beta$ value in the next time step ($\beta_{e,t,\tau+1}$) to be the maximum between the planned $\beta$ value and the edge capacity fraction that has already been allocated ($\frac{h^\tau_{e,t}(\mathbf{f})}{c_e}$). This approach is the common case and allows us to cope with capacity violations due to the approximate nature of the solver.

**Post-Processing LP:** However, it may be possible that the capacity violations due to the solver truly exceed edge capacity. This is more likely for the current time-step, wherein all of the edge capacities are available for allocation ($\beta_{e,t,t} = 1$) as well as for time-steps in the near future that have high $\beta$ values. One possibility is to try and repair the over-allocation by steering traffic from the edges where capacity is violated on to other edges and times. However, since the capacity violation can happen on any future edge, the optimization problem to repair would also have time as a dimension and can be large. Another alternative is to reject solutions that violate edge capacity, i.e., consider a given $(\boldsymbol{\alpha}, U)$ feasibility question to be infeasible even though the solver reports feasibility if it offers a flow assignment $\mathbf{f}$ that violates edge capacity. TEMPUS chooses this option. Due in part to such rejections the approximate solver can fail to fully allocate the edges in the current time-step even though flows that could use the capacity exist. Hence, after the searches for maximum $\boldsymbol{\alpha}$ and then maximum $U$ have concluded, TEMPUS uses a post-processing LP that aims to maximize the utility by allocating all of the unused capacity in the current time-step. Since this LP only relates to the current time-step, it is considerably smaller than the calendaring LP and can be solved quickly.

**High-Priority Requests:** As already mentioned in §3, high priority requests arrive in an online manner and *must* be satisfied. To incorporate highpri requests in $LP^\tau(\boldsymbol{\alpha}, U)$, TEMPUS adds a new request that arrives and ends in the current time-step, has demand equal to the cumulative demand of highpri requests, and requires full service, i.e., promise = 1. Further, for future time-steps ($t > \tau$), recall that TEMPUS sets aside some capacity for highpri requests ($\chi_{e,t}$). This can be done by replacing the corresponding $c_e$ with $(1-\chi_{e,t}) \cdot c_e$ in the above description of TEMPUS. TEMPUS infers $\chi_{e_t}$ based on historical usages of highpri traffic per-edge, per-time-of-day.

Since the $\chi$s are only estimations, it might be that when the true demands of highpri requests for the current time-step become known, they need more than the fraction set aside for them. As a consequence, satisfying the highpri requests fully may require

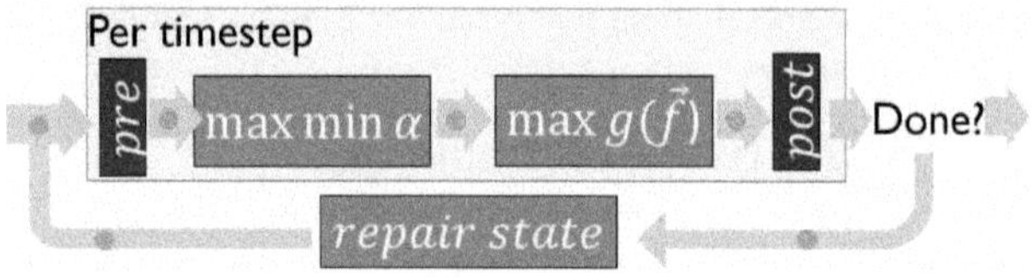


**Figure 3: TEMPUS's workflow**

| State | | |
|---|---|---|
| | $\{(a_i, b_i, d_i, D_i, s_i, t_i, P_i)\}$ | |
| | $y_{e,t}$ $\chi_{e,t}$ $h_{e,t}$ | edge |
| | $z_i$ $q_i$ $F_{i,\tau-1}$ $Q_{i,t}$ $\alpha_i$ | req. |
| | $r$ $U_{\tau-1}$ $U$ | utility |

**Figure 4: State kept by TEMPUS; at time-step $\tau$, for currently active requests $i \in R(\tau)$ and future time-steps $t \geq \tau$.**

lowering previously promised flow. As before, note that TEMPUS's under-allocation of future edges helps: in particular, the allocation in the previous time-step leaves some capacity unallocated on the edges in the current time-step ($1 - \beta_{e,\tau,\tau-1}$ fraction). If the over-use is smaller than this amount, nothing more needs to be done. If not, TEMPUS uses a small pre-process LP that considers only the current time-step and lowers pre-scheduled flow by the amount needed to accommodate the highpri requests while minimizing the effect on the promises already offered. As the name denotes, the pre-process LP runs first, at each time-step. Since the pre-process LP only considers the current time-step, it is small and quick. Further, when TEMPUS subsequently searches for best $\boldsymbol{\alpha}$ satisfying $LP^\tau(\boldsymbol{\alpha}, U)$, any requests that were impacted by the pre-process LP, and hence had their promises reduce, would be preferentially served, i.e., offered more flow at some future time-step. Finally, we observe that link and switch failures can also be modeled as if an additional highpri request arrives on each of the failed edges with demand equal to link capacity. Intuitively, this structure - ensure current time-step is feasible and then mitigate the impact on requests by giving them more flow on other paths or at other times - allows TEMPUS to accommodate apriori unknown amounts of highpri traffic with a small impact on promises to long-running transfers.

# 5. IMPLEMENTATION OF TEMPUS

So far, we have described the theoretical framework behind TEMPUS. In this section, we focus on some more practical aspects.

## 5.1 System overview

**Architecture.** Figure 3 describes how TEMPUS operates. At each time-step $\tau$, TEMPUS first attempts for fair allocation, i.e., maximize the minimum promise to all currently active requests (max min $\alpha_i$, as in §4.2). Then, to allocate any remaining bandwidth TEMPUS attempts to maximize total utility (as described in §4.2). Around these core pieces, are a few additional pieces: a *pre*-process LP that at each time step reduces pre-scheduled flows on edges where a higher-than expected volume of high-priority traffic causes allocation to exceed capacity (§4.2.3); a *post*-processing LP that allocates any further remaining bandwidth on the edges at time-step $\tau$ so as to improve total utility (as described in §4.2.3); and finally, a state *repair* step that changes the internal state variables from being a feasible solution to the current set of packing-covering constraints towards being a feasible solution to the new set of packing-covering constraints for the next time-step.

**State maintenance.** Figure 4 depicts the state maintained by TEMPUS. The first row is the input, the per-request tuple. The next three rows are TEMPUS's state per edge, per request and for total utility.

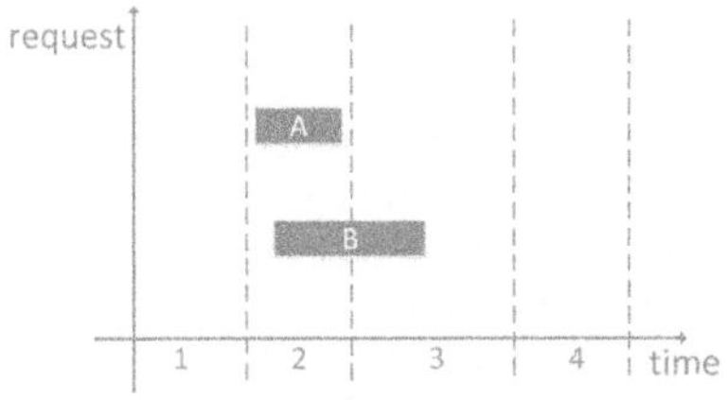


**Figure 5: An illustration of how TEMPUS partitions requests to threads. There is one thread per interval. $R_A$ is always assigned to thread 2 since it is only active in that interval. $R_B$ is assigned to either thread 2 or 3 with equal probability since it lies half in each of those intervals.**

Per edge, per time, TEMPUS retains the internal variable $y$ (defined in §4.1.1), the fraction of an edge's capacity that has been set aside for highpri traffic $\chi$ and the amount that has already been allocated $h$. Per request, TEMPUS retains internal variables related to its packing and covering constraints ($q, z$ respectively), the amount of flow already routed $F_{i,\tau-1}$, the promised fraction $\alpha_i$, and the amount of flow to be routed at each future time-step $t$ in order to achieve this promise $Q_{i,t}$. Similarly for utility, TEMPUS retains internal variable $r$, utility achieved so far $U_{i,\tau-1}$ and promised utility $U$. In particular, note that TEMPUS does not retain the flow assignment vector **f**, which has a value per edge, per time, per request; the above state represents everything needed for planning. *Repairing* state, refers to editing state at the end of current time-step to be appropriate for the next time-step. In particular, the internal variables $y, z, q, r$, are edited as per their definition in §4.1.1 to remove the effect of flow that has been routed in the current time-step. Newly arriving edges for time-step $\tau + W + 1$ are initialized with $y = 1$ indicating zero flow; similarly, newly arriving requests receive $z, q = 1$. Finally, we note that the state maintained by TEMPUS is $O(mW + W|R(\tau)|)$, where $m$ is the number of edges, $W$ is the window size that TEMPUS plans over and $R(\tau)$ is the set of requests that are active at time $\tau$. Of these, we believe $R(\tau)$ to be the largest; several hundred requests between each pair of datacenters. This is significantly smaller than the state used by a typical LP solver: per-edge (or per-path), per-request and per-time, namely $O(mW|R(\tau)|)$.

## 5.2 Parallelizing Young's algorithm

From Figure 4, observe that some of the state that TEMPUS has to keep can be partitioned by time ($y, \chi, h$) and the rest can be partitioned by request ($z, q, F, Q$). Further observe from Algorithm 2 that except for the values of $\sum y, \sum z, \sum q$ in the denominators of $(*)$, the remaining computation– finding a tuple $(i^*, p^*, t^*)$, routing additional flow for that request, editing the state etc.– can be done in parallel. Since the calendaring problem becomes harder the more time and more requests that one has to plan jointly, it would be very satisfying to parallelize the computation per-time and per-request; such a parallel version, if possible, could finish in constant time given enough threads.

We are able to achieve this goal partially; the overlap between requests' active times and the sums in the denominators of $(*)$ require synchronization. Step 1: we divide the total time into intervals and assign each to a different thread. The time-intervals are chosen so as to equalize the "load" (request count); (hence, intervals can have different lengths). As described in Fig. 5, requests that are active in multiple intervals are alternatively assigned to either range, with probability equal to the relative duration of the request in that time-interval. Step 2: we ask each thread, given a time interval and some requests, to make forward progress, e.g., $10^4$ iterations. While most threads make forward progress, we repeat these steps. Towards the end of the execution, where the number of unsatisfied requests is small, we switch to single-thread execution (the parallelization overhead dominates otherwise). Finally, to avoid contention between threads on the shared variables, we have the threads search for a feasible tuple $(i^*, t^*, p^*)$ and prepare a speculative update to the state variables; the actual update is performed quickly under an exclusive lock. We find speculation to succeed over 99.9% of the time and as we show in our evaluation on a single server, we find a roughly linear speedup up to 30 threads.

## 5.3 Efficient flow assignment

**Searching for a feasible tuple.** In principle, finding an $(i^*, t^*, p^*)$ tuple that satisfies $(*)$ (see Algorithm 2) can be hard. A simple random search over each of these values (request, time, path) can take a long time since not all tuples will satisfy $(*)$ esp: in later iterations of the algorithm. Instead, we observe that for each request, its *shortest path* has the smallest value of the left-hand-side (LHS) (path length is measured as $\sum_{e \in p} \frac{y_{e,t}}{c_e}$). Hence, if there exists a tuple that satisfies $(*)$, at least one of the shortest paths must satisfy $(*)$. Using this observation, we maintain a sorted list of the shortest paths through the network for each request, time-step. We then iterate over requests and check if their shortest path (overall) satisfies $(*)$. Note that the running complexity to find a feasible tuple is now the order of number of active requests $O(|R(\tau)|)$, whereas before it was much larger $O(|P_i|WR(\tau))$.

**Efficient updates to shortest path.** The shortest path data-structure has to be updated when path lengths change; for example, when new flow is allocated on an edge, the edge length $y_{e,t}$ changes. Observe that if some flow was allocated for $(i^*, t^*, p^*)$, the shortest-paths can change only for time $t^*$. Even better, since the edge lengths only increase, the shortest paths could only have changed for requests whose shortest path at $t^*$ has common edges with the path $p^*$ (whose flow has been augmented). By keeping appropriate data structures (e.g., for each $(e, t)$, the list of requests whose shortest path at time $t$ passes through $e$), this observation quickly updates the shortest paths that change in each iteration.

# 6. EVALUATION

## 6.1 Methodology

**Datasets:** We evaluate TEMPUS on the topology and traffic matrices from one of Microsoft's production wide area networks. Nodes in the graph are PoPs and edges are bundles of optical links. The network has 40 nodes and 280 edges. We also evaluate TEMPUS on larger synthetic topologies.

We collected sampled NetFlow data at every ingress into the WAN to obtain five-minute averages of traffic sent between PoPs (one day's worth of data overall). From discussions with cluster operators, we identified the portion of this traffic that is considered highpri. Recall that we model highpri traffic as an unpredictable amount of demand that arrives in each time step and has to be completely satisfied. The remaining traffic portion, which is the bulk of the bytes on the WAN, are attributed to large requests. While NetFlow traces do have TCP flow level information, we could not identify which of the flows belonged to a single request (e.g., moving a petabyte between datacenters). Instead, we interviewed cluster operators for typical distributions of the sizes of requests and the durations between their arrival and hard deadline. Given a traffic demand between a pair of PoPs, we repeatedly sample from these distributions to generate large transfer requests until their cumulative volume equals the observed traffic demand.

**Load factor:** To evaluate calendaring solutions under a wide range of network load, we scale the actual traffic demand matrix by a constant factor, that we call load factor.

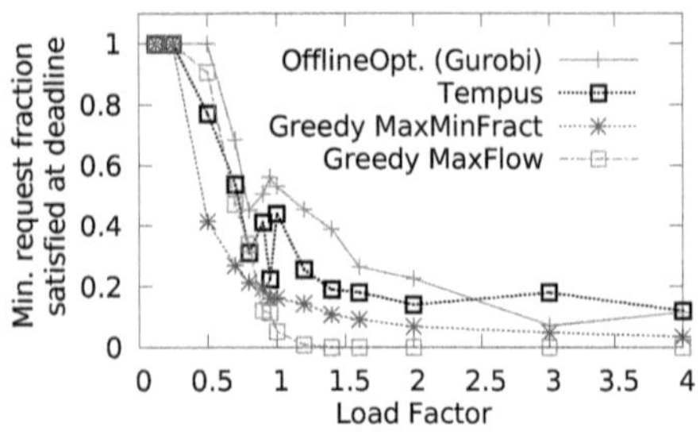


**Figure 6: Minimum request fraction satisfied post-facto.**

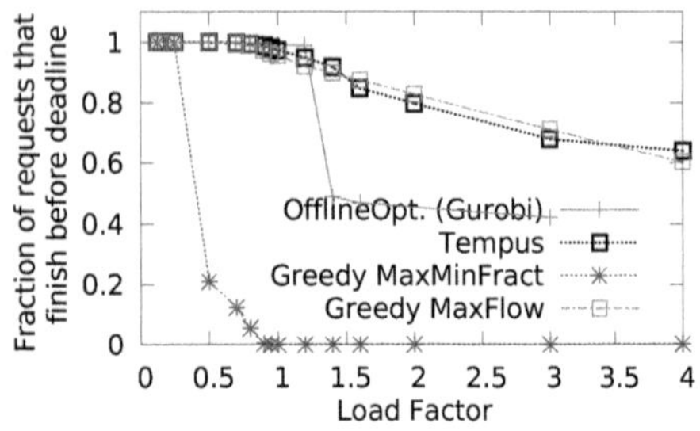


**Figure 7: Fraction of transfers that finish before deadline.**

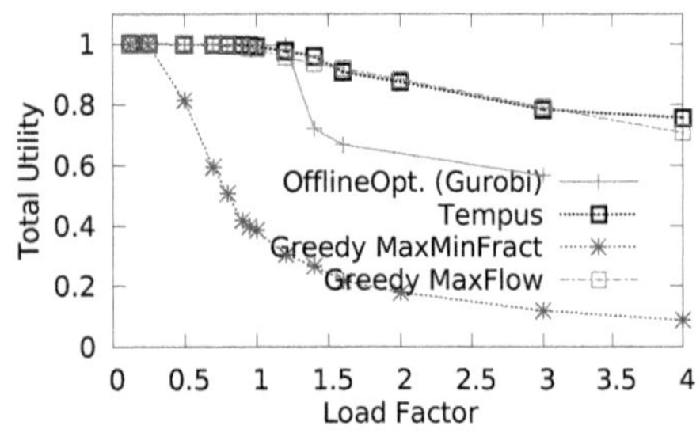


**Figure 8: Total utility.**

**Metrics:** We compare solutions on these metrics:

• **MinFract.** (or $\alpha$) This metric is the minimum of the fraction of request that is transferred before deadline. It bounds the worst-case behavior of a calendaring solution and also measures sensitivity towards unpredictable arrivals or load changes. An ideal calendaring scheme would offer the largest possible value of $\alpha$.

• **Requests finishing before deadline.** This metric measures how many requests finish on time. When the network load is low, carrying as much flow as possible will satisfy all (or most) deadlines. However, as the network load increases, finishing more requests on time requires carefully spreading traffic across available paths and time. Also, there is a tension between finishing more requests vs. offering a minimum guarantee to every request.

• **Total utility or $\delta$.** Whereas the above measure is binary, 1 when a request meets its deadline and 0 otherwise, this metric is a smoother measure of the total utility from carrying traffic. Recall that our design can handle arbitrary measures of utility, including the case where each request specifies, a non-negative number per timestep to depict the value per unit demand that is satisfied at that time step. Here, we use a simpler variant: the average fraction satisfied over all large transfers. A calendaring solution should maximize utility. However, there is a similar tension between maximizing $\alpha$ (the min. share of a request) versus maximizing $\delta$.

• **Promise.** A guarantee is only useful if provided pre-facto. Whereas $\alpha$ above measures the minimum post-facto fraction that each request gets served, with promise, we measure what the calendaring solution can guarantee ahead of time to each request. This is not relevant for offline solutions; their promise equals the best achievable fraction. For online schemes, however, where future arrivals of large requests and the remaining capacity after serving highpri transfers is unknown, it is challenging to specify a high promise. An ideal calendaring solution should offer as high a promise as possible, as early in a request's lifetime as possible and ensure that the promise does not decrease over request lifetime.

• **Running time, memory usage.** We are also interested in how long the different solutions take to run; how much memory they use; and how well these scale as the size of the problem increases.

**Compared schemes:**

• Offline Optimal (Gurobi): We formulate the calendaring solution as a sequence of two LPs over all requests and over all time-epochs. The first LP maximizes $\alpha$, and then the second LP maximizes $\delta$, where the optimal $\alpha$ obtained in the first LP is incorporated as a constraint ($\alpha$, $\delta$ defined above). Gurobi was the best performing of the commercially available LP solvers that we experimented with.

• TEMPUS: We built an incomplete implementation of TEMPUS. In particular, bounded time horizon has not been implemented. The *offline* variant does the same as above except by invoking Young's instead of an LP solver. The *online* variant is as described in §4.2. Also, we have implemented parallel versions as described.

• Greedy MaxFlow: This is an online solution. At each time step, this scheme first routes highpri traffic. Then, given all the un-satisfied demands, it uses an LP solver to maximize the total flow that can be served in the current time step. It does not plan into the future.

• Greedy MaxMinFract: This is an online solution similar to the above; the only difference is that the LP solver's goal is to maximize the minimum fraction served for all pending requests.

## 6.2 Value of calendaring

We compare the performance of online version of TEMPUS with online alternatives and the offline optimal. Figure 6 shows that at high load both the Greedy schemes have very small minimum offered service ($\alpha$). In fact, the $\alpha$ quickly reaches zero for Greedy MaxFlow; that is unlucky requests can receive no service at all. This is because both the Greedy schemes plan one timestep at a time. By planning into the future, we see that the online variant of TEMPUS continues to offer a high minimum service, closely approximating that achieved by the offline optimal.

Note that Gurobi could not compute the offline optimal for load factors above 1 because it could not finish within the time-limits imposed by Gurobi software. Sometimes looking for the best $\alpha$ would finish but not the second LP of maximizing $\delta$ given the best $\alpha$. The main issue is the degree of precision that the LP solvers operate at; lower precision values let the solver finish quickly but lead to poor answer quality. E.g., Gurobi has a parameter called optimalitytol; with the default sensitivity value of $10^{-6}$, maximizing $\alpha$ yields an $\alpha$ that is 2X smaller than the best possible value; setting sensitivity to $10^{-7}$ yields the best $\alpha$ but takes 5X more time. Throughout our evaluation, whenever Gurobi solver times-out, we re-run with progressively smaller sensitivity parameters. We believe that doing so is okay because running time is a challenge that cannot be neglected when looking at calendaring solutions. As we show later, TEMPUS finishes well within that time.

Figure 7 shows that even at high load factors, there is enough residual capacity after serving highpri traffic to finish most requests before their deadline. Between these two figures, it is interesting to note that the Greedy, single timestep planners, have a hard choice. Maximizing the minimum guarantee, such as Greedy MaxMinFract (shown with star markers) does, finishes very few flows before their deadline. This is because whenever some request has a large pending demand, MaxMinFract has to allocate more capacity

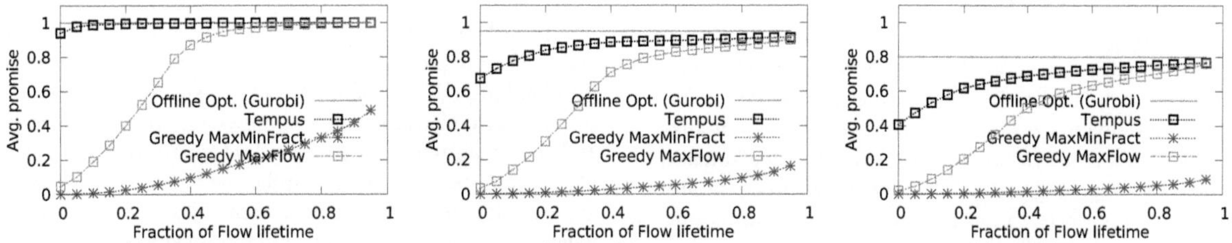


(a) Load factor 0.7 (b) Load factor 1.6 (c) Load factor 3

**Figure 9: How the promised fraction evolves over lifetime of requests? We show the average promise over all requests.**

| Instance. | # nodes ($n$) | # edges ($m$) | # transfers ($R$) | # timesteps ($T$) |
|---|---|---|---|---|
| prod. dataset | 40 | 280 | $10^4$ | 288 |
| E1 | 200 | 1000 | $10^4$ | 2000 |
| E2 | 200 | 1000 | $2 * 10^4$ | 2000 |
| E3 | 200 | 1000 | $2 * 10^4$ | 5000 |
| E4 | 200 | 1000 | $2.5 * 10^4$ | 5000 |
| E5 | 250 | 1250 | $3 * 10^4$ | 8000 |

**Table 2: Comparing Tempus with Gurobi on larger instances. For all instances, we choose 15 paths per src-dest pair; the transfer sizes and durations were scaled proportional to the number of timesteps, transfers such that the load factor remains around 0.4.**

to that request. Maximizing total flow, as Greedy MaxFlow (shown with light squares) does, finishes more flows before deadline but at the cost of significant unfairness ($\alpha$ =0 for load factors $\geq$ 1).

Figure 8 shows a similar trade-off. Whereas the Greedy schemes can only do one of these two well: finish more flows before deadline or offer a high minimum guarantee post facto, the online variant of Tempus does both well and is nearly the same as optimal.

Figure 9 shows how the promise evolves over the lifetime of a request. We see results at three different load factors; the promise value is averaged over all requests; the x axes plots the fraction of request lifetime. First, we see that Tempus begins with a high promise when the requests arrive, much higher than either version of Greedy. Second, due to the online nature of Tempus and the network smoothening, the promise gradually increases with time, as Tempus becomes more confident of how much capacity will be available in the future. The Greedy schemes can promise no more than the fraction that has already been served. Finally, we see that the best possible promise from the offline oracle reduces as the load factor increases. In all cases, Tempus reaches a promise that is over 80% of the best possible promise when the request is a fifth of its way into its lifetime (x=0.2). At high load factors, even when requests come close to their end, neither Greedy scheme offers as large an average promise as Tempus.

## 6.3 Computational costs, Scalability

Recall that one of our reasons behind using mixed packing covering solvers in Tempus is to scale to larger problem sizes. Figure 10 compares the running time and memory used by Gurobi with an offline variant of Tempus for larger instance sizes. Table 2 describes the instances. Notice that as proved in Theorem 3, the runtime of the online variant of Tempus is $O(\ln(mTK)(X_r+K)/\varepsilon^2)$ per timestep, the $\sum X_r$ over all timesteps is $O(mT+K)$ and the runtime of the offline variant is $O(\ln(mTk)(mT+k)/\varepsilon^2)$. Here, $k$ is the total number of requests whereas $K$ is the number that are active at each timestep; hence $K \leq k$. Hence, loosely speaking, the per timestep runtime of online Tempus is $\frac{1}{T}$ that of the offline variant. Gurobi ran on a 4 core 3.3GHz Intel Xeon E31240 with 16GB of memory. Tempus with 15 threads ran on an 8 core 2.5GHz Intel Xeon L5420 with 16 GB of memory. The latter is several years older; the disparity is because our Gurobi license was for a specific server. Our implementation of

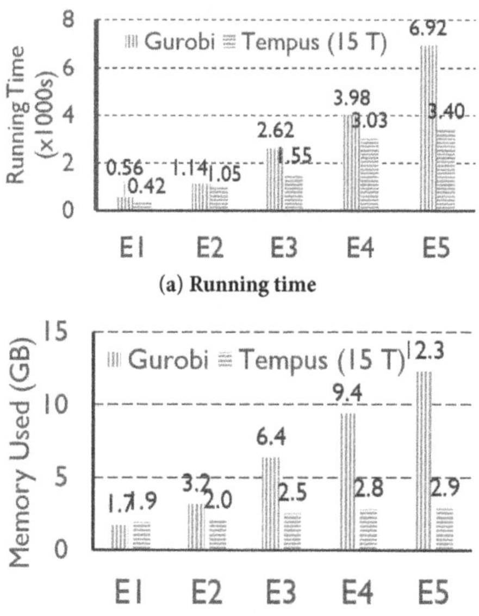


(a) Running time

(b) Memory usage

**Figure 10: Comparing the scalability of Tempus vs. Gurobi on the large instances shown in Table 2.**

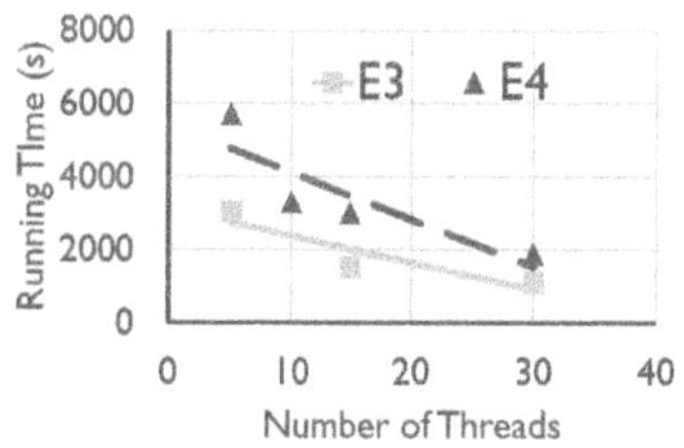


**Figure 11: Tempus's running time vs. number of threads.**

Tempus is in a high-level language that has garbage collection and is not optimized.

Regardless, we find that Tempus obtains comparable if not better running times than Gurobi. Further, Tempus uses significantly less memory. These gains are because our implementation has no variable that is indexed per time, per request, per path. Though such a variable exists in our formulation, we realize that the state needed for the packing covering problem is smaller (see §5.1 for details).

Finally, Figure 11 shows how the running time of Tempus changes when different numbers of threads are used. We see a sub-linear speedup. At 30 threads, the machine's CPU was consistently pegged at 100%. However, servers with up to 32 or more cores are available at modest prices hinting that Tempus can be sped up further. We take care to point out that our parallelization of Tempus is not the best possible; we attempt to but do not always ensure that the degree of parallelism is as much as the number of threads.

## 7. RELATED WORK

Traffic Engineering (TE) has been a long standing problem in networking. Early work focused on minimizing the maximum link utilization in order to avoid congestion. Some were adaptive [14]; some were oblivious to demands and network failures [1, 9]; some distributed traffic across paths [1, 14] while others computed suitable routing parameters (e.g., edge weights for OSPF equal cost multipath routing [9]). Recently [5, 6] consider the problem of sustaining different fairness criteria in a shared network. We note that to maximize return on investment inter-DC WANs run at nearly full utilization and hence, minimizing congestion does not apply. Further, prior work does not consider deadline SLAs for large transfers.

Traffic engineering for datacenter WANs has been a recent topic of research. NetStitcher [17] uses information about future bandwidth availability to move data between datacenters at low cost; it does not support deadlines for requests. B4 [13] and SWAN [11], designed by Google and Microsoft, respectively, focus on improving the utilization of the inter-DC WAN. The resource allocation policies offered therein can be classified as greedy/ one timestep, namely they do not compute long-term allocation schedules which are needed to offer deadline SLAs for long-running requests.

Deadlines have been considered in different subareas. Some prior work supports deadlines for flows within a datacenter by suitably modifying TCP or designing new transport protocols [4, 21, 23]. The calendaring problem is fundamentally different, as it operates at a much longer time scale and schedules requests which are aggregations of many flows. Other recent work considers deadlines for batch jobs in large clusters [7, 12, 19]. The algorithmic tools developed therein do not apply to the calendaring context mainly because we need to consider network routing in addition to scheduling.

Packing and covering problems have been considered extensively. Some algorithmic work adapts techniques from multi-commodity flow to general mixed packing and covering systems of inequalities [20] and proves that the running time of the algorithm depends only on the number of variables and constraints [10, 8]. Young [24] presented a further improvement. We extended Young to the online case, observed ways to speed-up the search for a feasible increment, to reduce memory footprint and also a novel parallelization method.

Finally, we note several fast algorithms for solving packing/covering linear programs, and specifically the CONCURRENT MULTICOMMODITY FLOW problem. Some of these works deal only with *pure* packing or *pure* covering constraints, e.g., [2, 18], whereas calendaring needs a *mixed* packing/covering LP. Some others [2, 3] take longer to converge when approximation error has to be small. Recall that $\varepsilon$ appears in bounds on the amount of violation in constraints; whereas the running time of Young's depends on $\varepsilon^{-2}$, those other works have running time proportional to $\varepsilon^{-5}$ and $\varepsilon^{-6}$, respectively. Even faster probabilistic algorithms exist [16], however they are more complex and do not always find a feasible solution.

## 8. CONCLUDING REMARKS

In this paper, we design TEMPUS, a novel WAN transfer framework, which schedules long-running transfers in space and time. This allows the network provider to accommodate both high priority traffic and long-running requests. TEMPUS uses an efficient online algorithm which incrementally utilizes a quick mixed packing-covering subroutine. Our simulation results demonstrate that TEMPUS clearly outperforms greedy state-of-the-art heuristics in terms of both transfer ratio guarantees and promise quality. Further, TEMPUS is efficient in terms of running time, memory usage, and update overhead, which we believe would make it an attractive framework for future traffic engineering systems.

While we focus here on making intra-org WAN transfers more efficient, we believe that the ideas in TEMPUS can be used in other contexts. For example, in the *public* cloud setting, where customers pay the cloud provider for data transfers, TEMPUS could be used to support new pricing frameworks where users specify data size, deadline and their willingness to pay. Customers can receive discounts for willingness to defer transfers, and providers can exploit price differentiation for more profits. More generally, TEMPUS can be reused whenever sequences of optimization problems, which change based on some underlying structure, have to be solved efficiently.

## Acknowledgements

We thank our shepherd Vyas Sekar and the SIGCOMM reviewers for useful comments.

## References

[1] D. Applegate and E. Cohen. Making Intra-Domain Routing Robust to Changing and Uncertain Traffic Demands. In *SIGCOMM*, 2003.

[2] B. Awerbuch and R. Khandekar. Stateless distributed gradient descent for positive linear programs. In *STOC*, 2008.

[3] B. Awerbuch and R. Khandekar. Greedy distributed optimization of multi-commodity flows. *Distributed Computing*, 2009.

[4] L. Chen et al. Towards minimal-delay deadline-driven data center tcp. In *HotNets*, 2013.

[5] E. Danna, A. Hassidim, H. Kaplan, A. Kumar, Y. Mansour, D. Raz, and M. Segalov. Upward max min fairness. In *INFOCOM*, 2012.

[6] E. Danna, S. Mandal, and A. Singh. A practical algorithm for balancing the max-min fairness and throughput objectives in traffic engineering. In *INFOCOM*, 2012.

[7] A. D. Ferguson et al. Jockey: Guaranteed Job Latency in Data Parallel Clusters. In *EuroSys*, 2012.

[8] L. K. Fleischer. Approximating fractional multicommodity flow independent of the num. commodities. *SIAM J. Discret. Math.*, 2000.

[9] B. Fortz and M. Thorup. Internet Traffic Engineering by Optimizing OSPF Weights in a Changing World. In *INFOCOM*, 2000.

[10] N. Garg and J. Könemann. Faster and simpler algorithms for multicommodity flow and fractional packing problems. *SIAM J. Comput.*, 2007.

[11] C.-Y. Hong et al. Achieving high utilization with software-driven wan. In *SIGCOMM*, 2013.

[12] N. Jain, I. Menache, J. Naor, and J. Yaniv. Near-optimal scheduling mechanisms for deadline-sensitive jobs in large computing clusters. In *SPAA*, 2012.

[13] S. Jain et al. B4: Experience with a globally-deployed software defined wan. In *SIGCOMM*, 2013.

[14] S. Kandula, D. Katabi, B. Davie, and A. Charny. Walking the tightrope: Responsive yet stable traffic engineering. In *SIGCOMM*, 2005.

[15] S. Kandula, I. Menache, R. Schwartz, and S. R. Babbula. Calendaring for Wide Area Networks (Extended Version), 2014.

[16] C. Koufogiannakis and N. E. Young. Beating simplex for fractional packing and covering linear programs. In *FOCS*, 2007.

[17] N. Laoutaris, M. Sirivianos, X. Yang, and P. Rodriguez. Inter-datacenter bulk transfers with netstitcher. In *SIGCOMM*, 2011.

[18] M. Luby and N. Nisan. A parallel approximation algorithm for positive linear programming. In *STOC*, 1993.

[19] V. Nagarajan et al. Flowflex: Malleable scheduling for flows of mapreduce jobs. In *Middleware*, 2013.

[20] S. Plotkin, D. Shmoys, and E. Tardos. Fast approximation algorithms for fractional packing and covering problems. *Math. Oper. Res.*, 1995.

[21] B. Vamanan et al. Deadline-Aware Datacenter TCP (D2TCP). In *ACM SIGCOMM*, 2012.

[22] H. Wang et al. COPE: Traffic Engineering in Dynamic Networks. In *ACM SIGCOMM*, 2006.

[23] C. Wilson et al. Better Never than Late: Meeting Deadlines in Datacenter Networks. In *SIGCOMM*, 2011.

[24] N. E. Young. Sequential and parallel algorithms for mixed packing and covering. In *FOCS*, 2001.

# Traffic Engineering with Forward Fault Correction

Hongqiang Harry Liu (Yale University) Srikanth Kandula Ratul Mahajan Ming Zhang David Gelernter (Yale University)

Microsoft Research

**Abstract—** Network faults such as link failures and high switch configuration delays can cause heavy congestion and packet loss. Because it takes time for the traffic engineering systems to detect and react to such faults, these conditions can last long—even tens of seconds. We propose forward fault correction (FFC), a proactive approach for handling faults. FFC spreads network traffic such that freedom from congestion is guaranteed under arbitrary combinations of up to $k$ faults. We show how FFC can be practically realized by compactly encoding the constraints that arise from this large number of possible faults and solving them efficiently using sorting networks. Experiments with data from real networks show that, with negligible loss in overall network throughput, FFC can reduce data loss by a factor of 7–130 in well-provisioned networks, and reduce the loss of high-priority traffic to almost zero in well-utilized networks.

**Categories and Subject Descriptors:** C.2.1 [**Computer Communication Networks**]: Network Architecture and Design–Network communications. C.2.3 [**Computer Communication Networks**]: Network Operations.
**Keywords:** Traffic Engineering; Congestion-Free; Fault Tolerance

## 1. Introduction

Centralized traffic engineering reduces network congestion and increases efficiency [1, 2, 3, 4, 5, 6]. In such systems, a TE controller frequently reconfigures the network to match current traffic demand. These reconfigurations enable the network to carry more traffic, thus enabling the operators to extract more value from the expensive infrastructure investment.

While centralized TE can be highly effective, it is unable to quickly react to faults in both the data and control planes. Data plane faults occur when a link or switch fails and stops forwarding packets. Another class of faults, which we call control plane faults, is where the controller fails to reconfigure a switch in a timely manner, even though the switch continues to forward packets (as previously configured). This fault can occur due to a host of factors, such as RPC (remote procedure call) failures, bugs in switch firmware or software, shortage of memory in the switch, and so forth.

Both classes of faults are common. Several studies have reported frequent link and switch failures in large networks [7, 8, 9]; in a wide area network that we study, a link fails every 30 minutes on average. Google reports both heavy delays and outright failures in configuring switches [1]. The percentage of configuration updates that failed was 0.1–1%. For switches from two different vendors, we observe a similar failure rate in our own experiments. In a network with a hundred switches, this failure rate implies the controller will commonly fail to configure at least some of them.

Data and control plane faults can cause heavy congestion and packet loss. When a data plane fault occurs, switches quickly move traffic to other available paths, but because this movement does not account for link capacity constraints, it can severely congest some links. Similarly, control plane faults cause congestion when a switch continues sending traffic on a link as per old configuration, while it was expected to move the traffic away. Our experiments show that data and control plane faults frequently lead to links getting 10–20% more traffic than their capacity. The resulting packet loss will hurt congestion-sensitive applications.

Today, relieving congestion due to these faults requires intervention by the TE controller. The downside of this approach is that interventions happen *after* congestion has occurred. Worse, they can take a long time because of the delay inherent to updating a large network, which stems from factors such as RPC delays, control load on switches, and the time to change forwarding rules. Updating a single switch rule can take a few seconds [1], and network-wide updates typically require updating many rules per switch.

We thus argue for proactively handling common fault scenarios. In particular, TE should spread traffic in the network such that no congestion occurs as long as the total number of faults is at most $k$ (a configurable bound). This guarantee should hold for arbitrary combinations of faults. Our view is inspired by forward error correction (FEC), in which a transmitted packet stream is modified such that all original packets can be recovered, without any reaction (e.g., retransmission) as long as the number of losses is up to $k$. Analogously, we call our approach forward fault correction (FFC).

Practically realizing FFC requires addressing two intertwined challenges—minimizing throughput loss and computational scalability. Just as FEC has overhead in terms of redundant information that is transmitted, FFC will have overhead in terms of link capacity set aside to tolerate faults. This overhead must be low for FFC to be acceptable. The computational challenge is that with $n$ potential faults, the number of combinations of up to $k$ faults is $\sum_{i=1}^{k} \binom{n}{i}$. With $n$=1000, a plausible number of links in a large network, and $k$=3, this number over $10^9$. Thus, enumerating all possible faults and considering their impact is intractable. Approximations may help reduce computational effort, but unless one is careful, they may result in high capacity overhead.

We address these challenges by first formulating FFC requirements as a linear program. This formulation is precise, which minimizes overhead, but has an intractably large number of constraints because of possible fault combinations. We then observe that these constraints can be transformed, with minimal loss in precision, to a "bounded M-sum" problem: the sum of any $M$ out of $N$ variables is bounded. Finally, we develop a method based on sorting networks [10], to efficiently encode this problem as $O(kn)$ linear constraints. For control plane FFC, our approach is optimal with


*SIGCOMM'14*, August 17–22, 2014, Chicago, Illinois, USA.

http://dx.doi.org/10.1145/2619239.2626314.

respect to overhead; for data plane FFC, it is optimal if the multiple paths that carry traffic between two switches are disjoint.

Our approach is flexible and applies to many TE scenarios. We show how it accommodates multiple traffic priorities, multi-step network updates [2], different TE objectives (*e.g.* fairness, maximizing throughput, and minimizing maximum link utilization), and handles control faults in traffic rate limiters [11, 12].

We evaluate FFC in a testbed and using simulations based on traffic and fault data from real networks. We find that it is valuable in a range of scenarios. In well-provisioned networks, as is common for ISPs today, FFC has negligible throughput overhead and reduces data loss by a factor of 7–130. In well-utilized networks that use multiple traffic priorities, as is common for inter-datacenter networks [1, 2], FFC protects high-priority traffic from almost all loss, again with negligible loss in total network throughput.

Fundamentally, FFC provides a novel control knob to network operators. Today, operators must either conservatively over-provision the network to guarantee the absence of congestion under faults or aggressively utilize the network [1, 2] at the risk of severe fault-induced congestion. FFC enables operating points that trade-off provisioning and congestion-risk in an informed manner, based on network characteristics and desired protection level.

## 2. Motivation

Many applications (e.g., Web search queries, online retail, multi-player games) are sensitive to congestion, and packet drops or long queuing delays hurt the user experience of these applications. FFC is motivated by the observations that data and control plane faults cause congestion and that reacting to these faults is slow. We illustrate these observations below. As is prevalent [1, 2, 3, 4] in networks with TE, we assume tunnel-based forwarding. One or more tunnels carry traffic between each ingress-egress switch pair; we call this traffic a *flow*. Relative weights configured at the ingress switch determine how the flow's traffic is split across tunnels.

### 2.1 Impact of data plane faults

When a link or switch fails, it impacts all tunnels traversing it. Upon detecting tunnel failures, ingress switches *rescale* traffic to the remaining tunnels in proportion to configured weights. Suppose a flow has 3 tunnels with splitting weights $(0.5, 0.3, 0.2)$. When the third tunnel fails, weights of $(\frac{0.5}{0.8}, \frac{0.3}{0.8}, 0)$ are used to split traffic. OpenFlow group tables can implement such rescaling [13].

Rescaling quickly restores connectivity but can leave the network in a congested state. For example, Figure 2(a) shows an initial traffic distribution with two flows: $\{s2, s3\} \rightarrow s4$. Dashed curves represent tunnels and numbers represent traffic volume they carry. When link $s2$-$s4$ fails and $s2$ rescales, the traffic distribution of Figure 2(b) emerges, in which link $s1$-$s4$ is heavily congested. Such congestion will persist until the TE controller can compute a new solution and configure the network, which can take tens of seconds (see below).

While this example was illustrative, Figure 1(a) characterizes congestion due to data plane faults for L-Net, a real network on which we provide more information in §8. This experiment uses topology and traffic data from the network, and it uses a standard TE algorithm (§4.1) to spread traffic every interval (5 minutes) across six tunnels per-flow. We fail randomly selected links or switches in each time interval and measure the maximum link oversubscription rate, i.e., the amount of traffic above capacity that arrives at the link. The graph plots the CDF of the oversubscription rate for the cases of 1–3 link failures and 1 switch failure. Even with a single link failure—which occurs every 30 minutes on average in this network—the link oversubscription rate is over 20% a quarter of the time (75th %-ile). For a 100 Gbps link, 20% over-

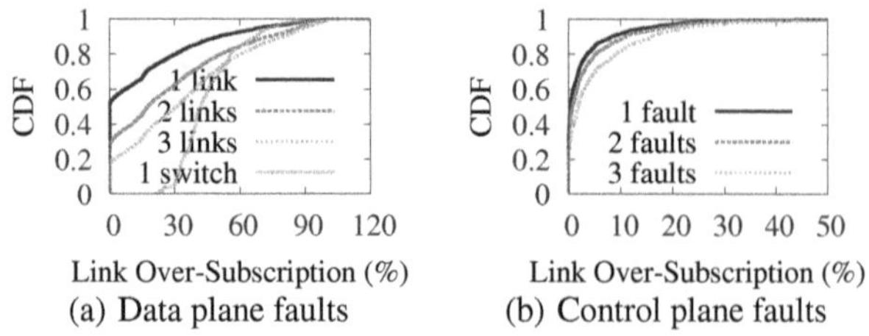


**Figure 1: Congestion due to faults in L-Net.**

subscription means that 120 Gbps traffic will arrive soon after a failure. Even with 100 MB buffer capacity, the switch will be unable to buffer even 50 ms of this traffic and applications will suffer a burst of high loss rate.

### 2.2 Impact of control plane faults

We now illustrate how a delay or failure in configuring a switch can cause congestion. Figure 3(a) shows a simple network with 4 flows: $s1 \rightarrow \{s2, s3\}$ and $\{s2, s3\} \rightarrow s4$. Assume that the controller wants to change the network configuration to Figure 3(b), to accommodate a new flow $s1 \rightarrow s4$. This change requires updating $s2$ and $s3$, to modify traffic split weights for their flows. If $s2$ does not update and continues to split traffic as before, link $s1$-$s4$ will be congested, as in Figure 3(c).

Figure 1(b) characterizes congestion in L-Net due to control plane faults. This experiment simulates a network update every interval based on the same TE algorithm as above. For each update, we inject control plane faults at randomly selected switches and measure the maximum link oversubscription rate. We see from the graph that, though control plane faults are less damaging than data plane faults, even a single fault—which can occur every 5 minutes if the fault rate is 1% and the network has 100 switches—can lead to an oversubscription of 10% a tenth of the time.

The example above assumes that all updates are sent to the switches in one shot; in another method, updates are sent in multiple steps to avoid transient congestion due to switches applying updates at different times [2]. To transition from Figure 3(a) to 3(b), possible steps are: 1) update traffic splitting ratios at $s2$ and $s3$; and 2) if that succeeds, update the rate of flow $s1 \rightarrow s4$. This way, no congestion will occur if $s2$ (or $s3$) fails to update. However, configuration failures will stall network updates because Step 2 cannot proceed until Step 1 finishes. They will also lower throughput since flow $s1 \rightarrow s4$ cannot start if Step 1 fails. FFC handles control plane faults for multi-step updates as well.

While this section focuses on switch configuration faults, in networks that control traffic rate [1, 2], a similar problem arises for rate limiter configuration as well. Congestion will occur if a rate limiter continues to send traffic at the older, higher rate. We show that FFC handles such faults as well.

### 2.3 Slow reaction to faults

Reactive approaches suffer from the fact that they start *after* congestion and loss has already started, and they can take a long time in large production networks. Figure 6(a) shows the distribution of rule update times in B4, based on Figure 12 and Table 4 of the paper [1]. It excludes switches for which configuration completely fails. It shows both RPC delays and the time to update a single forwarding rule. Typically, many rules per switch are updated during a network update; this number is commonly over 100 for L-Net.

While B4 is a complex system with many sources of delay and variability, we also quantify update delays in a controlled, lab environment using commodity switches. We issue rule update commands, while the switches have moderate background control load such as reading counters and running tunnel liveness detection pro-

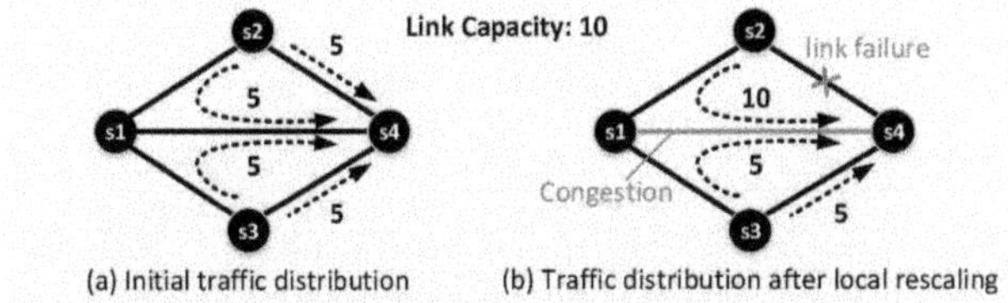


**Figure 2: Congestion due to a data plane fault.**

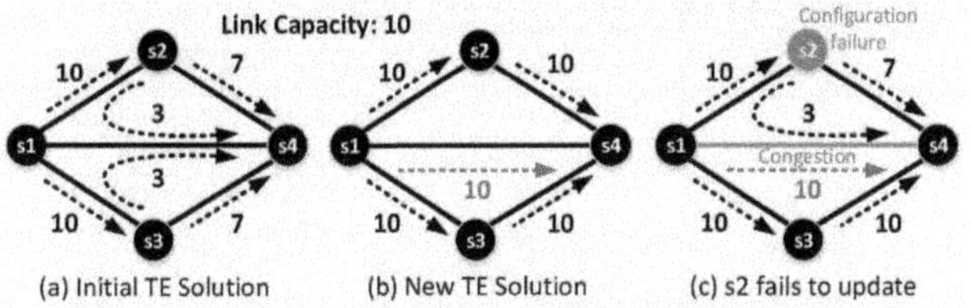


**Figure 3: Congestion due to a control plane fault.**

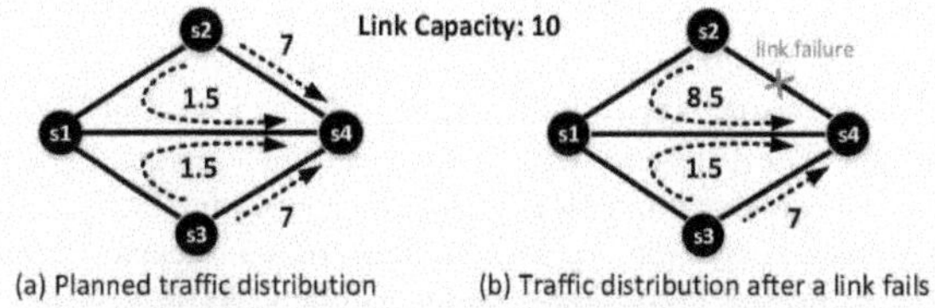


**Figure 4: FFC for link failures ($k = 1$)**

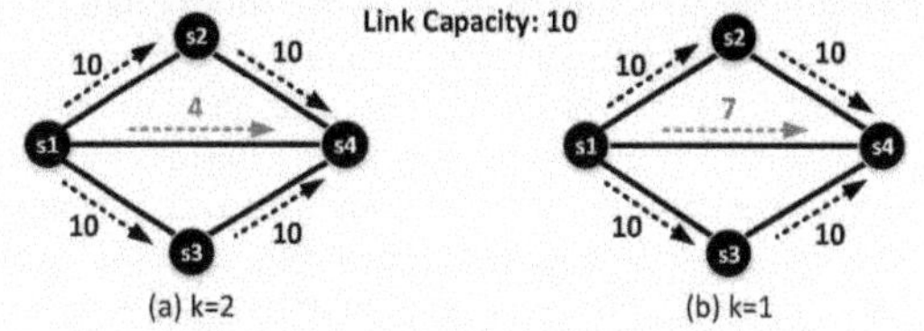


**Figure 5: FFC for control plane faults.**

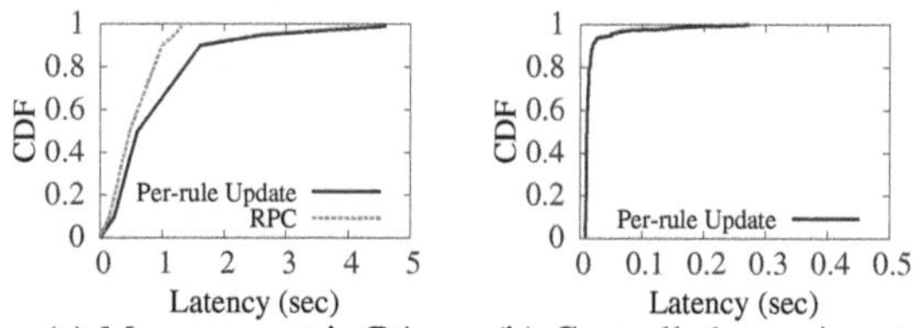


(a) Measurement in B4 (b) Controlled experiments

**Figure 6: Switch update latencies.**

tocol. (Forwarding load has no visible impact on rule update time.) The number and type of updates are drawn from those issued in `L-Net`. Figure 6(b) shows that the rule update time is still substantial. The median is 10 ms and the worst case is over 200 ms. For updating $R$ rules, the total update delay will be RPC delay + $R\times$ per-rule delay; we have confirmed this behavior experimentally. Ignoring RPC delay, for updating 100 rules, the median update delay for a switch will be 1 second and the worst case over 20 seconds. We will show that FFC provides significant benefit even when switch update characteristics mimic this simplified setting.

It may be possible to make reaction times faster, but it is fundamentally limited by factors such as network path latencies, overloaded switch CPUs, time to update forwarding tables,[1] and noise inherent to any production environment. We thus advocate an approach where common faults are handled proactively, and only big, rare faults are handle reactively.

## 3. FFC Overview and Challenges

Our goal is to develop proactive methods to handle data and control plane faults. Inspired by FEC, we develop the concept of FFC, which guarantees that no congestion will occur as long as the number of faults is at most (a configurable bound) $k$. Explicit fault detection or any reaction from the TE controller is not needed.

As the primary controls in FEC are the number of packets sent and their encoding, the primary controls in FFC are the amount of traffic entering a network and its spread. (Assume for now traffic injection is controlled; we consider networks without rate control later.) We illustrate below how these controls, with some overhead in terms of lower throughput, can proactively protect against faults.

### 3.1 FFC for control plane faults

We start with control plane faults because they are unique to centralized TE and have not been studied before. Control plane FFC guarantees that no congestion occurs as long as the number of switches that experience a configuration fault is up to $k$. To see how this guarantee may be achieved, let us revisit Figure 3, in which we wanted to update switches $s2$ and $s3$ to accommodate a new flow. If we try to update the network from Figure 3(a) to 3(b), in which flow $s1 \rightarrow s4$ sends 10 units of traffic, it is impossible to be robust against configuration failure of $s2$ or $s3$. However, the network configuration of Figure 5(a), in which $s1 \rightarrow s4$ sends 4 units of traffic, is robust to either one or both switches failing to configure. Thus, this traffic distribution is an example of FFC with $k$=2, where no congestion will occur if up to two switches fail to update.

The downside is that the network throughput is lower than what would have been in the absence of faults and FFC. However, this throughput overhead will be temporary if no further changes in traffic demand (or network topology) occur. In the example, once $s2$ and $s3$ are successfully configured, the flow $s1 \rightarrow s4$ will be allowed to increase its rate to 10 units in the next period. Even if temporary, lowered throughput is an overhead of robustness provided by FFC.

As with FEC, FFC overhead is lower for lower protection levels. In the example above, if robustness to the configuration failure of up to one switch ($k$=1) is desired, we can safely install the configuration of Figure 5(b), which supports 7 units of flow $s1 \rightarrow s4$. There will be no congestion if $s2$ or $s3$ (not both) fail to configure.

### 3.2 FFC for data plane faults

Data plane FFC guarantees no congestion occurs after rescaling when up to $k$ links or switches fail. To see how to achieve this, we revisit Figure 2, where congestion occurs when link $s2$-$s4$ fails. However, if we spread traffic as in Figure 4(a), any single link failure ($k = 1$) will not cause congestion. For example, if link $s2$-$s4$ fails, the traffic distribution after rescaling is shown in Figure 4(b).

Like control plane FFC, data plane FFC can also lower throughput. However, while the overhead of control plane FFC is borne only when the network is updated, the overhead of data plane FFC is persistent. The difference in the two cases is that when a link or switch fails, network capacity is reduced. To not congest after a failure, we must leave spare capacity to absorb the traffic that was being carried by the failed element.

### 3.3 Applying FFC

Operators use FFC by choosing the value of $k$, which can be different for the two types of faults. This choice allows them to make an informed trade-off between the risk of congestion due to faults and network throughput. For a fixed network capacity, higher values of $k$ may lower throughput but also lower the risk of congestion that can hurt congestion-sensitive applications.[2]

[1] Being based on TCAMs (ternary content addressable memory), forwarding tables are optimized for fast lookups, rather than fast updates [4]

[2] Throughput is lowered by rate limiting at end hosts [1, 2], not by dropping packets in the network, which to applications is indistinguishable from congestion. Packets dropped in the network generally hurt congestion-sensitive applications more than lim-

Throughput loss with FFC is not a given. First, in well-provisioned networks with ample spare capacity and in networks that do not rate control traffic, network throughput with and without FFC will be similar. The difference will be that FFC will strategically spread traffic in a way that guarantees protection against faults. Second, in networks that carry multi-priority traffic, the spare capacity that is needed to protect high-priority traffic can be used to carry lowest-priority (congestion-tolerant) traffic. Doing so leads to negligible loss in total throughput while protecting high-priority traffic (§8.4).

Finally, our FFC techniques have another use case. For a given traffic demand, they can precisely determine the link capacities needed for a desired level of protection from fault-induced congestion. Today, operators that want to minimize the risk of congestion tend to heavily over-provision the network, and even that does not provide any guarantee. We do not explore this use case in this paper, but enabling it requires straightforward modifications to the FFC constraints that we outline in the following sections.

### 3.4 Challenges and overview of techniques

Practical realization of FFC for arbitrary topologies and traffic demands poses two challenges. The first is the scalability with which robust traffic distributions can be computed. If there are $n$ network entities, and we want to be robust to up to $k$ of them failing, FFC has to deal with $\sum_{j=1}^{k}\binom{n}{j}$ failure cases. Thus, naive, enumeration-based approaches are computationally intractable for large networks. We must meet the computational challenge while meeting the second challenge of minimizing the loss in network throughput. If network throughput were not a concern, a trivially robust solution is to not carry any traffic.

We address these challenges by first formulating the conditions on traffic quantity and spread as linear constraints. While this formulation is precise, it has a large number of constraints. We then reduce these large number of constraints to a much smaller number by observing that the constraints can be transformed to what we call the "bounded M-sum" problem and all constraints in such a problem can be reduced to a single constraint on the largest (or smallest) M variables. Finally, we encode these variables using efficient linear expressions with the aid of sorting networks [10]. The result is an FFC formulation with $O(kn)$ constraints.

Our techniques exploit two properties of our setting. First, the impact of a fault is easy to model. If switch configuration fails, it sticks to its old configuration; if a link fails, ingress switches deterministically rescale traffic. This simplicity allows us to capture the conditions imposed by FFC using efficient, linear constraints. Second, while faults are common, the fault ratio (i.e., the fraction of elements that fail) is low. Thus, it suffices to guard against a small number of faults ($k$). Solving for high values of $k$ would be computationally intensive and impose a high throughput overhead.

## 4. Basic FFC Formulation

We now describe how to formulate and solve FFC for a basic TE setting. Our formulation is highly flexible, and in §5 we extend it to a range of other TE settings.

### 4.1 Basic TE (without FFC)

The basic TE problem can be formulated as follows, with key notations summarized in Table 1. The input is a graph $G$=$(V, E)$, where $V$ and $E$ are sets of switches and directed links between switches. Each link $e \in E$ has a capacity $c_e$. The traffic demand is a set of flows, where each flow $f$ is (aggregated) traffic from an ingress to an egress switch. The bandwidth demand of $f$ in a TE interval is $d_f$ and its traffic can be carried on a set of pre-established tunnels $T_f$.

iting their sending rate at source (to which they can adapt). For instance, detecting and recovering from a dropped TCP SYN takes time, which magnifies flow completion time for short transfers.

| | | |
|---|---|---|
| TE Input | $G$ | Network graph with switches $V$ and links $E$. |
| | F = $\{f\}$ | Flows aggregated by ingress-engress switches. |
| | $d_f$ | The bandwidth demand of $f$ in a TE interval. |
| | $c_e$ | The bandwidth capacity of link $e$. |
| | $T_f$ | The set of tunnels that are set up for flow $f$. |
| | $L[t, e]$ | 1 if tunnel $t$ uses link $e$ and 0 otherwise. |
| | $S[t, v]$ | 1 if tunnel $t$'s source is switch $v$ and 0 otherwise. |
| TE Output | $b_f$ | The granted bandwidth to flow $f$. |
| | $a_{f,t}$ | The bandwidth allocated for flow $f$ on tunnel $t$. |
| TE Others | $\beta_{f,t}$ | The upper-bound of flow $f$'s traffic. |
| | $w_{f,t}$ | The traffic splitting weight of flow $f$ on tunnel $t$. |
| FFC | $p_f$ & $p$ | The max number of $f$'s tunnels traverse a link. |
| | $q_f$ & $q$ | The max number of $f$'s tunnels traverse a switch. |
| | $k_c$, $k_e$, $k_v$ | The number of configuration, link and switch failures that FFC protects the network against. |
| | $\tau_f$ | The min number of $f$'s residual tunnels with up to $k_e$ link and $k_v$ switch failures. |

**Table 1: Key notations in FFC formulation.**

The TE output is bandwidth allocation $\{b_f|\forall f\}$ of each flow and how much of the flow can traverse each tunnel $\{a_{f,t}|\forall f, t \in T_f\}$. In networks where the flow rate cannot be controlled, the TE output is only the latter (and $b_f = d_f$).

The TE problem can be solved based on path-constrained multi-commodity flow problem [14], as follows:

$$\max \quad \textstyle\sum_{f\in F} b_f \tag{1}$$

$$\text{s.t.}\forall e \in E: \quad \textstyle\sum_{f\in F, t\in T_f} a_{f,t} L[t,e] \le c_e \tag{2}$$

$$\forall f \in F: \quad \textstyle\sum_{t\in T_f} a_{f,t} \ge b_f \tag{3}$$

$$\forall f \in F, t \in T_f: \quad 0 \le b_f \le d_f;\ 0 \le a_{f,t} \tag{4}$$

where the binary indicator $L[t, e]$ denotes if tunnel $t$ traverses link $e$. The TE objective in this formulation is to maximize network throughput (Eqn. 1). We consider other objectives in §5.3. Eqn. 2 states that no link should be overloaded, and Eqn. 3 states that the sum of the allocation of a flow across all its tunnels should not be less than its allocated rate.[3] Eqn. 4 states that the rate allocated to a flow should not exceed demand, and all variables are non-negative.

The formulation above captures TE for both wide area networks and data center networks (DCN). One difference is that in DCNs, given the larger scale, TE focuses only on large flows (elephants) and link capacity refers to what is not used by small flows (mice).

To implement the computed solution, the TE controller updates the flow's rate limiters to $\{b_f\}$ and ingress switches to use traffic splitting weights of $w_{f,t} = a_{f,t} / \sum_{t\in T_f} a_{f,t}$.

### 4.2 Modeling control plane faults

For control plane faults, the goal of FFC is to compute the new configuration ($\{b_f\}$, $\{a_{f,t}\}$) such that no congestion will occur as long as $k_c$ or fewer switches fail to update their old configuration ($\{b'_f\}$, $\{a'_{f,t}\}$). Another type of control plane fault is a failure to configure a rate limiter, which we will consider in §5.5. Let $\lambda_v$=1 denote a configuration failure for at least one of the flows with $v$ as the ingress switch; $\lambda_v$=0 denotes that configuration for *all* flows starting at $v$ succeeds. An individual case of control plane faults in the network can be represented by a vector $\boldsymbol{\lambda}$=$[\lambda_v | v \in V]$ that indicates the status of each switch. Thus, FFC that is robust to $k_c$ faults requires that the network have no overloaded link under the set of cases $\Lambda_{k_c} = \{\boldsymbol{\lambda} | \sum_{v\in V} \lambda_v \le k_c\}$.

This requirement can be captured as:

[3] Using '$\ge$' instead of '$=$' in Eqn. 3 simplifies the exposition of FFC for data plane faults. For TE without FFC, given the goal of maximizing $b_f$, using '$\ge$' is equivalent to using '$=$'.

$$\forall e \in E, \boldsymbol{\lambda} \in \Lambda_{k_c}: \sum_{v \in V}\{(1-\lambda_v)\hat{a}_{v,e} + \lambda_v \hat{\beta}_{v,e}\} \le c_e \tag{5}$$

where $\hat{a}_{v,e}$ is the total traffic that can arrive at link $e$ from flows starting at $v$ if there is no configuration fault. That is:

$$\forall v \in V, e \in E: \quad \hat{a}_{v,e} = \textstyle\sum_{f \in F, t \in T_f} a_{f,t} L[t,e] S[t,v] \tag{6}$$

where indicator $S[t, v]$ denotes if tunnel $t$'s source switch is $v$.

In Eqn. 5, $\hat{\beta}_{v,e}$ is the upper bound on link $e$ 's traffic from flows starting at $v$ when a fault occurs ($\lambda_v = 1$). That is:

$$\forall v \in V, e \in E: \quad \hat{\beta}_{v,e} = \textstyle\sum_{f \in F, t \in T_f} \beta_{f,t} L[t,e] S[t,v] \tag{7}$$

where $\beta_{f,t}$ is the upper bound on flow $f$'s traffic on tunnel $t$ when a faults occurs for $f$. Since we assume the updates in rate limiters are successful, $\beta_{f,t}$ can be modeled as:

$$\forall f \in F, t \in T_f: \quad \beta_{f,t} = \max\{w'_{f,t} b_f, a_{f,t}\} \tag{8}$$

where $w'_{f,t}$ is flow $f$'s splitting weight for tunnel $t$ in the old configuration (which is known).

Adding Eqns. 5–8 to the basic TE formulation can, in theory, find TE configurations that are robust to $k_c$ control plane faults. However, Eqn. 5 contains $|E| \sum_{j=1}^{k_c} \binom{|V|}{j}$ constraints because $\Lambda_{k_c}$ has $\sum_{j=1}^{k_c} \binom{|V|}{j}$ failures cases. Directly solving for so many constraints is computationally intractable. We outline in §4.4 how we reduce this problem to a smaller number of equivalent constraints.

### 4.3 Modeling data plane faults

For data plane faults, the goal of FFC is to compute flow allocations such that no congestion occurs even after up to $k_e$ links fail *and* up to $k_v$ switches fail. The guarantee is for link failures that are not incident on the failed switches. Since switch failures imply link failures, one could protect against them by considering only link failures [15]. But we explicitly consider switch failures because switches can have a large number of incident links; protecting against switch failures implicitly (using link failures) would require a high value of $k_e$. This approach would significantly hurt throughput because it will protect against arbitrary combinations of up to $k_e$ links, a much stronger condition than protecting against $k_e$ incident links on the same switch.

We model data plane FFC as follows. Let $\mu_e$=1 denote that link $e$ has failed, and $\eta_v$=1 denote that switch $v$ has failed; the indicator values are 0 otherwise. Then, a case of data plane fault can be represented by $(\boldsymbol{\mu}, \boldsymbol{\eta})$ in which vector $\boldsymbol{\mu} = [\mu_e | e \in E]$ and $\boldsymbol{\eta} = [\eta_v | v \in V]$. Thus, TE that is robust to $k_e$ link failures and $k_v$ switch failures requires that there is no overloaded link under the set of hardware failure cases $U_{k_e,k_v} = \{(\boldsymbol{\mu}, \boldsymbol{\eta}) | \sum_e \mu_e \le k_e, \sum_v \eta_v \le k_v\}$.

Recall that data plane faults can cause congestion because they alter traffic distribution over the network when ingress switches rescale traffic, that is, move it from the impacted to the residual tunnels for the flow. Given a fault case $(\boldsymbol{\mu}, \boldsymbol{\eta})$, we know the residual tunnels $T_f^{\boldsymbol{\mu},\boldsymbol{\eta}}$ of each flow $f$—those that do not traverse any failed link or switch. FFC requires that $f$'s residual tunnels be able to hold its allocated rate.

$$\forall f \in F, (\boldsymbol{\mu}, \boldsymbol{\eta}) \in U_{k_e,k_v}: \quad \textstyle\sum_{t \in T_f^{\boldsymbol{\mu},\boldsymbol{\eta}}} a_{f,t} \ge b_f \tag{9}$$

Further, if a flow $f$ has no residual tunnels ($T_f^{\boldsymbol{\mu},\boldsymbol{\eta}} = \emptyset$) under a failure case $(\boldsymbol{\mu}, \boldsymbol{\eta})$, its flow size $b_f$ should be fixed to 0.

Eqn. 9 also guarantees that no link will be overloaded:

LEMMA 1. *A TE configuration ($\{a_{f,t}\}$, $\{b_f\}$) that satisfies constraints Eqns. 2–4, 9 under fault case $(\boldsymbol{\mu}, \boldsymbol{\eta})$ causes no link overload after all ingress switches rescale.*

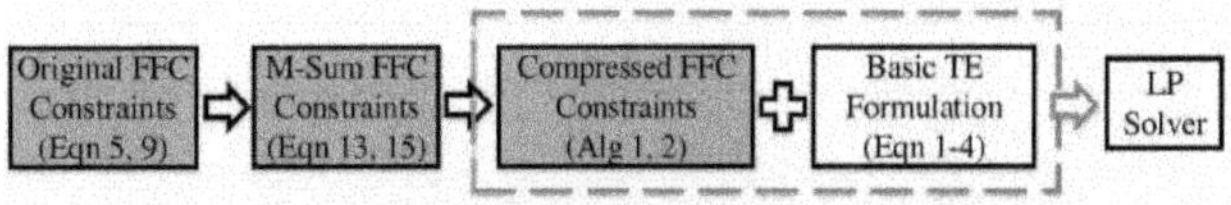


**Figure 7: Overall process for FFC-TE computation.**

PROOF. When a data plane failure case $(\boldsymbol{\mu}, \boldsymbol{\eta})$ happens, the traffic load of a flow $f$ on a residual tunnel $t \in T_f^{\boldsymbol{\mu},\boldsymbol{\eta}}$ is:

$$b_{f,t}^{\boldsymbol{\mu},\boldsymbol{\eta}} = \frac{a_{t,f}}{\sum_{t \in T_f^{\boldsymbol{\mu},\boldsymbol{\eta}}} a_{f,t}} * b_f \le \frac{a_{t,f}}{b_f} * b_f = a_{f,t} \tag{10}$$

which is directly derived from Eqn. 9. Therefore, we know the total traffic load on a link $e$ is:

$$\forall e \in E: \quad \textstyle\sum_{f, t \in T_f^{\boldsymbol{\mu},\boldsymbol{\eta}}} b_{f,t}^{\boldsymbol{\mu},\boldsymbol{\eta}} L[t,e] \le \sum_{f, t \in T_f} a_{f,t} L[t,e] \le c_e$$

which finishes the proof. □

As for control plane faults, adding these constraints to the basic TE will in theory yield a solution that is robust to data plane faults, but directly solving for these constraints is intractable given the large number of possible failure cases in $U_{k_e,k_v}$. Before describing how to solve these constraints, we briefly discuss how careful tunnel layout can improve robustness to data plane faults as well as reduce the overhead of data plane FFC.

**Robust tunnel layout** One observation from Eqn. 9 is that higher the number of residual tunnels, greater the network throughput. Thus, we can improve throughput by creating tunnels such that flows lose as few tunnels as possible when faults occur. Ideally, each flow would lose at most one tunnel upon a fault, but this guarantee requires switch-disjoint (and thus also link-disjoint) tunnels, which limits flows to a small number of tunnels in networks with low path diversity. That would in turn restrict network throughput, as more tunnels are better able to utilize network capacity.

To balance these needs, we recommend $(p, q)$ link-switch disjoint tunnels. For an individual flow, at most $p$ tunnels should traverse a link and at most $q$ tunnels should traverse a switch. The parameters $p$ and $q$ can be flow specific. Algorithms to find link and switch disjoint paths can be extended to find $(p, q)$ link-switch disjoint tunnels; we omit details for space constraints.

### 4.4 Efficiently solving FFC constraints

To tractably solve the large number of FFC constraints, we transform them to a "bounded M-sum" problem and then encode the transformed problem using a sorting network. Figure 7 shows the overall process of the FFC-TE computation.

#### *4.4.1 Transformation to bounded M-sum*

We define the *bounded M-sum* problem as: Given a set of $N$ variables, the sum of any $M$ of those should be less (or more) than a bound B. Formally, if $N_M$ is the set of all possible variable subsets with cardinality $\le M$, we have:

$$\forall S \in N_M: \sum_{n_i \in S} n_i \le B \tag{11}$$

The interesting aspects of this problem are: 1) FFC constraints can be transformed to it; and 2) while the original formulation has a large number of constraints, all of them are satisfied as long as one constraint involving the largest $M$ variables is satisfied. If $n^j$ is an expression for the $j$-th largest variable in $N$, all constraints above hold if:

$$\sum_{j=1}^{M} n^j \le B \tag{12}$$

Thus, if we can find efficient (linear) expressions for the largest $M$ variables in $N$, we can replace all original constraints with one constraint. Before showing how to find such expressions, we first show how to transform FFC constraints into bounded M-sum problem.

**Algorithm 1**: LargestValues($X$, $M$)

[Input] $X$: an array of variables
[Input] $M$: the number of largest values to extract
[Output] $Y$: an array of new variables in which $Y[i]$ $(0 \leq i \leq M)$ is the $i$th largest element in $X$
[Output] $C$: a set of constraints between $X$ and $Y$
$Y \leftarrow \emptyset; C \leftarrow \emptyset;$
// Pop $M$ largest variables from $X$.
**while** $|Y| < M$ **do**
  $y^*, X, C' \leftarrow$ BubbleMax($X$) ;
  $Y \leftarrow Y + \{y^*\}; C \leftarrow C + C'$ ;
**return** $Y, C$ ;

**Algorithm 2**: BubbleMax($X$)

1 [Input] $X$: an array of variables
2 [Output] $x^*$: a variable that represents $\max\{X\}$
3 [Output] $Y$: an array that represent $X \setminus \{x^*\}$
4 [Output] $C$: a set of constraints among $X$, $Y$ and $x^*$
5 $x^* \leftarrow X$.pop(); $Y \leftarrow \emptyset$; $C \leftarrow \emptyset$ ;
6 **while** $X \neq \emptyset$ **do**
7   $x \leftarrow X$.pop() ;
8   $x_{max}, x_{min} \leftarrow$ new variables ;
9   // Make two new constraints.
10   $c_1 \leftarrow 2 * x_{max} = x + x^* + |x - x^*|$ ;
11   $c_2 \leftarrow 2 * x_{min} = x + x^* - |x - x^*|$ ;
12   $x^* \leftarrow x_{max}; Y \leftarrow Y + \{x_{min}\}; C \leftarrow C + \{c_1, c_2\}$;
13 **return** $x^*, Y, C$ ;

**Control plane faults** Eqn. 5 of control plane FFC can be equivalently re-written as:

$$\forall e \in E, \boldsymbol{\lambda} \in \Lambda_{k_c} : \sum_{v \in V} \lambda_v(\hat{\beta}_{v,e} - \hat{a}_{v,e}) \leq c_e - \sum_{v} \hat{a}_{v,e} \qquad (13)$$

Let $D = \{\hat{\beta}_{v,e} - \hat{a}_{v,e} | v \in V\}$ and $d^j$ be the $j$th largest element in $D$. Since $\hat{\beta}_{v,e} - \hat{a}_{v,e} \geq 0$, Eqn. 13 is equivalent to

$$\forall e \in E : \sum_{j=1}^{k_c} d^j \leq c_e - \sum_{v} \hat{a}_{v,e} \qquad (14)$$

Thus, we have transformed the original $|E| \times |\Lambda_{k_c}|$ constraints into $|E|$ constraints, one for each link.

**Data plane faults** Assume that the tunnels of flow $f$ are $(p_f, q_f)$ link-switch disjoint. The values $(p_f, q_f)$ are computable for any given tunnel layout; the layout does not have to use the robust strategy above. Then, for any data plane fault case $(\boldsymbol{\mu}, \boldsymbol{\eta}) \in U_{k_e,k_v}$, the number of residual tunnels is no less than $\tau_f = |T_f| - k_e p_f - k_v q_f$. Suppose $a^j_{f,t}$ is the $j$th smallest (not largest) element in $A_f = \{a_{f,t} | t \in T_f\}$, then the following guarantees that all constraints in Eqn. 9 are satisfied:

$$\forall f : \ \sum_{j=1}^{\tau_f} a^j_{f,t} \geq b_f \qquad (15)$$

The guarantee holds because the left-hand side of Eqn. 15 is the worst-case rate allocation that flow $f$ can have from its residual tunnels under any case in $U_{k_e,k_v}$.

Unlike control plane faults, the transformation from Eqn. 9 to Eqn. 15 does not preserve equivalence. Satisfying Eqn. 15 satisfies Eqn. 9, but not vice versa. In the special cases link failures with link-disjoint tunnels and switch failures with switch-disjoint tunnels, the two are equivalent.

Interestingly, however, the imprecision of Eqn. 15 allows it to protect against fault cases beyond $U_{k_e,k_v}$. It essentially protects the network against any fault case where the number of tunnel failures is no more than $k_t = k_e p_f + k_v q_f$. Suppose $(p_f, q_f)$=(1, 3) and our desired protection level is up to 3 links failures and no switch failure ($k_e$=3, $k_v$=0), with Eqn. 15 we also simultaneously protect the network against one arbitrary switch failure and no link failure ($k_e$=0, $k_v$=1). We leverage this effect in our experiments.

### 4.4.2 Encoding for largest (or smallest) $M$ variables

We now explain how we express the largest $M$ variables as linear constraints. When added to other TE constraints, they help efficiently compute FFC traffic distribution.

Our method is based on sorting networks [10], which are networks of compare-swap operators that can sort any array of $N$ values. An example network to sort 4 values is shown in Figure 8(a). This network is based on the merge sort algorithm. Each compare-swap operator takes two inputs from left, and it moves the higher input upwards and the lower downwards.

The characteristic of sorting networks that we exploit is that the sequence of compare-swap operations is independent of the input, unlike many sorting algorithms (*e.g.* quick sort) where the next comparison depends on the outcome of previous ones. This characteristic allows us to encode the relationship between original variables and the $j$th largest element in them with linear expressions.

We also exploit that we are interested in only the largest $M$ values, rather than sorting them all, which allows us to use a partial network. Practical sorting networks require $O(N log(N)^2)$ compare-swap operators, while we use a partial network with $O(NM)$ operators. This difference is substantial since $N$ is large and $M$ is small in our setting—equivalent to the number of faults we guard against.

We base our network on bubble sort; unlike other algorithms, its premature termination after $M$ stages yields the largest $M$ values. Figure 8(b) illustrates our strategy for the case of finding the largest 2 of 4 values. The first stage finds the largest element, and the second finds the second largest.

Algorithm 1 shows the pseudo-code for generating expressions for the largest $M$ values. It operates in $M$ steps, and in each step, it builds an expression for the largest of the remaining values. Algorithm 2 shows the pseudo-code for building the expression for the largest value. Figure 8(c) shows a concrete example of Algorithm 2 in which $|x - x^*|$ in Lines 10 and 11 is encoded with linear formulations.

A similar approach can find the expressions for the smallest M values. The only difference is that compare-swap operators that push the lower (not higher) of the two values upwards are used.

### 4.4.3 Throughput and computational overhead

Our methods have the following properties with respect to throughput overhead: 1) Our control plane FFC scheme is optimal; and 2) Our data plane FFC scheme is optimal for the special cases of link failures with link disjoint tunnels and switch failures with switch disjoint tunnels. Optimal means that no other scheme will have lower overhead for the same degree of protection. We omit proofs from this paper due to space constraints.

The computational overhead of our methods can be characterized using the number of additional variables and constraints they introduce in the LP. The basic (non-FFC) TE problem has $2|F|+|E|$ constraints and $\sum_f |T_f| + |F|$ variables. Control plane FFC introduces $|E|$ constraints (Eqn. 14) plus up to $4k_c|V||E|$ constraints and up to $3k_c|V||E|$ variables to encode the partial sorting network. (Even though we show only 2 new variables and 2 constraints in Algorithm 2, multiplicative factors of 4 and 3 stem from converting the absolute values in Lines 10∼11 into standard linear constraints.) Data plane FFC introduces up to $|F| + 4\sum_f |T_f| \min\{|T_f| - \tau_f, \tau_f\}$ constraints and up to $3\sum_f |T_f| \min\{T_f - \tau_f, \tau_f\}$ variables. Recall that $\tau_f = |T_f| - k_e p_f - k_v q_f$.

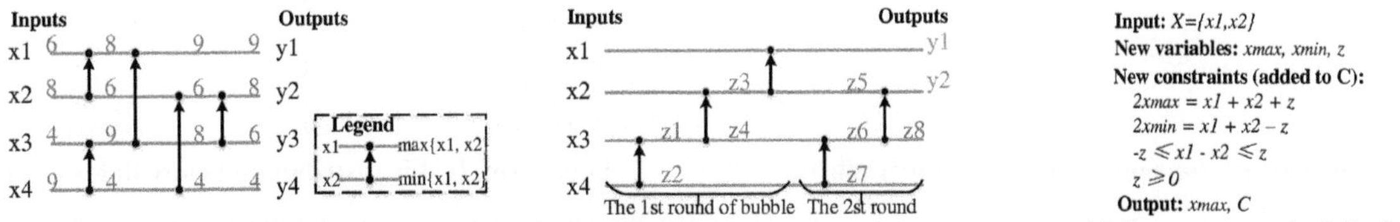


(a) An example of sorting networks (b) A network to find the largest-2 elements (c) A concrete example of Alg-2

**Figure 8: Sorting networks and finding largest elements among variables.**

## 4.5 Combined FFC for both faults types

To simultaneously protect against control and data plane faults, we simply include both types of constraints in TE computations. It will take three parameters $(k_c, k_e, k_v)$ and the guarantee is that no congestion will occur as long as switch configuration failures, link failures, and switch failures are up to $k_c$, $k_e$ , and $k_v$ , respectively.

A subtle issue can arise in combined protection settings right after data plane faults bigger than the protection level (*e.g.*, number of failed links $> k_e$). Due to such faults, some links may get congested and there may be no way to move traffic away from them while being also robust to control plane faults. For instance, assume that due to a big data plane fault, after rescaling, a link $e$ with capacity 10 gets 7 units of traffic each from three flows that start at different ingress switches. Moving the extra 11 units of traffic away from the link requires updating at least two switches. But if we are protecting against two control plane faults ($k_c$=2) planning for this movement is impossible; there would be no feasible solution to the FFC constraints. To handle this issue, we allow unprotected moves for overloaded links by setting $k_c$=0 for such links in Eqn. 5. In theory, overloaded links can arise after big control plane faults as well, but in our experience, such faults are unlikely to create congestion that is so severe that traffic cannot be moved in a manner that is robust to (further) control plane faults.

# 5. Extending Basic FFC

Our FFC formulation is not only efficient but also flexible. We now show how it extends to a wide range of TE settings.

## 5.1 Traffic with different priorities

Earlier, we assumed that all traffic has the same priority; some networks may use multiple priorities to differentiate between applications with different performance requirements [1, 2]. FFC can be extended to this setting to offer different levels of protections to different priorities. The TE solution for higher priority traffic is computed first with a custom protection level ($k_c^h$, $k_e^h$ and $k_v^h$), and the TE solution of lower priority traffic is computed next with its own protection level ($k_c^l$, $k_e^l$ and $k_v^l$). This cascading computation is already done to support multiple priorities [1, 2]; computation for lower priority traffic uses residual link capacity (not actually used higher priority traffic).

A requirement for the extension above is that the protection level for high priority should not be smaller ($k_x^h \geq k_x^l, x \in \{c, e, v\}$), which is a desirable property anyway. Otherwise, the FFC-TE for lower priorities may not have a feasible solution because the configuration for high priority traffic may violate FFC constraints.

## 5.2 Congestion-free updates

Some networks use multi-step updates to preclude transient congestion caused by different switches updating their configuration at different times [2, 16]. The basic idea is to find a chain of intermediate TE configurations $A^i$=$\{a^i_{f,t}\}(0 < i < m)$ that update the network from current configuration $A^0$ to the desired configuration $A^m$. The transition between each pair of adjacent TE configurations is guaranteed to be congestion free irrespective of the order in which the switches apply updates. Such intermediate TEs are found using the following key constraint:

$$\forall e \in E, i : \sum_v \max\{\hat{a}^{i-1}_{v,e}, \hat{a}^i_{v,e}\} \leq c_e \qquad (16)$$

This constraint captures the condition that each link $e$ should be able to accommodate the maximum traffic, across adjacent configurations, it gets from each ingress switch $v$. After computing the intermediate configurations, the TE controller updates the network step-by-step: $A^0 \rightarrow A^1 \ldots A^m$.

With congestion-free updates, control plane faults will not cause congestion, but will block the update process; the preceding step must complete before the next step can be taken. In this setting, FFC can ensure that the update can proceed from $A^{i-1}$ to $A^i$ as long as the cumulative number of faults (across all steps thus far) is $k_c$ or fewer. We can find such intermediate configurations by replacing Eqn. 16 with:

$$\forall e \in E, \lambda \in \Lambda_{k_c}, i :$$

$$\sum_v \lambda_v \max\{\beta^0_{v,e}, \ldots \beta^i_{v,e}\} + (1 - \lambda_v)\max\{\hat{a}^{i-1}_{v,e}, \hat{a}^i_{v,e}\} \leq c_e$$

This is a large number of constraints, but we can solve them efficiently by transforming them to the bounded M-sum problem (§4.4). We omit details for space constraints.

## 5.3 Optimizing for fairness

Earlier, we assumed that TE objective was to maximize network throughput; another common objective is fairness among flows [1, 2]. Fairness typically introduces more constraints in the TE problem, and simply including those constraints will yield FFC-TE with fairness. As a concrete example, consider the iterative approximate-max-min fair method of SWAN [2]. It solves the basic TE (Eqns. 1–4) multiple times, each time with an upper-bound on flow allocations ($b_f$). The bound is iteratively increased by multiplying it by a factor $\alpha$. The allocation of flows that are unable to reach the bound in a given iteration are frozen for future iterations, and the iterations continue until the bound goes above the maximum flow demand ($d_f$). This process ensures that flows with large demands cannot get a higher allocation until the allocation of other flows cannot be increased to at least that level. It yields flow allocations that are provably at most $\alpha$ away from true max-min fair allocation (which is computationally hard to calculate).

The same process can be used largely unmodified to compute TE solutions that are both fair and provide FFC. The only difference is that each iteration includes FFC-related constraints as well.

## 5.4 TE without flow rate control

In some networks, such as ISP backbones, controlling the rates of incoming flows is not possible. Instead of allocating flow rates, the goal of TE tends to be to configure the network such that maximum link utilization (MLU) is minimized while carrying the offered demand ($\{d_f\}$). The basic (non-FFC) network configuration ($\{a_{f,t}\}$) can be computed for this setting by replacing Eqns. 1 and 2 with the following objective function and constraint:

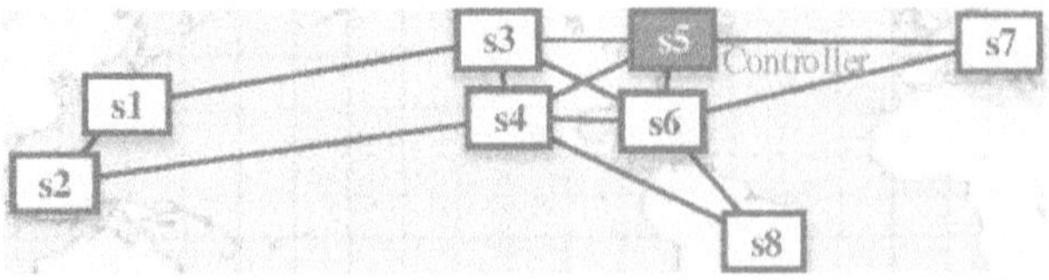

Figure 9: The network topology emulated in our testbed.

$$\begin{aligned} \text{min.} \quad & \Theta(u) \\ \text{s.t.} \forall e: \quad & u \geq \textstyle\sum_v \hat{a}_{v,e}/c_e \end{aligned}$$

where $u$ denotes MLU and $\Theta$ is a function of MLU that needs to be minimized. Eqn. 2, which limited the amount of traffic a link had to carry, is replaced because the offered demand may be higher than what is routable while honoring link capacities. In the equations above, $u$ is allowed to be higher than 1 (i.e., over-subscribed links).

To compute FFC configuration, constraints for data plane FFC stay the same, but control plane FFC requires changing the objective function and additional constraints, as follows:

$$\begin{aligned} \text{min.} \quad & \Theta(u) + \sigma\Theta(u_f) \\ \forall e \in E, \lambda \in \Lambda_{k_c}: \quad & u_f \geq \textstyle\sum_v \{\lambda_v \hat{\beta_{v,e}} + (1-\lambda_v)\hat{a}_{v,e}\}/c_e \end{aligned}$$

where $\sigma > 0$ is a coefficient that balances the importance of MLU in normal cases $u$ and MLU when faults occur $u_f$. These constraints can be solved using the method of §4.4.

## 5.5 Control plane faults for rate limiters

Earlier, we assumed that configuration updates for rate limiters always succeed; some networks may experience update failures for rate limiters as well. If ingress switches and rate limiters are updated independently, the traffic load of a flow on a tunnel can be a mix of old or new traffic splitting weights and old or new flow sizes. We can account for this by modifying Eqn. 8 to:

$$\beta_{f,t} = \max\{a'_{f,t}, b'_f w_{f,t}, b_f w'_{f,t}, a_{f,t}\} \qquad (17)$$

In some networks, the updates on switches and rate limiters are ordered to ensure that there is no congestion due to transient inconsistencies in flow sizes and tunnel weights [2]. The order is: if $f$'s size is increasing ($b'_f < b_f$), the traffic splitting weights at ingress switches are updated first and the rate limiter is updated after (and only if) that succeeds; otherwise, the rate limiter is updated first and the splitting weights are updated after that succeeds. Thus, if $b'_f < b_f$, the combination of new flow size and old weights ($b_f w'_{f,t}$) will not occur and $b'_f w_{f,t} < a_{f,t}$; similarly if $b'_f > b_f$, the combination of old flow size and new weights ($b'_f w_{f,t}$) will not occur and $b_f w'_{f,t} < a'_{f,t}$. We can then simplify Eqn. 17 to:

$$\beta_{f,t} = \max\{a'_{f,t}, a_{f,t}\} \qquad (18)$$

Besides simplifying the FFC formulation, ordering of updates on switches and rate limiters also helps lower the overhead of FFC. It reduces the number of possible traffic configurations for which we must be prepared.

## 5.6 Uncertainty in current TE

Earlier, we assumed that while computing the next TE configuration, the controller exactly knows the current configuration ($\{a'_{f,t}\}$, $\{b'_f\}$) of each flow. Sometimes, however, there may be uncertainty in the configuration of some flows, e.g., if update commands were sent in the last round to change configuration from ($\{a''_{f,t}\}, \{b''_f\}$) to ($\{a'_{f,t}\}, \{b'_f\}$) but the success of some updates could not be confirmed. In such an event, the configuration of the flow can be either ($\{a''_{f,t}\}, \{b''_f\}$) or ($\{a'_{f,t}\}, \{b'_f\}$).

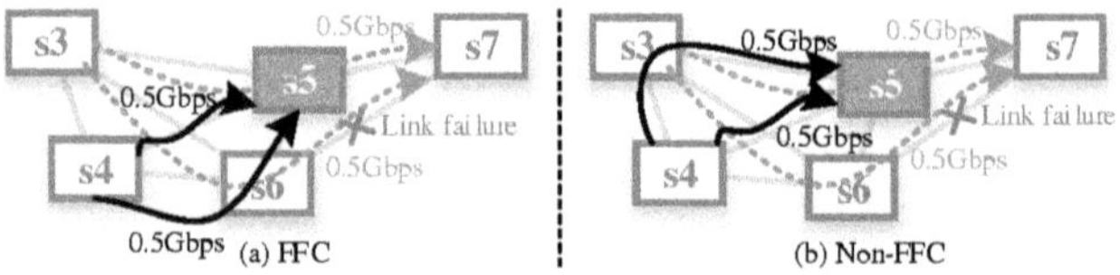

Figure 10: Traffic distribution before link s6-s7 fails.

We can explicitly account for this uncertainty in FFC computations. Suppose $\mathcal{F}$ is a set of flows with uncertain configurations. Instead of computing yet another configuration for them, we try to bring their configuration up-to-date and, in terms of link capacity allocation, we plan for them to be in either of the last two configurations. The following constraints capture this strategy:

$$\begin{aligned} \forall f \in \mathcal{F}, t \in T_f: \quad & b_f = b'_f; a_{f,t} = a'_{f,t} \\ \forall f \in \mathcal{F}, t \in T_f: \quad & \beta_{f,t} = \max\{a''_{f,t}, a'_{f,t}\} \end{aligned}$$

# 6. Implementation

Our FFC controller is implemented as a drop-in replacement for existing TE controllers. It takes as input traffic demand (per-priority ingress-egress flow), network topology, and current traffic, and produces the allocation of each flow and configuration for each switch. The additional configuration for our controller includes the protection level $(k_c, k_e, k_v)$ for each priority. It implements all the extensions in §5. We use Solver Foundation v3.0.2 with CPLEX plugin v12.5.0 as our LP solver.

Our implementation includes a few optimizations that lower computational burden without practically impacting FFC properties. For control plane FFC, observe that not all ingress switches have traffic on each link. Thus, in Eqn. 14, if a switch $v$ has no load on a link $e$ in the old TE, we ignore $v$ when considering the safety of $e$. Similarly, we also ignore switches that have little traffic load—less than 0.001% of capacity—on $e$ in the old TE because the impact of such switches not updating is negligible. For data plane FFC, we pick mice flows—those that collectively carry less than 1% of the traffic—and fix their tunnel bandwidth allocations with the constraint $a_{f,t} = \frac{b_f}{\tau_f}$, which suffices to satisfy Eqn. 15, rather than using sorting networks.

# 7. Testbed Evaluation

We begin our evaluation of FFC by first performing experiments on a testbed. These experiments show the value of FFC with real switches and actual delays in detecting and reacting to failures. The next section shows the value of FFC at scale using simulations with data from real networks.

Our testbed emulates a WAN with 8 sites spread across 4 continents, as shown in Figure 9. Each site has 5 servers that generate traffic and 1 WAN-facing switch (Arista 7050T). The capacity of every cross-site link is 1 Gbps. The TE controller is in New York ($s5$), and we emulate delays for control messages based on geographic distances. We update switch rules via a custom software agent running on the switches (which we have found to be more performant and reliable than the built-in software). We use *iperf* on the servers to generate UDP traffic flows with specified rates and measure packet loss according to both iPerf's server reports and the packet counters in the switches. All switches run link liveness detection protocol, and they report any failures to ingress switches. Upon hearing about a failure, ingress switches rescale traffic away from the impacted tunnels.

We conducted several experiments to study the behavior of FFC and non-FFC TE, but we present results only from a simple, representative experiment that illustrates their differences for a data

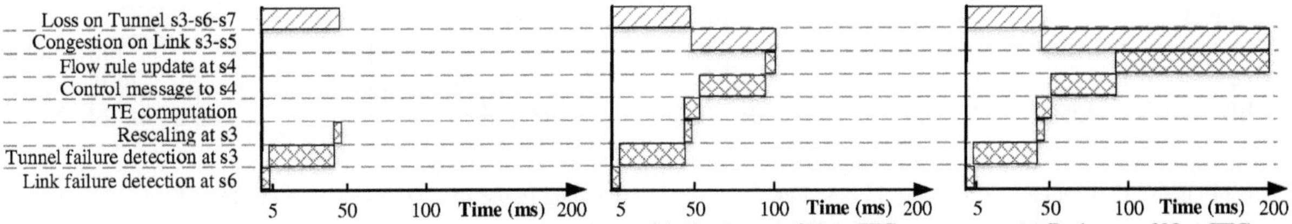


(a) FFC (b) Good case of Non-FFC (c) Bad case of Non-FFC

**Figure 11: Events with and without FFC during link failures.**

plane fault. This experiment has two flows, $s3 \to s7$ and $s4 \to s5$, each with demand 1 Gbps. Figure 10 shows how this traffic was spread in the case of FFC and non-FFC. The main difference is that FFC uses tunnel s4-s6-s5, instead of s4-s3-s5, to transmit 0.5 Gbps traffic, which provides protection against any single-link failure. We conducted many trials with this setup; in each we failed link s6-s7 and observed the ensuing events.

FFC behavior was consistent across trials. Figure 11(a) shows an example. The $x$-axis is a time line relative to when the link failure was injected and $y$-axis lists the events that could happen in a failure reaction. Shadowed blocks denote the start and end of the event. We see $s6$ detects link failure within 5 ms, and $s3$ hears about it within 45 ms. $s3$ rescales and moves all traffic to the residual tunnel within 2 ms. Packet loss on tunnel s3-s6-s7 stops immediately after that. We thus see that losses in FFC are a purely a function of the time it takes for fault detection and rescaling delay. We see that modulo propagation delay, which is fundamental, today's switches can detect faults and rescale quickly. FFC ensures that these activities suffice at eliminating congestion, and the TE controller does not need to react.

The situation is more complex in the non-FFC case. After s3 rescales, link s4-s5 will get congested as it starts getting 1.5 Gbps of traffic; see Figure 9(b). To remedy this, the TE controller computes a new solution in which s4 moves 0.5 Gbps of traffic to tunnel s4-s6-s5 and updates the switch s4. Figure 11(b) shows the best case for non-FFC in our trials, in which the update itself was quick (within 5 ms). We see rescaling-related loss on s3-s5 stops within 45 ms, given the propagation delay from the controller to the switch s4. Overall, the network was congested for twice the time compared to FFC. Figure 11(c) shows a bad case for non-FFC, in which the switch s4 took a long time to apply the update. Consequently, the congestion lasted for much longer.

## 8. Data-driven Evaluation

We now evaluate FFC with topology, traffic, and failure data from real networks. We first micro-benchmark its throughput and computation cost, then study its end-to-end impact in single- and multi-priority networks, and finally study its impact on update time for multi-step updates. We start by describing our data sources and experimental methodology.

### 8.1 Experimental methodology

**Networks** We experiment with two wide area networks. The first, which we call `L-Net`, has $O(50)$ sites globally with $O(100)$ switches and $O(1000)$ links. We have data on link capacities, traffic, and data plane faults for `L-Net`. To ensure that our results are robust to network topology, we also use B4's site-level topology with 12 sites [1], which we call `S-Net`. Since we do not know the internal details of `S-Net`, we assume that there are two switches per site, and each site-level link is composed of four 10 Gbps switch-level links between each of the four inter-site switch pairs.

**Traffic demand** We collect network traffic logs and aggregate it into ingress-egress flows. We partition time into 5-minute bins (the TE interval) and the demand of the flow for an interval is the average bandwidth it consumed. For `L-Net`, we use its traffic logs directly. For `S-Net`, we use traffic logs from another inter-datacenter network (not `L-Net`) and synthesize demand by mapping sites from the other network onto `S-Net`, as in earlier work [2].

For multi-priority experiments, we partition traffic into three priorities based on their source services. Following SWAN [2], high priority is for interactive services, which are highly sensitive to loss and delay; medium priority is for services that are less sensitive but are still impacted by packet loss (*e.g.* deadline-driven transfers); and low priority is for background services (*e.g.* data replications).

To understand the impact of network provisioning level, we study three cases. The first is a well-utilized network where capacity matches demand. To mimic this, we scale the demands of all flows (uniformly) such that 99% of demands per interval are satisfied. The results below refer to this case as traffic scale of 1. The other two cases are a well-provisioned network and an under-provisioned network, and we use traffic scales of 0.5 and 2 to mimic them.

In terms of relationship to practice, ISP networks are typically well-provisioned and use single priority traffic. Inter-datacenter networks are well-utilized and use multiple priorities to protect high priority traffic from short-term demand increases of lower priority traffic [1, 2].

**Failures and switch update models** For `L-Net`, we inject data plane faults as per logs from the network. For `S-Net`, we inject faults based on the per-link and per-switch failure probabilities derived from `L-Net` logs. We assume that it takes 5 ms for a switch to detect a link failure, and the time it takes for an ingress switch to hear about the failure and rescale depends on the propagation delay.

We consider two models of switch update behaviors. In the `Realistic` model, we use the update delay distribution reported for B4 (§2.3) and a configuration failure rate of 1%. In the `Optimistic` model, we use the update delay distribution we measured in a controlled environment (§2.3) and no configuration failures.

**TE approaches** We compare TE with and without FFC. Without FFC, when a link or switch fails, the TE controller immediately computes a new traffic distribution and updates the network. With FFC, the controller does not react to data plane faults unless it is on the edge of protection level. If the link protection level $k_e$=2, the controller reacts only after 2 links have failed. reaction logic is per-priority; when a given priority traffic is at the edge of protection level, only that traffic is re-adjusted. Both approaches use the same set of tunnels. We use (1, 3)-link-switch disjoint strategy to establish six tunnels for each flow. Except in the micro-benchmark experiments, if a flow's demand is not satisfied in an interval, the remaining bytes add to its demand in the next interval.

We evaluated both max-throughput and max-min fairness as TE objectives but present results only for the former. Results for the latter are qualitatively similar.

**Metrics** We use two metrics to capture the behavior of FFC:

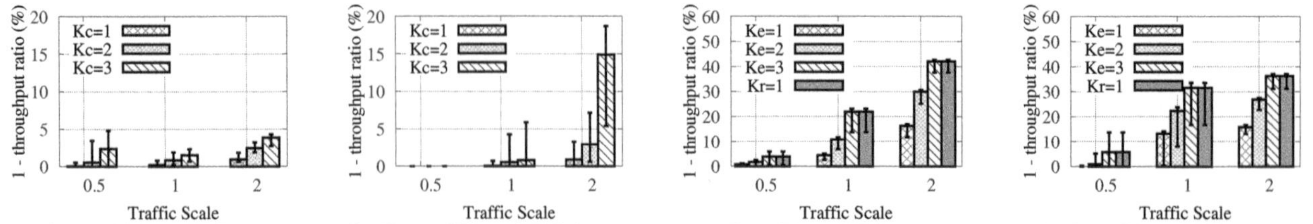

(a) Control Plane FFC (L-Net) (b) Control Plane FFC (S-Net) (c) Data Plane FFC (L-Net) (d) Data Plane FFC (S-Net)

**Figure 12: Throughput overhead of FFC. Bars show the 90th %-ile value and error bars show the 50th and 99th %-iles.**

*i) Throughput ratio* Network throughput with FFC versus without FFC. One minus this ratio is the overhead of FFC.
*ii) Data loss ratio* Bytes lost with FFC versus without FFC. We count bytes lost due to both blackholes and congestion. Blackhole losses occur during the time between when a link fails and when ingress switches rescale; all packets that traverse the failed link are considered lost in this period. Congestion losses are computed based on link capacity and the duration and degree to which the link is oversubscribed. This simple measure overestimates loss if traffic is congestion controlled, as such traffic will reduce sending rate in response to early losses. But it serves as a good proxy for capturing the intensity and duration of congestion, without requiring us to model the intricate relationship between loss and performance for a diverse set of applications.

## 8.2 Micro-benchmarks

**Throughput overhead** To micro-benchmark the overhead of FFC, we compute traffic distributions with and without it for successive TE intervals. In each interval, we exclude any unfinished data from previous intervals, so that both approaches operate on the same demand in each interval, independent of preceding allocations. Failure and switch models do not impact these experiments as we do not inject faults but study overhead when no faults happen.

Figures 12(a) and 12(b) show the overhead (1 - throughput ratio) of control plane FFC in isolation (no data plane FFC) for three protection levels. For each traffic scale, they plot three percentile values. We see that the overhead of control plane FFC is small—under 5% even at 90th percentile level for all but one setting—and, expectedly, increases with the protection level. We also see that the overhead generally increases with the traffic scale. As the network gets busier, it becomes harder to accommodate all traffic in a way that modifies traffic spread robustly. The results are similar for L-Net and S-Net.

Figures 12(c) and 12(d) show the overhead of data plane FFC for 1-3 links failures and 1 switch failure. Because we use (1, 3)-link-switch disjoint strategy to construct tunnels, the cases with $k_e$ = 3 and $k_v$ = 1 are identical. We see that the overhead is low at traffic scale 0.5 (a well-provisioned network), but it grows quickly as traffic scales and protection level increases.

Based on these results and that multiple link failures in a short amount of time and switch failures are uncommon (but do occur), we recommend using a protection level of $(k_c, k_e, k_v) = (2, 1, 0)$ in single-priority networks. In multi-priority networks, we recommend a higher protection level for high-priority flows. As the relative volume of this traffic is typically under 50%, FFC's overhead will still be small.

**Computation time** We benchmark computation time on an ordinary PC with Intel i5 M540 2.53 Ghz CPU (2 cores) and 4GB RAM. Table 2 lists the average computation time for FFC with different protection levels and without FFC. Because of the imprecision of Eqn. 15 (§4.4.1), FFC configuration of $(3, 3, 0)$ simultaneously provides protection for $(3, 0, 1)$. We use $(3, 0, 1) \cup (3, 3, 0)$ as a shorthand for this combined protection level. We see that even at a high protection level, FFC computation takes only 1.2 seconds for large network like L-Net.

| | FFC $(3, 3, 0) \cup (3, 0, 1)$ | FFC (2, 1, 0) | Non-FFC |
|---|---|---|---|
| L-Net | 1.2 sec | 0.3 sec | 0.05 sec |
| S-Net | 0.03 sec | 0.02 sec | 0.015 sec |

**Table 2: TE computation time with and without FFC.**

In contrast, we find that directly computing TE with the original FFC constraints (Eqns. 5 and 9) takes longer than 12 hours in each case. Such long computation time renders TE ineffective given that the traffic demands and network topology likely change before a solution is obtained.

## 8.3 Single-priority traffic

We now conduct end-to-end evaluation of FFC with realistic failure and switch models. This section focuses on the single-priority case, and the next on multi-priority case. Per above, we configure FFC as $(k_c, k_e, k_v) = (2, 1, 0)$.

Figure 13 shows the results for the two networks, the two switch models, and the three traffic scales. Focusing first on the case of well-provisioned networks (traffic scale 0.5), which is the common case for single-priority traffic, we see that throughput difference with and without FFC is negligible. At the same time, FFC offers 10–20 times reduction in data loss. We do not report absolute amount of lost data to maintain confidentiality for link capacities in L-Net. But we note that the loss is substantial—well above $O(100GB)$ per day—and in almost all cases of link oversubscription, the amount of data lost is well above typical buffer capacities.

For the case of well-utilized networks (traffic scale 1), we see that FFC carries over 90% of the traffic carried without FFC and cuts data loss by a factor of 7–130 (0.72–11.5%).

Closer inspection of lost data reveals that both with and without FFC, blackhole losses due to delay in rescaling after a link failure are negligible. With FFC, the primary factor behind losses is cases where the number of data plane faults is greater than the protection level. Without FFC, any control and data plane fault leads to congestive losses, and both types of faults contribute roughly equally.

Though the absolute amount of data loss is lower for the Optimistic switch model, we observe in Figure 13 that the relative gain of FFC is similar for both switch models. Thus, FFC helps even if switch updates times could be improved to those in controlled environments today and all configuration failures could be eliminated.

**Trade-off between throughput and data loss** Using link failures as an example, Figure 15 shows the tradeoff between data loss and throughput overhead as we change the protection level. This experiment uses the Realistic switch model and no protection from control plane faults or switch failures. For each traffic scale, the point at (100, 100) corresponds to no protection ($k_e = 0$) and successive points to the left correspond to increasing values of link protection. Expectedly, the less data we want to lose, the higher the throughput overhead, though throughput overhead grows slower than loss reduction (linear versus exponential).

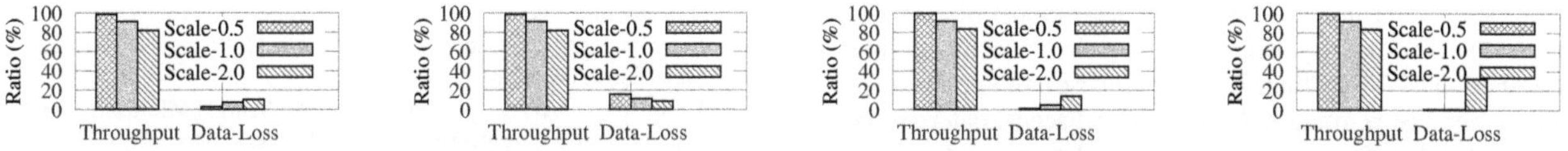


(a) `Realistic` on `L-Net` (b) `Optimistic` on `L-Net` (c) `Realistic` on `S-Net` (d) `Optimistic` on `S-Net`

**Figure 13: Throughput and data loss ratio for FFC with single-priority traffic.**

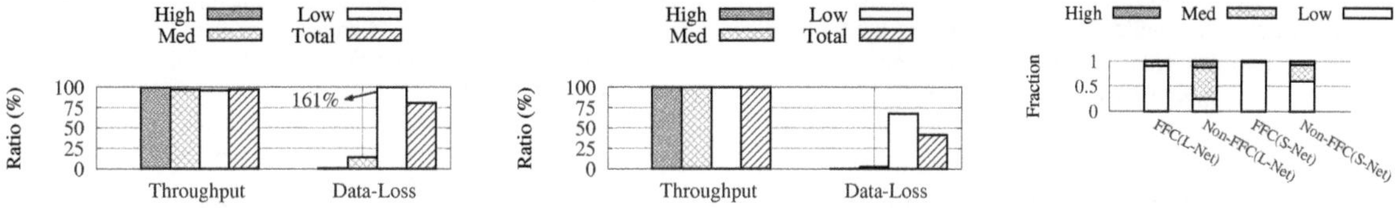


(a) `L-Net` (b) `S-Net` (c) Fractions of data loss

**Figure 14: Throughput and data loss ratio for FFC with multi-priority traffic with `Realistic` switch model.**

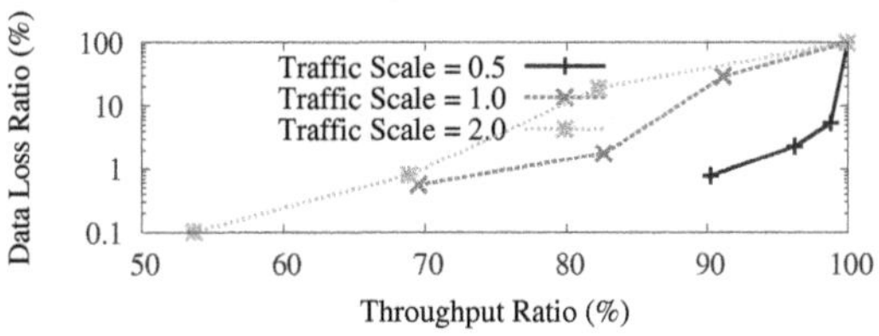


**Figure 15: The tradeoff of data loss and throughput.**

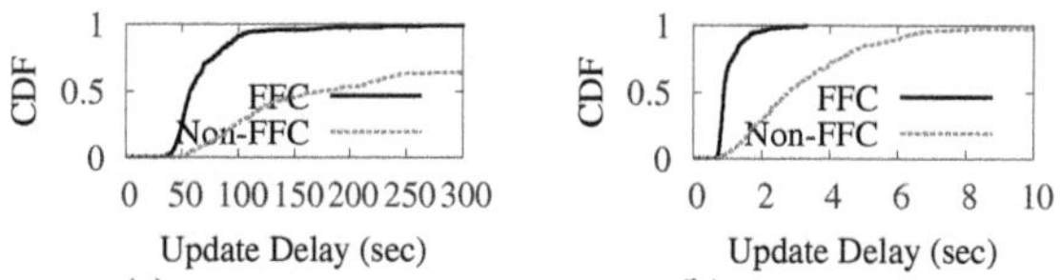


(a) `Realistic` (b) `Optimistic`

**Figure 16: Update time for congestion-free updates.**

## 8.4 Multi-priority traffic

We now consider multi-priority traffic. FFC offers the opportunity to provide greater protection for high-priority traffic with minimal loss in total throughput because low-priority traffic can be safely carried over the capacity that is set aside to protect high-priority traffic. When congestion occurs, priority queueing, which preferentially drops lower-priority packets, protects high-priority traffic as long as its rate does not exceed link capacity.

We use different protection levels for different priorities: $(k_c, k_e, k_v) = (3, 0, 1) \cup (3, 3, 0)$ for high-priority traffic to provide it strong protection, $(2, 1, 0)$ for medium priority, and $(0, 0, 0)$ for low priority. Thus, low priority traffic is not protected at all, which lets it use all network capacity.

Figure 14 shows the results for both networks. This experiment uses traffic scale of 1 (well-utilized network). In Figures 14(a) and 14(b), we see that the throughput ratio is close to 100%, for total traffic as well as for individual priorities. Recall that in a single-priority network, throughput ratio is 90% and loss ratio is 0.72–11.5% for this traffic scale. Given the basic FFC trade-off, the increase in total throughput for this multi-priority network must accompany a decrease in protection from congestion. The loss ratio for total traffic bears this out; it is 40–80%.

What is interesting, however, is the data loss ratios of different priorities. The high-priority traffic suffers almost no loss ($<$ 0.01%), and the loss has been concentrated towards low-priority traffic. The effect is extreme for `L-Net`, where low-priority traffic loses more bytes with FFC than without FFC.

Figure 14(c) shows the relative fraction of lost bytes for each priority. With FFC, there is negligible loss ($<$ 0.01%) for high-priority traffic and a small amount (2–7%) of loss for medium-priority traffic. In contrast, without FFC, 5–15% of the bytes lost are high-priority and 30–70% are medium-priority. Thus, priority queueing by itself is not sufficient to prevent congestion for high priority traffic. FFC provides strong protection without throughput loss.

## 8.5 Congestion-free network updates

We now consider the case of congestion-free, multi-step updates. Recall that in this setting, control plane faults do not lead to congestion losses, but network updates can be slow and can even stall. We evaluate the speed of network updates with and without FFC.

Figure 16 shows the results for `L-Net` for both switch models. With the `Realistic` model, without FFC, 40% of the updates do not finish within 300 seconds. Since that is the TE interval, it is the maximum time we wait for the update to finish. This poor performance stems from the fact that even a single switch that takes a long time or fails to update altogether hurts the update process. FFC allows for faster updates by being robust to a small number of control plane faults (in this case $k_c$=2). FFC provides significant reduction in update time even with the `Optimistic` model, in which there are no configuration failures, only occasional delays. The median and 99th percentile speedup is a factor of three.

Faster updates lead to a more nimble network that can quickly react to demands bursts. They can also improve throughput by enabling a shorter TE interval, which enables the network to handle shorter-term demand variations.

# 9. Related Work

We build upon the rich line of work in TE algorithms and systems. Researchers have studied various aspects of this problem, including $i$) how to implement close-to-optimal traffic distributions in different settings such as link-state routing [17], MPLS environments [18], and SDNs [1, 2, 19, 20]; $ii$) how to stably adapt to changing traffic demands [21, 22]; $iii$) how to reroute traffic after failures such that minimal changes are needed [23]; and $iv$) how to find efficient backup paths [24, 25].

For brevity, we focus below on proactive techniques to make TE robust. Our key contributions in this space are $i$) proactively handling control plane faults; and $ii$) proactively handling data plane faults in a way that is both robust to any combination of up to $k$ failures and works with today's commodity switches.

**Data plane faults** To prevent rescaling-induced congestion after a data plane fault, Suchara *et al.* [26] modify the ingress switch's rescaling behavior. Instead of simple proportional rescaling, tunnel splitting weights are based on the set of residual tunnels. These weights are pre-computed and configured at the switch. Unlike our data plane FFC, which protects against any combination of up to $k$

faults, this approach can handle only a modest number of potential failure cases as there are exponential number of residual tunnel sets.

For a distributed TE setting, R3 [15] proposes an approach for congestion-free fast re-route [27], in which adjacent routers route around failed links. The routing behavior is determined by a fast online computation, aided by offline computation that is done in advance. Like FFC, R3 protects against any combination of up to $k$ link failures. There are two key differences, however. Our constraint reduction framework handles both control and data plane faults; R3's approach handles only data plane faults (and we could not extend it to control plane faults). Second, while R3 mixes proactive and reactive elements, FFC is purely proactive, which is a better approach when control plane faults can occur.

Further, both works above [15, 26] require changes to the switch hardware or software. We build solely on existing primitives.

**Control plane faults** Dionysus enables faster network updates in the face of switch configuration delays and failures, by dynamically deciding the order in which rule updates are applied [28]. While it reduces update time in general, it does not address the fundamental limitations of reactive approaches—they kick in after congestion occurs and the slowest switch can bottleneck the update process—which we seek to address. FFC and Dionysus are complementary. The former ensures that reactions are not needed for common case faults, and the latter ensures that, when needed, reactions are fast.

**Demand uncertainty** In networks where incoming traffic rate is not controlled, oblivious routing [29] and COPE [30] compute TE configurations that are robust to changes in traffic demand or errors in demand prediction. They do not consider control and data plane faults which are our focus. An interesting area of future investigation is if our approach for control faults in rate limiting, which produce uncertainty in traffic entering the network, can be extended to handle demand uncertainty. That would enable a common framework for handling both faults and demand uncertainty.

## 10. Conclusions

We developed FFC methods that proactively protect a network from congestion and packet loss due to data and control plane faults. These methods have low overhead in terms of network throughput—even optimal in some cases—and are computationally efficient. Using testbed experiments and data from real networks, we showed how FFC is useful in a variety of settings. For instance, in well-provisioned networks, it can reduce packet loss by a factor of 7–130; in well-utilized networks that carry traffic with multiple priorities, it can reduce loss for high-priority traffic to almost zero, with negligible reduction in total network throughput.

**Acknowledgments** Mohan Nanduri helped collect data for our experiments; Mohit Singh suggested the use of sorting networks for constraint reduction; Meg Walraed-Sullivan, Vyas Sekar (our shepherd), and the anonymous reviewers provided valuable feedback on drafts of this paper. We thank them all.

## 11. References

[1] S. Jain, A. Kumar, S. Mandal, J. Ong, L. Poutievski, A. Singh, S. Venkata, J. Wanderer, J. Zhou, M. Zhu, J. Zolla, U. Hölzle, S. Stuart, and A. Vahdat, "B4: Experience with a Globally-deployed Software Defined Wan," in *SIGCOMM'13*.

[2] C.-Y. Hong, S. Kandula, R. Mahajan, M. Zhang, V. Gill, M. Nanduri, and R. Wattenhofer, "Achieving High Utilization with Software-driven WAN," in *SIGCOMM'13*.

[3] M. Al-Fares, S. Radhakrishnan, B. Raghavan, N. Huang, and A. Vahdat, "Hedera: Dynamic Flow Scheduling for Data Center Networks," in *NSDI'10*.

[4] A. R. Curtis, J. C. Mogul, J. Tourrilhes, P. Yalag, P. Sharma, and S. Banerjee, "Devoflow: Scaling Flow Management for High-Performance Networks," in *SIGCOMM'11*.

[5] D. Halperin, S. Kandula, J. Padhye, P. Bahl, and D. Wetherall, "Augmenting Data Center Networks with Multi-gigabit Wireless Links," in *SIGCOMM'11*.

[6] T. Benson, A. Anand, A. Akella, and M. Zhang, "MicroTE: Fine Grained Traffic Engineering for Data Centers," in *CoNext'11*.

[7] P. Gill, N. Jain, and N. Nagappan, "Understanding Network Failures in Data Centers: Measurement, Analysis, and Implications," in *SIGCOMM'11*.

[8] A. Markopoulou, G. Iannaccone, S. Bhattacharyya, C.-N. Chuah, Y. Ganjali, and C. Diot, "Characterization of Failures in an Operational IP Backbone Network," *IEEE/ACM Transactions Networking*, 2008.

[9] D. Turner, K. Levchenko, A. C. Snoeren, and S. Savage, "California Fault Lines: Understanding the Causes and Impact of Network Failures," in *SIGCOMM'10*.

[10] K. E. Batcher, "Sorting Networks and Their Applications," in *AFIPS'68 (Spring)*.

[11] B. Raghavan, K. Vishwanath, S. Ramabhadran, K. Yocum, and A. C. Snoeren, "Cloud Control with Distributed Rate Limiting," in *SIGCOMM'07*.

[12] H. Ballani, P. Costa, T. Karagiannis, and A. Rowstron, "Towards Predictable Datacenter Networks," in *SIGCOMM'11*.

[13] "OpenFlow 1.1." `http://www.openflow.org/documents/openflow-spec-v1.1.0.pdf`.

[14] S. Even, A. Itai, and A. Shamir, "On the Complexity of Timetable and Multicommodity Flow Problems," *SIAM Journal on Computing*, 1976.

[15] Y. Wang, H. Wang, A. Mahimkar, R. Alimi, Y. Zhang, L. Qiu, and Y. R. Yang, "R3: Resilient Routing Reconfiguration," in *SIGCOMM'10*.

[16] H. H. Liu, X. Wu, M. Zhang, L. Yuan, R. Wattenhofer, and D. Maltz, "zUpdate: Updating Data Center Networks with Zero Loss," in *SIGCOMM'13*.

[17] D. Xu, M. Chiang, and J. Rexford, "Link-state Routing with Hop-by-hop Forwarding Can Achieve Optimal Traffic Engineering," *IEEE/ACM Transactions on Networking*, 2011.

[18] A. Elwalid, C. Jin, S. Low, and I. Widjaja, "MATE: MPLS Adaptive Traffic Engineering," in *INFOCOM'01*.

[19] M. Casado, T. Koponen, S. Shenker, and A. Tootoonchian, "Fabric: A Retrospective on Evolving SDN," in *HotSDN'12*.

[20] A. R. Sharafat, S. Das, G. Parulkar, and N. McKeown, "MPLS-TE and MPLS VPNS with Openflow," in *SIGCOMM'11*.

[21] S. Kandula, D. Katabi, B. Davie, and A. Charny, "Walking the Tightrope: Responsive Yet Stable Traffic Engineering," in *SIGCOMM'05*.

[22] M. Kodialam, T. V. Lakshman, and S. Sengupta, "Efficient and Robust Routing of Highly Variable Traffic," in *HotNets'04*.

[23] D. Applegate, L. Breslau, and E. Cohen, "Coping with Network Failures: Routing Strategies for Optimal Demand Oblivious Restoration," in *SIGMETRICS'04*.

[24] K. Kar, M. Kodialam, and T. V. Lakshman, "Routing Restorable Bandwidth Guaranteed Connections Using Maximum 2-route Flows," *IEEE/ACM Transactions on Networking*, 2003.

[25] M. Kodialam, A. Member, T. V. Lakshman, and S. Member, "Dynamic Routing of Restorable Bandwidth-guaranteed Tunnels using Aggregated Network Resource Usage Information," *IEEE/ACM Transactions on Networking*, 2003.

[26] M. Suchara, D. Xu, R. Doverspike, D. Johnson, and J. Rexford, "Network Architecture for Joint Failure Recovery and Traffic Engineering," in *SIGMETRICS'11*.

[27] E. A. Atlas and E. A. Zinin, "Basic Specification for IP Fast Reroute: Loop-Free Alternates."

[28] X. Jin, H. H. Liu, R. Gandhi, S. Kandula, R. Mahajan, M. Zhang, J. Rexford, and R. Wattenhofer, "Dynamic Scheduling of Network Updates," in *SIGCOMM'14*.

[29] D. Applegate and E. Cohen, "Making Intra-domain Routing Robust to Changing and Uncertain Traffic Demands: Understanding Fundamental Tradeoffs," in *SIGCOMM'03*.

[30] H. Wang, H. Xie, L. Qiu, Y. R. Yang, Y. Zhang, and A. Greenberg, "COPE: Traffic Engineering in Dynamic Networks," in *SIGCOMM'06*.

# Dynamic Scheduling of Network Updates

Xin Jin† Hongqiang Harry Liu⋆ Rohan Gandhi^ Srikanth Kandula°
Ratul Mahajan° Ming Zhang° Jennifer Rexford† Roger Wattenhofer×

Microsoft Research° Princeton University† Yale University⋆ Purdue University^ ETH Zurich×

**Abstract—** We present Dionysus, a system for fast, consistent network updates in software-defined networks. Dionysus encodes as a graph the consistency-related dependencies among updates at individual switches, and it then dynamically schedules these updates based on runtime differences in the update speeds of different switches. This dynamic scheduling is the key to its speed; prior update methods are slow because they pre-determine a schedule, which does not adapt to runtime conditions. Testbed experiments and data-driven simulations show that Dionysus improves the median update speed by 53–88% in both wide area and data center networks compared to prior methods.

**Categories and Subject Descriptors:** C.2.1 [**Computer-Communication Networks**]: Network Architecture and Design—*Network communications*; C.2.3 [**Computer-Communication Networks**]: Network Operations—*Network management*

**Keywords:** Software-defined networking; network update

## 1. Introduction

Many researchers have shown the value of centrally controlling networks. This approach can prevent oscillations due to distributed route computation [1]; ensure that network paths are policy compliant [2, 3]; reduce energy consumption [4]; and increase throughput [5, 6, 7, 8, 9]. Independent of their goal, such systems operate by frequently updating the data plane state of the network, either periodically or based on triggers such as failures. This state consists of a set of rules that determine how switches forward packets.

A common challenge faced in all centrally-controlled networks is consistently and quickly updating the data plane. Consistency implies that certain properties should not be violated during network updates, for instance, packets should not loop (*loop freedom*) and traffic arriving at a link should not exceed its capacity (*congestion freedom*). Consistency requirements impose dependencies on the order in which rules can be updated at switches. For instance, for congestion freedom, a rule update that brings a new flow to a link must occur after an update that removes an existing flow if the link cannot support both flows simultaneously. Not obeying update ordering requirements can lead to inconsistencies such as loops, blackholes, and congestion.

Current methods for consistent network updates are slow because they are based on *static* ordering of rule updates [9, 10, 11, 12]. They pre-compute an order in which rules must be updated, and this order does not adapt to runtime differences in the time it takes for individual switches to apply updates. These differences inevitably arise because of disparities in switches' hardware and CPU load and the variabilities in the time it takes the centralized controller to make remote procedure calls (RPC) to switches. In B4, a centrally-controlled wide area network, the ratio of the 99th percentile to the median delay to change a rule at a switch was found to be over five (5 versus 1 second) [8]. Further, some switches can "straggle," taking substantially more time than average (e.g., 10-100x) to apply an update. Current methods can stall in the face of straggling switches.

The speed of network updates is important because it determines the agility of the control loop. If the network is being updated in response to a failure, slower updates imply a longer period during which congestion or packet loss occurs. Further, many systems update the network based on current workload, both in the wide area [8, 9] and the data center [5, 6, 7], and their effectiveness is tied to how quickly they adapt to changing workloads. For example, recent works [8, 9] argue for frequent traffic engineering (e.g., every 5 minutes) to achieve high network utilization; slower network updates would lower network utilization.

We develop a new approach for consistent network updates. It is based on the observations that $i$) there exist multiple valid rule orderings that lead to consistent updates; and $ii$) dynamically selecting an ordering based on update speeds of switches can lead to fast network updates. Our approach is general and can be applied to many consistency properties, including all the ones that have been explored by prior work [9, 10, 11, 12, 13].

We face two main challenges in practically realizing our approach. The first is devising a compact way to represent multiple valid orderings of rule updates; there can be exponentially many such orderings. We address this challenge using a dependency graph in which nodes correspond to rule updates and network resources, such as link bandwidth and switch rule memory capacity, and (directed) edges denote dependencies among rule updates and network resources. Scheduling updates in any order, while respecting dependencies, guarantees consistent updates.

The second challenge is scheduling updates based on dynamic behavior of switches. This problem is NP-complete in the general case, and making matters worse, the dependency graph can also have cycles. To schedule efficiently, we develop greedy heuristics based on preferring critical paths and strongly connected components in the dependency graph [14].

We instantiate our approach in a system called Dionysus and evaluate it using experiments on a modest-sized testbed and large-scale simulations. Our simulations are based on topology and traffic data from two real networks, one wide-area network and one data center network. We show that Dionysus improves the median network update speed by 53–88%. We also show that its faster updates lower congestion and packet loss by over 40%.


*SIGCOMM'14*, August 17–22, 2014, Chicago, IL, USA.

http://dx.doi.org/10.1145/2619239.2626307.

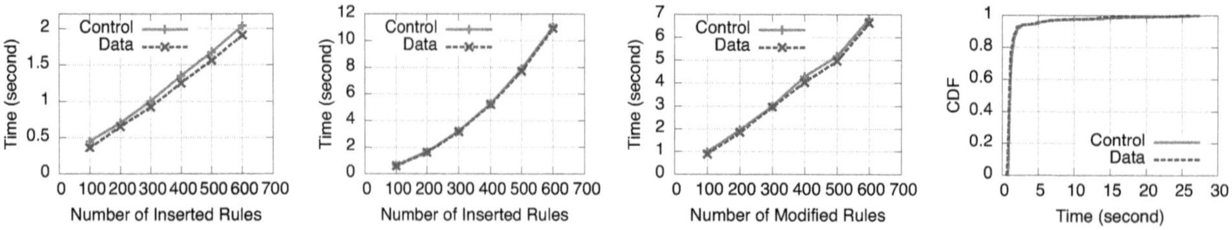


(a) (b) (c) (d)

**Figure 1: Rule update times on a commodity switch. (a) Inserting single-priority rules. (b) Inserting random-priority rules. (c) Modifying rules in a switch with 600 single-priority rules. (d) Modifying 100 rules in a switch with concurrent control plane load.**

## 2. Motivation

Our work is motivated by the observations that the time to update switch rules varies widely and that not accounting for this variation leads to slow network updates. We illustrate these observations using measurements from commodity switches and simple examples.

### 2.1 Variability in update time

Several factors lead to variable end-to-end rule update times, including switch hardware capabilities, control load on the switch, the nature of the updates, RPC delays (which include network path delays), etc. [7, 8, 15, 16]. To illustrate this variability, we perform controlled experiments on commodity switches. In these experiments, RPC delays are negligible and identical switch hardware and software are used, yet significant variability is evident.

The experiments explore the impact of four factors: $i$) the number of rules to be updated; $ii$) the priorities of the rules; $iii$) the types of rule updates (e.g., insertion vs. modification); and $iv$) control load on the switch. We measure switches from two different vendors and observe similar results. Figure 1 shows results for one switch vendor. We build a customized switch agent on the switch and obtain confirmation of rule updates in both the control and data planes. The control plane confirmation is based on the switch agent verifying that the update is installed in the switch's TCAM (ternary content addressable memory), and the data plane confirmation is based on observing the impact of the update in the switch's forwarding behavior (e.g., changes in which interface a packet is sent out on).

Figure 1(a) shows the impact of the number of rules by plotting the time to add different numbers of rules. Here, the switch has no control load besides rule updates, the switch starts with an empty TCAM, and all rule updates correspond to adding new rules with the same priority. We see that, as one might expect, that the update time grows linearly with the number of rules being updated, with the per-rule update time being 3.3 ms.

Figure 1(b) shows the impact of priorities. As above, the switch has no load and starts with an empty TCAM. The difference is that the inserted rules are assigned random priorities. We see that the per-rule update time is significantly higher than before. The slope of the line increases as the number of rules increase, and the per-rule update time reaches 18 ms when inserting 600 rules.

This variability stems from the fact that TCAM packing algorithms do different amounts of work, depending on the TCAM's current content and the type of operation performed. For instance, the TCAM itself does not encode any rule priority information. The rules are stored from top to bottom in decreasing priority and when multiple rules match a packet, the one with the highest place is chosen. Thus, when a new rule is inserted, it may cause existing rules to move in the table. Although the specific packing algorithms are proprietary and vary across vendors, the intrinsic design of a TCAM makes the update time variable.

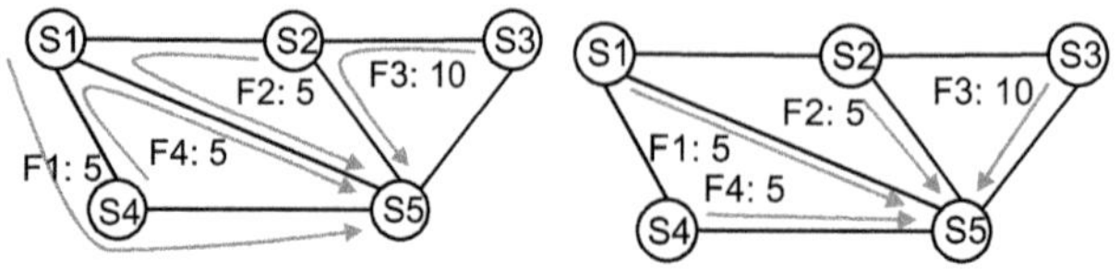


(a) Current State (b) Target State

**Figure 2: A network update example. Each link has 10 units of capacity; flows are labeled with their sizes.**

Figure 1(c) shows the impact of the type of rule update. Rather than inserting rules into an empty TCAM, we start with 600 rules of the same priority and measure the time for rule modifications. We modify only match fields or actions, not rule priorities. The graph is nearly linear, with a per-rule modification latency of 11 ms. This latency is larger than the per-rule insertion latency because a rule modification requires two operations in the measured switch: inserting the new rule and deleting the old rule.

Finally, Figure 1(d) shows the impact of control load, by engaging the switch in different control activities while updates are performed. Here, the switch starts with the 600 same-priority rules and we modify 100 of them. Control activities performed include reading packet and byte counters on rules with OpenFlow protocol, querying SNMP counters, reading switch information with CLI commands, and running BGP protocol (which SDN systems use as backup [8]). We see that despite the fact that update operations are identical (100 new rules), the time to update highly varies, with the 99th percentile 10 times larger than the median. Significant rule update time variations are also reported in [8, 16].

In summary, we find that even in controlled conditions, switch update time varies significantly. While some sources of this variability can be accounted for statically by update algorithms (e.g., number of rule updates), others are inherently dynamic in nature (e.g., control plane load and RPC delays). Accounting for these dynamic factors ahead of time is difficult. Our work thus focuses on adapting to them at runtime.

### 2.2 Consistent updates amid variability

We illustrate the downside of static ordering of rule updates with the example of Figure 2. Each link has a capacity of 10 units and each flow's size is marked. The controller wants to update the network configuration from Figure 2(a) to 2(b). Assume for simplicity that the network uses tunnel-based routing and all necessary tunnels have already been established. So, moving a flow requires updating only the ingress switch.

If we want a congestion-free network update, we cannot update all the switches in "one shot" (i.e., send all update commands simultaneously). Since different switches will apply the updates at different times, such a strategy may cause congestion at some links. For instance, if $S1$ applies the update for moving $F1$ before $S2$ moves $F2$ and $S4$ moves $F4$, link $S1$-$S5$ will be congested.

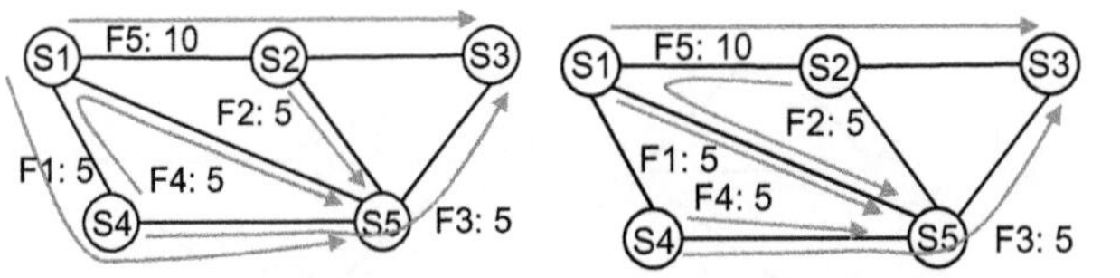


(a) Current State (b) Target State

**Figure 3: An example in which a completely opportunistic approach to scheduling updates leads to a deadlock. Each link has 10 units of capacity; flows are labeled with their sizes. If $F2$ is moved first, $F1$ and $F4$ get stuck.**

Ensuring that no link is congested requires us to carefully order the updates. Two valid orderings are:

Plan A: $[F3 \rightarrow F2]$ $[F4 \rightarrow F1]$

Plan B: $[F4]$ $[F3 \rightarrow F2 \rightarrow F1]$

Plan A mandates that $F2$ be done after $F3$ and $F1$ be done after $F4$. Plan B mandates that $F1$ be done after $F2$ and that $F2$ be done after $F3$. In both plans, $F3$ and $F4$ have no pre-requisites and can be done anytime and in parallel.[1]

Which plan is faster? In the absence of update time variability, if all updates take unit time, Plan A will take 2 time units and Plan B will take 3. However, with update time variability, no plan is a clear winner. For instance, if $S4$ takes 3 time units to move $F4$, and other switches take 1, Plan A will take 4 time units and Plan B will take 3. On the other hand, if $S2$ is slow and takes 3 time units to move $F2$, while other switches take 1, Plan A will take 4 time units and Plan B will take 5.

Now consider a dynamic plan that first issues updates for $F3$ and $F4$, issues an update for $F2$ as soon as $F3$ finishes, and issues an update for $F1$ as soon as $F2$ *or* $F4$ finishes. This plan dynamically selects between the two static plans above and will thus equal or beat those two plans regardless of which switches are slow to update. Practically implementing such plans for arbitrary network topologies and updates is the goal of our work.

## 3. Dionysus Overview

We achieve fast, consistent network updates through dynamic scheduling of rule updates. As in the example above, there can be multiple valid rule orderings that lead to consistent updates. Instead of statically selecting an order, we implement on-the-fly ordering based on the realtime behavior of the network and the switches.

Our focus is on flow-based traffic management applications for the network core (e.g., ElasticTree, MicroTE, B4, SWAN [4, 6, 8, 9]). As is the case for these applications, we assume that any forwarding rule at a switch matches at most one flow, where a flow is (a subset of) traffic between ingress and egress switches that uses either single or multiple paths. This assumption does not hold in networks that use wild-card rules or longest prefix matching. Increasingly, such rules are being moved to the network edge or even hosts [17, 18, 19], keeping the core simple with exact match rules.

The primary challenge is to tractably explore valid orderings. One difficulty is that there are combinatorially many such orderings. Conceivably, one may formulate the problem as an ILP (Integer Linear Program). But this approach would be too slow and does not scale to large networks with a lot of flows. Also it is static

[1]Some consistent update methods [9] use stages, a more rigid version of static ordering. They divide updates into multiple stages, and all updates in the previous stage must finish before any update in the next stage can begin. In this terminology, Plan A is a two-stage solution in which the first stage will update $F3$ and $F4$ and the second will update $F2$ and $F1$. Plan B is a three-stage solution. Since SWAN minimizes the number of stages, it will prefer Plan A.

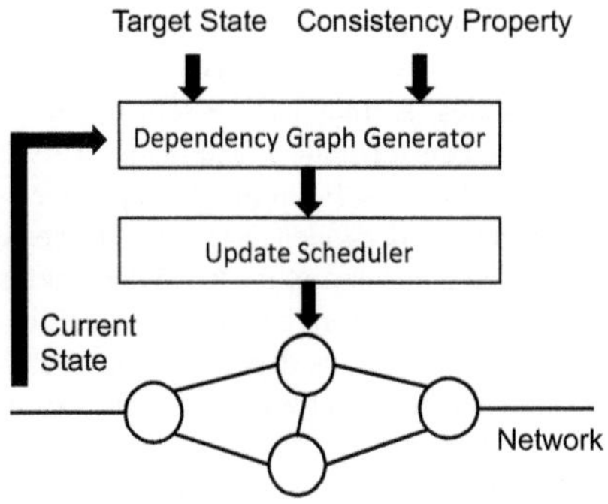


**Figure 4: Our approach.**

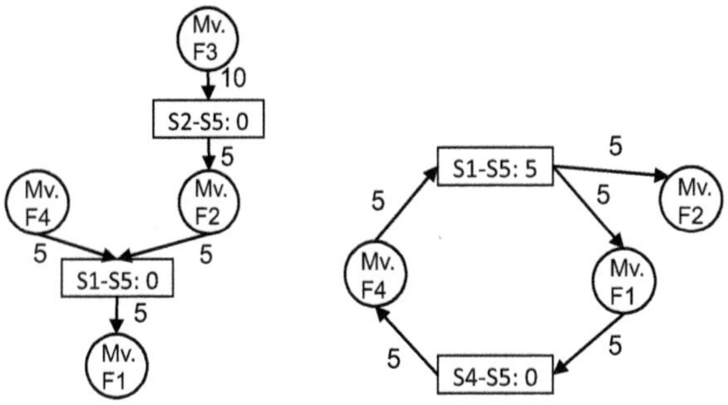


(a) Dependency graph for Figure 2 (b) Dependency graph for Figure 3

**Figure 5: Example dependency graphs.**

and not incrementally computable; one has to rerun the ILP every time the switch behaviors change. Another difficulty is that the extreme approach of being completely opportunistic about rule ordering does not always work. In such an approach, the controller will immediately issue any updates that are not gated (per consistency requirements) on any other update. While this approach works for the simple example in the previous section, in general, it can result in deadlocks (that are otherwise resolvable). Figure 3 shows an example. Since $F2$ can be moved without waiting for any other flow movement, an opportunistic approach might make that move. But at this point, we are stuck, because no flow can be moved to its destination without overloading at least some link. This is avoidable if we move other flows first. It is because of such possibilities that current approaches carefully plan transitions, but they err on the side of not allowing any runtime flexibility in rule orderings.

We balance planning and opportunism using a two-stage approach, shown in Figure 4. In the first stage, we generate a *dependency graph* that compactly describes many valid orderings. In the second stage, we schedule updates based on the constraints imposed by the dependency graph. Our approach is general in that it can maintain any consistency property that can be described using a dependency graph, which includes all properties used in prior work [8, 9, 11]. The scheduler is independent of the consistency property.

Figure 5(a) shows a simplified view of the dependency graph for the example of Figure 2. In the graph, circular nodes denote update operations, and rectangular nodes represent link capacity resources. The numbers within rectangles indicate the current free capacity of resources. A label on an edge from an operation to a resource node shows the amount of resource that will be released when the operation completes. For example, link $S2$-$S5$ has 0 free capacity, and moving $F3$ will release a capacity of 10 to it. Labels on edges from resource to operation nodes show the amount of free resource needed to conduct these operations. As moving $F1$ requires 5 free capacity on link $S1$-$S5$, $F1$ cannot move until $F2$ or $F4$ finishes.

Given the dependency graph in Figure 5(a), we can dynamically generate good schedules. First, we observe that $F3$ and $F4$ don't depend on other updates, so they can be scheduled immediately. After $F3$ finishes, we can schedule $F2$. Finally, we schedule $F1$ once *one* of $F2$ or $F4$ finishes. From this example, we see that the dependency graph captures dependencies but still leaves scheduling flexibility, which we leverage at runtime to implement fast updates.

There are two challenges in dynamically scheduling updates. The first is to resolve cycles in the dependency graph. These arise due to complex dependencies between rules. For example, Figure 5(b) shows that there are cycles in the dependency graph for the example of Figure 3. Second, at any given time, multiple subsets of rule updates can be issued, and we need to decide which ones to issue first. As described later, the greedy heuristics we use for these challenges are based on critical-path scheduling and the concept of SCC (strongly connected component) in graph theory.

## 4. Network State Model

This section describes the model of network forwarding state that we use in Dionysus. The following sections describe dependency graph generation and scheduling in detail.

The network $G$ consists of a set of switches $S$ and a set of directed links $L$. A flow $f$ is from an ingress switch $s_i$ to an egress switch $s_j$ with traffic volume $t_f$, and its traffic is carried over a set of paths $P_f$. The forwarding state of $f$ is defined as $R_f = \{r_{f,p} | p \in P_f\}$ where $r_{f,p}$ is the traffic load of $f$ on path $p$. The network state $NS$ is then the combined state of all flows, i.e., $NS = \{R_f | f \in F\}$. For example, consider the network in Figure 6(a) that is forwarding a flow across two paths, with 5 units of traffic along each. Here, $t_f = 10$, $P_f = \{p_1 = S_1S_2S_3S_5, p_2 = S_1S_2S_5\}$, and $R_f = \{r_{f,p_1} = 5, r_{f,p_2} = 5\}$.

The state model above captures both tunnel-based forwarding that is prevalent in WANs and also WCMP (weighted cost multi path) forwarding that is prevalent in data center networks. In tunnel-based forwarding, a flow is forwarded along one or more tunnels. The ingress switch matches incoming traffic to the flow, based on packet headers, and splits it across the tunnels based on configured weights. Before forwarding a packet along a tunnel, the ingress switch tags the packet with the tunnel identifier. Subsequent switches only match on tunnel tags and forward packets, and the egress switch removes the tunnel identifier. Representing tunnel-based forwarding in our state model is straightforward. $P_f$ is the set of tunnels and the weight of a tunnel is $r_{f,p}/t_f$.

In WCMP forwarding, switches at *every hop* match on packet headers and split flows over multiple next hops with configured weights. Shortest-path and ECMP (equal cost multipath) forwarding are special cases of WCMP forwarding. To represent WCMP routing in our state model, we first calculate the flow rate on link $l$ as $r_f^l = \sum_{l \in p, p \in P_f} r_{f,p}$. Then at switch $s_i$, the weight for next-hop $s_j$ is: $w_{i,j} = r_f^{l_{ij}} / \sum_{l \in L_i} r_f^l$ where $l_{ij}$ is the link from $s_i$ to $s_j$ and $L_i$ is the set of links starting at $s_i$. For instance, in Figure 6(a), $w_{1,2} = 1, w_{1,4} = 0, w_{2,3} = 0.5, w_{2,5} = 0.5$.

## 5. Dependency Graph Generation

As shown in Figure 4, the dependency graph generator takes as input the current state $NS_c$, the target state $NS_t$, and the consistency property. The network states includes the flow rate, and as in current systems [4, 6, 8, 9], we assume that flows obey this rate as a result of rate limiting or robust estimation. A static input to Dionysus is the rule capacity of each switch, relevant in settings where this resource is limited. Since Dionysus manages all rule additions and removals, it then knows how much rule capacity is available on each switch at any given time. This information is used such that rule capacity is not exceeded at any switch.

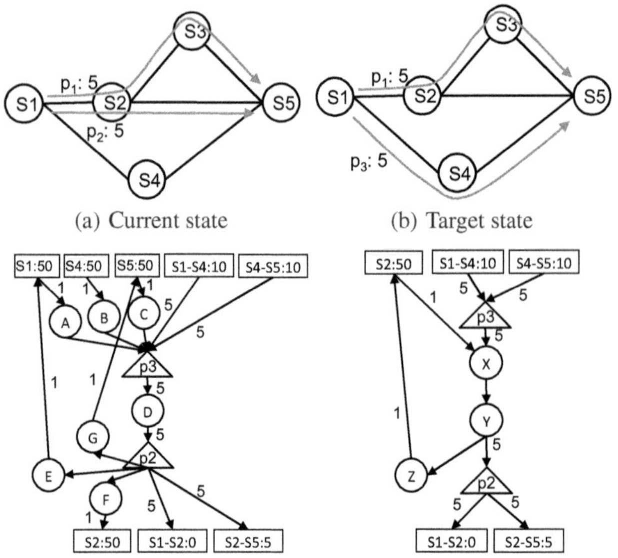

(a) Current state (b) Target state

(c) Dependency graph using tunnel-based rules (Table 1) (d) Dependency graph using WCMP-based rules (Table 2)

**Figure 6: Example of building dependency graph for updating flow $f$ from current state (a) to target state (b).**

| Index | Operation |
|---|---|
| A | Add $p_3$ at S1 |
| B | Add $p_3$ at S4 |
| C | Add $p_3$ at S5 |
| D | Change weight at S1 |
| E | Delete $p_2$ at S1 |
| F | Delete $p_2$ at S2 |
| G | Delete $p_2$ at S5 |

**Table 1: Operations to update $f$ with tunnel-based rules.**

| Index | Operation |
|---|---|
| X | Add weights with new version at S2 |
| Y | Change weights, assign new version at S1 |
| Z | Delete weights with old version at S2 |

**Table 2: Operations to update $f$ in WCMP forwarding.**

Given $NS_c$ and $NS_t$, it is straightforward to compute the set of operations that would update the network from $NS_c$ to $NS_t$. The goal of dependency graph generation is to inter-link these operations based on the consistency property. Our dependency graph has three types of nodes: *operation nodes*, *resource nodes*, and *path nodes*. Operation nodes represent addition, deletion, or modification of a forwarding rule at a switch, and resource nodes correspond to resources such as link capacity and switch memory and are labeled with the amount of resource currently *available*. An edge between two operation nodes captures an *operation dependency* and implies that the parent operation must be done before the child. An edge between a resource and an operation node captures a *resource dependency*. An edge from a resource to an operation node is labeled with the amount of resource that must be available before the operation can occur. An edge from an operation to a resource node is labeled with the amount of the resource that will be freed by that operation. There are no edges between resource nodes.

Path nodes help group operations and link capacity resources on a path. Path nodes can connect to operation nodes as well as to resource nodes. An edge between an operation and a path node

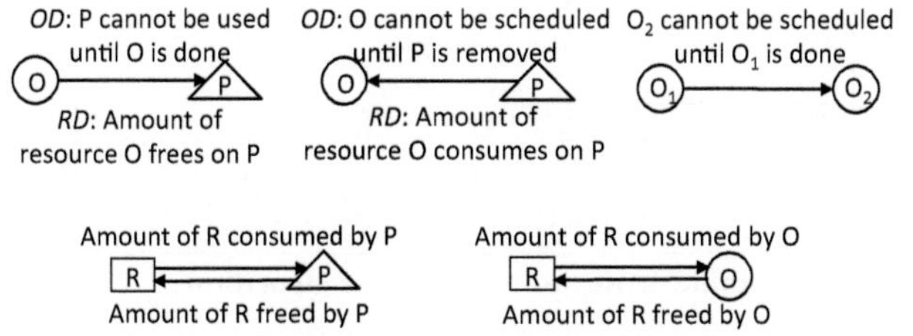


**Figure 7: Links and relationships among path, operation, and resource nodes; *RD* indicates a resource dependency and *OD* indicates an operation dependency.**

can be either an operation dependency (un-weighted) or a resource dependency (weighted). The various types of links connecting different types of nodes are detailed in Figure 7.

During scheduling, each path node that frees link resources has a label *committed* that denotes the amount of traffic that is moving away from the path; when the movement finishes, we use *committed* to update the free resource of its child resource nodes. We do not need to keep *committed* for path nodes that require resource, because we always reduce free capacity on its parent resource nodes first before we move traffic into the path.

In this paper, we focus on four consistency properties from prior work [13] and show how our dependency graphs capture them. The properties are $i)$ *blackhole-freedom*: no packet should be dropped at a switch (e.g., due to a missing rule); $ii)$ *loop-freedom*: no packet should loop in the network; $iii)$ *packet coherence*: no packet should see a mix of old and new rules in the network; and $iv)$ *congestion-freedom*: traffic arriving at a link should be below its capacity. We believe that our dependency graphs are general enough to describe other properties as well, which may be proposed in the future.

We now describe dependency graph generation. We first focus on tunnel-based forwarding without resource limits and then discuss WCMP forwarding and resource constraints.

**Tunnel-based forwarding:** Tunnel-based forwarding offers loop freedom and packet coherence by design; it is not possible for packets to loop or to see a mix of old and new rules during updates. We defer discussion of congestion freedom until we discuss resource constraints. The remaining property, blackhole freedom, is guaranteed as long as we ensure that $i)$ a tunnel is fully established before the ingress switch puts any traffic on it, and $ii)$ all traffic is removed from the tunnel before the tunnel is deleted.

A dependency graph that encodes these constraints can be built as follows. For each flow $f$, using $NS_c$ and $NS_t$, we first calculate the tunnels to be added and deleted and generate a path node for each. Then, we generate an operation node for every hop, adding an edge from each of them to the path node (or from the path node to each of them), denoting adding (or deleting) this tunnel at the switch. Then, we generate an operation node that changes the tunnel weights to those in $NS_t$ at the ingress switch. To ensure blackhole freedom, we add an edge from each path node that adds new tunnels to the operation node that changes tunnel weights, and an edge from the operation node that changes tunnel weights to each path node that deletes old tunnels.

We use the example in Figure 6 to illustrate the steps above. Initially, we set the tunnel weights on $p_1$ and $p_2$ with 0.5 and 0.5 respectively. In the target state, we add tunnel $p_3$, delete tunnel $p_2$, and change the tunnel weights to 0.5 on $p_1$ and 0.5 on $p_3$. To generate the dependency graph for this transition, we first generate path nodes for $p2$ and $p3$ and the related switch operations as in Table 1. Then we add edges from the tunnel-addition operations ($A$, $B$ and $C$) to the corresponding path node ($p3$), and edges to the tunnel-deletion operations ($E$, $F$ and $G$) from the corresponding path node ($p2$). Finally, we add an edge from the path node of the added path ($p3$) to the weight-changing operation ($D$) and from $D$ to the path node for the path to be deleted ($p2$). The resulting graph is shown in Figure 6(c). The resource nodes in this graph are discussed later.

**Algorithm 1** Dependency graph for packet coherence in a WCMP network

– $v_0$: old version number
– $v_1$: new version number
1: **for** each flow $f$ **do**
2: $\quad s^* = GetIngressSwitch(f)$
3: $\quad o^* = GenRuleModifyOp(s^*, v_1)$
4: $\quad$ **for** $s_i \in GetAllSwitches(f) - s^*$ **do**
5: $\quad\quad$ **if** $s_i$ has multiple next-hops **then**
6: $\quad\quad\quad o_1 = GenRuleInsertOp(s_i, v_1)$
7: $\quad\quad\quad o_2 = GenRuleDeleteOp(s_i, v_0)$
8: $\quad\quad\quad$ Add edge from $o_1$ to $o^*$
9: $\quad\quad\quad$ Add edge from $o^*$ to $o_2$

**WCMP forwarding:** With $NS_c$ and $NS_t$, we calculate for each flow the weight change operations that update the network from $NS_c$ to $NS_t$. We then create dependency edges between these operations based on the consistency property. Algorithm 1 shows how to do that for packet-coherence, using version numbers [10, 11]. In this approach, the ingress switch tags each packet with a version number and downstream switches handle packets based on the embedded version number. This tagging ensures that each packet either uses the old configuration or the new configuration, and never a mix of the two. The algorithm generates three types of operations: $i)$ the ingress switch tags packets with the new version number and uses new weights (Line 3); $ii)$ downstream switches have rules for handling the packets with the new version number and new weights (Line 6); and $iii)$ downstream switches delete rules for the old version number (Line 7). Packet coherence is guaranteed if Type $i$ operation occurs after Type $ii$ (Line 8) and Type $iii$ operations occur after Type $i$ (Line 9). Line 5 is an optimization; no changes are needed at switches that have only one next hop for the flow in both the old and new configurations.

We use the example in Figure 6 again to illustrate the algorithm above. For flow $f$, we need to update the flow weights at $S1$ from $[(S2, 1), (S4, 0)]$ to $[(S2, 0.5), (S4, 0.5)]$, and weights at $S2$ from $[(S3, 0.5), (S5, 0.5)]$ to $[(S3, 1), (S5, 0)]$. This translates to three operations (Table 2): add new weights with new version numbers at $S2$ (X), change to new weights and new version numbers at $S1$ (Y), and delete old weights at $S2$ (Z). We connect $X$ to $Y$ and $Y$ to $Z$ as shown in Figure 6(d).

Blackhole-freedom and loop-freedom do not require version numbers. For the former, we must ensure that every switch that may receive a packet from a flows always has a rule for it. For the latter, we must ensure that downstream switches (per new configuration) are updated before updating a switch to new rules [13]. These conditions are easy to encode in a dependency graph. For space constraints, we omit detailed description of graph construction.

**Resource constraints:** We introduce resource nodes to the graph corresponding to resources of interest, including link bandwidth and switch memory. These nodes are labeled with their current free amount or with infinity if that resource can never be a bottleneck.

We connect link bandwidth nodes with other nodes as follows. For each path node and bandwidth node for links along the path: if the traffic on the path increases, we add an edge from the bandwidth node to the path node with a label indicating the amount of traffic increase; if the traffic decreases, we add edges in the other direction. For a tunnel-based network, we add an edge from each path node on which traffic increases to the operation node that changes

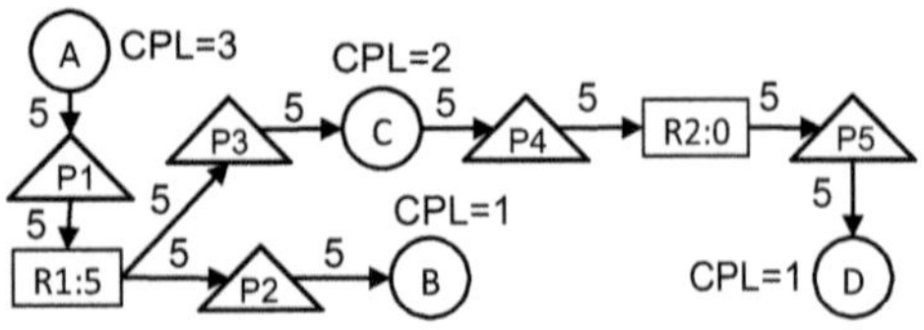


**Figure 8: Critical-path scheduling.** $C$ **has larger** $CPL$ **than** $B$**, and is scheduled.**

weight at the ingress switch with a label indicating the amount of traffic increase; similarly, we add an edge in the other direction if the traffic decreases. For a WCMP network, we add an edge from each path node on which traffic increases to each operation node that *adds weights with new versions* with a label indicating the amount of increase; similarly, we add an edge from the operation node that *changes weight at the ingress switch* to each path node on which traffic decreases with a label indicating the amount of decrease. This difference is due to that tunnels offer packet coherence by design, while WCMP networks need version numbers.

Connecting switch memory resource nodes with other nodes is straightforward. We add an edge from a resource node to an operation node if the operation consumes that switch memory with an weight indicating the amount of consumption; we add an edge from an operation node to a resource node if the operation releases that switch memory with an weight indicating the amount of release.

For example, in Figure 6(c) node $D$, which changes tunnel weights at $S1$, increases 5 units of traffic on $p_3$ which includes link $S1$-$S4$ and $S4$-$S5$, and decreases 5 units of traffic on $p_2$ which includes link $S1$-$S2$ and $S2$-$S5$. Node $A$ that adds tunnel $p_3$ consumes 1 rule at $S1$. In Figure 6(d), we link $p_3$ to $X$ and link $X$ to $Y$. $X$ and $Y$ essentially takes the same effect as $D$ in Figure 6(d).

**Post-processing:** After generating the dependency graph, we reduce it by deleting edges from non-bottlenecked resources. For each resource node $R_i$, we check the edges to its child nodes $N_j$. If the free resource $R_i.free$ is no smaller than $\sum_j l_{ij}$ where $l_{ij}$ is the edge weight, we delete all the edges from $R_i$ to its children and decrease the free capacity by $\sum_j l_{ij}$. The idea is that $R_i$ has enough free resource to accommodate all operations that need it, so it's not a bottleneck resource and the scheduling will not consider it. For example, if $S1$-$S4$ has over 5 units of free capacity, we can delete the edge from $S1$-$S4$ to $p_3$ in Figures 6(c) and 6(d).

## 6. Dionysus Scheduling

We now describe how updates are scheduled in Dionysus. First, we discuss the hardness of the scheduling problem, which guided our approach. Then, we describe scheduling algorithm for the special case where the dependency graph is a DAG (directed acyclic graph). Finally, we extend this algorithm to handle cycles.

### 6.1 The hardness of the scheduling problem

Scheduling is a resource allocation problem, that is, how to allocate available resources to operations to minimize the update time. For example, resource node $R1$ in Figure 8 has 5 units of free resource. It cannot cover both $B$ and $C$. We must decide to schedule $i)$ $B$, $ii)$ $C$, or $iii)$ part of $B$ and $C$. Every time we make a scheduling decision, we decide how to allocate a resource to its child operations and which parent operation to execute to obtain a resource. Additional constraints on scheduling are placed by dependencies between operations.

We can prove the following about network update scheduling; proofs of both theorems are in our technical report [20].

THEOREM 1. *In the presence of both link capacity and switch memory constraints, finding a feasible update schedule is NP-complete.*

| Symbol | Description |
|---|---|
| $O_i$ | Operation node $i$ |
| $R_j$ | Resource node $j$ |
| $R_j.free$ | Free capacity of $R_j$ |
| $P_k$ | Path node $k$ |
| $P_k.committed$ | Traffic that is moving away from path $k$ |
| $l_{ij}$ | Edge weight from node $i$ to $j$ |

**Table 3: Key notation in our algorithms.**

**Algorithm 2** ScheduleGraph($G$)

```
1: while true do
2:     UpdateGraph(G)
3:     Calculate CPL for every node
4:     Sort nodes by CPL in decreasing order
5:     for unscheduled operation node O_i ∈ G do
6:         if CanScheduleOperation(O_i) then
7:             Schedule O_i
8:     Wait for time t or for all scheduled operations to finish
```

The hardness stems from the fact that memory constraints involve integers and memory cannot be allocated fractionally. Scheduling is simpler if we only have link capacity constraints, but finding the fastest schedule is still hard because of the huge search space.

THEOREM 2. *In the presence of link capacity constraints, but no switch memory constraints, finding the fastest update schedule is NP-complete.*

### 6.2 Scheduling DAGs

We first consider the special case of a DAG. Scheduling a DAG is, expectedly, simpler:

LEMMA 1. *If the dependency graph is a DAG, finding a feasible update schedule is in P.*

While it is easy to find a feasible solution for a DAG, we want to find a fast one. Different scheduling orders lead to different finishing times. For example, if all operations take the same amount of time Figure 8, scheduling $C$ before $B$ will be faster.

We use *critical-path scheduling*. The intuition is that the critical path decides the completion time, and we thus want to schedule operations on the critical path first. Since resource nodes and path nodes in the dependency graph are only used to express constraints, we assign weight $w$=0 to them when calculating critical paths; for operation nodes, we assign weight $w$=1. With this, we calculate a critical-path length $CPL$ for each node $i$ as:

$$CPL_i = w_i + \max_{j \in children(i)} CPL_j \tag{1}$$

To calculate $CPL$ for all the nodes in the graph, we first topologically sort all the nodes and then iterate over them to calculate $CPL$ with Equation 1 in the reverse topological order. In Figure 8, for example, $CPL_D$=1, $CPL_C$=2, $CPL_B$=1, $CPL_A$=3. The CPL for each node can be computed efficiently in linear time.

Algorithm 2 shows how Dionysus uses CPL to schedule updates, with key notations summarized in Table 3. Each time we enter the scheduling phase, we first update the graph with finished operations and delete edges from unbottlenecked resources (line 2). Then, we calculate $CPL$ for every node (Line 3) and sort nodes in decreasing order of $CPL$ (Line 4). Then, we iterate over operation nodes and schedule them if their operation dependency and resource dependency are satisfied (Lines 6, 7). Finally, the scheduler waits for some time for all scheduled operations to finish before starting the next round (Line 10).

To simplify presentation, we first show the related pseudo code of $CanScheduleOperation(O_i)$ and $UpdateGraph(G)$ for tunnel-based networks and describe them below. Then, we briefly describe how the WCMP case differs.

**Algorithm 3** CanScheduleOperation($O_i$)

// **Add tunnel operation node**
1: **if** $O_i.isAddTunnelOp()$ **then**
2:   **if** $O_i.hasNoParents()$ **then**
3:     **return** true
4:   $R_j \leftarrow parent(O_i)$ // AddTunnelOp only has 1 parent
5:   **if** $R_j.free \geq l_{ji}$ **then**
6:     $R_j.free \leftarrow R_j.free - l_{ji}$
7:     Delete edge $R_j \rightarrow O_i$
8:     **return** true
9:   **return** false
// **Delete tunnel operation node**
10: **if** $O_i.isDelTunnelOp()$ **then**
11:   **if** $O_i.hasNoParents()$ **then**
12:     **return** true
13:   **return** false
// **Change weight operation node**
14: $total \leftarrow 0$
15: $canSchedule \leftarrow false$
16: **for** path node $P_j \in parents(O_i)$ **do**
17:   $available \leftarrow l_{ji}$
18:   **if** $P_j.hasOpParents()$ **then**
19:     $available \leftarrow 0$
20:   **else**
21:     **for** resource node $R_k \in parents(P_j)$ **do**
22:       $available \leftarrow min(available, l_{kj}, R_k.free)$
23:     **for** resource node $R_k \in parents(P_j)$ **do**
24:       $l_{kj} \leftarrow l_{kj} - available$
25:       $R_k.free \leftarrow R_k.free - available$
26:   $total \leftarrow total + available$
27:   $l_{ji} \leftarrow l_{ji} - available$
28: **if** $total > 0$ **then**
29:   $canSchedule \leftarrow true$
30: **for** path node $P_j \in children(O_i)$ **do**
31:   $P_j.committed \leftarrow min(l_{ij}, total)$
32:   $l_{ij} \leftarrow l_{ij} - P_j.committed$
33:   $total \leftarrow total - P_j.committed$
34: **return** $canSchedule$

**CanScheduleOperation (Algorithm 3):** This function decides if an operation $O_i$ is ready to be scheduled and updates the resource levels for resource and path nodes accordingly. If $O_i$ is a tunnel addition operation, we can schedule it either if it has no parents (Lines 2, 3) or its parent resource node has enough free resource (Lines 4–8). If $O_i$ is a tunnel deletion operation, we can schedule it if it has no parents (Lines 11–12); tunnel deletion operations do not have resource nodes as parents because they always release (memory) resources. If $O_i$ is a weight change operation, we gather all free capacities on the paths where traffic increases and moves traffic to them (line 14-34). We iterate over each parent path node and obtain the available capacity ($available$) of the path (Lines 16–27). This capacity limits the amount of traffic that we can move to this path. We sum them up to $total$, which is the total traffic we can move for this flow (Line 26). Then, we iterate over child path nodes (Lines 30–33). Finally, we decrease $P_j.committed$ traffic on path represented by $P_j$ (Line 31).

**UpdateGraph (Algorithm 4):** This function updates the graph before scheduling based on operations that successfully finished in the last round. We get all such operations and update related nodes in the graph (Lines 1–22). If the operation node adds a tunnel, we delete the node and its edges (Lines 2, 3). If the operation node deletes a tunnel, it frees rule space. So, we update the resource node (Lines 5, 6) and delete it (Line 7). If the operation node changes weight, for each child path node, we release resources to links on it (Lines 11–12) and delete the edge if all resources are released (Lines 13, 14). We reset the amount of traffic that is moving away from this path, $P_j.committed$, to 0 (Line 15). If we have moved all the traffic away from this path, we delete this path node (Lines 16, 17). Similarly, we check all the parent path nodes (Lines 18–20). If we have moved all the traffic into a path, we delete the path node (Lines 19, 20). Finally, if all parent path nodes are removed, the weight change for this flow finishes; we remove it from the graph (Line 22). After updating the graph with finished operations, we check all resource nodes (Lines 23–26). We delete edges from unbottlenecked resources (Lines 24–26).

**Algorithm 4** UpdateGraph($G$)

1: **for** finished operation node $O_i \in G$ **do**
  // **Finish add tunnel operation node**
2:   **if** $O_i.isAddTunneOp()$ **then**
3:     Delete $O_i$ and all its edges
  // **Finish delete tunnel operation node**
4:   **else if** $O_i.isDelTunnelOp()$ **then**
5:     $R_j \leftarrow child(O_i)$
6:     $R_j.free \leftarrow R_j.free + l_{ij}$
7:     Delete $O_i$ and all its edges // DelTunnelOp only has 1 child
  // **Finish change weight operation node**
8:   **else**
9:     **for** path node $P_j \in children(O_i)$ **do**
10:       **for** resource node $R_k \in children(P_j)$ **do**
11:         $l_{jk} \leftarrow l_{jk} - P_j.committed$
12:         $R_k.free \leftarrow R_k.free + P_j.committed$
13:         **if** $l_{jk} = 0$ **then**
14:           Delete edge $P_j \rightarrow R_k$
15:       $P_j.committed \leftarrow 0$
16:       **if** $l_{ij} = 0$ **then**
17:         Delete $P_j$ and its edges
18:     **for** path node $P_j \in parents(O_i)$ **do**
19:       **if** $l_{ji} = 0$ **then**
20:         Delete $P_j$ and its edges
21:     **if** $O_i.hasNoParents()$ **then**
22:       Delete $O_i$ and its edges
23: **for** resource node $R_i \in G$ **do**
24:   **if** $R_i.free \geq \sum_j l_{ij}$ **then**
25:     $R_i.free \leftarrow R_i.free - \sum_j l_{ij}$
26:     Delete all edges from $R_i$

**WCMP network:** Algorithms 3 and 4 for WCMP-based networks differ in two respects. First, WCMP networks do not have tunnel add or delete operations. Second, unlike tunnel-based networks that can simply change the weights at the ingress switches, WCMP networks perform a two-phase commit using version numbers to maintain packet coherence (node $X$ and $Y$ in Figure 6(d)). The code related to the weight change operation in the two algorithms has minor difference accordingly.

## 6.3 Handling cycles

Cycles in the dependency graph pose a challenge because inappropriate scheduling can lead to deadlocks where no progress can be made, as we saw for Figure 5(b) if $F2$ is moved first. Further, many cycles may intertwine together, which makes the problem even more complicated. For instance, $A$, $B$ and $C$ are involved in several cycles in Figure 9.

We handle dependency graphs with cycles by first transforming them into a virtual DAG and then using the DAG scheduling algorithm above. We use the concept of a strongly connected component (SCC), a subgraph where every node has a path to every other node [14]. One can think of an SCC as a set of intertwined cycles. If we view each SCC as a virtual node in the graph, then the graph becomes a virtual DAG, which is called the component graph in graph theory. We use Tarjan's algorithm [21] to efficiently find all SCCs in the dependency graph. Its time complexity is $O(|V|+|E|)$ where $|V|$ and $|E|$ are the number of nodes and edges.

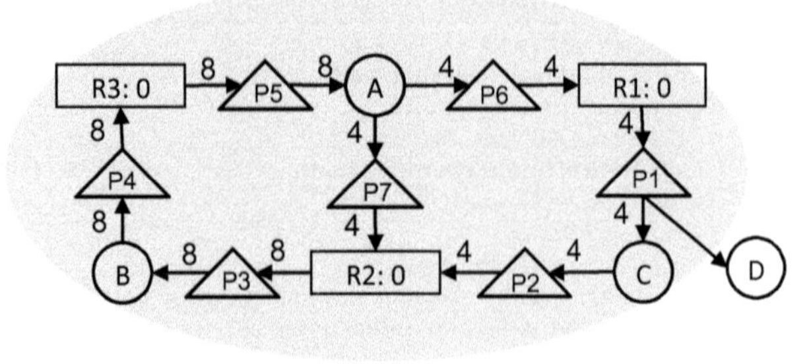


**Figure 9: A deadlock example where the target state is valid but no feasible solution exists.**

---

**Algorithm 5** RateLimit($SCC, k^*$)

1: $O^* \leftarrow$ weight change nodes $\in SCC$
2: **for** $i$=0 ; $i$<$k^*$ && $O^* \neq \emptyset$ ; $i$++ **do**
3: $\quad O_i \leftarrow O^*.pop()$
4: $\quad$ **for** path node $P_j \in children(O_i)$ **do**
$\quad\quad$ **// $f_i$ is the corresponding flow of $O_i$**
5: $\quad\quad$ Rate limit flow $f_i$ by $l_{ij}$ on path $P_j$
6: $\quad\quad$ **for** resource node $R_k \in children(P_j)$ **do**
7: $\quad\quad\quad R_k.free \leftarrow R_k.free + l_{ij}$
8: $\quad\quad$ Delete $P_j$ and its edges

---

With each SCC being a virtual node, we can use critical-path scheduling on the component graph. While calculating $CPLs$, we use the number of operation nodes in an SCC as the weight of the corresponding virtual node, which makes the scheduler prefer paths with larger SCCs.

We make two modifications to the scheduling algorithm to incorporate SCCs. The first is that the *for* loop at Line 5 in Algorithm 2 iterates over all nodes in the virtual graph. When a node is selected, if it is a single node, we directly call $CanScheduleOperation(O_i)$. If it is a virtual node, we iterate over the operation nodes in its SCC and call the functions accordingly. We use centrality [22] to decide the order of the iteration; the intuition is that a central node of an SCC is on many cycles, and if we can schedule this node early, many cycles will disappear and we can finish the SCC quickly. We use the popular outdegree-based definition of centrality, but other definitions may also be used. The second modification is that when path nodes consume link resources or tunnel add operations consume switch resources, they can only consume resources from nodes that either are in the same SCC or are independent nodes (not in any SCC). This heuristic prevents deadlocks caused by allocating resources to nodes outside the SCC ("Mv. F2") before nodes in the SCC are satisfied as in Figure 5(b).

**Deadlocks:** The scheduling algorithm resolves most cycles without deadlocks (§9). However, we may still encounter deadlocks in which no operations in the SCC can make any progress even if the SCC have obtained all resources from outside nodes. This can happen because (1) given the hardness of the problem, our scheduling algorithm, which is basically an informed heuristic, doesn't find the feasible solution among the combinatorially many orderings and gets stuck, or (2) there does not exist a feasible solution even if the target state is valid, like the example in Figure 9. One should note that deadlocks stem from the need for consistent network updates. Previous solutions face the same challenge but are much slower and cause more congestion than Dionysus (§9.4).

Our strategy for resolving deadlocks is to reduce flow rates (e.g., by informing rate limiters). Reducing flow rate frees up link capacity; and reducing it to zero on a path allows removal of the tunnel, which in turn frees up switch memory. Freeing up these resources allows some of the operations that were earlier blocked on resources to go through. In the extreme case, if we rate limit all the flows involved in the deadlocked SCC, the deadlock can be resolved in one step. However, this extreme remedy leads to excessive throughput loss. It is also unnecessary because often rate limiting a few strategically selected flows suffices.

We thus rate limit a few flows to begin with, which enables some operations in the SCC to be scheduled. If that does not fully resolve the SCC, we rate limit a few more, until the SCC is fully resolved. The parameter $k^*$ determines the maximum number of flows that we rate limit each time, and it controls the tradeoff between the time to resolve the deadlock and the amount of throughput loss. Algorithm 5 shows the procedure to resolve deadlocks for tunnel-based networks. It iterates over up to $k^*$ weight change nodes in the SCC, each of which corresponds to a flow (Lines 2–8). The order of iteration is based on centrality value as above. We can prove that as long as the target state is valid (i.e., no resource is oversubscribed), we can fully resolve a deadlock by calling the procedure by at most $\lceil O^*/k^* \rceil$ times. While we skip the formal proof, it is based on the observation that each time $RateLimit$ is called, followed by $ScheduleGraph$, the size of the SCC reduces by at least $k^*$ operation nodes. We find experimentally that often the number of steps needed is a lot fewer than this bound.

We use Figure 9 to illustrate deadlock resolution. Let $k^*$=1. The procedure first selects node $A$. It reduces 4 units of traffic on path $P6$ and 4 units on $P7$, which releases 4 units of free capacity to $R1$ and 4 units to $R2$, and deletes $P6$ and $P7$. At this point, node $A$ has no children and thus does not belong to the SCC any more. After this, we call $ScheduleGraph(G)$ to continue the update. It schedules $C$, and partially schedules $B$ (i.e., moves 4 units of traffic from path $P3$ to $P4$). After $C$ finishes, it schedules the remainded of operation $B$ and finishes the update. Finally, for node $A$ and its corresponding flow $f_A$, we increase its rate on $P5$ as long as $R3$ receives free capacity released by $P4$.

## 7. Implementation

We have implemented a prototype of Dionysus with 5,000+ lines of C# code. It receives current state from the network and target state from applications as input, generates a dependency graph, and schedules rule updates. We implemented dependency graph generators for both tunnel-based and WCMP networks and all the scheduling algorithms discussed above. For accurate control plane confirmations of rule updates (not available in most OpenFlow agents today), we run a custom software agent on our switches.

## 8. Testbed Evaluation

We evaluate Dionysus using testbed experiments in this section and using large-scale simulations in the next section. We use two update cases, a WAN TE case and a WAN failure recovery case. To show its benefits, we compare Dionysus against SWAN [9], a static solution.

**Methodology:** Our testbed consists of 8 Arista 7050T switches as shown in Figure 10(a). It emulates a WAN scenario. The switches are connected by 10 Gbps links. With the help of our switch agents, we log the time of sending updates and receiving confirmation. We use VLAN tags to implement tunnels and use prefix-splitting to implement weights when a flow uses multiple tunnels. We let $S2$ and $S4$ be straggler switches and inject 500 ms latency for rule updates on them. The remaining switches update at their own pace.

**WAN TE case:** In this experiment, the update is triggered by a traffic matrix change. TE calculates a new allocation for the new matrix, and we update the network accordingly. A simplified dependency graph for this update is shown in Figure 10(b). Numbers in the circles correspond to the switch to which the rule update is

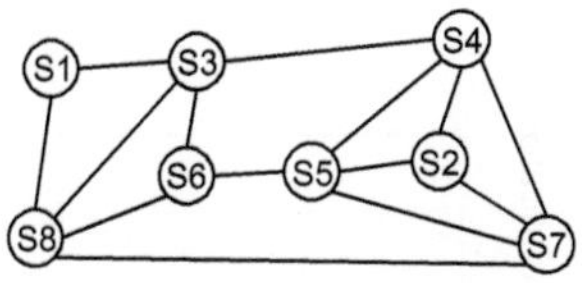


(a) Testbed topology

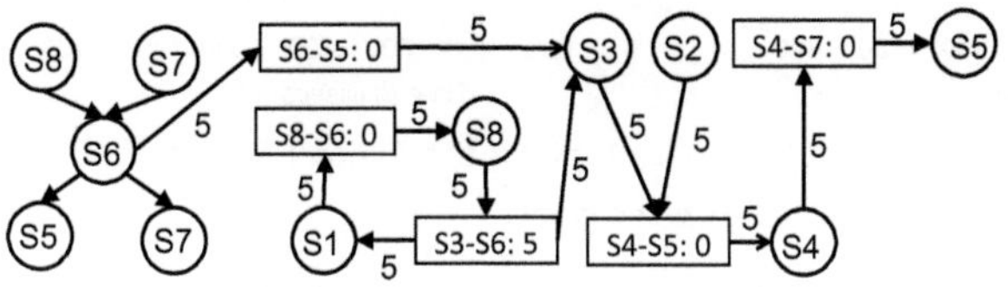


(b) Dependency graph for WAN traffic engineering case

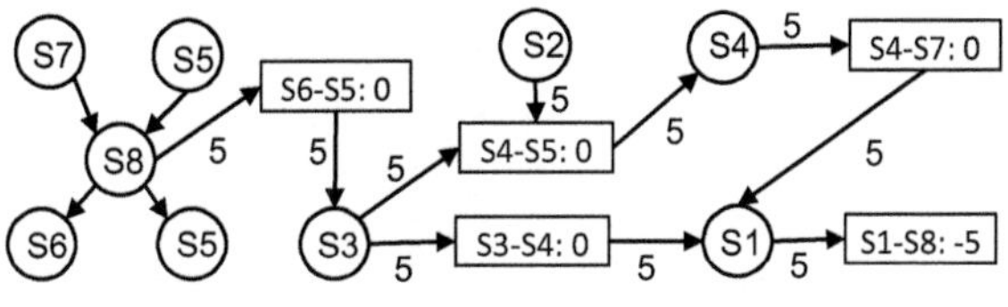


(c) Dependency graph for WAN failure recovery case

**Figure 10: Testbed setup. Path nodes are removed from the dependency graphs ((b) and (c)) for brevity.**

sent. For example, the operation node with annotation "S8" means a rule update at switch $S8$. The graph contains a cycle that includes nodes "S8", "S3-S6", "S1" and "S8-S6". Careless scheduling, e.g., one that schedules node "S3" before "S1" may cause a deadlock. There are also operation dependencies for this update: to move a flow at $S6$, we have to install a new tunnel at $S8$ and $S7$; after the movement finishes, we delete an old tunnel at $S5$ and $S7$.

Figure 11 shows the time series of this experiment. The x-axis is the time, and the y-axis is the switch index. A rectangle represents a rule update on a switch (y-axis) for some period (x-axis). Different rectangular patterns show different rule update operations (add rule, change rule, or delete rule). Rule updates on straggler switches, $S2$ and $S4$, take longer than those on other switches. But even on non-straggler switches, the rule update time varies—the lengths of the rectangles are not identical—between 20 and 100 ms.

Dionysus dynamically performs the update as shown in Figure 11(a). First it finds the SCC and schedules node "S1". It also schedules "S2", "S8" and "S7" as they don't have any parents. After they finish, Dionysus schedules "S6" and "S8", then "S3", "S5" and "S7". Rather than waiting for "S2," which is a straggler, Dionysus schedules "S4" after "S3" finishes—"S3" releases enough capacity for it. Finally Dionysus schedules "S5". The update finishes in 842 ms.

SWAN uses a static, multi-step solution to perform the update (Figure 11(b)). It first installs the new tunnel (node "S8" and "S7"). Then, it adjusts tunnel weights with a congestion-free plan with the minimal number of steps, as follows:

Step 1: "S1", "S6", "S2"
Step 2: "S4", "S8"
Step 3: "S3", "S5"

Due to stragglers $S2$ and $S4$, SWAN takes a long time on both Steps 1 and 2. Finally, SWAN deletes the old tunnel (node "S5" and "S7"). It does not start the tunnel addition and deletion steps with the weight change steps. The whole update takes 1241 ms, 47% longer than Dionysus.

**WAN failure recovery case:** In this experiment, the network update is triggered by a topology change. Link S3-S8 fails; flows that use this link rescale their traffic to other tunnels. This causes link S1-S8 to get overloaded by 50%. To address this problem, TE

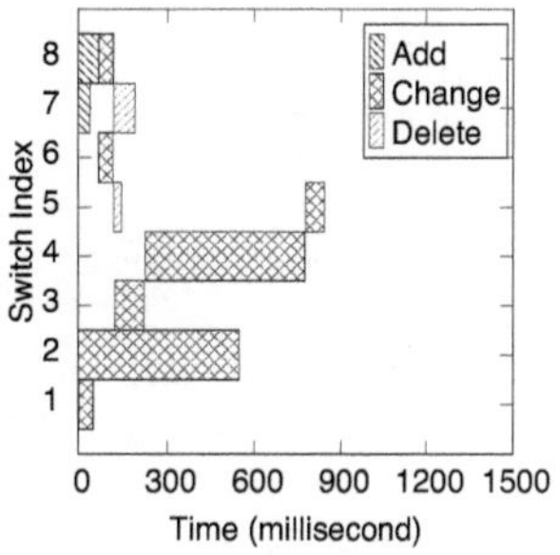


(a) Dionysus

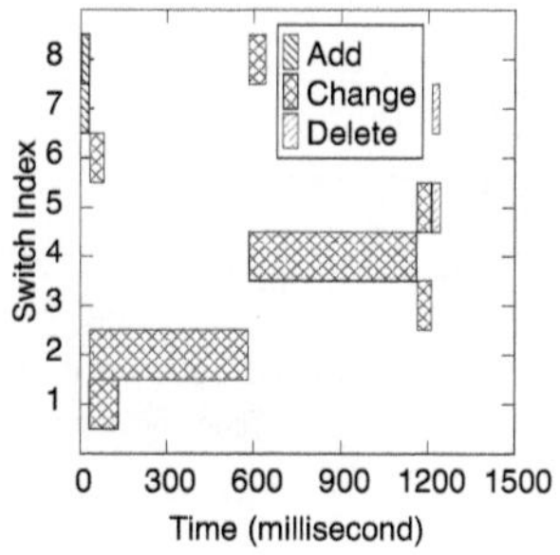


(b) SWAN

**Figure 11: Time series for testbed experiment of WAN TE.**

calculates a new traffic allocation that eliminates the link overload. The simplified dependency graph for this network update is shown in Figure 10(c). To eliminate the overload on link S1-S8, a flow at $S1$ is to be moved away, which depends on several other rule updates. Doing all the rule updates in one shot is undesirable as it may cause more link overloads and affect more flows. For example, if "S1" finishes faster than "S3" and "S4", then it causes 50% link overload on link S3-S4 and S4-S7 and unnecessarily brings congestions to flows on these links. We present extensive results in §9.3 to show that one-shot updates can cause excessive congestion.

Figure 12(a) shows the time series of the update performed by Dionysus. It first schedules nodes "S7", "S5" and "S2". After "S7" and "S5" finish, a new tunnel is established and it safely schedules "S8". Then it schedules "S3", "S5" and "S6". Although "S2" is on a straggler switch and is delayed, Dionysus dynamically schedules "S4" once "S3" finishes. Finally, it schedules "S1". It finishes the update in 808 ms, which eliminates the overload on S1-S8, as shown in Figure 12(c).

Figure 12(b) shows the time series of the update performed by SWAN. It first installs the new tunnel (node "S7" and "S5"), then calculates an update plan with minimal steps as follows.

Step 1: node "S2", node "S8"
Step 2: node "S3", node "S4"
Step 3: node "S1"

This static plan does not adapt, and it is delayed by straggler switches at both Steps 1 and 2. It misses the opportunity to dynamically re-order rule updates. It takes 1299 ms to finish the update and eliminate the link overload, 61% longer than Dionysus.

# 9. Large-Scale Simulations

We now conduct large-scale simulations to show that Dionysus can significantly improve update speed, reduce congestion, and effectively handle cycles in dependency graphs. We focus on congestion freedom as the consistency property, a particularly challenging property and most relevant for the networks we study.

## 9.1 Datasets and methodology

**Wide area network:** This dataset is from a large WAN that interconnects $O(50)$ sites. Inter-site links have tens to hundreds of Gbps capacity. We collect traffic logs on routers and aggregate them into site-to-site flows over 5-minute intervals. The flows are classified into 3 priorities: interactive, elastic and background [9]. We obtain 288 traffic matrices on a typical working day, where each traffic matrix consists of all the site-to-site flows in one interval.

The network uses tunnel-based routing, and we implement the TE algorithm of SWAN [9] which maximizes network throughput and approximates max-min fairness among flows of the same priorities. The TE algorithm produces the network configuration for successive intervals and we compute the time to update the network from one interval to the next.

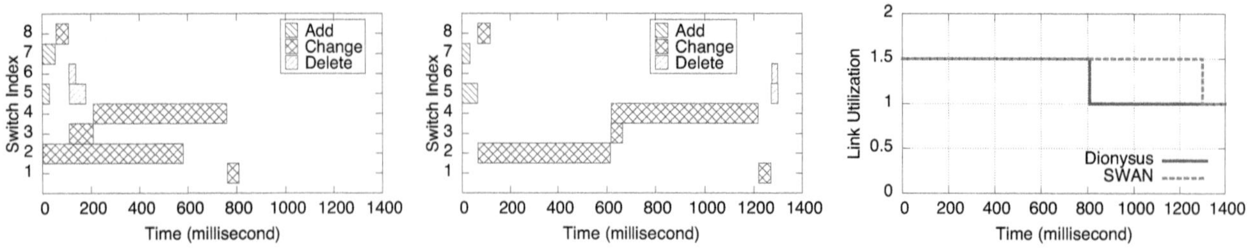


(a) Dionysus (b) SWAN (c) Link Utilization on Link $S1$-$S8$

**Figure 12: Time series for testbed experiment of WAN failure recovery.**

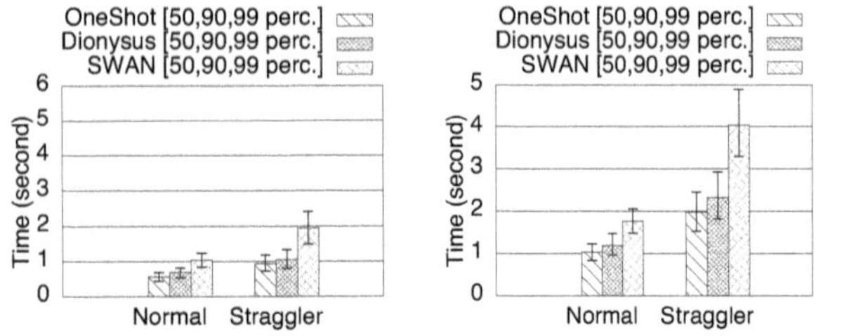


(a) WAN TE (b) Data center TE

**Figure 13: Dionysus is faster than SWAN and close to OneShot.**

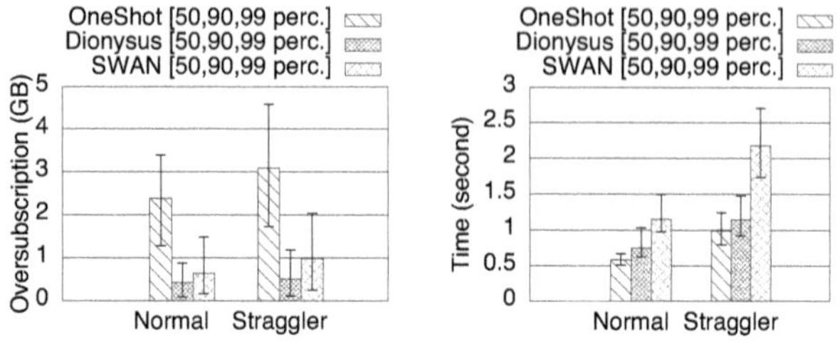


(a) Link Oversubscription (b) Update time

**Figure 14: In WAN failure recovery, Dionysus significantly reduces oversubscription and update time as compared to SWAN. OneShot, while fast, incurs huge oversubscription.**

**Data center network:** This dataset is from a large data center network with several hundred switches. The topoogy has 3 layers: ToR (Top-of-Rack), Agg (Aggeration), and Core. Links between switches are 10 Gbps. We collect traffic traces by logging the socket events on all servers and aggregate them into ToR-to-ToR flows over 5-minute intervals. As for the WAN, we obtain 288 traffic matrices for a typical working day.

Due to the large scale, we do elephant-flow routing [5, 6, 7]. We choose the 1500 largest flows, which account for 40–60% of all traffic. We use an LP to calculate their traffic allocation and use ECMP for other flows. This method improves the total throughput by up to 30% as compared to using ECMP for all flows. We run TE and update WCMP weights for elephant flows every interval. Since mice flows use default ECMP entries, nothing is updated for them.

For both settings, we leave 10% scratch capacity on links to aid transitions [9], and we use 1500 as switch rule memory size. This memory size means that the memory slack (i.e., unused capacity) is at least 50% in our experiments in §9.2 and §9.3. In §9.4, we study the impact of memory limitation by reducing memory size.

**Alternative approaches:** We compare Dionysus with two alternative approaches. First, *OneShot* sends all updates in one shot. It does not maintain any consistency, but serves as the lower bound for update time. Second, *SWAN* is the state-of-the-art approach in maintaining congestion freedom [9]. It uses a heuristic to divide the update into multiple phases based on memory constraints so that each intermediate phase can fit all rules in switches. SWAN may rate limit flows in intermediate phase as the paths in the network cannot carry all the traffic. Between consecutive phases, it uses a linear program to calculate a congestion-free multi-step plan based on capacity constraints.

**Rule update time:** The rule update time at switches is based on switch measurement results (§2). We show results in both *normal* setting and *straggler* setting. In the former case, we use the median rule update time in §2; in the latter case, we draw rule update time from the CDF in §2. We use 50 ms as RTT in WAN scenario.

## 9.2 Update time

**WAN TE:** Figure 13(a) shows the $50^{th}$, $90^{th}$, $99^{th}$ percentile update time across all intervals for the WAN TE scenario. Dionysus outperforms SWAN in both normal and straggler settings. In the normal setting, Dionysus is 57%, 49%, and 52% faster than SWAN in the $50^{th}$, $90^{th}$, $99^{th}$ percentile, respectively. The gain is mainly from pipelining: in every step, different switches receive different number of rules to update and thus takes different amount of time to finish. While SWAN has to wait for the switch with the most number of rules to finish, Dionysus begins to issue new operations as soon as some switches finish.

In the straggler setting, Dionysus reduces update time even more. It is 88%, 84%, and 81% faster than SWAN in the $50^{th}$, $90^{th}$, $99^{th}$ percentile, respectively. This advantage is because stragglers provide more opportunities for dynamic scheduling which SWAN cannot leverage. Dionysus also performs close to OneShot. It is only 25% and 13% slower than OneShot in the $90^{th}$ percentile in normal and straggler settings, respectively.

**Data center TE:** Figure 13(b) shows results for the data center TE scenario. Again, Dionysus significantly outperforms SWAN. In the normal setting, it is 53%, 48%, and 40% faster than SWAN in the $50^{th}$, $90^{th}$, and $99^{th}$ percentile; in the straggler setting, it is 81%, 74%, and 67% faster. Data center TE takes more time because it involves a two-phase commit across multiple switches for each flow; WAN TE only needs to update the ingress switch if all tunnels are established.

## 9.3 Link oversubscription

We use a WAN failure recovery scenario to show that Dionysus can reduce link oversubscription and shorten recovery time. We use the same topology and traffic matrices as in the WAN TE case. For each traffic matrix, we first use TE to calculate a state $NS_0$. Then we fail a randomly selected link, which causes the ingress switches to move traffic away from the failed tunnels to the remaining ones. For example, if flow $f$ originally uses tunnels $T_1$, $T_2$ and $T_3$ with weights $w_1$, $w_2$ and $w_3$ and the failed link causes $T_1$ to break, then $f$ carries its traffic using $T_2$ and $T_3$ with weights $w_2/(w_2+w_3)$ and $w_3/(w_2+w_3)$. We denote the network state that emerges after the failure and rescaling as $NS_1$. Since rescaling is a local action, $NS_1$ may have overloaded links. The TE calculates a new state

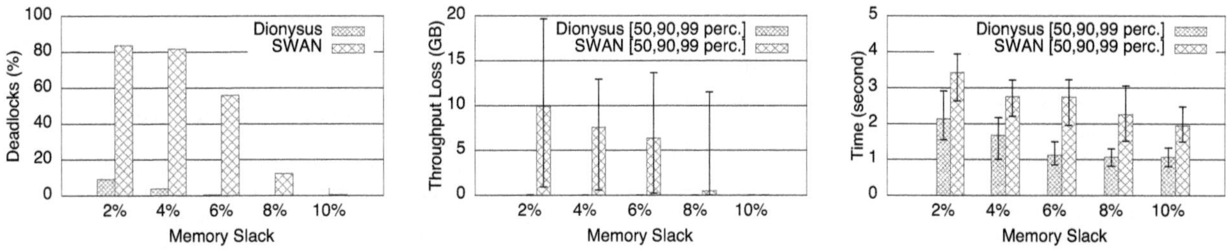


(a) Percentage of rate limited cases (b) Throughput Loss (c) Update Time

**Figure 16:** Dionysus **only occasionally runs into deadlocks and uses rate limiting, and experiences little throughput loss. It also consistently outperforms SWAN in update time.**

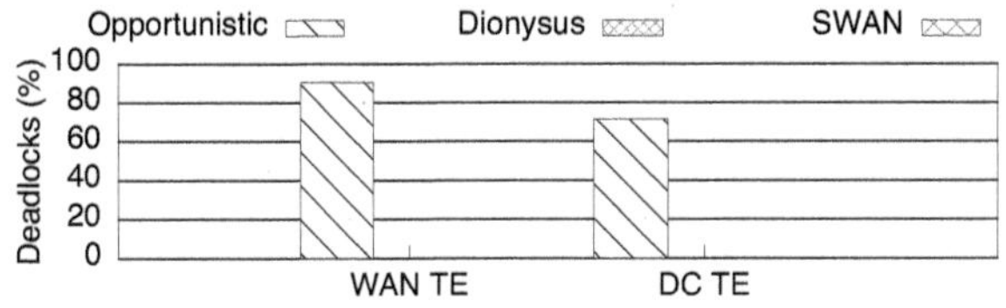


**Figure 15: Opportunistic scheduling frequently deadlocks.** Dionysus **and SWAN have no deadlocks.**

$NS_2$ to eliminate congestion. The network update that we study is the update from $NS_1$ to $NS_2$.

If the initial state $NS_1$ already has congestion, there will be no congestion-free update plan. For Dionysus and SWAN, we generate plans in which, during updates, no oversubscribed link carries more load than its current load. In such plans, the capacity of congested links is virtually increased to its current load, to make each link appear non-congested. For Dionysus, we increase the weight of overloaded links to the overloaded amount in $CPL$ calculation (Equation 1). Then, Dionysus will prefer operations that move traffic away from overloaded links. For SWAN, we use the linear program to compute the plan such that total oversubscription across all links is minimized at each step. Of all possible static plans, this modification makes SWAN prefer one that minimizes congestion quickly. OneShot operates as before because it does not care about congestion.

Figure 14 shows the update time and link oversubscription—the amount of data above capacity arriving at a link. Dionysus has the least oversubscription among the three. OneShot, while quick, has huge oversubscription. SWAN incurs 1.49 GB and 2.04 GB oversubscription in the $99^{th}$ percentile in normal and straggler settings, respectively. As even high-end switches today only have hundreds of MB buffer [23], such oversubscription will cause heavy packet loss. Dionysus reduces oversubscription to 0.88 GB and 1.19 GB, which are 41% and 42% less than SWAN. For update time, Dionysus is 45% and 82% faster than SWAN in the $99^{th}$ percentile in normal and straggler setting, respectively.

## 9.4 Deadlocks

We now study the effectiveness of Dionysus in handling circular dependencies, which can lead to deadlocks. First, we show that, as mentioned in §3, completely opportunistic scheduling can lead to frequent deadlocks even in a setting that is not resource-constrained. Then, we show the effectiveness of Dionysus in handling resource-constrained settings.

Figure 15 shows the percentage of network updates finished by Dionysus, SWAN, and an opportunistic approach without deadlocks, that is, without having to reduce flow rates during updates. The opportunistic approach immediately issues any updates that do not violate consistency (§3), instead of planning using a dependency graph. The data in the figure corresponds to the WAN and data center TE scenarios in §9.2, where the memory slack was over 50%. We do not show results for OneShot; it does not deadlock by design as it does not worry about consistency.

We see that planning-based approaches, Dionysus and SWAN, lead to no deadlocks, but the opportunistic approach deadlocks 90% of the time for WAN TE and 70% of the time for data center TE. It performs worse for WAN TE because the WAN topology is less regular than the data center topology, which leads to more complex dependencies.

We now evaluate Dionysus and SWAN in resource-constrained settings. To emulate such a setting, instead of using 1500 as memory size, we vary switch memory slack; 10% memory slack means we set the memory size as 1100 when the switch is loaded with 1000 rules. We show three metrics in the WAN TE setup: (1) the percentage of cases that deadlock and use rate limiting to finish the update, (2) the throughput loss caused by rate limiting (i.e., the product of the limited rate and the rate limited time), and (3) the update time. We set $k^*$=5 in Algorithm 5 for Dionysus.

Figure 16 shows the results for the straggler setting. The results with the normal setting are similar. Figure 16(a) shows the percentage of cases that use rate limiting under different levels of memory slack. Dionysus only occasionally runs into deadlocks and uses resorts to rate limiting more sparingly than SWAN. Even with only 2% memory slack, Dionysus uses rate limiting in fewer than 10% cases. SWAN, on the other hand, uses rate limiting in more than 80% of the cases. This difference is because the heuristics in Dionysus strategically account for dependencies during scheduling. SWAN uses simplistic metrics, such as the amount of traffic that a tunnel carries and the number of hops of the tunnel, to decide which tunnel to add or delete.

Figure 16(b) shows the throughput loss. The throughput loss with SWAN can be as high as 20 GB, while that with Dionysus is only tens of MB. Finally 16(c) shows the update time. Dionysus is 60%, 145%, and 84% faster than SWAN in the $90^{th}$ percentile under 2%, 6% and 10% memory slack respectively.

# 10. Related Work

In the domain of distributed protocols, there is a lot of work on avoiding transient misbehavior during network updates. Much focuses on maintain properties like loop-freedom for specific protocols or scenarios. For example, Francois *et al.* [24], John *et al.* [25] and Kushman *et al.* [26] focus on BGP, Francois *et al.* [27, 28] and Raza *et al.* [29] focus on link-state protocols, and Vanbever *et al.* [30] focus on migration from one routing protocol to another.

With the advent of SDN, many recent works propose solutions to maintain different consistency properties during network updates. Reitblatt *et al.* [11] provide a theoretical foundation and propose a two-phase commit protocol to maintain packet coherence. Katta *et al.* [12] and McGeer *et al.* [31] propose solutions to reduce the memory requirements to maintain packet coherence. SWAN [9], zUpdate [10] and Ghorbani and Caesar [32] provide solutions for congestion-free updates. Noyes *et al.* [33] propose a model checking based approach to generate update orderings that maintain invariants specified by the operator. Mahajan and Wattenhofer [13] present an efficient solution for maintaining loop freedom. As mentioned earlier, unlike these works, the key characteristic of our approach is dynamic scheduling, which leads to faster updates.

Mahajan and Wattenhofer [13] also analyze the nature of dependencies among switches induced by different consistency properties and outline a general architecture for consistent updates. We build on their work by developing a concrete system.

Some works develop approaches that spread traffic such that the network stays congestion-free after a class of common failures [34, 35], and thus no network-wide updates are needed to react to these failures. These approaches are complementary to our work. They help reduce the number of network updates needed. But network updates are still be needed to adjust to changing traffic demands and reacting to failures that are not handled by these approaches. Dionysus ensures that these updates will be fast and consistent.

## 11. Conclusion

Dionysus enables fast, consistent network updates in SDNs. The key to its speed is dynamic scheduling of updates at individual switches based on runtime differences in their update speeds. We showed using testbed experiments and data-driven simulations that Dionysus improves the median network update speed by 53%-88% over static scheduling. These faster updates translates to a more nimble network that reacts faster to events like failures and changes in traffic demand.

**Acknowledgements** We thank Srinivas Narayana, Meg Walraed-Sullivan, our shepherd Brighten Godfrey, and the anonymous SIGCOMM reviewers for their feedback on earlier versions of this paper. Xin Jin and Jennifer Rexford were partially supported by NSF grant TC-1111520 and DARPA grant MRC-007692-001.

## 12. References

[1] M. Caesar, D. Caldwell, N. Feamster, J. Rexford, A. Shaikh, and J. van der Merwe, "Design and implementation of a routing control platform," in *USENIX NSDI*, 2005.

[2] A. Greenberg, G. Hjalmtysson, D. A. Maltz, A. Myers, J. Rexford, G. Xie, H. Yan, J. Zhan, and H. Zhang, "A clean slate 4D approach to network control and management," *SIGCOMM CCR*, 2005.

[3] M. Casado, M. J. Freedman, J. Pettit, J. Luo, N. Gude, N. McKeown, and S. Shenker, "Rethinking enterprise network control," *IEEE/ACM Trans. Networking*, vol. 17, no. 4, 2009.

[4] B. Heller, S. Seetharaman, P. Mahadevan, Y. Yiakoumis, P. Sharma, S. Banerjee, and N. McKeown, "ElasticTree: Saving energy in data center networks.," in *USENIX NSDI*, 2010.

[5] M. Al-Fares, S. Radhakrishnan, B. Raghavan, N. Huang, and A. Vahdat, "Hedera: Dynamic flow scheduling for data center networks.," in *USENIX NSDI*, 2010.

[6] T. Benson, A. Anand, A. Akella, and M. Zhang, "MicroTE: Fine grained traffic engineering for data centers," in *ACM CoNEXT*, 2011.

[7] A. R. Curtis, J. C. Mogul, J. Tourrilhes, P. Yalagandula, P. Sharma, and S. Banerjee, "DevoFlow: Scaling flow management for high-performance networks," in *ACM SIGCOMM*, 2011.

[8] S. Jain, A. Kumar, S. Mandal, J. Ong, L. Poutievski, A. Singh, S. Venkata, J. Wanderer, J. Zhou, M. Zhu, *et al.*, "B4: Experience with a globally-deployed software defined WAN," in *ACM SIGCOMM*, 2013.

[9] C.-Y. Hong, S. Kandula, R. Mahajan, M. Zhang, V. Gill, M. Nanduri, and R. Wattenhofer, "Achieving high utilization with software-driven WAN," in *ACM SIGCOMM*, 2013.

[10] H. H. Liu, X. Wu, M. Zhang, L. Yuan, R. Wattenhofer, and D. A. Maltz, "zUpdate: Updating data center networks with zero loss," in *ACM SIGCOMM*, 2013.

[11] M. Reitblatt, N. Foster, J. Rexford, C. Schlesinger, and D. Walker, "Abstractions for network update," in *ACM SIGCOMM*, 2012.

[12] N. P. Katta, J. Rexford, and D. Walker, "Incremental consistent updates," in *ACM SIGCOMM HotSDN Workshop*, 2013.

[13] R. Mahajan and R. Wattenhofer, "On consistent updates in software defined networks," in *ACM SIGCOMM HotNets Workshop*, 2013.

[14] C. E. Leiserson, R. L. Rivest, C. Stein, and T. H. Cormen, *Introduction to Algorithms*. The MIT press, 2001.

[15] C. Rotsos, N. Sarrar, S. Uhlig, R. Sherwood, and A. W. Moore, "OFLOPS: An open framework for OpenFlow switch evaluation," in *Passive and Active Measurement Conference*, 2012.

[16] A. Ferguson, A. Guha, C. Liang, R. Fonseca, and S. Krishnamurthi, "Participatory networking: An API for application control of SDNs," in *ACM SIGCOMM*, 2013.

[17] Nicira, "Network virtualization for cloud data centers." `http://tinyurl.com/c9jbkuu`.

[18] M. Casado, T. Koponen, S. Shenker, and A. Tootoonchian, "Fabric: A retrospective on evolving SDN," in *ACM SIGCOMM HotSDN Workshop*, 2012.

[19] B. Raghavan, M. Casado, T. Koponen, S. Ratnasamy, A. Ghodsi, and S. Shenker, "Software-defined Internet architecture: Decoupling architecture from infrastructure," in *ACM SIGCOMM HotNets Workshop*, 2012.

[20] X. Jin, H. H. Liu, R. Gandhi, S. Kandula, R. Mahajan, M. Zhang, J. Rexford, and R. Wattenhofer, "Dionysus: Dynamic scheduling of network updates (extended version)," in *Microsoft Research Technical Report MSR-TR-2014-79*, 2014.

[21] R. Tarjan, "Depth-first search and linear graph algorithms," *SIAM Journal on Computing*, vol. 1, no. 2, 1972.

[22] M. Newman, *Networks: An Introduction*. Oxford University Press, 2009.

[23] Arista, "Arista 7500 series technical specifications." `http://tinyurl.com/lene8sw`.

[24] P. Francois, O. Bonaventure, B. Decraene, and P.-A. Coste, "Avoiding disruptions during maintenance operations on BGP sessions," *Network and Service Management, IEEE Transactions on*, vol. 4, no. 3, 2007.

[25] J. P. John, E. Katz-Bassett, A. Krishnamurthy, T. Anderson, and A. Venkataramani, "Consensus routing: The Internet as a distributed system," in *USENIX NSDI*, 2008.

[26] N. Kushman, S. Kandula, D. Katabi, and B. M. Maggs, "R-BGP: Staying connected in a connected world," in *USENIX NSDI*, 2007.

[27] P. Francois, M. Shand, and O. Bonaventure, "Disruption free topology reconfiguration in OSPF networks," in *INFOCOM*, 2007.

[28] P. Francois and O. Bonaventure, "Avoiding transient loops during the convergence of link-state routing protocols," *IEEE/ACM Trans. Networking*, vol. 15, no. 6, 2007.

[29] S. Raza, Y. Zhu, and C.-N. Chuah, "Graceful network state migrations," *IEEE/ACM Trans. Networking*, vol. 19, no. 4, 2011.

[30] L. Vanbever, S. Vissicchio, C. Pelsser, P. Francois, and O. Bonaventure, "Lossless migrations of link-state IGPs," *IEEE/ACM Trans. Networking*, vol. 20, no. 6, 2012.

[31] R. McGeer, "A safe, efficient update protocol for OpenFlow networks," in *ACM SIGCOMM HotSDN Workshop*, 2012.

[32] S. Ghorbani and M. Caesar, "Walk the line: Consistent network updates with bandwidth guarantees," in *ACM SIGCOMM HotSDN Workshop*, 2012.

[33] A. Noyes, T. Warszawski, and N. Foster, "Toward synthesis of network updates," in *Workshop on Synthesis (SYNT)*, 2013.

[34] Y. Wang, H. Wang, A. Mahimkar, R. Alimi, Y. Zhang, L. Qiu, and Y. R. Yang, "R3:resilient routing reconfiguration," in *ACM SIGCOMM*, 2010.

[35] H. H. Liu, S. Kandula, R. Mahajan, M. Zhang, and D. Gelernter, "Traffic engineering with forward fault correction," in *ACM SIGCOMM*, 2014.

# SDX: A Software Defined Internet Exchange

Arpit Gupta†, Laurent Vanbever⋆, Muhammad Shahbaz†, Sean P. Donovan†, Brandon Schlinker‡
Nick Feamster†, Jennifer Rexford⋆, Scott Shenker⋄, Russ Clark†, Ethan Katz-Bassett‡
†Georgia Tech ⋆Princeton University ⋄UC Berkeley ‡Univ. of Southern California

## Abstract

BGP severely constrains how networks can deliver traffic over the Internet. Today's networks can only forward traffic based on the destination IP prefix, by selecting among routes offered by their immediate neighbors. We believe Software Defined Networking (SDN) could revolutionize wide-area traffic delivery, by offering direct control over packet-processing rules that match on multiple header fields and perform a variety of actions. Internet exchange points (IXPs) are a compelling place to start, given their central role in interconnecting many networks and their growing importance in bringing popular content closer to end users.

To realize a Software Defined IXP (an "SDX"), we must create compelling applications, such as "application-specific peering"—where two networks peer only for (say) streaming video traffic. We also need new programming abstractions that allow participating networks to create and run these applications and a runtime that both behaves correctly when interacting with BGP and ensures that applications do not interfere with each other. Finally, we must ensure that the system scales, both in rule-table size and computational overhead. In this paper, we tackle these challenges and demonstrate the flexibility and scalability of our solutions through controlled and in-the-wild experiments. Our experiments demonstrate that our SDX implementation can implement representative policies for hundreds of participants who advertise full routing tables while achieving sub-second convergence in response to configuration changes and routing updates.

**Categories and Subject Descriptors:** C.2.1 [Computer-Communication Networks] *Network Architecture and Design*: Network Communications

**General Terms:** Algorithms, Design, Experimentation

**Keywords:** software defined networking (SDN); Internet exchange point (IXP); BGP

## 1 Introduction

Internet routing is unreliable, inflexible, and difficult to manage. Network operators must rely on arcane mechanisms to perform traffic engineering, prevent attacks, and realize peering agreements. Internet routing's problems result from three characteristics of the Border Gateway Protocol (BGP), the Internet's interdomain routing protocol:

- **Routing only on destination IP prefix.** BGP selects and exports routes for destination prefixes. Networks cannot make more fine-grained decisions based on the type of application or the sender.
- **Influence only over direct neighbors.** A network selects among BGP routes learned from its direct neighbors, and exports selected routes to these neighbors. Networks have little control over end-to-end paths.
- **Indirect expression of policy.** Networks rely on indirect, obscure mechanisms (*e.g.*, "local preference", "AS Path Prepending") to influence path selection. Networks cannot directly express preferred inbound and outbound paths.

These problems are well-known, yet incremental deployment of alternative solutions is a perennial problem in a global Internet with more than 50,000 independently operated networks and a huge installed base of BGP-speaking routers.

In this paper, we develop a way forward that improves our existing routing system by allowing a network to execute a far wider range of decisions concerning end-to-end traffic delivery. Our approach builds on recent technology trends and also recognizes the need for incremental deployment. First, we believe that Software Defined Networking (SDN) shows great promise for simplifying network management and enabling new networked services. SDN switches match on a variety of header fields (not just destination prefix), perform a range of actions (not just forwarding), and offer direct control over the data plane. Yet, SDN currently only applies to *intra*domain settings, such as individual data-center, enterprise, or backbone networks. By design, a conventional SDN controller has purview over the switches within a single administrative (and trust) domain.

Second, we recognize the recent resurgence of interest in Internet exchange points (IXPs), which are physical locations where multiple networks meet to exchange traffic and BGP routes. An IXP is a layer-two network that, in the simplest case, consists of a single switch. Each participating network exchanges BGP routes (often with a BGP route server) and directs traffic to other participants over the layer-two fabric. The Internet has more than 300 IXPs worldwide—with more than 80 in North America alone—and some IXPs carry as much traffic as the tier-1 ISPs [1, 4]. For example, the Open IX effort seeks to develop new North American IXPs with open peering and governance, similar to the models already taking root in Europe. As video traffic continues to increase, tensions grow between content providers and access networks, and IXPs are on the front line of today's peering disputes. In short, not only are IXPs the right place to begin a revolution in wide-area traffic delivery, but the organizations running these IXPs have strong incentives to innovate.

We aim to change wide-area traffic delivery by designing, prototyping, and deploying a software defined exchange (SDX). Contrary to how it may seem, however, merely operating SDN switches and a controller at an IXP does not automatically present a turnkey solution. SDN is merely a tool for solving problems, not the solution.


*SIGCOMM'14*, August 17–22, 2014, Chicago, IL, USA.

http://dx.doi.org/10.1145/2619239.2626300

In fact, running an SDN-enabled exchange point introduces many problems, ranging from correctness to scalability. To realize the SDX in practice, we must address the following four challenges:

- **Compelling applications.** The success of the SDX depends on identifying compelling wide-area traffic-delivery applications that are difficult to deploy today. We present four motivating applications: application-specific peering, inbound traffic engineering, server load balancing, and traffic redirection through middleboxes (Section 2).
- **Programming abstractions.** Participating networks need a way to create and run applications, without conflicting with each other or with the global routing system. Our SDX design presents each participating network with the illusion of its own virtual SDN switch that extends the footprint of its legacy network and enables flexible policies that interact safely with today's BGP (Section 3).
- **Scalable operation.** An SDX needs to support hundreds of participants, hundreds of thousands of IP prefixes, and policies that match on multiple packet-header fields—all while using conventional SDN switches. We show how to combine the policies of multiple participants and join them with the current BGP routes, while limiting rule-table size and computational overhead (Section 4).
- **Realistic deployment.** We have built a prototype and created two example applications (Section 5). Experiments demonstrate that our prototype scales (in terms of rule-table size and CPU time) to many participants, policies, and prefixes (Section 6).

We conclude with a discussion of related work (Section 7) and future possibilities (Section 8).

## 2 Wide-Area Traffic Delivery

We present four applications that the SDX enables. We describe how operators tackle these problems today, focusing in particular on the "pain points" for implementing these functions in today's infrastructure. We also describe how these applications would be easier to implement with the SDX. We revisit several of these examples throughout the paper, both demonstrating how the SDX makes them possible and, in some cases, deploying them in the wide area.

**Application-specific peering.** High-bandwidth video services like YouTube and Netflix constitute a significant fraction of overall traffic volume, so ISPs are increasingly interested in application-specific peering, where two neighboring AS exchange traffic only for certain applications. BGP does not make it easy to support such an arrangement. An ISP could configure its edge routers to make different forwarding decisions for different application packet classifiers (to identify the relevant traffic) and policy-based routing (to direct that traffic over a special path). For example, an ISP could configure its border routers to have multiple VRFs (virtual routing and forwarding tables), one for each traffic class, and direct video traffic via one VRF and non-video traffic through another. Still, such an approach forces the ISPs to incur additional routing and forwarding state, in proportion to the number of traffic classes, and configure these mechanisms correctly. SDX could instead install custom rules for groups of flows corresponding to specific parts of flow space.

**Inbound traffic engineering.** Because BGP performs *destination*-based routing, ASes have little control over how traffic *enters* their networks and must use indirect, obscure techniques (*e.g.*, AS path prepending, communities, selective advertisements) to influence how ASes reach them. Each of these existing approaches is limited: prepending cannot override another AS's local preference for outbound traffic control, communities typically only affect decisions of an immediate neighbor network, and selective advertisements pollute the global routing tables with extra prefixes. By installing forwarding rules in SDN-enabled switches at an exchange point, an AS can directly control inbound traffic according to source IP addresses or port numbers.

**Wide-area server load balancing.** Content providers balance client requests across clusters of servers by manipulating the domain name system (DNS). Each service has a single domain name (*e.g.*, `http://www.example.com/`) which resolves to multiple IP addresses for different backend servers. When a client's local DNS server issues a DNS request, the service's authoritative DNS server returns an IP address that appropriately balances load. Unfortunately, using DNS for server selection has several limitations. First, DNS caching (by the local DNS server, and by the user's browser) results in slower responses to failures and shifts in load. To (partially) address this problem, content providers use low "time to live" values, leading to more frequent DNS cache misses, adding critical milliseconds to request latency. Instead, a content provider could assign a single anycast IP address for a service and rewrite the destination addresses of client requests in the middle of the network (*e.g.*, at exchange points). SDX could announce anycast prefixes and rewrite the destination IP address to match the chosen hosting location based on any fields in the packet header.

**Redirection through middleboxes.** Networks increasingly rely on middleboxes to perform a wide range of functions (*e.g.*, firewalls, network address translators, load balancers). Enterprise networks at the edge of the Internet typically place middleboxes at key junctions, such as the boundary between the enterprise and its upstream ISPs, but large ISPs are often geographically expansive, making it prohibitively expensive to place middleboxes at every location. Instead, they manipulate the routing protocols to "steer" traffic through a fixed set of middleboxes. For example, when traffic measurements suggest a possible denial-of-service attack, an ISP can use internal BGP to "hijack" the offending traffic and forward it through a traffic scrubber. Some broadband access ISPs perform similar steering of a home user's traffic by routing all home network traffic through a scrubber via a VPN. Such steering requires ISPs to "hijack" much more normal traffic than necessary, and the mechanisms are not well-suited to steering traffic through a *sequence* of middleboxes. Instead, an SDN-enabled exchange point can redirect targeted subsets of traffic through one or more middleboxes.

## 3 Programming Abstractions

The SDX enables the operators of participating ASes to run novel applications that control the flow of traffic entering and leaving their border routers, or, in the case of remote participants, the flow of traffic destined for their AS. By giving each AS the illusion of its own virtual SDN switch, the SDX enables flexible specification of forwarding policies while ensuring isolation between different participants. SDX applications can base decisions on the currently available BGP routes, which offers greater flexibility while ensuring that traffic follows valid interdomain paths.

### 3.1 Virtual SDX Switch Abstraction

In a traditional exchange point, each participating AS typically connects a BGP-speaking border router to a *shared layer-two network* (a data plane for forwarding packets) and a *BGP route server* (a control plane for exchanging routing information). At an SDX, each AS can run SDN applications that specify flexible policies for dropping,

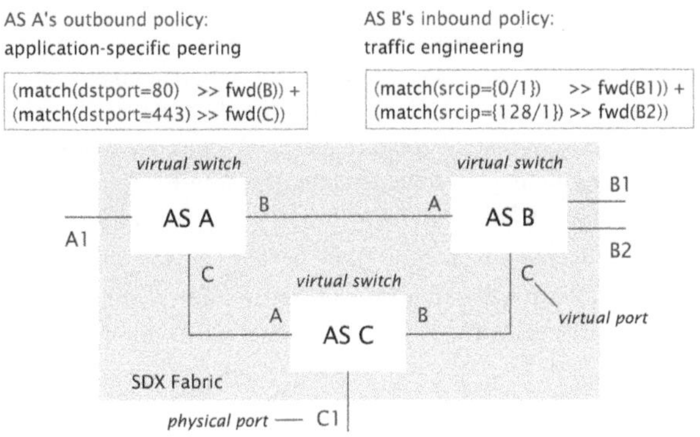


**(a)** *Virtual switch abstraction.*

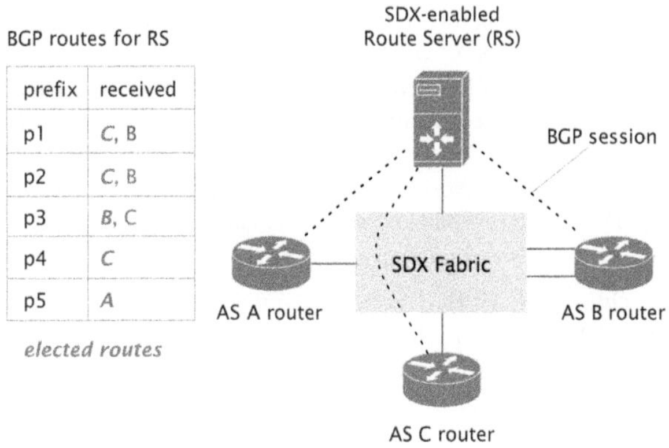


**(b)** *Integration with interdomain routes.*

**Figure 1:** *SDX programming abstractions.*

modifying, and forwarding the traffic. The SDX must then combine the policies of multiple ASes into a single coherent policy for the physical switch(es). To balance the desire for flexibility with the need for isolation, we give each AS the illusion of its own virtual SDN switch connecting its border router to each of its peer ASes, as shown in Figure 1a. AS A has a virtual switch connecting to the virtual switches of ASes B and C, where each AS can write forwarding policies as if it is the only participant at the SDX. Yet, AS A *cannot* influence how ASes B and C forward packets on their own virtual switches.

For writing policies, we adopt the Pyretic language [12] that supports declarative programming based on boolean predicates (that each match a subset of the packets) and a small set of actions (that modify a packet's header fields or location). A Pyretic policy maps a located packet (*i.e.*, a packet and its location) to a set of located packets. Returning the empty set drops the packet. Returning a set with a single packet forwards the packet to its new location. Finally, returning a set with multiple packets multicasts the packets. In contrast to vanilla Pyretic policies, we require participants to specify whether a policy is an *inbound* or an *outbound* policy. Inbound policies apply to the traffic entering a virtual switch on a virtual port from another SDX participant; outbound policies apply to the traffic entering a virtual switch on a physical port from the participant's own border router. In the rest of the paper, we omit this distinction whenever it is clear from context. We now present several simple examples inspired by Section 2.

**Application-specific peering.** In Figure 1a, AS A has an outbound policy that forwards HTTP traffic (destination port 80) and HTTPS traffic (destination port 443) to AS B and AS C, respectively:

```
(match(dstport = 80) >> fwd(B)) +
(match(dstport = 443) >> fwd(C))
```

The `match()` statement is a filter that returns all packets with a transport port number of 80 or 443, and the >> is the sequential composition operator that sends the resulting packets to the `fwd(B)` (or, respectively, `fwd(C)`) policy, which in turn modifies the packets' location to the corresponding virtual switch. The + operator corresponds to parallel composition which, given two policies, applies them both to each packet and combines their outputs. If neither of the two policies matches, the packet is dropped.

**Inbound traffic engineering.** AS B has an inbound policy that performs inbound traffic engineering over packets coming from ASes A and C:

```
(match(srcip = {0.0.0.0/1}) >> fwd(B1)) +
(match(srcip = {128.0.0.0/1}) >> fwd(B2))
```

AS B directs traffic with source IP addresses starting with 0 to B's top output port, and the remaining traffic (with source IP addresses starting with 1) to B's bottom output port. Under the hood, the SDX runtime system "compiles" A's outbound policy with B's inbound policy to construct a single policy for the underlying physical switch, such as:

```
(match(port=A1, dstport=80,
       srcip={0.0.0.0/1}) >> fwd(B1)) +
(match(port=A1, dstport=80,
       srcip={128.0.0.0/1}) >> fwd(B2))
```

that achieves the same outcome as directing traffic through multiple virtual switches (here, A and B's switches). This policy has a straightforward mapping to low-level rules on OpenFlow switches [12].

**Wide-area server load balancing.** An AS can have a virtual switch at the SDX *without* having any physical presence at the exchange point, in order to influence the end-to-end flow of traffic. For example, a content provider can perform server load balancing by dividing request traffic based on client IP prefixes and ensuring connection affinity across changes in the load-balancing policy [21]. The content provider might host a service at IP address `74.125.1.1` and direct specific customer prefixes to specific replicas based on their request load and geographic location:

```
match(dstip=74.125.1.1) >>
   (match(srcip=96.25.160.0/24) >>
       mod(dstip=74.125.224.161)) +
   (match(srcip=128.125.163.0/24) >>
       mod(dstip=74.125.137.139))
```

Manipulating packet forwarding at the SDX gives a content provider fast and direct control over the traffic, in contrast to existing indirect mechanisms like DNS-based load balancing. The content provider issuing this policy would first need to demonstrate to the SDX that it owns the corresponding IP address blocks.

## 3.2 Integration with Interdomain Routing

The ASes must define SDX policies in relation to the advertised routes in the global routing system. To do so, the SDX allows participating ASes to define forwarding policies relative to the current BGP routes. To learn BGP routes, the SDX controller integrates a route server, as shown in Figure 1b. Participants interact with the

SDX route server in the same way that they do with a conventional route server. The SDX route server collects the routes advertised by each participant BGP router and selects one best route for each prefix on behalf of each participant, and re-advertises the best BGP route on the appropriate BGP session(s). In contrast to today's route servers, where each participant learns and uses one route per prefix, the SDX route server allows each participant to forward traffic to all feasible routes for a prefix, even if it learns only one.

**Overriding default BGP routes.** Many ASes may be happy with how BGP computes routes for most of the traffic. Rather than requiring each AS to fully specify the forwarding policy for all traffic, the SDX allows each AS to rely on a default forwarding policy computed by BGP, overriding the policy as needed. In the example in Figure 1a, AS A's outbound policy for Web traffic (forwarding to AS B) applies only to Web traffic; all of the remaining traffic implicitly follows whatever best route AS A selects in BGP. This greatly simplifies the task of writing an SDX application: the simplest application specifies nothing, resulting in all traffic following the BGP-selected routes announced by the route server. The programmer need only specify the handling of any "non-default" traffic. For example in Figure 1b, AS A would forward any non-Web traffic destined to IP prefix $p_1$ or $p_2$ to next-hop AS C, rather than to AS B.

**Forwarding only along BGP-advertised paths.** The SDX should not direct traffic to a next-hop AS that does not want to receive it. In Figure 1b, AS B does *not* export a BGP route for destination prefix $p_4$ to AS A, so AS A should not forward any traffic (including Web traffic) for $p_4$ through AS B. To prevent ASes from violating these restrictions, and to simplify the writing of applications, the SDX only applies a `match()` predicate to the portion of traffic that is eligible for forwarding to the specified next-hop AS. In Figure 1, AS A can forward Web traffic for destination prefixes $p_1$, $p_2$, and $p_3$ to AS B, but not for $p_4$. Note that, despite not selecting AS B as the best route for destination prefix $p_1$ and $p_2$, AS A can still direct the corresponding Web traffic through AS B, since AS B does export a BGP route for these prefixes to AS A.

**Grouping traffic based on BGP attributes.** ASes may wish to express policies based on higher levels of abstraction than IP prefixes. Instead, an AS could handle traffic based on the organization managing the IP address (*e.g.*, "all flows sent by YouTube") or the current AS-PATH for each destination prefix. The SDX allows a policy to specify a match *indirectly* based on regular expressions on BGP route attributes. For example, an AS could specify that all traffic sent by YouTube servers traverses a video-transcoding middlebox hosted at a particular port (E1) at the SDX:

```
YouTubePrefixes =
          RIB.filter('as_path', .*43515$)
match(srcip={YouTubePrefixes}) >> fwd(E1)
```

The regular expression matches all BGP-announced routes ending in AS 43515 (YouTube's AS number), and generates the list of associated IP prefixes. The `match()` statement matches any traffic sent by one of these IP addresses and forwards it to the output port connected to the middlebox.

**Originating BGP routes from the SDX.** In addition to forwarding traffic along BGP-advertised paths, ASes may want the SDX to originate routes for their IP prefixes. In the wide-area load-balancing application, a remote AS D instructs the SDX to match request traffic destined to an anycast service with IP address 74.125.1.1. To ensure the SDX receives the request traffic, AS D needs to trigger a BGP route announcement for the associated IP prefix (`announce (74.125.1.0/24)`), and withdraw the prefix when it is no longer needed (`withdraw(74.125.1.0/24)`). AS D could announce the anycast prefix at multiple SDXs that each run the load-balancing application, to ensure that all client requests flow through a nearby SDX. Before originating the route announcement in BGP, the SDX would verify that AS D indeed owns the IP prefix (*e.g.*, using the RPKI).

**Integrating SDX with existing infrastructure.** Integrating SDX with existing IXP infrastructure and conventional BGP-speaking ASes is straightforward. Any participant that is physically connected to a SDN-enabled switch exchanges BGP routes with the SDX route server can write SDX policies; furthermore, an AS can benefit from an SDX deployment at a single location, even if the rest of the ASes run only conventional BGP routing. A participant can implement SDX policies for any route that it learns via the SDX route server, independently of whether the AS that originated the prefix is an SDX participant. Participants who are physically present at the IXP but do not want to implement SDX policies see the same layer-2 abstractions that they would at any other IXP. The SDX controller can run a conventional spanning tree protocol to ensure seamless operation between SDN-enabled participants and conventional participants.

## 4 Efficient Compilation

In this section, we describe how the SDX runtime system compiles the policies of all participants into low-level forwarding rules (Section 4.1). We then describe how we made that process efficient. We consider *data-plane* efficiency (Section 4.2), to minimize the number of rules in the switches, and *control-plane* efficiency (Section 4.3), to minimize the computation time under realistic workloads.

### 4.1 Compilation by Policy Transformation

The policies written by SDX participants are abstract policies that need to be joined with the BGP routes, combined, and translated to equivalent forwarding rules for the physical switch(es). We compile the policies through a sequence of syntactic transformations: (1) restricting policies according to the virtual topology; (2) augmenting the policies with BGP-learned information; (3) extending policies to default to using the best BGP route; and (4) composing the policies of all the participants into one main SDX policy by emulating multiple hops in the virtual topology. Then, we rely on the underlying Pyretic runtime to translate the SDX policy into forwarding rules for the physical switch.

**Enforcing isolation between participants.** The first transformation restricts the participant's policy so that each participant can only act on its own virtual switch. Each port on a virtual switch corresponds either to a physical port at the SDX (*e.g.*, *A*1 in Figure 1a) or a virtual connection to another participant's virtual switch (*e.g.*, port *B* on AS A's virtual switch in Figure 1a). The SDX runtime must ensure that a participant's outbound policies only apply to the traffic that it sends. Likewise, its inbound policies should only apply to the traffic that it receives. For example, in Figure 1a, AS A's outbound policy should only apply to traffic that it originates, not to the traffic that AS B sends to it. To enforce this constraint, the SDX runtime automatically augments each participant policy with an explicit `match()` on the participant's port; the port for the match statement depends on whether the policy is an inbound or outbound policy. For an inbound policy, the `match()` it refers to the participant's virtual port; for an outbound policy, it refers to the participant's physical ports. After this step, AS A's outbound and AS B's inbound policies in Figure 1(a) become:

```
PA = (match(port=A1) && match(dstport=80)
          >> fwd(B)) +
     (match(port=A1) && match(dstport=443)
          >> fwd(C))

PB = (match(port=B) && match(srcip={0/1})
          >> fwd(B1)) +
     (match(port=B) && match(srcip={128/1})
          >> fwd(B2))
```

For convenience, we use `match(port=B)` as shorthand for matching on any of B's internal virtual port.

**Enforcing consistency with BGP advertisements.** The second transformation restricts each participant's policy based on the BGP routes exported to the participant. For instance, in Figure 1, AS A can only direct traffic with destination prefixes $p_1$, $p_2$, and $p_3$ to AS B, since AS B did not export a BGP route for $p_4$ or $p_5$ to AS A. The SDX runtime generates a BGP filter policy for each participant based on the exported routes, as seen by the BGP route server. The SDX runtime then inserts these filters inside each participant's outbound policy, according to the forwarding action. If a participant AS A is forwarding to AS B (or C), the runtime inserts B's (or, respectively, C's) BGP filter before the corresponding forwarding action. After this step, AS A's policy becomes:

```
PA' = (match(port=A1) && match(dstport=80) &&
        (match(dstip=p1) || match(dstip=p2) ||
         match(dstip=p3))
      >> fwd(B)) +

      (match(port=A1) && match(dstport=443) &&
        (match(dstip=p1) || match(dstip=p2) ||
         match(dstip=p3) || match(dstip=p4))
      >> fwd(C))
```

AS B does not specify special handling for traffic entering its physical ports, so its policy `PB'` remains the same as `PB`.

**Enforcing default forwarding using the best BGP route.** Each participant's policy overrides the default routing decision for a select portion of the traffic, with the remaining traffic forwarded as usual. Each data packet enters the physical switch with a destination MAC address that corresponds to the BGP next-hop of the participant's best BGP route for the destination prefix. To implement default forwarding, the SDX runtime computes simple MAC-learning policies for each virtual switch. These policies forward packets from one virtual switch to another based on the destination MAC address and forward packets for local destinations on the appropriate physical ports. The default policy for AS A in Figure 1(a) is:

```
defA = (match(dstmac=MAC_B1) >> fwd(B)) +
       (match(dstmac=MAC_B2) >> fwd(B)) +
       (match(dstmac=MAC_C1) >> fwd(C)) +

       (match(port=A)  >>
         modify(dstmac=MAC_A1) >> fwd(A1))
```

The first part of the policy handles traffic arriving on A's physical port and forwards traffic to the participant with the corresponding destination MAC address. The second part of the policy handles traffic arriving from other participants and forwards to A's physical port. The runtime also rewrites the traffic's destination MAC address to correspond to the physical port of the intended recipient. For example, in Figure 1, A's diverted HTTP traffic for $p_1$ and $p_2$ reaches B with C1 as the MAC address, since C is the designated BGP next-hop for $p_1$ and $p_2$. Without rewriting, AS B would drop the traffic.

The runtime then combines the default policy with the corresponding participant policy. The goal is to apply `PA'` on all matching packets and `defA` on all other packets. The SDX controller analyzes `PA'` to compute the union of all match predicates in `PA'` and applies Pyretic's `if_()` operator to combine `PA'` and `defA`, resulting in policy `PA''`.

**Moving packets through the virtual topology.** The SDX runtime finally composes all of the augmented policies into one main SDX policy. Intuitively, when a participant *A* sends traffic in the SDX fabric destined to participant *B*, *A*'s outbound policy must be applied first, followed by *B*'s inbound policy, which translates to the sequential composition of both policies, (*i.e.*, `PA'' >> PB''`). Since any of the participant can originate or receive traffic, the SDX runtime sequentially composes the *combined* policies of all participants:

```
SDX = (PA'' + PB'' + PC'') >> (PA'' + PB'' + PC'')
```

When the SDX applies this policy, any packet that enters the SDX fabric either reaches the physical port of another participant or is dropped. In any case, the resulting forwarding policy within the fabric will never have loops. Taking BGP policies into account also prevent forwarding loops between edge routers. The SDX enforces two BGP-related invariants to prevent forwarding loops between edge routers. First, a participant router can only receive traffic destined to an IP prefix for which it has announced a corresponding BGP route. Second, if a participant router announces a BGP route for an IP prefix *p*, it will never forward traffic destined to *p* back to the SDX fabric.

Finally, the SDX runtime relies on the underlying Pyretic runtime to translate the SDX policy to the forwarding rules to install in the physical switch. More generally, the SDX may consist of *multiple* physical switches, each connected to a subset of the participants. Fortunately, we can rely on Pyretic's existing support for topology abstraction to combine a policy written for a single SDX switch with another policy for routing across multiple physical switches, to generate the forwarding rules for multiple physical switches.

## 4.2 Reducing Data-Plane State

Augmenting each participant's policy with the BGP-learned prefixes could cause an explosion in the size of the final policy. Today's global routing system has more than 500,000 IPv4 prefixes (and growing!), and large IXPs host several hundred participants (*e.g.*, AMS-IX has more than 600). The participants may have different policies, directing traffic to different forwarding neighbors. Moreover, composing these policies might also generate a "cross-product" of their predicates if the participants' policies match on different fields. For instance, in Figure 1a, AS A matches on `dstport`, and B on `srcip`. As a result, a naive compilation algorithm could easily lead to millions of forwarding rules, while even the most high-end SDN switch hardware can barely hold half a million rules [13].

Existing layer-two IXPs do not face such challenges because they forward packets based only on the destination MAC address, rather than the IP and TCP/UDP header fields. To minimize the number of rules in the SDX switch, the SDX (1) groups prefixes with the same forwarding behavior into an equivalence class and (2) implicitly tags the packets sent by each participant's border router using a virtual MAC address. This technique substantially reduces the number of forwarding rules, and works with unmodified BGP routers.

**Grouping prefixes into equivalence classes.** Fortunately, a participant's policy would typically treat a large number of IP prefixes the same way. For instance, in Figure 1, AS A has the same forwarding behavior for $p_1$ and $p_2$ (*i.e.*, send Web traffic via AS B, and send

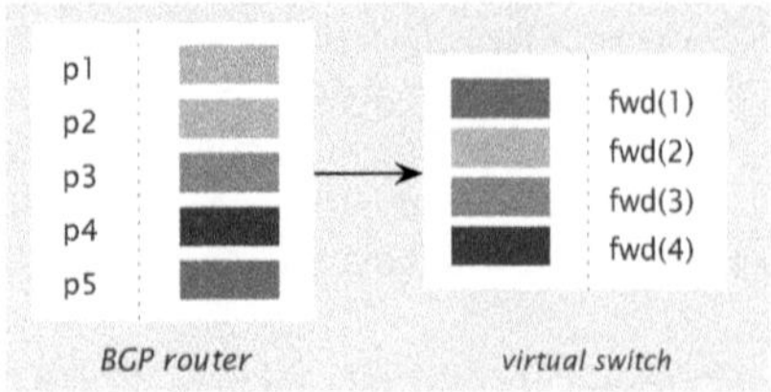


**Figure 2:** *Multi-stage FIB for each participant, where the first stage corresponds to the participant's border router and the second stage corresponds to the participant's virtual switch at the SDX.*

the rest via AS C). By grouping $p_1$ and $p_2$, we could implement the policy with only two forwarding rules, directing traffic to AS B and C, instead of the four currently required. We say that $p_1$ and $p_2$ belong to the same Forwarding Equivalence Class (FEC). An FEC is a set of IP prefixes that share the same forwarding behavior throughout the SDX fabric. Ideally, we would install the minimum set of forwarding rules for each FEC, which is equivalent to the number of forwarding actions associated with the FEC. Doing so requires a new way to combine prefixes; conventional IP prefix aggregation does not work because prefixes $p_1$ and $p_2$ might not be contiguous IP address blocks.

**Offloading tagging to the participants' border routers.** To group non-adjacent prefixes belonging to the same FEC, we introduce the abstraction of a multi-stage Forwarding Information Base (FIB) for each participant, as shown in Figure 2. The first table matches on the destination IP prefix and tags packets with the associated FEC. Then, a second table simply matches on the tag and performs the forwarding actions associated with the FEC. Using a multi-staged FIB substantially reduces the number of rules in the second table. The first table remains quite large because of the many IP prefixes. To address this challenge, we implement the first table using the participant's own border router. Each border router already maintains a forwarding table with an entry for each destination prefix, so we can realize our abstraction without any additional table space! Still, we need (1) a data-plane mechanism for tagging the packets and (2) a control-plane mechanism for the SDX to instruct the border router about which tag to use for each prefix. Ideally, the solution to both problems would be completely transparent to the participants, rather than requiring them to run or configure an additional protocol (*e.g.*, MPLS) for this purpose.

**Using the MAC address as data-plane tag and the BGP next-hop IP address for control-plane signaling.** The SDX runtime capitalizes on how BGP-speaking routers compute forwarding-table entries. Upon choosing a BGP route for a prefix $p$, a router (1) extracts the next-hop IP address from the BGP route announcement, (2) consults its ARP table to translate the IP address to the corresponding MAC address, and (3) installs a forwarding-table entry that sets the destination MAC address before directing the packet to the output port. Usually, this MAC address corresponds to the physical address of the next-hop interface. In the SDX though, we have the MAC address correspond to a virtual MAC address (VMAC)—the tag—which identifies the FEC for prefix $p$. The SDX fabric can then just match on the VMAC and perform the forwarding actions associated with the FEC. We refer to the BGP next-hop IP address sent to the border router as the *Virtual Next-Hop* (VNH). Finally, observe that we can assign the same VNH (and, hence, the same VMAC) to disjoint IP prefixes—the address blocks need not be contiguous.

In practice, the SDX runtime first pre-computes the FEC according to participant policies and assigns a distinct (VNH, VMAC) pair to each of them. It then transforms the SDX policies to match on the VMAC instead of the destination prefixes. Finally, it instructs the SDX route server to set the next-hop IP address (VNH) in the BGP messages and directs its own ARP server to respond to requests for the VNH IP address with the corresponding VMAC.

**Computing the virtual next hops.** Computing the virtual next-hop IP addresses requires identifying all groups of prefixes that share the same forwarding behavior, considering both default BGP forwarding and specific SDX policies. To ensure optimality, we want the groups of prefixes to be of maximal size; in other words, any two prefixes sharing the same behavior should always belong to the same group. The SDX runtime computes the FECs in three passes.

In the first pass, the SDX runtime extracts the groups of IP prefixes for which the default behavior is affected in the same way by at least one SDX outbound policy. Figure 1 shows that the group $\{p_1, p_2, p_3\}$ has its default behavior overridden by AS A's outbound policies, which forward its Web traffic to AS B. Similarly, the group $\{p_1, p_2, p_3, p_4\}$ has its default behavior overridden by AS A's outbound policies, which forward its HTTPS traffic to AS C. All of the prefixes except $p_5$ have their default behavior overridden.

In the second pass, the SDX runtime groups all the prefixes that had their default behavior overridden according to the default next-hop selected by the route server. In the previous example, prefixes $p_1, p_2, p_3, p_4$ will be divided into two groups: $\{p_1, p_2, p_4\}$ whose default next-hop is $C$ and $\{p_3\}$ whose default next-hop is $B$.

In the third pass, the SDX runtime combines the groups from the first two passes into one group $C = \{\{p_1, p_2, p_3\}, \{p_1, p_2, p_3, p_4\}, \{p_1, p_2, p_4\}, \{p_3\}\}$. It then computes $C'$ such that each element of $C'$ is the largest possible subset of elements of $C$ with a non-empty intersection. In the example above, $C' = \{\{p_1, p_2\}, \{p_3\}, \{p_4\}\}$ and is the only valid solution. Intuitively, $n$ prefixes belonging to the same group $C_i \in C$ either always appear altogether in a policy $P$, or do not appear at all—they share the same forwarding behavior. We omit the description of a polynomial-time algorithm that computes the Minimum Disjoint Subset (MDS).

Finally, observe that we do not need to consider BGP prefixes that retain their default behavior, such as $p_5$ in Figure 1. For these prefixes, the SDX runtime does not have to do any processing and simply behaves like a normal route server, which transmits BGP announcements with the next-hop IP address unchanged.

### 4.3 Reducing Control-Plane Computation

In this section, we describe how to reduce the time required for control-plane computation. Many of these operations have a default computation time that is exponential in the number of participants and thus does not scale as the number of participants grows. At a high level, the control plane performs three computation-intensive operations: (1) computing the VNHs; (2) augmenting participants' SDX policies; and (3) compiling the policies into forwarding rules. The controller performs these operations both during initialization and whenever SDX's operational state changes. We focus primarily on optimizing policy compilation, as this step is the most computationally intensive. We first describe optimizations that accelerate the initial computation. We then describe optimizations that accelerate incremental computation in response to updates (*i.e.*, due to changes in the available BGP routes or the SDX policies). We describe each optimization along with the insight that enables it.

#### 4.3.1 Optimizing initial compilation

SDX compilation requires composing the policies of every participant AS with every other participant's policy using a combination of sequential and parallel composition. Performing such compositions is time-consuming, as it requires inspecting each pair of policies involved to identify overlaps. As illustration, consider the final policy computed in Section 3, without considering default forwarding (for simplicity):

```
policy_composed =
  (PA'' + PB'' + PC'') >> (PA'' + PB'' + PC'')
```

Since the parallel-composition operator is distributive, the compiler can translate the policy into many pairs of sequential composition, combined together using parallel composition. Removing terms that apply the same policy in succession (*i.e.*, `PA'' >> PA''`) yields:

```
policy_composed =
  ((PA'' >> PB'')+(PA'' >> PC''))+
  ((PB'' >> PA'')+(PB'' >> PC''))+
  ((PC'' >> PA'')+(PC'' >> PB''))
```

Compiling this policy requires executing eleven composition operations—six sequential (two per line) and five in parallel—to combine the intermediate results together. Fortunately, a lot of these sequential and parallel composition can be avoided by exploiting three observations: (1) participant policies tend to involve only a subset of the participants; (2) participant policies are disjoint by design; and (3) many policy idioms appear multiple times in the final policy. The first observation reduces the number of sequential composition operations, and the second reduces the number of parallel composition operations. The third observation prevents compilation of the same policy more than once. With these optimizations, the SDX can achieve policy compilation with only three sequential compositions and no parallel compositions.

**Most SDX policies only concern a subset of the participants.** In the IXP traffic patterns we observe, a few IXP participants carry most of the traffic. Previous work has shown that about 95% of all IXP traffic is exchanged between about 5% of the participants [1]. We thus assume that most SDX policies involve these few large networks rather than all of the IXP participants. The SDX controller avoids all unnecessary compositions by only composing policies among participants that exchange traffic. In this example, AS B has no outbound policy, so compositions `(PB'' >> PA'')` and `(PB'' >> PC'')` are unnecessary. The same reasoning applies for AS C. The SDX controller therefore reduces the policy as follows:

```
policy_composed =
  (PA'' >> PB'') + (PA'' >> PC'') + (PC'' >> PB'')
```

which only involves three sequential composition operations.

**Most SDX policies are disjoint.** Parallel composition is a costly operation that should be used only for combining policies that apply to overlapping flow space. For policies that apply to disjoint flow spaces, the SDX controller can simply apply the policies independently, as no packet ever matches both policies. The policies are disjoint by design because they differ with respect to the virtual switch and port after the first syntactic transformation (*i.e.*, isolation). Also, the same observation applies within the policies of a single participant. We assume that the vast majority of participants would write unicast policies in which each packet is forwarded to one other participant. We do not prevent participants from expressing multicast policies, but we optimize for the common case. As a result, SDX policies that forward to different participants always differ with respect to the forwarding `port` and are also disjoint by construction.

| | AMS-IX | DE-CIX | LINX |
|---|---|---|---|
| **collector peers/total peers** | 116/639 | 92/580 | 71/496 |
| **prefixes** | 518,082 | 518,391 | 503,392 |
| **BGP updates** | 11,161,624 | 30,934,525 | 16,658,819 |
| **prefixes seeing updates** | 9.88% | 13.64% | 12.67% |

**Table 1:** *IXP datasets. We use BGP update traces from RIPE collectors [16] in the three largest IXPs—AMS-IX, DE-CIX, and LINX—for January 1–6, 2014, from which we discarded updates caused by BGP session resets [23].*

Returning to the previous example, none of the parallel compositions between `(PA'' >> PC'')`, `(PA'' >> PC'')`, and `(PC'' >> PB'')` are necessary, since each of them always applies on strictly disjoint portions of the flow space.

**Many policy idioms appear more than once in the global policy.** The reuse of various policy idioms results from the fact that participants exchange traffic with each other (and, more often than not, with the same participant). For instance, in an IXP where every participant sends to AS X, AS X's policies would be sequentially composed with all policies. Currently, the Pyretic compiler would recompile the same sub-policy multiple times. It would therefore compile `PA''`, `PB''`, and `PC''` twice. To accelerate compilation, the SDX controller memoizes all the intermediate compilation results before composing the final policy.

#### 4.3.2 Optimizing incremental updates

SDX compilation occurs not only at initialization time, but also whenever a change occurs in the set of available BGP routes after one or more BGP updates. Efficiently coping with these changes is important. The SDX runtime supports fast recompilation by exploiting three characteristics BGP update patterns: (1) prefixes that are likely to appear in SDX policies tend to be stable; (2) most BGP route changes only affect a small portion of the forwarding table; and (3) BGP route changes occur in bursts and are separated by large periods with no change at all. We draw these observations from a week-long analysis of BGP updates collected at BGP collectors in three of the largest IXPs in the world. Table 1 summarizes the data that we used for this analysis.

Based on these observations, we augmented the basic SDX compilation with an additional compilation stage that is invoked immediately whenever BGP routes change. The main recompilation algorithm is then executed in the background between subsequent bursts of updates. We tune the optimization to handle changes that result from BGP updates, because BGP updates are significantly more frequent than changes to the participants' SDX policies.

**Prefixes that are likely to appear in SDX policies tend to be stable.** Only about 10–14% of prefixes saw any BGP updates at all for an entire week, suggesting that most prefixes are stable. Furthermore, previous work suggests that the stable prefixes are also the same ones that carry the most traffic [15]. Hence, those stable prefixes are also the ones that are likely to be associated with SDX policies.

**Most BGP update bursts affect a small number of prefix groups.** Updates and best path changes tend to occur in bursts. In 75% of the cases, these update bursts affected no more than three prefixes. Over one week, we observed only one update burst that triggered updates for more than 1,000 prefixes. In the common case, the SDX thus only needs to recompute flow table entries for a few affected prefix groups. Even in cases where bursts are large, there is a linear

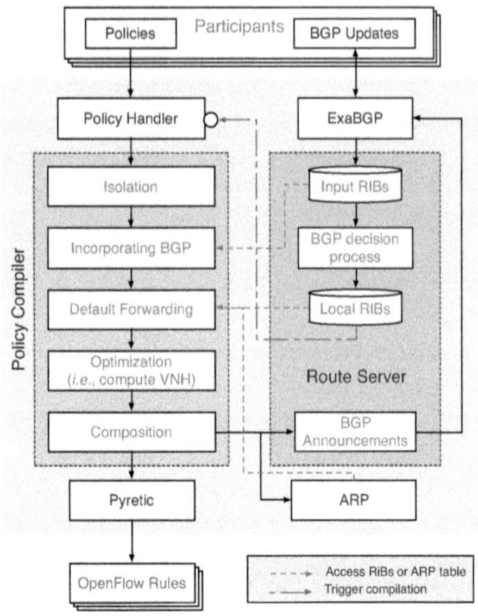


**Figure 3:** *The SDX controller implementation, which has two pipelines: a policy compiler and a route server.*

relationship between the burst size and recompilation time and, as we explain next, this recompilation can occur in the background.

**BGP bursts are separated by large periods with no changes, enabling quick, suboptimal reactions followed by background re-optimization.** We observed that the inter-arrival time between BGP update bursts is at least 10 seconds 75% of the time; half of the time, the inter-arrival time between bursts is more than one minute. Such large inter-arrival times enable the SDX runtime to adopt a two-stage compilation approach, whereby time is traded for space by combining: (1) a fast, but suboptimal recompilation technique, that quickly reacts to the updates; and (2) an optimal recompilation that runs periodically in the background.

The fast stage works as follows. Whenever there is a change in the BGP best path pertaining to a prefix $p$, the SDX immediately creates a new VNH for $p$ and recompiles the policy, considering only the parts related to $p$. It then pushes the resulting forwarding rules into the data plane with a higher priority. The computation is particularly fast because: (1) it bypasses the actual computation of the VNH entirely by simply assuming a new VNH is needed; (2) it restricts compilation to the parts of the policy related to $p$. In Section 6, we show that sub-second recompilation is achievable for the majority of the updates. Although the first stage is fast, it can also produce more rules than needed, since it essentially bypasses VNH optimization.

# 5 Implementation and Deployment

We now describe the implementation of the SDX controller, as well as our current deployment. We then describe several applications that we have implemented with the SDX. We describe one application with outbound traffic control (application-specific peering) and one with inbound traffic control (wide-area load balance).

## 5.1 Implementation

Figure 3 shows the SDX controller implementation, which has two main pipelines: a *policy compiler*, which is based on Pyretic; and a *route server*, which is based on ExaBGP. The policy compiler takes as input policies from individual participants that are written in Pyretic—which may include custom route advertisements from the participants—as well as BGP routes from the route server, and it produces forwarding rules that implement the policies. The route server processes BGP updates from participating ASes and provides them to the policy compiler and re-advertises BGP routes to participants based on the computed routes. We briefly describe the steps of each of these functions below.

**SDX policy compiler.** The policy compiler is a Pyretic process that compiles participant policies to forwarding rules. Based on the virtual SDX abstraction from the SDX configuration (*i.e.*, the static configuration of which ASes are connected to each other at layer two), the policy compiler isolates the policies that each AS writes by augmenting each policy with a `match` statement based on the participant's `port`. The compiler then restricts each participant's outbound policies according to the current BGP routing information from the route server and rewrites the participant policies so that the switch can forward traffic according to the default BGP policies. After augmenting the policies, the compiler then computes VNH assignments for the advertised prefixes. Finally, the compiler writes the participant policies where necessary, taking care to avoid unnecessary composition of policies that are disjoint and performing other optimizations such as caching of partial compilations, as described in Section 4.3. It then passes the policies to the Pyretic compiler, which generates the corresponding forwarding rules.

Because VNHs are virtual IP addresses, the controller also implements an ARP responder that responds to ARP queries for VNHs with the appropriate VMAC addresses.

**SDX route server.** We implemented the SDX route server by extending ExaBGP [5], an existing route server that is implemented in Python. As in other traditional route servers [2, 14], the SDX route server receives BGP advertisements from all participants and computes the best path for each destination prefix on behalf of each participant. The SDX route server also (1) enables integration of the participant's policy with interdomain routing by providing advertised route information to the compiler pipeline; and (2) reduces data-plane state by advertising virtual next hops for the prefixes advertised by SDX participants. The SDX route server recompiles the participants' policies whenever a BGP update results in changes to best routes for a prefix. When such an update occurs, the route server sends an event to the policy handler, which recompiles policies associated with the affected routing updates. The compiler installs new rules corresponding to the BGP update while performing the optimizations described in Section 4.3 in the background. After compiling the new forwarding rules, the policy compiler then sends the updated next-hop information to the route server, which marshals the corresponding BGP updates and sends them to the appropriate participant ASes.

## 5.2 Deployment

We have developed a prototype of the SDX [18] and a version that can be deployed using virtual containers in Mininet [7]. Figure 4 shows two setups that we have created in these environments for the purposes of demonstrating two applications: application-specific peering and wide-area load balance. For each use case, we explain the deployment setup and demonstrate the outcome of the running application. For both use cases, we have deployed an SDX controller (including route server) that is connected to an Open vSwitch software switch. The ASes that we have connected to the Open vSwitch at the exchange point are currently virtual (as our deployment has no peers that carry real Internet traffic), and these virtual ASes in turn establish BGP connectivity to the Internet via the Transit Portal [19]. The client generates three 1 Mbps UDP flows, varying the

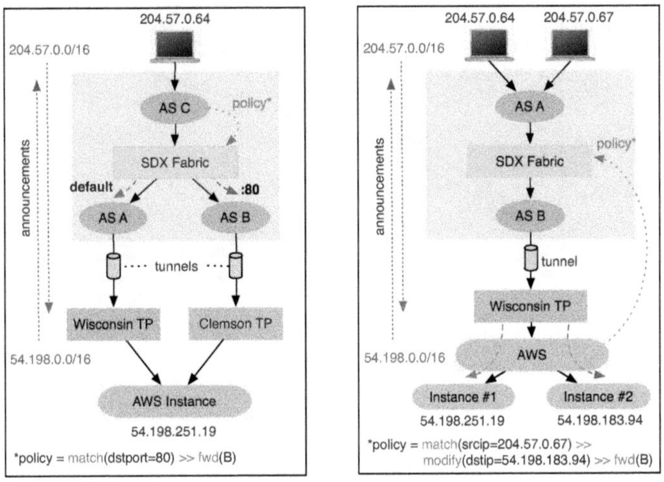


**(a)** *Application-Specific Peering.* **(b)** *Wide-Area Load Balance.*

**Figure 4:** *Setup for deployment experiments.*

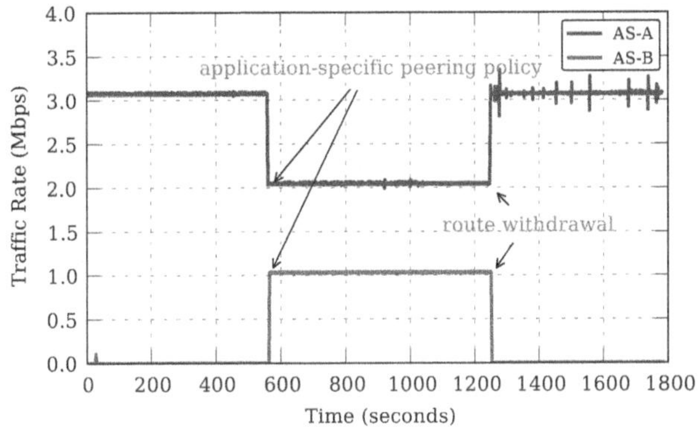


**(a)** *Application-specific peering.*

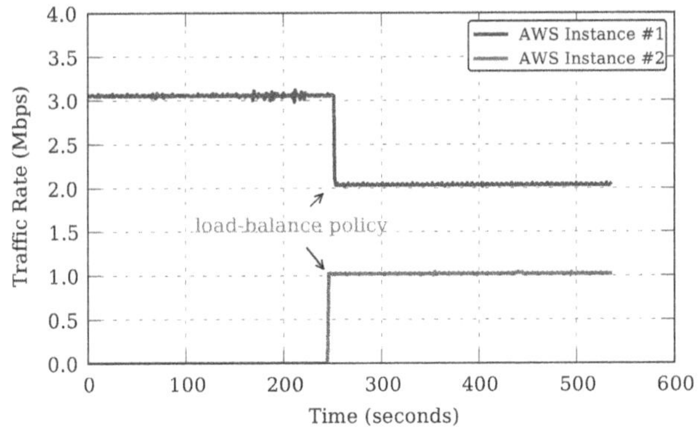


**(b)** *Wide-area load balance.*

**Figure 5:** *Traffic patterns for the two "live" SDX applications. (a) At 565 seconds, the AS C installs an application-specific peering policy, causing port 80 traffic to arrive via AS B. At 1253 seconds, AS B withdraws its route to AWS, causing all traffic to shift back to the path via AS A. (b) At 246 seconds, the AWS network installs a wide-area load balance policy to shift the traffic for source 204.57.0.67 to arrive at AWS instance #2.*

source and destination IP addresses and ports as required for the demonstrations below.

**Application-specific peering.** Figure 4a shows an SDX setup where we test the application-specific peering use-case described in Section 3. The example demonstrates several features of the SDX controller, including (1) the ability for a participant to control traffic flows based on portions of flow space other than destination IP prefix (*e.g.*, port number); and (2) the SDX controller's ability to guarantee correct forwarding that is in sync with the advertised BGP routes.

Transit Portal deployments at the University of Wisconsin and at Clemson University both receive a route to the Amazon prefix hosting our Amazon Web Services (AWS) instance. They distribute their routes to AS A and AS B, respectively. These ASes in turn send announcements to the SDX controller, which then selects a best route for the prefix, which it re-advertises to AS C. AS C's outbound traffic then flows through either AS A or AS B, depending on the policies installed at the SDX controller.

AS C, the ISP hosting the client, installs a policy at the SDX that directs all traffic to the Amazon /16 IP prefix via AS A, except for port 80 traffic, which travels via AS B. To demonstrate that the SDX controller ensures that the switch data plane stays in sync with the BGP control plane messages, we induce a withdrawal of the route announcement at AS B (emulating, for example, a failure). At this point, all traffic from the SDX to AWS travels via AS A. Figure ?? shows the traffic patterns resulting from this experiment and the resulting traffic patterns as a result of (1) installation of the application-specific peering policy; (2) the subsequent BGP route withdrawal.

**Wide-area load balancer.** The wide-area load balancer application also demonstrates the ability for a remote network to install a policy at the SDX, even if it is not physically present at the exchange. Figure 4b shows an SDX setup where an AWS tenant hosts destinations in two distinct AWS instances and wishes to balance load across those two destinations. The AWS tenant remotely installs a policy that rewrites the destination IP address for traffic depending on the source IP address of the sender. Initially, traffic from the clients of AS A directed towards the AWS tenant's instances traverses the SDX fabric unchanged and routed out to the Internet via AS B. After the AWS tenant installs the load-balance policy at the SDX, traffic that was initially destined only for AWS instance #1 is now balanced across both of the AWS instances. Figure ?? shows the traffic rates from the resulting experiment and how they evolve when the load balance policy is installed at the SDX. Although this deployment has only one SDX location, in practice the AWS tenant could advertise the same IP prefix via multiple SDX locations as an anycast announcement, thus achieving more control over wide-area load balance from a distributed set of locations.

## 6 Performance Evaluation

We now demonstrate that, under realistic scenarios, the SDX platform scales—in terms of forwarding-table size and compilation time—to hundreds of participants and policies.

### 6.1 Experimental Setup

To evaluate the SDX runtime, we provide realistic inputs to our compiler. We instantiate the SDX runtime with no underlying physical switches because we are not concerned with evaluating forwarding performance. We then install policies for hypothetical SDX participants, varying both their numbers and their policies. We derive policies and topologies from the characteristics of three large IXPs: AMS-IX, LINX, and DEC-IX. We repeat each experiment ten times.

**Emulating real-world IXP topologies.** Based on the characteristics of existing IXPs, we define a few static parameters, including the fraction of participants with multiple ports at the exchange, and the number of prefixes that each participant advertises. For example, at AMS-IX, approximately 1% of the participating ASes announce more than 50% of the total prefixes, and 90% of the ASes combined announce less than 1% of the prefixes. We vary the number of participants and prefixes at the exchange.

**Emulating realistic AS policies at the IXP.** We construct an exchange point with a realistic set of participants and policies, where each participant has a mix of inbound and outbound policies. Inbound policies include inbound traffic engineering, WAN load balancing, and redirection through middleboxes. Outbound policies include application-specific peering, as well as policies that are intended to balance transit costs. Different types of participants may use different types of policies. To approximate this policy assignment, we classify ASes as eyeball, transit, or content, and we sort the ASes in each category by the number of prefixes that they advertise. Since we do not have traffic characteristics, we use advertised prefixes as a rough proxy. Only a subset of participants exchange most of the traffic at the IXPs, and we assume that most policies involve the participants who carry significant amounts of traffic. We assume that the top 15% of eyeball ASes, the top 5% of transit ASes, and a random set of 5% of content ASes install custom policies:

*Content providers.* We assume that content providers tune outbound traffic policies for the top eyeball networks, which serve as destinations for the majority of traffic flows. Thus, for each content provider, we install outbound policies for three randomly chosen top eyeball networks. Occasionally, content providers may wish to redirect incoming requests (*e.g.*, for load balance), so each content provider installs one inbound policy matching on one header field.

*Eyeballs.* We assume that eyeball networks generally tune inbound traffic, and, as a result, most of their policies involve controlling inbound traffic coming from the large content providers. The eyeball networks install inbound policies and match on one randomly selected header field; they do not install any outbound policies. For each eyeball network, we install inbound policies for half of the content providers.

*Transit providers.* Finally, we assume that transit networks have a mix of inbound and outbound traffic-engineering policies to balance load by tuning the entry point. In our experiment, each transit network installs outbound policies for one prefix group for half of the top eyeball networks and installs inbound policies proportional to the number of top content providers. Again, the inbound policies match on one header field that we select at random, and outbound policies match on destination prefix group plus one additional header field.

In the following subsections, we show that the required forwarding rules and compilation time scale proportionally with the total number of policies for each participant.

## 6.2 Forwarding-Table Space

We first evaluate the number of prefix groups to implement a particular SDX policy, given a certain number of participants and prefixes. We then quantify the number of flow rules that result from a given number of prefix groups.

**Number of prefix groups.** We estimate the number of prefix groups (and hence, VNHs) that result when the participant ASes at the SDX apply policies to a certain number of prefixes. When policies involve portions of flow space other than destination IP address, the number of prefix groups can be larger than the number of participants times the number of next-hop IP addresses at the exchange, since the resulting policies can create more forwarding equivalence classes.

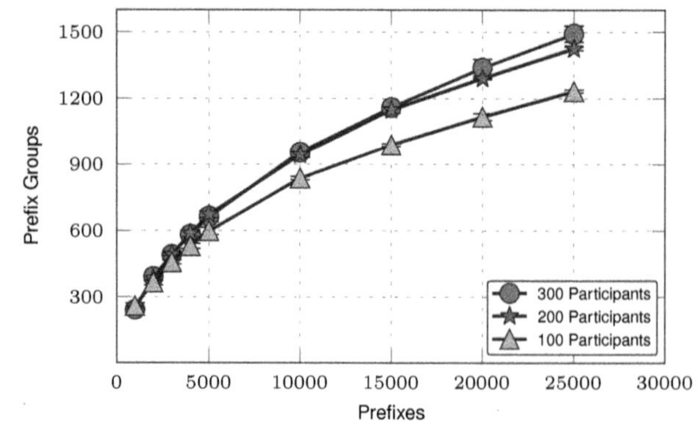


**Figure 6:** *Number of prefix groups as a function of the number of prefixes, for different numbers of participants.*

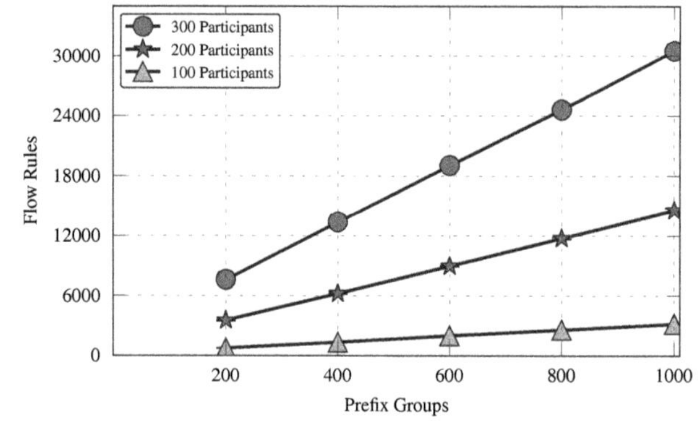


**Figure 7:** *The number of forwarding rules as a function of the number of prefix groups for different number of participants.*

To study the relationship between the number of prefixes and the number of prefix groups, we consider the approximately 300 ASes at AMS-IX which announce more than one prefix (about half of all ASes at the exchange). The results are similar for other large IXPs. Each experiment has two parameters, $N$ and $x$, defining the set of ASes that participate (the top $N$ by prefix count, for $N \in \{100, 200, 300\}$) and the set of prefixes with SDX policies ($|p_x| = x \in [0, 25000]$, selected at random from the default-free routing table). In a given experiment, for AS $i \in [1, \ldots, N]$, let $p_i$ be the set of prefixes announced by AS $i$, and let $p'_i = p_i \cap p_x$. We then run the minimum disjoint subset algorithm over the collection $P' = \{p'_1, \ldots, p'_N\}$, yielding the set of prefix groups.

Figure 6 shows that the number of prefix groups is sub-linear in the number of prefixes. As the number of prefixes to which SDX policies are applied increases, more prefixes are advertised by the same number of participants, thereby increasing the likelihood that the advertised prefixes are part of the same forwarding equivalence class. We also note that the number of prefix groups is significantly smaller than the number of prefixes, and that the ratio of prefix groups to prefixes decreases as the number of prefixes increases, indicating good scaling properties.

**Number of forwarding rules.** Figure 7 shows how the number of forwarding rules varies as we increase the number of prefix groups, for different numbers of participants. We select the number of prefix groups based on our analysis of the prefix groups that might appear in a typical IXP (Figure 6). We run the experiment as described above, selecting participant ASes according to common

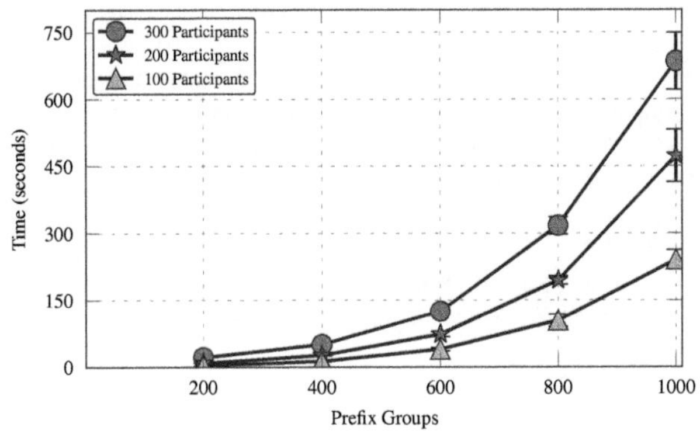


**Figure 8:** *Compilation time as a function of the number of prefix groups, for different numbers of participants.*

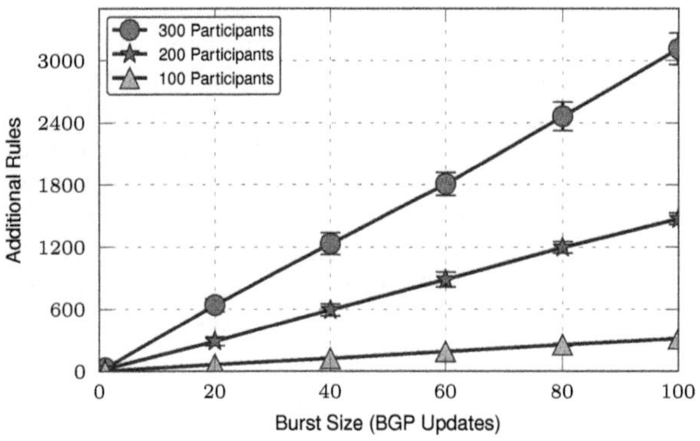


**Figure 9:** *Number of additional forwarding rules.*

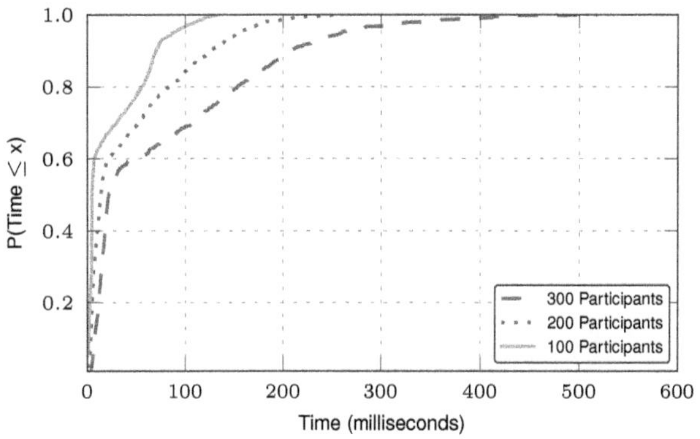


**Figure 10:** *Time to process a single BGP update for various participants.*

policies at IXPs. The number of forwarding rules increases roughly linearly with the number of prefix groups. Because each prefix group operates on a disjoint portion of the flow space, the increase in forwarding rules is linear in the number of prefix groups.

## 6.3 Compilation Time

We measure the compilation time for two scenarios: (1) *initial compilation time*, which measures the time to compile the initial set of policies to the resulting forwarding rules; and (2) *incremental compilation time*, which measures how long it takes to recompute when changes occur.

**Initial compilation time.** Figure 8 shows how the time to compute low-level forwarding rules from higher-level policies varies as we increase both the number of prefix groups and IXP participants. The time to compute the forwarding rules is on the order of several minutes for typical numbers of prefix groups and participants. The results also show that compilation time increases roughly quadratically with the number of prefix groups. The compilation time increases more quickly than linearly because, as the number of prefix groups increases, the interactions between policies of pairs of participants at the SDX also increases. The time for the SDX to compute VNHs increases non-linearly as the number of participants and prefix groups increases. We observed that for 1,000 prefix groups and 100 participants, VNH computation took about five minutes.

As discussed in Section 4.3, the SDX controller achieves faster compilation by memoizing the results of partial policy compilations. Supporting caching for 300 participants at the SDX and 1,000 prefix groups could require a cache of about 4.5 GB. Although this requirement may seem large, it is on the order of the amount of memory required for a route server in a large operational IXP today.

**Incremental compilation time.** Recall that in addition to computing an initial set of forwarding table rules, the SDX controller must recompile them whenever the best BGP route for a prefix changes or when any participant updates its policy. We now evaluate the benefits of the optimizations that we discussed in Section 4.3 in terms of the savings in compilation time. When new BGP updates arrive at the controller, the controller must recompute VNH IP addresses for the affected routes to establish new prefix groups.

Figure 9 shows the number of additional rules that are generated when a "burst" of BGP updates of a certain size arrives. These rules must reside in the forwarding table until the SDX controller recomputes the minimum disjoint set. The figure represents a worst-case scenario, whereby each BGP update results in a change to the best path and, hence, an additional VNH in the table, causing a number of additional forwarding rules that depends on the number of participants with policies installed. In practice, as we discussed in Section 4.3, not every BGP update induces changes in forwarding table entries. When a BGP update arrives, the SDX controller installs additional flow table rules for the affected flows and computes a new optimized table *in the background* to ultimately coalesce these flows into the smaller, minimal forwarding tables. As shown in Figure 10, re-computing the tables takes less than 100 milliseconds most of the time.

# 7 Related Work

We briefly describe related work in SDN exchange points, interdomain route control, and policy languages for SDNs.

**SDN-based exchange points.** The most closely related work is Google's Cardigan project [22], which shares our broad goal of using SDN to enable innovation at IXPs. Cardigan runs a route server based on RouteFlow [17] and uses an OpenFlow switch to enforce security and routing policies. The Cardigan project is developing a logical SDN-based exchange point that is physically distributed across multiple locations. Unlike the SDX in this paper, Cardigan does not provide a general controller for composing participant policies, offer a framework that allows IXP participants to write policies in a high-level language, or introduce techniques for scaling to handle a large number of participants and policies.

**Interdomain route control.** Previous work on applying SDN to interdomain routing has focused on how to use the separation of data and control planes to improve the manageability of routing within a single AS [8, 9]. Similarly, earlier work such as the Routing Control Platform (RCP) developed a BGP route controller for influencing route selection within a single AS and enabled various functions, such as re-routing traffic within an AS in the event of attack or traffic surge [3]. These systems apply SDN to help operators route interdomain traffic more efficiently within an AS, but they do not provide a way for *multiple* ASes to independently define policies which can then be composed into a single coherent forwarding policy for forwarding traffic *between* ASes. Previous work has also proposed outsourcing end-to-end path selection to third parties with an SDN controller [10, 11], but unlike SDX, these systems require ASes to modify their existing routing infrastructure.

**Policy languages for SDNs.** SDX takes advantage of recent advances in programming languages for SDNs that allow operators to express policies at a higher level of abstraction than flow rules [6, 12, 20]. In particular, Pyretic provides both topology abstraction and composition operators that we take advantage of when implementing the SDX policy compiler. It is worth pointing out, of course, that these languages only make it possible to implement something like the SDX—as discussed in Section 5, Pyretic is merely the language that we use to encode SDX policies, but the controller must first perform syntactic transformation and incorporate BGP routing information to ensure forwarding according to AS policies that is congruent with the BGP routes that the SDX participants advertise.

## 8 Conclusion

SDX can break the logjam on long-standing problems in interdomain routing by enabling entirely new policies with fine-grained control over packet handling. The SDX supports policies that match and act on multiple header fields, and allow ASes to have remote control over the traffic. The SDX addresses many of the challenges of an SDN-enabled IXP. The virtual switch abstraction ensures that ASes cannot see or control aspects of interdomain routing outside of their purview. Policy compilation allows the SDX controller to combine policies, resolving conflicts that arise between participants. The SDX policy compilation algorithm ensures that forwarding is consistent with BGP route advertisements; various optimizations ensure that SDX policies can be efficiently compiled to flow rules; and that these rules can be updated quickly when policies or BGP routes change. We have run experiments with the SDX in both controlled settings and in the wide area, and we have released a preliminary version of the SDX controller [18]. In ongoing work, we are working with a large regional IXP to deploy OpenFlow switches and our SDX controller for an initial deployment of interdomain routing applications beyond BGP.

As demand grows for more flexible data-plane functionality, we believe that BGP should also evolve to support richer patterns (beyond destination prefix) and actions (beyond selecting a single nexthop). We also envision that participant ASes might eventually write policies not only to control how traffic flows between ASes, but also to control how traffic flows through middleboxes (and other cloud-hosted services) along the path between source and destination, thereby enabling "service chaining" through middleboxes.

## Acknowledgments

We thank our shepherd Walter Willinger, Hyojoon Kim, João Luís Sobrinho, Jennifer Gossels, Darrell Newcomb, Michael Schapira, and the anonymous reviewers for comments. This research was supported by NSF awards CNS-1040705, CNS-1040838, CNS-1162112, CNS-1261462, and CNS-1261357. We thank Internet2 for their support and recognition with an Internet Innovation Award, the organizations that host Transit Portal nodes, and the GENI Project Office for supporting our ongoing deployment efforts.

## References

[1] B. Ager, N. Chatzis, A. Feldmann, N. Sarrar, S. Uhlig, and W. Willinger. Anatomy of a large European IXP. In *Proc. ACM SIGCOMM*, 2012.

[2] BIRD. `http://bird.network.cz/`.

[3] M. Caesar, D. Caldwell, N. Feamster, J. Rexford, A. Shaikh, and J. van der Merwe. Design and implementation of a routing control platform. In *Proc. USENIX NSDI*, 2005.

[4] Euro-IX Public Resources. `https://www.euro-ix.net/resources`.

[5] ExaBGP. `https://github.com/Exa-Networks/exabgp`.

[6] N. Foster, A. Guha, M. Reitblatt, A. Story, M. J. Freedman, N. P. Katta, C. Monsanto, J. Reich, J. Rexford, C. Schlesinger, A. Story, and D. Walker. Languages for software-defined networks. *IEEE Communications Magazine*, 51(2):128–134, 2013.

[7] B. Heller, N. Handigol, V. Jeyakumar, B. Lantz, and N. McKeown. Reproducible network experiments using container based emulation. In *Proc. ACM CoNEXT*, December 2012.

[8] C.-Y. Hong, S. Kandula, R. Mahajan, M. Zhang, V. Gill, M. Nanduri, and R. Wattenhofer. Achieving high utilization with software-driven WAN. In *Proc. ACM SIGCOMM*, 2013.

[9] S. Jain, A. Kumar, S. Mandal, J. Ong, L. Poutievski, A. Singh, S. Venkata, J. Wanderer, J. Zhou, M. Zhu, J. Zolla, U. Hölzle, S. Stuart, and A. Vahdat. B4: Experience with a globally-deployed software defined WAN. In *Proc. ACM SIGCOMM*, 2013.

[10] V. Kotronis, X. Dimitropoulos, and B. Ager. Outsourcing the routing control logic: Better Internet routing based on SDN principles. In *Proc. HotNets Workshop*, pages 55–60, 2012.

[11] K. Lakshminarayanan, I. Stoica, and S. Shenker. Routing as a service. Technical Report UCB/CSD-04-1327, UC Berkeley, 2004.

[12] C. Monsanto, J. Reich, N. Foster, J. Rexford, and D. Walker. Composing software defined networks. In *Proc. USENIX NSDI*, 2013.

[13] Noviflow. `http://noviflow.com/`.

[14] Quagga. `http://www.nongnu.org/quagga/`.

[15] J. Rexford, J. Wang, Z. Xiao, and Y. Zhang. BGP routing stability of popular destinations. In *Proc. Internet Measurment Workshop*, pages 197–202. ACM, 2002.

[16] RIPE Routing Information Service (RIS). `http://www.ripe.net/ris`.

[17] C. E. Rothenberg, M. R. Nascimento, M. R. Salvador, C. N. A. Corrêa, S. Cunha de Lucena, and R. Raszuk. Revisiting routing control platforms with the eyes and muscles of software-defined networking. In *Proc. HotSDN Workshop*, pages 13–18. ACM, 2012.

[18] SDX Controller. `https://github.com/sdn-ixp/sdx-platform`.

[19] V. Valancius, N. Feamster, J. Rexford, and A. Nakao. Wide-area route control for distributed services. In *Proc. USENIX Annual Technical Conference*, 2010.

[20] A. Voellmy, H. Kim, and N. Feamster. Procera: A language for high-level reactive network control. In *Proc. HotSDN Workshop*, 2012.

[21] R. Wang, D. Butnariu, and J. Rexford. OpenFlow-based server load balancing gone wild. In *Proc. HotICE Workshop*, March 2011.

[22] S. Whyte. Project CARDIGAN An SDN Controlled Exchange Fabric. `https://www.nanog.org/meetings/nanog57/presentations/Wednesday/wed.lightning3.whyte.sdn.controlled.exchange.fabric.pdf`, 2012.

[23] B. Zhang, V. Kambhampati, M. Lad, D. Massey, and L. Zhang. Identifying BGP routing table transfer. In *Proc. SIGCOMM MineNet Workshop*, August 2005.

# A Network-State Management Service

Peng Sun (Princeton) Ratul Mahajan Jennifer Rexford (Princeton)
Lihua Yuan Ming Zhang Ahsan Arefin

Microsoft

**Abstract—** We present Statesman, a network-state management service that allows multiple network management applications to operate independently, while maintaining network-wide safety and performance invariants. Network state captures various aspects of the network such as which links are alive and how switches are forwarding traffic. Statesman uses three views of the network state. In *observed state*, it maintains an up-to-date view of the actual network state. Applications read this state and propose state changes based on their individual goals. Using a model of dependencies among state variables, Statesman merges these *proposed states* into a *target state* that is guaranteed to maintain the safety and performance invariants. It then updates the network to the target state. Statesman has been deployed in ten Microsoft Azure datacenters for several months, and three distinct applications have been built on it. We use the experience from this deployment to demonstrate how Statesman enables each application to meet its goals, while maintaining network-wide invariants.

**Categories and Subject Descriptors:**
C.2.1 [**Computer-Communication Networks**]: Network Architecture and Design;
C.2.3 [**Computer-Communication Networks**]: Network Operations—*network management*

**Keywords:**
Network state; software-defined networking; datacenter network

## 1. Introduction

Today's planetary-scale services (e.g., search, social networking, and cloud computing) depend on large datacenter networks (DCNs). Keeping these networks running smoothly is difficult, due to the sheer number of physical devices, and the dynamic nature of the environment. At any given moment, multiple switches experience component failures, are brought down for planned maintenance or saving energy, are upgraded with new firmware, or are reconfigured to adapt to prevailing traffic demand. In response, DCN operators have developed an array of automated systems for managing the *traffic* (e.g., traffic engineering [12, 13], server load balancing [25], and network virtualization [17]) and the *infrastructure* (e.g., hardware power control for failure mitigation or energy saving [10, 30], switch firmware upgrade, and switch configuration management [4, 5]).


*SIGCOMM'14,* August 17–22, 2014, Chicago, Illinois, USA.
Copyright 2014 ACM 978-1-4503-2836-4/14/08 ...$15.00.
http://dx.doi.org/10.1145/2619239.2626298.

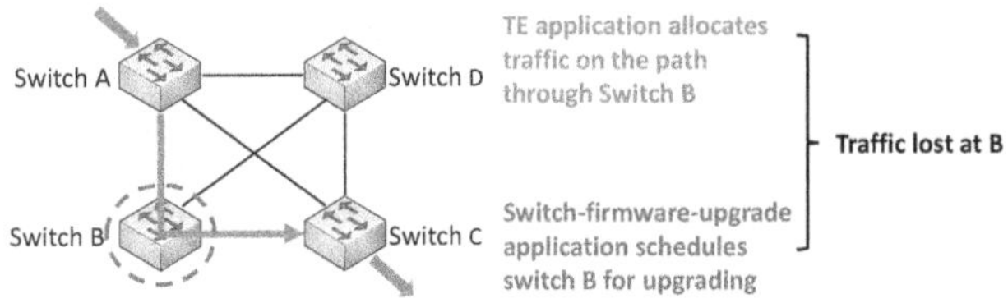


**Figure 1: Example of an application conflict**

Each management application is highly sophisticated in its own right, usually requiring several years to design, develop, and deploy. It typically takes the form of a "control loop" that measures the current state of the network, performs a computation, and then reconfigures the network. For example, a traffic engineering (TE) application measures the current traffic demand and network topology, solves an optimization problem, and then changes the routing configuration to match demand. These applications are complicated because they must work correctly even in the presence of failures, variable delays in communicating with a distributed set of devices, and frequent changes in network conditions.

Designing and running a single network management application is challenging enough; large DCNs must simultaneously run multiple applications—created by different teams, each reading and writing some part of the network state. For instance, both a TE application and an application to mitigate link failures need to run continuously to, respectively, adjust the routing configuration continuously and detect and resolve failures quickly.

These applications can conflict with each other, even if they interact with the network at different levels, such as establishing network paths, assigning IP addresses to interfaces, or installing firmware on switches. One application can inadvertently affect the operation of another. As an example in Figure 1, suppose a TE application wants to create a tunnel through the switch $B$, while a firmware-upgrade application wants to upgrade $B$. Depending on which action happens first, either the TE application fails to create the tunnel (because $B$ is already down), or the already-established tunnel ultimately drops traffic during the firmware upgrade.

Running multiple management applications also raises the risk of network-wide failures because their complex interactions make it hard to reason about their combined effect. Figure 2 shows an example where one application wants to shut down switch $AggB$ to upgrade its firmware, while another wants to shut down switch $AggA$ to mitigate packet corruption. While each application acting alone is fine, their joint actions would disconnect the ToRs (top-of-rack). To prevent such disasters, it is imperative to ensure that the collective actions of the applications do not violate certain network-wide invariants, which specify basic safety and performance requirements for the network. For instance, a pod of servers must not be disconnected from the rest of the datacenter, and there must be some minimum bandwidth between each pair of pods.

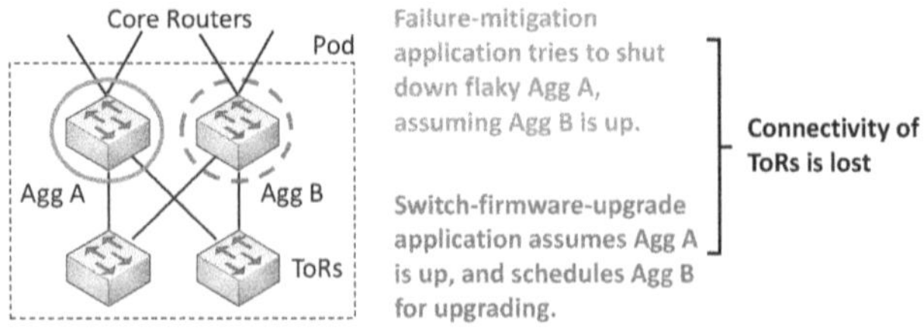


**Figure 2: Example of a safety violation**

DCN operators could conceivably circumvent the problems that stem from running multiple applications by developing a single application that performs *all* functions, e.g., combining TE, firmware upgrade, and failure mitigation. However, this monolithic application would be highly complex, and worse, it would need to be extended repeatedly as new needs arise. Thus, DCN operators need a way to keep the applications separate.

Another option is to have explicit coordination among applications. Corybantic [23] is one recent proposal that follows this approach. While coordination may be useful for a subset of applications, using it as a general solution to the problem of multi-application co-existence imposes high overhead on applications. It would require each application to understand the intended network changes of all others. To make matters worse, every time an application is changed or a new one is developed, DCN operators would need to test again, and potentially retrofit some existing applications, in order to ensure that all of them continue to co-exist safely.

We argue that network management applications should be built and run in a loosely coupled manner, without explicit or implicit dependencies on each other, and conflict resolution and invariant enforcement should be handled by a separate management system. This architecture would simplify application development, and its simplicity would boost network stability and predictability. It may forgo some performance gains possible through tight coupling and joint optimization. However, as noted above, such coupling greatly increases application complexity. Further, since applications may have competing objectives, a management system to resolve conflicts and maintain invariants would be needed anyway. We thus believe that loose coupling of applications is a worthwhile tradeoff in exchange for significant reduction in complexity.

In this paper, we present Statesman, a network-state management service that supports multiple loosely-coupled management applications in large DCNs. Each application operates by reading and writing some part of the network state at its own pace, and Statesman functions as the conflict resolver and invariant guardian. Our design introduces two main ideas that simplify the design and deployment of network management applications:

**Three views of network state (observed, proposed, target):** In order to prevent conflicts and invariant violations, applications cannot change the state of the network directly. Instead, each application applies its own logic to the network's *observed* state to generate *proposed* states that may change one or more state variables. Statesman merges all proposed states into one *target* state. In the merging process, it examines all proposed states to resolve conflicts and ensures that the target state satisfies an extensible set of network-wide invariants. Our design is inspired by version control systems like `git`. Each application corresponds to a different `git` user and (i) the observed state corresponds to the code each user "pulls", (ii) the proposed state corresponds to the code the user wants to "push", and (iii) the target state corresponds to the merged code that is ultimately stored back in the shared repository.

**Dependency model of state variables:** Prior work on abstracting network state for applications models the state as independent variable-value pairs [18, 19]. However, this model does not contain enough semantic knowledge about how various state variables are related, which hinders detection of conflicts and potential invariant violations. For example, a tunnel cannot direct traffic over a path that includes a switch that is administratively down. To ensure safe merging of proposed states, Statesman uses a *dependency model* to capture the domain-specific dependencies among state variables.

Statesman has been deployed in ten datacenters of Microsoft Azure for several months. It currently manages over 1.5 million state variables from links and switches across the globe. We have also deployed two management applications—switch firmware upgrade and link failure mitigation, and a third one—inter-datacenter TE—is undergoing pre-deployment testing. The diverse functionalities of these applications showcase how Statesman can safely support multiple applications, without hurting each other or the network. We also show that these benefits come with reasonably low overhead. For instance, the latency for conflict resolution and invariant checking is under 10 seconds even in the largest DCN with 394K state variables. We believe that our experience with Statesman can inform the design of future management systems for large production networks.

## 2. Statesman Model

In this section, we provide more details on the model of network state underlying Statesman, and how applications use that model.

### 2.1 Three Views of Network State

Although management applications have different functionalities, they typically follow a control loop of reading some aspects of the network state, running some computation on the state, and accordingly changing the network. One could imagine that each application reads and writes states to the network devices directly.

However, direct interaction between the network and applications is undesirable for two reasons. First, it cannot ensure that individual applications or their collective actions will not violate network-wide invariants. Second, reliably reading and writing network state is complex because of response-time variances and link or switch failures. When a command to a switch takes a long time, the application has to decide when to retry, how many times, and when to give up. When a command fails, the application has to parse the error code and decide how to react.

Given issues above, Statesman abstracts the network state as multiple variable-value pairs. Further, it maintains three different types of views of network state. Two of these are *observed state* (OS) and *target state* (TS). The OS is (a latest view of) the actual state of the network, which Statesman keeps up-to-date. Applications read the OS to learn about current network state. The TS is the desired state of the network, and Statesman is responsible for updating the network to match the TS. Any success or failure of updating the network towards the TS will be (eventually) reflected into the OS, from where the applications will learn about the prevailing network conditions.

The OS and TS views are not sufficient for resolving conflicts and enforcing invariants. If applications directly write to the TS, the examples in Figure 1 and 2 can still happen. We thus introduce the third type of view called *proposed state* (PS) that captures the state desired by applications. Each application writes its own PS.

Statesman examines the various PSes and detects conflicts among them and with the TS. It also validates them against a set of network-wide invariants. The invariants capture the basic safety and performance requirements for the network (e.g., the network should be physically connected and each pair of server pods should be able to survive a single-switch failure). The invariants are independent of what applications are running. Only non-conflicting and invariant-compliant PSes are accepted and merged into the TS.

## 2.2 Dependency Model of State Variables

Applications read and write different state variables of the network, e.g., hardware power, switch configuration, switch routing, and multi-switch tunneling. Statesman thus provides the state variables at multiple levels of granularity for applications' needs (more details are covered in §4, and Table 2 lists some examples).

But state variables are not independent. The "writability" of one state variable can depend on the values of other state variables. For example, when a link interface is configured to use the traditional control-plane protocol (e.g., BGP or OSPF), OpenFlow rules cannot be installed on that interface. In another example, when the firmware of a switch is being upgraded, its configuration cannot be changed and tunnels cannot be established through it. Thus, when proposing new values of state variables, conflicts can arise because a state variable in one application's PS may become unchangeable due to some *dependent* state variables in another application's PS. Requiring applications to understand the complex cross-variable dependency will go against our goal of running them in a loosely coupled manner. For instance, it will be difficult for a TE application to have to consider how one specific switch configuration affects its operation.

Therefore, Statesman does not treat network state as a collection of independent variables but includes a model of dependencies among them. These dependencies are used when checking for conflicts and invariant violations. Based on the dependency model, Statesman also exposes to applications the "controllability" of each state variable as an additional logical variable. Thus, an application can read only the state variables of interest and their controllability variables to decide whether it is able to propose new values for those variables of interest. For example, a TE application can read the "path" variable (i.e., a tunnel through multiple switches) and whether it is currently controllable, which is computed by Statesman based on various hardware and routing configurations of the switches along the path; the TE application does not need to reason about the related hardware and routing configurations itself.

## 2.3 Application Workflow

In the observed-proposed-target model, the workflow of management applications is simple. Each application reads the OS, runs its computational logic, and writes a newly generated PS. Statesman generates the new TS after resolving conflicts and invariant violations in the PSes and merging the accepted ones.

In this model, some application proposals may be rejected. Handling this rejection does not impose extra overhead on applications; even if interactions with the network were not mediated by Statesman, applications have to be prepared to be unable to update the network to the desired state (e.g., due to failures during the update process). When Statesman rejects a proposal, applications get detailed feedback on the reason for rejection (§5), at which point applications can propose a new PS in an informed manner.

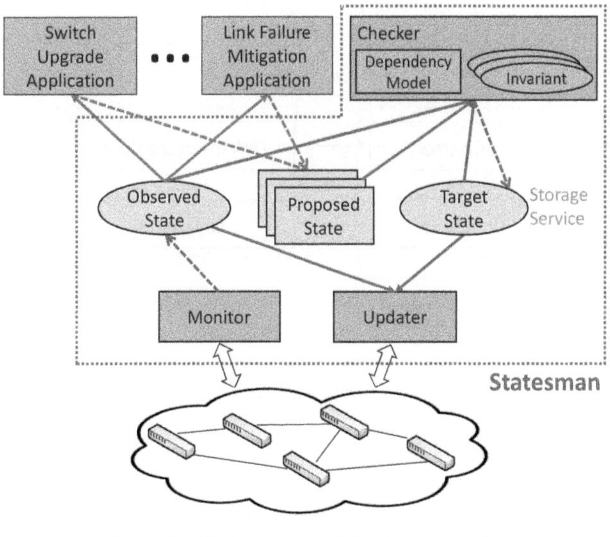


**Figure 3: Statesman architecture overview**

| Component | Input | Output |
|---|---|---|
| Monitor | Switch/link data | OS |
| Checker | OS<br>PSes<br>TS | TS |
| Updater | OS<br>TS | Switch update commands |

**Table 1: Input and output of each component in Statesman**

Per our desire for loose coupling, applications make proposals independently. It is thus possible that PSes of two applications frequently conflict or we do not compute a network state that satisfies all applications (even though such a state exists). In our experience with Statesman (so far), such cases are not common. Thus, we believe that the simplicity of loose coupling outweighs the complexity of tight coupling. In cases where coordination among two applications is highly beneficial, it may be done out of band such that applications make proposals after consulting each other. Done this way, most applications and the system as a whole stay simple, and the complexity cost of coordination is borne only in parts that benefit the most from the coordination.

# 3. System Overview

Figure 3 shows the architecture of Statesman. It has four components: storage service, checker, monitor, and updater. We outline the role of each below. The following sections present more details.

**Storage service** is at the center of the system. It persistently stores the state variables of OS, PS, and TS and offers a highly-available, read-write interface for other components and applications. It also handles all data availability and consistency issues, which allows all other components to be completely stateless—in each round of their operations, they just read the latest values of the needed state variables. This stateless mode of operation simplifies the design of the other components.

The checker, monitor, and updater independently interact with the storage service, and the latter two also interact with the network. Table 1 summarizes the input and output of each component.

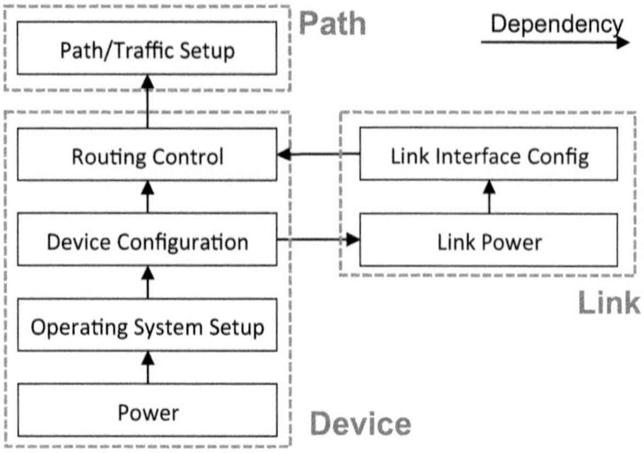


**Figure 4: Network state dependency model**

**Checker** plays a pivotal role of generating the TS. After reading the OS, PSes, and TS from the storage service, the checker first examines whether some PSes are applicable with respect to the latest OS (e.g., the proposed change may have already been made or cannot be made at all due to a failure). It then detects conflicts among PSes with the state dependency model and resolves them with one of two configurable mechanisms: last-writer-wins or priority-based locking. After merging the valid and non-conflicting PSes into the TS, the checker examines the TS for operator-specified invariants. It writes the TS to the storage service only if the TS complies with the invariants. It also writes the acceptance or rejection results of the PSes to the storage service, so applications can learn about the outcomes and react accordingly.

**Monitor** periodically collects the current network state from the switches and links, transforms it into OS variables, and writes the variables to the storage service. In addition to making it easy for other components and applications to learn about current network state, the monitor also shields them from the heterogeneity among devices. Based on the switch vendor and the supported technologies, it uses the corresponding protocol (e.g., SNMP or OpenFlow) to collect the network statistics, and it translates protocol-specific data to protocol-agnostic state variables. Other components and applications use these abstract variables without worrying about the specifics of the underlying infrastructure.

**Updater** reads the OS and TS and translates their difference into update commands that are then sent to the network. The updater is memoryless—it applies the latest difference between the OS and TS without regard to what happened in the past. Like the monitor, the updater handles how to update heterogeneous devices with a command template pool, and allows other components and applications to work with device- and protocol-agnostic state variables.

## 4. Managing Network State

We now describe the various aspects of Statesman in more details, starting with the network-state data model. We use the examples in Table 2 to illustrate how we build the state dependency model, and how to use and extend the model.

### 4.1 The State Dependency Model

Managing a DCN involves multiple levels of control. To perform the final function of carrying traffic, the DCN needs to be properly powered and configured. Statesman aims to support operations in the complete process of bringing up a large DCN from scratch to normal operations. In order to capture the relationship among the state variables at different levels of the management process, we use the state dependency model of Figure 4. We use the process of bootstrapping a DCN as an example to explain this model.

| Entity | Level in dependency | Example state variables | Permission |
|---|---|---|---|
| Path | Path/traffic setup | Switches on path<br>MPLS or VLAN config | ReadWrite<br>ReadWrite |
| Link | Link interface config | IP assignment<br>Control plane setup | ReadWrite<br>ReadWrite |
| | Link power | Interface admin status<br>Interface oper status | ReadWrite<br>ReadOnly |
| | N/A (counters) | Traffic load<br>Packet drop rate | ReadOnly<br>ReadOnly |
| Device | Routing control | Flow-link routing rules<br>Link weight allocation | ReadWrite<br>ReadWrite |
| | Device configuration | Mgmt. interface setup<br>OpenFlow agent status | ReadWrite<br>ReadWrite |
| | Operating system setup | Firmware version<br>Boot image | ReadWrite<br>ReadWrite |
| | Power | Admin power status<br>Power unit reachability | ReadWrite<br>ReadOnly |
| | N/A (counters) | CPU utilization<br>Memory utilization | ReadOnly<br>ReadOnly |

**Table 2: Example network state variables**

At the bottom of the dependency model is the power state of network devices. With the power cable properly plugged in and electricity properly distributed to the switches, we then need to control which switch operating system (i.e., firmware) runs. Running a functioning firmware on a switch is a prerequisite for managing switch configuration, e.g., use switch vendor's API to configure the management interface, boot up compatible OpenFlow agent, etc.

With device configuration states ready, we are able to control the link interfaces on the switch now. The fundamental state variable of a link is its being up or down. The configuration of a link interface follows when the link is ready to be up. There are various link-interface configuration states, such as IP assignment, VLAN setup, ECMP-group assignment, etc. Consider an example of control plane setup where a link interface can be configured to use the OpenFlow protocol or traditional protocols like BGP. For the chosen option, we need to set it up: either an OpenFlow agent needs to boot and take control of the link, or the BGP session needs to start with proper policies. These control plane states of the link determine whether and how the switch's routing can be controlled.

We can manage the routing states of the switches when all the dependent states are correct. We represent the routing state in a data structure of the flow-link pairs, which is agnostic to the supported routing protocols. For example, the routing states can map to the routing rules in OpenFlow or the prefix-route announcement or withdrawal in BGP. When applications change the value of the routing state variable, Statesman (specifically the updater) automatically translates the value to appropriate control-plane commands.

One level higher is the *path* state which controls tunnels through multiple switches. Creating a tunnel and assigning traffic along the path depend on all switches on the path having their routing states ready to manage. Again, Statesman is responsible for translating the path's states into the routing states of all switches on the path, and the application only needs to read or write the path states.

## 4.2 Using and Extending the Model

For simplicity, applications should not be required to understand all the state variables and their complex dependencies. They should be able to simply work with the subset of variables that they need to manage based on their goals. For instance, a firmware-upgrade application should be able to focus on only the *DeviceFirmwareVersion* variable. However, this variable depends on lower-level variables such as switch power state whose impact cannot be completely ignored; firmware cannot be upgraded if the switch is down.

We find that it suffices to represent the impact of these dependencies by using a logical variable that we call *controllability* and exposing it to applications. This boolean-valued variable denotes whether the parent state variable is currently controllable, and its value is computed by Statesman based on lower-level dependencies. For instance, *DeviceFirmwareVersion* is controllable only if the values of variables such as switch's power and admin states are appropriate. Now, the firmware-upgrade application can simply work with *DeviceFirmwareVersion* and *DeviceFirmwareVersionIsControllable* variables to finish its job.

To give another concrete example, the variable *DeviceConfigIsControllable* tells whether applications can change various state variables of switch configuration, such as the management interface setup. The value of *DeviceConfigIsControllable* is calculated based on whether the switch is powered up, whether the switch can be reachable via SSH/Telnet from the management network (indicating the firmware is functioning), and whether the switch is healthy according to the health criterion (e.g., CPU/memory utilizations are not continuously 100% for certain amount of time). Similarly, links have *LinkAdminPowerIsControllable* calculated with the *DeviceConfigIsControllable* of the two switches on the link's ends.

Exposing just the controllability variables makes the dependency model extensible. The functions calculating the controllability are implemented in the storage service. When a new state variable is added to Statesman, we just need to place it in the dependency model, i.e., find what state variables will be dependent of the new one. Then we modify the controllability functions of corresponding state variables to consider its impact. For applications that are not interested in the new variable, no modifications are needed.

# 5. Checking Network State

The checker plays a pivotal role in Statesman. It needs to resolve conflicts among applications and enforce network-wide invariants. Its design also faces scalability challenges when handling large networks. We first explain the state checking process and then describe techniques for boosting scalability of the checker. Figure 5 outlines the checker's operation.

## 5.1 Resolving Conflicts

Multiple types of conflicts can occur in the network state due to the dynamic nature of DCNs and uncoordinated applications:

- **TS–OS.** The TS can conflict with the latest OS when changes in the network render some state variables uncontrollable, although they have new values in the TS. For instance, if the OpenFlow agent on a switch crashes, which is reflected as *DeviceAgentBootStatus=Down* in the OS, any routing changes in the TS cannot be applied.
- **PS–OS.** When the checker examines a PS, the OS may have changed from the time that the PS was generated, and some variables in the PS may not be controllable anymore. For example, a PS could contain the new value of a *LinkEndAddress* variable, but when the checker reads the PS, the link may have been shut down for maintenance.
- **PS–TS.** The TS is essentially the accumulation of all accepted PSes in the past. A PS can conflict with the TS due to an accepted PS from another application. For example, assume that a firmware-upgrade application wants to upgrade a switch and proposes to bring it down; its PS is accepted and merged into the TS. Now, when a TE application proposes to change the switch's routing state, it conflicts with the TS even though the switch is online (i.e., no conflict with the OS).

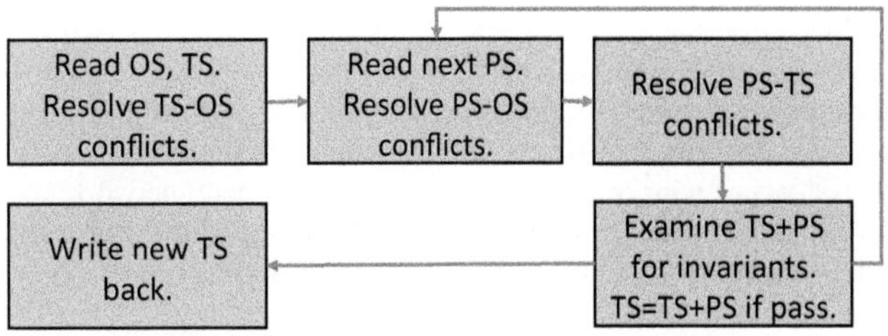


**Figure 5: Flow of the checker's operation**

The first two types of conflicts are because of the changing OS, which makes some variables in the PS or TS uncontrollable. To detect these conflicts, the checker reads the controllability values from the OS, which are calculated by the storage service based on the dependency model when relevant variable values are updated. It then locates the uncontrollable variables in the PS or TS. To resolve TS–OS conflicts, we introduce a flag called *SkipUpdate* for each variable in the TS. If set, the updater will bypass the network update of the state variable, thus temporarily ignoring the target value to resolve the conflict. The checker will clear the flag once the state variable is controllable again.

For uncontrollable state variables in a PS, the checker removes them from the PS, i.e., rejecting the part of PS that is inapplicable on the current network. The choice of partial rejection is a tradeoff between application's progress and potential side-effects of accepting a partial PS. The asynchrony between the application's and the checker's views of the OS is normal. By rejecting the whole PS due to a small fraction of conflicting variables, Statesman will be too conservative and will hinder application progress. We thus allow partial rejection. We have not yet observed any negative consequences in our deployment from this choice. In the future, we will extend the PS data structure such that applications can group variables. When a variable in a group is uncontrollable, the entire group is rejected, but other groups can still be accepted.

For PS–TS conflicts, which are caused by the conflicting application proposals, Statesman supports an extensible set of conflict resolution mechanisms. It currently offers two mechanisms. The basic one is last-writer-wins, in which the checker favors the value of state variable from the newer PS. The more advanced mechanism is priority-based locking. Statesman provides two levels of priorities of locks for each switch and link. Applications can acquire a low-priority or a high-priority lock before proposing a PS. In the presence of a lock, applications other than the lock holder cannot change the state variables of the switch or link; however, the high-priority lock can override the low-priority one. The choice of the conflict resolution mechanism is not system-wide and can be configured at the level of individual switches and links.

Although simple, these two conflict-resolution strategies have been proven sufficient for the applications that we have built and deployed thus far. In fact, we find from our traces that last-writer-wins is good enough most of the time since it is rare for two applications to compete for the same state variable head-to-head. For our intra-datacenter infrastructure, we configure the checker with the last-writer-wins resolution; for our inter-datacenter network, we have enabled the priority-based locking. If needed, additional resolution strategies (e.g., based on application identities) can be easily added to Statesman.

### 5.2 Choosing and Checking Invariants

Network-wide invariants are intended to ensure the infrastructure's operational stability in the face of application bugs or undesired effects of collective actions of multiple applications. They should capture minimum safety and performance requirements, independent of which applications are currently running.

**Choosing invariants:** This choice must balance two criterion. First, the invariant should suffice to safeguard the basic operations of the network—as long as it is not violated, most services using the network would continue to function normally. Second, the invariant should not be so stringent that it interferes with application goals. For instance, an invariant that all switches should be operational is likely too strict and interferes with a firmware-upgrade application.

Following the criterion above, we currently use two invariants in the checker. Both are application-agnostic and relate to the topological properties of the network. The first invariant considers network connectivity. It requires that every pair of ToR switches in the same datacenter are (topologically) connected and that every ToR is connected to the border routers of its DCN (for WAN connectivity). Here, we ignore the routing configurations on the switches (which could be that two ToRs cannot communicate) because applications can intentionally partition a DCN at the routing level for multi-tenant isolation.

The second invariant considers network capacity. We define the capacity between two ToRs in the same datacenter as maximum possible traffic flow between them based on the network topology. The invariant is that the capacity between $p\%$ of ToR pairs should be at least $t\%$ of their baseline, when all links are functional. The values of $p$ and $t$ should be based on level of capacity redundancy in the DCN, tolerance of the hosted services to reduced capacity, and implications of blocking a management application that violates the invariant. We currently use $p = 99$ and $t = 50$, i.e., 99% of the ToR pairs must have at least 50% of the baseline capacity.

Although Statesman currently maintains only two invariants, the set of invariants is extensible. As explained below, the invariant checking is implemented as a boolean function over a graph data structure that has the network topology and all state variables. It is straightforward to add more invariants by implementing new functions with the same interface. For example, some networks may add an invariant that requires the absence of loops and blackholes, which can be checked using the routing states of the switches.

**Checking invariants:** When checking whether the TS obeys the invariants, the checker first creates a base network graph using variable values from the OS. Then, it translates the difference between a variable's observed and target values into an operation on the network graph, e.g., bringing a switch offline, changing the routing state to the target value, etc. Finally, the invariant checking functions are run with the new network graph.

The invariant checking is invoked in two places. The first is when the checker reads the TS from the storage service. The TS was compliant when written but can be in violation when read due to changes in the network (i.e., the OS). While running the invariant checking as described above, the checker clears or sets the *SkipUpdate* flags in the TS respective of its compliance status.

The second place is when the checker tries to merge a PS into the TS after conflict resolution. The checker analyzes TS+PS, as if the PS was merged into the TS. If TS+PS passes the check, the PS is accepted and merged into the TS. Otherwise, the PS is rejected.

The acceptance or rejection (and reasons) for each PS is recorded by the checker into the storage service. We categorize the rejection reasons into three groups: state variable became uncontrollable; invariant was violated; and TS was unreachable. The reasons are encoded as machine-readable status code as values of a special state variable called *ProposalStatus* for each PS. Applications use the same interface as for reading the OS to read their PSes' status. They can then react appropriately (e.g., generate a new PS that resolves the conflicts with the latest OS).

### 5.3 Partitioning by Impact Group

The checker needs to read all the state variables in the OS and TS to examine conflicts and invariants every round of operation. The number of such variables across our infrastructure—the datacenters and the WAN that connects them—poses a scalability threat.

To help scale, we observe that the impact of state changes for a given switch or link is limited. For instance, changes to an aggregation switch in one datacenter do not affect the connectivity and capacity of ToRs in another datacenter. Similarly, changes to border routers in a datacenter do not impact the capacity and connectivity within the datacenter, though they do impact other datacenters' WAN reachability.

Based on this observation, we partition the checker's responsibility into multiple impact groups. We set up one impact group per datacenter and one additional group with border routers of all datacenters and the WAN links. These groups are independent with respect to the state checking process. In our deployment of Statesman, we run one instance of checker per impact group, which has enabled the state checking to scale (§8).

## 6. System Design and Implementation

We now describe in more details the design and implementation of Statesman. We start with the storage service, followed by the updater and monitor; we skip the checker as it was covered in details in §5. Figure 6 provides a closer look at various components in a Statesman deployment. Our implementation of Statesman has roughly 50 thousand lines of C# and C++ code, plus a number of internal libraries. At its core, it is a highly-available RESTful web service with persistent storage. Below, we also describe Statesman's read-write APIs.

### 6.1 Globally Available and Distributed Storage Service

The storage service needs to persistently and consistently store the network states. We thus use a Paxos-based distributed file system. However, two challenges prevent us from using a single big Paxos ring to maintain all the states for all our datacenters. The first is the datacenter reachability. Due to WAN failures, one datacenter may lose connectivity to all others, or two datacenters may not be able to reach each other. To protect Statesman from such failures, the storage instances need to be located in multiple datacenters.

A second challenge stems from the volume of state data. In DCNs, there are hundreds of thousands of switches and links, each

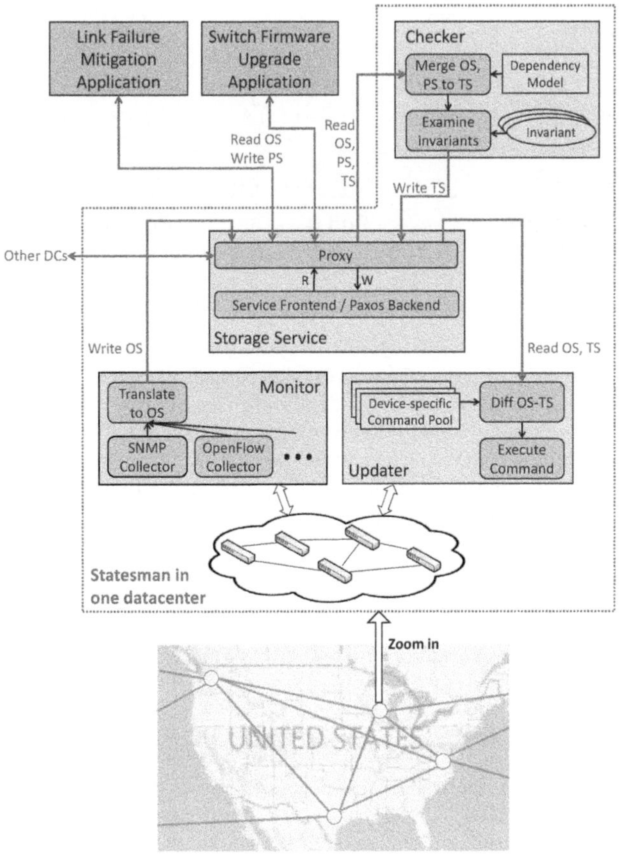


**Figure 6: Statesman system design**

with dozens of state variables. This scale results in millions of state variables (§8). Manipulating all variables in a single Paxos ring would impose a heavy message-exchange load on the file system to reach consensus over the data value. This impact worsens if the exchange happens over the WAN (as storage instances are located in multiple datacenters for reliability). WAN latencies will hurt the scalability and performance of Statesman.

Therefore, we break a big Paxos ring into independent smaller rings for each datacenter. One Paxos ring of storage instances is located in each datacenter, and it only stores the state data of the switches and links in that datacenter. In this way, Statesman reduces the scale of state storage to individual datacenter, and it lowers the impact of Paxos consensus by limiting message exchanges inside the datacenter.

Although the underlying storage is partitioned and distributed, we still want to provide a uniform and highly available interface for the applications and other Statesman components. These users of the storage service should not be required to understand where and how various state variables are stored.

We thus deploy a globally available proxy layer that provides uniform access to the network states. Users read or write network states of any datacenters from any proxy without knowing the exact locations of the storage service. Inside the proxy, we maintain an in-memory hash table of the switch and link names to corresponding datacenters for distributing the requests across the storage-service instances. The proxy instances sit behind a load balancer, which enables high availability and flexible capacity.

## 6.2 Stateless Update on Heterogeneous Devices

Network update is a challenging problem itself [12, 20, 28]. In the context of managing a large network, it becomes even more challenging for three reasons. First, the update process is device- and protocol-specific. Although OpenFlow provides a standard interface for changing the forwarding behaviors of switches, there is no standard interface today for management-related tasks such as changing the switch power, firmware, or interface configuration. Second, because of scale and dynamism, network failures during updates are inevitable. Finally, the device's response can be slow and dominate the application's control loop. Two aspects of the design of the Statesman updater help to address these challenges.

**Command template pool for heterogeneous devices:** The changes from applications (i.e., PSes) are device-agnostic network states. The updater translates the difference between a state variable's OS and TS values into device-specific commands. This translation is done using a pool of command templates that contains templates for each update action on each device model with supported control-plane protocol (e.g., OpenFlow or vendor-specific API). When the updater carries out an update action, it looks up the template from the pool based on the desired action and device details.

For instance, suppose we want to change the value of a switch's *DeviceRoutingState*. If the switch is an OpenFlow-enabled model, the updater looks up this model's OpenFlow command template to translate the routing state change into the insertion or deletion of OpenFlow rules, and issues rule update commands to the OpenFlow agent on the switch. Alternatively, if the switch is running a traditional routing protocol like BGP, the updater looks up the BGP command template to translate the routing state change into the BGP-route announcement or withdrawal.

**Stateless and automatic failure handling:** With all network states persistently stored by the storage service, the updater can be stateless and simply read the new values of OS and TS every round. This mode of operation makes the updater robust to failures in the network or in the updater itself. It can handle failures with an implicit and automatic retry. When any failure happens in one run of update, the state changes resulted by the failure reflect as a changed OS in the storage service. In the next run, the updater picks up the new OS which already includes the failure's impact, and it calculates new commands based on the new OS-TS difference. In this manner, the updater always brings the latest OS towards the TS, no matter what failures have happened in the process.

Being stateless also means that we can run as many updater instances as needed to scale, as long as we are able to coherently partition the work among them. In our current deployment, we run one instance per state variable per switch model. In this way, each updater instance is specialized for one task.

## 6.3 Network Monitors

The monitors collect the network states with various protocols from the switches, including SNMP and OpenFlow. The monitors then translate the protocol-specific data into the value of corresponding state variables, and write them into the storage service as the OS. We split the monitoring responsibility across many monitor instances, so each instance covers roughly 1,000 switches.

Currently the monitors run periodically to collect all switches' power states, firmware versions, device configurations, and various counters (and routing states for a subset of switches). For links, our monitors cover the link power, configuration, and counters like the packet drop rate and the traffic load.

| | | |
|---|---|---|
| GET | NetworkState/Read?Datacenter={*dc*}&Pool={*p*}<br>&Freshness={*c*}&Entity={*e*}&Attribute={*a*} | |
| POST | NetworkState/Write?Pool={*p*}<br>(Body is list of NetworkState objects in JSON) | |

**(a) HTTP Request**

| | | |
|---|---|---|
| Datacenter | *dc* | Datacenter name |
| Pool | *p* | OS, PS, or TS |
| Freshness | *c* | Up-to-date or bounded-stale |
| Entity | *e* | Entity name (i.e., switch, link, or path) |
| Attribute | *a* | State variable name |

**(b) Parameters**

**Table 3: Read-write APIs of Statesman**

### 6.4 Read-Write APIs

The storage service is implemented as a HTTP web service with RESTful APIs. The applications, monitors, updaters, and checkers use the APIs to read or write *NetworkState* objects from the storage service. A *NetworkState* object consists of the entity name (i.e., the switch, link, or path name), the state variable name, the variable value, and the last-update timestamp. The read-write APIs of Statesman are shown in Table 3.

There is a *freshness* parameter in the read API because Statesman offers different freshness modes for reading the network states. The up-to-date mode is for applications who are strict with the state staleness. For instance, the link-failure-mitigation application needs to detect link failures as soon as possible when the failures happen. Statesman also offers 5-minute bounded-staleness mode by reading from caches [27]. Many management applications do not need the most up-to-date network states and can safely tolerate some staleness in state data. For instance, the firmware-upgrade application needs to upgrade the switches within hours; it does not matter if the value of *DeviceFirmwareVersion* is slightly stale. By allowing such applications to read from caches, we boost the read throughput of Statesman. At the same time, applications that cannot tolerate staleness can use the up-to-date freshness mode.

## 7. Application Experiences

In this section, we present our experiences of running Statesman in Microsoft Azure. Statesman is now deployed in ten datacenters (DCs), and we have built two production and one pilot-stage applications on top of it. We first describe this deployment, and then use three representative scenarios to illustrate how Statesman facilitates the operations of management applications.

### 7.1 Statesman Deployment

Statesman currently manages ten geographically-distributed DCs of Microsoft Azure, covering all the switches and links in those DCs and the WAN connecting the DCs. The three applications that we have built leverage Statesman to manage different aspects (e.g., switches, links, and traffic flows) of our DCN.

- **Switch upgrade**: When a new version of firmware is released by a switch vendor, this application automatically schedules all the switches from the same vendor to upgrade by proposing a new value of *DeviceFirmwareVersion*. In the upgrade process, the checker of Statesman ensures that the DCN continues to meet the network-wide invariants.

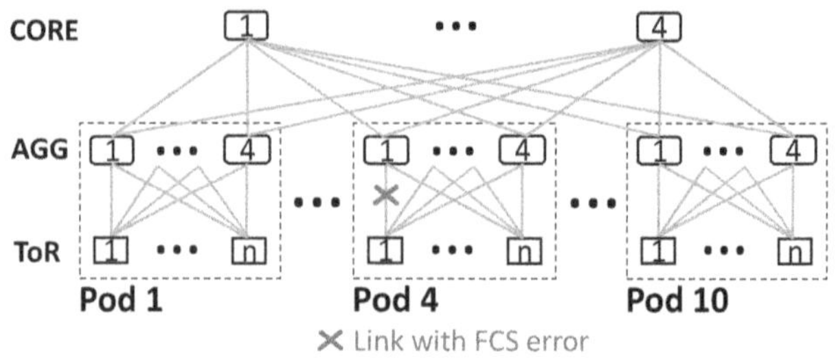


**Figure 7: Network topology for the scenario in §7.2**

- **Failure mitigation**: This application periodically reads the Frame-Check-Sequence (FCS) error rates on all the links. When detecting persistently high FCS error rates on certain links, it changes the *LinkAdminPower* state to shut down those faulty links to mitigate the impact of the failures [30]. The application also initiates an out-of-band repair process for those links, e.g., by creating a repair ticket for the on-site team.
- **Inter-DC TE**: As described in SWAN [12], Statesman collects the bandwidth demands from the *bandwidth brokers* sitting with the hosted services. In addition, the monitor of Statesman collects all the forwarding states, such as tunnel status and flow matching rules. Given this information, the TE application computes and proposes new forwarding states, which are then pushed to all the relevant routers by the Statesman updater.

The first two applications have been fully tested and deployed, while the third one is in pilot stage and undergoing testing.

We emphasize two issues on how applications interact with Statesman. First, they should understand that it takes time for Statesman to read and write a large amount of network states in large DCNs. Thus, their control loops should operate at the time scale of minutes, not seconds. Second, the applications should understand that their PSes may be rejected due to failures, conflicts, or invariant violations. Thus, they need to run iteratively to adapt to the latest OS and the acceptance or rejection of their previous PSes.

### 7.2 Maintaining Network-wide Invariants

We use a production trace to illustrate how Statesman helps two applications (switch-upgrade and failure-mitigation) safely coexist in intra-DC networks while maintaining the capacity invariant—99% of the ToR pairs in the DC should have at least 50% of their baseline capacity.

Figure 7 shows the topology for the scenario. It is a portion of one DC with 10 pods, where each pod has 4 Agg switches and a number of ToRs. The switch-upgrade application wants to upgrade all the 40 Aggs in a short amount of time. Specifically, it will upgrade the pods one by one. Within each pod, it will attempt to upgrade multiple Aggs in parallel by continuing to write a PS for one Agg upgrade until it gets rejected by Statesman.

In Figure 8, we pick one ToR from each pod, and organize the 10 ToRs from the 10 pods into 90 ToR pairs (10×9, excluding the originating ToR itself). On the Y-axis, we put the 9 ToR pairs originating from the same ToR/pod together. Essentially, Figure 8 shows how the network capacity between each ToR pair changes over time. Boxes A, B, and C illustrate how the network capacity temporarily drops when the switch-upgrade application upgrades the Aggs in Pod 1, 2, and 3 sequentially. To meet the 50%-capacity invariant, the switch-upgrade application can simultaneously upgrade up to 2 out of 4 Aggs, leaving at least 2 Aggs alive for traffic.

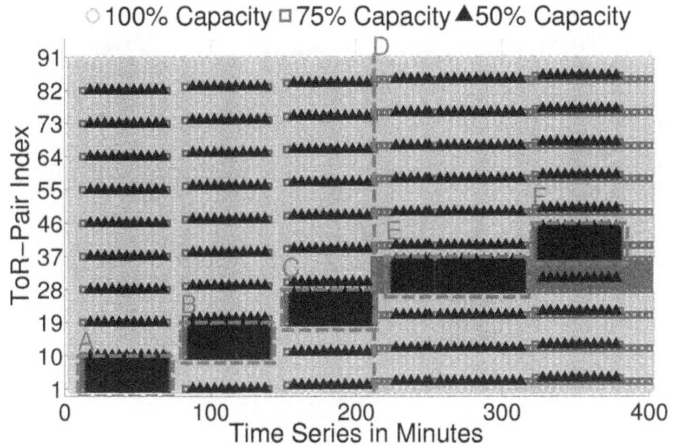


**Figure 8: Illustration of how the switch-upgrade and failure-mitigation applications interact through the checker. Y-axis: One ToR from each one of 10 pods to form directional ToR pairs, indexed by the originating ToR/Pod. A, B, C: The switch-upgrade application upgrades Pod 1, 2, 3 normally while the checker maintains an invariant that each ToR pair has at least 50% of baseline capacity. D: The failure-mitigation application detects a failing link $ToR_1$-$Agg_1$ in Pod 4 and shuts the link down. E: Due to the down link, upgrade of Pod 4 is automatically slowed down by the checker to maintain the capacity invariant. F: Upgrade of Pod 5 resumes the normal pattern.**

During the upgrade, the failure-mitigation application discovers persistently high FCS error rate on link $ToR_1$-$Agg_1$ in $Pod_4$. As a result, it shuts down this link at time D. Since one ToR-Agg link is down, the capacity of all $Pod_4$-related ToR pairs drops to 75%, which originate from $Pod_4$ (index # 28–36) or end at $Pod_4$ (index # 3, 12, 21, 40, 49, 58, 67, 76, & 85). When the switch-upgrade application starts to work on $Pod_4$, Statesman can only allow it to upgrade one Agg at a time to maintain the 50%-capacity invariant. Thus, as shown in box E, the switch-upgrade application automatically slows down when upgrading $Pod_4$. Its actual upgrade steps are $Agg_1$-$Agg_2$-together, then $Agg_3$, and finally $Agg_4$. Note that $Agg_1$ and $Agg_2$ can be upgraded in parallel, because link $ToR_1$-$Agg_1$ is already down and hence upgrading $Agg_1$ does not further reduce the ToR-pair capacity. The switch-upgrade application resumes normal speed when it upgrades $Pod_5$ in box F.

### 7.3 Resolving Application Conflicts

The inter-DC TE application is responsible for allocating inter-DC traffic along different WAN paths. Figure 9 shows the pilot WAN topology used in this experiment. This WAN inter-connects four DCs in a full mesh, and each DC has two border routers. The switch-upgrade application is also running on the WAN.

One recurring scenario is that we need to upgrade all the border routers while inter-DC traffic is on. This can lead to a conflict between the two applications: the switch-upgrade application wants to reboot a router for firmware upgrade, while the TE application wants the router to carry traffic. Without Statesman, the operators of the two applications have to manually coordinate, e.g., by setting up a maintenance window. During this window, the operators must carefully watch the upgrade process for any unexpected events.

With Statesman, the whole process becomes much simpler. When there is no upgrade, the TE application acquires the low-priority lock over each router, and changes the forwarding states as needed.

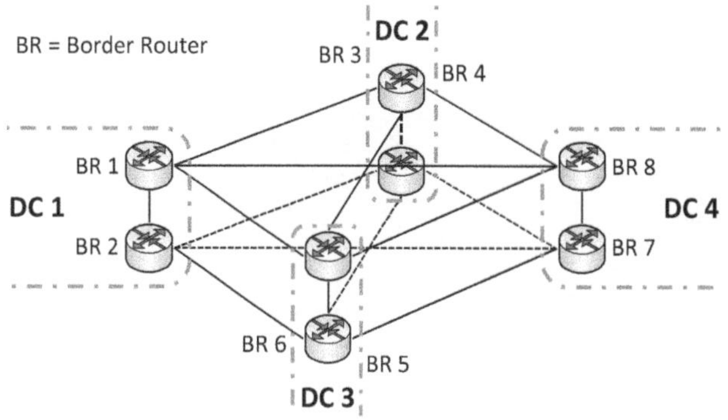


**Figure 9: WAN topology for the scenario in §7.3**

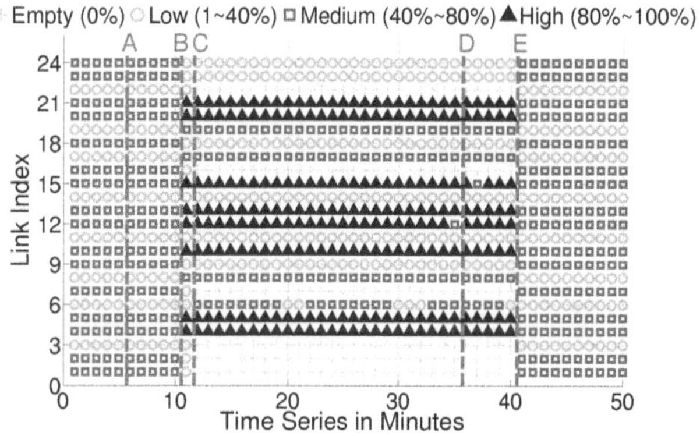


**Figure 10: Illustration of how Statesman resolves conflicts between the inter-DC TE and switch-upgrade applications. A: The switch-upgrade application acquires the high-priority lock of $BorderRouter_1$ ($BR_1$). B: The TE application fails to acquire the low-priority lock and moves traffic away from $BR_1$ to other links. C: The switch-upgrade application starts to upgrade $BR_1$ since traffic is zero. D: Upgrade of $BR_1$ is done. The switch-upgrade application releases the high-priority lock. E: The TE application re-acquires the low-priority lock of $BR_1$ and moves traffic back.**

When the switch-upgrade application wants to upgrade a router, it first acquires the high-priority lock over that router. Soon after, the TE application realizes that it cannot acquire a low-priority lock over the router, and it starts to shift traffic away from that router. Meanwhile, the switch-upgrade application keeps reading the traffic load of the locked router until the load drops to zero. At this moment, it kicks off the upgrade by writing a PS with a new value of *DeviceFirmwareVersion*. Once the upgrade is done, the switch-upgrade application releases the high-priority lock of the router, and proceeds to the next candidate.

We collected the traffic load data during one upgrade event in off-peak hours. Since the load patterns of different routers are similar, we only illustrate the upgrade process of $BorderRouter_1$ ($BR_1$). Figure 10 shows the time series of the link load (note that both applications run every 5 minutes). The Y-axis shows the 24 links (12 physical links × 2 directions) indexed by the originating router of each link. At time B, the TE application fails to acquire the low-priority lock over $BR_1$, since the high-priority lock of $BR_1$ was acquired by the switch-upgrade application at time A. So the TE application moves traffic away from $BR_1$. At time C, the load drops

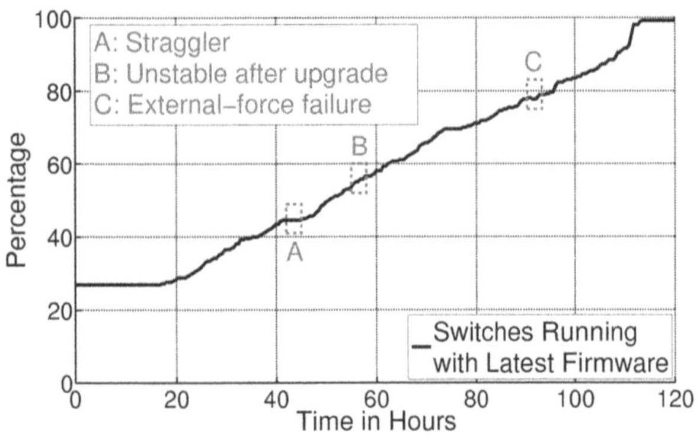


**Figure 11: Time series of firmware upgrade at scale**

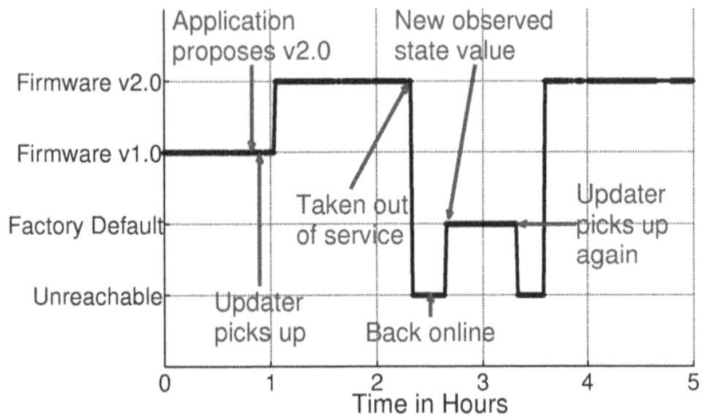


**Figure 12: External-force failure in firmware upgrade**

to zero on all the links originating from $BR_1$ (index # 1, 2, & 3) and ending at $BR_1$ (index # 7, 16, & 22). As expected, this increases the loads on the other links. After the switch-upgrade application finishes upgrading $BR_1$ and releases the high-priority lock at time D, the TE application successfully acquires the low-priority lock again at time E, and then moves traffic back to $BR_1$.

In this example, neither of the two applications needs to be aware of the other since conflict resolution and necessary coordination are automatically enabled by Statesman. We use locking as the conflict resolution strategy in the inter-DC case. So the TE application can move tunnels away from switches being upgraded before the upgrade process starts, rather than after (which would be the case with conflict resolution based on last-writer-wins). In the intra-DC case, we do not use tunnel-based TE, and neighboring routers can immediately reroute traffic when a switch is brought down for upgrade without warning.

### 7.4 Handling Operational Failures

In Statesman, an application outputs a PS instead of directly interacting with the network devices. Once the PS is accepted into the TS, Statesman takes the responsibility of (eventually) moving the network state to the TS. This simplifies the application design, especially in failure handling.

In this example, we show how the switch-upgrade application rolls out a new firmware to roughly 250 switches in several DCs in two stages. In the first stage, 25% of the switches are upgraded to test the new firmware. Once we are confident with the new firmware, the remaining 75% of the switches are upgraded in the second

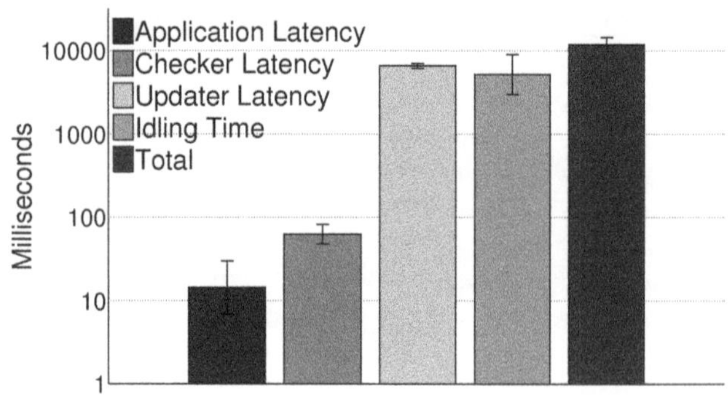


**Figure 13: End-to-end latency breakdown**

stage. Figure 11 illustrates the upgrade process, where the percentage of switches with new firmware gradually grows to 100% in about 100 hours. Here, the switch-upgrade application runs conservatively and upgrades one switch at a time.

During this process, Statesman automatically overcomes a variety of failures, which are highlighted in Figure 11. In box A, there is a straggling switch which takes 4 hours to upgrade; note the flat line in the figure. During the 4 hours, Statesman repeatedly tries to upgrade until it succeeds. This straggling happens because the switch has a full memory and cannot download the new firmware image. After some of the switch memory is freed up, the upgrade proceeds. In box B, a few switches become unstable after the upgrade, e.g., frequently flipping between on and off. This appears as a stair-shape line in Figure 11. Statesman automatically retries until the switches are stable with the new firmware.

Box C shows a failure case which involves human interventions. After a switch is upgraded, the operators take it out of service, and manually reset it to the factory-default firmware before returning it to production. This action causes the time-series line to slightly drop in Box C, and we zoom in the process in Figure 12. Once the switch is back to production, Statesman finds that the observed *DeviceFirmwareVersion* of one switch is the factory-default one. Since the firmware of the switch has been set to a new value in the TS, Statesman automatically redoes the firmware upgrade without any involvement from the switch-upgrade application.

## 8. System Evaluation

In this section, we quantify the latency and coverage of Statesman as well as the performance of checking, reading and writing network states.

**End-to-end latency:** Figure 13 shows Statesman's end-to-end latency measured by running the failure-mitigation application on a subset of our DCN. We manually introduce packet drops on a link, and let the failure-mitigation application discover the problem and then shut down the link. The end-to-end latency is measured from when the application reads the high packet drop rate of the link to when the faulty link is actually deactivated in the network. We break down the end-to-end latency into four portions:

- Application latency: from when the application reads the high packet drop rate to when it writes a PS for shutting down the faulty link.
- Checker latency: from when the checker reads the PS to when it finishes checking and writes a new TS.
- Updater latency: from when the updater reads the new TS to when it finishes shutting down the faulty link.

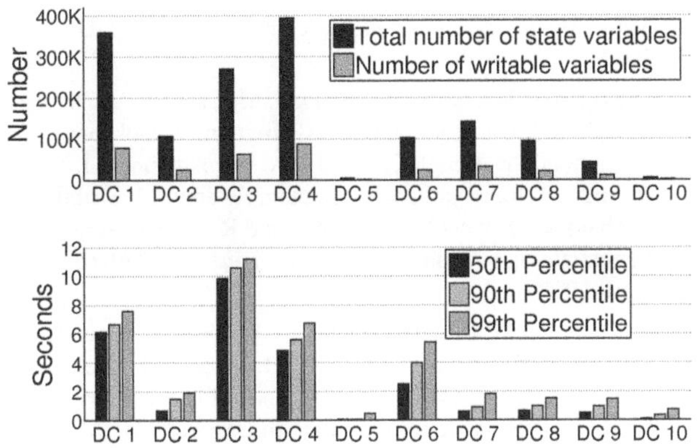


**Figure 14: Network state scale & checker performance**

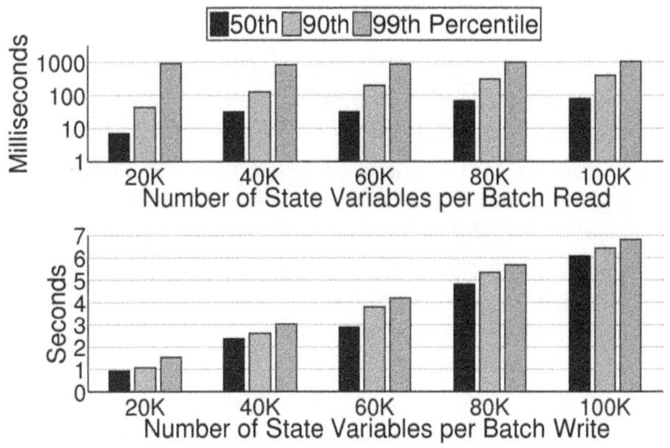


**Figure 15: Read-write micro-benchmark performance**

- Idling time: cumulative time when no one is running. It exists because the application, checker and updater run asynchronously (every 5 seconds in this experiment).

Figure 13 shows that the application and checker latencies are negligibly small, accounting for only 0.13% and 0.28% of the end-to-end latency on average. The main bottleneck is the time for the updater to apply the link-shutdown commands to the switch, which accounts for 57.7% of the end-to-end latency on average.

**Coverage:** Figure 14 shows the deployment scale and the checker latency across the ten DCs where Statesman is deployed. The number of state variables in each DC indicates its size. The largest DC (DC$_4$) has 394K variables and 7 out of 10 DCs have over 100K variables. The total number of variables managed by Statesman is currently 1.5 million and it continues to grow as Statesman expands to more DCs. Since only 23.4% of the variables are writable on average, the size of TS is correspondingly smaller than the OS.

**Checker latency:** Figure 14 also shows that one round of checking takes 0.5 to 7.6 seconds in most DCs. In the most complex DC (DC$_3$), the 99th-percentile of checking latency is 11.2 seconds.

**Read-write performance:** We stress-test the read-write performance of Statesman by randomly reading and writing varying numbers of state variables. Figure 15 shows that the 99th-percentile latency of reading 20K to 100K variables always stays under a second. Since the applications rarely read more than 100K variables at a time, Statesman's read speed is fast enough.

Figure 15 also shows that the write latency of Statesman grows linearly with the number of variables, and the 99th-percentile latency of writing 100K variables is under seven seconds. Since our largest DC has fewer than 100K variables in the TS, it takes less than 10 seconds to write the entire TS. In practice, the state-variable writers, e.g., applications, monitors, and checkers, rarely write more than 10K variables at a time. Hence, the write latency is usually around 500ms in our normal operations.

## 9. Related Work

Statesman descends from a long line of prior works on software-defined networking [1, 2, 3, 6, 8, 9, 22]. These works enable centralized control of traffic flow by directly manipulating the forwarding states of switches. In contrast, Statesman supports a wider range of network management functions (e.g., switch upgrade, link failure mitigation, elastic scaling, etc.).

Similar to Statesman, Onix [18, 19] and Hercules [16] provide a shared network-state platform for all applications. But these systems neither resolve application conflicts, in particular those caused by state variable dependency, nor enforce network-wide invariants.

Pyretic [24], PANE [7], and Maple [29] are recent proposals on making multiple applications coexist. Their target is again limited to traffic management applications. Their composition strategies are specific to such applications and do not generalize to the broader class of applications that we target at. Mesos [11] schedules competing applications using the cluster-resource abstraction, which is quite different from our network-state abstraction (e.g., no cross-variable dependency).

Corybantic [23] proposes a different way of resolving conflicts by letting each application evaluate other applications' proposals. As noted previously, such tight cross-application coordination, while sometimes beneficial, imposes enormous complexity on the application design and testing.

Another approach of hosting multiple applications is to partition the network into multiple isolated virtual slices as described in [17, 26]. Compared to the virtual topology model, our network-state model is more fine-grained and flexible. It allows multiple applications to manage different levels of states (e.g., power, configuration, and routing) on the same device.

There are also earlier works on invariant verification [14, 15, 21] for the network's forwarding state. In the future, we may incorporate some of these invariant checking algorithms into Statesman.

## 10. Conclusion

Statesman enables multiple loosely-coupled network management applications to run on a shared network infrastructure, while preserving network safety and performance. It safely composes uncoordinated and sometimes-conflicting application actions using three distinct views of network state, inspired by version control systems, and a model of dependencies among different parts of network state. Statesman is currently running in ten Microsoft Azure datacenters, along with three diverse applications.

**Acknowledgments:** We thank the Microsoft Azure Networking team, especially Murat Acikgoz, Jiaxin Cao, George Chen, Huoping Chen, Kamil Cudnik, Umesh Krishnaswamy, Guohan Lu, Shikhar Suri, Dong Xiang, and Chao Zhang, for helping develop Statesman and being early adopters. We also thank Chuanxiong Guo, Randy Kern, Dave Maltz, our shepherd Walter Willinger, and the SIGCOMM reviewers for feedback on the paper.

## 11. References


[1] M. Caesar, D. Caldwell, N. Feamster, J. Rexford, A. Shaikh, and J. van der Merwe. Design and Implementation of a Routing Control Platform. In *USENIX NSDI*, May 2005.

[2] M. Casado, M. J. Freedman, J. Pettit, J. Luo, N. McKeown, and S. Shenker. Ethane: Taking Control of the Enterprise. *ACM SIGCOMM CCR*, 37(4):1–12, August 2007.

[3] M. Casado, T. Garfinkel, A. Akella, M. J. Freedman, D. Boneh, N. McKeown, and S. Shenker. SANE: A Protection Architecture for Enterprise Networks. In *USENIX Security Symposium*, July 2006.

[4] C.-C. Chen, P. Sun, L. Yuan, D. A. Maltz, C.-N. Chuah, and P. Mohapatra. SWiM: Switch Manager For Data Center Networks. *IEEE Internet Computing*, April 2014.

[5] K. Chen, C. Guo, H. Wu, J. Yuan, Z. Feng, Y. Chen, S. Lu, and W. Wu. Generic and Automatic Address Configuration for Data Center Networks. In *ACM SIGCOMM*, August 2010.

[6] N. Feamster, J. Rexford, and E. Zegura. The Road to SDN. *ACM Queue*, 11(12):20:20–20:40, December 2013.

[7] A. Ferguson, A. Guha, C. Liang, R. Fonseca, and S. Krishnamurthi. Participatory Networking: An API for Application Control of SDNs. In *ACM SIGCOMM*, August 2013.

[8] A. Greenberg, G. Hjalmtysson, D. A. Maltz, A. Myers, J. Rexford, G. Xie, H. Yan, J. Zhan, and H. Zhang. A Clean Slate 4D Approach to Network Control and Management. *ACM SIGCOMM CCR*, 35(5):41–54, October 2005.

[9] N. Gude, T. Koponen, J. Pettit, B. Pfaff, M. Casado, N. McKeown, and S. Shenker. NOX: Towards an Operating System for Networks. *ACM SIGCOMM CCR*, 38(3):105–110, July 2008.

[10] B. Heller, S. Seetharaman, P. Mahadevan, Y. Yiakoumis, P. Sharma, S. Banerjee, and N. McKeown. ElasticTree: Saving Energy in Data Center Networks. In *USENIX NSDI*, April 2010.

[11] B. Hindman, A. Konwinski, M. Zaharia, A. Ghodsi, A. D. Joseph, R. Katz, S. Shenker, and I. Stoica. Mesos: A Platform for Fine-grained Resource Sharing in the Data Center. In *USENIX NSDI*, March 2011.

[12] C.-Y. Hong, S. Kandula, R. Mahajan, M. Zhang, V. Gill, M. Nanduri, and R. Wattenhofer. Achieving High Utilization with Software-driven WAN. In *ACM SIGCOMM*, August 2013.

[13] S. Jain, A. Kumar, S. Mandal, J. Ong, L. Poutievski, A. Singh, S. Venkata, J. Wanderer, J. Zhou, M. Zhu, J. Zolla, U. Hölzle, S. Stuart, and A. Vahdat. B4: Experience with a Globally-deployed Software Defined WAN. In *ACM SIGCOMM*, August 2013.

[14] P. Kazemian, G. Varghese, and N. McKeown. Header Space Analysis: Static Checking for Networks. In *USENIX NSDI*, April 2012.

[15] A. Khurshid, X. Zou, W. Zhou, M. Caesar, and P. B. Godfrey. VeriFlow: Verifying Network-wide Invariants in Real Time. In *USENIX NSDI*, April 2013.

[16] W. Kim and P. Sharma. Hercules: Integrated Control Framework for Datacenter Traffic Management. In *IEEE Network Operations and Management Symposium*, April 2012.

[17] T. Koponen, K. Amidon, P. Balland, M. Casado, A. Chanda, B. Fulton, I. Ganichev, J. Gross, P. Ingram, E. Jackson, A. Lambeth, R. Lenglet, S.-H. Li, A. Padmanabhan, J. Pettit, B. Pfaff, R. Ramanathan, S. Shenker, A. Shieh, J. Stribling, P. Thakkar, D. Wendlandt, A. Yip, and R. Zhang. Network Virtualization in Multi-tenant Datacenters. In *USENIX NSDI*, April 2014.

[18] T. Koponen, M. Casado, N. Gude, J. Stribling, L. Poutievski, M. Zhu, R. Ramanathan, Y. Iwata, H. Inoue, T. Hama, and S. Shenker. Onix: A Distributed Control Platform for Large-scale Production Networks. In *USENIX OSDI*, Vancouver, BC, Canada, October 2010.

[19] B. Lantz, B. O'Connor, J. Hart, P. Berde, P. Radoslavov, M. Kobayashi, T. Koide, Y. Higuchi, M. Gerola, W. Snow, and G. Parulkar. ONOS: Towards an Open, Distributed SDN OS. In *ACM SIGCOMM HotSDN Workshop*, August 2014.

[20] H. H. Liu, X. Wu, M. Zhang, L. Yuan, R. Wattenhofer, and D. Maltz. zUpdate: Updating Data Center Networks with Zero Loss. In *ACM SIGCOMM*, August 2013.

[21] H. Mai, A. Khurshid, R. Agarwal, M. Caesar, P. B. Godfrey, and S. T. King. Debugging the Data Plane with Anteater. In *ACM SIGCOMM*, August 2011.

[22] N. McKeown, T. Anderson, H. Balakrishnan, G. Parulkar, L. Peterson, J. Rexford, S. Shenker, and J. Turner. OpenFlow: Enabling Innovation in Campus Networks. *ACM SIGCOMM CCR*, 38(2):69–74, March 2008.

[23] J. Mogul, A. AuYoung, S. Banerjee, J. Lee, J. Mudigonda, L. Popa, P. Sharma, and Y. Turner. Corybantic: Towards Modular Composition of SDN Control Programs. In *ACM HotNets Workshop*, November 2013.

[24] C. Monsanto, J. Reich, N. Foster, J. Rexford, and D. Walker. Composing Software-defined Networks. In *USENIX NSDI*, April 2013.

[25] P. Patel, D. Bansal, L. Yuan, A. Murthy, A. Greenberg, D. A. Maltz, R. Kern, H. Kumar, M. Zikos, H. Wu, C. Kim, and N. Karri. Ananta: Cloud Scale Load Balancing. In *ACM SIGCOMM*, August 2013.

[26] R. Sherwood, G. Gibb, K.-K. Yap, G. Appenzeller, M. Casado, N. McKeown, and G. Parulkar. Can the Production Network Be the Testbed? In *USENIX OSDI*, October 2010.

[27] D. Terry. Replicated Data Consistency Explained Through Baseball. Technical Report MSR-TR-2011-137, Microsoft Research, 2011.

[28] L. Vanbever, S. Vissicchio, C. Pelsser, P. Francois, and O. Bonaventure. Seamless Network-wide IGP Migrations. In *ACM SIGCOMM*, August 2011.

[29] A. Voellmy, J. Wang, Y. R. Yang, B. Ford, and P. Hudak. Maple: Simplifying SDN Programming Using Algorithmic Policies. In *ACM SIGCOMM*, August 2013.

[30] X. Wu, D. Turner, C.-C. Chen, D. A. Maltz, X. Yang, L. Yuan, and M. Zhang. NetPilot: Automating Datacenter Network Failure Mitigation. In *ACM SIGCOMM*, August 2012.

# Rethinking Buffer Management in Data Center Networks

Aisha Mushtaq[1], Asad Khalid Ismail[2], Abdul Wasay[1],
Bilal Mahmood[1], Ihsan Ayyub Qazi[1], Zartash Afzal Uzmi[1]
[1]SBASSE, LUMS, Lahore, Pakistan, [2]UC, Santa Barbara, USA
aishaa.mushtaq@gmail.com, asad@cs.ucsb.edu, 14100117@lums.edu.pk,
mahmood.b07@gmail.com, ihsan.qazi@lums.edu.pk, zartash@lums.edu.pk

## ABSTRACT

Data center operators face extreme challenges in simultaneously providing low latency for short flows, high throughput for long flows, and high burst tolerance. We propose a buffer management strategy that addresses these challenges by isolating short and long flows into separate buffers, sizing these buffers based on flow requirements, and scheduling packets to meet different flow-level objectives. Our design provides new opportunities for performance improvements that complement transport layer optimizations.

## 1. INTRODUCTION

Many popular applications such as web search, advertising, and recommendation systems require low latency and high throughput from the underlying data center network [1]. Unfortunately, the completion times for latency-sensitive short flows in existing TCP-based deployments can be orders of magnitude larger than optimal [2]. This happens due to the *mixing* of short and long flows that have disparate performance expectations from the network fabric. As a result, short and long flows compete for a shared set of network resources (e.g., link capacity and switch buffers) in an adversarial manner. In particular, the buffer-filling nature of long-lived TCP flows often causes short flows to get queued up behind packets from long flows. In addition, the presence of long flows reduces the ability of switch buffers to absorb application-induced packet bursts that are common in data centers.

We propose MulBuff, a buffer management strategy that addresses the root cause of these problems that stem from the mixing of short and long flows. MulBuff uses three key design principles: (i) *segregation* of long flows and short flows into separate buffers, (ii) *sizing* of buffers based on flow requirements, and (iii) *scheduling* packets from these buffers to meet different flow-level objectives. We show that these principles complement each other and all are needed to achieve high performance across a wide range of scenarios.

Designs like MulBuff provide new opportunities for performance improvements that complement transport layer optimizations [1, 4, 5]. In particular, using MulBuff in conjunction with existing transports like DCTCP can provide significant performance benefits due to isolation of flows and by explicitly accounting for scenarios like incast. Our initial results show that TCP with MulBuff improves performance over DCTCP and achieves similar performance compared to pFabric [2].

## 2. FRAMEWORK DESIGN

MulBuff's key design insight is a principled handling of flows with heterogeneous requirements at a switch. End hosts using MulBuff mark each packet as belonging to the short flow queue or the long flow queue[1]. The MulBuff switch maps flows to queues, updates sizes of the short flow queue (to keep a bounded loss rate and low delay) and the long flow queue (to keep high utilization), and adjusts queue capacities based on the number of flows in each queue[2]. We now study the impact of buffer organization, sizing, and scheduling on MulBuff's performance and show that they must be considered in unison to maximize performance because a lack of principled consideration of one factor can override the benefits of the other.

*Buffer Organization:* MulBuff's segregation of flows with different requirements into seperate queues allows flows to achieve their desired performance without impacting other flows. Figure 2(a) shows the average flow completion time (AFCT) with TCP for two buffering policies as a function of network load. Observe that having a single common buffer for both short and long flows significantly increases the AFCT. This happens because of the increased queuing delays caused by long flows' packets filling up the buffer. On the other hand, using multiple buffers isolates the impact of long flows on short flows leading to lower AFCTs.

*Scheduling:* Allocating fixed capacities to queues can degrade performance when more flows get mapped to one queue compared to the other or when flows have different performance requirements (e.g., to minimize completion times, short flows should be prioritized). Thus to meet different flow-level objectives (e.g., minimize FCTs, fair sharing), each queue should be allocated capacity proportional to the number of ongoing flows and operator assigned weights. Figure 1(b) shows the AFCT for processor sharing (PS) across queues and weighted processor sharing (WPS) as a function of load. Observe that FCTs increase rapidly with load under PS. This happens because PS assigns equal capacity to both the queues irrespective of the number of flows in each queue, which causes the FCT of short flows to increase. However, with WPS, as rates are assigned based to the number of flows in each queue, it results in a graceful increase in FCT (see Figure 2(b)).

*Buffer Sizing:* The size of a buffer plays a key role in meeting the requirements of flows. For instance, latency-sensitive short flows often suffer TCP retransmission timeouts due to synchronized flow

[1]This is based on flow size information. If flow size is not known, it can be estimated using the amount of data sent so far [4].

[2]Note that MulBuff can use any number of queues.


*SIGCOMM'14,* August 17–22, 2014, Chicago, IL, USA.
ACM 978-1-4503-2836-4/14/08.
http://dx.doi.org/10.1145/2619239.2631462.

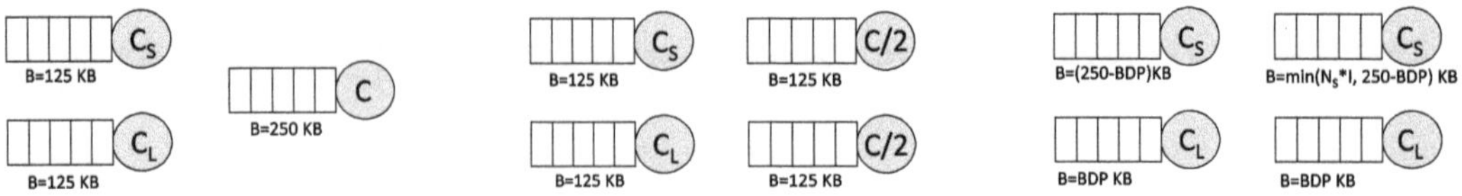


(a) Scenario A (b) Scenario B (c) Scenario C

**Figure 1: (a) Scenario A shows comparison of a single buffer with two buffers, (b) Scenario B shows comparison of static and dynamic link capacities (scheduling), and (c) Scenario C shows comparison of static and dynamic buffer sizing. Note that $B$ is the buffer size, $C$=1 Gbps is the link capacity, $C_S$ and $C_L$ are the capacities for the short and long buffers, respectively, and $N_S$ is the number of flows in the short buffer.**

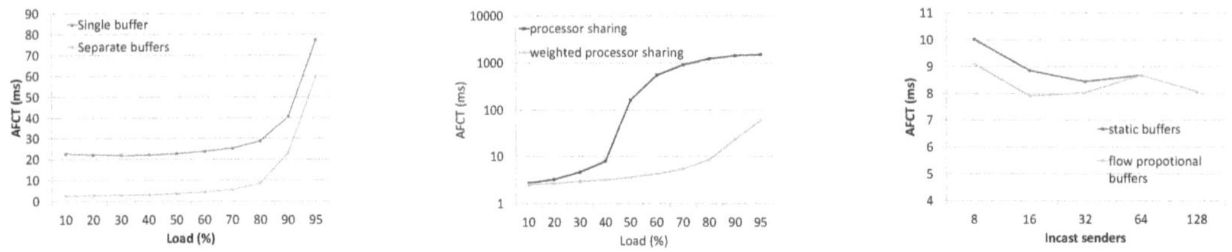


(a) Scenario A (b) Scenario B (c) Scenario C

**Figure 2: For each scenario in Fig. 1, comparison of AFCT for short flows as a function of load. For scenarios (a) and (b), flow sizes were drawn from the interval [2 KB,98 KB] using a uniform distribution while keeping two long-lived flows in the background as done in [4]. In case of (c), a 1 MB file was divided equally among the senders.**

arrivals. To prevent these timeouts and achieve a bounded loss rate, requires apportioning a certain amount of buffer space for each flow [3]. Thus MulBuff sizes buffers proportional to the number of flows for the short flow queue. For long flows to fully utilize the allocated capacity, the buffers must be large enough to prevent any queue underflow. Consequently, MulBuff sets the buffer size for the long flow queue to the bandwidth-delay product (BDP). Scenario C in Figure 1(c) compares the use of static and dynamic buffer sizing strategies. The static buffers setup uses BDP buffers for the long flows and (250-BDP) KB of buffer for the short flows. The other setup uses dynamic buffering for the short flow queue (for every new flow, the buffer size is increased by three packets and when a flow departs, it is decreased by three packets and the maximum size is capped at (250-BDP) KB. For these two setups, Figure 2(c) shows the AFCT results as a function of the number of senders in an ensuing incast. Observe that using dynamic buffering leads to improved FCTs especially when the number of senders are small as dynamic buffering helps in keeping small queues.

Overall, these results motivate the need to consider all these factors (buffer organization, scheduling, sizing) in unison.

**Evaluation:** Figure 3 shows the AFCT and the 99th percentile FCT for TCP with MulBuff, DCTCP, and pFabric on a 3-level tree topology in the network simulator (ns-2). Observe that MulBuff considerably improves performance over DCTCP and achieves similar performance compared to pFabric across a range of loads. Under incast, MulBuff's segregation ensures more headroom for short bursty flows, sizing allows dynamic allocation of buffers as flows arrive, and scheduling allows them to finish quickly (see Fig. 4(a)). Moreover, using MulBuff in conjunction with DCTCP provides up to 34% improvement in AFCT over DCTCP as shown in Fig. 4(b).

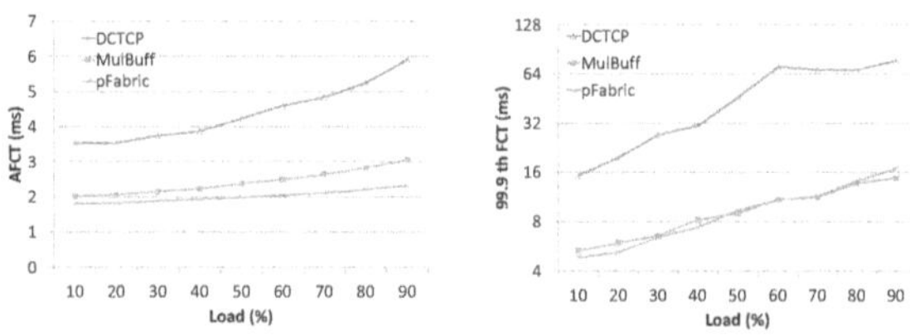


**Figure 3: Comparison of TCP-MulBuff with DCTCP and pFabric in terms of (a) AFCT, (b) 99.9th perc. FCT under the all-to-all scenario.**

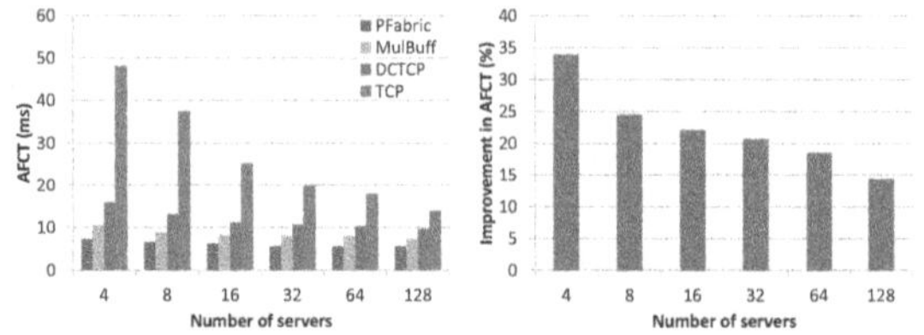


**Figure 4: (a) Performance under the (intra-rack) incast scenario and (b) Impact of using DCTCP with MulBuff.**

## 3. CONCLUSION AND FUTURE WORK

We make the following contributions in this paper: (a) We presented the design considerations needed for a buffer management strategy to achieve high performance across a range of data center workloads, (b) we presented a simple but novel solution that tackles buffer organization, sizing and scheduling, (c) we conducted evaluation of MulBuff in a typical data center environment. We are currently implementing MulBuff in the Click modular router. In the future, we plan to evaluate the effects of choosing arbitrary scheduling policies, and how MulBuff behaves in the presence of legacy switches. In addition, we plan to explore how MulBuff can help address problems like TCP Outcast.

## 4. REFERENCES

[1] ALIZADEH, M., GREENBERG, A., MALTZ, D., PADHYE, J., PATEL, P., PRABHAKAR, B., SENGUPTA, S., AND SRIDHARAN, M. Data center tcp (dctcp). In *SIGCOMM'10*.

[2] ALIZADEH, M., YANG, S., SHARIF, M., KATTI, S., MCKEOWN, N., PRABHAKAR, B., AND SHENKER, S. pfabric: Minimal near-optimal datacenter transport. In *SIGCOMM'13*.

[3] MORRIS, R. Scalable tcp congestion control. In *INFOCOM'00*.

[4] MUNIR, A., QAZI, I. A., UZMI, Z. A., MUSHTAQ, A., ISMAIL, S. N., IQBAL, M. S., AND KHAN, B. Minimizing Flow Completion Times in Data Centers. In *INFOCOM'13*.

[5] VAMANAN, B., HASAN, J., AND VIJAYKUMAR, T. N. Deadline-aware datacenter tcp (d2tcp). In *SIGCOMM'12*.

# VIRL: The Virtual Internet Routing Lab

Joel Obstfeld
Cisco Systems

Simon Knight
University of Adelaide/Cisco Systems

Ed Kern
Cisco Systems

Qiang Sheng Wang
Cisco Systems

Tom Bryan
Cisco Systems

Dan Bourque
Cisco Systems

## Abstract

The increasing demand to provide new network services in a timely and efficient manner is driving the need to design, test and deploy networks quickly and consistently. Testing and verifying at scale is a challenge: network equipment is expensive, requires space, power and cooling, and there is never enough test equipment for everyone who wants to use it! Network virtualization technologies enable a flexible environment for educators, researchers, and operators to create functional models of current, planned, or theoretical networks.

This demonstration will show VIRL — the Virtual Internet Routing Lab — a platform that can be used for network change validation, training, education, research, or network-aware applications development. The platform combines network virtualization technologies with virtual machines (VMs) running open-source and commercial operating systems; VM orchestration capabilities; a context-aware configuration engine; and an extensible data-collection framework. The system simplifies the process to create both simple and complex environments, run simulations, and collect measurement data.

## Categories and Subject Descriptors

C.2.3 [**Computer-Communication Networks**]: Network Operations—*Network Management*

## Keywords

Emulation; Simulation; Network Design; Network Modelling

## 1. INTRODUCTION

Operational data communication networks are complex, organic environments, where operations teams are challenged to maintain stability while being able to deploy new services or implement changes.


*SIGCOMM'14*, August 17–22, 2014, Chicago, IL, USA.
ACM 978-1-4503-2836-4/14/08.
http://dx.doi.org/10.1145/2619239.2631463.

Engineers who design and run the network must consider both new service requirements and the controlled evolution to support these requirements. Shadownets [1], where parallel networks are constructed to provide a facility to test changes, are one solution, however they are expensive and access is typically restricted.

The education sector teach networking concepts and principles to their students. The cost of commercial-grade networking equipment leads to high student-to-equipment ratios, which limits hands-on time per student. In many parts of the world, these costs are prohibitive, yet the skills are essential for the growth of the local IT economy. Practical exposure to networking improves skills and enhances knowledge retention. Networking simulation tools such as Mininet [4] provide a valuable learning environment but differ to production network environments. There is a role for both in network experimentation.

The 'DevOps' [2] approach to system administration introduces best practises from software engineering. As DevOps concepts gain traction in the networking arena, operators require a way to test proposed automation tools before deployment. Again, the high cost of networking equipment and the need to test and validate to reduce risk, have resulted in limited availability of access to test environments. To adopt this approach, engineers need solutions that provide test equipment on demand, rather than when available.

Virtualization is a common technology, but using it for network emulation requires VMs running production-level network operating systems, flexible networking for VMs, and orchestration of VMs and compute resources to run the simulation. Once launched, the virtual devices must be configured and managed.

## 2. SYSTEM OVERVIEW

Network emulation systems are available for both open-source [7], and commercial routing platforms [3, 5].

While such network emulation systems don't offer the data-plane forwarding performance or ASIC-level fidelity of production network hardware, they provide realistic control-plane and management-plane behavior, including the nuances of standards interpretations and software defects. Network VMs are not intended to emulate the hardware characteristics of physical network equipment, or to validate aspects such as convergence time, as timings can differ.

With high-performance CPUs available in x86 virtualization compute servers, network VMs can perform better than physical networking devices. The performance and scaling improvements in CPUs is motivating developments in Network Functions Virtualization (NFV), such as BGP Route-Reflectors. In many commercial networks, dedicated hardware devices were used for BGP route-reflection services: customers are now starting to deploy VMs to serve this function. Network emulation platforms can benefit from the development of these NFV VMs.

A data network is a series of network devices that operate in a collective manner — in network emulation, this requires the orchestration of network VMs and their communications links. A network design can be represented as a graph: a series of nodes and links, that must be translated into commands to instantiate the network VMs and connectivity.

VIRL aims to solve these problems. It has three core components: a simulation engine built on Openstack; a configuration engine, based on AutoNetkit [6]; and a User Interface for the design and operation of the simulated environment. The components can also be driven from third-party scripts via an XML-based topology file format, and REST APIs.

The simulation engine provides an API between OpenStack and the user interface, to start and stop individual VMs or simulations, and access status. The OpenStack Neutron networking module has been extended to allow VMs with large numbers of data interfaces.

Custom network device or server images can be added, enabling application-layer experiments across commercial-grade network devices. If a VM can run inside a supported hypervisor, it can be added to VIRL. This allows an understanding of how network and applications would behave in a production environment. Since OpenStack passes IP packets, systems such as Mininet can be integrated into the VIRL platform, combining SDN and traditional networks.

The configuration engine generates device configurations from the XML topology, with AutoNetkit extended to support more routing protocols, constructs such as BGP routing hierarchies and MPLS VPN service topologies, and Cisco network operating systems (IOS XR, IOS XE, NX-OS). As these are the operating systems used on production network hardware, the configurations can be easily adapted to physical devices — unlike the use of open-source routing stacks. The AutoNetkit visualization engine has been enhanced to show network layers and hierarchical relationships for protocols such as multi-protocol BGP and MPLS VPNs.

The user interface offers a point-and-click environment to construct a network topology, and annotate with information such as VM image or configuration attributes. The system also provides a data collection harness to pass data from the VMs, allowing topology data and network events to be collected for visualization and analysis.

## 3. SYSTEM USE

The platform has been used by commercial customers, including a large business and residential broadband service ISP in the UK, with BGP peering locations at many major UK Internet Exchange points. Their challenge was to plan and execute a major re-architecture of their BGP peering arrangements without impacting customer service.

Using VIRL, they constructed an accurate model of their core network control-plane, with VMs running IOS-XR using the same configuration as production routers, including over 12,000 lines of BGP policy entries. By injecting live BGP traffic feeds (over 700k paths) they could examine the impact of router configuration and policy changes on traffic flows. Engineers could conduct and record the step-by-step changes taking the BGP configuration from its original to desired target state, and examine the impacts on BGP prefix announcements and path-selections. The final VM configurations were used for the production network migration.

This customer significantly reduced the risks associated with a large-scale change and completed the project with a reduced timescale compared to previous projects. As the simulation can be readily instantiated as required, the constructed network model is also available for other projects.

Another customer used the VIRL platform to plan the introduction of MPLS Traffic Engineering to their network, and familiarise their operations staff with detailed configuration, operation and troubleshooting of MPLS-TE on production routers, running recent code releases. Engineers could log in to virtual routers and understand the impact of configurations, and perform 'break-fix' analysis, without the need for lab equipment.

Traditionally, experimenters have used open-source control-planes or other emulation techniques, rather than VMs using production network images. Access to systems using commercial images allows more realistic experimental results, and provides a richer set of network features.

The VIRL framework enables operators and researchers to easily run large-scale network simulations on real router images. It is being made available via a number of different programs, including one aimed at the research and education community, and another for developers and continuing education students.

## 4. DEMONSTRATION

The demonstration will show the workflow to create a network of VMs, set VM images and configuration attributes, using generating device configurations, and launching the resulting topology. It will demonstrate interacting with running VMs, and data capture, including WireShark and visualisation and graph export of run-time protocol topologies.

We would like to thank Christopher Hartley for editing suggestions, and contributions to the project by David Ward, Ian Wells, Mike O'Gorman, Ralph Schmieder, Bruce Pinsky, Miroslav Los and Brian Daugherty.

## 5. REFERENCES


[1] X. Chen, Z. Mao, and J. Van der Merwe. ShadowNet: a platform for rapid and safe network evolution. *USENIX Annual technical conference*, 2009.

[2] Damon Edwards. What is DevOps? http://dev2ops.org/2010/02/what-is-devops.

[3] GNS3. Graphical Network Simulator.

[4] N. Handigol, B. Heller, V. Jeyakumar, B. Lantz, and N. McKeown. Reproducible network experiments using container-based emulation. In *CoNEXT '12*, Dec. 2012.

[5] Juniper Networks, Inc. Junosphere User Guide.

[6] S. Knight, H. Nguyen, O. Maennel, I. Phillips, N. Falkner, R. Bush, and M. Roughan. An automated system for emulated network experimentation. In *CoNEXT '13*.

[7] M. Pizzonia and M. Rimondini. Netkit: network emulation for education. *Software: Practice and Experience*, 2014.

# SDX: A Software Defined Internet Exchange

Arpit Gupta†, Laurent Vanbever*, Muhammad Shahbaz†, Sean P. Donovan†, Brandon Schlinker‡
Nick Feamster†, Jennifer Rexford*, Scott Shenker◇, Russ Clark†, Ethan Katz-Bassett‡
†Georgia Tech *Princeton University ◇UC Berkeley ‡Univ. of Southern California

## Abstract

BGP severely constrains how networks can deliver traffic over the Internet. Today's networks can only forward traffic based on the destination IP prefix, by selecting among routes offered by their immediate neighbors. We believe Software Defined Networking (SDN) could revolutionize wide-area traffic delivery, by offering direct control over packet-processing rules that match on multiple header fields and perform a variety of actions. Internet exchange points (IXPs) are a compelling place to start, given their central role in interconnecting many networks and their growing importance in bringing popular content closer to end users. To realize a Software Defined IXP (an "SDX"), need new programming abstractions that allow participating networks to create and run these applications and a runtime that both behaves correctly when interacting with BGP and ensures that applications do not interfere with each other. We must also ensure that the system scales, both in rule-table size and computational overhead. In this demo, we show how we tackle these challenges demonstrating the flexibility and scalability of our SDX platform. The paper also appears in the main program [1].

**Categories and Subject Descriptors:** C.2.1 [Computer-Communication Networks] *Network Architecture and Design*: Network Communications

**Keywords:** software defined networking (SDN); Internet exchange point (IXP); BGP

## 1 Motivation

Today's Internet routing is unreliable, inflexible, and difficult to manage. Most of the problems are rooted in the Border Gateway Protocol's (BGP) mode of operations, which has three particularly annoying limitations: It *(i)* routes only on destination IP prefixes; *(ii)* can influence (not control!) direct neighbors only; *(iii)* provides an indirect way of controlling forwarding paths.

We believe that Software Defined Networking (SDN) can easily remove each of these limitations by enabling: *(i)* flexible forwarding policies on many different packet-header fields; *(ii)* remote control, as a SDN controller can receive control message from remote networks (on a bilateral basis); *(iii)* direct control on the forwarding paths by installing packet-processing rules directly in the data-plane.

Yet, simply deploying a few SDN switches here and there will not solve the problems of interdomain routing. Actually, improving Internet routing is–*and has always been*—a perennial problem in a world with 50,000 independently operated networks and a huge installed base of BGP routers.

We turn to Internet Exchange Points (IXPs) as a natural place to deploy new SDN-based inter-domain routing solutions. IXPs are topologically located at strategic positions—with most of the Internet traffic exchanged at around 300 IXPs around the globe. Even one deployment can therefore have a large impact. IXPs have also been particularly open to innovations, a direct consequence of the fact that they are usually managed by a handful of people. Finally, IXPs are large switched networks and some of them have already started to roll out SDN-enabled switching fabric.

Our goal in this project is therefore to improve wide-area traffic delivery by designing, prototyping, and deploying Software Defined Exchanges (SDX) throughout the world. SDX platforms remove the pain out of BGP by enabling their participants to realize fine-grained inter-domain policies easily, *without requiring any change to the existing protocol*.

## 2 Challenges

Designing SDX requires addressing a lot of challenges. Some of them are:

**Providing the right programming abstractions:** In SDX, multiple competing participants with conflicting goals share the same data-plane. SDX needs the right abstractions to balance the desire for flexibility with isolation. Our SDX platform provides each participant with the illusion of owning a (virtual) SDN switch, where other participants connect using a single link. This abstraction hides many details such as the underlying exchange topology. Moreover, this abstraction allows each AS to specify its own policies at the exchange independently from other ASes.

**Interacting with BGP to guarantee correctness:** SDX cannot let its participants define policies in a vacuum, without regard to how they relate to the global routing system. The SDX therefore gives participating ASes ways to define forwarding policies *relative* to the current BGP routes and ensure safe interaction with the existing routing system.

**Ensuring scalability:** SDX needs to support hundreds of participants, hundreds of thousands of IP prefixes, and policies that match on multiple packet-header fields—all while using FIB constrained SDN switches. To enable scalable operation, the SDX platform minimizes both the *space* (# of flow rules) and the *time* (time for policy compilation) complexities. SDX leverages existing control-plane signaling mechanism to reduce the data-plane state and domain-specific knowledge to speed up the compilation of policies.

**Enabling a realistic deployment:** We have built a SDX prototype and created multiple example applications [3] to demonstrate that our prototype scales to many participants, policies and prefixes.


*SIGCOMM'14*, August 17–22, 2014, Chicago, IL, USA.
Copyright 2014 ACM 978-1-4503-2836-4/14/08 ...$15.00.
http://dx.doi.org/10.1145/2619239.2631473

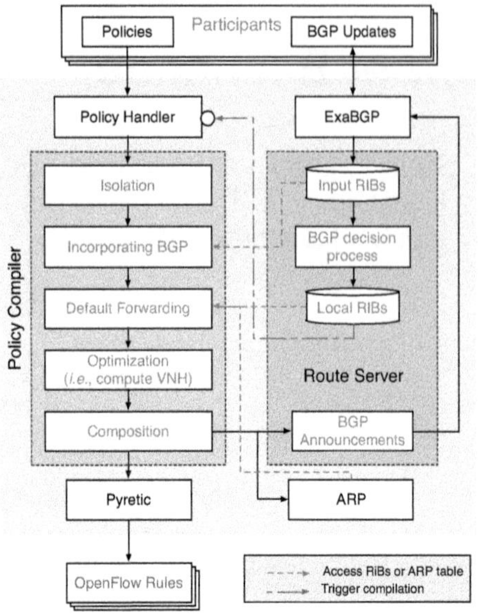


**Figure 1:** *The SDX controller implementation, which has two pipelines: a policy compiler and a route server.*

# 3 Implementation

The SDX consists of a switching fabric, BGP edge routers, and a SDX controller. Edge routers are unmodified and they simply establish normal eBGP sessions with the SDX controller, which also acts as a BGP Route Server. Participants send their policies written in Pyretic [2] to the SDX controller as JSON messages. The SDX controller implementation is divided into two processing pipelines (see Figure 1). One dealing with SDX policies (*Policy Compiler*), and the other with BGP routes (*Route Server*).

**Policy Compiler** takes Pyretic based policies of all the participants as input and produces aggregate forwarding rules. In the process, it augments the policies to *(i)* enable isolation; *(ii)* reduce data-plane state; *(iii)* and integrate with advertised BGP routes. Based on the virtual switch abstraction, the policy compiler isolates participants policies by augmenting them with additional `match` statements based on participant's physical/virtual ports. The compiler then restricts each participant's outbound policies according to advertised BGP routes. It also analyses each participant's policies to identify sets of prefixes sharing the exact same forwarding behavior and assigns one tag (Virtual Next-Hop) to each of them. It then rewrites the policies, replacing match on destination prefixes with match on tags instead. In the SDX, we use IP Next-Hop as tags and rely on BGP to provision (transparently) these tags in the participant edge routers directly. The SDX controller therefore also has an ARP-resolver to respond to queries for Virtual Next-Hop IP address. As a final step, the compiler composes policies of all the participants together to produce a set of forwarding rules. The policy handler also receives events from Route Server and from the participants whenever there is change in the best path for a prefix or in participant's policy, respectively.

**Route Server** performs the default functionality of a typical route server. It receives BGP advertisements from all the participants and computes the best paths on their behalf. It also: *(i)* provides the advertised route information to the compiler pipeline; *(ii)* advertises virtual next hops for each prefix rather than the physical ones; *(iii)* sends an event to the policy handler whenever best route to a prefix changes.

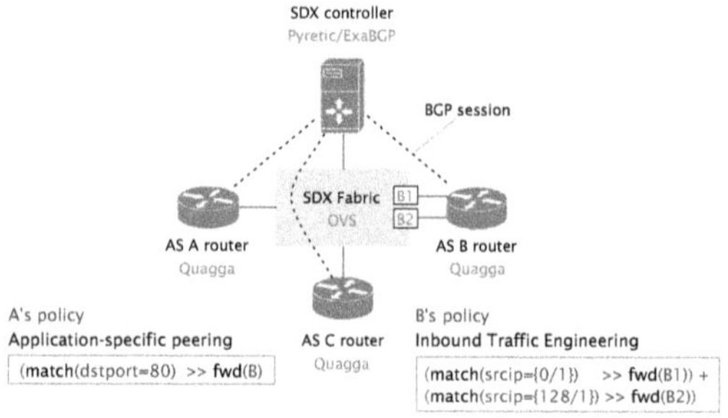


**Figure 2:** *Demonstration setup. By default, all traffic is sent to C. When A provides its policy, all HTTP traffic for the prefixes reachable via B is sent to B. This traffic is then load-balanced according to B's inbound policy.*

# 4 Demonstration Outline

The main goal of our demonstration is to highlight four major capabilities of SDX: *(i)* enabling participants to control the traffic flows based on the portions of flow space other than destination IP prefixes; *(ii)* enabling dynamic composition of participant's policies into a single set of coherent flow rules; *(iii)* minimizing the data-plane state by leveraging the existing BGP control-plane; *(iv)* guaranteeing correct forwarding behavior in sync with advertised BGP routes.

Figure 2 depicts our demonstration setup. It consists of a SDX controller (which includes a route server) connected to an Open vSwitch software (OVS) switch. We also have three BGP edge routers, running the Quagga routing engine, connected to the switch. These BGP routers belong to the participating ASes: *A*, *B*, and *C*. *B*'s router is connected via two input ports at SDX. *B* and *C* advertise prefixes $p_1$-$p_5$ and $p_1$-$p_{10}$ respectively to the SDX controller. For each prefix, the route server chooses the route via *C* as best. Policies are configured as shown in Figure 2. *A* sends uniformly distributed traffic for different sets of source/destination IP addresses and destination ports.

In our demonstration, we will start without any SDX policies. We will observe that all the traffic from *A* exits via *C*. Next, we will send *A*'s application specific policies to the controller. Now, we will observe *A*'s *HTTP* traffic leaving the switching fabric via *B*1. This demonstrates that SDX enables control over traffic flows beyond destination IP prefixes. We will also see that non-HTTP traffic for prefixes $p_1$-$p_5$ and all the traffic from prefixes $p_6$-$p_{10}$ still exits via *C*. This demonstrates that the SDX controller is in sync with the advertised BGP routes. We will now apply *B*'s inbound traffic engineering policies and will observe that half the *HTTP* traffic leave via port *B*1 and the remaining half via *B*2. This demonstrates how SDX composes policies of two participants with disparate high-level goals. In addition to this, we will also show the flow tables to demonstrate the efficacy of using Virtual Next Hops to reduce the number of flow rules in the data-plane.

## Acknowledgments

This research was supported by NSF awards CNS-1040705, CNS-1040838, CNS-1162112, CNS-1261462, and CNS-1261357.

## References

[1] A. Gupta, L. Vanbever, M. Shahbaz, S. P. Donovan, B. Schlinkler, N. Feamster, J. Rexford, S. Shenker, R. Clark, and E. Katz-Bassett. Sdx: A software defined internet exchange. In *SIGCOMM*, 2014.

[2] C. Monsanto, J. Reich, N. Foster, J. Rexford, and D. Walker. Composing software defined networks. In *Proc. USENIX NSDI*, 2013.

[3] SDX Controller. `https://github.com/sdn-ixp/sdx-platform`.

# Toward a Biometric-Aware Cloud Service Engine for Multi-Screen Video Applications


Han Hu
School of Computing
National Univ. of Singapore
Singapore 117417
huh@comp.nus.edu.sg

Yichao Jin
School of Computer Eng.
Nanyang Tech. University
Singapore 639798
YJIN3@e.ntu.edu.sg

Yonggang Wen
School of Computer Eng.
Nanyang Tech. University
Singapore 639798
ygwen@ntu.edu.sg

Tat-Seng Chua
School of Computing
National Univ. of Singapore
Singapore 117417
chuats@comp.nus.edu.sg

Xuelong Li
Center for OPTical IMagery
Analysis and Learning (OPTIMAL)
XIOPM of CAS, Xi'an 710119, China
xuelong_li@opt.ac.cn



## ABSTRACT

The emergence of portable devices and online social networks (OSNs) has changed the traditional video consumption paradigm by simultaneously providing multi-screen video watching, social networking engagement, etc. One challenge is to design a unified solution to support ever-growing features while guarantee system performance. In this demo, we design and implement a multi-screen technology to provide multi-screen interactions over wide area network (WAN). Furthermore, we incorporate face-detection technology into our system to identify users' bio-features and employ a machine learning based traffic scheduling mechanism to improve the system performance.



## Categories and Subject Descriptors

H.4.3 [**Communications Applications**]: Videotex; C.2.1 [**Network Architecture and Design**]: Network Communications

## Keywords

Cloud; Internet Video; Second Screen


## 1. INTRODUCTION

Owing to the popularity of mobile devices and online social networks, the traditional video watching experience has been dramatically changed, from a "laid-back" behavior into a "lean-forward" social engaged experience. In particular, two delightful features, including multi-screen and socialization, have been offered to video consumers. Multi-screen technology [2], also known as second-screen, provides a parallel companion device, whereby the user can engage in some other activities without interrupting the video watching. Socialization technology integrates social networking, including chatting, commenting, engaging OSNs, and so forth, into the video consumption.

However, it is a big challenge to build a unified solution to support the ever growing set of video-related features, while guarantee the efficiency and scalability. First, existing multi-screen technologies are only available in a limited local area network (LAN), lacking of a full-fledged multi-screen support. Second, user behavior under different video related applications varies case by case, resulting in performance degradation when the traditional access pattern based optimization mechanisms are applied.

In this work, we design and develop a multi-screen technology to provide multi-screen interactions over WAN. Our solution leverages cloud-based distributed service architecture and advanced virtual machine migration algorithm to provide scalable and economical multi-screen services for application deployment. Based on this invention, we implement a machine learning based system optimization mechanisms for content caching or prefetching, traffic classification, and virtual machine consolidation by utilizing users' bio-features in terms of gender, age, smile-degree, etc. The principal of our optimization mechanism is based on the observation that people with same gender or age will perform similarly in various applications [3][1]. For example, adult women are more likely to watch videos or post tweets that are related to fashion or personal topics, whereas men are more likely to enjoy sports or philosophical topics.

## 2. CLOUD CLONE BASED MULTI-SCREEN PLATFORM

Fig. 1 illustrates the system architecture of our multi-screen platform, which consists of three participants, including content sources, content consumers, and a cloud centric media network, serving as the multi-screen service engine to enable rich-media applications across multiple screens.

On the user side, one consumer typically has multiple associated screens, including mobile phone, pad, PC, TV, etc. In the case that the first screen (e.g., TV) does not have sufficient onboard resources for intelligent control and management, the second-screen devices will be attached to



*SIGCOMM'14*, August 17–22, 2014, Chicago, IL, USA.
ACM 978-1-4503-2836-4/14/08.
http://dx.doi.org/10.1145/2619239.2631430.

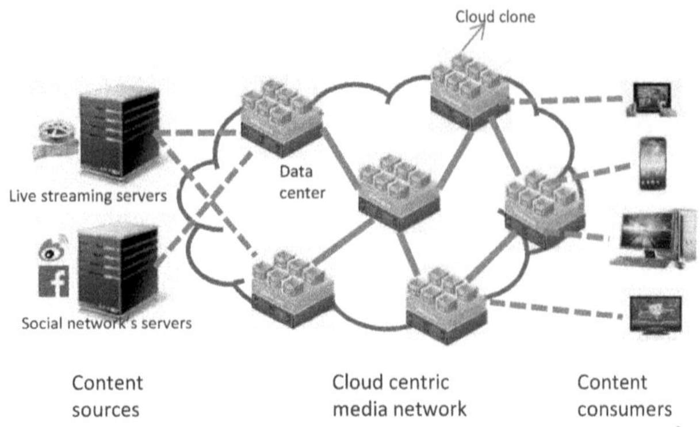


**Figure 1: System Architecture and Deployment of Cloud Clone based Multi-Screen Solution**

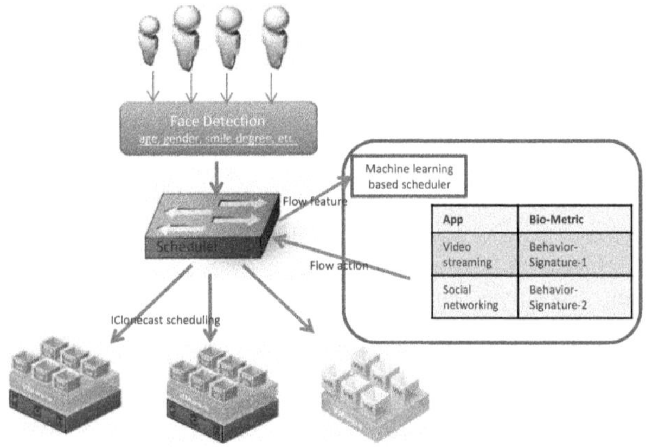


**Figure 2: Bio-Inspired Network Traffic Scheduling**

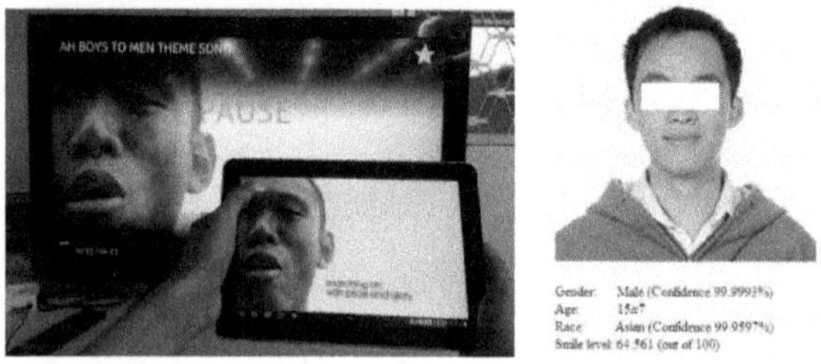

(a) Video transportation across multi-screens (b) Face detection

**Figure 3: Typical Features**

the first-screen device to provide the required intelligence. In the media cloud, each consumer will be incarnated by a dedicated virtual machine (called cloud clone) to control all the devices and orchestrate the multi-screen interactions. Specifically, the cloud clone manages all the real-time session information associated with the application session and migrate its location dynamically to best serve all the screens as the consumer switches the usage of active screen. Moreover, the set of cloud clones forms a stable P2P network for fast retrieval and convenient maintenance. It can also facilitate the multi-screen interactions among different consumers.

Since multiple screens from the same user are all connected to the same cloud clone, our multi-screen paradigm can work in both WAN and LAN. On the source side, the cloud clone gets different contents (e.g., live streaming contents, social media) according to its user's requests, and corresponding analysis. For example, when the user requests to watch an episode, the cloud clone not only streams the episode content itself, but also pre-fetches related social media data. Moreover, the set of cloud clones can collaborate for content sharing, media transcoding, etc.

## 3. BIO-INSPIRED SYSTEM OPTIMIZATION

Our multi-screen solution supports various video related applications, resulting in extremely complicated network dynamics. In addition to traditional system optimization mechanisms, we utilize users' bio-features to further improve the system performance. In particular, when a user logs into the system using a specific screen, the companion camera will take a snapshot of his face. We then employ the face detection technology to identify the age, gender, smile-degree of this user. Our system will automatically record the user behavior as well as the user bio-profile. These log data serve as the training set to mine the bio-related patterns. For example, how long an adult female will spend in watching a fashion video, and what topic she is browsing from online social networks. In this way, a flow table, consisting of three-item-tuple <bio-metric, application, signature>, can be generated for decision making. One potential strategy is to consolidate cloud clone corresponding to users with similar signature for power saving and content caching.

## 4. DEMO DESCRIPTION

Two features, including multi-screen video watching and face-detection based cloud clone initialization, of our demo in shown in Fig. 3. Using the first feature (as illustrated in Fig. 3 (a)), video transportation can be accomplished across multi-screens bi-directionally by just a flip action. In the second case (as shown in Fig. 3 (b)), we illustrate the face-detection results for subsequent cloud clone scheduling. Interested readers are referred to our online demo [1].

## 5. ACKNOWLEDGMENTS

This work is partially supported by the National Natural Science Foundation of China (Grant No: 61125106).

## 6. REFERENCES

[1] A. Finamore, M. Mellia, M. M. Munafò, R. Torres, and S. G. Rao. Youtube everywhere: Impact of device and infrastructure synergies on user experience. In *Proceedings of the 2011 ACM SIGCOMM conference on Internet measurement conference*, pages 345–360. ACM, 2011.

[2] Y. Jin, T. Xie, Y. Wen, and H. Xie. Multi-screen cloud social tv: transforming tv experience into 21st century. In *Proceedings of the 21st ACM international conference on Multimedia*, pages 435–436. ACM, 2013.

[3] Y.-C. Wang, M. Burke, and R. E. Kraut. Gender, topic, and audience response: an analysis of user-generated content on facebook. In *Proceedings of the SIGCHI Conference on Human Factors in Computing Systems*, pages 31–34. ACM, 2013.

[1] http://www.youtube.com/watch?v=NcP1AlOiyDc

# SDN-based Live VM Migration Across Datacenters

Jiaqiang Liu, Yong Li, Depeng Jin
Department of Electronic Engineering, Tsinghua University
liyong07@tsinghua.edu.cn

**Categories and Subject Descriptors:** C.2.1[Computer-Communication Networks]:Network Architecture and Design-*Network Communications*

**Keywords:** Virtual machine migration; software defined network

## 1. MOTIVATION

With the advances of server virtualization technology, virtual machines (VMs) are widely used to provide various services, where live VM migration becomes an important tool to manage these services. Especially, with the increasing trend of owning multiple datacenters by a single company, live VM migration across datacenters enables the administrators to carry out globally optimized resource control and management like cloud bursting [2].

Generally, migrating a virtual machine requires to copy the disk and memory from one server to another, and update the network to forward packets to the new location. Pre-copy strategy are usually used for disk and memory copy to reduce the service downtime. Ideally, two aspects of optimization can be used to improve the migration performance. The first is from the view of host, e.g., optimizing the algorithm that decides when to stop the pre-copy stage or eliminating redundancy of data transmissions through compression. The second is network based optimization, e.g., selecting the best path for data copy or optimizing the network update process to reduce service downtime.

However, as best as we know, most previous works [1, 2] only focus on the host based optimization, leaving the potential of network based optimization unexplored. The reason is the control of routing and network updating is distributed on every single forwarding device under traditional network architecture, making it hard to implement network based optimization. However, with the advances of Software-Defined Network (SDN) and the trend of its ubiquitous deployment in datacenters, it is able to control traffic forwarding and network update by running programs on the controller, which brings the opportunity to implement network based optimization.


*SIGCOMM'14,* August 17–22, 2014, Chicago, IL, USA.
ACM 978-1-4503-2836-4/14/08.
http://dx.doi.org/10.1145/2619239.2631431.

Motivated by the advantage SDN provides, in this demo, we design and implement a SDN based system for live VM migration across datacenters. By wildlife deployment and preliminary experimental results, we demonstrate its efficiency to support live VM migrations across datacenters.

## 2. KEY CHALLENGES AND SOLUTIONS

### 2.1 Control Across Datacenters

**Challenges:** Due to the constraint of security policy and requirement of scalability, each data center will have its own network controller. Implementing and optimizing VM migration across datacenters requires the coordination among them. For example, after migrating a VM from one datacenter to another one, both the original and destination datacenters require to update routing path to forward packets destined to the migrated VM to the new location. Besides, cloud manage system and network controller should also coordinate with each other, because cloud manage system owns the VMs' information and the controller also maintains VMs location information for traffic forwarding. Under the scenario of VM migration, if not well coordinated, they may have inconsistent view on a VM's location and lead to failure of service access.

**Solutions:** In accordance with SDN's spirit of centralized control, we use a global orchestrator for coordination among network controllers and cloud manage systems. Particularly, the global orchestrator maintains all VMs' location information, help to select the best paths for transferring the migration traffic, and control the network update process.

### 2.2 Communication Across Datacenters

**Challenges:** To maintain the active connections, a live migration always requires the migrated VM maintaining its original MAC and IP addresses. Considering live migration across datacenters, satisfying this requirement asks for support of distributing VMs within the same subnet to multiple datacenters, which needs to solve two problems, the first is how to deal with arp resolution request when the object host is located in another datacenter, the second is how to guarantee traffic of inter-data center communication is correctly routed through the Internet.

**Solutions:** L2VPN is usually used to extend a subnet to multiple geographically distributed datacenters. It is not efficient because all arp requests need to be broadcasted to every datacenter network and all required VPNs need to be pre-established. Therefore, we propose a SDN based solution. Specifically, we propose to use the network controller to respond with arp requests. To implement this, each net-

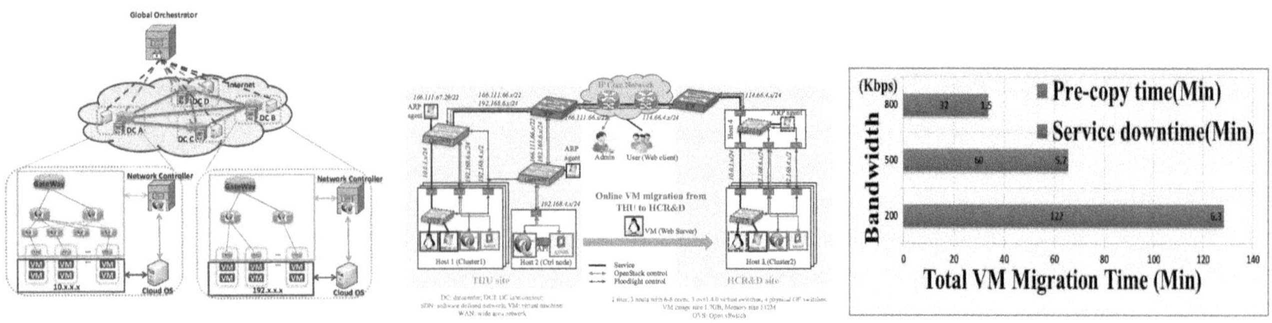


(a) (b) (c)

**Figure 1: (a) SDN VM migration system architecture; (b) Illustration for the system deployment; (c) Experimental Results.**

work controller maintains a table that records the mapping of IP and MAC addresses of devices in the datacenter it stays, and the global orchestrator maintains a similar table containing mapping information of all devices. Besides, we propose to use a programmable gateway at the edge of each datacenter to implement network address and port translation (NAPT) for inter-data center traffic. The specific rules of such translation is dynamically determined by the SDN controller.

# 3. SYSTEM DESIGN

Fig. 1(a) illustrates our proposed system architecture for live VM migration. Specifically, according to the above introduced solution, we deploy a global orchestrator to coordinate information sharing among the Cloud OSes and the network controllers, and deploy a programmable gateway to carry out NAPT to make sure that the packets forwarded to the Internet is compatible with the Internet protocol stacks. In the system, the Cloud OS is responsible for VM management like VM creation and migration, and the network controller directly connects to all OpenFlow enabled switches and makes routing decision on their delegation. Particularly, we note that OpenFlow switch support modifying packets header and thus use it to implement the programmable gateway.

In this system, we collaborate Cloud OS, network controller and global orchestrator to share information with each other to achieve a consistent view about VMs' condition and to improve VM migration performance. Specifically, when some events like VM creation or VM migration happen, the Cloud OS reports them with related configuration to the network controller and the global orchestrator. Besides, we use the network controller for proxy arp resolution, the required MAC addresses are learned from the reported events. If a request is about the VM located in another data center, the network controller will ask the orchestrator to get the corresponding MAC address.

Network-based optimization can be easily implemented on the controller in two aspects. First, the network controller is able to select the path with the most available bandwidth after receiving a migration request event. Second, the network controller can take out proactive network update. Specifically, the controller computes new routing paths and flow entries, and pre-update some flow tables in the migration stage rather than waiting for the VM initiated in the new place.

# 4. IMPLEMENTATION & DEMO

We implement and deploy above design on multi-site datacenter testbed. As shown in Fig. 1(b), the deployment consists two sites, THU site and HCR&D site, which are connected by public Internet. Floodlight is selected as the network controller, and OpenStack is used as the Cloud OS. The gateway is implemented using Open vSwitch (OVS). Particularly, we implement the network address translation logic as an application on the floodlight. Further, we leverage Quantum Plugin for OpenStack to report hosts information and VM migration events to the Floodlight, and we create a database on the orchestrator to store VM location information and mappings for network address translation. The interaction among the network controller and the orchestrator is implemented using REST APIs.

Our demonstration uses this prototype deployment to illustrate the effectiveness of SDN based live migration of virtual machines across THU site and HCR&D site. Specifically, to test the service downtime, we employ Iperf sending UDP traffic on the migrated VM to a user client, and measure the time period that the client does not receive the sent UDP packets as the service downtime. We illustrate some test results in Fig. 1(c), which shows the pre-copy time and service downtime under different network bandwidth used for migration. These results suggest that the prototype system is efficient to support live VM migration across datacenters even even when the datacenters are connected by the public Internet and the available bandwidth among them are rather low.

# 5. ACKNOWLEDGEMENT

This work is supported by National Basic Research Program of China (Grant No. 2013CB329105), National Nature Science Foundation of China (Grants No. 61301080, No. 91338102 and No. 61171065), China's Next Generation Internet (Grant No. CNGI-12-03-007), and Chinese National Major Scientific and Technological Specialized Project (Grant No. 2013ZX03002001).

# 6. REFERENCES

[1] T. HIROFUCHI, M. TSUGAWA, H. NAKADA, and T. KUDOH. A wan-optimized live storage migration mechanism toward virtual machine evacuation upon severe disasters. *IEICE TRANSACTIONS on Information and Systems*, 96(12):2663–2674, 2013.

[2] T. Wood, K. Ramakrishnan, P. Shenoy, and J. Van der Merwe. Cloudnet: dynamic pooling of cloud resources by live wan migration of virtual machines. In *ACM SIGPLAN Notices*, volume 46, pages 121–132. ACM, 2011.

# Characterizing Botnets-as-a-Service

Wentao Chang[1] An Wang[1] Aziz Mohaisen[2] Songqing Chen[1]
[1]Department of Computer Science, George Mason University [2]VeriSign Labs
{wchang7, awang10, sqchen}@gmu.edu amohaisen@verisign.com

**Categories and Subject Descriptors**
C.2.0 [**Computer Communication Networks**]: General—*data communications, security and protection.*
**General Terms**
Measurement, Security
**Keywords**
Botnet, measurement, collaborations

## 1. INTRODUCTION

Botnets are one of today's most challenging cybersecurity threats, and promise to remain a serious threat for many years to come.Bots today are not limited to sophisticated machines, such as servers and personal computers: recent DDoS attacks were reportedly utilizing fridges [3], and other massive scanning activities were using embedded devices, including IP monitoring cameras and security doors [5].

Driven by economical profit, botnets are arising in what has been coined as "Botnet-as-a-Service (BaaS)" [2]. Many of today's botnets are designed and developed to be loaned easily to third parties. Reportedly botnet controllers can make a large amount of money by loaning the service in the mature underground market [4]. Understanding such phenomena through analysis has been the goal of the research community for a while to develop effective defense mechanisms and to guide disinfections.

As the arms race between the malware developers and defenders is endless, it is essential to continuously track and understand the latest strategies of attackers in manipulating botnets for attacks. A timely understanding can provide important insights to guide the building of effective defenses. Therefore, we set to investigate modern botnets from the service perspective, focusing on its elasticity and stability.

Data analyzed in our study is obtained from the monitoring and attribution unit in a private security company that is located in the United States, with partnerships of traffic sharing across the globe. Malware samples used in launching various attacks are reverse engineered and labeled to a known malware family using best practices. A honeypot is then created to emulate the operation of the reverse-engineered malware sample that belongs to a given botnet and to enumerate all bots across the globe participating in that particular botnet. Traces of traffic associated with various botnets are then collected at various anchor points on the Internet, via the


*SIGCOMM'14,* August 17–22, 2014, Chicago, IL, USA.
ACM 978-1-4503-2836-4/14/08.
http://dx.doi.org/10.1145/2619239.2631464.

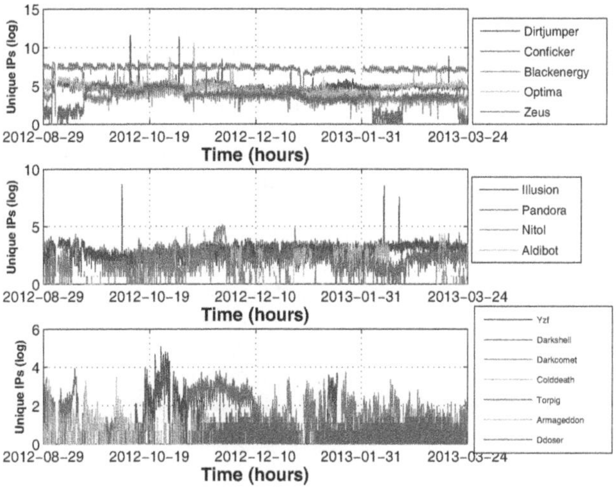


**Figure 1: Botnet stability of three groups (based on botnet size)**

cooperation of more than 300 ISPs, and analyzed to attribute and characterize attacks. The monitors of the company track temporal activities of 23 different known botnet families in the wild, and generate hourly log dumps from 08/29/2012 to 03/24/2013, a total of 207 days.

Our preliminary study reveals several interesting new trends of botnet management:

- Large botnets often maintain a dynamic stability: keep a stable number of live bots but also keep rotating individual bots.
- From the perspective of attack magnitude, large botnets are more elastic than small ones.
- There is a clear rising trend for botnets to collaborate on campaigns, concurrently or in turn.

## 2. BaaS CHARACTERIZATION

We briefly present some preliminary results of our BaaS analysis from the following three perspectives: stability, elasticity, and collaboration.

### 2.1 Botnet stability

Similar to the metrics used in [1], we define the botnet size as the total number of unique IPs that were once recruited in their lifetime by the specific botnet. We find that the botnet size of different families varies significantly. Based on the botnet size, we can classify them into 3 different groups from top to down: `large`, `medium` and `small` (Figure 1).

Figure 1 shows the simultaneous live bots along time for these three groups. Note the $y$-axis is in log scale. To some extent, the simultaneous live bots distribution along time can indicate the stability of the corresponding botnet family. As shown in the figure,

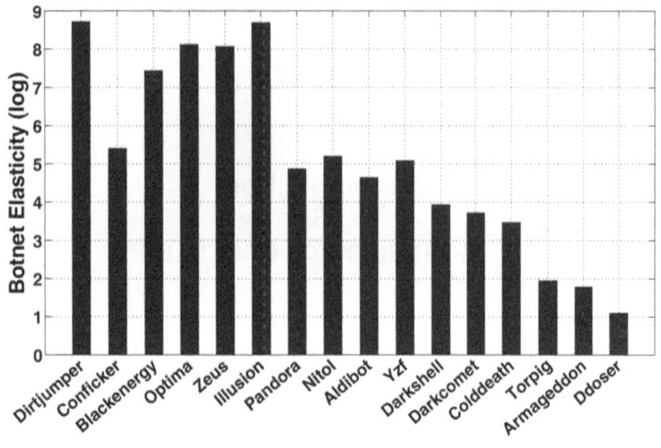


**Figure 2: Botnet Elasticity**

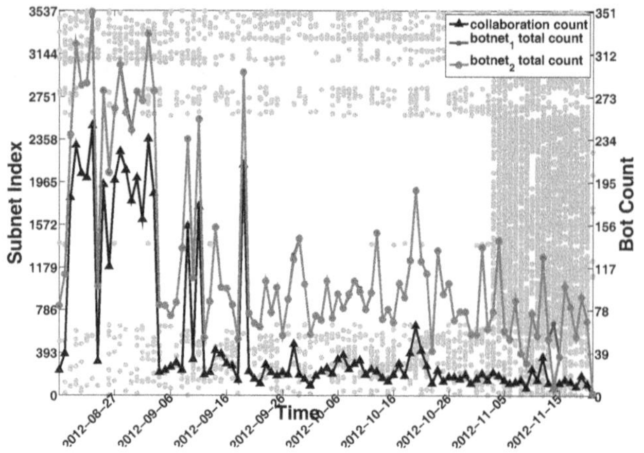


**Figure 3: Intra-family collaboration for Blackenergy**

besides the difference on the absolute numbers, the results indicate that the botnets in `large` group have maintained a relatively stable army of active bots with a few spikes, while there are more fluctuations in botnets in the `medium` and `small` groups. While this is kind of expected, it also raises a question on whether such stability in large botnets is due to the same sets of bots being active or more sophisticated strategies (e.g., bot rotation) have been used by botnets. Our further investigation (omitted due to space limit) indicates such stability is not static, but dynamic. That is, the live bots are being strategically rotated with a short online duration to maintain such dynamic stability.

## 2.2 Botnet elasticity

As Figure 1 shows, the number of live bots will surge within a very limited time frame, usually a couple of days, when the botnet is instructed to engage in certain attacks. In our observation, a well managed botnet could rapidly recruit new bots in the order of hundreds of thousands. This is another important perspective when we evaluate the potential of a botnet's attacking power, particularly as today botnets are moving towards BaaS. Therefore, we further define a metric `elasticity` of a botnet, which is the ratio of the maximum over the minimum number of simultaneously live bots.

Figure 2 shows the elasticity result for all families—sorted by size in descending order. As indicated by the figure, overall, the elasticity decreases with the decreasing botnet size. An exception is Conficker. As Figure 1 shows, compared to other large botnets, Conficker maintains a very stable army of bots. From the service perspective, the larger the elasticity value, the more capable a botnet is upon a demand for attacks. From the defense perspective, the more elastic a botnet, the harder to shut it down.

## 2.3 Service collaborations

For each family, we have a list of botnet identifiers derived from different malware signatures we detected during the 7 months, and we cross-compare the set of active bots from different botnet identifiers over time.

**Some collaborative attacks are concurrent.** Some different botnet identifiers within the same family have extremely high concurrent usage over the same set of bots. We speculate the attacker employs multiple botnets to launch the same attack. Figure 3 shows an example, demonstrating the collaborations of two botnets within the Blackenergy family. In this figure, the $x$-axis represents daily timestamps when collaboration happened, the $y$-axis on the left represents the index of subnet involved in the collaborations, and the $y$-axis on the right represents the the count of bots. For the scatter plot, each dot with different color shows which botnet the subnet belongs to at the time of collaborations, and cyan color indicates that they are employed concurrently by both botnets. Three curves for the total number of bots from each botnet and the number of collaborating bots are also plotted. From the collaboration curve and the total count curve, we can clearly see that activities of both botnets are well synchronized. Also, a dedicated group of bots that belong to both botnets are responsible for the surge events.

**Some botnets take turns in collaborative attacks.** We notice that some different botnet identifiers own a large number of the same bots, but those bots are rarely used concurrently. Instead, they were solely used by botnet 1 at a time, and later majority of those bots are transferred to botnet 2. We suspect the same set of bots are leveraged to participate in different campaigns. This temporal pattern suggests that different botnets could be controlled by the same botmaster. They are essentially the same botnet, with some difference in their code base that resulted in a different signature.

# 3. DISCUSSION

Botnets have been widely used for various Internet attacks. Driven by profit, "Botnet-as-a-Service (BaaS)" is on the rise. In this work, we set to examine botnets from the perspective of services, focusing on the service stability, elasticity, and collaborations. Our results indicate that to remain active and profitable, BaaS is very versatile and adaptive by constantly and continuously adopting new techniques, to evade from being detected and to better serve their underground customers. We are actively conducting in-depth analysis and we seek to offer more insights to the defense community in a timely manner.

This work is partially supported by NSF under grants CNS-0746649 and CNS-1117300.

# 4. REFERENCES

[1] M. Abu Rajab, J. Zarfoss, F. Monrose, and A. Terzis. A multifaceted approach to understanding the botnet phenomenon. In *IMC*, 2006.

[2] P. McDougall. Microsoft: Kelihos ring sold 'botnet-as-a-service'. `http://ubm.io/MtCSr7`, September 2011.

[3] M. Starr. Fridge caught sending spam emails in botnet attack. `http://bit.ly/1j5Jac1`, Jan 2014.

[4] M. Vicario. Four ways cybercriminals profit from botnets. `http://bit.ly/1elSIiP`, Nov 2010.

[5] Wikipedia. Carna botnet. `http://bit.ly/1slx1E6`, 2014.

# Aerial Wireless Localization Using Target-Guided Flight Route

Shaofeng Chen, Dingyi Fang, Xiaojiang Chen*, Tingting Xia, and Meng Jin
Northwest University, China
shaofeng.c.nwu@gmail.com,dyf@nwu.edu.cn
xjchen@nwu.edu.cn,xiatingt@gmail.com,mengj@stumail.nwu.edu.cn

## ABSTRACT

This poster presents GuideLoc, a highly efficient aerial wireless localization system that uses directional antennas mounted on a mini Multirotor Unmanned Aerial Vehicle (UAV) to enable detecting and positioning of targets. Taking advantage of angle and signal strength of frames transmitted from targets, GuideLoc can directly fly towards the targets with the minimum flight route and time. We implement a prototype of GuideLoc and evaluate the performance by simulations and experiments. Experimental results show that GuideLoc achieves an average location accuracy of 2.7 meters and reduces flight distance more than 50% compared with existing localization approaches using UAV.

Figure 1: GuideLoc in Localization.

## Categories and Subject Descriptors

C.2.1 [**Network Architecture and Design**]: Wireless communication

## Keywords

Wireless Localization; Flight Routes; Multi-rotor UAV

## 1. INTRODUCTION

It is extremely important for disaster rescue to quickly and accurately locate wireless devices of targets, as the higher efficiency is, the more life is saved. Some researchers have proposed Warwalking or Wardriving, which search for wireless targets by a person or a vehicle using a special wireless device. Unfortunately, it is impossible for vehicle and not convenient for people to access to the special places such as building roofs, which is inevitable in actual disaster rescue. Indeed, we search and rescue survivors from building debris after an earthquake, positioning them by localizing their active smart phones. Thus, researchers began to explore warflying tool which can fly to any point in open space and produce accurate location of the target wireless devices. Current warflying systems[1, 2], however, scan all target regions even in the absence of target according to fixed flight route, which have longer flight distances, leading to huge time and energy consumption.

This poster presents GuideLoc, a highly efficient target detection and localization system without requiring either infrastructure of cameras or training. The basic idea of GuideLoc is to estimate the angle of arrival (AoA) of frames transmitted from targets, using the received signal strength (RSS) on different directional antennas. Taking advantage of AoA, GuideLoc can directly fly towards the target without scanning target area in traversal patterns, which reduces the total flight distance and minimizes the search time.

## 2. GUIDELOC

To achieve this goal, we address the following challenges:

*(a) How to extract the angle and signal strength?* The traditional methods rely on rotating a single directional antenna or using a single steerable beam directional antenna to estimate the AoA. However, it is impossible for a moving UAV to gather frames on all directions exactly at the same location, thus the UAV has to fly very slowly and even needs to hover, which may not always be practical. Some researchers augment these methods by flying multiple times on the same route[3]. However, rotation of the antenna and repetitive flight consume too much energy, which is constrained by GuideLoc's battery life.

GuideLoc uses multiple fixed directional antennas, orienting along different directions, to connect to multiple radios on the moving UAV.

*(b) How to quickly determine whether GuideLoc has reached the area above the target?* To improve localization accuracy, we combine AoA with GPS: GuideLoc flies towards a target, we can get the coordinate of the target by the GPS of GuideLoc when the UAV reaches the area above the target.

When GuideLoc flies towards the target and gradually gets close to it, the RSS will become stronger whereas the

*Corresponding author


*SIGCOMM'14,* August 17–22, 2014, Chicago, IL, USA.
ACM 978-1-4503-2836-4/14/08.
http://dx.doi.org/10.1145/2619239.2631466.

RSS will become weaker.Therefore, the RSS (y-axis) and the GPS coordinate (x-axis) can form an x-y coordinate system, in which the coordinate value at the peak point of the waveform is the coordinate of the target. Unfortunately, to draw the waveform, UAV has to makes a round trip to the target, which wastes energy and reduces search efficiency. Therefore, how to quickly determine whether GuideLoc has reached the area above the target can be challenging.

Our solution to this problem is inspired by the feature that RSS values in different directions are almost the same, as GuideLoc reaches the area above the target. Firstly, the UAV flies towards the target and keeps capturing signals of this target. Secondly, if RSS values in different directions are not the same (Range of them is greater than 11dBm, this threshold value obtained by real experiments), GuideLoc updates AoA and makes slight adjustment to the flight direction. Finally, if those RSS values are almost the same, we can see the current GPS coordinate of GuideLoc as the target location.

*(c) How to plan the minimum flight distance with wireless signals of targets?*

**Range Partitioning:** To detect all targets, we need to divide the whole target area into $N \times N$ unit square, so that the communication range of GuideLoc can cover the unit square and the UAV can capture at least one packet from the target in each unit square. According to the above analysis, we can derive Theorem 1.

Theorem 1: If GuideLoc can detect all targets, the size of a unit $-N$ should meet the following formula,

$$\frac{\sqrt{d}}{R} \leq N < \frac{d}{vt} \qquad (1)$$

where, v is the maximum flight speed, d represents the side length of the target square area, R refers to the communication range of the plane where the UAV is, and t is the transmission interval of the target.

**Inter-region searching:** Our goal is to find a minimum distance of flight path in which GuideLoc flies through the center of each unit to detect all targets and returns to the starting point, which is the classic Traveling Salesman Problem. We use the Genetic Algorithm to solve this problem.

**Intra-region positioning:** When the UAV arrives at the center of the unit, we estimate the distances between targets and the center, according to a popular log-distance path loss (LDPL) model. If the estimated distance is less than $\lambda$, the target belongs to this unit. We set the threshold $\lambda$ to half of the unit's diagonal to enable the corresponding round regions of adjacent to have some overlap, which can effectively avoid leak detection for the targets at the edge of the unit.

When the UAV starts from the center of the current unit, how can we find a shortest flight route to locate each target and go to the end (the center of the next unit). This problem is not the classic TSP, as it doesn't need the UAV to return, at the same time the starting and end point are fixed, which inspired us to transfer it into a TSP problem. We estimate the locations of targets based on RSS and AoA, and assume that a virtual edge between the starting and end point is a tiny negative. Then we can use TSP algorithm to solve this problem and the resulting Hamiltonian cycle will definitely contain this virtual edge. After this virtual edge is deleted, as the weight of it is a constant, the rest edges will constitute a shortest path from the starting to the end and cover all the points, which solved our problem.

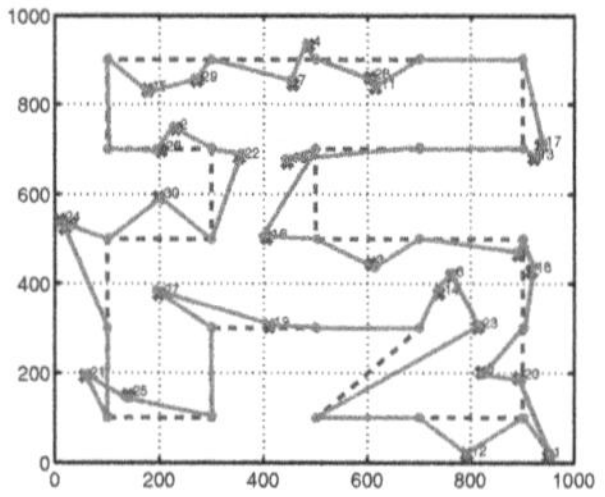

Figure 2: Flight route of GuideLoc

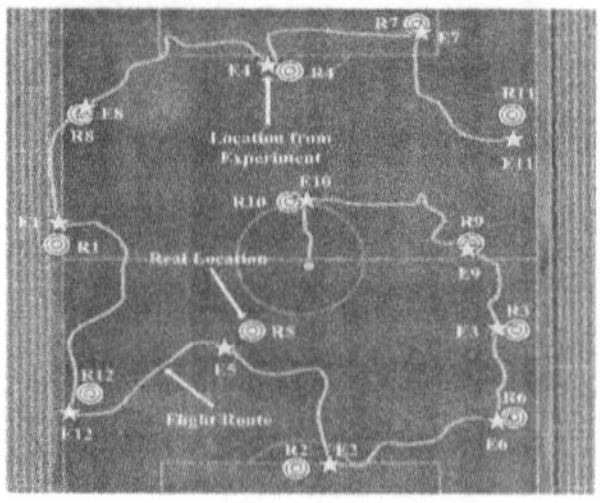

Figure 3: APs Identified by GuideLoc

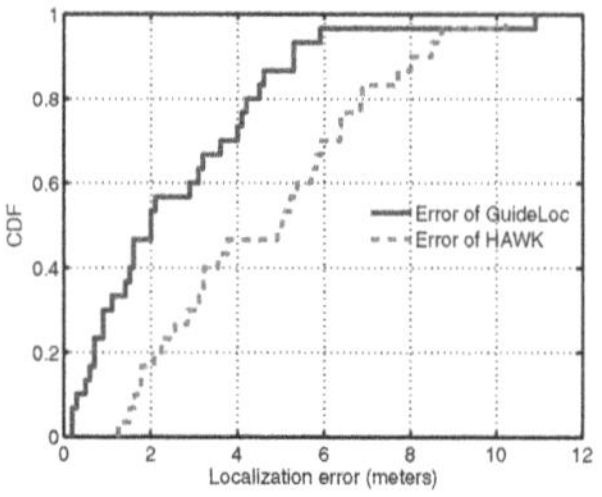


Figure 4: Localization errors for GuideLoc and HAWK

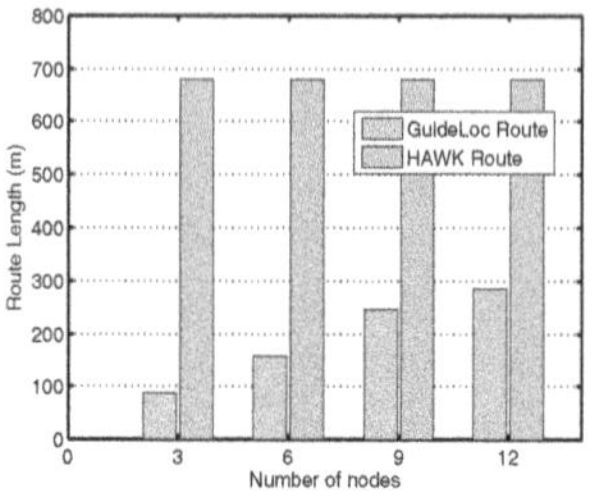


Figure 5: Route length for GuideLoc and HAWK

## 3. PRELIMINARY RESULTS

We implement a prototype of GuideLoc using the ArduCopter and the wireless nodes. Since GuideLoc currently has only a battery life for a 15-minutes flight, the simulation were used to validate the Theorem 1. The target area in the simulation is a $1km \times 1km$ square where 30 wireless nodes are randomly deployed. Figure 2 shows the unit squares (grid portion), flight route of GuideLoc (red solid line portion) and Hamilton cycle as the search order (blue imaginary line).

We conduct real-world field experiments to evaluate the performance of GuideLoc. In the experiments, 3,6, 9,12 wireless nodes are randomly distributed on the track field respectively. The main comparison points are HAWK[2], HAWK uses a level Moore curve 3 as flight route. Due to space limitation, Figure 3 only shows the 12 nodes' real and estimated locations and the flight route. Figure 4 shows the CDF curve of localization errors for GuideLoc and HAWK. We can achieve an accuracy of 2.7 meters on average. Figure 5 shows the total route length for GuideLoc and HAWK. Compared with HAWK, GuideLoc can greatly reduce the total flight distance so that it can rapidly locate targets.

## 4. ACKNOWLEDGMENTS

This work was supported by the NSFC(61170218, 61272461, 61373177,61070176,61202198), Project National Key Technology R&D Program 2013BAK01B02,the Key Project of Chinese Ministry of Education 211181.

## 5. REFERENCES

[1] Wireless aerial surveillance platform. Available at https://rabbit-hole.org/, 2011.

[2] Z. Liu, Y. Chen, B. Liu, C. Cao, and X. Fu. Hawk: An unmanned mini helicopter-based aerial wireless kit for localization. In *INFOCOM*, 2012.

[3] A. P. Subramanian, P. Deshpande, J. Gao, and S. R. Das. Drive-by localization of roadside wifi networks. In *INFOCOM*, 2008.

# An Educational Networking Framework for Full Layer Implementation and Testing

Keunhong Lee, Joongi Kim, Sue Moon
Department of Compute Science, KAIST
{khlee, joongi}@an.kaist.ac.kr, sbmoon@kaist.edu

## Categories and Subject Descriptors

C.2.2 [**Conputer-Communication Networks**]: Network Protocols—*Protocol verification*; D.2.5 [**Software Engineering**]: Testing and Debugging—*Testing tools*; K.3.2 [**Computers and Education**]: Computer and Information Science Education—*Computer science education, self-assessment*

## General Terms

Design, Verification

## Keywords

Educational Networking Framework, Full Layer Implementation, Automated Test Suite, Network protocols, TCP, IP

## 1 Introduction

In our computer science discipline, hands-on projects challenge students to build systems they learn in class. These projects have always been an integral part of our curricula. Kurose and Ross supplement their textbook on computer networking with Wireshark[1] labs and programming assignments for network application[3]. Wireshark labs help students to grasp quickly the workings of today's Internet via packet trace analysis without writing code. MYSOCK and STCP[2] have been used in undergrad networking courses for students to implement the socket API and a simplified TCP connection mechanism to work over simulated packet losses and reordering. Advanced graduate-level courses often include experiments with the network infrastructure. The popular network simulation tool, `ns2`[3], has accumulated an extensive set of protocol implementations in the past two decades, but the goal of `ns2` is to examine the protocol performance against other competing traffic. While `ns2` operates strictly in a simulated environment, emulab[4] and ONL (Open Network Laboratory) [2] offer an emulated networking environment with ease of access and configurability. VNS [1] and its successor Mininet [4] have empowered researchers with a container-based emulation environment that closely matches the performance of a real testbed with high fidelity.

Among the multitudes of protocol and networking tools, there lacks an environment where students can implement and test the full protocol layer in a realistic setting. In this poster we present ELSA (Educational Layered System with Auto-testing), a framework for students to implement TCP, IP, and routing protocols, and test against adversary implementations. We have designed ELSA, implemented it and are currently using it in CS341, an undergraduate computer networking course at KAIST. In the next section we present the design and main features of ELSA.

## 2 Design and Key Features

We have designed and implemented ELSA with the following educational goals in mind.

### 2.1 Complete experience on layered abstraction

To offer a complete experience on implementation of a layer in networking stacks, programming assignments should cover all of the following elements:

- demultiplexing calls from the lower layer (TCP)
- multiplexing calls from the upper layer (TCP)
- context management (IP and TCP)
- functions in protocol specification (IP and TCP)

We have designed the following hands-on projects to address the above elements:

- In the TCP layer, students are to implement connection establishment and tear-down. ELSA supports both reliable and unreliable modes for testing data transmission. Congestion and flow control of TCP is also part of the assignment. The challenge here is to manage multiple connections and their states in a single layer.
- The IP layer generates pcap-compatible logs[5] with the actual Ethernet packets instead of simulated data streams, which allows debugging and inspection via packet tracing tools such as Wireshark. This layer covers topics on route lookup, IP switching, persistent connection tests with the TCP layer and routing protocols (e.g., distance vector) under link failures.

[1]`http://www.wireshark.org/`
[2]`http://www.stanford.edu/class/cs244a/hw3/hw3.html`
[3]`http://www.isi.edu/nsnam/ns/`
[4]`http://www.emulab.net`

[5]MIME type *vnd.tcpdump.pcap*. See `http://www.iana.org/assignments/media-types/application/vnd.tcpdump.pcap`


*SIGCOMM'14*, August 17–22, 2014, Chicago, IL, USA.
ACM 978-1-4503-2836-4/14/08.
http://dx.doi.org/10.1145/2619239.2631467.

### 2.2 Complete experience over a network of hosts

The data link layer is implemented using Linux UDP sockets and a single host is realized as a single process. Students can build a network of hosts by having multiple ELSA processes either on a single machine or over a distributed environment. By replacing the virtual driver that implements the data link layer with a real user-level Ethernet device driver, we could turn ELSA into a barebone Linux networking stack. A network of four nodes connected in tandem is given to students as a reference network configuration.

## 3 Improvements from Experience

We have collected feedback from students and teaching assistants at the end of every semester when this framework was used. Here we summarize the comments, and describe our solutions in response to them.

**Comments from students:**

- **It was difficult to develop and test only one side of a coupled function.** Networking primitives are coupled with their counterparts. For example, the completion of connect() requires a correct implementation of accept() on the adversarial side. Students could not verify correctness of a partial, one-sided implementation.
- **Framework internals were not hidden from students.** Students had to understand the internal behaviours of the framework to write correctly working code. In particular, previous versions have exposed internal data structures for inter-layer communication. For example, students had to copy and manage underlying pipe file descriptors used by the framework when accept()-ing a new connection.

**Comments from TAs:**

- **Setting up a testing environment was time-consuming.** Setting up a multi-process virtual environment to grade an assignment was tedious, time-consuming, and not straightforward to automate.
- **Matching logs to the correct behavior was challenging.** Every student had to demonstrate the submitted code in person to the TA and ran through the log line by line with the TA in order to verify that the code was correct. It was almost impossible to find a needle in a haystack; investigating more than 1K lines of TCP implementation (e.g., 1187 LoC in a reference implementation[6]) was impractical when grading tens of students. Our practice was to check console outputs (logs) and let students explain what was going on. It was time-consuming and difficult to prove incorrectness when TAs were faced with verbose output.

**Our solutions:**

- **Combine multiple instances of function implementations:** ELSA enables incremental tests of coupled functions by combining multiple implementations of a single layer (e.g., TCP) in a single process. For example, ELSA combines both students' version of the TCP layer and a reference implementation in a single process for testing, which allows incremental and independent tests of every function.
- **Make the framework event-driven:** We reduce the amount of code to understand when beginning each assignment by adapting an event-driven structure. Students can receive events by implementing proper callback functions instead of polling events from the framework. This approach reduces the amount of skeleton code (we provide 84 lines of skeleton and 48 lines for header files). The skeleton resembles that of the linux driver code. As all the events are totally ordered, students can focus on the core functions rather than complicated synchronization issues.
- **Build an automated test suite for evaluation:** In order to reduce the effort that goes into grading, we have developed a complete test suite for all possible code execution paths in the TCP state transition diagram for network events such as packet reordering and losses. The test suite outputs grading results from a single issue of a command. Albeit it is almost an independent part of the framework, the test suit is the most time savior in our grading effort.

[6]The number of lines are measured with CLOC. See `http://cloc.sourceforge.net/`

## 4 Summary and Future Work

ELSA is an educational framework for transport and network layer implementation. Our improvements are based on eight years of accumulated lab expreiences. In Spring 2014 we are already benefitting from the improvements. We could cut the number of TAs by half for the class size 50% larger than last year. At the end of the semester we will release the framework as an open-source software and encourage other universities to try ELSA.

We have following plans for ELSA. First, we will extend our improvements to the IP layer. The current version of ELSA has reference implementations of the IP layer including fragmentation and reassembly, but lacks the automated test suite. Second, we are considering migrating ELSA's data link layer to a more general platform, such as Mininet or native Linux kernel. Third, we should extend the framework to include IPv6. With the address exhaustion of IPv4, IPv6 is gaining ground and educational networking systems should reflect this change.

## 5 Acknowledgments

ELSA is based on KENS (KAIST Educational Network System) developed by Junehwa Song and his students. The original motivation and design of KENS has been a great inspiration and we are greatly indebted. This work was supported by the Basic Science Research Program by the National Research Foundation of Korea (NRF) of MSIP (2014R1A2A1A01007580).

## 6 References

[1] M. Casado and N. McKeown. The virtual network system. In *ACM SIGCSE Bulletin*. ACM, 2005.

[2] J. DeHart, et al. The open network laboratory. In *ACM SIGCSE Bulletin*. ACM, 2006.

[3] J. F. Kurose and K. W. Ross. *Computer networking: a top-down approach featuring the Internet*. Pearson Education India, 2005.

[4] B. Lantz, et al. A network in a laptop: rapid prototyping for software-defined networks. In *ACM SIGCOMM HotNets*. ACM, 2010.

# DrawBridge—Software-Defined DDoS-Resistant Traffic Engineering

Jun Li
University of Oregon
Eugene, OR, USA
lijun@cs.uoregon.edu

Skyler Berg
University of Oregon
Eugene, OR, USA
skylerb@uoregon.edu

Mingwei Zhang
University of Oregon
Eugene, OR, USA
mingwei@cs.uoregon.edu

Peter Reiher
University of California
Los Angeles, CA, USA
reiher@cs.ucla.edu

Tao Wei
University of California
Berkeley, CA, USA
lenx.wei@gmail.com

## ABSTRACT

End hosts in today's Internet have the best knowledge of the type of traffic they should receive, but they play no active role in traffic engineering. Traffic engineering is conducted by ISPs, which unfortunately are blind to specific user needs. End hosts are therefore subject to unwanted traffic, particularly from Distributed Denial of Service (DDoS) attacks. This research proposes a new system called **DrawBridge** to address this traffic engineering dilemma. By realizing the potential of software-defined networking (SDN), in this research we investigate a solution that enables end hosts to use their knowledge of desired traffic to improve traffic engineering during DDoS attacks.

## Categories and Subject Descriptors

C.2.3 [**Computer-Communication Networks**]: Network Operations—*network management, network monitoring*; C.2.0 [**Computer-Communication Networks**]: General—*security and protection*; C.2.1 [**Computer-Communication Networks**]: Network Architecture and Design

## General Terms

Design, Management, Security

## Keywords

Traffic engineering; Software-defined networking; DDoS

## 1. PROBLEM STATEMENT

End hosts on today's Internet do not play an active role in traffic engineering. They have no means to control what traffic can be forwarded to them, how much traffic should be forwarded to them, and when traffic should be forwarded to them. Traffic engineering is totally the responsibility of their Internet Service Providers (ISPs).

An ISP must consider many factors when conducting traffic engineering, including the highly dynamic and unpredictable nature of Internet traffic, its resource capacity, its policy agreements with other ISPs, its service agreements with its customers, as well as its own desire to handle as much traffic as possible to make money. While many studies have addressed these factors, an ISP still faces a troubling dilemma: ISPs want to avoid possibly upsetting a customer's by dropping their traffic, however, much of the traffic may be unwanted by the customer.

This dilemma leads to problems familiar to end hosts, especially handling Distributed Denial of Service (DDoS) attack traffic that clogs the bandwidth or processing units of the end hosts, and sometimes impacts the ISP itself. For example, the DDoS against Spamhaus in March 2013—which may have been the largest DDoS to date—generated over 300 Gbps of attack traffic [1], enough to bring down almost any running service on the Internet that does not aggressively overprovision. More recently, in February 2014, an NTP-based DDoS generated over 400 Gbps of traffic [2], Many other similarly powerful attacks are feasible, posing a significant threaten to most hosts on today's Internet [3].

The recent rise of DDoS is in large part due to the use of a particularly potent breed of DDoS: the Distributed Reflective Denial of Service (DRDoS) attack. A DDoS is considered *reflective* if an attacker sends messages to so called *reflector* nodes with a spoofed IP address (the address of the desired victim), which in turn send response messages to the victim. With enough traffic from reflectors, the victims bandwidth will become saturated. Furthermore, the responses sent by the reflectors can be much larger than the queries sent by the attacker. This is referred to as *bandwidth amplification* because the attacker can use a small amount of attack bandwidth to generate a large amount of traffic.

In general, end hosts can determine if certain traffic is desired or not, but they are unable to inform upstream ISPs. ISPs can attempt to filter malicious traffic, but this is done blind to specific user needs. So end hosts can receive large volumes of traffic they know they do not want, ISPs could filter that traffic if they knew it was unwanted, but there is no effective communication between the party who knows what to do and the party that can do it.


*SIGCOMM'14*, August 17–22, 2014, Chicago, IL, USA.
ACM 978-1-4503-2836-4/14/08.
http://dx.doi.org/10.1145/2619239.2631469.

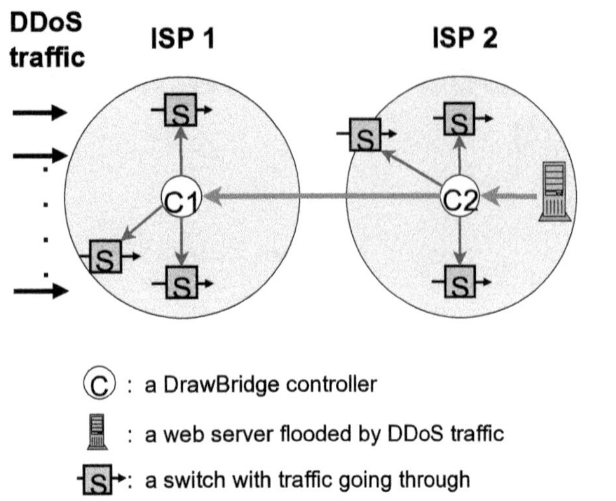


**Figure 1: An example of DrawBridge throttling DDoS traffic. A DrawBridge subscriber informs its DrawBridge controller what traffic to filter (red arrows), which then informs SDN switches to act on traffic filtering as instructed (blue arrows). Note in this example the web server is a subscriber of DrawBridge controller C2, and C2 is a subscriber of C1.**

## 2. DRAWBRIDGE ARCHITECTURE

Software-defined networking (SDN) has the potential to address the traffic engineering dilemma described in Section 1, through protocols such as OpenFlow [4]. We enhance SDN to perform the demanding task of handling high volume DDoS traffic. In particular, we devise an approach to blocking unwanted traffic while still letting desired traffic through. Due to its functional similarities to a castle's drawbridge, we call our approach **DrawBridge**.

DrawBridge enables an end host from within an ISP to act as a **subscriber** to express its traffic engineering rules and send them to a DrawBridge-enabled SDN controller in the ISP, referred to as a **DrawBridge controller**. The DrawBridge controller can further push such rules to the ISP's SDN switches where traffic will be filtered according to these rules, or another DrawBridge controller in an ISP upstream. In the latter case, the downstream controller will act as a subscriber to the upstream DrawBridge controller. Figure 1 shows how a potential victim can use DrawBridge to prevent itself from being flooded.

DrawBridge's architecture allows users, end hosts, or another ISP to subscribe to the traffic engineering service that an ISP's DrawBridge controller provides, and enables a DrawBridge subscriber to establish traffic engineering rules at the controller. This paradigm fundamentally changes the current paradigm of "blind" traffic engineering done by ISPs, enabling end hosts to express their needs and enabling ISPs to make informed traffic engineering decisions.

The primary function of a DrawBridge controller is to process and deploy traffic engineering rules. Upon receipt of new rules to deploy, a controller can verify the validity of rules, check if the rules can be aggregated with other rules, determine whether to deploy rules locally at switches of its own ISP, or push rules to ISPs upstream. It can further determine which local switches or upstream ISPs to deploy rules.

DrawBridge also supports a subscriber to be adaptive in dealing with traffic floods. Based on the traffic dynamics, a subscriber can decide on the fly what rules to establish at a DrawBridge controller. It can choose to receive all the traffic itself, or only a restricted set of traffic, or even nothing. Furthermore, if current rules do not seem effective in throttling DDoS traffic, the subscriber can adapt the rules and make them more restrictive. Not only can a subscriber express its rules when there is no DDoS, it can also do so when it is under stress.

## 3. OPEN ISSUES AND FUTURE WORK

Clearly, DrawBridge needs to support scalable handling of a potentially very large number of rules, speedy deployment of new rules, and secure handling of all operations. While still a research in progress, in our future work we will demonstrate how effective DrawBridge is in handling DDoS traffic. We will first apply DrawBridge to DRDoS traffic, and then use our experiences with DRDoS to expand DrawBridge's ability to handle more general DDoS traffic. We will also investigate security and deployment issues. In particular, we will consider what attackers can do to circumvent DrawBridge. We will design attacks which focus on attaining a high amplification and which cannot be easily blocked by the intended victim. After designing the attacks we will launch them against our networks to test both the success of the attack and the capabilities of the defense.

## 4. CONCLUSIONS

This research enhances SDN using an architectural design that allows users, end hosts, or another ISP to subscribe to the traffic engineering service that an ISP's controller provides, and enables a subscriber to establish traffic engineering rules at the controller. It further allows a controller to verify and process the traffic engineering rules, and deploy them at switches or upstream ISPs with the best location for filtering traffic. DrawBridge aims to handle these demanding traffic engineering tasks even when numerous victims are under high stress from DDoS traffic. It is designed to be scalable and efficient with high performance, as well as secure and easy to deploy with low cost. In our future work we will fully implement and comprehensively evaluate the DrawBridge architecture.

## 5. REFERENCES


[1] "Answers about recent DDoS attack on Spamhaus," http://www.spamhaus.org/news/article/695, Spamhaus, 2013.

[2] "Technical details behind a 400Gbps NTP amplification DDoS attack," http://blog.cloudflare.com/technical-details-behind-a-400gbps-ntp-amplification-ddos-attack.

[3] C. Rossow, "Amplification hell: Revisiting network protocols for DDoS abuse," in *the 21th Annual Network & Distributed System Security Symposium (NDSS)*, 2014, pp. 1–15.

[4] N. McKeown, T. Anderson, H. Balakrishnan, G. Parulkar, L. Peterson, J. Rexford, S. Shenker, and J. Turner, "Openflow: enabling innovation in campus networks," *ACM SIGCOMM Computer Communication Review*, vol. 38, no. 2, pp. 69–74, 2008.

# DesktopDC: Setting All Programmable Data Center Networking Testbed on Desk

Chengchen Hu, Ji Yang, Zhiming Gong, Shuoling Deng
Xi'an Jiaotong University
huc@ieee.org, {yangji, zhm.gong, dengshuoling2}@stu.xjtu.edu.cn

Hongbo Zhao
MeshSr Co. Ltd.
hongbo.zhao@meshsr.com

## Categories and Subject Descriptors

C.2.1 [**Computer-Communication Networks**]: Network Architecture and Design - Network communication, Network topology

## Keywords

OpenFlow, data center, programmable

## 1. INTRODUCTION

Software Defined Networking (SDN) is an emerging network architecture, which decouples the control plane from the physical network infrastructure and operates network with global abstraction of lower level network functionalities. SDN becomes very attractive to design a flexible and customized Data Center Networks (DCN) since Google had recently achieved huge impact by applying SDN to manage the inter-DC traffic [2]. The successful story when SDN met DCN in Google not only demonstrates the feasibility for deployment of SDN to large scale network, but also stimulates a research of SDN, especially in the context of DCN. However, it becomes quite challenging to realize and verify the research progress into practice or to emulate a whole SDN-compatible DCN, since it is costly to operate a Data Center (DC) testbed in a research lab and it is hard to modify the processing logic of a data path for the research and innovation purpose.

Although OpenFlow [3] is the de factor SDN protocol nowadays, which defines the interface between the data plane switches and the control plane controllers, new SDN architectures and protocols are proposed. Even for the OpenFlow itself, it keeps evolving and updates its specification in every a few months. Software OpenFlow Switches (OFS), *e.g.*, Open vSwitch, are easy to deploy and modify, but they are hard to guarantee the performance for wire-speed processing. Commercial OFS provide stable performance and sufficient network interfaces. However, they cannot be updated with evolving OpenFlow specifications and modified innovated processing logic. NetFPGA [4] is quite successful to open a way for changing the hardware logic through FPGA, but it also has limitations, e.g., a host server is further required, the logic resource is not enough for OFS processing, and bottleneck PCI interface between host CPU and NetFPGA (NetFPGA 1G version).

We have designed an all programmable SDN switch (named as ONetSwitch) and a DCN testbed on the desktop (named DesktopDC) based on ONetSwitch. The merits of DesktopDC are its small size, low power, and flexible programmability. Among many building cases, we briefly describe two of them in this paper: one is SDN based routing and the other is Hadoop based computing.


*SIGCOMM'14,* August 17–22, 2014, Chicago, IL, USA.
ACM 978-1-4503-2836-4/14/08.
http://dx.doi.org/10.1145/2619239.2631472.

## 2. DESIGN OF ONETSWITCH

ONetSwitch is a Zyqn-based embedded computing platform. The Zyqn chip is produced by Xilinx, which is constituted by both an ARM processor and a FPGA. Empowered by Zyqn, ONetSwitch is "all programmable", which means software programmable, gateware restructual, and hardware extensible.

Currently, ONetSwitch has two versions. The first version is ONetSwtich20. It has a 533MHz ARM Cortex-A9 dual core processor combined with a Artix FPGA in SoC, 512MB DDR3 SDRAM and 5 1G Ethernet ports. Four Ethernet ports are connected to FPGA and the rest is connected to the processor. Its size is about $13.5cm * 22.5cm * 1.5cm$. A second ONetSwitch45 model, which is first introduced in ONS 2014 [1], uses the Xilinx Zynq-7045 SoC integrating ARM Cortex-A9 dual core processor and Kintex-7 FPGA. ONetSwitch45 provides four SFP+ interfaces to support 10G links, four 1G Ethernet interfaces and commodity wireless adapter modules for 802.11 a/g/n. Its size is $18cm * 18cm * 1.5cm$.

An OpenFlow switch is implemented on ONetSwitch. As shown in Fig.1, this design of OpenFlow switch has a datapath with hybrid software and hardware design. The hardware part provides 8Gb/s packet header matching ability while the software part enables almost "unlimited" matching table size. The flow table lookup operation starts at the first table in hardware, which contains the hottest flow entries. If table miss in hardware, the packet will be sent to software datapath, which contains all the flow entries from controller. An OpenFlow agent is ported from the reference OpenFlow software switch to translate OpenFlow messages. Hardware Abstraction Layer (HAL) works between agent and hardware, which translates original flow entries from OpenFlow messages into the semantic-equivalent formats that optimize the switch performance.

Besides switch ability, ONetSwitch also has more resources for further use. A 64Gb/s DMA channel in the SoC connects software and hardware in various ways. The first way, configurable virtual Ethernet devices send packets to hardware datapath, which reduce latency and unnecessary matches. Another way helps to share computing resources by sending raw data from software to hardware.

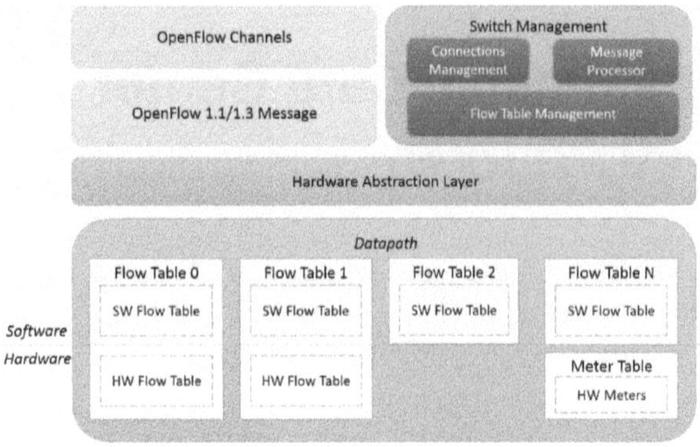


**Figure 1: OpenFlow switch implementation**

# 3. DESKTOPDC AND BUILDING CASES

Connected multiple ONetSwitches, we assemble a DCN testbed called DesktopDC, whose size makes it possible to put on the desktop. In DesktopDC, each ONetSwitch can work as both a computing node and a networking node, and both the computing and the networking functions can be fit either in ARM processor or FPGA, depending on the tradeoff between performance and flexibility. A DesktopDC can also be built with ONetSwitch45 only or mixing with two ONetSwitch models. In the example in Fig.2, the nodes were following a Fattree(4) topology.

**Figure 2: DesktopDC with Fat-Tree topology**

With this DesktopDC testbed, we set two building cases. In the first one, we emulate an OpenFlow based fault tolerance routing for DCN. Each ONetSwitch node in this experiment is served as an OpenFlow switch, as mentioned in the last section. All the ONetSwitches are directly connected to a Ryu OpenFlow controller where configurations and our fault tolerant routing application are performed. Two more servers are connected as client. In the first step, the routing application will collect physical topology of the DCN dynamically. In the second step, it maps the collected physical network topology with the blueprint. Even there are little malfunctions, the mapping process can identify the good ones for networking functions. Also, it equipped an ID learning mechanism, which helps to learn custom servers' physical ID (like MAC), logical ID (like IP) and its related physical locations. After completing of all the above work, the routing application will calculate a path based on the routing algorithm, and assign flow entries to switches. We have measured the average delay within 100 experiments. The time of topology collecting, ID mapping from blueprint to real network, and ID/address/flow table issuing time experiments are 1.5ms, 3.2ms and 0.29ms respectively. We simulate the network failure by disabling different links in the DesktopDC. A port-statistics OpenFlow message will be sent by the affected switches.

**Table 1: DesktopDC's Hadoop performance comparison**

| | ONetSwitch | x86 Server |
|---|---|---|
| Core Frequency | 533MHz | 3.3GHz |
| Boot | <10s | 50s |
| Job Duration | 192794ms | 13314ms |
| Node Power | 6.7W | 56.9W |
| Switch Power | – | 20W |
| Size | $13.5 * 22.5 * 1.5cm^3$ | $37.0 * 43.5 * 4.5cm^3$ |

On receiving the messages in the controller, routing application will figure out whether routing policy would suffers from the failure and if so, it recalculates all the lapsed paths and replace their entries with new ones. The path will recover in less than 500ms.

The second experiment tests Hadoop computing on DesktopDC, where we configure each node in DesktopDC as both computing node and networking node. For the testbed in Fig. 2, our Hadoop computing system will have at most 4Gbps bandwidth Ethernet for each node. In order to compare the power and computing with one single x86 based server, four ONetSwitch20 nodes are utilized. In the first stage, all the computing tasks are finished by ARM processors, meanwhile the rest resources form the OpenFlow based network connecting all ONetSwitches. A high bandwidth virtual Ethernet port transfers data to OpenFlow datapath, meanwhile, OpenFlow controller monitors and manages the data transfer to optimize bandwidth for jobs. Table.1 demonstrates that with elaborate design of computing management algorithm in controller, we can run a data center with hundreds of nodes on the desktop, without any concern about the power and space. In addition, the computing ability and power saving will be further improved by moving some dedicate computing to FPGA, which is our future work.

# 4. CONCLUSION

In this poster, we propose the DesktopDC, an all programmable and energy efficient SDN compatible innovation platform. Our initial experiments and demo exhibit the features of flexibility, capability, power saving. It provides the SDN datapath designs for fast SDN prototyping and verifications in both software and hardware.

# 5. ACKNOWLEDGEMENT

This paper is supported by 863 plan (2013AA013501), National Sci. and Tech. Major Project (no.2013ZX03002003-004), NSFC (61272459), Research Plan in Shaanxi Province (2013K06-38).

# 6. REFERENCES

[1] C. Hu, J. Yang, H. Zhao, and J. Lu. Design of all programmable innovation platform for software defined networking. In *Open Networking Summit 2014*, Santa Clara, CA, 2014.

[2] S. Jain, A. Kumar, S. Mandal, and Etal. B4: Experience with a globally-deployed software defined wan. In *Proceedings of the ACM SIGCOMM 2013*, pages 3–14, 2013.

[3] N. McKeown, T. Anderson, H. Balakrishnan, G. Parulkar, L. Peterson, J. Rexford, S. Shenker, and J. Turner. Openflow: enabling innovation in campus networks. *SIGCOMM Comput. Commun. Rev.*, 38(2):69–74, Mar. 2008.

[4] J. Naous, G. Gibb, S. Bolouki, and N. McKeown. Netfpga: reusable router architecture for experimental research. In *Proceedings of the ACM PRESTO '08*, pages 1–7, New York, NY, USA, 2008. ACM.

# Vidyut: Exploiting Power Line Infrastructure For Enterprise Wireless Networks

Vivek Yenamandra and Kannan Srinivasan
The Ohio State University

## ABSTRACT

Global synchronization across time and frequency domains significantly benefits wireless communications. Multi-Cell (Network) MIMO, interference alignment solutions, opportunistic routing techniques in ad-hoc networks, OFDMA etc. all necessitate synchronization in either time or frequency domain or both. This paper presents Vidyut, a system that exploits the easily accessible and ubiquitous power line infrastructure to achieve synchronization in time and frequency domains across nodes distributed beyond a single-collision domain. Vidyut uses the power lines to transmit a reference frequency tone to which each node locks its frequency. Vidyut exploits the steady periodicity of delivered power signal itself to synchronize distributed nodes in time.

We validate the extent of Vidyut's synchronization and evaluate its effectiveness. We verify Vidyut's suitability for wireless applications such as OFDMA and multi-cell MIMO by validating the benefits of global synchronization in an enterprise wireless network. Our experiments show a throughput gain of 8.2x over MegaMIMO, 7x over NEMOx and 2.5x over OFDMA systems.

## 1. INTRODUCTION

*Synchronization* significantly benefits wireless communication. Exciting new avenues of wireless communication require tight synchronization across distributed nodes in order to be realizable. For example, Network MIMO, a technology that scales the throughput of the network with the number of the transmitters, requires synchronization in frequency and time domains across all transmitters. Opportunistic ad-hoc routing techniques that exploit either sender (Sourcesync [14]) or receiver side diversity of the wireless medium require acceptable levels of time synchronization across the distributed routing nodes. Source coding techniques such as lattice coding techniques assume synchronization between the transmitters. Frequency and time synchronization are essential for implementing interference alignment solutions. While radio technology for individual nodes keeps continually improving (in terms of antenna technology, data processing capability etc.), in order to realize the previously mentioned wireless solutions the challenge of coordinating distributed nodes remains. One of the main challenges in this regard is achieving synchronization across distributed nodes.


*SIGCOMM'14,* August 17–22, 2014, Chicago, IL, USA.
Copyright 2014 ACM 978-1-4503-2836-4/14/08 ...$15.00.
http://dx.doi.org/10.1145/2619239.2626329 .

Global *time* synchronization techniques have been explored for sensor networks. However, these techniques achieve a time synchronization in the order of milliseconds, while Wi-Fi-like systems need synchronization in the order of nanoseconds [16]. Recent works have demonstrated frequency synchronization between distributed nodes for Network MIMO applications (MegaMIMO [15],Airsync [2]). However, these techniques are limited by the transmission range of a lead transmitter. MegaMIMO, for example, achieves distributed synchronization across a group of APs by having a lead AP among them transmit a pilot tone over the air. The remaining APs synchronize to the lead AP by referencing this pilot tone. However, the group of APs must be within the range of the lead AP. We refer to this group of APs as a *cluster*.

Vidyut utilizes power-lines to achieve synchronization between nodes distributed beyond a cluster. At its crux, Vidyut distributes a stable reference clock along the power-lines. APs distributed across space access this reference clock to synchronize their carrier clocks. Fig. 1(a) presents an example to highlight the difference of Vidyut from prior frequency synchronization techniques. This example illustrates the *distinct* advantage of Vidyut: Vidyut achieves frequency synchronization *across* clusters. This enables Network MIMO across clusters. Further, this example illustrates that throughput gain of our Vidyut implementation increases with the number of clusters as shown in Section 6.

There are many challenges in realizing Vidyut. First, the power distribution network of an enterprise has multiple electrical elements with distinct functionality. Fig. 2 shows the electrical network in an enterprise building. The reference frequency used in Vidyut has to propagate through all of these elements. Section 2 briefly discusses a typical power distribution network. Section 3 studies the propagation characteristics of these elements in order to make design decisions for Vidyut.

Second, a single reference frequency source on the power-lines for the entire enterprise network has a single point of failure: if the signal source fails so does Vidyut. Section 3 presents a distributed mechanism to provide a reliable synchronization signal on the power-line. Every Vidyut AP regenerates a reference clock and sends it back to the power-lines. This eliminates a single point failure for Vidyut.

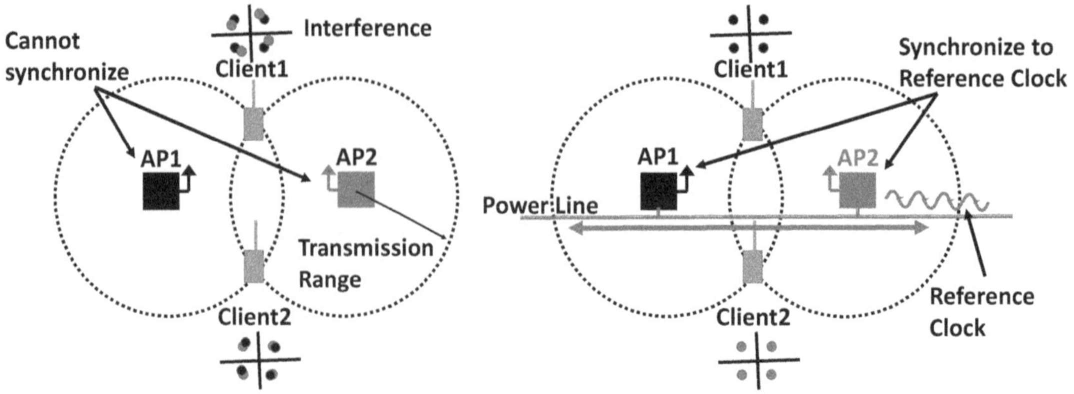


(a) Interference caused due to lack of synchronization.

(b) Achieving throughput gain by enabling Network MIMO.

**Figure 1: Motivating Vidyut: Access points (APs) outside of each other's transmission range cannot be synchronized using MegaMIMO [15] and NEMOx [21]. They form two distinct clusters. This causes interference when the APs simultaneously transmit. They need to take turns to avoid interference. In Vidyut, APs are synchronized using power-line. Simultaneous activation of APs enable interference-free Network MIMO. Vidyut enables cross-cluster synchronization and provides a linear throughput gain with increasing clusters.**

The example in Fig. 1(a) implicitly assumed time synchronization across the nodes. Vidyut borrows its time synchronization idea from the work published in [16]. Vidyut utilizes the stability of the time period of the power signal as a reference for time synchronization across distributed nodes. A fixed offset from the zero-crossing of the power signal is used as an event which each Vidyut node reports to a central server. The central server then computes the phase offset between Vidyut nodes. The technique is described in detail in Section 3.

## 1.1 Results

MegaMIMO reports that a phase mismatch of under 0.05 radians between a pair of transmitters results in negligible SNR degradation over all channel conditions. Vidyut provides frequency synchronization with a **mean phase mismatch of approximately 0.0218 radians** (over the duration of one 802.11g symbol). We observe a phase mismatch of under 0.05 radians in 90% of the experiments. Further, we verify that the frequency synchronization presented by Vidyut is steady over time by observing that the phase mismatch between Vidyut nodes does not deteriorate over 700 symbols (For a symbol duration of 4 $\mu$seconds).

Vidyut provides **time synchronization within 450 ns with a mean of approximately 225 ns**. While this variation is too high to support short guard intervals of 802.11n/ac standards (400ns), it is sufficient to support regular guard intervals of 802.11n/ac (800ns).

Our implementation of Vidyut provides a throughput gain of approximately 2x over MegaMIMO and NEMOx in the four node topology illustrated in Fig. 1(a). We simulate throughput gains for networks up to 20 clusters with four nodes per cluster. Vidyut presents a **throughput gain of up to 8.2x over MegaMIMO and 7x over NEMOx** for these networks.

Further, we compare a Vidyut backed OFDMA system with an OFDMA system of un-synchronized transmitters. We show a throughput gain of up to **2.5x** as the number of OFDMA transmitters increases to 7.

## 1.2 Contributions

To the best of our knowledge, this is the first solution to provide synchronization across multiple collision domains. We develop a simple, robust and scalable synchronization mechanism, Vidyut, and evaluate its applicability to provide *global* synchronization. We demonstrate the power signal as a cheap, available and stable resource for distributed time synchronization for Wi-Fi-type applications.

# 2. POWER-LINES AND DISTRIBUTION: A BACKGROUND

We look at the power distribution network and the power-line channel briefly before discussing Vidyut in detail.

## 2.1 Power Distribution

Power is typically delivered on three phases. Power on each phase is distributed from the substation to various buildings at a voltage of the order of 13KV. Typically, each building has a *large* three-phase transformer (with a power rating of around 500KVA) that steps down this voltage to around 480V or 240V on each phase to make it safe to distribute power within building premises. Further, the buildings have *smaller* three-phase transformers (power rating of around 65 KVA) that step down this voltage to 110V to deliver it to end appliances.

Our department building has eight floors. One *large* three-phase transformer (13KV/480V) with a typical power rating of 500 KVA sits outside the building to transform the power from the substation to a safer voltage to distribute within the building. The power from this transformer feeds two (480V/110V) three-phase transformers with a power rating of 65 KVA each. These two transformers are situated inside the building. Power from these two transformers is distributed throughout the building. One transformer feeds power to the first four floors while the other feeds the remaining four floors. Each phase is distributed on a physically isolated bus. Thus, power is delivered to each floor on three physically isolated buses.

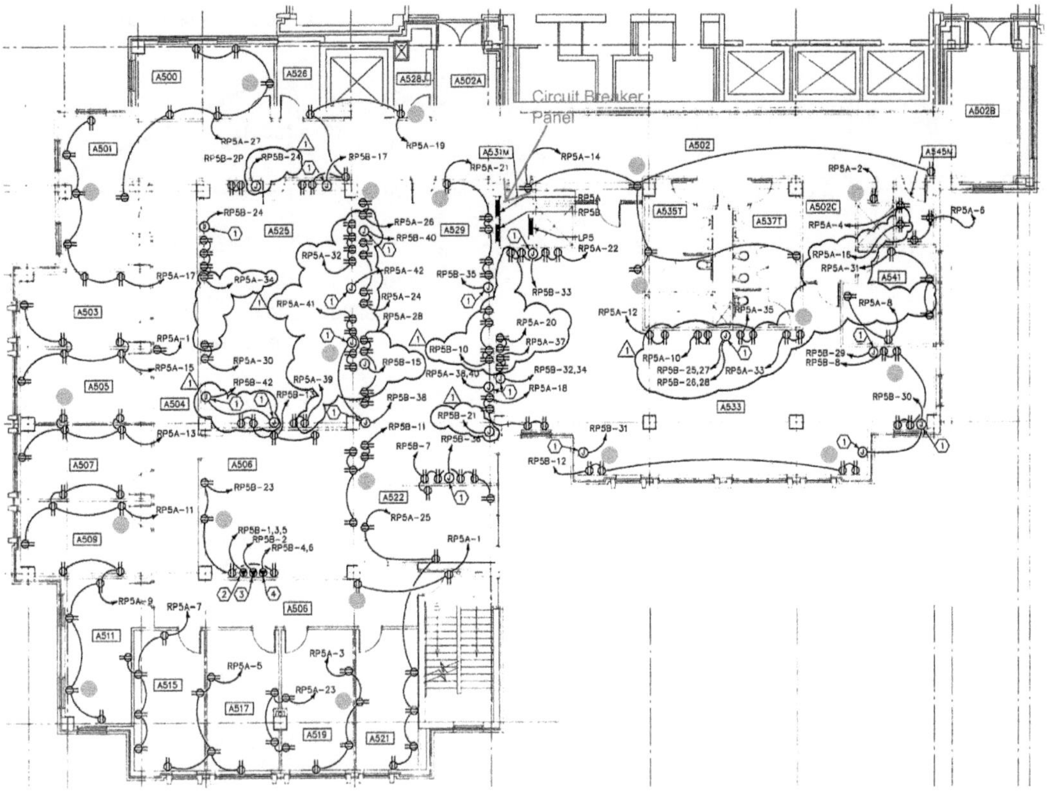


**Figure 2: Typical power distribution in a floor of a building. The free curves indicate circuits. Each circuit powers six to ten power outlets. The circuits branch from a circuit breaker panel (indicated in the figure). The branching itself is not explicitly indicated. The red circles adjacent to the power outlets indicate the power outlets accessed by Vidyut nodes. The power outlets cover all three phases and are live.**

Fig. 2 illustrates the power distribution network on one of the floors. As indicated in Fig. 2, power is distributed across each floor on different branches (circuits). Each branch typically powers six to ten power outlets. All power outlets connected to the same branch draw power on the same phase. All circuits on the same phase branch from a bus carry power at that phase. Thus, power outlets on the same phase but connected to different branches are connected together electrically at the bus carrying power at that phase. The three buses corresponding to the three distinct phases are housed in a *circuit breaker panel*. Each floor consists of two circuit breaker panels. Each circuit is connected to its bus through a circuit breaker. A circuit breaker is instrumental in isolating faulty circuits from disrupting power distribution on rest of the circuits.

The electrical routing of this building is a reasonable representation of typical electrical connections in a large building. Section 3 studies the implications of these electrical elements on Vidyut's design.

## 2.2 Power-Lines: The channel

The primary function of power-lines is to deliver power at 60 Hz. The capacitance and inductance presented by the power-lines are known to attenuate high frequency (of the order of MHz and beyond) signals and are thus *parasitic* at these frequencies. Besides the attenuation caused by power cables, the power lines are subject to multiple sources of noise. These include noise due to change in loading conditions, switching power supplies and simple background noise. While extensive literature studying the channel response [19, 20] and noise [13, 22] of power-lines exists, they have been studied from the perspective of achieving reliable power-line communication.

However, the objective of Vidyut is distinct from that of power-line communications (PLCs) in the following regard: Vidyut is only responsible for distributing a stable reference clock (a single tone) across the power-line network of an enterprise. Thus, when designing Vidyut, our primary concern is to find tones of frequencies that pass through the various electric circuit elements with minimal losses and **not** to find a band of frequencies that is most suitable for communicating data between two nodes with high throughput and/or high reliability.

Thus, in summary, we investigate the channel response of power-lines, the effect of loading and noise sources and the effect of electrical characteristics of circuit breaker panels, transformers, cross-phase physical isolation, etc. with the objective of finding a frequency tone that can be distributed across an enterprise network. Further, we make design decisions that enable the required synchronization to implement desirable applications such as Network MIMO, OFDMA, Interference Alignment etc.

# 3. Vidyut: DESIGN

Vidyut presents a suite of techniques to achieve synchronization over the span of an enterprise network. Vidyut uti-

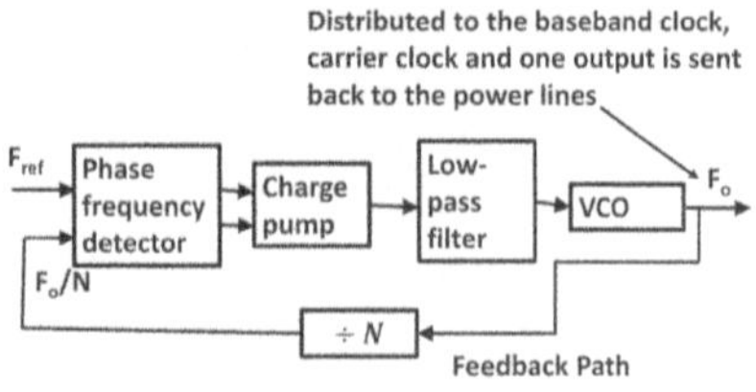


**Figure 3: Simplified block diagram of a PLL.**

lizes the power-line infrastructure to share a reference clock across the enterprise network. This section details the challenges presented by the power-lines to the distribution of this reference clock. Further, it presents the impact of these on the design decisions of Vidyut.

## 3.1 Frequency Synchronization

The opportunity presented by the power-line infrastructure is enticing for the following reasons. The infrastructure already exists and is accessible to majority of the nodes in an enterprise network. Thus, it presents an opportunity to achieve synchronization even between hidden nodes. The proposed solution would require no change in the MAC or higher layers for the purpose of achieving distributed synchronization since the solution is confined to the physical layer. Vidyut avails the power-line infrastructure to distribute a reference clock accessible to nodes in an enterprise network. Each node locks its own carrier frequency to this reference clock in phase to achieve frequency synchronization among distributed nodes. While the idea is straightforward, the following questions need to be tackled to use the power-lines to distribute a reference clock: What is the ideal frequency of the reference clock?

### *3.1.1 Determining the reference clock frequency*

Power is delivered at a stable frequency of 60 Hz (or 50 Hz). So then, the question arises: Why not use the power frequency itself as a reference? Which metric is indicative of the suitability of a reference clock for Vidyut? The answer to these questions can be better understood when the parameters affecting the performance of the frequency synthesizing element –the Phase Locked Loop (PLL)– are better understood. Fig.3 illustrates a simplified block diagram of a clock distribution circuit based on a PLL.

A Vidyut node synchronizes its baseband and carrier clocks to the reference frequency using a PLL in the clock distribution core. The PLL in the clock distribution core performs two functions: **(1)**Ensures that each clock output of the distribution core is phase locked to the reference frequency. **(2)** Multiplies the clock output by a pre-programmed factor to generate the desired output clock[1]. For example, the clock distribution core multiplies the reference clock of 10 MHz by 240 to generate a carrier clock output of 2.4GHz (which is then fed to the mixer to up-convert the baseband streams to RF or vice-versa).

Typically, a PLL consists of a **phase/frequency detector (PFD)** that generates a digital (or analog) signal directly proportional to the phase mismatch between the output of the PLL and the reference clock. This signal accumulates over time and feeds a voltage input to a **Voltage Controlled Oscillator (VCO)** to minimize the phase mismatch between its output and the reference clock. In addition, the PLL incorporates a low-pass filter to increase the stability of the PLL by preventing it from responding to sudden changes in the reference clock. This filter is referred to as the **loop filter**. All the components in the PLL have intrinsic noise characteristics. The phase noise of the PLL is one such metric that quantifies the accuracy with which the PLL synchronizes its output to the reference clock. Intuitively, as the multiplicating factor of the output clock increases, the intrinsic noise of the components of the PLL is exaggerated. Thus, when the reference clock is at a frequency of 60 Hz, to generate a carrier frequency of 2.4 GHz, the multiplicative factor is 40 million. This significantly degrades the phase noise of the PLL, well beyond the limits specified by the IEEE 802.11 standards. The 802.11a standard specifies a phase noise of the order of -95 dBc/Hz while the 802.11g standard specifies a phase noise of the order of -100 dBc/Hz [12].

[1]In practice, this effect is produced by dividing the clock output and feeding it back to the phase/frequency detector.

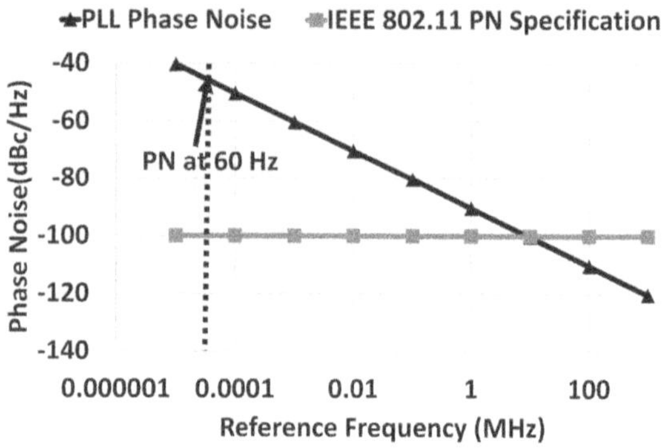


**Figure 4: Phase Noise of a typical PLL Frequency Synthesizer: The reference frequency and the frequency divider influence the output phase noise.**

Eq. 1 defines the relationship between the phase noise of AD9511(the PLL used in the clock distribution core of our Vidyut node implementation [1]) at a desired frequency with the frequency of the phase/frequency detector ($f_{PFD}$) and the multiplicative factor($N$) used to attain the desired frequency from $f_{PFD}$.

$$PhaseNoise(dBc/Hz) = -218 + 10log(f_{PFD}) + 20logN \tag{1}$$

Fig. 4 plots the phase noise of a PLL for a carrier frequency of 2.4 GHz as the reference frequency is swept from 10s of Hz to 1 GHz. As indicated in the figure, for reference frequencies below the order of a MHz, the PLL phase noise characteristic is degraded beyond phase noise specification provided by the IEEE 802.11 standard. Thus, frequencies below 1 MHz **cannot** provide an acceptable reference for Wi-Fi applications.

### *3.1.2 Characterizing Transformers*

At Vidyut's frequencies of interest (beyond 1 MHz), the two types of transformers discussed in Section 2 behave as filtering elements. Further, due to the construction of a transformer, it is also a site for electrical coupling between phases. Here, we characterize these phenomena.

**As a filtering element:** The transformers have a distinct filtering characteristic.We perform a series of experiments across transformers to measure the pass band characteristics of these transformers.

Transformers in the power distribution network are designed to transform power from one voltage to another at power frequency. At significantly higher operating frequencies, however, the transformer acts more as a filtering element than a power transformer. The copper windings and the ferrite core of the transformer introduce capacitive and inductive loads at high frequencies (of the order of MHz). The windings have an inductive response. The gap between the windings is capacitive in addition to the parasitic capacitance of the ferrite core. This load is *parasitic*.

First, we characterize the *large* 500 KVA, 30KV/95KV transformer. We connect two such transformers in a back-to-back configuration, i.e., connect the primary sides of the two transformers across all three phases. We evaluate the back-to-back configuration because Vidyut's reference signal has to traverse through two such transformers in such a configuration in order to be available to wireless nodes connected to the power outlets in enterprise buildings. We observe that this configuration attenuates signals (in the MHz range) below 8 MHz to the noise floor. From 8 MHz to 10 MHz however, the clock signal can be recovered on the primary side of the second transformer. At 10 MHz it presents a high attenuation of $\approx$ 23 dB.

Second, we characterize the filter response of 27 KVA, 240V/480V transformer. While this transformer is not of the same power rating as the *smaller* transformer in our department, it is approximately of the same size and thus is a reasonable representation of parasitics introduced by typical smaller transformers found within buildings. We inject a single tone on the primary side and we measure its power on the secondary side. The transformer acts as a notch filter in the frequency range between 1-10 MHz allowing frequencies below 3 MHz and frequencies above 9 MHz. The transformer is left de-energized for this experiment also. The filter response of the transformer is illustrated in the Fig. 6.

In summary, the large transformers (500 KVA) present high attenuation to high frequency signals, while the smaller transformers present notch filter characteristics with tolerable attenuation in the pass band. This suggests that if the smaller transformers draw power from different power sources, and thus through different large transformers, then distribution of Vidyut's reference across these smaller transformers will be unreliable due to the high attenuation introduced by the large transformers.

**As a phase coupling element:** Owing to the construction of a typical three phase transformer, it is also a site of coupling between phases. To evaluate the coupling between phases across a 500 KVA transformer, we inject a signal on the primary side of a de-energized transformer on a phase, say phase 1, and measure the signal on phase 2 and phase 3 on the primary side of the transformer. Then, we inject a single tone on a phase, say phase 1, on the primary side and measure the signal on phase 2 and phase 3 on the secondary side. The coupling response for the 500 KVA transformer and the 27 KVA transformer are illustrated in Fig. 5 and Fig. 6 respectively. The strong coupling across phases suggests that the transformers can route a reference clock on one phase to the other phases. Thus while a transformer plays a

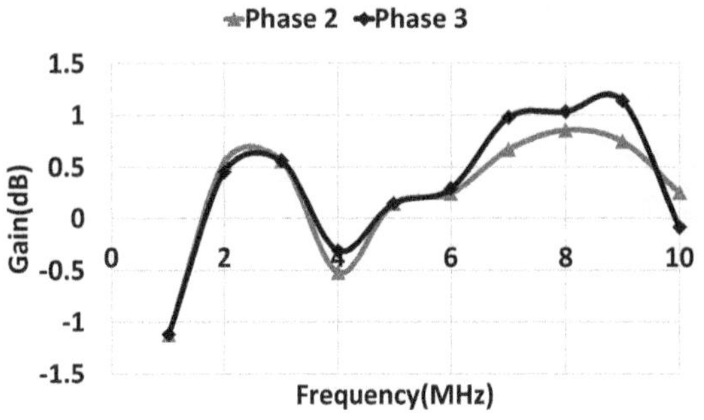


**Figure 5: Coupling response of 500KVA transformer.**

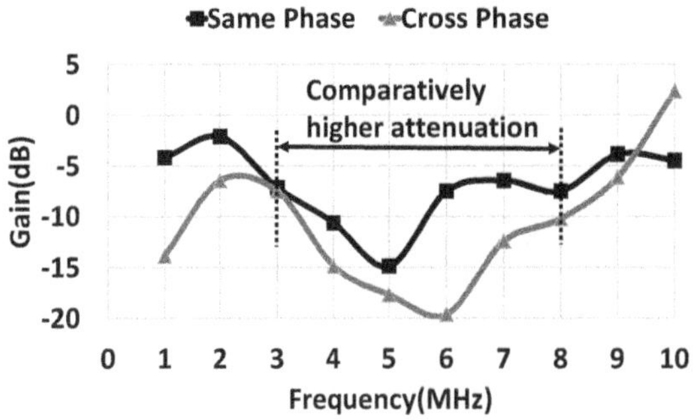


**Figure 6: Filter response of 27 KVA transformer.**

significant role in determining the frequency of the reference clock distributed around the building, it also presents a site of coupling between physically isolated phases.

Thus, both the transformers are sites of coupling between phases. The evaluation suggests that Vidyut's reference clock can be shared reliably across circuits connected to different smaller transformers as long as these transformers are connected to the same power source. These experiments to isolate the characteristics of the transformer were performed in a de-energized state for safety reasons. However, both the filter characteristics and phase coupling effectiveness are determined by the construction of the transformers alone. Therefore, these observations hold even when the transformers are powered.

### *3.1.3 Attenuation across power distribution network*

**Power-lines:** The power-lines are designed to carry power at 60 Hz. The cable material can introduce capacitance to the high frequency reference clock and cause attenuation of the reference clock. A lot of work has been done to study the attenuation introduced by power-lines to signals in the range of 10s and 100s of MHz [19]. Fig. 7 illustrates the attenuation caused by power cables across frequencies as a function of its length. A signal tone was injected into the power cable and measurements were taken at lengths of 10 feet, 100 feet and 200 feet. Fig. 7 illustrates a gradual increase in attenuation with length. However, the attenuation at 10 MHz is comparatively small.

**Circuit breaker panel:** The other site of attenuation in the power distribution network is the circuit breaker panel. The circuit breaker panel distributes power from a bus on to different circuits. Thus, the reference signal generated on one circuit is dispersed to all the circuits connected to that

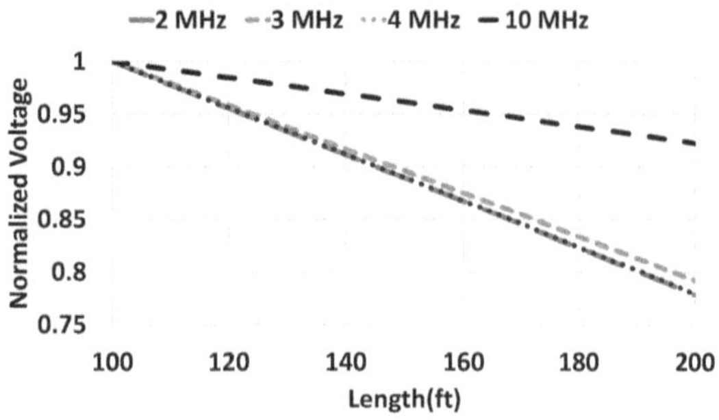


**Figure 7: Power cable attenuation vs length.**

bus in the circuit breaker panel. However, one advantage of transmitting a reference clock in the range of 10s of MHz is that the material between the buses in the circuit breaker panel presents reactive inductance that is *low* enough to allow for coupling across buses. Thus, the circuit breaker panel is another site of cross-phase coupling.

**Distributed Clock Regeneration:** To overcome the attenuation of power distribution network, every Vidyut node regenerates the reference clock and feeds it back on to the power-lines. It is the responsibility of each Vidyut node to ensure that the regenerated clock is phase locked to the reference clock. While it is possible for the regenerated clock to have a phase offset from the original reference clock, as long as the regenerated clock has the same frequency as that of the reference clock, the superposition of these two clocks only affects the duty cycle of the reference clock without affecting its frequency (unless the regenerated clock is out of phase with the reference clock, in which case the two signals destructively interfere). Thus, as long as the frequency of the reference clock remains unchanged, the synchronization between nodes is not affected.

#### *3.1.4 Noise in power-lines*

Power-lines experience multiple noise sources. Noise in power-lines can be classified into colored background noise (summation of all low-power noise sources), noise caused by the power-lines acting as antennas to broadcast radio signals, periodic impulsive noise caused by switched mode power supplies and asynchronous impulsive noise caused by changing load conditions on the power distribution network. The impulse and background colored noise have a very low power spectral density (PSD) in the MHz frequency band (-110dB$V^2$/Hz) [22]. The noise amplitude due to majority of the appliances at around 10 MHz is below -30 dBuV/$\sqrt{Hz}$ [13]. Thus, under most circumstances, the noise PSD at 10 MHz is within the acceptable phase noise (-90 to -100dBc/Hz) for a reference clock that is used to generate RF carriers for Wi-Fi applications.

While noise in power-lines is a concern for power-line communications, its influence on Vidyut is minimal. The reason for this can be understood by looking back at the working of the PLL. The PLL contains a low-pass filter, the loop filter, to minimize the responsiveness of the PLL to impulsive (high frequency) changes in the reference signal and thus increase its stability. Thus the power of broadband noise sources is constrained.

The PLL is a closed-loop network. Assuming the gain of the forward path is G and that of the feedback path is H (1/N:referring Fig. 3) the noise power at the output of the PLL due to the at the reference can be written using Equation 2.

$$noise_{output} = noise_{reference}\frac{G}{1+GH} \tag{2}$$

Outside the loop bandwidth, the contribution of the reference clock noise to the output is $\approx 0$ as $G \rightarrow 0$. Within the loop bandwidth, the noise power is limited by the bandwidth of the filter.

## 3.2 Time Synchronization

Vidyut utilizes the power frequency for the purpose of time synchronization. We define an offset, $\gamma$ from the start (zero crossing of the power cycle) of each period of a power cycle as a time reference for each node.

Each Vidyut node is equipped with a zero crossing detector. Once the nodes have their baseband and carrier clocks phase locked to the reference clock of Vidyut every node connected to the power distribution network measures the time period of the power cycle accurately within a resolution defined by the sampling frequency of the baseband clock. Thus, each Vidyut node can record the offset $\gamma$ from the start of the power cycle with an accuracy controlled by the time period of the baseband clock.

However, on an absolute scale, there is a time difference between the time each Vidyut node records the $\gamma$ offset. This difference is the same as the time it takes for the power signal to traverse the distance between the two nodes. Each Vidyut node can report the time instant it records a $\gamma$ offset to a central server that keeps track of the time at each of the nodes connected to it. Thus, upon receiving the time instant at which each node records the $\gamma$ offset, the central server can then let each node know its time-offset correction to ensure these nodes transmit simultaneously. This method is illustrated in Fig. 8.

However, if two nodes are close-by, then as illustrated in Fig. 2 the length of the electrical cables between the two nodes is, on most occasions low too. In these cases, the propagation delay of the power signal between the nodes can be assumed to be negligible and each node can use the event recorded at an offset $\gamma$ as a reference without any relative offset correction between the two nodes. The accuracy of Vidyut's time synchronization method is then limited by the accuracy with which the time period of the power frequency is measured at each node.

Finally, each Vidyut node needs to be given information regarding the phase of the power supply it is connected to. This information is necessary to correct for the constant phase offset between different phases. For instance, if phase A is considered the reference, nodes on phase B and phase C will have to include a phase offset correction of 120° and 240° respectively.

## 3.3 Power-line Interface

Fig. 9 illustrates a block diagram of Vidyut's interface circuit. Each Vidyut node extracts the reference clock signal from the power-lines as well as the power signal at a stepped down voltage. Vidyut's interface circuit consists of an isolation transformer (not indicated in Fig. 9) to protect the Vidyut node from the 110V of the power-lines. The stepped down voltage is fed to the zero crossing detector to achieve Vidyut's time synchronization.

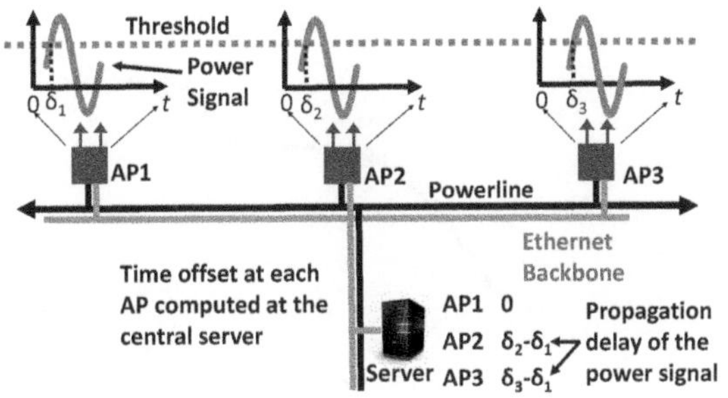


**Figure 8: Time synchronization methodology.**

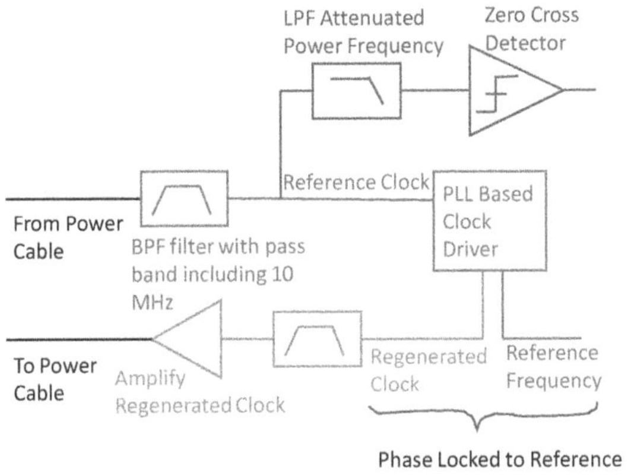


**Figure 9: Vidyut's power interfacing circuit.**

A second lead from the power-lines is band-pass filtered to obtain a copy of the reference clock signal with band-limited noise. This signal is fed as the reference clock to the PLL of the clock distribution core of Vidyut node. One output of the clock distribution core is used for baseband operations (baseband clock). The second output feeds the mixers in the RF front end that are used to up-convert the baseband signals to RF or vice versa. The third output, referred to as the *regenerated* clock, is sent back on to the power-lines. The regenerated clock is phase locked to the reference clock i.e. there is a constant phase offset between the reference and the regenerated clock. A repeater/regenerator module (this is a discrete IC and should not be confused with the Vidyut's regenerated clock output) can be used to ensure the regenerated and reference clock have the same frequency *and* phase. This is however, not mandatory.

# 4. IMPLEMENTATION

We implement each Vidyut node using NI-5791 radio front-ends. These front ends are each equipped with a PLL based clock distribution core (AD9511) that enables these nodes to synchronize their carrier and baseband clocks to an external reference clock. One output from NI-5791's clock core can be fed back on to the power-lines. While evaluating Vidyut we guarantee the presence of a reference clock when a Vidyut node is connected to the power-lines. We use a 10 MHz reference clock output from a signal generator, Agilent 8648C, as the default reference clock transmitted on to the power-lines. While we provide a default reference clock, it is not necessary for Vidyut to have a default reference clock to achieve distributed synchronization. Mechanisms can be developed to let nodes that do not *see* a reference clock to generate their own reference clock which can then be used by neighboring Vidyut nodes. However, since the focus of this paper is to establish the feasibility of Vidyut from the perspective of signal propagation and integrity, we assume we are given a reference clock. Each Vidyut node outputs its own clock on to the power-line medium. We interface the clocks of Vidyut node using the interface circuitry described in Section 3.

# 5. MICROBENCHMARK EVALUATION

We transmit a reference clock at 10 MHz through the power-lines for the purpose of synchronizing distributed nodes. While this is **not** the only frequency suitable for transmitting the reference clock, we choose 10 MHz following its favorable attenuation characteristics and ability to pass through transformers as detailed in the previous section. Further, the software defined radios used in our experiments accept a default external clock input of 10 MHz and is thus, convenient too.

## 5.1 Frequency Synchronization:

Frequency mismatch results in an increase in the noise floor of receivers. Recent work [15], simulated the effect of phase mismatch between two transmitters on the increase in noise floor at a receiver. It reported that for a phase mismatch under 0.05 radians (over the duration of a symbol), the increase in noise floor is negligible even at high SNR. We evaluate the accuracy of Vidyut's frequency synchronization and the effect of different design decisions of Vidyut on its frequency synchronization performance. We use the following method to estimate the phase mismatch of Vidyut's synchronization.

**Method:** Two Vidyut nodes are synchronized using the reference clock in the power-lines. The power-line medium between the two nodes is changed depending on the objective of the experiment. (Unless specified otherwise, these nodes are connected to a live power network, given in Fig. 2, and are thus subject to noise conditions and load variations typically experienced in a power network.) We assign one of these two nodes, the transmit node, to transmit a pilot tone, $F_{pilot}$, known to both nodes, over the air. The second node (receive node), placed within the transmission range of the transmit node receives the pilot tone as $F_{received}$. This node then computes the phase offset $\phi(t)$ between the received frequency and the transmitted frequency as a function of time using Eq. 3.

$$\phi(t) = (F_{received} - F_{pilot}) \times t + \phi(t_0) \qquad (3)$$

where $\phi(t_0)$ is the initial phase offset. The frequency mismatch is simply the slope of the phase offset as a function of time. Thus, perfect synchronization in frequency results in the phase offset variation being parallel to the time axis. We measure phase mismatch over the duration of $4\mu$ seconds (symbol duration defined in 802.11ac standard).

**Effect of distributed clock regeneration:** Each Vidyut node regenerates the reference clock and feeds it back on to the power-lines. As long as there is a constant phase offset between the reference clock and the regenerated clock and they are not out-of-phase, the frequency of the reference clock does not change. Fig. 10 plots the reference clock traversing the power-lines in both the time and frequency domain as the number of clock regenerators increases. The

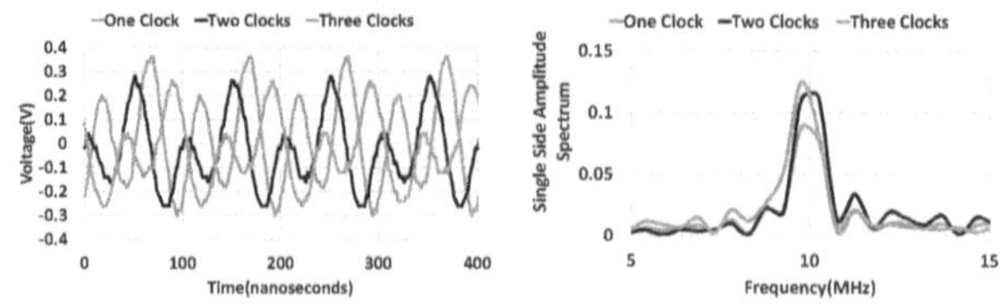


(a) Time Domain (b) Frequency Domain

**Figure 10: Effect of multiple reference clock sources.**

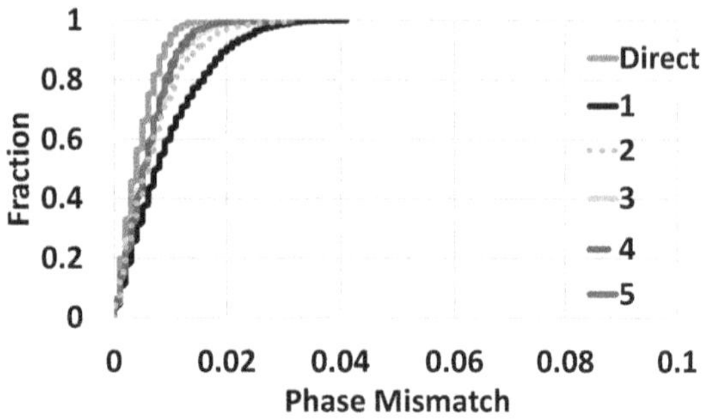


**Figure 11: Phase mismatch vs number of intermediate clock regenerations.**

reference clock frequency remains unaffected as the number of intermediate clock regenerators increase. However, each regeneration site still has a distinct phase noise characteristic. We evaluate the effect of the accumulation of phase noise as the number of regeneration sites increase.

***Method:*** The transmit and receive nodes are synchronized using Vidyut. We add an intermediate Vidyut node between the transmit and receive nodes and measure the phase mismatch between the transmit and receive node. We vary the number of intermediate Vidyut nodes from 0 to 5. For this experiment, all nodes are connected to the *live* power distribution network.

***Result:*** Fig. 11 plots the distribution of the phase mismatch between the transmit and receive nodes as the number of clock regenerators (intermediate nodes) between them is varied. Increasing the number of intermediate Vidyut nodes does not have a direct correlation on the phase mismatch between the transmit and receive nodes. This is because the phase noise of each PLL is random. Hence, the cumulative effect of the phase noise of individual nodes does not accumulate. Further, the phase mismatch distribution is well within the tolerable limits in terms of limiting SNR degradation at receivers. The phase mismatch for majority of the observations is under 0.04 radians.

**Power-line length:** We measure the phase mismatch between the transmit and receive nodes by varying the power-line length between these two nodes. On each occasion, the nodes and the power cable between them are connected to the *live* power network. We repeat the experiment by connnecting the Vidyut nodes to different power outlets (illustrated in Fig. 2). Fig. 12 plots the distribution of the phase mismatch between the nodes for different length of power-lines between them. As indicated in the figure, the phase mismatch distribution is largely independent of the length of the power-line between the nodes as the attenuation caused by the power-lines at this frequency is minimal.

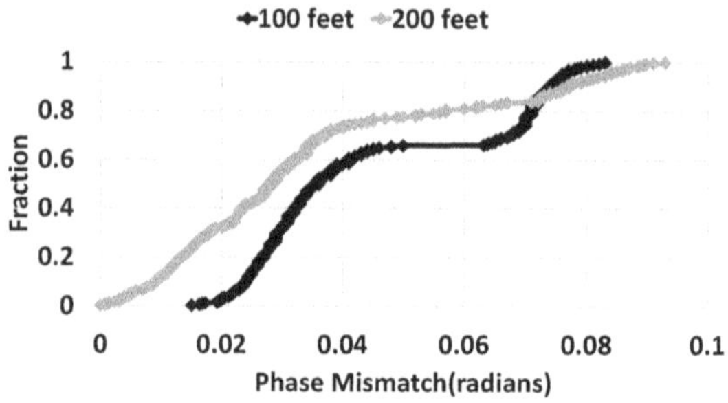


**Figure 12: Phase mismatch vs power cable length.**

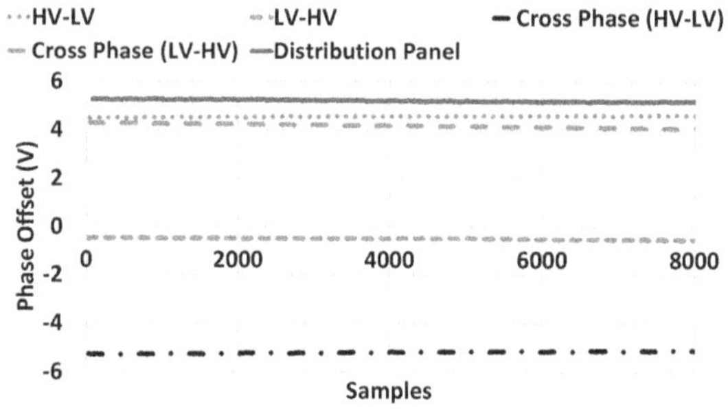


**Figure 13: Phase offset between Vidyut nodes on either side of typical elements found in the power grid (transformers/distribution panel). HV (High-Voltage) is the secondary side and LV (Low-Voltage) is the primary side in a step-up transformer.**

**Effect of Transformers/Circuit Breaker Panel:** We evaluate the phase mismatch caused by the frequency response of the transformer by placing the transmit and receive nodes directly across a de-energized transformer. We place the two nodes across the windings of the transformer on same as well as different phases. We perform the experiments on the 27 KVA transformer.

We also evaluate the effect of the circuit breaker panel on the phase mismatch across these two nodes by placing these nodes on different circuits along the same phase on a de-energized distribution panel. We ground all the unloaded circuits to mimic the effect of low-impedance presented by the circuit breaker panel. A qualitative estimate of the phase offset at the receive node for each configuration connected between the transmit and receive nodes is presented in Fig. 13. As illustrated in the figure, the phase offset over time is parallel to the time axis thus suggesting frequency synchronization between the two nodes.

**Synchronizing battery powered nodes:** We measure the effectiveness of Vidyut to synchronize mobile clients in the following experiment.

***Method:*** The transmit and receive nodes are connected to a *live* power network and synchronized using Vidyut. The location of the transmit and receive nodes is fixed. A third node, not connected to the power network (mobile), is placed within the transmission range of these two nodes. The transmit node transmits a pilot tone over the air at a frequency known to all the nodes, say pilot frequency. The mobile node listens to this pilot tone and computes the frequency offset between the transmit node and itself . Once computed, this node then transmits the pilot tone after accounting for

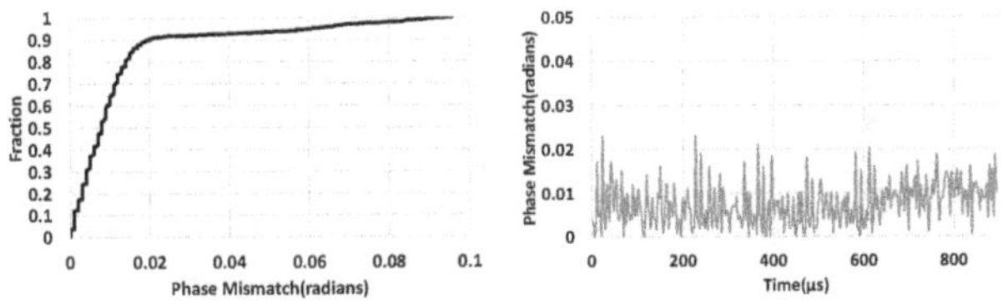

(a) Phase Mismatch Distribution (b) Phase Mismatch over time

**Figure 14: Effectiveness of Vidyut in synchronizing mobile nodes.**

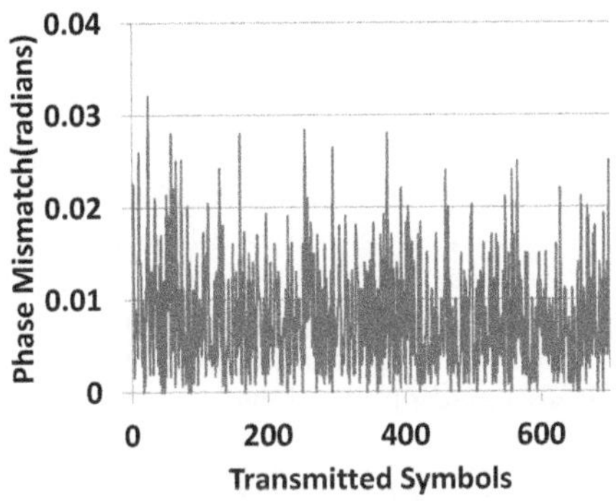


**Figure 15: Accumulated phase mismatch as the number of symbols (4$\mu$s) transmitted increases. The phase mismatch between two Vidyut nodes does not deteriorate as the number of symbols transmitted increases. As indicated, the accumulated phase mismatch over time is random since the phase noise distribution of each PLL is random.**

this frequency offset. The receive node, synchronized to the transmit node by Vidyut, computes the phase mismatch between the mobile node and itself by listening to the pilot frequency transmitted by the mobile node.

***Result:*** Fig. 14(a) plots the distribution of this phase mismatch. As before, the phase mismatch is calculated over the duration of one symbol (4$\mu$seconds). Fig. 14(b) plots the phase mismatch at the receive node over a time duration of 800$\mu$seconds. A flat phase mismatch over time indicates that the mobile node synchronizes itself to Vidyut's reference clock. Further, it indicates that the frequency offset between the free-running oscillator of the mobile node and the transmit node is relatively steady with time. This is useful in extending Vidyut for OFDMA type applications.

**Phase Mismatch vs Time:** We evaluate the phase mismatch between two Vidyut nodes as the number of symbols increases. We connect the transmit and receive nodes to a *live* power network and synchronize them using Vidyut. We fix the location of the transmit and receive nodes. We then track the accumulated phase mismatch between the transmit and receive nodes at the receive node with time. Fig. 15 plots the phase mismatch as a function of time. The phase mismatch is computed over the duration of the symbols transmitted. As indicated, the phase mismatch is relatively steady over time. This is because Vidyut nodes continuously relock to the common reference clock traversing the power-lines. Thus, the phase mismatch does not accumulate over time.

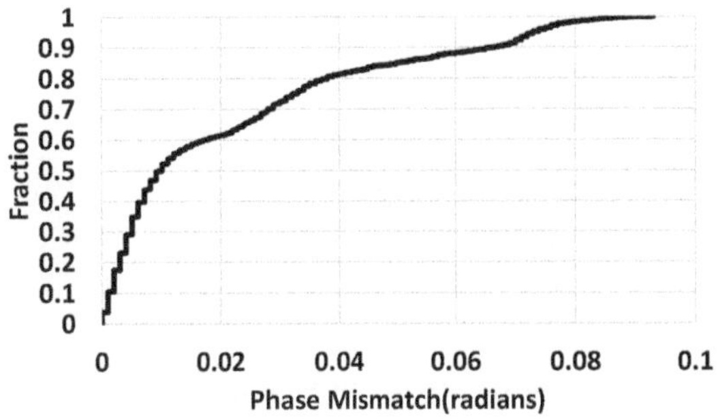


**Figure 16: CDF of phase mismatch between two nodes synchronized using Vidyut distributed randomly over the topology in Fig. 2.**

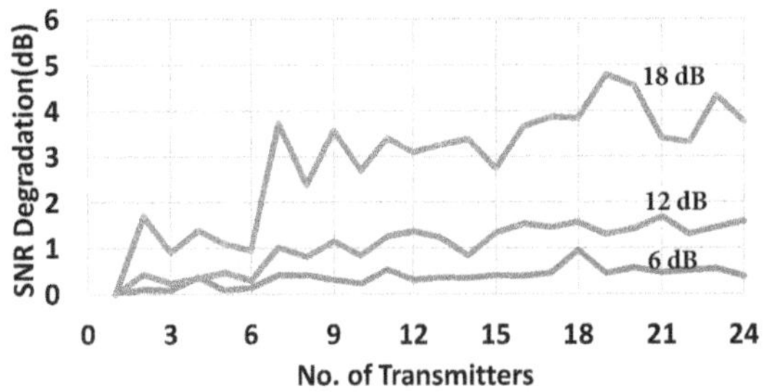


**Figure 17: SNR degradation due to phase mismatch across the transmitters as the number of transmitters is increased under different channel conditions.**

**Impact of Phase Mismatch:** Fig. 16 plots the phase mismatch distribution between two nodes synchronized by Vidyut. For each experiment, the nodes are connected to live power outlets randomly, across different phases and across the span of a floor in our department given in Fig. 2. The red circles in Fig. 2 indicate the power outlets to which the Vidyut nodes were connected. The experiment was carried out at different times of the day and thus the phase mismatch in Fig. 16 accounts for the various noise sources experienced in power-lines, different load conditions and the effect of the different electrical elements in the power distribution network. As indicated in Fig. 11, the distribution of the phase mismatch between two nodes synchronized by Vidyut is independent of the number of Vidyut nodes sharing the power-lines.

We estimate the increase in the noise floor at each receiver for the given phase mismatch distribution (Fig. 16) as the number of transmitters is increased. We plot the mean increase in the noise floor at each receiver as the number of transmitters synchronized by Vidyut is varied. Once we fix the number of transmitters, we vary the channel along three levels of SNR (6,12 and 18 dB). For each setting, we repeat the experiment a hundred times to establish the mean. The increase in noise floor at a receiver for different channel conditions is illustrated in Fig. 17. When the nodes perform Network MIMO using Vidyut in uniform channel conditions of 6dB SNR, the SNR degradation is negligible as the number of transmitters is increased. However, when the channel conditions are uniformly better, the average increase in SNR at each receiver as the number of transmitters is increased to 24 is $\approx$ 4dB.

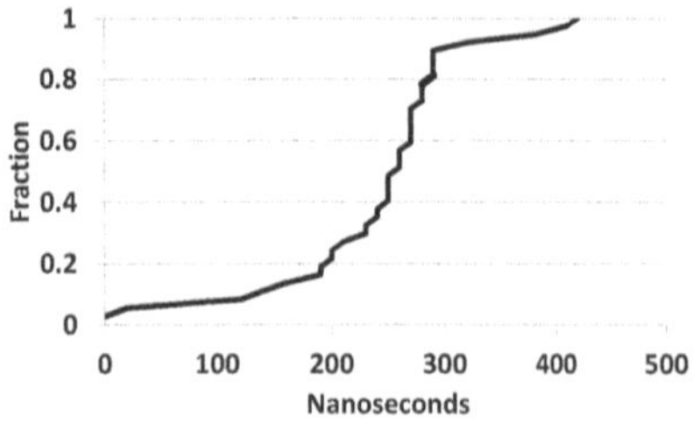


Figure 18: Variance in the power cycle zero crossing.

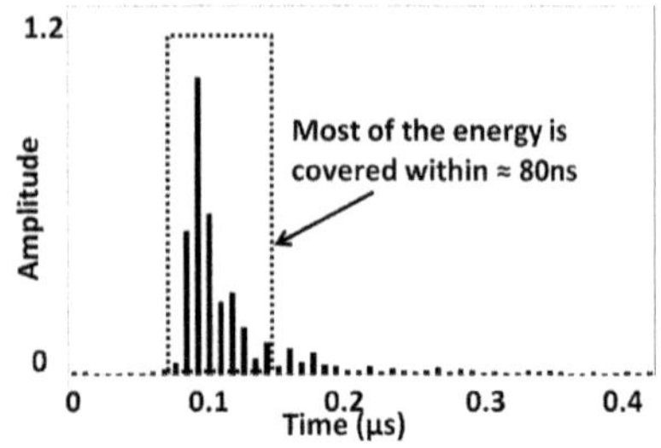


Figure 19: Capturing multipath in an indoor office environment.

## 5.2 Time Synchronization:

As discussed in the previous section, Vidyut utilizes the stable time period of power frequency as a reference for time across distributed nodes. Each node constructs a time averaged time period of the power cycle to filter out the impact of impulsive noise sources. We measure the variance in the zero crossing of the power cycle across random power outlets illustrated in Fig. 2.The cumulative distributed function (cdf) of this variance is illustrated in Fig. 18.

The distribution of the variance in the time period of the power cycle is almost Gaussian indicating the variation in the time period is due to random noise sources. The difference in time period between adjaced periods can be as high as $\approx$ 450 nanoseconds. The average variation in time period is $\approx$ 225 nanoseconds. Further, the measurement of the propagation delay of the power signal between two nodes can introduce errors. To correct for such errors, we provision an additional 100 nanoseconds.

The 802.11n makes a provision for two guard intervals: 400 ns(short) and 800 ns(typical). The intrinsic noise in the power-lines makes it hard for Vidyut nodes to operate with the short guard interval since the variation in the time reference itself exceeds the guard interval and leaves no further tolerance for multipath effects. We measure the multipath effects in a typical indoor enviroment in our lab. Our lab space includes multiple cubicles with metallic edges, metallic chairs and tables which all act as reflectors. The multipath profile of this environment is illustrated in Fig. 19. As indicated, most of the energy from multipath sources is covered at the receiver within 80 ns. Thus, even with an average variation of 225 ns, the Vidyut's time synchronization methodology should suffice as a method of time synchronization as the difference in signal paths at the receiver will be well within 800 ns.

## 5.3 Power:

The Agilent 8648C outputs a 10 MHz reference clock at an amplitude above $0.5V_{rms}$. This reference clock has been used to synchronize Vidyut nodes upto 200 feet away. Each NI-5791 based Vidyut node outputs a 2V peak-to-peak square clock output in phase to the reference clock traversing the power-lines. With this power we had no trouble synchronizing Vidyut nodes as far as two hundred feet away to enable Enterprise LAN based applications.

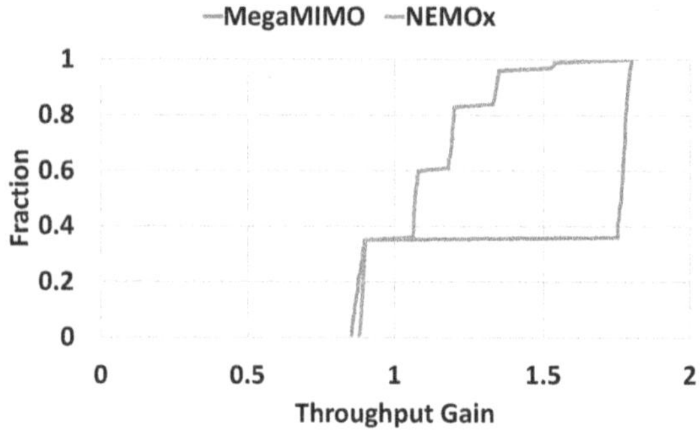


Figure 20: Throughput gain over MegaMIMO and NEMOx.

# 6. SYSTEM EVALUATION

The previous section quantifies the accuracy of Vidyut's synchronization in time and frequency domains. It analyzed the contribution of different elements of the power network and Vidyut's own clock circuitry to the synchronization. We now evaluate two Vidyut backed systems. First, we build an eight node Network MIMO type system. We distribute the eight node locations randomly across the area of a floor in our department illustrated in Fig. 2. For this setting, we analyze the throughput performance of Vidyut and compare it with MegaMIMO and NEMOx. Second, we build an eight node OFDMA type system and analyze Vidyut's distributed synchronization's effect on reliability of communication. For both experiments, the nodes are connected to power outlets of live networks and the experiments were performed during different times of the day. Thus the results presented include the effect of different loading conditions and noise sources experienced in power-lines.

**Network MIMO:** First, we define competing clusters as a set of those clusters (defined in Section 1) that has at least one client associated to every cluster in the set. We place Vidyut nodes at random locations illustrated in Fig. 2. For all locations, the nodes are synchronized using Vidyut. We place the nodes such that for every distribution of the nodes, we can group all the transmitting nodes into no more than two clusters. Also, a cluster is guaranteed at least one receiver for every node distribution. Fig. 20 plots the distribution of the throughput gain of Vidyut over MegaMIMO and NEMOx. Vidyut achieves a throughput gain of $\approx$ 1.8 times over MegaMIMO during approximately 65 % of the experiments. These are the instances where the nodes are placed in such a way that they form competing clusters. For almost, 60% of the experiments, the throughput gain of Vidyut over NEMOx is quite minimal. The reason for this is that the node density of our testbed is sparse.

We seek to determine the potential benefit of having synchronization beyond two clusters. Since the number of nodes required for bigger networks is prohibitively high, we run a MATLAB based simulation to evaluate the performance

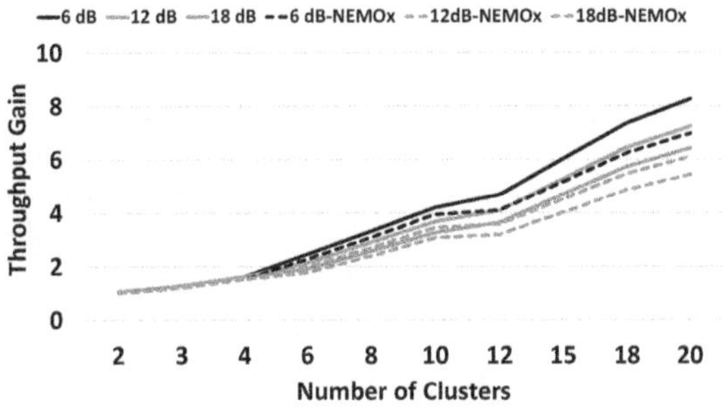


**Figure 21: Throughput gain for a Vidyut system compared to MegaMIMO and NEMOx as the number of clusters increases. The thick lines plot the throughput gain of Vidyut over MegaMIMO and the dotted lines over NEMOx.**

gains of Vidyut for networks with higher number of clusters. We assume every AP always has data to send to its clients. We compare the performance of Vidyut backed system with MegaMIMO and NEMOx backed systems. We group a set of clients with a cluster if every client is within the transmission range of at least one AP of that cluster. We implement a TDMA over CSMA type MAC for MegaMIMO and NEMOx systems, by letting all non competing clusters simultaneously transmit in each time slot. While implementing NEMOx, in case of competing clusters, we identify subsets of the competing clusters with distinct interference-free clients and let these APs transmit simultaneously. For the case of Vidyut, since all the APs are synchronized in time and frequency and since the data is sent from a single central server, all the APs can simultaneously send data without causing interference at unintended clients. The clusters and the clients are randomly placed. The number of clients is increased with the number of the clusters as well to ensure there is always a sink for the data demand. The experiment is repeated for 100 runs before increasing the number of clusters. For each run, we perform the experiment over three channel conditions. We assume uniform channel conditions over the span of the network. We let MegaMIMO and NEMOx transmit packets using the short guard interval. For Vidyut, we assume a long guard interval. Further, we account for the increase in noise power due to the phase mismatch of Vidyut.

Fig. 21 demonstrates the throughput benefit of Vidyut over MegaMIMO and NEMOx for larger networks as the number of clusters is increased. As indicated, the gain is negligible for two clusters since the network is sparse and thus the two clusters can simultaneously transmit without interfering with each other in the case of MegaMIMO and NEMOx, thus negating the benefit of Vidyut. However, as the number of clusters and clients increases, the network becomes more dense. Subsequently, the throughput gain of Vidyut system becomes more significant. Vidyut system with 20 clusters presents an average throughput gain of $\approx$ 8.1x over MegaMIMO system and $\approx$ 5.9x over NEMOx system. The simulation incorporates the imperfections in timing and frequency synchronization of a Vidyut system discussed in the previous section. The reduction in gain from an ideal implementation of such a system is indicated.

**OFDMA:** In our OFDMA implementation, each transmitter transmits on alternate subcarriers, i.e. if $Transmitter_1$ transmits on subcarrier $\alpha$, then $Transmitter_2$ transmits on subcarrier $\alpha+1$ and so on. We vary the number of OFDMA transmitters from three to seven. We perform the experiment in two states. First, we synchronize all the participating OFDMA transmitters using Vidyut. Second, we repeat the experiment with un-synchronized transmitters. When the transmitters are unsynchronized, inter carrier interference occurs thereby reducing the throughput of the OFDMA system. Fig. 22 illustrates the throughput gain of a Vidyut backed OFDMA system over an unsynchronized OFDMA system. Vidyut achieves a throughput gain of up to 2.5 times as the number of concurrent OFDMA transmitters is increased from three to seven.

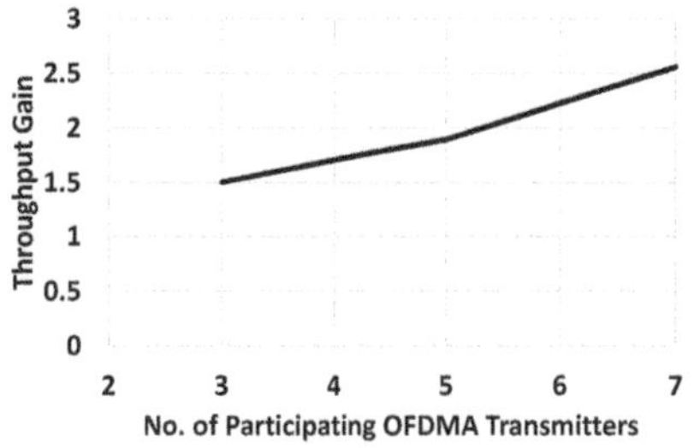


**Figure 22: Vidyut backed OFDMA systems show a throughput gain over unsynchronized free-running oscillators.**

# 7. RELATED WORK

**Time Synchronization:** Sourcesync [14] utilizes a synchronization header from a lead transmitter to synchronize transmissions between distributed concurrent transmitters in time domain. Sourcesync achieves time synchronization within 20ns. Sourcesync limits synchronization to nodes within a single collision domain. The work presented in [16] utilizes the electromagnetic radiations from the power frequency to synchronize distributed sensor nodes to enable coarse time synchronization in wireless sensor networks. The synchronization achieved is of the order of milliseconds which is not suitable for Wi-Fi-type applications.

**Frequency Synchronization:** Recently, practical implementations, MegaMIMO [15] and AirSync [2], have demonstrated time and frequency synchronization required for distributed MIMO applications. Both these techniques rely on a lead transmitter to transmit a synchronization header in the air. Thus, these implementations are applicable only to nodes within a single collision domain. NEMOx, [21], proposes a MAC that advocates opportunistic transmissions from APs within a competing cluster to interference-free clients.

**Power-line Communication:** The power-line medium is an emerging alternative to cellular and wireless media for Smart Grid, [6], as well as in-home broadband applications [5] [11]. Smart Grid PLC implementations operate in the 10-500 KHz band of the spectrum in The United States with a data rate in the order of 100s of Kbps [5] while in-home broadband PLC applications operate in the 2-86 MHz, [17]. While the communication range of this frequency range is much shorter than the KHz band used for Smart Grid applications, it achieves data rates of the order of a few 100s of

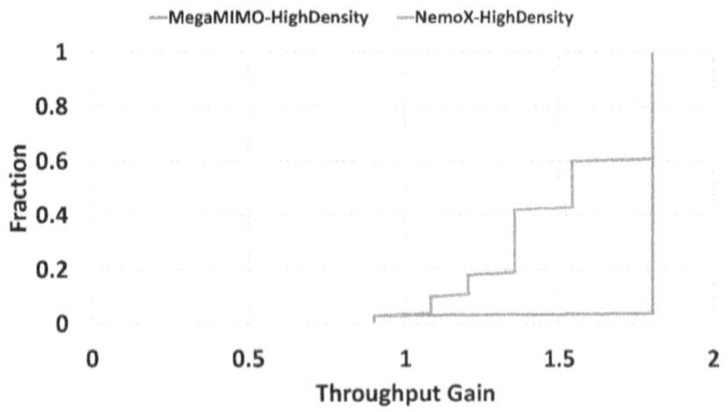


**Figure 23: Throughput gains of Vidyut in a two-cluster dense network.**

Mbps. The works in [3,18] explore extending the communication range of PLC using amplify-and-forward technique. While Vidyut requires each node to regenerate the reference clock, its objective is distinct from that of power-line communications in the following regard: Vidyut is only responsible for distributing a stable reference clock (a single tone) across the power-line network of an enterprise.

**Power-line assisted wireless communication:** SNUPI [4] utilizes the power-lines as an antenna to increase the transmission range for wireless sensor nodes. Vidyut directly injects the reference clock on to the power-lines. The work in [8] proposes PLC transmission schemes to assist sharing channel information between wireless relay nodes as well as with synchronization. Vidyut does not require its nodes to decode PLC packets. Instead, it achieves synchronization using the physical property of PLLs. Recent works studied PLC together with different wireless communication techniques to enhance performance of wireless networks [7,9,10]. In all these solutions, the power-lines are used to transmit data while Vidyut only transmits a reference clock.

## 8. DISCUSSION

We have demonstrated the feasibility of using power lines as a resource for achieving distributed synchronization across clusters. We demonstrated the throughput benefits of such synchronization from small to large networks. However, as pointed out in the previous section, when the network density is sparse, NEMOx in most cases will do as well, if not better than Vidyut (accounting for inaccuracies in the phase mismatch). Thus, one might be led to believe that Vidyut has benefits for only large networks with large number of clusters. While, we have not dealt with the problem of CSIT, it is a challenge in implementing a Network MIMO network. However, we point out that cross-cluster synchronization is critical even in small networks. The key, however, is for the network to have high density. Fig. 23 illustrates the throughput gain of Vidyut in one such two-cluster network. Thus, cross-cluster synchronization has significant benefits even for small networks.

**Effect of Vidyut on existing PLC:** The current state-of-the-art PLC standards employ OFDM with bit-loading schemes [17]. These standards specify a bandwidth of operation ranging from 2 MHz to 86 MHz using 3,455 subcarriers. The single-tone reference used for Vidyut will cause existing PLCs to skip one of its subcarriers. Therefore, the effect on PLCs will be insignificant.

One can consider a hybrid global synchronization technique that includes the long distance benefit of Vidyut with higher accuracy of other systems such as MegaMIMO. However, this is left as work for future research.

**Acknowledgment:** We thank our shepherd, Shyamnath Gollakota, for helping improve the quality of the paper. We thank Bob Carruth and others at Ohio State Utilities Development, Prof. Ertin and Prof. Wang for thoughtful discussions as well as providing equipment required to carry out some of the experiments.

## 9. REFERENCES

[1] Analog Devices. *AD9511:1.2 GHz Clock Distribution IC,PLL Core,Dividers, Delay Adjust, Five Outputs.* Rev. A.

[2] Balan, H. V., Rogalin, R., Michaloliakos, A., Psounis, K., and Caire, G. Airsync: Enabling distributed multiuser mimo with full spatial multiplexing. *CoRR abs/1205.6862* (2012).

[3] Cheng, X., Cao, R., and Yang, L. Relay-aided amplify-and-forward powerline communications. *Smart Grid, IEEE Transactions on 4*, 1 (March 2013), 265–272.

[4] Cohn, G., Stuntebeck, E., Pandey, J., Otis, B., Abowd, G. D., and Patel, S. N. Snupi: Sensor nodes utilizing powerline infrastructure. In *UBICOMP* (2010), ACM, pp. 159–168.

[5] Galli, S., Scaglione, A., and Wang, Z. For the grid and through the grid: The role of power line communications in the smart grid. *Proc. IEEE* (June 2011), 998–1027.

[6] Gungor, V., Sahin, D., Kocak, T., Ergut, S., Buccella, C., Cecati, C., and Hancke, G. Smart grid technologies: Communication technologies and standards. *Industrial Informatics, IEEE Trans. on* (2011).

[7] Ha, J. Y., Jeon, J., Lee, K., Heo, J., Kim, N., Kim, S. M., Kwon, W.-H., and Jin Jung, B. Design and implementation of convergence sub-layer for a heterogeneous home network. In *ISPLC* (2007).

[8] Kuhn, M., Berger, S., Hammerstrom, I., and Wittneben, A. Power line enhanced cooperative wireless communications. *Sel. Areas in Comm., IEEE J.* (2006).

[9] Lai, S., and Messier, G. The wireless/power-line diversity channel. In *IEEE Int. Conf. on Comm.(ICC)* (2010).

[10] Lai, S., and Messier, G. Using the wireless and plc channels for diversity. *Communications, IEEE Transactions on* (2012).

[11] Lin, Y.-J., Latchman, H., Lee, M., and Katar, S. A power line communication network infrastructure for the smart home. *Wireless Communications, IEEE* (2002).

[12] Maxim Integrated. *MAX2828/MAX2829: Single/Dual Band 802.11a/b/g World-Band Transceiver ICs.* Rev. 0.

[13] Meng, H., Guan, Y., and Chen, S. Modeling and analysis of noise effects on broadband power-line communications. *Power Del., IEEE Trans. 20*, 2 (April 2005), 630–637.

[14] Rahul, H., Hassanieh, H., and Katabi, D. Sourcesync: a distributed wireless architecture for exploiting sender diversity. In *SIGCOMM* (2010), ACM, pp. 171–182.

[15] Rahul, H., Kumar, S., and Katabi, D. MegaMIMO: Scaling Wireless Capacity with User Demands. In *SIGCOMM* (2012), ACM.

[16] Rowe, A., Gupta, V., and Rajkumar, R. R. Low-power clock synchronization using electromagnetic energy radiating from ac power lines. In *SENSYS* (2009), ACM, pp. 211–224.

[17] Schwager, A. An overview of the homeplug av2 technology. *Journal of Electrical and Computer Engineering 2013* (2013).

[18] Tan, B., and Thompson, J. Relay transmission protocols for in-door powerline communications networks. In *IEEE Int. Conf. on Comm. Work. (ICC)* (2011).

[19] Tlich, M., Zeddam, A., Moulin, F., and Gauthier, F. Indoor power-line communications channel characterization up to 100 mhz;part i: One-parameter deterministic model. *Power Del., IEEE Trans.* (July 2008), 1392–1401.

[20] Tlich, M., Zeddam, A., Moulin, F., and Gauthier, F. Indoor power-line communications channel characterization up to 100 mhz;part ii: Time-frequency analysis. *Power Del., IEEE Trans.* (July 2008), 1402–1409.

[21] Zhang, X., Sundaresan, K., Khojastepour, M. A. A., Rangarajan, S., and Shin, K. G. Nemox: Scalable network mimo for wireless networks. In *MOBICOM* (2013), ACM, pp. 453–464.

[22] Zimmermann, M., and Dostert, K. Analysis and modeling of impulsive noise in broad-band powerline communications. *Electromagnetic Compatibility, IEEE Trans.* (Feb 2002), 249–258.

# Wi-Fi Backscatter: Internet Connectivity for RF-Powered Devices

Bryce Kellogg, Aaron Parks, Shyamnath Gollakota, Joshua R. Smith, and David Wetherall
University of Washington
{kellogg, anparks, gshyam, jrsjrs, djw}@uw.edu

**Abstract–** RF-powered computers are small devices that compute and communicate using only the power that they harvest from RF signals. While existing technologies have harvested power from ambient RF sources (e.g., TV broadcasts), they require a dedicated gateway (like an RFID reader) for Internet connectivity.

We present *Wi-Fi Backscatter*, a novel communication system that bridges RF-powered devices with the Internet. Specifically, we show that it is possible to reuse existing Wi-Fi infrastructure to provide Internet connectivity to RF-powered devices. To show Wi-Fi Backscatter's feasibility, we build a hardware prototype and demonstrate the first communication link between an RF-powered device and commodity Wi-Fi devices. We use off-the-shelf Wi-Fi devices including Intel Wi-Fi cards, Linksys Routers, and our organization's Wi-Fi infrastructure, and achieve communication rates of up to 1 kbps and ranges of up to 2.1 meters. We believe that this new capability can pave the way for the rapid deployment and adoption of RF-powered devices and achieve ubiquitous connectivity via nearby mobile devices that are Wi-Fi enabled.

## Categories and Subject Descriptors

C.2.1 [**Network Architecture and Design**]: Wireless communication

## Keywords

Backscatter; Internet of Things; Energy harvesting; Wireless

## 1. Introduction

It is increasingly becoming feasible to perform low-end computing, sensing, and more recently communication [17] by harvesting power from ambient RF signals including TV, cellular, and Wi-Fi transmissions [26, 27, 22]. This technology is intriguing because it may be embedded inexpensively into everyday objects to help realize the pervasive vision of the "Internet of Things" [9]: objects that operate and communicate with each other when they are nearby, all without the need to ever plug them in or maintain batteries.

Existing technologies, however, lack the central component in this vision of an RF-powered Internet of Things: an ability to connect RF-powered devices to the Internet. Using conventional radio communication to achieve this connectivity is challenging, since it consumes orders of magnitude more power than is available in ambient RF [23]. Communication techniques like ambient backscatter [17] enable these devices to communicate with each other; but they create an isolated network disconnected from the Internet. A naïve solution is to develop and deploy special-purpose powered infrastructure devices, along the lines of RFID readers, that can connect the two networks. But deploying new support infrastructure adds cost and, more importantly, diminishes the key value-proposition of RF-powered systems — an ability to operate without dedicated power infrastructure.

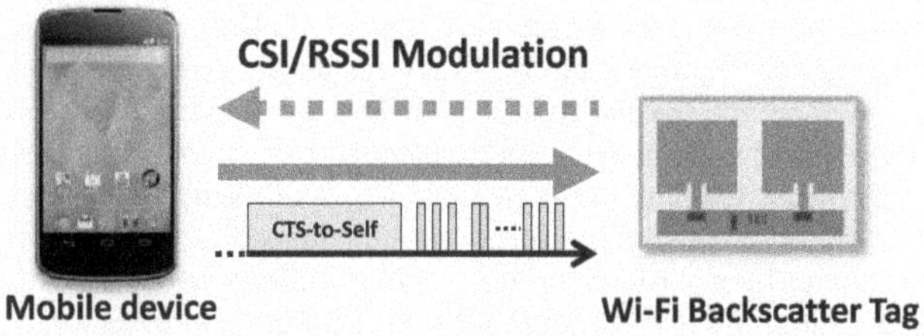


**Figure 1—Wi-Fi Backscatter at a high level.** The figure shows a Wi-Fi Backscatter tag (an RF-powered device) communicating with a Wi-Fi enabled mobile device. On the uplink, the Wi-Fi Backscatter tag conveys information by modulating the CSI and RSSI measurements received at the Wi-Fi device. On the downlink, the Wi-Fi device conveys information by encoding bits in the presence or silence of Wi-Fi packets. The Wi-Fi Backscatter tag uses its low-power Wi-Fi packet detector circuit to decode this information.

In this paper, we ask if it is possible to reuse existing infrastructure to connect these devices to the Internet. Specifically, we seek to design RF-powered devices that communicate directly with commodity Wi-Fi devices. A positive answer would pave the way for a rapid and simple deployment of the RF-powered Internet of Things by letting these devices connect to existing mobile phones and Wi-Fi APs. It would also expand the functionality of Wi-Fi networks in a new direction: from providing connectivity to existing Wi-Fi clients to a whole new class of battery-free devices.

Achieving this capability, however, is challenging since conventional low-power Wi-Fi transceivers require much more power than is available from ambient RF signals. Thus, it is not feasible for RF-powered devices to literally speak the Wi-Fi protocol. Conversely, since existing Wi-Fi devices are specifically designed to receive Wi-Fi signals, it is unclear how they would decode other kinds of signals from RF-powered devices.

We introduce *Wi-Fi Backscatter*, a novel communication system in which RF-powered "things" can communicate with off-the-shelf Wi-Fi devices. At a high level, a Wi-Fi Backscatter tag communicates with a Wi-Fi device by modulating its Wi-Fi channel. Since channel information including CSI and RSSI is widely available on commodity Wi-Fi devices, the Wi-Fi receiver can extract the modulated information by measuring the changes in its channel. To understand this in more detail, consider the Wi-Fi Backscatter tag and Wi-Fi enabled mobile device in Fig. 1. The Wi-Fi Backscatter tag communicates by modulating the Wi-Fi channel as seen by the mobile device. Specifically, it conveys a '1' and a '0' bit by either reflecting or absorbing the Wi-Fi packets received by the mobile device. The reflected signals change the per-packet CSI and RSSI


*SIGCOMM'14,* August 17–22, 2014, Chicago, IL, USA.
Copyright 2014 ACM 978-1-4503-2836-4/14/08 ...$15.00.
http://dx.doi.org/10.1145/2619239.2626319.

measurements, which the mobile device uses to decode messages from the Wi-Fi Backscatter tag.

We also enable downlink communication to the Wi-Fi Backscatter tag. While the mobile device can send Wi-Fi packets directly to the tag, the latter cannot decode Wi-Fi transmissions. Instead, Wi-Fi Backscatter relies on low-power circuit designs that can detect energy corresponding to a Wi-Fi packet (see §4.2). Specifically, as shown in the figure, the mobile device sends a pattern of short Wi-Fi packets — the presence (absence) of the short Wi-Fi packet encodes the '1' ('0') bit. The Wi-Fi Backscatter tag decodes this information by using our low-power energy detector to differentiate between the presence and absence of Wi-Fi packets. In §4, we develop the above ideas further and design Wi-Fi Backscatter to work in the presence of multiple Wi-Fi devices in the network.

To show the feasibility of our designs, we build prototype devices that are optimized to backscatter and harvest Wi-Fi signals at frequencies spanning the entire 2.4 GHz Wi-Fi band. We evaluate our prototype in various scenarios with commodity Wi-Fi devices including Intel Wi-Fi cards and the Wi-Fi infrastructure in our organization. We use the RSSI information that is widely available on commodity Wi-Fi devices. We also use the Intel CSI toolkit [13] to extract the finer grained CSI information. Our results show the following.

- The Wi-Fi devices can reliably decode information on the uplink at distances of up to 65 cm and 30 cm using CSI and RSSI information respectively. This is achieved at bit rates ranging from 100 bps to 1 kbps. The uplink range can be increased to more than 2.1 meters by performing coding at the Wi-Fi device.
- The uplink can operate using only the ambient Wi-Fi transmissions in the network. Specifically, the Wi-Fi device can use RSSI information extracted from all the packets transmitted by the AP in our organization to achieve uplink bit rates between 100 bps and 200 bps, depending on the network load.
- The prototype can detect Wi-Fi packets as short as 50 $\mu s$ at distances of up to 2.2 meters; this translates to a bit rate of 20 kbps on the downlink. The downlink range can be further extended to about 3 meters by reducing the bit rate to 5 kbps.

**Contributions:** We make the following contributions:

- We introduce a novel communication system that connects RF-powered devices (Wi-Fi Backscatter tags) to the Internet via existing Wi-Fi infrastructure.
- We design an uplink communication channel that allows Wi-Fi Backscatter tags to convey information to Wi-Fi devices by modulating the Wi-Fi channel information including CSI and RSSI.
- We design a downlink communication channel where Wi-Fi devices encodes information in the presence or absence of Wi-Fi packets; the Wi-Fi Backscatter tags use low-power circuits to detect Wi-Fi packets and decode this information.
- Finally, we build a hardware prototype for Wi-Fi Backscatter and demonstrate the first communication link between a Wi-Fi Backscatter tag and commodity Wi-Fi devices.

While the bit rates demonstrated in this paper are not high, we believe that the ability to communicate at even low rates between RF-powered devices and existing Wi-Fi infrastructure is a significant capability that would be critical for the commercial adoption of an RF-powered Internet of Things.

## 2. WI-FI BACKSCATTER OVERVIEW

Wi-Fi Backscatter is a novel communication system that enables RF-powered devices to communicate directly with commodity Wi-Fi devices. As shown in Fig. 2, Wi-Fi Backscatter has three main actors: a Wi-Fi reader, a Wi-Fi helper, and an RF-powered Wi-Fi Backscatter tag. In principle, the reader and helper can be any commodity Wi-Fi device, including routers and mobile devices. However, for ease of exposition, we consider a Wi-Fi client, such as a mobile phone, to be the reader and a Wi-Fi AP to be the helper device. We envision the RF-powered devices to be wireless sensor nodes that are embedded in everyday objects. The Wi-Fi Backscatter tags do not require any batteries and can harvest energy from ambient RF signals including TV, cellular, and Wi-Fi. We also note that Wi-Fi Backscatter can also be used to provide Internet connectivity to battery-free devices with other power harvesting sources including solar and mechanical energy.

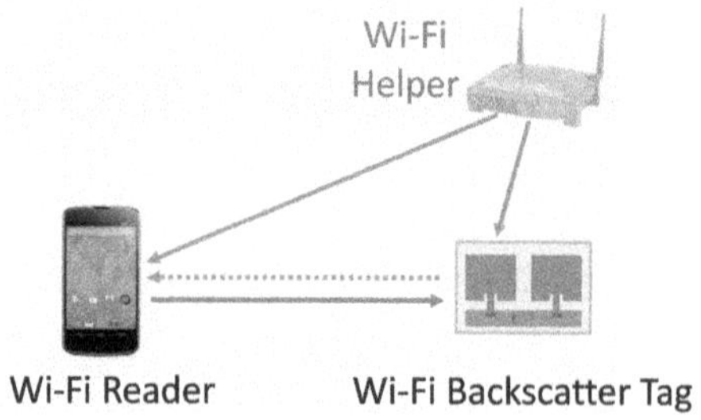


**Figure 2—Wi-Fi Backscatter Overview.** It has three actors: a Wi-Fi reader, a Wi-Fi helper, and a RF-powered device (Wi-Fi Backscatter tag). The reader and helper can be any commodity Wi-Fi device, including routers and mobile devices. The Wi-Fi reader leverages the channel information from the Wi-Fi helper's packets to decode the transmissions from the tag.

Wi-Fi Backscatter's communication has two main components: an uplink from the Wi-Fi Backscatter tag to the Wi-Fi reader and a downlink from the Wi-Fi reader to the Wi-Fi Backscatter tag. Wi-Fi Backscatter follows a request-response model, similar to RFID systems. Specifically, the Wi-Fi reader asks the Wi-Fi Backscatter tag for information on the downlink and receives a response on the uplink. In the presence of multiple Wi-Fi Backscatter tags in the vicinity, the interrogator can use protocols similar to EPC Gen-2 [2] to identify these devices and then query each of them individually. In this paper, however, we focus on establishing a communication link with a single Wi-Fi Backscatter tag.

At a high level, Wi-Fi Backscatter imitates RFID communication using a Wi-Fi device. Specifically, the Wi-Fi Backscatter tag communicates by modulating the transmissions from the Wi-Fi helper. The Wi-Fi reader decodes these transmissions by using the channel changes that are created on the received Wi-Fi packets. In principle, Wi-Fi Backscatter can have multiple Wi-Fi helper devices (e.g., multiple APs or other Wi-Fi client); in this paper, however, we focus on using a single Wi-Fi helper device. For the downlink, the Wi-Fi reader transmits directly to the Wi-Fi Backscatter tag by encoding information in short Wi-Fi packets interspersed by silence. The tag decodes these transmissions using a low-power circuit design that can detect energy from Wi-Fi packets.

In the rest of this paper, we describe the design of the Wi-Fi Backscatter uplink in §3 and the downlink in §4. We then generalize our description to work in the presence of multiple Wi-Fi devices in §5. Finally, we evaluate our prototype in various scenarios.

## 3. WI-FI BACKSCATTER UPLINK

Wi-Fi Backscatter enables communication on the uplink from an RF-powered device to the Wi-Fi reader. This is challenging however because it is not feasible for these devices to speak the Wi-Fi protocol. Instead we transmit data by modulating the Wi-Fi channel as seen in the Wi-Fi reader channel state information. In this section we describe the Wi-Fi Backscatter uplink in more detail.

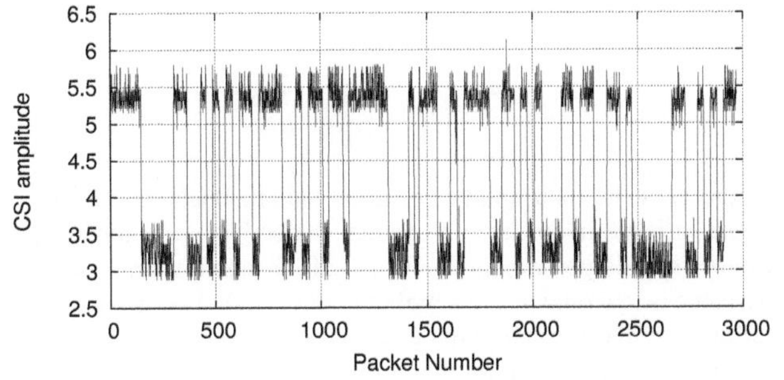


**Figure 3—Raw CSI measurements for a single Wi-Fi sub-channel in the presence of the Wi-Fi Backscatter tag 5 centimeters away.** The plot clearly shows a binary modulation on top of the CSI measurements.

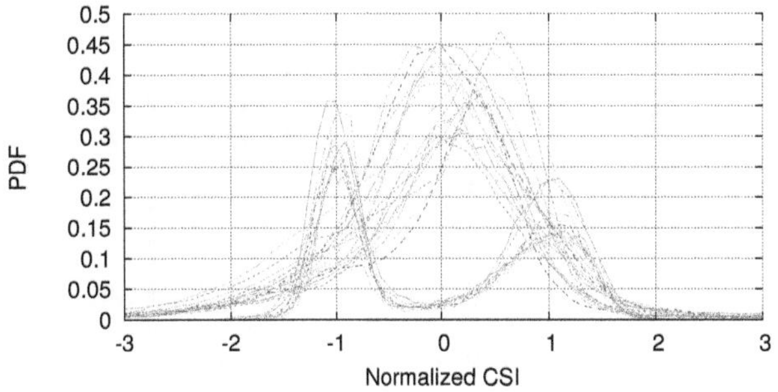


**Figure 4—PDF of normalized channel values for the 30 Wi-Fi sub-channels.** The plot shows diversity between sub-channels.

## 3.1 Modulating Wi-Fi Channel at the tag

The Wi-Fi Backscatter tag conveys information by modulating the Wi-Fi channel. To do this, it uses a low power switch that allows the antenna impedance to be modulated by a transmitted bit stream. The antenna's impedance affects the amount of signal that is reflected by the tag. By modulating this impedance, the tag can convey '1' and '0' bits. These switches consume less than 1 $\mu$W of power, which is negligible. Our prototype design optimizes the choice of the switch to operate well at frequencies spanning the entire 2.4 GHz Wi-Fi band.

The Wi-Fi Backscatter tag can in principle use a variety of antennas including monopoles and dipoles. For our prototype, we designed a special-purpose antenna for the Wi-Fi Backscatter tag that is capable of both impedance modulation as well as Wi-Fi energy harvesting. Specifically, we design a microstrip "patch" antenna, as the gain of this antenna can be relatively high with respect to its size. Our antenna design takes into consideration a key factor of system performance: the extent of radar cross section changes that the antenna is capable of achieving. The radar cross-section refers to the amount of incident Wi-Fi signals that can be reflected by an antenna; the contrast between the radar cross-section when the tag is reflecting versus not reflecting will determine the impact of the tag on a nearby Wi-Fi receiver. To improve the radar cross-section, we design an array of microstrip patches, each of which resonates at 2.4 GHz, but which act together to collaboratively scatter incident RF and therefore produce a larger change in the radar cross-section. Wi-Fi antenna design is a broad topic and one can use other antenna topologies that can significantly reduce the size of the antenna [18]. This, however, is not in the scope of this paper.

Finally, the minimum period with which our tag changes its impedance is larger than the duration of a Wi-Fi packet. That is, the duration of each transmitted bit is greater than the time it takes to transmit a few Wi-Fi packets. This ensures that the act of modulating does not change the channel within every Wi-Fi packet, thus allowing nearby Wi-Fi communication to proceed with minimal interference. We also note that the Wi-Fi Backscatter tag modulates the Wi-Fi channel only when queried by the reader. Further, the tag can adapt the modulation rate by increasing the duration of each bit, enabling our tag to adapt the resulting data rate to the Wi-Fi network traffic conditions (see §5).

## 3.2 Decoding algorithm at the Wi-Fi reader

Next, we describe how the Wi-Fi reader extracts the modulated Wi-Fi channel corresponding to the packets from the helper. To understand how the reflections at a Wi-Fi Backscatter tag affect the Wi-Fi channel, we run the following experiment. We place an Intel Wi-Fi Link 5300 card, which acts as a Wi-Fi reader, next to a Wi-Fi Backscatter tag. We configure the tag to modulate an alternating sequence of zero and one bits. The Wi-Fi reader downloads a 1 GB media file from a Linksys WRT54GL AP, which acts as a Wi-Fi helper. The helper is placed 5 meters away from the Wi-Fi Backscatter tag. Fig. 3 plots the CSI in Wi-Fi sub-channel 19 as a function of the packet number. The plot clearly shows a binary modulation on top of the captured channel measurements.

Our decoding algorithm extracts this modulated information in three main steps: (1) Signal conditioning to remove the variations in the channel measurements due to mobility in the environment, (2) Leveraging frequency diversity across the Wi-Fi sub-channels, and (3) Decoding the backscattered bits from the channel information.

**(1) Signal Conditioning.** The goal of this step is two-fold: 1) remove the natural temporal variations in the channel measurements due to mobility in the environment, and 2) normalize the channel measurements to map to -1 and +1 values. In particular, to remove the temporal variations, we subtract a moving average from the channel measurements at the Wi-Fi reader; the moving average is computed over a duration of 400 ms in our experiments. The above operation creates zero-mean channel measurements without the temporal variations. Next, we normalize these measurements such that the channel corresponding to a one bit from the Wi-Fi Backscatter tag maps to a +1 and that corresponding to a zero bit maps to a -1. Since we do not know the actual bits transmitted, we instead perform this normalization by computing the absolute values of the zero-mean channel measurements and then taking their average. We then divide the zero-mean channel measurements with this computed average to get the normalized channel values.

**(2) Exploiting Wi-Fi Frequency/Spatial Diversity.** Wi-Fi transmissions span a bandwidth of 20 MHz. At such a wide bandwidth, it is well known that the signals experience frequency diversity where the amplitude and the phase of the channel measurements vary significantly with the Wi-Fi OFDM subcarriers. Similarly, multipath issues result in similar variations across antennas. Thus, one would expect that some of the Wi-Fi subcarriers and antennas experience a stronger effect due to the reflections from the Wi-Fi Backscatter tag. To empirically check this effect, Fig. 4 plots the probability density functions (PDF) of the normalized channel values for each adjacent pair of the 60 Wi-Fi subcarriers (resulting in 30 "sub-channels") available from the Intel card. The PDF is computed over channel measurements taken across 42,000 Wi-Fi packets. Fig. 4 shows three main points: First, for about 30 percent of the Wi-Fi sub-channels, we see two Gaussian signals centered at +1 and -1; these represent the two-reflection states at the tag. Secondly, the variance in the channel measurements, i.e., noise, changes significantly with the sub-channel being used. Finally, some of the sub-channels do not see two distinct Gaussian signals. This corresponds to frequencies where the effect of backscatter is very weak, due to

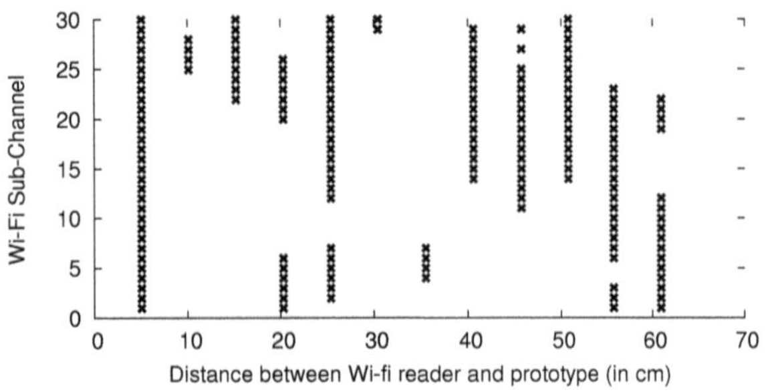


**Figure 5—Wi-Fi sub-channels with BER $< 10^{-2}$ at various distances.** For each Wi-Fi sub-channel, the figure shows the experiments where decoding using only that sub-channel achieves a bit error rate less than $10^{-2}$. The plot shows that the set of good sub-channels varies significantly with the position (and therefore multipath profile) of the Wi-Fi Backscatter tag.

multipath effects. Thus, we observe significant frequency diversity within the 30 Wi-Fi sub-channels even when the Wi-Fi Backscatter tag is placed next to the Wi-Fi reader.

We exploit this frequency diversity to increase the reliability of Wi-Fi Backscatter's uplink communication. Specifically, the Wi-Fi reader performs the following two steps:

*Step 1: Identify the good Wi-Fi sub-channels/antennas.* Ideally, if the combination of a set of Wi-Fi sub-channels and antennas that have a strong signal from the Wi-Fi Backscatter tag is consistent across locations, then we could decode the information from the tag using only that combination. The challenge however is that the set of "good" sub-channels and antennas varies significantly with the position of the tag. To empirically see this, we place the Wi-Fi Backscatter tag at different distances from the Wi-Fi reader and measure the channel information on all the Wi-Fi sub-channels. Fig. 5 shows the sub-channels where the Wi-Fi reader could decode the modulated information with a BER of less than $10^{-2}$ at a given distance. The figure shows that, in general, there are no Wi-Fi sub-channels that are consistently good. Thus, the Wi-Fi reader should independently extract the good sub-channel information for each uplink transmission.

To do this, the Wi-Fi reader uses correlation with a known preamble from the tag; the preamble is used by the tag at the beginning of each of its message transmission. Specifically, the Wi-Fi reader correlates with the preamble along every sub-channel (treating multiple antennas as additional sub-channels), while waiting for an incoming transmission from the tag. When a transmission arrives (which is identified by a peak in the correlation), the Wi-Fi reader sorts the sub-channels based on the correlation value. In particular, the sub-channels that correlate well with the preamble have a better signal from the Wi-Fi Backscatter tag than those that correlate poorly. The Wi-Fi reader picks the top ten "good" sub-channels based on this correlation method.

*Step 2: Combining information across the good Wi-Fi sub-channels.* A naive approach to do this is to simply add up the information across all the sub-channels. This is, however, not optimal because the noise variance may vary even across the good sub-channels. Instead the Wi-Fi reader combines the information across the sub-channels by computing a weighted average where sub-channels with low noise variance are given a higher weight, while those with higher noise variance are given a lower weight.

More formally, say $CSI_i$ is the normalized CSI computed on the $i$th good Wi-Fi sub-channel. The Wi-Fi reader performs a linear combination of the normalized CSI across these sub-channels by weighting them with the noise variance. Specifically, the reader computes the following summation:

$$CSI_{weighted} = \sum_{i=1}^{G} \frac{CSI_i}{\sigma_i^2}$$

where $G$ is the total number of good sub-channels, and $\sigma_i^2$ is the noise variance in the $i$th sub-channel. Effectively, the above equation gives a larger weight to Wi-Fi sub-channels where the noise variance is low (and hence a higher confidence). The above computation is similar to maximum ratio combining techniques [7] used in traditional communication that are known to be optimal for Gaussian noise. In scenarios where the Wi-Fi reader has multiple antennas, the above computation can be performed for each antenna and the summation can be taken across all the antennas.

**(3) Decoding bits from the Wi-Fi Backscatter tag.** To do this, the Wi-Fi reader can use a simple thresholding mechanism on $CSI_{weighted}$. Specifically, if $CSI_{weighted}$ is greater than zero, the receiver outputs a '1' and a '0' otherwise. We note the following:

- The CSI information provided by the off-the-shelf Wi-Fi devices is inherently noisy. To account for these noisy measurements, we add redundancy to our transmissions. Specifically, each bit transmitted by the tag corresponds to multiple channel measurements (i.e., received Wi-Fi packets) at the receiver. The Wi-Fi reader repeats the above procedure for all these channel measurements and uses a simple majority vote to compute the transmitted bits.
- Since the Wi-Fi medium is shared and bursty in nature, it is unlikely that every bit transmitted by the tag sees the same number of Wi-Fi packets (and the corresponding channel measurements). To account for this, we use the timestamp that is in every Wi-Fi packet header to accurately group Wi-Fi packets belonging to the same bit transmission. We then perform majority voting over the corresponding channel measurements.
- Finally, the Intel cards used in our experiments report spurious changes in the CSI once every so often. We see this behavior even in a static network with no mobility. To account for this spurious behavior, we use a hysteresis mechanism. Specifically, we use two thresholds, $Thresh_0$ and $Thresh_1$, corresponding to the 0 and 1 bits. The receiver outputs a one (zero) bit only when the received channel value is greater (smaller) than $Thresh_1$ ($Thresh_0$). We set the threshold values to be $\mu \pm \sigma^2$, where $\mu$ and $\sigma$ are the mean and standard deviation of $CSI_{weighted}$ computed across packets. The above heuristic works effectively in our experiments.

### 3.3 Decoding Using RSSI

While the 802.11n Wi-Fi specification requires per-subchannel channel state information to be made available on newer Wi-Fi chipsets, most existing chipsets only provide the RSSI information [5]. RSSI is a single metric that provides a measure of the cumulative Wi-Fi signal strength across all the sub-channels. In this section, we describe how the Wi-Fi reader can decode the reflected information from the Wi-Fi Backscatter tag using only RSSI.

To do this, we employ a decoding algorithm similar to that described earlier. Specifically, we perform signal conditioning, hysteresis, and thresholding to decode the information exactly as in the algorithm from §3.2. We note that depending on the Wi-Fi chipset, the RSSI information available is either a single value per packet or an RSSI value per antenna in the case of MIMO receivers. In scenarios with multiple RSSI channels (e.g., multiple antennas), we select the best RSSI channel using the maximum correlation mechanism. In particular, the receiver correlates with the packet preamble and picks the RSSI channel that has the maximum correlation value. Finally, we note that since RSSI is a single value that repre-

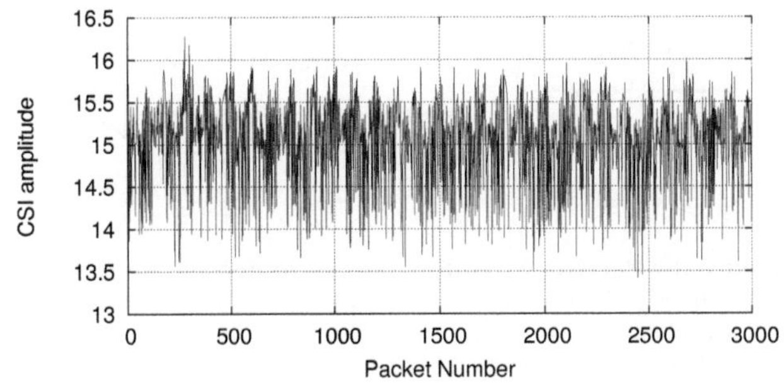


**Figure 6—Raw CSI measurements for a single Wi-Fi sub-channel in the presence of the Wi-Fi Backscatter tag one meter away.** The figure shows that at larger ranges, there are no longer two distinct levels in the CSI measurements. Thus, we need to design a different decoding mechanism to achieve higher ranges.

sents all Wi-Fi sub-channels and the RSSI bit resolution is limited, the BER performance is better with CSI information than RSSI.

### 3.4 Increasing Uplink Communication Range

The algorithm described so far assumes that the reflections from the Wi-Fi Backscatter tag create a distinctive difference in the channel values between a one and a zero bit. While such an algorithm is effective at small distances from the Wi-Fi reader (in our experiments up to 65 centimeters), it breaks down at larger distances. To see this, consider the channel measurements in Fig. 6, at a distance of two meters between the Wi-Fi Backscatter tag and the Wi-Fi reader. The figure shows that there are no two distinct levels in the channel measurements, which is in contrast to Fig. 3.

Wi-Fi Backscatter uses coding to increase its uplink communicate range. Specifically, the tag transmits two orthogonal codes of length $L$ each, to represent the one and the zero bits. The Wi-Fi reader correlates the channel measurements with the two codes and outputs the bit corresponding to the larger correlation value.

- Wi-Fi Backscatter repeats the above correlation operation on all the frequency sub-channels and picks the Wi-Fi sub-channels that provide the maximum correlation peaks.
- The communication range of the system can be increased by increasing the code length, $L$. This is because correlation with a $L$ bit long code provides an increase in the SNR that is proportional to $L$. Our evaluation shows that with a correlation length of 20 bits, the communication range can be increased to 1.6 meters. The uplink communication range can be further increased to 2.1 meters by increasing the correlation length to 150 bits..
- Since the tag still only transmits bits (now the bit duration expanded by $L$) and does not perform any decoding operations, the power consumption of the tag does not increase. The Wi-Fi reader on the other hand is a powered device and can perform the above correlation operations.

## 4. WI-FI BACKSCATTER DOWNLINK

Next, we describe how Wi-Fi Backscatter enables communication on the downlink from the Wi-Fi reader to a Wi-Fi Backscatter tag. The challenge in achieving this is that, on one hand, the reader can only transmit Wi-Fi packets; on the other hand, a Wi-Fi Backscatter tag cannot decode Wi-Fi transmissions. Instead, we design a novel circuit for the tag that can detect the energy during a Wi-Fi packet from a nearby transmitter. We then have the Wi-Fi reader encode information in the presence and absence of Wi-Fi packets. In the rest of this section, we describe the encoding mechanism at the Wi-Fi reader and the receiver design at the tag.

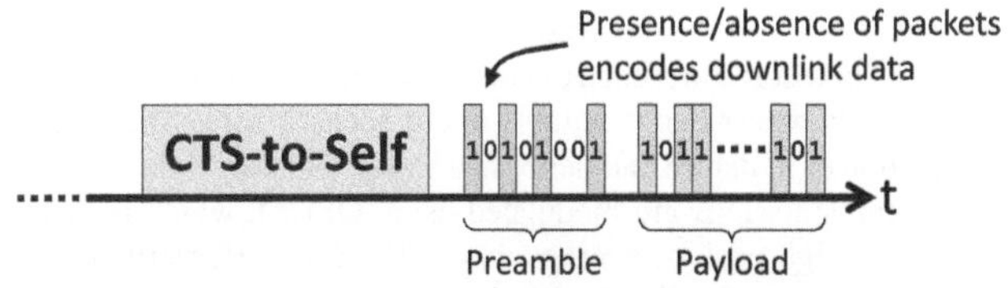


**Figure 7—Encoding information on the downlink.** the reader encodes a '1' bit with presence of a Wi-Fi packet and a '0' bit with silence (i.e., the absence of Wi-Fi packets). The duration of the silence period is set to be equal to that of the Wi-Fi packet. To enforce other Wi-Fi devices in the vicinity to not transmit during the silence periods, the Wi-Fi reader transmits a *CTS_to_SELF* packet before transmitting the message. The message consists of both the preamble bits and the payload bits (including the CRC).

### 4.1 Encoding at the Wi-Fi reader

The Wi-Fi reader encodes information using the presence or absence of a Wi-Fi packet. Specifically, as shown in Fig. 7, the reader encodes a '1' bit with presence of a Wi-Fi packet and a '0' bit with silence (i.e., the absence of Wi-Fi packets). The duration of the silence period is set to be equal to that of the Wi-Fi packet. To force other Wi-Fi devices in the vicinity to not transmit during the silence periods, the Wi-Fi reader transmits a *CTS_to_SELF* packet [10] before transmitting the encoded bits. *CTS_to_SELF* is a Wi-Fi message that forces 802.11-compliant devices to refrain for a specified time period. Wi-Fi Backscatter leverages this message to reserve the medium for the duration of its transmission to ensure that other Wi-Fi devices, unaware of the Wi-Fi Backscatter protocol, do not sense the medium as idle and transmit during the silence periods. We note the following key points:

- The current 802.11 standard only allows Wi-Fi devices to reserve the channel for up to a duration of 32 ms using the *CTS_to_SELF* packet. Thus, to maximize the number of bits transmitted within this duration, the Wi-Fi reader reduces the size of each Wi-Fi packet and the corresponding silence period. The smallest packet size possible on a Wi-Fi device is about 40 $\mu$s at a bit rate of 54 Mbps. Our receiver design in §4.2 can reliably detect Wi-Fi packets as small as 50 $\mu$s to a distance of more than two meters. Thus, the Wi-Fi reader can transmit a 64-bit payload message with a 16-bit preamble in 4.0 ms. We can transmit more bits by splitting them across multiple *CTS_to_SELF* packets.
- Since we assume a query-response model in this paper, if the Wi-Fi Backscatter tag does not respond to the Wi-Fi reader's query, the reader re-transmits its packet until it gets a response. More generally, the Wi-Fi Backscatter tag could also transmit ACK packets back to the Wi-Fi reader using the uplink communication in §3. The Wi-Fi Backscatter tag can reduce the overhead of the ACK packet by dropping the preamble and the address fields, and transmitting a single bit message.
- One may be worried that since Wi-Fi Backscatter's downlink messages occupy a considerable amount of time, they could affect the efficiency of Wi-Fi networks. While this certainly is a factor to be considered, there is growing evidence that Wi-Fi networks in typical home and office scenarios are under-utilized [24]. Thus, we believe that the spare Wi-Fi bandwidth can be used to communicate with Wi-Fi Backscatter devices.

### 4.2 Wi-Fi Backscatter tag receiver design

The goal of our receiver is to differentiate between the presence and absence of a Wi-Fi packet and decode the bits transmitted by the Wi-Fi reader. At a high level, we design a low-power Wi-Fi energy detection circuit that leverages the RF harvesting capabilities of our device. Traditional energy detection approaches compute the average energy in the received signal and use a highly sensitive receiver to detect the presence of energy on the wireless medium. This approach however is not suitable in our scenario since the receiver is low power in nature and hence has a very low sensitivity. Further, Wi-Fi transmissions are modulated using OFDM, which is known to have a high peak to average ratio [20]. Said differently, the average energy in the Wi-Fi signal is small, with occasional peaks spread out during the transmission.

Thus, the Wi-Fi Backscatter tag leverages a specially designed RF energy detector based on peak detection to decode information from the Wi-Fi Backscatter reader. As shown in Fig. 8, our receiver circuit has four main components: an envelope detector, a peak finder, a set-threshold circuit and a comparator. The role of the envelope detector circuit is to remove the carrier frequency (2.4 GHz) of the Wi-Fi transmissions. This is a standard circuit design similar to that used in RFID systems. We however tune the circuit elements to be optimal over the whole 2.4 GHz Wi-Fi frequency ranges.

The peak detector circuit captures and holds the peak amplitude of the received signal. It uses a diode, an operational amplifier, and a capacitor that can store the peak amplitudes as its charge. In order to adapt to time-varying channel conditions, it however does not hold this peak value indefinitely; the resistor network that is part of the set-threshold circuit allows the charge on the capacitor to slowly dissipate, effectively "resetting" the peak detector over some relatively long time interval. The output of this peak-detection circuit is halved to produce the actual threshold; this is performed by the capacitor element in the set-threshold circuit. Finally, the comparator takes two inputs: the threshold value and the received signal, and outputs a one bit whenever the received signal is greater than the threshold value and a zero bit otherwise.

We note that the receiver circuit described above can detect packets as small as 50 $\mu$s. Thus, it can differentiate Wi-Fi packet lengths up to that resolution. Specifically, since longer packets can be intuitively thought of as multiple small packets sent back-to-back without any gap, the Wi-Fi Backscatter tag outputs a continuous sequence of ones corresponding to each long packet. By counting the number of ones, Wi-Fi Backscatter can resolve the length of a Wi-Fi packet to a resolution of 50$\mu$s.

Further, the above circuit requires only a very small amount of power to operate (around 1 $\mu$W), and can therefore be left ON at all times. However, the microcontroller requires a relatively large amount of power (several hundred $\mu$W) in its active mode. To reduce overall power consumption, the Wi-Fi Backscatter tag keeps the microcontroller in a sleep state as much as possible by operating under two main modes:

- *Preamble detection mode.* The receiver spends most of its time in this mode detecting preambles at the beginning of potential reader transmissions. To reduce the power consumption of doing this, we leverage that there is no information in between the transitions of bits output by our receiver circuit. Thus, we keep the microcontroller asleep until a new transition occurs at the comparator's output. We then correlate the intervals between these transitions with the reference intervals for the preamble. If the transition intervals match the preamble, the receiver knows that a packet is about to begin and thus enters the next mode.
- *Packet decoding mode.* In this mode, the microcontroller again reduces the power consumption by sampling the signal only in the middle of each transmitted bit. Specifically, the microcontroller wakes up briefly to capture each sample, then sleeps until the next bit, thus saving considerable power. After the known packet length has expired, the microcontroller fully wakes up and attempts to decode the packet by performing operations such as framing and CRC checks for the Wi-Fi Backscatter messages transmitted on the downlink.

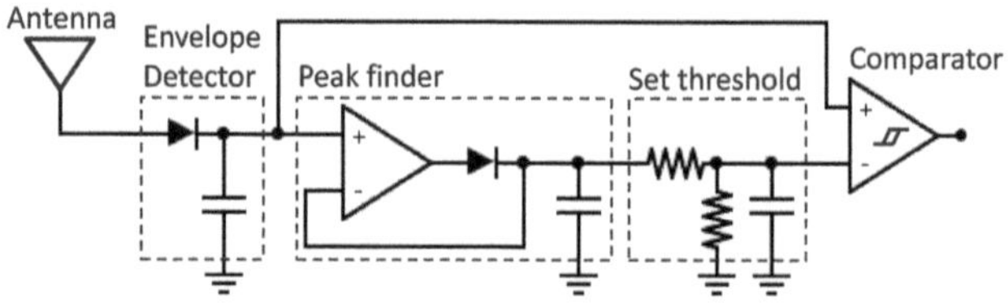


**Figure 8—Receiver circuit at the tag to decode the transmissions in Fig. 7.** The receiver has four main components: an envelope detector to remove the 2.4 GHz carrier frequency, a peak finder that stores the peak energy value of the Wi-Fi signals in its capacitor, a set-threshold circuit that halves the threshold values, and a comparator that outputs a one bit when the received energy is greater than the threshold value and a zero bit otherwise.

## 5. WI-FI BACKSCATTER IN A GENERAL WI-FI NETWORK

Typical Wi-Fi networks have multiple Wi-Fi devices that all share the same wireless medium; most of these devices are likely to be unaware of the Wi-Fi Backscatter protocol. Wi-Fi Backscatter's downlink design addresses the problem of multiple Wi-Fi devices by using a *CTS_to_SELF* packet that prevents other Wi-Fi devices from interfering with its transmissions. The presence of multiple Wi-Fi devices, however, is problematic for the uplink design in §3.

In particular, the Wi-Fi reader uses the channel measurements from the helper's packets to decode the information send by the Wi-Fi Backscatter tag. The assumption, however, is that for every bit sent by the Wi-Fi Backscatter tag, the Wi-Fi reader receives channel measurements from at least a few helper packets. Since Wi-Fi uses a random access MAC protocol, the number of packets per second transmitted from the Wi-Fi helper depends on the traffic in the network. Ideally, if the Wi-Fi Backscatter tag can identify the helper packets, it can ensure that there are an equal number of helper packets for each transmitted bit. This is however difficult since our Wi-Fi Backscatter tags cannot decode the Wi-Fi headers and hence cannot accurately identify the helper packets.

Wi-Fi Backscatter addresses this problem by having the Wi-Fi Backscatter device adapt its transmission rate for different network traffic loads. Specifically, the Wi-Fi reader computes the average number of packets the helper (e.g., an AP) can transmit for the current network conditions. Suppose the Wi-Fi helper can transmit, on average, $N$ packets per second given the current network load and suppose the Wi-Fi reader requires the channel information from $M$ packets to reliably decode each bit. Given these parameters, the rate at which the Wi-Fi Backscatter tag sends bits is given by $\frac{N}{M}$ bits per second. The Wi-Fi reader computes this bit rate and transmits this information in the query packet addressed to the Wi-Fi Backscatter tag. The latter uses this bit rate while transmitting bits on the uplink to the Wi-Fi reader. We note the following key points:

- *Dealing with bursty traffic.* While the above computation is based on the average statistics, Internet traffic in general is known for its bursty nature. Thus, it is unlikely that every bit from the Wi-Fi Backscatter tag affects the same number of helper packets. To address this problem, the Wi-Fi reader uses the timestamp information in the Wi-Fi header to bin the channel measurements to the correct bit boundaries. Further, the Wi-Fi reader provides conservative bit rate estimates to the Wi-Fi Backscatter device to minimize the probability of not receiving channel information for some of the transmitted bits.

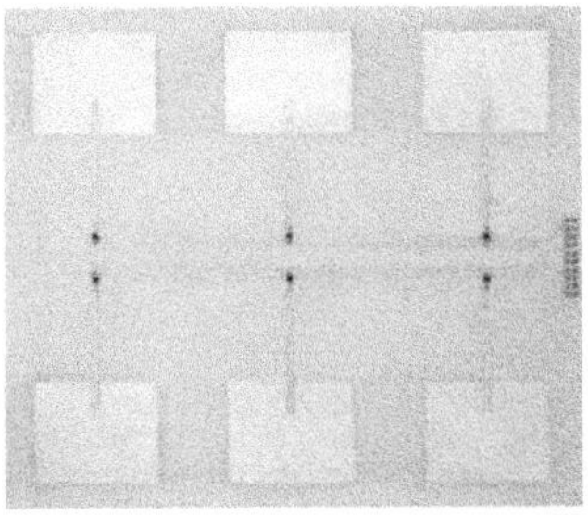

**Figure 9—Wi-Fi Backscatter prototype antenna.** The prototype antenna is designed to operate across the 2.4 GHz Wi-Fi channels and can both modulate the Wi-Fi channel as well as harvest RF signals. Our antenna consists of an array of six small micro-strip patch elements, each with dimensions 40.6 by 30.9 mm. We note that in principle, one can decrease the size of this antenna by using a number of other topologies that can achieve similar qualities. We use this topology due to its fabrication simplicity.

- *Leveraging traffic from all Wi-Fi devices.* In general, the Wi-Fi reader can leverage transmissions from all Wi-Fi devices in the network and combine the channel information across all of them to achieve a high data rate in a busy network. Since most of the traffic in a wireless network is downlink traffic [16], using the AP as a helper and leveraging its transmissions can eliminate the need for introducing additional traffic.
- *Using the AP's beacon packets.* The Wi-Fi reader can use the periodic beacon packets transmitted by Wi-Fi APs to decode the bits from the tag. Such an approach, while reducing the data rates, would have minimal overhead on the Wi-Fi network throughput. In §7.5, we evaluate the feasibility of this approach.

## 6. PROTOTYPE IMPLEMENTATION

We build a prototype of our Wi-Fi Backscatter tag that is optimized to operate across the 2.4 GHz Wi-Fi channels. The prototype has a 2.4 GHz antenna, shown in Fig. 9, that can both modulate the Wi-Fi channel and harvest RF signals. The harvesting circuit we use is similar to those proposed in prior systems [12, 26, 23]. Our antenna is comprised of an array of six elements, each of which is a small micro-strip patch that is connected to both an RF switch and a full-wave diode rectifier that provides RF-to-DC power conversion. The ADG902 RF switch [1] from Analog Devices was selected for its broad bandwidth, low power, and good switching isolation at 2.4 GHz. Skyworks SMS7630 RF detector diodes [4] were selected for their high rectification efficiency at low RF power levels. The antenna is connected to an MSP430G2553 running custom firmware with receive and transmit logic implementations.

On the uplink, a hardware timer module of the TI MSP430 microcontroller is used to generate a bit clock and drives a simple firmware module. Each packet consists of a Wi-Fi Backscatter preamble, payload and a postamble. The reader uses the preamble and postamble to recover the bit clock from the transmitted signals. We use a 13-bit Barker code that is known for its good autocorrelation properties [6]. For the downlink, we implement the circuit design in §4.2 that allows us to identify the presence of Wi-Fi packets. We implement the energy saving mechanisms as described in §4.2. Each packet has a preamble, a payload, and a postamble. We note that the power consumption of our transmit circuit is 0.65 $\mu$W, while that of the receiver circuit is 9.0 $\mu$W. Our results show that the Wi-Fi power harvester can continuously run both the transmitter and receiver from a distance of one foot from the Wi-Fi reader. Additionally, in a dual-antenna system with both Wi-Fi and TV harvesting, the full system could be powered with a duty cycle

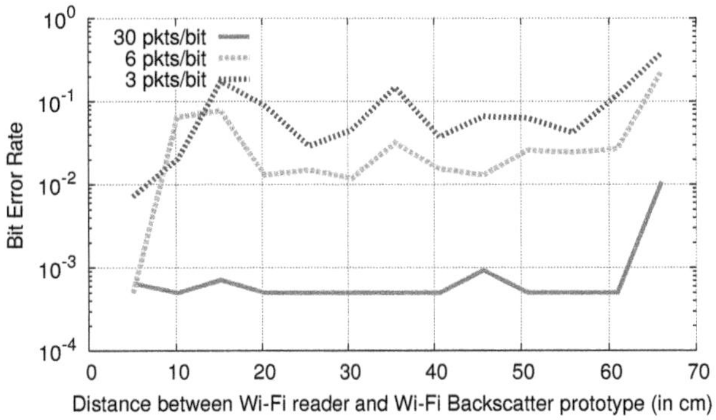


(a) CSI

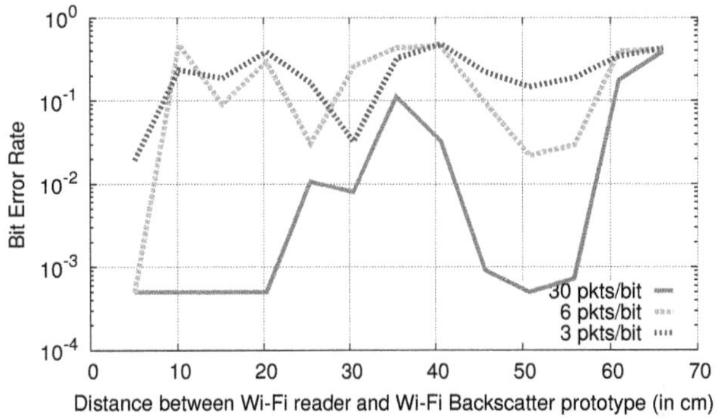


(b) RSSI

**Figure 10—Effect of distance on the uplink Bit Error Rate.** Figure (a) and (b) show the results when the Wi-Fi reader decodes using the CSI and RSSI information respectively. The figure also plots the BER for different number of packets per transmitted bit. The plots show that as the average number of Wi-Fi packets per bit increases, both the BER and the range improve. Further, the CSI measurements perform better than the RSSI. Finally, the receiver can decode with BERs less than $10^{-2}$ up to ranges of about 65 cm and 30 cm using CSI and RSSI respectively.

of around 50% at a distance of 10 km from a TV broadcast tower, independent of the distance from the Wi-Fi reader.

## 7. UPLINK EVALUATION

First, we evaluate Wi-Fi Backscatter's uplink communication from our prototype device to the Wi-Fi reader. We measure the impact of various parameters including the distance between our prototype and the Wi-Fi reader, the transmission rate of the Wi-Fi helper, and its distance from the prototype device.

### 7.1 Uplink BER versus Distance

We compute the uplink bit error rate (BER) observed at the Wi-Fi reader as a function of the distance from the prototype device. In this section, we focus on the efficiency of our decoding algorithm from §3.2 that is designed to operate at short ranges. Later in §10, we evaluate the long range uplink communication design from §3.4.

**Experiments.** We use Intel Link 5300 cards as both our Wi-Fi helper and reader devices. The devices are configured to run on Wi-Fi channel 6 in the 2.4 GHz range. The results for the other 2.4 GHz Wi-Fi channels are similar and are not presented for lack of space. We inject traffic from the Wi-Fi helper and configure the Wi-Fi reader to be in monitor mode. The helper is placed three meters away from the prototype device. The reader collects the CSI information for the helper's packets, using the Intel CSI Tool toolkit

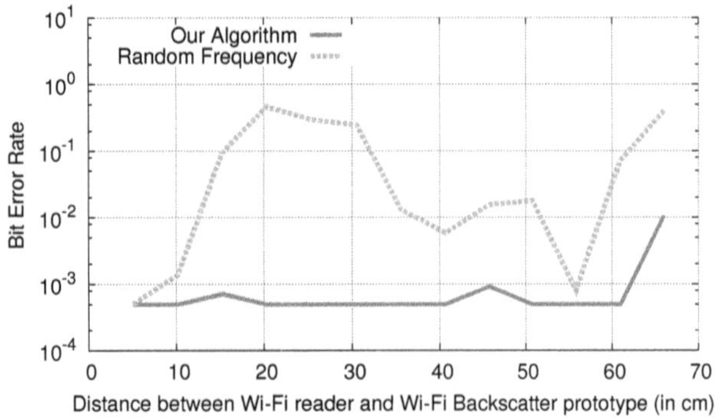


**Figure 11—Effect of frequency diversity on BER.** The figure shows the BER for two algorithms: one that randomly picks a Wi-Fi sub-channel and decodes, and the second is Wi-Fi Backscatter's algorithm that leverages frequency diversity to combine information across all the sub-channels. The figure shows that leveraging frequency diversity provides substantial benefits.

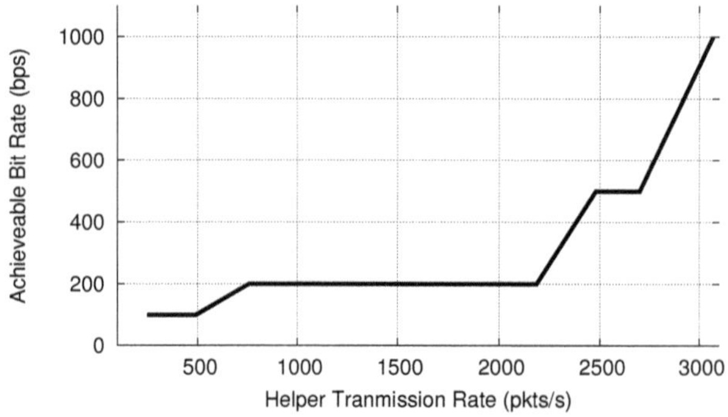


**Figure 12—Uplink Bit rate versus transmission rate at the Wi-Fi helper.** The average achievable bit rate is the maximum bit rate, amongst the tested rates of 100, 200, 500, and 1000 bits/s, that can be decoded at the Wi-Fi reader with a BER less than $10^{-2}$. The plot shows that the bit rate is around 100 bps and 1 kbps with transmission rates of 500 and 2070 packets/second.

from [13] on its three antennas. The Wi-Fi reader is configured to perform the algorithm in §3.2 that first identifies the good Wi-Fi sub-channels, combines them using maximum-ratio combining, and finally uses majority voting across channel measurements to decode the bits. We note that one of the antennas on our Intel device almost always reported significantly low CSI values. To avoid introducing bias, we included the CSI measurements from this antenna in our algorithm. The prototype device is set to transmit at various distances between five centimeters and 65 centimeters from the Wi-Fi reader. In each run of the experiment, the prototype device transmits a 90-bit payload message (including the Wi-Fi Backscatter preamble). We repeat the experiment 20 times at each distance value and compute the bit error rate (BER) by comparing the received bits with those transmitted across all the packet transmissions in the location. Since we transmit a total of 1800 bits, if we do not see any bit errors, we set the BER to $5 \times 10^{-4}$. The bit error rate depends on the average number of channel measurements for each bit; thus, we measure the BERs for different average number of Wi-Fi packets from the helper we use to represent each bit.

**Results.** Fig. 10(a) shows the BER as a function of the distance between the Wi-Fi reader and the prototype device. Fig. 10 (b) shows the corresponding results when using the RSSI information at the Wi-Fi reader, instead of CSI. The plots show the following:

- The BER increases with the distance between the prototype device and the Wi-Fi reader. This is expected because as the distance increases, the reflections from the prototype device experience higher attenuation and hence are more susceptible to noise.
- As the number of packets per bit increases, the BER significantly reduces. This is because with more packets per bit, the Wi-Fi reader receives more channel measurements and hence can achieve higher reliability using the majority voting procedure.
- The CSI information provides higher ranges and better BERs than the RSSI. This is because CSI gives us detailed channel information in each Wi-Fi OFDM sub-channel. In contrast, RSSI is a single value averaged across all the sub-channels. Thus, CSI values have more information and hence achieve lower BERs.
- Wi-Fi Backscatter can achieve distanced of up to 65 cms using an average of 30 packets/bit, with the CSI information. The RSSI information, on the other hand, provides a range of about 30 cms assuming a target BER of $10^{-2}$. In §10, we show how to increase this range further using our correlation mechanism.

**Effect of frequency diversity.** Next we evaluate the benefits of leveraging frequency diversity across all the Wi-Fi sub-channels. Specifically, we compare two main schemes:

*1. Random-Subchannel:* We pick a random Wi-Fi sub-channel and use it to decode bits from the prototype device.

*2. Our algorithm:* We use the algorithm described in §3.2 which picks the best Wi-Fi sub-channels, combines them using maximum-ratio combining, and then decodes bits from the prototype device.

Fig. 11 shows the BER results using the two algorithms for the case where we use 30 Wi-Fi packets per bit. The plot shows that using a random Wi-Fi sub-channel performs poorly and does not operate reliably at distances greater than 15 centimeters. In contrast, our algorithm significantly reduces the BER and also operates at much larger distances. This demonstrates that leveraging frequency diversity provides substantial benefits for our uplink channel.

## 7.2 Data Rate Versus Helper's Transmission Rate

The above set of experiments analyzes the achievable bit rate as a function of the average number of Wi-Fi packets required to represent each bit. The actual bit rate achieved, however, depends on the packet transmission rate at the Wi-Fi helper device. In this section, we measure the bit rate achieved by our system for different transmission rates at the Wi-Fi helper device.

**Experiments.** We fix the locations of the Wi-Fi reader (Intel Wi-Fi Link 5300 card) and the prototype device to be five centimeters away from each other. The Wi-Fi helper device (Intel Wi-Fi Link 5300 card) is again placed 3 meters away from the prototype device. We later present results for larger helper distance values. To change the number of packets transmitted per second at the helper device, we insert a delay between injected packets. In our network, which is running on the same Wi-Fi channel as our organization's Wi-Fi device, this results in a transmission rate between 240 and 3070 packets per second. For each of these transmission rates, the prototype device transmits at four different bit rates (100, 200, 500, and 1000 bits/sec). We measure the achievable bit rate by measuring the maximum bit rate at which the computed average BER is less than $10^{-2}$. We compute the average achievable bit rate by taking the mean of the achievable bit rates across multiple runs.

**Results:** Fig. 12 plots the achievable bit rate as a function of the Wi-Fi helper's transmission rate (packets per second). The plot shows that as the number of packets transmitted per second at the helper

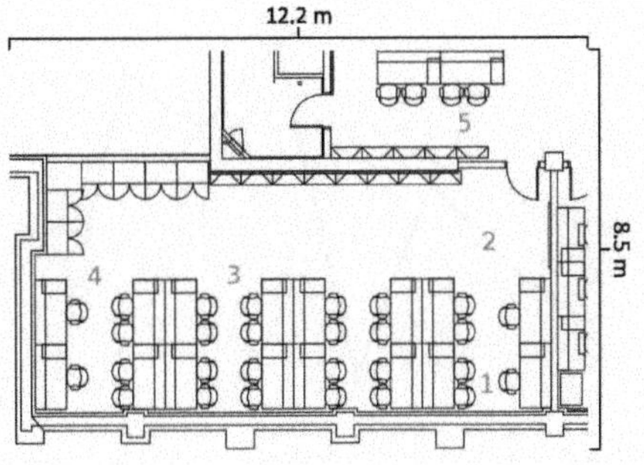


**Figure 13—Testbed with the tested locations.**

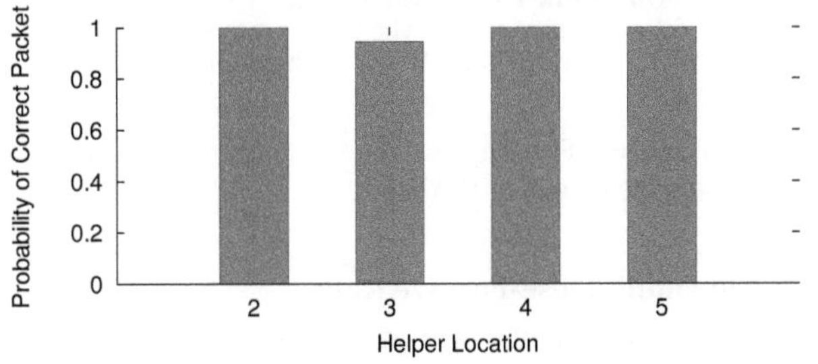


**Figure 14—Probability of receiving a correct packet on the uplink for the various helper locations shown in Fig. 13.** The figure shows that the Wi-Fi reader can decode packets even when the helper device is not in the same room (location 5). Further the uplink is fairly independent of the Wi-Fi helper location.

device increases, the achievable bit rate increases. The bit rate is around 100 bits/s at a helper transmission rate of 500 packets/s and is 1 kbps when the transmission rate is about 3070 packets/s. We note that these bit rates are more than sufficient for a majority of the sensing and Internet of Things applications.

## 7.3 Bit Rate Versus Wi-Fi Helper Location

Finally, we evaluate the effects of the Wi-Fi helper's location on the probability of decoding correct packets from the Wi-Fi Backscatter tag at the reader. To do this, we place the prototype device and the Wi-Fi reader (Intel Wi-Fi Link 5300 card) such that they are 5 centimeters away from each other, in location 1 in Fig. 13. We then place the Wi-Fi helper device (Intel Wi-Fi Link 5300 card) in locations 2-5 that span line-of-sight and non-line-of-sight scenarios and are at distances of 3-9 meters from the tag, as shown in Fig. 13. The average CSI values span 3-50 across these locations. Note that location 5 is in a different room from our prototype device. In each of our experiments, the prototype device transmits 20 packets at a bit rate of 100 bps. We compute the average packet delivery probability, i.e., the fraction of packets received correctly at the Wi-Fi reader, at each of the above locations.

Fig. 14 plots the packet delivery probability as a function of different Wi-Fi helper device locations. The figure shows that this probability is high across all the helper locations. We also note that the Wi-Fi reader can successfully decode our packets even when the helper device is not in the same room as our prototype device. This demonstrates that the communication capabilities on the uplink are fairly independent of the Wi-Fi helper location and depend only on the distance between the Wi-Fi reader and the prototype device.

## 7.4 Using Only Traffic on the Network

Our experiments so far create additional traffic on the network to communicate from the prototype device to the Wi-Fi helper. We

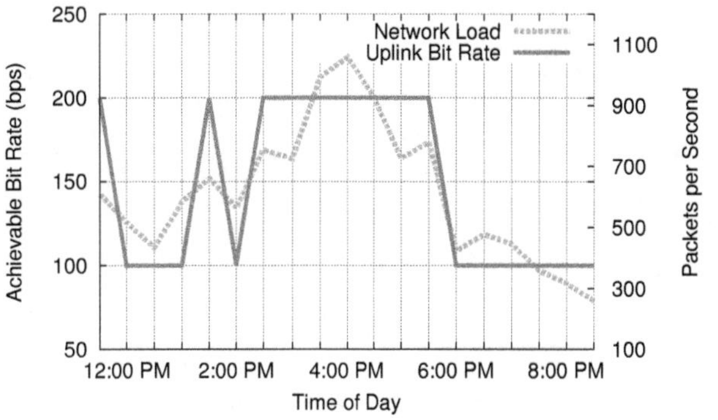


**Figure 15—Achievable uplink bit rate using ambient Wi-Fi packets in an office setting as a function of time.** The figure shows that the achievable bit rate is proportional to the number of packets on the network.

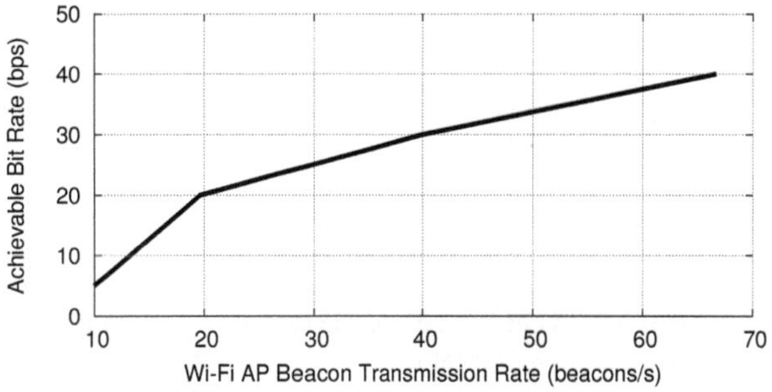


**Figure 16—Achievable uplink bit rate using only the periodic beacons from the AP (Wi-Fi helper).** The figure shows the feasibility of using only the beacon packets to establish the uplink.

evaluate the feasibility of uplink communication without the need for this additional traffic. Specifically, we run experiments in a lab environment in our organization by configuring the Wi-Fi helper to be in monitor mode and capturing all the packets transmitted by the organization's AP. We place the Wi-Fi reader (an Intel Wi-Fi Link 5300 card) at a fixed distance of five centimeters away from the prototype transmitter. We run experiments once every 10 minutes and compute the achievable uplink bit rate (the maximum rate at which the bit error rate at the Wi-Fi helper is less than $10^{-2}$). We also log the average number of Wi-Fi packets in the network as seen by our Wi-Fi reader device.

Fig. 15 plots the achievable bit rate as a function of time. For reference, we also plot the average number of all Wi-Fi packets as seen by the Wi-Fi helper device. The figure shows that the achievable bit rate is proportional to the number of packets on the network. This is because the better the Wi-Fi network utilization, the more the opportunities for the Wi-Fi reader to receive packets from the AP. Since the uplink bit rate depends on the transmission rate of the Wi-Fi helper device (which in our case is the AP), a better-utilized network results in higher data rates. The key point here is that we can establish the uplink communication channel without introducing additional traffic on the network.

## 7.5 Using only Beacon Packets

Finally, we check the feasibility of using only the periodic beacon messages from the AP. We use an Intel Wi-Fi Link 5300 card configured as the AP and an Intel Wi-Fi Link 5300 card as a Wi-Fi reader. The reader does not generate any traffic on the network and passively listens to the beacon messages periodically transmitted by the access point. No other device is associated with the access point,

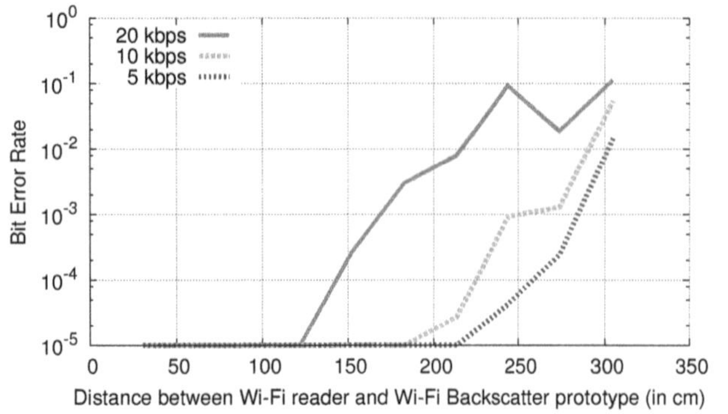


**Figure 17—Downlink Bit Error Rate Versus distance between Wi-Fi Backscatter tag and Wi-Fi reader.** The three bit rates correspond to Wi-Fi packets of length 50 $\mu$s, 100 $\mu$s, and 200 $\mu$s. The figure shows that at a target BER of $10^{-2}$, the prototype device can achieve bit rates of 20 kbps at distances of 2.13 m. The range can be increased to 2.90 m by decreasing the bit rate to 10 kbps.

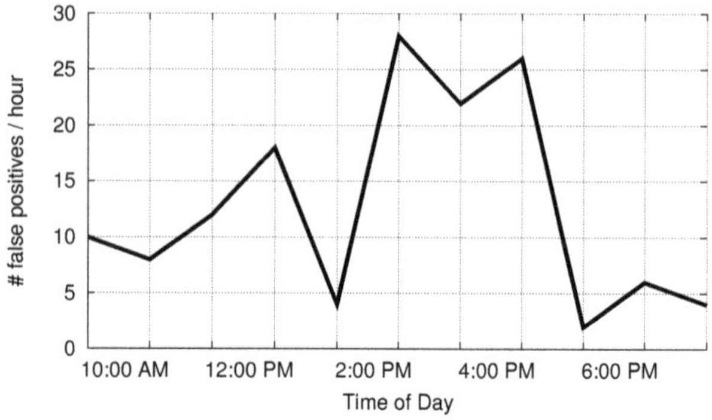


**Figure 18—Downlink False-positive rate.** The figure shows the number of false positive events where the prototype receiver confuses normal Wi-Fi traffic for a Wi-Fi Backscatter preamble.

but it operates on channel 6, which is the same frequency as our organization's Wi-Fi network. We run experiments from 2-3 PM on a weekday. We place the Wi-Fi Backscatter tag 5 centimeters away from the reader and compute the achievable bit rate by measuring the maximum rate at which the reader can decode the tag's transmissions at a BER less than $10^{-2}$. Since Intel cards do not currently provide CSI information for beacon packets, we again use RSSI for these experiments. We repeat the experiments for different beacon frequencies at the Wi-Fi AP. Fig. 16 shows that as expected the achievable bit rate increases with the beacon frequency. The key takeaway from these results, however, is that Wi-Fi Backscatter can establish uplink communication using only the AP's beacon packets and hence need no additional traffic to be generated on the network.

## 8. DOWNLINK EVALUATION

Next, we evaluate the performance of our downlink communication channel. Here, the Wi-Fi reader conveys information by encoding bits in the presence and absence of Wi-Fi packets. We evaluate the BER performance as well as the false-positive rate.

### 8.1 Downlink BER Versus Distance

We compute the bit error rate (BER) as a function of the distance between the Wi-Fi Backscatter tag and the Wi-Fi reader. At each distance, the Wi-Fi reader transmits a total of 200 kilobits to the Wi-Fi Backscatter tag across multiple transmissions. The transmit power at the reader is set to +16 dBm (40 mW). In each transmission, the reader encodes a '1' bit as the presence of a packet and a '0' bit as its absence. We run experiments with three different packet sizes of 50 $\mu$s, 100 $\mu$s, and 200 $\mu$s at the reader, corresponding to bit rates of 20 kbps, 10 kbps, and 5 kbps. The Wi-Fi Backscatter tag uses its thresholding circuit as described in §4.2 to decode the transmitted bits. We then compute the BER by comparing the decoded bits with the transmitted bits.

Fig. 17 plots the BER as a function of the distance. The plot shows the following:

- As expected, the BER increases with the distance between the Wi-Fi Backscatter tag and the reader. Similarly, the BER values are better at lower bit rates.
- Our prototype can efficiently identify Wi-Fi packets as small as 50 $\mu$s from nearby devices.
- At a target BER of $10^{-2}$, the Wi-Fi Backscatter downlink can achieve bit rates of 20 kbps at distances of 2.13 meters between the two devices. The range can be increased to 2.90 meters by decreasing the bit rate to 10 kbps.

### 8.2 Downlink False-Positive Rate

Finally, we measure the false-positive rate experienced by our downlink communication channel. We define the false-positive rate as the number of events per hour where, in the absence of a Wi-Fi Backscatter enabled Wi-Fi transmitter, our prototype device falsely detects the Wi-Fi Backscatter preamble in Fig. 7, and wakes up the microcontroller to perform decoding. To measure this, we place our receiver prototype 30 centimeters away from our network AP. To ensure that there is consistent traffic on the network, we stream music from Pandora [3] from one of the connected clients for the whole duration of the experiment. The receiver prototype is configured to log false-positive events, i.e., events when it detects the known preamble. We run our experiments during peak hours and configure our prototype to detect preambles where each bit is 50 $\mu$s.

Fig. 18 shows the number of false positive events per hour at our prototype receiver, as a function of the time of the day. The figure shows that the maximum false positive rate we observe in our setup is less than 30/hour. These low numbers are expected, because it is unlikely that normal Wi-Fi traffic generates a structure that matches the Wi-Fi Backscatter preamble in Fig. 7.

## 9. EFFECT OF REFLECTIONS ON WI-FI COMMUNICATION

Next, we evaluate the effects of the reflections created by our prototype device on communication between a Wi-Fi transmitter-receiver pair. Specifically, we stress-test the system when the Wi-Fi Backscatter tag is at close distances to the receiver.[1] Note that in practice, a Wi-Fi Backscatter device modulates only when queried by a Wi-Fi reader. However to stress-test the system, we set Wi-Fi Backscatter to continuously send bits at two different data rates of 1 kbps and 100 bps. Since Wi-Fi uses bit rate adaptation, we fix the Wi-Fi receiver and the prototype in location 1 in Fig. 13 and move the Wi-Fi transmitter across the remaining locations. The devices use their default bit rate adaptation algorithms. We use built in Wi-Fi of a Lenovo Thinkpad laptop as the transmitter and a Linksys WRT54GL AP as the receiver. In each run of the experiment, the Wi-Fi transmitter sends UDP packets for two minutes, and logs the throughput observed every 500 ms. We compute the average

[1]Note that we do not evaluate the effect of Wi-Fi Backscatter's downlink design on Wi-Fi traffic. Experimental evaluation of the effect of non Wi-Fi traffic on *CTS_to_SELF* and *CTS_to_SELF* on Wi-Fi traffic has been explored in prior work [10].

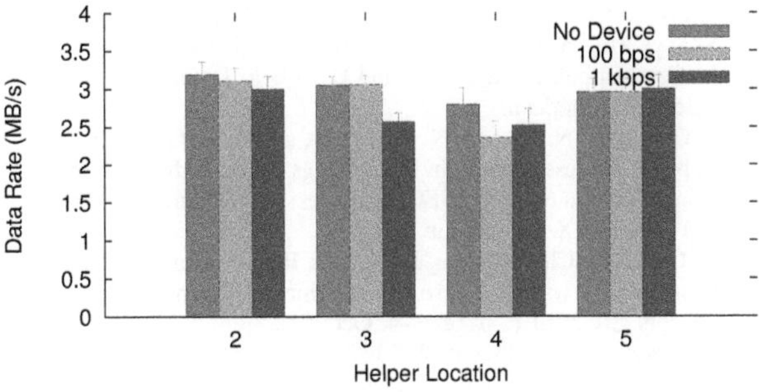


(a) Distance of 5 cm

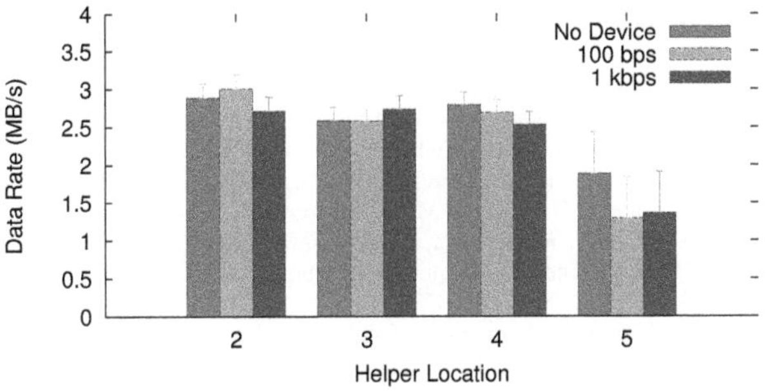


(b) Distance of 30 cm

**Figure 19—Effect of Wi-Fi Backscatter Uplink on Wi-Fi data rate.** The figure plots the data rates for different locations for the Wi-Fi transmitter placed in the testbed in Fig. 13. The Wi-Fi Backscatter prototype is configured to continuously modulate the Wi-Fi channel and the plots show the results for three scenarios: without the prototype, with the prototype modulating at 100 bps and 1 kbps. The plots show that Wi-Fi rate adaptation can easily adapt to the variations caused by the prototype transmitter.

throughput by computing the mean across the two minute duration. In each Wi-Fi transmitter location, we measure the average throughput both in the presence and absence of our prototype.

Fig. 19 (a) and (b) shows the average data rate as a function of the Wi-Fi transmitter location, for two different distance values between the prototype device and the Wi-Fi receiver. Each figure plots the data rates in three different scenarios: in the absence of the prototype, and when the prototype transmits at 100 bps and 1 kbps. The figures show that while there is variation in the observed data rate across these scenarios (most notably in location 5 where the experiments were performed with heavy Wi-Fi utilization due to the presence of a class in the adjacent room), they are mostly within the variance. We believe this is because Wi-Fi uses rate adaptation and can easily adapt for the small variations in the channel quality, resulting from the reflections from our prototype.

## 10. Evaluating Correlation Effects on Wi-Fi Backscatter Uplink Range

Finally, we evaluate the feasibility of extending Wi-Fi Backscatter's range on the uplink using the correlation technique in §3.4. Specifically, we place the Wi-Fi helper (an Intel Wi-Fi Link 5300 card) 3 meters away from the Wi-Fi reader (an Intel Wi-Fi Link 5300 card). The Wi-Fi Backscatter tag encodes zero and one bits using long code sequences of length $N$; the Wi-Fi reader correlates with these code sequences to decode the bits as described in §3.4. We vary the distance between the Wi-Fi reader and the prototype

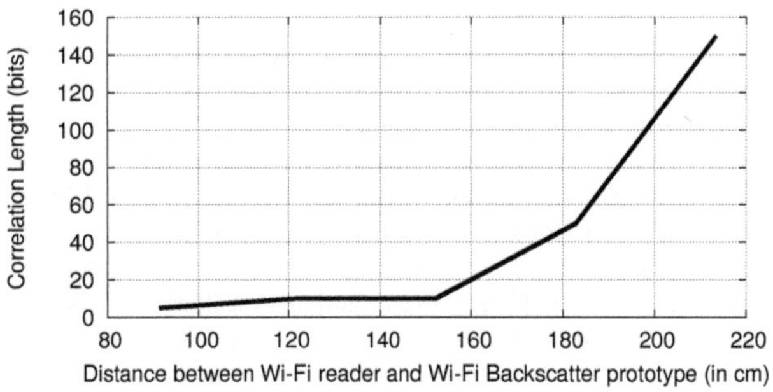


**Figure 20—Increasing the uplink range using the correlation mechanism in §3.4.** The figure shows that the range can be increased to more than 2 m by using long sequences to represent each transmitted bit and using correlation at the Wi-Fi reader.

and measure the correlation length at which the observed bit error rate at the Wi-Fi reader is less than $10^{-2}$.

Fig. 20 plots these correlation lengths as a function of the distance between the reader and our prototype. The figure shows that as the correlation length increases, the range at which Wi-Fi Backscatter's uplink operates also increases. Specifically, using a correlation length of 20 bits, we establish the uplink communication link at distances of about 1.6 meters between the Wi-Fi reader and the prototype. The required correlation length increases significantly with the distances between the Wi-Fi reader and the prototype. Specifically, at distances of 2.1 meters, we need a correlation length of about 150 bits. While this would reduce the effective bit rates achieved on the uplink, we emphasize that establishing a communication link between Wi-Fi Backscatter tags with existing Wi-Fi devices, albeit at a low rate, is beneficial for a large class of Internet-of-Things applications.

## 11. Related Work

Wi-Fi Backscatter is related to work on RFID systems [8, 28, 29], which use dedicated powered infrastructure (RFID readers) to provide power and enable communication with battery-free tags. The cost of deploying and maintaining such an infrastructure has tempered the adoption of these systems. In contrast, the key value proposition of RF-powered devices is that they can harvest ambient RF signals (e.g., TV, cellular, and Wi-Fi) and thus eliminate the need for dedicated infrastructure. Since traditional radio communication consumes significantly more power than is available in RF signals [23], it has thus far been challenging to connect these devices to the Internet. Wi-Fi Backscatter addresses this problem with a novel system that bridges RF-powered devices and the Internet.

Wi-Fi Backscatter is also related to recent work on ambient backscatter communication [17] that enables two RF-powered devices to communicate by scattering ambient TV signals. While ambient backscatter can enable a network of RF-powered devices to communicate with each other, it does not provide Internet connectivity. A naive option is to deploy powered infrastructure devices that are equipped with both ambient backscatter communication and traditional power-consuming radios, but this diminishes the key benefit of RF-powered systems; an ability to operate without dedicated infrastructure. Wi-Fi Backscatter enables RF-powered devices to communicate with existing Wi-Fi infrastructure, bringing us closer to the vision of an RF-powered Internet of Things.

Wi-Fi Backscatter also differs from both RFID and ambient backscatter systems in that these systems decode backscatter information from a single continuous signal source, i.e., an RFID reader or a TV tower. Further, the decoding is performed on custom hardware that is specially designed for this purpose. In contrast, this paper introduces a method to modulate the Wi-Fi channel and demonstrates that we can perform decoding on off-the-shelf Wi-Fi devices. Further, we show how to detect Wi-Fi packets and communicate using such a capability.

Finally, recent work has demonstrated the ability to harvest power from ambient signals including TV [26, 19, 15, 25], and cellular transmissions [27, 23]. More recently, researchers have demonstrated the ability to harvest energy from Wi-Fi transmissions [22, 21, 11]: [14] harvests and backscatters signals using transmissions from Agilent 89600 custom 2.4 GHz transceiver hardware and [22, 11] show the feasibility of power harvesting using signals from off-the-shelf Wi-Fi access points. Wi-Fi Backscatter builds on this work but is complimentary in that it transforms existing Wi-Fi signals into a communication medium for battery-free devices. Specifically, we are the first to establish a communication link between RF-powered devices and commodity Wi-Fi devices.

## 12. CONCLUSION

RF-powered devices hold the promise to realize a pervasive vision of the "Internet of Things" where devices may be embedded into everyday objects and can achieve computation, sensing, and communication, all without the need to ever plug them in or maintain batteries. This paper provides the critical component in this vision of RF-powered Internet of Things: an ability to connect RF-powered devices to the Internet.

We present Wi-Fi Backscatter, a novel communication system that bridges RF-powered devices with the Internet. We show that it is possible to reuse existing Wi-Fi infrastructure to provide Internet connectivity to RF-powered devices. We show the feasibility of our approach by building a hardware prototype and demonstrating the first communication link between an RF-powered device and commodity Wi-Fi devices. We run experiments with off-the-shelf Wi-Fi devices and achieve communication rates of up to 1 kbps and ranges of up to 2.1 m. We believe that this new capability is critical for the commercial adoption of RF-powered Internet of Things.

**Acknowledgements.** We would like to thank Ben Ransford, Vincent Liu, Rajalakshmi Nandakumar, Donny Huang, our shepherd Kyle Jamieson, and the anonymous SIGCOMM reviewers for their helpful comments. This research is funded in part by UW Commercialization Gap Fund, Qualcomm Innovation Fellowship, Washington Research Foundation gift, NSF, and University of Washington.

## 13. REFERENCES

[1] ADG902 RF switch datasheet. http://www.analog.com/static/imported-files/data_sheets/adg901_902.pdf.
[2] Epc class 1 generation 2 uhf rfid air interface specification. http://www.gs1.org/gsmp/kc/epcglobal/uhfc1g2/uhfc1g2_1_2_0-standard-20080511.pdf.
[3] Pandora. www.pandora.com.
[4] SMS7630 surface mount mixer and detector schottky diodes. http://www.skyworksinc.com/uploads/documents/Surface_Mount_Schottky_Diodes_200041W.pdf.
[5] Ieee standard for information technology– local and metropolitan area networks– specific requirements– part 11: Wireless lan medium access control (mac)and physical layer (phy) specifications amendment 5: Enhancements for higher throughput. IEEE Std 802.11n-2009 (Amendment to IEEE Std 802.11-2007 as amended by IEEE Std 802.11k-2008, IEEE Std 802.11r-2008, IEEE Std 802.11y-2008, and IEEE Std 802.11w-2009), pages 1–565, Oct 2009.
[6] R. Barker. Group synchronizing of binary digital sequences. Communication Theory, pages 273–287, 1953.
[7] D. Brennan. On the maximal signal-to-noise ratio realizable from several noisy signals. Proc. IRE, 43(10):1530, 1955.
[8] M. Buettner, R. Prasad, A. Sample, D. Yeager, B. Greenstein, J. R. Smith, and D. Wetherall. Rfid sensor networks with the intel wisp. In 6th ACM Conference on Embedded Network Sensor Systems, SenSys '08, pages 393–394, New York, NY, USA, 2008. ACM.
[9] N. Gershenfeld, R. Krikorian, and D. Cohen. The internet of things. Scientific American.
[10] S. Gollakota, N. Ahmed, N. Zeldovich, and D. Katabi. Secure in-band wireless pairing. In Proceedings of the 20th USENIX Conference on Security, SEC'11, pages 16–16, Berkeley, CA, USA, 2011. USENIX Association.
[11] K. Gudan, S. Chemishkian, J. Hull, M. Reynolds, and S. Thomas. Feasibility of wireless sensors using ambient 2.4ghz rf energy. In Sensors, 2012 IEEE, pages 1–4, Oct 2012.
[12] J. Hagerty, F. Helmbrecht, W. McCalpin, R. Zane, and Z. Popovic. Recycling ambient microwave energy with broad-band rectenna arrays. Microwave Theory and Techniques, IEEE Transactions on, 52(3):1014–1024, March 2004.
[13] D. Halperin, W. Hu, A. Sheth, and D. Wetherall. Tool release: gathering 802.11 n traces with channel state information. ACM SIGCOMM Computer Communication Review, 41(1):53–53, 2011.
[14] H. Ishizaki, H. Ikeda, Y. Yoshida, T. Maeda, T. Kuroda, and M. Mizuno. A battery-less wifi-ber modulated data transmitter with ambient radio-wave energy harvesting. In VLSI Circuits (VLSIC), 2011 Symposium on, pages 162–163, June 2011.
[15] Y. Kawahara, H. Lee, and M. M. Tentzeris. Sensprout: Inkjet-printed soil moisture and leaf wetness sensor. In Proceedings of the 2012 ACM Conference on Ubiquitous Computing, UbiComp '12, pages 545–545, New York, NY, USA, 2012. ACM.
[16] S. W. Kim, B.-S. Kim, and Y. Fang. Downlink and uplink resource allocation in ieee 802.11 wireless lans. Vehicular Technology, IEEE Transactions on, 54(1):320–327, 2005.
[17] V. Liu, A. Parks, V. Talla, S. Gollakota, D. Wetherall, and J. R. Smith. Ambient backscatter: wireless communication out of thin air. In SIGCOMM, 2013.
[18] D. Masotti, A. Costanzo, and S. Adami. Design and realization of a wearable multi-frequency rf energy harvesting system. In Antennas and Propagation (EUCAP), Proceedings of the 5th European Conference on, pages 517–520, April 2011.
[19] C. Mikeka, H. Arai, A. Georgiadis, and A. Collado. Dtv band micropower rf energy-harvesting circuit architecture and performance analysis. In RFID-Technologies and Applications (RFID-TA), 2011 IEEE International Conference on, pages 561–567, Sept 2011.
[20] H. Ochiai and H. Imai. On the distribution of the peak-to-average power ratio in ofdm signals. Communications, IEEE Transactions on, 49(2):282–289, Feb 2001.
[21] U. Olgun, C.-C. Chen, and J. Volakis. Wireless power harvesting with planar rectennas for 2.45 ghz rfids. In Electromagnetic Theory (EMTS), 2010 URSI International Symposium on, pages 329–331, Aug 2010.
[22] U. Olgun, C.-C. Chen, and J. Volakis. Design of an efficient ambient wifi energy harvesting system. Microwaves, Antennas Propagation, IET, 6(11):1200–1206, August 2012.
[23] A. N. Parks, A. P. Sample, Y. Zhao, and J. R. Smith. A wireless sensing platform utilizing ambient RF energy. In IEEE Topical Meeting on Wireless Sensors and Sensor Networks (WiSNet 2013), January 2013.
[24] R. Raghavendra, J. Padhye, R. Mahajan, and E. Belding. Wi-fi networks are underutilized. Technical report, Technical report, MSR, 2009.
[25] A. Sample and J. Smith. Experimental results with two wireless power transfer systems. In Radio and Wireless Symposium, 2009. RWS '09. IEEE, pages 16 –18, jan. 2009.
[26] R. Shigeta, T. Sasaki, D. M. Quan, Y. Kawahara, R. Vyas, M. Tentzeris, and T. Asami. Ambient rf energy harvesting sensor device with capacitor-leakage-aware duty cycle control. Sensors Journal, IEEE, 13(8):2973–2983, Aug 2013.
[27] H. Visser, A. Reniers, and J. Theeuwes. Ambient rf energy scavenging: Gsm and wlan power density measurements. In Microwave Conference, 2008. EuMC 2008. 38th European, pages 721–724, Oct 2008.
[28] J. Wang, H. Hassanieh, D. Katabi, and P. Indyk. Efficient and reliable low-power backscatter networks. In SIGCOMM, 2012.
[29] P. Zhang and D. Ganesan. Enabling bit-by-bit backscatter communication in severe energy harvesting environments. In NSDI, Berkeley, CA, 2014. USENIX.

# Turbocharging Ambient Backscatter Communication

Aaron N. Parks[†], Angli Liu[†], Shyamnath Gollakota, Joshua R. Smith
University of Washington
{anparks, anglil, gshyam, jrsjrs}@uw.edu
[†]Co-primary Student Authors

## ABSTRACT

Communication primitives such as coding and multiple antenna processing have provided significant benefits for traditional wireless systems. Existing designs, however, consume significant power and computational resources, and hence cannot be run on low complexity, power constrained backscatter devices. This paper makes two main contributions: (1) we introduce the first multi-antenna cancellation design that operates on backscatter devices while retaining a small form factor and power footprint, (2) we introduce a novel coding mechanism that enables long range communication as well as concurrent transmissions and can be decoded on backscatter devices. We build hardware prototypes of the above designs that can be powered solely using harvested energy from TV and solar sources. The results show that our designs provide benefits for both RFID and ambient backscatter systems: they enable RFID tags to communicate directly with each other at distances of tens of meters and through multiple walls. They also increase the communication rate and range achieved by ambient backscatter systems by 100X and 40X respectively. We believe that this paper represents a substantial leap in the capabilities of backscatter communication.

## CATEGORIES AND SUBJECT DESCRIPTORS

C.2.1 [**Network Architecture and Design**]: Wireless communication

## KEYWORDS

Backscatter; Internet of Things; Energy harvesting; Wireless

## 1. INTRODUCTION

The last decade has seen significant advances in wireless communication — Wi-Fi systems today can achieve bit rates as high as 300 Mbps [2] and cellular networks can operate at ranges of tens of kilometers [3]. These impressive rate and range capabilities have been made possible by communication primitives such as coding mechanisms and multi-antenna processing. These techniques, however, are not suitable for battery-free devices such as RFID tags and ambient power harvesting sensors: Existing multi-antenna designs consume power on the order of a few Watts [14]; this is orders of magnitude more power than is available on harvesting devices [24]. Similarly, coding techniques that enhance communication range and enable concurrent transmissions (e.g., CDMA) consume substantial power and computational resources that limit their applicability to low-power devices.


*SIGCOMM'14*, August 17–22, 2014, Chicago, IL, USA.
Copyright 2014 ACM 978-1-4503-2836-4/14/08 ...$15.00.
http://dx.doi.org/10.1145/2619239.2626312.

**Figure 1—Our Prototype** integrates both $\mu$mo and $\mu$code in a single design. It can operate using both RFID and TV transmissions.

The key reason for this is that these techniques assume the ability to perform complex digital signal processing — multi-antenna processing requires estimating channel parameters and performing operations such as matrix inversion; coding techniques (e.g., CDMA) require performing computationally expensive correlation and synchronization. These methods are infeasible on battery-free devices as obtaining a digital representation of a signal requires power-intensive ADCs, and performing computationally expensive tasks is also expensive in terms of power consumption.

In this paper, we ask if it is possible to achieve the benefits of these communication primitives on battery-free devices. The intuition we leverage is as follows: since the power-intensive nature of these techniques is due to their use of ADCs and digital computation, if we instead perform computation in the analog domain we can achieve orders of magnitude reduction in the power consumption. Using this as our guiding principle, we design two communication primitives for backscatter communication: *$\mu$mo*, a multi-antenna receiver that is powered using harvested energy, and *$\mu$code*, a low-power coding mechanism that enables large communication ranges and concurrent transmissions, and can be decoded using simple analog components on battery-free devices.

**$\mu$mo.** To understand our low-power multi-antenna design, consider the ambient backscatter [24] setting in Fig. 2 with two battery-free devices, Alice and Bob, where Bob communicates with Alice by backscattering the signals from the TV tower. Existing designs consider the TV transmissions to be noise, and hence achieve very low bit rates. Alice, however, can use multiple antennas to separate Bob's reflections from the direct TV signals, thus achieving significantly higher rates. The key challenge however is that conventional multi-antenna decoding hinges on estimating the amplitude and phase of the channel between the transmitters and the receive antennas. Since acquiring phase information is power-intensive, it is not available on backscatter devices [20]. This makes conventional multi-antenna decoding infeasible on backscatter devices.

To address this challenge, we present a multi-antenna technique that enables Alice's receiver to decode Bob's backscattered transmission without estimating the channel parameters. The intuition

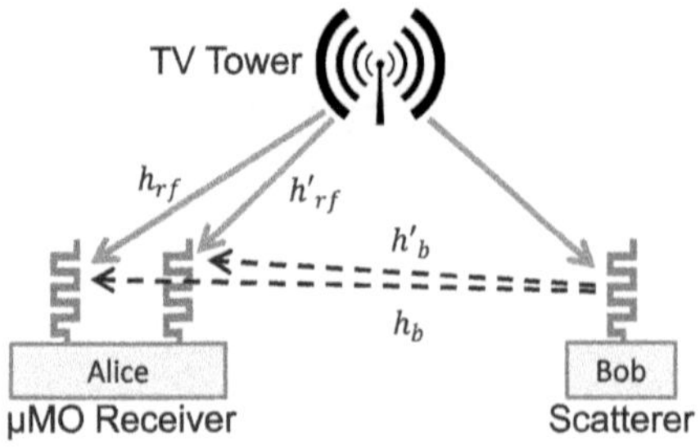


**Figure 2—$\mu$mo Decoding.** The two-antenna device, Alice, can decode Bob's backscattered information by separating the direct TV transmissions from the backscattered signals. $\mu$mo achieves this operation with neither channel estimation nor digital computation.

underlying our approach is best explained using an example. Let $s(t)$ be the signal from the TV tower and suppose Bob conveys '1' ('0') bit by reflecting (not reflecting) the TV signals. Alice now receives the following signals on its two antennas:

$$y_1(t) = h_{rf}s(t) + h_bBs(t)$$
$$y_2(t) = h'_{rf}s(t) + h'_bBs(t)$$

where $h_{rf}$,$h'_{rf}$ and $h_b$, $h'_b$ are the channels from the TV tower and Bob to the two antennas on Alice, respectively. Further, $B$ is 1 when Bob reflects the signals and is 0 otherwise.

$\mu$mo decodes the backscattered bits without estimating any channel parameters. Specifically, the receiver computes $\frac{y_1(t)}{y_2(t)}$ which is either $\frac{h_{rf}}{h'_{rf}}$ or $\frac{h_{rf}+h_b}{h'_{rf}+h'_b}$ depending on whether the backscattered bit is '0' or '1'. Thus, the receiver can decode the backscattered data without performing channel estimation. In §4 we explore the above idea further and describe how the above operation can be performed using simple analog components, without requiring digital computation.

**$\mu$code.** Coding mechanisms (e.g., CDMA) have been used in conventional radios to significantly increase the range of communication and enable concurrent transmissions. These techniques use pseudorandom codes to encode information at the transmitter; the receiver synchronizes with the transmit signal and decodes the information by correlating with the pseudorandom codes. The challenge in using these designs is that the correlation and synchronization operations are computationally expensive and are difficult to perform on backscatter devices.

To address this problem, we introduce a low-power coding scheme for backscatter communication that does not require synchronization. Our intuition is that periodic signals such as sinusoidal waves can be detected without the need for synchronization; thus we design $\mu$code to mimic a sine wave. Specifically, instead of using pseudorandom sequences, we use periodic sequences of alternating zeros and ones as the code. We show that such a design eliminates the need for synchronization operations at the receiver while providing large communication ranges. Further, the receiver can decode using only analog components, thus reducing its power consumption. Finally, we demonstrate that $\mu$code can also enable multiple concurrent transmissions in a network of battery-free devices, without the need for synchronization between transmitters.

We build multiple hardware prototypes (one of which is shown in Fig. 1) that integrate both $\mu$mo and $\mu$code in a single system. To demonstrate the benefits of our designs for backscatter communication, we build two different prototypes: the first prototype enables ambient backscatter communication using TV transmissions in the 539 MHz frequency range. The second prototype enables RFID tag-to-tag communication using RFID reader transmissions in the 915 MHz range. Note that tag-to-tag communication is a novel capability that is in contrast to conventional RFID systems, where the RFID tags communicate with the reader but not with each other. We run experiments in various line-of-sight and non-line-of-sight scenarios at various bit rates from 0.33 bps to 1 Mbps. Our experiments show the following:

- Our $\mu$mo prototype consumes 422 $\mu$W. In comparison, traditional Wi-Fi multi-antenna transceivers consume more than one Watt [14]. $\mu$code, on the other hand, consumes about 8.9 $\mu$W. At an ambient illuminance of 330 lux, we could continuously power $\mu$mo and $\mu$code using a photovoltaic array with an area of 8.28 square inches and 0.17 square inches, respectively. By using duty-cycling to reduce average power requirements, the prototypes can also operate on energy from ambient TV signals.
- $\mu$mo increases ambient backscatter's data rate by 100X from 10 kbps to 1 Mbps by providing multi-antenna cancellation; $\mu$code increases ambient backscatter's range by a factor of 40X from two feet to more than 80 feet through coding gain. This significantly expands the range of applications where ambient backscatter can be used.
- $\mu$code enables RFID tags to communicate with each other at distances of more than 80 feet and between different rooms that are separated by up to three walls. This reduces the need for deploying RFID readers throughout the environment, which is a substantial value proposition.

**Contributions:** We make the following contributions:

- We present $\mu$mo, the first multi-antenna interference cancellation design that can operate on backscatter devices. To do this, we introduce a multi-antenna decoding mechanism that does not require channel estimation and can be achieved using simple analog components.
- We present $\mu$code, a novel coding mechanism that can significantly increase the backscatter communication range and can be decoded on backscatter devices. Using $\mu$code we enable concurrent transmissions in a network of battery-free devices.
- Finally, we build hardware prototypes for $\mu$mo and $\mu$code and show that they significantly expand the capabilities of backscatter systems. Specifically, we provide orders of magnitude increase in the communication rate and range of ambient backscatter. We also enable RFID tag-to-tag communication at long ranges and in through-the-wall scenarios, which was previously not possible.

## 2. RELATED WORK

Our work is related to prior work in both conventional radio communication and backscatter communication:

**(a) Radio Communication:** There has been significant interest in multi-antenna systems and coding mechanisms to improve the performance of traditional Wi-Fi and cellular systems [36, 12, 40] . These techniques, however, require computationally expensive digital signal processing and power-consuming analog components (e.g., ADCs). In contrast, our work eliminates the need for ADCs and digital signal processing, and achieves multi-antenna cancellation and coding gains on backscatter devices.

Our work is also related to low-power MIMO radio designs [38, 8, 34, 18, 22]. These designs increase the energy efficiency of MIMO by optimizing the decoding algorithms [8, 34] and the processor designs [18, 22]. They operate in the digital domain, and thus require power-consuming ADCs. This makes them inapplicable to backscatter devices.

Prior work on low-power spread spectrum transceivers [25, 19, 26, 9, 11] has attempted to reduce the power consumption of digital operations such as synchronization and correlation. These systems use traditional radio architectures with power-consuming RF oscillators and ADCs that are not available on a backscatter device. In contrast, we are the first to design and implement CDMA-like codes on backscatter devices that do not require digital signal processing, and hence consume orders of magnitude less power.

Finally, our work is related to work in the area of analog signal processing [30, 32, 33]. Before the advent of digital processors, wireless communication was performed on analog circuits. Ultra-wide band communication and radar systems still use analog correlators to reduce the cost of hardware components [30, 31, 21]. We build on this foundational work but differ from it in that we are the first to apply this principle to achieve multi-antenna cancellation and channel coding benefits on backscatter devices. Further, we introduce algorithms, techniques, and circuits to achieve this goal.

**(b) Backscatter Systems:** There has been recent interest in improving the performance of backscatter communication [41, 6]. Recent work on ambient backscatter [24] enabled devices to communicate by backscattering existing RF signals like TV transmissions. However, current designs are limited to communication ranges of two feet and communication rates of 10 kbps. Similarly, work on RFID tag-to-tag communication [28] enabled two RFID tags to communicate with each other in the presence of an RFID reader at distances of up to 25 mm. Our work significantly improves the capabilities of these systems. Specifically, using $\mu$mo and $\mu$code, we demonstrate ambient backscatter communication at distances greater than 80 feet and communication rates of 1 Mbps using TV signals. We also show the feasibility of RFID tag-to-tag communication at distances of tens of meters, even when multiple walls separate the tags.

Recent work on MIMO RFID systems [15, 35, 23, 29, 4, 10] leverage multi-antenna capabilities to improve the throughput and reliability of RFID communication. These systems focus on the communication between a multi-antenna reader and a single-antenna backscatter device, and thus the computationally intensive and power-consuming MIMO operations are performed on the powered reader. Recent information theoretic work [13, 16, 17, 7] characterizes the diversity gains achieved by using multiple antennas on backscatter devices. In contrast, we introduce $\mu$mo, a novel multi-antenna technique that can decode the backscattered information by cancelling the interference from ambient signals. We believe that $\mu$mo is the first design and implementation of multi-antenna cancellation on a backscatter device.

Finally, prior work has proposed to use CDMA to address the problem of collisions in RFID networks [37, 5, 27, 39]. In these systems a code is assigned to each backscatter device, and the powered RFID reader correlates with the code to decode the transmitted data even in the face of collisions. These systems are however designed for uplink communication from the backscatter device to an RFID reader, and do not enable decoding on a low power backscattering device. In contrast, we present $\mu$code, the first coding mechanism that provides the benefits of CDMA and can be decoded on a backscattering device; we also show that $\mu$code can enable concurrent transmissions in a network of battery-free devices.

## 3. OUR DESIGN PRINCIPLE

Our goal is to design primitives that enhance wireless communication capabilities on battery-free devices. The key challenge in achieving this is that wireless primitives such as multi-antenna and coding use digital signal processing that requires power-intensive ADCs and computationally expensive digital operations. To address this challenge, we use the following guiding principle: eliminate the need for digital processing by enabling computation in the analog domain. Such an approach, as we show in the rest of the paper, can provide an order of magnitude reduction in the power consumption of these communication primitives.

In the rest of this paper, we describe $\mu$mo, our low-power multi-antenna backscatter receiver and show how it can improve the communication rate of ambient backscatter. We then describe $\mu$code, our low-power coding technique that is achieved using simple analog components, and show how it can be used to increase the communication range of backscatter systems. Finally, we show that our designs can be used to enable concurrent transmissions in a network of battery-free devices, without the need for synchronization.

## 4. $\mu$MO

We first motivate the need for multi-antenna cancellation in ambient backscatter systems and then describe the challenges in achieving $\mu$mo. We then describe our receiver design that addresses these challenges.

### 4.1 Motivation and Challenges

Multi-antenna designs are known to provide communication rate gains that are linear with the number of antennas at the receiver; linear improvements, however, might not be a compelling motivation for low-power designs. So we demonstrate next that multi-antenna cancellation can provide orders of magnitude communication rate improvements for ambient backscatter systems [24]. Ambient backscatter enables two battery-free devices, Alice and Bob, to communicate with each other by backscattering ambient signals in the environment (e.g., TV transmissions). This is in contrast to traditional backscatter systems (e.g., RFID), where the communication is between a battery-free tag and a powered RFID reader and works only in the presence of an RFID reader.

At a high level, the backscattering device encodes a '1' bit by reflecting the incident ambient signals and a '0' bit by absorbing them. The challenge in achieving this is that the ambient signals (e.g., TV) carry information and hence change significantly with time. Prior designs [24] average out the fast-changing TV transmissions to decode the backscattered signals. Averaging removes the variations inherent to the ambient signals, thus allowing the receiver to decode the backscattered signals.

The key issue with averaging, however, is that the backscattering device can transmit information only at a rate that is lower than that of the averaging. Specifically, if the receiver averages the TV transmissions over 100 ms, then the backscattering device can only transmit at a maximum rate of 10 bps. Similarly, if the receiver averages transmissions over one millisecond, then the maximum backscatter rate is 1 kbps. Since averaging must be done over a significant period of time to smooth out the variation in the TV transmissions, averaging does not allow rates much higher than 10 kbps [24]. Intuitively, this is because existing designs decode the backscattered information by considering the ambient signals (e.g., TV) as noise. Since the strength of the TV signal is significantly higher than that of the backscattering signal, the channel has a very low SNR and hence achieves a very low communication rate.

Using multiple antennas, one can eliminate interference from TV signals, and hence provide orders of magnitude higher bit rates.[1] To see this, consider the 2-antenna receiver in Fig. 2. Suppose $s(t)$ is the signal transmitted by an ambient RF source (e.g., TV tower) and that the backscattering device conveys a one bit by reflecting the TV signals and a zero bit by not reflecting them. Now, the receiver

[1]Note that we aim to use multiple antennas for interference cancellation rather than leverage them for antenna diversity. This is because while antenna diversity can reduce the amount of averaging required (e.g., halve it with a two antenna system) it does not eliminate the interference from TV signals.

receives the following signals on its two antennas.

$$y_1(t) = h_{rf}s(t) + h_bB(t)s(t)$$
$$y_2(t) = h'_{rf}s(t) + h'_bB(t)s(t)$$

where $h_{rf}, h'_{rf}$ and $h_b, h'_b$ are the channels from the RF source (TV tower) and the backscattering device respectively. In principle, if the receiver can estimate the channel parameters, $h_{rf}, h'_{rf}$ and $h_b, h'_b$, it would have two equations in two unknowns, $s(t)$ and $B(t)$; thus it can decode the backscattered information, $B(t)$ by performing a matrix inversion operation on the received signals.

Achieving the above operations on a backscatter device, however, is challenging for two main reasons:

- Channel estimation requires computing both the amplitude and phase on the receiver. Estimating the phase information requires the use of a local oscillator; an oscillator must operate at the carrier frequency, therefore consuming more power than is available. Thus backscatter devices do not have the phase information required to perform channel estimation.
- Decoding the backscattered signal is done by performing matrix inversion on a digital representation of the received signal. Digitizing the analog signals requires an 8-12 bit resolution ADC that operates at the communication rate; this again consumes more power than is available on a backscatter device.

### 4.2 $\mu$mo Decoding Algorithm

$\mu$mo can decode backscatter signals with neither phase information nor ADCs. In this section, we describe our algorithm to decode the backscatter signal without estimating the channel parameters. In the next section, we show how the algorithm can be achieved using only analog computation.

Our intuition is as follows: Since backscattering creates an additional reflection to the receiver, the effect of backscatter is to change the channel at the receiver. Further, since the reflected signal propagates by different distances to the two antennas at the receiver, the channel changes created on the two antennas are different. Thus, by comparing the relative channel changes across the two antennas, we can identify the bits transmitted by the backscattering device.

More formally, $\mu$mo first computes the amplitude of the received signal on the two antennas to get:

$$|y_1(t)| = |h_{rf}s(t) + h_bB(t)s(t)|$$
$$|y_2(t)| = |h'_{rf}s(t) + h'_bB(t)s(t)|$$

where $|a|$ represents the magnitude of $a$. Dividing the above equations, we have the following fraction:

$$\frac{|y_1(t)|}{|y_2(t)|} = \frac{|h_{rf} + h_bB(t)|}{|h'_{rf} + h'_bB(t)|}$$

Note that the above fraction is independent of the TV signal $s(t)$, and hence is not affected by the envelope fluctuations inherent in TV transmissions. Now, since the backscattered bits $B(t)$ are either '1' or '0', the above fraction gives us either $\frac{|h_{rf}|}{|h'_{rf}|}$ or $\frac{|h_{rf}+h_b|}{h'_{rf}+h'_b}$. Thus, the above fraction computation results in two different levels depending on whether the backscattered bit is a zero or a one.

To see the above computation in practice, we use a backscatter device to transmit an alternating sequence of zeros and ones at a rate of 1 *kbps*, by backscattering 539 MHz TV transmissions. We use a USRP equipped with two antennas separated by half a wavelength to capture the received digital signals from a distance of 3 feet. Fig. 3 (a) and (b) plot the received signal on each of the receive antennas. The figures show that it is difficult to see the backscattered signal in the presence of the TV transmissions. Fig. 3 (c) plots the result of dividing the received signals on the two antennas. The plot shows that now the alternating sequence of backscattered bits is visible, allowing the receiver to decode.

We note the following key points:

- The above computation does not guarantee that the output corresponding to a '1' bit is always greater than that corresponding to a '0' bit. In particular, the ratio of the amplitudes on the two antennas depends on $h_{rf}, h'_{rf}, h_b$, and $h'_b$, which change with device positions. To address this ambiguity, the receiver uses the preamble bits sent by the transmitter to extract the mapping.
- We note that while noise increases the BER at the receiver, it does not affect the correctness of the above equations. Further, in the above discussion, we assume that the channel is determined by a single channel parameter; since backscattering devices do not use oscillators, they are not frequency selective in their behavior. Thus it is reasonable to approximate the channel at the backscatter device as a single parameter.

### 4.3 $\mu$mo's Hardware Design

Next, we describe how $\mu$mo achieves the above algorithm using only simple analog components, thus eliminating the need for power-consuming components such as ADCs.

The $\mu$mo receiver has three main stages: 1) an envelope detection circuit that computes the amplitude of the received signal on each antenna, 2) an analog circuit that imitates the division operation to find the ratio of the signal envelopes received by the two antennas, and 3) a thresholding circuit that extracts the backscattered bits. We explain each of these components in detail.

*1) Envelope Detection Circuit.* The role of the envelope detector is to track the envelope of the received signal, while eliminating the carrier frequency (539 MHz in case of TV transmissions). The circuit in the figure uses passive components such as resistors, capacitors, and diodes and hence is ultra-low power in nature. The operating principle behind an envelope detector is similar to that used in an RFID tag: diodes act as switches that allow current to flow in the forward direction but not the reverse, capacitors are charge-storage elements and resistors regulate current flow. By choosing the appropriate values for these analog components, we can remove the carrier frequency (e.g., 539 MHz) and leave only the amplitude of the signal. As shown in Fig. 4, $\mu$mo performs the envelope detection computation on both the receiver antennas.

*2) Divider Circuit.* The next step is to divide the amplitudes received on the two antennas. Performing division in a low-power manner is not straightforward, particularly since analog dividers are not a commonly implemented primitive on low power devices. $\mu$mo employs simple logarithmic identities to split the division operation into several easily implemented steps, using the following mathematical trick:

$$\frac{a}{b} = e^{log(\frac{a}{b})} = e^{(log(a)-log(b))}$$

Specifically, to compute the quotient of two numbers $a$ and $b$ we can transform them into the logarithmic domain, subtract the two, and then exponentiate to get the result of the computation. $\mu$mo imitates the above math in the analog domain to perform division. In particular, $\mu$mo uses a log-amplifier on each of the receive signal envelopes to transform the signal amplitudes into the logarithmic domain. At a high level, log-amplifiers make use of the non-linear current-voltage (IV) relationship of a diode to convert a linear domain signal to a logarithmic representation. We then use an analog subtractor to compute the difference between the log-scale signal amplitudes on the two antennas. To get a true linear ratio signal, this difference would need to be transformed back into the linear

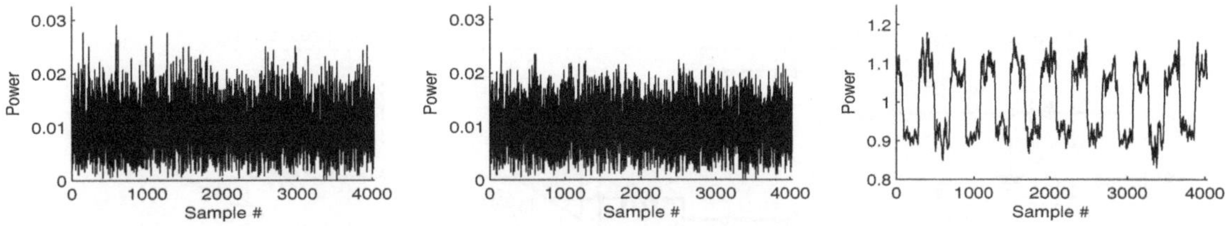


(a) Signal on the First Antenna (b) Signal on the Second Antenna (c) Result of $\mu$mo Division

**Figure 3—$\mu$mo on actual signals.** It is difficult to see the backscattered bits on the received signals at the two receiver antennas. Performing the division between the received signals on the two antennas, reveals the backscattered bits.

domain using an exponential amplifier (which would also make use of diode properties). However, because our next step is to perform a simple thresholding operation on the signal, we can make use of the fact that the log operation is monotonic and omit the exponential amplifier. Omitting this amplifier saves power by reducing the active component count, and does not impact the performance of the system as the simple thresholding operation is not impacted by the use of log domain signals.

*3) Thresholding Circuit.* The goal of this circuit is to distinguish between the two voltage levels at the output of the divider circuit. At a high level, the threshold circuit computes the mean of the two voltage levels, and outputs a one bit when the input is greater than the threshold and a zero bit otherwise. To compute this mean value, $\mu$mo uses an envelope detector as before. We use specific values for the resistors and the capacitors to compute the mean of the signal envelope. We then use a low-power comparator that outputs a one bit when the divider output is greater than the mean and a zero bit otherwise. As described in §4.2, the receiver uses a known preamble in the packet to flip the bits, if necessary, before decoding.

We note that the power consumption of analog components such as log-amplifiers and comparators depends on the bandwidth at which we would like our analog circuit to operate. The bandwidth of the analog circuit is defined as the maximum frequency that the circuit can process without severely attenuating the signals. In our case, we can set the analog bandwidth by selecting low-power amplifier and comparator components that can support a certain bandwidth. In our implementation, we build two different prototypes, one that operates at an analog bandwidth of 1 MHz and the other at an analog bandwidth of 1 kHz.

### 4.4 Putting Things Together

The discussion so far focuses on the physical layer of the $\mu$mo receiver. The backscatter transmitter uses the same physical layer as RFID systems to transmit messages with preambles and CRC checks. The transmitter can vary the transmitted bit duration and therefore the data rate. The receiver uses the low-power hardware design described above to decode messages, which are then validated by checking the CRC. The transmitter and the receiver use the same link layer mechanisms (including modulation and bit encoding) as prior backscatter systems. To conserve power, $\mu$mo's transmit hardware sends an alternating bit sequence long enough (8 bits in our implementation) to wake up the receiver's digital logic system, which then detects bit boundaries and performs framing.

## 5. $\mu$CODE

We first motivate the need for low-power coding designs for backscatter systems and then describe the challenges in achieving this goal. We then describe $\mu$code's encoding and decoding algorithms that address these challenges. Finally, we present our decoder hardware design that uses only analog components.

### 5.1 Motivation and Challenges

RFID systems have seen a limited adoption, mainly due to limited read range and the resulting requirement for a dense deployment of RFID readers to communicate with RFID tags. If we can enable the RFID tags to communicate with each other at long ranges, we can significantly extend the effective read range by creating a multi-hop network across the RFID tags. Another backscatter technology that is currently limited by range is ambient backscatter [24], which eliminates the need for RFID readers by backscattering ubiquitous ambient signals like TV transmissions. While ambient backscatter does achieve tag-to-tag communication, the communication range of existing work is limited to two feet, which significantly limits its applicability. Thus, increasing the range of backscatter communication is essential to improving the viability of these systems.

Coding mechanisms such as CDMA can in principle be used to increase the communication range of backscatter systems. These techniques use a string of pseudorandom bits called chips to encode information bits. For example, the transmitter could represent a zero bit by the chip sequence '101110111' and a one bit by the chip sequence '111011011'. The 1s and 0s in the above sequences are the chips used by the transmitter to encode the information. To decode these information bits, the receiver correlates the received signal with the chip sequence patterns and converts correlation peaks to data bits. To increase the communication range, the transmitter-receiver pair uses longer chip sequences that effectively increase the signal-to-noise ratio and hence enable long-range communication. Decoding such transmissions on a backscatter device is challenging for two main reasons:

- The correlation operation required at the receiver is both computationally expensive and requires power-consuming ADCs that are not available on a backscatter device.
- More important, performing synchronization at the receiver is expensive. Synchronization requires correlating the received signal with a chip sequence for every offset of the received signal. This is not only computationally expensive but also consumes much more power than is available on our target device.

So any code that is to be decoded on a backscatter device should satisfy two main properties: 1) It should not require an ADC or digital signal processing operations, and 2) It should work without the need for synchronization.

### 5.2 $\mu$code's Encoding and Decoding Algorithms

$\mu$code can achieve coding gains on the backscatter device without requiring synchronization operations at the receiver. To understand $\mu$code, we first explain the intuition using a simple sinusoidal wave; we then design the encoding and decoding algorithms to operate on the backscattered bits.

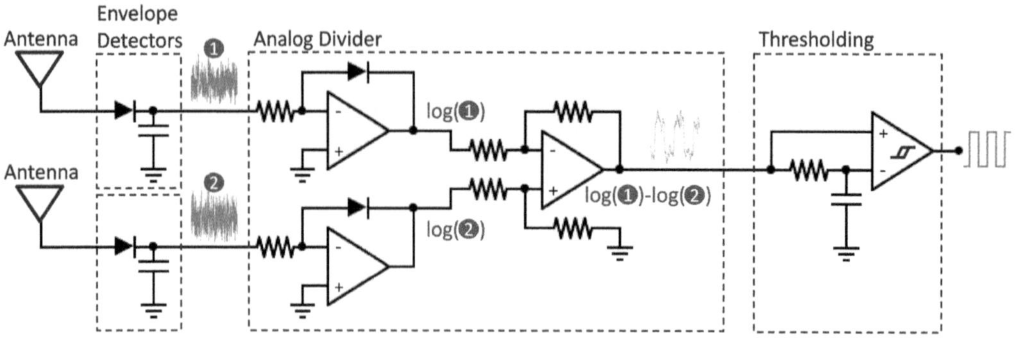


**Figure 4—$\mu$mo hardware design.** $\mu$mo performs the required computation using analog components. Specifically, $\mu$mo's hardware has three main components: an envelope detector that removes the carrier frequency (e.g., 539 MHz), an analog division circuit that divides the received signal on the two antennas, and finally a thresholding circuit that outputs the 0 and 1 bits.

Intuitively, instead of using a pseudorandom chip sequence, $\mu$code uses a periodic signal to represent the information. To see why this works, consider a periodic sinusoidal signal transmitted at a specific frequency. If the receiver knows the frequency of the sinusoidal signal, it can detect the signal without any phase synchronization with the transmitter. Specifically, suppose the transmitter sends a sine wave, $sin(ft+\phi)$, with a frequency $f$ and a phase offset $\phi$. One can easily detect the above sine wave without phase synchronization by performing a dot product operation with the sine and cosine basis functions at the same frequency to compute the In-phase (I) and Quadrature phase (Q) components:

$$I = \sum_{t=0}^{T} sin(ft+\phi)sin(ft)\,\Delta t = \frac{1}{2}sin(\phi)$$

$$Q = \sum_{t=0}^{T} sin(ft+\phi)cos(ft)\,\Delta t = \frac{1}{2}cos(\phi)$$

where $T$ is the duration over which the above dot product operation is computed.[2] Note that from the above equation,

$$|I|^2 + |Q|^2 = \frac{1}{2} \quad (1)$$

Since Eq. 1 is independent of the phase offset $\phi$ the receiver can detect the transmitted signal without the need for phase synchronization. Further, the receiver can increase its detection sensitivity by increasing the transmit signal duration, $T$. Thus, a simple periodic sine wave can be detected without requiring phase synchronization, and also provides a form of coding gain to increase reliability.

$\mu$code's design builds on the above intuition. However, since our backscatter transmitter has only two states and therefore cannot transmit sine waves, it instead uses a periodic alternating sequence of zeros and ones. Specifically, it encodes the one bit by the chip sequence $101010\cdots10$ and the zero bit by the chip sequence $000000\cdots00$.

Our decoder imitates the I and the Q computation above to detect the alternating one-zero sequence, without the need for synchronization. Specifically, it computes the in-phase component (I) by a dot-product operation with the chip sequence $101010\cdots10$ and the quadrature-phase component (Q) by a dot-product operation with a 90 degree offset chip sequence. This is similar to using the sine and the cosine function in the previous scenario. Note that a 90 degree offset is effectively a time offset of half a chip duration. To detect the presence of the alternating sequence of zeros and ones, the receiver then computes $|I| + |Q|$. This works independent of synchronization due to the following lemma:

LEMMA 5.1. *If the transmitter continuously sends an alternating sequence of zero and one chips and the receiver computes in-phase (I) and quadrature-phase (Q) components over any duration of N chips, then* $|I| + |Q| = N$.

The above lemma states that $|I| + |Q|$ is constant, independent of receiver synchronization (see appendix for the proof). Thus the receiver can detect an alternating sequence of zeros and ones by computing $|I| + |Q|$ over any duration of $N$ chips. To summarize:

**$\mu$code's Encoding Algorithm.** The transmitter uses the following chip sequences to represent the zero and one information bits:

$$1010\cdots N\cdots 10 \quad \textit{as bit } 1$$
$$0000\cdots N\cdots 00 \quad \textit{as bit } 0$$

where the chips are transmitted at a rate of $C$.

**$\mu$code's Decoding Algorithm.** The receiver computes $|I|+|Q|$ over a duration of $\frac{n}{3}$ chips. If the majority vote of three adjacent computations is greater than a threshold then the receiver outputs a 1, and a 0 otherwise. The threshold is computed by taking the average of the received signal over bits in the preamble at the beginning of the transmitted packet.

The transmitter can control both the chip rate $C$ and the chip length $N$ to achieve different bit rates. The chip rate determines the duration of each chip bit; a higher chip rate corresponds to smaller chip durations. Given a chip rate, longer chip lengths result in larger ranges since they increase the signal-to-noise ratio. We also show in §8 that by controlling these parameters, we can create orthogonal codes that do not require any synchronization and can enable multiple concurrent transmissions.

### 5.3 $\mu$code Hardware Design

Next we describe how $\mu$code achieves the above decoding algorithm in the analog domain, without the need for ADCs.

Specifically, as shown in Fig. 5, our receiver design has four main components: an envelope detector circuit, $|I|$ and $|Q|$ computation blocks, an addition circuit, and a thresholding circuit. The envelope detector circuit is the same as that described in §4 and is used to remove the carrier frequency (e.g., 539 MHz TV transmissions). We implement the addition operation with an analog adder circuit, and the thresholding circuit is similar to that used in §4.

[2] We replace the integration operation that is typically performed with summation, for ease of exposition.

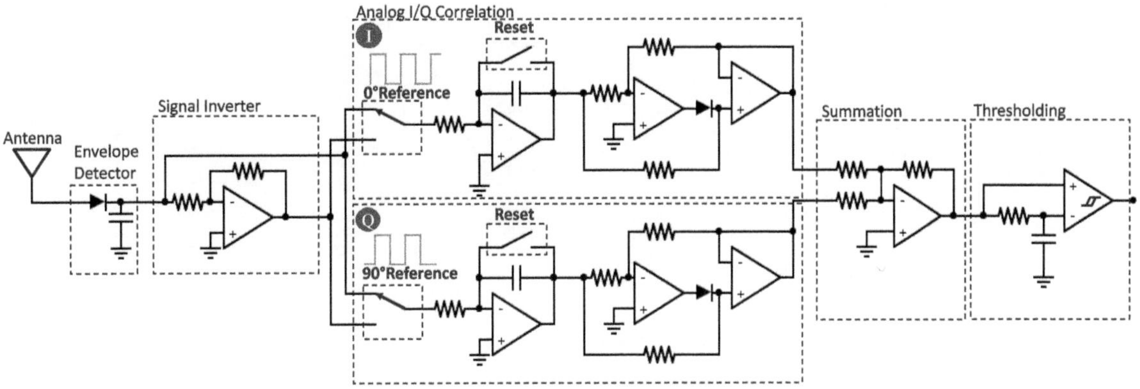


**Figure 5—$\mu$code hardware design.** Our hardware design performs the decoding operations using analog components, without the need for ADCs. The hardware system has three main components: I/Q correlation circuits that compute |I| and |Q|, a summation circuit that computes |I| + |Q|, and finally a thresholding circuit that outputs 0 and 1 bits.

We focus the rest of this discussion on the $|I|$ and $|Q|$ computation circuits. Note that, functionally, both operations are similar to a dot product operation, multiplying two signals and accumulating the result over a time period (in our case the chip length $N$). The only difference between the $|I|$ and the $|Q|$ computations is that the chip sequence $10 \cdots 10$ is offset by 90 degrees for the $|Q|$ computation. Thus, we focus on the $|I|$ computation circuit. At a high level, we achieve the dot product operation (which is a multiply-accumulate operation) using three key components. First, we send the received signal through an analog inverter to generate the inverted version of the input signal. We then use an analog switch that toggles between the inverted and the non-inverted signal every $T$ seconds, where $T$ is the duration of a chip. This effectively achieves the multiplication operation with the chip sequence. Finally, we use an analog integrator to accumulate the output of this multiplication operation and compute $|I|$. The reset function in Fig. 5 is used to reset the circuit every chip sequence length duration to repeat the computation for every transmitted bit.

## 5.4 Enabling multiple transmissions using $\mu$code

$\mu$code can also be used to enable concurrent transmissions in the network without the need to deal with collisions or random access. Specifically, we show in the appendix that $\mu$code satisfies the following property:

LEMMA 5.2. *A alternating zero-one chip sequence at a chip rate C is orthogonal to all chip sequences at a chip rate 2NC and chip length 2N, where N is a positive integer. The orthogonality property holds independent of the synchronization between the codes.*

The above lemma implies that transmitters with codes that satisfy the above condition do not interfere with each other. Further, one can create codes with rates $C, 2C, 4C, 8C, \cdots$ such that every pair of chip sequences satisfy the above condition. By setting a particular value for $C$ (say 100 Hz) and assigning different codes to different transmitter-receiver pairs, $\mu$code can be used to enable concurrent interference-free transmissions. In §8 we evaluate $\mu$code's ability to enable concurrent transmissions. One aspect of using different codes across transmitter-receiver pairs is the question of distributing these codes across the transmitters. Prior work on CDMA systems [27] has proposed a number of techniques including those that use collision-resistant hash functions to achieve this goal. In principle, we can combine $\mu$code's design with these existing solutions; evaluating this, however, is not in the scope of this paper.

## 6. FURTHER DISCUSSION

We discuss the following aspects of our design:

**(1) Bit Rate Adaptation.** $\mu$mo and $\mu$code each provide us with multiple bit rates; the transmitter-receiver pair can perform bit rate adaptation over all these rates to optimize the throughput and to account for channel fluctuations. We note that, for both systems, multiple bit rates can be achieved in hardware simply by changing timing parameters in the digital control logic. Our current prototype implementation allows us to pick different rates across $\mu$mo and $\mu$code. Designing bit rate adaptation algorithms however is not in the scope of this paper.

**(2) Interference with TV receivers.** While the receiver designs in this paper increase the range and rate of backscatter communication, the backscattering operation at the transmitter is the same as in prior designs. Specifically, we do not change the strength of the backscattered signal at the transmitter over prior designs, and thus create no additional interference at TV receivers. Thus, similar to [24], our system creates interference at the TV receiver only when it is closer than eight inches from the TV antenna.

**(3) Application to traditional RFID systems.** This paper is focused on enabling communication between battery-free devices using backscatter. However, our designs can also be used to increase the downlink rate and range from an RFID reader to a tag. Current RFID reader-tag systems do not operate across different rooms and are limited to communication ranges that are comparatively smaller; our designs can in principle also provide between-room capabilities to traditional RFID reader to tag links.

## 7. PROTOTYPE IMPLEMENTATION

To evaluate the performance of $\mu$mo and $\mu$code in practice, we designed and implemented the system on a printed circuit board as shown in Fig. 1. Our prototype integrates both the $\mu$mo and $\mu$code designs on a single board. Fig. 6 shows a block diagram of our receiver prototype; it is a fully reconfigurable platform controlled by firmware executed on the low power MSP430 microcontroller. Both the $\mu$mo and $\mu$code sections of the analog circuit are power-gated, i.e., they can be enabled or disabled easily to save power. Our prototype has the following features:

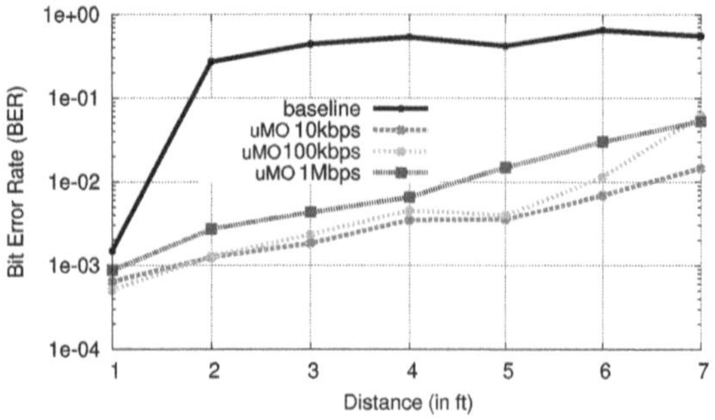


(a) -30 dBm TV Power at Transmitter

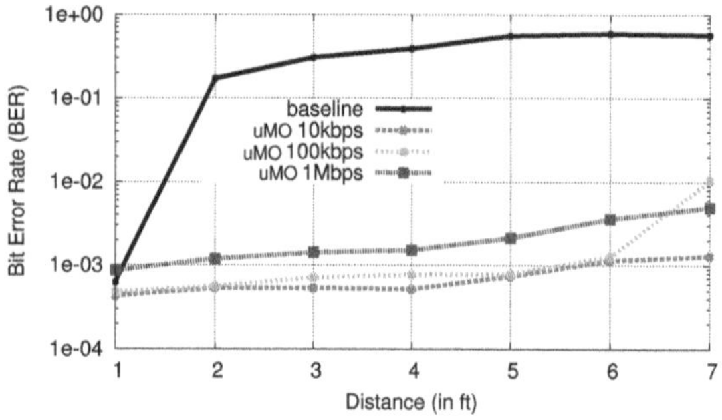


(b) -20 dBm TV Power at Transmitter

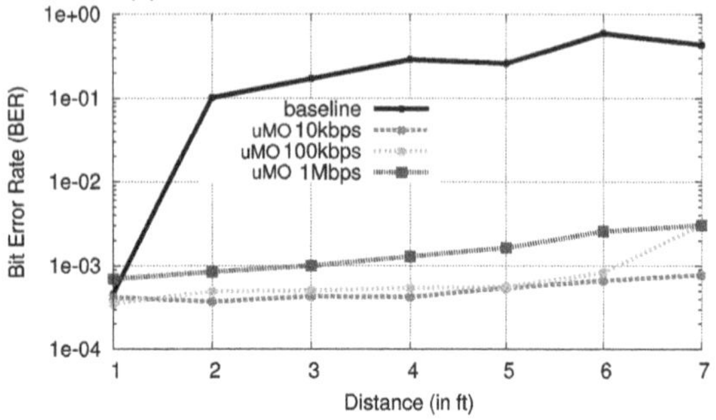


(c) -10 dBm TV Power at Transmitter

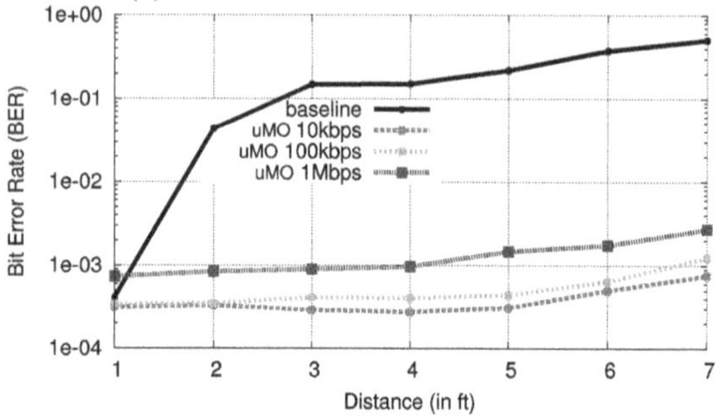


(d) 0 dBm TV Power at Transmitter

**Figure 7—$\mu$mo BER versus Distance.** The figure shows the bit error rate (BER) as a function of distance between the backscattering device and the receiver. The different plots correspond to different ambient RF power levels at the transmitter. The black solid line represents the baseline BER from existing ambient backscatter designs. The figure shows that $\mu$mo can enable data rates as high as 1 Mbps at distances between 4-7 feet. This translates to a 100X improvement in the data rates.

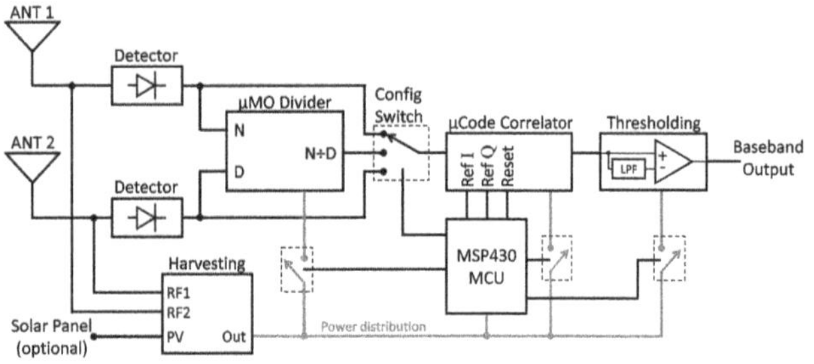


**Figure 6—Block diagram of our receiver prototype**

**Table 1—Power consumption of Analog Signal Processing**

| | Max. Rate | Range | Rx Power |
|---|---|---|---|
| $\mu$code | 1 kbps | >80 ft | 8.9 $\mu$W |
| $\mu$mo | 1 Mbps | 4 - 7 ft | 422 $\mu$W |

*1) Flexible switching between $\mu$mo and $\mu$code.* We use an ultra-low-power configuration switch as shown in the figure to route signals between two modes of operation: $\mu$mo and $\mu$code. When in $\mu$mo mode, the microcontroller directs the configuration switch to allow the output of the $\mu$mo divider to pass to the next decoding step. The $\mu$mo divider circuit is powered on, along with the thresholding circuit. When $\mu$mo is active, the $\mu$code correlator is bypassed internally by forcing it into a perpetual reset state, which effectively disables any impact from the correlation circuit.

When in $\mu$code mode, the switch is configured to route the signal from one of the two detectors to the correlator, allowing either of the two antennas to be selected as the signal source. The $\mu$code correlator is powered on, along with the thresholding circuit. The microcontroller generates the correlator's reference I and Q chip sequences as well as a periodic reset pulse that clears the correlation result after every chip sequence duration. Note that in our experiments, we use only one receive antenna to evaluate $\mu$code.

*2) Trading analog bandwidth for lower power consumption.* Every analog communication circuit has an constrained bandwidth, that is, there is a maximum baseband signal bandwidth that a receiver is capable of decoding. The analog bandwidth of a receiver is proportional to the maximum data rate that can be achieved using it. In our prototype, the analog bandwidth is determined by the capabilities of the operational amplifiers and other components we use to implement the analog processing. In general, higher bandwidth allows higher data rates but also increases power consumption.

We fabricate two prototypes: one that targets high-rate communication and consumes more power, and another that targets low-rate communication and consumes less power. Specifically, our high data rate prototype targets an analog bandwidth of 1 MHz. To achieve this we make use of the power-efficient TSV6390 operational amplifiers from ST Microelectronics in our signal processing circuits. For the final threshold comparison we use the NCS2200 comparator made by ON semiconductors. The low rate prototype, on the other hand, has an analog bandwidth of 1 kHz. To achieve this, we use the BU7265 operational amplifier from Rohm Semiconductor and the TS881 comparator from ST Microelectronics.

We use our high rate prototype to demonstrate $\mu$mo and our low rate prototype for $\mu$code. Table 1 shows the power consumption of their analog signal processing, including all the analog components. The table shows that $\mu$mo consumes about 422 $\mu$W of power; this is in contrast to traditional Wi-Fi MIMO implementations [14] that use more than one Watt for a two-antenna receiver. The power consumption numbers for $\mu$code are significantly lower at around 8.9 $\mu$W. We note that prior ambient backscatter designs use 0.54 $\mu$W of power but are significantly limited to less than two feet of communication range and 10 kbps of bit rates. The higher power consumption of our prototype, however, is not an issue since we use duty cycling to reduce the average power of these analog components, as described next. We also note that one can further reduce these power numbers by an order of magnitude by using application-specific integrated circuits (ASICs).

*3) Energy Harvesting and Duty Cycling.* Our prototype provides the ability to harvest energy from one or both of the following sources:

ambient TV energy, and solar power. In the case of an ambient RF energy harvesting supply, our prototype duty-cycles (periodically alternates between active and sleep states) to allow operation from such a low power source. With a typical TV harvesting power of 100 $\mu$W, our 1 MHz $\mu$mo device can operate 23% of the time, and the 1 kHz $\mu$code system can operate 100% of the time.

In the case of a solar photovoltaic power supply, we consider the area requirement of a typical-efficiency solar array such that it can provide sufficient power for continuous operation of $\mu$mo and $\mu$code circuits. To do this we measure the power output from an 2.75 by 1.38 inch thin film solar array (manufactured by PowerFilm Inc) in an environment with an illuminance of 330 lux. 330 lux is the minimal office and workplace illuminance specified by the Occupational Safety and Health Administration (OSHA) [1]. Given these measurements, $\mu$mo requires a 8.28 square inch solar array and $\mu$code requires a 0.17 square inch solar array to continuously operate in our office environment.

## 8. EVALUATION

We first evaluate the performance of $\mu$mo in an ambient backscatter scenario. We then evaluate $\mu$code for both ambient backscatter and RFID tag-to-tag communication in both line-of-sight and through-the-wall scenarios. Finally, we evaluate $\mu$code's ability to enable multiple concurrent transmissions.

### 8.1 Evaluating $\mu$mo

We evaluate $\mu$mo in an ambient backscatter scenario where two battery-free devices communicate by backscattering ambient TV transmissions. The state-of-the-art ambient backscatter system [24] achieves communication rates of up to 10 kbps at distances of less than two feet. As described in §4, our design can overcome the design limitation of [24] and achieve significantly higher ranges. To demonstrate this, we first evaluate the bit error rate (BER) as a function of distance for various transmitter data rates. We then evaluate the effects of antenna separation on the observed BER values.

#### *8.1.1 BER versus Distance*

We evaluate the bit error rate (BER) as a function of the distance between the two ambient backscatter devices.

*Experiments.* We perform the experiments using TV transmissions in the 539 MHz range. We use a single-antenna transmitter and our two-antenna receiver placed at different distances from each other. The two antennas at the receiver are separated by half a wavelength. We compute the bit error rate (BER) observed at the receiver as a function of the distance between the transmitter and the receiver. For each distance value, we repeat the experiments at ten different adjacent positions to account for multipath effects. We compute the average BER at each distance by averaging the BER across the ten locations. Since we are interested in demonstrating high rates, we use only our 1 MHz analog bandwidth prototype. We repeat the experiments for each of four different transmission rates: 1Mbps, 100 kbps, and 10 kbps. To quantify the effect of the TV signal strength on the BER, we measure the TV power level at our backscattering transmitter using a spectrum analyzer, and collect results for four different power levels of -30 dBm, -20 dBm, -10 dBm, and 0 dBm. To compare the results with existing systems, we replicate the design in [24] at a bit rate of 10 kbps and compute the BER as a function of distance for different transmit power levels.

*Results.* Figs. 7(a)-(d) give BER as a function of distance between the backscattering device and receiver for each of four TV power levels. Each plot shows the results for three $\mu$mo bit rates and the 10 kbps ambient backscatter design. The plots show the following:

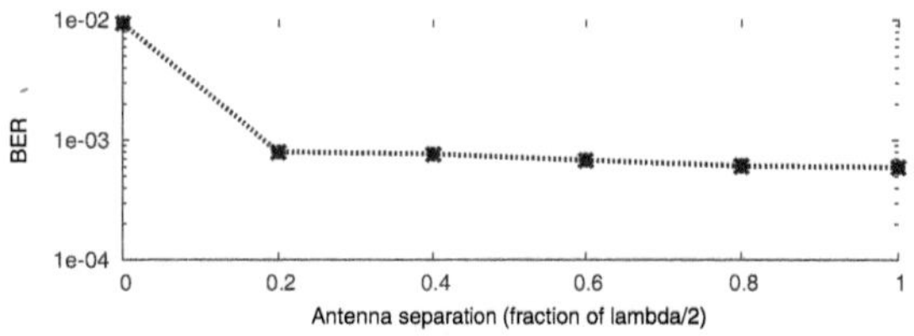


**Figure 9—Effect of separation between the antennas.** BER is given as a function of the antenna separation.

- The bit error rate increases as the distance between the transmitter and the receiver increases. In general, the BER increases with the bit rate. This is expected because at larger distances and higher transmission rates, noise starts affecting decodability. However, the BER values we measure for the $\mu$mo system are significantly lower than in prior work on ambient backscatter.
- As the TV power at the transmitter is reduced, the BER values across all the bit rates increase. This is because, at lower TV signal strengths, the backscatter signal power significantly reduces, decreasing the signal-to-noise ratio at the receiver. However, the BER values measured for $\mu$mo are less than $10^{-2}$ for distances up to 7 feet; this is true for all tested bit rates provided the TV power is greater than -20 dBm.
- At an operational BER of $10^{-2}$, $\mu$mo achieves bit rates of 1 Mbps at a distance of 4 ft across the considered ambient power range. Further, when the ambient power level is greater than -20 dBm, $\mu$mo achieves 1 Mbps at distances up to 7 ft. In comparison, a 10 kbps ambient backscatter device (our baseline) can only operate at distances less than two feet across all four power levels. We note that the BER for prior single-antenna ambient backscatter designs [24] is close to 50% at 1 Mbps data rates. This is because, as explained in §4.1, prior designs leverage averaging and hence the backscattering device can transmit information only at a rate that is lower than that of averaging. Since averaging must be done over a significant time period to smooth out variations in the TV transmissions, averaging-based designs [24] do not allow rates much higher than 10 kbps. In contrast, since $\mu$mo eliminates the variations in the TV transmissions using division, it can achieve a 100X improvement in the communication rate.

#### *8.1.2 BER Versus Antenna Separation*

Next, we evaluate the effect of receive antenna separation on $\mu$mo's ability to decode backscattered transmissions. To do this, we fix the positions of the transmitter and the receiver at a distance of three feet from each other. We vary the distance between the two antennas at the receiver from half a wavelength (0.9 feet) to zero feet. The transmitter uses a bit rate of 1 Mbps and is placed in locations where the average TV power is around -10 dBm. We then compute the BER as a function of the antenna separation at the receiver. Fig. 9 plots the results of our experiments. The plot shows that as expected the BER increases as the distance between the two antennas reduces. However, the BER does not see a significant increase until the antenna separation is less than 0.2 half-wavelengths (0.18 feet). This is because while in theory a half-wavelength separation is optimal, in practice smaller receive antenna separations also have good spatial diversity due to wireless multi-path.

We also note that, even when the antenna separation is zero, the BER is still $10^{-2}$. This is because, even at this minimal separation, the two antennas still experience a small phase difference that is sufficient to eliminate TV signal fluctuation and decode the backscattered signal.

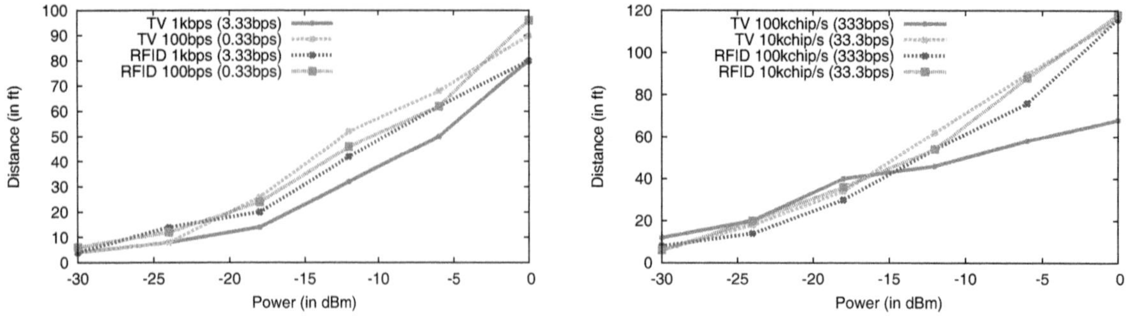


(a) With 1 kHz prototype (b) With 1 MHz prototype

**Figure 8—Communication range versus power in line-of-sight scenarios.** The plots show the communication range as a function of the power of the RFID and TV signals as seen by the backscattering device. We plot results for both our 1 kHz and 1 MHz prototypes.

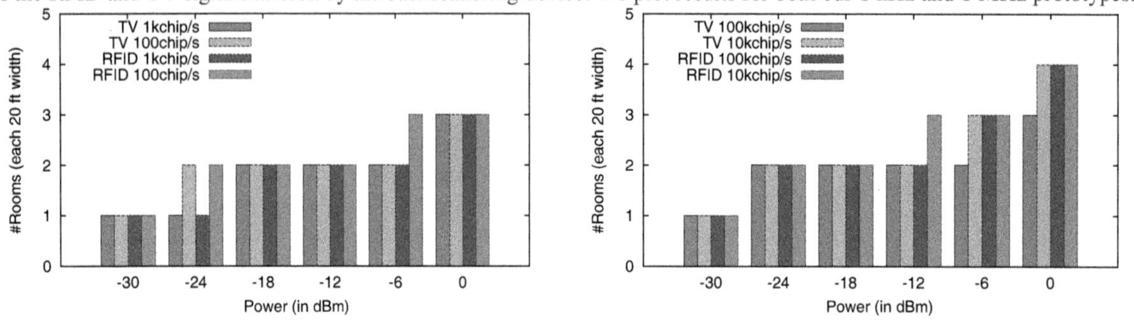


(a) With 1 kHz prototype (b) With 1 MHz prototype

**Figure 10—Communication range versus power in non-line-of-sight scenarios.** The receiver is moved away from the transmitter into different rooms as shown in Fig. 11. The y-axis represents the number of rooms where the BER is less than $10^{-2}$.

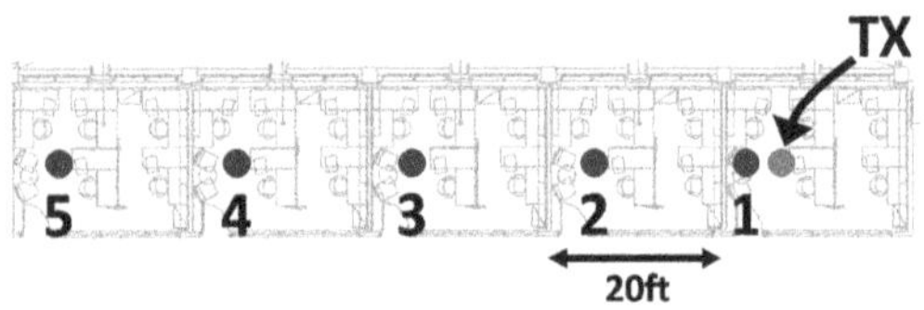


**Figure 11—Non-line-of-sight experiment locations.** We locate the transmitter in the middle of an office at point TX and move the receiver through several adjacent offices to determine the number of walls through which the system can continue to communicate. This is performed for both RFID tag-to-tag communication (continuous wave) and ambient backscatter (TV signal) scenarios.

## 8.2 Evaluating $\mu$code

Next, we evaluate the performance of $\mu$code in practice. As described in §5, $\mu$code achieves two main goals. First, it enables long range RFID tag-to-tag communication by backscattering signals from an RFID reader. Second, it enables ambient backscatter communication at ranges much greater than those demonstrated by existing systems. In this section, we evaluate these goals in both line-of-sight and non-line-of-sight scenarios.

### *8.2.1 In Line-of-Sight Scenarios*

Firstly, we evaluate $\mu$code for RFID tag-to-tag communication and ambient backscatter in line-of-sight scenarios.

*Experiments.* We run experiments in a large indoor space with dimensions 120 ft × 40 ft × 60 ft. We use both the 1 MHz and 1 kHz analog bandwidth receiver prototypes that implement $\mu$code. We pick chip rates of 100 chips/s and 1k chips/s on our 1 kHz bandwidth prototype and 10 kchips/s and 100 kchips/s on our 1 MHz bandwidth prototype. At every chip rate we use a chip length of 300 chips to represent an information bit. This combination of chip rates and chip lengths translates to bit rates of 0.33 bps, 3.33 bps, 33.3 bps, and 333 bps, respectively. We measure the range achieved by our system at different RF power levels for the RFID reader or TV signal as measured at our transmitter. To evaluate the benefits of RFID tag-to-tag communication in enable connectivity for tags far from the RFID reader, we place the transmitter (receiver) tag close to (far from) the RFID reader. We vary the power values from -30 dBm to 0 dBm by changing the position of the transmitter. For each combination of power level and transmitted bit rate, we measure the communication range between the transmitter and the receiver. To do this, we move the receiver away from the transmitter and note the distance at which the BER first goes below $10^{-2}$. Note that the receiver moves away from the RFID reader in all our experiments.[3] We repeat the above experiments with TV transmissions using our TV backscatter prototypes.

*Results.* Fig. 8 plots communication range as a function of the signal strength of the reader and TV transmissions as measured at the transmitter. Fig. 8(a) and (b) plot the results for our 1 MHz and 1 KHz prototypes, respectively. The plots show the following:

- On each of our 1 MHz and 1 kHz prototypes, the communication range is higher at lower bit rates. This observation holds for both our TV and RFID backscatter prototypes. This is expected because higher bit rates suffer from higher noise that limits the decoding capability at longer distances.
- Our 1 MHz analog hardware generally achieves higher ranges than our 1 kHz prototype. This is expected, as the 1 MHz hardware has a higher bandwidth and hence has less effective noise.
- The communication range increases with the power of the signal at the backscattering device. Using the 1 kHz prototype, RFID tags can communicate with each other at a rate of 3.33 bps at ranges greater than 90 feet given an incident RF power of 0 dBm. At an incident power level of -15 dBm, the communica-

[3] As the receiver moves away from the reader, it can receive neither transmissions nor power from the RFID reader. Our receiver can harvest power from solar and ambient TV signals in these scenarios.

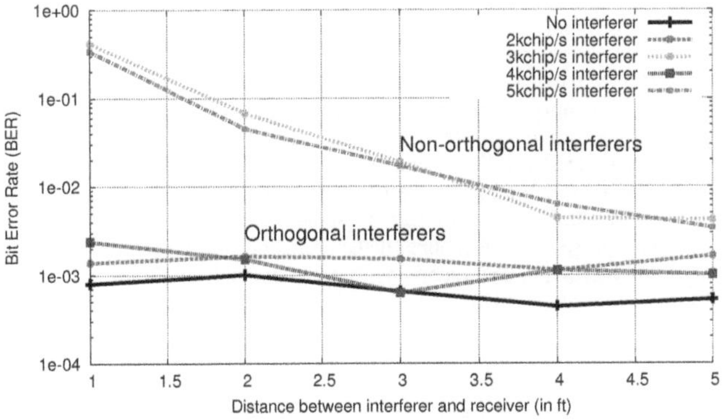


**Figure 12—Multiple concurrent transmissions.** We place an interferer close to a receiver configured to receive 1 kchips/s transmissions. We have the interferer transmit at 2 kchips/s and 4 kchips/s which are orthogonal codes and also at 3 kchips/s and 5 kchips/s which are non-orthogonal codes to 1 kchips/s. The plots show that the interferer increases the BER at the receiver when using non-orthogonal codes. The interference however is minimal with an interferer using orthogonal codes (2 kchips/s and 4 kchips/s).

tion range is over 30 feet with both TV and RFID transmissions. Such ranges are significantly higher than those achieved by existing systems.

### 8.2.2 In Non-Line-of-Sight Scenarios

Next, we evaluate $\mu$code's performance in non-line-of-sight scenarios. Conventional RFID technology is limited to line-of-sight scenarios and is not designed to work through walls or other occluding obstacles. $\mu$code achieves coding gains in a low-power manner that allows it to enable communication in through-the-wall scenarios. Specifically, we evaluate $\mu$code's ability to achieve both RFID tag-to-tag communication as well as ambient backscatter communication in through-the-wall scenarios.

*Experiments:* We run experiments in a through-the-wall scenario in our organization, as shown in Fig. 11. The testbed spans five rooms and is separated by double sheet-rock (plus insulation) walls with a thickness of approximately 5.7 inches. Each room is about 20 feet wide and contains typical furniture one would expect in an office (e.g., chairs, tables, couches, etc.). We fix the location of our single-antenna backscattering device as shown in the testbed. We then move our receiver prototype away from the transmitter, starting at a distance of one meter with the receiver in the same room as the backscattering device (no walls), then moving the receiver to different rooms increasingly distant from the transmitter. For our RFID tag-to-tag communication results, we place the backscattering device in the presence of an RFID reader and vary the RF signal power seen at the device. To evaluate an ambient backscatter scenario, we vary the TV signal power at the backscattering device.We also run experiments with both our 1 MHz and 1 kHz receiver prototypes and with different bit rates as before. For each power level observed at the transmitter, we note the number of walls through which the receiver can still decode the backscattered signal at a BER of less than $10^{-2}$.

*Results.* Fig. 10(a), and (b) plot the room number at which the system works, for both our 1 MHz and 1 kHz hardware. The plots show that while the devices cannot communicate through walls when the incident RF power is less than -25 dBm, through-wall communication is possible when the power level is greater than -25 dBm. This is true for both RFID tag-to-tag communication and ambient backscatter communication with TV signals. We believe this is a significant advancement in backscatter communication.

### 8.3 Evaluating Concurrent Transmissions with $\mu$code

As described in §5, $\mu$code can be used to enable concurrent transmission in the network without suffering from interference. Specifically, one can assign chip sequences that satisfy Lemma 5.2 to different transmitters, allowing them to transmit concurrently without interference. In this section, we evaluate the feasibility of achieving this in practice.

To do this, we place a transmitter and our receiver prototype at a fixed separation of 10 feet. The transmitter and receiver are configured to use a chip rate of 1 kHz and chip length of 300. We evaluate the effect of an interfering transmitter on the BER. Specifically, we place an interfering transmitter at different distances ranging from 1 feet to 5 feet away from our receiver. The interfering transmitter uses two sets of chip sequences: the first set has chip rates of 2kchips/s and 4kchips/s, and the second set has rates of 3kchips/s and 5kchips/s. The first set of chip rates are such that they satisfy the property in Lemma 5.2 and hence in theory should not interfere with the receiver. The chip rates in the second set, however, do not satisfy Lemma 5.2 and hence are expected to create interference.

Fig. 12 plots the computed BER values at the receiver as a function of distance from the interfering transmitter. The black solid line corresponds to the baseline results in the absence of an interfering transmitter. We show plots for the two sets of orthogonal (2 and 4 kchips/s) and non-orthogonal codes (3 and 5 kchips/s). The figure shows the following:

- As expected, the BER values corresponding to the non-orthogonal codes (3 and 5 kchips/s) are much higher than the baseline. Specifically, with a distance of one foot between the interference transmitter and receiver, the BER is close to 0.5 (which is similar to a random guess). The BER values improve as the distance from the interfering transmitter increases.
- The BER values for the orthogonal codes (2 and 4 kchips/s) are close to the baseline without the interfering device. This is true even when the interferer is as close as one foot away from the receiver. This demonstrates that $\mu$code can enable concurrent transmissions without significant interference at the receivers.

## 9. CONCLUSION

We present two novel communication primitives for backscatter communication systems: $\mu$mo, a multi-antenna cancellation receiver that operates on backscatter devices, and $\mu$code, a coding mechanism that provides the benefits of CDMA and can be decoded on backscatter devices. Using these communication primitives, we enable RFID tags to communicate directly with each other at distances of tens of meters and while separated by multiple walls. Further, we show that our designs can provide orders of magnitude increase in the communication rate and range of ambient backscatter systems. We believe that this paper represents a substantial leap forward in the capabilities of backscatter systems.

**Acknowledgements.** We would like to thank Ben Ransford, Vincent Liu, Rajalakshmi Nandakumar, Donny Huang, our shepherd Alex Snoeren, and the anonymous SIGCOMM reviewers for their helpful comments. This research is funded in part by UW Commercialization Gap Fund, Qualcomm Innovation Fellowship, Washington Research Foundation gift, and NSF.

## 10. REFERENCES

[1] Minimum illumination intensities in foot-candles. https://www.osha.gov/pls/oshaweb/owadisp.show_document?p_table=STANDARDS&p_id=10630.

[2] Ieee 802.11g standard, 2003. http://standards.ieee.org/getieee802/download/802.11g-2003.pdf.

[3] Ieee 802.21 standard, 2008. http://standards.ieee.org/getieee802/download/802.21-2008.pdf.
[4] C. Boyer and S. Roy. Backscatter communication and rfid: Coding, energy, and mimo analysis. Communications, IEEE Transactions on, 2013.
[5] M. Buettner. Backscatter Protocols and Energy-Efficient Computing for RF-Powered Devices. PhD thesis, 2013.
[6] M. Buettner, B. Greenstein, and D. Wetherall. Dewdrop: an energy-aware runtime for computational rfid. In NSDI, 2011.
[7] G. M. C. Angerer, R. Langwieser and M. Rupp. Maximal ratio combining receivers for dual antenna rfid readers. In Wireless Sensing, Local Positioning, and RFID, 2009.
[8] S. Chen and T. Zhang. Low power soft-output signal detector design for wireless mimo communication systems. In ISLPED, 2007.
[9] I. Chien C, Elgorriaga and M. C. Low-power direct-sequence spread-spectrum modem architecture for distributed wireless sensor networks. In ISLPED, 2001.
[10] C. Divarathne and N. Karmakar. Mimo based chipless rfid system. In RFID-TA, 2012.
[11] J. Ghalsari and A. Ferdosi. A direct sequence spread spectrum code acquisition circuit for wireless sensor networks. In International Journal of Electronics, 2011.
[12] S. Gollakota, F. Adib, D. Katabi, and S. Seshan. Clearing the rf smog: making 802.11 n robust to cross-technology interference. In SIGCOMM, 2011.
[13] J. Griffin and G. Durgin. Gains for rf tags using multiple antennas. Antennas and Propagation, IEEE Transactions on, 2008.
[14] D. Halperin, B. Greenstein, A. Sheth, and D. Wetherall. Demystifying 802.11n power consumption. In HotPower, 2010.
[15] C. He, X. Chen, Z. Wang, and W. Su. On the performance of mimo rfid backscattering channels. EURASIP Journal on Wireless Communications and Networking, 2012.
[16] C. He and Z. Wang. Gains by a space-time-code based signaling scheme for multiple-antenna rfid tags. In CCECE, 2010.
[17] C. He and Z. J. Wang. Closed-form ber analysis of non-coherent fsk in miso double rayleigh fading/rfid channel. Communications Letters, IEEE, 2011.
[18] J. Im, M. Cho, Y. Jung, Y. Jung, and J. Kim. A low-power and low-complexity baseband processor for mimo-ofdm wlan systems. Journal of Signal Processing Systems, 2012.
[19] I. Kang and A. N. Willson Jr. Low-power viterbi decoder for cdma mobile terminals. Solid-State Circuits, IEEE Journal of, 1998.
[20] B. Kellogg, V. Talla, and S. Gollakota. Bringing gesture recognition to all devices. In NSDI, 2014.
[21] O. Koistinen, J. Lahtinen, and M. T. Hallikainen. Comparison of analog continuum correlators for remote sensing and radio astronomy. Instrumentation and Measurement, IEEE Transactions on, 2002.
[22] E. Konguvel, J. Raja, and M. Kannan. Article: A low power vlsi implementation of 2x2 mimo ofdm transceiver with ici-sc scheme. International Journal of Computer Applications, 2013.
[23] R. Langwieser, C. Angerer, and A. Scholtz. A uhf frontend for mimo applications in rfid. In RWS, 2010.
[24] V. Liu, A. Parks, V. Talla, S. Gollakota, D. Wetherall, and J. R. Smith. Ambient backscatter: wireless communication out of thin air. In SIGCOMM, 2013.
[25] T. Long and N. R. Shanbhag. Low-power cdma multiuser receiver architectures. In SiPS, 1999.
[26] A. McCormick, P. Grant, J. Thompson, T. Arslan, and A. Erdogan. Low power receiver architectures for multi-carrier cdma. IEE Proceedings-Circuits, Devices and Systems, 2002.
[27] C. Mutti and C. Floerkemeier. Cdma-based rfid systems in dense scenarios: Concepts and challenges. In RFID, 2008.
[28] P. V. Nikitin, S. Ramamurthy, R. Martinez, and K. Rao. Passive tag-to-tag communication. In RFID, 2012.
[29] Y. Okunev, K. J. Powell, M. Arneson, and W. R. Bandy. System integration of rfid and mimo technologies. US Patent App. 11/294,464.
[30] S. Padin. A wideband analog continuum correlator for radio astronomy. Instrumentation and Measurement, IEEE Transactions on, 1994.
[31] S. Padin, J. K. Cartwright, M. C. Shepherd, J. K. Yamasaki, and W. L. Holzapfel. A wideband analog correlator for microwave background observations. Instrumentation and Measurement, IEEE Transactions on, 2001.
[32] R. Piechocki, J. Garrido, D. McNamara, J. McGeehan, and A. Nix. Analog mimo detector: the concept and initial results. In International Symposium on Wireless Communication Systems, 2004.
[33] Solar-Garrido, J. Picchocki, and D. McNamara. Analog mimo detection on the basis of belief propagation. In MWSCAS, 2006.
[34] T. Takahashi, A. T. Erdogan, T. Arslan, and J. Han. Low power layered space-time channel detector architecture for mimo systems. In Emerging VLSI Technologies and Architectures, 2006.
[35] K. Terasaki, K. Kinami, and N. Honma. Passive mimo transmission using load modulation. In ISAP, 2012.
[36] D. Tse and P. Viswanath. Fundamentals of wireless communication. Cambridge university press, 2005.
[37] J. Wang, H. Hassanieh, D. Katabi, and P. Indyk. Efficient and reliable low-power backscatter networks. In SIGCOMM, 2012.
[38] L. Wang and N. Shanbhag. Low-power mimo signal processing. VLSI Systems, IEEE Transactions on, 2003.
[39] L.-C. Wuu, Y.-J. Chen, C.-H. Hung, and W.-C. Kuo. Zero-collision rfid tags identification based on cdma. In International Conference on Information Assurance and Security, 2009.
[40] Q. Yang, X. Li, H. Yao, J. Fang, K. Tan, W. Hu, J. Zhang, and Y. Zhang. Bigstation: enabling scalable real-time signal processingin large mu-mimo systems. In SIGCOMM, 2013.
[41] P. Zhang and D. Ganesan. Enabling bit-by-bit backscatter communication in severe energy harvesting environments. In NSDI, 2014.

# APPENDIX

**A. Proof of Lemma 5.1** Say $2T$ is the duration of a chip and the amplitudes corresponding to the one and zero bits are $A_1$ and $A_2$. For simplicity let us assume that $A_1 > A_2$. Now say that chip sequence used to compute the in-phase component $I$ is $s$ seconds out of synchronization from the transmitted signal. Given these parameters we can write the following:

$$\begin{aligned} I &= -sA_1 + (2T - s)A_1 + sA_2 - (2T - s)A_2 \\ &= (2T - 2s)(A_1 - A_2) \end{aligned}$$

Now if $0 < s < T$, then the quadrature component $Q$ component over one two chips (01 sequence) is

$$\begin{aligned} Q &= -(T + s)A_1 + (T + s)A_1 + (T + s)A_2 - (T - s)A_2 \\ &= -2s(A_1 - A_2) \end{aligned}$$

Thus, $|I| + |Q| = 2T(A_1 - A_2)$. On the other hand, if $T < s < 2T$, then the quadrature component $Q$ is

$$\begin{aligned} Q &= (s - T)A_1 - (3T - s)A_1 - (s - T)A_2 + (3T - s)A_2 \\ &= (2s - 4T)(A_1 - A_2) \end{aligned}$$

In this case, again, $|I| + |Q| = 2T(A_1 - A_2)$. Therefore, for any $s$, $|I| + |Q| = t(A_1 - A_2)$. Furthermore, for $2N$ chips, the computation result will be $NT(A_1 - A_2)$, independent of synchronization. Finally, if $A_1 = 1, A_2 = 0$ and $T = 1/2$, then $|I| + |Q| = N$.

**B. Proof of Lemma 5.2** Our goal is to prove that a chip sequence with a code rate $R$ is orthogonal to one with a code rate $2NR$ and of chip length $2N$. First, within the time period of one chip with a chip rate $C$, there are $N$ complete alternating zero-one chips corresponding to the chip sequence with a chip rate $2NC$, independent of synchronization. Assuming that $A_1$ and $A_2$ are the amplitudes for bits one and zero, the computation for the 1 chip outputs $N(A_1 - A_2)$ or $-N(A_1 - A_2)$, and $-N(A_1 - A_2)$ or $N(A_1 - A_2)$ for 0 chip. Thus resulting in a sum of 0 when computed over two consecutive chips Similarly, the computation on the $Q$ path will output 0 as well for two consecutive chips. Thus, $|I| + |Q| = 0$ holds for a decoder tuned to chip rate $C$. Next, we look at the decoder for the chip sequence at rate $2NC$ and length $2N$. Within the time period of $2N$ chips at a rate of $2NC$, there is one complete 01 chip sequence corresponding to the chip rate of $C$, thus the correlation computation of $I$ and $Q$ are zero. Thus again $|I| + |Q| = 0$, proving our lemma.

# Geosphere: Consistently Turning MIMO Capacity into Throughput

Konstantinos Nikitopoulos[†] Juan Zhou[‡] Ben Congdon[‡] Kyle Jamieson[‡]

[†]5G Innovation Centre
University of Surrey
k.nikitopoulos@surrey.ac.uk

[‡]Department of Computer Science
University College London
{juan.zhou.12, ben.congdon.11, k.jamieson}@ucl.ac.uk

## ABSTRACT

This paper presents the design and implementation of Geosphere, a physical- and link-layer design for access point-based MIMO wireless networks that consistently improves network throughput. To send multiple streams of data in a MIMO system, prior designs rely on a technique called zero-forcing, a way of "nulling" the interference between data streams by mathematically inverting the wireless channel matrix. In general, zero-forcing is highly effective, significantly improving throughput. But in certain physical situations, the MIMO channel matrix can become "poorly conditioned," harming performance. With these situations in mind, Geosphere uses sphere decoding, a more computationally demanding technique that can achieve higher throughput in such channels. To overcome the sphere decoder's computational complexity when sending dense wireless constellations at a high rate, Geosphere introduces search and pruning techniques that incorporate novel geometric reasoning about the wireless constellation. These techniques reduce computational complexity of 256-QAM systems by almost one order of magnitude, bringing computational demands in line with current 16- and 64-QAM systems already realized in ASIC. Geosphere thus makes the sphere decoder practical for the first time in a $4 \times 4$ MIMO, 256-QAM system. Results from our WARP testbed show that Geosphere achieves throughput gains over multi-user MIMO of $2\times$ in $4 \times 4$ systems and 47% in $2 \times 2$ MIMO systems.

## Categories and Subject Descriptors

C.2.1 [**Network Architecture and Design**]: Wireless communication

## Keywords

MIMO; Distributed MIMO; Sphere Decoder

## 1. INTRODUCTION

One of the most important challenges in modern wireless networks is to meet many users' increasing demands for throughput. One example from the workplace or home is when tens of users are running video telephony sessions, resulting in a high demand for symmetric (uplink and downlink) bandwidth. One way of meeting the demand for more throughput is by a technique called *spatial multiplexing*. Networks that leverage spatial multiplexing increase capacity [58] and throughput by sending multiple data streams from different transmit antennas. If enough receiving antennas hear the resulting mixture of signals and channel conditions are favorable, such systems can deliver the multiple data streams simultaneously, in the same frequency bands and geographical spaces. Since multiple transmit and receive antennas are required, these systems are called *multiple-input, multiple-output* or *MIMO* systems, and are ubiquitous in wireless networks today. The throughput possible in these networks is determined, and thus constrained by, the number of available antennas at the access point (AP).


*SIGCOMM'14,* August 17–22, 2014, Chicago, Illinois, USA.

ACM 978-1-4503-2836-4/14/08 ...$15.00.
http://dx.doi.org/10.1145/2619239.2626301.

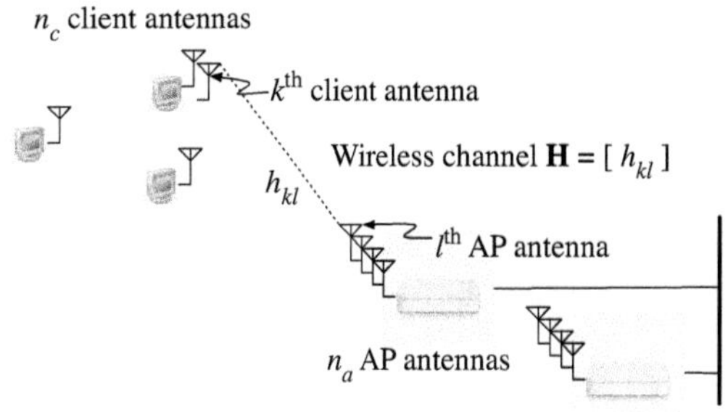


**Figure 1:** A MIMO wireless LAN with $n_c$ client antennas and $n_a$ AP antennas. Different clients and APs may transmit simultaneously, forming a MIMO system described by the channel matrix $\mathbf{H}$, whose entries characterize the wireless channel between a client's antenna and an AP's antenna.

The emergence of new applications for wireless networks such as video internet telephony, data backup, and wearables like Google Glass, is today shifting the ratio between uplink and downlink traffic towards the former. In an uplink multi-user MIMO setting, clients may simply send their own information streams to the access points (APs), which are connected by a wired network backhaul, as shown in Figure 1. While this frees clients from the need to cooperate, each of the $n_a$ receiving access point antennas then hears a mixture ($\mathbf{y}$) of signals sent from all $n_c$ transmit antennas ($\mathbf{x}$), where $\mathbf{y} = \mathbf{Hx} + \mathbf{w}$ with $\mathbf{H}$ being a matrix whose entries describe the channel between each client and AP antenna and $\mathbf{w}$ representing background noise. Then, the *capacity* for a specific signal to noise ratio (SNR) is [59]

$$C = \mathrm{E}\left[\log\det\left(\mathbf{I}_{n_a} + \frac{\mathrm{SNR}}{n_c}\mathbf{HH}^*\right)\right] \text{ bits/s/Hz.}$$

The question this paper considers is how to best turn this theoretical capacity into a practical throughput gain.

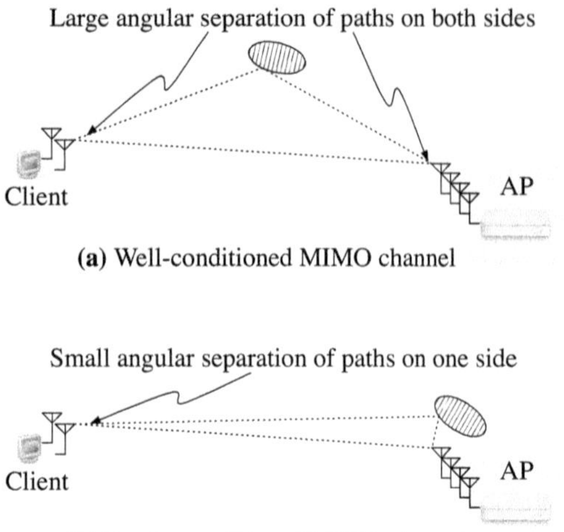


**(a)** Well-conditioned MIMO channel

**(b)** Poorly-conditioned MIMO channel

**Figure 2:** When reflectors are located solely in the vicinity of one of the endpoints of a MIMO link, the result is a very small angular separation of the energy arriving at the other end, and a poorly-conditioned channel matrix **H**.

The most frequent answer to this question is a demodulation scheme known as *zero-forcing*. In order to decouple interfering streams a zero-forcing receiver left-multiplies the received vector **y** with the inverse of matrix **H**, denoted $\mathbf{H}^{-1}$:

$$\mathbf{H}^{-1}\mathbf{y} = \mathbf{H}^{-1}\mathbf{H}\mathbf{x} + \mathbf{H}^{-1}\mathbf{w} = \mathbf{x} + \mathbf{H}^{-1}\mathbf{w}$$

Zero-forcing has been proposed as part of a way to accomplish spatial division multiplexing in SAM [56] and BigStation [67], null out aligned interference in IAC [21], and enable concurrent 802.11n transmissions in 802.11n$^+$ [35]. Together with a strategy for choosing which users will transmit together (*user selection*), it works well in these systems, achieving multiplicative increases in throughput, in line with expectations. But can spatial multiplexing systems achieve even greater throughput?

The *condition number* of **H**, $\kappa(\mathbf{H})$, answers this question in the positive. The condition number is a well-known metric from numeric linear algebra that measures the sensitivity of the system **H** to noise [33]. When the wireless channel to the access point is favorable as shown in Figure 2(a), the matrix **H** is well-conditioned (small $\kappa(\mathbf{H})$), and the noise term $\mathbf{H}^{-1}\mathbf{w}$ above is small. But when reflectors are located solely in the vicinity of one of the endpoints as shown in Figure 2(b), $\kappa(\mathbf{H})$ becomes large [59], and its matrix determinant small. Under these conditions, when a zero-forcing receiver multiplies what it hears by the inverted channel, it amplifies background noise and interference **w**, leading to bit errors and decreased throughput [12, 49].

While the theory above is well-established, the following open experimental question immediately arises. How often is the indoor MIMO channel poorly-conditioned? An experimental characterization of our indoor wireless testbed (§5.1) and prior experimental wireless studies outdoors [32] both show that zero-forcing systems will experience an SNR reduction of 10 dB on approximately 20% of $2 \times 2$ MIMO channels and one half of all $4 \times 4$ MIMO channels, causing a significant throughput decrease.

This paper presents the design, implementation, and evaluation of *Geosphere*, a system that closes the capacity gap that zero-forcing's noise amplification opens. Geosphere uses the *sphere decoder*, a decoder that returns the theoretical maximum-likelihood solution (*i.e.*, the one that minimizes the probability of detection errors).

The next section contains a primer on the sphere decoder, but in brief, the sphere decoder dramatically reduces the exponential (in terms of message length) asymptotic complexity of the maximum likelihood decoder by means of a tree search, and so is just now becoming practical for real systems. For example, in 2005, a $4 \times 4$ MIMO 16-QAM ASIC implementation achieved line rate over a 10 MHz frequency bandwidth [10], and then in 2012, a $4 \times 4$ MIMO 64-QAM ASIC implementation achieved 4G LTE line rates [64].

While the sphere decoder is practical today at the above rates, the search for higher throughputs is driving the use of even denser signal constellations. For example, 802.11ac devices already use 128- and 256-QAM constellations. Denser constellations are also prerequisite for adopting the promising new family of rateless codes [23, 42]. However, the challenge in adopting even denser constellations is that the sphere decoder's tree search has a branching factor equal to the size of the wireless constellation. This means that denser constellations necessitate a larger search space, with a corresponding increase in computation, overwhelming even the current state-of-the-art implementations mentioned above.[1] The challenge we tackle in this paper is to devise new tree traversal and tree pruning strategies that reduce the computational complexity the sphere decoder requires even with very dense constellations.

**Paper contributions.** Geosphere is a system for both multi-user and traditional[2] MIMO that incorporates two novel ways of reasoning about the geometry of signal constellations into the sphere decoder. Geosphere first: (a) contributes a new algorithm for determining the sphere decoder's search order (§3.1.1) and second (b) introduces a very efficient algorithm to prune the sphere decoder's search (§3.2) process, without sacrificing throughput. Geosphere is, to the best of our knowledge, the first system that makes $4 \times 4$ MIMO, 256-QAM communication practical. The paper also contributes the first, to our knowledge, rigorous experimental measurements of the conditioning of indoor MIMO wireless channels (§5.1).

**Roadmap.** We begin with a primer on sphere decoding (§2), setting up our subsequent discussion of Geosphere's design (§3). A performance evaluation follows, where we measure Geosphere's performance in trace-driven simulation, using wireless traces from a 15-node wireless testbed built with Rice WARP version 3 radios [43]. Here we show that Geosphere achieves substantial throughput gains over systems employing a combination of either zero-forcing or minimum mean-squared error successive interference cancellation (MMSE-SIC) decoding and user selection, and that in spatial-division multiplexing systems where many single-antenna clients transmit at the same time, Geosphere increases the per-user throughput. Results from our testbed show that Geosphere achieves average throughput gains of $2\times$ in $4 \times 4$ MIMO systems and 47% in $2 \times 2$ systems, while simultaneously requiring close to an order of magnitude less computation relative to the best known sphere decoder, bringing its computational demands in line with current systems already realized in ASIC and making SDR implementation possible. We then survey related work (§6) and conclude (§7).

## 2. PRIMER: THE SPHERE DECODER

This section provides essential background on the sphere decoder [2, 17], an algorithm able to determine the most-likely transmitted bits **x**

[1] For a $4 \times 4$ MIMO, 16-QAM system the sphere decoding tree has $6.6 \times 10^4$ nodes, while for 256-QAM it has $4.3 \times 10^9$ nodes.

[2] Geosphere also applies to the downlink, when both the AP and a single client are equipped with multiple antennas (*e.g.*, smart TVs).

in the MIMO system. Supposing transmitters send symbols chosen from a constellation $\mathcal{O}$ of size $|\mathcal{O}| = 2^Q$ (*i.e.*, $Q$ bits per symbol), such a solution, called the *maximum-likelihood* solution, finds

$$\mathbf{x}^* = \arg\min_{\mathbf{s}\in\mathcal{O}^{n_c}} \|\mathbf{y} - \mathbf{H}\mathbf{s}\|^2. \tag{1}$$

This is the solution that minimizes detection errors and therefore maximizes throughput. Unfortunately, the computational complexity of the exhaustive search in Equation 1 grows exponentially both in the message length and in the constellation size. For example, if we were to attempt to find the maximum-likelihood solution by exhaustive search, we would need to perform $|\mathcal{O}|^{n_c}$ Euclidean distance calculations. This means that for an OFDM system with 48 data sub-carriers, four antennas and a 4-QAM constellation, we would need to calculate approximately $10^4$ Euclidean distances, but in the same system sending with 64-QAM, we would need approximately $10^9$ distance calculations. Sphere decoding reduces this complexity while still finding the maximum-likelihood solution.

## 2.1 The sphere constraint

The sphere decoder constrains its search to only those possibilities $\mathbf{s}$ that lie within a hypersphere of radius $r$ about the received vector $\mathbf{y}$, as measured by the *Euclidean distance* $d(\mathbf{s})$. This is the *sphere constraint*:

$$d(\mathbf{s}) < r^2, \text{where } d(\mathbf{s}) = \|\mathbf{y} - \mathbf{H}\mathbf{s}\|^2. \tag{2}$$

Most sphere decoders begin with $r \leftarrow \infty$, and on finding a solution at distance $r' < r$ can safely set $r$ to $r'$ without the possibility of excluding the maximum-likelihood solution.

## 2.2 The tree

The sphere decoder recasts the maximum-likelihood problem (Equation 1) into a search in a tree of height $n_c$ (number of client antennas) and branching factor $|\mathcal{O}|$ (constellation size). Figure 3 shows an example for $n_c = 3$ and QPSK ($|\mathcal{O}| = 4$) to which we will subsequently refer. Each level $l$ of the tree corresponds to a decision on the value of the transmitted symbols from antennas $l$ through $n_c$, which we will term a *partial symbol vector* $\mathbf{s}^{(l)} = [s_l, s_{l+1}, \ldots, s_{n_c}]$. Formulating the problem as a tree search requires the channel matrix $\mathbf{H}$ to be triangularized using a QR decomposition [53] into $\mathbf{H} = \mathbf{QR}$, where $\mathbf{Q}$ (of dimension $n_a \times n_c$) has the property that $\mathbf{Q}^*\mathbf{Q} = \mathbf{I}$ and $\mathbf{R} = [r_{ij}]$ (of dimension $n_c \times n_c$) is *upper-triangular* (*i.e.*, has zeroes below its diagonal). We can then rewrite the received signal as

$$\widehat{\mathbf{y}} = \mathbf{R}\mathbf{s} + \mathbf{Q}^*\mathbf{w}, \text{where } \widehat{\mathbf{y}} = \mathbf{Q}^*\mathbf{y}, \tag{3}$$

and the Euclidean distances $d(\mathbf{s})$ as

$$d(\mathbf{s}) = K + \|\widehat{\mathbf{y}} - \mathbf{R}\mathbf{s}\|^2. \tag{4}$$

where $K$ is an independent constant that can be safely ignored. Since $\mathbf{R}$ is upper-triangular, we can now calculate *partial Euclidean distances* for the partial symbol vectors, starting at the top of the tree at level $n_c$. We label each branch in the tree with a non-negative *branch cost*

$$c(\mathbf{s}^{(l)}) = \left| \widehat{y}_l - \sum_{j=l}^{n_c} r_{lj} s_j \right|^2. \tag{5}$$

As we walk down the tree from the root, selecting a branch at level $l$ prepends a new symbol $s_l$ to $\mathbf{s}^{(l+1)}$, where $\mathbf{s}^{(l+1)}$ is the tentative solution constructed up to the level above. We calculate the partial Euclidean distance for all $\mathbf{s}^{(l)}$ as

$$d(\mathbf{s}^{(l)}) = d(\mathbf{s}^{(l+1)}) + c(\mathbf{s}^{(i)}). \tag{6}$$

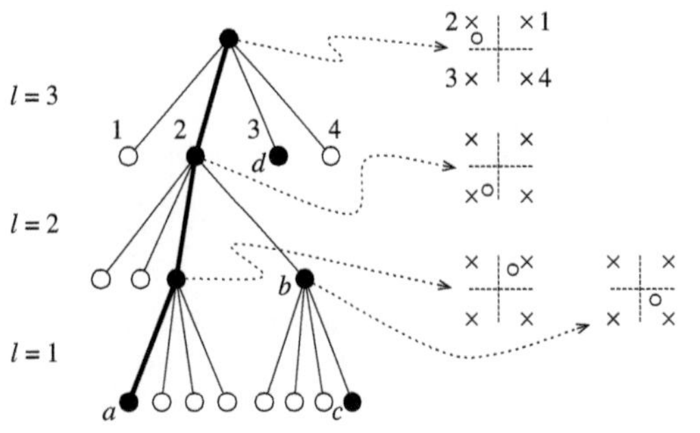


**Figure 3:** The sphere decoder operating on $n_c = 3$ transmit antennas, each sending a QPSK ($|\mathcal{O}| = 4$) symbol. Constellation points (denoted $\times$) and corresponding branches of the tree are numbered at the uppermost level ($l = 3$), and the received signal is denoted $\circ$. Visited nodes are colored black.

Since the branch cost is non-negative, the sphere decoder *prunes* all children below partial symbol $\mathbf{s}^{(l)}$ if

$$d(\mathbf{s}^{(l)}) \geq r^2, \tag{7}$$

as they will violate the sphere constraint. This pruning greatly reduces the number of solutions the sphere decoder needs to consider, but notice that further efficiencies are possible if we visit solutions closest to the maximum-likelihood solution earlier in our search. The efficiency of the sphere detector is thus to a large part determined by the tree-traversal strategy.

## 2.3 Traversing the tree

We begin with a depth-first tree-traversal strategy, as it is the approach we take in Geosphere for reasons that will become clear later. A refinement of a textbook depth-first tree traversal is to visit children of a tree node in ascending order of their partial Euclidean distances, an idea known as *Schnorr-Euchner* enumeration [46] after its inventors.

Continuing our example of Figure 3, conventional Schnorr-Euchner sphere decoders will first greedily follow the path to a leaf $a$ that minimizes partial Euclidean distance at each level (this path's branches are shown with thick lines in the figure). This entails computing distances for this path as well as all sibling nodes along the path (all nodes in this diagram). Upon reaching $a$, the decoder sets its sphere radius to $d(a)$ and backtracks up one level to check the node whose distance is second-closest, $b$. Let's assume that $d(b) < d(a)$; this means that the sphere decoder needs to expand $b$, search its children, and find the one with minimum distance ($c$). Once this is finished, the decoder backtracks up one level again to $l = 3$ and considers node $d$. Now $d(d) \geq d(a)$, so none of $d$'s children or siblings (note that the nodes are sorted) could possibly be the maximum-likelihood solution, so the sphere decoder terminates and returns $a$ as the maximum-likelihood solution.

It is clear that this pruning reduces the number of visited nodes, but reducing the number of visited nodes does not necessarily reduce processing requirements. In particular, the sorting requirement of Schnorr-Euchner enumeration is very computationally expensive for higher-order constellations (*e.g.*, 16- and 64-QAM), and can therefore compromise the sphere decoder's efficiency. In the foregoing example, in order to determine the node to visit we have fully enumerated and sorted all possibilities when we visited a node not violating the sphere constraint. This entails, at each step, calculating partial Euclidean distances for all possible children and then sorting

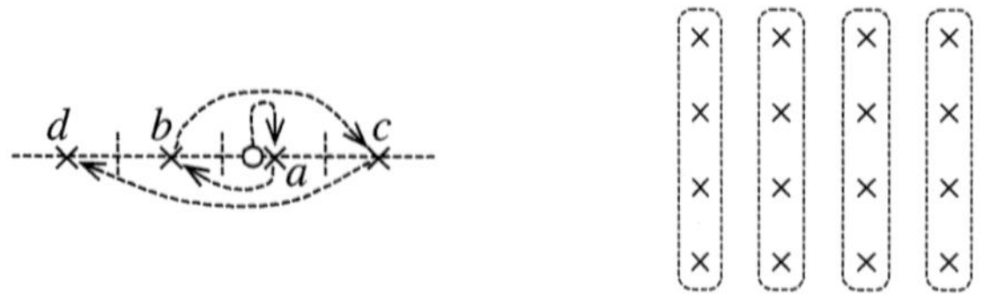


**Figure 4:** *Left:* The zigzag technique in a one-dimensional (PAM) constellation visits constellation points ($\times$) in increasing distance from the received symbol ($\circ$). *Right:* Dividing a 16-QAM constellation into four 4-PAM subconstellations.

them, a highly inefficient process, since we will spend processing power calculating distances for many nodes that we will never need to expand.

## 3. DESIGN

This section presents the design of Geosphere, starting from the enumeration technique we use in order to efficiently sort children of a node in the sphere decoder (§3.1), and continuing to describe an improved, novel, pruning technique (§3.2). Later (§5), we experimentally evaluate the relative gains of each to highlight the different roles the two techniques play under varying channel conditions.

### 3.1 Constellation point enumeration

The goal of Geosphere's enumeration technique is to determine the order that the sphere decoder should explore the set of constellation points $\mathcal{O}$, when it is considering which branch to expand at a particular node in the tree shown in Figure 3. We wish to explore constellation points in order of increasing branch cost, but the only soft information at our disposal is the received symbol.

However, since constellation distance is related to partial Euclidean distance by

$$c\left(\mathbf{s}^{(l)}\right) = |r_{ll}|^2 \left|\widetilde{\mathbf{y}}_l - s_l\right|^2 \qquad (8)$$

(where $\widetilde{\mathbf{y}}_l = \frac{\hat{y}_l - \sum_{j=l+1}^{n_c} r_{lj} s_j}{r_{ll}}$), it suffices to explore the constellation points in increasing Euclidean distance from the received symbol in the constellation itself, rather than as measured indirectly by the partial Euclidean distance metric.

If we were sending constellation points in one dimension (this is known as *pulse-amplitude modulation*, or *PAM*), the task is substantially easier, so we discuss this case first. Figure 4 *(left)* shows a PAM constellation comprised of four constellation points ($\times$) and a received symbol ($\circ$). To find the closest constellation point to the received symbol we compare the received symbol against the decision boundaries indicated by the vertical dotted lines in the figure (this procedure is called *slicing* the received symbol), and therefore order constellation point *(a)* first. The zigzag rule tells us to visit the next closest, unvisited constellation point from *(a)* in the direction of the received symbol; this is *(b)* in the figure. Subsequent applications of the same rule take us to *(c)* and then *(d)*.

#### *3.1.1 Two-dimensional zigzag enumeration*

Now let's consider the two-dimensional case. We are in fact seeking an approximation of an expanding ring search, starting at an arbitrary, continuous-valued received symbol point $\circ$. One inexact way of accomplishing this would be to partition the QAM constellation into PAM subconstellations as shown in Figure 4 *(left)*, and then zigzag "vertically" within each subconstellation. But this approach neglects the *in-phase* component of the received symbol.

**Algorithm (two-dimensional zigzag)**

1. Initialize a sorted priority queue $Q = \emptyset$, comprising constellation points (maintain $Q$ sorted by Euclidean distance to $\circ$ at all times).
2. Find the closest constellation point $a$ to the received symbol by slicing $\circ$ on the constellation's decision boundaries. constellation's decision boundaries). Calculate $a$'s Euclidean distance and enqueue $a \to Q$.
3. Dequeue $Q \to x$ and explore $x$'s children in the sphere decoder.
   (a) Zigzag vertically from $x$ with respect to $\circ$: call the result $z_v$. Calculate $z_v$'s Euclidean distance to $\circ$ and enqueue $z_v \to Q$.
   (b) Zigzag horizontally from $x$ with respect to $\circ$; call the result $z_h$. If no other constellation point in $z_h$'s PAM subconstellation is in $Q$, calculate $z_h$'s Euclidean distance to $\circ$ and enqueue $z_h \to Q$.
4. Go to Step 3.

**Figure 5:** Two-dimensional zigzag algorithm pseudocode.

So instead Geosphere first slices the received symbol to find the closest constellation point (call it $a$), and begins the two-dimensional zigzag from that exact constellation point. Note that the sphere decoder will then expand the branch corresponding to $a$ and search that subtree. Once the sphere decoder returns to the node whose constellation points we are sorting, should we zigzag horizontally or vertically? We try both, since we are trying to find the next-closest constellation point in (two-dimensional) Euclidean distance, with the exception that we avoid a horizontal zigzag if a constellation point from the target PAM subconstellation is already in our list of outstanding constellation points to explore. This ensures that we have at most one candidate constellation point per (vertical) PAM subconstellation.

Figure 5 shows the pseudocode for the algorithm. Notice that as a consequence of the two-dimensional zigzag rule, the algorithm needs a priority queue of length at most $\sqrt{|\mathcal{O}|}$. By only taking zigzag steps one constellation point at a time, the algorithm defers the Euclidean distance computation until as late as possible, often by which time the sphere decoder has pruned the relevant subtree (we demonstrate this later in the experimental evaluation).

**Example.** Figure 6 shows an example of the two-dimensional zigzag algorithm working in a 16-QAM constellation. In each frame, we show the 16-QAM constellation points ($\times$) alongside the received symbol ($\circ$), above the priority queue $Q$. In Step *(i)*, the slicer finds the closest constellation point to the received symbol, $a$. The sphere decoder explores $a$, zigzags vertically and horizontally, and enqueues $b$ and $c$, respectively in Step *(ii)*. Since $b$ is closer of $b$ and $c$ to $\circ$, in Step *(iii)* the algorithm explores and zigzags from $b$. But notice that a horizontal zigzag step from $b$ to $e$ would land in the same PAM subconstellation as a previously-explored constellation point ($c$). Consequently, we only zigzag vertically from $b$, enqueuing $d$. In Step *(iv)*, we explore and zigzag from $c$, picking up $e$ and visiting all four constellation points surrounding the received symbol (the closest to $\circ$) in Step *(v)*. Subsequent steps continue in the same manner, filling in the "expanding ring."

### 3.2 Geometrical pruning

We now turn to Geosphere's approach to pruning off whole sections of the sphere decoder's search tree, a key step in making the search process tractable in practice.

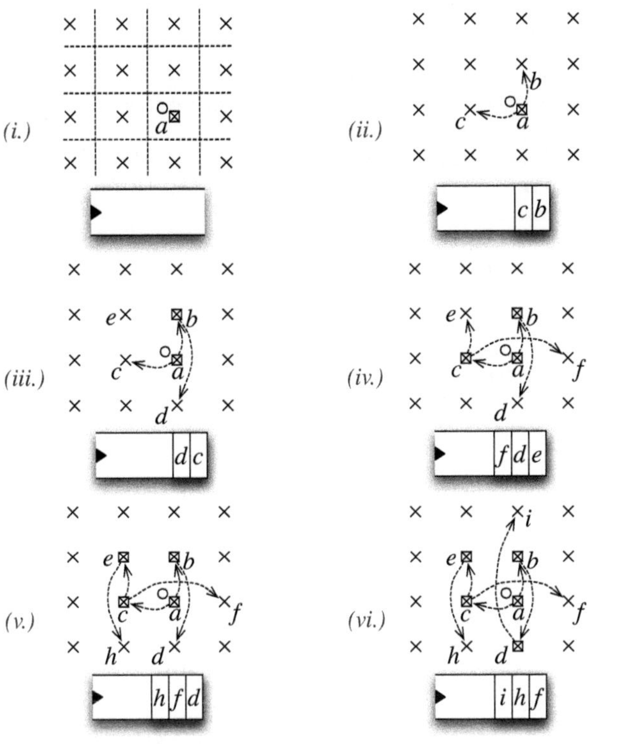


**Figure 6:** Geosphere's two-dimensional zigzag enumeration in the 16-QAM constellation. We denote constellation points $\times$, label points whose partial Euclidean distances have been computed, and denote points that have been explored ⊠.

Suppose that the sphere decoder has identified a currently-best candidate node $a$ (referring to Figure 7) somewhere in the tree, and now keeps track of the associated partial Euclidean distance $d(a)$. Recall from Section 2 that when the sphere decoder visits node $x$ elsewhere in the tree it considers whether or not to prune each branch emanating from $x$. The most straightforward way of doing this is to evaluate the exact branch cost $c\left(\mathbf{s}^l\right)$ for each, but this requires two multiplication operations and an addition.

Geosphere instead uses the constellation's geometry to establish a lower-bound on the exact branch cost, as shown in Figure 7. If the constellation point corresponding to the branch being tested is offset from the nearest constellation point by $d_I$ horizontally and $d_Q$ vertically, Geosphere computes

$$\hat{c}\left(\mathbf{s}^l\right) = \sqrt{(2d_I - 1)^2 + (2d_Q - 1)^2} \tag{9}$$

based on a fast table lookup indexed on $|d_I|$ and $|d_Q|$ and uses $\hat{c}(\cdot)$ instead of $c(\cdot)$ in its pruning decision. Since $\hat{c}(\cdot) \leq c(\cdot)$, pruning based on Equation (9) alone doesn't exclude the maximum-likelihood solution, but may expand more branches than pruning based on exact branch costs. Thus, if geometrical pruning fails to exclude a branch, we calculate the branch's exact cost and attempt to exclude the branch on that basis.

# 4. IMPLEMENTATION

We implement Geosphere on Rice WARP v3 radio hardware and WARPLab software. Using WARPLab, we implement OFDM modulation and demodulation using 4-, 16- and 64-QAM constellations. All clients send data using 1/2-rate convolutional coding (similar to recent 802.11 standards), and transmitted packets are limited in size to 500 Kbytes due to restrictions on the maximum packet size that WARPLab can handle.

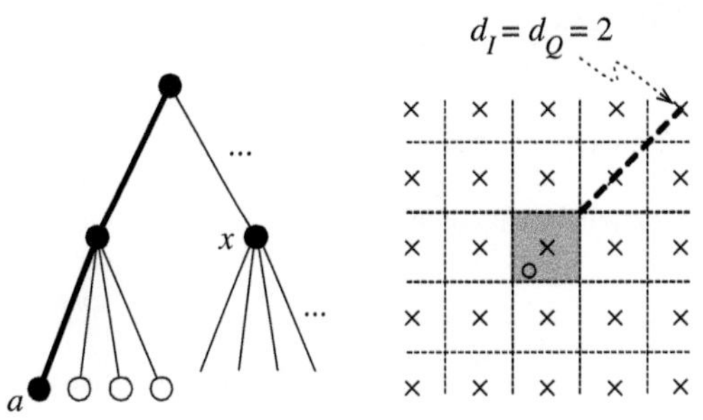


**Figure 7:** Geometrically lower-bounding the distance between received symbol $\circ$ and another constellation point at horizontal ($d_I$) and vertical ($d_Q$) offset two from the closest constellation point. Constellation points are spaced two units apart.

# 5. EVALUATION

In this section we measure Geosphere's throughput performance gains and computational complexity requirements in real indoor office conditions. First, we show that the indoor wireless channel is often quite poorly-conditioned, and that zero forcing-based techniques are leaving performance on the table. Then, in terms of throughput, we compare Geosphere with zero-forcing systems that attempt to intelligently adapt to poorly-conditioned MIMO channels by varying the number of antennas and spatial streams they use. Finally, we evaluate Geosphere's computational complexity, comparing it with the well established ETH depth-first sphere decoder [10], one the few efficient sphere decoders able to achieve maximum-likelihood performance. Table 1 summarizes the experimental results presented here.

**Testbed setup.** Our testbed consists of single-antenna clients and four-antenna APs, communicating over a 20 MHz wireless channel in the 5 GHz ISM band. The distance between consecutive AP antennas is about 20 cm (approximately $3.2\lambda$, where $\lambda$ is the wireless wavelength) so that the wireless channels from each AP antenna to a client are uncorrelated with each other, and so representative of antenna spacings above $\lambda$ indoors at 5 GHz [31].

We evaluate Geosphere in actual office conditions: Figure 8 shows the testbed environment, including the places we position APs and clients. Note that the topology includes both line-of-sight and non-line-of-sight paths due to furniture and people, but also due to transmissions penetrating through and reflecting off walls.

## 5.1 Channel characterization

As we mention above (§1), when the channel is well-conditioned, zero-forcing is a very efficient way to demultiplex the interfering streams. So, the experimental question that naturally arises is whether the channels we face in an indoor environment are typically well-conditioned. Or equivalently, is there throughput on the table for Geosphere?

**Methodology.** To answer this question we measure the MIMO channels corresponding to several concurrently transmitted streams across all OFDM subcarriers (*i.e.* on slightly different frequencies), and for many different positions of the clients and APs. Figure 8 shows their positions, with hollow circles and red triangles denoting client positions in this experiment, and squares denoting APs.

| Experiment | Section | Conclusion |
|---|---|---|
| Channel characterization | §5.1 | $2 \times 2$ indoor MIMO channels are poorly-conditioned 60% of the time; $4 \times 4$ indoor MIMO channels are almost always poorly-conditioned. |
| Throughput comparison | §5.2 | Geosphere achieves 2× throughput gains over multi-user MIMO for four AP antennas and four clients, (47% gain in the $2 \times 2$ case.) |
| Computational complexity | §5.3 | Geosphere reduces the required computation for the sphere decoder by nearly one order of magnitude over the ETH-SD sphere decoder ([25], *cf.* §5.3), making the sphere decoder practical for dense constellations. |

**Table 1:** A summary of the major experimental results in this paper.

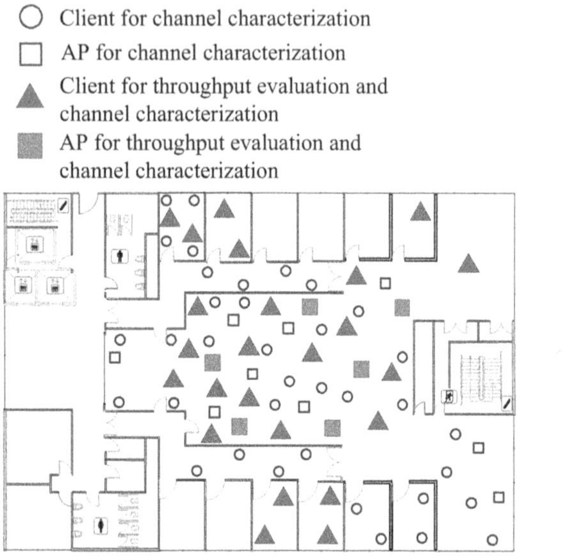


**Figure 8:** Floor plan of the office space housing the wireless testbed used in Geosphere's experimental evaluation.

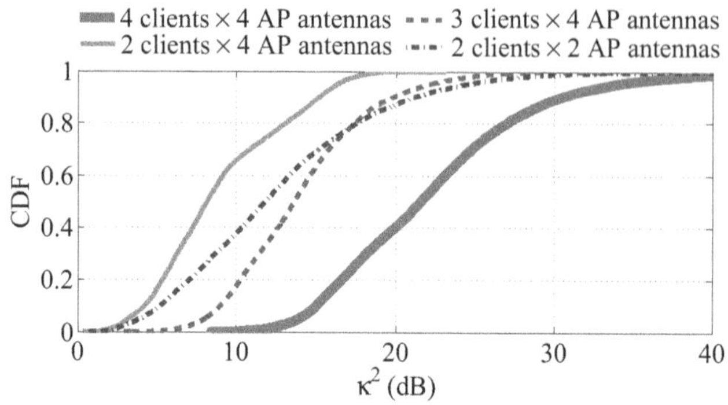


**Figure 9:** Cumulative distribution across testbed links, OFDM subcarriers, and spatial streams of $\kappa^2$ (decibels), the power of the MIMO channel condition number. Higher values of $\kappa^2$ indicate worse channel conditioning.

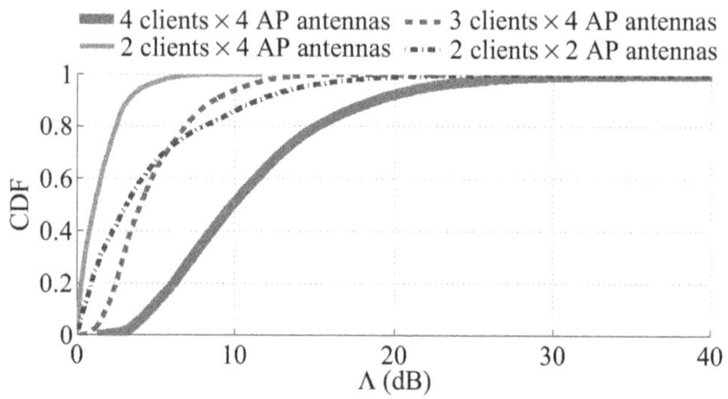


**Figure 10:** Cumulative distribution across testbed links and OFDM subcarriers of $\Lambda$, the SNR ratio degradation that the most-degraded user experiences for each particular link.

In order to characterize the channel we will use two metrics. The first is the square of the condition number $\kappa^2(\mathbf{H})$ which is a good upper-bound on the actual noise amplification due to zero-forcing [33]. However, this metric doesn't necessarily provide us with the actual performance difference between a zero-forcing system and one that uses a maximum-likelihood detector like Geosphere.

The metric of most interest is the signal-to-noise ratio (SNR) of the $k^{th}$ transmitted stream after being transmitted over the MIMO channel $\mathbf{H}$: $\frac{[\mathbf{H}^*\mathbf{H}]_{k,k}}{2\sigma^2}$. The SNR of the same stream after zero-forcing can be shown to be $\frac{1}{[(\mathbf{H}^*\mathbf{H})^{-1}]_{k,k}2\sigma^2}$. Thus, the SNR degradation for stream $k$ is $\lambda_k = \frac{[\mathbf{H}^*\mathbf{H}]_{k,k}}{[(\mathbf{H}^*\mathbf{H})^{-1}]_{k,k}}$.

We are interested in limiting the damage done to any particular user, and so we define our figure of merit $\Lambda$ to be the maximum over $\lambda_k$. In other words, $\Lambda$ denotes the worst (over clients) SNR degradation due to zero-forcing noise amplification.

**Results.** In Figure 9 and Figure 10 we show the cumulative distributions of $\kappa^2$ and $\Lambda$ respectively, partitioned by different numbers of clients and receive antennas at the AP. In the two-client, two receive antenna case (*i.e.*, $2 \times 2$), 60% of the links experience channels with condition numbers larger than 10 dB while in the $4 \times 4$ case, nearly all links are poorly conditioned.

To characterize the links in terms of the maximum SNR degradation that any particular user sees we refer to the cumulative distributions of $\Lambda$ (Figure 10). We observe that the use of zero-forcing will result in 30% of the MIMO channels experiencing an SNR degradation of more than 5 dB, while 90% of the channels will face such a degradation for $4 \times 4$ links. This shows that there are a significant number of situations where Geosphere can substantially increase throughput, especially when simultaneously serving more clients (increasing both the clients and receive antennas) as systems such as BigStation [67] do. From Figures 9 and 10, we also see that if we fix the number of receive antennas to a large number (*e.g.* four), we can achieve a better-conditioned channel by decreasing the number of clients transmitting simultaneously. For example, referring to the "2 clients × 4 AP antennas" curve in Figure 10, if only two clients transmit, the maximum degradation due to zero-forcing will be less than three decibels for 90% of the channels. That means we could sacrifice concurrency to reduce the degradation due to zero-forcing.

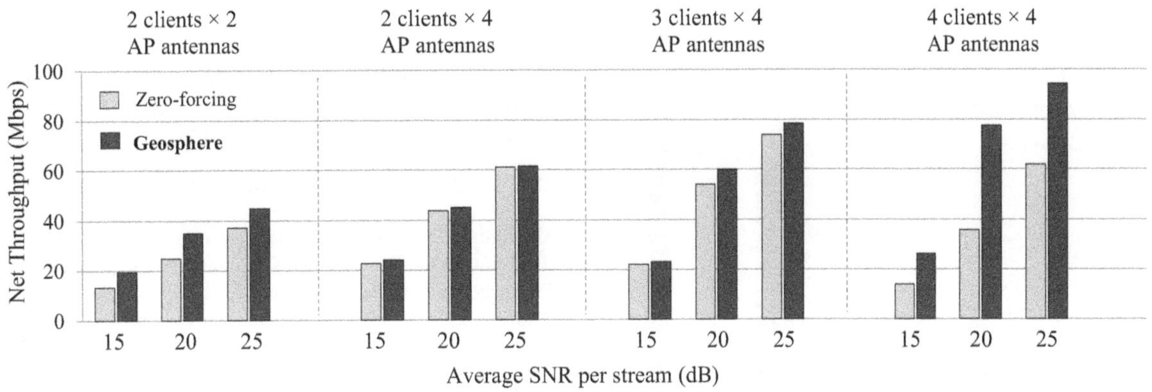


**Figure 11:** Experimental testbed throughput comparison between zero-forcing MIMO and Geosphere for different numbers of clients, number of AP antennas and SNRs.

Would this be a net benefit to throughput? We next examine this question in close detail.

## 5.2 System throughput

We now measure the uplink throughput that zero-forcing serving a network of clients, in comparison with Geosphere. The previous discussion shows that due to characteristics of the channel there is an opportunity for throughput improvement; we now test whether Geosphere can realize these gains in practice.

**Methodology.** We position clients and APs in a subset of the positions used for channel measurements, denoted by hollow circles and hollow squares respectively in Figure 8. We send data to the APs using various modulations to characterize performance at different transmission rates: we transmit 4-, 16- and 64-QAM constellations. We note that the channel is changing due to people walking nearby. We also note that for this subset of positions the condition number and the $\Lambda$ values of the links are smaller than those when all positions are included. Therefore, we are evaluating here a particularly challenging case for Geosphere.

We consider three SNR ranges, 15 dB $\pm$5 dB, 20 dB $\pm$ 5 dB, and 25 dB $\pm$5 dB, where the quoted SNR is the average SNR over all transmitted streams. Selecting users in a small SNR range around a specific value is a practical user selection method to keep the condition number small. Larger gains are expected for Geosphere's if the users are selected randomly. In addition, in lieu of implementing a rate adaptation algorithm, we show throughput results for the constellation that achieves the best average throughput for the corresponding range; this emulates ideal bit rate adaptation and makes the results independent of the rate adaptation method employed.

**Results.** In Figure 11 we show achieved throughput for different numbers of clients and receive antennas. We can see that Geosphere consistently provides better throughput than zero-forcing. Moreover, as expected, Geosphere's throughput gains increase with the condition number and $\Lambda$. In particular, for the $2 \times 2$ case, Geosphere can provide a throughput increase of up to 47%, while for the $4 \times 4$ case it can be more than two times faster.

Even in the most challenging case of two and three clients and an AP with four receive antennas (where channels are most often well-conditioned) Geosphere provides average gains of 6%. These throughput gains are consistent with what we expect from our channel characterization.

Since the condition number of a matrix becomes smaller with decreasing numbers of concurrently transmitting clients, another question we may ask is whether zero-forcing and an appropriate time-division scheduling strategy could equal Geosphere's performance, with fewer clients per timeslot. But Figure 11 shows that this is not in fact true. Geosphere with four clients and four receive antennas consistently provides better performance than a zero-forcing scheme which three transmitting clients, with throughput gains that can be up to 36% (at 20 dB SNR).

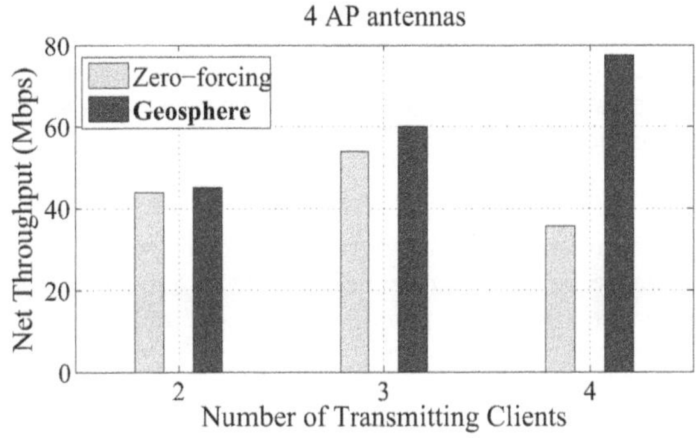


**Figure 12:** Experimental testbed throughput comparison between zero-forcing MIMO and Geosphere for different numbers of users accessing a four-antenna AP at the same time, at 20 dB SNR.

Figure 12 shows the achievable uplink throughput of zero-forcing and Geosphere for a four-antenna AP when we increase the number of clients at 20 dB. We see Geosphere achieves linear gains in throughput with the number of clients while zero-forcing does not. Therefore, with Geosphere we can increase the number of clients while keeping the throughput of each client unaffected, which is not feasible with zero-forcing.

### 5.2.1 *Comparison with MMSE-SIC detection*

The same effect can be seen in Figure 13, where we simulate a ten-antenna AP with different numbers of clients, again at 20 dB SNR. In these experiments we also consider MMSE-SIC receiver processing which orders users by descending SNR, then performs MMSE detection and interference cancellation successively for each user, an approach known to be capable of reaching multi-user capacity [59].

In Figure 13 we see that as long as we operate far from the maximum achievable throughput and only a limited number of clients are transmitting, all methods have similar performance. However,

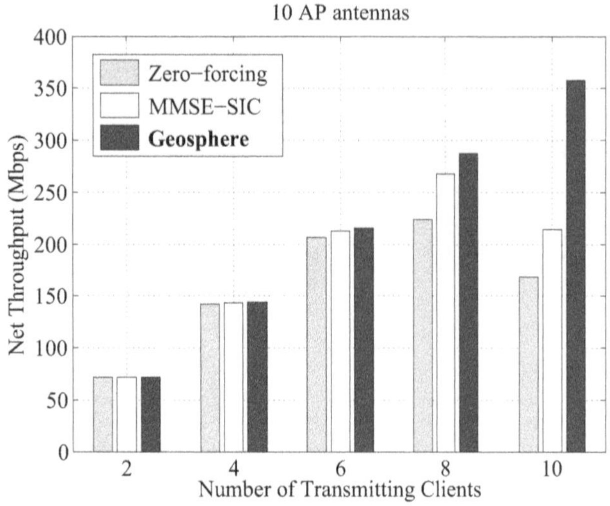


**Figure 13:** Simulation-based throughput comparison between zero-forcing MIMO, MMSE-SIC and Geosphere for different numbers of users accessing a ten-antenna AP at the same time over a Rayleigh fading channel.

for numbers of clients similar to the number of antennas, where the throughput becomes maximum, the performance difference between Geosphere and the other approaches increases, and Geosphere is almost two times faster for the $10 \times 10$ case.[3] We can also see that MMSE-SIC significantly outperforms zero-forcing, but despite its good information theoretical properties, in practice, it cannot optimize throughput due to error-propagation. In addition, SIC methods have a significant drawback compared to zero-forcing and Geosphere that limit their practicality. The decoding of the different users needs to be performed sequentially which linearly increases decoding latency.

## 5.3 Computational complexity

We now quantify the computation Geosphere requires. To this end, we compare Geosphere against the most efficient known depth-first sphere decoder implementation able to achieve maximum-likelihood performance; we denote this system *ETH-SD* in the following experimental results.

We base our implementation of ETH-SD on the VLSI implementation of Burg *et al.* [10], but instead of decomposing the constellation into a set of constant-amplitude phase-shift keying subconstellations as they do, we use the superior method of Hess *et al.* [25]. To determine the node to visit next, Hess' method splits the QAM constellation into horizontal subconstellations, performs an one-dimensional zigzag, and then compares Euclidean distances across all subconstellations. This approach is more efficient since for dense constellations it involves partitioning into fewer sub-constellations, hence is a more challenging comparison design point for Geosphere.

One frequently-used measure of computational complexity in the literature is the number of visited nodes in the sphere decoder tree. However since Geosphere performs some additional computation to avoid visiting nodes, we require a metric that captures this additional computation. Since the dominant part of the additional computation is partial Euclidean distance calculations, this metric tracks overall complexity accurately, and so we primarily use this metric in our evaluation, as is also common in the literature [40]. For completeness and additional insight into why Geosphere improves performance, we also report number of visited nodes.

Since in an OFDM system, MIMO processing takes place on a per subcarrier basis, we report the preceding metrics as needed per subcarrier, averaged across all subcarriers.

### *5.3.1 Testbed-based complexity evaluation*

**Methodology.** First we compare the complexity of Geosphere and ETH-SD for the live testbed experiments of the previous subsection. These complexity results measure the corresponding amount of computation required to obtain the throughput results we show in Figure 11.

**Results.** In Figure 14 we show the average number of partial Euclidean distance calculations for all experiments. We see that Geosphere is consistently less computationally demanding than ETH-SD, and the gains increase when SNR increases, due to fact that Geosphere is more efficient in dense constellations. In the 25 dB range, our computational savings can be up to 63%.

As noted above, the throughput gains of Geosphere are modest for well-conditioned channels. One might therefore be tempted to argue in favor of a system that switches back to zero-forcing when faced with a well-conditioned wireless channel. However, the above results show that Geosphere actually adjusts its computational complexity to the current SNR, and so complexity at high SNR is actually very small, obviating the need for a hybrid system.

### *5.3.2 Simulation-based complexity evaluation*

We now quantify the computation Geosphere requires with the purpose of convincing the reader that our system can achieve 256-QAM, $4 \times 4$ MIMO performance with a computational demand on par with 64-QAM sphere decoders currently implemented in ASIC. We also break down the complexity of each of Geosphere's two main components: two-dimensional zigzag enumeration (§3.1.1), and geometrical pruning (§3.2).

**Methodology.** Since the WARP platform's analog front end limits it to a maximum SNR of approximately 30 dB over the links in our testbed, for the following computational complexity experiments we perform simulations. To analyze the source of Geosphere's gains, we run the following two variants of our system:

1. *2D zigzag only*: Geosphere, running two-dimensional zigzag enumeration sorting without geometrical pruning.
2. *Full*: Geosphere's full design, including two-dimensional zigzag enumeration sorting and geometrical pruning.

We present both ***(a)*** trace-based simulation, driven by empirical MIMO channel measurements collected from our WARP testbed, and ***(b)*** simulation over a MIMO Rayleigh fading channel with independent, identically-distributed channel realizations sampled on a per-frame basis.[4]

**Results.** In Figure 15 we show complexity for an SNR such that each constellation reaches a frame error rate of approximately 10% (*e.g.*, approximately 27, 33 and 39 dB for the $2 \times 4$ measured channels and 16-, 64- and 256-QAM constellations, respectively). We examine two MIMO cases: In Figure 15(a) we show complexity for two clients and four AP antennas. In this case, complexity is relatively low, due to favorable MIMO channel conditioning, but at the cost of reduced throughput, since only two users transmit. We note that the complexity of ETH-SD increases with constellation

[3]The authors of BigStation [67] note a similar trend in their experimental results.

[4]This accurately quantifies performance over channels whose coherence times are greater than the time for one frame, *i.e.* driving speeds and slower.

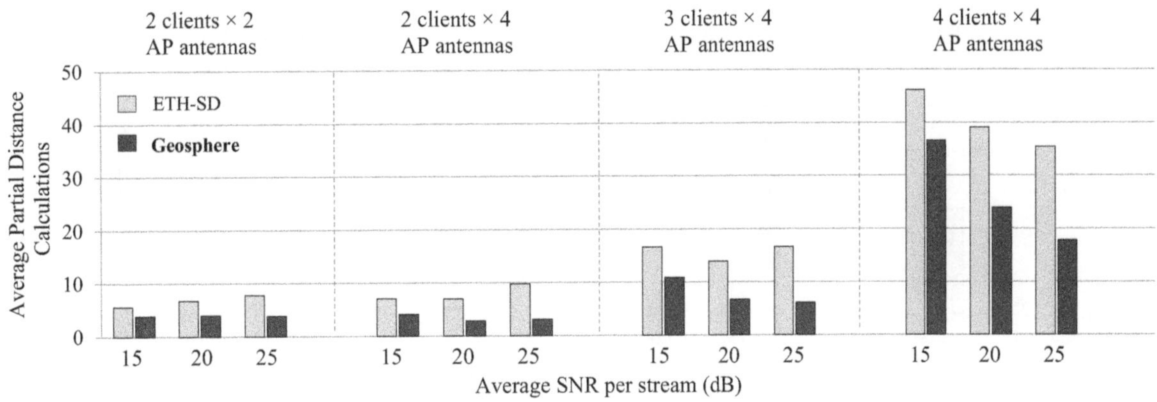


**Figure 14:** Complexity comparison between ETH-SD and Geosphere for different numbers of clients and AP antennas.

size, while the complexity of Geosphere is substantially smaller, independent of the constellation size, and comparable to the complexity of zero-forcing.[5] For the Rayleigh channel, Geosphere is 81% less complex than ETH-SD for the 256-QAM case, while the full Geosphere (with 2D zigzag and geometrical pruning) provides complexity gains of 27% compared to 2D-zigzag-only Geosphere.

Figure 15(b) shows complexity for four clients and four AP antennas, where we need to cope with more challenging MIMO channel conditions. For the $4 \times 4$ case we see that the complexity of ETH-SD (but not Geosphere) greatly increases with constellation size. As a result Geosphere is up to 70% less complex than ETH-SD for the Rayleigh channel. In addition we see that the zigzag algorithm is the main source of complexity improvement for large constellations, while early pruning provides complexity gains of 13–17%.

**Discussion.** In general, the effect of geometrical pruning becomes more apparent for better SNRs and channel conditions. For example, in any depth-first sphere decoder, we need $n_t$ partial Euclidean distance calculations to find the distance of the first candidate solution (first leaf). If this is the correct solution and it has a small Euclidean distance (as in the case of high SNR), a typical sphere decoder would require at least another $n_t - 1$ partial distance calculations to prune the rest of the tree. In contrast, geometrical pruning prunes the rest of the tree without any additional calculation. Therefore, if in the simulations above, we increase the SNR to reach target packet error rates of 1%, geometrical pruning reaches a 47% improvement compared to Geosphere with zigzag only.

Another significant characteristic of Geosphere is that since it and all leading practical sphere decoders (including ETH-SD) use the Schnorr-Euchner enumeration (§6), the number of visited nodes is the same for all of them. Therefore, Geosphere maintains the processing throughput of hardware architectures that process one node per clock cycle [10].

Finally, we also observe that while the collected channels are not Rayleigh distributed, the complexity results are in very good agreement. Empirically, this suggests that only the target bit error rate (and not channel fading statistics nor the operating SNR) determines the amount of computation required to decode.

# 6. RELATED WORK

Work on the sphere decoder has been extensive, and we are not the first to note the importance of and experimentally measure the condition number of the MIMO channel, or propose solutions for noise amplification. Here we discuss related work in these areas, in both the networked systems and communications theory communities, placing Geosphere into context and highlighting our contributions.

**Linear filtering.** We note that the classical minimum mean-squared error (MMSE) detector is an improvement on zero-forcing of similar complexity that balances between completely decoupling the interfering streams and amplifying noise. However, MMSE cannot provide substantial throughput gains compared to zero-forcing in the medium and the high signal-to-noise ratio regime [59]. Artés *et al.* [3] note the effect of the condition number on the zero-forcing decoder, and propose a linear filter that compensates for the distortion the zero-forcing decoder introduces, but their method does not maintain performance in larger constellations. Leveraging the power of the sphere decoder, Geosphere maintains performance while scaling to 256-QAM.

**SIC.** Successive interference cancellation (SIC) methods decode signals from the strongest interferers and subtract their effect on the other signals [69]. However, the efficacy of SIC is contingent on the information transmitted between users being sent at a rate that allows correct detection in the presence of uncancelled interference, a requirement which does not hold for a sphere decoders. Sayana *et al.* [45] use successive interference cancellation [59] and soft information to reduce the effects of noise amplification in a MIMO system, but their design is tied to a specific type of coding and modulation (bit-interleaved coded modulation), whereas Geosphere is generalizable to many different coding schemes, because it operates under the coding layer.

**Scheduling and user selection.** When the number of users is very large, zero-forcing combined with a user-selection strategy becomes asymptotically optimal [61]. Yoo and Goldsmith note the optimality of zero-forcing beamforming and propose a scheduling algorithm for a large number of users [68]. Chen and Wang analyze the interaction of zero-forcing and time-division scheduling techniques, proposing to select and schedule users so that noise amplification due to zero-forcing is lessened [12]. However, such approaches require a number of clients needing to send data that is *orders of magnitude* greater than the number of AP antennas, making them of limited applicability in a common case where a small number of clients (less than 10) saturate the wireless medium. With extremely large user numbers, the process of estimating and tracking the wireless channel to each also incurs non-negligible overhead. Furthermore,

[5]Zero-forcing requires $n_t \times n_r = 8$ complex multiplications, whereas Geosphere requires at most 10 complex multiplications (assuming that each partial distance calculation requires $n_t + 1$ multiplications).

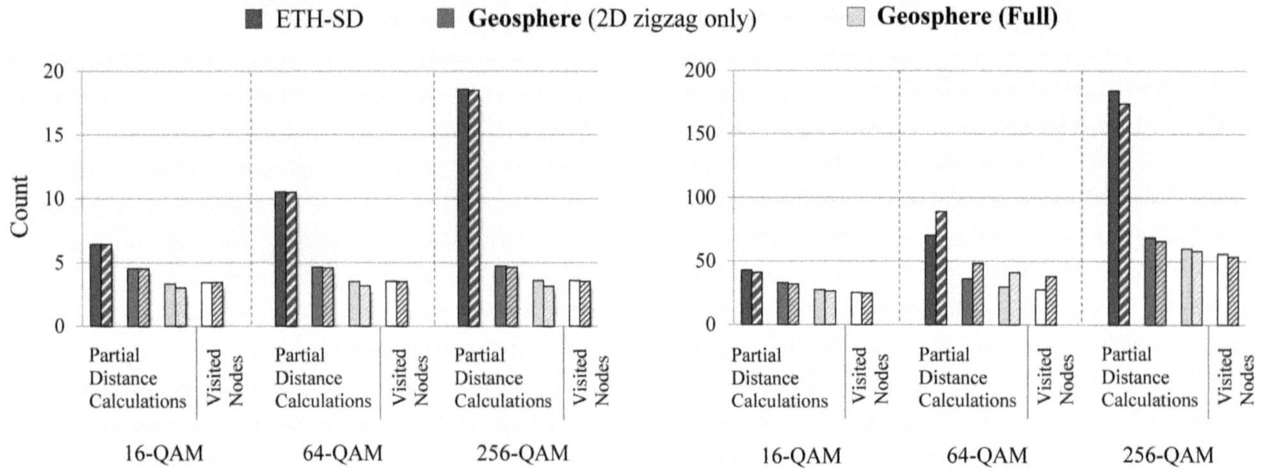


**(a)** Two clients and four AP antennas.

**(b)** Four clients and four AP antennas.

**Figure 15:** Simulation-based complexity comparison between ETH-SD and Geosphere. ***Solid bars:*** Simulated Rayleigh channel; ***striped bars:*** empirically measured channel. N.B.: each of the above sphere decoders visit the same number of nodes.

we have experimentally shown that Geosphere improves throughput consistently for both small and middling numbers of clients.

## 6.1 Sphere decoder optimizations

There is a large body of prior work that optimizes the performance of the sphere decoder. It roughly breaks down into proposals that simplify the Euclidean distance calculation (discussed next), optimize the order of visiting nodes, and prune the tree more aggressively.

**Simplified distance measures.** These proposals approximate Euclidean distance in the constellation with computationally simpler but less precise distance measures, to incrementally lower processing overhead [10, 25, 62]. However, such approaches increase the bit error probability while remaining impractical when sending dense constellations, and so Geosphere outperforms these approaches.

**Node ordering-based optimizations.** Chan and Lee [11] first proposed the frequently used radius update approach. However, their proposal doubles the height of the tree, making it impractical for implementation [10]. Zhao and Giannakis [70] generalize Schnorr-Euchner enumeration probabilistically, but by their own admission, their techniques are only beneficial in the high-SNR regime (> 22 dB). By comparison, Geosphere's techniques are effective over the entire common SNR range. Ghasemmehdi and Agrell [20] minimize the number of visited nodes, but also double tree height and require impractical amounts of memory.

Some prior work takes constellation geometry into account. Mennenga and Fettweis [37] propose an enumeration method that geometrically splits the I-Q space into sectors. However, their algorithm can accurately sort only the first eight nodes, resulting in decode errors and decreased throughput. As part of a $K$-best sphere decoder, Shabany *et al.* [48] propose an enumeration method superficially similar to Geosphere's two-dimensional zigzag. However, Geosphere's algorithm is superior, enumerating in Step 3(b) only if no other constellation point in $z_h$'s PAM subconstellation is in $Q$, yielding a significant reduction in partial distance calculations for dense constellations and depth-first sphere decoding. For example, when expanding a node to identify the child with the third smallest Euclidean distance, Geosphere needs four partial distance calculations while Shabany's needs five (25% more).

**Pruning-based optimizations.** Many proposals attempt to reduce complexity by probabilistically pruning tree branches unlikely to survive pruning. Work by Shim and Kang [50, 51] doubles decoder tree height and requires cumbersome tuning to tradeoff complexity with performance. Cui *et al.* propose statistical node pruning strategies [14, 15], but incur a significant loss of performance in order to achieve non-negligible complexity gains, making their proposals unsuitable for practical use. Stojnic *et al.* propose a pruning technique that requires solving a semi-definite problem on top of the usual sphere decoder search tree [52], but their technique is only appropriate for very low SNR (less than 6 dB), whereas Geosphere targets relatively higher SNR ranges and larger numbers of users. Gowaikar and Hassibi propose a related probabilistic pruning technique [22], but it achieves worst performance than the preceding proposal of Shim *et al.* [50].

**Breadth-first sphere decoders.** In contrast to depth-first sphere decoders, breadth-first sphere decoders have average complexity typically higher than depth-first approaches [10]. The fixed-complexity sphere decoder [5] is a specific type of breadth-first sphere decoder that initially searches the first $p$ levels of the tree, then plunges depth first, but using a branching factor of only one. Jaldén *et al.* show that the fixed-complexity sphere decoder can only asymptotically reach maximum-likelihood performance at high SNRs [30], with higher computational complexity than a depth-first approaches. Geosphere, on the other hand, reaches maximum-likelihood performance while significantly reducing computational complexity.

***K*-best sphere decoders.** $K$-best sphere decoders [13, 24, 34, 39, 47, 48, 63, 66] are depth-first sphere decoders that select the $K$ best branches at each level of the tree regardless of the sphere constraint or any other distance control policy. However, the choice of $K$ is speculative and increases with the order of the constellation, making $K$-best inappropriate for dense constellations. Furthermore, $K$ must be increased to accommodate the worst MIMO channel, making such schemes inefficient. To reduce complexity and increase parallelizability, Azzam and Ayanoglou [4] propose to reorder the channel matrix, but double its size (and thus the height of the sphere decoder tree) to accommodate practical QAM channels. Thus, the required complexity is is still very high.

**Channel condition-aware sphere decoders.** Maurer *et al.* propose a system that switches between zero-forcing and maximum-likelihood decoding via a threshold test on the channel condition number [36]. However, unlike Geosphere, they do not present experimental results with a real sphere decoder, and use random matrices rather than real MIMO wireless channel matrices, calling into question the practical applicability of their simulation-based results; also missing is a means of choosing the switching threshold. In a similar vein, Roger *et al.* [44] propose a sphere decoder that expands at most $K$ branches of each node in the decoding tree, varying $K$ based on $\kappa(\mathbf{H})$. Geosphere alleviates the need for such complex designs since it can automatically adjust its complexity to the condition of the channel, and can reduce it down complexities similar to zero-forcing. In addition, we present a full working system design and experimental evaluation in real indoor office conditions.

Su and Wassel [55] use a geometrically-inspired ordering of the MIMO channel matrix $\mathbf{H}$ before performing sphere decoding. However, the resulting computational savings vanish for average and high SNR values of practical interest.

**The generalized sphere decoder.** Generalized sphere decoders [16, 18, 19] are designed for situations where the number of transmit antennas exceeds the number of receive antennas, and so the MIMO channel matrix is rank deficient (as opposed to merely poorly-conditioned). However, these techniques don't increase capacity, since capacity increases with min $\{n_a, n_c\}$. But since these techniques use Schnorr-Euchner enumeration, Geosphere improves throughput and computational complexity synergistically.

## 6.2 MIMO channel condition measurements

While the MIMO channel condition number has been previously measured, published measurements are mostly associated with mobile cellular systems, and thus often taken outdoors (*e.g.*, Teague *et al.* [57], in the 2.16–2.18 GHz frequency band), indoors, but in a mobile cellular frequency band (*e.g.*, Kita *et al.* [32]), or in an unspecified environment (*e.g.*, Agilent Corp. [1]). Nonetheless, we note that the MIMO channel condition number distributions obtained in this related work are roughly comparable to our measurements (§1, §5), suggesting that the problem of poor channel conditioning occurs in general, in outdoor as well as indoor environments, and across the range of microwave frequencies.

Channel hardening [26, 29] refers to the linear increase in throughput possible in zero-forcing multi-user MIMO systems, when the number of antennas increases dramatically. This is due to the ability of the access point to select a set of antennas that results in a well-conditioned MIMO channel matrix. Among its results, this theoretical work shows that many more antennas than users are required to achieve linear throughput gains.

## 6.3 Downlink beamforming

In the downlink, sphere decoder-based techniques can be used at the transmitter in lieu of zero-forcing based precoding; this is known as *sphere encoder precoding* [6, 27, 38, 41]. This precoding, however, requires that APs track the wireless channel as they move, which adds complexity and becomes harder with increasing mobility. Nonetheless, since Geosphere's techniques are receiver-based, Geosphere is complementary to precoding: the two can achieve complementary performance gains if implemented together.

## 6.4 System designs

The Spinal codes [42] decoder resembles a breadth-first sphere decoder with a bounded branching factor at each level. However, Spinal codes uses a novel encoder design that improves performance. With regards to Geosphere, Spinal codes are designed for a point-to-point wireless channel, not the multi-antenna MIMO channel, but they may be extended to the MIMO channel in the future.

The authors of BigStation [67] have speculated that their zero-forcing multi-user MIMO access point may require more than 40 antennas (or 2× the number of users) in order to mitigate the problem of a MIMO channel hardening. In this context, our work on Geosphere offers an alternative solution to using many antennas and radios (with their associated costs) at the AP.

# 7. CONCLUSIONS AND FUTURE WORK

We have described Geosphere, a wireless multi-user MIMO system that consistently achieves higher uplink throughputs than similar systems based on zero-forcing. Geosphere makes the sphere decoder practical in real high-rate wireless systems (using dense constellations) with a geometrical approach based on soft information.

While Geosphere increases throughput, iterative soft receiver processing is required to reach MIMO capacity [28]. Such "soft-detectors" consist of several constrained maximum-likelihood problems and therefore the sphere decoder can be of use [9, 60]. State-of-the-art soft-input, soft-input sphere decoders [7, 8, 54, 65] are based on the ETH-SD approach, but their complexity remains prohibitive under dense constellations. Since Geosphere outperforms ETH-SD, a promising next step is to extend our techniques to this setting.

**Acknowledgements:** The research leading to these results has received funding from the European Research Council under the EU's Seventh Framework Programme (FP/2007-2013), ERC Grant Agreement n° 279976. We thank our shepherd Shyamnath Gollakota and the anonymous reviewers for their insightful feedback.

# 8. REFERENCES

[1] Agilent Technologies. MIMO Performance and Condition Number in LTE Test: App. Note, 2009.

[2] E. Agrell, T. Eriksson, A. Vardy, and K. Zeger. Closest point search in lattices. *IEEE Trans. Inf. Theory*, 48(8):2201–2214, Aug. 2002.

[3] H. Artés. Efficient detection algorithms for MIMO channels. *IEEE Tr. Sig. Proc.*, 51(11):2808–20, 2003.

[4] L. Azzam and E. Ayanoglu. Reduced complexity sphere decoding via a reordered lattice representation. *IEEE Tr. Comms.*, 57(9):2564–69, 2009.

[5] L. Barbero and J. Thompson. Fixing the complexity of the sphere decoder for MIMO detection. *IEEE Trans. on Wireless Comms.*, 7(6):2131–2142, 2008.

[6] M. Barrenechea et al. Implementation of complex enumeration for multiuser MIMO vector precoding. In *Proc. of Eur. Sig. Proc. Conf.*, 2011.

[7] F. Borlenghi et al. A 772 Mbit/s 8.81 bit/nJ 90 nm CMOS soft-input soft-output sphere decoder. In *Proc. of IEEE Asian Solid State Circ. Conf.*, 2011.

[8] F. Borlenghi et al. A 2.78 mm$^2$ 65 nm CMOS gigabit MIMO iterative detection and decoding receiver. In *Proc. of the ESSCIRC*, pages 65–68, 2012.

[9] J. Boutros et al. Soft-input soft-output lattice sphere decoder for linear channels. In *GLOBECOM*, 2003.

[10] A. Burg, M. Borgmann, M. Wenk, M. Zellweger, W. Fichtner, and H. Bolcskei. VLSI implementation of MIMO detection using the sphere decoding algorithm. *IEEE J. of Solid-State Circ.*, 40(7):1566–1577, 2005.

[11] A. Chan and I. Lee. A new reduced-complexity sphere decoder for multiple antenna sys. In *IEEE ICC*, 2002.

[12] C. Chen and L. Wang. On the performance of the zero-forcing receiver operating in the multiuser MIMO system with reduced noise enhancement effect. In *Proc. of IEEE Globecom*, 2005.

[13] S. Chen, T. Zhang, and Y. Xin. Relaxed K-best MIMO signal detector design and VLSI implementation. *IEEE Trans. on VLSI Sys.*, 15(3):328–337, 2007.

[14] T. Cui, S. Han, and C. Tellambura. Probability distribution based node pruning for sphere decoding. *IEEE Trans. on Veh. Tech.*, 62(4):1586–96, 2013.

[15] T. Cui, T. Ho, and C. Tellambura. Statistical pruning for near maxiumum likelihood detection of MIMO systems. In *IEEE ICC*, 2007.

[16] T. Cui and C. Tellambura. An efficient generalized sphere decoder for rank-deficient MIMO systems. *IEEE Comms. L.*, 9(5):423–5, 2005.

[17] M. Damen, H. El Gamal, and G. Caire. On maximum likelihood detection and the search for the closest lattice point. *IEEE T. Inf. Th.*, 49(10):2389–402, 2003.

[18] M. Damen et al. Generalized sphere decoder for asymmetrical space-time communication architecture. *IEEE Elec. L.*, 36(2):166–67, 2000.

[19] P. Dayal and M. Varanasi. A fast generalized sphere decoder for optimum decoding of under-determined MIMO systems. In *Proc. of Allerton Conf.*, 2003.

[20] A. Ghasemmehdi and E. Agrell. Faster recursions in sphere decoding. *IEEE T. Inf. Th.*, 57(6):3530–6, 2011.

[21] S. Gollakota, S. Perli, and D. Katabi. Interference alignment and cancellation. In *SIGCOMM*, 2009.

[22] R. Gowaikar and B. Hassibi. Statistical pruning for near-maximum likelihood decoding. *IEEE Tr. on Sig. Proc.*, 55(6):2661–75, 2007.

[23] A. Gudipati and S. Katti. Strider: Automatic rate adaptation and collision handling. In *SIGCOMM*, 2011.

[24] Z. Guo and P. Nilsson. Algorithm and implementation of the K-best sphere decoding for MIMO detection. *IEEE J. Sel. Areas Commun.*, 24(3):491–503, 2006.

[25] C. Hess et al. Reduced-complexity MIMO detector with close-to-ML error rate performance. In *ACM Great Lakes VLSI Symp.*, 2008.

[26] B. Hochwald, T. Marzetta, and V. Tarokh. Multiple-antenna channel hardening and its implications for rate feedback and scheduling. *IEEE Trans. on Info. Theory*, 50(9), Sept. 2004.

[27] B. Hochwald, C. Peel, and A. Swindlehurst. A vector-perturbation technique for near-capacity multiantenna multiuser communication. *IEEE Trans. on Comms.*, 53(3):537–544, 2005.

[28] B. Hochwald and S. Ten Brink. Achieving near-capacity on a multiple-antenna channel. *IEEE Trans. Comms.*, 51(3):389–399, Mar. 2003.

[29] B. Hochwald and S. Vishwanath. Space-time multiple access: Linear growth in the sum rate. In *Proc. of Allerton Conf.*, 2002.

[30] J. Jaldén, L. Barbero, B. Ottersten, and J. Thompson. The error probability of the fixed-complexity sphere decoder. *IEEE Tr. on Sig. Proc.*, 57(7):2711–20, 2009.

[31] P. Kafle et al. Spatial correlation and capacity measurements for wideband MIMO channels in indoor office environment. *IEEE Trans. on Wireless Comms.*, 7(5):1560–1571, 2008.

[32] N. Kita et al. Measurement of Demel condition number for 2x2 MIMO-OFDM channels. In *IEEE VTC*, 2004.

[33] E. Kreyszig. *Advanced Engineering Mathematics*. Wiley & Sons, Inc., 2006.

[34] Q. Li and Z. Wang. Improved K-best sphere decoding algorithms for MIMO systems. In *Proc. of IEEE Int. Symp. on Circuits and Sys.*, 2006.

[35] K. Lin, S. Gollakota, and D. Katabi. Random access heterogeneous MIMO networks. In *SIGCOMM*, 2011.

[36] J. Maurer, G. Matz, and D. Seethaler. Low-complexity and full-diversity MIMO detection based on condition number thresholding. In *IEEE ICASSP*, 2007.

[37] B. Mennenga and G. Fettweis. Search sequence determination for tree search based detection algorithms. In *IEEE Sarnoff Symp.*, 2009.

[38] M. Mohaisen and K. Chang. Fixed-complexity sphere encoder for multi-user MIMO systems. *Journal of Communications and Networks*, 13(1):63–69, 2011.

[39] S. Mondal et al. Design and implementation of a sort-free K-best sphere decoder. *IEEE Trans. on VLSI Sys.*, 18(10):1497–1501, 2010.

[40] K. Nikitopoulos et al. Complexity-efficient enumeration techniques for soft-input, soft-output sphere decoding. *IEEE Comms. L.*, 14(4):312–4, 2010.

[41] C. Peel et al. A vector-perturbation technique for near-capacity multiantenna multiuser communication. *IEEE Trans. on Comms.*, 53(1):195–202, 2005.

[42] J. Perry, P. Iannucci, K. Fleming, H. Balakrishnan, and D. Shah. Spinal codes. In *ACM SIGCOMM*, 2012.

[43] Rice Univ. Wireless Open Access Research Platform (WARP). http://warp.rice.edu/trac.

[44] S. Roger, A. Gonzalez, V. Almenar, and A. Vidal. Combined K-best sphere decoder based on the channel matrix condition number. In *IEEE ISCCSP*, 2008.

[45] K. Sayana, S. Nagaraj, and S. Gelfand. A MIMO zero-forcing receiver with soft interference cancellation for BICM. In *Proc. of the IEEE Workshop on Sig. Proc. Advances in Wireless Comms.*, 2005.

[46] C. Schnorr and M. Euchner. Lattice basis reduction: Improved practical algorithms and solving subset sum problems. *Math. Prog.*, 66(2):181–191, 1994.

[47] M. Shabany and P. Gulak. Scalable VLSI architecture for K-best lattice decoders. In *IEEE ISCAS*, 2008.

[48] M. Shabany, K. Su, and P. Gulak. A pipelined scalable high-throughput implementation of a near-ML K-best complex lattice decoder. In *IEEE ICASSP*, 2008.

[49] W. Shen et al. Rate adaptation for 802.11 multiuser MIMO networks. In *MobiCom*, 2012.

[50] B. Shim and I. Kang. Sphere decoding with a probabilistic tree pruning. *IEEE Trans. on Signal Processing*, 56(10):4867–4878, 2008.

[51] B. Shim and I. Kang. On further reduction of complexity in tree pruning based sphere search. *IEEE Trans. on Comms.*, 58(2):417–22, 2010.

[52] M. Stojnic et al. Further results on speeding up the sphere decoder. In *IEEE ICASSP*, 2006.

[53] G. Strang. *Introduction to Linear Algebra*. Wellesley-Cambridge Press, 4th edition, 2009.

[54] C. Studer and H. Bölcskei. Soft-input soft-output sphere decoding. In *IEEE ISIT*, 2008.

[55] K. Su and I. Wassell. A new ordering for efficient sphere decoding. In *IEEE ICC*, 2005.

[56] K. Tan et al. SAM: Enabling practical spatial multiple access in wireless LAN. In *MobiCom*, 2009.

[57] H. Teague et al. Field results on MIMO performance in UMB systems. In *IEEE VTC*, 2008.

[58] I. Telatar. Capacity of multi-antenna Gaussian channels. *Eur. Trans. Telecomms.*, 10(6):585–596, Dec. 1999.

[59] D. Tse and P. Viswanath. *Fundamentals of Wireless Communication*. Cambridge University Press, 2005.

[60] H. Vikalo, B. Hassibi, and T. Kailath. Iterative decoding for MIMO channels via modified sphere decoding. *IEEE Trans. on Wireless Comms.*, 3(6):2299–2311, 2004.

[61] J. Wang et al. User selection with zero-forcing beamforming achieves the asymptotically optimal sum rate. *IEEE Tr. on Sig. Proc.*, 56(8):3713–26, 2008.

[62] M. Wenk, L. Bruderer, A. Burg, and C. Studer. Area-and throughput-optimized VLSI architecture of sphere decoding. In *EEE/IFIP VLSI-SOC*, 2010.

[63] M. Wenk et al. K-best MIMO detection VLSI architectures achieving up to 424 Mbps. In *ISCC*, 2006.

[64] M. Winter et al. A 335 Mb/s 3.9 $mm^2$ 65 nm CMOS flexible MIMO detection-decoding engine achieving 4G wireless data rates. In *IEEE ISSCC*, 2012.

[65] E. Witte et al. A scalable VLSI architecture for SISO single tree-search sphere decoding. *IEEE Trans. on Circ. and Sys.*, 57(9):706–710, 2010.

[66] K. Wong et al. A VLSI architecture of a K-best lattice decoding algorithm for MIMO channels. In *ISCC*, 2002.

[67] Q. Yang et al. BigStation: Enabling scalable real-time signal processing in large MU-MIMO systems. In *SIGCOMM*, 2013.

[68] T. Yoo and A. Goldsmith. On the optimality of multiantenna broadcast scheduling using zero-forcing beamforming. *IEEE JSAC*, 24(3):528–541, 2006.

[69] A. Zanella, M. Chiani, and M. Win. MMSE reception and successive interference cancellation for MIMO systems with high spectral efficiency. *IEEE Trans. on Wireless Comms.*, 4(3):1244–1253, 2005.

[70] W. Zhao and G. Giannakis. Reduced complexity closest point decoding algorithms for random lattices. *IEEE Trans. on Wireless Comms.*, 5(1):101–111, 2006.

# Author Index

www.ingramcontent.com/pod-product-compliance
Ingram Content Group UK Ltd.
Pitfield, Milton Keynes, MK11 3LW, UK
UKHW051418290926
15471UKWH00009B/1667

9 781450 332606